CONTEMPORARY DRAMATISTS

Contemporary Writers of the English Language

Contemporary Poets

Contemporary Novelists
(including short story writers)

Contemporary Dramatists

Contemporary Literary Critics

CONTEMPORARY DRAMATISTS

FOURTH EDITION

WITH A PREFACE BY
RUBY COHN

EDITOR
D.L. KIRKPATRICK

CONSULTING EDITOR
JAMES VINSON

StJ

ST. JAMES PRESS
CHICAGO AND LONDON

For further information, write:
ST. JAMES PRESS
425 North Michigan Avenue
Chicago 60611, U.S.A.
or
3 Percy Street
London W1P 9FA, England

British Library Cataloguing in Publication Data
Contemporary dramatists.—4th ed.
1. Drama in English, 1945–. Biographical dictionaries
I. Kirkpatrick, D.L. (Daniel Lane), *1949–*
822′.914′09

ISBN 0–912289–62–7

First edition published 1973; second edition 1977
third edition 1982; fourth edition 1988
Reprinted 1989

Printed in Great Britain at
The Bath Press, Avon

CONTENTS

PREFACE

This volume contains well over three hundred entries for contemporary dramatists writing in English, thousands of miles apart. It might seem then that English drama is alive and well, but for that to be true, audiences should embrace drama. Do they? I have seen estimates ranging from one per cent of the population (of America) to five per cent (of England) who *ever* attend the theatre, but *regular* attendance thins down to decimals of decimals. Will these dramatists continue to write for a diminishing audience?

How different from the burgeoning drama of the Elizabethans. And yet Burbage and Henslowe may also have worried about theatre attendance. No language seems to sport more than one great age of drama, and other periods of English language drama have looked pale by contrast with the Elizabethan. In later times English theatre came to be a fabulous invalid, enjoying its several prognoses, diagnoses, and forecasts of doom. Such a forecast is again appropriate today, not because our contemporary drama is less skillful than that of any age since the Elizabethan, nor less plentiful. But because our drama, like that of no other period, has to survive in the noxious atmosphere of the mass media. Playwrights can defy the media, sidestep them, try to ignore them, or, as more often happens, use dramatic form as an entrée into the media, notably films and television.

In English-speaking countries, with their meagre theatre subsidies and their major technical resources, drama abounds on film and television. (Dublin's Abbey Theatre in 1922 became the first nationally subsidized theatre in the English language, whereas the subsidized Comédie Française dates from 1680.) If today's writer is inadequately nurtured by theatre or publisher, he can turn to the media. But few media graduates have contributed significant dramas to live theatre. Mass media drama tends to appeal to the most facile reactions of an audience, and yet the techniques of the media can broaden the palette of the stage playwright. Since writing the Preface to the first edition of *Contemporary Dramatists*, I have become aware of media writers who return sporadically but significantly to the stage and of Heathcote Williams's *AC/DC* which grounds a frenzied strength in the weaknesses of a media civilization. The theatre has always drawn upon other arts, crafts, and technologies, and it may arrive at a *modus vivendi* with the media.

Perhaps the *drama* is dying in the form we have known for some four hundred years—a fairly inflexible prompt copy which is eventually printed. However, the *theatre* today—with or without promptbook—must recognize its uniqueness in that live actors play before live audiences. Each actor has a single instrument, the body that includes the voice. And for all the experimentation with non-verbal sounds, the voice has recourse to words, which are the province of the dramatist.

English drama is coeval with the printing press, and response to drama has for centuries been cumulative, as a reader-spectator travels from stage to page and, all the more receptive, to stage again. This itinerary may be less frequent for today's spectators. Contemporary stage dialogue may include primitive non-verbal sounds and electronic post-verbal devices, but new dramas of verbal distinction are nevertheless being written and played. As long as that continues, in the full awareness of live theatre as a minority art, drama will endure.

Prognosis pronounced, whom do we actually have in a volume on contemporary dramatists writing in English? Since "contemporary" has been defined (for this volume) as biologically alive, we find curious neighbors. Some dramatists have spent successful years appealing to middle-class entertainment-seekers; others have tried to entertain while supporting worthy causes or baring social problems. As has been true for four hundred years, certain plays were written to provide scope for the special talents of a particular actor. None of this sounds contemporary in an age when we take it for granted that we will fly faster than sound.

I have seen many, many plays, and many kinds of plays in nearly forty years of theatre-going. It seems only yesterday that I saw *The Iceman Cometh* in a production advised by Eugene O'Neill. (It was actually 1946.) Or *The Apple Cart*, crackling wittily, only shortly after Bernard Shaw's witticisms had ceased to crackle. (It was actually 1953.) But yesterday is far away in contemporary theatre, so that Shaw and O'Neill belong to another age and another theatre language. And since this is true of master-playwrights, it is all the truer for their lesser colleagues. Even living playwrights are dead in today's theatre: a windy would-be Elizabethan, a once angry young man turned surly, a once fragile young lyricist turned coy, a reacher for tragedy resigned to routine comedy, or various squatters in the Abbey Theatre which nearly exploded under the impact of three different meteors. Such dramatists are less contemporary than Euripides or Shakespeare, not to mention John Whiting and Joe Orton, who died in mid-career. For there is no necessary convergence between biological and artistic life. I hope all playwrights live to be a hundred, but I cannot help exclaiming at some of the entries in this volume: "Is he still alive?"!

Since mid-century, we have seen specimens of English language theatre labelled epic, angry, kitchen sink, absurd, ridiculous, radical, third world, puppet, guerrilla, fact, nude, improvisational, perspectivist, alternative—all soon exploited by the mass media. It is small wonder that many of the contemporary dramatists in this volume seem either uncontemporary or undramatic, regardless of chronology or biology.

To shift abruptly to a positive note, we have among contemporary dramatists one giant, Samuel Beckett, who writes sometimes in English, sometimes in French, always in his own distinctive dramatic idiom. Beckett's plays are enduring masterpieces. They are also a terminus to the Western dramatic tradition, dissecting the parts of a play so that they can never again articulate innocently. Through the tension of play, Beckett probes the bases of Western culture—faith, reason, friendship, family. Through the skills of play, Beckett summarizes human action—word and pause, gesture and stillness, motion rising from emotion. Beckett's most celebrated play, *Waiting for Godot*, is striking in its stage presence. As Brecht called attention to the theatre, Beckett calls attention to the play as play. Often pitched as polar opposites, Brecht and Beckett both reacted against the dominant illusionist drama of their time and ours, so that it is no longer so dominant. In spite of their differences, Beckett resembles Brecht in precision of language at the textural level, and in integration of verbal rhythms into an original scenic whole.

Relentlessly digging his own way, Beckett has inspired two English-language playwrights, one on each side of the Atlantic, Harold Pinter and Edward Albee. From Beckett both younger dramatists have learned to convey the presence of stage action, without before or after, exposition or resolution. Pinter capitalizes on the unverifiability of a past, and Albee fits the past obliquely into the stage present. Both playwrights create the stage present through carefully crafted dialogue. Their characters speak in stylized patterns that draw upon colloquial phrases of contemporary speech. Unlike the realists with whom they are sometimes confused, they use repetition and cross-talk to probe beneath or beyond surface reality.

In their rejection of realism, other contemporary dramatists resemble Pinter and Albee. Since no stage designer can compete with the camera in photographic fidelity to surface appearance, many contemporary dramatists don't ask them to try. Departures from realism can be as diversified as John Arden's Brechtian songs in *The Ballygombeen Bequest*, Edward Bond's Ghost in *Lear*, the penitential geometry of Kenneth H. Brown's *The Brig*, the seasonal symbolism of Ed Bullins's *In the Wine Time*, the eternal sparring in María Irene Fornés's *Tango Palace*, the opportunity for improvisation in Paul Foster's *Tom Paine*, the drug metaphor in Jack Gelber's *The Connection*, the mythic dimension in Amiri Baraka's *Dutchman*, the documentary absurdism of James Saunders's *Next Time I'll Sing to You*, the stretch toward Artaud in Peter Shaffer's *The Royal Hunt of the Sun*, the manic rock monologues of Sam Shepard's *The Tooth of Crime*, the tribal magic of Derek Walcott's *Dream on Monkey Mountain*, the play organically within the play in Patrick White's *The Ham Funeral*. I am not saying that these plays are of equal quality, but I am saying that forays into non-realistic modes provide richer possibilities of theatricalizing the profundities of contemporary experience.

Provided that audiences come to see the plays.

RUBY COHN (1982)

EDITOR'S NOTE

The main part of *Contemporary Dramatists* includes entries on living English-language writers for the stage. There are also supplements on screenwriters, radio writers, television writers, musical librettists, and theatre groups, and an appendix of entries for some seven writers who have died since the 1950's but whose reputations are essentially contemporary.

The selection of writers in this book is based on the recommendations of the advisers listed on page xi, some of whom have helped with all four editions.

The entry for each writer consists of a biography, a complete list of produced and/or published plays and all other separately published books, and a signed essay. In addition, entrants were invited to comment on their work.

Original British and United States editions of all books have been listed; other editions are listed only if they are first editions. Details for a play first published in a magazine or anthology are not given if the play has been published later as a separate book or in a collection of the author; an acting edition of a play is not listed unless there is no trade edition. Librettos are listed among the plays. The first production, first productions in both Britain and the United States, as well as first productions in London and New York are listed. Reprints and revivals are not listed unless a revision of text or a change of title is involved. As a rule all books written about the entrant are listed in the Critical Studies section; the reviews and essays listed have been recommended by the entrant.

We would like to thank the entrants and contributors for their patience and cooperation in helping us compile this book.

ADVISERS

Arthur H. Ballet
Michael Benedikt
Eric Bentley
C.W.E. Bigsby
Herbert Blau
John Bowen
Katharine Brisbane
Constance Brissenden
Richard Christiansen
Harold Clurman
Ruby Cohn
John Robert Colombo
Albert Cook
Robert W. Corrigan
Tish Dace
W.A. Darlington
John Elsom
Richard Gilman
Otis L. Guernsey, Jr.
Carole Hayman
Ronald Hayman
Stanley Kauffmann
Naseem Khan
Laurence Kitchin
Richard Kostelanetz
Frank Marcus
E.A. Markham
Bonnie Marranca
Howard McNaughton
Benedict Nightingale
Richard Schechner
Alan Schneider
Michael T. Smith
John Spurling
Alan Strachan
J.L. Styan
Howard Taubman
John Russell Taylor
J.C. Trewin
Darwin T. Turner
Irving Wardle
Gerald Weales
B.A. Young

CONTRIBUTORS

Elizabeth Adams
Frances Rademacher Anderson
Addell Austin
Arthur H. Ballet
Clive Barker
Judith E. Barlow
Gene A. Barnett
David W. Beams
Joss Bennathan
Eugene Benson
Gerald M. Berkowitz
Misha Berson
Michael Bertin
C.W.E. Bigsby
Michael Billington
Sebastian Black
Walter Bode
John Bowen
Gaynor F. Bradish
Katharine Brisbane
Constance Brissenden
John Russell Brown
Joseph Bruchac
John Bull
Jarka M. Burian
Susan Carlson
Bernard Carragher
Ned Chaillet
D.D.C. Chambers
Richard Christiansen
William Coco
Ruby Cohn
Clare Colvin
Judy Cooke
David Copelin
Tish Dace
W.A. Darlington
Terence Dawson
Elin Diamond
Kathleen Dimmick
Reid Douglas
Tony Dunn
Arnold Edinborough
John Elsom
Mark W. Estrin
John V. Falconieri
Michael Feingold
Peter Fitzpatrick
Leonard Fleischer
Leah D. Frank
Melvin J. Friedman
Steven H. Gale
S.R. Gilbert
Lois Gordon
Martin Gottfried
Anthony Graham-White
Steve Grant
Frances Gray
Prabhu S. Guptara
Jonathan Hammond
Carole Hayman
Ronald Hayman

Dick Higgins
Errol Hill
Foster Hirsch
Harold Hobson
William M. Hoffman
Tess Hoffmann
Jorge A. Huerta
C. Lee Jenner
Burton Kendle
Helene Keyssar
Bruce King
Laurence Kitchin
H. Gustav Klaus
Richard Kostelanetz
John G. Kuhn
Jonathan Lamede
Bernd-Peter Lange
Paul Lawley
Michael T. Leech
Peter Lewis
Felicia Hardison Londré
Glenn Loney
Frank Marcus
E.A. Markham
Thomas B. Markus
John McCallum
Thomas J. McCormack
Arthur E. McGuinness
Howard McNaughton
Walter J. Meserve
Louis D. Mitchell
Christian H. Moe
Anne Morddel
Christopher Murray
Benedict Nightingale
Garry O'Connor
Marion O'Connor
Malcolm Page
Dorothy Parker
Rosemary Pountney
Henry Raynor
John M. Reilly
Sandra L. Richards
Andrew Rissik
James Roose-Evans
Ann Saddlemyer
Geoff Sadler
Arthur Sainer
Ellen Schiff
Elaine Shragge
Michael Sidnell
Christopher Smith
Michael T. Smith
A. Richard Sogliuzzo
Sandra Souchotte
John Spurling
Carol Simpson Stern
Alan Strachan
J.L. Styan
Elizabeth Swain
Alrene Sykes
John Russell Taylor
John Thomson
J.C. Trewin
Simon Trussler
Darwin T. Turner
Elaine Turner
Michelene Wandor
Daniel J. Watermeier
Gerald Weales
B.A. Young

CONTEMPORARY DRAMATISTS

Michael Abbensetts
George Abbott
Paul Ableman
Dannie Abse
Rodney Ackland
Ama Ata Aidoo
Edward Albee
William Alfred
Ted Allan
Robert Anderson
John Antrobus
Douglas Archibald
John Arden
George Axelrod
Alan Ayckbourn

Thomas Babe
James Baldwin
Janis Balodis
Amiri Baraka
Howard Barker
Peter Barnes
Samuel Beckett
Alan Bennett
Eric Bentley
Steven Berkoff
Barry Bermange
Kenneth Bernard
George Birimisa
Alan Bleasdale
Bridget Boland
Carol Bolt
Robert Bolt
Chris Bond
Edward Bond
Julie Bovasso
John Bowen
Howard Brenton
Lee Breuer
Kenneth H. Brown
Ed Bullins
John Burrows
Alexander Buzo
John Byrne

David Campton
Denis Cannan
Lewis John Carlino
Lonnie Carter
David Caute
Alice Childress
Caryl Churchill
Brian Clark
John Pepper Clark
Rick Cluchey
Barry Collins
Stewart Conn
Michael Cook
Ray Cooney
Ron Cowen
Richard Crane
David Cregan
Michael Cristofer
Beverley Cross
Mart Crowley

Sarah Daniels
Nick Darke
Robertson Davies
Jack Davis
Ossie Davis
Phillip Hayes Dean
Shelagh Delaney
Nigel Dennis
Keith Dewhurst
Charles Dizenzo
J.P. Donleavy
Rosalyn Drexler
Martin Duberman
Maureen Duffy
Andrea Dunbar
Nell Dunn
Christopher Durang
Lawrence Durrell
Charles Dyer

R. Sarif Easmon
Francis Ebejer
David Edgar
Obi B. Egbuna
Lonne Elder III
Barry England
Stanley Eveling
Tom Eyen

Jules Feiffer
David Fennario
Lawrence Ferlinghetti
Harvey Fierstein
Horton Foote
Richard Foreman
María Irene Fornés
James Forsyth
Paul Foster
Mario Fratti
Michael Frayn
David Freeman
David French
Bruce Jay Friedman
Brian Friel
Terence Frisby
Christopher Fry
Athol Fugard
Charles Fuller
George Furth

Frank Gagliano
Tom Gallacher
Herb Gardner
Shirley Gee
Jack Gelber
Pam Gems
William Gibson
Peter Gill
Frank D. Gilroy
John Godber
James Goldman
Steve Gooch
Charles Gordone
Clem Gorman
Ronald Gow
Jack Gray

John Gray
Simon Gray
Spalding Gray
Graham Greene
Trevor Griffiths
John Grillo
John Guare
A.R. Gurney, Jr.

Oliver Hailey
Wilson John Haire
John Hale
Roger Hall
Willis Hall
David Halliwell
Christopher Hampton
William Hanley
John Harding
David Hare
Ronald Harwood
Michael Hastings
William Hauptman
Tom Hendry
Beth Henley
James Ene Henshaw
John Herbert
James Leo Herlihy
Dorothy Hewett
Jack Hibberd
Errol Hill
Robert Hivnor
William M. Hoffman
Joan Holden
Margaret Hollingsworth
William Douglas-Home
John Hopkins
Israel Horovitz
Roger Howard
Donald Howarth
Tina Howe
Dusty Hughes
Ron Hutchinson
David Henry Hwang

Albert Innaurato

Ann Jellicoe
Len Jenkin
Errol John
Terry Johnson
Keith Johnstone

Lee Kalcheim
Garson Kanin
John B. Keane
Barrie Keeffe
Tom Kempinski
Peter Kenna
Adrienne Kennedy
Wendy Kesselman
Thomas Kilroy
Kenneth Koch
Harry Kondoleon
Arthur Kopit
Bernard Kops
H.M. Koutoukas

Ruth Krauss
Hanif Kureishi

Kevin Laffan
David Lan
Arthur Laurents
Bryony Lavery
Ray Lawler
Jerome Lawrence
Robert E. Lee
Mike Leigh
Hugh Leonard
Doris Lessing
Romulus Linney
Henry Livings
Robert Lord
Stephen Lowe
Doug Lucie
Peter Luke

Jackson Mac Low
Yulisa Amadu Maddy
David Mamet
Wolf Mankowitz
Emily Mann
Tony Marchant
Frank Marcus
William Mastrosimone
Ray Mathew
Mustapha Matura
Eugene McCabe
Michael McClure
Greg McGee
John McGrath
Tom McGrath
James McLure
Terrence McNally
Murray Mednick
Mark Medoff
Leonard Melfi
Ronald Millar
Arthur Miller
Jason Miller
Susan Miller
Ron Milner
Anthony Minghella
Adrian Mitchell
Julian Mitchell
Loften Mitchell
M.J. Molloy
Mavor Moore
Bill Morrison
John Mortimer
Tad Mosel
David Mowat
Iris Murdoch
Thomas Murphy
John Murrell
Joseph Musaphia

Bill Naughton
Richard Nelson
Ngugi wa Thiong'o
Peter Nichols
Lewis Nkosi
John Ford Noonan

Marsha Norman
Louis Nowra

Mary O'Malley
Michael O'Neill
John Osborne
Femi Osofisan
Alun Owen
Rochelle Owens

Louise Page
Stewart Parker
John Patrick
Robert Patrick
Caryl Phillips
John Pielmeier
Miguel Piñero
David Pinner
Harold Pinter
Alan Plater
Stephen Poliakoff
Sharon Pollock
Bernard Pomerance
Dennis Potter
David Pownall

David Rabe
Peter Ransley
James Reaney
Dennis J. Reardon
Barry Reckord
Renée
Trevor Rhone
Ronald Ribman
Jack Richardson
Anne Ridler
John Romeril
Ola Rotimi
David Rudkin
Willy Russell

Arthur Sainer
James Saunders
James Schevill
Murray Schisgal
Jeremy Seabrook
David Selbourne
Stephen Sewell
Alan Seymour
Anthony Shaffer
Peter Shaffer
Ntozake Shange
Wallace Shawn
Sam Shepard
Martin Sherman
Neil Simon
Beverley Simons
N.F. Simpson
Bernard Slade
Dodie Smith
Michael T. Smith
Wole Soyinka

Johnny Speight
Colin Spencer
John Spurling
David Starkweather
Barrie Stavis
Tom Stoppard
David Storey
Mike Stott
Efua Sutherland

George Tabori
Ted Tally
Ronald Tavel
Megan Terry
Peter Terson
Steve Tesich
Mervyn Thompson
Sue Townsend
William Trevor
Tsegaye Gabre-Medhin
David Turner

Peter Ustinov

Luis Valdez
Jean-Claude van Itallie
Gore Vidal

Derek Walcott
George F. Walker
Joseph A. Walker
Michelene Wandor
Douglas Turner Ward
Wendy Wasserstein
Keith Waterhouse
Arnold Weinstein
Michael Weller
Timberlake Wertenbaker
Arnold Wesker
Richard Wesley
John White
Patrick White
Ted Whitehead
Hugh Whitemore
Christopher Wilkinson
Heathcote Williams
Nigel Williams
David Williamson
Ted Willis
August Wilson
Doric Wilson
Lanford Wilson
Robert M. Wilson
Snoo Wilson
Charles Wood
Nicholas Wright
Olwen Wymark

Susan Yankowitz

Paul Zindel

Supplement 1: Screenwriters

Jay Presson Allen
Woody Allen
Edward Anhalt
George Axelrod
Robert Benton
DeWitt Bodeen
Robert Bolt
Richard Brooks
Robert Buckner
John Cassavetes
T.E.B. Clarke
Ian Dalrymple
Jules Dassin
I.A.L. Diamond
Philip Dunne
Julius Epstein
Bryan Forbes
Melvin Frank
Christopher Fry
Sidney Gilliat
Bo Goldman
William Goldman
Graham Greene
Albert Hackett
Joan Harrison
John Michael Hayes
Buck Henry
Garson Kanin
Lawrence Kasdan
Howard Koch
Stanley Kubrick
Ring Lardner, Jr.
Ernest Lehman
Ben Maddow
David Mamet
Joseph L. Mankiewicz
Wolf Mankowitz
Elaine May
David Newman
John Osborne
Norman Panama
Harold Pinter
Abraham Polonsky
Michael Powell
David Rabe
Frederic Raphael
Irving Ravetch
Jimmy Sangster
Alvin Sargent
John Sayles
Paul Schrader
Budd Schulberg
Lorenzo Semple, Jr.
Neil Simon
Curt Siodmak
Susan Sontag
Terry Southern
Stewart Stern
Oliver Stone
Jo Swerling
Daniel Taradash
Steve Tesich
Robert Towne
Billy Wilder

Supplement 2: Radio Writers

Douglas Adams
Rhys Adrian
John Arden
Howard Barker
Peter Barnes
Samuel Beckett
Barry Bermange
Rachel Billington
Frederick Bradnum
Angela Carter
Barry Collins
Michael Cook
Giles Cooper
Martin Crimp
Stephen Davis
Ian Dougall
Stephen Dunstone
Peter Everett
John Fletcher
Colin Free
Shirley Gee
Carey Harrison
Don Haworth
Susan Hill
Gabriel Josipovici
Barrie Keeffe
Anne Leaton
Gwendolyn MacEwen
Steve May
Mavor Moore
Joe Orton
Stewart Parker
Jennifer Phillips
Harold Pinter
David Pownall
Jonathan Raban
Derek Raby
Frederic Raphael
Martyn Read
Peter Redgrove
John Reeves
John P. Rooney
David Rudkin
Christopher Russell
Andrew Sachs
Michael Sadler
James Saunders
R.C. Scriven
Tom Stoppard
Rose Tremain
William Trevor
Elizabeth Troop
Michael Wall
Fay Weldon
George Woodcock
J. Michael Yates

Supplement 3: Television Writers

Jim Allen
Alan Bennett
Alan Bleasdale
Howard Brenton
Robin Chapman
Donald Churchill
Tom Clarke
Farrukh Dhondy
Nell Dunn
Clive Exton
Richard Eyre
John Finch
Wilfred Greatorex
Trevor Griffiths
Christopher Hampton
David Hare
Robert Holles
Arthur Hopcraft
Julia Jones
Nigel Kneale
Derek Marlowe
Troy Kennedy Martin
Peter McDougall
Ian McEwan
David Mercer
Julian Mitchell
John Mortimer
David Nobbs
Jeremy Paul
Stephen Poliakoff
Dennis Potter
Frederic Raphael
Graham Reid
Jack Rosenthal
David Rudkin
Jeremy Sandford
Howard Schuman
Mike Stott
Ken Taylor
Michael Wall
Fay Weldon
Colin Welland
Ted Whitehead
Donald Wilson

Supplement 4: Musical Librettists

George Abbott
Don Appell
Howard Ashman
Lionel Bart
Mark Bramble
William F. Brown
Al Carmines
Warren Casey
Jerome Chodorov
Betty Comden
C.C. Courtney
Beverley Cross
Gretchen Cryer
Ossie Davis
Donald Driver
Fred Ebb
Tom Eyen
Harvey Fierstein
William Finn
George Furth
William Gibson
James Goldman
John Gray
Adolph Green
Peggy Harmon
William Hauptman
Rupert Holmes
Jim Jacobs
Tom Jones
Garson Kanin
Larry L. King
Arthur Kopit
James Lapine
Arthur Laurents
Jerome Lawrence
Robert E. Lee
Joshua Logan
Stephen Longstreet
Joe Masteroff
Peter Masterson
Timothy S. Mayer
Terrence McNally
Thomas Meehan
Arthur Miller
Robert Nemiroff
Anthony Newley
Richard O'Brien
Sybille Pearson
Polly Pen
John R. Powers
James Rado
Gerome Ragni
Bob Randall
Tim Rice
Philip Rose
Budd Schulberg
Maurice Sendak
Ned Sherrin
Neil Simon
Bella Spewack
Joseph Stein
Richard Stilgoe
Peter Stone
Samuel Taylor
Garry Trudeau
Peter Udell
Melvin Van Peebles
Dick Vosburgh
Dale Wasserman
Jerome Weidman
John Weidman
Sandy Wilson
Aubrey Woods
Charlotte Zaltzberg

Supplement 5: Theatre Groups

Antenna Theater
At the Foot of the Mountain
ATC
Avon Touring Theatre Company
Black Theatre Co-operative
Bread and Puppet Theatre
CAST
Cheek by Jowl
DAC Theatre Company
Dell'Arte Players Company
Foco Novo Theatre Company
Footsbarn Theatre Company
Forkbeard Fantasy
Gay Sweatshop
Graeae
Hesitate and Demonstrate
Hidden Grin
Hull Truck Theatre Company
Impact Theatre Co-operative
Intimate Strangers
IOU Theatre
Joint Stock Theatre Group
The Living Theatre
Lumiere and Son
Mabou Mines
Modern Times Theater
Monstrous Regiment
Natural Theatre
New York Street Theater Caravan
Nightfire
Nightletter Theatre
No Theater
Omaha Magic Theatre
Paines Plough
The People Show
Performance Group
Performanceworks
Red Ladder Theatre
Roadside Theater
San Francisco Mime Troupe
7:84 Theatre Company
Shared Experience
Pip Simmons Theatre Group
Soon 3
Squat Theatre
Tara Arts Group
El Teatro Campesino
El Teatro de la Esperanza
Temba
A Traveling Jewish Theatre
Welfare State International
Women's Theatre Group
The Wooster Group

Appendix

Brendan Behan
Giles Cooper
Lorraine Hansberry
William Inge
David Mercer
Joe Orton
John Whiting

ABBENSETTS, Michael. British. Born in British Guiana (now Guyana), 8 June 1938; became British citizen, 1974. Educated at Queen's College, Guyana, 1952–56; Stanstead College, Quebec; Sir George Williams University, Montreal, 1960–61. Security attendant, Tower of London, 1963–67; staff member, Sir John Soane Museum, London, 1968–71. Resident playwright, Royal Court Theatre, London, 1974; Visiting Professor of Drama, Carnegie Mellon University, Pittsburgh, 1981. Recipient: George Devine award, 1973; Arts Council bursary, 1977; Afro-Caribbean award, 1979. Agent: Anthony Sheil Associates, 43 Doughty Street, London WC1N 2LF, England.

PUBLICATIONS

Plays

Sweet Talk (produced London, 1973; New York, 1974). London, Eyre Methuen, 1976.
Alterations (produced London and New York, 1978; revised version produced London, 1985).
Samba (produced London, 1980). London, Eyre Methuen, 1980.
In the Mood (produced London, 1981).
Outlaw (produced Leicester and London, 1983).
El Dorado (produced London, 1984).

Radio Plays: *Home Again*, 1975; *The Sunny Side of the Street*, 1977; *Brothers of the Sword*, 1978; *The Fast Lane*, 1980; *The Dark Horse*, 1981; *Summer Passions*, 1985.

Television Plays: *The Museum Attendant*, 1973; *Inner City Blues*, 1975; *Crime and Passion*, 1976; *Black Christmas*, 1977; *Roadrunner*, 1977; *Empire Road* series, 1977, 1979; *Easy Money*, 1982; *Big George Is Dead*, 1987.

Novel

Empire Road (novelization of television series). London, Panther, 1979.

*

Critical Study: "Taking Race for Granted" by Margaret Walters, in *New Society* (London), 16 November 1978.

Michael Abbensetts comments:

(1982) I once read something a black American playwright had written: he said his plays could not be understood by a white person. That is not the way I feel about my plays. It seems to me that if a play is good enough it should have something to say to everybody, once they are prepared to look for that something. However, having said that, I would like to add that I would never want to write a play that a black audience did not like, no matter how popular it was with a white audience. When my stage play *Alterations* was praised by critics of the *Sunday Times* and the *Financial Times*, it made me feel very pleased, but I was equally pleased that the reviewer in the *Jamaica Gleaner* liked the play as well.

Which brings me to the question I am sometimes asked. Why do I write so much for television? First, BBC-TV pays me well—okay, *reasonably* well—and second, my TV plays are bound to reach a larger black audience than my stage plays ever do.

Yet originally I had never even thought of writing for the theatre. Originally I wanted to be a novelist. Then while I was at university in Canada I saw a version of Osborne's *Look Back in Anger*, and suddenly I knew what I wanted to be—a playwright. So then I came to England. Other West Indians were coming to the UK to find jobs, I came here to find theatre. I'd read of a place called the Royal Court Theatre, and I vowed to myself to get one of my plays on there, even though, at that time, I hadn't even written a single play. Yet in time I did get a play on at the Royal Court, and I was made resident dramatist at the Court. A lot has happened to me since those first, heady days at the Royal Court Theatre.

* * *

The majority of black British playwrights emerged in the 1970's. Michael Abbensetts is quite simply the best of these. His first work to be widely noticed, a 1973 television play *The Museum Attendant*, struck the two notes that characterize all of his output. First, it worked out a tragic situation within a broad tradition of comedy; the humour arises primarily from incongruity, though there are fine instances of verbal felicity and wit. In the juxtaposition of tragedy and comedy Abbensetts goes back to English Renaissance drama, though the more immediate mentor is probably Albee. Second, his work stood out because it was practically the first time that television drama had shown an accurate slice of immigrant life. A whole generation of television sitcoms (*Love Thy Neighbour* and *Mixed Blessings* were then the latest) had taken race as their main, if not sole, theme. With their appalling racialist jokes, shown on the dubious grounds of "therapeutic value," these plays were deeply upsetting to many people. *The Fosters*, the only previous all-black comedy series, was welcomed by black people but showed its American origins too clearly to be more than an aperitif. *Gangsters*, another television series, also with racialist jokes and in an American blood-and-thunder movie tradition, was more controversial. Condemned as "vicious and vacuous," it was also praised for "somehow managing to suggest more of the corruption and reasons for racial tension than a score of more balanced and realistic programmes." It did not, however, affect the convention of cardboard blacks who were a "problem," or were pawns in arguments about British politics—e.g., in the automatic coupling of racism and fascism. Generally, blacks in plays were just plain stupid, as in *Curry and Chips* or *Till Death Us Do Part*. At best, the presence of blacks on television consoled a liberal conscience.

Abbensetts's achievement in presenting a black viewpoint on black life in Britain allowed his characters to emerge as fully human beings for the very first time in the history of British performing media. He provides an honest picture of the diversity of black people, with individuals as sincere, muddled, feckless, wicked, or wonderful as might come from any other group. In contrast to the work of otherwise fine black playwrights such as Mustapha Matura, Abbensetts's work is free from defensive clowning.

Abbensetts has said that *Black Christmas* constitutes his claim to be taken seriously as a writer. In it a West Indian family under the peculiar strains of life in Britain holds together only by sheer will; Abbensetts can be seen, then, as working also in a tradition of domestic drama, though "domestic" needs to be understood in its extended Third World rather than nuclear Western sense. The concentrated impact of the concerns of *Black Christmas* was spun out into two series called *Empire Road*. Slicker if slighter than the single play, this established Abbensetts with the public. In the second series, especially, he was able to match his writing to the personality and strength of the actors. *D.I.V.O.R.C.E.*, the seventh episode of the second series, is generally considered the best; and in its most praised section two of the characters, now drunk, reminisce about their life in Britain, and especially those experiences that are traumatic or hideous. Abbensetts often presents middle-aged characters haunted by memory, a device that enables him to add irony and bite to his plays. In *D.I.V.O.R.C.E.* that haunted hinterland of memory has a rich dramatic impact that itself comes to haunt viewers.

It is, however, the stage play *Alterations* that is Abbensetts's best complete work. Walker, a West Indian tailor, is desperately racing against the clock, trying to alter an immense number of trousers to sizes suitable for export to Japan: if he can finish this work, he will earn enough money in time to pay the deposit and begin to realize a life-long ambition of having his own shop. The pressures created by the situation impose a series of alterations in the lives, attitudes, and expectations of all the characters in the play: Walker himself, Horace and Buster, who intermittently help and hinder Walker, and Walker's discarded wife Darlene, to whom he is still attached in a strange West Indian way. All of Abbensetts's plays are, to a certain extent, parables. Though he tends to pack too much into his stage plays, they seem generally to be better constructed than his television plays.

His best television play is the recent *Big George Is Dead.* At Big George's funeral Tony appears, having returned prosperous from Tobago to repay the money he owes his former friend Boogie. For old times' sake, Tony and Boogie decide to relive their glorious past: back in the swinging sixties Boogie, Tony, and Big George were three black desperadoes calling themselves "the wild bunch." Identities forged on the frontline of Soho nightlife are tested in a London that now has punks, muggers, drug dealers. As the night wears on, the two become more and more immersed in the tragic sense of loss in their lives—particularly Tony, whose girlfriend married Boogie when Tony was forced to disappear to Tobago. Tony's son has been adopted by Boogie, and no-one wants the boy to realize the truth. Here is an understated, atmospheric play, finely testifying to Abbensetts's reluctant cleavage from his earlier comic mode, making it possible for him richly to explore the muted tragedies of everyday people, everyday lives.

Abbensetts was criticized earlier, by black and white activists, for his lack of political commitment. Over the years it has become clear that he does have a political vision, though it is not of course rendered in terms of British political allegiances. He has a larger vision of immigrant groups as incipiently one community, an all-embracing refuge which strengthens black people to tackle the problems presented by the alien white man's world in which they live. But Abbensetts also portrays the actualities of the relations between the different immigrant groups, as well as between generations, and raises the question of where this community is headed.

—Prabhu S. Guptara

ABBOTT, George (Francis). American. Born in Forestville, New York, 25 June 1887. Educated at Hamburg High School, New York; Rochester University, Rochester, New York, B.A. 1911; Harvard University, Cambridge, Massachusetts, 1912–13. Married 1) Ednah Levis in 1914 (died 1930), one daughter; 2) Mary Sinclair in 1946 (marriage dissolved 1951); 3) Joy Moana Valderrama in 1983. Founder, with Philip Dunning, Abbott-Dunning Inc., 1931–34. Recipient: Boston *Globe* award, 1912; Donaldson award, for directing, 1946, 1948, 1953, 1955; Tony award, 1955, 1956, 1960, and for directing, 1960, 1963, Special Tony, 1987; Pulitzer Prize, 1960; New York Drama Critics Circle award, 1960; Lawrence Langner award, 1976; City of New York Handel Medallion, 1976; Kennedy Center award, 1983. D.H.: Rochester University, 1961; H.H.D.: University of Miami, 1974. Address: 1270 Avenue of the Americas, New York, New York 10020, U.S.A.

Publications

Plays

The Head of the Family (produced Cambridge, Massachusetts, 1912).

Man in the Manhole (produced Boston, 1912).

The Fall Guy, with James Gleason (produced Milwaukee, 1924; New York, 1925; London, 1926). New York, French, 1928.

A Holy Terror: A None-Too-Serious Drama, with Winchell Smith (produced New York, 1925). New York, French, 1926.

Love 'em and Leave 'em, with John V.A. Weaver (also director: produced New York, 1926). New York, French, 1926.

Cowboy Crazy, with Pearl Franklin (produced New York, 1926).

Broadway, with Philip Dunning (also director: produced New York and London, 1926). New York, Doran, 1927.

Four Walls, with Dana Burnet (also director: produced New York, 1927). New York, French, 1928.

Coquette, with Ann Preston Bridgers (also director: produced New York, 1927; London, 1929). New York, Longman, 1928.

Ringside, with Edward A. Paramore, Jr., and Hyatt Daab (also director: produced New York, 1928).

Those We Love, with S.K. Lauren (also director: produced New York, 1930).

Lilly Turner, with Philip Dunning (also director: produced New York, 1932).

Heat Lightning, with Leon Abrams (also director: produced New York, 1933).

Ladies' Money (also director: produced New York, 1934).

Page Miss Glory (also director: produced New York, 1934).

Three Men on a Horse, with John Cecil Holm (also director: produced New York, 1935; London, 1936). New York, French, 1935.

On Your Toes, music and lyrics by Richard Rodgers and Lorenz Hart (also director: produced New York, 1936; London, 1937; revised version produced New York, 1983; London, 1984).

Sweet River, adaptation of the novel *Uncle Tom's Cabin* by Harriet Beecher Stowe (also director: produced New York, 1936).

The Boys from Syracuse, music and lyrics by Richard Rodgers and Lorenz Hart, adaptation of *A Comedy of Errors* by Shakespeare (also director: produced New York, 1938; London, 1963).

Best Foot Forward, with John Cecil Holm (also director: produced New York, 1941).

Beat the Band, with George Marion, Jr. (also director: produced New York, 1942).

Where's Charley?, music and lyrics by Frank Loesser, adaptation of the play *Charley's Aunt* by Brandon Thomas (also director: produced New York, 1948; London, 1958). London, French, 1965.

A Tree Grows in Brooklyn, with Betty Smith, adaptation of the novel by Smith (also director: produced New York, 1951).

The Pajama Game, with Richard Bissell, music by Richard Adler and Jerry Ross, adaptation of the novel *7½ Cents* by Bissell (also co-director: produced New York, 1954; London, 1955). New York, Random House, and London, Williamson Music, 1954.

Damn Yankees, with Douglass Wallop, music by Richard Adler and Jerry Ross, adaptation of the novel *The Year the Yankees Lost the Pennant* by Wallop (also director: produced New York, 1955; London, 1957). New York, Random House, 1956.

New Girl in Town, music and lyrics by Bob Merrill, adaptation of the play *Anna Christie* by Eugene O'Neill (also director: produced New York, 1957). New York, Random House, 1958.

Fiorello!, with Jerome Weidman, music and lyrics by Sheldon Harnick and Jerry Bock (also director: produced New York, 1959; Bristol and London, 1962). New York, Random House, 1960.

Tenderloin, with Jerome Weidman, music and lyrics by Sheldon Harnick and Jerry Bock, adaptation of the work by Samuel Hopkins Adams (also director: produced New York, 1960). New York, Random House, 1961.

Flora, The Red Menace, with Robert Russell, music and lyrics by John Kander and Fred Ebb (also director: produced New York, 1965).

Anya, with Guy Bolton, music and lyrics by Robert Wright and George Forrest, adaptation of the play *Anastasia* by Marcelle Maurette and Bolton (also director: produced New York, 1965).

Music Is, music by George Adler, lyrics by Will Holt, adaptation of *Twelfth Night* by Shakespeare (also director: produced Seattle and New York, 1976).

Tropicana, music by Robert Nassif, lyrics by Nassif and Peter Napolitano (also director: produced New York, 1985).

Screenplays: *The Saturday Night Kid*, with others, 1929; *Why Bring That Up?*, with others, 1929; *Half-Way to Heaven*, with Gerald Geraghty, 1929; *All Quiet on the Western Front*, with others, 1930; *The Sea God*, 1930; *Manslaughter*, 1930; *Stolen Heaven*, 1931; *Secrets of a Secretary*, with Dwight Taylor, 1931; *The Pajama Game*, with Richard Bissell, 1957; *Damn Yankees* (*What Lola Wants*), 1958.

Novels

Broadway (novelization of stage play), with Philip Dunning. New York, Doran, 1927; London, Hutchinson, 1928.

Tryout. Chicago, Playboy Press, 1979.

Other

Mister Abbott (autobiography). New York, Random House, 1963.

*

Theatrical Activities:
Director: **Plays**—most of his own plays, and *Lightnin'* by Winchell Smith and Frank Bacon, New York, 1918; *Chicago* by Maurice Watkins, New York, 1927; *Spread Eagle* by George S. Brooks and Walter S. Lister, New York, 1927; *Bless You, Sister* by John Meehan and Robert Riskin, New York, 1927; *Gentlemen of the Press* by Ward Morehouse, New York, 1928; *Jarnegan* by Charles Beahen and Garrett Fort, New York, 1928; *Poppa* by Bella and Sam Spewack, New York, 1928; *Louder, Please* by Norman Krasna, New York, 1931; *The Great Magoo* by Ben Hecht and Gene Fowler, New York, 1932; *Twentieth Century* by Ben Hecht and Charles MacArthur, New York, 1932, 1971; *The Drums Begin* by Howard Irving Young, New York, 1933; *John Brown* by Ronald Gow, New York, 1934; *Kill That Story* by Harry Madden and Philip Dunning, New York, 1934; *Small Miracle* by Norman Krasna, New York, 1934; *Jumbo* by Richard Rodgers and Lorenz Hart, New York, 1935; *Boy Meets Girl* by Bella and Sam Spewack, New York, 1935; *Brother Rat* by John Monks, Jr., and Fred F. Finklehoffe, New York, 1936; *Room Service* by John Murray and Allen Boretz, New York, 1937; *Angel Island* by Bernie Angus, New York, 1937; *Brown Sugar* by Bernie Angus, New York, 1937; *All That Glitters* by John Baragwanath and Kenneth Simpson, New York, 1938; *What a Life* by Clifford Goldsmith, New York, 1938; *You Never Know* by Cole Porter, New York, 1938; *The Primrose Path* by Robert Buckner and Walter Hart, New York, 1939; *Mrs. O'Brien Entertains* by Harry Madden, New York, 1939; *Too Many Girls* by George Marion, Jr., New York, 1939; *Ring Two* by Gladys Harlbut, New York, 1939; *The White-Haired Boy* by Charles Martin and Beatrice Kaufman, Boston, 1939; *The Unconquered* by Ayn Rand, New York, 1940; *Goodbye in the Night* by Jerome Mayer, New York, 1940; *Pal Joey* by John O'Hara, music by Richard Rodgers, lyrics by Lorenz Hart, New York, 1940; *Sweet Charity*, by Irving Brecher and Manuel Seff, New York, 1942; *Kiss and Tell* by F. Hugh Herbert, New York, 1943; *Get Away Old Man* by William Saroyan, New York, 1943; *A Highland Fling* by J.L. Galloway, New York, 1944; *Snafu* by Louis Solomon and Harold Buchman, New York, 1944; *On the Town* by Betty Comden and Adolph Green, New York, 1944; *Mr. Cooper's Left Hand* by Clifford Goldsmith, Boston, 1945; *Billion Dollar Baby* by Betty Comden and Adolph Green, New York, 1945; *One Shoe Off* by Mark Reed, New Haven, Connecticut, 1946; *Beggar's Holiday* by John La Touche (restaged), New York, 1946; *It Takes Two* by Virginia Faulkner and Sana Suesse, New York, 1947; *Barefoot Boy with Cheek* by Max Shulman, New York, 1947; *High Button Shoes* by Stephen Longstreet, music and lyrics by Jule Styne and Sammy Kahn, New York, 1947; *Look Ma, I'm Dancin'* by Jerome Lawrence and Robert E. Lee, music by Hugh Martin, New York, 1948; *Mrs. Gibbons' Boys* by Will Glickman and Joseph Stein, New York, 1949; *Tickets Please* (revue; restaged and rewritten), New York, 1950; *Call Me Madam* by Howard Lindsay and Russel Crouse, music and lyrics by Irving Berlin, New York, 1950; *Out of This World* by Dwight Taylor and Reginald Lawrence (restaged), New York, 1950; *The Number* by Arthur Carter, New York, 1951; *In Any Language* by Edmund Beloin and Harry Garson, New York, 1952; *Wonderful Town* by Joseph Fields and Jerome Chodorov, music by Leonard Bernstein, lyrics by Betty Comden and Adolph Green, New York, 1953; *Me and Juliet* by Richard Rodgers and Oscar Hammerstein II, New York, 1953; *Drink to Me Only* by Abram S. Ginnes and Ira Wallach, New York, 1958; *Once upon a Mattress* by Jay Thompson and others, New York, 1959; *Take Her, She's Mine* by Phoebe and Henry Ephron, New York, 1961; *A Call on Kuprin* by Jerome Lawrence and Robert E. Lee, New York, 1961; *A Funny Thing Happened on the Way to the Forum* by Burt Shevelove and Larry Gelbart, music and lyrics by Stephen Sondheim, New York, 1962, London, 1963; *Never Too Late* by Sumner Arthur Long, New York, 1962, London, 1963; *Fade Out—Fade In* by Betty Comden and Adolph Green, music by Jule Styne, New York, 1964; *Help Stamp Out Marriage* by Keith Waterhouse and Willis Hall,

New York, 1966; *Agatha Sue, I Love You* by Abe Einhorn, New York, 1966; *How Now, Dow Jones* by Max Shulman, New York, 1967; *The Education of Hyman Kaplan* by Benjamin Zavin, New York, 1969; *The Fig Leaves Are Falling* by Allan Sherman, New York, 1969; *Norman Is That You* by Ron Clark and Sam Bobrick, New York, 1970; *Winning Isn't Everything* by Lee Kalcheim, New York, 1978. **Films**—*The Carnival Man*, 1929; *The Bishop's Candlesticks*, 1929; *Why Bring That Up?*, 1929; *Half-Way to Heaven*, 1929; *The Sea God*, 1930; *Manslaughter*, 1930; *Stolen Heaven*, 1931; *Secrets of a Secretary*, 1931; *My Sin*, 1931; *The Cheat*, 1931; *Too Many Girls*, 1940; *Kiss and Tell*, 1945; *The Pajama Game* (co-director, with Stanley Donen), 1957; *Damn Yankees* (co-director, with Stanley Donen), 1958. **Television**—*U.S. Royal Showcase*, 1952.

Actor: **Plays**—"Babe" Merrill in *The Misleading Lady* by Charles Goddard and Paul Dickey, New York, 1913; in *The Queen's Enemies* by Lord Dunsany, New York, 1916; Henry Allen in *Daddies* by John L. Hobble,New York, 1918; Sylvester Cross in *The Broken Wing* by Charles Goddard and Paul Dickey, New York, 1920; in *Dulcy* by Marc Connelly and George S. Kaufman, toured, 1921; Texas in *Zander the Great* by Salisbury Field, New York, 1923; Sverre Peterson in *White Desert* by Maxwell Anderson, New York, 1923; Sid Hunt in *Hell-Bent fer Heaven* by Hatcher Hughes, New York, 1924; Steve Tuttle in *Lazybones* by Owen Davis, New York, 1924; Dynamite Jim in *Processional* by John Howard Lawson, New York, 1925; Dirk Yancey in *A Holy Terror*, New York, 1925; in *Cowboy Crazy*, New York, 1926; Frederick Williston in *Those We Love*, New York, 1930; title role in *John Brown* by Ronald Gow, New York, 1934; Mr. Antrobus in *The Skin of Our Teeth* by Thornton Wilder, New York, 1955.

* * *

George Abbott called his autobiography *Mister Abbott*, but *Mister Broadway* would have been more apt. Abbott notes: "From 1935 to this time [1963] I have, with the exception of a week or two, always had at least one play running on Broadway." Accepting without question the hit/flop mentality of the Broadway marketplace, Abbott is a professional showman whose canon is altogether undisturbed by the least suggestion of intellect. The Abbott production is a good show, a farce, a melodrama, a musical comedy; briskly paced, it is geared for the big laugh, the big climax, and its light-fingered, high-stepping rhythm naturally does not translate well to the library.

The Abbott play comes wrapped in two basic packages: the racy, slangy comedies and melodramas of the 1920's and 1930's, and the musical comedies of the 1940's and 1950's. In both kinds of plays, the colorful details of a milieu or particular way of life offer the appeal. Abbott's plots (Abbott almost always worked with a collaborator) are neither especially compelling nor well constructed. The "gimmick" is the milieu: the politics in *Fiorello!*, baseball in *Damn Yankees*, factory routine in *The Pajama Game*, the red-light district in *Tenderloin*. Sports, politics, the working class: the Abbott musical takes for its field of action a significant aspect of American life, only to reinforce popular myths of Americana. Relentlessly unexploratory, an Abbott show is indebted almost exclusively to the conventions of Broadway folklore. Entertainments like *The Pajama Game* and *Fiorello!* introduce a spurious kind of rebellious hero—a gal who wants the workers to get a raise, a mayor who tries to buck the compromises and corruptions of the political machine. But reinforcing rather than countering cliché, the shows ultimately leave the status quo unruffled. On the stage, aided by the music, and by the charm and élan of Abbott direction, the weaknesses of the books are camouflaged; on the page, unadorned, the plays are dreary, devoid not only of "ideas" but of spirit as well.

Abbott's earlier collaborations are much more flavorful. *Broadway*, a melodrama that combines prohibition, gang warfare, and the clichés of the backstage musical, is a lively and engaging portrait of an era. The earthy dialogue captures the lingo of the gangster and the entertainer; the slang has its own peculiar kind of melody, and the story—murder and retribution—is comfortably situated against the prohibition nightclub setting. *Three Men on a Horse* does for bookies what *Broadway* does for hoods: gives them the status of popular myth. This time the genre is farce rather than melodrama, but the same perky, accurate yet subtly stylized dialogue prevails. In less successful, but equally "contemporary" plays like *The Fall Guy* and *Love 'em and Leave 'em*, Abbott and his collaborators regard from the same sly angle other scenes of the 1920's. The fall guy goes wrong with some hoods, is caught and reprimanded, and returns chastened to his long-suffering wife. *Love 'em and Leave 'em* is a harsh portrait of a dame on the make; she'll go out with the highest bidder, the one who can give her the most diamonds and furs. Her schemes of self-advancement are set against the problems of the tenants of a working-class rooming house. The plays seem quaint today, but these glimpses into an America of the past retain their undignified comic and melodramatic energy. Artifacts of popular culture, the plays record the values and the aspirations and the setbacks and the sins of various character types of a turbulent and appealing era.

A shrewd practical man of the theatre, Abbott has given Broadway audiences what they have wanted to see, and he has entertained them more often, and over a longer period of time, than any other professional in the history of the American theatre. That is a revealing if not an especially happy statistic.

—Foster Hirsch

ABLEMAN, Paul. British. Born in Leeds, Yorkshire, 13 June 1927; brought up in New York. Attended King's College, University of London. Military service: 3 years. Married; one son. Agent: Jonathan Clowes Ltd., 22 Prince Albert Road, London NW1 7ST. Address: 36 Duncan House, Fellows Road, London N.W.3, England.

PUBLICATIONS

Plays

Even His Enemy, with Gertrude Macauley (as *Letters to a Lady*, produced London, 1951). London, French, 1948.
Help! (revue; produced London, 1963).
One Hand Clapping (revue; produced Edinburgh, 1964).
Dialogues (produced London, 1965).
Green Julia (produced Edinburgh and London, 1965; Washington, D.C., 1968; New York, 1972). London, Methuen, and New York, Grove Press, 1966.
Tests (sketches). London, Methuen, 1966.
Emily and Heathcliff (produced London, 1967).

Blue Comedy: Madly in Love, Hank's Night (produced London, 1968). London, Methuen, 1968; *Madly in Love* published in *Modern Short Comedies from Broadway and London*, edited by Stanley Richards, New York, Random House, 1969.
The Black General, adaptation of *Othello* (produced London, 1969).
And Hum Our Sword (produced London, 1973).
Little Hopping Robin (produced London, 1973).
The Visitor (produced London, 1974).
Windsor All-Sorts (produced London, 1977).

Radio Play: *The Infant*, 1974.

Television Plays: *Barlowe of the Car Park*, 1961; *That Woman Is Wrecking Our Marriage*, 1969; *Visits from a Stranger*, 1970; *The Catch in a Cold*, 1970; *The Wrong 'Un*, from a work by Michael Brett, 1983; *Love Song*, from a novel by Jeffrey Archer, 1985; *A Killing on the Exchange* series, 1987.

Novels

I Hear Voices. Paris, Olympia Press, 1957; London, New English Library, 1966.
As Near as I Can Get. London, Spearman, 1962.
Vac. London, Gollancz, 1968.
The Twilight of the Vilp. London, Gollancz, 1969.
Tornado Pratt. London, Gollancz, 1977.
Shoestring (novelization of television play). London, BBC Publications, 1979.
Porridge (novelization of screenplay). London, Pan, 1979.
Shoestring's Finest Hour. London, BBC Publications, 1980.
County Hall (novelization of television series). London, BBC Publications, 1981.
Hi-De-Hi (novelization of television series). London, BBC Publications, 1983.

Verse

Bits: Some Prose Poems. London, Latimer Press, 1969.

Other

The Mouth and Oral Sex. London, Running Man Press, 1969; as *The Mouth*, London, Sphere, 1972; as *The Sensuous Mouth*, New York, Ace, 1972.
Anatomy of Nakedness. London, Orbis, 1982; as *The Banished Body*, London, Sphere, 1984.
The Doomed Rebellion. London, Zomba, 1983.

Translator, with Veronica Hall, *Egypt*, by Simonne Lacourture. London, Vista, 1963.

* * *

Paul Ableman's dramatic output so far is small, but striking, both for the unpretentious wit of its dialogue and for the moral concern implicit in its characterization and plot. It is obviously too early to talk of "overriding themes," but one central concern would seem to be the difficulty of reconciling sexual fulfilment with good conscience and consideration for others. Certainly this is so in *Green Julia*, probably his most impressive piece to date, and as thoughtful a study of the hypocrisies of male sexuality as the modern theatre has produced.

There are only two characters onstage, Jake and Bob: the Julia of the title remains offstage throughout, a presence constantly invoked by them and, by the end of the play, a substantial one. Jake is leaving England, probably for a long time, and feels a faint guilt about Julia, the erratic, self-absorbed but generous divorcée he has made his mistress. Gradually, it becomes clear that he wants Bob, his best friend, to take her off his mind by taking her over. But Bob, who is the more morally pretentious of the two, affects both to despise her ("the most depraved old whore in Southern England") and to have a woman of his own. Not only will he reject the idea, he appears to resent it; and the verbal games the two men constantly play with each other (in which they imitate army officers, psychiatrists, university professors, anything capable of easy parody) become increasingly hostile. It is no longer possible to continue camouflaging their true feelings in such a way. Bob comes right out with: "What is your relationship with Julia? You never treat her, never help her or worry about her, hardly ever think about her except on the odd evenings when you happen to feel randy and she's available." This is clearly true; and yet, as we also gradually discover, Bob's stance is a fraud. He is inexperienced, anxious for sexual discovery, and likely to prove as unscrupulous as Jake in achieving it. The curtain falls on the arrival of Julia, who is evidently destined to be exploited by others until what promises to be a raddled and lonely old age.

By the end, the contrast between the jocular, harmless manner of these very ordinary young men and the callousness of their intentions is unmissable, and makes the play more than the light comedy it has at times pretended to be. With Ableman's other pieces on the same theme, however, there is no question of pretence. Both *Hank's Night* and *Madly in Love* leave a less bitter aftertaste, presumably because in each case mutual consent replaces exploitation and the tone can therefore remain good-humoured and amused. In *Madly in Love* an eccentric poet poses as a psychiatrist in the hope of losing his virginity by seducing a girl whose quirk is to obey every order she is given: the irony is that the shock of being told "make love to me" cures her, whereupon she freely gives herself to him in gratitude for his help. In *Hank's Night* two couples try to persuade themselves and each other to start an orgy, and fail lamentably until they give up the attempt, whereupon the thing actually happens, spontaneously and unselfconsciously. The moral of both plays, and perhaps also of *Green Julia*, may be that those who do not seek to manipulate others and bend them to their will may receive something the more satisfying for being offered freely and without constraint. In the most unpretentious way, Ableman's work is a criticism of the earnestness and anxiety that attaches to sex nowadays, with so many people regarding it, not as a means of cementing genuine relationships or even as a form of enjoyment, but as a mere proof of personal adequacy.

All these pieces are naturalistic, or nearly so: Ableman has also written some 50 surrealist sketches under the general title of *Tests*, some of which have been performed in *One Hand Clapping* and other revues, and most of which prove to have little more to offer than verbal invention and a vague aura of "absurdism." One speech, typical both in the apparent arbitrariness of its language and in its facetiousness, reads: "A mammal of an estuary saluted a kindly laundryman. With a yelp the match teetered. Pickle all laundrymen. Toast archipelagos as if to pronounce renounce." A few "tests" do, however, seem to have a subject, notably *Johnson*, a parody of military conventions, *She's Dead*, in which two characters parrot cliché responses to violence and death, and *Another Lovely Day*, in which the speakers seek to fox each other by shifting their names and personae. However he develops as a dramatist (and since the 1970's he has applied himself more to the novel), it seems clear that Ableman is strongest when he is handling material that, at least to some extent, engages him as a moralist.

—Benedict Nightingale

ABSE, Dannie. British. Born in Cardiff, Glamorgan, 22 September 1923. Educated at Marlborough Road Elementary School, Cardiff; St. Illtyd's College, Cardiff; University of South Wales and Monmouthshire, Cardiff; King's College, London; Westminster Hospital, London; qualified as physician 1950, M.R.C.S., L.R.C.P. Served in the Royal Air Force, 1951–54: Squadron Leader. Married Joan Mercer in 1951; one son and two daughters. Since 1954 specialist in charge of the chest clinic, Central London Medical Establishment. Senior Fellow in Humanities, Princeton University, New Jersey, 1973–74. Editor, *Poetry and Poverty* magazine, London, 1949–54. Since 1978 President, Poetry Society. Recipient: Foyle award, 1960; Welsh Arts Council award, for poetry, 1971, 1987, for play, 1980; Cholmondeley award, for poetry, 1985. Fellow, Royal Society of Literature, 1983. Agent: Anthony Sheil Associates, 43 Doughty Street, London WC1N 2LF. Address: 85 Hodford Road, London N.W.11, England; or, Green Hollows, Craig-yr-Eos Road, Ogmore-by-Sea, Glamorgan, South Wales.

PUBLICATIONS

Plays

Fire in Heaven (produced London, 1948). London, Hutchinson, 1956; revised version, as *Is the House Shut?* (produced London, 1964); revised version, as *In the Cage*, in *Three Questor Plays*, 1967.
Hands Around the Wall (produced London, 1950).
House of Cowards (produced London, 1960). Included in *Three Questor Plays*, 1967; in *Twelve Great Plays*, edited by Leonard F. Dean, New York, Harcourt Brace, 1970.
The Eccentric (produced London, 1961). London, Evans, 1961.
Gone (produced London, 1962). Included in *Three Questor Plays*, 1967; revised version, as *Gone in January* (produced Edinburgh, 1977; London, 1978), in *Madog* (Pontypridd, Glamorgan), 1981.
The Courting of Essie Glass (as *The Joker*, produced London, 1962; revised version, as *The Courting of Essie Glass*, broadcast 1975). Included in *Miscellany One*, 1981.
Three Questor Plays. Lowestoft, Suffolk, Scorpion Press, 1967.
The Dogs of Pavlov (produced London, 1969; New York, 1974). London, Vallentine Mitchell, 1973.
Funland (produced London, 1975).
Pythagoras (produced Birmingham, 1976; London, 1980). London, Hutchinson, 1979.

Radio Plays: *Conform or Die*, 1957; *No Telegrams, No Thunder*, 1962; *You Can't Say Hello to Anybody*, 1964; *A Small Explosion*, 1964; *The Courting of Essie Glass*, 1975.

Novels

Ash on a Young Man's Sleeve. London, Hutchinson, 1954; New York, Criterion, 1955.
Some Corner of an English Field. London, Hutchinson, 1956; New York, Criterion, 1957.
O. Jones, O. Jones. London, Hutchinson, 1970.

Verse

After Every Green Thing. London, Hutchinson, 1949.
Walking under Water. London, Hutchinson, 1952.
Tenants of the House: Poems 1951–1956. London, Hutchinson, 1957; New York, Criterion, 1959.
Poems, Golders Green. London, Hutchinson, 1962.
Dannie Abse: A Selection. London, Studio Vista, 1963.
A Small Desperation. London, Hutchinson, 1968.
Demo. Frensham, Surrey, Sceptre Press, 1969.
Selected Poems. London, Hutchinson, and New York, Oxford University Press, 1970.
Funland: A Poem in Nine Parts. Portland, Oregon, Portland University Press, 1971.
Corgi Modern Poets in Focus 4, with others, edited by Jeremy Robson. London, Corgi, 1972.
Funland and Other Poems. London, Hutchinson, and New York, Oxford University Press, 1973.
Lunchtime. London, Poem-of-the-Month Club, 1974.
Penguin Modern Poets 26, with D.J. Enright and Michael Longley. London, Penguin, 1975.
Collected Poems 1948–1976. London, Hutchinson, and Pittsburgh, University of Pittsburgh Press, 1977.
Way Out in the Centre. London, Hutchinson, 1981; as *One-Legged on Ice*, Athens, University of Georgia Press, 1983.
Ask the Bloody Horse. London, Hutchinson, 1986.

Recordings: *Poets of Wales*, Argo, 1972; *The Poetry of Dannie Abse*, McGraw Hill, n.d.; *Dannie Abse*, Canto, 1984.

Other

Medicine on Trial. London, Aldus, 1968; New York, Crown, 1969.
A Poet in the Family (autobiography). London, Hutchinson, 1974.
Miscellany One. Bridgend, Glamorgan, Poetry Wales Press, 1981.
A Strong Dose of Myself (essays). London, Hutchinson, 1983.
Under the Influence Of (lecture). Cardiff, University College of Wales, 1984(?).
Journals from the Ant-Heap. London, Hutchinson, 1986.

Editor, with Elizabeth Jennings and Stephen Spender, *New Poems 1956.* London, Joseph, 1956.
Editor, with Howard Sergeant, *Mavericks.* London, Editions Poetry and Poverty, 1957.
Editor, *European Verse.* London, Studio Vista, 1964.
Editor, *Corgi Modern Poets in Focus 1, 3, 5.* London, Corgi, 1971–73.
Editor, *Thirteen Poets.* London, Poetry Book Society, 1973.
Editor, *Poetry Dimension 2–5: The Best of the Poetry Year.* London, Robson, 1974–78; New York, St. Martin's Press, 1976–79; *The Best of the Poetry Year 6–7*, Robson, and Totowa, New Jersey, Rowman and Littlefield, 1979–80.
Editor, *Poetry Supplement, Christmas 1975.* London, Poetry Book Society, 1975.
Editor, *My Medical School.* London, Robson, 1978.
Editor, *Wales in Verse.* London, Secker and Warburg, 1983.
Editor, *Doctors and Patients.* Oxford, Oxford University Press, 1984.

Editor, with others, *Voices in the Gallery*. London, Tate Gallery Publications, 1986.

*

Critical Studies: interviews in *Jewish Quarterly* (London), Winter 1963–64, *Anglo-Welsh Review* (Tenby), Spring 1973, *Three Poets, Two Children* edited by Desmond Badham-Thornhill, Gloucester, Thornhill Press, 1975, *Guardian* (London), 31 January 1978, *Good Housekeeping* (London), May 1981, *The Poetry of Dannie Abse: Critical Essays and Reminiscences* edited by Joseph Cohen, London, Robson, 1983, and *Times* (London), 28 February 1983; "The Physician as Writer" edited by William Claire, in *Literature and Medicine* (Albany, New York), vol. 3, 1984; *Dannie Abse* by Tony Curtis, Cardiff, University of Wales Press, 1985.

* * *

Dannie Abse's work explores the conflicting elements of the human psyche, showing man at war with his own self-destructive urges. As a practising doctor and a Jew, he sees clearly the limitations of the known, and the frightening depths of the subconscious, the irrational tyranny and subservience that underlie the apparent normality of the world. As one who wears both the white coat of the physician, and the magician's purple cloak, he remains wary of the system, and its threat to the individual. Abse sees in institutionalized obedience a force that reduces men and women to objects, detecting in the manipulation of medical experiments those same dark impulses that led to the gas ovens of Auschwitz and Belsen. Memory of the Nazi holocaust colours his writing, recalled in his plays with their potent themes of choice, delusion, the assertion and denial of self, and unquestioning obedience to evil.

Abse is a poet first and foremost and his earliest venture into drama was a verse play, *Fire in Heaven*. Set in an occupied country, it depicts the terrible choice placed before the main character, Christian, who is ordered to kill his family, or have the entire village massacred. After a painful struggle with his conscience, Christian murders his family. The appalling nature of the decision, and the horror of the killing itself, are ably—and shockingly—evoked by the author, although *Fire in Heaven* seems at times to be more akin to poetry than drama. Abse later rewrote it in two prose versions where the contrast is less stark, the occupying soldiers and their commander shown not as monsters, but as human beings caught in a fearful dilemma. Even so, some aspects of the work fail to satisfy completely, with Christian's character over-idealized, and an excess of dialogue betraying the story's poetic origins.

Choice and illusion also feature in *House of Cowards*, a drama based on Abse's poem "Meeting." It centres on the expected visit of the Speaker to a drab, uninteresting town whose inhabitants see him as the answer to their prayers. Eager at his promised coming, they recreate his image in their minds to fit their own requirements. But the Speaker, like Beckett's Godot, does not arrive, although expected the following day. Abse's story bears too close a resemblance to that of Beckett, while his everyday treatment of a symbolic theme renders the work less than effective.

Far better is *The Dogs of Pavlov*, where Abse continues his investigation of choice, and submission to evil. Taking his theme from an actual psychological experiment, he presents a horrifying picture of outwardly normal people only too easily persuaded to inflict pain on their fellows in the interests of "science." The fraught love relationship between Kurt and Sally, whom Abse casts in the roles of victim and torturer, gives pointed emphasis to their situation, while clothing the horror in human terms. The fact that the "pain" is simulated, and the experiment a sham, does nothing to dispel its sinister implications. Abse views the godlike power of the doctors, their arbitrary manipulation of their subjects, as directly linked with the Nazi "experiments" and the concentration camps. Sally's final outburst, begging for death in the "electric chair," is a cry of anguish from a dehumanised victim whose own worst instincts have been realized. Abse displays assurance in the interplay and speech patterns of his characters, and in his use of the stage. *The Dogs of Pavlov* shows human beings operating to destructive effect inside the sheaths of their own illusory ideals.

Similar themes are explored in *Pythagoras*, perhaps Abse's finest play so far. The scene is set in a mental hospital, where a power struggle takes place between the superintendent and an eccentric patient whose individuality constitutes a challenge to his authority. A former stage magician, Pythagoras sees himself as a reincarnation of the Greek sage, whose knowledge combined science, medicine, and religious magic, disciplines whose segregation is embodied in Dr. Aquillus, the superintendent. In the course of the play Pythagoras adopts the persona of his rival, and in one amusing but significant scene a reporter mistakes him for the superintendent and Pythagoras promptly "recreates" Dr. Aquillus as a psychopath. The play is derived from Abse's poem *Funland*, in which Pythagoras dies after a bungled rebellion by the inmates. Here there is a more profound and striking denouement, with Pythagoras collapsing at the moment of confrontation, and recuperating as a "normal" person, shorn of his individuality and powers. Deluded or not, his "fall" is tragic, a triumph of white-coated order over intuitive creation. Abse expands the theme with consummate skill, putting over his dark message with sharp exchanges of dialogue and frequent gems of humour. Here the symbolic and the natural fit together without strain, though their revelation is often bleak, as in the utterance of the patient being "demonstrated" to the medical students: "Yes, I am dead, and this is hell."

Pythagoras is matched on a smaller scale by some of Abse's shorter works. This is true of *Gone*, a one-act play whose basis is a prevented attempt at suicide. Similarly, *The Eccentric*, another one-acter, presents the idea of self-assertion through eccentricity, showing in the figure of the shopkeeper Goldstein a man fulfilled through his idiosyncrasies. His apparent stupidity in refusing to sell customers what they want is revealed as a principle, of self-denial as an ennobling act. "God doesn't say yes to everything," Goldstein tells his young protégé. "Maybe that's what makes a man." Though slight, *The Eccentric* is a poised, appealing work, whose deeper meanings are expressed in clear, individualised speech.

As the descendant of a persecuted race, Abse evokes the horrors of the past. As a writer and healer, he links them to the tyrannies of our own time. His plays, though secondary to his poetic works, sound a warning note that we ignore at our peril.

—Geoff Sadler

ACKLAND, Rodney. British. Born in Westcliffe-on-Sea, Essex, 18 May 1908. Educated at Salesian College, 1915–16; Balham Grammar School, 1916–23; Central School of Speech Training and Dramatic Art, London. Married Mab Lonsdale (daughter of the playwright Frederick Lonsdale) in 1952 (died

1972). Salesman, Swan and Edgar, London, 1924; worked in the silks department, Stagg and Mantles, London, 1925, and in the advertising department, Vacuum Oil Company, London, 1925. Founder, with Roland Gillett, Kinsmen Pictures, 1946. Agent: Eric Glass Ltd., 28 Berkeley Square, London W1X 6HD, England.

PUBLICATIONS

Plays

Improper People (produced London, 1929). London, Heinemann, 1930.
Marion-Ella (produced London, 1930).
Dance with No Music (produced London, 1930). London, Deane, and Boston, Baker, 1933.
Strange Orchestra (produced London, 1931; New York, 1933). London, Gollancz, 1932.
Ballerina, music by Henry Sullivan, lyrics by Desmond Carter, adaptation of the novel by Eleanor Smith (produced London, 1933).
Birthday (produced London, 1934). London, French, 1935.
The White Guard, adaptation of a play by Michael Bulgakov (produced London, 1934).
The Old Ladies, adaptation of the novel by Hugh Walpole (produced London, 1935; as *Night in the House*, produced New York, 1935). London, Gollancz, and New York, French, 1935.
After October (produced London, 1936). London, Gollancz, 1936.
Plot Twenty-One (also director: produced London, 1936).
Yes, My Darling Daughter, adaptation of a work by Mark Reed (produced London, 1937).
The Dark River (as *Remembrance of Things Past*, produced London, 1938; as *The Dark River*, produced London, 1941). London, French, 1942.
Sixth Floor, adaptation of a play by Alfred Ghéri (produced London, 1939).
Blossom Time, music by Schubert (produced London, 1942).
The Diary of a Scoundrel, adaptation of a play by A.N. Ostrovsky (produced London, 1942; New York, 1956). London, Sampson Low, 1948.
Crime and Punishment, adaptation of a novel by Dostoevsky (produced London, 1946; New York, 1947). London, Sampson Low, and New York, Holt, 1948.
Cupid and Mars, with Robert G. Newton, adaptation of a story by Newton (produced London, 1947).
Before the Party, adaptation of a story by W. Somerset Maugham (produced London, 1949). London, French, 1950.
A Multitude of Sins, with Robert G. Newton (produced London, 1951).
The Pink Room; or, The Escapists (produced London, 1952).
A Dead Secret (produced London, 1957). London, French, 1958.
Farewell, Farewell, Eugene, adaptation of a work by John Vari (produced London, 1959; New York, 1960). London, French, 1960; New York, Dramatists Play Service, 1961.
The Other Palace (produced London, 1964).
Smithereens (produced Windsor, 1985).
Absolute Hell! (produced Richmond, Surrey, 1987).

Screenplays: *Number Seventeen*, with Alfred Hitchcock and Alma Reville, 1931; *Yellow Sands*, with Michael Barringer, 1938; *Bank Holiday* (*Three on a Weekend*), with Roger Burford and Hans Wilhelm, 1938; *Keep Smiling* (*Smiling Along*), with Val Valentine, 1938; *The Silent Battle* (*Continental Express*), with Wolfgang Wilhelm, 1939; *Young Man's Fancy*, with Roland Pertwee, 1939; *An Englishman's Home*, with others, 1939; *George and Margaret*, with Brock Williams, 1940; *A Call for Arms*, 1940; *Miss Grant Goes to the Door*, 1940; *Under Your Hat*, with Anthony Kimmins and L. Green, 1940; *Rush Hour*, with Arthur Boys, 1941; *49th Parallel* (*The Invaders*), with Emeric Pressburger, 1941; *Lady Be Kind*, with Arthur Boys, 1941; *Night Watch*, with Reg Graves, 1941; *Dangerous Moonlight* (*Suicide Squadron*), with Terence Young and Brian Desmond Hurst, 1941; *Hatter's Castle*, with Paul Merzbach and Rudolf Bernauer, 1941; *Uncensored*, with Terence Rattigan and Wolfgang Wilhelm, 1942; *The Hundred Pound Window*, with Abem Finkel and Brock Williams, 1943; *Thursday's Child*, with Donald Macardle, 1943; *The School Teacher*, 1944; *Love Story* (*A Lady Surrenders*), with Leslie Arliss and Doreen Montgomery, 1944; *Wanted for Murder*, with Emeric Pressburger, 1946; *Temptation Harbour*, with Victor Skutezky and Frederic Gotfurt, 1947; *Bond Street*, with Terence Rattigan and Anatole de Grunwald, 1948; *The Queen of Spades*, with Arthur Boys, 1949.

Other

The Celluloid Mistress; or, The Custard Pie of Dr. Caligari (autobiography), with Elspeth Grant. London, Wingate, 1954.

*

Critical Studies: article in *Theatre World* (London), January 1939; preface by Romain Fanvic to *The Dark River*, 1942; interview with Frank Granville-Barker, in *Plays and Players* (London), September 1957; articles by Norman Marshall, in *London Magazine*, April 1965, Hilary Spurling in *Spectator* (London), 22 November 1968, and Raymond Marriott in *Stage* (London), November 1968.

Theatrical Activities:
Director: **Plays**—*Plot Twenty-One*, London, 1936; *The Belle of New York* by Hugh Morton, London, 1942; *The Dark River*, London, 1943. **Films**—*Lady Be Kind*, 1941; *A Letter from Home*, 1942; *Thursday's Child*, 1943; *The School Teacher*, 1944.
Actor: **Plays**—Medvedieff in *The Lower Depths* by Gorky, London, 1924; roles with the Oxford Players, and Lubin, Zozim and The He-Ancient in *Back to Methuselah* by Shaw, Edinburgh, late 1920's; title role in *Young Woodley* by John van Druten, toured 1929; Young Man in *The Madonna of the Golden Hart* by Robert G. Newton, London, 1930; Charlie Clive in *The House with the Twisty Windows* by May Pakington, London, 1930; in *Recipe for Murder* by Arnold Ridley, toured, 1932; Joseph in *Musical Chairs* by Ronald Mackenzie, toured, 1933; Paul in *Ballerina*, London, 1933; Karl Opal in *Take Heed* by Leslie Reade, London, 1934; Tony Willow in *Birthday*, London, 1934; Lariossik in *The White Guard*, London, 1934; Tony in *Battle Royal* by Kim Peacock, London, 1934; Oliver Nashwick in *After October*, London, 1936; Henry T. Warner in *A Case of Murder* by John Sheppard, London, 1939. **Films**—*The Case of Gabriel Perry*, 1935; *Alibi*, 1942.

* * *

Rodney Ackland is one of those artists who, temporarily at least, lose on the swings what they have already lost on the roundabouts. In the 1930's when much of his best work was written and performed in small theatre clubs or for short runs in West End theatres, he was highly praised by critics, referred to as "the English Chekhov," but considered too high-brow to become a popular success. The enthusiastic notices for *Strange Orchestra* (directed by John Gielgud) cost Ackland his job with British International Pictures—the company saw no future in employing a serious writer. Now that fashions have changed and even Chekhov has become almost too respectable, Ackland is apt to be dismissed as "commercial," a practitioner of the "well-made play," for no better reason than that critics have learnt so to label a whole period in the English theatre.

His debt to Chekhov is unmistakable. Ackland's plays are organised as ant-heaps or hives in which a group of characters is arbitrarily gathered under one roof either by blood relationship (as in *Birthday* and *After October*) or by lodging together (as in *Strange Orchestra*), by belonging to the same club (*The Pink Room*), working on the same film (*The Other Palace*) or deliberately attempting to reconstruct the past (*The Dark River*). His characters have the same tendency as Chekhov's to follow separate lines of thought which surface abruptly in the middle of someone else's conversation, giving the same complex effect of mental isolation in the midst of physical conglomeration. And Ackland, like Chekhov, uses this effect to exploit the subtle range of emotional tones between comedy and tragedy—egotism, eccentricity, insensitivity, over-sensitivity shading down to loneliness, pathos and despair—intrinsic to the relationship between individuals and the more-or-less closed society of which they are part.

But the comparison with Chekhov will not go far beyond generalities. English middle-class metropolitan society of the period between the two World Wars had little in common with Russian rural society at the end of the 19th century and Ackland is a writer too faithful to his subject matter to follow Chekhov where he cannot lead. Even to use the word "society" in connection with Ackland's work rings false, since his characters are almost without exception those who have been tossed off the central wheel of their time and left lying at the edges, slightly bruised and spattered with mud, likely if they try to stand up again, as they consistently do, to be flung down flatter than before.

In his early play *Strange Orchestra* this process is somewhat too crudely demonstrated: a pair of lovers whose mutual devotion amounts to narcissism try to gas themselves; a girl jilted by a con-man goes blind as well. But, behind the obtrusively engineered story-line, the insecure, neurotic atmosphere of genteel seediness in furnished rooms—the world of Eliot's Prufock and of the typist in *The Waste Land*—is created by a careful accumulation of authentic detail. The play, like so many of Ackland's later and better ones, revolves around one of those elderly mother-figures, raffish, stalwart, broad-minded but none-too-bright, a giver and still more a taker of energy, who are perhaps his most recognisable contributions to the gallery of dramatic types.

Ackland's next play, *Birthday*, has no equal for its overtly humorous but finally savage portrait of a certain kind of English family life. The impenetrable selfishness of these people, the way they mask it as devotion to one another's interests, is expressed even in their appalling dog Jelly—surely the best part ever written for a dog—which has established such a tyranny of habit that its half-gnawed bones cannot be removed from the armchair without causing a scene. The play is weakened only by its heroine, whose attempt to escape from her family is too schematic, whose character is too unexplored, too fairy-tale, to stand up among so many realistic monsters.

No such weakness mars *After October*. It is the hero this time who has to bear the burden of a would-be escape, but although he is in himself a scarcely more realised character than the heroine of *Birthday*, his escape is altogether more tangible. The heroine of *Birthday* is dependent on love to take her away from lovelessness. The theatre is a good place for showing lovelessness and no one is better at it than Ackland, but love is another matter: even Shakespeare is apt to take refuge in formal passages about love rather than attempt a direct demonstration of the thing in action. But in *After October* the means of escape for the hero and all the other characters in his train is to be his success as a playwright. The essential tawdriness of this escape—to be rich and famous instead of poor and unknown—enables Ackland to treat his hero lightly and objectively, without in any way diminishing the pathos of his disillusionment. *After October* is alive with closely observed portraits of the hero's family and friends, including Oliver Nashwick, that doyen of surly poets, whose first words on entering through the window are: "You wish I hadn't come."

Ackland's masterpiece is undoubtedly *The Dark River*, originally entitled *Remembrance of Things Past*. Its themes and characters are easily recognisable from his earlier work, the plot still turns on a failed attempt at escape from a narrowly confined group of "throw-offs," but the play is somehow on a grander and more universal scale than his others. Is this simply because explosions and shouting fascists are heard off-stage, because the little boy spells out "Guernica" from a newspaper headline, because the hero is obsessed with persuading the British government to build deep air-raid shelters? Certainly one has more of a feeling of a large world beyond the wings than in his other plays. But the sense of sombre grandeur and universality is more intrinsic than this. The characters themselves, detailed, idiosyncratic portraits as always in Ackland's work, yet seem to cover more ground than before, to compose less a spectacle than an experience, drawing an audience into losses and defeats which temporarily stand for the audience's own, suggesting not simply that some unfortunates get caught in stagnant backwaters from which there is no escape, but that life itself is such a backwater when it is not infinitely worse, the approaching maelstrom that can be heard offstage.

For all the vagaries of fashion, there is not an English playwright this century more certain of being understood and loved by posterity than Rodney Ackland.

—John Spurling

AIDOO, (Christina) Ama Ata. Ghanaian. Born in Abeadzi Kyiakor in 1942. Educated at the University of Ghana, Legon (Institute of African Studies fellowship), B.A. (honours) 1964; Stanford University, California. Currently Lecturer in English, University of Cape Coast, Ghana. Address: Department of English, University of Cape Coast, Cape Coast, Ghana.

PUBLICATIONS

Plays

The Dilemma of a Ghost (produced Legon, 1964). Accra, Longman, 1965; New York, Macmillan, 1971.

Anowa. London, Longman, and New York, Humanities Press, 1970.

Novel

Our Sister Killjoy; or, Reflections from a Black-eyed Squint. London, Longman, 1977.

Short Stories

No Sweetness Here. London, Longman, 1970; New York, Doubleday, 1971.

Other

Dancing Out Doubts. Enugu, Nigeria, Nok, 1982.
Someone Talking to Sometime. Harare, Zimbabwe, College Press, 1985.

*

Critical Study: *Ama Ata Aidoo: The Dilemma of a Ghost* (study guide) by Jane W. Grant, London, Longman, 1980.

* * *

Although she has published only two plays, Ama Ata Aidoo is one of Africa's most significant playwrights. In both plays she handles situations which have become stock in African drama, but does so in such a way that the usual handling of them is unobtrusively shown to be shallow and conventional. Each goes beyond the commonplace opposition of European and African modes of life, of the modern and the traditional.

The stock situation in *The Dilemma of a Ghost* is the conflict between the "been-to"—the man who has gone to England—and the traditional ideas of his parents. The conflict is exacerbated by the ways of his American wife, Eulalie. An alien wife is also common in African drama, though she is usually white. Eulalie is black and her parents-in-law think it shameful that their son, Ato, has married the descendant of slaves. She finds the ways of his family rather primitive. Eulalie quarrels with her parents-in-law and both sides are increasingly humiliated. The parents, for example, cannot believe in contraception and try to make Eulalie undergo a ceremony to cure sterility. She takes to drink to escape her loneliness, and we expect Ato, who has been rather weakly trying to reconcile his wife and parents, to give her up and marry some girl from the village. This would be the standard pattern for the play to follow. Yet, in the end, it is the traditional ethic of hospitality that triumphs over other traditions that had led the family to take a hostile view of Eulalie. If blame is to be placed, it is upon Ato, for excusing each person's actions to the other instead of explaining them.

The writers of the colonial period, and many of their successors, proclaimed that the best of tradition should be matched with the best of modern ways. The significance of *The Dilemma of a Ghost* is that tradition as a whole is not set against modernity as a whole, and that the capacity for solution to the conflict is found within tradition—which is not presented to us as a monolith.

The concern in Aidoo's first play with the adjustment between different ways of life necessary in day-to-day living—rather than with the presentation of arguments, allegories, or demonstrations of rightness—prepares us for her second play. *Anowa* is perhaps the first historical play by an African in which the history is relegated to the background and made to serve the examination of a character. Anowa is a beautiful but wilful girl who refuses to marry the suitors of her parents' choice and marries a man whom they consider a good-for-nothing. The couple leave their home town and with her aid and ideas her husband, Kofi Ako, prospers mightily in trade with the British (who are represented in the play only by a picture of Queen Victoria). But Anowa finds wealth and the customary ideas of a woman's place confining, while Kofi finds his unconventional wife an increasing embarrassment. Finally, after a quarrel in which she guesses that the priest told Kofi that she had destroyed his manhood and that he half believes her to be a witch—a quarrel which they become aware has been overheard by Kofi's slaves—he shoots himself, she drowns herself.

Anowa is set in the late 19th century, and Aidoo uses the historical setting to give a fresh perspective to the call for a more liberated role for women in society. Anowa says,

> I hear in other lands a woman is nothing. And they let her know this from the day of her birth. But here, O my spirit mother, they let a girl grow up as she pleases until she is married. And then she is like any woman anywhere: in order for her man to be a man, she must not think, she must not talk.

African dramatists have often attacked the lack of status of women, but in a contemporary setting their indignation usually delivers dramatic tension and subtlety over to righteousness. But in the context of the 19th century the modern woman (Anowa) appears as an eccentric and a dramatic balance is regained.

Though this theme is dominant, others are important: the tensions of a childless marriage in a traditional society, and the intimation that all wrongs in the African past cannot be blamed upon colonialism. Anowa is modern in her uneasiness at her husband's accumulation of slaves. She is, he tells her, "too fond of looking for the common pain and the general wrong." It is in part perhaps because several of the themes common to African drama are combined that the impression is given that the play turns not around any one of them but around the character of Anowa.

Aidoo's plays have their faults: the narrative framework of *Anowa* is at times clumsy; the Americanisms of Eulalie unconvincing; and the position of Ato, inactive between Eulalie and his parents, awkward. *The Dilemma of a Ghost* takes its title from a song sung by two children:

> One early morning,
> When the moon was up
> Shining as the sun,
> I went to Elmina Junction
> And there and there,
> I saw a wretched ghost
> Going up and down
> Singing to himself
> "Shall I go
> To Cape Coast,
> Or to Elmina
> I don't know,
> I can't tell.
> I don't know,
> I can't tell."

The title of the play is quite enough of a hint that the song evokes the cultural tensions felt by the educated African; unfortunately Aidoo has Ato awake and tell how in his dream he saw himself as a small boy singing the song. Nevertheless,

Anowa suggests that Aidoo is learning, as many of her fellow-dramatists need to do, that something should be left for the spectator to find in a play for himself, that like a good teacher the playwright should evoke a response rather than set out everything explicitly.

—Anthony Graham-White

ALBEE, Edward (Franklin, III). American. Born in Virginia, 12 March 1928; adopted as an infant. Educated at Lawrenceville School; Valley Forge Military Academy, Pennsylvania; Choate School, Connecticut, graduated 1946; Trinity College, Hartford, Connecticut, 1946–47. Served in the United States Army. Radio writer, WNYC, office boy, Warwick and Legler, record salesman, Bloomingdale's, book salesman, G. Schirmer, counterman, Manhattan Towers Hotel, messenger, Western Union, 1955–58, all in New York; producer, with Richard Barr and Clinton Wilder, Barr/Wilder/Albee Playwrights Unit, later Albarwild Theatre Arts, and Albar Productions, New York. Founder, William Flanagan Center for Creative Persons, Montauk, Long Island, New York, 1971. U.S. cultural exchange visitor to the U.S.S.R. Recipient: Berlin Festival award, 1959, 1961; Vernon Rice award, 1960; Obie award, 1960; Argentine Critics award, 1961; Lola D'Annunzio award, 1961; New York Drama Critics Circle award, 1964; Outer Circle award, 1964; London *Evening Standard* award, 1964; Tony award, 1964; Margo Jones award, 1965; Pulitzer Prize, 1967, 1975; American Academy Gold Medal, 1980; Brandeis University Creative Arts award, 1983, 1984. D. Litt.: Emerson College, Boston, 1967; Litt. D.: Trinity College, 1974. Member, American Academy, 1966. Agent: William Morris Agency, 1350 Avenue of the Americas, New York, New York 10019. Address: 14 Harrison Street, New York, New York 10013, U.S.A.

PUBLICATIONS

Plays

The Zoo Story (produced Berlin, 1959; New York and London, 1960). Included in *The Zoo Story, The Death of Bessie Smith, The Sandbox*, 1960.

The Death of Bessie Smith (produced Berlin, 1960; New York and London, 1961). Included in *The Zoo Story, The Death of Bessie Smith, The Sandbox*, 1960.

The Sandbox (produced New York, 1960). Included in *The Zoo Story, The Death of Bessie Smith, The Sandbox*, 1960.

The Zoo Story, The Death of Bessie Smith, The Sandbox: Three Plays. New York, Coward McCann, 1960; as *The Zoo Story and Other Plays* (includes *The American Dream*), London, Cape, 1962.

Fam and Yam (produced Westport, Connecticut, and New York, 1960). New York, Dramatists Play Service, 1961.

The American Dream (produced New York and London, 1961). New York, Coward McCann, 1961; London, French, 1962.

Bartleby, with James Hinton, Jr., music by William Flanagan, adaptation of the story by Melville (produced New York, 1961).

Who's Afraid of Virginia Woolf? (produced New York, 1962; London, 1964). New York, Atheneum, 1962; London, Cape, 1964.

The Ballad of the Sad Café, adaptation of the story by Carson McCullers (produced New York, 1963; Worcester, 1969). New York and Boston, Atheneum-Houghton Mifflin, 1963; London, Cape, 1965.

Tiny Alice (produced New York, 1964; London, 1970). New York, Atheneum, 1965; London, Cape, 1966.

Malcolm, adaptation of the novel by James Purdy (produced New York, 1966). New York, Atheneum, 1966; London, Cape-Secker and Warburg, 1967.

A Delicate Balance (produced New York, 1966; London, 1969). New York, Atheneum, 1966; London, Cape, 1968.

Breakfast at Tiffany's, music by Bob Merrill, adaptation of the story by Truman Capote (produced Philadelphia, 1966).

Everything in the Garden, adaptation of the play by Giles Cooper (produced New York, 1967). New York, Atheneum, 1968.

Box and Quotations from Chairman Mao Tse-tung (as *Box-Mao-Box*, produced Buffalo, 1968; as *Box and Quotations from Chairman Mao Tse-tung*, produced New York, 1968). New York, Atheneum, 1969; London, Cape, 1970.

All Over (produced New York, 1971; London, 1972). New York, Atheneum, 1971; London, Cape, 1972.

Seascape (also director: produced New York, 1975; Kingston on Thames, Surrey, 1980). New York, Atheneum, 1975; London, Cape, 1976.

Counting the Ways (produced London, 1976; also director: produced Hartford, Connecticut, 1977). Included in *Two Plays*, 1977.

Listening (broadcast 1976; also director: produced Hartford, Connecticut, 1977; Coventry, 1977; New York, 1979). Included in *Two Plays*, 1977.

Two Plays: Counting the Ways and Listening. New York, Atheneum, 1977.

The Lady from Dubuque (produced New York, 1980). New York, Atheneum, 1980.

Lolita, adaptation of the novel by Vladimir Nabokov (produced Boston and New York, 1981). New York, Dramatists Play Service, 1984.

Plays:

1. *The Zoo Story, The Death of Bessie Smith, The Sandbox, The American Dream*. New York, Coward McCann, 1981.
2. *Tiny Alice, A Delicate Balance, Box and Quotations from Chairman Mao Tse-tung*. New York, Atheneum, 1982.
3. *Seascape, Counting the Ways, Listening, All Over*. New York, Atheneum, 1982.
4. *Everything in the Garden, Malcolm, The Ballad of the Sad Café*. New York, Atheneum, 1982.

The Man Who Had Three Arms (also director: produced Miami, 1982; New York, 1983).

Envy, in *Faustus in Hell* (produced Princeton, New Jersey, 1985).

Screenplay: *A Delicate Balance*, 1976.

Radio Play: *Listening*, 1976 (UK).

*

Bibliography: *Edward Albee at Home and Abroad: A Bibliography 1958–June 1968* by Richard E. Amacher and Margaret Rule, New York, AMS Press, 1970; *Edward Albee: An Annotated Bibliography 1968–1977* by Charles Lee Green, New York, AMS Press, 1980.

Critical Studies: *Edward Albee: Tradition and Renewal* by Gilbert Debusscher, translated by Anne D. Williams, Brussels, American Studies Center, 1967; *Edward Albee* by Richard E. Amacher, New York, Twayne, 1969, revised edition, 1982; *Edward Albee* by Ruby Cohn, Minneapolis, University of Minnesota Press, 1969; *Edward Albee: Playwright in Protest* by Michael E. Rutenberg, New York, Drama Book Specialists, 1969; *Albee* by C.W.E. Bigsby, Edinburgh, Oliver and Boyd, 1969, New York, Chip's Bookshop, 1978, and *Edward Albee: A Collection of Critical Essays* edited by Bigsby, Englewood Cliffs, New Jersey, Prentice Hall, 1975; *Edward Albee* by Ronald Hayman, London, Heinemann, 1971, New York, Ungar, 1973; *From Tension to Tonic: The Plays of Edward Albee* by Anne Paolucci, Carbondale, Southern Illinois University Press, 1972; *Edward Albee: The Poet of Loss* by Anita M. Stenz, The Hague, Mouton, 1978; *Who's Afraid of Edward Albee?* by Foster Hirsch, Berkeley, California, Creative Arts, 1978; *Edward Albee: An Interview and Essays* edited by Julian N. Wasserman, Houston, University of St. Thomas, 1983; *Edward Albee* by Gerald McCarthy, London, Macmillan, 1987.

Theatrical Activities:
Director: several of his own plays.

* * *

Since emerging with his extraordinary one-act plays in the late 1950's, Edward Albee has become the most internationally successful American dramatist since Tennessee Williams and Arthur Miller first came to attention in the 1940's. But his career bears more resemblance to that other and earlier American playwright Eugene O'Neill. Like O'Neill's, his one-act plays first brought him acclaim; like O'Neill in *Mourning Becomes Electra* and other marathon adventures, he turned in *Who's Afraid of Virginia Woolf?* to a play of unusual length; like O'Neill he became interested in experimenting with new dramatic forms. But unlike O'Neill, whose stature is based upon his brilliant dramatic concepts or blueprints for plays that seem in their working out largely unwritten, Albee can surely *write*. Indeed, it is his ear for dialogue, from the glittering and seemingly casual tone of his earlier plays to the heightened rhetoric of more recent work, that is one of his principal characteristics. It is in fact as a writer that O'Neill is so vulnerable and Albee particularly triumphs. But there is yet another, rather ironic connection between O'Neill and Albee. As the late Alan Schneider, who had been Albee's principal director, correctly remarked, if the Actors Studio Theater had chosen in 1962 to open its first season with the scintillating *Virginia Woolf*, which was available to it, rather than O'Neill's backward-looking *Strange Interlude*, the whole course of the American theater might have been—indeed it would have been—altered for the better. There might even still be an Actors Studio Theater.

Albee's accomplishment, like that of any major writer, presents a pattern of development and has its own inner logic and cohesion. Critics who are puzzled by the later plays and admire the earlier ones should remember that when Albee was finishing *Virginia Woolf* he announced in a speech at Harvard that he was already planning two additional full-length plays, *Tiny Alice*, produced in 1964, and *The Substitute Speaker*, later renamed *The Lady from Dubuque*, which did not appear until 1980. And it is that death-figure, with her connotations of Ibsen's Lady from the Sea, who suggests the controlling concern in that group of preoccupations that in differing patterns inform his plays: "all of the values were relative save one... 'Who am I?'" All of Albee's plays in some way probe this question, and the search is usually worked out through family relationships involving real or imagined parents and children, measured by death, and frequently framed by religious or irreligious allusions. In the early and personally felt one-act plays that culminate in that brilliant tour de force *Virginia Woolf* this quest is energized by the presence of mysterious young men, indirect figures who are and are not sons: "the van man" who is "the American dream," the Angel of Death in *Sandbox*, the imaginary son killed in *Virginia Woolf*. These figures, initially introduced and placed into perspective by remembered youth in *The Zoo Story*, together with Mommy and Daddy, George, Martha, Grandma, and their subsequent variations, compose a kind of Albee family portrait, and in the world of games, songs, and children's books, from that unforgettable outing at the beach in his poetic, finest play *The Sandbox* to the new doll house in *Tiny Alice*, offspring and parents, both real and imagined, find themselves in the same terrifying dark/light.

Among the individual plays themselves *Virginia Woolf* is Albee's greatest public success. From the moment at the play's outset when George and Martha stumble into a dark room until hours later, with a death at dawn, they are exposed to where they really are. *Who's Afraid of Virginia Woolf?* is a richly connotative triumph. The pun in its title brings together at once the play's combination of songs and games, adults and children, terror and death, life and art; the three acts, each with its own title, recalls the form of the one-act plays and expands their concerns into a common structure; the names, with their ironic reference to the founding but childless first family, become a frightening comment upon the sterility and illusion inherent in the American dream; and the references to Jesus that casually but deliberately open and close the first act compare the imaginary son to the most extraordinary of all sons of exceptional parentage. And in *Virginia Woolf* there is not only all of "this" but "so much more."

The rhetorically heightened plays that follow are more distanced, more formal in design, and in a sense dramatize the implied or indirect action more common to the lyric poem, a form of writing Albee had already exploited in other ways in *The Sandbox*. The screens in *All Over* which conceal the dying tycoon from his extended family, waiting and reacting in the foreground, visualize the method. Among these later plays *A Delicate Balance*, with its motivating but unseen terror, creates a metaphor between the very form of drama selected, drawing-room comedy, and a way of life. Both require a mastery of precarious equilibrium. In *Tiny Alice* the world of the play itself becomes indirect and anti-realistic as Julian, the imaginary young man grown up or come to life, explores in metaphysical games D.H. Lawrence impulses amid the shifting dimensions and identities of *Alice in Wonderland* and *Through the Looking-Glass*. The later *The Lady from Dubuque* is a play of haunting echoes, and reiterates the uncertainty of parent-child relationships and the chill of death against the sounds of forced revels from earlier rooms.

Each of these plays, of course, explores dramatic form, explorations that reach their technical climax in *Box-Mao-Box*, and the movement they represent, with the exception of the more recent and strange dramatic monologue *The Man Who Had Three Arms*, toward this more objective kind of drama had actually been signaled when Albee first decided to alternate original plays with adaptations. If the plays that have resulted have been less popular with public and critics (though two of them, including the pastoral interlude *Seascape*, have won the Pulitzer Prize), they are no less striking or original. They have their own proud and frosty brilliance. And as one considers both the earlier and later Albee plays as a group, it is clear that as we wait "at this place for the fall of night" no other contemporary American dramatist has in such an extensive body of work told us more about *who* we are—or seem to be.

—Gaynor F. Bradish

ALFRED, William. American. Born in New York City, 16 August 1922. Educated at Brooklyn College, B.A. 1948; Harvard University, Cambridge, Massachusetts, M.A. 1949, Ph.D. 1954. Served in the United States Army, 1943–46. Associate editor, *American Poet*, Brooklyn, 1942–44. Instructor, 1954–57, Assistant Professor, 1957–59, Associate Professor, 1959–63, and since 1963 Professor of English, Harvard University. Recipient: Brooklyn College Literary Association award, 1953; Amy Lowell traveling poetry scholarship, 1956; Brandeis University Creative Arts award, 1960; American Academy grant, 1965. Agent: Luis Sanjurjo, International Creative Management, 40 West 57th Street, New York, New York 10019. Address: 31 Athens Street, Cambridge, Massachusetts 02138, U.S.A.

PUBLICATIONS

Plays

The Annunciation Rosary. Matawan, New Jersey, Sower Press, 1948.

Agamemnon (produced Cambridge, Massachusetts, 1953). New York, Knopf, 1954.

Hogan's Goat (produced New York, 1965). New York, Farrar Straus, 1966; revised version, as *Cry for Us All*, with Albert Marre, music by Mitch Leigh (produced New York, 1970).

The Curse of an Aching Heart, music by Claibe Richardson (produced Chicago, 1979; New York, 1982). New York, French, 1983.

Holy Saturday (produced Boston, 1980). Published in *Canto* (Andover, Massachusetts), vol. 3, no. 1, 1979–80.

Other

Editor, with others, *Complete Prose Works of John Milton 1.* New Haven, Connecticut, Yale University Press, 1953; London, Oxford University Press, 1954.

Translator, *Beowulf*, in *Medieval Epics.* New York, Modern Library, 1963.

*

Manuscript Collections: Houghton Library, Harvard University, Cambridge, Massachusetts; Brooklyn College Library.

William Alfred comments:

I write plays because I love people the way dog-lovers love dogs, indiscriminately, and want to capture as many as I can in all their baffled splendor.

* * *

"It is a fearful thing to love what death can touch." These words are uttered by Cassandra in poet-playwright William Alfred's blank verse version of the tragedy of Agamemnon. Yet they come not from Homer nor Aeschylus; they were found on an ancient Vermont gravestone. The desperate sense of irremediable loss, both restrained and simple in this phrasing, is typical of Alfred's best dialogue in his *Agamemnon.* It is at once economic, poetic, and dramatically effective. In reading or in playing, one does not have the vaguely disquieting feeling that Alfred's characters are speaking English translations of Sophocles or Anouilh. They are all too human, which at times diminishes the magnitude of the tragic experience, especially when the dramatic diction tries to evoke a kind of realism. Cassandra says to Agamemnon on the voyage back from Troy: "A penny for your thoughts." Had she said "drachma" instead, it would still be jarring.

Central to Alfred's idea of the events is Agamemnon's guilty concealment of the true manner of his daughter Iphigenia's death at Aulis. On ship-board, he has the tongue cut from a man who dares to utter the truth. He keeps it from Cassandra, who divines it. Clytemnestra has been told her daughter died of fever, but her oldest adviser actually saw the ritual slaying. Her co-regents have said nothing of this, anxious to preserve order in the kingdom. Aegisthus, in an awkward situation he'd like to escape from, feels used. The action moves back and forth from the palace to Agamemnon's ship, as the moment of reunion approaches. When Clytemnestra finally discovers the truth, she goes down to the courtyard to receive—and to murder—her husband and Cassandra. This action is heard from offstage by her advisers—and the audience.

It's curious that Alfred observes this nicety of the Attic Greek theatre—scenes of horror offstage—when he is much more Shakespearean in his alternation of locales and intercutting of developing plotlines. He certainly makes thoughtful use of the soliloquy, but there are moments in the play when poetic ruminations detract from the potential power of the approaching confrontation by further foreshadowing it or by delaying it needlessly. Part of the problem is that Alfred is a poet first and a playwright second. That he is also a distinguished academic lends strength to his resources in rhetoric and cultural allusion, but this may have made him less spontaneous as a dramatist.

Periodically, there comes a fervent cry for the "return of poetry to the theatre," as though the victory of prose on stage were some kind of debasing of the drama. T.S. Eliot—who later said he'd learned playwriting at the public's expense—and Christopher Fry were hailed in the 1940's as new champions of the verse drama. The danger to the theatre in such cyclic surgings of desire for poetry on stage is that poetry-lovers and their favorite poets—encouraged to write for the theatre—will be more interested in images and devices than in characterisation and dramatic structure. When Alfred's tragic tale of ambition and deceit in *fin de siècle* Brooklyn, *Hogan's Goat*, was initially produced by the American Place Theatre which then specialized in staging works by poets and novelists, it was praised for its poetic virtues.

What made *Hogan's Goat* interesting to audiences, beyond its lilting Brooklyn Irish diction and homely but arresting images, was, however, its strong plot and vivid characters. As in *Agamemnon*, Alfred's tragic hero, Matthew Stanton, has concealed a terrible truth from his young wife. His vaunting political ambitions are brought low with the threat of blackmail, and he kills his wife in a frenzy when she tries to leave him, having learned their marriage isn't legal, that he was the kept man of a powerful woman whom he abandoned cruelly. There is power in the conflicts; complexity in the characters. Alfred's dialogue captures the idioms and rhythms of the Brooklyn Irish in the 1890's. *Hogan's Goat* recreates a bygone era in New

York City's ethnic and political history in a vividly dramatic way. Best of all for ordinary audiences, the flow of Irish speech—heightened though it often is—is seldom perceived as poetry, but rather as passionate diction.

The critical and popular acceptance of *Hogan's Goat* led to a Broadway musical version, *Cry for Us All*, which failed. The essential failure was not in Alfred's drama, but in Albert Marre's notion that, with music by Mitch Leigh, this might be another Broadway hit like *Man of La Mancha*, also produced by Marre. As with the disappointing musical *Zorba!*, *Hogan's Goat* should have been an opera.

This disappointment didn't deter Alfred from offering Broadway in 1982 a charming suite of explorations among the Brooklyn Irish and their friends, *The Curse of an Aching Heart*. Subtitled "An Evening's Comedy," it is also a verse play, with some appealing songs by Alfred and music by Claibe Richardson. But the work failed to win a critical majority or a long run. Nonetheless, it remains a wryly and comically honest evocation of growing up in the big city in the 1920's and after. Its link with *Hogan's Goat* is its revelation of the hopes and defeats of descendants of figures noted in the earlier drama. It is not a sequential narrative; with a Prologue (1942) which looks backward, five one-act plays are offered, showing various stages in the lives of Frances Anna Duffy Walsh, her uncle Jo Jo, and their neighbors, friends, and lovers. The five mini-dramas are: *Friday Night Dreams Come True—1923; Clothes Make the Woman—1925; The Curse of an Aching Heart—1927; All Saints, All Souls—1935*; and *Holy Saturday—1942*. (The last play has been published and produced separately as well as *en suite*.) When Jo Jo inadvertently lets Fran know he is strongly attracted to her—even as he rages against her boyfriends, it shocks her. Until the end of the plays, when he's old and helpless and a healing occurs between them, she refuses to speak to him. These plays are not only an effective exercise in nostalgia, recreating games, folklore, values, prejudices, and style of the 1920's, 1930's, and 1940's, but they are also moving accounts of human strivings for contact and affection.

—Glenn Loney

ALLAN, Ted. Canadian. Born Alan Herman in Montreal, Quebec, 25 January 1916. Educated at Baron Byng High School, Montreal. Served in the International Brigade during the Spanish Civil War: Colonel. Married Kate Schwartz in 1939 (divorced 1966); one daughter and one son. Store clerk, 1933–34; Montreal correspondent, Toronto *Daily Worker*, 1935; radio, television, and film actor; lived in London for nearly 30 years, now lives in Toronto and Los Angeles. Recipient: Canada Council grant, 1956, 1970, Senior Arts grant, 1974, and travel grant, 1974; Berlin Film Festival Golden Bear, 1985; Stephen Leacock award, for fiction, 1985. Agent: Mike Zimring, William Morris Agency, 151 El Camino, Beverly Hills, California 90212, U.S.A.

PUBLICATIONS

Plays

The Money Makers (produced Toronto, 1954; as *The Ghost Writers*, produced London, 1955).
Legend of Pepito, adaptation of a story by B. Traven (produced London, 1955).
Double Image, with Roger MacDougall, based on a story by Roy Vickers (produced London, 1956). London, French, 1957.
The Secret of the World (produced London, 1962).
Oh What a Lovely War, with the Theatre Workshop (produced London and New York, 1964). London, Methuen, 1965.
Chu Chem: A Zen Buddhist-Hebrew Musical, music and lyrics by Mitch Leigh, Jack Haines, and Jack Wohl (produced Philadelphia, 1966).
My Sister's Keeper (as *I've Seen You Cut Lemons* produced London, 1969; revised version, as *My Sister's Keeper*, produced Lennoxville, Quebec, 1974; New York, 1979). Toronto, Toronto University Press, 1976.
Love Streams, and The Third Day Comes (produced Los Angeles, 1984).
Lies My Father Told Me (produced New York, 1986). Toronto, Playwrights, 1984.

Screenplays: *1001 Arabian Nights*, with others, 1959; *The Webster Boy*, with Leo Marks, 1962; *Fuse*, 1970; *Them Damned Canadians*, 1973; *Lies My Father Told Me*, 1975; *Love Streams*, with John Cassavetes, 1984.

Radio Plays: *Canadian Mental Health* series, 1953; *Coloured Buttons*, 1958; *The Good Son*, 1969.

Television Plays: *Willie the Squowse*, 1954; *Go Fall in Love*, 1955; *Early to Braden* series, 1957–58; *Legend of Paradiso*, 1960; *Flowers at My Feet*, 1968.

Novels

This Time a Better Earth. London, Heinemann, and New York, Morrow, 1939.
Quest for Pajaro (as Edward Maxwell). London, Heinemann, 1957.
Chu Chem: A Zen Buddhist-Hebrew Novel. Montreal, Editions Quebec, 1973.
Lies My Father Told Me (novelization of screenplay; as Norman Allan). New York, New American Library, 1975.
Love Is a Long Shot. Toronto, McClelland and Stewart, 1984; London, Hale, 1986.

Short Stories

Don't You Know Anybody Else? Family Stories. Toronto, McClelland and Stewart, 1985.

Other

The Scalpel, The Sword: The Story of Dr. Norman Bethune, with Sydney Gordon. Boston, Little Brown, 1952; London, Hale, 1954; revised edition, New York, Monthly Review Press, 1973.
Willie the Squowse (for children). Toronto, McClelland and Stewart, and London, Cape, 1977; New York, Hastings House, 1978.

*

Ted Allan comments:

(1977) I find it difficult to appraise my work. At some moments I think they are the most underestimated plays of the 20th century. At other moments I think they all need to be rewritten.

They have been praised and damned but have not attained the fame I sought for them, with the exception of *Oh What a Lovely War*. But here my pleasure is mixed, for the director-producer threw out my main plot, kept my peripheral scenes, rewriting most of them, took my name off the play in England, and gave writing credits to a few hundred people, to indicate that nobody *wrote* it. I consider my original version a theatrical tour de force and hope to get it produced one day under a new title: *Smith and Schmidt*, directed by someone who will do it as I wrote it.

Outside of *Gog and Magog*, which began life as *Double Image*, and which ran for a year in London and almost five years in Paris, none of my plays ever achieved commercial success.

The Secret of the World (my major opus), which told the story of three generations of a Montreal family (the head of which goes mad), did get wild critical hosannas from most of London's critics, but was panned by Canadian critics when it was performed at Lennoxville in 1976.

I've Seen You Cut Lemons probed the problem of alleged insanity in those we, the so-called normal, like to call abnormal. It was cruelly savaged by most of London's critics. That sent me brooding for a few years and to writing screenplays. I will return to playwriting next year, after I finish a new screenplay, which will provide me with the wherewithal to write for the theatre.

I consider *Chu Chem* the happiest of my plays although it died an untimely death after six performances in Philadelphia. I keep hoping it will one day get the kind of imaginative production it needs. (We had an elderly and beloved lead who couldn't remember his lines. The poor man died soon after the play did.)

My wildest fantasy is called *Willie the Squowse*, which nobody wants to produce, although it's been done on both radio and television. I have a horrible feeling that my plays will start getting produced all over the world to be acclaimed with noisy popularity after I am dead. If that is the price I must pay to get my plays produced, I agree. I have decided to die before I am ninety. This is a concession, for I had planned to live to a hundred. When I finally go, I will let you know.

(1988) I'm finding it easier to appraise my work now that I have rewritten *The Secret of the World* for the thousandth time. With the off-Broadway production of *Lies My Father Told Me* and a scheduled production of *Willie the Squowse* I feel less neglected.

* * *

With his high octane forcefulness and his formidable technical expertise, Ted Allan is a playwright who has been undeservedly neglected in the London theatre since *The Secret of the World* was produced at Stratford East in 1962. His two-hander *I've Seen You Cut Lemons* is a far more interesting piece of theatrical writing than *Two for the Seesaw*, for instance, a two-character play which enjoyed considerable success.

The Secret of the World is rather like a Canadian *Death of a Salesman*, with the life of the central family set in a context of direct involvement in union politics during and after the upheaval caused by Khrushchev's revelations about Stalin. Chris Alexander (or Sam Alexander as he became at Stratford East) is an idealistic union leader who fails to get re-elected when he breaks with the Communist Party, and, from being successful, busy and well-liked, declines further into loneliness, ineffectuality, and near-madness. He is too honest to take advantage of an opportunity to get big money from a bus company in settlement of an accident claim, and hopes instead to make a fortune out of a crackpot invention—cufflinks joined by elastic, so that shirts can be put on without unfastening them.

The play's emotional brew is a very rich one. The interlocking emotional problems of Chris's father, wife, son, daughter, and brother-in-law are all boiled up together, and the resulting soup would possibly be more digestible with a little more comedy and a little less meat. But there is an admirable sureness of touch in creating theatrical effects, even if this is done without letting the characters be conscious enough of their own theatricality. The old father is rather like a Montreal version of Ibsen's Old Ekdal. But the decline of Chris is powerfully plotted, and, even when it is too obvious that Allan is trying to tug at the audience's heartstrings, the tugs are not usually fumbled.

In family plays especially an over-rich emotional mixture is often due to the presence of too much autobiographical material and too much residue of the guilt that family pressures create. The suspicion one has that Allan is drawing directly on his own experience is strengthened when we see how much Sarah in *I've Seen You Cut Lemons* resembles Susan in *The Secret of the World* and when we hear her recalling incidents we actually saw in the earlier play—the mother, for instance, shouting "I believe in God, I believe in God! Atheists. Communists," outside the door of a room in her house where the Young Communist League was holding a meeting.

I've Seen You Cut Lemons is a more controlled, more economical play, which succeeds in sustaining tension all through the action by focusing on different aspects and different phases of a semi-incestuous brother-sister relationship. The action is set in the London bachelor flat of a Canadian university lecturer. His sister is a few years younger than he is. Like Susan, Sarah is a painter but she blames the relationship with her brother for her partially deliberate failure to make more use of her talent, which they both regard as a very considerable one.

They both have children from broken marriages. As the action starts he is on the point of taking his son to Corsica for a holiday, when she arrives unexpectedly, discharged early from the hospital. He lets her stay in the flat, judging her mental health to be sufficiently restored to stand up to a period of loneliness. Later, of course, he will regret this. When he returns she tries harder and harder to monopolise his life, untruthfully informing his girlfriend (who is also called Susan) that they are having an incestuous relationship, and going all out to convince him that this is what he really wants as much as she does. Allan's dialogue measures up well to the difficult task of registering her oscillations between lucidity and hallucination, and it even convinces us that she could play on her brother's guilt feelings cleverly enough to make him believe that her sanity could be fully and permanently restored if only he would devote a month of his life to looking after her. The play ends touchingly as she voluntarily goes back to hospital and he emerges from the purgatory of their time together a wiser man than he was before.

Allan has also written prolifically for the screen and television, and he collaborated with Roger MacDougall on the stage play *Double Image*. He has also written *Chu Chem*, which he describes as a Zen Buddhist-Hebrew Musical Comedy. It owes as much to Brecht as to Zen Buddhism, and the ingredients do not quite jell, but there are some very amusing moments. The most inspired theatrical image is a seesaw with buckets attached to either end. A rock is put into one, and the villagers have to "balance the budget" by putting jewels and gold into the other.

—Ronald Hayman

ANDERSON, Robert (Woodruff). American. Born in New York City, 28 April 1917. Educated at Phillips Exeter Academy, Exeter, New Hampshire, 1931–35; Harvard University, Cambridge, Massachusetts, 1935–42, A.B. (magna cum laude) 1939, M.A. 1940. Served in the United States Naval Reserve, 1942–46: Lieutenant; Bronze Star. Married 1) Phyllis Stohl in 1940 (died 1956); 2) the actress Teresa Wright in 1959 (divorced 1978). Actor, South Shore Players, Cohasset, Massachusetts, summers 1937 and 1938. Assistant in English, Harvard University, 1939–42; teacher, Erskine School, Boston, 1941; teacher of playwriting, American Theatre Wing, New York, 1946–51, and Actors Studio, New York, 1955–56; member of the faculty, Salzburg Seminar in American Studies, 1968; writer-in-residence, University of North Carolina, Chapel Hill, 1969, and University of Iowa Writers Workshop, Iowa City, 1976. Member of the Playwrights Producing Company, 1953–60; President, New Dramatists Committee, 1955–56, and Dramatists Guild, 1971–73; member of the Board of Governors, American Playwrights Theatre, 1963–79. Since 1965 member of the Council, and since 1980 Vice-President, Authors League of America. Recipient: National Theatre Conference prize, 1945; Rockefeller fellowship, 1946; Writers Guild of America award, for screenplay, 1970. Agent: Luis Sanjurjo, International Creative Management, 40 West 57th Street, New York, New York 10019. Address: Roxbury, Connecticut 06783, U.S.A.

PUBLICATIONS

Plays

Hour Town, music and lyrics by Anderson (produced Cambridge, Massachusetts, 1938).
Come Marching Home (produced Iowa City, 1945; New York, 1946).
The Eden Rose (produced Ridgefield, Connecticut, 1949).
Sketches in *Dance Me a Song* (produced New York, 1950).
Love Revisited (produced Westport, Connecticut, 1951).
All Summer Long, adaptation of the novel *A Wreath and a Curse* by Donald Wetzel (produced Washington, D.C., 1952; New York, 1954). New York, French, 1955.
Tea and Sympathy (produced New Haven, Connecticut, and New York, 1953; London, 1957). New York, Random House, 1953; London, Heinemann, 1957.
Silent Night, Lonely Night (produced New Haven, Connecticut, and New York, 1959). New York, Random House, 1960.
The Days Between (produced Dallas, 1965; New York, 1979). New York, Random House, 1965.
You Know I Can't Hear You When the Water's Running (produced New York, 1967; London, 1968). New York, Random House, 1967.
I Never Sang for My Father (produced Philadelphia, 1967; New York, 1968; London, 1970). New York, Random House, 1968; screenplay published, New York, New American Library, 1970.
Solitaire/Double Solitaire (produced New Haven, Connecticut, Edinburgh, and New York, 1971). New York, Random House, 1972.
Free and Clear (produced New Haven, Connecticut, 1983).

Screenplays: *Tea and Sympathy*, 1956; *Until They Sail*, 1957; *The Nun's Story*, 1959; *The Sand Pebbles*, 1966; *I Never Sang for My Father*, 1970.

Radio and Television Plays: *David Copperfield, Oliver Twist, Vanity Fair, The Glass Menagerie, Trilby, The Old Lady Shows Her Medals, The Petrified Forest, The Scarlet Pimpernel, A Farewell to Arms, Summer and Smoke, Arrowsmith*, and other adaptations, 1946–52; *The Patricia Neal Story*, 1980.

Novels

After. New York, Random House, and London, Barrie and Jenkins, 1973.
Getting Up and Going Home. New York, Simon and Schuster, 1978.

*

Bibliography: *The Apprenticeship of Robert Anderson* by David Ayers, unpublished dissertation, Columbus, Ohio State University, 1969.

Manuscript Collection: Harvard University Theatre Collection, Cambridge, Massachusetts.

Critical Studies: *Playwrights Talk about Playwriting* edited by Lewis Funke, Chicago, Dramatic Publishing Company, 1975; *Robert Anderson* by Thomas Adler, Boston, Twayne, 1978; "A Dramatist's Inner Space," in *Dramatists Guild Quarterly* (New York), Spring 1979; *The Strands Entwined* by Samuel Bernstein, Boston, Northeastern University Press, 1980.

Robert Anderson comments:

(1973) It is difficult and dangerous for a writer to talk about his own work. He should move on to whatever he is impelled to write about next without looking back and trying to analyze his work. Recently I read a doctoral thesis written about me and my plays. In many ways I wish I hadn't read it. I don't think it is wise for a writer to think about his "continuing themes" and recurring attitudes.

When I was near the end of writing *Tea and Sympathy*, my first wife begged me to tell her something of the subject of my new play. (I never discuss my work with anyone while I am writing.) I gave in and simply told her it took place in a boys' school. She said, "Oh, my God, not another play about a boys' school!" This almost stopped me. At that moment I hadn't been consciously aware that I had written other (unproduced) work with a boys' school background. I simply knew that I wanted to write that play. My wife's making me aware that I had worked that vein before almost stopped me from finishing the play.

People sometimes say, "Why don't you write about something besides marriage?" Strangely, it is only after I have finished a play that I am aware that I have written again about marriage. Each time I start a play, I certainly don't have the feeling that I am going over old ground. I feel I have something new and different nagging at me to be written. I do not consciously say, "This is my theme. I have done it reasonably well before. Let's try it again."

And these "plays about marriage" are seldom just that. *Solitaire/Double Solitaire* was not about marriage in the present and in the future, as some critics described it. It was about the loneliness of being alone and the loneliness of marriage. *The Days Between* was not about an academic marriage on the rocks but about a man who was ruining his life and his marriage by being unable to live the ordinary, unexciting days of life, "the days between." Marriage is often the arena of the plays, but not always the real subject matter.

As a matter of fact, the plays are rarely "about" what critics say they are about. *Tea and Sympathy* has always been described as "a play about homosexuality." In effect, it has nothing to do with homosexuality. It has to do with an unjust charge of homosexuality and what follows such a charge. It has to do with responsibility, which must extend beyond giving tea and sympathy; it has to do again with loneliness; it has to do with questioning some popular definitions of manliness; and, most important, it has to do with judgment by prejudice . . . and a great deal more, I hope.

You Know I Can't Hear You When the Water's Running was said to be "about" sex. The plays were told in terms of sex, but they were not about sex. As Elia Kazan said when he first read the manuscript, "They're about the same things as your other plays except this time it came out funny and sad." They are very sad plays. As Walter Kerr said of them, "Laugh only when it hurts."

I seem to have written largely about the family, or rather to have used the family as the arena. By and large English critics feel that American playwrights rather overwork this area of concern. Still, our three finest plays are, probably, *The Glass Menagerie, Death of a Salesman*, and *Long Day's Journey into Night.* I am glad that Williams, Miller, and O'Neill didn't scare when and if someone said to them, "not another play about the family!"

I have been amused that I have sometimes been considered a "commercial" playwright. I am amused because each of my plays has had an enormous struggle to get on. Nobody has thought of them as "commercial" till after they were successful. *Tea and Sympathy* was turned down by almost every producer and was on its way back into my files when the Playwrights Company optioned it and started me on my career. *You Know I Can't Hear You When the Water's Running* was turned down by everyone until two new producers "who didn't know any better" took a chance on it. I waited something like seven years before someone "took a chance" on *I Never Sang for My Father.* I think I can't be blamed for being amused when I hear myself described as "commercial," especially inasmuch as three of my plays have premiered in very non-commercial regional theatres, one opened off-Broadway, and one launched The American Playwrights Theatre, a project which seeks to get the plays of "established" playwrights into the regional and college theatres rather than into Broadway theatres.

At various times in my youth I wanted to be an actor and a poet. I acted in college and summer theatres, and I was elected Harvard Class Poet on graduation. I think it is only natural that with these two "bents" I should end up a playwright, because in playwriting one finds the same kind of compression and essentialization one finds in poetry. Poems and plays are both the tips of icebergs.

Finally, I admire form. I took a course at Harvard with Robert Frost. One evening he was asked why he didn't write free verse. He replied, "I don't like playing tennis with the net down." I think that a great deal of the excitement in the theatre comes from using the limitations of the theatre creatively. Most plays, when they are adapted as movies, "opened up," lose their effectiveness, because part of their attraction was the way the playwright had found intensity and a creative impulse in dealing with the limitations of the theatre. Compare the play and the film of *Our Town.* I believe that form can be challenged, changed, stretched. But some kind of form seems to me of the essence of theatre.

I would wish that a person coming on my plays for the first time would not have any preconceived idea as to what they are "about." Each reader or spectator is a new collaborator, and he will, in a sense, write his own play and arrive at his own meanings, based on his own experience of life.

(1988) It has never been easier to get a play done someplace. It has never been more difficult to get a play done where a playwright can earn enough money to write the next play. Many years ago I wrote something which has been endlessly quoted and is still true: "You can make a killing in the theatre but not a living." If I had not been able to write movies and television from time to time, I could not have continued as a playwright. Most playwrights I know are moonlighters. When *Tea and Sympathy* was done in 1953, it cost forty thousand dollars to produce, with Elia Kazan, Jo Mielziner, and Deborah Kerr, all superb and expensive talents. I am told that my six character new play, *The Kissing Was Always the Best*, will probably cost close to a million dollars to produce on Broadway. I try not to think about this.

* * *

Robert Anderson first received limited recognition as a playwright in 1945 when his play *Come Marching Home* was awarded first prize in a National Theatre Conference contest. This was followed five years later by *Love Revisited* which was performed at the Westport County Playhouse. But it was Alan Schneider's Washington Arena production of *All Summer Long* that really marked his emergence as a writer of genuine power and considerable subtlety. Though it was not particularly well received when it eventually reached Broadway two years later, the success of *Tea and Sympathy* had by then established Anderson's reputation as a skilful and impressive playwright.

All Summer Long is a sensitive if somewhat portentously symbolic play about the loss of illusions and the inevitable dissolution of beauty, love, and innocence. The family, which is the focus for this elegy on human weakness, live beside a river which is slowly eroding the bank under their home—a none-too-subtle image of the collapse of genuine feeling within the family itself. Willie, the youngest boy, is on the verge of adolescence and his brother Don, a college sports star crippled in a motor accident, tries to protect him from his own emerging sexuality and from the cynicism and bitterness of the rest of the family, though ironically Don is unable to come to terms with the change in his own life. Anderson piles on the agony, with parents who no longer care for each other or their children, and a girl who tries to produce an abortion by throwing herself on an electrified fence. Though Willie and Don spend the summer trying to build a wall to hold out the threatening floodwaters, the forces of nature can no more be controlled on this level than they can in the lives of individuals growing more self-centered and lonely as they grow older. The play ends as the house collapses—an obvious image of the family itself which has long since disintegrated in human terms.

Though he has never since relied on such a melodramatic climax Anderson's work is never entirely free of a certain dramatic overstatement. In *All Summer Long* Don is not only a crippled sports star, itself something of a cliché, but the accident which caused his injury had been a result of his father's inadequacy. Similarly, in a later play, *Silent Night, Lonely Night*, a child dies because her mother is at that very moment preoccupied with reading a letter which reveals her husband's adultery. Her subsequent plunge into insanity is, perhaps, understandable, but serves to create a melodramatic setting for what is otherwise a subtle examination of human need. Nowhere, however, does Anderson control this tendency better than in what remains his best play, *Tea and Sympathy*, though even here there is a certain lack of subtlety in his portrait of a callous father and a weak and therefore vindictive schoolmaster who may well share the very sexual deviancy which he denounces in others.

Tea and Sympathy was Anderson's Broadway debut and earned him a deserved reputation for confronting delicate and even contentious issues with courage and effect—a reputation which he himself was to parody in his later *You Know I Can't Hear You When the Water's Running*. The play is concerned with the plight of a 17-year-old boy in a New England boarding school who is accused of being homosexual. Unsure of himself and tormented by his fellow pupils, he turns to his housemaster's wife, whom he loves with adolescent passion and anguish. Horrified by her husband's inhumanity and genuinely concerned for the fate of the young boy, she finally allows him to make love to her—the only way she can see him regaining his sexual self-confidence and his faith in other people. The boy's father, long since divorced, has never offered his son the slightest affection while his housemaster punishes the boy for his own suppressed fears. As a perceptive indictment of the witch-hunt the play was produced at a particularly appropriate moment, the height of the McCarthy era. But it is a great deal more than this and despite the rather casual psychological assumptions which underlie the portraits of both father and housemaster the play was a perceptive comment on the failure of compassion in a society which demanded conformity as the price of acceptance.

Anderson's next play, *Silent Night, Lonely Night*, again dealt with the anguish of those who are deprived of the affection and understanding of those who should be closest to them. Katherine, temporarily separated from a husband whom she has just discovered to be unfaithful, finds herself alone in a New England inn on Christmas Eve. Upset and lonely she dines with another guest whose wife is in a nearby mental hospital—driven there by his own infidelity. For this one night they manage to overcome their sense of guilt and self-concern in order to offer one another the momentary consolation of true compassion. The simple symmetry of the structure underlines the justice of those who see Anderson primarily as a constructor of well-made plays, but despite this and despite the melodramatic nature of the man's personal history the play remains a delicate study which compares well with Anderson's earlier work.

His next production, four one-act comedies presented under the title *You Know I Can't Hear You When the Water's Running*, was not staged until eight years later. Lightweight sketches which partly depend on and partly satirize the new vogue for sexual explicitness, they show little of his earlier sensitivity or skill. The same nostalgic regret for the decay of love and the passing of youth is manifested in two of the plays, "The Footsteps of Doves" and "I'll Be Home for Christmas," but now it becomes the subject of rather tasteless jokes. The spectacle of Anderson mocking his earlier convictions is not an altogether attractive one, for the humour of the plays derives from precisely that cynical worldly-wise detachment which he had previously seen as the enemy of the human spirit. When he briefly comes close to a moment of true pathos, in "I'll Be Home for Christmas," the integrity of the scene is lost in the sophisticated banter of the rest of the play.

I Never Sang for My Father does little to redeem the weakness of this composite play. Centering on the almost neurotic need of a son to win the love of a bitter and virtually senile father, it reveals not only the terrifying gaps which can open up between those who should be drawn to one another by all the ties of natural affection and concern, but also the desperate absence of love in a world full of people who choose to shelter and exile themselves in the fragile shell of their own personalities. Yet, despite the emotive nature of his subject, Anderson fails, in the last resort, to establish the tension which he creates as anything more than a pathological study—a compassionate and detailed examination of individuals who, despite the familiarity of their situations, remain case studies rather than evocative projections of a universal state.

In some respects Anderson suggests comparison with dramatists like William Inge, Carson McCullers, and Tennessee Williams. Like them he has chosen to describe the plight of those whose romantic dreams founder on the harsh realities of modern life. Emotionally scarred and sexually vulnerable, his protagonists try to find their way in a world which frightens and dismays them. In *All Summer Long* and *Tea and Sympathy* the central figure, appropriately enough, is an adolescent—for the boy confronting sexuality and cruelty for the first time serves to emphasise simultaneously the ideals of youth and the cynicism and disillusionment of middle age. For Anderson this contrast constitutes the key to individual anguish and the mainspring of a pathos which he seems to regard as the truest expression of human experience. Clearly this is the stuff of which nostalgia and sentimentality are made and his work is open to both charges. Where Tennessee Williams balances his regret for the destruction of the innocent and the romantic with a grudging regard for the "Promethians" who dominate their surroundings, Anderson offers only a romantic regret that things cannot be other than they are. Where Inge and McCullers see the growth away from innocence into experience as a painful but necessary human process, Anderson tends to see it as the first stage in the extinction of genuine feeling and human compassion. If some people can sustain their innocence into maturity they do so, in his world it seems, only at the cost of their ability to act. It is a paradox which he is content to identify rather than examine with the kind of subtlety which Williams had brought to *The Glass Menagerie* and *Orpheus Descending*.

—C.W.E. Bigsby

ANTROBUS, John. British. Born in Woolwich, London, 2 July 1933. Educated at Bishop Wordsworth Grammar School, Salisbury; Selhurst Grammar School, Croydon; King Edward VII Nautical College; Royal Military Academy, Sandhurst, Camberley, Surrey. Served in the British Army, East Surrey Regiment, 1952–55. Married Margaret McCormick in 1958 (divorced 1980); two sons and one daughter. Apprentice Deck Officer, Merchant Navy, 1950–52; supply teacher and waiter, 1953–54. Since 1955 free-lance writer. Recipient: George Devine Award, 1970; Writers Guild award, 1971; Arts Council bursary, 1973, 1976, 1980, 1982. Lives in London. Agent: Deborah Rogers Ltd., 49 Blenheim Crescent, London W11 2EF, England.

PUBLICATIONS

Plays

The Bed-Sitting Room, with Spike Milligan (also co-director: produced London, 1963). Walton on Thames, Surrey,

Hobbs, 1970; revised version, as *The Bed-Sitting Room 2* (also director: produced London, 1983).
Royal Commission Review (produced London, 1964).
You'll Come to Love Your Sperm Test (also director: produced Edinburgh and London, 1965). Published in *New Writers 4*, London, Calder and Boyars, 1965.
Cane of Honour (produced London, 1965).
The Missing Links (televised 1965; produced London, 1977). Included in *Why Bournemouth? and Other Plays*, 1970.
Trixie and Baba (produced London, 1968). London, Calder and Boyars, 1969.
Why Bournemouth? (produced London, 1968). Included in *Why Bournemouth? and Other Plays*, 1970.
Captain Oates' Left Sock (produced London, 1969). London, French, 1974.
An Evening with John Antrobus (produced London, 1969).
Why Bournemouth? and Other Plays. London, Calder and Boyars, 1970.
An Apple a Day (televised 1971; produced London, 1974). Included in *Why Bournemouth? and Other Plays*, 1970.
Stranger in a Cafeteria, in *Christmas Present* (produced Edinburgh, 1971).
The Looneys (produced Edinburgh, 1971; London, 1974).
Crete and Sergeant Pepper (produced London, 1972).
The Dinosaurs, and Certain Humiliations (produced Edinburgh, 1973; London, 1974).
The Illegal Immigrant (produced London, 1974).
Mrs. Grabowski's Academy (produced London, 1975).
They Sleep Together (produced Leicester, 1976).
Sketches in *City Delights* (revue; produced Oxford, 1978; London, 1980).
Jonah (also director: produced Cambridge, 1979).
Hitler in Liverpool, One Orange for the Baby, Up in the Hide (produced London, 1980). London, Calder, and New York, Riverrun Press, 1983.
When Did You Last See Your Trousers?, with Ray Galton, adaptation of a story by Galton and Alan Simpson (produced Mold, Clwyd, 1986; London, 1987).

Screenplays: *Carry on Sergeant*, with Norman Hudis, 1958; *Idol on Parade*, 1959; *Jazzboat*, with Ken Hughes, 1960; *The Wrong Arm of the Law*, with others, 1962; *The Big Job*, with Talbot Rothwell, 1965; *The Bed-Sitting Room*, with Charles Wood, 1969.

Radio Writing: *Idiot Weekly* and *The Goon Show* series; *Brandy, Brandy*, 1972; *LMF* (*Lack of Moral Fibre*), 1976; *Haute Cuisine*, 1977; *The Lie*, 1978; *In a Dry Place*, 1986.

Television Writing: *The Army Game* series; *Bootsie and Snudge* series; for Eric Sykes, Arthur Haynes, Frankie Howerd, Jimmy Wheeler shows; *Lenny the Lion Show*, 1957; *Variety Inc. Show*, 1957; *For the Children Show*, 1957; *Early to Braden* series, 1957; *The April 8th Show* (*Seven Days Early*), 1958; *The Deadly Game of Chess*, 1958; *The Missing Links*, 1965; *An Apple a Day*, 1971; *Don't Feed the Fish*, 1971; *Marty Feldman Show*, 1972; *Milligan in All Seasons*, with Spike Milligan, 1974; episode in *M*A*S*H*, 1980 (USA); episode in *Too Close for Comfort*, 1984 (USA); *The Last Laugh Before T.V. AM*, with Spike Milligan, 1985.

Other (for children)

The Boy with Illuminated Measles. London, Robson, 1978.
Help! I Am a Prisoner in a Toothpaste Factory. London, Robson, 1978.
Ronnie and the Haunted Rolls Royce. London, Robson, 1982.
Ronnie and the Great Knitted Robbery. London, Robson, 1982.

*

Manuscript Collection: Mugar Memorial Library, Boston University.

Theatrical Activities:
Director: **Plays**—*The Bed-Sitting Room* (co-director, with Spike Milligan), London, 1963; *You'll Come to Love Your Sperm Test*, Edinburgh and London, 1965; *Savages* by Christopher Hampton, Aalsburg, Denmark, 1973; *Jonah*, Oxford, 1979; *One Orange for the Baby*, London, 1980; *The Bed-Sitting Room 2*, London, 1983.
Actor: **Plays**—*You'll Come to Love Your Sperm Test*, Edinburgh and London, 1965; *An Evening with John Antrobus*, London, 1969; Glendenning in *The Contractor* by David Storey, London, 1970; *Hitler in Liverpool*, London, 1980. **Film**—*Raising the Wind* (*Roommates*), 1961. **Radio**—*The Missing Links*, 1986. **Television**—*Squaring the Circle* by Tom Stoppard, 1986.

* * *

John Antrobus wrote his first play, *The Bed-Sitting Room*, with Spike Milligan; and though Antrobus's range has broadened, all his work has retained characteristics which are as well examined through this first play as through any other.

World War III, apparently caused by a "Nuclear Misunderstanding," mutates Lord Fortnum of Alamein into the bed-sitting room of the title. His doctor moves into the premises instead of curing his patient, a trendy vicar in a Victorian bathing costume performs a marriage service by reading from *Lady Chatterley's Lover*, and Harold Wilson becomes a parrot. It is a surrealist mock-heroic fable, then, a shell-distorted mirror to an absurd society. The Milligan element is clearly crucial; like that of *The Goon Show*, its humour may or may not be tasteful, and its vaudeville cross-talk moves from brilliant lunacy to dead trivialities. It remains hilarious—indeed it must be one of the funniest plays to come out of modern England—and it cocktails gentleness with blasphemy, pathos, beauty, desperation, and innocent reverence. The exuberance of the play gives way to tenderness in the scene at the end in which a mother cries, "Give me back my baby." But Goonishness is a fraught context for simple or naive sincerity, especially where it leads to immediate wish-fulfilment. Muddling through the ineptitude of the protagonists and the play is a strong moral concern addressed to the perennially urgent question of human survival. The play's satire, directed against politicians, vicars, advertising men, and all other regulators of modern man, is clearly rooted in Britain—as is its refusal to take itself seriously.

Ambivalences and tensions are rife in all of Antrobus's plays, and it is unclear whether these result from mere self-indulgence or from a lack of critical sense. At its worst, Antrobus's indiscipline leads to monotony, flabbiness, and garrulity; at his best Antrobus bids fair to rival Pinter; and usually, in spite of his lack of clarity and faults of his dramatic structure, Antrobus manages to be profoundly disturbing and stimulating. From a formal or technical point of view, his best work has been for radio. He is among the half dozen radio dramatists who manage to produce work which both understands and exploits the distinctive nature of radio as a medium. Antrobus is best known, however, for his work on television where both *The Army Game* and *Bootsie and Snudge* have acquired immortality.

His Christian conversion, though a conversion to Jesus rather than to dogma or denomination, seemed out of character to observers who could only see in his work brilliant if anarchic satire of the Establishment. Lying just under that hard and polished surface has been a concern, usually expressed through irony, with the deepest issues of our time: the problems posed by the "advances" of science, the nature of militarism, whether anything differentiates normalcy from madness, pretence and honesty in human relationships, the wolfish and sheepish character of such religion as is tolerated (or connived at) by those in cultural and political power, However, his conversion seems to have had no discernible effect on his work—or is the relatively conservative form of *Crete and Sergeant Pepper* part of a search for a new synthesis that is as yet only partly evident? If Antrobus can find a structure for his pyrotechnic fluidity, and grow the body of his work from that inner womb or heart which is clearly sensitive to moral and even spiritual issues, we may find his genius properly revealed instead of the individual, energetic, and zany playwright whom we have seen so far.

—Prabhu S. Guptara

ARCHIBALD, (Rupert) Douglas. Citizen of Trinidad and Tobago. Born in Port-of-Spain, 25 April 1919. Educated at Queen's Royal College, Port-of-Spain, 1928–35; McGill University, Montreal, Bachelor of Engineering (Civil) 1946. Served in the 2nd Battalion, Trinidad Light Infantry, 1938–40: Sergeant; in the Canadian Army Reserve, 1943–45: 2nd Lieutenant. Married Maureen Wedderburn Berry in 1953; one daughter and one son. Student engineer, Trinidad Government Railways, 1935–41; riot policeman, 1937, and platoon commander, 1940–41, Trinidad Special Police; assistant maintenance engineer, Trinidad Government Railways, 1946–48; in private practice as a consulting civil engineer, 1949–63 and 1969–83; editor, *Progress* magazine, 1952; member of the Editorial Board, *Clarion* newspaper, 1954–56; general manager, Trinidad and Tobago Telephone Service, 1963–68; Managing Director, Trinidad and Tobago Telephone Company Ltd., 1968–69; Chairman of the Railway Board, Trinidad, 1963–65; Chairman of the Central Water Distribution Authority, Trinidad and Tobago, 1964–65; Vice-Chairman of the Public Transport Service Corporation, Trinidad and Tobago, 1965–67; Director, Trinidad Engineering and Research Ltd., 1970–83. Tutor in Creative Writing, University of the West Indies, St. Augustine, Trinidad, 1971, 1973, 1975. Founding member, later Vice-President and President, Readers and Writers Guild of Trinidad and Tobago, 1948–54; member, Engineering Institute of Canada, 1953; founding member, 1958, later Vice-President and President, and Fellow, 1974, Association of Professional Engineers of Trinidad and Tobago; President, Historical Society of Trinidad and Tobago, 1967–80. Recipient: Theatre Guild award, 1962. Address: 3 St. Andrew's Avenue, Fairways, Maraval, Trinidad and Tobago.

PUBLICATIONS

Plays

Junction Village (produced Port-of-Spain, 1954; London, 1955). Mona, University of the West Indies, 1958.

Anne-Marie (produced Port-of-Spain, 1958; London, 1976). St. Augustine, Trinidad, University of the West Indies, 1967.

The Bamboo Clump (produced Port-of-Spain, 1962). Mona, University of the West Indies, 1967.

The Rose Slip (produced Port-of-Spain, 1962). Mona, University of the West Indies, 1967.

Old Maid's Tale (produced Port-of-Spain, 1965). Mona, University of the West Indies, 1966.

Island Tide (produced San Fernando, Trinidad). Mona, University of the West Indies, 1972.

Defeat with Honour. Mona, University of the West Indies, 1977.

Back of Beyond (produced Port-of-Spain, 1984).

Radio Plays: *That Family Next Door* series and *Island Tide* series, 1973.

Television Play: *My Good Friend Justice*, 1974.

Novel

Isidore and the Turtle. St. Augustine, University of the West Indies, 1977.

* * *

Douglas Archibald is concerned with the decay of rural society in Trinidad. We see something of the old bourgeois order in *Anne-Marie*, set on an estate 50 miles from Port-of-Spain towards the end of the last century. Here, James Fanshawe and his Spanish-descended neighbour, Pedro Meijas, bemoan the fact that they are not the men their fathers were. Their estates are being run down, they have no male heirs and if they make their housekeepers pregnant, it is not to perpetuate the old line. *Old Maid's Tale* is a sentimental extension of this world where "Aunt Hetty," last of the Macdougals, brings romantic young lovers together over tea and cucumber sandwiches, recalling the lovers of her own youth—who exist only in her imagination.

Men in this society abdicate responsibility, and this is also the basic fact of life in the village, cut off equally from the town and from the plantation. In *The Bamboo Clump* the hypochondriac Charles Mackenzie is master of the house in name only. He has ignored his family, neglected his 30-acre cocoa estate, and done little in the last five years but sit on a bench in his garden. As a result, his son Dennis, like every other West Indian youth unable to emigrate, adopts supposedly United States dress (this was before Black Power!) and drifts towards trouble with the police. His daughter Drina is an intolerable prude and is being trained for her projected schoolteacher's career by the usual caricature spinster. When she fails her exams, there seems no way to stop Li Fat (the middleaged Chinese shopkeeper from whom they'd been getting credit) claiming her as his wife. To stop the rot, Charles finally (and improbably) asserts himself.

But the men are fighting a losing battle. In *Junction Village* the matriarchal society has arrived. The action centres round the household of Grannie Gombo who, past 90, is apparently dying. The neighbours (including Bobo and Lizzy, also in their

90's) gather for the wake, but are on their guard as Grannie has tried this trick before. As they wait, the granddaughters discuss Grannie's money, and Bobo relives the many conquests of his youth—counting Granny and Lizzy among them. Bobo is now treated as a harmless nuisance, but when he echoes the dying cry of all the other nonagenarian men, from Baba in *Anne-Marie* to Bucket in *The Rose Slip*, we are genuinely disturbed. Archibald shows us that their fear isn't only of a cold bath and the poor house, but of the loneliness and loss of power and respect which afflict the old. And they abound in these villages. Bobo reflects that

> dere was a time w'en Ah wus strong, an' me arm wus like iron. Den pipple use to fear me an' Ah use ter walk in an' out a whey Ah did want. . . . Ah had moh bed dan one to sleep in dose days. Now me strenk gorn. One day it leave me sudden, jus' like dat an' dey begin to push me aroun' an aroun'. Dese days me bones hurtin' me somet'ing bad and me t'roat alweys dryin' up. . . .

This is unsettling, also, because there seems so little compensating vitality among the youth. In the fishing village of *Island Tide* the three generation family of Mr. Paps, his son Copy Cat, and his grandson Uncle Look Up, suggests a sort of evolution in reverse—somewhat like R.S. Thomas's hill farmers. Of the two young men in *Junction Village*, one is a fool addicted to long words, and the other is a violent lout who hides under the dying woman's bed to escape detection from the police—there is energy here but ill-directed. However, there is comic relief as Grannie Gombo returns to life and demands food. There's nothing like this to lighten the drudgery of the city dwellers in *The Rose Slip*. Men, young and old, have been reduced to children; the women are harassed by their landlord, and in spite of their prayer meetings, can't feed their children. There is no relief in sight.

Archibald's social concern is serious enough. The plays suggest that a lack of paternal grip in all its forms leads to disintegration. But there is a certain old-fashioned view of social order in that things are measured against the loss of past certainties rather than explored for their present potential. It is a determinism which eschews experiment, and is reflected at its worst in the characterization. The caricatures—of the spinster, the black Englishman, the druggist using long words, etc.—work beautifully; but when in play after play, *individuals* fail to break through this "type casting" either of their aspirations or of their diction, the result is an overall complacency that confirms old prejudices.

—E.A. Markham

ARDEN, John. British. Born in Barnsley, Yorkshire, 26 October 1930. Educated at schools in Barnsley; Sedbergh School, Yorkshire, 1944–48; King's College, Cambridge, 1950–53, B.A. in architecture 1953; Edinburgh College of Art, 1953–55, diploma in architecture 1955. Served in the British Army Intelligence Corps, 1949–50: Lance-Corporal. Married the actress Margaretta Ruth D'Arcy in 1957; five sons (one deceased). Architectural assistant, London, 1955–57; full-time writer from 1958. Fellow in Playwriting, Bristol University, 1959–60; Visiting Lecturer in Politics and Drama, New York University, 1967; Regents Lecturer, University of California, Davis, 1973; writer-in-residence, University of New England, Armidale, New South Wales, 1975. Founder, Committee of 100 anti-nuclear group, 1961; chairman, *Peace News* pacifist weekly, London, 1966–70; co-founder, Corrandulla Arts Centre, County Galway, Ireland, 1973; founding member, Theatre Writers' Group (now Theatre Writers' Union), 1975. Recipient: BBC Northern Region prize, 1957; Encyclopaedia Britannica prize, 1959; *Evening Standard* award, 1960; Trieste Festival award, 1961; Vernon Rice award, 1966; John Whiting Award, 1973. Lives in Galway. Agent: Margaret Ramsay Ltd., 14-A Goodwin's Court, London WC2N 4LL, England.

PUBLICATIONS

Plays

All Fall Down (produced Edinburgh, 1955).

The Waters of Babylon (produced London, 1957; New York, 1965). Included in *Three Plays*, 1964.

When Is a Door Not a Door? (produced London, 1958). Included in *Soldier, Soldier and Other Plays*, 1967.

Live Like Pigs (produced London, 1958; New York, 1965). Published in *New English Dramatists 3*, London, Penguin, 1961; in *Three Plays*, 1964.

Serjeant Musgrave's Dance: An Unhistorical Parable (produced London, 1959; San Francisco, 1961; New York, 1966). London, Methuen, 1960; New York, Grove Press, 1962; revised version (produced London, 1972).

The Happy Haven, with Margaretta D'Arcy (produced Bristol and London, 1960; Kingston, Rhode Island, 1963; New York, 1967). Published in *New English Dramatists 4*, London, Penguin, 1962; in *Three Plays*, 1964.

Soldier, Soldier (televised 1960). Included in *Soldier, Soldier and Other Plays*, 1967.

The Business of Good Government: A Christmas Play, with Margaretta D'Arcy (also co-director: as *A Christmas Play*, produced Brent Knoll, Somerset, 1960; New York, 1970; as *The Business of Good Government*, produced London, 1978). London, Methuen, 1963; New York, Grove Press, 1967.

Wet Fish (televised 1961). Included in *Soldier, Soldier and Other Plays*, 1967.

The Workhouse Donkey: A Vulgar Melodrama (produced Chichester, 1963). London, Methuen, 1964; New York, Grove Press, 1967.

Ironhand, adaptation of a play by Goethe (produced Bristol, 1963). London, Methuen, 1965.

Armstrong's Last Goodnight: An Exercise in Diplomacy (produced Glasgow, 1964; London, 1965; Boston, 1966). London, Methuen, 1965; New York, Grove Press, 1966.

Ars Longa, Vita Brevis (for children), with Margaretta D'Arcy (produced London, 1964). Published in *Eight Plays 1*, edited by Malcolm Stuart Fellows, London, Cassell, 1965.

Three Plays. London, Penguin, 1964; New York, Grove Press, 1966.

Play Without Words (produced Glasgow, 1965).

Fidelio, adaptation of a libretto by Joseph Sonnleithner and Friedrich Treitschke, music by Beethoven (produced London, 1965).

Left-Handed Liberty: A Play about Magna Carta (produced London, 1965; Boston, 1968). London, Methuen, 1965; New York, Grove Press, 1966.

Friday's Hiding, with Margaretta D'Arcy (produced Edinburgh, 1966). Included in *Soldier, Soldier and Other Plays*, 1967.

The Royal Pardon; or, The Soldier Who Became an Actor (for children), with Margaretta D'Arcy (also co-director: produced Beaford, Devon, 1966; London, 1967). London, Methuen, 1967.
Soldier, Soldier and Other Plays. London, Methuen, 1967.
The True History of Squire Jonathan and His Unfortunate Treasure (produced London, 1968; New York, 1974). Included in *Two Autobiographical Plays*, 1971.
The Hero Rises Up: A Romantic Melodrama, with Margaretta D'Arcy (also co-director: produced London, 1968). London, Methuen, 1969.
The Soldier's Tale, adaptation of a libretto by Ramuz, music by Stravinsky (produced Bath, 1968).
Harold Muggins Is a Martyr, with Margaretta D'Arcy and the Cartoon Archetypical Slogan Theatre (produced London, 1968).
The Bagman; or, The Impromptu of Muswell Hill (broadcast 1970). Included in *Two Autobiographical Plays*, 1971.
Two Autobiographical Plays. London, Methuen, 1971.
Two Hundred Years of Labour History, with Margaretta D'Arcy (produced London, 1971).
Granny Welfare and the Wolf, with Margaretta D'Arcy and Roger Smith (produced London, 1971).
My Old Man's a Tory, with Margaretta D'Arcy (produced London, 1971).
Rudi Dutschke Must Stay, with Margaretta D'Arcy (produced London, 1971).
The Ballygombeen Bequest, with Margaretta D'Arcy (produced Belfast and London, 1972; New York, 1976). Published in *Scripts 9* (New York), September 1972; revised version, as *The Little Gray Home in the West: An Anglo-Irish Melodrama* (produced Birmingham, 1982), London, Pluto Press, 1982.
The Island of the Mighty: A Play on a Traditional British Theme, with Margaretta D'Arcy (produced London, 1972; section produced, as *Handful of Watercress*, New York, 1976). London, Eyre Methuen, 1974; in *Performance* (New York), 1974.
The Devil and the Parish Pump, with Margaretta D'Arcy (produced Galway, 1974).
The Crown Strike Play, with Margaretta D'Arcy (produced Galway, 1975).
The Non-Stop Connolly Show: A Dramatic Cycle of Continuous Struggle in Six Parts, with Margaretta D'Arcy (also co-director: produced Dublin, 1975; London, 1976). London, Pluto Press, 5 vols., 1977–78; 1 vol. edition, London, Methuen, 1986.
Sean O'Scrudu, with Margaretta D'Arcy (produced Galway, 1976).
The Mongrel Fox, with Margaretta D'Arcy (produced Galway, 1976).
No Room at the Inn, with Margaretta D'Arcy (produced Galway, 1976).
Silence, with Margaretta D'Arcy (produced Galway, 1977).
Mary's Name, with Margaretta D'Arcy (produced Galway, 1977).
Blow-in Chorus for Liam Cosgrave, with Margaretta D'Arcy (produced Galway, 1977).
Plays 1 (includes *Serjeant Musgrave's Dance, The Workhouse Donkey, Armstrong's Last Goodnight*). London, Eyre Methuen, 1977; New York, Grove Press, 1978.
Vandaleur's Folly: An Anglo-Irish Melodrama, with Margaretta D'Arcy (also co-director: produced Lancaster, 1978). London, Eyre Methuen, 1981.
Pearl: A Play about a Play Within the Play (broadcast 1978). London, Eyre Methuen, 1979.
The Old Man Sleeps Alone (broadcast 1982). Published in *Best Radio Plays of 1982*, London, Methuen, 1983.
The Mother, with Margaretta D'Arcy, adaptation of a play by Brecht (produced London, 1984).
The Making of Muswell Hill, with Margaretta D'Arcy (produced London, 1984).

Radio Plays: *The Life of Man*, 1956; *The Bagman*, 1970; *Keep These People Moving!* (for children), with Margaretta D'Arcy, 1972; *Pearl*, 1978; *To Put It Frankly*, 1979; *Don Quixote*, from the novel by Cervantes, 1980; *The Winking Goose* (documentary), 1982; *Garland for a Hoar Head*, 1982; *The Old Man Sleeps Alone*, 1982; *The Manchester Enthusiasts*, with Margaretta D'Arcy, 1984.

Television Plays: *Soldier, Soldier*, 1960; *Wet Fish*, 1961; *Sean O'Casey: Portrait of a Rebel* (documentary), with Margaretta D'Arcy, 1973 (Ireland).

Novel

Silence among the Weapons: Some Events at the Time of the Failure of a Republic. London, Methuen, 1982; as *Vox Pop: Last Days of the Roman Republic*, New York, Harcourt Brace, 1983.

Other

To Present the Pretence: Essays on the Theatre and Its Public. London, Eyre Methuen, 1977; New York, Holmes and Meier, 1979.

*

Critical Studies: *John Arden* by Ronald Hayman, London, Heinemann, 1968, New York, Ungar, 1972; *Theatre Language: A Study of Arden, Osborne, Pinter, and Wesker* by John Russell Brown, London, Allen Lane, and New York, Taplinger, 1972; *John Arden* by Simon Trussler, New York, Columbia Universtiy Press, 1973; *John Arden* by Glenda Leeming, London, Longman, 1974; *Arden: A Study of His Plays* by Albert Hunt, London, Eyre Methuen, 1974; *Anger and Detachment: A Study of Arden, Osborne, and Pinter* by Michael Anderson, London, Pitman, 1976; *John Arden* by Frances Gray, London, Macmillan, and New York, Grove Press, 1982; *John Arden* by Malcolm Page, Boston, Twayne, 1984, and *Arden on File* edited by Page, London, Methuen, 1985.

Theatrical Activities:
Director, with Margaretta D'Arcy: several of his own plays.
Actor: **Plays**—Wise Man in *A Christmas Play*, Brent Knoll, Somerset, 1960; Constable in *The Royal Pardon*, Beaford, Devon, 1966; Mr. Muggins in *Harold Muggins Is a Martyr*, London, 1968.

John Arden comments:

(1977) At the present time the gap between the playwright and the active life of the theatre seems as wide as it has ever been: and it shows no sign of closing. Figures such as the director and the scenic designer, whose relevance to good dramatic writing is at best marginal, have increased their power and influence in no small measure during the past few years: and they stand ominously between playwright and actors, inhibiting proper communication. The *content* of new plays is obscured and neutralized by over-emphasis on aesthetic theatrical *form*.

The dependence of the dramatic art upon subsidies from public funds has given rise to a bureaucratic intransigence on the part of directors, who are too often administrators as well, and are becoming less and less inclined to take the necessary risks demanded by adventurous and expanding experiment. The problem is similar to that faced by Ben Jonson in the 1620's, when he struck out against the dominance of Inigo Jones as designer-director of court entertainment, and lost his battle. The result of Jones's victory was the securing by the monarchy of the complete allegiance of the theatrical profession, followed by the closure of the theatres during the Cromwellian revolution. The playwrights, as a trade-grouping, never again recaptured the position of artistic strength and poetic potency which they had attained at the beginning of the 17th century. To forestall an equivalent disaster today, the modern dramatists must attempt two apparently contradictory tasks. 1) They must abandon their solitary status and learn to combine together to secure conditions-of-work and artistic control over the products of their imagination. 2) They must be prepared to combine not only with their fellows, but also with *actors*. It is not enough for the occasional author to *direct*; playwrights should be members of theatrical troupes, and take part in all aspects of production. In order to achieve goal 2), goal 1) must first be arrived at. The authors together must establish the importance of their written work as an essential *internal* element of the theatre, and then, individually, they must become absorbed into the theatre themselves as co-workers.

I am aware that these requirements go against all current trends. But the current trends are running towards the complete death of the modern drama. Remember, Shakespeare and Molière regarded themselves as men of the theatre rather than *literary* figures: and I believe it to be no accident that their works remain unequalled in the Western tradition.

* * *

John Arden is generally acknowledged to be one of the major playwrights of the modern British theatre. Ironically, however, while praise is lavished on his breaking of the forms of realism—his open staging; his bold, poetic language; his grand, compelling characters; his resonant visual imagery—the content of his plays is often treated with bemusement and confusion. Ironic because a moment's consideration suggests that changes in form by necessity signal changes in perspective and concern. Alternative forms imply alternative preconceptions not only about what the theatre is about but also about its subject matter.

Realism, for example, assumes the individual's personal experience as both its source and goal; it invites the audience to get closer to the psychology and emotions of the central characters, while at the same time presents morality as a basic dichotomy, moving the audience in the direction of overt and generalized judgements, the desirable vs. the undesirable. The confusions about what Arden's plays "mean" seem to stem from the assumption that, whatever the form of the play, it will somehow end up elaborating human emotion, eliciting sympathy, and making a clear moral stand—especially if it appears to deal with social and political issues. However, the illustrative purposes of realism belong to realism, and Arden's change of form implies a change of purpose.

Take *Serjeant Musgrave's Dance*: argument rages about whether Arden is for or against pacifism. But the question becomes irrelevant if a more inclusive view of the whole play is taken. Obviously, the play is not pro-war. Indeed, it is based on the assumption that war is undesirable; Arden assumes his audience will begin on this premise. No argument is set up in the play either for or against war or for or against pacifism. The discussion is simply never entered into. Pacifism may be a burning 20th-century issue, but Arden, or any other playwright, is under no obligation to pass judgement on it directly. In *Serjeant Musgrave's Dance*, pacifism is the context, not the content, of the play. Pacifism states the terms by which the relationship between the means and the ends are elaborated.

The very fact that war has negative value in the play and that it is assumed the audience accepts this is an indication that the play is not about the dichotomy between war-mongering and pacifism. We are meant to agree that Musgrave's aim is desirable, that his intentions could not be more positive. Our attention is thus turned from his intentions to his actions, from his desired end, which we share, to his means, which, in turn, produce their own ends, ends which contradict these excellent intentions. Through Musgrave we see the process by which even the finest of intentions becomes corrupted by the means employed for its accomplishment.

We are introduced to Musgrave indirectly, through the effect he has on others. This prepares us to look toward action, not explanation, to judge by effect, not rationale. His soldiers prepare us for a man to look up to: organized, commanding, demanding respect. Because of his uniform and his confident manner, Musgrave attracts our respect for the qualities our society admires: order, organization, "God fearing," and, above all, logic. But these are the very qualities which drive him to his horrifying conclusion. When Musgrave—steeped in a simple fundamental religious belief, a soldier's training, a life of careful order and authority and, above all, a complete faith in logical thought—is confronted with the horrifying chaos of war (to which he has devoted his life), he inevitably uses these means, the only ones he has, to create a plan to annihilate war. His solution is neat, ordered, totally logical and has, in his eyes, the blessing of God. His intentions are good; the result, insane and destructive. Even Musgrave's insight that the source of war lies with ordinary people who let their husbands and sons become cannon fodder, has a certain validity, but his method of eradicating war is not only unacceptable but futile. Killing 25 villagers will never eradicate war.

The opposition set up in *Serjeant Musgrave's Dance* is not between war and peace but between social ideals of order, organization, and logic and the "messy scribbling" of day-to-day existence, the erratic demands of emotion and need. At the opposite extreme from Musgrave stands the Bargee, an unattractive picture of daily survival unhampered by principle and design. Near Musgrave, the Major and Parson, organizing fumblingly for their own ends. In the middle, the women and the miners with their needs, passions, and inconsistencies, and morals based more on experience than ideals. The play provides an analysis of the social precepts of order and reason as they are superimposed on the chaos of ordinary life.

Serjeant Musgrave's Dance also challenges the realist premise that good intentions mitigate behavior and that reason can solve all human problems by calling reason into question. What is important about Annie, for example, is not that she will sleep with any man, but that her act of lovemaking is an act of warmth and revivification. Arden is neither promoting nor condemning promiscuity, but contrasting the effect of Annie's actions with the imposed purity of Musgrave's orderliness.

Arden's vision is essentially anarchic. Ideals of organization and reason distort human life. War itself is the result of imposed ordering on human existence. The entrance of the dragoons to restore "order" and save us from Musgrave may bring some relief, but it also brings an inescapable sense of failure.

The playwright's organization subverts the audience's preconceptions of order. Arden's use of the open stage, his ballads and heightened language, his frequent placing of more than one character at the centre of a play are devised to turn attention away from personalization and simple morality toward an examination of how these moral precepts function in practice. In *The Workhouse Donkey*, for example, it is fruitless to complain that none of the politicians is blameless. "Misgoverned," says Sweetman, "Oh, its not exactly misgoverned. Its just the wrong lot are the governors, that's all." The play assumes that power corrupts. The difference between Labour and Tory is not which is corrupt, but what form their corruption takes and to what end. Indeed, the involvement in this cosily untidy world of Feng, the incorruptible policeman, takes us into an examination of the consequences of obsessive morality imposed on an imperfect world. As Arden says, Feng's absolute integrity causes infinitely more damage than Butterthwaite's bumbling dishonesty could ever manage. Feng lacks warmth and an understanding of the catch-as-catch-can living that is the very breath of life, whereas it is Butterthwaite's warmth and human failings that endear him to us, despite his imperfections. By assuming a world of general imperfection, Arden attempts to turn attention away from abstract ideals of simplistic morality and towards the effect of these ideals being put into practice without regard for the fundamental anarchy of daily living.

Arden's theatrical devices distance the audience from the characters so the characters might be seen as active members of working societies. No better or worse than any others, these societies run, as all do, on moral precepts that have their weaknesses and strengths. When one of these little worlds is confronted by another which does not share its assumptions, the characters find themselves in extreme situations which threaten their social preconceptions. The consequences and effects of these actions dramatize the complex relationships between the individual and society, between social ideals and their practical application, between means and end.

Live Like Pigs can be read as a confrontation between two ways of living, acceptable enough in themselves, but mutually destructive in confrontation. But this pattern is most richly and tragically elaborated in *Armstrong's Last Goodnight*. Through Lindsay and Armstrong the weaknesses and inner workings of their societies are set in relief. Neither Armstrong nor Lindsay is a villain. Each is the perfect representative of his society, but their worlds are different, with different ways of ordering and interpreting life, different moral concepts, different ideals. Both enlist our sympathy: Armstrong, leader in an individualist world of action; Lindsay, spokesman of the King of an integrated world of reason. Each society, in its own terms, is perfectly viable, but they are totally incompatible.

Though both live in Scotland, Lindsay and Armstrong inhabit realities so different they can hardly speak to each other. The way each sees and evaluates the world excludes the world of the other. (When Lindsay tells Armstrong's wife he has come from the King, she answers "What King would that be?" Even such a simple concept as "King" is not shared.) The scenes of the play are juxtaposed to emphasize the misinterpretations and incompatibilities. The use of the stage itself—with James's court on one side and Armstrong's castle on the other—presents a visual image of the distance between the two worlds. Clothing imagery elaborates the social symbols of value and role and marks the opposing experiences of the characters. It is not that one is right and one wrong, but rather that each, though wholly consistent within itself, is totally incompatible with the other. Yet, Lindsay's quest is to integrate the two.

Both societies have justifiable organizations and moral precepts which serve as strengths as well as weaknesses. These weaknesses are forced to the surface in the confrontation. Armstrong's individualism leads him to his death. Lindsay's belief in reason is entirely negated as the reasonable, organized society destroys Armstrong and the world he represents. We are not asked to judge the moral precepts informing these two worlds so much as to wonder at the fact that despite their opposing orders and moralities, they resort to the same exact manner of dealing with threats to their own security—Wamphrey and Armstrong are executed on the same tree. Neither vision is intrinsically superior to the other. Attention is turned from the superficialities of abstract moral judgement to the exacting examination of the execution of moral ideals in an imperfect world.

Arden's formal changes in theatre imply criticism of the preconceptions that are fundamental to realist forms of narrative. They demand a shift from simplistic moralizing to dramatic investigation, a transfer both in life and theatre from idealized expectations and easy judgements to responsible application and political analysis that goes beyond the simple taking of sides. The best of his later plays, those written for radio, make full use of the vast canvas offered by the medium and continue Arden's unblinkered investigation of the individual in his social/historical setting, including, hardly surprisingly, the question of the artist's function in his society.

—Elaine Turner

AXELROD, George. American. Born in New York City, 9 June 1922. Served in the United States Army Signal Corps during World War II. Married 1) Gloria Washburn in 1942 (divorced 1954), two sons; 2) Joan Stanton in 1954, one daughter. Film director and producer. Recipient: Writers Guild of America West award, for screenplay, 1962. Agent: Irving Paul Lazar Agency, 211 South Beverly Drive, Beverly Hills, California 90212, U.S.A.

PUBLICATIONS

Plays

Sketches, with Max Wilk, in *Small Wonder* (produced New York, 1948).

The Seven Year Itch: A Romantic Comedy (produced New York, 1952; London, 1953). New York, Random House, 1953; London, Heinemann, 1954.

Will Success Spoil Rock Hunter? (also director: produced New York, 1955). New York, Random House, 1956.

Goodbye Charlie (also director: produced New York, 1959). New York, French, 1959.

Souvenir, with Peter Viertel (produced Los Angeles, 1975).

Screenplays: *Phffft!*, 1954; *The Seven Year Itch*, with Billy Wilder, 1955; *Bus Stop*, 1956; *Rally 'round the Flag, Boys* (uncredited), 1958; *Breakfast at Tiffany's*, 1961; *The Manchurian Candidate*, 1962; *Paris When It Sizzles*, 1963; *How to Murder Your Wife*, 1964; *Lord Love a Duck*, with Larry H. Johnson, 1966; *The Secret Life of an American Wife*, 1968; *The Lady Vanishes*, 1979; *The Holcroft Covenant*, with Edward Anhalt and John Hopkins, 1982.

Radio Writer: *Midnight in Manhattan* program, 1940; material for *Grand Old Opry*, 1950–52.

Television Writer: for *Celebrity Time*, 1950.

Night Club Writer: *All about Love*, New York, 1951.

Novels

Beggar's Choice. New York, Howell Soskin, 1947; as *Hobson's Choice*, London, Elek, 1951.
Blackmailer. New York, Fawcett, 1952; London, Fawcett, 1959.
Where Am I Now—When I Need Me? New York, Viking Press, and London, Deutsch, 1971.

*

Theatrical Activities:
Director: **Plays**—*Will Success Spoil Rock Hunter?*, New York, 1955; *Once More, With Feeling* by Harry Kurnitz, New York, 1958; *Goodbye Charlie*, New York, 1959; *The Star-Spangled Girl* by Neil Simon, New York, 1966. **Films**—*Lord Love a Duck*, 1966; *The Secret Life of an American Wife*, 1968.

* * *

The playwriting career of George Axelrod well illustrates that dramatist of particular wit and imagination who manages to create marketable products for Broadway tastes and, for a brief period, enjoys the fame and fortune that successful commercial comedy brings. His brief period was the decade of the 1950's. *The Seven Year Itch* ran nearly three years in New York, with 1,141 performances and *Will Success Spoil Rock Hunter?* lasted a year and had 444 performances. Prior to his first success he had learned his trade writing for radio and television. Since this decade of playwriting he has had some success as a director, effectively directing such plays as Neil Simon's *The Star-Spangled Girl* for an audience acceptance that he was no longer able to reach as a dramatist.

In the history of American comic drama Axelrod might be mentioned as the author of two plays which say something about American tastes and attitudes during that post-World War II decade when audiences enjoyed a semi-sophisticated joke along with a semi-realistic view of themselves. Although the period for this enjoyment continued under the aegis of Neil Simon, Axelrod's imagination for such playwriting dried up. A later novel, *Where Am I Now—When I Need Me?*, is an artless attempt to capitalize on current free expression in writing as well as a kind of pathetic admission. In the span of theatre history in America the decade of the 1950's will be considered undistinguished and Axelrod's contribution will be measured, if at all, as an instance of conscious yet effective technique on the Broadway scale of carefully analysed entertainment.

Axelrod's success as a dramatist came with his ability to write clever, simply structured comedy that seemed a bit outrageous or naughty at first but was generally acceptable and comforting. Liberal circles have labelled him a writer of right-wing comedy in which right-wing morality always triumphs and have considered his success a disturbing feature of American comedy. Such observations have their place in history, but it is nonetheless true that such conservative comedy has a rich reputation in American comedy and for a decade Axelrod's polished and carefully tailored plays were the most imaginative of these slim pieces of professionally manufactured theatre. His plays satisfied an audience's needs. *The Seven Year Itch* tells of a New York businessman, Richard Shermans, who combines a humorous reluctance and eagerness as he spends a night with a girl after his wife has left the hot city for the summer months. *Will Success Spoil Rock Hunter?* toys with the Faustus theme as George MacCawley sells his soul ten percent at a time for fame, fortune and certain pleasures. But Axelrod always emphasized a definite, if sometimes late, morality. Richard is funny because his reluctance, his ineptness, and his remorse contrast hilariously with his view of himself as a seducer. At the final curtain a likeable hero emerges from an educational experience; even the girl, who slept with him because he could not be serious with her, begins to think that marriage should be worth a try. George also eats his cake and has it to enjoy. His fantasies are dramatically fulfilled, and he does not lose his soul. In this manner Axelrod presented safe, conservative entertainment that would run for at least a year. A few years later it is out of date, and with another generation it has lost most of its appeal.

Technically, Axelrod used the accepted devices of unpretentious comic entertainment. Verbal and visual jokes were a major part of a play's success with an audience. Perhaps that is why Axelrod has since substituted directing for playwriting. Topicality in the jokes was as much a part of a play's success as it was an appeal to snobbishness in the audiences. There are numerous local references to New York, and names were dropped in almost every scene. Obviously, Axelrod studied his audiences, considering them knowledgeable but not overly bright. Certain gags in *Will Success Spoil Rock Hunter?*—the positioning of the "Scarlet Letter" on a scantily clad model and the impossibility of making love in the sand—are repeated, and the staircase in *The Seven Year Itch*, described as giving "the joint a kind of Jean-Paul Sartre quality," is further explained as having "no exit." In *The Seven Year Itch* Axelrod enlivened his presentation with dramatic devices such as fantasy sequences, flashbacks, and soliloquies. Throughout all of his plays, ridiculing, making witty comments, and satirizing man and his society are standard ploys for humor. But Axelrod is neither innovator nor reformer, merely a professional entertainer. He satirized the usual things—the movies, psychiatrists, rental-novel sex, certain kinds of decadence, and so on. He had nothing to say to any thoughtful person, and he scarcely took himself seriously, suggesting as he did a thorough and comfortable acceptance of all that he ridiculed in his plays. John Gassner referred to his work as "imaginative fluff," and as such it has appeal for certain theatre audiences at certain times.

—Walter J. Meserve

AYCKBOURN, Alan. British. Born in London, 12 April 1939. Educated at Haileybury, Hertford, 1952–56. Married Christine Roland in 1959; two sons. Stage manager and actor, Donald Wolfit's company, in Edinburgh, Worthing, Leatherhead, Scarborough, and Oxford, 1956–57; actor and manager, Stephen Joseph Theatre-in-the-Round, Scarborough, Yorkshire, 1957–62; associate director, Victoria Theatre, Stoke-on-Trent, Staffordshire, 1962–64; drama producer, BBC Radio, Leeds, 1964–70. Since 1970 artistic director, Stephen Joseph Theatre-in-the-Round; since 1986 associate director, National Theatre, London. Recipient: *Evening Standard* award, 1974, 1975, 1978, 1985; Olivier award, 1985. D.Litt.:

Hull University, 1981. C.B.E. (Commander, Order of the British Empire), 1987. Agent: Margaret Ramsay Ltd., 14-A Goodwin's Court, London WC2N 4LL, England.

PUBLICATIONS

Plays

The Square Cat (as Roland Allen) (produced Scarborough, 1959).
Love after All (as Roland Allen) (produced Scarborough, 1959).
Dad's Tale (for children; as Roland Allen) (produced Scarborough, 1960).
Standing Room Only (as Roland Allen) (also director: produced Scarborough, 1961).
Xmas v. Mastermind (produced Stoke-on-Trent, 1962).
Mr. Whatnot (also director: produced Stoke-on-Trent, 1963; revised version produced London, 1964).
Relatively Speaking (as *Meet My Father*, produced Scarborough, 1965; as *Relatively Speaking*, produced London, 1967; New York, 1984). London, Evans, and New York, French, 1968.
The Sparrow (also director: produced Scarborough, 1967).
How the Other Half Loves (also director: produced Scarborough, 1969; London, 1970; New York, 1971). London, Evans, and New York, French, 1972.
Countdown, in *We Who Are about to...*, later called *Mixed Doubles* (produced London, 1969). London, Methuen, 1970.
Ernie's Incredible Illucinations (for children; produced London, 1971). London, French, 1969; in *The Best Short Plays 1979*, edited by Stanley Richards, Radnor, Pennsylvania, Chilton, 1979.
The Story So Far (also director: produced Scarborough, 1970; revised version, as *Me Times Me Times Me*, produced Leicester, 1971; revised version, as *Family Circles*, produced Richmond, Surrey, 1978).
Time and Time Again (also director: produced Scarborough, 1971; London, 1972). London, French, 1973.
Absurd Person Singular (also director: produced Scarborough, 1972; London, 1973; New York, 1974). Included in *Three Plays*, 1977.
Mother Figure, in *Mixed Blessings* (produced Horsham, Sussex, 1973).
The Norman Conquests: Table Manners, Living Together, Round and Round the Garden (also director: produced Scarborough, 1973; London, 1974; Los Angeles and New York, 1975). London, Chatto and Windus, 1975; New York, Grove Press, 1979.
Absent Friends (also director: produced Scarborough, 1974; London, 1975; New Haven, Connecticut, 1977). Included in *Three Plays*, 1977.
Confusions: Mother Figure, Drinking Companion, Between Mouthfuls, Gosforth's Fête, A Talk in the Park (also director: produced Scarborough, 1974; London, 1976). London, French, 1977.
Jeeves, music by Andrew Lloyd Webber, adaptation of works by P.G. Wodehouse (produced London, 1975).
Bedroom Farce (also director: produced Scarborough, 1975; London, 1977; New York, 1979). Included in *Three Plays*, 1977.
Just Between Ourselves (also director: produced Scarborough, 1976; London, 1977; Princeton, New Jersey, 1981). Included in *Joking Apart, Ten Times Table, Just Between Ourselves*, 1979.
Three Plays. London, Chatto and Windus, 1977; New York, Grove Press, 1979.
Ten Times Table (also director: produced Scarborough, 1977; London, 1978; Cleveland, 1983). Included in *Joking Apart, Ten Times Table, Just Between Ourselves*, 1979.
Joking Apart (also director: produced Scarborough, 1978; London, 1979). Included in *Joking Apart, Ten Times Table, Just Between Ourselves*, 1979.
Men on Women on Men, music by Paul Todd (produced Scarborough, 1978).
Joking Apart, Ten Times Table, Just Between Ourselves. London, Chatto and Windus, 1979; augmented edition, as *Joking Apart and Other Plays* (includes *Sisterly Feelings*), London, Penguin, 1982.
Sisterly Feelings (also director: produced Scarborough, 1979; London, 1980). With *Taking Steps*, London, Chatto and Windus, 1981.
Taking Steps (also director: produced Scarborough, 1979; London, 1980; Houston, 1983; New York, 1986). With *Sisterly Feelings*, London, Chatto and Windus, 1981.
Suburban Strains, music by Paul Todd (also director: produced Scarborough, 1980; London, 1981). London, French, 1982.
First Course, music by Paul Todd (also director: produced Scarborough, 1980).
Second Helping, music by Paul Todd (also director: produced Scarborough, 1980).
Season's Greetings (also director: produced Scarborough and London, 1980; revised version, also director: produced London, 1982; Berkeley, California, 1983; New York, 1985). London, French, 1982.
Way Upstream (also director: produced Scarborough, 1981; London, 1982). London, French, 1983.
Making Tracks, music by Paul Todd (also director: produced Scarborough, 1981; London, 1983).
Me, Myself, and I, music by Paul Todd (also director: produced Scarborough, 1981).
Intimate Exchanges (also director: produced Scarborough, 1982; London, 1984). London, French, 2 vols., 1985.
A Trip to Scarborough, adaptation of the play by Sheridan (also director: produced Scarborough, 1982).
Incidental Music (produced Scarborough, 1983).
It Could Be Any One of Us (also director: produced Scarborough, 1983).
The Seven Deadly Virtues, music by Paul Todd (also director: produced Scarborough, 1984).
The Westwoods (also director: produced Scarborough, 1984; London, 1987).
A Game of Golf (produced London, 1984).
A Chorus of Disapproval (also director: produced Scarborough, 1984; London, 1985). London, Faber, 1986.
Woman in Mind (also director: produced Scarborough, 1985; London, 1986; New York, 1987). London, Faber, 1986.
Boy Meets Girl, music by Paul Todd (also director: produced Scarborough, 1985).
Girl Meets Boy, music by Paul Todd (also director: produced Scarborough, 1985).
Mere Soup Songs, music by Paul Todd (also director: produced Scarborough and London, 1986).
A Small Family Business (also director: produced London, 1987).
Henceforward (also director: produced Scarborough, 1987).

Television Play: *Service Not Included* (*Masquerade* series), 1974.

Other

Conversations with Ayckbourn, with Ian Watson. London, Macdonald, 1981.

*

Critical Studies: *Theatre in the Round* by Stephen Joseph, London, Barrie and Rockliff, 1967; *The Second Wave* by John Russell Taylor, London, Methuen, and New York, Hill and Wang, 1971; *Post-War British Theatre* by John Elsom, London, Routledge, 1976, revised edition, 1979; *The New British Drama* by Oleg Kerensky, London, Hamish Hamilton, 1977, New York, Taplinger, 1979; *Alan Ayckbourn* by Michael Billington, London, Macmillan, 1983, New York, Grove Press, 1984.

Theatrical Activities:
Director: **Plays**—numerous productions at Victoria Theatre, Stoke-on-Trent, and Stephen Joseph Theatre, Scarborough, including *Miss Julie* by Strindberg, *Pygmalion* by Shaw, *A Man for All Seasons* by Robert Bolt, *Patriotic Bunting* and *Tishoo* by Brian Thompson, *Time and the Conways* by J.B. Priestley, *The Crucible* by Arthur Miller, *The Seagull* by Chekhov, *Thark* and *Rookery Nook* by Ben Travers, and many of his own plays; National Theatre, London: *Way Upstream*, 1982, *A Chorus of Disapproval*, 1985, *Tons of Money* by Will Evans and Valentine, 1986, *A View from the Bridge* by Arthur Miller, 1987, and *A Small Family Business*, 1987. **Radio**—more than 100 productions, Leeds, 1964–70, and subsequently.
Actor: **Plays**—roles with Stephen Joseph's touring company: The Cook in *Little Brother, Little Sister* by David Campton, Newcastle-under-Lyme, 1961; Victoria Theatre, Stoke-on-Trent: Fred in *The Birds and the Wellwishers* and Robert in *An Awkward Number* by William Norfolk, Aston in *The Caretaker*, James in *The Collection*, and Ben in *The Dumb Waiter*, by Harold Pinter, title role in *O'Flaherty, V.C.* by G.B. Shaw, Roderick Usher in *Usher* by David Campton, Bill Starbuck in *The Rainmaker* by N. Richard Nash, The Crimson Gollywog in *Xmas v. Mastermind*, The Count in *The Rehearsal* by Anouilh, Vladimir in *Waiting for Godot* by Beckett, Thomas More in *A Man for All Seasons* by Robert Bolt, Jordan in *The Rainbow Machine* and Anderson in *Ted's Cathedral* by Alan Plater, Jerry Ryan in *Two for the Seesaw* by William Gibson, Mr. Manningham in *Gaslight* by Patrick Hamilton, The Interrogator in *The Prisoner* by Bridget Boland, and A Jew and Martin del Bosco in *The Jew of Malta* by Marlowe, 1962–64.

* * *

In the early part of Alan Ayckbourn's career, discussion often turned on his method of playwriting, announcing a title and then, three or four days before rehearsals were due to start, shutting himself away to write. Ayckbourn responded by stressing that he was only a dramatist once a year, occasionally twice, and was primarily a director, of the Stephen Joseph Theatre-in-the-Round in Scarborough. (He cleverly, and uniquely, appeared in print, presenting his view of his writings, in *Conversations with Ayckbourn*, ahead of any books of criticism.)

Ayckbourn's early plays, such as *Relatively Speaking* and *Time and Time Again*, are polished and amusing. (As Ayckbourn's titles rarely point unmistakeably to the content, distinguishing between the plays is initially difficult.) His distinctive ingenuity is first shown in *How the Other Half Loves*, in which a couple attend two different dinner parties, on different days, at the same time. *Absurd Person Singular* has its three scenes on three consecutive Christmas Eves, in three different kitchens, featuring the same three married couples: a fastidious tidiness. *The Norman Conquests* is a trilogy about the events of one weekend; it shows what is happening in a dining-room, sitting-room, and garden. The plays are designed to make sense in any order, or indeed if only one is seen. *Bedroom Farce* somehow steers eight people into three on-stage bedrooms. *Sisterly Feelings* has alternative second and third acts (the choice of which is to be played determined by tossing a coin at the end of Acts 1 and 2) leading to the same fourth act. *Taking Steps* is set on different floors of a three-storey house, but "really" there is only one floor. In *It Could Be Any One of Us* Ayckbourn essays the comedy thriller, with five different endings convicting each of the suspects. *Intimate Exchanges* has two first acts, four second acts, eight third acts, and 16 fourth acts. Each episode concludes with a choice, and Ayckbourn has written the scenes for both choices. Further, the time between acts is always five days, then five weeks and finally five years, and the fourth acts are all in a churchyard, variously following weddings, christenings, funerals, and Harvest Festivals. To make his task even harder, the whole is for one actor and one actress, playing two or three parts in every version.

Ayckbourn's first attempt to write, in his phrase, "a truly hilarious dark play" is *Absurd Person Singular.* In the middle act a woman attempts suicide by several methods, while a stream of kind visitors fail to see her misery and instead clean her oven and mend her light. The comic-sinister ending has an obnoxious man dictatorially imposing party games on a group who want nothing to do with him. In *Absent Friends*, Ayckbourn's most restrained and sombre work, five people gather for a Saturday afternoon tea party to cheer Colin, whom they have not seen for some years and whose fiancée drowned two months before. Colin proves to be cheerful, which exposes the unhappiness of the rest.

Just Between Ourselves was Ayckbourn's first "Winter Play," written for January production when "the pressure that had always been on me to produce a play suited primarily to a holiday audience was no longer there." In this work he shows how a well-meaning husband drives his wife to insanity through relentless cheerfulness and optimism. The second scene ends with a disastrous tea party at which everyone tries not to focus on the forgotten birthday cake and the likelihood of accidents by the tense wife. In the extraordinary climax of the third scene, wildly funny and deeply tragic, the wife goes insane. While her husband has become entangled inside the car with the steering-wheel, seat belts, and a neighbouring woman, to whom he is demonstrating it, his wife quarrels with her mother-in-law and pursues her with a roaring electric drill. The car horn "blasts loudly and continuously," then a birthday cake is carried in and lights are switched on "bathing the scene in a glorious technicolour." Four months later the wife is seen again, sitting silent in the garden in January. Throughout this chilling scene she stares out blankly, speechless, motionless, as grim an image as any in Beckett.

Joking Apart sets its four scenes on special occasions: Guy Fawkes Night, Boxing Day, an 18th-birthday party. The scenes are four years apart, so the seven characters are seen over 12 years, from their twenties to their thirties. *Joking Apart* studies winners and losers, a likeable, generous, hospitable couple (who, significantly, have never bothered to get married) and their circle. Ayckbourn illuminates the sadness intrinsic to the way the world has born winners, and the less obvious fact that other people shrink through contrasting themselves with the winners. Similar emotional bleakness, and the same misgivings about the married state, are found in *The Story So Far* and *Season's Greetings*.

Two plays represent changes of direction. *Way Upstream* is about three couples struggling with a cabin cruiser on a week's river trip. As their journey is to Armageddon Bridge, allegory is intended: the decent, unassertive moderates (perhaps Social Democrats) eventually realise they must fight authoritarianism, capitalism, and the idle rich. *Woman in Mind* extends what has been called Comedy of Pain. Hit on the head by a garden rake, a concussed wife copes with her unsympathetic family and fantasizes an ideal family as well—which may not be as delightful as it seems. As her husband is a vicar, Ayckbourn is alluding to the failings of religion, with central themes of dislocation and unfulfilled existences.

Michael Billington in 1974 tried to place Ayckbourn as "a left-wing writer using a right-wing form; even if there is nothing strident, obvious or noisy about his socialism, it is none the less apparent that he has a real detestation for the money-grubber, the status-seeker and the get-rich-quicker." Martin Bronstein emphasises the feminism: "He's the only contemporary playwright who shows the real plight of the average woman in today's world." Ayckbourn himself has never admitted to such intentions; instead he speaks of examining "the Chekhovian field, exploring attitudes to death, loneliness, etc.—themes not generally dealt with in comedy." All Ayckbourn's work is amusing and ingenious; his greatest moments are those that combine laughs and true seriousness about the human condition—or at least the present condition of the English middle classes.

—Malcolm Page

BABE, Thomas. American. Born in Buffalo, New York, 13 March 1941. Educated at high school in Rochester, New York; Harvard University, Cambridge, Massachusetts, B.A. 1963 (Phi Beta Kappa), graduate work, 1965–68; St. Catharine's College, Cambridge (Marshall scholar, 1963–65), B.A. 1965; Yale University School of Law, New Haven, Connecticut, J. D. 1972. Married Susan Bramhall in 1967 (divorced 1976), one daughter. Operated the Summer Players, Agassiz Theatre, Cambridge, Massachusetts, with Timothy S. Mayer, 1966–68; speechwriter for John Lindsay, Mayor of New York, 1968–69. Recipient: CBS-Yale fellowship; Guggenheim fellowship, 1977; Rockefeller grant, 1978; National Endowment for the Arts fellowship, 1983. Agent: Lantz Office, 888 Seventh Avenue, New York, New York 10106. Address: 103 Hoyt Street, Darien, Connecticut 06820, U.S.A.

PUBLICATIONS

Plays

Kid Champion, music by Jim Steinman (produced New York, 1974). New York, Dramatists Play Service, 1980.

Mojo Candy (produced New Haven, Connecticut, 1975).

Rebel Women (produced New York, 1976). New York, Dramatists Play Service, n.d.

Billy Irish (produced New York, 1977). New York, Dramatists Play Service, 1982.

Great Solo Town (produced New Haven, Connecticut, 1977). New York, Dramatists Play Service, 1981.

A Prayer for My Daughter (produced New York, 1977; London, 1978). New York, French, 1977.

Fathers and Sons (produced New York, 1978). New York, Dramatists Play Service, 1980.

Taken in Marriage (produced New York, 1979). New York, Dramatists Play Service, 1979.

Daniel Boone (for children; produced on tour, 1979).

Salt Lake City Skyline (produced New York, 1980). New York, Dramatists Play Service, 1980.

Kathleen (produced New York, 1980; revised version, as *Home Again, Kathleen*, produced Baltimore, 1981; New York, 1983).

The Wild Duck, adaptation of a play by Ibsen, translated by Erik J. Friis (produced New York, 1981).

Buried Inside Extra (produced New York and London, 1983). New York, Dramatists Play Service, and London, Methuen, 1983.

Planet Fires (produced Rochester, New York, 1985).

Screenplays: *The Sun Gods*, with Mike Wadleigh, 1978; *The Vacancy*, 1979; *Kid Champion*, 1979.

Radio Plays: *Hot Dogs and Soda Pop*, 1980; *The Volunteer Fireman*, 1981; *One for the Record*, 1986.

Ballet Scenarios: *When We Were Very Young*, music by John Simon, New York, 1980; *Twyla Tharp and Dancers*, 1980.

*

Manuscript Collection: Harvard University Theatre Collection, Cambridge, Massachusetts.

Theatrical Activities:
Director: **Plays**—*Two Small Bodies* by Neal Bell, New York, 1977; *Justice* by Terry Curtis Fox, New York, 1979; *Marmalade Skies* by M. Z. Ribalow, New York, 1983; *The Pornographer's Daughter* by Terry Curtis Fox, Chicago, 1984; *Life and Limb* by Keith Reddin, New York, 1985; *Voices in the Head* by Neal Bell, New York, 1986.

Thomas Babe comments:

(1982) My position as an American playwright has been realized in the tension between a longing for eternal verities and my perverse desire, like any writer who thinks he's worth his salt, to complicate things. I've gotten in a lot of critical trouble on my native turf, most of which I've tried to weather, because when you push at the edges of things that people really care about, you find the breaking point. This is not to say what I've written is best; only to mention that the theater, in bad money times, has become more conservative in its choices as the funding has dried up while ticket prices go on rising. I've never gotten a prize, and I don't expect one, but I would love to continue to work. And that is all the impetus behind what I've done—that, and a few bucks for the bills. There is a myth that has been promulgated about the suffering of American playwrights; it is neither true nor fair to their ability to survive.

I most suspect that the ability to survive is what's behind the best work done by my contemporaries in the last decade, and nearly every one of them has upped the ante every time out.

* * *

The strains of inheritance are pulled tightly through Thomas Babe's plays. Personal and social links between parents and children tie generations together into a moment of history. His first plays explicitly turned on a pivot of historical transition, but more recently he has narrowed his focus to the intimate links between parents and children.

The first plays—*Fathers and Sons, Rebel Women*, and *Salt Lake City Skyline*—centered on American figures who can be seen as either culture heroes or historical avatars. Wild Bill Hickok, General William Sherman, and Joe Hill, respectively are used to focus on a time in American history when a particular aspect of American culture died and another was born.

In *Great Solo Town*, which juxtaposes adolescent society with Robert Kennedy's assassination, and *Taken in Marriage*, which reunites two sisters at an aborted marriage, Babe moved toward the intimacy of *A Prayer for My Daughter*. These plays focus on the bases of personal relationships: honesty, trust, love, and loyalty, with an almost microscopic intensity. In *A Prayer for My Daughter*, two policemen bring in Sean and his "daughter"-epigone Jimmy for interrogation about a murder. During this, Sergeant Kelly's daughter calls, with a gun in her mouth, threatening to kill herself. Kelly refuses to go to her, staying rather to question his suspects. Jimmy, who also has a daughter, is fascinated by Kelly's apparent lack of feeling, and the more concerned Jimmy becomes, the more Kelly transfers his feelings to the boy, culminating in a brief erotic episode between them.

Kelly's coldness toward his daughter and his warmth toward Jimmy are both part of a distinctly contemporary search for ties that don't bind. When Kelly tries to explain why he did not go to his daughter, he speaks of the relief he feels now that she is dead, because there are no more complications. At last, he says, their relationship can be pure, unadulterated by temporal problems:

> I don't want anything from her, except that I'm her father and she's my daughter, and that will never get removed. ... It's more like a thing I read about Alfred [sic] Einstein ... who said when he was a kid he read a lot of dead scientists and authors and said he didn't feel alone, he didn't think he ever would feel alone, because those dead guys were his unloseable friends. That's how I think of her, my daughter, my unloseable friend.

Babe explores this search for an objective basis for intimate emotions freely in *A Prayer for My Daughter*, as well as in the more recent plays *Home Again, Kathleen* and (to some extent) *Buried Inside Extra*. In the latter play, however, the relationship between the city editor of a major metropolitan daily newspaper, Jake Bowsky, his wife, and his daughter (who again never appears) is enclosed in a melodramatic plot. The newspaper, printing its final edition, is threatened with an atomic bomb, and the resulting narrative complications slow the play and weigh heavily on the personal revelations, which in themselves fail to weld the parts of play together. Although Babe is capable of poignant and provocative scenes, he has yet to find the dramatic structures and situations that will allow him to focus his talent for dialogue and feeling.

—Walter Bode

BALDWIN, James (Arthur). American. Born in New York City, 2 August 1924. Educated at Public School 139, Harlem, New York, and De Witt Clinton High School, Bronx, New York, graduated 1942. Worked as handyman, dishwasher, waiter, and office boy in New York, and in defense work, Belle Meade, New Jersey, in early 1940's; full-time writer from 1943; lived in Europe, mainly in Paris, 1948–56. Member, Actors Studio, New York, National Advisory Board of CORE (Congress on Racial Equality), and National Committee for a Sane Nuclear Policy. Recipient: Saxton fellowship, 1945; Rosenwald fellowship, 1948; Guggenheim fellowship, 1954; American Academy award, 1956; Ford fellowship, 1958; National Conference of Christians and Jews Brotherhood Award, 1962; George Polk Award, 1963; Foreign Drama Critics award, 1964; Martin Luther King, Jr., Award (City University of New York), 1978. D.Litt.: University of British Columbia, Vancouver, 1963. Member, American Academy, 1964. *Died 30 November 1987.*

PUBLICATIONS

Plays

The Amen Corner (produced Washington, D.C., 1955; New York, Edinburgh, and London, 1965). New York, Dial Press, 1968.

Blues for Mister Charlie (produced New York, 1964; London, 1965). New York, Dial Press, 1964; London, Joseph, 1965.

One Day, When I Was Lost: A Scenario Based on "The Autobiography of Malcolm X." London, Joseph, 1972; New York, Dial Press, 1973.

A Deed from the King of Spain (produced New York, 1974).

Screenplay: *The Inheritance*, 1973.

Novels

Go Tell It on the Mountain. New York, Knopf, 1953; London, Joseph, 1954.

Giovanni's Room. New York, Dial Press, 1956; London, Joseph, 1957.

Another Country. New York, Dial Press, 1962; London, Joseph, 1963.

Tell Me How Long the Train's Been Gone. New York, Dial Press, and London, Joseph, 1968.

If Beale Street Could Talk. New York, Dial Press, and London, Joseph, 1974.

Just above My Head. New York, Dial Press, and London, Joseph, 1979.

Short Stories

Going to Meet the Man. New York, Dial Press, and London, Joseph, 1965.

Verse

Jimmy's Blues: Selected Poems. London, Joseph, 1983; New York, St. Martin's Press, 1986.

Other

Notes of a Native Son. Boston, Beacon Press, 1955; London, Joseph, 1964.
Nobody Knows My Name: More Notes of a Native Son. New York, Dial Press, 1961; London, Joseph, 1964.
The Fire Next Time. New York, Dial Press, and London, Joseph, 1963.
Nothing Personal, photographs by Richard Avedon. New York, Atheneum, and London, Penguin, 1964.
A Rap on Race, with Margaret Mead. Philadelphia, Lippincott, and London, Joseph, 1971.
No Name in the Street. New York, Dial Press, and London, Joseph, 1972.
A Dialogue: James Baldwin and Nikki Giovanni. Philadelphia, Lippincott, 1973; London, Joseph, 1975.
Little Man, Little Man (for children). London, Joseph, 1976; New York, Dial Press, 1977.
The Devil Finds Work: An Essay. New York, Dial Press, and London, Joseph, 1976.
The Price of a Ticket: Collected Nonfiction 1948–1985. New York, St. Martin's Press, and London, Joseph, 1985.
The Evidence of Things Not Seen. New York, Holt Rinehart, 1985; as *Evidence of Things Not Seen*, London, Joseph, 1986.

*

Bibliography: "James Baldwin: A Checklist 1947–1962" by Kathleen A. Kindt, and "James Baldwin: A Bibliography 1947–1962" by Russell G. Fischer, both in *Bulletin of Bibliography* (Boston), January–April 1965; *James Baldwin: A Reference Guide* by Fred L. and Nancy Standley, Boston, Hall, 1980.

Critical Studies: *The Furious Passage of James Baldwin* by Fern Eckman, New York, Evans, 1966, London, Joseph, 1968; *James Baldwin: A Critical Study* by Stanley Macebuh, New York, Third Press, 1973, London, Joseph, 1975; *James Baldwin: A Collection of Critical Essays* edited by Keneth Kinnamon, Englewood Cliffs, New Jersey, Prentice Hall, 1974; *James Baldwin: A Critical Evaluation* edited by Therman B. O'Daniel, Washington, D.C., Howard University Press, 1977; *James Baldwin* by Louis H. Pratt, Boston, Twayne, 1978; *James Baldwin* by Carolyn W. Sylvander, New York, Ungar, 1980.

Theatrical Activities:
Director: **Film**—*The Inheritance*, 1973.

* * *

One of the best known contemporary authors in the United States, James Baldwin is least known as a dramatist. He was admired in the 1950's for the style and thought of his novels, the semi-autobiographical *Go Tell It on the Mountain* and *Giovanni's Room*, and for his personal and literary essays, first published in "little" avant-garde magazines, then collected as *Notes of a Native Son.* During the early 1960's, as increased attention was directed to the civil rights movement, Baldwin became recognized as a leading spokesman for black Americans. In a novel (*Another Country*) and two collections of essays (*Nobody Knows My Name* and *The Fire Next Time*), Baldwin seemed to articulate eloquently and persuasively the bitterness, the alienation, and the despair of black Americans. Some critics felt that Baldwin's statements reached a pinnacle in his first widely known drama, *Blues for Mister Charlie.* With an eye towards John Osborne and other British dramatists, some critics argued that Baldwin was "America's angriest young man." Just as few critics have recognized Baldwin's interest in drama, so most have missed the continuous message of the one-time preacher. In drama, as in his other writing, Baldwin repeatedly preaches that people must love and understand other people if they wish to save the world from destruction.

Born and raised in New York City, Baldwin, the eldest of nine children, suffered in childhood from the oppression of Depression poverty and the religious enthusiasm of a fanatically devout father. During his youth he wavered between the church and literature. Undoubtedly influenced by his stepfather, at least seeking to please him, Baldwin became a teenaged minister in a faith which viewed romance (in literature or in life) as a snare for the godly. In junior high school, however, Baldwin had been a member of the literary society advised by Countee Cullen, the famous black poet and novelist. The opposing forces, Baldwin has written, met in a climactic confrontation when an excessively long sermon from the minister of Baldwin's church threatened to prevent Baldwin's attendance at a play for which he had tickets. When the minister chose to make an example of the quietly departing Baldwin, Baldwin became convinced that he could not endure the rigors of the faith. From this point Baldwin embraced literature as a faith with an emphasis upon the creed of love for fellow man.

After graduation from De Witt Clinton High School, Baldwin worked as a waiter while he tried to write a novel. With assistance from Richard Wright, the most famous black American novelist of the time, he secured a Saxton award, which temporarily relieved his financial needs. Despite occasional publication in little magazines, however, Baldwin increasingly despaired of his position as a black man and writer in the white-oriented United States. In 1948, he left for France, where, during the next ten years, he established a limited reputation as a creative writer and literary critic (the latter based partly on his rejection of Richard Wright, his former benefactor, as a novelist who sacrificed art to a message of social protest) and persuaded himself that he had discovered his identity.

As early as 1957 Baldwin had made a dramatic adaptation of his novel *Giovanni's Room*, the story of a white American who discovers and surrenders to his latent homosexuality. Baldwin's recognition as a dramatist did not come until the season of 1963–64 when *Blues for Mister Charlie* became the controversial sensation of the New York stage while the quieter *The Amen Corner*, first produced at a black college in Washington, D.C., was receiving a professional production on the west coast. In both plays he tried to infuse the vitality of life which he felt to be missing from American drama.

Written after Baldwin had taken his first trip to Mississippi, to participate in civil rights demonstrations, *Blues for Mister Charlie* is based in part on two actual incidents. In one, a 14-year-old black youth from Chicago was tortured and killed while visiting his grandparents in Mississippi. The reason given by one killer was that the youth allegedly had flirted with a white woman. Although one murderer freely admitted the crime and a second did not deny it, both were acquitted by an all-white jury. In a second incident, a black man was killed by a white man. The reason was rumored to be the fact that the black man protested against the white man's using the black man's wife as a concubine.

In *Blues for Mister Charlie* Baldwin focused on Richard Henry, a young black entertainer, who, after succumbing to dope, has returned bitter and frustrated to his Mississippi home. Within a short period of time, Henry becomes involved in an altercation with Lyle Britton, a white man known to have killed another black who objected to surrendering his wife to Britton's sexual exploitation. Britton kills Henry, is tried, and is acquitted.

Although some critics denounced the play as melodramatic and excessively bitter, Baldwin's major theme—his recurrent theme—is found in the tragedy of two secondary figures, who see the destruction of their hope for love between the races. One is a white journalist who, unlike his neighbors, has no prejudices against blacks. Once, in fact, he loved a black woman and wanted to marry her. At the critical moment in the play, however, this white "liberal" betrays himself and his black friends because, although he knows that Britton is guilty, he cannot force himself to testify that Lyle's wife—a southern white woman—is lying. The second tragic figure is the Reverend Meridian Henry. All of his adult life, Henry has worked to improve the condition of his people by peaceful means. Even after his son's murder, he continues to urge black youths to limit themselves to non-violent protests in the manner of Mahatma Gandhi and Martin Luther King, Jr. After the acquittal of his son's murderer, however, the Christian minister decides that, in the future, he and other blacks need to carry their guns even to church to protect themselves from the savages in their community.

The Amen Corner is the story of a woman minister who is forced to realize that love and compassion for human beings are more important than a fanatically rigid enunciation of God's law. After deserting her husband because he was inadequate to her needs after the death of their second child, Sister Margaret has become a minister who insists that members of her congregation and her son dedicate themselves to continuous sanctity. The return of her husband, who is dying, precipitates conflict by inspiring rebellion in her son and her congregation. By the end of the play, Margaret has been compelled to remember how human and loving she had been before the ministry. Now that she has regained compassison for human frailty, she is truly prepared for the first time to lead a congregation. But it is too late. Her son leaves her, her husband dies, and she can find no words to maintain her control over the faction of the congregation which has decided to replace her.

—Darwin T. Turner

BALODIS, Janis (Maris). Australian. Born in Tully, Queensland, 21 September 1950. Educated at Townsville College of Advanced Education, Queensland, teaching diploma 1970; James Cook University, Townsville, 1973; East 15 Acting School, Loughton, Essex, 1976–77. Married Pauline Walsh in 1982; one son and one daughter. Primary school teacher, Tully, 1971, and Bambaroo, 1972, Queensland; assistant stage manager, Queensland Theatre Company, Brisbane, 1974; civil servant, Brisbane, 1975; teacher and director, East 15 Acting School, 1977–79. Since 1979 free-lance writer, Sydney. Recipient: Australia Literature Board grant, 1981, 1983, and fellowship, 1985, 1987; Victorian Premier's award, 1986. Agent: Hilary Linstead and Associates, 223 Commonwealth Street, Surry Hills, New South Wales 2010. Address: 35 George Street, Redfern, New South Wales 2016, Australia.

PUBLICATIONS

Plays

Backyard (produced Sydney, 1980).
Happily Never After (produced Brisbane, 1982).
Beginning of the End (produced Darwin, 1982).
Summerland (produced Brisbane, 1984).
Too Young for Ghosts (produced Melbourne, 1985). Sydney, Currency Press, 1985.
Wet and Dry (produced Darwin, 1986). Sydney, Currency Press, 1987.

Television Play: *A Step in the Right Direction*, 1981.

* * *

Janis Balodis was brought up in rural North Queensland, the Australian son of Latvian parents, and he is distinguished from his fellow Australian playwrights on both counts: he is the first child of that generation of European displaced persons who came to Australia under the postwar immigration scheme to reach the front rank of our theatre writers; and he is the first Queenslander of his generation to do so. His background is that of a frontier society and his plays, not surprisingly, are inhabited by men and women cut off from their origins who cling together for self-preservation and irrationally engage with a mutual destiny which they variously attempt to oppose or assimilate.

This theme is present in two minor allegorical works with local political overtones, *Happily Never After* and *Summerland*, both written for the TN Company in Brisbane. In the first a group of characters from the tales of the Brothers Grimm gather to rewrite their stories more favourably; but are murdered severally in plots of self-interest. In the second, Sinbad the Sailor is narrator of a tale of a beggar transformed into a millionaire by learning to love himself. First he cheats and defrauds his way to power, then by experience he comes to terms with the good and the bad within himself. But the sense of deracination, of malevolent intervention in the laws of man and nature, is more significantly present in the three plays upon which Balodis's reputation rests: *Backyard, Too Young for Ghosts*, and *Wet and Dry*.

The setting of *Backyard* is a shabby house in a small Queensland country town. The inhabitants are Pencil, a sugar-mill worker, his wife Merlene, and her sister Dorothy; their relationship is based largely on long familiarity and fear of change. Merlene regularly leaves home, but never town, and when she goes Pencil takes Dorothy to bed. This betrayal comes to light when Dorothy becomes pregnant; and the play ends in a distorted, half-comic violence. Central to the theme is Sandshoeboots, an elderly backyard abortionist who sees herself as the instrument of a vengeful female God. On her first entrance she presents Pencil with the corpse of a pigeon she claims he shot; and the body follows the action like a talisman, becoming at one point an image of the aborted foetus. Written in a dense regional vernacular, the play shares with the early plays of Sam Shepard its portrayal of an inbred community.

Backyard is a chamber work; Balodis's next play, *Too Young for Ghosts*, advances the dual theme of destiny and survival onto an epic scale. A group of refugees gather in a Stuttgart camp in 1947 to decide their future. One man has become a black marketeer, one has returned from the front, grossly deformed by injuries; the third is his wife's lover. The women have been surviving as best they can, mainly on the spoils from American GIs. Later we find the group in a tin shed in North Queensland, working out their two-year government bond as cane-cutters. Their struggles with labour, loneliness, and the intractable language, climate, and culture are counterpointed with the colonial explorations of the German explorer Ludwig Leichhardt, who died in 1848 while attempting to cross northern Australia. The setting is an open stage and the structure complex and inventive: the action moves back and forward in time on an emotional pendulum while the actors perform in rotation the roles of the immigrants and the explorers. *Too Young for Ghosts* is a dense, demanding play with the inevitable thrust of tragedy.

Balodis's next stage play, probably his finest to date, makes an unexpected leap into comedy of manners. *Wet and Dry*, as the name implies, is a play of contrasts, using the language of comedy to hold emotion at bay while it examines the plight of urban men and women at war with nature—displaced persons in the urban middle class.

Pam and George are in their thirties. He is an estate agent, she a nurse; they have been unable to conceive a child. George is cynical, alienated: he buries himself in his work. When his young brother Alex comes to stay—an honest, disingenuous type of country worker—Pam decides that he will father her baby. Alex flees to Darwin, sets up with a pragmatic older woman and funds her hysterectomy. But finally Pam and Alex get together in a tropical storm and the result is a son with which both men now find they must—painfully—come to terms. Bisecting the play is a cyclone fence (another intervention in nature) which from scene to scene keeps at bay rabbits, neighbours, and the would-be suicides at Sydney's famous landmark, the Gap. The title refers in the first instance to the two seasons of tropical Australia and the opposing poles of north and south, bush and city; but more significantly it refers to the parallel struggle between nature and "civilisation" in which the characters are engaged. *Wet and Dry* is one of the finest examples of a particularly indigenous form of urban comedy in which the characters batten down with tight, elegant, ironic dialogue emotions, natural disasters, and an ungovernable country to which white Australians are only now becoming reconciled.

—Katharine Brisbane

BARAKA, Amiri. American. Born Everett LeRoi Jones in Newark, New Jersey, 7 October 1934; took name Amiri Baraka in 1968. Educated at Central Avenue School, and Barringer High School, Newark; Rutgers University, New Brunswick, New Jersey, 1951–52; Howard University, Washington, D.C., 1953–54, B.A. in English 1954. Served in the United States Air Force, 1954–57. Married 1) Hettie Roberta Cohen in 1958 (divorced 1965), two daughters; 2) Sylvia Robinson (now Amina Baraka) in 1967, five children; also two stepdaughters and one other daughter. Teacher, New School for Social Research, New York, 1961–64, and summers, 1977–79, State University of New York, Buffalo, Summer 1964, and Columbia University, New York, 1964 and Spring 1980; Visiting Professor, San Francisco State College, 1966–67, Yale University, New Haven, Connecticut, 1977–78, and George Washington University, Washington, D.C., 1978–79. Assistant Professor, 1980–82, Associate Professor, 1983–84, and since 1985 Professor of Africana Studies, State University of New York, Stony Brook. Founder, *Yugen* magazine and Totem Press, New York, 1958–62; editor, with Diane di Prima, *Floating Bear* magazine, New York, 1961–63; founding director, Black Arts Repertory Theatre, Harlem, New York, 1964–66. Since 1966 founding director, Spirit House, Newark; involved in Newark politics: member of the United Brothers, 1967, and Committee for Unified Newark, 1969–75; Chairman, Congress of Afrikan People, 1972–75. Recipient: Whitney fellowship, 1961; Obie award, 1964; Guggenheim fellowship, 1965; Dakar Festival prize, 1966; Rockefeller grant, 1981; National Endowment for the Arts award, for poetry, 1981; Before Columbus Foundation award, 1984. D.H.L.: Malcolm X College, Chicago, 1972. Member, Black Academy of Arts and Letters. Address: Department of Africana Studies, State University of New York, Stony Brook, New York 11794-4340, U.S.A.

PUBLICATIONS (earlier works as LeRoi Jones)

Plays

A Good Girl Is Hard to Find (produced Montclair, New Jersey, 1958; New York, 1965).

Dante (produced New York, 1961; as *The 8th Ditch*, produced New York, 1964). Included in *The System of Dante's Hell*, 1965.

The Toilet (produced New York, 1964). With *The Baptism*, New York, Grove Press, 1967.

Dutchman (produced New York, 1964; London, 1967). With *The Slave*, New York, Morrow, 1964; London, Faber, 1965.

The Slave (produced New York, 1964; London, 1972). With *Dutchman*, New York, Morrow, 1964; London, Faber, 1965.

The Baptism (produced New York, 1964; London, 1971). With *The Toilet*, New York, Grove Press, 1967.

Jello (produced New York, 1965). Chicago, Third World Press, 1970.

Experimental Death Unit #1 (also director: produced New York, 1965). Included in *Four Black Revolutionary Plays*, 1969.

A Black Mass (also director: produced Newark, 1966). Included in *Four Black Revolutionary Plays*, 1969.

Arm Yrself or Harm Yrself (produced Newark, 1967). Newark, Jihad, 1967.

Slave Ship: A Historical Pageant (produced Newark, 1967; New York, 1969). Newark, Jihad, 1967.

Madheart (also director: produced San Francisco, 1967). Included in *Four Black Revolutionary Plays*, 1969.

Great Goodness of Life (A Coon Show) (also director: produced Newark, 1967; New York, 1969). Included in *Four Black Revolutionary Plays*, 1969.

Home on the Range (produced Newark and New York, 1968). Published in *Drama Review* (New York), Summer 1968.

Police, published in *Drama Review* (New York), Summer 1968.

The Death of Malcolm X, in *New Plays from the Black Theatre*, edited by Ed Bullins. New York, Bantam, 1969.

Four Black Revolutionary Plays. Indianapolis, Bobbs Merrill, 1969; London, Calder and Boyars, 1971.

Insurrection (produced New York, 1969).

Junkies are Full of (SHHH ...), and Bloodrites (produced Newark, 1970). Published in *Black Drama Anthology*, edited by Woodie King and Ron Milner, New York, New American Library, 1971.

BA-RA-KA, in *Spontaneous Combustion: Eight New American Plays*, edited by Rochelle Owens. New York, Winter House, 1972.

Columbia the Gem of the Ocean (produced Washington, D.C., 1973).

A Recent Killing (produced New York, 1973).

The New Ark's a Moverin (produced Newark, 1974).

The Sidnee Poet Heroical (also director: produced New York, 1975). New York, Reed, 1979.
S-1 (also director: produced New York, 1976). Included in *The Motion of History and Other Plays*, 1978.
The Motion of History (also director: produced New York, 1977). Included in *The Motion of History and Other Plays*, 1978.
The Motion of History and Other Plays (includes *S-1* and *Slave Ship*). New York, Morrow, 1978.
What Was the Relationship of the Lone Ranger to the Means of Production? (produced New York, 1979).
At the Dim'crackr Convention (produced New York, 1980).
Boy and Tarzan Appear in a Clearing (produced New York, 1981).
Weimar 2 (produced New York, 1981).
Money: A Jazz Opera, with George Gruntz, music by Gruntz (produced New York, 1982).
Primitive World, music by David Murray (produced New York, 1984).

Screenplays: *Dutchman*, 1967; *Black Spring*, 1967; *A Fable*, 1971.

Novel

The System of Dante's Hell. New York, Grove Press, 1965; London, MacGibbon and Kee, 1966.

Short Stories

Tales. New York, Grove Press, 1967; London, MacGibbon and Kee, 1969.

Verse

Spring and Soforth. New Haven, Connecticut, Penny Poems, 1960.
Preface to a Twenty Volume Suicide Note. New York, Totem-Corinth, 1961.
The Dead Lecturer. New York, Grove Press, 1964.
Black Art. Newark, Jihad, 1966.
A Poem for Black Hearts. Detroit, Broadside Press, 1967.
Black Magic: Collected Poetry 1961–1967. Indianapolis, Bobbs Merrill, 1969.
It's Nation Time. Chicago, Third World Press, 1970.
In Our Terribleness: Some Elements and Meaning in Black Style, with Fundi (Billy Abernathy). Indianapolis, Bobbs Merrill, 1970.
Spirit Reach. Newark, Jihad, 1972.
Afrikan Revolution. Newark, Jihad, 1973.
Hard Facts. Newark, Peoples War, 1976.
Selected Poetry. New York, Morrow, 1979.
AM/TRAK. New York, Phoenix Book Shop, 1979.
Reggae or Not! Bowling Green, New York, Contact Two, 1982.
Thoughts for You! Nashville, Winston Derek, 1984.

Other

Cuba Libre. New York, Fair Play for Cuba Committee, 1961.
Blues People: Negro Music in White America. New York, Morrow, 1963; London, MacGibbon and Kee, 1965.
Home: Social Essays. New York, Morrow, 1966; London, MacGibbon and Kee, 1968.
Black Music. New York, Morrow, 1968; London, MacGibbon and Kee, 1969.
Trippin': A Need for Change, with Larry Neal and A.B. Spellman. Newark, Cricket, 1969 (?).
A Black Value System. Newark, Jihad, 1970.
Gary and Miami: Before and After. Newark, Jihad, n.d.
Raise Race Rays Raze: Essays since 1965. New York, Random House, 1971.
Strategy and Tactics of a Pan African Nationalist Party. Newark, National Involvement 1971.
Beginning of National Movement. Newark, Jihad, 1972.
Kawaida Studies: The New Nationalism. Chicago, Third World Press, 1972.
National Liberation and Politics. Newark, Congress of Afrikan People, 1974.
Crisis in Boston!!!! Newark, Vita Wa Watu-People's War Publishing, 1974.
Afrikan Free School. Newark, Jihad, 1974.
Toward Ideological Clarity. Newark, Congress of Afrikan People, 1974.
The Creation of the New Ark. Washington, D.C., Howard University Press, 1975.
Selected Plays and Prose. New York, Morrow, 1979.
Spring Song. Privately printed, 1979.
Daggers and Javelins: Essays 1974–1979. New York, Morrow, 1984.
The Autobiography of LeRoi Jones/Amiri Baraka. New York, Freundlich, 1984.
The Artist and Social Responsibility. N.p., Unity, 1986.

Editor, *Four Young Lady Poets*. New York, Totem-Corinth, 1962.
Editor, *The Moderns: New Fiction in America*. New York, Corinth, 1963; London, MacGibbon and Kee, 1965.
Editor, with Larry Neal, *Black Fire: An Anthology of Afro-American Writing*. New York, Morrow, 1968.
Editor, *African Congress: A Documentary of the First Modern Pan-African Congress*. New York, Morrow, 1972.
Editor, with Diane di Prima, *The Floating Bear: A Newsletter, Numbers 1–37*. La Jolla, California, Laurence McGilvery, 1974.
Editor, with Amina Baraka, *Confirmation: An Anthology of African American Women*. New York, Morrow, 1983.

*

Bibliography: *LeRoi Jones (Imamu Amiri Baraka): A Checklist of Works by and about Him* by Letitia Dace, London, Nether Press, 1971; *Ten Modern American Playwrights* by Kimball King, New York, Garland, 1982.

Manuscript Collection: Howard University, Washington, D.C.

Critical Studies: *From LeRoi Jones to Amiri Baraka: The Literary Works* by Theodore Hudson, Durham, North Carolina, Duke University Press, 1973; *Baraka: The Renegade and the Mask* by Kimberly W. Benston, New Haven, Connecticut, Yale University Press, 1976, and *Imamu Amiri Baraka (LeRoi Jones): A Collection of Critical Essays* edited by Benston, Englewood Cliffs, New Jersey, Prentice Hall, 1978; *Amiri Baraka/LeRoi Jones: The Quest for a Populist Modernism* by Werner Sollors, New York, Columbia University Press, 1978; *Amiri Baraka* by Lloyd W. Brown, Boston, Twayne, 1980; *To Raise, Destroy, and Create: The Poetry, Drama, and Fiction of Imamu Amiri Baraka (LeRoi Jones)* by Henry C. Lacey, Troy, New York, Whitston, 1981; *Theatre and Nationalism: Wole Soyinka and LeRoi Jones* by Alain Ricard, Ife-Ife, Nigeria, University of Ife Press, 1983; *Amiri Baraka: The Kaleidoscopic Torch* edited by James B. Gwynne, New York, Steppingstones Press, 1985.

Theatrical Activities:
Director: several of his own plays.

Amiri Baraka comments:
My work changes as I change in a changing world.

* * *

The debut of Amiri Baraka (LeRoi Jones) on the New York stage was an enviable personal success for the young playwright. In March 1964 when three one-act plays at different off-Broadway locales introduced Baraka to city audiences, black theatre in America knew it had found a compelling voice summoning black playwrights to a new and urgent mission.

The first of these plays, *The 8th Ditch* (staged semi-professionally at the New Bowery Theatre), closed by action of civic authorities after a few days. Its fate foretold the playwright's continuing quarrel with officialdom. His second play, *The Baptism* (given two performances at the Writers' Stage), with its deliberate satire of subjects held sacred and taboo, served notice of Baraka's determination ruthlessly to strip the hypocritical masks that society wears to protect its vested interests. But it was in his third play and first professional production, *Dutchman* (presented at the Cherry Lane Theatre), that Baraka found his authentic voice to delineate a clearly perceived mission. That mission is nothing less than the cultural liberation of the black man in white America.

Dutchman, hailed by critic Clayton Riley as "the finest short play ever written in this country," spoke lucidly to black Americans of the savage destruction of their cultural identity should they continue to imitate or to flirt with an alien, though dominant, white lifestyle. White establishment critics, impressed with the power of the play but largely ignoring its fundamental revolutionary message, praised Baraka's "fierce and blazing talent"; the *Village Voice* awarded *Dutchman* an Obie as the best American play of the season.

Overnight Baraka became the top cultural freedom-fighter of black America. Before he could properly assume this role, however, he had to win credibility by first liberating himself. Aged 29, university educated, and an air force veteran, Baraka belonged to a group of young Greenwich Village intellectuals, the beat generation of the troublesome 1960's, influenced by writers like Allen Ginsberg and Jack Kerouac. He was already a published poet, essayist, and sometime editor of an underground literary journal. He had married a Jewish woman, Hettie Cohen, and the marriage had produced two daughters. Paradoxically, the acknowledged new leader of the black cultural revolution had elected to share his life with a representative of the decaying and corrosive white culture which he condemned. The dilemma had to be speedily resolved.

Baraka's next professional production consisted of two plays. *The Slave*, a two-act drama, and *The Toilet*, another one-acter, staged at the St. Mark's Playhouse in December 1964. *The Slave*, although it purports to speak of a coming race war between black and white and is called by Baraka "a fable," is frankly autobiographical in intent. Walker Vessels, a tall, thin Negro leader of a black army, enters the home where his former white wife, their two children, and her second husband are living together, apparently quite happily. The husband is a white liberal-minded professor who had taught Vessels in college. After a long, excoriating harangue in which he renounces his former life, Vessels shoots the white man, watches with indifference as his ex-wife is hit by a falling beam, and departs as shells from his black revolutionary forces demolish the house while the cries of children in an upstairs room mingle with the boom of guns and the shriek of falling debris. *The Toilet*, a curious work of teenage brutality and homosexual love set in a school lavatory, hints at the possibility of black and white coming together at some future time after the black man has earned his manhood and self-respect by defeating the white.

These two revolutionary plays were followed by an even more lurid and propagandistic work when *Experimental Death Unit #1* was staged at the St. Mark's Playhouse in New York in March 1965. In this short play Baraka concentrates on a night-time encounter between two white homosexuals and a black whore in a seamy section of the city. The climax occurs when a death unit of marching black militants enters and executes the three degenerates. The men are beheaded and their heads stuck on pikes at the head of the procession. The black liberation army, Baraka seems to say, has a duty to rid society not only of the oppressor but also of the collaborator. Black skin does not save one from the due penalty for betraying the revolution.

Writing of this second group of plays, white critics who a few months ago had hailed the rising star of playwright Baraka were now confounded. He had rejected the blandishments of popular (white) success held out to him and had become, to them, a bitter dramatist and violent propagandist preaching race hatred in virulent terms. Their attitude in the main confirmed Baraka's suspicions that the white culture would allow nothing but what it approved of to have credence and value.

Having declared his artistic independence, Baraka was now ready to deal with his personal life. A month after the production of *Experimental Death Unit #1*, he imitated the actions of his fictitious character, Walker Vessels, by breaking with his past life. He left his white wife and two children, moved to Harlem, and founded what he called the Black Arts Repertory Theatre School. The aim of the school was to train and showcase black theatrical talent, as well as teach classes in remedial reading and mathematics. It lasted for only a short time. Supportive funding from the U.S. Office of Economic Opportunity ceased once the initial grant was exhausted and this setback coupled with internal problems forced an early closing of the theatre. But the idea of a black arts movement did not die. In its short life in Harlem, Baraka's Black Arts Group proved, in the words of Larry Neal, "that the community could be served by a valid and dynamic art [and] that there was a definite need for a cultural revolution in the black community."

Similar black arts groups were formed on the west coast; the idea sparked movements in Detroit, Philadelphia, Jersey City, New Orleans, and Washington, D.C. On many college campuses across the nation, black arts programs were started and festivals held. The black cultural revolution was in fact taking place. In a forum on Black Theatre held at the Gate Theatre, New York, in 1969, Baraka articulated the philosophic premise of the movement, giving credit to Ron Karenga of San Francisco for having helped in its formulation. Black art, he affirmed, is collective, functional, and committed since it derives from the collective experience of black people, it serves a necessary function in the lives of black people (as opposed to the useless artifacts of most white art that adorn museums), and is committed to revolutionary change.

The short-lived Harlem-based theatre produced only one new play by Baraka: *Jello*, a hard-hitting satire on the once popular Jack Benny radio program advertising this product. The play, rejected by at least one established publisher because of its attack on a well-known stage personality, was performed on the streets of Harlem by the Black Arts Group. The straightforward plot casts Rochester, Benny's chauffeur and stereotype black handyman, as a militant who demands and gets full redress for years of subservience and oppression. In this play Baraka is less interested in attacking the white man than in erasing the myth of black inferiority which decades of white-controlled entertainment have helped to perpetuate. From this point Baraka was more conscious of addressing a black audience in his plays. His main characters were black, and whitey became either the symbolic beast whose ritualistic death is necessary for the emergence of black consciousness and nationhood, or else whitey will be pilloried mercilessly as completely irrelevant to the black struggle. Baraka declared:

> The artist must represent the will, the soul of the black community. [His art] must represent the national spirit and the national will. . . . We don't talk about theatre down here, or theatre up there as an idle jest but because it is necessary to pump live blood back into our community.

When the Black Arts Repertory Theatre closed in 1966, Baraka transferred the operational base of his cultural movement from Harlem to his native Newark in New Jersey. He rented a three-story building on Stirling Street, known as Spirit House, and formed the Spirit House Movers, a group of non-professional actors who performed his plays as well as the plays of other black writers. Baraka spent a year teaching at San Francisco State College where he was exposed to the influence of the young black nationalist, Ron Karenga. Then he returned to Newark determined to practice some of the liberating ideas which he advocated in his works.

In January 1969 he formed the Committee for Unified Newark dedicated to the creation of a new value system for the Afro-American community. Aspects of this new system of values are evidenced in the wearing of traditional African dress, the speaking of Swahili language as much as English, the rejection of Christianity as a Western religion that has helped to enslave the minds of black people and the adoption of the Kawaida faith in its stead, and finally the assumption of Arabic names in place of existing Christian names. Jones became a minister of Kawaida faith and adopted his new name of Amiri Baraka prefixed by the title Imamu (Swahili for Spiritual Leader).

Baraka's work continues to dwell on themes of black liberation and the need to create a new black sensibility by alerting audiences to the reality of their lives in a country dominated by a culture that Baraka passionately believes to be alien and hostile to blacks. The urgent need to root out white ways from the hearts and minds of black people is constantly reiterated. White error is seen in *A Black Mass* as the substitution of thought for feeling, as a curiosity for anti-life. In *Home on the Range* the white family speaks a gibberish of unintelligible sounds and gazes glasseyed at the television box like robots of the computer society they have created. The devils in *Bloodrites* eat of the host and chant a litany of love immediately after attempting to shoot blacks in a glaring indictment of the hypocrisy of Christianity.

Baraka graphically dramatizes the problem by personifying the evil white lifestyle in the form of a devil or beast that must be slain if blacks are to gain their freedom. In *A Black Mass*, a play based on an Islamic fable, one of a trio of magicians persists in creating a wild white beast that he believes he can tame through love. The beast goes on a rampage and destroys everything in sight, including the magicians. *Madheart* has a Devil Lady who keeps a mother and sister of the Black Man in thrall, worshipping whiteness. In *Bloodrites*, whites are gun-toting devils that masquerade as artists, musicians, and hipsters to seduce blacks struggling towards spiritual reconstruction.

Baraka has been accused of preaching race hatred and violence as a way of life. In 1967 he was given the maximum sentence of three years in prison by a county judge for possession of revolvers during the Newark riots, a conviction that was condemned as victimization by the American Council of Civil Liberties and was later overturned by a higher court. It is true that violence permeates his plays, that Baraka seems to revel in bloodletting, but the intensity of his feeling and the power of his language have the effect of lifting violence to the level of a holy war against evil forces of supernatural potency. When the Devil Lady in *Madheart* boasts that she can never die, the Black Man responds "you will die only when I kill you" whereupon he stabs her several times, impales her with a stake and arrows, abuses her, stomps on her dead face, and finally drops her body into a deep pit from which smoke and light shoot up. Such needless overkill can only be understood in terms of magic and ritual.

Ritual, in fact, is the crucible that helps to transform the melodramatic incident in Baraka's plays into significant drama. Clay, the young black hounded by the vampire Lula in a subway train in *Dutchman*, realizes that the murder of a white is the only cure for the black man's neuroses, but he is too ingrained in white middle-class values to perform the rite that will liberate him. He dies as a result. Not so Walter Vessels in *The Slave*. When he shoots Easley, the white liberal professor, the latter's last words are "Ritual drama, like I said, ritual drama." Similarly, when Court Royal, the weak-kneed assimilationist in *Great Goodness of Life* is forced to shoot his militant son, this too is a rite that must be performed, "a rite to show that you would be guilty, but for the cleansing rite." In keeping with his philosophy that black theatre must be functional, Baraka has sought to make his plays identify with his audiences in form as well as content. Thus, *Bloodrites* calls for the sacrifice of a chicken whose blood is sprinkled into the audience. In *Police* the white cops are required to eat chunks of flesh from the body of the black policeman who has killed a member of his race and is forced by the black community to commit suicide. Such ritualistic acts reinforce the magical dimension of the struggle in which black people are engaged.

A second medium of identification is language. Baraka, the poet and littérateur, deliberately reaches for the vernacular and idiom of the urban black to pound home his message. *The Slave* is a fine example of the way in which college-educated Walker Vessels rejects the elegant but alienating discourse of which he is capable for the unifying language of the ghetto. The language in *Police* is pruned and compressed to a single drumbeat, with the syncopation and lyricism associated with that pervasive black musical instrument. The process of creating a new and appropriate language for black drama is pushed further in *Slave Ship* where the narrative element relies heavily on action and music rather than language, and where Yoruba instead of English is used in the first part of the production.

Finally, in his capacity as Spiritual Leader, Baraka uses the stage as a pulpit from which he exhorts his audiences to carry his message for revolutionary thinking and action into their daily lives. The Black Man in *Madheart* urges the audience to "think about themselves and about their lives when they leave this happening." A concluding narration in *A Black Mass* reminds the audience that the beasts are still loose in the world and must be found and slain. *Junkies* begins with an address by an Italian dope dealer who informs the audience that he succeeds by getting "niggers to peddle dope." The audience at *Police* are expected to leap on stage at one point of the play and join the characters in demanding vengeance on the black cop who shot and killed a black brother.

Baraka's theatre is blatantly agit-prop drama exalted to an elemental plane. Apart from *Slave Ship* the structure of his plays remains conventional but the dynamic of message, the boldness of conception, and the lyricism of language give his dramas a fierceness on the stage that defies complacency. Critics may praise or damn him, but Baraka is no longer writing for critical acclaim. Neither does he write for posterity, so it is irrelevant to conjecture whether his plays will last. They have brought hope and vision of a better life to millions of Americans, and they have infused the theatre with a new vitality and veered it closer to the lives of people. Such achievements are enough to win Baraka a permanent place in the annals of the American and world theatre.

—Errol Hill

BARKER, Howard. British. Born in London, 28 June 1946. Educated at Battersea Grammar School, London, 1958–64; Sussex University, Brighton, 1964–68, M.A. in history 1968. Married Sandra Law in 1972; one son. Resident dramatist, Open Space Theatre, London, 1974–75. Recipient: Arts Council bursary, 1971; Sony award, Society of Authors award, and Italia prize, all for radio play, 1985. Agent: Judy Daish Associates, 83 Eastbourne Mews, London W2 6LQ. Address: 57 Freshfield Road, Brighton, Sussex, England.

PUBLICATIONS

Plays

Cheek (produced London, 1970). Published in *New Short Plays 3*, London, Eyre Methuen, 1972.
No One Was Saved (produced London, 1971).
Edward: The Final Days (produced London, 1971).
Faceache (produced London, 1971).
Alpha Alpha (produced London, 1972).
Private Parts (produced Edinburgh, 1972).
Skipper, and My Sister and I (produced London, 1973).
Rule Britannia (produced London, 1973).
Bang (produced London, 1973).
Claw (produced London, 1975; New York, 1976). With *Stripwell*, London, Calder, 1977.
Stripwell (produced London, 1975). With *Claw*, London, Calder, 1977.
Wax (produced Edinburgh and London, 1976).
Fair Slaughter (produced London, 1977). London, Calder, 1978; with *Crimes in Hot Countries*, New York, Riverrun Press, 1985.
That Good Between Us (produced London, 1977). With *Credentials of a Sympathizer*, London, Calder, 1980; New York, Riverrun Press, 1981.
The Love of a Good Man (produced Sheffield, 1978; revised version produced Oxford and London, 1980). With *All Bleeding*, London, Calder, 1980; New York, Riverrun Press, 1981.
The Hang of the Gaol (produced London, 1978). With *Heaven*, London, Calder, 1982.
The Loud Boy's Life (produced London, 1980). Included in *Two Plays for the Right*, 1982.
Birth on a Hard Shoulder (produced Stockholm, 1980). Included in *Two Plays for the Right*, 1982.
No End of Blame: Scenes of Overcoming (produced Oxford, London, and New York, 1981). London, Calder, 1981; New York, Riverrun Press, 1982.
The Poor Man's Friend (produced Bridport, Dorset, 1981).
Two Plays for the Right. London, Calder, and New York, Riverrun Press, 1982.
Victory: Choices in Reaction (produced London, 1983). London, Calder, and New York, Riverrun Press, 1983.
A Passion in Six Days (produced Sheffield, 1983). With *Downchild*, London, Calder, and New York, Riverrun Press, 1985.
The Power of the Dog (produced Brentford, Middlesex, 1984; London, 1985). London, Calder, and New York, Riverrun Press, 1985.
Don't Exaggerate (produced London, 1984). London, Calder, 1985; New York, Riverrun Press, 1986.
Scenes from an Execution (broadcast 1984). With *The Castle*, London, Calder, 1985; New York, Riverrun Press, 1986.
Crimes in Hot Countries (produced London, 1985). With *Fair Slaughter*, London, Calder, 1984; New York, Riverrun Press, 1985.
Downchild (produced London, 1985). With *A Passion in Six Days*, London, Calder, and New York, Riverrun Press, 1985.
The Castle (produced London, 1985). With *Scenes from an Execution*, London, Calder, 1985; New York, Riverrun Press, 1986.
Pity in History (televised 1985; produced Edinburgh, 1986). With *Women Beware Women*, New York, Riverrun Press, 1987.
Women Beware Women, adaptation of the play by Thomas Middleton (produced London, 1986; New York, 1987). London, Calder, 1986; with *Pity in History*, New York, Riverrun Press, 1987.

Screenplays: *Made*, 1972; *Rape of Tamar*, 1973; *Aces High*, 1976.

Radio Plays: *One Afternoon on the North Face of the 63rd Level of the Pyramid of Cheops the Great*, 1970; *Henry V in Two Parts*, 1971; *Herman, with Millie and Mick*, 1972; *Scenes from an Execution*, 1984.

Television Plays: *Cows*, 1972; *The Chauffeur and the Lady*, 1972; *Mutinies*, 1974; *Pity in History*, 1985.

Verse

The Breath of the Crowd. London, Calder, 1986; New York, Riverrun Press, 1987.

*

Critical Studies: *The New British Drama* by Oleg Kerensky, London, Hamish Hamilton, 1977, New York, Taplinger, 1979; *Stages in the Revolution* by Catherine Itzin, London, Eyre Methuen, 1980; *Dreams and Deconstructions* edited by Sandy Craig, Ambergate, Derbyshire, Amber Lane Press, 1980; "Howard Barker Issue" of *Gambit* (London), vol. 11, no. 41, 1984.

Theatrical Activities:
Director: **Play**—*Don't Exaggerate*, Edinburgh, 1986.

* * *

Caustic wit, temporary utopias, and complex plots are the distinguishing features of Howard Barker's work. His plays over the last 15 years have engaged all the political flash-points—the failure of social democracy, feminism, nuclear militarism—of our times, but his oblique approach and his subversion of political stereotypes have disorientated ideologues and critics of both the centre and the left. Nevertheless Barker has an audience, and one which is growing. The 1985 season of three plays at the Royal Shakespeare Company's Pit theatre was a sell-out. The earliest play, *Crimes in Hot Countries* (written 1978), portrays a lethargic island-colony which is abruptly energized by the arrival of a businessman, three whores, a (disguised) Government inspector, and a magician. Their varied talents combine to transform the constitution into a utopia of dignified equality, whose ideals are sardonically undercut by a cold, astringent militarist who bears a remarkable resemblance to T. E. Lawrence. Democracy is eventually put down by two comic-sinister British agents, but the play demonstrates that there exists a hunger for ideas, argument, and alternative social structures among the most unlikely combinations of persons.

Downchild (written 1980) castigates the betrayals of postwar Labour politicians and focusses this critique through the figure of Downchild himself, alias Lord Cocky, gossip columnist of the *Daily World*. Holidaying in Devon with his criminal lover Stoat, he finds himself with a mystery to solve. There are screams at night under the full moon and the ghost of the previous lord of the nearby manor appears to Downchild. The present incumbent, "Knobby" Dicker, is near insanity and the last of the line. He is guarded by Roy Scadding, ex-Labour Prime Minister, and Ann Heyday, a powerful Cabinet colleague. Downchild alternatively triumphs over and is humiliated by Scadding, the ghost turns out to be the local vicar, and Downchild buys the child of Dicker's liaison with a local village girl. The climax of the play is a horrific scene where Downchild threatens to throw the child over a cliff unless Scadding can envisage some meaningful future for it. The labour politician weeps—"I do declare," says Downchild, "it's salt, not piss"—and admits he can't, Downchild hurls the child over the edge but it is caught by Stoat who has hidden on the rock-face. Downchild is beaten to the ground by the grandparents but, dying, still defies conventions to the end. "I shan't recall my sins and suck them . . .," he declares. "No dignity. No wisdom. Serenity. Or peace. Kick to the finish." Downchild, socialist gossip columnist, without Party and sexually deviant, is the crossroads where all contradictions meet.

The third play of this trilogy, *The Castle*, is the most recent. Completed in 1984, its central clash is between men who have just returned from the Crusades, and their women who, in their absence, have feminised their demesne. Religion and property have been abolished, and Ann, the Lady of the Manor, and Skinner, a feminist witch, have a passionate lesbian love which transcends anything the men could offer. Ann's husband Stucley is enraged by this peaceful revolution and gets his Arab architect Krak to design the largest castle ever built. This will be his instrument for remilitarising his estate. Ann defects to the males through a passion for Krak, and Skinner, in revenge, sexually mutilates the castle-builder Holiday. While Ann colludes with the men, Skinner is their intransigent enemy. "Where there are buildings," she insists to Ann, "there are whores . . . and what was peace and simple is dirt and struggle, and where there was a field to stand up straight in there is a loud and frantic city. Stucley will make a city of this valley. . . ." She is unbroken by the torture before her trial for Holiday's murder, she resists the punishment inflicted on her, and when Krak defects to the feminist camp, Stucley's power is broken and Skinner is handed the keys to the castle. Whether she will assume power, and how she will exercise it, is left deliberately ambiguous at the end. The theme of nuclear war is almost a cliché in many naturalist plays today, but through his oblique, mediaeval setting Barker here dramatises, not only this theme, but also all our contemporary confusions about war, gender, knowledge, and desire.

Barker has used other historical periods as analogues for today's concerns. *Victory* is set in 1660 when, with the restoration of Charles II, the Cromwellian republicans are being hunted out. Among them is Bradshaw, wife of the chief regicide, whose search for the dismembered body of her husband is also a journey of harsh discovery that utopian ideals have to be sacrificed to the imperatives of bare survival, Barker's familiar wit is brilliantly deployed throughout, particularly in the hilarious scene where the new trading class gives Charles II a lesson in economics in the vaults of the Bank of England. But Barker also shows his ability to write passages of lyrical plangency as in the Duchess of Devonshire's lament for impossible tranquillity and innocence at the beginning of Act 2. *Scenes from an Execution*, set in 16th-century Venice, dramatises the perennial struggle between artistic autonomy and state control. Galactia is the best painter in Venice. She has been commissioned to paint the battle of Lepanto and thereby glorify the Venetian state. What her work reveals is arrogance masked as humility, violence masquerading as peace, and absurdity as the undersurface of dignity. Both her friends and her enemies are alienated by her unwavering execution of the true state of affairs, but neither prison nor isolation break her intransigence. Her appeal is to a third party—the public. The painting is a great success, the Doge, who hated it, now praises it, and Galactia is welcomed among the ruling elite. Can even honest success, Barker asks, be neutralised by state trickery?

There remain plays by Barker which have yet to receive an adequate production in Britain. *The Power of the Dog* is a fascinating enactment of the interplay between politics, sex and aesthetics by the middle strata of the Red Army in the aftermath of Yalta. Stalin is entertained by an awful Scots comedian, and everyone's perceptions of the real are destabilised by the wandering Hungarian model, Ilona. This play cuts more rapidly from idea to idea than any other play by Barker and really demands an ensemble trained in Brechtian expressionism. Barker's earlier plays, from *Claw* to *The Loud Boy's Life*, were sufficiently distinguished to ensure him a prominent position among the writers of his generation. But his output during the 1980's shows him to be the most intelligent and most talented playwright of our times.

—Tony Dunn

BARNES, Peter. British. Born in London, 10 January 1931. Educated at Stroud Grammar School, Gloucestershire. Served in the Royal Air Force, 1949–50. Married Charlotte Beck in 1961. Worked for the London County Council, 1948 and 1950–53; critic, *Films and Filming*, London, 1954; story editor, Warwick Films, 1956. Recipient: John Whiting Award, 1969; *Evening Standard* award, 1969; Olivier Award, 1985. Agent: Margaret Ramsay Ltd., 14-A Goodwin's Court, London WC2N 4LL. Address: 7 Archery Close, Connaught Street, London W2 2BE, England.

Publications

Plays

The Time of the Barracudas (produced San Francisco, 1963).
Sclerosis (produced Edinburgh and London, 1965).
The Ruling Class: A Baroque Comedy (produced Nottingham, 1968; London, 1969; Washington, D.C., 1971). London, Heinemann, and New York, Grove Press, 1969.
Leonardo's Last Supper, and Noonday Demons (produced London, 1969; *Noonday Demons* produced Los Angeles, 1977). London, Heinemann, 1970.
Lulu, adaptation of plays by Frank Wedekind, translated by Charlotte Beck (also co-director: produced Nottingham and London, 1970). London, Heinemann, 1971.
The Alchemist, with Trevor Nunn, adaptation of the play by Jonson (produced Nottingham and London, 1970; revised version produced Stratford-on-Avon and London, 1977).
The Devil Is an Ass, adaptation of the play by Jonson (also co-director: produced Nottingham, 1973; revised version produced Edinburgh, 1976).
The Bewitched (produced London, 1974). London, Heinemann, 1974.
The Frontiers of Farce, adaptation of the plays *The Purging* by Feydeau and *The Singer* by Wedekind (also director: produced London, 1976; *The Purging* produced New York, 1980). London, Heinemann, 1977.
For All Those Who Get Despondent (cabaret), adaptation of works by Brecht and Wedekind (also director: produced London, 1976; revised version, as *The Two Hangmen: Brecht and Wedekind*, broadcast 1978).
Antonio, adaptation of the plays *Antonio and Mellida* and *Antonio's Revenge* by Marston (broadcast 1977; also co-director: produced Nottingham, 1979).
Laughter! (produced London, 1978). London, Heinemann, 1978.
The Devil Himself (revue), adaptation of a play by Wedekind, music by Carl Davis and Stephen Deutsch (also director: produced London, 1980).
Barnes' People: Seven Monologues (broadcast 1981). Included in *Collected Plays*, 1981.
Collected Plays (includes *The Ruling Class, Leonardo's Last Supper, Noonday Demons, The Bewitched, Laughter!, Barnes' People*). London, Heinemann, 1981.
Somersaults (revue; also director: produced Leicester, 1981).
Barnes' People II: Seven Duologues (broadcast 1984). London, Heinemann, 1984.
Red Noses (produced London, 1985; Chicago, 1987). London, Faber, 1985.
Scenes from a Marriage, adaptation of a play by Feydeau (produced London, 1986).
The Real Long John Silver and Other Plays: Barnes' People III (as *Barnes' People III*, broadcast 1986). London, Faber, 1986.

Screenplays: *Violent Moment*, 1959; *The White Trap*, 1959; *Breakout*, 1959; *The Professionals*, 1960; *Off-Beat*, 1961; *Ring of Spies* (*Ring of Treason*), with Frank Launder, 1963; *Not with My Wife You Don't*, with others, 1966; *The Ruling Class*, 1972.

Radio Plays: *My Ben Jonson*, 1973; *Eastward Ho!*, from the play by Jonson, Chapman, and Marston, 1973; *Antonio*, 1977; *The Two Hangmen: Brecht and Wedekind*, 1978; *A Chaste Maid in Cheapside*, from the play by Middleton, 1979; *Eulogy on Baldness*, from work by Synesius of Cyrene, 1980; *For the Conveyance of Oysters*, from a work by Gorky, 1981; *The Soldier's Fortune*, from the play by Thomas Otway, 1981; *The Atheist*, from the play by Thomas Otway, 1981; *Barnes' People*, 1981; *The Singer*, from a work by Wedekind, 1981; *The Magician*, from a work by Gorky, 1982; *The Dutch Courtesan*, from the play by Marston, 1982; *A Mad World, My Masters*, from the play by Middleton, 1983; *Barnes' People II*, 1984; *The Primrose Path*, from a play by Feydeau, 1984; *A Trick to Catch the Old One*, from the play by Middleton, 1985; *The Old Law*, from the play by Middleton and Rowley, 1986; *Woman of Paris*, from a work by Henri Becque, 1986; *Barnes' People III*, 1986; *No End to Dreaming*, 1987; *The Magnetic Lady*, from the play by Jonson, 1987.

Television Play: *The Man with a Feather in His Hat*, 1960.

*

Critical Studies: *Jenseits des Absurden* by Martin Esslin, Vienna, Europaverlag, 1973; *The Theatre of Peter Barnes* by Bernard F. Dukore, London, Heinemann, 1981; *Landmarks of Modern British Drama: The Plays of the Sixties* edited by Roger Cornish and Violet Ketels, London, Methuen, 1986.

Theatrical Activities:
Director: **Plays**—several of his own plays; *Bartholomew Fair* by Jonson, London, 1978 and 1987. **Film**—*Leonardo's Last Supper*, 1977.

Peter Barnes quotes from his programme note for *The Ruling Class*, 1968:

The aim is to create, by means of soliloquy, rhetoric, formalized ritual, slapstick, songs, and dances, a comic theatre of contrasting moods and opposites, where everything is simultaneously tragic and ridiculous. And we hope never to consent to the deadly servitude of naturalism or lose our hunger for true size, weight, and texture.

* * *

Peter Barnes is one of the most consistently exciting and inventive of contemporary playwrights, a savage satirist and a glorious free-booter of past theatrical styles. Some of the more obvious influences are discernible in the adaptations of work by Marston, Jonson, and Wedekind—and in particular a magnificent version of Wedekind's *Lulu* plays. He is as implacably opposed to the dominant theatrical mode of naturalism as he is to the perpetuation of the status quo in the world in which he writes. His chief weapon is comedy, but a comedy always on the verge of nightmare. He first came to prominence with *The Ruling Class* in 1968—a play in which the delusion of the latest in a long line of insane Earls of Gurney that he is Christ serves as a perfectly reasonable representation of the continued appropriation of power by a self-perpetuating ruling class.

The play—the plot of which concerns the efforts of the Earl's relations to get a male heir from him before having him certified—is a free-wheeling farcical broadside on ruling-class excesses. However, a pervading sense of disgust at the way things are is never balanced by any suggestion of a way out of the impasse. The only character who might seriously threaten the perpetuation of the old order is the butler, an ill-defined revolutionary completely unable to leave the world of privilege he would destroy despite the acquisition of a substantial inheritance from the previous Earl. And this fascination with the ostensible object of attack is something that he shares with the play itself. For all its venom Barnes seemed at this juncture unable to do more than pick away at the scab.

Subsequently the humour would be increasingly less cosy and the visions of society far bleaker. His plays were to offer an excess of blood, vomit, and excrement, guaranteed to offend the conventional West End audience (as is clearly intended), without ever offering the kind of positive analysis that might appeal to a more politically engaged audience. His work thus falls between the two extremes of contemporary theatre, and as a result he has quite unfairly continued to struggle for productions. Indeed, it took him seven years to get his recent play *Red Noses* on.

After *The Ruling Class* Barnes moved away from an albeit fantasy version of the contemporary world, and his later plays offer a series of nightmare visions of climactic moments of earlier "civilisation" inhabited by characters who speak a variety of inventive and historically unlocatable languages in ways which make the link between present crisis and past roots something never less than urgent and disturbing. In *Leonardo's Last Supper* the great artist comes to in a filthy charnel-house where he has been carried having been prematurely declared dead. His joy at his resurrection, and at the further works of genius he will now be able to leave the world, is not shared by the wretched family. They had seen their contract for the burial of the famous man as a way to worldly fame and success, and they simply carry on with the arrangements having first ensured a real corpse by plunging Leonardo headfirst into a bucket of excrement, urine and, vomit. The wonders of the Renaissance mean nothing to this self-dependent family unit, and the working model of the basic precepts of capitalist enterprise that they provide acts also as a demonstration of the way in which all that is represented by the aspirations of such as Leonardo is built on the usually mute sufferings of other such socially insignificant people.

In *The Bewitched* Barnes turned to a key moment in modern European history, the problems over the succession to the grotesquely inbred Philip IV of Spain. The effect of the transference of power on the lives of the powerless throughout Europe is dramatically heightened by the Court's own total lack of concern for them, all interest being centered on explanations of, and attempts to rectify, the ruler's impotence. It is a world in which spiritual salvation is sought for in the torture chamber and in the *auto-da-fé*, as the political fate of Europe is decided by the crazy attempts of the institutions of church and state to create a rightful heir from the seed of an impotent and degenerate imbecile. The central metaphor that links a mad incapacity with political power is here used to far more telling effect, and the result is one of the most thrilling and disturbing plays of the modern period.

And in *Laughter!* he was to push the process a stage further with a series of carefully prepared theatrical shocks. Part 1 takes us back to another account of the insanity of rule, this time in the court of Ivan the Terrible. Terrifyingly comic though it is, it leaves the audience quite unready for what is to follow. Part 2 opens in an office which is dominated by an eight-foot high stretch of filing cabinets and in which a poster of Hitler is prominent on the wall. As the dialogue develops, the audience is invited to laugh as the bureaucrats fight for power and status among themselves, even as it becomes increasingly apparent that the office is responsible for organising the finer details of the extermination programme at Auschwitz.

And then the wall of filing cabinets opens to reveal an interior of gassed corpses being violently stripped of valuables by a Sanitation Squad in gas-masks—the dry statistics of the files are suddenly metamorphosed in a grotesque masque of death. The audience has thrust at them the reality behind the language of a petty officialdom that carries out the insane demands of its rulers without questioning or ever properly looking at what is being administered. That Barnes should then finish his play with an Epilogue in which two Jewish stand-up comedians go through their paces at the Concentration Camp Christmas Concert is evidence of a writer who is prepared to tread a more dangerous tightrope than any of his contemporaries.

With *Red Noses* he moved back into more distant history, continuing his exploration of the potential of "laughter" as a weapon against oppression. In the midst of a plague-torn Europe a group of self-appointed, and Papally sanctioned, Red Noses take on the role of theatrical clowns—acting out their parts on a politically repressive stage. They form an alliance with other more politically active groups in response to Barnes's own question: "Can we ever get laughter from comedy which doesn't accept the miseries of life but actually helps to change them? . . . Laughter linked with revolution might be the best of both worlds." But by the end of this remarkable play the passing of the plague is accompanied by the inevitable restoration of the old order of church and state. The question that Barnes raises ever more urgently about the ability of the writer to bring about change remains an open one. It is to be hoped that the British theatre will not have to wait so long this time for the playwright's further thoughts.

—John Bull

BECKETT, Samuel (Barclay). Irish. Born near Dublin, 13 April 1906. Educated at Portora Royal School, County Fermanagh; Trinity College, Dublin, B.A. in French and Italian 1927, M.A. 1931. Worked at the Irish Red Cross Hospital, St. Lô, France, 1945. Married Suzanne Deschevaux-Dumesnil in 1961. French teacher, Campbell College, Belfast, 1928; Lecturer in English, École Normale Supérieure, Paris, 1928–30; Lecturer in French, Trinity College, Dublin, 1930–31. Closely associated with James Joyce in Paris in the late 1920's and 1930's. Settled in Paris in 1937 and has written chiefly in French since 1945; translates his own work into English. Recipient: *Evening Standard* award, 1955; Obie award, 1958, 1960, 1962, 1964; Italia prize, 1959; International Publishers Prize, 1961; Prix Filmcritice, 1965; Tours Film prize, 1966; Nobel Prize for Literature, 1969; National Grand Prize for Theatre (France), 1975; New York Drama Critics Circle citation, 1984. D.Litt.: Dublin University, 1959. Member, German Academy of Art; Companion of Literature, Royal Society of Literature, 1984; Member, Aosdána, 1986. Address: c/o Editions de Minuit, 7 rue Bernard-Palissy, 75006 Paris, France.

Publications

Plays

Le Kid, with Georges Pelorson (produced Dublin, 1931).

En Attendant Godot (produced Paris, 1953). Paris, Minuit, 1952; translated by Beckett as *Waiting for Godot: Tragicomedy* (produced London, 1955; Miami and New York, 1956), New York, Grove Press, 1954; London, Faber, 1956.

Fin de partie: suivi de Acte sans paroles, music by John Beckett (produced London, 1957). Paris, Minuit, 1957; translated by Samuel Beckett as *Endgame: A Play in One Act; Followed by Act Without Words: A Mime for One Player* (*Endgame* produced New York and London, 1958; *Act Without Words* produced New York, 1960), New York, Grove Press, and London, Faber, 1958.

All That Fall (broadcast 1957; produced Santa Barbara, California, 1965). New York, Grove Press, and London, Faber, 1957.

Krapp's Last Tape (produced London, 1958; New York, 1960). With *Embers*, London, Faber, 1959; in *Krapp's Last Tape and Other Dramatic Pieces*, 1960.

Embers (broadcast 1959). With *Krapp's Last Tape*, London, Faber, 1959; in *Krapp's Last Tape and Other Dramatic Pieces*, 1960.

Act Without Words II (produced New York, 1959; London, 1960). Included in *Krapp's Last Tape and Other Dramatic Pieces*, 1960; in *Eh Joe and Other Writings*, 1967.

La Manivelle/The Old Tune (bilingual edition), adaptation of the play by Robert Pinget. Paris, Minuit, 1960; Beckett's text only (broadcast 1960), in *Plays 1*, by Pinget, London, Calder, 1963; in *Three Plays*, by Pinget, New York, Hill and Wang, 1966.

Krapp's Last Tape and Other Dramatic Pieces (includes *All That Fall, Embers, Act Without Words I* and *II*). New York, Grove Press, 1960.

Happy Days (produced New York, 1961; London, 1962). New York, Grove Press, 1961; London, Faber, 1962; bilingual edition, edited by James Knowlson, Faber, 1978.

Words and Music, music by John Beckett (broadcast 1962). Included in *Play and Two Short Pieces for Radio*, 1964; in *Cascando and Other Short Dramatic Pieces*, 1968.

Cascando, music by Marcel Mihalovici (broadcast in French, 1963). Included in *Dramatische Dichtungen 1*, Frankfurt, Suhrkamp, 1963; translated by Beckett as *Cascando: A Radio Piece for Music and Voice* (broadcast 1964; in *Beckett 3*, produced London, 1970; produced New York, 1976), included in *Play and Two Short Pieces for Radio*, 1964; in *Cascando and Other Short Dramatic Pieces*, 1968.

Play (as *Spiel*, produced Ulm-Donau, 1963; as *Play*, produced New York and London, 1964). Included in *Play and Two Short Pieces for Radio*, 1964; in *Cascando and Other Short Dramatic Pieces*, 1968.

Play and Two Short Pieces for Radio. London, Faber, 1964.

Eh Joe (televised 1966; produced New York, 1978). Included in *Eh Joe and Other Writings*, 1967; in *Cascando and Other Short Dramatic Pieces*, 1968.

Va et vient: Dramaticule (as *Kommen und Gehen*, produced Berlin 1966; as *Va et vient*, also director: produced Paris, 1966). Paris, Minuit, 1966; translated by Beckett as *Come and Go: Dramaticule* (produced Dublin and London, 1968; New York, 1974), London, Calder and Boyars, 1967; in *Cascando and Other Short Dramatic Pieces*, 1968.

Eh Joe and Other Writings (includes *Act Without Words II* and *Film*). London, Faber, 1967.

Cascando and Other Short Dramatic Pieces (includes *Words and Music, Eh Joe, Play, Come and Go, Film*). New York, Grove Press, 1968.

Film. New York, Grove Press, 1969; London, Faber, 1972.

Breath (part of *Oh! Calcutta!*, produced New York and Glasgow, 1969; London, 1970). Included in *Breath and Other Shorts*, 1971.

Breath and Other Shorts (includes *Come and Go, Act Without Words I* and *II*, and the prose piece *From an Abandoned Work*). London, Faber, 1971.

Not I (produced New York, 1972; London, 1973). London Faber, 1973; in *First Love and Other Shorts*, 1974.

Ghost Trio (as *Tryst*, televised 1976). Included in *Ends and Odds*, 1976.

That Time (produced London and Washington, D.C., 1976; New York, 1977). London, Faber, 1976; in *Ends and Odds*, 1976.

Footfalls (also director: produced London and Washington, D.C., 1976; New York, 1977). London, Faber, 1976; in *Ends and Odds*, 1976.

Ends and Odds: Eight New Dramatic Pieces (includes *Not I, That Time, Footfalls, Ghost Trio, Theatre I* and *II, Radio I* and *II*). New York, Grove Press, 1976; as *Ends and Odds: Plays and Sketches* (includes *Not I, That Time, Footfalls, Ghost Trio, . . . but the clouds . . ., Theatre I* and *II, Radio I* and *II*), London, Faber, 1977.

Rough for Radio (broadcast 1976). As *Radio II*, included in *Ends and Odds*, 1976.

Theatre I and II (produced London and New York, 1985). Included in *Ends and Odds*, 1976.

A Piece of Monologue (produced New York, 1980). Included in *Rockaby and Other Short Pieces*, 1981; in *Three Occasional Pieces*, 1982.

Rockaby (produced Buffalo, New York, and New York City, 1981; London, 1982). Included in *Rockaby and Other Short Pieces*, 1981; in *Three Occasional Pieces*, 1982.

Rockaby and Other Short Pieces. New York, Grove Press, 1981.

Ohio Impromptu (produced Columbus, Ohio, 1981; New York, 1983; Edinburgh and London, 1984). Included in *Rockaby and Other Short Pieces*, 1981; in *Three Occasional Pieces*, 1982.

Catastrophe et autres dramaticules: Cette fois, Solo, Berceuse, Impromptu d'Ohio. Paris, Minuit, 1982.

Three Occasional Pieces. London, Faber, 1982.

Quad (as *Quadrat 1 +2*, televised in German, 1982; as *Quad*, televised 1982). Included in *Collected Shorter Plays*, 1984.

Catastrophe (produced Avignon, 1982; New York, 1983; Edinburgh and London, 1984). Included in *Collected Shorter Plays*, 1984.

Nacht und Träume (televised 1983). Included in *Collected Shorter Plays*, 1984.

What Where (as *Was Wo*, produced Graz, Germany, 1983; produced in English, New York, 1983; Edinburgh and London, 1984). Included in *Collected Shorter Plays*, 1984.

Collected Shorter Plays. London, Faber, and New York, Grove Press, 1984.

Ohio Impromptu, Catastrophe, and What Where. New York, Grove Press, 1984.

The Complete Dramatic Works. London, Faber, 1986.

Screenplay: *Film*, 1965.

Radio Plays: *All That Fall*, 1957; *Embers*, 1959; *The Old Tune*, from a play by Robert Pinget, 1960; *Words and Music*, 1962; *Cascando*, 1963; *Rough for Radio*, 1976.

Television Plays: *Eh Joe*, 1966; *Tryst*, 1976; *Shades* (*Ghost Trio, Not I, . . . but the clouds . . .*), 1977; *Quadrat 1 + 2*, 1982 (Germany); *Quad*, 1982; *Nacht und Träume*, 1983.

Novels

Murphy. London, Routledge, 1938; New York, Grove Press, 1957.

Molloy. Paris, Minuit, 1951; translated by Beckett and Patrick Bowles, Paris, Olympia Press, and New York, Grove Press, 1955; London, Calder and Boyars, 1966.

Malone meurt. Paris, Minuit, 1951; translated by Beckett as *Malone Dies*, New York, Grove Press, 1956; London, Calder, 1958.

L'Innommable. Paris, Minuit, 1953; translated by Beckett as *The Unnamable*, New York, Grove Press, 1958.
Watt (written in English). Paris, Olympia Press, 1953; New York, Grove Press, 1959; London, Calder, 1963.
Molloy, Malone Dies, The Unnamable. London, Calder, 1960.
Comment c'est. Paris, Minuit, 1961; translated by Beckett as *How It Is*, New York, Grove Press, and London, Calder, 1964.
Mercier et Camier. Paris, Minuit, 1970; translated by Beckett as *Mercier and Camier*, London, Calder and Boyars, 1974; New York, Grove Press, 1975.

Short Stories and Texts

More Pricks Than Kicks. London, Chatto and Windus, 1934; New York, Grove Press, 1970.
Nouvelles et Textes pour rien. Paris, Minuit, 1955; translated by Beckett and Richard Seaver as *Stories and Texts for Nothing*, New York, Grove Press, 1967; in *No's Knife*, 1967.
From an Abandoned Work. London, Faber, 1958.
Imagination morte imaginez. Paris, Minuit, 1965; translated by Beckett as *Imagination Dead Imagine*, London, Calder and Boyars, 1965.
Assez. Paris, Minuit, 1966; translated by Beckett as *Enough*, in *No's Knife*, 1967.
Bing. Paris, Minuit, 1966; translated by Beckett as *Ping*, in *No's Knife*, 1967.
Têtes-Mortes (includes *D'Un Ouvrage Abandonné, Assez, Bing, Imagination morte imaginez*). Paris, Minuit, 1967; translated by Beckett in *No's Knife*, 1967.
No's Knife: Collected Shorter Prose 1945–1966 (includes *Stories and Texts for Nothing, From an Abandoned Work, Enough, Imagination Dead Imagine, Ping*). London, Calder and Boyars, 1967.
L'Issue. Paris, Georges Visat, 1968.
Sans. Paris, Minuit, 1969; translated by Beckett as *Lessness*, London, Calder and Boyars, 1971.
Séjour. Paris, Georges Richar, 1970.
Premier Amour. Paris, Minuit, 1970; translated by Beckett as *First Love*, London, Calder and Boyars, 1973.
Le Dépeupleur. Paris, Minuit, 1971; translated by Beckett as *The Lost Ones*, London, Calder and Boyars, and New York, Grove Press, 1972.
The North. London, Enitharmon Press, 1972.
Abandonné. Paris, George Visat, 1972.
Au loin un oiseau. New York, Double Elephant Press, 1973.
First Love and Other Shorts. New York, Grove Press, 1974.
Fizzles. New York, Grove Press, 1976.
For to End Yet Again and Other Fizzles. London, Calder, 1976.
All Strange Away. New York, Gotham Book Mart, 1976; London, Calder, 1979.
Four Novellas (*First Love, The Expelled, The Calmative, The End*). London, Calder, 1977; as *The Expelled and Other Novellas*, London, Penguin, 1980.
Six Residua. London, Calder, 1978.
Company. London, Calder, and New York, Grove Press, 1980.
Mal vu mal dit. Paris, Minuit, 1981; translated by Beckett as *Ill Seen Ill Said*, London, Calder, and New York, Grove Press, 1982.
Worstward Ho. London, Calder, and New York, Grove Press, 1983.

Verse

Whoroscope. Paris, Hours Press, 1930.
Echo's Bones and Other Precipitates. Paris, Europa Press, 1935.
Gedichte (collected poems in English and French, with German translations). Wiesbaden, Limes, 1959.
Poems in English. London, Calder, 1961; New York, Grove Press, 1963.
Poèmes. Paris, Minuit, 1968.
Collected Poems in English and French. London, Calder, and New York, Grove Press, 1977; revised edition, as *Collected Poems 1930–1978*, Calder, 1984.

Other

"Dante . . . Bruno. Vico . . Joyce," in *Our Exagmination round His Factification for Incamination of Work in Progress.* Paris, Shakespeare and Company, 1929; London, Faber, 1936; New York, New Directions, 1939.
Proust. London, Chatto and Windus, 1931; New York, Grove Press, 1957; with *Three Dialogues with Georges Duthuit*, London, Calder, 1965.
Bram van Velde, with Georges Duthuit and Jacques Putman. Paris, Georges Fall, 1958; translated by Beckett and Olive Classe, New York, Grove Press, 1960.
A Samuel Beckett Reader. London, Calder and Boyars, 1967.
I Can't Go On: A Selection from the Work of Samuel Beckett, edited by Richard Seaver. New York, Grove Press, 1976.
Disjecta: Miscellaneous Writings and a Dramatic Fragment, edited by Ruby Cohn. London, Calder, 1983; New York, Grove Press, 1984.
Collected Shorter Prose 1945–1980. London, Calder, 1984.
Happy Days: The Production Notebook, edited by James Knowlson. London, Faber, 1985; New York, Grove Press, 1986.

Translator, *Anthology of Mexican Poetry*, edited by Octavio Paz. Bloomington, Indiana University Press, 1958; London, Thames and Hudson, 1959.
Translator, with others, *Selected Poems*, by Alain Bosquet. New York, New Directions, 1963.
Translator, *Zone*, by Guillaume Apollinaire. Dublin and London, Dolmen Press-Calder and Boyars, 1972.
Translator, *Drunken Boat*, by Arthur Rimbaud, edited by James Knowlson and Felix Leakey. Reading, Whiteknights Press, 1977.

*

Bibliography: *Samuel Beckett: His Works and His Critics: An Essay in Bibliography* by Raymond Federman and John Fletcher, Berkeley, University of California Press, 1970 (through 1966); *Samuel Beckett: Checklist and Index of His Published Works 1967–1976* by Robin John Davis, privately printed, 1979.

Manuscript Collections: University of Texas, Austin; Ohio State University, Columbus; Washington University, St. Louis; Dartmouth College, Hanover, New Hampshire; Reading University, England.

Critical Studies (selection): *Samuel Beckett: A Critical Study*, New York, Grove Press, 1961, London, Calder, 1962, revised edition, Berkeley, University of California Press, 1968, and *A Reader's Guide to Samuel Beckett*, New York, Farrar Straus, and London, Thames and Hudson, 1973, both by Hugh Kenner; *Samuel Beckett: The Comic Gamut*, New Brunswick, New Jersey, Rutgers University Press, 1962, *Back to Beckett*, Princeton, New Jersey, Princeton University Press, 1974, and *Just Play: Beckett's Theater*, Princeton University Press, 1980, all by Ruby Cohn, and *Samuel Beckett: A Collection of Criticism*, New York, McGraw Hill, 1975, and *Waiting for Godot: A Selection of Critical Essays*, London, Macmillan, 1987, both edited by Cohn; *Samuel Beckett* by William York Tindall, New York, Columbia University Press, 1964; *Beckett* by Richard N. Coe, Edinburgh, Oliver and Boyd, 1964, as *Samuel Beckett*, New York, Grove Press, 1964; *Samuel Beckett: A Collection of Critical Essays* edited by Martin Esslin, Englewood Cliffs, New Jersey, Prentice Hall, 1965; *Samuel Beckett's Art* by John Fletcher, London, Chatto and Windus, and New York, Barnes and Noble, 1967, and *Beckett: A Study of His Plays* by Fletcher and John Spurling, London, Eyre Methuen, and New York, Hill and Wang, 1972, revised edition, Eyre Methuen, 1978, as *Beckett the Playwright*, Methuen, and New York, Farrar Straus, 1985; *Beckett at 60: A Festschrift* edited by John Calder, London, Calder and Boyars, 1967; *Samuel Beckett* by Ronald Hayman, London, Heinemann, 1968, New York, Ungar, 1974, revised edition, Heinemann, 1980; *Samuel Beckett Now: Critical Approaches to His Novels, Poetry, and Plays* edited by Melvin J. Friedman, Chicago, University of Chicago Press, 1970; *Angels of Darkness: Dramatic Effect in Samuel Beckett* by Colin Duckworth, London, Allen and Unwin, 1972; *Beckett the Shape Changer* edited by Katharine J. Worth, London, Routledge, 1975; *Art and the Artist in the Works of Samuel Beckett* by Hannah Case Copeland, The Hague, Mouton, 1975; *Samuel Beckett's Dramatic Language* by James Eliopulos, The Hague, Mouton, 1975; *Beckett and Broadcasting: A Study of the Works of Samuel Beckett for and in Radio and Television* by Clas Zilliacus, Abo, Finland, Abo Akademi, 1976; *Samuel Beckett* by John Pilling, London, Routledge, 1976, and *Frescoes of the Skull: The Later Prose and Drama of Samuel Beckett* edited by Pilling and James Knowlson, London, Calder, 1979, New York, Grove Press, 1980; *Beckett/Beckett* by Vivian Mercier, New York, Oxford University Press, 1977, London Oxford University Press, 1979; *A Student's Guide to the Plays of Samuel Beckett* by Beryl S. Fletcher, London, Faber, 1978, revised edition, with John Fletcher, 1985; *Samuel Beckett: A Biography* by Deirdre Bair, New York, Harcourt Brace, and London, Cape, 1978; *Samuel Beckett: The Critical Heritage* edited by Raymond Federman and Lawrence Graver, London, Routledge, 1979; *The Samuel Beckett Manuscripts: A Critical Study* by Richard L. Admussen, London, Prior, 1979; *The Transformations of Godot* by Frederick Busi, Lexington, University Press of Kentucky, 1980; *Accommodating the Chaos: Samuel Beckett's Nonrelational Art* by J. E. Dearlove, Durham, North Carolina, Duke University Press, 1982; *Samuel Beckett: Humanistic Perspectives* edited by Morris Beja, S. E. Gontarski, and Pierre Astier, Columbus, Ohio State University Press, 1983, and *The Intent of Undoing in Samuel Beckett's Dramatic Texts* by Gontarski, Bloomington, Indiana University Press, 1985, and *On Beckett: Essays and Criticism* edited by Gontarski, New York, Grove Press, 1986; *Samuel Beckett* by Charles Lyons, New York, Grove Press, 1983; *Beckett's Theaters: Interpretations for Performance* by Sidney Homan, Lewisburg, Pennsylvania, Bucknell University Press, 1984; *Samuel Beckett and the Meaning of Being: A Study in Ontological Parable* by Lance St. John Butler, London, Macmillan, and New York, St. Martin's Press, 1984; *Beckett on File* edited by Virginia Cooke, London, Methuen, 1985; *Understanding Beckett: A Study of Monologue and Gesture in the Works of Beckett* by Peter Gidal, London, Macmillan, and New York, St. Martin's Press, 1986; *Beckett at 80/Beckett in Context* edited by Enoch Brater, New York, Oxford University Press, 1986, and *Beyond Minimalism: Beckett's Late Style in the Theater* by Brater, New York, Oxford University Press, 1987; *Samuel Beckett* by Linda Ben-Zvi, Boston, Twayne, 1986; *As No Other Dare Fail: For Samuel Beckett on His 80th Birthday*, London, Calder, and New York, Riverrun Press, 1986; *The Broken Window: Beckett's Dramatic Perspective* by Jane Alison Hale, West Lafayette, Indiana, Purdue University Press, 1987; *Beckett's Later Fiction and Drama: Texts for Company* edited by James Acheson and Kateryna Arthur, London, Macmillan, 1987.

Theatrical Activities:
Director: **Plays**—*L'Hypothèse* by Robert Pinget, Paris, 1965; *Come and Go*, Paris, 1966; *Endgame*, Berlin, 1967; *Krapp's Last Tape*, Berlin, 1969 and 1977, Paris, 1970, London, 1978; *Happy Days*, Berlin, 1971, London, 1979; *Waiting for Godot*, Berlin, 1975, London, 1984; *Krapp's Last Tape* and *Not I*, Paris, 1975; *That Time*, Berlin, 1976; *Footfalls*, London and Berlin, 1976, Paris, 1978; *Play*, Berlin, 1978. **Television** (Germany)—*Eh Joe*, 1966, 1979; *Quadrat 1+2*, 1982; *Nacht und Träume*, 1983; *Was Wo* (*What Where*), 1986.

* * *

Poet, novelist, playwright, Samuel Beckett is most widely celebrated for his drama, which is a large and varied body of work—two mime plays, six radio plays, one movie, six television scripts, one actorless play, and 17 dramas for speaking actors in the theatre. Ten pieces were written in French and nine subsequently translated into English by Beckett; the others were composed directly in English. French or English, Beckett's diverse dramas concentrate human experience into highly theatrical images.

Beckett's first play, *Le Kid* (not extant), parodied Corneille's *Cid* for a Trinity College audience. Written 16 years later, but unproduced and unpublished, his second play, *Eleuthéria*, parodies the well-made play with its three acts developed through climaxes to resolution. Act 1 satirizes the Krap family with its several aches and pains, but their worst pain is their son Victor who has gone to live in "sordid inertia." "Victor's father dies between Acts 1 and 2, and in Act 2 the Krap family and friends try to lure Victor back to bourgeois respectability. In Act 3 complications are resolved when Victor firmly declares his independence: "Liberty is seeing yourself dead." For that unattainable liberty—the eleutheria of the title—Victor spurns both middle-class life and romantic suicide. In dramatizing the familiar theme of a misunderstood young man, Beckett stuffs his dialogue into a familiar structure. It is therefore astonishing that within a year Beckett had written *Waiting for Godot* (in French).

Waiting for Godot is divided into two acts, and the second seems to repeat the first: at dusk Gogo and Didi meet to wait for Godot. Pozzo and Lucky arrive, stop a while, and then leave. As night falls, a boy announces that Godot will come not today but tomorrow. This "tragicomedy" rests on the account of the crucifixion in the gospel of St. Luke, as summarized by St. Augustine: "Do not despair: one of the thieves was saved. Do not presume: one of the thieves was damned." The two thieves are Didi and Gogo; the two thieves are Pozzo and Lucky. And each spectator wonders whether he is saved thief or damned thief.

The four nationalities evoked by the characters' names—Slavic Vladimir, French Estragon, Italian Pozzo, English Lucky—suggest a composite portrait of an international Everyman. Though the printed text does not specify their costumes,

Vladimir and Estragon wear the black suit and derby of music hall or silent films, and their antics arouse sympathetic laughter. The other couple, Pozzo and Lucky, wear elaborate but dated clothes, and their actions arouse horror as well as laughter. Grotesque Pozzo and Lucky confront endearing Didi and Gogo; for all the volumes of exegesis that have been written about the play, its theatricality rests on this confrontation of two couples during the endless wait for the mysterious Godot. While the two friends wait, their activities accumulate into a life, which mirrors and criticizes the activities of most lives. What is distinctively new about *Godot* is the inextricable union of its method and its madness; stage words and gestures are comically and excruciatingly concrete; stage words and gestures are metaphysically meaningful, but the play's meaning is evanescent as a firefly.

After 1950 Beckett has found it increasingly difficult to write in any genre. His fourth play, *Endgame*, was nearly two years in the writing—again in French. Its single act takes place in a "shelter," a living and dying room of a family. In some ways the family is ordinary, with its quarrels and attachments; in most ways the family is extraordinary, being the last of the human race. The members of this family have no family name, but each of the four family members has a four-letter name meaning nail: Nell puns on English nail as Clov puns of French *clou*; Nagg abbreviates German Nagel as Hamm abbreviates Latin *hamus*. Nailhood seems to represent humanity, stick figures topped with a head. Hamm, however, is also an abridgement of hammer, which drives the nails on the stage board. He is chief actor and director of the sado-masochistic play of *Endgame*. Nagg and Nell are Hamm's parents, but Clov is variously called his son, menial, creature, and dog. After Clov claims to sight another character—a small boy—he prepares to leave the family shelter. At the end of the play, however, Clov stands in the doorway, as at the beginning. And Hamm curtains his face as at the beginning. The play plays full circle: the shelter still offers protection from world catastrophe, the endgame does not yet end, the stage lives are not quite finished, and the play will presumably be repeated on another night. More rigorous than *Godot*, with fewer music hall routines, *Endgame* rests more gravely on an economy of purposeless play. Words are echoic and actions are repetitive in the few moments before life fades into nothingness.

After the stringent suffering of *Endgame*, Beckett penned the mime play *Act Without Words*, in which the mute figure painfully learns the futility of motion. The radio play *All That Fall* peoples the Irish town of Boggshill through sound alone. Experience with the mime play and radio play contributed to Beckett's next stage play, *Krapp's Last Tape*, his first complete theatre piece written directly in English. The invisible voice of radio is committed to tape in *Krapp's Last Tape*, while the lone character on stage plays much of his role in mime. At 69 Krapp is addicted to bananas that constipate him, to alcohol that undermines him, to desire for women in fact and in fantasy. 69-year-old Krapp listens to a tape recorded on his 39th birthday, in which he laments his addiction to bananas and alcohol, and lingers over his farewell to a loved woman. In that tape Krapp speaks of a tape made ten or twelve years earlier, in which he recalls his constipation and his weakness for alcohol and women. Finally, Krapp broods while the tape-recorder records silence. *Krapp's Last Tape* is a dramatic record of aging, with death imminent.

Beckett's subsequent drama dissolves the familiar world into the context of an eternal void. *Happy Days* (written in English) shows Winnie literally sinking into her grave, returning to dust. And yet she prattles cheerfully under a blazing sun. Winnie uses four main resources in living through what she repeatedly designates as her happy day—the stage props, her husband Willie, the composition of a story, and the recollections that seem to be involuntary and through which thread fragments of quotations from English verse. By Act II Winnie is buried p to her neck, and her resources are reduced; her face is her only prop, she tries to tell her story, she vainly addresses her husband, and the grasps for lines of verse. Indomitable, she is rewarded with the most startling climax in all Beckett's drama—the entrance of her husband Willie on all fours, in morning clothes. Despite Winnie's encouragement, Willie fails to reach her, but he does manage to utter a single syllable—"Win"—at once her name and a mockery of their lives of loss. In the final tableau Willie's hand is poised between Winnie and revolver. Unsmiling, husband and wife look at one another as the curtain falls on this happy day that summarizes her life.

In shorter plays Beckett etches the human condition ever more sharply. The radio play *Embers* pits human embers against the inhuman timeless sea. The mime play *Act Without Words II* contrasts the slow gestures of a thinker with the swift movements of a doer, to show the same result or non-result. The stage play *Play* views a lovers' triangle from the perspective of eternity. *Words and Music* and *Cascando*, radio plays, play words and music against a creator who attempts to blend them meaningfully. *Film*, a movie, and *Eh Joe*, a television play, use and mock the camera upon which their genres depend. *Come and Go* plays the circularity of time in three minutes, and *Breath* plays the brevity of life in thirty seconds.

After several years devoted to fiction and directing, Beckett returned to drama. These late stage plays inquire into the mechanics and meaning of theatre—figures playing against background, light against sound, words against stillness or motion. Ingeniously deploying a technique that I call "theatereality," he blends his fictional portraits into the physical reality of the theatre. Thus, a light beam and buzzing in the discourse of Mouth of *Not I* become a theatre spotlight and the words of the discourse. Similarly, in *That Time*, we see the head of a white-haired old man, and we hear of a white-haired old man in two of the three voice-strands that finally dissolve "that time" into no time. The very title *Footfalls* describes what we hear and see in the theatre, but we also hear *about* them in the dialogue between a visible pacing woman and an invisible woman, who narrate and dramatise mother/daughter dialogues. *Rockaby* also engraves the titular action on the audience eyes, while a voiceover tells *about* a woman who retraces the way of her mother from a world outside into a cradling rocker/grave. *A Piece of Monologue is* a piece of monologue about a man, a lamp his height, and the corner of a bed, which is also what we see on stage. *Ohio Impromptu* confronts us with two identical white-haired, black-coated men, Listener and Reader who reads aloud about a listener and reader—the last staging to date of theatereality, which crystallizes in an image our several perceptions. Imagery is more narrow and relentless in the television plays *Ghost Trio*, *. . . but the clouds . . .*, and *Quad*. In the first two, stark black and white reveals the tension between description and music, portraiture and poetry; wordless, *Quad* is a flurry of motion—with and without colour—about a mysterious centre. *Catastrophe* blends politics and aesthetics in a parody piece about the staging of a catastrophic victim. *Nacht und Träume* televises a dream, and *What Where* translates from theatre to television the old Beckett questions about being and the words it takes.

Beckett's plays are at once play and parable, words and images, immediate and durable.

—Ruby Cohn

BEKEDEREMO, J.P. Clark. See **CLARK, John Pepper.**

BENNETT, Alan. British. Born in Leeds, Yorkshire, 9 May 1934. Educated at Leeds Modern School, 1946–52; Exeter College, Oxford, 1954–57 (Open Scholar in History), B.A. (honours) 1957. National Service: Joint Services School for Linguists, Cambridge and Bodmin. Temporary junior lecturer in history, Magdalen College, Oxford, 1960–62. Recipient: *Evening Standard* award, 1961, 1968, 1971, 1985 (for screenplay); Tony award, 1963; Guild of Television Producers award, 1967; Broadcasting Press Guild award, for television play, 1984; Royal Television Society award, 1984, 1986. Agent: Anthony Jones, A.D. Peters Ltd., 10 Buckingham Street, London WC2N 6BU, England.

PUBLICATIONS

Plays

Beyond the Fringe, with others (produced Edinburgh, 1960; London, 1961; New York, 1962). London, Souvenir Press, and New York, Random House, 1963.
Forty Years On (produced Manchester and London, 1968). London, Faber, 1969.
Sing a Rude Song (additional material), book by Caryl Brahms and Ned Sherrin, music by Ron Grainer (produced London, 1969).
Getting On (produced Brighton and London, 1971). London, Faber, 1972.
Habeas Corpus (produced Oxford and London, 1973; New York, 1975). London, Faber, 1973.
The Old Country (produced Oxford and London, 1977). London, Faber, 1978.
Office Suite (includes *Green Forms*—televised as *Doris and Doreen*—and *A Visit from Miss Prothero*; televised 1978; produced London, 1987). London, Faber, 1981.
Enjoy (produced London, 1980). London, Faber, 1980.
Objects of Affection and Other Plays for Television (includes *Objects of Affection: Our Winnie, A Woman of No Importance, Rolling Home, Marks,* and *Say Something Happened*; and *A Day Out, Intensive Care, An Englishman Abroad*). London, BBC Publications, 1982.
A Private Function (screenplay). London, Faber, 1984.
Forty Years On, Getting On, Habeas Corpus. London, Faber, 1985.
The Writer in Disguise (television plays; includes *Me, I'm Afraid of Virginia Woolf; Afternoon Off; One Fine Day; All Day on the Sands; The Old Crowd*; and an essay). London, Faber, 1985.
Kafka's Dick (produced London, 1986). Included in *Two Kafka Plays*, London, Faber, 1987.
The Insurance Man (televised 1986). Included in *Two Kafka Plays*, London, Faber, 1987.
Prick Up Your Ears (screenplay). London, Faber, 1987.
Talking Heads (televised 1987). London, BBC Publications, 1987.

Screenplays: *A Private Function*, 1984; *Prick Up Your Ears*, 1987.

Radio Play: *Uncle Clarence*, 1986.

Television Plays: *On the Margin* series, 1966; *A Day Out*, 1972; *Sunset Across the Bay*, 1975; *A Little Outing*, 1977; *A Visit from Miss Prothero*, 1978; *Me, I'm Afraid of Virginia Woolf*, 1978; *Doris and Doreen*, 1978; *The Old Crowd*, 1979; *Afternoon Off*, 1979; *One Fine Day*, 1979; *All Day on the Sands*, 1979; *Intensive Care*, 1982; *Objects of Affection* (5 plays), 1982; *An Englishman Abroad*, 1983; *The Insurance Man*, 1986; *Talking Heads* (6 monologues), 1987.

*

Theatrical Activities:
Actor: **Plays**—in *Better Late* (revue), Edinburgh, 1959; in *Beyond the Fringe*, Edinburgh, 1960, London, 1961, and New York, 1962; Archbishop of Canterbury in *The Blood of the Bambergs* by John Osborne, London, 1962; Reverend Sloley-Jones in *A Cuckoo in the Nest* by Ben Travers, London, 1964; Tempest in *Forty Years On*, London, 1968; Mrs. Swabb in *Habeas Corpus*, London, 1974. **Films**—*Long Shot*, 1980; *The Secret Policeman's Ball*, 1986. **Radio**—in *The Great Jowett* by Graham Greene, 1980; *Dragon* by Don Haworth, 1982. **Television**—Augustus Hare in *Famous Gossips*, 1965; in *On the Margin*, 1966; Denis Midgley in *Intensive Care*, 1982; Shallow in *The Merry Wives of Windsor*, 1982; Housemaster in *Breaking Up*, 1986; in *Fortunes of War*, 1987.

* * *

> . . . when we play language games,
> we do so rather in order to find
> out what game it is we are
> playing.
>
> —*Beyond the Fringe*

Whatever their ostensible subjects, Alan Bennett's plays consistently dramatize man's desire to define himself and his world through teasingly inadequate language, whether conventional adages, women's magazine prose, government jargon, or quotations from the "Greats." The rich parodies that result simultaneously mock and honor this impulse to erect linguistic safeguards in a frightening world. Bennett's comedy invariably respects his characters, from intellectuals to the northern ladies for whom "Conversation is a conspiracy," and who talk in "speech as mannered and dramatic as Restoration comedy" ("Introduction" to *Office Suite*).

In *Beyond the Fringe* both Bennett's monologues and sketches with Peter Cook, Jonathan Miller, and Dudley Moore focus on the game cliché, which trivializes the supposedly serious, yet suggests that even inane values are better than none (such conservatism ballasts the Headmaster's epigram in *Forty Years On*: "Standards are always out of date. That is what makes them standards"). A supposed lecture by the Duke of

Edinburgh illustrates the precariousness of metaphorical language as well as an underlying desire for decency: "This business of international politics is a game. . . . It's a hard game, it's a rough game . . . sometimes, alas, it's a dirty game, but the point about a game, surely, is that there's no need to take it seriously. . . ." Other *Fringe* sketches brilliantly question the limits of discourse: a prison governor rebukes a condemned man who rejects an analogy between capital punishment and public school caning, "Come along, now, you're playing with words." Just as this semantic comedy foreshadows later plays like Hampton's *The Philanthropist* and Stoppard's *Jumpers*, "Aftermyth," a *Fringe* sketch on Britain during the Blitz, seems the spiritual parent of the many parodies of wartime England during the early 1970's. Bennett illuminates both the hilarious perversion of political rhetoric and the profound need to find attractive equivalents for painful reality.

The Headmaster in *Forty Years On*, an ingenious play-within-a-play focusing on the annual performance by the boys and faculty of Albion School, indulges in similar rhetoric: "The more observant among you will have noticed that one of Bombardier Tiffin's legs was not his own. The other one, God bless him, was lost in the Great War. Some people lost other things, less tangible perhaps than legs, but no less worthwhile—they lost illusions, they lost hope, they lost faith. . . ." *Forty Years On* organizes a series of skits, similar in tone to "Aftermyth," on the cultural and political life of 20th-century England. Wicked portraits of culture heroes like Virginia Woolf and T.E. Lawrence are both outrageously unfair and deadly accurate. The best sketch is the Wilde pastiche in which Lady Dundowne, played by one of the masters in drag, advises her nephew to marry his spinster mother: "the arrangement seems to tidy that I am surprised it does not happen more often in society"—a perfect spoof of the archetypal Wilde plot and wit. "But then all women dress like their mothers, that is their tragedy. No man ever does. That is his," a parody of Wildean paradox, resonates with additional meaning from the elaborate pattern of homosexual allusion in the play; in this representative public school world, witty hyperbole equals literal statement. Bennett exposes the simultaneous idiocy and seductiveness of language on all levels, from the folk-wisdom of a nanny to the devious rhetoric of Chamberlain, while the rude singing of the rugby team both undercuts and elevates the idealized game metaphor of the school anthem. Though only the Headmaster emerges as a character, the cast of stereotypes is suitable for what is essentially a comic allegory of English life.

Getting On, an ambitious Chekhovian comedy, involves a fortyish Labour MP, George Oliver, whose nostalgia for stability ("What we crave in life is order") and linguistic skill link him with the Headmaster. His precarious illusion of order depends on an innocence of the sexual and political realities of his world: his son by a first marriage, his young second wife, and a Conservative homosexual MP form a strange triangle; his West Indian constituent who claimed that neighbors were poisoning her dog is not mad, as he had believed. Reality seems too complex for his categorizing, analytical mind, and, despite his belief in logic and language, he concludes, after a hilariously unsuccessful attempt to order a taxi, "Words fail me." Though continually confronted with proof of the pointlessness of work, George persists with established values (his only radical action, from an English viewpoint, is throwing a bucket of water at a dog that perpetually fouls his doorstep). Yet, as the punning title suggests, the ultimate reward for hard work is aging and death.

All the characters represent different stages of development/decay, sometimes a bit schematically, yet the play flatters only with a sentimentalized portrait of George's son (Bennett was clearer-eyed about the young in *Forty Years On*). George's comic logorrhea offends almost everyone (the stage directions state: "He is deeply misanthropic man, hence his jokes"). Yet, since the play is ambiguous about the sources of this compulsion, he remains a man who can joke about anything, a facility useful in a politician, but insufficient as an index to character. Though some of the comic bits are so funny that they almost weaken the dramatic tension ("Can't have pouffs in the Conservative Party. No seat would be safe"), *Getting On* is an impressive attempt to subordinate laughter to mood and theme.

Habeas Corpus, which focuses on a sadly lecherous, aging GP in Hove, somewhat uneasily balances a well-made farce plot with Bennett's verbal comedy, more elegiac than ever amid a frenzy of trouserless men, missed assignations, and a spinster with an artificial bust. The wit, frequently obsessed with the decline of England or of individual Englishmen, often slows down the crucial pacing of the farce, which, in turn, sometimes undercuts the impact of Bennett's parodies. The wistful tone of the comedy is apparent in the doctor's lament for his lacerated sensibility: "They parade before me bodies the color of tripe and the texture of junket. Is this the image of God, this sagging parcel of vanilla blancmange hoisted day after day on to the consulting table? Is this the precious envelope of the soul?" Though such disillusionment does not stop his pursuit of a nubile young patient, his later reference to "the long littleness of life" as he prepares to examine her attests to the general elegiac note of the play. This mood derives partly from the songs and verses, like those in Auden's verse plays, that allow characters to comment directly to the audience, as the action stops: "So if you get your heart's desire,/Your longings come to pass,/Remember in each other's beds,/It isn't going to last." The resulting vaudeville atmosphere, however effective, softens the hard lines of the farce, a form that Bennett wisely abandoned in the plays that followed.

The Old Country, another comic elegy on the continuing decline of England, initially puzzles the viewer with its tricky setting, a country house outside Moscow in which a British defector, Hilary, and his wife, Bron, have tried to recreate the England he betrayed. A visit from Hilary's sister and her husband, Duff, ostensibly in Russia to lecture on Forster, brings the offer of a return to an England Hilary will no longer recognize. Hilary and Duff, former Cambridge men like Bennett, conduct a typical loving yet satirical analysis of Forster *dicta* like "Only connect." While such material would have produced a self-contained skit in *Fringe* days, it is now a dramatically useful index to the complex attitudes of Englishmen toward their origins.

In the debate over the desirability of return, when Bron asks where in England they could leave their doors unlocked for long periods, her sister-in-law replies, "Wiltshire once. Not any more. There are muggers in Malmesbury." Hilary attempts a more balanced assessment of the overall situation: "No Gamages. No Pontins. No more trains from Kemble to Cirencester. No Lyons. On the other hand I read of the Renaissance of the small bakery; country breweries revive. Better bread, better beer. They come from Florence to shop in Marks and Spencer. It is not an easy decision." But Bron angrily rejects this supposed objectivity as another instance of his ability to argue both sides simultaneously. Certainly Hilary does seem the archetypal Bennett verbal juggler as he tries to define the English response to experience with a complex litany of familiar allusions: "Irony is inescapable. We're conceived in irony. We float in it from the womb. It's the amniotic fluid. It's the silver sea. It's the waters at their priestlike task washing away guilt and purpose and responsibility. Joking but not joking. Caring but not caring. Serious but not serious." *The Old Country*, Bennett's most successful play since *Forty Years On*, dramatizes the dangerous moral and political consequences of this semantic playfulness.

Bennett's more recent work attests to his versatility in demonstrating a similar decline among less sophisticated characters in the England of his Leeds origins. *Green Forms*, one of two television plays collected as *Office Suite*, satirizes the attempts of government workers to define the unknown with comforting jargon. Perplexed by the computerization of the system and the expendability of employees and whole offices, the workers display typical linguistic resourcefulness: "Southport is being wound down. . . . Wound down. Wound up. Phased out anyway. I hope she hasn't been made . . . you know. . . . Well . . . redundant. I wouldn't like to think she's been made redundant; she was very nicely spoken." *A Visit from Miss Prothero*, the second one-acter, abounds in cozy malice as a retired bureaucrat gradually realizes the worthlessness of his life's work. In his world, gossip masquerades as folk-wisdom (Miss Prothero comments on an associate's eczema: "The doctor thinks it's nerves. I think it's those tights. Man-made fibers don't do for everybody. I pay if I wear crimplene").

Enjoy depicts a typical northern family, the son a transsexual social worker, the daughter a prostitute ("She's exceptional. You won't find girls like Linda stood on every street corner"), while the parents await the demolition of their home and speculate on their future residence: "It's a maisonette. They're built more on the human scale. That's the latest thing now, the human scale." Excerpts from Novello and Handel comment ironically on the action, as Mom and Dad learn that their house will be recreated as "A shrine laden with the relics of the recent past and a testimonial to the faith that one day the world will turn and the past come back into its own. . . ." Unfortunately, no authentic unifying tone emerges from the play's blend of folk comedy, parody, and satire on deranged social planners. That the old life with its family betrayals and vulgarities does not merit preservation, except as an historical curiosity, weakens concern for the fates of the couple, though there are affecting moments. This play, less successful than *The Old Country* and *Getting On*, is nevertheless proof of Bennett's developing dramatic ambition and consistently brilliant exploration of language as an index to human aspiration and folly.

—Burton Kendle

BENTLEY, Eric (Russell). American. Born in Bolton, Lancashire, England, 14 September 1916; moved to the United States, 1939; became citizen, 1948. Educated at Bolton School; Oxford University, B.A. 1938, B.Lit. 1939; Yale University, New Haven, Connecticut, Ph.D. 1941. Married 1) Maja Tschernjakow (marriage dissolved); 2) Joanne Davis in 1953; twin sons. Taught at Black Mountain College, North Carolina, 1942–44, and University of Minnesota, Minneapolis, 1944–48; Brander Matthews Professor of Dramatic Literature, Columbia University, New York, 1952–69; free-lance writer, 1970–73; Katharine Cornell Professor of Theatre, State University of New York, Buffalo, 1974–82. Since 1982 Professor of Comparative Literature, University of Maryland, College Park. Charles Eliot Norton Professor of Poetry, Harvard University, Cambridge, Massachusetts, 1960–61; Fulbright Professor, Belgrade, 1980. Drama critic, *New Republic*, New York, 1952–56. Recipient: Guggenheim fellowship, 1948; Rockefeller grant, 1949; American Academy grant, 1953; Longview award, for criticism, 1961; Ford grant, 1964; George Jean Nathan Award, for criticism, 1967; CBS fellowship, 1976; Obie award, 1978; Theater Festival gold medal, 1985. D.F.A.: University of Wisconsin, Madison, 1975; Litt.D.: University of East Anglia, Norwich, 1979. Member, American Academy of Arts and Sciences, 1969. Agent: Jack Tantleff, 360 West 20th Street, New York, New York 10011; or, Joy Westendarp, International Copyright Bureau, 26 Charing Cross Road, Suite 8, London WC2H 0DG, England. Address: 194 Riverside Drive, Apartment 4-E, New York, New York 10025, U.S.A.

Publications

Plays

A Time to Die, and A Time to Live: Two Short Plays, adaptations of plays by Euripides and Sophocles (as *Commitments*, produced New York, 1967). New York, Grove Press, 1967.

Sketches in *DMZ Revue* (produced New York, 1968).

The Red White and Black, music by Brad Burg (produced New York, 1970). Published in *Liberation* (New York), May 1971.

Are You Now or Have You Ever Been: The Investigation of Show-Business by the Un-American Activities Committee 1947–1958 (produced New Haven, Connecticut, 1972; New York, 1973; Birmingham, 1976; London, 1977). New York, Harper, 1972.

The Recantation of Galileo Galilei: Scenes from History Perhaps (produced Detroit, 1973). New York, Harper, 1972.

Expletive Deleted (produced New York, 1974). Published in *Win* (New York), 6 June 1974.

From the Memoirs of Pontius Pilate (produced Buffalo and New York, 1976). Included in *Rallying Cries*, 1977.

Rallying Cries: Three Plays (includes *Are You Now or Have You Ever Been, The Recantation of Galileo Galilei, From the Memoirs of Pontius Pilate*). Washington, D.C., New Republic Books, 1977; as *Are You Now or Have You Ever Been and Other Plays*, New York, Grove Press, 1981.

The Kleist Variations: Three Plays. Baton Rouge, Louisiana, Oracle Press, 1982.
1. *Wannsee* (produced Buffalo, 1978).
2. *The Fall of the Amazons* (produced Buffalo, 1979).
3. *Concord* (produced Buffalo, 1982).

Larry Parks' Day in Court (produced New York, 1979).

Lord Alfred's Lover (produced Gainesville, Florida, 1979). Toronto, Personal Library, 1981; in *Monstrous Martyrdoms*, 1985.

Monstrous Martyrdoms: Three Plays (includes *Lord Alfred's Lover, H for Hamlet, German Requiem*). Buffalo, Prometheus, 1985.

Other

A Century of Hero-Worship: A Study of the Idea of Heroism in Carlyle and Nietzsche, with Notes on Other Hero-Worshipers of Modern Times. Philadelphia, Lippincott, 1944; as *The Cult of the Superman*, London, Hale, 1947.

The Playwright as Thinker: A Study of Drama in Modern Times. New York, Reynal, 1946; as *The Modern Theatre: A Study of Dramatists and the Drama*, London, Hale, 1948.

Bernard Shaw: A Reconsideration. New York, New Directions, 1947; London, Hale, 1950; revised edition as *Bernard*

Shaw 1856–1950, New Directions, 1957; as *Bernard Shaw*, London, Methuen, 1967.
In Search of Theater. New York, Knopf, 1953; London, Dobson, 1954.
The Dramatic Event: An American Chronicle. New York, Horizon Press, and London, Dobson, 1954.
What Is Theatre? A Query in Chronicle Form. New York, Horizon Press, 1956; London, Dobson, 1957.
The Life of the Drama. New York, Atheneum, 1964; London, Methuen, 1965.
The Theatre of Commitment and Other Essays on Drama in Our Society. New York, Atheneum, 1967; London, Methuen, 1968.
What Is Theatre? Incorporating "The Dramatic Event" and Other Reviews 1944–1967. New York, Atheneum, 1968; London, Methuen, 1969.
Theatre of War: Comments on 32 Occasions. New York, Viking Press, and London, Eyre Methuen, 1972.
The Brecht Commentaries 1943–1980. New York, Grove Press, and London, Eyre Methuen, 1981.
The Pirandello Commentaries. Lincoln, University of Nebraska Department of Modern Languages and Literatures, 1985.
The Brecht Memoir. New York, Performing Arts Journal Publications, 1986.

Editor, *The Importance of "Scrutiny": Selections from "Scrutiny," A Quarterly Review, 1932–1948*. New York, G.W. Stewart, 1948.
Editor and Part Translator, *From the Modern Repertory*. Denver, University of Denver Press, series 1 and 2, 1949–52; Bloomington, Indiana University Press, series 3, 1956.
Editor, *The Play: A Critical Anthology*. New York, Prentice Hall, 1951.
Editor, *Shaw on Music*. New York, Doubleday, 1955.
Editor and Part Translator, *The Modern Theatre*. New York, Doubleday, 6 vols., 1955–60.
Editor and Part Translator, *The Classic Theatre*. New York, Doubleday, 4 vols., 1958–61.
Editor and Translator, *Let's Get a Divorce! and Other Plays*. New York, Hill and Wang, 1958.
Editor and Part Translator, *Works of Bertolt Brecht*. New York, Grove Press, 1961—.
Editor and Part Translator, *The Genius of the Italian Theatre*. New York, New American Library, 1964.
Editor, *The Storm over "The Deputy."* New York, Grove Press, 1964.
Editor, *Songs of Bertolt Brecht and Hanns Eisler. . . .* New York, Oak, 1966.
Editor, *The Theory of the Modern Stage: An Introduction to Modern Theatre and Drama*. London, Penguin, 1968.
Editor and Part Translator, *The Great Playwrights: Twenty-Five Plays with Comments by Critics and Scholars*. New York, Doubleday, 2 vols., 1970.
Editor, *Thirty Years of Treason: Excerpts from Hearings before the House Committee on Un-American Activities 1938–1968*. New York, Viking Press, 1971.
Editor and Translator, *Dramatic Repertoire*. New York, Applause, 1985—.

Translator, *The Private Life of the Master Race*, by Brecht. New York, James Laughlin, 1944.
Translator, *Parables for the Theatre: The Good Woman of Setzuan, and The Caucasian Chalk Circle*, by Brecht. Minneapolis, University of Minnesota Press, 1948; revised edition, University of Minnesota Press, and London, Oxford University Press, 1965.
Translator, with others, *Naked Masks: Five Plays*, by Pirandello. New York, Dutton, 1952.
Translator, *Orpheus in the Underworld* (libretto), by Hector Crémieux and Ludovic Halévy. New York, Program Publishing Company, 1956.
Translator, *The Wire Harp*, by Wolf Biermann. New York, Harcourt Brace, 1968.

Recordings (Folkways): *Bentley on Brecht*, Riverside, 1963; *Brecht Before the Un-American Activities Committee*, 1963; *A Man's a Man*, Spoken Arts, 1963; *Songs of Hanns Eisler*, 1965; *The Elephant Calf/Dear Old Democracy*, 1967; *Bentley on Biermann*, 1968; *Eric Bentley Sings The Queen of 42nd Street*, 1974.

*

Manuscript Collection: Boston University Library.

Theatrical Activities:
Director: **Plays**—*Sweeney Agonistes* by T.S. Eliot, Salzburg, 1949; *Him* by E.E. Cummings, Salzburg, 1950; *The House of Bernarda Alba* by García Lorca, Dublin, 1950; *The Iceman Cometh* (co-director) by Eugene O'Neill, Zurich, 1950; *Purgatory* by W.B. Yeats, and *Riders to the Sea* and *The Shadow of the Glen* by J.M. Synge, U.S. tour, 1951; *The Good Woman of Setzuan* by Brecht, New York, 1956.

Eric Bentley quotes from an interview with Jerome Clegg:
Clegg: Why on earth did you have to write a play? For you are nothing if not critical.
Bentley: Maybe the impulse was to write a counter-play.
Clegg: Counter to what?
Bentley: A (good) performance of the Anouilh Antigone—in its integrity, not in the Galantiere adaptation-distortion—had riled me. So I had to write a "correct" Antigone; set Anouilh straight. The same with Brecht.
Clegg: Meaning?
Bentley: He made such absurd demands upon his people. What else could Mother Courage have done?
Clegg: Galileo?
Bentley: Brecht wilfully chose to misunderstand him. The recantation could not possibly be taken as a betrayal of Marxism.
Clegg: So it was historical correctness you were after? Oh, you and your scholarly background!
Bentley: Rubbish. There would be no possible "historical correctness" for Antigone. It is a human correctness that interests me. Telling a story more honestly—truer to *our* time, if you will, not necessarily truer to some other time.
Clegg: Someone had called your dramatic works "no nonsense plays."
Bentley: Can one tell the Jesus story without nonsense? There would be no precedents.
Clegg: The New Testament nonsense?
Bentley: A very over-rated book.
Clegg: "Better than the New Testament"—is that a good description of your Jesus-Pilate play?
Bentley: I hope so. Shaw spoke of himself as "better than Shakespeare" with something like that in mind.
Clegg: He also put a question mark after the phrase.
Bentley: As I do.
Clegg: What was your first play? I want to know how all this got started.

Bentley: Which is the wickedest of all your wicked questions.
Clegg: Answer it.
Bentley: My first play wasn't a play of mine at all, it was other people's plays.
Clegg: Especially Bertolt Brecht's.
Bentley: Actually, my first-play-that-was-really-someone-else's-play was not a Brecht, it was a Meilhac and Halévy.
Clegg: Who dey?
Bentley: Jacques Offenbach. The first time I launched out on my own was when I re-did the libretto to Offenbach's *Orpheus* for the New York City Opera Company.
Clegg: Everyone loved it.
Bentley: The press hated it. Except the communist paper.
Clegg: So you took up the Commie cause in *Are You Now or Have You Ever Been?*
Bentley: Well, that was some centuries later, and it wasn't the commie cause.
Clegg: But you do champion causes. What came next?
Bentley: Lord Alfred's Lover?
Clegg: Exactly. Your gay liberation play.
Bentley: Touché.
Clegg: After which I lose you. No causes but lots of Heinrich von Kleist.
Bentley: My three Kleist Variations. In which lots of Kleist got thrown overboard—and not all causes were forgotten . . .
Clegg: No?
Bentley: No! Didn't you interview me on this point, and isn't your interview the Preface to the Kleist Variations, published sometime, somewhere?
Clegg: Is it? Oh, yes. What's your latest?
Bentley: Another gay item.
Clegg: But prompted by a non-gay item, Schnitzler's *Reigen? La Ronde?*
Bentley: Transposed to the 1970's and New York. Round two.

* * *

First some facts. Eric Bentley just turned 70. Though he is known as a critic and scholar of the stage, he sees himself primarily as a playwright.

He began writing plays in the late 1960's. The period of the Vietnam war saw his private and professional life in turmoil as well, and it released something in him. In a self-defining act, he walked away from his easy chair at Columbia University and kissed academic austerity goodbye. In retrospect it is clear that criticism and the academy could no longer fully satisfy his radical's conscience. Ever the searcher, his critical style became plainer, more direct, in a word, naked, while his playwriting prompted the voice that scholarship had subdued.

So he changed, but the perception of him lags behind. To the extent that he is viewed solely as a critic, his ambitions as a dramatist are complicated, if not frustrated. But as the author and editor of some 60 books on theatre—several of which are considered classics—it is a predicament he can hardly avoid. What is unfair, however, is the assumption current in our culture that a good critic can't be a good playwright, and what is worse, the further assumption that a good critic should stick to criticism, and the corollary, that if he doesn't it's a decline. Such misconceptions are occasionally voiced, even by those who should know better, sometimes by those who don't know better, not having seen or read Bentley's plays.

But if Bentley gambled, doesn't he deserve to be met half way? His risk warrants a critical appraisal, for though it may come as news to some, he has written 15 plays. And in his own words, "The drama lies precisely in the chance of total fiasco."

For all practical purposes, his playwriting career was launched by a question provoked by his personal life, one which became the title to his best known play, his treatment of the Un-American Activities Committee, *Are You Now or Have You Ever Been.* By dropping the final words—"A Communist"—from the historical record, Bentley hints at a larger concern, which is ultimately existential, a matter of honest living. "Are you yourself," he asks his characters, and by extension the audience, "or do you allow others or a political hierarchy to define your acts?" It is an issue Bentley hasn't avoided—least of all when confronting the implications of his homosexuality or the consequences of the Vietnam war—and it is the center of a cluster of dramas. Radiating from this core of concern is his talent for creating the illusion of history on stage—the feeling that an audience has of eavesdropping on a past that implicates the moment significantly; and his flair for dialectics—the way he makes and marshalls passionate thought. This is the universe of *A Time to Die, and A Time to Live, The Recantation of Galileo Galilei, From the Memoirs of Pontius Pilate,* and *Lord Alfred's Lover.* Each affords an original interpretation of radical will, as Antigone, Peleus, Galileo, Yeshu (Jesus), and Oscar Wilde discover themselves through the courage to resist oppression, a sometimes meager, but often meaningful human victory.

From the late 1970's to 1985, Bentley worked on *The Kleist Variations.* His obsession with Heinrich von Kleist for more than half a decade is a puzzle the biographers and historians will have to solve. But one thing is obvious; where the earlier dramas asked "are you now or have you ever been," the *Variations* ask "now that you are can you live?" Let me explain. It takes no dramatist to announce the planet's precarious condition. If anything, the collision with Armageddon is taken for granted. Which worries Bentley, not so much because the world will end, but because it most certainly will if we proceed on the belief. It also explains his polemic against chic pessimism and phoney optimism. He suggests instead that we may be overlooking something of importance, namely, a human hope founded on love that can help lighten our days. That the phrase "hope founded on love" sticks in the throat just confirms the malady. *Concord, Wannsee, The Fall of the Amazons,* and *German Requiem*—especially the middle two—are wondrous enactments of our spiritual state.

Wannsee is a "variation" on Kleist's *Cathy of Heilbronn,* which Bentley recreates as a play within a play. The outer action, or frame, portrays Kleist on the night of his suicide observing his play with the help of a ministering angel. What he sees is a madcap medieval morality illuminated by the purity of a quest and darkened by the shadow of a death. Little Cathy pursues her dream of love until it becomes reality. Through forest and along the mist-laden way, she overcomes an indifferent lover, an obtuse father, the machinations of a comic trio of Teutonic knights and a rival's evil. At her journey's end, just when she is joined with her lover, Kleist kills himself; and *Wannsee* suspends the optimism of the one act against the pessimism of the other, as the angel sounds out: "Hope Hope Hope." This metaphysical slapstick tragedy is a unique creation that shows Bentley facing his own despair.

The Fall of the Amazons is more concerned with love as the triumph over aggressive sexuality. Set before the walls of Troy, it pits Achilles against the Amazon Queen, Penthesilea, while the Greeks, primarily Ulysses, serve as the engines of a machismo fate that distorts all attempts at trust between the sexes. By looking back to a time where men and women might have been whole, Bentley subverts our sexual wars with a utopian yearning for what might be. Again, there is nothing like it on the contemporary horizon.

When Bentley's dramas are staged they invariably provoke discussion, often controversy. His latest, *Round 2*, is no exception, and it has generated its share, even before being staged. Using Arthur Schnitzler's *La Ronde* as inspiration, Bentley replaces the image of Gay Vienna at the turn of the century with an image of Gay New York, only now the people playing around are homosexuals in the pre-Aids 1970's. It took courage for a homosexual identified with Gay Rights candidly to depict the sexual relations between men at a time when they are under fire and demanding "positive images" of gay life. The daisy-chain of seductions has panache and pathos—it is finally oppressive in its insistence and lack of love, and it confirms Bentley's observation "That there is something radically deficient in the personal relations of this society." The writing has a street-smart metallic edge, and all of its sadness and hate imply their opposites: a vision of homosexuals as no better or worse than the rest of us, a vision of life that tolerates the possibility of happiness.

—Michael Bertin

BERKOFF, Steven. British. Born in Stepney, London, 3 August 1937. Educated at schools in Stepney; Hackney Downs Grammar School, London; Webber-Douglas Academy of Dramatic Art, London, 1958–59; École Jacques Lecoq, Paris, 1965. Married Shelley Lee in 1976. Actor in repertory in Nottingham, Liverpool, Coventry, and at Citizens' Theatre Glasgow, for six years. Since 1973 founding director, London Theatre Group. Recipient: Los Angeles Drama Critics Circle award, for directing, 1983. Agent: Joanna Marston, Rosica Colin Ltd., 1 Clareville Grove Mews, London SW7 5AH, England.

PUBLICATIONS

Plays

The Penal Colony, adaptation of a story by Kafka (produced London, 1968).
Metamorphosis, adaptation of a story by Kafka (produced London, 1968; Los Angeles, 1982). With *The Trial*, Ambergate, Derbyshire, Amber Lane Press, 1981.
The Trial, adaptation of a novel by Kafka (produced in the Netherlands, 1971; London, 1973). With *Metamorphosis*, Ambergate, Derbyshire, Amber Lane Press, 1981.
Agamemnon, adaptation of a play by Aeschylus (produced London, 1971; revised version produced London, 1976). Included in *East, Agamemnon, The Fall of the House of Usher*, 1977.
Knock at the Manor Gate, adaptation of a story by Kafka (produced Falmer, Sussex, and London, 1972).
Miss Julie Versus Expressionism, adaptation of a play by Strindberg (produced London, 1973).
Lunch (as *Mr. Prufrock's Songs*, produced London, 1974; revised version, as *Lunch*, produced London, 1981). Included in *West, Lunch, Harry's Christmas,* 1985.
The Fall of the House of Usher, adaptation of the story by Poe (produced Edinburgh, 1974; London, 1975). Included in *East, Agamemnon, The Fall of the House of Usher*, 1977.
East (produced Edinburgh and London, 1975). Included in *East, Agamemnon, The Fall of the House of Usher*, 1977.
East, Agamemnon, The Fall of the House of Usher. London, Calder, 1977; New York, Riverrun Press, 1982.
Greek (produced London, 1980; Los Angeles, 1982; New York, 1983). With *Decadence*, London, Calder, 1982; New York, Riverrun Press, 1983.
West (produced London, 1980). Included in *West, Lunch, Harry's Christmas*, 1985.
Decadence (produced London, 1981). With *Greek*, London, Calder, 1982; New York, Riverrun Press, 1983.
Harry's Christmas (produced London, 1985). Included in *West, Lunch, Harry's Christmas*, 1985.
The Tell-Tale Heart, adaptation of the story by Poe (produced London, 1985).
West, Lunch, Harry's Christmas. London, Faber, and New York, Grove Press, 1985.
Kvetch, and Acapulco (produced Los Angeles, 1986; *Kvetch* produced New York, 1987). London, Faber, 1986; New York, Grove Press, 1987.
Sink the Belgrano! (produced London, 1986). With *Massage*, London, Faber, 1987.

Short Stories

Gross Intrusion and Other Stories. London, Calder, and Dallas, Riverrun Press, 1979.

*

Theatrical Activities:
Director: **Plays**—all his own plays; *Macbeth*, London, 1970; *The Zoo Story* by Edward Albee, Newcastle upon Tyne, 1973.
Actor: **Plays**—most of his own plays; Gentleman Caller in *The Glass Menagerie* by Tennessee Williams, London, 1971; title role in *Hamlet*, London, 1980. **Films**—*A Clockwork Orange*, 1971; *Barry Lyndon*, 1975; *The Passenger*, 1975; *Joseph Andrews*, 1977; *McVicar*, 1980; *Outland*, 1981; *Octopussy*, 1983; *Beverly Hills Cop*, 1984; *Rambo: First Blood, Part II*, 1985; *Revolution*, 1985; *Absolute Beginners*, 1986; *Under the Cherry Moon*, 1986. **Television**—*Charlie Was a Rich Man*, 1981; *Sins*, 1987.

* * *

Ideals are commonplace on the fringes of the theatre. Only success is likely to call them into question. Steven Berkoff's work was notable for its integrity when the bulk of it was produced through struggles for subsidy and with a handful of dedicated collaborators. His consistency of vision and highly individual modes of expression brought him a loyal audience, whether he was confronting the demands of Shakespeare's *Hamlet* as performer and star, presenting his own vivid interpretations of Kafka or Poe, or offering his own profane and violently metrical original plays. Though theatrically sophisticated, his work earned its credibility as a kind of street poetry reflecting the obscene argot of East London. The remarkable thing about Berkoff's development as a playwright in the 1980's, when he became an international film star and appeared in several of Hollywood's most successful movies, has been his faithful extension of his earlier style—and his utterly fearless expression of outrage at the behaviour of the establishment, political and artistic.

Berkoff very early in his career chose some difficult masters, admiring the discipline and formal skills of Bertolt Brecht as playwright and director, and admiring the way Brecht was able to develop his technique through his own company, the Berliner Ensemble. His next master was Antonin Artaud, and all his theatrical work demonstrates Artaud's dedication to using the theatre as a visceral art, drawing its energy from "the lower echelons of the body," from sexual and primal urges which can unleash profound feelings in actor and spectator. He once described his relationship with Artaud in clearly sexual terms when he said, "since I started with Artaud I've never flirted with anyone else."

Like the Living Theatre, however, and rather unlike Artaud, Berkoff has found the primal physicality of the theatre a means for expressing political ideas. His disgust at Britain's conduct during the Falklands War is dramatized in his 1986 play *Sink the Belgrano!*, a diatribe in punk-Shakespearean verse which depicts Britain's Prime Minister, Margaret Thatcher, as a character called Maggot and which chronicles in obscene language what he sees as the government's cynical decision to sink Argentina's battleship as it sailed away from the exclusion zone around the Falkland Islands.

Sink the Belgrano! makes no concessions to the sensibilities of his admirers who know him only for his film work as a cold villain. He scourges the audience with violent language, and, as in his earliest work, demands of his actors extreme physical acts, portraying the dying sailors in screams and formalized agony while his indictment of the government is expressed through the loose poetic speech which has become his trademark. With the coarse language comes a coarse comedy, burlesquing the conventions of polite society. However hard Berkoff hits out, he seeks to entertain.

Being the expression of a single idea, which has already been well documented, his Falklands play is unlikely to have the lasting life of much of his other work. His earliest dramatizations, for instance, have continued to receive productions, including revivals by Berkoff himself. His adaptation of Kafka's *Metamorphosis*, originally tailored to his own athletic performance as the man who is transformed into a giant insect, has proved exceptionally durable and paved the way for his particular use of the human body and voice as the prime elements in his productions. His key concern is the expression of the text through physical images which imprint themselves on the audience's memory. Visionary as his adaptations might be, however, it is Berkoff's original writing which is of most interest, and which is proving most influential.

East, the play in which he first gave a violent representation to his vision of London life, has become a model to younger playwrights seeking to escape the limits of conversational drama. In this play he mingles a Cockney corruption of Elizabethan-styled verse with sexual and aggressive prose speeches. The play is structured somewhat as a story of growing up in London's East End, with fights and fornication as major themes, and the extreme imagery frequently grows into lyrical fantasias. "If I write a bit rationally, I know I fail. For instance, when I talk about a motorbike in *East*, it has to be the best, the shiniest. When I talk about a phallus, it is the largest. ... Everything has to be extreme."

His whole vision of drama is of extremes, demonstrated again in his North London reworking of the *Oedipus Tyrannus* of Sophocles which he called *Greek*. "In *Greek* every speech is an extreme feeling; of tenderness, of passion, of hate." Typically, despite the extremity of feeling when his hero, Eddie, discovers he has married his mother, Berkoff dispenses with the tragic ending and lets Eddie continue as her husband. Love, wherever you find it, is something worth keeping. It is by borrowing such themes as the Oedipus story and submitting them to his own vision that Berkoff achieves much of his intensity, and even in *Sink the Belgrano!* there are constant playful borrowings from Shakespeare.

Decadence was his first full-scale assault on the ruling classes, though his distaste for middle-class values was early evident in his comic vulgarization of the insect's family in *Metamorphosis*. Gluttony and the buggery of public schools are indulgences ideally suited to gross physical imagery, and the coarse poetry he provides for his couple in evening dress is potently expressed by the man as if the words were vomit.

In *Harry's Christmas* Berkoff supplied a bitter corrective to the holiday spirit with his one-man play about a man whose loneliness leads him each year to recycle the few Christmas cards he has ever collected. Like his other work, the play is designed for sharp physical interpretations of the world rather than representations, and despite his work in Hollywood, his plays are still intended to tap the full potentiality of actors and clear away the trivial routines and reenactments of ordinary activity. Through his use of dialogue and monologues, "acting becomes a compulsive medium because I can touch primeval forces and release them—madness and maybe enlightenment."

—Ned Chaillet

BERMANGE, Barry. British. Born in London, 7 November 1933. Educated at an art school in Essex, 1947–52. National service, 1952–54. Married Maurine Jewel Bright in 1961. Assistant designer, Perth Repertory Company, Scotland, 1955; actor and assistant stage manager, Swansea Repertory Company, 1956. Recipient: Arts Council bursary, 1964; Ohio State University award, 1967; German Critics award, 1968; Karl Sczuka prize (Germany), 1981. Address: 35 Alexandra Park Road, London N10 2DD, England.

PUBLICATIONS

Plays

No Quarter (broadcast 1962; produced London, 1964). Included in *No Quarter and the Interview*, 1969.

Nathan and Tabileth (broadcast 1962; produced Edinburgh and London, 1967). With *Oldenberg*, London, Methuen, 1967.

The Cloud (produced London, 1964).

Four Inventions (includes *The Dreams, Amor Dei, The After-Life, The Evenings of Certain Lives*) (broadcast 1964–65; produced London, 1969).

Oldenberg (televised 1967; produced Edinburgh and London, 1967). With *Nathan and Tabileth*, London, Methuen, 1967.

The Interview (televised 1968; produced London, 1969). Included in *No Quarter and The Interview*, 1969.

Invasion (televised 1969). Included in *No Quarter and The Interview*, 1969.

No Quarter and The Interview (includes *Invasion*). London, Methuen, 1969.

Scenes from Family Life (televised 1969; produced Leatherhead, Surrey, 1974). Published in *Collection: Literature for the Seventies*, edited by Gerald and Nancy S. Messner, Boston, Heath, 1972.

Warcries (broadcast 1981; produced Donaueschingen, 1981).

The Soldiers (broadcast 1985; produced Frankfurt-am-Main, 1985).

The Dreams, Warcries, Klänge am Mikrophon (produced Kassel, 1987).

Radio Plays: *The Voice of the Peanut*, 1960; *Never Forget a Face*, 1961; *No Quarter*, 1962; *A Glass of Lemonade*, 1962;

Nathan and Tabileth, 1962; *The Imposters* series, 1962; *Four Inventions*, 1964–65; *The Mortification*, 1964; *The Detour*, 1964; *Paths of Glory*, from the novel by Humphrey Cobb, 1965; *Letters of a Portuguese Nun*, 1966; *As a Man Grows Older*, 1967; *Neues vom Krieg*, 1969 (Germany); *S.O.S.*, 1977 (Netherlands), 1978 (UK); *Social Welfare*, 1979; *Warcries*, 1981 (Germany), *Four Inventions* (*Reconstruction 1*), 1983 (Netherlands); *Klänge am Mikrophon*, 1985 (Germany); *The Soldiers*, 1985 (Germany); *Testament*, 1985 (Germany); *Le Désir*, 1986 (Germany); *Radioville*, 1987 (Germany); *Der gelbe Klang*, 1987 (Germany); *Annulamento*, 1987 (Germany).

Television Plays: *Oldenberg*, 1967; *The Interview*, 1968; *Tramp*, 1968 (Germany); *Invasion*, 1969; *Scenes from Family Life*, 1969; *International*, 1976; *Stars*, 1976.

*

Critical Studies: "Amor Dei" by Peter Faecke, in *Neues Hörspiel: Essays, Analysen, Gespräche* edited by Klaus Schöning, Frankfurt-am-Main, Suhrkamp, 1970; *Das englische "Radioplay" seit 1945: Typen, Themen, und Formen,* Berlin, Schmidt Verlag, 1978, *Barry Bermange: Eine Beschreibung seines Buhnen-, Funk-, und Fernsehdramatischen Werken*, Tubingen, Narr Verlag, 1986, and *Ut Pictura/Musica Poesis: Radiokomposition von Barry Bermange,* Giessen, Hoffman Verlag, 1986, all by Horst Priessnitz; "Warcries" in *Kirche und Rundfunk 82*, 24 October 1981.

Theatrical Activities:
Director: most of his own plays.

* * *

The most remarkable characteristic of Barry Bermange's style as a dramatist is his ability to convey a powerful, universal theme with the utmost economy of means. His early plays (originally written for the stage) were first produced on radio, a medium ideally suited to capture the full evocativeness of the language, the symbolic power of the stories and the graceful accuracy of each carefully calculated effect. Indeed a live audience sometimes seems to disturb the precise timing on which his plays depend: there is too little room for laughter or any other spontaneous reaction. Bermange has sometimes been compared to Beckett and Ionesco: and his plots are occasionally reminiscent of the Theatre of the Absurd. In *No Quarter*, for example, a fat man and a quiet man seek lodging in a mysterious collapsing hotel: and eventually huddle together in a dark upper storey room, hoping that nothing will happen to them if they stay quite still. But Bermange's dialogue, unlike Ionesco's, rarely exploits for its own sake. His images do not carry the logic-shattering irrelevance of Dadaism. The plain meaning of *No Quarter* is also too apparent: the fat man and the quiet man represent two recognizable human reactions to the fear that their world is disintegrating. Nor is Bermange an iconoclastic writer. The collapsing hotel is not symbolic, say, of religion falling apart. Unlike the writers of the Absurd, Bermange does not delight in pointing out the nonsense of cherished institutions: nor are his stories tantalizingly ridiculous. He doesn't attempt to give a pleasing *frisson* to the rational mind by rubbing it up the wrong way. The themes of his plays are usually coherent and indeed logical, although they may contain many ambiguities. Bermange is a writer who defies easy categorizing simply because he chooses each technique carefully to express most directly his underlying themes. His plays can be absurdist: they can be naturalistic: they can even include carefully manoeuvred "happenings." But the styles have always been selected for their appropriateness, not from any *a priori* assumptions about Theatre or Dramatic Art.

In the same way he chooses his different styles with care, so Bermange distils each effect to its essential elements. Like Marguerite Duras, he sometimes presents an apparently small incident observed in precise detail: and separates it from all the surrounding life until it exists in a significant isolation. In *The Interview* eight men wait in an outer office, before being interviewed for a job. The audience never learns what the job is or who is finally selected. The play is solely concerned with the applicants' reactions to each other: and the small details—one man reading a newspaper, another looking at a picture—manage to convey an almost intolerable atmosphere of suspicion and rivalry. In *Nathan and Tabileth*, an elderly couple feed the pigeons in the park, return home and spend the evening by the fire. They are visited by a young man, Bernie, who says he is their grandson, although they do not recognize him, and who talks of relatives they have forgotten. When Bernie leaves, the couple go to bed: and "darkness comes." Bermange manages to capture in the rambling repetitive dialogue and in the intense short soliloquies the shifting concentration of the old. Certain details—the hired boats on the lake, the pigeons, and the glowing fire— emerge in sharp focus: others slide into a grey and closing background. The timing of the play is calculated to break up the normal pace of events: the old people do not think consecutively and the audience is not allowed to do so. Sometimes they ramble on about the past: sometimes they try to cope with the present, with the breaking of a plate, with a scratched hand. No other contemporary play—with the possible exception of Beckett's *Happy Days*—conveys with such agonizing plausibility the experience of old age.

The Interview and *Nathan and Tabileth* are both basically naturalistic plays: the observable details have been carefully selected and arranged to provide a particular impact—but these details are convincing on the level of external reality. In *Oldenberg*, however, Bermange caricatures the main characters. A man and a woman decide to let a room in their house. The tenant is a stranger, Oldenberg, whom they have never even met. At first they make considerable efforts to furnish the room comfortably: but then the possibility occurs to them that their tenant may not be *English*. In a fit of xenophobia, they destroy and desecrate the room they have so carefully prepared. But the stranger when he arrives is English—and blind. *Oldenberg* is an allegory about the way in which people long for change but are afraid of the unfamiliar—of invasion. By using some of the techniques of Absurdist writers, Bermange heightens the contradictory emotions caused by the intrusions of visitors.

But perhaps Bermange's most extraordinary achievement was to compile four "sound inventions," originally for radio, but which were afterwards presented at the Institute of Contemporary Arts in London—through loudspeakers in a darkened auditorium. The inventions were recorded extracts of interviews with ordinary men and women—about their dreams, their reflections on old age, their beliefs or scepticisms about God and the After-life. The speeches were carefully edited into short revealing phrases, "orchestrated" with electronic music and finally presented as totally original music-drama works. In these inventions, Bermange's remarkable gifts for ordering sound effectively—both ordinary speech patterns and electronic effects—were allied to themes which could scarcely have been expressed effectively any other way. He invented a new form of radio and theatrical experience: and the only possible contemporary parallel would be with Berio's music-drama for Italian radio. With equal ingenuity, Bermange also wrote an improvisatory work for television, *Invasion*, where a dinner party is gradually submerged by the images of Vietnam, flickering across a television screen. Bermange's inventiveness, his assurance in handling different styles and media, and the powerful intensity of his chosen themes have won him a unique position among British dramatists. No other writer can rival him for controlled daring and insight into the potentialities of experimental drama.

—John Elsom

BERNARD, Kenneth. American. Born in Brooklyn, New York, 7 May 1930. Educated at City College of New York, B.A. 1953; Columbia University, New York, M.A. 1956, Ph.D. 1962. Served in the United States Army, 1953–55: Private. Married Elaine Reiss in 1952; two sons and one daughter. Instructor, 1959–62, Assistant Professor, 1962–66, Associate Professor, 1967–70, and since 1971 Professor of English, Long Island University, Brooklyn. Advisory editor, 1973–75, assistant editor, 1976–78, and since 1979 fiction editor, *Confrontation*, Brooklyn. Vice-President, New York Theatre Strategy, 1972–79. Recipient: Rockefeller grant, 1971, 1975; Guggenheim fellowship, 1972; Creative Artists Public Service grant, 1973, 1976; National Endowment for the Arts grant, for fiction, 1977; Arvon poetry prize, 1980. Address: 800 Riverside Drive, New York, New York 10032, U.S.A.

PUBLICATIONS

Plays

The Moke-Eater (produced New York, 1968). Included in *Night Club and Other Plays*, 1971.

The Lovers, published in *Trace* (London), May 1969; in *Night Club and Other Plays*, 1971.

Marko's: A Vegetarian Fantasy, published in *Massachusetts Review* (Amherst), Summer 1969.

Night Club (produced New York, 1970). Included in *Night Club and Other Plays*, 1971.

The Monkeys of the Organ Grinder (produced New Brunswick, New Jersey, and New York, 1970). Included in *Night Club and Other Plays*, 1971.

The Unknown Chinaman (produced Omaha, Nebraska, 1971). Published in *Playwrights for Tomorrow 10*, edited by Arthur H. Ballet, Minneapolis, University of Minnesota Press, 1973.

Night Club and Other Plays (includes *The Moke-Eater, The Lovers, Mary Jane, The Monkeys of the Organ Grinder, The Giants in the Earth*). New York, Winter House, 1971.

Mary Jane (also director: produced New York, 1973). Included in *Night Club and Other Plays*, 1971.

Goodbye, Dan Bailey, published in *Drama and Theatre* (Fredonia, New York), Spring 1971.

The Magic Show of Dr. Ma-Gico (produced New York, 1973). Published in *Theatre of the Ridiculous*, edited by Bonnie Marranca and Gautam Dasgupta, New York, Performing Arts Journal Publications, 1979.

How We Danced While We Burned (produced New York, 1974).

King Humpy (produced New York, 1975). Published in *2Plus2* (Lausanne, Switzerland), 1985.

The Sensuous Ape, published in *Penthouse* (New York), September 1975.

The Sixty Minute Queer Show, music by John Braden (produced New York, 1977).

La Justice; or, The Cock That Crew, music by John Braden (produced New York, 1979).

La Fin du Cirque (produced New York, 1984). Published in *Grand Street* (New York), 1982.

The Panel (produced New York, 1984).

Play with an Ending; or, Columbus Discovers the World (produced New York, 1984).

Short Stories

Two Stories. Mount Horeb, Wisconsin, Perishable Press, 1973.

The Maldive Chronicles. New York, Performing Arts Journal Publications, 1987.

*

Manuscript Collections: Lincoln Center Library of the Performing Arts, New York; University of Minnesota, Minneapolis.

Critical Studies: introduction by Michael Feingold to *Night Club and Other Plays*, 1971; "A Collaboration: Kenneth Bernard and John Vaccaro" by Gerald Rabkin, in *Performing Arts Journal* (New York), Spring-Summer 1978; *The Original Theatre of New York* by Stefan Brecht, Frankfurt am Main, Suhrkamp, 1978; *Contemporary American Dramatists 1960–1980* by Ruby Cohn, London, Macmillan, and New York, Grove Press, 1982.

Theatrical Activities:
Director: **Play**—*Mary Jane*, New York, 1973.

Kenneth Bernard comments:

I like to think of my plays as metaphors, closer to poetic technique (the coherence of dream) than to rational discourse. I am not interested in traditional plot or character development. My plays build a metaphor; when the metaphor is complete, the play is complete. Within that context things and people do happen. I would hope the appeal of my plays is initially to the emotions only, not the head, and that they are received as spectacle and a kind of gorgeous (albeit frightening) entertainment. The characters in my plays can often be played by either men or women (e.g., *The Moke-Eater, Night Club*): only a living presence is necessary, one who reflects the character component in the play rather than any aspect of non-stage individuality: they are instruments to be played upon, not ego-minded careerists: they must "disappear" on stage. More important than technique, etc., are passion and flexibility. The defects of this preference are offset by strong directorial control: each play in effect becomes a training program. My plays use music, dance, poetry, rhetoric, film, sounds and voices of all kinds, costume, color, make-up, noise, irrationality, and existing rituals to give shape (e.g., the auction, the magic show). The audience must be authentically pulled into the play in spite of itself. It must not *care* what it all means because it is enjoying itself and feels itself involved in a dramatic flow. What remains with the audience is a totality, the metaphor, from which ideas may spring—not ideas from which it has (with difficulty) to recreate the dramatic experience.

* * *

Kenneth Bernard's major plays have been produced mainly by the Play-House of the Ridiculous, under John Vaccaro's direction. This collaboration provides the best avenue of approach to an understanding of Bernard's plays. The "Ridiculous" style, with its shrilly pitched, frenzied extravagance, its compulsively and explicitly sexual interpretation of every action, the elaborate makeup and costumes that lend confusion to the antics of transvestites of both sexes, the general aura of bleakness and violence that adds despair to even the company's most optimistic productions—that style is a reasonable physicalization of the world Kenneth Bernard evokes.

The two interlocking themes of Bernard's drama are cruelty and entertainment. His characters are perpetually threatening each other with tortures, mutilations, particularly painful modes of execution, and these vicissitudes are constantly placed in a theatrical "frame" of some sort, as intended for the amusement of a group, or of the torture-master, or of the audience itself, implicated by its silent consent to the proceedings. In Bernard's first full-length work, *The Moke-Eater*, the setting is a prototypical American small town, the hero the stock figure of a traveling salesman, desperately ingenuous and jaunty, who suddenly finds himself, when his car breaks down, confronting the sinister, inarticulate townspeople and their malevolent boss, Alec. Alec alternately cajoles and bullies the salesman into submitting to a humiliating series of charades, nightmarish parodies of small-town hospitality, climaxing in his realization that he is trapped when he drives off in the repaired auto, only to have it break down outside the next town . . . which turns out to be exactly the same town he has just left. (In the Ridiculous production, an additional frisson was added to the salesman's re-entrance by having the townspeople, at this point, attack and eviscerate him—a fate which Alec describes earlier in the play as having been inflicted on a previous visitor.)

Later plays by Bernard present the spectacle of cruelty with the torturer, rather than the victim, as protagonist. *Night Club* displays Western civilization as a hideous, inept cabaret show, controlled by an androgynous master of ceremonies named Bubi, who, like Alec in *The Moke-Eater*, cajoles and bullies both audience and performers into humiliating themselves. In fact, the theatre audience first sees the company performing the show as a parody of itself: the grotesque nightclub acts all emerge out of the "audience," which meanwhile cheers, catcalls, attacks the club's one waitress, and generally behaves boorishly. The acts themselves include a ventriloquist (male) trapped in a virulent love-hate relationship with his dummy (female), who spouts obscenities; a juggler (recalling the "Destructive Desmond" of Auden and Isherwood's *The Dog Beneath the Skin*) who throws valuable antiques into the air and declines to catch them; an impersonator, obsessed with his own virility, whose imitations veer from a sex-starved southern belle to a sadistic Nazi; and "The Grand Kabuki Theatre of America," which lends the patina of Japanese ceremoniousness to a vulgar soap-opera-like story about a pregnant college girl. Eventually, the nightclub show culminates, at Bubi's behest, in mass copulation by the "audience," accompanied by the William Tell Overture; for a climax, the one member of the audience who declines to perform is summarily dragged onstage and decapitated, while he repeatedly screams, "The menu says there's no cover charge!" In a similar vein, Bernard's *The Magic Show of Dr. Ma-Gico* is a series of violent encounters, more courtly in tone but just as unpleasant, based on fairy-tale and romance themes. (A maiden, to test her lover's fidelity, transforms herself into a diseased old crone and forces him to make love to her; a king is challenged to pick up a book without dropping his robe, orb, and scepter; in both cases the man fails.) *Auction* (unproduced) is a surreal, aleatory version of a rural livestock auction, whose items include a pig-woman and an invalid who sells off his vital organs one by one. The world-picture contained in these plays is essentially that of a continuous nightmare, and while the surface action and language change (Bernard's language is exceptionally varied in texture, going from the loftiest politeness to the most degraded abuse), the emotional thrust of the material is constantly the same: towards revealing the sheer ludicrous horror of existence. In his collaboration with the Play-House of the Ridiculous, Bernard has carried the Artaudian project of raising and exorcizing the audience's demons about as far as it is likely to get through the theatrical metaphor.

—Michael Feingold

BIRIMISA, George. American. Born in Santa Cruz, California, 21 February 1924. Attended school to the ninth grade; studied with Uta Hagen at the Herbert Berghof Studios, New York. Served in the United States Naval Reserve during World War II. Married Nancy Linden in 1952 (divorced 1961). Worked in a factory, as a disc jockey, health studio manager, clerk, salesman, bartender, page for National Broadcasting Company, bellhop; counterman, Howard Johnson's, New York, 1952–56; typist, Laurie Girls, New York, 1969–70. Artistic director, Theatre of All Nations, New York, 1974–76. Recipient: Rockefeller grant, 1969. Address: 627 Page Street, Apartment 27, San Francisco, California 94117, U.S.A.

PUBLICATIONS

Plays

Degrees (produced New York, 1966).
17 Loves and 17 Kisses (produced New York, 1966).
Daddy Violet (produced Ann Arbor, Michigan, and New York, 1967). Published in *Prism International* (Vancouver), 1968.
How Come You Don't Dig Chicks? (produced New York, 1967). Published in *The Alternate* (San Francisco), January 1981.
Mister Jello (produced New York, 1968; London, 1969; revised version produced New York, 1974).
Georgie Porgie (produced New York, 1968). Published in *More Plays from Off-Off-Broadway*, edited by Michael T. Smith, Indianapolis, Bobbs Merrill, 1972.
Adrian (produced New York, 1974).
Will the Real Yoganga Please Stand Up? (produced New York, 1974).
A Dress Made of Diamonds (produced Los Angeles, 1976).
Pogey Bait! (produced Los Angeles, 1976; New York, 1977). Published in *Drummer*, 1977.
A Rainbow in the Night (produced Los Angeles, 1978).
A Rose and a Baby Ruth (produced San Francisco, 1981).

*

Manuscript Collection: Joe Cino Memorial Library, Lincoln Center Library of the Performing Arts, New York.

Theatrical Activities:
Director: **Plays**—*The Bed* by Robert Heide, New York, 1966; *The Painter* by Burt Snider, New York, 1967; *Georgie Porgie*,

New York, 1971; *A Buffalo for Brooklyn* by Anne Grant, Corning, New York, 1975.

George Birimisa comments:

(1973) I write about the people I know. At this point in my life many of my friends are homosexual. I try to write honestly about them. In writing honestly about them I believe that my plays (in particular *Georgie Porgie*) mirror the terror of a schizophrenic society that is lost in a world of fantasy. In *Daddy Violet* I believe I showed how the individual's fantasy can lead to the burning of women and children in Vietnam. The problem with my plays is that many critics label them as homosexual plays. In the United States we live at the edge of a civilization that is near the end of the line. I feel that it is important for me to throw away every fantasy and get down into the total terror of this insane society. Only then can I truly write a play that is God-affirming, that is full of light. In my new play, tentatively titled *It's Your Movie*, I'm trying to write about the only alternative left in a demonic society—the nitty-gritty love of brother for brother and sister for sister. I know I must go through the passions of the flesh before I can break through to love my brother and sister. Anything else is an illusion. I also believe that the American male is terrified of his homosexuality and this is one of the chief reasons why he is unable to love his brother. His repression creates fires of the soul and this is translated into wars and violence. If all the "closet queens" would step out into the sunshine it would be a different country. I believe the above is what I write about in my plays.

(1977) At last I have discovered that four letter word LOVE. My early plays were screams of anger and rage. I was really screaming at myself because I was a microcosm of the good and evil of the western world, and I finally realize that it is possible to walk through death and destruction, and care . . . really care.

* * *

George Birimisa's early play *Daddy Violet* is built on a series of cathartic acting exercises which, through a process of association and hallucinatory transformation, evoke a battle in the Vietnam war. The cruelty and destruction of the war are connected, using a technique based on improvisation, with the actor's self-loathing and sexual immaturity.

Birimisa is a fiercely moral writer; his plays are filled with compassionate rage against needless suffering, furious impatience with the human condition, desperately frustrated idealism. He links the pain of human isolation to economic and social roots.

Mister Jello starts out with a mixed bag of characters: a waspish aging transvestite, a bitchy social worker, a dreamy boy flower child, a business-like prostitute, and fat, foolish Mister Jello, who likes to pretend to be a little boy and have the prostitute as his mommy discipline him. Birimisa sets their antagonisms in perspective by reference to the social philosopher Henry George.

Georgie Porgie is a series of vignettes about homosexual relationships, almost all bitter and ugly in tone, interspersed with choral episodes quoted from Friedrich Engels. The contrast between Engels's idealistic vision of human liberty and Birimisa's variously stupid, contemptible, pitiful, self-despising characters, all imprisoned in their own compulsions, is powerful and painful.

Birimisa's writing is often crude, the language vulgar, the humor cruel, the events shocking; the author has been preoccupied with psychic pain and the consequences of neurotic patterns, and his work makes up in self-examining integrity and emotional intensity what it eschews of seductiveness and beauty. In 1976 he made what is for Americans a mythic move from East to West, from New York first to Los Angeles, then to San Francisco. In the more affirmative pre-Aids climate of gay liberation there, he attempted to go beyond the rage and desperation of the earlier plays to a more positive view: *Pogey Bait!* was well received in Los Angeles and ran for several months.

—Michael T. Smith

BLEASDALE, Alan. British. Born in Liverpool, Lancashire, 23 March 1946. Educated at St. Aloysius Infant and Junior schools, Huyton, Lancashire, 1951–57; Wade Deacon Grammar School, Widnes, Lancashire, 1957–64; Padgate Teachers Training College, teachers certificate 1967. Married Julia Moses in 1970; two sons and one daughter. Teacher, St. Columbus Secondary Modern School, Huyton, 1967–71, King George V School, Gilbert and Ellice Islands, 1971–74, and Halewood Grange Comprehensive School, Lancashire, 1974–75; resident playwright, Liverpool Playhouse, 1975–76, and Contact Theatre, Manchester, 1976–78; joint artistic director, 1981–84, and associate director, 1984–86, Liverpool Playhouse. Recipient: Broadcasting Press Guild award, 1982; Royal Television Society award, 1982; BAFTA award, 1982; *Evening Standard* award, for musical, 1985. Lives in Liverpool. Agent: Harvey Unna and Stephen Durbridge Ltd., 24–32 Pottery Lane, London W11 4LZ, England.

PUBLICATIONS

Plays

Fat Harold and the Last 26 (produced Liverpool and London, 1975).

The Party's Over (produced Liverpool, 1975).

Scully, with others, adaptation of the novel by Bleasdale (produced Liverpool, 1975).

Franny Scully's Christmas Stories, with Kenneth Alan Taylor (produced Liverpool, 1976).

Down the Dock Road (produced Liverpool, 1976).

It's a Madhouse (produced Manchester, 1976). With *Having a Ball*, London, Faber, 1986.

Should Auld Acquaintance (produced Manchester, 1976).

No More Sitting on the Old School Bench (produced Manchester, 1977). Todmorden, Yorkshire, Woodhouse, 1979.

Crackers (produced Leeds, 1978).

Pimples (produced Manchester, 1978).

Love Is a Many Splendoured Thing (for children; produced Redditch, Worcestershire, 1986). Published in *Act I*, edited by David Self and Ray Speakman, London, Hutchinson, 1979.

Having a Ball (produced Oldham, Lancashire, and London, 1981). With *It's a Madhouse*, London, Faber, 1986.

Boys from the Blackstuff (televised 1982). London, Hutchinson, 1985.

Young People Today (sketch), in *The Big One* (produced London, 1983).

Scully, adaptation of his own novel (televised 1984). London, Hutchinson, 1984.

Are You Lonesome Tonight? (produced Liverpool and London, 1985). London, Faber, 1985.

The Monocled Mutineer, adaptation of the book by William Allison and John Fairley (televised 1986). London, Hutchinson, 1986.
No Surrender: A Deadpan Farce (screenplay). London, Faber, 1986.

Screenplay: *No Surrender*, 1987.

Television Plays: *Early to Bed*, 1975; *Dangerous Ambition*, 1976; *Scully's New Year's Eve*, 1978; *The Black Stuff*, 1980; *The Muscle Market*, 1981; *Boys from the Blackstuff* series, 1982; *Scully* series, from his own novel, 1984; *The Monocled Mutineer*, 1986.

Novels

Scully. London, Hutchinson, 1975.
Who's Been Sleeping in My Bed? London, Hutchinson, 1977; revised edition, as *Scully and Mooey*, London, Corgi, 1984.

*

Critical Studies: *Dossier 20*, London, British Film Institute, 1984; *Boys from the Blackstuff: The Making of Television Drama* by Bob Millington and Robin Nelson, London, Comedia, 1986.

Alan Bleasdale comments:

I try *never* to look back and examine my work. I don't re-read the script or watch the video once the piece is finished. For what it's worth, I don't think a writer should know what he or she is doing! That's for the audience or critic to judge. I do know, however, that since I was a child all I have ever wanted was to be good and to do good. I should have been a social worker.

Notes such as these can sometimes become a playwright's first and last line of defence or explanation: "This is what my plays really mean!" My only explanation and defence lie between the first and last curtain.

Finally, the only three quotations I have ever managed to learn off by heart: "Any victim demands allegiance" (Graham Greene, *The Heart of the Matter*). "All my humor is based on destruction and despair. If the whole world was tranquil, without disease and violence, I'd be standing on the breadline, right behind J. Edgar Hoover" (Lenny Bruce). "Too much talking stinks up the room" (Duke Ellington).

* * *

Although he had been writing for the theatre since the mid-1970's, it was his television series *Boys from the Blackstuff* that brought Alan Bleasdale wide recognition. In five successive episodes he traced, with mordant irony, the despair and madness of a group of unemployed Liverpool men and their families. The central battle is between the individual and the state. The unemployed struggle to supplement their dole money with casual earnings on building sites and in dockyards; the Department of Employment, the social services, and the police combine to corral their clients within the government regulations. Farce turns into tragedy which reverts to farce. While cars skid, crash, and overturn on Malloy's illegal building site at the end of the first episode, Snowy Malone, the plasterer who takes pride in his skills, falls to his death trying to escape the dole officials. Elsewhere Chrissie Todd shoots his rabbits for food, Yosser Hughes is rescued from drowning by the police he's assaulted, and the sanctimonious priest at George Malone's funeral finishes up vomiting his whiskey down a grid after the reception. Bleasdale has no more sentimental regard for his characters than they have for each other. The children are as uncompromising as the parents. The scene where Yosser's daughter Ann Marie butts the social worker Veronica is as comic as it is shocking.

Snowy's death is echoed by that of his father in the last episode. George Malone is respected throughout the community as a socialist and a battler for citizens' rights, but the structure of Bleasdale's series questions radically whether the Malones' ideology of class solidarity is still relevant to 1980's Britain. The Malones have some analysis of why mass unemployment has returned. Chrissie, Yosser, Dixie, and the rest have only their native wits which, unsupported by any community or educational training, can flip over into hallucination. Yosser Hughes is a monomaniac, and his white face, staring red-rimmed eyes, and monotonous cry of "Gizza job" and "I can do that" immediately became the nation's most dramatic vision of unemployed misery. Chrissie's wife Angie sees clearly that jokes are not enough: "if you don't laugh, you'll cry—I've heard it for years—this stupid soddin' city's full of it," but when she screams at her husband to fight back she has no more idea than he about how it can be done.

Bleasdale's view of the professional classes is equally acerbic. *Having a Ball*, a stage play of 1981, counterpoints the reactions of three men, Lenny, Ritchie, and Malcolm, waiting in hospital for vasectomies. They are all middle class and they are all terrified. With a woman surgeon and Malcolm's wife Doreen contemptuous of his Territorial Army "bravery," the play exposes not woman, but man, as victim. And with three simultaneous areas for stage action, the Waiting Room, the Preparation Room, and the Operating Theatre, Bleasdale exploits all the possibilities for farcical encounters and concealments. But there is no harmonious resolution. The play ends with Lennie, like Yosser, screaming in despair. Through wit, mockery, and a kind of trickster role-playing, he has exposed his own and everyone else's pretensions to control and confidence. "Most of us are cowards most of the time," he remarks. "Until we have no choice. And all the choices seem to be going." This is Bleasdale's savage double bind which Chrissie expresses in *Boys from the Blackstuff* as "It's a way of life. The only trouble is, it's no way to live."

With *Are You Lonesome Tonight?*, Bleasdale moves away, to his cost, from his familiar territory of the North West of England. Elvis Presley, in his last hours at Graceland, has the successes and betrayals of life portrayed to him upstage. He drools over his mother, curses Colonel Parker, and comes over as a good ol' southern boy of musical genius who was led astray by unscrupulous agents. Other accounts of Elvis's last years depict a drug-ridden, gun-obsessed monster, but Bleasdale was determined that this should be a tribute to what he called the "working class hero" of his youth. It was a West End hit, but it remains unique among Bleasdale's plays for its sentimentality and uncritical adulation. The London production was memorable, not for the writing, but for the electrifyingly accurate rendition of Elvis's great early hits by Simon Bowman.

In 1986 Bleasdale returned to his strengths, anti-heroism and farce, with a 4-part television series *The Monocled Mutineer*, and a film *No Surrender*. The tricky career of Percy Toplis, a World War I conscript, is the subject of the series. He leads an uprising of conscripted men against their atrocious conditions in the Etaples training camp in 1917. But he also impersonates officers and thoroughly enjoys their life of gambling, drinking, and whoring. Percy Toplis is neither demogogue nor ideologue. On several occasions he refuses to be called either a hero or a socialist. He is a working-class rebel who refuses all the clichés of such a figure. And he doesn't "lead" the Etaples uprising in any conventional way. Rather he finds himself in a situation where he can inflict the maximum of mayhem on a class which he both hates and simulates. "Don't get angry," he advises; "get even." Toplis is no Scarlet Pimpernel of the workers. After the war he is a poor man still hunted for his role at Etaples. He thinks he can live off a rich widow, but finds she's as big a poser as he is. Naturally he falls in love with her. When he rejoins the army it's not just to get rich by black-marketing army supplies. He admits he doesn't seem able to function outside that structure of command. Its rigidity creates his flexibility. He's not therefore the roving outsider of the romantic tradition. To be that you have to have the money and class Toplis hasn't got and never will have. The agents of the state finally eliminate this cultural hybrid on a deserted Cumbrian road, but his girlfriend's pregnancy indicates that he may be reborn. What Bleasdale has intuited is that Toplis's combination of cynicism, courage, and style is the true basis for oppositional politics in 1980's Britain. The man who invents himself from the debris all around him is the man who anticipates the new patterns of life.

No Surrender begins, continues, and ends in debris. A new manager comes to take over a decrepit nightclub in Liverpool and finds it has been double-booked by two parties of Old Age Pensioners, one Catholic and the other Protestant. Infiltrated into this gathering is a Loyalist gunman on the run. Insults escalate from the verbal to the physical, the geriatrics take strength from the fires of religious fanaticism, and the film finishes in a mayhem of fists, bottles, the police, and the Fancy Dress competition. With this "deadpan farce" Bleasdale shows himself as adept at visual as verbal wit and confirms his status as the most talented of the new generation of Merseyside writers.

—Tony Dunn

BOLAND, Bridget. British. Born in London, 13 March 1913. Educated at the Convent of the Sacred Heart, Roehampton, 1921–31; Oxford University, 1932–35, B.A. (honours) in politics, philosophy, and economics 1935. Served in the Auxiliary Territorial Service, 1941–46: Senior Commander; produced morale-orientated plays for the troops, with three companies of actors, 1943–46. Film writer from 1937. *Died 19 January 1988.*

PUBLICATIONS

Plays

The Arabian Nights (produced Nottingham, 1948).
Cockpit (produced London, 1948). Published in *Plays of the Year 1*, London, Elek, 1949.
The Damascus Blade (produced Edinburgh, 1950).
Temple Folly (produced London, 1951). London, Evans, 1958.
The Return (as *Journey to Earth*, produced Liverpool, 1952; as *The Return*, produced London, 1953). London, French, 1954.
The Prisoner (produced London, 1954). Published in *Plays of the Year 10*, London, Elek, 1954; New York, Dramatists Play Service, 1956.
Gordon (produced Derby, 1961). Published in *Plays of the Year 25*, London, Elek, 1962.
The Zodiac in the Establishment (produced Nottingham, 1963; as *Time Out of Mind*, produced Guildford, Surrey, 1970). London, Evans, 1963.
A Juan by Degrees, adaptation of a play by Pierre Humblot (produced London, 1965).

Screenplays: *Spies of the Air*, with A.R. Rawlinson, 1939; *Laugh It Off*, with Austin Melford, 1940; *Old Mother Riley in Society*, with others, 1940; *Gaslight* (*Angel Street*), with A.R. Rawlinson, 1940; *This England*, with A.R. Rawlinson and Emlyn Williams, 1941; *Freedom Radio* (*A Voice in the Night*), with others, 1941; *He Found a Star*, with Austin Melford, 1941; *The Lost People*, with Muriel Box, 1949; *Prelude to Fame*, 1950; *The Fake*, with Patrick Kirwan, 1953; *The Prisoner*, 1955; *War and Peace*, with others, 1956; *Constantino il Grande* (*Constantine and the Cross*), with others, 1961; *Damon and Pythias*, 1962; *Anne of the Thousand Days*, with John Hale, 1970.

Radio Play: *Sheba*, 1954.

Television Play: *Forever Beautiful*, 1965.

Novels

The Wild Geese. London, Heinemann, 1938.
Portrait of a Lady in Love. London, Heinemann, 1942.
Caterina. London, Souvenir Press, 1975; New York, St. Martin's Press, 1976.

Other

Old Wives' Lore for Gardeners, with Maureen Boland. London, Bodley Head, 1976; New York, Farrar Straus, 1977.
Gardener's Magic and Other Old Wives' Lore. London, Bodley Head, and New York, Farrar Straus, 1977.
At My Mother's Knee. London, Bodley Head, 1978.

Editor, *The Lisle Letters: An Abridgement* (from 6-vol. edition edited by Muriel St. Clare Byrne). London, Secker and Warburg, and Chicago, University of Chicago Press, 1983.

*

Bridget Boland comments:

Although I hold a British passport I am in fact Irish, and the daughter of an Irish politician at that, which may account for a certain contrariness in my work. Many playwrights have become screenwriters: so I was a screenwriter and became a playwright. Most women writers excel on human stories in domestic settings: so I am bored by domestic problems and allergic to domestic settings. I succeed best with heavy drama (*The Prisoner*), so I can't resist trying to write frothy comedy (*Temple Folly*).

By the time you have written half a dozen plays or so you begin to realize you are probably still trying to write the one you started with. However different I begin by thinking is the theme of each, I find that in the end every play is saying: "Belief is dangerous"—the theme of *Cockpit*. In *The Damascus Blade*, which, produced by Laurence Olivier and with John Mills and Peter Finch in the cast, yet contrived to fold on its short pre-London tour, I tried to put across the theme by too complicated a paradox. An Irishman descended from a long line of soldiers of fortune holds that you must not kill for what you believe in, but that a man must be prepared to die for something, if only the belief of someone else. Having offered his sword to the foreign forces of extreme right and extreme left in turn, he ends by dying as bodyguard to the child of a prostitute, trying to keep it for her from its father—and realises that in spite of all his/my theories he has come to believe in the justice of her cause: man—alas, God—is like that.

* * *

In 1948 Bridget Boland was well ahead of her time as a playwright. *Cockpit* was one of the early forerunners of the vogue for environmental theatre which was to spread to England from off-Broadway in the 1960's. It was a play which boldly turned its back on everything that was normal in the English theatre of the time, including insularity. Its way of coming to grips with the problem of Displaced Persons in post-war Europe was to use the whole auditorium to create a theatrical image of a D.P. assembly centre, which itself served as an image of the chaos on the continent, with masses of bewildered hopeless people uprooted from where they belonged. Unsuspecting London theatregoers arriving at the Playhouse found themselves faced with a curtain painted in Germanic style and with notices in various European languages forbidding them to fight or carry firearms. The dialogue began incomprehensibly: a quarrel in Polish between two women fighting over a saucepan. Two English soldiers take charge, appearing from the back of the stalls, shouting orders and questions, treating the whole audience like D.P.'s forcing them to feel uncomfortably involved in the action.

The discomfort becomes most acute at the climax of the play. Behind the drawn curtains of one of the boxes a man is gravely ill. A Polish Professor tells the English Captain that it may be a case of bubonic plague. The theatre has to be sealed off. Armed guards are stationed at the exits and the suspense is sustained while they wait for a doctor to arrive and then while they wait for the news that it was a false alarm. If the play ran for only 58 performances it cannot have been because it failed to make an impact.

On the face of it, the subject of *The Return* could hardly have been more contrasted—a nun's return to the modern world after 36 years of seclusion in a convent. This is difficult material, but well dramatized it could have produced fascinating insights both into the mind of the woman and into the changes which had overtaken the world that surrounded her since she last saw it—in 1913. The play is by no means a complete failure: it has some very touching moments. But it fails to do justice to its subject because, unlike *Cockpit*, it fails to find a way of making the audience participate in the raw experience. It relies too much on dialogue which analyses and describes.

The part of the nun is quite well-written, but on leaving the convent she goes to live with a nephew and his wife, who are both sentimentally and unconvincingly characterized, while the chaplain and the man who runs a youth club where the nun does voluntary work are seen very superficially. The problem of dramatizing the impact the modern world makes on the woman's mind is largely side-stepped. What we get instead is a plot in which a series of misunderstandings are peeled off to reveal an unrealistic core of human goodness.

In spite of several forays into the past (like *Gordon*, an old-fashioned drama about Gordon and the siege of Khartoum) Boland is at her best in writing about post-war Europe, and her best play is still *The Prisoner*, which seems to have been inspired partly by the trial of the Hungarian Cardinal Mindszenty and partly perhaps by Arthur Koestler's novel *Darkness at Noon*, which presents a similar relationship between a political prisoner in a Communist country and his interrogator, though in Koestler the sympathetic interrogator is replaced half way through the action by a callous and unintelligent party-liner of peasant stock. In *The Prisoner* it is the Cardinal whose origins are proletarian, while the Interrogator is a clever aristocrat who has joined the Party. The dialogue gives clear definition to the stages in the close personal relationship that develops between the two adversaries, who like and respect each other. Most of the cut and thrust is verbal, but there are some highly theatrical climaxes, as when a coffin is brought in containing the apparently dead body of the Cardinal's mother. The revelation that she has only been anaesthetized is followed by the threat that she will be killed if he does not sign the confession his captors want.

Not only the two central parts but also that of the main warder provide excellent opportunities for actors, and the physical breakdown of the Cardinal is particularly rewarding. The main flaw in the writing is a lapse into sentimentality when the Interrogator is made to repent, revealing that in destroying his victim he has also destroyed his faith in his own work. But the damage this does to the play is almost compensated for by a fine twist at the end. The death sentence is repealed and the Cardinal, whose confession has discredited him, knows that it will be more difficult for him to live than to die.

—Ronald Hayman

BOLT, Carol (née Johnson). Canadian. Born in Winnipeg, Manitoba, 25 August 1941. Educated at the University of British Columbia, Vancouver, 1957–61, B.A. 1961. Married David Bolt in 1969; one son. Researcher, Dominion Board of Statistics, London School of Economics, Market Facts of Canada, and Seccombe House, 1961–72; dramaturge, 1972–73, and Chairwoman of the Management Committee, 1973–74, Playwrights Co-op, Toronto; dramaturge, Toronto Free Theatre, 1973; writer-in-residence, University of Toronto, 1977–78. Recipient: Canada Council grant, 1967, 1972; Ontario Arts Council grant, 1972, 1973, 1974, 1975. Agent: Great North Artists, 345 Adelaide Street West, Toronto, Ontario M5V 1R5. Address: 76 Herbert Avenue, Toronto, Ontario, Canada.

PUBLICATIONS

Plays

I Wish (as Carol Johnson) (produced Toronto, 1966). Published in *Upstage and Down*, edited by D.P. McGarity, Toronto, Macmillan, 1968.

Daganawida (produced Toronto, 1970).

Buffalo Jump (as *Next Year Country*, produced Regina, Saskatchewan, 1971; as *Buffalo Jump*, produced Toronto, 1972). Toronto, Playwrights, 1972.

My Best Friend Is Twelve Feet High (for children), music by Jane Vasey (produced Toronto, 1972). With *Tangleflags*, Toronto, Playwrights, 1972.

Cyclone Jack (for children; produced Toronto, 1972). Toronto, Playwrights, 1972.

Gabe (produced Alcoma, Ontario, 1972). Toronto, Playwrights, 1973.

Tangleflags (for children; produced Toronto, 1973; St. Louis, 1977). With *My Best Friend Is Twelve Feet High*, Toronto, Playwrights, 1972; published separately, 1974.
The Bluebird, adaptation of a story by Marie d'Aulnoy (produced Toronto, 1973).
Pauline (produced Toronto, 1973).
Maurice (for children; produced Toronto, 1973). Toronto, Playwrights, 1975.
Red Emma, Queen of the Anarchists (produced Toronto, 1974). Toronto, Playwrights, 1974.
Shelter (produced Toronto, 1974). Toronto, Playwrights, 1975.
Finding Bumble (for children; produced Toronto, 1975).
Norman Bethune: On Board the S.S. Empress of Asia (produced Gravenhurst, Ontario, 1976).
Okey Doke (produced Kingston, Ontario, 1976).
Buffalo Jump, Gabe, Red Emma. Toronto, Playwrights, 1976.
One Night Stand (produced Toronto, 1977). Toronto, Playwrights, 1977.
Desperadoes (produced Toronto, 1977).
TV Lounge (produced Toronto, 1977).
Star Quality (produced Louisville, 1980). Excerpt published in *Acta Victoriana* (Toronto), vol. 102, no. 2, 1978.
Deadline (produced Toronto, 1979).
Escape Entertainment (produced Toronto, 1981). Toronto, Playwrights, 1982.
Love or Money (produced Blyth, Ontario, 1981).

Radio Play: *Fast Forward*, 1976.

Television Plays: *A Nice Girl Like You* (*Collaborators* series), 1974; *Distance*, 1974; *Talk Him Down*, 1975.

*

Carol Bolt comments:

(1977) I've had a lot of opportunity to work in the theatre in the last four years, with twelve new plays commissioned. Much of this work has been inspired by the theatrical community, particularly work being done at the Toronto Free Theatre and the Théâtre Passe Muraille.

The plays often deal with "political" subjects, the characters often want to change the world, but I think my preoccupation is with the adventure, rather than the polemic, of politics. I think a play like *Red Emma* is about as political as *The Prisoner of Zenda*.

I'm interested in working in new forms of musical comedy and epic romance and in creating (or recreating) characters who are larger than life or mythic.

I'm also interested in exploring, recording, recreating, and defining Canadian concerns, characters, histories, cultures, identities. I want to create plays for this country, whether the plays are about the lost moments in Canada's past (like *Buffalo Jump*), whether they offer another view of an American mythic figure (like *Red Emma*), or whether they play at creating Canadian archetypes (*Shelter*).

I don't think this kind of cultural nationalism is parochial. I think our differences are our strengths, not our weaknesses, nationally and internationally, so I think the argument that if a Canadian play is any good the Americans or British will be happy to tell us via Broadway or the West End is specious and muddle-headed. I don't think Canadians will say anything of interest to the world until we know who Canadians are.

* * *

Through her prolific contribution to Canadian theatre Carol Bolt has shaped a unique form of social documentary using factual reference material to gain access to an imaginative Canadian mythology. Her best early plays are cohesive, rich in entertainment and dramatic values, politically inspired but romantically motivated, and imbued with a keen, sometimes riotous sense of social injustice.

Central to *Buffalo Jump*, *Gabe*, and *Red Emma* is an interest in combining theatrical styles and methods: a fluid interchange of locations loosely defined by props and emotional intensities, quick episodic scene changes, direct audience address, and the use of song to develop action or as a divertissement. This willing exhibition of the theatrical process can also be found in Bolt's approach to children's plays.

Both her adult and children's plays have a common free-form fluctuation of time, place, and space, enhanced by a strong entertainment factor which smooths abrupt or unlikely transitions with song, special lighting changes, or the emphasis of a significant prop—the train in *Buffalo Jump* or the banner of anarchy in *Red Emma*. This montage format partly results from rewriting plays in a creative collaboration with the directors and actors during the rehearsal period. *Buffalo Jump* (which originated as a revue called *Next Year Country*) and the young people's plays *Cyclone Jack* and *My Best Friend Is Twelve Feet High* were formed completely in rehearsal.

These ongoing transformations of original material also sift fiction, or rather an imaginative interpretation, into factual details aiming at a conscious redefinition of the time-blurred outlines of historical figures. Bolt has stated she would rather be interesting than accurate and rather be one-sided than give a well-rounded viewpoint honed to dullness.

The central character in *Buffalo Jump*, for example, a play about the disastrous on-to-Ottawa trek of unemployed Vancouver men during the Great Depression, combines two Canadian heroes, "Red" Walsh and "Slim" Evans, united for dramatic purposes into the single character Red Evans. A character develops not necessarily from what *is* true but from what *might* be true as the playwright understands it. The creation of myth and the reshaping of myth is more important to Bolt than the documentation of history. As she has said, "Myth is more appealing than fact. It postulates that heroism is possible, that people can be noble and effective and change things . . . what we were doing in *Buffalo Jump* was making those characters tragic heroes. It was the same with the great Native Indian runner Tom Longboat, the central character of *Cyclone Jack* and others."

Buffalo Jump, a political and social indictment of Canadian society of the 1930's, manages to be a less serious work than either *Gabe* or *Red Emma*. The play borrows from the mythology of the old west for its central metaphor, equating the workers protest march to Ottawa with a herd of buffalo about to be stampeded off a cliff. With its explicit breakdown between villains and heroes, the play might have become a modern melodrama were it not for its cut-up, cartoon style.

Gabe, based on the story of Louis Riel, the doomed Métis Indian leader of the Riel Rebellion, and his comrade in arms, Gabriel Dumont, is a constant interplay between memory images and the reality of the lives of the two modern namesakes who are the main characters of the play. The original Riel and Dumont have been refined by time into spiritual heroes who provide a constant source of romantic inspiration. Says the modern-day Louis of his historic counterpart: "Louis Riel! Was the maddest, smartest, bravest Métis bastard ever wrote his own treaty. Ever fought for the rights of his people. For their land. Fought for representation. For his people and their children." In spite of courageous poses, the figures from the past did not achieve their political ideals or their romantic fantasies. The modern-day Louis must function within the context of a failed mythology. Where there was once a battle at Batoche there's now a sports day and a camp meeting. And Louis has just finished a jail sentence.

Red Emma is more focussed, dealing with one aspect of the life of the revolutionary Emma Goldman. Although the play is the least concerned with Canadian content, its style and sensibility link it with *Buffalo Jump* and *Gabe*. Structurally, the play draws upon a fluid intermingling of scenes and juxtaposes caricature with real people. While Emma and her fellow anarchists are portrayed as full-blooded characters, Henry Clay Frick is a stereotyped capitalist oppressor, backed up by a duo of one-dimensional Pinkerton men who might have stepped from a vaudeville routine.

Set in New York in 1890, *Red Emma* glorifies the myth of freedom fighters, "the people and the things they can wish for, the beautiful radiant things." The clue to an interpretation of *Red Emma* lies in the sub-title, "Queen of the Anarchists." The Emma of this story is a young, idealistic woman given to histrionic poses and flamboyant gestures. But she is also a staunch supporter of women's emancipation, declaring "Woman's development . . . must come from and through herself . . . freeing herself from the fear of public opinion and public condemnation will set a woman free, will make her a force hitherto unknown in the world."

Bolt's first attempt to come to real terms with such assumptions began tentatively with *Shelter*, the adult play following *Red Emma.* Dealing with five women, the social rituals of a funeral, wedding, and election campaign, and one woman's decision to run for office, *Shelter* shields its concerns with comedy. Painful decisions and reactions are given an almost surrealistic stylization, absurdity tops reality, and the women tend to be representative types instead of fully developed, deeply felt human beings. *Shelter* was followed by *One Night Stand*, Bolt's most aggressively modern play to date. In this award-winning play, Daisy, a young, lonely woman, celebrates her birthday with Rafe, a charming stranger who punctuates his lies with country and western songs. The consequences of their brief encounter—murder—are chillingly realistic.

—Sandra Souchotte and Constance Brissenden

BOLT, Robert (Oxton). British. Born in Sale, Manchester, Lancashire, 15 August 1924. Educated at Manchester Grammar School, graduated 1940; Manchester University, 1943, 1946–49, B.A. (honours) in history 1949; Exeter University, 1949–50, teaching diploma 1950. Served in the Royal Air Force, 1943–44; in the Royal West African Frontier Force, 1944–46: Lieutenant. Married 1) Celia Ann Roberts in 1949 (marriage dissolved 1967), one son and two daughters; 2) the actress Sarah Miles in 1967 (divorced 1976), one son; 3) Ann, Lady Queensberry in 1980 (divorced 1985). Office boy, Sun Life Assurance Company, Manchester, 1942; schoolmaster, Bishopsteignton, Devon, 1950–51, and Millfield School, Street, Somerset, 1952–58. Recipient: *Evening Standard* award, 1957, for screenplay, 1987; New York Drama Critics Circle award, 1962; BAFTA award, 1962, 1966; Oscar, 1966, 1967; New York Film Critics award, 1966; Golden Globe award, for screenplay, 1967, 1987. LL.D.: Exeter University, 1977. C.B.E. (Commander, Order of the British Empire), 1972. Agent: Margaret Ramsay Ltd., 14-A Goodwin's Court, London WC2N 4LL, England.

PUBLICATIONS

Plays

A Man for All Seasons (broadcast 1954; produced London, 1960; New York, 1961). London, Heinemann, 1960; New York, Random House, 1962.
The Last of the Wine (broadcast 1955; produced London, 1956).
The Critic and the Heart (produced Oxford, 1957).
Flowering Cherry (produced London, 1957; New York, 1959). London, Heinemann, 1958.
The Tiger and the Horse (produced London, 1960). London, Heinemann, 1961.
Gentle Jack (produced London, 1963). London, Heinemann, and New York, Random House, 1965.
The Thwarting of Baron Bolligrew (produced London, 1965; Chicago, 1970; New York, 1978). London, Heinemann, 1966; New York, Theatre Arts, 1967.
Doctor Zhivago: The Screenplay Based on the Novel by Boris Pasternak. London, Harvill Press, and New York, Random House, 1966.
Brother and Sister (produced Brighton, 1967; revised version produced Bristol, 1968).
Vivat! Vivat Regina! (produced Chichester and London, 1970; New York, 1972). London, Heinemann, 1971; New York, Random House, 1972.
State of Revolution (produced London, 1977). London, Heinemann, 1977.

Screenplays: *Lawrence of Arabia*, 1962; *Doctor Zhivago*, 1965; *A Man for All Seasons*, 1966; *Ryan's Daughter*, 1970; *Lady Caroline Lamb*, 1973; *The Bounty*, 1984; *The Mission*, 1986.

Radio Plays: *The Master*, 1953; *Fifty Pigs*, 1953; *Ladies and Gentlemen*, 1954; *A Man for All Seasons*, 1954; *Mr. Sampson's Sundays*, 1955; *The Last of the Wine*, 1955; *The Window*, 1958; *The Drunken Sailor*, 1958; *The Banana Tree*, 1961.

*

Critical Study: *Robert Bolt* by Ronald Hayman, London, Heinemann, 1969.

Theatrical Activities:
Director: **Film**—*Lady Caroline Lamb*, 1973.

* * *

"Inevitable," as Robert Bolt pointed out in the introduction to his most recently produced play, *State of Revolution*, "is the favourite word of Marx and Lenin. Their pages are spattered with it. Yet they are spattered too with fervent praise and bitter blame and urgent exhortation." This tension between the ideal as incorporated in a detached, quasi-scientific viewpoint (or in other manifestations) and private needs for self-expression, links the otherwise diverse and apparently unrelated themes of Bolt's important plays. In his first stage play to be produced, *The Critic and the Heart*, over-contrived though it is in the Somerset Maugham mould (Bolt consciously adopted *The Circle* as his model) the issues raised by two similar couples in the pattern of dependent artist and suffering, supportive woman, resolve themselves into alternative courses of action: art, here, is the ideal, the demands it makes on those close to the artist, its lowering contradiction. Like Marx, artists want to embody a truth, but their lives are often tragic contradictions of this.

Flowering Cherry, Bolt's most resounding stage success prior to *A Man for All Seasons*, embodies the detachment of the dreamer who cannot relate to ordinary office life. Cherry, again, has to choose whether he wants just the substance of his dream to remain true, or the actual orchard itself to exist, with all its attendant, real problems. His wife, Isobel, is unable to understand this. Ultimately Cherry is found to be inadequate (it was Ralph Richardson's larger-than-life quality which realized the fantasy inherent in Bolt's intentionally ordinary and scaled-down conception of Cherry).

Bolt's next play, *The Tiger and the Horse*, is a far more intellectual exercise, hinging on whether the wife of a Master of a college should sign a petition against the atom bomb and thereby jeopardize her husband's hope to succeed as Vice-Chancellor (it mirrored Bolt's own experience as one of the original members of Bertrand Russell's Committee of 100, when he served a short prison sentence). In *A Man for All Seasons* the opposition of the ideal to the politics of the state carries further the notion of love as the only thing that can rescue people from isolation. Thomas More is perfection of behaviour—as Bolt said, "This is why people like the play. They think 'Thank Christ, somebody can do it. I may not be able to, but life *can* be that perfect.' And he didn't do anything that you or I couldn't have done." It is More's adamantine sense of his own self—he is a good, an irreproachable man—which makes him refuse to go beyond a certain point, as he himself says when arguing with Thomas Cromwell, "Yes, a man's soul is his self!"

Gentle Jack, Vivat! Vivat Regina!, and *State of Revolution* show Bolt developing his fastidious craftsmanship more and more along Brechtian lines, though totally repudiating, in spite of former Marxist beliefs, Brecht's political values. The first's fairy-tale methods confused and alienated audiences, but the second, with its stronger integration of theatrical effect and its return to a broad historical canvas, brought back Bolt's reputation nearly to the peak it enjoyed when Paul Scofield was playing Thomas More. *State of Revolution*, performed at the National Theatre in 1977, with Michael Bryant as Lenin, betrays in its uneasy title too great a concentration of effort made by Bolt to find popular qualities in Gorky, Stalin, Trotsky, and Lenin himself. The subject's size is daunting, but Bolt does, with a culminating effort of intellectual power, prove his point that Lenin was an admirable man, "possessed by a terribly wrong idea," as well as providing rich ironic sidelights to history. But to whom, exactly, is he proving it? *State of Revolution*, overstocked with giants, lacks those essentially witty and English qualities that inform Bolt's best work. We are not so far away from Kronstadt that, as Shakespeare could with Rome, we can turn it into contemporary poetry.

—Garry O'Connor

BOND, Chris(topher Godfrey). British. Born in Sussex in 1945. Child actor; educated at the Central School of Speech and Drama, and the Drama Centre, both London. Married to the writer Claire Luckham. Actor, 1968–70, and resident dramatist, 1970–71, Victoria Theatre, Stoke-on-Trent, Staffordshire; artistic director, Everyman Theatre, Liverpool, 1976–78; director, Liverpool Playhouse, 1981–83. Since 1984 director, Half Moon Theatre, London. Recipient: Arts Council grant, 1970. Agent: Blanche Marvin, 21-A St. John's Wood High Street, London NW8 7NG; or, Lou Coulson, 37 Berwick Street, London W.1. Address: Half Moon Theatre, 213 Mile End Road, London E.1, England.

PUBLICATIONS

Plays

Sweeney Todd, The Demon Barber of Fleet Street (produced Stoke-on-Trent, 1970; London, 1973). London, French, 1974.

Mutiny (produced Stoke-on-Trent, 1970).

Shem's Boat (for children; produced Stoke-on-Trent, 1971).

Downright Hooligan (produced Stoke-on-Trent, 1972; London, 1978).

Tarzan's Last Stand (produced Liverpool, 1973).

Judge Jeffreys (produced Exeter, 1973; London, 1976).

The Country Wife, adaptation of the play by William Wycherley (produced Liverpool, 1974).

Under New Management (produced Liverpool, 1975).

The Cantril Tales, with others (produced Liverpool, 1975).

George, in *Prompt One*, edited by Alan Durband. London, Hutchinson, 1976.

Scum: Death, Destruction, and Dirty Washing, with Claire Luckham (produced London, 1976).

Good Soldier Scouse (produced Liverpool, 1976).

The Beggar's Opera, based on the play by John Gay (also director: produced Liverpool, 1977).

A Tale of Two Cities, adaptation of the novel by Dickens (produced Liverpool, 1981).

Dracula (also director: produced London, 1984).

Spend, Spend, Spend, with Claire Luckham, adaptation of the television play by Jack Rosenthal (also director: produced London, 1985).

All the Fun of the Fair, with John McGrath and others (also director: produced London, 1986).

Novel

You Want Drink Something Cold. London, Joseph, 1969.

*

Theatrical Activities:

Director: **Plays**—*Flying Blind* by Bill Morrison, Liverpool, 1977, New York, 1979; *The Beggar's Opera*, Liverpool, 1977; *Stags and Hens* by Willy Russell, Liverpool, 1978; *Trafford Tanzi* by Claire Luckham, London, 1981 (and U.S. version, *Teaneck Tanzi*, New York, 1983); *Blood Brothers* by Willy Russell, Liverpool and London, 1983; *Dracula*, London, 1984; *Sweeney Todd* by Hugh Wheeler and Stephen Sondheim (musical adaptation of Bond's play), London, 1985; *Scrap!* by Bill Morrison, London, 1985; *Spend, Spend, Spend*, London, 1985; *Destiny* by David Edgar, London, 1985; *All the Fun of the Fair*, London, 1986; *Moll Flanders* by Claire Luckham, London, 1986; *Love on the Plastic* by Julia Schofield, London, 1987; *As Is* by William M. Hoffman, London, 1987; *Macbeth*, London, 1987.

* * *

Chris Bond is one of several British dramatists who grew up under the spell of Joan Littlewood's Theatre Workshop in Stratford, East London. In his case, however, a primary attraction to the theatre began almost from his cradle. His parents had run a touring company after World War II, and Bond himself was a child actor, playing at the Shakespeare Memorial Theatre, Stratford-on-Avon, from the age of 11. He grew to love the rough-and-tumble of acting life, the performing skills and the ability to contact audiences at all levels of appreciation; and in his plays he loves to throw in effects which grab the attention—songs, dances, pieces of mime, and simple stage tricks, such as the enlarged washing machine in *Under New Management* which "Harold MacMillan" mistakes for a Mini car and thus gets spun around with the rest of the laundry.

But the direction of his work, its more serious side, derives from Littlewood. Bond has written social and historical documentaries, such as *Under New Management* and *Judge Jeffreys*, and he seeks his audiences primarily from the young, working-class, left-wing public. Although not an overtly political writer, there is a strong vein of socialist thought within his work, which sometimes emerges into didactic messages but more usually is reflected in the handling of his themes—the caricatures of establishment authority, the sympathies with the underprivileged and downtrodden.

The clearest and most striking example of this tendency is *Downright Hooligan*, first produced at the Victoria Theatre, Stoke-on-Trent, where Bond was resident dramatist. The central character, Ian Rigby, is a sort of contemporary Wozzeck, whose eyes, deep-set beneath a granite forehead, suggest a Neanderthal mentality. Permanently out of work, a fixture in the betting shop, Ian is surrounded by a society whose logical illogicalities he cannot comprehend. His mother bawls at him for masturbating in his bedroom, while her lover winks at him and tells him dirty jokes. He accidentally kills the school hamster and sticks drawing pins in its eyes to decorate the body. His headmaster is appalled by the atrocity—but he doesn't know that Ian has just paid his last respects to his grandmother, whose dead drawn face has been padded out with clutches of her own hair. One form of decorating the dead is socially acceptable—Ian's treatment of the hamster is not. Confronted by the unpredictability of society, Ian asserts himself by hitting out savagely at an elderly man and is brought before the courts as a downright hooligan.

Thus, Bond, without glamourising his hero-victim, places the blame for his behaviour upon society at large; and some critics have claimed that his impression of the repressive social forces is simplistic, belonging too much to a "them" and "us" mentality. While his portrait of Ian Rigby's background is telling and convincing, and was presented with marvellous detail by the Stoke company, *Under New Management* is almost a cartoon, agit-prop documentary, showing 12 cretinous general managers—one dressed as a schoolboy clutching a teddy bear—messing up the Fisher-Bendix factory on the outskirts of Liverpool, until the heroic workers, faced by mass redundancy, take over. It was a thoroughly lively, enjoyable production, but inevitably one-sided, partly because Bond had deliberately not interviewed anyone from the management while conducting his research.

By trying to make his plays immediately entertaining, Bond also falls into the trap which snared some of Littlewood's productions. There is too much outer fun, too little inner content. The scenes are short and sketch-like, sometimes extended by horseplay, separated by songs and little dances, and the connecting themes are either lost or so heavily stressed that they seem merely repetitive. In the hands of a highly disciplined company, such as that of Stoke or of the old Liverpool Everyman, where Bond became artistic director, this music-hall mixture could be pulled into a tight shape. His plays usually require the concentration supplied by a firm director and an experienced team.

While striving for a casual, easy-going and lighthearted approach to the theatre, Bond in fact usually demands great restraint and professionalism from his performers—an apparent contradiction which not all directors have realised. There was a luckless production of *Judge Jeffreys* at Stratford East, where the script seemed as banal as the performances; and *Tarzan's Last Stand*, about Enoch Powell the "ape man," seemed to miss its very broad, satirical target by not taking Powell's arguments sufficiently seriously. Bond (like a somewhat similar writer of social documentaries, Alan Plater) has yet to find perhaps that dramatic structure within which his talents and social insights can be best expressed.

—John Elsom

BOND, Edward. British. Born in London, 18 July 1934. Educated at Crouch End Secondary Modern School, 1944–49. Served in the British Army, 1953–55. Married Elisabeth Pablé in 1971. Member of the English Stage Company Writers Group, Royal Court Theatre, London, from 1958. Founding member, Theatre Writers' Group (now Theatre Writers' Union), 1975; Northern Arts Literary Fellow, universities of Newcastle upon Tyne and Durham, 1977–79; resident writer, University of Essex, Colchester, 1982; Visiting Professor, University of Palermo, Italy, 1983. Recipient: George Devine Award, 1968; John Whiting Award, 1968; Obie award, 1976. D.Litt.: Yale University, New Haven, Connecticut, 1977. Agent: Margaret Ramsay Ltd., 14-A Goodwin's Court, London, WC2N 4LL, England.

PUBLICATIONS

Plays

The Pope's Wedding (produced London, 1962). Included in *The Pope's Wedding* (collection), 1971.

Saved (produced London, 1965; New Haven, Connecticut, 1968; New York, 1970). London, Methuen, and New York, Hill and Wang, 1966.

A Chaste Maid in Cheapside, adaptation of the play by Middleton (produced London, 1966).

Three Sisters, adaptation of a play by Chekhov (produced London, 1967).

Narrow Road to the Deep North (produced Coventry, 1968; London and Boston, 1969; New York, 1972). London, Methuen, and New York, Hill and Wang, 1968.

Early Morning (produced London, 1968; New York, 1970). London, Calder and Boyars, 1968; New York, Hill and Wang, 1969; revised version in *Plays 1*, 1977.

Sketch in *The Enoch Show* (produced London, 1969).

Black Mass, part of *Sharpeville Sequence: A Scene, A Story, and Three Poems* (produced London, 1970). Included in *The Pope's Wedding* (collection), 1971; in *The Best Short Plays 1972*, edited by Stanley Richards, Philadelphia, Chilton, 1972.

Passion (produced London, 1971; New Haven, Connecticut, 1972). Published in *New York Times*, 15 August 1971; with *Bingo*, London, Eyre Methuen, 1974.

Lear (produced London, 1971; New Haven, Connecticut, 1973). London, Methuen, and New York, Hill and Wang, 1972.

The Pope's Wedding (collection; includes *Sharpeville Sequence* and the stories "Mr. Dog" and "The King with Golden Eyes"). London, Methuen, 1971.

The Sea (produced London, 1973; Chicago, 1974; New York, 1975). London, Eyre Methuen, 1973; with *Bingo*, New York, Hill and Wang, 1975.

Bingo: Scenes of Money and Death (and Passion) (produced Exeter, Devon, 1973; London, 1974; Cleveland, 1975; New York, 1976). London, Eyre Methuen, 1974; with *The Sea*, New York, Hill and Wang, 1975.

Spring Awakening, adaptation of a play by Wedekind (produced London, 1974; New York, 1978). Chicago, Dramatic Publishing Company, 1979; London, Eyre Methuen, 1980.

The Fool: Scenes of Bread and Love (produced London, 1975; Washington, D.C., 1976). With *We Come to the River*, London, Eyre Methuen, 1976; published separately, Chicago, Dramatic Publishing Company, 1978.

We Come to the River: Actions for Music, music by Hans Werner Henze (produced London, 1976). With *The Fool*, London, Eyre Methuen, 1976.

The White Devil, adaptation of the play by Webster (produced London, 1976).

A-A-America: Grandma Faust, and The Swing (produced London, 1976). Included in *A-A-America, and Stone*, 1976.

Stone (produced London, 1976; New York, 1981). Included in *A-A-America, and Stone*, 1976; in *Performing Arts Journal* (New York), Fall 1977.

A-A-America, and Stone. London, Eyre Methuen, 1976; revised edition, 1981.

Plays (revised versions):

1. *Saved, Early Morning, The Pope's Wedding*. London, Eyre Methuen, 1977.
2. *Lear, The Sea, Narrow Road to the Deep North, Black Mass, Passion*. London, Eyre Methuen, 1978.
3. *Bingo, The Fool, The Woman*. London, Methuen, 1987.

The Woman: Scenes of War and Freedom (also co-director: produced London, 1978; Baltimore, 1983). London, Eyre Methuen, 1979 (includes stories); New York, Hill and Wang, 1979.

The Bundle: Scenes of Right and Evil; or, New Narrow Road to the Deep North (produced London, 1978; New Haven, Connecticut, 1979). London, Eyre Methuen, 1978; Chicago, Dramatic Publishing Company, 1981.

The Worlds (also director: produced Newcastle upon Tyne and London, 1979). With *The Activists Papers*, London, Eyre Methuen, 1980.

Restoration: A Pastoral, music by Nick Bicât (also director: produced London, 1981). London, Eyre Methuen, 1981; revised version, with *The Cat*, Methuen, 1982.

Summer: A European Play (also director: produced London, 1982; New York, 1983). London, Methuen, and Chicago, Dramatic Publishing Company, 1982.

Summer, with Fables, and Service: A Story. London, Methuen, 1982.

Derek (produced Stratford-on-Avon, 1982; London, 1984). With *Choruses from After the Assassinations*, London, Methuen, 1983.

The Cat (opera libretto), music by Hans Werner Henze, adaptation of a work by Balzac (as *Die englische Katze*, produced Schwetzingen, West Germany, 1983; as *The English Cat*, produced Santa Fe, 1985; New York, 1986; Edinburgh, 1987). With *Restoration*, London, Methuen, 1982; as *The English Cat: A Story for Singers and Instrumentalists*, Mainz and London, Schott, 1983.

After the Assassinations (produced Colchester, Essex, 1983). Choruses published with *Derek*, London, Methuen, 1983.

The War Plays: A Trilogy (includes *Red, Black and Ignorant; The Tin Can People; Great Peace*) (*Red, Black and Ignorant* produced London, 1984; *The Tin Can People* produced Birmingham, 1984; also director: trilogy produced London, 1985). London, Methuen, 2 vols., 1985.

Human Cannon (produced Edinburgh, 1986). London, Methuen, 1985.

Burns (for children; produced Birmingham, 1986).

Screenplays: *Blow-up*, with Michelangelo Antonioni and Tonino Guerra, 1967; *Laughter in the Dark*, 1969; *Michael Kohlhaas*, with others, 1969; *The Lady of Monza* (English dialogue), 1970; *Walkabout*, 1971; *Nicholas and Alexandra*, with James Goldman, 1971; *Fury*, with Antonio Calenda and Ugo Pirro, 1973.

Ballet Scenario: *Orpheus*, music by Hans Werner Henze, Stuttgart and New York, 1979.

Verse

The Swing Poems. London, Inter-Action, 1976.

Theatre Poems and Songs, edited by Malcolm Hay and Philip Roberts. London, Eyre Methuen, 1978.

Poems 1978–1985. London, Methuen, 1987.

*

Critical Studies: *Edward Bond* by Simon Trussler, London, Longman, 1976; *The Plays of Edward Bond* by Richard Scharine, Lewisburg, Pennsylvania, Bucknell University Press, 1976; *The Plays of Edward Bond: A Study* by Tony Coult, London, Eyre Methuen, 1977, revised edition, 1979; *Edward Bond: A Companion to the Plays*, London, TQ Publications, 1978, and *Bond: A Study of His Plays*, London, Eyre Methuen, 1980, both by Malcolm Hay and Philip Roberts, and *Bond on File* edited by Roberts, London, Methuen, 1985; *Edward Bond: A Study of His Plays* by Delia Donahue, Rome, Bulzoni, 1979; *Edward Bond* by David L. Hirst, London, Macmillan, 1985, New York, Grove Press, 1986.

Theatrical Activities:

Director: **Plays**—*Lear*, Vienna, 1973; *The Woman* (co-director, with Sebastian Graham-Jones), London, 1978; *The Worlds*, Newcastle upon Tyne and London, 1979; *Restoration*, London, 1981; *Summer*, London, 1982; *The War Plays*, London, 1985.

Actor: **Plays**—Aighard in *One Leg over the Wrong Wall* by Albert Bernel, London, 1960; Christ in *Black Mass*, London, 1970.

* * *

Edward Bond writes the most lapidary language of today's English theatre, absorbing dialects, pastiches, metaphors, and questions into a rich mineral vein. Pithy phrases, swift scenes, and vivid characters are his building-blocks for what he calls Rational Theatre, dedicated to the creation of a rational society. Far from agit-prop, however, his plays range through history and legend, as well as the contemporary scene.

The early plays of surface realism shock by their pointless murders: young Scopey throttles an old hermit at the end of *The Pope's Wedding*; a group of youths stone a baby to death in the middle of *Saved*; at the beginning of *The Sea* Colin drowns while Hatch watches idly from the shore. However, confrontation with these deaths involves radical action on the part of Bond's protagonists. Behind its provocative title *The Pope's Wedding* dramatizes a young man's vain effort fully to understand another human being. Step by step, Scopey abandons companions, wife, job, in order to spend his time with an old hermit to learn "What yoo 'ere for?" Even in the old man's coat, communing with his corpse, he never learns.

As the title *Saved* suggests, Len is more successful. A loner, Len does not share in the bored activities of London youths who gamble, steal, fornicate. They rub a baby's face in its diaper, then pitch stones into its carriage while Len, perhaps the baby's father, watches. The baby dies, and only later does Len admit: "Well, I should a stopped yer." Rejected by the baby's mother, flirting briefly with the grandmother, Len the loner is finally "saved" by the grandfather's barely articulate plea for him to remain in their household.

The Sea opens with Colin's drowning while his friend Willie pleads vainly for help from Evens, a drunken recluse, and Hatch, a paranoid coast-guard watchman. Later Willie barely escapes a murderous attack by Hatch, who believes him to be an enemy from outer space. Despite his grief at Colin's death, contrasted with the satirized indifference of the townspeople, Willie comes to see that "The dead don't matter." Persuading Colin's fiancée to leave the town with him, he swims in the sea after his dead friend's seaside funeral. Cumulatively, through these apparently realistic plays "Life laughs at death."

For the most part, Bond resembles Brecht in analyzing contemporary social injustice through parables based on legend or history. Since both playwrights see war as the cruellest social injustice, Bond explores that violence in violent plays. *Narrow Road to the Deep North* takes place in 19th-century Japan. Basho, the protagonist, follows the narrow road to the deep north in order to study solitude, but he learns that "enlightenment is where you are." And where he is necessitates a choice between two evils, an English invader or a homegrown warlord. Choosing the former, he obliquely causes the suicide of his young disciple. As the play ends, Basho is Prime Minister, his disciple falls disembowelled, and a stranger emerges from the river. Each man must make his own decisions in a time of war, and life goes on.

Of all Bond's protagonists, his Lear experiences the hardest enlightenment. From Shakespeare Bond borrows the large tragic conception intensified by grotesque humor. By way of Shakespeare, Bond re-enforces his own dramatic concern with moral responsibility. As in Shakespeare, Lear is an absolute autocrat. Instead of dividing his kingdom, Bond's Lear encloses it within a wall built by forced labor. Lear's two daughters foment war, and both meet violent deaths. A composite of Kent and the Fool, Bond's Gravedigger's Boy has a wife named Cordelia. After the Boy is shot and his wife raped by the daughter's soldiers, his Ghost accompanies Lear on an infernal descent through madness and blindness. The Gravedigger's Boy's Ghost is slain, Lear attains wisdom, and Cordelia attains power as head of a new autocracy. At the old home of the twice killed Gravedigger's Boy, Lear speaks out against Cordelia's wall. In spite of his age, he then tries physically to dismantle the wall, but he is shot. Like Shakespeare's Lear, he has learned compassion, but he has also learned the necessity for socially responsible action.

In a later war parable Bond looks back to the cultural roots of the Western tradition—the Trojan War. *The Woman* (or "Scenes of War and Freedom") is a panoramic drama with Trojan Hecuba as its protagonist. Part 1, set at the walls of Troy, condenses and revises Homer's *Iliad* to show a capitalist Greece attacking a feudal Troy ruled by Hecuba. Ismene, wife of the Greek commander Hero, speaks out so passionately for peace and mercy that she is buried alive in the Trojan wall. Part 2, set on an unnamed island 12 years later, finds blind Hecuba caring for her adopted daughter, the mentally crippled Ismene. War encroaches upon freedom when the Greeks invade the island. After wise old Hecuba perpetrates a ruse for freedom, she is killed in a storm. Ismene, crippled in mind, and a miner, crippled in body, face the new day together, strangers on an island.

Bond's non-war plays deriving from history and legend zigzag sharply from comic to tragic tone. *Early Morning* puns on mourning, but the play is grotesquely hilarious in its exposé of Victorian social injustice. Proper Queen Victoria has Siamese twin sons, Crown Prince George and the protagonist Arthur. The Queen matches the former to Florence Nightingale whom she then rapes. Prince Albert, Disraeli, and Gladstone all plot against the Queen. By mid-play the whole cast is dead in Heaven, where the main activity is cannibalism, but all flesh regenerates. Arthur alone refuses to accept heavenly habit, starving himself to a second death.

Suicide also closes the grimmer *Bingo*, whose protagonist is William Shakespeare in retirement at Stratford. Aware that the land enclosure spreads starvation for its victims, Shakespeare nevertheless fails to oppose enclosure so long as his own investments are guaranteed. After a visit from drunken Ben Jonson, Shakespeare's disgust at cruelties of his fellowmen shifts to self-disgust at his own failure to act: "How long have I been dead?" He answers the question by taking poison.

Like *Bingo, The Fool* indicts the cruelties of an acquisitive society. But unlike *Bingo*'s Shakespeare, The Fool, who is poet John Clare, is exploited by his social "betters." Not only does he lose his money, his poems, and his evanescent mistress, but also his sanity. Though Bond only sketches his two protagonist poets, Shakespeare and Clare, he dramatizes their society with deft economy.

Restoration dramatizes the life and death of another kind of fool, the honest servant Bob in the world of Restoration fops. Elegant, witty Lord Are deigns to marry a businessman's daughter for her dowry. She in turn has married him for entrance into the social whirl—an entrance he refuses her. In a preposterous scene she haunts him as a sourly unblithe spirit; he stabs her dead and persuades faithful Bob to take the blame. In spite of the courage and protests of Bob's black wife, he is hanged for the crime he did not commit. The status quo is restored in this drama that exposes the dirty underside of the world of Restoration comedy, without denying its charm. *Summer* stages a private story and the trilogy *The War Plays* a post-atomic epic in impassioned pleas for social responsibility.

Bond's violent scenes and cruel humor at first attracted attention rather than appreciation, but he has gradually gathered admirers of his moral commitment theatricalized with verve and economy. Speaking against the Theatre of the Absurd—"Life becomes meaningless when you stop *acting* on the things that concern you most"—Bond has called his work the Rational Theatre. Instead of preaching a rational gospel, however, he fills an almost bare stage with whole societies from which and against which heroes arise, who learn through their suffering to act responsibly. This resembles the *pathos-mathos* of classical tragedy, but it is translated into a modern godless world.

—Ruby Cohn

BOVASSO, Julie (Julia Anne Bovasso). American. Born in Brooklyn, New York, 1 August 1930. Educated at City College of New York, 1948–51. Married 1) George Ortman in 1951 (divorced 1958); 2) Leonard Wayland in 1959 (divorced 1964). Founder (director, producer, actress), Tempo Playhouse, New York, 1953–56. Teacher, New School for Social Research, New York, 1965–71, Brooklyn College, New York, 1968–69, and Sarah Lawrence College, Bronxville, New York, 1969–74; playwright-in-residence, Kentucky Wesleyan University, Owensboro, 1977. President, New York Theatre Strategy. Recipient: Obie award, Best Actress, and Best Experimental Theatre, 1956; Triple Obie award, Best Playwright-Director-Actress, 1969; Rockefeller grant, 1969, 1976; New York Council on the Arts grant, 1970; Guggenheim fellowship, 1971; Public Broadcasting Corporation award, 1972; Vernon Rice award, for acting, 1972; Outer Circle award, for acting, 1972. Agent: Helen Harvey Associates, 410 West 24th Street, New York, New York 10011, U.S.A.

PUBLICATIONS

Plays

The Moon Dreamers (also director: produced New York, 1967; revised version produced New York, 1969). New York, French, 1972.

Gloria and Esperanza (also director: produced New York, 1968; revised version produced New York, 1970). New York, French, 1973.

Schubert's Last Serenade (produced New York, 1971; Dewsbury, Yorkshire, 1976). Published in *Spontaneous Combustion: Eight New American Plays*, edited by Rochelle Owens, New York, Winter House, 1972.

Monday on the Way to Mercury Island (produced New York, 1971).

Down by the River Where Waterlilies Are Disfigured Every Day (produced Providence, Rhode Island, 1972; New York, 1975).

The Nothing Kid, and Standard Safety (also director: produced New York, 1974). *Standard Safety* published, New York, French, 1976.

Super Lover, Schubert's Last Serenade, and The Final Analysis (also director: produced New York, 1975).

*

Theatrical Activities:
Director: **Plays**—many of her own plays; and at Tempo Playhouse, New York: *The Maids* by Jean Genet, 1953, *The Lesson* by Eugène Ionesco, 1955, and *The Typewriter* by Jean Cocteau, *Three Sisters Who Were Not Sisters* by Gertrude Stein, *Escurial* by Michel de Ghelderode, and *Amédée* by Eugène Ionesco, 1956; *Boom Boom Room* by David Rabe, New York, 1973.
Actress: **Plays**—A Maid in *The Bells* by Leopold Lewis, New York, 1943; Gwendolyn in *The Importance of Being Earnest* by Wilde, New York, 1947; title role in *Salome* by Wilde, New York, 1949; Belissa in *Don Perlimplin* by García Lorca, New York, 1949; Lona Hessel in *Pillars of Society* by Ibsen, New York, 1949; title role in *Hedda Gabler* by Ibsen, New York, 1950; Emma in *Naked* by Pirandello, New York, 1950; Countess Geschwitz in *Earth Spirit* by Wedekind, New York, 1950; Zinida in *He Who Gets Slapped* by Andreyev, New York, 1950; title role in *Faustina* by Paul Goodman, New York, 1952; Anna Petrovna in *Ivanov* by Chekhov, San Francisco, 1952; Tempo Playhouse, New York: Margot in *The Typewriter* by Jean Cocteau, 1953, Madeleine in *Amédée* by Eugène Ionesco, 1955, Claire, 1955, and Solange, 1956, in *The Maids* by Jean Genet, and The Student in *The Lesson* by Eugène Ionesco, 1956; Henriette in *Monique* by Dorothy and Michael Blankfort, New York, 1957; Luella in *Dinny and the Witches* by William Gibson, New York, 1959; The Wife in *Victims of Duty* by Eugène Ionesco, New York, 1960; Lucy and Martha in *Gallows Humor* by Jack Richardson, New York, 1961; Mistress Quickly in *1 Henry IV*, Stratford, Connecticut, 1963; Madame Rosepettle in *Oh Dad, Poor Dad*... by Arthur Kopit, Cincinnati, 1964; Mrs. Prosser in *A Minor Miracle* by Al Morgan, New York, 1965; Fortune Teller in *The Skin of Our Teeth* by Thornton Wilder, Cincinnati, 1966; Madame Irma in *The Balcony* by Jean Genet, Baltimore, 1967; Agata in *Island of Goats* by Ugo Betti, and Constance in *The Madwoman of Chaillot* by Giraudoux, Cincinnati, 1968; Gloria in *Gloria and Esperanza*, New York, 1970; The Mother in *The Screens* by Jean Genet, New York, 1971. **Films**—*Willie and Phil*, 1980; *The Verdict*, 1982; *Daniel*, 1983. **Television**—Rose in *From These Roots* series, 1958–60; Pearl in *The Iceman Cometh* by O'Neill, 1960; *Just Me and You*, 1978; *The Last Tenant*, 1978; *King Crab*, 1980; *The Gentleman Bandit*, 1981; *Doubletake*, 1985; and other performances in *U.S. Steel Hour, The Defenders*, and other series, 1958–63.

* * *

The Bovasso world is highly orchestrated; the work appears to be driven, indeed hounded, by an ideological aesthetic. Julie Bovasso, one of America's more interesting actresses, becomes as playwright a kind of mad mathematician, marshalling people and events into lunatic propositions and hallucinatory equations. The work sometimes marches to a drumbeat, sometimes sidles up to you, sometimes stridently calls out to the heavens, sometimes chuckles to itself. Throughout, there is the strong sense of the child infiltrating the grown-up theatre breathlessly, stealthily while the adults are asleep, relocating the furniture, putting bells on the cat, all to see how it will come out, to see whether the cunning proposition will prove itself.

The Moon Dreamers, one of Bovasso's earlier pieces, uses as the core of its narrative a simple situation in which wife, husband, and mistress can't agree as to who is to vacate the apartment. But into the situation, Bovasso, with a sense of increasing lunacy, introduces the wife's mother (Jewish), a lawyer (specified as dark-haired) who turns out to be the wife's second cousin, a doctor who turns out to be a childhood admirer of the wife's, an Indian chief who turns out to be a Japanese Buddhist, and a chief of police who turns out to be a French midget. Doctor, Lawyer, Indian chief, as well as Jewish momma and Gallic Fuzz. All these argue and split hairs in an increasingly complicated situation that on its surface is humorous but nevertheless suggests it is going somewhere other than farce. Around this core, Bovasso adds another layer, what she designates as an "Epic" world as opposed to the

"Personal" world. The characters of the Epic world are in shadows, there is barely dialogue for them and they seem to exist principally as witnesses. But there are dozens of them, soldiers, black stockbrokers, gangsters, belly dancers, snake dancers, Spanish royalty. The domestic squabble is thus both knotted with what we might call the presence of banal archetypes and overseen by graver archetypes until it simply ceases to be what it has been. That is, it seems to become nothing that we can intellectually comprehend—until the end when the appearance of the astronaut, a kind of deus ex machina, makes a comprehensive statement about humanity—but rather something that we must allow to wash over us if we want to continue sensing it at all. Any information seems to be taken out of our hands and we must become like children or Martians witnessing an unknown world.

Monday on the Way to Mercury Island is filled with both dialogue and silent actions that recur numerous times, sometimes repeated identically, sometimes with variations. As in *Moon Dreamers*, these are sometimes banal and sometimes extraordinary. But even the banal elements usually suggest something beyond themselves. The repetition tends to ritualize these sounds and movements without providing a philosophical base. A formal, austere aesthetic seems to be at work. The ritual tends here to make the theatre more into play, a relentlessly earnest if also whimsical play. But there appears to be a political thesis at work. Servants and peasants rise at last against socialite masters. The latter are painted as corrupt and soft, the former as steadfast and hard. But even here the intellectual content seems subordinate to the flowering theatrics, to the rhythms and colors of spectacle.

Down by the River Where Waterlilies Are Disfigured Every Day is another vast landscape, another epic with vivid theatrics. The Bovasso trait of mixed, merged, or transferred identities is strong here. Phoebe and Clement, lovers for many years, exchange clothes and then sexes. Count Josef, leader of the established order, is at work on a statue of Pango, head of the revolutionary forces, breathing life and the qualities dear to him into the figure that is attempting to end his own life. Revolt is strong here. Overturned lives, overturned order. In *Monday* the peasants end by burying the aristocrat. In *Waterlilies* the children toss the old world onto a garbage heap in the town square. But again one has the sense that the playing out of the act takes precedence over the intellectual meaning of the act, that the logic of aesthetics and of form is ultimately the prime mover.

—Arthur Sainer

BOWEN, John (Griffith). British. Born in Calcutta, India, 5 November 1924. Educated at Queen Elizabeth's Grammar School, Crediton, Devon; Pembroke College, Oxford (editor, *Isis*), 1948–51; St. Antony's College, Oxford (Frere Exhibitioner in Indian Studies), 1951–53, M.A. 1953; Ohio State University, Columbus, 1952–53. Served in the Mahratha Light Infantry, 1943–47: Captain. Assistant editor, *Sketch* magazine, London, 1953–56; copywriter, J. Walter Thompson Company, London, 1956–58; head of the copy department, S.T. Garland Advertising, London, 1958–60; script consultant, Associated Television, London, 1960–67; drama producer, Thames Television, London, 1978–79, London Weekend Television, 1981–83, and BBC, 1984. Recipient: Society of Authors travelling scholarship, 1986. Agent: (fiction) Elaine Greene Ltd., 31 Newington Green, London N16 9PU; (theatre) Margaret Ramsay Ltd., 14-A Goodwin's Court, London WC2N 4LL. Address: Old Lodge Farm, Sugarswell Lane, Edgehill, Banbury, Oxfordshire OX15 6HP, England.

PUBLICATIONS

Plays

The Essay Prize, with A Holiday Abroad and The Candidate: Plays for Television. London, Faber, 1962.
I Love You, Mrs. Patterson (produced Cambridge and London, 1964). London, Evans, 1964.
The Corsican Brothers, based on the play by Dion Boucicault (televised 1965; revised version produced London, 1970). London, Methuen, 1970.
After the Rain, adaptation of his own novel (produced London, 1966; New York, 1967). London, Faber, 1967; New York, Random House, 1968; revised version, Faber, 1972.
The Fall and Redemption of Man (as *Fall and Redemption*, produced London, 1967; as *The Fall and Redemption of Man*, produced New York, 1974). London, Faber, 1968.
Silver Wedding (televised 1967; revised version, produced in *We Who Are about to . . .*, later called *Mixed Doubles*, London, 1969). London, Methuen, 1970.
Little Boxes (includes *The Coffee Lace* and *Trevor*) (produced London, 1968; New York, 1969). London, Methuen, 1968; New York, French, 1970.
The Disorderly Women, adaptation of a play by Euripides (produced Manchester, 1969; London, 1970). London, Methuen, 1969.
The Waiting Room (produced London, 1970). London, French, 1970; New York, French, 1971.
Robin Redbreast (televised 1970; produced Guildford, Surrey, 1974). Published in *The Television Dramatist*, edited by Robert Muller, London, Elek, 1973.
Diversions (produced London, 1973). Excerpts published in *Play Nine*, edited by Robin Rook, London, Arnold, 1981.
Young Guy Seeks Part-Time Work (televised 1973; produced London, 1978).
Roger, in *Mixed Blessings* (produced Horsham, Sussex, 1973). Published in *London Magazine*, October–November 1976.
Florence Nightingale (as *Miss Nightingale*, televised 1974; revised version, as *Florence Nightingale*, produced Canterbury, 1975). London, French, 1976.
Heil Caesar!, adaptation of *Julius Caesar* by Shakespeare (televised 1974). London, BBC Publications, 1974; revised version (produced Birmingham, 1974), London, French, 1975.
Which Way Are You Facing? (produced Bristol, 1976). Excerpts published in *Play Nine*, edited by Robin Rook, London, Arnold, 1981.
Singles (produced London, 1977).
Bondage (produced London, 1978).
The Inconstant Couple, adaptation of a play by Marivaux (produced Chichester, 1978).
Spot the Lady (produced Newcastle upon Tyne, 1981).
The Geordie Gentleman, adaptation of a play by Molière (produced Newcastle upon Tyne, 1987).

Radio Plays: *Digby* (as Justin Blake, with Jeremy Bullmore), 1959; *Varieties of Love* (revised version of television play *The First Thing You Think Of*), 1968; *The False Diaghilev*, 1987.

Television Plays: created the *Garry Halliday* series; episodes in *Front Page Story, The Power Game, Wylde Alliance*, and *The Villains* series; *A Holiday Abroad*, 1960; *The Essay Prize*, 1960; *The Jackpot Question*, 1961; *The Candidate*, 1961; *Nuncle*, from the story by John Wain, 1962; *The Truth about Alan*, 1963; *A Case of Character*, 1964; *Mr. Fowlds*, 1965; *The Corsican Brothers*, 1965; *Finders Keepers*, 1967; *The Whole Truth*, 1967; *Silver Wedding*, 1967; *A Most Unfortunate Accident*, 1968; *Flotsam and Jetsam*, 1970; *Robin Redbreast*, 1970; *The Guardians* series (7 episodes), 1971; *A Woman Sobbing*, 1972; *The Emergency Channel*, 1973; *Young Guy Seeks Part-Time Work*, 1973; *Miss Nightingale*, 1974; *Heil Caesar!*, 1974; *The Treasure of Abbot Thomas*, 1974; *The Snow Queen*, 1974; *A Juicy Case*, 1975; *Brief Encounter*, from the film by Noël Coward, 1976; *A Photograph*, 1977; *Rachel in Danger*, 1978; *A Dog's Ransom*, from the novel by Patricia Highsmith, 1978; *Games*, 1978; *The Ice House*, 1978; *The Letter of the Law*, 1979; *Dying Day*, 1980; *The Specialist*, 1980; *A Game for Two Players*, 1980; *Dark Secret*, 1981; *Honeymoon*, 1985.

Novels

The Truth Will Not Help Us: Embroidery on an Historical Theme. London, Chatto and Windus, 1956.
After the Rain. London, Faber, 1958; New York, Ballantine, 1959.
The Centre of the Green. London, Faber, 1959; New York, McDowell Obolensky, 1960.
Storyboard. London, Faber, 1960.
The Birdcage. London, Faber, and New York, Harper, 1962.
A World Elsewhere. London, Faber, 1965; New York, Coward McCann, 1967.
Squeak: A Biography of NPA 1978A 203. London, Faber, 1983; New York, Viking, 1984.
The McGuffin. London, Hamish Hamilton, 1984; Boston, Atlantic Monthly Press, 1985.
The Girls: A Story of Village Life. London, Hamish Hamilton, 1986; New York, Atlantic Monthly Press, 1987.

Other (for children)

Pegasus. London, Faber, 1957; New York, A.S. Barnes, 1960.
The Mermaid and the Boy. London, Faber, 1958; New York, A.S. Barnes, 1960.
Garry Halliday and the Disappearing Diamonds [*Ray of Death*; *Kidnapped Five*; *Sands of Time*; *Flying Foxes*] (as Justin Blake, with Jeremy Bullmore). London, Faber, 5 vols., 1960–64.

*

Manuscript Collections: Mugar Memorial Library, Boston University; (television works) Temple University Library, Philadelphia.

Critical Studies: *Writers on Themselves*, London, BBC Publications, 1964; "The Man Behind *The Disorderly Women*" by Robin Thornber, in *Guardian* (London), 19 February 1969; "Like a Woman They Keep Coming Back To" by Ronald Hayman, in *Drama* (London), Autumn 1970; "Bowen on the Little Box" by Hugh Hebert, in *Guardian* (London), 6 August 1971; "Author/Director," in *London Magazine*, December 1971, and "*The Guardians*: A Post Mortem," in *Plays and Players* (London), January 1972, both by Bowen.

Theatrical Activities:
Director: **Plays**—at the London Academy of Music and Dramatic Art since 1967; *The Disorderly Women*, Manchester, 1969, London, 1970; *Fall and Redemption*, Pitlochry, Scotland, 1969; *The Waiting Room*, London, 1970.
Actor: **Plays**—in repertory in North Wales, summers 1950–51; Palace Theatre, Watford, Hertfordshire, 1965.

John Bowen comments:

My plays, like my novels, are distinguished by a general preoccupation with myth (*The Truth Will Not Help Us, After the Rain, A World Elsewhere, Fall and Redemption, The Disorderly Women, Robin Redbreast*), and mainly with one particular myth, that of the Bacchae, which in my reading represents the conflict between Apollonian and Dionysiac ways of living more than the mere tearing to pieces of a Sacred King. This theme, the fight in every human being and between beings themselves, rationality against instinct, is to be found somewhere in almost everything I have written.

Another common theme is of manipulation, one person using another or others, not always consciously, and sometimes "for their good." This theme has been most clearly expressed politically in the episodes I wrote for the television series *The Guardians*, and in my novel *A World Elsewhere*. A third common theme, allied to the other two, is that of self-deceit.

I think of plays as constructions (as all literary forms are, but plays and poems perhaps most), and enjoy theatricality. I like movement; plays are not talk, but action, though the talk may *be* action. I think that the cinema and television have helped the theatre in the 20th century to rediscover some of the mobility it had in the 16th. Though I like above all naturalistic acting, I hate naturalistic settings, and try to avoid waits for scene changes: in most of my plays, the scenes flow into each other by a shift of light.

I have been influenced by Ibsen and Chekhov, probably by Coward, Anouilh, Pirandello and Shaw. Of 20th-century directors, I have most admired Sir Tyrone Guthrie.

* * *

Before his first major stage success, with *After the Rain* in 1966, John Bowen was already well known as a novelist and theatre critic for the then prestigious *London Magazine*. His theatre columns of that period reveal a sympathetic understanding of a large variety of dramatic modes, and so it is unsurprising that his own plays have been criticised for stylistic eclecticism. Though *After the Rain* was based on one of Bowen's novels, its theatricality was immediately seen to reflect Weiss's *Marat/Sade*, particularly in the way that each member of the cast is presented as being a criminal deviant hypnotised into the therapeutic re-enactment of events related to the great deluge of the late 20th century. The metatheatrical dimension is not developed at all, however, and Bowen's deeper interest emerges as lying in the use of archetype, particularly through sometimes startling diachronic collations. *After the Rain* displays the emblems of epic theatre from the start: a bare stage with a lectern, minimal props, placards identifying locations, and the first character (a Lecturer) delivering his opening lines to the lighting technician. All the barriers of the conventional theatre seem to have dissolved. But within a few seconds the Lecturer is referring to "life in 1968" as something prehistoric; elastic time has suddenly soared beyond the audience's experience. Early in the second act there appears a character whom audience members (but not the characters) recognise as Noah, and time bounces back violently in the other direction. The nine prisoner/characters, ostensibly drifting on a raft in the 1970's, find themselves in an arena in which the mythological merges with the futuristic, and a primitive theocracy is generated by necessity—although the Lecturer's scepticism is continually apparent. Satire of varying strengths has been directed at the figures on the raft—stock types from the 1960's—and Noah, on his first appearance, seems also a target for iconoclastic ridicule. However, it quickly becomes apparent that the Noah myth is not one of regeneration but of fossilisation; the ark is full of rotting animals, and Noah survives alone as a demented Ancient Mariner, persecuted by the anonymous gods, crazed by drinking the blood of the Shetland pony. For the protection of humanity, the ark is incinerated with Noah aboard. A new totalitarian myth is, of course, emerging, but for the audience there remains the question of whether Arthur, the autocrat of the raft society, has annihilated the Noah myth or assimilated it. The ending differs in the 1972 revised version, but essentially in both versions Arthur's divinity is challenged when he demands the sacrifice of the first baby born, and the result is a duel, with the death of the god and the birth of the new society which presents the play; at the same time, however, roles are also broken and the play ends with the insistence that the theatre has been invaded by reality.

Bowen's fascination with what he calls "myth" seems to derive from its defiance of chronology and conventional concepts of causation. His adaptation of Boucicault's *The Corsican Brothers* for television and then for the stage seems to have been stimulated by the telepathic link between the twins, and thus between Corsican and Parisian society; but the play also drops the morality of melodrama into a Brechtian limbo, heralded by the hobby-horses of the first episode and developed by numerous flippantly sardonic songs, culminating in a "Moral Finale." *Fall and Redemption* seems to consist of an iconoclastic pilfering of quaint details from the Mystery Cycles to create an acting exercise for LAMDA students, and its termination with the crucifixion (rather than Doomsday, where all the English cycles end) was interpreted as insensitivity to form; yet its Brechtian rationale is evident at least when Cain and Abel are joined by a talking horse, and inescapable in the ending, where the actors help Jesus off the cross and then come forward for applause. In another myth play for LAMDA, *The Disorderly Women*, Bowen knew that he was joining numerous playwrights of the 1960's in attempting a contemporary adaptation of *The Bacchae*; yet he was also trying to give a relatively sympathetic portrayal of Pentheus, as a ruler committed to moderation, a principle neither understood by his father nor respected by Dionysus, whose cynicism, Bowen's introduction suggests, is substantiated by Auschwitz, Hiroshima, and Vietnam.

In the 1970's Bowen's interests and techniques developed variously, with *Singles*, a comedy about sexual mercenaries, achieving a modest London critical success. The dilemma of Pentheus was expanded and domesticated in a play which did not reach London, *Which Way Are You Facing?*, a cerebral but aggressively theatrical contribution to the history of the problem play, from the sympathetic perspective of the control room of the Samaritans, monitoring the unloveliest of humanity in every corner of the auditorium. By contrast, in the much-praised *Robin Redbreast* Bowen exploits the savagery of myth which leaps from prehistory into the life of a television script editor; the dialogue of the final scene even includes a reference to *The Golden Bough*, but the structure of this play depends on psychological realism and its main impact is that of a thriller. In fact, although Bowen is best known for plays based on myth using techniques of epic theatre, he learned his dramatic craft writing for television, and his early plays (notably *A Holiday Abroad*) show a mastery of the subtleties of realism. One of his mature plays, *The Coffee Lace*, has even been interpreted as naturalistic in its portrayal of six veteran actors who have hermetically sealed themselves off from the world after a major theatrical failure ten years previously; however, they are also fossilised grotesques, very similar in their situation to the figures of *After the Rain*. Ambivalent it may be, but the play, with its companion piece *Trevor*, must dispel the common complaint that Bowen is a humourless writer; the gentle comedy in the portrayal of the social cripples in *The Coffee Lace* is rich but compassionate.

—Howard McNaughton

BRENTON, Howard. British. Born in Portsmouth, Hampshire, 13 December 1942. Educated at Chichester High School; St. Catharine's College, Cambridge, B.A. (honours) in English 1965. Married Jane Fry in 1970; two sons. Stage manager in several repertory companies; resident dramatist, Royal Court Theatre, London, 1972–73. Recipient: Arts Council bursary, 1969, 1970; John Whiting Award, 1970; *Evening Standard* award, 1977, 1985. Agent: Margaret Ramsay Ltd., 14-A Goodwin's Court, London, WC2N 4LL, England.

PUBLICATIONS

Plays

Ladder of Fools (produced Cambridge, 1965).
Winter, Daddykins (produced Dublin, 1965).
It's My Criminal (produced London, 1966).
A Sky-Blue Life, adaptation of stories by Gorky (produced London, 1967; revised version produced London, 1971).
Gargantua, adaptation of the novel by Rabelais (produced Brighton, 1969).
Gum and Goo (produced Brighton, 1969; London, 1971). Included in *Plays for Public Places*, 1972.
Revenge (produced London, 1969). London, Methuen, 1970.
Heads, and The Education of Skinny Spew (produced Bradford, 1969; London, 1970). Included in *Christie in Love and Other Plays*, 1970.
Christie in Love (produced Brighton and London, 1969; Chicago, 1981). Included in *Christie in Love and Other Plays*, 1970.
Christie in Love and Other Plays. London, Methuen, 1970.
Fruit (produced London, 1970).
Wesley (produced Bradford, 1970). Included in *Plays for Public Places*, 1972.
Scott of the Antarctic; or, What God Didn't See (produced Bradford, 1971). Included in *Plays for Public Places*, 1972.
Lay By, with others (produced Edinburgh and London, 1971). London, Calder and Boyars, 1972.
Hitler Dances (produced Edinburgh and London, 1972). London, Methuen, 1982.
Plays for Public Places. London, Eyre Methuen, 1972.
How Beautiful with Badges (produced London, 1972).
England's Ireland, with others (produced Amsterdam and London, 1972).
Measure for Measure, adaptation of the play by Shakespeare (produced Exeter, Devon, 1972).
A Fart for Europe, with David Edgar (produced London, 1973).

The Screens, adaptation of a play by Jean Genet (produced Bristol, 1973).
Brassneck, with David Hare (produced Nottingham, 1973). London, Eyre Methuen, 1974.
Magnificence (produced London, 1973). London, Eyre Methuen, 1973.
Mug (produced Manchester, 1973).
The Churchill Play: As It Will be Performed in the Winter of 1984 by the Internees of Churchill Camp Somewhere in England (produced Nottingham, 1974; London, 1979). Included in *Plays 1*, 1986.
The Saliva Milkshake, adaptation of the novel *Under Western Eyes* by Conrad (televised 1975; produced London, 1975; New York, 1978). London, TQ Publications, 1977.
Government Property (produced Aarhus, Denmark, 1975).
Weapons of Happiness (produced London, 1976; Buffalo, 1983). London, Eyre Methuen, 1976.
Epsom Downs (produced London, 1977). London, Eyre Methuen, 1977.
Deeds, with others (produced Nottingham, 1978). Published in *Plays and Players* (London), May and June 1978.
Sore Throats (produced London, 1979; St. Louis, 1983; New York, 1985). With *Sonnets of Love and Opposition*, London, Eyre Methuen, 1979.
The Life of Galileo, adaptation of a play by Brecht (produced London, 1980). London, Eyre Methuen, 1980.
The Romans in Britain (produced London, 1980). London, Eyre Methuen, 1980; revised version, Methuen, 1982.
Plays for the Poor Theatre (includes *The Saliva Milkshake, Christie in Love, Heads, The Education of Skinny Spew, Gum and Goo*). London, Eyre Methuen, 1980.
A Short Sharp Shock!, with Tony Howard (produced London, 1980). With *Thirteenth Night*, London, Eyre Methuen, 1981.
Thirteenth Night (produced London, 1981). With *A Short Sharp Shock!*, London, Eyre Methuen, 1981.
Danton's Death, adaptation of a play by Georg Büchner (produced London, 1982). London, Methuen, 1982.
The Thing (for children; produced Brackley, Northamptonshire, 1982).
Conversations in Exile, adaptation of a work by Brecht (produced London, 1982).
The Genius (produced London, 1983; Los Angeles, 1984). London, Methuen, 1983.
Sleeping Policemen, with Tunde Ikoli (produced London, 1983). London, Methuen, 1984.
Bloody Poetry (produced Leicester and London, 1984; New York, 1987). London, Methuen, 1985.
Pravda: A Fleet Street Comedy, with David Hare (produced London, 1985). London, Methuen, 1985.
Plays 1 (includes *Christie in Love, Magnificence, The Churchill Play, Weapons of Happiness, Epsom Downs, Sore Throats*). London, Methuen, 1986.
Dead Head (televised 1986). London, Methuen, 1987.

Screenplay: *Skin Flicker*, 1973.

Television Plays: *Lushly*, 1972; *The Saliva Milkshake*, 1975; *The Paradise Run*, 1976; *A Desert of Lies*, 1984; *Dead Head* serial, 1986.

Verse

Notes from a Psychotic Journal and Other Poems. Privately printed, 1969.

*

Critical Studies: interview with Peter Ansorge, in *Plays and Players* (London), February 1972; *New British Political Dramatists* by John Bull, London, Macmillan, and New York, Grove Press, 1984.

Theatrical Activities:
Actor: **Plays**—with the Brighton Combination, 1969.

* * *

"It took me a long time", said Howard Brenton after reading English at Cambridge, "to get over being taught literature in that way." While at Cambridge Brenton wrote a long unworkable play called *Ladder of Fools*, but it was not until joining Brighton Combination as actor and writer in 1968 that he began to find his feet in the theatre. Adapting Rabelais's *Gargantua* for a group show led Brenton to experiment with style, and a shoestring budget while writing *Gum and Goo* in 1969 taught him to write with concentration: "the limitations became a kind of freedom," he told Peter Ansorge (*Plays and Players*, February 1972). His first full-length play, *Revenge*, was produced by the Royal Court Theatre Upstairs in 1969 and he subsequently worked with Portable Theatre, writing *Lay By* and *Brassneck* in collaboration with David Hare and others.

In 1970 Brenton won the John Whiting Award for *Christie in Love*. The Rillington Place murderer is treated naturalistically, as a lover in search of a love-object, while the police are essentially non-naturalistic. In a prefatory note to the play Brenton describes his technique as "a kind of dislocation, tearing up one style for another, so the proceedings lurch and all interpretations are blocked," giving the audience "a sense of moral vertigo." The Royal Court Theatre presented Brenton's *Magnificence* in 1973, while he was resident dramatist there. *Magnificence* turns on the impossibility of taking effective action against the establishment. In the final scene a would-be revolutionary, newly released from prison, fails to assassinate a cabinet minister because his gelignite mask has fused. When he tosses the mask away it explodes, killing both himself and his victim, a final ineffectual act.

Brenton's early settings range from the South Pole (*Scott of the Antarctic*) to Epsom racecourse on Derby day (*Epsom Downs*), via an internment camp (*The Churchill Play*) and a crisp factory (*Weapons of Happiness*). The plays are anarchic. *The Churchill Play*, for example, shows an army-operated internment camp for recalcitrant trade union members, in the Britain of 1984. Fascism lives, Brenton implies, warning against the possibility of a totalitarian Britain. *Weapons of Happiness* presents a black and white world of bosses and workers in which (with heavy symbolism) the workers flee literally down the drain. The boss comments: "Children of the Revolution? I want them to ... to bleed like pigs in a ditch." Brenton's characters become signposts for good and evil. He describes the costumes for *Scott of the Antarctic* as "Huge, gangling, gaudy apparitions—like adverts stepped down from the billboards of some rubbish world." It is strip-cartoon technique, Brechtian in style.

Brenton has emerged as a major political dramatist and his work has been increasingly in demand over the past decade from theatres such as the National, the Royal Shakespeare Company, and the Royal Court. The National Theatre production of *The Romans in Britain* (which caused a furore due to its prosecution by Mary Whitehouse) is a serious exploration of the dubious nature of Empire-building. Brenton uses the homosexual rape of a Druid priest by a Roman soldier as an illustration of this theme, and in the second act shows the results of British incursions into Ireland. The play is not, as suggested in the trial, merely a celebration of violence and degradation.

Brenton's latest work has included the translation and adaptation of Brecht's *Galileo* and Büchner's *Danton's Death* both for the National Theatre—for which he also wrote with David Hare the enormously successful Fleet Street satire *Pravda* (Russian for "truth"). The newspaper tycoon Lambert Le Roux cynically manipulating his "foundry of lies" is one of Brenton's major characterisations. *A Short Sharp Shock!* (written with Tony Howard) is a hilarious satire in which virtually the entire Tory cabinet is identified by name:

> Sir Keith Joseph —There are a lot of people in this country who through no fault of their own are working-class. I do hope this applies to no-one here tonight . . .

Other plays have experimented with technique. Brenton commented to the director Barry Kyle at an RSC workshop, for example, that in *Thirteenth Night* "the plot of *Macbeth* is like a marker: I tried to bury that in my play." Similarly *The Genius* owes something to the plot of *Galileo*, which Brenton had translated three years earlier. The play concerns a mathematician who, having discovered a formula which if used to make a bomb would mark the end of the universe, attempts to bury his knowledge. *The Genius* ends in a strong CND protest at the Newbury Women's Camp. Brenton's most innovative experiment is his collaboration with Tunde Ikoli for Foco Novo in which both men wrote entirely separate plays, set in Peckham, about the same six characters. Working with their director, Roland Rees, the two plays were intercut to form the curiously dreamlike play *Sleeping Policemen*. Also for Foco Novo Brenton wrote *Bloody Poetry*, which (via the tangled relations of Byron, Shelley, Mary Godwin, and Claire Clairemont) discusses the problems of the artist seeking to overturn the moral order in a bourgeois society—problems clearly within his own experience.

—Rosemary Pountney

BREUER, Lee. American. Born in Philadelphia, Pennsylvania, 6 February 1937. Educated at University of California, Los Angeles, B.A. 1958; San Francisco State University. Married Ruth Maleczech in 1978; two children. Director, San Francisco Actors' Workshop, 1963–65; free-lance director in Europe, 1965–70. Since 1970 co-artistic director, Mabou Mines, New York; since 1982 staff director, New York Shakespeare Festival; co-artistic director, Re Cher Chez studio. Teacher, Yale University School of Drama, New Haven, Connecticut, 1978–80, Harvard University Extension, Cambridge, Massachusetts, 1981–82, and New York University, 1981–82. Board member, Theatre Communications Group, New York. Recipient: Obie award, 1978, 1980, 1984; Creative Artists Public Service grant, 1980; National Endowment for the Arts fellowship, 1980, 1982; Rockefeller grant, 1981; Los Angeles Drama Critics Circle award, 1986. Lives in New York City. Agent: Lynn Davis, Davis-Cohen Associates, 513-A Avenue of the Americas, New York, New York 10011. Address: Mabou Mines, c/o Performing Arts Journal, 325 Spring Street, Suite 318, New York, New York 10013, U.S.A.

PUBLICATIONS

Plays

The Red Horse Animation, music by Philip Glass (produced New York, 1970; revised version, produced New York, 1972). Published in *The Theatre of Images*, edited by Bonnie Marranca, New York, Drama Book Specialists, 1977.

The B-Beaver Animation, music by Philip Glass, adaptation of a work by Samuel Beckett (produced Waterford, Connecticut, and New York, 1974).

The Saint and the Football Players (produced New York, 1976).

The Lost Ones, adaptation of the fiction by Samuel Beckett (produced New York, 1977).

The Shaggy Dog Animation (produced New York, 1977).

A Prelude to Death in Venice (produced New York, 1980; Edinburgh and London, 1982). Published in *New Plays USA 1*, edited by James Leverett, New York, Theatre Communications Group, 1982.

Sister Suzie Cinema, music by Bob Telson (produced New York, 1980; Edinburgh and London, 1982). New York, Theatre Communications Group, 1986.

The Gospel at Colonus, music by Bob Telson, adaptation of *Oedipus at Colonus* by Sophocles (produced Edinburgh and London, 1982; New York, 1983).

Hajj (produced New York, 1983). Published in *Wordplays 3*, New York, Performing Arts Journal Publications, 1984.

Animations: A Trilogy for Mabou Mines. New York, Performing Arts Journal Publications, 1986.

*

Theatrical Activities:

Director: **Plays**—all his own plays; *The House of Bernarda Alba* by García Lorca, San Francisco, 1963; *Mother Courage* by Brecht, Paris, 1967; *The Messingkauf Dialogues* by Brecht, Edinburgh, 1968; *Play* by Samuel Beckett, Paris, 1969, New York, 1970; *Come and Go* by Samuel Beckett, New York, 1975; *Mr. Frivolous* by Wallace Shawn, New York, 1976; *Earth Spirit* by Wedekind, New Haven, Connecticut, 1976(?); *Sunday Childhood Journeys to Nobody at Home* by Arthur Sainer, New York, 1980; *Lulu* by Wedekind, Cambridge, Massachusetts, 1980; *The Tempest*, New York, 1981; *From the Point of View of the Salt* by Liza Lorwin, New York, 1986.

Actor: **Play**—in *Wrong Guys* by Ruth Maleczech, New York, 1981.

Choreographer: **Play**—*Measure for Measure*, New York, 1976.

* * *

Lee Breuer is a dramatist as well as auteur-director, and was artistic head of the Mabou Mines experimental theatre company in New York until 1975, when the group became a collective, of which he is still a member. His "performance poems," as he calls his playtexts, merge the American tradition of the self-conscious, extended lyric poem (Whitman, Ginsberg) with the main tendencies of European modern drama. After beginning his directorial work with the San Francisco Actors' Workshop, Breuer studied with the Berliner Ensemble and with Grotowski, so he knows both "presence" and the complexities of presentational form.

The greater part of Breuer's dramatic writing is structured in the form of a labyrinthine monologue that he then "animates" in a richly physicalized stage setting and performance.

The monologues telescope many identities into a single voice that in turn splices together fragments of many linguistic worlds: street language, colloquialisms, phrases from sports, science, Latin, spiritualism, etc., and above all pop imagery from the movies and the media. Through juxtaposition he develops a complex mode of irony which perhaps has its origins in Beckett, whose work he has directed in innovative productions. Dominated by a sophisticated use of punning, Breuer's irony allows the poem and its speakers to subvert the efficacy of the expressive language of emotion without denying the reality of the emotion itself. Breuer's approach to dramatic language plays with the illusions of performance, emphasized by the *bunraku* puppets he so admires and often uses in his stagings of the poems.

His early poems are brief modernist beast fables in the Kafka manner, in which the animal figure tells a human story. A single voice is taken up by several performers to project a fragmented self. *The Red Horse Animation* is an interior monologue about a lone voice seeking a shape for its life, as performers gyrate in evocation of a message-carrying horse. In its struggle the horse's life is stifled by the father's ethos of drudge-work and money. Just as the voice starts to feel mind and imagination coming together, the image of the horse—and potential poet—tears itself apart and dissolves into silence. *The B-Beaver Animation* tells of a stutterer—the artist who can't get his words out. He seeks to build a dam to protect his Missus and The Brood, who function as a chorus for his thoughts, which are dammed up with the detritus of his everyday experience, his learning, and his fantasies.

While working on these Animations, Breuer experimented with performance art, and both lines of work converged during the late 1970's, culminating in the hours-long *The Shaggy Dog Animation.* Here two distinct voices speak for a pair of *bunraku*-style puppets in American contemporary dress, supported by live performers who animate the puppets' bodies and their words. The story is that of the exploitative John Greed who falls in love with a faithful woman who calls herself Your Dog Rose. She submits to him as one of the "bitches of the city" who are "prisoners of love." Her shaggy-dog life includes a trip to Venice, California, for moviemaking, and a return to New York where she enters the art world. At her opening she shows a painted fireplug, and the art establishment comes down on her for seeing only the surface of things. She goes on to have puppies, and in a last bitter street fight with John, she ends it with him. Still, their voices merge to become one voice, as powerful in memory as they were in life.

With *A Prelude to Death in Venice* Breuer's stagings shift to solo performance, here with a triple persona: of a puppeteer (Bill); the puppet John Greed; and the movie agent Bill Morris. Expanded from a brief section of *Shaggy Dog*, life is presented as a succession of late-night calls into a pair of city street payphones which frame the figure like the two thieves framed Christ on Golgotha. He suffers the indignities of family and the movie world, with tirades to Mother, his Agent (who's "into producing reality" and is in fact himself), and finally his father. Throughout, Thomas Mann's *Death in Venice* provides an overlay of imagery and ironic contrast. Exasperated by his failed plan to shoot a movie in Venice, California, Bill the puppeteer kills John his puppet-self and thus is able to call down his father and deliver himself to momentary freedom.

A monologue of even greater complexity emerges with *Hajj*, in which an American actress seated at her make-up table summons the memory of her East European father who committed suicide. They sleep together, suffer together, and he shoots himself before she can repay the money she borrowed from him, which stands for an emotional debt, too. In this fateful recollection that is her version of the traditional Moslem's trip to ancient Mecca, her father's image is superimposed upon her own, and even upon that of her son—all through a sophisticated interaction of live performer, mask, film, and video imagery. No unmasking will separate their identities, for they vibrate within one another.

Beginning in 1980, Breuer initiated a series of experiments in music-theatre with the composer Bob Telson, aiming for a synthesis of popular and high art on the order of the Brecht-Weill collaborations. Their first piece was *Sister Suzie Cinema*, a brief "Doo-Wop Opera" in which young black singers dream of a union with images on a movie-house screen. Imagination becomes reality as the ground gives way and they ride to their paradise on a huge airplane wing.

In a major experiment with Telson, *The Gospel at Colonus*, Breuer rips the Oedipus story from its Greek context and thrusts it into the world of exultation that is American black gospel singing. While this radical adaptation maintains the central events and figures of Sophocles's final masterpiece, it augments the Greek conventions with the black preacher's dramaturgy of chanting and shouting together with an onstage congregation. By the end, the audience too joins this great chorus, standing, clapping, and joyously singing along.

In these jubilant displays, music and song now have led Breuer to worlds of dramatic reconciliation. But even here, as in all his work, Breuer's poetry of the theatre is predicated upon a radical synthesis of performance genres—illusory play that also is a feat of illumination.

—William Coco

BROWN, Kenneth H. American. Born in Brooklyn, New York, 9 March 1936. Educated at a preparatory school in Brooklyn. Served in the United States Marine Corps, 1954–57. Mail clerk, 1951–54; bartender and waiter, New York and Miami, 1958–63; bank clerk, New York, 1960; cigarette salesman, New York, 1961; resident playwright, Living Theatre, New York, 1963–67; private tutor, 1966–69, and resident playwright, 1968–69, Yale University School of Drama, New Haven, Connecticut; Visiting Lecturer (improvisational acting), Hollins College, Virginia, 1969; Visiting Lecturer (history of theatre), Hunter College, New York, 1969–70; Associate Professor in Performance (theatrical production), University of Iowa, Iowa City, 1971. Recipient: Venice Film Festival gold medal, 1964; Rockefeller fellowship, 1965, and grant, 1967; ABC-Yale University fellowship, 1966, 1967; Guggenheim fellowship, 1966; Creative Artists Public Service grant, 1974. Agent: Rick O'Shea, 72 Second Street, Garden City, New York 11530. Address: 150 74th Street, Brooklyn, New York 11209, U.S.A.

PUBLICATIONS

Plays

The Brig (produced New York, 1963; London, 1964). New York, Hill and Wang, and London, Methuen, 1965.
Devices (produced New York, 1965).
The Happy Bar (produced New York, 1967).
Blake's Design (produced New Haven, Connecticut, 1968; New York, 1974). Published in *The Best Short Plays 1969*, edited by Stanley Richards, Philadelphia, Chilton, 1969.

The Green Room (produced Iowa City, 1971).
The Cretan Bull (produced Waterford, Connecticut, 1972; New York, 1974).
Nightlight (produced Hartford, Connecticut, 1973; London, 1974). New York, French, 1973.

Screenplays: *The Brig*, 1965; *Devices*, 1967.

Novel

The Narrows. New York, Dial Press, 1970.

*

Manuscript Collection: New York Public Library.

Kenneth H. Brown comments:

I began as a playwright quite by accident. It was the best means to convey my experiences as a confined prisoner in a Marine Brig. All my plays since have been either direct or symbolic representations of my life experiences. As such, I have been classified by one theatre historian as an accidental playwright, a title I gladly accept since I adhere to the belief that all things of personal import in my life have come about as a result of pure chance. I do not take to writing as a daily chore that must be done. It is, for me, a labor of love and, as such, I engage in it only when moved to do so. As I get older, I am constantly amazed by the body of works accumulated through this philosophy.

* * *

Although Kenneth H. Brown has published poetry and a novel, *The Narrows*, his most significant achievements to date have been in drama. *The Brig*, a stark and appalling indictment of militarism, stamped Brown as one of the more gifted and experimental of American dramatists of the 1960's. It placed him in a tradition with Artaud and proved him able to create what neither Artaud nor Ionesco accomplished, "theatre of cruelty" complete with a metaphysics of language. His next published play, *Blake's Design*, gave further support to the belief that Brown was a dramatist who defied labels. Moving away from the stark, purposefully flat prose of *The Brig*, Brown played with the catchy rhythms of vaudeville, embellished his prose giving it a lyrical quality, and turned away from naturalism to expressionism. Of *The Cretan Bull*, Brown says he produced a "very funny play about complete strangers who meet in Central Park at dawn and confront a very odd set of circumstances." Again Brown went in new directions, experimenting with another style, and exploring different themes.

Though *The Brig* and *Blake's Design* are very different, they share many common elements. In both, an egalitarianism makes Brown select characters for his drama who reflect the ethnic and racial mix that makes up American society. In both Brown draws on music and popular songs: in *Blake's Design* the songs and dances are handled in a manner reminiscent of a vaudeville skit; in *The Brig* music is subverted and becomes an instrument of torture. The sarcastic, strident, sneering tone of a guard's voice is played contrapuntally against a clear, impersonal, unaffected voice. The breaking of a command is answered by its own often inaudible flat echo. The hideous dissonant martial music that is the tool of the fascist or authoritarian state, the kind of music that breaks a man's mind and makes him crawl like a maggot at any command, is produced by clashing garbage can lids together as if they were cymbals. Yet more hellish music derives from the sound of a voice resonating against a toilet bowl as one of the prisoners, using the cubicle as his confessional, cries out his litany of wrongs in obedience to the guard's orders. Dance, too, figures in the plays. In *Blake's Design* Muvva and Zack sing of Zack's necrophilia with his dead, black wife while they do a soft shoe dance. In *The Brig* dance is a ritual in which the prisoners suffer repeatedly at the hands of the guards. The dance is one where men shrink, recoil, and double-over in response to the quick, sharp blows delivered by the truncheons of the Warden or the guards. This violent dance pattern is varied with a pattern of running across the stage and halting at every white line in conformity with the procedure outlined in the *Marine Corps Manual*. Finally, both plays employ a point of view that is reminiscent of naturalism. A dispassionate exact observer records precisely the world in all its minutiae as if the reality being depicted were a hard surface that can only be penetrated once it has been fully sounded. But for all these seeming similarities, the plays are, in fact, very different, both in style and in theme.

The Brig is a blatantly political play, or rather, "concept of theater," as Brown would have it called. A penal institute in Camp Fuji, the brig is the place where Marines are sent to be punished for any infraction of military orders. The set of the play duplicates as nearly as possible the specifications of the brig and its actions reenact the rules that govern its workings as set down in the *Marine Corps Manual*. The play opens with the waking of the prisoners at dawn and it closes with the putting out of the light at night. Between dawn and night, we see the prisoners repeat again and again the same gestures and motions as they are forced to dress and undress, eat and march, clean and stand at attention, for no other reason than to fulfill an order and submit to power. Nameless (they are called by number—only the guards have names), the prisoners grovel, crawl, abuse themselves, whimper silently, and try desperately to carry out any order to the letter while the military guards sadistically delight in finding new indignities for them to suffer and new punishments for their supposed failures. The discipline is without restraint or reason. Senselessly the prisoners are humiliated, beaten, and abused. The only logic that governs events is the relentless logic of power and physical force. In the course of the day, one prisoner is released, a new one enters, and a third is released to an even worse form of institutional imprisonment, the asylum. Number 26, after two weeks in the brig which follows upon 16 years of honorable military service, finds himself, against all orders and common sense, crying out his name, James Turner, and in so doing demonstrating that in the brig seemingly sane behavior is in fact insane. For two hours, the senses of the audience are assaulted as the prisoners are hollered at and harassed by the guards. Plot and character development in the ordinary sense are absent from the play. Language, stripped of all warmth, finally negates itself. The members of the audience are left responding to sounds, intonations, incantations, and not denotative meanings. They experience an agony of feeling which derives from the immediacy of the violence unleashed both on the stage and in themselves and which has little reference to the world of reason that has systematically been destroyed by the extremes to which it has been pushed on the stage.

Blake's Design depicts Zack's struggle to free himself from both his past—the black woman whose dead body he has slept with for ten years—and his illusions—Blake, or call him God, is one of them—in order to tell his son the truth, live in the present, and move out of his dark basement apartment upstairs and into the light. Zack's mulatto son, Sweek, and his two women, Muvva, with whom he has shared his bed, dead wife, and son for ten years, and Modrigal, his half-oriental mistress, all talk rather self-consciously throughout the play about man's weakness, his lies, and that part of himself which he does not know or understand and so calls God, or Blake, in an effort at understanding. The play ends when Zack unburdens himself, tells the truth, closes the door on his past, and mounts the stairs. The symbolism is rather obvious and the long talks about Blake tend to be tiresome, but the characters themselves are well imagined and the quick staccato exchanges between Sweek and Zack and the shuffling dances and songs save the play.

Brown's talents are considerable; he was one of the few genuinely original American dramatists to emerge in the early 1960's.

—Carol Simpson Stern

BULLINS, Ed. American. Born in Philadelphia, Pennsylvania, 2 July 1935. Educated in Philadelphia public schools; at William Penn Business Institute, Philadelphia; Los Angeles City College, 1958–61; San Francisco State College, 1964–65. Served in the United States Navy, 1952–55. Married Trixie Warner. Playwright-in-residence and associate director, New Lafayette Theatre, New York, 1967–73; producing director, Surviving Theatre, New York, from 1974; writers unit co-ordinator, New York Shakespeare Festival, from 1975; Mellon Lecturer, Amherst College, Massachusetts, from 1977. Editor, *Black Theatre* magazine, New York, 1969–74. Recipient: Rockefeller grant, 1968, 1970, 1973; Vernon Rice award, 1968; American Place grant, 1968; Obie award, 1971, 1975; Guggenheim grant, 1971, and fellowship, 1976; Creative Artists Public Service grant, 1973; National Endowment for the Arts grant, 1974; New York Drama Critics Circle award, 1975, 1977. D.L.: Columbia College, Chicago, 1976. Address: 932 East 212th Street, Brooklyn, New York 10469, U.S.A.

PUBLICATIONS

Plays

Clara's Ole Man (produced San Francisco, 1965; New York, 1968; London, 1971). Included in *Five Plays*, 1969.
How Do You Do? (produced San Francisco, 1965; London, 1969; New York, 1980). Mill Valley, California, Illuminations Press, 1965.
Dialect Determinism; or, The Rally (produced San Francisco, 1965). Included in *The Theme Is Blackness*, 1973.
The Theme Is Blackness (produced San Francisco, 1966). Included in *The Theme Is Blackness*, 1973.
It Has No Choice (produced San Francisco, 1966; London, 1968). Included in *The Theme Is Blackness*, 1973.
A Minor Scene (produced San Francisco, 1966; London, 1968). Included in *The Theme Is Blackness*, 1973.
The Game of Adam and Eve, with Shirley Tarbell (produced Los Angeles, 1966).
In New England Winter (produced New York, 1967). Published in *New Plays from the Black Theatre*, edited by Bullins, New York, Bantam, 1969.
In the Wine Time (produced New York, 1968). Included in *Five Plays*, 1969.
A Son, Come Home (produced New York, 1968). Included in *Five Plays*, 1969.
The Electronic Nigger (produced New York and London, 1968). Included in *Five Plays*, 1969.
Goin' a Buffalo: A Tragifantasy (produced New York, 1968). Included in *Five Plays*, 1969.
The Corner (produced Boston, 1968; New York, 1972). Included in *The Theme Is Blackness*, 1973.
The Gentleman Caller (produced New York and London, 1969). Published in *A Black Quartet*, edited by Clayton Riley, New York, New American Library, 1970.
Five Plays. Indianapolis, Bobbs Merrill, 1969; as *The Electronic Nigger and Other Plays*, London, Faber, 1970.
We Righteous Bombers (as Kingsley B. Bass, Jr.), adaptation of a work by Camus (produced New York, 1969).
The Man Who Dug Fish (produced Boston, 1969; New York, 1970). Included in *The Theme Is Blackness*, 1973.
Street Sounds (produced New York, 1970). Included in *The Theme Is Blackness*, 1973.
The Helper (produced New York, 1970). Included in *The Theme Is Blackness*, 1973.
A Ritual To Raise the Dead and Foretell the Future (produced New York, 1970). Included in *The Theme Is Blackness*, 1973.
The Fabulous Miss Marie (produced New York, 1970). Published in *The New Lafayette Theatre Presents*, edited by Bullins, New York, Doubleday, 1974.
Four Dynamite Plays: It Bees Dat Way, Death List, The Pig Pen, Night of the Beast (produced New York, 1970; *It Bees Dat Way* produced London, 1970). New York, Morrow, 1971.
The Duplex: A Black Love Fable in Four Movements (produced New York, 1970). New York, Morrow, 1971.
The Devil Catchers (produced New York, 1970).
The Psychic Pretenders (produced New York, 1972).
You Gonna Let Me Take You Out Tonight, Baby (produced New York, 1972).
Next Time, in *City Stops* (produced New York, 1972).
House Party, music by Pat Patrick, lyrics by Bullins (produced New York, 1973).
The Theme Is Blackness: The Corner and Other Plays (includes *Dialect Determinism, or, The Rally; It Has No Choice; The Helper; A Minor Scene; The Theme Is Blackness; The Man Who Dug Fish; Street Sounds*; and the scenarios and short plays *Black Commercial No. 2, The American Flag Ritual, State Office Bldg. Curse, One-Minute Commercial, A Street Play, A Short Play for a Small Theatre*, and *The Play of the Play*). New York, Morrow, 1973.
The Taking of Miss Janie (produced New York, 1975). Published in *Famous Plays of the '70's*, New York, Dell, 1980.
The Mystery of Phyllis Wheatley (produced New York, 1976).
I Am Lucy Terry (for children; produced New York, 1976).
Jo Anne!!! (produced New York, 1976).
Home Boy, music by Aaron Bell, lyrics by Bullins (produced New York, 1976).
Daddy (produced New York, 1977).
Sepia Star; or, Chocolate Comes to the Cotton Club, music and lyrics by Mildred Kayden (produced New York, 1977).
Storyville, music and lyrics by Mildred Kayden (produced La Jolla, California, 1977; revised version produced Washington, D.C., 1979).
Michael (also director: produced New York, 1978).
C'mon Back to Heavenly House (produced Amherst, Massachusetts, 1978).
Leavings (produced New York, 1980).
Steve and Velma (produced Boston, 1980).

Screenplays: *Night of the Beast*, 1971; *The Ritual Masters*, 1972.

Novel

The Reluctant Rapist. New York, Harper, 1973.

Short Stories

The Hungered One: Early Writings. New York, Morrow, 1971.

Verse

To Raise the Dead and Foretell the Future. New York, New Lafayette Publications, 1971.

Other

Editor, *New Plays from the Black Theatre.* New York, Bantam, 1969.

Editor, *The New Lafayette Theatre Presents: Plays with Aesthetic Comments by 6 Black Playwrights.* New York, Doubleday, 1974.

*

Bibliography: *Ten Modern American Playwrights* by Kimball King, New York, Garland, 1982.

Critical Study: *Drumbeats, Masks, and Metaphor: Contemporary Afro-American Theatre* by Geneviève Fabre, translated by Melvin Dixon, Cambridge, Massachusetts, Harvard University Press, 1983.

Theatrical Activities:
Director: **Play**—*Michael*, New York, 1978.
Actor: **Play**—role in *The Hotel Play* by Wallace Shawn, New York, 1981.

Ed Bullins comments:

I write plays for a number of reasons but the most simple and direct truth of the matter is that it is my work.

* * *

Though he is the most prolific, and one of the most active, figures in black American theater, Ed Bullins resists close identification with the prominent contemporary styles. With Black House and Black Arts/West in San Francisco he participated in projects to create a revolutionary theater; yet, at the same time he was capable of satirizing revolutionary ideologues in *Dialect Determinism.* He can adapt the mode of realism for his Twentieth-Century Cycle, but deflect a critic's attempt to discern its autobiographical theme with the remark that specific reference is not apt for symbolic writing like his own. Bullins's statements are often, in fact, less a commentary than an enactment of the theatrical devices of black language. There is the pretended innocence of "shuckin" that allows him to deny association with militants, the inflated language of the put-on self-description ("Ed Bullins, at this moment in time, is almost without peer in America—black, white or imported"), and the ironic humor producing elaborate games about racial stereotypes in and around his plays. Like the originators of those linguistic techniques Bullins stays loose so that he can survive the pressures of the moment and continue to evolve through performance after performance.

The best known of his works are set in the 1950's, a period that matches historically the personal deracination of the characters. They are urban people completely divorced from the southern past, the soil, and traditional culture. Shown without the coloration of myth in either their own or their creator's consciousness, they are neither idealized folk primitives so dearly beloved in the past to friendly white writers on the Negro, nor the agents of imminent revolution ardently desired by some black spokespersons. Their ghetto is both physical and moral. Excluded from accomplishments beyond those of subsisting they cannot transcend private passion or see any possibility of redemption in community. In *Clara's Ole Man*, for instance, a young student hoping to make out with a woman stumbles into a cast of grotesques who fulfill a projected sense of menace by calling in a street gang to beat him senseless.

The Twentieth-Century Cycle—about which Bullins says, in his put-on voice "there is already talk of this collective project surpassing greatness in its scope, though the work is not that astonishing, relative to Bullins' abilities"—develops its first installment, *In the Wine Time*, from a prologue in which a male narrator lyrically describes the beautiful woman who represents the goals he innocently hopes to achieve. As counterpoint the body of the play reveals through its slowly moving dialogue of a summer evening the disappointments of the youth's exhausted aunt, the frustrated hopes of her husband, and the diversion of their ambitions into a contest over the boy. Structured as an initiation play, *In the Wine Time* carries the protagonist to a point where he destroys his own future with an act of casual violence. *In New England Winter* picks up the leading character, now free from the prison sentence he receives for the pointless assault in the previous play, and juxtaposes him to yet another young man and group of small-time hustlers. Scenes of a planned robbery intermix with memories of a love idyll that is at first attractive, like the prologue of *In the Wine Time*, and is then revealed to have been a period of desperate escape. The human needs people have for each other issue in sadomasochistic relationships, gratuitous brutality, and a deadly lack of sustained feeling.

With *The Duplex*, subtitled *A Black Love Fable in Four Movements,* the theme of the cycle is fully established: the impossibility of love, and by implication broader community, and the reflexive self-destruction of character. Again the movement is of a young man gaining experience in the social world. Steve Benson hesitates between submission to the anodynes of alcohol and sex and the resolution to direct his own life. The forces for submission are so powerful that hesitation seems the only plausible action for him in the brief time of the play; self-sufficiency would be too unlikely. Application of the playwright's naturalism is so overwhelming that race hardly seems the point of the plays in the cycle, though it certainly provides the circumstances that prod characters along their desperate ways. Cast out and angry they invert their creativity: social insignificance releases energy in violence and sexual dominance; the contempt of an external society is mirrored in a lumpen style and contempt for life itself.

Still, Bullins stops short of dehumanizing his characters. In *The Fabulous Miss Marie* the vital and vulgar heroine demonstrates the vigor that sustains humanity, and in the other cycle plays Bullins rejects either a portrayal of characters as victims or the easy sentiment of pity, equally dehumanizing. His identification with the plight of his people in the industrial slums of the northeastern cities and sunshine ghettoes of southern California instead advances the idea that the public world we know in terms of social and economic problems is lived in the experience of personal troubles and private feelings. If the inhabitants of the 1950's ghetto appear to be trapped, it is because Bullins sees in politics and the philosophy of art no release for their humanity. We have got to see the problem, he says, in the depths of personality before we can honestly propose any solution.

The dramaturgy of Bullins's cycle, as well as such a pre-cycle play as *Goin' a Buffalo*, exploits the entire theatrical ambience for effect. The decor of *Goin' a Buffalo* consists of all-white walls and a crimson carpet. The set of *The Duplex* is a non-realistic gradation of planes that contest with the realism of the dramatic action and dialogue to give credence to the view that the plays are, indeed, intended to be seen symbolically. Nearly all the plays call for musical accompaniment attuned to situation and shifting lighting effects to spot significant relationships, while the directions for movements on stage suggest choreography.

In the late 1970's Bullins carried his interest in the associated stage arts into collaboration on the musicals *Storyville* and *Sepia Star*. At other times in his career he wrote sketches, one-act plays, children's dramas, scenarios, even radio commercials. In this variety of production one sees the historical problem of the black playwright searching for a sympathetic audience. The expectations of white playgoers subtly educe, even against a writer's will, some accommodation, or else they create a strong need for defiance. Meanwhile blacks who share the writer's cultural experience and language find their theater in the events of the church and other institutions, rather than on Broadway which for more reasons than one has been called the great white way. In an approach to the latter part of the problem Bullins became involved in the Black Arts Alliance on the west coast and, then, invested ten years' time in New York attempting to establish in the contemporary city the New Lafayette Theatre as a successor to the original Lafayette Stock Company that laid the foundations of black legitimate theater from 1917 to 1932.

The creation of such political plays as those collected in *Four Dynamite Plays* can also be understood as part of Bullins's effort to engender in audiences the conviction that drama can be the arena for serious examination of black values. *Death List* from this collection portrays a rifleman intoning indictments of popular leaders while the play's other character, Blackwoman, explains the extenuating circumstances of each alleged betrayal of black interests. Getting no response to her pleas for mercy Blackwoman asks if the potential assassin himself is not the actual enemy of the people. There is no resolution of the opposition. The action simply ends with the offstage sound of shots; presumably it is time for the audience to debate the issue.

Bullins's confrontation of the white members of his dual audience generally takes the form of instructive, but not necessarily didactic, writing. The cycle plays are works meant to inform whites as much as to produce recognition for blacks. Then, too, a play such as *Daddy* can be taken, as it was by New York reviewers, to be an exploration of the feelings animating the man who abandons his family to better himself and the substitute father who replaces him. The abstracts of social science quantify the behavior that produces broken homes; Bullins tries to humanize it.

The theater has taken a breather from militancy, and Bullins has assumed a retrospective attitude toward the revolutionary period. *House Party* satirizes political figures, and *The Taking of Miss Janie* converts the politics of the 1960's into a drama of inter-racial rape. All-black theater, too, seems to be a thing of the past for Bullins. Though there are several active companies in America, and New York's Negro Ensemble Company looks to be the genuine successor to the famous American Negro Theater of the 1940's, as well as the old Lafayette Players, Bullins sees community theater in a drift. For the present at least the outlet for his remarkable productivity will be the mainstream American theater. He has been supervising the playwrights workshop of the New York Shakespeare Festival, recovering the roots of black show business for musical theater, and trying to shape his instructional plays into the style of domestic drama. Bullins will stay loose, avoid getting backed into a corner, and survive to give the American stage in one or another of its forms his intensely dramatic vision.

—John M. Reilly

BURROWS, John. British. Born in London, 19 November 1945. Educated at Manchester University, B.A. in drama. Agent: Michael Imison Playwrights, 28 Almeida Street, London N1 1TD, England.

PUBLICATIONS

Plays

For Sylvia, with John Harding (produced London, 1972). Published in *The Best Short Plays 1978*, edited by Stanley Richards, Radnor, Pennsylvania, Chilton, 1978.
The Golden Pathway Annual, with John Harding (produced Sheffield, 1973; London, 1974). London, Heinemann, 1975.
Loud Reports, with John Harding and Peter Skellern (produced London, 1975).
Dirty Giant, with John Harding, music by Peter Skellern (produced Coventry, 1975).
The Manly Bit, with John Harding (produced London, 1976).
Son of a Gun, with Sidewalk Theatre Company (produced London, 1976).
Cash Street, with Sidewalk Theatre Company (produced London, 1977).
Sketches in *Some Animals Are More Equal* (produced London, 1977).
Restless Natives, music by Rick Lloyd (produced London, 1978).
Dole Queue Fever, music by Rick Lloyd (produced London, 1978).
Sketches in *City Delights* (produced Oxford, 1978; London, 1980).
Freedom Point, music by Rick Lloyd (produced London, 1979).
The Last Benefit (produced London, 1980).
One Big Blow, music by Rick Lloyd (produced Bradford, 1980; London, 1981).
The Checkpoint, with the People Show (produced London, 1983).
Wartime Stories, music by Andrew Dickson, lyrics by Burrows (produced London, 1984).
It's a Girl!, music by Andy Whitfield (produced Lancaster and London, 1987).

Radio Writing: *The Heath and Me*, 1985.

Television Plays: *Do You Dig It?*, with John Harding, 1976; *Not the Nine O'Clock News* series, 1980.

*

Theatrical Activities:
Director: **Plays**—several of his own plays, and *Big Square Fields* by John McGrath, London, 1979; *The Garden of England* by Peter Cox, Sheffield and London, 1985.

Actor: Several of his own plays, and television plays, including *Talkin' Blues* by Nigel Williams, 1977

* * *

John Burrows and John Harding are two actors who evolved a distinctive revue-style to look at British class society and the effect its various myths have had on some of the inhabitants of that society. *For Sylvia* satirises gently and almost nostalgically the post-war myth-making of such 1950's epics as *The Dam Busters* and *Reach for the Sky*. Burrows, in the original production, played the central part of the pilot hero while Harding played everybody else. It was a very accurate re-creation and parody of that genre of film, performed with sensitivity and affection.

But *The Golden Pathway Annual* is a more considerable work. It revolves around Michael Peters, a member of the postwar grammar school generation, and traces him from his childhood, the son of a working-class George and Enid, through primary school, the 11-plus examination, grammar school, university, and out to the prospect of graduate unemployment. Again, Burrows played the central role in the first production, while Mark Wing-Davey and Maggie McCarthy played his parents and Harding everybody else. It is written in a series of short scenes—"Dad comes home from the war," "Michael at school," "The Coronation," "The Famous Five." *The Golden Pathway Annual* is a motif for the whole play—an annual sold by a slick salesman to Michael's gullible parents for Michael's "education" and the trigger to Michael's fantasies, both in boyhood and early adolescence. We see him imagine himself as one of Enid Blyton's very middle-class "Famous Five" and then, a few years later, ironically realize this fantasy's bourgeois content. The play is a gently ironic satire on the rise of the post-war meritocracy and is beautifully evocative for anyone (like me) of that generation.

Their third play, *Loud Reports*, done this time with pop singer Peter Skellern, is about a blimpish brigadier, Corfe-Prater, and his resolute refusal to come to terms with modern-day social realities, whether it be the depression in the 1930's, the advent of the Welfare State in the 1940's, or affluence in the 1950's. Suez is a brief reminder of former glories, while he staggers on into the 1960's. It is less original than *The Golden Pathway Annual*, though scarcely less entertaining.

—Jonathan Hammond

BUZO, Alexander (John). Australian. Born in Sydney, New South Wales, 23 July 1944. Educated at the Armidale School, New South Wales, 1956–60; International School of Geneva, 1962; University of New South Wales, Sydney, 1963–65, B.A. 1965. Married Merelyn Johnson in 1968; two daughters. Salesman, David Jones Ltd., Sydney, 1960; messenger, E.L. Davis and Company, Sydney, 1961; storeman-packer, McGraw-Hill Book Company, Sydney, 1967; clerk, New South Wales Public Service, Sydney, 1967–68; resident playwright, Melbourne Theatre Company, 1972–73; writer-in-residence, Sydney Teachers College, 1980. Recipient: Australian Literature Society gold medal, 1972; Commonwealth Literary Fund fellowship, 1973; Australia Council Literature Board grant, 1974, 1978. Agent: June Cann Management, P.O. Box 1577, North Sydney, New South Wales 2060. Address: 14 Rawson Avenue, Bondi Junction, New South Wales 2022, Australia.

PUBLICATIONS

Plays

The Revolt (produced Sydney, 1967).

Norm and Ahmed (produced Sydney, 1968; London, 1974). Included in *Norm and Ahmed, Rooted, and The Roy Murphy Show*, 1973.

Rooted (produced Canberra, 1969; Hartford, Connecticut, 1972; London, 1973). Included in *Norm and Ahmed, Rooted, and The Roy Murphy Show*, 1973.

The Front Room Boys (produced Perth, 1970; London, 1971). Published in *Plays*, Melbourne, Penguin, 1970.

The Roy Murphy Show (produced Sydney, 1971; London, 1983). Included in *Norm and Ahmed, Rooted, and The Roy Murphy Show*, 1973.

Macquarie (produced Melbourne, 1972). Sydney, Currency Press, 1971.

Tom (produced Melbourne, 1972; Washington, D.C., 1973). Sydney and London, Angus and Robertson, 1975.

Batman's Beach-head, adaptation of a play by Ibsen (produced Melbourne, 1973).

Norm and Ahmed, Rooted, and The Roy Murphy Show: Three Plays. Sydney, Currency Press, and London, Eyre Methuen, 1973.

Coralie Lansdowne Says No (produced Adelaide, 1974). Sydney, Currency Press, and London, Eyre Methuen, 1974.

Martello Towers (produced Sydney, 1976). Sydney, Currency Press, and London, Eyre Methuen, 1976.

Vicki Madison Clocks Out (produced Adelaide, 1976; Louisville, 1980).

Makassar Reef (produced Melbourne and Seattle, 1978). Sydney, Currency Press, 1978.

Big River (produced Adelaide, 1980). With *The Marginal Farm*, Sydney, Currency Press, 1985.

The Marginal Farm (produced Melbourne, 1983). With *Big River*, Sydney, Currency Press, 1985.

Screenplay: *Rod*, 1972.

Radio Plays: *File on Rod*, 1972; *Duff*, 1980; *In Search of the New Class*, 1982; *East of Singapore*, 1986.

Television Writing (animated films): *A Christmas Carol*, 1982, *Great Expectations*, 1983, *David Copperfield*, 1984, and *The Old Curiosity Shop*, 1985, all from works by Dickens.

Novel

The Search for Harry Allway. Sydney, Angus and Robertson, 1985.

Other

Tautology: I Don't Want to Sound Incredulous But I Can't Believe It. Melbourne, Penguin, 1981; revised edition, as *Tautology Too*, 1982.

Meet the New Class. Sydney, Angus and Robertson, 1981.

Editor (Australian edition), *Real Men Don't Eat Quiche*, by Bruce Feirstein. Sydney, Angus and Robertson, 1982.

*

Manuscript Collections: Mitchell Library, Sydney; National Library, Canberra.

Critical Studies: introduction by Katharine Brisbane to *Norm and Ahmed, Rooted, and The Roy Murphy Show*, 1973; *After "The Doll": Australian Drama since 1955* by Peter Fitzpatrick, Melbourne, Arnold, 1979; *Alexander Buzo's Rooted and Norm and Ahmed: A Critical Introduction* by T.L. Sturm, Sydney, Currency Press, 1980, and "Alexander Buzo: An Imagist with a Personal Style of Surrealism" by Sturm and "Aggressive Vernacular" by Roslyn Arnold, both in *Contemporary Australian Drama* edited by Peter Holloway, Currency Press, 1981; interview in *Southerly* (Sydney), March 1986.

Theatrical Activities:
Director: **Play**—*Care* by Daniel Hughes, Sydney, 1969.
Actor: **Plays**—*The Alchemist* by Jonson, Sydney, 1966; *Macbird* by Barbara Garson, Sydney, 1967.

Alexander Buzo comments:

My plays are, I hope, realistic poetic comedies set in contemporary times. They are not naturalistic. The mentality behind them could be described as humanist. Magritte is my favourite painter. When I started writing, the Theatre of the Absurd was a big influence. I place emphasis on verbal precision and visual clarity, and am not terribly interested in group anarchy. I believe in literacy, professionalism, and niceness. Nearly all my plays concentrate on one central character having problems with what's around and about.

* * *

Alexander Buzo's first short play, *Norm and Ahmed*, was something of a landmark on the route to the contemporary form of the Australian play. It was only a decade from Ray Lawler's *Summer of the Seventeenth Doll* and seven years from Alan Seymour's *The One Day of the Year*, each of them regarded as quintessential Australian plays. But *Norm and Ahmed*, though not apparently revolutionary in form, gathered up a number of new popular influences which began to take the new writers in a different direction.

Norm, a middle-aged, lonely, and unimaginative storeman, stops Ahmed, a Pakistani student, on a street corner one night and engages him in reluctant conversation. Norm's character has drawn on caricatures of the conservative returned serviceman and portraits like Barry Humphries's Sandy Stone and Seymour's Alf Cook from *The One Day of the Year*. Buzo gives their xenophobia and their rigid daily rituals a new aspect by placing them in confrontation with an Asian hinterland. Norm's strikingly aggressive-defensive attitude, quite unprovoked by Ahmed, is crystallised in the final moment. Norm proffers his hand in farewell and when Ahmed takes it, Norm smashes his head.

This is the only real moment of violence in all of Buzo's writing. After that he moves into the middle class for his context; the violence turns inward into verbal persecution.

In common with other playwrights, in the late 1960's Buzo was attracted by the variety of vernacular language and the loose rhythms of Australian life. Play by play he developed towards a comedy of manners which makes one listen afresh to familiar phrases and to his satirical embroidery of the colourful cliché. It has been said with justice that if his characters stopped talking they would scream: Buzo uses language both as a weapon against and as a shield between his people and an unpleasant or mundane reality.

For Buzo is more than a satirist. Behind the writing there are loneliness and a belief that in an older society with a stronger base of religious or social dogma things might be different. The absence of religious influence in Buzo's work is almost unique among contemporary Australian playwrights. In its place is a strong poetic response to nature which the characters express in unguarded moments. Without exception Buzo's figures are alienated. Both Norm and Ahmed are aliens in the same land, trying fruitlessly to understand it. Bentley, the timid but ambitious public servant in *Rooted*, is singled out for persecution in the schoolboy gang games of the young executives for no better reason than that he is a bore. Beneath the parody of adolescent manners, the comic-strip structure of the scenes, and the jargon of the beach, the art gallery, and the public service, *Rooted* is an allegory of every young man's sense of inadequacy in a society that has no roots but other people's acceptance. In *The Front Room Boys*, which satirically records in 12 scenes the tribal rituals of a city office, all the front room boys are hunted by the unexplained power of the back room boys and in turn hunt each other. In *Tom* Buzo gives us a manufactured hero, an oil exploration troubleshooter who speaks in monosyllables and is surrounded by the camp followers of big business while his wife suffers suburban neurosis and toothache.

In *Macquarie* Buzo abandons satire to deal with an early governor of New South Wales whose idealistic liberalism led to his downfall at the hands of the conservative power group. And in *Coralie Lansdowne Says No*, his most serious comedy of manners, a high flying young rebel facing a bleak future on the other side of thirty settles for a tiresome public servant who offers durability. All of these characters are misfits, aliens like Norm in their own world, and they are swallowed up by the unquestioning values of their too-modern society.

Buzo continues to pursue this problem of rootlessness in *Martello Towers* and *Makassar Reef*, the first about the immigrant consciousness in urban Australia, the second about the migrant habits of those who touch down in the resorts of Indonesia. The setting of *Martello Towers* is an island holiday house on the Hawkesbury River, near Sydney, where Edward Martello and his estranged wife and their parents gather by accident. The family is aristocratic, two generations Australian, but still with roots in Trieste; old Martello has come to beg for a grandchild who will continue the family name. Edward says no, there are plenty of Martellos in the phone book. None of the family is happy, though they have their comforts and their brief contact with the earth and the water. They are as alienated as Norm.

This is the last of the fierce, bitter Buzo wit in the theatre, and the last of the rebelliousness. With his most recent works, *Big River* and *The Marginal Farm*, Buzo has entered a new phase, abandoning the brittleness for an overt romanticism in his examination of his characters' allegiance to their environment; and emerges with the realisation that, when men and women put down their roots in the land, they find themselves not owners but servants of it.

Big River is a portrait of Australia at Federation, moving imperceptibly from the dramatic action of a frontier community to the gentler preoccupations of suburbia. The central image is the River Murray which divides Victoria from New South Wales; and the protagonist a young widow returning to her father's vineyard for his funeral. As members of the family go their separate ways we see Adele remain, her high-flying life force captured and domesticated into a quiet contentment. A similar prey of circumstances is Toby, the heroine of *The Marginal Farm*, who takes a job as governess in Fiji in a moment of romantic restlessness. Overwhelmed at first by the beauty of the sugar cane island, she soon finds her new community a band of itinerants who one by one fly away, leaving her stranded, clinging half-heartedly to the Indian lover she has taken on an impulse of defiant individualism.

Recently Buzo has moved away from the theatre to journalism, political and social satire and novel writing.

—Katharine Brisbane

BYRNE, John. British. Born in Paisley, Renfrewshire, Scotland, 6 January 1940. Educated at St. Mirin's Academy and Glasgow School of Art, 1958–63. Married Alice Simpson in 1964; one son and one daughter. Graphic designer, Scottish Television, Glasgow, 1964–66; designer, A.F. Stoddard, carpet manufacturers, Elderslie, 1966–68. Writer-in-residence, Borderline Theatre, Irvine, Ayrshire, 1978–79, and Duncan of Jordanstone College, Dundee, 1981; associate director, Haymarket Theatre, Leicester, 1984–85. Theatrical set and costume designer. Recipient: *Evening Standard* award, 1978. Agent: Margaret Ramsay Ltd., 14-A Goodwin's Court, London WC2N 4LL, England. Address: 3 Castle Brae, Newport-on-Tay, Fife, Scotland.

PUBLICATIONS

Plays

Writer's Cramp (produced Edinburgh and London, 1977; revised version, produced London, 1980; New York, 1986). Published in *Plays and Players* (London), December 1977.

The Slab Boys Trilogy (originally called *Paisley Patterns*). London, Penguin, 1987.

1. *The Slab Boys* (produced Edinburgh and London, 1978; Louisville, 1979; New York, 1980). Glasgow, Scottish Society of Playwrights, and New York, French, 1981; revised version, Edinburgh, Salamander Press, 1982.
2. *Cuttin' a Rug* (as *The Loveliest Night of the Year*, produced Edinburgh, 1979; revised version, as *Threads*, produced London, 1980; as *Cuttin' a Rug*, produced London, 1982). *Threads* published in *A Decade's Drama: Six Scottish Plays*, edited by Richard and Susan Mellis, Todmorden, Lancashire, Woodhouse, 1981; *Cuttin' a Rug* published Edinburgh, Salamander Press, 1982.
3. *Still Life* (produced Edinburgh, 1982). Edinburgh, Salamander Press, 1982.

Normal Service (produced London, 1979). Published in *Plays and Players* (London), May-June 1979.

Hooray for Hollywood (produced Louisville, 1980).

Babes in the Wood, music by John Gould, lyrics by David Dearlove (produced Glasgow, 1980).

Cara Coco (produced Irvine, Ayrshire, 1981).

Candy Kisses (produced London, 1984).

The London Cuckolds, adaptation of the play by Edward Ravenscroft (produced Leicester and London, 1985). London, French, 1986.

Radio Plays: *The Staffie* (version of *Cuttin' a Rug*); *A Night at the Alex*, 1981; *The Nitshill Writing Circle*, 1984.

Television Plays: *The Butterfly's Hoof*, 1978; *Big Deal* (*Crown Court* series), 1984; *Tutti Frutti* series, 1987.

Novel

Tutti Frutti (novelization of TV series). London, BBC Publications, 1987.

*

Theatrical Activities:
Designer (sets, costumes, and/or posters): **Plays**—*The Cheviot, The Stag, and the Black Black Oil* by John McGrath, Edinburgh and tour, 1973; *The Fantastical Feats of Finn MacCool* by Sean McCarthy, Edinburgh, 1974; *Writer's Cramp*, London, 1980; *Heaven and Hell* by Dusty Hughes, Edinburgh, 1981; *The Number of the Beast* by Snoo Wilson, London, 1982; *The Slab Boys Trilogy*, Edinburgh and London, 1982; *Other Worlds* by Robert Holman, 1982; *La Colombe* by Gounod, Buxton, Derbyshire, 1983; *McQuin's Metamorphosis* by Martyn Hobbs, Edinburgh, 1984; *The Cherry Orchard* by Chekhov, Leicester, 1984; *A Midsummer Night's Dream*, Leicester, 1984; *Candy Kisses*, London, 1984; *Dead Men* by Mike Stott, Edinburgh, 1985; *The London Cuckolds*, Leicester, 1985; *The Marriage of Figaro* by Mozart, Glasgow, 1986.

John Byrne comments:

(1982) I think I was 11 or 12 when I wrote my first piece . . . not for the theatre, although it was highly dramatic . . . about a cat that gets squashed under a bus. Accompanied by a linocut showing the young master in tears alongside the open coffin, it appeared in the pages of the school magazine. A slow fuse had been lit. 25 years later (in 1976) I wrote my first stage play, *Writer's Cramp*, a scherzo in J Minor for trio. This was followed by *The Slab Boys* (part 1 of a trilogy) based (but heavily embroidered) upon my own experience of working as a retarded teenager in the design studio of a carpet factory. Next came *Normal Service*, in the original draft densely packed with all sorts of motley stuffs like the haggis, but subsequently "opened up" for the stage, again based (however loosely) on a working experience, this time in television. I was trying in *Normal Service* to write a comedy without jokes, a comedy of manners, of character, the relationships within and without the office, the characters' attitudes towards one another, towards their own and each others' spouses, to their work. I can't be certain I've got the skill to cram all of that into two hours or so, which is part of the reason for my writing the aforementioned trilogy (in which the protagonists in Parts 1 and 2 are moved on 20-odd years in Part 3). In effect *The Slab Boys* trilogy will be one long play in three acts. In *Hooray for Hollywood* I transplanted the hero (F.S. McDade) of *Writer's Cramp* from Paisley to Los Angeles and looked on with mounting alarm as he proceeded to behave quite predictably. This was a ten-minute piece (part of an anthology) commissioned by the Actors' Theatre of Louisville. The distaff side of *Writer's Cramp, Cara Coco* (at present being rewritten), was presented by Borderline Theatre Co. in Scotland. Just now I am working on a play set in another country (other than Scotland, that is) and on one set in another time (not based on personal experience).

* * *

John Byrne was born in Paisley, a suburb of Glasgow, in 1940 and draws heavily on his past experiences and his Scottish upbringing and adolescence for his stage writing. Unlike many of his contemporaries Byrne didn't have any success as a writer until early middle age. This success came in 1977 with his first play, *Writer's Cramp*, which transferred to London from the

Edinburgh Festival and was subsequently revived. Until then Byrne had earned his living as a designer and painter, having studied art before spells in carpet manufacture and in television, periods on which he was to draw in subsequent plays. Byrne had dealings with the trendy world of art and pop music, particularly in the swinging 1960's when he had an exhibition in London and was even accorded a profile in one of the Sunday supplements. Byrne *also* designed LP covers and dust jackets for contemporaries such as comedian Billy Connolly and singer Gerry Rafferty and worked as a scene painter with the celebrated Scottish touring group 7:84. His contempt for the art world has led him to quit it for good and embrace the theatrical world not only as an alternative source of inspiration but, in his view, as a superior way of life. Nevertheless his painter's preoccupation with detail and his gifts of observation are stamped boldly on his work for the stage.

Writer's Cramp is an often very funny and accurate extended literary joke which parodies the styles and pretensions of arty Scotland, through the life and times of one Francis Seneca McDade. McDade, a writer, painter, and belle lettrist as well as a loveable but irredeemable mediocrity, is shown progressing from disaster to disaster: prep school, prison, literary Oxford, and swinging London, before his final demise clutching a hard-won but rather irrelevant wad of bank notes. Included among the send-ups and satires which intersperse the scenes in question are an article on Work-shy Pensioners and a disastrous musical on Dr. Spock, the latter like much of McDade's canon not advanced much further than the planning stage. However, McDade does acquire brief fame in the 1960's as an artist following a typical review from the art critic of the *Scottish Field*, one Dermot Pantalone: "When I quizzed the artist as to why so many of his pictures were painted on Formica using household brushes, his answer was to pick up a pot of Banana Yellow Deep Gloss Enamel and proceed to draw the outline of a giraffe on my overcoat. . . ." McDade and his world of poseurs and eccentrics were a rather easy target for Byrne's obvious comic and linguistic gifts. His second play, first seen at the Traverse Theatre in Edinburgh, and later in London and on television, was a very different affair. *The Slab Boys* is a lively piece of social realism cum situation comedy set in the paint-mixing room of a Glasgow carpet factory in 1957, and it draws heavily on Byrne's own past as an apprentice. The play, fiercely idiomatic and full of pungent one-liners and shop-floor banter, details a working day, in particular that of three very different apprentices: Phil, the small young rebel with a secret urge to be a painter; Spanky, the heavy and slow pal of Phil's; and Hector, shy and domiciled with an over-protective mother. It is Hector's attempt to make himself ready and presentable for the forthcoming staff dance which provides the piece with most of its narrative drive, although it is Byrne's gift for recreating the trends and preoccupations of the period (from hit parade to comic book heroes and hairstyles) and his raucous sense of character and speech which made the play such a success.

Certainly Byrne's subsequent plays have also revealed an interest in character over narrative. *Threads* (originally *The Loveliest Night of the Year*) takes the action of *The Slab Boys* on to the evening of the "staffie" or firm dance. The dialogue is similarly colloquial, strident, and often witheringly amusing, but the action runs out of steam and relies on a series of farcical encounters in the dark which are poor compensation for the loss of the setting of the marvelously evocative slab room in the first play. Nevertheless Byrne still manages to provide the occasional telling visual effect (such as the glaring imprint of a flat iron on the back of Phil's otherwise immaculate white tuxedo).

Normal Service, which equally obviously draws on Byrne's experiences (this time as a designer for Scottish Television in the early 1960's), is set in the design room of such an organisation during a weekend in 1963 when the station's special tenth anniversary programme is due to be recorded. It depicts the internecine strife of the assembled workers who range from a cowardly, trendy media man with a kilt, to a decrepit and hilariously unsuccessful repair man, a weedy expectant father to a demonic trade-union official of Italian descent who declares war every time he answers a ringing phone. Indeed in the resulting chaos the characters and their interplay holds more sway over the audience than any development of storyline or message about technology and the chaotically minded people who service it daily.

Byrne's last substantial stage work, *Candy Kisses*, shows that his comic terrain can extend beyond Glasgow or London. It is set in 1963 in Italy where the visit of Pope Paul VI to Perugia is greeted with murderous intent by a demented fascist professor and two youthful locals with differing degrees of commitment to a Trotskyist terror group. There are varying supports: an East Coast American art student meets a draft-dodging West Coast twerp; a German fraulein attempts restoration of a Perugino fresco. Cleverly the local Italians speak with either Scots, Welsh, or Irish accents, a device which further isolates the cultural imperialists and foreigners. The plot unravels like a plate of spaghetti, although the play is hardly as substantial.

Byrne may not have kept up his steady output for the stage (though there is an amusing but insubstantial radio satire, *The Nitshill Writing Circle* which takes us back to *Writer's Cramp* territory) but he was acclaimed in 1987 for his television series *Tutti Frutti*, a whacky saga of an ageing Scottish rock-soul band on the road which starred among others one of the original Slab Boys, Robbie Coltrane. Perhaps this is the future direction for one of Britain's more engaging and unpretentious comic talents.

—Steve Grant

CAMPTON, David. British. Born in Leicester, 5 June 1924. Educated at Wyggeston Grammar School, 1935–41, matriculation 1940. Served in the Royal Air Force, 1942–45; in the Fleet Air Arm, 1945–46. Clerk, City of Leicester Education Department, 1941–49, and East Midlands Gas Board, Leicester, 1949–56. Recipient: Arts Council bursary, 1958; British Theatre Association Whitworth prize, 1975, 1978, 1985; Japan Prize, for radio play, 1977. Agent: ACTAC (Theatrical and Cinematic) Ltd., 16 Cadogan Lane, London S.W.1. Address: 35 Liberty Road, Glenfield, Leicester LE3 8JF, England.

PUBLICATIONS

Plays

Going Home (produced Leicester, 1950). Manchester, Abel Heywood, 1951.
Honeymoon Express (produced Leicester, 1951). Manchester, Abel Heywood, 1951.
Change Partners (produced Leicester, 1952). Manchester, Abel Heywood, 1951.
Sunshine on the Righteous (produced Leicester, 1953). London, Rylee, 1952.

The Laboratory (produced Leicester and London, 1954). London, J. Garnet Miller, 1955.
Want a Bet? (produced Leicester, 1954).
Ripple in the Pool (produced Leicester, 1955).
The Cactus Garden (produced Reading, Berkshire, 1955). London, J. Garnet Miller, 1955.
Dragons Are Dangerous (produced Scarborough, 1955).
Idol in the Sky, with Stephen Joseph (produced Scarborough, 1956).
Doctor Alexander. Leicester, Campton, 1956.
Cuckoo Song. Leicester, Campton, 1956.
The Lunatic View: A Comedy of Menace (includes *A Smell of Burning, Then . . ., Memento Mori, Getting and Spending*) (produced Scarborough, 1957; New York, 1962; *Then . . .* produced London, 1980). Scarborough, Studio Theatre, 1960; *A Smell of Burning, and Then . . .* published New York, Dramatists Play Service, 1971.
Roses round the Door (as *Ring of Roses*, produced Scarborough, 1958). London, J. Garnet Miller, 1967.
Frankenstein: The Gift of Fire, adaptation of the novel by Mary Shelley (produced Scarborough, 1959). London, J. Garnet Miller, 1973.
Little Brother, Little Sister (produced Newcastle-under-Lyme, 1961; London, 1966). Leicester, Campton, 1960.
A View from the Brink (playlets; produced Scarborough, 1960). Section entitled *Out of the Flying Pan* included in *Little Brother, Little Sister and Out of the Flying Pan*, 1970.
Four Minute Warning (includes *Little Brother, Little Sister, Mutatis Mutandis, Soldier from the Wars Returning, At Sea*) (produced Newcastle-under-Lyme, 1960; *Soldier from the Wars Returning* produced London, 1961; *Mutatis Mutandis* produced London, 1967). Leicester, Campton, 4 vols., 1960.
Funeral Dance (produced Dovercourt, Essex, 1960). London, J. Garnet Miller, 1962.
Sketches in *You, Me and the Gatepost* (produced Nottingham, 1960).
Sketches in *Second Post* (produced Nottingham, 1961).
Passport to Florence (as *Stranger in the Family*, produced Scarborough, 1961). London, J. Garnet Miller, 1967.
The Girls and the Boys (revue; produced Scarborough, 1961).
Silence on the Battlefield (produced Dovercourt, Essex, 1961). London, J. Garnet Miller, 1967.
Sketches in *Yer What?* (produced Nottingham, 1962).
Usher, adaptation of the story "The Fall of the House of Usher" by Poe (also director: produced Scarborough, 1962; London, 1974). London, J. Garnet Miller, 1973.
Incident (produced 1962). London, J. Garnet Miller, 1967.
A Tinkle of Tiny Bells (broadcast 1963; produced Cumbernauld, Dumbartonshire, 1971).
Comeback (produced Scarborough, 1963; revised version, as *Honey, I'm Home*, produced Leatherhead, Surrey, 1964).
Don't Wait for Me (broadcast 1963; produced London, 1963). Published in *Worth a Hearing: A Collection of Radio Plays*, edited by Alfred Bradley, London, Blackie, 1967.
Dead and Alive (produced Scarborough, 1964). London, J. Garnet Miller, 1983.
On Stage: Containing Seventeen Sketches and One Monologue. London, J. Garnet Miller, 1964.
Resting Place (broadcast 1964; in *We Who Are about to . . .*, later called *Mixed Doubles*, produced London, 1969). London, Methuen, 1970.
The End of the Picnic (broadcast 1964; produced Vancouver, British Columbia, 1973). Included in *Laughter and Fear*, 1969.
The Manipulator (broadcast 1964; shortened version, as *A Point of View*, produced 1964; as *The Manipulator*, produced 1968). London, J. Garnet Miller, 1967.
Cock and Bull Story (produced Scarborough, 1965).
Where Have All the Ghosts Gone? (broadcast 1965). Included in *Laughter and Fear*, 1969.
Split Down the Middle (broadcast 1965; produced Scarborough, 1966). London, J. Garnet Miller, 1973.
Two Leaves and a Stalk (produced 1967). London, J. Garnet Miller, 1967.
Angel Unwilling (broadcast 1967; produced 1972). Leicester, Campton, 1972.
More Sketches. Leicester, Campton, 1967.
Ladies' Night: Four Plays for Women (includes *Two Leaves and a Stalk, Silence on the Battlefield, Incident, The Manipulator*). London, J. Garnet Miller, 1967.
Parcel (broadcast 1968). London, French, 1979.
The Right Place (produced 1970). Leicester, Campton, 1969.
Laughter and Fear: 9 One-Act Plays (includes *Incident, Then . . ., Memento Mori, The End of the Picnic, The Laboratory, A Point of View, Soldier from the Wars Returning, Mutatis Mutandis, Where Have All the Ghosts Gone?*). London, Blackie, 1969.
On Stage Again: Containing Fourteen Sketches and Two Monologues. London, J. Garnet Miller, 1969.
The Life and Death of Almost Everybody (produced London, 1970). Leicester, Campton, 1971; New York, Dramatists Play Service, 1972.
Now and Then (produced 1970). Leicester, Campton, 1973.
Little Brother, Little Sister; and Out of the Flying Pan. London, Methuen, and New York, Dramatists Play Service, 1970.
Timesneeze (produced London, 1970). London, Eyre Methuen, 1974.
Wonderchick (produced Bristol, 1970).
Jonah (produced Chelmsford, Essex, 1971). London, J. Garnet Miller, 1972.
The Cagebirds (produced Tunbridge Wells, Kent, 1971; London, 1977). Leicester, Campton, 1972.
Provisioning (produced London, 1971).
Us and Them (produced 1972). Leicester, Campton, 1972.
Carmilla, adaptation of a story by Le Fanu (produced Sheffield, 1972). London, J. Garnet Miller, 1973.
Come Back Tomorrow. Leicester, Campton, 1972.
In Committee. Leicester, Campton, 1972.
Three Gothic Plays (includes *Frankenstein, Usher, Carmilla*). London, J. Garnet Miller, 1973.
Eskimos, in *Mixed Blessings* (produced Horsham, Sussex, 1973). Included in *Pieces of Campton*, 1979.
Relics (produced Leicester, 1973). London, Evans, 1974.
An Outline of History (produced Bishop Auckland, County Durham, 1974). Leicester, Campton, 1981.
Everybody's Friend (broadcast 1974; produced Edinburgh, 1975). London, French, 1979.
Ragerbo! (produced Peckleton, Leicestershire, 1975). Leicester, Campton, 1977.
The Do-It-Yourself Frankenstein Outfit (produced Birmingham, 1975). London, French, 1978.
George Davenport, The Wigston Highwayman (produced Countesthorpe, Leicestershire, 1975).
What Are You Doing Here? Leicester, Campton, 1976.
No Go Area. Leicester, Campton, 1976.
One Possessed (broadcast 1977). Leicester, Campton, 1977.
Oh, Yes It Is! (produced Braunston, Northamptonshire, 1977).
Zodiac, music by John Whitworth (produced Melton Mowbray, Leicestershire, 1977). London, French, 1978.

The Great Little Tilley (produced Nottingham, 1978).
After Midnight, Before Dawn (produced Leicester, 1978). London, French, 1978.
Dark Wings (produced Leicester, 1978). Leicester, Campton, 1980.
Pieces of Campton (dialogues; includes *According to the Book, At the Door, Drip, Eskimos, Expectation, Strong Man Act, Sunday Breakfast, Under the Bush, Where Were You Last Winter?*). Leicester, Campton, 1979.
Who Calls? (produced Dublin, 1979). London, French, and Chicago, Dramatic Publishing Company, 1980.
Under the Bush (produced London, 1980). Included in *Pieces of Campton*, 1979.
Attitudes (produced Stoke-on-Trent, 1981). Leicester, Campton, 1980.
Freedom Log. Leicester, Campton, 1980.
Star-station Freedom (produced Leicester, 1981).
Look—Sea, and Great Whales. Leicester, Campton, 1981.
Who's a Hero, Then? Leicester, Campton, 1981.
Apocalypse Now and Then (includes *Mutatis Mutandis* and *The View from Here*) (produced Leicester, 1982).
Olympus (produced Leicester, 1983).
But Not Here (produced Leicester, 1983). Leicester, Campton, 1984.
Two in the Corner (includes *Reserved, En attendant François, Overhearings*). Leicester, Campton, 1983.
En attendant François (produced Chelmsford, Essex, 1984). Included in *Two in the Corner*, 1983.
Who's Been Sitting in My Chair? (produced Chelmsford, Essex, 1984).
So Why? Leicester, Campton, 1984.
Mrs. Meadowsweet (as *Mrs. M.*, broadcast 1984; revised version, as *Mrs. Meadowsweet*, produced Ulverston, Lancashire, 1985). London, French, 1986.
Cards, Cups, and Crystal Ball (produced Broadway, Worcestershire, 1985). Leicester, Campton, 1986.
Singing in the Wilderness (produced Leicester, 1985). London, French, 1986.
Our Branch in Brussels. London, French, 1986.

Radio Plays: *A Tinkle of Tiny Bells*, 1963; *Don't Wait for Me*, 1963; *The Manipulator*, 1964; *Alison*, 1964; *Resting Place*, 1964; *The End of the Picnic*, 1964; *Split Down the Middle*, 1965; *Where Have All the Ghosts Gone?*, 1965; *Angel Unwilling*, 1967; *The Missing Jewel*, 1967; *Parcel*, 1968; *Boo!*, 1971; *Now You Know*, 1971 (Italy); *Ask Me No Questions* (Germany); *Holiday, As Others See Us, So You Think You're a Hero, We Did It for Laughs, Deep Blue Sea?, Isle of the Free, You Started It, Good Money, You're on Your Own, Mental Health, We Know What's Right, When the Wells Run Dry, Our Crowd, Nice Old Stick Really, On the Rampage, Victor, Little Boy Lost*, and *Tramps* (all in *Inquiry* series), from 1971; *Everybody's Friend*, 1974; *One Possessed*, 1977; *I'm Sorry, Mrs. Baxter*, 1977; *Our Friend Bimbo*, 1978, *Three Fairy Tales*, 1979, and *Bang! Wham!*, 1979 (all Denmark); *Community* series (5 episodes for schools), 1979; *Peacock Feathers*, 1982; *Kahani Apni Apni* series, 1983; *Mrs. M.*, 1984.

Television Plays: *One Fight More*, with Stephen Joseph, 1956; *See What You Think* series, 1957; *Starr and Company* (serialization), 1958; *Tunnel under the World*, 1966; *Someone in the Lift*, 1967; *The Triumph of Death*, 1968; *A Private Place*, 1968; *Liar*, 1969; *Time for a Change*, 1969; *Slim John*, with others, 1971; *The Bellcrest Story*, 1972; *People You Meet*, 1972.

Other (for children)

Gulliver in Lilliput. London, University of London Press, 1970.
Gulliver in the Land of the Giants. London, University of London Press, 1970.
The Wooden Horse of Troy. London, University of London Press, 1970.
Modern Aesop Stories. Kuala Lumpur, Oxford University Press, 1976.
Vampyre, from a story by John Polidori. London, Hutchinson, 1986.
Frankenstein. London, Hutchinson, 1987.

*

Critical Studies: *Anger and After* by John Russell Taylor, London, Methuen, 1962, revised edition, 1969, as *The Angry Theatre*, New York, Hill and Wang, 1962, revised edition, 1969; *The Disarmers* by Christopher Driver, London, Hodder and Stoughton, 1964; "Comedy of Menace" by Irving Wardle, in *The Encore Reader*, London, Methuen, 1965; *Laughter and Fear* edited by Michael Marland, 1969; *Investigating Drama* by Kenneth Pickering, Bill Horrocks, and David Male, London, Allen and Unwin, 1974.

Theatrical Activities:
Director: **Play**—*Usher*, Scarborough, 1962.
Actor: **Plays**—roles with Stephen Joseph's Theatre in the Round, Scarborough and on tour, 1957–63, including Petey in *The Birthday Party* by Harold Pinter, Birmingham, 1959, Old Man in *Memento Mori*, London, 1960, Polonius in *Hamlet*, Newcastle-under-Lyme, 1962, Noah in *The Ark* by James Saunders, Scarborough, 1962, and Harry Perkins in *Comeback*, Scarborough, 1963; Cinquemani in *The Shameless Professor* by Pirandello, London, 1959; Bread in *The Blue Bird* by Maeterlinck, London, 1963.

David Campton comments:

Realizing that a play in a drawer is of no use to anyone, and that, being an ephemeral thing, it will not wait for posterity to catch up with it, I have always written with production in mind.

The circumstances of production have varied from the village hall, through radio and television, to the West End stage. (Though representation on that last has been confined to one-act plays and sketches.) This has also meant that my plays have varied in kind from domestic comedy, through costume melodrama to—as Irving Wardle coined the phrase—"comedy of menace."

My profession is playwriting, and I hope I approach it with a professional mixture of art and business. The art of playwriting is of prime importance; I hope I have never relegated it to second place. I have never written a play "because it might sell." Everything I have written has been clamouring to be written and as long as I have been able to make marks on paper, there has always been a queue of a dozen or more ideas waiting their turn to achieve solid form. But an idea can always be developed towards a particular medium, be it experimental theatre in the round or an all-female group performing in a converted schoolroom.

I dislike pigeonholes and object to being popped into one. However, one label that might fit is the title of an anthology of my plays: *Laughter and Fear*. This is not quite the same as comedy of menace, which has acquired a connotation of theatre of the absurd. It is in fact present in my lightest domestic comedy. It seems to me that the chaos affecting everyone today—political, technical, sociological, religious, etc., etc.—is so all-pervading that it cannot be ignored, yet so shattering that it can only be approached through comedy. Tragedy demands firm foundations; today we are dancing among the ruins.

* * *

David Campton is a prolific writer of short plays. The nine plays in *Laughter and Fear* include some of the best of them. *On Stage* and *On Stage Again* are collections of revue-length sketches, and many of his short plays are slight, akin to those traditional short stories that present two or three characters, reveal some significant event in their past to explain their present eccentricities, and end with an unexpected twist. In *Where Have All the Ghosts Gone?*, for example, a sensible young man intrudes on a drunken widow looking for his girlfriend, who has been too ashamed of her mother to bring him home. The mother does her best to break their attachment with a suicide attempt. She is dependent on her daughter, but also blames her for the death of her husband in a car crash, though the daughter was only five years old at the time, and now plays upon her sense of guilt. The young man, however, proposes to the daughter, and in an epilogue the mother tells the audience that the house and garden are restored and she is grandmother to twins. But the twist is still to come: "Just one big happy family. In fact to see me now, you'd never imagine... No, you'd never imagine that I was once a real person."

This is typical Campton territory: the crumbling house, or dowdy flat; the middle-aged or elderly middle-class woman in reduced circumstances as central character (one collection is *Ladies' Night: Four Plays for Women*); and for theme the fight to maintain independence and defend one's individuality, whether unsuccessfully, as in *Where Have All the Ghosts Gone?*, or successfully, as in *The Manipulator*, in which a Volpone-like bedridden woman uses gossip to blackmail, manipulate, and ensure that her daughters do not move her out of her flat. Since Campton's plays exploit the aching articulacies of the middle classes rather than the working-class inarticulacies explored by Pinter, Bond, and Stephen Lowe, it is not surprising that a number of his plays have had radio productions.

Yet from his earliest work with Stephen Joseph's Theatre-in-the-Round in Scarborough, Campton has played with the inherent theatricality of the stage experience. This is particularly true of some of his more recent plays. In *The Life and Death of Almost Everybody*, a stage sweeper conjures characters from his imagination whom he then has trouble controlling. The committee of *In Committee*, meeting onstage, becomes aware, but refuses to acknowledge, that there is an audience present—even when "audience members" one by one replace committee members. And in *Who's a Hero, Then?* the stage is divided into an area representing a club and an "imagination area." At the club Norm is criticized for apparently letting his friend drown; each of his critics enters the imagination area in turn—through which the drowning man's cries ring each time—and does no better. The artificiality of the theatre experience is also implicit in *Timesneeze*, a play for youth performed by the National Theatre in 1970, in which a time-machine moves the hero to different places and periods.

Another kind of theatricality that Campton exploits, more successfully, is linguistic. Like Pinter, he plays with proverbs, catch-phrases, and clichés. *On Stage* includes four sketches about teenagers in which such phrases as "See you around" are by their repetition filled with all that is not being expressed. The committee members in *In Committee* are so tangled in procedural jargon that we never learn what the committee is considering. And in the high-level diplomatic encounter of *Out of the Flying Pan* the words themselves become garbled.

Campton acknowledges the influence of the Theatre of the Absurd. Ionesco's Jack, who demands a bride who is well-endowed, is first cousin to the new father who in *Mutatis Mutandis* has to break the news to his wife of their baby's precocious development of a full head of hair (green), teeth (pointed), and tail. The baby has inherited his eyes—fine brown eyes, all three of them. Similarly reminiscent of Ionesco is *Getting and Spending*, which follows a couple's progress from marriage to old age, pursuing mutual dreams that lead to the offstage proliferation of cots and prams in the nursery, while their dreams distract them from ever actually producing offspring.

It is when the absurd serves Campton's social conscience that he produces his best plays. *Incident* is a parable on racial prejudice, in which an inn refuses admission to a weary traveller because no one named Smith is to be admitted. The most interesting aspect of the play is the way in which Campton shows how Miss Smith's companion is drawn into negotiating a compromise, only to be (rightly) abandoned by Miss Smith. In *Soldier from the Wars Returning* a soldier boasts to a barmaid of his exploits and she hands him an eye-patch, a crutch, and so on, until he leaves the bar a cripple: a parable about war and perhaps an externalizing of the hidden psychological wounds that war inflicts on all participants. *Then...* is a nuclear-holocaust play. A physics teacher and the reigning Miss Europe are the sole survivors; despite the social conventions that they strive to follow, feelings that neither has ever had time for flow between them, but they dare not remove the brown paper bags they wear over their heads. These absurdly slight means of protection, like children's masquerades, and their unperturbedly conventional responses to meeting, convey the frailty and limited vision of human beings, commenting more effectively in ten minutes on the threat of nuclear war than any large-scale television dramatization of the future.

Of Campton's full-length plays, the swift-moving *Jonah*, commissioned for performance at Chelmsford Cathedral in 1971, is the most interesting. Jonah is called on to warn everyone, from businessmen to the cathedral's cleaners, of the imminent destruction of their sinful city. He resists the call, knowing he will be laughed at, and the destruction occurs—though, he and the audience learn, only in a private vision for him. He calls upon people to reform, and they do. But they begin to demand when the destruction will occur and goad Jonah into declaring a date and time. No destruction occurs. No one blames Jonah for false prophecy but at the end of the play he feels humiliated: he has devoted his life to justice and punishment, not to the mercy God has shown. The play could easily be performed with one professional as Jonah and amateurs in the numerous other parts.

Campton is an unfashionable playwright. In an age that finds critically interesting the tough-minded and difficult, the crabbed or elliptical, his inventions seem facile, sometimes workaday, especially in his full-length plays, and sometimes whimsical. His characters are usually articulate, understand each other fairly well, and his humane messages are clear. Some of his short plays deserve repeated production.

—Anthony Graham-White

CANNAN, Denis. British. Born Dennis Pullein-Thompson in Oxford, 14 May 1919; son of the writer Joanna Cannan; brother of the writers Christine, Diana, and Josephine Pullein-Thompson. Educated at Eton College. Served in the Queen's Royal Regiment, 1939–45: mentioned in despatches. Married 1) Joan Ross in 1946 (marriage dissolved), two sons and one daughter; 2) Rose Evansky in 1965. Worked in repertory companies, 1937–39; actor at Citizens' Theatre, Glasgow, 1946–48. Address: 43 Osmond Road, Hove, East Sussex BN3 1TF, England.

PUBLICATIONS

Plays

Max (produced Malvern, Worcestershire, and London, 1949).
Captain Carvallo (produced Bristol and London, 1950). London, Hart Davis, 1952.
Colombe, adaptation of the play by Jean Anouilh (produced London, 1951). London, Methuen, 1952.
Misery Me! A Comedy of Woe (produced London, 1955). London, French, 1956.
You and Your Wife (produced Bristol, 1955). London, French, 1956.
The Power and the Glory, with Pierre Bost, adaptation of the novel by Graham Greene (produced London, 1956; New York, 1958). New York, French, 1959; revised version (produced Edinburgh, 1980).
Who's Your Father? (produced London, 1958). London, French, 1959.
US, with others (produced London, 1966). Published as *US: The Book of the Royal Shakespeare Production US/Vietnam/US/Experiment/Politics . . .*, London, Calder and Boyars, 1968; as *Tell Me Lies . . .*, Indianapolis, Bobbs Merrill, 1968.
Ghosts, adaptation of the play by Ibsen (produced London, 1967).
One at Night (produced London, 1971).
Les Iks, with Colin Higgins, based on *The Mountain People* by Colin Turnbull (produced Paris, 1975; as *The Ik*, produced London and Minneapolis, 1976).
Dear Daddy (produced Oxford and London, 1976; Philadelphia, 1982). London, French, 1978.

Screenplays: *The Beggar's Opera*, with Christopher Fry, 1953; *Alive and Kicking*, 1959; *Don't Bother to Knock* (*Why Bother to Knock*), with Frederic Raphael and Frederic Gotfurt, 1961; *Tamahine*, 1963; *Sammy Going South* (*A Boy Ten Feet Tall*), 1963; *The Amorous Adventures of Moll Flanders*, with Roland Kibbee, 1965; *A High Wind in Jamaica*, with Stanley Mann and Ronald Harwood, 1965; *Mayerling*, with Terence Young, 1968.

Radio Plays: *Headlong Hall*, from the novel by Peacock, 1950; *The Moth and the Star*, from *Liber Amoris* by Hazlitt, 1950; *The Greeting*, from the work by Osbert Sitwell, 1964.

Television Plays: *Heaven and Earth*, with Peter Brook, 1956; *One Day at a Time*, 1977; *Home-Movies*, 1979; *Fat Chance*, from a story by Robert Bloch, 1980; *Picture of a Place*, from a work by Doug Morgan, 1980; *The Best of Everything*, from the novel by Stanley Ellin, 1981; *Way to Do It*, from a work by Jack Ritchie, 1981; *By George!*, 1982; *The Absence of Emily*, from a work by Jack Ritchie, 1982; *The Memory Man*, from a story by Henry Slesar, 1983; *The Last Bottle in the World*, from a story by Stanley Ellin, 1986.

*

Theatrical Activities:
Actor: **Plays**—Richard Hare in *East Lynne*, based on Mrs. Henry Wood's novel, Henley-on-Thames, 1936; roles in repertory theatres, 1937–39; Citizens' Theatre, Glasgow: Hjalmar in *The Wild Duck* by Ibsen, Valentine in *You Never Can Tell* by Shaw, and Hsieh Ping Quei in *Lady Precious Stream* by S.I. Hsiung, and other roles, 1946–48; Ajax and Reporter in *These Mortals* by H.M. Harwood, London, 1949; Sempronius in *The Apple Cart* by Shaw, Malvern, 1949; Kneller in *In Good King Charles's Golden Days* by Shaw, 1949; The Widower in *Buoyant Billions* by Shaw, Malvern and London, 1949, Oliver in *As You Like It*, Bristol, 1950; title role and Octavius in *Julius Caesar*, Bristol 1950; Samuel Breeze in *A Penny for a Song* by John Whiting, London, 1951; Harold Trewitt in *All the Year Round* by Neville Croft, London, 1951. **Film**—*The Beggar's Opera*, 1953. **Television**—*The Rose Without a Thorn*, 1948; *Buoyant Billions*, 1949.

* * *

Denis Cannan is the kind of dramatist who always has a tough time of it in the English theatre: one who attempts to mix the genres. His forte, particularly in the early 1950's, was intelligent, satirical farce, much closer to the world of Giraudoux and Anouilh than that of Rattigan and Coward. After a period of prolonged silence, he dropped the comic mask and launched a couple of direct, frontal assaults on the values of our society; but he still seems a dramatist of manifest talent who has been critically undervalued and unfairly neglected by the public.

Like so many postwar English dramatists, he started out as an actor working his way round the quality repertory companies (Glasgow, Malvern, Bristol); and his first play, *Max*, was in fact staged at the 1949 Malvern Festival when he was also playing three key Shavian roles. The work is of interest now chiefly because it established the theme that was to preoccupy him for several years to come, the barren, life-destroying conflict between opposing ideologies. But it was an uncharacteristic work in that it explored the theme in slightly melodramatic terms.

Cannan really came into his own with *Captain Carvallo*, presented the following year at the St. James's under Laurence Olivier's management. This is an absolutely delightful play, a witty, bubbling farcical comedy about the absurdities of military conflict. Set behind the lines of an unspecified occupied territory, it confronts a pair of ineffectual, peace-loving partisans with a philandering enemy officer in a remote farmhouse. The enemy Captain is interested only in seducing the farm-owner's wife: the partisans, though ordered to kill the Captain, are concerned only with keeping him alive. But, although the tone of the play is light, it makes the perfectly serious point that the only sane attitude to life is to preserve it at all costs.

Misery Me!, which had a short run at the Duchess in 1955, is likewise the work of a man who, in Kenneth Tynan's words, "despises politics and is in no humour for war." And again Cannan puts to the test the English love of categorisation by encasing his theme within a light, semi-farcical framework. The setting is a moth-eaten Arcadian tavern: and the basic conflict is between a Communist and a Capitalist each determined to slay the other. Both hit on the idea of employing a suicidal young intellectual as a hired assassin and so we see two great powers forcing weapons on a man bent only on self-destruction: a resonant and neatly satirical idea in the cold-war atmosphere of mid-1950's Europe. The weakness of the play is that the characters are abstractions invented to illustrate a theme and that the play's affirmation of life boils down in the end to an endorsement of romantic love: but again Cannan shows himself capable of satirising the contemporary condition and of expressing ideas within a popular format.

His other plays of the 1950's were rather less ambitious. *You and Your Wife* was about two fractious married couples trying to sort out their problems while held captive by a couple of gangsters; *The Power and the Glory* was a proficient adaptation (done in conjunction with Pierre Bost) of the Graham Greene novel about a whiskey-priest; and *Who's Your Father?* was an ingenious farce about a snobbish nouveau-riche couple and their daughter's irresponsible fiancé.

But, after a long absence from the theatre, Cannan only surfaced again as joint writer of the Royal Shakespeare Company's corporately devised Vietnam show, *US*. His precise contribution is difficult to disentangle. But we do know that he was author of Glenda Jackson's scorching and passionate indictment of the non-involvement of the English in anything happening outside their shores and that he wrote a very specific attack on the fact that Vietnam is a "reasonable" war. "It is," he said, "the first intellectuals' war. It is run by statisticians, physicists, economists, historians, psychiatrists, mathematicians, experts on everything, theorists from everywhere. Even the atrocities can be justified by logic." In the 1950's Cannan's attack on war had been comic and oblique: now it was impassioned and direct.

One at Night attacks certain aspects of our society with punitive vigour and sharp intelligence, if not with the greatest technical skill. Its hero is a middle-aged ex-journalist and advertising man seeking discharge from a mental institution to which he has been committed after having sexual relations with a girl under 16. He argues to the middle-class hospital tribunal that, far from corrupting an innocent, he has enlarged the girl's emotional experience: but he is steadfastly refused a discharge after shattering the tribunal's complacency by uncovering the hidden fears and frailties of its individual members. What gives the play its urgency is the feeling that Cannan isn't simply exploring a fashionable intellectual thesis (only the mad are sane) but that he is sharing with us a lived-through experience. And he makes, with some power, the point that in our society it is the scramble for wealth and material possessions that increases the incidence of insanity, but that it's the self-same scramble that produces the instant cure-alls and panaceas. It's precisely the point made, in fact, by Ken Loach's film, *Family Life*.

As a dramatist, Cannan has obviously changed course radically. Where once he wrapped his message up in farce and fantasy, he now lays it right on the line. Where once he adopted a deliberately apolitical stance, he now writes with a definite sense of commitment. But, whatever the profound changes in his style and attitude, he still writes with a bristling intelligence and pungent wit. For that reason one hopes the theatre will hear more from him.

—Michael Billington

CARLINO, Lewis John. American. Born in New York City, 1 January 1932. Educated at El Camino College, California; University of Southern California, Los Angeles, 1956–60, B.A. (magna cum laude) in film 1959 (Phi Beta Kappa), M.A. in drama 1960. Served in the United States Air Force, 1951–55. Married Denise Jill Chadwick; three children from previous marriage. Recipient: British Drama League prize, 1960; Huntington Hartford fellowship; Yaddo fellowship; Rockefeller grant. Lives in California. Agent: Gilbert Parker, William Morris Agency, 1350 Avenue of the Americas, New York, New York 10019, U.S.A.

PUBLICATIONS

Plays

The Brick and the Rose: A Collage for Voices (produced Los Angeles, 1957; New York, 1974; London, 1985). New York, Dramatists Play Service, 1959.
Junk Yard. New York, Dramatists Play Service, 1959.
Used Car for Sale. New York, Dramatists Play Service, 1959.
Objective Case (produced Westport, Connecticut, and New York, 1962). With *Mr. Flannery's Ocean*, New York, Dramatists Play Service, 1961.
Mr. Flannery's Ocean (includes *Piece and Precise*) (produced Westport, Connecticut, 1962). With *Objective Case*, New York, Dramatists Play Service, 1961.
Two Short Plays: Sarah and the Sax, and High Sign. New York, Dramatists Play Service, 1962.
The Beach People (produced Madison, Ohio, 1962).
Postlude, and Snowangel (produced New York, 1962).
Cages: Snowangel and Epiphany (produced New York, 1963; Leicester, 1964; *Epiphany* produced London, 1974). New York, Random House, 1963.
Telemachus Clay: A Collage for Voices (produced New York, 1963). New York Random House, 1964.
Doubletalk: Sarah and the Sax, and The Dirty Old Man (produced New York, 1964; *Sarah and the Sax* produced London, 1971). New York, Random House, 1964.
The Exercise (produced Stockbridge, Massachusetts, 1967; New York, 1968). New York, Dramatists Play Service, 1968.

Screenplays: *Seconds*, 1966; *The Fox*, with Howard Koch, 1967; *The Brotherhood*, 1968; *Reflection of Fear*, with Edward Hume, 1971; *The Mechanic*, 1972; *Crazy Joe*, 1973; *The Sailor Who Fell from Grace with the Sea*, 1976; *I Never Promised You a Rose Garden*, with Gavin Lambert, 1977; *The Great Santini*, 1980; *Resurrection*, 1981.

Television Plays: *And Make Thunder His Tribute* (*Route 66* series), 1963; *In Search of America*, 1971; *Doc Elliot* (pilot), 1972; *Honor Thy Father*, from the novel by Gay Talese, 1973; *Where Have All the People Gone?*, with Sandor Stern, 1974.

Novels

The Brotherhood. New York, New American Library, 1968.
The Mechanic. New York, New American Library, 1972.

*

Theatrical Activities:
Director: **Films**—*The Sailor Who Fell from Grace with the Sea*, 1976; *The Great Santini*, 1980; *Class*, 1983.

* * *

Between June, 1963 and May, 1964—less than a year's time—four one-act plays and one full-length work by Lewis John Carlino were produced off-Broadway in New York. They ranged from the vast talent and imagination of *Telemachus Clay* to the burgeoning maturity of *Cages* to the unfulfilled *Doubletalk*. With these plays, Carlino established himself as an American playwright of exceptional quality and promise. The theatre did not hear from him again for four years, as he turned to screenwriting (*Seconds, The Brotherhood*). In 1968 he made his Broadway debut with the sloppy and self-indulgent *The Exercise*, and the catastrophe seems to have driven him permanently from the theatre.

If critics, financial uncertainty, and the unpredictable duration of a play's run are the theatre's risks, however, film writing has its own dangers. Like too many artistic writers caught up in the American commercial maelstrom, Lewis John Carlino was lost in the hurly-burly of a marketplace too busy to notice or care. Nevertheless, the originality and craftsmanship of his stage work endure. He is a playwright who should not forget or be forgotten.

His first notable New York production was a bill of one-act plays—*Cages*. The curtain raiser, *Snowangel*, is a minor look at a constricted intellectual and an earthy prostitute, spelling out the predictable point. The main work of the program, however, is devastating.

Called *Epiphany*, it is about an ornithologist who is discovered by his wife in a homosexual act. In reaction he turns into a rooster. The Kafkaesque metaphor is theatrically powerful, visually striking, and provocative in context. But as he becomes that rooster, clucking and strutting, it turns out that he is laying eggs. Having really wanted to be a hen, he has suffered a breakdown only to find his wife all too willing to strip the coxcomb from the mask he has donned. He need no longer pretend to virility. She turns him into a female and stays to keep him that way.

Although the play came at a time when every other drama seemed to condemn women as man's arch-enemy, Carlino's imaginative story and powerful structure transcended the cliché. The dramatic scheme is faultless and the writing is for actors—something too few playwrights seem capable of doing.

As is often the case, a well received play generates production of a writer's earlier work and, within six months, Carlino's *Telemachus Clay* was presented off-Broadway. One could only again ponder the judgment of producers for here was a drama of tremendous poetry, artistry and stage life—a drama that would never have been presented had it not been for the notices *Cages* received.

Like so many first plays, *Telemachus Clay* is a story of the artist as a young man, in this case drawn parallel to Odysseus's son. It is subtitled *A Collage for Voices*, as indeed it is, the actors perched on stools, facing the audience. The 11 of them play a host of characters, changing time and location with the magic of poetry weaving the fabric of story, thought, event, and emotion in overlapping dialogue and sound.

This is a device that risks pretension and artiness, but in *Telemachus Clay* it succeeds on the sheer beauty of language and the structural control. There are thoughts and dreams, flashbacks, memories, overheard conversation—a score of effects beyond conventional structure and justifying the form. Like *Cages* the play suffers from immature message making, but like it, too, there is a marvellous sense of theatre, of dialogue, of fantasy, and of humor.

Doubletalk underlined the flaws rather than the strengths of these earlier plays—instead of picking up on his technical finesse, strong dialogue, and sense of stage excitement, Carlino stumbled on his inclination toward point-making and his trouble with plots. These two one-act plays used coy notions instead of stories—an old Jewish lady having a chance meeting with a black musician; a virgin having a chance meeting with an aged poet. This coyness came to a head with *The Exercise*—a play about actors, improvisations, reality, and theatricality that threatened to bring Pirandello from his grave if only to blow up New York's Actors Studio, to which this play was virtually a bouquet.

The work output is slim, certainly inconsistent, and no peak of development was ever achieved. Yet, Carlino's playwriting is unmistakably artistic. Its uncertain flowering is tragically representative of too many American writers for the stage.

—Martin Gottfried

CARTER, Lonnie. American. Born in Chicago, Illinois, 25 October 1942. Educated at Loyola University, Chicago, 1960–61; Marquette University, Milwaukee, B.A. 1964, M.A. 1966; Yale University School of Drama, New Haven, Connecticut (Molly Kazan Award, 1967; Shubert Fellow, 1968–69), M.F.A. 1969. Married Marilyn Smutko in 1966 (divorced 1972). Taught writing at Marquette University, 1964–65, Yale University School of Drama, 1974–75, Rockland Community College, Suffern, New York, University of Connecticut, Storrs, and New York University, 1979–86; Jenny McKean Moore Fellow, George Washington University, Washington, D.C., 1986–87. Recipient: Peg Santvoord Foundation fellowship, 1969, 1970; Guggenheim fellowship, 1971; National Endowment for the Arts grant, 1974, 1983; CBS Foundation grant, 1974; Connecticut Commission on the Arts grant, 1976; Open Circle award, 1978; PEN grant, 1978. Address: Cream Hill Road, West Cornwall, Connecticut 06796, U.S.A.

PUBLICATIONS

Plays

Adam (produced Milwaukee, 1966).
Another Quiet Evening at Home (produced New Haven, Connecticut, 1967).
If Beauty's in the Eye of the Beholder, Truth Is in the Pupil Somewhere Too (produced New Haven, Connecticut, 1969).
Workday (produced New Haven, Connecticut, 1970).
Iz She Izzy or Iz He Ain'tzy or Iz They Both, music by Robert Montgomery (produced New Haven, Connecticut, 1970; New York, 1972). Included in *The Sovereign State of Boogedy Boogedy and Other Plays*, 1986.
More War in Store, and Time Space (produced New York, 1970).
Plumb Loco (produced Stockbridge, Massachusetts, 1970).
The Big House (produced New Haven, Connecticut, 1971).
Smoky Links (produced New York, 1972).
Watergate Classics, with others (produced New Haven, Connecticut, 1973). Published in *Yale/Theatre* (New Haven, Connecticut), 1974.

Cream Cheese (produced New York, 1974).
Trade-Offs (produced New Haven, Connecticut, 1976; New York, 1977).
Bleach (produced Chicago, 1977).
Bicicletta (produced New York, 1978). Included in *The Sovereign State of Boogedy Boogedy and Other Plays*, 1986.
Victoria Fellows (produced Baltimore, 1978).
Sirens (produced New York, 1979).
The Sovereign State of Boogedy Boogedy (produced Chicago, 1985; New York, 1986). Included in *The Sovereign State of Boogedy Boogedy and Other Plays*, 1986.
The Sovereign State of Boogedy Boogedy and Other Plays (includes *Iz She Izzy or Iz He Ain'tzy or Iz They Both, Waiting for G, Bicicletta, Necktie Party*). West Cornwall, Connecticut, Locust Press, 1986.

Radio Plays: *Certain Things about the Trombone*, 1982; *Lulu*, 1983.

Television Play: *From the Top*, 1976.

* * *

While Lonnie Carter was studying playwriting at Yale University School of Drama he spent most of his time not writing plays, but rather attending movie retrospectives of Buster Keaton, Charlie Chaplin, the Marx Brothers, and W.C. Fields. Spending hours watching these classic comedies, he saw something in the basic physiognomy of the characters that he was trying to do verbally in his own plays. He then decided to write his own slapstick farce, *The Big House*, using a Marx Brothers film as a springboard.

Employing the original plot of the film, in which three conmen take over a prison and lock up the warden, he used the film's basic characters of Groucho, a cockney Chico, Harpo, and a minister made up to look like Chaplin. Carter's only additions were a few songs and dances. Basically what Carter ended up with was a hodge-podge of 1920's and 1930's movie comedies. The play is filled with low comedy hijinks, pratfalls galore, and very broad burlesque humor. The action proceeds at such a furious pace that by the middle of the second act the audience is out of breath and the playwright out of plot. The main trouble with Carter's *The Big House* lies in the plot and structure. It would have been fine as a one-act play or mini-musical, but it didn't work as a full-length play.

The most popular play Carter has written is called *Iz She Izzy or Iz He Ain'tzy or Iz They Both*. It had its premiere at Yale in 1970, and has since been performed regularly by university and high school drama groups. *Izzy* is set in a chaotic contemporary courtroom where a schizoid judge (Justice "Choo-Choo" Justice; half-male and half-female) is on trial for having committed the premeditated murder of his female self. In *Izzy* Carter once again uses many familiar movie gags, and supplements the action by songs with lovely lyrics that show off his audacious wit. A good example is the song sung by the frustrated Justice (Choo-Choo) Justice near the end of the play: "I'd like to have a baby/A lass or little laddie/But when it saw its mommy/Would it say 'Daddy'?"

Smoky Links is about a revolution on a mythical Scottish golf course. The main revolutionary is a symbolic Oriental golf pro who threatens the whole club while turning the Scottish accent around with his Oriental pronunciation.

In *Smoky Links*, as in most of his plays, Carter wrestles with the subject of justice. All of his main characters, Wolfgang Amadeus Gutbucket in *The Big House*, Justice (Choo-Choo) Justice in *Izzy*, and the Oriental Golf Pro in *Smoky Links*, are in some way frustrated by the law. But the characters' attitude towards justice and the law remains mostly ambiguous, except in the case of the Marx Brothers in *The Big House*. The Marx Brothers are dyed in the wool anarchists and never offer any alternative except total disruption.

Except for the highly derivative *The Big House*, Carter's sharp humor and verbal somersaults remind one more of Restoration comedy or the satires of Rabelais than the oldtime Hollywood comedies. The influence of films is strong, but Carter has also a special, quite obvious talent that has yet to be developed to its fullest extent.

—Bernard Carragher

CAUTE, (John) David. British. Born in Alexandria, Egypt, 16 December 1936. Educated at Edinburgh Academy; Wellington College, Crowthorne, Berkshire; Wadham College, Oxford, M.A. in modern history, D.Phil. 1962; Harvard University, Cambridge, Massachusetts (Henry Fellow), 1960–61. Served in the British Army, in Africa, 1955–56. Married 1) Catherine Shuckburgh in 1961 (divorced 1970), two sons; 2) Martha Bates in 1973, two daughters. Fellow, All Souls College, Oxford, 1959–65; Visiting Professor, New York University and Columbia University, New York, 1966–67; Reader in Social and Political Theory, Brunel University, Uxbridge, Middlesex, 1967–70; Regents' Lecturer, University of California, 1974; Benjamin Meaker Visiting Professor, University of Bristol, 1985. Literary and arts editor, *New Statesman*, London, 1979–80. Deputy Chairman, 1979–80, and Co-Chairman, 1981–82, Writers Guild of Great Britain. Recipient: London Authors' Club award, 1960; Rhys Memorial Prize, 1960. Address: 41 Westcroft Square, London W6 0TA, England.

Publications

Plays

Songs for an Autumn Rifle (produced Edinburgh, 1961).
The Demonstration (produced Nottingham, 1969; London, 1970). London, Deutsch, 1970.
The Fourth World (produced London, 1973).

Radio Plays: *Fallout*, 1972; *The Zimbabwe Tapes*, 1983; *Henry and the Dogs*, 1986.

Television Documentary: *Brecht & Co.*, 1979.

Novels

At Fever Pitch. London, Deutsch, 1959; New York, Pantheon, 1961.
Comrade Jacob. London, Deutsch, 1961; New York, Pantheon, 1962.
The Decline of the West. London, Deutsch, and New York, Macmillan, 1966.
The Occupation. London, Deutsch, 1971; New York, McGraw Hill, 1972.
The Baby Sitters (as John Salisbury). London, Secker and Warburg, and New York, Atheneum, 1978.
Moscow Gold (as John Salisbury). London, Futura, 1980.

The K-Factor. London, Joseph, 1983.
News from Nowhere. London, Hamish Hamilton, 1986.

Other

Communism and the French Intellectuals 1914–1960. London, Deutsch, and New York, Macmillan, 1964.
The Left in Europe since 1789. London, Weidenfeld and Nicolson, and New York, McGraw Hill, 1966.
Fanon. London, Fontana, and New York, Viking Press, 1970.
The Illusion. London, Deutsch, 1971; New York, Harper, 1972.
The Fellow-Travellers. London, Weidenfeld and Nicolson, and New York, Macmillan, 1973.
Collisions: Essays and Reviews. London, Quartet, 1974.
Cuba, Yes? London, Secker and Warburg, and New York, McGraw Hill, 1974.
The Great Fear: The Anti-Communist Purge under Truman and Eisenhower. New York, Simon and Schuster, and London, Secker and Warburg, 1978.
Under the Skin: The Death of White Rhodesia. London, Allen Lane, and Evanston, Illinois, Northwestern University Press, 1983.
The Espionage of the Saints: Two Essays on Silence and the State. London, Hamish Hamilton, 1986.
Left Behind: Journeys into British Politics. London, Cape, 1987.

Editor, *Essential Writings*, by Karl Marx. London, MacGibbon and Kee, 1967; New York, Macmillan, 1968.

*

Critical Studies: *Anger and After* by John Russell Taylor, London, Methuen, 1962, revised edition, 1969, as *The Angry Theatre*, New York, Hill and Wang, 1962, revised edition, 1969; "Rebels and Their Causes" by Harold Hobson, in *Sunday Times* (London), 23 November 1969; "Keeping Our Distance" by Benedict Nightingale, in *New Statesman* (London), 28 November 1969; in *Plays and Players* (London), February 1970; in *Times* (London), 22 July 1971.

David Caute comments:

With one exception, my plays have all been public plays. A "public" play, like a "private" play, is of course populated by individual characters with distinctive personalities, but the real subject lies elsewhere, in some wider social or political issue. Obviously the most elementary problem for the public playwright is to present characters who are not merely ciphers or puppets—words much cherished by critics hostile to didactic theatre.

Songs for an Autumn Rifle, written in 1960, is shaped in the spirit of banal realism. By the time I wrote my next play, *The Demonstration*, seven years later, my attitude towards both fiction and drama had changed. While the necessity of commitment still imposed itself, the old forms of naturalism, realism, and illusionist mimesis seemed incompatible with our present-day knowledge about language and communication. (These ideas are developed more fully in *The Illusion*, 1971.) One is therefore working to achieve a form of self-aware or dialectical theatre which is not only about a subject, but also about the play itself as a presentation—an inevitably distorting one—of that subject. The intention is to stimulate in the audience a greater critical awareness, rather than to seduce it into empathy and catharsis. In my view, for example, the lasting impact of Brecht's *Arturo Ui* consists less in what the play tells us about Hitler than what it tells us about *knowing about Hitler*.

The kind of writing I have in mind must pay far more attention to the physical possibilities of the theatre than did the old realism or well-made play. But whereas the author was once dictator, the modern playwright finds his supremacy challenged by directors or groups of actors. Up to a point this is healthy. But only up to a point! (See my "Author's Theatre," the *Listener*, 3 June 1971.)

One of my plays, *The Fourth World*, is different: a very private play, and, I hope a funny one. It was conceived and delivered all within a week.

* * *

While concern with social and political issues is no longer as rare among English dramatists as it was in the 1940's and early 1950's, there are still very few who are as deeply committed as David Caute, or as deeply interested either in European politics or in committed European playwrights like Sartre. Caute's first play, *Songs for an Autumn Rifle*, was a direct response to the dilemma that the Russian treatment of the 1956 Hungarian uprising created for members of the Party. The central character is the editor of a British Communist newspaper torn between his duty to the Party and his duty to the truth as relayed to him by an honest correspondent. On a personal level he is being pressured by his wife, who is not a Party member, by the doctrinaire daughter of a Party leader who works on his paper and is in love with him, and—indirectly—by his son, a National Serviceman who brings the Cyprus question into the play, first going to military prison for refusing to serve there, then submitting to an Intelligence Officer's persuasions and later being killed.

The play plunges right into its subject matter, with several scenes set in Hungary, showing the disillusioned correspondent of the English paper in argument not only with the Hungarian rebels but with Russian soldiers, whose attitudes are not altogether at one with the orders they have to carry out.

The Demonstration is a much more sophisticated piece of playmaking dramatising the problems of student revolution in terms of drama students at a university who rebel against the play their Professor gives them to perform, insisting on substituting a play about their own experience of repressive authoritarianism at the university. Their play has the same title as the play we are watching, and we are often jerked from one level of theatrical reality to another, when, for instance, a scene between the Women's Dean and a student turns out to be a scene between two students, one of whom is playing the Woman's Dean but can come out of character to make comments on her.

There is a very funny scene of rehearsing a sequence of the Professor's play ironically representing a confrontation between a bearded guerrilla and a single peasant, with interruptions from the students playing the parts, objecting that a bourgeois audience could take comfort from the satire. There is also an effective climax to the whole play when the police constables fail to respond to the Professor's orders to remove the handcuffs from the students they have arrested and the Superintendent's moustache fails to come off when he pulls at it. Reality has taken over.

But there is more theatrical exploitation than dramatic exploration of the no-man's-land between reality and illusion, and the play is not fuelled to fulfil the Pirandellian promise of its first few scenes. There are three main flaws. One is that the basic statement it is making seems to have been too rigidly predetermined instead of being evolved during the course of the writing. The second is that while there is an admirable sympathy in general for the victims of our society—black women not admitted to hairdressing shops, students whose liberty is curtailed by rules that stem from pre-Victorian puritanism—there is not enough sympathy for the private predicaments of the characters, who remain too much like stereotypes. This applies even to the central character, Professor Bright. Caute (who himself resigned from All Souls the year after he helped to organise the Oxford Teach-In on Vietnam) has no difficulty in understanding the dilemma of a son who deplores the rule-worshipping bigotry of the university authorities but still cannot side with the rebellious students against them. So it may be a kind of personal modesty that makes him keep pulling Steven Bright away from the centre of the action. Or it may be the technical failure to provide a character Steven can confide in. Or it may be a determination to focus on social and political rather than personal problems. But his failure to project Steven's ambivalence results in the third flaw—the lack of a firm moral and structural centre. In Act 2 Steven keeps disappearing to leave the stage free for the student actors. He makes two reappearances as an actor himself, in disguise. In the first he is not recognized until after he has made a long speech—an effective *coup de théâtre*. But this does not reveal enough of what he is feeling. Instead he is crowded out by a host of peripheral characters. The stage direction at the beginning of Act 2 Scene 2 tells us that his "maliciously creative hand" can be detected in the presence on the stage of the hippies and drop-outs who reject the political aims of the student revolutionaries, and that he is seen prowling about taking occasional notes and photographs. This is not enough. He should be holding the play together and carrying it forward, even when he is left by the students who take the initiative away from him.

—Ronald Hayman

CHILDRESS, Alice. American. Born in Charleston, South Carolina, 12 October 1920. Educated at schools in Harlem, New York; Radcliffe Institute for Independent Study (scholar), 1966–68, graduated 1968. Married to the musician Nathan Woodard; one daughter. Actress and director, American Negro Theatre, New York, 1941–52; columnist ("Here's Mildred"), Baltimore *Afro-American*, 1956–58. Artist-in-residence, University of Massachusetts, Amherst, 1984. Recipient: Obie award, 1956; Woodward School Book award, 1975; Paul Robeson award, for screenplay, 1977; Virgin Islands Film Festival award, 1977; Radcliffe Graduate Society medal, 1984; African Poets Theatre award, 1985; Audelco award, 1986; Harlem School of the Arts Humanitarian award, 1987. Agent: Flora Roberts Inc., 157 West 57th Street, New York, New York 10019, U.S.A.

PUBLICATIONS

Plays

Florence (also director: produced New York, 1949). Published in *Masses and Mainstream* (New York), October 1950.
Just a Little Simple, adaptation of stories by Langston Hughes (produced New York, 1950).
Gold Through the Trees (produced New York, 1952).
Trouble in Mind (produced New York, 1955). Published in *Black Theatre: A Twentieth-Century Collection of the Work of Its Best Playwrights*, edited by Lindsay Patterson, New York, Dodd Mead, 1971.
Wedding Band (produced Ann Arbor, Michigan, 1966; New York, 1972). New York, French, 1974.
The World on a Hill, in *Plays to Remember*. New York, Macmillan, 1968.
Young Martin Luther King (produced on tour, 1969).
String, adaptation of a story by Maupassant (produced New York, 1969). With *Mojo*, New York, Dramatists Play Service, 1971.
Wine in the Wilderness (televised 1969; produced New York, 1976). New York, Dramatists Play Service, 1970.
Mojo (produced New York, 1970). With *String*, New York, Dramatists Play Service, 1971.
When the Rattlesnake Sounds (for children). New York, Coward McCann, 1975.
Let's Hear It for the Queen (for children). New York, Coward McCann, 1976.
Sea Island Song (produced Charleston, South Carolina, 1977).
Gullah (produced Amherst, Massachusetts, 1984).
Moms: A Praise Play for a Black Comedienne, music and lyrics by Childress and Nathan Woodard (produced New York, 1987).

Screenplay: *A Hero Ain't Nothin' But a Sandwich*, 1977.

Television Play: *Wine in the Wilderness*, 1969.

Novel

A Short Walk. New York, Coward McCann, 1979.

Other

Like One of the Family: Conversations from a Domestic's Life. New York, Independence, 1956.
A Hero Ain't Nothin' But a Sandwich (for children). New York, Coward McCann, 1973.
Rainbow Jordan (for children). New York, Coward McCann, 1981.

Editor, *Black Scenes: Collections of Scenes from Plays Written by Black People about Black Experience*. New York, Zenith, 1971.

*

Critical Studies: articles by Gayle Austin and Polly Holliday, in *Southern Quarterly* (Hattiesburg, Mississippi), Spring 1987.

Theatrical Activities:
Director: **Play**—*Florence*, New York, 1949.
Actress: **Plays**—Dolly in *On Strivers Row* by Abram Hill, New York, 1940; Polly Ann in *Natural Man* by Theodore Browne, 1941; Blanche in *Anna Lucasta* by Philip Yordan, New York, 1944.

* * *

The career of Alice Childress evidences the difficulty of earning major recognition in the world of theatre. Despite an Obie award, international production of her work, collegiate and professional recognition of her play *Wedding Band*, and a Harvard appointment to the Radcliffe Institute, Childress, a talented actress, director, and writer, has not received the attention lavished on some of her more sensational or more controversial contemporaries.

Born in Charleston, South Carolina, and brought up in Harlem, she began her career in theatre by studying acting with the American Negro Theatre. During the 12 years she worked with that company as actress, director, and author, Childress supported herself with a variety of jobs. The struggle to maintain the dream of a career in theatre forms the theme of *Florence*, a short story subsequently adapted into a play. In the most telling incident of the play, a black mother, angered by a white woman's assumption that security as a domestic is ample opportunity for a black woman, encourages her daughter to continue to seek her dream regardless of the cost.

The best known of Childress's other plays are *Gold Through the Trees, Just a Little Simple, Trouble in Mind*, and *Wedding Band*. Even a brief account of some of these reveals the variety of her interests. *Just a Little Simple* is a dramatic adaptation of Langston Hughes's *Simple Speaks His Mind*, a collection of dialogue narratives focused on Jesse B. Semple ("Simple"), a black man characterized by pride and keen insight into the follies of prejudice and hypocrisy. *Wedding Band*, the drama of an interracial romance, featured Ruby Dee in a Professional Theatre Production at the University of Michigan and Eartha Kitt in the New York production. *Like One of the Family* is a series of satiric monologues by a black domestic who, in temperament and character, might be considered a soul sister of Simple. *Black Scenes*, an anthology of scenes from plays by black authors, is a collection intended for people who wish to use scenes from black experience for auditions or classroom study.

In several respects, her most interesting play is *Trouble in Mind*, which reveals the difficulties experienced by blacks as performers and as images in American theatre. The story takes place during a rehearsal of a play which the white director praises as a powerful and controversial protest against lynching. The director, who identifies himself as a liberal, does not perceive that the theme is outdated, the images of whites are polemically flattering, and the images of blacks are demeaning. Consequently, the black performers, seeking theatrical work to support themselves and further their dreams, must decide whether to withdraw from the play or to abet the perpetuation of derogatory stereotypes of black people.

—Darwin T. Turner

CHURCHILL, Caryl. British. Born in London, 3 September 1938. Educated at Trafalgar School, Montreal, 1948–55; Lady Margaret Hall, Oxford, 1957–60, B.A. in English 1960. Married David Harter in 1961; three sons. Resident dramatist, Royal Court Theatre, London, 1974–75. Recipient: Richard Hillary Memorial Prize, 1961; Obie award, 1982, 1983; Susan Smith Blackburn Prize, 1983; *Time Out* award, 1987. Agent: Margaret Ramsay Ltd., 14-A Goodwin's Court, London WC2N 4LL. Address: 12 Thornhill Square, London N.1, England.

PUBLICATIONS

Plays

Downstairs (produced Oxford, 1958; London, 1959).
Having a Wonderful Time (produced Oxford and London, 1960).
Easy Death (produced Oxford, 1962).
The Ants (broadcast 1962). Published in *New English Dramatists 12*, London, Penguin, 1968.
Schreber's Nervous Illness (broadcast 1972; produced London, 1972).
Owners (produced London, 1972; New York, 1973). London, Eyre Methuen, 1973.
Perfect Happiness (broadcast 1973; produced London, 1974).
Moving Clocks Go Slow (produced London, 1975).
Objections to Sex and Violence (produced London, 1975). Published in *Plays by Women 4*, edited by Michelene Wandor, London, Methuen, 1985.
Light Shining in Buckinghamshire (produced Edinburgh and London, 1976). London, Pluto Press, 1978.
Vinegar Tom (produced Hull and London, 1976). London, TQ Publications, 1978.
Traps (produced London, 1977; Chicago, 1982). London, Pluto Press, 1978.
Floorshow, with others (produced London, 1978).
Cloud Nine (produced Cardiff and London, 1979; New York, 1981). London, Pluto Press, 1979.
Three More Sleepless Nights (produced London, 1980; San Francisco, 1984).
Top Girls (produced London and New York, 1982). London, Methuen, 1982; revised version, Methuen, and New York, French, 1984.
Fen (produced Wivenhoe, Essex, London, and New York, 1983). London, Methuen, 1983.
Softcops (produced London, 1984). London, Methuen, 1984.
Midday Sun, with Geraldine Pilgrim, Pete Brooks and John Ashford (produced London, 1984).
Plays 1 (includes *Owners, Vinegar Tom, Traps, Light Shining in Buckinghamshire, Cloud Nine*). London, Methuen, 1985.
A Mouthful of Birds, with David Lan (produced Birmingham and London, 1986). London, Methuen, 1987.
Softcops, and Fen. London, Methuen, 1986.
Serious Money (produced London and New York, 1987).

Radio Plays: *The Ants*, 1962; *Lovesick*, 1967; *Identical Twins*, 1968; *Abortive*, 1971; *Not, Not, Not, Not, Not Enough Oxygen*, 1971; *Schreber's Nervous Illness*, 1972; *Henry's Past*, 1972; *Perfect Happiness*, 1973.

Television Plays: *The Judge's Wife*, 1972; *Turkish Delight*, 1974; *The After Dinner Joke*, 1978; *The Legion Hall Bombing*, 1978; *Crimes*, 1982.

* * *

Caryl Churchill is probably the most widely published woman playwright in Britain. Her writing career has spanned different media, beginning with radio plays in the 1960's, moving into theatre and television in the 1970's. Her stage plays have been particularly associated with the Royal Court Theatre, but in the mid-1970's she also worked collaboratively with groups, involving a workshop approach to creating plays as well as continuing to write in the more conventional individual mode. Her work spans a range of thematic and formal concerns—linear time and space, the nature of imagined reality—as well as (more recently) wider social and political questions, the latter through her work with Monstrous Regiment and Joint Stock theatre companies.

Her first major stage play, *Owners*, already shows an awareness of the relationship between property ownership, power, and personal exploitation. Reversing the conventional sexual patterns of power, Marion, the main character, is a ruthless property owner, "emasculating" her butcher husband Clegg who takes out his frustrations in sexual and fantasy violence. The play is redolent of the imagery of death, violence, and frustration, as we watch a network of individuals, none of whom have control over their lives. Marion is almost an Ortonesque character, grotesque in the havoc she wreaks; in terms of Churchill's later receptivity to feminism, Marion is more of a male fantasy of female power—de-sexed, monolithic. But the play's power lies in its grasp of the pain of individual characters, written in a spare, poetic, and colloquial idiom that is Churchill's distinction as a stylist. (Her 1987 hit *Serious Money* is written in hilarious couplets.)

Objections to Sex and Violence shows a more explicit interest in socio-political questions. Two sisters meet one another on a seaside-postcard beach; one is a putative terrorist, the other a suburbanite. The play is a vehicle for the debate between the two, with subsidiary characters who are cartoon exemplars of British reaction and repression.

By the mid-1970's Churchill was moving into a new phase with her work, with two "collaborative" plays, both set in the 17th century. *Light Shining in Buckinghamshire* was written for Joint Stock and is a "history" play about the millennial fervour which gripped groups of people during the social upheavals of the time. It includes dramatised documentary material on the merits of freedom and democracy, and is the most overtly political play of ideas she has written to date. *Vinegar Tom*, written for Monstrous Regiment, is by contrast a delicate play about the irrational persecution of women as witches, in which contemporary songs are juxtaposed with the historical material. The combination of styles seems an over-ingenuous appeal to Brechtian alienation techniques, so that the crudity of the songs sits ill on the subtlety of the spoken play. It also has the effect of dividing the audience—the songs are sexually aggressive, aimed (not necessarily consciously) at the men in the audience, while the play itself is sympathetic and accessible to both men and women.

Traps was performed at the Royal Court, although it was in fact written before the two "collaborative" plays. It is Churchill's most exciting and complex foray into the nature of theatrical form—with sections replayed, characters changing their relationships to one another. Formally the play is a set of variations on the theme of the way individuals locate themselves in time and space, teetering sometimes on the edge of sanity, a poignant exploration (though with a rather hastily sentimental end) of the way people define their own realities.

Cloud Nine was again written for Joint Stock, and attempted a more ambitious exploration of sexual politics. The first half, set in Victorian colonial Africa, moves at a semi-farcical pace, showing the relationship between the ideology of imperialism and personal/sexual repression and guilt. The second half leaps a hundred years in historical time, with the characters aging 25 years, a device which is meant to draw parallels between sexual morality then and today. However, the second half is little more than a parade of libertarian life-styles (often movingly drawn), which does not match the sureness of the first half in either form or content. Formally again the play is often daring—the actor playing the paterfamilias in the first half plays a little girl in the second half, to test the audience's responses to gender roles—but the play is an uneasy whole.

Top Girls explores women's existential life decisions across the centuries. The first long scene is notionally set in a restaurant, where a successful businesswoman (Marlene) from the present entertains a group of random women from the past, including Pope Joan and the traveller Isabella Bird. The play then moves into Marlene's life; her present success in business is counterpointed with the emotional chaos of her past; an unresolved conflict with her sister, and an illegitimate and slightly retarded daughter. The play ends with a powerful argument between the two sisters, taking up one of the themes in *Objections to Sex and Violence*. The play makes no judgement on either sister, simply presenting them as having made different choices.

Softcops has an all-male cast, in contrast with the all-female cast of the previous play. It is an elaborate demonstration of some contemporary ideas about "soft" state control, but set in 19th-century France and based on the memoirs of a policeman and a criminal. Both are revealed to share similar characteristics, showing a collusion between the legal and the illegal. The play quotes Bentham and Foucault, and ends with a brief summary of the circular arguments which show that the desire to control unacceptable behaviour can itself lead to formulations of ideas which do not make any sense.

Fen is set in a small rural community in East Anglia, and was also written with Joint Stock. The play lays out a picture of a bleak, barely surviving community, personally unhappy, where the unacceptable (the single woman, the lovers) are ostracised by the community. The theme of fear and superstition from *Vinegar Tom* reappears here, as do the vain and momentary attempts of people to find a space for personal happiness, as in *Traps*. While the picture is poignant and often sympathetic, there is something a little uncomfortable in such a relentlessly bleak picture which occasionally reduces the characters to ciphers in a landscape. But the play is less an analysis of the politics of rural life than a platform on which Churchill returns to some of her familiar themes. Ownership here (unlike that in *Owners*) is merely a backdrop against which a more deep-rooted emotional pessimism and romanticism are poignantly displayed.

Churchill has been receptive to the influences of feminism and the democratic working methods of fringe theatre; she has come to write more consciously about women, and to see her concerns as part of a wider political context. Her more recent work has also included a sympathy towards working-class experience. Her dialogue is spare and telling, her interest in form continuing; she is interested in the way people can attain moments of liberation through the imagination, the vision, the momentary utopia (such as the end of *Traps*), and this gives her an ambivalent attitude to political change. Her work touches again and again on the issues of sexual and class power and on the solutions individuals find for themselves—and her plays alternate between the philosophical and the political in a way that few women writers have achieved. It will be interesting to see whether her future work centers on the philosophical or the political.

—Michelene Wandor

CLARK, Brian (Robert). British. Born in Bournemouth, Hampshire, 2 June 1932. Educated at Merrywood Grammar School, Bristol; Redland College of Education, Bristol, teaching certificate 1954; Central School of Speech and Drama, London, 1954–55; Nottingham University, B.A. (honours) in English 1964. Served in the Royal Corps of Signals, 1950–52. Married 1) Margaret Paling in 1961, two sons; 2) Anita Modak in 1983, one stepson and one stepdaughter. Schoolteacher, 1955–61 and 1964–68; Staff Tutor in Drama, University of Hull, 1968–72. Founder, Amber Lane Press, Ashover, Derbyshire, 1978–79, Ambergate, Derbyshire, 1980–81, and Oxford since 1982. Recipient: *Evening Standard* award, 1978. Agent: Judy Daish Associates, 83 Eastbourne Mews, London W2 6LQ, England.

PUBLICATIONS

Plays

Lay By, with others (produced Edinburgh and London, 1971). London, Calder and Boyars, 1972.
England's Ireland, with others (produced Amsterdam and London, 1972).
Truth or Dare? (produced Hull, 1972).
Whose Life Is It Anyway? (televised 1972; revised version produced London and Washington, D.C., 1978; New York, 1979). Ashover, Derbyshire, Amber Lane Press, 1978; New York, Dodd Mead, 1979.
Post Mortem (produced London, 1975). Published in *Three One-Act Plays*, Ashover, Derbyshire, Amber Lane Press, 1979.
Campion's Interview (produced London, 1976; New York, 1978–79).
Can You Hear Me at the Back? (produced London, 1979). Ashover, Derbyshire, Amber Lane Press, 1979.
Switching in the Afternoon; or, As the Screw Turns (produced Louisville, 1980).
Kipling (produced London and New York, 1984).
All Change at the Wells, with Stephen Clark, music by Andrew Peggie (produced London, 1985).
The Petition (produced New York and London, 1986). Oxford, Amber Lane Press, 1986.

Screenplay: *Whose Life Is It Anyway?*, with Reginald Rose, 1981.

Television Plays: *Ten Torrey Canyons*, 1972; *Play in a Manger*, 1972; *Whose Life Is It Anyway?*, 1972; *Achilles Heel*, 1973; *Operation Magic Carpet*, 1973; *A Follower for Emily*, 1974; *Easy Go*, 1974; *An Evil Influence*, 1975; *The Saturday Party*, 1975; *The Eleventh Hour*, with Clive Exton and Hugh Whitemore, 1975; *Parole*, 1976; *A Working Girl*, 1976; *Or Was He Pushed*, 1976; *The Country Party*, 1977; *There's No Place . . .*, 1977; *Happy Returns*, 1977; *Cat and Mouse*, 1977; *A Swinging Couple* (*Crown Court* series), 1977; *Out of Bounds* series, with Jim Hawkins, 1977; *Mirage*, with Jim Hawkins, 1978; *Houston, We Have a Problem*, with Jim Hawkins, 1978; *Telford's Change* series, 1979; *Horse Sense* (*All Creatures Great and Small* series), 1979; *Late Starter*, 1985; *Lord Elgin and Some Stones of No Value*, with others, 1985.

Other

Group Theatre. London, Pitman, 1971; New York, Theatre Arts, 1972.
Out of Bounds (for children; novelization of television series), with Jim Hawkins. London, BBC Publications, 1979.

* * *

Having taught drama in a university and written on group theatre, Brian Clark began his career as a playwright by collaborating with a number of younger radical dramatists on the anti-establishment political shockers *Lay By* and *England's Ireland* for Portable Theatre. There is no little irony in the fact that at about the same time he was writing the original television version of *Whose Life Is It Anyway?*, a play which six years later was to become the great "serious" West End hit of the late 1970's. Such was the critical and popular success of this play that it may be considered to have representative status. Here, it seemed, was a serious writer whose handling of an issue of contemporary relevance was, however entertaining, uncompromised by commercial success.

Whose Life Is It Anyway? concerns the claim by a man who lies in a hospital bed after a road accident, paralyzed from the neck down, to his right to die—that is, to commit suicide by choosing to be taken off the life-support machine. As its title suggests, the play's interest is in the moral argument, which culminates in the good-humored legal confrontation between the specialist, for whom life is an absolute, and the patient, who claims the right to choose suicide (eventually winning his case). The personal relationships between the patient, Ken, and the hospital staff are economically handled and often touching, and the play provides the opportunity for a virtuoso performance of an unusual kind in the central role (Tom Conti's performance was a major factor in its success in London). The dialogue, alert, witty, and highly polished, is one of the play's most attractive features, yet its particular quality points to a major dramatic limitation. Clark is interested only in those elements of his chosen dramatic situation which can readily be verbalized. His dialectical resource is impressive, but the most interesting things about the paralyzed Ken's situation are those matters—most of them to do with psychological states—that are on the edges of the moral and legal dialectics. Ken has chosen to have his life ended and seeks to enforce his wishes with wit and pertinacity, but what of the frustration, anger, depression, and eventual self-resignation that he must be presumed to have experienced? The legal case turns on his mental state, yet psychology is unimportant to the play itself. The arguments are there, but what of the *experience* of being paralyzed?

The problem of verbalization is even more acute in Clark's second full-length stage play, *Can You Hear Me at the Back?*, though here, in a very different situation, the dramatist shows himself to be continually aware of that problem. The play deals with the attempts of the middle-aged chief architect of a New Town to break out of a professional and personal (marital) impasse. The professional planner feels that his life is "planned," devoid of spontaneity (his ideal is a "planned spontaneity"). Although he finally leaves his wife, he has previously refused to take the easy way out by going away with his best friend's wife, who has confessed her love for him. The character himself is aware that he fits only too well the self-pitying cliché of the discontented middle-class white-collar menopausal male, just as he acknowledges that the slickness and facility of his way of speaking is the verbal equivalent of what he abhors about his profession: in both cases a disorderly reality is made to submit to neat abstractions. Yet the necessary critique of the middle-class ethos represented—of which luxuriant self-scorn and guilt are an essential part—is entirely absent. Clark's own failure to reveal in the play a valid alternative way of speaking to that of his main character means that the only perspective on middle-class disillusionment offered by the work is that of the middle-class represented within it.

Implicit in Clark's attempts to combine moral argument with popular theatrical appeal is a keen awareness of an essentially middle-class liberal audience. This emerges explicitly in the quasi-biographical one-man show written for Alec McCowen, *Kipling*. Confronted by an audience composed largely of what he would term "wishy-washy liberals," and resisting crustily any demand for self-revelation, Kipling launches out on "a non-stop elegy of self-justification." The show invites the projected (liberal) audience to re-examine inherited assumptions about Kipling and to question its own beliefs and convictions; yet at least one reviewer saw it as an "accomplished exercise in audience ingratiation," carefully neutralizing a potentially disturbing subject.

Much the same could be said (and was) of Clark's most recent piece, a two-hander called *The Petition*. Here Clark returns to the issue-play mode of *Whose Life Is It Anyway?*, except that in this instance the connection between the public issue ("in a way, the Bomb is the only thing worth writing about") and the private context is not ready-made. Clark's way of making it is thoroughly conventional. The discovery by a retired General that his wife has signed an anti-nuclear petition published in the *Times* prompts disclosure of her terminal illness and of an old sexual infidelity. Arguments about nuclear confrontation and the threat of universal annihilation are thus seen within the context of a purgative conflict within marriage. The characteristic facility of the dialogue tends only to confirm the cosy domestication of a disturbing issue (though the performances of Rosemary Harris and John Mills in London were remarkable). Reviewers mentioned William Douglas-Home and Terence Rattigan.

—Paul Lawley

CLARK, John Pepper. Now writes as J.P. Clark Bekederemo. Nigerian. Born in Kiagbodo, 6 April 1935. Educated at Warri Government College, Ughelli, 1948–54; University of Ibadan, 1955–60, B.A. (honours) in English 1960, and graduate study (Institute of African Studies fellowship), 1963–64; Princeton University, New Jersey (Parvin Fellowship). Married to Ebun Odutola Clark; three daughters and one son. Information officer, Government of Nigeria, 1960–61; head of features and editorial writer, Lagos *Daily Express*, 1961–62; Research Fellow, 1964–66, and Professor of African Literature, 1966–85, University of Lagos. Founding editor, *Horn* magazine, Ibadan; co-editor, *Black Orpheus*, Lagos, from 1968. Founding member, Society of Nigerian Authors. Agent: Andrew Best, Curtis Brown, 162–168 Regent Street, London W1R 5TB, England.

PUBLICATIONS

Plays

Song of a Goat (produced Ibadan, 1961; London, 1965). Ibadan, Mbari, 1961; in *Three Plays*, 1964; in *Plays from Black Africa*, edited by Fredric M. Litto, New York, Hill and Wang, 1968.

Three Plays. London, Oxford University Press, 1964.

The Masquerade (produced London, 1965). Included in *Three Plays*, 1964.

The Raft (broadcast 1966; produced New York, 1978). Included in *Three Plays*, 1964.

Ozidi. Ibadan, London, and New York, Oxford University Press, 1966.

The Bikoroa Plays (as J.P. Clark Bekederemo) (includes *The Boat, The Return Home, Full Circle*) (produced Lagos, 1981). Oxford, Oxford University Press, 1985.

Screenplay: *The Ozidi of Atazi*.

Radio Play: *The Raft*, 1966.

Verse

Poems. Ibadan, Mbari, 1962.

A Reed in the Tide: A Selection of Poems. London, Longman, 1965; New York, Humanities Press, 1970.

Casualties: Poems 1966–68. London, Longman, and New York, Africana, 1970.

Urhobo Poetry. Ibadan, Ibadan University Press, 1980.

A Decade of Tongues: Selected Poems 1958–1968. London, Longman, 1981.

State of the Union (as J.P. Clark Bekederemo). London, Longman, 1985.

Other

America, Their America. London, Deutsch-Heinemann, 1964; New York, Africana, 1969.

The Example of Shakespeare: Critical Essays on African Literature. London, Longman, and Evanston, Illinois, Northwestern University Press, 1970.

The Hero as a Villain. Lagos, University of Lagos Press, 1978.

Editor and Translator, *The Ozidi Saga*, by Okabou Ojobolo. Ibadan, University of Ibadan Press, 1977.

*

Critical Study: *A Critical View of John Pepper Clark's "Three Plays"* by Martin Banham, London, Collins, 1985.

* * *

There is in Africa today the opportunity—felt sometimes as an obligation—for those who belong to the small elite of educated men to play more than one role in society. The same was true of the European Renaissance, and, as the diversity of his activities and publications indicates, John Pepper Clark is a Renaissance man. He has not dedicated himself to the theatre in the way that Wole Soyinka and Efua Sutherland have. Because his energies are scattered, and because his first full-length play was such a departure, to assess his work as a whole is difficult. It may even be that, when his writing career is over, it will be as a poet rather than as a playwright that he seems important.

Clark's best play is probably his first, *Song of a Goat*. The plot is simple: Zifa has lost his virility and his wife Ebiere, in her frustration, turns to make love with his younger brother, Tonye. Zifa is furious, seeking to kill Tonye, who, however, hangs himself. Shamed by his own sterility and by his brother's death, Zifa walks into the sea, drowning himself.

The virtues of the play flow directly from this strong situation. Unfortunately, Clark seeks to shape the play along the lines of Greek tragedy. The self-consciousness of this attempt is typified by the play's title and by the neighbour's function as a Greek chorus. This adds a portentousness to the psychological restlessness of his characters that Clark, here and elsewhere, can suggest so well.

Clark's second play, *The Masquerade*, deals with the son whom Ebiere conceived with Tonye. The son, Tufa, is to marry; as the marriage is about to be celebrated, his parentage is disclosed; his strong-willed affianced, Titi, will not give him up and is shot by her father, who mistakenly thinks she has given herself to Tufa before the marriage ceremony; and in a fight with her father Tufa is accidentally killed, too. Like Oedipus, Tufa is ignorant until halfway through the play of the circumstances of his parentage. Unlike Oedipus, however, Tufa has committed no act which continues the crime of his parents' generation. And so the tragedy has a sense of arbitrariness about it. The sense of the author pushing beyond what a short play will bear is strongest in the character of the mother, whom events drive mad and who, cradling a cat, sings a ditty which sadly lacks the relevance of mad Ophelia's songs:

> Fresh fish at tuppence
> Who'll buy fresh, oh,
> Fresh fish at tuppence.

The play is full of echoes of Shakespeare's great lovers, and one suspects that the play was written as a sophisticated exercise—although any sense of irony remains the author's, uncommunicated to audiences.

The third of Clark's short, poetic plays is *The Raft*. Here the flurry of onstage action of the earlier plays is abandoned. Four men float down a river on a raft of timbers over which they have no control. During the play, one gets chopped up by the propellers of a passing ship to which he swims, and another floats away when the raft splits. As the play ends, the last two are floating out of the mouth of the river in a thick fog. Whatever the characters symbolize—certainly the human condition, and perhaps the four Regions of which Nigeria was then composed—the play is largely an exercise in character revelation, abounding in set-piece descriptions of their past experiences.

Poetic adornment, in the form of set-pieces, increases in each of the short plays. The language itself, however, develops away from a poeticism reminiscent of Christopher Fry and Gerard Manley Hopkins. Clark has always been capable of simple diction which is yet rich with suggestions, as at the opening of *Song of a Goat*:

> Masseur —Your womb
> Is open and warm as a room:
> It ought to accommodate many.
> Ebiere —Well, it seems like staying empty.
> Masseur —An empty house, my daughter, is a thing
> Of Danger. If men will not live in it
> Bats or grass will, and that is enough
> Signal for worse things to come in.
> Ebiere —It is not my fault. I keep my house
> Open by night and day
> But my lord will not come in.

Yet it is only in *Ozidi* that he has resisted the temptation to embroider and has maintained rich but simple language throughout. *Ozidi* is an adaptation of a traditional drama of the Ijaw—among whom all his plays are set. His other plays all have admirably tight structures, but this could hardly be expected of an adaptation from an epic that lasts seven days. It is Clark's first full-length play and he may be deliberately seeking a looser form; certainly, gone with the tight structure is the sense of the playwright's tight control over the characters.

Ozidi has links with Clark's earlier plays: a curse upon a family, bizarrely bloody events, a son obliged to pursue a fate determined by his father. Yet it is, one presumes, a transitional work—though transitional to what is unclear.

—Anthony Graham-White

CLUCHEY, (Douglas) Rick(land). American. Born in Chicago, Illinois, 5 December 1933. Served in the United States Army, 1949–51. Married Teri Cluchey in 1951; one son and one daughter. Convicted of armed robbery in 1955: sentenced to life imprisonment at San Quentin State Prison, California; paroled, 1966. Founder and executive director, San Quentin Prison Theatre Group, 1957–66.

PUBLICATIONS

Plays

The Cage (produced San Quentin, California, 1965; New York, 1970; London, 1973). San Francisco, Barbuire Press, 1970.
The Wall Is Mama (produced Edinburgh and London, 1974).
The Bug, with R.S. Bailey (produced Edinburgh, 1974).

*

Theatrical Activities:
Director: **Plays**—*In the Zone* by Eugene O'Neill, *Hughie* by Eugene O'Neill, *The Caretaker* by Harold Pinter, *Deathwatch* by Jean Genet, *Krapp's Last Tape* by Samuel Beckett, *The Cage, The Wall Is Mama, The Iceman Cometh* by Eugene O'Neill, *The Execution of Eddie Slovik, Escurial* by Michel de Ghelderode, and *Don Juan in Hell* by Shaw, 1957–75; *Endgame* by Beckett, London, 1978.
Actor: **Plays**—in his own directed plays, and in *Stalag 17* by Donald Bevan and Edmund Trzcinski, *Time Limit* by Henry Denker and Ralph Berkey, *Room Service* by John Murray and Allen Boretz, *Of Mice and Men* by John Steinbeck, *Inherit the Wind* by Jerome Lawrence and Robert E. Lee, *Brother Orchid, Waiting for Godot* by Samuel Beckett, *The Dock Brief* by John Mortimer, *Endgame* by Samuel Beckett, *The Advocate* by Robert Noah, *The Brig* by Kenneth H. Brown, *The Dumb Waiter* by Harold Pinter, *People Need People* by H.F. Greenberg, *Krapp's Last Tape* by Samuel Beckett, and *The Bug*, 1957–77; 5 roles in *Edmond* by David Mamet, New York, 1982.

Rick Cluchey comments:

(1977) I became involved with theatre while serving time at San Quentin. Prior to November 1957, no live drama had been seen within the walls of the prison since the turn of the century when Sarah Bernhardt's troupe entertained the convicts. Thus, when the San Francisco Actors Workshop production of Samuel Beckett's *Waiting for Godot* was taged in our north dining hall, the several hundred inmates who saw the play fairly howled their satisfaction, and the Warden gave his approval to the formation of our own drama group. Our theatrical program took time developing. Drama activity was in the main looked upon as something for sissies and homosexuals, child molesters and rapists. This attitude took time to overcome, but the program gradually gained acceptance and approval. Since no female was allowed to participate, and no inmates were allowed to impersonate females, we were limited to plays with all-male casts.

I began as an actor, and for several years (with the help of Al Mandell and, later, Ken Kitch of the San Francisco Actors Workshop) studied acting and directing. Since plays were difficult to find, I began to investigate possibilities of adapting plays for our use. I discovered that the plays of Beckett appeared void of any expository elements and seemed to take on wholly their own reality. There followed a period of several years when we experimented with the works of Beckett, producing *Waiting for Godot, Endgame*, and *Krapp's Last Tape*. We staged productions twice a year for the general public, and weekly for inmates. Martin Esslin visited the workshop in 1963 and was impressed that we were preparing John Mortimer's *The Dock Brief*, and sent us Mrozek's early play *Out at Sea*, which we also produced. Other productions were Solzhenitsyn's *One Day in the Life of Ivan Denisovich* and Kenneth H. Brown's *The Brig*.

Throughout the decade of theatre activity at San Quentin, the inmates themselves were directly responsible for all aspects of production. Outside professional assistance was welcome and warmly received, but only on an advisory level. As a theatre the workshop was committed to social and political themes; oddly the focus of much of this activity, although censored by the prison staff, seemed to point to conditions outside the walls of our own prison. But certainly prison as such was an on-going theme, although nothing could directly be said of our own four-walled hell.

Sadly the San Quentin workshop was closed down in 1967, though almost all of the convicts who'd worked to bring the program to fruition had already been paroled. In May 1967 the first outside production of the Quentin group was staged in Walnut Creek, California, the beginning of a ten-year journey.

* * *

Though Rick Cluchey has lived in relative freedom since December 1966, when he was paroled from his life sentence, he remains metaphorically in prison. Not only is the underworld the subject of his three plays, but he responds as director to confined spaces in which passions rise to explosion. Innocent of orthography and syntax, he writes of the world he knows in the idiom he knows.

While Cluchey was still in San Quentin prison, he composed *The Cage* for performance by the prison theatre group. "We asked the Warden for permission to perform the play," recalls Cluchey, "and he said fine—as long as it isn't about my prison." So Cluchey set his play in France, and the Warden exclaimed after the performance: "I had no idea French prisons were so bad." Though Cluchey had read Genet, the prison was his very own.

Cluchey has reworked the play, but the kernel remains invariant: Jive, a college graduate charged with murdering his girlfriend, is imprisoned in the same "cage" as three lifers—ex-prize fighter Doc, crippled homosexual Al, and mad Hatchet. Both Doc and Al make advances to the newcomer, but Hatchet, whose insanity takes a virulently religious form, places Jive on trial. Hatchet's two cell-mates are accustomed to lending themselves to his fixations and they play Jive's defense counsel and prosecuting attorney. Hatchet is both judge and executioner, finally sentencing Jive to death and strangling him on stage. As Hatchet washes his murderous hands in the toilet-bowl, he addresses the gods: "I have done your will," but then points into the audience to conclude the play: "Your will."

The Wall Is Mama is nominally set outside prison, in the shady darkness of Mother's Bar on the Bowery in New York City. However, the characters have been in prison and are still caged by their criminal past. Duke, a black heroin user and dealer, claims to have kicked dope and is encouraged by his ex-mistress, bar owner Bea. However, two white members of the dope ring believe he has siphoned off heroin for his own use, and they torture him to reveal its whereabouts. Nearly unconscious with pain, Duke nevertheless defies them until Bea seizes their gun and drives them from her bar. In Act 2, several hours later, a homosexual addict seduces a Marine in the presence of Duke, Bea, and a pseudo-preacher. The Marine addresses Duke much as did the gang killers. In a dope trance, Duke then reverts to childhood, seeing Bea as his mother. As she cuddles him, the white killers shoot both. For these rejects of society, the wall *is* mama.

The Bug, written with R.S. Bailey, a San Quentin colleague, is a work in progress. A woman is harassed by obscene phone calls. Two policemen hide in an adjoining apartment, with electronic equipment that will ostensibly identify the source of the calls. But the play merges invasion of privacy into alleged obscenity.

Circumstances have walled Cluchey's life, but he has exchanged the enclosed space of prison for the enclosed space of theatre—an exchange that has liberated him and deepened public perception of prison-fostered brutalities.

—Ruby Cohn

COLLINS, Barry. British. Born in Halifax, Yorkshire, 21 September 1941. Educated at Heath School, Halifax, 1953–61; Queen's College, Oxford. Married Anne Collins in 1963; two sons and one daughter. Teacher, Halifax Education Committee, 1962–63; journalist, Halifax *Evening Courier*, 1963–71. Recipient: Arts Council bursary, 1974; Edinburgh Festival award, 1980. Agent: Lemon and Durbridge Ltd., 24 Pottery Lane, London W11 4LZ, England.

PUBLICATIONS

Plays

And Was Jerusalem Builded Here? (produced Leeds, 1972).
Beauty and the Beast (for children; produced Leeds, 1973).
Judgement (produced Bristol, 1974; London, 1975; Chicago and New York, 1980). London, Faber, 1974; revised version, Ambergate, Derbyshire, Amber Lane Press, 1980.
The Strongest Man in the World (produced Nottingham, 1978; London, 1980). London, Faber, 1980.
Toads (produced Nottingham, 1979).
The Ice Chimney (produced London, 1980).
King Canute (broadcast 1985). Published in *Best Radio Plays of 1985*, London, Methuen, 1986.
Atonement (produced London, 1987).

Radio Play: *King Canute*, 1985.

Television Plays: *The Lonely Man's Lover*, 1974; *The Witches of Pendle*, 1975; *Dirty Washing*, 1985; *Land*, 1987.

* * *

Any script for solo theatre makes extraordinary demands on the creative resources of the performer, especially when, as is common with the genre, there is a virtual absence of stage directions. So Barry Collins's major work, *Judgement*, is deservedly also associated with the actors who have turned the 150-minute monologue into an engrossing theatrical debate: Peter O'Toole, Colin Blakely, and Richard Monette, to name the most successful of those who have done it in a dozen countries. Collins explains that the genesis of *Judgement* lay in an anecdote in George Steiner's epilogue to *The Death of Tragedy* concerning a war atrocity that suggests that God has grown weary of the savagery of man, and, in withdrawing His presence, has precluded tragedy. In the anecdote, a group of imprisoned Russian officers during World War II, abandoned by the Germans, resort to cannibalism; two survivors found by the advancing Russian forces are given a good ("decent") meal and then shot, which, with the incineration of their monastery prison, obliterates the evidence of man's potential for bestiality. Collins infers (though Steiner does not say this) that the survivors were insane, and projects his play from the hypothesis that one of them preserved his sanity, to be able, "dressed in white hospital tunic and regulation slippers," to deliver his Socratic apology to his judges (the theatre audience). His implicit crime is not cannibalism (his fellow survivor would be equally culpable), but sanity: he will "defend obscenities that should strike reason dumb." At the end of the argument, the speaker insists on his right to return to active service, and speaks of himself as someone who has suffered greatly for his country.

That the play is polemical few would doubt; in fact, one way of responding to the speaker's sophistry is interpreting it as the manufacture of the warrior-hero. Theatrically, the play is also something of a milestone, in that it may be seen as an extreme form of naturalism, in which the laboratory animal finds a voice and articulates its experiences before its extermination. This reading is supported by the context that Steiner gives the story: before the Germans left, they released some of their starving police dogs on the prisoners, so that the behaviour is seen as conditioned on various animals. Read in this light, the play poses the question which obsessed writers from Cicero to Zola: what is there about man that places him above the brute beasts? That a taboo has been violated is taken for granted by the judges, whose tribal mentality insists that a scapegoat must be found so that the existence of the taboo may be reinforced, and the dignity of man reasserted; thus in the theatre there is the uncanny atmosphere of a voice coming from "the other side," voicing extraterrestrial mysteries, rather as was presented in the medieval Harrowing of Hell or *Danse Macabre* dramas.

Collins's second attempt at a full-length monologue, *The Ice Chimney*, deals with an attempt by Maurice Wilson at a solo assault on Everest in 1936, and is thus another case of human fortitude braced against superhuman afflictions. Wilson's stature as a man of principle allows a sustained expositional analysis of the circumstances that led to his heroics, but the play never generates the urgency of *Judgement*, and its development seems an awkward amalgam of Milton, Auden, and Golding. In this play, Collins's socialism is not organic to the action, and commitment appears to be to the self rather than to the society.

Though best known for monologues, Collins has also written several large-cast works of epic theatre which articulate dilemmas of socialism with a Brechtian flamboyance and a sometimes Hegelian complexity. His loose documentary about the Luddites, *And Was Jerusalem Builded Here?*, required two choruses, actors with circus skills and singing ability, projections, and costumes based on Tarot cards. Nevertheless, the play does focus on one key character, a pamphleteer, on whom is centred a perplexing array of social and domestic responsibilities. Collins's most successful large-cast play has been *The Strongest Man in the World*, a parable for the theatre about Ivan Shukhov, a Russian miner who wins an Olympic weightlifting title as a consequence of being made to take steroids. The echoes of *Samson Agonistes* in *The Ice Chimney* become rather more explicit here, as the dissident protagonist is initially discovered back in the mines, considering the aetiology of his present condition of muscle-bound impotence, both physical and ideological. The argument of the play does have a close affinity with that of *Judgement*, because Shukhov is acutely conscious of his own state as a (former) Soviet hero descended from a line of such heroes; the retribution visited on him is, again, extreme, and critics have been, predictably, divided in interpreting this as either a portrait of normal Soviet practice or a black cartoon inflating a commonplace to an enormity. Collins's stagecraft would support the latter view.

—Howard McNaughton

CONN, Stewart. British. Born in Glasgow, Scotland, 5 November 1936. Educated at Kilmarnock Academy and Glasgow University. National Service: Royal Air Force. Married Judith Clarke in 1963; two sons. Since 1962 radio drama producer, currently Head of Drama (Radio), BBC, Edinburgh. Literary adviser, Edinburgh Royal Lyceum Theatre, 1973–75. Recipient: Eric Gregory award, for poetry, 1963; Scottish Arts Council Poetry Prize and Publication Award, 1968, award, 1979; *Scotsman* prize, 1981. Lives in Edinburgh. Agent: Harvey Unna and Stephen Durbridge Ltd., 24–32 Pottery Lane, London W11 4LZ, England.

PUBLICATIONS

Plays

Break-Down (produced Glasgow, 1961).
Birds in a Wilderness (produced Edinburgh, 1964).
I Didn't Always Live Here (produced Glasgow, 1967). Included in *The Aquarium, The Man in the Green Muffler, I Didn't Always Live Here,* 1976.
The King (produced Edinburgh, 1967; London, 1972). Published in *New English Dramatists 14*, London, Penguin, 1970.
Broche (produced Exeter, 1968).
Fancy Seeing You, Then (produced London, 1974). Published in *Playbill Two*, edited by Alan Durband, London, Hutchinson, 1969.
Victims (includes *The Sword, In Transit*, and *The Man in the Green Muffler*) (produced Edinburgh, 1970). *In Transit*, published New York, Breakthrough Press, 1972; *The Man in the Green Muffler*, included in *The Aquarium, The Man in the Green Muffler, I Didn't Always Live Here*, 1976.
The Burning (produced Edinburgh, 1971). London, Calder and Boyars, 1973.
A Slight Touch of the Sun (produced Edinburgh, 1972).
The Aquarium (produced Edinburgh, 1973). Included in *The Aquarium, The Man in the Green Muffler, I Didn't Always Live Here*, 1976.
Thistlewood (produced Edinburgh, 1975). Todmorden, Lancashire, Woodhouse, 1979.
Count Your Blessings (produced Pitlochry, Perthshire, 1975).
The Aquarium, The Man in the Green Muffler, I Didn't Always Live Here. London, Calder, 1976.
Play Donkey (produced Edinburgh, 1977). Todmorden, Lancashire, Woodhouse, 1980.
Billy Budd, with Stephen Macdonald, adaptation of the novel by Melville (produced Edinburgh, 1978).

Hecuba (produced Edinburgh, 1979).
Herman (produced Edinburgh, 1981; London, 1986).

Radio Plays: *Any Following Spring,* 1962; *Cadenza for Real*, 1963; *Song of the Clyde*, 1964; *The Canary Cage*, 1967; *Too Late the Phalarope*, from the novel by Alan Paton, 1984.

Television Plays: *Wally Dugs Go in Pairs*, 1973; *The Kite*, 1979; *Blood Hunt*, 1986.

Verse

Thunder in the Air. Preston, Lancashire, Akros, 1967.
The Chinese Tower. Edinburgh, M. Macdonald, 1967.
Stoats in the Sunlight. London, Hutchinson, 1968; as *Ambush and Other Poems*, New York, Macmillan, 1970.
Corgi Modern Poets in Focus 3, with others, edited by Dannie Abse. London, Corgi, 1971.
An Ear to the Ground. London, Hutchinson, 1972.
Under the Ice. London, Hutchinson, 1978.
In the Kibble Palace. Newcastle upon Tyne, Bloodaxe, 1987.

Other

Editor, *New Poems 1973–74*. London, Hutchinson, 1974.

*

Manuscript Collection: Scottish National Library, Edinburgh.

Critical Studies: interviews with James Aitchison in *Scottish Theatre* (Edinburgh), March 1969, Allen Wright in *The Scotsman* (Edinburgh), 30 October 1971, and Joyce McMillan in *Scottish Theatre News* (Glasgow), August 1981; *Towards the Human* by Iain Crichton Smith, Edinburgh, M. Macdonald, 1987.

Theatrical Activities:
Director: **Radio**—many plays, including *Armstrong's Last Goodnight* by John Arden, 1964; *The Anatomist* by James Bridie, 1965; *My Friend Mr. Leakey* by J.B.S. Haldane, 1967; *Mr. Gillie* by James Bridie, 1967; *Happy Days Are Here Again* by Cecil P. Taylor, 1967; *Wedderburn's Slave*, 1980, and *The Telescope Garden*, 1986, both by Douglas Dunn; *Losing Venice* by John Clifford, 1986; *Dirt under the Carpet* by Rona Munro, 1987.

Stewart Conn comments:

(1973) My plays are about human beings, and about the dilemma of human choice. I interpret this dilemma in moral terms, and visualize the characters in the plays, and their relationships, as revolving around it. As Camus wrote (in *The Plague*), "On this earth there are pestilences and there are victims, and it's up to us, so far as possible, not to join forces with the pestilences." If there is a through line in what I have written so far, it might be a reminder that we do not live our lives in isolation—but that how we behave involves, and may cause hurt to, other people. At the same time the plays are explorations: they pose questions, rather than pretending to provide any easy answers. I do not wish to impose a set of values on an audience; but like to think what I write might induce them to reassess their own. At the same time I am concerned with theatricality and with the use of words in the theatre, as also with the attempt to provide an instructive metaphor for the violence and betrayal, large and small, with which we must come to terms, within ourselves and in our society.

(1982) I find the above all rather pretentious—and rather than "comment" again I would prefer simply to get on with the plays: that is hard enough. "We must remember who we are . . ." (Lopakhin in *The Cherry Orchard*). Perhaps my main aim now is to send the audience out into the night, ideally both transformed and entertained, in time for the last bus!

* * *

Stewart Conn is a poet as well as a dramatist, and his best plays, like *The King, The Sword* and *The Burning*, reveal this lyrical side. Of his full-length plays *Broche and I Didn't Always Live Here* are little more than solid, competent pieces of dramatic craftsmanship; but *The Aquarium* and *The Burning* are both of considerable merit.

The Aquarium is set in a lower-middle-class Scottish home and depicts a classical father-son confrontation. The father is imbued with the puritanical work ethic and has clearly defined attitudes and beliefs, based on an old-fashioned morality, that he attempts to impose on his teenage son. The son is restless, unsure of himself and tentative in his approach to life, an attitude which is reflected in his flitting from job to job. Not unnaturally, he resists his father's attempts to make him conform, and they needle and taunt each other, with the mother ineffectually intervening, until matters come to a head when the father attempts to give his son a beating. This action triggers the son into a final breakaway from his family environment. The oppressive family atmosphere is particularly well and truthfully observed in this play, and the characters have a depth and power to them that belie their slightly clichéd conception. More than any other play of his, *The Aquarium* reveals the influence of Arthur Miller, a playwright he greatly admires.

The Burning is perhaps his most impressive work to date. It deals with the 16th-century power struggle between James VI of Scotland and his cousin, the Earl of Bothwell, and its theme can be deduced from Bothwell's line to James near the end of the play: "We are the upper and nether millstones, you and I. One way or another, it is those trappt in the middle must pay the price." The play is essentially about the brutality exercised toward those caught in the middle of any struggle for religious or political power, James standing for the divine right of kings, Bothwell for self-expression and individual freedom. But both treat the people under them as expendable and use them as pawns to advance their own positions. A subsidiary theme is that of witchcraft and superstition, but it is firmly placed within the context of the battle between authority and anarchy. The characters are vibrant with life, and reflect the underlying moral and ethical problems posed by a commitment to one side or the other, in a powerful and an exact way. Another remarkable feature of the play is the hard, sinewy Scottish language, which cleverly contrives to give an impression of late 16th-century speech.

Count Your Blessings revolves around Stanley, a man on the brink of death looking back over his past life and regretting the lost opportunities for fulfilling his potentialities. A particularly powerful scene shows him as a boy berating his schoolmaster father for caving in to pressure from his headmaster employer and reneging on his commitment to address a Communist Party rally in the 1930's on the effect of government cuts in education. *Thistlewood* is an impressionistic study of the 1820 Cato Street conspiracy of a group of radicals to assassinate the British Cabinet. The play draws modern parallels in the continuing struggle between conservatism and radicalism in our society.

Of Conn's short plays *The King* is a beautifully observed picture of two men fighting each other for the same girl, with a seduction scene between Attie and Lena that is replete with an unsentimental lyricism in the language. His trio of short plays, *Victims* (*The Man in the Green Muffler, In Transit*, and *The Sword*), are sharply and concisely drawn pictures of situations whose implications reverberate in the mind. The first play deals with an encounter between two pavement artists, one of whom has replaced someone who has died; the second is a macabre, Pinteresque exercise in violence, between two men and an intruder whom they slowly dominate; and *The Sword*, the best of the three, is a spooky psychological study of a man and a boy, both obsessed, for different reasons, with the idea of military glory. The characterisation in all of the plays is minutely and precisely accurate, qualities reflected in the taut dialogue, with strong lyrical undertones (particularly in *The Sword*), and the craftsmanlike attention to form.

The metaphorical connotations of Conn's best plays are strengthened by his feeling for dramatic construction, his understanding of individual psychology, and his basic interest in violence and its causes, both individual and in society at large. Allied with his quality of lyricism, these give his plays a peculiar power and depth.

—Jonathan Hammond

COOK, Michael. Canadian. Born in London, England, 14 February 1933; emigrated to Canada, 1966; became citizen, 1971. Educated at boarding schools near London to age 15; Nottingham University College of Education, 1962–66, T.T.C. (honours) in English 1966. Served in the Royal Electrical and Mechanical Engineers, and later in the Intelligence Corps, 1949–61: Staff Sergeant. Married 1) Muriel Horner in 1951 (marriage dissolved 1966), eight children; 2) Janis Jones in 1967 (divorced 1973), two children; 3) Madonna Decker in 1973, four children. Farm worker and waiter, 1948–49; steelworker and farm worker, 1961–62; schoolteacher, 1966. Specialist in Drama, 1967–70, Lecturer, 1970–74, Assistant Professor, 1974–79, and since 1979 Associate Professor of English, Memorial University, St. John's, Newfoundland. Drama critic, St. John's *Evening Telegram*, 1967–77; artistic director, St. John's Summer Festival, 1969–76; host of the weekly television review *Our Man Friday*, St. John's, 1973; playwright-in-residence, Banff Festival, Alberta, 1978. Member of the Editorial Board, *Canadian Theatre Review*, Downsview, Ontario, from 1973; Governor, Canadian Conference of the Arts, Ottawa, 1975–79; Vice-President, Guild of Canadian Playwrights, 1978–80; member of the Newfoundland and Labrador Arts Council, 1979–82. Also actor on stage, radio, and television, mainly in character roles. Recipient: Canada Council Senior Arts grant, 1973, 1979; Labatt award, 1974, 1975, 1978, 1979; Queen's Silver Jubilee Medal, 1979; Newfoundland and Labrador Government award, 1985. Agent: Playwrights Union of Canada, 8 York Street, 6th Floor, Toronto, Ontario M5J 1R2. Address: Department of English, Memorial University, P.O. Box 4200, St. John's, Newfoundland A1C 5S7, Canada.

PUBLICATIONS

Plays

The J. Arthur Prufrock Hour (revue; also director: produced St. John's, Newfoundland, 1968).

Tiln (broadcast 1971; produced Toronto, 1972). With *Quiller*, Toronto, Playwrights, 1975.

Colour the Flesh the Colour of Dust (also director: produced St. John's, Newfoundland, 1971). Toronto, Simon and Pierre, 1972.

The Head, Guts, and Soundbone Dance (produced St. John's, Newfoundland, 1973). St. John's, Breakwater, 1974.

Jacob's Wake (produced St. John's, Newfoundland, 1974; Fox Island, Washington, 1980). Vancouver, Talonbooks, 1975.

Quiller (produced St. John's, Newfoundland, 1975). With *Tiln*, Toronto, Playwrights, 1975.

Therese's Creed (produced Montreal, 1977; London, 1982). Toronto, Playwrights, 1976.

The Fisherman's Revenge (for children; produced Trinity Bay, Newfoundland, 1976). Toronto, Playwrights, 1985.

Not as a Dream (produced Halifax, Nova Scotia, 1976). Toronto, Playwrights, 1976; New York, Doubleday, 1979.

Tiln and Other Plays (includes *Quiller* and *Therese's Creed*). Vancouver, Talonbooks, 1976.

On the Rim of the Curve (produced Gander, Newfoundland, 1977). Included in *Three Plays*, 1977.

Three Plays (includes *On the Rim of the Curve; The Head, Guts, and Soundbone Dance; Therese's Creed*). Portugal Cove, Newfoundland, Breakwater, 1977.

The Gayden Chronicles (produced Lennoxville, Quebec, 1977; Waterford, Connecticut, 1978). Toronto, Playwrights, 1979.

The Apocalypse Sonata (produced Regina, Saskatchewan, 1980).

The Deserts of Bohemia (produced San Francisco, 1980).

The Terrible Journey of Frederick Dunglass (broadcast 1982). Published in *Canadian Theatre Review* (Downsview, Ontario), Fall 1986.

The Great Harvest Festival (produced Stratford, Ontario, 1986).

Radio Plays: *How to Catch a Pirate*, 1966; *A Walk in the Rain*, 1967; *No Man Can Serve Two Masters*, 1967; *The Concubine*, 1968; *Or the Wheel Broken*, 1968; *The Truck*, 1969; *A Time for Doors*, 1969; *The Iliad* (for children), from the poem by Homer, 1969; *A Midsummer Night's Dream*, from the play by Shakespeare, 1970; *To Inhabit the Earth Is Not Enough*, 1970; *Journey into the Unknown*, 1970; *Ballad of Patrick Docker*, 1971; *Tiln*, 1971; *Apostles for the Burning*, 1972; *There's a Seal at the Bottom of the Garden*, 1973; *An Enemy of the People*, from a play by Ibsen, 1974; *Love Is a Walnut*, 1975; *Travels with Aunt Jane* series (1 episode), 1975; *The Producer, The Director*, 1976; *Knight of Shadow, Lady of Silence*, 1976; *Ireland's Eye* (*The Best Seat in the House* series), 1977; *The Gentleman Amateur*, 1978; *All a Pack o' Lies*, 1979; *The Hunter*, 1980; *The Preacher*, 1981; *The Terrible Journey of Frederick Dunglass*, 1982; *The Sweet Second Summer of Kitty Malone*, from the novel by Matt Cohen, 1983; *This Damned Inheritance*, 1984; *The Bailiff and the Women*, 1984; *The Ocean Ranger*, 1985; *The Saddest Barn Dance Ever Held*, 1985; *The Hanging Judge*, 1985; *The Moribundian Memorandum*, 1986.

Television Plays: *In Search of Confederation*, 1971; *Daniel My Brother, The C.F.A.*, and *The Course of True Love* (all in *Up at Ours* series), 1979–80.

Novel

The Island of Fire. Toronto, Doubleday, 1980.

*

Bibliography: by Don Rubin, in *Canadian Theatre Review* (Downsview, Ontario), Fall 1977.

Manuscript Collection: University of Calgary Library, Alberta.

Critical Studies: "On the Edge: Michael Cook's Newfoundland Trilogy" by Brian Parker, in *Canadian Literature* (Vancouver), Summer 1980; *The Work: Conversations with English-Canadian Playwrights* by Robert Wallace and Cynthia Zimmerman, Toronto, Coach House Press, 1982; *Major Plays of the Canadian Theatre 1934–1984* edited by Richard Perkyns, Toronto, Irwin, 1984 (includes bibliography).

Theatrical Activities:
Director: **Plays**—in St. John's, Newfoundland: *Antigone* by Jean Anouilh, 1967; *The Queen and the Rebels* by Ugo Betti, 1967; *Mother Courage* by Brecht, 1968; *The J. Arthur Prufrock Hour*, 1968; *Bousille et les justes* by Gratien Gélinas, 1968; *Play* by Beckett, Labrador City, 1969; *Our Town* by Thornton Wilder, Labrador City, 1969; *Endgame* by Beckett, 1970; *The Geisha*, 1970; *Colour the Flesh the Colour of Dust*, 1971; *Hamlet*, 1972; *1 Henry IV*, 1973; *Macbeth*, 1974; *The Merchant of Venice*, 1975; *The Head, Guts, and Soundbone Dance*, Regina, Saskatchewan, 1977; *A Funny Thing Happened on the Way to the Forum* by Burt Shevelove, Larry Gelbart, and Stephen Sondheim, 1978; *Juno and the Paycock* by Sean O'Casey, 1980 and 1982; *Therese's Creed*, 1980.

Michael Cook comments:

(1977) The basic source of inspiration for my stage plays has been, and I suspect will continue to be, the people and the environment of Newfoundland. The environment is startlingly dramatic; the people the inheritors of moral, social, and economic conflicts that have existed (in many instances, destructively) for three centuries. Specifically, the head-on conflict with technology has, in years of Confederation with Canada, lifted the material prosperity and hopes of the nation but has undermined the fabric of community and social life which made survival possible and gave the island its unique identity. The people, mainly of Irish and West of England origins, maintained for centuries the rich dialects, the fatalistic humour, the careless command of a savage environment that historians might associate with their forebears, the sailors of Nelson's navy, the fodder of Wellington's army. Escaping the brutal caste system of Europe they developed, despite crippling economic circumstances, a heroic individualism. Add to this a language colourful, rich, musical, scatological, varying in accent from Bay to Bay, full of the power of ancient metaphors, and I think it becomes obvious why, at times, I feel like a celebrant at a peculiarly rich, but obviously threatened, ceremony of a way of life in which individuals struggle with the timeless questions of worth and identity against an environment which would kill them if it could.

As in all such environments—the wild Coast of Clare, the weeping Hebrides, the granite coast of Cornwall—there is much in man that responds to the land in all its moods. There are, balancing energy and joy and spoken communion, madness and superstition and violence and repression and anger. There is an overwhelming sense of frustration as bureaucrats and technocrats condone the rape of the oceans.

It seems that what has occurred in Newfoundland has, or will, occur everywhere in North America. Newfoundland is the continent in microcosm. And yet, because of this vastly reduced scale, it is still possible to conceive and portray men and women in the grip of great forces, changes, emotions that are in direct conflict with everything they know and understand. There is no diffusion here through the silt of great cities. No. The changes occur where the sea still runs, where the land provides evidence of ancient struggles, and the aged provide eloquent testimony of traditional patterns of survival. I pay attention, therefore, to the realistic, the specific, the concern with the known identity and the agonised recognition of a different kind of survival. I like to think that my work speaks to the condition of all men who have only recently come to realise that somewhere in the transition between rural and industrial man they left behind a portion of their souls.

(1988) My rather gloomy forecast (above) has come true. The ocean is dying, overfishing and greed have seen to that; the quest and lust for oil have turned the traditional lifestyle about-face; and the media revolution has delivered the *coup de grâce*: metaphor and richness of dialect are all but extinct, and parking lots and four-lane highways are all the rage. Without realising it I was called upon to chronicle the death throes of a dying culture. Of all my plays, *Jacob's Wake* chronicles that most explicitly.

* * *

Michael Cook's plays are passionate, extravagant, intensely linked with his environment. His home is Newfoundland, a province that has always been and will always remain unconquerable. Nothing can stop the winds and tides which wrack its coastlines year in and year out. Its people must forever struggle against its unpredictable climate and unyielding nature. It is this struggle which gives Cook his inspiration; he defines and hones it to a sharp, indelible edge.

Cook's heroes are often brutal, tough men. They would be despicable if the playwright did not delineate for us, in the most human of terms, their plight. They are brutal because the land is brutal, tough because that is the only way they can survive. In poetic terms, with the "million sea birds" screeching overhead, with the wind rising and falling, Michael Cook creates characters of passionate intensity.

In his first stage play, *Colour the Flesh the Colour of Dust*, the author looks to the historical past. Set in St. John's in 1762, it is the story of a garrison long forgotten by England. The men are bitter and worn-out; the women coarsened by misery and want. The Captain, defeated by "the rock," reveals its power: "I've watched, year after year. People build. Then fire. Or drowning. Or famine. Or disease. Or just—failure of the spirit. Somebody else comes and carts the house away, for timber or firewood. The thin scrub marches across the cleared land. The flake rots into the sea. . . . I have seen places where people once lived, where the land no longer bears the scar. It It makes me frightened." The French come and go, the poor get poorer, the rich flourish, heroes die, the women remain to bear a new generation. The story is melodramatically predictable but the script is notable because it shows us, for the first time, both Cook's essential understanding and his sensitive poetic abilities.

In *The Head, Guts, and Soundbone Dance*, a splitting room, where fish are cut and cleaned, is the setting. Once the lively centre of Newfoundland industry, it has now become a mausoleum for three old die-hards, Skipper Pete, his retarded son Absalom, and his son-in-law John. They live in the past, knowing yet refusing to accept the truth . . . there are no more fish. The Skipper is intractable to the point of obsessiveness, but, in spite of the power of his refusal to let the past go and face the realities of the future, John has already begun to realize their fate. "Oh yis," he says to the unrelenting Skipper, "We'll go down round to St. John's and there we'll sell our season's catch. Six fish. It's alright to get drunk here because this is us. And I don't mind. But I'm dying, Skipper. And so is ye. And the trouble is the god damn place has died afore us. We can't git that out of our guts, can we?" When a young, bright boy falls off the dock, neither John nor Pete moves to save him, locked as they are in their dreams of the past. It is only the final cruel blow of this death, once comprehended, that compels John to leave. The Skipper refuses to acknowledge his departure; he remains stern and unforgiving, like "the rock."

The Head, Guts, and Soundbone Dance is not totally believable—once again because of its melodramatic overtones. Nevertheless, it can be played successfully. It moves well, heightened (as is *Colour the Flesh the Colour of Dust*) with song, ribald humour, and cathartic insight. And one can never ignore the language, with its colloquialisms and intimacy.

The past weighs heavily on all of Cook's characters. In both *Quiller* and *Tiln*, a pair of one-acts which follow *The Head, Guts, and Soundbone Dance*, the protagonists of the same names struggle with a tide of memories. Quiller, his wife and friend dead, lives on alone in his outport house. He rails against his neighbours, lusts comically but pathetically after a young widow, retraces his past, volubly communes with God and chats with his dead wife. Quiller's comprehension is slow in coming, but like John's, inevitable. "It's not the same," says John, and Quiller repeats the motif, "I'm still here. And they is still there, but it ain't the same." His monologue reveals the direction of his life, both to the audience and to himself and he finally comes to a holy realization—man is fire and water, not dust. He gives thanks for this insight which enables him to accept the tragedy of his son's death, "All dese years since Amos died I've been troubled. Didn't make sense ye see. . . . We ain't dust, Lord. That's what it is, I've been foolish . . . Dat's a powerful piece of knowledge ye give me. . . ."

Tiln also traces a life to a realization about death, but unlike Quiller's Tiln's is full of despair. The difference, perhaps, is that while Quiller talks to God, Tiln thinks he is God. He shouts at the seagulls overhead, "You may shit on my Kingdom, but I am still God. Tiln . . . God of the wilderness . . . I am Lord of the Universe still. . . ." Tiln's Universe is the sea which surrounds the lighthouse where he has lived for an apparent eternity. But not completely alone. Ten years before, Fern came, a man half-dead, tossed up by the waves, to share Tiln's existence. Now Fern lies dying, begging Tiln for a few humble prayers from the Book to ease his passing. Tiln acts half-crazed, refusing Fern's request, packing him into a salt barrel to preserve his body before he's even dead, shooting off a rifle by his companion's head. "You were not listening Fern. Pay attention, I warn you." Then comes the shock of death. . . . He roars in pain and cradles Fern's head in his arms, crying out in anguish, "You've cheated me Fern. . . . You've cheated me . . ." as the lights fade. It is a moment as powerful in its despair as Quiller's was in its joy.

In spite of the dynamic poetry and indelible passions of the one-acts, Cook's full-length play, *Jacob's Wake*, must be considered the tour de force of his work to date. Whereas the one-acts were virtual monologues, *Jacob's Wake* has a cast of seven. The occasion is Easter, and the sons—Brad, a defrocked minister, Lonz, a local gambler and pimp, and Wayne, a politician whose government falls during the course of the play—join their parents, spinster Aunt, and bed-ridden Grandfather, the Skipper, to pass the holidays. There is nothing holy in this reunion. The Father agonizes over his failure as a son; the Aunt plots to get the Skipper into a mental institution; Lonz forges his Father's name on the committal certificate in return for governmental favours. Brad, crazed by the fact that he once seduced a girl who later killed herself and his baby, runs into a blinding snowstorm, coatless and hatless. The plot is complex and the agonies almost unrelenting but the playwright is in control, and the result is moving, detonating theatre. The home—the ship—is running aground, wracking itself on the ice, sinking with a roar.

What is remarkable about the play, indeed about all Cook's plays, is that the characters display a ribald, often wry humour which constantly challenges the grimness of their lives. This is the Newfoundlander's unfailing antidote to stress. The humour of Cook's plays, biting though it may be, makes the tragedy of his characters accessible. Life is a struggle, but what makes his people "Gods and Heroes" is that they can mock their fate. They are a strong people, caught by a strong yet sensitive writer.

In *The Gayden Chronicles*, a historical drama set in the 18th century, William Gayden, a British farm boy conscripted by force into the navy, grows up to become a one-man revolution. Taking Tom Paine as his guide to freedom, Gayden struggles without complete success to overcome his own impoverished background and the century itself, with its cruelty and bitter political conflicts. As Gayden awaits his execution for murder and mutiny, he recreates his life and loves—of freedom, women, the poor and oppressed. Panoramic but not entirely successful in its goals, *The Gayden Chronicles* continues Cook's passionate obsessions.

—Constance Brissenden

COONEY, Ray(mond George Alfred). British. Born in London, 30 May 1932. Educated at Alleyn's School, Dulwich, London. Served in the Royal Army Service Corps, 1950–52. Married Linda Ann Dixon in 1962; two sons. Actor from 1946; theatrical director and producer from 1965; since 1966, director, Ray Cooney Presentations Ltd., London; since 1983 director and artistic director, Theatre of Comedy Company, London. Address: 1/3 Spring Gardens, London SW1A 2BD, England.

Publications

Plays

Dickory Dock, with Tony Hilton (produced Richmond, Surrey, 1959).

One for the Pot, with Tony Hilton (produced Wolverhampton, 1960; London, 1961). London, English Theatre Guild, 1963.

Who Were You with Last Night?, with Tony Hilton (produced Windsor, 1962).

How's Your Father? (produced Richmond, Surrey, 1963).

Chase Me, Comrade! (produced London, 1964). London, English Theatre Guild, and New York, Dramatists Play Service, 1966.

Charlie Girl, with Hugh and Margaret Williams, music and lyrics by David Heneker and John Taylor (produced London, 1965). London, Chappell, 1972.

Bang Bang Beirut; or, Stand by Your Bedouin, with Tony Hilton (produced Guildford, Surrey, 1966; as *Stand by Your Bedouin*, produced London, 1967). London, English Theatre Guild, 1971.

Not Now, Darling, with John Chapman (produced Richmond, Surrey, 1967; London, 1968; also director: produced New

York, 1970). London, English Theatre Guild, 1970; New York, Dramatists Play Service, 1971.
My Giddy Aunt, with John Chapman (produced Wolverhampton, 1967; London, 1968). London, English Theatre Guild, 1970.
Move Over, Mrs. Markham, with John Chapman (produced Richmond, Surrey, 1969; also director: produced London, 1971). London, English Theatre Guild, and New York, French, 1972.
Why Not Stay for Breakfast?, with Gene Stone (produced Westcliff-on-Sea, Essex, 1970; also director: produced London, 1973). London, French, 1974.
Come Back to My Place, with John Chapman (produced Westcliff-on-Sea, Essex, 1973).
There Goes the Bride, with John Chapman (produced Birmingham and London, 1974). London, English Theatre Guild, 1975.
Her Royal Highness...?, with Royce Ryton (also director: produced London, 1981).
Two into One (produced Leicester, 1981; also director: produced London, 1984). London, French, 1985.
Run for Your Wife (also director: produced London, 1983). London, French, 1984.
Wife Begins at Forty, with Arne Sultan and Earl Barret (also director: produced Guildford, Surrey, and London, 1985). London, French, 1986.
An Italian Straw Hat, adaptation of a play by Eugène Labiche (also director: produced London, 1986).

Screenplays: *Not Now Comrade*, 1977; *There Goes the Bride*, with Terence Marcel, 1980; *Why Not Stay for Breakfast?*, with Terence Marcel, 1985.

Radio Plays: *Tale of the Repertory Actor*, 1971; *Mr. Willow's Wife*, with John Chapman, 1972.

Television Plays (with Tony Hilton): *Boobs in the Wood*, 1960; *Round the Bend* (*Dial Rix* series), 1962.

*

Theatrical Activities:
Director: **Plays**—many of his own plays, and *Thark* by Ben Travers, London, 1965; *In at the Death* by Duncan Greenwood and Robert King, London, 1967; *Press Cuttings* by Shaw, 1970; *The Mating Game* by Robin Hawdon, London, 1972; *Birds of Paradise* by Gaby Bruyère, London, 1974; *See How They Run* by Philip King, London, 1984; *Pygmalion* by Shaw, London, 1984; *Three Piece Suite* by Richard Harris, Hornchurch, Essex, 1986; *Holiday Snap* by Michael Pertwee, Guildford, Surrey, 1986. **Films**—*Not Now Darling*, with David Croft, 1973; *Not Now Comrade*, with Harold Snoad, 1977; *There Goes the Bride*, 1980.
Actor: **Plays**—role in *Song of Norway* by Milton Lazarus, Robert Wright, and George Forrest, London, 1946; *Calcutta in the Morning* by Geoffrey Thomas, London, 1947; Larkin in *The Hidden Years* by Travers Otway, London, 1948; roles in repertory companies, 1952–56; *Dry Rot* by John Chapman, London, 1956; Corporal Flight in *Simple Spymen* by John Chapman, London, 1958; *One for the Pot*, London, 1961; Detective-Sergeant Trotter in *The Mousetrap* by Agatha Christie, London, 1964; Simon Sparrow in *Doctor at Sea* by Ted Willis, London, 1966; David Prosser in *Uproar in the House* by Anthony Marriott and Alistair Foot, London, 1967; Nicholas Wainwright in *Charlie Girl*, London, 1968; Timothy Westerby in *There Goes the Bride*, London, 1975; Willoughby Pink in *Banana Ridge* by Ben Travers, London, 1976; *Two into One*, Leicester, 1981, and Guildford, Surrey, 1985; *Run for Your Wife*, Guildford, Surrey, 1983. **Films**—*Not Now Darling*, 1973; *Not Now Comrade*, 1977.

* * *

From the time of his first success with *One for the Pot* in 1960, Ray Cooney has sought to perfect his "talent to amuse." As one who has mastered the techniques of farce in the role of actor and producer, as well as writer, he is perhaps more qualified than most; certainly his varied abilities enable him to assess the likely response from the market-place, as well as the ivory tower, and the past 20 years have seen an increasingly imaginative use of his craft.

Farce is Cooney's chosen medium, and one in which he excels. Traditionally, its success depends less on characterisation or psychological insight than on swift and continuous action. Cooney's plays invariably fulfil these technical demands. Starting with a humdrum situation—a forthcoming society wedding, the collection of a mink coat, the decorating of an upmarket flat—the plays rapidly develop into a maze of misunderstandings, with the impending threat of potentially disastrous confrontations. Cooney shows great skill with his plots, neatly gauging the accelerating pace and eventual climax, matching the action with a brittle, fragmented dialogue. He is also adept at exploiting such stock devices as the aside to the audience, Gilbert's comments on his partner Arnold in *Not Now, Darling* being a typical—and effective—example. A similar device is used in the same play, when Arnold, confronted by a succession of irate spouses and girlfriends about to discover "proof" of infidelity, is repeatedly reduced to hurling the "evidence"—usually underwear—out of the window. Read cold from a script, the effect appears tedious and mechanical. Onstage it works, lending added emphasis to the humour of the situation.

Repetition is a key element in Cooney's farces, the threat of discovery or catastrophic encounter continually recurring as the comic tension heightens and the possibilities grow more disastrous. *Run for Your Wife* has its bigamous taxi-driver hero striving desperately to prevent the meeting of his two wives, his position rendered more comic by the use of a split stage which reveals both women and their thoughts at the same time. *Run for Your Wife* is one of Cooney's most striking works, the action ably measured, the wit of the matching dialogue astute and keen. The same is true of *Not Now, Darling* and *Move Over, Mrs. Markham*, which show Cooney at his best. Like most of his plays, they are aimed at an upper-middle-class audience—"the tired businessman," as one reviewer puts it—and this is reflected in the locations, the former set in a high-class furrier's, the latter in "a very elegant top floor London flat." In *Not Now, Darling* Cooney contrasts the lecherous Gilbert and the prim Arnold in an escalating series of encounters as the former's amorous intrigues come home to roost. (Arnold's "I refuse to put all my bags in one exit!" must be one of Cooney's funniest lines.) *Move Over, Mrs. Markham* involves a publisher's family and friends and their liaisons, its climax a hilarious scene where a prudish best-selling author is persuaded to sign for the firm by the publisher's wife, while the publisher himself (as the butler) makes constant interruptions. All three plays are deftly executed, the interplay of character and situation sure and precise, the climaxes carefully weighted for maximum comic impact. *There Goes the Bride* is not quite equal to them. Polly Perkins, the 1920's flapper invisible to everyone but the dazed Timothy, is an overworked device, and the play lacks the "ordinariness" of Cooney's best settings. More effective is the Australian father-in-law, Babcock, in his role as that stock figure, the "funny foreigner."

Farce, like the "tired businessman," is not noted for its taste, and Cooney's plays are no exception. On the face of it, there would appear to be nothing very funny about Lebanon, but *Bang Bang Beirut* (produced in 1966) manages to wring comedy from the subject, much as Croft and Perry's *'Allo, 'Allo* has done with wartime France. Just as farce admits no un-funny locations, Cooney also regards minorities as fair game. The "funny foreigner" is repeatedly met with in his plays, either in person or by proxy, as with Linda's awful Austrian imitation in *Move Over, Mrs. Markham*. Cooney seems to find homosexuality unbelievably amusing, and makes repeated use of its possibilities. The apparent "relationship" of Philip Markham and his partner is milked for laughs, the irony being their "discovery" by the effetely dressed Alistair, of whom Cooney seems unduly anxious to reassure us that "underneath his slightly arty exterior lurks a virile male." The bigamous husband of *Run for Your Wife* pretends to be gay himself at one point, and another camp character also makes an appearance. Many would contend that this kind of humour is on a par with racist jokes, and that the author is playing for easy laughs. No doubt Cooney, as a performer, would contend that there is no such thing. While for some his jibes go too far, it is perhaps wrong to level such criticism at a form noted for its lack of pity.

Cooney, one feels, is not a particularly innovative writer. Rather, he is a master technician, a skilled manipulator of the conventions of his medium, where he operates to best effect. Attempts to move outside, as in *Why Not Stay for Breakfast?*, have been less satisfying. Within the limitations of his form, Cooney is altogether more impressive. Whether one laughs quite as loudly as the average businessman, or winces on occasion, the fact remains that Cooney is one of the most capable, and consistently successful, writers in the medium of farce.

—Geoff Sadler

COWEN, Ron(ald). American. Born in Cincinnati, Ohio, 15 September 1944. Educated at the University of California, Los Angeles, B.A. in English 1966; Annenberg School of Communications, University of Pennsylvania, Philadelphia, 1967–68. Taught classes in theatre at New York University, Fall 1969. Associate Trustee, University of Pennsylvania. Recipient: Wesleyan University fellowship, 1968; Vernon Rice award, 1968; Emmy award, 1986, and Peabody award, 1986, for television play. Lives in Pacific Palisades, California. Agent: William Morris Agency, 151 El Camino, Beverly Hills, California 90212, U.S.A.

PUBLICATIONS

Plays

Summertree (produced Waterford, Connecticut, 1967; New York, 1968). New York, Random House, 1968.
Valentine's Day (produced Waterford, Connecticut, 1968; revised version, music by Saul Naishtat, produced New York, 1975).
Saturday Adoption (televised 1968; produced New York, 1978). New York, Dramatists Play Service, 1969.
Porcelain Time (produced Waterford, Connecticut, 1972).
The Book of Murder (televised 1974). New York, Dramatists Play Service, 1974.
Lulu, adaptation of plays by Wedekind (produced New York, 1974; as *Inside Lulu*, produced New York, 1975).

Television Plays: *Saturday Adoption*, 1968; *The Book of Murder*, 1974; *Paul's Case*, from the story by Willa Cather, 1977; *I'm A Fool*, from the story by Sherwood Anderson, 1979; *An Early Frost*, with Daniel Lipman, 1985.

* * *

The ethical crisis arising from America's involvement in the Vietnam war was a major concern for American writers in the 1960's. *Summertree*, the most successful American play of the decade to deal with this subject, was written by Ron Cowen at the age of twenty. (David Rabe's *The Basic Training of Pavlo Hummel* and *Sticks and Bones* may prove to be more significant works, but they appeared after the initial national tension over the war had peaked.) *Summertree*, which was widely produced and made into a Hollywood film, was perhaps successful more because of its timeliness than its intrinsic worth.

The play is an excessively sentimental telling of an inconsequential young man's death and life in Vietnam. As the protagonist (Young Man) lies fatally wounded under a jungle tree, he hallucinates flashback episodes from his civilian and military experience: sometimes he is twenty, sometimes he is ten. The jungle tree becomes the backyard tree in which he once built a treehouse. His recollections are of his Mother and Father, his Girl and his Buddy (Soldier). These characters are drawn by Cowen in broad strokes that critics of the production were prone to see as American archetypes: the essential constellation of personae. A critic of a less emotionally charged era is prone to see them as uninspired caricatures.

The play's most successful attribute is its three-act, cinematic structure which provides a degree of dramatic irony and gives the play substance. Its least successful is its banal dialogue. When the Young Man says to his father, late in the final act, "I want to tell the back yard goodbye," there is a cloying sentimentality which renders the moment bathetic. Yet for an audience tired of both the brutality of the war and the hysteria of the anti-war protests which shook the land in 1967, the play (and even its dialogue) struck sympathetic chords.

The play is a product of its cultural climate in yet another sense. It was written by Cowen while he was a student at the University of Pennsylvania. When the play was first presented, in the summer of 1967 at the Eugene O'Neill Memorial Theatre Foundation in Waterford, Connecticut, it underwent major re-writings at the request of its director. As it was prepared for New York production by the Repertory Theater of Lincoln Center, additional changes were introduced. The play—far more than the average commercial project—became the reflection of many concerned persons' attitudes towards the war. Small wonder it found a receptive ear and was awarded the Vernon Rice award for that turbulent year. (When the movie script was being prepared this procedure got out of control. Cowen wrote a first screenplay, Rod McKuen was hired to do a second, and the shooting script was finally the work of Hollywood pros Edward Hume and Stephen Yafa. The final script owes shockingly little to Cowen's initial intentions, images, or characters.)

Cowen's subsequent career has been somewhat erratic. In 1968 *Saturday Adoption* was telecast on CBS Playhouse and in 1974 ABC aired *The Book of Murder*. Both were critical failures. The first dealt with a socially conscious young man's failures to change the world through his father's money or his pupil's achievements; the second is a coy murder mystery. Cowen's trademarks are easily seen in both: the cinematic structure, the sentimental and nostalgic tone, the domestic circumstance, the conflict over money. His weaknesses are in evidence as well: the badly motivated actions, the clichéd characters, and the clumsy dialogue which the critic for *Variety* called "goody two-shoes language." *I'm a Fool*, a television adaptation of Sherwood Anderson's story, was more successful, and *An Early Frost* won an Emmy award.

Cowen has completed subsequent stage scripts, but none has been given major production. He assisted on the book for *Billy* which flopped on Broadway in 1968. His musical *Valentine's Day* was show-cased at the Manhattan Theatre Club in 1975 but reviewed as an "unsatisfying experience." It included the Cowensque line, "I want to tell the apartment goodbye." *Inside Lulu* was a banal work, loosely based on the Wedekind plays, and created by Section Ten, the off-off-Broadway improvisational group. Cowen was their literary collaborator.

In retrospect, *Summertree* appears very much to be in the tradition of television soap opera and it is appropriate that Cowen should continue to write for the televison medium. As long as his language, characters and situations remain banal, autobiographical, and domestic it is unlikely he will produce a major work. *Summertree* appears to have been less the work of a *wunderkind* than a timely reflection of a culture's anxieties.

—Thomas B. Markus

CRANE, Richard (Arthur). British. Born in York, 4 December 1944. Educated at St. John's School, Leatherhead, Surrey, 1958–63; Jesus College, Cambridge, 1963–66, B.A. (honours) in classics and English 1966, M.A. 1971. Married Faynia Jeffery Williams in 1975; two sons and two stepdaughters. Actor and director: founder member, Brighton Combination and Pool, Edinburgh. Fellow in Theatre, University of Bradford, Yorkshire, 1972–74; resident dramatist, National Theatre, London, 1974–75; Fellow in Creative Writing, University of Leicester, 1976; literary manager, Royal Court Theatre, London, 1978–79; dramaturg, Tron Theatre, Glasgow, 1983–84. Since 1980 associate director, Brighton Theatre. Since 1973 member of the Board of Directors, Edinburgh Festival. Recipient: Edinburgh Festival award, 1973, 1974, 1975, 1977, 1980; Thames Television bursary, 1974; Arts Council bursary, 1979. Agent: Margaret Ramsay Ltd., 14-A Goodwin's Court, London WC2N 4LL, England.

PUBLICATIONS

Plays

Footlights Revue, with others (produced Cambridge, 1966).
Three Ugly Women (produced Cork and London, 1967).
The Tenant (produced Edinburgh, 1971; London, 1972).
Crippen (produced Edinburgh, 1971).
Tom Brown (produced Bradford, 1971).
Decent Things (produced Edinburgh, 1972; London, 1973).
The Blood Stream (produced Edinburgh, 1972).
Mutiny on the Bounty, music by Chris Mitchell (produced Bradford, 1972; revised version produced Brighton, 1980).
Bleak Midwinter (produced Edinburgh, 1972).
David, King of the Jews, music by Chris Mitchell (produced Bradford, 1973).
Thunder: A Play of the Brontës (produced Ilkley, Yorkshire, 1973; London, 1978). London, Heinemann, 1976.
Examination in Progress (produced Edinburgh, 1973).
Secrets (produced Belfast, 1973; London, 1974).
The Pied Piper, music by Chris Mitchell (produced Bradford, 1973).
The Quest, music by Chris Mitchell (produced Edinburgh, 1974).
The Route of All Evil (produced Edinburgh, 1974).
Humbug; or, A Christmas Carol Backwards, music by Milton Reame-James (produced Bracknell, Berkshire, 1974).
Mystery Plays (produced Bracknell, Berkshire, 1974).
The King (produced Bradford, 1974).
The Bradford Revue (produced Edinburgh, 1974).
Mean Time (produced London, 1975).
Venus and Superkid (for children), music by Milton Reame-James (produced London, 1975).
Clownmaker (produced Edinburgh, 1975; London and Westport, Connecticut, 1976; New York, 1982).
Bloody Neighbours (produced London, 1975).
Manchester Tales (produced Manchester, 1975).
Gunslinger: A Wild West Show, music by Joss Buckley (produced Leicester, 1976; London, 1977). London, Heinemann, 1979.
Nero and the Golden House (produced Edinburgh, 1976).
The Perils of Bardfrod, with David Edgar (produced Bradford, 1976).
Satan's Ball, adaptation of a novel by Mikhail Bulgakov (produced Edinburgh, 1977; Berkeley, California, 1984).
Gogol (produced Brighton, 1978; London, 1979; New York, 1983).
Vanity, adaptation of *Eugene Onegin* by Pushkin (produced Edinburgh, 1980; London, 1983).
Sand (produced Brighton, 1981).
The Brothers Karamazov, adaptation of a novel by Dostoevsky (produced Edinburgh and London, 1981).
Burke and Hare (produced Glasgow, 1983).
The Possessed, with Yuri Lyubimov, adaptation of a novel by Dostoevsky (produced Paris and London, 1985).
Mutiny!, with David Essex, music by Essex (produced London, 1985).
Envy, adaptation of a novel by Yuri Olesha (produced Edinburgh, 1986).
Soldier Soldier, adaptation of a work by Tony Parker (produced Edinburgh, 1986).
Pushkin (produced Edinburgh and London, 1987).

Screenplay: *Sebastian and the Seawitch* (for children), 1976.

Radio Plays: *Decent Things*, 1984; *Optimistic Tragedy*, from play by Vsevolod Vishnevsky, 1986.

Television Plays: *Nice Time* series, 1968–69; *The Billy West Show*, 1970; *Rottingdean*, 1980.

Recordings: *Mutiny!*, Phonogram, 1983, and Telstar, 1985 (and singles *Tahiti*, 1983, and *Welcome*, 1984, both Phonogram).

*

Critical Studies: in *Vogue* (London), October 1977; *Yorkshire Arts Association Magazine*, February–March 1979.

Theatrical Activities:
Director of plays in Bradford, Edinburgh, and London, and actor from 1966 in London and in repertory, on television, and in films.

* * *

With *The Brothers Karamazov* in 1981, Richard Crane finally became a dramatist with a London reputation (and, indeed, a reputation in the Soviet Union). Not that he had been previously unseen in London. As a resident playwright with the Royal Court and with the National Theatre, he had initiated productions in the capital. Several of his plays, after establishing reputations elsewhere, had made their way into London. But *The Brothers Karamazov* was more than just a confirmation of his literary potential: it was an affirmation of the importance of his collaboration with his wife, the director Faynia Williams, and a remarkable demonstration of his absorption in Russian writing.

Before turning to *The Brothers Karamazov* and Dostoevsky, Crane had presented a string of confrontations with Russian writers, including Bulgakov, Gogol, and Pushkin. They had followed investigations into British legends, English literature, and religion. At one point, he had even written a children's play called *Venus and Superkid* which was described as a "transgalactic rock supershow based on Greek legend." His wide interests were channeled into Russian literature through his relationship with Faynia Williams, but not before several remarkable productions had made their way from Bradford University to the Edinburgh Festival Fringe.

These plays showed the dramatic breadth of Crane's stage vision, which had already ranged from a music-hall impression of the murderer Crippen, to *Thunder*, a retelling of the Brontë family story, and *David, King of the Jews*, performed at Bradford Cathedral in 1973. His 1974 script for Bradford University, *The Quest*, offered the first serious rumblings of significant talent—in part because it was technically overambitious—and it was the Edinburgh Fringe success of that year. In the play he retold the legend of Arthurian England, with opposing factions divided into prose and poetry speakers while the audience witnessed the rise and destruction of Camelot as if watching a jousting tournament.

The following year, which also saw the production of *Bloody Neighbours* in the National Theatre's studio season at the ICA Theatre, produced *Clownmaker*. It tells the story of the relationship between Diaghilev and Nijinsky, and it was marked by shattering stage effects in Faynia Williams's production. The Ballets Russes forms the backdrop for the portrait of Diaghilev as puppet-master, and the struggles of Nijinsky to establish a separate existence create the dramatic moments. Diaghilev produces Nijinsky's first sign of animation, by providing the impetus to dance, and Nijinsky's rebellion against his homosexual relationship with Diaghilev provokes a virtual earthquake. Memorable scenes and moments of evocative dialogue did not quite jell into a total success, but the sheer theatricality was refreshing and unusual.

His adaptation of Bulgakov's novel *The Master and Margarita* appeared two years later, after a series of somewhat less ambitious works. Called *Satan's Ball*, the play marked his first serious use of Russian material and formed a vast satirical and erotic canvas for Williams's staging, again on the Edinburgh Fringe. The next collaboration was on a markedly reduced scale: a monologue, originally performed by Crane himself in a production by Williams for their own small company, the Brighton Actors' Workshop. Again, the subject was Russian, the title the name of the author, *Gogol*, with material taken from Gogol's writing, particularly "The Overcoat," and from Gogol's life. His intention was to contrast the inner life with the outer appearance, to present the spiritual substance simultaneously with the surface indications and contradictions of the body, the clothes, and the published writing.

Before *The Brothers Karamazov* promoted him to the official Edinburgh Festival, Crane and Williams produced *Vanity* on the Fringe in 1980. It was a further investigation of Russian writing, described as a "response to *Eugene Onegin*," and it cleared the way for the official invitation in 1981, which resulted in the London season and a tour of the Soviet Union.

The distinction of *The Brothers Karamazov* as an adaptation for the stage lies largely in the lucid retention of the moral and metaphysical ambiguities of Dostoevsky's novel. The originality of the work is largely in the ingenious structural emphases which significantly alter the tone of the original. Crane transforms introspective guilt into heady confessions, with each son eagerly displaying the reasons for which he might possibly have murdered his father. A familiarity with the novel helps clarify the multiple actions, but the multiple role-playing of each character is theatrically engaging on its own. There is a playfulness in giving each of the four actors a principal characterization, then diverting them to play old Fyodor (always in a fur coat) or lounging women, which provides moment to moment entertainment. Crane thrives on challenges, and more often than not meets them with original theatrical solutions.

The main thrust of Crane's work remains his collaborations with his wife, often with student actors, but his most visible production was his collaboration with the pop star and actor David Essex on a West End musical based on *Mutiny on the Bounty*. *Mutiny!* had the merit of dispensing with the standard image of the leading mutineer, Fletcher Christian, as a recognizable hero. He was approached rather as a confused Romantic, longing for equality between officers and enlisted men. Unfortunately, Essex's contributions were all too visible, keeping him moodily in view as sailors were flogged and and involving him in erotic caresses with his island lover at every available chance.

Crane's most important collaboration was with the exiled Soviet director Yuri Lyubimov on his European co-production of a dramatization of Dostoevsky's *The Possessed*. The production reflected the director's highly personal vision of the book, but Crane's use of language was equally personal and the heightened imagery came as much from his concentrated English as from the director's vivid staging. Other projects, from a lively dramatization of the Soviet classic *Envy*, for the 1986 Edinburgh Festival to a radio version of the classic Soviet drama by Vsevolod Vishnevsky, *Optimistic Tragedy*, have continued to explore the riches of Russian writing, an area he has made his own.

—Ned Chaillet

CREGAN, David (Appleton Quartus). British. Born in Buxton, Derbyshire, 30 September 1931. Educated at the Leys School, Cambridge, 1945–50; Clare College, Cambridge, 1952–55, B.A. in English 1955. Served as an Acting Corporal in the Royal Air Force, 1950–52. Married Ailsa Mary Wynne Willson in 1960; three sons and one adopted daughter. Head of English, Palm Beach Private School, Florida, 1955–57; Assistant English Master, Burnage Boys' Grammar School, Manchester, 1957; Assistant English Master and Head of Drama, 1958–62, and part-time drama teacher, 1962–67, Hatfield School, Hertfordshire; salesman, and clerk at the Automobile Association, 1958. Worked with Royal Court Theatre Studio, London, 1964, 1968, and Midlands Arts Centre, Birmingham, 1971; conducted three-week studio at the Royal Shakespeare Company Memorial Theatre, Stratford-on-Avon, 1971. Member of the Drama Panel, West Midlands Arts Association, 1972, and Eastern Arts, 1980. Recipient: Arts Council bursary, 1966, 1975, 1978, and grant, 1971; Foyle award, 1966. Agent: Margaret Ramsay Ltd., 14-A Goodwin's Court, London WC2N 4LL. Address: 76 Wood Close, Hatfield, Hertfordshire, England.

PUBLICATIONS

Plays

Miniatures (produced London, 1965). London, Methuen, 1970.
Transcending, and The Dancers (produced London, 1966). London, Methuen, 1967.
Three Men for Colverton (produced London, 1966). London, Methuen, 1967.
The Houses by the Green (produced London, 1968). London, Methuen, 1969.
A Comedy of the Changing Years (produced London, 1969).
Arthur, in *Playbill One*, edited by Alan Durband. London, Hutchinson, 1969.
Tipper (produced Oxford, 1969).
Liebestraum and Other Pieces (produced Birmingham, 1970). Included in *The Land of Palms and Other Plays*, 1973.
Jack in the Box; and If You Don't Laugh, You Cry (produced Birmingham, 1971). Included in *The Land of Palms and Other Plays*, 1973.
The Daffodil, and Sentimental Value (produced Birmingham, 1971).
How We Held the Square: A Play for Children (produced Birmingham, 1971; London, 1974). London, Eyre Methuen, 1973.
The Land of Palms (produced Dartington, Devon, 1972). Included in *The Land of Palms and Other Plays*, 1973.
George Reborn (televised 1973; produced Richmond, Surrey, 1973; London, 1977). Included in *The Land of Palms and Other Plays*, 1973.
Cast Off (produced Sheffield, 1973).
Pater Noster (in *Mixed Blessings*, produced Horsham, Sussex, 1973). Published in *Play Nine*, edited by Robin Rook, London, Arnold, 1981.
The Land of Palms and Other Plays (includes *Liebestraum; George Reborn; The Problem; Jack in the Box; If You Don't Laugh, You Cry*). London, Eyre Methuen, 1973.
The King (produced London, 1974).
Tina (produced Richmond, Surrey, 1975). With *Poor Tom*, London, Eyre Metheun, 1976.
Poor Tom (produced Manchester, 1976). With *Tina*, London, Eyre Methuen, 1976.
Tigers (produced Richmond, Surrey, 1978).
Young Sir (produced Richmond, Surrey, 1979).
Red Riding Hood (produced Stoke-on-Trent, 1979).
Getting It Right (produced Hatfield, Hertfordshire, 1980).
A Name Is More Than a Name, in *Play Nine*. edited by Robin Rook. London, Arnold, 1981.
Jack and the Beanstalk (pantomime), music by Brian Protheroe (produced London, 1982).
The Sleeping Beauty (pantomime), music by Brian Protheroe (produced London, 1983). London, French, 1984.
Red Ridinghood (pantomime), music by Brian Protheroe (produced London, 1984). London, French, 1986.
Crackling Angels (produced Beaminster, Dorset, 1987).

Radio Plays: *The Latter Days of Lucy Trenchard*, 1974; *The Monument*, 1978; *Hope*, 1979; *Inventor's Corner*, 1979; *The Joking Habit*, 1980; *The True Story of the Public School Strike 1990*, 1981; *Diana's Uncle and Other Relatives*, 1982; *The Spectre*, 1983; *The Awful Insulation of Rage*, 1986.

Television Plays: *That Time of Life*, 1972; *George Reborn*, 1973; *I Want to Marry Your Son*, 1973; *Pipkins*, with Susan Pleat, 1974; *Reluctant Chickens*, 1982; *Events in a Museum*, 1983; *Goodbye Days*, 1984; *A Still Small Shout*, 1985.

Novel

Ronald Rossiter. London, Hutchinson, 1959.

*

Critical Studies: *The Second Wave* by John Russell Taylor, London, Methuen, and New York, Hill and Wang, 1971; article by Timothy J. Kidd, in *British Dramatists since World War II* edited by Stanley Weintraub, Detroit, Gale, 1982.

David Cregan comments:

1. I am a socialist because there is no other reasonable thing to be. However, all problems, as well as all interesting thoughts, seem to stem from that one position. How much does the individual matter and how much the community? Can a contemporary community ever avoid becoming systematized, and anyway how much less traumatic is it living unsystematically than systematically? How simplistic can a government be before it must be opposed totally? If material poverty produces spiritual poverty, which, with special exceptions, it does, can material wealth produce spiritual wealth? How important *is* spiritual wealth, and on what does its value depend? Can the elevation of one working class be justified if it is achieved at the expense of another working class? If freedom is no longer a meaningful conception (and it only achieves any meaning by being opposed to some form of tyranny), which qualified freedom is the most important? Of thought or from hunger? If leaders are bad, are institutions worse? What is the basic nature of man as opposed to the animals, and can it be improved?

I doubt if any of this appears overtly in any of my writing, though the head of steam is always provided by acute anxieties felt on one score or another among these and similar peculiarly 20th-century questions.

2. Since for me the best plays seem to *be* rather than to be *about*, I personally prefer the episodic forms in which characters may be presented quickly and variously, so that the architecture provides the major insights.

3. Since I have this delight in form, I find no pleasure or virtue in personal rhetoric, self-indulgent self-revelation, or absolute naturalism.

4. Delight in construction also biases me against any form of expressionism or abstract symbolism, and increasingly I use songs, jazz, and a rough poetry spoken to music for various constructional purposes.

5. Since construction of the kind so far indicated is frequently a question of rhythm, there is a "playful" quality about my work. It has a musical quality, each scene sounding forward to another. This means the plays should be acted with a care for their surface, and anyone who acts them for any individual significance, the same shall surely lose it. There are frequently large alterations in emotional stance needed between the giving and receiving of the words, and there is much pleasure in watching this.

6. I have been much influenced by farce, Ibsen, Brecht, Beckett, and the directors I have been associated with at The Royal Court. Also by the intensely magical understanding of comedy shown by Keith Johnstone.

7. I am the fourth and youngest son of a an Irish shirt manufacturer. My father fought and was gassed in World War I, and sought peace and prosperity in a small Derbyshire town, where he pursued a quiet Protestant way of life. My brothers fought, and one died, in World War II, I was largely brought up by a young working-class nursemaid.

8. A writer's notes about himself are alas more revealing when they fail to confirm the impression of his work than when they succeed. This happens to more of us than is generally supposed.

* * *

In David Cregan's earliest play, *Miniatures*, the deputy headmaster says "If only one knew what every mind was thinking. If one had their habits of thought one could put in train the running of the school the way it ought to go. That's the way of achieving what is democratically best for everyone. One must have their minds, or else it is coercion." The common theme of Cregan's plays is the struggle for power and the manipulation of social conventions to achieve it. A more or less closed society that has developed its own conventions is often the setting: a school in *Miniatures* and again in *Tina*, a small town in *Three Men for Colverton*, an oasis in *The Land of Palms*, a boarding house in *Poor Tom*. In other plays the characters act as if in a closed society: in *The Dancers*, in which a middle-aged quintet dance and pair off in various combinations, and the "cozy circle" of two mutually adulterous couples of *Liebestraum*—but where, when Jane does not find herself attracted to her husband's lover's husband, the others fear that she will seek a lover elsewhere, in which case "we'll find ourselves part of a larger community before we know where we are, with all the loss of sovereignty that will entail."

Often in Cregan's plays one set of conventions is brought into conflict with another. In his most complex play, *Three Men for Colverton*, the leader of a trio of evangelists seeks to take control of the town from the domineering Mrs. Carnock. She believes Colverton "was meant to be a stagnant pool . . . and stagnant it will remain." The uncompromising vision of the evangelists, who "hate every lubricant of living" and decry "the stern virility of man [etiolated] in the black night of consumer goods," threatens the indulgence and manipulation of human relationships by which she maintains her dominance. Other power-seekers are the liberal vicar and an Anglican monk who uses the confessional to his own advantage.

Where existing conventions are strained or broken, new conventions are invented. In *Liebestraum* the adulterous relationships are regularized. A strict alternation of days for sleeping with one's marriage partner and with one's lover is threatened by Jane's uncertain feelings; when she does fulfil everyone's expectations by completing the sexual cross-partnering she does so on the wrong day and is denounced for her carnality. In *The Land of Palms* some British have set up a community of peace and harmony at an oasis. Three British ex-Foreign Legionnaires arrive with their military values. In *Transcending*, a short play of wonderful verve, a teenage girl escapes from the world of her parents and two of her neighbours, a young man and an older widower, all of whom have a role to offer her, by appearing at the end of the play dressed as a nun—escaping by invoking a different set of conventions.

There are in Cregan's plays instinctive non-conformists. In *Miniatures* the climactic scene reveals the music teacher sitting in his store closet surrounded by all the items that have been stolen around the school. He later tries to hang himself. In *The Land of Palms* the soldier who cannot adapt to the oasis community kills himself. In *Three Men for Colverton* one of the evangelists is homosexual. He declares, "One is one and all alone and ever more shall be so. Two bodies don't make one, two minds don't make one, and I'm one." In the last scene he throws himself from a clocktower and dies. Not borne up by angels, this individualist has unwittingly destroyed the leading evangelist's power. Meanwhile, Mrs. Carnock has died, and perhaps the play's other nonconformist, a teacher who fornicates with his pupils, will establish "that dreary venture, the Arts Centre," which Mrs. Carnock had opposed, as "an act of existential heroism." In much the same spirit he will marry his latest, pregnant teenage mistress.

In Cregan's more recent short plays the nonconformists are the central characters. Tina, a teacher, dresses in jeans and leather jacket to try to reach an abused ten-year-old, whom Cregan has ironically named Dawn. In *Poor Tom* Tom murders the owner of the boarding-house to prevent him selling it. In each play much of the interest is in how the other characters react to this tearing of the social fabric.

Cregan writes dry, wry comedies. Introducing *Three Men for Colverton* he writes that "the situations of most of the characters are too painful to make me laugh. However, most of the people are themselves aware of the silliness of their positions, and this frequently leads them to act in a sillier way than ever." So it is in all his plays. The characters' self-consciousness effects a certain distancing from the audience. They often introduce themselves to the audience and sing choruses together. In *Three Men for Colverton* they move the revolving platforms Cregan envisions as setting. In *The Dancers* different records are put on and taken off, accompanied by lighting changes, while in the brief comedy *George Reborn* the characters conduct an orchestra in snatches from well-known classical works.

The Houses by the Green is more farcical than his other full-length plays. It is a Plautine or *commedia* farce, offering the battle of two elderly men, the Commander and Mervyn Molyneux, who live in adjacent houses, for the hand of Molyneux's adopted daughter Susan, and their besting by her young lover, the servingman Oliver whom they share. Molyneux woos Susan disguised as his own friend; the Commander does likewise. Neither is aware of the other's deception. Disguised as a land developer, Oliver threatens both with their community's destruction. Even Susan disguises herself, as the developer's trollop; Oliver, puzzled, tells the audience "I must be impersonating a real person." Traditional forgiveness and marriage promises end the play when Susan, untraditionally pregnant, "is suddenly sick at the side of the stage."

—Anthony Graham-White

CRISTOFER, Michael. Pseudonym for Michael Procaccino. American. Born in White Horse, New Jersey, 22 January 1945. Educated at Catholic University, Washington, D.C., 1962–65; American University, Beirut, 1968–69. Recipient: Los Angeles Drama Critics Circle award, for acting, 1973, for playwriting, 1975; Pulitzer Prize, 1977; Tony award, 1977; Obie award, for acting, 1980. Address: c/o Dramatists Play Service, 440 Park Avenue South, New York, New York 10016, U.S.A.

PUBLICATIONS

Plays

The Mandala (produced Philadelphia, 1968).
Plot Counter Plot (produced New York, 1971).
Americomedia (produced New York, 1973).
The Shadow Box (produced Los Angeles, 1975; New York, 1977; London, 1979). New York, French, 1977.
Ice (produced Los Angeles, 1976; New York, 1979).
Black Angel (produced Los Angeles, 1978; New York, 1982). New York, Dramatists Play Service, 1984.
C.C. Pyle and the Bunyon Derby (produced Gambier, Ohio, 1978).
The Lady and the Clarinet (produced Los Angeles, 1980; New York, 1983). New York, Dramatists Play Service, 1985.

Screenplays: *Falling in Love*, 1985; *The Witches of Eastwick*, 1987.

Theatrical Activities:
Director: **Plays**—*Candida* by Shaw, New York, 1981; *Forty-Deuce* by Alan Bowne, New York, 1981.
Actor: **Plays**—roles at the Arena Stage, Washington, D.C., 1967–68, Theatre of Living Arts, Philadelphia, 1968, and Beirut Repertory Company, Lebanon, 1968–69; in *Yegor Bulichov* by Gorky, New Haven, Connecticut, 1970–71; Jules in *The Justice Box* by Michael Robert Davis, New York, 1971; *The Tooth of Crime* by Sam Shepard, Los Angeles, 1973; *Ajax* by Sophocles, Los Angeles, 1974; Colin in *Ashes* by David Rudkin, Los Angeles, 1976; *The Three Sisters* by Chekhov, Los Angeles, 1976; *Savages* by Christopher Hampton, Los Angeles; Trofimov in *The Cherry Orchard* by Chekhov, New York, 1976; Charlie in *Conjuring an Event* by Richard Nelson, New York, 1978; title role in *Chinchilla* by Robert David MacDonald, New York, 1979. **Films**—*An Enemy of the People*, 1976; *The Little Drummer Girl*, 1984. **Television**—*Sandburg's Lincoln*, 1975; *Crime Club*, 1975; *The Last of Mrs. Lincoln*, 1975; *The Entertainer*, 1976; *Knuckle*, 1976.

* * *

Michael Cristofer's development as a playwright, a development that includes *Plot Counter Plot*, *The Mandala*, and *Americomedia* and climaxed with *The Shadow Box* (Pulitzer Prize and Tony Award), is as instructive a lesson in how to become a playwright as *The Shadow Box* is an exciting addition to recent American drama. Like Harold Pinter and certain other contemporary dramatists, Cristofer is a gifted actor—and, with the Circle in the Square production of Shaw's *Candida*, director—and his own practical experience with theater is everywhere apparent in the play's skillful theatricality. In addition his association with the Mark Taper Forum and its director Gordon Davidson has provided a unifying center. The coalescence of three one-act plays through a series of workshops into a single contrapuntal drama, *The Shadow Box* is a process seldom possible without a secure producing environment.

The play, apparently based upon the terminal illness of two friends and Kubler-Ross's research into the state of mind of dying patients, demonstrates how the shadow of death intensifies life, merges individuality into community, and reduces times and places into a single here and now. Perhaps reflecting its origin as three draft one-act plays, *The Shadow Box* is built upon threes. Cristofer presents a trinity of characters, each surrounded by two other characters important in his personal life: Joe, a blue-collar worker, his wife, and adolescent son; Brian, an extravagant writer-intellectual, his lover, and his former wife; and Felicity, a lady of uncertain age, and both her spinster daughter and her dead daughter whose imaginary letters keep her alive. The play's set seems also to be in triplicate: three vacation cottages in the woods in a medically and psychologically controlled estate for the dying, each cottage with "*A front porch, a living room area, and a large kitchen area.*" But it is through the set's omnipresent visual image, and the constant cross-cutting this makes possible, that death's power to reduce diversity to communality and a common ground is constantly reiterated: the three cottages are in effect presented as one, and the trio of characters, who never actually meet, alternately inhabit, as the lights go down and come up, the various playing areas. The pastoral setting and the domesticity made possible by the cottage also unobtrusively place death in the context of external nature and the echoes of everyday life.

If Cristofer has a sure theatrical sense and a feeling for essential dimensions of the human experience, he also has a sense for the other indispensable ingredient of drama: language. Like a number of recent dramatists he has deliberately attempted to reverse the trend toward non-verbal theater—really the concern of dance—that characterized so much drama in the 1960's and early 1970's. The movement made important contributions but forgot the necessity to be memorably articulate. Cristofer's concern for verbal complexity is apparent immediately in the title *The Shadow Box*. In modern drama especially, titles index a play's concerns, and this one works on several complementary levels of reference. It refers to a late 19th-century device in which figures were superimposed against a chosen landscape or setting. The stationary quality of such scenes and their arbitrary arrangement express the predetermined situation of the terminally ill who are placed in a deliberately arranged environment. The term, which refers as well to a method of covering a motion picture screen so that film can be shone in daylight, expresses the play's analysis of the usually unseen, and the verb "to shadow box" connotes a fight, like the fight with death, which is ultimately an illusion. If the play begins with an emphasis upon words, it ends with an extraordinary "coda" in which life is celebrated in the face of death. The characters speak in choral fashion exchanging brief words and phrases and conclude with repetitions of the affirmative "Yes" and the final "This moment."

Ice is set in a cabin in Alaska and shows a trio of characters caught in a situation that symbolizes death in life. The subsequent *Black Angel* and *The Lady and the Clarinet* have now been seen in New York, but these somewhat counterpart plays do not sustain the promise of *The Shadow Box*. The former studies a man, Martin Engel, an apparent Nazi war criminal, and analyzes "hate," and the latter is a portrait of a woman, Luba, and her experiences with "love." Both plays interestingly suppress facts and narrative clarity and make use of simultaneous time, but in neither case are the central characters themselves created in enough depth or uniqueness to occasion or to support the playwright's relentless analyses of them. But these plays do continue Cristofer's important interest in the collaborative arts of theater.

—Gaynor F. Bradish

CROSS, (Alan) Beverley. British. Born in London, 13 April 1931; son of the theatrical manager George Cross and the actress Eileen Williams. Educated at the Nautical College, Pangbourne, Berkshire, 1944–47; Balliol College, Oxford, 1952–53. Served in the Royal Naval Reserve, 1944–48; British Army, 1948–50. Married 1) Elizabeth Clunies-Ross in 1955 (marriage dissolved), two daughters; 2) Gayden Collins in 1965 (marriage dissolved), one son; 3) the actress Maggie Smith in 1975. Seaman, Norwegian Merchant Service, 1950–52; actor, Shakespeare Memorial Theatre Company, 1954–56; production assistant for children's drama, BBC Television, 1956. Drama consultant, Stratford Festival Theatre, Ontario, 1975–80. Recipient: Arts Council grant, 1957, and award, 1960. Agent: Curtis Brown, 162–168 Regent Street, London W1R 5TB, England.

PUBLICATIONS

Plays

One More River (produced Liverpool, 1958; London, 1959; New York, 1960). London, Hart Davis, 1959.

The Singing Dolphin (for children), based on an idea by Kitty Black (produced Oxford, 1959; London, 1963). With *The Three Cavaliers*, London, Hart Davis, 1960.

Strip the Willow (produced Nottingham and London, 1960). London, Evans, 1961.

The Three Cavaliers (for children; produced Birmingham, 1960). With *The Singing Dolphin*, London, Hart Davis, 1960.

Belle; or, The Ballad of Dr. Crippen, with Wolf Mankowitz, music by Monty Norman (produced London, 1961).

Boeing-Boeing, adaptation of a play by Marc Camoletti (produced Oxford, 1961; London, 1962; New York, 1965). London, Evans, and New York, French, 1967.

Wanted on Voyage, adaptation of a play by Jacques Deval (produced Canterbury, 1962).

Half a Sixpence, music by David Heneker, adaptation of the novel *Kipps* by H.G. Wells (produced London, 1963; New York, 1965). London, Chappell, 1967; Chicago, Dramatic Publishing Company, n.d.

The Mines of Sulphur, music by Richard Rodney Bennett (produced London, 1965; New York, 1968). Published in *Plays of the Year 30*, London, Elek, 1965.

The Pirates and the Inca Gold (produced Sydney, 1966).

Jorrocks, music by David Heneker, adaptation of novels by R.S. Surtees (produced London, 1966). London, Chappell, 1968.

All the King's Men (for children), music by Richard Rodney Bennett (produced Coventry and London, 1969). London, Universal Editions, 1969.

Phil the Fluter, with Donal Giltinan, music and lyrics by David Heneker and Percy French (produced London, 1969).

Victory, music by Richard Rodney Bennett, adaptation of the novel by Joseph Conrad (produced London, 1970). London, Universal Editions, 1970.

The Rising of the Moon, music by Nicholas Maw (produced Glyndebourne, Sussex, 1970). London, Boosey and Hawkes, 1971.

Catherine Howard (televised 1970). Published in *The Six Wives of Henry VIII*, edited by J.C. Trewin, London, Elek, 1972; revised version (produced York, 1972), London, French, 1973.

The Crickets Sing (produced Devizes, Wiltshire, 1971). London, Hutchinson, 1970.

The Owl on the Battlements (for children; produced Nottingham, 1971).

Where's Winkle? (for children; produced Liverpool, 1972).

The Great Society (produced London, 1974).

Hans Christian Andersen, with John Fearnley and Tommy Steele, music and lyrics by Frank Loesser (produced London, 1974; revised version produced London, 1976). New York, Music Theatre International, 1978.

The Mask of Orpheus, music by Nicholas Maw. London, Boosey and Hawkes, 1976.

Happy Birthday, adaptation of a play by Marc Camoletti (produced Brighton, 1978; London, 1979). London, French, 1980.

Haworth: A Portrait of the Brontës (produced Stratford, Ontario, 1978; Birmingham, 1981). Toronto, Theatrebooks, 1978.

The Scarlet Pimpernel, adaptation of the novel by Baroness Orczy (produced Chichester, Sussex, and London, 1985).

Miranda, adaptation of a play by Goldoni (produced Chichester, 1987).

Screenplays: *Jason and the Argonauts*, with Jan Read, 1963; *The Long Ships*, with Berkely Mather, 1964; *Genghis Khan*, with Clarke Reynolds and Berkely Mather, 1965; *Half a Sixpence*, 1967; *The Donkey Rustlers*, 1969; *Mussolini: Ultimo Atto* (*Mussolini: The Last Act*), with Carlo Lizzani, 1972; *Sinbad and the Eye of the Tiger*, 1977; *The Clash of the Titans*, 1981.

Television Plays: *The Nightwalkers*, 1960; *The Dark Pits of War*, 1960; *Catherine Howard*, 1970; *March On, Boys!*, 1975; *A Bill of Mortality*, 1975; *Miss Sugar Plum*, 1976 (Canada); *The World Turned Upside Down*, 1976 (USA).

Novels

Mars in Capricorn. London, Hart Davis, and Boston, Little Brown, 1955.

The Nightwalkers. London, Hart Davis, 1956; Boston, Little Brown, 1957.

*

Critical Studies: *Anger and After* by John Russell Taylor, London, Methuen, 1962, revised edition, 1969, as *The Angry Theatre*, New York, Hill and Wang, 1962, revised edition, 1969; introduction by J.C. Trewin to *The Mines of Sulphur*, in *Plays of the Year 30*, London, Elek, 1965.

Theatrical Activities:
Director: **Plays**—*Boeing-Boeing*, Sydney, 1964; *The Platinum Cat* by Roger Longrigg, London, 1965.
Actor: **Plays**—Agamemnon in *Troilus and Cressida*, Oxford,

1953; Soldier in *Othello*, Stratford-on-Avon, 1954; Mr. Fox in *Toad of Toad Hall* by A.A. Milne, London, 1954; Balthazar in *Much Ado about Nothing*, London, 1955; Herald in *King Lear*, London, 1955.

Beverley Cross comments:

Four main divisions of work: 1) for the commercial theatre, viz., books for musicals, boulevard comedies (i.e., *Boeing-Boeing, Half a Sixpence*); 2) librettos for modern opera (i.e., *Mines of Sulphur, Rising of the Moon*); 3) comedies and librettos for children (i.e., *Three Cavaliers, All the King's Men, Owl on the Battlements*); 4) fantasy movies (i.e., *Jason and the Argonauts, Clash of the Titans*, etc.).

Since 1969 has lived mostly abroad—in Greece, France, the US, and Canada—working on 4).

* * *

Beverley Cross has become best known as a writer of books for popular musicals (*Half a Sixpence, Jorrocks*) and of librettos for operas (*Victory, The Rising of the Moon*). He has also translated a highly successful boulevard farce (*Boeing-Boeing*), contributed one of the better episodes to a highly successful television series, *The Six Wives of Henry VIII* (*Catherine Howard*), written several lively, if less obviously successful, plays for children, and a small number of commercially unsuccessful plays for adults. What generalisations can be made on the basis of such a spread of work?

First, that at his best he is capable of writing a vigorous, muscular, masculine dialogue which many more pretentious writers might envy. Second, that he is particularly interested in a spirit of adventure that (he feels) no longer exists in the contemporary world, and, consequently, in the character of the adventurer himself. It is significant that many of his works are set in other periods: the light children's play, *The Singing Dolphin*, among pirates in the 18th century, the serious opera, *The Mines of Sulphur*, in a remote country house at about the same time. This latter work, with its forceful language and vivid portrayal of a murderer who traps a troupe of wandering actors and is then trapped by them, shows Cross at his strongest. Another work is set in the future:

> No planes to spoil the view. No trippers to litter the grass. No stinking petrol fumes to poison the air. No silly women to bitch away your time with their gossip and intrigue Nothing to read, nothing to see. Complete freedom for the first time in my life. It's wonderful!

That is spoken by a character in *Strip the Willow*, a rather inconclusive quasi-Shavian comedy of ideas involving a tiny group of survivors of nuclear desolation, deep in the English countryside, living on their wits while the Russians and Americans divide the world between them; but the sentiment could be Cross's own.

He has written only one artistically successful play for adults; and that is his first, *One More River*, which occurs (characteristically) in a ship moored in a backwater on another continent and involves (characteristically) a mutiny. The seamen, among whom egalitarian notions have been circulating, turn on an unpopular officer and hang him, on false suspicion of having caused the death of one of their number. But they haven't the ability to exercise power, and are ignominiously forced to get an apprentice officer to navigate them upriver. The story is excitingly told, and some of the characterisation, notably of a self-satisfied, popularity-seeking bosun, is as good as some of it is melodramatic; but what makes the play interesting is its unfashionable viewpoint. Carefully, logically, it suggests that absolute democracy is mob-rule: some men are superior to others, and the others must submit to their authority. It is, of course, possible to pick holes in the argument as it emerges, for instance by pointing out that Cross does not face the possibility that the seaman's apparent inferiority may be less innate than the result of an unjust environment; but the achievement stands. *One More River* is one of the very few intelligent right-wing plays that the modern theatre has produced.

—Benedict Nightingale

CROWLEY, Mart. American. Born in Vicksburg, Mississippi, 21 August 1935. Educated at St. Aloysius High School, Vicksburg; Catholic University, Washington, D.C., graduated 1957. Worked for Martin Manulis Productions, 1963, and Four Star Television, 1964; secretary to the actress Natalie Wood, 1964–66; from 1979 producer of the television series *Hart to Hart*. Agent: International Creative Management, 40 West 57th Street, New York, New York 10019. Address: 1355 North Laurel Avenue, Los Angeles, California, U.S.A.

PUBLICATIONS

Plays

The Boys in the Band (produced New York, 1968; London, 1969). New York, Farrar Straus, 1968; London, Secker and Warburg, 1969.
Remote Asylum (produced Los Angeles, 1970).
A Breeze from the Gulf (produced New York, 1973). New York, Farrar Straus, 1974.

Screenplay: *The Boys in the Band*, 1970.

Television Play: *There Must Be a Pony*, from the novel by James Kirkwood, 1986.

* * *

Michael, the host of the homosexual birthday party in Mart Crowley's highly successful *The Boys in the Band*, through whose agency it becomes a shattering summation of all ironic birthdays, is also a character in Crowley's other two plays, *Remote Asylum* and *A Breeze from the Gulf*. In *The Boys in the Band*, in the aftermath of his drunken manipulation and mockery of his friends, Michael's hysterical guilt quiets into the memory of his father dying in his arms with the last words, "I don't understand any of it. I never did." In *Remote Asylum* this scene is re-enacted at an exotic clifftop mansion in Acapulco, where Michael is a guest. The wealthy American owner, Ray, mute from cancer and abjectly mothered by his wife, Irene, with furtive liquor and a shrine to the Madonna his sole remaining prerogatives, expires in Michael's arms as Michael speaks the confession-absolution for him. Finally, in *A Breeze from the Gulf* the original scene is enacted as Michael's father, Teddy, the insecure, conventionally Catholic owner of a pool hall who jocularly took a drink "just to be somebody," dies of alcoholism cradled in his son's arms. Since

Michael's father is diminutive whether as "Daddy" or Teddy, his wife Loraine has taken to Demerol and to the protective and flirtatious smothering of her son, expressed in the adolescent Michael's asthma. Though Michael depends on Teddy and Teddy's God to keep his mother well, both let him down. At the climax of the first act, when Teddy threatens to have Loraine committed, Michael cracks a gin bottle over his head and curses God for betraying the bargain in which Michael stopped masturbating for his mother's sake. Thus Crowley's recurring image is of the death or bafflement of the masculine principle, not least in Michael himself.

The Boys in the Band was a sensational success in New York and was soon filmed. Although conventional in form, depending on a naturalistic verve in the styles with which the homosexual subculture disports itself, it marks a breakthrough in dramatizing that milieu from within. Its perspective of the comforting if not always comfortable camaraderie of a gay circle allows Crowley to project the internal conflict of the homosexual in the sphere and relationships in which it arises, besides exploiting the native mix of defiant role-playing and wry self-consciousness. Crowley may be said to invert the older pattern in that the outsider in this ensemble play is the one heterosexual character. Historically the importance of the play is that, in the idiom of its characters, it brings out of the closet the species of male bitch (in Eric Bentley's word) or that generic ambivalence notoriously felt but dissembled in the plays of Williams and Albee. Significantly these dramatists are integrated into Crowley's dialogue as the upper end of the camp culture with which his characters identify.

The homosexuals assembled in a smart New York duplex are demonstrative in several senses, ranging from giddy effeminacy through a pair of more masculine and stable lovers, a black, and a dumb hustler hired for $20 as a birthday present, to the host Michael, preoccupied with his thinning hair and feckless lifestyle, remembering his possessive mother and weak father, and drinking heavily until his self-hatred is turned on the others in the second-act "game." The unexpected presence of Michael's heterosexual college friend Alan focuses the fantasy of the straight man who can be had, and he is the intended victim of the game in which Michael compels the others to telephone the one individual they have truly loved. With surprising candor the game is evidence for a view of homosexuality as the dissimulated impulse to emasculate other men. The tables are turned on Michael when Alan calls his wife and when the lovers Hank and Larry repair the breach of jealousy by sentimentally phoning each other, but what lingers from this epiphany of love is the disembodiment of the telephone as an acute symbol of the severance of love and carnal expression which is the homosexual's plight, of the promiscuous Larry no less than the dehumanized hustler, Cowboy. Possibly the limitation of the play is that, beyond the desperate fraternity of the group, it finds no better image of love with which to transcend the self-centeredness and compulsion of sex. Michael says at the end, "You show me a happy homosexual and I'll show you a gay corpse." The dialogue preserves a witty flash and bite and refuses to solemnize the gambits of gay life, except for a persistent referent of self-pity, but intellectually, for all its epigrammatic edge and tartness, the camp ambience is a kind of glamorizing soft-focus suggestive of Hollywood models like Mankiewicz's *All about Eve* (which one of the boys can recite verbatim). In the end the dialogue is all about "Evelyn," the archetypal guilty mother who loved her son for his failures.

In *Remote Asylum* Michael depends on liquor and pills and a familial relationship with the lovers Diana and Tom, whom he accompanies to the Acapulco retreat of the older Americans Irene and Ray. Both Diana and Tom are flying from broken marriages, and the latter, a golden boy of tennis, is nearly as infantile as Michael. But the terrible example of the emasculating Irene, in whose barrenness and barren luxury the maternal haven is exposed for good and all, inspires Tom to a knowledge that responsibility as well as love is necessary for survival. And even Michael, after identifying with the dying Ray both as father and father confessor, flees the mad asylum of Irene. This play recalls Tennessee Williams in its vivid coastal scene and bizarre symbolism—the towers rising above the terrace set, the recurrent cry of a baby for which there appears to be no explanation (though Michael claims to be a ventriloquist), the magnified shadow of a rat, and the grotesquely cackling and jangling homosexual Mexican servants "La Damita" and "El Dorado," who cavort in obscene travesty of the Americans, of sex itself, and savagely beat Michael in the drained swimming pool. The pool, scene also of lovemaking between Diana and Tom in which Irene voyeuristically shares from atop her tower, is the ironic womb of Michael's yearnings. Simultaneously the audience hears Diana climaxing, the sleeping moans of the drunken Ray, and the cry of the baby. Set against masculine debility and the neuter freaks of Irene's household is the primitive virility of the native chauffeur Carlos who, besides befriending the helpless Ray, secretes and protects his peasant girl-wife and baby, and in the end coolly sells his body to Irene, meeting her on equal if ambiguous terms.

A Breeze from the Gulf, a three-character play spanning ten years of family life in a Mississippi town, also recalls Williams in the neurotic, drug-dependent Loraine, particularly in the final scene where she is being readied for the sanatorium and in her last speech about moments of happiness as "a breeze from the gulf." For that matter, in the miasma of alcohol and drugs, comparisons arise with O'Neill. And the familiarity of the basic situation lends itself to Michael's compact summary in the other two plays. The ineffectual Teddy censures his son's spelling and stands by while Loraine bathes, babies, and woos Michael. Loraine's own weakness—social insecurity, hypochondria, and dependence on drugs—becomes the classic feminine mode of domination.

But for all this, and the increasing extremities of conflict, the play has a remarkable integrity of felt experience owing to the naturalness, thrift, and energy of Crowley's dialogue. The first act is a lyric evocation of the family bond regardless of warps, of the intimate rites and instinctive if groping affirmations that, however universal, are *sui generis* in the matrix Michael "remembers." The irony of the second act is that Michael, out of his crucible of dependency and with now the addition of rankling resentments, must return from college to take bitter responsibility for both his parents. In the brutal duel of the final scene he compels Loraine to make her perennial trip to the sanatorium. Sex remains the fatality in Crowley's world, but here it is indivisible from love, and by that token the moral center passes from the self-pity of *The Boys in the Band* to the compassion of which Teddy speaks. This also he does not "understand," but where his last words have been objectified with harrowing and poignant force, it is the authentic form and distillate of Crowley's play.

Crowley's most recent work is a television play, *There Must Be a Pony*, based on the novel by James Kirkwood. This drama of a flamboyant aging actress, her relationship to her sensitive son and to a new lover with whom the teenager also identifies, seems continuous with the Crowley ambience: Hollywood and Tennessee Williams. Though the lover's masculine strength and appeal, the much-needed *reliable* quality, appear to derive from his being outside the tinsel show-business world of mother and son, in the end he lets them down, his so positive role in their lives proving a "role" in the wrong sense, a false identity which undermines the good he has done and finally destroys him. So there is the familiar ambiguity of the masculine model, the familiar letdown, possibly the irony that for all her instability and excesses the actress is more "real" than the rational people on whom she depends.

—David W. Beams

DANIELS, Sarah. British. Born in London in 1957. Writer-in-residence, Royal Court Theatre, London, 1984. Recipient: George Devine Award, 1983. Agent: Judy Daish Associates, 83 Eastbourne Mews, London W2 6LQ, England.

PUBLICATIONS

Plays

Penumbra (produced Sheffield, 1981).
Ripen Our Darkness (produced London, 1981). With *The Devil's Gateway*, London, Methuen, 1986.
Ma's Flesh Is Grass (produced Sheffield, 1981).
The Devil's Gateway (produced London, 1983). With *Ripen Our Darkness*, London, Methuen, 1986.
Masterpieces (produced Manchester and London, 1983). London, Methuen, 1984; revised version (produced London, 1984), 1984, revised version, 1986.
Neaptide (produced London, 1986). London, Methuen, 1986.
Byrthrite (produced London, 1986). London, Methuen, 1987.

* * *

While it is possible with most plays to laugh or feel anger or delight only vaguely aware that one's feelings are being shared (or not), the work of Sarah Daniels seems to draw from the audience emotions almost tangible in their specificity—anger, shock, rejection, or partisanship—which themselves affect the climate in which the play is being performed. This springs partly from the subject matter: Daniels treats controversial issues such as pornography, marital violence, the rights of lesbian mothers. But it is also prompted by the plays' form. Michelene Wandor remarks that "her sense of structure is unformed" and that "she veers in style between sit-com cliché, earnest naturalism, and unintegrated polemic," and Daniels does indeed outrage many conventional expectations of what a play should be; but audiences seem divided between those who see this as a failing and those who find it her most theatrically exciting quality.

Take, for example, Scene 9 of *Ripen Our Darkness*. It is sandwiched between two scenes which require, and get, very delicate handling. In Scene 8 two sisters meet; Julie, the elder has left home and her violent father, the younger has stayed on. Now she needs advice and the relationship begins tentatively to re-form itself. In Scene 10 we see Julie again, as part of a loving lesbian couple. Scene 9 itself is about ten seconds long, a melodramatic tableau in which Julie's mother remarks flatly to her younger daughter "Your father's choked to death on a scone." It is a laugh line, a cheery deus ex machina which will make possible some improvements in both sisters' lot. Daniels does not shirk the long-term effects of family violence—this lucky accident does not provide all the answers and even raises new problems which are sensitively treated. But by erupting into near-farce she displaces the prevalent notion of marital violence as a "problem" to be treated on "both sides" rather than as a crime men commit.

Daniels frequently dislocates our assumptions in this way. In her first play, *Penumbra*, it becomes slowly apparent that the setting is in the future: the sexual and economic violence to which the central female characters are subjected is not a one-off horror but a part of a developing and systematic pattern of oppression. At the end of the play one of the women makes it clear that the pattern is already starting to form. "They changed our language. It wasn't ours anyway. Women who led alternative lives were 'obstructionist' and 'reactionary.' It hasn't changed anything much . . . we were always abnormal—the enemy."

This dislocation effect counterpoints Daniels's increasing use of central characters who initially accept the status quo orthodoxy. They start by attempting to change one aspect of society—nuclear weapons, pornography—only to discover that its whole fabric of patriarchy is rotten. One of her most effective plays, *Masterpieces*, centres on a nice young social worker, Rowena; we see her trying to sort out a job for a client, coping with an embarrassing dinner party, and, smug in her own married life, persuading her husband to show her the sort of pornographic magazine he sees at work. These naturalistic scenes are framed by the trial of Rowena for murder. At first this seems to be a nightmare, a projection of her worst fears. Gradually Daniels reveals that the trial is real, that it is taking place in present time and that the other scenes flash back to the events which triggered the killing of a man on a station platform. Rowena is gradually shown to be one of a number of victims of the pornography about which she is initially so light-hearted. The male characters who profess to enjoy it and be unaffected by it are all seen to treat women as objects: through direct use of force, through abuse of their authority at work, through "humour" which actually provides an outlet for the agression inherent in their marital relationships. All the women gradually come to the conclusion that pornography is just one aspect of male exploitation that also manifests itself in economic and social terms. But, as the play shows, they are powerless to change things rapidly enough. Rowena becomes increasingly angry about the impact of pornography on her own life and the lives of her woman friends until, like many social workers, she has to view a snuff movie; her reaction to it is murderous rage arbitrarily vented on the first man who approaches her. The court refuses to believe that a pornographic film really has this potential power over its audience; it thus takes up the same position as the consumers of it. It is only at this point that Daniels forces us to confront what pornography really is as the already sentenced Rowena describes the film to a policewoman. The details are profoundly shocking; they create a silence among the audience that persists a long time. Rowena can change nothing; it is, Daniels seems to imply, up to us. And to change the society that produced the film is, in the end, to change its structure from top to bottom.

—Frances Gray

DARKE, Nick. British. Born in Wadebridge, Cornwall, 29 August 1948. Educated at Newquay Grammar School, Cornwall; Rose Bruford College, Sidcup, Kent, 1967–70, diploma 1970. Has two sons. Actor in repertory, Belfast, 1970; actor and director, Victoria Theatre, Stoke-on-Trent, Staffordshire,

1971–79. Recipient: George Devine Award, 1979. Agent: Margaret Ramsay Ltd., 14-A Goodwin's Court, London WC2N 4LL. Address: St. Julians, Sevenoaks, Kent TN15 0RX, England.

PUBLICATIONS

Plays

Mother Goose (pantomime; also director: produced Stoke-on-Trent, 1977).
Never Say Rabbit in a Boat (produced Stoke-on-Trent, 1978).
Landmarks (produced Chester and London, 1979).
A Tickle on the River's Back (produced London, 1979).
Summer Trade (produced Ilfracombe, Devon, 1979).
High Water (produced Newcastle upon Tyne and London, 1980). Published in *Plays Introduction*, London, Faber, 1984.
Say Your Prayers, music by Andrew Dickson (produced Plymouth and London, 1981).
The Catch (produced London, 1981).
The Lowestoft Man (produced on tour, 1982).
The Body, music by Guy Woolfenden (produced London, 1983). London, Methuen, 1983.
Cider with Rosie, adaptation of the work by Laurie Lee (produced Manchester, 1983).
The Earth Turned Inside Out (produced St. Austell, Cornwall, 1984).
Bud (produced Newcastle upon Tyne and London, 1985).
The Oven Glove Murders (produced London, 1986).
The Dead Monkey (produced London, 1986).
Ting Tang Mine (produced St. Austell, Cornwall, 1987; revised version produced London, 1987).

Radio Plays: *Foggy Anniversary*, 1979; *Lifeboat*, 1981.

Television Play: *Farmers Arms*, 1983.

*

Theatrical Activities:
Director: **Plays**—Victoria Theatre, Stoke-on-Trent: *Mother Goose, Man Is Man* by Brecht, *The Miser* by Molière, *Absurd Person Singular* by Alan Ayckbourn, *The Scarlet Pimpernel*, and *A Cuckoo in the Nest* by Ben Travers, 1977–79.
Actor: roles in more than 50 plays, Victoria Theatre, Stoke-on-Trent.

Nick Darke comments:

I consider my seven years as an actor to have been an apprenticeship for writing plays. By appearing in over 50 productions of new plays, classics, documentaries, children's plays, and community road-shows I learned first hand the difference between good and bad dialogue, how to create characters and construct a world for the play to exist in. Most of my plays make people laugh, but I try to make an audience question its laughter. I have a low boredom threshold, and my interest in my plays lasts for exactly as long as it takes me to write them. I have strong ideas about how they should be cast and directed, and I watch them in performance to see how the audience reacts. After that my interest wanes and the next one has to be different in every respect to the last. I write quickly: the quicker it's written, the better the play. I think about a play for far longer than it takes me to write it. I type as fast as my brain works, so I dispense with the longhand stage and work straight onto the keyboard. I read my work out loud as I write it. For this reason I have to work entirely alone and out of earshot. I don't just mouth what I've written, if a scene demands decibels I supply them. If it's funny, I laugh. To see an audience laugh at something as much as I did when I first thought of it is a pleasure only another playwright could understand. I judge the success of my plays from the audience's response. My agent reads and sees my work, and I disregard her advice at my peril; she is my most valuable critic. I don't know what is a good play and what isn't. I don't know what makes some people like a play and others not. Some nights a whole audience will dislike a play, the next night they'll love it, with no perceptible change in the performance. My plays tend to be ambiguous, and because the style alters with each one, nobody knows what to expect. This makes for hair-raising volatility which I don't like, but can't help. My advice to a budding playwright: Cultivate your sense of rhythm, and never go into rehearsal without a good ending.

* * *

Nick Darke, who started his theatrical career as an actor at the Victoria Theatre, Stoke-on-Trent, seems to launch himself into writing plays rather as if he were working on new roles. Energetic, versatile, imaginative, inventive, eclectic, insatiably hungry for identifications which let him disappear into a disguise, he slips unrecognisably from one style, one period, one setting to another. *The Dead Monkey* is set in contemporary California, *Ting Tang Mine* goes back to an early 19th-century Cornish copper-mining community, *A Tickle on the River's Back* takes place on a Thames barge, while the setting for *The Oven Glove Murders* is a Soho film production company. Darke lodges himself in contrasting idioms like an actor who is good at accents.

His plays, almost without exception, contain sequences which are extremely suspenseful, and others which are extremely funny, but even in his best plays, such as *The Body* and *The Dead Monkey*, the writing sometimes sinks too far below the level he is capable of achieving. The funniest sequences in *The Body* occur in the first half, which climaxes in a hilarious scene involving a muddy, half-naked corpse, a farmer who is also muddy and half-naked because he is impersonating the corpse, a cat which has just been strangled, a rat-trap, an old man wearing a gas-mask, an old woman who believes she may have been touched by divinity, three farmers who speak verse in unison and a policeman who is trying to arrest all the villagers simultaneously. Less amusing and more suspenseful, the second half of the play, set in an American airbase, works towards a climax that centres on the probability of a nuclear explosion as a young Cornish farmer, brainwashed into believing he is an American soldier, brandishes a loaded machine gun and hesitates about whether to obey the orders of a sane sergeant or a demented lieutenant who has been tied up and blindfolded but not—this was the sergeant's mistake—gagged.

The plot also introduces a rector who dresses as a Mandarin, realising that his parishioners pay no more attention to him than they would to a Chinaman. They do listen if he harangues them in Chinese, but all this is not entirely irrelevant to the plot because it convinces the psychopathic lieutenant (who suspects reds under the unlikeliest of beds) that Chinese infiltration is converting the villagers to Maoism. The solution is to ask them whether they're Communist and shoot them if they deny it.

Darke's hostility to nuclear weapons, Americans, policemen, soldiers, and capitalism is rather generalised, and his writing sags under its heavy burden of literary influences and bizarre jokes. The most obvious debt is to Brecht, who was himself indebted to Kipling for the three soldiers in *Mann ist Mann* who brainwash a civilian into taking on the identity of a missing comrade. The play also seems to have been influenced by the Auden and Isherwood of *The Dog Beneath the Skin*, by the Stoppard of *After Magritte*, and by the T.S. Eliot of the verse plays.

The Dead Monkey is a funnier, more consistent play, more accomplished, less patchy, less eclectic, though the rhythms of Tennessee Williams and Edward Albee are sometimes audible. We also feel that, as in some of the morbid *coups de théâtre* of *The Body*, Darke is trying to make us shudder. The play opens with the monkey dead on the table. Later on in the act we learn that Dolores, the wife of an unsuccessful commercial traveller, has been supplementing her income by performing sexual tricks with the monkey. Towards the end of the act the monkey, which may have died from the physical strain, is cooked and eaten by husband and wife.

It must be conceded though, that even if Darke is trying too hard to shock, he is succeeding better than any young playwright since Stephen Poliakoff and that the play is still richer in surprising dramatic twists than in shock effects. The plot pulls the couple through a taxing series of changing situations so that, as in a play by Strindberg, they each become almost like a new person as they react to changes in their partner. Lingering love gradually gives way to implacable hatred, but the savagery of Hank's physical attack on Dolores takes us by surprise. Eventually we see her lying dead on the table in the same position as the monkey, but the aggressive husband then starts talking to his dead wife, apologising, pleading with her to come back, reminding her of what she said after the animal's death—perhaps it was looking down on them. Perhaps she is now, while he pulls the dead body off the table and clings to it as if dancing.

Like the imaginary child in Albee's *Who's Afraid of Virginia Woolf?* the monkey and the Macedonian curly pig they adopt to replace it are emblems of what is missing from their relationship, but the borrowing is unimportant in comparison with the success achieved in the sharply written sequences of marital bickering and in the chemical changes that occur in Dolores's personality and in the relationship when a well-paid job lifts her into a position financially superior to Hank's. An acute observer of the effects that money and social prestige have on sexual relationships, Darke is already starting to take his eclecticism into his stride.

—Ronald Hayman

DAVIES, (William) Robertson. Canadian. Born in Thamesville, Ontario, 28 August 1913. Educated at Upper Canada College; Queen's University, Kingston, Ontario; Balliol College, Oxford, 1936–38, B.Litt. 1938. Married Brenda Mathews in 1940; three daughters. Teacher and actor, Old Vic Theatre School and Repertory Company, London, 1938–40; literary editor, *Saturday Night*, Toronto, 1940–42; editor and publisher, *Examiner*, Peterborough, Ontario, 1942–63. Since 1960 Professor of English, since 1962 Master of Massey College, and since 1981 Master Emeritus, University of Toronto. Governor, Stratford Shakespeare Festival, Ontario, 1953–71; member, Board of Trustees, National Arts Centre. Recipient: Ottawa Drama League prize, 1946, 1947; Dominion Drama Festival prize, for play, 1948, 1949, for directing, 1949; Leacock Medal, 1955; Lorne Pierce Medal, 1961; Governor-General's Award, for fiction, 1973; World Fantasy Convention award, for fiction, 1984; City of Toronto Book award, 1986; Canadian Authors' Association award, for fiction, 1986; Banff Centre award, 1986; Toronto Arts Lifetime Achievement Award, 1986; U.S. National Arts Club Medal of Honor, 1987 (first Canadian recipient). LL.D.: University of Alberta, Edmonton, 1957; Queen's University, 1962; University of Manitoba, Winnipeg, 1972; University of Toronto, 1981; D.Litt.: McMaster University, Hamilton, Ontario, 1959; University of Windsor, Ontario, 1971; York University, Toronto, 1973; Mount Allison University, Sackville, New Brunswick, 1973; Memorial University of Newfoundland, St. John's, 1974; University of Western Ontario, London, 1974; McGill University, Montreal, 1974; Trent University, Peterborough, Ontario, 1974; University of Lethbridge, Alberta, 1981; University of Waterloo, Ontario, 1981; University of British Columbia, Vancouver, 1983; University of Santa Clara, California, 1985; D.C.L.: Bishop's University, Lennoxville, Quebec, 1967; LL.D.: University of Calgary, Alberta, 1975; D.Hum.Litt.: Rochester University, Rochester, New York, 1983. Fellow, Balliol College, Oxford, 1986, and Trinity College, Toronto, 1987. Fellow, Royal Society of Canada, 1967, and Royal Society of Literature, 1984; Honorary Member, American Academy, 1981 (first Canadian elected). Companion, Order of Canada, 1972. Agent: Curtis Brown, 10 Astor Place, New York, New York 10003, U.S.A. Address: Massey College, 4 Devonshire Place, Toronto, Ontario M5S 2E1, Canada.

PUBLICATIONS

Plays

A Play of Our Lord's Nativity (produced Peterborough, Ontario, 1946).

Overlaid (produced Peterborough, Ontario, 1947). Included in *Eros at Breakfast and Other Plays*, 1949.

The Voice of the People (produced Montreal, 1948). Included in *Eros at Breakfast and Other Plays*, 1949.

At the Gates of the Righteous (produced Peterborough, Ontario, 1948). Included in *Eros at Breakfast and Other Plays*, 1949.

Hope Deferred (produced Montreal, 1948). Included in *Eros at Breakfast and Other Plays*, 1949.

Fortune, My Foe (produced Kingston, Ontario, 1948). Toronto, Clarke Irwin, 1949.

Eros at Breakfast (produced Ottawa, 1948). Included in *Eros at Breakfast and Other Plays*, 1949.

Eros at Breakfast and Other Plays. Toronto, Clarke Irwin, 1949.

At My Heart's Core (produced Peterborough, Ontario, 1950). Toronto, Clarke Irwin, 1950.

King Phoenix (produced Peterborough, Ontario, 1950). Included in *Hunting Stuart and Other Plays*, 1972.

A Masque of Aesop (for children; produced Toronto, 1952). Toronto, Clarke Irwin, 1952; in *Five New One-Act Plays*, edited by James A. Stone, London, Harrap, 1954.

A Jig for the Gypsy (produced Toronto and London, 1954). Toronto, Clarke Irwin, 1954.

Hunting Stuart (produced Toronto, 1955). Included in *Hunting Stuart and Other Plays*, 1972.

Leaven of Malice, adaptation of his own novel (as *Love and Libel; or, The Ogre of the Provincial World*, produced Toronto and New York, 1960; revised version, as *Leaven of Malice*, produced Toronto, 1973). Published in *Canadian Drama* (Waterloo, Ontario), vol. 7, no. 2, 1981.
A Masque of Mr. Punch (for children; produced Toronto, 1962). Toronto, Oxford University Press, 1963.
Centennial Play, with others (produced Lindsay, Ontario, 1967). Ottawa, Centennial Commission, 1967.
Hunting Stuart and Other Plays (includes *King Phoenix* and *General Confession*), edited by Brian Parker. Toronto, New Press, 1972.
Brothers in the Black Art (televised 1974). Vancouver, Alcuin Society, 1981.
Question Time (produced Toronto, 1975). Toronto, Macmillan, 1975.
Pontiac and the Green Man (produced Toronto, 1977).

Television Play: *Brothers in the Black Art*, 1974.

Novels

The Salterton Trilogy. Toronto and London, Penguin, 1986.
Tempest-Tost. Toronto, Clarke Irwin, 1951; London, Chatto and Windus, and New York, Rinehart, 1952.
Leaven of Malice. Toronto, Clarke Irwin, 1954; London, Chatto and Windus, and New York, Scribner, 1955.
A Mixture of Frailties. Toronto, Macmillan, London, Weidenfeld and Nicolson, and New York, Scribner, 1958.
The Deptford Trilogy. Toronto and London, Penguin, 1983.
Fifth Business. Toronto, Macmillan, and New York, Viking Press, 1970; London, Macmillan, 1971.
The Manticore. Toronto, Macmillan, and New York, Viking Press, 1972; London, Macmillan, 1973.
World of Wonders. Toronto, Macmillan, 1975; New York, Viking Press, 1976; London, W.H. Allen, 1977.
The Rebel Angels. Toronto, Macmillan, 1981; New York, Viking Press, and London, Allen Lane, 1982.
What's Bred in the Bone. Toronto, Macmillan, and New York, Viking, 1985; London, Viking, 1986.

Short Stories

High Spirits: A Collection of Ghost Stories. Toronto and London, Penguin, 1982; New York, Viking Press, 1983.

Other

Shakespeare's Boy Actors. London, Dent, 1939; New York, Salloch, 1941.
Shakespeare for Young Players: A Junior Course. Toronto, Clarke Irwin, 1942.
The Papers of Samuel Marchbanks (revised editions). Toronto, Irwin, 1985; New York, Viking, 1986; London, Viking, 1987.
The Diary of Samuel Marchbanks. Toronto, Clarke Irwin, 1947.
The Table Talk of Samuel Marchbanks. Toronto, Clarke Irwin, 1949; London, Chatto and Windus, 1951.
Marchbanks' Almanack. Toronto, McClelland and Stewart, 1967.
Renown at Stratford: A Record of the Shakespearean Festival in Canada 1953, with Tyrone Guthrie. Toronto, Clarke Irwin, 1953.
Twice Have the Trumpets Sounded: A Record of the Stratford Shakespearean Festival in Canada 1954, with Tyrone Guthrie. Toronto, Clarke Irwin, 1954; London, Blackie, 1955.
Thrice the Brinded Cat Hath Mew'd: A Record of the Stratford Shakespearean Festival in Canada 1955, with Tyrone Guthrie. Toronto, Clarke Irwin, 1955.
A Voice from the Attic. New York, Knopf, 1960.
The Personal Art: Reading to Good Purpose. London, Secker and Warburg, 1961.
Stephen Leacock. Toronto, McClelland and Stewart, 1970.
What Do You See in the Mirror? Agincourt, Ontario, Book Society of Canada, 1970.
The Revels History of Drama in English VI: 1750–1880, with others. London, Methuen, 1975.
One Half of Robertson Davies: Provocative Pronouncements on a Wide Range of Topics. Toronto, Macmillan, 1977; New York, Viking Press, 1978.
The Enthusiasms of Robertson Davies, edited by Judith Skelton Grant. Toronto, McClelland and Stewart, 1979.
Robertson Davies, The Well-Tempered Critic: One Man's View of Theatre and Letters in Canada, edited by Judith Skelton Grant. Toronto, McClelland and Stewart, 1981.
The Mirror of Nature (lectures). Toronto, University of Toronto Press, 1983.

Editor, *Feast of Stephen: An Anthology of Some of the Less Familiar Writings of Stephen Leacock*. Toronto, McClelland and Stewart, 1970; as *The Penguin Stephen Leacock*, London, Penguin, 1981.

*

Bibliography: by John Ryrie, in *The Annotated Bibliography of Canada's Major Authors 3* edited by Robert Lecker and Jack David, Downsview, Ontario, ECW Press, 1981.

Manuscript Collection: Massey College, University of Toronto.

Critical Studies: *Robertson Davies* by Elspeth Buitenhuis, Toronto, Forum House, 1972; *4 Canadian Playwrights* by Mavor Moore, Toronto, Holt Rinehart, 1973; *Robertson Davies* by Patricia A. Morley, Agincourt, Ontario, Gage, 1977; "Robertson Davies Issue" of *Journal of Canadian Studies* (Peterborough, Ontario), February 1977, and of *Canadian Drama* (Waterloo, Ontario), vol. 7, no. 2, 1981; *Stage Voices* edited by Geraldine C. Anthony, Toronto, Doubleday, 1978; *Robertson Davies* by Judith Skelton Grant, Toronto, McClelland and Stewart, 1978; *Here and Now 1* edited by John Moss, Toronto, NC Press, 1979; "The Master of the Unseen World" by Judith Finlayson, in *Quest* (Toronto), vol. 8, no. 4, 1979; *Canadian Writers and Their Work* edited by Robert Lecker, Jack David, and Ellen Quigley, Downsview, Ontario, ECW Press, 1985; *Robertson Davies, Playwright: A Search for the Self on the Canadian Stage* by Susan Stone-Blackburn, Vancouver, University of British Columbia Press, 1985.

Theatrical Activities:
Actor: **Plays**—Lord Norfolk in *Traitor's Gate* by Morna Stuart, London, 1938; Stingo in *She Stoops to Conquer* by Oliver Goldsmith, London, 1939; Archbishop of Rheims in *Saint Joan* by Shaw, London, 1939; roles in *The Taming of the Shrew* by Shakespeare, London, 1939.

Robertson Davies comments:

My plays are cast in the form of comedy because they are intended in general to be criticisms of society, even when they are set in an age other than our own; and, as I believe our age to be one of comedy and melodrama rather than one of tragedy, I have chosen to write plays that are comedies with a substantial melodramatic strain.

* * *

Although better known and certainly more widely acclaimed as a novelist and man-of-letters, Robertson Davies is one of Canada's foremost contemporary dramatists.

His earliest plays set the tone and style and introduced the themes that Davies has explored for almost 40 years. *Overlaid* and *The Voice of the People*, set in contemporary postwar Canada, *At the Gates of the Righteous*, set in Upper Canada in 1860, and *Hope Deferred*, set in 17th-century Quebec, are gentle, social satires attacking Canadian materialism and a penchant for the utilitarian and their converse philistinism towards art, imagination, intellectualism—culture in general. All of these plays are short—one-act in length—straightforward and essentially realistic in character portrayal, language, and structure.

Retaining the same satirical tone and realistic style, Davies elaborates on these themes in his first full-length play, *Fortune, My Foe*. The émigré puppeteer Szabo persists in pursuing his art despite rejection by and even ridicule from the Kingston establishment, but in so doing he encourages young Nicholas Hayward to remain in Canada rather than accept a more lucrative offer from an American university. For Davies, Canadians may be narrow and culturally malnourished, but there is promise in the younger generation. *At My Heart's Core*, set in Upper Canada during the Rebellion of 1837, is a more complex and ambiguous play, but the conflict between practicality and imagination, science and art, cultural philistinism and cultural aspiration is a central theme. As the drunken Irish Bard, Phelim, says, "We're the song birds that aren't wanted in this bitter land, where the industrious robins and the political crows get fat, and they not with a tuneful chirp among the lot of 'em."

With the founding of the Stratford Shakespearean Festival in 1953 and a general expansion of arts activities in the 1950's, Davies's attacks on Canadian cultural philistinism and provincialism became less creditable and relevant. In *A Jig for the Gypsy* he turned his attention to politics, the pretensions of the middle class, and the relationship between passionate, romantic love and marriage. Although set in Wales in 1885 and including among its cast of characters a gypsy fortune teller and a Welsh conjuror, the dramatic situation, characters, and even particular lines are clearly intended to reflect contemporary Canadian attitudes and personalities.

As he notes in his Preface to the play, romance and politics are not strange bedfellows: "The ambitions and actions of politicians, if one does not stand too near to them, are powerfully romantic, especially if they belong to a reform party with strong convictions about the perfectability of mankind through political action. To me there is nothing odd about linking politics with fortune-telling in a play; they have been too often linked in reality, even in Canada." The last sentence is a direct reference to Prime Minister Mackenzie King (1874–1950) who reportedly regularly consulted fortune-tellers.

Davies has also long been concerned in mankind's inner life and, especially, in Jung's psychological theories about spiritual heredity or the "collective unconscious." He introduced these ideas in his early allegorical play, *Eros at Breakfast*, subtitled "A Psychosomatic Interlude." Moreover, this play also revealed Davies's interest in dramatic techniques and forms that are more theatricalist and less realistic, such as the morality play, the masque, and the extravaganza.

King Phoenix, for example, is an allegorical fantasy centering on the mythical Old King Cole; *Hunting Stuart* is a "romance of heredity" in which a contemporary Canadian civil servant, Henry Benedict Stuart, is transformed—transmigrated actually—into his illustrious ancestor, Bonnie Prince Charlie, with delightfully witty results; and *General Confession* is a historical comedy of ideas in which the main characters, Casanova, Voltaire, Cagliostro, and Amalie or the Ideal Beloved serve as Jung's archetypical *self, persona, shadow*, and *anima*. All three plays, furthermore, exploit the energy of the actor and the magic and spectacle inherent in theatrical presentation. *King Phoenix* features lavish, Druidical costumes, properties, settings, and ceremonies; *General Confession* includes magical transformations and appearances and an elaborate 18th-century mise-en-scène; while *Hunting Stuart* to be effective demands a certain histrionic virtuosity from the actor playing Stuart/Prince Charlie.

Davies's *A Masque of Aesop* and *A Masque of Mr. Punch*, modeled after Jonson's masques, and written for performance by the boys of Upper Canada College Preparatory School, employ a wide range of dramatic techniques and comic devices, including parody, satire, slapstick, song, farcical verse dialogue, and Punch and Judy shows. Though intended for amateur performance, they nevertheless continue Davies's serious purpose in exposing pretensions both in art and life, while creating a vision of better society achieved through inner peace and self-knowledge.

Leaven of Malice, adapted from Davies's novel, and subtitled "A Theatrical Extravaganza," while using no formal scenery and few props, does include a number of masked figures as in the Japanese *bunraku* who manipulate elements of costuming and large printed signs, an elaborate five-part dream sequence, and a spectacular wedding procession at the finale.

In *Question Time* Davies attempted to combine or synthesize his social and political concerns with his interests in spiritual development. The central character, Peter MacAdam, is Canada's Prime Minister. He is the lone survivor of a plane crash in the Arctic, Les Montagnes de Glace, and the action of the play takes place in his delirious mind as he is ministered to by an unorthodox, Edinburgh-trained Eskimo shaman. The major confrontation takes place in a fantastical mock parliament. This ironic, allegorical drama is both an individual and, in that the PM also represents Canada, a national self-examination. Davies, in a program note for the Toronto St. Lawrence Centre's production in 1975, wrote that the play was about "what power may do to a man and what that man in his turn does to the people around him and to the country he leads . . . Canada is gravely misshaped by its reluctance to come to terms with its inmost self and to find that inmost self in its land. . . ." *Question Time* also calls for fairly elaborate scenic spectacle, including a large television screen, various Arctic sound effects, the appearance of a gigantic bear, and the transformation of Les Montagnes de Glace into the Canadian House of Commons.

Davies's latest play, *Pontiac and the Green Man*, based loosely on the 1768 court martial of major Robert Rogers (the Green Man of the title because he and his ranger regiment wore green jackets instead of the traditional British scarlet), also calls for an examination of Canadian individual and collective identity. It is also structured as a play-within-a-play, since excerpts from Rogers's own *Ponteach; or, The Savage of America* are staged during the trial.

Critical response to Davies's plays has been decidedly "mixed." For example, Herbert Whittaker in the Toronto *Globe and Mail* (26 February 1975) called *Question Time* "a glittering polemic of a play," while Urjo Kareda in the Toronto

Star (26 February 1975) labeled it "a disappointment" and "a disaster," but he conceded that it was "a very grand, ambitious, and idiosyncratic disaster of the order that only Robertson Davies could have created . . . a failure with a master's signature on it." Similarly *Pontiac and the Green Man* was described by McKenzie Porter in the Toronto *Sun* (28 October 1977) as "a play full of Shavian paradox, with wit, profundity and grief, a play evoking sudden gusts of laughter, sudden chills of pity, a play rich in cutting satire on soldiers, lawyers, academics, actors, writers, women in general and even critics who, figuratively and literally, are seen to ride in the clouds." Bryan Johnson of the *Globe and Mail* (27 October 1977) labeled it "a hopeless muddle," while Gina Mallet of the *Star* (7 November 1977) walked out after two hours failing to find any "redeeming artistic importance."

These reactions to Davies's recent efforts are undoubtedly extreme, but his earlier plays also provoked varying critical responses. While many have admired his witty dialogue, original plots, strong characterizations, and thought-provoking themes, others have found his plays overwritten, too literary, obscure, old-fashioned, labored, sexist, and conservative.

The term most often applied to Davies's style is "Shavian" (or sometimes "Neo-Shavian"). Indeed, with his Celtic love of language, his interest in social and political ideas, his exploration of the life of the spirit, his ironic point of view, and his experimentations with various dramatic techniques and forms, there is much that Davies shares with Shaw. Davies concedes Shaw's influence (as well as Pinero's, Jonson's, and Goldsmith's), but he denies that he has ever consciously imitated a Shavian play. Davies has not written for the theatre since 1977, preferring the novel to the play, and recognizing perhaps that his style of drama is unfashionable in present-day Canada. A future generation may take a different point of view, however, and revive these plays of considerable theatricality, power, and insight.

—Daniel J. Watermeier

DAVIS, Jack (Leonard). Australian; member of Bibbulmun tribe. Born in Perth, Western Australia, 11 March 1917. Educated at Yarloop State School; Perth Technical College. Worked as a stockman in North West Australia; director, Aboriginal Centre, Perth, 1967–71; managing editor, Aboriginal Publications Foundation, 1972–77; joint editor, *Identity* magazine, Perth, 1973–79; teacher of creative writing, Murdoch University, Western Australia. Director and President, Aboriginal Advancement Council, 1967 and 1972; first Chairman, Aboriginal Lands Trust, 1971; President, Aboriginal Writers and Dramatists Association, 1980–84; member, Australia Council Aboriginal Arts Board, from 1983. Recipient: British Empire Medal, 1977; Weickhardt award, 1980; Sidney Myer award, 1985; Australian Writers Guild award, 1986. D.Litt.: Murdoch University, 1985. A.M. (Member, Order of Australia), 1985. Agent: Hilary Linstead and Associates, 223 Commonwealth Street, Surry Hills, New South Wales 2010. Address: 22 Knutsford Avenue, Rivervale, Western Australia 6103, Australia.

PUBLICATIONS

Plays

The Dreamers (produced 1973; revised version produced Perth, 1982; Portsmouth, Hampshire, 1987). With *Kullark (Home)*, Sydney, Currency Press, 1982.

Kullark (Home) (produced 1978). With *The Dreamers*, Sydney, Currency Press, 1982.

No Sugar (produced Perth, 1985). Sydney, Currency Press, 1986.

Honeyspot (for children; produced Adelaide, 1985).

The Mini and the Leprechaun (for children; produced 1986).

Verse

The First-Born and Other Poems. Sydney and London, Angus and Robertson, 1970.

Jagardoo: Poems from Aboriginal Australia. Sydney, Methuen, 1977.

Other

Editor, with Bob Hodge, *Aboriginal Writing Today: Papers from the First National Conference of Aboriginal Writers.* Canberra, Australian Institute of Aboriginal Studies, 1985.

* * *

Jack Davis was 56 years old before he tried his hand at playwriting and over 60 before he gained a professional production. He had published short stories and two books of poetry; but as a black activist in Australia he discovered late in life that the theatre was the right forum for his work.

His early childhood was spent in the forest country of southwest Western Australia and his young adult life on sheep stations in the northern Gascoigne region. But part of his early life was also spent at the Moore River Native Settlement under the notorious Western Australian Aboriginal Protection Act, which once forced blacks on to government reserves, banned fraternisation with whites, and separated families for the purpose of educating the children in the white way of life. These experiences are the material of his poetry and plays.

Since he first came to national attention with his play *Kullark* in 1978 his work has focused on bridging the gap of understanding between black and white values. For this he has received many awards from the white community, including an Hon. D.Litt and the Order of Australia. He is not the first Aboriginal to have worked in the theatre but he is the first to produce a body of work at the forefront of Australian drama; and his plays have been the occasion for creating in Western Australia a training ground for black actors and a growing demand for their performances.

Davis's first playwriting was *The Dreamers*, a short piece performed by an amateur group in 1973; it was later revised into a full-length work. A meeting with the director Andrew Ross, then working in Perth, led to the production of *Kullark* in 1979, and to a long professional association which has had an important influence upon Davis's new direction as a writer. *Kullark* is a polemical work which gathers together a variety of Aboriginal experiences at the hands of whites: fatal misunderstandings in the early settlement period; evacuation of blacks from country towns during the Depression; life under the protection laws; the granting of citizenship rights to returned soldiers; and the round of grog, poverty, and prison which has customarily made up Aboriginal family life on the fringes of white society. What stands out from the basic narrative form of this early work is the revelations it makes about the life he knows: the indigenous humour, the forbearance, the brawling acts of frustration, instinctively expressed in comic/dramatic dialogue.

These qualities show a marked advance in Davis's next play, *The Dreamers*, a domestic drama of the Wallitch family: two school-age children coping with a white education system; two layabouts on the dole and one ambitious young public servant; a dispirited father and a mother who, like all the women in Davis's plays, bears the heat and burden of the day. Uncle Worru, patriarch and storyteller, is the family's link with their Aboriginal identity and heritage, and his death brings the play to a close. As he fades from his surroundings, his spirit retreats into his tribal past. This atavistic theme mingles with the modern in the form of a tribal dancer who haunts old Worru's thoughts and ritually signals his passing, demonstrating to his white audience that the familial and telepathic links of the old society are still an important element in black consciousness today.

No Sugar returns to the theme of black oppression on the Moore River Native Settlement in a fuller and more refined form. The Millimurras are a happy-go-lucky family who live in a tent on the Northam reserve, about 60 miles east of Perth. Their peace is disrupted when they are ordered to Moore River, where they are subjected to many indignities in the name of hygiene and Christianity. Jimmy, the uncle, is a rebel and humorist who keeps the family's spirits up until he dies at an Australia Day ceremony; Gran is a reprobate who plays the system; and in the centre is the love story of Joe and Mary, who run away back to the old free life.

Concurrent with *No Sugar* came *Honeyspot*, a children's play about a white ranger's daughter and a black family who rendezvous in the bush to invent a dance for the girl's ballet examination. Each side is at sea with the other's form of dance, and together they learn a mutual accommodation.

The simple story illustrates Davis's steadfast intent: to interpret the public and private nature of his people for the white community. He writes toughly, with political purpose, but without bitterness; with a great faith in the younger generation and a natural dramatic flair, in the European sense, for capturing the lives of his black characters. His whites—soldiers and settlers in *Kullark*, paternalistic public servants, police, and itinerant unemployed in *No Sugar*—are not so distinctive. They serve either as caricatures or foils to support the main action: the two groups live in strictly separate societies. With his new children's play, *The Mini and the Leprechaun*, he takes a firm step towards unification. Here for the first time Davis brings together the soul of both Australias as Aboriginal and Celtic sprites preside over the destinies of their black and white charges.

—Katharine Brisbane

DAVIS, Ossie. American. Born in Cogdell, Georgia, 18 December 1917. Educated at Waycross High School, Georgia; Howard University, Washington, D.C., 1935–39; studied acting with Paul Mann and Lloyd Richards. Served in the United States Army, 1942–45: surgical technician. Married Ruby Ann Wallace (i.e., the actress Ruby Dee) in 1948; two daughters and one son. Janitor and clerk, 1938–41; member of the Rose McClendon Players, Harlem, New York, 1940–42; then writer, actor, and director; off-Broadway stage manager, 1954–55; co-host, *Ossie Davis and Ruby Dee Story Hour* and *With Ossie and Ruby* television programs. Recipient: Frederick Douglass Award, 1970; Emmy award, for acting, 1970; American Library Association Coretta Scott King Award, for children's book, 1979. Agent: The Artists Agency, 10000 Santa Monica Boulevard, Suite 305, Los Angeles, California 90067. Address: P.O. Box 1318, New Rochelle, New York 10802, U.S.A.

PUBLICATIONS

Plays

Goldbrickers of 1944 (produced in Liberia, 1944).
Alice In Wonder (produced New York, 1952; revised version, as *The Big Deal*, produced New York, 1953).
Purlie Victorious (produced New York, 1961). New York, French, 1961; revised version, with Philip Rose and Peter Udell, music by Gary Geld, as *Purlie* (produced New York, 1970), New York, French, 1970.
Curtain Call, Mr. Aldridge, Sir (produced New York, 1963). Published in *The Black Teacher and the Dramatic Arts*, edited by William R. Reardon and Thomas D. Pawley, Westport, Connecticut, Negro Universities Press, 1970.
Escape to Freedom: A Play about Young Frederick Douglass (for children; produced New York, 1976). New York, Viking Press, 1978.
Langston (for children). New York, Delacorte Press, 1982.
Bingo!, with Hy Gilbert, music by George Fischoff, lyrics by Gilbert, adaptation of a play by William Brashler (also director: produced New York, 1985).

Screenplays: *Gone Are the Days!*, 1963; *Cotton Comes to Harlem*, with others, 1970; *Black Girl*, with J.E. Franklin, 1973; *Countdown at Kusini*, with others, 1976.

Television Writing: *Schoolteacher*, 1963; *Just Say the Word*, 1969; *Today Is Ours*, 1974; *For Us the Living*, 1983; scripts for *Bonanza*; *NYPD; East Side, West Side*; and *The Eleventh Hour* series.

*

Theatrical Activities:
Director: **Plays**—*Take It from the Top* by Ruby Dee, New York, 1979; *Bingo!*, New York, 1985. **Films**—*Cotton Comes to Harlem*, 1970; *Kongi's Harvest*, 1970; *Black Girl*, 1973; *Gordon's War*, 1973; *Countdown at Kusini*, 1976. **Television**—*The Perpetual People Puzzle* (co-director), 1972; *Today Is Ours*, 1974.
Actor: **Plays**—in *Joy Exceeding Glory*, New York, 1941; title role in *Jeb* by Robert Ardrey, New York, 1946; Rudolf in *Anna Lucasta* by Philip Yordan, toured, 1947; Trem in *The Leading Lady* by Ruth Gordon, New York, 1948; Lonnie Thompson in *Stevedore* by George Sklar and Paul Peters, New York, 1948; Stewart in *The Smile of the World* by Garson Kanin, New York, 1949; Jacques in *The Wisteria Trees* by Joshua Logan, New York, 1950, 1955; Jo in *The Royal Family* by George S. Kaufman and Edna Ferber, New York, 1951; Gabriel in *The Green Pastures* by Marc Connelly, New York, 1951; Al in *Remains to be Seen* by Howard Lindsay and Russel Crouse, New York, 1951; Dr. Joseph Clay in *Touchstone* by William Stucky, New York, 1953; The Lieutenant in *No Time for Sergeants* by Ira Levin, New York, 1955; Cicero in *Jamaica* by E.Y. Harburg and Fred Saidy, New York, 1957; Walter Lee Younger in *A Raisin in the Sun* by Lorraine Hansberry, New York, 1959; Purlie in *Purlie Victorious*, New York, 1961; Sir Radio in *Ballad for Bimshire* by Loften Mitchell, New York, 1963; in *A Treasury of Negro World Literature*, toured, 1964; Johannes in *The Zulu and the Zayda* by Howard DaSilva and Felix Leon, New York, 1965; *Take it from the Top* by Ruby

Dee, New York, 1979; Midge in *I'm Not Rappapart* by Herb Gardner, New York, 1987. **Films**—*No Way Out*, 1950; *Fourteen Hours*, 1951; *The Joe Louis Story*, 1953; *The Cardinal*, 1963; *Gone Are the Days!*, 1963; *Shock Treatment*, 1964; *The Hill*, 1965; *A Man Called Adam*, 1966; *The Scalphunters*, 1968; *Slaves*, 1969; *Sam Whiskey*, 1969; *Let's Do It Again*, 1975; *Countdown at Kusini*, 1976; *Hot Stuff*, 1980; *Harry and Son*, 1984; *Avenging Angel*, 1985. **Television**—*The Green Pastures* (*Showtime* series), 1951; *The Emperor Jones* (*Kraft Theater* series), 1955; *The Defenders* series, 1961–65; *Death Is the Door Price* (*The Fugitive* series), 1966; *The Outsider*, 1967; *The Third Choice* (*The Name of the Game* series), 1969; *Night Gallery* series, 1969; *Teacher, Teacher*, 1969; *The Sheriff*, 1971; *Billy: Portrait of a Street Kid*, 1980; *Roots: The Next Generation*, 1981; *King*, 1981; *The Tenth Level*, 1984; and *Seven Times Monday, The Doctors, The Nurses, Twelve O'Clock High, Bonanza, Hawaii Five-O*, and *All God's Children* series.

* * *

Ossie Davis is extraordinary on two counts. Loften Mitchell says in *Black Drama*, "For this tall, intelligent, graying, proud man came into the theater, interested in writing. Fortunately and unfortunately, it was learned that he is a good actor—a phenomenon rare for a writer, and detrimental as well. Mr. Davis went on to job after job working regularly as a Negro actor, never quite getting as much writing done as he wanted to do." But, despite his greater acclaim as director and actor, two of his plays are lasting contributions to dramatic literature.

The early 1950's were difficult years for black playwrights to try to get their works produced. One of the plays that did happen to make the boards—directed and produced in September 1952, in Harlem by the playwright and his friends, Maxwell Glanville, Julian Mayfield, and Loften Mitchell among others—was Davis's *Alice in Wonder*. The production, impoverished as it was, also included two of Mayfield's one-acters, *A World Full of Men* and *The Other Foot*. At the Elks Community Theater the talented group of spirited black artists "ushered in a hit show with few people in the audience" (Loften Mitchell in the *Crisis*, March 1972). Eventually Davis's charming play was optioned off to Stanley Greene and was produced successfully in downtown New York. Davis later expanded it into a full piece, *The Big Deal*.

Alice in Wonder—a reputable beginning for a gifted man—is a delightful piece. It is set in upper Harlem ("cadillac country," as Davis calls it). Alice (Ruby Dee in the original production) sees her husband Jay (Maxwell Glanville) given a sizeable contract by one of the leading television networks. In the meantime, Alice's brother (Ed Cambridge) has involved himself in a number of political affairs—one of which is an effort to restore the passport of a militant black singer. The network director asks Jay to go to Washington to testify before a government committee and to denounce the singer. Complications arise and Alice—who refuses to compromise her principles—sees that Jay is about to "sell out." She packs up and leaves. The ethos of this play is racial tension and all that it means, and it showed what Davis could do as a writer.

Purlie Victorious—warmly received by the alert New York critics at the Cort Theater, 29 September 1961—moved beyond an embryonic idea of laughter as a cure to racial bigotry, and became a dramatic experiment, and an artistic dream. The play is farcical, mocking, sparkling, resounding in ethnic wit, rapid, and unyielding as satire. Purlie Judson, a man of impatience, with a flowery evangelical style, moved by messianic mission for his race ("Who else is they got?") goes South determined to turn Big Bethel (an old barn) back into a church as an integrated symbol of freedom. Every racial cliché of southern life—and northern life for that matter—the white pro-Confederate Colonel, the Jim Crow system, the "colored" mammy and all that that image brings to mind, the Uncle Tom figures, the plantation store, the parochial cops, the stalking country sheriff, the NAACP, the Supreme Court, the church—and all that it symbolizes in both the white man's and the black man's psychology—integration, constitutional rights—are given a Swiftian examination. *Purlie Victorious* is a series of irresistible mirrors in which men are forced to see the folly of hatred, the insanity of bigotry, and the fruitlessness of racial supremacy theories. As Davis himself says (in *Contemporary Drama*, edited by Clinton T. Oliver and Stephanie Sills, 1971), "What else can I do but laugh? . . . The play is an attempt, a final attempt to hold that which is ridiculous up to ridicule—to round up all the indignities I have experienced in my own country and to laugh them out of existence."

The dialogue is scintillating, poetic, and realistic. There are many puns, ironic uses of idiomatic expressions, and an acute awareness of the black American's sense of melody and rhythm. The satire is sharply focused with the clever use of malapropisms and misnomers: "This is outrageous—This is a catastrophe! You're a disgrace to the Negro profession! . . . That's just what she said all right—her exactly words . . . When I think of his grandpaw, God rest his Confederate soul, hero of the Battle of Chickamauga—. . . My ol' Confederate father told me on his deathbed: Feed the Negroes first—after the horses and cattle—and I've done it evah time! . . . You know something, I've been after these Negroes down here for years: Go to school, I'd say, first chance you get—take a coupla courses in advanced cotton picking. But you'd think they'd listen to me: No sireebob. By swickety!" Like many other comic works *Purlie Victorious* is an angry play. Davis allows his anger to smolder through a gem-lit comedy, and he permits his work to romp and bound through southern settings and bromidic racial situations of the most impoverished and demeaning variety. But Davis is ever in control. Like Molière he knows that people laugh at beatings, mistaken identities, disguises, clever repartee, buffoonery, indecency, and themselves when taken off guard. Thus the satire—ever corrective in the hands of an artist—is both crude and polished in aiming its fire at personal and general prejudices.

The struggle to keep the mask in place in comedy becomes a conflict between intelligence and character, craft and habit, art and nature. In Davis's principles of writing and performing there is a beautiful balance between poetry and realism.

—Louis D. Mitchell

DEAN, Phillip Hayes. American. Born in Chicago, Illinois. Educated at schools in Pontiac, Michigan. Taught acting at the University of Michigan, Ann Arbor. Recipient: Dramatists Guild Hull-Warriner Award, 1972; Drama Desk award, 1972. Address: c/o Dramatists Play Service, 440 Park Avenue South, New York, New York 10016, U.S.A.

PUBLICATIONS

Plays

This Bird of Dawning Singeth All Night Long (produced New York, 1968). New York, Dramatists Play Service, 1971.

The Sty of the Blind Pig (produced New York, 1971). New Dramatists Play Service, 1972.
American Night Cry (includes *Thunder in the Index, This Bird of Dawning Singeth All Night Long, The Minstrel Boy*) (produced New York, 1974). *Thunder in the Index* and *The Minstrel Boy* published New York, Dramatists Play Service, 1972.
Freeman (produced New York, 1973). New York, Dramatists Play Service, 1973.
The Owl Killer. New York, Dramatists Play Service, 1973.
Every Night When the Sun Goes Down (produced Waterford, Connecticut, 1974; New York, 1976). New York, Dramatists Play Service, 1976.
If You Can't Sing, They'll Make You Dance (also director: produced New York, 1978).
Paul Robeson (produced New York and London, 1978). New York, Doubleday, 1978.

*

Theatrical Activities:
Director: **Play**—*If You Can't Sing, They'll Make You Dance*, New York, 1978.

* * *

Phillip Hayes Dean, who had been working intermittently as a playwright since the 1950's, emerged as a dramatist to watch when the Negro Ensemble Company produced *The Sty of the Blind Pig* late in 1971. The title is the name of the red-light house in which Blind Jordan, one of the last of the blind street singers, was born and which he describes in a graphic passage as a place of blood and violence and the "smell of butchered pig." (Pork would figure more directly as an image of black self-corruption in *Every Night When the Sun Goes Down.*) Blind Jordan's presence emphasizes the condition of the other three characters, whose worlds are collapsing: Weedy, the acid-tongued churchwoman, sure of her own righteousness despite a years-long affair with her minister, who goes on the annual convocation to Montgomery just in time for the 1955 bus boycott and finds the new church unrecognizable; her brother Doc, who imagines that if he can get a little money together he can become Sportin' Jimmy Sweet again in a Memphis that has disappeared; and Alberta, Weedy's daughter. She is the central figure in the play, a woman caught between a past she never really had and a future she cannot embrace; at the end, she assumes the voice and manner of her mother. The off-stage event, the burgeoning civil rights movement, is putting an end to whatever community Weedy and Doc know although the characters never see anything other than a bunch of "young folks" with "nappy hair" heading South for some reason. The most effective scene in *The Sty of the Blind Pig* is the one in which Alberta re-enacts a funeral service in which her fervor is clearly sexual, a mark of the personal and social repression in which she lives, but the strength of the piece lies in the characters as a group, the querulous sense of family even in a state of disintegration, and in the mysterious and disquieting presence of Blind Jordan.

The three plays that make up *American Night Cry*, some of which predate *The Sty of the Blind Pig*, are fables of white fear and black oppression, images of mutuality which end in madness, murder, and suicide. *Thunder in the Index, This Bird of Dawning Singeth All Night Long*, and *The Minstrel Boy* are all long on accusation, but the confrontations, despite Dean's talent for grostesque gamesplaying, are too obviously in the service of the ideational thrust of the plays. The programmatic quality of the work and the assumption of inevitable violence prepare the way for the Moloch plays. Both *Freeman* and *Every Night When the Sun Goes Down* are set in Moloch, a small industrial city in Michigan obviously suggested by Pontiac, where Dean lived for a time, but appropriately named Moloch because that god was worshipped through the sacrificial burning of children; both plays end in fire. *Freeman* is a family play in which the titular protagonist is an ambitious and bright man constantly defeated by his inability to work in the practical world of compromise, thwarted by his working-class family, his frightened wife, and his foster brother, who has become a successful doctor. In the end, he torches the community center that he sees as a symbol of accommodation to white power and is saved from arrest at the cost of incarceration in a mental hospital. A more fully developed version of the main character in *Thunder in the Index*, Freeman is interesting dramatically as a man whose best impulses are self-destructive and harmful to those around him. Such a description may be an act of white liberal co-option, softening Dean for the mainstream of American theater, for the play is more ambiguous about Freeman. It suggests, primarily through the belated understanding of his father, that Freeman is not an instance of black hubris but of a man driven mad by an uncongenial society whose final act of violence is the inevitable end of his frustrated quest. Certainly, such a reading is suggested by *Every Night When the Sun Goes Down.* Set in a decrepit bar-hotel, peopled by whores, pimps, drunks, and crazies, it brings Blood back from prison, inspirited by a new sense of self, as a prophet who enlists this motley crew in a firebomb attack on their own environment. "And God gave Noah the Rainbow sign. No more water, the fire next time."

Paul Robeson is an unusual play in the Dean canon unless one sees the destruction of the political activist in the second act as the inevitable end of the black hero who outwitted the forces of oppression in Act 1 to become a football star, a lawyer, a famous singer and actor. Yet the celebratory frame of the play belies so Dean-like a movement. Neither convincingly Paul Robeson nor effectively Phillip Hayes Dean, it remains an anomaly in the playwright's work perhaps because Dean had his dramatic image forced on him by Robeson's biography. One of Dean's theatrical virtues is that he has a knack for non-realistic fables in which his best characters have room to develop realistically. At his weakest, the expected development never takes place; such is the case with *If You Can't Sing, They'll Make You Dance*, in which an unlikely triangle allows the protagonist's ineffectuality to expose his macho self-image. At the other extreme is *The Sty of the Blind Pig*, in which the fable, implicit in Alberta's wondering if Blind Jordan was "ever really here," gains power from those who act it out. It is not that "every character comes from some man or woman," as Dean has said, but that every character becomes a man or woman. The other plays lie between these two, at their strongest when invention and idea are less visible than the people who embody them.

—Gerald Weales

DELANEY, Shelagh. British. Born in Salford, Lancashire, 25 November 1939. Educated at Broughton Secondary School. Has one daughter. Worked as salesgirl, usherette, and photographer's laboratory assistant. Recipient: Foyle New Play award, 1959; Arts Council bursary, 1959; New York Drama

Critics Circle award, 1961; BAFTA award, 1962; Robert Flaherty Award, for screenplay, 1962; Encyclopaedia Britannica award, 1963; Writers Guild award, for screenplay, 1969; Cannes Film Festival award, 1985. Fellow, Royal Society of Literature, 1985. Agent: Tessa Sayle, 11 Jubilee Place, London SW3 3TE, England.

PUBLICATIONS

Plays

A Taste of Honey (produced London, 1958; New York, 1960). London, Methuen, and New York, Grove Press, 1959.

The Lion in Love (produced Coventry and London, 1960; New York, 1963). London, Methuen, and New York, Grove Press, 1961.

The House That Jack Built (televised 1977; produced New York, 1979). London, Duckworth, 1977.

Screenplays: *A Taste of Honey*, with Tony Richardson, 1961; *The White Bus*, 1966; *Charlie Bubbles*, 1968; *Dance with a Stranger*, 1985.

Radio Plays: *So Does the Nightingale*, 1981; *Don't Worry about Matilda*, 1983.

Television Plays: *Did Your Nanny Come from Bergen?*, 1970; *St. Martin's Summer*, 1974; *The House That Jack Built* series, 1977; *Find Me First*, 1981.

Other

Sweetly Sings the Donkey. New York, Putnam, 1963; London, Methuen, 1964.

* * *

Shelagh Delaney's *A Taste of Honey* has a single set of a room in a lodging house, and three main characters, a mother, a schoolgirl daughter, and a homosexual art student. Each woman has an affair with a man. Helen, the mother, goes off with hers returning only when Jo, the daughter, is about to give birth to the child of her boyfriend, a black sailor who has long since left without trace. In the last scene, Geoffrey, the art student who has been mothering Jo, leaves the women alone together. Joan Littlewood first presented the play in 1958 at the Theatre Royal, Stratford East, London, and provided the model for many subsequent productions. There was a jazz trio which accompanied entrances and provided support for songs. The actors played directly to the audience wherever possible, especially Avis Bunnage as Helen. So the action had vitality and continuous interest, and the dialogue and characterisation rang clearly; repetitions were strongly marked. So produced, the action seems both lively and inevitable: and the audience is encouraged to see the implications about education, housing, and need for affection that underline the writing. The three main characters have dialogue, especially in shorter speeches, that rings both true and unexpectedly. More than this, Jo, who is portrayed as only a little younger than her 19-year-old creator, has speeches of sensitive irony: "I'm contemporary . . . aren't I, though, Geoff? I really live at the same time as myself, don't I?"

Delaney's second play, *The Lion in Love*, followed two years afterwards and at once her ambitions became clearer. The set is both a public place and the interior of a house. The cast is large and is involved in many interwoven stories; at one time, the stage is busy with buying and selling in a market. Almost all the characters are conscious of social change and most have views to express about it. There is a bearded prophet who distributes pamphlets. Some songs, dances, and conscious joking again enliven the action, but the main story-line is very slight—Frank may leave one woman for another, and doesn't—and the author's sympathetic presentation of her characters can scarcely provide enough dramatic interest and excitement. Again the presentation of a young girl is the most convincing element, but Peg is not given a main part in the action: her story is simply that she falls into a dazed love for a young boy and may go away with him.

Since these two plays Delaney has written chiefly for television and films; her screenplay for *Dance with a Stranger* was a notable success.

—John Russell Brown

DENNIS, Nigel (Forbes). British. Born in Bletchingley, Surrey, 16 January 1912. Educated at Plumtree School, Southern Rhodesia; Odenwaldschule, Germany. Married 1) Mary-Madeleine Massias, two daughters; 2) Beatrice Ann Hewart Matthew in 1959. Secretary, National Board of Review of Motion Pictures, New York, 1935–36; assistant editor and book reviewer, *New Republic*, New York, 1937–38; staff book reviewer, *Time*, New York, 1940–59; drama critic, 1960–63, and joint editor, 1967–70, *Encounter*, London; staff book reviewer, *Sunday Telegraph*, London, 1961–82. Recipient: Houghton Mifflin-Eyre and Spottiswoode award, for fiction, 1950; Royal Society of Literature Heinemann Award, for non-fiction, 1966. Fellow, Royal Society of Literature, 1966. Address: c/o A.M. Heath, 40–42 William IV Street, London WC2N 4DD, England.

PUBLICATIONS

Plays

Cards of Identity, adaptation of his own novel (produced London, 1956). Included in *Two Plays and a Preface*, 1958.

The Making of Moo (produced London, 1957; New York, 1958). Included in *Two Plays and a Preface*, 1958.

Two Plays and a Preface. London, Weidenfeld and Nicolson, 1958; New York, Vanguard Press, 1959.

August for the People (produced Edinburgh and London, 1961). London, French, 1962.

Radio Play: *Swansong for 7 Voices*, 1985.

Novels

Boys and Girls Come Out to Play. London, Eyre and Spottiswoode, 1949; as *A Sea Change*, Boston, Houghton Mifflin, 1949.

Cards of Identity. London, Weidenfeld and Nicolson, and New York, Vanguard Press, 1955.

A House in Order. London, Weidenfeld and Nicolson, and New York, Vanguard Press, 1966.

Verse

Exotics: Poems of the Mediterranean and the Middle East. London, Weidenfeld and Nicolson, 1970; New York, Vanguard Press, 1971.

Other

Dramatic Essays. London, Weidenfeld and Nicolson, 1962; Westport, Connecticut, Greenwood Press, 1978.
Jonathan Swift: A Short Character. New York, Macmillan, 1964; London, Weidenfeld and Nicolson, 1965.
An Essay on Malta. London, Murray, 1972; New York, Vanguard Press, 1974.

* * *

Nigel Dennis has written only three plays: *Cards of Identity, The Making of Moo*, and *August for the People*. This is regrettable since he specializes in satirical, dehumanized comedy of a kind rare in modern English drama; and since, whatever the formal defects of his work, he at least has something to say. His output as a novelist and literary critic has been comparably slender; but, although the quantity is small, through all his work there can be heard the distinctive, iconoclastic tone of the funniest right-wing English satirist since Evelyn Waugh.

Underlying all his plays is a profound conviction that men are willing robots who can be readily manipulated. It first surfaced in *Cards of Identity* which he adapted from his own highly acclaimed novel and which was one of the first works to be staged by George Devine when the English Stage Company began its historic tenancy of the Royal Court Theatre in 1956. The play's theme is the Pirandellian one that human personality is neither absolute nor immutable; and it's demonstrated through the activities of a fraudulent trio (reminiscent of the principal figures of Jonson's *The Alchemist*) who take over a vacant country house in order to alter people's identities. Their weapon is the mumbo-jumbo of psychotherapy and hypnotism and their aim to cram the largest number of mutually exclusive qualities into the same new personality.

Like the novel, the play is full of dazzling set pieces; but Dennis is unable to bind them together with a strong enough plot. The result is like looking at a collection of unstrung jewels. However, one can almost forgive the invertebrate structure for the sake of a sub-Greene whisky-priest's soliloquy proving that religious experience is inseparable from the deepest debauchery and arriving at the conclusion "I stink, therefore I am"; of the absurdist scene in which the Co-Wardens of the Badgeries discover that their only function is to parade an imaginary badger on state occasions. The play has all the heartlessness of good satire: what it lacks is the structure to support its attack on manipulable humanity.

By the time he wrote *The Making of Moo*, however, Dennis had clearly learned a good deal; for this attack on organised Christianity and the gullibility of its believers is neatly and ingeniously constructed. In the first act a civil engineer and his wife, situated in some colonial outpost, invent a new religion based on the Highway Code. In the second act the new religion of Moo has so asserted itself that its creators have become fanatical believers in it even to the extent of making human sacrifices. In the third act Moo is a successful, worldly, benign religion and it is up to the son of its creators to usher in another era of reformatory murder and bloodshed.

Historically the play is significant in that it was the first outright attack on religion ever to be presented on the English stage. And there is no gainsaying the sincerity of Dennis's belief that all religions are built on a foundation of pain, torture and blood: the second-act curtain involving the ritual slaughter of a pair of casual English visitors is meant in deadly earnest. But the play lacks the full blasphemous force of, say, Buñuel's *Viridiana* or Genet's *The Balcony* for the simple reason that Dennis denies the existence and power of God. Blasphemy, to be effective, paradoxically depends on belief. For a self-styled "history of religion" the play is also woefully incomplete, offering little more than three arbitrarily chosen stages in the development of any religious cult. But even if the play is lightweight and elliptical, it still has a considerable power to shock (the substitution of toast and tomato juice for the bread and wine of Communion causes a particular frisson) and has the merit of being a genuine pioneering work. For all its faults, it occupies an important niche in the history of English drama.

Having attacked in his first two works people who readily change their personalities at anyone's bidding and those who happily follow any half-baked new religion, in *August for the People* Dennis went the whole hog and assaulted the democratic principle as such. His protagonist is a sceptical, ironic owner of a stately home who rudely attacks the average man at a public dinner and in consequence finds his privacy invaded by an ever-swelling army of day-trippers and reporters. The more he abuses the common man and the hollowness of his illusions, the greater his notoriety and success until he too finds himself acting out a role for the benefit of the public. And the shame of this drives him mad.

Intellectually, the play is seriously flawed: it attacks the press, for instance, as an example of the abuse of democracy conveniently ignoring the fact that the British popular press is not democratically controlled. Theatrically, it is also weakened by the fact that it tries to contain a Shavian extravaganza inside a naturalistic framework. Yet once again Dennis shows considerable audacity in attacking deeply cherished beliefs and proves that he is a considerable verbal stylist in the Coward tradition. Like his other work, *August for the People* had a short run at the Royal Court (with Rex Harrison in the principal role) but has not been much played elsewhere; and it seems a pity Dennis has been a theatrical exile ever since he provided a necessary satirical corrective to the sentimentality and woolly-mindedness of so much contemporary drama.

—Michael Billington

DEWHURST, Keith. British. Born in Oldham, Lancashire, 24 December 1931. Educated at Rydal School, 1945–50; Peterhouse, Cambridge, 1950–52, B.A. (honours) in English 1953. Married 1) Eve Pearce in 1958 (divorced 1980), one son and two daughters; 2) Alexandra Cann in 1980. Yarn tester, Lancashire Cotton Corporation, Romiley, Cheshire, 1953–55; sports writer, Manchester *Evening Chronicle*, 1955–59; presenter, Granada Television, 1968–69, and *Review* arts programme, BBC, 1972; arts columnist, the *Guardian*, London, 1969–72. Writer-in-residence, West Australian Academy of Performing Arts, Perth, 1984. Recipient: Japan Prize, for television play, 1968. Agent: London Management, 235 Regent Street, London W1A 2JT, England.

Publications

Plays

Running Milligan (televised 1965). Published in *Z Cars: Four Scripts from the Television Series*, edited by Michael Marland, London, Longman, 1968.

Rafferty's Chant (produced London, 1967). Published in *Plays of the Year 33*, London, Elek, 1967.
The Last Bus (televised 1968). Published in *Scene Scripts*, edited by Michael Marland, London, Longman, 1972.
Pirates (produced London, 1970).
Brecht in '26 (produced London, 1971).
Corunna! (produced London, 1971).
Kidnapped, adaptation of the novel by Robert Louis Stevenson (produced Edinburgh, 1972).
The Miser, adaptation of a play by Molière (produced Edinburgh, 1973).
The Magic Island (produced Birmingham, 1974).
The Bomb in Brewery Street (produced Sheffield, 1975).
One Short (produced Sheffield, 1976).
Luggage (produced London, 1977).
Lark Rise, adaptation of works by Flora Thompson (produced London, 1978). Included in *Lark Rise to Candleford*, 1980.
The World Turned Upside Down, adaptation of the work by Christopher Hill (produced London, 1978).
Candleford, adaptation of works by Flora Thompson (produced London, 1979). Included in *Lark Rise to Candleford*, 1980.
Lark Rise to Candleford (includes *Lark Rise* and *Candleford*). London, Hutchinson, 1980.
San Salvador (produced Louisville, 1980).
Don Quixote, adaptation of the novel by Cervantes (produced London, 1982). Oxford, Amber Lane Press, 1982.
Batavia (produced Perth, Western Australia, 1984).

Screenplay: *The Empty Beach*, 1985.

Radio Plays: *Drummer Delaney's Sixpence*, 1971; *That's Charlie George Over There*, 1972; *Dick Turpin*, 1976; *Mother's Hot Milk*, 1979.

Television Plays: *Think of the Day*, 1960; *A Local Incident*, 1961; scripts for *Z Cars* series, 1962–67; *Albert Hope*, 1962; *The Chimney Boy*, 1964; *The Life and Death of Lovely Karen Gilhooley*, 1964; *The Siege of Manchester*, 1965; *The Towers of Manhattan*, 1966; *Softly Softly* series, 1967, 1975–76; *The Last Bus*, 1968; *Men of Iron*, 1969; *Why Danny Misses School*, 1969; *It Calls for a Great Deal of Love*, 1969; *Helen*, from the play by Euripides, 1970; *The Sit-In*, 1972; *Lloyd-George*, 1973; *End Game*, 1974; *The Great Alfred* (*Churchill's People* series), 1975; *Our Terry*, 1975; *Just William* series, from books by Richmal Crompton, 1977; *Two Girls and a Millionaire*, 1978; *The Battle of Waterloo*, 1983; *What We Did in the Past*, 1986; *Joe Wilson* series, from short stories by Henry Lawson, 1987 (Australia); and for *Knight Errant, Skyport, Love Story, Front Page Story, The Villains, The Emigrants, Dominic*, and *Juliet Bravo* series.

Novels

Captain of the Sands. New York, Viking Press, 1981; London, Cape, 1982.
McSullivan's Beach. London, Angus and Robertson, 1986.

*

Keith Dewhurst comments:

One day in June 1986 I walked into a discount bookshop in Sydney and flicked through an encyclopaedic television guide compiled by Leslie Halliwell, whom I remember with gratitude from my Cambridge days (when he managed the Rex Cinema), and the critic Philip Purser. Two of my own television plays were accorded entries: *Men of Iron* and *The Siege of Manchester*, which had an asterisk admitting it to "Halliwell's Hall of Fame." This stunned me, in an amiable sort of way, and seems to me to be a classic example of the random fates that await the plays people write.

The Siege of Manchester was a broken-backed epic, for which I have a very soft spot, as I suppose one does for anything half-regretted, and I am delighted that Philip Purser remembers it, but it does not seem to me to be in the same class as some other television plays I have written, such as *Albert Hope, It Calls for a Great Deal of Love, Our Terry, Lloyd-George, Men of Iron* itself, and an episode of *Juliet Bravo* called *Oscar*.

Similarly, *Lark Rise*, which was performed at the National Theatre and subsequently in various countries around the world has, I hazard, been recognised as an interesting piece, and the one in which the director Bill Bryden and myself best expressed a modern genre—the promenade play with music, that tries to make the theatre an event again. Yet the plays by which one arrived at that destination, especially *Corunna!*, aren't even in a vestibule of fame. They're out in the car park, where it's pissing with rain.

This damp obscurity I attribute mainly to the plays in question never having been published. Nor was *The Bomb in Brewery Street*, which additionally suffered from radical chic reviewers who thought that, being set in the Belfast troubles, it should provide solutions that eluded Elizabeth I, Oliver Cromwell, Henry Grattan, Gladstone, Parnell, Lloyd-George, and de Valera. In fact it is a funny and carefully researched work whose sub-text clearly favours colonial disengagement, and I wish I could hustle it into *somebody's* "Hall of Fame," but I don't suppose I will.

I can, however, close with an appropriate "Hall of Fame" reminiscence. There was an extra in *The Siege of Manchester* who was supposed to be dead in a battle scene but kept getting up. Four years later, when the director Herbert Wise and I were working on *Men of Iron*, we met this same extra in the studio corridor, clearly wearing a costume for our new play.

Herbert gripped my wrist and said: "It's George!"

George said: "Hello, Mr. Wise. I never thought I'd work for you again!"

"You wouldn't have," said Herbert, "if I'd remembered your other name."

Maybe the car park does have consolations, after all.

* * *

Keith Dewhurst is a highly skilled and conscientious dramatic craftsman. He has been prepared to write in a number of different dramatic styles, readily accepting the challenges of working for the technically demanding medium of television and of preparing for the stage adaptations of works of fiction which a large proportion of his audience already know well and love in their original form. For television he has adopted the realistic manner which is the current norm for popular entertainment, but for the stage he has often preferred to experiment with ideas taken up from Bertolt Brecht's "epic theatre," with the illusion of reality broken in order to facilitate a more direct address to the audience and to accommodate subjects which might prove unduly resistant to conventional treatment. As well as scaling down his work so that it fits comfortably on to the small screen, Dewhurst has used a number of different forms of staging, including arena style, the thrust stage with the audience seated to either side of a long ramp, and what he calls "promenade production" which goes a long way towards abolishing the traditional—or to be more accurate, the 19th-century—distinction between the public and the actors in order to create (if need be at the cost of some spoiling of the sight lines that used to be thought so important) a greater degree of intimacy and involvement. Music is not treated as a mere incidental or just to emphasise atmosphere; it serves as an essential part of the dramatic presentation in many instances. Dewhurst never loses sight of the need for the theatre to entertain, but when he comments on this he is not just repeating a commonplace and far less is he making the facile distinction of some old-fashioned critics between a theatre of entertainment and a theatre of ideas. Instead, he insists that drama can and ought to be an artistic medium which appeals to a wide range of people in a number of different ways. In this, as in his choice of dramatic mentor, Dewhurst proclaims a wide sympathy with the great mass of humanity.

His talents and his sympathy are clearly revealed in *Running Milligan*, an outstanding contribution to the BBC's epoch-making series *Z Cars*. Milligan is shown leaving prison, let out on parole to attend his wife's funeral. The policemen on patrol see him, and their immediate suspicions set the perspectives of a tragedy that is inevitable. At home Milligan predictably finds no support and cannot resist the crazy temptation of trying to run away. It is to no avail, and Barlow, who has presided over the usual police station subplot, arrives to arrest him. To some extent this is conventional enough, but Dewhurst contrives to bring out all the pathetic helplessness of Milligan, suggesting that the blame lies not with him but with his impossible situation and that society's response to his problems is no less bungling and ineffectual than his own efforts at escape. The dialogue is pared down to essentials, but in a scene near the end when Milligan tries to comfort a drink-sodden tramp whose memory is fuddled by memories of fighting in the war by telling him a fairy story, there is a sudden and disturbingly apt touch of poetry.

Rafferty's Chant, which was produced at the Mermaid Theatre, London, has a great deal more humour in its portrayal of the life and downfall of a wonderfully plausible con man in the used car trade. The dialogue is crisp and laconic, but there is a wonderful touch of romance in Rafferty's patter as he sells old bangers as if they were dream machines. The skimpy plot of this play that has more than a touch of farce to it is no more than a thread to hold together closely observed characters in a number of sketches that explore their motivations as they try to cope with one of those vitally important little matters in present-day life, the buying of a car. As we laugh with Rafferty at mankind's foibles there is no more danger of our taking any more seriously than he does the stern words he imagines a judge speaking to him before pronouncing a stiff sentence for preying on gullibility.

Following a line of development that probably owes its origins to the experiments of the French director Jean-Louis Barrault and which was certainly influenced to some extent by the work of Ariane Mnouchkine whose production of *1789* with the Théâtre du Soleil he witnessed at the Cartoucherie de Vincennes, Paris, Dewhurst has done some of his most original work in adaptations. *Corunna!*, for instance, dramatises episodes from the Napoleonic War as a ballad opera with no more than five actors reinforced by a five-piece rock band. *Kidnapped*, after Robert Louis Stevenson, was also notable for its freedom of dramatic treatment. If the problem with *Don Quixote* was an excess of text, that with *Lark Rise*, after Flora Thompson's celebrated portrait of village life in Victorian Oxfordshire, was a lack of narrative and a consequent lack of a clear central focus of attention. Dewhurst does not try to remedy this. His approach is rather to let the images of the village and its people develop before the eyes of the audience so that the succession of glimpses may add together almost as they do when we look in on real life. In this way *Lark Rise* serves as a prelude to the rather more obviously shaped *Candleford*. The texts do not read particularly well, but that criticism is no more just here than when it is levelled at television scripts. Flora Thompson's book, like the novels of Cervantes or Stevenson, remains intact for those who wish to read it. Dewhurst's aim is to find a dramatic representation of these works which functions in performance with all the different means of communication that are available in the theatre when, without the trammels and clutter of old-fashioned realism, the imagination is engaged and provoked into providing whatever may be sensed as needed to colour the pictures that are sketched before our eyes. The success of the productions of *Lark Rise* and *Candleford* is ample justification for the enterprise that Dewhurst has embarked upon.

—Christopher Smith

DIZENZO, Charles (John). American. Born in Hackensack, New Jersey, 21 May 1938. Educated at New York University, B.A. 1962. Married Patricia Hines in 1964. Instructor in Playwriting, New York University 1970–71, and Yale University, New Haven, Connecticut, 1975–76. Recipient: Yale University-ABC fellowship, 1966, and CBS fellowship, 1975; Guggenheim fellowship, 1967; National Endowment for the Arts grant, 1972. Agent: Helen Harvey Associates, 410 West 24th Street, New York, New York 10011. Address: 106 Perry Street, New York, New York 10014, U.S.A.

PUBLICATIONS

Plays

The Drapes Come (televised 1965; produced New York, 1965; Liverpool, 1973; London, 1982). New York, Dramatists Play Service, 1966; in *Off-Broadway Plays 1*, London, Penguin, 1970.

An Evening for Merlin Finch (produced New York, 1968; Coventry, 1969). New York, Dramatists Play Service, 1968; in *Off-Broadway Plays 1*, London, Penguin, 1970.

A Great Career (produced New York, 1968). New York, Dramatists Play Service, 1968.

Why I Went Crazy (produced Westport, Connecticut, 1969; New York, 1970; as *Disaster Strikes the Home*, produced Edinburgh, 1970; London, 1971).

The Last Straw, and Sociability (produced New York, 1970). New York, Dramatists Play Service, 1970.

Big Mother and Other Plays (includes *An Evening for Merlin Finch* and *The Last Straw*). New York, Grove Press, 1970.

Big Mother, music by John Braden (produced New York, 1974). Included in *Big Mother and Other Plays*, 1970.

Metamorphosis, adaptation of works by Kafka (produced New York, 1972).

The Shaft of Love (produced New York, 1975).

Television Play: *The Drapes Come*, 1965.

Other

Phoebe (for children), with Patricia Dizenzo. New York, Bantam, 1970.

* * *

Charles Dizenzo's plays were first produced in the off-off-Broadway workshop movement of the 1960's. Since then they have been presented by the Repertory Company of Lincoln Center, the David Merrick Arts Foundation, and the American Place Theater in New York, and in theatres in Europe.

A good example of Dizenzo's work is a pair of one-act comedies first presented at Lincoln Center's experimental Forum Theater. The first play, *A Great Career*, is an office play built on the assumption that office life is impossible, but that for all the meaningless work and the petty quarrels among employees, the office is as much "womb as tomb," or, as the heroine snarlingly calls it as the play opens, "a home away from home." It is about a harried clerical worker named Linda who has a report to prepare. During the course of the action she explodes, gets herself fired, and then realizing that there is no place else to go that is not the same she literally begs to be taken back. This description makes the play sound more painful than funny, and Dizenzo obviously wants his audience to hang on to that side of the story. The ending certainly encourages them to. We see Linda crawling around the stage picking up the papers that she scattered during her defiant scene, as a fellow employee tells her about the new bookkeeper who tried to commit suicide unsuccessfully in the men's room. In *A Great Career* Dizenzo shows the emasculating nature of office life by having men play women and women turning out to be men.

In *An Evening for Merlin Finch* the sterility of the office gives way to the silent violence of the home. Darlene Finch, an insensitive middle-class middle-American housewife, is plagued by a vengeful mother who materializes in the shape of her son Merlin. This becomes her vision of hatred and guilt. As he demonstrates in all of his plays Dizenzo is fascinated with the normality within a sick society. His plays point up the compromises which sink the soul of modern man into a dismal acceptance of everyday predicaments. Merlin, the focus of concern, is forced to play his bassoon for company. Each observation his parents make is a body blow and each gesture of contact a refusal. Merlin's life turns out to be an eternal adolescence andas he blows away on his bassoon his slim identity evaporates before our eyes. His mother's ignorance and hostility continuously undercut the comic image of Merlin's silly instrument. Here Dizenzo's dry black humor together with a carefully constructed situation exposes and explodes the Finches' severely distorted family life.

Another Dizenzo play which in its own bizarre and comic way explodes the quiet violence of family life is *Disaster Strikes the Home* (also presented under the title *Why I Went Crazy*). In this play Dizenzo submerges his audience into a complete and outrageous comic world. Once again the sexes are changed: wives are played by men, husbands by women. The reversal is not a gimmick, but a surrealistic view of sexual strangulation that exists in the American household. Dizenzo counterpoints these outlandish images with careful, and empty, colloquial speech. The violent role reversals that take place in weak marriages epitomize Dizenzo's nightmare view of American family life.

Dizenzo's playwriting is always startlingly inventive and for the most part consistently amusing. By distorting the real world he illuminates the dark emotional silences between people which is something many contemporary playwrights attempt but seldom achieve. Although his writing has none of the manicured edge of Albee's or Ionesco's, and in places is in serious need of tightening, Dizenzo has a keen ear for the truthful phrase and a fine farceur's instinct for pace. His theatrical vision is controlled and iconoclastic; he imitates no one, relying totally on his own creative talents, thereby fostering a theatrical voice which is both unique and thoroughly American.

—Bernard Carragher

DONLEAVY, J(ames) P(atrick). Irish. Born in Brooklyn, New York, United States, 23 April 1926; became Irish citizen, 1967. Educated at a preparatory school, New York; Trinity College, Dublin. Served in the United States Naval Reserve during World War II. Married 1) Valerie Heron (divorced), one son and one daughter; 2) Mary Wilson Price in 1970, one daughter and one son. Recipient: London *Evening Standard* award, 1961; Brandeis University Creative Arts award, 1961; American Academy award, 1975. Address: Levington Park, Mullingar, County Westmeath, Ireland.

PUBLICATIONS

Plays

The Ginger Man, adaptation of his own novel (produced London and Dublin, 1959; New York, 1963). New York, Random House, 1961; as *What They Did in Dublin, with The Ginger Man: A Play*, London, MacGibbon and Kee, 1962.

Fairy Tales of New York (produced Croydon, Surrey, 1960; London, 1961; New York, 1980). London, Penguin, and New York, Random House, 1961.

A Singular Man, adaptation of his own novel (produced Cambridge and London, 1964; Westport, Connecticut, 1967). London, Bodley Head, 1965.

The Plays of J.P. Donleavy (includes *The Ginger Man, Fairy Tales of New York, A Singular Man, The Saddest Summer of Samuel S*). New York, Delacorte Press, 1972; London, Penguin, 1974.

The Beastly Beatitudes of Balthazar B, adaptation of his own novel (produced London, 1981; Norfolk, Virginia, 1985).

Radio Play: *Helen*, 1956.

Novels

The Ginger Man. Paris, Olympia Press, and London, Spearman, 1955; New York, McDowell Obolensky, 1958; complete edition, London, Corgi, 1963; New York, Delacorte Press, 1965.

A Singular Man. Boston, Little Brown, 1963; London, Bodley Head, 1964.

The Saddest Summer of Samuel S. New York, Delacorte Press, 1966; London, Eyre and Spottiswoode, 1967.

The Beastly Beatitudes of Balthazar B. New York, Delacorte Press, 1968; London, Eyre and Spottiswoode, 1969.

The Onion Eaters. New York, Delacorte Press, and London, Eyre and Spottiswoode, 1971.

A Fairy Tale of New York. New York, Delacorte Press, and London, Eyre Methuen, 1973.

The Destinies of Darcy Dancer, Gentleman. New York, Delacorte Press, 1977; London, Allen Lane, 1978.

Schultz. New York, Delacorte Press, 1979; London, Allen Lane, 1980.

Leila. New York, Delacorte Press, and London, Allen Lane, 1983.

DeAlfonce Tennis: The Superlative Game of Eccentric Champions: Its History, Accoutrements, Conduct, Rules and Regimen. London, Weidenfeld and Nicolson, 1984; New York, Dutton, 1985.

Are You Listening Rabbi Löw? London, Viking, 1987.

Short Stories

Meet My Maker the Mad Molecule. Boston, Little Brown, 1964; London, Bodley Head, 1965.

Other

The Unexpurgated Code: A Complete Manual of Survival and Manners, drawings by the author. New York, Delacorte Press, and London, Wildwood House, 1975.

Ireland: In All Her Sins and in Some of Her Graces. London, Joseph, and New York, Viking, 1986.

Bibliography: by David W. Madden, in *Bulletin of Bibliography* (Westport, Connecticut), September 1982.

Critical Study: *J.P. Donleavy: The Style of His Sadness and Humor* by Charles G. Masinton, Bowling Green, Ohio, Popular Press, 1975.

* * *

Although J.P. Donleavy is better known as a novelist, he has adapted his own novels, *The Ginger Man* and *A Singular Man*, into plays which have received fairly successful productions, and his original stage play, *Fairy Tales of New York*, won the *Evening Standard* Most Promising Playwright Award for 1961. In adjusting to the medium of the theatre, Donleavy faced two particular problems. His prose style is rich, idiosyncratic, and of a quality to encourage cult enthusiasms: but to what extent could this verbal power be incorporated into stage dialogue without leaving the impression of over-writing? His novels too are usually written from the standpoint of one man, an anti-hero such as Sebastian Dangerfield or George Smith: but in a play the audience is necessarily aware of other characters, simply because they're on the stage. If the central character talks too much, the audience's sympathy may be drawn towards the reactions of other people to him. A single angle of vision, easy to maintain in a novel, is often hard to achieve in the theatre, which is a multi-dimensional medium.

Donleavy's first play, *The Ginger Man*, revealed an uncertain control of these difficulties. The story concerns Sebastian Dangerfield, an impoverished American living with his English wife, Marion, in Dublin. He is supposedly studying law at Trinity College: but his main efforts are direct towards staving off creditors, avoiding the responsibilities of fatherhood, and raking together enough money to get drunk. In the novel Sebastian's sheer wildness, his refusal to settle down, is exciting: it is an archetypal rebellion against dreary conformity. But in the play, we are unavoidably aware of the pain Sebastian causes others—particularly Marion who leaves him, and the genteel spinster, Miss Frost, whom he seduces. And the fine uninhibited imagination of Sebastian, which provides so much fun in the book, is in the play relentlessly controlled by the physical surroundings of the set: the squalid flat at One Mohammed Road, the prim suburban house at 11 Golden Vale Park. "*The Ginger Man*," concluded Richard Gilman, "desperately requires: song, dance, lyrical fragments, voices from nowhere, shapes, apparitions, unexplainable gestures." In the format of a naturalistic play, it lost many of the qualities which made the book so remarkable. Even the theme seemed less original: the relationship between O'Keefe and Sebastian recalled the boozing friendship between Joxer and "Captain" Boyle in O'Casey's *Juno and the Paycock*.

Fairy Tales of New York is much more successful: a sequence of four related anecdotes, which almost seems to continue the ginger man's career. An American returns to his native city, with his English wife who dies on the voyage. Cornelius Christian is in the same state of desolation, harassed by poverty, guilty and grief-stricken, which faced Sebastian at the close of the earlier play. The four scenes illustrate Cornelius's gradual rehabilitation: the burial of his wife and his job at the funeral parlour, his entry into the American business world, his work-outs at a gymnasium and finally his successful (though imaginary) conquest of a snobbish head-waiter and an embarrassed girlfriend. Unlike Sebastian, however, Cornelius is a reserved quiet man—observing others and sometimes poking gentle fun at them: and this changed role for the central character, together with the much greater flexibility of form, allows Donleavy's great gifts for caricature, witty dialogue, and buoyant fun to be more evident. Nor are the episodes as unrelated and superficial as they may appear. Donleavy stresses the contrast between the democratic ideals of American society with the rigidly class-structured and snobbish habits: Christian is employed because he's been to Europe and acquired "breeding"—he dazzles the head-waiter, who refused to serve him because he wore peach shoes, by dressing as a visiting Eastern potentate wearing no shoes at all. The spurious emotionalism of the funeral parlour is related to Christian's moving grief: and the sheer falseness of an over-commercialized society is exposed with a delicate skill that only Evelyn Waugh and Edward Albee have matched.

Although *A Singular Man* lacks some of the moral seriousness (and fun) of *Fairy Tales of New York*, it too is a rewarding play: centered around the life of a fairly successful New York businessman, George Smith, his friendships and affairs with three women, Ann Martin, Sally Tomson, and Shirl. Smith is a fall guy, always missing out on the opportunities he dreams about. "The only time the traffic will stop for me," he confesses to Shirl, "is when I'm dead." His sexual fantasies focus on Sally Tomson, a gorgeous secretary, protected by her tough-guy brother and many other lovers. Her death at the end of the play, just before her marriage to a rich tycoon, crystallizes Smith's sense of cosmic defeat. But Smith never quite gives up hope: and his resilience through successive embarrassments and failures provides the mainspring for the play. *A Singular Man* is similar in construction to *Fairy Tales of New York*: a sequence of 12 anecdotal scenes, which work both on the level of isolated and very amusing revue sketches, and together as a group, the insights of one episode being carried forward to the next, until the full picture emerges both of the society and the central man. In the first scene, Smith opts out of conversation with a boring friend by answering just "Beep beep"; in the seventh, he tries the same tactics with Shirl, only to discover that his relationship with her is too charged and complex to admit such an evasion.

Donleavy's style of humour is reminiscent both of *New Yorker* cartoons and of the American dramatist Murray Schisgal, whose plays are also popular in Britain. But his jokes are never flippant—although they sometimes seem whimsical. They succeed because they're based on detailed observation and a rich command of language. Although as a dramatist, he may not yet have lived to the promise of *Fairy Tales of New York*, he remains one of the most potentially exciting dramatists now at work.

—John Elsom

DREXLER, Rosalyn. American. Born in New York City, 25 November 1926. Self-educated. Married Sherman Drexler in 1946; one daughter and one son. Painter, sculptor, singer, and wrestler; taught at the University of Iowa, Iowa City, 1976–77. Recipient: Obie award, 1965, 1979, 1985; Rockefeller grant, 1965 (2 grants), 1968, 1974; *Paris Review* fiction prize, 1966; Guggenheim fellowship, 1970; Emmy award, 1974. Agent: (drama) Helen Harvey Associates, 410 West 24th Street, New York, New York 10011; (literary) Georges Borchardt Inc., 136 East 57th Street, New York, New York 10022, U.S.A.

PUBLICATIONS

Plays

Home Movies; and Softly, and Consider the Nearness, music by Al Carmines (produced New York, 1964). Included in *The Line of Least Existence and Other Plays*, 1967.

Hot Buttered Roll (produced New York, 1966; London, 1970). Included in *The Line of Least Existence and Other Plays*, 1967; with *The Investigation*, London, Methuen, 1969.

The Investigation (produced Boston and New York, 1966; London, 1970). Included in *The Line of Least Existence and Other Plays*, 1967; with *Hot Buttered Roll*, London, Methuen, 1969.

The Line of Least Existence (produced New York, 1967; Edinburgh, 1968). Included in *The Line of Least Existence and Other Plays*, 1967.

The Line of Least Existence and Other Plays. New York, Random House, 1967.

The Bed Was Full (produced New York, 1972). Included in *The Line of Least Existence and Other Plays*, 1967.

Skywriting, in *Collision Course* (produced New York, 1968). New York, Random House, 1968.

Was I Good? (produced New York, 1972).

She Who Was He (produced New York, 1973).

The Ice Queen (produced Boston, 1973).

Travesty Parade (produced Los Angeles, 1974).

Vulgar Lives (produced New York, 1979).

The Writers' Opera, music by John Braden (produced New York, 1979).

Graven Image (produced New York, 1980).

Starburn, music by Michael Meadows (produced New York, 1983).

Room 17-C (produced Omaha, 1983).

Delicate Feelings (produced New York, 1984).

Transients Welcome (includes *Room 17-C, Lobby, Utopia Parkway*) (produced New York, 1984). New York, Broadway Play Publishing, 1984.

A Matter of Life and Death (produced New York, 1986).

Novels

I Am the Beautiful Stranger. New York, Grossman, 1965; London, Weidenfeld and Nicolson, 1967.

One or Another. New York, Dutton, 1970; London, Blond, 1971.

To Smithereens. New York, New American Library, 1972; London, Weidenfeld and Nicolson, 1973; as *Submissions of a Lady Wrestler*, London, Mayflower, 1976.

The Cosmopolitan Girl. New York, Evans, 1975.

Dawn: Portrait of a Teenage Runaway (as Julia Sorel). New York, Ballantine, 1976.

Alex: Portrait of a Teenage Prostitute (as Julia Sorel). New York, Ballantine, 1977.

Rocky (novelization of screenplay; as Julia Sorel). New York, Ballantine, 1977.

See How She Runs (novelization of screenplay; as Julia Sorel). New York, Ballantine, 1978.

Starburn: The Story of Jenni Love. New York, Simon and Schuster, 1979.

Forever Is Sometimes Temporary When Tomorrow Rolls Around. New York, Simon and Schuster, 1979.

Bad Guy. New York, Dutton, 1982.

Other

Rosalyn Drexler: Intimate Emotions. New York, Grey Art Gallery, 1986.

*

Rosalyn Drexler comments:

I try to write with vitality, joy, and honesty. My plays may be called absurd. I write to amuse myself. I often amuse others.

Almost all my reviews have been excellent, but I am not produced much. It seems that every theatre wants to premiere a play. (That's how they get grants.) Therefore, if a play is done once, good or bad, that's it for the playwright—unless she is Ibsen, Shaw . . . etc.

Playwriting is my first love, I'm considered established, but I have just begun.

* * *

Rosalyn Drexler came to prominence as a novelist anc playwright at a time when the absurdist symbolism of Albe was very much in vogue. Her own work of the 1960's has some times been called "pop art", and it has also been billed a "An Evening of Bad Taste"; whichever, it seems very mucl a reaction against the intellectualism and pretentiousness whicl surrounded the "theatre of the absurd." One historian of th absurd has even contrasted one of Drexler's incontinent senil hedonists with Beckett's Molloy.

Bad taste is often both the subject and the style of Drexler' plays, manipulating the audience into compromising corners *The Investigation* seems to be a simple if not naive parabl about a police interrogation of an adolescent murder suspec a timid, purtianical boy who is eventually bullied by the polic into suicide. Some critics found it a fashionable tract again police brutality, and hence a very slight work. The characte are, as usual in Drexler, two-dimensional, but the boy is s colourless that he is unattractive even as a sympathy objec The detective, on the other hand, is so resourceful that h techniques of sadistic attrition become the theatrical dynam and the boy's suicide is the act of a spoil-sport. Much of tl detective's imaginative energy is invested in verbal reconstru tion of the grotesque rape and murder, putting the boy in tl central role. As the audience receives no evidence from a external source, there remains the possibility that the fac which the detective narrates may be correct, and that wh appears to be his sadism is in fact nausea at an outrageo crime. In the second scene there is a surprising technical tw when the murder victim's twin sister introduces herself to the audience and volunteers to re-enact the crime, using a boyfriend of hers as the accused boy. That this is parodic is obvious—they congratulate each other on their performances and show no sadness that a girl has been killed—but the mechanics of the parody are obscure. Does the scene represent the detective's hypothesis? or the boy's nightmare? or public assumptions about what happens when repression meets precociousness? The only possibility to be eliminated is that the scene shows what really happened. When questions like these are left open at the end of a play, the author can hardly be accused of triteness.

If questions are generated prodigally, Drexler also seems to have many techniques for ensuring that her plays do not become too meaningful; the title-piece for her collection, *The Line of Least Existence*, may consist of profundity or malapropism. Verbal vandalism certainly does exist in that play, but so also does an utterly unpretentious playfulness, in which words are discovered and traded just for their phatic values. Because Drexler's dramatic world is never remotely naturalistic, the reference of words is often totally unclear; one wonders whether "least existence" actually defines the dramatic cosmos as a sort of limbo, especially when at the end the central character, with a heroic irresponsibility, commits his wife and himself to a mental asylum. In *Hot Buttered Roll* Mr. Corrupt Savage, a senile bedridden billionaire, exercises his waning appetites with the assistance of a call girl and an amazonian bodyguard who from time to time throws him back into bed. The cast also includes two pimps—a "purveyor of girly girls," and a "purveyor of burly girls"—but the essential action seems to be in a bunker, where all connections and relationships have been severed and the use of appetite is tentative and vicarious. As with the detective in *The Investigation*, the more disgusting parts of the dialogue sometimes have a vatic quality, so that the appeal is often in its vagueness or suggestiveness. Thus the play's central image is never clearly stated: that of man as a sort of transplant patient, his faculties being monitored externally, his needs being canvassed through a huge mail-order system, and his responses being tested by the bizarre performances by the call-girl at the foot of the bed. Very similar in rationale is *Softly, and Consider the Nearness*, in which a woman uses a television set as a surrogate world of experience.

In a later play, *Skywriting*, there are only two characters, and their referential functions are trimmed back even further: the unnamed Man and Woman seem to be archetypes, and as such make this an important work, a transition from the pop plays of the 1960's towards the mythical work of the 1970's. Beyond the fact that the diction seems closer to Drexler's Bronx than to Eden, the play is not located in any time or place. The two characters, segregated on either side of the stage, argue about the possession of a huge (projected) picture post-card of clouds. As in the plays of Sam Shepard, the sky is perceived as a fantasy arena, and the characters instinctively take a territorial attitude to it, invading each other's minds as they defend their sexuality. This is a very clever and economical play, in which the primordial merges with the futuristic before dissolving in a throw-away ending. *She Who Was He* investigates the world of myth and ritual in an exotic, distant past: the style is lavish and operatic, but the play is weakly structured in terms of suspense, and its action has no apparent bearing on the world of the audience. In her Obie-winning *The Writers' Opera* Drexler returns to her more familiar mode, the perversely illogical collage of stereotypical items. The pretentiousness and fickleness of the art world is the satirical target in this play, and this world is reflected in the domestic behaviour of the central characters, where a transsexual finds himself in an Oedipal relationship with his son. Such events differ only in degree from the ingredients of her first stage success, *Home Movies*, where outrageous farcical grotesquerie revolves round the prodigal and inventive sexuality of the characters. There, as throughout Drexler's large output of plays, novels, and novelisations, her most characteristic trait, the ridiculous pun, typifies an author who defies serious critical assessment.

—Howard McNaughton

DUBERMAN, Martin (Bauml). American. Born in New York City, 6 August 1930. Educated at Yale University, New Haven, Connecticut, 1948–52, B.A. 1952 (Phi Beta Kappa); Harvard University, Cambridge, Massachusetts, 1952–57, M.A. 1953, Ph.D. 1957. Tutor, Harvard University, 1955–57; Instructor and Assistant Professor (Morse Fellow, 1961–62), Yale University, 1957–62; Assistant Professor, 1962–65, Associate Professor, 1965–67, and Professor of History, 1967–71, Princeton University, New Jersey. Since 1971 Distinguished Professor, Lehman College, City University of New York. Recipient: Bancroft Prize, for history, 1962; Vernon Rice award, 1964; American Academy award, 1971. Address: 475 West 22nd Street, New York, New York 10011, U.S.A.

PUBLICATIONS

Plays

In White America (produced New York, 1963; London, 1964). Boston, Houghton Mifflin, 1964; London, Faber, 1965.
Metaphors, in *Collision Course* (produced New York, 1968). New York, Random House, 1968.
Groups (produced New York, 1968).
The Colonial Dudes (produced New York, 1969). Included in *Male Armor*, 1975.
The Memory Bank: The Recorder, and The Electric Map (produced New York, 1970; *The Recorder* produced London, 1974). New York, Dial Press, 1970.
Payments (produced New York, 1971). Included in *Male Armor*, 1975.
Soon, music by Joseph Martinez Kookoolis and Scott Fagan, adaptation of a story by Kookoolis, Fagan, and Robert Greenwald (produced New York, 1971).
Dudes (produced New York, 1972).
Elagabalus (produced New York, 1973). Included in *Male Armor*, 1975.
Male Armor: Selected Plays 1968–1974 (includes *Metaphors, The Colonial Dudes, The Recorder, The Guttman Ordinary Scale, Payments, The Electric Map, Elagabalus*). New York, Dutton, 1975.
Visions of Kerouac (produced New York, 1976). Boston, Little Brown, 1977.

Screenplays: *The Deed*, 1969; *Mother Earth*, 1971.

Other

Charles Francis Adams 1807–1886. Boston, Houghton Mifflin, 1961.
James Russell Lowell. Boston, Houghton Mifflin, 1966.

The Uncompleted Past (essays). New York, Random House, 1969.
Black Mountain: An Exploration in Community. New York, Dutton, 1972; London, Wildwood House, 1974.
About Time: Exploring the Gay Past. New York, Seahorse, 1986.

Editor, *The Antislavery Vanguard: New Essays on the Abolitionists*. Princeton, New Jersey, Princeton University Press, 1965.

* * *

In White America was first produced in October 1963, at a time of great optimism in American social consciousness. It was the era of the New Frontier. The play was an immediate, sustained, and internationally acclaimed success. Its author, however, was a playwright by avocation only, and his subsequent theatrical productivity has proven to reflect his true profession in subject matter, theory of communication, and evolution. Martin Duberman is a Professor of History at Lehman College, a professional historian of recognized accomplishment, and author of several works in that field: *James Russell Lowell, Charles Francis Adams, The Uncompleted Past, Black Mountain: An Exploration in Community*, and *About Time*.

In White America is less a "play" in any traditional literary sense than an "evening of theatre"—it is an assemblage of documents from the history of the black American's experience of 200 years' suffering. As an historical event reflecting the social fabric of its time, the piece is significant, and at the time of its presentation it was a moving experience for all audiences. It weaves together dialogues, documents, songs, and narration with impressive sensitivity for theatrical construction and it suggests a possible form for playwrights to explore. In a 1963 essay, "Presenting the Past," Duberman argued that "the past has something to say to us . . . a knowledge of past experience can provide valuable guidelines, though not blueprints, for acting in the present." Clearly his professional concern for history provided him with his subject matter (he did not create material; he selected, edited, and shaped it). His teaching duties, moreover, led him to a belief in the theatrical and dramatic potential of oral communication: a lecturer can be more than informative. "The benefits of a union between history and drama," Duberman wrote, "would not by any means be all on one side. If theater, with its ample skill in communication, could increase the immediacy of past experience, history, with its ample material on human behavior, could broaden the range of theatrical testimony." In his preface to the printed play he added, "I chose to tell this story on the stage, and through historical documents, because I wanted to combine the evocative power of the spoken word with the confirming power of historical fact." It was the assessment of critics of the time that Duberman had succeeded in all respects. The play stimulated an awakening social consciousness, was vital in the enactment, and communicated its thesis most effectively.

In the late 1960's Duberman's attitudes towards the uses of the past and the efficacy of wedding history to theatre began to change. Perhaps the disenchantment of the New Left that followed the Kennedy and King assassinations influenced his thinking. His work for the theatre abandoned the path suggested by *In White America*, and he began to write fiction-invented drama.

Male Armor collects seven plays written between 1968 and 1974. Two are full-length. Four of the one-acts, had been published previously. None had received successful production in the commercial theatre. In his introduction to the collection, Duberman professes that the plays explore a common theme, "What does it mean to be a 'man'?" The collection's title, he explains, is meant to recall Wilhelm Reich's concept of "character armor"—the devices we employ to protect ourselves from our own energy, particularly our sexual energy. Each of the plays investigates the way we build protective roles which then dominate us. For Duberman, the way to destroy these confining roles is, apparently, androgyny, either practiced or metaphorical.

Metaphors, The Electric Map, and *The Recorder* are all highly literate sparrings between consenting adults which explore the themes of power struggle and homosexuality. In *Metaphors* a young applicant to Yale University nearly seduces his admissions interviewer. *The Electric Map* and *The Recorder*, which had an unsuccessful off-Broadway production under the title *The Memory Bank*, are also duologues. The former is set before an elaborate, electrified map of the Battle of Gettysburg, and self-consciously uses this visual analogue to puff up a foolish domestic quarrel between two brothers into what the author hopes will be something akin to universality. There is a predictable undertone of latent homosexuality to the trite and poorly motivated action. *The Recorder* is an interview of the friend of a great man by an academician-historian. In it, Duberman is intrigued by the ineffectiveness and inaccuracy of historical inquiry, and the play unquestionably reflects his growing disenchantment with the study of history, as well as his growing use of sexuality as a dramatic subject. By the time of these plays, Duberman was referring to himself as "more a writer than a historián."

The newest play in *Male Armor* is *Elagabalus*, a six-scene realistic play about Adrian, a self-indulgent and affluent androgynist. Duberman writes, "Adrian is playful and daring. His gaiety may be contaminated by petulance and willfulness, but he *is* moving toward an *un*-armored territory, moving out so far that finally he's left with no protection against the traditional weaponry brought to bear against him . . . other than the ultimate defense of self-destruction." In his quest for self, Adrian stabs himself fatally in the groin, and the final image the writer offers is a gratuitous freeze-frame from the porno film "Big Stick" in which a teenage girl sucks sensuously on a popsicle. This reader was reminded of the adage that many people (Adrian? Duberman?) who are looking for themselves may not like what they find. Adrian is a boring character whose self-destruction does not seem significant.

The Uncompleted Past is a collection of Duberman's critical and historical essays which concludes with an expression of his disenchantment with the study of history and reveals why his theatrical development had moved towards fiction (in which area he appears undistinguished) and away from the documentary (in which his initial acclaim was achieved). He writes,

> For those among the young, historians and otherwise, who are chiefly interested in changing the present, I can only say . . . they doom themselves to bitter disappointment if they seek their guides to action in a study of the past. Though I have tried to make it otherwise, I have found that a "life in history" has given me very limited information or perspective with which to understand the central concerns of my own life and my own times.

It seems probable that *In White America* will stand as Duberman's major writing for the theatre, and that it will prove more significant as an event of cultural history than as either an innovation in theatrical form or the first work in the career of a significant playwright—thus belying the very attitudes towards history and theatre which Duberman has recently held.

—Thomas B. Markus

DUFFY, Maureen (Patricia). British. Born in Worthing, Sussex, 21 October 1933. Educated at Trowbridge High School for Girls, Wiltshire; Sarah Bonnell High School for Girls; King's College, London, 1953–56, B.A. (honours) in English 1956. Schoolteacher for five years. Co-founder, Writers Action Group, 1972; Joint Chairman, 1977–78, and since 1985, President, Writers Guild of Great Britain; Chairman, Greater London Arts Literature Panel, 1979–81; Vice-Chairman, British Copyright Council, 1981–86; since 1982 Chairman, Authors Lending and Copyright Society; Vice-President, Beauty Without Cruelty. Recipient: City of London Festival Playwright's Prize, 1962; Arts Council bursary, 1963, 1966, 1975; Society of Authors travelling scholarship, 1976. Fellow, Royal Society of Literature, 1985. Agent: Jonathan Clowes Ltd., 22 Prince Albert Road, London NW1 7ST. Address: 18 Fabian Road, London SW6 7TZ, England.

PUBLICATIONS

Plays

The Lay-Off (produced London, 1962).
The Silk Room (produced Watford, Hertfordshire, 1966).
Rites (produced London, 1969). Published in *New Short Plays 2*, London, Methuen, 1969.
Solo, Olde Tyme (produced Cambridge, 1970).
A Nightingale in Bloomsbury Square (produced London, 1973). Published in *Factions*, edited by Giles Gordon and Alex Hamilton, London, Joseph, 1974.

Radio Play: *Only Goodnight*, 1981.

Television Play: *Josie*, 1961.

Novels

That's How It Was. London, Hutchinson, 1962; New York, Dial Press, 1984.
The Single Eye. London, Hutchinson, 1964.
The Microcosm. London, Hutchinson, and New York, Simon and Schuster, 1966.
The Paradox Players. London, Hutchinson, 1967; New York, Simon and Schuster, 1968.
Wounds. London, Hutchinson, and New York, Knopf, 1969.
Love Child. London, Weidenfeld and Nicolson, and New York, Knopf, 1971.
I Want to Go to Moscow: A Lay. London, Hodder and Stoughton, 1973; as *All Heaven in a Rage*, New York, Knopf, 1973.
Capital. London, Cape, 1975; New York, Braziller, 1976.
Housespy. London, Hamish Hamilton, 1978.
Gor Saga. London, Eyre Methuen, 1981; New York, Viking Press, 1982.
Scarborough Fear (as D.M. Cayer). London, Macdonald, 1982.
Londoners: An Elegy. London, Methuen, 1983.
Change. London, Methuen, 1987.

Verse

Lyrics for the Dog Hour. London, Hutchinson, 1968.
The Venus Touch. London, Weidenfeld and Nicolson, 1971.
Actaeon. Rushden, Northamptonshire, Sceptre Press, 1973.
Evesong. London, Sappho, 1975.
Memorials of the Quick and the Dead. London, Hamish Hamilton, 1979.
Collected Poems. London, Hamish Hamilton, 1985.

Other

The Erotic World of Faery. London, Hodder and Stoughton, 1972.
The Passionate Shepherdess: Aphra Behn 1640–1689. London, Cape, 1977; New York, Avon, 1979.
Inherit the Earth: A Social History. London, Hamish Hamilton, 1980.
Men and Beasts: An Animal Rights Handbook. London, Paladin, 1984.

Editor, with Alan Brownjohn, *New Poetry 3.* London, Arts Council, 1977.
Editor, *Oroonoko and Other Stories*, by Aphra Behn. London, Methuen, 1986.

Translator, *A Blush of Shame*, by Domenico Rea. London, Barrie and Rockliff, 1968.

*

Manuscript Collection: King's College, University of London.

Critical Studies: by Dulan Barber, in *Transatlantic Review 45* (London), Spring 1973; *Guide to Modern World Literature* by Martin Seymour-Smith, London, Wolfe, 1973, as *Funk and Wagnalls Guide to Modern World Literature*, New York, Funk and Wagnalls, 1973.

Maureen Duffy comments:

(1973) I began my first play in my third year at university, finishing it the next year and submitting it for the *Observer* playwriting competition of 1957–58. I had done a great deal of acting and producing at school and at this stage my aim was to be a playwright as I was already a poet. I wrote several more plays and became one of the Royal Court Writers Group which met in the late 1950's to do improvisations and discuss problems. I have continued to write plays alternately with novels and every time I am involved in a production I swear I will never write anything else. From early attempts to write a kind of poetic social realism I have become increasingly expressionist. *Solo, Olde Tyme* and *Rites* are all on themes from Greek mythology. *Megrim*, the play I am working on at present, is a futurist study of racialism and the making of a society. I believe in theatrical theatre including all the pantomime elements of song, dance, mask and fantasy and in the power of imagery.

* * *

Maureen Duffy is firmly established as one of the foremost novelists of her generation. During the past 25 years she has also written plays; the fact that these, with the possible exception of *Rites*, have not yet received the recognition they deserve is due quite as much to an absence of a fortuitous conjunction of circumstance typical of the theatre and necessary for the achievement of success, as to the demands made on the audience by the author.

Duffy's plays are not "easy." They are densely written, pitched between fantasy and realism, and have allegorical undertones. At the centre of her work lie three short plays derived from Greek myths: The Bacchae (*Rites*), Narcissus (*Solo*), and Uranus (*Olde Tyme*).

Rites, which first appeared in an experimental programme of plays presented by the National Theatre, is set in a ladies' public lavatory, presided over by the monstrous Ada (*Agave*). Duffy describes it as a black farce. She use a chorus of modern prototypes—three office girls, a cleaner, an old tramp—and involves them in situations both modern (a girl's attempted suicide in a cubicle) and parallel to the myth. Her Dionysus is a boy doll, brought in by two women and examined with gloating curiosity; her Pentheus a transvestite lesbian, dressed like a man. She is brutally murdered as a consequence of entering this exclusive women's domain, and disposed of in the incinerator for sanitary towels. It helps to know *The Bacchae*, but it is by no means essential. The strength of the play resides in the power of the writing, the violence of its situations, and the deliberate "Peeping Tom" element.

In *Solo* her Narcissus is a man, reflecting on his image in a bathroom mirror: again a deft blending of the modern and the ancient mythical.

Olde Tyme, which deals with the castration of Uranus, is in many ways her most interesting and original play, but dramatically the least convincingly realized. It is studded with brilliant, Pirandellian ideas. Her hero is a television tycoon, keeping his employees in slavish dependence. He sustains his confidence with the help of cherished memories of his mother, a queen of the Music Halls. The slaves get their chance to revolt when he hires a derelict theatre and forces them to recreate an old Music Hall evening, with his mother as the star. This he plans to film and preserve for posterity.

Sexual fantasies are enacted, and at last his "mother" appears and punctures with her revelations the whole basis of the tycoon's life. He is destroyed ("castrated") and his minions take over. There are echoes here of Jean Genet's *The Balcony*, but the play's effectiveness is undermined by the lack of credibility of the characters. To dehumanize a three-dimensional character and make him two-dimensional will engage an audience's emotions, but you cannot flatten caricatures.

Among Duffy's other works for the stage are *The Silk Room*, which chronicles the gradual disintegration of a pop group, and a play about François Villon. The unproduced *Megrim* is an expressionist, futuristic fantasy about a secluded society. It combines the nightmarish quality of Fritz Lang's film *Metropolis* with the intellectual daring of the discussions contained in Shaw's late extravaganzas. To these Duffy has added a human, mainly sexual dimension of her own. It makes a rich but probably undigestible concoction.

More modestly, and entirely successfully, *A Nightingale in Bloomsbury Square* shows us Virginia Woolf going though a lengthy creative stocktaking prior to suicide before a spectral audience consisting of Sigmund Freud and Vita Sackville-West. It is an interrupted monologue, written with great sympathy and power.

Duffy is a writer of fierce originality and imaginative depth; hopefully, she will take the opportunity at some point to prove herself to a wider public as a dramatist, too.

—Frank Marcus

DUNBAR, Andrea. British. Born in Bradford, Yorkshire, 22 May 1961. Educated at Buttershaw Comprehensive School, Bradford. Has two daughters and one son. Recipient: George Devine Award, 1981. Address: 7 Edge End Gardens, Buttershaw, Bradford, West Yorkshire BD6 2BB, England.

PUBLICATIONS

Plays

The Arbor (produced London, 1980; New York, 1983). London, Pluto Press, 1980.

Rita, Sue, and Bob Too (produced London, 1982). London, Methuen, 1982.

Shirley (produced London, 1986).

Screenplay: *Rita, Sue, and Bob Too*, 1987.

* * *

Andrea Dunbar is unique: an original voice, not waving but shouting from the underclass of the North of England, a class that is jobless, school-less, and money-less. Her plays, not so much slices as hacksaw chunks, expose rough life on a Bradford council estate, where family violence is the norm, drinking and fighting the main entertainments, and you're odd one out if you haven't been sexually abused by the time you are 12. Dunbar writes, not as a middle-class voyeur, but as an active protagonist, and it is this which gives her plays a bleak truthfulness and rich vein of humour. Dunbar's characters, particularly the women, have a resilience and wit that make their actions funny and moving, as well as shocking.

Her first and still most famous play, described family life on a breezeblock estate inappropriately named The Arbor by some town planner with a sense of humour. A young girl becomes pregnant and her family react in various ways. Her father, a drunken bully, beats her up; her mother, a put-upon but still spirited woman, tries ineptly to help. Her brothers, sisters, and neighbours join in the family battles, which eventually rage up and down the entire street. The girl is sent away to a mother-and-baby home where she learns sums in the morning and nappy changing in the afternoon and comes up against a very different class of people. Figures of authority punctuate this play, as in all Dunbar's others. Social workers, teachers, policemen all attempt to interfere and alter the course of the girl's life. Dunbar sees them as through the small end of the telescope, not necessarily with hostility but with curiosity. They inhabit another world, strange and distant from the lives of the main protagonists. Some of Dunbar's wittiest scenes lie in the addressing of authority across a major gap in life experience.

In *Rita, Sue, and Bob Too* a married man has sex with two under-age girls, who then compete with each other and with his wife for his favours. Again, violence is never far (a couple of lagers, usually) from the surface, and often quickly erupts. The men visit it upon the women, the women upon each other. It's a fact of life, no better or worse than any other. A black eye or broken tooth is proof of love. Or at least of possession. Thrills in this environment consist of what comes cheap—beer, glue, and sex, with a preference for the last as it comes cheapest of all. But if a girl falls pregnant, she's on her own and she's a sissy if she can't cope.

In *Shirley* Dunbar examines for the first time the relationship between two women. Shirley and her mother, at violent odds with each other at the start of the play, screaming abuse in the presence of their respective alarmed and embarrassed lovers, end by arriving at a tacit understanding of and agreement with each other. Throughout their desperate rows, fuelled by jealousy and the struggle for power over poor and barren territory, the bond between them is evident. They hate and love each other and have a whole range of explicit curses to demonstrate their passion.

Passion is the keynote of all Dunbar's plays. There's nothing tame or reasoned about them. The major passions are rage, envy, spite, jealously, and sexual desire. The action proceeds through emotion in a culture which revolves around grabbing what you can, before you are toothless and hairless and old before your time. The plays rarely move outside the boundaries of the estate with its pubs, chippies, bedrooms, and streets. All of life, for its inhabitants, is contained in this isolated cube. They have little apparent curiosity for the outside world and scorn the ways of those not of their kind. Their life may be brutal but it has its mores and niceties like any other, and strangers ignore them at their peril.

Dunbar has entered the world of film with a Channel Four film of *Rita, Sue, and Bob Too* and another BBC project on the way. She has not been to date a prolific writer, preferring to live life first and art second, but it will be interesting to see what effect media attention will have on her work. Will film producers take over as authority figures and the affairs of continuity girls be detailed on her ruthless pages? On the whole, I think not. Dunbar remains devoted to the world which created her, the fights and feuds of which charge her work. I think her development will be in the direction of examining more fully the relationships between female friends, as they struggle to assert themselves in a society more devoted to basic chauvinism than seems possible in these post-feminist times. Women have no rights here other than those they kick and bite for. Above all they respect, no, revere, the power of the male, although it be the power to bruise, impregnate, and terrify them. This was not Ripper country for nothing. Nevertheless, these women rise to challenge the terms of their existence and express their anarchy. They cheek policemen, flout the education officer, spit at the social worker. Dunbar has created a band of bloodied but unbowed women whose raw existence is supported, not by the men in their lives, but by the offer of survival techniques from other women: their friends and mothers who've been there before.

—Carole Hayman

DUNN, Nell (Mary). British. Born in London in 1936. Educated at a convent school. Married the writer Jeremy Sandford in 1956; three children. Recipient: Rhys Memorial Prize, for fiction, 1964; Susan Smith Blackburn Prize, 1981; *Evening Standard* award, 1982; Society of West End Theatre award, 1982. Agent: Curtis Brown, 162–168 Regent Street, London W1R 5TB. Address: 10 Bell Lane, Twickenham, Middlesex, England.

PUBLICATIONS

Plays

Steaming (produced London, 1981; Stamford, Connecticut, and New York, 1982). Ambergate, Derbyshire, Amber Lane Press, 1981; New York, Limelight, 1984.

Sketches in *Variety Night* (produced London, 1982).

I Want, with Adrian Henri, adaptation of their own novel (produced Liverpool, 1983; London, 1986).

Screenplay: *Poor Cow*, with Ken Loach, 1967.

Television Play: *Up the Junction*, from her own stories, 1965.

Novels

Poor Cow. London, MacGibbon and Kee, and New York, Doubleday, 1967.

The Incurable. London, Cape, and New York, Doubleday, 1971.

I Want, with Adrian Henri. London, Cape, 1972.

Tear His Head off His Shoulders. London, Cape, 1974; New York, Doubleday, 1975.

The Only Child: A Simple Story of Heaven and Hell. London, Cape, 1978.

Short Stories

Up the Junction. London, MacGibbon and Kee, 1963; Philadelphia, Lippincott, 1966.

Other

Talking to Women. London, MacGibbon and Kee, 1965.

Freddy Gets Married (for children). London, MacGibbon and Kee, 1969.

Editor, *Living Like I Do.* London, Futura, 1977; as *Different Drummers*, New York, Harcourt Brace, 1977.

* * *

Nell Dunn was best known in the 1960's and 1970's as a chronicler of the lives of working-class women. The child of a securely middle-class background, with a convent school education, she became fascinated by the haphazard lives of women who existed without the safety net of money or education to sustain them. In 1963 she published a collection of short stories, *Up the Junction*, which consisted of vignettes of life she had observed it among the young in Clapham. The book, which she later adapted for television, emphasised the vitality and sharpness of perception of the women, together with their acceptance of the fate life had mapped out for them—a few short butterfly days, followed by a hopeless and unrewarding existence.

In her first novel, *Poor Cow*, Dunn centred on one woman, Joy, whose life from early on is set on a downward spiral. At 22 she has gone through one broken marriage and has a young son, Jonny. As her own life deteriorates, she transfers her hopes onto her son, trusting that his life, at least, will be better. Her epitaph on her own is: "To think when I was a kid I planned to conquer the world and if anyone saw me now they'd say. 'She's had a rough night, poor cow.'" A film was made of the book by director Ken Loach, with Carol White in the leading role.

Dunn's stage play, *Steaming*, continues her fascination with working-class women and with the character on whom Joy was based in particular: the woman who lives for freedom and fun, but in reality remains a prisoner of her lack of self-confidence and the hard brutalities of life. Josie, the "Joy" figure, is lively, earthy, enjoys leading her men a dance, but invariably ends up the worse for it. "How come I always get hit on the left side?" she asks, after yet another beating up.

Steaming is set in a London Turkish bath, which provides Dunn with the background for what she is best at—women talking among themselves, without the constraints of a male presence. The only male, the caretaker of the Baths, is dimly glimpsed through a glass door, unable to enter the female domain. The six characters are a mixture of age and class. Apart from Josie, there is Mrs. Meadow, a repressive mother, who will not let her retarded, overweight daughter take her "plastics" off, even in the shower. There are two middle-class women—Jane, a mature student with a bohemian past, and Nancy, who shops at Peter Jones and whose husband has just left her after 22 years of marriage. The Baths are presided over by Violet, in her forties, who has worked there as attendant for 18 years and who is threatened with early retirement if the Council goes ahead with its intention to close the building.

Not a great deal happens in the play, but the humour and conversation sustain the evening. Without their clothes, and in the steamy companionship of the Baths, the women develop a sisterhood that transcends class barriers. The new entrant, Nancy, at first nervous of the milieu, is drawn in and at one point breaks down and talks about her broken marriage and the pressures that have kept her dependent on a man. Josie reveals that her seeming sexual freedom is also tied to dependence on a man's finances. Their campaign against the closure of the Baths gives them a new lease of life, and by the end Josie, after making a brilliant, if disregarded, speech at a public meeting, says she is going to get an education; Nancy, the rejected wife, announces she is "going to get fucked"; and Dawn asserts herself against her over-protective mother.

Whether this ending is anything more than a way of giving an upbeat finale to the play is a matter for debate, and Dunn's characters will probably find they are not able to change their lives greatly after their temporary euphoria. The dialogue of the working-class women has far more of a ring of truth about it than the dialogue of the middle-class women, but the author has always found a richness and rhythm in working-class speech that she fails to find in the more educated voice. *Steaming* can be regarded as a gentle piece of female consciousness-raising. It must also be one of the few feminist plays to have brought large numbers of male chauvinists in, attracted by the fact that the cast members are nude for much of the time.

I Want, written in 1972 in collaboration with Adrian Henri, is about a love affair between a well-bred, convent-educated girl but "with the devil in her" and a scholarship boy from a Liverpool terrace home. They meet in the 1920's and the play charts the course of their relationship over the next 60 years. It has moments of humour, but lacks the strength of *Steaming*. Dunn also wrote a book of interviews, *Talking to Women*, published in 1965. It is of interest for its recording of the stirrings of "female consciousness" among divergent women. The interviewees included a talented young actress and a rich upper-class hippy who owned an esoteric clothes shop. Both of them are now dead, and one wonders what has happened to the rest. A sequel for Dunn, perhaps?

—Clare Colvin

DURANG, Christopher (Ferdinand). American. Born in Montclair, New Jersey, 2 January 1949. Educated at Harvard University, Cambridge, Massachusetts, 1967–71, A.B. in English 1971; Yale University School of Drama, New Haven, Connecticut, 1971–74, M.F.A. in playwriting 1974. Drama teacher, Southern Connecticut College, New Haven, 1975, and Yale University, 1975–76. Recipient: CBS fellowship, 1975; Rockefeller grant, 1976; Guggenheim grant, 1979; Obie award, 1980, 1985; Lecomte de Nouy Foundation grant, 1981; Dramatists Guild Hull-Warriner Award, 1985. Agent: Helen Merrill Ltd., 361 West 17th Street, New York, New York 10011, U.S.A.

PUBLICATIONS

Plays

The Nature and Purpose of the Universe (produced Northampton, Massachusetts, 1971; New York, 1975). Included in *The Nature and Purpose of the Universe; Death Comes to Us All, Mary Agnes; 'dentity Crisis*, 1979.

'dentity Crisis (as *Robert*, produced Cambridge, Massachusetts, 1971; as *'dentity Crisis*, also director: produced New Haven, Connecticut, 1975; London, 1986). Included in *The Nature and Purpose of the Universe; Death Comes to Us All, Mary Agnes; 'dentity Crisis*, 1979.

Better Dead Than Sorry, music by Jack Feldman, lyrics by Durang (produced New Haven, Connecticut, 1972; New York, 1973).

I Don't Generally Like Poetry But Have You Read "Trees"?, with Albert Innaurato (produced New Haven, Connecticut, 1972; New York, 1973).

The Life Story of Mitzi Gaynor; or, Gyp, with Albert Innaurato (produced New Haven, Connecticut, 1973).

The Marriage of Bette and Boo (produced New Haven, Connecticut, 1973; revised version produced New York, 1979). New Haven, Connecticut, Yale/Theatre, 1973; revised version (produced New York, 1985; London, 1987), New York, Dramatists Play Service, 1985.

The Idiots Karamazov, with Albert Innaurato, music by Jack Feldman, lyrics by Durang (produced New Haven, Connecticut, 1974). New Haven, Connecticut, Yale/Theatre, 1974; augmented edition, New York, Dramatists Play Service, 1981.

Titanic (produced New Haven, Connecticut, 1974; New York, 1976). New York, Dramatists Play Service, 1983.

Death Comes to Us All, Mary Agnes (produced New Haven, Connecticut, 1975). Included in *The Nature and Purpose of the Universe; Death Comes to Us All, Mary Agnes; 'dentity Crisis*, 1979.

When Dinah Shore Ruled the Earth, with Wendy Wasserstein (produced New Haven, Connecticut, 1975).

Das Lusitania Songspiel, with Sigourney Weaver, music by Mel Marvin and Jack Gaughan (produced New York, 1976; revised version produced New York, 1976; revised version produced New York, 1980).

A History of the American Film (produced Hartford, Connecticut, 1976; New York, 1978). New York, Avon, 1978.

The Vietnamization of New Jersey (produced New Haven, Connecticut, 1977). New York, Dramatists Play Service, 1978.

Sister Mary Ignatius Explains It All for You (produced New York, 1979; London, 1983). New York, Dramatists Play Service, 1980.

The Nature and Purpose of the Universe; Death Comes to Us All, Mary Agnes; 'dentity Crisis: Three Short Plays. New York, Dramatists Play Service, 1979.

Beyond Therapy (produced New York, 1981; revised version produced New York and London, 1982). New York, French, 1983.
The Actor's Nightmare (produced New York, 1981; London, 1983). With *Sister Mary Ignatius Explains It All for You*, New York, Dramatists Play Service, 1982.
Christopher Durang Explains It All for You (includes *The Nature and Purpose of the Universe, 'dentity Crisis, Titanic, The Actor's Nightmare, Sister Mary Ignatius Explains It All for You, Beyond Therapy*). New York, Avon, 1982.
Baby with the Bathwater (produced Cambridge, Massachusetts, and New York, 1983; Colchester, Essex, 1984). New York, Dramatists Play Service, 1984.
Sloth, in *Faustus in Hell* (produced Princeton, New Jersey, 1985).
Laughing Wild (produced New York, 1987).

Screenplay: *Beyond Therapy*, with Robert Altman, 1987.

Television Writing: *Comedy Zone* series; *Carol Burnett Special.*

*

Theatrical Activities:
Director: **Play**—*'dentity Crisis*, New Haven, Connecticut, 1975.
Actor: **Plays**—at Yale University School of Drama, New Haven, Connecticut—Gustaf in *Urlicht* by Albert Innaurato, 1971, Darryl in *Better Dead Than Sorry*, 1972, Performer in *The Life Story of Mitzi Gaynor; or, Gyp*, 1973, Bruce in *Happy Birthday, Montpelier Pizz-zazz* by Wendy Wasserstein, 1974, and Emcee in *When Dinah Shore Ruled the Earth*, 1975; at Yale Repertory Theatre—Chorus in *The Frogs* by Burt Shevelove and Stephen Sondheim, 1974, Student in *The Possessed* by Camus, 1974, and Alyosha in *The Idiots Karamazov*, 1974; Performer in *I Don't Generally Like Poetry But Have You Read "Trees"?*, New York, 1973; Performer in *Das Lusitania Songspiel*, New York, 1976, 1976, 1980; Young Cashier in *The Hotel Play* by Wallace Shawn, New York, 1981; Matt in *The Marriage of Bette and Boo*, New York, 1985. **Film**—*The Secret of My Success*, 1987.

* * *

Handsomely surviving a Catholic boyhood in New Jersey and Ivy League education at Harvard and Yale (M.F.A. in playwriting), Christopher Durang has been critically ranked in the top echelon of American playwrights. Most of his plays have been popular with regional and off-the-mainline theatres, and reflect their author's penchant for parody with favorite targets being drama and film, literature, American social history and popular culture, parochial religion, and the middle-class family. National recognition arrived with the 1978 Broadway production on *A History of the American Film*. Most critics applauded Durang's satiric skills that coalesced in this inventive multi-leveled profile of the films and social history of the last 50 years.

Using a revue-type format and song lyrics by Durang, *American Film* trots out the clichés, stereotypes, and superficial attitudes toward events that bombarded American culture from *Orphans of the Storm* to *Earthquake*. The characters interchange as screen spectators and actors, as we follow the thorny path of the naively innocent heroine from poverty with a callous Cagney-like lover through speakeasies, prison, high society, wartime, to heavenly ascension. The play spoofs specific films of the 1930's and 1940's, film genres, and screen stars representing our personified ideals of toughness or innocence. And the audience watches itself identifying with the black and white morality of the western, the jingoism of World War II, and the neurotic narcissism of the postwar period. More than a revue with some skits wearing thin by the second act, this satiric farce is impudently effective.

Literature and drama, respectively, fall under attack in *The Idiots Karamazov*, written with Albert Innaurato, and *The Vietnamization of New Jersey*. The first is an irreverent send-up of Dostoevsky's novel and western literature's great books; its action combines chaotic slapstick with a profusion of literary allusions comprehensible largely to the cognoscenti. Displaying sharper comedic ability, the second play is an absurdist parody of David Rabe's anti-Vietnam play *Sticks and Bones* and of American anti-war dramas thrusting collective guilt upon docile audiences. Comic recognition, however, rests too heavily on knowledge of Rabe's drama.

The theatre and drama as satirical subjects again surface in *The Actor's Nightmare*, a hilarious curtain-raiser in which a befuddled accountant clad as Hamlet, without benefit of lines or rehearsal, finds himself on stage in a phantasmagoric play whose actors veer from Coward's *Private Lives* and Beckett plays to *Hamlet* and Robert Bolt's *A Man for All Seasons*. Ultimately thrust into a scene from the last play, the baffled hero becomes Sir Thomas More facing a suddenly realistic execution, and despite his last minute, out-of-character recanting, is not seen on stage for the curtain call—an end resembling that of Tom Stoppard's Rosencrantz and Guildenstern.

Setting his sights on personal relationships and the deficiencies of psychiatrists, Durang in *Beyond Therapy* chronicles the tale of two Manhattan singles in their thirties, a bisexual male lawyer and a female journalist concerned about getting herself married, who meet through a personals ad. The curious couple are ineptly coached through a courtship of insults, rejections, and threats by their respective psychiatrists: the woman's shrink, a male chauvinist who seduces his female patients, and the man's, a daffy lady who constantly carries a Snoopy doll and confuses words. In a more optimistic ending than Durang normally gives, the couple jointly reject their therapists and consider having a continued relationship perhaps even leading to marriage. There is a dazzling display of funny lines and jokes on contemporary mores, gender identity, and psychiatry. Credibility is stretched with two such divergent lovers even considering a relationship, a problem not mitigated by the lack of a final resolution scene or a well-developed farcical plot to connect the many short two-character scenes. Yet these shortcomings have not prevented the play from becoming a favorite with community and regional theatres.

Dogmatic parochial education receives barbs in Durang's Obie-winning *Sister Mary Ignatius Explains It All for You*. The title character is a sin-smelling teaching nun who tyrannizes her students. During a lecture she is interrupted by the return of four former students who loathe her. The group ranges from a happy homosexual and unwed mother to a rape victim and a suicidal alcoholic; their recriminations rouse the nun to shoot them, and class servility is restored. The satire is sharp and wildly funny in this gem of black humor.

Absurdist portraits of the American family particularly abound in five Durang plays. *The Nature and Purpose of the Universe, Death Comes to Us All, Mary Agnes*, and *'dentity Crisis* are three short black comedies treating victimized females losing life, sanity, or identity at the hands of callous families and the traditional Catholic view of women. Although losing their bite in farcical chaos, the plays project subjects more maturely developed in two later works. The first is *Baby with the Bathwater*, a satirical farce on parenting in which two self-absorbed parents idiotically raise a male child (confusing his true gender for 15 years) who survives to young adulthood desperate to avoid his own upbringing's mistakes when becoming a father himself. The play's string of cartoon-like scenes progressively pall, despite the satirical feast they offer, and would profit from sharper variety and a greater buttressing of reality. More effective is the revised (1985) Obie-winning *The Marriage of Bette and Boo*, a trenchantly amusing dissection of the contemporary Catholic family. In 33 inventive scenes related by the family's only son and treated with farcical brilliance, a marriage moves through three decades of alcoholism, divorce, surrounding relatives representing failures of the married and single state, and a priest who dodges counsel-session questions by imitating frying bacon. At the center stand the dypsomaniac Boo and the dimwit Bette, who persists after a first surviving child producing stillborn babies against medical advice. Admitting an Autobiographical connection, the playwright gives us the outrageously satiric view of society that characterizes his best work.

Durang's work rises above collegiate-like preciosity to reveal a gifted satirist and farceur whose American absurdist view of the world is most delightfully successful when he furnishes a floor of reality under the dance of his characters. As a satirist writing for the stage, he is a member of an endangered species who deserves the theatre's nurturing if he is to continue to flourish. He is a needed talent in the American theatre.

—Christian H. Moe

DURRELL, Lawrence (George). British. Born in Julundur, India, 27 February 1912; brother of the zoologist and writer Gerald Durrell. Educated at the College of St. Joseph, Darjeeling, India; St. Edmund's School, Canterbury, Kent. Married 1) Nancy Myers in 1935 (divorced 1947); 2) Eve Cohen in 1947 (divorced); 3) Claude Durrell in 1961 (died 1967); 4) Ghislaine de Boysson in 1973 (divorced 1979); two daughters (one deceased). Has had many jobs, including jazz pianist (Blue Peter nightclub, London), automobile racer, and real estate agent; lived in Corfu, 1934–40; editor, with Henry Miller and Alfred Perlès, *The Booster* (later *Delta*), Paris, 1937–39; columnist, *Egyptian Gazette*, Cairo, 1941; editor, with Robin Fedden and Bernard Spencer, *Personal Landscape*, Cairo, 1942–45; special correspondent in Cyprus for the *Economist*, London, 1953–55; editor, *Cyprus Review*, Nicosia, 1954–55. Taught at the British Institute, Kalamata, Greece, 1940. Foreign Service press officer, British Information Office, Cairo, 1941–44; press attaché, British Information Office, Alexandria, 1944–45; director of Public Relations for the Dodecanese Islands, Greece, 1946–47; director, British Council Institute, Cordoba, Argentina, 1947–48; press attaché, British Legation, Belgrade, 1949–52; director of Public Relations for the British Government in Cyprus, 1954–56. Andrew Mellon Visiting Professor of Humanities, California Institute of Technology, Pasadena, 1974. Has lived in France since 1957. Recipient: Duff Cooper Memorial Prize, 1957; Foreign Book Prize (France), 1959; James Tait Black Memorial Prize, 1975; Cholmondeley award, for poetry, 1986. Fellow, Royal Society of Literature, 1954. Address: c/o Grindlay's Bank, 13 St. James's Square, London SW1Y 4LF, England.

PUBLICATIONS

Plays

Sappho: A Play in Verse (produced Hamburg, 1959; Edinburgh, 1961; Evanston, Illinois, 1964). London, Faber, 1950; New York, Dutton, 1958.
Acte (produced Hamburg, 1961). London, Faber, 1964; New York, Dutton, 1965.
An Irish Faustus: A Morality in Nine Scenes (produced Hamburg, 1963). London, Faber, 1963; New York, Dutton, 1964.
Judith (shortened version of screenplay), in *Woman's Own* (London), 26 February–2 April 1966.

Screenplays: *Cleopatra*, with others, 1963; *Judith*, with others, 1966.

Radio Script: *Greek Peasant Superstitions*, 1947.

Television Scripts: *The Lonely Roads*, with Diane Deriaz, 1970; *The Alexandrians*, 1970; *The Search for Ulysses* (Canada); *Spirit of Place: Lawrence Durrell's Greece*, 1976, and *Lawrence Durrell's Egypt*, 1978.

Recordings: *The Love Poems*, Spoken Arts; *Ulysses Come Back: Sketch for a Musical* (story, music, and lyrics by Durrell), Turret Records, 1970.

Novels

Pied Piper of Lovers. London, Cassell, 1935.
Panic Spring (as Charles Norden). London, Faber, and New York, Covici Friede, 1937.
The Black Book: An Agon. Paris, Obelisk Press, 1938; New York, Dutton, 1960; London, Faber 1973.
Cefalû. London, Editions Poetry London, 1947; as *The Dark Labyrinth*, London, Ace, 1958; New York, Dutton, 1962.
The Alexandria Quartet. London, Faber, and New York, Dutton, 1962.
 Justine. London, Faber, and New York, Dutton, 1957.
 Balthazar. London, Faber, and New York, Dutton, 1958.
 Mountolive. London, Faber, and New York, Dutton, 1958.
 Clea. London, Faber, and New York, Dutton, 1960.
White Eagles over Serbia. London, Faber, and New York, Criterion, 1957.
The Revolt of Aphrodite. London, Faber, 1974.
 Tunc. London, Faber, and New York, Dutton, 1968.
 Nunquam. London, Faber, and New York, Dutton, 1970.
The Avignon Quincunx:
 Monsieur; or, The Prince of Darkness. London, Faber, and New York, Viking Press, 1974.
 Livia; or, Buried Alive. London, Faber, 1978; New York, Viking Press, 1979.
 Constance; or, Solitary Practices. London, Faber, and New York, Viking Press, 1982.
 Sebastian; or, Ruling Passions. London, Faber, 1983; New York, Viking, 1984.
 Quinx; or, The Ripper's Tale. London, Faber, and New York, Viking, 1985.

Short Stories

Zero, and Asylum in the Snow. Privately printed, 1946; as *Two Excursions into Reality*, Berkeley, California, Circle, 1947.

Esprit de Corps: Sketches from Diplomatic Life. London, Faber, 1957; New York, Dutton, 1959.
Stiff Upper Lip: Life among the Diplomats. London, Faber, 1958; New York, Dutton, 1959.
Sauve Qui Peut. London, Faber, 1966; New York, Dutton, 1967.
The Best of Antrobus. London, Faber, 1974.
Antrobus Complete. London, Faber, 1985.

Verse

Quaint Fragment: Poems Written Between the Ages of Sixteen and Nineteen. London, Cecil Press, 1931.
Ten Poems. London, Caduceus Press, 1932.
Ballade of Slow Decay. Privately printed, 1932.
Bromo Bombastes: A Fragment from a Laconic Drama by Gaffer Peeslake. London, Caduceus Press, 1933.
Transition. London, Caduceus Press, 1934.
Mass for the Old Year. Privately printed, 1935.
Proems: An Anthology of Poems, with others, edited by Oswald Blakeston. London, Fortune Press, 1938.
A Private Country. London, Faber, 1943.
The Parthenon: For T.S. Eliot. Privately printed, 1945 (?).
Cities, Plains, and People. London, Faber, 1946.
On Seeming to Presume. London, Faber, 1948.
A Landmark Gone. Privately printed, 1949.
Deus Loci. Ischia, Italy, Di Maio Vito, 1950.
Private Drafts. Nicosia, Cyprus, Proodos Press, 1955.
The Tree of Idleness and Other Poems. London, Faber, 1955.
Selected Poems. London, Faber, and New York, Grove Press, 1956.
Collected Poems. London, Faber, 1960; revised edition, Faber, and New York, Dutton, 1968.
Penguin Modern Poets 1, with Elizabeth Jennings and R.S. Thomas. London, Penguin, 1962.
The Poetry of Lawrence Durrell. New York, Dutton, 1962.
Beccaffico/Le Becfigue (English, with French translation by F.-J. Temple). Montpellier, France, La Licorne, 1963.
A Persian Lady. Edinburgh, Tragara Press, 1963.
Selected Poems 1935–1963. London, Faber, 1964.
The Ikons and Other Poems. London, Faber, 1966; New York, Dutton, 1967.
Faustus: A Poem. Privately printed, 1970.
The Red Limbo Lingo: A Poetry Notebook. London, Faber, and New York, Dutton, 1971.
On the Suchness of the Old Boy. London, Turret, 1972.
Vega and Other Poems. London, Faber, and Woodstock, New York, Overlook Press, 1973.
Lifelines. Edinburgh, Tragara Press, 1974.
Selected Poems, edited by Alan Ross. London, Faber, 1977.
Collected Poems 1931–1974, edited by James A. Brigham. London, Faber, and New York, Viking Press, 1980.

Published Lyrics (music by T.W. Southam): *Walking in My Sleep* (as Larry Dell), Athens, Gaetanos, 1945; *Nemea,* London, Augener, 1950; *Lesbos,* London, Oxford University Press, 1967; *Nothing Is Lost, Sweet Self,* London, Turret, 1967.

Other

Prospero's Cell: A Guide to the Landscape and Manners of the Island of Corcyra. London, Faber, 1945; with *Reflections on a Marine Venus,* New York, Dutton, 1960.
Key to Modern Poetry. London, Peter Nevill, 1952; as *A Key to Modern British Poetry,* Norman, University of Oklahoma Press, 1952.
Reflections on a Marine Venus: A Companion to the Landscape of Rhodes. London, Faber, 1953; with *Prospero's Cell,* New York, Dutton, 1960.
Bitter Lemons (on Cyprus). London, Faber, 1957; New York, Dutton, 1958.
Art and Outrage: A Correspondence about Henry Miller Between Alfred Perlès and Lawrence Durrell, with an Intermission by Henry Miller. London, Putnam, 1959; New York, Dutton, 1961.
Groddeck (on Georg Walther Groddeck). Wiesbaden, Limes, 1961.
Briefwechsel über "Actis", with Gustaf Gründgens. Hamburg, Rowohlt, 1961.
Lawrence Durrell and Henry Miller: A Private Correspondence, edited by George Wickes. New York, Dutton, and London, Faber, 1963.
La Descente du Styx (English, with French translation by F.-J. Temple). Montpellier, France, La Murène, 1964; as *Down the Styx,* Santa Barbara, California, Capricorn Press, 1971.
Spirit of Place: Letters and Essays on Travel, edited by Alan G. Thomas. London, Faber, and New York, Dutton, 1969.
Le Grand Suppositoire (interview with Marc Alyn). Paris, Belfond, 1972; as *The Big Supposer,* London, Abelard Schuman, 1973; New York, Grove Press, 1975.
The Happy Rock (on Henry Miller). London, Village Press, 1973; Belfast, Maine, Bern Porter, 1982.
The Plant-Magic Man. Santa Barbara, California, Capra Press, 1973.
Blue Thirst. Santa Barbara, California, Capra Press, 1975.
Sicilian Carousel. London, Faber, and New York, Viking Press, 1977.
The Greek Islands. London, Faber, and New York, Viking Press, 1978.
A Smile in the Mind's Eye. London, Wildwood House, 1980; New York, Universe, 1982.
Literary Lifelines: The Richard Aldington-Lawrence Durrell Correspondence, edited by Harry T. Moore and Ian S. MacNiven. New York, Viking Press, and London, Faber, 1981.
The Durrell-Miller Letters 1935–1980 (correspondence with Henry Miller), edited by Ian S. MacNiven. New York, New Directions, 1987.

Editor, with Robin Fedden and Bernard Spencer, *Personal Landscape: An Anthology of Exile.* London, Editions Poetry London, 1945.
Editor, *A Henry Miller Reader.* New York, New Directions, 1959; as *The Best of Henry Miller,* London, Heinemann, 1960.
Editor, *New Poems 1963.* London, Hutchinson, 1963.
Editor, *Poems,* by Wordsworth. London, Penguin, 1972.

Translator, *Six Poems from the Greek of Sekilianos and Seferis.* Privately printed, 1946.
Translator, with Bernard Spencer and Nanos Valaoritis, *The King of Asine and Other Poems,* by George Seferis. London, Lehmann, 1948.
Translator, *The Curious History of Pope Joan,* by Emmanuel Royidis. London, Verschoyle, 1954; revised edition, as *Pope Joan: A Romantic Biography,* London, Deutsch, 1960; New York, Dutton, 1961.
Translator, with others, *Selected Poems,* by Alain Bosquet. Athens, Ohio University Press, 1973.
Translator, *Three Poems of Cavafy.* Edinburgh, Tragara Press, 1980.

*

Bibliography: *Lawrence Durrell: An Illustrated Checklist* by Alan G. Thomas and James A. Brigham, Carbondale, Southern Illinois University Press, 1983.

Manuscript Collections: University of California, Los Angeles; University of Illinois, Urbana.

Critical Studies: *The World of Lawrence Durrell* edited by Harry T. Moore, Carbondale, Southern Illinois University Press, 1962; *Lawrence Durrell* by John Unterecker, New York, Columbia University Press, 1964; *Lawrence Durrell* by John A. Weigel, New York, Twayne, 1965; *Lawrence Durrell: A Study* (includes bibliography by Alan G. Thomas), London, Faber, 1968, New York, Dutton, 1969, revised edition, Faber, 1973, and *Lawrence Durrell*, London, Longman, 1970, both by G.S. Fraser; *Alexandria Still: Forster, Durrell, and Cavafy* by Jane Lagoudis Pinchin, Princeton, New Jersey, Princeton University Press, 1977; *Deus Loci: Lawrence Durrell Newsletter* (Kelowna, British Columbia), since 1977; "Lawrence Durrell Issue" of *Labrys 5* (London), 1979; *Critical Essays on Lawrence Durrell* edited by Alan Warren Friedman, Boston, Hall, 1986.

*   *   *

Lawrence Durrell's plays explore the nature of love and the nature of reality and suggest that the two are interdependent. The protagonists of his poetic dramas love, suffer, and speculate on the meaning of an absurd universe. They learn that all passion is suspect, all happiness fleeting, and that a stoical acceptance of these truths may bring wisdom. Life cannot be understood but neither can it be evaded: Durrell's heroes are romantics, allowing themselves to feel acutely, in isolation.

All three plays centre on a search for absolute truth and suggest that it can be found only in the extremes of experience. Petronius Arbiter bleeds to death at the end of *Acte* and voices his contentment with suicide; it is for him the summation of philosophy. "Yes, it is possible to become an adept of reality." Similarly Faustus, returned from hell fire, describes its great attraction for him in the following terms:

For the first time I knew I was in reality.
Most of the time
We are not, d'you see; life is a conditional state
And reality prime.

Their attitudes suggest that an authentic statement about the human condition can be achieved but at a high cost, the total disintegration of accepted forms and beliefs. It is an idea which Durrell has expressed in his prose narratives, experimenting with style and structure in ways which reflect the bewildering contradictions of experience. His plays have a more formal framework, written in blank verse, based on classical myth and legend. They describe madness, vampirism, incest—morbid and fantastic subjects which are characteristic of his writing.

Sappho, Acte, Faustus: all are creatures of the ancient world, whose lives provide ample scope for the exuberance of Durrell's imagination. *Sappho* is a fine study of palace intrigue, an evocation of a past civilization and a credible portrait of a real woman. Sappho's origins are mysterious; we learn that she was orphaned in an earthquake, found by the philosopher Minos, and educated by him to become the unacknowledged ruler of Lesbos. She is loved by twin brothers, Phaon, who retreats from the world, and Pittakos, who seeks to conquer it as a soldier. Neither can satisfy Sappho, who described her nature, and that of all poets, as being beyond human love.

Born old, we turn away from men and women:
Hermaphrodites of conscience, copulating with ourselves.

Pittakos sends her a severed arm from battle, still bearing a golden bracelet; this is the only tribute that power can bring the artist. Phaon dives into the submerged city under the harbour of Lesbos and retrieves evidence which brings his mistress disaster; her parentage is discovered and it appears that she has married her own father, the punishment for which is exile. Pittakos, who becomes Tyrant, refuses to let Sappho's children accompany her from the island, and her son dies in his care. The action now resembles that of a Jacobean tragedy, dominated by the macabre and by the theme of revenge. Sappho brings about the death of both brothers but it is a bitter victory; she is elected Tyrant, thus losing her freedom as an artist but not the isolation of that role. She is reunited with her daughter and can only lament:

Everyone is afraid of me
All that I could not solicit of love
I gained at last in fear.

Durrell's *An Irish Faustus* is a reinterpretation of the Faust myth, unorthodox and in part comic, since this is Faust placed in County Galway. The traditional story is here reversed; Faustus sets the pace for the devil and goes to hell "dragging the cringing Mephisto with him." There is a plenty of gothic horror and melodrama but much of the dialogue is in a lighter vein as in the scenes with the pardoner, Martin, whose methods of selling relics differ little from the methods of the modern salesman:

While nothing I ever say is quite true
Nothing is quite false; I keep a sense of proportion
I am what you might call a perfectly balanced man.

Faustus has certainly lost his soul by the end of the play but this is not expressed in terms of brimstone or heaven relinquished: he has to abandon the language of scientific enquiry for that of the card sharper. Magic becomes another confidence trick.

Acte is the story of a tragic passion, a love affair between a Scythian princess and the Roman general Fabius who takes her as hostage to Nero's Rome. Acte has been blinded by the conquerors and raped by a leader of her own primitive people; she has pathos and beauty and, it is hinted, a dark knowledge which can grow only from such extreme suffering. She resembles Justine and Clea, two characters from Durrell's *Alexandria Quartet*: indeed the whole play echoes that work. Acte and her lover are caught up in a political intrigue over which they have no control, pawns in a game, prisoners in a city of corruption. At night, the princess meets "the arch-poet" Nero in the cellars of his palace, calms his fears, and feeds him soup. The Emperor listens to her, as he listens to Petronius Arbiter, but their influence cannot restrain the excesses of his madness. Acte is doomed and her epitaph spoken by Petronius as he himself faces death:

One could see that she would lose her life
In some thoughtless and tragic pageant. She belonged to art!

Durrell's plays, like those of other postwar dramatists writing in blank verse, are not aimed at the commercial theatre; his interest in the bizarre and the grandiose places him outside the main current of contemporary drama. However, his themes are in many ways those of his contemporaries, although their expression is not. Durrell's luxuriance is the reverse coin to Beckett's brevity; but both playwrights are concerned with metaphysics, both appear deeply pessimistic, both write at opposite poles of the same tradition, that of debased romanticism.

—Judy Cooke

DYER, Charles (Raymond). British. Born in Shrewsbury, Shropshire, 7 July 1928. Educated at the Highlands Boys' School, Ilford, Essex; Queen Elizabeth's School, Barnet, Hertfordshire. Served in the Royal Air Force, 1944–47: Flying Officer. Married Fiona Thomson in 1959; three sons. Actor and director; Chairman and artistic director, Stage Seventy Productions Ltd. Address: Old Wob, Gerrards Cross, Buckinghamshire, England.

PUBLICATIONS

Plays

Clubs Are Sometimes Trumps (as C. Raymond Dyer) (produced Wednesbury, Staffordshire, 1948).
Who on Earth! (as C. Raymond Dyer) (produced London, 1951).
Turtle in the Soup (as C. Raymond Dyer) (produced London, 1953).
The Jovial Parasite (as C. Raymond Dyer) (produced London, 1954).
Single Ticket Mars (as C. Raymond Dyer) (produced Bromley, Kent, 1955).
Time, Murderer, Please (as C. Raymond Dyer) (produced Portsmouth, Hampshire, and London, 1956). London, English Theatre Guild, 1962.
Wanted—One Body! (as C. Raymond Dyer) (produced on tour, 1956). London, English Theatre Guild, 1961.
Poison in Jest (as C. Raymond Dyer) (produced Oxford, 1957).
Prelude to Fury (as C. Raymond Dyer) (produced London, 1959).
Red Cabbage and Kings (as R. Kraselchik) (produced Southsea, Hampshire, 1960).
Rattle of a Simple Man (produced London, 1962; New York, 1963). London and New York, French, 1963.
Gorillas Drink Milk, adaptation of a play by John Murphy (produced Coventry, 1964).
Staircase (produced London, 1966; New York, 1968). London, Penguin, 1966; New York, French, 1967.
Mother Adam (produced York, 1971; also director: produced London, 1971). London, Davis Poynter, 1972.
A Hot Godly Wind (produced Manchester, 1975). Published in *Second Playbill 3*, edited by Alan Durband, London, Hutchinson, 1973.
Futility Rites (produced in Germany, 1980).
Lovers Dancing (produced London, 1983). Oxford, Amber Lane Press, and New York, French 1984.

Screenplays: *Rattle of a Simple Man*, 1964; *Staircase*, 1969; *Brother Sun and Sister Moon*, 1970.

Novels

Rattle of a Simple Man. London, Elek, 1964.
Charlie Always Told Harry Almost Everything. London, W.H. Allen, 1969; as *Staircase; or, Charlie Always Told Harry Almost Everything*, New York, Doubleday, 1969.

*

Manuscript Collection: Manchester Central Library.

Critical Studies: in *Sunday Times* (London), 14 April 1966, 5 December 1971, and 29 April 1973; *Drama* (London), Winter 1967; *L'Avant Scène* (Paris), 15 January 1968; *New Yorker*, 20 January 1968; *Sipario* (Rome), August 1969; *Irish Tatler* (Dublin), December 1969.

Theatrical Activities:
Director: **Plays**—in London, Amsterdam, Rotterdam, Paris, Berlin; recently, *Mother Adam*, London, 1972, Stratford-on-Avon and London, 1973, Paris, 1981 and 1986.
Actor: **Plays**—roles in 250 plays; debut as Lord Harpenden in *While the Sun Shines* by Terence Rattigan, Crewe, Cheshire, 1947; Duke in *Worm's Eye View* by R.F. Delderfield, London and tour, 1948–50; Digger in *The Hasty Heart* by John Patrick, toured 1950; Wilkie in *No Trees in the Street* by Ted Willis, toured, 1951; Turtle in *Turtle in the Soup*, London, 1953; Launcelot Gobbo in *The Merchant of Venice*, London, 1954; Freddie Windle in *The Jovial Parasite*, London, 1954; Maitre d'Hotel in *Room for Two* by Gilbert Wakefield, London, 1955; Keith Draycott in *Pitfall* by Falkland L. Cary, London, 1955; Dr. John Graham in *Suspended Sentence* by Sutherland Scott, London, 1955; Horace Grimshaw in *The Imperfect Gentleman* by Harry Jackson, London, 1956; Wishee Washee in *Aladdin*, London, 1956; Syd Fish in *Painted Sparrow* by Guy Paxton and E.V. Hoile, Cork, Ireland, 1956; Flash Harry in *Dry Rot* by John Chapman, London and tour, 1958; Shylock in *The Merchant of Venice*, Bromley, Kent, 1959; Viktor in *Red Cabbage and Kings*, Southsea, Hampshire, and tour, 1960; Percy in *Rattle of a Simple Man*, London, 1963; Mickleby in *Wanted—One Body!*, Guildford, Surrey, 1966. **Films**—include *Cuptie Honeymoon*, 1947; *Naval Patrol*, 1959; *The Loneliness of the Long Distance Runner*, 1962; *Rattle of a Simple Man*, 1964; *The Knack*, 1965; *How I Won the War*, 1967. **Television**—*Hugh and I* series, 1964; Charlie in *Staircase*, 1986.

Charles Dyer comments:

Outside bedtime, no one truly exists until he is reflected through the mind of another. We exist only as we think of us. We are not real except in our own tiny minds according to our own insignificant measurement of thought.

Animals adapt to their inadequacies without shame or discernible consciousness. Eventually, they wither to nothing, wagging their minds behind them, and die unsurprised—like frogs. Man is different, and is measured according to breadth of chest, amount of hair, inside leg, bosom and backside. He is insulted by death. He cares. And he cares more about what is seen than is hidden; yet unseen differences have greatest emotional effect.

Such as loneliness.

And I write about loneliness.

Obviously, Man is progressing towards a life, a world of Mind. Soon. Soon, in terms of creation. But with physicalities dismissed, the mind is lonelier than ever. Mind was God's accident. An unfortunate bonus. We should be more content as sparrows, spring-fluttering by the clock; a sudden day, tail-up;

then the cock-bird, and satisfaction matter-of-factually; a search for straw; eggs and tomorrow automatic as the swelling of string in water. It happens for sparrows, that is all! Anything deeper is Mind. And Mind is an excess over needs. Therefore Mind is loneliness.

Rattle of a Simple Man and *Staircase* and *Mother Adam* form a trilogy of loneliness, three plays enacted on Sundays. Bells are so damned lonely. Duologues, they are, because two seems the most sincere symbolic number, especially as man plus woman may be considered physically One. My plays have no plots, as such. Action cannot heal loneliness: it is cured only by *sharing* an action, and is emphasised by reduction of plot. And reduction of stage setting—which should, I feel, be expendable once the play is written. I detail a setting for the preparation of each duologue, that its dialogue may relate to a particular room; then, as a casting reflects its mould, the setting becomes irrevocably welded into and between the lines. The potency of these duologues is greater in drapes.

They reprimand me, occasionally, for handicapping my characters either physically or mentally: Cyrenne the prostitute and Percy, male virgin, in *Rattle of a Simple Man*; schizophrenic Adam and arthritical Mammles in *Mother Adam*; homosexual Charlie and nakedly-bald Harry in *Staircase*. And as the Trilogy grew, I locked them into barber shops and attics, depriving them even of a telephone to outside realities. This was a private challenge; yet what interest in an even face? what fault in a crooked smile? I love the courage of my imperfect characters, I despair with them—so small in a world of mindless faces, and faceless minds driving science to God's borders. In *Staircase*, man plus man situation, Charlie and Harry are lost without one another. But Charlie is too proud to admit such a fatal interdependence. He patronises Harry, taunts him, and drops "exciting" names which are anagrams of his own; he refuses to reflect anything of Harry; thus, Harry becomes an anagram, too; and even me, as their author. Charlie, Harry and me, become one; because there is no reality until we are reflected through someone else's eyes.

My characters have hope with their imperfections. They are dismayed by today's fading simplicity; today's lack of humility—no one ever wrong, always an excuse; kissing footballers without respect for the losers; and people who, from the safety of secret conscience, dismiss others as "them."

Man's disease is loneliness; God's is progress.

* * *

The opening performance of Charles Dyer's *Rattle of a Simple Man* was given at the Garrick Theatre on 19 September 1962. I had heard that it consisted of a dialogue between a mug and a tart, and, knowing nothing of Dyer's delicacy and integrity, assumed it would be full of equivocal situations. Before the end of the first act I realized I was in the presence of a new and valid talent, possessed to an astonishing degree of the capacity to find pearls among swine. In drunken football fans, in middle-aged, failing homosexual hairdressers, and the half-paralysed relics of tambourine-banging religiosity, Dyer finds not the débris of humanity, but unforgettable gleams of tenderness and self-sacrifice:

Cyrenne —Been on holiday?
Percy —I went to Morecambe. There were lots of married couples at the digs.
They took a fancy to me. I was always making them laugh. It was marvellous. I think I'll go somewhere else next year, though.

Dyer shows his skill in changing, by the simplest words, the whole mood of a scene. Once can tell the very moment the light went out for Percy.

For many years Dyer travelled the country as an actor in provincial productions of London successes; and in Percy's unhappy seaside memories there may well be recollections of drab theatrical lodgings. The two homosexual barbers in *Staircase* are exceptionally bitter on this subject:

Charlie —Even me honeymoon was a—a—a holocaust: one night of passion and food-poisoning for thirteen. Maggots in the haddock, she claimed.
(Harry giggles)
Oh, I was laughing, dear. Yes. What! Lovely—your blushing bride all shivering and turgid in the promenade shelter; hurricanes whipping the shingle. Couldn't even paddle for a plague of jelly-fish.

Dyer considers and reconsiders every aspect of his work, and does not let it go until he has got out of it everything that it contains. Unlike most other eminent contemporary dramatists he is ready, even delighted, to discuss his work, its meaning, and its origin. It is clear that what he puts into his plays is but a small part of his knowledge of the people he writes about. He has written two novels, which have had considerable success, and both are treatments of themes dealt with in his plays, *Rattle of a Simple Man* and *Staircase*. Most people suppose that the novels are rewritings of the plays, but this is not true. The novels are the original work, and the plays follow after.

Thus, though *Rattle of a Simple Man* has an effect similar to that of the *nouveau roman* in that it leaves the audience with a question unanswered, Dyer is really at the opposite pole from writers like Alain Robbe-Grillet and Marguerite Duras. They leave questions open because their philosophy tells them that human knowledge is limited, whereas Dyer ends with an uncertainty only because the wealth of information with which he could resolve it would blur the clear outline of what he wishes to say.

Long before the end of *Rattle* we understand and love Cyrenne and Percy. They are characters, bruised, resilient, and in their ridiculous way curiously dignified, who make for righteousness, because they manifest sympathy and consideration for others. They are in fact people of honour.

That they are so is the basis of Dyer's outlook on the drama. He writes his plays, which are spare and austere in form, according to a classic formula of abiding power. The question with Dyer is not what his characters appear to be, but what they will do in the circumstances in which he places them. It is in my opinion a mistake to consider *Staircase* as primarily a study of homosexuality. Essentially it is a study of how under great stress a man's character may crumble, and then rebound to a level it never attained before.

Dyer is in fact the complement to Anouilh, whom in many ways he rivals in theatrical expertise. Whereas with bitter distress Anouilh discovers the sordidness of purity, Dyer—in this resembling Maupassant—comes upon purity in sordidness. Against dispiriting odds, people are capable of behaving unexpectedly well. This is one reason why Dyer's work is so much more exhilarating than that of even his most distinguished contemporaries. He is a dramatist who indulges neither in self-pity nor in recrimination.

In *Staircase*, presented by the Royal Shakespeare Company 1966–67, Dyer did a very curious thing. He gave his own name to the character played by Paul Scofield. This was the introduction of his theory that everybody is alone. He carries his theme into *Mother Adam*, but in *Staircase* all characters, on and off-stage, are woven into patterns of the name Charles Dyer. It is a dramatic device to pinpoint the lack of substance in a man-man relationship where Charlie could not exist without Harry, nor Harry without Charlie. All is loneliness. And each without the other, says Dyer, would be like "a golfer holing-in-one by himself. Nobody to believe him. Nobody to prove his moment ever truly existed." Dyer is at his best when dealing with commonplace aspects of life, and discerning in them the emotional depths of their apparent shallowness. There is something both ludicrous and touching in the way Harry broods over the distresses he suffered as a scout master. Patrick Magee brought real humanity to his task of making tea for Scofield's Dyer, prissy, pampered, pomaded, a ruined god, awaiting a summons for indecent behaviour. To his lurking terror, Mr. Scofield gave a fine touch of injured vanity.

The actor who plays this splendid part—one of the best in modern drama—can be riveting, revolting, and masterly all at the same time: in his sudden bursts of panic, in his vain boastings of a largely imaginary past as a pantomime dame, in his irritability, and in his readiness, in his own terror, to wound his pitiably vulnerable companion.

Mother Adam is Dyer's most ambitious play. Adam's paralysed mother is a tyrant of extreme power, and she brings it to bear on her son, who longs—he thinks—to escape and marry. Despite its consciousness that, in one of Dyer's shining phrases, "There aren't so many silk-loined years," the play is as full of laughter as it is of heartbreak. Its dialogue is rich in curious eloquence and stirring images.

Fine as these things are, it is not in them that Dyer's mastery is to be found, but in his capacity to hold in his mind two conflicting rights, and to see, with a true compassion, that their confrontation cannot be resolved. It is because of this capacity that he has written in *Mother Adam* one of the few tragedies of our time. Adam cannot be free unless his mother is deserted; his mother cannot be cared for unless her son's life is ruined. It is this situation that Charles Dyer observes with a dancing eye and a riven heart.

I say, with the same absolute confidence with which I wrote of Pinter's *The Birthday Party* in 1958, that in the history of the contemporary theatre *Mother Adam* will rank as a masterpiece.

Dyer had previously written two fine and successful plays: *Rattle of a Simple Man* and *Staircase*. *Mother Adam* is better than either. It is more disturbing; it has deeper resonances; it is more beautifully written, with an imagination at once exotic and desperately familiar; it has a profounder pity, and a more exquisite falling close.

Loneliness haunts Dyer's imagination. Is there any solution to this terrible problem? Dyer says there is. Loneliness is the product of selfishness, and where no selfishness is, there is no loneliness. The condition of unselfishness is not easy to attain. It is within reach only of the saints. But sanctity is not an unattainable goal. We should all aim for it.

In *Mother Adam* Dyer seeks the continuing theme of Oneness. Man and mother, almost to the edges of Oedipus. The moment when Adam falls to his knees at the bedside, hugging his mother, dragging her crippled knuckles to his face, begging "Hung me! hug me! I dream of love. I need love," should represent the climax, not only of *Mother Adam*, but of the whole Loneliness Trilogy.

In two of his plays Dyer deals with subjects which, when the plays were first produced, were considered daring. The Lord Chamberlain made 26 cuts in *Staircase*, including the scene in which Harry explains his hatred of the physical side of life. The *Report on Censorship 1967* mentioned *Staircase* throughout 25 of its two hundred pages. Dyer likes to feel he is ahead of trends, but not excessively so: "In terms of eternity, the interval between Adam and Eve's nakedness and the Moment when God cast them forth in animal skins is but a finger click. The serious, most important period is what happens *after* they put on clothes."

We clothe our inadequacies. This is what Dyer's plays are all about.

—Harold Hobson

EASMON, R(aymond) Sarif. Sierra Leonean. Received M.B. and B.S. degrees. Practising doctor. Address: 31 Bathurst Street, Freetown, Sierra Leone.

PUBLICATIONS

Plays

Dear Parent and Ogre (produced Ibadan, Nigeria, 1961). London and New York, Oxford University Press, 1964.

The New Patriots. London, Longman, 1966.

Novel

The Burnt-Out Marriage. London, Nelson, and New York, Humanities Press, 1967.

Short Stories

The Feud and Other Stories. London, Longman, 1981.

* * *

With his unfailing sense of the comic potential in any situation, it seems likely that R. Sarif Easmon is, as Bernth Lindfors puts it, "the first African offspring of Oscar Wilde and Noël Coward." His witty, urbane plays deal with the romance of politics and the politics of romance—two areas dear to the heart of an African audience—and they move with the grace of a dancer from one finely choreographed scene to the next.

There has been some criticism of the language used by Easmon's "upper class" characters, a pure Oxford English of the type which has proven so satisfying to a generation of word-conscious and Western-educated Africans. Yet when one sees one of Easmon's plays in production there is no doubt that the language is perfectly suited to both the personalities and the social positions of the characters. After all, not all Africans speak continually in proverbs. Moreover, when Easmon introduces characters from different social backgrounds he fits their speech to their class. One need only compare the words of Dauda Touray, the "parent and ogre" of Easmon's first play—"Our gratitude shall transcend champagne, Saidu!"—with those of the hired ruffian Charles Randall—"Lord 'ave mercy—Oh! For de name way me daddy and mammy gave me!"—to see the difference.

There is nothing stock about the characters in Easmon's delightful comedies. The two roguish politicians of his second play, *The New Patriots*, who are struggling for the hand of the same woman are as alive as Dauda Touray, the main character of *Dear Parent and Ogre*, yet they are not in any way a copy of the earlier character. Easmon's figures have unorthodox turns to their nature. Sekou, the young hero of *Dear Parent and Ogre*, is a son of a Yalie, a class given over to singing (quite literally) the praises of the noble Touray family, yet he has found success in Europe as a recording star and has returned, replete with impeccable French and Rolls-Royce, to claim the hand of Dauda's daughter.

Because they deal with the themes of a new Africa, an Africa where the two suitors can be a descendant from former slaves on the one hand and from a lowly class of minstrels on the other, an Africa where champagne, moonlight, Joloff rice, and hired thugs can be blended into a scene of high comedy, Easmon's plays have attracted large audiences whenever they have been performed in West Africa. Because Easmon manages, while developing these themes, to present us with vital human characters and situations which have larger universal implications, it seems safe to say that his appeal need not be limited to African audiences.

—Joseph Bruchac

EBEJER, Francis. Maltese. Born in Dingli, 28 August 1925. Educated at Lyceum Grammar School, Valletta, 1934–39; University of Malta, Msida, 1942–43; St. Mary's College, Twickenham, Middlesex, 1948–50. Served as an English-Italian interpreter with the British 8th Army, Tripolitania, 1943–44. Married Jane Cauchi Gera in 1947; two sons (one deceased) and one daughter. Teacher, 1944–48, and school principal, 1950–77; Malta Education Department. Since 1976 Guest Lecturer, University of Malta. Recipient: Malta Amateur Film Circle award, for acting, 1959; International PEN (English Centre) fellowship, 1961; Fulbright travel grant (USA), 1961; Cheyney award, for producing, 1964; Dublin Television Festival award, for documentary, 1969; Malta Literary Award, 1971, 1976, 1983, 1985; Phoenicia Trophy (Malta), 1982; Medal of Honor (Avignon), 1986. Agent: Eulama, via Torino 135, 1–00184 Rome, Italy; or, Peter Miller Agency, 1021 Avenue of the Americas, New York, New York 10018, U.S.A. Address: 3 Nivea Court, Swieqi Valley, St. Andrews, Malta.

PUBLICATIONS

Plays

Is-Sejha ta' Sarid (Sarid's Summons) (broadcast 1950; produced Valletta 1966). Included in *Id-Drammi 1*, 1965.

Cpar fix-Xemx (Fog in the Sun) (broadcast 1950). Published in *Lehen il-Malti* (Msida), April–December 1952.

Bwani (broadcast 1951; revised version produced Valletta, 1974). Included in *Id-Drammi 1*, 1965.

Iz-Zjara (The Visit) (broadcast 1952). Included in *Id-Drammi 1*, 1965.

Ix-Xorti ta' Mamzell (Mamzell's Luck) (broadcast 1953; produced Floriana, 1982). Included in *Id-Drammi 1*, 1965.

Sefora (broadcast 1954; produced Valletta, 1984). Included in *Id-Drammi 6*, 1984.

Loghba (The Game) (broadcast 1954). Included in *Id-Drammi 6*, 1984.

Rewwixta tas-Swaba' (Revolt of the Fingers) (broadcast 1955). Included in *Id-Drammi 6*, 1984.

Vaganzi tas-Sajf (produced Valletta, 1962). Included in *Id-Drammi 2*, 1970; translated by Ebejer as *Summer Holidays*, in *Collected English Plays 3*, 1980.

Boulevard (produced Valletta, 1964). Included in *Id-Drammi 2*, 1970; translated by Ebejer as *Boulevard*, in *Collected English Plays 2*, 1980.

Id-Drammi ta Francis Ebejer (The Plays of Francis Ebejer):
1. *Iz-Zjara, Is-Sejha ta' Sarid, Bwani, Ix-Xorti ta' Mamzell.* Privately printed, 1965.
2. *Menz, Boulevard, Vaganzi tas-Sajf.* Privately printed, 1970.
3. *Il-Hadd Fuq Il-Bejt, L-Imnarja Zmien il-Qtil, L-Imwarrbin.* Valletta, KKM, 1973.
4. *Hitan.* Valletta, KKM, 1974.
5. *Meta Morna tal-Mellieha, Vum-Barala-Zungarè, Karnival.* Valletta, KKM, 1977.
6. *Sefora, Filfla Minn Wara Hajt* (Filfla from Behind a Wall), *Morru Sejhu lill-Werrieta, Rewwixta tas-Swaba', Loghba, X'Ma Kixifx il-Hajt.* Valletta, Mid-Med, 1984.
7. *Il-Gahan ta' Bingemma, Il-Mutur, It-Telefonata, L-Ghajta, F'Hagar Qim, In-Nasba.* Valletta, Ministry of Education, 1985.

Menz (produced Valletta, 1967). Included in *Id-Drammi 2*, 1970; translated by Ebejer as *Menz*, in *Collected English Plays 2*, 1980.

The Cliffhangers (produced Valletta, 1968). Included in *Collected English Plays 3*, 1980; translated by the author into Maltese as *L-Imwarrbin* (produced Valletta, 1974), in *Id-Drammi 3*, 1973.

Hefen Plus Zero (broadcast 1970; produced Coventry, 1981). Included in *Collected English Plays 3*, 1980.

Hitan (Walls) (televised 1970; produced Valletta, 1983). Included in *Id-Drammi 4*, 1974.

Il-Hadd Fuq Il-Bejt (Sunday on the Roof) (produced Valletta, 1971). Included in *Id-Drammi 3*, 1973.

L-Imnarja Zmien il-Qtil (Imnarja Is a Time for Killing) (produced Valletta, 1973). Included in *Id-Drammi 3*, 1973.

Vum-Barala-Zungarè (produced Valletta, 1973). Included in *Id-Drammi 5*, 1977.

X'Ma Kixifx il-Hajt (What the Wall Didn't Reveal) (televised 1973). Included in *Id-Drammi 6*, 1984.

Bloody in Bolivia (produced Floriana, 1975). Included in *Collected English Plays 1*, 1980.

Meta Morna tal-Mellieha (When We Went to Mellieha) (produced Valletta, 1976). Included in *Id-Drammi 5*, 1977.

Karnival (Carnival) (produced Valletta, 1977). Included in *Id-Drammi 5*, 1977.

Id-Dar tas-Soru (The Nun's House) (televised 1977–78). Valletta, KKM, 1977.

Golden Tut (produced Valletta, 1979; London, 1981). Included in *Collected English Plays 2*, 1980.

Morru Sejhu lill-Werrieta (Go and Call the Inheritors) (televised 1979). Included in *Id-Drammi 6*, 1984.

Collected English Plays:
1. *Mark of the Zebra, Cleopatra Slept (Badly) Here, Bloody in Bolivia.* Valletta, Aquilina, 1980.
2. *Boulevard, Golden Tut, Hour of the Sun, Menz.* Valletta, Aquilina, 1980.
3. *Saluting Battery, The Cliffhangers, Hefen Plus Zero, Summer Holidays.* Valletta, Aquilina, 1980.

Il-Gahan ta' Bingemma (The Jester of Bingemma) (produced Valletta, 1985). Included in *Id-Drammi 7*, 1985.
Il-Mutur (The Motorbike) (produced Hal Far, 1985). Included in *Id-Drammi 7*, 1985.
It-Telefonata (The Telephone Call) (produced Hal Far, 1985). Included in *Id-Drammi 7*, 1985.
L-Ghajta (The Shout) (produced Hal Far, 1985). Included in *Id-Drammi 7*, 1985.
F'Hagar Qim (At Hagar Qim) (produced Hal Far, 1985). Included in *Id-Drammi 7*, 1985.
In-Nasba (The Trap) (produced Valletta, 1985). Included in *Id-Drammi 7*, 1985.

Radio Plays: *Is-Sejha ta' Sarid*, 1950; *Cpar fix-Xemx*, 1950; *Bwani*, 1951; *Il-Karba ta' l-Art* (The Cry of the Earth), 1951; *L-Ghassiesa ta' l-Alpi* (The Guardian of the Alps), 1951; *Iz-Zjara*, 1952; *Tieqa Bla Qamar* (Window Without Moon), 1952; *Ix-Xorti ta' Mamzell*, 1953; *Majjistral* (Mistral), 1953; *Sefora*, 1954; *Loghba*, 1954; *Dawra-Durella* (Ring-a-Ring-a-Rosy), 1954; *Rewwixta tas-Swaba'*, 1955; *Hemm Barra* (Out There), 1955; *Il-Bidu Jintemm* (End of the Beginning), 1955; *'Il Hinn mill-Biza'* (Beyond Fear), 1956; *Izfen, Ors, Izfen* (Dance, Bear, Dance), 1956; *Elsie*, 1956; *It-Triq ghal Tyburn* (The Road to Tyburn), 1957; *L-Imjassra ta' Fotheringay* (The Prisoner of Fotheringay), 1957; *Mixtieq il-Kenn* (Shelter Wanted), 1957; *Hefen Plus Zero*, 1970 (Italy).

Television Plays: *Hitan*, 1970; *X'Ma Kixifx il-Hajt*, 1973; *Persuna Qieghda Tigi Investigata Dwar . . .* (A Person Is Being Interrogated Regarding . . .), 1974; *Id-Dar tas-Soru* series, 1977–78; *Morru Sejhu lill-Werrieta*, 1979.

Novels

A Wreath for the Innocents. London, MacGibbon and Kee, 1958; as *A Wreath of Maltese Innocents*, Malta, Bugelli, 1981.
Evil of the King Cockroach. London, MacGibbon and Kee, 1960; as *Wild Spell of Summer*, Malta, Union Press, 1968.
In the Eye of the Sun. London, Macdonald, 1969.
Come Again in Spring. Malta, Union Press, 1973; New York, Vantage Press, 1979.
Requiem for a Malta Fascist. Valletta, Aquilina, 1980.
Leap of Malta Dolphins. New York, Vantage Press, 1982.
Il-Harsa ta' Ruzann (Ruzann's Glance). Valletta, KKM, 1985.

Other

Translator, *The Lamplighter*, by Anton Buttigieg. Portree, Isle of Skye, Aquila, 1977.

*

Bibliography: in *Id-Drammi 7*, 1985.

Manuscript Collections: National Library of Malta, Valletta; University of Malta Library, Msida.

Critical Studies: article by Hella Jean Bartolo, in *Canadian Theatre Review* (Downsview, Ontario), Summer 1975; "The Bicultural Situation in Malta" by Ebejer, in *Individual and Community in Commonwealth Literature* edited by Daniel Massa, Msida, University of Malta, 1979; article by Arthur Pollard, in *ACLALS Bulletin 2* (St. Lucia, Queensland), January 1979; "The Malta Theatre Connection" by Adrian Rendle, in *Contemporary Review* (London), 1980.

Theatrical Activities:
Director: **Plays**—most of his own plays; *Marching Song* by John Whiting, 1963, *The Boy Friend* by Sandy Wilson, 1965, and *The Rope Dancers* by Morton Wishengrad, 1975, all Valletta.

Francis Ebejer comments:

While I have written all my novels, except one, in English, the majority of my plays are in my native language, Maltese. Most of my plays deal with universal themes and universal humankind; in the others, universal themes are applied to a specific society, the Mediterranean-Maltese, within a cosmopolitan context. In other words, I have tried to explain life on an island steeped in antiquity yet a member of the modern world, and eying the future through the geopolitical, military, industrial, and cross-cultural concerns in the central Mediterranean.

A recurrent theme is the function and influence of the past upon the present of, as the case may be, the private individual or the colonized country striving for and trying to understand independence; in either case, the interaction of past and present might provide glimpses of alternative futures.

If it may appear that I have treated certain themes from a philosophical and/or sociological angle, all that is secondary to the attention I try to give to actual lives lived by three-dimensional people with their psychological, moral, and ethical strengths and weaknesses, integralities and contradictions.

For instance, if a character is isolated in certain psychological and moral patterns of alienation, the exercise takes on the workings of analogy, or allegory, in so far as the character comes to represent the self-flawed image of a country—in our case, Malta itself, which became a sovereign state only recently after a long history of colonization, beginning with the Phoenicians and ending with the British.

In those plays that most specifically deal with Mediterranean-Maltese society I have on several occasions gone in search of a sense of identity and continuity right to the bed-rock of Mediterranean cultures, to "the sacred groves of the goat-god and the mother-goddess"—an ethos which is still a palpable omnipresence in Catholic Malta: one wonders, in fact, whether this is as paradoxical as it may seem, since religions and pagan cults in the Mediterranean have always interlocked.

In my English plays, on the other hand, such Mediterranean aspects are touched upon only here and there, or for the most part intermittently felt, leaving me freer to explore and concentrate more upon actual relationships among disparate people caught in (semi-)existentialist conditions of life.

Thus: guilt and expiation in both the pagan sense and the Christian (*The Cliffhangers*); the various levels of freedom, starting from the snug serflike desire for non-freedom—let others do the caring!—and working upwards to freedom in responsibility (*Bloody in Bolivia*); individual and societal consciences in a conformist society (*Menz*); impotence in the face of oppression (*Saluting Battery*); the way humans at large seem destined, because of some inherent blind perversity, to miss one chance after another of a reasonably lasting fulfilment (*Boulevard*); loneliness caused by self-delusion (*Golden Tut*); the individual of vision, however weak to start with, in an entropic society (*Hefen Plus Zero*); completely ignoring, or missing, the truth about oneself to one's own and others' detriment (*Summer Holidays*); genuine and fake identities, with particular reference to those induced by the theatre itself (*Cleopatra Slept (Badly) Here*); role-reversal under the influence of strange new places and diverted desires (*Hour of the Sun*); the black-white tension in an artist trying to make some sense of his own contradictions while not really wishing them resolved: he discerns in such an eventual symbiosis, or synthesis, a threat to his art, to his essential self (*Mark of the Zebra*).

* * *

Francis Ebejer began as a Maltese language dramatist, later writing novels and plays in English, and has continued to create in both languages. Four of his eleven *Collected English Plays* are translated from Maltese. His plays fluctuate, often during scenes within a single work, between naturalism, expressionism, symbolism, and the absurd. The four modes correspond to the various kinds of significance in the plays: the deterministic, the psychological, the social-political, and the philosophical. His early radio plays in Maltese are represented by *Hefen Plus Zero* with its science-fiction futuristic setting and philosophical themes. Moving to the theatre with *Summer Holidays*, he already had assembled many of the ingredients of his later drama, including settings so indistinct as to universalize the events while being applicable to Malta. Probably influenced by Strindberg's later plays, the dominant naturalism unexpectedly changes into expressionism and symbolism. The characters, as in *The Cliffhangers* and *Hour of the Sun* live in an apparent paradise, but bring their own hell with them. Obsessed with their past, guilt, private relations, and delusions of free choice, they are blind to the external dangers which will destroy them, the enemy soldiers literally at the door. Throughout the plays ideas of freedom are tested. While society threatens personal liberty, such freedom is often an illusion, mere adolescent rebellion, unaware of the limitations imposed by reality; isolation and role playing must be overcome through social commitment, especially to the freedom of others.

Mark of the Zebra concerns a writer whose work is unsuccessful because of an inability to reconcile sexual desires with ideals of purity; such confusion leaves him unable to write convincingly of human passions. The symbolist-absurd *Boulevard*, regarded as the start of modern Maltese theatre, reveals people continually repeating the same patterns in their life. The lack of contact between the characters reflected in incongruous, stylized dialogue, and their failure to take advantage of second chances, result in a pessimistic vision of humankind, condemned eternally to the same cycles of experience.

Set in unspecified or unlikely locations, using highly repetitive dialogue filled with such abstract moral and psychological terms as "fear" and "conscience," the plays are populated by stereotypes and caricatures who at first have no more depth than the cardboard figures used in *Menz* to suggest crowds and the "people." Such plays begin as witty exercises in the manipulation of role and power relationships, but they suddenly deepen into powerful revelations of the way emotions developed in childhood continue to influence behaviour. Comic farce erupts into a psychodrama of frantic searches for mothers, violent rebellions against fathers, murderous hatreds and stunning collapses of will. There are also Sartre-influenced existentialist implications as the surreal goonery uncovers relationships between the personal and the socio-political. *Menz* combines the comic theatre of the absurd with symbolism to show why the desire for freedom is betrayed as much by the emotional damage of the past as by social and political pressures to conform. The seemingly totally alienated Menz, symbol of freedom, is easily overcome by Ludilla B., the Governor, seductress and Mediterranean matriarch who, wearing a female lion tamer's outfit of silver tights and high black, green-sequined boots, entices him into betraying his sympathizers and letting her take care of all his decisions. As Menz's individuality leaves him he rapidly becomes senile; he says, "I'm indeed in my mother's house." The only freedom left for him is death.

In *Bloody in Bolivia* three Englishmen and an Englishwoman, absurdly attempting to sell insurance in Bolivia during a civil war, try to remain neutral, but cannot help becoming involved. While the government treats the four as possible spies, two of them are held hostage by the guerrillas, the leader of whom is the rebellious son of the dictator. Although the son's rebellion is motivated by personal obsessions, Captain Berger, who secretly works against the government for communal liberty, is a hero, as is the guerrilla leader's sister, who lives fully by risking her life for her brother. In these political plays where characters appear two-dimensional and behaviour rapidly changes, symbols give the events significance. Berger collects butterflies (symbols of beautiful freedom), while in *Saluting Battery* the ancient cannon, which the old man takes care of and which is fired as part of the rebellion, signifies sexual impotence as well as an attempted last stand for freedom. The symbolism structures what might otherwise seem mere absurdity and translates apparently arbitrary, inconsequential events into a criticism of confused, misdirected, empty lives. Not having sincerity of purpose, the characters betray themselves and others, falsely proclaim their liberty, and collapse into dependence. In *Saluting Battery* Charles, who after his dismissal from the state council leads the revolutionaries, becomes the spokesman for conformity once he is restored to his former position.

The way people are influenced by the roles they play is seen in *Hour of the Sun*, where Diana passes her discontent with marriage to Marion by having the latter imitate her. The farcical comedy of *Cleopatra Slept (Badly) Here* also concerns role-playing which, as in most of Ebejer's work, is shown as dishonest and self-defeating. The insults, advice, comments traded between the characters in the plays are similar to the nonsense game which bonds the two lonely young women in *Golden Tut*, who drive away a young man who might have redeemed them from isolation.

The use of visual symbols, sudden dramatic displays of emotion, character parts built on role-playing, and other kinds of theatricality reflects Ebejer's experience as an actor and director. His scripts suggest the kind of lighting to be used, point to significant moments of timing for entrances, and are built around such effective theatrical techniques as contrasting characters, unexpected reversals of roles, and clear parallels or contrasts between opening and concluding scenes. They are highly self-conscious plays which allude to acting and theatre while offering a surprisingly complete analysis of the human condition.

—Bruce King

EDGAR, David. British. Born in Birmingham, Warwickshire, 26 February 1948. Educated at Oundle School, Northamptonshire, 1961–65; Manchester University, 1966–69, B.A. (honours) in drama 1969. Reporter, Bradford *Telegraph and Argus*, Yorkshire, 1969–72; Yorkshire Arts Association Fellow, Leeds Polytechnic, 1972–73; resident playwright, Birmingham Repertory Theatre, 1974–75; Lecturer in Playwriting, Birmingham University, 1974–78. Since 1984 literary adviser, Royal Shakespeare Company. Recipient: John Whiting Award, 1976; Bicentennial Exchange fellowship, 1978; Society of West End Theatre award, 1980; New York Drama Critics

Circle award, 1982; Tony award, 1982. Lives in Birmingham. Agent: Michael Imison Playwrights, 28 Almeida Street, London N1 1TD, England.

PUBLICATIONS

Plays

Two Kinds of Angel (produced Bradford, 1970; London, 1971). Published in *The London Fringe Theatre*, edited by V.E. Mitchell, London, Burnham House, 1975.
A Truer Shade of Blue (produced Bradford, 1970).
Still Life: Man in Bed (produced Edinburgh, 1971; London, 1972).
The National Interest (produced on tour, 1971).
Tedderella (produced Edinburgh, 1971; London, 1973).
Bloody Rosa (produced Edinburgh, 1971).
Acid (produced Bradford, 1971).
Conversation in Paradise (produced Edinburgh, 1971).
The Rupert Show (produced on tour, 1972).
The End (produced Bradford, 1972).
Excuses, Excuses (produced Coventry, 1972; London, 1973; as *Fired*, produced Birmingham, 1975).
Rent; or, Caught in the Act (produced on tour and London, 1972).
State of Emergency (also director: produced on tour and London, 1972).
Not with a Bang But a Whimper (produced Leeds, 1972).
Death Story (produced Birmingham, 1972; New York and London, 1975).
The Road to Hanoi, in *Point 101* (produced London, 1972).
England's Ireland, with others (produced Amsterdam and London, 1972).
A Fart for Europe, with Howard Brenton (produced London, 1973).
Gangsters (produced London, 1973).
Up Spaghetti Junction, with others (produced Birmingham, 1973).
Baby Love (produced Leeds and London, 1973).
The Case of the Workers' Plane (produced Bristol, 1973; shorter version, as *Concorde Cabaret*, produced on tour, 1975).
Operation Iskra (produced on tour and London, 1973).
Liberated Zone (produced Bingley, Yorkshire, 1973; London, 1974).
The Eagle Has Landed (televised 1973; produced Liverpool, 1973).
Man Only Dines (produced Leeds, 1974).
The Dunkirk Spirit (produced on tour, 1974).
Dick Deterred (produced London, 1974; New York, 1983). New York, Monthly Review Press, 1974.
The . . . Show (produced Bingley, Yorkshire, 1974).
O Fair Jerusalem (produced Birmingham, 1975). Included in *Plays 1*, 1987.
The National Theatre (produced London, 1975).
Summer Sports: Beaters, Cricket, Shotputters, Cross Country, Ball Boys (produced Birmingham, 1975; as *Blood Sports*, produced London, 1976; revised version of *Ball Boys* produced London, 1977). *Ball Boys* published London, Pluto Press, 1978; in *The Best Short Plays 1982*, edited by Ramon Delgado, Radnor, Pennsylvania, Chilton, 1982.
Events Following the Closure of a Motorcycle Factory (produced Birmingham, 1976).
Destiny (produced Stratford-on-Avon, 1976; London, 1977). London, Eyre Methuen, 1976; revised version (produced London, 1985), Methuen, 1986.
Welcome to Dallas, J.C., adaptation of a play by Alfred Jarry (produced London, 1976).
The Perils of Bardfrod, with Richard Crane (produced Bradford, 1976).
Saigon Rose (produced Edinburgh, 1976; New York, 1982). Included in *Plays 1*, 1987.
Wreckers (produced Exeter and London, 1977). London, Eyre Methuen, 1977.
Our Own People (produced London, 1977).
Mary Barnes (produced Birmingham, 1978; London, 1979; New Haven, Connecticut, 1980). London, Eyre Methuen, 1979; revised version, Methuen, 1984.
The Jail Diary of Albie Sachs, adaptation of the work by Sachs (produced London, 1978; New York, 1979). London, Collings, 1978.
Teendreams, with Susan Todd (produced Bristol and London, 1979). London, Eyre Methuen, 1979.
The Life and Adventures of Nicholas Nickleby, adaptation of the novel by Dickens (produced London, 1980; New York, 1981). New York, Dramatists Play Service, 2 vols., 1982.
Maydays (produced London, 1983). London, Methuen, 1983; revised version, 1984.
Entertaining Strangers: A Play for Dorchester (produced Dorchester, Dorset, 1985; revised version produced London, 1987). London, Methuen, 1986.
That Summer (produced London, 1987). London, Methuen, 1987.
Plays 1 (includes *The Jail Diary of Albie Sachs, Mary Barnes, Saigon Rose, O Fair Jerusalem, Destiny*). London, Methuen, 1987.

Screenplay: *Lady Jane*, 1986.

Radio Play: *Ecclesiastes*, 1977.

Television Plays: *The Eagle Has Landed*, 1973; *Sanctuary*, from his play *Gangsters*, 1973; *I Know What I Meant*, 1974; *The Midas Connection*, 1975; *Censors*, with Hugh Whitemore and Robert Muller, 1975.

*

Theatrical Activities:
Director: **Plays**—*State of Emergency*, tour and London, 1972; *The Party* by Trevor Griffiths (co-director, with Howard Davies), London, 1985.

David Edgar comments:

Balzac defined his role as being "the secretary of French society." Since the late 1950's a group (or rather groups) of stage playwrights have aspired to the same function within the British polity. They've done so in a variety of forms: from the traditional social-realism of writers like Arnold Wesker, via the epic theatre plays of John Arden to the absurdist, symbolist drama of early Howard Brenton and Edward Bond.

Since the mid-1970's, the "post-68" generation of radical playwrights—most of whom are university trained and of a literary bent—have become increasingly distanced from the theatre of their youth: a theatre in which strong visual imagination informed a bewildering variety of theatrical devices and languages. The "house style" of that generation became increasingly conservative, oscillating between traditional social-realism and satire.

I think that in the 1980's we need to recapture the sense of festival that ran through our work in the late 1960's/early

1970's. In the same way that agit-prop ceased to be able to address the complexities of the 1970's, so the cerebral ironies of the 1970's cannot address the issues of the 1980's, in particular, the great subject of the collapse of the industrial society and the re-formation of the cities. Feminist theatre has already broken the bounds of realism: it's time for the rest of us to follow.

* * *

A glance at the titles of David Edgar's many plays of the early 1970's will suggest readily enough to anyone who was aware of the chief social and political issues of the time in Britain (and not only there) the nature of his early work. Edgar himself has described his work with General Will between 1971 and 1974 as "pure unadulterated agit-prop," designed to convey information in an entertaining way and from a socialist standpoint by using satirically the forms of popular culture—pantomime, comic strip, and the like. The aim was to elucidate political and economic conditions in general by reference to particular incidents. In 1973–74 Edgar turned from agit-prop to "become a social realist," feeling the necessity to "inculcate consciousness" more forcefully and in so doing to create a truly radical "theatre of public life." Several documentary plays preceded *Destiny* which, through television and radio adaptations, brought his work before the widest possible audience (though he is well aware of the problematic nature of the "mass" audience).

Edgar describes *Destiny* as having an "agit-prop structure"—the dramatic unit is, as in Brechtian epic theatre, the presentational scene rather than the traditional long act—but it is the creation of convincing characters (without the "psychologism" which is anathema to the socialist playwright) rather than demonstration-room puppets which enables it to communicate so powerfully a sense of crisis. Though the play spans in epic fashion the period from 1947 (the year of Indian Independence and the consequent return home of the colonial army) to the mid-1970's, its main action takes place against the background of a West Midland by-election campaign and the concurrent unofficial strike of Asian workers at a local foundry. The growth of the fascist Nation Forward party, through the power of its racist rhetoric to manipulate widely differing groups and individuals into a shallow yet dangerous unit of purpose, is coolly examined, and its relation to Conservatism in its many varieties precisely analyzed. Nation Forward gains increasing popular support and the new, tough Toryism, bitter at the loss of empire, shakes off old-style sentimental-paternalist Conservatism, secretly joining forces with the fascists in order to break the Asian strike and to ensure a formidable economic basis for the hard right. The cruel irony of its final plot-twist crystallizes the play's message in terms of the individual: the pathetic local antique dealer (and before that, soldier in India) whose misdirected bitterness had driven him to join Nation Forward and who—as their adopted candidate in the by-election—has been exploited by the party to such good effect, finds out by accident that his shop was taken away from him not by Jewish property speculators (as his mentors had insinuated) but by the same businessmen who are now concluding a secret agreement with his own party leaders.

Wreckers (written for and with 7 : 84) and *Teendreams* (written with Susan Todd for the feminist group Monstrous Regiment) confirm Edgar's continuing belief in the validity and usefulness of collectively devised agit-prop-type work in the late 1970's. His best work of this period, however, shows a growing interest in the relation between politics and psychology—especially the psychology of suffering. This interest emerges first in *The Jail Diary of Albie Sachs*, an adaptation yet very much Edgar's own play. For the Jewish lawyer Albie, detained under the "90-day" law in his native South Africa, the suffering inflicted upon him by the state is merely destructive, depriving him of moral strength and crushing his will to political action; yet for the eponymous heroine of *Mary Barnes* the suffering caused by mental illness is something to be gone *through* (in her case in a Christ-like way). Alternative therapy, unlike conventional psychiatry, helps her to "go through" her schizophrenia towards the attainment of a stable self. In this way she becomes capable, as many "normal" people are not, of real human relationships. The play avoids the simplistic rubric of the anti-psychiatry fashion of the 1960's—that only the mad are truly sane—while at the same time allowing an implicit socio-political critique to emerge from Mary's schizophrenia and the treatment of it. Yet it is also honest about the dilemmas and conflicts within the alternative community and the causes of its eventual dissolution.

Since his adaptation of the immensely popular and widely seen *Nicholas Nickleby* (for the Royal Shakespeare Company), Edgar has continued to work on plays with and for particular groups, most recently with *Entertaining Strangers*. Written as a community play for Dorchester (by a "stranger" and on the subject of the rightness of "entertaining strangers" of different kinds), this is nonetheless a rich dramatic text in its own right, sharing significant formal characteristics with a slightly earlier play, Edgar's most important one of the 1980's so far, *Maydays*.

By way of an epic structure resembling that of *Destiny* (though without the feel of agit-prop), *Maydays* deals with the course of socialism since World War II. With special concentration on the impact of the crucial dates 1956 and 1968, and ending in the election year of 1979, the play attempts to articulate the shifting relations between history, ideology, and personal belief and commitment by charting the ironically interconnected progress of three men: the radical son of a vicar who becomes a Trotskyist but who, in the aftermath of 1968, grows disillusioned, is ejected from the party, and ends up in the 1980's Tory think-tank; a working-class communist who, feeling himself to have been born too late and into the wrong class, comes in the 1970's to embrace unquestioningly the authoritarian nationalism of the hard right; and a Russian army officer who, having been jolted by his experience in Hungary in 1956, is imprisoned as a dissident in the 1970's, then exiled to the West—where he finds his views being co-opted and himself used by the same right-wing authoritarian grouping. The play ends with two very different acts of protest: the subtle disruption by the Russian exile, Lermontov, of a public function organized by the right to honour him; and the stand of the women on Greenham Common. The many ironies built into the plot(s) are characteristic of Edgar's drama as a whole. Their pointedness and inevitability are intensified by the rich pattern of echo and counterpoint—in both phrase and idea—that is created by the continuous juxtaposition of the three narrative strands. The intensity is both dialectical and emotional: in a play which (among other things) examines the opposition in political discourse between thought and feeling, Edgar succeeds in provoking both.

—Paul Lawley

EGBUNA, Obi B(enedict). Nigerian. Born in 1938. Educated at a university in England; University of Iowa, Iowa

City, M.A. in English; Howard University, Washington, D.C., Ph.D. in English. Taught in France and the U.S.A.; former director of State Writers Workshop and of ECBS Television, Enugu. Address: c/o Fourth Dimension Publishing, 179 Zik Avenue, P.O. Box 553, Enugu, Anambra State, Nigeria.

PUBLICATIONS

Plays

Divinity (broadcast 1965). Published in *New Africa* (London), August, September 1965.
The Anthill. London and New York, Oxford University Press, 1965.
Wind Versus Polygamy (broadcast 1966; produced Dakar, 1966).
Theatre of Power (produced Copenhagen, 1967).
The Agony (produced London, 1970).

Radio Plays: *Divinity*, 1965; *Wind Versus Polygamy*, 1966; *Daughters of the Sun*, 1970.

Novels

Wind Versus Polygamy: Where "Wind" Is the "Wind of Change" and "Polygamy" Is the "Change of Eves." London, Faber, 1964; as *Elina*, London, Fontana, 1978.
The Madness of Didi. London, Fontana, 1980.
The Rape of Lysistrata. Enugu, Fourth Dimension, 1980.

Short Stories

Daughters of the Sun and Other Stories. London, Oxford University Press, 1970.
Emperor of the Sea and Other Stories. London, Fontana, 1974.
The Minister's Daughter. London, Fontana, and New York, Watts, 1975.
Diary of a Homeless Prodigal. Enugu, Fourth Dimension, 1976.
Black Candle for Christmas. Enugu, Fourth Dimension, 1980.

Other

The Murder of Nigeria: An Indictment. London, Panaf, 1968.
Destroy This Temple: The Voice of Black Power in Britain. London, MacGibbon and Kee, and New York, Morrow, 1971.
The ABC of Black Power Thought. Apapa, Nigeria, di Nigro Press, 1973.

* * *

Although Obi B. Egbuna's efforts as a dramatist include a number of radio dramas and a play entitled *Wind Versus Polygamy*, his light and frothy comedy *The Anthill* remains the only drama which he has published as such, his earlier works having been rewritten into short stories and a novel. It seems that Egbuna has chosen well, for of all his dramatic works *The Anthill* seems to be the most entertaining and the best constructed, displaying the sort of witty comedy which has made Wilde's *The Importance of Being Earnest* a perennial favorite.

In his tale of a young African painter, Bobo, who for some reason paints only anthills, Egbuna draws a number of characters (all of whom, except for Bobo, are British and white) who are just substantial enough to interest us and just stock enough to be taken less than seriously—which is necessary in any comedy which centers around a series of deaths, two real and one pretended. Even the landlady mother of the young British soldier, Tommy, who dies from a heart attack when confronted by Bobo, does not seem to be overly disturbed by her own son's death. She is more concerned that people admire her appendix, which she keeps in a jar on her mantel.

Egbuna presents us with a full house of coincidences—that the policeman who visits their room just happens to be the father of the girl who has matrimonial intentions on Bobo's friend Nigel, that Tommy dies because Bobo resembles a young African whose death Tommy caused while stationed in Tongo (Bobo's home country), that Bobo is the deceased African's twin brother, and so on. But such coincidences are as in keeping with this kind of frolic as are the puns, which flow fast and freely. The verdict of the judge that Tommy's death was his own fault—"All young British soldiers must behave like English gentlemen at home and abroad. Under no circumstances must you kill a man to whom you are not properly introduced"—is the perfect sort of climax to a story which another writer might have turned into a heavy-handed tragedy.

Underneath it all, of course, there is a deep undercurrent of seriousness. Comedy is the other side of the mask of tragedy. Egbuna himself is a serious writer—as *Destroy This Temple*, essays written while he was locked in an English prison, indicates. His other plays have dealt with the conflict between tribal ways and Christianity and the resultant agonies in the hearts of young men who are the sons of Christian Africans but advocates of Black Power. When Egbuna has Bobo describe himself as "a typical Tongolese gentleman . . . a dedicated vindicator of African personality and I've got my Anglo-Saxon political and academic titles to prove it," the laughter is as bitter as it is sweet.

—Joseph Bruchac

ELDER, Lonne, III. American. Born in Americus, Georgia, 26 December 1931. Educated at New Jersey State Teachers College (now Trenton State College); Yale University School of Drama, New Haven, Connecticut (John Hay Whitney Fellow and American Broadcasting Company Television Writing Fellow, 1965–66; John Golden Fellow and Joseph E. Levine Fellow in film-making, 1967). Served in the United States Army, 1952. Married Judith Ann Johnson in 1969; two sons. Worked as a docker, waiter, and professional gambler; coordinator of the Playwrights-Directors Unit, Negro Ensemble Company, New York, 1967–69; writer, Talent Associates, New York, 1968; writer/producer, Cinema Center Films, Hollywood, 1969–70; writer, Universal Pictures, Hollywood, 1970–71, and Radnitz/Mattel Productions, Hollywood, 1971; writer/producer, Talent Associates, Hollywood, 1971; writer, MGM Pictures and Columbia Pictures, Hollywood, 1972. Recipient: Stanley Drama award, 1965; American National Theatre Academy award, 1967; Outer Circle award, 1970; Vernon Rice award, 1970; Stella Holt Memorial Playwrights Award, 1970. Address: c/o Farrar Straus and Giroux, 19 Union Square West, New York, New York 10003, U.S.A.

PUBLICATIONS

Plays

Ceremonies in Dark Old Men (produced New York, 1965; revised version produced New York, 1969). New York, Farrar Straus, 1969.
Charades on East 4th Street (produced Montreal, 1967). Published in *Black Drama Anthology*, edited by Woodie King and Ron Milner, New York, New American Library, 1971.
Seven Comes Up—Seven Comes Down (produced New York, 1977–78).

Screenplays: *Sounder*, 1972; *Melinda*, 1972; *Sounder Part 2*, 1976; *Bustin' Loose*, with Roger L. Simon and Richard Pryor, 1981.

Television Plays: *Camera 3* series, 1963; *The Terrible Veil*, 1964; *NYPD* series, 1967–68; *McCloud* series, 1970–71; *A Woman Called Moses*, from a book by Marcy Heidish, 1978.

*

Manuscript Collection: Boston University.

Theatrical Activities:
Actor: **Plays**—Bobo in *A Raisin in the Sun* by Lorraine Hansberry, New York, 1959; Clem in *Days of Absence* by Douglas Turner Ward, New York, 1965.

* * *

Lonne Elder III, a black American playwright, has involved himself in a sufficient variety of activities that his own career might serve as the subject of a drama. Born in Georgia, he has spent most of his life in New York and New Jersey, where he has supported himself by working on the docks, waiting tables, gambling professionally, and promoting political causes. Under the influence of Douglas Turner Ward, he abandoned his interest in writing poetry and fiction to concentrate on drama.

Elder gained some attention for the one-act *Charades on East 4th Street*, commissioned by New York City's Mobilization for Youth Inc., which was performed at Expo 67 in Montreal. A thesis drama, *Charades* urges young blacks to combat the oppression of corrupt police by legal means rather than by violence. Elder's best known stage play, however, is *Ceremonies in Dark Old Men*, which was produced professionally in 1969 by the Negro Ensemble Company of New York City.

Elder, like Ward, articulates an argument of many black American dramatists that, in order to develop fully as artists in professional theatre, they must be able to write for an audience sympathetic towards and informed about black life. Without the existence of such an audience, black dramatists are denied opportunity by producers who, believing that most American theatre-goers are indifferent or hostile to serious drama about blacks, will risk money only on exotic or sensational presentations. Black dramatists are further restricted if they must write for an audience which, ignorant of actual black life, evaluates black American plays according to their fidelity to clichés and false stereotypes. Like the serious white American playwright, the argument continues, the black dramatist desires to test his skill in revealing the nuances, the subtleties, and the complexities of the life he knows; he resents any effort to require him instead to write a primer for beginning readers.

Although Elder's works have been presented before interracial groups, Elder has written them with the assumption that his audience is empathetic and informed. In *Ceremonies in Dark Old Men*, for instance, Elder did not follow the pattern of many black dramatists who write for uninformed, white audiences. Although he wrote *Ceremonies* in the midst of a period in which black Americans actively crusaded for their rights as citizens, Elder did not plead the justice of their cause, nor did he capitalize upon the sensationalism of black-white confrontations. Unlike some of his contemporaries, he did not seek to promote integration by suggesting that his characters were identical to white Americans except for skin color. On the other hand, he did not try to exaggerate the differences between his characters and other Americans. Instead, he artistically created the story of the Parkers, a black family enervated by individual weaknesses and by a collective sense of the inability of blacks to prosper in a white-oriented society.

The mother of the family has died from overwork. The father, Russell B. Parker, a former vaudeville entertainer, hides from the world while he relives the transitory successes of his earlier life. Theo, an academically talented son, has stopped attending school because he believes that education does not benefit black Americans; he hides in dreams of becoming an artist. A second son, Bobby, is a petty thief. The only full-time worker in the family, Adele, the daughter, bolsters her self-image by complaining that she is the financial support of the family. Nevertheless, her failure to accept a challenge to leave the family reveals that her own insecurities cause her to prefer to cling to a crumbling household rather than face the responsibilities of an independent life outside the home.

When Adele Parker insists that the three males secure jobs, her father is forced to admit to himself that years of humiliation by whites when he was a performer have rendered him psychologically incapable of re-experiencing such humiliation as an employee. The family is further weakened by its decision to participate in a scheme to secure money by exploiting and defrauding the black community. Encouraged by having money to spend, Russell Parker seeks his lost youth in a young girl who eventually betrays him for a younger man. As the play ends, Parker, deaf to the reality that his son Bobby has been killed while attempting robbery, rejoices in his first victory in the checkers games which he has regularly lost to a friend.

—Darwin T. Turner

ENGLAND, Barry. British. Born in London, 16 March 1934. Educated at Downside School, Bath. Served in the British Army, 1950–52. Married Diane Dirsztay in 1967; one son and one daughter. Actor in provincial repertory companies, films, and television. Recipient: Arts Council grant; Author's Club award, 1968. Agent: Patricia Macnaughton, Macnaughton Lowe Representation, 200 Fulham Road, London SW10 9PN, England.

PUBLICATIONS

Plays

End of Conflict (produced Coventry, 1961). London, Evans, 1964.
The Big Contract (produced Coventry, 1963).

The Damn Givers (produced Coventry, 1964).
Conduct Unbecoming (produced Bristol and London, 1969; New York, 1970). London, Heinemann, and New York, French, 1971.

Television Plays: *The Sweet War Man*, 1966; *The Move after Checkmate*, 1966; *An Experience of Evil*, 1966; *You'll Know Me by the Stars in My Eyes*, 1966; *The Man Who Understood Women*, 1967.

Novel

Figures in a Landscape. London, Cape, and New York, Random House, 1968.

*

Barry England comments:

I am a storyteller. I revere economy and precision.

* * *

Barry England is best known for one play, *Conduct Unbecoming*. The play's well-deserved success was no doubt partly due to its unfashionably gripping story, with some help perhaps from its fashionable period setting—British India in the 1880's—and its dashing red uniforms. But, although England's approach to his subject matter is a little reminiscent of the equally unfashionable Rattigan's in *The Winslow Boy*, in that he treats a moral conflict in which there is little doubt from the outset who is right and who is wrong, *Conduct Unbecoming* is more than a simple moral tract as it is more than a thriller.

England's dramatic method is that of "putting the screws on." The dramatist chooses a completely enclosed situation, fills it with mutually conflicting characters and then deftly tightens the situation until the pips squeak. In the form of plotting, this method is inevitably an ingredient in almost every sort of play. But it is a question of where the weight of the play finally rests. Do the characters, the stage images, the philosophical, political, or social themes spill over the framework and more or less conceal it? Are they subservient to it, as in farces, thrillers, and court-room dramas? Or almost miraculously created from it, as in Racine or middle-period Ibsen?

It is quite difficult to decide where the weight falls in *Conduct Unbecoming*. An image such as the pig-sticking episode in the second scene makes a most powerful impression in its own right, but loses force for being meticulously absorbed into the final twists of the plot: there is not enough left over to expand in the mind of the audience. For all the subtlety and unexpectedness of the characters, the plot never ceases to contain them, and its neat finish seems to put them away in a box and shut the lid on them. As for England's theme, it is so organic to his method that one must ask whether he has chosen the method to explore the theme or the theme to suit the method.

His earlier plays *End of Conflict* and *The Damn Givers* argue for the primacy of the theme. *End of Conflict* is another army play, set in the New Territories of China at the time of the Korean War. Like *Conduct Unbecoming* its situation arises from the introduction of a new officer into the Mess. Its plotting is looser than that of the later play, but its theme is almost identical—the clash of an individual, still experimental code of behaviour with a traditional, collective code. For all its apparent rigidity, the army's code is shown to be flexible enough to allow good men to behave well. Indeed in *End of Conflict* the real hero is not the liberal-minded rebel who causes disaster by his inexperienced good intentions, but the liberal-minded and experienced conformist. In *Conduct Unbecoming* this clash and its outcome are more complex, but again it is the officer with "bourgeois principles" of honour who triumphs, saving the rebel from himself at the same time as restoring a true sense of honour to the regiment, whose collective pride and inflexibility had corrupted it.

The Damn Givers is a much less convincing piece, perhaps because a group of pleasure-loving socialites makes a less coherent collective than a regiment. The misfit here is a young sex-starved academic and the clash is between his awakened idea of lasting love—after he has slept with the voracious Lady Jane Moore-Fuller-Bracke—and the collective's idea of sex as one pleasure among others to be taken on the trot. England's own lack of conviction in this variation on his basic theme seems to be reflected both in the shadowy characters and the too predictable plot.

Nevertheless, it does seem clear that England's theme comes first. Because it is well defined—there is no suggestion of the infinite perplexities of life beyond the enclosed societies England studies—it is almost perfectly served by a tightly geared plot. The characters too are emanations of the theme, in the sense that their passions stop at discovering the honourable mode of conduct within a given set of rules. But since, at least in the setting of an officers' Mess in the heyday of the British Raj, such people are entirely credible, they can develop an individuality well beyond the limitations of the morality or the cliffhanger. The real strength of *Conduct Unbecoming* is in its delicately orchestrated character studies. One would like to see what England could do with a contemporary story—there are after all plenty of enclosed collectives to choose from.

—John Spurling

EVELING, (Harry) Stanley. British. Born in Newcastle upon Tyne, Northumberland, 4 August 1925. Educated at Rutherford College; Samuel King's School; King's College, Durham University (William Black Noble Student, 1950–51), B.A. (honours) in English 1950, B.A. (honours) in philosophy 1953; Lincoln College, Oxford, D. Phil. 1955. Served in the Durham Light Infantry, 1944–47. Married to Kate Eveling. Assistant Lecturer, Department of Logic and Metaphysics, King's College, University of Aberdeen, 1955–57; Lecturer, Department of Philosophy, University College of Wales, Aberystwyth, 1957–60. Senior Lecturer, 1960–83, and since 1984 Teaching Fellow in Philosophy, University of Edinburgh. Since 1970 television critic, the *Scotsman*, Edinburgh. Recipient: Earl Grey fellowship, 1955. Agent: Harvey Unna and Stephen Durbridge Ltd., 24–32 Pottery Lane, London W11 4LZ, England. Address: 30 Comely Bank, Edinburgh EH4 1AJ, Scotland.

PUBLICATIONS

Plays

The Balachites (produced Edinburgh, 1963). With *The Strange Case of Martin Richter*, London, Calder and Boyars, 1970.
An Unspeakable Crime (produced London, 1963).
Come and Be Killed (produced Edinburgh, 1967; London, 1968). With *Dear Janet Rosenberg, Dear Mr. Kooning*, London, Calder and Boyars, 1971.

The Strange Case of Martin Richter (produced Glasgow, 1967; London, 1968). With *The Balachites*, London, Calder and Boyars, 1970.
The Lunatic, The Secret Sportsman, and the Woman Next Door (produced Edinburgh, 1968; London, 1969). With *Vibrations*, London, Calder and Boyars, 1970.
Dear Janet Rosenberg, Dear Mr. Kooning (produced Edinburgh and London, 1969; New York, 1970). With *Come and Be Killed*, London, Calder and Boyars, 1971.
Vibrations (produced Edinburgh, 1969; London, 1972). With *The Lunatic, The Secret Sportsman, and the Woman Next Door*, London, Calder and Boyars, 1970.
Dracula, with others (produced Edinburgh, 1969; London, 1973).
Mister (produced Edinburgh, 1970; London, 1971). London, Calder and Boyars, 1972.
Sweet Alice (as *Jakey Fat Boy*, produced New York 1970; as *Sweet Alice* produced Edinburgh and London, 1971). Published in *Plays and Players* (London), March 1971.
Better Days, Better Knights (produced Edinburgh, 1971; London, 1972).
Our Sunday Times (produced Edinburgh and London, 1971).
Oh Starlings (produced Edinburgh, 1971). Published in *Plays and Players* (London), March 1971.
The Laughing Cavalier (produced London, 1971).
He Used to Play for Hearts, in *Christmas Present* (produced Edinburgh, 1971).
Caravaggio, Buddy (produced Edinburgh, 1972; London, 1977).
Union Jack (and Bonzo) (produced Edinburgh and London, 1973).
Shivvers (produced London, 1974).
The Dead of Night (produced Edinburgh, 1975).
The Buglar (sic) *Boy and His Swish Friend* (produced Edinburgh, 1983). Edinburgh, Salamander Press, 1983.

Radio Plays: *Dance ti Thy Daddy*, 1964; *The Timepiece*, 1965; *A Man Like That*, 1966; *The Devil in Summer*, with Kate Eveling, from a play by Michel Faure, 1971; *The Queen's Own*, 1976.

Television Play: *Ishmael*, 1973.

Verse

(*Poems*). Oxford, Fantasy Press, 1956.

Other

The Total Theatre. Edinburgh, Heriot Watt University, 1972.

*

Manuscript Collections: Brandeis University, Waltham, Massachusetts; National Library of Scotland, Edinburgh.

Stanley Eveling comments:

My plays seem, very roughly speaking, to oscillate between reality and unreality, between moral dramas and plays in the absurdist, or, better, Dickensian, tradition. I hanker after the former and still think that *Mister*, a sort of dramatic interface between the fantastic and the real, is the play that says most, though it doesn't have the inventive duplicity and cunning of *Dear Janet* and some others.

If I had to say what theme hovers around in all, it would be that they all seem to have something to do with beleaguered human beings, most often male ones, in circumstances that precisely don't call for his (or her) particular virtues. In *Mister*'s case these are heroic virtues, Nelsonian virtues; in the case of the Oblomovian Jim in *Come and Be Killed*, it is as if he were called upon to exercise the "wrong" virtues, mundane virtues that go with domesticity and responsibility, like asking Shelley to wash the nappies or the Ford Cortina, or so Jim construes it. Alec, in *Dear Janet*, is asked to play a romantic role in a young girl's dream as she is required to fulfil a dreamed-up bit of him. In *The Buglar Boy and His Swish Friend* (the most complicated play, perhaps), the characters themselves, called down from the eternal library of the imagination, attempt and fail to fulfil the tragic requirements of the play's theme, attempt and fail to take on a tragic role at a time, in an age, and with qualities that belong to comedy. This is as close as I want to get. In an as yet unproduced play, *Impossible People*, I see that the theme is that of a man called upon to perform the last male role, that of being subservient to his wife's genius. Naturally he does not succeed.

What is "ridiculous" or "absurd" is that the wrong qualities are also the right qualities, that tragic predicaments happen in comic circumstances, that is, outside the environment which would give them tragic significance. As Janet says of her own work, at the end of the play, it is carried along on "the last ripple left by the receding impulse of tragedy."

* * *

Stanley Eveling is a prolific and at first sight a somewhat baffling playwright: he writes in a variety of styles and almost always adopts a veiled, even blurred approach to his subject matter. But although he is a professional moral philosopher as well as a playwright and although his characters often involve themselves in philosophical argument and speculation, his plays are by no means intellectual, in the sense of being elaborately constructed to act as working models of some abstract thesis. Eveling's approach is veiled not because he is hiding the machinery, but on the contrary because he himself seems to write in the act of watching the machinery at work; he sits almost painfully close to the characters, feels them rather than thinks them, and uses one style or another, as he might use one stage or another, as at most a temporary accommodation for his stubborn and chaotic material.

This material is presented in its simplest versions in the two plays *Come and Be Killed* and *Dear Janet Rosenberg, Dear Mr. Kooning*. The first concerns an abortion, the second an abortive relationship between an ageing novelist and his female fan. The muddled, narrowly confined, squalid situations in which the characters find themselves in both plays are compounded by their own muddled, limited, and selfish reactions. "You're not wicked, you're just ignorant," says one character to another in *Come and Be Killed*: this might be a motto for all Eveling's work. Creation in general is messy, cruel, blind, and the lords of creation are no more and no less: in *The Balachites*, Eveling shows a pair of innocents, a modern Adam and Eve, corrupted not by Satan but by the ghosts of dead men; in his nearest thing to an "absurdist" play, *The Lunatic, The Secret Sportsman, and the Woman Next Door*, he shows the pathetic innocence of mental and sexual aberration.

Naturally the idea of there being such creatures as "heroes" in such a world is a fruitful source of still further pain and confusion. The story of Donald Crowhurst, who made it appear that he was winning the *Sunday Times* single-handed yacht race round the world, but turned out to have disappeared, almost certainly overboard, without ever having sailed beyond the Atlantic, forms the basis of Eveling's play *Our Sunday*

Times. But he extends the story, as the title implies, to cover a much more widespread form of bogus heroism, of cheaply bought superiority over trivial circumstances, the vicarious act of reading newspapers or watching television. The play's effect is weakened by this attempt at generalization; Eveling steps back too far from his characters. But *Mister*, in which he again treats a would-be sailor-hero, the owner of an antique shop who acts out his fantasy of being Lord Nelson, with the unfortunate complication of having a Lady Hamilton on the premises who is not content with a sexual relationship confined to fantasy, is perhaps Eveling's best play. It is certainly his saddest and funniest, his finest example of what Janet Rosenberg calls "the curious mixture of farce and misery which is the slight ripple left by the receding impulse of tragedy."

Nevertheless, although Eveling's dramatic outlook is on the whole more sad than angry, reminiscent of those world-weary but intermittently kindly doctors in Chekhov's plays, he has written at least one pay in which the mixture of farce and misery is replaced by that of savage humour and despair. In *The Strange Case of Martin Richter* a German industrialist employs three ex-Nazis as household servants, not realizing or not caring what this means for his butler, who is of "Swebish" origin and whose father was murdered during the Third Reich for being "Swebish." The butler's solution is to pretend that he himself was a prominent Nazi, claim acquaintance with Hitler, constitute himself "Leader" of a neo-Nazi party and pretend to eliminate the industrialist for being "Swebish." The play ends, after several twists of fortune and a marvellously composed drunken party, with everything as it was, the industrialist once more on top of the evil heap. *Martin Richter* is the nearest thing in Eveling's work to a straight political and moral fable. It is compact and clear, a powerful and bitterly comic outcry against the nastiness, brutishness, and shortness of human life.

The more recent plays *Shivvers, Caravaggio, Buddy*, and *The Dead of Night* all deal with suicide in one form or another. The central character of *Shivvers*, having for a time assuaged his own sense of guilt by imposing vicious behaviour on a vicar and a whore, commits suicide when they shake off his domination. *Caravaggio, Buddy* is an ambitious comic fantasy—an episodic quest play somewhat reminiscent of *Peer Gynt*—whose hero fails in many attempts to commit suicide and ends up reconciled with society. The play's complex and carefully controlled shifts of style establish in dramatic rather than intellectual terms the reality and humanity of the misfit as against the unreality and inhumanity of the "organized." It is full of delightful comic inventions, such as the colloquy between Buddy and a Yeti on the slopes of Mount Everest, while just off-stage innumerable international expeditions make more or less disastrous assaults on the summit. *The Dead of Night* is a sombre piece—enlivened by a German general trying to disguise himself as a woman—set beside Hitler's bunker in Berlin and featuring the arch-suicide himself.

All three plays show Eveling sharpening his lines and clarifying his construction without losing his closeness to the characters. His themes remain in the same, but his methods of exploring them are growing more precise and versatile.

—John Spurling

EYEN, Tom. American. Born in Cambridge, Ohio, 14 August 1941. Educated at Ohio State University, Columbus, 1957–61, B.A. in English 1961; American Academy of Dramatic Arts, New York, 1961–62. Married Lisa Giradeux in 1963; three sons. Taught drama for Metropolitan Television Arts, New York, 1962; also worked as a publicity agent. Founder, Theatre of the Eye (affiliated with the La Mama group), New York, 1967; director, sometimes under the pseudonym of Jerome Eyen or Roger Short, Jr.; director and writer, Theatre of Big Dreams, 1982–83. Recipient: Rockefeller grant, 1967; Guggenheim fellowship, 1970; Tony award, 1982; NAACP award, 1982. Agent: Bridget Aschenberg, International Creative Management, 40 West 57th Street, New York, New York 10019. Address: 95 Horatio Street, New York, New York 10014, U.S.A.

PUBLICATIONS

Plays

Frustrata, The Dirty Little Girl with the Paper Rose Stuck in Her Head, Is Demented! (produced New York, 1964).
The White Whore and the Bit Player (produced New York, 1964; revised version, as *The White Whore and the Bit Players*, produced New York, 1969; London, 1970). Included in *Sarah B. Divine! and Other Plays*, 1971.
My Next Husband Will Be a Beauty! (produced New York, 1964). Included in *Sarah B. Divine! and Other Plays*, 1971.
Court (produced New York, 1965).
Why Hannah's Skirt Won't Stay Down; or, Admission 10¢ (produced New York, 1965; London, 1970). Included in *Sarah B. Divine! and Other Plays*, 1971.
Can You See a Prince?, music by Bill Elliott (produced New York, 1965).
The Last Great Cocktail Party (produced New York, 1965).
The Demented World of Tom Eyen (produced New York, 1965).
Cinderella Revisited, music by Bill Elliott (produced New York, 1965).
Miss Nefertiti Regrets, music by Eyen and Ilene Berson (produced New York, 1965).
Give My Regards to Off-Off-Broadway (produced New York, 1966; revised version produced New York, 1966; as *Power, Greed, and Self-Destruction in America*, produced New York, 1987).
Sarah B. Divine!, music by Jonathan Kramer (produced New York, 1967; revised version produced Spoleto, Italy, 1967; with additional material by Pam Gems, produced London, 1973). Included in *Sarah B. Divine! and Other Plays*, 1971.
Grand Tenement/November 22nd, music by Jonathan Kramer (produced New York, 1967). Included in *Sarah B. Divine! and Other Plays*, 1971.
When Johnny Comes Dancing Home Again (produced New York, 1968).
The Kama Sutra (An Organic Happening) (produced New York, 1968; revised version, as *The No Plays: Paradise Later; Fantasies and Smaller Peaces; Frankenstein's Wife; Antigone Meets Dionysus for Lunch; Oh, Cowfucker!*, produced New York, 1969; revised version, as *The Kama Sutra*, produced New York, 1969). Included in *Sarah B. Divine! and Other Plays*, 1971.
Who Killed My Bald Sister Sophie? or, Thank God for Small Favors! (produced New York, 1968). Included in *Sarah B. Divine! and Other Plays*, 1971.
Alice Through a Glass Lightly, music by Jonathan Kramer (produced New York, 1968).
Caution: A Love Story (produced New York, 1969).

4 Noh Plays (produced New York, 1969).
Lana Got Laid in Lebanon (produced New York, 1970; revised version, as *The Dirtiest Show in Town*, produced New York, 1970; London, 1971).
Gertrude Stein and Other Great Men (produced New York, 1970).
Areatha in the Ice Palace; or, The Fully Guaranteed Fuck-Me Doll (produced New York, 1970; London, 1973). Included in *Sarah B. Divine! and Other Plays*, 1971.
What Is Making Gilda So Gray?; or, It Just Depends on Who You Get (produced New York, 1970). Included in *Sarah B. Divine! and Other Plays*, 1971.
Sarah B. Divine! and Other Plays (includes *Three Sisters from Springfield, Illinois:* 1. *Why Hannah's Skirt Won't Stay Down,* 2. *Who Killed My Bald Sister Sophie?,* 3. *What Is Making Gilda So Gray?; Areatha in the Ice Palace; The Kama Sutra* [*An Organic Happening*]; *My Next Husband Will Be a Beauty; The Death of Off-Broadway* [*A Street Play*]; *The White Whore and the Bit Player; Grand Tenement/November 22nd*). New York, Winter House, 1971; as *Ten Plays*, New York, French, 1977(?).
Rachel Lily Rosenbloom and Don't You Ever Forget It, with Paul Jabara, music by Jabara (also director: produced New York, 1973).
Ms. Nefertiti (also director: produced New York, 1973).
2008½: A Spaced Oddity, music by Gary William Friedman (produced New York, 1974).
Women Behind Bars (produced New York, 1974; London, 1977). New York and London, French, 1975.
Dirtiest Show II, music by Henry Krieger (produced New York, 1975).
The Neon Woman (produced New York, 1978).
Independence Day, in *Holidays* (produced Louisville, 1979).
Dreamgirls, music by Henry Krieger (produced New York, 1981).

Television Plays: *Mary Hartman, Mary Hartman* series, 1976–77; *Milliken Show*, 1977–78; *Bette Midler TV Special*, 1977; *Melody of the Glittering Parrot*, 1980.

*

Theatrical Activities:
Director and designer of most of his own plays; director: *Tour de Four* (revue), New York, 1963.

* * *

Unique among the generation of dramatists who started out in the Greenwich Village coffee houses, basements, lofts, and church halls of the 1960's, Tom Eyen has gone on to achieve—with *Dreamgirls*—big-time smash commercial success. Before that he had written or helped to write 140 scripts for *Mary Hartman, Mary Hartman*, a television series that attracted an enormous "in" audience. Asked if he had known he was going in this direction, he replies, "Always!" Ellen Stewart, he says, told him from the start that he belonged on Broadway.

Beginning small at the Caffe Cino, Eyen developed a distinctive method and voice, combining often corny, emotionally raw material with sharply satirical humor and presenting it in a form that leaps about in time and space. He has a fondness for the vulgar, a tenderness for the grotesque, a special feeling for the poignance behind the glitz. Beneath the openly exploitative, often crass surfaces of his plays and their commitment to entertaining at all costs, Eyen makes felt a darker, possibly truer view of the world and compassion for its victims. One of his frequent themes has been the confrontation between a powerful woman and a narcissistic male. His characters are lonely, reaching out to others with an intensity that too often frightens them away.

An affinity for irony and shock effect was evident from the start. *The White Whore and the Bit Player* explores the mind of a woman who was groomed by a movie studio for stardom and then relegated to bit parts. (Like many of his contemporaries, Eyen uses the Hollywood images he grew up with as a basic imaginative resource.) The conceit of the play is to show the woman twinned: simultaneously the beautiful, apparently virginal young woman whoring after fame, and her older self, who is dressed as a nun but crazy and corrupt within. The play occurs in the moment of the woman's death and moves through her life in flashbacks.

Another early play, *Why Hannah's Skirt Won't Stay Down*, is set in the funhouse at Coney Island, where Hannah gets her thrills by standing over the airhole, and Arizona, a handsome, vapid young man, admires himself in the multiple mirrors. In "real life" Hannah works as a cashier in a sleazy movie theatre and lives alone, but these two lost and lonely souls make some contact through their fantasies.

Hannah reappears in *Who Killed My Bald Sister Sophie?*, the story of a door-to-door cosmetics saleswoman, and *What Is Making Gilda So Gray?* The playwright tended to refine these complex, demanding structures through a number of productions, and right through the middle 1970's he was enormously prolific. He formed a company he called the Theatre of the Eye, and in more than two dozen plays explored a range of subjects and styles.

Eyen soon started bringing music into his plays, and he won some commercial viability with *The Dirtiest Show in Town.* A satirical response to the sex-oriented shows featuring nude actors that were then the fad in New York, it also unequivocally was one of them. The title is ironic. The play's themes are sex and environmental pollution, and the presentation was strikingly bright and clean. The stage was all white, and the actors, wholesome looking, beautiful young men and women, were dressed all in white when not nude.

Dreamgirls, which retains all of Eyen's quirky angle of vision but turns up the intensity, is dazzling theatre. The subject of black soul singers de-Negrifying their art in order to succeed in the white world has enough depth and reality to sustain powerful, complex feelings, and in collaboration with the director-choreographer Michael Bennett, Eyen sharpened his stagecraft to a dynamic, irresistible perfection. The show is the ultimate in slick and moves with exhilarating speed and freedom, and it transcends itself by the nitty-gritty density of the experience it so forcefully projects.

—Michael T. Smith

FEIFFER, Jules (Ralph). American. Born in the Bronx, New York, 26 January 1929. Educated at James Monroe High School, New York; Art Students' League, New York, 1946; Pratt Institute, Brooklyn, 1947–48, 1949–51. Served as a cartoon animator and graphic artist in the United States Army Signal Corps, 1951–53: Private. Married 1) Judith Sheftel in 1961 (separated 1971, divorced 1983), one daughter; 2) Jennifer Allen in 1983, one daughter. Assistant to the cartoonist Will Eisner, 1946–51 (ghostwriter, *The Spirit* comic, 1949–51); drew cartoon *Clifford*, 1949–51; free-lance cartoonist and artist, 1951–56. Since 1956 cartoonist (*Feiffer*), *Village Voice*, New York, and since 1959 syndicated in other newspapers and magazines. Faculty member, Yale University School of Drama, New Haven, Connecticut, 1973–74. President, Dramatists Guild Foundation, 1982–83. Since 1976 director, Corporation of Yaddo, Saratoga Springs, New York. Recipient: Oscar, for cartoon, 1961; George Polk Memorial Award, 1962; London Theatre Critics award, 1968; Obie award, 1968; Outer Circle award, 1968, 1969; Pulitzer Prize, for cartoon, 1986. Address: c/o Andrews McMeel and Parker, 4900 Main Street, Kansas City, Missouri 64112, U.S.A.

PUBLICATIONS

Plays

The Explainers (produced Chicago, 1961; New York, 1964).
Crawling Arnold (produced Spoleto, London, and Cambridge, Massachusetts, 1961; New York, 1979). Published in *Best Short Plays of the World 1958–1967*, edited by Stanley Richards, New York, Crown, 1968.
The World of Jules Feiffer (produced Hunterdon Hills, New Jersey, 1962).
Interview, published in *Harper's* (New York), June 1962.
You Should Have Caught Me at the White House, published in *Holiday* (Indianapolis), June 1963.
Little Murders (produced New Haven, Connecticut, 1966; London and New York, 1967). New York, Random House, 1968; London, Cape, 1970.
The Unexpurgated Memoirs of Bernard Mergendeiler (produced Los Angeles, 1967; New York, 1968; Glasgow, 1969; London, 1972). Published in *Collision Course*, New York, Random House, 1968.
God Bless (produced New Haven, Connecticut, and London, 1968). Published in *Plays and Players* (London), January 1969.
Feiffer's People (produced Edinburgh and London, 1968; Los Angeles, 1971).
Dick and Jane, in *Oh! Calcutta!* (produced New York, 1969; London, 1970). New York, Grove Press, 1970.
The White House Murder Case (produced New York, 1970). New York, Grove Press, 1970.
Munro (produced New York, 1971).
Carnal Knowledge: A Screenplay. New York, Farrar Straus, and London, Cape, 1971.
Silverlips, in *VD Blues* (televised 1972). New York, Avon, 1973.
Watergate Classics, with others (produced New Haven, Connecticut, 1973).
Cohn of Arc, published in *Partisan Review* (New Brunswick, New Jersey), vol. 40, no. 2, 1973.
Knock, Knock (produced New York, 1976). New York, Hill and Wang, 1976.
Hold Me! (produced New York, 1977). New York, Dramatists Play Service, 1977.
Grown Ups (produced Cambridge, Massachusetts, and New York, 1981). New York, French, 1982.
A Think Piece (produced New York, 1982).

Screenplays: *Munro* (animated cartoon), 1960; *Carnal Knowledge*, 1971; *Little Murders*, 1971; *Popeye*, 1980.

Television Plays: *VD Blues*, with others, 1972; *Kidnapped* (*Happy Endings* series), 1975.

Novels

Harry, The Rat with Women. New York, McGraw Hill, and London, Collins, 1963.
Ackroyd. New York, Simon and Schuster, 1977; London, Hutchinson, 1978.
Tantrum: A Novel-in-Cartoons. New York, Knopf, 1979; London, Sidgwick and Jackson, 1980.

Other

Sick, Sick, Sick. New York, McGraw Hill, 1958; London, Collins, 1959.
Passionella and Other Stories. New York, McGraw Hill, 1959; London, Collins, 1960.
The Explainers. New York, McGraw Hill, 1960; London, Collins, 1961.
Boy, Girl. Boy, Girl. New York, Random House, 1961; London, Collins, 1962.
Hold Me! New York, Random House, 1963.
Feiffer's Album. New York, Random House, 1963.
The Unexpurgated Memoirs of Bernard Mergendeiler. New York, Random House, 1965; London, Collins, 1966.
The Penguin Feiffer. London, Penguin, 1966.
Feiffer on Civil Rights. New York, Anti-Defamation League of B'nai B'rith, 1966.
Feiffer's Marriage Manual. New York, Random House, 1967.
Pictures at a Prosecution: Drawings and Text from the Chicago Conspiracy Trial. New York, Grove Press, 1971.
Feiffer on Nixon: The Cartoon Presidency. New York, Random House, 1974.
Jules Feiffer's America from Eisenhower to Reagan, edited by Steven Heller. New York, Knopf, and London, Penguin, 1982.
Outer Space Spirit 1952, with Will Eisner and Wallace Wood, edited by Denis Kitchen. Princeton, Wisconsin, Kitchen Sink Press, 1983.
Marriage Is an Invasion of Privacy and Other Dangerous Views. Fairway, Kansas, Andrews McMeel and Parker, 1984.
Feiffer's Children. Fairway, Kansas, Andrews McMeel and Parker, 1986.

Editor, *The Great Comic Book Heroes*. New York, Dial Press, 1965; London, Allen Lane, 1967.

* * *

Jules Feiffer is, first of all, a cartoonist. Long before he began to write plays, he had made a reputation as a satirist with an uncanny knack for catching the psychological, social, and political clichés which are the refuge and the cross of the college-educated middle class that provides him with an audience as well as a subject matter. His talent has always been as much verbal as visual; his ear as good as his hand. His cartoons are ordinarily strips in which two characters pursue a conversation, panel by panel, until the congenial platitudes dissolve into open aggression, naked greed, impotence, ineffectuality, pain; a variation is the strip in which a single figure—I almost said performer—speaks directly to the reader. The line between this kind of cartoon and the revue sketch is a narrow one, and a great many of Feiffer's early cartoons have crossed that line. Most of the material in *Feiffer's People* and *Hold Me!* presumably began as cartoon dialogue. Even those short works written for the theatre—*Dick and Jane*, the Feiffer sketch from *Oh! Calcutta!*, or the early one-acter *Crawling Arnold*—seem little more than extended cartoons with the stage directions standing in for the drawing.

Inevitably, Feiffer's full-length plays have been viewed—and condemned in some cases—as the work of a cartoonist. There is justice in the viewing, if not in the condemnation, for—as so often with satirists—Feiffer works in terms of stereotypes, of those figures identified by a single idiosyncrasy or a pattern of related compulsions. Even the two young men in *Carnal Knowledge* are societal types rather than psychological studies, although the labels by which we identify them may be written in the kind of psychological language that one expects to find in the balloons of Feiffer's cartoons. Feiffer tends to see his figures as more realistic than my description suggests. Just before the off-Broadway revival of *Little Murders*, Feiffer told an interviewer (*New York Times*, 26 January 1969) that his characters "are very, very real to me. I care about them as people." Yet, elsewhere in the same interview, he identified the family in the play as "a nice, Andy Hardy type family," and the Hardy family films were straight stereotype. If we read *real* in the Feiffer quotation as *true*—that is, identifiable—then the characters are real, as Andy Hardy is, as the figures in his cartoons are; we look at them and say, *oh yes, I know him*, meaning, *oh, yes, I know the type*.

The important thing about Feiffer as a playwright is that he produces unified dramatic structures—related, in some of their elements, to his cartoons and to revue sketches—in which apparently disparate material is held together by a controlling idea. In *Little Murders* the random violence that is the ostensible subject is simply the most obviously theatrical evidence of a general collapse that is reflected in technological malfunction (the failed electricity) and the impotence of traditional power-and-virtue figures (the comic turns of the judge, the detective, the priest). When Feiffer's nice American family begins to shoot people on the street, the event is not so much a culmination of the action as an open statement of what has been implicit all through the play. That last scene; the disintegration, physical and political, in *The White House Murder Case*; the sexual ignorance, and failure, that calls itself "Carnal Knowledge"—all these suggest that Feiffer has about as black a view of American society and of human possibility as one can find in the contemporary theatre.

After *Knock, Knock*, an uncharacteristic fantasy of commitment, *Grown Ups* comes home to familiar Feiffer territory with a self-pitying protagonist, faced with personal and professional collapse and a parental support system which is the presumed cause of his misery; on stage, his daughter, used as a weapon by all the adults, is something of a trial for the audience, but the television version of the play, ending with the camera on the little girl, successfully emphasizes the child as victim and the continuity of loving destructiveness within the family. *A Think Piece* concentrates on the trivia of daily existence to show, as the author says, "the nothingness that constitutes so much of our lives."

—Gerald Weales

FENNARIO, David. Canadian. Born David William Wiper in Montreal in 1947. Educated at Dawson College, Montreal, 1969–71. Married Elizabeth Fennario in 1976; one child. Playwright-in-residence, Centaur Theatre, Montreal, from 1973. Co-founder, Cultural Workers Association. Recipient: Canada Council grant, 1973; Chalmers award, 1979. Address: c/o Centaur Theatre Company, 453 St. François Xavier Street, Montreal, Quebec H2Y 2TI, Canada.

PUBLICATIONS

Plays

On the Job (produced Montreal, 1975). Vancouver, Talonbooks, 1976.
Nothing to Lose (produced Montreal, 1976). Vancouver, Talonbooks, 1977.
Toronto (produced Montreal, 1978).
Without a Parachute, adaptation of his own book (produced Toronto, 1978).
Balconville (produced Montreal, 1979; Bath and London, 1981). Vancouver, Talonbooks, 1980.
Changes, adaptation of his journal *Without a Parachute* (produced Ottawa, 1980).
Moving (produced Montreal, 1983).
Blue Mondays, poems by Daniel Adams. Verdun, Quebec, Black Rock Creations, 1984.

Other

Without a Parachute (journal). Privately printed, 1972; Toronto, McClelland and Stewart, 1974.

* * *

It is difficult to consider David Fennario's work without reference to the man himself. Many contemporary artists are clearly present in their work, but in Fennario's case the connections between the author, his social and educational background, his politics and values, and the plays themselves are so clear and so central that a discussion based on an autobiographical premise becomes more useful than it might be in the case of a playwright who absents himself more convincingly from his creations.

Fennario comes from an immigrant, working-class area of Montreal, Canada's second largest and most cosmopolitan city. As a member of this sub-culture, he learned to be street-wise and to survive in a city divided between French and English factions and further stressed by an increasingly obvious and vocal ethnic mosaic. His personal story, which was dramatized in a one-man show, *Changes*, has become a literary artifact itself, since it was the initial and unexpected publication of his diary memoir, *Without a Parachute*, which led Fennario to an unprecedented residency with a theatre company, the production of his first play, and an immediate popular success. This strangely extended sense of self has become characteristic of Fennario's plays: *On the Job* and *Balconville* move further from it than, say, *Nothing to Lose*, where a protagonist exactly like the author returns to a slum exactly like his home and talks to friends exactly like his own about what it has been like to become a famous playwright and media personality, but even these plays exhibit the familiar setting, figures, and tone of the author's actual background. When he moves further from it, in the play *Toronto*, where he not only sets aside his own territory but moves across the border into Anglo-Saxon Canada, he writes his least convincing play and, interestingly enough, the only one not to enjoy popular and financial success.

On the Job establishes the themes central to Fennario's writing. Set in the packing room of a clothing manufacturing factory on Christmas Eve, the play is incited by a special rush order from the Eaton department store, a huge megabusiness which becomes a symbol of the Canadian Establishment (in this, as in other Canadian writing). The order requires that the shipping crew remain through the usual half-day holiday and brings to the surface the workers' feelings of exploitation and powerlessness. It also allows their various representative personalities to emerge: the old worker, aware of his political weakness, hopes only to retain his salary until retirement; the foreman, a Quebecois who has risen to a position of impotent power in the English management, hopes to protect his uncomfortable position; the young punk wishes only to drink, play, and avoid working; the young radical tries to inspire his fellow labourers into revolution and organizes an illegal strike which ends with the employees being fired.

The notion of revolution is pivotal, as it introduces Fennario's political ideology. His is a Marxist, anarchist viewpoint, and he leads his characters to a realization of the need for change without providing the audience with a clear suggestion of what that change should be. The political discussion among the men is reproduced in extremely effective dialogue; Fennario's ear for the dialects of Montreal is authentic, and the powerful, vernacular language accounts, in large part, for his local success.

The play is full of vulgar songs, fights, props, and business, and, in production, is lively and engaging. In print, it suffers from a political vision which seems shallow and a situation which has been explored before.

Balconville is Fennario's most popular play, having broken attendance records in a number of productions and having elicited ecstatic reviews from newspaper critics. More recently literary critics have begun to consider this success and have attributed it more to the relation of the play to the social milieu of its city and its bold experiment in bilingualism than to an intrinsic excellence in the drama itself.

The play is set in Point St. Charles, the working class district so familiar in Fennario's work. In this setting, cleverly represented on stage by two double-storied apartment buildings with balconies which face each other, family groups of English and Quebecois workers display the characteristics of representative types, the common traits of the milieu and the linguistic and social differences between the French and English within an otherwise similar society. These people cannot afford to travel south to the sun in the freezing winter or away from the inner city in the humid summer, and so "vacation" in "Balconville," the crowded verandah's of their tenements. Here, each observes the other, and petty jealousies and language barriers explode under pressure into family and social hatreds. The symbolism for Canadian society is obvious and is amplified in the dialogue by the use of untranslated passages from each language. The theatrical effect of this bilingualism is significant—while the characters cannot understand one another, neither can large portions of the audience and the viewer is trapped by the dialogue into participating in a dramatic distillation of the frustrations of a nation with two languages. (It also allows Montreal audiences, who love the play, to enjoy a linguistic inside joke against other Canadians who are noticeably less bilingual.)

Once again, the characters fulfill political stereotypes of little depth: the slum landlord and politician are monsters; the unemployed are self-destructive victims of capitalist exploitation. The ending, in which the *quartier* burns down, is a facile statement of revolution and an easy way out for the playwright. On the other hand, the figures are more rounded than those of *On the Job*: in Thibault, Fennario creates a clown in the best dramatic tradition, and the rhythms of the dialogue, punctuated by hauntingly lonely guitar music, are well-crafted and disciplined.

In *Balconville* and his other plays Fennario repeatedly demonstrates his laudable command of language and his keen ability to observe. He also shows a growing command of his craft. Now he needs to venture into new territory.

—S.R. Gilbert

FERLINGHETTI, Lawrence (Mendes-Monsanto). American. Born in Yonkers, New York, 24 March 1919; lived in France, 1920–24. Educated at Riverside Country School, 1927–28, and Bronxville Public School, 1929–33, both New York; Mount Hermon School, Greenfield, Massachusetts, 1933–37; University of North Carolina, Chapel Hill, B.A. in journalism 1941; Columbia University, New York, 1947–48, M.A. 1948; the Sorbonne, Paris, 1948–49, Doctorat de l'Université 1949. Served in the United States Naval Reserve, 1941–45: Lieutenant Commander. Married Selden Kirby-Smith in 1951 (divorced 1976); one daughter and one son. Worked for *Time* magazine, New York, 1945–46; French teacher, San Francisco, 1951–53. Co-founder, 1952, with Peter L. Martin, and since 1955 owner, City Lights Bookstore, and editor-in-chief, City Lights Books, San Francisco. Delegate, Pan American Cultural Conference, Concepción, Chile, 1960. Also a painter: individual show—Ethel Guttmann Gallery, San Francisco, 1985. Recipient: Etna-Taormina Prize (Italy), 1968. Address: City Lights Books, 261 Columbus Avenue, San Francisco, California 94133, U.S.A.

PUBLICATIONS

Plays

The Alligation (produced San Francisco, 1962; New York, 1970). Included in *Unfair Arguments with Existence*, 1963.

Unfair Arguments with Existence: Seven Plays for a New Theatre (includes *The Soldiers of No Country*, *Three Thousand Red Ants*, *The Alligation*, *The Victims of Amnesia*, *Motherlode*, *The Customs Collector in Baggy Pants*, *The Nose of Sisyphus*). New York, New Directions, 1963.

The Customs Collector in Baggy Pants (produced New York, 1964). Included in *Unfair Arguments with Existence*, 1963.

The Soldiers of No Country (produced London, 1969). Included in *Unfair Arguments with Existence*, 1963.

3 by Ferlinghetti: Three Thousand Red Ants, The Alligation, The Victims of Amnesia (produced New York, 1970). Included in *Unfair Arguments with Existence*, 1963.

Routines (includes 13 short pieces). New York, New Directions, 1964.

Novel

Her. New York, New Directions, 1960; London, MacGibbon and Kee, 1967.

Verse

Pictures of the Gone World. San Francisco, City Lights, 1955.
A Coney Island of the Mind. New York, New Directions, 1958.
Tentative Description of a Dinner Given to Promote the Impeachment of President Eisenhower. San Francisco, Golden Mountain Press, 1958.
One Thousand Fearful Words for Fidel Castro. San Francisco, City Lights, 1961.
Berlin. San Francisco, Golden Mountain Press, 1961.
Starting from San Francisco. New York, New Directions, 1961; revised edition, 1967.
Penguin Modern Poets 5, with Allen Ginsberg and Gregory Corso. London, Penguin, 1963.
Where Is Vietnam? San Francisco, City Lights, 1965.
To Fuck Is to Love Again; Kyrie Eleison Kerista; or, The Situation in the West; Followed by a Holy Proposal. New York, Fuck You Press, 1965.
Christ Climbed Down. Syracuse, New York, Syracuse University, 1965.
An Eye on the World: Selected Poems. London, MacGibbon and Kee, 1967.
After the Cries of the Birds. San Francisco, Dave Haselwood, 1967.
Moscow in the Wilderness, Segovia in the Snow. San Francisco, Beach, 1967.
Repeat After Me. Boston, Impressions Workshop, 1967(?).
Reverie Smoking Grass. Milan, East 128, 1968.
The Secret Meaning of Things. New York, New Directions, 1968.
Fuclock. London, Fire, 1968.
Tyrannus Nix? New York, New Directions, 1969; revised edition, 1973.
Back Roads to Far Towns after Basho. Privately printed, 1970.
Sometime During Eternity. Conshohocken, Pennsylvania, Poster Prints, 1970(?).
The World Is a Beautiful Place. Conshohocken, Pennsylvania, Poster Prints, 1970(?).
The Illustrated Wilfred Funk. San Francisco, City Lights, 1971.
A World Awash with Fascism and Fear. San Francisco, Cranium Press, 1971.
Back Roads to Far Places. New York, New Directions, 1971.
Love Is No Stone on the Moon: Automatic Poem. Berkeley, California, Arif Press, 1971.
Open Eye, with *Open Head*, by Allen Ginsberg. Melbourne, Sun, 1972; published separately, Cambridge, Massachusetts, Pomegranate Press, 1973.
Constantly Risking Absurdity. Brockport, New York, State University College, 1973.
Open Eye, Open Heart. New York, New Directions, 1973.
Populist Manifesto. San Francisco, Cranium Press, 1975; revised edition, San Francisco, City Lights, n.d.
Soon It Will Be Night. Privately printed, 1975(?).
The Jack of Hearts. San Francisco, City Lights, 1975(?).
Director of Alienation. San Francisco, City Lights, 1975(?).
The Old Italians Dying. San Francisco, City Lights, 1976.
Who Are We Now? New York, New Directions, 1976.
White on White. San Francisco, City Lights, 1977.
Adieu à Charlot. San Francisco, City Lights, 1978.
Northwest Ecolog. San Francisco, City Lights, 1978.
The Sea and Ourselves at Cape Ann. Madison, Wisconsin, Red Ozier Press, 1979.
Landscapes of Living and Dying. New York, New Directions, 1979.
The Love Nut. Lincoln, Massachusetts, Penmaen Press, 1979.
Mule Mountain Dreams. Bisbee, Arizona, Bisbee Press Collective, 1980.
A Trip to Italy and France. New York, New Directions, 1981.
The Populist Manifestos, Plus an Interview with Jean-Jacques Lebel. San Francisco, Grey Fox Press, 1981.
Endless Life: The Selected Poems. New York, New Directions, 1981.
Over All the Obscene Boundaries: European Poems and Transitions. New York, New Directions, 1984.

Recordings: *Poetry Readings in "The Cellar,"* with Kenneth Rexroth, Fantasy, 1958; *Tentative Description of a Dinner to Impeach President Eisenhower and Other Poems*, Fantasy, 1959; *Tyrannus Nix? and Assassination Raga*, Fantasy, 1971; *The World's Greatest Poets 1*, with Allen Ginsberg and Gregory Corso, CMS, 1971; *Lawrence Ferlinghetti*, Everett-Edwards, 1972.

Other

Dear Ferlinghetti/Dear Jack: The Spicer-Ferlinghetti Correspondence. San Francisco, White Rabbit Press, 1962(?).
The Mexican Night: Travel Journal. New York, New Directions, 1970.
A Political Pamphlet. San Francisco, Anarchist Resistance Press, 1975.
Literary San Francisco: A Pictorial History from Its Beginnings to the Present Day, with Nancy J. Peters. San Francisco, City Lights, 1980.
An Artist's Diatribe. San Diego, Atticus Press, 1983.
Leaves of Life: Fifty Drawings from the Model. San Francisco, City Lights, 1983.
Seven Days in Nicaragua Libre, photographs by Chris Felver. San Francisco, City Lights, 1984.

Editor, *Beatitude Anthology.* San Francisco, City Lights, 1960.
Editor, with Michael McClure and David Meltzer, *Journal for the Protection of All Beings 1* and *3*. San Francisco, City Lights, 2 vols., 1961–69.
Editor, *City Lights Journal.* San Francisco, City Lights, 4 vols., 1963–78.
Editor, *Panic Grass*, by Charles Upton. San Francisco, City Lights, 1969.
Editor, *The First Third*, by Neal Cassady. San Francisco, City Lights, 1971.
Editor, *City Lights Anthology.* San Francisco, City Lights, 1974.
Editor, with Nancy J. Peters, *City Lights Review 1.* San Francisco, City Lights, 1987.

Translator, *Selections from Paroles by Jacques Prévert.* San Francisco, City Lights, 1958; London, Penguin, 1963.
Translator, with Anthony Kahn, *Flowers and Bullets, and Freedom to Kill*, by Yevgeny Yevtushenko. San Francisco, City Lights, 1970.
Translator, with Richard Lettau, *Love Poems*, by Karl Marx. San Francisco, City Lights, 1977.
Translator, with Francesca Valente, *Roman Poems*, by Pier Paolo Pasolini. San Francisco, City Lights, 1986.

*

Bibliography: *Lawrence Ferlinghetti: A Comprehensive Bibliography to 1980* by Bill Morgan, New York, Garland, 1982.

Manuscript Collection: Bancroft Library, University of California, Berkeley.

Critical Studies: *Ferlinghetti: A Biography* by Neeli Cherkovsky, New York, Doubleday, 1979; *Lawrence Ferlinghetti: Poet-at-Large* by Larry Smith, Carbondale, Southern Illinois University Press, 1983.

* * *

Poet of the Beat Generation, Lawrence Ferlinghetti has published two volumes of short plays in prose. Ferlinghetti's plays, like his poems, are influenced by French Existentialist attitudes to love and death, but, like his fellow Beats, he replaces French Existentialist commitment by disaffiliation. Even before he turned to plays, Ferlinghetti "performed" his poems, sometimes with jazz accompaniment. His first volume of plays, *Unfair Arguments with Existence*, uses a casual American idiom for depicting existence as we know it in modern industrial society. The progression of the seven plays in this volume is from the roughly realistic to the distinctly symbolic. The next to last play is a monologue, and the last play spurns all dialogue, striving for a more improvisational effect.

In the longest Argument with Existence, *The Soldiers of No Country*, a 60-year-old priest and a 20-year-old deserter compete for the love of 35-year-old Erma. Watching this grotesque triangle in a womblike cave are many silent people who fall, one by one, to the ground. After the priest's victory, Erma stumbles out of the cave, and the deserter threatens the priest. Though the play seems to end in ubiquitous death, a baby cries within the cave, implying the possibility of rebirth.

Hope is fainter in the next two Arguments. *Three Thousand Red Ants* is an associational conversation between Fat and Moth, a married couple in bed. At the end Fat turns binoculars on the audience and exclaims that he sees a breakthrough, to which his wife replies under the bedclothes: "Your own! Humpty Dumpty!" In *The Alligation* Ladybird is fixated on her pet alligator, Shooky, though a Blind Indian warns her that this is dangerous. When Ladybird stretches full length on Shooky, he rolls over on top of her, and the Blind Indian calls to the audience for help. Both plays pose audience help as an implicit question.

Influenced by the Theatre of the Absurd, the next three Arguments are extended metaphors for the human condition. In *The Victims of Amnesia* a Night Clerk converses with a woman shown at four stages of diminishing age—Marie, Young Woman, Girl, Baby—all embraced in the name Mazda. At the play's end the Night Clerk *cum* Fate inveighs against all life, as the play explodes into smashing light bulbs of many sizes. But finally a single small bulb flickers in the dark before the theatre lights come up. Similarly, *Motherlode* theatricalizes the undimmed faith of a dying miner, even after the crass commercial Schmucks have despoiled the land. After the miner's death, with Schmuck triumphant, the birds still call "Love! Love!" *The Customs Collector in Baggy Pants* is set on a lifeboat "full of flush-toilets which we call civilization." Assailed by a storm outside and the storm of flushing toilets on the boat, the Customs Collector shouts his determination not to die or capitulate. Ferlinghetti punctuates the Absurd with hope.

In *The Nose of Sisyphus*, however, hope is all but extinguished. In a playground that is a metaphor for the world, Sisyphus uses his false nose to try to push a globe up a slide, while assorted human beings try to scale a jungle gym. Though Sisyphus cannot persuade the people to help him, he does succeed in leading their chants. But a whistle-blowing Big Baboon slides down the slide, toppling Sisyphus, frightening the people, and robbing Sisyphus of globe and nose. Alone on stage, the Big Baboon tosses the false nose into the audience. At best, one can hope for another Sisyphus to arise from the audience.

The Nose of Sisyphus is the last play in *Unfair Arguments with Existence*, and Ferlinghetti incorporates it as the last of the 13 pieces in his second volume of plays, *Routines*. He defines a routine as

> a song and dance, a little rout, a routing-out, a run-around, a "round of business or amusement": myriads of people, herds, flowerbeds, ships and cities, all going through their routines, life itself a blackout routine, an experimental madness somewhere between dotage and megalomania, lost in the vibration of a wreckage (of some other cosmos we fell out of).

All 13 Routines focus on visual metaphors, but they read rhythmically, with the free flexible rhythms of Ferlinghetti's poems. Their subjects are love, death, and the totalitarian establishment. Just before *The Nose of Sisyphus* appears *Bore*, a call to action: "Routines never end; they have to be broken. This little routine to end all routines requires the formation of a worldwide society dedicated to the non-violent disruption of institutionalized events." Play tries to infiltrate life in Ferlinghetti's final play.

—Ruby Cohn

FIERSTEIN, Harvey (Forbes). American. Born in Brooklyn, New York, 6 June 1954. Educated at Pratt Institute, Brooklyn, B.F.A. 1973. Drag performer and actor from 1970: professional debut at Club 82 and La Mama Experimental Theatre Club, New York, 1971; roles in more than 60 plays and in several films. Recipient: Rockefeller grant; Ford grant; Creative Artists Public Services grant; Obie award, 1982; Tony award, 1983 (for writing and acting), 1984; Oppenheimer award, 1983; Drama Desk award, 1983 (for writing and acting); Dramatists Guild Hull-Warriner Award, 1983; Los Angeles Drama Critics Circle award, 1984. Agent: George Lane, William Morris Agency, 1350 Avenue of the Americas, New York, New York 10019, U.S.A.

PUBLICATIONS

Plays

In Search of the Cobra Jewels (produced New York, 1972).
Freaky Pussy (produced New York, 1973).
Flatbush Tosca (produced New York, 1975).
Torch Song Trilogy (produced New York, 1981; London, 1985). New York, Gay Presses of New York, 1981; London, Methuen, 1984.
  The International Stud (produced New York, 1978).
  Fugue in a Nursery (produced New York, 1979).
  Widows and Children First! (produced New York, 1979).
Spookhouse (produced New York, 1982; London, 1987). Published in *Plays International* (London), July 1987.
La Cage aux Folles, music and lyrics by Jerry Herman, adaptation of the play by Jean Poiret (produced Boston and New York, 1983; London, 1986).

Manny and Jake (produced New York, 1987).
Safe Sex (includes *Manny and Jake*, *Safe Sex*, *On Tidy Endings*) (produced New York, 1987). New York, Atheneum, 1987.

* * *

Torch Song Trilogy, the gay playwright Harvey Fierstein's epic about the life and loves of drag queen Arnold Beckoff, is remarkable not only because it won numerous awards, but also because it marks one of the few times in history when homosexuality has been depicted on stage as a normal, healthy lifestyle. In *The Boys in the Band*, for example, the famous line, "You show me a happy homosexual and I'll show you a gay corpse," basically summed up the attitudes about homosexuals not only in theatre but also in film, until *Torch Song Trilogy* crossed over to become award-winning mainstream popular theatre.

The beginning for *Torch Song Trilogy* was 2 February 1978, when *The International Stud* opened off-off-Broadway at La Mama Theatre to such acclaim that its run was extended to a larger off-Broadway house. *The International Stud* is the first part in the *Trilogy*, and although it is a complete play unto itself, it sets up plot and character development for the trilogy. We are introduced to Arnold Beckoff (originally played by Fierstein himself), a drag entertainer whose life and loves are the melody of *Torch Song*. Arnold meets and falls in love with the bisexual Ed, who ultimately leaves him for Laurel, thereby setting the stage for *Fugue in a Nursery*. *The International Stud* contains one of the funniest and most touching explicit sex scenes in recent theater history (although there is no nudity)—when the rejected, brokenhearted Arnold makes his first foray into the backroom of the International Stud bar.

In the middle play in the trilogy, *Fugue in a Nursery*, Ed and Laurel invite Arnold and his new lover, Alan, to spend a weekend in the country. "Isn't this civilized," Laurel crows, as the seeds of destruction are sown in the furrows of everyone's relationships. Like *Stud*, *Fugue* did so well it transferred to a larger theater and also created a popular demand to find out how Arnold was going to cope with the rest of his life. The third play, *Widows and Children First!*, also opened at La Mama. Of the three, this is the most artistically mature. Arnold has grown up emotionally, and the characters are forced to take stock of who they are and what they want out of life and from each other. As *Torch Song Trilogy*, these three wildly popular plays moved together to Broadway in 1982.

Fierstein is a witty, clever writer, who has an unerring ear for truthful dialogue. However, the wide appeal of *Torch Song Trilogy* is due more to the fact that although Arnold is a flamboyant drag queen, he wants the same things from life that even the most conservative long for; the characters in the trilogy aspire to simple domesticity. As Fierstein says, "Nobody has guilt in *Torch Song*, and the straight people aren't unrealistically understanding. From my viewpoint, what else is there in this world to want but to have a job you don't hate too much, an apartment you can afford, and somebody to share it with."

Prior to the success of the three plays that make up the trilogy, Fierstein had gained a reputation in off-off-Broadway theaters and clubs as a female impersonator and author of outrageously camp pieces such as *In Search of the Cobra Jewels*, subtitled "An Archeomystical Poeseurie in Two Short Acts." This play is reputed to have been inspired by a job Fierstein took cleaning the cluttered, cockroach-infested apartment of the playwright Harry Koutoukas. It was quickly followed by the successful *Freaky Pussy*, in which Fierstein acted the part of a transvestite prostitute working out of a subway men's room. *Flatbush Tosca*, which he also wrote as an acting vehicle for himself, is an updated, transvestite version of the Puccini opera. The partly autobiographical *Torch Song Trilogy* came about when the breakup of a love affair left Fierstein so depressed that he was considering suicide. He wrote the play instead.

While starring on Broadway in *Torch Song Trilogy*, Fierstein began working on a musical adaptation of *La Cage aux Folles*, the French play by Jean Poiret from which two movies had already been made. In Fierstein's version, it is the insensitivity of the heterosexual son that disrupts the harmony of the family unit. That the "mother" and "father" are both men is almost incidental to the basic theme of the musical. Again, as in *Torch Song Trilogy*, homosexuals are shown as normal people, in this case, ordinary parents with a difficult child.

His next play was the short-lived *Spookhouse*, a drama about a gay social worker whose efforts to help a pathological family are a nightmare of ineptitude. The excessiveness of the metaphor—the horrible family in question lives over the spookhouse at Coney Island—gets in the way of the story about rape, incest, murder, and the urban poor. It is, without the overbearing special effects, unbelievable and uninvolving. Fierstein has returned to La Mama to try out his latest plays, three one acts: *Manny and Jake*, *Safe Sex*, and *On Tidy Endings*, presented under the title *Safe Sex*. The plays deal with various aspects of how human beings are dealing, or not dealing, with the fact of the Aids virus.

Thousands of young Jewish boys leave Brooklyn every year and become successful at a variety of jobs—business administration, medicine, teaching, truck driving, art, dope peddling, even playwriting. But only Harvey Fierstein left Brooklyn to become a world-famous homosexual and Tony Award-winning actor and playwright.

—Leah D. Frank

FOOTE, (Albert) Horton (Jr.). American. Born in Wharton, Texas, 14 March 1916. Educated at the Pasadena Playhouse Theatre, California, 1933–35; Tamara Daykarhanova Theatre School, New York, 1937–39. Married Lillian Vallish in 1945; two daughters and two sons. Actor with American Actors Theatre, New York, 1939–42; theatre workshop director and producer, King-Smith School of Creative Arts, 1944–45, and manager, Productions Inc., 1945–48, both Washington, D.C. Recipient: Oscar, for screenplay, 1963, 1983. D.Litt.: Austin College, Sherman, Texas, 1987; Drew University, Madison, New Jersey, 1987. Lives in New York City. Agent: Lucy Kroll Agency, 390 West End Avenue, New York, New York 10024, U.S.A.

Publications

Plays

Wharton Dance (produced New York, 1940).
Texas Town (produced New York, 1941).
Out of My House (also co-director: produced New York, 1942).
Only the Heart (produced New York, 1942). New York, Dramatists Play Service, 1944.
Two Southern Idylls: Miss Lou, and The Girls (produced New York, 1943).
The Lonely (produced New York, 1943).

Goodbye to Richmond (produced New York, 1943).
Daisy Lee, music by Bernardo Segall (produced New York, 1944).
Homecoming, In My Beginning, People in the Show, The Return (produced Washington, D.C., 1944).
Themes and Variations (produced Washington, D.C., 1945?).
Celebration (produced New York, 1948).
The Chase (produced New York, 1952). New York, Dramatists Play Service, 1952.
The Trip to Bountiful (televised 1953; produced New York, 1953; London, 1956). New York, Dramatists Play Service, 1954.
The Midnight Caller (televised 1953; produced New York, 1958). New York, Dramatists Play Service, 1959.
John Turner Davis (televised 1953; produced New York, 1958). Included in *A Young Lady of Property*, 1955.
The Dancers (televised 1954; produced Los Angeles, 1963). Included in *A Young Lady of Property*, 1955.
The Traveling Lady (produced New York, 1954). New York, Dramatists Play Service, 1955.
A Young Lady of Property: Six Short Plays (includes *A Young Lady of Property, The Dancers, The Old Beginning, John Turner Davis, The Death of the Old Man, The Oil Well*). New York, Dramatists Play Service, 1955.
Harrison, Texas: Eight Television Plays (includes *The Dancers, The Death of the Old Man, Expectant Relations, John Turner Davis, The Midnight Caller, The Tears of My Sister, The Trip to Bountiful, A Young Lady of Property*). New York, Harcourt Brace, 1956.
Flight (televised 1957). Published in *Television Plays for Writers*, edited by A. S. Burack. Boston, The Writer, 1957.
Old Man, adaptation of a story by Faulkner (televised 1958). Included in *Three Plays*, 1962.
Roots in a Parched Ground (as *The Night of the Storm*, televised 1960). Included in *Three Plays*, 1962.
Tomorrow, adaptation of the story by Faulkner (televised 1960). Included in *Three Plays*, 1962.
Three Plays. New York, Harcourt Brace, 1962.
The Screenplay of To Kill a Mockingbird. New York, Harcourt Brace, 1964.
Gone with the Wind, music and lyrics by Harold Rome, adaptation of the novel by Margaret Mitchell (produced London, 1972; Los Angeles, 1973).
The Roads to Home (includes *The Dearest of Friends, A Nightingale, Spring Dance*) (produced New York, 1982). New York, Dramatists Play Service, 1982.
Courtship (produced Louisville, 1984). Included in *Courtship, Valentine's Day, 1918*, 1987.
Tomorrow (television play) and *Tomorrow* (screenplay), in *Tomorrow and Tomorrow and Tomorrow* (also includes Faulkner's story "Tomorrow"), edited by David G. Yellin and Marie Conners. Jackson, University Press of Mississippi, 1985.
The Road to the Graveyard (produced New York, 1985).
Blind Date (produced New York, 1986). New York, Dramatists Play Service, 1986.
Lily Dale (produced New York, 1986).
The Widow Claire (produced New York, 1986).
Courtship, Valentine's Day, 1918. New York, Grove Press, 1987.

Screenplays: *Storm Fear*, 1955; *To Kill a Mockingbird*, 1962; *Baby, The Rain Must Fall*, 1964; *Hurry Sundown*, with Thomas Ryan, 1966; *Tomorrow*, 1972; *Tender Mercies*, 1983; *1918*, 1984; *The Trip to Bountiful*, 1985; *On Valentine's Day*, 1985; *Courtship*, 1986.

Television Plays: *Ludie Brooks*, 1951; *The Travelers*, 1952; *The Old Beginning*, 1952; *The Trip to Bountiful*, 1953; *A Young Lady of Property*, 1953; *The Oil Well*, 1953; *Rocking Chair*, 1953; *Expectant Relations*, 1953; *The Death of the Old Man*, 1953; *The Tears of My Sister*, 1953; *John Turner Davis*, 1953; *The Midnight Caller*, 1953; *The Dancers*, 1954; *The Shadow of Willie Greer*, 1954; *The Roads to Home*, 1955; *Drugstore: Sunday Noon*, 1956; *Flight*, 1957 (UK title: *Summer's Pride*, 1961); *Member of the Family*, 1957; *Old Man*, 1958; *Tomorrow*, 1960; *The Shape of the River*, 1960; *The Night of the Storm*, 1960; *The Gambling Heart*, 1964; *The Displaced Person*, from a story by Flannery O'Connor, 1977; *Barn Burning*, from the story by Faulkner, 1980; scripts for *Gabby Hayes Show*, 1950–51.

Novel

The Chase. New York, Rinehart, 1956.

*

Theatrical Activities:
Director: **Plays**—*Out of My House* (co-director, with Mary Hunter and Jane Rose), New York, 1942; *Goodbye to Richmond*, New York, 1946.
Actor: **Plays**—role in *The Eternal Road* by Franz Werfel, New York, 1937; with One-Act Repertory Company: Robert Emmet in *The Coggerers*, Lorenzo in *The Red Velvet Goat*, and Chief Outourou's Brother in *Mr. Banks of Birmingham*, New York, 1939; *Railroads on Parade*, New York, 1939; *Yankee Doodle Comes to Town*, toured, 1940; *The Fifth Column* by Ernest Hemingway, New York, 1940; Pharmacist in *Texas Town*, New York, 1941.

* * *

Since the 1940's, Horton Foote has been writing realistic plays about small-town families in southeastern Texas. Foote portrays ordinary citizens going about their daily business, suffering and enduring the rhythms and events of life. An accomplished creator of semi-rural atmosphere, Foote does not manipulate events to illustrate a premise; instead, he shows the details (both humdrum and exciting) of the passage of time, and the slow, unsteady forging of character under powerful social pressures. As a playwright Foote is unusually conscious of the virtues of patience. In his dramatic world attempts to force the pace of change—or to retard it—invite disaster.

A conservative artist, Foote ignores recent innovations in dramatic subject matter, form, or technique. His vignettes are rarely flashy or "theatrical." Foote never condescends to his characters, and his plays contain no special pleading for them. Onstage events may seem so simple, so routine, that Foote has been accused of substituting endless exposition for action. However, the placid surface of his genteel slices-of-life may conceal vivid psychological depths.

Many of Foote's plays began as films or television dramas. Some of his screen work survives the transition to three-dimensional life by virtue of strong conflicts or memorable characters, but a few of Foote's adaptations feel awkward and physically cramped on stage. Certain slight but crucial moments in the lives of these characters are less compelling without close-ups or evocative music on a sound track. Certain audiences find his low-key realism unremarkable and dreary, but Foote's accessibility, sly humor, and lack of pretension have won him many partisans among meat-and-potatoes theatregoers.

A typical Foote play may include several of the following elements: the sensitive children of parents who are separated, divorced, or clearly unsuited to each other must undergo some rite of passage that inches them toward adulthood. That state, while desirable, is not sentimentalized: Foote's grown-ups can behave childishly, engaging in emotional blackmail and power-tripping, while hiding deep feelings from themselves as well as from each other. Education and culture are viewed with suspicion by "practical" but smug, hidebound characters. The unpredictable weather, the capriciousness of disease and the vulnerable economy of East Texas in this century's early decades form the background to Foote's drama. In every generation such influences buffet families whose inner resources are as precarious as their bank balances. Footloose characters yearn for roots while their inert relatives yearn to wander; both Leaving Home and Coming Home are major themes. Foote's people endure harsh lives, submit to their fate, accept what life has to offer them. They find what heroism they can in hanging on, in trying over and over again, in refusing to cry over spilt milk. Pathos and passive suffering, alleviated by mild irony and a lightly satiric eye, are hallmarks of Foote's dramatic world.

Among Foote's most characteristic plays are *The Trip to Bountiful* and the trilogy *Courtship*, *Valentine's Day*, and *1918*. In *The Trip to Bountiful* Carrie Watts, a poor but proud widow, shares a Houston apartment with her hard-working but passive son Ludie and his wife Jessie Mae. Brassy, selfish, and lazy, Jessie Mae insists on controlling Mrs. Watts's small income. Her mother-in-law's habits irritate Jessie Mae, and she thinks the old woman is crazy for wanting to return to Bountiful—the tiny town she came from years ago. Mrs. Watts hides her government check from Jessie Mae and sets off on an exhausting bus trip to Bountiful. Unfortunately, the little town is defunct. Her old friend Callie Davis, Bountiful's last resident, was buried the day before. Meanwhile, Jessie Mae and Ludie have tracked her down, and are on their way to get her. A sympathetic sheriff drives Mrs. Watts to her old house, now derelict and sagging. When Ludie shows up, he and his mother discuss their long-ago decision to leave the land for the city—and how that choice now seems to have been disastrous for them. Bowing to the inexorability of change, Mrs. Watts makes peace with Jessie Mae, agreeing to all her daughter-in-law's demands. She says goodbye to Bountiful forever.

The trilogy, part of Foote's projected nine-play *The Orphans' Home* cycle, deals with the marriage and early manhood of Horace Robedaux—the cycle's central character, based on an ancestor of Foote's. His lawyer father dead of alcoholism, his mother remarried and moved to Houston, Horace has a reputation as a penniless rake who will never amount to much. But slowly and steadily, without fanfare, Horace turns himself into a respected citizen of Foote's fictional Harrison, Texas. A hard worker in various retail businesses, Horace has a natural kindness of heart that quietly knits the torn fabric of several families beside his own. In *Courtship*, set in 1915, Horace wins Elizabeth Vaughn despite her father's strong opposition to the match. Set on Christmas Eve of 1917, *Valentine's Day* offers a comparison of Horace and Elizabeth's strong marriage with a variety of offstage events. Their growing happiness contrasts with the venality and hopelessness displayed by other families in the community. In *1918* the influenza epidemic strikes both Horace and Jenny, the Robedaux's small daughter. Horace recovers, but Jenny dies. Elizabeth bears another child, and the devastated couple admit their love for each other even as they express their bitter sense of loss. Meanwhile, World War I ends, and Horace and Elizabeth accept their lot.

—David Copelin

FOREMAN, Richard. American. Born in New York City, 10 June 1937. Educated at Scarsdale High School, Scarsdale, New York; Brown University, Providence, Rhode Island, 1955–59, B.A. 1959; Yale University Drama School, New Haven, Connecticut, 1959–62, M.F.A. 1962. Married Amy Taubin in 1962 (divorced 1971). Writer with New Dramatists and Actors Studio, both New York, 1962–65; associate director, Film-Maker's Cinematheque, New York, 1967–68. Since 1968 founding director, Ontological-Hysteric Theatre, New York. Recipient: Obie award, 1970, 1973, 1976, 1986 (for directing); National Opera Institute grant, 1971; National Endowment for the Arts grant, 1972, 1974; Creative Artists Public Service grant, 1972, 1974; Rockefeller grant, 1974; Guggenheim fellowship, 1975. Agent: George Ashley, 325 Spring Street, New York, New York 10012. Address: 152 Wooster Street, New York, New York 10012, U.S.A.

PUBLICATIONS

Plays

Angelface (also director: produced New York, 1968).
Elephant-Steps, music by Stanley Silverman (also director: produced Lenox, Massachusetts, 1968; New York, 1970).
Ida-Eyed (also director: produced New York, 1969).
Real Magic in New York, music by Stephen Dickman (produced New York, 1969).
Total Recall: Sophia = (Wisdom) Part 2 (also director: produced New York, 1970).
Dream Tantras for Western Massachusetts, music by Stanley Silverman (also director: produced Lenox, Massachusetts, 1971).
HcOhTiEnLa; or, Hotel China (also director: produced New York, 1971). Excerpts published in *Performance 2* (New York), April 1972.
Evidence (also director: produced New York, 1972; selection, as *15 Minutes of Evidence*, produced New York, 1975).
Dr. Selavy's Magic Theatre, music by Stanley Silverman, lyrics by Tom Hendry (also director: produced Lenox, Massachusetts, and New York, 1972; Oxford, 1978).
Sophia = (Wisdom) Part 3: The Cliffs (also director: produced New York, 1972). Published in *Performance 6* (New York), May–June 1973.
Particle Theory (also director: produced New York, 1973).
Honor (also director: produced New York, 1973).
Classical Therapy; or, A Week under the Influence ... (also director: produced Paris, 1973).
Pain(t) (also director: produced New York, 1974).
Vertical Mobility: Sophia = (Wisdom) Part 4 (also director: produced New York, 1974). Published in *Drama Review 63* (New York), June 1974.
RA-D-IO (Wisdom); or, Sophia = (Wisdom) Part 1, music by David Tice (produced New York, 1974).
Pandering to the Masses: A Misrepresentation (also director: produced New York, 1975). Published in *The Theatre of Images*, edited by Bonnie Marranca, New York, Drama Book Specialists, 1975.
Hotel for Criminals, music by Stanley Silverman (also director: produced New York, 1975).
Rhoda in Potatoland (Her Fall-starts) (also director: produced New York, 1975).
Thinking (One Kind) (produced San Diego, 1975).
Le Théâtre de Richard Foreman, edited by Simone Benmussa and Erika Kralik. Paris, Gallimard, 1975.
Plays and Manifestos, edited by Kate Davy. New York, New York University Press, 1976.
Livre de Splendeurs (Part I) (produced Paris, 1976).
Lines of Vision, music by George Quincy, lyrics by María Irene Fornés (produced New York, 1976).
Slight (produced New York, 1977).
Book of Splendors (Part II): Book of Levers: Action at a Distance (also director: produced New York, 1977). Published in *Theater* (New Haven, Connecticut), Spring 1978.
Blvd. de Paris (I've Got the Shakes) (produced New York, 1978).
The American Imagination, music by Stanley Silverman (produced New York, 1978).
Luogo + Bersaglio (Place + Target) (produced Rome, 1979).
Madame Adare, music by Stanley Silverman (produced New York, 1980).
Penguin Touquet (also director: produced New York, 1981).
Café Amérique (produced Paris, 1982).
Egyptology: My Head Was a Sledgehammer (produced New York, 1983).

George Bataille's Bathrobe (produced Paris, 1984).
Miss Universal Happiness (also director: produced New York, 1985).
Reverberation Machines: The Later Plays and Essays. Barrytown, New York, Station Hill Press, 1985.
Africanis Instructus, music by Stanley Silverman (also director: produced New York, 1986).
The Cure, music by Foreman (produced New York, 1986).

Screenplays: *Out of the Body Travel*, 1975; *City Archives*, 1977; *Strong Medicine*, 1978.

*

Manuscript Collections: Lincoln Center Library of the Performing Arts, New York; Anthology Film Archives, New York.

Critical Studies: "Richard Foreman's Ontological-Hysteric Theatre" by Michael Kirby, in *Drama Review* (New York), June 1973; *Richard Foreman and the Ontological-Hysteric Theatre* by Kate Davy, Ann Arbor, Michigan, UMI Research Press, 1981.

Theatrical Activities:
Director: **Plays**—most of his own plays (also designer); *The Threepenny Opera* by Brecht, New York, 1976; *Stages* by Stuart Ostrow, New York, 1978; *Don Juan* by Molière, Minneapolis, 1981; *Three Acts of Recognition* by Botho Strauss, New York, 1982; *Die Fledermaus* by Johann Strauss, Paris, 1984; *Dr. Faustus Lights the Lights* by Gertrude Stein, Paris, 1984; *Golem* by H. Levick, New York, 1984; *My Life My Death* by Kathy Acker, Paris, 1985; *The Birth of the Poet* by Kathy Acker, New York, 1985; *Largo Desolato* by Václav Havel, New York, 1986.

Richard Foreman comments:

In 1968 I began to write for the theatre which I wanted to see, which was radically different from any style of theatre that I had seen. In brief, I imagined a theatre which broke down all elements into a kind of atomic structure—and showed those elements of story, action, sound, light, composition, gesture, in terms of the smallest building-block units, the basic cells of the perceived experience of both living and art-making.

The scripts themselves read like notations of my own process of imagining a theatre piece. They are the evidence of a kind of effort in which the mind's leaps and inventions may be rendered as part of a process not unique to the artist in question (myself) but typical of the building-up which goes on through all modes of coming-into-being (human and non-human). I want to refocus the attention of the spectator on the intervals, gaps, relations and rhythms which saturate the objects (acts and physical props) which are the "givens" of any particular play. In doing this, I believe the spectator is made available (as I am, hopefully, when writing) to those most desirable energies which secretly connect him (through a kind of resonance) with the foundations of his being.

* * *

Richard Foreman's statement "I have developed a style that shows how it is with us, in consciousness. I don't speak in generalities. I show the mind at work, moment-by-moment" is perhaps the best starting point from which to approach his theatre. His plays eschew plot, characters, development, and even emotions in the attempt to dramatize the process of thinking itself. Each moment in the theatre corresponds to a moment in consciousness, and the relationships between them, or between the moments in the theatre, may not be immediately obvious. In *Rhoda in Potatoland* actors discuss writing, but digress to a dinner of potatoes. As in any train of thought ("Do you think using the associative method," says Foreman's Voice in *Pandering to the Masses*. "Everybody does you know."), potatoes become part of the freight, and the play begins to compare everything to a potato. After a digression for an all-girl band and a shoe store, a sign announces "THE RETURN OF THE POTATOES" and with the entrance of four human-sized potatoes, the Voice says

> Now this is where the interesting part of the
> evening begins. Everything up to now was
> Recognizable.
>
> Now, however
> The real potatoes are amongst us
> And a different kind of understanding is possible
> for anybody who wants a different kind of
> understanding.

Thereafter "potato" becomes a kind of counter, a word that can replace another word or form comparisons and links with other objects. Even when the word is replaced by other words, Foreman follows the linguistic philosophy of Ludwig Wittgenstein, as he interprets it: "Use anything, to mean anything, but the system must have a rigor."

To perform consciousness rigorously, Foreman developed techniques which allow tight control over the presentation. His plays are performed by untrained actors (many of whom reappear from one play to the next), who speak their lines flatly, without inflection. In some of the performances, the actors only murmur key words of their pre-recorded dialogue. Their words are frequently repeated, their sentences broken into fragments, and their phrases echoed by another character. While they do not perform a character, their gestures are also repeated in a hieratic style until they lose their original significance and acquire a new one from the course of the play.

Although there are no sets, the visual side of Foreman's theatre is crucial. Backdrops are used to present a fleeting image, to introduce a stray thought. Small stages reproduce the larger scene, and the actors themselves freeze into tableaux. Strings, ropes, and pieces of wood or paper stretch across the stage, link props or actors, or divide the stage into smaller frames. Buzzers, lights, and noises create other aural and visual "frames," to isolate words and actions.

No description of this odd theatre can suggest the power that these slow, measured plays can build. As the performances progress, the incomprehensible actions and incidents take their place in an overall design, not with a logical inevitability, but with a psychological appropriateness. As in Gertrude Stein's landscape plays, dialogue and incident are meant to be seen all together and simultaneously, not as a sequential development. A part of the power of the plays arises from the effort of the spectator in deciphering each individual moment like the facet in a Cubist painting, and then assembling them into a whole.

Foreman has described his plays as being what happens in his mind as he is writing a play. Recently, however, he has been increasingly directing other playwright's works, and it is possible that this expansion of his artistic universe is infecting his playwriting. *Egyptology* hints at a real setting (Egypt), and includes Louis XIV, who may have come from Foreman's having directed Molière's *Don Juan. Miss Universal Happiness* topically includes Central American guerrillas even as it asserts that "the self you seek is inside you." *The Cure* not only provides a moment of emotional contact, but even a hesitant attempt at synthesis and statement: "The pain is the cure," says one of the characters. All of this is undoubtedly happening in Foreman's mind, and while we may debate whether such a detailed presentation of one man's mind is appropriate to the theatre, that is precisely the kind of debate Foreman would enjoy: "The play's over. You're left with your own thoughts. Can you really get interested in them or are they just occurring."

—Walter Bode

FORNÉS, María Irene. American. Born in Havana, Cuba, 14 May 1930; emigrated to the United States, 1945; became citizen, 1951. Educated in Havana public schools. Lived in Europe, 1954–57; painter and textile designer; costume designer, Judson Poets Theatre and New Dramatists Committee productions, 1965–70; teacher at the Teachers and Writers Collaborative, New York, privately, and at numerous drama festivals and workshops, from 1965. President, New York Theatre Strategy, 1973–80. Recipient: Whitney fellowship, 1961; Centro Mexicano de Escritores fellowship, 1962; Office for Advanced Drama Research grant, 1965; Obie award, 1965, 1977, 1979, 1982, 1984, 1985; Cintas Foundation fellowship, 1967; Yale University fellowship, 1967, 1968; Rockefeller fellowship, 1971, 1985; Guggenheim fellowship, 1972; Creative Artists Public Service grant, 1972, 1975; National Endowment for the Arts grant, 1974; American Academy award, 1985. Agent: Helen Merrill Ltd., 361 West 17th Street, New York, New York 10011. Address: 1 Sheridan Square, New York, New York 10014, U.S.A.

PUBLICATIONS

Plays

The Widow (produced New York, 1961). Published, as *La Viuda*, in *Teatro Cubano*, Havana, Casa de las Américas, 1961.
Tango Palace (as *There! You Died*, produced San Francisco, 1963; as *Tango Palace*, produced New York, 1964; revised version produced Minneapolis, 1965). Included in *Promenade and Other Plays*, 1971.
The Successful Life of Three: A Skit for Vaudeville (produced Minneapolis and New York, 1965). Included in *Promenade and Other Plays*, 1971.
Promenade, music by Al Carmines (produced New York, 1965; revised version produced New York, 1969). Included in *Promenade and Other Plays*, 1971.
The Office (produced New York, 1966).
A Vietnamese Wedding (produced New York, 1967). Included in *Promenade and Other Plays*, 1971.
The Annunciation (also director: produced New York, 1967).
Dr. Kheal (produced New York, 1968; London, 1969). Included in *Promenade and Other Plays*, 1971.
The Red Burning Light; or, Mission XQ3 (produced Zurich, 1968; New York, 1969). Included in *Promenade and Other Plays*, 1971.
Molly's Dream music by Cosmos Savage (produced Lenox, Massachusetts, 1968; also director: produced New York, 1968). Included in *Promenade and Other Plays*, 1971.
Promenade and Other Plays. New York, Winter House, 1971; revised edition, New York, Performing Arts Journal Publications, 1987.
The Curse of the Langston House, in *Baboon!!!* (produced Cincinnati, 1972).
Dance, with Remy Charlip (also co-director: produced London, 1972).
Aurora, music by John FitzGibbon (also director: produced New York, 1974).
Cap-a-Pie, music by José Raúl Bernardo (also director: produced New York, 1975).
Lines of Vision (lyrics only), book by Richard Foreman, music by George Quincy (produced New York, 1976).
Washing (produced New York, 1976).
Fefu and Her Friends (also director: produced New York, 1977). Published in *Wordplays 1*, New York, Performing Arts Journal Publications, 1980.
Lolita in the Garden, music by Richard Weinstock (also director: produced New York, 1977).
In Service (also director: produced Padua Hills, California, 1978).
Eyes on the Harem (also director: produced New York, 1979).
Blood Wedding, adaptation of a play by García Lorca (produced New York, 1980).
Evelyn Brown: A Diary (also director: produced New York, 1980).
Life Is Dream, adaptation of a play by Calderón, music by George Quincy (also director: produced New York, 1981).
A Visit, music by George Quincy (also director: produced Padua Hills, California, and New York, 1981).
The Danube (also director: produced Padua Hills, California, 1982; New York, 1983). Included in *Plays*, 1986.
Mud (also director: produced Padua Hills, California, and New York, 1983; revised version, also director: produced Omaha, 1985). Included in *Plays*, 1986.
Sarita, music by Leon Odenz (also director: produced New York, 1984). Included in *Plays*, 1986.
Abingdon Square (produced Seattle, 1984).
The Conduct of Life (also director: produced New York, 1985). Included in *Plays*, 1986.
Cold Air, adaptation of a play by Virgilio Piñera (also director: produced New York, 1985).
Drowning, adaptation of a story by Chekhov, in *Orchards* (produced Urbana, Illinois, 1985; New York, 1986). New York, Knopf, 1986.
The Trial of Joan of Arc on a Matter of Faith (also director: produced New York, 1986).
Lovers and Keepers, music by Tito Puente and Ferrando Rivas, lyrics by Fornés (also director: produced New York, 1986).
Art, in *Box Plays* (produced New York, 1986).
The Mothers (also director: produced Padua Hills, California, 1986).
Plays. New York, Performing Arts Journal Publications, 1986.

*

Manuscript Collection: Lincoln Center Library of the Performing Arts, New York.

Critical Studies: interviews with Rob Creese in *Drama Review* (New York), December 1977, with Gayle Austin in *Theatre Times* (New York), March 1984, with Allen Frame in *Bomb* (New York), Fall 1984, and with Scott Cummings in *Theater* (New Haven, Connecticut), Winter 1985; "The Real Life of María Irene Fornés," in *Theatre Writings* by Bonnie Marranca, New York, Performing Arts Journal Publications, 1984; "Creative Danger" by Fornés, in *American Theatre* (New York), September 1985; preface by Susan Sontag to *Plays*, 1986.

Theatrical Activities:
Director: **Plays**—several of her own plays; *Exiles* by Ana Maria Simo, New York, 1982.

*   *   *

A loose, objectifying abstraction or the opacity of realized detail, rather than plot, is the likely pivot of a María Irene Fornés script. Reviews have ranged from annoyed to ecstatic. By 1982 Fornés's plays, designs, lyrics, and directing represented "Sustained Achievement" and earned her a special Obie. For more than 20 years she has walked the stylistic edges of the avant garde and experimental theatre—especially since *Tango Palace*, *The Successful Life of Three* for the Open Theatre, and the script and lyrics for *Promenade*. Despite the currency of her form (*Dr. Kheal*) and, often, her themes (*The Danube*), her plays refuse to settle for "reductively psychological and ... sociological explanations" (Susan Sontag's phrase) as the underlying truth. Even the fairly consistent if selective realism of *Fefu and Her Friends*, *Mud*, *Sarita*, *Cold Air*, and *The Conduct of Life* moves with the odd undulations of an idiosyncratic human heart (and mind) and can give rise to the magic startlings of her considered theatricality. From the first, Fornés's broad and playful sense of attention and of verbal and visual images poked audiences with freakishly or theatrically exalted characters, both innocent and experienced. In her later, seriously passionate plays, comic provocations of a laugh or grimace still reveal a fresh point of view. Fornés, a poignant and humorous playwright, frequently gives the theatrical experience a wise twist or the dramatic event a twist of wisdom.

The professor's ridiculous harangue in *Dr. Kheal* and the antic symbiosis of sadism and masochism in life and art that locks the naive Leopold and the strenuous Isidore into *Tango Palace* now seem too familiar as comic-didactic theatre pieces. Their respective modes and theme are more fully realized in the songs and the Crosby-Hope *Road*-show format of *Promenade*. In their journey from cell back to cell, from womb to tomb or tomb to womb, prisoners 105 and 106 must constantly trick or elude the pursuing Jailer—a dumb, sexually overactive beast. Tunnelling out into a snooty Banquet, 105 and 106 meet Miss Cake, ally themselves with the Servant (she seeks the meaning of life), and escape after robbing the rich guests who nod off after stupid self-indulgence. Mother, seeking her long-lost babes, joins the lengthening line of their pursuers. She and the fugitives play a tender double Pietà with two Soldiers on the Battlefield, before the tyrannical Mayor sends them all back to jail to escape again. The cruelty and criminality are casual. After the Servant's fond farewell and Mother's tucking-in, the prisoners remain alone—like everyone else, neither informed nor changed by their adventures.

The more raucous roadshow of *The Red Burning Light* lacks the simple effectiveness of audience participation offered by *A Vietnamese Wedding*. The frantic points of the "telling" farce-musical are less persuasively anti-war than the dignified ceremony and participation. Equally direct by denser, *The Danube* creates a more bloated horror out of America's naive, almost innocent international policies and wars. From 1938 till whenever, in Budapest, a very nice Paul and a sweet Eve meet with Basic Sentences in units (scenes) of Hungarian-English lessions; Paul stays and they marry, decline with mysterious sickness, blame each other. The last two lessons, most difficult to learn, are repeated as puppet shows and human scenes until Paul and Eve, contorted and red-spotted, exit together to the murder-suicide of a white-flash explosion of pistol shot or nuclear blast.

The Cuban-American playwright adds to positive dual-cultural understanding in her translation-adaptation of *Cold Air*, Piñera's family chronicle of grinding poverty from 1940 to 1958 in Havana. These cultural roots enrich her own *Sarita* that tells of Sarita's incinerating, self-destructive passion for Julio. Trapped in poverty and the South Bronx, between Cuban and American values and Catholic-pagan gods, she tries from age 13 in 1939 to follow her mind away from Julio but can't, despite his ruthless betrayals and her "nice" new husband Mark's understanding. Sarita hates herself ever more deeply, as momentary vignettes and songs lead her to stab her lover-destroyer to death in 1947. Mark clasps her hand in the hospital. Some hope?

Movie timing and allusion activate a young couple and an older man through ten semi-burlesque scenes of *The Successful Life of Three*, as their looks at each other (He "disdainful"; She "stupid") become part of the dialogue. *Molly's Dream* uses the bar-setting of Hollywood westerns and Molly's Dietrich-like pose to ridicule various forms of machismo and romance, but it arrives at the poignant missed-chance-for-love as Molly dozes and Young Man re-enters without his five Hanging (-on) Women, notices her, and leaves without waking her.

The intricate human relationships among Mae and Lloyd (both 25) and the older, semi-literate Henry are compassionately realized in *Mud*, one of Fornés's best plays. Behind the ignorant, repetitious, brutal language, both Mae and Lloyd yearn for nourishment and to nourish: dinner, health, sex, learning. Trying to recreate themselves out of the red mud they are moving into a new phase, as reflected in the actors' exiting one scene to pivot visibly in the doorway to re-enter for the next. Mae brings in the meaner-spirited Henry to read a pamphlet about Lloyd's sickness and to teach her to read. Not wanting to live like an animal, Mae mistakes Henry for "heaven"; Lloyd weeps but learns to read, cure himself, and nurture Henry who becomes greedy, mocking, and crippled. Mae tries to flee the destructive combat of Henry and Lloyd ("Lloyd is good, Henry. And this is his home"), but Lloyd chases, shoots her, and brings her back, bleeding. A similar gunshot ends the bright agony of *Fefu and Her Friends* and the brutal agony of *The Conduct of Life*.

In *Fefu and Her Friends* seven already accomplished women arrive to plan with Fefu a panel presentation on education. Fefu considers herself, alternately, bright and "loathsome," certainly "outrageous"—which she proves by shooting a rifle (only blanks?) at her husband through the window. He falls and dusts himself off; men are lucky. Only female dancers are without the heavy insides, observes Julia, crippled and dying of a malady and hallucinations. Even the ferocious Fefu who must, for her own self-respect and survival, save Julia, cannot do so. Fefu shoots again outside and Julia dies with blood on her forehead. In her *Performing Arts Journal* interview Fornés explains her effective device for bringing viewers into real intimacy with her characters: after watching the first scene, the audience is quartered and led into rooms with the actors who play four revealing scenes four times each, before all return to the auditorium for the last scene. *Fefu* is a mature play, ripe with nuance and mystery.

The Conduct of Life shows women in three roles in relation to Orlando, 33, who rises as state torturer on the mutilated bodies and minds of his victims. He ridicules the intellectual and spiritual aspirations of his wife Leticia, who tolerates his humiliations and betrayals. He rapes, enslaves, tortures, and installs in his cellar, as a servant, 12-year-old Nena who "receives" those who hurt her "since maybe they are in worse pain than me." He ignores or mocks the servant Olimpia who seethes with anger but will survive. It is the women's play, especially Leticia's. She does learn some independence and political science but remains petulantly childish with Olimpia and grovelling toward her husband; she resists knowledge of evil, especially his, and adapts rather than takes action. When the torture comes home to her breast, she accepts her responsibility, her identity with both Orlando and his victims, shoots him and gives Nena the gun to shoot her. No solution, but a fascinating theatrical exploration of the consequences of moral distancing in human actions.

—John G. Kuhn

FORSYTH, James (Law). British. Born in Glasgow, Lanark, 5 March 1913. Educated at Glasgow High School, graduated 1930; Glasgow School of Art, diploma in drawing and painting 1934. Married 1) Helen Steward in 1938 (divorced 1953), two sons; 2) Louise Tibble in 1955. Served in the Scots Guards, 2nd Monmouthshire Regiment, 1940–46: Captain, Battalion Adjutant; Bronze Cross of the Netherlands. Worked with the General Post Office Film Unit, 1937–40; dramatist-in-residence, Old Vic Company: worked with the Old Vic School and the Young Vic, 1946–48; dramatist-in-residence, Howard University, Washington, D.C., 1962; guest director and lecturer, Tufts University, Medford, Massachusetts, 1963; Distinguished Professor-in-Residence, Florida State University, Tallahassee, 1965; director, Tufts University Program in London, 1967–71. Since 1972 artistic director, The Forsyths' Barn Theatre, Ansty, Sussex. Member of the Executive Council, League of Dramatists and Radio Writers Association, 1954–64; founding member, Theatres Advisory Council. Recipient: Arts Council bursary, 1980. Agent: Cecily Ware, 19c John Spencer Square, London N1 2LZ; or, Harold Freedman, Brandt and Brandt, 1501 Broadway, New York, New York 10036, U.S.A. Address: Grainloft, Ansty, Haywards Heath, Sussex RH17 5AG, England.

PUBLICATIONS

Plays

Trog (broadcast 1949; produced Coventry, 1959; Tallahassee, Florida, 1964).
Brand, adaptation of the play by Ibsen (broadcast 1949; produced London, 1964). London, Heinemann, and New York, Theatre Arts, 1960.
The Medicine Man (produced London, 1950).
Emmanuel: A Nativity Play (broadcast 1950; produced London and New York, 1960). London, Heinemann, 1952; New York, Theatre Arts, 1963.
Héloïse (broadcast 1951; produced Southsea, Hampshire, and London, 1951; New York, 1958). Included in *Three Plays*, 1957; New York, Theatre Arts, 1958.
The Other Heart (broadcast 1951; produced London, 1952; also director: produced Medford, Massachusetts, 1963). Included in *Three Plays*, 1957; New York, Theatre Arts, 1964; revised version, as *Villon*, music by Gardner Read (produced New Orleans, 1981).
Adelaise (broadcast 1951; produced Ashburton, Devon, 1953). Included in *Three Plays*, 1957.
Three Plays. London, Heinemann, 1957.
The Pier (televised 1957; produced Bristol, 1958).
The Road to Emmaus: A Play for Eastertide. London, Heinemann, 1958; New York, Theatre Arts, 1972.
Joshua, music by Franz Waxman (produced Dallas, 1960). New York, Ricordi, 1959.
Dear Wormwood, adaptation of *The Screwtape Letters* by C.S. Lewis (produced Brighton, 1965). Chicago, Dramatic Publishing Company, 1961; as *Screwtape*, 1973.
Fifteen Strings of Money, adaptation of a play by Guenther Weisenhorn based on a story by Chu Su-chen (produced Pitlochry, Perthshire, 1961).
Everyman (produced Coventry, 1962).
Defiant Island (produced Washington, D.C., 1962). Chicago, Dramatic Publishing Company, 1975.
Seven Scenes for Yeni (produced Boston, 1963).
Cyrano de Bergerac, adaptation of the play by Edmond Rostand (produced Sarasota, Florida, 1963; London, 1967; New York, 1968). Chicago, Dramatic Publishing Company, 1968.
If My Wings Heal (produced Stroud, Gloucestershire, 1966).
Four Triumphant (televised 1966; as *Festival of Four*, produced Ansty, Sussex, 1976).
What the Dickens, adaptation of the novel *The Pickwick Papers* by Dickens (produced Ansty, Sussex, 1974).
Lobsterback (produced Boston and Ansty, Sussex, 1975).
No Crown for Herod (as *Christmas at Greccio*, produced Ansty, Sussex, 1976). Chicago, Dramatic Publishing Company, 1977.
The Play of Alban (produced St. Albans, 1977).
"N" for Napoleone (produced Ansty, Sussex, 1978).
When the Snow Lay Round About (broadcast 1978; as *Wenceslas*, produced Ansty, Sussex, 1980).
A Time of Harvest (produced Ansty, Sussex, 1981; as *The Threshing Floor*, broadcast 1982).

Screenplays: *The End of the Road*, with Geoffrey Orme, 1954; *Francis of Assisi*, with Eugene Vale and Jack Thomas, 1961.

Radio Plays: *The Bronze Horse*, 1948; *Trog*, 1949; *Brand*, 1949; *Emmanuel*, 1950; *Seelkie*, music by Brian Easdale, 1950; *The Other Heart*, 1951; *Adelaise*, 1951; *Héloïse*, 1951; *The Nameless One of Europe*, 1951; *For He's a Jolly Good Fellow*, 1952; *Pig*, 1953; *The Festive Spirit*, 1955; *Lisel*, 1955; *Christophe*, 1958; *Every Pebble on the Beach*, 1963; *When the Snow Lay Round About*, 1978; *The Threshing Floor*, 1982.

Television Plays: *Old Mickmack*, 1955; *The Pier*, 1957; *Underground*, from a novel by Harold Rein, 1958; *Four Triumphant*, 1966; *The English Boy*, 1969; *The Last Journey*, 1972; *The Old Man's Mountain*, 1972.

Other

Tyrone Guthrie: A Biography. London, Hamish Hamilton, 1976.
Back to the Barn. Anstey, Sussex, Grainloft, 1986.

*

Manuscript Collection: Lincoln Center Library of the Performing Arts, New York.

Theatrical Activities:
Director: **Play**—*The Other Heart*, Medford, Massachusetts, 1963.

James Forsyth comments:

(1982) The plays themselves being the playwright's *more than* personal statement to the public, I am reluctant to make other statements. I say "more than personal" and I say "play-*wright*" (not playwrite) for these reasons: That Theatre, where it is more than a show for Entertainment or Propaganda purposes, is an Art—an all-arts Art—and in Art the thing wrought out of the raw material is a thing in itself and speaks for itself. I *wright* for the Theatre as a performing place for the Art of Theatre, a tough and practical and popular art. The *writing* of the playwright is only the recording art which ends up with a script. The script ends up with "the thing itself" which is the event, the production. And it is all *wrought* out of the many arts of the playwright in the fields of sight, sound, touch, etc., realized in any playhouse by all the contributory arts of those who were once, and accurately, referred to as "artistes."

I had started life as an artist painter and sculptor, and my apprenticeship to the art of the theatre, with the Old Vic Company of Guthrie and Olivier, gave me a taste for the all-arts theatre and also for epic theatre. I am a playwright because I have found that the live event of the play is the best occasion in the world for the communion with—the sharing of artistic experience with—an audience; and the art of Theatre is the best medium for creation of the concepts worth sharing.

But the all-arts theatre is a hard road in a world of theatre brutally constricted by cash considerations, a constriction relieved only a bit by subsidy of certain playhouses and the heroism of "fringe" and "off-off" companies. That is why I have directed, for the last ten years, my own plays in my own barn which is a natural playhouse with an enthusiastic audience and a company of so-called "amateurs" who have become professed to the Art of Theatre to a professional degree. But in turning away in some despair from the world of the professional theatre and showbiz in its present state to this limited but real local success in the art, I have not of course "made a living" from it, which begins to make this statement more "personal" than necessary. But by the subsidy of an Arts Council bursary I have been able to complete what could be my most important play, *The Spanish Captain*.

*   *   *

Craft is fundamental to all art, although not all craftsmen are artists, any more than every artist is a craftsman. Indeed today, as artists are promoted by PRs, craft has become somewhat unfashionable. Hence the well-made play has, of recent years, come to be regarded as something slightly old-fashioned. Yet the virtue of a well-made play is that it knows how to tell a story, how to hold an audience, and this is an essential part of the dramatist's craft.

James Forsyth is such a playwright and this term is perhaps the most pat of all for an author who has himself said (January 1972): "I have yet to wright my best play. And 'wright' is right, I am not a 'dramatist,' I am a 'playwright.' Drama is the stuff, plays are the works, and I am professed to works."

His works are prolific, a steady output over the years, from the Old Vic production of *The Other Heart* to a television series on the patron saints of England, Scotland, Ireland and Wales, to *The Last Journey*, a 90-minute television play on Tolstoy.

The Other Heart is one of Forsyth's strongest and most powerfully constructed plays and full of excellent small character studies such as that of Marthe, the servant, who when asked why she risks her life in coming to Paris during the plague replies, "I need to help." In the character of the romantic poet, François Villon, Forsyth catches marvellously the impetuosity of young love, and the radiant recklessness of the visionary and poet. They are qualities that seem to attract him again and again. While he is drawn to "wrighting" plays about historical characters, it is noticeable how many of them are variations upon the theme of "a pair of starcrossed lovers." In this play we have Villon and Catherine de Vausselles; we have also Francis and Clare in *If My Wings Heal*, Héloïse and Abelard in *Héloïse*; in *The Last Journey*, a study of the last days of Tolstoy, Forsyth has written brilliantly of the tragic gap between a husband and wife.

The clash of the idealist with reality is perhaps, however, the profoundest recurring theme in all Forsyth's work. It has attracted him to a powerful adaptation of Ibsen's *Brand*, and in *If My Wings Heal* he sets out to explore the conflict between St. Francis of Assisi, the creative artist, poet, visionary, and Brother Elias, the ambitious administrative genius of the Franciscan Order. It was Brother Elias who wanted to turn the Friars Minor into the most powerful order within the Church, "for the sake of possession, for the possession of power." As one of the Friars remarks, "It was never Brother Francis's idea that we should be other than small bands, always on the move. We were to be the salt which is scattered."

This is a tougher and less sentimental rendering of the story of Francis of Assisi than the *Little Plays of St. Francis* by Laurence Housman, or the five-act devotional drama by Henri Ghéon, *The Marriage of St. Francis*. Only the scene of the stigmata fails. Perhaps it is an impossibility—to put on the stage a mystical experience. Perhaps only a major poet, such as T.S. Eliot, whose insight into the transcendental was close to that of the great mystics themselves, could really tackle such a scene. If Forsyth is a playwright proven he is, I think, a poet *manqué*. His weakest writing stems almost always from a tendency to poeticize, to lapse into obvious rhyming blank verse. Yet in theatre terms one can see what he is about for the steady beat and rhythm of these passages serve to carry the story forward.

David, *Andrew*, *Patrick*, and *George* (*Four Triumphant*) are four full-length plays, envisaged as a cycle, to be performed over two days. They embody not merely the history of the four patron saints but are a study of the pioneers of Christianity. Each play is self-sufficient, and yet each gains from its relation to the others.

Perhaps Forsyth's most memorable play is *Defiant Island*, the true story of Henri Christophe, the first black king of Haiti. It is a deeply moving tragedy of an idealist who is led astray by his fanatical devotion to his own ideals, so that the man is destroyed at the expense of the image of himself as the first black monarch. Finally, when Napoleon insists on "nothing less than the total extinction of every adult black, male and female," Henri Christophe, who had naively believed that all men could meet in equal justice, has to admit to himself, "I asked too much. It is a fault in me."

Henri Christophe, Brand, Abelard, Villon, Francis of Assisi are all portraits of men of thought suffused with passion; they are the solitary visionaries, the reckless romantics, the uncomfortable reformers; in the true sense of the word they are heroes. Forsyth belongs to that great tradition of bardic poets, who sang the exploits and epics of heroes. It is a tradition that is at present a little out of fashion, but fashions change and the wheel comes full circle. When that happens Forsyth will find he has wrought his best play.

—James Roose-Evans

FOSTER, Paul. American. Born in Penns Grove, New Jersey, 15 October 1931. Educated at schools in Salem, New Jersey; Rutgers University, New Brunswick, New Jersey, 1950–54, B.A. 1954; St. John's University Law School, New York, 1954, 1957, 1958. Served in the United States Naval Reserve, 1955–57. Since 1962 co-founder and President, La Mama Experimental Theater Club, New York. U.S. Department of State lecturer, 1975, 1976, 1977; Fulbright lecturer, Brazil, 1980; taught at University of California, San Diego, 1981, and New York University, 1983. Recipient: Rockefeller fellowship, 1967; Irish Universities award, 1967, 1971; New York Drama Critics Circle award, 1968; Creative Artists Public Service grant, 1972, 1974; National Endowment for the Arts grant, 1973; Arts Council of Great Britain award, 1973; Guggenheim fellowship, 1974; Bulandra Foreign Play award, 1983. Address: 242 East 5th Street, New York, New York 10003, U.S.A.

PUBLICATIONS

Plays

Hurrah for the Bridge (produced New York, 1962; Edinburgh, 1967). Bogotá, Colombia, Canal Ramirez, 1965; in *Balls and Other Plays*, 1967.
The Recluse (produced New York, 1964; Edinburgh, 1967). Included in *Balls and Other Plays*, 1967.
Balls (produced New York, 1964; Edinburgh, 1967). Included in *Balls and Other Plays*, 1967.
The Madonna in the Orchard (produced New York, 1965). Published as *Die Madonna im Apfelhag*, Frankfurt, Fischer, 1968; as *The Madonna in the Orchard*, New York, Breakthrough Press, 1971; in *Elizabeth I and Other Plays*, 1973.
The Hessian Corporal (produced New York, 1966; Edinburgh, 1967). Included in *Balls and Other Plays*, 1967.
Balls and Other Plays. London, Calder and Boyars, 1967; New York, French, 1968.
Tom Paine (produced New York, 1967; expanded version produced Edinburgh and London, 1967; New York, 1968). London, Calder and Boyars, 1967; New York, Grove Press, 1968.
Heimskringla; or, The Stoned Angels (televised 1969; produced New York, 1970). London, Calder and Boyars, and New York, French, 1970.
Satyricon (produced New York, 1972). Published in *The Off-Off-Broadway Book*, edited by Bruce Mailman and Albert Poland, Indianapolis, Bobbs Merrill, 1972; in *Elizabeth I and Other Plays*, 1973.
Elizabeth I (produced New York, 1972; London, 1973). New York, French, 1972; in *Elizabeth I and Other Plays*, 1973.
Elizabeth I and Other Plays. London, Calder and Boyars, 1973.
Silver Queen Saloon (as *Silver Queen*, music by John Braden, lyrics by Foster and Braden, produced New York, 1973; revised version, as *Silver Queen Saloon*, produced New York, 1978; London, 1982). New York, French, 1976; with *Marcus Brutus*, London, Calder, 1977.
Rags to Riches to Rags (produced New York, 1974).
Marcus Brutus (produced Springfield, Massachusetts, 1975). New York, French, 1976; with *Silver Queen Saloon*, London, Calder, 1977.
A Kiss Is Just a Kiss (televised 1980; produced New York, 1983).
The Dark and Mr. Stone 1–3 (produced New York, 1985–86).

Screenplay: *Cinderella Story*, 1985.

Television Plays: *Heimskringla, or, The Stoned Angels*, 1969; *A Kiss Is Just a Kiss*, 1980 (Denmark); *Mellon*, 1980; *Smile*, 1981; *The Cop and the Anthem*, from the story by O. Henry, 1984.

Short Stories

Minnie the Whore, The Birthday Party, and Other Stories. Caracas, Venezuela, Zodiaco, 1962.

*

Manuscript Collection: Lincoln Center Library of the Performing Arts, New York.

Critical Studies: *The New Bohemia* by John Gruen, New York, Shorecrest, 1966; "The Theatre of Involvement" by Richard Atcheson, in *Holiday* (New York), October 1968; "The World's a Stage," in *MD Publications* (New York), October 1968; *Foster, Robbe-Grillet, Bergson: Teatro, Novela, Tiempo* by Gustavo Majia, unpublished doctoral dissertation, University of the Andes, Bogotá, 1969; *Up Against the Fourth Wall* by John Lahr, New York, Grove Press, 1970; *Le Nouveau Théâtre Américain* by Franck Jotterand, Paris, Seuil, 1970; *Selvsyn-Aktuel Litteratur og Kulturdebat* by Elsa Gress, Copenhagen, Gyldendal, 1970; *Now: Theater der Erfahrung* by Jens Heilmeyer and Pia Frolich, Cologne, Schauberg, 1971; *The Off-Off-Broadway Book* edited by Bruce Mailman and Albert Poland, Indianapolis, Bobbs Merrill, 1972.

* * *

The theatrical reputation of Paul Foster essentially belongs to the 1960's, when, as a highly innovative contributor to the off-off-Broadway movement, he showed greater audacity than Albee and at one stage appeared to be the mentor to the emergent Sam Shepard. The diversity of Foster's early work is much greater than his often-argued debt to Beckett would suggest. As well as abstraction, symbolism, and existentialism—for which European models may be suggested—his plays up to *Tom Paine* all have a highly idiosyncratic lyrical vein which was peculiarly suited to the ensemble techniques of the La Mama Experimental Theater Club, where all his best work was premiered. In *Hurrah for the Bridge* an old waif, pulling a cart piled high with junk, appears to be victimised by an expressionistic group of leather-jacketed urban predators, though their autonomy is demonstrated by his eventual death at their hands, at which point he is visited by the down-and-out angel he idolises. *The Recluse* is more distinctively American in style, in its presentation of an old basement grotesque accompanied by her semi-animate mannequins and her pet cat, stuffed, which she hides in a drawer and keeps the best milk for. Foster's sympathies with the Happening and kinetic art, hinted at in these earliest plays, become rather more explicit in *Balls*, strictly a puppet play in which two pendant table tennis balls swing in and out of light; human representation comes only through recorded voices over, a nostalgic dialogue between the only two cadavers remaining in a coastal cemetery which is being eroded by the sea.

Foster's first approach to an ostensibly non-fictional subject was in *The Hessian Corporal*, subtitled "a one-act documentary play," but more like a parable for the theatre on the theme of the immorality of war, historicised to the Hessian recruitment of 1776. Though this was an important new development for Foster, it differs from his later "historical" works in that its focus is not a famous individual; his concern here is with the exploited nonentity, and the play has a social resonance which approaches the sentimental, although its relevance to Vietnam disguised this in the premiere. However, even Foster's most famous play, *Tom Paine*, is only superficially a historical portrait in any sense; in the face of surging ensemble playing and an insistent line of lyrical narrative, individuality crystallises only briefly before dissolving back into a faceless, collective context. The play poses questions about individuality; it presents conflicting elements in the traditional portrait of Paine, the visionary and the alcoholic, but by theatricality (such as fragmenting Paine and sharing him among several actors) there arises the implicit question whether such elements can coexist in the world of history or whether such a Paine is just a monster from myth. Several prominent critics felt that the play was not about a person but about a way of looking at a society, about collective impulses towards revolution. Paine himself is, theatrically and metatheatrically, a trigger device for common-sense reappraisal of the world that matters, a world which comes into focus haphazardly through the blurring devices of Paine's alcoholism and the ensemble performance.

Nor is *Elizabeth I* any more a history play or documentary. Again, two actors play the title role, but not this time to achieve schizoid characterisation; one actress does Queen Elizabeth, while the other does Elizabeth the Player Queen, a member of an itinerant company presenting a fairy-tale, cartoon-style play about the queen in the late 16th century. A few episodes, such as those concerning the death of Mary of Scotland, have some urgency, but the sterner tone and historical momentum of *Tom Paine* are all but absent; the play is generally much more frolicsome, and there is no sense of continuity between the events depicted and the world of the modern audience. A similar tone of historical vandalism permeates an earlier television play, *Heimskringla*, in which Leif Eriksson's discovery of Newfoundland is presented initially with the aura of a dramatised saga, with a massed choric incantation generating the action; however, an anachronistic flippancy soon permeates the action, with a diagram showing how to fill the stage with bubbles, and by the second-act "love-in" all intellectual pretensions have been abandoned. From this perspective, *Satyricon* would seem an almost logical development for Foster: a stage embellishment of Petronius's work in which the decadence of the *Cena* is supplemented by appearances from various Bacchantes, Petronius himself, and Nero and Agrippina (who together enact the Foundation of Rome, the emperor playing Romulus while she plays the she-wolf). The comic grotesquerie of this play moves beyond cartoon caricature into theatrical pop art, an appropriate contribution to the Theatre of the Ridiculous. A later play with a Roman setting, *Marcus Brutus*, attempts to return to an individual focus, but again fails to target the play on contemporary issues.

Foster's subsequent plays have been diverse, and have included film scripts, but the stylistic assurance that marked his work up to *Tom Paine* has not been seen again. His sole work to attract substantial critical interest has been *A Kiss Is Just a Kiss* in which Humphrey Bogart sits centre stage and splices together personal memory and public film clips. Bogey seems intended—like Tom Paine—to offer a lens to our world, but in performance the play has lacked cohesion. Foster has never been a playwright in any conventional sense; he has been a literary collaborator in group-developed work, and his idiosyncratic habit of writing stage directions as imperatives defies any acceptance of his scripts as literature.

—Howard McNaughton

FRATTI, Mario. American. Born in L'Aquila, Italy, 5 July 1927; emigrated to the United States, 1963; became citizen, 1974. Educated at Ca'Foscari University, Venice, 1947–51, Ph.D. in language and literature 1951. Served in the Italian Army, 1951–52: Lieutenant. Married 1) Lina Fedrigo in 1953 (marriage dissolved); 2) Laura Dubman in 1964; three children. Translator, Rubelli publishers, Venice, 1953–63; drama critic, *Sipario*, Milan, 1963–66, *Paese Sera*, Rome, 1963–73, *L'Ora*, Palermo, 1963–73, and since 1963 *Ridotto*, Venice. Taught at Adelphi University, Garden City, New York, and New School for Social Research, New York, 1964–65, Columbia University, New York, 1965–66, and Hofstra University, Hempstead, New York, 1973–74. Since 1968 member of the Department of Romance Languages, Hunter College, New York. Recipient: RAI-Television prize, 1959; Ruggeri prize, 1960, 1967, 1969; Lentini prize, 1964; Vallecorsi prize, 1965; Unasp-Enars prize, 1968; Arta-Terme award, 1973; Eugene O'Neill award, 1979; Richard Rodgers award, 1980. Agent: Samuel French Inc., 45 West 25th Street, New York, New York 10010. Address: 145 West 55th Street, Apartment 15D, New York, New York 10019, U.S.A.

Publications

Plays

Il Campanello (produced Milan, 1958). Published in *Ridotto* (Venice), 1958; as *The Doorbell* (produced New York, 1970; London, 1972), in *Ohio University Review* (Athens), 1971.

La Menzonga (The Lie) (produced Milan, 1959). Published in *Cynthia* (Florence), 1963.

A (produced Rome, 1965). Published in *Ora Zero* (Rome), 1959; translation in *Fusta* (New Jersey), 1976.

La Partita (The Game) (produced Pesaro, 1960). Published in *Ridotto* (Venice), 1960.

Il Rifiuto (produced Mantua, 1960). Published in *Il Dramma* (Turin), October 1965; as *The Refusal* (produced New York, 1972; London, 1973), in *Races*, 1972.

In Attesa (produced La Spezia, 1960). Rome, EIST, 1964; as *Waiting* (produced New York, 1970), in *Poet Lore* (Boston), Autumn 1968.

Il Ritorno (produced Bologna, 1961). Published in *Ridotto* (Venice), 1961; as *The Return* (produced New York, 1963; London, 1972), New York, French, n.d.

La Domanda (The Questionnaire) (produced La Spezia, 1961). Published in *La Prora* (Rome), 1962.

Flowers from Lidice, published in *L'Impegno* (Bari), 1961; in *Dramatics* (Cincinnati), October 1972.

L'Assegno. Cosenza, Pellegrini, 1961; translated by Adrienne S. Mandel as *The Third Daughter* (produced New York, 1978), New York, French, n.d.
Confidenze (produced Rome, 1962). Rome, EIST, 1964; as *The Coffin* (produced New York, 1967), in *Four Plays*, 1972.
Gatta Bianca al Greenwich (produced Rome, 1962). Published in *Il Dramma* (Turin), March 1962; as *White Cat*, in *Races*, 1972.
Il Suicidio (produced Spoleto, 1962). Published in *Cynthia* (Florence), 1962; as *The Suicide* (produced New York, 1965; London, 1973), New York, French, n.d.
La Gabbia (produced Milan, 1963). Published in *Cynthia* (Florence), 1962; as *The Cage* (produced New York, 1966), in *The Cage, The Academy, The Refrigerators*, 1977.
The Academy (produced New York, 1963). As *L'Accademia*, Rome, EIST, 1964; as *The Academy*, in *The Cage, The Academy, The Refrigerators*, 1977.
La Vedova Bianca (produced Milan, 1963). Published in *Ridotto* (Rome), 1972; as *Mafia* (produced Tallahassee, Florida, 1966), Newark, Delaware, Proscenium Press, 1971.
La Telefonata (produced Rome, 1965). Rome, EIST, 1964; as *The Gift* (produced New York, 1966; London, 1972), in *Four Plays*, 1972.
I Seduttori (produced Venice, 1972). Published in *Il Dramma* (Turin), 1964; as *The Seducers*, music and lyrics by Ed Scott (produced New York, 1974), with *The Roman Guest*, Rome, Ora Zero, 1972.
I Frigoriferi (produced Pistoia, 1965). Published in *Ora Zero* (Udine), 1964; as *The Refrigerators* (produced New York, 1971), in *The Cage, The Academy, The Refrigerators*, 1977.
Le Spie (produced Pescara, 1967). Published as *The Spies*, in *Fusta* (New Jersey), 1978.
Eleonora Duse (produced Sarasota, Florida, 1967; New York, 1980). New York, Breakthrough Press, 1972.
Il Ponte (produced Pesaro, 1967). Published in *Ridotto* (Rome), 1967; as *The Bridge* (produced New York, 1972; London, 1980), New York, McGraw Hill, 1970.
The Victim (produced Sacramento, California, 1968; New York, 1973). As *La Vittima*, Rome, Lo Faro, 1972; as *The Victim*, in *Eleonora Duse, The Victim, Originality*, 1980.
Che Guevara (produced Toronto, 1968; New York, 1971). Published in *Enact* (New Delhi), April 1970.
Unique (produced Baltimore, 1968). Published in *Ann Arbor Review* (Ann Arbor, Michigan), 1971.
L'Amico Cinese (produced Fano, 1969). Published in *Ridotto* (Rome), 1969; as *The Chinese Friend* (produced New York, 1972), in *Enact* (New Delhi), October 1972.
L'Ospite Romano (produced Pesaro, 1971). Rome, ENARS, 1969; as *The Roman Guest*, with *The Seducers*, Rome, Ora Zero, 1972.
La Panchina del Venerdi (produced Milan, 1970); as *The Friday Bench* (produced New York, 1971), in *Four Plays*, 1972.
Betrayals. Cosenza, Pellegrini, 1970; in *Drama and Theatre* (Fredonia, New York), 1970.
The Wish (produced Denton, Texas, 1971; London, 1972). Included in *Four Plays*, 1972.
The Other One (produced New York, 1971). Included in *Races*, 1972.
The Girl with a Ring on Her Nose (produced New York, 1971). Published in *Janus* (Seaside Park, New Jersey), 1972.
Too Much (produced New York, 1971). Published in *Janus* (Seaside Park, New Jersey), 1972.
Cybele (produced New York, 1971).
The Brothel (produced New York, 1972). Published in *Mediterranean Review* (Orient, New York), 1971.
The Family (produced New York, 1972). Published in *Enact* (New Delhi), October 1972.
Four Plays. Houston, Edgemoor, 1972.
Three Minidramas, published in *Janus* (Seaside Park, New Jersey), 1972.
Rapes (produced New York, 1972). Included in *Races*, 1972.
Races: Six Short Plays (includes *Rapes, Fire, Dialogue with a Negro, White Cat, The Refusal, The Other One*). Newark, Delaware, Proscenium Press, 1972.
Dialogue with a Negro (produced New York, 1975). Included in *Races*, 1972.
Notti d'amore, published in *Tempo Sensibile* (Novara), July 1972.
The Letter (produced New York, 1978). Published in *Tempo Sensibile* (Novara), September 1972; in *Wind* (Kentucky), 1974.
Teatro Americano (includes *Fuoco, Sorelle, Violenze, Famiglia*). Casale Monferrato, Tersite, 1972.
L'Ungherese (produced Florence, 1974). Published in *Tempo Sensibile* (Novara), 1972.
The 75th (produced Florence, 1974; New York, 1980). Published in *Arcoscenico* (Rome), January 1972; in *Dramatika* (New York), 1976.
Dolls No More (produced London and Lafayette, Indiana, 1975). Published in *Drama and Theatre* (Fredonia, New York), Winter 1972–73.
Chile 1973 (produced Parma and New York, 1974). Published in *Enact* (New Delhi), October, November, and December 1973; in *Parola del Popolo* (Chicago), 1974.
New York: A Triptych (produced New York, 1974).
Patty Hearst, published in *Enact* (New Delhi), 1975; in *Parola del Popolo* (Chicago), 1975.
Madam Senator, music and lyrics by Ed Scott (produced New York, 1975).
Originality (produced New York, 1975). Included in *Eleonora Duse, The Victim, Originality*, 1980.
The Only Good Indian . . ., with Henry Salerno (produced New York, 1975). Published in *Drama and Theatre* (Fredonia, New York), 1975.
Tania, music by Paul Dick (produced New York, 1975).
Two Centuries, with Penelope Bradford (produced New York, 1976).
Kissinger (produced California, 1976). Published in *Enact* (New Delhi), 1976.
Messages, published in *Dramatika* (New York), 1976.
The Cage, The Academy, The Refrigerators. New York, French, 1977.
Lunch with Fratti: The Letter, Her Voice, The Piggy Bank (produced New York, 1978). *The Piggy Bank* published in *Scholia Satyrica* (Tampa, Florida), 1977.
La Croce di Padre Marcello. Turin, Elle Di Ci, 1977.
The Biggest Thief in Town (produced New York, 1978).
Birthday. New York, French, n.d.
David, Son of Sam, published in *Ars-Uomo* (Rome), 1978.
Six Passionate Women, published in *Enact* (New Delhi), 1978.
Two Women (produced New York, 1981). Published in *Zone Press* (New York), 1978.
Sette Commedie. Frascati, Tusculum, 1979.
The Fourth One (produced New York, 1980).
Caccia al Morto, Mafia. Frascati, Tusculum, 1980.
The Pill (produced New York, 1980). Published in *Scholia Satyrica* (Tampa, Florida), 1980.
Eleonora Duse, The Victim, Originality. New York, French, 1980.
Nine, book by Arthur Kopit, music and lyrics by Maury Yeston, adaptation of the screenplay *8½* by Federico Fellini (produced

Waterford, Connecticut, 1981; New York, 1982). New York, French, 1983.

Half, published in *Other Stages* (New York), 1981.

Elbow to Elbow, adaptation of a play by Glauco Disalle (produced New York, 1982).

Il Pugnale Marocchino (produced L'Aquila, 1982). L'Aquila, Teatrama, 1982.

Viols, Feu (two plays) (produced Paris, 1983).

Translations for Italian television: plays by David Shaw, Reginald Rose, Thomas W. Phipps, R.O. Hirson, J.P. Miller.

Verse

Volti: Cento Poesie (Faces: 100 Poems). Bari, Mariano, 1960.

*

Bibliography: in *Ora Zero* (Udine), 1972; in *Four Plays*, 1972.

Manuscript Collection: Lincoln Center Library of the Performing Arts, New York.

Critical Studies: by Robert W. Corrigan, in *New Theatre of Europe II*, New York, Dell, 1964, and in *Masterpieces of the Modern Italian Theatre*, New York, Collier Macmillan, 1967; by Paul T. Nolan, in *Ora Zero* (Udine), 1972, and in *La Vittima*, 1972; *Mario Fratti* by Jane Bonin, Boston, Twayne, 1982; "Italian-American Playwrights on the Rise" by G.C. Di Scipio, in *Journal of Popular Culture* (Bowling Green, Ohio), Winter 1985.

* * *

Mario Fratti arrived in New York in 1963 as foreign correspondent for the Italian press. He had already achieved some distinction in Italy as a playwright, and made his American debut that same year with a production of *The Academy* and *The Return* at the Theatre De Lys, starring Ron Liebman. Although a critical success, this first production failed to establish Fratti as an important New York playwright. Undaunted, Fratti continued writing prolifically. Translations of his plays appeared in prominent American literary journals and anthologies; his words were produced throughout the United States and abroad, and were evaluated in several academic studies. Fratti was a phenomenon: a European playwright based in New York achieving national and international recognition without being produced in New York. While most playwrights struggled to "crack" the New York theatrical scene, Fratti imposed himself upon the city by the weight of his international success (more than 300 productions).

Fratti is fascinated with the idea of life as theatre. Existing in an unknowable universe, caught in social systems beyond his control, man becomes an actor wearing an endless array of public and private masks as a means of survival. In such a world, deceit, treachery, and violence are commonplace. While this theme is explored by other modern writers, Fratti is unique for embracing clarity rather than obscurity in the theatre, convinced that the playwright must be the "quintessence of clarity" both for the actor and the audience. Otherwise, he is only "an hysterical poet talking to himself in front of a mirror." Fratti's rich theatrical imagination and impeccable craftsmanship assure clarity.

Comparable to the plots of the commedia dell'arte, many of his plays hinge on a deception, but the results are frequently pathetic or tragic rather than comic. While the characters are passionate, and the situation tense, the structure is coldly logical and tight, progressing like a mystery thriller: the audience's sympathies shift from one character to another; each seems to be on the side of right and the truth is elusive. However, the conclusion is not the revelation of a murderer but a provocative idea regarding the human condition. "I want to open a door in the minds of the audience," states Fratti.

In *The Cage*, Cristiano's pessimism is convincing and his isolation seems justified. Ultimately, however, his moralizing proves destructive; his murder of Pietro, the presumably cruel husband, is the megalomaniacal act of a man who would play God with other peoples' lives. Sanguemarcio, the invalid degenerate of *The Coffin*, pays to hear lurid tales of violence and perversion, aided by his trusted friend, Paoletto, who provides him with storytellers. But the tales are lies; Paoletto is a thief and parasite using the old degenerate for profit. Sanguemarcio dies when he discovers that his one trusted friend was just another of life's frauds. Fratti, however, never moralizes: deceived and deceiver are caught in a hopeless struggle for survival.

The dominant metaphor in Fratti's plays is the trap: characters trapped in situations which they attempt to escape from by violence or deception. Most of the plays are set indoors: oppressive rooms, a cage: concretized images of entrapment. Even the short, percussive titles of his plays suggest traps that have been sprung. But Fratti is not another modern pessimist. While dramatizing life's *Inferno*, he believes in man's basic goodness: "I believe in man, man notwithstanding." In *The Bridge*, a courageous policeman risks his life to save potential suicide victims, recalling a biblical parable that it is better to save one lost sheep than keep a flock. The Priest of *The Roman Guest* learns a new liberalism in America, confronts a prejudiced mob, and returns to Italy with a more profound sense of Christianity. *Che Guevara* is a heroic yet realistic depiction of the Argentinean revolutionary, a man who views his actions as expedient rather than superhuman, necessary steps toward the positive evolution of society.

Fratti also has a subtle sense of comedy. Works such as *The Academy* and *Waiting* are humorous explorations of deceit and self deception. In *The Academy*, set in postwar Italy, a fascist attempts to revenge himself upon America by maintaining an academy for gigolos in pursuit of wealthy American women. The heroine of *Waiting* feigns docility in order to lure her seducer into marriage and then punish him by making his future life a hell. *The Refrigerators*, a dark comedy, is a bizarre parable of contemporary American life and technology, a unique departure from the essential realism of Fratti's drama. Transvestism and perversion are rampant, and the madcap events have a Marx Brothers quality.

America has had a significant influence on Fratti: "This society with all its problems and conflicts is fascinating. It's the ideal society for a modern dramatist." He now writes in English as well as Italian, and evidences a remarkable ear for American dialogue: a terseness and directness that suit the compactness of his dramatic structure. Living in the heart of Manhattan's theatre district, Fratti is continually stimulated by the city, inspired by the most seemingly insignificant event or occurrence around him. "I am a great observer. Faces are incredibly revealing. Just an expression can give me an idea for a play." He describes the scene that provided him with the idea for *The Chinese Friend*, a one-act masterpiece of racial prejudice, filled with nuances regarding America's foreign policy in the Far East: "A very handsome, and elegantly attired American family passed me on the street. They seemed to be overly solicitous to a Chinese gentleman, who was, apparently, their guest."

Thematically, cynicism has tended to override Fratti's humanism in recent years. The world is too much with him of late, embittered by the cruelty, violence, and obsessive war mentality in the post-Vietnam period. But he remains deeply concerned about the poor, the underdog, the perennially helpless victims of life's more skilful and deceptive players. A recurring metaphor is exposure: men and women enmeshed in a futile battle of the sexes, exposing their penchant for foolishness, deceit, and treachery. In his darker plays, the exposure concerns buried guilts, jealousies, hatreds that end in senseless tragedy.

In the comedy *Six Passionate Women* voyeurism and self exposure dominate the lives of the film industry characters of the play. A man hater, appropriately named Mrs. Gunmore, sets out to avenge herself upon the film director, Nino, for what she regards as the male chauvinism and contempt for women evident in his work. *Nine* also centers on the travails of a film director, Guido Contini, but he is treated more sympathetically than Nino. "Sometimes I neglect you," Guido tells his suffering wife; but asks her to forgive him for his waywardness and exposure of their private life on film; it is his way of "creating and recreating." Adapted from Fellini's $8\frac{1}{2}$, *Nine* dramatizes the central character's attempts toward self-understanding by exploring his guilts, desires, fantasies through his characters. The work also satirizes the film industry's incongruous marriage of crass materialism and art through the character of the German financier, Weissnicht, who backs Guido's latest film.

The Third Daughter and *Birthday* are two dark plays concerned with the theme of a father's incestuous desire for his daughter. In *The Third Daughter* Ilario decides to avenge himself upon his adulterous wife by having the offspring of her infidelity, their third daughter Alda, have an affair with a young man, thus destroying her purity, and so torment his wife. The sordid tale is complex in its implications regarding family ties, hatreds, jealousies, desires. Ilario's actual daughters are acting out their own love-hate relationship with their father: hating him for his cruel treatment of their mother, and for his preferring his stepsister to them. He has not only denied them paternal love, but aroused their jealousy, based upon their own repressed incestuous desires. *Birthday* is a fascinating dramatization of incest that becomes madness. A father annually enacts the imagined return of his runaway daughter on her birthday. Women are brought in to assume the role coached by the servant, who encourages them to please the man, and satisfy his incestuous desires.

In *The Piggy Bank* deception and exposure again prevail. A clever prostitute frightens off clients, who have paid in advance, by pretending to have venereal disease; she uses her victims, and is in turn used by her husband; a vicious game of survival with no real winners. *The Letter* is one of Fratti's short chamber plays; excellent acting vehicles—brief, intense, ambivalent.

Fratti is one of off-off Broadway's most frequently performed playwrights, a tribute to his originality and willingness to explore uncomfortable truths about contemporary life. He finds fertile ground for his drama in the most apparently insignificant moments in the passing scene of everyday life, and has a notebook filled with ideas for plays. "Look, I'll never be able to use them all in my lifetime." Let's hope he's wrong.

—A. Richard Sogliuzzo

FRAYN, Michael. British. Born in Mill Hill, London, 8 September 1933. Educated at Sutton High School for Boys; Kingston Grammar School, Surrey; Emmanuel College, Cambridge, B.A. 1957. Served in the Royal Artillery and Intelligence Corps, 1952–54. Married Gillian Palmer in 1960; three daughters. Reporter, 1957–59, and columnist, 1959–62, the *Guardian*, Manchester and London; columnist, the *Observer*, London, 1962–68. Recipient: Maugham Award, 1966; Hawthornden Prize, 1967; National Press award, 1970; *Evening Standard* award, for play, 1976, 1981, 1983, 1985; Society of West End Theatre award, 1977, 1982; British Theatre Association award, 1981, 1983; Olivier Award, 1985; New York Drama Critics Circle award, 1986. Honorary Fellow, Emmanuel College, 1985. Agent: Elaine Greene Ltd., 31 Newington Green, London N16 9PU, England.

Publications

Plays

Zounds!, with John Edwards, music by Keith Statham (produced Cambridge, 1957).
The Two of Us (includes *Black and Silver*, *The New Quixote*, *Mr. Foot*, *Chinamen*) (produced London, 1970; Ogunquit, Maine, 1975; *Chinamen* produced New York, 1979). London, Fontana, 1970; *Chinamen* published in *The Best Short Plays 1973*, edited by Stanley Richards, Radnor, Pennsylvania, Chilton, 1973; revised version of *The New Quixote* (produced Chichester, Sussex, and London, 1980).
The Sandboy (produced London, 1971).
Alphabetical Order (produced London, 1975; New Haven, Connecticut, 1976). With *Donkeys' Years*, London, Eyre Methuen, 1977.
Donkeys' Years (produced London, 1976). With *Alphabetical Order*, London, Eyre Methuen, 1977.
Clouds (produced London, 1976). London, Eyre Methuen, 1977.
The Cherry Orchard, adaptation of a play by Chekhov (produced London, 1978). London, Eyre Methuen, 1978.
Balmoral (produced Guildford, Surrey, 1978; revised version, as *Liberty Hall*, produced London, 1980; revised version, as *Balmoral*, produced Bristol, 1987). London, Methuen, 1987.
The Fruits of Enlightenment, adaptation of a play by Tolstoy (produced London, 1979). London, Eyre Methuen, 1979.
Make and Break (produced London, 1980; Washington, D.C., 1983). London, Eyre Methuen, 1980.
Noises Off (produced London, 1981; New York, 1983). London, Methuen, 1982; New York, French, 1985.
Three Sisters, adaptation of a play by Chekhov (produced Manchester and Los Angeles, 1985; London, 1987). London, Methuen, 1983.
Benefactors (produced London, 1984; New York, 1985). London, Methuen, 1984.
Wild Honey, adaptation of a play by Chekhov (produced London, 1984; New York, 1986). London, Methuen, 1984.
Number One, adaptation of a play by Jean Anouilh (produced London, 1984).
Plays 1 (includes *Alphabetical Order*, *Donkeys' Years*, *Clouds*, *Make and Break*, *Noises Off*). London, Methuen, 1986.
The Seagull, adaptation of a play by Chekhov (produced Watford, Hertfordshire, 1986). London, Methuen, 1986.
Clockwise (screenplay). London, Methuen, 1986.

Uncle Vanya, adaptation of a play by Chekhov. London, Methuen, 1987.

Screenplay: *Clockwise*, 1986.

Radio Play: *Exchange*, from a play by Yuri Trifonov, 1986.

Television Plays and Documentaries: *Second City Reports*, with John Bird, 1964; *Jamie, On a Flying Visit*, 1968; *One Pair of Eyes*, 1968; *Birthday*, 1969; *Beyond a Joke* series, with John Bird and Eleanor Bron, 1972; *Laurence Sterne Lived Here* (*Writers' Houses* series), 1973; *Imagine a City Called Berlin*, 1975; *Making Faces*, 1975; *Vienna: The Mask of Gold*, 1977; *Three Streets in the Country*, 1979; *The Long Straight* (*Great Railway Journeys of the World* series), 1980; *Jerusalem*, 1984.

Novels

The Tin Men. London, Collins, 1965; Boston, Little Brown, 1966.
The Russian Interpreter. London, Collins, and New York, Viking Press, 1966.
Towards the End of the Morning. London, Collins, 1967; as *Against Entropy*, New York, Viking Press, 1967.
A Very Private Life. London, Collins, and New York, Viking Press, 1968.
Sweet Dreams. London, Collins, 1973; New York, Viking Press, 1974.

Other

The Day of the Dog (*Guardian* columns). London, Collins, 1962; New York, Doubleday, 1963.
The Book of Fub (*Guardian* columns). London, Collins, 1963; as *Never Put Off to Gomorrah*, New York, Pantheon, 1964.
On the Outskirts (*Observer* columns). London, Fontana, 1967.
At Bay in Gear Street (*Observer* columns). New York, Fontana, 1967.
Constructions (philosophy). London, Wildwood House, 1974.
Great Railway Journeys of the World, with others. London, BBC Publications, 1981; New York, Dutton, 1982.
The Original Michael Frayn: Satirical Essays, edited by James Fenton. Edinburgh, Salamander Press, 1983.

Editor, *The Best of Beachcomber*, by J.B. Morton. London, Heinemann, 1963.

*

Critical Study: introduction by Frayn to *Plays 1*, 1986.

* * *

A former columnist for the *Guardian* and the *Observer*, Michael Frayn has both extended and broadened his scope since his first West End play, *The Two of Us*. To call this a play is perhaps an exaggeration: it consists of four short pieces, each built round a couple. Three of the pieces are duologues; the first, in which a married pair abroad on holiday take it in turn to be subjugated by their howling infant, is little more than an extended revue sketch, with the baby becoming like the proverbial hot brick passed from hand to hand. The second is a spirited conversation piece between an electronics engineer and his girlfriend, where the frenzied talk is reminiscent of *Design for Living*, and where the plot's design is minimal. The third, *Mr. Foot*, has a middle-aged pair probing one another's mildly absurd anxieties, with more substance to the situation, possibly, than a pure *farceur* might have used. The final, longest, and most substantial offering, *Chinamen*, has a host and hostess waiting for and receiving their dinner guests, resulting in confusion that makes it the highlight of the quartet. Frayn was clearly feeling his way with *The Two of Us* and later revised the sketch *The New Quixote*.

In *The Sandboy*, Frayn's first full-length play, attention is again focused on an omnipresent couple, this time within a more distinctive framework. A city planner's private life is invaded by an army of television cameras. They are symbolized by a fat slug of an electric cable which slides off the forestage and forms a kind of umbilicus joining the audience to the stage. But the framework is little more than plasterboard for Frayn's wit to decorate. The subject is happiness. Phil always falls on his feet. Every telephone call brings good news, and the television unit is an excuse for him to bounce into an apologia of good fortune. A woman from across the street disrupts this with a private marital grief. Phil becomes her grief's compère. Every time something really might happen, he jumps in with a clever inhibitory explanation. The conclusion of *The Sandboy* would seem to be that happiness and unhappiness balance themselves out chemically, and people find out how happy they are by seeing how unhappy others are: a limited view and, to use a favourite word of Phil's, "metabolic." Like *The Two of Us*, this play is characterized by amusing and extremely well observed bouts of repartee, but little by way of a reversal of fortune comes along to bring the play to a crisis, even a comic one. Repeated bouts of garrulity tend to wear thin.

In *Alphabetical Order* Frayn turns directly to projecting his own journalistic experience. The play is set in the cutting library of a small provincial newspaper and at once the specialist wit Frayn lines up on the situation lifts it quite out of the class of the previous works. The first act introduces a new arrival, Leslie, into the office and in the tradition of occupational comedy her acclimatization to other members of the staff provides the opportunity for witty lines. There is Geoffrey, the messenger, "in and out all the time" with a word for everybody. He insists on supplying Leslie with a clean hand towel. John, the leader writer from Oxford ("was it All Saints?") takes a shine to Leslie, meanwhile turning every sentence he utters into a peroration. His parenthetic meanderings cover every subject from global density to local Indian nosh. "I'm merely being a channel through which an unasked question can get itself asked," he observes of himself. Then there is Lucy, the library chief, who keeps the place bungling along with happy ineptitude. She sets to and reforms the library, as well as the lives of those who work there, and when the job is nearing completion the paper goes bankrupt and closes down. This gives rise to a splendid comic climax of frustration, where Frayn can indulge fully his gift for verbal invention and farcical action, with sallies into the realm of higher meaning.

Clouds again shows Frayn sticking firmly to known territory, as well as to the multiple-character channels of invention comic playwrights—with the notable exception of Molière—like to employ. Three reporters are on a tour of Cuba—Cuba being a blue sky represented by a stage cloth and six chairs. The interaction between their journalistic competitiveness, their own individual needs, and the subject matter of their assignments, the Cubans themselves, provides many triggers both for situation comedy and a more serious comment of a political nature—in a socialist country the trio share a common and spoilt Western ethos—and of a mildly philosophical kind.

There is, *Clouds* underlines, a difference between factual and imaginative reporting.

Make and Break is a more ambitious piece set in a high-rise hotel in Frankfurt. During a business convention a suite is given over to a display of movable British walls: these provide the light, frenzied, and farcical action though the more crucial focus of the play is of a moment of dying. *Make and Break* is a step forward in so far as Frayn manages to achieve in Garrard, his competitive salesman (competition, as in *Clouds*, is a recurrent comic theme), a memorable monster of the species.

In the 1980's, in a career of consistently high quality, Frayn has repeated his earlier West End successes with *Noises Off* and *Benefactors*. The first is an intricate farce which explores the farce genre itself with spectacular invention and relentless high spirits: the work of a master who has brought to his observation of the process of putting on a play the same eye for detail and comic discrepancy between aspiration and practical reality he showed, with regard to journalism, in *Alphabetical Order*.

Benefactors is a much darker work, a study of two couples, David and Jane, Colin and Sheila, whose lives, over a 15-year span, rise and decline in fugue-like variations on the theme of human dependence. The dramatic impetus is created by the proposed re-development of Basuto Road, a rundown Victorian residential area in S.E. 15, for which David, an architect, has the job of designing a new scheme. Jane takes pity on Sheila, unhappily married to Colin, a struggling journalist and part-time encyclopaedist, and engages her to help David. This stimulates jealousy in Colin who, finally, leaves Sheila, moving into a "squat" in Basuto Road where he engages in campaigning against David's plan to build two 50-storey blocks.

Benefactors switches back and forth in time with admirable deftness and concentration, while each of the four characters emerges, by the end, into an acceptance of the relativity of human happiness. Frayn has also adapted two Chekhov plays, *Three Sisters* and *Wild Honey* (the latter, Chekhov's first play, was formerly called *Platonov*, after its protagonist).

—Garry O'Connor

FREEMAN, David. Canadian. Born in Toronto, Ontario, 7 January 1945; palsied from birth. Educated at Sunnyview School, Toronto, to grade 10; McMaster University, Hamilton, Ontario (news features editor, university newspaper), 1966–71, B.A. in political science 1971. Public relations officer, IBM, Don Mills, Ontario, 1970. Recipient: Ontario Council for the Arts grant, 1971; Canada Council grant, 1972, 1974; Chalmers award, 1973; Drama Desk award, 1974. Agent: John Goodwin and Associates, 4235 Avenue de l'Esplanade, Montreal, Quebec H2W 1T1, Canada.

PUBLICATIONS

Plays

Creeps (produced Toronto, 1971; Washington, D.C., and New York, 1973; Edinburgh, 1979; London, 1981). Toronto, University of Toronto Press, 1972; New York and London, French, 1975.

Battering Ram (produced Toronto, 1972; New York, 1975). Toronto, Playwrights, 1972.

You're Gonna Be Alright, Jamie-Boy (produced Toronto, 1974; New York, 1977). Vancouver, Talonbooks, 1974.

Flytrap (produced Montreal, 1976). Toronto, Playwrights, 1980.

*

David Freeman comments:

(1973) *Creeps* is an autobiographical play which takes place one afternoon in the men's washroom of a sheltered workshop for the cerebral palsied. It has four main characters: Tom, Jim, Pete, and Sam. The four congregate in the washroom in order to get away from such menial and boring tasks as sanding blocks, separating nuts and bolts, folding boxes, and weaving rugs. The main conflict is between Tom, who considers himself an abstract artist and wants to leave the workshop to devote more time to his painting, and Jim, who has recently been promoted to office work and would prefer that Tom stay in the workshop where life is less complicated. Pete is lazy and is content to let the world wait on him, while Sam is bitter, cruel, foul-mouthed, and lecherous. This afternoon they talk about sexual frustration, broken dreams, and rage at a society which has condemned them to the mercy of false charity and at themselves for accepting it. The play came out of my own experiences in such a place ten years ago, for I myself am afflicted with cerebral palsy. My latest play, *Battering Ram*, also deals with a handicapped person, but is quite different in that it deals with the problems of sexual frustration and loneliness more explicitly. At this writing, I am at work on a screenplay, *The Poker Player*, which deals with handicapped teenagers at camp. I hope you don't think I'm in a rut, because I intend soon to start work on a play where the characters are only emotionally disabled—and not physically.

(1977) *You're Gonna Be Alright, Jamie-Boy* and *Flytrap* deal with emotionally handicapped characters, not those who are physically handicapped.

* * *

David Freeman's world is one of cripples, both physical and psychological, and one which mirrors the equally crippled morality, aspirations, and institutions of the "real" world which surrounds his fictional one and which causes or assists in the deforming of his various victims. It follows, therefore, that his characters and plots are naturalistic, although dramatic hyperbole often breaks into the otherwise naturalistic conception in the form of stereotype leading to caricature, as in *You're Gonna Be Alright, Jamie-Boy*, or of intensely theatrical and fantastic vignettes superimposed on the plot, as in the circus interludes of *Creeps*. The result in *Creeps* is the creation of a shockingly powerful dramatic vehicle for Freeman's bitter but balanced attack on his audience, its physical normality, its ignorance of the humiliation experienced by an adult trapped in the crippled body of a hideous child, and, finally and most unrelentingly, on its pity. It is in the dramatic rather than thematic elements that Freeman most devastatingly exposes the shallow and self-gratifying attempts of the charitable institutions to invade this "sheltered" world. In its virtually terroristic design, the play hurls its washroom set, sexual frustration, unremittingly obscene language, and grotesque mime at the audience in a *coup de théâtre* which the more controlled and mature later plays cannot approach. This design is so compelling and dramatically so powerful that in production, the audience, stunned by Freeman's ferocity, accepts elements—the exaggeration of the foul language, for example—

which it would not credit in print. In the later plays, where his personal anger becomes less acute, Freeman cannot assume the same overwhelmed acceptance by his audience; regrettably, he sometimes does.

Battering Ram reworks the theme of sexual frustration, and in its removal of the physically repulsive, loses much of the dramatic strength of *Creeps*. Still, the play makes an arresting statement and, more importantly, builds it around a full characterization of the protagonist. In this focus and its largely successful execution, Freeman evidences his growth as a playwright, moving as he does into more literary and less personal devices. The play is also a movement into the more commercial theatre, employing themes which become more popular as they become less personal.

In *You're Gonna Be Alright, Jamie-Boy* Freeman creates a play in the neo-naturalistic school which became popular in Canadian drama in the 1970's. Unfortunately, in moving completely from his physically crippled familiars, Freeman created rather clichéd North American types working out a predictable pattern based on the emptiness of television-oriented lives. After the strength of the earlier plays, this reworking of a commonplace situation seems facile; in many respects it seems more like a first play than the third in a series. In its investigation of the psychology of the characters, however, it holds together well given the shallow range of personality each exhibits. Freeman looks at stereotypical characters but he looks at them reasonably well, especially through his dialogue which often picks up the verve of *Creeps* and sometimes leaps into moments of real comedy and pathos.

His fourth play, *Flytrap*, moves further into the realm of the commercial and it does so with considerable success. In its first production in Montreal, the play was called "straightforward, well crafted, entertaining and unpretentious" (Myron Galloway in the *Montreal Star*, 3 May 1976) and it has been seen as a significant example of a movement in contemporary Canadian theatre away from self-consciously social themes and into middle-class issues with a broad base of appeal. This is particularly interesting in the case of Freeman because of the very specialized concerns of *Creeps* which had previously obsessed him. The dramatic tone and staging of the play also differs: it moves at a leisurely pace through the struggle of a married but childless couple to come to terms with the new presence in their troubled marriage of a surrogate son of mature years. This strange triangle is explored without the bombast of the early work (until the end, at least, when the principals finally fight out their frustration) and the treatment is much lighter and more ironic than in the previous plays. The critical dilemma is to determine whether a more controlled discussion of average material is more or less laudable than an uncontrolled scream through the highly unusual and astonishing world of *Creeps*.

Freeman has proved himself a professional man of the theatre; he has not, however, yet matched the brilliance of his first play and that has exposed him to negative comment from those who will never be satisfied until he matches its energy but in a fully mature framework. The development of the plays to date suggests that Freeman is capable of doing just that and when he does, he will create a play of great significance.

—S.R. Gilbert

FRENCH, David. Canadian. Born in Coley's Point, Newfoundland, 18 January 1939. Educated at Harbord Collegiate High School; Oakwood Collegiate High School, Toronto, graduated 1958; studied acting at Al Saxe Studio, Toronto, 1958, Pasadena Playhouse, California, 1959, and Lawlor School of Acting, Toronto, 1960. Married Leslie Grey in 1978. Actor in Toronto, 1960–65; post office worker, 1971–72. Recipient: Chalmers award, 1973; Lieutenant-Governor's award, 1974; Canada Council grant, 1974, 1975; Dora award, 1985; Canadian Authors Association award, 1986. Agent: Lois Berman, 240 West 44th Street, New York, New York 10036, U.S.A. Address: c/o Tarragon Theatre, 30 Bridgman Avenue, Toronto, Ontario M5R 1X3, Canada.

PUBLICATIONS

Plays

Leaving Home (produced Toronto, 1972; New York, 1974). Toronto, New Press, 1972; New York and London, French, 1976.

Of the Fields, Lately (produced Toronto, 1973; New York, 1980). Toronto, Playwrights, 1973; New York, French, 1977.

One Crack Out (produced Toronto, 1975; New York, 1978). Toronto, Playwrights, 1975.

The Seagull, adaptation of a play by Chekhov (produced Toronto, 1977). Toronto, Playwrights, 1977.

Jitters (produced Toronto and New Haven, Connecticut, 1979). Toronto, Playwrights, 1980.

The Riddle of the World (produced Toronto, 1981).

Salt-Water Moon (produced Toronto, 1984; Costa Mesa, California, 1985; Edinburgh, 1986). Toronto, Playwrights, 1985.

Radio Plays: *Angeline*, 1967; *Invitation to a Zoo*, 1967; *Winter of Timothy*, 1968.

Television Plays: *Beckons the Dark River*, 1963; *The Willow Harp*, 1964; *A Ring for Florrie*, 1964; *After Hours*, 1964; *Sparrow on a Monday Morning*, 1966 (USA); *A Token Gesture*, 1970; *A Tender Branch*, 1972; *The Happiest Man in the World*, from a short story by Hugh Garner, 1972; scripts for *Razzle Dazzle* children's series.

* * *

The first of David French's stage plays, *Leaving Home*, concerns the sense of displacement and frustration of a family of Irish immigrants who have been torn, not once, but twice from their roots, first from Ireland to Newfoundland and then from Newfoundland to Toronto. They carry with them the luggage of their past—Catholic-Protestant antagonisms, family loyalties and bitter dissension, a salty vituperation, and a habit of convivial overdrinking. Because of the double displacement, the past has become meaningless, yet the older generation retain it and struggle to relate it to the future. The play's theme is the ancient one of a son's need to free himself from his father, paralleled and reinforced by the theme of the alienation of the immigrant from his children in the new land.

The Mercer family organization is not unlike that in Arthur Miller's *Death of a Salesman*, with Mary Mercer loving but ineffectual in her efforts to keep the family peace and protect her husband, Jacob, and eldest son, Ben, from hurting each other. Jacob's life has been damaged by a brutal, uncaring father, the early death of his mother, and an interrupted education. In Ben, Jacob dreams of living again, successful in some socially esteemed profession and with a warm father-son relationship, yet he sneers at the university education, which is his son's path to a better life.

The action of the play takes place in the Mercer kitchen and parlour, rendered with an effect of cramped and unlovely realism, on the wedding day of the younger son, Billy, who has gotten his high school girlfriend pregnant. Significantly she is Catholic, and the daughter of Minnie Jackson, a sweetheart of Jacob's youth, a woman he did not marry because of her religion and because of her randy and slip-shod behaviour, which still both attracts and repels him. Instead he married Protestant Mary, pretty, austere, and middle-class. The wedding triggers off a series of painful reminiscences and violent reactions in Jake, not against Billy, who is marrying a Catholic, abandoning school and the traditional prejudices of the Irish in general, but against Ben, whose leaving home Jacob regards with anguish as the death of all his hopes.

The sequel to this play, *Of the Fields, Lately*, deals with Ben's return home after two futile years in the prairies, summoned ostensibly for the funeral of his aunt, but actually because of the growing frailty of his father. The play is permeated with the sense of death, but the funeral device does not create as tight a dramatic unity as the wedding in *Leaving Home*. The same temperamental antagonisms arise between Jacob and Ben, completing their alienation, shown by the use of soliloquies of reminiscence by both characters at the beginning of the play and by Ben alone after his father's death in the end. This single departure from realism frames the play declaring symbolically at the opening and reaffirming at the closing the sense of isolation felt by each character.

Yet rejection and alienation are not the whole story. Jake has a vitality lacking in his sons, although it has been warped into boasting, empty heroics at his job, and heavy drinking. Ben instinctively recognizes his father's superiority to him and feels a dogged sense of duty and even respect for Jacob, but cannot bear to be enslaved by Jacob's disappointments and dead values.

The realism of the first two plays is pushed to greater extremes in French's third, *One Crack Out*, which deals with the tawdry life of petty criminals and pool hall gamblers. The set is divided between the squalid pool hall and adjoining lavatory, and the equally squalid bedsitting room of Charlie, a pool shark, and his wife, Helen, a stripper. These claustrophobic interiors, plus eleven short scenes tumbling upon one another, build up tension as the deadline approaches when Charlie must pay the Collector the $3,000 he owes or get his hands broken.

As all his efforts to raise the money by borrowing and hustling fail, Charlie emerges as not only devious and frantic, but also as one who is capable of loyalty and unselfish feeling. With his losing streak ended through an act of pure devotion by Helen, he is able to resolve his problem in his own terms by a duel of skill. In creating Charlie's dilemma and preventing any avenue of escape, French has over-plotted the play and its emotional power is diffused by melodramatic effects such as the breathlessly approaching deadline, the complication of Charlie's sexual impotence with his wife, and the unprepared-for conversion of the Collector to accepting Charlie's challenge debt. Despite the fact that this play is less strong than French's first two, it marks a forward step in his development by moving away from the autobiographical into an invented, objective world.

French's first comedy was *Jitters*, the title of which reflects the feelings of a group of Canadian actors as they rehearse a play which they expect to be seen by an important New York director who they hope will pave their way to Broadway, the necessary seal of success in Canada. During the action they reveal the uncertainty and inferiority felt by Canadian artists in the shadow of the U.S.A.

The play begins with a trompe d'oeil effect of a play-within-a-play which the audience thinks is the real thing for the first several minutes until the director leaps up from a theatre seat calling "cut, cut!" This sudden break from "theatrical" harmony to "real life" rivalry in the past points up the personal antagonism between Jessica, who has star billing, and Patrick, the leading actor, who is outraged that his long successful career in Canada counts for less than Jessica's two flops on Broadway. It is her former director in New York who operates as a kind of nemesis, increasing both the hopes and jitters of everyone including the playwright. The director's ultimate non-attendance of the performance is the final irony of Canadian-American relations, in theatre as in everything, underscoring the Canadian sense of American imperviousness and indifference.

In *Salt-Water Moon*, his most recent work, French returns to Newfoundland and autobiographical themes with a play which precedes *Leaving Home* in time by depicting the courtship of Jacob Mercer and Mary Snow. Set on the front porch and in the yard of the summer home of the local MP, where Mary is in service, confined to the 90-minute running time of the action (there is no intermission), the play focusses narrowly on Jacob and Mary, their frustrated love, their poverty, their poignant struggle in different ways to help their families: Mary to save her sister from the brutality of an orphan asylum, and Jacob to spare his father the humiliation of being "in collar," a pernicious employment system devised by the local fishing bosses.

The play's tension arises not from suspense about whether the lovers will finally resolve their differences, but how they will do it. Their meeting after a year's absence begins in recrimination—hers for his sudden departure, and his for her becoming engaged to his arch-enemy's son. The evening proceeds with a series of explanations which reveal their experience of suffering, death, and poverty, along with their strength and tenacity. It ends with harmony being reestablished under the "salt-water moon." As always French's dialogue is affecting and funny, nostalgic and poetic with the resonance of Newfoundland Irish idiom.

—Dorothy Parker

FRIEDMAN, Bruce Jay. American. Born in New York City, 26 April 1930. Educated at De Witt Clinton High School, Bronx, New York; University of Missouri, Columbia, 1947–51, Bachelor of Journalism 1951. Served in the United States Air Force, 1951–53: Lieutenant. Married Ginger Howard in 1954 (divorced 1977); three children. Editorial director, Magazine Management Company, publishers, New York, 1953–66. Visiting Professor of Literature, York College, City University, New York, 1974–76. Address: P.O. Box 746, Walter Mill, New York 11976, U.S.A.

PUBLICATIONS

Plays

23 Pat O'Brien Movies, adaptation of his own short story (produced New York, 1966).

Scuba Duba: A Tense Comedy (produced New York, 1967). New York, Simon and Schuster, 1968.
A Mother's Kisses, music by Richard Adler, adaptation of the novel by Friedman (produced New Haven, Connecticut, 1968).
Steambath (produced New York, 1970). New York, Knopf, 1971.
First Offenders, with Jacques Levy (also co-director: produced New York, 1973).
A Foot in the Door (produced New York, 1979).

Screenplays: *Stir Crazy*, 1980; *Splash*, with others, 1984.

Novels

Stern. New York, Simon and Schuster, 1962; London, Deutsch, 1963.
A Mother's Kisses. New York, Simon and Schuster, 1964; London, Cape, 1965.
The Dick. New York, Knopf, 1970; London, Cape, 1971.
About Harry Towns. New York, Knopf, 1974; London, Cape, 1975.
Tokyo Woes. New York, Fine, 1985.

Short Stories

Far from the City of Class and Other Stories. New York, Frommer-Pasmantier, 1963.
Black Angels. New York, Simon and Schuster, 1966; London, Cape, 1967.
Let's Hear It for a Beautiful Guy and Other Works of Short Fiction. New York, Fine, 1984.

Other

The Lonely Guy's Book of Life. New York, McGraw Hill, 1978.

Editor, *Black Humor*. New York, Bantam, and London, Corgi, 1965.

*

Critical Study: *Bruce Jay Friedman* by Max F. Schulz, New York, Twayne, 1974.

Theatrical Activities:
Director: **Play**—*First Offenders* (co-director, with Jacques Levy), New York, 1973.

* * *

It has always been the temptation of fiction writers to turn to the theatre. From Balzac through Henry James 19th-century novelists tried their hand at playwriting, with quite mixed results. Most of us are now interested in only one of Balzac's plays, *Mercadet*, and that probably because of its influence on *Waiting for Godot*. James's plays are readily available in Leon Edel's fine edition but only specialists seem to bother to read them. The same is true for most of the plays of the other 19th-century novelists-turned-dramatist. This rule-of-thumb applies also to certain of our contemporaries: Saul Bellow and John Hawkes, for example, have turned from first-rate fiction to the theatre; the results have been somewhat frustrating and disappointing.

The case of Hawkes is instructive because his plays seem largely extensions of his novels and elaborate on certain of their themes. Hawkes had already published four superb novels by the time he brought out his collection of plays, *The Innocent Party*, in 1966. It would seem that he turned to the theatre only after he felt his position as a novelist was fairly assured. Bruce Jay Friedman appeared to follow the same pattern although he turned to playwriting earlier in his career than Hawkes. The change from fiction to drama was also managed, from all indications, with fewer problems. *Scuba Duba* and *Steambath* are clearly more stageable, if less literary, than Hawkes's plays.

But like the plays in *The Innocent Party* Friedman's work for the theatre is thematically very much tied to his fiction. *Scuba Duba* and *Steambath* use the ambience, character types, and other literary props familiar to readers of Friedman's novels and collections of stories. Guilt, failure, and frustration are words which come to mind when we look at any part of his *oeuvre*.

Scuba Duba bears the subtitle "a tense comedy"; so might almost anything else Friedman has written because laughs come always at the expense of overbearing psychic pain in all of his work. Harold Wonder, the 35-year-old worrier who uses a scythe as a more aggressive kind of security blanket, has rented a chateau in the south of France. As the play opens he laments the fact that his wife has just run off with a black man. Harold's urban Jewish intonation is evident even in his first speech: "I really needed this. This is exactly what I came here for." He feels the need to communicate his *tsuris* to anyone who will listen. An attractive young lady, Miss Janus, is all too willing to help out, but Harold—like most of Friedman's other heroes—seems especially drawn to his psychiatrist and his Jewish mother. The former, aptly named Dr. Schoenfeld, who appears in the first act as a "cut-out" and returns in the flesh in Act 2, warns him in accustomed psychiatric fashion: ". . . you've never once looked at life sideways . . ." Harold's mother seems cut from the same cloth as the mothers in Friedman's novels *Stern*, *A Mother's Kisses*, and *The Dick*. Harold speaks to her long-distance and the telephone conversation which follows should be familiar to readers of the fiction of Philip Roth, Wallace Markfield, Herbert Gold, and other American Jewish writers. Harold's mother's voice is perfectly tuned: "That's all right, Harold. I'll just consider that my payment after thirty-six years of being your mother."

As the play develops the stage gets more and more crowded. A namedropping French landlady, an American tourist who demands proximity to a Chinese restaurant, a thief with an aphoristic turn ("All men are thieves"), an anti-American gendarme, a "wild-looking blonde" named Cheyenne who prefers "Bernie" Malamud and "those urban Jews" to C.P. Snow—all appear at one time or other. The main confrontation occurs in the second act when Harold's wife appears, followed shortly by two black men, one of whom is her lover. Harold's reaction involves much of the ambivalence experienced by Friedman Jews when in the company of blacks. The hero of Friedman's first novel, for example, went out of his way to express an affection he was never certain was compelling enough: ". . . Stern, who had a special feeling for all Negroes, hugged him [Crib] in a show of brotherhood."

Harold, *schlemiel* that he is, ends up by losing his wife and vows to "get started in my new life." Stern and Kenneth LePeters (the hero of *The Dick*) make similar resolutions and LePeters even goes to the point of leaving his wife and planning an extended trip with his daughter.

Friedman has been grouped with the so-called black humorists on several occasions. In a foreword he wrote for a collection of stories, *Black Humor* (which included his own story "Blank Angels"), he remarked: "There *is* a fading line between fantasy and reality ..." This is evident in *Scuba Duba* but perhaps even more in *Steambath*. Almost half way through the first act, the protagonist Tandy makes the shocked discovery: "... We're dead? Is that what you were going to say? That's what I was going to say. That's what we are. The second I said it, I knew it. Bam! Dead! Just like that! Christ!" Until this point in the play all indications are of a *real* steambath; then everything suddenly dilates into symbol and "fantasy," with no noticeable change in the dramatic movement. (John Hawkes used the steambath in the fifth chapter of his novel *The Lime Twig* with somewhat the same symbolical intent.)

Tandy is clearly not quite ready for death and protests the Attendant's (read God) decision through the remainder of the play. He seems very like Kenneth LePeters at the end of *The Dick*. He is on the verge of doing this he likes—writing a novel about Charlemagne, working for a charity to help brain-damaged welders, courting a Bryn Mawr girl who makes shish kebab—after divorcing his wife and giving up his job "teaching art appreciation over at the Police Academy." Tandy shares his frustration with a blonde girl named Meredith in somewhat the way Harold Wonder shared his plight, conversationally, with Miss Janus in *Scuba Duba*.

Max Schulz, in a very good book on the American Jewish novel, *Radical Sophistication*, speaks of Friedman's manner as having something "of the stand-up comic." This is especially noticeable in *Steambath*. Its humor favors the incongruous and unlikely. One can almost hear Woody Allen pronouncing some of the lines with considerable relish, like Tandy's incredulous response when he realizes that God is a Puerto Rican steambath attendant or when he discovers what he stands to lose by being dead: "No more airline stewardesses ... *Newsweek* ... Jesus, no more *Newsweek*."

Much of the humor has to do with popular culture. Bieberman, who makes intermittent appearances, is very much taken with the actors and baseball players of the 1940's. Other characters refer to the impact made by such essentials of television as the David Frost Show and pro football (American style). Names of every variety, including those of defeated political candidates (Mario Procaccino) and editors of magazines (Norman Podhoretz), are introduced incongruously and irreverently in the conversations. Theodore Solotaroff believes that

> nostalgia has a particular attraction for many Jewish writers: some of them, like Gold or Bruce Jay Friedman or Wallace Markfield or Irwin Faust, seem to possess virtually total recall of their adolescent years, as though there were still some secret meaning that resides in the image of Buster Brown shoes, or Edward G. Robinson's snarl, or Ralston's checkerboard package.

How much to the point of this remark is *Steambath*!

There is a good deal of the spirit of the second-generation American Jew in Friedman's plays as well as in his novels. He has caught this verbal rhythm and pulse beat in much the way that Philip Roth and Woody Allen have.

—Melvin J. Friedman

FRIEL, Brian (Bernard Patrick Friel). Irish. Born in Killyclogher, County Tyrone, 9 January 1929. Educated at St. Columb's College, Derry, 1941–46; St. Patrick's College, Maynooth, 1946–49, B.A. 1949; St. Mary's Training College (now St. Joseph's College of Education), Belfast, 1949–50. Married Anne Morrison in 1954; four daughters and one son. Schoolteacher in primary and intermediate schools in Derry, 1950–60. Since 1960 full-time writer: founder, with Stephen Rea, Field Day Theatre Company, Northern Ireland, 1980. Observer, for five months in 1963, Tyrone Guthrie Theatre, Minneapolis. Recipient: Irish Arts Council Macauley fellowship, 1963; Christopher Ewart-Biggs Memorial Award, 1982. D.Lit.: Rosary College, Chicago; University of Ulster, Coleraine; D.Litt.: National University of Ireland, Dublin, 1983. Member, Irish Academy of Letters, 1972, Aosdana, 1983, and Irish Senate, 1987. Agent: Curtis Brown, 162–168 Regent Street, London W1R 5TB, England; or, International Creative Management, 40 West 57th Street, New York, New York 10019, U.S.A. Address: Drumaweir House, Greencastle, County Donegal, Ireland.

PUBLICATIONS

Plays

The Francophile (produced Belfast, 1960; as *The Doubtful Paradise*, produced Belfast, 1960).
The Enemy Within (produced Dublin, 1962). Dublin, Gallery Press, and Newark, Delaware, Proscenium Press, 1979.
The Blind Mice (produced Dublin, 1963; Belfast, 1964).
Philadelphia, Here I Come! (produced Dublin, 1964; New York, 1966; London, 1967). London, Faber, 1965; New York, Farrar Straus, 1966.
The Loves of Cass McGuire (broadcast 1966; produced New York, 1966; Belfast, 1968; London, 1970). London, Faber, and New York, Farrar Straus, 1967.
Lovers: Part One: Winners; Part Two: Losers (produced Dublin, 1967; New York, 1968; London, 1969). New York, Farrar Straus, 1968; London, Faber, 1969.
Crystal and Fox (produced Dublin, 1968; Los Angeles, 1970; New York, 1973). London, Faber, 1970; with *The Mundy Scheme*, New York, Farrar Straus, 1970.
The Mundy Scheme (produced Dublin and New York, 1969). With *Crystal and Fox*, New York, Farrar Straus, 1970.
The Gentle Island (produced Dublin, 1971). London, Davis Poynter, 1974.
The Freedom of the City (produced Dublin, London, and Chicago, 1973; New York, 1974). London, Faber, 1974; New York, French, 1979.
Volunteers (produced Dublin, 1975). London, Faber, 1979.
Living Quarters (produced Dublin, 1977; New York, 1983). London, Faber, 1978; in *Selected Plays*, 1984.
Faith Healer (produced New York, 1979; London, 1981). London, Faber, 1980; in *Selected Plays*, 1984.
Aristocrats (produced Dublin, 1979). Dublin, Gallery Press, 1980; in *Selected Plays*, 1984.
Translations (produced Derry, 1980; New York and London, 1981). London, Faber, 1981; in *Selected Plays*, 1984.
American Welcome (produced Louisville and New York, 1980). Published in *The Best Short Plays 1981*, edited by Stanley Richards, Radnor, Pennsylvania, Chilton, 1981.
Three Sisters, adaptation of a play by Chekhov (produced Derry, 1981). Dublin, Gallery Press, 1981.

The Communication Cord (produced Derry, 1982; London, 1983; Seattle, 1984). London, Faber, 1983.
Selected Plays (includes *Philadelphia, Here I Come!*; *The Freedom of the City*; *Living Quarters*; *Aristocrats*; *Faith Healer*; *Translations*). London, Faber, 1984; Washington, D.C., Catholic University of America Press, 1986.
Fathers and Sons, adaptation of a novel by Turgenev (produced London, 1987). London, Faber, 1987.

Screenplay: *Philadelphia, Here I Come!*, 1970.

Radio Plays: *A Sort of Freedom*, 1958; *To This Hard House*, 1958; *The Founder Members*, 1964; *The Loves of Cass McGuire*, 1966.

Short Stories

The Saucer of Larks. New York, Doubleday, 1962; London, Gollancz, 1963.
The Gold in the Sea. London, Gollancz, and New York, Doubleday, 1966.
A Saucer of Larks: Stories of Ireland (selection). London, Arrow, 1969.
Selected Stories. Dublin, Gallery Press, 1979.
The Diviner. Dublin, O'Brien Press, and London, Allison and Busby, 1983.

Other

Editor, *The Last of the Name*, by Charles McGlinchey. Belfast, Blackstaff Press, 1986.

*

Bibliography: *Ten Modern Irish Playwrights* by Kimball King, New York, Garland, 1979.

Critical Studies: *Brian Friel* by D.E.S. Maxwell, Lewisburg, Pennsylvania, Bucknell University Press, 1973; *Brian Friel: The Growth of an Irish Dramatist* by Ulf Dantanus, Gothenburg, Sweden, Gothenburg Studies in English, 1985, London, Faber, 1987.

* * *

Brian Friel is now, perhaps unfairly, generally thought of in terms of *Translations*. Recognised as a sensitive, sympathetic (and, when needed, unflinching) dramatist, but without any one piece, except *Philadelphia, Here I Come!*, that sparked immediately in the mind, he came up suddenly with *Translations*. This moved during 1981 from the small stage at Hampstead to a full-scale production in the Lyttelton Theatre of the National.

Still, much had happened before that. Friel, who had been a teacher, became a full-time writer when he was about 30 and presently had stories published in the *New Yorker*. His early plays, done in Belfast and Dublin and set in Ireland, were not important, but with the rhythms of their dialogue and their bittersweetness—a term that would be inseparable from Friel—they showed the way that he was going. He would first emerge as an uncommon writer with *Philadelphia, Here I Come!* which took two years to reach New York where it was an immediate and long-running success, and three to reach London where it was acclaimed, but less strongly. The principal figure is a young Irishman, Gareth O'Donnell, emigrating to the United States like so many of his countrymen. His private life has been luckless; his public image is resolutely hopeful. As O'Neill did in *Days Without End*, with his businessman and doppelgänger, but never with any similar intensity, Friel splits his main character into two selves, representing the private and public sides of his life. They are played by the same actor and the ensuing serio-comedy—for Gareth and his alter ego—is ingeniously unstrained.

We might say that Friel himself, as a dramatist, is two people: one who will not minimise disaster, and another who is sympathetic, wistful, and (with his feeling for history) often absorbed by the past. Certainly much of the work has an innate wistfulness, *The Loves of Cass McGuire*, for example, set in an Irish old folks' home where one of the tougher inmates realises, like other dreamers, that she has been a prey to illusion. *Lovers* is a double bill, one piece about ardent and tragic adolescents, the other about a middle-aged pair whose loving is constantly interrupted by an invalid upstairs. In *Crystal and Fox* (the title stands for a former variety act) the husband, Fox, seeks hopelessly, and without regard for others, to work again by himself, as in his youth.

Of Friel's later plays, *The Freedom of the City* considers the anguished political scene in Ulster. *Faith Healer*, also acted in London at the Court Theatre, wavers badly because the dramatist—customarily assured—has tried to break his narrative (that of an itinerant faith-healer, his sorely tried wife, and their manager) into four consecutive monologues. The plot itself could be absorbing: the tragedy of the healer whose occasional gift can bewilder him (as on a night in South Wales); the wanderings across remoter Britain; the loss of the wife's child, stillborn, somewhere up in Sutherland; and a final terror, suggested rather than described, outside a pub in Donegal. Much of the writing is crisply first-rate with such imaginative passages as the incantation of the place names; but it is the construction that fails: we want to see the characters together, and we never do.

Translations so startled one of London's leading drama critics that he described it, after its first night at Hampstead, as a masterpiece. This is a valuable word that the play hardly deserves though it is sharply original and often exciting. Its scene is an Irish "hedge-school' in a corner of Donegal 150 years ago, one of those traditional evening schools in which the Gaelic-speaking peasants learned the classical tongues but no English. There is disaster when Royal Engineers on an ordnance survey arrive in the village where Englishmen must be intrusive foreigners. Friel has handled the language problem subtly, for though English is all we hear, we are never in doubt whether the characters are speaking English or Gaelic. This is a striking piece of theatrical legerdemain. The writing throughout has an easy flow; but the last act, with its rising tragedy, becomes curiously blurred: it does need clarification. Probably we can take the play as an analogy, from a distance, to the situation in Ulster today. Unusual though it is in conception and often in treatment, one is left with a certain disappointment.

One has to say that more sharply about *The Communication Cord* which reached London in 1983 (it had been done in Derry during the previous year) upon the small stage of the Hampstead Theatre where *Translations* had also been seen. The link between the two pieces is that both are set in Donegal though with a century-and-a-half between them. The action of *The Communication Cord*, established in a "restored" cottage of a remote "townland," is resolutely farcical; the people cannot communicate with each other, and halfway through the night the cast is in a tangle that might have satisfied the English *farceur* Ben Travers, though he would have done more with it than Friel, whose talents are astray in this medium. Still, we understand why the author has a single word in his programme glossary: "gulder," to talk loudly. And there is a good final black-out when the cottage roof seems to have disintegrated and a heavy beam crashes down to the alarm of all on stage, especially a man who for reasons of his own has fastened himself to the wall by a chain-collar once intended for a cow. This is the second time that Friel uses the joke: his first victim is a pompous Senator with a passion for everything tiresomely folk-historical. Most of the work falls to a solemn young lecturer in linguistics who has been lent the cottage briefly in a complex plan to help his career. Friel has some mischievous fun with him, but the play as a whole is a farce (from a distorted Ireland) that seldom comes to life.

—J.C. Trewin

FRISBY, Terence. British. Born in New Cross, London, 28 November 1932. Educated at Dobwalls Village School; Dartford Grammar School; Central School of Speech Training and Dramatic Art, London, 1955–57. Married Christine Vecchione in 1963 (divorced); one son. Worked as a salesman, capstan lathe operator, factory hand, waiter, chauffeur, chucker-out at the Hammersmith Palais, etc.; since 1957 professional actor; also a producer. Resident director, New Theatre, Bromley, Kent, 1963–64. Agent: Harvey Unna and Stephen Durbridge Ltd., 24–32 Pottery Lane, London W11 4LZ. Address: 72 Bishops Mansions, Bishops Park Road, London SW6 6DZ, England.

PUBLICATIONS

Plays

The Subtopians (also director: produced London, 1964). London, French, 1964.
There's a Girl in My Soup (produced London, 1966; New York, 1967). London and New York, French, 1968.
The Bandwagon (produced London, 1969). London, French, 1973.
It's All Right If I Do It (produced Leicester and London, 1977). London, French, 1977.
Seaside Postcard (also director: produced London, 1977). London, French, 1978.

Screenplay: *There's a Girl in My Soup*, 1970.

Television Plays: *Guilty*, 1964; *Public Eye* series, 1964; *Take Care of Madam*, 1965; *Adam Adamant* series, 1966; *More Deadly Than the Sword*, 1966; *Don't Forget the Basics*, 1967; *Lucky Feller* series, 1976.

*

Critical Studies: *Anger and After* by John Russell Taylor, London, Methuen, 1962, revised edition, 1969, as *The Angry Theatre*, New York, Hill and Wang, 1962, revised edition, 1969; *The Season* by William Goldman, New York, Harcourt Brace, 1969, revised edition, New York, Limelight, 1984.

Theatrical Activities:
Director: **Plays**—in various repertory companies, including plays at Bromley, Kent, 1963–64; *The Subtopians*, London, 1964; *Seaside Postcard*, London, 1977.
Actor (as Terence Holland, 1957–66): **Plays**—over 200 roles in repertory theatres in Bromley, Guildford, Lincoln, Richmond, York; London debut as Charlie Pepper in *Gentleman's Pastime* by Marion Hunt, 1958; in *A Sense of Detachment* by John Osborne, London, 1973; *X* by Barry Reckord, London, 1974; Clive Popkiss in *Rookery Nook* by Ben Travers, London, 1979; Father Mullarkey in *Once a Catholic* by Mary O'Malley, toured, 1980–81 and 1986; Birdboot in *The Real Inspector Hound* by Tom Stoppard, and Leslie in *Seaside Postcard*, toured, 1983–84; Archie Rice in *The Entertainer* by John Osborne, Sonning, Berkshire, 1984; David Bliss in *Hay Fever* by Noel Coward, Manchester, 1985; other roles in London and on tour. **Television**—*Play School*; *It Must Be Something in the Water* by Alan Plater, 1973; *When the Boys Come Out to Play* by Richard Harris, 1974; *Leeds—United!* by Colin Welland, 1974.

* * *

Terence Frisby's first play, *The Subtopians*, was greeted with eulogies when, in 1964, it was seen for the first time. It was, critics decided, funny but complex, accurately worked out, deeply felt in spite of its genuine comedy, serious in intention but almost painfully hilarious, and it had an unbreakable grip on the realities of social life in the 1960's.

Frisby was 32 when *The Subtopians* arrived to signal a newcomer whose gifts were, to say the least, so interesting that his future activities were sure to demand close attention. Part at least of the technical neatness of his first play was due to his training at the Central School of Speech Training and Dramatic Art and to his work as an actor in repertory, musicals, and films, as an entertainer in night clubs and cabaret, and as a director. There is a solid foundation of technique beneath the sometimes unkind observation and harsh comedy.

In 1966 *There's a Girl in My Soup* brought Frisby one of the greatest commercial successes in the modern theatre, running for six years in the West End and, at the same time, pleasing most of the critics. Like *The Subtopians*, it has beautifully efficient machinery and precision of observation. Its hero has the sort of position in life—he is an expert on food, writing for intellectual periodicals—which once would have pointed him out as a figure of fun but, in 1966, assured an audience that he was a leader of thought and fashion whose familiarity with the best restaurants is intrinsically romantic and enviable. Thus he is in a position to follow an exhausting, eventful career as an amorist whose endless successes are with the young who find his expertise, and the attitude towards him of those whose efforts he criticises, altogether glamorous. It is less the dialogue or anything explicit in the play than the form it takes and the succession of events which indicate that behind the parade of insatiable appetite for change and his pride in his sexual prowess he is at the same time both lonely and uncertain of his attractiveness to those whom he regards as victims. Frisby naturally chooses to study the girl whose victim he becomes, in whose life he is only a pleasant interlude. The "trendiness" and "contemporaneity" of *There's a Girl in My Soup* carried the play round a triumphal tour of the world's theatres, with productions not only throughout the English-speaking theatre but in most European countries as well as in Turkey, Israel, and Mexico.

The course of events which led to the production of Frisby's third play, *The Bandwagon*, rose out of his success as a script writer. *Guilty*, a one-off piece for the BBC in 1964, was followed by a comedy, *Don't Forget the Basics*, for Independent Television and contributions to various series, notably to *Public Eye*, which at its best gave an almost continental seediness to the activities of a provincial private detective, and *Adam Adamant*, in which adventure stories which might almost have come to birth in a boys' comic were treated with unusual and preposterous elegancies and elaborations. *The Bandwagon*, originally *Some Have Greatness Thrust upon Them*, was to be one of BBC television's socially conscious Wednesday Plays. It chose to imagine the situation of a stupid, ugly, graceless teenage girl, a member of a family of almost appalling fecundity—her mother and her sister are both pregnant when the play begins—who discovers that, though unmarried, she is to become the mother of quintuplets. Her fecundity, before drugs inducing multiple births had won any special attention, reaches the ears of popular newspapers, who make her a heroine, and television, which interviews her. The interview comes to an end when Aurora (the most unfortunately named heroine) explains the physiological misinformation and ignorance that are responsible for her plight. Frisby's refusal to alter a line which, the BBC believed, would give unnecessary offence, led to the Corporation's refusal to produce the play.

The BBC was, perhaps, entirely wrong. The line—"My friend Syl told me it was safe standing up"—is all of a piece—with a matter-of-fact simplicity which makes Aurora almost unexploitable. Aurora is manoeuvred into marriage, and has to be hurried from the church into childbed; and so have her mother and sister. The play belongs to the tradition of broad farce, and its final scene, as the women-folk depart from the alter in agonized haste, sacrifices the precarious dignity and simplicity which have won the sympathy of the audience. *The Bandwagon*, in the good old days of curtain-raisers, could have stopped at its natural end, the silent, almost unnerving confrontation of two essentially pathetic victims of exploitation, Aurora and her husband-to-be, and have retained its integrity.

Although *The Bandwagon* seemed, when it was new, likely to follow Frisby's earlier plays and become an outstanding success, it did not do so. Possibly its depressing social milieu and its unfriendly view of what we have been taught to call the "media," as well as its combination of farce with serious moral concern, simply bothered audiences who found Aurora to be no more than a heroine of farce. In the same way, neither *It's All Right If I Do It*, and *Seaside Postcard* won any startling success. Frisby's gift for comic incident and comic dialogue, obviously rooted in a serious view of society, has not, perhaps, found its audience when it applies itself to areas outside the provinces and the glossy West End world of *There's a Girl in My Soup*.

—Henry Raynor

FRY, Christopher. British. Born Christopher Fry Harris in Bristol, 18 December 1907. Educated at Bedford Modern School, 1918–26. Served in the Non-Combatant Corps, 1940–44. Married Phyllis Marjorie Hart in 1936; one son. Teacher, Bedford Froebel Kindergarten, 1926–27; actor and office worker, Citizen House, Bath, 1927; schoolmaster, Hazelwood School, Limpsfield, Surrey, 1928–31; secretary to H. Rodney Bennett, 1931–32; founding director, Tunbridge Wells Repertory Players, 1932–35; lecturer and editor of schools magazine, Dr. Barnardo's Homes, 1934–39; director, 1939–40, and visiting director, 1945–46, Oxford Playhouse; visiting director, 1946, and staff dramatist, 1947, Arts Theatre Club, London. Also composer. Recipient: Shaw Prize Fund award, 1948; Foyle Poetry Prize, 1951; New York Drama Critics Circle award, 1951, 1952, 1956; Queen's Gold Medal for Poetry, 1962; Royal Society of Literature Heinemann award, 1962. D.A.: Manchester Polytechnic, 1966. Fellow, Royal Society of Literature. Agent: ACTAC Ltd., 16 Cadogan Lane, London S.W.1. Address: The Toft, East Dean, near Chichester, West Sussex PO18 0JA, England.

PUBLICATIONS

Plays

Youth and the Peregrines (produced Tunbridge Wells, Kent, 1934).

She Shall Have Music (lyrics only, with Ronald Frankau), book by Frank Eyton, music by Fry and Monte Crick (produced London, 1934).

To Sea in a Sieve (as Christopher Harris) (revue; produced Reading, 1935).

Open Door (produced London, 1936). Goldings, Hertfordshire, Printed by the Boys at the Press of Dr. Barnardo's Homes, n.d.

The Boy with a Cart: Cuthman, Saint of Sussex (produced Coleman's Hatch, Sussex, 1938; London, 1950; New York, 1953). London, Oxford University Press, 1939; New York, Oxford University Press, 1951.

The Tower (produced Tewkesbury, Gloucestershire, 1939).

Thursday's Child: A Pageant, music by Martin Shaw (produced London, 1939). London, Girls' Friendly Society, 1939.

A Phoenix Too Frequent (produced London, 1946; Cambridge, Massachusetts, 1948; New York, 1950). London, Hollis and Carter, 1946; New York, Oxford University Press, 1949.

The Firstborn (broadcast 1947; produced Edinburgh, 1948). Cambridge, University Press, 1946; New York, Oxford University Press, 1950; revised version (produced London, 1952; New York, 1958), London and New York, Oxford University Press, 1952, 1958.

The Lady's Not for Burning (produced London, 1948; New York, 1950). London and New York, Oxford University Press, 1949; revised version, 1950, 1958.

Thor, With Angels (produced Canterbury, 1948; Washington, D.C., 1950; London, 1951). Canterbury, H.J. Goulden, 1948; New York, Oxford University Press, 1949.

Venus Observed (produced London, 1950; New York, 1952). London and New York, Oxford University Press, 1950.

Ring round the Moon: A Charade with Music, adaptation of a play by Jean Anouilh (produced London and New York, 1950). London and New York, Oxford University Press, 1950.

A Sleep of Prisoners (produced Oxford, London and New York, 1951). London and New York, Oxford University Press, 1951.

The Dark Is Light Enough: A Winter Comedy (produced Edinburgh and London, 1954; New York, 1955). London and New York, Oxford University Press, 1954.

The Lark, adaptation of a play by Jean Anouilh (produced London, 1955). London, Methuen, 1955; New York, Oxford University Press, 1956.

Tiger at the Gates, adaptation of a play by Jean Giraudoux (produced London and New York, 1955). London, Methuen, 1955; New York, Oxford University Press, 1956; as

The Trojan War Will Not Take Place (produced London, 1983), Methuen, 1983.
Duel of Angels, adaptation of a play by Jean Giraudoux (produced London, 1958; New York, 1960). London, Methuen, 1958; New York, Oxford University Press, 1959.
Curtmantle (produced in Dutch, Tilburg, Netherlands, 1961; Edinburgh and London, 1962). London and New York, Oxford University Press, 1961.
Judith, adaptation of a play by Jean Giraudoux (produced London, 1962). London, Methuen, 1962.
The Bible: Original Screenplay, assisted by Jonathan Griffin. New York, Pocket Books, 1966.
Peer Gynt, adaptation of the play by Ibsen (produced Chichester, 1970). London and New York, Oxford University Press, 1970.
A Yard of Sun: A Summer Comedy (produced Nottingham and London, 1970; Cleveland, 1972). London and New York, Oxford University Press, 1970.
The Brontës of Haworth (televised 1973). London, Davis Poynter, 2 vols., 1974.
Cyrano de Bergerac, adaptation of the play by Edmond Rostand (produced Chichester, 1975). London and New York, Oxford University Press, 1975.
Paradise Lost, music by Penderecki, adaptation of the poem by Milton (produced Chicago, 1978). London, Schott, 1978.
Selected Plays (includes *The Boy with a Cart*, *A Phoenix Too Frequent*, *The Lady's Not for Burning*, *A Sleep of Prisoners*, *Curtmantle*). Oxford and New York, Oxford University Press, 1985.
One Thing More, or, Caedmon Construed (produced Chelmsford, Essex, 1986).

Screenplays: *The Beggar's Opera*, with Denis Cannan, 1953; *A Queen Is Crowned* (documentary), 1953; *Ben Hur*, 1959; *Barabbas*, 1962; *The Bible: In the Beginning*, 1966.

Radio Plays: for *Children's Hour* series, 1939–40; *The Firstborn*, 1947; *Rhineland Journey*, 1948.

Television Plays: *The Canary*, 1950; *The Tenant of Wildfell Hall*, 1968; *The Brontës of Haworth* (four plays), 1973; *The Best of Enemies*, 1976; *Sister Dora*, from the book by Jo Manton, 1977.

Verse

Root and Sky: Poetry from the Plays of Christopher Fry, edited by Charles E. and Jean G. Wadsworth. Cambridge, Rampant Lions Press, and Boston, Godine, 1975.

Other

An Experience of Critics, with *The Approach to Dramatic Criticism* by W.A. Darlington and others, edited by Kaye Webb. London, Perpetua Press, 1952; New York, Oxford University Press, 1953.
The Boat That Mooed (for children). New York, Macmillan, 1966.
Can You Find Me: A Family History. London, Oxford University Press, 1978; New York, Oxford University Press, 1979.
Death Is a Kind of Love (lecture). Cranberry Isles, Maine, Tidal Press, 1979.
Genius, Talent and Failure (lecture). London, King's College, 1987.

Translator, *The Boy and the Magic*, by Colette. London, Dobson, 1964.

Incidental Music: *A Winter's Tale*, London, 1951; recorded by Caedmon.

*

Bibliography: by B.L. Schear and E.G. Prater, in *Tulane Drama Review 4* (New Orleans), March 1960.

Manuscript Collection: Harvard University Theatre Collection, Cambridge, Massachusetts.

Critical Studies: *Christopher Fry: An Appreciation*, London, Nevill, 1950, and *Christopher Fry*, London, Longman, 1954, revised edition, 1962, both by Derek Stanford; *The Drama of Comedy: Victim and Victor* by Nelson Vos, Richmond, Virginia, John Knox Press, 1965; *Creed and Drama* by W.M. Merchant, London, SPCK, 1965; *The Christian Tradition in Modern British Verse Drama* by William V. Spanos, New Brunswick, New Jersey, Rutgers University Press, 1967; *Christopher Fry* by Emil Roy, Carbondale, Southern Illinois University Press, 1968; *Christopher Fry: A Critical Essay*, Grand Rapids, Michigan, Eerdmans, 1970, and *More Than the Ear Discovers: God in the Plays of Christopher Fry*, Chicago, Loyola University Press, 1983, both by Stanley M. Wiersma.

Theatrical Activities:
Director: **Plays**—*How-Do, Princess?* by Ivor Novello, toured, 1936; *The Circle of Chalk* by James Laver, London, 1945; *The School for Scandal* by Sheridan, London, 1946; *A Phoenix Too Frequent*, Brighton, 1950; *The Lady's Not for Burning*, toured, 1971; and others.
Actor: **Plays**—in repertory, Bath, 1937.

Christopher Fry comments:

The way a man writes for the theatre depends on the way he looks at life. If, in his experience, direction and purpose seem to be all-pervading factors, pattern and shape are necessary to his writing. The verse form is an effort to be true to what Eleanor, in *Curtmantle*, calls "the silent order whose speech is all visible things." No event is understandable in a prose sense alone. Its ultimate meaning (that is to say, the complete life of the event, seen in its eternal context) is a poetic meaning. The comedies try to explore a reality behind appearances. "Something condones the world incorrigibly" says Thomas Mendip in *The Lady's Not for Burning*—in spite of the "tragic" nature of life. The problem, a long way from being solved, is how to contain the complexities and paradoxes within two hours of entertainment: how to define the creative pattern of life without the danger of dogmatic statement. Dogma is static; life is movement. "La vérité est dans une nuance."

* * *

Christopher Fry's work was doubtless overrated in the fruitful years of *The Lady's Not for Burning* and *A Sleep of Prisoners*; it is most certainly underrated today. This is in part due to an integrity and consistency in the work of a playwright who has pursued his own style of the serio-comic and chosen to ignore fashion. It is as if Beckett and the theatre of the absurd had not existed, nor Brecht and the practice of epic theatre with its oblique devices of structure and technique, nor the socially and politically committed drama following Osborne's *Look Back in Anger*; and Fry's reputation has paid the price. It remains to be seen whether his neglect of contemporary trends matters in the final verdict.

In his last original stage play, *A Yard of Sun*, Fry is still writing in that highly idiosyncratic, all-but-verse idiom of loose pentameters which drew attention to his earliest plays. Characteristically mixing the colloquial and the allusive, a minor character can say, "I pick words gingerly like a rose out of thorns," and at a stroke equalizes his role with that of a major, thus by prosaic kitchen-sink standards making all the parts equally literate and classless. Or Angelino Bruno, one of the two central characters whose families are unexpectedly united after World War II, can come out with a startling turn of expression which fixes and underscores the general statement of the stage:

> What a settling-up God's having this week!
> Both of us within two days. Well, once
> The bit's between His teeth things start to move.

Although it may not bear close analysis as poetry on the page, verbal panache of this kind keeps Fry's stage alive when a situation is static. It is often spendthrift with the necessary economy of the action, and the idiom which refreshed the grim postwar years and dazzled the critics can now seem irrelevant, even facile.

But Fry was seeking a spiritual idiom for a contemporary and unobtrusively Christian verse drama after T.S. Eliot had prepared the ground with *Murder in the Cathedral* (1935) and *The Family Reunion* (1939). Where Eliot was concerned to find a spare and unobtrusive verse form designed to control the speech and movement on a stage of modern martyrs, Fry, in a less certain style but with more sense of the stage, aimed with abandon at a general mood to match his themes. There are moments in *A Sleep of Prisoners*, possibly the best anti-war play of its period, when the verse achieves the richness of both tonal and physical embodiment of the stage moment while exploring a verbal idea:

> How ceaseless the earth is. How it goes on.
> Nothing has happened except silence where sound was,
> Stillness where movement was . . .

These lines are spoken by the figure of Adam just after he has witnessed the murder of Abel his son, and they enact both the father's horror and the scene's meaning.

Where, however, Eliot's profundity of vision carried him through his own inadequacies as a dramatist—notably his inability to create character which did not suffer the atrophy of symbolism—Fry came to lean on an explosive central situation fruitful in itself. This situation might lack the qualities of conflict, tension, and development, yet still be capable of holding attention. Thus *A Sleep of Prisoners* consists of a pattern of re-enacted Old Testament stories chosen to illustrate facets of the idea of violence. Each story is not only informed by the audience's own memories of the Bible, but also, because it is dreamed by a modern soldier held prisoner in a church, is automatically granted a contemporary relevance: within the structure of the play the spectator himself works to supply the missing factor in the dramatic equation, and the teaching element of a morality play is actively deduced by our application of the fiction to the fact. Nevertheless, this play suffers, as only morality plays can, from the static preconception by which morality characters tend to be fixed in their symbolic attitudes.

This play in its time startled and delighted audiences by the free use of its church setting, where at a glance the chancel could be Adam's jungle or the pulpit Abraham's mountain: as they were for *Murder in the Cathedral*, audiences were both theatregoers and congregation, and were unusually exercised by the multiplicity of association felt within the performance. There are no such props for a dramatic experience in Fry's other plays, although in *The Boy with a Cart*, a simple mystery play of spontaneous charm, *The Firstborn*, exploring the tragic dilemma of Moses and the Plagues, and *Curtmantle* he draws upon legend and history in parallel attempts to bring the remote closer to home. *Curtmantle*, too neglected a play, was his most sustained attempt at a serious character study: this chronicle play of Henry II in conflict with his Archbishop Becket is set out in a sequence of vivid episodes more in the simple manner of Bolt's episodic *A Man for All Seasons* than with the prismatic counterpoint of Brecht's epic theatre, the scenes designed to illustrate the wit, the wisdom, and the complex passions of the title part as Henry searches for a rational unity of divinie and secular law.

Fry creates a drama of colour and flair, choosing a situation for its imaginative potential, often one of implicit crisis involving a clash of strong, bright personalities. His situation enables him to demonstrate a compassionate affirmation of life—an optimism which inevitably seemed escapist beside the bleak absurdist landscape of the postwar years, in spite of the tragic mode of *The Firstborn*, *Thor, With Angels* (the 1948 Canterbury Festival play) and *The Dark Is Light Enough*, plays which exemplify Fry's philosophy of maturing through crisis:

> We reach an obstacle, and learn to overcome it;
> our thoughts or emotions become knotted, and we
> increase ourselves in order to unknot them; a
> state of being becomes intolerable, and, drawing
> upon a hidden reserve of spirit, we transform it.

But he is nevertheless remembered for those early comedies of mood touched with the wit and fantasy by which he could express his most gentle and humane thinking. The prototype for this kind of comedy, and still the most regularly revived, was the one-act, *A Phoenix Too Frequent*. This was taken from the ancient tale of the young Roman widow romantically committed to a fast to the death in her husband's tomb, until she and an equally romantic young soldier agree to substitute the husband's body for the corpse the soldier was guarding with his life. With the lightest of touches, the widow decides for life, and youth and love supplant social convention and death: a joyful illustration of the life-force at work.

The spring-time comedy that made Fry's name and competed for London's attention with Eliot's *The Cocktail Party* in 1949 was his best-known play *The Lady's Not for Burning*, an extension of the style and spirit of *A Phoenix Too Frequent*. His verbal pyrotechnics were at their most assured, and the medieval colour on his stage lifted the play into a rarefied atmosphere that forced comparison with Giraudoux and the lighter Anouilh of *L'Invitation au château* (which Fry was later to translate beautifully as *Ring round the Moon*). A simple crisis again sets the play in motion, when one Thomas Mendip, desiring but denied death, is confronted with Jennet Jourdemayne, who wants to live but must die as a witch. She envies his deathwish, he her "damnable mystery," until, to test his sincerity and her courage, Fry impudently arranges for them one last "joyous" evening together before Jennet's execution. The result is to dramatize with graceful irony Fry's sense of cosmic purpose.

His other plays designed to celebrate the seasons followed irregularly in an unpredictable range of moods, some unexpectedly sombre: *Venus Observed* (autumn), *The Dark Is Light Enough* (winter) and *A Yard of Sun* (summer). *Venus Observed* was a comedy of middle-aged disillusionment, but pleasingly balanced and without fashionable cynicism. However, *The Dark Is Light Enough* selects the year of revolutions, 1848, for its darker setting, and secures its unity in the compassionate and gracious presence of an Austrian countess, a part created by Edith Evans. With the Countess's "divine non-interference" it is demonstrated

how apparently undemandingly
She moves among us; and yet
Lives make and unmake themselves in her
neighbourhood
As nowhere else.

Thus the theme is one of providence, and, through the wisdom of the Countess as she recognizes the imminence of death, embodies the necessity of our respect for every human personality in its touch of grace.

To set side by side plays as contrasting as *The Lady's Not for Burning* and *The Dark Is Light Enough* is inescapably to be impressed by Fry's versatility, and by the integrity of a writer who uses his chosen medium as a way of searching out his personal philosophy whether in the vein of farce or tragedy, spring or winter. Eliot notwithstanding, Fry's is the most sustained attempt in English to write an undogmatic Christian drama in modern times.

—J.L. Styan

FUGARD, (Harold) Athol (Lannigan). South African. Born near Middleburg, Cape Province, 11 June 1932. Educated at Marist Brothers College, Port Elizabeth, 1938–45; Port Elizabeth Technical College, 1946–50; University of Cape Town, 1950–53. Married Sheila Meiring in 1956; one daughter. Seaman, S.S. *Graigaur*, 1953–54; journalist, Port Elizabeth *Evening Post*, 1954; reporter, South African Broadcasting Corporation, Port Elizabeth and Cape Town, 1955–57; clerk, Fordsburg Native Commissioner's Court, Johannesburg, 1958; stage manager and publicity agent, National Theatre Organization, 1958; worked as cleaner in London, 1960. Co-founder, Circle Players theatre workshop, Cape Town, 1957, African Theatre Workshop, Sophiatown, 1958–59, New Africa Group, Brussels, 1960, Ijinle Company, London, 1966, and The Space experimental theatre, Cape Town, 1972. Since 1963 director, Serpent Players, Port Elizabeth. Recipient: *New York Times* award, 1965; Obie award, 1971; London Theatre Critics award, 1974; Locarno Film Festival Ernest Artaria Award, 1977; Berlin Film Festival Golden Bear, 1980; Yale University fellowship, 1980; New York Drama Critics Circle award, 1981; London *Evening Standard* award, 1984; Common Wealth award, 1984; Drama League award, 1986. D.Litt.: University of Natal, Durban, 1981; Rhodes University, Grahamstown, 1983; University of Cape Town, 1984; D.F.A.: Yale University, New Haven, Connecticut, 1983; D.H.L.: Georgetown University, Washington, D.C., 1984. Agent: Esther Sherman, William Morris Agency, 1350 Avenue of the Americas, New York, New York 10019, U.S.A. Address: P.O. Box 5090, Walmer, Port Elizabeth, South Africa.

PUBLICATIONS

Plays

No-Good Friday (also director: produced Johannesburg, 1958; Sheffield, 1974). Included in *Dimetos and Two Early Plays*, 1977.

Nongogo (also director: produced Cape Town, 1959; Sheffield, 1974; New York, 1978). Included in *Dimetos and Two Early Plays*, 1977.

The Blood Knot (also director: produced Johannesburg, 1961; London, 1963; New York, 1964). Cape Town, Simondium, 1963; New York, Odyssey Press, 1964; in *Three Port Elizabeth Plays*, 1974.

Hello and Goodbye (also director: produced Johannesburg, 1965; New York, 1968; Leicester, 1971; London, 1973). Cape Town, Balkema, 1966; in *Three Port Elizabeth Plays*, 1974.

The Coat (produced Port Elizabeth, 1966). With *The Third Degree*, by Don MacLennan, Cape Town, Balkema, 1971.

People Are Living There (produced Glasgow, 1968; also director: produced Cape Town, 1969; New York, 1971; London, 1972). Cape Town, Buren, 1969; London, Oxford University Press, 1970.

The Occupation: A Script for Camera, in *Ten One Act Plays* edited by Cosmo Pieterse. London, Heinemann, 1968.

Boesman and Lena (also director: produced Grahamstown, 1969; revised version produced New York, 1970; London, 1971). Cape Town, Buren, 1969; New York, French, 1972; London, Oxford University Press, 1973.

Orestes (produced Cape Town, 1971). Published in *Theatre One: New South African Drama*, edited by Stephen Gray, Johannesburg, Donker, 1978.

Statements after an Arrest under the Immorality Act (also director: produced Cape Town, 1972; London, 1974; New York, 1978). Included in *Statements*, 1974.

Sizwe Bansi Is Dead, with John Kani and Winston Ntshona (also director: as *Sizwe Banzi Is Dead*, produced Cape Town, 1972; as *Sizwe Bansi Is Dead*, produced London, 1973; New Haven, Connecticut, and New York, 1974). Included in *Statements*, 1974; in *Two Plays*, 1976.

The Island, with John Kani and Winston Ntshona (also director: as *Die Hodoshe Span* produced Cape Town, 1973; as *The Island* produced London, and New York, 1974). Included in *Statements*, 1974; in *Two Plays*, 1976.

Three Port Elizabeth Plays: The Blood Knot, Hello and Goodbye, Boesman and Lena. New York, Viking Press, and London, Oxford University Press, 1974.

Statements: Three Plays. London, Oxford University Press, 1974.

Dimetos (also director: produced Edinburgh, 1975; revised version produced Nottingham, London, and New York, 1976). Included in *Dimetos and Two Early Plays*, 1977.

Two Plays: Sizwe Bansi Is Dead, and The Island, with John Kani and Winston Ntshona. New York, Viking Press, 1976.

Dimetos and Two Early Plays. London, Oxford University Press, 1977.

The Guest: An Episode in the Life of Eugène Marais, with Ross Devenish (as *The Guest at Steenkampskraal* televised 1977). Johannesburg, Donker, 1977.

A Lesson from Aloes (also director: produced Johannesburg, 1978; New Haven, Connecticut, New York, and London, 1980). New York, Random House, and Oxford, Oxford University Press, 1981.
Boesman and Lena, and Other Plays (includes *The Blood Knot, People Are Living There, Hello and Goodbye*). London, Oxford University Press, 1978.
The Drummer (produced Louisville, 1980).
"Master Harold" and the Boys (also director: produced New Haven, Connecticut, and New York, 1982; London, 1983). New York, Knopf, 1982; Oxford, Oxford University Press, 1983.
Marigolds in August (screenplay), with Ross Devenish. Johannesburg, Donker, 1982.
The Road to Mecca (produced New Haven, Connecticut, 1984; London, 1985). London, Faber, 1985.
A Place with the Pigs (also director: produced New Haven, Connecticut, 1987).
Selected Plays (includes *"Master Harold" and the Boys, The Blood Knot, Hello and Goodbye, Boesman and Lena*). Oxford, Oxford University Press, 1987.

Screenplays: *Boesman and Lena*, 1973; *Marigolds in August*, with Ross Devenish, 1980.

Television Plays: *Mille Miglia*, 1968 (UK); *The Guest at Steenkampskraal*, with Ross Devenish, 1977.

Novel

Tsotsi. Johannesburg, Donker, and London, Collings, 1980; New York, Random House, 1981.

Other

Notebooks 1960–1977, edited by Mary Benson. Johannesburg, Donker, and London, Faber, 1983; New York, Knopf, 1984.

*

Bibliography: *Athol Fugard: A Bibliography, Biography, Playography* by Russell Vandenbroucke, London, TQ Publications, 1977; *Athol Fugard: A Source Guide* by Temple Hauptfleisch, Johannesburg, Donker, 1982.

Manuscript Collection: National English Literary Museum, Rhodes University, Grahamstown.

Critical Studies: *Athol Fugard* by Stephen Gray, Johannesburg, McGraw Hill, 1982; *Athol Fugard* by Dennis Walder, London, Macmillan, 1984, New York, Grove Press, 1985; *Truths the Hand Can Touch: The Theatre of Athol Fugard* by Russell Vandenbroucke, New York, Theatre Communications Group, 1985.

Theatrical Activities:
Director: **Plays**—many of his own plays; *The Cure*, adaptation of *Mandragola* by Machiavelli, Grahamstown, 1963; *Woyzeck* by Georg Büchner, South Africa, 1964; *Antigone* by Sophocles, Cape Town, 1965; *The Trials of Brother Jero* by Wole Soyinka, London, 1966.
Actor: **Plays**—roles in most of his own plays in South Africa; Okkie the Greek in *A Kakamas Greek* by David Herbert, Brussels, 1960; Morrie in *The Blood Knot*, New York, 1962 and 1985, London, 1966; *A Place with the Pigs*, New Haven, Connecticut, 1987. **Films**—*Boesman and Lena*, 1973; *Meetings with Remarkable Men*, 1979; *Marigolds in August*, 1980; *Gandhi*, 1982; *The Killing Fields*, 1984. **Television**—*The Blood Knot*, 1967 (UK); *The Guest at Steenkampskraal*, 1977.

* * *

Athol Fugard is a playwright in the fullest sense of the word: he is a builder of plays in the way that a shipwright is a builder of ships. For a particular moment in the 1970's he was able to harness his multiple accomplishments as actor, dramatist, and director and fashion plays, partly through collaboration, that spoke of the furnace of conflicts in South Africa with humour and force. Even after Fugard left South Africa to build a new base in the United States, his plays continued to examine his native land, and by continuing to direct them himself, he continued to control the shape and expression of his ideas far more than most writers.

Some of the plays of the 1970's were every bit as *written* as his earliest successes such as *The Blood Knot*. Thus, *Statements after an Arrest under the Immorality Act*, examining the carnal relations between a man and a woman whose contact was forbidden under the racial laws of South Africa, was a fully scripted drama. But during that period his most significant plays were the two that he wrote in collaboration with the black African actors Winston Ntshona and John Kani, *Sizwe Bansi Is Dead* and *The Island*.

Those plays opened a dialogue with the world presenting, as *The Blood Knot* had done earlier, such theatrically exact metaphors for South Africa's racial strife that the human situation transcended the politics while at the same time illuminating the nature of the conflict. In addition the final shape of the plays, with many roles performed by two actors, was to provide an economical model for further explorations of the South African situation, such as those by Barney Simon and Percy Mtwa. *Sizwe Bansi* remains a particularly powerful statement about the effect of repression on individuals subjected to South Africa's laws. Its examination of the problem of individual identity gives a haunting, nearly mythological power.

The South African division of humanity into three groups—whites, coloureds, and blacks—always had its absurdities as well as its tragedies. *Sizwe Bansi* seizes on both aspects, beginning with an actual death and ending with a symbolic transfer of identities with a dead man; in a society where access was determined by bureaucratic interpretations of race and by the possession of the right identity card, a new card could mean a new life.

Fugard's expansion of the idea into a full-length play was given additional reality through the improvisational work of Kani and Ntshona under his direction. They contributed in a similar way to *The Island*, which is set in a prison, and they undoubtedly endowed both plays with elements of speech and observed details that deepened the impact. There is none the less a dominant sense of form that evokes the two brothers of *The Blood Knot*, one light-skinned and one black, who share an identity while appearing different to the world. It is Fugard's clear theatrical structuring, combined with an exceptional literacy, that gives each of his plays a recognizable voice.

While most of his plays operate within the context determined by the politics and racial situation in South Africa, and most of his characters, regardless of race, are victims of those policies, he has extended his work equally bravely into mythic dimensions. *Dimetos*, which was commissioned by the Edinburgh Festival and subsequently performed in London, followed some of his most political pieces and attempted to explore a mythic fragment which had lodged itself in his memory. He explored it in contemporary dress, with lengthy literal discussions, around the subject of a guilty love, but while the touch of a major playwright was always evident it was a considerably more literary touch than in his more specifically South African works.

However, unlike any other playwright of comparable stature, Fugard has identified the work of the Polish director Jerzy Grotowski as a major influence on his own work. Grotowski was notable for extending the physical and vocal range of actors, and for productions which obscured the language and texts at their centres. In a similar manner, one of the major experiments made by Fugard in Cape Town was almost completely physical. He describes this experiment, *Orestes*, as "an experience which lasted about eighty minutes and which had a 'text' of about four hundred words. The rest was space, silence, and action."

Neither *Orestes* nor *Dimetos* could be described as typical; rather they are extremes of Fugard's approach to theatre and might be explored further if he did not obviously find the problems and contradictions of his country so pressing. The work beginning with *A Lesson from Aloes* (1978) is far more representative of his usual concerns, and prepared the way for the discursively personal dramas, *"Master Harold" and the Boys* and *The Road to Mecca* which appeared in the 1980's.

Reflecting back to notes he had made in 1961, *A Lesson from Aloes* was based on actual people caught in the closing trap of apartheid. It graphically and poignantly examined the decision of an Afrikaner of conscience who decides to cling to South Africa, drawing what sustenance he can from his native earth, while he bids farewell to a Cape Coloured friend who has been forced out. The play clearly suggested Fugard's private debate on the importance and effectiveness of remaining bound to South Africa, but *"Master Harold" and the Boys* was to bring an even more personal expression of conflict, being the self-confessedly true story of his own temptation into the assertion of racial superiority when he was a boy. The irony in the title, with the "master" being a foolish youth and the "boys" being African men of wit, generosity, and sympathy, is a statement of Fugard's guilt, and the play gruellingly accepts responsibility for an unforgiveable act of contempt to men who had befriended him.

The Road to Mecca, like *A Lesson from Aloes*, was more of a biographical portrait than autobiography, but the sub-text was always the intolerant society of South Africa. His eccentric heroine, modelled on a woman who had reached her seventies while building her own extremely private version of Mecca, faces the pressure of the repressive community in her village of New Bethlehem, in the Great Karoo. When they wish to confine her to an old people's home, she turns for support to a young woman friend who is finding it hard to come to grips with a recent abortion and her meeting with an African woman and child she encountered on the road to New Bethlehem.

Nothing Fugard has written declines to the didactic, and though he remains a political author of the first rank, he is even more consistently a humanist. The body of his work is a glowing testament to the human spirit.

—Ned Chaillet

FULLER, Charles (H., Jr.). American. Born in Philadelphia, Pennsylvania, 5 March 1939. Educated at Villanov University, 1956–58, and La Salle College, 1965–67, both Philadelphia. Served as a petroleum lab technician in the Unite States Army in Japan and Korea, 1959–62. Married Miriar A. Nesbitt in 1962; two sons. Bank loan collector, counselo at Temple University, and city housing inspector, all Philadephia, 1960's; co-founder and co-director, Afro-American Ar Theatre, Philadelphia, 1967–71; writer and director, *The Blac Experience* program, WIP Radio, Philadelphia, 1970–71. Recpient: Creative Artists Public Service grant, 1975; Rockefelle grant, 1976; National Endowment for the Arts grant, 197 Guggenheim fellowship, 1977; Obie award, 1981; Audelc award, 1981, 1982; Pulitzer Prize, 1982; New York Drama Cr tics Circle award, 1982; Outer Circle award, 1982; Hazeli award, 1983; Mystery Writers of American Edgar Allan Po Award, for screenplay, 1985. D.F.A.: La Salle College, 198 Villanova University, 1983. Lives in Philadelphia. Agen Esther Sherman, William Morris Agency, 1350 Avenue of th Americas, New York, New York 10019, U.S.A.

PUBLICATIONS

Plays

The Village: A Party (produced Princeton, New Jersey, 196 as *The Perfect Party*, produced New York, 1969).
The Rise, in *New Plays from the Black Theatre*, edited by E Bullins. New York, Bantam, 1969.
In My Many Names and Days (produced New York, 1972).
Candidate (produced New York, 1974).
In the Deepest Part of Sleep (produced New York, 1974).
First Love (produced New York, 1974).
The Lay Out Letter (produced Philadelphia, 1975).
The Brownsville Raid (produced Waterford, Connecticu 1975; New York, 1976).
Sparrow in Flight, music by Larry Garner, based on a conce by Rosetta LeNoire (produced New York, 1978).
Zooman and the Sign (produced New York, 1980). Ne York, French, 1982.
A Soldier's Play (produced New York, 1981; Edinburg 1984). New York, Hill and Wang, 1982.

Screenplay: *A Soldier's Story*, 1984.

Television Plays: *Roots, Resistance, and Renaissance* serie 1967; *Mitchell*, 1968; *Black America* series, 1970–71; *The S Is Gray*, from the story by Ernest J. Gaines (*American Sho Story* series), 1980.

* * *

An angry, consuming energy which propels the protagoni towards violence, an irony which humanizes him while depri ing the viewer of easy categorizations: these elements chara terize Charles Fuller's style. Within an American theat tradition Fuller's work both acknowledges the seminal positi of Amiri Baraka and extends the vision of the tumultuo 1960's beyond a rigid, racial schematization which in conferri upon blacks the status of victims of oppression, seeming robbed them of any responsibility for or power over the circur stances in which they found themselves.

A former bank loan collector, college counsellor, and ci housing inspector, Fuller initially gained a measure of nation recognition in 1976 with *The Brownsville Raid*. Though presently out of circulation, the play is of interest because it prefigures the approach adopted in the later *A Soldier's Play*. *The Brownsville Raid* is a dramatization of the investigation into a 1906 shooting spree which culminated in President Teddy Roosevelt's unwarranted, dishonorable discharge of an entire black infantry brigade. With historical accounts as his starting point, Fuller skilfully interweaves a "whodunnit" plot with a compelling portrait of a black corporal who has his faith in the Army shattered when he refuses to comply with his officers' demand for a scapegoat. Both black and white men are presented with strengths and faults; what emerges is a composite picture of men and a society whose vision is distorted by racism.

In both *Zooman and the Sign* and *A Soldier's Play* racism appears not as a specific, external event to which the black protagonists must react; rather, its negative values have been so internalized that, propelled by their own frantic despair, the characters move relentlessly towards self-destruction. In the first play, about a father's search for his daughter's killer, a knife-toting, drug-running, 15-year-old casually admits to the audience at the outset that he is the killer. Although Zooman attempts to mask a mounting sense of entrapment with calculated bravado, his direct conversations with the audience about familial disintegration, unwanted homosexual encounters, and detention for uncommitted crimes characterize him as an alienated youth whose experiences have taught him that "niggahs can't be heroes," that blacks seemingly have no control over the atrophy engulfing their families and communities. These monologues, delivered in a street-wise, frenetic style which is nonetheless reminiscent of black toast traditions and Muhammad Ali's alliterative poetry, have the effect of humanizing Zooman, of placing him in a context where his asocial behavior becomes more understandable, and his affinity to the larger society more apparent.

Just as Zooman believes that blacks are helpless, so too do the neighbors of the slain girl, for no one will come forth as witnesses to the crime. The father's erecting a sign accusing them of moral complicity triggers only hostile recriminations from the neighbors and argument within the family itself. Symbolic of a community's failure to foster a more active, ennobling sense of its own possibilities, the sign occasions the final violence wherein Zooman is accidentally killed in his attempt to tear it down. Another black child lies dead in the street, another family grieves, and another sign goes up as momentary monument to incredible waste.

An ultimately pervasive irony, which empties the landscape of possible victors and reveals instead a society maimed by racism, is equally evident in *A Soldier's Play*. Unlike Zooman, Sergeant Waters espouses the black middle-class values of hard work, education, and racial pride as the means of self-advancement. Like Zooman, Waters, in seeking a sphere in which to exercise a masculine sense of control and dignity, has had only limited success, for he operates within the segregated Army of World War II. The search for his killer triggers a series of flashbacks which reveal him as a vicious, petty tyrant bent upon literally ridding the race of all those blues-singing, hoodoo-oriented men who he says prevent advancement; yet, they also create a measure of sympathy for this ambitious man, consumed by misplaced faith, self-hatred, and guilt.

The eventual identification of two black recruits as Waters's murderers defies the expectation, carefully nurtured by the playwright, that overt white hostility is the motivating factor. Additionally, it raises questions concerning the definition of justice, for the infantrymen have just received their long-awaited orders to ship out, in effect being granted license to kill in Europe a tyranny similar to what Waters represents at home. Compounding the irony further, Fuller provides a postscript which subverts the dramatic experience: the investigating officer reveals that the entire incident is recorded in military documents as meaningless black-on-black crime; Waters is inadvertently listed as an heroic war casualty; and the entire company is destroyed in combat. Thus, the Army learns nothing from this sorry episode.

To date, Fuller's dramatic world is dominated by driven, destructive men trying to carve out a viable place within a hostile environment. Though his characters inhabit a bleak landscape, his audiences need not: through the dramatic experience they can appreciate how racism distorts an entire society and choose to stop the human destruction.

—Sandra L. Richards

FURTH, George. American. Born George Schweinfurth in Chicago, Illinois, 14 December 1932. Educated at Northwestern University, Evanston, Illinois, B.S. in speech 1954; Columbia University, New York, 1955–56, M.F.A. 1956. Served in the United States Navy, 1958–62. Stage, film, and television actor from 1956; member of the Drama Department, University of Southern California, Los Angeles, 1979. Recipient: New York Drama Critics Circle award, 1970; Outer Circle award, 1970; Drama Desk award, 1970; Tony award, 1971. Agent: Broder Kurland and Webb, 8439 Sunset Boulevard, Los Angeles, California 90069. Address: 3030 Durand Drive, Hollywood, California 90068, U.S.A.

PUBLICATIONS

Plays

Company, music and lyrics by Stephen Sondheim (produced New York, 1970; London, 1972). New York, Random House, 1970.

Twigs (includes *Emily*, *Celia*, *Dorothy*, *Ma*) (produced New York, 1971; Coventry, 1973). New York, French, 1972.

The Act, music by John Kander, lyrics by Fred Ebb (produced New York, 1977).

Merrily We Roll Along, music and lyrics by Stephen Sondheim, adaptation of the play by George S. Kaufman and Moss Hart (produced New York, 1981; London, 1983).

The Supporting Cast (produced New York, 1981). New York, French, 1982.

Precious Sons (produced New York, 1986).

*

Manuscript Collection: Northwestern University School of Speech, Evanston, Illinois.

Theatrical Activities:

Director: **Play**—*The Supporting Cast*, Chicago, 1986.

Actor: **Plays**—Jordan in *A Cook for Mr. General* by Steve Gethers, New York, 1961; Skip in *Tadpole* by Jules Tasca, Los Angeles, 1973; Butter in *Tiny Alice* by Edward Albee. **Films**—*The Best Man*, 1964; *The New Interns*, 1964; *A Rage to Live*, 1965; *A Very Special Favor*, 1965; *The Cool Ones*,

1967; *Games*, 1967; *Tammy and the Millionaire*, 1967; *The Boston Strangler*, 1968; *How to Save a Marriage—And Ruin Your Life*, 1968; *Nobody's Perfect*, 1968; *P.J.*, 1968; *What's So Bad about Feeling Good?*, 1968; *Butch Cassidy and the Sundance Kid*, 1969; *Myra Breckinridge*, 1970; *Blazing Saddles*, 1974; *Shampoo*, 1975; *Airport '77*, 1977; *Cannonball Run*, 1981; *MegaForce*, 1982; *The Man with Two Brains*, 1983; *Doctor Detroit*, 1983. **Television**—*Tammy*, *Broadside*, *Mary Hartman, Mary Hartman* and *The Dumplings* series.

* * *

George Furth's career to date, his book for Stephen Sondheim's *Company* excepted, has been a tantalising series of near misses. Adroit as his work is, especially when he has risked innovations with the actual form of mainstream playwriting, he has rarely strayed from the narrow range of concerns that can occupy the successful Broadway play.

Twigs is essentially four one-act plays with a linking thread, providing a versatile actress with the chance to play three different sisters and their mother in the course of the evening. Taking its title from Alexander Pope ("Just as the twig is bent, the tree's inclined"), the plays are set in four different kitchens all on the same prior-to-Thanksgiving Day. All the sisters have their problems, seen mainly through a comedic lens, although the slick lines and sight-gags of the first playlet in which the garrulous recently-widowed Emily finds a possible new romance are in sharp contrast to the second, in which Celia, married to a crudely unfeeling slob whose ex-army buddy joins them for Thanksgiving, trembles on the verge of another nervous breakdown. This play begins in a vein of rumbustious comedy but gradually reveals an undertow of bleak pain. Furth does not always have time to paint in the subtlest of brush strokes, one of the hazards of the one-act format; perhaps unsurprisingly, the most successful episode is the final one in which the sisters' terminally ill Mother, a formidable old lady, decides that before she dies the "Pa" with whom she has lived for so long will do right by her and marry her. The ensuing wedding scene with an understandably flustered priest may be fairly broad comedy but it has a gleeful relish, skirting the boundaries of taste, which fuels it with zest.

Furth, with an actor's background, gives all his cast good opportunities, as well as providing a virtuoso showcase for the central performer. The play had a moderate Broadway success, which was more than he achieved with *The Supporting Cast*. Set in a luxurious Malibu beachhouse, with a bushfire and a minor earthquake among the traumas of the day, the play is happiest in the realms of a wisecracking or visual comedy; it milks a recurring sight-gag of characters walking into glass patio doors, and the dialogue is crammed with sardonic one-liners, the most pungent coming from the sharp-tongued Mae. Like all the characters, all friends of first-time novelist Ellen whose novel's publication requires waivers from the real-life prototypes of her characters, Mae represents East Coast unease with Californian living ("Someone must have tipped this country on its end and everything that wasn't screwed down fell into California," as Florrie from Brooklyn puts it). The play's slight plot rests on the mixed reactions to the book before outrage turns to ego-preening; aiming for a high-octane zany comedy the play becomes progressively more desperate in its contrivances simply to keep events moving.

All of which made Furth's most recent play perhaps somewhat surprising. *Precious Sons* managed only a short run, even in a Broadway season starved of good new plays. It has many of the hallmarks of an autobiographical play: set in Furth's native Chicago in the summer of 1949, it is a solidly naturalistic play centered on the lower-middle-class household of Fred Small, hard-working and tough father in poor health, Bea his slapdash, indomitably optimistic wife, and their two very different sons (the younger with dreams of becoming an actor, the elder sneaking off to wed his Prom sweetheart), for both of whom Fred is desperate for better lives. It is a long, and sometimes flawed play (somewhat confused over Bea's motives at crucial points, especially her attitude to a projected promotion of Fred's) but offering magnificent acting opportunities, particularly in the loving, brawling volatile relationship between Fred and Bea. The play, set as it is in 1949, inevitably recalls the playwrights of that period—Inge, Miller, Williams (indeed Williams figures strongly in the story, with Freddy the younger son auditioning for the touring company of *A Streetcar Named Desire*, producing a wonderful scene in which Bea has to read Blanche to Freddy's Newspaper Boy)—but deserved a more considered critical reaction than the faint praise it received on Broadway.

Furth has had considerable success with his streamlined books for various musicals including *Company* (although *The Act* required little more than linking dialogue between Liza Minnelli's numbers) but there are signs in his work to date that there is possibly a major play yet to come from him.

—Alan Strachan

GAGLIANO, Frank (Joseph). American. Born in Brooklyn, New York, 18 November 1931. Educated at Queens College, New York, 1949–53; University of Iowa, Iowa City, B.A. 1954; Columbia University, New York, M.F.A. 1957. Served in the United States Army, 1954–56. Married Sandra Gordon in 1958; one son. Free-lance copywriter, New York, 1958–61; promotion copywriter, McGraw-Hill Text-Film Division, New York, 1962–65. Associate Professor of Drama, Florida State University, Tallahassee, 1969–72; Lecturer in Playwriting and director of the E.P. Conkle Workshop, University of Texas, Austin, 1972–75. Since 1975 Benedum Professor of Playwriting, University of West Virginia, Morgantown. Visiting Professor, University of Rhode Island, Providence, 1975. Recipient: Rockefeller grant, 1965, 1966; Wesleyan University-O'Neill Foundation fellowship, 1967; National Endowment for the Arts grant, 1973; Guggenheim fellowship, 1974. Lives in Pittsburgh. Agent: Cristine Beato, Videosyncrasy, 6671 Sunset Boulevard, Hollywood, California 90028. Address: Theatre Arts Center, University of West Virginia, Morgantown, West Virginia 26506, U.S.A.

PUBLICATIONS

Plays

Night of the Dunce (as *The Library Raid*, produced Houston, 1961; revised version, as *Night of the Dunce*, produced New York, 1966). New York, Dramatists Play Service, 1967.

Conerico Was Here to Stay (produced New York, 1965). Included in *The City Scene*, 1966.

The City Scene (includes *Paradise Gardens East* and *Conerico Was Here to Stay*) (produced New York, 1969). New York, French, 1966.

Father Uxbridge Wants to Marry (produced Waterford, Connecticut, and New York, 1967). New York, Dramatists Play Service, 1968.
The Hide-and-Seek Odyssey of Madeleine Gimple (produced Waterford, Connecticut, 1967). New York, Dramatists Play Service, 1970.
The Prince of Peasantmania (*Inny*), music by James Reichert (produced Waterford, Connecticut, 1968; revised version produced Milwaukee, 1970).
Big Sur (televised 1969; revised version produced Tallahassee, Florida, 1970). New York, Dramatists Play Service, 1971.
In the Voodoo Parlour of Marie Laveau: Gris-Gris, and The Comedia World of Byron B (produced Waterford, Connecticut, 1973; as *Gris-Gris, and The Comedia World of Lafcadio Beau*, produced New York, 1974; revised version, as *Voodoo Trilogy*, produced New York, 1977; revised version, as *In the Voodoo Parlour of Marie Laveau*, produced New York, 1983).
Congo Square, music by Claibe Richardson (produced Providence, Rhode Island, 1975).
The Resurrection of Jackie Cramer, music by Raymond Benson (produced Providence, Rhode Island, and New York, 1976).
The Private Eye of Hiram Bodoni (produced New York, 1978).
The Total Immersion of Madeleine Favorini (produced Las Vegas, Nevada, 1981).
San Ysidro (cantata), music by James Reichert (produced Milwaukee, 1985).
From the Bodoni County Songbook Anthology, Book 1 (produced Morgantown, West Virginia, 1986).

Television Play: *Big Sur*, 1969.

*

Manuscript Collections: Lincoln Center Library of the Performing Arts, New York; O'Neill Theatre Center Library, Waterford, Connecticut.

Critical Studies: *Stages: The Fifty-Year Childhood of the American Theatre* by Emory Lewis, Englewood Cliffs, New Jersey, Prentice Hall, 1969; *The Nature of Theatre* by Vera M. Roberts, New York, Harper, 1971.

Frank Gagliano comments:

My whole effort in dramatic writing has been to keep a center while allowing myself the freedom of following any *seemingly* absurd path that seems to make sense. Form and impulse; the artist's great tightrope act. My favorite playwrights are Shakespeare, Georg Büchner, Chekhov, Verdi, and Bach.

* * *

Frank Gagliano is an experimental artist, uncompromising in his quest for a dramatic form that synthesizes his passion for music, language, and metaphysical themes of Christian idealism in an age of terror, disorder, perversion, and violence. "Mindlessness scares me and I'm in a mindless age," cries the heroine of *The Total Immersion of Madeleine Favorini.* Her words express the playwright's own torment. But Gagliano resembles a medieval dramatist, theatricalizing the terrors of hell to effect salvation, yet fascinated by the evils he deplores. In his plays, images of decay, violence, and death prevail over those of transcendence and salvation.

Gagliano is at war with himself. His drama is often an unresolved battleground of contradictory themes, language, and structure; winged allegories soar toward some unperceived light, burdened by the very demons they hope to evade. It is a brilliant, painful quest for truth, a journey for playwright and spectator in which the ridiculous and sublime combine in uneasy balance. Gagliano never plays it safe, and that is his great virtue as an artist.

His two-act opera, *Inny*, exemplifies the allegories of his earlier work. The dominant metaphor is that of the odyssey toward some form of self-realization, though the play's structure is far more logical and compact than that of his later plays. Innocent, "Inny," rightful heir to the throne of Peasantmania, is prevented from ruling by forces of political, social, and religious corruption that dominate the country. In his struggle to obtain power, Inny journeys from innocence to wisdom. Despite the evils endured, Inny remains spiritually pure, a Christ on the throne ready to suffer for man's transgressions and leading him to salvation: "I must stay . . . I'll never understand this—the ones who chased me, beat me, betrayed me . . . I love them all."

Inny is a grand operatic spectacle of pageants, processions, dances, choruses, battles; an entourage of jaded, cruel aristocrats, hags, heroines, fools, and a wise jester, symbol of art, who ultimately dies a horrid death with Inny's beloved, Glorabella. The dominant image of the play is a huge, foreboding eye that hangs overhead: "God's surrealistic yo-yo?" cries the jester, "but where's the string?" Is the horror heaven sent, the cruel plaything of a less than benign God, or the devil's toy? The ultimate answers are beyond us; all we know for certain is that man pursues senseless evil. The innocent and wicked suffer alike. All we can hope for is that wise, beneficent, courageous leaders like Inny may ultimately triumph.

The Private Eye of Hiram Bodoni is a flawed, sprawling work intended for television, part comedy, part surrealistic nightmare. Bodoni, a private eye, is hired to discover the cause of the unexplained death of the star of a television soap opera. However, the plot is merely a device to explore the lives of the characters through their personal recollections, flashbacks, a fantasies. Although it offers some imaginative visual images and poetic dialogue, the play is confused and unresolved.

In the Voodoo Parlour of Marie Laveau, "an unsung chamber opera," is a three-character play in which a man and woman seek help and revenge from a voodoo sorceress. Under Marie Laveau's spell, the two characters give vent to nightmare and sexual fantasy:

> I wish that was me
> being humped by a donkey
> while the chic of New Orleans
> marveled at me.

The woman's gross allusion revolts the man, who dreams of pure, idealized love. Verbal images of lurid sexuality dominate the play's language, but never gratuitously, only as essential to theme and action. Marie Laveau's parlor is a microcosm of New Orleans at the turn of the century, a city of Mardi Gras, witchcraft, perversion, racial hatred, and violence. The play gains its intensity by the very limitations of its theme. Rather than Gagliano's usual depiction of the characters' torments as symptomatic of a vaster social malaise, *Marie Laveau* is concentrated on the characters as ends in themselves. The parallel to 19th-century melodramatic plots of love and revenge is deliberate—a self-contained world of passion, violence, and death. The settings and costumes are simple yet theatrically effective: a bare space, masks, skulls, bizarre headgear, the horrid implements of the voodoo ritual. The hypnotic spell of the ritual is perfectly suited to Gagliano's odyssey metaphor, the evocation of nightmare and fantasy. Through an imaginative use of scenery, costumes, and operatic dialogue, Gagliano creates a Genet-like transcendence through evil. *Marie Laveau* is powerful drama that lends itself naturally to music.

In *The Total Immersion of Madeleine Favorini* Gagliano again uses the metaphor of the journey into self through a protagonist's total immersion in fantasy, nightmare, and dreams. Madeleine, a timid librarian locked in a gynecologist's stirrups for two weeks, wanders back in fantasy to Sicily, land of her ancestors. On her journey she encounters various forms and characters: a Stalactite, the Wax Prometheus, the Goddess Materna. The actress playing Madeleine transforms herself into each of them (the other actor and actress also assume a variety of identities). Madeleine becomes imbued with the Dionysian and Christian spirit of this ancient land, an earth mother absorbing all humanity into her giant womb. In a brilliant sequence of dialogue, Madeleine and her deceased grandfather, Pazzotesto (Crazy Head), rhapsodize over the wonders of basil that covers the landscape of Sicily, creeping "up from the bottom of the green Mediterranean ... on the beach ... the roads, rooftops. The toilets have basil seats. The bells of the great cathedrals are covered with basil and cushion their clang." At the conclusion of the play, Madeleine is freed from the restrictions of the harsh, decadent society that nurtured her. She ascends to freedom on a crescendo of pure language. "Yes! Yes! I know what I want. I know what I mean! I want to become—language! Language!"

These final moments of the play seem to represent Gagliano's desire to free himself from the limits of drama. This work is a form of theatricalized literature or poetry rather than drama. Action becomes the exploration of character and theme instead of the resolution of some essential dramatic conflict. Gagliano's emphasis upon language as the dominant structural element of his drama can become excessive and unfocused. He has a tendency to use dialogue for the sheer richness of sound and imagery. Yet, his dialogue can also be stirring or even frightening, revealing a character's desperate need for freedom and salvation. Gagliano's drama is in transition, and its direction is unclear, but he remains one of the most daring, imaginative, and poetic playwrights of the American theatre.

—A. Richard Sogliuzzo

GALLACHER, Tom. British. Born in Alexandria, Dunbartonshire, Scotland, 16 February 1934. Writer-in-residence, Pitlochry Festival Theatre, Perthshire, 1975–78, and Royal Lyceum Theatre, Edinburgh, 1978–80. Recipient: Scottish Arts Council award, 1986. Agent: Michael Imison Playwrights, 28 Almeida Street, London N1 1TD, England.

PUBLICATIONS

Plays

Our Kindness to Five Persons (produced Glasgow, 1969). Glasgow, Scottish Society of Playwrights, 1980.
Mr. Joyce Is Leaving Paris (produced London, 1970; revised version produced Dublin, 1971; London, 1972; New York, 1978). London, Calder and Boyars, 1972.
Revival! (produced Dublin, 1972; London, 1973). With *Schellenbrack*, Glasgow, Molendinar Press, 1978.
Three to Play: Janus, Pastiche, Recital (produced Montrose, Angus, 1972; *Recital* produced London, 1973).
Schellenbrack (produced London, 1973). With *Revival!*, Glasgow, Molendinar Press, 1978.
Bright Scene Fading (produced London, 1973).
The Only Street (produced Dublin and London, 1973). Glasgow, Scottish Society of Playwrights, 1980.
Personal Effects (produced Pitlochry, 1974).
A Laughing Matter (produced St. Andrews, 1975).
Hallowe'en (produced Dundee, 1975). Glasgow, Scottish Society of Playwrights, 1980.
The Sea Change (produced Edinburgh, 1976). Glasgow, Scottish Society of Playwrights, 1980.
A Presbyterian Wooing, adaptation of the play *The Assembly* by Archibald Pitcairne (produced Pitlochry, 1976).
The Evidence of Tiny Tim, with Joan Knight (produced Perth, 1977).
Wha's Like Us—Fortunately (produced Dundee, 1978).
Stage Door Canteen, with John Scrimger (produced Perth, 1978).
Deacon Brodie, adaptation of the play by Robert Louis Stevenson and W. E. Henley (produced Edinburgh, 1978).
An Enemy of the People, adaptation of a play by Ibsen (produced Edinburgh, 1979).
Jenny (produced Pitlochry, 1979). London, French, 1980.
Natural Causes (produced Perth, 1980).
The Father, adaptation of a play by Strindberg (produced Dundee, 1980).
A Doll's House, adaptation of a play by Ibsen (produced Edinburgh, 1980).
The Parole of Don Juan (produced Perth, 1981).
The Treasure Ship, adaptation of the play by John Brandane (produced Pitlochry, 1981).
The Wild Duck, adaptation of a play by Ibsen (produced Perth, 1987).

Radio Plays: *Progress to an Exile*, 1970; *The Scar*, 1973; *Hunting Shadows*, 1975; *The Man with a Hatchet*, 1976; *Portrait of Isa Mulvenny*, 1978; *Perfect Pitch*, 1979; *Store Quarter*, 1983; *Personal Effects*, 1986; *The Previous Tenant*, 1986.

Television Plays: *The Trial of Thomas Muir*, 1977; *If the Face Fits*, 1978.

Novels

Apprentice. London, Hamish Hamilton, 1983.
Journeyman. London, Hamish Hamilton, 1984.
Survivor. London, Hamish Hamilton, 1985.
The Wind on the Heath. London, Hamish Hamilton, 1987.

Short Stories

Hunting Shadows. Helensburgh, Jeffrey, 1981.
The Jewel Maker. London, Hamish Hamilton, 1986.

Other

The Way to Write for the Stage. London, Elm Tree, 1987.

*

Tom Gallacher comments:

Mainly, the plays deal with exceptions. Sometimes the exceptions are artists; sometimes it is another kind of outsider, a genius, a catalyst, or a singular man. All of them are in some way seeking to extend the meaning of their lives or the boundaries of reality.

An illustration of this can be gained from my book *The Jewel Maker* which is a fictional account of a playwright at work. There it is made clear how the work is influenced by people and events, and how the conflict of illusion and reality extends the boundaries of the human spirit. That is the testing ground where human evolution continues to progress.

All the plays celebrate the individual. The protagonists are unmoved by Class, Party, or Movement but they are acutely conscious of the interior actions of emotion, spirit, and reason. The crises—whether sad or funny—are person to person. The conflict in comedy and drama arises from an effort to make a workable connection—between the accepted and the potential, between what we are and what we may be, between what is degrading and what is exalting.

"Only connect" was the motto which E.M. Forster placed as guardian over his novel *Howards End.* I can't think of a better motto for a writer because the motto leads to a concept of great courage and enterprise. The characters in my plays do not always master the concept or gain its acceptance by others. But if they go down they go down knowing which way is forward.

* * *

At the end of Tom Gallacher's first play, *Our Kindness to Five Persons*, an alcoholic Glaswegian author pours himself another drink and proposes a solitary toast: "Should auld acquaintance be forgot and *never* brought to mind? Yes. Please God. Yes." The play has just demonstrated a denial of the prayer; but the question, and the artist's special rights of adjudication over it, are the constant threads through the plays Gallacher has written since.

Gallacher's preoccupation with art and artist is immediately obvious on the surfaces of his plays. Writers are the central characters of at least half of them, and Gallacher often points a passage of dialogue towards the epigrammatic use of a quotation, or builds a scene around the recitation of poetry or the singing of ballads. Literary sources and models are of even greater substantive and structural importance for some of Gallacher's work. *The Sea Change* and the short radio play *The Scar* are both dream-plays-within-plays in which the stuff of the central character's imagination comes from Shakespeare. *A Presbyterian Wooing* descends from literary obscurity: *The Assembly*, a Jacobite's dramatic satire on the ecclesiastical politics and personal morals of the Edinburgh Kirk. Trimmed and embroidered into a neo-Restoration comedy of sexual hypocrisy, *A Presbyterian Wooing* demonstrates Gallacher's sensitivity to earlier dramatic modes and his ability to tune his invention and idiom to the same key. The same knack belabours Ibsen's dramaturgy and Kierkegaard's ontology in *Revival!*, the aim of which seems to be to tease the audience into reading the complete works of both Scandinavians. In *Hallowe'en*, on the other hand, Fraser's account of that ritual in pagan times is compactly reincarnated in contemporary Glasgow, and the literary *drame à clé* is cleanly unlocked in the dialogue.

The thematic purposes to which Gallacher puts these and other of his "auld acquaintance" in literature are remarkably repetitive, though the dramatic techniques he uses vary considerably. He is occupied unto the edge of obsession with the dual nature of the remembered past—omnipresent in influence and irretrievable in fact. Every one of his original plays is in large measure focussed upon the relationship between dramatic past and present. In some cases, a radical time change is built into the play, its point of departure being the out-of-time introduction of the central character. *The Sea Change, Bright Scene Fading*, and the unproduced *A Lady Possessed* are all constructed as flashbacks in time and space through the consciousness of that character, while *Mr. Joyce Is Leaving Paris* brings the personages of Joyce's past to the front of his present consciousness. The other plays, while preserving naturalistic time schemes and the convention of the fourth wall, investigate events and relationships anterior to the action of the play, reenact them or exorcise them.

For Gallacher the memory that matters is the artistic statement of a perception about personal experience. Such a statement stands for him as evidence of the essentials of observed and observer, and as an imposition of order and connexion among these essentials. "Witness" and "pattern" are the terms which often turn up in the dialogue; another is "signpost," an indication of where someone has been and a directive to those who follow. When the plays incorporate such overt expositions of their author's understanding of art, it is not surprising that several draw attention to their own artificiality, nor that so many celebrate the triumph of artistic insight—over technology, biographical data, time, and the perceptions of the pedestrian majority of mankind.

Though the penultimate victory supplies him with some fairly strong stuff, Gallacher finds his best dramatic material in the last. Only here does he create any real competition, and only here are his aesthetic concerns communicated by more than interpretative glosses and plot gimmickry. The axis along which Gallacher most characteristically depicts these conflicts is that of an intense relationship between a gifted figure and a sympathetic sibling or comrade left behind: James and Stanislaus Joyce in *Mr. Joyce Is Leaving Paris*, Martin and Richard in *The Only Street*, and Otto and Steve in *Bright Scene Fading*. The high price of giftedness also hovers over the presentation of parent-child, husband-wife, and mentor-pupil relationships in these and other plays, but Gallacher plays a better game for higher stakes when he is dealing with doubles and shadows.

Gallacher's own practice of art as witness and as pattern is apparent in his plays and illuminates some of their more idiosyncratic aspects. His writing of dialogue is distinguished on the one hand by an accurate reproduction of spoken rhythms, with particularly precise variations for local, professional, social, and even situational idiom, and on the other hand by a wit which specializes in paradoxes, perfect squelches, and the literalisation of abstractions and figures of speech. Gallacher rarely loses this balance of an attentive ear and orderly invention.

Gallacher's patterning of his materials betrays a taste for symmetry, a mastery of plot mechanics, and an ability to exploit exposition, complication, reversal, and resolution in traditional well-made ways or to invert them for the sake of emphasis. (The exceptions to this rule of flexibility are found in his act-endings; he seems incapable of placing an interval anywhere but on the edge of a cliff in the plot.) His fascination with pattern is perhaps most easily perceived in miniature in the tidy and playful plots of his three one-acts for three players (*Janus, Recital*, and *Pastiche*). The patterning is, however, so apparent in the full-length plays as well that it is impressively ironic that Gallacher's best and best-known play should be, superficially, his most untidy: *Mr. Joyce Is Leaving Paris.* The second half of this play saw production first. Its order is not dictated by traditional dramaturgy but, as is pointed out by one of the figures which haunt the ageing Joyce, by the order of events at an Irish wake. That the "corpse" is the sole survivor of the wake is a good instance of how Gallacher can plot a joke to great thematic purpose. The order of the first half, set much earlier in Joyce's career but written slightly later in

Gallacher's, is one of the playwright's confrontations of gifted and ungifted, moving from mutual challenge, though routines long familiar to both, towards acceptance. Though Stanislaus turns up, much muted, in the second half, the two patterns converge only through the consciousness of Joyce—formal confirmation of his (and, behind him, Gallacher's) claim to sole mastery of the remembered situations.

Mr. Joyce Is Leaving Paris in fact typifies Gallacher's dramatic writing as a whole as well as at its best. The qualitative difference between its parts is the difference between commendably accomplished craftsmanship and irresistibly imaginative insight. An analogous difference may be discerned in the use of theatrical resources. To these Gallacher is always attentive, using them to supplement the scripted action and dialogue in his fourth-wall dramas and pulling off some stunning isolated effects in the process. At best, however, Gallacher makes the technical parts of theatrical production indispensable to his dramatic statement. The lighting in the second half of *Mr. Joyce Is Leaving Paris*, for example, and the set for *The Sea Change* serve as visual indices to the central character's control of his memories and thus as evidence of the truth of his vision. In *The Sea Change* that vision, despite its ingenious presentation, remains derivative and diffuse. But when, as in the second half of *Mr. Joyce Is Leaving Paris*, Gallacher aligns tradition and his individual talent in perfect focus, he creates a resonant work.

—Marion O'Connor

GARDNER, Herb(ert). American. Born in Brooklyn, New York, 28 December 1934. Educated at the High School of Performing Arts, New York, graduated 1952; Carnegie Institute of Technology, Pittsburgh; Antioch College, Yellow Springs, Ohio. Married the actress Rita Gardner in 1957. Cartoonist: created *The Nebbishes* syndicated cartoon strip. Recipient: Screenwriters Guild award, 1966; Tony award, 1986; Outer Circle award, 1986; John Gassner Award, 1986. Lives in New York City. Address: c/o Samuel French Inc., 45 West 25th Street, New York, New York 10010, U.S.A.

PUBLICATIONS

Plays

The Elevator (produced New York, 1952). New York, French, 1952.

A Thousand Clowns (produced New York, 1962; London, 1964). New York, Random House, 1962.

The Goodbye People (produced New York, 1968). New York, Farrar Straus, 1974; revised version (produced Los Angeles and New York, 1979), included in *A Thousand Clowns, Thieves, The Goodbye People*, 1979.

Who Is Harry Kellerman and Why Is He Saying Those Terrible Things about Me? (screenplay). New York, New American Library, 1971.

Thieves (produced New York, 1974). Included in *A Thousand Clowns, Thieves, The Goodbye People*, 1979.

Love and/or Death (produced New York, 1979).

A Thousand Clowns, Thieves, The Goodbye People. New York, Doubleday, 1979.

I'm Not Rappaport (produced Seattle and New York, 1985; Birmingham and London, 1986). New York, French, 1987.

Screenplays: *A Thousand Clowns*, 1965; *Who Is Harry Kellerman and Why Is He Saying Those Terrible Things about Me?*, 1971; *Thieves*, 1976.

Television Play: *Happy Endings*, with others, 1975.

Novel

A Piece of the Action. New York, Simon and Schuster, 1958; London, W.H. Allen, 1959.

* * *

Critics keep trying to point out serious ideas in Herb Gardner's plays, but the playwright consistently wards off their attempts with a comic flourish. Clearly a thoughtful man, obviously stimulated by certain prevailing attitudes of mankind, he insists that he is a writer of comedy and that his objective is to entertain audiences. Surely this is a noble and inspiring trait in a modern dramatist, particularly during a period in history when social issues are forcibly intruded into theatres at every opportunity. Unlike Robert Sherwood who, though concerned with the human condition, hid his serious thoughts behind a facade of light comedy, the like-minded Gardner looks carefully around and, like Chekhov, is genuinely amused by what he sees—the fancied and futile attempts of man to escape the real world, the indefatigable quality of old age. Gardner, then, proceeds to use the comic techniques that bring his plays to Broadway—*A Thousand Clowns, The Goodbye People, Thieves*, and *I'm Not Rappaport.*

The world that seems funny to Gardner, however, sometimes arrests the attention of others as extremely sad. There is Max Silverman in *The Goodbye People.* This exuberant but completely unrealistic old gentleman wants to erase 20 years from passing time, rebuild his hot-dog stand on Coney Island, and bring his "Hawaiian Ecstasies" to an eager public. Moreover, he wants to do this in February, so convinced is he that his dreams can awaken "ecstasy" in a dull world. There is old Nat in *I'm Not Rappaport*, a defiant, irascible Jewish radical who refuses to be intimidated by either the establishment or the underworld and rejects any movement that intrudes upon his independence. There are all the pathetic people around the apartment building in *Thieves*, each with a problem to which no one listens, each a thief and each being robbed by passing time. And from *A Thousand Clowns* there are Murray who is tortured by the world he sees, Leo who wants to believe in himself but cannot, and Arthur who purposefully surrenders to the establishment but survives. He catches the wind and goes with it. Mainly, Gardner's characters appear to catch the cold wind straight in their faces, defiantly, stubbornly, and disastrously—and die, in one sense or another, romantically and in the glow of stage sentiment.

The comic appeal of Gardner's plays comes from his mastery of comic technique and his philosophy as a writer. Although not a storyteller and, as his plays show, somewhat contemptuous of traditional plotting in a play, he likes to hear people talk. He is also a dreamer who, like Nat, can make up little scenes which may appear as a line, a speech, or an incident—a joke, a monologue, or an episode. Like Max Silverman, Gardner does not believe in standing around and watching. One must act, wage battle even while knowing that victory is impossible. Like Murray he is afraid of "dying alive." Although called a "laureate of losers," Gardner has a sense of comic balance that contradicts this description. He sees humor, not sadness. Losers stand around; fighters keep the soul alive, and Gardner's characters, synthetic and romanticized or caricatured as they may be, are ever hopeful, even in their fantastic, ridiculous, or childishly recalcitrant attempts to escape whatever worlds surround them. Gardner sees his people as survivors, and in juxtaposing their acts with those of others in the world he experiences he creates dramatic tension in silly-serious, comic-tragic, and pathetic-horrible situations while revealing a real comic irony.

Structurally, Gardner's plays include a lavishly encumbered stage and a love story. As visual metaphors there are the incredibly messy room in *A Thousand Clowns*, the beach that sprouts fireworks in *The Goodbye People*, the terrace in *Thieves*, and the bench in *I'm Not Rappaport.* Gardner truly loves the long monologue, the quick repartee of stand-up comedians, and the one-line gag. Jewish humor, local New York humor, visual jokes, absurd comparisons, and the unexpected retort vie for attention in a selected accumulation of odd people. In *Thieves* a character complains that "all I ever got from this neighborhood was four knife scars, two broken noses and a fruitcake wife! And they all hurt when it rains." Gardner's comedies are assuredly enhanced by good actors: his monologues are a comedian's food and wine; his dialogue can be as sprightly and as touching as the actor can create. Music also is significant in his plays to please or assault the ear as the clutter on stage may accost the eye. Within this grand expression of comic theatre where dreams cannot be answered but believing in dreams is deemed necessary, Gardner presents his characters, mainly in episodes involving the rituals of lovemaking in the modern world. Then, he stops; conclusions are not his métier.

The comic possibilities that have brought Gardner success, however, may also serve to limit his acceptance with future audiences. During the 1960's, for example, audiences applauded the rebellious youth's single-minded escape into fantasy from a real world where they found people living as "fakes." Audiences of the 1980's are more interested in contending with this real world. Carlton, the young thief in *Thieves*, is not funny to them, nor is Sally, who contends seriously and unsuccessfully with a stubbordly inhuman father. It is scarcely funny to a generation concerned with people starving in the streets that the doorman is not sleeping but dead. Gardner presents father-daughter relationships in *The Goodbye People, Thieves*, and *I'm Not Rappaport*, each one funny to him, each one geared to the comic sense of a different audience. In his most recent play he catches the pathos as well as the comedy and with this development in his dramaturgy may advance beyond the comic banter of temporal pleasure.

—Walter J. Meserve

GEE, Shirley (née Thieman). British. Born in London, 25 April 1932. Educated at Frensham Heights, Farnham, Surrey; Webber-Douglas Academy of Dramatic Art, London. Married Donald Gee in 1965; two sons. Stage and television actress, 1952–66. Member of the Radio Committee, Society of Authors, 1980–82. Since 1986 member of the Women's Committee, Writers Guild. Recipient: *Radio Times* award, 1974; Pye award, for radio play, 1979; Sony award, for radio play, 1983; Susan Smith Blackburn Prize, 1984; Samuel Beckett Award, 1984. Agent: John Rush, David Higham Associates, 5–8 Lower John Street, London W1R 4HA. Address: 28 Fernshaw Road, London SW10 0TF, England.

Publications

Plays

Typhoid Mary (broadcast 1979; produced London, 1983). Published in *Best Radio Plays of 1979*, London, Eyre Methuen, 1980.

Never in My Lifetime (broadcast 1983; produced London, 1984; Stamford, Connecticut, 1987). Published in *Best Radio Plays of 1983*, London, Methuen, 1984.

Ask for the Moon (produced London, 1986). London, Faber, 1987.

Radio Plays: *Stones*, 1974; *The Vet's Daughter*, from the novel by Barbara Comyns, 1976; *Moonshine*, 1977; *Typhoid Mary*, 1979; *Bedrock*, 1979; *Men on White Horses*, from the novel by Pamela Haines, 1981; *Our Regiment* (documentary), 1982; *Never in My Lifetime*, 1983.

Television Plays: *Long Live the Babe*, 1984; *Flights*, 1985.

*

Critical Studies: *British Radio Drama* edited by John Drakakis, London, Cambridge University Press, 1981; *The Way to Write Radio Drama* by William Ash, London, Elm Tree, 1985.

Theatrical Activities:
Actress: roles with Worthing, Hull, Malvern, and other repertory companies, and in more than 100 television plays and series episodes, 1952–66.

Shirley Gee comments:

I really don't like to make statements about my work; I hope those who see or hear the plays will have the freedom to draw their own conclusions. However, I'll try. I suppose I write to try to understand. To make sense out of chaos. To confront some terrors. I wonder what particular individuals might do trapped in a particular public event or social context. I watch them grapple, try to come to terms, fight to find the meaning of their lives. Often they are in a besieged landscape: the dead in *Stones;* Mary the typhoid carrier, imprisoned, in *Typhoid Mary*; British soldiers and Irish nationals in Belfast in *Never in My Lifetime*; the Victorian laceworkers and present-day sweatshop workers in *Ask for the Moon.* They are tyrannised by fear or poverty or loneliness or war. Their individual needs and desires run counter to the needs and desires of society, and must be sacrificed to that society. Still, they behave with love and courage. They save one another despite themselves. They beam a little light into a dark world. I wonder what I would have done, had I been in their place.

* * *

The list of women playwrights who have won major awards is, although increasing daily, not long, and one might expect Shirley Gee's name to be better known. Sadly, it is easy to account for her comparative lack of fame: most of her work has been written for radio, the most critically neglected medium of the past few decades. In Gee's case this is doubly unfortunate, for her radio experience is what gives her work for the stage its special vitality.

The radio playwright enjoys virtually unlimited freedom of approach; as long as he or she can unlock the listener's imagination anything is possible. Radio allows all kinds of spatial and temporal jumps; it is possible to create and instantly change the scenery, flash backwards or forwards in time, simply by the use of a few words or a snatch of song. Gee has always been one of the most technically authoritative of radio writers, and it was perhaps the triple accolade given to her radio play *Typhoid Mary*—a Giles Cooper award, a Pye award, a Special Commendation in the Italia prize—that prompted the Royal Shakespeare Company to stage the play and discover that its darting, fragmented structure worked onstage with verve and power.

Typhoid Mary is Mary Mallon, the tragic Irish immigrant who unwittingly spread the disease around New York at the beginning of the century. Instead of narrating her story straightforwardly, Gee creates a kaleidoscope of fragments: in one brief scene, for example, disembodied voices chant sensationalist newspaper headlines ("Calamity Cook Kills Wholesale"), a lawyer pronounces on her status in dry legal prose, a chorus sings "Molly Malone" to the accompaniment of spoons, and Mary in the midst speaks of her pain and grief as if she was in her own living room.

This lively variety of styles (from naturalism to the surreal) provides an analysis of her plight from several simultaneous angles. The spoon music stresses her background as struggling immigrant desperate to make good in a new world, and the humming of "Molly Malone" counterpoints this; Mary is already enshrined in popular song and in the popular imagination as a killer. The crude unthinking bias against her is fed by the press and allowed by the law. In fact Gee allows us in a few seconds to see Mary with the whole of American society ranged against her, with a vividness and compression naturalistic techniques would never permit.

For all its liveliness *Typhoid Mary* remained a study of a tragic individual without wider resonance. Gee's next ambitious work, also originating in radio, showed her wrestling with political drama. *Never in My Lifetime* opens shatteringly with the shooting of two British soldiers in a Belfast disco, then flashes backwards and forwards in time to explain the motives behind the shooting and its consequences. We follow the lives of the soldiers—Charlie, badly wounded, with a pregnant wife, and Tom, who dies—and the girls who lured them into ambush—the terrorist Maire, and Tess who is sleeping with Tom and joins Maire to save her own life when this becomes known to the IRA. By juxtaposing past and present, snatches of song, and snippets of Belfast life, Gee creates their lives and evokes unforgettably the grief of their loved ones. On a less personal level, however, the play is not so satisfying. The breadth and daring of the structure give the misleading impression that the play is presenting the fullest possible spectrum of Belfast politics. In fact, the cards are stacked. The only voice to speak for the Republican cause, for instance, is the voice of terrorism. Through the violent and twisted Maire, not just this killing but the whole concept of Irish nationhood is associated with a chain of ugly and sexually perverse imagery, contrasting with the wholesome lyricism of the naive Tess. The soldiers are described taking part in a brutal attack, but it is not shown, whereas the disco incident is terrifyingly realised. Essentially the play takes a pro-British stance while presenting itself as a slice of life; it seems that Gee is not fully in control of her material.

Ask for the Moon, however, shows a clearer political direction, and also translates the techniques of radio into striking visual terms. It shows simultaneously two generations of workers, Victorian lacemakers and women in a modern sweat shop. Gee's talent for conveying the texture of working life does more than lament their exploitation; she also shows how working conditions are structured to prevent unionisation. A lacemaker is forced to provide her child with opium so that the group will not slow up production; an old sweatshop hand steals another's piece-work to escape the sack. Gee makes it clear that this is forced on them despite real comradeship and caring and pride in their work. There is a touching moment when time barriers are broken and both groups join in wonder to admire a wedding veil that has cost one woman her eyesight. The women have no illusions about why they betray one another, and in the final anger of one of them, at first blind rage and then quiet planning for her own future, there is a hint that they are learning at last how to change.

—Frances Gray

GELBER, Jack. American. Born in Chicago, Illinois, 12 April 1932. Educated at the University of Illinois, Urbana, B.S. in journalism 1953. Married Carol Westenberg in 1957; one son and one daughter. Writer-in-residence, City College, New York, 1965–66; Adjunct Professor of Drama, Columbia University, New York, 1967–72. Since 1972 Professor of Drama, Brooklyn College, City University of New York. Recipient: Obie award, 1960, for directing, 1972; Vernon Rice award, 1960; Guggenheim fellowship, 1963, 1966; Rockefeller grant, 1972; National Endowment for the Arts grant, 1974; CBS-Yale fellowship, 1974. Address: Department of English, Brooklyn College, Bedford Avenue and Avenue H, Brooklyn, New York 11210, U.S.A.

PUBLICATIONS

Plays

The Connection (produced New York, 1959; London, 1961). New York, Grove Press, 1960; London, Faber, 1961.

The Apple (produced New York, 1961). New York, Grove Press, 1961.

Square in the Eye (produced New York, 1965). New York, Grove Press, 1966.

The Cuban Thing (also director: produced New York, 1968). New York, Grove Press, 1969.

Sleep (produced New York and Edinburgh, 1972). New York, Hill and Wang, 1972.

Barbary Shore, adaptation of the novel by Norman Mailer (also director: produced New York, 1973).

Farmyard, adaptation of a play by Franz Xaver Kroetz (also director: produced New Haven, Connecticut, 1975). Published in *Farmyard and Four Other Plays*, by Kroetz, New York, Urizen, 1976.

Rehearsal (also director: produced New York, 1976).

Starters (produced New Haven, Connecticut, 1980).

Screenplay: *The Connection*, 1962.

Novel

On Ice. New York, Macmillan, 1964; London, Deutsch, 1965.

*

Bibliography: *Ten Modern American Playwrights* by Kimball King, New York, Garland, 1982.

Critical Studies: *Seasons of Discontent* by Robert Brustein, New York, Simon and Schuster, 1965, London, Cape, 1966; *Les U.S.A.: A la Recherche de Leur Identité* by Pierre Dommergues, Paris, Grasset, 1967; *Tynan: Right and Left* by Kenneth Tynan, London, Longman, 1967, New York, Atheneum, 1968; *Now: Theater der Erfahrung* edited by Jens Heilmeyer and Pia Frolich, Cologne, Schauberg, 1971; *The Living Theatre* by Pierre Biner, New York, Avon, 1972; *Theatricality* by Elizabeth Burns, New York, Harper, 1972; *Off Broadway* by Stuart Little, New York, Coward McCann, 1972; *People's Theatre in Amerika* by Karen Taylor, New York, Drama Book Specialists, 1973; introduction by Richard Gilman to *The Apple, and Square in the Eye*, New York, Viking Press, 1974.

Theatrical Activities:
Director: **Plays**—several of his own plays, and works at Lincoln Center, New Theatre Workshop, and the American Place Theatre, including *The Kitchen* by Arnold Wesker, 1966, *Kool Aid* by Merle Molofsky, 1971, *The Kid* by Robert Coover, 1972, *The Chickencoop Chinaman* by Frank Chin, 1972, *Eulogy for a Small-Time Thief* by Miguel Piñero, 1977, and *Seduced* by Sam Shepard, 1979; *Indians* by Arthur Kopit, London, 1968; *The Man and the Fly* by José Ruibal, New York, 1982; *The House of Ramon Iglesia* by José Rivera, New York, 1983; *The Dolphin Position* by Percy Granger, New York, 1983; *Mink on a Gold Hook* by James Ryan, New York, 1986.

* * *

Jack Gelber, playwright, award-winning director, and teacher, has had one of the most important and innovative careers in contemporary American drama, and in discussing this career there are two aspects of it that must be taken into account: the kind of influence his plays had upon the improvisational and group drama of the 1960's and early 1970's, and the particular vision the plays themselves present.

The most influential of his plays is *The Connection*, produced by the Living Theatre in 1959, and its theatrical characteristics introduce the Gelber technique: the play and production represent, or seem to represent, an attack upon the "written" play. The usual authority figures of playwright and producer are parodied, plot is suppressed, and improvisation takes their place as the actors, supposedly junkies and musicians drawn from everyday life, improvise a play from their personal lives to the complementary accompaniment of Charlie Parker-type jazz. Dramatic time is ambiguous and also improvised, with the specifically allocated length of the musical passages its clearest measure. Gelber deliberately avoids detailed psychological characterization and concentrates upon communal, representative figures although three of the characters, with specific functional roles, are especially vivid: Cowboy, the "connection" who incites the events; Sister Salvation, the unexpected guest who places the play in perspective; and Leach, the everyman of the play's world who overdoses on heroin. This "spontaneous" making of a play, the seemingly improvised action with its jazz accompaniment, the use of photographers to validate another version of the happenings, the interaction with the spectators, all combine to break down the usual relationship between actors and audience, reality and illusion, play and life. The subsequent group theater movement with its distrust of authority, its emphasis upon spontaneity and community, and its attack upon the text was clearly foreshadowed, even partly suggested, by the success of Gelber's play. But it is important to note that *The Connection* is itself a carefully written text.

Gelber's subsequent plays explore and expand these characteristics of *The Connection. The Apple* is communal and without central characters; its action is deliberately ambiguous and chaotic; and the actors shift in and out of character and participation. *Square in the Eye* is a family play about Ed Stone, a teacher, his wife, the children, and grandparents. Here various theatrical styles, including stand-up comedy and movies, undermine realism, and the chronology of events is purposefully disrupted. In *Sleep* two sleep scientists replace the playwright; the world of the play is a sleep laboratory; time is measured in sleep cycles; and the hero Gil, whose dreams coalesce into a kind of psychological action, proves on examination to be an average everyman. His sleeping and dreams, which correspond to the waking sleep of the addicts in *The Connection*, question the nature of reality, and in the play's most important speech one of the scientists expands the ambiguity into social statement: "The fact is that we have wired up a scientifically selected sample of the entire population and we have found, I know you won't believe this, we have found that they are technically asleep." In *Rehearsal*, publicly admired by several of his fellow dramatists, a play is in rehearsal; the nervous director cannot control the performance; and the producer is an incompetent alcoholic. The theater itself becomes the setting as the play emerges from the "interpolated" digressions initiated by the actors.

These formal characteristics suggest, of course, a view of life, and it is his second play, *The Apple*, that most clearly provides its symbol. The play invites the audience to make what it will of the apple and its connotations are many, but the biblical reference to what Milton calls "the fruit of that forbidden tree" is inescapable. The Gelber dramatic world describes a society that seems to have begun with a mythic expulsion, a communal and pragmatic place without heroes where man has become his ordinary self and disappointment and death are inevitable. It is a world where a secure reality is generally illusory and a world where drugs and call it sleep become the refuge of the human imagination which cannot recall it to order.

Gelber's writing, like the title of his best known play, has many connections, connections with the contemporary theater and the world it reflects, and he is paradoxically both the American playwrights' playwright and the chronicler of the American everyman.

—Gaynor F. Bradish

GEMS, (Iris) Pam(ela, née Price). British. Born in Bransgore, Dorset, 1 August 1925. Educated at Brockenhurst County High School, 1936–41; Manchester University, 1946–49, B.A. (honours) in psychology 1949. Served in the Women's Royal Naval Service, 1944–46. Married Keith Gems in 1949; two sons, including the writer Jonathan Gems, and two daughters. Research assistant, BBC, London, 1950–53. Agent: ACTAC, 16 Cadogan Lane, London S.W. 1, England.

PUBLICATIONS

Plays

Betty's Wonderful Christmas (for children; produced London, 1972).

My Warren, and After Birthday (produced London, 1973).
The Amiable Courtship of Miz Venus and Wild Bill (produced London, 1973).
Sarah B. Divine! (additional material), by Tom Eyen, music by Jonathan Kramer (produced London, 1973).
Go West Young Woman (produced London, 1974).
Up in Sweden (produced Leicester, 1975; London, 1980).
Dusa, Fish, Stas, and Vi (as *Dead Fish*, produced Edinburgh, 1976; as *Dusa, Fish, Stas, and Vi*, produced London, 1976; Los Angeles, 1978; New York, 1980). London, French, and New York, Dramatists Play Service, 1977.
The Project (produced London, 1976).
Guinevere (produced Edinburgh and London, 1976).
The Rivers and Forests, adaptation of a play by Marguerite Duras (produced London, 1976).
My Name Is Rosa Luxemburg, adaptation of a play by Marianne Auricoste (produced London, 1976).
Franz into April (produced London, 1977).
Queen Christina (produced Stratford-on-Avon, 1977; London, 1979; revised version produced London, 1982). London, St. Luke's Press, 1982.
Piaf (produced Stratford-on-Avon and London, 1978; New York, 1981). Ashover, Derbyshire, Amber Lane Press, 1979; New York, French, 1983.
Ladybird, Ladybird (produced London, 1979).
Sandra (produced London, 1979).
Uncle Vanya, adaptation of a play by Chekhov (produced London, 1979; San Francisco, 1983). London, Eyre Methuen, 1979.
A Doll's House, adaptation of a play by Ibsen (produced Newcastle upon Tyne, 1980).
Sketches in *Variety Night* (produced London, 1982).
The Treat (produced London, 1982).
Aunt Mary (produced London, 1982). Published in *Plays by Women 3*, edited by Michelene Wandor, London, Methuen, 1984.
The Cherry Orchard, adaptation of a play by Chekhov (produced Leicester, 1984).
Loving Women (produced London, 1984). Included in *Three Plays*, 1985.
Camille, adaptation of a play by Dumas fils (produced Stratford-on-Avon, 1984; London, 1985; New Haven, Connecticut, 1987). Included in *Three Plays*, 1985.
Pasionaria, music by Paul Sand, lyrics by Gems and Sand (produced Newcastle upon Tyne, 1985).
Three Plays (includes *Piaf, Camille, Loving Women*). London, Penguin, 1985.
The Danton Affair, adaptation of a work by Stanislawa Przybyszewska (produced London, 1986).

Television Plays: *A Builder by Trade*, 1961; *We Never Do What They Want*, 1979.

*

Theatrical Activities:
Actress: **Film**—*Nineteen Eighty-Four*, 1984.

* * *

Pam Gems's writing career began when she moved to London with her family in 1970. First, the fringe was hungry for new plays; second, she became involved with younger women in the new wave of feminism. Her first play was an autobiographical extravaganza staged at the Cockpit Theatre—*Betty's Wonderful Christmas*. She followed this with two monologue plays at the Almost Free Theatre—*My Warren* and *After Birthday*, one about a woman living alone in a bedsitter, the other about a working-class girl who had just miscarried—both on the themes of woman's survival in extremis.

The Amiable Courtship of Miz Venus and Wild Bill was written for the first Women's Theatre Season at the Almost Free Theatre in London. Gems's play took a satirical look at extreme masculine and feminine attitudes. Although Gems is very wary of being described as a "feminist" writer, clearly the concerns of younger feminists struck a chord with her own interest in women's lives in her plays. Perhaps the clearest expression of this is in *Queen Christina*, which she began writing in 1974 and which was produced by the Royal Shakespeare Company at the Other Place in Stratford in 1977 (the first play by a woman to be staged there). Although sprawling, it is an ambitious and unusual attempt at an epic play by and about a woman. Christina is a Renaissance woman, brought up as a boy for the Swedish throne. When the court begins to worry about her successor, pressure is brought to bear on her to marry and behave "like a woman." Christina does not want to lose her freedom, and refuses to be limited by gender. But she finds this refusal creates a problem in a world where individuals are expected to conform to norms of gender behaviour. Her quest for emotional security turns on the wider questions of what it means to live as a "male," or to live as a "female." Christina leaves the choice of motherhood until too late, and for Gems (who has described this as a "uterine" play) this dilemma is a central concern which she explored more thoroughly than any other woman playwright writing in the 1970's.

Dusa, Fish, Stas, and Vi moved from a fringe production at the Edinburgh Festival in 1976 through a production at the Hampstead. Theatre Club to the Mayfair Theatre in the West End. Here Gems explored contemporary women's experience; four women share a flat—Fish, who commits suicide after the breakup of a love affair, Dusa, whose children have been "kidnapped" by their father, Stas, a part-time call-girl, and Vi, an anorexic faddist. In it Gems expresses a suspicion about the power of organised politics to change personal lives, while recording in a realistic television-style episodic structure the lives of four women.

In *Piaf*, the most successful of her plays, Gems continues her exploration of women's life choices through the saga of Edith Piaf, from street sparrow to rich chanteuse. Gems's Piaf is a woman who never loses the feel of her gutter origins, despite her almost orgasmic satisfaction from becoming a highly paid singing star. Piaf claims sexual as well as economic independence, assuming a hungry, active sexuality to match that of any man. Structurally the play is little more than an extended monologue, punctuated by songs, in which other characters come and go.

Aunt Mary is an entirely different departure for Gems, a gentle and mischievously inventive piece about two transvestite men who write romantic novels under a pseudonym, and provide a haven for lonely social outcasts. Their lives are dictated by images from old movies, and their idyll is interrupted by a brutal media lady who wants to grab them for a television programme. The play is about the way notions of style shape people's lives, but it is also about sexual freedom, affection, and dependence, with extra bonuses, such as a satirical cameo about a young modernist macho poet. *Aunt Mary* is an undervalued play.

Loving Women is actually an expansion of an earlier play, *The Project*, which, while it develops that play's theme of middle-class social-worker pretension, ends up somewhat overblown, and not as effective in reaching its mark as the earlier version.

Camille, based on the famous Dumas play, recounts the tale of the beautiful courtesan Marguerite Gautier, and her doomed love for Armand Duval. Like Piaf, Camille is strong-minded, sexually independent, and only allows herself to succumb to destroying the affair when she is blackmailed because of her illegitimate child. Here Gems returns to one of her continuing preoccupations: the relationship of women to motherhood—fraught and hedged around in the modern world. This very much influenced her rewritten version of *Queen Christina*, which, while it became a much tighter script, was reduced to a helpless cry from the queen for the fact that she had been deprived of motherhood. While this is a potent theme, it actually detracts from the power of the original, sprawling as it was, in its genuine questioning of gender roles across the board.

So far Gems has been essentially a social realist writer, whose work is marked by a distinctive approach to class and to women. All her major plays have been woman-centred, about the specificity of being female with the values which Gems holds important. Among these are an independent heterosexuality, a need for motherhood, and an individualistic attachment to the values of working-class survival. Organised politics is treated with suspicion in *Dusa*, and particularly acerbically in *The Project* which satirises trendy middle-class do-goodism. Her writing is sometimes over-blown, but as a woman writer whose experience spans two generations she is continually receptive to new ideas, and the development of her work has been exciting to watch.

—Michelene Wandor

GIBSON, William. American. Born in New York City, 13 November 1914. Educated at the City College of New York, 1930–32. Married Margaret Brenman in 1940; two sons. Since 1966 co-founding President, Berkshire Theatre Festival, Stockbridge, Massachusetts. Recipient: Harriet Monroe Memorial Prize (*Poetry*, Chicago), 1945; Sylvania award, for television play, 1957. Agent: Flora Roberts Inc., 157 West 57th Street, New York, New York 10019. Address: Stockbridge, Massachusetts 01262, U.S.A.

PUBLICATIONS

Plays

I Lay in Zion (produced Topeka, Kansas, 1943). New York, French, 1947.

Dinny and the Witches: A Frolic on Grave Matters (produced Topeka, Kansas, 1945; revised version produced New York, 1959). With *The Miracle Worker*, New York, Atheneum, 1960.

A Cry of Players (produced Topeka, Kansas, 1948; New York, 1968). New York, Atheneum, 1969.

The Ruby (as William Mass), libretto based on the play *A Night at an Inn* by Lord Dunsany, music by Norman Dello Joio. New York, Ricordi, 1955.

The Miracle Worker: A Play for Television (televised 1957). New York, Knopf, 1957; stage version (produced New York, 1959; London, 1961), with *Dinny and the Witches*, New York, Atheneum, 1960; published separately London, French, 1960.

Two for the Seesaw (produced New York and London, 1958). Published in *The Seesaw Log: A Chronicle of the Stage Production*, New York, Knopf, 1959; London, Corgi, 1962.

Golden Boy, with Clifford Odets, adaptation of the play by Odets, music by Charles Strouse, lyrics by Lee Adams (produced New York, 1964). New York, Atheneum, 1965.

American Primitive (as *John and Abigail*, produced Stockbridge, Massachusetts, 1969; as *American Primitive*, produced Washington, D.C., 1971). New York, Atheneum, 1972.

The Body and the Wheel: A Play Made from the Gospels (produced Lenox, Massachusetts, 1974). New York, Atheneum, 1975.

The Butterfingers Angel, Mary and Joseph, Herod the Nut, and the Slaughter of 12 Hit Carols in a Pear Tree: A Christmas Entertainment (produced Lenox, Massachusetts, 1974; London, 1979; New York, 1980). New York, Dramatists Play Service, 1975.

Golda (produced New York, 1977). Published as *How to Turn a Phoenix into Ashes: The Story of the Stage Production, with the Text, of Golda*, New York, Atheneum, 1978; *Golda* published London, French, 1978.

Goodly Creatures (produced Washington, D.C., 1980).

Monday after the Miracle (produced Pretoria, South Africa, Charleston, South Carolina, and New York, 1982; Northampton, 1986). New York, Atheneum, 1983.

Handy Dandy (produced New York, 1984).

Raggedy Ann and Andy, music and lyrics by Joe Raposo (produced Albany, New York, 1984; as *Rag Dolly*, produced Albany, 1985; as *Raggedy Ann*, produced New York City, 1986).

Screenplays: *The Cobweb*, 1954; *The Miracle Worker*, 1962.

Television Play: *The Miracle Worker*, 1957.

Novel

The Cobweb. New York, Knopf, and London, Secker and Warburg, 1954.

Verse

Winter Crook. New York, Oxford University Press, 1948.

Other

A Mass for the Dead. New York, Atheneum, 1968.

A Season in Heaven, Being a Log of an Expedition after That Legendary Beast, Cosmic Consciousness. New York, Atheneum, 1974.

Shakespeare's Game. New York, Atheneum, 1978.

* * *

William Gibson began as a novelist and poet, earning a reputation with a bestselling novel (*The Cobweb*) and a collection of verse (*Winter Crook*). An early playwriting interest resulted in a short verse drama about the Apostle Peter (*I Lay in Zion*), well-tailored for church groups, which predicted larger dramas to come.

Gibson's first success on the Broadway stage came in 1958 with *Two for the Seesaw*, a two-character drama about an embittered and lonely Nebraska lawyer in New York, separated from his wife, and his affair with a generous-hearted Bronx gamine down on her luck as a dancer. Although mutual love and dependency develop between these two disparate people, the lawyer's home ties are strong enough ultimately to draw him back to his wife. The drama's chief appeal lies in its engaging portrait of the dancer, whose colorful individuality and guileless love in the face of what she realizes is a doomed relationship grasps one's attention and sympathy. The role marked the author's uncommon ability to create strong parts for women and brought recognition to the actress Ann Bancroft who continued to portray other Gibson heroines. The play won praise from the critics and a substantial Broadway run resulting in a film contract for Gibson. Later it was adapted by others as the basis of the successful musical *Seesaw*. In *The Seesaw Log* Gibson chronicles with liveliness the page-to-stage odyssey of *Two for the Seesaw* in which he reveals his disenchantment with the professional production process without minimizing the significant contribution of his collaborators.

In 1959 Gibson's short-lived off-Broadway production of *Dinny and the Witches*, a satirical fantasy with song whose good intentions exceeded its effectiveness, was followed by his greatest success: *The Miracle Worker*. Originally written as a teleplay, the biography-drama portrays the teacher Anne Sullivan's turbulent but triumphant struggle to free her savagely recalcitrant pupil, Helen Keller, from the prison of a sightless and soundless body. Encompassing the time it takes the young teacher to gain mastery over the seemingly ungovernable child in order to teach her language, the play is brought to a poignant resolution when Helen, having had her hand repeatedly doused under the water pump, excitedly discovers the connection between words and things as she writes the word "water" in her teacher's palm. Somewhat uneven and clumsy structure results from an insufficient transformation of the drama from its television form. Although critics faulted the play for its sentimentality and deficiencies in craft, they and the public agreed on its theatrical impact in presenting a compassionate portrait of the heroic teacher who made possible the greatness of Helen Keller. The play's success led to a 1962 film scripted by Gibson. Less critically successful was the 1982 sequel *Monday after the Miracle*, which focuses on the lively courtship and marriage of Anne Sullivan, still Helen Keller's companion and protector 17 years later, to the journalist John Macy, who comes to live in the Boston-area household of the two women and unavoidably disturbs their dependent relationship. Macy, unable to subordinate his private and professional needs to the now famous and articulate Helen, who is first in his wife's priorities and also sexually awakened by his presence, must leave. Critically indicted for being less emotionally powerful in material and effect than its predecessor, this thoughtful play about the difficult choices between duty and happiness offers compelling characterizations of its three leading figures and deserved better than its brief Broadway run.

Extending his experience in 1965 by collaborating on the book for a musical version of Clifford Odets's *Golden Boy*, Gibson transforms the white violinist-turned-boxer hero into a non-musical black pugilist. Aided by Sammy Davis, Jr. in the title role and a well-adapted book, the musical's New York production won moderate success.

A return to biography in the late 1960's was marked both by *American Primitive*, a lively documentary portraying John and Abigail Adams through their letters over three stormy years, and *A Cry of Players*, Gibson's dramatization of young Will Shakespeare's scantily recorded Stratford years and those of his wife Anne, who emerges as a full-bodied character enlisting our compassion. Young Will is characterized as a restless, free-living profligate, frustrated by the limitations of his village and the constricting ties of his family, who survives public punishment for poaching to join Will Kempe's troupe of players for the destiny that awaits him in London. That critics validly observed that the writer's penchant for poetic speech was marred by his lapses into either pretentious or prosaic dialogue and did not offer sufficient approval to let the play endure on Broadway, did not diminish the drama's popularity with community and college theatres.

Less successful than his other ventures into biography, Gibson's *Golda* offers the decisive days of the Arab-Israeli Yom Kippur War of 1973 as a dramatic frame to surround an episodic portrait of Israel's Golda Meir. As the Prime Minister deals with strategy crises and conflicting generals, she recalls in a series of flashbacks key public and private moments in her life stretching from her childhood to her ultimately troubled marriage and strong commitment to Zionism. Despite several strong scenes and a periodically enlivening profile of the protagonist's humor and humanity, the play failed to compress sufficiently the abundant scope of the material and to disclose the private person behind the public one. Yet Gibson merits credit for attempting to dramatize so worthy and so difficult a subject who was then still living.

In the 1980's Gibson wrote two works considerably slighter than *Monday after the Miracle*: *Handy Dandy*, a thematically pointed comedy about a conservative judge and a radical anti-armaments nun constantly brought into his court; and the book for the musical *Raggedy Ann*, concerning a doll springing to life to solve a sick young girl's parental problems, whose 1986 New York production lasted only briefly.

Gibson's work in several media demonstrates both his literary and dramatic gifts, which have resulted in some important plays of sensitivity and substance. Largely successful in dramatizing actual figures, Gibson has secured his place in American letters as an effectual writer of biography-drama.

—Christian H. Moe

GILL, Peter. British. Born in Cardiff, Glamorgan, 7 September 1939. Educated at St. Illtyd's College, Cardiff. Actor, 1957–65; associate director, Royal Court Theatre, London, 1970–72; director, Riverside Studios, Hammersmith, London, 1976–80. Since 1980 associate director, National Theatre, London, and since 1984 director, National Theatre Studio. Recipient: Belgrade International Theatre Festival prize, for directing, 1968; George Devine Award, 1968; British Theatre Association award, for directing, 1985. O.B.E. (Officer, Order of the British Empire), 1980. Agent: Margaret Ramsay Ltd., 14-A Goodwin's Court, London WC2N 4LL. Address: National Theatre, South Bank, London SE1 9PX, England.

PUBLICATIONS

Plays

The Sleepers Den (produced London, 1965; revised version produced London, 1969). With *Over Gardens Out*, London, Calder and Boyars, 1970.

A Provincial Life, adaptation of a story by Chekhov (produced London, 1966).

Over Gardens Out (produced London, 1969). With *The Sleepers Den*, London, Calder and Boyars, 1970.

The Merry-Go-Round, adaptation of the play by D.H. Lawrence (produced London, 1973). London, Theatreprint, 1973.

Small Change (produced London, 1976). With *Kick for Touch*, London, Boyars, 1985.
The Cherry Orchard, adaptation of a play by Chekhov (produced London, 1978).
Kick for Touch (produced London, 1983). With *Small Change*, London, Boyars, 1985.
In the Blue (produced London, 1985).
As I Lay Dying, adaptation of the novel by Faulkner (produced London, 1985).
Mean Tears (produced London, 1987). Published in *Plays International* (London), August 1987.

*

Theatrical Activities:
Director: **Plays**—all his own plays, and *A Collier's Saturday Night* by D. H. Lawrence, London, 1965, 1968; *The Dwarfs* by Harold Pinter, Glasgow, 1966; *The Ruffian on the Stair* by Joe Orton, London, 1966; *O'Flaherty, V. C.* by Shaw, London, 1966; *The Local Stigmatic* by Heathcote Williams, London, 1966; *The Soldier's Fortune* by Thomas Otway, London, 1967; *The Daughter-in-Law* by D. H. Lawrence, London, 1967, 1968, and Bochum, 1972; *Crimes of Passion* by Joe Orton, London, 1967, 1972; *June Evening* by Bill Naughton, toured, 1967; *The Widowing of Mrs. Holroyd* by D. H. Lawrence, London, 1968; *Life Price* by Michael O'Neill and Jeremy Seabrook, London, 1969; *Much Ado about Nothing*, Stratford, Ontario, 1969; *Hedda Gabler* by Ibsen, Stratford, Ontario, 1970; *Landscape and Silence* by Harold Pinter, New York, 1970; *The Duchess of Malfi* by Webster, London, 1971; *Macbeth*, Stratford, Ontario, 1971; *Cato Street* by Robert Shaw, London, 1971; *A Midsummer Night's Dream*, Zurich, 1972; *Crete and Sergeant Pepper* by John Antrobus, London, 1972; *Twelfth Night*, Stratford-on-Avon, 1974; *Fishing* by Michael Weller, New York, 1975; *The Fool* by Edward Bond, London, 1975; *As You Like It*, Nottingham and Edinburgh, 1975, London, 1976; *The Changeling* by Middleton and Rowley, London, 1978; *Measure for Measure*, London, 1979; *Julius Caesar*, London, 1980; *Scrape Off the Black* by Tunde Ikoli, London, 1980; *A Month in the Country* by Turgenev, London, 1981; *Don Juan* by Molière, London, 1981; *Much Ado about Nothing*, London, 1981; *Major Barbara* by Shaw, London, 1982; *Danton's Death* by Georg Büchner, London, 1982; *Tales from Hollywood* by Christopher Hampton, 1983; *Venice Preserv'd* by Thomas Otway, London, 1984; *Antigone*, London, 1984; *Fool for Love* by Sam Shepard, London, 1984; *A Twist of Lemon* by Alex Renton, London, 1985; *The Garden of England* by Peter Cox, 1985; *Bouncing* by Rosemary Wilton, London, 1985; *The Marriage of Figaro* by Mozart, Leeds, 1987. **Television**—*Girl* by James Robson, 1973; *Grace* by David Storey, 1974; *A Matter of Taste* by Alex La Guma, 1974; *Fugitive* by Sean Walsh, 1974; *Hitting Town* by Stephen Poliakoff, 1976.
Actor: **Plays**—Customer in *Last Day in Dreamland* by Willis Hall, London, 1959; Plato in *The Trial of Cob and Leach* by Christopher Logue, London, 1959; Mangolis in *The Kitchen* by Arnold Wesker, London, 1959; Marcus and A Postcard Seller in *This Way to the Tomb* by Ronald Duncan, London, 1960; Silvius in *As You Like It*, 1962; in *The Caucasian Chalk Circle* by Brecht, London, 1962. **Films**—*H.M.S. Defiant* (*Damn the Defiant!*), 1962; *Zulu*, 1964.

* * *

For Peter Gill, playwriting has always been incidental to his profession as director. Indeed, he is still better known as the director who first realised the theatrical potential of D.H. Lawrence's plays than as the author of any of his own works, all of which he has also directed. His special skill, both as director and as dramatist, derives from the naturalistic exploitation of subtext, usually in association with relatively inarticulate proletarian characters, so that the simplest domestic situations are weighted and economically developed for their dramatic potential. *The Sleepers Den* illustrates this method well. The Shannon family, immured in an apparently condemned Cardiff slum flat, suffers variously from claustrophobia and agoraphobia; cornered, defensive, and scared to come to grips with their real dangers, they gradually expose themselves to emotional decomposition until their whole pattern of life collapses. The subtext becomes of paramount importance because of the characters' severely limited capacity even to begin to understand their problems. The Shannons are a fragmented family: an adult brother and sister, their bedridden mother, and a daughter. There is no explanation of how this situation has evolved, and there is no evidence that anyone understands it; across the three generations, power and defense are manipulated by trivial—but effective—gestures of bribery, blackmail, and threatening. Two outsiders—a debt collector and a Catholic social worker—function as catalysts to the situation, but the revelations which are offered seem ridiculous irrelevancies; the brother confesses to the social worker that he has been doing overtime and not telling his sister, and no one seems to understand the seriousness of court action for debt. It is clear that the characters' mental state is a reflection of their environment, that their lethargy and low self-esteem have a century of conditioning behind them. The dramatic crisis comes at the end of the second act, when the sister barricades herself inside the flat as a response to a situation which is too complicated for her to understand, let alone solve; the very short last act consists in her ignoring the pleadings of her brother and the daughter, who are now forced to sleep with friends. In Gill's 1969 production it was clear that old Mrs. Shannon is dead in the last act, so that the sister has shut herself in with the corpse. The interpretation is available that, far from presenting a grotesque family incident, the play suggests a recurrent pattern, with the now insane sister usurping her dead mother's role at the end, where a hereditary family state of introverted lethargy is on the verge of re-enactment. The ambiguous omission of an apostrophe from the play's title, which has been observed in all editions, may be calculated to hint at this.

The single sealed-in set of *The Sleepers Den* is an ideal laboratory for naturalism, but in *Over Gardens Out* Gill developed similar assumptions about character evolution, but set the action in two domestic and several exterior locations. Again, several generations are represented, and surprise and vagueness about the processes of physical decay and growth are intermittently felt; but the structures of authority and rebellion between the generations are relatively unambiguous here, and mindless behaviour, though plentiful, seems attributable to individual characters rather than collective. This means that particular anti-social gestures can be isolated as particular problems, so that even through some of the severities of the action a rich vein of wry comedy persists. The central characters are two adolescent Cardiff boys of widely differing propensities (though both are intellectually limited) whose leisure hours are filled with acts of vandalism which range from the trivial to the alarming. The picaresque tone of this play is more typical of the 1960's than is *The Sleepers Den*, but the play does show an advance in terms of its warmly sympathetic characterisation.

A very similar technique is deployed more adventurously in *Small Change*, where two Cardiff boys are again followed through boyhood and adolescence into manhood; for the premier, Gill even used one of the lead actors from *Over Gardens Out* (and would use him again in *Kick for Touch*). Such an expansive chronology means that the play's naturalistic cogency is not comparable with the earlier plays, and Gill allows himself rather more intelligent and perceptive characters, who deliver nostalgic, poetical monologues, the quality of which has been questioned by critics. However, by 1976 Gill could include a climactic scene of adult anagnorisis and recrimination, in which the boyhood relationship is explicitly perceived as homosexual.

Gill's later plays use very similar material, dissected with increasingly audacious techniques. *Kick for Touch* has two Cardiff brothers, war babies, reminiscing haphazardly across a kitchen table; a woman who is married to one of them and has been the lover of both, is the linking device for a series of interior monologues and duologues, with uninvolved characters simply moving a yard or two away and freezing. Again, there is a bond of something approaching love between the men, but the finale does not pivot on this but on the mystery of a domestic tragedy. *In the Blue* has only two male characters, homosexuals, one of whom is articulate and educated. The technical novelty of this play consists in the hypothetical reinterpretation of scenes, alternative performances introduced just by the word 'OR', so that there is some uncertainty as to which version represents actuality and which fantasy. Gill's naturalism has here been obscured completely; the play is almost purely expressionistic.

Gill has also written and directed numerous successful adaptations, but mention should be made of one heroic failure because its technical effrontery resembles that of his original plays. *As I Lay Dying* theatricalises the innovative narrative method of Faulkner's novel, resulting in a pattern of monologues, with varying perspectives being traded across the body of the characters' mother. The jigsaw of monologues epitomises a tedency in Gill's plays, and the maternal catalyst is also recurrent, especially in *Small Change*.

—Howard McNaughton

GILROY, Frank D(aniel). American. Born in New York City, 13 October 1925. Educated at De Witt Clinton High School, Bronx, New York; Dartmouth College, Hanover, New Hampshire, B.A. (magna cum laude) 1950; Yale University School of Drama, New Haven, Connecticut, 1950–51. Served in the United States Army, 1943–46. Married Ruth Dorothy Gaydos in 1954; three sons. Since 1964, member of the Council, and President, 1969–71, Dramatists Guild, New York. Recipient: Obie award, 1962; Outer Circle award, 1964; Pulitzer Prize, 1965; New York Drama Critics Circle award, 1965; Berlin Film Festival Silver Bear, 1971. D.Litt.: Dartmouth College, 1966. Lives in Monroe, New York. Address: c/o Dramatists Guild, 234 West 44th Street, New York, New York 10036, U.S.A.

PUBLICATIONS

Plays

The Middle World (produced Hanover, New Hampshire, 1949).

A Matter of Pride, adaptation of the story "The Blue Serge Suit" by John Langdon (televised 1957). New York, French, 1970.

Who'll Save the Plowboy? (produced New York, 1962; London, 1963). New York, Random House, 1962.

The Subject Was Roses (produced New York, 1964). New York, French, 1962; included in *About Those Roses; or, How Not to Do a Play and Succeed, and the Text of "The Subject Was Roses,"* New York, Random House, 1965.

Far Rockaway (televised 1965). With *That Summer—That Fall*, New York, Random House, 1967.

That Summer—That Fall (produced New York, 1967). With *Far Rockaway*, New York, Random House, 1967.

The Only Game in Town (produced New York, 1968). New York, Random House, 1968.

Present Tense (includes *Come Next Tuesday, Twas Brillig, So Please Be Kind, Present Tense*) (produced New York, 1972). New York, French, 1973.

The Next Contestant (produced New York, 1978). New York, French, 1979.

Dreams of Glory (produced New York, 1979). New York, French, 1980.

Last Licks (produced New York, 1979; as *The Housekeeper*, produced Brighton and London, 1982).

Real to Reel (produced New York, 1987).

Screenplays: *The Fastest Gun Alive*, with Russell Rouse, 1956; *Texas John Slaughter*, 1958; *Gunfight at Sandoval*, 1959; *The Gallant Hours*, with Beirne Lay, Jr., 1960; *The Subject Was Roses*, 1968; *The Only Game in Town*, 1969; *Desperate Characters*, 1971; *From Noon till Three*, 1976; *Once in Paris*, 1978; *The Gig*, 1985.

Television Plays: *A Matter of Pride*, 1957; *Who Killed Julie Greer?* and *Up Jumped the Devil* (*Dick Powell Show*), 1960–61; *Far Rockaway*, 1965; *The Turning Point of Jim Malloy*, 1975; *Gibbsville* series, from stories by John O'Hara, 1976; *Nero Wolfe*, from the novel *The Doorbell Rang* by Rex Stout, 1979; *Burke's Law* series; and since 1952 plays for *U.S. Steel Hour, Omnibus, Kraft Theater, Studio One, Lux Video Theatre*, and *Playhouse 90*.

Novels

Private. New York, Harcourt Brace, 1970.

From Noon till Three: The Possibly True and Certainly Tragic Story of an Outlaw and a Lady Whose Love Knew No Bounds. New York, Doubleday, 1973; as *For Want of a Horse*, London, Coronet, 1975.

Other

Little Ego (for children), with Ruth G. Gilroy. New York, Simon and Schuster, 1970.

*

Theatrical Activities:

Director: **Films**—*Desperate Characters*, 1971; *From Noon till Three*, 1976; *Once in Paris*, 1978; *The Gig*, 1985. **Television**—*The Turning Point of Jim Malloy* (pilot film), 1975; *Gibbsville* series, 1976; *Nero Wolfe*, 1979.

* * *

Frank D. Gilroy's bittersweet comedies consider men and male rituals: their alienation and loneliness, their difficulty communicating with and understanding women, and their insecurities in dealing with one another.

In Gilroy's first commercial success, *Who'll Save the Plowboy?*, the characters set the pattern of relationships found in his later work. Gilroy introduces us to three lives characterized by frustration, failure, and an inability to communicate honestly. Albert, the Plowboy of the title, and Helen, his wife, confront Larry, the now-dying man who saved the Plowboy's life during the war. Albert builds a castle of lies to impress his war buddy with non-existent postwar success and accomplishment, with fantasies of a happy marriage, and an imaginary strong and healthy son. Albert struts through the script like a rooster who doesn't notice that the hen house is empty. In *Plowboy* Gilroy begins to delineate the little humiliations, the deceits, and the burdensome pretenses of being a man. He also introduces us to the sexually unresponsive, adulterous woman who talks incessantly about insignificant and inappropriate things. These are the characters who populate all of Gilroy's work. In spite of *Plowboy*'s exposition and plot development, the shorthand that will become a trademark of a Gilroy script is apparent: the short, snappy repartee; the one-liner insights; the quick expressions of anger and bitterness.

The Subject Was Roses won the Pulitzer Prize and is still the epitome of his style and thematic concerns. Elegant in its spareness, this play all but eliminates plot and concentrates on a moment of precisely outlined dramatic time. The World War II experiences of Timmy, another veteran, are a backdrop for the parental battlefield in his home, where his warring parents alternately use him as the cannon with which to shoot one another down. Gilroy hones his ability to communicate a complex set of emotions by focusing in exquisite detail on ordinary objects. When Nettie's waffles stick in the waffle iron, spoiling the first breakfast she's made her son in three years, her tears have less to do with a hungry son than they do with her fear of ruining an already tenuous mother-son relationship, her sense of inadequacy as a woman, and her inability to cope with losing her baby to an adult world.

Because of their terror of exposing their inner selves, Gilroy's characters are divided rather than united by emotions. They smash into one another and spin away without pausing to examine the damage. Toward the end of *The Subject Was Roses*, Timmy says: "I suspect that no one's to blame.... Not even me." This disavowal of any responsibility for the mess they've made of their lives is a common factor among all of Gilroy's characters.

Impressed with his Pulitzer Prize and subsequent personal publicity, Gilroy admits to having felt a pressure to write something worthy of all his new-found fame. The result was the disastrous *That Summer—That Fall*, in which he tried to wed the Phaedra and Hippolytus legend to modern characters living in Manhattan's Little Italy. The play had 12 performances, and as Gilroy now says: "It proved that a boy from the Bronx shouldn't mess with the Greeks." That experience released him from what he perceived as the burden of being a Pulitzer Prize-winning playwright, and enabled him to return to his own ideas and terse dramaturgy.

It is in his one-act plays that Gilroy is best able to concentrate the power of his simple descriptive style. He takes an incident and rapidly sets time, mood, and place by zeroing in on the minutest detail. In *The Next Contestant*, for example, a man who is about to be married becomes a guest on a television game show, and is challenged to call up an ex-girlfriend, who knows he's engaged, and get a date with her. If he achieves his goal, he will win a washer and dryer, a bedroom suite, a radio, television, stereo, wall-to-wall carpeting, luggage, an all-expenses-paid vacation in Miami Beach, and more. The heart of this very short play is the quick and emotionally painful telephone conversation between the contestant and the jilted ex-girlfriend. Gilroy shows the manipulation, the deceit, and the subsequent devastating disillusionment.

Gilroy is an idea man more than a plot man, and this can and does hinder him in his full-length work. *Last Licks* presents a variation on his stock characters who are involved with a one-act's worth of idea. A father, a son, and, in this case, the father's mistress, present a typical Gilroy triangular relationship filled with deception, emotional and physical sadism, drinking bouts, and tales of extramarital affairs.

Gilroy builds entire lives around rebuke and repentance. *Last Licks* is resplendent with repressed emotions and bitter speeches. Like so many of his plays, it is an often comic, but more often quite painful skirmish between the sexes, in which the primary sympathy is with the men's involvement with the world and with each other.

—Leah D. Frank

GODBER, John (Harry). British. Born in Upton, Yorkshire, 15 May 1956. Educated at Minsthorpe High School, South Elmsall, Yorkshire; Bretton Hall College, West Bretton, Yorkshire, 1974–78, Cert. Ed. 1977, B. Ed. (honours) 1978; Leeds University, 1978–79, M.A. in theatre 1979, graduate study, 1979–83. Teacher, Minsthorpe High School, 1981–83. Since 1984 artistic director, Hull Truck theatre company. Recipient: Edinburgh Festival award, 1981, 1982, 1984; Olivier Award, 1984; Los Angeles Drama Critics Circle award, 1986. Address: Hull Truck, Spring Street Theatre, Spring Street, Hull, Yorkshire HU2 8RW, England.

PUBLICATIONS

Plays

A Clockwork Orange, adaptation of the novel by Anthony Burgess (produced Edinburgh, 1980; London, 1984).
Cry Wolf (produced Rotherham, Yorkshire, 1981).
Cramp (produced Hull, 1981; revised version, music by Tom Robinson and Hereward K, produced Edinburgh and London, 1986).
E.P.A. (produced Hull, 1982).
Happy Jack (produced Hull, 1982; London, 1985).
Young Hearts Run Free: Ideas Towards a Play (produced West Bretton, Yorkshire, 1983).
September in the Rain (produced Edinburgh, 1983; London, 1984; New York, 1985).
Bouncers (produced Edinburgh and London, 1984; Los Angeles, 1986). With *Shakers*, London, Chappell, 1987.
Up 'n' Under (produced Edinburgh and London, 1984). Oxford, Amber Lane Press, 1985.
Shakers, with Jane Thornton (produced Hull and London, 1985). With *Bouncers*, London, Chappell, 1987.
Up 'n' Under II (produced Edinburgh, 1985).
Blood, Sweat and Tears (produced Hull and London, 1986).
The Ritz (televised 1987; as *Putting on the Ritz*, produced Leicester, 1987).

Teechers (produced Edinburgh and London, 1987).

Television Plays: series scripts for *Grange Hill*, 1981–83, *Brookside*, 1983–84, and *Crown Court*, 1983; *The Rainbow Coloured Disco Dancer*, from work by C.P. Taylor, 1984; *The Ritz* series, 1987; *The Continental*, 1987.

*

Theatrical Activities:
Director: **Plays**—all of his own plays; *Imagine* by Stephen Jeffreys, *Hedda Gabler* by Ibsen, and *The Dock* by Phil Woods, Hull, 1987.

* * *

John Godber is very clear about his particular theatrical style: "the dancer and not the poet is the father of the theatre." Reading his plays gives little sense of the energy and pace of the pieces in performance, an energy and pace deriving from his resolute refusal to separate the role of writer from that of director. His involvement with the Hull Truck company has been a happy one. Hull Truck's commitment to productions based on contemporary and community-related issues, and their long pedigree of theatre derived from improvisation and intense collaboration between writer and actors, have allowed Godber to experiment with an exhilarating mixture of theatrical techniques. The result has been some of the funniest and most enjoyable evenings available in the theatre in recent years.

Plot in Godber's work is kept to a minimum, and frequently the plays have a strong if deliberately jokey documentary feel to them. In *Bouncers* the action takes place at a provincial disco—where the events of a typical night are interspersed with flashback scenes of anxious preparation for the great night out by the lads and girls. Nothing particularly unusual occurs. The bouncers rehearse various degrees of aggression towards the punters, copious amounts of tears, beer, and vomit are spilt, and the characters are united in a macabre attempt to shut off the grim realities of their lives—an attempt that will be, as always, doomed. All the many characters (both male and female) are played by the same four male bouncer actors, and the effect is to enlarge the comic potential of the events but also to stress its non-particularity. Godber is not interested in creating unique psychologically realised characters. They are representative, standing in for an audience that may very well proceed from the theatre to such a disco—particularly since Godber is intent on attracting audiences that would not normally regard theatre as a part of their cultural experience. The club acts as a loose symbolic location of the contemporary world at play: the patrons are looking for a dream-world of alcoholic oblivion and easy sex, and find instead a continuation of the daytime regime, ruled over by arbitrary bouncers free to admit or refuse entrance to a fun palace in which there are strict rules about dress, an expensive bar, and complete limitations on the celebration of any conceivable excess.

Shakers, written with Jane Thornton, changes the sexual perspective. Set in a provincial wine bar run by four waitresses who again play all the other (male and female) characters, it offers an even bleaker account of the urge to escape. We see four young girls at work in the supermarket, fantasising about the birthday party to come, agonising over the choice of clothes, and seeing as the limit of their dreams the joy of actually working in a cocktail bar. But the life at Shakers presented by the four waitresses is no different from any other work situation. The hours are long, the pay is bad, and sexual harassment is not only rife, but is effectively encouraged by the unseen management. That the waitresses are the better able to analyse their situation than their male counterparts in *Bouncers* is typical of Godber's work. His strong feminist line demands this distinction. His plays are all about politically marginalised people, failures and victims of the system; for the women victimisation is made worse by their sense of being underdogs in a world of underdogs, and they are given a stronger oppositional voice.

The pace of the productions, and the constant role switching does little to disguise, however, a certain literalness of political analysis. Everything fits too neatly into place. Godber's concentration on marginalised characters in an urban wasteland brings with it an inability to look beyond the boundaries of marginalisation—although it must be admitted that in performance this is a weakness that is less apparent than on more sober reflection. For these reasons his most successful play to date is *Up 'n' Under*, for here Godber has been able to use the build-up to and the actual enactment on stage of a Rugby League Sevens match as a far less prosaic metaphor of a modern world of male competition and machismo. Down-at-heels Arthur is conned into a large bet with a bent but successful businessman that he cannot train the worst amateur pub team in Yorkshire to beat the top dogs, the Cobblers Arms from Castleford. Arthur's players are dragged, understrength and unwilling, into a training programme supervised by (horror of horrors!) a woman, and the scene is set for a *Rocky*-style conclusion—and Arthur's favourite movies are the *Rocky* series—in which the underdog gets up off his backside at the last possible moment and wins. The presentation of the game, with seven actors (including their female trainer) involved in actual play provides an exciting example of total theatre. Tension as to the outcome is kept up throughout. This is not Hollywood, however, and our heroes lose by the odd point. But Godber's characters, though inveterate losers, always retain an optimistic strain and the play ends with the team planning a double-or-nothing bet on the result of a replay—a match which duly takes place in *Up 'n' Under II*. And this time ... well, find out for yourself.

—John Bull

GOLDMAN, James. American. Born in Chicago, Illinois, 30 June 1927; brother of the writer William Goldman. Educated at the University of Chicago, Ph.B. 1947, M.A. 1950; Columbia University, New York, 1950–52. Served in the United States Army, 1952–54. Married 1) Marie McKeon in 1962 (divorced 1973), one daughter and one son; 2) Barbara Deren in 1975. Since 1966 member of the Council, Dramatists Guild, and since 1967 member of the Council, Authors League of America. Recipient: Oscar, 1969; Writers Guild of America West award, 1969. Agent: Sam Cohn, International Creative Management, 40 West 57th Street, New York, New York 10019, U.S.A.

PUBLICATIONS

Plays

They Might Be Giants (produced London, 1961).

Blood, Sweat and Stanley Poole, with William Goldman (produced New York, 1961). New York, Dramatists Play Service, 1962.
A Family Affair, with William Goldman, music by John Kander (produced New York, 1962).
The Lion in Winter (produced New York, 1966; London, 1969). New York, Random House, and London, French, 1966.
Follies, music and lyrics by Stephen Sondheim (produced New York, 1971; revised version produced Manchester, 1985; London, 1987). New York, Random House, 1971.
Robin and Marian (screenplay). New York, Bantam, 1976.

Screenplays: *The Lion in Winter*, 1968; *They Might Be Giants*, 1970; *Nicholas and Alexandra*, with Edward Bond, 1971; *Robin and Marian*, 1976; *Oliver Twist*, 1983; *White Nights*, with Eric Hughes, 1985.

Television Plays: *Evening Primrose*, music by Stephen Sondheim, 1966; *Anna Karenina*, with Simon Langton, from the novel by Tolstoy, 1985.

Novels

Waldorf. New York, Random House, 1965; London, Joseph, 1966.
The Man from Greek and Roman. New York, Random House, 1974; London, Hutchinson, 1975.
Myself as Witness. New York, Random House, 1979; London, Hamish Hamilton, 1980.

* * *

James Goldman at his best is a second-rate Neil Simon: both are dramatists who entertain rather than engage their audiences. Whether he is writing situation comedies (in collaboration with his brother), *A Family Affair* and *Blood, Sweat and Stanley Poole*, historical dramas, *The Lion in Winter* and *Nicholas and Alexandra*, or a musical, *Follies*, his work is always predictable, never ranging outside of the already-tested limits of the form. Only his skillful handling of dialogue occasionally redeems his plays, but even this cannot compensate for his deficiency in imagination, nor can it conceal that his characters are stock, plots mechanical, and themes imperfectly realized.

A Family Affair and *Blood, Sweat and Stanley Poole* play like the pseudo-comedies that could be seen between 6 and 10 p.m. any weeknight on American television throughout the late 1950's and early-to-middle 1960's. One concerns itself with the bustle and bickering that typically occurs when two families attempt to plan a wedding and the guardian of the bride wants a simple, elegant "family affair" while the mother of the groom longs for something a bit fancier. The other involves an army officer, 1st Lieutenant Stanley Poole, who has been bribing the education officer, Malcolm, with goods from the supply room to pass him on the army proficiency tests. The hero-of-the-day is Private Robert Oglethorpe who runs a "cram" course for the army officers, making it possible for Poole to replace the pilfered supplies, free himself from his bondage to Malcolm, and retain his military rank by passing the proficiency exams. The plot is mechanical, the jokes are stale, the characters too familiar, and the situation—Oglethorpe's classroom for the army's dunderheads—plays like a classroom scene from *Our Miss Brooks* or *Sergeant Bilko*, replete with all the cute gimmicks and mnemonics that teach the adult student to learn the names of the five Great Lakes or to recognize "the Symphony that Schubert wrote and never finished." Even the two Goldmans' sense of theatricality falters in this play. The slapstick accident where the good guys mangle and mutilate the villainous Captain Malcolm's coveted Jag takes place off-stage and can only be recounted, supposedly hilariously, by the conspirators on the stage. The climax of the play comes when the clumsy Private Oglethorpe, who previously got headaches whenever even the word "bayonet" was mentioned, catches the rifle Malcolm throws at him and brilliantly executes the manual of arms. The first action better fits a movie or television program than a play; the second simply lacks enough intrinsic importance to carry even the climax of a silly piece of canned comedy.

Goldman finds better success in another genre, the history or chronicle play, which had its revival in the 1960's with *Luther*, *Lawrence of Arabia*, and most successfully, *A Man for All Seasons*. Well done, the chronicle play examines and revitalizes characters from the past whose significance is unchallenged. It brings the past to life and, more importantly, it shows how the present has worked upon the past making it relevant. Goldman, however, seems to have overlooked this most important aspect of historical drama. It is not surprising that the dramatist of *They Might Be Giants* left the contemporary world and looked to the past to supply him with the heroes he sought, but it is regrettable that he only went to the past to acquire material and not to relate it to modern concerns. In *The Lion in Winter* Henry II of England and Eleanor of Aquitaine engage in a battle of wits as each attempts to outdo the other and settle the questions of succession, which son will marry the king's mistress, and which son will inherit the Vexin and Aquitaine. Henry, the aging monarch, still the roaring, regal lion, seeks to possess both his mistress and his wife and both their lands in order to pass England and that portion of France which is England's to John, his youngest and weakest son. Eleanor fights fiercely to hold Henry, and, failing that, to guarantee that England and her precious Aquitaine are willed to Richard Coeur de Lion. Geoffrey, the middle and cleverest son, plays brother against brother and son against father as he, too, struggles to protect what he believes should be his own. Alais, the lovely mistress, is pawn to Henry and his aged and imprisoned wife throughout the play. The dialogue in the play is witty, intelligent, pithy, and often mercurial. Henry and Eleanor alternately rage at each other and ask each other for pity in a manner reminiscent of George and Martha's quarrels in *Who's Afraid of Virginia Woolf?* But finally, the play is too contrived, the games of oneupmanship grow stale, and the audience begins to doubt that anything so real as the fate of the kingdom is at stake. The Christmas Court ends in a stalemate; the question of succession is postponed to another year; Eleanor and Henry conclude acknowledging to each other that their real enemy is time and that it will win. Goldman, meanwhile, seems to have forgotten that there was ever a real historical question raised in the play. History, and not the play, is left to tell us how the question of succession was resolved. The natures of the regal pair and not succession seem to have been the stuff of the play, but Goldman never demonstrates why these natures matter or who this King and Queen are.

More recently Goldman tried his hand at musical comedy; but he seems no more likely to be successful with this form than with the others. The book for *Follies* suffers from the same flaws that plagued his earlier works. The occasion is a reunion called by an impresario of the Weismann Follies' girls. Back to the crumbling music hall that had its heyday thirty years earlier come the showgirls who had danced for the era between the two wars. Among the guests are two girls, Sally and Phyllis, and their husbands, Buddy and Ben. As the evening progresses, we watch these pairs when they were young and in love, thirty years ago, and now, when they are old and discontented and flirting with the possibility that they can undo time and their marriages and return to the men who had jilted them before they married so long ago. The soap opera tale can be guessed. After an evening in which the couples dance and sing down memory lane and exorcize their regrets in a Follies Loveland, the couples leave their fancied past and return to drab realities and each other. The lyrics and music do much to redeem the play, and the gauzy interplay of past and present, shadows and substance, is visually well-handled and extremely well-suited to a musical that has taken sentimentality and nostalgia for its theme. A revised version of *Follies*, which Goldman and Stephen Sondheim worked on together, was a 1987 hit in London.

Goldman's difficulty in creating fully realized characters of his own fresh imagining and his lack of a significant theme continue to plague his work.

—Carol Simpson Stern

GOOCH, Steve. British. Born in Surrey, 22 July 1945. Educated at the Emanuel School, London, 1956–63; Trinity College, Cambridge, 1964–67, B.A. (honours) in modern languages 1967; St. John's College, Cambridge (Harper-Wood Scholar), 1967; Birmingham University, 1968–69. Assistant editor, *Plays and Players* magazine, London, 1972–73; resident dramatist, Half Moon Theatre, London, 1973–74, Greenwich Theatre, London, 1974–75, Solent People's Theatre, Southampton, 1981–82, Theatre Venture, London, 1983–84, and Croydon Warehouse Theatre, Surrey, 1986. Recipient: Arts Council bursary, 1973; Thames Television award, 1974. Agent: Margaret Ramsay Ltd., 14-A Goodwin's Court, London WC2N 4LL, England.

PUBLICATIONS

Plays

The NAB Show (produced Brighton, 1970).
Great Expectations, adaptation of the novel by Dickens (produced Liverpool, 1970).
Man Is Man, adaptation of the play by Brecht (produced London, 1971; New Haven, Connecticut, 1978).
It's All for the Best, adaptation of the novel *Candide* by Voltaire (produced Stoke-on-Trent, 1972; London, 1979).
Big Wolf, adaptation of a play by Harald Mueller (produced London, 1972). London, Davis Poynter, 1972.
Will Wat; If Not, What Will? (produced London, 1972). London, Pluto Press, 1975.
Nicked (produced Exeter, 1972).
The Mother, adaptation of a play by Brecht (produced London, 1973). London, Eyre Methuen, 1978.
Female Transport (produced London, 1973; Louisville, 1975; New York, 1976). London, Pluto Press, 1974.
Dick (produced London, 1973).
The Motor Show, with Paul Thompson (produced Dagenham, Essex, and London, 1974). London, Pluto Press, 1975.
Cock-Artist, adaptation of a play by Rainer Werner Fassbinder (produced London, 1974). Published in *Gambit 39–40* (London), 1982.
Strike '26, with Frank McDermott (produced London, 1975).
Made in Britain, with Paul Thompson (produced Oxford, 1976).
Landmark (as *Our Land Our Lives*, produced London, 1976; revised version, as *Landmark*, produced Wivenhoe, Essex, 1980). Colchester, Theatre Action Press, 1982.
Back-Street Romeo (produced London, 1977).
Rosie, adaptation of a play by Harald Mueller (also director: produced London, 1977).
The Women Pirates: Ann Bonney and Mary Read (produced London, 1978). London, Pluto Press, 1978.
In the Club (produced London, 1979).
Future Perfect, with Michelene Wandor and Paul Thompson (produced on tour, 1980).
Fast One (produced Southampton, 1982). Southampton, Solent People's Theatre, 1982.
Fuente Ovejuna, adaptation of the play by Lope de Vega (produced London, 1982).
Flotsam, adaptation of a play by Harald Mueller (produced Croydon, Surrey, 1985). Published in *Gambit 39–40* (London), 1982.
Home Work, adaptation of a play by Franz Xaver Kroetz, published in *Gambit 39–40* (London), 1982.
Taking Liberties (produced London, 1984).
Good for You (produced Leicester, 1985).
Mister Fun (produced Sheffield and London, 1986).
Star Turns (produced Croydon, Surrey, 1987).

Radio Plays: *The Kiosk*, from a play by Ludvík Aškenazy, 1970; *Delinquent*, from a play by Harald Mueller, 1978; *Santis*, from a play by Martin Walser, 1980; *What Brothers Are For*, 1983.

Other

All Together Now: An Alternative View of Theatre and the Community. London, Methuen, 1984.

Translator, *Poems and Ballads*, by Wolf Biermann. London, Pluto Press, 1977.
Translator, with Paul Knight, *Wallraff, The Undesirable Journalist*, by Günter Wallraff. London, Pluto Press, 1978; New York, Overlook Press, 1979.

*

Critical Studies: interviews in *Renaissance and Modern Studies* (Nottingham), 1977, and *Hard Times 12* (Berlin), 1980; *Alternativen im britischen Drama der Gegenwart* by Günther Klotz, Berlin, Akademie, 1978; *Stages in the Revolution* by Catherine Itzin, London, Eyre Methuen, 1980; "The Surveyor and the Construction Engineer" by Gooch, in *Theatre Quarterly 36* (London), 1980.

Theatrical Activities:
Director: **Plays**—*Work Kills!* by Bruce Birchall, London, 1975; *Consensus* by Michael Gill, London, 1976; *Rosie*, London, 1977; *Night Shift* by John Derbyshire, London, 1983.

Steve Gooch comments:

My work is mainly about working-class experience and history, and for a working-class audience and readership. Its intention is to align itself with the most developed and progressive sections of the working-class movement in Britain and elsewhere. To this end it draws on traditions of thought from the working-class movement, both in Britain and abroad. It also draws freely on innovations in style and dramatic technique from working-class culture everywhere, in an experimental attempt to find a new socialist, humanist theatre.

* * *

In contrast to other playwrights of the British 1968 generation, Steve Gooch has not, in spite of being a very prolific and versatile writer, found a firm foothold in either the major subsidised theatre companies or the mass media. This is not due to a lack of talent or of successful productions of his plays or even to a decline of the British alternative theatre scene, but rather to Gooch's adherence to a theatre for the community. A great deal of artistic energy, from the beginning of Gooch's career as a writer for the stage, has gone into the mediation, by translations or adaptations, of plays and theatrical ideas from the Romance and German languages. Gooch shows particular skill in his translations of the earlier Brecht and of those contemporary playwrights (Kroetz, Harald Mueller, Martin Walser) whose preoccupation with political aspects of subjectivity mirrors his own, but he has also adapted classics like Dickens, Voltaire, Lope de Vega, and Terence.

In his original work for the stage Gooch early on found a congenial venue in the Half Moon Theatre in London's East End. One of the first results of their workshop projects was Gooch's dramatization, as *Will Wat; If Not, What Will?*, of Wat Tyler's 1381 peasants' uprising, the first proto-socialist movement in English history. In this attempt "to show what the history books usually leave out" Gooch draws on contemporary documents and alternative versions of medieval history to present the peasants' point of view in their opposition to royal militarism and exploitation by old feudal and emerging merchant interests. The play acutely balances the eventual defeat of the peasants led by John Ball and Wat Tyler against the positive growth of self-awareness of an oppressed class. History is brought on stage as a collective process whose dramaturgy has to preempt individual identification by anti-illusionist techniques such as double casting, songs, and quotes from historical documents. Similar Brechtian techniques are employed in Gooch's next historical play, also produced by the Half Moon Theatre, *Female Transport.* Again, it is history from below, this time in the more familiar scenery of early 19th-century Britain. The play gives a realistic account of the voyage to Australia of six female convicts who gradually win through to an insight into the necessity of resistance against a patriarchal class society. This socialist-feminist line in Gooch's work is elaborated in an early text that ended up as a Royal Shakespeare Company production of *The Women Pirates: Ann Bonney and Mary Read.* In this epic portrait of two historical women at the turn of the 18th century, Gooch charts, in a loose configuration of scenes interspersed with many songs, a successful if seemingly peripheral liberation from hegemonic law and morality.

While developing his Brechtian style of historical plays with a socialist, humanist, and feminist slant, Gooch collaborated on some theatrical projects that concerned sections of the contemporary working class in a more direct way. It was here that Gooch came nearest to his declared aim of writing "about working-class experience and history, and for a working-class audience and readership." In *The Motor Show* (written with Paul Thompson) Gooch tried to create a working-class community theatre from within. After local research at the Dagenham Ford plant by the group called Community Theatre, the play turned into a 24-scene documentation, in a deft cartoon-like style mixing documentary, realistic, and music hall elements, of 60 years of struggle between the Ford Company and their workers. The Community Theatre failed to set itself up in Dagenham, but the unashamedly agit-prop techniques—rescued from preachiness by witty dialogue—of *The Motor Show*, largely retained in *Strike '26* and in *Made in Britain* (a documentary about British Leyland, again written with Paul Thompson), became a model for many similar attempts by other writers. In *Our Land, Our Lives* Gooch's concern with issues involving specifically contemporary communities was placed on a more general level by being given a fictional focus in a reunion of young married people in a village barn that had served them as a meeting-place in their schooldays. The play shows the encroachment of agribusiness on traditional village life, but in the reworking of it with Essex University Theatre (under the title *Landmark*) it came to include the theme of nuclear threat. In the revised version the fields against whose sale the young people have been rallying opposition are bought up by the Ministry of Defence to be converted into a site for nuclear missiles.

In the new austerity of the 1980's Gooch has apparently redefined the range of his dramatic themes, even though he has remained faithful to the small companies and theatre groups of the dwindling alternative circuit. The move away from agit-prop didacticism is obvious even in his recent *Taking Liberties*, written in the genre of the historical play which lends itself most readily to political discourse with clear-cut messages. In this play we get an unusually broad social panorama, from patricians to plebeians, bound up in the radical agitation of the late 18th century. The carnivalesque action here focuses on the mock election of a Mayor of Garratt and reflects John Wilkes's creation of a new type of populist politics involving the London masses. The play also indicates a change in the post-1979 political atmosphere in that it does not so much rescue the utopian perspectives from the historical setting but ends in the temporary defeat of plebeian aspirations for political participation. The widening of thematic range and intended appeal finds expression in a reappropriation of realist and even naturalist theatrical approaches. This development accompanies the synthesis in Gooch's conception of his own work between John McGrath's purist reliance on popular traditions and David Edgar's more eclectic attitude towards mainstream theatrical codes. The new approach characterizes even a play with a seemingly exotic setting like *Fast One*, in which a merchant seaman is caught up in an international intrigue about the sale of arms in an unspecified South American country.

Mister Fun, written for a Sheffield-based touring group, goes even further in the direction of a naturalist tradition that the author had never completely excluded from his theatre language. The play concentrates on the lives of a young couple working on a traditional fairground. The action shows the inevitable take-over of the fair by the electronics branch of the leisure industry after a local council's abortive attempts to give it a permanent site. This process is traced in its divisive effects on the young couple's lives. In their drifting apart the girl achieves some degree of independence, whereas the eponymous hero becomes a kind of walking ad for what was once popular entertainment but which now usurps people's work and minds.

—Bernd-Peter Lange

GORDONE, Charles (Edward). American. Born in Cleveland, Ohio, 12 October 1925. Educated at Elkhart High School, Indiana; University of California, Los Angeles; Los Angeles State College (now University), B.A. in drama 1952; New York University Television Workshop. Served in the United States Air Force. Married Jeanne Warner in 1959; two sons and three daughters. Instructor, Cell Block Theatre, Yardville and Bordontown prisons, New Jersey, 1977–78; taught playmaking, New School for Social Research, New York, 1978–79. Founder, with Godfrey Cambridge, Committee for the Employment of Negro Performers, 1962. Recipient: Obie award, for acting, 1964; Pulitzer Prize, 1970; New York Drama Critics Circle award, 1970; Vernon Rice award, 1970; American Academy award, 1971. Address: 17 West 100th Street, New York, New York 10025, U.S.A.

PUBLICATIONS

Plays

A Little More Light Around the Place, adaptation of the novel by Sidney Easton (produced New York, 1964).
No Place to Be Somebody: A Black-Black Comedy (also director: produced New York, 1967). Indianapolis, Bobbs Merrill, 1969.
Gordone Is a Muthah (miscellany; produced New York, 1970). Published in *The Best Short Plays 1973*, edited by Stanley Richards, Radnor, Pennsylvania, Chilton, 1973.
Baba-Chops (produced Los Angeles, 1974; New York, 1975).
The Last Chord (produced New York, 1976).
A Qualification for Anabiosis (produced New York, 1978; revised version, as *Anabiosis*, produced St. Louis, 1979).

*

Manuscript Collection: Schomburg Collection, New York.

Critical Study: "Yes, I Am a Black Playwright, But . . ." by Gordone, in *New York Times*, 25 January 1970.

Theatrical Activities:
Director: **Plays**—about 25 plays, including *Rebels and Bugs*, 1958, *Faust* by Goethe and *Peer Gynt* by Ibsen, 1959, and *Tobacco Road* by Erskine Caldwell, *Three Men on a Horse* by George Abbott and John Cecil Holm, *Detective Story* by Sidney Kingsley, *Hell Bent fer Heaven* by Hatcher Hughes, and Eugene O'Neill's "Sea Plays," 1960; *No Place to Be Somebody*, 1967 (and later productions); *Leaving Home* by Marcia Haufrecht, 1978; *After Hours* by Virgil Richardson (co-director, with Lucien Fiiyer), 1981.
Actor: **Plays**—in *Fortunato*; Logan in *The Climate of Eden* by Moss Hart, 1952; in *Mrs. Patterson* by Greer Johnson and Charles Sebree, 1957; The Valet in *The Blacks* by Jean Genet, 1961; George in *Of Mice and Men* by Steinbeck, 1964; Jero in *The Trials of Brother Jero* by Wole Soyinka, 1967; in *Gordone Is a Muthah*, 1970. **Television**—*The Climate of Eden*, 1961.

Charles Gordone comments:
Always the search for IDENTITY.

* * *

Charles Gordone first came to public attention as an actor in the tumultuous 1961 New York production of Genet's *The Blacks*. In addition to Gordone, the cast for that production included James Earl Jones, Cicely Tyson, Godfrey Cambridge, and Cynthia Belgrave. Like the first production of *A Raisin in the Sun, The Blacks* inspired most of its cast members to continue and extend the 1960's renaissance of black theater. As a member of the cast of *The Blacks*, Gordone was deeply involved in discussions of the politics of the play and of the relationship of theater to the black movement.

Although Gordone continued to work in and around theater throughout the 1960's, it was not until 1969, with the first production of his major play, *No Place to Be Somebody*, that his voice was clearly heard. Gordone had difficulty finding a producer for the play until Joseph Papp agreed to do it. The productions quickly won public and critical applause. Gordone received a Drama Desk award as one of the three most promising playwrights of the year, and the play received the Pulitzer Prize.

No Place to Be Somebody aptly fits a category or genre of drama defined by W.E.B. Du Bois early in this century: it is a "play of the contact of black and white." More than most plays by black American dramatists, and certainly more than most plays of the late 1960's, *No Place to Be Somebody* quickly establishes a world in which black characters and white characters not only inhabit the same space but come into direct conflict with each other. Johnny Williams, the owner of Johnny's bar where the play is set, is a young, angry black man who is obsessed with "Charlie fever," the play's organizing metaphor for black rage against white power. Johnny's rage does not take a strictly separatist form; some of his most important and ambiguous relationships are with vulnerable whites. He serves as the abusive pimp for two prostitutes—one black, the other white. He has an affair with the white, liberal college daughter of a lawyer who holds information useful to Johnny. He employs as bartender a white man whose dreams of being a "black" musician are undermined both by his ethnicity and his drug addiction. Since all of these white characters are weak and dependent on Johnny, we can read his contact with whites as a mode of reverse cultural exploitation; that is true of the structure of the relationships, but, within each one, there is at least a moment when Johnny reveals enough human concern to suggest that something in addition to power is at stake. The complexities of Johnny's motivations are only hinted, however, and could be taken in a number of directions in performance.

Johnny's foil and eventually his foe is Gabe, a "fair-skinned" black man who plays a role and a half as unemployable actor and the author of the play-in-progress. Gabe haunts Johnny's bar from its internal and external fringes. As a Brechtian narrator, Gabe initiates each scene with a commentary on the play's intentions and limitations; he informs us, for example, that *No Place to Be Somebody* is not a social protest play. Gabe is not satisfied in his external role; he enters the world of the play, in disguise one might say, as an actor-poet who distracts and provokes the company at the bar but can not get cast in any other show in town because he is neither white nor black enough in appearance. Gabe's voice opposes Johnny's "Charlie fever" throughout the play, but his voice does not suffice. In the end, Gabe kills Johnny, and in so doing destroys both his black brother and the character created by the playwright-at-work.

No Place to Be Somebody is an unabashedly derivative play whose sources make odd and only sometimes harmonious bedfellows. The constrained barroom setting of the play is reminiscent of *The Lower Depths, The Iceman Cometh*, and *The Time of Your Life*; expressionistic conventions such as Gabe's lyrics and rhapsodies and Machine Dog, a materialized hallucination, interrupt the interactions on stage much as they do in the plays of Tennessee Williams and Ed Bullins; Gabe's final speeches and his appearance costumed as a black woman in mourning recall Baraka's *Dutchman* and Hawthorne's sin-laden Puritans. As many reviewers commented, the play also manages to accelerate its activity so that we find ourselves suddenly confronted with melodrama replete with an over-abundance of on-stage corpses.

In *No Place to Be Somebody* Gordone took on the difficult task of writing a drama that would at once illuminate the complex and discordant responses of black Americans to white American culture and would embrace what he himself called the "broader human context." In the 1970's he moved to the midwest and continued his struggle to "tell the story of the human comedy" through directing for the theater. His later writing includes an attempt to extend the form of the American musical with a musical version of *No Place to Be Somebody*. *Anabiosis* explores his tendency to "get sidetracked," and has been revised several times.

—Helene Keyssar

GORMAN, Clem (Brian Gorman). Australian. Born in Perth, Western Australia, 18 October 1942. Educated at St. Louis School, 1955–56, and Aquinas College, 1957–60, both Perth; University of Sydney, 1963–67, B.A., Dip.Ed.; Polytechnic of Central London, diploma in arts administration 1975. Married Sandra Dent in 1967 (divorced 1986). Free-lance stage manager and theatre administrator, Sydney, 1967–68: founder, Australian Free Theatre Group; co-founder, *Masque* theatre magazine, 1968; lived in London, 1970–79; deputy administrator, Round House Trust, London, 1975–76; administrator, Moving Being dance company, Cardiff, 1976–77; administrator, Australian National Playwrights Conference, Sydney, 1982; Lecturer in Playwriting, Victorian College of the Arts, Melbourne, 1984, and Adelaide University, 1985; training officer, Australian Book Publishers Association, Sydney, 1986. Since 1966 free-lance journalist. Recipient: Australia Council Literature Board grant, 1980, and fellowship, 1981. Agent: Anthony Williams, 55 Victoria Street, Potts Point, New South Wales 2011. Address: 505/3 Greenknowe Avenue, Potts Point, New South Wales 2011, Australia.

PUBLICATIONS

Plays

I Love You Sailor (produced London, 1976).
Let Me In, I'm a Friend of the Band (produced London, 1978).
A Manual of Trench Warfare (produced Adelaide, 1978). Sydney, Currency Press, 1979.
The Harding Women (produced Adelaide, 1980). With *A Night in the Arms of Raeleen*, Sydney, Currency Press, 1983.
The Motivators (produced Sydney, 1981). Montmorency, Victoria, Yackandandah, 1983.
A Night in the Arms of Raeleen (produced Melbourne, 1982). With *The Harding Women*, Sydney, Currency Press, 1983.
A Fortunate Life, adaptation of the autobiography by A.B. Facey (produced Melbourne, 1984).
The Journey Home (for children; produced Adelaide, 1985).
A Face from the Street (produced Canberra, 1985).
The Last Night-Club. Montmorency, Victoria, Yackandandah, 1985.

Screenplay: *The Swans Away* (documentary), 1986.

Other

The Book of Ceremonies. Bottisham, Cambridgeshire, Whole Earth Tools, 1969; revised edition, as *Making Ceremonies*, 1972; revised edition, as *The Book of Ceremony*, 1972.
Making Communes: Survey/Manual. Bottisham, Cambridgeshire, Whole Earth Tools, 1971.
People Together. St. Albans, Hertfordshire, Paladin, 1975.
Backstage Rock: Behind the Scenes with the Bands. London, Pan, 1978.

*

Manuscript Collection: University of Queensland Press, St. Lucia.

Clem Gorman comments:

It may be—and a writer is not necessarily the best person to know—that my work is about the struggle between the female and male sides of my own nature.

* * *

Though it was only in 1978 with *A Manual of Trench Warfare* that he achieved recognition as an Australian playwright, Clem Gorman had been working in the Australian and English theatre since the mid-1960's and had written books on several aspects of the counter-culture as well as organising an experimental Sydney group theatre. In view of this background, his original published plays are surprising in that they are stylistically muted, mostly using a naturalistic structure of human relationships broken only by intermittent songs and direct audience address. Moreover, in his plays with male subjects the ostensible central theme is the traditional Australian one of mateship, questioned, tested, and analysed but not absolutely rejected. *A Manual of Trench Warfare* actually begins with a male chorus of Australian voices singing a hymn to mateship, an assertion of both working-class and nationalistic solidarity, and the first scene opens with a young soldier alone in a trench at Gallipoli writing a letter to his mother about how he killed the Turk who had killed his mate. A new trenchmate, a more garrulous Irish larrikin soldier, brings a new bond in terms of whisky, anti-authoritarianism, and comradeship in battle, but gradually Gorman's focus shifts from this traditional model of mateship to an examination of the support system which evolves between the two men and which is ultimately expressed in physical love. In the poignant final scene the Australian's patriotism has been completely displaced by his loyalty to his dying Irish mate, to the extent that he offers to shoot the corporal who has interrupted their love-making.

In *A Night in the Arms of Raeleen* the solitary female character is a catalyst for the delusory concept of mateship which twenty years previously had bound together the four males who are now having a reunion, trying to regress to their Bodgie identities in talk and dress. Raeleen, however, has recently told herself that she has got to make her "own support system now," and she defiantly asserts the sober values of middle age, forcing the men away from mutual congratulation and myth-mongering, towards a rudimentary awareness of themselves and their needs. A series of monologues from various characters, done direct to the audience under a single spotlight, shows how with a brutal cauterising of emotions Raeleen was used as the pivotal commodity in their adolescent camaraderie. But the naturalistic context of these addresses shows her emergent self-knowledge dissolving all relationships and the whole support structure, forcing them all to find independence, as a precondition for new, honest relationships. In *The Harding Women* all three characters are female, held together by their various relationships to the dead paterfamilias, dramaturgically a male equivalent of Raeleen, whom they have known as wife, as housekeeper/mistress, and as daughter. Each character has at least three monologues and songs which deal with personal crises and explain how the present situation of distrust and exploitation evolved; for these, the widow dresses in clothes of the early 1960's and speaks accusingly to her dead husband, while the other two women speak direct to the audience in a more reflective manner. A Strindbergian web of entrapment is sketched, with the acerbic hypochondriac mother venting her histrionic bitterness on the housekeeper, who had been paradoxically snared by the dead man's intended generosity, and on the daughter, who feels an irrational piety towards her mother even though she can state, "I don't need a man to look after me. I don't need a support system except my friends and colleagues at work. I don't need a system of beliefs to buttress me." But both mother and daughter have a chemical dependence, on alcohol and dope, and the ending is intensely pessimistic because, whereas the reunion at Raeleen's occurred once in twenty years, never to be repeated, for the Harding women it is an annual ritual with no prospect of relief or resolution, at least until another death occurs.

The playwright Jack Hibberd has astutely observed that the Harding mother "embodies the awful oppressiveness of the 1950's in Australia," and she has a strong affinity to a recurrent type in the plays and novels of Patrick White of that period of "the great Australian emptiness." Gorman's pessimism is reinforced because that oppressiveness has invaded and infected the 1970's, and this implication underlies the ironies of his other major work, a stage adaptation of A. B. Facey's autobiography, *A Fortunate Life*. Here, Old Bert narrates from the stage the story of his life which is episodically acted out by a large cast; the narrator's persistence in refusing to see that the extraordinary saga of abandonment and deprivation is anything other than fortunate, coupled with a simplistic delivery style and a magnification of the most meagre happiness, brings an extreme pathos. Even at Gallipoli, where Bert sees the deaths of not only his mate but also his brother, there is expression of neither anger nor grief, and when his son is killed in World War II Bert's response does not go beyond losing faith in God. The terrible stoicism which accepts oppressiveness ironically belies Gorman's assertion that Australians "are a very direct and often publicly emotional people." The impregnable satisfaction of the old Facey, the obdurate larrikin, would have few answers to the emotional directness of the middle-aged Raeleen.

—Howard McNaughton

GOW, Ronald. British. Born in Heaton Moor, near Manchester, Lancashire, 1 November 1897. Educated at Altrincham Grammar School, Cheshire; Manchester University, B.Sc. 1922. Served in the British Army, 1918–19. Married the actress Wendy Hiller in 1937; one daughter and one son. Worked as a chemist and schoolmaster; educational film producer. Agent: Laurence Fitch Ltd., 4 New Burlington Place, London W1X 2AS. Address: 9 Stratton Road, Beaconsfield, Buckinghamshire HP9 1HR, England.

PUBLICATIONS

Plays

Breakfast at Eight (produced Altrincham, 1920). London, French, 1921.
The Sausage (produced Altrincham). London and New York, French, 1924.
Under the Skull and Bones: A Piratical Play with Songs (produced Altrincham). London, Gowans and Gray, and Boston, Baker, 1929.
Higgins: The Highwayman of Cranford (produced Altrincham). London, Gowans and Gray, and Boston, Baker, 1930.
Henry; or, The House on the Moor (produced Altrincham). London, Gowans and Gray, and Boston, Baker, 1931.
Five Robin Hood Plays (includes *The King's Warrant, The Sheriff's Kitchen, All on a Summer's Day, Robin Goes to Sea, The Affair at Kirklees*). London, Nelson, 1932.
The Golden West (produced Altrincham). London, Gowans and Gray, and Boston, Baker, 1932.
The Vengeance of the Gang (produced Altrincham). London, Gowans and Gray, and Boston, Baker, 1933.
Plays for the Classroom (text). London, Murray, 1933.
O.H.M.S. (produced Altrincham, 1933). London, Deane, 1933.
Gallows Glorious (produced Altrincham and London, 1933; as *John Brown*, produced New York, 1934). London, Gollancz, 1933.
My Lady Wears a White Cockade (produced London, 1934). London, Garamond Press, 1935.
Love on the Dole, adaptation of the novel by Walter Greenwood (produced Manchester, 1934; London, 1935; New York, 1936). London, Cape, 1935; New York, French, 1936.
Compromise. London, Deane, and Boston, Baker, 1935.
The Marrying Sort. London, Garamond Press, and Boston, Baker, 1935.
The Miracle on Watling Street: A Play for the Open Air. London, Dickson and Thompson, 1935.
Men Are Unwise, adaptation of the novel by Ethel Mannin (produced London, 1937).
Ma's Bit o' Brass, based on the screenplay *Lancashire Luck* (produced Colwyn Bay and London, 1938; as *Lovejoy's Millions*, produced London, 1938). London, Deane, and Boston, Baker, 1938.
Scuttleboom's Treasure. London and New York, French, 1938.
Grannie's a Hundred. London, Deane, and Boston, Baker, 1939.
The Lawyer of Springfield (broadcast 1940). London, Deane, and Boston, Baker, 1949.
Jenny Jones, music by Harry Parr Davies, adaptation of stories by Rhys Davies (produced London, 1944).

Tess of the D'Urbervilles, adaptation of the novel by Thomas Hardy (produced London, 1946).

Jassy, adaptation of the novel by Norah Lofts (produced Wimbledon, 1947).

Ann Veronica, adaptation of the novel by H.G. Wells (produced London, 1949). London, French, 1951; revised version, with Frank Wells, music by Cyril Ornadel, lyrics by David Croft (produced London, 1969).

The Full Treatment, with Robert Morley (produced London, 1953).

The Edwardians, adaptation of the novel by V. Sackville-West (as *Weekend in May*, produced Windsor, 1959; as *The Edwardians*, produced London, 1959). London, French, 1960.

Mr. Rhodes (produced Windsor, 1961).

A Boston Story, adaptation of the novel *Watch and Ward* by Henry James (as *Watch and Ward*, produced Windsor, 1964; revised version, as *A Boston Story*, produced London, 1968). London, Theatre Guild, 1969.

This Stratford Business, adaptation of stories by Henry James (produced Cheltenham, 1971).

The Friendship of Mrs. Eckley (produced Cheltenham, 1975).

The Old Jest, adaptation of the novel by Jennifer Johnston (produced Brighton, 1980).

Screenplays: *The Man Who Changed His Mind*, 1928; *The Glittering Sword*, 1929; *Southern Roses*, 1936; *Lancashire Luck*, with A.R. Rawlinson, 1937; *Mr. Smith Carries On*, 1937; *Jig Saw*, 1942.

Radio Plays: *The Lawyer of Springfield*, 1940; *Enter, Fanny Kemble*, 1940; *Front Line Family* series, during World War II; *Mr. Darwin Comes Ashore*, 1941; *Patience on a Monument*, 1944; *Westward Ho!* (serialization), from the novel by Charles Kingsley, 1953; *Lorna Doone* (serialization), from the novel by R.D. Blackmore, 1954.

Television Play: *Trumpet in the Clouds*, 1955.

*

Ronald Gow comments:

The question I am being asked is "what makes me tick as a playwright?" I was brought up near Manchester with the strong belief that the Gaiety Theatre was the greatest thing that ever happened there—even greater than the Hallé—and that Brighouse, Monkhouse, and Houghton were not only household words but shining examples. We knew them all and I had even acted with the author of *Hindle Wakes*. I was definitely stage-struck and when we built a theatre in my home town I cared little whether I shifted scenery or acted or took tickets at the door. After many one-act plays and a desperate wish to be a shining example myself I began to look around for something to be angry about. Most of my plays had some compelling obsession in them. When I wrote about Bonnie Prince Charlie it became anti-war and anti-romantic. Result, a mere six weeks at the Embassy. Next play about John Brown, whose soul went marching on, brought the audience cheering to their feet at the old Shaftesbury. But a bitter anti-slavery bias and an austere title (*Gallows Glorious*) were no good in that temple of musical comedy. Two weeks. (Two nights in New York.) I was trying to write an anti-unemployment play (three million of them) but fortunately read Walter Greenwood's *Love on the Dole* and decided to dramatize that instead. Marriage necessitated making money, with no axes to grind, resulting in comedies like *Ma's Bit o' Brass* and various film scripts and a great deal of propaganda radio and film work during the war (*Front Line Family*). Success with adapting novels led to London productions of *Tess of the D'Urbervilles, Ann Veronica, The Edwardians*, and *A Boston Story* from a Henry James novel.

* * *

Ronald Gow is a very modest man. Questioned about his work, he will say that any claim to distinction as a playwright that he may have achieved is due rather to his ability as an adaptor of borrowed plots to stage production than as an inventor of original stories. He will say this with a deprecating air, as of one ready to admit that he is operating on an artistic level rather below the highest.

How he can take this view, seeing that he is following the lead given by the most inveterate plot-borrower of them all, William Shakespeare, is not clear. One suspects Gow of being over-modest; and suspicion becomes certainty when a close critical look at his whole range of dramatic writings reveals that his early original plays were no less distinguished than his subsequent adaptations. Simply, they were less popular.

A reason for this can easily be found. Gow was educated at the grammar school at Altrincham in Cheshire, a town with easy access to Manchester. His subject was science, and his objective a B.Sc. degree at Manchester University; but during his schooldays the institution in that city which chiefly excited his interest was the Gaiety Theatre, where Miss Horniman had installed her famous regime and a whole group of angry young men were writing for her a whole series of realistic plays about social injustices of the time.

Gow, violently stage-struck, worshipped at the feet of these dramatists, came to know some of them (Harold Brighouse, Stanley Houghton, and the older Alan Monkhouse), and made up his mind that when the time came he would follow their example; meanwhile he became an enthusiastic amateur actor.

Fortunately for him, there lay at his very door the means to make the theatre an absorbing hobby without too much encroachment on the more serious business of earning a living. An amateur dramatic society at Altrincham, the Garrick, was fast becoming (and, incidentally, is still) one of the leaders in its own field. In the period after World War II when the professional stage was given over almost wholly to glittering frivolity and the general playgoing public asked for nothing better, the task of keeping a more serious theatre alive fell to amateurs who, organized and led by the newly formed British Drama League, rose nobly to the call.

As the movement gathered force and a large public responded, men like Gow found their hobby growing into something very like a profession. He himself, now a young man with his science degree behind him, working first as research chemist and then as schoolmaster, was in his spare time wholly at the Garrick Theatre's service. He acted for it, wrote for it, shifted scenery, took money at the doors. For several years he was its secretary; and when it decided to build itself its own playhouse, he even laid bricks for it. By the time when, at 33 or so, he decided to try his luck as a professional dramatist, he had had a fuller training for the craft than most.

True to the principles he had learnt as a boy, he now looked for social injustices to write about. This was easy enough so far as themes went, for he had as sharp a sense of the follies and injustices of human life as any of the Horniman dramatists whose disciple he was. Unlike them, however, he had a natural sense of period, and was apt to look to the past for his plots.

From the first, there was no question of the excellence of Gow's writing, and he soon had a play accepted for West End production. This was *Gallows Glorious*, which told the story of that John Brown whose soul, in the song, goes marching on. It was produced at the old Shaftesbury Theatre in 1933, and the first-night audience received it with rapturous applause and a standing ovation. But the Shaftesbury (destroyed by German bombs in World War II) was a big house to fill, and the general public, which was not in the mood for period pieces anyhow, showed no interest in John Brown whatever. The play limped along for two weeks and then had to be taken off.

A rather similar experience in the following year with an anti-romantic and anti-war play about Bonnie Prince Charlie must have taught him the lesson that a man writing a play-with-a-purpose should choose to set his action in the immediate present, for he next sat down to write about unemployment, the chief problem of the moment. While engaged on this he happened to read Walter Greenwood's novel *Love on the Dole*, and decided to dramatize Greenwood's story instead of going on with his own.

The great success of this play changed Gow's whole life. It made a name not only for him but for Wendy Hiller, the aspiring young actress who played his heroine and whom, in 1937, he married. It also brought him sharply to the notice of Pinewood film studios and the BBC, with the ironic result that he was, practically speaking, lost to the stage for nine years or so. Indeed, his next two stage plays, *Ma's Bit o' Brass* and *Tess of the D'Urbervilles* were both adapted to the stage from filmscripts of his own.

Ma's Bit o' Brass, a light-hearted exercise in the Lancashire idiom, ranks rather uneasily among Gow's original pieces. It never quite reached the West End, but it toured successfully and became a favourite among "Reps" and amateurs. Its author now regards it with a kind of rueful gratitude.

He wrote the film version of *Tess* for his wife, who during the war was invited to play this part in Hollywood. He himself did not quite "see" her in the part, and advised her against taking it—and, indeed, it was not one of her greatest successes. But she did well enough for John Burrell to want her to do it on the London stage, and to invite Gow to write the play. His next three West End productions—*Ann Veronica, The Edwardians* and the very delightful *A Boston Story*—were adaptations (as was his latest play, *The Old Jest*) but *The Friendship of Mrs. Eckley* is an original story about the Brownings.

—W.A. Darlington

GRAY, Jack. Canadian. Born in Detroit, Michigan, United States, 7 December 1927. Educated at primary and secondary schools in Ontario; Queen's University, Kingston, Ontario; University of Toronto, B.A., M.A. Married Araby Lockhart in 1952; three sons and two daughters. Assistant editor, *Maclean's Magazine*, Toronto, 1953–57; executive director and resident playwright, Neptune Theatre, Halifax, Nova Scotia, 1963; Professor of Integrated Studies, University of Waterloo, Ontario, 1969–71; Secretary General, Canadian Theatre Centre, Toronto, 1971–73; President, Association of Canadian Television and Radio Artists (ACTRA), 1978–82; special consultant on cultural policy, Department of Communications, Ottawa, 1982–83; President, League for Canadian Communications, 1984. President, International Writers Guild, and John Gray Productions Ltd.; editor, Canadian Play Series, University of Toronto Press. Agent: Elspeth Cochrane Agency, 11-13 Orlando Road, London SW4 0LE, England. Address: 65 Pine Street, Brockville, Ontario K6V 1G6, Canada.

PUBLICATIONS

Plays

Bright Sun at Midnight (produced Toronto, 1957).
Ride a Pink Horse, music by Louis Applebaum (produced Toronto, 1958).
The Teacher (produced Stratford, Ontario, 1960).
Chevalier Johnstone (as *Louisbourg*, produced Halifax, 1964; revised version, as *Chevalier Johnstone*, produced Halifax, 1966). Toronto, Playwrights, 1972.
Emmanuel Xoc (produced Toronto, 1965).
Godiva! (produced Coventry, 1967).
Susannah, Agnes, and Ruth (broadcast 1969). Toronto, Playwrights, 1972.
Striker Schneiderman (produced Toronto, 1970). Toronto, University of Toronto Press, 1973.

Radio Plays: *To Whom It May Concern*, 1958; *The Lost Boy*, 1959; *Susannah, Agnes, and Ruth*, 1969; *The Cracker Man*, 1970; *And I Mayakovsky*, 1976.

Television Plays: *The Ledge*, 1959 (UK); *The Glove*, 1961 (UK); *Man in Town*, 1962; *The Enemy*, 1962 (UK); *The Guard*, 1963; *Miss Hanago*, 1964 (UK).

Other

The Third Strategy: A Canadian Primer of Sensible Proposals for the Solution of Insoluble Problems, with André Fortier. Ottawa, Canadian Conference of the Arts, 1984.

*

Manuscript Collection: Metropolitan Toronto Library.

Theatrical Activities:
Director: **Play**—*Clap Hands* (revue), London, 1962.

* * *

Jack Gray is a Shavian with a taste for the baroque. Most of his plays inhabit the world of witty altercation—to the detriment, occasionally, of their dramatic form. But they are on the whole well made, and the aphoristic quality of many of the speeches indicates more than superficial wit. In *Susannah, Agnes, and Ruth* the repartee is brittle:

Ian —He'll never get over it.
Susannah —He never got over being born.

But it is more than brittle. Gray has listened to the ghastly maxims of middle-class Methodism with an attentive ear. "Don't be smart" or "A responsible parent can never be said to be interfering." Both speak for the world of O'Neill's *Ah, Wilderness!* with all the exuberance removed—a world in which we expect to hear that "the Attorney-General says that dancing on Sunday must stop in Ontario." This is only just the day before yesterday, and it does Gray credit not only that he can capture it so exactly without cause or rancour but that he can give to Susannah (the grandmother figure who is its spokesman) a toughness and a life that even the men in the play have missed. In a passage reminiscent of Strether's impassioned speech to Little Bilham in Henry James's *The Ambassadors*, Bob, one of the uncles, says to Ruth: "We've evaded life—sidestepped it—it's like a dance—one-two-sidestep—one-two-step aside. . . . Don't be like we are, Ruth—take hold of life." But it is Susannah more than the rest who realizes the importance of seizing upon life and denying death. She rebukes the simpering vicar who speaks of her son and others as having died heroic deaths in France in World War I:

> They did not. They died dirty, lonely blasphemous deaths. Each year on that anniversary, Mr. Smith, I take off my mourning, I wear my gayest clothes. It's all I can do to protest the shallow sham you men make of life. It's how I would meet God—singing! We must never celebrate such deaths.

It is this festivity in the face of bleakness and heroism in spite of itself that characterize the lead in Gray's later play *Striker Schneiderman*—probably his best-known work. But there is a set-piece quality about the play, a sense of its being written for an occasion or to a prescription that does not allow it to be much more than an entertaining piece of theatre. Its elements are too predictable, even down to the tailor joke from *Endgame*.

This criticism is valid to some degree for *Chevalier Johnstone* as well, but although it too seems very much written for an occasion (not to say for television) it has a greater toughness about it, and the ending seems somehow less forced. Part of this is due to the hard-headedness of the dialogue—the absence of sentimentality and Jewish melodrama—and part to a sense that the world described, though it is two centuries away from our own, is closer to our preoccupations than are those of Schneiderman. The play has a curiously Brechtian quality—partly the result no doubt of the rapid shifting of scenes and the extravagant stage directions: "We lose the woods and stream and follow them as they walk back to, and then through, the fortress." But this Brechtian character is most obvious in the restraint of sentiment by a wit that keeps us off. This wit is directed against our prejudices—of flabby democracy and literary superstition, for instance. "I'm an Indian, not a gentleman," says Samuel, the scout who attaches himself to Johnstone while repulsing any foolish notion of mere equality. And in response to Johnstone's explanation that he reads for his recreation, "Pascal . . . Molière. And, of course, Voltaire," Drucour, his superior, asks "What do you do for healthy recreation?"

Emmanuel Xoc and *The Teacher* both suffer from flaws not so evident in the other plays. In fact, in spite of some turns of phrase in *Emmanuel Xoc*—"fifty years' caution in a man is a kink"—the play is not a good omen. It is like a combination of Puccini's *Gianni Schicchi* and Tennessee Williams's *The Milk Train Doesn't Stop Here Anymore*. But its host of characters—Tweedie, Xoc, Baptist, Fink, Fingers, Arnold, and Morgan—is too much like something out of an old Bowery Boys film for us to take the play as more than a sort of baroque exercise.

There is a similar element of fantasy in *The Teacher* (like *Emmanuel Xoc*, it has a ghost), though the fantasy is not grotesque but lyrical in a way that easily becomes sentimental. Indeed there is a studied quality about the play that, coupled with the absence of the sort of wit so evident in the later plays, gives it an unfortunate flatness. Its gestures are both towards Dylan Thomas's *Under Milk Wood* and Joyce's *The Dead*, but it fails to get beyond the sort of artificial melodrama—complete with folksongs—that used to be the favorite of the CBC.

Fortunately Gray has come a great way since then. His later plays show both an eye for detail and an ear for wit that are badly needed. None of his plays so far is great, but some of them are very good indeed.

—D.D.C. Chambers

GRAY, John. Canadian. Born in Ottawa, Ontario, 26 September 1946. Educated at Mount Allison University, Sackville, New Brunswick, B.A. 1968; University of British Columbia, Vancouver, M.A. in theatre 1972. Has two sons. Founding director, Tamahnous Theatre, Vancouver, 1971–74; free-lance director, 1972–76: directed 40 productions throughout Canada. Recipient: Los Angeles Drama Critics Circle award, 1981; Governor-General's award, 1983. Address: 3392 West 37th Avenue, Vancouver, British Columbia V6N 2V6, Canada.

PUBLICATIONS

Plays

Salty Tears on a Hangnail Face (lyrics only, with Jeremy Long), book by Long, music by Gray (produced Vancouver, 1974).
18 Wheels, music and lyrics by Gray (also director: produced Toronto, 1977).
Billy Bishop Goes to War, music and lyrics by Gray (also director: as *Billy Bishop*, produced Vancouver, 1978; as *Billy Bishop Goes to War*, produced Washington, D.C., New York, and Edinburgh, 1980; London, 1981). Vancouver, Talonbooks, 1981.
Rock and Roll (also director: produced Ottawa, 1981). Published in *Canadian Theatre Review* (Downsview, Ontario), Summer 1982.
Bongo from the Congo (for children; produced Vancouver, 1982).
Balthazaar and the Mojo Star (produced Vancouver, 1982).
Better Watch Out, You Better Not Die (produced Halifax, Nova Scotia, 1983).
Don Messer's Jubilee (produced Halifax, Nova Scotia, 1984).
The B.C. Review (produced Vancouver, 1986).

Screenplays: *Billy Bishop Goes to War*, 1982; *The King of Friday Night*, 1984.

Novel

Dazzled. Toronto, Irwin, 1984.

Other

Recording: *Billy Bishop Goes to War*, Tapestry, 1979.

*

Critical Studies: "John Gray's Progress" by Judy Steed, in *Toronto Life*, May 1981; *The Work: Interviews with English-Canadian Playwrights* by Robert Wallace and Cynthia Zimmerman, Toronto, Coach House Press, 1982; *Second Stage: The Alternative Theatre Movement in Canada* by Renate Usmiani, Vancouver, University of British Columbia Press, 1983; article by

David Cruise, in *Atlantic Insight* (Halifax, Nova Scotia), August 1983.

Theatrical Activities:
Director: **Plays** (selection)—most of his own plays; *The Bacchae* by Euripides, Vancouver, 1972; *Dracula Two*, Vancouver, 1974; *The Tempest*, Vancouver, 1974; *Bull Durham* by Jeremy Newson, Toronto, 1974; *Canadian Heroes Series 1* (co-director with Paul Thompson), Toronto, 1975; *Preparing* by Beverley Simons (co-director with Buzz Bense), Vancouver, 1975; *The Imaginary Invalid* by Molière, Vancouver, 1975; *Herringbone* by Thomas Cone, Vancouver, 1975 and 1976, and Lennoxville, Quebec, 1978.
Composer: music for all his own plays, and: *Bull Durham* by Jeremy Newson, Toronto, 1974; *The Imaginary Invalid* by Molière, Vancouver, 1975; *The False Messiah* by Rick Salutin, Toronto, 1975; *The Horsburgh Scandal* by Betty Jane Wylie, Toronto, 1976; *1837: The Farmer's Revolt* by Rick Salutin, Toronto, 1976; *The Farm Show* by Theatre Passe Muraille (music with Jimmy Adams), Toronto, 1976; *The Olympics Show* by Theatre Passe Muraille, Toronto, 1976; *The Great Wave of Civilization* by Herschel Hardin, Lennoxville, Quebec, 1976; *Money* by Rick Salutin, Toronto, 1976; *Le Temps d'une vie* by Roland Lepage, Toronto, 1978.

John Gray comments:

I write populist musicals in which regional and Canadian themes are placed in the broader context of the world and the human spirit. In *18 Wheels* the Canadian truck driver is the central focus for the Canadian preoccupation with physical distance and the enormous space between things and people. *Billy Bishop Goes to War* is about the World War I flying ace, and explores the various ironies that result from colonial success in an imperial war. *Rock and Roll* is about youth culture in a small Canadian town in the 1960's, from the point of view of the local rock and roll band. *Better Watch Out, You Better Not Die* is a satire on left-right attitudes in the face of old age and violent death. *Bongo from the Congo* is an afro musical about a man's search for a mystical African animal and for the grace that that animal both embodies and bestows. *Balthazaar and the Mojo Star* is a nativity jazz musical about the odyssey of a Parthian magus. *Don Messer's Jubilee* is a musical about traditional rural culture: its purpose, how it develops, and how it is destroyed in favour of international stereotypes. *Dazzled*, the novel, is a comic Bildungsroman, a cultural satire in which a Vancouver ex-hippie makes the adjustment from the romanticism of the 1960's to the neoconservatism of the 1970's. As he makes the adjustment he attempts to see beyond the media hallucinations of both eras and to understand what is really going on around him.

* * *

Although he can be said to belong to the large school of playwrights who chronicle Canadian social and political history, John Gray strikingly differs from other such playwrights in style and, often, in subject matter. He searches for signifiers of the Canadian psyche and finds them not only in conventional heroes like the World War I aviator Billy Bishop, but in an array of small-town heroes—band leaders, high school rock music stars—who speak directly to the audience's local identification with the social and musical rhythms of its country. The fact that Gray writes pop musical theatre is not coincidental to the success his work has found with audiences: the national sense he presents is young, unsure, energetic, and discordant; his theatrical design itself forms a major part of the social myths he creates. His is a satirical vision, but it is satire full of affection for the small-town ethos he replicates. He presents documentary history, but as Jamie Portman says, "this kind of history is part cartoon, part musical hall." While his early work, in plays such as *18 Wheels* (a musical about truckers), presents issues and sounds to be heard throughout North America, there is a steady movement through the work to more particularly Canadian images and attitudes. In his recent play *Don Messer's Jubilee* Gray attempts, not always successfully, to make an icon of a homely CBC variety programme which ran on radio and television for 40 years and which, Gray suggests, is part of the Canadian personality, even if viewers of Gray's own age deplored it in their teens as old-fashioned and corny.

Gray first came to major international attention with his second musical, *Billy Bishop Goes to War*, a one-man show about the most celebrated Canadian war-time aviator. Accompanied by a pianist who doubles as occasional foil (Gray himself in the early productions), the narrator/actor impersonates 18 characters, including Bishop. The debt is obvious to the improvisational technique of Paul Thompson's Theatre Passe Muraille, in whose ensemble Gray worked as a young musician and from which influence *18 Wheels* first grew. In *Billy Bishop*, however, Gray finds his own voice both in the score and in his reading of history, an interpretation of Bishop which is endearing while iconoclastic. It is the irony of this play that while showing Bishop to be, as Gray puts it, "a sort of small town juvenile delinquent who, though just scraping to survive and hang on, became the toast of London," he makes him a hero of tremendous power and appeal. In Gray's version, Bishop becomes the peculiar hero most suited to the Canadian self-image, a hero who is swept into fame almost against his will, but who is not, in the end, unaware of his new status, nor above using it to his own advantage. Bishop realizes "I really was Number One now," but his enjoyment of the adulation does not change him or endow him with any new sense of personal purpose; in this sense he is a hero without guile, perhaps even the "hero as anti-hero" which Allan Massie called him in the *Scotsman.* He is also still the small-town boy, able to call himself "a dignitary," but ever aware, as the character Trenchard reminds him, that he is "A colonial dignitary, Bishop. There is a difference." He remains, as his sophisticated London benefactress, Lady St. Helier sings, "a typical Canadian/You're modesty itself." Indeed, as Bishop himself comments, "Nobody starts no wars on Canada/Where folks tend to wish each other well." It is only "once . . . in the air, [Bishop] felt a lot better. In fact, [he] felt like a King." In this complex characterization Gray has captured a personality who seeks for security in the knowledge that he is second-best and yet who, alone in an environment he can control, can scream "at the top of my lungs, I win, I WIN, I WIN!" Such a hero appeals—as the astounding commercial success of this play attests—to the Canadian sense of self. Its similar success in other Commonwealth countries and its commercial failure in New York, despite marked critical support, underlines the point: in his subtle portrait Gray has captured a hero for the colonial mind.

The play exploits its economical design: the sparse set and multiple characterizations force an audience to imagine most of the action and, in doing so, compel its involvement. The pace, the comic and often cruel caricatures, the sentiment, bravado, and charm of the protagonist, the adventure of a World War I setting, and the acting tour de force required of the principal actor all work together to engage an audience. Gray capitalizes well on his single actor; when, for example, he has him read letters from home (a device which could be simply trite), Gray can count on the audience responding to the loneliness of the only person on stage. And if that character is also likeable, embodies fears and hopes with which the audience can empathize—and if he sings and makes airplane noises—the resulting relationship is certain to be intense and positive.

In *Rock and Roll* Gray presents personal memoir in a play about the members of a small-town rock and roll band meeting again in middle age to restage their youth while preparing for a reunion concert. The script exists largely to allow the music to tell the story, as it does in *18 Wheels*, but the songs are Gray's best work to date, and the predictable plot is happily lost in the highly theatrical staging and hard-driving rock music. The show is pure nostalgia for those who were teenagers in the 1950's. It displays a spectrum of easy emotion—love, jealousy, a manic sense of humour, the pathos of ruined dreams, and the triumph of maturity over adolescent insecurities—and if the play can be criticized for its failure to develop any emotion (or, in fact, any plot event) past the surface, it survives in performance because the pace of the mood swings is naturalistic to the teenage characters and appropriate to the highly wrought emotions of those caught up in memory, and because the design of the play is episodic, built around the musical numbers. The play is great fun to watch, and like *Billy Bishop* presents involved patterns of music and action, establishing Gray as firmly in control of score and staging.

In *Don Messer's Jubilee* Gray is more self-conscious about memory, more intent upon exploring the reasons for the cancellation of the popular television show than in truly recreating one of Messer's old programmes. But in his version of the old show, he presents an entertainment which Martin Knelman in *Saturday Night* calls "a lot livelier than an evening of true Messer music would be"; Gray is guilty himself of polishing the hero and giving him more "big time" glitz. In doing so, however, Gray is clearly myth-making as playwrights have always done; he seeks to secure popular social myth in a contemporary aesthetic and thereby make it accessible, if no longer quite real, to new generations. Like the folkloric fiddler whom Don Messer represents, Gray provides a mimetic link for Canadian audiences to their memories and national values, a link which often seems more potent than that provided by non-musical writers of documentary drama. The phenomenal success Gray has enjoyed with Canadian audiences may, indeed, result not only from his keen sense of current style and commercial appeal, but from a singular ability to capture, as *scop*, the temperament of his nation.

—S.R. Gilbert

GRAY, Simon (James Holliday). British. Born on Hayling Island, Hampshire, 21 October 1936. Educated at a school in Montreal; Westminster School, London; Dalhousie University, Halifax, Nova Scotia, 1954–57, B.A. (honours) in English 1957; Trinity College, Cambridge, 1958–61, B.A. (honours) in English 1961, M.A. Married Beryl Mary Kevern in 1965; one son and one daughter. Harper-Wood Student, 1961–62, and research student, 1962–63, Trinity College; Lecturer in English, University of British Columbia, Vancouver, 1963–64; Supervisor in English, Trinity College, 1964–66; Lecturer in English, Queen Mary College, London, 1965–85. Since 1964 editor, *Delta* magazine, Cambridge. Recipient: *Evening Standard* award, 1972, 1976; New York Drama Critics Circle award, 1977. Honorary Fellow, Queen Mary College, 1985. Lives in London. Agent: Judy Daish Associates, 83 Eastbourne Mews, London W2 6LQ, England.

PUBLICATIONS

Plays

Wise Child (produced London, 1967; New York, 1972). London, Faber, 1972.

Molly (as *Death of a Teddy Bear*, televised 1967; revised version, as *Molly*, produced Watford, Hertfordshire, and London, 1977; New York, 1978). Included in *The Rear Column and Other Plays*, 1978; in *The Rear Column, Dog Days, and Other Plays*, 1979.

Sleeping Dog (televised 1967). London, Faber, 1968.

Spoiled (televised 1968; produced Glasgow, 1970; London, 1971; New York, 1972). London, Methuen, 1971.

Dutch Uncle (produced Brighton and London, 1969). London, Faber, 1969.

Pig in a Poke (televised 1969). With *Close of Play*, London, Eyre Methuen, 1980.

The Idiot, adaptation of a novel by Dostoevsky (produced London, 1970). London, Methuen, 1971.

Butley (produced Oxford and London, 1971; New York, 1972). London, Methuen, 1971; New York, Viking Press, 1972.

Man in a Side-Car (televised 1971). Included in *The Rear Column and Other Plays*, 1978; in *The Rear Column, Dog Days, and Other Plays*, 1979.

Otherwise Engaged (produced Oxford and London, 1975; New York, 1977). Included in *Otherwise Engaged and Other Plays*, 1975.

Plaintiffs and Defendants (televised 1975). Included in *Otherwise Engaged and Other Plays*, 1975.

Two Sundays (televised 1975). Included in *Otherwise Engaged and Other Plays*, 1975.

Otherwise Engaged and Other Plays. London, Eyre Methuen, 1975; New York, Viking Press, 1976.

Dog Days (produced Oxford, 1976). London, Eyre Methuen, 1976; in *The Rear Column, Dog Days, and Other Plays*, 1979.

The Rear Column (produced London and New York, 1978). Included in *The Rear Column and Other Plays*, 1978; in *The Rear Column, Dog Days, and Other Plays*, 1979.

The Rear Column and Other Plays. London, Eyre Methuen, 1978.

The Rear Column, Dog Days, and Other Plays. New York, Viking Press, 1979.

Close of Play (produced London, 1979; New York, 1981). With *Pig in a Poke*, London, Eyre Methuen, 1980; published separately, New York, Dramatists Play Service, 1982.

Stage Struck (produced London, 1979; Chicago, 1984). London, Eyre Methuen, 1979; New York, Seaver, 1981.

Quartermaine's Terms (produced London, 1981; New Haven, Connecticut, 1982; New York, 1983). London, Eyre Methuen, 1981; revised version, Methuen, and New York, French, 1983.

Chapter 17 (produced Guildford, Surrey, 1982).

Tartuffe, adaptation of the play by Molière (produced Washington, D.C., 1982).

The Common Pursuit: Scenes from Literary Life (produced London, 1984; New Haven, Connecticut, 1985; also co-director: produced New York, 1986). London, Methuen, 1984.

Plays 1 (includes *Butley, Otherwise Engaged, The Rear Column, Quartermaine's Terms, The Common Pursuit*). London, Methuen, 1986.
Melon (produced London, 1987). London, Methuen, 1987.
After Pilkington (televised 1987). London, Methuen, 1987.

Screenplays: *Butley*, 1976; *A Month in the Country*, 1987.

Radio Play: *Up in Pigeon Lake*, from his novel *Colmain*, 1963 (Canada).

Television Plays: *The Caramel Crisis*, 1966; *Death of a Teddy Bear*, 1967; *A Way with the Ladies*, 1967; *Sleeping Dog*, 1967; *Spoiled*, 1968; *Pig in a Poke*, 1969; *The Dirt on Lucy Lane*, 1969; *Style of the Countess*, 1970; *The Princess*, 1970; *Man in a Side-Car*, 1971; *Plaintiffs and Defendants*, 1975; *Two Sundays*, 1975; *After Pilkington*, 1987.

Novels

Colmain. London, Faber, 1963.
Simple People. London, Faber, 1965.
Little Portia. London, Faber, 1967.
A Comeback for Stark (as Hamish Reade). London, Faber, 1968.

Other

An Unnatural Pursuit and Other Pieces: A Playwright's Journal. London, Faber, 1985; New York, St. Martin's Press, 1986.

Editor, with Keith Walker, *Selected English Prose.* London, Faber, 1967.

*

Theatrical Activities:
Director: **Plays**—*Dog Days*, Vienna, 1980; *The Common Pursuit* (co-director, with Michael McGuire), New York, 1986.

* * *

Simon Gray's plays have appeared regularly in the West End since *Wise Child* opened in 1967, shocking its London audience. *Butley*, in 1971, secured Gray's reputation as a gifted, popular playwright. Gray's detractors were quick to give most of the credit to the superior actors and directors—including Alec Guinness, Simon Ward, Alan Bates, and Harold Pinter—who lent their talents to his plays. In 1979, in a particularly nasty review, James Fenton of the *Sunday Times*, announced that Gray had committed "public suicide" in his thriller *Stage Struck*, and gloated that *Close of Play*, an "overblown domestic tragedy," had itself closed at the Lyttelton in less than ten days. *Quartermaine's Terms*, an international success, was similarly savaged by a San Francisco radio reviewer. Not one quick to forget or forgive slights, Gray opens his playwright's journal, *An Unnatural Pursuit and Other Pieces*, quoting the critic's words: "Ladies and Gentlemen, the play's the thing, as Shakespeare put it. But Ladies and Gentlemen, there isn't a play here! No play at all, ladies and gentlemen." Later in the same book, Gray defiantly boasts that his new play, *The Common Pursuit*, like *Quartermaine's Terms*, "has no plot." In the new play, entitled ambiguously after F.R. Leavis's book, Gray takes revenge upon his unkindly reviewers and includes a rude joke at the expense of the *Sunday Times*. Upon hearing that "Nappies" Harrop has been appointed theatre critic, one of his characters marvels at the *Times*'s choice, concluding that "apparently they're impressed by his lack of qualifications." Gray feared that this line would cost him dearly, and if his account of the play's reviews and fate is accurate, his fears were warranted. Ultimately, his producers backed out of the plans to move the play from the Lyric in Hammersmith to the West End. Cruel notices have dogged Gray's career, but his plays have generally fared well with audiences, and his best are important plays by any standard. He is a witty, intelligent, literary playwright with a flair for the topical and a gift for creating memorable characters. Butley's savage wit, Simon Hench's arch reserve, Quartermaine's kindly vacancy live long after the details of the play have been forgotten. Gray's skillful control of dialogue—witty, derisive, colloquial, syntactically lively, and often irreverent—rarely fails him. His portraits of academics and the life of the literarily inclined belong beside Kingsley Amis's *Lucky Jim*. Gray's negative critics fault him for his lack of "magnanimity of spirit and largeness of vision." No doubt his often corrosive humor contributes to this judgement, but his poignant depiction of Quartermaine ought to go a long way towards silencing those who argue that he lacks heart. If anything, he feels too keenly and requires humor to make life more tolerable.

Gray has had more than his share of flops. His adaptation of Dostoevsky's *The Idiot* entertained his audience but left the critics immodestly displaying their expertise on the Russian master while ignoring Gray's talents. *Dutch Uncle* was depressing; the critics deplored its lack of taste. *Spoiled*, with its touching exploration of a homosexual encounter between pupil and teacher, simply failed to stir any interest. *Close of Play* did not work.

Butley, on the other hand, was a stunning success, capturing the bitchiness, vanity, and all-too-fragile ego of a thoroughly jaundiced university lecturer. The protagonists of *Otherwise Engaged* and *Stage Struck* shared many of the traits that made Ben Butley unforgettable. Both plays had long runs in the West End. Gray's thrillers are not period pieces and they lack the marvelous visual effects which made Paul Giovanni's Sherlock Holmes play *The Crucifer of Blood* such a favorite. Instead, they depend on the ingenuity of their plots and the psychological intricacies of their characters for their success. Gray's domestic comedies compare favorably with Alan Ayckbourn's, but with the exception of *Quartermaine's Terms*, they have the same limitations. They pander to popular taste, make too much of sexual peccadilloes, be they between members of the same or of the opposite sex, and lack love. None equals Peter Shaffer's *Black Comedy*.

In *Otherwise Engaged* and *Dog Days*, as well as in the television plays *Two Sundays* and *Plaintiffs and Defendants*, Gray allows the characters of one play to slip into the others while the situation remains fairly constant. In *Otherwise Engaged* a snobbish, Oxford-educated editor, Simon Hench, lives with his schoolteacher wife, Beth, and their annoying tenant, David. On a day when Simon hopes to listen quietly to Wagner while his wife is away on an outing with her foreign students and a colleague, Ned, Simon in fact has many visitors. An interruption by his tenant is followed by an unexpected visit by his brother. Next his boisterous friend, Jeff, and his current mistress, Davina, barge in. Finally, Simon is confronted by an old schoolmate who accuses him, rightly, of having an affair with Joanna, a young lady in Simon's office who is in fact betrothed to the schoolmate. In the course of the day the old rivalries between the brothers are explored; Simon is propositioned by the bare-breasted Davina after she quarrels with Jeff; and Simon learns that his wife has been having an affair with Ned and now, pregnant, wants to marry him. At the play's close, Jeff and Simon turn on *Parsifal*. *Dog Days* offers a variant of the same situation with different names. Peter is the junior editor whose wife, Hilary, is having an affair that threatens to destroy the marriage. His brother, Charles, is married to a vegetarian earth-mother, Alison, who has produced four children and is expecting more. After accusing Hilary of "replacing mechanical sex with spontaneous frigidity," Peter walks out to join Joanna. When pre-coital depression mars his affair, he returns contrite to Hilary who will no longer have him. Peter and Charles live a dog's life, both grovelling to people they loathe, both dependent on others in ways they had not predicted. Hilary, like Beth, cannot contemplate spending any more years in a marriage with a man who neither likes himself nor her. In the two television plays about Peter and Charles, the marriages withstand Peter's infidelities and Alison's endless cooing.

The Rear Column, a fascinating play, is based on Stanley's march to the relief of Emin Pasha in 1887 and the fate of the rear column and the five white men left behind in the encampment in the Congo with three hundred "niggers" inside and hoards of cannibals without. The play is about Major Barttelot who, left to guard the rear column, ends up flogging, shooting, and eating the natives while Jameson, the British naturalist left behind with him, also loses all moral purpose. In his final decadence, he watches a "nigger girl" killed, cooked, and eaten so that he can sketch the rite of cannibalism with the same care he used to sketch the African birdlife.

Gray's plays are peopled with men discontented with themselves and ill-suited to the roles they find themselves in. Often these men are homosexuals. Transvestism (*Wise Child*), bondage (*Sleeping Dog*), and sado-masochistic games (*Sleeping Dog, Dutch Uncle*, and *Stage Struck*) are the acts they resort to in their self-loathing. Butley has married to escape his homosexuality only to leave his wife six months later and return to his male student/lover turned colleague. Butley constantly belittles his wife, colleagues, and lover. Ultimately his corrosive humor drives them all away leaving him too worn out and full of self-dislike to initiate yet another affair with one of his students. Butley uses words to kill. Although he cuts to the quick those who need or love him, ultimately it is he who is the victim. The nasty cut on his chin that he dabs at throughout the play physicalizes the depth of his self-dislike. Mr. Godboy, the protagonist of *Dutch Uncle*, courts punishment at the hands of a police constable noted for his strict ways. Mr. Godboy is unsuccessful in his attempt to gas his wife and upstairs tenant, but he does experience vicariously the humiliations practiced by the constable. In *Molly* Molly and her lover kill her rich, old husband—a man whose habit of spanking his "naughty" wife finally infuriates the lover. In *Sleeping Dog* a retired colonial officer torments a West Indian for being too familiar with his wife. He chains the Jamaican in the cellar of his English house, makes him confess to crimes against his wife and to homosexuality, and finally forces the man to service his wife. *Stage Struck* develops the cat-and-mouse game of *Dutch Uncle* into an extravagant panoply of stage tricks masterminded by the stage-director husband who uses suicide and murder to revenge himself upon his domineering actress wife.

Quartermaine's Terms and *The Common Pursuit* depart in significant ways from the mode of *Butley* although both take schoolteachers and literary types for their characters. Whereas Butley and Simon Hench use language and wit trenchantly—Butley to lash out, deflecting his self-hatred against others, Hench more sparingly as an armor to prevent others from touching him—Sir John Quartermaine, teacher in a Cambridge public school training foreign boys in English, is a man of halting phrases, few words, and nearly vacant silences. While the play traces the fortunes of the school and its small staff, we witness Sir John's retreat from his world into a drowsy sleep where he can no longer remember when or what he is teaching, nor even remember the swans on the pond near his aunt's home. He drifts in and out of reminiscences, weaving the words of Yeats's "The Wild Swans at Coole" with his own vague memories, reproducing in his own diminished way the sense of radical dislocation and displacement of Yeats's poem. Gray's treatment of Quartermaine and the staff is richly comic. The plotting and character delineation are Chekhovian. Mr. Meadle is the play's Two-and-Twenty-Misfortunes; Quartermaine's yearnings for another era echo Anya's and Gaev's nostalgia in *The Cherry Orchard*; the characters in the play cannot remember each others' names; they murmur reassuring pleasantries to each other while underneath they are confused and hurting. Melanie is a frustrated spinster driven to kill her sickly, hatred-ridden mother and does penance through her Christian conversion. Mr. Meadle, the accident-prone new instructor from the North Country, struggles desperately to secure both a permanent position in the school and a wife. There is a liberal sprinkling of marital infidelities and complications in the play, and it contains the suicide which has become standard in Gray's plays. But its texture is different. It is lyrical and deeply moving. Quartermaine's plight is poignant. When he is finally dismissed by Windscape, the new principal, on the eve of the Christmas break, it is wrenching. All of Windscape's reasons for his actions are legitimate: Quartermaine has not been teaching for years; the old principals simply carried him on, not having the heart to do anything else. Gray makes us realize at one level that it is unconscionable to pretend that Quartermaine has a role to play in an instructional institution; on the other hand, he makes us want to ask, "why not let him linger in the staff lounge, teaching almost not at all, rather than displace him utterly?" Gray crafts the final scene so skillfully that we are forced to balance the conflicting needs of the situation. The gentle goodnight exchanged between the two men followed by Quartermaine's lapse into silence ends the play. Echoes of Yeats's poem hover in the air. It is Gray's most perfect ending.

The Common Pursuit departs from *Butley* in its treatment of time and its reliance on cinematic techniques for its staging and its plot development. Gray calls it a play about friendship, "English, middle-class, Cambridge-educated friendship." He has remarked that its control of time—it covers 20 years and closes with a scene set 15 minutes later than its opening scene, 20 years before—grew out of the television play *Two Sundays*. Critics have mistakenly traced it to Pinter's play *Betrayal*, written a number of years after *Two Sundays*. Although *The Common Pursuit* is episodic, tracing the fortunes of the Cambridge friends and their literary enterprise, many of its characters are the typical academic misfits and literary opportunists that figured in *Butley* and *Otherwise Engaged*. Unlike the protagonists of a number of Gray's other plays, Stuart is not the hub around which the action revolves. Simon Hench, Butley, and, curiously, Sir John Quartermaine, dominate their plays. Stuart is what Gray calls "the spine of the play," but the play's sweeping movement over the lives of the six Cambridge friends is more akin to the structure of Virginia Woolf's novel *The Waves* than it is to the structure of his other plays. Gray rightly sensed that the play might be too precious, too literary, and too elitist to please the public, but it is an effective evening of theatre, and the depiction of the group of writers, editors, scholars, and publishers is adept. Its control of time is superb and its startling epilogue a stunning piece of theatre.

Gray is among Britain's most talented playwrights, well schooled in his craft, original, and able to create unforgettable characters.

—Carol Simpson Stern

GRAY, Spalding. American. Born in Providence, Rhode Island, 5 June 1941. Educated at Fryeburg Academy, Maine; Emerson College, Boston, B.A. 1965. Actor in summer stock, Cape Cod, Massachusetts, and in Saratoga, New York, 1965–67; with Performance Group, New York, 1969–75; founder, with Elizabeth LeCompte, the Wooster Group, New York, 1975. Recipient: National Endowment for the Arts fellowship, 1977; Rockefeller grant, 1980; Guggenheim fellowship, 1985; Obie award, 1985. Agent: Suzanne Gluck, International Creative Management, 40 West 57th Street, New York, New York 10019. Address: c/o The Wooster Group, Box 654, Canal Street Station, New York, New York 10013, U.S.A.

PUBLICATIONS

Plays and Monologues

Scales (also director: produced Northampton, Massachusetts, 1966; New York, 1975).
Sakonnet Point, with Elizabeth LeCompte (produced New York, 1975).
Rumstick Road, with Elizabeth LeCompte (also co-director: produced New York, 1977).
Nayatt School, with Elizabeth LeCompte (produced New York, 1978).
Three Places in Rhode Island (includes *Sakonnet Point, Rumstick Road, Nayatt School*), with Elizabeth LeCompte (produced New York, 1978).
Point Judith: An Epilog, with Elizabeth LeCompte (produced New York, 1979).
Sex and Death to the Age 14 (produced New York, 1979). Included in *Sex and Death to the Age 14* (collection), 1986.
Booze, Cars, and College Girls (produced New York, 1979). Included in *Sex and Death to the Age 14*, 1986.
India and After (America) (produced New York, 1979).
Nobody Wanted to Sit Behind a Desk (produced New York, 1980). Included in *Sex and Death to the Age 14*, 1986.
A Personal History of the American Theater (produced New York, 1980).
Interviewing the Audience (produced New York, 1981).
47 Beds (produced New York, 1981). Included in *Sex and Death to the Age 14*, 1986.
In Search of the Monkey Girl, with Randal Levenson (produced New York, 1982). New York, Aperture, 1982.
8 × Gray (produced New York, 1982).
Swimming to Cambodia, parts 1 and 2 (produced New York, 1984; London, 1985). New York, Theatre Communications Group, 1985; included in *Swimming to Cambodia: The Collected Works*, 1987.
Travels Through New England (produced Cambridge, Massachusetts, 1984).
Rivkala's Ring, adaptation of a story of Chekhov, in *Orchards* (produced Urbana, Illinois, 1985; New York, 1986). New York, Knopf, 1986.
Terrors of Pleasure: The House (produced Cambridge, Massachusetts, 1985; New York, 1986; London, 1987). Included in *Sex and Death to the Age 14*, 1986.
Sex and Death to the Age 14. New York, Random House, 1986; augmented edition, including *Swimming to Cambodia*, parts 1 and 2, as *Swimming to Cambodia: The Collected Works*, London, Pan, 1987.

Screenplay: *Swimming to Cambodia*, 1987.

Television Play: *Bedtime Story*, with Renée Shafransky, 1987.

*

Theatrical Activities:
Director: **Plays**—*Scales*, Northampton and Amherst, Massachusetts, 1966; *Rumstick Road* (co-director, with Elizabeth LeCompte), New York, 1977.
Actor: **Plays**—roles in all of his own plays and in numerous other plays; Hoss in *The Tooth of Crime* by Sam Shepard, New York, 1973; role in *North Atlantic* by Jim Strahs, New York, 1984. **Films**—*The Killing Fields*, 1984; *True Stories*, 1986; *Swimming to Cambodia*, 1987. **Television**—*Bedtime Story*, 1987.

* * *

Like Eugene O'Neill—also a New England playwright—Spalding Gray creates histrionic exorcisms of private demons. Such an autobiographical dramatist that he cheerfully admits to narcissism, Gray—again like O'Neill—in his early work is obsessed with his family and with doctors. Although Gray's subjects have evolved into his more recent experiences, his work always, unabashedly, is about himself. An actor before he began writing roles, Gray appears in his pieces as well.

Gray began the creation of personal plays in collaboration with the director Elizabeth LeCompte, with whom he constructed four works named after places from his boyhood. *Sakonnet Point* recalls discontinuous images of his preschool summer beach vacations; it's as non-verbal as the infant Gray. This quiet piece built around objects and simple activities contrasts to the often frenetic and noisy *Rumstick Road*, which includes tape recordings of actual family members and of the psychiatrist who treated his mother prior to her suicide. So important are the recordings that the operator of the tape machine sits above the set in full view. Below is a doctor's examination table and to either side a room. One, containing a window through which we see a tent, is associated primarily with Gray's re-enacted past, while the other, containing a screen and slide projector, is associated more often with Gray's probing the past by stimulating his memories with mementos and tapes. The most interesting is a recording of the insensitive doctor, who tells Gray his mother's insanity is hereditary, "but don't be frightened."

Although still more fragmented and surreal, the third of Gray's *Three Places in Rhode Island*, called, after a childhood school, *Nayatt School*, begins with a seemingly straightforward lecture on T. S. Eliot's *The Cocktail Party*, from which Gray and LeCompte's script derives at least half its dialogue. While it deconstructs the Eliot play, *Nayatt School*'s imagery remains that of *Rumstick Road*: a red tent, insanity, death, Christian Science's suspicion of doctors, and preservation of past experience on tapes, film and records—though the latter eventually are destroyed. Gray's earnest academician, a pedant intoning without passion his passion for the Eliot play, sits at a long table midway between the audience above and playing space below, where one of the rooms in *Rumstick Road* has been turned around, so we peer into it through the window. From quiet beginnings, *Nayatt School* increases its speed, ferocity, iconoclasm and discontinuity. Farce chases punctuate scenes with a mad doctor and a parody of a horror film in which a scientist lets a giant blob of protoplasm run amok ("Get me a rewrite man quick—it's still growing"). Mindless antisocial amenities of alcohol, cigarettes, and disco music are partaken by children dressed as sophisticated adults, until characters strip and—literally—climb the walls.

Even more apocalyptic is the Gray and LeCompte part of the Rhode Island trilogy's epilogue, *Point Judith* (which also incorporates a send-up of machismo by Jim Strahs called *Rig*). Once more recur the red tent and the room frame, preservation of the past on records and film, windows which invite us in yet cut us off, and madness—this time in part by deconstruction of O'Neill's *Long Day's Journey into Night*, drowned out by a buzzer, wind, and Berlioz and accompanied by frantic farce in which objects (particularly a reversed vacuum cleaner billowing exhaust), writhing ribbons of light, and whirling bodies create cataclysmic discord. As a quieter coda, a film of men dressed as nuns and the trademark room frames concludes the piece.

After *Point Judith* Gray tired of fragmentation and deconstruction. In search of a controlled narrative form, he returned to the monologue format he'd employed in the opening of *Nayatt School* and constructed three intensely personal solo pieces. In these and his subsequent experiments in unilateral repartee, Gray reflects upon such intimate, often embarrassing details of his private life as what sort of things he did with his penis at the age of twelve. (A variation is *Interviewing the Audience*, in which, after speaking candidly of his own life, he grills spectators upon *their* experiences.) Although he condenses time and occasionally embellishes details, Gray does not fabricate. "A poetic journalist," as he terms himself, he may rearrange events to increase the humor or drama, but candor compels him to confess in *Swimming to Cambodia* (about corruption, both national and personal) that he vomited on the beach, made half as much money as others in *The Killing Fields*, was obsessed about losing his money, and patronized prostitutes. *Terrors of Pleasure* examines memories of being outfoxed by a con artist and of humiliation in Hollywood.

Whereas in those monologues Gray is largely victimized, in others he reveals his ineptitude at getting laid. Among his Woody Allen-style anxiety tales about bumbling towards the sack and fumbling in it is his ineffectual attempt to escape his confirmed heterosexuality in sex with another man. "I figured no one will know about it," Gray muses—and 200 spectators laugh.

This self-deprecatory raconteur who carries a dozen "public memories" around in his head—a nearly Homeric achievement—writes of shame—"pretty hard to maintain in New York City"—and pain, of fear, freaks, and failure, of embarrassment, banality, discomfort, and death, of greed and exploitation. With minimalist means, he confronts his paranoia and, employing a Buddhist idea, he recycles negative energy, a healing process for us as well as for him.

—Tish Dace

GREENE, Graham. British. Born in Berkhamsted, Hertfordshire, 2 October 1904. Educated at Berkhamsted School; Balliol College, Oxford. Served in the Foreign Office, London, 1941–44. Married Vivien Dayrell-Browning in 1927; one son and one daughter. Staff member, the *Times*, London, 1926–30; movie critic, 1937–40, and literary editor, 1940–41, *Spectator*, London. Director, Eyre and Spottiswoode, publishers, London, 1944–48, and The Bodley Head, publishers, London, 1958–68. Member, Panamanian Canal Treaty Delegation to Washington, 1977. Recipient: Hawthornden Prize, 1941; James Tait Black Memorial Prize, 1949; Shakespeare Prize (Hamburg), 1968; Thomas More Medal, 1973; Dos Passos Prize, 1980; City of Madrid Medal, 1980; Jerusalem Prize, 1981; Ruben Dario Medal (Nicaragua), 1987. Litt.D.: Cambridge University, 1962; D.Litt.: Edinburgh University, 1967; Oxford University, 1979. Honorary Fellow, Balliol College, 1963. Honorary Citizen, Anacapri, 1978. Companion of Honour, 1966; Chevalier, Legion of Honour (France), 1967; Grand Cross, Order of Balboa (Panama), 1983; Commandant, Order of Arts and Letters (France), 1984; Companion of Literature, Royal Society of Literature, 1984; O.M. (Order of Merit), 1986. Address: c/o The Bodley Head, 32 Bedford Square, London WC1B 3EL, England.

PUBLICATIONS

Plays

The Living Room (produced London, 1953; New York, 1954). London, Heinemann, 1953; New York, Viking Press, 1954.

The Potting Shed (produced New York, 1957). New York, Viking Press, 1957; revised version (produced London, 1958), London, Heinemann, 1958.

The Complaisant Lover (produced London, 1959; New York, 1961). London, Heinemann, 1959; New York, Viking Press, 1961.

Three Plays (includes *The Living Room, The Potting Shed, The Complaisant Lover*). London, Mercury, 1961.

Carving a Statue (produced London, 1964; New York, 1968). London, Bodley Head, 1964.

The Third Man: A Film, with Carol Reed. London, Lorrimer Films, 1968; New York, Simon and Schuster, 1969; revised version (original script), Lorrimer Films, 1984.

Alas, Poor Maling, adaptation of his own story (televised 1975). Published in *Shades of Greene*, London, Bodley Head-Heinemann, 1975.

The Return of A.J. Raffles: An Edwardian Comedy Based Somewhat Loosely on E.W. Hornung's Characters in "The Amateur Cracksman" (produced London, 1975). London, Bodley Head, 1975; New York, Simon and Schuster, 1976.

Yes and No, and For Whom the Bell Chimes (produced Leicester, 1980). London, Bodley Head, 1983.

The Great Jowett (broadcast 1980). London, Bodley Head, 1981.

Collected Plays (includes *The Living Room, The Potting Shed, The Complaisant Lover, Carving a Statue, The Return of A.J. Raffles, The Great Jowett, Yes and No, For Whom the Bell Chimes*). London, Penguin, 1985.

Screenplays: *The First and the Last* (*21 Days*), 1937; *The New Britain*, 1940; *Brighton Rock* (*Young Scarface*), with Terence Rattigan, 1947; *The Fallen Idol*, with Lesley Storm and William Templeton, 1948; *The Third Man*, with Carol Reed, 1950; *The Stranger's Hand*, with Guy Elmes and Giorgio Bassani, 1954; *Loser Takes All*, 1956; *Saint Joan*, 1957; *Our Man in Havana*, 1960; *The Comedians*, 1967.

Radio Play: *The Great Jowett*, 1980.

Television Play: *Alas, Poor Maling*, 1975.

Novels

The Man Within. London, Heinemann, and New York, Doubleday, 1929.
The Name of Action. London, Heinemann, 1930; New York, Doubleday, 1931.
Rumour at Nightfall. London, Heinemann, 1931; New York, Doubleday, 1932.
Stamboul Train. London, Heinemann, 1932; as *Orient Express*, New York, Doubleday, 1933.
It's a Battlefield. London, Heinemann, and New York, Doubleday, 1934; revised edition, London, Heinemann, 1948; New York, Viking Press, 1962.
England Made Me. London, Heinemann, and New York, Doubleday, 1935; as *The Shipwrecked*, New York, Viking Press, 1953.
A Gun for Sale: An Entertainment. London, Heinemann, 1936; as *This Gun for Hire*, New York, Doubleday, 1936.
Brighton Rock. London, Heinemann, 1938; as *Brighton Rock: An Entertainment*, New York, Viking Press, 1938.
The Confidential Agent: An Entertainment. London, Heinemann, and New York, Viking Press, 1939.
The Power and the Glory. London, Heinemann, 1940; as *The Labyrinthine Ways*, New York, Viking Press, 1940.
The Ministry of Fear: An Entertainment. London, Heinemann, and New York, Viking Press, 1943.
The Heart of the Matter. London, Heinemann, and New York, Viking Press, 1948.
The Third Man. New York, Viking Press, 1950.
The Third Man, and The Fallen Idol. London, Heinemann, 1950.
The End of the Affair. London, Heinemann, and New York, Viking Press, 1951.
Loser Takes All. London, Heinemann, 1955; New York, Viking Press, 1957.
The Quiet American. London, Heinemann, 1955; New York, Viking Press, 1956.
Our Man in Havana: An Entertainment. London, Heinemann, and New York, Viking Press, 1958.
A Burnt-Out Case. London, Heinemann, and New York, Viking Press, 1961.
The Comedians. London, Bodley Head, and New York, Viking Press, 1966.
Travels with My Aunt. London, Bodley Head, 1969; New York, Viking Press, 1970.
The Honorary Consul. London, Bodley Head, and New York, Simon and Schuster, 1973.
The Human Factor. London, Bodley Head, and New York, Simon and Schuster, 1978.
Doctor Fischer of Geneva; or, The Bomb Party. London, Bodley Head, and New York, Simon and Schuster, 1980.
Monsignor Quixote. London, Bodley Head, and New York, Simon and Schuster, 1982.
The Tenth Man. London, Bodley Head-Blond, and New York, Simon and Schuster, 1985.

Short Stories

The Basement Room and Other Stories. London, Cresset Press, 1935.
The Bear Fell Free. London, Grayson, 1935.
24 Short Stories, with James Laver and Sylvia Townsend Warner. London, Cresset Press, 1939.
Nineteen Stories. London, Heinemann, 1947; New York, Viking Press, 1949; augmented edition, as *Twenty-One Stories*, London, Heinemann, 1954; New York, Viking Press, 1962; selection, as *Across the Bridge and Other Stories*, Bath, Chivers, 1981.
A Visit to Morin. London, Heinemann, 1959.
A Sense of Reality. London, Bodley Head, and New York, Viking Press, 1963.
May We Borrow Your Husband? and Other Comedies of the Sexual Life. London, Bodley Head, and New York, Viking Press, 1967.
The Collected Stories of Graham Greene. London, Bodley Head–Heinemann, 1972; New York, Viking Press, 1973.
How Father Quixote Became a Monsignor. Los Angeles, Sylvester and Orphanos, 1980.

Verse

Babbling April. Oxford, Blackwell, 1925.
For Christmas. Privately printed, 1951.

Other

Journey Without Maps. London, Heinemann, and New York, Doubleday, 1936.
The Lawless Roads: A Mexican Journey. London, Longman, 1939; as *Another Mexico*, New York, Viking Press, 1939.
British Dramatists. London, Collins, 1942; included in *The Romance of English Literature*, New York, Hastings House, 1944.
The Little Train (for children; published anonymously). London, Eyre and Spottiswoode, 1946; as Graham Greene, New York, Lothrop, 1958.
Why Do I Write? An Exchange of Views Between Elizabeth Bowen, Graham Greene, and V.S. Pritchett. London, Marshall, and New York, British Book Centre, 1948.
After Two Years. Privately printed, 1949.
The Little Fire Engine (for children). London, Parrish, 1950; as *The Little Red Fire Engine*, New York, Lothrop, 1953.
The Lost Childhood and Other Essays. London, Eyre and Spottiswoode, 1951; New York, Viking Press, 1952.
The Little Horse Bus (for children). London, Parrish, 1952; New York, Lothrop, 1954.
The Little Steamroller: A Story of Adventure, Mystery, and Detection (for children). London, Parrish, 1953; New York, Lothrop, 1955.
Essais Catholiques, translated by Marcelle Sibon. Paris, Editions de Seuil, 1953.
In Search of a Character: Two African Journals. London, Bodley Head, 1961; New York, Viking Press, 1962.
The Revenge: An Autobiographical Fragment. Privately printed, 1963.

Victorian Detective Fiction: A Catalogue of the Collection Made by Dorothy Glover and Graham Greene. London, Bodley Head, 1966.
Collected Essays. London, Bodley Head, and New York, Viking Press, 1969.
A Sort of Life (autobiography). London, Bodley Head, and New York, Simon and Schuster, 1971.
The Virtue of Disloyalty. Privately printed, 1972.
The Pleasure-Dome: The Collected Film Criticism 1935–40, edited by John Russell Taylor. London, Secker and Warburg, 1972; as *Graham Greene on Film: Collected Film Criticism 1935–1940*, New York, Simon and Schuster, 1972.
The Portable Graham Greene, edited by Philip Stratford. New York, Viking Press, 1973; London, Penguin, 1977.
Lord Rochester's Monkey, Being the Life of John Wilmot, Second Earl of Rochester. London, Bodley Head, and New York, Viking Press, 1974.
Ways of Escape. London, Bodley Head, 1980; New York, Simon and Schuster, 1981.
J'Accuse: The Dark Side of Nice (bilingual edition). London, Bodley Head, 1982.
A Quick Look Behind: Footnotes to an Autobiography. Los Angeles, Sylvester and Orphanos, 1983.
Getting to Know the General: The Story of an Involvement. London, Bodley Head, and New York, Simon and Schuster, 1984.
Graham Greene Country, paintings by Paul Hogarth. London, Pavilion-Joseph, 1986.

Editor, *The Old School: Essays by Divers Hands.* London, Cape, 1934.
Editor, *The Best of Saki.* London, Lane, 1950; New York, Viking Press, 1961.
Editor, with Hugh Greene, *The Spy's Bedside Book: An Anthology.* London, Hart Davis, 1957.
Editor, *The Bodley Head Ford Madox Ford.* London, Bodley Head, 4 vols., 1962–63.
Editor, *An Impossible Woman: The Memories of Dottoressa Moor of Capri.* London, Bodley Head, 1975; New York, Viking Press, 1976.
Editor, the Hugh Greene, *Victorian Villainies: Four Classic Victorian Tales.* London, Viking, 1984; New York, Viking, 1985.

*

Bibliography: *Graham Greene: A Checklist of Criticism* by J.D. Vann, Kent, Ohio, Kent State University Press, 1970; *Graham Greene: A Descriptive Catalog* by Robert H. Miller, Lexington, University Press of Kentucky, 1978; *Graham Greene: A Bibliography and Guide to Research* by R.A. Wobbe, New York, Garland, 1979; *Graham Greene: An Annotated Bibliography of Criticism* by A.F. Cassis, Metuchen, New Jersey, Scarecrow Press, 1981.

Manuscript Collection: Humanities Research Center, University of Texas, Austin.

Critical Studies (selection): *Graham Greene and the Heart of the Matter* by Marie Mesnet, London, Cresset Press, 1954; *Graham Greene* by Francis Wyndham, London, Longman, 1955, revised edition, 1958; *Graham Greene* by John Atkins, London, Calder, and New York, Roy, 1957, revised edition, London, Calder and Boyars, 1966, New York, Humanities Press, 1967; *The Labyrinthine Ways of Graham Greene* by Francis Leo Kunkel, New York, Sheed and Ward, 1960, revised edition, Mamaroneck, New York, Appel, 1973; *Graham Greene* by David Pryce-Jones, Edinburgh, Oliver and Boyd, 1963, New York, Barnes and Noble, 1968; *Graham Greene: Some Critical Considerations* (includes bibliography by N. Brennan) edited by Robert O. Evans, Lexington, University of Kentucky Press, 1963; *Graham Greene* by A.A. DeVitis, New York, Twayne, 1964, revised edition, 1986; *Graham Greene* by David Lodge, New York, Columbia University Press, 1966; *Graham Greene: A Critical Essay* by Martin Turnell, Grand Rapids, Michigan, Eerdmans, 1967; *Graham Greene: The Aesthetics of Exploration* by Gwenn R. Boardman, Gainesville, University of Florida Press, 1971; *Graham Greene the Entertainer* by Peter Wolfe, Carbondale, Southern Illinois University Press, 1972; *Graham Greene: A Collection of Critical Essays* edited by Samuel Hynes, Englewood Cliffs, New Jersey, Prentice Hall, 1973; *The Other Man: Conversations with Graham Greene* by Marie Françoise Allain, London, Bodley Head, and New York, Simon and Schuster, 1983; *Graham Greene* by John Spurling, London, Methuen, 1983; *Graham Greene* by Richard Kelly, New York, Ungar, 1985; *The Achievement of Graham Greene* by Grahame Smith, Brighton, Sussex, Harvester Press, 1985, New York, Barnes and Noble, 1986.

Theatrical Activities:
Actor: **Film**—*La Nuit americaine* (*Day for Night*), 1973.

* * *

Graham Greene was approaching his fiftieth birthday and generally accepted as one of the few outstanding novelists of the age when, in 1953, his first play, *The Living Room,* was produced. Three years later, John Osborne's *Look Back in Anger* inaugurated a revolution in the English theatre, but Greene's later plays were obviously uninfluenced by the outburst of new activity and the exploration of new styles and themes.

As a novelist, Greene has developed new and effective narrative techniques, but his almost cinematic cutting and timing of scenes have been fed into the tradition. When he turned to the theatre, fulfilling ambitions which (he explained in the Preface to *Three Plays*) had been with him since his schooldays, he turned to the traditional disciplines of the well-made play. He found "a fascination in unity" and designed his plays to preserve traditional theatrical virtues. The results are elegantly made for all their harshness, economical and precise; their interest is always in the matter expressed, not in the development of new means of expression.

Greene's range has always been limited; he has a few obsessive themes to which he tends to return always with new and sharper intensities. He is concerned primarily about the relation of man—not generalised, abstract man but whatever individual happens to demand his attention—to God, and secondly about men's relationship to each other. *The Complaisant Lover*, a comedy, restricts itself to his secondary theme; its tone is not happy but, at times, distressing; its solution to a difficult moral problem is by no means conventional and its observation of average sensual life is not designed to comfort an audience. For all her clandestine love affair with a possessive bookseller, Mary Rhodes loves her dentist husband (the domestic clown, the practical joker who is most at home in the mental world of his prep-school son) no less than she loves her lover.

The play might easily become a commonplace domestic tragedy; Rhodes might carry out his suicide plan, but it is his wife's needs which persuade him to abandon it: if she wants a husband and a lover, she must have both for the sake of her happiness; it is the adulterer who finds the solution outrageous until Rhodes persuades him that to love is to give the beloved what she needs.

The Complaisant Lover is Greene's *Comédie humaine*; in his first play, *The Living Room*, he returns to the idea of a Catholic suicide without repeating the ideas of his novel *The Heart of the Matter*. Rose Pemberton, who kills herself because her life can bring only unhappiness to the people she loves, is the centre round which others—her old aunts and her crippled uncle who can no longer function as a priest—revolve in a life which rejects the truth and refuses to acknowledge the fact of death. Rose's suicide compels them to do so; in a sense, it offers them salvation. The rules, the crippled priest explains, are man's rules, man's attempt to make God's will into comprehensible law; decisions rest ultimately with God. It is not only *The Heart of the Matter* but *Brighton Rock* and *The Power and the Glory* which are somehow involved in *The Living Room*, but it is a remarkably gentle, emotionally simple work to have come from a writer so wittily harsh as Greene.

The Potting Shed is harsh in Greene's accustomed way, and it seems that it won less respect than it deserves because it is rooted in a supernatural event. Its central character, as a boy, hanged himself but was restored to life because a priest sacrificed his faith to bring the boy back. Greene's own unsparing criticism of the play is that the "hollowness" of the man who had been dead is less convincingly treated than the "hollow man" he had explored in the novel *A Burnt-Out Case*, but nothing in the novel compares with the tragedy of the priest who found that God took him quite seriously and destroyed his capacity for faith when the boy was given life again. Greene could have quoted again the line of the old priest at the end of *Brighton Rock*, and offered another reflection on "the appalling strangeness of the mercy of God." Nothing in *A Burnt-Out Case* is so moving as the prospect of warmth returning to the play's spiritually dead central figure.

Carving a Statue, Greene wrote in the Preface to its published version, is neither "symbolic" nor "theological," and he has some caustic fun at the expense of critics who found its symbolism and theology obscure while they should have been regarding it as a play of direct statements which means no more than is seen and heard on the stage. A bad sculptor—Greene was thinking, he wrote, of Benjamin Robert Hayden, who killed himself when he awoke from a dream of impossible greatness—has given his life to the making of a statue to God the Father. Everything except his dreams is sacrificed to his task; he knows that his work—though he does not realize its worthlessness—is a refuge from the pressures he would suffer if he abandoned a task he has no notion of how to complete. His friends, his adolescent son's happiness, a dumb girl's life, are all destroyed. Greene draws no moral and offers no comment.

The Return of A.J. Raffles came as a disappointment after these plays. Witty and lightly treated, almost a sub-Wildean pastiche, it sets E.W. Hornung's upper-class burglar into more imposing social circumstances than his creator envisaged for him; Raffles is involved in the quarrel of Lord Alfred Douglas with the Marquis of Queensberry; Edward VII appears as an unconscious *deus ex machina*. But there is no sense, in this play, that the Society burglar is blaspheming the standards by which he lives; the late-20th century, perhaps, sees nothing outrageous in the idea of a gentleman-thief, and the seamier side of Edwardian society, thus exposed, turns Raffles from a kind of unaltruistic Robin Hood into one of the corrupt in a corrupt society. *Yes and No, and For Whom the Bell Chimes* is another easy-going play in which Greene exploits a certain elegance of technique almost, it seems, for its own sake, without any of the obsessive compulsions which had given force to his earlier works.

Though Greene's plays do not offer technical or stylistic experiments but live as their author's expression in traditional dramatic form of the essential preoccupation of all his work, one thing—and again it is traditional—should be said of them. They create personalities—the crippled priest of *The Living Room*, the hollow man who returned from the dead in *The Potting Shed*, and the sculptor of *Carving a Statue*—which demand and reward fine acting, as do the husband and lover of *The Complaisant Lover*. They translate into terms of theatre the strangeness and haunting power which belong to Greene's novels. Inescapably, they are religious plays in which men are able to see that they live inescapably and often terrifyingly in the presence of God.

—Henry Raynor

GRIFFITHS, Trevor. British. Born in Manchester, Lancashire, 4 April 1935. Educated at St. Bede's College, Manchester, 1945–52; Manchester University, 1952–55, B.A. in English 1955; studied for external M.A. from 1961. Served in the British Army, Manchester Regiment, 1955–57: Infantryman. Married Janice Elaine Stansfield in 1960 (died 1977); one son and two daughters. Teacher of English and games in a private school, Oldham, Lancashire, 1957–61; Lecturer in Liberal Studies, Stockport Technical College, Cheshire, 1962–65; further education officer, BBC, Leeds, 1965–72. Co-editor, *Labour's Northern Voice*, 1962–65, and series editor for Workers Northern Publishing Society. Recipient: BAFTA award, for screenplay, 1982. Lives in Boston Spa, Yorkshire. Agent: A.D. Peters Ltd., 10 Buckingham Street, London WC2N 6BU, England.

PUBLICATIONS

Plays

The Wages of Thin (produced Manchester, 1969; London, 1970).

The Big House (broadcast 1969; produced Newcastle upon Tyne, 1975). With *Occupations*, London, Calder and Boyars, 1972.

Occupations (produced Manchester, 1970; London, 1971; New York, 1982). With *The Big House*, London, Calder and Boyars, 1972; revised version, published separately, London, Faber, 1980.

Apricots (produced London, 1971). With *Thermidor*, London, Pluto Press, 1978.

Thermidor (produced Edinburgh, 1971). With *Apricots*, London, Pluto Press, 1978.

Lay By, with others (produced Edinburgh and London, 1971). London, Calder and Boyars, 1972.

Sam, Sam (produced London, 1972; revised version produced London, 1978). Published in *Plays and Players* (London), April 1972.

Gun (also director: produced Edinburgh, 1973).

The Party (produced London, 1973; revised version produced Coventry, 1974). London, Faber, 1974.

All Good Men (televised 1974; produced London, 1975). Included in *All Good Men, and Absolute Beginners*, 1977.

Comedians (produced Nottingham and London, 1975; New York, 1976; revised [women's] version produced Liverpool, 1987). London, Faber, and New York, Grove Press, 1976; revised version, Faber, 1979.

The Cherry Orchard, adaptation of a play by Chekhov, translated by Helen Rappaport (produced Nottingham, 1977). London, Pluto Press, 1978.

All Good Men, and Absolute Beginners: Two Plays for Television. London, Faber, 1977.

Through the Night, and Such Impossibilities: Two Plays for Television. London, Faber, 1977.

Deeds, with others (produced Nottingham, 1978). Published in *Plays and Players* (London) May and June 1978.

Country: A Tory Story (televised 1981). London, Faber, 1981.

Sons and Lovers, adaptation of the novel by D.H. Lawrence (televised 1981). Nottingham, Spokesman, 1982.

Oi for England (televised 1982; produced London, 1982). London, Faber, 1982.

Real Dreams, adaptation of the story "Revolution in Cleveland" by Jeremy Pikser (also director: produced Williamstown, Massachusetts, 1984; London, 1986). London, Faber, 1987 (includes "Revolution in Cleveland" by Pikser).

Judgement over the Dead: The Screenplay of The Last Place on Earth, adaptation of a book by Roland Huntford (as *The Last Place on Earth*, televised 1985). London, Verso, 1986.

Fatherland (screenplay). London, Faber, 1987.

Screenplays: *Reds*, with Warren Beatty, 1981; *Fatherland*, 1987.

Radio Plays: *The Big House*, 1969; *Jake's Brigade*, 1971.

Television Plays: *Adam Smith* series (as Ben Rae), 1972; *The Silver Mask*, from a story by Horace Walpole (*Between the Wars* series), 1973; *All Good Men*, 1974; *Absolute Beginners* (*Fall of Eagles* series), 1974; *Don't Make Waves* (*Eleventh Hour* series), with Snoo Wilson, 1975; *Through the Night*, 1975; *Bill Brand* series, 1976; *Sons and Lovers*, 1981; *Country*, 1981; *Oi for England*, 1982; *The Last Place on Earth*, 1985.

Other

Tip's Lot (for children). London, Macmillan, 1972.

*

Manuscript Collection: British Film Institute, London.

Critical Study: *Powerplays: Trevor Griffiths in Television* by Mike Poole and John Wyver, London, British Film Institute, 1984.

Theatrical Activities:
Director: **Plays**—*Gun*, Edinburgh, 1973; *Real Dreams*, Williamstown, Massachusetts, 1984.

* * *

Trevor Griffiths is unique for the remarkable consistency with which he has probed into critical phases and issues of the international labour movement. Earlier social and political dramatists portrayed individual labour struggles or dealt with the brutal consequences of fascism, but never before have the crucial questions of socialist strategy and morality been so forcefully examined on the stage. Griffiths does not discuss the desirability of socialism, or its moral superiority over capitalism—that issue appears to him settled. What he analyses are the different positions hammered out by various brands of socialism and communism, and the personal dilemmas arising out of absorbing engagement in one of these movements.

Significantly, Griffiths started with a number of plays about Continental rather than British points of crisis. *Occupations* is set in Turin at the height of the revolutionary upsurge after World War I when factories were taken over and soviets formed in many Italian cities. The play shows the workers of Turin addressed in two moving speeches by Gramsci, but its focus is less on the confrontation between capital and labour than on the controversy between Gramsci and Kabak, a secret envoy of the Comintern, over the correct estimate and handling of the situation. Kabak, who has the experience and prestige of a successful revolution behind him, stands for a communist *realpolitik*; Gramsci, by contrast, embodies a hesitant, if fervent revolutionary idealism, which is always guided by a consideration, even love, for the people he leads.

The strategic differences between these two exponents of communism are also reflected in their personal outlooks. At the end Kabak leaves behind his mistress, who is dying of cancer; Gramsci goes to Sardinia to attend to his sister on her deathbed. The political and the personal, it is suggested, should not be seen as separate concerns. This dual perspective is also expressed by the play's title (Griffiths has a predilection for succinct, ambiguous titles), which refers not only to the action taken by the Fiat workers, but also to the private undertakings of the protagonists.

One of several future historical developments hinted at towards the end of *Occupations* is Stalinism. It can be seen germinating in Kabak's ruthless pragmatism and is summed up in Gramsci's ominous words: "Treat masses as expendable, as fodder, during the revolution, you will always treat them thus." *Thermidor* gives us a glimpse of Soviet Russia in the throes of Stalinism, during the purges of 1937. This one-act play is named after the summer month of the French revolutionary calendar, in which Robespierre himself fell victim to the Terror he had unleashed in the defence of the Revolution. Here it is Anya, formerly a loyal member of the Communist Party, who will disappear in the cellars of the NKVD. The play shows her at the mercy of her interrogator, Yukhov, who twists her sentences and fabricates absurd charges. Here there is even less doubt than in the altercations between Gramsci and Kabak as to where the author's sympathies lie. Yukhov's phrase "Enemies ... are no longer people" disqualifies him and a whole system from speaking in the name of a humanist socialism. But when Anya finally pleads innocent and Yukhov asks the rhetorical question "Are you?," this is as much the voice of the author, who cannot absolve a once diligent and influential party member like Anya of historical guilt.

In contrast to these two analytical and descriptive plays *The Party* introduces an ironical note. An assortment of non-communist and almost exclusively non-working-class leftists meet at the instigation of a progressive television producer, Joe Shawcross, to discuss the possibilities of joint revolutionary action in Britain, all against the backdrop of Parisian students mounting the barricades in May 1968. The ironic nature of the whole radical-chic congregation, and the impotence of the British (intellectual) left, are suggested from the beginning through the appearance, in the Prologue, of Groucho Marx musing at a picture of his political namesake, and Joe's masturbation prior to the arrival of the leftist partygoers. Neither of the two conflicting analyses of the situation offered by a sociology lecturer and a veteran Trotskyist respectively (the latter pointing to the necessity of building *the* Party) is entirely wrong, but equally neither is free of empty revolutionary phrase-making and worn-out slogans, as the debunking comments of an accidentally present drunken writer point out.

Occupations, Thermidor, and *The Party* were all conceived and written for the stage. So was *Comedians*, which is often regarded as Griffiths's best work. It is certainly his funniest, even though one finds oneself often painfully aware of the impropriety of one's laughs. For this is a comedy about the social uses of stand-up comedy, and of working-class entertainment, a comedy about the proper function of the performer and, by implication, of the dramatist. Humour for Griffiths is too serious a business to be left in the hands of mindless word-jugglers who insult people's intelligence or pander to ethnic and sexual stereotypes.

Since the mid-1970's Griffiths's career has, however, been primarily and deliberately that of a television playwright. Few critics and scholars have appreciated this decision, and some on the left have even accused him of opportunism. The author has sought this medium out of a deep conviction that a socialist dramatist today cannot afford only to address the theatre-goer, whether in the West End or the fringe. While the one kind of theatre reaches only a middle-class audience, the other too often ends by preaching to the converted. For the vast majority of the population "drama in a dramatised society" (Raymond Williams) like ours means television drama, and as one character in *Through the Night* puts it: "whoever does not reach the capacity of the common people and fails to make them listen to him, misses his mark."

Yet what Griffiths has called the "strategic penetration" of the central channel of communication proved initially difficult. *Such Impossibilities*, commissioned by the BBC as part of a series entitled *The Edwardians*, was rejected, ostensibly on grounds of cost, but more probably because its hero, the militant labour leader Tom Mann, and its theme, the 1911 transport strike in Liverpool, a social conflict of almost civil-war like dimensions, fitted awkwardly into an ancestral gallery composed of such establishment figures as Baden-Powell, Horatio Bottomley, and Charles Stewart Rolls.

Not surprisingly, therefore, *All Good Men*, Griffiths's first major produced television play, shows the author fully alert to the power of the medium to forge consensus and to mystify. The television producer who wants to conduct an interview with the elderly Labour politician Edward Waite, a former Cabinet Minister now to be made a peer, is attacked by William, the politician's son, precisely for his seemingly disinterested, value-free pose. William, a left-wing research student, is equally critical of the historical record of the Labour Party, and the dispute between father and son over its successes, as the former sees it, or purely minor reforms ultimately solidifying capitalism, as the latter argues, forms the climax of the play. But true to his now familiar oppositional set-up, Griffiths, though sharing many of William's reservations about "Labourism," distributes the arguments fairly evenly. Moreover, Waite—like so many of Griffiths's totally committed figures—has paid a heavy price for his lifelong dedication to working-class politics. He has been deserted by his wife and is now betrayed by his son, who supplies the interviewer with compromising material about his father's past, not out of personal vindictiveness but in order to bring the internal political machinations of the Labour Party into the open.

All Good Men, like its 11-part successor *Bill Brand*, questions the parliamentary road to socialism, and scrutinises the role of the Labour Party, without writing off either completely. But as the revolutionary optimism of much of the British socialist drama of the 1970's subsided and experienced a definite check under the realities of Thatcher's Britain, Griffiths found other themes more pertinent, among them the situation of unemployed urban youths (*Oi for England*) and the construction of national myths (*The Last Place on Earth*).

Country, Griffiths's strongest play of the 1980's, is about a significant "moment" in the history of British socialism, namely Labour's landslide victory in 1945. But it looks at it from an unexpected angle, an upper-class estate in Kent, where the members of the Carlion dynasty have assembled for the annual family gathering, at which a successor to the ageing Sir Frederic, baronet and Chairman of the Board of the Carlion brewery empire, will have to be found. As the devastating election results come in, and the common people themselves symbolically lay claim to the property by trespassing and occupying a barn, incredulity and consternation alternate with wrath. But Philip, one Carlion not affected by the general stupefaction, an outsider among the pretenders for the succession not least because of his bohemian lifestyle, now energetically assumes responsibility. Philip's victory over the "old gang," his efficient and smooth dealing with the squatters, indicates the capacity of the ruling class to renew itself and adapt to unforeseen circumstances—a point already made in *Occupations*, where the Fiat manager envisages a whole paternalistic welfare programme as a palliative against future social unrest.

Griffiths's work also includes screenplays. Chief among these are *Reds* (directed by Warren Beatty) about the American journalist John Reed's involvement in the October Revolution, and *Fatherland* (directed by Ken Loach), an intriguing story of German partition and a songmaker's search for his father, who left the GDR for the West 30 years before his son.

With *Real Dreams* Griffiths has lately returned to the stage—and to an earlier preoccupation. Like *The Party*, this play about the American student movement in the late 1960's highlights the feelings of isolation and frustration behind the leftward move of many intellectuals. The attempt of a commune of white middle-class students to move out of the protected world of the campus and form a fighting alliance with Puerto Rican working people fails dismally, hampered as it is by all kinds of ethnic, cultural, sexist, and psychic blocks. But the play ends on an optimistic note: the real historical contradictions are dissolved into an anticipatory dream of perfect unity, grace, and victory—all symbolised by a trance-like Tai-Chi exercise. The limitations and self-indulgence as well as the potential power and promise of this phase of radicalism are thus brought alive. If the conclusion appears somewhat forced, the play demonstrates once again Griffiths's masterly building up of tension, and testifies to his continuing concern for the global struggle for liberation.

—H. Gustav Klaus

GRILLO, John. British. Born in Watford, Hertfordshire, 29 November 1942. Educated at Watford Boys Grammar School 1954–61; Trinity Hall, Cambridge, 1962–65, B.A. in history 1965. Professional actor: in Lincoln, Glasgow, Farnham, Brighton, London. Resident dramatist, Castle Theatre, Farnham, Surrey, 1969–70; literary associate, Soho Theatre Club, London, 1971. Recipient: Arts Council bursary, 1965. Agent (for acting): Howes and Prior Ltd., 66 Berkeley House, Hay Hill, London W.1, England.

PUBLICATIONS

Plays

Gentlemen I . . . (produced Cambridge, 1963; London, 1968).
It Will Come or It Won't (produced Dublin, 1965).
Hello Goodbye Sebastian (produced Cambridge, 1965; London, 1968). Published in *Gambit 16* (London), 1970.
The Downfall of Jack Throb (produced London, 1967).
The Fall of Samson Morocco (produced London, 1969).
Oh Everyman Oh Colonel Fawcett (produced Farnham, Surrey, 1969).
Mr. Bickerstaff's Establishment (produced Glasgow, 1969; expanded version, produced London, 1972).
History of a Poor Old Man (produced London, 1970).
Number Three (produced Bradford and London, 1970). Published in *New Short Plays*, London, Methuen, 1972.
Blubber (produced London, 1971).
Zonk (produced London, 1971).
Food (produced London, 1971).
Will the King Leave His Tea Pot (produced Edinburgh and London, 1971).
George and Moira Entertain a Member of the Opposite Sex to Dinner (produced Edinburgh and London, 1971).
The Hammer and the Hacksaw, in *Christmas Present* (produced Edinburgh, 1971).
Christmas Box, and Civitas Dei (produced London, 1972).
Snaps (*Civitas Dei, Days by the River, MacEnery's Vision of Pipkin*) (produced London, 1973).
Crackers (produced London, 1973).
Mr. Ives' Magic Punch and Judy Show (produced London, 1973).

Television Play: *Nineteen Thirty Nine*, 1973.

*

Critical Study: by Germaine Greer, in *Cambridge Review*, 29 May 1965.

Theatrical Activities:
Actor: **Plays**—Theatre Royal, Lincoln: Dabble in *Lock Up Your Daughters* by Bernard Miles, Billy Bones in *Treasure Island* by Jules Eckert Goodman, Poet in *Five to a Flat* by Valentine Kataev, Ingham in *Little Malcolm and His Struggle Against the Eunuchs* by David Halliwell, roles in *Beyond the Fringe*, Andrei in *The Three Sisters* by Chekhov, Clarence in *2 Henry IV*, Max in *The Homecoming* by Harold Pinter, Jopplin in *A Shouting in the Streets* by Elizabeth Dawson, and Rusty Charley in *Guys and Dolls* by Abe Burrows and Jo Swerling, 1966–67; Brighton Combination: Old Man in *Hello Goodbye Sebastian* and Rasputin in *The Rasputin Show* by Michael Almaz, 1968; Royal Court Theatre, London: Verlaine in *Total Eclipse* by Christopher Hampton, 1968, roles in *Erogenous Zones* by Mike Stott, 1969, Perowne in *AC/DC* by Heathcote Williams, 1970, Reporter and Deaf and Dumb Man in *Lulu* by Peter Barnes, 1971, and Marx in *Anarchist* by Michael Almaz, 1971; Glendower in *1 Henry IV*, Glasgow, 1969; Castle Theatre, Farnham: Eddy in *Tango* by Mrozek, Millionaire in *Cliffwalk* by Sebastian Shaw, Fawcett in *Oh Everyman Oh Colonel Fawcett*, and Don Pedro in *Much Ado About Nothing*, 1969–70; Soho Theatre Club, London: Nurse in *Number Three*, 1970, Thug in *Dynamo* by Christopher Wilkinson, 1971, and Recorder in *Inquisition* by Michael Almaz, 1971; Mr. Bickerstaff in *Mr. Bickerstaff's Establishment*, London, 1972; Doc in *The Tooth of Crime* by Sam Shepard, London, 1972; Sergeant Kite in *The Recruiting Officer* by Farquhar, Hornchurch, Essex, 1972; Dr. Rank in *A Doll's House* by Ibsen, Greenwich, 1972; Poltrone in *The Director of the Opera* by Anouilh, Chichester, 1973; Gremio in *The Taming of the Shrew*, London, 1974; Ashley Withers in *The End of Me Old Cigar* by John Osborne, London, 1975. **Films**—*The F and H Film; Dynamo; Firefox*, 1982; *Brazil*, 1985. **Television**—*Brideshead Revisited*, 1981; *Chessgame*, 1983; *Dog Ends*, 1984; *Blott on the Landscape*, 1985.

John Grillo comments:

(1973) Aspects of my work include 1) A writing out of private obsessive fantasies and an attempt to excite the audience by parading on the stage that which is forbidden. 2) The plays are firmly based in the lower-middle-class morality and culture of my childhood. 3) Influence of theatrical innovators and fantasists such as Ionesco and Jarry. 4) Influence of television and film. Before the age of twenty I had visited the theatre perhaps half a dozen times. 5) I do not know how my work will develop but I hope it will become more public, less private, more realistic, less fantastic.

* * *

John Grillo is the Alfred Jarry of modern British theatre: a clown dramatist whose plays mingle outrageous solemnity with knockabout comedy and a Rabelaisian relish for dirty jokes. His stories have the simplicity of Punch and Judy shows. Bickerstaff (in *Mr. Bickerstaff's Establishment*) murders his sleep-walking wife as an alternative to committing suicide. Emboldened by this desperate deed, he tries to take over the underworld of pimps, thugs, and prostitutes: but finally the Forces of the Law—and his wife's ghost—catch up with him and condemn him to death. Bickerstaff (like Punch) escapes and decides to "emigrate—to Beirut": where his yearning for the fleshpots of the East can be satisfied. The Nurse (in *Number Three*) is a male fascist orderly in a mental hospital, preserving a solemn repressive dignity before a torrent of sexual insults from his worst patient, Three. The King (in *Will the King Leave His Tea Pot*) retires from the Affairs of State—and his frustrated thinning wife—into a huge womb-like tea-pot: thus causing the utmost consternation among his subjects, who lose all sense of protocol. These anecdotes are told in the style of children's stories. The characters are dressed like cartoons: Bickerstaff is a "fat man with a drooping bedraggled moustache"—like Crippen. The Queen (in *Will the King Leave His Tea Pot*) "wears a long silver dress, which is frayed at the edges, a necklace of pearls, several of which are missing and two or three of which are molars." The dialogue mainly consists of torrential speeches, where wild puns, extreme thought-associations, and an almost innocent scatology provide buoyant, idiosyncratic fun. The characters talk at each other—rather than to or with—and any change in mood is underlined by asides to the audience. When the Nurse, who is trying to persuade Three to go to bed, changes his tactics, he tells the audience that he is doing so. "Poor Nurse is worried because Number Three is such a bad boy. Nurse is a very sensitive man and he cries when Number Three plays him up . . . (aside) This is called 'Making the patient feel guilty.'"

This overtness in handling the story, the dialogue, the bawdiness, and the characters gives Grillo's plays an ingenuous charm. Grillo is an actor—as well as a dramatist—and he has a performer's instinct for bizarre, shock tactics. As an actor, he has worked extensively with fringe theatre in Britain: in the rudimentary pub theatres of London and the student theatre clubs. His plays are designed to require little in the way of staging, but to rely on actor-audience contact, in the style of music hall. He is one of the rare dramatists to exploit the essential roughness, the slapdash circumstances of fringe theatre: and therefore his plays work particularly well in pubs. Nor is the humour as unsophisticated as may appear. Grillo delights in choosing apparently "serious" themes and placing them in comic-strip settings. In his longest and perhaps most ambitious play, *Hello Goodbye Sebastian*, Grillo tells the story of an apprentice gravedigger, Sebastian, who longs for a better life and refuses to fill in a grave, because the old man whose wife occupies it believes in the resurrection of the dead. Sebastian's home life however is an unhappy one. His mother, Mary, and the lodger, Charlie, are living off his earnings: and their sex life dominates the household arrangements. Sebastian can't leave his job—to become a barber—because his mother doesn't want him to: it would destroy the precarious balance of her affair. And so Sebastian finally resigns himself to being a gravedigger: and in the final scene, he fills in the grave of the old man's wife. The allegorical overtones of Grillo's story relate it to the Theatre of the Absurd and to Ionesco's plays in particular. The suppression of innocence and adolescent hope leads to a death-centredness. Sebastian at the end of the play fills up the grave with unnecessary relish: "Half a pound of worms, landlord, down the hatch. Pound of filth, landlord. Coming, sir, down the hatch!" But this "serious" theme is handled with a flippant lightness, which does not, however, prevent the allegory from being both noticeable and important to the success of the play.

Grillo's cheerful irreverence has a habit of misfiring in the wrong surroundings. He was once the resident dramatist/actor with a repertory theatre in Farnham, a quiet country town in the South of England. His comic-strip version of the Everyman story caused the greatest possible local outrage. "They called the play," remembers Grillo, "lavatorial, smutty, schoolboyish, nihilistic, unnecessarily cruel, and what's more my acting stank." Nor was he at ease in the portentous atmosphere of avant-garde theatre clubs, which may be one reason why his plays have been under-rated by British critics. His best productions have perhaps come with the talented fringe group, Portable Theatre, who included *Zonk* and *Food* in their 1971 repertoire. Zonk is an extraordinary family comedy, involving a mother, Dora (a man in drag), a domineering father, Bone, a son, and a substitute Dora (an attractive woman in her early forties). The son's antagonism towards his father and his yearnings for sex with his mother provide a comic interpretation of Oedipalism. The son eventually disgusts the father by sucking milk from his mother's artificial penis. Not all of Grillo's plays are, however, equally extreme. His *History of a Poor Old Man* is a mock-melancholic monologue of an old man arrested for soliciting in a lavatory.

Grillo's great quality as a dramatist is that his sense of fun is infectious. The jokes tumble over each other and the uninhibitedness of the bawdry creates an easy relaxation in the theatre. He breaks down the over-solemn atmosphere of playgoing and brings back a childlike delight in trying anything once. His plays are unique, and have stayed fresh and exuberant. His technical range is severely limited, but within these limits his imagination is exhilarating.

—John Elsom

GUARE, John (Edward). American. Born in New York City, 5 February 1938. Educated at Joan of Arc Elementary School, and St. John's Preparatory School, New York; Georgetown University, Washington, D.C., 1956–60, A.B. 1960; Yale University School of Drama, 1960–63, M.F.A. 1963. Served in the United States Air Force Reserve, 1963. Married Adele Chatfield-Taylor in 1981. Assistant to the manager, National Theatre, Washington, D.C., 1960; member, Barr/Wilder/Albee Playwrights Unit, New York, 1964; founding member, Eugene O'Neill Playwrights Conference, Waterford, Connecticut, 1965; playwright-in-residence, New York Shakespeare Festival, 1976–77; Adjunct Professor of Playwriting, Yale University, 1978. Council member, Dramatists Guild, 1971; Vice-President, Theatre Communications Group, 1986. Recipient: ABC-Yale University fellowship, 1966; Obie award, 1968, 1971; *Variety* award, 1969; Cannes Film Festival award, for screenplay, 1971; New York Drama Critics Circle award, 1971, 1972; Tony award, 1972, 1986; Joseph Jefferson award, 1977; Venice Film Festival Golden Lion, National Society of Film Critics award, New York Film Critics Circle award, and Los Angeles Film Critics award, all for screenplay, 1980; American Academy Award of Merit Medal, 1981; New York Institute for the Humanities fellowship, 1987. Lives in New York City. Address: c/o R. Andrew Boose, Collyer and Boose, 1 Dag Hammarskjold Plaza, New York, New York 10017-2299, U.S.A.

PUBLICATIONS

Plays

Theatre Girl (produced Washington, D.C., 1959).

The Toadstool Boy (produced Washington, D.C., 1960).

The Golden Cherub (produced New Haven, Connecticut, 1962?).

Did You Write My Name in the Snow? (produced New Haven, Connecticut, 1963).

To Wally Pantoni, We Leave a Credenza (produced New York, 1965).

The Loveliest Afternoon of the Year, and Something I'll Tell You Tuesday (produced New York, 1966; *The Loveliest Afternoon of the Year* produced London, 1972). New York, Dramatists Play Service, 1968.

Muzeeka (produced Waterford, Connecticut, 1967; New York and Edinburgh, 1968; London, 1969). Included in *Off-Broadway Plays*, London, Penguin, 1970; in *Cop-Out, Muzeeka, Home Fires*, 1971.

Cop-Out (produced Waterford, Connecticut, 1968; New York, 1969). Included in *Off-Broadway Plays*, London, Penguin, 1970; in *Cop-Out, Muzeeka, Home Fires*, 1971.

Home Fires (produced New York, 1969). Included in *Cop-Out, Muzeeka, Home Fires*, 1971.

Kissing Sweet (televised 1969). With *A Day for Surprises*, New York, Dramatists Play Service, 1971.

A Day for Surprises (produced New York, 1970; London, 1971). With *Kissing Sweet*, New York, Dramatists Play Service, 1971.

The House of Blue Leaves (produced New York, 1971). New York, Viking Press, 1972.

Two Gentlemen of Verona, with Mel Shapiro, music by Galt MacDermot, lyrics by Guare, adaptation of the play by Shakespeare (produced New York, 1971; London, 1973). New York, Holt Rinehart, 1973.

Cop-Out, Muzeeka, Home Fires. New York, Grove Press, 1971.
Taking Off (screenplay), with others. New York, New American Library, 1971.
Optimism; or, The Misadventures of Candide, with Harold Stone, based on a novel by Voltaire (produced Waterford, Connecticut, 1973).
Rich and Famous (produced Lake Forest, Illinois, 1974; New York, 1976). New York, Dramatists Play Service, 1977.
Marco Polo Sings a Solo (produced Nantucket, Massachusetts, 1976; revised version produced New York, 1977). New York, Dramatists Play Service, 1977.
Landscape of the Body (produced Lake Forest, Illinois, and New York, 1977). New York, Dramatists Play Service, 1978.
Take a Dream (produced New York, 1978).
Bosoms and Neglect (produced Chicago and New York, 1979). New York, Dramatists Play Service, 1980.
In Fireworks Lie Secret Codes (produced in *Holidays*, Louisville, 1979; also director: produced separately, New York, 1981). New York, Dramatists Play Service, 1981.
Nantucket series:
Lydie Breeze (produced New York, 1982). New York, Dramatists Play Service, 1982.
Gardenia (produced New York, 1982; London, 1983). New York, Dramatists Play Service, 1982.
Women and Water (produced Los Angeles, 1984; revised version produced Washington, D.C., 1985).
Three Exposures (includes *The House of Blue Leaves, Landscape of the Body, Bosoms and Neglect*). New York, Harcourt Brace, 1982.
Hey, Stay a While, music by Galt MacDermot, lyrics by Guare (produced Chicago, 1984).
Gluttony, in *Faustus in Hell* (produced Princeton, New Jersey, 1985).
The Talking Dog, adaptation of a story by Chekhov, in *Orchards* (produced Urbana, Illinois, 1985; New York, 1986). New York, Knopf, 1986.
The House of Blue Leaves and Two Other Plays (includes *Landscape of the Body* and *Bosoms and Neglect*). New York, New American Library, 1987.

Screenplays: *Taking Off*, with others, 1971; *Atlantic City*, 1980.

Television Play: *Kissing Sweet* (*Foul!* series), 1969.

*

Manuscript Collection: Beinecke Library, Yale University, New Haven, Connecticut.

Critical Study: article and checklist by John Harrop, in *New Theatre Quarterly 10* (Cambridge), May 1987.

Theatrical Activities:
Director: **Play**—*In Fireworks Lie Secret Codes*, New York, 1981.

* * *

John Guare has not been particularly prolific over a writing career that spans a quarter of a century, and he has received relatively little critical acclaim recently. Moreover, much of his canon, especially his early plays, is too outrageous in conception (even during the period of the Theatre of the Absurd) to be considered mainstream American drama or to achieve popular acceptance. However, Guare remains one of the most interesting, innovative, and imaginative playwrights now at work.

Guare's *The Loveliest Afternoon of the Year* and *Something I'll Tell You Tuesday* attracted attention when they ran at the off-off-Broadway Caffe Cino in New York City in 1966, and within the next five years he received both national recognition and several prestigious awards for his work. Since his early success, Guare has continued to write for the stage, but his potentiality has never been fulfilled. There are probably two main reasons for this. First, his early work was characterized by startling plot twists, and, second, when he moved away from his inventive approach to the more conventional later works, he lost the underlying, animating verve that enlivened and made his first plays unique, and he began to create dramas with a soap opera tone. In moving from the woman-eating stone lion in *A Day for Surprises* to the bomb in the elevator in *The House of Blue Leaves*, Guare simultaneously moved from fantastic images that captured the essentials of American life to the merely bizarre surface nature of his society. While the lost-dream motif is important and there are a few special signature touches in *The House of Blue Leaves*, the essence of the play is not as emotionally gripping as its forerunner. Even less moving are Guare's attempts to examine American culture in a historical context in the Nantucket series. In establishing a metaphor for the decline of American spirituality in these plays, Guare adopted the tone and dialogue of O'Neill's dramas about similar subjects, and as a result, his own particular dramatic trademarks diminished even further. Ironically, as he becomes a better writer, he becomes less unique.

Muzeeka is a short sketch, complete with Pinter-like dialogue and blackouts (compare *The Basement*) and stage devices reminiscent of those employed by Brecht and Wilder. The protagonist prepares to take over the world when his musically transmitted message impinges directly on the cortical overlay of everyone in America. Instead, he ends up on the front lines in Vietnam, hoping that in spite of all the people whom he has killed there, he will return to a life where Muzeeka will "massage my brain and convince me I didn't do anything wrong." Man's lack of contact with his world is also the subject of the short television play, *Kissing Sweet*, in which Guare attacks social ills by using television commercial clichés to produce an absurdist slice of life in which the characters are so involved with the social necessity for breath mints that they are unable to comprehend that the pollution they create is destroying them. Even more farfetched is the premise that informs *A Day for Surprises*: two librarians (presumably from the New York Public Library) discover that they love one another after the 28,000 pound stone statue of a lion moves from its stand in front of the library and devours the man's fiancée in the Ladies' Room.

The House of Blue Leaves is generally considered Guare's best and most important play. It is also the first of his more conventional endeavors. In the Foreword to the published version of the play, Guare explains his aims. Since the action of the drama includes would-be song-writer Artie's unconsummated affair with Bunny conducted in front of his wife, Bananas, as well as Bananas's mental instability and an attempt by their A.W.O.L. son to blow up the Pope (resulting in the death of two nuns and a film starlet), and assorted satirical comments on all aspects of American culture from politics to religion to the arts, such an explanation is useful. More than anything, Guare states, he is interested in how people avoid humiliation, for he thinks that "avoiding humiliation is the core of tragedy and comedy and probably of our lives." He is concerned with how people react when it becomes clear that their publicly announced dreams can never be realized. To some extent the play is autobiographical, Guare admits, and is based on the Pope's New York City visit in 1965. More importantly, though, Guare reveals the attitude that is the impulse behind much of his writing: "one night at the National Theatre I saw Laurence Olivier do [Strindberg's] *Dance of Death* and the next night ... saw him in [Feydeau's] *A Flea in Her Ear*. The savage intensity of the first blended into the maniacal intensity of the second, and somewhere in my head *Dance of Death* became the same play as *A Flea in Her Ear*. Why shouldn't Strindberg and Feydeau get married... and *The House of Blue Leaves* be their child?" It is no wonder that Guare, whose two favorite plays are *Gypsy* and *The Homecoming*, sees a dichotomy in contemporary American society and that he relies on non-conventional devices to express his insights.

Rich and Famous is an amusing albeit slight piece. Bing Ringling is a writer who is about to see his first play produced (it is the 843rd that he has written). The play is related to Guare's other works in two ways: it is about a protagonist confronting his dreams and his suffocating life; it is also about the theatre, and Guare's production notes indicate that the "show is a performance piece." In theme it looks forward; in style it looks backward.

With *Marco Polo Sings a Solo* Guare returns more forcefully to the offbeat subject matter and black humor of his pre-*The House of Blue Leaves* plays. The play is set in Spring 1999 and examines the foibles of this century. The plot involves, among other matters, an astronaut's semen being transmitted by nuclear bolts to impregnate his wife who has been kidnapped and taken to the White House; a formula for a cure for cancer; and a sex-change operation. This play, Guare explains in an Author's Note, is an extension of the theme explored in *The House of Blue Leaves*. The earlier play had been about "limits: people limited by a lack of talent, limited economically ... emotionally ... geographically," so he wanted to examine people who had everything in the world *except* limits.

The presentation of *Landscape of the Body* reflects Guare's theatricality and originality with its montage of flashbacks, fade-ins, and a cabaret-like use of songs. The violence present in Guare's other plays is prevalent here again in his exploration of the themes of alienation and human relationships.

Bosoms and Neglect contains the most passionate sub-text of all of Guare's plays. This is because it is one of the few plays in which the weight of his meaning is carried by the characterization. There are only three characters involved: Henny, who has been suffering from cancer for two years while the disease literally devours her breast; Scooper, her son, who is in psycotherapy; and Deirdre, a woman whose life is divided between reading literature and sessions with Dr. James, the never-seen psychiatrist whose services she shares with Scooper. The key to the drama is found in the characters' need to connect with another human on a more than superficial basis, and their desperate attempts to overcome the neglect that they have experienced throughout their lives as they try to make that connection. In the end, Scooper and Deirdre connect minimally and Henny, unaware, remains abandoned. Needs have been exposed, but it is unlikely that they can be met.

The pyrotechnical theatrics and cabaret turns of *Landscape of the Body* are gone; what is left is the distilled essence of what was epitomized in Betty's movement toward Holahan. The characters are conscious of their motivation—Scooper admits to Deirdre that "I just wanted to connect to you." Guare reinforces this theme even in his stage directions, as when Henny and her son "*connect hands*." The word neglect reappears constantly, too: Deirdre likes to read "neglected authors"; Henny's husband died and a suitor neglected her; Scooper was neglected as a child and he neglects his mother. The symbolism of the diseased breast, the breast that nursed Scooper, was his "first connection," and which has been neglected until it is destroyed, revolves around the parent-child relationship, yet the thematic implications are far broader and encompass the nurturing characteristics of human relationships. The strength of this drama lies in its examination of the human condition as opposed to commenting on the failings of society. Guare's distinctive brand of humor is present in *Bosoms and Neglect*, but it is not as pervasive as in his other works. At the same time, this is his best and most powerful play.

Lydie Breeze, Gardenia, and *Women and Water* metaphorically trace the disintegration of American spirituality. In a sense, they are a step backward for Guare, who uses characters here for symbolic purposes instead of exploiting characterization that focuses on the individual. The difference is what distinguishes psychology from history. *Lydie Breeze* depicts the life led by the members of a Nantucket Island commune in 1895, 20 years after a series of events that vitally affected everyone involved. The play is filled with references to those events, so the audience is aware of what happened, but there is no real understanding of why things occurred. *Gardenia*, set in the same locale but 20 years earlier, functions as a flashback for *Lydie Breeze*. During the Civil War, Lydie was a nurse in an army hospital where she cared for three wounded friends, Joshua, Dan, and Amos. The four share a dream fostered by Lydie, and create a utopian settlement, Aipotu, after the war. What develops is a tale of greed, perverted dreams, and revenge in which spouses, lovers, and sons are infected, often maliciously, with syphilis—each infected character trying to exact revenge by infecting the loved one of whoever infected them. *Women and Water* moves back in time to the original meeting of the characters in the Civil War hospital and serves to unify the three-play series by establishing the highly idealistic impulse that lies behind the quartet's decision to implement their idyllic version of Brook Farm. The overall conceptual movement is from where they are to where they came from. In the minds of the characters, the highly symbolic events referred to in *Lydie Breeze* are related to moral decay; in *Gardenia* the events are depicted, and it is obvious that while they may reflect American culture, it is also evident that what transpires derives from the base nature of the individuals themselves. Whether a commentary on a society or on human nature, these plays present a dark and bleak portrait. As in O'Neill's *Mourning Becomes Electra* and *Desire under the Elms*, hope and potential are tragically destroyed by a combination of fate and the emotional weaknesses. Guare's tone and conclusions are remarkably similar to O'Neill's. In spite of the bizarre revelations, then, *Lydie Breeze, Gardenia*, and *Women and Water* are workmanlike mainstream dramas.

The sense of the fantastic that characterizes Guare's vision of 20th-century America is epitomized in brilliant flashes of black humor matched among his contemporaries only by Kopit in the United States and Orton in England. Unfortunately, these moments are not sustained throughout Guare's canon. There are occasions in the later plays when he comes to rely more on dialogue than *coups de théâtre*, and his dialogue is accomplished and even approaches the cadences and resonances of Pinter's writing. There can be no doubt that Guare's dramas have a theatrical impact; he understands and uses the potentials of the stage, and his dramas play very well. Too many of them, however, are too short to allow the development of serious ideas beyond the level of one-liners, and even in his longer dramatic works his characterizations tend to be only moderately successful. Many of his characters are insufficiently realized to capture the audience's interest, and with few exceptions they are not fully enough drawn to permit identification—rather they seem to be cartoon caricatures. At this point in his career, Guare remains a competent playwright with a dramatic flair for unexpected plot twists that provide an evening's entertainment.

—Steven H. Gale

GURNEY, A(lbert) R(amsdell), Jr. American. Born in Buffalo, New York, 1 November 1930. Educated at St. Paul's School, Concord, New Hampshire, 1944–48; Williams College, Williamstown, Massachusetts, 1948–52, B.A. 1952; Yale University School of Drama, New Haven, Connecticut, 1955–58, M.F.A. 1958. Served in the United States Naval Reserve, 1952–55. Married Mary Goodyear in 1957; two sons and two daughters. Since 1960 member of the Faculty, and since 1970 Professor of Literature, Massachusetts Institute of Technology, Cambridge. Recipient: Drama Desk award, 1971; Rockefeller grant, 1977; National Endowment for the Arts award, 1982. D.D.L.: Williams College, 1984. Agent: Gilbert Parker, William Morris Agency, 1350 Avenue of the Americas, New York, New York 10019. Address: 74 Wellers Bridge Road, Roxbury, Connecticut 06783, U.S.A.

PUBLICATIONS

Plays

Three People, in *The Best Short Plays 1955–56*, edited by Margaret Mayorga. Boston, Beacon Press, 1956.
Turn of the Century, in *The Best Short Plays 1957–58*, edited by Margaret Mayorga. Boston, Beacon Press, 1958.
Love in Buffalo (produced New Haven, Connecticut, 1958).
The Bridal Dinner (produced Cambridge, Massachusetts, 1962).
The Comeback (produced Cambridge, Massachusetts, 1965). New York, Dramatists Play Service, 1967.
The Rape of Bunny Stuntz (produced Cambridge, Massachusetts, 1966; New York, 1967; Richmond, Surrey, 1976). London, French, 1976.
The David Show (produced Tanglewood, Massachusetts, 1966; New York, 1968). New York, French, 1968.
The Golden Fleece (produced New York, 1968; London, 1982). Published in *The Best Short Plays 1969*, edited by Stanley Richards, Philadelphia, Chilton, 1970.
The Problem (produced Boston, 1969; London, 1973; New York, 1978). New York, French, 1968; London, French, 1973.
The Open Meeting (produced Boston, 1969). New York, French, 1969.
The Love Course (produced Boston, 1970; New York, 1973; London, 1974). Published in *The Best Short Plays 1970*, edited by Stanley Richards, Philadelphia, Chilton, 1971; published separately, London, French, 1976.
Scenes from American Life (produced Tanglewood, Massachusetts, 1970; New York, 1971). Included in *Four Plays*, 1985.
The Old One-Two (produced Waltham, Massachusetts, 1973; London, 1974). New York, French, 1971; London, French, 1976.
Children, suggested by the story "Goodbye, My Brother" by John Cheever (produced London, 1974; Richmond, Virginia, and New York, 1976). London, French, 1975; included in *Four Plays*, 1985.
Who Killed Richard Cory? (produced New York, 1976). New York, Dramatists Play Service, 1976; revised version, as *Richard Cory* (produced Williamstown, Massachusetts, 1984), 1985.
The Middle Ages (produced Los Angeles, 1977; New York, 1982). Included in *Four Plays*, 1985.
The Wayside Motor Inn (produced New York, 1977). New York, Dramatists Play Service, 1978.
The Golden Age, suggested by the story "The Aspern Papers" by Henry James (produced London, 1981; New York, 1984). New York, Dramatists Play Service, 1985.
What I Did Last Summer (produced New York, 1981). New York, Dramatists Play Service, 1983.
The Dining Room (produced New York, 1982; London, 1983). London, French, 1982; included in *Four Plays*, 1985.
Four Plays. New York, Avon, 1985.
The Perfect Party (produced New York, 1986; London, 1987). New York, Dramatists Play Service, 1986.
Another Antigone (produced San Diego, 1986; New York, 1987).
Sweet Sue (produced Williamstown, Massachusetts, 1986; New York, 1987).

Screenplay: *The House of Mirth*, 1972.

Television Play: *O Youth and Beauty*, from a story by John Cheever, 1979.

Novels

The Gospel According to Joe. New York, Harper, 1974.
Entertaining Strangers. New York, Doubleday, 1977; London, Allen Lane, 1979.
The Snow Ball. New York, Arbor House, 1985.

*

Manuscript Collection: Sterling Library, Yale University, New Haven, Connecticut.

A.R. Gurney, Jr., comments:

What attracts me about the theatre are its limitations as well as its possibilities. Indeed, its best possibilities may lie in its limitations. I am as much concerned about what to leave out as about what to put in. Offstage characters and events give a kind of pressure and resonance to what is shown onstage. In fact, offstage comprises the infinite possibilities and resources of film and television. Anyone who writes plays these days is forced to explore the very restrictions of this enduring old medium. I am particularly drawn to it because I like to write about people who themselves are beginning to stretch out and push against the walls.

* * *

In recent years A.R. Gurney, Jr.'s reputation in his native America has risen sharply and his work also continues to be performed in Britain. This has been partly due to changes in the organisation of the American theatre. After Gurney's first full-length play, *Scenes from American Life*, was produced at the Forum Theatre at Lincoln Center in 1971, he had virtually nowhere else to go with his work after the Center regime changed, especially at a time when his main concern—WASP manners and mores—was out of fashion. But with a changing society that produced the Yuppie generation, Gurney's plays (especially *The Dining Room* which marked his breakthrough in the U.S.) finally found their audiences. He also formed a continuing and productive link with the Playwrights' Horizon group in New York. His work continues to expand the technical skill and that fascination with theatrical flexibility that has marked it from the outset.

Scenes from American Life is, as the title implies, a kind of montage of Americana. With a small cast including an on-stage pianist linking scenes, it uses an almost cinematic technique of dissolving and overlapping scenes to build up a series of WASP life from the 1930's to the immediate future—a christening, a debutante dance, a modern Encounter Therapy session, and so on. Its ingenious structure at points recalls Thornton Wilder, but in its concern with archetypal American rituals and family ties, not to mention the device of an offstage character (the omnipresent Snoozer), the play indicated that Gurney had his own voice.

Offstage characters dominate his one-act plays to a great extent: *The Golden Fleece* is about a suburban couple, friends of Jason and Medea, whom the audience never sees, and in the very funny *The Open Meeting* a discussion group discovers startling new relationships while awaiting the arrival of a vanished founder member. Much of their edge derives from characters who never appear; as in Greek drama, the Gods remain offstage but people are influenced by them (or, as Gurney has said "people find their gods in other people"), and Gurney often uses or adapts classical motifs. *The Love Course* and *The Old One-Two* are both sharp satires on liberal-academic attitudes, but *The Old One-Two* develops a strain of Plautine farce as a hip young college Dean discovers an unexpected relationship with his adversary, an old-fashioned professor.

Children, first produced in London during the fallow years at home for Gurney, was "suggested by" John Cheever's 1940's story "Goodbye, My Brother"; the story, like the play, takes place in a New England summer home and has a violent confrontation between two brothers, a crucial offstage event in the play. In structure the play is much tighter than *Scenes from American Life*, covering one Saturday on a July 4th weekend in the lives of a well-to-do WASP family vacationing at their Massachusetts summer home. It is a deceptively simple study of the tensions in the family caused by the eldest son, Pokey, who rules his family as an offstage presence (only one of the offstage "Gods" in the piece—the dead father is a kind of God to all the characters). In a long final speech the Mother reverses her decision to re-marry and talks to Pokey (finally visible as a shadow on the terrace on which the play passes) casting him out to preserve the family. The scene is a fitting summation to the play which subtly exposes (not least in its aptly sparse dialogue, devoid of metaphor) a culture in erosion.

Who Killed Richard Cory?, an exploration around a WASP lawyer who in middle age finds "liberation," is a more confident handling of the techniques of *Scenes from American Life*, confirming Gurney's special ability to suggest the unease under the surface of average American life. Even more confident was *The Dining Room*, a long-running New York success later produced widely in regional theatres and abroad, a sign that Gurney's world was less recondite than it had seemed when he began his career. The dining room in which the play is set represents many such rooms in different places and times from the Depression to the present; the play is both a dissection of and an elegy to a civilisation in flux, a world centred round rituals and family occasions. Using a small cast to represent a large canvas of characters—children, patriarchs, servants, and adulterous adults alike—its stagecraft is breathtakingly assured. It can move from sharply observed social comedy as a Thanksgiving lunch collapses into disarray when the grandmother slides into happy senility to a poignant late scene in which an upright dying father instructs his son in the arrangements for his funeral.

Gurney continues to be encouragingly prolific. *What I Did Last Summer* is a touching and often very funny play centred round an adolescent boy spending a wartime summer with his mother and family on the Canadian borders, befriending a dynamic eccentric woman while the family's father—another of Gurney's potent offstage presences—is away in the Pacific. Less successful was *The Golden Age*, an updated version of "The Aspern Papers," faintly reminiscent of the kind of star-vehicle play of Gurney's childhood. Despite an intriguing central situation—Henry James's Juliana transformed into Isobel Hastings Hoyt, fabled New York legend, possibly the original of Daisy in *The Great Gatsby* and possessor of Fitzgerald manuscripts—the play never quite worked either in London or New York (despite Constance Cummings and Irene Worth, respectively), mainly because of Gurney's inability to create a satisfactory character for his variation on James's investigative scholar. But he was quickly back to form with both *Another Antigone*, a full-length return to the culture-clash world of his academic background one-act plays, and *The Perfect Party*, a successful example of that rarity, an American artificial comedy of manners. Set in the house of a college professor hosting what he plans as "the perfect party" reflecting late 20th-century American life, the event to be reviewed by a critic from "a leading New York newspaper," the play spirals into Wildean comedy as the professor, to keep the beautiful critic's interest, finds himself embroiled in a plot with distinct echoes of *The Importance of Being Earnest.* His latest play, *Sweet Sue*, which uses two actresses to play different aspects of the central character, had a run on Broadway; it looks as if Gurney's wilderness years are over.

—Alan Strachan

HAILEY, Oliver. American. Born in Pampa, Texas, 7 July 1932. Educated at the University of Texas, Austin, B.F.A. 1954; Yale University School of Drama, New Haven, Connecticut (Phyllis S. Anderson Fellow, 1960, 1961), M.F.A. 1962. Served in the United States Air Force, 1954–57; Captain in the Reserve. Married Elizabeth Ann Forsythe in 1960; two daughters. Feature writer, Dallas *Morning News*, 1957–59; story editor, *McMillan and Wife* television series, 1972–74; creative consultant, *Mary Hartman, Mary Hartman* television series, 1976–77; co-producer, *Another Day* television series. Recipient: Vernon Rice award, 1963; Writers Guild award, for television writing, 1982. Agent: Shirley Bernstein, Paramuse Artists Associates, 1414 Avenue of the Americas, New York, New York 10019. Address: 11747 Canton Place, Studio City, California 91604, U.S.A.

Publications

Plays

Hey You, Light Man! (produced New Haven, Connecticut, 1962; New York, 1963; Bromley, Kent, 1971). Published

in *The Yale School of Drama Presents*, edited by John Gassner, New York, Dutton, 1964.
Child's Play: A Comedy for Orphans (produced New Haven, Connecticut, 1962).
Home by Hollywood (produced New London, Connecticut, 1964).
Animal (produced New York, 1965). Included in *Picture, Animal, Crisscross*, 1970.
Picture (produced New York, 1965). Included in *Picture, Animal, Crisscross*, 1970.
First One Asleep, Whistle (produced New York, 1966). Frankfurt, Fischer, 1967.
Who's Happy Now? (produced Los Angeles, 1967; New York, 1969). New York, Random House, 1969.
Crisscross (produced Los Angeles, 1969). Included in *Picture, Animal, Crisscross*, 1970.
Picture, Animal, Crisscross: Three Short Plays. New York, Dramatists Play Service, 1970.
Orphan (produced Los Angeles, 1970).
Continental Divide (produced Washington, D.C., 1970). New York, Dramatists Play Service, 1973.
Father's Day (produced Los Angeles, 1970; New York, 1971). New York, Dramatists Play Service, 1971; revised version (produced New York, 1979; London, 1987), 1981.
For the Use of the Hall (produced Providence, Rhode Island, 1974; New York, 1977). New York, Dramatists Play Service, 1975.
And Where She Stops Nobody Knows (produced Los Angeles, 1976).
Red Rover, Red Rover (produced Minneapolis, 1977; New York, 1983). New York, Dramatists Play Service, 1979.
And Furthermore (produced Pittsburgh, 1977).
Triptych (produced Los Angeles, 1978).
I Can't Find It Anywhere, in *Holidays* (produced Louisville, 1979).
I Won't Dance (produced Buffalo, 1980; New York, 1981). New York, French, 1982.
And Baby Makes Two (produced Los Angeles, 1981).
About Time (produced Los Angeles, 1982). Published in *A.M./P.M.*, New York, Dramatists Play Service, 1983.
Round Trip (produced Kalamazoo, Michigan, 1984).
The Father, adaptation of a play by Strindberg (produced Philadelphia, 1984). New York, Dramatists Play Service, 1984.
Kith and Kin (produced Dallas, 1986).

Screenplay: *Just You and Me, Kid*, with Leonard Stern, 1979.

Television Plays: *McMillan and Wife* series (9 episodes), 1971–74; *Sidney Shorr: A Girl's Best Friend*, 1981; *Isabel's Choice*, 1981.

*

Critical Study: *Showcase One* by John Lahr, New York, Grove Press, 1969.

Oliver Hailey comments:

(1973) My plays are primarily the attempt to take a serious theme and deal with it comedically. Though the idea for a particular play often begins as something quite serious, I try not to start writing until I have found a comic point of view for the material.

In the case of my play that is most autobiographical, *Who's Happy Now?*, it took ten years to find that comic attitude. There had been nothing particularly funny about my childhood—and yet I felt that to tell the story without a comic perspective was to put upon the stage a story too similar to many that had been seen before. With the comic perspective came the opportunity for a much fresher approach to the material—and also, strangely, it allowed me to deal with the subject on a much more serious level than I would have risked otherwise.

Because, finally, my plays are an attempt to entertain—and when they cease to entertain—no matter how "important" what I am trying to say—they fail as plays.

* * *

Despite considerable early promise Oliver Hailey has yet to achieve either critical or commercial success in the theatre. While some of his plays have been well received in university and regional playhouses, the full-length works presented in New York City all had brief runs.

Hey You, Light Man!, written and first produced at Yale University, contrasts the reality-stained world of banal domesticity with the more glamorous role-playing offered by the stage. Hailey's hero, an unhappily married actor named Ashley Knight, flees from his dreadful family to live on a stage set. There he meets a lonely young widow who has fallen asleep during a performance and is locked in the theatre. Lula Roca's husband, a stagehand, was accidentally killed by some falling equipment and her three children were all lost at a national park. One fell into a waterfall at the same time that another fell off a mountain. A third was taken by a bear. Ashley and Lula, an unlikely pair, change the direction of each other's life. Lula's experience with the illusory world of the stage permits her to develop her imaginative powers so as to face the future with new hope. Ashley, on the other hand, for whom reality could only be dreary, sees in Lula new possibilities in life off the stage and is able to make a final escape from his domestic prison. Much of the play's humor and charm stems from Lula's endearing innocence, but Hailey's somewhat redundant elaboration of his illusion vs. reality theme weakens the play. A number of oddball characters appear, but the playwright's straining for an eccentric originality is apparent. At times, however, his dialogue achieves the intended poetic effect, and his tender concern for his odd couple results in some touching moments.

First One Asleep, Whistle, which had only one performance on Broadway, reflects some of the same concerns as *Hey You, Light Man!* but lacks its offbeat charm. The milieu is again theatrical, the heroine an actress in television commercials. She has a daughter by a man not her husband and during the course of the play has an affair with a married man. This time her lover is an emotionally immature actor who is separated from his wife. As in *Light Man* the lovers eventually part, the actor returning to his wife, unaware that his mistress is pregnant. Elaine, the actress, has somehow been strengthened by this latest affair and remains confident that she will survive without a man. The ill-fated romance is complicated by the presence of Elaine's seven-year-old daughter whose innocent responses to her mother's unconventional life are the principal sources of the play's occasional humor. While Hailey avoids a sentimental "happy" ending, his characters are never very interesting and the play remains at the level of semi-sophisticated soap opera.

Who's Happy Now? also deals with domestic difficulties, but the setting is far removed from the urbane New York scene. The play takes place in Texas during the years 1941–55 and focuses on the confused reactions of a young man to the bizzare relationship between his parents. His father, a strong-willed and crude butcher, has managed to keep both his wife and mistress happy, despite the efforts of his son to alter the situation. The mistress, a waitress named Faye Precious, has lost her husband as a result of a freak accident and respects her butcher/lover (aptly named Horse) despite his continuing affection for his wife. The hero is an aspiring songwriter, his ambition inspiring disgust in Horse, and the play is a kind of comic variation of the Oedipal struggle. *Who's Happy Now?* contains some diverting musical numbers, but the mixture of irony and sentiment results in a confused tone. The frame of the play involves the hero attempting to explain to his mother, through the medium of drama, what he really felt about his parents. Such a device seems intended to point out the disparity between actual experience and its painful, often inaccurate, recreation on stage, a theme Hailey deals with elsewhere. There are other theatrical techniques that serve to distance the audience from potentially mawkish material, but the effects, while at times inventive, ultimately manage to make a play too diffuse in impact. Despite Hailey's genuine ironic gifts, his play suffers from the lack of a firm larger design.

Continental Divide is closer to pure farce as it contrasts a wealthy couple from Long Island with the down-at-heel parents of their future son-in-law. The latter couple are visitors from their native Arkansas and the juxtaposition of rich and poor in mined of its limited potential for original insight and humor. Mr. John, the father of the groom, had killed his first wife and during the course of the play manages to wound his host twice. There are other farcical events, and whatever satiric thrusts intended by the playwright are subordinated to the broad comic effects.

Hailey's best play, *Father's Day*, despite some highly favorable reviews, ran for only one performance on Broadway. It marked a return to the urbane New York scene, and the dialogue has a pungency and bite. The characters are three divorced couples briefly reunited on Father's Day. The play focuses primarily on the complex feelings of the women, as it uncovers their ambivalent desires for both independence and security. The comic tone on the surface barely conceals the pathos of their situation, and the play has a toughminded quality normally absent in a conventional sex comedy. The characters, especially the women, are sharply drawn and while *Father's Day* at times suffers from an overly eager attempt to be topical, the playwright's verbal energy is sufficient to sustain the work. Hailey demonstrates his usual compassion and refusal to impose standard moral judgments. Here he has avoided his tendency to employ striking, if redundant or irrelevant, theatrical effects. At the close of the play, there is a reference to Chekhov's *The Three Sisters* suggesting that Hailey saw a parallel to is unhappy trio in the Russian classic. While *Father's Day* lacks the depth and resonance of Chekhov's work, its tenderness and its willingness to understand the bitterness and frustration of unfulfilled lives make the parallel not altogether inapt.

In addition to his full-length plays, Hailey has written several shorter works. *Picture*, a labored one-act play or "demonstration" is similar to *Who's Happy Now?* in its concern with the problems in recreating the past through the medium of drama. *Crisscross* is a strained sketch in which Santa Claus is crucified by his father, a carpenter resentful of his son's desire for independence. *Animal* is a brief, but effective, monologue by a mother desperately struggling to impose her will on her rebellious daughter.

It is perhaps too early to make any definitive judgment on Hailey's playwriting career. What does seem evident at this point is that he has failed in his efforts at employing conventional commercial formulas to sustain an often original point of view. Despite his refusal to provide emotionally satisfying conclusions to his plays, his dramas seem too designed to please, too eager to be charming and clever. His major themes appear rooted in the dislocations of family life and while he is often adept in revealing the sadness beneath the laugh, the shifting tone of his plays results in uncertain dramatic effects. The characters are ultimately "liberated," although their freedom contains no guarantee of happiness or security. Hailey's fondness for obvious comic devices prevents the emergence of the genuine artist he at times reveals himself to be.

—Leonard Fleischer

HAIRE, Wilson John. British. Born in Belfast, Northern Ireland, 6 April 1932. Educated at Clontonacally Elementary School, Carryduff, County Down, 1939–46. Married 1) Rita Lenson in 1955 (marriage dissolved) five children; 2) Sheila Fitz-Jones in 1974 (marriage dissolved); 3) Karen Mendelsohn in 1979 (marriage dissolved). Actor, Unity Theatre, London, 1962–67; co-director, Camden Group Theatre, London, 1967–71; resident dramatist, Royal Court Theatre, London, 1974, and Lyric Theatre, Belfast, 1976. Recipient: George Devine Award, 1972; *Evening Standard* award, 1973; Thames Television award, 1974; Leverhulme fellowship, 1976. Address: 61 Lulot Gardens, London N19 5TS, England.

Publications

Plays

The Clockin' Hen (produced London, 1968).

The Diamond, Bone and Hammer; and Along the Sloughs of Ulster (produced London, 1969).

Within Two Shadows (produced London, 1972; New York, 1974). Published in *Scripts 9* (New York), September 1972; published separately, London, Davis Poynter, 1973.

Bloom of the Diamond Stone (produced Dublin, 1973). London, Pluto Press, 1979.

Echoes from a Concrete Canyon (produced London, 1975).

Lost Worlds: Newsflash, Wedding Breakfast, Roost (produced London, 1978). London, Heinemann, 1978.

Worlds Apart, with J.P. Dylan (produced Glasgow, 1981).

Television Plays: *Letter from a Soldier*, 1975; *The Dandelion Clock*, 1975.

*

Wilson John Haire comments:

I first began writing about Northern Ireland back in 1960. I wrote three short stories for a monthly paper called the *Irish Democrat*. My first story was called "Refuge from the Tick-Man" and I went under the pen name of "Fenian." "Fenian" is a derogatory name for Catholic in Northern Ireland. When I began writing the story of how my family fled the city of Belfast for the countryside to escape the debt collectors I became proud of that name. To me it meant someone who resists corruption and sectarian bullying. The editor of the paper persuaded me to use my real name for my second story

"The Screening"—a teenage boy, pretending to be a Protestant, survives interrogation and taunts about Catholicism and gets the job for which he is applying. The third story was "The Beg." "Beg" is bag or sack in Ulster dialect. The local shipyard sheds a quarter of its workers, and the story is told through the eyes of an apprentice carpenter.

I took to writing drama in 1968 with a one-act play *The Clockin' Hen*. A broody hen hatches out her eggs under a darkening sky—in 1968 the Reverend Paisley attempts to lead a demonstration, with protection, through a Catholic ghetto and is resisted. A Catholic and Protestant are put on trial. The Catholic sees no hope of justice in a court that openly loathes him.

After that I wrote *The Diamond, Bone and Hammer, and Along the Sloughs of Ulster.* It is a sort of "Fear and Misery in the Third Reich." This play sequence was produced at the Hampstead Theatre, and later transfered to the Unity Theatre. This was not a professional production, and no reviewer appeared except for D.A.N. Jones of the *Listener*, who gave it an intelligent review. It was this one and only review that made me want to go on writing.

On opening night, Friday, 8 August 1969, the Bogside riots began, and Ulster became a topic of conversation in London. On 12 April 1972 *Within Two Shadows* opened at the Royal Court Theatre. The media said it was the first play on the Ulster crisis to open in London. I come from a parentage of both Catholic and Protestant. I saw this as the "two shadows" in my life, and I told the tale from within the family.

Though I have not had a London production of my work recently it still continues to be alive and well within the colleges and universities in the English-speaking world. At the moment I am hoping to write some drama for radio. I have a love for language and I am hoping that radio will give me the facilities that the old Royal Court Theatre once gave.

*   *   *

Wilson John Haire, born in the Shankill Road, Belfast, the son of a Catholic mother and a Protestant father, has drawn much of the background material for his plays from that stark area of the tortured city. Even when the actual turmoil of Northern Ireland is not part of a play, as in *Echoes from a Concrete Canyon*, we can still feel the claustrophobic atmosphere of an unfriendly town beyond the walls of a lonely flat. Four of Haire's plays, however, are set against the background of sectarian violence, bigotry, and loneliness. He conveys the tragedy of Ulster more directly and vividly than any other contemporary playwright, drawing upon memories which reach far back into his childhood.

Haire is not a polemical writer. Political ideas interest him, particularly as part of the environments from which they come, but he is concerned more with the nature and extent of Ulster's suffering than with easy moralising. His best known play, *Within Two Shadows*, is also the most autobiographical. It deals with a working-class Belfast family, dog-eared with poverty, and torn apart by prejudices which they try to exclude but which gradually eat into their lives. In the play the mother is a Protestant, the father a Catholic, and we feel that both, at some time in their lives, have made conscientious efforts to leap over the religious barriers which divide them. But the pressure of events, the opinions of their neighbours, and the growing violence are too much for them. They try to stay away from conflict, if only to protect their children; but the children are growing up, now teenagers, and quick to enter into the rivalries, as part of their puppy-play but with fangs bared.

In *Bloom of the Diamond Stone* Haire shows what could almost have been the beginnings of that marriage, a Romeo and Juliet love affair, where the young couple from opposite sides fall in love and then have to battle against their families, the restrictions set at work, and the rigid outlooks of their former friends. In both plays Haire conveys a sense of inner honesty and goodness corrupted by circumstance. In that way, he can be an optimistic writer. His characters are not vicious in themselves, only made so by a historical backlog of revenge, fear, and defensiveness. To that extent, Ulster's torment seems the result of a curable mixture of follies, rather than the dark nightmare of the soul as other dramatists, including David Rudkin, have sometimes presented it. The British soldier searching for a "terrorist" in *Bloom of the Diamond Stone* is shown to be a likeable human being, until his fears and his job prompt him to be otherwise.

But the follies extend in all directions. They are sometimes rooted in sheer lack of understanding of the awfulness of the situation. In his first television play, *Letter from a Soldier*, Haire merely describes a soldier's effort to make his family in England understand what a tour of duty in Ulster is like. His second, *The Dandelion Clock*, concerns the particular problems facing a young girl growing up in Belfast. What sort of future can she plan for herself? The problems, however, are not just ones of comprehension. They also stem from the social organisation which is out of touch with the lives people lead.

The Clockin' Hen, Haire's first stage play, concerns a court case in which two shipyard workers of different religions are put on trial, following a Paisleyite demonstration in 1966. How do they react to the presence of the Law? Do they regard Law in any meaningful sense? And if they do not, where does an Ulsterman go? "Emotionally," Haire has said, "I am a Catholic, but intellectually I am a Protestant." This conflict is reflected in his plays. Haire perceives the need for a formal social order, but is ympathetic to the resentments caused by the existing one. To be out of touch with society, to defy, ignore, or simply have an engrained distrust of the ordering forces which are there, is equivalent to "dropping out." Haire's sympathy with Irish drop-outs, tramps, and drunkards is shown in *The Latchicoes of Fort Camden*, an unperformed play set in a London dosshouse.

Haire's skill as a dramatist reveals the strength and weaknesses of someone who chooses subjects so close to his personal experience. He can write vigorously and directly, usually naturalistically, but without the detachment needed to ensure that his plays have a clear form and that each point is made dramatically and concisely. He has indicated an intention to break away from his concentration on Northern Ireland; but in *Echoes from a Concrete Canyon*, which concerns the mental breakdown of a woman living with her daughter in a block of flats and estranged from her husband, the clotted verbosity which often accompanies autobiography is still present. Lightening touches of humour are rare; and the frequent poeticisms add heaviness rather than variety to the language. Haire in time may gain maturity as a dramatist by becoming less dependent on his background, but he may lose the force of reality which adds power to his Ulster plays. He speaks as a witness and a survivor of a continuing drama of stupidity, cruelty, and resentment. That, so far, has been his main role, and not an insignificant one, in contemporary British theatre.

—John Elsom

HALE, John. British. Born in Woolwich, Kent, 5 February 1926. Educated at army schools in Egypt, Ceylon, and Malta; Borden Grammar School, Sittingbourne, Kent; Royal Naval College, Greenwich. Served in the Fleet Air Arm, 1941–51: boy apprentice to petty officer, later commissioned. Married Valerie June Bryan in 1950; one son and one daughter. Stage hand, stage manager, and electrician, in variety, touring, and repertory companies, 1952–55; founder, and artistic director, Lincoln Theatre, 1955–58; artistic director, Arts Theatre, Ipswich, 1958–59 and Bristol Old Vic, 1959–61; free-lance director, 1961–64; member of the Board of Governors, 1963–71, associate artistic director, 1968–71, and resident playwright, 1975–76, Greenwich Theatre, London. Since 1964 free-lance writer and director. Agent: Harvey Unna and Stephen Durbridge, Ltd., 24–32 Pottery Lane, London W11 4LZ, England.

PUBLICATIONS

Plays

The Black Swan Winter (as *Smile Boys, That's the Style*, produced Glasgow, 1968; as *The Black Swan Winter*, also director: produced London, 1969). Published in *Plays of the Year 37*, London, Elek, 1970.
It's All in the Mind (also director: produced London, 1968).
Spithead (also director: produced London, 1969). Published in *Plays of the Year 38*, London, Elek, 1971.
Here Is the News (produced Beaford, Devon, 1970).
Lorna and Ted (also director: produced London, 1970).
Decibels (produced Liverpool, 1971). Published in *Prompt Three*, edited by Alan Durband, London, Hutchinson, 1976.
The Lion's Cub (televised 1971). Published in *Elizabeth R*, edited by J.C. Trewin, London, Elek, 1971.
In Memory of . . . Carmen Miranda (also director: produced London, 1975).
Love's Old Sweet Song (also director: produced London, 1976).
The Case of David Anderson, Q.C. (produced Manchester, 1980; London, 1981).

Screenplays: *The Mind of Mr. Soames*, with Edward Simpson, 1969; *Anne of the Thousand Days*, with Bridget Boland, 1970; *Mary Queen of Scots*, 1972.

Radio Writing: *Micah Clarke* series, 1966.

Television Plays: *The Rules That Jack Made*, 1965; *The Noise Stopped*, 1966; *Light the Blue Touch Paper*, 1966; *Thirteen Against Fate* series, 1966; *Samson and Delilah, Strike Pay*, and *Her Turn*, all from short stories by D.H. Lawrence, 1966–67; *The Queen's Traitor* (5 parts), 1967; *Retreat*, 1968; *The Picnic*, 1969; *The Distracted Preacher*, 1969; *The Lion's Cub*, 1971; *The Bristol Entertainment*, 1971; *Anywhere But England*, 1972; *Ego Hugo: A Romantic Entertainment*, 1973; *The Brotherhood*, 1975; *An Impeccable Elopement*, 1975; *Goodbye America*, 1976; *The Grudge Fight*, from his own novel, 1981.

Novels

Kissed the Girls and Made Them Cry. London, Collins, 1963; Englewood Cliffs, New Jersey, Prentice Hall, 1966.
The Grudge Fight. London, Collins, 1964; Englewood Cliffs, New Jersey, Prentice Hall, 1967.
A Fool at the Feast. London, Collins, 1966.
The Paradise Man. London, Rapp and Whiting, and Indianapolis, Bobbs Merrill, 1969.
Mary, Queen of Scots (novelization of screenplay). London, Pan, 1972.
The Fort. London, Quartet, 1973.
The Love School. London, Pan, 1974; New York, St. Martin's Press, 1975.
Lovers and Heretics. London, Gollancz, 1976.
The Whistle Blower. London, Cape, 1984; New York, Atheneum, 1985.

*

Theatrical Activities:
Director: **Plays**—about 150 plays in Lincoln, Ipswich, Bristol and elsewhere, including several of his own plays, and *An Enemy of the People* by Arthur Miller, Lincoln, 1958; *Cyrano de Bergerac* by Edmond Rostand, Bristol, 1959; *The Merry Wives of Windsor*, London, 1959; *The Tinker* by Laurence Dobie and Robert Sloman, Bristol and London, 1960; *The Rehearsal* by Anouilh, Bristol and London, 1961; *The Killer* by Ionesco, Bristol, 1961; *Sappho* by Lawrence Durrell, Edinburgh, 1961; *Mother Courage* by Brecht, Hiram, Ohio, 1966. **Television**—about 16 plays, 1961–64, including *The Fruit at the Bottom of the Bowl* by Ray Bradbury, and *Drill Pig* by Charles Wood; *The Rules That Jack Made*, 1965. **Recordings**—13 Shakespeare plays, including *The Taming of the Shrew, Richard II* and *Henry V*, FCM Productions.

John Hale comments:

Until I was asked to write this introduction I had not considered what, if anything, my plays have in common.

Once, in the first flush of being published, I was incautious enough to write earnestly about my motives and aims as a writer. It is painful even at this distance to read that piece. So having considered the plays and come to some conclusions I shall keep them to myself and try to avoid repeating the error of that first article.

I am both a playwright and a novelist. The plays and novels are written alternately when I can afford the luxury of the time. I buy the time with television plays and film scripts. If I have anything to say only part of it is in the plays: all of it, whatever it is, is in the plays and the novels taken together.

* * *

As a playwright, John Hale seems to share what is a common quality of actors, the ability to take up a theme, immerse himself in it, work it out, and leave it: recognizably the same actor is performing, if your concern is to look for him, yet the characters are different creations. Where other writers may work through and within an obsession, in some cases (Strindberg and Tennessee Williams) becoming trapped by it, so that their plays are like a series of studies of some vast central object too large to be contained in any one play, Hale seems to make a fresh start in each case, as if he were to say, "Here is my subject. I give myself to it. I use *this* particular piece of my own experience for it. I build it from inside, and shape it from the outside. I have made a play. I move on."

The Black Swan Winter, Hale's first stage play, was written after his own father's death, and uses memories of his father and himself. In a later play, *Love's Old Sweet Song*, Hale and his father appear again, and his grandfather also, but as supporting characters in what seems to be primarily an appalled examination of two castrating women, mother and daughter jointly devoted to the destruction of all the men around them. His novel *The Grudge Fight* used his experience of the navy, and when he wanted to return to the subject in *Spithead* he used instead the secondary experience of history. *It's All in the Mind* is his only excursion into politics, *Lorna and Ted* the only one into Suffolk, and his one-act monologue *In Memory of . . . Carmen Miranda* the only one into Samuel Beckett country, which is just as well since he seems not to be happy there.

Yet there is a moral being, Hale himself, who made all this work, even though he is modest as well as moral, and requires one to search for him. *Kissed the Girls and Made Them Cry, The Black Swan Winter*, and *Love's Old Sweet Song* all share a theme, the attempt to get back into one's past and find out what went wrong. The shadow of his father, a warrant officer in the Regular Army, lies upon his work and is shown in Hale's concern for fairness and his admiration of discipline, most of all self-discipline: if Forster can be boiled down to "Only connect," then John Hale's two words are "Soldier on." Fairness for him means most of all fairness to other people, a decent recognition of the right to difference, but it can also mean (*Lorna and Ted*) fairness to oneself, an assertion of one's own rights, and an acceptance of responsibility.

Hale's plays are well-made in the manner, nowadays common, of a television play (or a play by Shakespeare), with a number of scenes running into each other, and a fragmented set. They are thoughtful, observed, humane, and only rarely self-indulgent. Their fault (commonly found in company with these virtues) is an occasional over-explicitness: Hale's characters, like Priestley's, too often say what they should only mean, though this is not a fault of *Lorna and Ted*, which is his most interesting play so far. He seems always to have been happiest when writing duologues (too many characters at once appear to worry him), and in this two-hander, with only a non-speaking voluptuous lady in support, his construction has been most at ease, most relaxed, least stiff.

—John Bowen

HALL, Roger (Leighton). New Zealander. Born in England, 17 January 1939. Educated at University College School, London, 1952–55; Victoria University, Wellington, 1963–68, M.A. (honours). Married Mavis Dianne Sturm in 1968; one daughter and one son. Worked in insurance, as a wine waiter, in factories, and as a teacher before becoming a free-lance writer and editor. Teaching fellow, University of Otago, Dunedin, 1979–86; guest artist, New Mexico State University, Las Cruces, 1983. Recipient: Arts Council of New Zealand travel grant, 1975; Robert Burns fellowship, University of Otago, 1977, 1978. Agent: Douglas Rae Management, 28 Charing Cross Road, London WC2H 0DB, England; or, Playmarket, P.O. Box 9767, Wellington, New Zealand.

PUBLICATIONS

Plays

Glide Time (produced Wellington, 1976; as *Roll On, Friday*, produced Southampton, England, 1985). Wellington, Victoria University Press, 1978.

Middle-Age Spread (produced Wellington, 1977; London, 1979). Wellington, Victoria University Press, 1978; London, French, 1980.

State of the Play (produced Wellington, 1978). Wellington, Victoria University Press, 1979.

Cinderella (produced Auckland, 1978).

Robin Hood (produced Auckland, 1979).

Prisoners of Mother England (produced Dunedin, 1979). Wellington, Playmarket, 1980.

Captain Scrimshaw in Space (for children). Adelaide, Rigby, 1979; London, Arnold, 1981.

How the Crab Got a Hard Back (for children), adaptation of a West Indian folktale. Adelaide, Rigby, 1979; London, Arnold, 1981.

Fifty-Fifty (produced Auckland, 1981). Wellington, Victoria University Press, 1982.

The Rose (produced Auckland, 1981).

The Quiz (broadcast 1982; produced Dunedin, 1983). Published in *On Stage 1*, edited by David Dowling, Auckland, Longman Paul, 1983.

Hot Water (produced Auckland, 1982). Wellington, Victoria University Press, 1983.

Footrot Flats, music by Philip Norman, lyrics by A.K. Grant, based on works by Murray Ball (produced Christchurch, 1983). Wellington, Playmarket, 1984.

Multiple Choice (produced Las Cruces, New Mexico, 1983; Guildford, Surrey, 1984).

Dream of Sussex Downs (produced Auckland, 1986).

Love Off the Shelf, music by Philip Norman, lyrics by A.K. Grant (produced Dunedin, 1986).

The Hansard Show, songs by Nigel Eastgate and John Drummond (produced Wellington, 1986).

Radio Plays: *Gliding On* series, 1977–80; *Hark, Hark, The Harp!*, 1981; *Last Summer*, 1981; *The Quiz*, 1982.

Television Plays: *Clean Up*, 1972; *The Bach*, 1974; *Some People Get All the Luck*, 1974; *The Reward*, 1974; *Gliding On* series, 1982–86; and series episodes for *In View of the Circumstances*, 1970–71, *Pukemanu*, 1972, and *Buck House*, 1974.

*

Manuscript Collections: Alexander Turnbull Library, Wellington; Hocken Library, University of Otago, Dunedin.

* * *

Before his first major stage successes in 1976–77, Roger Hall had extensive experience in scripting satirical revues for television and stage, and techniques evident in this early work recur throughout most of his full-length plays. The professionalism with which Hall manipulates and qualifies his audience's comic response is remarkable, and his best known trait is the resonant one-liner. However, the main critical interest in his development lies in the structuring of comic incidentals into an organic and often cogent piece of satirical realism.

The title of *Glide Time* refers to a system of flexible working hours available to some New Zealand public servants, and much of the action involves a group of bureaucratic menials preserving a modicum of dignity and ambition by trivial gestures of anarchy and independence. The world of the office, where the whole play is set, is drawn with considerable detail; almost all audiences have close knowledge of this world, and so the satirical target is easily accessible and eminently violable. It is through characterisation, however, that Hall achieves a texture that is much more complex than his early satire, with the anxieties of several characters generating a poignancy that lasts beyond the somewhat contrived resolution.

Middle-Age Spread revolves around a dinner party hosted by a placidly normal schoolteacher who has recently retreated from the only infidelity of his life; both wife and mistress are at the party, and the affair is dramatised through intermittent flashbacks. The main energy source for the immediate action is a sourly perverse teachers' college lecturer, a constant irritant whose final gesture of revealing the facts of the affair ends the play. Again, a poignancy remains. Several of the characters have been emotionally brutalised, and the adult devastation is paralleled by an adolescent pregnancy, though the children neither appear on stage nor contribute significantly to the action. The reverberations in the younger generation thus have an air of melodramatic contrivance, and there is some disparity in the depth of characterisation among the adults; the hostess in particular verges on a caricatured domestic tyrant whose insensitivity, it is implied, has precipitated the affair.

The success of Hall's first two full-length plays was enormous. Both had numerous professional productions and revivals, *Glide Time* was developed into a number of radio and television series, and *Middle-Age Spread* had a long London run as well as being made into a feature film. Inevitably, this success to an extent eclipsed Hall's next few plays, but there also seems to be a drain on his energy evident in *State of the Play*, an attempt at a more serious mode, in which a once-successful dramatist conducts a weekend seminar with amateur playwrights. The situation accidentally precipitates various exercises in self-discovery, but it remains something of a cliché and none of the characters has the vitality that audiences expected after the earlier plays. *Prisoners of Mother England*, on the other hand, develops a secondary theme from *Glide Time* (migration) into an unpretentious but technically audacious piece of satirical comedy in which eight English migrants are followed through a decade of attempted adjustment to New Zealand life. Many of the 59 scenes echo revue technique, but this splintering effect relates well to the central theme of cultural fragmentation.

Fifty-Fifty has one domestic set (in London), and seems tailored to West End norms. The central character is an unassertive middle-aged failure abandoning his bachelor flat in the face of divorce. The slight plot is economically scripted, and there is an effective balance of interest among the characters, but the imprecision of the play's social location means that it lacks any possibility of a satirical edge. By contrast, the 50-minute *The Rose* mobilises the full panoply of satirical aggression against the political and social face of New Zealand, specifically in the context of the 1981 Springbok rugby tour. The style is unsubtle, caricature is used extensively, and the theatrical impact was very much occasional; the script defies critical assessment, but it is important evidence of Hall's serious side.

Hall's subsequent work has varied considerably but has not included another major success except for *Footrot Flats*, a stage musical developed from a popular New Zealand cartoon strip (Hall did not script the film of the same title). *Hot Water* is unadulterated farce which incidentally pinpoints various farcical mannerisms which infiltrated earlier plays. An American, a Maori, a Scotsman, an Englishwoman, and a few New Zealanders converge on a Taupo holiday home; the whole action is in the over-populated living room (with no less than six doors), and revolves around a businessman's quest to bag a trout, a deer, a swordfish and a woman within 24 hours. The situational farce is crude and untidily resolved, and the matriarch seems very close to the hostess of *Middle-Age Spread*. *Multiple Choice* veers back to the more serious, with its theme of individuality in education. With many short scenes and a minimal functional set, it also accommodates a good deal of comedy and touches of farce which temper its tendency towards the thesis play. Derived from Chekhov's *Three Sisters*, *Dream of Sussex Downs* is a realistic and sometimes sombre study of English expatriates in Wellington in the 1950's. Inevitably, there are echoes of *Prisoners of Mother England*, but the atmosphere of retrenchment is much more sustained and claustrophobic. Acknowledgement of a source in Chekhov can, however, only work to such a play's disadvantage, and the characterisation often seems trite.

The *Footrot Flats* collaboration with Norman and Grant was repeated in *Love Off the Shelf*, ostensibly a play about a literary researcher writing True Love romances to finance serious research, but essentially a musical parody of the popular genre. It is a slight work. More propitious is *The Hansard Show*, another musical, but ingeniously derived from New Zealand's parliamentary archives, filtering many aspects of the country's emergent national identity through the lenses of politics. The images range from the grotesque to the compassionate, providing a rich field for satire and irony, and perhaps substantiating Hall's insistence that he is at heart a serious playwright.

—Howard McNaughton

HALL, Willis. British. Born in Leeds, Yorkshire, 6 April 1929. Educated at Cockburn High School, Leeds. National Service 1947–52: radio playwright for the Chinese Schools Department of Radio Malaya. Married 1) the actress Jill Bennett in 1962 (marriage dissolved 1965); 2) Dorothy Kingsmill-Lunn (marriage dissolved); 3) Valerie Shute in 1973; four sons. Lives in Oakworth, West Yorkshire. Recipient: *Evening Standard* award, 1959. Agent: London Management, 235 Regent Street, London W1A 2JT, England.

Publications

Plays

Final at Furnell (broadcast 1954). London, Evans, 1956.

Poet and Pheasant, with Lewis Jones (broadcast 1955; produced Watford, Hertfordshire, 1958). London, Deane, and Boston, Baker, 1959.

The Gentle Knight (broadcast 1957; produced London, 1964). London, Blackie, 1966.

The Play of the Royal Astrologers (produced Birmingham, 1958; London, 1968). London, Heinemann, 1960.

Air Mail from Cyprus (televised 1958). Published in *The Television Playwright: Ten Plays for BBC Television*, edited by Michael Barry, London, Joseph, and New York, Hill and Wang, 1960.

The Long and the Short and the Tall (produced Edinburgh, 1958; London, 1959; New York, 1962). London, Heinemann, 1959; New York, Theatre Arts, 1961.

A Glimpse of the Sea, and Last Day in Dreamland (produced London, 1959). Included in *A Glimpse of the Sea: Three Short Plays*, 1961.

Return to the Sea (televised 1960; produced London, 1980). Included in *A Glimpse of the Sea: Three Short Plays*, 1961.

Billy Liar, with Keith Waterhouse, adaptation of the novel by Waterhouse (produced London, 1960; Los Angeles and New York, 1963). London, Joseph, 1960; New York, Norton, 1961.

Chin-Chin, adaptation of the play by François Billetdoux (produced London, 1960).

A Glimpse of the Sea: Three Short Plays. London, Evans, 1961.

Celebration: The Wedding and The Funeral, with Keith Waterhouse (produced Nottingham and London, 1961). London, Joseph, 1961.

Azouk, with Robin Maugham, adaptation of a play by Alexandre Rivemale (produced Newcastle upon Tyne, 1962).

England, Our England, with Keith Waterhouse, music by Dudley Moore (produced London, 1962). London, Evans, 1964.

Squat Betty, with Keith Waterhouse (produced London, 1962; New York, 1964). With *The Sponge Room*, London, Evans, 1963.

The Sponge Room, with Keith Waterhouse (produced Nottingham and London, 1962; New York, 1964). With *Squat Betty*, London, Evans, 1963; in *Modern Short Plays from Broadway and London*, edited by Stanley Richards, New York, Random House, 1969.

All Things Bright and Beautiful, with Keith Waterhouse (produced Bristol and London, 1962). London, Joseph, 1963.

Yer What? (revue), with others, music by Lance Mulcahy (produced Nottingham, 1962).

The Days Beginning: An Easter Play. London, Heinemann, 1964.

The Love Game, adaptation of a play by Marcel Achard, translated by Tamara Lo (produced London, 1964).

Come Laughing Home, with Keith Waterhouse (as *They Called the Bastard Stephen*, produced Bristol, 1964; as *Come Laughing Home*, produced Wimbledon, 1965). London, Evans, 1965.

Say Who You Are, with Keith Waterhouse (produced Guildford, Surrey, and London, 1965). London, Evans, 1966; as *Help Stamp Out Marriage* (produced New York, 1966), New York, French, 1966.

Joey, Joey, with Keith Waterhouse, music by Ron Moody (produced Manchester and London, 1966).

Whoops-a-Daisy, with Keith Waterhouse (produced Nottingham, 1968). London, French, 1978.

Children's Day, with Keith Waterhouse (produced Edinburgh and London, 1969). London, French, 1975.

Who's Who, with Keith Waterhouse (produced Coventry, 1971; London, 1973). London, French, 1974.

The Railwayman's New Clothes (televised 1971). London, French, 1974.

They Don't All Open Men's Boutiques (televised 1972). Published in *Prompt Three*, edited by Alan Durband, London, Hutchinson, 1976.

Saturday, Sunday, Monday, with Keith Waterhouse, adaptation of a play by Eduardo De Filippo (produced London, 1973; New York, 1974). London, Heinemann, 1974.

The Card, with Keith Waterhouse, music and lyrics by Tony Hatch and Jackie Trent, adaptation of the novel by Arnold Bennett (produced Bristol and London, 1973).

Walk On, Walk On (produced Liverpool, 1975). London, French, 1976.

Kidnapped at Christmas (for children; produced London, 1975). London, French-Heinemann, 1975.

Stag-Night (produced London, 1976).

Christmas Crackers (for children; produced London, 1976). London, French-Heinemann, 1976.

Filumena, with Keith Waterhouse, adaptation of a play by Eduardo De Filippo (produced London, 1977; New York, 1980). London, Heinemann, 1978.

A Right Christmas Caper (for children; produced London, 1977). London, French-Heinemann, 1978.

Worzel Gummidge (for children), with Keith Waterhouse, music by Denis King, adaptation of stories by Barbara Euphan Todd (produced Birmingham, 1980; London, 1981). London, French, 1984.

The Wind in the Willows, music by Denis King, adaptation of the story by Kenneth Grahame (produced Plymouth, 1984; London, 1985).

Treasure Island, music by Denis King, adaptation of the novel by Robert Louis Stevenson (produced Birmingham, 1984).

Lost Empires, with Keith Waterhouse, music by Denis King, adaptation of the novel by J.B. Priestley (produced Darlington, County Durham, 1985).

The Water Babies, adaptation of the novel by Charles Kingsley (produced Oxford, 1987).

Screenplays: *The Long and the Short and the Tall* (*Jungle Fighters*), with Wolf Mankowitz, 1961; with Keith Waterhouse—*Whistle Down the Wind*, 1961; *The Valiant*, 1962; *A Kind of Loving*, 1963; *Billy Liar*, 1963; *West Eleven*, 1963; *Man in the Middle*, 1963; *Pretty Polly* (*A Matter of Innocence*), 1967; *Lock Up Your Daughters*, 1969.

Radio Plays: *Final at Furnell*, 1954; *The Nightingale*, 1954; *Furore at Furnell*, 1955; *Frenzy at Furnell*, 1955; *Friendly at Furnell*, 1955; *Fluster at Furnell*, 1955; *Poet and Pheasant*, with Lewis Jones, 1955; *One Man Absent*, 1955; *A Run for the Money*, 1956; *Afternoon for Antigone*, 1956; *The Long Years*, 1956; *Any Dark Morning*, 1956; *Feodor's Bride*, 1956; *One Man Returns*, 1956; *A Ride on the Donkeys*, 1957; *The Calverdon Road Job*, 1957; *The Gentle Knight*, 1957; *Harvest the Sea*, 1957; *Monday at Seven*, 1957; *Annual Outing*, 1958; *The Larford Lad*, 1958; *The Case of Walter Grimshaw*, with Leslie Halward, 1958.

Television Plays: *Air Mail from Cyprus*, 1958; *Return to the Sea*, 1960; *On the Night of the Murder*, 1962; *The Ticket*, 1969; *The Railwayman's New Clothes*, 1971; *The Villa Maroc*, 1972; *They Don't All Open Men's Boutiques*, 1972; *Song at Twilight*, 1973; *Friendly Encounter*, 1974; *The Piano-Smashers of the Golden Sun*, 1974; *Illegal Approach*, 1974; *Midgley*, 1975; *Match-Fit*, from a story by Brian Glanville, 1976; *A Flash of Inspiration*, 1976; *Secret Army* series, 1977; *The Fuzz* series, 1977; *Hazell Gets the Boot* (*Hazell* series), 1979; *Danedyke Mystery*, from a work by Stephen Chance, 1979; *National Pelmet*, 1980; *Minder* series, 1980–86; *Christmas Spirits*, 1981; *Stan's Last Game*, 1983; *The Road to 1984*, 1984; *The Bright Side* series, 1985; *The Return of the Antelope*, and *The Antelope Christmas Special*, from his own stories, 1986; with Keith Waterhouse—*Happy Moorings*, 1963; *How Many Angels*, 1964; *Inside George Webley* series, 1968; *Queenie's Castle* series, 1970; *Budgie* series, 1971–72; *The Upper Crusts* series, 1973; *Three's Company* series, 1973; *By Endeavour Alone*, 1973; *Billy Liar* series, 1973–74; *Briefer Encounter*, 1977; *Public Lives*, 1977; *Worzel Gummidge* series, from stories by Barbara Euphan Todd, 1979.

Novel

The Fuzz (novelization of TV series). London, Coronet, 1977.

Other

They Found the World (for children), with I.O. Evans. London and New York, Warne, 1960.
The Royal Astrologer: Adventures of Father Mole-Cricket or the Malayan Legends (for children). London, Heinemann, 1960; New York, Coward McCann, 1962.
The A to Z of Soccer, with Michael Parkinson. London, Pelham, 1970.
The A to Z of Television, with Bob Monkhouse. London, Pelham, 1971.
My Sporting Life. London, Luscombe, 1975.
The Incredible Kidnapping (for children). London, Heinemann, 1975.
The Summer of the Dinosaur (for children). London, Bodley Head, 1977.
The Television Adventures [and *More Television Adventures*] *of Worzel Gummidge* (for children), with Keith Waterhouse. London, Penguin, 2 vols., 1979; complete edition, as *Worzel Gummidge's Television Adventures*, London, Kestrel, 1981.
Worzel Gummidge at the Fair (for children), with Keith Waterhouse. London, Penguin, 1980.
Worzel Gummidge Goes to the Seaside (for children), with Keith Waterhouse. London, Penguin, 1980.
The Trials of Worzel Gummidge (for children), with Keith Waterhouse. London, Penguin, 1980.
Worzel's Birthday (for children), with Keith Waterhouse. London, Penguin, 1981.
New Television Adventures of Worzel Gummidge and Aunt Sally (for children), with Keith Waterhouse. London, Sparrow, 1981.
The Last Vampire (for children). London, Bodley Head, 1982.
The Irish Adventures of Worzel Gummidge (for children), with Keith Waterhouse. London, Severn House, 1984.
The Inflatable Shop (for children). London, Bodley Head, 1984.
Dragon Days (for children). London, Bodley Head, 1985.
The Return of the Antelope (for children). London, Bodley Head, 1985.
The Antelope Company Ashore [*At Large*] (for children). London, Bodley Head, 2 vols., 1986–87.
Worzel Gummidge Down Under (for children), with Keith Waterhouse. London, Collins, 1987.
Spooky Rhymes (for children). London, Hamlyn, 1987.

Editor, with Keith Waterhouse, *Writers' Theatre*. London, Heinemann, 1967.
Editor, with Michael Parkinson, *Football Report: An Anthology of Soccer*. London, Pelham, 1973.
Editor, with Michael Parkinson, *Football Classified: An Anthology of Soccer*. London, Luscombe, 1975.
Editor, with Michael Parkinson, *Football Final*. London, Pelham, 1975.

* * *

Willis Hall and Keith Waterhouse have written so many stage plays and television and film scripts over nearly 30 years that critics are wont to regard them as the stand-by professionals of British theatre. Their technical skill has never been doubted—but their artistry and originality often have. They were both born in Leeds in 1929 and have therefore shared a similar Yorkshire background. Both were successful individually before their long-standing collaboration began. Hall's *The Long and the Short and the Tall* was premiered by the Oxford Theatre Group in 1958: and was described by Kenneth Tynan as "the most moving production of the [Edinburgh] festival." Waterhouse's novel, *Billy Liar*, was well received in 1957. The stage version of *Billy Liar* was their first joint effort, and its success in London (where it helped to establish the names of the two actors who played the title role, Albert Finney and Tom Courtenay) encouraged them to continue in the vein of "purely naturalistic provincial working-class comedy," to quote T.C. Worsley's description. *Celebration, All Things Bright and Beautiful*, and *Come Laughing Home*, together with the one-act plays *The Sponge Room* and *Squat Betty*, allowed critics to regard them as the true successors of Stanley Houghton and Harold Brighouse: and this convenient label stuck to their work, until 1965, when their farce, *Say Who You Are*, set in Kensington and concerning a middle-class *ménage à quatre*, proved an unexpected success of the season. This lively and (in some respects) ambitious sexual comedy demonstrated that their talents were not confined to one style of humour nor their sense of place to the North of England. When this barrier of mild prejudice was broken, it was remembered that Hall was responsible for perhaps the best British adaptation of a contemporary French comedy, Billetdoux's *Chin-Chin* (1960), that both had contributed widely to revues and satirical programmes (such as the BBC's *That Was the Week That Was*) and had written modern versions of Greek tragedies (such as Hall's *Afternoon for Antigone*). Their range as writers and their sophistication obviously extended beyond the narrow limits which brought them their reputations.

Nor is technical skill so common a quality among contemporary dramatists that it can be dismissed as unimportant. Hall and Waterhouse have the merits of good professionals. When they write satirically, their polemic is sharp, witty, and to the point. When they write naturalistically—whether about a provincial town in Yorkshire, a seaside amusement arcade, the war in Malaya, or Kensington—they take the trouble to know the surroundings in detail: and this groundwork enables them to discover possibilities which other writers overlook. *Celebration*, for example, presents two contrasting family events—a marriage and a funeral set in a working-class suburb of a Yorkshire town. There is no main story to hold the episodes together, nor a theme, nor even a clearly identifiable climax. But the play triumphs because the distinctive flavour of each "celebration" is captured and because the 15 main characters are each so well drawn. The slender threads of continuity which bind the episodes together reveal a sensitive insight into the nature of the society. The first act is about the wedding preparations in the backroom of a pub: Rhoda and Edgar Lucas are determined to do well by their daughter, Christine, who is marrying Bernard Fuller. But Rhoda has decided to economize by not employing Whittaker's, the firm in the town who specialize in weddings. Her efforts to ensure that the wedding breakfast doesn't let her daughter down are helped and hindered by the other members of the family: but despite the tattiness of the scene, the collapsible tables, the grease-proof paper and the dirty cups, the audience eventually is drawn to see the glowing pride and family self-importance which surround the event. Christine and Bernard survey the transformed room at the end of the act: and their contented happiness justifies the efforts. The second act is about the funeral of Arthur Broadbent, Rhoda's great-uncle and the best known eccentric of the family, who has been living in sin for years with May Beckett. The funeral is over and the pieties continue in the living room of the Lucas's house. But the family doesn't wish to acknowledge May Beckett, until she invades the house both physically (since they try to prevent her from coming) and emotionally, by expressing a grief which the conventional sentiments of the family cannot match. May's nostalgic tribute to her lost lover—so carefully prepared for in the script and emerging with an easy naturalness—is one of the truly outstanding moments of postwar British naturalistic drama: to rank with Beatie's speech at the end of Wesker's *Roots*.

This assured handling of naturalistic details is a feature of all their best plays. What other writers would have used the pub and the telephone box as so important a part of a sex comedy, replacing the more familiar stage props of a settee and a verandah? Or caught the significance of a back yard for a lonely introvert like Billy Liar? Or surrounded the pregnant unmarried girl, Vera Fawcett, in *Come Laughing Home*, with a family whose stultifying complacency offered a convincing example of the waste land from which she is trying unsuccessfully to escape? With this unusual skill in capturing an exact milieu, Hall and Waterhouse are also adept at writing those single outstanding roles which actors love to play. The part of Private Bamforth in *The Long and the Short and the Tall* gave Peter O'Toole his first opportunity—which he seized with relish: Hayley Mills was "discovered" in their film, *Whistle Down the Wind*, with the then underrated actor, Alan Bates. Hall and Waterhouse were once criticised for writing "angry young man" parts without providing the psychological insight or rhetoric of Osborne's Jimmy Porter. John Russell Taylor wrote that

> the central characters, Bamforth and Fentrill [in *Last Day in Dreamland*], are almost identical: the hectoring angry young man who knows it all and stands for most of the time in the centre of the stage, aquiver as a rule (whether the situation warrants it or not) with almost hysterical intensity, berating the other characters, who in each case, rather mysteriously, accept him as a natural leader and the life and soul of the party. The indebtedness to *Look Back in Anger* is unmistakable. . . .

This description may apply to Fentrill, whose anger at the run-down amusement arcade seems somewhat strained since he's not forced to stay there: less so to Bamforth, whose bitterness derives from claustrophobic jungle war: and scarcely at all to the other main characters of their plays. The distinctive strength of their protagonists lies not in their volubility nor their character complexities, but in their reactions to unsympathetic surroundings. Vera Fawcett is not a stock rebel: Billy Liar doesn't rebel at all—he's too satisfied with fantasies about escape. Unlike John Osborne, Hall and Waterhouse rarely offer "mouthpiece" characters, people whose insight and rhetoric about their own problems justify their presence on the stage. Their central characters emerge from their surroundings: the environment shapes the nature of their rebellion. Their dilemmas are a typical part of their societies: and are not superimposed upon their families as a consequence of too much intelligence or education.

A fairer criticism of their work might run along these lines: while their dialogue is always lively and accurate, it rarely contains flashes of intuition. Much of the humour of *Celebration, Billy Liar*, and *Say Who You Are* depends upon carefully calculated repetition. The characters are sometimes given verbal catch-phrases—Eric Fawcett teases his son Brian endlessly for ordering "whisky and Scotch" in a pub—but more frequently are given habits which become irritating after a time. Eric Fawcett's life centres around making model boats (in *Come Laughing Home*); Edgar continually chides Rhoda for not arranging the wedding through Whittaker's, while his son Jack greets every newcomer with the same question, "Lend us a quid?" Often the reiteration makes a valid dramatic point—if only to illustrate the poverty of the relationships: but sometimes it seems just an easy way of establishing a person, by constantly reminding the audience of an obsession. Hall and Waterhouse often fail to reveal any deeper cause behind the nagging habit: and this lack of depth prevents the characters from seeming sympathetic. In *Say Who You Are* the two men, David and Stuart, are both self-opinionated male chauvinists: credible enough but rather uninteresting because they have so little self-knowledge. Valerie, who invents a marriage so that she can have an affair without getting too involved, is a more engaging creation—but she too seems superficial when we learn that her objections to marriage rest on a dislike of "togetherness"—"toothbrushes nestling side by side"—and on little else. Sometimes when Hall and Waterhouse try to give an added dimension to their characters, the effect seems strained: when Vera Fawcett resigns herself to an arid future with her family from whom she cannot escape, she says "I wanted to reach out for something, but I couldn't reach far enough. It's something you need—for living—that I haven't got. I haven't really looked, but I wanted to, I was going to." This statement of her defeat doesn't dramatically match or rise to the opportunity which the play provides for her.

This superficiality has often been explained as the reverse side of the authors' facility; writers who produce so many scripts can't be expected to be profound as well. But there may be another reason. Hall and Waterhouse share a remarkable sense of form and timing, which partly accounts for the success of *Say Who You Are* and *Celebration.* David and Sarah go to two different telephones at the same time, intending to ring each other up—with the result that the numbers are always engaged and they jump to the wrong conclusion. The scenes are based on a clever use of parallels and counterpoint: but this also depends on the characters behaving with a mechanical predictability. We know what they're really going to do, and the fun comes from seeing their stock reactions fail to achieve the expected results. The formalism of the scripts, in short, sometimes prevents the characters from having an independent life: and this is the result, not so much of technical facility, as of an over-zealous care in the construction which shortsightedly ignores other possibilities. Despite these limitations, however, Hall and Waterhouse have an expertise which few other writers of the new wave of British drama can match and which accounts for the continuing popularity of their best plays.

—John Elsom

HALLIWELL, David (William). British. Born in Brighouse, Yorkshire, 31 July 1936. Educated at Bailiff Bridge Elementary School; Victoria Central Secondary Modern School, Rastrick; Hipperholme Grammar School; Huddersfield College of Art, Yorkshire, 1953–59; Royal Academy of Dramatic Art, London, diploma 1961. Founder, with Mike Leigh, Dramagraph production company, London, 1965; director and committee member, Quipu group, London, 1966–76; Visiting Fellow, Reading University, 1969–70; literary manager, 1976, and resident dramatist, 1976–77, Royal Court Theatre, London; resident dramatist, Hampstead Theatre, London, 1978–79. Co-director, Vardo Productions Ltd. Recipient: *Evening Standard* award, 1967; John Whiting Award, 1978. Fellow, Royal Society of Literature. Agent: Phil Kelvin, Goodwin Associates, 12 Rabbit Row, London W8 4DX. Address: 8 Crawborough Villas, Charlbury, Oxford OX7 3TS, England.

PUBLICATIONS

Plays

Little Malcolm and His Struggle Against the Eunuchs (produced London, 1965). London, French, 1966; as *Hail Scrawdyke!* (produced New York, 1966), New York, Grove Press, 1967.
A Who's Who of Flapland (broadcast 1967; produced London, 1969). Included in *A Who's Who of Flapland and Other Plays*, 1971.
The Experiment, with David Calderisi (also co-director: produced London and New York, 1967).
A Discussion (produced Falmouth, 1969). Included in *A Who's Who of Flapland and Other Plays*, 1971.
K.D. Dufford Hears K.D. Dufford Ask K.D. Dufford How K.D. Dufford'll Make K.D. Dufford (produced London, 1969). London, Faber, 1970.
Muck from Three Angles (produced Edinburgh and London, 1970). Included in *A Who's Who of Flapland and Other Plays*, 1971.
The Girl Who Didn't Like Answers (produced London, 1971).
A Last Belch for the Great Auk (produced London, 1971).
A Who's Who of Flapland and Other Plays. London, Faber, 1971.
An Amour, and A Feast (produced London, 1971).
Bleats from a Brighouse Pleasureground (broadcast 1972; also director: produced London, 1972).
Janitress Thrilled by Prehensile Penis (also director: produced London, 1972).
An Altercation (also director: produced London, 1973).
The Freckled Bum (also director: produced London, 1974).
Minyip (also director: produced London, 1974).
Progs (also director: produced London, 1975).
A Process of Elimination (also director: produced London, 1975).
Meriel the Ghost Girl (televised 1976; also director: produced London, 1982). Published in *The Mind Beyond*, London, Penguin, 1976.
Prejudice (also director: produced Sheffield, 1978; as *Creatures of Another Kind*, produced London, 1981).
The House (produced London, 1979). London, Eyre Methuen, 1979.
A Rite Kwik Metal Tata (produced Sheffield and London, 1979).
Was It Her? (broadcast 1980; also director: produced London, 1982).
Wychways along the Evenlode (produced Chipping Norton, Oxfordshire, 1986).
The Tomato Who Grew into a Mushroom (produced on Oxfordshire tour, 1987).

Radio Plays: *A Who's Who of Flapland*, 1967; *Bleats from a Brighouse Pleasureground*, 1972; *Was It Her?*, 1980; *Spongehenge*, 1982; *Grandad's Place*, 1984; *Shares of the Pudding*, 1985; *Do It Yourself*, 1986.

Television Plays: *A Plastic Mac in Winter*, 1963; *Cock, Hen and Courting Pit*, 1966; *Triptych of Bathroom Users*, 1972; *Blur and Blank via Checkheaton*, 1972; *Steps Back*, 1973; *Daft Mam Blues*, 1975; *Pigmented Patter*, 1976, and *Tree Women of Jagden Crag*, 1978 (*Crown Court* series); *Meriel the Ghost Girl* (*The Mind Beyond* series), 1976; *There's a Car Park in Witherton*, 1982; *Speculating about Orwell*, 1983; *Arrangements*, 1985; *Doctor Who* series (2 episodes), 1985.

*

Theatrical Activities:
Director: **Plays**—Quipu group: many of his own plays, and *The Dumb Waiter* by Harold Pinter, *Keep Out, Love in Progress* by Walter Hall, *The Stronger* by Strindberg, and *A Village Wooing* by Shaw, 1966; *The Experiment* (co-director, with David Calderisi), London and New York, 1967; *A Day with My Sister* by Stephen Poliakoff, Edinburgh, 1971; *The Hundred Watt Bulb* by George Thatcher, *I Am Real and So Are You, A Visit from the Family*, and *Crewe Station at 2 A.M.* by Tony Connor, 1972; *The Only Way Out* by George Thatcher, 1973; *We Are What We Eat* by Frank Dux, *The Knowall* by Alan C. Taylor, and *The Quipu Anywhere Show* (co-director, with Gavin Eley), London, 1973; *The Last of the Feinsteins* by Tony Connor, London, 1975; *Paint* by Peter Godfrey, London, 1977; *Lovers* by Brian Friel, Kingston, Surrey, 1978.

Actor: **Plays**—Vincentio in *The Taming of the Shrew* and Seyton in *Macbeth*, Nottingham, 1962; Hortensio in *The Taming of the Shrew*, Leicester, 1962; Sydney Spooner in *Worm's Eye View* by R.F. Delderfield, Colchester, 1962; General Madigan in *O'Flaherty, V.C.* by Shaw, and Jim Curry in *The Rainmaker* by N. Richard Nash, Stoke-on-Trent, 1962; Hero in *The Rehearsal* by Anouilh, Pozzo in *Waiting for Godot* by Beckett, and the Common Man in *A Man for All Seasons* by Robert Bolt, Stoke-on-Trent, 1963; Scrawdyke in *Little Malcolm and His Struggle Against the Eunuchs*, London, 1965; Jackson McIver in *The Experiment*, London, 1967; Policeman in *An Altercation*, London, 1973; Botard in *Rhinoceros* by Ionesco, London, 1974; Frankie in *Birdbath* by Leonard Melfi, Bristol, 1975. **Films**—*Defence of the Realm*, 1986; *Mona Lisa*, 1986. **Radio**—Landlord in *Spongehenge*, 1982.

David Halliwell comments:

(1977) When I wrote a statement for the last edition of this book, I said very firmly that I would write only multiviewpoint plays in future. I spoke with the desperate certainty of a man about to crumble. The obsession with multiviewpoint was a product of severe identity disturbances which came to a climax early in 1974. I stopped writing completely and sought other means of resolving my conflicts. One of these, putting plays together by means of improvisation, was very salutary in that it was extremely social. In my new writing, I wish to develop a style of my own which will be organic, which will juxtapose different levels of human activity and which will be entertaining. A style which to some extent has evolved through multiviewpoint but is not multiviewpoint. A style achieved through the precise voicing of each character and each modality of character. The text of the play being a score from which actors perform. I feel an analogy with jazz, particularly jazz since the bop revolution of the early 1940's. What I have in mind is very much a performer's style which can, if necessary, be presented anywhere with absolutely no mechanical equipment.

* * *

David Halliwell's dramatic territory is Flapland; his perennial subject, the Hitler syndrome; the motive force of his central characters, that childish outburst of King Lear's: "I will do such things,/What they are, yet I know not, but they shall be/The terrors of the earth." Malcolm Scrawdyke, the hero of *Little Malcolm and His Struggle Against the Eunuchs*, models himself explicitly on the early Hitler, except that he wears a Russian anarchist's greatcoat in place of Hitler's raincoat. Expelled from art school, Scrawdyke enlists three variously inadequate siblings into his Party of Dynamic Erection, plans a ludicrous revenge (which never gets beyond the fantasy stage) on the man who expelled him, and succeeds only in two petty, but nonetheless unpleasant, acts of terror: the "trial" of his most articulate and independent sibling, and the beating-up of a girl who has taunted him with sexual cowardice. Scrawdyke is only a phantom Hitler, his rabble-rousing speeches are confined to the inside of his Huddersfield garret and his grasp of reality so tenuous as to constitute little danger even to his specific enemies, let alone the community at large. But the hero of Halliwell's other full-length play, *K.D. Dufford Hears K.D. Dufford Ask K.D. Dufford How K.D. Dufford'll Make K.D. Dufford*, who actually wears a raincoat, sets his sights lower than Scrawdyke: his recipe for instant notoriety is to murder a child and he is entirely successful. Halliwell makes an ambitious attempt in this play not simply to suggest the interplay between fantasy and reality, but actually to display it, chapter and verse, on the stage, with several different versions of each scene—the real event compared with the event as imagined to his own advantage by K.D. Dufford and by each of the other main characters.

Halliwell explores the possibilities and limitations of this device in a series of short plays—*Muck from Three Angles, A Last Belch for the Great Auk, Bleats from a Brighouse Pleasureground*, and *Janitress Thrilled by Prehensile Penis*. The effect is often clumsy and ultimately superfluous since the shades of fantasy and reality pursue one another with such unerring clarity through his virtuoso monologues, that an audience must grow restive at being told by means of explicit technical devices what it has already grasped implicitly through intense dramatic sympathy.

For, however faceless, talentless, witless, loveless, lacking in courage and moral compunction these characters may be, Halliwell's comic view of them makes them irresistibly sympathetic. Something similar happens in the plays of Halliwell's contemporary Joe Orton, as well as in those of the master from whom they both learnt, Samuel Beckett. The fact that these characters would be, if met in real life, virtually subhuman, certainly pitiable or despicable to an extreme degree, is beside the point. In Halliwell's, as in Orton's and Beckett's plays, they are exaggerated dramatic representations of universal human weaknesses; and Halliwell has found and shown that, in this age of overpopulation and social disorientation, we are peculiarly vulnerable to paranoia. In *The Experiment*, partly devised by himself, partly improvised by the actors, Halliwell acted an avant-garde theatrical director "of international repute" rehearsing his company in "a modern epic translated from the Icelandic entitled *The Assassination of President Garfield*." The efforts of this director to drive his cast towards the nadir of art, to discover in the purposeless murder of a forgotten American politician deeper and deeper levels of insignificance, satirized the gullibility of audiences as much as the inflated self-admiration of certain members of the theatrical profession, but they were above all a direct demonstration of Halliwell's own special subject: the banal striving to be the unique, the insignificant the significant, the squalid reality the dream of power.

In his lightest and most charming play, *A Who's Who of Flapland*, originally written for radio but successfully translated to lunch-time theatre, Halliwell closes the circle by confronting one paranoiac with another, his equal if not his master at the gambits and routines of Flapland. Here, as in *Little Malcolm*, Halliwell relies entirely on his mastery of dramatic speech, using his native industrial Yorkshire idiom as a precision instrument to trace complex patterns of aggression, alarm, subterfuge, humiliation, triumph, surrender. The more recent plays *A Rite Kwik Metal Tata, The House*, and *Prejudice*, are all what one might call "polyphonic" developments of this technique, adding, for example, a cockney girl and an upper-class MP to the Yorkshire characters in *Metal Tata* and a Bradford Pakistani and an exiled Zulu to those in *Prejudice*. *The House*, set in a country mansion requisitioned as a hospital during World War I, is the least successful, since Halliwell's command of regional idioms is not matched by any sense of period, and the action is too desultory. But in *Prejudice* and *Metal Tata* the plots are strong enough to allow him to turn his characters all round and inside out in relation to each other without losing the momentum of the play. Of course this is only what the best playwrights have always done, but good methods decay into tired conventions and it is now clear that Halliwell's struggle over the past two decades has been to remove the dead wood and reconstitute traditional polyphonic drama in the fresh terms of his own ideas and idiosyncrasies.

—John Spurling

HAMPTON, Christopher (James). British. Born in Fayal, the Azores, 26 January 1946. Educated at schools in Aden and Alexandria, Egypt; Lancing College, Sussex, 1959–63; New College, Oxford, 1964–68, B.A. in modern languages (French and German) 1968, M.A. Married Laura de Holesch in 1971; two daughters. Resident dramatist, Royal Court Theatre, London, 1968–70. Recipient: *Evening Standard* award, 1970, 1984, 1986; Los Angeles Drama Critics Circle award, 1974; Olivier award, 1986. Fellow, 1976, and since 1984 council member, Royal Society of Literature. Agent: Margaret Ramsay Ltd., 14-A Goodwin's Court, London WC2N 4LL. Address: 2 Kensington Park Gardens, London W.11, England.

PUBLICATIONS

Plays

When Did You Last See My Mother? (produced Oxford and London, 1966; New York, 1967). London, Faber, and New York, Grove Press 1967.

Marya, adaptation of a play by Isaak Babel, translated by Michael Glenny and Harold Shukman (produced London, 1967). Published in *Plays of the Year 35*, London, Elek, 1969.

Total Eclipse (produced London, 1968; Washington, D.C., 1972; New York, 1974). London, Faber, 1969; New York, French, 1972; revised version (produced London, 1981), Faber, 1981.

Uncle Vanya, adaptation of a play by Chekhov, translated by Nina Froud (produced London, 1970). Published in *Plays of the Year 39*, London, Elek, 1971.

The Philanthropist: A Bourgeois Comedy (produced London, 1970; New York, 1971). London, Faber, 1970; New York, French, 1971; revised version, Faber, 1985.

Hedda Gabler, adaptation of a play by Ibsen (produced Stratford, Ontario, 1970; New York, 1971; London, 1984). New York, French, 1971.

A Doll's House, adaptation of a play by Ibsen (produced New York, 1971; London, 1973). New York, French, 1972.

Don Juan, adaptation of a play by Molière (broadcast 1972; produced Bristol, 1972; Chicago, 1977). London, Faber, 1974.

Savages (produced London, 1973; Los Angeles, 1974; New York, 1977). London, Faber, 1974; revised version, London, French, 1976.

Treats (produced London, 1976; New York, 1977). London, Faber, 1976.

Signed and Sealed, adaptation of a play by Georges Feydeau and Maurice Desvallières (produced London, 1976).

Able's Will (televised 1977). London, Faber, 1979.

Tales from the Vienna Woods, adaptation of a play by Ödön von Horvath (produced London, 1977; New Haven, Connecticut, 1978). London, Faber, 1977.

Ghosts, adaptation of a play by Ibsen (produced on tour, 1978). London, French, 1983.

Don Juan Comes Back from the War, adaptation of a play by Ödön von Horvath (produced London, 1978; New York, 1979). London, Faber, 1978.

The Wild Duck, adaptation of a play by Ibsen (produced London, 1979). London, Faber, 1980; New York, French, 1981.

Geschichten aus dem Wiener Wald (screenplay), with Maximilian Schell. Frankfurt, Suhrkamp, 1979.

After Mercer, based on works by David Mercer (produced London, 1980).

The Prague Trial, adaptation of a work by Patrice Chereau and Ariane Mnouchkine (produced Paris, 1980).

A Night of the Day of the Imprisoned Writer, with Ronald Harwood (produced London, 1981).

The Portage to San Cristobal of A.H., adaptation of the novel by George Steiner (produced London and Hartford, Connecticut, 1982). London, Faber, 1983.

Tales from Hollywood (produced Los Angeles, 1982; London, 1983). London, Faber, 1983.

Tartuffe; or, The Impostor, adaptation of the play by Molière (produced London, 1983). London, Faber, 1984.

Les Liaisons Dangereuses, adaptation of the novel by Choderlos de Laclos (produced Stratford-on-Avon, 1985; London, 1986; New York, 1987). London, Faber, 1985.

Screenplays: *A Doll's House*, 1973; *Geschichten aus dem Wiener Wald* (*Tales from the Vienna Woods*), with Maximilian Schell, 1981; *Beyond the Limit* (*The Honorary Consul*), 1983; *The Good Father*, 1986.

Radio Plays: *2 Children Free to Wander* (documentary), 1969; *Don Juan*, 1972; *The Prague Trial 79*, from a work by Patrice Chereau and Ariane Mnouchkine, 1980.

Television Plays: *Able's Will*, 1977; *The History Man*, from the novel by Malcolm Bradbury, 1981; *Hotel du Lac*, from the novel by Anita Brookner, 1986.

*

Critical Study: *Theatre Quarterly 12* (London), October–December 1973.

Theatrical Activities:
Actor: **Play**—role in *When Did You Last See My Mother?*, Oxford, 1966.

* * *

Les Liaisons Dangereuses coyly preserves the original French title of an epistolary novel adroitly dramatized by Christopher Hampton—to applause both on Broadway and in the West End (after a small-scale opening in Stratford's Other Place). The title—French or English—aptly summarizes Hampton's own theatrical focus. Although Hampton is not an overtly political playwright, he suggests that one of the dangers to the self-absorbed partners of their liaison is their very indifference to politics.

At age 18, while still an Oxford undergraduate (reading French and German) Hampton composed his first play, *When Did You Last See My Mother?* It received a bare-boards Sunday night production at the Royal Court Theatre and was immediately snapped up for the West End. Hampton's cruel and articulate protagonist adheres to the Angry tradition established by John Osborne, but all three of Hampton's characters are involved in dangerous liaisons—a love-hate ménage of teenage boys, a brief affair between one of the boys and the mother of the other. Unlike Broadway's *Tea and Sympathy*, the latter emotion is absent from Hampton's stage. In six swift, pitiless scenes, the teenage lovers circle back to their ménage—after the automobile accident in which the self-reproachful mother is killed. The play's titular question is never posed; instead, Hampton's title for the final scene colloquially conveys its worldweary tone: "Down the Snake to Square One."

In *Total Eclipse* the cruelly brilliant teenager is the French poet Arthur Rimbaud, who formed a dangerous liaison with Paul Verlaine, a married poet nearly twice his age. Hampton steeped himself in scholarly sources for their two-year relationship, in order to dramatize its tempestuous quality, again in six scenes. This time it is Verlaine who pivots from wife to lover, again and again, until Mme. Verlaine divorces him. Lies, drink, and drugs exacerbate the avidity of the homosexual liaison, which erupts twice into violence: Rimbaud coolly stabs Verlaine's hands, and on another occasion Verlaine accidentally shoots Rimbaud in the hand—and is imprisoned for two years. Hampton's final scene bears witness to his title, since both poetic talents suffer total eclipse; a derelict Verlaine is visited by the sister of the dead Rimbaud, and he fantasizes an idyllic liaison. Although these two early plays show a family resemblance, *Total Eclipse* benefits from the frame of an aged, haunted Verlaine, who opens and closes Hampton's play in treacherous memory.

In spite of Hampton's three productions by the age of 21, he toyed with the idea of graduate study after taking his degree in 1968, whereupon Bill Gaskill created for him the position of resident dramatist at the Royal Court, with a slender income and no duties. Hampton proceeded to work simultaneously on translations, adaptations, and his own *The Philanthropist*, conceived as a rebuttal to Molière's *Le Misanthrope*. As the latter is an aristocratic comedy in rhyme, Hampton's play is a bourgeois comedy in prose. Since the protagonist Philip is a philologist as well as philanthropist, Hampton has marked him thrice as a lover (the translation of philo). True to Hampton's focus, Philip involves himself in dangerous liaisons—with the woman he wants to marry and with a woman who does not attract him. Spurned by both, he starts a wooing letter to still a third woman. By the end of the play, all love rejected, Philip reaches into a drawer for a gun, but when he pulls the trigger, a flame shoots out to light his cigarette. It will be a slower death, with sophisticated London as an analogue of the desert island to which Molière's misanthrope resolved to flee.

Incisive and obliquely moral about the worlds of his experience, Hampton reaches out globally in *Savages*, his most ambitious drama. Triggered by the genocide of Brazilian Indians, *Savages* indicts cultured Europeans and radical South Americans for their complicity in the systematic decimation of the natives in order to acquire their land. Painting on a large canvas, Hampton parallels the public tragedy with a private one. A British Embassy official and minor poet, significantly named West, is taken hostage by Brazilian radicals who hope to trade him for their imprisoned colleagues. As the confinement of West stretches on, Hampton shows us the past in flashback—Embassy dinners, an anthropologist's distress, a pious and callous American mission, mercenaries who kill wholesale, preparations for the ceremonial gathering of Indian tribes, West's poems based on Indian legends. Then abruptly, the two plots coalesce in disaster. A bourgeois radical proves his revolutionary fervor by shooting West. A light plane bombs the Indians at their ceremony, and the pilot descends to shoot survivors. But the pilot burns all trace of the massacre, whereas West, dead, becomes a hero of the media. The Indians are gone, but Hampton's play honors them theatrically.

Hampton retreated to another lover's triangle in *Treats*. A private term for sexual favors, the title points to the desires of two different men for Ann, married to the psychologically sadistic Dave, and intermittently living with the flaccid Patrick. When the play ends, Ann has replaced Patrick with Dave, and the sado-masochistic merry-go-round will presumably continue.

While producing these plays, Hampton worked on an unusually wide range of translations—Ibsen, Chekhov, Molière, and the lesser-known Austrian playwright Ödön von Horvath, who fired his imagination. Fleeing to Paris after the *Anschluss*, Horvath was killed at the age of 37 when a freak storm felled a tree under which he had taken shelter. In *Tales from Hollywood* Hampton invents a life for Horvath among the anti-Nazi Central European refugees in Hollywood. Mixing both easily and uneasily with the Mann family, Brecht, and others, Horvath is unable to toe any party line, as he is unable to fulfill any woman's needs. Unlike earlier Hampton heroes, Horvath is too humane and compassionate for dangerous liaisons. He withdraws from his putative afterlife, and is killed instantly by the falling tree, as recorded in history. Underplayed both in England and America, this searching ahistorical drama has yet to receive the production it deserves.

Hampton is a playwright in the old English sense of the word "wright"—a craftsman who hones his tools even as he moulds increasingly large structures. As witty as his contemporaries, Hampton is more serious than most of them in his incisive dramas of cruelties of our private and public lives.

—Ruby Cohn

HANLEY, William. American. Born in Lorain, Ohio, 22 October 1931. Educated at Cornell University, Ithaca, New York, 1950–51; American Academy of Dramatic Arts, New York, 1954–55. Served in the United States Army, 1952–54. Married 1) Shelley Post in 1956 (divorced 1961); 2) Patricia Stanley in 1962 (divorced 1978); two daughters. Recipient: Vernon Rice award, 1963; Outer Circle award, 1964. Agent: Georges Borchardt Inc., 136 East 57th Street, New York, New York 10022. Address: 179 Ivy Hill Road, Ridgefield, Connecticut 06877, U.S.A.

PUBLICATIONS

Plays

Whisper into My Good Ear (produced New York, 1962; London, 1966). Included in *Mrs. Dally Has a Lover and Other Plays*, 1963.

Mrs. Dally Has a Lover (produced New York, 1962). Included in *Mrs. Dally Has a Lover and Other Plays*, 1963.

Conversations in the Dark (produced Philadelphia, 1963).

Mrs. Dally Has a Lover and Other Plays. New York, Dial Press, 1963.

Today Is Independence Day (produced Berlin, 1963; New York, 1965). Included in *Mrs. Dally Has a Lover and Other Plays*, 1963.

Slow Dance on the Killing Ground (produced New York, 1964). New York, Random House, 1964.

Flesh and Blood (televised 1968). New York, Random House, 1968.

No Answer, in *Collision Course* (produced New York, 1968). New York, Random House, 1968.

Screenplay: *The Gypsy Moths*, 1969.

Radio Play: *A Country Without Rain*, 1970.

Television Plays: *Flesh and Blood*, 1968; *Testimony of Two Men*, with James and Jennifer Miller, from the novel by Taylor Caldwell, 1977; *Who'll Save Our Children*, from a book by Rachel Maddox, 1978; *The Family Man*, 1979; *Too Far to Go*, from stories by John Updike, 1979; *Father Figure*, 1980; *Moviola: The Scarlett O'Hara War* and *The Silent Lovers*, from the novel by Garson Kanin, 1980; *Little Gloria . . . Happy at Last*, from the book by Barbara Goldsmith, 1982; *Something about Amelia*, 1984; *Celebrity*, 1984.

Novels

Blue Dreams; or, The End of Romance and the Continued Pursuit of Happiness. New York, Delacorte Press, and London, W.H. Allen, 1971.

Mixed Feelings. New York, Doubleday, 1972.

Leaving Mt. Venus. New York, Ballantine, 1977.

* * *

With a trio of one-act plays and one full-length drama William Hanley achieved a reputation in American drama which seems to have satisfied him. During a three-year period he made his appearance, created a play—*Slow Dance on the Killing Ground*—which not only reflected relevant contemporary issues but provided three acting vehicles, and disappeared from the New York theatre scene.

In spite of some serious dramaturgical weaknesses in his work Hanley was one of the few American playwrights who infused a certain amount of vitality into American drama of the early 1960's. His one-act plays are somewhat unstructured, talky, two-character plays. They are essentially conversations, but they involve perceptive thought, poetic tenderness, and the problems and feelings of generally believable people. Hanley's major concern is communication, that sometimes impossible connection between two people. Language, therefore, is important to him and his plays occasionally show a too luxuriant use of it, just as these same plays become overly concerned with discussion. Understandably, then, his sense of humanity, which is allied to his feelings for communication, frequently erupts in a distasteful sentimentality. He believes in the optimism which such sentiment suggests, however; and although his characters would seem to stumble around in an unhappy world, they do see something better. It is this vague idea of something better which he once explained as the major thought he wished his audiences for *Slow Dance on the Killing Ground* would take with them. It was a shrewd comment, however, for throughout man's history such points of view have not only been acceptable but ardently desired, especially in the theatre.

Whisper into My Good Ear presented the conversation of two old men who are contemplating suicide but change their minds. One can find a good ear for his problems: friends have value. Hanley's most popular one-act play. *Mrs. Dally Has a Lover*, is a conversation between a middle-aged Mrs. Dally and her 18-year-old lover. Before they part as the curtain falls and their affair ends the difficulty of conversation is dramatized as they are drawn in and out of their respective psychological shells. The sympathy created in this play for Mrs. Dally is further explored in *Today Is Independence Day* where she talks with her husband Sam who almost leaves her but decides to stay. Mrs. Dally also makes decisions about her own attitudes, and, although the ending of the play is sad and essentially unhappy, it is an affirmation of living.

The same comment can be made for *Slow Dance on the Killing Ground*, his only full-length Broadway success. (*Conversations in the Dark*, a discussion of the problems of husband-wife infidelity, closed in Philadelphia.) Act 1 of *Slow Dance* introduces us to three characters. None of the three—a young black genius, a middle-class white girl, a Jew who has denied his heritage and his family—can escape the violence of the world, that killing ground. In Act 2 each is unmasked, and in Act 3 a mock trial shows each one guilty. Although the play suggests that nothing can be done, there is a cohesiveness among the characters, a joint decision toward commitment and responsibility on this "killing ground," which tends to remove the play from sentimental and simply clever melodrama. Instead Hanley's insight into his characters and his obvious theme of contemporary significance have challenged critics to see *Slow Dance* as a quite substantial theatre piece.

—Walter J. Meserve

HARDING, John. British. Born in Ruislip, Middlesex, 20 June 1948. Educated at Pinner Grammar School; Manchester University, 1966–69, B.A. (honours) in drama 1969. Married Gillian Heaps in 1968; one son. Agent: Michael Imison Playwrights, 28 Almeida Street, London N1 1TD, England.

PUBLICATIONS

Plays

For Sylvia, with John Burrows (produced London, 1972). Published in *The Best Short Plays 1978*, edited by Stanley Richards, Radnor, Pennsylvania, Chilton, 1978.

The Golden Pathway Annual, with John Burrows (produced Sheffield, 1973; London, 1974). London, Heinemann, 1975.

Loud Reports, with John Burrows and Peter Skellern (produced London, 1975).

Dirty Giant, with John Burrows, music by Peter Skellern (produced Coventry, 1975).

The Manly Bit, with John Burrows (produced London, 1976).

Television Play: *Do You Dig It?*, with John Burrows, 1976.

*

Theatrical Activities:

Actor: **Plays**—all his own plays, and *Jack and Beanstalk*, Bromley, Kent, 1969; Whitaker in *The Long and the Short and the Tall* by Willis Hall, London, 1970; Pantalone in *Pinocchio* by Brian Way, London, 1971; James in *My Fat Friend* by Charles Laurence, London, 1972; Antipholus in *The Comedy of Errors*, Hornchurch, Essex, 1973; Sir Andrew Aguecheek in *Twelfth Night*, Sheffield, 1974; *Donkeys' Years* by Michael Frayn, London, 1976; Actors Company, London: *The Importance of Being Earnest* by Wilde and *Do You Love Me?* by R.D. Laing, 1977–78; *The Circle* by W. Somerset Maugham, Chichester and tour, 1978; National Theatre, London: *The Double Dealer* by Congreve, *Strife* by Galsworthy, *The Fruits of Enlightenment* by Tolstoy, *Undiscovered Country* by Tom Stoppard, *Richard III*, and *Amadeus* by Peter Shaffer, 1978–81; *Miranda* by Beverley Cross, Chichester, 1987. **Television**—*Man of Mode* by Etherege, 1980; *Baby Talk* by Nigel Williams, 1981.

* * *

See the essay on John Burrows and John Harding.

HARE, David. British. Born in Bexhill, Sussex, 5 June 1947. Educated at Lancing College, Sussex; Jesus College, Cambridge, M.A. 1968. Married Margaret Matheson in 1970 (divorced 1980); two sons and one daughter. Founding director, Portable Theatre, Brighton and London, 1968–71; literary manager, 1969–70, and resident dramatist, 1970–71, Royal Court Theatre, London; resident dramatist, Nottingham Playhouse, 1973; director, Joint Stock Theatre Company, 1975–80; founder, Greenpoint Films, 1982. Since 1984 associate director, National Theatre, London. Since 1981 member of the Council, Royal Court Theatre. Recipient: *Evening Standard* award, 1971, 1985; Rhys Memorial Prize, 1975; USA/UK Bicentennial fellowship, 1977; BAFTA award, 1979; New York Drama Critics Circle award, 1983; Berlin Film Festival Golden Bear, 1985. Agent: Margaret Ramsay Ltd., 14-A Goodwin's Court, London WC2N 4LL. Address: 33 Ladbroke Road, London W.11, England.

PUBLICATIONS

Plays

Inside Out, with Tony Bicât, adaptation of the diaries of Kafka (also director: produced London, 1968).

How Brophy Made Good (produced London, 1969). Published in *Gambit 17* (London), 1971.

What Happened to Blake? (produced London, 1970).

Slag (produced London, 1970; New York, 1971). London, Faber, 1971.

The Rules of the Game, adaptation of a play by Pirandello (produced London, 1971).

Deathsheads, in *Christmas Present* (produced Edinburgh, 1971).

Lay By, with others (produced Edinburgh and London, 1971). London, Calder and Boyars, 1972.
The Great Exhibition (produced London, 1972). London, Faber, 1972.
England's Ireland, with others (also director: produced Amsterdam and London, 1972).
Brassneck, with Howard Brenton (also director: produced Nottingham, 1973). London, Eyre Methuen, 1974.
Knuckle (produced Oxford and London, 1974; New York, 1975). London, Faber, 1974; revised version, 1978.
Fanshen, adaptation of the book by William Hinton (produced London, 1975; Milwaukee, 1976; New York, 1977). London, Faber, 1976.
Teeth 'n' Smiles, music by Nick Bicât, lyrics by Tony Bicât (also director: produced London, 1975; Washington, D.C., 1977). London, Faber, 1976.
Plenty (also director: produced London, 1978; Washington, D.C., 1980; New York, 1982). London, Faber, 1978; New York, New American Library, 1985.
Deeds, with others (produced Nottingham, 1978). Published in *Plays and Players* (London), May and June 1978.
Licking Hitler (televised 1978). London, Faber, 1978.
Dreams of Leaving (televised 1980). London, Faber, 1980.
A Map of the World (also director: produced Adelaide, Australia, 1982; London, 1983; New York, 1985). London, Faber, 1982; revised version, 1983.
Saigon: Year of the Cat (televised 1983). London, Faber, 1983.
The Madman Theory of Deterrence (sketch), in *The Big One* (produced London, 1983).
The History Plays (includes *Knuckle, Licking Hitler, Plenty*). London, Faber, 1984.
Pravda: A Fleet Street Comedy, with Howard Brenton (also director: produced London, 1985). London, Methuen, 1985.
Wetherby (screenplay). London, Faber, 1985.
The Asian Plays (includes *Fanshen, Saigon: Year of the Cat, A Map of the World*). London, Faber, 1986.
The Bay at Nice, and Wrecked Eggs (also director: produced London, 1986; New York, 1987). London, Faber, 1986.
The Knife (opera), music by Nick Bicât, lyrics by Tim Rose Price (also director: produced New York, 1987).

Screenplays: *Wetherby*, 1985; *Plenty*, 1985.

Television Plays: *Man above Men*, 1973; *Licking Hitler*, 1978; *Dreams of Leaving*, 1980; *Saigon: Year of the Cat*, 1983.

*

Critical Studies: by John Simon, in *Hudson Review* (New York), 1971; *The New British Drama* by Oleg Kerensky, London, Hamish Hamilton, 1977, New York, Taplinger, 1979; *Dreams and Deconstructions* edited by Sandy Craig, Ambergate, Derbyshire, Amber Lane Press, 1980; *Stages in the Revolution* by Catherine Itzin, London, Eyre Methuen, 1980.

Theatrical Activities:
Director: **Plays**—*Inside Out*, London, 1968; *Christie in Love* by Howard Brenton, Brighton and London, 1969; *Purity* by David Mowat, Canterbury, 1969; *Fruit* by Howard Brenton, London, 1970; *Blow Job* by Snoo Wilson, Edinburgh and London, 1971; *England's Ireland*, Amsterdam and London, 1972; *The Provoked Wife* by Vanbrugh, Watford, Hertfordshire, 1973; *Brassneck*, Nottingham, 1973; *The Pleasure Principle* by Snoo Wilson, London, 1973; *The Party* by Trevor Griffiths, tour, 1974; *Teeth 'n' Smiles*, London, 1975; *Weapons of Happiness* by Howard Brenton, London, 1976; *Devil's Island* by Tony Bicât, Cardiff and London, 1977; *Plenty*, London, 1978, New York, 1982; *Total Eclipse* by Christopher Hampton, London, 1981; *A Map of the World*, Adelaide, 1982, London, 1983, New York, 1985; *Pravda*, London, 1985; *The Bay at Nice, and Wrecked Eggs*, London, 1986; *King Lear*, London, 1986; *The Knife*, New York, 1987. **Film**—*Wetherby*, 1985. **Television**—*Licking Hitler*, 1978; *Dreams of Leaving*, 1980; *Saigon: Year of the Cat*, 1983.

* * *

Of all the playwrights of his generation, David Hare has proved to be the most assimilable and protean talent. As a filmmaker he has both directed and written *Wetherby*, a film in the tradition of his earlier television film *Licking Hitler*. As a stage director he has recently produced a National Theatre *King Lear* with Anthony Hopkins and in New York an opera, *The Knife*, on the theme of transsexualism. His stage work since 1978 shows no sign of abeyance: *A Map of the World, Pravda*, co-written with Howard Brenton, and the recent double bill *The Bay at Nice* and *Wrecked Eggs* have all been successful at the National Theatre where *Pravda*, his first collaboration since *Brassneck* in 1973, broke all box-office records. Hare has admitted to a love of filmmaking but his considerable talents show no signs of being lost to the theatre.

Hare was introduced to the theatre through Portable Theatre, which he co-founded with his Cambridge friend Tony Bicât in 1968. Certainly Hare started off purely as a director and claims that only the non-appearance of a Portable-commissioned play made him start writing, his first work being a comedy, *How Brophy Made Good.* Hare's contribution to contemporary theatre begins in earnest in 1974 with *Knuckle*, a piece written for the progressive West End producer Michael Codron, although two early plays, *Slag* and *The Great Exhibition*, are of some interest. The first is a Genet-style sexual comedy in which three women, seemingly ensconsed within a girls public school, rhetoricise about various burning topics of the day, women's rights and revolutionary feminism prominent among them. Hare has always been very much the wit of his generation, and *Slag* is typical in its tendency to send up the more vulnerable sections of radical chic as much as its more reactionary counterparts. Also typical are the literary elements in the writing: on one level *Slag* is a parody of the opening scenes of *Love's Labour's Lost.* Hare admits that *The Great Exhibition* came out of his experience as literary manager of the Royal Court, and it can be seen on one level as a technically assured send-up of the archetypal Royal Court play: working-class Labour MP, disillusioned with public and private life, takes to exposing himself on Clapham Common while employing a private detective to trail his middle-class wife.

In *Knuckle* Hare's powers take on a new, developing turn—a formally inventive comedy that transposes the affluent world of Raymond Chandler's Los Angeles to the smarter echelons of Surrey society while concerning itself with the corrupting effects of capitalism. Curly Delafield is an international arms dealer who returns home to investigate the disappearance of his sister Sarah. In the course of his investigation Curly exposes the monied values of his father's society and falls for a friend of Sarah's, Jenny, only to lose her in the end because of a lie. *Knuckle* is a muscular piece of writing, an affectionate parody of the clipped, labyrinthine thriller (Curly drinks lemonade at the bar) and of parental discord (his stockbroker father barely acknowledges the existence of his children while being engrossed in the novels of Henry James), and a biting comment on the damaging effect of acquisitive lifestyles on potentially worthwhile lives. Indeed Curly, who refuses finally to act on his knowledge, gives a rather bizarre defence of his occupation of gun-runner, both as a service to world peace and as a reaction to his father's more respectable form of exploitation.

Curly's father, Patrick—the play's real survivor—talks at one point of the value of tact: "it's not a question of talent. It's a question of noise." The statement is echoed in *Teeth 'n' Smiles*, which was a hit at the Royal Court where it marked the new directorial regime of Nicholas Wright and Robert Kidd. It depicts one madcap, self-destructive night in the life of a rock band whose fortunes are on the decline and whose terminal gig takes them to a Cambridge May Ball in 1969, a ready-made symbol of 1960's optimism on the slide. Maggie, the lead singer, is perpetually caught between bouts of drunken catatonia and egocentric nihilism while the other musicians concern themselves with deliberately mindless, time-consuming games or establish hatred for their student audience. "I would rather busk in a VD clinic," says the bass player, Peyote at one point, and indeed Peyote, a veritable drugs and sex machine, turns out finally to be the only real victim—dying of a drugs-related inhalation of vomit four years after the action of the play, his death told by the use of slides.

The representatives of the dreaded university consist of a put-upon porter, Snead, who reappears at the end of the first act to instigate a drug bust, and a medical student called Anson, a safe figure of mockery who is given some LSD after attempting to interview Maggie for the college magazine and is carried off to hospital after an abortive bout of hallucinatory sex behind the cricket pavilion. The play is certainly fascinating in its concern with youthful idealism and its potentiality for waste. Arthur, a young songwriter who had earlier dropped out of university life, represents the kind of moral earnestness which on a more academic level typifies the university he has come to despise, but Arthur's romantic love for Maggie is itself a self-sustaining illusion little different in essence from her own gesture in taking the rap for the drugs offence without complaint. Indeed although the group insults the punters, steals a few trinkets, and even sets fire to the champagne tent, the values of Cambridge remain intact—indeed the only real survivor of the group's entourage is their manager, Saraffian.

Before *Teeth 'n' Smiles* Hare adapted William Hinton's *Fanshen*, a book about the transformation of a tiny Chinese village after the Mao revolution, for Joint Stock, which, like Portable Theatre, Hare had helped found. The play, a marvellous Chinese box with ingenious doubling up of actors, was a great success despite being about a remote culture and community, but certainly marks a diversion in Hare's career to date.

Plenty is in many ways Hare's most ambitious and certainly his most heroic play. Hare, like many writers of his generation, has always been fascinated by what he believes to be a great waste of resources and talent which arose from our inability to come to terms with the passions generated by World War II. Indeed *Plenty* is a companion piece (even to having the same actress, Kate Nelligan, in both central roles) to his television film *Licking Hitler*, which depicted the loss of innocence of an upper-class young woman engaged on propaganda work at a secret establishment with, among others a tough journalist from a poverty-stricken Scottish background. The theme of *Licking Hitler*, as well as *Plenty*, might be "We may have won the war, but we have lost the peace." Indeed in *Plenty* Susan, the heroine, is shown in her progress towards a kind of inspired insanity from 1943 when she served as a young SOAS courier to 1962 and a brief reunion in Blackpool with a young officer she last met in wartime France. It's a catalogue of wasted talents. In between she has drifted aimlessly through jobs in advertising and the civil service, has tried unsuccessfully to have a child by a working-class acquaintance whom she shoots at, and finally marries a lacklustre diplomat, Brock, abandoning him at the close of the play and giving their Knightsbridge home to a Battered Wives organisation run by an old bohemian friend, Alice.

As a vehicle for Kate Nelligan the play worked tremendously, but as with *Teeth 'n' Smiles* Hare's attempt to relate the social history of postwar Britain to the personal psychology of his central characters was less successful. In *Teeth 'n' Smiles* his picture of wet students in antagonism to hostile, working-class musicians seems a little pat—one would have expected far more mutual admiration and certainly far more general optimism at the time than Hare supposes. In *Plenty* Hare's most successful moral questions are concerned with the decline of diplomacy: Brock's own boss, Darwin, is shown failing to recover from the treachery of Suez while his later superior, Charleson, seems concerned only with the rules: "Behaviour is all," he intones when Susan threatens suicide in order to save Brock's crumbling diplomatic career.

In *A Map of the World*, set against the background of a Unesco conference on world poverty held in Bombay, hostilities are declared between two very different observers of mankind: Victor Mehta, an urbane right-wing Indian novelist loosely inspired by V.S. Naipul, and Stephen Andrews, a young radical journalist. The confrontation is triggered off by an American visitor, Peggy Whitton. Though Hare uses the alienating device of a film set to break up the naturalism of the piece, the highspot is a passionate and intellectually forceful debate between the two men which explores the West's commitment, or lack of it, and guilt or lack of it, in its relationship with the Third World. As usual, Hare fills out the debate with personal intrigue and emotional relationships, and Mehta's wit is typically scorching on occasion.

Hare and Brenton's *Pravda* is a massive Jonsonian city comedy in the tradition of their earlier *Brassneck*, in which the field of vision is Fleet Street and the parlous state of British journalism. Though keenly researched the play has become a *cause célèbre* for certain newspapers, notably both the *Times* and the *Sunday Times* whose proprietor Rupert Murdoch, an Australian, is known to be the source for their monstrously villainous central character, Lambert Le Roux, whose rise up the journalistic ladder in Britain is also somewhat similar to Murdoch's own. Lambert, a great bull-necked South African says at one point that he has "broken their toys," and as with Jonson's own plays it seems that most of the energies of the authors have gone into villainies. The token good guys, and notably the female characters, are very weak, and eventually the play runs out of steam in a bid to prove that in the Street of Shame everyone has a price. But it is also immensely funny and Hare's contribution seems to have been his usually choice epigrammatic sense of humour against Brenton's flair for the shocking and theatrical. Accurate or not, it's the most popular success that either playwright has had so far.

Hare keeps up his workrate with *The Bay at Nice* and *Wrecked Eggs* which though set respectively in Russia and America are linked by their exploration of the elusive nature of freedom in whatever kind of society the individual lives. The first is more of a glorified essay; the second, accurate in its potrayal of the yuppie generation, effortlessly captures the aspirations of modern Americans reacting against the earlier liberal ethos of the 1960's but still well short of finding solutions to the problems of life.

—Steve Grant

HARWOOD, Ronald. British. Born Ronald Horwitz in Cape Town, South Africa, 9 November 1934. Educated at Sea Point Boys' High School, Cape Town; Royal Academy of Dramatic Art, London. Married Natasha Riehle in 1959; one son and two daughters. Joined Donald Wolfit's Shakespeare Company in London, 1953: actor, 1953–59; presenter, *Kaleidoscope* radio programme, 1973, and television series *Read All about It*, 1978–79, and *All the World's a Stage*, 1984; artistic director, Cheltenham Festival, 1975; Visitor in Theatre, Balliol College, Oxford, 1986. Chairman, Writers' Guild of Great Britain, 1969; member of the Literature Panel, Arts Council of Great Britain, 1973–78. Recipient: Royal Society of Literature Winifred Holtby Prize, for fiction, 1974; *Evening Standard* award, 1980. Fellow, Royal Society of Literature, 1974. Agent: Judy Daish Associates, 83 Eastbourne Mews, London W2 6LQ, England.

PUBLICATIONS

Plays

Country Matters (produced Manchester, 1969).
One Day in the Life of Ivan Denisovich (screenplay). London, Sphere, 1970; New York, Ballantine, 1971.
The Good Companions, music by André Previn, lyrics by Johnny Mercer, adaptation of the novel by J.B. Priestley (produced London, 1974). London, Chappell, 1974.
The Ordeal of Gilbert Pinfold, adaptation of the novel by Evelyn Waugh (produced Manchester, 1977; London, 1979). Oxford, Amber Lane Press, 1983.
A Family (produced Manchester and London, 1978). London, Heinemann, 1978.
The Dresser (produced Manchester and London, 1980; New York, 1981). Ambergate, Derbyshire, Amber Lane Press, 1980; New York, Grove Press, 1981.
A Night of the Day of the Imprisoned Writer, with Christopher Hampton (produced London, 1981).
After the Lions (produced Manchester, 1982). Oxford, Amber Lane Press, 1983.
Tramway Road (produced London, 1984). Oxford, Amber Lane Press, 1984.
The Deliberate Death of a Polish Priest (produced London 1985). Oxford, Amber Lane Press, 1985.
Interpreters: A Fantasia on English and Russian Themes (produced London, 1985). Oxford, Amber Lane Press, 1985.
J.J. Farr (produced Bath and London, 1987).

Screenplays: *The Barber of Stamford Hill*, 1962; *Private Potter*, with Casper Wrede, 1962; *A High Wind in Jamaica*, with Denis Cannan and Stanley Mann, 1965; *Drop Dead Darling* (*Arrivederci, Baby!*), with Ken Hughes, 1966; *Diamonds for Breakfast*, with N.F. Simpson and Pierre Rouve, 1968; *Eyewitness*, 1970; *Cromwell*, with Ken Hughes, 1970; *One Day in the Life of Ivan Denisovich*, 1972; *Operation Daybreak*, 1975; *The Dresser*, 1984; *The Doctor and the Devils*, 1986.

Radio Play: *All the Same Shadows*, from his own novel, 1971.

Television Plays: *The Barber of Stamford Hill*, 1960; *Private Potter*, with Casper Wrede, 1961; *Take a Fellow Like Me*, 1961; *The Lads*, 1963; *Convalescence*, 1964; *Guests of Honour*, 1965; *The Paris Trip*, 1966; *The New Assistant*, 1967; *Long Lease of Summer*, 1972; *The Guests*, 1972; *A Sense of Loss* (documentary on Evelyn Waugh), with John Selwyn, 1978; *The Way Up to Heaven*, 1979, *Parson's Pleasure*, 1986, and *The Umbrella Man*, 1986 (all in *Tales of the Unexpected* series); *Evita Péron*, 1981; *Mandela*, 1987.

Novels

All the Same Shadows. London, Cape, 1961; as *George Washington September, Sir!*, New York, Farrar Straus, 1961.
The Guilt Merchants. London, Cape, 1963; New York, Holt Rinehart, 1969.
The Girl in Melanie Klein. London, Secker and Warburg, 1969; New York, Holt Rinehart, 1973.
Articles of Faith. London, Secker and Warburg, 1973; New York, Holt Rinehart, 1974.
The Genoa Ferry. London, Secker and Warburg, 1976; New York, Mason Charter, 1977.
César and Augusta. London, Secker and Warburg, 1978; Boston, Little Brown, 1979.

Short Stories

One. Interior. Day. Adventures in the Film Trade. London, Secker and Warburg, 1978.

Other

Sir Donald Wolfit, C.B.E.: His Life and Work in the Unfashionable Theatre. London, Secker and Warburg, and New York, St. Martin's Press, 1971.
All the World's a Stage. London, Secker and Warburg, 1984; Boston, Little Brown, 1985.
Mandela. London, Boxtree, and New York, New American Library, 1987.

Editor, with Francis King, *New Stories 3*. London, Hutchinson, 1978.
Editor, *A Night at the Theatre*. London, Methuen, 1982.
Editor, *The Ages of Gielgud: An Actor at Eighty*. London, Hodder and Stoughton, and New York, Limelight, 1984.

*

Theatrical Activities:
Actor: **Plays**—with Donald Wolfit's Shakespeare Company in London: roles in *Macbeth, The Wandering Jew* by E. Temple Thurston, *The Taming of the Shrew, 1 Henry IV, Hamlet, Volpone* by Jonson, *Twelfth Night, A New Way to Pay Old Debts* by Massinger, and *The Clandestine Marriage* by Garrick and Colman, 1953; Third Jew in *Salome* by Oscar Wilde, London, 1954; Captain Arago in *The Strong Are Lonely* by Fritz Hochwalder, London, 1955; repertory seasons in Salisbury and Chesterfield.

* * *

It is still too early to seek any particular pigeon-hole for Ronald Harwood in the theatre. Maybe one will never be found. He is not in the least polemical, simply a novelist and dramatist, brought up as an actor, whose already long list of works—novels, television plays, screenplays, stage plays—

have no common denominator except a natural dramatic sense coupled with an acute sense of character. So far in the theatre he is regarded principally for *The Dresser*, which triumphed in both London and New York after a premiere in Manchester's theatre-in-the-round at the Royal Exchange, and is likely to remain a minor classic of the period. *The Dresser* derives from Harwood's days with the last of the actor-managers, Donald Wolfit, though he denies that the principal figure is to be taken as a portrait of Sir Donald himself. In the circumstances, of course, hints have to be inescapable; but the play is a study of an old and dictatorial Shakespearian, almost an elegy, richly theatrical, for a lost period of the stage.

Before *The Dresser* Harwood's plays—two of them also bred at the Royal Exchange in Manchester—were relatively unimportant. *The Ordeal of Gilbert Pinfold* was an able dramatisation of Evelyn Waugh's late novel about the invalid who is harassed on a cruise by the figments of his imagination. *A Family*, which in 1978 came down to the Haymarket in London, powerfully cast, left one feeling that the play should have been re-worked as a novel. Expert technician though he is, Harwood seems here to be cramped: it is hard to get on terms with a family that, in a book, might have had an immediate and plausible life. The piece is designed to show that a family, however suffocatingly possessive, can hold allegiance to the last; but this one seldom coalesces in the theatre in spite of a redoubtable portrait of a doctor son.

Far better in every way is *The Dresser* in which Harwood recreates with astonishing fidelity a part of the English theatre that had all but vanished when he caught it as a youth. It echoes from the past, from the end of the actor-managers' world, a touring Shakespearian company in the middle of World War II. The manager here is called simply "Sir." At a third-rate provincial theatre he is acting King Lear on what proves to be the last night of his life; doubtless he knows that it is when he is forcing himself to make Lear's entrance. If we like (though the analogy should not be extended) we can equate the Shakespearian tragedy with another story, played out in dressing-room and wings and momentarily among the oak-cleaving thunderbolts of an air-raid.

Harwood, as a young man not long in England from South Africa, was Donald Wolfit's dresser besides being an actor. But "Sir," we must insist, is not a portrait of Wolfit. The part is a mosaic, a symbol, of the lost managers, those often remarkable men who were sworn to the classical repertoire and to the high tradition of performance. We can think of several names that might fit into the mosaic—no one man with the unhappier qualities of Harwood's supreme egotist. The piece is a tale of the relationship between actor and dresser: between a difficult and complex veteran who, long ago, "donned the purple" (as they used to say about actor-management) and a youngish man (Norman) who has watched over him almost unflappably, always protectively. Lonely himself, he gives everything—and, he finds, without requital—to the man he serves. There are other, lesser people—the leading lady, for example, who has long been Sir's mistress, and a member of the company who is promoted to Lear's Fool—but the play, one of the most notable of its period, rests upon the doomed manager and his dresser. These are parts likely now to be established among permanent possessions of the late 20th-century English theatre.

One cannot say that about *After the Lions* which, like *The Dresser* (to which it might be regarded almost as a companion piece) was done at the Royal Exchange, Manchester; it did not transfer. Here, too, there is a falling star and a backstage associate, though in this narrative the star is none other than Sarah Bernhardt (at the grim period of her career when her leg was amputated), and the backstage—or, rather, offstage—figure is Pitou, her secretary. He wants her to retire and not to face a humiliating American tour; she is obstinate, and her obstinacy succeeds. This is a skilfully organised but artificial piece, lacking the atmospherics of *The Dresser*.

Tramway Road, Harwood's next work and a narrative both moving and disturbing, was far better. It returned him to the Cape Town of his youth is a play that should have gone farther than the Lyric, Hammersmith, where it had a brief London run. The place and date are Cape Town, 1951; two of its principal characters are a pair of married English exiles, unremittingly at odds. He is what would have been known once as a "remittance man"; she, shrewish and frustrated, has been an operetta singer. The other major personage, who does not appear after the first act, is a South African youth learning elocution from the Englishman and buoyed by hopes of a London drama school. These hopes are vain because under the new laws of 1951 he is "re-classified" as a half-caste and his future is shattered. Faced by the youth's problem, the husband acts with unforgivable weakness. The play, written with uncompromising truth and decision, is, in effect, a collision between wistfulness for the no longer attainable and shock at the cruelty of a world of bigots. The Tramway Road of the title, near which the English couple lives, belonged in those days to the Cape Coloureds.

During the following year, 1985, Harwood had two new plays. The first, done on the London fringe at the Almeida in Islington, was a straight modern documentary, *The Deliberate Death of a Polish Priest*, taken from the transcripts of the trial of the murderers of Father Jerzy Popieluszko, something dramatic enough in its twists and sophistries to be left to speak for itself. *Interpreters*, which followed, but at a West End theatre where it had a long run, could hardly have been more different: an unusual "commercial" comedy, ingeniously and expertly managed, and roughly about a pair of interpreters and the renewed love affair carried on in the intervals of their professional duties. The occasion is a visit of the Soviet President to England. Everything, down to menus for the State banquet, must be considered carefully at the Foreign Office. The interpreters, facing each other at the conference table, are the English translator Nadia (who is of Russian descent) and the passionate Viktor, who is Russian and who had had an affair with her in New York ten years before. The rejuvenated alliance cannot last, but Harwood has outlined it wittily and vigorously, whether in Whitehall or in the Kensington flat where Nadia's 93-year-old grandmother, once with the Ballets Russes, watches events and the interpreters have to interpret each other. Though the play does not entirely sustain its first promise, Harwood has designed it with a truth and zest often fully transmitted.

—J.C. Trewin

HASTINGS, Michael (Gerald). British. Born in Lambeth, London, 2 September 1938. Educated at Alleyn's School, 1949–53; apprentice, Kilgour French and Stanbury, bespoke tailors, London, 1953–56. Married Victoria Hardie in 1975; two sons and one daughter from previous marriage. Recipient: Arts Council award, 1956; Encyclopaedia Britannica award, 1965; Maugham award, 1972; Writers Guild award, 1972; Emmy award, 1973; British Screenwriters Guild award, 1975; *Evening Standard* award, 1979. Fellow, Royal Geographical Society. Agent: Jonathan Clowes Ltd., 22 Prince Albert Road,

London NW1 7ST. Address: 2 Helix Gardens, London S.W.2, England.

PUBLICATIONS

Plays

Don't Destroy Me (produced London, 1956; New York, 1957). London, Nimbus, 1956.
Yes, and After (produced London and New York, 1957). Included in *Three Plays*, 1966.
The World's Baby (produced London, 1965). Included in *Three Plays*, 1966.
Lee Harvey Oswald: A Far Mean Streak of Indepence Brought on by Negleck (as *The Silence of Lee Harvey Oswald*, produced London, 1966). London, Penguin, 1966.
Three Plays (includes *Don't Destroy Me; Yes, and After; The World's Baby*). London W.H. Allen, 1966.
The Silence of Saint-Just (produced Brighton, 1971). London, Weidenfeld and Nicolson, 1970.
The Cutting of the Cloth (produced London, 1973).
For the West (Uganda) (produced London, 1977). Included in *Three Plays*, 1980.
Gloo Joo (produced London, 1978). Included in *Three Plays*, 1980.
Full Frontal (produced London, 1979). Included in *Three Plays*, 1980.
Carnival War (as *Carnival War a Go Hot*, produced London, 1979). With *Midnite at the Starlite*, London, Penguin, 1981.
Midnite at the Starlite (as *Midnight at the Starlight*, televised 1980; as *Midnite at the Starlite*, produced Birmingham, 1981). With *Carnival War*, London, Penguin, 1981.
Three Plays. London, Penguin, 1980.
Two Fish in the Sky (produced New York, 1982).
The Miser, adaptation of a play by Molière (produced Cambridge, 1982).
Tom and Viv (produced London, 1984; New York, 1985). London, Penguin, 1985.
Going to a Party (for children; produced London, 1984).
The Emperor, with Jonathan Miller, adaptation of a novel by Ryszard Kapuscinski (also co-director: produced London, 1987). London, Penguin, 1988.

Screenplays: *Bedtime*, 1968; *The Nightcomers*, 1972.

Television Plays: *Sucker*, 1961; *The Game*, 1961, revised version, 1973; *Adam's Game*, 1964; *For the West (Congo)*, 1965; *Blue as His Eyes the Tin Helmet He Wore*, 1967; *Camille '68*, 1968; *Ride, Ride*, 1970; *The Search for the Nile* (documentary), with Derek Marlowe, 1971; *Auntie Kathleen's Old Clothes*, 1977; *Murder Rap*, 1980; *Midnight at the Starlight*, 1980; *Michael Hastings in Brixton* (documentary), 1980; *Stars of the Roller State Disco*, 1984.

Novels

The Game. London, W.H. Allen, 1957; New York, McGraw Hill, 1958.
The Frauds. London, W. H. Allen, 1960; New York, Orion Press, 1961.
Tussy Is Me: A Romance. London, Weidenfeld and Nicolson, 1970; New York, Delacorte Press, 1971.
The Nightcomers. New York, Delacorte Press, 1972; London, Pan, 1973.
And in the Forest the Indians. London, Hodder and Stoughton, 1975.

Short Stories

Bart's Mornings and Other Tales of Modern Brazil. London, Hodder and Stoughton, 1975.

Verse

Love Me, Lambeth, and Other Poems. London, W.H. Allen, 1961.

Other

The Handsomest Young Man in England: Rupert Brooke: A Biographical Essay. London, Joseph, 1967.
Sir Richard Burton: A Biography. London, Hodder and Stoughton, 1978.

*

Manuscript Collections: Princeton University, New Jersey; University of Texas, Austin.

Theatrical Activities:
Director: **Play**—*The Emperor* (co-director, with Jonathan Miller), London, 1987.

* * *

Michael Hastings's first play was produced at the now defunct New Lindsey Theatre in Notting Hill when he was only 18, winning him instant fame as one of the youngest dramatists ever to have had his work performed. *Don't Destroy Me* showed an ear for the casual but revealing remark, though the dialogue was never fully controlled. Hastings's second play, *Yes, and After*, was three times as long (i.e., four and a half hours), indicating an increasing ease with the medium. It was also a mature work in many respects. He exploited his ability at dialogue, his minor characters were well observed, and, significantly, the female characters came at least as fully to life as the male ones: the daughter in this play is one of his finest creations. Both these plays were considered significant additions to the new drama of the angry young men.

Hastings returned to the stage only after nine years. For five years he had not written at all, having spent time educating himself while living frugally in France, Germany, and Spain. That education was less digested, in dramatic terms, than was desirable: *The World's Baby* is a sceptical chronicle of British life from the 1920's to the 1950's. The central character, Anna, begins as a Dionysian dispenser of sex. While her Cambridge boyfriends change as a result of wartime experiences, Anna's anti-bourgeois convictions remain intact. Hastings's Jewish and working-class background might lead one to expect sympathy with Anna's views, but their effect is pitilessly to transform her from charming (if childish) impetuousness to menopausal crankiness. Is Anna to be seen as a victim of circumstances, as a symbol of her times, or simply as an individual? She is a little of each but not enough of any to be quite convincing. If Hastings's technique had not grown any more coherent, he certainly had come better to understand how people behave under emotional stress.

Hastings discovered the vein which he was to mine most successfully with his first popular success, *The Silence of Lee Harvey Oswald*. The playwright's background had given him an undeniable instinct for character, his self-education gave him a sense of what is topical, and he rightly focussed on the person rather than on history. He had read through the 26-volume Warren Commission Report, but the purpose of his play was to understand what was enigmatic in the alleged assassin. Structured on Oswald's declining marriage, the play's emotional power is generated by the explosive brutality of Oswald's treatment of his wife. When she attempts to desert him, their sense of loneliness and exhaustion, which prompts Oswald to plead with her for her return, is equally tellingly handled. The play moves from verbatim transcripts of evidence by Oswald's wife and mother, to dramatisations of episodes described by them. The two women hold different views of the man, his mother believing him to be a framed CIA agent, his wife thinking that he killed Kennedy to gain notoriety. (The play's popularity may have also come from the perpetually appealing techniques and suspense of cross-examination, which has a key place in the technique of the play.) The two views are, however, presented flatly. Oswald remains impenetrable, and Hastings's concern for truth is precisely what prevents the play from achieving the insight of art.

In his play on Saint-Just, Hastings violently couples the documentary material with invented dialogue about twisted revolutionary heroes. Saint-Just's powerful and mysterious silence for the 30 hours preceding his execution is made into the play's crucial anti-climax, showing Hastings at his technically adventurous best. *For the West*, on Idi Amin, is a better blend of documentary and imaginative material, and it is assisted by a large part of it taking place in Amin's dreams.

In the third stage of his playwriting career, Hastings was preoccupied with racial themes. *Gloo Joo* and *Carnival War* are perhaps the best known of the plays on these themes, but Hastings's, undoubtedly serious concern is undercut by the farcical mode in which he chooses to treat strongly divisive issues. *Carnival War* combines larking about the Notting Hill Carnival with buffoonery aimed against the police, reminiscent of some of Hastings's earlier plays, especially the television play *Blue as His Eyes the Tin Helmet He Wore*. Notwithstanding this, Hastings's plays about black people have enjoyed considerable success in Africa and the Caribbean.

Tom and Viv is based on the allegation that T.S. Eliot's first wife Vivien Haigh-Wood was committed to an asylum not because she was a lunatic but because, emotionally troubled as she was, she indulged in behaviour that Eliot and his Bloomsbury friends found embarrassing. The controversial nature of this thesis was compounded by the uncertainty regarding its factual basis. History will reveal the truth of the matter. This satirical and sometimes sickening play succeeds as a startling recreation of the period and of period characters, eloquently portraying the savagery of the two societies that destroyed Viv: the landed merchant class of her origin and her husband's glittering literary set who considered her a boor.

Hastings is a dramatist of ever-widening range (extended even further in his recent *The Emperor*), but he still seems in search of a completely congenial dramatic form; there remains a gulf between the inner and outer worlds of his plays.

—Prabhu S. Guptara

HAUPTMAN, William (Thornton). American. Born in Wichita Falls, Texas, 26 November 1942. Educated at Wichita Falls Senior High School, graduated 1961; University of Texas, Austin, B.F.A. in drama 1966; Yale University School of Drama, New Haven, Connecticut, M.F.A. in playwriting 1973. Married 1) Barbara Barbat in 1968 (divorced 1977), one daughter; 2) Marjorie Erdreich in 1985, one son. Performer with Cadillac Cowboys rockabilly band, La Jolla, California, Summer 1985. Recipient: CBS grant, 1976; National Endowment for the Arts grant, 1977; Obie award, 1977; Guggenheim grant, 1978; Boston Theatre Critics Circle award, 1984; Tony award, 1985; San Diego Drama Critics Circle award, 1985; Drama-Logue award, 1986. Agent: Ellen Neuwald, 905 West End Avenue, New York, New York 10025. Address: 240 Warren Street, Apartment E, Brooklyn, New York 11201, U.S.A.

Publications

Plays

Heat (produced New Haven, Connecticut, 1972; revised version produced New York, 1974). New York, French, 1977.

Shearwater (produced New Haven, Connecticut, 1973; New York, 1974). Published in *Performance* (New York), vol. 1, no. 5, March–April 1973.

Domino Courts (produced New York, 1975). With *Comanche Cafe*, New York, French, 1977.

Comanche Cafe (produced New York, 1976). With *Domino Courts*, New York, French, 1977.

The Durango Flash (produced New Haven, Connecticut, 1977).

Big River, music and lyrics by Roger Miller, adaptation of the novel *Adventures of Huckleberry Finn* by Mark Twain (produced Cambridge, Massachusetts, 1984; New York, 1985). New York, Grove Press, 1986.

Gillette (produced Cambridge, Massachusetts, 1985; revised version produced La Jolla, California, 1986). New York, Theatre Communications Group, 1985.

Television Play: *A House Divided* series (3 episodes), 1981.

*

William Hauptman comments:

I find as I get older I'm more interested in writing what I know about, and what I really know about is working class, because that's where I'm from. . . . When you get older you realize that there's a reason why the forms exist; they've been created by a process that's hundreds of years long. Story and character are still the most important things. The style comes and goes, but stories about people remain.

* * *

There is a remarkable wholeness about William Hauptman's dramatic writing that transcends the working-class milieu in which his plays are set. His characteristic preoccupations surface even in *Big River*, his Tony award-winning book for the 1985 Broadway musical based upon Mark Twain's *Adventures of Huckleberry Finn*. An awareness of the outdoors, the land, and forces of nature permeates this writing and generates some striking scenic images. That visual sensibility is supplemented by his strongly imagistic use of sound: the distant dog bark that ends *Domino Courts*, the low rumble that seems to comment upon Carroll's line "Now we can have some peace and quiet, right, honey?" in *Heat*, a passing train, the howl of a coyote, droning cicadas, and specific musical selections that often mock a character's pipe dreams.

All of his plays are episodically constructed; like the early Tennessee Williams, Hauptman might be better described as a "scenewright" than a playwright. That loose construction, however, is metaphorically appropriate for these studies of characters infected by wanderlust. The car on the road or the raft on the river offer them an aimless mobility that might bring "the answer" to drifters like Huck and Jim in *Big River*, Mickey and Bobby in *Gillette*, and Roy in *Domino Courts*, or to those who merely dream of travel, like Ronnie in *Comanche Cafe* and Joe Billy in *Heat*. Above all, Hauptman's characters seem to be in search of their own identities. Huck Finn declares in song his determination "to be nobody but himself." "Hell—let's be ourselves," Floyd pleads with Roy, whom he accuses of flaunting a "phony personality." In *Heat* Carroll says, "I've got a club. When you belong you can be anyone you want." Mickey, the fortyish drifter in *Gillette*, says "You look at that town and you see all the towns that ever were, and every person you've ever been. . . . There's somebody inside me who's bigger and better than I've ever been yet." But his young friend Bobby, a novice on the road, seeks to define himself in terms of an occupation.

Friendship between two men is the basis for all of Hauptman's full-length plays as well as for the one-act *Domino Courts*. Huck and Jim, Mickey and Bobby, Carroll and Harley, and Floyd and Roy all experience a pattern of alternating closeness and estrangement in their relationships. Each craves self-sufficiency but fears loneliness. The pattern is reiterated structurally by an alternation of scenes set in town with scenes set on the river or prairie or desert. When they are in town, the men feel trapped and have to get away from "civilization"; but out in the country, with the town's lights twinkling in the distance, they feel as if they are missing out on some action. Similarly, they are often torn between their need for freedom and their desire for the comfort of a woman's love. Mickey sums up the conflict most of them have faced: "Long time ago, I decided not to go for the house and kids. I was going for the other dream—freedom and a big score at the end of the road."

Women cause the greatest stress on the men's friendships. *Gillette* deals most directly with this problem, for both Mickey and Bobby must choose between binding themselves to the women who seem to be so right for them or remaining buddies as before. In *Domino Courts* Floyd and Roy get at each other through their women. In both of these plays and in *Heat*, the men often behave like little boys showing off for the women or for each other. They speak of "staying up all night" as if it were a special affirmation of manhood. Between women this sort of bonding is rare in Hauptman's plays; they are usually too afraid of losing their man. Occasionally that wariness will be dissolved in a spontaneous appreciation of "something in common," as in *Heat* when Susan and Billie find that they have both shoplifted. They devote much effort to learning, as Ronnie says in *Domino Courts*, "how to deal with men," even as they tell each other: "Don't cry, honey, no man's worth it." It is a major breakthrough when a woman like Jody in *Gillette* learns that she need not be dependent upon a man.

Hauptman's best writing to date is probably *Gillette*, about a couple of oil rig roughnecks who dream of making "big coin" in a northeastern Wyoming boom town. Originally published in Theatre Communications Group's "Plays in Process" series in 1985, it was extensively revised by Hauptman for its 1986 production at La Jolla Playhouse. *Variety*'s review sums up the appeal of this compelling portrait of blue-collar America: "It is earthy, rousing, contemporary and tough-minded—a very funny, well-written, well-staged, well-played serious comedy with a Saroyanesque strain in oddly touching moments. And like Saroyan, Hauptman's long suit is dialog and the creating of strong, highly individual, often eccentric characters."

—Felicia Hardison Londré

HENDRY, Tom (Thomas Best Hendry). Canadian. Born in Winnipeg, Manitoba, 7 June 1929. Educated at Bishop Taché School and Norwood Collegiate Institute, St. Boniface, Manitoba; Kelvin Technical High School, Winnipeg, graduated 1947; University of Manitoba, Winnipeg, 1947; Manitoba Institute of Chartered Accountants, admitted to membership 1955. Married 1) Irene Chick in 1958 (divorced 1963); 2) Judith Carr in 1963; two sons and one daughter. Owner, Thomas Hendry, C.A., 1956–58, and partner, Hendry and Evans, 1958–61, Winnipeg; founder and partner, Theatre 77, Winnipeg, 1957–58; manager and producer, Rainbow Stage, Winnipeg, 1958–60; founder and general manager, Manitoba Theatre Centre, Winnipeg, 1958–63; secretary-general, Canadian Theatre Centre, Toronto, 1964–69; editor, *Stage in Canada*, Toronto, 1965–69; literary manager, Stratford Festival, Ontario, 1969, 1970; founding director, Playwrights Co-op, 1971–79 and Playwrights Canada, 1979–82, Toronto; co-founder and producer, Toronto Free Theatre, 1971–82; co-founder, Banff Playwrights Colony, and head of the Playwriting Department, Banff Centre, Alberta, 1974–76; audit officer, Department of National Revenue, Toronto, 1982–84; chairman, Task Force on National Arts Centre, Ottawa, 1986. Consultant, 1984–85, and since 1985 policy director, Toronto Arts Council; since 1986 Barker Fairley Distinguished Visitor in Canadian Culture, University College, Toronto. Recipient: Canada Council travel grant, 1963, Senior Arts grant, 1973, and grant, 1977; Centennial Medal, 1967; Lieutenant-Governor's medal, 1970; Queen's Silver Jubilee Medal, 1977; Toronto Drama Bench award, 1982. Fellow, Bethune College, York University, Downsview, Ontario, 1978. Address: 34 Elgin Avenue, Toronto, Ontario M5R 1G6, Canada.

PUBLICATIONS

Plays

Do You Remember? (televised 1954; revised version, music by Neil Harris, produced Winnipeg, 1957).
Trapped! (for children; produced Winnipeg, 1961).
Do Not Pick the Flowers (mime play; produced Winnipeg, 1962).
All about Us (revue), with Len Peterson, music by Allan Laing (produced Winnipeg, 1964).
Fifteen Miles of Broken Glass (televised 1966). Published in *A Theatre Happening*, Toronto, Nelson, 1968; revised version (produced Toronto, 1970), Toronto, Playwrights, 1972.
Satyricon, music by Stanley Silverman, adaptation of the work by Petronius (produced Stratford, Ontario, 1969).
How Are Things with the Walking Wounded? (as *The Walking Wounded*, produced Lansing, Michigan, 1970; as *How Are Things with the Walking Wounded?*, produced Toronto, 1972). Toronto, Playwrights, 1972.
That Boy—Call Him Back (produced Lansing, Michigan, 1970; Toronto, 1971). Published in *Performing Arts in Canada* (Toronto), Winter 1972.
You Smell Good to Me, and Séance (produced Toronto, 1972). Toronto, Playwrights, 1972.

The Missionary Position (produced Vancouver, 1972). Toronto, Playwrights, 1972.
Dr. Selavy's Magic Theatre (lyrics only), with Richard Foreman, music by Stanley Silverman (produced Lenox, Massachusetts, and New York, 1972; Oxford, 1978).
Aces Wild, music by Hendry and Stephen Jack, lyrics by Hendry (also director: produced Hamilton, Ontario, 1972).
Friends and Lovers (includes *You Smell Good To Me* and *The Missionary Position*). Toronto, Playwrights, 1972.
Gravediggers of 1942, music by Stephen Jack, lyrics by Hendry (produced Toronto, 1973; London, 1984). Toronto, Playwrights, 1973.
The Dybbuk (lyrics only), book by John Hirsch, music by Allan Laing, adaptation of the play by S. Ansky (produced Winnipeg, 1974; Los Angeles, 1975). Winnipeg, Peguis, 1975.
Naked at the Opera (produced Banff, Alberta, 1975). Toronto, Co-opera, 1976.
A Memory of Eden (produced Banff, Alberta, 1975).
Apart from Everything, Is Anything the Matter? (produced Banff, Alberta, 1975).
Byron, music by Stephen Jack (produced Toronto, 1976).
Confidence (produced Banff, Alberta, 1976).
Séance II, published in *Quarry* (Kingston, Ontario), Winter 1978–79.
Hogtown: Toronto the Good, music by Paul Hoffert (produced Toronto, 1981).
East of the Sun, West of the Moon (produced Toronto, 1986).

Screenplays: *Box Car Ballet* (documentary), 1955; *A City in White* (documentary), 1956; *A House Divided* (documentary), 1957; *The Day the Freaks Took Over*, 1972; *Aces Wild*, 1974; *Private Places*, with Ron Kelly, 1976.

Radio Plays: *Wolf, Adolph, and Benito*; *The Steps Behind Her*; *Sea and Sky*, 1951–59.

Television Plays: *Do You Remember?*, 1954; *The Anniversary*, from short story by Chekhov, 1965; *Fifteen Miles of Broken Glass*, 1966; *Last Man on Horseback*, 1969; *I Was Never in Kharkov*, 1972; *Pickles*, 1976; *Royal Suite* series (3 episodes), 1976; *Santa Claus from Florida*, 1976; *King of Kensington* series (6 episodes), 1977–78, 1981; *Welcome to Canada*, 1977; *The Central Tech Tiger*, 1977; *Volcano*, 1978; *Please Say You're Real*, 1978.

Other

The Canadians (on English-Canadian theatre). Toronto, Macmillan, 1967.
Theatre in Canada: A Reluctant Citizen. Toronto, Committee for an Independent Canada, 1972.
Cultural Capital: The Care and Feeding of Toronto's Artistic Assets. Toronto, Toronto Arts Council, 1985.

*

Manuscript Collections: Public Archives of Canada, Ottawa; Toronto Public Library.

Critical Study: *The Work: Conversations with English-Canadian Playwrights* by Robert Wallace and Cynthia Zimmerman, Toronto, Coach House Press, 1982.

Theatrical Activities:
Director: **Play**—*Aces Wild*, Hamilton, Ontario, 1972.
Actor: roles in *The Jacksons and Their Neighbours* and other radio and television series, early 1950's.

Tom Hendry comments:

I cannot explain why I write plays, or why I choose the subjects that I do. The people in the plays reflect the people in my life—mostly they are outsiders. Paradoxically, I believe that if you examine anyone closely you will find that in some important area of his life he is an outsider, a non-participant. I believe that civilized society is a system of institutionalized violence directed at the individuals who make it up, and that to some extent each of us is aware of and opposes this violence. I believe that how people behave is as important as why they behave as they do. I believe that the damage we do to each other will only abate and finally cease when more perfect forms of communication—akin to ESP—are discovered and taught to everyone. Therefore I believe that dreams and nightmares and fairy tales are the only things worth writing or writing about. My plays say what I have to say.

* * *

Tom Hendry fills the plays from his most prolific period of writing for the stage with articulate and sophisticated characters, with artists, models, *literati*, and successful businessmen. His is a world of chic parties, brittle dialogue, liquor, drugs, and sexual freedom of a marked homosexual ambiance—a world of falsity. In expressing a set of attitudes typical of young urbanites of the 1970's, these plays also present central themes and figures which can be found in Hendry's earliest plays and which recur in the more recent work. In this world of stereotypes, the very shallowness of the fictional personalities is true to the real world they represent, and Hendry draws them accurately: his world is less erudite than is Waugh's, but it is also less guilty and self-indulgent than is Crowley's and, therefore, more credible. At times, Hendry draws elements out of even these predictable characters that bring them to life, but the strains of the mannered drawing-room comedy are more than reminiscent and when Hendry is imitative he is as shallow as his characters and as boring. In a play like *How Are Things with the Walking Wounded?* an unevenness arises between those sections which work out an original pattern and those which seem superimposed snatches of Noël Coward, a difficulty in integrating material (especially lyrics) which persists through the later musical collaborations. This is unfortunate, since a maturation of craft can be seen through this period and, apart from the sense of *déjà vu* which besets it, *Walking Wounded* is a fine play. Unfortunately also, Simone is correct in remarking of herself and her fellow characters, "we do tend to talk a lot, darling."

The plays produced at the Toronto Free Theatre rework the related themes of the outsider, the "non-participant" as Hendry has called him, and the prostitute he becomes in a world based on selling out as a solution to loneliness or failure. The figure first appears in the television play *Fifteen Miles of Broken Glass* in the person of an under-aged air force cadet who is left out when the war ends three years before he can join it. The bombing of Hiroshima ends the protagonist's heroic dreams, forcing him to connect with reality. The outsider becomes representative of Canada in this war play and, more strongly, in the later *Gravediggers of 1942*, which overlays a campy musical comedy subplot on the shocking events of the Dieppe raid. Here the thesis is a more intellectual statement of the Hendry theme, with the prostitution symbolically extended to a cynical self-destruction of the Canadian psyche in the person of the ingenue Judy who finally capitulates to

Hitler's offers of wealth and power. Kept outside the principal action and sacrificed by stronger powers, made as ineffectual as the naive Canadian kids in the subplot trying to become part of the war effort by putting on a show to sell war bonds, "Our Lady of the Peace Tower" accepts one solution to being outside: she learns to prostitute herself. By doing so, she completes the series of characters in *You Smell Good to Me, The Missionary Position*, and *Walking Wounded*; seen from various vantages, Albert-Steven-Willy is the same character and Regan-Rene-Barbara-Judy, although they display different external characteristics and even genders are simply facets of the hustler figure.

Gravediggers suffers from often clumsy lyrics and an uneven relationship of song to plot, a problem which caused the later musical collaboration *Hogtown: Toronto the Good* to fail in production though its concept is sound and its scale ambitious. *Hogtown* presents a dialectic on the legislation of public morality, and, once again, it presents the struggle as a battle between the establishment and the outsider. Once again, that outsider is a prostitute—a famous brothel keeper from Toronto's past. Like *Gravediggers* and a series of musical collaborations since *Satyricon*, this play attempts to join a debate on heroism through often hopeless action (a theme explored most completely in *Byron*) to the apparatus of the Broadway musical. Each of these entertainments is an exciting cooperative project, but each remains in need of further revision and completion; Hendry has not yet achieved the complex mix of cynicism and froth he seeks, has not yet brought his highly interrelated plays together to produce the one play to which all the others point.

Hendry now works as an arts administrator and has recently prepared a pivotal report on cultural funding. He has turned away from writing for the stage, but has recently adapted *Fifteen Miles of Broken Glass* to film.

—S.R. Gilbert

HENLEY, Beth (Elizabeth Becker Henley). American. Born in Jackson, Mississippi, 8 May 1952. Educated at Southern Methodist University, Dallas, B.F.A. 1974; University of Illinois, Urbana, 1975–76. Actress, Theatre Three, Dallas, 1972–73, with Southern Methodist University Directors Colloquium, 1973, and with the Great American People Show, New Salem, 1976; teacher, Dallas Minority Repertory Theatre, 1974–75. Recipient: Pulitzer Prize, 1981; New York Drama Critics Circle award, 1981; Oppenheimer award, 1981. Lives in Los Angeles. Agent: Gilbert Parker, William Morris Agency, 1350 Avenue of the Americas, New York, New York 10019, U.S.A.

PUBLICATIONS

Plays

Am I Blue? (produced Dallas, 1973; revised version produced Hartford, Connecticut, 1981; New York, 1982). New York, Dramatists Play Service, 1982.

Crimes of the Heart (produced Louisville, Kentucky, 1979; New York, 1980; London, 1983). New York, Viking Press, 1982.

The Miss Firecracker Contest (produced Los Angeles, 1980; London, 1982; New York, 1984). New York, Dramatists Play Service, 1985.

The Wake of Jamey Foster (produced Hartford, Connecticut, and New York, 1982). New York, Dramatists Play Service, 1983.

The Debutante Ball (produced Costa Mesa, California, 1985; New York, 1987).

The Lucky Spot (produced New York, 1987).

Screenplays: *The Moon Watcher*, 1983; *True Stories*, with Stephen Tobolowsky, 1986; *Crimes of the Heart*, 1987; *Nobody's Fool*, 1987.

* * *

A compassion for human frailties coupled with a balanced apprehension of man's progress through life as both comic and pathetic helped bring Beth Henley a Pulitzer Prize for her first full-length play. Thoughtful, concerned, and sympathetic rather than philosophical, *Crimes of the Heart* exudes an aura of naivety and ingenuousness that gives it an epic quality. God is in Heaven, but somehow things are not always right for the MaGrath sisters who try in their honestly humorous fashion to find hope and happiness in unlikely situations. As Meg says toward the end of the play, "We've just got to learn how to get through these real bad days here." This compelling play dealing with family affections and human fears, unpretentious and utterly authentic, was an auspicious beginning for a young playwright. Maintaining that level of creativity has been her constant challenge.

One of Henley's fine attributes is her ability to interest her audience immediately in a variety of concerns. In each of her three major plays—*Crimes of the Heart, The Wake of Jamey Foster*, and *The Miss Firecracker Contest*—she structures her first act in such a way that events, haphazardly revealed it would appear and carefully juxtaposed, create a suspense and frequently bizarre comic excitement that is extremely effective on stage. In Act 1 of *Crimes of the Heart*, for example, exposition is slowly provided concerning Lenny's birthday, Babe's shooting of Zackery, and the illness of Old Granddaddy. By degrees in *The Wake of Jamey Foster* the audience learns about the situation leading to the wake—that Marshael's husband died, that he was kicked in the head by a cow, that he had left Marshael four months earlier to live with another woman, that divorce papers have been filed, and that his coffin is the cheapest pine box Marshael could find. Along with this carefully measured exposition, Henley further enhances her plot and reveals her characters through a variety of little stories. In *Crimes of the Heart* there is the story of Lenny and Charlie, the story of Babe and Dog, of Mama and the cat. Less subtly intruded into the text of *The Wake of Jamey Foster* are the stories Pixrose, Collard, and Marshael tell of their most embarrassing moments in order to encourage an embarrassed Kathy to leave the bathroom. The technique, however, remains a favorite one with Henley as she splices stories and actions to good effect.

Henley's comic sense of life is most effectively revealed in *Crimes of the Heart*. There, with beautiful simplicity, she juxtaposes in line and scene the terror of life with the reality of the passage and finds hope and possible joy for all. Although the presence of death is a contributing impulse in the plot of each play—Old Granddaddy and Billy Boy in *Crimes of the Heart*, Jamey in *The Wake of Jamey Foster*, Aunt Ronelle in *The Miss Firecracker Contest*—Henley considers it with the fine sense of proportion that sanity requires. As a natural event, death can be humorous, pathetic, or irritating, a selection of human responses which Henley cleverly emphasizes in her plays. It is, in fact, the progressive difference in these responses that best shows Henley's change in attitude and writing style. The influence of Old Granddaddy, along with Meg's determination and Lenny's birthday wish, suggests the hope and happiness that infiltrate the climax of *Crimes of the Heart.* The villains of the play—if there are any—are clearly defeated: Zackery's fate is sealed and Chick is up a tree. In the later plays this comic approach to human existence fades away.

Only the first act of *The Wake of Jamey Foster* offers comedy similar to that in *Crimes of the Heart.* In subsequent scenes the comedy is less inspired and more farcical—the pie episode and the drunken name-calling. The characters hate; they are all unfulfilled. Bitterness creeps in with their drinking, and as they reveal their anger and angst, all vestiges of Henley's earlier comic charm disappear. They are villains to themselves, but this villainy subsides at the final curtain as hope replaces the despair of the unfulfilled. In *The Miss Firecracker Contest* there is very little of the fresh and ingenuous humor of *Crimes of the Heart*, perhaps because there are few fresh and ingenuous people in the play. Death is still a presence as Carnelle, the unsuccessful candidate for the contest, exclaims: "They say everyone's gonna be dying someday. I believe it, too." The "desperate futility of life," however, is the major issue: with Elain who is afraid she is "missing everything in the world," with Delmount who wonders "why we are living," with Carnelle who does not know "what you can, well, reasonably hope for in life." To which Mac Sam responds: "Not much, baby, not too damn much." There is also a villain in this play—Mama or Aunt Ronelle—a "mean" woman whose effect upon her children was destructive. Although there is more pathos than comedy in the play, and few light moments, Henley persists in supplying a hopeful climax for all of her characters.

Henley's plays are still set in Mississippi—Hazelhurst, Canton, and Brookhaven. There is still a southern flavor to her characters, who reappear in all her plays. There are the strange and violent people (Babe, Marshael, Delmount), the rebels who want to find satisfaction (Meg, Collard, Carnelle), the unfulfilled (Lenny, Kathy, Elain). Throughout her plays Henley is at her best in scenes with women who long for freedom, love to remember the past, and tend to be sentimental and gossipy. It is unfortunate, however, that in recent work she appears to have replaced her balanced and beautifully simple and natural comedy with a pathos that is mainly supported by a less sensitive, if robust, humor.

—Walter J. Meserve

HENSHAW, James Ene. Nigerian. Born in Calabar, 29 August 1924. Educated at Christ the King College, Onitsha; National University of Ireland, Dublin, M.B. 1949; University of Wales, T.D.D. 1954. Married Caroline Nchelem Amadi in 1958; five sons and three daughters. Physician: medical consultant to Government of Eastern Nigeria, 1955–78: controller of medical services in Southern Eastern State (now Cross River State), 1968–72, and senior consultant on tuberculosis control, Rivers State, 1973–78. Member, National Council on Health, 1968–72, and Nigerian Medical Council, 1970–72. Recipient: Henry Carr Memorial Cup, 1953. Knight, Order of St. Gregory the Great, 1965; Officer, Order of the Niger, 1977. Address: Itiaba House, Calabar Road, Calabar, Nigeria.

PUBLICATIONS

Plays

This Is Our Chance: Plays from West Africa (includes *The Jewels of the Shrine, A Man of Character, This Is Our Chance*). London, University of London Press, 1957; *The Jewels of the Shrine* published in *Plays from Black Africa*, edited by Fredric M. Litto, New York, Hill and Wang, 1968.

Children of the Goddess and Other Plays (includes *Companion for a Chief* and *Magic in the Blood*). London, University of London Press, 1964.

Medicine for Love. London, University of London Press, 1964.

Dinner for Promotion. London, University of London Press, 1967.

Enough Is Enough: A Play of the Nigerian Civil War (produced Benin City, Nigeria, 1975). Benin City, Ethiope, 1976.

A Song to Mary Charles, Irish Sister of Charity (produced Owerri, 1981). Calabar, Etewa, 1984.

* * *

Although James Ene Henshaw has been criticized for the "simplicity" of his plays, he is undoubtedly one of the most frequently produced playwrights in West Africa. Part of the reason for this may be found in his statement that he has chosen to write "to the African audience," feeling that "the problem of how to get African countries or tribes to understand each other" is far more important than "explaining the African to the non-African." Like George Bernard Shaw, Henshaw envisions his entertaining plays as having a positive impact on his society. (Also, like Shaw, Henshaw prefaces his plays with long introductions which are more essay than introduction.)

Presenting us with situations drawn from the heart of contemporary Africa, Henshaw invariably manages to bring off his comic confrontations in such a way that the good are rewarded, the wrong are both chastened and instructed, and the audiences are sent home remembering the uproarious scenes Henshaw is so adept at staging. His characters win immediate recognition and response from his audiences and range from juju priests and old maiden aunts who attempt to use magic in order to ensure success in a nephew's bid for political office to two friends who cheerfully employ all manner of treachery against each other to win promotion and the hand of the boss's daughter.

True, Henshaw's plays do not delve into the psychological depths or the metaphysical speculations of Soyinka's, but this is part of the reason for Henshaw's success—he knows his depth and keeps to it, writing competent, well-staged, sophisticated African comedies. In his own way, Henshaw is as important to the dramatic diversity and liveliness of Africa as is a genius such as Soyinka.

Moreover, like a number of other African writers, Henshaw is developing new directions in the use of the English language by non-westerners. He mentions his concern with the use of "mixed English" and employs it in his plays. Pidgin English, ungrammatical (but quite understandable) popular usages, phrases which result from the transliteration of African idioms into English and the Queen's speech itself are all a vital part of the language Henshaw ably employs.

From the first, with plays written primarily for use by schools, Henshaw has been a popular and influential dramatist throughout most of anglophone Africa. There seems little doubt that this will continue to be so in the future.

—Joseph Bruchac

HERBERT, John. Pseudonym for John Herbert Brundage. Canadian. Born in Toronto, Ontario, 13 October 1926. Educated in public schools, 1932–43; Art College of Ontario, Toronto, 1947–49; New Play Society School of Drama, Toronto, 1955–58; Volkoff Ballet School, Toronto, 1956; National Ballet School of Canada, 1957. Commercial artist, Toronto, 1943–46; served 6-month sentence in reformatory, Guelph, Ontario, 1946; worked at various jobs in the U.S.A., 1947, 1950–54; artistic director, Adventure Theatre, 1960–62, and New Venture Players, 1962–65, both Toronto; artistic director and producer, Garret Theatre Company, Toronto, 1965–71; artistic director, Medusa Theatre, 1972–74; associate editor, Arteditorial Company, Toronto, 1975–82; resident dramatist and associate director, Smile Company, Toronto, 1984–85. Lecturer in Drama, Ryerson Polytechnical School, Toronto, summers 1969–70, York University, Downsview, Ontario, Summer 1972, New College, University of Toronto, summers 1973–76, Three Schools of Art, Toronto, 1975–81, and Tappa School of Art, 1982–83. Dancer, Garbut Roberts's Dance Drama Company; actor, dancer, and set and costume designer with other companies. Recipient: Dominion Drama Festival Massey Award, 1968 (refused); Chalmers award, 1975. Agent: Ellen Neuwald Inc., 905 West End Avenue, New York, New York 10025, U.S.A. Address: Suite B-1, 1050 Yonge Street, Toronto, Ontario M4W 2L1, Canada.

PUBLICATIONS

Plays

They Died with Their Boots On: A Marsh-Melodrama (produced Canoe Lake, Ontario, 1942).
Private Club (also director: produced Toronto, 1962).
A Household God (also director: produced Toronto, 1962).
A Lady of Camellias, adaptation of a play by Dumas fils (also director: produced Toronto, 1964).
Closer to Cleveland (also director: produced Toronto, 1967).
Fortune and Men's Eyes (produced New York, 1967; London, 1968). New York, Grove Press, 1967; in *Open Space Plays*, edited by Charles Marowitz, London, Penguin, 1974.
World of Woyzeck, adaptation of a play by Georg Büchner (also director: produced Toronto, 1969).
Beer Room (produced Toronto, 1970). Included in *Some Angry Summer Songs*, 1976.
Close Friends (produced Toronto, 1970). Included in *Some Angry Summer Songs*, 1976.
Born of Medusa's Blood (also director: produced Toronto, 1972).
Omphale and the Hero (produced Toronto, 1974). Published in *Canadian Theatre Review 3*, (Toronto), Summer 1974.
Some Angry Summer Songs (includes *Pearl Divers, Beer Room, Close Friends, The Dinosaurs*) (also director: produced Toronto, 1974). Vancouver, Talonbooks, 1976.

Screenplay: *Fortune and Men's Eyes*, 1971.

Other

Belinda Wright and Jelko Yuresha (biography). London, Kaye Bellman, 1972.

*

Manuscript Collection: University of Waterloo, Ontario.

Critical Studies: by Nathan Cohen, in *Canadian Writing Today* edited by Mordecai Richler, London, Penguin, 1970; "Damnation at Christmas" by Ann P. Messenger, in *Dramatists in Canada* edited by W.H. New, Vancouver, University of British Columbia Press, 1972; "Sexuality and Identity in *Fortune and Men's Eyes*" by Neil Carson, in *Twentieth Century Literature* (Los Angeles), July 1972.

Theatrical Activities:
Director: **Plays**—*Mourning Becomes Electra* by O'Neill, Toronto, 1957; Adventure Theatre, Toronto: *The Chalk Garden* by Enid Bagnold, 1961, and *Dear Brutus* by J.M. Barrie, 1962; New Venture Players, Toronto: *Private Club* and *A Household God*, 1962, and *A Lady of Camellias*, 1964; Garret Theatre, Toronto: *The Maids* by Jean Genet and *Escurial* by Michel de Ghelderode, 1965, *The Sea Gull* by Chekhov, 1966, *Closer to Cleveland*, 1967, *Doberman* by David Windsor and *Gin Rummy* by S. Bordenvik, 1968, and *World of Woyzeck*, 1969; *Born of Medusa's Blood*, Toronto, 1972; *Some Angry Summer Songs*, Toronto, 1974; *The Gnädiges Fräulein* by Tennessee Williams, Toronto, 1976; *Close Friends*, Toronto, 1976.
Actor: **Plays**—Shylock in *The Merchant of Venice*, Toronto, 1939; Thisbe in *A Midsummer Night's Dream*, Toronto, 1939; Juliet in *Romeo and Juliet*, Toronto, 1949; Father in *The Monkey's Paw* by W.W. Jacobs and L.N. Parker, Toronto, 1941; Farmer in *The Arkansas Traveller*, Toronto, 1942; Singer in *The Rising of the Moon* by Lady Gregory, Canoe Lake, Ontario, 1942; Carmen in *They Died with Their Boots On*, Canoe Lake, Ontario, 1942; Dancer in *Paris after Midnight* by Betty Rohm, Canadian tour, 1953; Tom in *The Glass Menagerie* by Tennessee Williams, Toronto, 1956; Octavius and Doctor in *The Barretts of Wimpole Street* by Rudolf Besier, Toronto, 1957; Orin in *Mourning Becomes Electra* by O'Neill, Toronto, 1957; Trigorin in *The Sea Gull* by Chekhov, Toronto, 1958; Dr. Sloper in *The Heiress* by Ruth and Augustus Goetz, Toronto, 1958; Professor Tobin in *The Druid Circle* by John van Druten, Toronto, 1959; Mental Patient in *The Wall* by Vyvyan Frost, Toronto, 1960; Rhangda in *A Balinese Legend* by Garbut Roberts, Toronto, 1967; title role in *The Gnädiges Fräulein* by Tennessee Williams, Toronto, 1976.

John Herbert comments:

(1973) My life in theatre goes back as far as I can remember, for I fell in love with the art as a small child. I saw Leonide Massine dance the Cuban Sailor in a production of *Gaîté Parisienne* with a touring company. I saw and heard some of the greatest artists of the theatre at Toronto's Royal Alexandra, in the days when all artists of magnitude travelled the world for us, and I have never lost my passion as a member of the audience. I visit the theatre constantly to see and hear what others are thinking, feeling, and doing. Occasionally, the original thrilling convulsion of surprise returns, as when the Bolshoi Ballet dances, or when Laurence Olivier plays the father in O'Neill's *Long Day's Journey into Night*, or whenever I encounter a new young voice in the theatre, whether it belong to playwright, director, or player. I cannot say that I care more about writing a play than for directing, acting, designing, or dancing. I try to live in the theatre as one would revel as a swimmer in the ocean. The tides must always be felt, powerful, endless, timeless, and terrible as life itself.

* * *

John Herbert's reputation as the *enfant terrible* of Canadian drama arose almost entirely from the acclaim with which his *Fortune and Men's Eyes* was first greeted. That it was well written and without the worst aspects of nationalistic theatre recommended it highly to audiences weary of the sentimental quest for the great Canadian play.

Having said that, though, it is necessary to say that *Fortune and Men's Eyes* is not a great play. Its attractions are that it can easily be performed by a small cast with a modest competence and few resources for sets. Its weakness is that, for all its Sartrean setting, it is sentimental in another way—in its depictions of good and evil in "Western" terms. Smitty, the first-time criminal, who is at the center of the play, is essentially a Victorian character. He is corrupted not by defects present in his own character but by the circumstances of his confinement. In fact, we have very little sense of what sort of person he is, and in that sense his transformation from bewildered innocence to black awareness is artificial. His last speech—"I'll pay you all back"—reminds us of Malvolio's "I'll be revenged on the whole pack of you." But the comparison reveals the thinness of the conflict.

Something of this artifice is manifested in Smitty's diction. To Mona, the Blanche DuBois of this underworld whose brutalization is the moment of Smitty's awakening, he says, "You keep your secrets, like Greta Garbo—under a hat." And his revulsion from Mona is too articulate for the character that he is meant to be: "Let me out of here! I'll go to the bloody concert—anywhere—where there is life."

It is the tendency toward caricature that weakens the play and exposes it as trading both in a fashionable subject and on the need for social reform. Neither of these things would in itself have prevented the play from retaining some permanent stature—Ibsen's *Ghosts* is an example of similar defects—were it not for the fact that the characters seem manufactured. Mona is too weak, and "her" penchant for great books too exaggerated. (It is from "her" attempt to make analogies between the banal life of Kingston Pen and Shakespeare's relation to Southampton that the somewhat precious title comes.) Queenie is credible enough as a caricature queen but not as a person. "Her" vocabulary is just not credible. "Does Macy's bother Gimbel's?" is not a phrase that we believe he, as a Canadian, in a Canadian prison, would use. The author is coming through. It is, in fact, in precisely this absence of particular places and definable voices that the play is weakest. To be everywhere is to be nowhere.

This is not to say that the play is without dramatic force. In its first production and again in its London premiere, it was shocking in the forthrightness of its language and action. But more than shock and a passable narrative are required in a play of stature. And not even these are present in *Omphale and the Hero*, where an archetypal whore-meets-hustler situation is the venue for a great deal of bathetic language and a plot that creaks at every joint. It is sad to see Herbert's talent wasted on bad Tennessee Williams.

—D.D.C. Chambers

HERLIHY, James Leo. American. Born in Detroit, Michigan, 27 February 1927. Educated at Black Mountain College, North Carolina, 1947–48; Pasadena Playhouse, California, 1948–50; Yale University School of Drama, New Haven, Connecticut (RCA Fellow), 1956–57. Served in the United States Naval Reserve, 1945–46: petty officer. Taught playwriting at City College, New York 1967–68; Distinguished Visiting Professor, University of Arkansas, Fayetteville, 1983. Lives in Los Angeles. Agent: Jay Garon-Brooke Associates, 415 Central Park West, New York, New York 10025, U.S.A.

PUBLICATIONS

Plays

Streetlight Sonata (produced Pasadena, California, 1950).

Moon in Capricorn (produced New York, 1953).

Blue Denim, with William Noble (produced New York, 1958; Swansea, Wales, 1970). New York, Random House, 1958.

Crazy October, adaptation of his story "The Sleep of Baby Filbertson" (also director: produced New Haven, Connecticut, 1958).

Terrible Jim Fitch (produced Chicago, 1965; London, 1973).

Stop, You're Killing Me (includes *Terrible Jim Fitch; Bad Bad Jo-Jo; Laughs, Etc.*) (produced Boston, 1968; New York, 1969; *Bad Bad Jo-Jo* produced London, 1970; *Laughs, Etc.* produced London, 1973). New York, Simon and Schuster, 1970.

Novels

All Fall Down. New York, Dutton, 1960; London, Faber, 1961.

Midnight Cowboy. New York, Simon and Schuster, 1965; London, Cape, 1966.

The Season of the Witch. New York, Simon and Schuster, and London, W.H. Allen, 1971.

*

Short Stories

The Sleep of Baby Filbertson and Other Stories. New York, Dutton, and London, Faber, 1959.

A Story That Ends with a Scream and Eight Others. New York, Simon and Schuster, 1967; London, Cape, 1968.

Other

The Sleep of Reason, photographs by Lyle Bongé. Highlands, North Carolina, Jargon, 1974.

*

Manuscript Collection: Boston University.

Theatrical Activities:

Director: **Play**—*Crazy October*, New Haven, Connecticut, 1958.

Actor: **Plays**—roles at the Pasadena Playhouse, California; in *The Zoo Story* by Edward Albee, Boston and Paris, 1961; title role in *Terrible Jim Fitch*, Chicago, 1965. **Films**—*In the French Style*, 1963; *Four Friends* (*Georgia's Friends*), 1981.

* * *

So I'll get on a bus to Hell.
Which will probably be
another San Pedro—or Times
Square or Tia Juana or
Dallas—and I'll make out all
right. I can make out in places
like Hell. I've had practice.

—*Terrible Jim Fitch*

Embattled innocence and vulnerable corruption, often shading into each other, define the limits of James Leo Herlihy's drama. The innocent, struggling in a hostile society they inadvertently threaten, sometimes perish, sometimes triumph, and occasionally become embodiments of the corruption they once challenged. In Herlihy's unpublished fantasy *Moon in Capricorn*, Jeanne Wilkes has an actual star in her heart, a condition producing untrammelled happiness, often objectified in her tendency toward impromptu dancing. Such behavior causes incomprehension, pain, and hostility in those around her (including a typical Herlihy psychotic cripple), and ultimately Jeanne's own death. Another unpublished play, *Crazy October*, derived from Herlihy's story "The Sleep of Baby Filbertson," focuses on a mother who tyrannizes her simple-minded son until he unearths a literal family skeleton that could destroy her, a reversal suggesting both the victory of innocence and its transmutation into corrupt power. Despite the presence of Tallulah Bankhead in a showy role, the play failed to reach New York, perhaps because the conventional plotline, which punishes the wicked Mrs. Filbertson, lacked an irony consistent with the black-comic atmosphere and characterizations.

Herlihy's least representative play, *Blue Denim*, written in collaboration with William Noble, was both a critical and financial success and became a popular film. In some ways the archetypal version of the misunderstood adolescent theme of the 1950's, *Blue Denim* partially transcends the genre through clever scenic symbolism and a sympathetic portrait of the adults. The setting, the Detroit home of Major Bartley, his wife, their 23-year-old daughter Lillian, and 15-year-old son Arthur, provides simultaneous views of both the main-floor existence of the family and the basement refuge of Arthur and his friends, Janet and Ernie, a combination hideaway and copy of the adult world upstairs (the boys' beer parodies the Major's serious brandy drinking). Though the play fails to explore the full possibilities of the semi-underground life of the adolescents, the setting suggests that their rebellion (the sexual union of Janet and Arthur, Janet's abortion, the boys' forgery to help pay for the abortion) will be short-lived. The young are already aping their elders.

The bluejeans of the title, a familiar image in Herlihy, stress Arthur's sexual vulnerability (in Herlihy's novels like *Midnight Cowboy* and *All Fall Down* the garment displays sexual aggressiveness or commercial availability). The innocence of Arthur and Janet causes her pregnancy and encounter with a shady abortionist. However, the painful experience does not destroy the youngsters, nor turn them into variants of the abortionist or Lillian's gangster suitor. Ultimately, Arthur and Janet will become part of the world of the Major, a muted version of Herlihy's familiar grotesque, whose "game leg" results not from 18 years army service but from a ludicrous fall on a department store escalator. Though Arthur seems the logical protagonist and achieves an insight into his relationship with his parents, Janet's plight generates more interest; unfortunately, most of her anguish occurs offstage, and Arthur's once-removed reactions seem too inarticulate to reveal either his own feelings or to echo Janet's. Thus, in a sense, Major Bartley, the faintly ridiculous, faintly grotesque personification of the American Legion outlook, emerges as the focal figure and the catalyst in Arthur's maturation. Though the Major's sudden prominence unbalances the play, his changing role seems designed less to please a predominantly middle-aged Broadway audience than to convey the decency latent in such a man: his belief that feeding Arthur huge quantities of food will effect the desired reconciliation may be simplistic, but works convincingly in the play and amusingly underscores Arthur's youthfulness.

Herlihy's next dramatic work, *Stop, You're Killing Me*, is a collection of three one-act plays that experiment in varying ways with the monologue and attempt to create a nightmare vision of a violent America. In *Laughs, Etc.*, a single-character play in the Ruth Draper tradition, Gloria, the middle-aged wife of a lawyer, reminisces to unseen friends and husband about her recent party at which she fed vicariously off the lives of some East Village neighbors and the young female addict they had befriended. Gloria's nastiness inadequately disguises a vulnerability stemming from her childlessness, the source of her quasi-sexual, quasi-maternal obsession with her "safe" homosexual neighbors. Gloria's stress on her essential purity, as she describes the effect of a popular song heard across the courtyard, is predictably ludicrous: "It was as if we were all seven again, and taking our first Holy Communion together. There was this feeling of the oneness of humanity, the sort of thing Dostoevski raved about." However, the irony becomes obtrusive when Gloria, having spent generously for the party, refuses to provide $35 in drug money for the girl, who dies the next day from the forced withdrawal. Not only is it difficult to understand why none of the men living in an expensive building could find the necessary money, but it is also difficult to accept the play's assessment of the girl as a violated innocent whom only Gloria sees as grotesque: "Then Michael said, Gloria, I hope you'll try to bring her out, will ya? Try to get to know her a little? She's very worthwhile, she has all kinds of original thoughts, insights, ideas, she has her own little window on the world." This view seems as falsely sentimentalized as Gloria's reaction to the song. Despite Gloria's shallowness and bitchery, it is easy to share her indignation at the charge that ". . . this same dreadful Gloria is responsible for shelling out thirty-five smackeroos to save the life of every drug fiend in Manhattan." The play fails to make a $35 drug purchase an index either to the girl's purity or Gloria's compassion, and seems a rigged attempt to flay the would-be hip bourgeois. Since Gloria's auditors apparently respond to her lines, the monologue does not intensify her sense of isolation and remains merely a technical exercise.

Bad Bad Jo-Jo begins with what is essentially a telephone monologue by Kayo Hathaway, creator of the pop novel and movie figures, Bad Bad Jo-Jo and Mama, allegorical right-wing dispensers of violent law and order in a mother-dominated society. A poster depicts them as "a little old lady with tiny eyeglasses and sensible shoes leading an enormous apelike young man by a chain. The young man wears an Uncle Sam hat that is too small for him." The play parodies the Frankenstein myth when two young men invade Kayo's home and don the garb of Jo-Jo and Mama in order to murder their creator ritualistically. Though Kayo protests, "Is it really and truly necessary to point out to you that I do not kill people? I am in show business," he is responsible for the violence he commercializes. The play, least effective of the three because of its predictable conclusion and use of camp humor to satirize a camp culture hero like Kayo, merely dwells on varieties of corruption and creates neither a sense of justice at Kayo's death, nor sufficient irony to define the climax as more than an exercise in sadism.

Terrible Jim Fitch, Herlihy's best play, focuses on a man who robs churches, a character with rich folklore resonance and the allegorical dimensions of Spenser's Kirkrapine. In a variation of Strindberg's method in *The Stronger*, Jim addresses his monologue to the silent, but responsive Sally Wilkins, a former singer whose face he once scarred in a fit of rage. The motel room setting helps build a powerful sense of Jim's loneliness and frustration, as he half-threatens, half-begs a reaction from Sally:

> What am I talking about, Sal, something about sleeping in cars? Help me! Answer me, goddam you. . . . Some

day, some day, lady, you are not gonna answer me, and God help—I got it! Sleeping in cars! One night in a saloon in Key West, I got in a fist fight and when it was daylight I went to sleep in a car and had this dream about philosophy. There! I remembered—without anybody helping me.

Jim eventually loses his battle for control in the face of loneliness heightened by Sally's unspoken hostility (her behavior underlines the effectiveness of the monologue); but Jim is sometimes capable of raw tenderness: "If I was God, I'd hear you." However, his final plea apparently goes unanswered and leads to Sally's death: "Come on Sally, let me quit now. I'm beggin you. What's my name? Just say what my name is. You don't have to call me darling with it, but just say that one thing. Say my name. Once." The play illuminates Jim's blend of "criminal mentality" and vulnerability, and implies their genesis without sociological jargon or condescension. The inevitability of the conclusion heightens the tension and helps create that fusion of corruption and innocence toward which all Herlihy's plays aspire.

—Burton Kendle

HEWETT, Dorothy (Coade). Australian. Born in Perth, Western Australia, 21 May 1923. Educated at Perth College; University of Western Australia, Perth, 1941–42, 1959–63, B.A. 1961, M.A. 1963. Married Lloyd Davies in 1944 (marriage dissolved 1949), one son (deceased); lived with Les Flood, 1950–59, three sons; married Merv Lilley in 1960, two daughters. Millworker, 1950–52; advertising copywriter, Sydney, 1956–58; Senior Tutor in English, University of Western Australia, 1964–73. Writer-in-residence, Monash University, Melbourne, 1975, University of Newcastle, New South Wales, 1977, Griffith University, Nathan, Queensland, 1980, La Trobe University, Bundoora, Victoria, 1981, and Magpie Theatre Company, Adelaide, 1982. Poetry editor, *Westerly* magazine, Nedlands, Western Australia, 1972–73. Member of the Editorial Board, *Overland* magazine, Melbourne, since 1970, and *Sisters* magazine, Melbourne, since 1979; since 1979 editor and director, Big Smoke Books, and review editor, *New Poetry*, both Sydney. Member of the Communist Party, 1943–68. Recipient: Australian Broadcasting Corporation prize, for poetry, 1945, 1965; Australia Council grant, 1973, 1976, 1979, 1981, 1984; Australian Writers Guild award, 1974, 1982; International Women's Year grant, 1976. Agent: Hilary Linstead and Associates, 223 Commonwealth Street, Surry Hills, New South Wales 2010. Address: 195 Bourke Street, Darlinghurst, New South Wales 2011, Australia.

PUBLICATIONS

Plays

Time Flits Away, Lady (produced 1941).
This Old Man Comes Rolling Home (produced Perth, 1966; revised version produced Perth, 1968). Sydney, Currency Press, 1976.
Mrs. Porter and the Angel (produced Sydney, 1969).
The Chapel Perilous; or, The Perilous Adventures of Sally Banner, music by Frank Arndt and Michael Leyden (produced Perth, 1971). Sydney, Currency Press, 1972; London, Eyre Methuen, 1974.
Bon-Bons and Roses for Dolly (produced Perth, 1972). With *The Tatty Hollow Story*, Sydney, Currency Press, 1976.
Catspaw (produced Perth, 1974).
Miss Hewett's Shenanigans (produced Canberra, 1975).
Joan, music by Patrick Flynn (produced Canberra, 1975). Montmorency, Victoria, Yackandandah, 1984.
The Tatty Hollow Story (produced Sydney, 1976). With *Bon-Bons and Roses for Dolly*, Sydney, Currency Press, 1976.
The Beautiful Miss Portland, published in *Theatre Australia* (Sydney). November-December and Christmas 1976.
The Golden Oldies (produced Melbourne, 1976; London, 1978). With *Susannah's Dreaming*, Sydney, Currency Press, 1981.
Pandora's Cross (produced Sydney, 1978). Published in *Theatre Australia* (Sydney), September-October 1978.
The Man from Mukinupin (produced Perth, 1979). Sydney, Currency Press, 1980.
Susannah's Dreaming (broadcast 1980). With *The Golden Oldies*, Sydney, Currency Press, 1981.
Golden Valley (for children; produced Adelaide, 1981). With *Song of the Seals*, Sydney, Currency Press, 1985.
The Fields of Heaven (produced Perth, 1982).
Song of the Seals (for children), music by Jim Cotter (produced Adelaide, 1983). With *Golden Valley*, Sydney, Currency Press, 1985.
Christina's World (opera libretto; produced Sydney, 1983).

Screenplays: *For the First Time*, with others, 1976; *Journey among Women*, with others, 1977; *The Planter of Malata*, with Cecil Holmes, 1983.

Radio Plays: *Frost at Midnight*, 1973; *He Used to Notice Such Things*, 1974; *Susannah's Dreaming*, 1980.

Novel

Bobbin Up. Sydney, Australasian Book Society, 1959; revised edition, London, Virago Press, 1985.

Short Stories

The Australians Have a Word for It. Berlin, Seven Seas, 1964.

Verse

What about the People, with Merv Lilley. Sydney, Realist Writers, 1962.
Windmill Country. Sydney, Edwards and Shaw, 1968.
The Hidden Journey. Newnham, Tasmania, Wattle Grove Press, 1969.
Late Night Bulletin. Newnham, Tasmania, Wattle Grove Press, 1970.
Rapunzel in Suburbia. Sydney, New Poetry, 1975.
Greenhouse. Sydney, Big Smoke, 1979.
Journeys, with others, edited by Fay Zwicky. Melbourne, Sisters, 1982.

Other

Editor, *Sandgropers: A Western Australian Anthology*. Nedlands, University of Western Australia Press, 1973.

*

Manuscript Collections: Australian National Library, Canberra; Fisher Library, University of Sydney; Flinders University, Adelaide, South Australia.

Critical Studies: "Quest or Question? Perilous Journey to the Chapel" by Reba Gostand, in *Bards, Bohemians, and Bookmen* edited by Leon Cantrell, St. Lucia, University of Queensland Press, 1976; "Confession and Beyond" by Bruce Williams, in *Overland* (Sydney), 1977; *After "The Doll"* by Peter Fitzpatrick, Melbourne, Arnold, 1979; *Contemporary Australian Playwrights* edited by Jennifer Palmer, Adelaide, University Union Press, 1979; interview with Jim Davidson, in *Meanjin* (Melbourne), 1979; articles by Brian Kiernan and Carole Ferrier, in *Contemporary Australian Drama* edited by Peter Holloway, Sydney, Currency Press, 1981.

* * *

It is hard to be indifferent to the work of Dorothy Hewett. Everything she has goes into it, provoking in the observer anger, distaste, admiration, extravagant praise and partisanship, and, on two occasions, threat of court action. First a poet, author of one important novel and much left-wing journalism, she turned to playwriting in 1965. Her materials are the female psyche and the burden that men and society lay on the romantic imagination and the artistic soul. She disclaims any autobiographical intention, bending her mind as she does to the universal experience of the artist as woman through her own painful experience of the role; but it is nevertheless true that most of her characters can be identified by a style of language and imagery that refers noticeably to her own life and literary experience.

The progress of her work shows a steady motion from dramatic narrative to ritual poetry; and much of the discomfort she causes stems from her defiant intrusion of the private nature of the poetic experience into the naked public arena of the theatre.

Her first play, *This Old Man Comes Rolling Home*, remains her most immediately accessible and contains some of her best dramatic writing. It is the story of a household of communist activists in Redfern, an inner Sydney suburb, in the early 1950's, the fierce time of the unsuccessful attempt by Sir Robert Menzies to ban the Communist Party. The play was a response to her own time in Redfern and is an acknowledgement of what she calls her "love affair with the working class."

Two early dramatic influences were Patrick White and Tennessee Williams both of them moving out of realism towards a poetic interpretation of the ordinary man. Like them but in her own way she has since progressed into a landscape not "real" in the accepted sense but born of and reflecting the mind and sensibilities of Hewett and her characters. She made a leap into this landscape with *Mrs. Porter and the Angel*, a play in which a deranged woman teacher wanders through the gathering dark to the houses of her colleagues in search of an imaginary dog. The play is replete with black dog images of impotence and closet sexuality, of men and women destroying each other out of their own fantasies. And yet the play adds up to a kind of celebration of the good and evil in them all: it shares the optimism of *This Old Man*, a comedy of poverty which pays tribute to the force of life and laughter.

Journeys are endemic to Hewett's writing. The major journey to date is that taken by Sally Banner in *The Chapel Perilous*, her most widely performed play. In it she audaciously compares to the questing of Malory's heroes a woman's search for spiritual truth through literary striving, sexual adventures, marriage, communism, and public recognition. In *Bon-Bons and Roses for Dolly* her heroine is a teenager of the 1940's, indulged by her emotionally starved parents and grandparents and fed on the fairy floss of the Hollywood movie. In Act 2 Dolly returns, middle-aged, to the now crumbling Crystal Palace—a meeting of two empty and neglected monuments to second-hand dreams.

Hewett's rock opera *Catspaw* in different style offers a drop-out guitar player in search of the real Australia. In a ribald grand parade of legendary characters the author postulates that most of these enlightened minds were stick-in-the-mud conservatives.

The Tatty Hollow Story and *Joan* return to the theme of the female predicament and demonstrate how women rise to the roles men create for them. The former ritually brings together the five lovers of the mysterious Tatty Hollow, whom each remembers in a different fantasy. At last, in retaliation for what she sums up as a wasted life, Tatty takes revenge on them and dissolves—and the play with her—into a poetic madness. *Joan* is the Joan of Arc story as a rock opera with four eponymous heroines—Joan the peasant, Joan the soldier, Joan the witch, and Joan the saint.

The Golden Oldies, a savage mood piece on the round of domestic duty and mutual exploitation which is the lot of many women, emerges in retrospect as a turning point for Hewett's imagination, an exorcism of the past. Leaving us with the image of an old woman's death and her daughter sifting through the flotsam of a lifetime, Hewett moves away from her exploration of isolation towards unifying the elements of life. In the work which follows she begins to live down the old defiance and absorb the destructive forces, which had hitherto preoccupied her, into a total creative vision.

Pandora's Cross is a nostalgic attempt to rally the old creative forces of the once bohemian Kings Cross, today a haunt of drug addicts and racketeers. The play contains some of her best poetry but suffers, like other work from this middle period, from unresolved dramatic action. In 1979, however, the challenge of writing a festive work for the Western Australian sequicentennial celebrations, drew from her a play which changed her fortunes and reconciled her with the State of her birth. *The Man from Mukinupin* mingles childhood memories of the wheat-farming district in which she grew up with a dense education in Shakespeare and the English and Australian Romantics. The play is set during World War I, and she brings to the story of a grocer's daughter and her sweetheart, and of their darker siblings, a half-Aboriginal whore and her outcast lover, a world view of the good and evil forces over which the mad water diviner Zeek Perkins presides, Prospero-like, in a parched but magical land.

This was the beginning of what has come to be known as Hewett's pastoral period, which produced in close succession *Susannah's Dreaming*, a radio play about the tragic intrusion of adult brutality into the magical sea-world of a retarded innocent; *The Fields of Heaven*, about the takeover of a farming community by an ambitious escapee from Mussolini's Italy; and two children's plays, *Golden Valley*, set in the wheatfields, and *Song of the Seals*, set in a mystical sub-Antarctic bay, which use the forces of nature, in the form of people transmuted into birds and fish, to fight the intrusion of acquisitive outsiders into their rural harmony.

Hewett's work is informed by a strongly literary background and an incorrigible romanticism which contrasts oddly with her critical armoury. Part of the romanticism is an attention-getting daring and a determination to prove that life can be beautiful—a desire so strong in some plays that the energy consumes an often shaky structure. The source of her romanticism can be traced to the artistic isolation of her girlhood in Western Australia and her private schooling which together encouraged poetry and idealism. Her long allegiance to the Communist Party was an emotional, even a religious commitment, which, after her expulsion in 1968, left her isolated, bereft of beliefs and newly aware of her mortality—a sense confirmed by the senility and death of her mother. These factors are strongly represented in the work of her middle period and come to an end with the sudden force of *The Man from Mukinupin*. Hewett's subsequent works still take the same journey through idealism to understanding but they carry a new optimism and a new acceptance of the follies of life; a new recognition of the splendour and the resilience of the human spirit.

—Katharine Brisbane

HIBBERD, Jack (John Charles Hibberd). Australian. Born in Warracknabeal, Victoria, 12 April 1940. Educated at Marist Brothers College, Bendigo, Victoria; University of Melbourne, M.D. 1964. Married 1) Jocelyn Hibberd in 1969 (divorced 1977), one daughter and one son; 2) Evelyn Krape in 1978, one son. Practising physician, 1965–66, 1970–73, and since 1986. Member, Australia Council Theatre Board, 1977–79; first President, Melbourne Writers' Theatre; editor, "Performing Arts in Australia" issue of *Meanjin*, Melbourne, 1984. Currently wine columnist, Melbourne *Age*. Recipient: Australia Council fellowship, 1973, 1977, 1981. Agent: Almost Managing, P.O. Box 34, Carlton, Victoria 3053, Australia.

PUBLICATIONS

Plays

Brain Rot (produced Carlton, Victoria, 1967; augmented version produced Melbourne, 1968). Section *Who?* published in *Plays*, Melbourne, Penguin, 1970; *Just Before the Honeymoon* in *Kosmos II* (Clayton, Victoria), 1972; *One of Nature's Gentlemen* in *Three Popular Plays*, 1976; selections in *Squibs*, 1984.

White with Wire Wheels (produced Melbourne, 1967). Published in *Plays*, Melbourne, Penguin, 1970.

Dimboola: A Wedding Reception Play (produced Carlton, Victoria, 1969). Melbourne and London, Penguin, 1974.

Marvellous Melbourne, with John Romeril (produced Melbourne, 1970). Published in *Theatre Australia* (Potts Point, New South Wales), July-September 1977.

Customs and Excise (also director: produced Carlton, Victoria, 1970; augmented version, as *Proud Flesh*, produced Carlton, Victoria, 1972).

Klag (produced Melbourne, 1970).

Aorta (produced Melbourne, 1971).

A Stretch of the Imagination (also director: produced Carlton, Victoria, 1972; London, 1982; Richmond, Virginia, 1983). Sydney, Currency Press, 1973; London, Eyre Methuen, 1974.

Women!, adaptation of a play by Aristophanes (produced Carlton, Victoria, 1972).

Captain Midnight V.C., music by Lorraine Milne (produced Carlton, Victoria, 1973). Montmorency, Victoria, Yackandandah, 1984.

The Architect and the Emperor of Assyria, adaptation of a play by Fernando Arrabal (produced Carlton, Victoria, 1974).

The Les Darcy Show (produced Adelaide, 1974). Included in *Three Popular Plays*, 1976.

Peggy Sue; or, The Power of Romance (produced Carlton, Victoria, 1974; revised version produced Melbourne, 1983). Montmorency, Victoria, Yackandandah, 1982.

Goodbye Ted, with John Timlin (produced 1975). Montmorency, Victoria, Yackandandah, 1983.

A Toast to Melba (also director: produced Adelaide, 1976). Included in *Three Popular Plays*, 1976.

The Overcoat, music by Martin Friedel, adaptation of a story by Gogol (produced Carlton, Victoria, 1976; London, 1978). With *Sin*, Sydney, Currency Press, 1981.

Three Popular Plays. Melbourne, Outback Press, 1976.

Memoirs of a Carlton Bohemian, published in *Meanjin* (Melbourne), no. 3, 1977.

Sin (opera libretto), music by Martin Friedel (produced Melbourne, 1978). With *The Overcoat*, Sydney, Currency Press, 1981.

A Man of Many Parts (produced Perth, 1980).

Mothballs (produced Melbourne, 1981). Published in *Meanjin* (Melbourne), no. 4, 1980.

Liquid Amber (produced Wodonga, Victoria, 1982). Included in *A Country Quinella*, 1984.

Lavender Bags, published in *Aspect*, no. 25, 1982.

Glycerine Tears (produced Melbourne, 1983; London, 1985). Published in *Meanjin* (Melbourne), no. 4, 1982.

Squibs: A Collection of Short Plays (includes selections from *Brain Rot* and *Asian Oranges, A League of Nations, The Three Sisters, Death of a Traveller*). Brisbane, Phoenix, 1984.

A Country Quinella: Two Celebration Plays (includes *Dimboola* and *Liquid Amber*). Melbourne, Penguin, 1984.

Death Warmed Up, published in *Scripsi* (Melbourne), vol. 2, no. 4, 1984.

Odyssey of a Prostitute, published in *Outrider* (Indooroopilly, Queensland), 1985.

Other

The Barracker's Bible: A Dictionary of Sporting Slang, with Garrie Hutchinson. Melbourne, McPhee Gribble, 1983.

Translator, *Le vin des amants: Poems from Baudelaire*. Toorak, Victoria, Gryphon, 1977.

*

Manuscript Collections: Australian National Library, Canberra; Melbourne University Archives; La Trobe University Library, Bundoora, Victoria; Eunice Hanger Collection, University of Queensland, St. Lucia.

Critical Studies: "Snakes and Ladders" by Margaret Williams, in *Meanjin* (Melbourne), no. 2, 1972; "Assaying the New Drama" by A.A. Phillips, in *Meanjin* (Melbourne), no. 2, 1973; *After "The Doll"* by Peter Fitzpatrick, Melbourne, Arnold, 1979; interviews in *Contemporary Australian Playwrights* edited by Jennifer Palmer, Adelaide, University Union Press, 1979, *Sideways from the Page* by Jim Davidson, Sydney, Fontana, 1983, and with Elizabeth Perkins in *Linq* (Townsville, Queensland), vol. 11, no. 1, 1983; articles by Peter Pierce, Charles Kemp, and Paul McGillick, in *Contemporary Australian Drama* edited by Peter Holloway, Sydney, Currency Press, 1981.

Theatrical Activities:
Director: **Plays**—several of his own plays, and *Bedfellows* by Barry Oakley, Carlton, Victoria, 1975.

Jack Hibberd comments:

(1977) I have striven over the last ten years to write specifically of an Australian experience on matters of social aberration and folly, history, politics, popular myth, and individual torment. As a playwright, I believe implacably in the necessity for practical involvement in theatre. Though my plays do not evolve out of laboratory and workshop situations, I believe theatre is the best context in which to attempt dramaturgical diversity and innovation.

(1988) Over the last ten years I have been less concerned to write specifically of Australian experience but more sweepingly of human conduct in a context of comico-tragic formal experiment, especially in my monodramas and other theatrical sorties into the actor-audience farce.

* * *

In the introduction to his *Three Popular Plays*, Jack Hibberd explained what Popular Theatre suggested to him: "... a theatre of accessibility that is above all Australian in theme and substance, a theatre for the populace that deals with legendary figures and events, perennial and idiosyncratic rituals, mythically implanted in the nation's consciousness. It is a form of folk theatre without being folksy. It is a theatre of gum without being gumnut.... It can usefully intermingle celebration with satire, fun with gravity, fiction with information, ignorance with politics, slang with poetry." This remains a fair description of the best of Hibberd's own work. Several of his better known plays deal with legendary figures (*A Toast to Melba, The Les Darcy Show*) and ritual (*White with Wire Wheels, Dimboola, A Stretch of the Imagination*), and his style could be described as "slang with poetry." (He is not interested in psychological explanation, which he describes as "a form of realism in the theatre, which I am totally opposed to.") Conscious of (white) Australians as "pragmatic newcomers to an alien land," he feels that Australia is lacking in both history and long-term common tradition, and he is committed to "creating a culture, building a culture." Hibberd is not the first Australian playwright to see the dramatist as mythmaker—Douglas Stewart declared many years ago that "The playwright creates the myths by which the people live"—but he was central to a wave of myth-making in Australian drama in the late 1960's and the 1970's.

Hibberd's best known play, *A Stretch of the Imagination*, was early accorded the status of Australian classic. It is a play for one actor—the first of several such plays that Hibberd was to write. Here again he has probably been influential, for in recent years the one-actor play has become almost an Australian tradition, and the many playwrights who have written successfully in the form include Blair, Dickins, Motherwell, Oakley, Romeril, and Spears. Monk O'Neill, the solitary protagonist of *A Stretch of the Imagination*, lives alone in a dilapidated corrugated iron hut on the top of One Tree Hill, apparently near to death. He acts out a series of memories, which may be fantasies, of his encounters with men, women, and animals; in every case he is, in his own eyes, the hero, and the episodes cover a wide range of Australian myth. Margaret Williams says in her introduction to the Currency edition of the play that Monk O'Neill is "a distillation of the Australian legend of pioneer, old fossicker, footie hero, womaniser and a solitary hero pitted against the land," and to these I would add the most recent urban accretions of man-about-town and scholar. The play is shaped by ritual as Monk performs a whole series of superficially meaningless tasks, which presumably give some order to his solitary life: changing his clothes, fussing with the clock, altering his will, going through his possessions, urinating. As usual with Hibberd, the play is both celebratory and critical, and audience reaction to the panorama of Monk's experiences normally ranges through amusement, shock, compassion, and respect for his genuine stoicism.

A Man of Many Parts is also a play for one actor; the hero, Noah Hope, is in fact an actor and is described as "a valetudinarian of grizzled and berserk mien, much given to wild changes of mood, as well as sighs and palsied gestures." To date the play has proved less successful in production than *A Stretch of the Imagination*. Hibberd's most popular plays are probably *Dimboola* and *A Toast to Melba. Dimboola*, normally performed in theatre restaurants, takes the audience as guests to a country wedding reception, with bad food, excruciating vocal renditions, lewd telegrams, and a bridal party which becomes inebriated in record time. In this theatre piece Hibberd shows two complementary facets of social ritual: ritual as a trip, and ritual as providing us with a role to play and a sense of community; *Dimboola* is both social celebration and social satire. *A Toast to Melba*, like *The Les Darcy Show*, is about an Australian folk hero (in this case heroine) turned into a typical Hibberd larrikin, with an iconoclasm that is more apparent than real.

Hibberd is a playwright of paradoxes. He is a passionate devotee of the live theatre (he speaks of "the intimate black magic yet sense-drenched volatility of live performance in the context of social occasion") as opposed to the "synthetic media" of television and cinema. And yet, at least on the strength of *A Stretch of the Imagination*, he can be described as one of the most literary of Australian playwrights, a maker of myths and provocative images, with a wide-ranging vocabulary and a love of words, which encompasses appreciation of both subtle, precise meaning and deliberately appalling puns ("Conjunctivitis. As they say at funerals"). He has a Pinter-like appreciation of place names, and the ability to invest the most banal with a sense of mystery: Ultima, Echuca, Bundaberg, Sunraysia, Leongatha. In the end, however, his plays are highly physical, frequently violent, and with a good deal of knockabout farce. Particularly characteristic of Hibberd is the humour which is at the same time funny—and breath-takingly painful.

—Alrene Sykes

HILL, Errol (Gaston). American. Born in Trinidad, 5 August 1921; naturalized U.S. citizen. Educated at the Royal Academy of Dramatic Art, London, diploma 1951; University of London (British Council Scholar), diploma in dramatic art 1951; Yale University, New Haven, Connecticut, B.A., M.F.A., D.F.A. 1966. Married Grace L.E. Hope in 1956; four children. Drama tutor, University of the West Indies, Kingston, Jamaica, 1952–58; creative arts tutor, University of the West Indies, Trinidad, 1958–65; Teaching Fellow in Drama, University of Ibadan, Nigeria, 1965–67; Associate Professor of Drama, City University, New York, 1967–68. Associate Professor of Drama, 1968–69, and since 1969 Willard Professor of Drama and Oratory and Chairman of the Drama Department, Dartmouth College, Hanover, New Hampshire. Chancellor's Distinguished Professor, University of California, Berkeley, 1983. Founder, Whitehall Players, Trinidad; editor, Caribbean Plays series, University of the West Indies, 1954–65. Since 1971 editor, *ATA Bulletin of Black Theatre*, Washington,

D.C. Recipient: Rockefeller fellowship, 1958, 1959 and teaching fellowship, 1965–67; Theatre Guild of America fellowship, 1961; Bertram Joseph Award for Shakespeare Studies, 1985; Barnard Hewitt Award, for theatre history, 1985; Guggenheim fellowship, 1985. Address: Department of Drama, Dartmouth College, Hanover, New Hampshire 03755, U.S.A.

PUBLICATIONS

Plays

Oily Portraits (as *Brittle and the City Fathers*, produced Trinidad, 1948). Port-of-Spain, Trinidad, University of the West Indies, 1966.
Square Peg (produced Trinidad, 1949). Port-of-Spain, Trinidad, University of the West Indies, 1966.
The Ping Pong: A Backyard Comedy-Drama (broadcast 1950; produced Trinidad, 1953). Port-of-Spain, Trinidad, University of the West Indies, 1955.
Dilemma (produced Jamaica, 1953). Port-of-Spain, Trinidad, University of the West Indies, 1966.
Broken Melody (produced Jamaica, 1954). Port-of-Spain, Trinidad, University of the West Indies, 1966.
Wey-Wey (produced Trinidad, 1957). Port-of-Spain, Trinidad, University of the West Indies, 1958.
Strictly Matrimony (produced New Haven, Connecticut, 1959; London, 1977). Port-of-Spain, Trinidad, University of the West Indies, 1966; in *Black Drama Anthology*, edited by Woodie King and Ron Milner, New York, New American Library, 1971.
Man Better Man (produced New Haven, Connecticut, 1960; London, 1965; New York, 1969). Published in *The Yale School of Drama Presents*, edited by John Gassner, New York, Dutton, 1964; in *Plays for Today*, edited by Hill, London, Longman, 1986.
Dimanche Gras Carnival Show (produced Trinidad, 1963).
Whistling Charlie and the Monster (carnival show; produced Trinidad, 1964).
Dance Bongo (produced New York, 1965). Port-of-Spain, Trinidad, University of the West Indies, 1966; in *Caribbean Literature: An Anthology*, edited by G.R. Coulthard, London, University of London Press, 1966.

Radio Play: *The Ping Pong*, 1950 (UK).

Other

The Trinidad Carnival: Mandate for a National Theatre. Austin, University of Texas Press, 1972.
Why Pretend? A Conversation about the Performing Arts, with Peter Greer. San Francisco, Chandler and Sharp, 1973.
Shakespeare in Sable: A History of Black Shakespearean Actors. Amherst, University of Massachusetts Press, 1984.

Editor and Contributor, *The Artist in West Indian Society: A Symposium.* Port-of-Spain, Trinidad, University of the West Indies, 1964.
Editor, *A Time and a Season: 8 Caribbean Plays.* Port-of-Spain, Trinidad, University of the West Indies, 1976.
Editor, *Three Caribbean Plays for Secondary Schools.* Port-of-Spain, Trinidad, Longman, 1979.
Editor, *The Theater of Black Americans: A Collection of Critical Essays.* Englewood Cliffs, New Jersey, Prentice Hall, 2 vols., 1980.
Editor, *Plays for Today.* London, Longman, 1986.

*

Theatrical Activities:
Director: **Plays**—more than 120 plays and pageants in the West Indies, England, the United States, and Nigeria.

Actor: **Plays**—more than 40 roles in amateur and professional productions in the West Indies, England, the United States, and Nigeria.

Errol Hill comments:

I was trained first as an actor and play director. I began writing plays when it became clear to me, as founder of a Trinidad theatre company (the Whitehall Players, later merged with the New Company to become the Company of Players), that an indigenous West Indian theatre could not exist without a repertoire of West Indian plays. The thrust of my work as playwright has been to treat aspects of Caribbean folk life, drawing on speech idioms and rhythms, music and dance, and to evolve a form of drama and theatre most nearly representative of Caribbean life and art. As drama tutor for the University of the West Indies I carried this message to every part of the Caribbean and have written plays by way of demonstrating what could be done to provide a drama repertoire for Caribbean theatre companies.

* * *

Errol Hill demonstrates a remarkable talent in two separate but closely associated artistic fields—namely, playwriting and literary criticism. Presently Chairman of the Department of Drama at Dartmouth College, he is the author of one-act plays and full-length dramas; he has edited the Caribbean Plays series and is the author of many articles and reports. *The Trinidad Carnival: Mandate for a National Theatre* is a definitive contribution to the study of a rich folklore.

Man Better Man, Hill's most outstanding theatrical success, tells of a young suitor for the hand of Petite Belle Lily. The suitor's method is to challenge the village stick-fighting champion to a decisive duel. The young lover resorts to the supernatural means of his vibrant culture. He goes to the village obeahman, Diable Papa, and is subsequently cheated by the quack magician. He receives a herb, "Man Better Man"—a known cure which guarantees invincibility. With characteristic humility, Hill once wrote to me the following explanation:

> It [*Man Better Man*] was for me little more than an experiment in integrating music, song, and dance into dramatic action, and using the calypso form with its rhymed couplets to carry the rhythm and make the transitions occur more smoothly. . . . I never had an orchestral score of the music for the play. Since most of it is traditional-based, with a few numbers "composed by me," . . . I simply provided a melodic line and left it to each production to create their own orchestration. Much of the music should appear to be improvised anyway with, ideally, the musicians carrying their instruments as part of the chorus on stage.

Hill's play celebrates, in a ritualized form, the triumphal pleasure of comedy. Richard F. Shepard said in the *New York Times* (3 July 1969): "Mr. Hill has encapsuled an authentic folk tale flavor, letting us know something about a people, his people, whose history antedates steel drum bands. It is quaint, yet not condescending; ingenuous, yet not silly." On the surface the musical play gleams with a tropical panache; beneath are the threatened subtleties and hidden meanings. Thus that magic, that mystery which the festive Greeks knew very well, is engaged—no, released—by Hill on a richly set

Caribbean stage. The connection between the author's skill in portraying effects obtained by the juxtaposition of the real with the assumed—one of the several functions of comedy—and his symbolic comic vision is the dynamic element of this work.

C.L.R. James was deeply moved when Hill produced and directed a lengthy skit in Trinidad of dramatic, musical, festive, and political impact. He observed that the audience enjoyed it while "the authorities" did not approve. Hill's venture to me is completely West Indian, and completely Greek. Sir William Ridgeway in *The Origin of Tragedy* (1910) and *The Dramas and Dramatic Dances of Non-European Races* (1915) could have been speaking of West Indian drama as well as Greek tragedy when he states that the heavy emphasis on ghosts, burial rites, and ancestor worship could not be derived from such a deity as Dionysus alone. The art must be related to hero and ancestor worship and the cult of the dead. For example, in *Man Better Man* Hannibal, Calypsonian, enjoys a position roughly analogous to the Anglo-Saxon court *scop*. He immortalizes the island's heroes in song, and his repertoire constitutes a veritable oral chronicle. Pogo's homeric cataloguing of famous stick-fighters displays the continuity of the heroic tradition. Villagers manifest an awareness that they see tradition-in-the-making. "Excitement for so/More trouble and woe/A day to recall/When you grow old."

Medieval courtly conventions are carried off to the Caribbean setting in the most graceful and lyrical moods. Courtly love comes forward and all action stems from Tim Briscoe's desire to win a woman's affection through a demonstration of physical prowess. He expresses his longing in courtly love terms for Petite Belle Lily. Tim displays those familiar symptoms of "heroes"—the conventional lover's malady—when he says "I cannot eat by day, come the night/Cannot sleep, what a plight." Petite Belle Lily shows her indifference—perhaps medieval, perhaps Petrarchan—to her lover's sorry state which is so fitting and proper to her courtly heroine-like state. The stick-fight itself—traditionally accompanied by a calinda—between Tim and Tiny Sata is reminiscent of a medieval tournament whose proceedings are governed by ritualized and rigid customs. Aspects of trial-by-combat are ever-present, along with strong emphasis on personal honor and its defence. Indeed, stick-fighting is envisioned among these island dwellers as a folk institution. The fighter is a true folk hero, like Beowulf or Achilles, who embodies not only the primitive drive of the islanders, but also the qualities which they esteem most highly—physical courage, prowess in battle, personal honor. The reigning champion becomes a personification of the communal ideal.

The tension between Diable Papa—a fake and a counterfeit who, by means of voodoo, makes money from the primitive fears of the people—and Portagee Joe supplies the intellectual focus of the drama. The obeahman—the holder of all the local rituals, spells, and incantations—represents the power of illusion and mass deception. Portagee Joe, who successfully challenges Diable Papa's authority, is the typical "village atheist"—whose cynicism or rationalism keeps him outside the circle of communal belief. "The social significance of the play lies in the relationship between Portagee Joe and his customers: They were not 'niggers' to him and he is not 'white' to them," writes Mrs. Stanley Jackson, in a letter to the *New York Times*. "A man could be judged as a man seventy years ago in Trinidad. . . . The author of *Man Better Man* knew his material extremely well."

Lastly, Diable Papa, who is a fraud, nevertheless reflects some picaresque influences. He is reminiscent of the medieval and Tudor horrific-comic depiction of stock diabolic figures. But the obeahman is balanced against the broader irony of the play's resolution. Tim Briscoe qua anti-hero, although defeated, emerges as a hero in spite of himself. Diable Papa, confounded by supposedly "supernatural" happenings and spectral visitations, is actually victimized by the very beliefs he has fostered in the villagers.

The drama is a picture of thoughtful delight. The audience—even the reader—becomes an extension of the stage. One cannot help recalling throughout the work Michael Rutenberg's advice to directors: "Break through the proscenium!" The ceremonial interaction of chorus, dancers, actors, and calypsonian sequences—responsorial in nature (counter-melodies are used by Diable Papa and Minee)—and the lively verse—incantatorial in quality and reflecting the natural rhythmic delivery of the West Indian speech pattern—all go to picture and reemphasize the profundity of life, dying, and existence when tragic and comic values meet in confrontation.

—Louis D. Mitchell

HIVNOR, Robert (Hanks). American. Born in Zanesville, Ohio, in 1916. Educated at the University of Akron, Ohio, A.B. 1936; Yale University, New Haven, Connecticut, M.F.A. 1946; Columbia University, New York, 1952–54. Served in the United States Army, 1942–45. Married Mary Otis in 1947; two sons and one daughter. Political cartoonist and commercial artist, 1934–38; Instructor, University of Minnesota, Minneapolis, 1946–48, and Reed College, Portland, Oregon, 1954–55; Assistant Professor, Bard College, Annandale-on-Hudson, New York, 1956–59. Recipient: University of Iowa fellowship, 1951; Rockefeller grant, 1968. Address: 420 East 84th Street, New York, New York 10028, U.S.A.

PUBLICATIONS

Plays

Martha Goodwin, adaptation of the story "A Goat for Azazel" by Katherine Anne Porter (produced New Haven, Connecticut, 1942; revised version broadcast, 1959).

Too Many Thumbs (produced Minneapolis, 1948; New York, 1949; London, 1951). Minneapolis, University of Minnesota Press, 1949.

The Ticklish Acrobat (produced New York, 1954). Published in *Playbook: Five Plays for a New Theatre*, New York, New Directions, 1956.

The Assault upon Charles Sumner (produced New York, 1964). Published in *Plays for a New Theatre: Playbook 2*, New York, New Directions, 1966.

Love Reconciled to War (produced Baltimore, 1968). Published in *Break Out! In Search of New Theatrical Environments*, edited by James Schevill, Chicago, Swallow Press, 1973.

"I" "Love" "You" (produced New York, 1968). Published in *Anon* (Austin, Texas), 1971.

DMZ (includes the sketches *Uptight Arms, How Much?, "I" "Love" "You"*) (as Osbert Pismire and Jack Askew; produced New York, 1969).

A Son Is Always Leaving Home, in *Anon* (Austin, Texas), 1971.

*

Critical Studies: "The Pleasure and Pains of Playgoing" by Saul Bellow, in *Partisan Review* (New York), May 1954; *The Theatre of the Absurd* by Martin Esslin, New York, Doubleday, 1961, London, Eyre and Spottiswoode, 1962, revised edition, London, Penguin, 1968, Doubleday, 1969; *American Drama since World War II* by Gerald Weales, New York, Harcourt Brace, 1962; *The New American Arts* edited by Richard Kostelanetz, New York, Horizon Press, 1965; by Albert Bermel, in *New Leader* (New York), 1966; by A.W. Staub, in *Southern Review* (Baton Rouge, Louisiana), Summer 1970.

* * *

The economics of theatre are all too cruel to art: because a play costs so much more to produce than, say, a novel, many important texts are rarely, if ever, presented. Those particularly victimized by such economic discrimination include older playwrights who have neither the time nor energy necessary to launch non-commercial productions on their own. There is no doubt, in my judgment, that Robert Hivnor has written two of the best and most original American postwar dramas, but it is lamentable that our knowledge of them, as well as his reputation, must be based more upon print than performance and that lack of incentive keeps yet other plays half-finished. The first, called *Too Many Thumbs*, is more feasible, requiring only some inventive costuming and masks to overcome certain difficulties in artifice. It tells of an exceptionally bright chimpanzee, possessed of a large body and a small head, who in the course of the play moves up the evolutionary ladder to become, first, an intermediate stage between man and beast, and then a normal man and ultimately a god-like creature with an immense head and a shrivelled body. The university professors who keep him also attempt to cast him as the avatar of a new religion, but unending evolution defeats their designs. Just as Hivnor's writing is often very funny, so is the play's ironically linear structure also extremely original (preceding Ionesco's use of it in *The New Tenant*), for by pursuing the bias implicit in evolutionary development to its inevitable reversal, the play coherently questions mankind's claim to a higher state of existence. *The Ticklish Acrobat* is a lesser work, nonetheless exhibiting some true originality and typically Hivnorian intellectual comedy; but here the practical difficulty lies in constructing a set whose period recedes several hundred years in time with each act.

Hivnor is fundamentally a dark satirist who debunks myths and permits no heroes; but unlike other protagonist-less playwrights, he is less interested in absurdity than comprehensive ridicule. *The Assault upon Charles Sumner* is an immensely sophisticated history play, regrettably requiring more actors and scenes than an unsubsidized theatre can afford, and an audience more literate than Broadway offers. Its subject is the supreme example of liberal intellectuality in American politics—the 19th-century Senator from Massachusetts, Charles Sumner, who had been a distinguished proponent of abolition and the Civil War. Like Sumner's biographer David Donald, Hivnor finds that Sumner, for all his saintliness, was politically ineffectual and personally insufferable. The opening prologue, which contains some of Hivnor's most savage writing, establishes the play's tone and thrust, as it deals with the funeral and possible afterlife of the last living Negro slave. "Sir, no American has ever been let into heaven." "Not old Abe Lincoln?" the slave asks. "Mr. Lincoln," Sumner replies, "sits over there revising his speech at the Gettysburg. . . ."

Extending such negative satire, Hivnor feasts upon episodes and symbols of both personal and national failure, attempting to define a large historical experience in a single evening. While much of the imagery is particularly theatrical, such as repeating the scene where Preston Brooks assaults Sumner with a cane, perhaps the play's subject and scope are finally closer, both intrinsically and extrinsically, to extended prose fiction.

—Richard Kostelanetz

HOFFMAN, William M. American. Born in New York City, 12 April 1939. Educated at the City University, New York, 1955–60, B.A. (cum laude) in Latin 1960 (Phi Beta Kappa). Editorial assistant, Barnes and Noble, publishers, New York, 1960–61; assistant editor, 1961–67, and associate editor and drama editor, 1967–68, Hill and Wang, publishers, New York; literary adviser, *Scripts* magazine, New York, 1971–72; Visiting Lecturer, University of Massachusetts, Boston, Spring 1973; playwright-in-residence, American Conservatory Theatre, San Francisco, 1978, and La Mama, New York, 1978–79. Since 1980 Star Professor, Hofstra University, Hempstead, New York. Recipient: MacDowell Colony fellowship, 1971; Colorado Council on the Arts and Humanities grant, 1972; Carnegie Fund grant, 1972; PEN grant, 1972; Guggenheim fellowship, 1974; National Endowment for the Arts grant, 1975, 1976; Drama Desk award, 1985; Obie award, 1985; New York Foundation for the Arts grant, 1985. Lives in New York City. Agent: Luis Sanjurjo, International Creative Management, 40 West 57th Street, New York, New York 10019, U.S.A.

Publications

Plays

Thank You, Miss Victoria (produced New York, 1965; London, 1970). Published in *New American Plays 3*, edited by Hoffman, New York, Hill and Wang, 1970.
Saturday Night at the Movies (produced New York, 1966). Published in *The Off-Off-Broadway Book*, edited by Albert Poland and Bruce Mailman, Indianapolis, Bobbs Merrill, 1972.
Good Night, I Love You (produced New York, 1966).
Spring Play (produced New York, 1967).
Three Masked Dances (produced New York, 1967).
Incantation (produced New York, 1967).
Uptight! (produced New York, 1968).
XXX (produced New York, 1969; as *Nativity Play*, produced London, 1970). Published in *More Plays from Off-Off-Broadway*, edited by Michael T. Smith, Indianapolis, Bobbs Merrill, 1972.
Luna (also director: produced New York, 1970). As *An Excerpt from Buddha*, published in *Now: Theater der Erfahrung*, edited by Jens Heilmeyer and Pia Frolich, Cologne, Schauberg, 1971.
A Quick Nut Bread to Make Your Mouth Water (also director: produced New York, 1970). Published in *Spontaneous Combustion: Eight New American Plays*, edited by Rochelle Owens, New York, Winter House, 1972.
From Fool to Hanged Man (produced New York, 1972). Published in *Scenarios* (New York), 1982.
The Children's Crusade (produced New York, 1972).
Gilles de Rais (also director: produced New York, 1975).

Cornbury, with Anthony Holland (produced New Haven, Connecticut, 1977). Published in *Gay Plays*, edited by Hoffman, New York, Avon, 1979.
The Last Days of Stephen Foster (televised 1977). Published in *Dramatics* (Cincinnati), 1978.
A Book of Etiquette, music by John Braden (produced New York, 1978; as *Etiquette*, produced New York, 1983).
Gulliver's Travels, music by John Braden, adaptation of the novel by Swift (produced New York, 1978).
Shoe Palace Murray, with Anthony Holland (produced San Francisco, 1978). Published in *Gay Plays*, edited by Hoffman, New York, Avon, 1979.
The Cherry Orchard, Part II, with Anthony Holland (produced New York, 1983).
As Is (produced New York, 1985; London, 1987). New York, Random House, 1985.

Television Writing: *Notes from the New World: Louis Moreau Gottschalk*, with Roger Englander, 1976; *The Last Days of Stephen Foster*, 1977; *Whistler: 5 Portraits*, 1978.

Verse

The Cloisters: A Song Cycle, music by John Corigliano. New York, Schirmer, 1968.
Wedding Song. New York, Schirmer, 1984.

Other

Editor, *New American Plays 2, 3* and *4*. New York, Hill and Wang, 3 vols., 1968–71.
Editor, *Gay Plays: The First Collection*. New York, Avon, 1979.

*

Manuscript Collections: University of Wisconsin, Madison; Lincoln Center Library of the Performing Arts, New York.

Theatrical Activities:
Director: **Plays**—*Thank You, Miss Victoria*, New Brunswick, New Jersey, 1970; *Luna*, New York, 1970; *A Quick Nut Bread to Make Your Mouth Water*, New York, 1970, Denver, 1972; *XXX*, New York, 1970; *First Death* by Walter Leyden Brown, New York, 1972; *Gilles de Rais*, New York, 1975.
Actor: **Plays**—Frank in *The Haunted Host* by Robert Patrick, New York, 1964; Cupid in *Joyce Dynel* by Robert Patrick, New York, 1969; Twin in *Huckleberry Finn*, New York, 1969. **Film**—*Guru the Mad Monk*, 1970.

William M. Hoffman comments:

(1982) In 1980 the Metropolitan Opera commissioned me to write a libretto for their 1983–84 season. The composer chosen was John Corigliano. We decided to complete the trilogy of operas on Figaro, using Beaumarchais's last play, *La Mère coupable* (*The Guilty Mother*), as our port of embarkation.

This libretto capped a decade of work with historical materials. My subjects included Gilles de Rais, the actual Bluebeard of 15th-century France; *Gulliver's Travels* and Emily Post's *Book of Etiquette* (1934 edition), in musical adaptation; James McNeill Whistler, Stephen Foster, and Louis Moreau Gottschalk, in plays for television; and Jesus.

My three collaborations with Anthony Holland were also historically founded. *Cornbury* is based on the life of the transvestite English governor of New York in the early 18th century. *Shoe Palace Murray* is located in New York in the 1920's. And *Cherry Orchard, Part II* is set in Russia of the 1905–17 era.

But now after finishing the libretto, I have returned to the more personal material of my earliest plays, which all took place in contemporary times. I am currently working on a semiautobiographical play and a novel set in my neighborhood, SoHo.

* * *

William M. Hoffman's early work *Spring Play* is about a young man leaving home, girlfriend, and innocence and coming to New York City, where he meets a variety of exciting, corrupting people and experiences, and comes to some grief in his growing up. The style of the play is romantic and poetic, a kind of hallucinatory naturalism. Since then Hoffman has edited several anthologies of new American plays, and his awareness of contemporary styles and modes of consciousness is reflected in his own work. *Thank You, Miss Victoria* is a brilliant monologue in which a mother-fixated young business executive gets into a bizarre sado-masochistic relationship on the telephone. *Saturday Night at the Movies* is a bright, brash comedy, and *Uptight!* a musical revue. The eccentrically titled play *XXX* has as characters Jesus, Mary, Joseph, the Holy Ghost, and God. It retells the story of Jesus's life in a personal, free-form, associative, hip, provocatively beautiful fashion. The play is conceived as an ensemble performance for five actors. *Luna* is a light show. *A Quick Nut Bread to Make Your Mouth Water* is an ostensibly improvisatory play for three actors constructed in the form of a recipe, and the nut bread is served to the audience at the finish of the performance. In one production the author himself directed, he incorporated a group of gospel singers into the play.

Hoffman has explored forms other than drama, seeking a renewal of dramatic energies, attempting to expand theatrical possibilities and the audience's awareness. *From Fool to Hanged Man* is a scenario for pantomime, based on imagery from the Tarot. By contrast with much of Hoffman's earlier work, which made a point of the possibility of enlightenment, in which innocence was rewarded at least with edifying experience, here the innocent hero moves blindly, almost passively, through a bleak succession of destructive encounters and is finally hanged. The beauty of the work only emphasizes its despair. Characteristically, the forces at work are not worldly or political but seem to exist in the individual state of mind. *The Children's Crusade* is another dance-pantomime of naive and sentimental innocence brought down by the mockery and hostility of the corrupt, historically worn-out world. The theme parallels a widespread shift of attitude in the United States; to follow Hoffman's work is to observe a representative contemporary consciousness.

Although *Gilles de Rais* embraces depravity, most of Hoffman's subsequent work treats lighter subjects. In this vein are *The Cherry Orchard, Part II, Shoe Palace Murray*, and *Cornbury*, all collaborations with Anthony Holland. *The Cherry Orchard, Part II* is a political satire, incorporating lyrical and melodramatic elements, which opens and closes with the final moments of Chekhov's play and co-opts the character of Irina from *The Three Sisters*. It traces the evolution between 1903 and 1918 of a group of Moscow intellectuals from Tolstoyan pacifists to Bolsheviks. Comedies both, *Shoe Palace Murray* takes place in a New York footwear store in 1926, while *Cornbury* dramatizes the life of an early governor of New York, a transvestite who ruled in Queen Anne's leftover clothing. With the songwriter John Braden, Hoffman has also written two musicals, *Gulliver's Travels* and *A Book of Etiquette*. Another musical project—suggested by the third play in Beaumarchais's trilogy *The Guilty Mother*—is the libretto to *A Figaro for Antonia* for the composer John Corigliano, commissioned by the Metropolitan Opera.

As Is returns to serious matters: the mysterious and, so far, incurable illness Aids, which in America has struck male homosexuals particularly hard. Blending humor with rage and sorrow, playing freely with time and place, *As Is* makes its larger social commentary within the context of an old-fashioned love story—only here the lovers are gay men, one of whom has a fatal, infectious disease. Hoffman's most popular play to date, *As Is* transferred from the Circle Repertory Company to Broadway.

—Michael T. Smith and C. Lee Jenner

HOLDEN, Joan. American. Born in Berkeley, California, 18 January 1939. Educated at Reed College, Portland, Oregon, B.A. 1960; University of California, Berkeley, M.A. 1964. Married 1) Arthur Holden in 1958 (divorced); 2) Daniel Chumley in 1968, three daughters. Waitress, Claremont Hotel, Berkeley, 1960–62; copywriter, Librairie Larousse, Paris, 1964–66; research assistant, University of California, Berkeley, 1966–67. Since 1967 playwright, publicist, 1967–69, and business manager, 1978–79, San Francisco Mime Troupe. Editor, Pacific News Service, 1973–75; Instructor in Playwriting, University of California, Davis, 1975, 1977, 1979, 1983, 1985, 1987. Recipient: Obie award, 1973; Rockefeller grant, 1985. Address: San Francisco Mime Troupe, 855 Treat Street, San Francisco, California 94110, U.S.A.

PUBLICATIONS

Plays

L'Amant Militaire, adaptation of a play by Carlo Goldoni, translated by Betty Schwimmer (produced San Francisco and New York, 1967). Published in *The San Francisco Mime Troupe: The First Ten Years*, by R.G. Davis, Palo Alto, California, Ramparts Press, 1975.

Ruzzante; or, The Veteran, adaptation of a play by Angelo Beolco, translated by Suzanne Pollard (produced Hayward, California, 1968).

The Independent Female; or, A Man Has His Pride (produced Los Angeles, 1970). Included in *By Popular Demand*, 1980.

Seize the Time, with Steve Friedman (produced San Francisco, 1970).

The Dragon Lady's Revenge, with others (produced San Francisco, 1971; New York, 1972). Included in *By Popular Demand*, 1980.

Frozen Wages, with Richard Benetar and Daniel Chumley (produced San Francisco, 1972). Included in *By Popular Demand*, 1980.

San Fran Scandals, with others (produced San Francisco, 1973). Included in *By Popular Demand*, 1980.

The Great Air Robbery (produced San Francisco, 1974).

Frijoles; or, Beans to You, with others (produced San Francisco, 1975). Included in *By Popular Demand*, 1980.

Power Play (produced San Francisco, 1975).

False Promises/Nos Engañaron (produced San Francisco, 1976; New York, 1978). Included in *By Popular Demand*, 1980.

The Loon's Rage, with Steve Most and Jael Weisman (produced on tour, 1977). Published in *West Coast Plays 10* (Berkeley, California), Fall 1981.

The Hotel Universe, music by Bruce Barthol (produced La Rochelle, France, 1977).

By Popular Demand: Plays and Other Works by The San Francisco Mime Troupe (includes *False Promises/Nos Engañaron; San Fran Scandals; The Dragon Lady's Revenge; The Independent Female; Frijoles; Frozen Wages* by Holden, and *Los Siete* and *Evo-Man*). San Francisco, San Francisco Mime Troupe, 1980.

Factperson, with others (produced San Francisco, 1980). Published in *West Coast Plays 15–16* (Berkeley, California), Spring 1983.

Americans; or, Last Tango in Huahuatenango, with Daniel Chumley (produced Dayton, Ohio, and London, 1981; New York, 1982).

Factwino Meets the Moral Majority, with others (produced San Francisco, 1981; New York, 1982). Published in *West Coast Plays 15-16* (Berkeley, California), Spring 1983.

Factwino vs. Armaggedonman (produced San Francisco, 1982). Published in *West Coast Plays 15-16* (Berkeley, California), Spring 1983.

Steeltown, music by Bruce Barthol (produced San Francisco, 1984; New York, 1985).

1985, with others (produced San Francisco, 1985).

Spain/36, music by Bruce Barthol (produced Los Angeles, 1986).

The Mozamgola Caper, with others (produced San Francisco, 1986).

*

Manuscript Collection: University of California, Davis.

Critical Studies: "*Hotel Universe*: Playwriting and the San Francisco Mime Troupe" by William Kleb, in *Theater* (New Haven, Connecticut), Spring 1978; "Joan Holden and the San Francisco Mime Troupe," in *Drama Review* (New York), Spring 1980, and *New American Dramatists 1960–1980*, London, Macmillan, and New York, Grove Press, 1982, both by Ruby Cohn.

Joan Holden comments:

I write political cartoons. For years, I was ashamed of this. I agreed meekly with those critics who said, "*mere* political cartoons." To please them, and led astray by well-wishers who'd say, "You can do more—you could write *serious* plays," I've tried my hand, from time to time, at realism. Each time I've been extremely impressed, at first, with the solemnity of what I've written. Rereading those passages, I always find I've written melodrama. The fact is, I'm only inspired when I'm being funny. Writing comedy is not really a choice: it's a quirk. On a certain level, making things funny is a coward's way of keeping pain at arm's length. But that same distance allows you to show certain things clearly: notably, characters' social roles, their functions in history. These generalities, not the specifics which soften them, interest caricaturists—who have serious reasons for being funny, and in whose ranks I now aspire to be counted.

For 20 years, I've written for a permanent company, for particular actors, directors, and composers, and in collaboration with them. This has put conditions on my writing; it has also supplied a nearly constant source of ideas, and a wonderful opportunity to learn from mistakes.

* * *

Joan Holden has been the principal playwright of the San Francisco Mime Troupe, which has always performed with words as well as gesture. Chance led to this association. During the Vietnam war the Mime Troupe director (before it became a collective) wished to update Goldoni's *Amante Militare*, and Troupe member Arthur Holden volunteered his wife, who based her script on the Troupe's familiar *commedia* style with racial stereotypes. From the first company reading of the script, Holden knew that she wanted to be a playwright.

The Holden/Goldoni *Military Lover/L'Amant Militaire* drew large audiences to nearly fifty park performances. Shortly after producing the play, Holden wrote: "Comedy, which in its basic action always measures an unsatisfactory reality against its corresponding ideal, may be the revolutionary art form *par excellence*." It became Holden's art form *par excellence*, pitting satirized Establishment figures of unsatisfactory reality against the satisfactory dream of working-class harmony and celebration.

After the Mime Troupe went collective in 1970, *The Independent Female* expressed the new spirit. *Commedia* characters gave way to those of soap opera with satiric telltale names—Pennybank for a business tycoon, Heartright for a junior executive, Bullitt for a militant feminist. A pair of lovers is faced with an obstacle to their marriage—soap opera. But subverting the genre, Holden identifies the obstacle as the young ingénue's growing independence. Instead of dissolving the obstacle for a happy curtain clinch, Holden sees a happy ending in sustained feminist revolt which the audience is asked to link to working class revolt. Now nearly two decades old, the play has proved popular with many groups.

The Dragon Lady's Revenge is grounded in another popular form, the comic strip, with assists from Grade B movies, and its intricate plot involves the corrupt American ambassador in Long Penh, his soldier son, a CIA agent Drooley, and the titular Dragon Lady, as well as the honest native revolutionary Blossom. Holden shifted from global to local politics with *San Fran Scandals* blending housing problems into vaudeville. Science fiction and detective story were then exploited for *The Great Air Robbery*.

The San Francisco Mime Troupe was made up mainly of members of the white middle class, committed to social change. In the mid-1970's they actively recruited Third World members, and Holden's scripts from that time reflect their new constituency. *Frijoles* (Spanish for beans) zigzags from a Latin American couple to a North American couple, joining them at a food conference in Europe, and joining them in identical class interests. As *Frijoles* travels through space, *Power Play* travels through time in order to indict the anti-ecological monopoly of the Pacific Gas and Electric Company.

By 1976, America's bicentennial year, Holden was in firm command of her style: a specific issue attacked through a popular art form; simple language and clean story line; swift scenes often culminating in a song. The group wished to present a play on the uncelebrated aspects of American history—the role of workers, minorities, women. Based on collective research, Holden scripted *False Promises*, which deviated from her usual satiric formula in presenting heightened realism of working-class characters. They continue to appear in subsequent plays, but Holden never sentimentalizes them.

In *Steeltown* she experiments with time to dramatize creeping consumerism eroding worker solidarity. *Spain/36* is a prodigiously ambitious musical in which world leaders in masks sacrifice common people to the monster of Fascism. Local or international, Holden theatricalizes events with comic verve.

—Ruby Cohn

HOLLINGSWORTH, Margaret. Canadian. Born in London, England, in 1940; emigrated to Canada, 1968; became citizen, 1974. Educated at Hornsey High School, London; Loughborough School of Librarianship, Leicestershire, A.L.A.; Lakehead University, Thunder Bay, Ontario (Gold Medal), B.A. 1972; University of British Columbia, Vancouver, M.F.A. in theatre and creative writing 1974. Journalist, editor, librarian, and teacher in England, 1960–68; chief librarian, Fort William Public Library, Ontario, 1968–72. Since 1972 free-lance writer. Assistant Professor, David Thompson University Centre, Nelson, British Columbia, 1981–83; writer-in-residence, Stratford Festival Theatre, Ontario, 1986. Recipient: Chalmers award, 1983. Lives in Toronto. Address: c/o Playwrights Union of Canada, 8 York Street, 6th Floor, Toronto, Ontario M5J 1R2, Canada.

Publications

Plays

Bushed (produced Vancouver, 1973). With *Operators*, Toronto, Playwrights, 1981.

Operators (produced Vancouver, 1974; revised version produced 1981). With *Bushed*, Toronto, Playwrights, 1981.

Dance for My Father. Vancouver, New Play Centre, 1976.

Alli Alli Oh (produced Vancouver, 1977). Toronto, Playwrights, 1979.

The Apple in the Eye (broadcast 1977; produced Vancouver, 1983). Included in *Willful Acts*, 1985.

The Writers Show (revue), with others (produced Vancouver, 1978).

Mother Country (produced Toronto, 1980). Toronto, Playwrights, 1980.

Ever Loving (produced Victoria, British Columbia, 1980). Toronto, Playwrights, 1981.

Islands (produced Vancouver, 1983). Toronto, Playwrights, 1983.

Diving (produced Vancouver, 1983). Included in *Willful Acts*, 1985.

War Babies (produced Victoria, British Columbia, 1984). Included in *Willful Acts*, 1985.

It's Only Hot for Two Months in Kapuskasing (produced Toronto, 1985).

Willful Acts (includes *The Apple in the Eye, Ever Loving, Diving, Islands, War Babies*). Toronto, Coach House Press, 1985.

The Green Line (produced Stratford, Ontario, 1986).

Radio Plays: *Prairie Drive, As I Was Saying to Mr. Dideron, Wayley's Children*, and *War Games*, from 1973; *The Apple in the Eye*, 1977; *Webster's Revenge*, 1977.

Television Plays: *Ole and All That*, 1968 (UK); *Sleepwalking* (*AirWaves* series), 1986.

*

Critical Study: introduction by Ann Saddlemyer to *Willful Acts*, 1985.

Margaret Hollingsworth comments:

My work is very wide-ranging in style and subject. Constantly recurring themes are the search for a home, sex roles and sexual stereotypes, and war. My latest plays are *The Green Line* which is set on the green line in Beirut, and *Marked for Marriage*, a 3-act farce set against the background of the survival games which are an extremely popular pseudo-military outdoor activity among Canadian men.

Some of my more experimental work, such as *Prim and Duck, Mama and Frank*, has yet to get beyond the workshop production stage, since there are very few outlets for experimental work in Canada at this time.

* * *

Margaret Hollingsworth presents woman exploring, projecting, provoking, and sometimes escaping from the need to come to terms with herself and her environment. Neither peripheral nor passive, she is yet aware that while she observes others, she herself is not always noted, and until she acts, she will not be seen or heard. Like the heroine of "Widecombe Fair," one of Hollingsworth's recent short stories, she has been granted full rights of citizenship but remains an English-speaking alien. And from this isolated point of view she must carve out both a space and a language in order to build her world.

Sometimes that point of view is split between the external, ostensibly "real" world in which a role is imposed upon her, and the—to her—truer reality from which she looks out: Gemma, in *The Apple in the Eye*, for example, recognizes all too clearly the distinction between her husband Martin's ordered, reductive, factually objective universe and her own expansive, encircling, imaginative inner life, and actually watches herself deftly weave the one through the other. In *Islands*, on the other hand, both Alli and Muriel deliberately reject that outer world, refusing to cope with it on any level: Alli elects madness where, her mind in "cold storage," she does not have to apologize for her actions and words because she is "sick" and so can move freely, untouched, through the lives of others, while Muriel retires into isolation, seeking a self-sufficiency where she runs no risk of hurting others, or herself.

Sometimes the imaginative inner world is surrealistically imposed on the framework of the outer life, as in *Diving*, where Viveca can safely compose the male/female, mother/daughter relationships into new metaphorical patterns. At other times the external structure is wilfully destroyed in order to achieve the inner dream, just as Luce fends off Chuck in *Ever Loving* to create her own independent life in the new world; but the obverse too is, threateningly, always there, and in the same play the other two war brides, Ruth and Diana, find their hopes and plans overwhelmed and submerged in the strange, new, and demanding environments of their husbands.

And sometimes, as in *War Babies*, that inner world becomes a mirror, reflecting the pain and oppressiveness of separation and the constant struggle to bridge two isolations: "I thought I'd try to put you in my position, so you'd really know how it feels," Esme explains as she writes a play about her life with Colin from the other side of the looking glass.

But always, in all of Hollingsworth's plays, it is this mental landscape one notices first, and then the need for a relationship with it, the need in fact to feel at home. "Home comes in again and again in my work," Hollingsworth admits. "It's about relating to the place that you're in and finding a place for yourself in a foreign environment."

Home also means sharing, talking to each other, above all, listening. "I get the feeling you two should talk more," the nurse Paddy tells Colin in *War Babies*. "We talk all the time," protests Colin. "Real talk," replies Paddy. And so they do talk all the time—to themselves, to each other, to the audience. Hollingsworth's characters are fluent to the limit of endurance, pushing words, images, ideas to the wall in their effort to be heard and felt. For "real talk" requires not only listening but emotional engagement. Words, feelings, questions, listening—all must be managed into a pattern of familiarity before one can feel safe. "We're always trying to contain ... look for limits," the playwright Esme has her creation Colin 2 say. "Without limits, we go mad, don't we?"

It is on the brink of this precipice that most of Hollingsworth's characters live. Indeed, *Islands* takes characters from an even earlier stage life, *Alli Alli Oh*, and pushes them over the edge. At the end of that earlier one-act play, Alli escapes into madness in order to run away from a relationship that has gone nerve-rendingly wrong, leaving Muriel to deal with a calving cow and a farm she cannot manage on her own. Now, six months later, in *Islands*, Muriel has achieved an uneasy truce with her environment, but the stage directions, in describing a setting that is only "roughly finished," reflect the tenuousness of her new-found stability. In the end some things are accomplished: Alli's uninhibited frankness serves as a catalyst towards honesty, and Rose must confront the fact of her daughter's lesbianism. But the calm of the play's conclusion is not completely reassuring, and we suspect that no man—or woman—can be an island. *Alli Alli Oh* and its companion piece *Islands* are both set on an island off the west coast of British Columbia, an environment Hollingsworth herself enjoyed for some years and repeatedly returns to.

In *Mother Country*, which also has a west coast setting, the themes of home and belonging are set in a larger context still of culture and country. *Ever Loving*, which received its first production the same year (but at the other end of the country) as *Mother Country*, further explores the problems of belonging, through the lives of three immigrants thrown up by the tide of war.

Hollingsworth's work for the theatre ranges from full-length plays with conventional stage settings and large casts to miniatures with one, two, or three characters; from comedies of situation and character to fantasy voyages through strange mental landscapes. In *Bushed*, two retired immigrant workers meet each day in the laundromat and against the rhythm of sheet-folding, humming machines, and the ceaseless mimed action of housewives, weave their own fantasies, dream their own dreams. *Operators*, like *Bushed*, is set in northern Ontario (the region Hollingsworth first settled in after emigrating from England); like *Bushed*, it reflects the inner worlds of workers—this time two women on factory night shift—as they try to build a friendship without communicating the facts of their daily lives. *The Apple in the Eye* and *Diving* pursue this more lyrical, abstract aspect of Hollingsworth's work, reflecting her long training in writing for radio and her keen ear for nuances of speech and both regional and cultural differences.

Written with stylishness and wit from a woman's point of view, Hollingsworth's plays are not rigidly feminist; rooted in place, they are not restrictively regional. They speak both of Canada and the human condition.

—Ann Saddlemyer

HOME, William Douglas-. British. Born in Edinburgh, 3 June 1912; brother of the political leader Alec Douglas-Home (Baron Home of the Hirsel). Educated at Eton College, 1927–32; New College, Oxford, 1932–35, B.A. in history 1935; Royal Academy of Dramatic Art, London, 1935–37. Served in the Royal Armoured Corps, 1940–44: Captain; court-martialled and imprisoned for 8 months, 1944–45. Married Rachel Brand (Baroness Dacre) in 1951; one son and three daughters. Progressive Independent Candidate for Parliament, Cathcart Division, Glasgow, April 1942, Windsor Division of Berkshire, June 1942, and Clay Cross Division of Derbyshire, April 1944; Liberal Candidate, South Edinburgh, 1957. Since 1971 Chairman, Farnham Repertory Trust, Surrey. Agent: Laurence Evans, International Creative Management, 388 Oxford Street, London W1N 9HE. Address: Derry House, Kilmeston, Hampshire SO24 0NR, England.

PUBLICATIONS

Plays

Great Possessions (produced London, 1937).
Passing By (produced London, 1940).
Now Barabbas . . . (produced London, 1947). London, Longman, 1947.
The Chiltern Hundreds (produced London, 1947). London, French, 1949; as *Yes, M'Lord* (produced New York, 1949), New York, French, 1949.
Ambassador Extraordinary (produced London, 1948).
Master of Arts (produced Brighton and London, 1949). London, French, 1951.
The Thistle and the Rose (produced London, 1949). Included in *The Plays of William Douglas Home*, 1958.
Caro William (produced London, 1952).
The Bad Samaritan (produced Bromley, Kent, 1952; London, 1953). London, Evans, 1954.
The Manor of Northstead (produced London, 1954). London, French, 1956.
The Reluctant Debutante (produced Brighton and London, 1955; New York, 1956). London, Evans, 1956; New York, French, 1957.
The Iron Duchess (produced Brighton and London, 1957). London, Evans, 1958.
The Plays of William Douglas Home (includes *Now Barabbas . . ., The Chiltern Hundreds, The Thistle and the Rose, The Bad Samaritan, The Reluctant Debutante*). London, Heinemann, 1958.
Aunt Edwina (produced Eastbourne, Sussex, and London, 1959). London, French, 1960.
Up a Gum Tree (produced Ipswich, 1960).
The Bad Soldier Smith (produced London, 1961). London, Evans, 1962.
The Cigarette Girl (produced London, 1962).
The Drawing Room Tragedy (produced Salisbury, 1963).
The Reluctant Peer (produced London, 1964). London, Evans, and New York, French, 1965.
Two Accounts Rendered: The Home Secretary and Lady J.P. 2 (produced London, 1964).
A Friend Indeed (produced Windsor, 1965; London, 1966). London, French, 1966.
Betzi (produced Salisbury, 1965; revised version produced London, 1975). London, French, 1977.
The Queen's Highland Servant (produced Salisbury, 1967; London, 1968).
The Secretary Bird (produced Manchester and London, 1968). London, French, 1969.
The Grouse Moor Image (produced Plymouth, 1968).
The Bishop and the Actress (televised 1968). London, French, 1969.
The Editor Regrets (televised 1970; produced London, 1978). London, Evans, 1979.
Uncle Dick's Surprise (produced Salisbury, 1970).
The Jockey Club Stakes (produced London, 1970; Washington, D.C., 1972; New York, 1973). London, French, 1971.
The Douglas Cause (produced Nottingham and London, 1971).
Lloyd George Knew My Father (as *Lady Boothroyd of the By-Pass*, produced Boston, Lincolnshire, 1972; as *Lloyd George Knew My Father*, produced London, 1972; Washington, D.C., 1974). London, French, 1973.
In the Red (as *The Bank Manager*, produced Boston, Lincolnshire, 1972; as *In the Red*, produced London, 1977). London, French, 1978.
At the End of the Day (produced Guildford, Surrey, and London, 1973).
The Dame of Sark (produced Oxford and London, 1974). London, French, 1976.
The Lord's Lieutenant (produced Farnham, Surrey, 1974).
The Kingfisher (produced Brighton and London, 1977; Baltimore and New York, 1978). London, French, 1981.
Rolls Hyphen Royce (produced London, 1977).
The Perch (produced Pitlochry, 1977).
The Consulting Room (produced Winchester, 1977).
Four Hearts Doubled (produced Windsor, 1982).
Her Mother Came Too (produced Leatherhead, Surrey, 1982).
The Golf Umbrella (produced Birmingham, 1983). London, English Theatre Guild, 1984.
David and Jonathan (produced Farnham, Surrey, 1984; as *And as for Jonathan*, produced Worthing, Sussex, 1985; as *Marriage Rites*, produced Windsor, 1986).
After the Ball Is Over (produced London, 1985).
Portraits (produced Malvern, Worcestershire, and London, 1987).

Screenplays: *Sleeping Car to Trieste*, with Allan Mackinnon, 1948; *For Them That Trespass*, with J. Lee-Thompson, 1949; *The Chiltern Hundreds* (*The Amazing Mr. Beecham*), with Patrick Kirwan, 1949; *Your Witness* (*Eye Witness*), with Hugo Butler and Ian Hunter, 1950; *Made in Heaven*, 1952; *The Colditz Story*, with others, 1955; *The Reluctant Debutante*, 1959; *Follow That Horse!*, with Howard Mason and Alfred Shaughnessy, 1960.

Television Plays: *The Bishop and the Actress*, 1968; *The Editor Regrets*, 1970; *On Such a Night*, 1974; *You're All Right, How Am I?*, 1981.

Verse

Home Truths. London, Lane, 1939.

Other

Half-Term Report: An Autobiography. London, Longman, 1954.

Mr. Home, Pronounced Hume: An Autobiography. London, Collins, 1979.

Sins of Commission (memoirs). Wilton, Wiltshire, Russell, 1985.

Editor, *The Prime Ministers.* London, Robson, 1985.

*

Theatrical Activities:

Actor: **Plays**—with the Brighton Repertory Company, 1937; Brian Morellian in *Bonnet over the Windmill* by Dodie Smith, London, 1937; Johnny Greystroke in *Plan for a Hostess* by Thomas Browne, London, 1938; Pym in *The Chiltern Hundreds*, London, 1948; Jimmy Broadbent in *The Reluctant Debutante*, London, 1955; Colonel Ryan in *Aunt Edwina*, Brighton, 1960.

* * *

Audiences in the West End and in the provinces have been chuckling at William Douglas-Home's light-hearted comedies ever since the end of World War II. In *The Chiltern Hundreds* the accurate but affectionate portrayal of the odd characters of an upper-class family serves as the background to a wry comment on changing political and social conditions with a plot that gets close to turning elections into a game of musical chairs. In this there is some reflection of the playwright's own experiences as a parliamentary candidate and a good deal of tongue-in-cheek comment on the political scene by one who knew it well. But the success of the play probably owed more to the witty dialogue and the warm humanity revealed in Home's response to a gallery of British eccentrics as a pretty American girl looks on making pert comments. He had, in fact, found a formula that was to serve him well, even if, for a while, influential critics were to inveigh against what they solemnly stigmatised as incorrigible frivolity.

The Reluctant Debutante is pure froth, presenting, within a tradition that looks back to Oscar Wilde, the eternal pentangle when a girl "comes out" in the London season: a put-upon father ruefully counts the cost of a flat, expensive dresses, and an extravagant party, his wife plunges into match-making with Machiavellian determination, the pretty daughter is constantly afraid of getting out of her depth, and there are a pair of bachelors. The outcome is perfectly predictable, but there is just enough suspense to create the plot which serves as a framework for a succession of entertaining episodes reflecting the way audiences like to think the upper classes behave. The generation gap, like taxation, is just one of those facts of life you have to put up with, and love still makes the world go round in a whirl that always seems unique to those involved for the first time. *The Jockey Club Stakes* depicts the world that its author came to know well when he owned a racehorse. The venerable institution that controls the turf is shown as the domain of bumbling ex-officers who somehow muddle through in a world of uncertain values where everybody wants to place an each-way bet on the main chance.

Lloyd George Knew My Father—which has nothing to do with the Liberal statesman apart from the fact that the nonsense parody of "Onward Christian Soldiers" is sung at one point—begins with the potentially serious issue of a landowner's wife threatening to commit suicide if a by-pass is built through the estate. Disaster is easily averted, but not before Home has paraded a cavalcade of military types with his usual verve and thickened the plot with farcical elaborations. Similar comments apply to *Aunt Edwina* which takes as its starting point the sex-change which a retired colonel undergoes when he takes some hormone pills that the vet had prescribed for his horse. The natural embarrassment this causes soon dissolves into good-humoured hilarity. Home milks the situation for every laugh while avoiding anything like indecency. What distinguishes this play and his other comedies is a warm sympathy for humanity even in absurd situations as people struggle to be themselves in a world that changes in ways they could barely understand even if they tried to do so.

Home sometimes shows a more serious side. *The Secretary Bird* contains some genuine emotion, though the general tone of this account of a modern man caught between his wife and his secretary is humorous. The early prison drama *Now Barabbas . . .*, reflecting its author's spell "inside," is a powerful psychological drama presented with a technique that seems more advanced than we usually find in the comedies. Tensions grow as a condemned man waits to learn whether he has been reprieved, as the governor discovers that he must tell the bad news that he has not, as the warders become tetchy, and as the prisoners, from a wide variety of backgrounds, interact with one another in a situation not of their making. *The Thistle and the Rose* is a chronicle play set at the time of the Battle of Flodden, quite deftly planned though undermined by problems over appropriate language. Scotland also provides the basis for *The Queen's Highland Servant* which treats Queen Victoria's friendship with her Scottish gillie, John Brown. Home treats this delicate topic with sympathy and human understanding, finding the widowed queen a lonely woman in need of friendship. Similar sensitivity, and the same interest in developing the possibilities of a historical subject, can be found in *The Dame of Sark* which explores the human side of the German occupation of the Channel Islands.

Home has a remarkable lightness of touch and generally chooses to treat his themes in a light-hearted way. Behind all this, though, lies a very professional technique, and though he records that he quite often wrote successful plays at very high speed, he was able to do so only because he had so much practical experience of the stage. After education at Eton and Oxford, where he read history, he trained at the Royal Academy of Dramatic Art, and his life has been devoted to the theatre. Though he soon gave up acting, he knows what will work on stage, and he takes special care to write dialogue which runs easily. It has the naturalness that comes only when it is written by a playwright who has taken pains to observe how people speak and has then carefully honed their language to make it sufficiently compressed for use on stage. Nowhere is his skill better demonstrated than in the telephone conversations in, for instance, *The Reluctant Debutante.* His plots move fast, almost like French farces, and if the endings are not the strongest part of the plays, by that time nobody is going to care very much. Home is, as his life and his two volumes of autobiography reveal, a man of serious conviction, though he was never averse from enjoying himself. In his comedies he has created a picture of British social life in the postwar era which may well be of interest to social historians, but he did not quarrel with a public that wanted to come to the theatre to be entertained and amused. Like Denry, the hero of Arnold Bennett's *The Card*, he has not been ashamed to be identified with "the great cause of cheering us all up."

—Christopher Smith

HOPKINS, John (Richard). British. Born in London, 27 January 1931. Educated at Raynes Park County Grammar School; St. Catharine's College, Cambridge, B.A. in English. Served in the British Army (national service), 1950–51. Married 1) Prudence Balchin in 1954; 2) the actress Shirley Knight in 1970; two daughters. Worked as television studio manager; writer, BBC Television, 1962–64. Since 1964 free-lance writer. Recipient: two Screenwriters Guild awards. Agent: William Morris Agency Ltd., 31-32 Soho Square, London W1V 6AP, England. Address: Hazelnut Farm, R.F.D. 1, Fairfield, Connecticut 06430, U.S.A.

PUBLICATIONS

Plays

A Place of Safety (televised 1963). Published in *Z Cars: Four Scripts From the Television Series*, edited by Michael Marland, London, Longman, 1968.
Talking to a Stranger: Four Television Plays (includes *Anytime You're Ready I'll Sparkle, No Skill or Special Knowledge Is Required, Gladly My Cross-Eyed Bear, The Innocent Must Suffer*) (televised 1966). London, Penguin, 1967.
A Game—Like—Only a Game (televised 1966). Published in *Conflicting Generations: Five Television Plays*, edited by Michael Marland, London, Longman, 1968.
This Story of Yours (produced London, 1968; New Haven, Connecticut, 1981). London, Penguin, 1969.
Find Your Way Home (produced London, 1970; New York, 1974). London, Penguin, 1971; New York, Doubleday, 1975.
Economic Necessity (produced Leicester, 1973; New York, 1976).
Next of Kin (produced London, 1974).
Losing Time (produced New York, 1979). New York, Broadway Play Publishing, 1983.

Screenplays: *Two Left Feet*, with Roy Baker, 1963; *Thunderball*, with Richard Maibaum, 1965; *The Virgin Soldiers*, with John McGrath and Ian La Fresnais, 1969; *Divorce—His, Divorce—Hers*, 1972; *The Offence*, 1973; *Murder by Decree*, 1980; *The Holcroft Covenant*, with George Axelrod and Edward Anhalt, 1982; *The Power*, with John Carpenter and Gerald Brach, 1983.

Television Plays: *Break Up*, 1958; *After the Party*, 1958; *The Small Back Room*, 1959; *Dancers in Mourning*, 1959; *A Woman Comes Home*, 1961; *A Chance of Thunder* (6 parts), 1961; *By Invitation Only*, 1961; *The Second Curtain*, 1962; *Look Who's Talking*, 1962; *Z Cars* series (53 episodes), 1962–65; *The Pretty English Girls*, 1964; *I Took My Little World Away*, 1964; *Parade's End* (serialization), from the novel by Ford Madox Ford, 1964; *Time Out of Mind*, 1964; *Houseparty* (ballet scenario), 1964; *The Make Believe Man*, 1965; *Fable*, 1965; *Horror of Darkness*, 1965; *A Man Like Orpheus*, 1965; *Talking to a Stranger* (4 parts), 1966; *Some Place of Darkness*, music by Christopher Whelen, 1966; *A Game—Like—Only a Game*, 1966; *The Gambler* (serialization), from a novel by Dostoevsky, 1968; *Beyond the Sunrise*, 1969; *The Dolly Scene*, 1970; *Some Distant Shadow*, 1971; *That Quiet Earth*, 1972; *Walk into the Dark*, 1972; *The Greeks and Their Gifts*, 1972; *A Story to Frighten the Children*, 1976; *Double Dare*, 1976; *Fathers and Families* (6 plays), 1977; *Smiley's People*, with John le Carré, from the novel by le Carré, 1982.

* * *

With well over 50 scripts for the television series *Z Cars*, and several short television plays behind him, John Hopkins is not primarily a writer for the stage. It was on the newer medium that his reputation was made, and continues to stand at its highest. Indeed, one important critic called his tetralogy, *Talking to a Stranger*, "the first authentic masterpiece written directly for television," and there must be many others who, though perhaps charier of the word "masterpiece," would agree that no finer dramatic work has yet been seen on it. It is undeniably impressive in itself: it also makes a helpful introduction to the first plays Hopkins was subsequently to write for the theatre, *This Story of Yours* and *Find Your Way Home*.

Each of the four plays involves approximately the same day, and each is written from the stance of a different member of the same family, the father, the mother, and their two grown-up children, Alan and Teresa. All are characterised in striking depth; all, with the possible exception of the son, are thoroughly self-absorbed, more inclined to talk in monologue than dialogue; all, again except for him, stand in danger of being overwhelmed by their own self-destructive feelings; all, including him, are lonely and dissatisfied. The tetralogy opens with Teresa, bustling with frantic neurosis, and ends with the mother, dead by her own hand, and, between the two, Hopkins avoids none of the emotional collisions and unpleasantness that his plot generates. Where most contemporary writers would hedge, or tread warily, or retreat into irony, he strides in wholeheartedly and sometimes repetitively, using straightforward, unpretentious, naturalistic language. Not surprisingly, he has been accused of dramatic overstatement, even melodrama.

But "melodrama" occurs when a writer presents extremes of feeling which are neither justified by his material nor empathetically understood by himself. In *Talking to a Stranger* the emotions on display are no more than the "objective correlative" of the dramatic situation, so painstakingly assembled; and, equally, Hopkins has a thorough grasp of the people he has created. He gives the impression of knowing, instinctively, how they would react to any new event. The question is: can we say as much for his stage plays? And the proper answer would seem to be: not quite.

This Story of Yours seems almost to be accusing Hopkins's scripts for *Z Cars* of romanticizing their subject, the police (though in fact they were widely admired for their wry realism). It is a study of the mind of Detective-Sergeant Johnson, trapped in an unfulfilling marriage and at once disgusted and fascinated by work that, characteristically, Hopkins describes in lurid detail. He breaks, and, in a scene of considerable dramatic intensity, beats to death an alleged child rapist: an act that is doubly self-destructive, since it wrecks his career and since it is clearly a way of sublimating his loathing for his own hideous thoughts and corrupt desires. *Find Your Way Home* mainly concerns two homosexuals, one young, unhappy, and apparently a part-time prostitute, the other a married man, and ends with them settling down seriously to live together, having confessed their mutual love. By bringing on a distraught wife, and by accentuating the crudity and sadness of the homosexual subculture, Hopkins is at pains to make this decision as difficult as possible. But his view evidently is that it is the right one. The older man has "found his way home," to a more honest and fulfilling way of life.

From this, it will be seen that Hopkins's view of the world is bleak: and what seems "melodramatic" in his work is often only his way of emphasizing his belief that people are lonely and perverse, full of black thoughts and longings. If a relationship is capable of any success at all, which is doubtful, it can be only after each partner has accepted his own and the other's emotional inadequacies, as the protagonists of *Find Your Way Home* are beginning to do. It is an outspoken, unfashionable moral stance which, to be persuasive, may need the more thorough characterisation we find in *Talking to a Stranger*. There are psychological gaps left open in the stage plays, and notably in *Find Your Way Home*, whose scheme forces Hopkins to the dubious assumption that a young man who has gone very far in self-destructive promiscuity may be capable of sustained affection in a mature relationship. Hopkins achieves his effects by accumulating the emotional evidence as thickly as he can, and may therefore need more space, more time, than other contemporary writers in order to do so.

—Benedict Nightingale

HOROVITZ, Israel (Arthur). American. Born in Wakefield, Massachusetts, 31 March 1939. Educated at the Royal Academy of Dramatic Art, London, 1961–63; City College, New York, M.A. in English 1972. Married 1) Elaine Abber in 1959 (marriage annulled 1960); 2) Doris Keefe in 1961 (divorced 1972), one daughter and two sons; 3) Gillian Adams in 1981, twin daughter and son. Stage manager, Boston and New York, 1961–65; playwright-in-residence, Royal Shakespeare Company, London, 1965; Instructor in Playwriting, New York University, 1967–69; Professor of English, City College, 1968–73; Fanny Hurst Professor of Theatre, Brandeis University, Waltham, Massachusetts, 1973–75. Founder, New York Playwrights Lab, 1977; founder, 1980, and producer and artistic director, Gloucester Stage Company, Massachusetts. Columnist, *Magazine Littéraire*, Paris, 1971–77. Recipient: Obie award, 1968, 1969; Rockefeller fellowship, 1969; Vernon Rice award, 1969; Drama Desk award, 1969; *Jersey Journal* award, 1969; Cannes Film Festival Jury prize, 1971; New York State Council of Arts fellowship, 1971, 1975; National Endowment for the Arts fellowship, 1974, 1977; American Academy award, 1975; Fulbright fellowship, 1975; Emmy award, 1975; Christopher award, 1976; Guggenheim fellowship, 1977; French Critics prize, 1977; Los Angeles Drama Critics Circle award, 1980; Goldie award, 1985; Eliot Norton prize, 1986. Agents: Jonathan Sand, Writers and Artists Agency, 162 West 56th Street, New York, New York 10019, U.S.A.; Patty Detroit, International Creative Management, 8899 Beverly Boulevard, Los Angeles, California 90069, U.S.A.; Margaret Ramsay Ltd., 14-A Goodwin's Court, London WC2N 4LL, England.

PUBLICATIONS

Plays

The Comeback (produced Boston, 1958).
The Death of Bernard the Believer (produced South Orange, New Jersey, 1960).
This Play Is about Me (produced South Orange, New Jersey, 1961).
The Hanging of Emanuel (produced South Orange, New Jersey, 1962).
Hop, Skip, and Jump (produced South Orange, New Jersey, 1963).
The Killer Dove (produced West Orange, New Jersey, 1963).
The Simon Street Harvest (produced South Orange, New Jersey, 1964).
The Indian Wants the Bronx (produced Waterford, Connecticut, 1966; New York and Watford, Hertfordshire, 1968; London, 1969). Included in *First Season*, 1968; in *Off-Broadway Plays*, London, Penguin, 1970.
Line (produced New York, 1967; London, 1970; revised version produced New York, 1971). Included in *First Season*, 1968.
It's Called the Sugar Plum (produced Waterford, Connecticut, 1967; New York and Watford, Hertfordshire, 1968; London, 1971). Included in *First Season*, 1968; in *Off-Broadway Plays*, London, Penguin, 1970.
Acrobats (produced New York, 1968; London, 1980). New York, Dramatists Play Service, 1971.
Rats (produced New York, 1968; London, 1969). Included in *First Season*, 1968.
Morning (in *Chiaroscuro* produced Spoleto, Italy, 1968; in *Morning, Noon, and Night* produced New York, 1968). Published in *Morning, Noon and Night*, New York, Random House, 1969.
First Season: Line, The Indian Wants the Bronx, It's Called the Sugar Plum, Rats. New York, Random House, 1968.
The Honest to God Schnozzola (produced Provincetown, Massachusetts, 1968; New York, 1969). New York, Breakthrough Press, 1971.
Leader (produced New York, 1969). With *Play for Trees*, New York, Dramatists Play Service, 1970.
Play for Trees (televised 1969). With *Leader*, New York, Dramatists Play Service, 1970.
Shooting Gallery (produced New York, 1971). With *Play for Germs*, New York, Dramatists Play Service, 1973.
Dr. Hero (as *Hero*, produced New York, 1971; revised version, as *Dr. Hero*, produced Great Neck, New York, 1972; New York City, 1973). New York, Dramatists Play Service, 1973.
The Wakefield Plays (produced New York, 1978). Included in *The Wakefield Plays* (collection), 1979.

1. *Alfred the Great* (also director: produced Paris and Great Neck, New York, 1972; New York City, 1973). New York, Harper, 1974.
2. *Our Father's Failing* (produced Waterford, Connecticut, 1973; New York 1974).
3. *Alfred Dies* (produced New York, 1976).

Play for Germs (in *VD Blues*, televised 1972). With *Shooting Gallery*, New York, Dramatists Play Service, 1973.
The First, The Last, and the Middle: A Comedy Triptych (produced New York, 1974).
The Quannapowitt Quartet (produced New Haven, Connecticut, 1976). 3 plays in *The Wakefield Plays* (collection), 1979.

1. *Hopscotch* (also director: produced Paris and New York, 1974; London, 1980). With *The 75th*, New York, Dramatists Play Service, 1977.
2. *The 75th* (produced New York, 1977). With *Hopscotch*, New York, Dramatists Play Service, 1977.
3. *Stage Directions* (produced New York, 1976; Richmond, Surrey, 1978). With *Spared*, New York, Dramatists Play Service, 1977.
4. *Spared* (also director: produced Paris and New York, 1974). With *Stage Directions*, New York, Dramatists Play Service, 1977.

Turnstile (produced Hanover, New Hampshire, 1974).
The Primary English Class (produced Waterford, Connecticut, 1975; also director: produced New York, 1975; Richmond, Surrey, 1979; London, 1980). New York, Dramatists Play Service, 1976.
Uncle Snake: An Independence Day Pageant (produced New York, 1975). New York, Dramatists Play Service, 1976.
The Reason We Eat (produced Stamford, Connecticut, and New York, 1976).
The Lounge Player (produced New York, 1977).
Man with Bags, adaptation of a play by Eugène Ionesco, translated by Marie-France Ionesco (produced Baltimore, 1977). New York, Grove Press, 1977.
The Former One-on-One Basketball Champion (produced New York, 1977). With *The Great Labor Day Classic*, New York, Dramatists Play Service, 1982.
Cappella, with David Boorstin, adaptation of the novel by Horovitz (produced New York, 1978).
The Widow's Blind Date (produced New York, 1978). New York, Theatre Communications Group, 1981.
Mackerel (produced Hartford, Connecticut, 1978; revised version produced Washington, D.C., 1978). Vancouver, Talonbooks, 1979.
A Christmas Carol: Scrooge and Marley, adaptation of the story by Dickens (produced Baltimore, 1978). New York, Dramatists Play Service, 1979.
The Good Parts (produced New York, 1979). New York, Dramatists Play Service, 1983.
The Great Labor Day Classic (in *Holidays*, produced Louisville, 1979; produced separately New York, 1984). With *The Former One-on-One Basketball Champion*, New Dramatists Play Service, 1982.
The Wakefield Plays (collection; also includes *The Quannapowitt Quartet* except for *The 75th*). New York, Avon, 1979.
Sunday Runners in the Rain (produced New York, 1980).
Park Your Car in Harvard Yard (produced New York, 1980).
Henry Lumper (produced Gloucester, Massachusetts, 1985).
Today, I am a Fountain Pen, adaptation of stories by Morley Torgov (produced New York, 1986).
A Rosen by Any Other Name, adaptation of a novel by Morley Torgov (produced New York, 1986).
The Chopin Playoffs, adaptation of stories by Morley Torgov (produced New York, 1986).
North Shore Fish (produced Gloucester, Massachusetts, 1986; New York, 1987).
The Year of the Duck (produced Portland, Maine, 1986).

Screenplays: *Machine Gun McCain* (English adaptation), 1970; *The Strawberry Statement*, 1970; *Believe in Me* (*Speed Is of the Essence*), 1970; *Alfredo*, 1970; *The Sad-Eyed Girls in the Park*, 1971; *Camerian Climbing*, 1971; *Acrobats*, 1972; *Fast Eddie*, 1980; *Fell*, 1982; *Berta*, 1982; *Author! Author!*, 1982–83; *Light Years*, 1985.

Television Plays: *Play for Trees*, 1969; *VD Blues*, with others, 1972; *Start to Finish*, 1975; *The Making and Breaking of Splinters Braun*, 1976; *Bartleby the Scrivener*, from the story by Melville, 1978; *A Day with Conrad Green*, from a story by Ring Lardner, 1978; *The Deer Park*, from the novel by Norman Mailer, 1979.

Novels

Cappella. New York, Harper, 1973.
Nobody Loves Me. Paris, Minuit, 1975; New York, Braziller, 1976.

*

Manuscript Collections: Lincoln Center Library of the Performing Arts, New York; Sawyer Free Library, Gloucester, Massachusetts.

Critical Studies: *Thirty Plays Hath November* by Walter Kerr, New York, Simon and Schuster, 1969; *Opening Nights* by Martin Gottfried, New York, Putnam, 1970; *The Playmakers* by Stuart W. Little and Arthur Cantor, New York, Dutton, 1970, London, Reinhardt, 1971; in *Études Anglaises* (Paris), Summer 1975.

Theatrical Activities:
Director: **Plays**—several of his own plays in English and French, and *Chiaroscuro: Morning, Noon and Night*, by Horovitz, Leonard Melfi, and Terrence McNally, Spoleto, Italy, 1968. **Film**—*Acrobats*, 1972. **Television**—*VD Blues*, 1972.
Actor: **Film**—*The Strawberry Statement*, 1970.

Israel Horovitz comments:

(1988) Much of life has changed for me.

I used to aspire to run 10 kilometers under 30 minutes. Breaking 40 minutes for the same distance is now quite satisfactory.

My family and my work remain as they were to me before: holy.

* * *

Israel Horovitz had been working as a writer for a number of years, but it seemed as if he suddenly burst upon the New York scene in 1967 when the successful productions of four of his one-act plays established him as a brilliant new American playwright, and a socially committed artist. Like several other off-off-Broadway playwrights of the 1960's, Horovitz worked closely with actors and profited from their experimentation and dedication to ensemble productions. His plays were ensemble pieces, not star vehicles.

Although intensely concerned about the social issues facing America, Horovitz remains objective about the playwright's art. "If a play has pristine concept—if you have a clear concept of what the hell you're writing about before you sit down to write, you have a chance of writing a good play." His structure is clear, compact, and logical. Theme is implicit and didacticism is eschewed. His plays are impact not message plays, brutally realistic in their exposure of the American malaise. Even his two parable plays, *Line* and *Rats*, are basically realistic in style. Horovitz has an extraordinary ear for dialogue and has found poetry in the harsh language of the slum dweller and juvenile delinquent.

Line is a grotesque allegory of the American success myth; five characters struggle by the use of force or guile to gain first place on a line leading nowhere. In the course of their struggles, each alternately gains and loses first place. The mad contest is perpetuated by the young man, Stephen, who delights in belittling the combatants. He has an insane desire to die younger than his idol, Mozart, and is forever singing Figaro's aria from *The Marriage of Figaro*: "Cleverly, hitting, planning, and scheming, I'll get the best of the hypocrite yet." Like the wily barber, Stephen is not above using a little deception himself in his battle against hypocrisy. Ultimately, in an attempt to commit suicide and defeat his opposition, Stephen eats the line, but retches it up involuntarily. Each of the combatants grabs the pieces from his mouth, and rush to separate parts of the stage to be first on their own individual lines, a vivid stage metaphor of isolation and meaningless power struggles. Stephen rushes off in a fit of joy, liberated by a renewed sense of the absurdity of the human condition.

The only jarring moment in this otherwise imaginative allegory is Stephen's monologue revealing his inner conflict—a conventional bit of psychological realism, but too brief to weaken the play. Steven's bathetic monologue is quickly terminated by the promiscuous Molly, who scorns his need for a "mommy." Molly has used sex as a means of tormenting her husband, and also winning the game. She coarsely declares that she had "them" (the men), thus maintaining her dominance in the battle of the sexes, which is as meaingless as the desire to be first.

The work that overwhelmed the critics and achieved fame for Horovitz was *The Indian Wants the Bronx*, a genre classic of violence. It was one of the most gripping productions of the off-Broadway theatre of the 1960's, introducing the brilliant young actor, Al Pacino, and offering a stirring performance by John Cazale as the Indian.

A non-English speaking East Indian is lost somewhere in the city and is attempting to get to his son's home in the Bronx. Two juvenile delinquents discover the Indian, and proceed to tease, torment, and beat him. They have a strange mixture of love and hatred for the Indian: pity for his helplessness and contempt for him as a foreigner, referring to him as "Turkie" and "elephant." He becomes a convenient scapegoat for their own self-hatred. Their treatment of the Indian is terrifying, leading to what seems to be his inevitable murder. The Indian's frantic pleadings in his native language intensify the diabolical mood of the play.

Ultimately, the two youths cut the wire of the telephone receiver as well as the Indian's hand and then run off. The play ends on a tableau—the Indian holding the receiver toward the audience, sobbing and uttering his few words of English: "How are you? You're welcome. Thank you. Thank you"—a more effective piece of business than actually murdering the Indian. His pathetic appeal to the audience is a grim reminder of the city's apathy toward violence.

It's Called the Sugar Plum is a cynical one-act situation comedy: a slight work with some funny lines and two zany characters. Zuckerman has accidentally killed a fellow Harvard student. He is acquitted by the court, but the deceased's fiancée (or so she claims), Joanna, calls upon Zuckerman and accuses him of murder. Initially agonizing over her lover's death, Joanna soon rhapsodizes over Zuckerman's romantic occupation as a part-time butcher in a slaughterhouse. Ultimately, the masks are removed: both characters had hoped the accident would bring them notoriety, but were disappointed by the minimal coverage they received in the local papers. The play satirizes the self-righteousness of certain people who are as fundamentally self-seeking as the rest of crass America. Despite the revelation of the actual motivations, Zuckerman and Joanna begin romanticizing their relationship. With the flicker of a light bulb, lust is converted into true love.

The Honest to God Schnozzola is something of a departure from the fundamental realism of Horovitz's drama: an unnerving study of fantasy and reality set in a German bar, and adorned with suitably decadent trimmings—a smoke filled atmosphere, a dwarf, a whore, a male transvestite, and two American television executive types. The style is presentational: asides to the audience, songs, dances, and filmic plot structure using flashbacks, blackouts, tableau freezes, and a flexible use of lighting reminiscent of a camera cut. The two executives are on a brief European vacation, and have left their wives at home. Although the men dislike each other, their jobs force them into an artificial friendship. Emotionally weak and insecure, they make the conventional declaration of virility of immature American males. One of them, Jimmy, described as "a small man with a large nose," maintains Jimmy Durante as an alter ego (hence the title of the play): "I wanted to be something special. I became Jimmy Durante."

The plot has a bizarre twist. On the previous evening, Jimmy has been duped into having anal intercourse with the transvestite, Athenia, believing he was female. Tortured by this experience, Jimmy is determined that his associate, Johnny, should experience the same degradation. Johnny is comparably deceived, and Jimmy later maliciously reveals Athenia's sexual identity.

There is a deliberate ambiguity inherent in the plot. Were the men ignorant of Athenia's sexual identity? Is their suffering actually a guilt reaction for having fulfilled their own homosexual desires? Is the play allegorical—post-war Germany's revenge on the American supermen—or a commercially appealing tale of perversion cloaked in seriousness?

Horovitz's description of *Line* as "comedy of displacement" provides a key to his dramatic technique: situations in which characters cleverly or brutally attempt to displace their competition in a vivious game of survival. Most of his plays begin in a mood of relative calm (except *Rats*) which is quickly shattered by the arrival of another character. Fleming is contentedly singing and sitting on his line when Stephen arrives and begins the insane game of displacement. Joanna invades Zuckerman's privacy and accuses him of murder, but the play really deals with a success struggle in which each character believes himself to have been displaced by the press notoriety of the other. Murphy and Joey torment the Indian as a means of vindicating themselves for their own displacement from society. Jebbie and Bobby, the two Harlem rats, battle for territory, each attempting to dispace the other. Jimmy and Johnny veer from the "straight" world by a fleeting homosexual experience, a displacement effected through clever disguise.

Horovitz's more recent work represents a departure from his somewhat formalized technique of displacement, being more experimental in form and style. Rather than realistic or parable plays of social malaise, he focuses on plays of character introspection and mental disorientation: dark chamber pieces of fragmented dialogue, staccato rhythms, monologues, or silent interaction. His characters are impelled helplessly into the vortex of their own mental disorientation.

In the Wakefield trilogy, Horovitz probes into the roots of his own psyche by dramatizing the adventures of Alfred, a celebrated citizen of Wakefield, Massachusetts, who returns to this small town to unravel the confusing narrative of his past. *Alfred the Great*, the first play of the trilogy, is a complex dramatic structure uniting farce, allegory, and psychoanalysis. Alfred encounters his childhood sweetheart, Margaret, in her sitting room, resulting in a painful yet amusing situation of nostalgia, awkwardness, and ultimately diabolical revenge effected by her jealous husband, Will.

In *Our Father's Failing*, Alfred visits his aged Father in an insane asylum and discovers the dark secret of his past: as a boy he stabbed and murdered his mother and her lover. In order to protect his son, Alfred's father declared himself the murderer; the court pronounced him insane and committed him to the asylum. Despite this somewhat melodramatic revelation, the play avoids the pitfalls of stock psychological drama: it is a dark comedy, exploring the complex undercurrents of love and hostility existing between a father and son. The most inspired aspect of the play is Horovitz's comic treatment of the hostile relationship existing between the father and his old crony Sam: a badinage of insult, innuendo, and non sequiturs.

Alfred reappears as the character merely described as "The Man" in the one act monologue, *Spared* (part of the *Quannapowitt Quartet*), another dark comedy, in which he narrates his bizarre, unsuccessful attempts at suicide or euthanasia. Despite his longing for death, fate keeps him alive.

Horovitz's outstanding success remains *The Primary English Class*, a zany farce set in a classroom where a sexually repressed and highly neurotic young woman attempts to teach English to a group of foreigners. Two narrators translate the foreign dialogue, revealing the absurdity of the young teacher's dark suspicions of her students' innocent motivations and sincere desire to understand and communicate with her.

—A. Richard Sogliuzzo

HOWARD, Roger. British. Born in Warwickshire, 19 June 1938. Educated at Dulwich College, London; Royal Academy of Dramatic Art, London, 1956–57; Bristol University, 1958; University of Essex, Colchester, M.A. 1976. National Service in Royal Armoured Service Corps, 1958: sentenced to imprisonment for refusal to wear uniform: dishonourable discharge. Married Anne Mary Zemaitis in 1960; one son. Teacher, Nankai University, Tientsin, China, 1965–67; manager, Collets Bookshop, Peterborough, 1967–68, and Bookshop 85, London, 1968–72; teacher, Peking University, 1972–74; playwright-in-residence, Mercury Theatre, Colchester, 1976; Arts Council Fellow in Creative Writing, University of York, 1976–78; Henfield Writing Fellow, University of East Anglia, Norwich, 1979. Since 1979 Lecturer, and founding director, Theatre Underground, and since 1980 editor, New Plays series, University of Essex. Member, Council of Management, Society for Anglo-Chinese Understanding, and Editorial Committee, *China Now* magazine, London, 1970–72. Since 1978 member of the Editorial Committee, *Platform* magazine, Manchester; since 1980 founder, Theatre Action Press, Colchester. Recipient: Arts Council bursary, 1975. Address: Department of Literature, University of Essex, Wivenhoe Park, Colchester, Essex CO4 3SQ, England.

PUBLICATIONS

Plays

Bewitched Foxes Rehearsing Their Roles (produced London, 1968).
New Short Plays 1, with Leonard Melfi and Carey Harrison (includes *The Carrying of X from A to Z, Dis, The Love Suicides at Havering, Seven Stages on the Road to Exile*). London, Methuen, 1968.
Fin's Doubts (produced London, 1969). Privately printed, 1968.
The Love Suicides at Havering (produced London, 1969). Included in *New Short Plays 1*, 1968.
The Carrying of X from A to Z (produced Papua New Guinea, 1971). Included in *New Short Plays 1*, 1968.
Dis (produced York, 1971). Included in *New Short Plays 1*, 1968.
Seven Stages on the Road to Exile (produced Carlisle, 1970). Included in *New Short Plays 1*, 1968.
Season (produced London, 1969).
Simon Murdering His Deformed Wife with a Hammer (produced London, 1969).
The Meaning of the Statue (produced London, 1971). Included in *Slaughter Night and Other Plays*, 1971.
Writing on Stone (produced London, 1971). Included in *Slaughter Night and Other Plays*, 1971.
Slaughter Night and Other Plays: The Meaning of the Statue, The Travels of Yi Yuk-sa to the Caves at Yenan, Returning to the Capital, Writing on Stone, Korotov's Ego-Theatre, Report from the City of Reds in the Year 1970, The Drum of the Strict Master, The Play of Iron, Episodes from the Fighting in the East, A New Bestiary. London, Calder and Boyars, 1971.
The Travels of Yi Yuk-sa to the Caves at Yenan (produced Colchester, 1976). Included in *Slaughter Night and Other Plays*, 1971; in *Scripts 4* (New York), February 1972.
The Drum of the Strict Master (produced Colchester, 1976). Included in *Slaughter Night and Other Plays*, 1971.
Korotov's Ego-Theatre (produced Edinburgh, 1978). Included in *Slaughter Night and Other Plays*, 1971.
Episodes from the Fighting in the East (produced Edinburgh, 1978). Included in *Slaughter Night and Other Plays*, 1971; in *Scripts 4* (New York), February 1972.
Report from the City of Reds in the Year 1970 (produced Cambridge, 1978). Included in *Slaughter Night and Other Plays*, 1971.
The Auction of Virtues, in *Point 101* (produced London, 1972). Published in *Y* (York), 1977.
Sunrise. Peking, Peking University, 1973.
Klöng 1, Klöng 2, and the Partisan (produced Colchester, 1976).
Notes for a New History (produced Colchester, 1976).
The Tragedy of Mao in the Lin Piao Period (produced London, 1976).
The Great Tide (produced Colchester, 1976).
A Feast During Famine (produced London, 1977).
Travelling Players of the Dawn (produced York, 1977).
The Play of Margery Kempe (produced York and London, 1978).
Women's Army (produced Nottingham and London, 1978).
Joseph Arch (produced London, 1978).
Queen (produced Alsager, Cheshire, 1979).
Memorial of the Future: A Rag (produced Norwich, 1979). With *The Society of Poets*, Colchester, Theatre Action Press, 1979.
The Society of Poets: A Grotesquery (produced Norwich, 1979). With *Memorial of the Future*, Colchester, Theatre Action Press, 1979.
A Break in Berlin (produced Colchester, 1979). Colchester, Theatre Action Press, 1981.
The Siege (produced Colchester, 1981). Published as *The Violent Irruption and Terrible Convulsions of the Siege During the Late Lamentable Civil War at Colchester in the Year 1648*, Colchester, Theatre Action Press, 1981.
White Sea (produced Colchester, 1982).
Partisans (produced Colchester, 1983). London, Actual Size, 1983.
The Speechifier, published in *Double Space*, no. 2, 1984–85.
Contact (produced Nottingham, 1985).

Novels

A Phantastic Satire. Bala, Merioneth, Chapple, 1960.
From the Life of a Patient. Bala, Merioneth, Chapple, 1961.

Short Stories

Four Stories, with *Twelve Sketches*, by Tony Astbury. London, Mouthpiece, 1964.
Ancient Rivers. Warwick, Greville Press, 1984.

Verse

To the People.... London, Mouthpiece, 1966.
Praise Songs. Tientsin, Tianjin Ribao, and London, Mouthpiece, 1966.

Other

The Technique of the Struggle Meeting. London, Clandestine, 1968.
The Use of Wall Newspapers. London, Clandestine, 1968.
The Hooligan's Handbook: Methods of Thinking and Action. London, Action, 1971.
Method for Revolutionary Writing. London, Action, 1972.
Mao Tse-tung and the Chinese People. London, Allen and Unwin, and New York, Monthly Review Press, 1977.
La théâtre chinois contemporain. Brussels, La Renaissance du Livre, 1978; as *Contemporary Chinese Theatre*, London, Heinemann, 1978.

Editor, *Culture and Agitation: Theatre Documents*. London, Action, 1972.

*

Critical Studies: *Contradictory Theatres* edited by Leslie Bell, Colchester, Theatre Action Press, 1985; "The Dramatic Sense of Life: Theatre and Historical Simulation" by Howard, in *New Theatre Quarterly* (Cambridge), no. 3, 1985.

Roger Howard comments:

(1973) In revolutionary war, plays are performed to show scenes of the struggle in which fighters who actually took part replay their "parts" as examples to other fighters. Their short, instructional plays go back over the battle just ended in order to point out the lesson to be learnt for the next round. They educate by showing the audience—other fighters—the significance of their actions.

Such drama is deeply rooted in the day-to-day work experience of the people. It captures their imagination because it closely expresses themselves. At the same time it is a higher form of artistic expression than mere realism, because it shows the people's actions in their relationship to the new, evolving, and advancing socialist morality. Their plays are agitation in the service of the people's advance and an aid in the overthrow of the old society.

My short plays are part of the same process. Preparing for the situation where there will be open military warfare, they are agitational plays in the wider war which engulfs us all, the war between classes which takes many forms and which will not cease until classes cease. Each play is located at a point where a certain stage of development in struggle has been reached, and where the choices are open as to what the following stage should be.

The point reached at the opening of each play may be either a victory or a defeat for revolutionary advance. The body of the play then develops the initial point by showing the contending sides and conflicting interests, giving visual and verbal guidelines from the particular instance to the wider significance in the form of interpolated screen captions, extended sound words, lyrical or didactic verses, or actual physical combat.

The characters are shown in their class as well as in their individual roles; they are individuals who express class positions in the way they think, speak, act, and interact. Their conflicts therefore elicit humour, grotesquery, poetry, reason, tragedy, and decision.

The resolution of the conflicts between the characters, as of those within one character, is resolution not of a "personality" to his "destiny" or of the "mind" to the "universe," still less of the "underdog" to his "station in life." It is a resolution that will give the revolutionary protagonist, the positive character, his due as the man who has history on his side in an era when capitalism is in decline and the many forces of socialism are in the ascendant. It is therefore as resolution of *ideas*, by which the conscious, active man triumphs over the slave in man, whether it be in himself or in others. For some, the resolution comes as a condemnation: they are the negative characters, the reactionaries, backward rejects of history. For others, the resolution comes too late; for them they have their message to pass on to a new generation. For all our mistakes, man is learning to advance. The point of resolution in each play is therefore an ideological point, to be perceived as such by the audience.

So the characters of the plays are representations of contradictory class position as they appear in individual human beings. This gives the positive characters greater dimensions than those of mere self-contained, alienated individuals at odds with society for their own sake, just as in life itself the activists of revolution are so much greater figures than those who merely talk about it or those who use socialism for their personal advantage.

Our oppression will last for as long as we remain afraid; if only we act, we lose our fear. Oppressors tremble when they lose their grip on our terror. The revolutionary characters in my plays are heroic because they are no longer afraid. And they are no longer afraid because they have become conscious. They know that as active workers, conscious of class, they hold the future in their hands. I warm to those men and women in our century who, raising the people to raise themselves, and growing thus in stature, have reminded mankind of its dignity. My heart is stung when I hear of their deeds; they are few of them famous and most suffered great privation and even death. My plays can hardly emulate their lives but they are some sort of small monuments, not for us to gaze at and pity, but to stir us to action. They rescue from the great killings some memorials of actions that teach us to kill more precisely in future: our killers.

(1977) The idea of people as doers, as much as sufferers, has been pushed into the background in much of recent drama that has become academically respectable, from Ibsen to Beckett. The idea that people are capable of directing their future more completely has been neglected.

In my short plays I have introduced prototypes of such representative men and women. The transition I am now making from short to full-length plays will give the idea of renewal more scope. The first long play, *The Tragedy of Mao in the Lin Piao Period*, is a 19-scene construction of the shifts in the relationship between two men striving to remake men and themselves. Then follows a trilogy on turning points in English history, from tribalism to feudalism, to capitalism, and to socialism.

(1982) The trilogy—*The Earth-Founding, The Force in the Land* and *The Great Tide*—has expanded into a series of full-length historical plays which now includes *Bread, Meat and Higher Learning* about the Marian suppression of the protestants, *The Siege* about clashes of inner self and outer self-interest in the radical debates of the English Civil War at the time of the Siege of Colchester (a play commissioned by the Mercury Theatre), and *Joseph Arch* about the founding of the agricultural workers' union. In these plays and in *A Break in Berlin* I have attempted to develop a method of characterisation that dialectically relates the inner person to his or her outer status in historical change, relying increasingly heavily on a dynamic use of dialogue as "spoken action" to present multi-dimensional and many-layered representations of characters caught in their personal "moments" inside the "movement" of changing societies. I still use a variety of dramatic forms—comic extravaganza in *Queen*, a study of the psychological effects of rule on the personality of Elizabeth II; epic in *Joseph Arch*, now expanded into a 37-scene play retitled *The Weight of Many Masters*; comic grotesquery in *The Society of Poets*; naturalism in *A Break in Berlin*; dynamic verbal-action theatre in *The Siege*. I have developed a notion of socialist tragedy which attempts to use a method of writing plays to show the processes of a person's life in terms of the extent to which he or she must submit to necessity and the extent to which he or she remains free (and willing) to act. *The Force in the Land, The Tragedy of Mao*, *A Break in Berlin* and *The Siege* are examples of such attempts. Increasingly I have felt the need to bring my critical, scholarly, and theoretical work on theatre, which has appeared largely in journals, together with the practice of production and the teaching of ideas of theatre. My work at Essex University is to do with the idea content of new English theatre writing and I have initiated a New Plays Scheme whereby each year M.A. drama students are given the opportunity of working on the production of a play with a specially commissioned theatre writer. I have founded the Theatre Underground in this connection in order to explore the possibility of a materialist and dialectical method of theatre writing and production practice. Theatre Underground's productions are of new English and overseas plays which have to do with representing, in a variety of theatre forms and by dialectical characterisation, a dramatic appraisal of men and women in their personal and their social lives in the connections of their personae to the wider forces of their time. The Theatre Underground scripts published in Essex University New Plays series—*A Break in Berlin* was the first—are accompanied by production notes and introductory material which provide a discourse about the play both as a piece of dramatic literature and as a theatre piece for performance. In Theatre Underground work my own ideas develop alongside the work of others whose research and practice is in overlapping areas and who have become involved in the concepts embodied by Theatre Underground. My plans for the future include plays about George Stephenson, Hitler, Ernst Toller and early English socialists; and a play about the rise and tribulations of the "alternative" theatre of the 1970's.

(1988) My exploration of socialist tragedy has extended to five new plays. *White Sea*, an ironic drama with music, traces the effects of their labour on the consciousness of a group of theatre workers helping to dig the White Sea Canal in the Soviet Union in the early 1930's. The "tragedy of expediency" occurs where Stalinist social and political euphoria, associated with the Five-Year Plan, meets the necessities of material reality—and plain human inadequacies. *Partisans* is a series of grotesque and savage scenes in the comic and disturbing life of a freedom-seeking actress in the English "alternative" theatre of the 1960's and 1970's. She turns from drugs to terrorism and goes from prison to a peace camp before gaining a sense of her own identity as that of a victim's mental and emotional dissolution in a surrounding pre-nuclear chaos. The published edition contains a short essay by Charles Lamb on aspects of the play's dramaturgy. This "tragedy of liberation," whose main character, Cindy, bears some resemblance to Gerda in *A Break in Berlin* and Margery in *The Play of Margery Kempe* in her tortured questing, was followed by a tragedy of confinement, *The Speechifier*. Based on *The Orator*, a play by the Lithuanian writer Kazys Saja, the play is set in the family apartment of the ghost-writer of a Leader of a tyrannical state. The writer loses himself in obedience to his master, achieving a most perfect acquiescence rewarded when his family is gassed, trapped in their flat. *Britannia* (unproduced) is a dream play about the state of England. Christian Wager embarks on a journey of self-exposure from early-mediaeval hermetic spirituality, through Tudor state-forming and Victorian empire-building to Thatcherite monetarist opportunism, before learning how an intellectual has to conform to the powers-that-be. This latterday Faust is chided by his female double, Wager 2, for not learning from a regicide who at least had the nobleness to crown with his own suicide his repeated failure through the ages to remove the monarch, while Wager signs a deal with the King ensuring merely his own degenerate survival. *Contact* is a four-hander in 17 scenes, a contemporary tragedy of romantic love in a Europe divided by ideologies and united in oppportunism. A young Polish woman and an English poet have a brief affair across the borders, an idealistic contact which collapses in a bitter war of self-interest.

All these plays reflect a new idea of tragedy in which human drives reach the limits imposed on them by necessity in one form or another. They reflect a notion of a tragic moment as resulting from a collision that is socially produced as well as personally motivated. Much of the theory attached to these ideas is published in *Contradictory Theatres*, a collection of essays and documentation about the work of the Theatre Underground at Essex University, which also contains essays by other hands on *A Break in Berlin* and *White Sea*.

* * *

Roger Howard is a genuine original, whose plays combine an essentially Maoist political stance with a range of diverse and ecclectic styles, including Brechtian epic theatre, slapstick, music hall, and cartoon theatre. In his introductory essay to his collection *Slaughter Night* he makes the point that, in the present political situation, it is the playwright's task to divide and agitate, not to help in the creation of culture, which is part of the "deep sleep" our rulers want to impose on us. His plays are sharp, clear, and carry out this task of division with an admirable precision, though their form is very far from being conventional agitational socialist realism. This essay, which of necessity considers the plays more as cultural objects than as means of heightening political consciousness, is an exercise in contradictions, an example of the dialectical relationship between politics and art; but it is true to say that the best of the plays do work on an artistic and aesthetic level over and above their directly political one.

Howard's plays fall into three distinct phases. First, there are the lyrical pre-China pieces, like *Season* and *Simon Murdering His Deformed Wife with a Hammer*, which propagate a William Morris-type socialism through semi-abstract poetic characters and language. *Season* shows the struggle between urban and rural values; while *Simon* shows a young man trying to educate his wife to his own level of political consciousness, failing and murdering her as a result. Then come more complex plays, like *The Love Suicides at Havering*, which shows a group of people attempting to overcome their psychological inhibitions as a necessary precondition to achieving a revolutionary situation, and *Fin's Doubts*, which shows in symbolist form the full cycle of a revolution. A group of revolutionaries overthrow an era of reactionary repression, achieve the first stages of a revolution, and impose temporary authoritarian measures to consolidate its achievements; by a process of bureaucratic ossification this authoritarianism becomes permanent, and the whole cycle starts off again.

Howard went to China as a teacher for two years and the result can be seen in the artistically and politically more mature plays in *Slaughter Night.* The title play juxtaposes Sauer, the Dog King, and the Writer, a nice, cosy arrangement with the Writer reflecting Sauer's interests through his works until two Wolves and an Outlaw show him the error of his ways. *The Meaning of the Statue* shows a young man in conversation with the statue of a general. Essentially, it is about the loss of spontaneity and fluidity in a revolutionary situation occasioned by its bureaucratic organisation, symbolised by the youth being shot by the statue and being put, in the same fixed position, in the statue's place. *Returning to the Capital* uses the characters of Seami Motokiyo and his son, the fashioners of the first Noh plays, to point the differences between and consequences of being a reformist, like Seami, and a revolutionary. *Writing on Stone* is about a couple romanticising the past in lyrical images and being afraid to face up to the implications of the present. *Korotov's Ego-Theatre* shows the irrelevance and sterility of individualist concepts of art in a revolutionary situation; *Episodes from the Fighting in the East*, the erratic progress of a revolution and the shifts of power that take place within it; while *A New Bestiary* hilariously satirises, through animal imagery, types of people pretending to be revolutionaries who are in fact, without realizing it, on the revolutionaries' side. They all use language and sound in a most original way.

The Tragedy of Mao in the Lin Piao Period examines the ideological differences between Mao and the PLA commander-in-chief Lin (who was killed in an air crash in 1971 while fleeing to Moscow) and their origins in the civil war struggles of the 1930's. It is a subtle stylistic mixture of realism and a kind of heightened poetry, which in its totality gives some idea of how China's peasant-based socialism has evolved.

Howard has been little performed as yet; his plays are, however, eminently actable and stageable. They condense more into their brief spans, both in thought and style, than most full-length plays.

—Jonathan Hammond

HOWARTH, Donald. British. Born in London, 5 November 1931. Educated at the Grange High School for Boys, Bradford; Esme Church Northern Children's Theatre School, 1948–51. Stage manager and actor in various repertory companies, 1951–56. Literary manager, Royal Court Theatre, London, 1975–76. Recipient: Encyclopaedia Britannica award, 1961; George Devine Award, 1971. Agent: Margaret Ramsay Ltd., 14-A Goodwin's Court, London WC2N 4LL, England.

PUBLICATIONS

Plays

Lady on the Barometer (also co-director: produced London, 1958; as *Sugar in the Morning,* produced London, 1959).

All Good Children (produced Bromley, Kent, 1960; also director: produced London, 1964). London, French, 1965.

Secret of Skiz, adaptation of a play by Zapolska (produced Bromley, Kent, 1962).

A Lily in Little India (televised 1962; also director: produced London, 1965). London, French, 1966.

Ogodiveleftthegason (also director: produced London, 1967).

School Play, in *Playbill One*, edited by Alan Durband. London, Hutchinson, 1969.

Three Months Gone (produced London, 1970). London, French, 1970.

Othello Sleges Blankes, adaptation of the play by Shakespeare (also director: produced Cape Town, 1972).

Scarborough (also director: produced Cape Town, 1972).

The Greatest Fairy Story Ever Told, adaptation of a play by Kathleen Housell-Roberts (also director: produced New York, 1973).

Meanwhile, Backstage in the Old Front Room (produced Leeds, 1975).

Ibchek (also director: produced Grahamstown, South Africa, 1979).

Adventures of a Black Girl, adaptation of the novel *Adventures of a Black Girl in Her Search for God* by Shaw (also director: produced Cape Town, 1980).

Screenplay: *Gates to Paradise*, 1968.

Television Plays: *A Lily in Little India*, 1962; *Stanley*, 1972.

*

Critical Study: introduction by Michael Billington to *New English Dramatists 9*, London, Penguin, 1966.

Theatrical Activities:
Director: **Plays**—several of his own plays, and *This Property Is Condemned* by Tennessee Williams, London, 1960; *Miniatures* by David Cregan, London, 1965; *Play Mas* by Mustapha Matura, London, 1974; *Mama, Is Terry Home for Good?* by James Edward Shannon, Johannesburg, 1974; *Parcel Post* by Yemi Ajibade, London, 1976; *Rum an' Coca Cola* by Mustapha Matura, London, 1976, New York, 1977; *Waiting for Godot* by Beckett, London, Cape Town, and New York, 1981.
Actor: **Plays**—roles in reportory, 1951–56; Salvation Army Captain in *Progress to the Park* by Alun Owen, London, 1959.

Donald Howarth comments:
Art is what you don't do. Less is more.

* * *

One of the pleasures of reading through Donald Howarth's earlier plays in sequence—*Sugar in the Morning, All Good Children, A Lily in Little India, Ogodiveleftthegason*, and *Three Months Gone*—is the pleasure of seeing a playwright finding his way to an individual and successful compromise between naturalism and freewheeling expressionism by dint of returning again and again to the same themes and the same characters but never to the same style. He has worked hard, and at its worst his writing is laborious, but he has been capable from the beginning of sustaining passages of comedy which deftly combine truthfulness with elegant and compelling theatrical rhetoric. Finally, in *Three Months Gone*, he achieved a sureness of touch that enables him to tie fantasy material down to solid surfaces and to draw dividends from all his earlier stylistic experiments. *Ogodiveleftthegason* is the play in which he takes the most expressionistic short cuts and spans over the greatest amount of human experience. It is his least successful play, though, not because it is the least comic or the least realistic, but because it is the most shapeless and the least able to gain an audience's sympathy for the characters or sustain its interest in them—partly because their identity keeps changing. *Three Months Gone*, while no less remote from the slow development of the conventional naturalistic three-act play, has a storyline strong enough to keep the colourful balloons of fantasy that both main characters fly tethered securely to a solid matter-of-factness.

Mrs. Broadbent, the sexually frustrated landlady in *Sugar in the Morning*, and Grannie Silk, her obstinately vulgar, cheerful, warm-hearted, interfering mother, are both rough prototypes of Mrs. Hanker in *A Lily in Little India* and *Three Months Gone*, who combines the main characteristics of both of them without having Mrs. Broadbent's pretensions to gentility or her ineptness at finding food for her sexual appetites. A clear picture of suburban life emerges in *Sugar in the Morning* but much of the basic energy is spent on drawing it. Decisions about which lodgers to take, clipping the privet hedge, arguments about noisy radios and washing hung up outside windows, rent collecting, drinking cups of tea in the landlady's room, hurrying for the twenty-to-eight bus, finding a shilling for the gas meter, discussing whether to have a baby—in using episodes like these as its currency, the play makes them all seem equally important. None of the characters in *Sugar in the Morning* reappears in *All Good Children* but Rev. Jacob Bowers and his daughter and son, Anna and Maurice, are in both *All Good Children* and *A Lily in Little India*, which introduces Mrs. Hanker and her son Alvin, who are to reappear in *Three Months Gone*, together with Anna and Maurice. The whole of the action of *All Good Children* is set in a converted farmhouse in South Yorkshire, but the 60-year-old minister is about to retire and to move his family to the suburb where we find them in the two subsequent plays. The new theme introduced in *All Good Children*, which will recur persistently in the later work, is the relationship between Protestant morality and sexual deprivation. Jacob Bowers, now a devout anti-sensualist, has been very different when younger, and became a minister only because of guilt feelings after his affair with a minister's daughter had caused the old man's death. Unlike his younger brother, Clifford, who has been more of a conformist, Maurice has reacted violently against his Puritanic upbringing and becomes a sailor. His letters, with their juicy descriptions of local brothels, have been Anna's main life-line, and the love she feels for Maurice verges on the incestuous, but after her mother's death, caused by an on-stage fall down a staircase, she rejects her chance of breaking out of the family cage and condemns herself, after 20 years of imprisonment, to staying with her father.

The plot of *All Good Children* is developed mostly through speeches that rake over the past. *A Lily in Little India* is a less Ibsenite play, and physical action bulks larger in it. The action, like the stage, is divided between the Bowers' house and the Handers'. We see Anna waiting on the old father who has spoiled her life by his narrowness, and writing letters to the brother through whom she is still vicariously living; in the other house a selfishly sensual landlady is trapping a reluctant postman into an affair regardless of the harm done to her sensitive son, who finds happiness only in growing a lily and in his encounters with Anna. When the mother, poised on a ladder outside his bedroom window, threatens to destroy his beloved lily, he throws water in her face causing her to fall backwards, and moves into Anna's house when his mother goes to hospital. The characters win considerable sympathy and interest, and there are some very funny and some very touching moments, but the comedy and the seriousness do not quite balance or reinforce each other as one comes to feel they should and, though the dialogue has been praised by Michael Billington (in his Introduction to the Penguin *New English Dramatists 9*) as "a just sufficiently heightened version of ordinary speech," it sinks sometimes into self-consciousness and just occasionally into sentimentality.

But the dialogue of *Three Months Gone* is virtually unflawed. The rapid shifts in and out of Anna's fantasies, and later Alvin's, give Howarth the opportunity to penetrate funnily but compassionately their private views of themselves, each other, and the two other main characters, Maurice and Mrs. Hanker, who are sexually so much more robust. There is a hilarious scene in which Mrs. Hanker, bullying Alvin to find the pluck to make Anna marry him, makes him propose to her while she pretends to be Anna, and this is followed by a sequence in which Maurice makes a pass at him under guise of teaching him how to make a woman submit. The audience's uncertainty about which sequence represents fantasy, which reality, is often an advantage.

The later plays are different and less successful. *The Greatest Fairy Story Ever Told* is a skittish pantomime full of arch chinoiserie. There are characters called Much Too Yin and Too Much Yang and jokes about Pon-Ting's fabric hall and the Royal Courtyard. *Meanwhile, Backstage in the Old Front Room* is highly serious, ambitiously moving further away from naturalism than any of Howarth's earlier works. It leans on both Beckett and Genet: *Endgame* is feminised in the relationship between the dominating old woman who never leaves her wheelchair and the blind younger women, possibly her daughter, who lives with her. The power games and the extremism in making the characters speak out their thoughts are reminiscent of Genet's *The Maids*. The influence is domesticated into a family setting, but not altogether digested.

—Ronald Hayman

HOWE, Tina. American. Born in New York City, 21 November 1937. Educated at Sarah Lawrence College, Bronxville, New York, B.A. 1959; Chicago Teachers College, 1963–64. Married Norman Levy in 1961; one son and one daughter. Since 1983 Adjunct Professor, New York University. Recipient: Rosamond Gilder award, 1983; Rockefeller grant, 1983; Obie award, 1983; Outer Critics Circle award, 1983, 1984; John Gassner Award, 1984; National Endowment for the Arts grant, 1984. Agent: Flora Roberts Inc., 157 West 57th Street, New York, New York 10019. Address: 333 West End Avenue, New York, New York 10023, U.S.A.

PUBLICATIONS

Plays

Closing Time (produced Bronxville, New York, 1959).
The Nest (produced Provincetown, Massachusetts, 1969; New York, 1970).
Museum (produced Los Angeles, 1976; New York, 1977). New York, French, 1979.

Birth and After Birth, in *The New Women's Theatre*, edited by Honor Moore. New York, Random House, 1977.
The Art of Dining (produced Washington, D.C., and New York, 1979). New York, French, 1980.
Appearances (produced New York, 1982).
Painting Churches (produced New York, 1983). New York, French, 1984.
Three Plays (includes *Museum, The Art of Dining, Painting Churches*). New York, Avon, 1984.
Coastal Disturbances (produced New York, 1986). New York, French, 1987.

*

Tina Howe comments:

The motivating factor in all my works is a hopeless infatuation with extravagance. To me, the theater is an arena for celebrating excess—outrageous settings, lush language, and intense emotions. The three constants that keep popping up in my plays are art, food, and the sight gag.

* * *

Tina Howe is a marvelously perceptive observer of contemporary mores, and much of the pleasure one receives from her plays comes from her comic skewering of pretentious amateur art critics, couples moaning orgasmically over the yuppie menu of their dreams, and thoroughly enlightened parents thoroughly unable to cope with their monstrous four-year-old. At their best, however, her comedies probe beneath the surface to reveal the inextricable mixture of the humorous and horrific to which modern culture—including art, ritual, and table manners—is a barely adequate response.

Although it already hints of better things to come, *The Nest* is the least satisfying of Howe's six full-length plays. The influence of Ionesco and Beckett, whose work Howe admires, is evident here in the use of repeated scenes as well as in the heavy reliance on verbal and physical farce. Still, this play about a trio of female roommates lacks the satirical and emotional bite of her subsequent creations even as it offers glimpses of her prodigious imagination.

"Family life has been over-romanticized; the savagery has not been seen enough in the theatre and in movies," Howe once complained. She attempts to fill this gap with *Birth and After Birth*, a sometimes hilarious, often frightening portrait of the Apples. As their name implies, the Apples (including a four-year-old son played by an adult actor) are a parody of the TV-fare all-American family, continually declaring how happy they are and continually belying this claim. What keeps *Birth and After Birth* from being simply another satire on Ozzie and Harriet is not only Howe's accurate portrait of the physical and emotional brutality inherent in family life but her disturbingly negative exploration of why women choose to have—or not to have—children. Despite the often broad slapstick, *Birth and After Birth* is one of Howe's darkest comedies.

Museum is less a plotted play than a wonderful series of comic turns as visitors—singly and in groups—wander through an exhibit entitled "The Broken Silence." As Howe has acknowledged in interviews, all of her plays are about art, and *Museum* examines the complex interrelationships among creator, creation, and viewers. On one level, *Museum* reveals what fools art makes of us (witness the young woman painstakingly copying an all-white canvas); on another level, however, it shows that artworks cannot fully exist except in the presence of an audience, foolish or not. Finally, in one of the comically horrific monologues that seem an essential part of the Howe landscape, a museum-goer recounts a foraging expedition she took with Agnes Vaag, a young artist represented in the show but never seen on stage. The story reveals the frightening, non-rational roots of art. Vaag, at once a mysterious being who makes "menacing constructions" out of animal carcasses and a ludicrous figure who lugs suitcases through state parks, may well be Howe's archetypal artist.

Another loosely knit comedy, *The Art of Dining* combines Howe's obsession with food (first manifest in *The Nest*) and her concern with art and its consumption. Because the fragility of art is a repeated motif throughout Howe's canon, in a sense food is for her the ultimate artistic medium: it must be destroyed to be appreciated. Set in a restaurant, *The Art of Dining* contains one of Howe's most brilliant creations, Elizabeth Barrow Colt, a wonderfully comic and pathetic figure who embodies every cliché about writers; comfortable only in the world of the imagination, she's a genius with a pen but a total failure with a soup spoon. In *The Art of Dining*'s spectacular conclusion—all the restaurant guests gathered around a flaming platter of crepes tended by the female chef—Howe uses Elizabeth to point out the connection between art and ritual as well as the redemptive power of artistic creation, a theme that runs through several of Howe's works.

Howe's biggest critical success to date is *Painting Churches*, in some ways her most conventional play as well as one of her most lyrical. Returning to the favorite subject of the American playwright—the nuclear family—Howe gives us a comedy about the necessity of acceptance: a daughter accepting the inevitable decline of her aging parents, parents accepting their daughter as a capable adult (and artist). Howe's quirky sense of humor and her distinctive verbal and visual idiom mark the work as uniquely her own, however familiar her starting point. Although Howe denies that she is an autobiographical writer, there is obviously a kinship between the playwright and Mags Church, the young artist who learns that the portrait she is painting of her parents reveals her as well as them. In a moving final tour-de-force that erases the line between Mags' painting and Howe's play, the stripped-bare stage becomes the portrait, the aging characters rescued from decline for the space of a magical moment.

Howe favors unusual settings—a museum, a restaurant kitchen—and the beach locale of her latest play, *Coastal Disturbances*, is as much metaphor as place: like human beings and their relationships, the sand and ocean remain essentially the same over millennia yet change from moment to moment. The main character is a young woman photographer; appropriately, the play is divided into numerous short scenes that rely heavily on visual effects—resembling, in other words, a sequence of snapshots. Although the central situation, a love triangle, is not Howe's most original, her verbal and especially her visual wit are amply in evidence.

Howe has acknowledged her debt to Absurdist writers, a debt more apparent in her earlier work than in her most recent plays. Like many other American playwrights, Howe doesn't quite share the nihilistic vision of her European counterparts; although salvation is transitory and more likely to be aesthetic than religious or social, there are moments of redemption in most of her plays. Her work has grown in emotional depth over the years and her focus on art and the artist has become stronger. Women artists are her favored protagonists: she writes from a clearly female perspective even if not from a consistently feminist one. Howe's comedies reveal a playwright with a fine sensitivity to the terrors of existence, a splendidly anarchic sense of humor, and a willingness to take risks on the stage.

—Judith E. Barlow

HUGHES, Dusty. British. Born in Boston, Lincolnshire, 16 September 1947. Educated at Queen Elizabeth Grammar School, Wakefield, Yorkshire, 1957–65; Trinity Hall, Cambridge, 1965–68, M.A. (honours) in English. Has one daughter. Director, Birmingham Repertory Theatre, 1970–72; theatre editor, *Time Out*, London, 1973–76; artistic director, Bush Theatre, London, 1976–79; script editor, *Play for Today* series, BBC Television, 1982–84. Member, Arts Council Drama panel, 1975–80. Recipient: London Theatre Critics award, 1980; Edinburgh Festival award, 1981. Agent: Margaret Ramsay Ltd., 14-A Goodwin's Court, London WC2N 4LL, England.

PUBLICATIONS

Plays

Grrr (produced Edinburgh, 1968).
Commitments (produced London, 1980). With *Futurists*, London, Faber, 1986.
Heaven and Hell (produced Edinburgh and London, 1981).
Molière; or, The Union of Hypocrites, adaptation of a play by Mikhail Bulgakov (produced Stratford-on-Avon, 1982; London, 1983). London, Methuen, 1983.
From Cobbett's Urban Rides, in *Breach of the Peace* (produced London, 1982).
Bad Language (produced London, 1983).
Philistines, adaptation of a play by Maxim Gorky (produced Stratford-on-Avon, 1985; London, 1986). Oxford, Amber Lane Press, 1985; New York, Applause, 1986.
Futurists (produced London, 1986). With *Commitments*, London, Faber, 1986.
Jenkin's Ear (produced London, 1987). London, Faber, 1987.

Screenplays: *Cries from the South*, 1986; *In Hiding*, 1987.

*

Theatrical Activities:
Director: **Plays**—Bush Theatre, London: *The Soul of the White Ant* by Snoo Wilson, 1976; *Blood Sports* by David Edgar, 1976; *Vampire* by Snoo Wilson, 1977; *Happy Birthday, Wanda June* by Kurt Vonnegut, Jr., 1977; *In at the Death* by Snoo Wilson and others, 1978; *A Greenish Man* by Snoo Wilson, 1978; *Wednesday* by Julia Kearsley, 1978.

* * *

Dusty Hughes emerged in the 1980's with several dramatic works to his credit and more to come. An early experience with the left-wing's not having transformed him into a "good Bolshevik" has shaped the subject and concerns of his produced plays. The plays pursue a theme of disenchantment with the Marxist-Socialist ideal turned sour or repressive, as well as with middle-class aspirations which disclose emptiness and produce social and personal inertia.

Standing as immediate examples are Hughes's three best works: *Commitments, Futurists*, and an adaptation, *Molière; or, The Union of Hypocrites*.

Commitments introduces a small group of left-wing activists in 1973 using as live-in headquarters the London flat of a tolerant bourgeois dilettante reluctant to join their cause. Forming a focal and substantially dimensionalized triumvirate are the charming but undirected benefactor, an actress strongly committed to "the Party," and her working-class actor-lover. Fellow workers drop in as the group discusses politics and strategies and performs menial Party tasks, while outside the 1974 Labour government comes to power owing little to the Party's efforts or workers. Malaise affects the group's interrelationships: the flat-owner, motivated to become politically active, now ends up returning to his wastrel ways persuaded that the Party is "authoritarian and not a little unrealistic"; and the politically committed actress loses her lover, who returns to his wife. The drama offers a trenchant picture of disillusioned leftists whose cause and commitments have seemed wasted effort.

In *Futurists* Hughes takes us to 1921 post-revolution Petrograd, where great and mediocre artists, journalists, political hacks, striking sailors, and Bolshevik informers mingle in a sweaty nightclub. The drama centers on the Futurist poets—the famous figures of Mandelstam, Mayakovsky, Anna Akhmatova, and others are vividly recreated—who are drawn together by a fervent revolutionary belief that they have something to say but are initially unaware that their individualistic, unconventional thought and expression will eventually doom them. They proclaim their art and reveal their loss of equilibrium in the excitement of revolutionary confusion, while beyond the nightclub the revolution has gone wrong. The poets have relied for protection on their hero Gorky, friend of Lenin, who presides over them like a one-man arts council, but finds he cannot save them from the firing squads or being otherwise silenced. In the new society the artist is an endangered species: the mediocre survive, the talented grow silent or die. Central to the action, the tubercular Gorky becomes a tragic figure losing his self-assured belief that "people don't kill poets" as he becomes increasingly powerless to help his friends and is even warned by Lenin to leave the country. Hughes fills his characters and their world with vibrant life and a dire meaning, tellingly visualized in the 1986 London production as the colorfully grotesque Futurist trappings of the artists' cabaret are progressively stripped away to reveal the ominous black and red banners of Stalin. Yet with Anna Akhmatova's final recitation of a forbidden poem, Hughes reminds us that poetry outlasts revolutions.

That the playwright was drawn to adapt Mikhail Bulgakov's *Molière* is understandable. The play focuses on Molière's relationship to Louis XIV, as a sardonic paradigm of the Russian Bulgakov's position as a writer under Stalin, who in 1936 banned the play after seven performances. Hughes, in portraying a freethinking Molière incurring the wrath of Mother Church in mounting *Tartuffe* and suffering its banishment and his own fall from grace, demonstrates how the artist must demean himself before tyrannical and faction-influenced authority. Rejecting his long-time mistress Madeleine for a disastrous marriage with her supposed younger sister, Molière is informed upon by a dismissed actor in his company. This allows the religious cabal unscrupulously to engineer Molière's fall from favor by extracting Madeleine's confession that his wife is actually their mutual daughter, thus forcing the King's disapproval and his capitulation to their condemnation of the artist.

The lively portrait of Moilière, who switches from the impetuous actor-manager-writer backstage to a grovelling sycophant when in the presence of his sovereign, is both dramatically powerful, if perhaps historically exaggerated (as is the use of the unproven incest rumor), and thematically lucid. Molière underestimates the power of church and state with its near-omnipotent king and informer-ridden society resembling Stalinist Russia. The play is effective as theatre and as political statement.

The vapid inertness of middle-class values infecting the generations underscores two further works. *Bad Language*, a comedy about university undergraduates touched by the malady of sameness, is a wryly affectionate survey of Cambridge life while lightly giving a perceptive glimpse of empty contemporary mores. Adapting Gorky's flawed yet compelling first play, Hughes in *Philistines* incisively presents a blackly comic portrait of a turn-of-the-century *petit bourgeois* Russian provincial family unable to change their ineffectual lives—foreshadowing the national upheaval to follow.

Each new work helps to establish Hughes as a playwright committed to creating dramas of substance that thoughtfully examine or offer parallels to the socio-political tapestry of his time.

—Christian H. Moe

HUTCHINSON, Ron. British. Born near Lisburn, County Antrim, Northern Ireland; brought up in Coventry, Warwickshire. Educated at schools in Coventry. Worked at various jobs, including fish gutter, carpet salesman, scene shifter, and bookseller, all Coventry; clerk, Ministry of Defence and Ministry of Labour, Coventry; social worker and claims investigator, Department of Health and Social Security, Coventry, 5 years. Resident writer, Royal Shakespeare Company, London, 1978–79. Recipient: George Devine Award, 1978; John Whiting Award, 1984. Agent: Judy Daish Associates, 83 Eastbourne Mews, London W2 6LQ, England.

PUBLICATIONS

Plays

Says I, Says He (produced Sheffield, 1977; London, 1978; New York, 1979). Part 1 published in *Plays and Players* (London), March and April 1978; complete play published Newark, Delaware, Proscenium Press, 1980.
Eejits (produced London, 1978).
Jews/Arabs (produced London, 1978).
Anchorman (produced London, 1979).
Christmas of a Nobody (produced 1979).
The Irish Play (produced London, 1980).
Into Europe (produced London, 1981).
Risky City (broadcast 1981; produced Coventry, 1981).
The Dillen, adaptation of a work by Angela Hewins (produced Stratford-on-Avon, 1983).
Rat in the Skull (produced London, 1984; New York, 1985). London, Methuen, 1984.
Mary, After the Queen, with Angela Hewins (produced Stratford-on-Avon, 1985).
Curse of the Baskervilles, from a story by Arthur Conan Doyle (produced Plymouth, 1987).

Radio Plays: *Roaring Boys*, 1977; *Murphy Unchained*, 1978; *There Must Be a Door*, 1979; *Motorcade*, 1980; *Risky City*, 1981.

Television Plays: *Twelve Off the Belt*, 1977; *Deasy Desperate*, 1979; *The Last Window Cleaner*, 1979; *The Out of Town Boys*, 1979; *Deasy*, 1979; *The Winkler*, 1979; *Bull Week*, 1980; *Bird of Prey* series, 1982 and 1984; *Connie* series, 1985; *The Marksman*, from the novel by Hugh C. Rae (*Unnatural Causes* series), 1987.

Novel

Connie (novelization of television series). London, Severn House, 1985.

* * *

The value of Ron Hutchinson's drama to date derives from his consistent concentration on the Irish experience *outside* Ireland—an experience which serves in his plays to crystallize native Irish problems. The focus is only incidentally social in character. *Risky City* offers a forceful account, in the form of deathbed flashbacks, of the wasting of a Coventry–Irish youth by his inner-city environment, but his experience is not presented as a specifically Irish one. More characteristic is Hutchinson's first stage play, *Say I, Says He*, in which the "Old Firm" of two picaresque Ulster navvies, the "roaring boy" Hannafin and the "clean-shave" Phelan, leave their terrorist siblings, and the beautiful dancer for whose hand they are rivals, to conquer London. Financial success for Phelan (gained, ironically, not without obscure threats of Ulster-style violence) attracts the attention of the terrorists, but turns out to be illusory, a matter of the "gab." Reunited, the two plan to leave for England again but are gunned down.

With its musical numbers (some of them uproariously obscene, all of them broadly ironic), *Says I, Says He* resembles a navvies' version of Stewart Parker's *Catchpenny Twist*—another Irish play in which the aspiring heroes ultimately fail to escape political violence. Where Parker has musicians, Hutchinson, as his title suggests, has talkers—but they are no less *performers*: the play consists of a series of comic sketch-episodes (in which the humour is not often a matter of inflection) crowned by Phelan's final fibbing performance ("You took *me* in. With *your* act"). However, in this play Hutchinson is content to revel in his characters' gift of the gab rather than to reflect upon it. The comedy is not of the serious kind.

Eejits also focuses on performers. But here the four violently argumentative members of a London-based Ceilidh band are not under threat from terrorists; rather they carry their nationa-l(ist) factionalism around with them. The same predicament receives thorough and hilarious treatment, again in connection with a performance, in *The Irish Play*. In a broken-down Midlands Irish club, the embattled President O'Higgins, striving to retain his control and dignity in the face of the machinations of the opposing Roche faction, endorses the presentation of a nationalistic historical play (agit-prop Ferguson) as part of his plan to endow the bibulous membership with a "historical perspective." As to history, he discovers that "it's all around us, that's the trouble," when, in debate, committee, and finally rehearsal, the ancient alignments of civil war emerge: "Constitutionals versus Hill-men"; Collins versus De Valera; Kerry versus Wexford. In a comic metaphor of internecine self-destruction, the building is jointly wrecked by the warring factions, leaving only the bewildered step-dancer who "plays recorder and dances in the rubble."

The play-writer Ruari in *The Irish Play* declares that he is "trying to understand my country ... my countrymen ... myself." Hutchinson himself has said of his most successful and best play, *Rat in the Skull*: "I wanted to write this play to sort out my personal reactions to what is going on in Ireland. ... You find out who you are in the process." Certainly this feels like a work energized by a personal imperative. For perhaps the first time, Hutchinson's abrasively comic dialogue and his preoccupation with performance are concentrated into a sustained scrutiny of the self-awareness and self-understanding catalyzed within an Irishman by his presence in England. The theme is not new for this writer, but the power is.

Rather than a plot, *Rat in the Skull* presents a situation and poses a question. The framework is not naturalistic. Under a screen, showing clinical photographs of Michael Patrick De Valera Demon Bomber Roche after his clinical beating-up by Detective-Inspector Nelson of the Royal Ulster Constabulary in Paddington Green police station, are played out the interrogation of Roche by Nelson which led up to the beating, and the consequent interviews, by the Irish "specialist" Superintendent Harris, of Nelson and of the young policeman detailed to be present at the interrogation. The case had been "stitched up," and Nelson had come to London only because of the possibility of the prisoner's turning informer; so why the very deliberative act of violence? The weary Harris reaches for extenuating personal circumstances (an unfaithful wife and a recently dead father), persuading Nelson to accept an "unfit discharge," but neither he nor the baffled, indifferent Constable Naylor can conceive of the complex relation between history and personal identity which renders these Irishmen intimate in conflict—to the exclusion of the Englishman—and which alone points to the explanation. Nelson's fierce parodies of sectarian rhetoric and his sudden changes of tone and address turn the interrogation into a terrible comic performance—one calculated not only to "get inside" and break Roche but also to discomfit an English public which, he senses, stereotypes him in the role of "unclean" Paddy. As Naylor, the "audience" to the interrogation, says: "Roche hasn't said a word the sod, but he's straight man to Nelson ... it's him and Roche on me." But Nelson is also inflicted with the performer's self-scrutinizing distance. The eponymous rat-in-the-skull images the doubt and self-awareness that persuade him to "break step" for the first time with his Protestant forebears by acknowledging, through this calculated gesture of violence, that he is not a state-sanctioned fighter in a "Holy War" but rather one of "two fellas in a ditch, clubbing each other, till the one dropped dead." *Rat in the Skull* capitalizes thematically on the talent for punchy, stylized dialogue that has always been apparent in Hutchinson's work for both stage and television (*Bird of Prey* and *Connie*), and in so doing enriches that most vital tradition within Irish drama—its concern with the nature and power of rhetoric.

—Paul Lawley

HWANG, David Henry. American. Born in Los Angeles, California, 11 August 1957. Educated at Stanford University, California, 1975–79, A.B. in English 1979; Yale University School of Drama, New Haven, Connecticut 1980–81. Married Ophelia Y.M. Chong in 1985. Recipient: Drama-Logue award, 1980, 1986; Obie award, 1981; Golden Eagle award, for television writing, 1983; Rockefeller fellowship, 1983; Guggenheim fellowship, 1984; National Endowment for the Arts fellowship, 1985. Lives in Los Angeles. Agent: Paul Yamamoto and William Craver, Writers and Artists Agency, 70 West 36th Street, New York, New York 10018, U.S.A.

Publications

Plays

FOB (produced Stanford, California, 1978; New York, 1980). Included in *Broken Promises: Four Plays*, 1983.
The Dance and the Railroad (produced New York, 1981; in *Broken Promises*, produced London, 1987). Included in *Broken Promises: Four Plays*, 1983.
Family Devotions (produced New York, 1981). Included in *Broken Promises: Four Plays*, 1983.
Sound and Beauty (includes *The House of Sleeping Beauties* and *The Sound of a Voice*) (produced New York, 1983; *The House of Sleeping Beauties* in *Broken Promises*, produced London, 1987). *The House of Sleeping Beauties* included in *Broken Promises: Four Plays*, 1983; *The Sound of a Voice* published New York, Dramatists Play Service, 1984.
Broken Promises: Four Plays. New York, Avon, 1983.
Rich Relations (produced New York, 1986).
As the Crow Flies (produced Los Angeles, 1986).
Broken Promises (includes *The Dance and the Railroad* and *The House of Sleeping Beauties*) (produced London, 1987).

*

Theatrical Activities:
Director: **Plays**—*A Song for a Nisei Fisherman*, 1980, and *The Dream of Kitamura*, 1982, both by Philip Kan Gotanda, San Francisco.

David Henry Hwang comments:

I'm interested in the dust that settles when worlds collide. Sometimes these worlds are cultural, as in my explorations of a Chinese past meeting an American present. Sometimes they are spiritual, as in *Rich Relations*, where the gung-ho materialism of a California family struggles with its Christian mysticism. Most of the time I also try to walk the fine line between tragedy and comedy. I'm fascinated by America as a land of dreams—people pursue them and hope some day to own one.

* * *

"I am going to America because of its promises," says Steve in *FOB*, David Henry Hwang's first play, but the line is followed by a dismissal of possibility. *Broken Promises* is the overall title Hwang gave to the collection of his first four plays, an accurate indication of one of the major themes of his work. Historically, the promise that was broken for so many Chinese immigrants was the dream of the Gold Mountain, an America where fortunes could be picked up off the street. The new arrivals, who came in the mid-19th century to build the railroad, were used and dismissed and sent to scramble for survival in an alien and unfriendly society. Survive some of them did and flourish, but Hwang, the son of Chinese immigrants, conventionally educated at choice American universities, is interested not only in the broken promises of the past. He is concerned about the loss implicit in an embracing of the emblems of American success and the tensions embodied in being a hyphenated person, a Chinese-American.

There is some ambiguity about the Steve who speaks the line above. Is he the wealthy young man from Hong Kong, come for an American education, or is he, as his obsessed wiping of the table suggests, the 19th-century immigrant he conjured in a monologue preceding the line? Both are outsiders, and Hwang wants to suggest a continuity of exclusion/inclusion for Chinese in America. His strategy for presenting that idea is characteristic of all his work—not the particular device but the use of non-realistic elements. His characters are not developed in the conventional Western way, the accumulation of psychological detail. They emerge through formal presentational modes as varied as Chinese opera (*The Dance and the Railroad*) and the television sitcom (*Family Devotions*). Neither the opera nor the sitcom is allowed to retain its classic form, however, for artistically as well as ideationally Hwang is preoccupied with the ground on which the hyphenated American struggles to define himself.

In a comic lecture at the beginning of *FOB*, Dale, the second-generation Chinese-American, explains that the ABC (American Born Chinese) are "sworn enemies" of the FOB (Fresh Off the Boat) in a denigrating speech which suggests the way established European immigrants early in the century dismissed the greenhorns whose dress, manners, speech might inhibit their own movement toward assimilation. *FOB* is a three-way struggle among Dale, who is accepted—almost—as something other than "a Chinese, a yellow, a slant, a gook"; Grace, his first-generation cousin who has been in the States since she was a child; and Steve, the bumptious newcomer. Steve, who is sometimes the hero Gwan Gung as well as immigrants of earlier generations, and Grace, who on occasion becomes Fa Mu Lan, the Woman Warrior, go off together at the end of the play. Their pairing suggests that the Chinese in America must hold onto some sense of their being Chinese, but it is instructive that they are heading for a fashionable disco in a rented limousine. There is a similar but more moving cross-over in *The Dance and the Railroad*, in which Lone tries to separate himself from his fellow workers—"dead men," he calls them—by going to the mountaintop to practice the movements of Chinese opera. Ma, who wants both to dance with Lone and to be one of "the guys" down below, is allowed to perform as the hero of his own story in an improvised opera that celebrates the victory of the Chinese workers in a strike for more pay. The opera, in which Lone dances the various forces which oppose Ma, is both comic and touching, a retention of the past that uses the vocabulary of traditional art to place Ma heroically if ironically in an American context. Lone, less naive than Ma, stays to dance alone for "the last time" before he goes to join the men whom he no longer sees as dead. In *Family Devotions* it is the visiting uncle from the mainland, more Chinese than Communist, who teaches his great nephew that, before he can escape the twin traps of materialism and Christianity which his family represents, he must recognize his face—reflected in the back of the violin that will open his path to the future—and carry his Chinese self into his American world. The broad comedy of the piece, the caricature in both the militantly Christian old women and the gadget-ridden achievers in the middle generation, was disconcerting to some playgoers who had responded to the more austere *The Dance and the Railroad*, particularly when the ritual verbal battle at the end led to the death of the old women. Yet, *Family Devotions*, for all the surface differences, is of a piece, thematically and dramaturgically, with the earlier plays.

More recently, Hwang has been working with Japanese settings, which means that, as Chinese and as American, he is outside his material. The result—the two plays that make up *Sound and Beauty*—reflects a distancing that brings the non-realistic elements in his work into even greater prominence. *The House of Sleeping Beauties* combines the writing of Kawabata's novel of that title with the author's suicide to produce a meditation on aging. *The Sound of a Voice*, an encounter between a woman who lives alone in the forest and the man who fails to kill her as a witch, is a confrontation that is dependent on movement, light, sound, and color as much as on Hwang's words. The Japanese aura of the piece is a fascinating facade through which can be seen a much more widely accessible fable of conflicting, converging desires and the failure implicit in them. Hwang, no longer a theatrical FOB, is clearly extending his range.

—Gerald Weales

INNAURATO, Albert. American. Born in Philadelphia, Pennsylvania, 2 June 1947. Educated at Temple University, Philadelphia, B.A.; California Institute of the Arts, Valencia, B.F.A. 1972; Yale University School of Drama, New Haven, Connecticut, M.F.A. 1975. Playwright-in-residence, Playwrights Horizons, New York, 1983; Adjunct Professor, Columbia University, New York, and Princeton University, New Jersey, 1987. Recipient: Guggenheim grant, 1975; Rockefeller grant, 1977; Obie award, 1977; National Endowment for the Arts grant, 1986. Agent: George Lane, William Morris Agency, 1350 Avenue of the Americas, New York, New York 10019. Address: 325 West 22nd Street, New York, New York 10011, U.S.A.

PUBLICATIONS

Plays

Urlicht (produced New Haven, Connecticut, 1971; New York, 1974). Included in *Bizarre Behavior*, 1980.

I Don't Generally Like Poetry But Have You Read "Trees"?, with Christopher Durang (produced New Haven, Connecticut, 1972; New York, 1973).

The Life Story of Mitzi Gaynor; or, Gyp, with Christopher Durang (produced New Haven, Connecticut, 1973).

The Transfiguration of Benno Blimpie (produced New Haven, Connecticut, 1973; New York, 1975; London, 1978). New Haven, Connecticut, Yale/Theatre, 1976; London, TQ Publications, 1977.

The Idiots Karamazov, with Christopher Durang, music by Jack Feldman, lyrics by Durang (also director: produced New Haven, Connecticut, 1974). New Haven, Connecticut, Yale/Theatre, 1974; augmented edition, New York, Dramatists Play Service, 1981.

Earth Worms (produced Waterford, Connecticut, 1974; New York, 1977). Included in *Bizarre Behavior*, 1980.

Gemini (produced New York, 1976). New York, Dramatists Play Service, 1977.

Ulysses in Traction (produced New York, 1977). New York, Dramatists Play Service, 1978.

Passione (also director: produced New York, 1980). New York, Dramatists Play Service, 1981.

Bizarre Behavior: Six Plays (includes *Gemini, The Transfiguration of Benno Blimpie, Ulysses in Traction, Earth Worms, Urlicht, Wisdom Amok*). New York, Avon, 1980.

Coming of Age in SoHo (also director: produced Seattle and New York, 1984; revised version produced New York, 1985). New York, Dramatists Play Service, 1985.

*

Theatrical Activities:

Director: **Plays**—*The Idiots Karamazov*, New Haven, Connecticut, 1974; *Passione*, New York, 1980; *The Transfiguration of Benno Blimpie*, New York, 1983; *Herself as Lust*, New York, 1983; *Coming of Age in SoHo*, Seattle 1984, New York, 1984 and 1985.

Actor: **Play**—*I Don't Generally Like Poetry But Have You Read "Trees"?*, New York, 1973.

* * *

In his Introduction to his collection of plays *Bizarre Behavior* the extraordinarily talented Albert Innaurato expresses understandable annoyance at the frequency with which critics misunderstand his plays or insist upon discussing connections between them. But to misread is always the critic's risk and to search out the connections, when they do indeed exist, one of his obligations. When considered together, Innaurato's individual plays delineate, as the work of such an important and promising dramatist must, a unique, powerfully held vision of the human condition. This vision is characterized by the skillful manipulation of vividly contrasting dramatic elements that ignite the plays' tensions and yield to their reconciliations. Most prominent among these are satiric farce, comedy, and pathos; the beauty-and-the-beast combination of the grotesque and the beautiful; and the religious and the blasphemous. Among a rather extensive list of more specific dualities are his characters' outward appearances and contrasting inner realities; their often "bizarre behavior" and their rather different inner impulses; and a frequent doubling of times and places that parallel these dichotomies of character and action. Innaurato also explores the psychological terrain of sexual ambiguity, seems to exploit aspects of the disease of overeating, bulimia, with the necessary purgation, here Aristotelian rather than Roman-orgy in nature, and from music borrows the concepts of aria and counterpoint.

The multiple dualities of *Gemini*, his most commercially successful play, with a run of over four years at a small Broadway house, are indicated by the title from which the hero Francis Geminiani, "plump" and "a little clumsy," derives his name. At the time of his 21st birthday, his fellow Harvard students, the attractive and very WASP Judith Hastings and her freshman younger brother, arrive for an unexpected visit to his Italian and Catholic South Philadelphia home. At his symbolic coming of age, climaxed by a disastrous birthday feast, Francis is forced to investigate openly his inner life and to admit that he is attracted emotionally not only to the sister but to her brother as well. But despite the potential pathos of the central situation, as Harvard and South Philadelphia, his college friends and his overfed, rough-talking, but good-hearted neighbors collide, the results are a raucous comic festival, as lively as an Italian street *festa* and funnier than anything Neil Simon could devise. In *Passione* Innaurato returns to South Philadelphia to explore the emotional problems of a middle-aged couple and to contrast the parents with their happy son, a clown, who is incongruously married to the fat lady of the circus.

Innaurato's most recent, more interesting, and less successful play *Coming of Age in SoHo* is a kind of counterpart or sequel to *Gemini* and brings to the foreground some of its preoccupations. The hero Bartholomew Dante has left his wife to write in a loft in SoHo and like his predecessor also comes of age, this time at 36. There is again much wild humor, triggered here by his wife's South Philadelphia family headed by her father, the Mafia don Cumbar' Antonio, and the unexpected entrance of three boys, the brothers Odysseus ("WASP culture") and Trajan from St. Paul's and Harvard, and his own forgotten son Puer, the result of a long-ago affair with a German terrorist. But the play's intent is serious. The brothers with their classical names, poor Puer ("boy" and the *puer* complex) who seeks a brother and finds his father, and the Dante-Beatrice allusions index the play's assemblage of elements of what might be called the *gemini* concept: the linkage of narcissism, dual or ambivalent identity, and creativity. Aspects of this concept underlie Albee's much earlier *The American Dream* and are present in the plays of Peter Shaffer, particularly *Equus*.

But the brilliant, darkly beautiful *The Transfiguration of Benno Blimpie*, Innaurato's finest work thus far, belongs to a differently imagined South Philadelphia than *Gemini* and is more characteristic of his other plays. The fat, unattractive Benno, with his delicate inner life, is eating himself to death. As he controls the play's dramatic time, he comments upon and verbally participates in scenes of his past emotional yearnings and rejections. The play ends with a startling cannibalistic image as Benno, before the quick black-out, "*lowers the meat cleaver as though to cut off some part of himself.*"

The same dark intensity is present in *Earth Worms*, one of the most wildly imaginative plays by any recent dramatist. Arnold Longese, the sexually ambiguous hero, manages to beget a child with a country girl from the south. He brings her back to South Philadelphia, and there they are surrounded by his blind grandmother who lives on the floor, two transvestites, and a group of hustlers. At the end of the play the grandmother dies, the family home is becoming a whorehouse, and the hero is mutilated by three vindictive nuns. Ingredients for an unintended comedy? Perhaps. But here they combine into Magritte-like fragments of a vivid tragicomic nightmare. The short play *Urlicht* belongs to a similar dramatic world, features outrageously comic religious situations, and is peopled in part by incongruous nuns.

Innaurato's plays clearly make allusions to his awareness of the grandeur and comedy of the classical past. *Gemini* and *Ulysses in Traction*, with its implications of inhibited enterprise, make the suggestions in their titles; the mad nuns who become like giant cockroaches as they swarm over the hero of *Earth Worms* recall the Furies. But in their effects the plays bring to mind that modern gothic playwright Michel de Ghelderode, and they seem more properly gothic and medieval. Francis in *Gemini* and Arnold in *Earth Worms* wander like modern everymen through their distorted worlds, and Innaurato's most memorable characters resemble frightening or wildly comic gargoyles. But in familiar phrases from Shakespeare and Yeats, most of his characters have "that within which passeth show": they have Dionysus's "beating heart" rather than stone "in the midst of all."

—Gaynor F. Bradish

JELLICOE, (Patricia) Ann. British. Born in Middlesbrough, Yorkshire, 15 July 1927. Educated at Polam Hall, Darlington, County Durham; Queen Margaret's, Castle Howard, Yorkshire; Central School of Speech and Drama, London (Elsie Fogarty Prize, 1947), 1944–47. Married 1) C.E. Knight-Clarke in 1950 (marriage dissolved 1961); 2) Roger Mayne in 1962, one son and one daughter. Actress, stage manager, and director, in London and the provinces, 1947–51; founding director, Cockpit Theatre Club, London, 1952–54; lecturer and director, Central School of Speech and Drama, 1954–56; literary manager, Royal Court Theatre, London, 1973–75; founding director, Colway Theatre Trust 1978–85. O.B.E. (Officer, Order of the British Empire), 1984. Agent: Margaret Ramsay Ltd., 14-A Goodwin's Court, London WC2N 4LL, England.

PUBLICATIONS

Plays

Rosmersholm, adaptation of the play by Ibsen (also director: produced London, 1952; revised version produced London, 1959). San Francisco, Chandler, 1960.

The Sport of My Mad Mother (also co-director: produced London, 1958). Published in *The Observer Plays*, London, Faber, 1958; revised version, London, Faber, 1964; with *The Knack*, New York, Dell, 1964.

The Lady from the Sea, adaptation of a play by Ibsen (produced London, 1961).

The Knack (also co-director: produced Cambridge, 1961; London, 1962; Boston, 1963; New York, 1964). London, Encore, and New York, French, 1962.

The Seagull, with Adriadne Nicolaeff, adaptation of a play by Chekhov (produced London, 1964).

Der Freischütz, translation of the libretto by Friedrich Kind, music by Weber (produced London, 1964).

Shelley; or, The Idealist (also director: produced London, 1965). London, Faber, and New York, Grove Press, 1966.

The Rising Generation (produced London, 1967). Published in *Playbill 2*, edited by Alan Durband, London, Hutchinson, 1969.

The Giveaway (produced Edinburgh, 1968; London, 1969). London, Faber, 1970.

You'll Never Guess (also director: produced London, 1973). Included in *3 Jelliplays*, 1975.

Two Jelliplays: Clever Elsie, Smiling John, Silent Peter, and A Good Thing or a Bad Thing (also director: produced London, 1974). Included in *3 Jelliplays*, 1975.

3 Jelliplays (for children; includes *You'll Never Guess; Clever Elsie, Smiling John, Silent Peter; A Good Thing or a Bad Thing*). London, Faber, 1975.

Flora and the Bandits (also director: produced Dartington, Devon, 1976).

The Reckoning (also director: produced Lyme Regis, Dorset, 1978).

The Bargain (also director: produced Exeter, 1979).

The Tide (also director: produced Axminster, Devon, 1980).

The Western Women, music by Nick Brace, adaptation of a story by Fay Weldon (also co-director: produced Lyme Regis, Dorset, 1984).

Other

Some Unconscious Influences in the Theatre. London and New York, Cambridge University Press, 1967.

Devon: A Shell Guide, with Roger Mayne. London, Faber, 1975.

Community Plays: How to Put Them On. London, Methuen, 1987.

*

Theatrical Activities:
Director: **Plays**—*The Confederacy* by Vanbrugh, London, 1952; *The Frogs* by Aristophanes, London, 1952; *Miss Julie* by Strindberg, London, 1952; *Rosmersholm* by Ibsen, London, 1952; *Saint's Day* by John Whiting, London, 1953; *The Comedy of Errors*, London, 1953; *Olympia* by Ferenc Molnar, London, 1953; *The Sport of My Mad Mother* (co-director, with George Devine), London, 1958; *For Children* by Keith Johnstone, London, 1958; *The Knack* (co-director, with Keith Johnstone), London, 1962; *Skyvers* by Barry Reckord, London, 1963; *Shelley*, London, 1965; *You'll Never Guess*, London, 1973; *Two Jelliplays*, London, 1974; *A Worthy Guest* by Paul Bailey, London, 1974; *Six of the Best*, London, 1974; *Flora and the Bandits*, Dartington, Devon, 1976; *The Reckoning*, Lyme Regis, Dorset, 1978; *The Bargain*, Exeter, 1979; *The Tide*, Axminster, Devon, 1980; *The Poor Man's Friend* by Howard Barker, Bridport, Dorset, 1981; *The Garden* by Charles Wood, Sherborne, Dorset, 1982; *The Western Women* (co-director, with Chris Fog and Sally-Ann Lomax), Lyme Regis, Dorset, 1984; *Entertaining Strangers* by David Edgar, Dorchester, Dorset, 1985.

* * *

The major plays by new young writers in London between 1956 and 1959 included *Look Back in Anger, The Birthday Party, Roots, Serjeant Musgrave's Dance, A Resounding Tinkle, The Long and the Short and the Tall, Flowering Cherry, Five Finger Exercise, The Hostage, A Taste of Honey*—and Ann Jellicoe's *The Sport of My Mad Mother* at the Royal Court, the heart of this activity.

Since this impressive debut, Jellicoe has written only three other full-length stage plays, two of them slight. The 16 brief scenes of *Shelley* take the poet from his Oxford years, through two marriages, to Harriet Westbrook and Mary Godwin, to his drowning in Italy. *Shelley*, subtitled "the Idealist," is written as though for a 19th-century touring company of twelve: heavy, walking gentleman, juvenile, and so on. Jellicoe remarks that as a writer she is tackling a new set of problems here, working "within a set narrative framework—partly for the sheer technical discipline involved." Shelley interests her because he is very young, and trying to be good: "the problems of goodness which are so much more interesting than those of evil." He is tragic because of "his blindness to the frailty of human nature." *Shelley* is a flat work, with conspicuous explanatory sections in which the poet talks like a letter or tract.

The Giveaway turns on a suburban housewife who wins a competition prize of ten years' supply of cornflakes (which are conspicuously on stage); she has had to pretend to be under 14. While the only production may not have done it justice, *The Giveaway* seems to be a clumsy attempt to write a farce, with a hint of satire on consumerism and a touch of the kind of non-verbal comedy Jellicoe had written earlier.

Jellicoe's best play, *The Knack*, is an exuberant, liberating, youthful comedy. Three young men share a flat: Tolen (he has only this one curious name), who has "the knack" of success with women; likeable Colin, who lacks it and envies Tolen; and the garrulous Tom, half outside the sex war. Enter Nancy, a lost, gawky, 17-year-old Northerner, looking for the YWCA, who will give Tolen a chance to demonstrate his knack. The staccato, repetitive dialogue skims along like jazz, and is sometimes hard to follow on the page. A bed provides comic business (they pretend it is a piano), as do entries through the window. An undercurrent is Tolen's Nazi characteristics, and whether negotiation is possible with such people. (The film, scripted by Charles Wood and directed by Richard Lester, is substantially changed, and also great fun.)

Jellicoe's *succès d'estime, The Sport of My Mad Mother*, is much more unusual and demanding. This is about four London teenagers and three people they come across, a liberal American, a retarded girl of 13, and Greta, an Australian who comes to represent also the Hindu goddess of destruction and creation, Kali. Yet character, plot, dialogue hardly matter. This is a piece to be brought to life by a director, and, to make reading really difficult, stage-directions are few. The form is non-linear; Jellicoe writes in the Preface to the revised text of 1964 that the play "was not written intellectually according to a prearranged plan. It was shaped bit by bit until the bits felt right in relation to each other and to the whole. It is an anti-intellect play not only because it is about irrational forces and urges but because one hopes it will reach the audience directly through rhythm, noise and music.... Very often the words counterpoint the action or intensify the action by conflicting with it." *The Sport of My Mad Mother* is highly original (especially for Britain and for the 1950's) in its Artaudian use of ritual, in its stress on physical expressiveness, in its use of speech and drums for rhythms, in its audacious non-literary form and apparent shapelessness, and in its search for the roots of arbitrary violence. Proper recognition and appreciation will require a readily available film version, as yet unmade.

In 1972 Jellicoe told Carol Dix in the *Guardian*: "Directing, as I see it, is an interpretative art, and writing is a creative art, and it's a bloody relief not to have to be creative any longer. The impulse to create is linked with the aggressive instinct."

A ten-year silence ended when in 1978 Jellicoe moved to Lyme Regis, Dorset; she has since staged seven community plays in the southwest. These ambitious works involve many local people (up to 180 onstage), use the town as the setting and have a promenade production. Jellicoe wrote the first, *The Reckoning*, about the Monmouth Rebellion of 1685. Allen Saddler described it in *Plays and Players*: "It is all action. The mayor and his cronies scramble about in a frenzy, people rush by in terror, beg for mercy or confide strange secrets in your ear. A girl who is pregnant by a Catholic finds herself in a strange dilemma, proclamations are read from various parts of the hall. Soldiers burst in. Bands play. Prisoners are dragged off screaming. Brawls break out just where you are standing. Events proceed so quickly that there is no time to examine the Catholic or the Protestant case." *The Western Women*, about the part played by women in the siege of Lyme in the Civil War, was re-written by Jellicoe from a script by Fay Weldon. Another local history piece, *The Bargain*, concerned Judge Jeffreys and was commissioned by the Southwest Music Theatre. Jellicoe in her essay in *Women and Theatre* writes of the satisfaction of this community activity: "It was extraordinary, the people of Lyme, in rehearsal and in performance, watching a play about themselves. There is a unique atmosphere. It's partly the promenade style of performance, partly that the play is specially written for the town, but it has never failed, that excitement, they just go wild.... What I love about it is slowly building something in the community."

Jellicoe appears unlikely to return to the Royal Court, or to the West End, as her fulfilment now comes from her community work in the West Country.

—Malcolm Page

JENKIN, Len (Leonard Jenkin). American. Born in New York City, 2 April 1941. Educated at Columbia University, New York, 1958–64, 1969–71, B.A. in English 1962, M.A. 1964, Ph.D. in English 1972. Has one daughter. Lecturer in English, Brooklyn College, New York, 1965–66; Associate Professor of English, Manhattan Community College, 1967–79. Since 1980 Associate Professor, Tisch School of the Arts, New York University. Since 1983 associate artistic director, River Arts Repertory Company, Woodstock, New York. Recipient: Yaddo fellowship, 1975; National Endowment for the Arts fellowship, 1979, 1982; Rockefeller fellowship, 1980; Christopher award, 1981; American Film Festival award, 1981; Creative Artists Public Service grant, 1981; Obie award, 1981 (for writing and directing), 1984; MacDowell fellowship, 1984; Guggenheim fellowship, 1987. Agent: Flora Roberts Inc., 157 West 57th Street, New York, New York 10019. Address: 110 Bleecker Street, Apartment 22-C, New York, New York 10012, U.S.A.

PUBLICATIONS

Plays

Kitty Hawk (produced Stratford, Connecticut, 1972; New York, 1974; London, 1975).

Grand American Exhibition (produced New York, 1973).

The Death and Life of Jesse James (produced Los Angeles, 1974; New York, 1978).

Mission (produced New York, 1975).

Gogol: A Mystery Play (also director: produced New York, 1976). Published in *Theatre of Wonders: Six Contemporary American Plays*, edited by Mac Wellman, Los Angeles, Sun and Moon Press, 1986.

Kid Twist (produced San Francisco, 1977; New York, 1983).

New Jerusalem (produced New York, 1979).

Limbo Tales (includes *Highway, Hotel, Intermezzo*) (also director: produced New York, 1980; London, 1982). New York, Dramatists Play Service, 1982.

Five of Us (produced Seattle, 1981; New York, 1984). New York, Dramatists Play Service, 1986.

Dark Ride (also director: produced New York, 1981). New York, Dramatists Play Service, 1982.

Candide; or, Optimism, adaptation of the novel by Voltaire (produced Minneapolis, 1982). New York, Theatre Communications Group, 1983.

My Uncle Sam (also director: produced New York, 1983). New York, Dramatists Play Service, 1984.

A Country Doctor, adaptation of a story by Kafka (also director: produced San Francisco, 1983; New York, 1986).

Madrigal Opera, music by Philip Glass (produced Los Angeles, 1985).

American Notes (also director: produced Los Angeles, 1986; New York, 1987).

A Soldier's Tale, adaptation of a libretto by Ramuz, music by Stravinsky (produced New York, 1986).

Screenplays: *Merlin and Melinda*, 1977; *Blame It on the Night*, 1985.

Television Plays: *More Things in Heaven and Earth*, 1976, and *See-Saw*, 1977 (*Family* series); *Road Show* (*Visions* series), 1976; *Eye of the Needle* (*Quincy* series), 1977; *Games of Chance* (*Incredible Hulk* series), 1979; *Family of Strangers*, 1980.

Novel

New Jerusalem. Los Angeles, Sun and Moon Press, 1986.

Other

Editor, with Leonard Allison and Robert Perrault, *Survival Printout*. New York, Random House, 1973.

*

Theatrical Activities:
Director: some of his own plays.

Len Jenkin comments:

I always like the opening: the houselights fade, the room goes black, the voices around me quiet, the first lights come up in the toybox, and the figures start to move.

Once that's over, for something to hold me, as author or audience, there needs to be a continuing sense of *wonder*, as powerful as that in fairy tales, moonlight, or dreams. This can be present in any sort of work for the stage—realistic to sublimely outrageous—and it's a quality that can't be fused into or onto something with clever staging or sideways performances. Its gotta be there, in the text and through and through.

The other thing that needs to be there for what I'd consider to be "Theatre" to exist is what I call *heart*. This doesn't mean I want to look at people struggling bravely through their emotional problems. It means that the author is not primarily an entertainer; that he/she is instead a preacher, and a singer, and a human being. And that the deep twined nature of what binds us and what makes us free is going to be out there on the stage.

What I try to make when I write or direct is the same as what I value when I'm looking at the stage as audience—and that's also the same as what I respond to when I see or feel it in the "actual" world: moments (and the roads toward and away from them) where the life within breaks through, where it signals out through language, object, gesture; where the bubble breaks, and all the cold air or all the heat within escapes with a whoosh, right at me... this doesn't need to happen in a noisy way, though it can—it's also able to be quite quiet, and still. Like a lot of writers, I often suspect I'm telling the same story over and over, till the day (I hope) when I get it right... and sometimes it seems as if each work is a very different sort of step: dance backwards, or forward, or to the side....

The competition—movies and TV—labors under a big disadvantage: it needs to make things that appeal to a huge segment of the population, because its production costs are so pleasingly enormous. However, the movies and TV do one thing right: with the exception of some reruns and a few revival houses in college towns, they don't show work by the dead to be seen by the living, and they don't try to be engaging classrooms, or an innovative sort of museum.

I want to see theatre energetically stomping around the U.S.A. Rent 7–11s, and put on plays by the highway (the plays already offered at the 7–11 are pretty good, and the lighting is amazing). I want to see tractor-trailers full of men in hats and beautiful women, pulling into town and setting up on the high school football field. I'll be glad to be in the cab of the first truck in line—the one that says "ALIVE" in a bullet on its side.

* * *

Len Jenkin writes of self-conscious theatricality. In *Gogol* a stage direction ends the opening address to the audience:

> Gogol lifts his bloody hand up to his face, and draws on himself in blood, a bright red circle on each cheek. He smears his face over with blood. He laughs. A giant turtle enters, moving very slowly. It has a small saddle on its back. As it passes Gogol, he mounts it, facing the audience. The turtle, never varying its pace, carries him off. The stage is bare. It darkens.

Is this the turtle of Chinese philosophy, which bears the world on its back? The audience will know neither this nor why the central character is named Gogol. Indeed, seven scenes later Gogol will ask "have they (*gesture toward audience*) learned anything?" and his mistress will reply "Don't make jokes."

The central characters of *Gogol*, *Five of Us*, *Dark Ride*, and *My Uncle Sam* are all artists of a kind: a playwright, a writer who is more successful at writing pornographic romances pseudonymously than the artistic novel in his desk drawer, the translator of a meaningless and quite possibly fake Chinese mystical work, and the salesman of trick novelties designed to surprise and startle people. The last character might speak for Jenkin when he says "These gags break the rules in people's heads. If there weren't any rules, I'd be outta business." Jenkin plays with theatrical conventions and seems to disclaim any deeper intentions. As ten characters repeat, one after another, at the end of *Dark Ride*, "I'm not interested in philosophy. Just tell me how it ends."

Jenkin shares with some other contemporary American playwrights, the most notable of whom is Sam Shepard, an interest in monologues and anecdotes, in the forms of popular culture, and in the use of popular songs (or of Mozart in *Gogol*) as an ironic counterpoint to the action. But he is alone in writing what might be called *drames noirs*. *Gogol*, *Dark Ride*, and *My Uncle Sam* all portray rather absurd quests in which gangsters or police dog the footsteps of the central character as he stumbles toward an unclear goal. All have narrator figures and an episodic structure full of seedy eccentrics who typically offer the audience an introductory account of themselves. *My Uncle Sam*, indeed, has various levels of commentary upon the action: from the Author; from his Uncle Sam in old age, looking back on his youthful escapade; from Sam when young, as he enacts the quest; from an audio cassette from the Universal Detective Agency that instructs him step by step; and from a series of Narrators dressed appropriately for the successive settings.

It may be significant that the least successful of Jenkin's published plays is the most conventional in form. *Five of Us* intercuts the monologues of a mentally slow epileptic with the quarrels of a young writer and his girlfriend, an anthropologist who is about to depart for a year in Sri Lanka, both tense about the impact of this separation on their relationship. This uncertainty, and the arrival of one friend of each gender, leads one to expect sexual re-partnering as a catalyst to intensifying psychological exploration. Instead, the two men attempt to burglarize the epileptic's next-door apartment. The dilemma of what to do with the awakened neighbor is posed at some length, but ends in his convenient but arbitrary death in an epileptic fit. The audience may infer from the title and the professions of the two women, anthropologist and nurse, a lesson about man's (in)humanity to man.

By contrast, *Gogol* and *Dark Ride* keep to a cool and ironic tone of narrative. Through the Translator, Jenkin seems to mock himself:

> You torture your mind to find modern equivalents for what seems to be ancient wisdom, and you end up revealing the seemingly obscure and certainly repetitious conversations of military officers, or peasants, or hotel-keepers, fishermen, senile nuns at roadside shrines. It's indicative of the fate of serious scholarship in our time that, for the pittance Mr. Zendavesta pays me, I continue to struggle with this impossibly recalcitrant text.
>
> However, there is one dim light. Structure. I'm fairly sure this book presupposes, as a frame device, the existence of a group of companions, who were originally ten in number. Whether these characters relate to actual people, or are pure inventions, I have no idea. The author seems obsessed with their moving from place to place like peripatetic shadows.

Jenkin indeed presents his characters as shadow puppets, the playthings of their author. In *Gogol* the second half of the play takes place at a private performance Gogol stages for the hypnotist Mesmer, with a woman in torn jeans bound by cardboard chains to a cardboard dungeon wall. In the course of the evening Mesmer is encouraged to kill Pontius Pilate, or an actor representing him, in play, and then to kill Gogol in reality—only to find himself addressed as Gogol in the final scene by police inspector Bucket and thanked for getting rid of Mesmer. In *Dark Ride* the characters end up in a stately dance at an oculists' convention in Mexico City. No one, presumably, can see any better at an oculists' convention than anywhere else. And, more than with most dramatists, what we see in Jenkin's play is left to us.

—Anthony Graham-White

JOHN, Errol. Citizen of Trinidad and Tobago. Recipient: *Observer* prize, 1957; Guggenheim fellowship, 1958. Agent: Fraser and Dunlop Scripts Ltd., 91 Regent Street, London W1R 8RU. England.

PUBLICATIONS

Plays

Moon on a Rainbow Shawl (produced London, 1958). London, Faber, 1958; revised version (produced New York, 1962), Faber, 1963; New York, Grove Press, 1966.

The Tout. Port-of-Spain, Trinidad, University of the West Indies, 1966.

Force Majeure, The Dispossessed, Hasta Luego: Three Screenplays. London, Faber, 1967.

Television Plays: *For the Children* series, 1952; *The Emperor Jones*, 1953; *Teleclub*, 1954; *Dawn*, 1963; *The Exiles*, 1969.

*

Theatrical Activities:
Director: **Play**—*Moon on a Rainbow Shawl*, London, 1986.
Actor: **Plays**—roles in many plays, including Lester in *Anna Lucasta* by Philip Yordan, London, 1953; Paul Prescott in *Local Colour* by Joan Sadler, London, 1954; The Negro in *The Respectable Prostitute* by Jean-Paul Sartre, London, 1954; Nubian Slave in *Salome* by Oscar Wilde, London, 1954; Jeremy in *South* by Julien Green, London, 1955; Honey Camden Brown in *The Member of the Wedding* by Carson McCullers, London, 1957; at the Old Vic Theatre, London: Prince of Morocco in *The Merchant of Venice*, 1962, title role in *Othello*, 1962, and Barnardine in *Measure for Measure*, 1963. **Films**—*The Nun's Story*, 1959; *The Sins of Rachel Cade*, 1961; *PT 109*, 1963; *Man in the Middle*, 1964; *Guns at Batasi*, 1964; *Assault on a Queen*, 1966. **Television**—role in *A Man from the Sun*, 1956.

* * *

Errol John's main theme is escape, and in *Moon on a Rainbow Shawl*, as well as the screenplays *The Dispossessed* and *Hasta Luego*, we see the various traps which destroy those who remain. These Caribbean plays come from a world of linguistic vitality, of improvised music and assorted animal noises all seeming to wage war on nature.

The trap in *Moon on a Rainbow Shawl* is the Trinidad backyard of a prostitute exhibiting her American sailors; of a poor "respectable" woman who goads her broken husband into theft and jail; and of the pregnant girl now abandoned, who settles for the protection of an old rack-renting landlord. From this mess Ephraim escapes. Ephraim is a young handsome trolleybus driver in line for promotion to inspector, but who rejects this way out as illusory. His single-mindedness causes him to brush aside the girl he's just made pregnant, recalling the time he put his foster-mother in a home to die after she had got in the way.

But at least he gets out, which is more than those on the run in the Spanish-Caribbean pressure-cooker of *The Dispossessed* achieve. The religious stranglehold is fiercer here and thus the extended family becomes one of the main battlefields. For a fisherman's son like Lou Delvado, who doesn't want to take over his father's boat, the only outlet, apart from crime, seems to be to put "classy" girls on their backs to prove he is as good as they are. But there is a limit to this. He organizes a robbery which results in the death of an old woman, and is eventually stabbed by his crippled father before he can escape. The number of fatherless children who blight the lives of young girls in these plays cannot be dismissed as a pre-pill relic, but is more part of the general lack of tidiness in human relationships prevalent in the society.

In three other plays, *Force Majeure, Dawn*, and *The Exiles*, John shows us the effects of having escaped the trap. There is no continuation of the Ephraim story of *Moon on a Rainbow Shawl*. Those who make it into exile are fairly successful artists and academics: the implication must be that the numerous Ephraims will sink without a trace. John now widens the area of rootlessness to include American blacks. In *Force Majeure* we meet the ex-bus driver who, having adopted the literary name of Robert Rademaeker, has risen to New York glossy magazine fame, and is brought to London by his new agent Scott Linehard to conquer the film world. (Here he meets his ex-wife, now a successful singer living in Rome.) Everything is provided for Rademaeker's comfort in England, including Scott's Mustang, Scott's flat, and Scott's fiancée, Christa. It all turns out to be a big con, of course, for Scott is white and Jewish, and wants to destroy the arrogance of the black Rademaeker for the smugness of all blacks who've climbed out of the gutter (there is no film contract) and he also wants to punish his German girlfriend (and her aunt) by letting a black loose in the house. As Scott reveals this, he escapes being murdered by Rademaeker only by the discovery of Christa's suicide. In *The Exiles* it is middle-class West Indians who are trying to adapt to new surroundings—Kester McWilliams, white-looking Trinidad Professor of History on an exchange to Keele telling his students how it really happened with the slaves; his artist sister attempting suicide in a London flat (which she shares with a French-Sicilian model) because her lover called her a black woman; and their dark-skinned cousin, retracing his steps to the last war with his wife's $60,000 insurance money. More interesting is *Dawn* where the Ivy League All-American writer Wayne Coty actually finds roots in Africa. Wayne is on a Manhattan assignment to an Africa on the verge of revolution. At an awkward party of German and Portuguese residents, he meets Salena (an American friend of his earlier days in Paris). On their visit across country to Salena's Dutch farmer-employer, Erik Van Den Hoorn, they witness Africans being shot; and Wayne is insulted by the police. All this makes him more receptive to the servant in the Van Den Hoorn's household who takes Wayne to a village and shows him evidence of white brutality (an old man with an arm chopped off and tongue torn out). From here on, however, the play collapses under much talk about roots and then limps on to the contrived disclosure that Salena is really black; that it is time for them both to stop running, and return to fight in their own country.

Middle-class West Indians (and that includes the artists) have always had a certain amount of mobility. That's probably the strongest theme of romance in West Indian fiction. But what of the poor man who insists on being treated like a human being, and who finds it impossible to live either at home, or to escape abroad? Is there any answer but revolution?

—E.A. Markham

JOHNSON, Terry. British. Born 20 December 1955. Educated at Queens School, Bushey, Hertfordshire; University of Birmingham, 1973–76, B.A. in drama 1976. Actor in late 1970's, and director. Recipient: *Evening Standard* award, 1983. Lives in London. Agent: Phil Kelvin, Goodwin Associates, 12 Rabbit Row, London W8 4DX, England.

PUBLICATIONS

Plays

Amabel (produced London, 1979).
Days Here So Dark (produced Edinburgh and London, 1981).
Insignificance (produced London, 1982; New York, 1986). London, Methuen, 1982.
Bellevue (produced on tour, 1982).
The Idea (produced Bristol, 1983).
Unsuitable for Adults (produced London, 1984; Costa Mesa, California, 1986). London, Faber, 1985.
Cries from the Mammal House (produced Leicester and London, 1984).
Tuesday's Child, with Kate Lock (televised 1985; produced London, 1986). London, Methuen, 1987.

Screenplays: *Insignificance*, 1985; *Killing Time*, 1985; *Way Upstream*, 1987.

Television Plays: *Time Trouble*, 1985; *Tuesday's Child*, with Kate Lock, 1985.

*

Terry Johnson comments:

Writing is very hard. Six months of one's life, somewhat at risk mentally, to produce a play. Then forty minutes of a critic's life spent deciding if anyone should go and see it or not. More often than not, they persuade the audience to stay at home, so few people hear.

I have to acknowledge a certain success, but the combined efforts of the critic and the myopic theatre manager, resulting in one's words being echoed in empty halls, have slowly turned off the tap. If there is to be no audience, how can there be more plays?

* * *

Boldness of conception and a subtle control in execution are richly combined in Terry Johnson's drama. Thus *Insignificance*, despite all the potential for lurid sensation in a scenario which brings together an Einstein-figure, a Marilyn Monroe-figure, a Joe DiMaggio-figure, and a Senator McCarthy-figure in a New York hotel room in 1953, impresses as a sustained dramatic scrutiny, within a basically naturalistic framework, of the nature of celebrity and of the human need for celebrities. It is a play about wants. The far-from-dumb-blond Actress arrives at the Professor's hotel room wanting to talk to him, to prove her knowledge (of his theories especially), and finally to sleep with him; the Ballplayer wants the Actress to come home and *make* a home; the Senator, meanwhile, wants the Professor to co-operate with him and his committee, and to back an anti-Soviet nuclear programme. The Professor himself wants only to be left alone to retreat with his calculations about the shape of the universe. He it is who articulates a Theory of *existential* Relativity, concerning the need of each individual to feel a centre of identity which in modern Western culture results in the erection of "false gods" as guarantors and measures of personal wholeness—the neon-lit image of the Actress's famous skirt-blown-up pose; the Ballplayer immortalized on a million bubble-gum cards; the omniscient Professor dubbed "True Child of the Universe." Yet the Actress, whose desperate desire for a child is thwarted even within the play itself (she miscarries when the Senator strikes her), ultimately recognizes the despair implicit in the Professor's refusal to confront his own fear—of an impending nuclear devastation for which he feels responsible. The repulsive Senator, self-proclaimed "gentleman and . . . solipsist," is the extreme embodiment of the "madman's scheme of things" that the Professor and the Actress, in their different ways, both diagnose as general: so convinced is he of a self-centred universe that he can claim to have *invented* them all to fulfil his purposes.

The ability of Johnson fully and powerfully to *dramatize* complex ideas and arguments is also evident in the more recent *Unsuitable for Adults*. The setting—an upstairs pub-theatre in Soho—is very different from that of *Insignificance*, but the concentration is again upon a vital lack of personal identity in modern culture. The resolution is gender-based. The feminist alternative comedian Kate attempts to convince the asthmatic lunchtime stripper Tish of her unthinking collusion with a culture which turns women into images and potential objects of violence; but Kate's real *experience* of feminism and her extrication from her own hopeless involvement with Nick, a brilliant impressionist whose pretence and avoidance of moral responsibility in his private life are an extension of his act, can take place only with self-acknowledgement and self-understanding. While the other acts—Tish's schoolgirl strip, Nick's impressions, the magician Keith's feeble escapism—provide images of fantasy or compensation for an audience which as a result of that remains "captive," Kate attempts aggressively to confront both them and herself with her scabrous Lenny Bruce-style act (a considerable opportunity for the performer). But her routine gradually falls apart, and verbal violence comes to a cathartic physical climax when she deliberately mutilates a finger: "the body turns against the mind and says, 'Enough. I want to stop this now.'" In the play's Epilogue Kate withdraws to a Dartmoor cottage with Tish (who is recovering from a serious asthma attack). The performances are over, and the stripping is now a discovery of truth, both moral and physical: it reveals an essentially *natural* identity in which both women partake.

The very considerable philosophical ambition of *Insignificance* and *Unsuitable for Adults* is fully disclosed only as the carefully worked dramatic pattern of each play becomes apparent. Each is notable for a stylistic texture which is varied and flexible, natural and uninsistent; climaxes are violent, but there are no shocks of structure or style. In *Cries from the Mammal House*, however, there is a clear relation between philosophical ambition and theatrical experiment. Hitherto in Johnson's work, metaphor has provided a crucial means of dialectical organization within a broadly naturalistic structure; but now a single, diagnostic dramatic metaphor is proposed at the outset and subsequently explored in a theatrical mode replete with bizarre detail, blackly comic juxtaposition, and stylistic variation. The point of reference is expressionism—in plot as in style. When a half-Celtic bastard bird-conservationist arrives at the zoo kept by his brother for the funeral of their father, the zoo's founder, he finds it in a state of terminal decay. Despite the efforts of his wife, Anne (who falls in love with the visitor), the despairing brother Alan is impotent to reverse the trend of death and morbid preservation begun by the morally corrupt founding father himself, and the zoo is sold. Renewal comes only after the "Birdman" David has undertaken a "dreamlike" journey to Mauritius in search of the pink pigeon and returns to England, having experienced the company of strange colonial survivors and kidnap by a Creole tribe, with a real live Dodo. The zoo animals have by now been killed, prior to his suicide, by Alan; but as the play ends, David and Anne, together with her daughter Sally (formally traumatized but now released) and his three Mauritian companions, plan a "new lease of life" for the zoo—under the sign not of the decadent Western father but of an Eastern enlightenment (and with the "absurd cry" of the Dodo). Dialectic has here given way to symbol, and the resulting theatrical effect confirms the range as well as the scale of Johnson's dramatic abilities.

—Paul Lawley

JOHNSTONE, Keith. British. Born in Brixham, Devon. Married to Ingrid Johnston. Director of the Theatre Studio, 1965–66, and associate director, 1966, Royal Court Theatre, London; director, Theatre Machine Improvisational Group; taught at Royal Academy of Dramatic Art, London, and Statens Teaterskole, Copenhagen. Currently Associate Professor of Drama, University of Calgary. Co-director, Loose Moose Theatre Company, Calgary. Address: Department of Drama, University of Calgary, Calgary, Alberta T2N 1N4, Canada.

PUBLICATIONS

Plays

Brixham Regatta, and For Children (produced London, 1958).
Gloomy Go Round (produced London, 1959).
Philoctetes, adaptation of the play by Sophocles (produced London, 1964).
Clowning (produced London, 1965).
The Performing Giant, music by Marc Wilkinson (also co-director: produced London, 1966).
The Defeat of Giant Big Nose (for children; also director: produced on Welsh tour, 1966).
Instant Theatre (produced London, 1966).
Caught in the Act (produced London, 1966).
The Time Machine (produced London, 1967).
The Martians (produced London, 1967).
Moby Dick: A Sir and Perkins Story (produced London, 1967).
Wakefield Mystery Cycle (also director: produced Victoria, British Columbia, 1968).
Der Fisch (also director: produced Tübingen, 1971).
The Last Bird (produced Aarhus, Denmark, 1973). Toronto, Playwrights, 1981.
Shot by an Elk (produced Kingston, Ontario, 1974).
Robinson Crusoe (produced Calgary, Alberta, 1976).

Other Plays: *The Nigger Hunt*, 1959; *The Cord; Home; Live Snakes and Ladders; The Loose Moose Hamlet.*

Other

Impro: Improvisation and the Theatre. London, Faber, and New York, Theatre Arts, 1979; revised edition, London, Eyre Methuen, 1981.

*

Theatrical Activities:
Director: **Plays**—*Eleven Plus* by Kon Fraser, London, 1960; *The Maimed* by Bartho Smit, London, 1960; *The Triple Alliance* by J.A. Cuddon, London, 1961; *Sacred Cow* by Kon Fraser, London, 1962; *Day of the Prince* by Frank Hilton, London, 1962, 1963; *The Pope's Wedding* by Edward Bond, London, 1962; *The Knack* by Ann Jellicoe (co-director, with Jellicoe), London, 1962; *Edgware Road Blues* by Leonard Kingston, London, 1963; *The Cresta Run* by N.F. Simpson, London, 1965; *The Performing Giant* (co-director, with William Gaskill), London, 1966; *The Defeat of Giant Big Nose*, Welsh tour, 1966; *Wakefield Mystery Cycle*, Victoria, British Columbia, 1968; *Der Fisch*, Tübingen, 1971; *Waiting for Godot* by Beckett, Alberta, 1972.

Keith Johnstone comments:
(1973) I began writing plays when the Royal Court commissioned me in 1957. They were about physical sensations, often sensations experienced in infancy, expressed in visual images.

When I began writing again in 1966 it was only to provide suitable scripts for improvisors and short "entertainment" pieces. Most of my work from 1965 to 1970 was with my group

Theatre Machine. We toured in many parts of England, gave demonstrations to teachers and trainee teachers, and hammered out an effective formula. *Instant Theatre* was the Theatre Machine in an early show. We were the only British group to be invited to Expo 67 in Montreal, and toured in Denmark, Germany, Belgium, Yugoslavia, and Austria.

I am at present writing an account of my improvisational methods, and am returning to writing "real" plays. *Brixham Regatta* was given a Sunday night production at the Mermaid in about 1969 and it looked O.K. to me. This has made me feel that there might be some point in trying a serious work again.

I dislike "sets." I think theatre should be popular. I think theatre should "freak-out" the audience rather than offer conversation pieces. Favourite play—*Do It* performed by the Pip Simmons Group.

* * *

Keith Johnstone's work has been relatively little exposed and it can hardly be claimed that he has had much direct influence on the British theatre; but in a more subtle and pervasive manner, his work played an important role in the British theatre of the 1960's. To a large extent this was initially confined to his work at the Royal Court for the English Stage Company during one of its most creative periods. Associated with the Court from 1957, he was a co-director of the 1965–66 season and director of the Theatre Studio, from which emerged Johnstone's Theatre Machine group, whose work, based on improvisations, has influenced a large number of younger English actors and writers.

The first efforts of the Court Studio to gain widespread attention consisted of a 1965 Christmas show, *Clowning*. Designed for both children and adults, each performance was unpredictable and different, basing itself on mime and improvisation exercises orginated in the Court's acting classes. Its theme, broadly, was the making of clowns, examining whether and how they can be trained. Taking a few basic situations from which the actors could take off into improvisation, the show intriguingly experimented with that sense of the unexpected and dangerous which Johnstone evidently sees as a major clowning skill, in its concentration on the immediacy of the theatrical moment. Some aspects of this work were elaborated in Johnstone's most interesting play to date, *The Performing Giant*, produced in a double-bill with Cregan's *Transcending* at the Court in 1966. The play received a poor reception at the time; critics seemed to lack a critical vocabulary with which to cope with a kind of theatre which later many other experimental groups were to make easier for them. Basically the play is an allegory of the adolescent's attempt to understand the mysteries and puzzles of the outside world as well as the processes of the developing body; a group of pot-holers encounter a giant and explore the terrain of his inside as a potential tourist Disneyland only to have the giant rebel and defeat them with the aid of the female pot-holer with whom he falls in love. To most critics the play seemed merely strange and extravagant; charging it with whimsical obscurity in its initial premise, they missed the denseness of the developing fantasy and the way in which Johnstone's allegory worked, not as a planned series of concepts but as an immediate theatrical experience, using a loose basic structure as a starting-point in a manner parallel to the work of another Court dramatist, Ann Jellicoe, in *The Sport of My Mad Mother*. It would be interesting to see *The Performing Giant* revived, for it is a more important play than was noticed at the time.

Johnstone's other work in England has been mainly in the shape of further Theatre Machine shows, each one progressively more adventurous, or of adaptations (such as his excellent version of Sophocles's *Philoctetes*). His sense of the possibilities of theatre, coupled with his ability to work within the terms of fantasy without sentimentality or whimsy, marks him as an original voice too rarely heard.

—Alan Strachan

JONES, LeRoi. See **BARAKA, Amiri.**

KALCHEIM, Lee. American. Born in Philadelphia, Pennsylvania, 27 June 1938. Educated at Trinity College, Hartford, Connecticut, B.A.; Yale University School of Drama, New Haven, Connecticut, one year. Recipient: Rockefeller grant, 1965; Emmy award, 1973. Agent: International Creative Management, 40 West 57th Street, New York, New York 10019. Address: 38 West 9th Street, New York, New York 10011, U.S.A.

PUBLICATIONS

Plays

A Party for Divorce (produced New York, 1963).

Match Play (produced New York, 1964). Published in *New Theatre in America*, edited by Edward Parone, New York, Dell, 1965.

. . . And the Boy Who Came to Leave (produced Minneapolis, 1965; New York, 1973). Published in *Playwrights for Tomorrow 2*, edited by Arthur H. Ballet, Minneapolis, University of Minnesota Press, 1966.

An Audible Sigh (produced Waterford, Connecticut, 1968).

The Surprise Party (produced New York, 1970).

Who Wants to Be the Lone Ranger (produced Los Angeles, 1971).

Hurry, Harry, with Jeremiah Morris and Susan Perkis, music by Bill Weeden, lyrics by David Finkle (produced New York, 1972).

Prague Spring (produced Providence, Rhode Island, 1975; New York, 1976).

Win with Wheeler (produced Waterford, Connecticut, 1975). New York, French, 1984.

Winning Isn't Everything (produced New York, 1978).

Breakfast with Les and Bess (produced New York, 1982). New York, French, 1984.

Friends (produced New York, 1983).

Television Plays: *Reunion*, 1967; *Let's Get a Closeup of the Messiah*, 1969; *Trick or Treat*, 1970; *All in the Family* series, 1971–72; *Is (This) Marriage Really Necessary*, 1972; *The Class of '63*, 1973; *The Bridge of Adam Rush*, 1974; *The Comedy Company*, 1978; *Marriage Is Alive and Well*, 1980.

*

Lee Kalcheim comments:

I am a realist. So, my plays are realistic. Comic. Dramatic. Strongly based on characters. I grew up with the realistic writers of the 1950's. Found myself sitting in the middle of the avant garde movement with an inherited style. And then as the theatre began to be less faddish (in New York) it became apparent that I could indeed maintain my love of character—of reality—and survive as a playwright. My work in improvisational theatre and film began to broaden my work. My later work became more fragmented or filmlike. Less ... livingroomish. But I realized that for all the excitement of theatrical effects (I have tried various experiments with mixed media), the thing that still moved me most, standing in rehearsal watching my plays, were those one to one scenes. Those scenes where two people faced each other, wanting something from each other. Those scenes where something happened between people. They washed out all the media effects, or unusual transitions, or whatever. They were theatre at its strongest. And I suppose I keep coming back to those in my plays. I do write film. But I keep coming back to the theatre for the excitement of those live, vibrant scenes—that put flesh and blood out there in front of you.

* * *

"It makes me very sad and very happy to be a playwright," was Lee Kalcheim's answer to a request for a statement which could introduce this piece about him. It serves well. Kalcheim is indeed a melancholy and a joyful chronicler. But what made him almost unique among the American dramatists of his generation was his ability to bustle, hustle, and earn his own way *as a writer*. While most "young playwrights" are weaving their tortured ways through the mazes of foundations and endowments and theatre boards seeking grants, honoraria, subsistences, and other encouraging hand-outs, Kalcheim energetically and quite successfully went into the *business* of writing.

He has a good mind and that intelligence which reflects both cool observations and warm insights into the characters he creates. More than storytelling, Kalcheim is people-telling. His plays, he says, are about "human ideas": as a playwright he is less concerned with the usual ideas *per se* than he is with the humanness of those ideas, with the humanity which generates those ideas.

Moreover, as even a quick reading or viewing of his work for the stage reveals, Kalcheim is fascinated by human loneliness. What for other, more abstract writers is a concern with the condition of loneliness, for Kalcheim becomes both a compassionate and an uninvolved concern for the human being as an alone creature: yes, both passionate and uninvolved, both sad and happy. People trying—desperately, lazily, sadly, hopefully, hilariously, pathetically, ridiculously—to make contact with other people is what his plays not only are but are about.

At the end of *An Audible Sigh*, one of the characters, Gale, says, "You see ... I want to be loved, but I don't want to have strings attached." And there, indeed, is the rub. Kalcheim's people are lonely, loving but afraid of being loved and even of being un-lonely. They sometimes seem to enjoy their loneliness and find sanctuary in their states of not being loved. Driven in part by fear of being possessed and by desire to possess, the characters are intensely vulnerable. Their bulwarks seem all terribly sturdy and well-planned but facing in the wrong direction.

In play after play, Kalcheim examines these qualities. Even more personally, he exhibits a unique ability to watch and be part of the action, *and* to double the effect, to watch the watchers (himself included) and the actors. Again and again, Kalcheim seems to be writing much the same play—each time in a different guise but each time about the same qualities, sensibilities. If these feelings and events are indeed his own experiences (love, divorce, joining, separation, regret, hope, need, fear, tenacity, escape), he is quite excellent at turning that experience into theatrical action, because Kalcheim the writer is a very astute observer of Kalcheim the man.

Moreover, his technique works unusually well: he juxtaposes comedy and drama with almost metronomic regularity, but at the critical heart of the matter is a much more important and profound juxtaposition: The Fear of Death poised against An Immortality Assured, if one may capitalize such sentiments anymore.

Kalcheim has been writing since he was eleven years old, and he says that when his first playlet was produced, he wept at the recognition of his own voice "up there." If he has turned now more and more to film and television to earn a living, his first and enduring love is perhaps not a person (ironically) but the theatre. As with many media writers, Kalcheim plays the game of running down his own television writing, but nonetheless he speaks with justified pride about the way his voice is now heard "up there."

—Arthur H. Ballet

KANIN, Garson. American. Born in Rochester, New York, 24 November 1912. Educated at local schools to age 15; attended American Academy of Dramatic Arts, New York, 1932–33. Served in the United States Army Signal Corps, 1941–42: Private; Air Force, 1942–43, and the Office of Strategic Services, 1943–45: Captain, on Staff on SHAEF (European Theatre Operations). Married the actress and playwright Ruth Gordon in 1942 (died 1985). Jazz musician, Western Union messenger, stock boy and advertising proofreader at Macy's, New York, burlesque comedian, and summer camp social director, 1929–32; assistant to the playwright and director George Abbott, *q.v.*, 1935–37; radio interviewer and actor; on production staff, Samuel Goldwyn Productions, Hollywood, 1937–38. Since 1938 free-lance director and producer: formed Kanin Productions, 1967. Recipient: New York Film Critics Circle award, 1945; Oscar, for documentary, 1946; Sidney Howard Memorial Award, 1946; Donaldson Award, for play and direction, 1946; American Academy of Dramatic Arts Award of Achievement, 1958. Agent: William Morris Agency, 1350 Avenue of the Americas, New York, New York 10019. Address: 200 West 57th Street, New York, New York 10019, U.S.A.

PUBLICATIONS

Plays

Born Yesterday (also director: produced New York, 1946; London, 1947). New York, Viking Press, 1946.

The Smile of the World (also director: produced New York, 1949). New York, Dramatists Play Service, 1949.

The Rat Race (also director: produced New York, 1949). New York, Dramatists Play Service, 1950.

The Live Wire (also director: produced New York, 1950). New York, Dramatists Play Service, 1951.

The Amazing Adèle, adaptation of a play by Pierre Barillet and Jean-Pierre Grédy (also director: produced Westport, Connecticut, 1950).
Fledermaus, adaptation of the libretto by Haffner and Genée, music by Johann Strauss, lyrics by Howard Dietz (also director: produced New York, 1950). New York, Boosey and Hawkes, 1950.
The Good Soup, adaptation of a play by Félicien Marceau (also director: produced New York, 1960).
Do Re Mi, music and lyrics by Jule Styne, Betty Comden, and Adolph Green, adaptation of his own novel (also director: produced New York, 1960; London, 1961).
A Gift of Time, adaptation of *Death of a Man* by Lael Tucker Wertenbaker (also director: produced New York, 1962). New York, Random House, 1962.
Come On Strong, based on his own stories (also director: produced New York, 1962). New York, Dramatists Play Service, 1964.
Remembering Mr. Maugham, adaptation of his own book (produced New York, 1966).
Adam's Rib, with Ruth Gordon (screenplay). New York, Viking Press, 1972.
Dreyfus in Rehearsal, adaptation of a play by Jean-Claude Grumberg (also director: produced New York, 1974). New York, Dramatists Play Service, 1983.
Peccadillo (also director: produced St. Petersburg, Florida, 1985).

Screenplays: *Woman of the Year* (uncredited), 1942; *The More the Merrier* (uncredited), 1943; *From This Day Forward*, with Hugo Butler, 1946; *Born Yesterday* (uncredited), 1950; *It Should Happen to You*, 1953; *The Girl Can't Help It*, with Frank Tashlin and Herbert Baker, 1957; *The Rat Race*, 1960; *High Time*, 1960; *Where It's At*, 1969; *Some Kind of a Nut*, 1969; with Ruth Gordon—*A Double Life*, 1947; *Adam's Rib*, 1949; *The Marrying Kind*, 1952; *Pat and Mike*, 1952.

Television Plays: *An Eye on Emily, Something to Sing About*, and *The He-She Chemistry* (*Mr. Broadway* series), 1963–64; *Josie and Joe; Hardhat and Legs*, with Ruth Gordon, 1980; *Scandal*, 1980.

Novels

Do Re Mi. Boston, Little Brown, 1955.
Blow Up a Storm. New York, Random House, 1959; London, Heinemann, 1960.
The Rat Race. New York, Pocket Books, and London, Ace, 1960.
Where It's At. New York, New American Library, 1969.
A Thousand Summers. New York, Doubleday, 1973; London, Hart Davis MacGibbon, 1974.
One Hell of an Actor. New York, Harper, 1976; London, Barrie and Jenkins, 1979.
Moviola: A Hollywood Saga. New York, Simon and Schuster, 1979; London, Macmillan, 1980.
Smash. New York, Viking Press, 1980; London, Macmillan, 1981.
Cordelia? New York, Arbor House, 1982; London, Severn House, 1983.

Short Stories

Cast of Characters: Stories of Broadway and Hollywood. New York, Atheneum, 1969.

Other

Remembering Mr. Maugham. New York, Atheneum, and London, Hamish Hamilton, 1966.
Tracy and Hepburn: An Intimate Memoir. New York, Viking Press, 1971; London, Angus and Robertson, 1972.
Hollywood: Stars and Starlets, Tycoons and Flesh-Peddlers, Movie-Makers and Moneymakers, Frauds and Geniuses, Hopefuls and Has-Beens, Great Lovers and Sex Symbols. New York, Viking Press, 1974; London, Hart Davis MacGibbon, 1975.
It Takes a Long Time to Become Young. New York, Doubleday, and London, Prior, 1978.
Together Again! The Stories of the Great Hollywood Teams. New York, Doubleday, 1981; as *Great Hollywood Teams*, London, Angus and Robertson, 1982.

*

Theatrical Activities:
Director: **Plays**—assistant director, to George Abbott, of *Three Men on Horse* by Abbott and John Cecil Holm, New York, 1935, *Boy Meets Girl* by Bella and Sam Spewack, New York, 1935, *Brother Rat* by John Monks, Jr., and Fred F. Finklehoffe, New York, 1936, and *Room Service* by John Murray and Allen Boretz, New York, 1937; director of *Hitch Your Wagon* by Sidney Holloway, New York, 1937; *Too Many Heroes* by Dore Schary, New York, 1937; *The Ragged Path* by Robert E. Sherwood, New York, 1945; *Years Ago* by Ruth Gordon, New York, 1946; *Born Yesterday*, New York, 1946; *How I Wonder* by Donald Ogden Stewart, New York, 1947; *The Leading Lady* by Ruth Gordon, New York, 1948; *The Smile of the World*, New York, 1949; *The Rat Race*, New York, 1949; *The Amazing Adèle*, Westport, Connecticut, 1950; *The Live Wire*, New York, 1950; *Fledermaus*, New York, 1950, 1966; *Into Thin Air* by Chester Erskine, London, 1955; *The Diary of Anne Frank* by Frances Goodrich and Albert Hackett, New York, 1955; *Small War on Murray Hill* by Robert E. Sherwood, New York, 1957; *A Hole in the Head* by Arnold Schulman, New York, 1957; *The Good Soup*, New York, 1960; *Do Re Mi*, New York, 1960, London, 1961; *Sunday in New York* by Norman Krasna, New York, 1961; *A Gift of Time*, New York, 1962; *Come On Strong*, New York, 1962; *Funny Girl* by Isobel Lennart, New York, 1964; *I Was Dancing* by Edwin O'Connor, New York, 1964; *A Very Rich Woman* by Ruth Gordon, New York, 1964; *We Have Always Lived in the Castle* by Hugh Wheeler, New York, 1966; *Remembering Mr. Maugham*, Los Angeles, 1969; *Idiot's Delight* by Robert E. Sherwood, Los Angeles, 1970; *Dreyfus in Rehearsal*, New York, 1974; *Ho! Ho! Ho!* by Ruth Gordon, Stockbridge, Massachusetts, 1976; *Peccadillo*, St. Petersburg, Florida, 1985. **Films**—*A Man to Remember*, 1938; *Next Time I Marry*, 1938; *The Great Man Votes*, 1939; *Bachelor Mother*, 1939; *My Favorite Wife*, 1940; *They Knew What They Wanted*, 1940; *Tom, Dick and Harry*, 1941; *Night Shift, Fellow Americans*, and *Ring of Steel* (documentaries), 1942; *Woman of the Year*, 1942; *German Manpower* (documentary), 1943; *Night Stripes* (documentary), 1944; *Battle Stations* (documentary), 1944; *A Salute to France* (*Salut à France*) (documentary), with Jean Renoir, 1944; *The True Glory* (documentary), with Carol Reed, 1945; *Where It's At*, 1969; *Some Kind of Nut*, 1969. **Television**—*Born Yesterday*, 1956.
Actor: **Plays**—Tommy Deal in *Little Ol' Boy* by Albert Bein, New York, 1933; Young Man in *Spring Song* by Bella and Sam Spewack, New York, 1934; Red in *Ladies' Money* by George Abbott, New York, 1934; Al in *Three Men on a Horse* by George Abbott and John Cecil Holm, New York, 1935;

Izzy Cohen in *The Body Beautiful* by Robert Rossen, New York, 1935; Green in *Boy Meets Girl* by Bella and Sam Spewack, New York, 1935; Vincent Chenevski in *Star Spangled* by Robert Ardrey, New York, 1936; Garson Kanin in *Remembering Mr. Maugham*, Los Angeles, 1969. **Film**—*Bachelor Mother*, 1939. **Radio**—*March of Times* news re-enactments, *The Goldbergs, Aunt Jenny's Real Life Stories, The Theatre Guild on the Air, Five-Star Final, The NBC Theatre, The Honeymooners—Grace and Eddie*, 1935–37.

* * *

For the critic of American theatre Garson Kanin remains a dramatist of a single play. After gaining some reputation as an actor and as a director, he wrote *Born Yesterday*, his first and only successful play. Mainly, the play is hokum and sweet sentiment, the stock-in-trade of the commercial comic dramatist, but in this work Kanin also showed perception as a comic satirist which he, unfortunately, never repeated. In *Born Yesterday* the traditional dumb blonde is provided with a variant reading which gives her a substance that one accepts even when recognizing the play's flimsy quality. Educated by a *New Republic* correspondent, she realizes that the junk-man tycoon who keeps her is endangering the country. And with her teacher, she defeats him, providing a memorable stage exit in such a way that the play makes a comment on the state of the nation.

Never again has Kanin found the right combination for an effective theatre piece. Generally, he has employed the same devices as his colleagues writing comedies for the New York stage, but his tricks have not worked properly, and he has not provided good or interesting story lines or carefully created characters. Topicality and local color have been major devices in his plays—name dropping of places, movie stars, dramatists, and so on. He likes the stage joke, usually visual as well as verbal, as well as the quick one-line gag. As a good director of his own plays as well as plays by others, he emphasizes stage business, prop gimmicks, and well-paced dialogue. None of these techniques is, of course, unusual even in good plays, but without interesting characters and plots and some good wit such devices or techniques become ineffective.

In 1949 Kanin wrote and directed both *The Rat Race*, the rather tired story of a beaten down dancer and an optimistic saxophone player, and an equally tepid play called *The Smile of the World*. The next year he offered *The Live Wire*. In this play he shows how a pretty good fellow is unintentionally saved from marrying a gold digger by a loud-mouthed, self-indulgent heel who makes everyone hate him and yet reaches the success that they all want. If there were a serious note in the play, one might call the dramatist bitter, but it is all patently thin and meaningless. From this point Kanin began to spend his time directing or writing stories. Then in 1962 he provided New York audiences with two plays—both characteristically his and both too slight to be considered by historians of the drama. *A Gift of Time* was a dramatization of a novel. A man discovers that he has an inoperable cancer, and Kanin dramatizes that "gift of time" the man is given before death takes him. Although the action is not completely sentimentalized, the thinness of the characters and the ineffective episodic narrative make the action meaningless and the climax, as the wife helps her husband slash his wrists, both improbable and theatrically unpleasant. *Come On Strong* brings only a slight twist to the tired plot: boy meets girl but girl marries other man who dies, later boy meets girl who has now become hard and commercial, boy meets girl again in the third act, convinces her of her original charm, and all ends happily.

More than most American dramatists Kanin has divided his career between writing (fiction, plays, essays) and practical theatre (acting and directing). But he has been truly outstanding in neither art. Rather, he merges with the mass of dramatists who produce the daily theatrical fare, rising to recognizable height only in *Born Yesterday*.

—Walter J. Meserve

KEANE, John B(rendan). Irish. Born in Listowel, County Kerry, 21 July 1928. Educated at Saint Michael's College, Listowel, graduated 1947. Married Mary O'Connor in 1955; three sons and one daughter. Chemist's assistant, 1946–51; street sweeper and furnace operator, Northampton, England, 1952–54. Since 1955 pub owner-operator, Listowel. Weekly columnist Limerick *Leader* and Dublin *Evening Herald*. Since 1973 President, Irish PEN. D.Litt: Trinity College, Dublin, 1977; D.F.A.: Marymount Manhattan College, New York, 1984. Address: 37 William Street, Listowel, County Kerry, Ireland.

PUBLICATIONS

Plays

Sive (produced Listowel, County Kerry, 1959; London, 1960). Dublin, Progress House, 1959; Elgin, Illinois, Performance, n.d.

Sharon's Grave (produced Cork, 1960; New York, 1961). Dublin, Progress House, 1960; Elgin, Illinois, Performance, n.d.

The Highest House on the Mountain (produced Dublin, 1961). Dublin, Progress House, 1961.

Many Young Men of Twenty (produced Cork, 1961; London, 1987). Dublin, Progress House, 1961; in *Seven Irish Plays 1946–1964*, edited by Robert Hogan, Minneapolis, University of Minnesota Press, 1967.

No More in Dust (produced Dublin, 1962).

Hut 42 (produced Dublin, 1963). Dixon, California, Proscenium Press, 1963.

The Man from Clare (produced Cork, 1963). Cork, Mercier Press, 1963.

The Year of the Hiker (produced Cork and Chicago, 1964). Cork, Mercier Press, 1964.

The Field (produced Dublin, 1965; New York, 1976). Cork, Mercier Press, 1967.

The Roses of Tralee (produced Cork, 1966).

The Rain at the End of the Summer (produced Cork, 1967). Cork, Mercier Press, 1967.

Big Maggie (produced Cork, 1969; New York, 1973). Cork, Mercier Press, and New York and London, French, 1969.

Faoiseamh (produced Dublin, 1970). Dublin, Avel Linn, n.d.

The Change in Mame Fadden (produced Cork and Chicago, 1971). Cork, Mercier Press, 1973.

Moll (produced Killarney, County Kerry, 1971; New York, 1977). Cork, Mercier Press, 1971.

The One-Way Ticket (produced Listowel, County Kerry, 1972). Elgin, Illinois, Performance, 1972.

Values: The Spraying of John O'Dovey, Backwater, and The Pure of Heart (produced Cork, 1973; *The Pure of Heart* produced London, 1985). Cork, Mercier Press, 1973.

The Crazy Wall (produced Waterford, 1973). Cork, Mercier Press, 1974.
Matchmaker (produced Dublin, 1975).
The Good Thing (produced Limerick, 1976). Cork, Mercier Press, 1976; Newark, Delaware, Proscenium Press, 1978.
The Buds of Ballybunion (produced Cork, 1979). Cork, Mercier Press, 1979.
The Chastitute (produced Dublin, 1980). Cork, Mercier Press, 1981.

Radio Plays: *Barbara Shearing*, 1959; *A Clutch of Duckeggs*, 1970; *The War Crime*, 1976 (UK); *The Talk Specific*, 1979; *The Battle of Ballybooley*, 1980.

Novel

The Bodhrán Makers. Dingle, County Kerry, Brandon, 1986.

Short Stories

Death Be Not Proud and Other Stories. Cork, Mercier Press, 1976.
More Irish Short Stories. Cork, Mercier Press, 1981.

Verse

The Street and Other Poems. Dublin, Progress House, 1961.

Other

Strong Tea. Cork, Mercier Press, 1963.
Self-Portrait. Cork, Mercier Press, 1964.
Letters of a Successful T.D. [*an Irish Parish Priest, an Irish Publican, a Love-Hungry Farmer, a Matchmaker, an Irish Civic Guard, a Country Postman, an Irish Minister of State*]. Cork, Mercier Press, 8 vols., 1967–78.
The Gentle Art of Matchmaking. Cork, Mercier Press, 1973.
Is the Holy Ghost Really a Kerryman? Cork, Mercier Press, 1976.
Unlawful Sex and Other Testy Matters. Cork, Mercier Press, 1978.
Stories from a Kerry Fireside. Cork, Mercier Press, 1980.
Unusual Irish Careers. Cork, Mercier Press, 1982.
Man of the Triple Name. Dingle, County Kerry, Brandon, 1984.
Owl Sandwiches. Dingle, County Kerry, Brandon, 1985.

*

Bibliography: *Ten Modern Irish Playwrights* by Kimball King, New York, Garland, 1979.

Critical Studies: in *Seven Irish Plays 1946–1964* edited by Robert Hogan, Minneapolis, University of Minnesota Press, 1967, and *After the Irish Renaissance* by Hogan, University of Minnesota Press, 1967, London, Macmillan, 1968; *Fifty Years Young: A Tribute to John B. Keane* edited by John M. Feehan, Cork, Mercier Press, 1979.

John B. Keane comments:

I regard the playwright of today as a man who must speak for his people, to speak up and to speak out, to say what vested interests, politicians, and big business are afraid to say. I believe that men should be tried for not speaking out when doing so would benefit their fellows and ultimately save lives. Those guilty of not doing so are criminals in every sense of the word. Most men have moral courage, but moral courage without skill to impose one's views is like a steed without a rider. I feel strongly about exploring the ills of modern Ireland and the world, for the anguish of our times is the Frankenstein monster that has been created by our convenient and long silences. We reap this anguish because we have encouraged its growth by pulling the bedclothes over our heads, hoping that the ogres might go away and that dawn might purify all. That is why we are fast approaching a post-Christian era. This is why speaking out early and often is so essential if there is to be a decent quality of life. I look to life as it is lived around me and listen to a language that is living. It would be against my nature to ignore a living speech and a living people. I sometimes feel I would die without these to sustain me. Playwriting is my life. Just as a tree spreads its roots into the earth, I spread my recording impulses around the breasts of my people and often into their very cores. People need to be recorded, to be witnessed; they expect and deserve it. I feel a responsibility to my people, a duty to portray them accurately and with dignity lest they are falsely delineated. There is a lot of love and humour in my plays, for without love and humour there is nothing. Where there is love there is every virtue you care to think of: love begets all that is great and constant. Think of that word "constant." That's what love is. That is the rock to which I have anchored myself, and I think my best is to come.

* * *

Despite his reputation in Ireland as a dramatist, essayist, publican, and raconteur, John B. Keane is little known outside Ireland. Unlike many other Irish writers, Keane has chosen not to leave home but to remain in Listowel, the small market town in rural north Kerry where he was born and educated and where he has for thirty years operated John B. Keane's Public House. Not surprisingly, his best plays, *Sive, Sharon's Grave, The Field* and *Big Maggie*, are those which deal with rural Irish experience. The nightly drama at his pub provides a rich source of situation, character, and theme. Keane possesses a natural understanding of Irish countrymen. He knows the rhythm of their language and their lives. One never doubts that the problems he dramatizes are real problems in rural Ireland—emigration (*Many Young Men of Twenty*), arranged marriages (*Sive*), class conflict (*The Rain at the End of the Summer*), the breakdown of families (*Big Maggie, The Crazy Wall*), the disposition of land (*Sharon's Grave*), and the conflict of tribal and national loyalties (*The Field*).

In nearly all his plays Keane is concerned with the intimidation and exploitation of the weak by the strong, and with the insensitive, brutal, and often terrifying nature of this exploitation. In his earlier plays, perhaps up to *The Rain at the End of the Summer*, the power of violence and intimidation is limited by the greater power of a Christian providence which judges evil acts and promises justice, if not in this world, then in the next. The brutalization of the young orphan Sive by those who would force her into an unwanted arranged marriage with the doddering lecher Sean Dota will be punished. The tinkers Pats Bocock and Carthalawn lament Sive's untimely death and their choric songs promise the ultimate justice which Kean's Irish Catholic audience would have expected.

Similarly in *Sharon's Grave* the bullying Dinzie Colee, who tries to seize the land from his defenseless cousin, meets a horrible but "just" fate at the end of the play. Even in Keane's most violent play, *The Field*, in which "The Bull" McCabe beats to death a young stranger who has outbid him for title to a four-acre field, there is the sense that justice will prevail.

The murderer survives, but so does his conscience: "That's the way of the world. The grass won't be green over his grave when he'll be forgot by all . . . forgot by all except me!"

Keane's more recent plays have taken a darker, more ironic, and therefore more modern view of exploitation and violence. *Big Maggie* opens in a graveyard with Maggie sitting on a gravestone listening to the sound of the dirt being thrown down on her husband's coffin. Keane is suggesting here the finality of death and in the play he offers no traditional palliatives for the inevitability of age and for the mulish actions of a mother who drives away her four grown children in the name of domestic economy. Big Maggie prevails; she has her possessions intact. But her things mean nothing. She is alone and she has willed it so.

The Rain at the End of the Summer and *Moll* both suggest the darker moral vision of *Big Maggie*. Moll, housekeeper in an Irish rectory, has the tenacity and self-centeredness of Maggie. She copes with a succession of venal pastors in a Christian house which is indifferent to God. *Rain*, one of Keane's best-made plays, is a domestic tragedy which develops with a *Lear*-like inevitability the change in fortune of an old man who begins utterly confident of his family's love and ends rejected and defeated, muttering empty commands to a daughter who has given up her religious vocation to remain with him. The play in no way provides an ultimate justice which would make sense of such human suffering. Joss O'Brien, like Lear, has experienced "this tough world."

In *The Crazy Wall* Keane seems to be moving in new directions, but he remains preoccupied with the breakdown of traditional Christian values. More obviously autobiographical than any of his earlier plays—the central figure is a schoolmaster and one of his sons wants to be an actor—*The Crazy Wall* is set in rural Ireland during World War II. Michael Barnett, convinced that the stone wall which he is building will gain him the privacy he desires, becomes instead more exposed and more vulnerable. He cannot maintain the psychological walls which he has built against human relations. His vulnerability results in a powerful and cathartic encounter with his wife at the end of the play in which truths are told and possibilities develop for a deeper and more genuine love. Keane develops these human possibilities in a context which rejects pious platitudes. Barnett's final line, the last line of the play—"God always comes up trumps in the morning"—is surely ironic. Much closer to the moral center of *The Crazy Wall* and very likely to Keane's own values are the words of Moses McCoy, a poor wanderer who has lost his wife and two sons and who will not be appeased by traditional Christian consolation. "What fool says God is good? God is no damned good, never was and never will be world without end."

—Arthur E. McGuinness

KEEFFE, Barrie (Colin). British. Born in London, 31 October 1945. Educated at East Ham Grammar School, London. Married 1) Dee Truman in 1969 (divorced 1979); 2) the writer Verity Bargate in 1981 (died 1981), two stepsons; 3) Julia Lindsay in 1983. Actor, at Theatre Royal Stratford East, London, 1964, and National Youth Theatre, 3 years; reporter, *Stratford and Newham Express*, London, to 1969, and for news agency to 1975; dramatist-in-residence, Shaw Theatre, London (Thames TV Playwright scheme), 1977, and Royal Shakespeare Company, 1978. Since 1986 associate writer, Theatre Royal Stratford East. Since 1977 member of the Council, National Youth Theatre; since 1978 member of the Board of Directors, Soho Poly Theatre, London. Recipient: French Critics prize, 1978; Mystery Writers of America Edgar Allan Poe Award, for screenplay, 1982. Agent: Harvey Unna and Stephen Durbridge Ltd., 24–32 Pottery Lane, London W11 4LZ; or, Gilbert Parker, William Morris Agency, 1350 Avenue of the Americas, New York, New York 10019, U.S.A. Address: 110 Annandale Road, London SE10 0JZ, England.

PUBLICATIONS

Plays

Only a Game (produced London, 1973).

A Sight of Glory (produced London, 1975).

Gimme Shelter: Gem, Gotcha, Getaway (*Gem* produced London, 1975; *Gotcha* produced London, 1976; trilogy produced London, 1977; New York, 1978). London, Eyre Methuen, 1977; New York, Grove Press, 1979.

My Girl (produced London, 1975).

A Certain Vincent, with Jules Croiset, adaptation of letters of Vincent Van Gogh (also director: produced Amsterdam and London, 1975).

Scribes (produced Newcastle upon Tyne, 1975; London, 1976; New York, 1977).

Here Comes the Sun (produced London, 1976). Published in *Act 3*, edited by David Self and Ray Speakman, London, Hutchinson, 1979.

Barbarians: A Trilogy: Killing Time, Abide with Me, In the City (*Abide with Me* produced London, 1976; trilogy produced London, 1977). London, Eyre Methuen, 1978.

Up the Truncheon (produced London, 1977).

A Mad World, My Masters (produced London, 1977; San Francisco, 1978; revised version produced London, 1984). London, Eyre Methuen, 1977.

Frozen Assets (produced London and San Francisco, 1978; revised version produced London, 1987). London, Eyre Methuen, 1978.

Sus (produced London, 1979; New York, 1983). London, Eyre Methuen, 1979.

Heaven Scent (broadcast 1979). Published in *Best Radio Plays of 1979*, London, Eyre Methuen, 1980.

Bastard Angel (produced London, 1980). London, Eyre Methuen, 1980.

Black Lear (produced Sheffield, 1980).

She's So Modern (produced Hornchurch, Essex, 1980).

Chorus Girls, music by Ray Davies (produced London, 1981).

A Gentle Spirit, with Jules Croiset, adaptation of a story by Dostoevsky (also director: produced Amsterdam, 1981; London, 1982).

The Long Good Friday (screenplay). London, Methuen, 1984.

Better Times (produced London, 1985). London, Methuen, 1985.

Screenplay: *The Long Good Friday*, 1981.

Radio Plays: *Good Old Uncle Jack*, 1975; *Pigeon Skyline*, 1975; *Self Portrait*, 1977; *Heaven Scent*, 1979.

Television Plays: *The Substitute*, 1972; *Nipper*, 1977; *Not Quite Cricket*, 1977; *Champions*, 1978; *Hanging Around*, 1978; *Waterloo Sunset*, 1979; *No Excuses* series, 1983; *King*, 1984.

Recording: *A Certain Vincent*, RCA; *No Excuses*, CBS.

Novels

Gadabout. London, Longman, 1969.
No Excuses (novelization of his television series). London, Methuen, 1983.

Other

Editor, *The 1984 Verity Bargate Award Short Plays.* London, Methuen, 1985.
Editor, *The Verity Bargate Award New Plays 1986.* London, Methuen, 1987.

*

Theatrical Activities:
Director: **Plays**—*A Certain Vincent*, Amsterdam and London, 1975; *A Gentle Spirit*, Amsterdam, 1981, London, 1982.

* * *

In the days when Barrie Keeffe worked for a local newspaper in East London, one of his assignments was the astrology column which, even more than most astrology columns, was a piece of total imagination written under the by-line of "Kay Sera." The random assignment of different fates to his readers must have given Keeffe's employers some indication of his developing dramatic gifts, but it was another assignment which profoundly coloured his future work. At the end of an interview with the pro-censorship campaigner Mary Whitehouse, later to be the recognizable target of his satire *She's So Modern*, he asked her who the people were that she professed to speak for. With a metaphorical pat on the head, she replied: "Ordinary, decent people; like you and me." The plays which followed that interview, whether comedies or dramas, frequently troubled Mrs. Whitehouse, particularly when broadcast on television, but Keeffe's explorations of British racism and alienated youth certainly followed his own concerns with decency. What is remarkable, for a writer so very much of his time and place, is how successful the plays have been in other countries and how they have endured.

In 1987, Barrie Keeffe found that *Frozen Assets*, his play written for the Royal Shakespeare Company in 1978, was being revived and revalued. His radio version of the play, somewhat less profane but no less powerful than the stage version, was being broadcast by the BBC in his own updated adaptation, and stage revivals were being scheduled in acknowledgement that the basic story of a borstal boy on the run in London had survived with its comical cynicism intact. Indeed, the picture the play paints of East London as a community destroyed by property speculation was provided with additional poignancy in the wake of the yuppie invasion of dockland.

Similarly, 1986 saw revivals of his 1977 trilogy of one-act plays, *Gimme Shelter*, which included the play *Gotcha* about a schoolboy who held his teachers hostage with matches held over the open petrol tank of a motorcycle. The arguments in that play had not dated, nor had the level of resentment he had first measured in schools from which pupils were being dumped, unprepared, into a society which could not provide them with jobs. Another apparently topical play, *Sus*, about a black man arrested under the now abolished "sus" law where people could be held by the police on grounds of suspicion alone, has also survived the progress of time and continues to appear in various productions, both in Britain and abroad, though it was very specifically set on the night of Margaret Thatcher's first electoral victory. At the heart of its survival is the recognizable human pain of the man falsely accused of his wife's death.

Despite the continued interest in and the undoubted influence of Keeffe's early plays, the flood of stage plays from the 1970's had subsided to a trickle by the mid-1980's. The plays that appeared in the 1980's were notably different from the scripts of the 1970's, as with the short-lived musical he wrote with Ray Davies of the Kinks, *Chorus Girls*, a political entertainment taken from an obscure comedy by Aristophanes, *Thesmophoriazousai.* Similar in some ways to the satirical comedy he wrote in 1977 for the Joint Stock Company, *A Mad World, My Masters* (with the title and the spirit of the free-flowing plot borrowed from the Jacobean writer Thomas Middleton), the play tapped a classical source for a very current inspiration and concerned the kidnapping of Prince Charles by dedicated feminists. Ill-directed, the play had only a local success at the Theatre Royal, Stratford East, the theatre for which it was designed. None the less it was witty, often uproariously so, with several excellent songs from Davies, and its presentational format was a breakthrough in Keeffe's technique which seems to have prepared the way for further musical theatre collaborations, including a promised Davies-Keeffe collaboration on *Around the World in Eighty Days.*

The play which followed four years later, *Better Times*, was another departure, part documentary about East London's historical Poplar Rent Strike and again part East End comedy in the mood of *A Mad World, My Masters.* Meticulous in its re-creation of the courtroom scenes and backroom dramas surrounding an important moment in British socialist history, and admirable for it, the most telling demonstration of Keeffe's talent was in the imaginary scenes with his patented version of an East End Keystone Cop. Though cheered by his East London audiences, the play was received with bemusement by several of his critics. It has often been the wayward force of his comedy which has bewildered reviewers, but the touch of absurdism in his work remains another of the qualities which keeps the apparently topical subject matter of the plays alive.

Keeffe's work has long benefitted from associations with specific companies, beginning with the National Youth Theatre and achieving a major impetus from the late Verity Bargate's support at London's Soho Poly Theatre. It was in that small venue that both his youth trilogies, *Gimme Shelter* and *Barbarians*, were developed, and something of the claustrophobic power of those pictures of aimless young Londoners can probably be ascribed to their original performance space which he exploited to its full. The trilogies boldly gave his inarticulate and angry young men a rich imagistic language, both abusive and tender, which has been much imitated by younger writers. Keeffe, however, has varied his dramatic offerings much more than his followers and his own influences range visibly from Plautus—the twins in *She's So Modern*—to Chekhov.

Bastard Angel, probably Keeffe's most important play, was written for the Royal Shakespeare Company. Belying its own gutsy story of a female rock singer rattling painfully through despair in the mansion which she bought in order to humiliate servants who had humiliated her when she was a young singer, the play took its inspiration from Chekhov's *Platonov*, and key images from each of the four acts of the Russian play have been retained. More cataclysmic by far than the Chekhov original, with the rock star entering into a sexual relationship with her own son, the play manages to retain autumnal beauty in the midst of violent events and blasting music. The later television version, *No Excuses*, carried the story further but lacked the focus of the stage version which is a major work.

With the success of his screenplay *The Long Good Friday*, a film which seized the initiative from American crime movies to mingle East End villainy, the IRA, international crime, and a unique political perspective, Keeffe moved into the rank of writers constantly courted by Hollywood. Prior to that he had contributed notably to British television, particularly with his audacious comedy *Waterloo Sunset*, with its portrait of an elderly white woman who walks out of an old folks home and moves in with a black family in South London. His short prize-winning radio play, *Heaven Scent*, about crime and perfume, is a model of radio technique and beautifully demonstrates his own gift for characterization and storytelling. Keeffe also wrote the novel version of *No Excuses*, providing interesting commentary on the intentions of the story, but losing the touch of Chekhov which made the original play so powerful. With his exuberant language and uninhibited vision of the potential of the stage, his greatest gifts are theatrical and his influence continues to grow.

—Ned Chaillet

KEMPINSKI, Tom. British. Born in London, 24 March 1938. Educated at Hall School; Abingdon Grammar School; Cambridge University (open scholar). Married. Actor, 1960–71. Recipient: London Drama Critics award, 1980. Agent: Anthony Sheil Associates, 43 Doughty Street, London WC1N 2LF, England.

PUBLICATIONS

Plays

The Peasants Revolt (produced Essex, 1971).
The English Civil War (produced London, 1972).
Moscow Trials (produced London, 1972).
Pageant of Labour History (4 plays; produced London, 1973).
The Ballad of Robin Hood, with Roger Smith (produced London, 1973).
October, with Roger Smith (produced 1973).
Sell-Out (1931), with Roger Smith, music by Kempinski and Smith (produced London, 1974).
Flashpoint (as Gerrard Thomas) (produced London, 1978).
What about Borneo? (produced London, 1978).
The Workshop, adaptation of a play by Jean-Claude Grumberg (produced London, 1979; as *The Workroom*, produced New Haven, Connecticut, 1982).
Japanese Noh Plays (for children; produced Leicester, 1979).
Mayakovsky, adaptation of a work by Stefan Schütz (produced London, 1979).
Duet for One (produced London, 1980; New York, 1981). London, French, 1981.
Dreyfus, adaptation of the play by Jean-Claude Grumberg (produced London, 1982).
The Beautiful Part of Myself (produced Watford, Hertfordshire, 1983).
Life of Karl Marx, with Roger Smith (produced London, 1984).
Self-Inflicted Wounds (produced Mold, Clwyd, 1985).
Separation (produced London, 1987).

Screenplay: *Duet for One*, with Jeremy Lipp and Andrei Konchalovsky, 1987.

*

Tom Kempinski comments:

There are two kinds of oppression in the world: the oppression of one group in society by another, and the oppression of one part of a person by another part of the same person. I write about both kinds, because I have experienced both—and also studied and struggled to change both.

My historical plays are influenced by English radio comedy of the 1950's, and include songs and music which I compose.

My "personal" plays are characterised by attempts to penetrate beneath the surface of people's deeds to their inner, and often concealed motives. These plays are written in a "naturalistic" "style," and—in a country that keeps a stiff upper lip (since 1800?) in order not to show weakness to wogs, niggers, wops, and other human beings which Britain has conquered—are found to be just a touch emotional.

Top people—whether parents or dictators—prefer lies of all kinds, because they invent these lies to maintain their superior status in the world.

* * *

Tom Kempinski writes about strong people under unbearable pressure, charting the process of their bravely resisted but inevitable collapse. Stephanie Abrahams in *Duet for One* is a classical musician struck down by multiple sclerosis and compelled to face a life without the music that has been the centre of it; Isaac Cohen in *Self-Inflicted Wounds* is a dedicated Nazi-hunter who finds his courage faltering when it comes time to publish his research; Carter in *Flashpoint* is a wise-cracking soldier whose method of coping with army routine is tested in a crisis.

Given these outlines, it is not surprising that Kempinski's plays sometimes skirt the edge of soap opera and melodrama. *Duet for One*, which consists entirely of Stephanie's sessions with an overly wise psychologist, follows a predictable emotional outline, at least in part: one knows from the minute she enters bravely denying a psychological problem that she will eventually break down and cry, "I-can never-never-play-the-the-the-violin again" (it happens at the end of Act 1), just as one can predict that the laconic psychologist will eventually make an eloquent pull-yourself-together speech (Act 2). *Self-Inflicted Wounds* is also a bit schematic in the way that Cohen's affair with a young girl and his own family secrets are twisted back on the main plot to be used against him by his enemies. And the action of *Flashpoint*, which involves an armed soldier going berserk and taking his platoon hostage in an attempt to stop the execution of a deserter, threatens to lose sight of its ideas in the melodramatic action.

But these dangers, not always avoided, are almost inevitable, given Kempinski's determination to find the sources and limits of his protagonists' strength. Notably, the process is not simple or direct, and the discoveries made are complex and sometimes surprising. Stephanie Abrahams does not go from bold defiance to simple despair—that predictable breakdown is only the end of the first act. Kempinski sees that despair is a step, not a conclusion; it is followed by self-denial and self-abasement, as Stephanie tries to convince herself that she doesn't care about her loss of dignity and self-control; by self-deceit, as the fear of losing her husband is raised to deflect the psychologist from deeper probing; and only then by the loss of all defenses and the admission of the very elementary fears that everything else was covering, an admission that Kempinski sees as the bravest step of all and the basis for hope.

Similarly, Cohen's perplexing hesitancy to publish the damning results of his research is not explained or exposed simply. Each revelation is a little more true than the one before it, but not itself the entire truth. Even at the end, when Cohen admits that he might have deliberately sabotaged himself by giving his enemies the means to discredit him, his reasons are a subtle mixture of weakness and strength, betrayals of his own morality and higher affirmations of it. And Carter is also shown to be more complex than one might first expect: his wise-guy attitude does not keep him from being the strongest participant in the hostage crisis or bar him from sympathy for his weaker comrades. It is only after the crisis is over and he learns how those outside had manipulated both gunman and hostages that Carter momentarily breaks, showing in his sense of betrayal a core of faith in the military that his sneers had hidden.

Duet for One is the strongest of Kempinski's plays, partly because of the exciting role it offers a sensitive actress, and to a great extent because making the "enemy" a disease frees him from having to create melodramatic events; the play's attention is entirely on Stephanie's internal struggle. Kempinski is also more in control of this more tightly focussed story. *Self-Inflicted Wounds* is at least partly about the evils of Nazism and Neo-Nazism, and *Flashpoint* about the British military presence in Northern Ireland, and Kempinski's own personal feelings on these subjects are clearly so strong that they tempt him toward the soapbox and diffuse the plays' dramatic energies.

—Gerald M. Berkowitz

KENNA, Peter (Joseph). Australian. Born in Sydney, New South Wales, 18 March 1930. Educated at the Christian Brothers' School, Lewisham, New South Wales. Actor and singer; member, Australian Elizabethan Theatre Trust, 1956–59; worked as window dresser and salesman; lived in London, 1960–64, 1966–71. Writer-in-residence, New South Wales Institute of Technology, Broadway, 1979. Recipient: General Motors-Holden prize, 1959; Australia Council grant, 1973, 1975. Agent: Curtis Brown, 27 Union Street, Paddington, New South Wales 2021, Australia.

PUBLICATIONS

Plays

The Slaughter of St. Teresa's Day (produced Sydney, 1959). Sydney, Currency Press, 1972; London, Eyre Methuen, 1973.
Talk to the Moon (produced London, 1963). Included in *Talk to the Moon, Listen Closely, Trespassers Will Be Prosecuted*, 1977.
Muriel's Virtues (also director: produced Sydney, 1966).
Listen Closely (produced Sydney, 1972). Included in *Talk to the Moon, Listen Closely, Trespassers Will Be Prosecuted*, 1977.
A Hard God (produced Sydney, 1973). Sydney, Currency Press, and London, Eyre Methuen, 1974; revised version, Currency Press, 1982.
Mates (produced Sydney, 1975; London, 1976). Published in *Drag Show*, Sydney, Currency Press, 1977.
Trespassers Will Be Prosecuted (produced Sydney, 1976; Cleveland, 1982). Included in *Talk to the Moon, Listen Closely, Trespassers Will Be Prosecuted*, 1977.
Talk to the Moon, Listen Closely, Trespassers Will Be Prosecuted. Sydney, Currency Press, 1977.
The Cassidy Album: A Hard God, Furtive Love, An Eager Hope (produced Adelaide, 1978). *Furtive Love* published Sydney, Currency Press, 1980.

Screenplays: *The Umbrella Woman*, 1982; *The Good Wife*, 1987.

Television Plays: *Goodbye, Gloria, Goodbye*, 1964; *Miles Away* (*The Emigrants* series), 1976 (UK).

*

Manuscript Collection: Eunice Hanger Collection, University of Queensland, St. Lucia.

Critical Studies: *After "The Doll"* by Peter Fitzpatrick, Melbourne, Arnold, 1979; *Contemporary Australian Playwrights* edited by Jennifer Palmer, Adelaide, University Union Press, 1979; "Peter Kenna's *A Hard God*" by Frank Bladwell, in *Southerly* (Sydney), no. 2, 1979; articles by John McCallum and Barry Oakley, in *Contemporary Australian Drama* edited by Peter Holloway, Sydney, Currency Press, 1981.

Theatrical Activities:
Director: **Play**—*Muriel's Virtues*, Sydney, 1966.
Actor: **Radio**—*Portia Faces Life* and *Life Can Be Beautiful* series.

* * *

The work of Peter Kenna spans two movements in Australian playwriting and expresses the radical changes which took place in that country's theatre between the 1950's and the 1970's. From childhood a working actor and a private writer, Kenna first came to national notice as a playwright in 1959 with *The Slaughter of St. Teresa's Day*. At that time he was one of a cluster of new playwrights, among them Ray Lawler, Alan Seymour, Ric Throssell, Ru Pullen, and Richard Beynon, who reflected the flush of hope accorded by the establishment of Australia's first subsidising body for the performing arts, the Australian Elizabethan Theatre Trust.

The Slaughter of St. Teresa's Day is a comedy drama about an underworld party that ends in violence. It was inspired by the then queen of the Sydney madams, Tilly Devine, but its style owes more to the Hollywood movies and to Tennessee Williams, whose influence on the Australian theatre in the 1950's and 1960's was significant. The play survives today, despite its theatrical contrivances, for the warm Irish exuberance of its characterisation.

The true source of this play and of all his work to date has been Kenna's family. Eleventh of 13 children of a Sydney carpenter, Kenna stems from Irish farming stock who settled in New South Wales at the beginning of the century. Kenna grew up within the sound of stories of country and urban working class life as the relatives came and went. These people inspired *Talk to the Moon*, an urban drama about a disappointed woman whose restlessness places strain on her children and on her dying husband. They inspired *Listen Closely*, a comedy of country manners in which the conventions of the teenage generation confront those of their parents.

Kenna spent most of the 1960's in Britain; it was when he returned home to settle in 1971 that his work developed to its present maturity. The new playwrights by this time had discarded the conventions in which the plays like *The Slaughter of St. Teresa's Day* had been bred in favour of looser, more personal dramatic structures based on rhythms more familiar to Australian life and language. Out of this climate Kenna wrote three largely autobiographical plays about a working-class Catholic family, the Cassidys.

In the first play, *A Hard God*, set in 1945, the home of Dan and Aggie Cassidy is invaded by Dan's brothers, Martin, an eccentric poet and anti-communist activist, whose estranged wife has "got religion," and Paddy, a weak charmer whose rebellious wife Sophie is pursuing him with a razor. Dan's painful, ultimately terminal illness is forced to take second place to the absurd domestic problems of his feckless family. And in contrapuntal movement is a brief, guilt-ridden affair between 16-year-old Joe Cassidy and his friend Jack Shannon. The play is about time, which hurts and heals, about dislocation from ancestral roots, and is an indictment of a superstitious form of Catholicism that lacks compassion.

In the second play, *Furtive Love*, the time is the 1950's and Joe an established actor, playwright, and homosexual in a company exhausted at the end of a long tour. The sense of uprootedness that pervades *A Hard God* is here channelled into an investigation of personal identity expressed through the image of the itinerant actor. As their disbandment approaches, the company clings together, their predicament personified in the character of the amnesiac Ned, who keeps his biography, cut out of a theatre programme, in his pocket to remind himself of who he is. The central image of the last act is a group photograph, which confirms their need to capture the image of themselves before they dissolve into vacancy.

While Joe is the constant in the three plays he is the observer rather than the protagonist. In the third play, *An Eager Hope*, Joe is in his thirties, his health failing from incipient kidney disease as he tries to pull together his new play. As his fortune wanes, that of his charming and worthless brother rides high. *An Eager Hope* is Kenna's hard submission to a hard God. Joe's time, he says at the end of the play, is not yet come.

Kenna's plays are about love, particularly familial bonds in their variety: possessiveness, self-sacrifice, a reluctance to tell the truth. Pivotal to most of his work is a maternal figure whose life force, for good or evil, dominates the action. The finest of these creations is Aggie Cassidy in the centre of *A Hard God* and *An Eager Hope*—a loving, pragmatic woman who believes first in her family and secondly in her God.

His short play *Mates* is a light comment on aspects of love which brings into perspective the self-deception behind the lost souls who people Kenna's world. An old shearer on holiday in the city is led in the pre-dawn hours by a dream of lost youth to the site of a former brothel, now a night club. The old man, a transvestite singer, his footballer friend, and a retired prostitute expose by degrees that their varied sexual relations have taught them nothing about human relationships: four uncomprehending souls in a house of illusion. If one can sum up the themes of Kenna's work to date, they turn on the delicate balance between the need to exploit others for comfort against the world and the need to give comfort and make one's peace with God.

—Katharine Brisbane

KENNEDY, Adrienne (Lita, née Hawkins). American. Born in Pittsburgh, Pennsylvania, 13 September 1931; grew up in Cleveland, Ohio. Educated in Cleveland public schools; Ohio State University, Columbus, B.A. in education 1953; Columbia University, New York, 1954–56. Married Joseph C. Kennedy in 1953 (divorced 1966); two sons. Joined Edward Albee's workshop in 1962. Lecturer in Playwriting, Yale University, New Haven, Connecticut, 1972–74, Princeton University, New Jersey, 1977, and Brown University, Providence, Rhode Island, 1979–80; Chancellor's Distinguished Lecturer, University of California, Berkeley, 1986. Member of the Board of Directors, PEN, 1976–77. Recipient: Obie award, 1965; Guggenheim fellowship, 1967; Rockefeller grant, 1967, 1969, 1973; New England Theatre Conference grant; National Endowment for the Arts grant, 1972; CBS-Yale fellowship, 1973; Creative Artists Public Service grant, 1974. Address: 325 West 89th Street, New York, New York 10024, U.S.A.

PUBLICATIONS

Plays

Funnyhouse of a Negro (produced New York, 1964; London, 1968). New York, French, 1969.

The Owl Answers (produced Westport, Connecticut, and New York, 1965). Included in *Cities in Bezique*, 1969.

A Beast's Story (produced New York, 1965). Included in *Cities in Bezique*, 1969.

The Lennon Play: In His Own Write, with John Lennon and Victor Spinetti, adaptation of works by John Lennon (produced London, 1967; revised version produced London, 1968; Albany, New York, 1969). London, Cape, 1968; New York, Simon and Schuster, 1969.

A Lesson in Dead Language (produced New York and London, 1968). Published in *Collision Course*, New York, Random House, 1968.

A Rat's Mass (produced New York and London, 1970). Published in *New Black Playwrights*, edited by William Couch, Jr., Baton Rouge, Louisiana State University Press, 1968.

Boats (produced Los Angeles, 1969).

Sun: A Poem for Malcolm X Inspired by His Murder (produced London, 1969). Published in *Scripts 1* (New York), November 1971.

Cities in Bezique: 2 One-Act Plays: The Owl Answers and A Beast's Story. New York, French, 1969.

An Evening with Dead Essex (produced New York, 1973).

A Movie Star Has to Star in Black and White (produced New York, 1976). Published in *Wordplays 3*, New York, Performing Arts Journal Publications, 1984.

Orestes and Electra (produced New York, 1980).

Black Children's Day (produced Providence, Rhode Island, 1980).

A Lancashire Lad (for children; produced Albany, New York, 1980).

Other

People Who Led to My Plays (memoirs). New York, Knopf, 1987.

*

Adrienne Kennedy comments:

My plays are meant to be states of mind.

* * *

As black power gathered strength in America in the 1960's, the dramatist Adrienne Kennedy, who is black, was discovering more uses for the word Negro. She marks the beginnings of celebratory blackness with *Funnyhouse of a Negro* in which a woman's personal history of miscegenation, rape, and madness inscribes the larger history of black experience in white America, a history that Americans now sanitize and democratize under the rubric "race relations." Kennedy makes no totalizing claims to represent anyone, but the play's motifs resonate sharply in collective history.

In her New York apartment, Kennedy's "Negro-Sarah" enshrines an enormous statue of Queen Victoria and, in the course of the play, splits into a hunchbacked Jesus, the Duchess of Hapsburg, the African liberation leader Patrice Lumumba, and even Queen Victoria—each denoted as "One of Herselves." This is history and identity in a funnyhouse of distorted mirrors whose reflections are as unthinkable in racist America emerging from the 1950's as Sarah herself, child of a white woman raped by her missionary black husband in Africa. Slowly Sarah's incarnations emerge from darkness to narrate bits of the original trauma: the missionary zeal of the father who "wanted the black man to rise from colonialism," the mother who "didn't want him to save the black race and spent her days combing her hair ... and would not let him touch her in their wedding bed and called him black," the daughter conceived in violence, who rejects the father but resembles him and watches her mother lapse into madness, then death, the remembered sign for which is hair falling out.

Throughout the play, shining hairless skulls appear in dialogue and enacted fantasy until Sarah tries to stifle her father's (and her race's) claim on her by bludgeoning him with an ebony mask. Yet he returns: "He keeps returning forever, coming back ever and keeps coming back forever." Sarah's white friends whose (Victorian) culture "keep [her] from reflecting too much upon the fact that [she is] a Negro" cannot protect her from this returning and recurring repressed racial memory, signified by the repeated sound of knocking and the obsessively repeated images of fallen hair, kinky and straight, on a white pillow; of yellowness, the sickly white color of Sarah's skin; of swarming ravens and of death's-heads. The expressionistic funnyhouse of Sarah's memory defies linear logic. Her father hangs himself—or does not—in two versions of the story, but the last play image shows Sarah herself hanged, reclaimed by the jungle that engulfs the stage. Sarah's split subjectivity bears the scars of Afro-American history; her identification with her mother and murderous repression of her father's culture engage the discourses of feminism and psychoanalysis, and reveal the desire and exclusion embodied in Kennedy's "Negro."

The Owl Answers brilliantly extends these issues through the laminated identities of Kennedy's protagonist, She who is Clara Passmore who is the Virgin Mary who is the Bastard who is the Owl, whose history generates another violently skewed family romance, this time with a poor black mother and the "Richest White Man in the Town." Gradually a story emerges of a bastard daughter of miscegenous union, adopted by the Reverend Passmore, renamed Clara, but who carries her black mother's color and a passion for her white father's culture, "the England of dear Chaucer, Dickens and dearest Shakespeare," whose works she reads as a child in the Passmore library, and later disseminates as a "plain, pallid" schoolteacher in Savannah, Georgia. The glorious fathers of literary history merge with those of Christian myth as God's white dove (associated with Reverend Passmore's preaching) replaces the jungle father's black ravens in *Funnyhouse*. Her black mother called a whore, the adopted Clara identifies with the Virgin Mary, but in a fantasy visit to England the white fathers who have colonized her desire refuse Clara access to St. Paul's where she imagines burying her own white father, and lock her in the Tower of London. Rejected by her father, but unable to bury or repress him, Clara is imprisoned in her own history. In the play's associative logic the Tower is also a New York subway car in which the adult Clara, lost in guilt and rage, picks up a Negro man, introduces herself as Mary, addresses him as God, and tries to stab him.

The surrealistic Tower (dominant white culture) and the High Altar (sacrificial Christianity) are the phallic edifices against which Clara Passmore measures her being. Ultimately she transforms into the screeching Owl, symbol of her black mother and her criminal origins: "The Owl was ⟨my] beginning." Although her adopted status allows her to "pass more," Clara belongs to the owls as she cannot belong to the world of "Buckingham Palace, ... the Thames at dusk, and Big Ben" or the "Holy Baptist Church ... on the top of the Holy Hill." Near the end of the Play, Clara kneels to pray: "I call God and the Owl answers."

This summary conveys nothing of Kennedy's surrealistic spectacle: "There is the noise of the train, the sound of moving steel on the track." "The WHITE BIRD's wings should flutter loudly"—a cacophony that should evoke, says Kennedy, "a sense of exploding imprisonment."

Two shorter works, *A Lesson in Dead Language* and *A Rat's Mass*, add new elements of Kennedy's bestiary. In the first Western culture in the form of a Latin lesson and a schoolteacher, costumed from waist up as a White Dog, and Christian doctrine in the form of enormous statues of Jesus, Joseph, Mary, two Wise Man, and a shepherd, instruct and overwhelm seven little girls, whose initiation into menstruation marks them (and their white dresses) as guilty. In *A Rat's Mass* redemptive authority resides in a schoolmate, Rosemary, who refuses to expiate the incestuous crime of Brother and Sister Rat; and the sister goes mad. In this as in all of Kennedy's beautifully crafted plays, cultural exclusion translates into sexual terror and guilt, the signs of "Negro" womanhood.

Funnyhouse of a Negro won an Obie, but Kennedy's work is rarely discussed or performed in the United States.

—Elin Diamond

KESSELMAN, Wendy (Ann). American. Teaching Fellow, Bryn Mawr College, Pennsylvania, 1987. Also a composer and songwriter. Recipient: Meet the Composer grant, 1978, 1982; National Endowment for the Arts fellowship, 1979; Sharfman award, 1980; Susan Smith Blackburn Prize, 1980; Playbill award, 1980; Guggenheim fellowship, 1982; McKnight fellowship, 1985. Agent: George Lane, William Morris Agency, 1350 Avenue of the Americas, New York, New York 10019; or, Jane Annakin, William Morris Agency Ltd., 31–32 Soho Square, London W1V 6AP, England. Address: P.O. Box 680, Wellfleet, Massachusetts 02667, U.S.A.

PUBLICATIONS

Plays

Becca (for children), music and lyrics by Kesselman (produced New York, 1977).

Maggie Magalita (produced Washington, D.C., 1980; New York, 1986). New York, French, n.d.
My Sister in This House, music by Kesselman (produced Louisville and New York, 1981; revised version produced Leicester and London, 1987). New York, French, 1982.
Merry-Go-Round (produced Louisville, 1981; New York, 1983).
I Love You, I Love You Not (one-act version produced Louisville, 1982; New York, 1983; full-length version produced St. Paul, 1986; New York, 1987).
The Juniper Tree: A Tragic Household Tale, music and lyrics by Kesselman (produced Stockbridge, Massachusetts, 1982; New York, 1983). New York, French, 1985.

Fiction (for children)

Franz Tovey and the Rare Animals. New York, Quist, 1968.
Angelita. New York, Hill and Wang, 1970.
Slash: An Alligator's Story. New York, Quist, 1971.
Joey. New York, Lawrence Hill, 1972.
Time for Jody. New York, Harper, 1975.
Emma. New York, Doubleday, 1980.
There's a Train Going by My Window. New York, Doubleday, 1982; London, Hodder and Stoughton, 1983.
Flick. New York, Harper, 1983.

*

Critical Study: "Wendy Kesselman: Transcendence and Transformation" by Jay Dickson, in *Harvard Advocate* (Cambridge, Massachusetts), 1986.

Theatrical Activities:
Actress: **Play**—role in *The Juniper Tree*, New York, 1983.

* * *

Wendy Kesselman began her writing career as an author of children's books. Her sensitivities to the fears, fantasies, and problems of childhood permeate her six plays, and women and girls are her dominant characters. The past as shaper of the present is a recurring theme, as is loneliness, sometimes resulting in aberrant behaviour, or sometimes eased by simple acts of faith, personal discovery, or inner resolve.

Becca is a musical for which Kesselman wrote the book, music and lyrics, as she did for *The Juniper Tree.* (She is also the composer of a score for *The Caucasian Chalk Circle.*) *Becca* is a children's piece whose characters include a collection of unhappy caged pets, horribly neglected by a troubled ten-year-old boy, Jonathan. He is equally beastly to his sister, Becca, terrorising her into pretending to be a doll and shoving her into a dark closet when she rebels. Here she is terrified by three witches, two giant rats, a snake, and a spider complete with web. Recovering from her nightmare (or was it?), she effects the escape of the animals by demanding a simple act of faith, "Trust in your Daydreams," and then challenges Jonathan, who finally learns the lesson of love. Songs dominate the play with only minimal dialogue, and imaginative staging and costuming are demanded. Kesselman draws the audience into the vivid and scary world of the animals and children, with no loving parent or fairy godmother to put things right. Becca does this through her own inner resources, as do so many of Kesselman's anguished characters.

Kesselman describes *The Juniper Tree* as a play with music. It is also related to story theatre. Almost half of the play is in the form of songs and, but for brief sections of dialogue, the rest of the play is presented in first-person narration given by the different characters from their own perspectives, creating counterpoint and contrast. A distancing effect is also achieved. Taken from a Grimm fairy tale, *The Juniper Tree* is a story of viciousness and violence, transcended by innocence and love, and an act of plain vengeance. A stepmother kills her stepson and serves him up as a soup to his unsuspecting father. The Stepmother convinces her daughter that she is responsible for the boy's death. Distracted, the girl gathers up the boy's bones and sits under the juniper tree where the boy's beautiful mother is buried. The girl's steadfastness secures the boy's resurrection. Kesselman vividly and poetically portrays the loneliness of the widower, the haunting memories of the beautiful wife, the quiet devotion and growing jealousy of the stepmother, the confused children, the girl's final agony, and her faith which brings reconciliation.

Reconciliation is another recurring theme in Kesselman's plays, movingly exemplified in *Maggie Magalita*, the story of a young Latin American girl's assimilation into the culture of New York. In contrast to the two plays discussed above, it is a realistic play with psychologically motivated characters. The arrival in New York of Maggie's non-English-speaking grandmother revives for Maggie the pains of her own cultural adjustment, and she flounders between rage and embarrassment at her grandmother's old-world ways and stubbornness with the language, and tenderness and love towards the old woman who had nurtured her in her early childhood. Kesselman punctuates the present-day scenes with Maggie's "voice-over" memories of singing with her grandmother in Latin America, and memories of the taunts and cruelties of her young peers when she herself was trying to learn the language and ways of New York. It is a moving play, tinged with gentle humour derived from its clearly drawn characters.

In *My Sister in This House* Kesselman develops the technique of cross-cut scenes more fully. Different locations frequently appear on stage at the same time with simultaneous action, and the dialogue is picked up first in one place, then another. The transitions are fluid, creating counterpoint and tension. Based on a true story, the play is set in Le Mans, France, between 1925 and 1933 and concerns two young sisters who take up domestic employment in the home of the wealthy Mme. Danzard and her unmarried daughter. Tensions mount between all four characters, leading to the bloody climax when the sisters brutally murder their employers. The power of the play lies in the haunting but inexplicit neuroses of the four women, oppressed by their prescribed and inescapable roles in their society. Kesselman's dramaturgical strength often lies in what she leaves unexplained and it is particularly so in this play, where she creates an atmosphere of mystery, of tortured, lonely souls with volcanic passions, corseted in by their time and circumstance. We don't totally understand the course of events and therein lies the horror and power of the play.

In *Merry-Go-Round*, a short one-act piece, much is also left unexplained. Daisy and Michael appear to have just met again after several years and, in Daisy's apartment, they re-enact scenes from their shared childhood. The scene fades in and out of the past and the present. Nothing is certain. Why didn't Michael show up for their suicide pact? Was that what it was? Was Michael's father having an affair with Daisy's mother? Which parent discovered them in their undressing game? Is the whole play an acting-out of sexual fantasy? Again Kesselman creates fear and tension, tinged with humour, out of the unexplained. Yet she commands attention because within the fantasy world there is the integrity of truth.

I Love You, I Love You Not, in its realistic style and intergenerational theme, most resembles *Maggie Magalita.* Daisy, an adolescent, visits her grandmother, a holocaust survivor. Nana's patience, understanding, and, above all, her sense of adventure and fun, penetrate Daisy's stubborn recalcitrance. She is troubled by her quarreling parents and their lack of understanding towards her, but the renewed intense bond between her and her grandmother is a powerful healer.

Without writing feminist tracts, Kesselman effectively focuses on women, their bonds, their troubles, and their triumphs. While childhood or adolescent agonies and lonely or disturbed characters are common to her work, she balances her serious themes by her sense of dramatic humour, particularly in the two most realistically treated plays. Her clear affection for her characters gives them vital dimensions. Kesselman is at ease in different theatrical styles and perhaps it is her musician's ear that is behind her effectiveness with language. Her range includes the crisp narrative of *The Juniper Tree*, the rich lyrics of the two musicals, the selective hyper-realism of *Merry-Go-Round* and the naturalism of *Maggie Magalita* and *I Love You, I Love You Not.* Even in these two plays, however, there is a sense of a paring-down, leaving much unsaid, which adds to the poignancy and power of her work.

—Elizabeth Swain

KILROY, Thomas. Irish. Born in Callan, County Kilkenny, 23 September 1934. Educated at Christian Brothers School, Callan; St. Kiernan's College, Kilkenny; University College, Dublin, 1953–59, B.A. 1956, Higher Diploma in Education 1957, M.A. in English 1959. Married 1) Patricia Cobey in 1963 (divorced 1980), three sons; 2) Julia Lowell Carlson in 1981. Headmaster, Stratford College, Dublin, 1959–64; Visiting Lecturer in English, University of Notre Dame, Indiana, 1962–63; Visiting Professor of English, Vanderbilt University, Nashville, 1964–65; Assistant Lecturer, Department of Modern English and American Literature, University College, Dublin, 1965–73; lecturer, School of Irish Studies, Dublin, 1972–73. Visiting Professor, Sir George Williams University and McGill University, both Montreal, 1973, University College, Galway, 1975–76 and 1979, Dartmouth College, Hanover, New Hampshire, 1976, University College, Dublin, 1977–78, and Bamberg University, West Germany, 1984; Examiner in Modern English, Trinity College, Dublin, and Thomond College, Limerick, 1983. Recipient: *Guardian* prize, for fiction, 1971; Royal Society of Literature Heinemann award, for fiction, 1972; Irish Academy prize, 1972; American-Irish Foundation award, 1974; Arts Council of Ireland bursary, 1976; Bellagio Study Centre grant, 1986; Rockefeller grant, 1986. Fellow, Royal Society of Literature, 1972; Member, 1973, and Member of the Council, 1979, Irish Academy of Letters; Member, Aosdana, 1986. Agent: Margaret Ramsay Ltd., 14-A Goodwin's Court, London WC2N 4LL, England. Address: Department of Modern English, University College, Galway, Ireland.

PUBLICATIONS

Plays

The Death and Resurrection of Mr. Roche (produced Dublin, 1968; London, 1969; New York, 1978). London, Faber, and New York, Grove Press, 1969.

The O'Neill (produced Dublin, 1969).

Tea and Sex and Shakespeare (produced Dublin, 1976).

Talbot's Box (produced Dublin and London, 1977). Dublin, Gallery Press, and Newark, Delaware, Proscenium Press, 1979.

The Seagull, adaptation of a play by Chekhov (produced London, 1981). London, Eyre Methuen, 1981.

Double Cross (produced Derry and London, 1986). London, Faber, 1986.

Radio Plays: *The Door*, 1967; *That Man, Bracken*, 1986.

Television Plays: *Farmers*, 1978; *The Black Joker*, 1981.

Novel

The Big Chapel. London, Faber, 1971.

Other

Editor, *Sean O'Casey: A Collection of Critical Essays.* Englewood Cliffs, New Jersey, Prentice Hall, 1975.

*

Bibliography: *Ten Modern Irish Playwrights* by Kimball King, New York, Garland, 1979.

Critical Studies: articles by Christopher Murray, in *Ireland Today* (Dublin), 1982, and by Gerald Dawe, in *Theatre Ireland 3* (Belfast), 1982; "The Fortunate Fall: Two Plays by Thomas Kilroy" by Anthony Roche, in *The Writer and the City* edited by Maurice Harmon, Gerrard's Cross, Buckinghamshire, Smythe, 1984; "A Haunted House: The Theatre of Thomas Kilroy" by Frank McGuinness, in *Irish Theatre Today* edited by Barbara Hayley and Walter Rix, Würzburg, Königshausen & Neumann, 1985.

* * *

Thomas Kilroy is probably best known on both sides of the Atlantic for *The Death and Resurrection of Mr. Roche*, a tragicomedy which demonstrates his flair for funny yet trenchant dialogue in a style reminiscent of O'Casey. In this play, as well as in his historical portraits of Matt Talbot in *Talbot's Box* and William Joyce and Brendan Bracken in *Double Cross*, his characters are strongly defined, and his sense of dramatic structure is adroit. He is quite eclectic in his dramaturgy; his plays have little in common except an apparent rejection of the strong naturalistic tradition of many Abbey playwrights. His first play, *Mr. Roche*, is basically realistic in style, while his second, *The O'Neill*, is a historical work about Owen Roe O'Neill, the Irish opponent of Queen Elizabeth I. *Talbot's Box* is a penetrating psychological study notable for its use of expressionistic devices. *Tea and Sex and Shakespeare* is a thin comedy which teeters on the edge of absurdist theater. *Double Cross*, Kilroy's most recent work, is a curious dramatic diptych, a study of two political opposites who figured prominently in the propaganda battles of England and Germany in World War II. Some of Kilroy's themes are traditionally Irish; others are universal (e.g., the "aloneness" of spiritual isolation).

In *The Death and Resurrection of Mr. Roche* an all-male drinking party seemingly turns tragic when one of the group dies suddenly, or so it appears. Kelley, a mid-thirties civil servant of peasant background, has extended a casual invitation to assorted patrons of Murray's Bar to return to his small, desolate Dublin flat for further drinking. Last to arrive is Mr. Roche, the oldest of the lot and a known homosexual to whom Kelley is openly hostile. After they are even further into their cups, they begin to torment him, and he "dies" suddenly after they have forced him into a cubbyhole of a cellar. While two of the drinkers, Doc and Kevin, are out attempting to dispose of the body, Kelley and Seamus have what is thematically the most significant scene of the play. In an account of a sexual encounter with Roche, Kelley reveals his homosexual tendencies, and Seamus confesses he is trapped in marriage to a girl whose "sameness is beginning to drive me mad." At a carefully chosen moment, Doc and Kevin reappear with a very live Mr. Roche and an explanation that never quite includes how Doc could have pronounced him dead in the first place.

The central theme is the stultifying effect—the spiritual and cultural sterility—that contemporary urban life has had on young Irish men who were able to leave small family farms and villages and make careers in Dublin. They are descendants of the early "peasant play" characters who, unconsciously at least, longed to leave behind the hard life on the land, the narrow provinciality of the village, and the stifling influence of parents and clergy for the headier life of Dublin, England, or America. Kilroy's Irish are cousins to Brian Friel's Gar who leaves the small family business for the United States in *Philadelphia, Here I Come!* The father-son conflict, the Irish generational gap, is well behind Kilroy's characters; they have made their escape and feel lucky. However, they have, as they sadly admit, lost contact with their families. Kelley thinks he has a very good job, and Seamus, with whom he grew up, is proud of being a teacher and, until he thinks about it, is happily married. Their reunion over several pints becomes a melancholy soul-baring in which Seamus admits that he is not just attempting to recapture the pleasure of their last reunion two years ago. "Twas more like I was trying to get back to ten years ago. What was healthy then is sick now.... Why haven't you changed even a little? ... You're in the same situation as you were when you came to Dublin—" Kelley angrily insists that he's "the success of my family," while Seamus concludes sadly that he's "as happy as ever I'll be." Their conversation concludes with Kelley's unwelcome revelation that he had, in fact, invited Roche to the apartment before and that once they had had sexual relations.

Homosexuality is Kilroy's second theme, along with Irish hypocrisy. Kelley's hostile attitude toward Roche is made clear quite early to underline his hypocrisy: "I won't let the likes of him over that step...." After Roche's "death," Kelley is terrified that their acquaintance will come out: "Prison I can take. It's the bad name that leaves me wake at the knees." However, Roche is, in Kevin's words, "not a bad auld skin." In fact, Roche speaks for Kilroy in a plea for sympathy and understanding for all his characters, for homosexuality is here the playwright's metaphor for "aloneness." Through Roche, Kilroy strongly condemns their lifestyle, their drinking bouts to assuage loneliness and uncertainty, the waste of their lives. When Kelley condescendingly rejects Roche's sympathy, the homosexual makes a plea for all of them: "We all need sympathy now and again.... There's little comfort as it is, in this world.... Who am I or you to deny someone the single object which makes each day bearable?"Writing in 1968, Irving Wardle praised *Mr. Roche* as "the most important new work ever presented by the Dublin Theatre Festival."

Tea and Sex and Shakespeare was Kilroy's contribution to the 1976 Dublin Festival and has not been published. It involves the fantasies of a blocked writer named Brien. In one fruitless day spent in his Dublin attic workroom, he plays out his dreams involving his wife, Elmina, who is, in fact, at work; his neighbor, Sylvester, who finds him a nuisance but fancies his wife; his comic landlady and her nubile daughter, Deirdre, to whom he is tutor; and finally Mummy and Daddy, his in-laws, who might have escaped from a short play by Edward Albee. Brien's dream world centers around dramatic suicides and seductions, with dialogue quoted or paraphrased from Shakespeare, the subject of his tutorials with the buxom Deirdre. The plot and characters are exceedingly thin. The play ends on a poignantly serious note as the long-suffering wife remonstrates with Brien: "You build your absurd jokes around you like a high wall so that no one can reach you," she charges. Brien responds that he is only trying to say "I'm alone." Her reply—"And who in this world isn't alone?" reiterates the theme of spiritual isolation that Kilroy mined far more effectively and dramatically in *Talbot's Box.* This comedy of the frustrated, haunted creative person is only moderately successful.

Talbot's Box rarely matches the humor of *Mr. Roche*, but in its central character there is a highly effective study of religious zealotry, a subject the dramatist had dealt with in his novel *The Big Chapel* a few years earlier. Matt Talbot was a Dublin workman and mystic who died in 1925, and as early as 1931 a movement was underway for his canonization. On his death, it was discovered that for many years he had been wearing heavy chains and cords around his body, arms, and legs and that some of the rusty chains had sunk into the flesh. The play is an inquiry into the psyche of Talbot. The action comes through four actors who portray a variety of different roles, with costume changes made on stage. The playwright touches a number of social bases: for example, Talbot's role in the Transport Strike of 1913 sets his unique vision against the background of labor troubles, just as his encounters with the Church demonstrate that in his zealous humiliation of the flesh he is as unmanageable as Shaw's St. Joan. In the key scene of the play, Talbot tells the priest, "I knows the darkness! ... 'Tis in every man, woman 'n child born inta the world." For him, "the darkness is Gawd," and "there's no peace till ya walk through it inta some kinda light." The humiliation of the flesh is "only the way for me to know the darkness of me own body." In Kilroy's own words *Talbot's Box* is a play "about aloneness, its cost to the person and the kind of courage required to sustain it."

Kilroy's next work for the stage was a highly effective adaptation of Chekhov's *The Seagull.* Now set on an estate in the West of Ireland, this transplanted Russian classic shows no signs of a sea-change in its passage from one predominantly rural, 19th-century culture to another.

Double Cross is concerned with the problem of "doubleness or doubling, ... the way things repeat themselves in life or attract their opposites." This is the "basis of acting or role-playing," Kilroy writes in an introduction, as well as the impetus behind "the universal desire ... to make up and tell stories, thereby inventing a reality which may reflect everyday life but is still distinct from it." *Double Cross* attempts "to move along the lines from role-playing and fiction-making to the act of political treason." William Joyce, born in Brooklyn in 1906, arrived in England (via Ireland and Northern Ireland) in 1921. By 1933 he had become a member of Sir Oswald Mosley's British Union of Fascists. In 1939 he went to Germany where he joined German Radio. Before the year was out, he had become the infamous Lord Haw-Haw, probably Goebbels's best known radio commentator and apologist for the Nazi regime. Kilroy finds Joyce's "opposite" in Brendan Bracken, born 1901 in Tipperary, who by dint of systematic cultivation of the rich, famous, aristocratic, and politically powerful, rose, by 1939, to be Churchill's Parliamentary Private Secretary at the Admiralty and, by 1941, to be Minister of Information, whose responsibility it was to counteract the effect of Lord Haw-Haw's broadcasts.

Double Cross is divided into two halves: "The Bracken Play: London" and "The Joyce Play: Berlin." The first scene of "the Bracken Play" introduces both Joyce and Bracken (played by the same actor) as well as an actor and actress who both narrate and play a variety of characters, most notably Churchill and Lord Beaverbrook and the two women in the lives of Joyce and Bracken. Structurally, each play is made up of a series of free-flowing scenes which chronicle, in the case of Bracken, his political maneuverings and his affair with a woman called Popsie, while still allowing him to look back at his modest beginnings in Ireland and ahead to his own death (by cancer) in 1958. Joyce's "Berlin Play" focuses on his relations with his second wife, Margaret, and an interview (after his capture by the Allies) with Lord Beaverbrook. He was hanged as a war criminal in 1946.

For Kilroy this is a play about "two men who invented themselves," Bracken as an actor on the English political scene of the late 1930's and the war years, and Joyce as "a creator of fictions" driven to an invented self by a "deep, angry impatience" with life. Both came of unremarkable Irish backgrounds; both invented lives for themselves in English society; both tried to imitate his oppressor, Joyce by his anti-British propaganda, and Bracken by his very "English" attitude toward Ireland. Each of the plays is a tour de force for both the dramatist and the actor, with the first being the better of the two. Yet, as Irving Wardle wrote in the London *Times*, Kilroy's idea that "social play-acting in some way leads to fascism and treason" is not effectively projected. However, the play remains a fascinating study of "doubles/opposites." Kilroy followed *Double Cross* with a radio play on the same subject—or the Bracken half of it—called *That Man, Bracken*, which is an effective distillation of material used in the earlier work.

—Gene A. Barnett

KOCH, Kenneth. American. Born in Cincinnati, Ohio, 27 February 1925. Educated at Harvard University, Cambridge, Massachusetts, A.B. 1948; Columbia University, New York, M.A. 1953, Ph.D. 1959. Served in the United States Army, 1943–46. Married Mary Janice Elwood in 1955; one daughter. Lecturer in English, Rutgers University, New Brunswick, New Jersey, 1953–54, 1955–56, 1957–58, and Brooklyn College, 1957–59; director of the Poetry Workshop, New School for Social Research, New York, 1958–66. Lecturer, 1959–61, Assistant Professor, 1962–66, Associate Professor, 1966–71, and since 1971 Professor of English, Columbia University. Associated with *Locus Solus* magazine, Lans-en-Vercors, France, 1960–62. Recipient: Fulbright fellowship, 1950, 1978; Guggenheim fellowship, 1961; National Endowment for the Arts grant, 1966; Ingram Merrill Foundation fellowship, 1969; Harbison award, for teaching, 1970; Frank O'Hara prize (*Poetry*, Chicago), 1973; American Academy award, 1976. Address: Department of English, 414 Hamilton Hall, Columbia University, New York, New York 10027, U.S.A.

PUBLICATIONS

Plays

Bertha (produced New York, 1959). Included in *Bertha and Other Plays*, 1966.

The Election (also director: produced New York, 1960). Included in *A Change of Hearts*, 1973.

Pericles (produced New York, 1960). Included in *Bertha and Other Plays*, 1966.

George Washington Crossing the Delaware (in *3 × 3*, produced New York, 1962; produced separately, London, 1983). Included in *Bertha and Other Plays*, 1966.

The Construction of Boston (produced New York, 1962). Included in *Bertha and Other Plays*, 1966.

Guinevere; or, The Death of the Kangaroo (produced New York, 1964). Included in *Bertha and Other Plays*, 1966.

The Tinguely Machine Mystery; or, The Love Suicides at Kaluka (also co-director: produced New York, 1965). Included in *A Change of Hearts*, 1973.

Bertha and Others Plays (includes *Pericles, George Washington Crossing the Delaware, The Construction of Boston, Guinevere; or, The Death of the Kangaroo, The Gold Standard, The Return of Yellowmay, The Revolt of the Giant Animals, The Building of Florence, Angelica, The Merry Stones, The Academic Murders, Easter, The Lost Feed, Mexico, Coil Supreme*). New York, Grove Press, 1966.

The Gold Standard (produced New York, 1969). Included in *Bertha and Other Plays*, 1966.

The Moon Balloon (produced New York, 1969). Included in *A Change of Hearts*, 1973.

The Artist, music by Paul Reif, adaptation of the poem "The Artist" by Koch (produced New York, 1972). Poem included in *Thank You and Other Poems*, 1962.

A Little Light (produced Amagansett, New York, 1972).

A Change of Hearts: Plays, Films, and Other Dramatic Works 1951–1971 (includes the contents of *Bertha and Other Plays*, and *A Change of Hearts; E. Kology; The Election; The Tinguely Machine Mystery; The Moon Balloon; Without Kinship; Ten Films: Because, The Color Game, Mountains and Electricity, Sheep Harbor, Oval Gold, Moby Dick, L'Ecole Normale, The Cemetery, The Scotty Dog*, and *The Apple; Youth*; and *The Enchantment*). New York, Random House, 1973.

A Change of Hearts, with David Hollister (produced New York, 1985). Included in *A Change of Hearts* (collection), 1973.

Rooster Redivivus (produced Garnerville, New York, 1975).

The Art of Love, adaptation of his own poem (produced Chicago, 1976).

The Red Robins, adaptation of his own novel (produced New York, 1978). New York, Performing Arts Journal Publications, 1979.

The New Diana (produced New York, 1984).

Popeye among the Polar Bears (produced New York, 1986).

Screenplays: *The Scotty Dog*, 1967; *The Apple*, 1968.

Novel

The Red Robins. New York, Random House, 1975.

Short Stories

Interlocking Lives, with Alex Katz. New York, Kulchur Press, 1970.

Verse

Poems. New York, Tibor de Nagy, 1953.

Ko; or, A Season on Earth. New York, Grove Press, 1960.
Permanently. New York, Tiber Press, 1960.
Thank You and Other Poems. New York, Grove Press, 1962.
Poems from 1952 and 1953. Los Angeles, Black Sparrow Press, 1968.
When the Sun Tries to Go On. Los Angeles, Black Sparrow Press, 1969.
Sleeping with Women. Los Angeles, Black Sparrow Press, 1969.
The Pleasures of Peace and Other Poems. New York, Grove Press, 1969.
Penguin Modern Poets 24, with Kenward Elmslie and James Schuyler. London, Penguin, 1973.
The Art of Love. New York, Random House, 1975.
The Duplications. New York, Random House, 1977.
The Burning Mystery of Anna in 1951. New York, Random House, 1979.
From the Air. London, Taranman, 1979.
Days and Nights. New York, Random House, 1982.
Selected Poems 1950–1982. New York, Random House, 1985.
On the Edge. New York, Viking, 1986.

Other

John Ashbery and Kenneth Koch (A Conversation). Tucson, Interview Press, 1965(?).
Wishes, Lies, and Dreams: Teaching Children to Write Poetry. New York, Random House, 1970.
Rose, Where Did You Get That Red? Teaching Great Poetry to Children. New York, Random House, 1973.
I Never Told Anybody: Teaching Poetry Writing in a Nursing Home. New York, Random House, 1977.

Editor, with Kate Farrell, *Sleeping on the Wing: An Anthology of Modern Poetry, with Essays on Reading and Writing.* New York, Random House, 1981.
Editor, with Kate Farrell, *Talking to the Sun: An Illustrated Anthology of Poems for Young People.* New York, Holt Rinehart, 1985; London, Viking Kestrel, 1986.

*

Theatrical Activities:
Director: **Plays**—*The Election*, New York, 1960; *The Tinguely Machine Mystery* (co-director, with Remy Charlip), New York, 1965.

* * *

Kenneth Koch is a genuine man of letters, though that epithet seems inappropriate for a writer whose natural instincts are comic and parodic. In addition to writing much first-rate poetry and some striking fiction, he has been one of America's best teachers of writing—not only inspiring several promising younger poets, but also popularizing the idea of poetry writing in elementary education. His book *Wishes, Lies, and Dreams* details his own experience in the New York City public schools, and thus establishes a pedagogical example that is currently imitated all over the United States. Koch has also written short plays over the past three decades, most of which originated as responses to his personal experience as a graduate student of literature, a college professor, a serious poet, and a participant in the New York art scene. Perhaps because of their occasional inspiration, many of these shorter works remained too attached to their original circumstances to be presented again. His second collection, *A Change of Hearts*, includes several new pieces, all of which are typically Kochian, none particularly better than his past work.

On one hand, Koch is an absurdist and a giggler, incapable of taking anything too seriously, whose plays exploit situations and/or subjects for their available humor. On the other, he is a "New York School" poet capable of extraordinary acoherent (as distinct from incoherent) writing, such as the marvelous nonsense of these concluding lines from his early play, *Pericles*:

> And we stood there with pure roots
> In silence in violence one two one two
> Will you please go through that again
> The organ's orgasm and the aspirin tablet's speechless
> spasm.

In structure, his plays tend to be collections of related sketches, strung together in sequences of varying duration, allowing imaginative leaps between the scenes. The best also reveal his debt, both as playwright and as poet, to the French surrealists and dadaists.

Bertha and Other Plays collects most of Koch's early works in chronological order. The very best, *George Washington Crossing the Delaware*, originated as a response to Larry Rivers's painting of the same title (and the play is appropriately dedicated to the artist). Koch's compressed historical play ridicules several kinds of clichés: the myths of American history, the language of politicians, war films, military strategies, patriotism, and much else. The theme of Koch's multiple burlesques, here and elsewhere, is that the accepted familiar versions are no more credible than his comic rewritings. The play also reveals Koch's love of Apollinaire's great poem *Zone* (1918) by scrambling space and time. The British general refers at one point to "the stately bison," which did not enter popular mythology until the 19th-century and certainly could not be seen on the East Coast; and the play takes place in "Alpine, New Jersey," which is nowhere near the Delaware River.

In the ten short-short scenes of his earlier mini-epic, *Bertha*, whose text runs less than ten pages, Queen Bertha of Norway uses power to assuage her evident madness, attacks Scotland only to halt at the frontier, shoots lovers for their sins, only to win the confidence, nonetheless, of both her armies and their captives. (The historical source of this burlesque is less obvious than for *George Washington*, but several possibilities come to mind.) Koch's book also includes *Guinevere*, an early work with some marvelous nonsense writing; and "Six Improvisational Plays," four of which are prose texts that suggest a performance (much like a script for a "happening"); and the book closes with scenes from *Angelica*, an opera about 19th-century French poetry that was written for the American composer Virgil Thomson but never performed.

Koch's more recent plays are likewise filled with marvelous moments. In *The New Diana*, essentially a satire of the myth of poets and their muses, he has live turkeys appear, speaking indigenous language: CAGED TURKEY: Mishiki wai nowuga gan! Ish tang. TURKEY ON TABLE: Nai shi mai ghee itan, korega. *Popeye among the Polar Bears*, likewise a series of vignettes, has the wit and representational freedom we've come to associate with Koch's verse plays. *The Red Robins* is, by contrast, an adaptation of Koch's sole novel, published a few years before; it differs from other Koch theater in having considerably longer speeches.

In the mid-1980's he developed a working relationship with Barbara Vann and her colleagues at the Medicine Show, a New York Off-Broadway theater, which produced an operatic version of *A Change of Hearts* (from his second collection). For them he has very recently been finishing *A Thousand*

Avant-Garde Plays, a title so delicious it would seem conducive to his best writing.

Whereas Koch is clearly a major American poet, he is not yet a major playwright. The best one can say about his dramatic texts is that they are unique in the ways that all major work is unique. They are radical enough for Ruby Cohn to write (in *New American Dramatists 1960–1980*, 1982), "I find the plays of poet Kenneth Koch, which I have never seen performed, too childish to examine in a book intended for adults." Such dismissal would not occur unless Koch's texts took risks with theatrical language and yet, to my senses, they don't take enough risks within their premises and don't sustain their innovations to sufficient length. There is nothing in Koch's theater equal to his two book-length poems, *When the Sun Tries to Go On* (written in 1953, but not published until 1969) and *Ko; or, A Season on Earth*—but symptoms of such ambition abound in his work. It should also be noted that Koch, like his poetic colleagues John Ashbery and Frank O'Hara (both of whom also wrote plays), belongs to the counter-tradition of American playwriting—a theatre of poets and novelists that emphasizes not naturalism but fantasy; not character but circumstance; not events but essence.

—Richard Kostelanetz

KONDOLEON, Harry. American. Born in New York City, 26 February 1955. Educated at Hamilton College, Clinton, New York (Bradley Playwriting Prize, 4 times), 1974–77, B.A. 1977; Yale University, New Haven, Connecticut (Kazan Award, 1979, 1980), M.F.A. 1981. Member, playwrights and directors unit, Actors Studio, New York, 1978–80, and Manhattan Theatre Club, 1982–84. Instructor in Playwriting, New School for Social Research, 1983–84, and Columbia University, 1985–87, both New York. Recipient: International Institute of Education fellowship, 1977; Oppenheimer award, 1983; Obie award, 1983; New York Foundation for the Arts grant, 1984; National Endowment for the Arts grant, 1985. Agent: George Lane, William Morris Agency, 1350 Avenue of the Americas, New York, New York 10019, U.S.A.

PUBLICATIONS

Plays

The Cote d'Azur Triangle (produced New York, 1980). New York, Vincent FitzGerald, 1985.
The Brides, music by Gary S. Fagin (also director: produced Stockbridge, Massachusetts, 1980; as *Disrobing the Bride*, also director: produced New York, 1981). Published in *Wordplays 2*, New York, Performing Arts Journal Publications, 1982.
Rococo (produced New Haven, Connecticut, 1981).
Andrea Rescued (produced New York, 1982). Montclair, New Jersey, Caliban Press, 1987.
Self Torture and Strenuous Exercise (produced New York, 1982). Published in *The Best Short Plays 1984*, edited by Ramon Delgado, Radnor, Pennsylvania, Chilton, 1984.
Slacks and Tops (produced New York, 1983). New York, Dramatists Play Service, 1983.
Christmas on Mars (produced New York, 1983). New York, Dramatists Play Service, 1983.
The Vampires (produced Seattle, 1984; also director: produced New York, 1984). New York, Dramatists Play Service, 1984.
Linda Her, and The Fairy Garden (produced New York, 1984). New York, Dramatists Play Service, 1985.
Anteroom (produced New York, 1985). New York, Dramatists Play Service, 1985.

Television Play: *Clara Toil*, 1982.

Novel

The Whore of Tjampuan. New York, Performing Arts Journal Publications, 1987.

Verse

The Death of Understanding. Montclair, New Jersey, Caliban Press, 1986.

*

Theatrical Activities:
Director: **Plays**—*The Brides*, Stockbridge, Massachusetts, 1980; *Disrobing the Bride*, New York, 1981; *The Vampires*, New York, 1984; *Rich Relations* by David Henry Hwang, New York, 1986.

* * *

With just a handful of plays, Harry Kondoleon has mapped out a territory where the brittle wit of high comedy of manners and the breakneck plot-twists of farce fuse with the primal fears, monstrous egotism, and logic of dreams. There, the bedrock of social existence—loving partnerships, family life, the company of friends—are depicted as barely preferable to purgatory. There is no suggestion that these are bourgeois constraints. The elemental world—as represented by children (dead and alive) and fairies—is viewed as damaged and damaging. No one is innocent in this world. Salvation is not a possibility. It is a measure of Kondoleon's unique—one is tempted to say warped—perspective that all this is presented as hilarious.

A voice out of bedlam wailing of love and loss, to the formal rhythm of the tango: this is Screamin' Jay Hawkins's rendition of "I Put a Spell on You." This song is integral to *The Vampires* (but could serve as anthem to any Kondoleon play). Zivia, a zombie 13-year-old, plays it as she wanders around her aunt and uncle's chic home, mainlining heroin and wondering what happened to her brother. Dispatching her to an ashram only creates new problems. Meanwhile, her elders are establishing aberrant and obnoxious behaviour as normative. Particularly notable is Uncle Ian, who has taken to sleeping during the day and biting his wife in the neck at night.

Linda Her is set in a sparse bedroom on a humid night in a summer cottage upstate somewhere. Carol walks out on her sleeping husband, his daughter, her best friend. She does this because Linda Her, the most popular girl in her husband's nursery class, died. Some years ago. ". . . I picture her so clearly. This very beautiful, bright girl, who everyone likes, with her whole life ahead of her and then one day many years later boom you find out she doesn't exist anymore—isn't that scary?" asks Carol. And goes.

Linda Her is the curtain raiser and complement to *The Fairy Garden*. The stark bedroom is replaced with a lush garden and the ornate lives of its inhabitants. Mimi and Roman are men and lovers and best friends with Dagny who is married to Boris, but he is old and ugly and she wants to live with her boyfriend The Mechanic. So Dagny cuts off Boris's head. Luckily a fairy appears who restores Boris's head to his shoulders and elopes with him. (The Fairy, it should be noted, is more fond of diamonds than Zsa Zsa Gabor and charges for wishes granted.) Mimi leaves Roman for Dagny which leaves The Mechanic to seduce Roman except that Roman prefers the agony of being alone to the pain of being dependent and vulnerable.

This is soap opera taken to demented and dislocating extremes. Everyone acts out of boredom, malice, and self-interest, communicating only to feed and confirm their obsessive urges. "I thought Boris was kind of cute in a boyish innocent kind of way, and he'd be fun to kiss and hold for a few minutes," the Fairy tells Roman while predicting that Mimi and Dagny—who have torn Roman's world apart—will be together, "A week, two weeks, maybe even a month." Kondoleon takes groups at crisis point, but though the group fragments and realigns, no change occurs. The pace merely accelerates.

When asked his wish, Roman (Kondoleon's most fully realized character) replies, "I want the world to disappear," and—in a remarkable visual coup—the Fairy (kind of) obliges. Like Carol's flight into the unknown or Ian's vampirism, Roman is yearning for a state of otherness, in a world where death—or at least oblivion—is preferable to life suffused with loss.

This does not sound like the stuff of comedy. Yet there has been no playwright this side of Joe Orton who relishes the awfulness of people in the way Kondoleon does. This mordant delight is contagious. There is also the vicarious thrill of observing characters totally unfettered by propriety. Best of all there is the dialogue, where the barbed wisecrack and the hysterical outburst attain new heights of elegance and wit. With all this to delight in, it is a shame that there is a tinge of misogyny. For no apparent reason, the female characters are even more horrendous than the male.

Kondoleon's outlandish vision is usually taken as satirical but could equally be his perception of reality. This ambiguity only serves to make the plays more complex and interesting. Like the creature in *Alien*, Kondoleon has burst forth, spewing the entrails of American domestic comedy in his wake. He is the most arresting playwright at work in America today.

—Joss Bennathan

KOPIT, Arthur (Lee). American. Born in New York City, 10 May 1937. Educated at Lawrence High School, New York, graduated 1955; Harvard University, Cambridge, Massachusetts, A.B. (cum laude) 1959 (Phi Beta Kappa). Married to Leslie Ann Garis; two sons and one daughter. Playwright-in-residence, Wesleyan University, Middletown, Connecticut, 1975–76; Adjunct Professor of Playwriting (CBS fellowship), 1977–80, Yale University, New Haven, Connecticut. Since 1982 has taught playwriting workshop at City College, New York. Since 1982 Council member, Dramatists Guild. Recipient: Vernon Rice award, 1962; Outer Circle award, 1962; Guggenheim fellowship, 1967; Rockefeller grant, 1968, 1977; American Academy award, 1971; National Endowment for the Arts grant, 1974; Wesleyan University Center for the Humanities fellowship, 1974; Italia prize, for radio play, 1979. Lives in Connecticut. Agent: Luis Sanjurjo, International Creative Management, 40 West 57th Street, New York, New York 10019, U.S.A.

PUBLICATIONS

Plays

The Questioning of Nick (produced Cambridge, Massachusetts, 1957; New York, 1974; London, 1981). Included in *The Day the Whores Came Out to Play Tennis and Other Plays*, 1965.

Gemini (produced Cambridge, Massachusetts, 1957).

Don Juan in Texas, with Wally Lawrence (produced Cambridge, Massachusetts, 1957).

On the Runway of Life, You Never Know What's Coming Off Next (produced Cambridge, Massachusetts, 1957).

Across the River and into the Jungle (produced Cambridge, Massachusetts, 1958).

To Dwell in a Place of Strangers, Act 1 published in *Harvard Advocate* (Cambridge, Massachusetts), May 1958.

Aubade (produced Cambridge, Massachusetts, 1958).

Sing to Me Through Open Windows (produced Cambridge, Massachusetts, 1959; revised version produced New York, 1965; London, 1976). Included in *The Day the Whores Came Out to Play Tennis and Other Plays*, 1965.

Oh Dad, Poor Dad, Mamma's Hung You in the Closet and I'm Feelin' So Sad: A Pseudoclassical Tragifarce in a Bastard French Tradition (produced Cambridge, Massachusetts, 1960; London, 1961; New York, 1962). New York, Hill and Wang, 1960; London, Methuen, 1962.

Mhil'daim (produced New York, 1963).

Asylum; or, What the Gentlemen Are Up To, And As for the Ladies (produced New York, 1963; *And As for the Ladies* produced, as *Chamber Music*, London, 1971). *Chamber Music* published in *The Day the Whores Came Out to Play Tennis and Other Plays*, 1965.

The Conquest of Everest (produced New York, 1964; London, 1980). Included in *The Day the Whores Came Out to Play Tennis and Other Plays*, 1965.

The Hero (produced New York, 1964; London, 1972). Included in *The Day the Whores Came Out to Play Tennis and Other Plays*, 1965.

The Day the Whores Came Out to Play Tennis (produced Cambridge, Massachusetts, 1964; New York, 1965). Included in *The Day the Whores Came Out to Play Tennis and Other Plays*, 1965.

The Day the Whores Came Out to Play Tennis and Other Plays. New York, Hill and Wang, 1965; as *Chamber Music and Other Plays*, London, Methuen, 1969.

Indians (produced London, 1968; Washington, D.C., and New York, 1969). New York, Hill and Wang, 1969; London, Methuen, 1970.

An Incident in the Park, in *Pardon Me, Sir, But Is My Eye Hurting Your Elbow?*, edited by Bob Booker and George Foster. New York, Geis, 1968.

What's Happened to the Thorne's House (produced Peru, Vermont, 1972).

Louisiana Territory; or, Lewis and Clark—Lost and Found (also director: produced Middletown, Connecticut, 1975).

Secrets of the Rich (produced Waterford, Connecticut, 1976). New York, Hill and Wang, 1978.

Wings (broadcast 1977; produced New Haven, Connecticut, and New York, 1978; London, 1979). New York, Hill and Wang, 1978; London, Eyre Methuen, 1979.

Nine (book), music and lyrics by Maury Yeston, from an adaptation by Mario Fratti of the screenplay *8½* by Federico Fellini (produced Waterford, Connecticut, 1981; New York, 1982). New York, French, 1983.
Good Help Is Hard to Find (produced New York, 1981). New York, French, 1982.
Ghosts, adaptation of a play by Ibsen (produced New York, 1982; Southampton, 1986). New York, French, 1984.
End of the World (produced New York, 1984; as *The Assignment*, produced Southampton, 1985). New York, Hill and Wang, and London, French, 1984.

Radio Play: *Wings*, 1977.

Television Plays: *The Conquest of Television*, 1966; *Promontory Point Revisited*, 1969.

*

Bibliography: *Ten Modern American Playwrights* by Kimball King, New York, Garland, 1982.

Critical Study: *Sam Shepard, Arthur Kopit, and the Off Broadway Theater* by Doris Auerbach, Boston, Twayne, 1982.

Theatrical Activities:
Director: **Plays**—*Oh Dad, Poor Dad, Mamma's Hung You in the Closet and I'm Feelin' So Sad*, Paris, 1963; *Louisiana Territory*, Middletown, Connecticut, 1975. **Television**—*The Questioning of Nick*, 1959.

* * *

"Do I exaggerate?" asks Michael Trent in his first speech in *End of the World*. "Of course. That is my method. I am a playwright." The line is a comic one which becomes ironic in the face of a theme—the prospect of global annihilation—which turns even the grandest theatrical exaggeration into austere understatement. Out of context, the words provide a suitable description of the way Arthur Kopit works.

At 23, fresh out of Harvard, Kopit escaped—or appeared to escape—the cocoon of university production when *Oh Dad, Poor Dad, Mamma's Hung You in the Closet and I'm Feelin' So Sad* was published by a house that specializes in serious drama and went on to production in London and New York. A fashionable success, it established Kopit as a dramatist, but it also saddled him with the label "undergraduate playwright" which stayed with him long after the playfulness of *Oh Dad* had given way to the mixed-genre method that marks his best and most complex plays. One reason the epithet stuck is that the work that immediately followed *Oh Dad* lacked the flash of that play and offered little substance in consolation. *The Day the Whores Came Out to Play Tennis and Other Plays*, which contained some of his student work along with his post-*Oh Dad* efforts, seemed to confirm the critics who saw him simply as a clever young man noodling around.

Such a judgment is far too dismissive. Although some of *Oh Dad*'s games—the parody references to Tennessee Williams, for instance—seem too cute in retrospect, it is an early indication of the dramatic virtues that have become increasingly apparent in Kopit's work: a facility with language, an ear for the clichés of art and life, an eye for the effective stage image (the waltz scene in which Madame Rosepettle breaks Commodore Roseabove, for instance), a strategic use of caricature, the talent for being funny about a subject that is not at all comic. All of these are in evidence in *Oh Dad* and all of them are in the service of a serious theme (or one that seemed serious in 1960)—the emasculation of the American male by the too protective mother, the iron-maiden temptress and the little girl as seducer.

In an interview in *Mademoiselle* (August 1962), Kopit said, "Comedy is a very powerful tool . . . You take the most serious thing you can think of and treat it as comically as you can." Although he invoked Shaw, *Oh Dad* is the immediate reference. Since then, he has thought of more serious things—war, death, nuclear destruction—and has treated them seriously. And comically, as *Indians* and *End of the World* indicate. The Bantam edition of *Indians* (1971) prints a long interview with John Lahr in which Kopit identifies his play as a response to "the madness of our involvement in Vietnam," but he chose to approach the subject obliquely, going back to the eviction of the American Indian from his land. The play shows the distance between official words and deeds, the power of platitude and the way in which myths are made and used. The central figure is Buffalo Bill, who begins as a friend of the Indians and ends—a star of his own show—as an apologist for slaughter. The play moves back and forth between comic and serious scenes, from the broad farce of the play within the play and the cartoon Ol' Time President to the powerful accusatory ending in which the Wild West Show is invaded by the dead Indians. For some, the funny scenes fit uncomfortably with the solemn subject matter, but they are not simply entertaining decoration. The comedy is thematic. The disastrous production of the Ned Buntline melodrama at the White House is both an instance of the creation of myth and a critique of it.

End of the World is a similar fusion of genres. It concerns a playwright who is commissioned to write a play about the dangers of nuclear proliferation—as Kopit was, in fact—and finds that he can only do so by writing a play about a playwright who . . . The parody private-eye frame of the play (the playwright as detective), the agents' lunch at the Russian Tea Room and the three interviews in which the rationale of nuclear stockpiling and scenarios of destruction are presented as comic turns are all central to the play's assumption that there are personal, artistic, and official ways of not facing up to the impending horror. What Michael Trent learns in the play is that all the nuclear strategists know the situation is hopeless but do not believe what they know, and that he was chosen to write the play because, like the men he interviews, he has an attraction to evil and destruction. A painful and funny play, it provides no solution, only an insistence on the probability of catastrophe and, unlike the conventional post-bomb melodrama, no promise of rebirth.

If *Indians* and *End of the World* share dramatic method, *Wings* is an indication of Kopit's unpredictability. There are funny lines in the play, but it is primarily a lyric exploration of death. It is about a woman who suffers a stroke, struggles to make her fragmented speech fit her still coherent thoughts and, after a second stroke, becomes eloquent as she sees herself flying into the unknown. A wing-walker in her youth, her profession/art provides the main metaphor for her final sense of exhilarating discovery. The play evokes both the concerned narrowness of medicine's perception of the woman and the imagination that continues to carry her above her stammering exasperation with herself and those around her. It is an indication—along with *Indians* and *End of the World*—that Kopit is wing-walking far above the bravura flight of *Oh Dad*.

—Gerald Weales

KOPS, Bernard. British. Born in London, 28 November 1926. Educated in London elementary schools to age 13. Married Erica Gordon in 1956; four children. Has worked as a docker, chef, salesman, waiter, lift man, and barrow boy. Writer-in-residence, London Borough of Hounslow, 1980–82; Lecturer in Drama, Spiro Institute, 1984–85. Recipient: Arts Council bursary 1957, 1975; C. Day Lewis fellowship, 1980. Agent: David Higham Associates, 5–8 Lower John Street, London W1R 4HA. Address: 35 Canfield Gardens, Flat 1, London N.W.6, England.

PUBLICATIONS

Plays

The Hamlet of Stepney Green (produced Oxford, London and New York, 1958). London, Evans, 1959.
Goodbye World (produced Guildford, Surrey, 1959).
Change for the Angel (produced London, 1960).
The Dream of Peter Mann (produced Edinburgh, 1960). London, Penguin, 1960.
Stray Cats and Empty Bottles (produced Cambridge, 1961; London, 1967).
Enter Solly Gold, music by Stanley Myers (produced Wellingborough, Northamptonshire, and Los Angeles, 1962; London, 1970). Published in *Satan, Socialites, and Solly Gold: Three New Plays from England*, New York, Coward McCann, 1961; in *Four Plays*, 1964.
Home Sweet Honeycomb (broadcast 1962). Included in *Four Plays*, 1964.
The Lemmings (broadcast 1963). Included in *Four Plays*, 1964.
Four Plays (includes *The Hamlet of Stepney Green, Enter Solly Gold, Home Sweet Honeycomb, The Lemmings*). London, MacGibbon and Kee, 1964.
The Boy Who Wouldn't Play Jesus (for children; produced London, 1965). Published in *Eight Plays: Book 1*, edited by Malcolm Stuart Fellows, London, Cassell, 1965.
David, It Is Getting Dark (produced Rennes, France, 1970). Paris, Gallimard, 1970.
It's a Lovely Day Tomorrow, with John Goldschmidt (televised 1975; produced London, 1976).
More Out Than In (produced on tour and London, 1980).
Ezra (produced London, 1981).
Simon at Midnight (broadcast 1982; produced London, 1985).

Radio Plays: *Home Sweet Honeycomb*, 1962; *The Lemmings*, 1963; *Born in Israel*, 1963; *The Dark Ages*, 1964; *Israel: The Immigrant*, 1964; *Bournemouth Nights*, 1979; *I Grow Old, I Grow Old*, 1979; *Over the Rainbow*, 1980; *Simon at Midnight*, 1982; *Trotsky Was My Father*, 1984.

Television Plays: *I Want to Go Home*, 1963; *The Lost Years of Brian Hooper*, 1967; *Alexander the Greatest*, 1971; *Just One Kid*, 1974; *Why the Geese Shrieked*, and *The Boy Philosopher*, from stories by Isaac Bashevis Singer, 1974; *It's a Lovely Day Tomorrow*, with John Goldschmidt, 1975; *Moss*, 1975; *Rocky Marciano Is Dead*, 1976; *Night Kids*, 1983.

Novels

Awake for Mourning. London, MacGibbon and Kee, 1958.
Motorbike. London, New English Library, 1962.
Yes from No-Man's Land. London, MacGibbon and Kee, 1965; New York, Coward McCann, 1966.
The Dissent of Dominick Shapiro. London, MacGibbon and Kee, 1966; New York, Coward McCann, 1967.
By the Waters of Whitechapel. London, Bodley Head, 1969; New York, Norton, 1970.
The Passionate Past of Gloria Gaye. London, Secker and Warburg, 1971; New York, Norton, 1972.
Settle Down Simon Katz. London, Secker and Warburg, 1973.
Partners. London, Secker and Warburg, 1975.
On Margate Sands. London, Secker and Warburg, 1978.

Verse

Poems. London, Bell and Baker Press, 1955.
Poems and Songs. Northwood, Middlesex, Scorpion Press, 1958.
An Anemone for Antigone. Lowestoft, Suffolk, Scorpion Press, 1959.
Erica, I Want to Read You Something. Lowestoft, Suffolk, Scorpion Press, and New York, Walker, 1967.
For the Record. London, Secker and Warburg, 1971.

Other

The World Is a Wedding (autobiography). London, MacGibbon and Kee, 1963; New York, Coward McCann, 1964.
Neither Your Honey nor Your Sting: An Offbeat History of the Jews. London, Robson, 1985.

Editor, *Poetry Hounslow.* London, Hounslow Civic Centre, 1981.

*

Manuscript Collections: University of Texas, Austin; Indiana University, Bloomington.

* * *

Bernard Kops's work is informed by tension between the despair—not for himself, but for humanity—from which suicide beckons, and a redeeming joy of life. Contradictions inform such poems as "Shalom Bomb," "Sorry for the Noise—We're Dancing," and "First Poem," which injoins "let's dance upon the desolation." Despite his clarity of vision about the mess we're making of the world and the death which awaits us—necessarily as individuals, with increasing probability collectively as well—Kops's celebratory rejoinder sets to dancing the feet of those high-spirited people who populate his novels and poems and plays.

Although occasionally mislabeled a kitchen-sink realist, Kops writes neither gritty nor cozy domestic drama. More often presentational than representational, offering parables upon human nature, his plays are theatrical poetry employing language—in its rhythms, rhymes, word play, and word choice—and conflicts not so much contemporary as timeless.

Unlike other "poetic" playwrights, however, Kops creates not a rarefied atmosphere but robust crackpots, energetic con-artists and their gullible targets, and colorful characters whose values he satirizes even as he nudges them towards reform and affirmation of life. A writer poised between tears and laughter, Kops has increasingly emphasized palpable passion; of late he leaves spectators more often touched than chuckling.

Kops frequently depicts old people made anxious by mortality, yet he emphasizes the imperative to live. Although such plays as *Just One Kid, Change for the Angel, Goodbye World*, and *It's a Lovely Day Tomorrow* don't flinch from death snatching people prematurely or tempting them to end their own lives, Kops holds up those characters who harbor a death wish as negative examples not to be emulated. Thus Danny Todd's initial respect for independent lives in *Home Sweet Honeycomb* is commendable, and his ultimate embrace of the firing squad which killed his brother signifies his dehumanization. Sam Levy and Peter Mann both learn through their skirmishes with death to embrace life. Appreciating only on his death bed that he's let life slip by, Sam in *The Hamlet of Stepney Green* returns as a ghost to inspire love of life in his son. Peter Mann grows from a lad convinced nothing's worth living for to exuberance about life. An anti-nuclear and anti-war play, *The Dream of Peter Mann* makes a compelling argument against mass destruction; life is worth living. The remarkable black comedy *The Lemmings* likewise carries in its criticism of suicide implicit affirmation. After Norman and Iris follow their parents into the water, the sound of seagulls and sea devastates us because they should have lived.

Frequently Kops dramatizes means of surviving bereavement or failure. Moss chooses life in the face of grief for his beloved grandson. Moss survives by taking up painting and giving away his money, while Harry of *Rocky Marciano Is Dead* maintains his independence by nurturing the potential of a black boxer. *The Lost Years of Brian Hooper* and *Simon at Midnight* likewise demonstrate the efficacy of hopes and dreams in combating futility and fear of death; without them, life is meaningless.

Repeatedly interfering with these characters' happiness are their wealth and/or greed. The miser Moss has agonized over the loss of his sweet-shop profits to thieving kids; his salvation lies in divesting himself of his fortune. Sam Levy and Peter Mann have been distracted from life's beauty by pursuit of riches from pickled-herring or shrouds. The successful right-wing writer in *David, It Is Getting Dark* is driven so far as to plagiarize the work of a Jewish writer living in penury. The title character of *Enter Solly Gold*, as he fleeces a family of vulgar snobs, releases them from materialism to enjoyment of life. *The Boy Who Wouldn't Play Jesus* dramatizes a Christmas lesson about giving which turns the boy into a social activist. Distressed that Christianity "hasn't really happened yet," he appeals to the cast members' consciences and cancels the nativity play. As long as children are starving, Jesus cannot be born.

For many years Kops's work displayed ambivalence towards women. Although occasionally rapturous about romantic love, Kops gives David Levy and Peter Mann traditional women who want nothing in life but to sacrifice themselves for their mates. His men most often are hen-pecked or neglected or part of a bickering couple in a marriage not exactly made in heaven. His sons fall victim to overbearing mothers who smother them or even—in *Home Sweet Honeycomb* and *The Lemmings*—send them to their deaths. Such stereotypes of domineering mothers and controlling wives have, however, given way in several recent Kops plays to more fully developed women. The runaway in *Night Kids* who resorts to prostitution to survive inspires compassion both when she's on the streets and as she returns to her indifferent parents. Leading female characters in the unproduced *Some of These Days* (about Sophie Tucker) and *Kafe Kropotkin* (about an anarchist collective) even show signs of autonomy and competence.

Kops's masterpiece *Ezra* attempts to reconcile Ezra Pound's poetic genius with the fascism and anti-semitism he espoused. Playful in tone and fluid in structure, *Ezra* dramatizes Pound's postwar imprisonment. Mocking his situation and those who accuse him of treason with snatches of pop songs, Pound chats with Mussolini and Vivaldi. Not a one-dimensional villain, Pound argues in his defense: "A poet listens to his own voice." Implicitly, Kops condemns the confiscation of Pound's literary manuscripts as evidence and defends his right to free expression. After his release, troubled by his former views, Pound goes to the Ghetto Vecchio in Venice, where he appeals to the Jews there to vouch for him. As he is answered only by the wind, Pound cannot understand why the houses are empty. Kops appears to forgive the poet's complicity in genocide out of a humanity which the poet cannot discover in himself until too late, when Pound reaches a chilling anagnorisis, a recognition that those Jews he loved have perished because of policies he championed.

—Tish Dace

KOUTOUKAS, H.M. American. Born in Endicott, New York, 4 June 1947. Educated at Harpur College, Binghamton, New York; Maria Ley-Piscator Dramatic Workshop, New School for Social Research, New York, 1962–65; Universalist Life Church, Modesto, California, Ph.D. Associated with the Electric Circus and other theatre groups in New York; founder Chamber Theatre Group, New York. Recipient: Obie award, 1966; National Arts Club award; Professional Theatre Wing award. Agent: Nino Karlweis, 250 East 65th Street, New York, New York 10021. Address: c/o Judson Church, Washington Square, New York, New York 10012, U.S.A.

PUBLICATIONS

Plays

The Last Triangle (produced New York, 1965).
Tidy Passions; or, Kill, Kaleidoscope, Kill (produced New York, 1965). Published in *More Plays from Off-Off-Broadway*, edited by Michael T. Smith, Indianapolis, Bobbs Merrill, 1972.
All Day for a Dollar (produced New York, 1966).
Medea (produced New York, 1966).
Only a Countess (produced New York, 1966).
A Letter from Colette (also director: produced New York, 1966).
Pomegranada, music by Al Carmines (produced New York, 1966).
With Creatures Make My Way (produced New York, 1967).
When Clowns Play Hamlet (also director: produced New York, 1967).
View from Sorrento (produced New York, 1967).
Howard Kline Trilogy (produced New York, 1968).
Christopher at Sheridan Squared (produced New York, 1971).
French Dressing (revue), with others (produced New York, 1974).
Grandmother Is in the Strawberry Patch (produced New York, 1974).

The Pinotti Papers (produced New York, 1975).
One Man's Religion (produced New York, 1975).
Star Followers in an Ancient Land, music by Tom O'Horgan and Gale Garnett (also director: produced New York, 1975).
The Legend of Sheridan Square (produced New York, 1976).
Turtles Don't Dream (also director: produced New York, 1977).
Too Late for Yogurt (also director: produced New York, 1978).
The Butterfly Encounter, music by David Forman (produced New York, 1978).

*

Theatrical Activities:
Director: **Plays**—several of his own plays.

* * *

H.M. Koutoukas wrote a very large number of plays—several dozen—in the decade beginning about 1963. Most of them he produced himself in a wide variety of situations. He is the quintessential off-off-Broadway dramatist: in addition to showing his work in the usual coffee houses, churches, and lofts, he put on plays in art galleries, concert halls, movie theatres, and, on commission, at parties as private entertainment for the rich. He gained a considerable though largely underground following, but this did not bring him readier access to stages. The theatre scene has changed, there is less personal rapport between producers and artists, more commercial pressure, and since the mid-1970's Koutoukas's output has declined.

His plays have a special tone and flavor that are all his own and immediately recognizable. He often writes in verse, and the characters and situations are the product of a highly fanciful imagination and an elaborately refined sensibility. Most of his plays are designated "camps" rather than drama or comedies, and the style is flamboyantly romantic, idiosyncratic, sometimes self-satirizing, full of private references and inside jokes, precious, boldly aphoristic, and disdainful of restrictions of sense, taste, or fashion. Koutoukas is perhaps the last of the aesthetes. Underlying the decoration, his characteristic themes concern people or creatures who have become so strange that they have lost touch with ordinary life, yet their feelings are all the more tender and vulnerable—the deformed, the demented, the rejected, the perverse.

Medea is an adaptation of the Greek play in which the action is set in a laundromat, and in the author's production Medea was played by a man. On the surface a ridiculous notion, the play vividly articulates the situation of a woman from a more primitive, natural, expressive culture trapped among the over-civilized, calculating Greeks and conveys a sympathetic insight into her desperation. The characters in *Tidy Passions; or, Kill, Kaleidoscope, Kill* include a high priestess and several witches of a broken-down cobra cult, a dying dove, Narcissus, and Jean Harlow, who proclaims, "Glamour is dead." *With Creatures Make My Way* is set in a sewer where the single character, neither man nor woman, finally consummates an eternal love with a passing lobster. *A Letter from Colette*, in the naturalistic mode, sweetly tells of romance between an aging woman and a handsome young delivery boy. *Pomegranada* opens in the Garden of Eden and is about tarnish. *Christopher at Sheridan Squared* is an hallucinatory documentary about the Greenwich Village street where Koutoukas has lived for years.

These are some of the exotic and poignant special worlds that Koutoukas creates and explores. His plays are heroic in spirit and fiercely compassionate. He should be remembered as one of the most original dramatists of his time.

—Michael T. Smith

KRAUSS, Ruth (Ida). American. Born in Baltimore, Maryland, 25 July 1911. Educated in public elementary schools; at Peabody Institute of Music, Baltimore; New School for Social Research, New York; Maryland Institute of Art, Baltimore; Parsons School of Art, New York, graduate. Married David Johnson Leisk (i.e., the writer Crockett Johnson) in 1940 (died 1975). Address: c/o Scholastic Books, 730 Broadway, New York, New York 10003, U.S.A.

PUBLICATIONS

Poem-Plays

The Cantilever Rainbow. New York, Pantheon, 1965.
There's a Little Ambiguity Over There among the Bluebells and Other Theatre Poems. New York, Something Else Press, 1968.
If Only. Eugene, Oregon, Toad Press, 1969.
Under Twenty. Eugene, Oregon, Toad Press, 1970.
Love and the Invention of Punctuation. Lenox, Massachusetts, Bookstore Press, 1973.
This Breast Gothic. Lenox, Massachusetts, Bookstore Press, 1973.
If I Were Freedom (produced Annandale-on-Hudson, New York, 1976).
Re-examination of Freedom (produced Boston, 1976). West Branch, Iowa, Toothpaste Press, 1981.
Under 13. Lenox, Massachusetts, Bookstore Press, 1976.
When I Walk I Change the Earth. Providence, Rhode Island, Burning Deck, 1978.
Small Black Lambs Wandering in the Red Poppies (produced New York, 1982).
Ambiguity 2nd (produced Boston, 1985).

Productions include *A Beautiful Day, There's a Little Ambiguity Over There among the Bluebells, Re-Examination of Freedom, Newsletter, The Cantilever Rainbow, In a Bull's Eye, Pineapple Play, Quartet, A Show, A Play—It's a Girl!, Onward, Duet* (or *Yellow Umbrella*), *Drunk Boat, If Only, This Breast*, many with music by Al Carmines, Bill Dixon, and Don Heckman, produced in New York, New Haven, Boston, and other places, since 1964.

Fiction (for children)

A Good Man and His Good Wife. New York, Harper, 1944; revised edition, 1962.
The Carrot Seed. New York, Harper, 1945.
The Great Duffy. New York, Harper, 1946.
The Growing Story. New York, Harper, 1947.
Bears. New York, Harper, 1948.
The Happy Day. New York, Harper, 1949.
The Big World and the Little House. New York, Schuman, 1949.
The Backward Day. New York, Harper, and London, Hamish Hamilton, 1950.

The Bundle Book. New York, Harper, 1951.
A Hole Is to Dig: A First Book of First Definitions. New York, Harper, 1952; London, Hamish Hamilton, 1963.
A Very Special House. New York, Harper, 1953.
I'll Be You and You Be Me. New York, Harper, 1954.
How to Make an Earthquake. New York, Harper, 1954.
Charlotte and the White Horse. New York, Harper, 1955; London, Bodley Head, 1977.
Is This You? New York, Scott, 1955.
I Want to Paint My Bathroom Blue. New York, Harper, 1956.
The Birthday Party. New York, Harper, 1957.
Monkey Day. New York, Harper 1957.
Somebody Else's Nut Tree and Other Tales from Children. New York, Harper, 1958.
A Moon or a Button. New York, Harper, 1959.
Open House for Butterflies. New York, Harper, and London, Hamish Hamilton, 1960.
"Mama, I Wish I Was Snow" "Child, You'd Be Very Cold." New York, Atheneum, 1962.
Eye Nose Fingers Toes. New York, Harper, 1964.
The Little King, The Little Queen, The Little Monster, and Other Stories You Can Make Up Yourself, illustrated by the author. New York, Scholastic, 1966.
This Thumbprint: Words and Thumbprints, illustrated by the author. New York, Harper, 1967.
Little Boat Lighter Than a Cork. Westport, Connecticut, and New York, Magic Circle Press-Walker, 1976.
Minestrone: A Ruth Krauss Selection, illustrated by the author. New York, Greenwillow, 1981.

Verse (for children)

I Can Fly. New York, Simon and Schuster, 1950.
A Bouquet of Littles. New York, Harper, 1963.
What a Fine Day for . . ., music by Al Carmines. New York, Parents' Magazine Press, 1967.
I Write It. New York, Harper, 1970.
Everything under a Mushroom. New York, Four Winds Press, 1974.
Somebody Spilled the Sky. New York, Greenwillow, 1979.

*

Manuscript Collection: Dupont School, Wilmington, Delaware.

Ruth Krauss comments:

All the "works"—or "plays"—are essentially poems—with an approach from the words themselves, rather than ideas, plot, etc. (This division cannot be made in so cut-and-dried a fashion.) The interpretation is *mostly* left completely to the director—i.e., one line can be made to take dozens of forms in actual presentation.

Part of the philosophy behind this is: say *anything*—and leave it to the director to see what happens. This does not always work out for the best—depending on the director.

* * *

The nature of Ruth Krauss's work is that it is bursting with health, bursting with greenery, with fresh promise. This nutritional assault, this vitality asserts itself beyond all the emotions of the day, all of which, sadness, wistfulness, and hilarity, appear ephemeral beside the steady residue of glowing good health.

But health seems to issue from a steadying optimism and a kind of bravery, an ability to look the universe in the eye. Nothing cannot be looked at, nothing is so awful that it cannot be faced, perhaps mended, always accepted.

But the world that she sees appears to be without serious menace, without horror; it appears to be essentially benign, so that in effect what Krauss faces is what she perhaps nearsightedly envisions. The bursting sense to her work is matched by a quieter sense, one of comic wistfulness. And one of whimsy. The world viewed in comic tranquillity.

I recall a series of Krauss whimsies. A number of years ago the Hardware Poets, long since gone not only from Manhattan but from the planet, presented an evening of her works which, if memory doesn't betray me, had the generic term of seven-second plays. I may be inventing this name but they certainly *felt* like seven-second plays. They were little, exploding, comic pellets which appeared exploded and disappeared in dazzling succession for many long minutes. Or what appeared, to be many long minutes. They were delightful charmers, about nothing that I can now possibly recall, except the essential sense of them—comic energy organisms, dramatic meteorites which lasted long enough to be retained forever in the spirit.

My sense of Krauss's work is that it consists of fragmented interruptions in the more sombre concourse of human events, healthy winks from over the fence. The fragments give off the sense also of interrupting shards of sunlight in a universe grown perceptibly greyer as the years go on. Here are excerpts from a Krauss fragment, a monologue called *If Only* which Florence Tarlow, a performer with an especially dry wit, delivered with comic gravity at the Judson Poets Theatre in New York:

If only I was a nightingale singing
If only I was on my second don't-live-like-a-pig week
If only the sun wasn't always rising behind the next hill
If only I was the flavor of tarragon
If only I was phosphorescence and a night phenomena at sea
If only Old Drainpipe Rensaleer as we used to call him hadn't hit bottom in Detroit the time he made a fancy dive and got absentminded and forget to turn and all his shortribs got stove in he got sucked down the drainpipe because the grate wasn't on
If only I didn't have to get up and let our dog out now
If only the glorious day in April because it has no beginning or end that all Flatbush had awaited impatiently between creation and construction had come
If only I was Joyce and had written Finnegans Wake only then I'd be gone

If only somebody would kiss me on the back of the neck right now

If only those degraded bastards hadn't monkeyed around with the Oreo Sandwich pattern

Krauss is a playwright to turn to when both the flesh and spirit grow weak.

—Arthur Sainer

KUREISHI, Hanif. British. Born in London, 5 December 1954. Educated at King's College, University of London, B.A. in philosophy. Writer-in-residence, Royal Court Theatre, London, 1981 and 1985–86. Recipient: George Devine Award,

1981; *Evening Standard* award, for screenplay, 1985. Agent: Sheila Lemon, Lemon and Durbridge Ltd., 24 Pottery Lane, London W11 4LZ, England.

PUBLICATIONS

Plays

Soaking the Heat (produced London, 1976).
The Mother Country (produced London, 1980).
The King and Me (produced London, 1980). Included in *Outskirts, The King and Me, Tomorrow—Today!*, 1983.
Outskirts (produced London, 1981). Included in *Outskirts, The King and Me, Tomorrow—Today!*, 1983.
Tomorrow—Today! (produced London, 1981). Included in *Outskirts, The King and Me, Tomorrow—Today!*, 1983.
Cinders, from a play by Janusz Glowacki (produced London, 1981).
Borderline (produced London, 1981). London, Methuen, 1981.
Artists and Admirers, with David Leveaux, from a play by Alexander Ostrovsky (produced London, 1982).
Birds of Passage (produced London, 1983). Oxford, Amber Lane Press, 1983.
Outskirts, The King and Me, Tomorrow—Today! London, Calder, and New York, Riverrun Press, 1983.
Mother Courage, adaptation of a play by Brecht (produced London, 1984).
My Beautiful Laundrette (screenplay; includes essay "The Rainbow Sign"). London, Faber, 1986.
Sammy and Rosie Get Laid (screenplay). London, Faber, 1988.

Screenplays: *My Beautiful Laundrette*, 1985; *Sammy and Rosie Get Laid*, 1988.

Radio Plays: *You Can't Go Home*, 1980; *The Trial*, from a novel by Kafka, 1982.

* * *

Hanif Kureishi is often assumed to be a purely Asian writer, but for the most part his earlier plays look at events through the eyes of characters who are white. Kureishi himself was born in London of mixed parentage, with an English mother and Pakistani father. He grew up without feeling that he was different from his classmates and has always thought of himself as an Englishman. However, the need for an Asian voice in contemporary theatre and the current concern with problems that affect Asians have caused him to examine that other aspect of his heritage.

After two early plays produced in 1980, *The Mother Country* at Riverside Studios and *The King and Me* (about a couple's obsession with Elvis Presley) at the Soho Poly, Kureishi's more ambitious play *Outskirts* received a production at the Royal Shakespeare Company Warehouse in 1981. It centres on two men who grew up together in the straggling suburbs around Orpington and on the eventual divergence of their lives. Del, who has always tagged along with the more dominant Bob, makes the break from their dead-end working-class background and trains as a teacher. Bob, who leaves school early for a well-paid job, finds himself on the unemployment scrap-heap. In his bitterness, he turns to the National Front where, he says, "We're strong men, together. Men worn down by waiting. Abused men. Men with no work. Our parents made redundant. Now us. . . ." But the racialism he expresses now is a reminder of an evening ten years ago when he and Del had beaten up a Pakistani. On that occasion, Del had taken the initiative in violence, and the shadow of that incident haunts him now that he is a respectable teacher.

Outskirts has an awkwardness of construction in the way it moves from past to present and back again, and the appearance at intervals of Bob's mother is not always successfully dealt with. But nonetheless, Kureishi gets inside the skin of young men who thought, with the end of school and a wage packet each week, that the world was theirs: "I tell you," says Bob, "it's all waiting for a boy like me. Cars, clothes, crumpet." Kureishi also illuminates the lot of the women. Bob's wife, Maureen, returns from having had an abortion rather than bring up a child in a home with no money, to be told by Bob's mother, who is prematurely old, "You did the right thing. Sometimes I wish I'd done the same. I know it's wicked to say that. But I think it. I do."

In *Borderline*, written after a workshop collaboration with Joint Stock and produced at the Royal Court in 1981, Kureishi turns to the problems of Asian immigrants. The idea of writing about Asians in Britain came from the Court's artistic director, Max Stafford-Clark, and Kureishi was at first nervous of writing from outside his own experience. His misgivings proved unnecessary, and with the combination of several weeks of meeting and talking with Asians in Southall, and the inspiration of his imagination and his own past, he was able to write a play about the Asian dilemma in England. For him, writing about Pakistanis in England is also a way of writing about the English and the way England has changed.

Borderline is concerned with the lives of several Asians who are trying to survive in an indifferent or hostile community. An English observer, Susan, a journalist writing an article on Asians in England, takes the role at times of commentator on what Kureishi himself heard during his research: "All the people I've spoken to have been beaten or burnt or abused at some time. You speak to them, they say they like England, it is democratic, or just or good. And then say what's been done to them here. Such viciousness in England." The play also deals with conflict among the Asians—those who try to maintain an Asian way of life, and those who adopt English morals and attitudes. The parents of Amina decide to send her back to an arranged marriage in Pakistan, but she realises that she has become English and, whether she likes it or not, England is her home.

Birds of Passage deals with a lower middle-class family in Sydenham who have fallen on hard times. There are resonances of *The Cherry Orchard* as the family are forced to sell their house to an Asian former lodger. The father of the family, a self-educated Labour councillor, does not realise times have changed until he loses his job. His daughter, despite her education, has taken to prostitution on the side, and his wife's sister and her husband, at one time affluent on the proceeds of selling central heating, suddenly find that the bottom has dropped out of the market. Kureishi writes about his ineffectual characters with affection, and there is what amounts to a hymn of praise to suburbia from the father. "Out here we live in peace, indifferent to the rest of the world. We have no sense of communal existence but we are tolerant, not cruel." The least sympathetic character is the Asian, Asif, the spoilt, indolent son of rich parents. Asif despises poor Pakistani immigrants and is smugly upwardly mobile. The play is not primarily about racial attitudes, but about the effect of the recession on people in Britain who believed in the optimism of the 1960's and now have to face the workless 1980's.

Kureishi's script for the film *My Beautiful Laundrette* brought him to the attention of a wider public. A small-budget movie, directed by Stephen Frears, it caught the imagination of critics and audiences. Several of the characters and situations of his stage plays are enlarged on here. The outwardly modest but sexually experienced Amina of *Borderline* has her counterpart in the film, as does the amoral young entrepreneur Asif of *Birds of Passage*, while the intense and, in the film's case, homosexual, relationship of the two boys who grew up together echoes the relationship of Del and Bob in *Outskirts*.

—Clare Colvin

LAFFAN, Kevin (Barry). British. Born in Reading, Berkshire, 24 May 1922. Married Jeanne Lilian Thompson in 1952; three sons. Repertory actor and director until 1950; director of productions, Pendragon Company, 1950–52, and Everyman Theatre Company, 1953–58, both Reading. Recipient: ATV Television award, 1959; Irish Life award, 1969; National Union of Students award, 1969; *Sunday Times* award, 1970. Agent: ACTAC (Theatrical and Cinematic) Ltd., 16 Cadogan Lane, London S.W.1, England.

PUBLICATIONS

Plays

Ginger Bred (as Kevin Barry) (produced Reading, 1951).
The Strip-Tease Murder (as Kevin Barry), with Neville Brian (produced Reading, 1955).
Winner Takes All (as Kevin Barry) (produced Reading, 1956).
First Innocent (as Kevin Barry) (produced Reading, 1957).
Angie and Ernie, with Peter Jones (produced Guildford, Surrey, 1966).
Zoo Zoo Widdershins Zoo (produced Leicester, 1969). London, Faber, 1969.
It's a Two-Foot-Six-Inches-above-the-Ground World (produced Bristol, 1969; London, 1970). London, Faber, 1970.
The Superannuated Man (produced Watford, Hertfordshire, 1971).
There Are Humans at the Bottom of My Garden (produced London, 1972).
Adam and Eve and Pinch Me, adaptation of the story by A.E. Coppard (produced East Midlands, 1974).
Never So Good (produced London, 1976).
The Wandering Jew (produced London, 1978).
The Dream of Trevor Staines (produced Chichester, 1983).

Screenplays: *It's a Two-Foot-Six-Inches-above-the-Ground World* (*The Love Ban*), 1973; *The Best Pair of Legs in the Business*, 1973.

Radio Play: *Portrait of an Old Man*, 1961.

Television Plays: *Lucky for Some*, 1969; *The Best Pair of Legs in the Business*, 1969; *You Can Only Buy Once*, 1969; *Castlehaven* series, 1970; *Kate* series, 1970; *A Little Learning*, 1970; *The Designer*, 1971; *Decision to Burn*, 1971; *Fly on the Wall* (trilogy), 1971; *The General*, 1971; *Emmerdale Farm*, 1972, 1977; *Justicer* series, 1973; *The Reformer*, 1973; *Getting Up*, 1973; *Beryl's Lot* series, with Bill McIlwraith, 1973, 1977; *After the Wedding Was Over*, 1975; *It's a Wise Child*, 1975; for Bud Flanagan programme.

* * *

Anybody leaving the theatre after the first performance of Kevin Laffan's *Zoo Zoo Widdershins Zoo* would probably have been amazed to discover that the writer was a man in his forties. Laffan's study of a group of young people—the eldest are in their early twenties—sharing a house and everything in it while refusing to work and turning to petty crime—shop-lifting, robbing telephone booths, and cheating gas meters—when money is scarce, seems to have come exactly out of the way of life it re-creates.

Laffan, however, was born in 1922 and *Zoo Zoo Widdershins Zoo* was his first real success. It won an award from the National Union of Students, which wanted a play for production in universities. If the occasion of the play suggested its theme, only Laffan's complete understanding of his characters, their idioms, attitudes and rejection of social responsibility, can account for the play's authenticity and for its cool, morally neutral tone. It captures and makes comprehensible a gaiety which seems to grow out of the apparently depressing life-style these people have adopted. Cleverly, it is a play entirely about a minute community, and there is a feeling that the audience, as well as the squatters is betrayed when the couple whose house has become a home for the group manoeuvre the others out and, suddenly, revert to conventional bourgeois habits.

Zoo Zoo Widdershins Zoo is almost plotless, carefully designed to seem as aimless as the way of life it observes, and its alternations of intensity and relaxation are all conveyed in the limited, inexplicit dialogue which exploits its young people's idiom.

This was by no means Laffan's first play. He began his career in the theatre as an actor; with others, he helped to found the Everyman Theatre Company in Reading and in 1959 won an award from ATV for a television play *Cut in Ebony* which was never produced because it deals, in terms of comedy, with problems of race and colour. Laffan, abandoning acting and direction, earned the time to write plays by undertaking any other writing that would pay, including a not very successful series of television programmes for the comedian Bud Flanagan. His television plays, *Lucky for Some, You Can Only Buy Once*, and *The Best Pair of Legs in the Business*, however, established him as a playwright in this medium, and *Castlehaven*, a television serial doing for a Yorkshire community what *Coronation Street* did for Lancashire, became a fixed part of commercial television schedules outside London.

Laffan's stage play *Angie and Ernie* was produced outside London. *The Superannuated Man* won an Irish Life award in 1969 but was produced only in 1971. But *Zoo Zoo Widdershins Zoo*, after its university production, was given a successful commercial production in London and impressed the critics, with the result that *It's a Two-Foot-Six-Inches-above-the-Ground World*, first seen at the Theatre Royal, Bristol, was able to travel to London and make a distinct impression there; it considers, in a very individual tone of toughly angry, affectionate hilarity, the effects on a young Catholic husband and wife of their Church's refusal to permit any means of birth control. Catholics complained that Laffan's play misrepresents the Church's attitude, but in its own terms, as a work for the theatre, it is entirely successful.

The marriage of a young Liverpool Catholic is falling into ruins; his wife, a Protestant girl who was converted to Catholicism only in order to marry him, has provided him with three sons; another child would probably kill her, while sexual abstinence, which suits the wife even less than it suits the husband, is destroying the marriage. The voice of the Church is transmitted by a young priest who expresses the Catholic prohibition at its most extreme and unyielding. A totally permissive view is offered by an outsider—a van driver making a delivery at the middle son's Catholic primary school. The father's prudery had prevented him from teaching his children anything about their physical functions, so that the van driver's use of the school lavatory, arousing the child's interest in an adult masculine body, costs the unfortunate driver—an energetic and undeviating lecher—his job.

These people argue their cases with great energy, and the play dresses the situation in continual high spirits. When all else fails, the wife's surreptitiously acquired and so far unused collection of contraceptive pills comes in useful; they can, for example, be mistaken for aspirins. It would not be fair to accuse Laffan of pulling his punches in the interests of good taste or of scrupulous intellectual fairness in his presentation of opposed points of view. He is, however, far more deeply involved through his emotions than through any desire to solve intellectual arguments, and under the hard-edged hilarity of its presentation, there is a touching awareness of the painful situation of two simple, good, likeable people trapped by the husband's earnest conviction.

Laffan's progress has been slow. *There Are Humans at the Bottom of My Garden* did not rival the success of its predecessor, and his later work for television, notably the skillfully written *Emmerdale Farm* and the more predictable *Justicer* series, won a loyal television following without suggesting any of the tougher moral and social implications of his work for the theatre. A handful of television plays and two unusual comedies, differing so widely in tone and aim as *Zoo Zoo Widdershins Zoo* and *It's a Two-Foot-Six-Inches-above-the-Ground World*, suggest that his other plays deserve careful study by some enterprising theatre manager.

—Henry Raynor

LAN, David. South African. Born in Cape Town, 1 June 1952. Educated at the University of Cape Town, 1970–72, B.A. in English 1972; London School of Economics, 1973–76, B.Sc. in social anthropology 1976, Ph.D. 1983. Moved to England, 1972; lived in Zimbabwe, 1980–82. Member of the Editorial Board, *Journal of Southern African Studies*, Oxford. Recipient: John Whiting Award, 1977; George Orwell Memorial Award, 1982. Agent: Margaret Ramsay Ltd., 14-A Goodwin's Court, London WC2N 4LL, England.

PUBLICATIONS

Plays

Painting a Wall (produced London, 1974; New York, 1980). London, Pluto Press, 1979.
Bird Child (produced London, 1974).
Paradise (produced London, 1975).
Homage to Been Soup (produced London, 1975).
The Winter Dancers (produced London, 1977; Los Angeles, 1978; New York, 1979).
Not in Norwich (produced London, 1977).
Red Earth (produced London, 1978).
Sergeant Ola and His Followers (produced London, 1979). London, Methuen, 1980.
Flight (produced Stratford-on-Avon, 1986; London, 1987). London, Methuen, 1987.
A Mouthful of Birds, with Caryl Churchill (produced Birmingham and London, 1986). London, Methuen, 1987.

Television Play: *The Sunday Judge*, 1985.

Other

Guns and Rain: Guerrillas and Spirit Mediums in Zimbabwe. London, Currey, and Berkeley, University of California Press, 1985.

*

Theatrical Activities:
Director: **Plays**—*A New Way to Pay Old Debts* by Massinger, Cape Town, 1971; *The Sport of My Mad Mother* by Ann Jellicoe, Cape Town, 1972.

* * *

David Lan is a South African, so he begins with a subject. His one-acter *Painting a Wall* and his full-length play *Bird Child* both deal with aspects of South African life—which is to say, with aspects of apartheid. The first is slight, impressionistic, a short story. Two coloured men and an Indian paint a wall, helped by a coloured boy. The Indian has lost his child, and makes a botched attempt at suicide by drinking paint. The boy runs away. The men paint pictures on the wall, but must paint over them. They talk, and paint. The wall is finished. They leave. In *Bird Child* all but one of the characters (and that a small part) are white, quasi-hippie students and friends of students, in collision with the police. In protesting against the denial of freedom to her mother's maid, the heroine discovers the nature of freedom for herself. All the other protagonists of the play are locked by the system into sets of predetermined attitudes. Though the structure falls to pieces by the end, this is Lan's most accessible play, particularly in his handling of Krou, the Colonel of Police, an intelligent, logical, and resourceful man, by no means a target for the scoring of easy liberal points.

But a single subject will not do for a serious artist, and Lan's next two plays, *Homage to Been Soup* and *Paradise*, both presented by the Theatre Upstairs at the Royal Court in 1975, represent his attempt to find a way on. The first is again a one-acter only twelve manuscript pages long, a mere technical exercise, sterile except in so far as it has allowed its author to grow. *Paradise* is more ambitious, Lan's most interesting play so far, though botched in the execution. He appears to have been inspired by Goya's *Horrors of War*, and has set the play in Northern Spain in 1808, the year of Bonaparte's invasion. His characters—deserters from the French army, Spanish peasants and their landlord, his wife and school-mistress daughter—have no particularity of time and place, and the play might more suitably have been set in a non-particular Whiting-land, into which his two most successful images, a simpleton who teaches the others his private unintelligible non-language, and the birds which move their nests from trees about to be chopped down, might more successfully fit. Nevertheless, again Lan's concern with the nature of freedom ("You begin by giving people their freedom. Then you pick up a gun, if they won't voluntarily do what you want."—my paraphrase) is noble, his images striking, and his own search for a language, fuller than the stylized short sentences of the two earlier plays to allow him to express more complex ideas, is admirable.

A new direction came with the two following plays, *The Winter Dancers* (John Whiting Award) and *Sergeant Ola and His Followers*, again both presented by the Royal Court. Lan studied at the London School of Economics, earning a doctorate in social anthropology, and both plays make use of anthropological material, for *The Winter Dancers* the work of Boas on the Kwakiutl of Vancouver Island, for *Sergeant Ola* Peter Worsley's research into cargo cults in Papua-New Guinea. A major concern of both plays is with ritual and magic; both make the statement explicit in *The Winter Dancers*, "White men are eating up the world." In *The Winter Dancers* the shaman, Carver, knows that he cures the sick by trickery and sleight of hand. Others believe in his power; only he knows that he has none. Yet the cures are genuine. When finally he comes to believe in his own power, and the need for it against the white men, he loses it, and is killed by a madman's daughter. In *Sergeant Ola* there is no power any more in the people but only in the "wetmen," who have taken away the people's ancestors, and offered them Adam and Eve instead. The wetmen have all the cargo (riches), and the people are merely offered pay (which is not cargo) for doing the wetmen's work—while the wetmen manifestly do no work at all. The attempts of the people to make cargo come again by ignorant imitation, amounting to parody, of what they have observed of the wetmen's ways is both comic and piteous, and the play established Lan securely in the first rank of the playwrights of his generation.

In 1980 he went to Zimbabwe to live and work with the Shona and complete his doctoral thesis; his book *Guns and Rain* has already become a textbook for students of anthropology. His next play, *Flight*, was mounted by the Royal Shakespeare Company at their studio theatre in Stratford. It is more complex than any of Lan's previous plays; the narrative is neither strong nor straightforward. The action moves in time between 1930, when a Jewish family flees from persecution in Lithuania, to 1980, when the next generation is getting out of Zimbabwe. The title and a prologue to the play seem to suggest that its theme is the perpetual uprooting, rooting elsewhere, and again uprooting of the Jews under persecution, but my own view is that the title may be ironic, and the real flight may be from political reality, that centuries of persecution have made the Jews politically aware and active but have also contributed to the development of a family loyalty which occludes political vision and vitiates action. Because of its complexity, the play demands to be seen more than once, which is not always a good quality in plays. A later dramatic work, *A Mouthful of Birds*, written with Caryl Churchill, and staged by the RSC on tour, is imagistic in manner, consisting of many short scenes. Clearly Lan intends to continue to experiment in form and theme. He is never likely to write an uninteresting play, preferring always to stretch an audience than to satisfy.

—John Bowen

LAURENTS, Arthur. American. Born in Brooklyn, New York, 14 July 1918. Educated at Cornell University, Ithaca, New York, B.A. 1937. Served in the United States Army, 1940–45: Sergeant; radio playwright, 1943–45 (Citation, Secretary of War, and *Variety* radio award, 1945). Stage director. Director, Dramatists Play Service, New York, 1961–66. Council member, Dramatists Guild, from 1955. Recipient: American Academy award, 1946; Sidney Howard Memorial Award, 1946; Tony award, for play, 1967, for directing, 1984; Vernon Rice award, 1974; Golden Globe award, 1977; Screenwriters Guild award, 1978; Sydney Drama Critics award, for directing, 1985. Agent: Shirley Bernstein, Paramuse Artists, 1414 Avenue of the Americas, New York, New York 10019. Address: Dune Road, Quogue, New York 11959, U.S.A.

PUBLICATIONS

Plays

Now Playing Tomorrow (broadcast 1939). Published in *Short Plays for Stage and Radio*, edited by Carless Jones, Albuquerque, University of New Mexico Press, 1939.

Western Electric Communicade (broadcast 1944). Published in *The Best One-Act Plays of 1944*, edited by Margaret Mayorga, New York, Dodd Mead, 1944.

The Last Day of the War (broadcast 1945). Published in *Radio Drama in Action*, edited by Erik Barnouw, New York, Farrar and Rinehart, 1945.

The Face (broadcast 1945). Published in *The Best One-Act Plays of 1945*, edited by Margaret Mayorga, New York, Dodd Mead, 1945.

Home of the Brave (produced New York, 1945; London, 1948; as *The Way Back*, produced London, 1949). New York, Random House, 1946.

Heartsong (produced New Haven, Connecticut, 1947).

The Bird Cage (produced New York, 1950). New York, Dramatists Play Service, 1950.

The Time of the Cuckoo (produced New York, 1952). New York, Random House, 1953.

A Clearing in the Woods (produced New York, 1957). New York, Random House, 1957; revised version, New York Dramatists Play Service, 1960.

West Side Story, music by Leonard Bernstein, lyrics by Stephen Sondheim (produced New York, 1957; London 1958). New York, Random House, 1958; London, Heinemann, 1959.

Gypsy, music by Jule Styne, lyrics by Stephen Sondheim, adaptation of a book by Gypsy Rose Lee (produced New York 1959; also director: produced London, 1973). New York Random House, 1960.

Invitation to a March (also director: produced New York, 1960 Hereford, 1965). New York, Random House, 1961.

Anyone Can Whistle, music by Stephen Sondheim (also director: produced New York, 1964; Cheltenham, Gloucestershire, 1986). New York, Random House, 1965.

Do I Hear a Waltz?, music by Richard Rodgers, lyrics by Stephen Sondheim (produced New York, 1965). New York Random House, 1966.

Hallelujah, Baby!, music and lyrics by Jule Styne, Betty Comden, and Adolph Green (produced New York, 1967). New York, Random House, 1967.

The Enclave (also director: produced Washington, D.C., and New York, 1973). New York, Dramatists Play Service 1974.

Scream (also director: produced Houston, 1978).

The Madwoman of Central Park West, with Phyllis Newman music by Peter Allen and others, adaptation of the play *M*

Mother Was a Fortune Teller by Newman (also director: produced Buffalo and New York, 1979).
A Loss of Memory (produced Southampton, New York, 1981). Published in *The Best Short Plays 1983*, edited by Ramon Delgado, Radnor, Pennsylvania, Chilton, 1983.

Screenplays: *The Snake Pit*, with Frank Partos and Millen Brand, 1948; *Rope*, with Hume Cronyn, 1948; *Anna Lucasta*, with Philip Yordan, 1949; *Caught*, 1949; *Anastasia*, 1956; *Bonjour Tristesse*, 1958; *The Way We Were*, 1973; *The Turning Point*, 1977.

Radio Plays: *Now Playing Tomorrow*, 1939; *Hollywood Playhouse, Dr. Christian, The Thin Man, Manhattan at Midnight*, and other series, 1939–40; *The Last Day of the War, The Face, Western Electric Communicade*, and other plays for *The Man Behind the Gun, Army Service Force Presents* and *Assignment: Home* series, 1943–45; *This Is Your FBI* series, 1945.

Television Script: *The Light Fantastic*, 1967.

Novels

The Way We Were. New York, Harper, 1972; London, W.H. Allen, 1973.
The Turning Point. New York, New American Library, 1977; London, Corgi, 1978.

*

Manuscript Collection: Brandeis University, Waltham, Massachusetts.

Theatrical Activities:
Director: **Plays**—*Invitation to a March*, New York, 1960; *I Can Get It for You Wholesale* by Jerome Weidman, New York, 1962; *Anyone Can Whistle*, New York, 1964; *The Enclave*, Washington, D.C., and New York, 1973; *Gypsy*, London, 1973, New York, 1974; *My Mother Was a Fortune Teller* by Phyllis Newman, New York, 1978; *Scream*, Houston, 1978; *The Madwoman of Central Park West*, Buffalo and New York, 1979; *So What Are We Gonna Do Now?* by Juliet Garson, New York, 1982; *La Cage aux Folles* by Jean Poiret, adapted by Harvey Fierstein, Boston and New York, 1983, Sydney, 1985, London, 1986.

Arthur Laurents comments:
Too much of today's theatre brings "The Emperor's New Clothes" to my mind. Style is considered content; formlessness is considered new technique; character is reduced to symbol and/or type; and story has been banished—not necessarily a loss—in favor of incident which is usually too thin and too undramatic to fuse an entire play. Moreover, the dominant tone is modish pessimism or militancy, both of which can be as sentimentally romantic as effulgent optimism.

All a matter of taste, of course. My own is for a heightened theatricality and for new forms—but I still believe that form is determined by content and requires control. I want characters in a play, I want to be emotionally involved; I want social content; I want language and I want a *level* of accessibility. (I suspect obscurantism of being the refuge of the vague, the uncommitted, and the chic.) Although I do not demand it, I prefer optimism—even if only implied. For I think man, naturally evil or not, is optimistic. Even the bleakest has hope: why else does he bother to write?

For the United States, for New York, I want subsidized theatres with permanent companies playing repertory. I think that is the most important need of the American playwright and would be of the greatest aid in his development.

* * *

One of the most promising dramatists appearing immediately after World War II was Arthur Laurents. His first success in New York, *Home of the Brave*, showed both his skill as a dramatist and his insight into human nature as he dramatized the ethnic and individual problems of a Jewish soldier in a battle situation. During the following 15 years Laurents wrote four plays—*The Bird Cage, The Time of the Cuckoo, A Clearing in the Woods*, and *Invitation to a March*—which continued to demonstrate his theatrical powers and his inclination to write serious drama. Unfortunately, in neither area—theatricality or intellectual penetration—was he able to sustain or develop a first-rate drama for the American commercial theatre. Perhaps he recognized either the personal or public impasse. At any rate, toward the end of this period Laurents had begun to devote more of his talents to musical comedy with considerable success. His creation of the books for *West Side Story* and *Gypsy* gave these musicals the careful integration and character development which distinguish them among modern musicals. During the next decade he collaborated on musicals but without significant success, and seemed to abandon his career in legitimate drama—a disappointment for critics who had felt his earlier promise.

Laurents's seriousness as a dramatist was most evident in the themes that he chose to develop. The fearful uncertainties of the lonely person trying to find a meaningful identity in a world full of frustrations and strangers—this is a dominant theme in his works. Generally, his major character was trying to discover the essentials of love which Laurents seemed to believe would lead to a revelation of self. Although his psychological penetration into his major characters suggests a generally acute perception of humanity, his dramatized solutions tend more consistently toward theatricality than a probing concern for mankind. In other words, the problems that he considers—a person's fears, frustrations, feeling of alienation—place Laurents among those seriously concerned with modernity, but his insistence that sex is fundamental to all such problems limits both his psychology and his insight.

In three of his four plays since his initial success his major characters have been women whose psychological problems have driven them toward disaster. (The other play, *The Bird Cage*, tells the story of Wally, a vicious egomaniac and owner of a night club, whose abuse of everyone stems from his own sexual frustrations.) In *The Time of the Cuckoo* Leona Samish is that warm but lonely woman whose pathos rests in her inability to know and have faith in herself or accept the love of others. Sorry for herself and bitter towards life and thus unable to get what she most desires, she is that dangerous person who destroys. Virginia, the heroine of *A Clearing in the Woods*, sees herself as that destroyer although she wants desperately to be loved. Discovering that someone does truly care, she can work toward a position where she accepts both herself and the real world around her. *Invitation to a March* tells of a girl who, at first, wants to "march" along with the ordinary world and its seemingly inherent problems of love, sex, and divorce. But she changes, rejects the "march" and finds love with one who said "come dance with me." Uncharacteristically for a Laurents play, a strongly made decision becomes the climax of this one, and perhaps both the author and his characters abandon the ordinary world as idealism seems a possible alternative to drudgery. Unfortunately, no further step has been dramatized.

Although Laurents has not been an innovator in technical theatre, he has courageously employed distinctive techniques in his plays. While *The Bird Cage* employs a rather obvious use of theatrical symbol, the "clearing in the woods" with its "magic circle" is well integrated into the structure of the play where three characters—Ginna, Nora, Jigee—act out particular ages in the heroine's life and tease her with her inability to accept what "they" contribute to her present problems. The frequent "front" delivery to the audience in an attempt to indicate unspoken and personal feelings was unsuccessful even in a semi-fantasy such as *Invitation to a March*. Music becomes a dominant part of several of his plays, as might be expected of a dramatist interested in musical comedy. In all of Laurents's theatre works his care in the creation of his characters is a major asset. Whether in musical comedy or straight drama, through an integration of theme and theatrical technique Laurents has tried to express his views on psychological and social life in the modern world.

—Walter J. Meserve

LAVERY, Bryony. British. Born in Wakefield, Yorkshire, 21 December 1947. Educated at the University of London, 1966–69, B.A. (honours) in English 1969. Artistic director, Les Oeufs Malades, 1976–78, Extraordinary Productions, 1979–80, and Female Trouble, 1981–83, all London. Since 1985 resident dramatist, Unicorn Theatre for Young People, London. Agent: Jonathan Clowes Ltd., 22 Prince Albert Road, London NW1 7ST. Address: 40 Ridgdale Street, London E3 2TW, England.

PUBLICATIONS

Plays

Of All Living (produced London, 1967).
Days at Court (produced London, 1968).
Warbeck (produced London, 1969).
I Was Too Young at the Time to Understand Why My Mother Was Crying (also director: produced London, 1976).
Sharing (also director: produced London, 1976).
Germany Calling, with Peter Leabourne (produced London, 1976).
Grandmother's Footsteps (also director: produced London, 1977).
The Catering Service (also director: produced London, 1977).
Floorshow, with others (produced London, 1978).
Helen and Her Friends (also director: produced London, 1978).
Bag (also director: produced London, 1979).
The Wild Bunch (for children; produced London, 1979).
Sugar and Spice (for children; produced Ipswich, Suffolk, 1979).
Unemployment: An Occupational Hazard? (for children; also director: produced London, 1979).
Gentlemen Prefer Blondes, adaptation of the novel by Anita Loos (produced London, 1980).
The Joker (for children; also director: produced London, 1980).
The Family Album (also director: produced London, 1980).
Missing (also director: produced Colchester, Essex, and London, 1981).
Zulu, with Patrick Barlow (produced London, 1981).
Female Trouble (cabaret; produced London, 1981).
The Black Hole of Calcutta (produced London, 1982).
Gotterdammerung; or, Twilight of the Gods, with Patrick Barlow and Susan Todd (produced London, 1982).
For Maggie, Betty and Ida, music by Paul Sand (produced London, 1982).
More Female Trouble (cabaret), music by Caroline Noh (produced London, 1982).
Uniform and Uniformed, and Numerical Man (broadcast 1983). Published in *Masks and Faces*, edited by Dan Garrett, London, Macmillan, 1984.
Hot Time (produced London, 1984).
Calamity (produced London, 1984).
Origin of the Species (produced Birmingham, 1984; London, 1985).
The Wandsworth Warmers (cabaret; also director: produced London, 1984).
The Zulu Hut Club (for children; produced London, 1984).
The Wandsworth Warmers Christmas Carol Concert (also director: produced London, 1985).
Over and Out (also director: produced on tour, 1985).
Snakes (produced London, 1985).
Witchcraze (produced London, 1985).
Getting Through (additional lyrics only), by Nona Shepphard, music by Helen Glavin (produced on tour, 1985; London, 1987).
Unbridled Passions (also director: produced London, 1986).
Sore Points (for children; produced London, 1986).
Mummy, with Sally Owen and L. Ortolja (produced London, 1987).
Madagascar (for children; also director: produced London, 1987).
The Headless Body, music by Stephanie Nunn (produced London, 1987).

Radio Plays: *Fire the Life-Giver*, 1979; *Changes at Work* series, 1980; *Uniform and Uniformed*, 1983; *Numerical Man*, 1983.

Television Plays: *Revolting Women* series, with others, 1981.

*

Critical Study: "But Will Men Like It; or, Living as a Feminist Writer Without Committing Murder" by Lavery, in *Women and Theatre* edited by Susan Todd, London, Faber, 1984.

Theatrical Activities:
Director: **Plays**—most of her own plays; *More Female Trouble* (revival), London, 1983; *Homelands: Under Exposure* by Lisa Evans, and *The Mrs. Docherties* by Nona Shepphard (co-director, with Shepphard), London, 1985.

* * *

Bryony Lavery trained and worked as a schoolteacher, then became a feminist playwright. In spite of her real talent for dialogue and comedy, the didacticism of the schoolteacher and the inevitable polemic of the political purist tend to crush the light out of her plays. More seriously, they seem unable to develop beyond cluttered, undisciplined jumbles of sketches, songs, dances, and comic monologues, with incomplete characterizations, superficiality, and inconclusive, abrupt endings.

With two performers, Jessica Higgs and Gerard Bell, Lavery started in 1976 a fringe theatre company, Les Oeufs Malades, which toured the country performing her plays. *Grandmother's Footsteps* is a collection of songs and routines, in old music hall style. Two women, Iris and Crystal, share a flat, in which there is a giant fortune wheel. They challenge each other to games of wit, determined by the wheel. Both cheat. Iris is capable of some cruelty. *The Catering Service* is an allegory on the evils of paramilitarism and fanatics. *Helen and Her Friends* tells the story of a young woman dying in hospital as her horrified friends drift away. The simple point that fear of death strains loyalty is lightened with some very funny, absurdly humorous moments. *Bag* is probably the weakest of the plays of this era. Another play about friendship, it examines five people on a camping trip together. Nick and Bella hope to revitalize their marriage. Bella's best friend, Stella, wouldn't mind bedding Nick. Zoe and Lizzy observe and fall down, respectively. The overlapping dialogue and jokes finally yield the thin moral that one must first love one's self before being able to love friends. *The Family Album* dabbles in psychoanalysis with the examination of the hell of childhood violence, and shows Lavery firmly settled in the unfortunate habit of taking on larger themes than she can handle. Death, friendship, child abuse, are all, after the jokes, brushed away with platitudes.

In the early 1980's Lavery began to write for the feminist theatre companies Monstrous Regiment and the Women's Theatre Group. *Female Trouble*, probably her most successful play, gives the messages and morals in songs and sketches, some of them among her funniest. In one, a woman addicted to men is trying to kick her forty-men-a-day habit. In another, the last man on earth is locked up in a rocket and shot into outer space. In a third, the cast simply stand and make funny faces at the audience. "A play is a wonderful, nutty, fruity cake," Lavery has written.

She also wrote, a bit simplistically, that she was tired of her women characters being losers who say "Yes, but..." instead of winners who say "Yes, and...." *Missing* is a mix of dream sequences and reminiscences of three women who say "Yes, and...." They like to read thrillers, and suddenly find themselves "missing," mysteriously locked up in cells. They plan and bravely execute their escape, liberating their female jailer as well. This jailer ends the play with a hymn to sisterhood, praising the wonders of the world women could create, if only they could organize.

Parallel to her feminist works, Lavery has also written numerous plays for children which, in many ways, strike a better balance between her humor and her moralizing. *Hot Time* was written over a weekend for a group of unemployed young people. Centered around the Flagg family, it depicts the problems of divided loyalties within a family during the General Strike of 1926. Lavery's position as resident dramatist at the Unicorn Theatre for Children in London produced *Madagascar*, about a girl and her grandmother who in a series of games conjure up foreign lands, complete with natives. *The Wild Bunch* has adolescents learning about the pains of sexual stereotyping, while *Uniform and Uniformed* warns against unthinking conformity. The family entertainment *The Headless Body* uses magic tricks and illusions, as well as songs and audience participation, to find out which of the freaks in a travelling circus committed murder.

A more recent theme in the adult plays has been women in history. *For Maggie, Betty and Ida* creates the intimate atmosphere of a grandmother's storytelling. The stories told are of the suffering of women through the centuries, from the ugliest woman in the world to Anne Boleyn. *Calamity* purports to tell the truth about pioneer women in the Wild West, or at least to create better myths. Quiet Kate leaves her oppressive husband, Madame Mustache is a card sharp and murderess, and Calamity Jane is a tough drinker who pens warm letters to her daughter. (The recent discovery of these letters was an inspiration for the play.) *Witchcraze* uses the familiar material of women persecuted as witches.

Lavery's trademarks are wit, songs, sketches, cabaret, even the occasional use of magic and rope tricks, all hampered by lack of structure and depth. One suspects that she sees herself as a feminist Brecht. She could, with a little structure and consistency, be an excellent feminist Coward.

—Anne Morddel

LAWLER, Ray(mond Evenor). Australian. Born in Footscray, Melbourne, Victoria, in 1921. Left school at age 13. Married Jacklyn Kelleher; three children. Worked in a foundry, 1934–45; actor, Sid Turnbull's Melbourne Repertory Company, 1946–49; actor and producer, National Theatre Company, Melbourne, 1950–54; director, Union Theatre Repertory Company, Melbourne University, 1954–55; lived in Denmark, England, and mainly in Ireland, early 1960's–1975; director and literary adviser, Melbourne Theatre Company, 1976–86. Recipient: Playwrights Advisory Board prize, 1955; London *Evening Standard* award, 1958. O.B.E. (Officer, Order of the British Empire), 1981. Agent: Curtis Brown, 27 Union Street, Paddington, New South Wales 2021, Australia.

PUBLICATIONS

Plays

Cradle of Thunder (produced Melbourne, 1949).
Summer of the Seventeenth Doll (produced Melbourne, 1955; London, 1957; New York, 1958). London, Angus and Robertson, and New York, Random House, 1957.
The Piccadilly Bushman (produced Melbourne, 1959; Liverpool, 1965). London, Angus and Robertson, 1961.
The Unshaven Cheek (produced Edinburgh, 1963).
A Breach in the Wall (televised 1967; produced Canterbury, Kent, 1970).
The Man Who Shot the Albatross (produced Melbourne, 1972).
Kid Stakes (produced Melbourne, 1975). Included in *The Doll Trilogy*, 1978.
Other Times (produced Melbourne, 1976). Included in *The Doll Trilogy*, 1978.
The Doll Trilogy (includes *Kid Stakes, Other Times, Summer of the Seventeenth Doll*). Sydney, Currency Press, 1978.
Godsend (produced Melbourne, 1982).

Television Plays: *A Breach in the Wall*, 1967; *Sinister Street* serial, from the novel by Compton Mackenzie, 1968; *Cousin Bette* serial, from the novel by Balzac, 1971; *The Visitors* serial, from the novel by Mary McMinnies, 1972; *Two Women* serial, from a novel by Alberto Moravia, 1972; *Mrs. Palfrey at the Claremont*, from the novel by Elizabeth Taylor, 1973; *After the Party*, from the story by W. Somerset Maugham, 1974; *Seeking the Bubbles* (*The Love School* series), 1975; *True Patriots All*, 1975; *Husband to Mrs. Fitzherbert*, 1975.

*

Theatrical Activities:
Actor: **Play**—Barney Ibbot in *Summer of the Seventeenth Doll*, Melbourne, 1955, London, 1957.

* * *

Ray Lawler's reputation as one of Australia's most distinguished playwrights is still based largely on one extremely successful play, *Summer of the Seventeenth Doll*. The play came at a crucial time, not only for the narrow world of the Australian theatre but for Australian culture generally. The 1950's were a time of national self-consciousness, when former ideas of "Australianness" were being, to a certain extent, reassessed. The *Doll* took the traditional legend of the laconic, hard-bitten Australian bushman, which had been an important part of the national self-image since the 1890's, and dragged it, almost literally, kicking and screaming into the cities to face the realities of postwar urban Australia.

The play had a sudden popular impact when it first appeared. Its warm portrayal of distinctive bush and city character-types was greeted with delighted recognition by middle-class audiences for whom the original legend had in fact only ever been an exotic dream. The two tough cane-cutters, Roo and Barney, who come down from the Queensland cane-fields each year to spend the "lay-off" season whooping it up in Melbourne, represented a vanishing national type with whom the city audiences liked to identify.

The *Doll* shows these two legendary characters failing to deal with the new urban Australia. The romantic dream of the lay-offs—times of innocent loving fun for the men and their barmaid girlfriends—is already beginning to fail as the play opens. Olive, Roo's woman, tries to sustain her vision of a nobler life than that which the "soft city blokes" have to offer, and she clings to it even when it brings personal tragedy for her, but the world of the soft city blokes wins, practically if not emotionally. For contemporary audiences, perhaps, the portrayal of Olive as a foolish woman who refuses to grow up (confirmed in the expanded *The Doll Trilogy*) has dated. There is some justice in her claim to have found a serious alternative to marriage, but after a series of reversals at the end we are left with a final ironic triumph of the legend, as Roo and Barney stagger out to head back north, leaving Olive alone in her grief.

The *Doll*'s appeal, even for foreign audiences who know nothing of the bush legend, is based in the solid, old-fashioned virtues of well-made realism: detailed and consistent characterisation, a wonderfully rich use of vernacular, and a complex and carefully plotted action. These were virtues which Lawler showed he was still a master of when he came, 20 years after the original appearance of the *Doll*, to write the two additional plays which make up the trilogy, *Kid Stakes* and *Other Times*.

The extraordinary success of the *Doll* meant that Lawler's next plays, before the completion of the trilogy, were bound to be received with disappointment. *The Piccadilly Bushman* is a technically competent play which explores the self-image of an Australian expatriate actor who has achieved success as an actor in England and returns to confront what he now sees as his embarrassing "colonial" past. *The Man Who Shot the Albatross* is an historical play about a much-treated subject in Australian drama: the colonial Governor Bligh, struggling to deal with mutinous local bigwigs, and haunted by the memory of the other more famous mutineers on the *Bounty*. The play presents its subject largely in terms of personal conflict between Bligh and the politically astute landowner, John Macarthur—avoiding any wider historical or political exploration. For this reason, perhaps, it seemed rather old-fashioned in 1972. Neither of these two plays has had much impact in the Australian theatre.

Lawler lived abroad during the great upsurge in Australian drama of the early 1970's, but he returned in the mid-1970's to produce two plays which revived his reputation: *Kid Stakes* and *Other Times*. These plays are set prior to the *Doll*. They go back to the first and the ninth "lay-offs," introducing the appealing character of Nancy, whose memory so dominates the *Doll*, and generally filling in the background to what had by the mid-1970's become a well-known and well-loved part of the national heritage. *Kid Stakes* is a play of great charm. Its delightful portrait of an innocent young Australian society before World War II showed Lawler at his full strength, lamenting the loss of a simpler world. *Other Times*, set during the war, in winter, is written in a minor key, introducing a note of bitterness which anticipates the tragedy of the *Doll*.

The effect of the trilogy, ironically, was to lessen the impact of the original play. The new plays take so much trouble to plant hints anticipating the action of the *Doll* that the brilliant Ibsenite exposition in the original becomes rather pointless and the story and characters move into a new world of sophisticated soap opera. Again, however, the warmth and richness with which these familiar characters are developed make this one of the most charming works in the New Wave of Australian drama.

In 1982 Lawler produced his first major work since the trilogy, *Godsend*. The "godsend" is the discovery in a small rural church in Kent of the lost tomb of St. Thomas à Becket. Each of the four central characters—a traditionalist Catholic bishop, the Anglican Archbishop, an idealistic parson, and his agnostic wife—has a different interest in the holy remains, and through their conflict the play explores the nature of religious faith and the difficulties of sustaining it. Stylistically the play is a departure from the well-made realism of *The Doll Trilogy*, especially in its complex use of direct audience address. It is the work of a mature dramatist, with accomplished skills, which has not yet had the impact it deserves.

Lawler's place in the development of Australian drama is still assured by the *Doll*. If he has never repeated that success, it is perhaps partly because his dramatic interests have become less relevant to the issues which now involve Australian audiences, but he remains one of the most technically capable of all Australian dramatists, and one who has contributed some of the best-loved characters in the culture.

—John McCallum

LAWRENCE, Jerome. American. Born Jerome Lawrence Schwartz in Cleveland, Ohio, 14 July 1915. Educated at Ohio State University, Columbus, B.A. 1937; University of California, Los Angeles, 1939–40. Director of summer stock, Connellsville, Pennsylvania, then Pittsfield, Massachusetts, summers 1934–37; reporter and telegraph editor, Wilmington, *News-Journal*, Ohio, 1937; editor, New Lexington *Daily News*, Ohio, 1937–38; continuity editor, KMPC Radio, Beverly Hills, California, 1938, 1939; senior staff writer, Columbia Broadcasting System, Hollywood and New York, 1939–41; scenario writer, Paramount Pictures, Hollywood, 1941. Expert Consultant to the Secretary of War during World War II: co-founder of Armed Forces Radio Service, and radio correspondent in

North Africa and Italy (wrote and directed the official Army-Navy programs for D-Day, VE Day and VJ Day). Since 1942 partner, Lawrence and Lee, and since 1955 President, Lawrence and Lee Inc., New York and Los Angeles. Founder and National President, Radio Writers Guild; co-founder and President, American Playwrights Theatre; co-founder and judge, Margo Jones Award; founder and Board member, Writers Guild of America; Council member, Dramatists Guild and Authors League of America; member of the Advisory Board, Eugene O'Neill Foundation, American Conservatory Theatre, Board of Standards of the Living Theatre, and Ohio State University School of Journalism. Professor, Banff School of Fine Arts, Alberta, Canada, 1950–53; Member, U.S. State Department Cultural Exchange Panel, 1962–70. Master Playwright, New York University, 1967, 1968; Visiting Professor of Playwriting, Ohio State University, 1969; Lecturer, Salzburg Seminar in American Studies, 1972; Visiting Professor, Baylor University, Waco, Texas, 1976; Professor of Playwriting, University of Southern California, Los Angeles, 1984–86. Contributing editor, *Dramatics* magazine, Cincinnati. Recipient: New York Press Club award, 1942; *Radio-TV Life* award, 1948, 1952; Peabody award, 1949, 1952; *Radio-TV Mirror* award, 1952, 1953; *Variety* award, 1954, 1955; Donaldson award, 1955; Outer Circle award, 1955; British Drama Critics award, 1960; Moss Hart Memorial Award, 1967; Ohio State University Centennial award, 1970, and Alumni medal, 1985; American Theatre Association award, 1979; International Thespian Society Directors award, 1980; Valentine Davies award, 1984. D.H.L.: Ohio State University, 1963; D.Litt.: Fairleigh Dickinson University, Rutherford, New Jersey, 1968, College of Wooster, Ohio, 1983; D.F.A.: Villanova University, Pennsylvania, 1969. Agent: Robert Freedman Dramatic Agency, 1501 Broadway, New York, New York 10036; or, Ben Benjamin, International Creative Management, 8899 Beverly Boulevard, Los Angeles, California 90048. Address: 21056 Las Flores Mesa Drive, Malibu, California 90265, U.S.A.

PUBLICATIONS

Plays

Laugh, God!, in *Six Anti-Nazi One-Act Plays*. New York, Contemporary Play Publications, 1939.

Tomorrow, with Budd Schulberg, in *Free World Theatre*, edited by Arch Oboler and Stephen Longstreet. New York, Random House, 1944.

Inside a Kid's Head, with Robert E. Lee, in *Radio Drama in Action*, edited by Erik Barnouw. New York, Farrar and Rinehart, 1945.

Look, Ma, I'm Dancin', with Robert E. Lee, music by Hugh Martin, conceived by Jerome Robbins (produced New York, 1948).

The Crocodile Smile, with Robert E. Lee (as *The Laugh Maker*, produced Hollywood, 1952; revised version, as *Turn on the Night*, produced Philadelphia, 1961; revised version, as *The Crocodile Smile*, also director: produced Flatrock, North Carolina, 1970). New York, Dramatists Play Service, 1972.

Inherit the Wind, with Robert E. Lee (produced Dallas and New York, 1955; London, 1960). New York, Random House, 1955; London, Four Square, 1960.

Shangri-La, with Robert E. Lee and James Hilton, music by Harry Warren, adaptation of the novel *Lost Horizon* by Hilton (produced New York, 1956). New York, Morris Music, 1956.

Auntie Mame, with Robert E. Lee, adaptation of the work by Patrick Dennis (produced New York, 1956; London, 1958). New York, Vanguard Press, 1957; revised version, music by Jerry Herman, as *Mame* (produced New York, 1966; London, 1969), New York, Random House, 1967.

The Gang's All Here, with Robert E. Lee (produced New York, 1959). Cleveland, World, 1960.

Only in America, with Robert E. Lee, adaptation of the work by Harry Golden (produced New York, 1959). New York, French, 1960.

A Call on Kuprin, with Robert E. Lee, adaptation of the novel by Maurice Edelman (produced New York, 1961). New York, French, 1962.

Sparks Fly Upward, with Robert E. Lee (as *Diamond Orchid*, produced New York, 1965; revised version, as *Sparks Fly Upward*, produced Dallas, 1967). New York, Dramatists Play Service, 1969.

Live Spelled Backwards (produced Beverly Hills, California, 1966). New York, Dramatists Play Service, 1970.

Dear World, with Robert E. Lee, music by Jerry Herman, based on *The Madwoman of Chaillot* by Giraudoux (produced New York, 1969).

The Incomparable Max, with Robert E. Lee (also director: produced Abingdon, Virginia, 1969; New York, 1971). New York, Hill and Wang, 1972.

The Night Thoreau Spent in Jail, with Robert E. Lee (produced Columbus, Ohio, and 154 other theatres, 1970). New York, Hill and Wang, 1970.

Jabberwock: Improbabilities Lived and Imagined by James Thurber in the Fictional City of Columbus, Ohio, with Robert E. Lee (produced Columbus, Ohio, 1972). New York, French, 1974.

First Monday in October, with Robert E. Lee (also director: produced Cleveland, 1975; New York, 1978). New York, French, 1979.

Screenplays, with Robert E. Lee: *My Love Affair with the Human Race*, 1962; *The New Yorkers*, 1963; *Joyous Season*, 1964; *The Night Thoreau Spent in Jail*, 1972; *First Monday in October*, 1982.

Radio Plays: *Junior Theatre of the Air* series, 1938; *Under Western Skies* series, 1939; *Nightcap Yarns* series, 1939, 1940; *Stories from Life* series, 1939, 1940; *Man about Hollywood* series, 1940; *Hollywood Showcase* series, 1940, 1941; *A Date with Judy* series, 1941, 1942; *They Live Forever* series, 1942; *Everything for the Boys* series, 1944; *I Was There* series; with Robert E. Lee—*Columbia Workshop* series, 1941–42; *Armed Forces Radio Service Programs*, 1942–45; *The World We're Fighting For* series, 1943; *Request Performance* series, 1945–46; *Screen Guild Theatre* series, 1946; *Favorite Story* series, 1946–49; *Frank Sinatra Show*, 1947; *Dinah Shore Program*, 1948; *The Railroad Hour*, 1948–54; *Young Love* series, 1949–50; *United Nations Broadcasts*, 1949–50; *Halls of Ivy* series, 1950–51; *Hallmark Playhouse* series, 1950–51; *Charles Boyer Show*, 1951; other free-lance and special programs, 1941–50.

Television Plays: *Lincoln, The Unwilling Warrior*, 1975; with Robert E. Lee—*The Unexpected* series, 1951; *Favorite Story* series, 1952–53; *Song of Norway*, 1957; *West Point*, 1958; *Actor*, music by Billy Goldenburg, 1978.

Other

Oscar the Ostrich (for children; as Jerome Schwartz). New York, Random House, 1940.

Actor: The Life and Times of Paul Muni. New York, Putnam, 1974; London, W.H. Allen, 1975.

Editor, *Off Mike: Radio Writing by the Nation's Top Radio Writers*. New York, Essential, 1944.

*

Manuscript Collections: Lawrence and Lee Theatre Research Institute, Ohio State University, Columbus; Lincoln Center Library of the Performing Arts, New York; Kent State University, Ohio; Widener Library, Harvard University, Cambridge, Massachusetts; Ziv-United Artists film and transcription library.

Critical Study: "The Greatest Sport in the World" (interview with Christopher Meeks), in *Writer's Digest* (Cincinnati), March 1986.

Theatrical Activities:
Director: **Plays**—*You Can't Take It with You*, by George S. Kaufman and Moss Hart, *The Imaginary Invalid* by Molière, *Anything Goes* by Howard Lindsay and Russel Crouse, *The Green Pastures* by Marc Connelly, *Boy Meets Girl* by Bella and Sam Spewack, *H.M.S. Pinafore* and *The Pirates of Penzance* by Gilbert and Sullivan, and *Androcles and the Lion* by Shaw, in summer stock, 1934–37; *Mame*, Sacramento, California, 1969; *The Incomparable Max*, Abingdon, Virginia, 1969; *The Crocodile Smile*, Flatrock, North Carolina, 1970; *The Night Thoreau Spent in Jail*, Dublin, 1972; *Jabberwock*, Dallas, 1974; *Inherit the Wind*, Dallas, 1975; *First Monday in October*, Cleveland, 1975.

Jerome Lawrence comments:

Robert E. Lee and I have been called by various critics: "the thinking man's playwrights." In our plays and in our teaching we have attempted to be part of our times. We have done all we can to encourage truly national and international theatre, not confined to a few blocks of real estate in Manhattan or London's West End. Thus, we have sought to promote the growth of regional and university theatres through the formation of American Playwrights Theatre, to bring new and vital and pertinent works to all of America and all of the world.

It has been my privilege to travel to more than a hundred countries, often on cultural-exchange missions. At home, through the years, we have tried to encourage new and untried playwrights, stimulating their work through teaching and through the annual Margo Jones Award.

In our plays we have hoped to mirror and illuminate the problems of the moment—but we have attempted to grapple with universal themes, even in our comedies. We have tried for a blend between the dramatic and the entertaining: our most serious works are always leavened with laughter (*Inherit the Wind* is an example) and our seemingly frivolous comedies (*Auntie Mame, Mame, Jabberwock*) have sub-texts which we hope say something important for the contemporary world.

We are lovers of the living theatre and intend to continue working and living in it.

* * *

"Eatable things to eat and drinkable things to drink," comments a shocked character in Dickens's short story "Mugby Junction," describing a visit to France. The British railway station buffet is the object of Dickens's scorn, and the news that French railways provide edible and easily assimilated food causes the staff of Mugby Junction's restaurant to come close to catatonic fits.

Many a critic, professional *or* amateur, might, in snobbish chorus, make similar comments about the works of collaborators Jerome Lawrence and Robert E. Lee. "Playable plays to play—or readable plays to read!" might be their disbelieving cry. The expressions of disapproval and disdain might be almost as extreme as those of the 19th-century railway grotesques, for both playability and readability are cardinal points of the works of Lawrence and Lee. Their plots are tight, their characters cleanly developed, their dialogue smooth. Actors like them for they present strong speeches and well developed scenes, and although this might be considered old-fashioned playwriting it is clear that audiences like it too. Their most successful work, *Inherit the Wind* (first presented at the National Theatre in New York, April 1955, after a run in Dallas under a great encourager of new talent, Margo Jones) was the third longest-running serious play in the history of Broadway. It is based on the famous Scopes Trial in Tennessee (the "Monkey Trial") when Darwinism and traditional religion had a head-on crash in a rural American setting. It featured Paul Muni and Ed Begley, who made the dialogue of this solid courtroom drama flow back and forth like a mounting tide. The script is very readable; although not deep it is most engaging in a theatrical, if not an intellectually involving way. The effect of putting two great contemporary orators, pitted one against the other, as the core of the play makes for compelling speeches, and the device of the trial itself provides a rounded dramatic vehicle, still open-ended enough to allow one of the protagonists to stand at the end weighing copies of the Bible and Darwin while planning the appeal. Today's audience (even though we would like to think ourselves beyond quaint beliefs) can still become emotionally involved over God versus gorilla. Good and forceful fare, it has been produced around the world.

Many of the works of Lawrence and Lee are lighter, mirroring their ability to zero in on the essentially sentimental underbelly of the average Broadway audience. Their evident enjoyment of the sentimental is one of their secrets. By far the largest part of the Broadway audience is out for fun, a pleasurable look at the land of never-never, which is why the musical when successful is always such a huge money-spinner. Lawrence and Lee pull off a clever trick with *Inherit the Wind* for it has many elements of the musical, yet gives patrons the self-importance of feeling they have seen something serious. They are also at home in creating an impossible character like *Auntie Mame*, first produced in New York in 1956. This giddy American dame was adored onstage, although she probably would not have been tolerated for more than a moment beyond Manhattan or Wilshire Boulevard. Many of the members of the audience would have come from suburban patios like the satirized Upsons (whose house in Connecticut is called "Upson Downs"—Lawrence has a weakness for rather ponderous puns in conversation and his own California house is called "Writers to the Sea") but the social comment is kept gentle and the medicine is never too strong. An amusing evening and intended to be nothing more no doubt, yet for this writer the play only sparked into life when Beatrice Lillie played the part in the London production.

Auntie Mame became the very successful musical *Mame* (May 1966) which Lawrence and Lee also wrote, featuring the then relatively unknown Angela Lansbury. Their collaboration on a monolithic musical called *Dear World* based on the Giraudoux play *The Madwoman of Chaillot* was less successful. However, it's hard to find fault with writers when faced with the complexities of producing musicals in New York City where music, lyrics, choreography, special songs, production numbers, direction, elaborate costumes, and staggering scenery—along with equally staggering costs—seem often to overwhelm the basic book.

Nevertheless Lawrence and Lee seem happier when they are away from the big-time musical stage, as witness their commitment to a play entitled *The Night Thoreau Spent in Jail*. This play, first presented at Ohio State University in 1970, is an interesting experiment. Some years ago, intent on trying to circumvent the sterile Broadway scene where serious plays are concerned, the partners set up American Playwrights Theatre in Columbus, Ohio. It was a deliberate move away from New York in a laudable attempt to develop new audiences for serious drama, with the plays of dramatists, known and unknown, presented in a new "circuit"—the network of resident and university theatres across America. Each writer was guaranteed a number of *different* productions in various spots on this new circuit and many were produced before Lawrence and Lee launched one of their own—*Thoreau*, a subject of particular interest to young audiences, for it deals with one of the first cases of civil disobedience in America. Later collaborations include *Jabberwock* and *First Monday in October*.

Their hand with humour can, unfortunately, be a little heavy, and when tackling such a delicate exponent of the art as Max Beerbohm in *The Incomparable Max* they became caught in a morass that was anything but Maxian. There are times when the pair cleaves dangerously close to the jungle of clichés.

Lawrence and Lee collaborate easily—each has a veto, "but it's a positive one" says Lawrence. They both feel they can, and do, learn from criticism. Their contribution to American drama is perhaps most significant when one looks at the number of nations that know them from the many translations of their principle works. *Inherit the Wind* has been translated into 28 different languages while the citizens of Ireland, Israel, Holland, Germany, Bangladesh, and Russia, among others, have been given an eye-opening view of a Yankee philosopher's protest in *Thoreau*.

—Michael T. Leech

LEE, Robert E(dwin). American. Born in Elyria, Ohio, 15 October 1918. Educated at Northwestern University, Evanston, Illinois; Drake University, Des Moines, Iowa; Ohio Wesleyan University, Delaware, 1935–37. Served in the United States Army, 1942–45: Expert Consultant to the Secretary of War, 1942; co-founder, Armed Forces Radio Service; writer-director, Armed Forces Radio Service, Los Angeles, 1942–45: Special Citation, Secretary of War, 1945. Married Janet Waldo in 1948; one son and one daughter. Astronomical observer, Perkins Observatory, Delaware, Ohio, 1936–37; director, WHK-WCLE Radio, Cleveland, 1937–38; director, Young and Rubicam, New York and Hollywood, 1938–42; Professor of Playwriting, College of Theatre Arts, Pasadena Playhouse, California, 1962–63. Since 1942 partner, Lawrence and Lee, and since 1955 Vice-President, Lawrence and Lee Inc., New York and Los Angeles; since 1966, Lecturer, University of California, Los Angeles. Co-founder and judge, Margo Jones Award; co-founder, American Playwrights Theatre. Recipient: New York Press Club award, 1942; City College of New York award, 1948; *Radio-TV Life* award, 1948, 1952; Peabody award, 1949, 1952; *Radio-TV Mirror* award, 1952, 1953; *Variety* award, 1954, 1955; Donaldson award, 1955; Outer Circle award, 1955; British Drama Critics award, 1960; Moss Hart Memorial Award, 1967. Lit.D.: Ohio Wesleyan University, 1962; M.A.: Pasadena Playhouse College of Theatre Arts, 1963; H.H.D.: Ohio State University, Columbus, 1979; Litt.D.: College of Wooster, Ohio, 1983. Agent (Attorney): Martin Gang, 6400 Sunset Boulevard, Hollywood, California 90028. Address: 15725 Royal Oak Road, Encino, California 91436, U.S.A.

PUBLICATIONS

Plays

Inside a Kid's Head, with Jerome Lawrence, in *Radio Drama in Action*, edited by Erik Barnouw. New York, Farrar and Rinehart, 1945.

Look, Ma, I'm Dancin', with Jerome Lawrence, music by Hugh Martin, conceived by Jerome Robbins (produced New York, 1948).

The Crocodile Smile, with Jerome Lawrence (as *The Laugh Maker*, produced Hollywood, 1952; revised version, as *Turn on the Night*, produced Philadelphia, 1961; revised version, as *The Crocodile Smile*, produced Flatrock, North Carolina, 1970). New York, Dramatists Play Service, 1972.

Inherit the Wind, with Jerome Lawrence (produced Dallas and New York, 1955; London, 1960). New York, Random House, 1955; London, Four Square, 1960.

Shangri-La, with Jerome Lawrence and James Hilton, music by Harry Warren, adaptation of the novel *Lost Horizon* by Hilton (produced New York, 1956). New York, Morris Music, 1956.

Auntie Mame, with Jerome Lawrence, adaptation of the work by Patrick Dennis (produced New York, 1956; London, 1958). New York, Vanguard Press, 1957; revised version, music by Jerry Herman, as *Mame* (produced New York, 1966; London, 1969), New York, Random House, 1967.

The Gang's All Here, with Jerome Lawrence (produced New York, 1959). Cleveland, World, 1960.

Only in America, with Jerome Lawrence, adaptation of the work by Harry Golden (produced New York, 1959). New York, French, 1960.

A Call on Kuprin, with Jerome Lawrence, adaptation of the novel by Maurice Edelman (produced New York, 1961). New York, French, 1962.

Sparks Fly Upward, with Jerome Lawrence (as *Diamond Orchid*, produced New York, 1965; revised version, as *Sparks Fly Upward*, produced Dallas, 1967). New York, Dramatists Play Service, 1969.

Dear World, with Jerome Lawrence, music by Jerry Herman, based on *The Madwoman of Chaillot* by Giraudoux (produced New York, 1969).

The Incomparable Max, with Jerome Lawrence (produced Abingdon, Virginia, 1969; New York, 1971). New York, Hill and Wang, 1972.

The Night Thoreau Spent in Jail, with Jerome Lawrence (produced Columbus, Ohio, and 154 other theatres, 1970). New York, Hill and Wang, 1970.

Jabberwock: Improbabilities Lived and Imagined by James Thurber in the Fictional City of Columbus, Ohio, with Jerome Lawrence (produced Columbus, Ohio, 1972). New York, French, 1974.

Ten Days That Shook the World, based on reports from Russia by John Reed (also director: produced Los Angeles, 1973).

First Monday in October, with Jerome Lawrence (produced Cleveland, 1975; New York, 1978). New York, French, 1979.
Sounding Brass (produced New York, 1975). New York, French, 1976.

Screenplays, with Jerome Lawrence—*My Love Affair with the Human Race*, 1962; *The New Yorkers*, 1963; *Joyous Season*, 1964; *The Night Thoreau Spent in Jail*, 1972; *First Monday in October*, 1982; with John Sinn—*Quintus*, 1971.

Radio Plays: *Empire Builders* series, 1938; *Opened by Mistake*, 1940; *Flashbacks* series, 1940–41; *Three Sheets to the Wind*, 1942; *Task Force*, 1942; *Ceiling Unlimited*, 1942; *Meet Corliss Archer*, 1942; *Suspense*, 1943; *The Saint* 1945; with Jerome Lawrence—*Columbia Workshop* series, 1941–42; *Armed Forces Radio Service Programs*, 1942–45; *The World We're Fighting For* series, 1943; *Request Performance* series, 1945–46; *Screen Guild Theatre* series, 1946; *Favorite Story* series, 1946–49; *Frank Sinatra Show*, 1947; *Dinah Shore Program*, 1948; *The Railroad Hour*, 1948–54; *Young Love* series, 1949–50; *United Nations Broadcasts*, 1949–50; *Halls of Ivy* series, 1950–51; *Hallmark Playhouse* series, 1950–51; *Charles Boyer Show*, 1951; other free-lance and special programs, 1941–50.

Television Plays: *A Colloquy with Paul*, 1961; with Jerome Lawrence—*The Unexpected* series, 1951; *Favorite Story* series, 1952–53; *Song of Norway*, 1957; *West Point*, 1958; *Actor*, music by Billy Goldenburg, 1978.

Other

Television: The Revolution. New York, Essential, 1944.

*

Manuscript Collections: Lawrence and Lee Theatre Research Institute, Ohio State University, Columbus; Lincoln Center Library of the Performing Arts, New York; Kent State University, Ohio.

Critical Study: "The Greatest Sport in the World" (interview with Christopher Meeks), in *Writer's Digest* (Cincinnati), March 1986.

Theatrical Activities:
Director: **Plays**—*Only in America*, Los Angeles, 1960; *The Night Thoreau Spent in Jail*, Los Angeles, 1970; *The Gang's All Here*, Los Angeles, 1972; *Ten Days That Shook the World*, Los Angeles, 1973.

Robert E. Lee comments:

The devil's name is Dullness. An eraser is sometimes more essential than a pencil. But merely to entertain is fatuous. Writing for today is really writing for yesterday; I try to write for tomorrow.

* * *

See the essay on Jerome Lawrence and Robert E. Lee.

LEIGH, Mike. British. Born in Salford, Lancashire, 20 February 1943. Educated at North Grecian Street County Primary School; Salford Grammar School; Royal Academy of Dramatic Art, London, 1960–62; Camberwell School of Arts and Crafts, London, 1963–64; Central School of Art and Design, London, 1964–68; London Film School, 1965. Married the actress Alison Steadman in 1973; two sons. Founder, with David Halliwell, Dramagraph production company, London, 1965; associate director, Midlands Arts Centre for Young People, Birmingham, 1965–66; actor, Victoria Theatre, Stoke-on-Trent, Staffordshire, 1966; assistant director, Royal Shakespeare Company, 1967–68; lecturer, Sedgley Park and De La Salle colleges, Manchester, 1968–69, and London Film School, 1970–73. Recipient: Chicago Film Festival and Locarno Film Festival awards, for screenplay, 1972; George Devine Award, 1974; *Evening Standard* award, 1982. Agent: A.D. Peters Ltd., 10 Buckingham Street, London WC2N 6BU, England.

PUBLICATIONS

Plays

The Box Play (produced Birmingham, 1965).
My Parents Have Gone to Carlisle (produced Birmingham, 1966).
The Last Crusade of the Five Little Nuns (produced Birmingham, 1966).
Waste Paper Guard (produced Birmingham, 1966).
NENAA (produced Stratford-on-Avon, 1967).
Individual Fruit Pies (produced Loughton, Essex, 1968).
Down Here and Up There (produced London, 1968).
Big Basil (produced Manchester, 1969).
Epilogue (produced Manchester, 1969).
Glum Victoria and the Lad with Specs (produced Manchester, 1969).
Bleak Moments (produced London, 1970).
A Rancid Pong (produced London, 1971).
Wholesome Glory (produced London, 1973).
The Jaws of Death (produced Edinburgh, 1973; London, 1978).
Dick Whittington and His Cat (produced London, 1973).
Babies Grow Old (produced Stratford-on-Avon, 1974; London, 1975).
The Silent Majority (produced London, 1974).
Abigail's Party (produced London, 1977). With *Goose-Pimples*, London, Penguin, 1983.
Ecstasy (produced London, 1979).
Goose-Pimples (produced London, 1981). With *Abigail's Party*, London, Penguin, 1983.

Screenplay: *Bleak Moments*, 1972.

Television Plays: *A Mug's Game*, 1973; *Hard Labour*, 1973; *The Permissive Society*, 1975; *Nuts in May*, 1976; *Knock for Knock*, 1976; *The Kiss of Death*, 1977; *Who's Who*, 1979; *Grown-Ups*, 1980; *Home Sweet Home*, 1982; "Five Minute Plays": *The Birth of the 2001 FA Cup Final Goalie, Old Chums, Probation, A Light Snack*, and *Afternoon*, all 1982; *Meantime*, 1983; *Four Days in July*, 1985.

*

Critical Study: *The Improvised Play: The Work of Mike Leigh* by Paul Clements, London, Methuen, 1983.

Theatrical Activities:
Director and designer of all his own plays.

* * *

Improvisational or "devised" theatre has come of age during the last two decades, as presented by Mike Bradwell of Hull Truck, the northern based touring group, Les Blair both on stage and television, Sheila Kelly and Sarah Pia Anderson, particularly at the Bush Theatre, and even two directors, John Chapman and Tim Fywell, whose slice of Sheffield life, *Safe House* came to the ICA in London from the Yorkshire steel town's Crucible Theatre studio. Yet none of these theatre workers would deny that Mike Leigh is the oldest and the best in this business, someone who started more than 20 years ago and has worked in the form in film, on television, and on the stage.

It has been argued that Leigh's form of theatre doesn't really count as textual or "given," but there is nothing flabby, loosely improvisational, or self-indulgent about his working method, and all plays are finally scripted—his 1977 success *Abigail's Party* has indeed been a success with amateur dramatic groups via French's acting edition.

What Leigh's work does attempt is a distillation from carefully arranged acting exercises into character and then "plot," the latter worked out from interactions between actors in "role" who may not have worked together before and whose initial meeting may come in a "real" context—in a pub, in the back of a taxi, in the street. Leigh, for instance, has instructed his actors to learn Arabic, to walk around a large Midlands town carrying heavy shopping and a hoover, and to find their way to a remote Dorset caravan site on a motorbike posing as "greasers" (motorbike fans). Solitary improvisation is the starting point—to begin with he works with performers individually (after careful process of selection—he looks in particular for a strong sense of humour and regional geography) asking them to develop a character around someone they know, and to stay in that character, particularly when they are on their own, for as long as several months. What happens next is the all-important bringing together of the actors.

Leigh, the son of a doctor, was born near Manchester and studied at the Royal Academy of Dramatic Art before taking a course at Camberwell School of Arts in the early 1960's. Indeed, it was life drawing which gave him the idea for a theatre based on detail and experience, his coaching at RADA striking him as being stultifying and bookish. After film school he joined the Midlands Art Centre in Birmingham and tried out his method on teenagers while waiting for a full-time company which had been slow to materialize. Then came stints at the Royal Shakespeare Company as assistant to Peter Hall and work with both the East 15 Acting School and with the Manchester Youth Theatre. He devised plays with titles like *Individual Fruit Pies* and *My Parents Have Gone to Carlisle* (an early variant on *Abigail's Party*) and directed the original six-hour version of David Halliwell's *Little Malcolm and His Struggle Against the Eunuchs*.

Leigh's first considerable achievement as a deviser came in 1974 with his RSC production at Stratford-on-Avon's Other Place of *Babies Grow Old*, a piece about a group of young Midlands doctors, their motivations and their patients, who included an arthritic old lady and a soldier who'd had his leg shot off—Leigh encouraged the actors in question to improvise freely on their characters before drawing them into the medical arena (one character had a "father" who changed from being a stiff military figure to a rather cold clinical professor of medicine).

After another piece, *The Silent Majority*, Leigh's most popular stage play (he had spent a good deal of the intervening period working in television on grainier, more subdued pieces) came some three years later with *Abigail's Party* which was also televised in an adapted form. The play in question poses one of the most insistent questions in Leigh's work: does he patronise his characters? *Abigail's Party* is centred around a brassy, atavistic matron called Beverley, a beautician whose kitsch and lurid drawing-room provides a battleground for her relationship with her estate-agent husband Laurence who after a night of argument, high activity, and alcohol as well as much viciously satirical talk about "art" (Laurence keeps Dickens on the shelf for the look of the covers rather than for the content) dies in horribly graphic manner from a heart attack. Other guests at the event include a sullen former-footballer and his gruesome wife, a nurse whom he seems to have married out of duty and moral necessity (cf. *Who's Afraid of Virginia Woolf?*), as well as the mother of the Abigail of the title who has arrived at Beverley's to "escape" her adolescent daughter's party, alarming offstage accounts of which permeate the banter. The performance of Leigh's wife, Alison Steadman, as Beverley won her plaudits and even awards but there were accusations that Leigh was merely putting some rather unattractive aspiring middle-class people under the microscope and indeed making them squirm under the tweesers. However, Bernard Levin writing in the *Sunday Times* saw the play as a deeply disturbing but successful comment on a society bereft of spiritual values and the immense loneliness of people looking for something to fill the void left by the decline of Christian values.

Since *Abigail's Party* Leigh's most notable pieces for the stage have been *Ecstasy* and *Goose-Pimples*, the latter providing him with his first West End transfer. *Ecstasy*, which is set in the extremely claustrophobic and depressing bedsitter of a thirty-ish single woman living in the Birmingham area, was a harrowing and elongated study in loneliness in which moments of crassness (including a long sequence of after-pub song-singing which Leigh refused to edit) were interspersed with tense episodes such as that in which Jean, the central character, is forced into sex with a boyfriend who has no interest in her beyond the perfunctory act. There was also a haunting climax in which Jean and an old, rather ridiculous friend from Corby give vent to their inner feelings of loneliness and despair. But *Ecstasy* was certainly not one of Leigh's most harmonious pieces of theatre.

Goose-Pimples is set in a more affluent setting, the Dollis Hill flat of a car dealer whose croupier lodger, Jackie, brings back a lonely Arab businessman (though not an oil sheik as is first thought) who in time mistakes the place for a brothel and, through a series of misunderstandings, proceeds to try to pay for drinks and later for the services of the croupier herself. It's very much a reversal of the farce mechanism to make a point about ideas of hospitality and our treatment of people more vulnerable than ourselves. Not only is Jackie cajoled into bed by the car salesman but he and a male friend from work proceed to abuse and finally humiliate the Arab by drugging his drink. On the way there are some very amusing jokes on the theme of linguistic misunderstanding with the Arab, Muhammed, patting the furniture everytime anyone says "Cheers!" Several eminent Arabs accused Leigh of painting a picture of them as drunken, lecherous, and obsessed with gambling, but indeed Leigh was more concerned with exposing the ignorance and innate superiority many Britishers still feel towards non-Europeans, as well as their predatory attitude towards women whose honour they still pretend to cherish.

Leigh's output is split between television and the stage, and certainly in his stage work he exhibits a more exaggerated and exhibitionist turn than is generally noticeable in his films. His popularity remains one of his biggest assets (his television work has attracted audiences of up to 4 million) as well as his love of detail and authenticity, an impulse which is never totally submerged by his strong sense of the ridiculous and the grimly pathetic.

—Steve Grant

LEONARD, Hugh. Pseudonym for John Keyes Byrne. Irish. Born in Dublin, 9 November 1926. Educated at Presentation College, Dun Laoghaire, 1941–45. Married Paule Jacquet in 1955; one daughter. Civil servant, Dublin, 1945–59; script editor, Granada Television, Manchester, 1961–63; literary editor, Abbey Theatre, Dublin, 1976–77; programme director, Dublin Theatre Festival, 1978–80. Recipient: Italia Prize, for television play, 1967; Writers Guild of Great Britain award, 1967; Tony award, 1978; New York Drama Critics Circle award, 1978; Outer Circle award, 1978; Vernon Rice award, 1978. D.H.L.: Rhode Island College, Providence, 1980. Agent: Harvey Unna and Stephen Durbridge Ltd., 24–32 Pottery Lane, London W11 4LZ, England. Address: 6 Rossaun, Pilot View, Dalkey, County Dublin, Ireland.

PUBLICATIONS

Plays

The Italian Road (produced Dublin, 1954).
The Big Birthday (produced Dublin, 1956).
A Leap in the Dark (produced Dublin, 1957).
Madigan's Lock (produced Dublin, 1958; London, 1963; Olney, Maryland, 1970).
A Walk on the Water (produced Dublin, 1960).
The Passion of Peter Ginty, adaptation of the play *Peer Gynt* by Ibsen (produced Dublin, 1961).
Stephen D, adaptation of the works *A Portrait of the Artist as a Young Man* and *Stephen Hero* by James Joyce (produced Dublin, 1962; London, 1963; New York, 1967). London, Evans, 1965.
Dublin One, adaptation of the stories *Dubliners* by James Joyce (produced Dublin, 1963).
The Poker Session (produced Dublin, 1963; London, 1964; New York, 1967). London, Evans, 1963.
The Family Way, adaptation of a play by Eugène Labiche (produced Dublin, 1964; London, 1966).
The Late Arrival of the Incoming Aircraft (televised 1964). London, Evans, 1968.
A View from the Obelisk (televised 1964; in *Scorpions*, produced Dublin, 1983).
The Saints Go Cycling In, adaptation of the novel *The Dalkey Archives* by Flann O'Brien (produced Dublin, 1965).
Mick and Mick (produced Dublin, 1966; as *All the Nice People*, produced Olney, Maryland, 1976; New York, 1984). London, French, 1966.
A Time of Wolves and Tigers (televised 1967; produced in *Irishmen*, Olney, Maryland, and Dublin, 1975). Included in *Suburb of Babylon*, 1983.
The Quick, and The Dead (produced Dublin, 1967).
The Au Pair Man (produced Dublin, 1968; London, 1969; New York, 1973). Published in *Plays and Players* (London), December 1968; New York, French, 1974.
The Barracks, adaptation of the novel by John McGahern (produced Dublin, 1969).
The Patrick Pearse Motel (produced Dublin and London, 1971; Olney, Maryland, 1972; New York, 1984). London, French, 1972.
Da (produced Olney, Maryland, and Dublin, 1973; London, 1977; New York, 1978). Newark, Delaware, Proscenium Press, 1976; revised version, London, French and New York, Atheneum, 1978.
Summer (produced Olney, Maryland, and Dublin, 1974; London, 1979; New York, 1980). London, French, 1979.
Suburb of Babylon (includes *A Time of Wolves and Tigers, Nothing Personal, The Last of the Last of the Mohicans*) (as *Irishmen*, produced Olney, Maryland, and Dublin, 1975). London, French, 1983.
Some of My Best Friends Are Husbands, adaptation of a play by Eugène Labiche (produced London, 1976).
Liam Liar, adaptation of the play *Billy Liar* by Keith Waterhouse and Willis Hall (produced Dublin, 1976).
Time Was (produced Dublin, 1976). Included in *Da, A Life, Time Was*, 1981.
A Life (produced Dublin, 1979; London and New York, 1980). London, French, 1980; New York, Atheneum, 1981.
Da, A Life, Time Was. London, Penguin, 1981.
Kill (produced Dublin, 1982).
Scorpions (includes *A View from the Obelisk, Roman Fever, Pizzazz*) (produced Dublin, 1983).
The Mask of Moriarty, based on characters by Arthur Conan Doyle (produced Dublin, 1985; Leicester, 1987).

Screenplays: *Great Catherine*, 1967; *Interlude*, with Lee Langley, 1967; *Whirligig*, 1970; *Percy*, with Terence Feely, 1970; *Our Miss Fred*, 1972.

Radio Plays: *The Kennedys of Castlerosse* series.

Television Plays: *The Irish Boys* (trilogy), 1962; *Saki* series, 1962; *A Kind of Kingdom*, 1963; *Jezebel Ex-UK* series, 1963; *The Second Wall*, 1964; *A Triple Irish*, 1964; *Realm of Error*, 1964; *My One True Love*, 1964; *The Late Arrival of the Incoming Aircraft*, 1964; *Do You Play Requests?*, 1964; *A View from the Obelisk*, 1964; *The Hidden Truth* series, 1964; *Undermind* series, 1964; *I Loved You Last Summer*, 1965; *Great Big Blond*, 1965; *Blackmail* series, 1965; *Public Eye* series, 1965; *Simenon* series: *The Lodger* and *The Judge*, 1966; *Insurrection* (8 parts), 1966; *Second Childhood*, 1966; *The Retreat*, 1966; *Silent Song*, from a story by Frank O'Connor, 1966; *The Liars* series, 1966; *The Informer* series, 1966; *Out of the Unknown* series, 1966–67; *A Time of Wolves and Tigers*, 1967; *Love Life*, 1967; *Great Expectations* (serialization), from the novel by Dickens, 1967; *Wuthering Heights* (serialization), from the novel by Emily Brontë, 1967; *No Such Things as a Vampire*, 1968; *The Corpse Can't Play*, 1968; *A Man and His Mother-in-Law*, 1968; *Assassin*, 1968; *Nicholas Nickleby* (serialization), from the novel by Dickens, 1968; *Conan Doyle* series: *A Study in Scarlet* and *The Hound of the Baskervilles*, 1968; *Hunt the Peacock*, from a novel by H.R.F. Keating, 1969; *Talk of Angels*, 1969; *The Possessed* (serialization), from a novel by Dostoevsky, 1969; *Dombey and Son* (serialization), from the novel by Dickens, 1969; *Somerset Maugham* series: *P & O*, 1969, and *Jane*, 1970; *A Sentimental Education* (serialization), from a novel by Flaubert, 1970; *The Sinners* series, 1970–71; *Me Mammy* series, 1970–71; *White Walls and Olive Green Carpets*, 1971; *The Removal Person*, 1971; *Pandora*, 1971; *The Virgins*, 1972; *The Ghost of Christmas Present*, 1972; *The Truth Game*, 1972; *Tales from the Lazy Acres* series, 1972; *The Moonstone* (serialization), from the novel by Wilkie Collins, 1972; *The Sullen Sisters*, 1972; *The Watercress Girl*, from the story by H.E. Bates, 1972; *The Higgler*, 1973; *High Kampf*, 1973; *Milo O'Shea*, 1973; *Stone Cold Sober*, 1973; *The Bitter Pill*, 1973; *Another Fine Mess*, 1973; *Judgement Day*, 1973; *The Travelling Woman*, 1973; *The Hammer of God, The Actor and the Alibi, The Eye of Apollo, The Forbidden Garden, The Three Tools of Death*, and *The Quick One* (*Father Brown* series), 1974; *London Belongs to Me*, from the novel by Norman Collins, 1977; *Bitter Suite*, 1977; *Teresa, The Fur Coat*, and *Two of a Kind*, from stories by Sean O'Faolain, 1977; *The Last Campaign*, from the novel *The Captains and the Kings* by Jennifer Johnston, 1978; *The Ring and the Rose*, 1978; *Strumpet City*, from the novel by James Plunkett, 1980; *The Little World of Don Camillo*, from a novel by Giovanni Guareschi, 1981; *Good Behaviour*, from a work by Molly Keane, 1983; *O'Neill* series, 1983; *The Irish R.M.* series, 1985; *Hunted Down*, from a story by Dickens, 1985; *Troubles*, 1987.

Other

Leonard's Last Book (essays). Enniskerry, County Wicklow, Egoist Press, 1978.
A Peculiar People and Other Foibles (essays). Enniskerry, County Wicklow, Tansy, 1979.
Home Before Night: Memoirs of an Irish Time and Place. London, Deutsch, 1979; New York, Atheneum, 1980.
Leonard's Year (journalism). Dublin, Canavaun, 1985.

*

Bibliography: *Ten Modern Irish Playwrights* by Kimball King, New York, Garland, 1979.

Theatrical Activities:
Actor: **Play**—in *A Walk on the Water*, Dublin, 1960.

Hugh Leonard comments:

(1973) Being an Irish writer both hampers and helps me: hampers, because one is fighting the preconceptions of audiences who have been conditioned to expect feyness and parochial subject matter; helps, because the writer can utilise a vigorous and poetic idiom which enables him to combine subtlety with richness. Ireland is my subject matter, but only to the degree in which I can use it as a microcosm; this involves choosing themes which are free of Catholicism and politics, both of which I detest, and which deprive one's work of applicability outside Ireland.

For many years I was obsessed with the theme of betrayal (*A Walk on the Water* and *The Poker Session*)—its effects and its inevitability. My work then began to reflect a preoccupation with defining and isolating the essence of the new prosperity, which I used as the subject for satire (*The Patrick Pearse Motel* and *Thieves*, as yet unproduced). By and large—and after the event—my work reflects Ibsen's observation that to be a writer is to sit in judgment on oneself; and perhaps for this reason I now want to write a play which, like *A Walk on the Water* and *Pandora*, is autobiographical. Like most writers I am involved in seeking a form. A play takes me a long time to write, and my methods involve—partly deliberately, partly because of how I work—various subterranean levels. At times this leads to an excess of cleverness, stemming perhaps from a lack of faith in one's own powers. Now that I have learned both the requirements and the uses of the dramatic form I would like to use a simplicity of style combined with visual situations—the image in my mind is the scene in which Lavinia confronts her mother across her father's corpse in *Mourning Becomes Electra*.

Like all writers who achieve middle-age, I am conscious of having wasted time, and also of having at last arrived at a sense of identity. Ideally, I would now like to write my "failures"; i.e., plays written as pure acts of self-expression, without any hope of their being staged. I am conscious that my main faults are the cleverness (in the structural sense) which I have mentioned and at times an irresponsible sense of comedy, which is not so much out of place as inclined to give my work an unintended lightness. These faults at least I know and can guard against. I regard myself as an optimist, and the theme that emerges from my plays is that life is good if it is not misused. But this is only an impression which—again after the event—I have gleaned from revisiting my work. As Moss Hart has said, one begins with two people on a stage, and one of them had better say something pretty damn quick! One starts to write, and one's own character and beliefs—not consciously defined—shapes, limits, enriches, pauperises, and defines one's work. Choice of subject and form are the cartridge case which contains the bullet. A play is an accident: often one writes the right play at the wrong time in one's life, and vice-versa; often one begins to write it that vital fraction in time before it has ripened in one's skull—or a moment too late, when it has gone cold. One goes on trying.

* * *

In the masterful autobiography of his early years, *Home Before Night*, Hugh Leonard tells of his gradual progress into the stifling prize of a job in the Irish civil service. The book is an eloquent statement of reconciliation, exploring his illegitimacy and family relationships, and is a rich lode of characters, full of personalities that are developed further in his plays. There is a passage toward the end where he records his first serious experience of theatre-going, when he visited the Abbey's production of Sean O'Casey's *The Plough and the Stars*. His prose crystallizes that experience, communicating the personal epiphany that made him a playwright. Rushing from the theatre to a train, he found himself in a compartment with a courting couple, sulking at his presence: "The pair of them could strip to their skins for all he cared. He looked away from them through the window and saw his reflection in the dark glass. It was amazing how calm he looked. His breath in the unheated compartment threw a mist upon the glass, but even then he could see, as if it was out there by the tracks, the door he would escape through."

Since O'Casey Irish playwrights have made Ireland their major subject. Leonard has claimed his place in that tradition, but there are essential differences, and he has always looked for broader applicability. He works mainly through the emergent middle classes of Ireland, with conflicts more suburban than urban and politics and religion as mere ghosts in the background. They are, of course, inescapable ghosts.

His best plays explore the characters of his own life, and stretch from *A Walk on the Water* to *A Life*, with 20 years of experience between the plays and a rare, deepening texture that demonstrates his own increased understanding of the past. Memory is also the form of many of his adaptations, including his first international success, *Stephen D*, a dramatization of James Joyce's autobiographical books. Using both *A Portrait of the Artist as a Young Man* and Joyce's earlier, more straightforward version of the book, *Stephen Hero*, Leonard showed his sympathy for the metaphysical flight of Dedalus—Joyce's own exile from church, family, and Ireland—as directly as if telling his own story.

His earliest plays found him more within the Irish dramatic tradition, even showing a concern with politics, but the form of *A Leap in the Dark* suggested his alienation from the violent course Irish politics often took. On a New Year's Eve in Dublin, a father and son fall out over the new troubles in Northern Ireland, with the son opposing the violence so completely that his best friend tries to show the reasoning behind the border raids by confessing his own part in them. The son, Charles, then discovers that another raid is in the making and sets out to inform the police. On his return to the house, he is shot.

It is rare that such scenes are depicted in Leonard's work, but his private path has wandered in many directions. After his start in theatre, writing plays for the Dublin Theatre Festival, he learned the disciplines of prolificacy by writing a serial called *The Kennedys of Castlerosse* for commercial radio. He went from Irish radio to British television, editing scripts, writing dramas and churning out numerous series. In the midst of that work, and while providing a steady stream of original plays for the stage, he continued adapting the work of other writers. Before *Stephen D*, there was the Irish *Peer Gynt*, which he called *The Passion of Peter Ginty*. Flann O'Brien's surreal humour in *The Dalkey Archives* went to the stage as *The Saints Go Cycling In* and *Billy Liar* was transformed into an Irish play for the Abbey as *Liam Liar*.

Leonard, who is known to most of Ireland as Jack Byrne, or plain Jack, since they reject the pseudonym of Hugh Leonard, is quick to point out that an Irish literary movement is when two playwrights are on speaking terms. Nonetheless he has found himself at the centre of Irish letters on several occasions, including the stormy year he spent as literary manager of the Abbey and during his spell of literary management as one of the directors of the important Dublin Theatre Festival. Those positions were dignified by his presence, for there is no doubt that he is a major playwright of international importance.

For a long time he had a rewarding relationship with a theatre in Olney, Maryland, just outside Washington, D.C. Plays such as *The Patrick Pearse Motel* and *Da* were mounted in Olney well before New York took notice. New York, however, finally did with *Da* what London regularly refused to do with Leonard's critically well-regarded work; it gave him a major popular success.

The play is a joyous one, undisguisedly about the death of Leonard's own stepfather, the Da of the title. At the father's death the son flies from London to Dublin for the funeral, only to find that the old man wanders in to discuss the funeral and claim his place in his stepson's heart and mind. Leonard links past and present with the son's younger self, who is also on hand, reliving the traumas of adolescence, fighting it out with his mother, and getting furiously annoyed with his Da. The memories of the past and the details of the present, which include putting the meagre effects of the father into order, are so ingeniously layered that farce, understanding, and frustrated fury all manage to coexist, and, from Leonard's precise evocation of individuals at different points in time, the love that comes from understanding is conveyed.

A minor figure from *Da* is the character of Drumm, a man who figures in the autobiography as the civil servant who brings Leonard into the civil service. In *Da* he complains of "tummy trouble" which is revealed as cancer in the next memory play, *A Life*. Again, past and present coexist, with Drumm irascibly trying to make his peace with the girl he failed to marry in his youth while witnessing his younger self making all the original mistakes that foretold his old age as a bundle of attitudes and principles. The delicacy of Leonard's imagery and the richness of his comedy deflects the maudlin potential of the story, and the affirmation of life is reflected even in the final sentence when Drumm confronts the imminence of death and says to his wife, "Let's make a start." In those plays, Leonard is a writer at the height of his powers and he confirms his ability to extend the specific to a large audience: it is as if he were a master of the spectator's memories as well as his own.

A spectacular Dublin story about money siphoned out of Leonard's accounts saw to it that Leonard spent the greater part of his time for a few years after *A Life* concentrating on the more lucrative expression of films, but he never abandoned the theatre. His most notable advance was *Kill*, a dinner-party metaphor about Irish politics with some acidly presented characters all too recognizable to the Irish audience. His presentation of the Irish government as covert collaborators with terror alienated some of his audience, but not permanently. His Sherlock Holmes adventure, *The Mask of Moriarty*, was the hit of the 1985 Dublin Theatre Festival despite a notorious interview with the play's leading actor which gave away the twist in the play before it opened.

—Ned Chaillet

LESSING, Doris (May, née Tayler). British. Born in Kermansha, Persia, 22 October 1919; moved with her family to Banket, Southern Rhodesia, 1924. Educated at Dominican Convent School, Salisbury, Southern Rhodesia, 1926–34. Married 1) Frank Charles Wisdom in 1939 (divorced 1943), one son and one daughter; 2) Gottfried Lessing in 1945 (divorced 1949), one son. Au pair, Salisbury, 1934–35; telephone operator and clerk, Salisbury, 1937–39; typist, 1946–48; journalist, Cape Town *Guardian*, 1949; moved to London, 1950; secretary, 1950; member of the Editorial Board, *New Reasoner* (later *New Left Review*), 1956. Recipient: Maugham Award, for fiction, 1954; Médicis Prize (France), 1976; Austrian State Prize, 1981; Shakespeare Prize (Hamburg), 1982; W. H. Smith Literary Award, 1986. Associate Member, American Academy, 1974; Honorary Fellow, Modern Language Association (USA), 1974. Agent: Jonathan Clowes Ltd., 22 Prince Albert Road, London NW1 7ST, England.

PUBLICATIONS

Plays

Before the Deluge (produced London, 1953).
Mr. Dollinger (produced Oxford, 1958).
Each His Own Wilderness (produced London, 1958). Published in *New English Dramatists*, London, Penguin, 1959.
The Truth about Billy Newton (produced Salisbury, Wiltshire, 1960).
Play with a Tiger (produced Brighton and London, 1962; New York, 1964). London, Joseph, 1962; in *Plays by and about Women*, edited by Victoria Sullivan and James V. Hatch, New York, Random House, 1973.
The Storm, adaptation of a play by Alexander Ostrovsky (produced London, 1966).
The Singing Door (for children), in *Second Playbill 2*, edited by Alan Durband. London, Hutchinson, 1973.

Television Plays: *The Grass Is Singing*, from her own novel, 1962; *Care and Protection* and *Do Not Disturb* (both in *Blackmail* series), 1966; *Between Men*, 1967.

Novels

The Grass Is Singing. London, Joseph, and New York, Crowell, 1950.
Children of Violence:
Martha Quest. London, Joseph, 1952; with *A Proper Marriage*, New York, Simon and Schuster, 1964.
A Proper Marriage. London, Joseph, 1954; with *Martha Quest*, New York, Simon and Schuster, 1964.
A Ripple from the Storm. London, Joseph, 1958; with *Landlocked*, New York, Simon and Schuster, 1966.
Landlocked. London, MacGibbon and Kee, 1965; with *A Ripple from the Storm*, New York, Simon and Schuster, 1966.
The Four-Gated City. London, MacGibbon and Kee, and New York, Knopf, 1969.
Retreat to Innocence. London, Joseph, 1956; New York, Prometheus, 1959.
The Golden Notebook. London, Joseph, and New York, Simon and Schuster, 1962.
Briefing for a Descent into Hell. London, Cape, and New York, Knopf, 1971.
The Summer Before the Dark. London, Cape, and New York, Knopf, 1973.
The Memoirs of a Survivor. London, Octagon Press, 1974; New York, Knopf, 1975.
Canopus in Argos: Archives:
Shikasta. London, Cape, and New York, Knopf, 1979.
The Marriages Between Zones Three, Four, and Five. London, Cape, and New York, Knopf, 1980.
The Sirian Experiments. London, Cape, and New York, Knopf, 1981.
The Making of the Representative for Planet 8. London, Cape, and New York, Knopf, 1982.
The Sentimental Agents. London, Cape, and New York, Knopf, 1983.
The Diaries of Jane Somers. New York, Vintage, and London, Joseph, 1984.
The Diary of a Good Neighbour (as Jane Somers). London, Joseph, and New York, Knopf, 1983.
If the Old Could—(as Jane Somers). London, Joseph, and New York, Knopf, 1984.
The Good Terrorist. London, Cape, and New York, Knopf, 1985.

Short Stories

This Was the Old Chief's Country. London, Joseph, 1951; New York, Crowell, 1952.
Five: Short Novels. London, Joseph, 1953.
No Witchcraft for Sale: Stories and Short Novels. Moscow, Foreign Language Publishing House, 1956.
The Habit of Loving. London, MacGibbon and Kee, and New York, Crowell, 1957.
A Man and Two Women. London, MacGibbon and Kee, and New York, Simon and Schuster, 1963.
African Stories. London, Joseph, 1964; New York, Simon and Schuster, 1965.
Winter in July. London, Panther, 1966.
The Black Madonna. London, Panther, 1966.
Nine African Stories, edited by Michael Marland. London, Longman, 1968.
The Story of a Non-Marrying Man and Other Stories. London, Cape, 1972; as *The Temptation of Jack Orkney and Other Stories*, New York, Knopf, 1972.
Collected African Stories. New York, Simon and Schuster, 1981.
1. *This Was the Old Chief's Country*. London, Joseph, 1973.
2. *The Sun Between Their Feet*. London, Joseph, 1973.
(*Stories*), edited by Alan Cattell. London, Harrap, 1976.
Collected Stories: To Room Nineteen and *The Temptation of Jack Orkney*. London, Cape, 2 vols., 1978; as *Stories*, New York, Knopf, 1 vol., 1978.

Verse

Fourteen Poems. Northwood, Middlesex, Scorpion Press, 1959.

Other

Going Home. London, Joseph, 1957; revised edition, London, Panther, and New York, Ballantine, 1968.
In Pursuit of the English: A Documentary. London, MacGibbon and Kee, 1960; New York, Simon and Schuster, 1961.
Particularly Cats. London, Joseph, and New York, Simon and Schuster, 1967.
A Small Personal Voice: Essays, Reviews, Interviews, edited by Paul Schlueter. New York, Knopf, 1974.
The Wind Blows Away Our Words (on Afghanistan). London, Pan, 1987.
Prisons We Choose to Live Inside. London, Cape, 1987.

*

Bibliography: *Doris Lessing: A Bibliography* by Catharina Ipp, Johannesburg, University of the Witwatersrand Department of Bibliography, 1967; *Doris Lessing: A Checklist of Primary and Secondary Sources* by Selma R. Burkom and Margaret Williams, Troy, New York, Whitston, 1973; *Doris Lessing: An Annotated Bibliography of Criticism* by Dee Seligman, Westport, Connecticut, Greenwood Press, 1981; *Doris Lessing: A Descriptive Bibliography of Her First Editions* by Eric T. Brueck, London, Metropolis, 1984.

Critical Studies (selection): *Doris Lessing* by Dorothy Brewster, New York, Twayne, 1965; *Doris Lessing*, London, Longman, 1973, and *Doris Lessing's Africa*, London, Evans, 1978, New York, Holmes and Meier, 1979, both by Michael Thorpe; *Doris Lessing: Critical Studies* edited by Annis Pratt and L.S. Dembo, Madison, University of Wisconsin Press, 1974; *Notebooks/Memoirs/Archives: Reading and Re-reading Doris Lessing* edited by Jenny Taylor, London and Boston, Routledge, 1982; *Doris Lessing* by Lorna Sage, London, Methuen, 1983; *Doris Lessing* by Mona Knapp, New York, Ungar, 1984; *Doris Lessing* edited by Eve Bertelsen, Johannesburg, McGraw Hill, 1985; *Critical Essays on Doris Lessing* edited by Claire Sprague and Virginia Tiger, Boston, Hall, 1986.

* * *

In any theatre, a deal of talent must go to waste, especially among playwrights, but it is a great pity that Doris Lessing's career as a playwright should have been abortive. One of the failures of George Devine's successful regime at the Royal Court was its failure to help her to go on from *Each His Own Wilderness*, which was given a Sunday night production in 1958.

Though it was dismissed by many of the critics as a novelist's play can so readily be dismissed, simply by describing it as "a novelist's play," in fact it was remarkably free from the flaws that might have been expected—flat characters, over-leisurely development, verbal analysis written out as dialogue, lack of dramatic drive. Lessing had, on the contrary, a very keen instinct for how to ignite a situation theatrically.

By building the play around a mother-son conflict and empathising successfully with the son, she steered clear of the pitfall of subordinating all the other characters to the woman she could most easily identify with. Myra Bolton is an attractive, middle-aged campaigner for left-wing causes, warm, well-meaning, but gauche in human relationships, liable to inflict unintended pain not only on her son but on the three men in the play she has had relationships with—two of her own generation, one of her son's. The muddles and misunderstandings of these involvements are all developed in a way that contributes richly to the play's dramatic texture, and the untidiness we see on the set—the hall of her London house—contributes visually to the impression of an inability to keep things under control.

The men are all well characterized—the sad, ageing, lonely politician, the architect trying to embark on a new marriage with a young girl, the opportunistic 22-year-old son of a woman friend, and above all Tony, the son, who returns from National Service to find Myra did not know which day to expect him. His pained anger at his own inability to commit himself to any outside reality and at the lack of understanding between them mounts effectively through the play, reaching a climax when he discovers that Myra has sold the house he loves more than anything, intending to help him by raising money to set him up on his own in a flat. It may be a well-made play but it is made remarkably well, with an unusual talent for keeping a number of relationships simultaneously on the boil, and it catches the flavour of the life of left-wing intellectuals in the 1950's. Showing private people devoting their lives protesting about public issues, Lessing successfully merges personal and political themes. Like the characters in John McGrath's play, these people are all "plugged-in to history."

Lessing had started writing for the theatre five years earlier, in 1953, and of the three plays she turned out *Mr. Dollinger* was also produced in 1958, earlier in the year, at the Oxford Playhouse, and *The Truth about Billy Newton* was produced in 1960 at Salisbury. But the only play of hers to receive a full-scale London production was *Play with a Tiger* which was written in 1958 and had a seven-and-a-half week run at the Comedy in 1962 with Siobhan McKenna as the central character, who is, unfortunately, very much more central than any of the characters in *Each His Own Wilderness*.

Lessing was determined to turn her back on both naturalism and realism. "It is my intention," she wrote in a 1963 note on the play,

> that when the curtain comes down at the end, the audience will think: Of course! In this play no one lit cigarettes, drank tea or coffee, read newspapers, squirted soda into Scotch, or indulged in little bits of "business" which indicated "character." They will realize, I hope, that they have been seeing a play which relies upon its style and its language for its effect.

But it starts off naturalistically in an underfurnished room with a litter of books and cushions, paraffin heaters, a record player, and a telephone. There are also sound effects of traffic noises. Anna Freeman is a woman of "35 or so" who lives as a literary freelance, has a son by a broken marriage and has recently decided not to marry an Englishman who is about to settle for a safe job on a woman's magazine. She is in love with an American Jew who would never settle and if she had been entertaining ideas of marrying him, these would be killed off in Act 1 by the visit of a nice young American girl who announces that she is going to have Dave's baby.

The play's starting points, in other words, are all naturalistic and there is even a naturalistic cliché neighbour who fusses about an invisible cat. But towards the end of Act 1 the walls disappear, and though the neighbour is going to reappear and the play is still going to make gestures towards satisfying the audience expectations that its first half-hour has aroused, its centre has been shifted. With only a few interruptions from other characters, about 62 pages of the 92-page script are taken up with a dialogue between Anna and Dave. But the language and the style cannot depart completely from those of the naturalistic beginning. Some of the writing in it is very good, some of it bad and embarrassing, especially when they play games reminiscent of the psychoanalytical situation.

Even the best sections of the dialogue, which make a defiant and articulate declaration of rights on behalf of the woman against the male predator, tend to generalize the play away from its roots in the specific predicament of a specific woman. In reacting against naturalism, Lessing is renouncing all its disciplines, some of which were very useful to her in *Each His Own Wilderness*. *Play with a Tiger* may look more like a public statement and it was seized on by feminist groups, whose performances unbalanced the central relationship by failing to give Dave equal weight with Anna. Lessing complained about this in a 1972 postscript, but the fault is basically in the play, which is really more private than *Each His Own Wilderness*, and more self-indulgent, in that the dialogue is spun too directly out of personal preoccupations.

—Ronald Hayman

LINNEY, Romulus. American. Born in Philadelphia, Pennsylvania, in 1930. Educated at Oberlin College, Ohio, A.B. 1953; Yale University School of Drama, New Haven, Connecticut, M.F.A. 1958. Served in the United States Army, 1954–56. Actor and director in stock for 6 years; stage manager, Actors Studio, New York, 1960; has taught at the Manhattan School of Music, University of North Carolina, Chapel Hill, University of Pennsylvania, Philadelphia, Brooklyn College, Princeton University, New Jersey, Columbia University, New York, Hunter College, New York, and Connecticut College, New London. Recipient: National Endowment for the Arts grant, 1974; Obie award, 1980; Guggenheim fellowship, 1980; Mishima prize, for fiction, 1981; American Academy award, 1984; Rockefeller fellowship, 1986. Lives in New York City. Agent: Gilbert Parker, William Morris Agency, 1350 Avenue of the Americas, New York, New York 10019, U.S.A.

PUBLICATIONS

Plays

The Sorrows of Frederick (produced Los Angeles, 1967; Birmingham, 1970; New York, 1976). New York, Harcourt Brace, 1966.

The Love Suicide at Schofield Barracks (produced New York, 1972). With *Democracy and Esther*, New York, Harcourt

Brace, 1973; one-act version (produced Louisville, 1984), in *The Best Short Plays 1986*, edited by Ramon Delgado, New York, Applause, 1986.

Democracy and Esther, adaptation of the novels by Henry Adams (as *Democracy*, produced Richmond, Virginia, 1974; revised version produced Milwaukee, 1975). With *The Love Suicide at Schofield Barracks*, New York, Harcourt Brace, 1973; as *Democracy*, New York, Dramatists Play Service, 1976.

Holy Ghosts (produced New York, 1974). With *The Sorrows of Frederick*, New York, Harcourt Brace, 1977.

The Seasons, Man's Estate (produced New York, 1974).

Appalachia Sounding (produced on tour, 1975).

Old Man Joseph and His Family (produced New York, 1977). New York, Dramatists Play Service, 1978.

Childe Byron (produced Richmond, Virginia, 1977; revised version produced Louisville, New York, and London, 1981). New York, Dramatists Play Service, 1981.

Just Folks (produced New York, 1978).

The Death of King Philip, music by Paul Earls (produced Boston, 1979). New York, Dramatists Play Service, 1984.

Tennessee (produced New York, 1979). New York, Dramatists Play Service, 1980.

El Hermano (produced New York, 1981). New York, Dramatists Play Service, 1981.

The Captivity of Pixie Shedman (produced New York, 1981). New York, Dramatists Play Service, 1981.

Goodbye, Howard (produced New York, 1982). Included in *Laughing Stock*, 1984.

Gardens of Eden (produced New York, 1982).

F.M. (also director: produced Philadelphia, 1982; New York, 1984). Included in *Laughing Stock*, 1984.

April Snow (produced Costa Mesa, California, 1983; New York, 1987).

Laughing Stock (includes *Goodbye, Howard*; *F.M.*; *Tennessee*) (produced New York, 1984). New York, Dramatists Play Service, 1984.

Wrath, in *Faustus in Hell* (produced Princeton, New Jersey, 1985).

Sand Mountain (includes *Sand Mountain Matchmaking* and *Why the Lord Come to Sand Mountain*) (produced New York, 1986). New York, Dramatists Play Service, 1985.

A Woman Without a Name (produced Denver, 1986). New York, Dramatists Play Service, 1986.

Pops (produced New York, 1986). New York, Dramatists Play Service, 1987.

Heathen Valley, adaptation of his own novel (produced Denver, 1986).

Television Plays: *The 34th Star*, 1976; episodes for *Feelin' Good* series, 1976–77.

Novels

Heathen Valley. New York, Atheneum, 1962; London, Cassell, 1963.

Slowly, By Thy Hand Unfurled. New York, Harcourt Brace, 1965; London, Cassell, 1966.

Jesus Tales. San Francisco, North Point Press, 1980.

Other

Editor, with Norman A. Bailey and Domenick Cascio, *Ten Plays for Radio*. Minneapolis, Burgess, 1954.

Editor, with Norman A. Bailey and Domenick Cascio, *Radio Classics*. Minneapolis, Burgess, 1956.

*

Manuscript Collection: Lincoln Center Library for the Performing Arts, New York.

Theatrical Activities:
Director: **Play**—*F.M.*, Philadelphia, 1982.

Romulus Linney comments:

My plays and novels are drawn from either historical subjects or memories of my childhood in Tennessee and North Carolina, or direct personal experiences.

* * *

Romulus Linney has worked at the writer's trade as playwright, novelist, and television scriptwriter. His dramatic writing thus far has garnered awards and resulted in more than 15 plays produced on and off Broadway, in American regional theatres, and abroad. Widely ranging in subject and structure, Linney's plays mark a distinctive writer of uncommon literacy.

Linney often develops in his dramas a pattern of action in which his protagonists enter or mature in environments where they confront values repressive of their own worth as individuals. Usually tempted or victimized by such values, these characters experience them while testing or evaluating them against their own needs and beliefs and ultimately reaching a decision to accept or reject them. This pattern is evident in at least six plays: *The Love Suicide at Schofield Barracks*, *Democracy*, *Holy Ghosts*, *A Woman Without a Name*, *Tennessee*, and *The Sorrows of Frederick*.

Within the framework of a military inquiry, *The Love Suicide at Schofield Barracks* reveals the events behind the bizarre double suicide of an army general and his wife in 1970 in Hawaii at a Schofield Barracks Officers' Club party. As witnesses testify, a compassionate portrait emerges of a patriotic professional soldier whose beliefs become so shattered by Vietnam that with his wife he perpetrates—in the guise of a classic Japanese drama—a ritualistic suicide symbolizing disapproval of the war and America's conduct. The play generates considerable tension as the event is finally pieced together, and makes a strong statement about war and individual responsibility for national morality. Linney also wrote an equally powerful one-act version preserving the original's skillfully orchestrated characters.

Democracy, a combined dramatization of two Henry Adams 19th-century novels, introduces a wealthy widow and an agnostic photographer, two attractive and intelligent women who in 1875 enter Washington's Presidential society during the corruption-ridden Grant administration, to be charmed and courted by, respectively, a powerful senator rationalizing corruption as necessary to democracy and an attractive clergyman who is convinced that hypocrisy is acceptable in a helpmate. Although tempted to marry, the women courageously reject the men whose beliefs they abhor, and depart. Major characters are richly drawn; the values of 19th-century American democracy are examined in a manner provocative and dramatic.

In *Holy Ghosts* a runaway wife flees a boorish husband to find sanctuary with a Pentecostal sect whose members seek redemption from self-loathing by surviving the suicidal handling of poisonous snakes. When the husband angrily comes to reclaim his newly converted wife and lets his low self-esteem turn him into a convert during the cult's ritual, the wife abandons her conversion and leaves, resolving to achieve independence and self-realization. This theatrically intriguing drama of redemption colorfully recreates the rural southern milieu and its dispossessed. Also rising above domestic strife and despair by achieving self-recognition is the title character in *A Woman Without a Name*, a drama adapted from Linney's novel *Slowly, By Thy Hand Unfurled*. She is an uneducated, small-town southern wife and mother tormented both by her turn-of-the-century family's afflictions (ranging from illness and incest to death) and by its unfair calumny of her regarding its travails. With despairing self-doubt she records memories of family experiences in a journal as characters come forward re-enacting events and interacting with her as participant, and progressively becomes more literate and liberated as she absolves herself of guilt and discovers her self-worth when her integrity earns her leadership in the Women's Temperance Movement. Starkly yet imaginatively conceived, the play paints a compelling portrait of feminine endurance and self-discovery. Similarly effective, the Obie-winning *Tennessee*, set in 1870, portrays an elderly Appalachian woman, her family's sole survivor, who recalls her youth and realizes her late husband had cheated her of independence by tricking her into a frontier marriage's stern service. The richly rounded protagonist and vividly detailed exposition create a definitive world of the past with present parallels. (Appearing in a short-play trilogy collectively entitled *Laughing Stock*, *Tennessee* accompanies two efficacious comedies: *Goodbye, Howard*, about three sisters' confused death-watch over a brother; and *F. M.*, focusing on a talented rough-diamond student writer who shocks dilettante classmates in a creative writing course.)

The Sorrows of Frederick offers a psychological portrait of Prussia's philosopher-king Frederick the Great. Introduced as a snarling, sardonic septuagenarian, Frederick recalls his life when journeying homeward to bury a beloved dog after irrationally dismissing an army before battle. In a series of sharply etched scenes, Linney unravels the chronicle of a father-dominated prince who as a king forsakes great artistic and intellectual gifts to pursue power and finds himself a victim of his life at its end. Enriched by elevated dramatic language and full characterizations, the drama revivifies Frederick and, like the plays already discussed, exemplifies Linney's concern with characters resolving their destinies by their choice of values.

Apparent in Linney's work is a penchant for comedy, romance, and the one-act form, demonstrated by two collective works of short plays: *Sand Mountain* and *Pops*. Strong in homespun humor, *Sand Mountain* encompasses two Appalachian folklore yarns about, respectively, a discriminating young widow who rejects a bragging band of eligible men for a truth-telling widower, and the visit of a humanly disguised Jesus and St. Peter to a mountaineer family. *Pops*, consisting of six amusingly thoughtful one-acts, treats forms of love, young and old, from the romantic to the aesthetic. Among the collection's funniest works are those of a progeny-opposed oldsters' romance (*Tonight We Love*) and a 10th-century abbess's defense of Hrosvitha's, and her own, right to create art (*Ave Maria*). The entire collection is comedically rich.

A writer of substance and range, Linney creates plays that crackle with challenging issues and theatricality, and evince by the spectrum of their structural variety an imaginative craftsman. He is a major talent among contemporary dramatists.

—Christian H. Moe

LIVINGS, Henry. British. Born in Prestwich, Lancashire, 20 September 1929. Educated at Park View Primary School, 1935–39; Stand Grammar School, Prestwich (scholarship), 1940–45; Liverpool University, 1945–47, read Hispanic studies. Served in the Royal Air Force, 1950–52. Married Judith Francis Carter in 1957; one son and one daughter. Worked for Puritex, Leicester, then actor with Theatre Royal, Leicester, and many repertory companies; associated with the BBC programme *Northern Drift*. Recipient: *Evening Standard* award, 1961; Encyclopaedia Britannica award, 1965; Obie award, 1966. Agent: Harvey Unna and Stephen Durbridge Ltd., 24–32 Pottery Lane, London W11 4LZ. Address: 49 Grains Road, Delph, Oldham, Lancashire OL3 5DS, England.

PUBLICATIONS

Plays

Stop It Whoever You Are (produced London, 1961). Published in *New English Dramatists 5*, London, Penguin, 1962.

Big Soft Nellie (as *Thacred Nit*, produced Keswick, Cumberland, 1961; as *Big Soft Nellie*, produced Oxford and London, 1961). Included in *Kelly's Eye and Other Plays*, 1964.

Nil Carborundum (produced London, 1962). Published in *New English Dramatists 6*, London, Penguin, 1963.

Kelly's Eye (produced London, 1963). Included in *Kelly's Eye and Other Plays*, 1964.

There's No Room for You Here for a Start (televised 1963). Included in *Kelly's Eye and Other Plays*, 1964.

The Day Dumbfounded Got His Pylon (broadcast 1963; produced Stoke-on-Trent, 1965). Published in *Worth a Hearing: A Collection of Radio Plays*, edited by Alfred Bradley, London, Blackie, 1967.

Kelly's Eye and Other Plays. London, Methuen, and New York, Hill and Wang, 1964.

Eh? (produced London, 1964; Cincinnati and New York, 1966). London, Methuen, 1965; New York, Hill and Wang, 1967.

The Little Mrs. Foster Show (produced Liverpool, 1966; revised version, also director: produced Nottingham, 1968). London, Methuen, 1969.

Brainscrew (televised 1966; produced Birmingham, 1971). Published in *Second Playbill 3*, edited by Alan Durban, London, Hutchinson, 1973.

Good Grief! (includes *After the Last Lamp, You're Free, Variable Lengths, Pie-Eating Contest, Does It Make Your Cheeks Ache?, The Reasons for Flying*) (produced Manchester, 1967). London, Methuen, 1968.

Honour and Offer (produced Cincinnati, 1968; London, 1969). London, Methuen, 1969.

The Gamecock (produced Manchester, 1969). Included in *Pongo Plays 1–6*, 1971.

Rattel (produced Manchester, 1969; London, 1974). Included in *Pongo Plays 1–6*, 1971.

Variable Lengths and Longer: An Hour of Embarrassment (includes *The Reasons for Flying, Does It Make Your Cheeks Ache?*) (produced London, 1969).

The Boggart (produced Birmingham, 1970). Included in *Pongo Plays 1–6*, 1971.

Conciliation (produced Lincoln, 1970; London, 1971). Included in *Pongo Plays 1–6*, 1971.

The Rifle Volunteer (produced Birmingham, 1970; London, 1971). Included in *Pongo Plays 1–6*, 1971.

Beewine (produced Birmingham, 1970; London, 1971). Included in *Pongo Plays 1–6*, 1971.
The ffinest ffamily in the Land (produced Lincoln, 1970; London, 1972). London, Methuen, 1973.
You're Free (produced London, 1970).
GRUP (televised 1970; produced York, 1971).
Mushrooms and Toadstools (produced London, 1970). Included in *Six More Pongo Plays*, 1974.
Tiddles (produced Birmingham, 1970). Included in *Six More Pongo Plays*, 1974.
Pongo Plays 1–6. London, Methuen, 1971; revised versions, music by Alex Glasgow, 1976.
This Jockey Drives Late Nights, adaptation of a play by Tolstoy (produced Birmingham, 1972; London, 1980). London, Eyre Methuen, 1972; revised version, 1976.
Daft Sam (televised 1972; produced London, 1976). Included in *Six More Pongo Plays*, 1974.
The Rent Man (produced Stoke-on-Trent, 1972). Included in *Six More Pongo Plays*, 1974.
Cinderella: A Likely Tale, adaptation of the story by Perrault (produced Stoke-on-Trent, 1972; London, 1973). London, Dobson, 1976.
The Tailor's Britches (produced Stoke-on-Trent, 1973). Included in *Six More Pongo Plays*, 1974.
Glorious Miles (televised 1973; produced Sheffield, 1975).
Jonah (produced Manchester, 1974). London, Pulpit Press, 1975.
Six More Pongo Plays Including Two for Children (includes *Tiddles, The Rent Man, The Ink-Smeared Lady, The Tailor's Britches, Daft Sam, Mushrooms and Toadstools*). London, Eyre Methuen, 1974.
Jack and the Beanstalk, music by Alex Glasgow (produced London, 1974).
Jug, adaptation of a play by Heinrich von Kleist (produced Nottingham, 1975; revised version produced London, 1986).
The Astounding Adventures of Tom Thumb (for children; produced London, 1979).
Don't Touch Him, He Might Resent It, adaptation of a play by Gogol (produced Chipping Norton, Oxfordshire, 1984).
This Is My Dream: The Life and Times of Josephine Baker (produced London, 1987).

Radio Plays: *After the Last Lamp*, 1961; *The Weavers*, from a play by Hauptmann, 1962; *The Day Dumbfounded Got His Pylon*, 1963; *A Public Menace*, from the play by Ibsen, 1964; *Nelson Cape Requests the Pleasure*, 1967; *The Government Inspector*, from a play by Gogol, 1969; *The Dobcross Silver Band* (documentary), 1971; *The Red Cockerel Crows*, from a play by Hauptmann, 1974; *A Most Wonderful Thing*, 1976; *Crab Training*, 1979; *Urn*, 1981; *The Moorcock*, 1981.

Television Plays: *The Arson Squad*, 1961; *Jack's Horrible Luck*, 1961; *There's No Room for You Here for a Start*, 1963; *A Right Crusader*, 1963; *Brainscrew*, 1966; *GRUP*, 1970; *Daft Sam*, 1972; *Glorious Miles*, 1973; *Shuttlecock*, 1976; *The Game*, from the play by Harold Brighouse, 1977; *The Mayor's Charity*, 1977; *Two Days That Shook the Branch*, 1978; *We Had Some Happy Hours*, 1981; *Another Part of the Jungle* and *I Met a Man Who Wasn't There* (*Bulman* series), 1985.

Short Stories

Pennine Tales. London, Methuen, 1983.
Flying Eggs and Things: More Pennine Tales. London, Methuen, 1986.

Other

That the Medals and the Baton Be Put on View: The Story of a Village Band 1875–1975. Newton Abbot, Devon, David and Charles, 1975.

*

Critical Study: *Anger and After* by John Russell Taylor, London, Methuen, 1962, revised edition, 1969, as *The Angry Theatre*, New York, Hill and Wang, 1962, revised edition, 1969.

Theatrical Activities:
Director: **Plays**—*Stop It Whoever You Are*, Nottingham; *The Little Mrs. Foster Show*, Nottingham, 1968; *Trinity Tales* by Alan Plater, Sheffield.
Actor: **Plays**—with the Century Theatre, the Midland Theatre Company, Coventry, Theatre Workshop, Stratford East, and other repertory and London theatres. **Radio**—*Northern Drift* (miscellany). **Television**—*Cribbins, Livings and Co.*, 1976; *Get the Drift*, 1976; *Night People* by Alan Plater, 1978.

Henry Livings comments:

To me, a show is an opportunity for communal imaginings, actors and audience together, for which I provide the material. When I first wrote plays, I felt there weren't enough plays which were fun, and that plot and naturalism were overwhelming the other aspects (fun, magic, social observation, the sculptural kinetics, the social connection that can be set up in a theatre); I now feel that I neglected story too much: I still feel it's better to know the story beforehand—if we're wondering what happens next, how can we pay attention to what's happening now?—but I try to steal a good story as well. I would like to make plays that are neither a simple narrative nor a flat picture, but a complete experience to carry out of the building, so that we could look around us with new eyes and say "Oh yes, that's right." For this I go mostly for laughter, because for me laughter is the shock reaction to a new way of looking at something: even a pun questions our security in the solidity of words. I also believe that we are what we do, rather than having some kind of permanent identifiable reality: the materials of art, observation, ritual, symbol, gesture, community give us a chance to focus for a moment, and then go forward with fresh hope that we matter and that what we do signifies. For this reason again I try to choose as a principal character or characters someone who isn't normally a big deal in our thinking—not that I'm not interested in power, as we all are, but that I want to see how it works and on whom. I have only once had the worm turning (in *Stop It*), and then only on Mrs. Warbeck, the scold, which is good gag; but have frequently shown the humble to be indestructible—which I consider to be a fair observation of what goes on: we do survive, in our millions, in spite of famine, war, and pestilence.

* * *

An actor with Joan Littlewood's Theatre Workshop, as well as numerous repertory companies throughout the country, Henry Livings has had plays produced by the English Stage Company, the Royal Shakespeare Company, and Theatre Workshop itself. His first play, *Stop It Whoever You Are*, misleadingly described as a "North Country farce" in one book, is in fact a mixture of farce and fantasy with social overtones—a combination which has characterized most of Livings's work.

In plays like *Big Soft Nellie*, his televison play *There's No Room for You Here for a Start, Eh?*, and *Honour and Offer*, he pitches a bewildered and socially inept individual against the forces of authority and permits him a minor victory. But this is not the conventional social battlefield and the victory is doubtful and even ironic. The issues are trivial and absurd, the characters are reduced to caricature and the farcical elements permitted to extend into a fantasy which subverts any social commitment. If this is social drama it is social drama refracted by the surreal. The settings are recognizably real; the characters who inhabit them are unreal, parodies of the social types which they represent. Indeed, far from insisting on humanist values in these plays, Livings seems to regard man as irretrievably ridiculous. His moments of fulfilment are brief and farcically trivial; his claims for dignity derisively ironic. In *Big Soft Nellie* Stanley, a partly demented television mechanic, is given a lyrical speech in which he describes the progress of the Royal Highlander train towards London, a train which seems to shout "this is what it's for" as it surges down the main line. But when this miracle of engineering reaches the capital "who gets out? . . . Fellers! That's all . . . Crumpled, little people!" It is these very crumpled little people who are the subject of his plays and, with the exception of his more realistic work, he deals with them in a way which they cannot understand, waging battles which only serve to underline their own insignificance.

As a social dramatist, Livings offers no solutions except an anarchic resistance to any authority—a refusal to serve the machine. But the individuals who do resist tend to be portrayed, as are William Warbeck in *Stop It Whoever You Are*, Valentine Brose in *Eh?*, Len in *There's No Room for You Here for a Start*, and Stanley in *Big Soft Nellie*, as at least marginally deranged. The fact that they nonetheless constitute a contrast with the self-important representatives of the establishment indicates Livings's social objectives but fails, finally, to validate them. The ending of *Eh?*, in which the machine explodes while everyone sits around eating narcotic mushrooms, typifies the collapse of this social dimension. Livings seems unwilling to concede any potential for meaningful action or to grant any substance to character. If everything is equally absurd then there is no room for social commitment and no point in distinguishing the vitally subversive from the debilitatingly conformist. The ruler and the ruled are ultimately interchangeable—as they had seemed clearly enough to the Samuel Beckett of *Waiting for Godot*. And yet Livings seems to see a distinction while proving unable to define the nature of that distinction or to grant it any real significance. As a result his characters constantly threaten to become merely figures of fun—wholly so in a play like *The ffinest ffamily in the Land*, in which the humour derives in part from the middle-class pretensions of working-class characters (itself a patronising form of humour), and in part from the willing acquiescence of these characters in the most outrageous of suggestions—an echo of *The Homecoming*, which underlines Livings's debt to Pinter as his earlier work had emphasised the influence of N.F. Simpson. But where Simpson is a farceur with no real social pretensions, and Pinter a metaphysician intent on examining the nature of human relationships and the pressure of existence itself, Livings is too content to play for laughs while implying a satirical dimension which could be sustained only if there was some evidence of the dramatist himself occupying an identifiable moral world of his own. The evidence that he does indeed grant value to integrity and humanity, that he does regard the individual who sustains his own values in the face of authority as being potentially heroic, is clear enough from plays like *Nil Carborundum* and *Kelly's Eye* and from the satirical energy of *The Little Mrs. Foster Show*. But his reliance, elsewhere, on characters who are little more than music hall patsies creates a drama which, astute in its use of linguistic incongruities and visual humour, lacks the fundamental seriousness which distinguishes the work of writers like Beckett and Pinter.

The Little Mrs. Foster Show is an exception because here the elements of fantasy, the music hall format, the savage caricatures become totally functional, for the play is a pitiless examination of human nature and an attack on the tasteless display of brutality for public entertainment. When a member of the audience walked out of the Nottingham Playhouse production complaining that, "It's not a play at all! It's a nightmare," he came remarkably close to stating the play's central theme and method. As Livings himself remarked,

> It's no pleasure to me so to offend a customer that he leaves his seat; but I'm bound to feel a little proud that I could tell a story of our time in such a way that in spite of having repellent atrocity and horror daily under our satiated noses, at least one man felt its impact afresh. . . . Reading a newspaper or listening to radio or watching television, we guzzle in horror, boredom, jokes etc. as they come; by setting these experiences on the stage we made quite a lot of people take notice.

The play presents the experiences of a white mercenary in Africa as a stage show, complete with atrocity photographs hired at $20 a set. But the violence of the war itself, briefly sketched but familiar enough to a modern audience even in the theatrical form in which it is presented, is finally secondary to Livings's contempt for those who display their inhumanity through a seemingly limitless ability to absorb horror as though it were designed for its entertainment value. Indeed here, and in later short plays like *Pie-Eating Contest* and *Does It Make Your Cheeks Ache?*, he denounces those who contrive to create spectacle out of human anguish. If this raises questions about his art this play remains, nonetheless, one of his more effective and consistent works.

It is, indeed, in military conflict that human nature is seen at its most naked and it is perhaps not without significance that one of his earliest plays, *Nil Carborundum*, a basically naturalistic play produced in 1962 by the Royal Shakespeare Company, should have been set in an RAF camp. But his concern here is less with man's capacity for brutality than with the pointless waste of a life designed to serve the interests of authority without questioning its purpose. It is a play, moreover, which shows a compassionate understanding even of the weakest and most vacillating characters virtually absent from all of his work with the exception of the lyrical *Kelly's Eye*. His theme is expressed in the typically humorous title, *Nil Carborundum*—don't let them grind you down. And if this is essentially the motto of all of his work it has a validity here which it is difficult to maintain in plays which see no real human resource for such resistance. Of course the inanities of service life, the strict delineation of social position, the harnessing of human energy to serve the interests of a self-justifying system arguably constitute an appropriate image of society at large and Livings's play should not be seen as a comment only on the nature of military service. When he describes the patent absurdities of a military exercise in which people perform their prescribed roles with no clear understanding of the purpose or progress of the attack, he is equally describing a society in which individuals are likewise required to conform to socially defined identities. The only possible response is that offered by the unit cook who is described as "cockily cheerful" and "resilient" and who continues to cook his chips as the battle rages around him.

The following year *Kelly's Eye*, performed by the Royal Court Theatre, offered another portrait of resilience, but Livings's view of human nature in this play is already considerably darker and the resilience now simply a form of desperate resistance. It is a demonstration of his growing conviction that "inside we are scarlet, raw, bloody." The play is set in 1936 and 1939, a time which Livings describes as "an evil time" when men demonstrated "apathy in the face of cruelty and the will to destroy." Kelly himself is a murderer but a man who has come to understand both himself and his society, which seems infected with the same spirit which had led him to kill his best friend. His own youthful conviction that "if I hit the first feller hard enough the others'd lie down by themselves" is clearly now enshrined in the principles of a nation which is itself on the verge of war. That Kelly comes to learn the need for compassion suggests little hope, for he in turn is destroyed by the single-minded and callous vengefulness of society. We are left with the narrator's observation that "Kelly is hollow, inferior and evil" and that "the only thing that can recommend him to us is his humanity, which we share and so must love."

The play is a powerful work, combining a lyric sublety with emotional force. Nothing Livings has written since has approached this level of explicit statement. The confident humanism of *Nil Carborundum* has dissipated and this perhaps explains the apparent contempt which seems implicit in the caricatures of the other plays—a contempt never entirely neutralized by his humour or by the anarchic eccentricity which seems to be the only strategy which the individual can adopt in the face of social pressure. Indeed, the eccentricity is perhaps itself a product of that pressure and the caricature as much a consequence of the deadly power of an inhuman society. The high-rise apartment block which is the setting of *The ffinest ffamily in the Land* is an entirely appropriate setting for a family so totally detached from all conventional values and isolated from other human contact.

The series of "Pongo Plays," short works based on Japanese Kyogen plays and stories culled from folklore, suggests a continuation of his moral ambivalence. These delightfully humorous sketches feature Sam Pongo, a cunning Lancashire weaver, who scores a series of victories over authority, in the person of the Master, and over anyone else gullible enough to be taken in by his quick wits and plausible patter. Livings creates a hero, in other words, who can successfully challenge the system only because he is aware of human fallibility and can manipulate it to his advantage.

Whether it be with the participant of a pie-eating contest who competes in order to forget her lost lover, or a ventriloquist who is controlled by his dummy, Livings creates a disconcerting world in which the pain of living is embodied in distorted characters. If the humour of his plays is never quite sufficient to neutralize a more fundamental sense of despair, nevertheless the resulting tension expresses essentially the same sense of ambivalence which one finds in other contemporary writers from Wesker to Orton, from Pinter to Bond. Livings's particular gift to the English theatre lies in his capacity to reproduce on stage the colour and energy of the comic strip. His work has all the virtues and vices of the form.

—C.W.E. Bigsby

LORD, Robert. New Zealander. Born in Rotorua, in 1945. Writer-in-residence, Mercury Theatre, Auckland, 1973. Member of the Editorial Board, *Act* magazine, Wellington, 1970–74. Recipient: Katherine Mansfield award, for short story, 1969; Arts Council of New Zealand travel bursary, 1974. Agent: Gilbert Parker, William Morris Agency, 1350 Avenue of the Americas, New York, New York 10019; or, Playmarket, P.O. Box 9767, Wellington, New Zealand. Address: 250 West 85th Street, Apartment 14-J, New York, New York 10024, U.S.A.

PUBLICATIONS

Plays

It Isn't Cricket (produced Wellington, 1971). Published in *Act 15* (Wellington), November 1971.
Moody Tuesday (broadcast 1972). Wellington, New Zealand Broadcasting Corporation, 1972.
Meeting Place (produced Wellington, 1972; New York, 1975). Published in *Act 18* (Wellington), December 1972.
Balance of Payments (produced Wellington, 1972). Published in *Can't You Hear Me Talking to You?*, edited by Alrene Sykes, St. Lucia, University of Queensland Press, 1978.
Nativity (produced Auckland, 1973).
Blood on My Sprigs (broadcast 1973; as *I'll Scream If I Want To*, produced Provincetown, Massachusetts, 1976).
Well Hung (produced Wellington and Providence, Rhode Island, 1974; revised version, as *Cop Shop*, produced Toronto, 1979; as *Country Cops*, produced Wellington, 1985; New York, 1986).
Heroes and Butterflies (produced Auckland, 1974).
Dead and Never Called Me Mother (produced Waterford, Connecticut, 1975).
Glitter and Spit (produced Ranfurly, 1982). Published in *Act 27* (Wellington), May 1975.
The Kite Play (produced Wellington, 1979).
Unfamiliar Steps (produced Christchurch, 1983; as *Bert and Maisy*, produced Sydney, 1984; San Diego, 1985).
The Travelling Squirrel (produced New York, 1985).
China Wars (produced New York, 1985).

Screenplays: *The Day We Landed on the Most Perfect Planet in the Universe*, 1981; *Pictures*, with John O'Shea and Michael Black, 1982.

Radio Plays: *Moody Tuesday*, 1972; *Friendship Centre*, 1972; *Blood on My Sprigs*, 1973; *Body in the Park*, 1976; *Sergei's Strawberry Surprise*, 1979.

*

Critical Study: *New Zealand Drama 1930–1980* by John Thomson, Auckland, Oxford University Press, 1984.

* * *

Robert Lord has tried a variety of types of play. There is the exaggerated farce, with a touch of the macabre (Joe Orton's name has been mentioned), of which *Balance of Payments* and *Well Hung* are examples; there is an example of what is ostensibly a political drama; and there is the play, sometimes much more original in method, which explores the way personality is affected by varying human relationships, as happens in *It Isn't Cricket* and *Meeting Place*, and in his more recent work.

Well Hung, Lord's most popular piece, is not altogether typical. It was written in part to prove to himself and to his critics that he could handle conventional plot. It makes fun of the sexual exploits and problems of officers in a small country police station whose activities are endangered by outside investigation of a local murder. The quite amoral capital made of double entendre, from the title of the piece on, hardly pretends to offer more than easy entertainment, but the effect is almost destroyed by the late introduction of melodrama with its simple but insistent black and white morality. A substantially revised version, first called *Cop Shop* and then *Country Cops*, attempted without much success to update the original.

Lord's excursion into political drama, written with a nod in the direction of Edward Bond, appears to embody a more complex morality. But *Heroes and Butterflies*, a study of the effects of a political rebellion, with side dressings of sexual frustration, is overweighted with portentous symbolism, and lacks the sharpness of setting and speech which might give it a local habitation, if not in reality, then at least in the mind. What strength it has lies in the private not the public lives of its characters. Lord is not a satirist nor a champion of a better way of life. He has said he does not believe the theatre to be the vanguard of revolution, and in any case his more serious purpose in writing plays has been to heighten one's perceptions of one's relations with others. When he reviewed Donald Howarth's play *Three Months Gone* in 1970, Lord noted approvingly how this work existed beyond the bounds of formal unities, and said, "It is the realization that Alvin never really decided where he was at or who he was that lingers, and of course these are decisions that very few of us make." This comment could stand as an epigraph to Lord's most characteristic work.

It Isn't Cricket presents a middle-class couple and their friends talking to one another about one another, and reveals how they describe things differently in different circumstances. It isn't cricket to cheat at games, but do the same rules apply in the much more complex game of life? Only one lie is shown up in the course of the play to be a socially unacceptable falsehood, but there is a whole range of usually barely conscious prevarication, used as the speaker wants to please or win sympathy from or indeed hurt his or her auditor. Lord is less interested than, say, Pinter in why people lie and does not build a plot out of what they try to gain by it: he simply shows what an entertaining pattern can be made of demonstrating how it goes on.

Pattern rather than plot also shapes *Meeting Place*, a play which has so far proved difficult to present to an audience, but which is undoubtedly Lord's most ambitious and intriguing piece. What interests him here is the way people's personalities can be affected, and perhaps even defined, by their relationship to others; how in extreme emotional circumstances (in this play it is sexual assault of one sort or another) character can for a while alter beyond recognition. What seems to remain constant is the cycle, set in motion as pairs of characters group and regroup. This is a play which more than any of the others "exists beyond the bounds of formal unities."

In two recent works, *The Kite Play* and *Bert and Maisy* (the latter originally written as *A Family Portrait* and then called *Unfamiliar Steps*), obscurity is not an issue—if anything, these plays are too straightforward. But Lord has listened to the rhythms of domestic chit-chat with an ear sharpened by close observation of Pinter, and he puts to theatrical use the varying dynamics of conversation, fascinated by the way it has a life of its own which seems at times even independent of the wishes of any of the individuals speaking. In *Bert and Maisy* retired parents relive the leaving home of their only son. The original short divertimento-like movements skilfully shaped out of empty chatter are still there, but there is also a larger shape which allows the surface comedy of conversational inanities to build to an unexpected human depth. An experienced Wellington cast in 1986 demonstrated the play's potential before enthusiastic audiences—Lord's greatest success for over ten years.

—John Thomson

LOWE, Stephen. British. Born in Nottingham, 1 December 1947. Educated at the University of Birmingham, 1966–70, B.A. (honours) in English 1969. Actor and director, Stephen Joseph Theatre-in-the-Round, Scarborough, Yorkshire, 1975–78; Senior Lecturer, Dartington College of Arts, Devon, 1978–82; resident playwright, Riverside Studios, London, 1984. Since 1984 artistic director, Meeting Ground Theatre Company, Nottingham. Recipient: George Devine Award, 1977. Agent: Goodwin Associates, 12 Rabbit Row, London W8 4DX, England.

PUBLICATIONS

Plays

Comic Pictures (includes *Stars* and *Cards*) (produced London, 1972; revised version produced Scarborough, 1976; London, 1982). *Cards* published London, French, 1983; *Stars* included in *Moving Pictures: Four Plays*, 1985.

Touched (produced Nottingham, 1977). Todmorden, Yorkshire, Woodhouse, 1977; revised version (produced London, 1981; New York, 1982), London, Eyre Methuen, 1981.

Shooting, Fishing and Riding (produced Scarborough, 1977).

Sally Ann Hallelujah Band (produced Nottingham, 1977).

The Ragged Trousered Philanthropists, adaptation of the novel by Robert Tressell (produced Plymouth and London, 1978). London, Joint Stock, 1978; revised version (produced London, 1983), London, Methuen, 1983.

Fred Karno's Bloody Circus (produced London, 1980).

Moving Pictures (as *Glasshouses*, produced London, 1981; as *Moving Pictures*, produced Leeds, 1985). Included in *Moving Pictures: Four Plays*, 1985.

Tibetan Inroads (produced London, 1981). London, Eyre Methuen, 1981.

Strive (produced Exeter, 1983). Included in *Moving Pictures: Four Plays*, 1985.

The Trial of Frankenstein (produced Plymouth, 1983).

Seachange (produced London, 1984). Included in *Moving Pictures: Four Plays*, 1985.

Keeping Body and Soul Together (produced London, 1984). Published in *Peace Plays 1*, edited by Lowe, London, Methuen, 1985.

Moving Pictures: Four Plays. London, Methuen, 1985.

Desire (produced Nottingham, 1986).

Demon Lovers (produced Loughborough, Leicestershire, 1987).

The Storm, adaptation of a play by Alexander Ostrovsky (produced London, 1987).

Television Plays: *Cries from a Watchtower*, 1979; *Shades*, 1982; *Kisses on the Bottom*, 1985; *Albion Market* series, 1986.

Other

Editor, *Peace Plays 1*. London, Methuen, 1985.

*

Critical Studies: "Letters from a Workshop: *The Ragged Trousered Philanthropists*," in *Dartington Papers 2* (Totnes, Devon), 1978, and "Peace Plays: Peace as a Theatrical Concern," in *Englische Amerikanische Studien* (Munich), nos. 3–4, 1986, both by Lowe.

Stephen Lowe comments:

The best introductions to my work are, of course, the plays. But some central concerns, or obsessions, are clear even to me, and have taken me into plays set in the past, and into plays set on the other side of the world—in Tibet. One concern is to explore moments of real change in society, to discover perhaps an optimistic vision that might inspire us through the present moment of change. A large number of them *I* would call political love stories; these have often led me into an exploration of "inner language" through dreams and fairy and folk tale elements.

As Joyce pointed out, there are probably only three subjects worth writing about—politics, religion, and sex. I have discovered in my work that the clear divisions between these create a false perspective, and the interrelation of all these elements is, to me, a crucial theatrical concern, in both form and content.

* * *

Stephen Lowe has many of the gifts a Good Fairy could give, more than most of his contemporaries. He has intelligence, learning, authority, curiosity, and daring. Although he maintains a deep attachment to his roots in Nottingham, both the place and the people, he is ready to push out into areas of ideas, and even geography (Tibet in *Tibetan Inroads*, Asia Minor in *Seachange*) which other British dramatists are often reluctant to enter. He is in this sense European, as Edward Bond is, but his intelligence is more rigorous than Bond's, and more fastidious—which is where the Fairy Carrabosse may have made her malicious contribution to his christening, as to John Whiting's, for fastidiousness is an ambiguous gift for a dramatist. Even in such achieved plays as *Touched*, *Moving Pictures* (both set in Nottingham), and *Tibetan Inroads*, Lowe's talent is sometimes more illustrative than dramatic, the energy sporadic instead of sustained, and *Seachange* seems an almost entirely undramatic piece, like a prose-poem. This is not to suggest that Lowe is incapable of energy, but it is more likely to be sustained through a scene or a powerful speech such as those at the end of *Keeping Body and Soul Together*; only in *The Ragged Trousered Philanthropists*, adapted from Robert Tressell's novel, is it sustained throughout the play. In general it might be said that the structures of Lowe's plays have usually been imposed, not organic, and that he may not find himself fully as a playwright until he succeeds in becoming a little less intentional, and allows his unconscious to call a few more of his tunes.

—John Bowen

LUCIE, Doug. British. Born in Chessington, Surrey, 15 December 1953. Educated at Tiffin Boys' School, 1965–72; Worcester College, Oxford, 1973–76, B.A. (honours) in English 1976. Resident playwright, Oxford Playhouse Company, 1979–80; visiting playwright, University of Iowa, Iowa City, 1980. Agent: Michael Imison Playwrights, 28 Almeida Street, London N1 1TD, England.

PUBLICATIONS

Plays

John Clare's Mad, Nuncle (produced Edinburgh, 1975).
Rough Trade (also director: produced Oxford, 1977).
The New Garbo (produced Hull and London, 1978).
We Love You (also director: produced London, 1978).
Oh Well (also director: produced Oxford, 1978).
Heroes (also director: produced Edinburgh and London, 1979).
Fear of the Dark (produced London, 1980).
Poison (also director: produced Edinburgh, 1980).
Strangers in the Night (produced London, 1981).
Hard Feelings (produced Oxford, 1982; London, 1983). With *Progress*, London, Methuen, 1985.
Progress (produced London, 1984; New Haven, Connecticut, 1986). With *Hard Feelings*, London, Methuen, 1985.
The Key to the World (produced Leicester and London, 1984).
Force and Hypocrisy (produced London, 1986).
Fashion (produced Stratford-on-Avon, 1987). Published in *Plays International* (London), June 1987.

Television Plays: *A Class of His Own*, 1984; *Funseekers*, with Nigel Planer, 1987.

*

Theatrical Activities:
Director: **Plays**—some of his own plays; student productions of *The Duchess of Malfi* by Webster, *The Comedy of Errors*, and *Hitting Town* by Stephen Poliakoff.
Actor: **Plays**—*We Love You*, London, 1978; *Oh Well*, Oxford, 1978.

* * *

Wherever people congregate there will be rich pickings for those with an ear for the nuances of speech and a nose for the ridiculous. Since comedy of manners was invented, the drawing room has provided the playwright with a suitable microcosm for bourgeois society. Where once there were drawing rooms there are now communal living spaces. At some point in the last decade Doug Lucie moved into yours or mine. He has captured the social mores and hypocrisies of a particular social strata—at university and beyond—and pilloried us on stage for our general amusement and embarrassed recognition.

Lucie has not dealt exclusively with the cynicism, power games, and capacity for self-delusion of his contemporaries. *The New Garbo* anticipated the present interest in the actress Frances Farmer. *Strangers in the Night* flirted with a lurid expressionism redolent of mid-period Sam Shepard. But it is as the persistent chronicler of his peers that Lucie has gained his reputation. *We Love You* dealt with adolescent rebel posturing. *Heroes* showed six undergraduates in a shared house in Oxford and contrasted them with a different group living there ten years before. *Hard Feelings* is set in Brixton in 1981. Inside another shared house they bicker and pose. Outside, they riot. *Progress* is marriage and careers and sexual politics. Will is a Channel 4 researcher; Ronee is a social worker. What with the lodger, the battered wife they adopt, the phone calls from Ronee's lesbian lover, and Will's men's group ("We're trying to change our attitudes by being open and supportive without resorting to traditional, hierarchical structures"), their living room achieves honorary communal status.

Lucie's plays unfold with an ease and grace which belie a precise construction and rigorous comic technique. Lucie has an insidious way with his exposition; scenes end at precisely the right moment—the structure never sags; the comic effect derives from incongruous juxtaposition and savage undercutting. With a good designer to capture the latest nuances of interior decor and personal accessories, an evening at a Lucie play can provide an irresistible but excruciating portrait of the way we carry on, as our foibles are exposed in a relentlessly funny and viciously acute way.

Is it replication or exaggeration? There are those who say Lucie lacks subtlety. True, he assembles predictable characters in unsurprising combinations. *Progress* is a title with heavy-handed irony. In *Hard Feelings* the living room blinds are always down, which is perhaps an overemphatic metaphor. But unless Lucie aspires to subtlety, lack of it is neither here nor there. One cannot scourge discreetly. Yet who is being scourged and why? It may be that Lucie feels himself an interloper in the world he describes, but his sympathies are always with the outsider, regardless of their actions and attitudes. When Tone, the outsider in *Hard Feelings*, bellows, "people aren't kind of things, they're people," he articulates the author's—and the audience's—outrage. But in *Progress* the outsiders are Mark and Lenny. Mark is a gutter-press journalist with a spectacular line in sexist banter. Lenny uses his wife "as a sparring partner and she doesn't box." He also rapes her. Being bereft of privilege or pretense does not accord integrity by default, and it seems untypically naive of Lucie even to hint that this is the case.

I do not think, as some do, that Lucie is trivial, but he often trivialises. Comedy of manners is, almost by definition, concerned with surfaces. Too often the dictates of this comic form constrain Lucie. When human beings are reduced to plot functionaries, however brilliantly, it is difficult to care much about what happens to them. Points are half-raised then abandoned, lest the pace slacken. Despite his huge talent, Lucie often seems wilfully insubstantial.

It is possible that Lucie will transcend the civilizing parameters he has set himself and attain the corroscating heights of great satire. Interestingly, his recent play *The Key to the World* moved out of the drawing room and towards a more humane and less comic vision. Whatever direction Lucie takes, he is a dramatist of rare wit and exceptional powers of observation.

—Joss Bennathan

LUKE, Peter (Ambrose Cyprian). British. Born in St. Albans, Hertfordshire, 12 August 1919. Educated at Eton College; Byam Shaw School of Art, London; Atelier André Lhote, Paris. Served in the Rifle Brigade, in the Western Desert, Italy, and Northwest Europe, 1940–46: Military Cross, 1944. Married 1) Carola Peyton-Jones (died); 2) Lettice Crawshaw (marriage dissolved), one son (deceased) and one daughter; 3) the actress June Tobin in 1963, two sons and three daughters. Sub-editor, Reuters, 1946–47; worked in the wine trade, 1947–57; book critic, *Queen* magazine, London, 1957–58; story editor, *Armchair Theatre* programme, 1958–60, and editor, *Bookman* programme, 1960–61, and *Tempo* arts programme, 1961–62, all for ABC Television, London; drama producer, BBC Television, London, 1963–67. Since 1967 free-lance writer, producer, and director: director, Gate Theatre, Dublin, 1977–80. Recipient: Italia prize, for television production, 1967; Tony award, 1969. Agent: Harvey Unna and Stephen Durbridge Ltd., 24–32 Pottery Lane, London W11 4LZ, England.

PUBLICATIONS

Plays

Hadrian VII, based on *Hadrian the Seventh* and other works by Frederick Rolfe, "Baron Corvo" (produced Birmingham, 1967; London, 1968; New York, 1969). Published as *The Play of Hadrian VII*, London, Deutsch, 1968; New York, Knopf, 1969.

Bloomsbury (produced London, 1974). New York and London, French, 1976.

Rings for a Spanish Lady, adaptation of a play by Antonio Gala (also director: produced Dublin, 1977).

Proxopera, adaptation of the novel by Benedict Kiely (produced Dublin, 1978).

Married Love: The Apotheosis of Marie Stopes (produced Leatherhead, Surrey, 1985).

Yerma, adaptation of the play by García Lorca (produced London, 1987).

Radio Play: *Nymphs and Satyrs Come Away*, 1985.

Television Writing: *Small Fish Are Sweet*, 1959; *Pig's Ear with Flowers*, 1960; *Roll On, Bloomin' Death*, 1961; *A Man on Her Back*, from story by William Sansom, 1966; *The Devil a Monk Wou'd Be*, from a story by Daudet, 1967; *Anach Cuan: The Music of Sean O Riada*, 1967; *Black Sound—Deep Song: The Andalusian Poetry of Federico García Lorca*, 1968; *Honour, Profit, and Pleasure*, with Anna Ambrose, 1985.

Novel

The Other Side of the Hill. London, Gollancz, 1984.

Short Stories

Telling Tales: The Short Stories of Peter Luke. The Curragh, County Kildare, Goldsmith Press, 1981.

Other

Sisyphus and Reilly: An Autobiography. London, Deutsch, 1972.

Paquito and the Wolf (for children). The Curragh, County Kildare, Goldsmith Press, 1981.

The Mad Pomegranate and the Praying Mantis: An Andalusian Adventure. London, Mantis Press, 1984.

Editor, *Enter Certain Players: Edwards-MacLiammóir and the Gate 1928–1978*. Dublin, Dolmen Press, 1978.

*

Critical Studies: by Ronald Bryden in *Observer* (London), 21 April 1968; by Harold Hobson in *Sunday Times* (London), 21 April 1968; "Peter Luke Used to Be a Television Producer. Then He Escaped" by Luke, in *Listener* (London), 12 September 1968; by Clive Barnes in *New York Times*, 9 January

1969; "*Hadrian VII* Is Alive and a Hit" by John Chapman, in *San Francisco Examiner*, 5 October 1969.

Theatrical Activities:
Director: **Plays**—*Hadrian VII*, Dublin, 1970; *Rings for a Spanish Lady*, Dublin, 1977. **Television**—*Hamlet at Elsinore*, 1963; *A Passage to India*, 1966; *Silent Song*, 1967; *Anach Cuan: The Music of Sean O Riada*, 1967; *Black Sound—Deep Song: The Andalusian Poetry of Federico Garciá Lorca*, 1968.

Peter Luke comments:

(1977) To write an introduction to my work as a playwright is difficult because to date there is relatively little of it. I did not write my first play until I was nearly forty. The oeuvre, such as it is to date, consists of four original plays for television and one dramatization of a novel by William Sansom for the same medium. In addition there are two films d'auteur commissioned by the BBC. They are respectively, and perhaps significantly, about a musician and a poet. Then there is the stage play, *Hadrian VII*, which was first written in 1961 but was not produced until 1967. *Bloomsbury*, produced by Richard Cottrell in 1974, ran for only five weeks due to the American recession as it affected Throgmorton Street and the tourist trade and a petulant notice from Harold Hobson (anagram: Dora Snobhol). (1988: Since then *Married Love* has had an airing, but has not yet reached the West End.)

I would like to be able to give some indication of the direction in which I think I am going, but this is difficult. Certainly I am more than ever interested in poetry, which is not to say that I am immediately contemplating a play in verse. But if I can see a development in my work, it is towards the articulate. Language is my preoccupation and I feel that the theatre, now as in the past, and quite irrespective of present day vogues and trends, should be the place to use it in.

The choice of medium was made for me. My father, Harry Luke, was a writer but early on I decided that I wanted to paint and I had already spent two years studying when the war broke out in 1939. Nineteen—nearly twenty—years later, in 1959, my first television play, *Small Fish Are Sweet*, starring Donald Pleasence and Katherine Blake, was produced. Several others followed hard upon. What happened in between is told in an essay in autobiography, *Sisyphus and Reilly*.

I did not intend to become a playwright. It happened by accident. I do not even now consider myself to be solely a writer of plays, though I suppose few writers can have been so fortunate as to have had an international success on the scale of *Hadrian VII*. Indeed, how many playwrights have had a major success which began as a flop? Thanks to Hadrian, however, I am now free to write what I want to and my intention for the foreseeable future is to alternate plays with books. This I find very therapeutic and my one concern now is that the results will justify the therapy, and that the therapy will give me a long life in which to write a great deal more.

*   *   *

Peter Luke was almost 40 when, in 1958, he became a story editor for ABC Television, and began writing televison plays. In 1963, he joined the BBC, with whom he stayed until 1967. Since then he has worked as a free-lance writer, producer, director, and translator, as well as writing a historical novel, short stories, and two autobiographical reminiscences.

In 1967 Luke adapted Frederick Rolfe's novel, *Hadrian the Seventh*, for the stage. In an otherwise faithful rendering, he made one major change. In the novel, the protagonist is a young man called George Arthur Rose. Luke has described his play as "a biography of Rolfe himself in terms of his 'Hadrian' fantasy."

Hadrian VII begins with Rolfe being visited by two bailiffs. They present him with a writ, resulting from a series of petty debts, which he refuses to sign. Left alone to his "imagining," he fantasizes that the two bailiffs are a Bishop and a Cardinal come to persuade him to accept ordination. They invite him to Rome, where he learns that he has been elected Pope. He calls himself Hadrian VII, and immediately announces his intention of dissolving the "temporal" Church and selling the Vatican's treasure and real estate. The cardinals are outraged. Meanwhile, Jeremiah Sant, who knew Rolfe before his election, tries to wheedle money out of him. Hadrian refuses to give him any, but offers to help save his soul instead. Sant thereupon draws a revolver and shoots Hadrian, who dies requesting that Sant be forgiven his crime. The final scene shows the bailiffs confiscating Rolfe's belongings, among them the manuscript of his masterpiece. The play's enormous success in the late 1960's can be attributed to two factors. The contrast between the "real" Rolfe in his seedy garret and Rolfe as he imagines himself is dramatically very effective; and the theme—individuality vs. authority—is perennial.

Luke's next play, *Bloomsbury*, portrays the group of friends which surrounded Lytton Strachey, as seen through the eyes of Virginia Woolf. Towards the end of the play, she says: "Yes, I have created an art form out of them all. . . . I have orchestrated their movements like the waves." Although the concept is clever, the various relationships and attitudes explored lack the dramatic interest of his previous work.

Proxopera—a coinage for "operation proxy"—is adapted from a novel by Benedict Kiely, who described his story as "a condemnation of the interference by violent men in the lives of the innocent." A group of IRA gunmen are holding a family at gunpoint. They threaten to kill the women and child if Binchey, a retired schoolmaster, does not drive a bomb into town for them. He agrees, and sets off to do so, but when he sees his town in the early morning light, he can't bring himself to aid in the murder of any of its citizens. He tells two soldiers what he is carrying. They rescue his family, but Binchey dies of a heart attack after safely exploding the bomb.

Married Love: The Apotheosis of Marie Stopes opens lightheartedly, contrasting Stopes's academic brilliance and her emotional immaturity. After chasing a Japanese professor to no avail, she marries a man who is impotent. As a result, she comes to think that contraception could be used to produce a better species. George Bernard Shaw persuades her that it would be better employed to help women to avoid unwanted pregnancies. Her subsequent achievement in promoting contraception is set against her sense of personal emptiness. Early in the play, she tells Shaw: "I only know that I haven't got something that I feel I ought to have." She never acquires it. She never settles; is never satisfied. The play maintains a fine balance between comedy and domestic tragedy. It is certainly Luke's best work since *Hadrian VII*.

Ez, commissioned by the Hampstead Theatre Company (and not yet produced), is about the non-trial for treason of Ezra Pound. The first act is set in a cage in a Pisan prison; the second, in St. Elizabeths hospital in Washington where Pound spent more than a decade. Some of Pound's best work belongs to this period, but Luke is more concerned with the contradictions inherent in his character: an egotist, he would share his scraps of food with a cat; a racist, he made friends easily with blacks. He emerges as a victim of a genius inseparable from irresponsibility. But when he is eventually released, he is no longer so sure that what he believed in was right. His confession that he was at fault brings the play to a close. It is a plea for tolerance.

Luke has also written many successful television plays and documentaries, from *Small Fish Are Sweet* in 1959, to *Honour, Profit, and Pleasure*, about Handel, co-written with Anna Ambrose, in 1985. And he has made two excellent translations from the Spanish. *Rings for a Spanish Lady*, from a prize-winning play by Antonio Gala, is the story of how El Cid's widow, who represents Spain, is compelled by the king to forego her love for Don Minaya and accept her widowhood. Luke describes his translation of Lorca's *Yerma* as "the first unbowdlerized version."

Although Luke's subjects vary widely, their themes are closely related. In all his plays, the main character's dreams or plans are threatened by a society which has no place for his or her kind of individuality. His work is a call for greater understanding between individuals.

—Terence Dawson

MAC LOW, Jackson. American. Born in Chicago, Illinois, 12 September 1922. Educated at the University of Chicago, 1939–43, A.A. 1941; Brooklyn College, New York, 1955–58, A.B. (cum laude) in Greek 1958. Formerly married to the painter Iris Lezak; two children. Free-lance music teacher, English teacher, translator, and editor, 1950–66; reference book editor, Funk and Wagnalls, 1957–58, 1961–62, and Unicorn Books, 1958–59; copy editor, Alfred A. Knopf, 1965–66, all in New York. Member of the editorial staff, and poetry editor, 1950–54, *Why?* (later *Resistance*), a pacifist-anarchist magazine; Instructor, American Language Institute, New York University, 1966–73; poetry editor, *WIN* magazine, New York, 1966–75. Recipient: Creative Artists Public Service grant, 1973, 1976; PEN grant, 1974; National Endowment for the Arts fellowship, 1979. Address: 42 North Moore Street, New York, New York 10013, U.S.A.

PUBLICATIONS

Plays

The Marrying Maiden: A Play of Changes, music by John Cage (produced New York, 1960).
Verdurous Sanguinaria (produced New York, 1961). Baton Rouge, Louisiana, Southern University, 1967.
Thanks: A Simultaneity for People (produced Wiesbaden, 1962).
Letters for Iris, Numbers for Silence (produced Wiesbaden, 1962).
A Piece for Sari Dienes (produced Wiesbaden, 1962).
Thanks II (produced Paris, 1962).
The Twin Plays: Port-au-Prince, and Adams County, Illinois (produced New York, 1963). New York, Mac Low and Bloedow, 1963.
Questions and Answers . . .: A Topical Play (produced New York, 1963). New York, Mac Low and Bloedow, 1963.
Asymmetries No. 408, 410, 485 (produced New York, 1965).
Asymmetries, Gathas and Sounds from Everywhere (produced New York, 1966).
A Vocabulary for Carl Fernbach-Flarsheim (produced New York, 1977). New York, Mac Low, 1968.

Performance Scores and Broadsides (published New York, Mac Low): *A Vocabulary for Sharon Belle Mattlin [Vera Regina Lachman, Peter Innisfree Moore]*, 1974–75; *Guru-Guru Gatha*, 1975; *1st Milarepa Gatha*, 1976; *1st Sharon Belle Mattlin Vocabulary Crossword Gatha*, 1976; *Homage to Leona Bleiweiss*, 1976; *The WBAI Vocabulary Gatha*, 1977, revised edition, 1979; *A Vocabulary Gatha for Pete Rose*, 1978; *A Notated Vocabulary for Eve Rosenthal*, 1978; *Musicwords (for Phill Niblock), 1978; A Vocabulary Gatha for Anne Tardos*, 1980; *Dream Meditation*, 1980; *A Vocabulary Gatha for Malcolm Goldstein*, 1981; *1st [2nd] Happy Birthday, Anne, Vocabulary Gatha*, 1982; *Unstructured Meditative Improvisation for Vocalists and Instrumentalists on the Word "Nucleus,"* 1982; *Pauline Meditation*, 1982; *Milarepa Quartet for Four Like Instruments*, 1982; *The Summer Solstice Vocabulary Gatha*, 1983; *Two Heterophonics from Hereford Bosons 1 and 2*, 1984; *Phonemicon from Hereford Bosons 1*, 1984.

Radio Writing: *Dialog unter Dichtern/Dialog among Poets*, 1982; *Thanks/Danke*, 1983; *Reisen/Traveling*, 1984 (all Germany); *Locks*, 1984.

Composer: incidental music for *The Age of Anxiety* by W.H. Auden, produced New York, 1954; for *The Heroes* by John Ashbery, produced New York, 1955.

Verse

The Pronouns: A Collection of 40 Dances—for the Dancers—6 February—22 March 1964. New York, Jackson Mac Low, 1964; London, Tetrad Press, 1970.
August Light Poems. New York, Caterpillar, 1967.
22 Light Poems. Los Angeles, Black Sparrow Press, 1968.
23rd Light Poem: For Larry Eigner. London, Tetrad Press, 1969.
Stanzas for Iris Lezak. Barton, Vermont, Something Else Press, 1972.
4 Trains, 4–5 December 1964. Providence, Rhode Island, Burning Deck, 1974.
36th Light Poem: In Memoriam Buster Keaton. London, Permanent Press, 1975.
21 Matched Asymmetries. London, Aloes, 1978.
54th Light Poem: For Ian Tyson. Milwaukee, Membrane Press, 1978.
A Dozen Douzains for Eve Rosenthal. Toronto, Gronk, 1978.
Phone. New York, Printed Editions, 1978.
Asymmetries 1–260: The First Section of a Series of 501 Performance Poems. New York, Printed Editions, 1980.
Antic Quatrains. Minneapolis, Bookslinger, 1980.
From Pearl Harbor Day to FDR's Birthday. College Park, Maryland, Sun and Moon, 1982.
"Is That Wool Hat My Hat?" Milwaukee, Membrane Press, 1983.
Bloomsday. Barrytown, New York, Station Hill Press, 1984.
French Sonnets, Composed Between January 1955 and April 1983. Tucson, Black Mesa Press, 1984.
The Virginia Woolf Poems. Providence, Rhode Island, Burning Deck, 1985.
Representative Works 1938–1985. New York, Roof, 1986.

*

Critical Studies: "Jackson Mac Low Issue" of *Vort 8* (Silver Spring, Maryland), 1975, and *Paper Air* (Blue Bell, Pennsylvania), vol. 2, no. 3, 1980.

Theatrical Activities:
Actor: **Plays**—in *Tonight We Improvise* by Pirandello, New York, 1959, and other plays.

* * *

Jackson Mac Low is recognized as America's leading dramatist of the aleatoric school, which uses chance-structured materials and is best known by its principal musical exponent, John Cage. Mac Low's works for the theatre have been performed in the U.S.A., Canada, West Germany, Brazil and England, although few have ever been commercially published in a complete form.

Mac Low's original interest was musical composition, though after 1939 he became increasingly involved in poetry. During the 1940's Mac Low contributed to such anarchist publications as *Now, Why?* (later called *Resistance*) and was poetry editor for *WIN*, for the Workshop In Nonviolence. Most of his poems are, however, designed for live performance and Mac Low has described himself as a "Writer and Composer of Poetry, Music, Simultaneities, and Plays."

The most active phase of his theatre activity begins with Prester John's Company in New York in 1949 (one of the most interesting early off-off-Broadway groups), as co-director and actor in various Paul Goodman plays, and continues in a long association with the Living Theatre beginning in 1952, originally as composer for productions of John Ashbery's *The Heroes*, W.H. Auden's *The Age of Anxiety*, etc., but also as an actor, and eventually as dramatist.

The major phase of his dramatic corpus begins also with his association with the Living Theatre and, at about the same time, with John Cage. There are two sets of "Biblical Poems" and a "Biblical Play," performed in 1955, and a major play called *Lawrence*, based on writings by D.H. Lawrence. These pieces are extremely static and resemble Gagaku oratorios of words. The climax of this group of works is *The Marrying Maiden* performed in repertoire by the Living Theatre in 1960–61 with a sound score by John Cage. This play is totally lyrical and abstract, and it includes actions to be determined by the performers using a randomizing process. The Living Theatre's production was extremely conventional and inappropriate; it failed to bring out the uniqueness of the piece which was, as a result, unpublished except as an acting script and has not been performed since. About the works of this time, Mac Low has written:

> All during the 1940's and 1950's, many poems of mine in all modes express a pacifistic and libertarian political viewpoint strongly related to religious attitudes derived from Taoism, Buddhism, and mystical Judaism (Chassidism and Cabala).... These religious and political views, along with the more libertarian schools of psychotherapy [e.g. Paul Goodman], helped make me receptive to the use of chance operations and to the interpenetration of art works and the environment....

Mac Low's performance works are structured as social models in which each participant participates as a co-equal and direction is self-guidance and by working-out, rather than being along doctrinaire, authoritarian, or imposed-visionary lines. The sound of the lines is as important as the sense (the sound often *is* the sense), resulting in a uniquely musical theatre experience.

After *The Marrying Maiden* the plays become more choric—there is action, usually in unison and repetitive—though the texts remain more musical than semantic. As with *Lawrence*, the pieces take their names from some aspect of their source material. For instance, one major work of this period is *Verdurous Sanguinaria*, which is derived from a botanical text on wild flowers. Another is *The Twin Plays*, mentioned before, two plays with identical action in all respects, but one of which uses combinations of the letters in the name "Port-au-Prince" and the other proverbs collected from "Adams County Illinois" which become the names for their respective plays. Another of these works is *Questions and Answers Incredible Statements the Litany of Lies Action in Freedom Statements and Questions All Round Truth and Freedom in Action; or, Why Is an Atom Bomb Like a Toothbrush? A Topical Play* which takes political texts reflecting Mac Low's views, treats it as a litany, then randomizes the actions.

Simultaneous with Mac Low's theatre work (and not necessarily completely separate from it) Mac Low's poems were developing in parallel blocks. There are early works such as *Peaks and Lamas* (1957, included in the magazine *Abyss*, Spring 1971). There is *Stanzas for Iris Lezak*, a massive cycle of over 400 pages, written more or less immediately after *The Marrying Maiden* and in some ways paralleling it. And at the end of *Stanzas*, the work develops into the *Asymmetries*, another large cycle (unpublished in any complete form but, like the Iris Lezak stanzas, often performed). These poems are overwhelmingly ear-oriented. They include long silences, difficult to approximate on a printed page apart from performance. They may be "poetry" but they partake of theatre, especially of the heard elements. Many are "simultaneities," by Mac Low's term, but theatre in fact.

Starting in the late 1950's the theatre of Happenings began to develop, with its emphasis on the simple image. The acme of Happenings was the Fluxus group, which performed in Europe, Japan, and the U.S.A. many works by George Brecht, Ben Vautier, Ay-o, Dick Higgins, Bob Watts, Wolf Vostell, Yoko Ono, Chieko Shiomi, and others. In 1962 and the years immediately following, the Fluxus group published and performed a number of Mac Low pieces. Mac Low's third major body of performance works relates to the Fluxus kind of piece. Many of these pieces, such as *Thanks* or *Questioning*, have sets of directions and intentions as scripts, and these are filled in improvisatorially by the performer. Others, such as the *Gathas* (a series begun in 1961), are purely choric "simultaneities," in which the readers read the sounds in any direction. Still other performance pieces are "buried" in other cycles, such as the *8th Light Poem* which is a scenario, written in a fairly typical Happenings vein. There also exist film scenarios from this period and in this style, the best known of which is *Tree* in which the cameraman is asked to photograph a tree, unmoving and static, through a day.

Mac Low's cycle of odes, highly personal poems in classical form, do not use chance in any direct way and suggest a more direct and semantic phase in his work.

—Dick Higgins

MADDY, Yulisa Amadu. Sierra Leonean. Born in Freetown, 27 December 1936. Educated at schools in Sierra Leone;

Rose Bruford College, Sidcup, Kent, diploma 1965; City of London University, postgraduate diploma in arts administration; research fellow, Leeds University, from 1986. Married Abibatu Kamara in 1986; six children. Worked for Sierra Leone Railways; radio producer, Denmark and Britain, early 1960's; director and dancer, Comedia Hus, Copenhagen, 1966; director and actor, British Council Theatre, Freetown, 1968–69; tutor in drama and African literature, Evelyn Hone College, University of Zambia, Lusaka, 1969–70; artistic director, Keskidee Arts Centre, London, 1971–73; acting director, Sierra Leone Ministry of Tourism and Culture, Freetown, 1974–77; instructor in dance and drama, Morley College, London, 1979–80; Fellow in Theatre Arts, Ibadan University, Nigeria, 1980–81; Senior Lecturer in Performing Arts, Ilorin University, Nigeria, 1981–83; Visiting Professor of Performing Arts, Special Education Resource Center, Bridgeport, Connecticut, 1983–85; Fulbright Senior Scholar, University of Maryland, College Park, and Morgan State College, Baltimore, 1985–86. Since 1986 artistic director, Gbakanda Afrikan Tiata, Leeds. Recipient: Sierra Leone National Arts Festival prize, for fiction, 1973; Gulbenkian grant, 1978; Edinburgh Festival award, 1979. Address: 19 Francis Street, Leeds, Yorkshire LS7 4BY, England.

PUBLICATIONS (early works as Pat Amadu Maddy)

Plays

Alla Gbah (produced London, 1967). Included in *Obasai and Other Plays*, 1971.
Obasai and Other Plays. London, Heinemann, 1971.
Gbana-Bendu (produced London, 1973; Baltimore, 1986). Included in *Obasai and Other Plays*, 1971.
Yon-Kon (televised 1982; produced Bridgeport, Connecticut, 1984). Included in *Obasai and Other Plays*, 1971.
Life Everlasting (produced London, 1972). Published in *Short African Plays*, edited by Cosmo Pieterse, London, Heinemann, 1972.
Big Breeze Blow (produced Freetown, 1974). Privately printed, 1984.
Take Tem Draw di Rope (produced Freetown, 1975).
Put for Me (produced Freetown, 1975).
Nah We Yone Dehn See (produced Freetown, 1975).
Big Berrin (in Krio: Big Death) (produced Freetown, 1976; Washington, D.C., 1984). Privately printed, 1984.
A Journey into Christmas (produced Ibadan, 1980).
Drums, Voices and Words (produced London, 1985).

Radio Plays: *If Wishes Were Horses*, 1963 (UK); and plays for Cross River Broadcasting, Sierra Leone Broadcasting, and Zambia Broadcasting.

Television Writing: *Saturday Night Out* series, 1980 (Nigeria); *Yon-Kon*, 1982 (Nigeria); and plays for Sierra Leone Broadcasting.

Novel

No Past, No Present, No Future. London, Heinemann, 1973.

Short Stories

Ny Afrikansk Prose, edited by Ulla Ryum. Copenhagen, Vendelkaer, 1967.

*

Critical Study: *The Development of African Drama* by Michael Etherton, London, Hutchinson, 1982.

Theatrical Activities:
Director: **Plays**—all of his own plays; *The Trials of Brother Jero* by Wole Soyinka, Copenhagen, 1966, Freetown, 1969; *Theatre of Power* by Obi B. Egbuna, Copenhagen, 1967; *The Road* by Wole Soyinka, Freetown, 1968, Lusaka, 1970; *Dalabani* by Mukhtarr Mustapha, London, 1972; *Anansi and Bra Englishman* by Manley Young, London, 1972; *Onitsha Market Play*, London, 1973; *Cherry and Wine* by Jimi Rand, London, 1973; *Sighs of a Slave's Dream* by Lindsey Barrett, London, 1973; *Alla Gbah*, Freetown, 1974; *Gbakfest* (National Theatre Festival), Freetown, 1976; *Pulse* by Alem Mezgebe, London, 1979, Ibadan, 1980; *The Refund*, Ilorin, Nigeria, 1982; *The Chattering and the Song* by Femi Osofisan, Ilorin, Nigeria, 1983; *Gbana-Bendu*, Ilorin, Nigeria, 1983; *12 Days at the Round House*, London, 1986. **Television**—*Saturday Night Out* series, 1980; *Yon-Kon*, 1982.
Actor: **Plays**—Chume in *The Trials of Brother Jero* by Wole Soyinka, Copenhagen, 1966; Student in *Theatre of Power* by Obi B. Egbuna, Copenhagen, 1967; Professor in *The Road* by Wole Soyinka, Freetown, 1968, Lusaka, 1970; Brother Jero in *The Trials of Brother Jero*, Freetown, 1969; *Dalabani* by Mukhtarr Mustapha, London, 1972; *Life Everlasting*, London, 1972; *Onitsha Market Play*, London, 1973; *Sighs of a Slave's Dream* by Lindsey Barrett, London, 1973; *Alla Gbah*, Freetown, 1974; *Big Breeze Blow*, Freetown, 1974; *Take Tem Draw di Rope*, Freetown, 1975; *Put for Me*, Freetown, 1975; *Nah We Yone Dehn See*, Freetown, 1975; Awoko in *Big Berrin*, Freetown, 1976, Washington, D.C., 1984; Dictator in *Pulse* by Alem Mezgebe, London, 1979, Ibadan, 1980; *A Journey into Christmas*, Ibadan, 1980; Bobby in *Big Breeze Blow*, Ibadan, 1981; Student in *The Refund*, Ilorin, Nigeria, 1982; *Drums, Voices and Words*, London, 1985; *12 Days at the Round House*, London, 1986; Shadow in *Gbana-Bendu*, Baltimore, 1986. **Television**—Pagu in *Yon-Kon*, 1982.

Yulisa Amadu Maddy comments:

To make a statement introducing my work as a playwright is not easy for I am still asking questions which have yet to be answered; questions which demand honest, direct, and altruistic answers from publishers, critics, distributors, and a great many institutions and individuals. These people have yet to come to terms with the history, traditions, social, political, and economic background of this playwright; who and what he is; what he represents—this African from the so-called Third World.

I have always held Dylan Thomas in great esteem, not only because he was a great poet but because without him, the world would never have known, experienced, and enjoyed the wealth of knowledge and greatness in Amos Tutuola's Yoruba folktale, *The Palm-Wine Drinkard*. Tutuola's work, written in his own cryptic pidgin English, was looked upon with disdain and rejected as non-literary by his own countrymen and other African men of letters ("Euro-Afros"). Things haven't changed much—or have they? I am very happy that I am recognised as an "Afrikan Writer"; but first as a Sierra Leonean. I do not strive to satisfy American or European academics, researchers or Africanists. My direction is Africa—the people; whatever I write identifies with the people I know, from whom I came.

It will never be easy for most critics to be enthusiastic about my plays because they cannot discuss my characters without destroying them. My critics expose their own limitations with regard to their ignorance of the grassroots, the vital human relationships that I share very closely with those characters in their own world.

I took to creative writing, especially playwriting, because it gives me the freedom to experiment with the senses and emotions, the foibles and frailties of people, but mostly because I enjoy probing the fears, jealousies, greed, and power that influence their lives. Fools I detest; nonetheless, I prefer them to the religious hypocrite, the bigoted politician, the insincere academic poser. My fascination and sympathy have always been with and for the rejects, the down-trodden, and the over-zealous who fail only because they believe and follow blindly. Even the truth must be proved. When I wrote my first play, *If Wishes Were Horses*, while a student at Rose Bruford College, I was mocked, ridiculed, and laughed at. When the play was accepted and broadcast by the BBC African Service it dawned on me that the mockery and laughter were the incentive, inspiration, and encouragement I needed which I never got from my tutors and those elites of my own kind. So I have continued to write.

It is true that my plays speak out on behalf of the masses. My protagonists are drawn mostly from among the underdogs, the underprivileged. I caution against despair, apathy, and inertia. I urge them to come to terms with the realities of the world they live in, to use their common sense, plan their own strategies, and take individual and collective decisions as men and women in control of their own principles, not those dictated to them. They should be people who respect themselves—who understand their indigenous traditions, love their country, are ready to make sacrifices, even to die for it; are willing to make mistakes and ready to correct those mistakes: all of which leads to individual freedom and self-determination. From this basis they are prepared to face the world as men and women in control of their own destinies.

If posterity judges my work adversely, as some critics have done, the youth will always be there to prove it wrong. I believe in the young and unafraid Africans. For them, I will continue to write as I feel and like and want.

* * *

Mixing absurdist comedy, ritualistic theatre, and Brechtian alienation effects with dialect, African proverbs, satire, political and social allusions, a rich, highly poetic stage language, parodies (especially of Christian missionary songs), and his own songs, Yulisa Amadu Maddy has tried to move beyond elite art to a popular yet political theatre for the African urban population. From European fringe theatre of the 1960's he returned to Africa, where he has increasingly worked in pidgin English and local languages. His published plays are similar to his partly autobiographical novel, *No Past, No Present, No Future*, in being critical of the characters and their actions and in not choosing sides between them. The plays present highly stylized versions of representative African social problems but offer no solutions. Maddy aims to demystify and raise consciousness.

The early one-act play *Yon-Kon* contains many of the ingredients developed at more length in his other works, including the relationship of personal freedom to communal activity. Although the setting is an African prison (details suggest Maddy has Sierra Leone in mind), it is symbolic of the prison of the world in which the convicts are forced to keep up an absurd, endless march "Right, left, left, right." A store clerk who has been sentenced to two weeks imprisonment objects to the march and is hurt by the others who demand that he respect Yon-Kon, their leader, who makes them chant "We must not steal, we must not fight, we must obey the laws." When the new convict continues to assert his rights, he is attacked and after a struggle is accused of killing another prisoner who probably died from a weak heart. When Yon-Kon asks for £200 to have the prison doctor testify that the dead man died of a stroke, the clerk foolishly says he will trust justice. He is unjustly sentenced to a further seven years imprisonment for manslaughter and loses his life savings as a consequence.

Yon-Kon illustrates both the insecurity of a life of routine, and the ways in which law responds to money, prestige, and the views of the community. The new convict believes in bourgeois ideals of truth, justice, and personal rights, but he cannot survive the cruelty and absurdity of the world as represented by the prison, where power and leadership are more important than truth. Bully, leader, cynic, hypocrite, middleman between the prisoners and prison officials, leader of a criminal gang, enforcer of prison discipline, Yon-Kon appears adjusted to the reality of his environment: "I don't feel free outside. I will never feel free or enjoy anything outside prison. Prison was built for people like me. I will always make new friends there. I will have people to command." At the play's end he is once more making the others march "Right, left, left, right," while the convicts chant "We must behave—as good citizens should."

Alla Gbah, possibly influenced by Camus's *L'Étranger*, portrays the last hours of Joko Campbell, a 27-year-old student condemned to death for killing his mistress. Maddy is here particularly concerned with the relationship of love to freedom. Joko ran away from home as his mother made him feel helpless, "like a child." Claiming not to have time for the "ethics of decadent puritan society" he falls in love with a Mrs. Manly, a woman of his mother's age who is notorious for seducing students. He idealizes her, and finds in his love a way of transforming his dull, purposeless existence into a new life; but when he catches her making love to another man Joko kills her in defence of his manhood. Although Joko is a Dostoevskian hero who defines himself by "creating and killing," his notions are tested by a moral realism. Rejecting "money, education, morals, society," Joko wants to find "Love, selfless love. Freedom" and "Above all, happiness' among the underprivileged. But despite his proud defiance, as the play ends he is alone in his cell with one hour to live, frightened, crying "I need you mother." Independence means learning the hard facts of life through trial and error.

Obasai, another short play, is a farcical yet hard-boiled portrait of modern African society. It concerns the decision of a tough village schoolboy to leave his mother, brother, and "good society" to join some swindlers in creating a new life for himself as a fisherman. Women, as in all Maddy's plays, seem seductively threatening, hypocritical, agents of conformity, whom the protagonist must reject. As society is corrupt there is little to choose between the good and the swindlers. The dialogue often takes on the power of Jacobean satire: "Easy, Dad. He's a real punk. Look how he's running to meet the bitch. She wears his trousers and he wears her frock." Maddy's dramas are Jonsonian comedies where crooked characters play upon and bring out the hypocrisy of society, while the attractiveness of the swindlers puts the audience's own values into question.

A common Maddy target is the African ruling class, especially the Europeanized Creole elite of Sierra Leone, which is contrasted to the downtrodden labourers and peasants through whose eyes the dramatist attempts to see reality. The long play *Gbana-Bendu*, with its wry, arch, exaggerated, melodramatic style, is concerned with the robbery of Africa by the governing elite and the improbability of the people in a democracy willingly ridding themselves of their oppressors. The attempt by two drunken tramps to save a virgin from being sacrificed becomes symbolic of the condition of Africa. The traditional masqueraders are revealed to be thieves who rob the people's houses during ceremonies, and keep the sacrificial maidens for their own sexual use. The rhetoric of tradition and convention sanctifies their misdeeds. When she refuses to be saved from the sacrifice and claims that she must fulfil her duty, the virgin at first appears a symbol for the self-repression of traditional Africa. In a surprising twist, however, we learn that she is in cahoots with the chief masquerader, whom she loves; she uses her supposed loyalty to convention as a means to trick others. Although Maddy demystifies both traditionalist and nationalist rhetoric, the ending of the play becomes confusing, as the tramps are unreliable and might be making up the explanations they offer. In a final irony, as the tramps discuss whether they are becoming corrupted by others, they are themselves trapped by the crowd.

Many of Maddy's later plays in Krio and pidgin have not been published. *Big Berrin*, for which he was imprisoned, concerns corruption in Sierra Leone and the hopeless condition of the urban poor. According to Michael Etherton in *The Development of African Drama* (1982), the central character is a schoolteacher who, not having been paid for months, creates his own church through which he can exploit others. The play shows that the local politicians, businessmen, religious leaders, and other members of the establishment have continued the ways of the colonial powers in robbing the people.

—Bruce King

MAMET, David (Alan). American. Born in Flossmoor, Illinois, 30 November 1947. Educated at Rich Central High School; Francis W. Parker School; Goddard College, Plainfield, Vermont, B.A. in English 1969; Neighborhood Playhouse School, New York, 1968–69. Married Lindsay Crouse in 1977; one daughter. Actor in summer stock, 1969; stage manager, *The Fantasticks*, New York, 1969–70; Lecturer in Drama, Marlboro College, Vermont, 1970; artist-in-residence, Goddard College, 1971–73; founder and artistic director, St. Nicholas Company, Plainfield, Vermont, 1972, and St. Nicholas Players, Chicago, 1974–76; faculty member, Illinois Arts Council, 1974; Visiting Lecturer, University of Chicago, 1975–76 and 1979, and New York University, 1981; Teaching Fellow, Yale University School of Drama, New Haven, Connecticut, 1976–77; associate artistic director, Goodman Theatre, Chicago, 1978–84; associate director, New Theater Company, Chicago, 1985. Contributing editor, *Oui* magazine, 1975–76. Recipient: Joseph Jefferson award, 1974; Obie award, 1976, 1983; New York State Council on the Arts grant, 1976; Rockefeller grant, 1976; CBS-Yale University fellowship, 1977; New York Drama Critics Circle award, 1977, 1984; Outer Circle award, 1978; Society of West End Theatre award, 1983; Pulitzer Prize, 1984; Dramatists Guild Hull-Warriner Award, 1984; American Academy award, 1986. Agent: Howard Rosenstone, Rosenstone/Wender, 3 East 48th Street, 4th Floor, New York, New York 10017, U.S.A.

PUBLICATIONS

Plays

Lakeboat (produced Marlboro, Vermont, 1970; revised version produced Milwaukee, 1980). New York, Grove Press, 1981.

Duck Variations (produced Plainfield, Vermont, 1972; New York, 1975; London, 1977). With *Sexual Perversity in Chicago*, New York, Grove Press, 1978; in *American Buffalo, Sexual Perversity in Chicago, Duck Variations*, 1978.

Mackinac (for children; produced Chicago, 1972?).

Marranos (produced Chicago, 1972–73?).

The Poet and the Rent: A Play for Kids from Seven to 8:15 (produced Chicago, 1974). Included in *Three Children's Plays*, 1986.

Squirrels (produced Chicago, 1974). New York, French, 1982.

Sexual Perversity in Chicago (produced Chicago, 1974; New York, 1975; London, 1977). With *Duck Variations*, New York, Grove Press, 1978; in *American Buffalo, Sexual Perversity in Chicago, Duck Variations*, 1978.

American Buffalo (produced Chicago, 1975; New York, 1976; London, 1978). New York, Grove Press, 1977; in *American Buffalo, Sexual Perversity in Chicago, Duck Variations*, 1978.

Reunion (produced Louisville, 1976; New York, 1979; London, 1981). With *Dark Pony*, New York, Grove Press, 1979.

The Woods (also director: produced Chicago, 1977; New York, 1979; London, 1984). New York, Grove Press, 1979.

All Men Are Whores (produced New Haven, Connecticut, 1977). Included in *Short Plays and Monologues*, 1981.

A Life in the Theatre (produced Chicago and New York, 1977; London, 1979). New York, Grove Press, 1978.

The Revenge of the Space Pandas; or, Binky Rudich and the Two-Speed Clock (produced Chicago, 1977). Included in *Three Children's Plays*, 1986.

Dark Pony (produced New Haven, Connecticut, 1977; New York, 1979; London, 1981). With *Reunion*, New York, Grove Press, 1979.

The Water Engine: An American Fable (produced Chicago and New York, 1977). With *Mr. Happiness*, New York, Grove Press, 1978.

Prairie du Chien (broadcast 1978; produced New York, 1985; London, 1986). Included in *Short Plays and Monologues*, 1981.

American Buffalo, Sexual Perversity in Chicago, Duck Variations: Three Plays. London, Eyre Methuen, 1978.

Mr. Happiness (produced New York, 1978; London, 1984). With *The Water Engine*, New York, Grove Press, 1978.

Lone Canoe; or, The Explorer, music and lyrics by Alaric Jans (produced Chicago, 1979).

The Sanctity of Marriage (produced New York, 1979). With *Reunion* and *Dark Pony*, New York, French, 1982.

Shoeshine (produced New York, 1979). Included in *Short Plays and Monologues*, 1981.

A Sermon (also director: produced New York, 1981; London, 1987). Included in *Short Plays and Monologues*, 1981.

Short Plays and Monologues (includes *All Men Are Whores, The Blue Hour: City Sketches, In Old Vermont, Litko, Prairie du Chien, A Sermon, Shoeshine*). New York, Dramatists Play Service, 1981.

Edmond (produced Chicago and New York, 1982; London, 1985). New York, Grove Press, 1983; London, Methuen, 1986.

The Disappearance of the Jews (produced Chicago, 1983).

Glengarry Glen Ross (produced London, 1983; Chicago and New York, 1984). New York, Grove Press, and London, Methuen, 1984.

Red River, adaptation of a play by Pierre Laville (produced Chicago, 1983).

Five Unrelated Pieces (includes *Two Conversations*; *Two Scenes*; *Yes, But So What*) (produced New York, 1983). Included in *Dramatic Sketches and Monologues*, 1985.
The Dog (produced 1983). Included in *Dramatic Sketches and Monologues*, 1985.
Film Crew (produced 1983). Included in *Dramatic Sketches and Monologues*, 1985.
4 A.M. (produced 1983). Included in *Dramatic Sketches and Monologues*, 1985.
Vermont Sketches (includes *Pint's a Pound the World Around*, *Deer Dogs*, *Conversations with the Spirit World*, *Dowsing*) (produced New York, 1984). Included in *Dramatic Sketches and Monologues*, 1985.
The Frog Prince (produced Louisville, 1984; New York, 1985). Included in *Three Children's Plays*, 1986.
The Spanish Prisoner (produced Chicago, 1985).
The Shawl (produced Chicago and New York, 1985; London, 1986). With *Prairie du Chien*, New York, Grove Press, 1985.
The Cherry Orchard, adaptation of a play by Chekhov (produced Chicago, 1985). New York, Grove Press, 1987.
Cross Patch (broadcast 1985). Included in *Dramatic Sketches and Monologues*, 1985.
Goldberg Street (broadcast 1985). Included in *Dramatic Sketches and Monologues*, 1985.
Vint, adaptation of a story by Chekhov, in *Orchards* (produced Urbana, Illinois, 1985; New York, 1986). New York, Knopf, 1986.
Dramatic Sketches and Monologues (includes *Five Unrelated Pieces*, *The Power Outrage*, *The Dog*, *Film Crew*, *4 A.M.*, *Food*, *Pint's a Pound the World Around*, *Deer Dogs*, *Columbus Avenue*, *Conversations with the Spirit World*, *Maple Sugaring*, *Morris and Joe*, *Steve McQueen*, *Yes*, *Dowsing*, *In the Mall*, *Cross Patch*, *Goldberg Street*). New York, French, 1985.
Goldberg Street: Short Plays and Monologues. New York, Grove Press, 1985.
Three Children's Plays. New York, Grove Press, 1986.
Speed-the-Plow (produced New York, 1987).
House of Games (screenplay). New York, Grove Press, 1987.

Screenplays: *The Postman Always Rings Twice*, 1981; *The Verdict*, 1982; *The Untouchables*, 1987; *House of Games*, 1987.

Radio Plays: *Prairie du Chien*, 1978; *Cross Patch*, 1985; *Goldberg Street*, 1985.

Other

Writing in Restaurants (essays). New York, Viking, 1986; London, Faber, 1988.
The Owl (for children), with Lindsay Crouse. N.p., Kipling Books, 1987.

*

Bibliography: *Ten Modern American Playwrights* by Kimball King, New York, Garland, 1982.

Critical Studies: *David Mamet* by C.W.E. Bigsby, London, Methuen, 1985; *David Mamet* by Dennis Carroll, London, Macmillan, and New York, St. Martin's Press, 1987.

Theatrical Activities:

Director: **Plays**—*Beyond the Horizon* by O'Neill, Chicago, 1974; *The Woods*, Chicago, 1977; *Twelfth Night*, New York, 1980; *A Sermon*, New York, 1981. **Film**—*House of Games*, 1987.

* * *

David Mamet announced his arrival as a significant playwright in the American theater in 1974 with the first scene of his first professionally produced full-length play, *Sexual Perversity in Chicago*. The scene, a rhapsodic, free-form account by a young man recounting his incredible sexual exploits of the night before, was filled with a jazzy, explosive use of coarse street language that immediately stamped the then-26-year-old writer as a fresh, invigorating force in drama. This consummate use of the argot of the underbelly of American society—and more particularly its Chicago subspecies—has been prominent in many Mamet works ever since, from the petty hoodlum bravado of *American Buffalo* in 1975 to the triumphant real estate sales pitches of *Glengarry Glen Ross*, his Pulitzer Prize drama of 1983. This keen use of down-and-dirty talk is more than a playwright's sharp ear for dialogue at work, however. It is an attempt by the author to shape and distill dialogue—even language of the lowest, most common variety spoken by characters of the lowest, most common variety—into a poetry for the theater.

Born and raised in the Chicago area, Mamet brought to his first plays the energy and innovation he had discovered while working as a youngster in the small experimental theaters of Chicago and at Second City, the improvisational comedy cabaret that has served as a breeding ground for so many actors and writers. Several of his early plays—including *Duck Variations*, *Sexual Perversity in Chicago*, and *A Life in the Theatre*—were dominated by the techniques of Second City's blackout sketches, in which comic and dramatic epiphanies were achieved in swift, economical language and in situations involving only a couple of characters. Other early influences were the ever-present Samuel Beckett and Harold Pinter, whose use of dramatic pauses, hesitations, and false starts as an integral part of stage dialogue is also evident in Mamet's own American rhythms.

Mamet's attempts to use prosaic language poetically have achieved wildly variable results. In a realistic context, his dialogue seems pungent and fresh, but his efforts to create a less realistic, more abstract vision of theater frequently have made his poetic flights seem forced and false. *Lone Canoe* was almost laughed off the stage in a disastrous premiere in 1979 because the play with music, about a 19th-century explorer who finds peace (and subsequently loses it) in the wilds amid the natural ways of the Indians, inflated the contrast of harassed, civilized man with the natural beauties of the Indians' life into a pretentious, pseudo-operatic style. *Edmond*, a brilliant exploration of urban hell through one man's journey into an underground of sex and violence, stripped away realism in favor of an abstract, impressionistic presentation that created a powerful, surreal world of dark despair. It was a noble, ambitious, and beautifully designed work in its premiere in Chicago; but it was a critical flop off-Broadway, and its failure, a hard blow to the playwright, at least partly accounted for his return to the more familiar territory of *Glengarry Glen Ross*, which contained complex, sophisticated plotting but was basically a further, refined exploration of the themes he had introduced in *American Buffalo*. (*The Spanish Prisoner*, another brief excursion into near-abstraction in language, was so dense that audiences found it nearly incomprehensible.)

There are political repercussions in Mamet's plays. Both *American Buffalo* and *Glengarry Glen Ross* contain implicit criticism of capitalistic exploitation as reflected in the wheelings and dealings of the plays' grifters and con men. *The Water Engine*, "an American fable" set in Chicago in 1933 during the Century of Progress World's Fair, dealt specifically with the swallowing up of a young, idealistic inventor by evil fat cats who want to keep his miraculous water engine from ruining their trade.

But the most telling, most important battles and victories in Mamet's plays occur on the basic, personal levels of individual relationships. The bonds of friendship, family, and love are crucial in Mamet's world, and when they are broken, the world collapses for his characters. When Donny, the owner of the junk shop in *American Buffalo*, breaks the ongoing union he has forged with Bobby, the hophead kid who looks at him as a father, in favor of the scheme for quick bucks dreamed up by the two-bit crook Teach, the result is ruinous for their friendship. A betrayal of trust similarly haunts the driven salesmen in *Glengarry Glen Ross*. The failure of personal commitments is at the heart of sadness among the young people of both *Sexual Perversity in Chicago* and *The Woods*, the two-character romance that is Mamet's most personal and intimate study of man–woman relationships. The breaking up of family ties is again specifically addressed in two poignant companion pieces, *Dark Pony* and *Reunion*. The former is a sweet, sad reverie for a father and his young daughter, while the latter is a bitter encounter between the same two persons years later. In *Edmond* the Everyman hero's initial walk-out on the social and sexual ties of his marriage plunges him into the nightmare of disarray that he discovers in the city's underworld. The play's final scene, in which the imprisoned Edmond finds peace at last in a new master–slave relationship with the hulking black men in his prison cell, is Mamet's comment on the enduring need for such personal commitments, and the state to which they have come in today's chaotic society.

While Mamet is fatalistic about society at large, he is zestful and joyous in dealing with individuals who are secure in their professional and personal relationships. Very early in his career, while still in college, he established his own group, the St. Nicholas Company, composed of close friends and colleagues, and he often works within a family framework of designers, actors, and directors (most notably, Gregory Mosher, who has staged the majority of Mamet's theater premieres) whose work he knows and trusts. *The Poet and the Rent*, a comedy written in 1974 when the author and his friends were desperately searching for money to pay their own rents as struggling theater artists in Chicago, lightly and sweetly celebrates this union of care and concern that good professionals feel in sharing their trials and accomplishments.

A Life in the Theatre is at once a charming and thoughtful salute to the people who toil in the theater. As it traces the change in relationships between an experienced, older actor and the talented young man who has his whole career ahead of him, the play reveals a knowledge of and affection for the joys and idiosyncrasies of the profession. In fact, Mamet's language is at its most imaginative and vital when professionals are at work. The super spieler salesman Richard Roma in *Glengarry Glen Ross* has several dazzling arias in which he spins off mesmerizing monologues of obscenities, aborted phrases, and ungrammatical sentences. The rough dialogue of the men in *Lakeboat* expertly establishes their character and history in vigorous, economical strokes, as does the similar shop talk of the two actors in *A Life in the Theatre*.

Despite his pleasure in working in films (as screenwriter, most recently of *The Untouchables*, and as writer and director of *House of Games*), Mamet's allegiance to the theater remains strong. A prolific writer, he continues to pile up scenes and scripts, sometimes as short as a few pages. His best work in theater may lie ahead.

—Richard Christiansen

MANKOWITZ, (Cyril) Wolf. British. Born in London, 7 November 1924. Educated at East Ham Grammar School, London; Downing College, Cambridge, M.A. in English 1946. Served as a volunteer coal miner and in the British Army during World War II. Married Ann Margaret Seligmann in 1944; four sons. Play and film producer: with Oscar Lewenstein, 1955–60; independently, 1960–70; with Laurence Harvey, 1970–72. Owner, Pickwick Club restaurant, London, 1963–70; also antique and art dealer. Moved to Ireland in 1971. Since 1982 Adjunct Professor of English, University of New Mexico, Albuquerque. Honorary Consul to the Republic of Panama in Dublin, 1971. Recipient: Society of Authors award, for poetry, 1946; Venice Film Festival prize, 1955; BAFTA award, 1955, 1961; Oscar, for screenplay, 1957; Film Council of America Golden Reel, 1957; *Evening Standard* award, 1959; Cork Film International Critics Prize, 1972; Cannes Film Festival Grand Prize, 1973. Address: The Bridge House, Ahakista, Durrus, near Bantry, County Cork, Ireland; or, 2322 Calle Halcon, Santa Fe, New Mexico 87505, U.S.A.

PUBLICATIONS

Plays

Make Me an Offer, adaptation of his own novel (televised 1952; revised version, music and lyrics by Monty Norman and David Heneker, produced London, 1959).

The Bespoke Overcoat (produced London, 1953). London, Evans, 1954; New York, French, n.d.

The Baby, adaptation of a work by Chekhov (televised 1954; produced London, 1981). Included in *Five One-Act Plays*, 1955.

The Boychik (produced London, 1954).

It Should Happen to a Dog (televised 1955; produced Princeton, New Jersey, 1967; London, 1977). Included in *Five One-Act Plays*, 1955.

Five One-Act Plays. London, Evans, 1955; New York, French, n.d.

The Mighty Hunter (produced London, 1956). Included in *Five One-Act Plays*, 1955.

The Last of the Cheesecake (produced London, 1956). Included in *Five One-Act Plays*, 1955.

Expresso Bongo, with Julian More, music and lyrics by David Heneker and Monty Norman (produced London, 1958). London, Evans, 1960.

Belle; or, The Ballad of Dr. Crippen, with Beverley Cross, music by Monty Norman (produced London, 1961).

Pickwick, music and lyrics by Cyril Ornadel and Leslie Bricusse, adaptation of the novel by Dickens (produced London, 1963).

Passion Flower Hotel, music and lyrics by Trevor Peacock and John Barry, adaptation of the novel by Rosalind Erskine (produced London, 1965).

The Samson Riddle (produced Dublin, 1972; as *Samson and Delilah*, produced London, 1978). London, Vallentine Mitchell, 1972.
Jack Shepherd, music by Monty Norman (produced Edinburgh, 1972; as *Stand and Deliver*, produced London, 1972).
Dickens of London (televised 1976). London, Weidenfeld and Nicolson, 1976; New York, Macmillan, 1977.
The Hebrew Lesson (screenplay). London, Evans, 1976.
The Irish Hebrew Lesson (produced London, 1978; New York, 1980).
Iron Butterflies (produced Albuquerque, 1985). Two acts published in *Adam International Review* (London), 1984.

Screenplays: *Make Me an Offer*, with W.P. Lipscomb, 1954; *A Kid for Two Farthings*, 1955; *The Bespoke Overcoat*, 1955; *Trapeze*, 1955; *Expresso Bongo*, 1959; *The Two Faces of Dr. Jekyll* (*House of Fright*), 1960; *The Millionairess*, with Ricardo Aragno, 1960; *The Long and the Short and the Tall* (*Jungle Fighters*), with Willis Hall, 1961; *The Day the Earth Caught Fire*, with Val Guest, 1961; *Waltz of the Toreadors*, 1962; *Where the Spies Are*, with James Leasor and Val Guest, 1965; *Casino Royale*, with John Law and Michael Sayers, 1967; *La Vingt-cinquième Heure* (*The Twenty-fifth Hour*), 1967; *The Assassination Bureau*, with Michael Relph, 1969; *Bloomfield* (*The Hero*), with Richard Harris, 1970; *Black Beauty*, with James Hill, 1971; *The Hebrew Lesson*, 1972; *Treasure Island*, with Orson Welles, 1973; *The Hireling*, 1973; *Almonds and Raisins* (documentary), 1983.

Television Plays: *Make Me an Offer*, 1952; *The Baby*, 1954; *The Girl*, 1955; *It Should Happen to a Dog*, 1955; *The Killing Stones*, 1958; *Love Is Hell*, 1966; *Dickens of London* series, 1976; *Have a Nice Death*, from the story by Antonia Fraser (*Tales of the Unexpected* series), 1984.

Novels

Make Me an Offer. London, Deutsch, 1952; New York, Dutton, 1953.
A Kid for Two Farthings. London, Deutsch, 1953; New York, Dutton, 1954.
Laugh Till You Cry: An Advertisement. New York, Dutton, 1955; included in *The Penguin Wolf Mankowitz*, 1967.
My Old Man's a Dustman. London, Deutsch, 1956; as *Old Soldiers Never Die*, Boston, Little Brown, 1956.
Cockatrice. London, Longman, and New York, Putnam, 1963.
The Biggest Pig in Barbados: A Fable. London, Longman, 1965.
Raspberry Reich. London, Macmillan, 1979.
Abracadabra! London, Macmillan, 1980.
The Devil in Texas. London, Royce, 1984.
Gioconda. London, W.H. Allen, and New York, Freundlich, 1987.
The Magic Cabinet of Professor Smucker. London, W.H. Allen, 1988.

Short Stories

The Mendelman Fire and Other Stories. London, Deutsch, and Boston, Little Brown, 1957.
Expresso Bongo: A Wolf Mankowitz Reader. New York, Yoseloff, 1961.
The Blue Arabian Nights: Tales of a London Decade. London, Vallentine Mitchell, 1973.
The Day of the Women and the Night of the Men: Fables. London, Robson, 1977.

Verse

XII Poems. London, Workshop Press, 1971.

Other

The Portland Vase and the Wedgwood Copies. London, Deutsch, 1952.
Wedgwood. London, Batsford, and New York, Dutton, 1953; revised edition, London, Barrie and Jenkins, 1980.
Majollika and Company (for children). London, Deutsch, 1955.
ABC of Show Business. London, Oldbourne Press, 1956.
A Concise Encyclopedia of English Pottery and Porcelain, with R.G. Haggar. London, Deutsch, and New York, Hawthorn, 1957.
The Penguin Wolf Mankowitz. London, Penguin, 1967.
The Extraordinary Mr. Poe: A Biography of Edgar Allan Poe. London, Weidenfeld and Nicolson, and New York, Summit, 1978.
Mazeppa: The Lives, Loves, and Legends of Adah Isaacs Menken: A Biographical Quest. London, Blond and Briggs, and New York, Stein and Day, 1982.

*

Theatrical Activities:
Director: **Film**—*The Hebrew Lesson*, 1972.

Wolf Mankowitz comments:

There have been some quite good notes and notices on odd works of mine from time to time, but I really could not give details. Let's just say that they all agreed that I was somewhat over-diversified and altogether too varied, and generally speaking, pragmatic, which means, I suppose, opportunistic in the way one tends to be if one is a professional writer. Lately my writing has been described as erudite, sophisticated, always funny, sometimes bizarre—so whether I'm getting better or worse, I am certainly continuing. I have never considered myself to be a playwright. I think of myself as a storyteller, and I tend to use whatever form the story seems to me to require.

* * *

In his early novels and short stories Wolf Mankowitz displayed a sure grasp of the dramatic, that sense of character and situation which makes for good theatre. *Make Me an Offer* and *A Kid for Two Farthings* are both simple, direct narratives, sensitive and funny; it was natural enough to see them transcribed for the stage and the screen. Since then, Mankowitz has joyfully embraced show biz at all levels; he has become an impresario, he is a screenwriter who adapts his own scripts and those of others, and he has put every form of popular entertainment on celluloid. The films to which he has contributed range in their appeal from the glamorous (*The Millionairess*) to the horrific (*The Two Faces of Dr. Jekyll*), from adventure (*The Day the Earth Caught Fire*) to schmaltz (*Black Beauty*).

Mankowitz has certainly found his spiritual home in Shaftesbury Avenue but that hasn't shaken his allegiance to the basic principles of storytelling first learnt in the East End; he still employs a powerful mixture of cynicism and sentiment, still reveres the past, still delights in patterns of speech and idiosyncrasies of behaviour. At a guess, his central character in *Make*

Me an Offer is something of a self-portrait. "Who knew better than he that nothing is given, that everything passes, the woods decay. He was the ultimate human being. He resigned himself to make a profit." *Expresso Bongo* is a further comment on commercialisation, a musical set in Soho, where the promoters of pop live in the continued hope of overnight successes, sudden fortune.

Of Mankowitz's one-act plays, *The Bespoke Overcoat* has always attracted praise for its technical skill and depth of feeling. It is published together with four smaller pieces, one entitled *It Should Happen to a Dog*, another, *The Last of the Cheesecake*. As one might expect, these are anecdotes of Jewish life, poignant, comic, and shrewd. *The Bespoke Overcoat* is something more, a celebration of that stubborn reverence for life which the good adhere to, however desperate their circumstances. Morry the tailor ("a needle like Paganini") can never give his friend the longed-for overcoat, since Fender has died in poverty. But human values are not negated by death: this truth is triumphantly stated in Morry's speeches and, at the close of the play, in his chanting of the Kaddish. Pathos is the dominant mood in another early play, *The Boychik*; this is a study of hopeless ambition, that of an elderly actor who, with his son, dreams of reopening the decaying theatre where he was once a star.

Mankowitz has made an important contribution to postwar drama, which is not always acknowledged by those who distrust box office success. His picture of Jewish life is convincing for its realism and memorable for its use of symbolism, as in *A Kid for Two Farthings*. He has eschewed the avant garde but is nevertheless a highly sophisticated playwright who understands the traditions of the European theatre and has worked against the parochialism of the English stage.

—Judy Cooke

MANN, Emily. American. Born in Boston, Massachusetts, 12 April 1952. Educated at Radcliffe College, Cambridge, Massachusetts, B.A. in English 1974 (Phi Beta Kappa); University of Minnesota, Minneapolis (Bush Fellow), 1974–76, M.F.A. in theater arts 1976. Married Gerry Bamman in 1981; one son. Associate director, Guthrie Theatre, Minneapolis, 1978–79; resident director, BAM Theater Company, Brooklyn, New York, 1981–82. Recipient: Obie award, 1981 (for writing and directing); Guggenheim fellowship, 1983; Rosamond Gilder Award, 1983; National Endowment for the Arts grant, 1984, 1986; Creative Artists Public Service grant, 1985; McKnight fellowship, 1985; Dramatists Guild award, 1986; Playwrights USA award, 1986. Lives in Grandview-on-Hudson, New York. Agent: George Lane, William Morris Agency, 1350 Avenue of the Americas, New York, New York 10019, U.S.A.

Publications

Plays

Annulla, An Autobiography (as *Annulla Allen: The Autobiography of a Survivor*, also director: produced Minneapolis, 1977; revised version, as *Annulla, An Autobiography*, produced St. Louis, 1985). New York, Theatre Communications Group, 1985.

Still Life (also director: produced Chicago, 1980; New York, 1981; Edinburgh and London, 1984). New York, Dramatists Play Service, 1982.

Execution of Justice (produced Louisville, 1984; also director: produced New York, 1986). New York, French, 1986.

Nights and Days, adaptation of a play by Pierre Laville, published in *Avant-Scène* (Paris), July 1984.

*

Theatrical Activities:

Director: **Plays**—*Cold* by Michael Casale, Minneapolis, 1976; *Ashes* by David Rudkin, Minneapolis, 1977, and Cincinnati, 1980; *Annulla Allen*, Minneapolis, 1977; *Surprise, Surprise* by Michel Tremblay, Minneapolis, 1978; *On Mount Chimborazo* by Tankred Dorst, Minneapolis, 1978; *Reunion* and *Dark Pony* by David Mamet, Minneapolis, 1978; *The Glass Menagerie* by Tennessee Williams, Minneapolis, 1979; *He and She* by Rachel Crothers, New York, 1980; *Still Life*, Chicago, 1980, New York, 1986; *Oedipus the King* by Sophocles, New York, 1981; *A Tantalizing* by William Mastrosimone, Louisville, 1982; *The Value of Names* by Jeffrey Sweet, Louisville, 1982, and Hartford, Connecticut, 1984; *A Weekend near Madison* by Kathleen Tolan, Louisville and New York, 1983; *Execution of Justice*, Minneapolis, 1985, New York, 1986; *A Doll's House* by Ibsen, Hartford, Connecticut, 1986; *Hedda Gabler* by Ibsen, La Jolla, California, 1987.

* * *

Emily Mann has referred to her work as "theatre of testimony." Documentary drama is her métier, and recent history has provided her subjects ranging from the horrors of war, to peacetime violence, to the revolution in gender roles and sexual politics. Her first three stage plays are based wholly or in part on interviews with the people whose stories she tells.

Annulla, An Autobiography is the prototype. Mann visited the protagonist, a survivor of Nazism, in 1974, and the work hews so closely to what the playwright heard in Annulla Allen's London kitchen that she credits her as co-author. The short play turns Annulla's own words into an uninterrupted monologue. Annulla's privileged girlhood in Galicia is a distant memory, eclipsed by the Nazi terror. Her self-assurance and unsemitic good looks helped her escape the camps and rescue her Jewish husband from Dachau. Now widowed, she cares for a demanding invalid sister. However compelling her harrowing story, Annulla insists, "It is not me who is interesting, it is my play." An enormous manuscript covers her kitchen table, stage center. Annulla's play argues for global matriarchy as the solution to evil and barbarism. "If women would only start thinking, we could change the world," she observes, declaring women incapable of the monstrous acts of Hitler or Stalin.

Still, Annulla is unable to read out representative passages from her work in progress. The manuscript is so disorganized and the need to get dinner for her ailing sister so pressing that she loses patience sifting through the jumbled pages. Therein lies Mann's point. However reasoned Annulla's thesis or promising her creativity, she is chronically distracted by more traditional female roles and by the anxieties and guilt which stem from her terrible past. Annulla can no more impose order on her play than she can on her life. Mann does not try to do that for her. In setting down the unmediated monologue of this scarred but plucky woman, Mann makes a statement about her own role. *Annulla* testifies to the freedom for creativity exercised by the playwright who recognizes that, by sheer accident of time and place, she was spared the life of her co-author and subject.

In *Still Life* Mann again draws on interviews with real people who become the *dramatis personae*. She calls this work a documentary, specifying that it be produced with that genre's characteristic objectivity. That tone is the first of the ironies that mark this work about the virulent psychic and emotional conditioning suffered by a Vietnam veteran and about the troubled society to which he returns. As a Marine, Mark learned that he could kill civilians as easily as enemy soldiers. After the war, he cannot get rid of the memory of having wielded power over life and death. His obsession is alternately the source of rage, guilt, and physical pleasure. Incapable of talking either to those who were not in Vietnam, or to those who were, Mark turns to drugs, crime, and domestic violence. He is not too self-centered to appreciate that his wife, Cheryl, whom he abuses, is as much of a casualty of the war years as he. Cheryl wants to return to the securities of a traditionalism more alive in her memories than in post-1960's America. She longs to play the roles her mother did, noting that, except in wartime, it is women who protect men—a point of view strikingly antithetical to that of Annulla Allen. Mark's mistress Nadine has done battle with all manner of "naughtiness." "A woman with many jobs and many lives," in Mann's words, Nadine describes herself as being so busy that she sleeps with her shoes on. The observation is metaphoric. Nadine steps over troubled waters, never feeling the cold or agitation, and never plunging beneath the surface. Mark can tell Nadine his ugly truths, for absolutely nothing offends, disturbs, or even touches her.

Still Life is staged so as to make palpable the lack of genuine communication between Mark, who lives in the past, Cheryl, who yearns for an unrealizable future, and Nadine, who hovers above an unexamined present. The three characters sit side by side behind a table, like members of a panel discussion—or witnesses at a trial. They talk about, but rarely to, one another, their intersecting speeches often juxtaposed ironically. So, for example, Nadine's innocence about her near fatal pregnancies overlaps the ingenuous Cheryl's shock in coming upon Mark's pictures of war casualties. Projections on a screen behind the actors underscore the hopelessness of anyone's enjoying the full understanding of others. Gruesome pictures of horribly mutilated war injured, for instance, illustrate Mark's inability to talk to his parents who supported the war. Indeed, this seething play whose self-possessed characters never touch one another on stage ironically reflects a society where people, however uncommunicating, are continually in violent and destructive collision.

The notion of the audience as jury, implicit in *Still Life*, is central to *Execution of Justice*. Significantly, the work was commissioned by the Eureka Theatre of San Francisco. Its subject is the 1978 murder of George Moscone, Mayor of San Francisco, and Harvey Milk, a City Supervisor and the first avowed homosexual voted into high public office. The play brings to the stage the case of the People against Dan White, the assassin. It demonstrates the instability of White, who had been elected a City Supervisor, resigned, changed his mind, and, when Moscone refused to reappoint him to his former post, vented his rage by shooting him and Milk. Mann bases her script on the transcript of the trial, reportage, extensive interviews with some of the principals, as well as what she calls in a prefatory note "the street." The play neatly synthesizes background pertinent to the case, such as the evolution in the social and political spheres caused by the migration to San Francisco of a large homosexual population. It recreates the climate of fear provoked by the mass deaths in Jonestown, Guyana, and the reputed connections between James Jones and liberal elements in San Francisco. The play captures effectively the unprecedented violence that stalked American political life in the 1970's.

As the testimony piles up, one appreciates the implausible defense arguments (e.g., the famous "Twinkies defense," which attributed criminal behavior to the accused's junk food diet) and its unlikely claim that the murders were purely politically and not homophobically motivated. *Execution of Justice* shows that what was really on trial was conservative values, outraged and threatened by the growing power of the gay community. The use of video projections and film clips from documentaries intensify the passions of the trial; the inclusion of reporters and photographers heightens its immediacy. Though Mann treats this explosive material with an even hand, there is no question that she wants the audience as jury to find that Dan White's conviction and light jail sentence for the lesser charges of voluntary manslaughter amount to the miscarriage of justice referred to in the play's title.

In addition to her work for the stage, Mann has written two screenplays (neither yet produced). *Naked* (1985), based on the book by Jo Giese Brown, is subtitled *One Couple's Intimate Journey Through Infertility*. *Fanny Kelly* (1985) dramatizes the true story of an intrepid pioneer woman captured by the Sioux. Both these scripts are distinguished by tight, suspenseful plots as well as the credible characterizations that Mann has made her signature.

—Ellen Schiff

MARCHANT, Tony. British. Born in London, 11 July 1959. Educated at St. Joseph Academy School. Recipient: Edinburgh Festival award, 1982. Agent: Lemon and Durbridge Ltd., 24 Pottery Lane, London W11 4LZ, England.

PUBLICATIONS

Plays

Remember Me? (produced London, 1980).

Thick as Thieves (includes *London Calling* and *Dealt With*) (produced London, 1981). London, Methuen, 1982.

Stiff (produced London, 1982).

Raspberry (produced Edinburgh and London, 1982). Included in *Welcome Home, Raspberry, The Lucky Ones*, 1983.

The Lucky Ones (produced London, 1982). Included in *Welcome Home, Raspberry, The Lucky Ones*, 1983.

Welcome Home (produced Hemel Hempstead, Hertfordshire, and London, 1983). Included in *Welcome Home, Raspberry, The Lucky Ones*, 1983.

Welcome Home, Raspberry, The Lucky Ones. London, Methuen, 1983.

Lazydays Ltd. (produced London, 1984).

The Attractions (produced London, 1987).

Television Play: *Reservations*, 1985.

*

Tony Marchant comments:

I started writing at twenty, and for the past seven or eight years I have written about my generation in various situations—

unemployed, trapped in office conformity, at war, in a state of sexual confusion. The experiences of my characters differ vastly: from having fought in the Falklands (*Welcome Home*) to confronting the "stigma" of infertility (*Raspberry*). Generally the plays are about people attempting to confound the expectations of their environment. They are mostly excluded from the mainstream of society, but suffer from its judgement. They all question these judgements and ultimately defy them. Theirs is a plea for dignity.

* * *

Tony Marchant's work so far marks him as the spokesman for people not normally given a voice. His earliest plays toured schools and youth clubs and he has tended to work in theatres which have a strong sense of community, such as the Theatre Royal at Stratford East, a regular clientele, such as the Soho Poly, or for touring companies like Paines Plough—in short in intimate locations which allow his greatest strengths free play. He has a sharp eye for the minutiae of characterisation, allied to the ability to endow his characters with a high level of articulacy that still seems to keep within the bounds of naturalism. *Thick as Thieves*, for example, shows a group of unemployed London teenagers; the first part, *London Calling*, depicts them merely wandering about flirting with the notion of casual violence; but there is also a clear sense that at least some of them are thinking out their situation in a remarkably organised way. They take on the unthinking prejudices of Pimple, a mate who is toying with the ideas of the National Front; but while they are clear about who not to blame for their situation, they cannot conceive of a way out and their very real linguistic energy is dissipated in destructive self-parody. They are only too aware that they are prime subjects for well-meaning, ineffectual documentary: when Pimple remembers bonfires on the tatty dump that is now their social space, Paul responds sardonically "Our heritage—building things with rubbish and setting light to 'em." The idea of waste is made overt in the second play, *Dealt With*, in which Paul and the others confront a personnel officer who has rejected him; they harass him without much effect and the play ends with the boys on the run from the security guard, except for Paul, now on the verge of suicide. Here the focus is split: on the one hand there is a simple clash between the deprived and the prosperous, on the other a contrast between the dreams with which Paul invests this confrontation and the inadequacy of the personnel officer as a target for his rage. Marchant sometimes seems lost between the two and the somewhat melodramatic ending looks like a way of dodging the issue.

In his play about the Falklands aftermath, *Welcome Home*, we are shown a group of young men who have found at least a temporary alternative—the Army. Marchant gives a scrupulous account of both the benefits and the cost of that alternative on a personal level. In the discipline of the "cherry berets" the boys have found both self-image and self-respect. They have developed a comradeship which can show itself in uproarious horseplay but also in their care that a comrade's funeral shall turn out well. In return the Army demands not just their lives but also the right to control their self-expression. As the Corporal points out, the funeral is part of their public duty to be heroes "as advertised on TV"; when one of them messes up the discipline of the procession he isn't simply punished by the Army for violating its image—he assists the process, breaking down from pure shame. The Corporal treats him with savage violence, but his motivation is not the reflex action of a man addicted to "bull"; it is rather a clumsy attempt at shock therapy, an attempt to help while staying within the permitted boundaries of the Para image; this, Marchant implies, is the real cost of the Army as an outlet for youthful energy and courage—the damage it does to the best human instincts.

Raspberry is perhaps the clearest celebration of the human ability to transcend immediate oppression. Two women share a gynaecological ward—one for an abortion, the other for yet another operation for her infertility. Despite the insensitivity of the system that has flung them together, symbolised by the hostility of the nurse towards the young abortion patient, they achieve a close and mutually comforting relationship. Lacking any common ground, they unite against their surroundings in an almost surreal spirit. What starts as a near-quarrel turns, in the face of an angry nurse, to a mischievous assertion that they have been playing games; this then becomes something like fact as they improvise a "party" to transform the grimness of the pre-operation evening; this leads in turn to a genuine relationship; the moment when they hold each other in the face of their shared pain is a touching moment of theatre. This ability to show the play instinct at work in the unlikeliest settings, and the comradeship arising out of it, is perhaps Marchant's major strength. At present the naturalism of his sets and plots precludes a close analysis of the underlying politics. One simply accepts that, unjust as it is, this is the present situation. However, he shows clearly the resources that are there to fight it; the linguistic energy of his characters is a lively symbol of human energy in the face of oppression. For change to occur, Marchant implies, that energy needs only to be harnessed.

—Frances Gray

MARCUS, Frank (Ulrich). British. Born in Breslau, Germany, 30 June 1928; emigrated to England in 1939. Educated at Bunce Court School, Kent (evacuated to Shropshire), 1939–43; St. Martin's School of Art, London, 1943–44. Married Jacqueline Sylvester in 1951; one son and two daughters. Secretary, salesman, and manager, T.M.V. Ltd., London, 1944–54; manager, Marshal's Antiques (Silver), London, 1954–65. Actor, director, and scenic designer, Unity Theatre, Kensington, London; founder, International Theatre Group. Theatre critic, the *Sunday Telegraph*, London, 1968–78; regular contributor to *Plays and Players*, London, *London Magazine*, and *Dramatists Guild Quarterly*, New York. Since 1984 television critic, *Plays International*, London. Recipient: *Evening Standard* award, 1965; *Plays and Players* award, 1965; *Variety* award, 1966. Agent: Margaret Ramsay Ltd., 14-A Goodwin's Court, London WC2N 4LL. Address: 8 Kirlegate, Meare, near Glastonbury, Somerset BA6 9TA, England.

PUBLICATIONS

Plays

Minuet for Stuffed Birds (also director: produced London, 1950).

Merry-Go-Round, adaptation of a play by Schnitzler (as *Reigen—La Ronde*, produced London, 1952). London, Weidenfeld and Nicolson, 1953.

The Man Who Bought a Battlefield (produced London, 1963).

The Formation Dancers (produced London, 1964; revised version, produced London, 1971). Published in *Plays of the Year 28*, London, Elek, 1965.

The Killing of Sister George (produced Bristol and London, 1965; New York, 1966). London, Hamish Hamilton, 1965; New York, Random House, 1967.
Cleo (produced Bristol, 1965). Excerpt, as *Cleo and Max*, published in *London Magazine*, February 1966.
The Window (televised 1966; produced London, 1969; New York, 1973). London, French, 1968; New York, French, 1970.
Studies of the Nude (produced London, 1967).
Mrs. Mouse, Are You Within? (produced Bristol and London, 1968). Published in *Plays of the Year 35*, London, Elek, 1969.
The Guardsman, adaptation of a play by Ferenc Molnár (produced Watford, Hertfordshire, 1969; London, 1976; New York, 1980). London, Eyre Methuen, 1978.
Blank Pages: A Monologue (televised 1969; also director: produced London, 1972; New York, 1973). London, French, 1973; in *The Best Short Plays 1974*, edited by Stanley Richards, Radnor, Pennsylvania, Chilton, 1974.
Notes on a Love Affair (produced London, 1972). Published in *Plays of the Year 42*, London, Elek, 1973.
Christmas Carol (produced London, 1972; New York, 1973; as *Carol's Christmas*, produced London, 1975).
Keyholes (produced New York, 1973).
Beauty and the Beast (produced Oxford, 1975). Published in *Plays of the Year 46*, London, Elek, 1978.
Anatol, adaptation of the play by Schnitzler (produced London, 1976). London, Methuen, 1982.
Portrait of the Artist (mime; produced London, 1976).
Blind Date: An Anecdote (produced London, 1977). London, French, 1977; in *The Best Short Plays 1979*, edited by Stanley Richards, Radnor, Pennsylvania, Chilton, 1979.
The Ballad of Wilfred II (produced London, 1978).
The Merman of Orford (mime; produced Niagara-on-the-Lake, Ontario, 1978).
The Weavers, adaptation of a play by Gerhart Hauptmann (produced London, 1980). London, Eyre Methuen, 1980.
La Ronde, with Jacqueline Marcus, adaptation of a play by Schnitzler (televised 1982). London, Methuen, 1982.
From Morning to Midnight, adaptation of a play by Georg Kaiser (produced London, 1987).

Screenplays: *The Snow Tiger*, 1966; *The Formation Dancers*, 1972.

Radio Plays: *The Hospital Visitor*, 1979; *The Beverley Brooch*, 1981; *The Row over La Ronde*, 1982.

Television Plays: *Liebelei*, 1954; *The Window*, 1966; *A Temporary Typist*, 1966; *The Glove Puppet*, 1968; *Blank Pages*, 1969; *Carol's Story*, 1974; *La Ronde*, with Jacqueline Marcus, 1982.

*

Manuscript Collection: Boston University Libraries.

Critical Studies: "The Plays of Frank Marcus" by Irving Wardle, in *London Magazine*, March 1966; "The Comedy is Finished" by Marcus, in *London Magazine*, June–July 1971.

Theatrical Activities:
Director: **Plays**—*House of Regrets* by Peter Ustinov, London, 1948; *The Servant of Two Masters* by Carlo Goldoni, London, 1949; *Minuet for Stuffed Birds*, London, 1950; *The Broken Jug* by Heinrich von Kleist, London, 1950; *Husbands and Lovers* by Ferenc Molnár, London, 1950; *The Man of Destiny* by Shaw, London, 1950; *Reigen* (*La Ronde*) by Arthur Schnitzler, London, 1952; *Georges Dandin* by Molière, London, 1953; *This Property Is Condemned* by Tennessee Williams, London, 1953; *The Killing of Sister George*, toured, 1967; *Blank Pages*, London, 1972.
Actor: **Plays**—The General in *House of Regrets* by Peter Ustinov, London, 1948; Silvio in *The Servant of Two Masters* by Carlo Goldoni, London, 1949; title-role in *The Man with the Flower in His Mouth* by Pirandello, London, 1950; Priest in *The Broken Jug* by Heinrich von Kleist, London, 1950; Napoleon in *The Man of Destiny* by G.B. Shaw, London, 1950; Orlando in *Angelica* by Leo Ferrero, London, 1951; The Son in *My Friend, The Enemy* by Sheila Hodgson, London, 1952.

* * *

A quality that has distinguished all Frank Marcus's mature plays is his sympathetic, though not sentimental, understanding of the behaviour of women in love, using the word "love" in its widest possible sense. The examination of feminine amatory practice in its various forms has been his theme in play after play. In two of them, *Cleo* and *Notes on a Love Affair*, it furnishes virtually the whole material of the plot.

Marcus's first play to achieve any kind of commercial success was *The Formation Dancers*, a light-hearted foursome in which one man borrows another man's mistress for a brief episode. His wife, to reclaim his fidelity, feigns an affair with this other man. The plot, in fact, is triviality itself; but two points are worth observing. One is the insistence that it is the two women who are always in command. The other is the drawing of the mistress, a Chelsea demi-beatnik of a type more common in 1964 (the date of the play) than now, who recurs several times in later work.

A much more detailed portrait of what is pretty well the same character appears in *Cleo*. This play is a theme and variations; the protagonist, that same demi-beatnik, as intelligent as she is footloose, is observed in a series of encounters with assorted men. (It may be significant that in 1953 Marcus published a translation of Schnitzler's *Reigen*, best known as the film *La Ronde*.) In this play it is clear that woman is unarguably the dominant sex, even if her dominance cannot always insure her against disaster. A later play, *Studies of the Nude*, was a developed version of one of the episodes from *Cleo*. Schnitzler's *Anatol*, adapted by Marcus ten years after *Cleo*, gives an idea of where he got the story from, only here the sexes are reversed.

Between *The Formation Dancers* and *Cleo* came what is certainly Marcus's most imaginative play so far, *The Killing of Sister George*. This is a penetrating study of a lesbian love affair. The "masculine" woman of the association is a once-successful actress whose career has dwindled to a steady part in a radio soap opera from which the producers now intend to drop her. She shares her life with a girl who appears to be merely young and silly, but who is later revealed as not so young and mentally retarded, the object not only of love but of a genuinely charitable beneficence. It is the younger girl, however, who at the end of the play has moved into a greater happiness and left the older woman on the brink of despair: the dominance is once again attributed to the weaker vessel. This play, in which the events mark an almost uninterrupted sequence of sadness, is nevertheless hilariously funny throughout: an imaginative masterpiece. Its sensitivity was somewhat obscured in a subsequent film version, in which Marcus did not have a hand.

After *Sister George*, Marcus's next piece dealt with characters almost defiantly ordinary. This was *Mrs. Mouse, Are*

You Within?, once more a comedy of which the storyline is unrelieved tragedy. It is set among mildly trendy middle-class people in London, and once again there is a strong female part at the core, though on this occasion, for once, she is a character to whom things happen rather than a character who makes things happen. What happens is that she becomes pregnant by a passing association with a black neighbour. The lover decamps; the boring man to whom she has been engaged for eight years is so stuffy that she sends him away; and her Marxist landlord, in whom she has never felt much interest, makes a proposal of marriage to which she agrees from the depths of her despair.

The ordinariness of the characters is an asset to the play, in that vast misfortunes seem vaster when they light on little people. But *Mrs. Mouse* has not quite the imaginative spark of *Sister George* nor the wit of *The Formation Dancers*, though there is plenty of good comedy and real pathos in it. The *Cleo* character is once more recognisable in the heroine's younger sister.

Notes on a Love Affair is more romantic and less comic than any of Marcus's previous work. In this, a woman novelist stuck on a play sets up a love affair between a former lover of hers and a colourless girl who works for her dentist, so that she may observe their mutual reactions. As so often, the experiment progresses through realms of comedy to final heartbreak. The play does not mark any advance on Marcus's part, unless in his willingness to adopt the Pirandellian shift of having his heroine explain directly to the audience what she is doing. But it is a moving play, and contains two fine parts for actresses.

Marcus has also made several adaptations, including a stylish translation of Molnar's *The Guardsman*, and written several plays for television, one of which, a short two-hander called *The Window*, has also been seen in the theatre. There is some significance in the Molnar translation. If there is any detectable influence in Marcus's work, it is in Molnar and Schnitzler that you will find it.

—B.A. Young

MASTROSIMONE, William. American. Born in Trenton, New Jersey, 19 August 1947. Educated at Pennington Preparatory School, New Jersey, 1963–66; Tulane University, New Orleans, 1966–70; Rider College, Trenton, New Jersey, 1973–74, B.A. in English 1974; Rutgers University, New Brunswick, New Jersey, 1974–76, M.F.A. 1976. Recipient: Los Angeles Drama Critics Circle award, 1982; Outer Circle award, 1983; John Gassner Award, 1983. Agent: George Lane, William Morris Agency, 1350 Avenue of the Americas, New York, New York 10019. Address: 715 First Avenue West, Apartment 202, Seattle, Washington 98119, U.S.A.

PUBLICATIONS

Plays

The Woolgatherer (produced New Brunswick, New Jersey, 1979; New York, 1980; London, 1985). New York, French, 1981.

Extremities (produced New Brunswick, New Jersey, 1980; New York, 1982; London, 1984). New York, French, 1984.

A Tantalizing (produced Louisville, 1982). New York, French, 1985.

Shivaree (produced Seattle, 1983). New York, French, 1984.

The Undoing (produced Louisville, 1984).

Nanawatai (produced in Norwegian, Bergen, Norway, 1984; produced in English, Los Angeles, 1985). New York, French, 1986.

Tamer of Horses (produced New Brunswick, New Jersey, 1985; revised version produced Los Angeles, 1986; revised version produced Seattle, 1987).

Cat's-Paw (produced Seattle, 1986). New York, French, 1987.

The Understanding (produced Seattle, 1987).

Screenplay: *Extremities*, 1986.

*

Manuscript Collection: Boston University.

* * *

When *Extremities* opened off-Broadway in 1982, it proved to be one of the most controversial plays of the season, on or off Broadway. Some critics suggested that William Mastrosimone's tense drama about a would-be rapist and his implacable woman captor attracted audiences because there wasn't more powerful fare available. Some dismissed the play as an exercise in old-fashioned melodrama, with onstage violence to whet the visual appetites of jaded television viewers. Actually, Mastrosimone, inspired by a 55-year-old woman rape victim—as he explained in "The Making of Extremities," had touched a raw nerve among theatre-goers in general and women in particular. The fear of and revulsion against, violent, vicious, and unprovoked sexual attacks were very real. That angry or unbalanced male members of some minority groups were perceived as the usual rapists found resonance in the play, whose very disturbed potential ravisher is named Raul. This, some suggested, was invoking racial stereotypes, and confronting a seemingly helpless young woman, Marjorie, with this cunning, shifty criminal seemed a deliberate attempt to exploit current fears.

This is unfair to Mastrosimone, although he clearly cares more for victims' rights and safety than he does for those of wrong-doers. In *Extremities* the naked threat of violence and violation is presented almost immediately, but fortunately Marjorie is able to turn the tables and take Raul captive. His deviousness and threats, as the play progresses, make her decide—driven by rage—to kill him and bury the body in her garden. Her roommates return and react variously, suggesting standard social reactions to such a situation when it is merely hypothetical. At the close, there is a catharsis—somewhat schematic—for both Raul and Marjorie, but it offers no magic solutions to the problem. In addition to the exercise of physical violence on stage, Mastrosimone offers audiences a tightly constructed cat-and-mouse plot, whose outcome is not easily guessed. What is especially appealing, however, as in other Mastrosimone plays, is his ability not only to capture the rhythms and idioms of conversation of various social groups, but also to make them the proper expression of his characters. David Mamet is often praised for his ear for common or raffish speech; Mastrosimone is also adept, but in a different way. Where Mamet's characters may seem involved in an aimless stream-of-consciousness, Mastrosimone's are generally trying to achieve some end, to move the plot forward at the very least.

In *The Woolgatherer*, there is almost no major plot action. Rose, a fragile, disturbed girl, who displaces her terrors and misadventures on a mythical friend, Brenda, brings home Cliff, a trucker looking for a sexual encounter. Their banter—his jocular, angry, or uncomprehending; hers tense, poetic, pained—are the substance of the play, as they come to know and trust each other. The title refers to her collection of men's sweaters, begged from previous visitors. *A Tantalizing*, a one-act play, is also a two-character exercise, but this time it's the man, Ambrose, who is unbalanced. Dafne, a young woman who has watched this once well-dressed, confident lawyer spend his days in a parking lot, doing imaginary business on a disconnected telephone he carries with him, has brought him to her apartment, though it's not clear why. No matter what comforts or refreshments she offers him, he is peremptory, corrective, fussy, revealing reasons for his failure in life. At the close, she succeeds in getting him to lay aside his ragged clothing for some of her late father's fine garb.

Mastrosimone can manipulate three or more characters on stage at the same time, with effective exchanges of dialogue, but he seems to prefer confrontations between two people, with others brought on—if at all—only when required by the plot. *Shivaree* has echoes of *Butterflies Are Free*, with the difference that Chandler, its protagonist, is hemophiliac, not blind. His overprotective mother drives a cab to pay the bills, while he saves ice-cream money to pay for a session with a prostitute. He finds himself and romance, however, with a neighboring exotic dancer named Shivaree.

Nanawatai deals with the fates of a Soviet tank-team, trapped in a mountain cul-de-sac by Afghan rebels. The title is supposedly the tribal word for sanctuary: once uttered, enemies must protect the one who begs it. A Russian soldier claims it and is spared. Later, his former comrades do so as well, but implacable Afghan women, impatient with the seeming softness of their men, slaughter the helpless Soviets. Interestingly, this was premiered in Norway rather than the United States.

Cat's-Paw goes beyond *Extremities* in dealing with topical terrors and in subtly satirizing American manners and mores. Jessica Lyons, a weekend television anchor-woman, who wants a major news scoop to improve her position, is brought blindfolded to make a television interview with Victor, who has just blown up a car loaded with explosives outside the Environmental Protection Agency in Washington, D.C. He and his small group are using terror tactics to protest government failures to protect the public from toxic wastes. To that end, he's kidnapped a culpable minor EPA official, David Darling, whom he threatens to kill. Lyons's past television coups have shown her unblinking in the face of horrors; Victor hopes to use her talents to get his message to the world and, perhaps, blow up the White House as she reports the event on television. The willingness of the media to exploit—or to trivialize—horrors to win audiences, the very real threat of toxic wastes and official coverups, and the various aspects of terrorism are all effectively used dramatically. It's especially provocative that the maniacal killer seems to espouse all the pieties of the Sierra Club and be willing to destroy unknown innocents for the greater good of mankind. The verbal sparring between Victor and Lyons is notable; the situation, cinematic.

In *The Undoing* there are overtones of Tennessee Williams: Lorraine Tempesta, who runs a chicken-slaughtering and dressing shop, drinks too much, longs for a man, and harasses her dating daughter. A year before, her husband Leo had been killed in a terrible traffic accident; at the site, she laughed. Now she's overcome with guilt. Into the shop comes a one-eyed man who wants to help out. He proves to be the driver of the other wrecked car, come to make amends. There's also a kind of Greek-Italian chorus, two old women, Mrs. Corvo and Mrs. Mosca.

Tamer of Horses combines elements familiar in other Mastrosimone plays. Childless Ty and Georgiane have taken a youthful black offender, Hector, as a foster child. Ty, orphaned and separated from his brother Sam, who died young as a criminal, wants to give another youth in trouble a chance for a new life. Ty, who is a classics teacher, reaches Hector through a retelling of *The Iliad*, but he cannot break him of old thieving, lying ways. Especially chilling is Hector's recreation of a subway mugging. Touched by the two and their caring, Hector nonetheless departs. With his talent for authentic ethnic dialogue and his apparent belief that one cannot even teach a *young* dog new tricks, Mastrosimone has found a voice and themes for the audiences of his time.

—Glenn Loney

MATHEW, Ray(mond Frank). Australian. Born in Sydney, New South Wales, 14 April 1929. Educated at Sydney Boys' School; Sydney Teacher's College, 1947–49. Schoolteacher in New South Wales, 1949–51; free-lance journalist, 1951–52; staff member, Commonwealth Scientific and Independent Research Organisation, Sydney, 1952–54; tutor and lecturer, Workers Education Association, University of Sydney, 1955–60; left Australia in 1961, and has lived in London, Italy, and New York. Recipient: Commonwealth Literary Fund grant, 1951, 1956; Arts Council of Great Britain bursary, 1960. Address: c/o Currency Press, P.O. Box 452, Paddington, New South Wales 2021, Australia.

PUBLICATIONS

Plays

Church Sunday (produced Ballarat, Victoria, 1950).
We Find the Bunyip (produced Sydney, 1955). Published in *Khaki, Bush and Bigotry*, St. Lucia, University of Queensland Press, 1968; as *Three Australian Plays*, Minneapolis, University of Minnesota Press, 1969.
Lonely Without You (produced Hobart, 1957).
The Bones of My Toe (produced Brisbane, 1957). Published in *Australian One-Act Plays 1*, edited by Eunice Hanger, Adelaide, Rigby, 1962.
A Spring Song (produced Brisbane, 1958; Edinburgh and London, 1964). St. Lucia, University of Queensland Press, 1961.
Sing for St. Ned (produced Brisbane, 1960).
The Life of the Party (produced London, 1960).

Radio Plays: *The Love of Gotama*, 1952; *The Medea of Euripides*, 1954.

Novel

The Joys of Possession. London, Chapman and Hall, 1967.

Short Stories

A Bohemian Affair. Sydney, Angus and Robertson, 1961.
The Time of the Peacock, with Mena Abdullah. Sydney, Angus and Robertson, 1965; New York, Roy, 1968.

Verse

With Cypress Pine. Sydney, Lyre-Bird Writers, 1951.

Song and Dance. Sydney, Lyre-Bird Writers, 1956.
South of the Equator. Sydney, Angus and Robertson, 1961.

Other

Miles Franklin. Melbourne, Landsdowne Press, 1963.
Charles Blackman. Melbourne, Georgian House, 1965.

* * *

By the time Ray Mathew's first important play, *We Find the Bunyip*, was produced he had been a schoolteacher, radio scriptwriter, university tutor, and poet. Before leaving Australia to live in Italy five years later he had published his second and third volumes of poetry, one minor and three full-length plays, as well as having written most of the short stories later collected in *A Bohemian Affair*. The fourth major play was written a year later, the novel in 1965–66.

One of the dimensions used in surveying a playwright's work is the breadth of his technical resource, another the innovations which arose from his experimental structures. On both Mathew scores unusually well.

Technically he is the most sophisticated playwright Australia has produced. His range of dramatic devices, particularly in the area of dialogue, is remarkable and it is difficult to find any instance where a structure obtrudes or is used merely as dramatic ornamentation. Even in *Sing for St. Ned*, which uses some expressionistic devices to achieve alienation, the technical means to Mathew's end remain in control, always revealing rather than distracting from his sub-text.

Mathew's work as a poet had material influence on his drama, many of his more interesting sequences using modes common to both. His dialogue is based on idiomatic syntax, built into rhythmical blocks with caesurae and stresses placed as they are by the sub-group to which each character belongs. This leaves the impression of real speech but creates a denser texture and much broader emotional range.

Repetition is a favourite device, sometimes used to reinforce the texture of ostensibly colloquial chatter, sometimes to establish key phrases without obvious emphasis, frequently to restore significance to devalued words. In *We Find the Bunyip* the key word "happy" occurs thirty times, in as many emotional colours, in one short stretch of dialogue—its original coinage is re-established and it takes a final, ironic, value with considerable impact. In performance the point of the sub-text is clearly established but both the use of the device and the rather formal structure of the sequence go unnoticed.

Mathew's ability to create freshly observed characters, his avoidance of stereotype and his lack of condescension give him much in common with those older playwrights, Lawler, Seymour, Beynon, and Sumner Locke Elliott who, using more conventional moulds, were working in Australia during the same period.

Both *A Spring Song* and *We Find the Bunyip* are closely related to biographical sources, a point which perhaps gives each its authoritative, unforced grasp of the value systems in Australian provincial life. In each play the young middle-class schoolmaster is plummeted among those with whom he appears to have little in common: instead of using them to look on in anger or play the quasi-narrator, Mathew has both characters interact with their new setting, sometimes in wry puzzlement, always with compassion and delight. The myth of Australian egalitarianism is not invoked, neither is there a single extraneous gag for the benefit of the middle-class audience at the expense of the humble.

The very rapid modification of emotional colour necessary in Mathew dialogue is typical of a later period of playwriting than that in which it was conceived. What might now be dismissed as "pinteresque" was written before Pinter was published. Equally innovatory in the middle 1950's, when it was written, was *Sing for St. Ned*, one of the earliest plays to use extensive sequences in which the cast was encouraged to use the techniques of improvisation. Originally intended for college and university use, this play developed a number of devices now taken for granted in educational theatre. Simultaneous discovery is as common in the arts as in science, logical innovation often arising from experiments in several test-tubes.

Mathew's plays do not "read" well, largely because they depend more on the Chekhovian interaction of characters than upon a strong plot line and resolution. On the printed page his deliberately unsensational vocabulary (much closer to Australian reality than to stereotype stage-Australian vernacular) and the subtle flexibility of his emotional colours both contribute to the same difficulty. The doyenne of Australian drama critics, Eunice Hanger, was the first to perceive Mathew's substantial technical resource, other commentators having often missed the carefully concealed technique. Some find the plays unattractive because Mathew does not attempt to capitalize, as a later crop of playwrights have, on the popular Australian sociological and psychological myths.

Mathew's work was not maximised, either quantitatively or qualitatively, at its point of origin. His characteristic qualities needed to be confirmed and consolidated by major Australian directors and actors. When staged in England, with that form of Cockney-cum-Loamshire which passes there for an Australian dialect, the plays—perhaps predictably—failed.

His work remains one of the many basic resources which Australia's heavily subsidized non-commercial management has failed to exploit.

—Reid Douglas

MATURA, Mustapha. Citizen of Trinidad and Tobago. Born in Trinidad, 17 December 1939. Educated at Belmont Boys Roman Catholic Intermediate School, 1944–53. Married Mary Margaret Walsh in 1964; three children. Worked as an office boy and in a solicitor's firm, 1954–57, stocktaker in hotel, 1958–59, insurance salesman, 1959–60, and tally clerk on the docks, 1960–61, all in Trinidad; moved to England, 1961; hospital porter, 1961–62, display assistant in a cosmetic factory, 1962–65; stockroom assistant in a garment factory, 1966–70. Founding chairman, Black Theatre Co-operative, London, 1978. Recipient: Arts Council bursary, 1971; John Whiting Award, 1972; George Devine Award, 1973; *Evening Standard* award, 1975; *Caribbean Times* award, for directing, 1982. Agent: Judy Daish Associates, 83 Eastbourne Mews, London W2 6LQ, England.

PUBLICATIONS

Plays

Black Pieces (includes *Party*, *Indian*, *Dialogue*, *My Enemy*) (produced London, 1970). With *As Time Goes By*, London, Calder and Boyars, 1972.

As Time Goes By (produced Edinburgh and London, 1971). With *Black Pieces*, London, Calder and Boyars, 1972.
Bakerloo Line (produced London, 1972).
Nice (produced London, 1973). Included in *Nice, Rum an' Coca Cola, and Welcome Home Jacko*, 1980.
Play Mas (produced London, 1974; New York, 1976). London, Marion Boyars, 1976.
Black Slaves, White Chains (produced London, 1975).
Bread (produced London, 1976).
Rum an' Coca Cola (produced London, 1976; New York, 1977). Included in *Nice, Rum an' Coca Cola, and Welcome Home Jacko*, 1980.
More, More (produced London, 1978).
Another Tuesday (produced London, 1978).
Independence (produced London, 1979). Included in *Play Mas, Independence, and Meetings*, 1982.
Welcome Home Jacko (produced London, 1979; New York, 1983). Included in *Nice, Rum an' Coca Cola, and Welcome Home Jacko*, 1980.
A Dying Business (produced London, 1980).
Nice, Rum an' Coca Cola, and Welcome Home Jacko. London, Eyre Methuen, 1980.
One Rule, music by Victor Romero and John Laddis (produced London, 1981).
Meetings (produced New York, 1981; also director: produced London, 1982). New York, French, 1982; included in *Play Mas, Independence, and Meetings*, 1982.
Play Mas, Independence, and Meetings. London, Methuen, 1982.
The Playboy of the West Indies (produced Oxford and London, 1984).

Screenplay: *Murders of Boysie Singh*, 1972.

Television Plays: *No Problem* series, with Farrukh Dhondy, 1983; *There's Something Wrong in Paradise*, 1984; *Black Silk* series, with others, 1985.

*

Theatrical Activities:
Director: **Plays**—*Meetings*, London, 1982; *Fingers Only* by Yemi Ajibade, London, 1982.

Mustapha Matura comments:

In my writing I have tried to examine the effects of colonialism, political and psychological, on the colonisers and the colonised, hoping that in the magic process of theatre these experiences will lead to eventual liberation.

* * *

The prolific Mustapha Matura was hailed as "the most perceptive and humane black dramatist presently writing in Britain" by Benedict Nightingale as early as 1979. Matura's earlier plays were taken up by the Royal Court and Theatre Upstairs and by the different sections of the London fringe represented by the ICA, the Almost Free, and the Bush. His *Play Mas* was the only work by a Caribbean writer to transfer to the West End. In 1978 Matura co-founded the Black Theatre Co-operative with Charlie Hanson; the Co-op has produced his *Welcome Home Jacko* and *One Rule*. Matura has gained wider exposure in the 1980's through television scripts: a musical examining black politics through Kid Creole's shipwreck in the Caribbean, *There's Something Wrong in Paradise*; a series about a black barrister in London, devised with Rudy Narayan, *Black Silk*; and a Channel 4 comedy series about five young blacks, *No Problem*, written with Farrukh Dhondy. The 40-minute *Black Slaves, White Chains* is a curiosity in his work, an allegory in which three manacled slaves are discouraged from escape by tempters who offer sex, religion, and books. Two finally accept an offer of work, leaving the third still defiant. Matura's other plays are best divided into those set among West Indians living in England and plays set in the Caribbean.

As Time Goes By is the most entertaining of the former group. It concerns a plausible Trinidadian East Indian mystic and con-man, a Jonsonian rogue, living in Notting Hill, who solves everyone's problems, for a fee. Other characters include the West Indian father worried that his son has turned into a cockney skinhead and the white hippie couple who steal the con-man's best "pot." His wife longs to return to Trinidad: "Trinidad en much but is we own is a heaven compared to dis. . . . Look, child, is five years I here and every night a go ter bed a pray dat when a open my eyes in de morning a go see de sun shining, home." Matura wants his comedy taken seriously: "*As Time Goes By* is about a black man living in this country and how he's escaping from the realities of being a black man and not looking at the world, this country, in any political context. A lot of it is about his escapism and how he's pretending and not being himself, not being black, not being his own true identity." The jokes and high spirits cover a desperation and near-despair about the struggle to make a bare living in a hostile environment.

Welcome Home Jacko looks at unemployed boys in a run-down London youth club, who profess faith in rastafarianism but are eventually forced, by the return of Jacko from prison, into a more accurate perception of their blackness. *Play Mas* is one of Matura's more ambitious dramas of change in Trinidad. The first half presents Samuel working as a dogsbody in a tailor's shop, being pushed around by his East Indian bosses, mother and son. The time is the early 1950's with the Peoples' National Movement emerging. Samuel goes to a political meeting instead of sweeping the floor, and is sacked. Play Mas, the Carnival, arrives and people revel in the streets in striking costumes. The second half is set several years later, after independence. Samuel has become the local police chief, seeking the source of arms coming to guerrillas on the island. A State of Emergency could prevent Carnival, but Samuel is persuaded to lift the ban, and the Carnival provides an apparent happy ending.

Rum an' Coca Cola has only two characters, composers of calypsos, on a Trinidad beach. The very form of calypso is shown to be degraded by the need to perform "Rum an' Coca Cola," with its refrain, "working for the Yankee dollar." As usual with Matura, the surface lightness is deceptive: he feels passionately about the state of his own part of the Third World.

"In *Independence*," writes Matura in his Author's Note, "I wanted to show that colonialism is a state of mind as well as a political reality and to examine the conflicts created by the leftovers of such attitudes." In this drama two barmen in an old, little-used hotel offer contrasting views. The older clings to memories of the good old days when the hotel was full of tourists while the younger wants to be a farmer and completely discard the colonialism which lingers with the hotel—which the older finally burns down.

Meetings focuses on another facet of independent Trinidad: the successful, though they have riches as well as self-government, are, in Matura's words, "people living outside their landscape, with problems that neither inheritance can solve."

Meetings is about an affluent Americanized couple, seen in their sterile labour-saving kitchen, enjoying a Mercedes, air-conditioning, and a swimming-pool. Both lead a hectic life of business meetings. The man, however, influenced by a new young cook in the household, discovers a preference for traditional foods, breadfruit and coconut leaves. This leads to growing commitment to his roots, talking to old people with tales of slave revolts, and to taking part in a shango, an ecstatic African-based ritual—to the horror of his wife, who says that she did not marry a monkey-man. She, meanwhile, sinks into the corruption that follows selling illegally imported cigarettes, and satire turns to tragedy.

The Playboy of the West Indies is an audacious re-writing of J.M. Synge's classic. Matura moves the location from County Mayo to the remote Trinidadian fishing village of Mayaro, so one outpost of the English-speaking world becomes another. Widow Quin becomes Mama Benin, the shebeen becomes a rum-shop, and the local girls bring gifts of molasses and fresh-water oysters. The time is 1950; many men are emigrating and the girls fear they will not find husbands. Synge's eloquent Irish poetry becomes a racy, idiomatic, earthily comic Caribbean speech.

Matura has remarked: "I respond differently to each new play I write. . . . So it would be less than accurate, and misleading, to find one common perception throughout my work." Matura's subjects are the state of former black colonies and of blacks in Britain, usually treated with apparent lightness, and with a mastery of all the possibilities of West Indian speech.

—Malcolm Page

McCABE, Eugene. Irish. Born in Glasgow, Scotland, 7 July 1930. Educated at Castleknock College, Dublin; University College, Cork, B.A. 1953. Married Margôt Bowen in 1955; one daughter and three sons. Since 1955 farmer in County Monaghan. Chairman, Patrick Kavanagh Society, 1970–73. Recipient: *Irish Life* award, 1964; Prague Festival award, for television play, 1974; Irish Critics award, for television play, 1976; Royal Society of Literature Winifred Holtby prize, for fiction, 1977; Reading Association of Ireland award, for children's book, 1987. Agent: Macnaughton Lowe Representation, 200 Fulham Road, London SW10 9PN, England. Address: Drumard, Clones, County Monaghan, Ireland.

PUBLICATIONS

Plays

The King of the Castle (produced Dublin, 1964; New York, 1978). Dublin, Gallery Press, and Newark, Delaware, Proscenium Press, 1978.
Breakdown (produced Dublin, 1966).
Pull Down a Horseman (produced Dublin, 1966). With *Gale Day*, Dublin, Gallery Press, 1979.
Swift (produced Dublin, 1969).
Victims (trilogy; includes *Cancer*, *Heritage*, *Victims*), adaptation of his own fiction (televised 1976; produced Belfast, 1981). Cork, Mercier Press, 1976; *Cancer* published Newark, Delaware, Proscenium Press, 1980.
Roma, adaptation of his own story (televised 1979). Dublin, Turoe Press, 1979.
Gale Day (televised 1979; produced Dublin, 1979). With *Pull Down a Horseman*, Dublin, Gallery Press, 1979.

Television Plays: *A Matter of Conscience*, 1962; *Some Women on the Island*, 1966; *The Funeral*, 1969; *Victims* (trilogy), 1976; *Roma*, 1979; *Gale Day*, 1979; *Music at Annahullion*, from his own short story, 1982; *The Year of the French*, with Pierre Lary, from the novel by Thomas Flanagan, 1983.

Novel

Victims: A Tale from Fermanagh. London, Gollancz, 1976.

Short Stories

Heritage and Other Stories. London, Gollancz, 1978.

Other

Cyril: The Quest of an Orphaned Squirrel (for children). Dublin, O'Brien Press, 1986.

* * *

Eugene McCabe's output is small: one could wish for more plays from such a talent. In recent years he has turned more to fiction and television as his media, winning much acclaim for his adaptation of Thomas Flanagan's best-selling historical novel *The Year of the French*. As playwright, McCabe belongs to the 1960's, when he was instrumental, together with such dramatists as Brian Friel, Thomas Murphy, and John B. Keane, in revitalizing the moribund Irish theatre (symptomatic of which was the Abbey Theatre's ultra-conservatism at this period).

McCabe's plays have a forthrightness that must be seen in the context of theatrical and cultural conditions in an Ireland emergent from isolationism and about to come to terms with changes and challenges brought by television, the EEC, air travel, and an affluence deriving from unprecedented industrial development. *The King of the Castle* challenged certain taboos in Irish society by presenting for contemplation the spectacle of a childless couple goaded by social attitudes towards sex and fertility into hiring a surrogate father. The setting is a farm in County Monaghan, where Scober Mac Adam is harvesting and has many hired hands and petty farmers in assistance. A proud and powerful figure, Scober is all too sensitive to the mocks and jeers of those who look on his pretty wife Tressa and fault Scober for her childlessness. The imagery and atmosphere of the harvest reinforce Scober's bitter sense of sterility, and unknown to Tressa he encourages a young labourer, Matt Lynch, to think of her as in need of him. When she discovers the monstrous notion that Scober has planned, Tressa, a sympathetic character, is shattered. Ironically, Scober has succeeded only in driving her further away from him than ever, while the mockery of the "chorus" of Hardy-esque locals is not silenced but increased. Written with sensitivity as well as appropriate frankness, this play is McCabe's greatest claim to attention as a dramatist. It is, one might say, an Irish *Desire under the Elms*. It won for McCabe the prestigious *Irish Life* award.

Two unpublished plays followed: *Breakdown* and *Swift*. Neither was a success. *Breakdown*, a play about the new Ireland of big business deals and shady ethical standards, could nevertheless be regarded as rather old-fashioned in its moral approach, "pure Ibsen through the idiom," as the *Irish Times* reviewer put it. *Swift* was a major production at the Abbey, with Tyrone Guthrie directing, Tanya Moisiewitch designing, and Micheál MacLiammóir from the Gate Theatre starring as Swift. The *Irish Times* reviewer described the play as "an episodic, impressionistic chronicle" and found it somewhat tedious, in spite of (or can it have been because of?) the stars descending amid the homely Abbey company. The subsequent television adaptation of *Swift* indicated that the proper medium for McCabe's main theme, Swift's madness, was film rather than theatre. But in tackling the theme for the stage he was joining a long and distinguished line of Irish dramatists fascinated by the mysteries of Swift's biography: Yeats, Lord Longford, and Denis Johnston, for example.

The greater success on television of *Swift* may have inclined McCabe towards that medium and away from the stage. Yet he did, in fact, write once more for the stage with *Gale Day*, a short play about Patrick Pearse. This was written at a time when revisionist historians were depicting Pearse as less than heroic, and, indeed, seriously flawed. *Gale Day* puts Pearse on trial and presents him as sympathetic and courageous in spite of the charges laid against him. This play makes a pendant to an earlier short piece in which Pearse and James Connolly hold a debate over the true nature of Irish republicanism, *Pull Down a Horseman*. McCabe does not take sides between the romantic idealist and the socialist.

With his three-part television drama on the Northern Ireland situation, *Cancer*, *Heritage*, and *Victims*, McCabe reached a wider audience with enormous success. Using fiction that McCabe had either already published or was about to publish, these plays carried a documentary quality that was both new and powerful on Irish television. From his native vantage point in the border county of Monaghan adjoining the rural population of Fermanagh that is sharply divided on sectarian lines, McCabe can communicate through codes of language and skilful subtext startling and even shocking insights into the ways violence blasts through coexistence and undermines human feeling. As one character puts it in *Heritage*: "men who don't want to hate are pushed to it" and must take sides. McCabe probably said all he wanted to say about the Northern Ireland tragedy in these three plays. Subsequently, he wrote a simple study of a tramp figure, an Irish Mad Tom, in *Roma*, based on a story with the same title already published in *Heritage and Other Stories*. The confused mind of the old man could be seen as an image of Irish consciousness strained by the twin forces of loyalty to traditional pieties and the necessity to see and accept changes in moral standards when doors are opened to foreign influences. The concern with "breakdown" under one kind of strain or another has been McCabe's enduring theme as a playwright, and it is found again even in so minor a piece as *Roma*.

—Christopher Murray

McCLURE, Michael (Thomas). American. Born in Marysville, Kansas, 20 October 1932. Educated at the University of Wichita, Kansas, 1951–53; University of Arizona, Tucson, 1953–54; San Francisco State University, B.A. 1955. Married Joanna Kinnison in 1954; one daughter. Assistant Professor, 1962–77, Associate Professor, 1977, and since 1978 Professor, California College of Arts and Crafts, Oakland. Playwright-in-residence, American Conservatory Theatre, San Francisco, 1975; Associate Fellow, Pierson College, Yale University, New Haven, Connecticut, 1982. Editor, with James Harmon, *Ark II/Moby I*, San Francisco, 1957. Recipient: National Endowment for the Arts grant, for poetry, 1967, 1974; Guggenheim fellowship, for poetry, 1973; Magic Theatre Alfred Jarry award, 1973; Rockefeller fellowship, 1975; Obie award, 1978. Agent: Helen Merrill Ltd., 361 West 17th Street, New York, New York 10011. Address: 264 Downey Street, San Francisco, California 94117, U.S.A.

PUBLICATIONS

Plays

!The Feast! (produced San Francisco, 1960). Included in *The Mammals*, 1972.

Pillow (produced New York, 1961). Included in *The Mammals*, 1972.

The Growl, in *Four in Hand* (produced Berkeley, California, 1970; produced separately New York, 1976). Published in *Evergreen Review* (New York), April–May 1964.

The Blossom; or, Billy the Kid (produced New York, 1964). Milwaukee, Great Lakes Books, 1967.

The Beard (produced San Francisco, 1965; New York, 1967; London, 1968). Privately printed, 1965; revised version, New York, Grove Press, 1967.

The Shell (produced San Francisco, 1970; London, 1975). London, Cape Goliard Press, 1968; in *Gargoyle Cartoons*, 1971.

The Cherub (produced Berkeley, California, 1969). Los Angeles, Black Sparrow Press, 1970.

The Charbroiled Chinchilla: The Pansy, The Meatball, Spider Rabbit (produced Berkeley, California, 1969). Included in *Gargoyle Cartoons*, 1971.

Little Odes, Poems, and a Play, The Raptors. Los Angeles, Black Sparrow Press, 1969.

The Brutal Brontosaurus: Spider Rabbit, The Meatball, The Shell, Apple Glove, The Authentic Radio Life of Bruce Conner and Snoutburbler (produced San Francisco, 1970; *The Meatball* and *Spider Rabbit* produced London, 1971; New York, 1976; *The Authentic Radio Life of Bruce Conner and Snoutburbler* produced London, 1975). Included in *Gargoyle Cartoons*, 1971.

The Pansy (produced London, 1972). Included in *Gargoyle Cartoons*, 1971.

Gargoyle Cartoons (includes *The Shell*, *The Pansy*, *The Meatball*, *The Bow*, *Spider Rabbit*, *Apple Glove*, *The Sail*, *The Dear*, *The Authentic Radio Life of Bruce Conner and Snoutburbler*, *The Feather*, *The Cherub*). New York, Delacorte Press, 1971.

Polymorphous Pirates: The Pussy, The Button, The Feather (produced Berkeley, California, 1972). *The Feather* included in *Gargoyle Cartoons*, 1971.

The Mammals (includes *The Blossom*, *!The Feast!*, *Pillow*). San Francisco, Cranium Press, 1972.

The Grabbing of the Fairy (produced Los Angeles, 1973). St. Paul, Truck Press, 1978.

The Pussy, The Button, and Chekhov's Grandmother; or, The Sugar Wolves (produced New York, 1973).

McClure on Toast (produced Los Angeles, 1973).

Gorf (produced San Francisco, 1974). New York, New Directions, 1976.

Music Peace (produced San Francisco, 1974).

The Derby (produced Los Angeles, 1974; revised version produced New York, 1981).

General Gorgeous (produced San Francisco, 1975; Edinburgh, 1976). New York, Dramatists Play Service, 1982.

Two Plays. Privately printed, 1975.
Sunny-Side Up (includes *The Pink Helmet* and *The Masked Choir*) (produced Los Angeles, 1976). *The Pink Helmet* included in *Two Plays*, 1975; *The Masked Choir* published in *Performing Arts Journal* (New York), August 1976.
Minnie Mouse and the Tap-Dancing Buddha (produced San Francisco, 1978). Included in *Two Plays*, 1975.
Two for the Tricentennial (includes *The Pink Helmet* and *The Grabbing of the Fairy*) (produced San Francisco, 1976).
Range War (produced Tucson, 1976).
Goethe: Ein Fragment (produced San Francisco, 1977). Published in *West Coast Plays 2* (Berkeley, California), Spring 1978.
Josephine the Mouse Singer, adaptation of a story by Kafka (produced New York, 1978). New York, New Directions, 1980.
The Red Snake (produced San Francisco, 1979).
The Mirror (produced Los Angeles, 1979).
Coyote in Chains (produced San Francisco, 1980).
The Velvet Edge. Privately printed, 1982(?).
The Beard, and VKTMS: Two Plays. New York, Grove Press, 1985.

Television Play: *The Maze* (documentary), 1967.

Novels

The Mad Cub. New York, Bantam, 1970.
The Adept. New York, Delacorte Press, 1971.

Verse

Passage. Big Sur, California, Jonathan Williams, 1956.
Peyote Poem. San Francisco, Wallace Berman, 1958.
For Artaud. New York, Totem Press, 1959.
Hymns to St. Geryon and Other Poems. San Francisco, Auerhahn Press, 1959.
The New Book: A Book of Torture. New York, Grove Press, 1961.
Dark Brown. San Francisco, Auerhahn Press, 1961.
Two for Bruce Conner. San Francisco, Oyez, 1964.
Ghost Tantras. Privately printed, 1964.
Double Murder! Vahrooooooohr! Los Angeles, Wallace Berman, 1964.
Love Lion, Lioness. Privately printed, 1964.
13 Mad Sonnets. Milan, East 128, 1964.
Poisoned Wheat. Privately printed, 1965.
Unto Caesar. San Francisco, Dave Haselwood, 1965.
Mandalas. San Francisco, Dave Haselwood, 1965.
Dream Table. San Francisco, Dave Haselwood, 1966.
Love Lion Book. San Francisco, Four Seasons, 1966.
Hail Thee Who Play: A Poem. Los Angeles, Black Sparrow Press, 1968; revised edition, Berkeley, California, Sand Dollar, 1974.
Muscled Apple Swift. Topanga, California, Love Press, 1968.
Plane Pomes. New York, Phoenix Book Shop, 1969.
Oh Christ God Love Cry of Love Stifled Furred Wall Smoking Burning. San Francisco, Auerhahn Press, 1969(?).
The Sermons of Jean Harlow and the Curses of Billy the Kid. San Francisco, Four Seasons, 1969.
The Surge: A Poem. Columbus, Ohio, Frontier Press, 1969.
Hymns to St. Geryon, and Dark Brown. London, Cape Goliard Press, 1969; San Francisco, Grey Fox Press, 1980.
Lion Fight. New York, Pierrepont Press, 1969.
Star. New York, Grove Press, 1971.
99 Theses. Lawrence, Kansas, Tansy Press, 1972.
The Book of Joanna. Berkeley, California, Sand Dollar, 1973.
Transfiguration. Cambridge, Massachusetts, Pomegranate Press, 1973.
Rare Angel (writ with raven's blood). Los Angeles, Black Sparrow Press, 1974.
September Blackberries. New York, New Directions, 1974.
Solstice Blossom. Berkeley, California, Arif Press, 1974.
Fleas 189–195. New York, Aloes, 1974.
A Fist Full (1956–1957). Los Angeles, Black Sparrow Press, 1974.
On Organism. Canton, New York, Institute of Further Studies, 1974.
Jaguar Skies. New York, New Directions, 1975.
Man of Moderation: Two Poems. New York, Hallman, 1975.
Flea 100. New York, Hallman, 1975.
Antechamber. Berkeley, California, Poythress Press, 1977.
Antechamber and Other Poems. New York, New Directions, 1978.
Fragments of Perseus. New York, Jordan Davies, 1978.
Letters. New York, Jordan Davies, 1978.
The Book of Benjamin, with Wesley B. Tanner. Berkeley, California, Arif, 1982.
Fragments of Perseus (collection). New York, New Directions, 1983.
Specks. Vancouver, Talonbooks, 1985.
Fleas 180–186. Berkeley, California, Les Ferriss, 1985.
Selected Poems. New York, New Directions, 1986.

Other

Meat Science Essays. San Francisco, City Lights, 1963; revised edition, San Francisco, Dave Haselwood, 1967.
Freewheelin' Frank, Secretary of the Angels, as Told to Michael McClure by Frank Reynolds. New York, Grove Press, 1967; London, New English Library, 1974.
Scratching the Beat Surface. Berkeley, California, North Point Press, 1982.

Editor, with David Meltzer and Lawrence Ferlinghetti, *Journal for the Protection of All Beings 1* and *3*. San Francisco, City Lights, 2 vols., 1961–69.

*

Bibliography: *A Catalogue of Works by Michael McClure 1956–1965* by Marshall Clements, New York, Phoenix Book Shop, 1965.

Manuscript Collections: Simon Fraser University, Burnaby, British Columbia; University of California, Berkeley.

Critical Studies: "This Is Geryon," in *Times Literary Supplement* (London), 25 March 1965; interview in *San Francisco Poets* edited by David Meltzer, New York, Ballantine, 1971, revised edition, as *Golden Gate*, San Francisco, Wingbow Press, 1976; "Michael McClure Symposium" in *Margins 18* (Milwaukee), March 1975.

Theatrical Activities:
Actor: **Films**—*Beyond the Law*, 1968; *Maidstone*, 1971.

Michael McClure comments:

Theatre is an organism of poetry—weeping, and laughing, and crying, and smiling, and performing superhuman acts—on a shelf in space and lit with lights.

* * *

Michael McClure's curious and highly personal amalgams of Artaud, pop art playfulness, surrealism, and Eastern mysticism seek to bridge the Romantic gap, to join the mind and body in what he calls *spiritmeat*. His first attempt in this ambitious project was a succès de scandale, *The Beard*, in which two archetypes of American dreams, Jean Harlow and Billy the Kid, confront each other outside time and place. Harlow's challenge, "Before you can pry any secrets from me, you must first find the real me! Which one will you choose?" counterpoints Billy's "You're divine," and "You're a bag of meat," two McClurean identities. *The Beard* avoids the implied metaphysics of meaty divinity, since rational argument could only intensify the split between the senses and the spirit. Instead, Billy and Harlow's verbal duel becomes increasingly sexual and violent, pulsating to an ecstatic climax rather than a resolution.

McClure has tried to extend our concept of what humanity is, first by emphasizing man's animality. *!The Feast!* was written in grahr language, sound-poetry based on animal grunts, growls, howls and groans, which gradually evolved into mystical imagery:

> There's no light in the closed rose but a tiny black cherub sleeps there and sings to the creatures that walk in the cliffs of the Lily's pollen, moving from shadow to light in the drips of rain. The seen is as black as the eye seeing it.

At its best, such language is difficult to sustain in the theatre, and for *Gargoyle Cartoons* and subsequent plays up to *Minnie Mouse and the Tap-Dancing Buddha* McClure returned to the more direct statement of *The Beard*. These plays present his metaphysics in what is almost a parody of Beat slang: "from the moment of birth till the hour we're zapped and boogie to the grave, we're thoroughly enwrapped in the realms of being. How can we know nothing, and know especially that even nothing isn't something, if there's always *Being* there?" Although these bald statements have little dramatic value, the best of the plays are oddly unsettling glimpses of human nature, and humans and nature. The combination spider and rabbit of *Spider Rabbit* wanders absent-mindedly onstage, and decides to show and tell. Producing a head from his bag, he saws it open: "BOY AM I HUNGRY! This is the brain of a soldier. BOY, do I hate war. (The head quivers as Spider Rabbit proceeds to eat it with the spoon.) I'M OUT OF CARROTS. BOY, DO I HATE WAR." Few of the plays blend social satire and sight gag so sharply, but they all have a reckless playfulness, a freedom to explore the theatre's sensuous possibilities and the audience's expectations about the theatre.

Despite their frequent childishness, McClure felt these plays illustrated the universe's basic nature, which embraces the silly and shallow as well as the profound. More recently, however, he decided "I'd carried that stream of comedies where the universe created the plays to an extreme that completed my expectations and satisfactions in that mode. So at this time, I've nothing further to say in that vein." Since then (about 1978), his work has focused largely on the relation of art to society. In *Goethe: Ein Fragment*, Mephistopheles offers a callow, arrogant young Goethe a deal: if Goethe will write a play that immortalizes the devil, the playwright will receive a second life. This alternate life is the play called *Faust*, and with this arrangement, McClure plays with the relative importance of the artist and his creation. Not only is the devil a more sympathetic character than Goethe, both of them frequently become subordinate to the play *Faust*. As Mephistopheles says, "Everything real or imagined exists everywhere at once," and McClure suggests that what is imagined is less mortal than ordinary reality, a state that is performed behind a scrim in *Goethe: Ein Fragment*.

Like *Goethe* and the clumsy *The Red Snake* (based on James Shirley's 1641 *The Cardinal*), McClure's *Josephine the Mouse Singer* is drawn from existing literature, Kafka's delicate and eloquent short story. The play won an Obie award for its script before it was produced in New York, and its best dialogue is the narration taken directly from Kafka. However, McClure effectively dramatizes the central problem: Is Josephine's art, brilliant as it is, more important than the dull grey mouse society? Josephine, proud and demanding, is willing to break all the rules of society in order to give it better art, but at the same time she threatens to destroy it. Neither, Kafka nor McClure is foolhardy enough to try to resolve this dilemma, but in dramatizing it, McClure produced some of the best writing of his career.

—Walter Bode

McGEE, Greg(ory William). New Zealander. Born in Oamaru, 22 October 1950. Educated at Waitaki Boys High School; University of Otago, Dunedin, LL.B. 1973. Married Mary Davy; one daughter. Literary fellow, University of Auckland, 1982. Agent: Playmarket, P.O. Box 9767, Wellington. Address: 8 John Street, Ponsonby, Auckland 2, New Zealand.

PUBLICATIONS

Plays

Foreskin's Lament (produced Auckland, 1980). Wellington, Victoria University Press, 1981.
Tooth and Claw (produced Wellington, 1983). Wellington, Victoria University Press, 1984.
Out in the Cold (produced Auckland, 1983). Wellington, Victoria University Press, 1984.
Whitemen (produced Auckland, 1986).

Television Plays: *Free Enterprise*, 1982; *Mortimer's Patch* series, 1984; *Roche* series, 1985.

*

Greg McGee comments:

The colour, vitality, humour, and general excess I have tried to bring to my work, particularly *Foreskin's Lament*, *Out in the Cold*, and *Whitemen*, are reactions against the traditional literary perception of New Zealand as a dull, grey, colourless place which forced most of our writers and artists into cultural exile. Even those who stayed, like Frank Sargeson, seem in their work to share this "colonial" view of New Zealand as culturally bankrupt. It has been a view that has been too easily accepted by our novelists and short story writers, many of whom felt unable to work here.

I have no such difficulties and I glory in the idiosyncrasies of a very inventive New Zealand colloquial English. The burgeoning Maori writing presence does not seem to be having any difficulties, either, in throwing off the yoke of what, after all, was a very pakeha (white) perception of this land.

* * *

From its first production in 1980, Greg McGee's *Foreskin's Lament* was immediately recognised as the most strident piece of confrontational realism in New Zealand drama. For some theatre-goers, the play was simply about rugby: the first act set in a changing room on practice night, the second act at a party after the Saturday match. Most people, however, also followed the argument of the character nicknamed Foreskin, that the rugby player is "the heart and bowels" of New Zealand society, the greatest influence on New Zealand law and ethics; rugby, with its associations of brutality and insensitivity, thus becomes a metaphor for New Zealand life, the "larger game." The team is a herd, which represents a society, and the action essentially consists of an individual detaching himself from the herd, articulating his independence, and then being absorbed back into the herd. Foreskin's mission is not to undermine rugby or destroy the team, of which he is the (valued) fullback; he simply wants to encourage them to play better rugby, to teach them a primitive altruism on the field. The coach, whose ethic is to "kick shit out of everything above grass height," protests that he "does not understand the meaning of the word" altruism, and in the second half of the play Foreskin's defeat is reflected in his retreat into the coach's language. As Foreskin realises that his stance is hopeless, he moves into his "lament," which begins as a parody of a formal speech at the party (echoing the speech which the acting captain made at the start of the act), although the subject now is the death of a team-mate; gradually, the speech turns into a more general threnody for the lost heroes of New Zealand rugby, and the style becomes increasingly poetical, with invented verbs of loss and fragmentation. The stance of the individual against the collective has obvious parallels in Ibsen and Bond, and the central action (a villainous scheme against the captain, resulting in his death) is the stuff of sporting melodrama. However, McGee's depiction of the bonds which give cohesion to the team, and the nuances of language in which the slogans are asserted, questioned, and reasserted, constitute the finest piece of social realism in New Zealand drama to that point. (The published script of *Foreskin's Lament* is based on the version used in the premiere productions; McGee has subsequently modified the play considerably, and the performance script held by his agents does not even contain the final poetical "lament.")

McGee's second play, *Free Enterprise*, was a disappointment, a television situation comedy about the thwarting of a cafe owner. His next two stage plays, however, were much more substantial. *Tooth and Claw* is set in a law office (McGee's own profession), with a large central screen serving sometimes as a window (suggesting that events in the city are being monitored from the executive tower) and sometimes a depiction of the lawyer's mental state, illustrating his anxieties, for his own reflective scrutiny. Before the first lines of dialogue, a black-and-white screen image of civic anarchy, being viewed in dismay by the lawyer, suggests that there is again to be a metaphorical expansion of the action; however, it also becomes clear that there is really disorder in the streets, and that the lawyer's nightmare is derived from a recent incident in which he was actually assaulted and robbed by a Maori activist (who expressionistically appears on stage as a mime). The immediate action consists of politely veiled blackmail from a former student flatmate who is now a speculator and entrepreneur, manipulations which are reflected in two senior law partners as well. The guilty past is analysed and confessed in clinical detail, a method which contrasts strongly with the remarkable vagueness with which the wider present and imminent future are depicted.

In the same year as *Tooth and Claw*, *Out in the Cold* was premiered as a stage play, although its outline was already familiar from McGee's short story of the same title. Summarised, it sounds like a situation comedy: Judy, a former student and now a solo mother, tries to pass herself off as a man to get a well-paid heavy labouring job in the chamber at the local freezing works. The imminent general peripeteia which will occur when her real identity is discovered—as it is transparently obvious it will be—means that there is a good deal of comic suspense pivoting on the inevitable rethinking of attitudes. However, like rugby in the earlier play, the meat works is here a metaphor for Kiwi masculinity—or the packaging of masculinity—and the facility with which it can be penetrated and possibly punctured means that the overt comedy is supported by rich implicit ironies. A 1985 television version began with a brief introduction without dialogue in which Judy, sunbathing naked, got up, cut her hair and dressed as a man before going to the employment room at the freezing works; this clarified some of the possible early ambiguities in the stage version, and generated strong sympathy with Judy from the start. The screen also allowed meticulous coverage of the butchery process, and the camera dwelt on the labyrinthine concrete expanses of the works, which became even more clearly a physical correlative to a bizarre social system.

McGee's fourth stage play, *Whitemen*, was a resounding critical and commercial failure, and has not been published. However, such has been the continuing impact of his earlier works that several companies have successfully mounted second productions, exploring different approaches.

—Howard McNaughton

McGRATH, John (Peter). British. Born in Birkenhead, Cheshire, 1 June 1935. Educated at Alun Grammar School, Mold, Wales; St. John's College, Oxford (Open Exhibitioner), 1955–59, Dip.Ed. Served in the British Army (national service), 1953–55. Married Elizabeth MacLennan in 1962; two sons and one daughter. Farm worker, Neston, Cheshire, 1951; play reader, Royal Court Theatre, London, and television writer and director, 1959–65. Since 1971 founder and artistic director, 7:84 Theatre Company (divided into Scottish and English companies, 1973); since 1983 founding director, Freeway Films. Judith E. Wilson Fellow, Cambridge University, 1979. Agent: Margaret Ramsay Ltd., 14-A Goodwin's Court, London WC2N 4LL. Address: 7:84 Theatre Company Scotland, 31 Albany Street, Edinburgh EH1 3QN, Scotland.

PUBLICATIONS

Plays

A Man Has Two Fathers (produced Oxford, 1958).
The Invasion, with Barbara Cannings, adaptation of a play by Arthur Adamov (produced Oxford and Edinburgh, 1958).
The Tent (produced Edinburgh and London, 1958).
Why the Chicken (produced Edinburgh, 1959; revised version produced on tour, 1960).

Tell Me Tell Me (produced London, 1960). Published in *New Departures* (London), 1960.
Take It (produced London, 1960).
The Seagull, adaptation of a play by Chekhov (produced Dundee, 1961).
Basement in Bangkok, music and songs by Dudley Moore (produced Bristol, 1963).
Events While Guarding the Bofors Gun (produced London, 1966). London, Methuen, 1966.
Bakke's Night of Fame, adaptation of the novel *A Danish Gambit* by William Butler (produced London, 1968). London, Davis Poynter, 1973.
Comrade Jacob, adaptation of the novel by David Caute (produced Falmer, Sussex, 1969).
Random Happenings in the Hebrides; or, The Social Democrat and the Stormy Sea (produced Edinburgh, 1970). London, Davis Poynter, 1972.
Sharpeville Crackers (produced London, 1970).
Unruly Elements (includes *Angel of the Morning*, *Plugged-in to History*, *They're Knocking Down the Pie-Shop*, *Hover Through the Fog*, *Out of Sight*) (produced Liverpool, 1971; *Plugged-in to History*, produced London, 1971; *Out of Sight*, *Angel of the Morning*, *They're Knocking Down the Pie-Shop*, and *Hover Through the Fog*, produced London, 1972). *Angel of the Morning*, *Plugged-in to History* and *They're Knocking Down the Pie-Shop*, published as *Plugged-in*, in *Plays and Players* (London), November 1972.
Trees in the Wind (also director: produced Edinburgh and London, 1971; New York, 1974).
Soft or a Girl (produced Liverpool, 1971; revised version, as *My Pal and Me*, also director: produced Edinburgh, 1975).
The Caucasian Chalk Circle, adaptation of a play by Brecht (produced Liverpool, 1972).
Prisoners of the War, adaptation of the play by Peter Terson (produced Liverpool, 1972).
Underneath (also director: produced Liverpool, 1972; London, 1978).
Serjeant Musgrave Dances On, adaptation of the play *Serjeant Musgrave's Dance* by John Arden (produced Stirling, 1972).
Fish in the Sea, music by Mark Brown (produced Liverpool, 1972; revised version produced London, 1975). London, Pluto Press, 1977.
The Cheviot, The Stag, and the Black, Black Oil (also director: produced Edinburgh, 1973). Kyleakin, Isle of Skye, West Highland Publishing, 1973; revised version, 1975; revised version, London, Eyre Methuen, 1981.
The Game's a Bogey (also director: produced Aberdeen, 1974). Edinburgh, Edinburgh University Student Publications, 1975.
Boom (also director: produced Golspie, Sutherland, 1974; revised version produced Aberdeen, 1974). Published in *New Edinburgh Review*, August 1975.
Lay Off (also director: produced Lancaster and London, 1975).
Little Red Hen (also director: produced Edinburgh, 1975; London, 1976). London, Pluto Press, 1977.
Oranges and Lemons (also director: produced Amsterdam, 1975; Birmingham, 1977).
Yobbo Nowt, music by Mark Brown (also director: produced York and London, 1975; as *Mum's the Word*, produced Liverpool, 1977; as *Left Out Lady*, produced New York, 1981). London, Pluto Press, 1978.
The Rat Trap, music by Mark Brown (also director: produced Amsterdam and London, 1976).
Out of Our Heads, music by Mark Brown (also director: produced Aberdeen, 1976; London, 1977).
Trembling Giant (English version) (produced Lancaster, 1977).
Trembling Giant (Scottish version) (also director: produced Dundee and London, 1977).
The Life and Times of Joe of England (also director: produced Basildon, Essex, and London, 1977).
Big Square Fields, music by Mark Brown (produced Bradford and London, 1979).
Joe's Drum (also director: produced Aberdeen, 1979). Aberdeen, People's Press, 1979.
Bitter Apples, music by Mark Brown (produced Liverpool, 1979).
If You Want to Know the Time (produced London, 1979).
Swings and Roundabouts (also director: produced Aberdeen, 1980). Included in *Two Plays for the Eighties*, 1981.
Blood Red Roses (also director: produced Edinburgh, 1980; London, 1981; revised version produced Liverpool, 1982). Included in *Two Plays for the Eighties*, 1981.
Two Plays for the Eighties. Aberdeen, People's Press, 1981.
Nightclass, music by Rick Lloyd (also director: produced Corby, Northamptonshire, and London, 1981).
The Catch, music by Mark Brown (produced Edinburgh, 1981).
Rejoice!, music by Mark Brown (produced Edinburgh and London, 1982).
On the Pig's Back, with David MacLennan (produced Kilmarnock, Ayrshire, 1983).
The Women of the Dunes (produced in Dutch, Ijmuiden, Netherlands, 1983).
Women in Power; or, Up the Acropolis, music by Thanos Mikroutsikos, adaptation of plays by Aristophanes (also director: produced Edinburgh, 1983).
Six Men of Dorset, music by John Tams, adaptation of a play by Miles Malleson and Harry Brooks (produced Sheffield and London, 1984).
The Baby and the Bathwater: The Imperial Policeman (produced Cumbernauld, Dunbartonshire, 1984; revised version produced Edinburgh, 1985; London, 1987).
The Albannach, music by Eddie McGuire, adaptation of the novel by Fionn MacColla (produced Edinburgh, 1985).
Behold the Sun (opera libretto), with Alexander Goehr, music by Goehr (produced Duisburg, West Germany, 1985).
All the Fun of the Fair, with others (produced London, 1986).

Screenplays: *Billion Dollar Brain*, 1967; *The Bofors Gun*, 1968; *The Virgin Soldiers*, with John Hopkins and Ian La Fresnais, 1969; *The Reckoning*, 1970; *Blood Red Roses*, 1986.

Television Plays: scripts for *Bookstand* series, 1961; *People's Property* (*Z Cars* series), 1962; scripts for *Tempo* series, 1963; *Diary of a Young Man* series, with Troy Kennedy Martin, 1964; *The Entertainers* (documentary), 1964; *The Day of Ragnarok*, 1965; *Mo* (documentary), 1965; *Shotgun*, with Christopher Williams, 1966; *Diary of a Nobody*, with Ken Russell, from the novel by George and Weedon Grossmith, 1966; *Orkney*, from stories by George Mackay Brown, 1971; *Bouncing Boy*, 1972; *Once upon a Union*, 1977; *The Adventures of Frank*, from his play *The Life and Times of Joe of England*, 1979; *Sweetwater Memories* (documentary), 1984; *There Is a Happy Land*, 1987.

Other

A Good Night Out: Popular Theatre: Audience, Class and Form. London, Eyre Methuen, 1981.

Translator, with Maureen Teitelbaum, *The Rules of the Game* (screenplay), by Jean Renoir. London, Lorrimer, 1970.

*

Bibliography: by Malcolm Page, in *New Theatre Quarterly* (Cambridge), November 1985.

Critical Studies: *Disrupting the Spectacle* by Peter Ansorge, London, Pitman, 1975; *British Theatre since 1955* by Ronald Hayman, London and New York, Oxford University Press, 1979; *Stages in the Revolution* by Catherine Itzin, London, Eyre Methuen, 1980; *Dreams and Deconstructions* edited by Sandy Craig, Ambergate, Derbyshire, Amber Lane Press, 1980; "Three Socialist Playwrights" by Christian W. Thomsen, in *Contemporary English Drama* edited by C.W.E. Bigsby, London, Arnold, and New York, Holmes and Meier, 1981, and "The Politics of Anxiety" by Bigsby, in *Modern Drama* (Toronto), December 1981; *Modern Scottish Literature* by Alan Bold, London, Longman, 1983; interview with Oscar Moore, in *Plays and Players* (London), April 1983.

Theatrical Activities:
Director: **Plays**—many of his own plays, and *Bloomsday* by Allan McClelland, Oxford, 1958; *The Birds* by Aristophanes, Oxford, 1959; Live New Departures series of plays, 1961–64; *The Eccentric* by Dannie Abse, London, 1961. **Television**—*Bookstand* series, 1961; *The Compartment* by Johnny Speight, 1961; *Z Cars* series (8 episodes), 1962; *The Fly Sham* by Thomas Murphy, 1963; *The Wedding Dress* by Edna O'Brien, 1963; *The Entertainers* (documentary), 1964; *The Day of Ragnarok*, 1965; *Mo* (documentary), 1965; *Shotgun* by McGrath and Christopher Williams, 1966; *Double Bill* by Johnny Speight, 1972; *Z Cars: The Final Episode*, 1978; *The Adventures of Frank*, 1979; *Come to Mecca* by Farrukh Dhondy, 1983; *Blood Red Roses*, 1986.

John McGrath comments:

(1973) My plays, I now realize, have been from the beginning about the relationship of the individual to other individuals and thence to history. They have pursued this theme in many ways, poetic, comic, tragic, realistic, and latterly more and more freely. Music is now coming to play a more important part in my plays, to help break through the barriers of naturalism which I can no longer tolerate. My work has never suited London (West End) audiences or ways of thinking: it is now being seen by working-class audiences from Orkney to Plymouth, and by young audiences all over the country in the new university theatres and art labs and studio theatres, via the 7:84 Theatre Company. I have also benefited from a thriving relation with the Everyman Theatre, Liverpool, under the direction of Alan Dosser, as previously from working with directors as perceptive and helpful as Ronald Eyre, Anthony Page, and Richard Eyre in Edinburgh.

My plays are not difficult to approach, although they tend to have many levels of meaning embedded fairly deeply under them as well as on the surface. The key, if key is needed, is a growing political consciousness allied to a growing feeling for individual human beings, with all the contradictions that alliance involves.

* * *

The enormity of John McGrath's contribution to the field of contemporary drama will probably never be fully realised, largely because of the way in which he has latterly chosen to direct his energies. Active in the theatre as an undergraduate writer, he immediately went on to earn a place in history as one of the key developers of the dominant mode of modern television naturalism—during his time with the BBC he was jointly responsible for the hugely influential *Z Cars* series. Rejecting a full-time career in television, he turned first to the conventional professional theatre. After *Events While Guarding the Bofors Gun*, a play deriving from his own experience in Army National Service in the 1950's, linkable thematically and in stature with Wesker's *Chips with Everything*, he produced *Bakke's Night of Fame*, an adaptation of a novel, as well as working on a number of screenplays, including that for his own *The Bofors Gun*.

Interest in the political consciousness of his characters was apparent from the outset but the demands of television and the conventional professional theatre for a well-crafted play with a resolved narrative proved inhibiting. The sense of class confrontation and ideological moulding in *The Bofors Gun*, for instance, is never matched by any strand in the play which suggests a way out of the fatalistically conceived framework of plot and society. What McGrath sought was a way of presenting individuals in conflict with their social context, but in ways which suggested the possibility of change through self-education and experience. This was to involve him in a conscious turning away from the conventional theatre with what he saw as, at best, its minimally questioning analysis of capitalist society. The problem for him was as much that of audience as theatrical style: "the audience has changed very little in the theatre, the social requirements remain constant, the values remain firmly those of acceptability to a metropolitan middle-class audience, with an eye to similar acceptability on the international cultural market."

The real break with his past—and a consistent turning away from the politically restricting naturalistic mode—came in 1968. McGrath had started work on the first of a long series of plays about Scotland's history and its struggles, *Random Happenings in the Hebrides*. The play was to deal with the attempts of a young Scottish Labour MP to work for change for his island community within the confines of the parliamentary system. In the middle of writing the play, the barricades went up in Paris, and McGrath went over, rethought the play, placing a greater emphasis on a non-parliamentary oppositional strategy—but seeing all the time the conflict between the need for political organisation and the immediacy of action that he had witnessed in France. It was a theme that was to dominate much of his later work, taking him progressively further away from naturalism and into various models of agit-prop theatre in pursuit of an audience that could be defined in terms of its political potential rather than its interest in the theatre as such.

By 1970, when *Random Happenings* was first produced, McGrath had started a formative period of work with the Liverpool Everyman—including a series of playlets about contemporary Britain, *Unruly Elements* (later retitled *Plugged-in to History*). In 1971 McGrath founded 7:84, a socialist theatre group intent on taking plays into the kind of non-theatrical venues shunned by the conventional theatrical establishment. Since then he has worked largely in Scotland producing a string of plays dealing with Scottish Socialist strategy in a variety of historical and contemporary contexts—with the occasional production for the English off-shoot of 7:84. Productions have varied from the didactic intensity of the first 7:84 piece, *Trees in the Wind*, to offerings, such as the political pantomime *Trembling Giant*, that make use of the loosest of narrative structures to put across a deliberately crude analysis. McGrath's clear awareness of the dangers of arguing for an impossibly simple solution to a highly complex problem—the dilemma of all revolutionaries living in a non-revolutionary age—is brilliantly articulated in the humour and wit of the plays, frequently inviting the audience into the never self-contained discourse. The general method is summed up well by Joe's tongue-in-cheek invitation to the audience to retake its seats after the interval in *Joe's Drum*, a play written in response to the election of a Conservative administration and the failure of the Scottish Assembly vote. They are assured that they should not be frightened off by the fear of weighty material. "It's yer ain true story told in biased argument, highly selective history and emotional folksong. Are ye all back that's comin' back? Right—lock the doors."

McGrath's—and 7:84's—insistence on a theatre that should not only offer enlightenment but entertainment is a key part of the plays' acceptance. McGrath has moved progressively away from the kind of consumer society cultural parody that has proved a staple of so much agit-prop theatre—as in the "Beat the System" television show in *The Game's a Bogey*—in search of popular cultural roots that oppose those offered by the consumerist system. The use of the Highland ceilidh form for the first Scottish 7:84 tour of *The Cheviot, The Stag, and the Black, Black Oil*, gave McGrath the structure of a traditional evening entertainment through which to tell the story of the exploitation of Scotland throughout history up to the oil boom. In subsequent plays he was to make the link between the music as part of an oppositional cultural history and the need to question contemporary representations a major part of each show's dynamics.

McGrath's is a questioning development of agit-prop, and his conclusions are usually open-ended, witnessing a small personal achievement perhaps but not proclaiming the imminence of revolutionary change. And in this context, his depiction of the particular dilemma of women caught in the dual webs of capitalism and a male-oriented ideology has emerged as a major theme in his work. In *Joe's Drum* the wife is a continual presence, chipping away at masculine vanities, and in a play such as *Yobbo Nowt* all the emphasis is placed on the struggles of a wife after she has ejected the unfeeling husband. Her discovery of the way in which the system operates against the "have-nots" parallels her own discovery of individual potential, and the play ends with another small personal leap forward.

McGrath has continued to produce work at a prolific rate—with, as always, a central interest in the way in which the individual can operate against the increasingly sophisticated and endlessly elastic models of late capitalist society. The overall effect is to suggest the way in which the various manifestations of authority and oppression are part of a single system and thus linkable, as they are from one play to another—each then becoming just one in a series of views through different windows of a part of the same enormous construction inside. In *Blood Red Roses* he traces the political struggles of Bessie from the 1950's to the present day; she is the latest member of what is by now a very large political family assured of an audience away from the subsidised and commercial theatres of London where reputations are made. A popular writer in a genuine sense, McGrath will continue to be active long after the reputations of many participants in what he sees as an integral part of the capitalist system have been forgotten.

—John Bull

McGRATH, Tom. British. Born in Rutherglen, Lanarkshire, 23 October 1940. Educated at Glasgow University, degree in drama and English. Married; four daughters. Director, Third Eye Centre, Glasgow; founding editor, *International Times* underground newspaper, London, 1960's; writer-in-residence, Traverse Theatre, Edinburgh, and University of Iowa, Iowa City. Also a jazz pianist. Agent: Michael Imison Playwrights, 28 Almeida Street, London N1 1TD, England.

Publications

Plays

Laurel and Hardy (produced Edinburgh, 1976; as *Mr. Laurel and Mr. Hardy*, produced London, 1976).
The Hard Man, with Jimmy Boyle (produced Edinburgh and London, 1977). Edinburgh, Canongate, 1977.
The Android Circuit (produced Edinburgh, 1978).
Sisters (produced London, 1978; revised version produced Southampton, 1985).
Animal (produced Edinburgh, 1979).
The Innocent (produced London, 1979).
1-2-3: Who Are You Anyway?, Very Important Business, Moondog (produced Edinburgh and London, 1981).
The Phone Box (for children; produced on tour, 1983).
Pals (produced Cumbernauld, Dunbartonshire, 1984).
Kora (produced Edinburgh, 1986).
Thanksgiving (produced Glasgow, 1986).
Private View, with Mhairi Grealis (produced Edinburgh, 1987).

Radio Play: *The Silver Darling*, from the novel by Neil Gunn, 1982.

Television Plays: *The Nuclear Family*, 1982; *Blowout*, 1984; *The Gambler*, 1984; *End of the Line*, 1984.

Composer: music for *The Great Northern Welly Boot Show*, book by Tom Buchan, lyrics by Billy Connolly, Edinburgh and London, 1972.

* * *

For a long time, the original success of Tom McGrath's most completely achieved play, *Animal*, kept it out of circulation in England. Although the hit of the 1979 Edinburgh Festival, when it was presented as an official offering by the Traverse Theatre, it was snapped up by American entrepreneurs and the English rights were blocked. The absurdity of such absolute control was reflected by its middling success when it was finally produced south of the Scottish border long after its ecstatic notices. None the less, it remains his most dazzling theatrical conceit.

Originally mounted in an ascending structure of scaffolds and platforms, the play observed the drama of life in a colony of apes, with the intrusive presence of zoologists observing them. The real spectacle and abiding image of the play was the movement and inter-relationships of the apes themselves. With the animals portrayed by loose-limbed actors and actresses, the effect was of life observed through a series of mirrors. The animals were watched by the humans, while the apes aped the humans they were watching. Insights and comedy came through the parallel dramas, and, ironically, dramatic communication was hindered most by the necessity of speech among the humans.

Before becoming a dramatist, McGrath was himself an outside observer of sorts. He edited Britain's most influential counter-cultural periodical, *International Times*, part of the exploding drug culture of the 1960's. That experience was brought to his play for the Royal Shakespeare Company, *The*

Innocent, which followed a progression from the use of drugs for pleasure to addiction and withdrawal in an attempt to consider the implications of a selfish pursuit of pleasure on the dreams of the lost "alternative society." It was the first of his plays even to suggest personal experience and observation, and most of his work through the 1970's was notable for his wide-ranging interests. Science fiction and dramatized biography were perhaps the strongest elements.

His first play, which appeared at the Edinburgh Festival in 1976 and later transferred to London, was *Mr. Laurel and Mr. Hardy*, a private view of the off-screen life of the best comic team of the first Hollywood era. McGrath takes the ambitious route of showing both lives independently as well as matching his two actors for some of the on-screen routines. For McGrath, the attraction of Stan Laurel is obviously his Glasgow beginnings, but Oliver Hardy is given equal biographical substance. The play is notable for its contemplation of the team's pathetic final years, with Laurel alone, still writing routines for himself and his old partner, but speaking both parts.

McGrath's second play, a violent dramatization of the life of a reformed Glasgow gangster, appeared the following year. *The Hard Man* was written with Jimmy Boyle, who told the story under his own name in the book *A Sense of Freedom*, which McGrath had a hand in. The story is essentially an odyssey through childhood and gang warfare in the Glasgow slums, culminating in a criminal career which included brutal murder. There is a further dimension to the story, which could tell of Boyle's rehabilitation in prison and his emergence as a sculptor. The play does not go that far; rather it provides a form of ritual re-enactment of the street violence which accentuates key moments in the life of Johny Byrne, the fictional Boyle. Inside prison, jailed for murder, Byrne remains the fiercely proud street-fighter, resisting the regimentation and sadism of the prison and finally reaching a peculiar transcendence in a cramped cage where he squats and smears excrement over himself.

That power was missing from McGrath's fantasy *The Android Circuit*, and from his portrait of three girls growing up in London's East End, *Sisters*. Moments of that force are again visible in a trilogy which he wrote for the Traverse and BBC radio, *1-2-3*, which McGrath described as "plays about male identity written from a feminist viewpoint by a man." The plays are chiefly connected by a cast of three (two men and a woman), and the first play, *Who Are You Anyway?*, blazes a trail of gender confusion as male love and bonding are transferred to love of a woman. The final play appears to pick up the thread of *The Innocent* and shows the two men and woman reinventing a myth about woman as witch, or specifically as priestess of the moon. *Moondog* begins with a dropout Scot pictured in his chosen solitude in the Highlands, greeting the morning with a chant before being interrupted by an old friend who comes bearing unwanted business propositions. A further interruption is in the form of the woman who arrives with a different purpose, in the nature of human sacrifice.

The trilogy failed in London, but found an audience for the same production at the Toronto Theatre Festival of 1981 and McGrath himself spent a year at the University of Iowa directing the Playwrights' Workshop there. Returning to Scotland, he returned to Scottish themes, notably with *Kora*, a documentary drama about the struggle of tenants in a Dundee housing estate to improve conditions, but filled with flashes of McGrath's theatrical invention and optimism. The American experience was satirically reflected through his short play, *Thanksgiving*, written for Glasgow's Tron Theatre. As part of a trilogy including plays by other Glasgow-based writers, it was designed to accommodate original music by Edward McGuire, but rather more theatrically made use of the spectral presence of the musicians as he dissected the consumerism of America's Thanksgiving Day, with a bossy television set and a woman reasonably declaring her love for two men during "the year of the Ayotallah." It passes more as amused observation than enlightening comment, and if his work in the 1980's is less visible than his work of the 1970's, it is similarly diverse and sympathetic.

—Ned Chaillet

McLURE, James. American. Born in Louisiana. Address: c/o Dramatists Play Service, 440 Park Avenue South, New York, New York, 10016, U.S.A.; or, Chappell Plays Ltd., 129 Park Street, London W1Y 3FA, England.

PUBLICATIONS

Plays

Lone Star (produced Louisville and New York, 1979; London, 1980). New York, Dramatists Play Service, 1980.
Pvt. Wars (produced New York, 1979; London, 1980). New York, Dramatists Play Service, 1980.
1959 Pink Thunderbird (includes *Lone Star* and *Laundry and Bourbon*) (produced Princeton, New Jersey, 1980).
Laundry and Bourbon (produced Ashland, Oregon, 1980; London, 1986). New York, Dramatists Play Service, 1981.
The Day They Shot John Lennon (produced Princeton, New Jersey, 1983). New York, Dramatists Play Service, 1984.
Thanksgiving (produced Louisville, 1983).
Wild Oats: A Romance of the Old West, adaptation of the play by John O'Keeffe (produced Los Angeles, 1983). New York, Dramatists Play Service, 1985.
Lahr and Mercedes (produced Denver, 1984).
The Very Last Lover of the River Cane (produced Louisville, 1985).

*

Theatrical Activities:
Actor: **Plays**—in *The Death and Life of Jesse James* by Len Jenkin, New York, 1978; *Music Hall Sidelights* by Jack Heifner, New York, 1978.

* * *

James McLure is a playwright and actor who became recognized for two one-acts, *Lone Star* and *Pvt. Wars*, that were produced on Broadway in 1979. It is *Lone Star* that best characterizes the nature and dilemma of McLure's favorite protagonist: a southwestern country bumpkin, good ole boy veteran who returns as an adult to a tamer and duller world which both baffles and bores him. This character or his counterpart, appearing in several McLure plays, is a displaced romantic unable to function well in an adult world that no longer operates by his values.

Set in the littered backyard of a small-town Texas bar, *Lone Star* focuses on the swaggering figure of Roy, a former high school hero now back in town after a hitch in Vietnam and not adjusting well. He drinks Lone Star beer and gasses with his hero-worshipping but slower younger brother about his military and amorous exploits and his three loves: his wife, his country, and his 1959 pink Thunderbird convertible. At the evening's end only one love is left intact, for Roy learns that his brother has slept with his young wife and that his cherished Thunderbird has been borrowed and demolished by a fatuous hardware store clerk ever jealous of Roy. Though the symbols of Roy's youth are destroyed or tarnished, he bounces back at the conclusion dimly realizing he can no longer merely muse on the past. Validly praised by critics for its earthy humor and the salty regional idiom of its roistering language, the short play represents McLure at his most effective.

Less successful than its companion piece, *Pvt. Wars* is a black comedy set in an Army hospital where three recuperating Vietnam veterans tease, torment, and even solace each other to disguise their anxiety about returning to the uncertainties of civilian life. Like *Lone Star*'s Roy, they will have to confront a different world. The trio includes a Georgia hillbilly (Gately) given to fiddling with a dead radio, a street-wise hipster (Silvio) addicted to "flashing" nurses even though he is now possibly impotent, and a prissy rich kid (Natwick) who misses his mother. The men's encounters, depicted in 12 sketch-like scenes, project an off-beat humor; but the play's episodic structure forces too fragmentary a quality on the action and characters.

Conceived as a companion piece to *Lone Star* and set in the latter's same mythical Texas town at the home of Roy and his wife Elizabeth, *Laundry and Bourbon* is a short comedy introducing three women on a hot summer afternoon. Elizabeth, the intelligent young lady of the house, folds laundry and sips bourbon while chatting with a gabby neighbor, Hattie. Their talk is interrupted by the self-righteous and unwelcome Amy Lee, the gossipy wife of the hardware clerk met in *Lone Star*. Amidst self-generated bits of gossip, Amy Lee purposefully blurts out that Roy has been seen with another woman. Displaying an inner strength and an understanding of her husband's turmoil since returning from Vietnam, Elizabeth realizes Roy's need for her and her love for him and resolves to be waiting for him when he returns home whatever the opinion of others. In this comedy McLure's humor, characters, and dialogue are richly successful. It stands alongside *Lone Star* as the playwright's strongest work.

Wild Oats is a loose adaptation of John O'Keeffe's 18th-century comedy of the same name keeping the plot structure of the original while transferring the action's locale and characters to the legendary American Old West. The plot and characters are a send-up of old-fashioned melodrama's clichés and stereotypes involving long-lost sons found and forgiven, long-estranged parents reunited, and mistaken identities ultimately revealed. While *Wild Oats* suffers from a surfeit of complications and characters, it yet emerges as an amusing theatrical romp disclosing its author's promising hand for theatricality and parody.

The Day They Shot John Lennon is comprised of a series of encounters between a group of strangers gathered at the New York City site of John Lennon's assassination. The disparate group, whose motives vary from curiosity and shock to theft, includes the veterans Silvio and Gately (of *Pvt. Wars*) now out of Army hospital and practicing pickpockets. Caught in a theft, Gately reveals his serious mental disturbance and Silvio his protective overseeing of his friend. The total group's interaction throughout point up the assassination's larger significance: that violence and ugliness continue to exist in the communal soul and are too soon forgotten even when witnessed. McLure credibly portrays contemporary urbanites with point and poignancy, demonstrating that his territory goes beyond the southwest.

That he is an actor as well as a writer contributes to McLure's strengths, which include a sharp eye for character, a gifted ear for regional idiomatic speech, and an uncommon comic flair extending to the examination of American myths and mores. If he can stretch effectively beyond the one-act form in which he is most comfortable, McLure should have a productive future.

—Christian H. Moe

McNALLY, Terrence. American. Born in St. Petersburg, Florida, 3 November 1939. Educated at schools in Corpus Christi, Texas; Columbia University, New York (Evans Traveling Fellow, 1960), 1956–60, B.A. in English 1960 (Phi Beta Kappa). Stage manager, Actors Studio, New York, 1961; tutor to John Steinbeck's children, 1961–62; film critic, *Seventh Art*, New York, 1963–65; assistant editor, *Columbia College Today*, New York, 1965–66. Since 1981 Vice-President, Dramatists Guild. Recipient: Stanley award, 1962; Guggenheim fellowship, 1966, 1969; Obie award, 1974; American Academy award, 1975. Agent: Rosenstone/Wender, 3 East 48th Street, 4th Floor, New York, New York 10017. Address: 218 West 10th Street, New York, New York 10014, U.S.A.

Publications

Plays

The Roller Coaster published in *Columbia Review* (New York), Spring 1960.

And Things That Go Bump in the Night (as *There Is Something Out There*, produced New York, 1962; revised version, as *And Things That Go Bump in the Night*, produced Minneapolis, 1964; New York, 1965; London, 1977). Published in *Playwrights for Tomorrow 1*, edited by Arthur H. Ballet, Minneapolis, University of Minnesota Press, 1966.

The Lady of the Camellias, adaptation of a play by Giles Cooper based on the play by Dumas fils (produced New York, 1963).

Next (produced Westport, Connecticut, 1967; New York, 1969; London, 1971). Included in *Sweet Eros, Next, and Other Plays*, 1969.

Tour (produced Los Angeles, 1967; New York, 1968; London, 1971). Published in *Collision Course*, New York, Random House, 1968.

Botticelli (televised 1968; produced Los Angeles, 1971; London, 1972). Included in *Sweet Eros, Next, and Other Plays*, 1969; in *Off-Broadway Plays 2*, London, Penguin, 1972.

Sweet Eros (produced Stockbridge, Massachusetts, and New York, 1968; London, 1971). Included in *Sweet Eros, Next, and Other Plays*, 1969; in *Off-Broadway Plays 2*, London, Penguin, 1972.

¡Cuba Si! (produced Provincetown, Massachusetts, and New York, 1968). Included in *Sweet Eros, Next, and Other Plays*, 1969.

Witness (produced New York, 1968; London, 1972). Included in *Sweet Eros, Next, and Other Plays*, 1969.

Noon (in *Chiaroscuro* produced Spoleto, Italy, 1968; in *Morning, Noon, and Night*, produced New York, 1968). Published in *Morning, Noon, and Night*, New York, Random House, 1968.

Apple Pie (includes *Next, Tour, Botticelli*). New York, Dramatists Play Service, 1969.
Last Gasps (televised 1969). Included in *Three Plays*, 1970.
Bringing It All Back Home (produced New Haven, Connecticut, 1969; New York, 1972). Included in *Three Plays*, 1970.
Sweet Eros, Next, and Other Plays. New York, Random House, 1969.
Three Plays: ¡Cuba Si!, Bringing It All Back Home, Last Gasps. New York, Dramatists Play Service, 1970.
Where Has Tommy Flowers Gone? (produced New Haven, Connecticut, and New York, 1971). New York, Dramatists Play Service, 1972.
Bad Habits: Ravenswood and Dunelawn (produced East Hampton, New York, 1971; New York City, 1974). New York, Dramatists Play Service, 1974.
Let It Bleed, in *City Stops* (produced New York, 1972).
Whiskey (produced New York, 1973). New York, Dramatists Play Service, 1973.
The Ritz (as *The Tubs*, produced New Haven, Connecticut, 1973; revised version, as *The Ritz*, produced New York, 1975). Included in *The Ritz and Other Plays*, 1976.
The Ritz and Other Plays (includes *Bad Habits, Where Has Tommy Flowers Gone?, And Things That Go Bump in the Night, Whiskey, Bringing It All Back Home*). New York, Dodd Mead, 1976.
Broadway, Broadway (produced New York, 1978).
It's Only a Play (produced New York, 1982).
The Rink, music by John Kander, lyrics by Fred Ebb (produced New York, 1984; Manchester, 1987). New York, French, 1985.
The Lisbon Traviata (produced New York, 1985).
Frankie and Johnny in the Claire de Lune (produced New York, 1987).

Screenplay: *The Ritz*, 1976.

Television Plays: *Botticelli*, 1968; *Last Gasps*, 1969; *The Five Forty-Eight*, from the story by John Cheever, 1979; *Mama Malone* series, 1983.

* * *

Terrence McNally is one of the finest comic dramatists writing for the English-speaking stage. Like all comic writers of genuine importance and lasting potential, he understands the nature of comedy: its shimmering, ephemeral surface caught in a certain uniqueness of style; its paradoxical undercurrent of shifting, larger, darker connotations. In a period in which the comic tradition from the Restoration through Shaw has seemed decimated, he has in American drama demonstrated the subtle intelligence of its survival.

McNally's career had its symbolic beginning perhaps in the Actors Studio Playwrights Unit when a passage from *And Things That Go Bump in the Night* was performed and appreciated by a rather distinguished group of people, and this play, performed in its complete form later on Broadway, introduces the personal McNally characteristics: a vivid sense of contemporary attitudes and interests, which he extends just beyond expectation; an expansion of characters, action, and setting from vivid individuality to the communal; and the universalizing of the seemingly different, the apparently unusual, through the wise and seductive tolerance of comedy. And to these characteristics must be added a McNally special dimension: the influence of his well known and erudite appreciation of opera, with its duets, trios, ensembles, its disguises, its mistaken identities, and its frequent preoccupation with the possibilities of *la maledizione*.

And Things That Go Bump involves a strange family consisting of Grandfa, Fa, a mother who tapes messages to the world, and two children with operatic names, Sigfrid and Lakme. They live in a kind of cellar house protected from the terrifying outside world by an electric fence. The outside world is the direct focus of attention in McNally's picaresque play *Where Has Tommy Flowers Gone?* as Tommy, the innocent to whom things happen, wanders through New York City, which is transformed into a kind of familiar-unfamiliar wilderness. But McNally's two best plays—and there are some excellent one-act plays as well—are *Bad Habits* and *The Ritz*.

In *Bad Habits* the communal is represented by two sanatoriums, each figuring in one half of the play. Ravenswood is completely permissive, and it is presided over by a kindly figure, Jason Pepper, M.D., who tolerates the idiosyncrasies of his patients. Dunelawn is the exact opposite, with a dictatorial although non-verbal director, and patients strapped into wheelchairs. Both plays are wonderfully funny, filled with rich eccentricities of behavior and with vaudeville devices reminiscent of "crazy house" routines, and despite their "bad habits" the patients at both charming places are quite happy. But there is, as always in McNally's plays, that disquieting under-surface which is brilliantly articulated by the outrageous comedy itself. In fact the polarities of "treatment" at the two institutions suggest these inherent polarities of the comic method.

The Ritz, his most popular play, a Broadway and motion picture success, is surely one of the most hilarious plays in modern American drama. It opens with a death scene that recalls Puccini's *Gianni Schicchi* and with a curse, and the comic permutations of *la maledizione* permeate the play as a Mafia boss into garbage, his sister, and her chubby and luckless husband all find themselves in a bathhouse in New York. The play is constantly visual, and the disguises and mistaken identities multiply to an appropriately razzle-dazzle conclusion. And the dialogue which accompanies these shenanigans—"We'll pretend you're him and I'm me and the real you is under the bed"—is the language of farce comedy at its quickest and best.

Recently McNally has expanded his range with three new, contrasting works. His book for the intimate musical *The Rink* is unusually taut and dramatic for this genre of popular writing. Here an about-to-be-demolished roller palace in a decaying amusement park provides the arena for a confrontation and reconciliation of the daughter Angel and her mother Anna and also triggers the many flashbacks which expand the action in time. *The Lisbon Traviata* is a tragicomedy about a writer, Stephen, and his friends. The title refers to a pirated recording of Maria Callas in Lisbon; the record provides the principal continuity in the "comic" first act and then gives way to "The Humming Chorus" of *Butterfly* which accompanies the love-death scene in Act 2, a curtain scene set up surreptitiously in Act 1 with deadly precision. *It's Only a Play*, a farce, returns to more familiar ground and is filled with references to current theater and personalities. It consists mainly of gossipy fun, which is, after all, the point.

In a theater—in a world, for that matter—always in need of wit and intelligence, Terrence McNally is a very special asset indeed.

—Gaynor F. Bradish

MEDNICK, Murray. American. Born in Brooklyn, New York, 24 August 1939. Educated at Fallsburg Central School, New York; Brooklyn College, 1957–60. Artistic co-director, Theatre Genesis, New York, 1970–74. Since 1978 artistic director, Padua Hills Playwrights Workshop and Festival, California. Playwright-in-residence, Florida State University, Tallahassee, 1972, State University of New York, Buffalo, 1973, California State University, Long Beach, 1973, La Verne College, California, 1978–82, and Pomona College, Claremont, California, 1983, 1984. Recipient: National Endowment for the Arts grant, for poetry, 1967; Rockefeller grant, 1968, 1972; Obie award, 1970; Guggenheim grant, 1973; Creative Artists Public Service grant, 1973. Address: 2242 Lake Shore Avenue, Los Angeles, California 90039, U.S.A.

PUBLICATIONS

Plays

The Box (produced New York, 1965).
The Mark of Zorro (produced New York, 1966).
Guideline (produced New York, 1966).
Sand (produced New York, 1967; London, 1970). Published in *The New Underground Theatre*, New York, Bantam, 1968.
The Hawk: An Improvisational Play, with Tony Barsha (produced New York, 1967). Indianapolis, Bobbs Merrill, 1968.
Willie the Germ (produced New York, 1968). Published in *More Plays from Off-Off-Broadway*, edited by Michael T. Smith, Indianapolis, Bobbs Merrill, 1972.
The Hunter (produced New York, 1968). Indianapolis, Bobbs Merrill, 1969.
The Shadow Ripens (also director: produced San Diego and New York, 1969).
The Deer Kill (produced New York, 1970). Indianapolis, Bobbs Merrill, 1971.
Cartoon (produced New York, 1971).
Are You Lookin'? (also director: produced New York, 1973).
Black Hole in Space (produced New York, 1975).
Taxes (also director: produced New York, 1976). Published in *Wordplays 3*, New York, Performing Arts Journal Publications, 1984.
The Coyote Cycle (7 plays) (also director: produced Los Angeles, 1978–80; complete cycle produced Santa Fe, 1984). Published in *West Coast Plays* (Berkeley, California), 1981; *Coyote V: Listening to Old Nana*, in *Plays from Padua Hills*, edited by Mednick, Claremont, California, Pomona College, 1983.
Solomon's Fish (produced New York, 1979).
The Actors' Delicatessen, with Priscilla Cohen (produced New York, 1984).
Scar (also director: produced San Francisco, 1985).
Zohar (also director: produced Los Angeles, 1985).
The Pitch (produced San Francisco, 1985). Published in *Articles*, 1986.

Television Plays: *Iowa*, 1977; *Blessings*, 1978.

Other

Editor, *Plays from Padua Hills*. Claremont, California, Pomona College, 1983.

*

Theatrical Activities:
Director: **Plays**—several of his own plays, and *Blue Bitch* by Sam Shepard, New York, 1973.
Actor: **Plays**—*The Actors' Delicatessen*, New York, 1984; *Zohar*, Los Angeles, 1985.

* * *

Murray Mednick is one of the important American dramatists who came of age in the 1960's. In the decade beginning in 1965 he produced some dozen plays, developing increasing technical strength, clarity, and complexity and extending his vision with passionate conviction. His plays and the worlds they evoke are often dominated by ugly, crushing economic and personal pressures that lie behind the American pretense of equality and social justice. The humor is often bitter. Another recurring theme has been the attempt to place contemporary experience in the context of native American myth.

Mednick did most of his early work at Theatre Genesis, a church-sponsored theatre on the lower East Side in New York. A poet before turning to drama, he wrote several one-act plays in the mid-1960's, then moved on to larger forms. *Sand* shows an aging, used-up American couple who are visited by a formal Ambassador, their horrible regressive stupor unbroken by the news that their son is dead in the (Vietnam) war. The dead soldier's body is brought in at the end on a meat hook. *Willie the Germ* is about a down-and-out man working as a dishwasher for a grotesque family of Coney Island freaks who endlessly seduce him into incomprehensible machinations that always get him into trouble. He yearns to escape but is kept in his place by put-downs and an invisible electric force field operated by an anonymous Button-Pusher in the audience. At the end he is destroyed and castrated by the monstrous representatives of "society."

Mednick has also created plays with groups of actors, using improvisation to draw material from their lives and imaginations into a form devised by the dramatist. *The Hawk* is a play about a drug pusher and his victims. The victims' self-revealing monologues were developed by the actors and framed in a formal, ritualistic structure. The play employed a novel and experimental set of technical acting devices and was remarkably successful in shaping very loose, idiosyncratic material within an elegantly disciplined and cohesive form. *The Shadow Ripens* was based on an Eskimo legend and embodied the idea of descending to dangerous non-rational depths of being in quest of wisdom and authenticity.

Similar themes were pursued in subsequent plays: *Are You Lookin?*, a fragmented, highly subjective study of the effect of heroin on personal emotional life, and *The Coyote Cycle*, plays drawn from American Indian stories.

The Hunter shows a hip, tight friendship between two men. They are united by a common enemy, a middle-aged hunter obsessed with the Civil War, whom they nail to a tree; and driven to mutual mistrust by a woman. Though the play has a contemporary setting, its place in space and time is kept ambiguous. The events are spare, elusive, mysterious, moving always toward a visionary plane of perception. *The Deer Kill*, another long play, focuses on a sincere, honest young man trying to live virtuously and simply, having moved from the city to an old farm. His good nature and well-being are assaulted from all sides—by crazed friends from the city, one of whom kills himself, by his unfaithful wife, and by the local authorities, because his dog has killed a deer. The play is more realist than Mednick's earlier work, a clear, rich, and affecting study of a struggle to live morally in contemporary America.

Black Hole in Space received such a demoralized production in New York that it completely escaped notice. But it is the most remarkable of his plays—a bold effort to push the theatre into esoteric meaning. It is like three plays at once, three transparent plays superimposed on each other—a science-fiction thriller, a dream-like segment of autobiography, and a pure metaphysical speculation. Mednick uses theatre as a free poetic medium, and the dark intensity of his vision, as well as the intelligence of his forms, fuses the layers into one picture: it is the priest cutting out the human heart and offering it to the sun. But such a spectacle makes great demands—and requires a willing theatre.

—Michael T. Smith

MEDOFF, Mark (Howard). American. Born in Mount Carmel, Illinois, 18 March 1940. Educated at the University of Miami, 1958–62, B.A. 1962; Stanford University, California, 1964–66, M.A. 1966. Married Stephanie Thorne in 1972 (second marriage); three daughters. Supervisor of publications, Capitol Radio Engineering Institute, Washington, D.C. 1962–64. Instructor, 1966–71, Assistant Professor, 1971–74, Associate Professor, 1974–79, since 1979 Professor of Drama (currently Head of the Department of Theatre Arts), since 1975 dramatist-in-residence, and since 1982 artistic director, American Southwest Theatre Company, all at New Mexico State University, Las Cruces. Chairman of the Awards Committee, American College Theatre Festival, 1985–86. Recipient: Drama Desk award, 1974, 1980; New Mexico State University Westhafer award, 1974; Obie award, 1984; John Gassner Award, 1974; Joseph Jefferson award, for acting, 1974; Guggenheim fellowship, 1974; Tony award, 1980; Outer Circle award, 1980; New Mexico Governor's award, 1980; Society of West End Theatre award, 1982. D.H.L.: Gallaudet College, Washington, D.C., 1981. Agent: Gilbert Parker, William Morris Agency, 1350 Avenue of the Americas, New York, New York 10019. Address: Department of Theatre Arts, New Mexico State University, Las Cruces, New Mexico 88003, U.S.A.

PUBLICATIONS

Plays

The Wager (produced Las Cruces, New Mexico, 1967; New York, 1974). New York, Dramatists Play Service, 1975.

Doing a Good One for the Red Man (produced Las Cruces, New Mexico, 1969). Included in *Four Short Plays*, 1974.

The Froegle Dictum (produced Albuquerque, New Mexico, 1971). Included in *Four Short Plays*, 1974.

The War on Tatem (produced Las Cruces, New Mexico, 1972). Included in *Four Short Plays*, 1974.

The Kramer (produced San Francisco, 1972). New York, Dramatists Play Service, 1976.

When You Comin Back, Red Ryder? (produced New York, 1973). New York, Dramatists Play Service, 1974.

The Odyssey of Jeremy Jack (for children), with Carleene Johnson (produced Las Cruces, New Mexico, 1975). New York, Dramatists Play Service, 1974.

Four Short Plays (includes *The Froegle Dictum*, *Doing a Good One for the Red Man*, *The War on Tatem*, *The Ultimate Grammar of Life*). New York, Dramatists Play Service, 1974.

The Wager: A Play, and Doing a Good One for the Red Man, and The War on Tatem: Two Short Plays. Clifton, New Jersey, James T. White, 1975.

The Halloween Bandit (produced Huntington, New York, 1976; New York City, 1978).

The Conversion of Aaron Weiss (produced Minneapolis, 1977).

Firekeeper (produced Dallas, 1978).

The Last Chance Saloon (also director: produced Las Cruces, New Mexico, 1979).

Children of a Lesser God (produced Los Angeles, 1979; New York, 1980; London, 1981). New York, Dramatists Play Service, 1980; Ambergate, Derbyshire, Amber Lane Press, 1982.

The Hands of Its Enemy (produced Los Angeles, 1984; New York, 1986).

The Majestic Kid, music by Jan Scarborough, lyrics by Medoff and Scarborough (produced San Francisco, 1985).

Kringle's Window (produced Las Cruces, New Mexico, 1985).

The Heart Outright (produced Santa Fe, 1986).

Screenplays: *Good Guys Wear Black*, with Bruce Cohn and Joseph Fraley, 1978; *When You Comin' Back, Red Ryder?*, 1979; *Off Beat*, 1986; *Apology*, 1986; *Children of a Lesser God*, with Hesper Anderson, 1987.

Radio Plays: *The Disintegration of Aaron Weiss*, 1979.

*

Theatrical Activities:

Director: **Plays**—*When You Comin Back, Red Ryder?*; *Waiting for Godot* by Samuel Beckett; *The Effect of Gamma Rays on Man-in-the-Moon Marigolds* by Paul Zindel; *Jacques Brel Is Alive and Well and Living in Paris*; *The Birthday Party* by Harold Pinter; *One Flew over the Cuckoo's Nest* by Dale Wasserman; *Equus* by Peter Shaffer; *The Wager*; *The Hotel Baltimore* by Lanford Wilson; *Head Act* by Mark Frost; *The Hold Out* by Tony Stafford; *Xmor* by Jan Scarborough and Barbara Kerr; *Vanities* by Jack Heifner; *A Flea in Her Ear* by John Mortimer; *Deadline for Murder*.

Actor: **Plays**—Andrei Bolkonski in *War and Peace*; Marat in *Marat/Sade* by Peter Weiss; Pozzo in *Waiting for Godot* by Samuel Beckett; Teddy in *When You Comin Back, Red Ryder?*; Harold Gorringe in *Black Comedy* by Peter Shaffer; Bro Paradock in *A Resounding Tinkle* by N.F. Simpson; Lenny Bruce in *The Soul of Lenny Bruce*; Dysart in *Equus* by Peter Shaffer; Deeley in *Old Times* by Harold Pinter; Scrooge in *A Christmas Carol*; Bellman in *The Hands of Its Enemy*, Los Angeles, 1984.

Mark Medoff comments:

My work is simply a reflection of my own spirit, my fears, sorrows, and fires.

* * *

Mark Medoff's characters are nostalgic, hoping for redemption in the face of a disappearing way of life. This life exists in various forms: in some of Medoff's plays we mourn the lost idealism of the 1960's, in some the disappearing myth of the west. In all of them characters are defending against a changing world, whether through violence, verbal wit, or the hope of love.

The Kramer is a dream play depicting a power-hungry young man's seemingly gratuitous attempt to take over a secretarial school and simultaneously transform the lives of everyone in it. In a touch of rather heavy-handed symbolism Kramer's profile is marred by a cancerous mole. The men in his way—the obligatory conservative supervisor, the unambitious secretary Artie Malin—are no match for Kramer's cynicism, his verbal game-playing, or his eventual transition from verbal to physical violence. Or the women either. Kramer's persuasiveness is based on his apparent ability to know, verbatim, the past lives of his antagonists. He easily persuades Judy Uichi to leave her Japanese amputee husband on the grounds that: "the idealism of your youth having dissipated, he's a lodestone around your neck." Equally as easily he persuades Artie Malin to leave his unattractive wife, Carol May. Ironically, it is Carol May, who seems to be Kramer's weakest opponent, who is actually his only true adversary. Carol May is the only character who seems capable of genuine feeling, and it is her voice that we remember: "You understand you're trying to drown me. . . . Why are you doing this? . . . Is it me—or is it that you just want to destroy things? . . . Haven't you ever loved another person very, very much?"

Teddy in *When You Comin Back, Red Ryder?* is, like Kramer, a figure of violence who far exceeds everyone around him in both intelligence and physical strength. But Teddy is a more complex character. Though initially his disruption of the New Mexico diner appears as gratuitous as Kramer's takeover, it becomes evident that Teddy's real threat is not only his violence but also his ability to destroy the illusions around which lives are constructed. Teddy shares Kramer's uncanny insight into others' pasts, and his readings of people are both cruel and accurate. If Teddy is evil he is also a catalyst for change, forcing decisions and realizations that have long been avoided. In addition, Medoff allows an insight that we don't get into Kramer: we see what Teddy is mourning. Calling himself one of the "disaffected" youth, he asks of the old western heroes, "What in the hell happened to those people?" and announces at the end of the play, "This is the last dance then, gang. Time's gone and I'm gonna ride off into the sunrise." Teddy's tragedy is both his misused brilliance and his ability to accept life's divergence from myth.

The Wager is in many ways a transition between Medoff's earlier works and *Children of a Lesser God*. John Leeds shares with Kramer and Teddy the qualities of violence, verbal wit, and cruel if brilliant insight. But the violence here is transformed to suggest emotional vulnerability. As in *The Kramer* the protagonist's only real match is a woman. The verbal pyrotechnics between Leeds and Honor are clearly a defense against their attraction to one another. Leeds's ability to overcome this defensiveness, even if with great resistance, and Honor's recognition that words are often destructive to understanding suggest greater depth of character than that possessed by any of Medoff's earlier protagonists, and, in addition, for Medoff, a change of key.

The singular quality of *Children of a Lesser God* is its lyricism, relying on the same fluid and dream-like staging employed in *The Kramer*. The play begins and ends in James's memory. James, like his predecessors, is bright and somewhat disaffected, a former Peace Corps volunteer who tells us, "I saved Ecuador." Unlike his predecessors, he retains in the face of the cynicism of his somewhat stereotypical supervisor and students at a school for the non-hearing both some measure of idealism and an openness to feeling, although his tendency to what Robert Brustein has called "pop psychoanalysis" can become annoying. Also unlike his predecessors, James shares the stage. He has a co-protagonist.

Sarah Norman, one of James's non-hearing students, who signs because she will not speak, provides the play with much of its lyrical eloquence. The relationship between James and Sarah, initially a power struggle between teacher and student, becomes a love affair and then reverts to a power struggle. The issues Medoff explored in earlier works are now complicated by the conflict between power and feeling. James acknowledges the inherent ambiguity of his motives: do they stem from a desire to help or a desire to control? Sarah, for her part, is "determined to preserve her wholeness inside a deaf world . . . deafness . . . is a condition of being 'other,' and this otherness has its sufficient rewards." She signs to James: "I live in a place you can't enter. It's out of reach. . . . Deafness isn't the opposite of hearing, as you think. It's a silence full of sound . . . ." Their final confrontation is a recognition of simultaneous love and difference—a difference that is, despite love, irresolvable, James acknowledging: "Yes, I'm a terrific teacher: Grow, Sarah, but not too much. Understand yourself, but not more than I understand you. Be brave, but not so brave you don't need me anymore," and Sarah: "I'm afraid I would just go on trying to change you. We would have to meet in another place; not in silence or in sound but somewhere else. I don't know where that is now."

The play's eloquence is, paradoxically, inherent in its characters' inability to make themselves understood. The fact is that the two protagonists speak separate languages. Although this linguistic difference is muted by James's simultaneous translation of Sarah's signing, the play does give an indication, at least, of the imperative to understand those who are "inarticulate" in our language. Those who are non-vocal, Medoff suggests, do not necessarily have nothing to say. The struggle to be heard is a common theme, and Brustein, in his review, expresses his irritation, calling the play "a chic compendium of every extant cliché about women and minority groups. . . ." But the frequency with which a theme is explored does not necessarily relate to its importance; if anything the repetition of an idea may indicate the necessity of coming to terms with it. Gerald Weales has written of this play that: "Since no marriage—however close, however loving—can make two people one . . . the special cases of James, as teacher, and Sarah, as unwilling pupil, can become metaphors for any marriage." James's final nostalgia for a love that is real and yet not realizable is at the heart of the play's poignance, a poignance the later screenplay, by resorting to a happy ending, fails to retain.

Two later plays by Medoff are less successful in their reiteration of earlier themes. Aaron, in the musical *The Majestic Kid*, is like Leeds, concerned with issues of love and distance, with lost idealism. But the characters are unrealized. Aaron's love affair with Lisa is abrupt and therefore unimportant. It is difficult to know how to take the Laredo Kid, a movie character brought to life who knows all the old western plots by heart—movie as karma?—but cannot decipher the present script. And the ideological and political concerns of Aaron's long-time lover and co-worker, A.J., jar with her flip one-liners. *The Hands of Its Enemy* also concerns a woman who cannot hear. But *Enemy* is more conceptional than *Children*, a play within a play which juxtaposes a psychological exploration of the characters of a playwright and her director with the rehearsal process for their play. The central theme again centers around issues of distance and the need to trust, but here the struggle is at times cloying and overdone.

At his weakest Medoff may occasionally go too far in one direction or the other, becoming either gratuitous or overly sentimental. But in his best plays he is able to combine a frighteningly realistic depiction of the cruelties we wittingly or unwittingly commit with a simultaneous acknowledgement of our tremendous vulnerability.

—Elizabeth Adams

MELFI, Leonard (Anthony). American. Born in Binghamton, New York, 21 February 1935. Educated at Binghamton Central High School; St. Bonaventure University, New York, 1956–57; American Academy of Dramatic Arts. Worked as a waiter and carpenter; lecturer, New York University, 1969–70. Columnist ("Notes of a New York Playwright"), *Dramatists Guild Quarterly*, New York. Recipient: Eugene O'Neill Memorial Theatre Foundation award, 1966; Rockefeller grant, 1966, 1967; Guggenheim fellowship, 1978. Lives in New York City. Agent: Helen Harvey Associates, 410 West 24th Street, New York, New York 10011, U.S.A.

PUBLICATIONS

Plays

Lazy Baby Susan (produced New York, 1965).
Sunglasses (produced New York, 1965).
Pussies and Rookies (produced New York, 1965).
Ferryboat (produced New York, 1965). Included in *Encounters*, 1967.
Birdbath (produced New York, 1965; Edinburgh, 1967; London, 1969). Included in *Encounters*, 1967; in *New Short Plays 1*, London, Methuen, 1968.
Times Square (produced New York, 1966; Edinburgh and London, 1967). Included in *Encounters*, 1967.
Niagara Falls (produced New York, 1966; revised version produced Los Angeles, 1968; London, 1976). Published in *New Theatre for Now* (*New Theatre in America 2*), edited by Edward Parone, New York, Dell, 1971.
Lunchtime (produced New York, 1966; London, 1969). Included in *Encounters*, 1967.
Halloween (produced New York, 1967; London, 1969). Included in *Encounters*, 1967.
The Shirt (produced New York, 1967). Included in *Encounters*, 1967.
Encounters: 6 One-Act Plays. New York, Random House, 1967.
Disfiguration (produced Los Angeles, 1967).
Night (in *Chiaroscuro* produced Spoleto, Italy, 1968; in *Morning, Noon, and Night*, produced New York, 1968). Published in *Morning, Noon, and Night*, New York, Random House, 1969.
Stars and Stripes, in *Collision Course* (produced New York, 1968). New York, Random House, 1968.
Stimulation (produced New York, 1968; London, 1969).
Jack and Jill (produced New York, 1968; revised version, produced as part of *Oh! Calcutta!*, New York, 1969; London, 1970). New York, Grove Press, 1969.
The Breech Baby (produced New York, 1968).
Having Fun in the Bathroom (produced New York, 1969).
The Raven Rock (produced New York, 1969).
Wet and Dry, and Alive (produced New York, 1969).
The Jones Man (produced Provincetown, Massachusetts, 1969).
Cinque (produced London, 1970; New York, 1971). Published in *Spontaneous Combustion: Eight New American Plays*, edited by Rochelle Owens, New York, Winter House, 1972.
Ah! Wine! (produced New York, 1974).
Beautiful! (produced New York, 1974).
Horse Opera, music by John Braden (produced New York, 1974).
Sweet Suite (produced New York, 1975).
Porno Stars at Home (produced New York, 1976). New York, French, 1980.
Eddie and Susanna in Love (produced New York, 1976).
Fantasies at the Frick; or, (The Guard and the Guardess) (produced New York, 1976). New York, French, 1980.
Butterfaces (produced New York, 1977).
Taxi Tales (five plays; produced New York, 1978). Included in *Later Encounters*, 1980.
Rusty and Rico, and Lena and Louie (produced New York, 1978). Included in *Later Encounters*, 1980.
Later Encounters: Seven One-Act Plays (includes *Taxi Tales—Taffy's Taxi, Tripper's Taxi, Toddy's Taxi, The Teaser's Taxi, Mr. Tucker's Taxi—Rusty and Rico, Lena and Louie*). New York, French, 1980.
Amorous Accidents (produced Los Angeles, 1981).
The Dispossessed (produced New York, 1982).
Eve Is Innocent (produced New York, 1983).
Rosetti's Apologetics, music by Mark Hardwick (produced New York, 1983).
The Little Venice Makes a Good Drink (produced Binghamton, New York, 1985).
Lily Lake (produced Binghamton, New York, 1986).

Screenplay: *La mortadella* (*Lady Liberty*), 1971.

Television Plays: *The Rainbow Rest*, 1967; *Puck! Puck! Puck!*, 1968; *What a Life!*, 1976.

*

Critical Study: *American Playwrights: A Critical Survey* by Bonnie Marranca and Gautam Dasgupta, New York, Drama Book Specialists, 1981.

Theatrical Activities:
Actor: **Plays**—Knute Gary in *Beautiful!*, New York, 1974; Room Service in *Sweet Suite*, New York, 1975; Richard DeRichard in *The Dispossessed*, New York, 1982; Rosetti in *Rosetti's Apologetics*, New York, 1983. **Films**—*La mortadella* (*Lady Liberty*), 1971; *Rent Control*, 1983.

Leonard Melfi comments:

A personal statement introducing my plays?

Well . . . "I borrow from life and pay back my debt by giving my imagination."

Or, maybe . . . "Plays about my fellow human beings in and out of trouble, like all of us at various times. In other words: celebrating the human condition, the miracle and mystery of life, no matter what."

Or, maybe . . . "I take people who wake up in the morning and ask themselves: 'Are you happy?', and then they answer immediately to themselves: 'Yes, I am!' . . . and I throw them together with the other group, who, when they ask themselves the very same question, always answer immediately: 'No, I'm not!' (There's always a play in that situation!)."

Why I feel so great about writing plays (among other certain reasons)? Well, once in my father's roadhouse restaurant and bar in Upstate New York where I grew up, a bunch of hunters walked in to drink and eat and my father was behind the bar. One of the men asked: "By the way: what does your son down in New York City do anyway?" And my father smiled and proudly replied (he had gone as far as the sixth grade): "My son does the same thing that Shakespeare did!"

* * *

It's just like a sort of Utopia ... all those windows with all those people behind all of those windows: living and breathing and trying to love too. Well, I just love it all, my dear Louie Pussycat! All of them trying like holy hell and holy heaven to be wholly holy happy as much as it's humanly possible in all of our rather only half-happy lives instead of our wholly happy lives. . . !

Lena of *Lena and Louie* shows the best and the worst of Leonard Melfi's playwriting. The exuberance and visionary optimism are as typical of his work as the shallow sentiment and flabby prose. Although Melfi has never fulfilled the promise of his early plays, and may have reneged on it, he has consolidated his dramatic territory and remained constant to it.

Melfi gained his first foothold in theatre when he began writing one-act plays for Ellen Stewart's Cafe La Mama, one of the birthplaces of off-off-Broadway. To fit the one-act form, Melfi stripped his characters of all but one or two qualities, usually the need for love or the need for sex, or both. Similarly, the plays of *Encounters* revolved around those brief moments when human contact becomes possible. Such moments are particularly rare in large cities, and Melfi's plays are as New York as pavement, filled with specific references to the city and its people. Presented at La Mama, they were always on intimate terms with their audiences.

The plays range in style from a necessarily narrowed realism to a highly stylized fantasy occasionally reminiscent of Michael McClure's cartoon plays. *Birdbath*, one of Melfi's best known plays, brings together a superficially composed young man and an excessively nervous young woman who can speak of little but her mother. Their encounter brings out the man's obsessive need to write and the woman's murder of her mother that morning, and the bond between them that results from these revelations brings them together, and the play ends with Frankie's valentine to Velma. In contrast, *Times Square* is a masque-like fantasy about the people who inhabit New York's most offensive block of sex-shows and other adult temptations. The characters, however, are childlike, hopeful dreamers whose innocence is only confirmed by the fluid, anything-can-happen life of Times Square. When the angelic Melissa Sobbing is hit by a car, she is revivified with a kiss, and for a moment Times Square really is a street of dreams.

Melfi's world has its nightmares too, which come with a sudden violence that counterpoints oddly its romance. In *Encounters* the violence exploded into the romance with a sharpness and suddenness that enriched the plays. In *Later Encounters* and Melfi's longer plays the dark side of New York has been increasingly absorbed and softened by the light. Although Lena and Louie freeze to death in Central Park, their deaths are an apotheosis. They die "in each other's arms, with the two most beautiful smiles on their faces: smiling like one has never seen smiling ever before in one's life; smiling smiles that told of things like, well, things like . . . forever!"

Melfi's longer plays are essentially enlarged one-acts, with small casts and limited aims. In *Porno Stars at Home* the characters begin an evening with their facades intact, smoothly congratulating themselves on their style and dash. Before the evening is out, they've reduced their styles to shreds, and are trying desperately to put them back together. Unfortunately, their psychological strip uncovers little of interest, little more than "Baby, all I do all of the time is to try and not be scared anymore, that's all," or "I just want something to hang on to before it's too late." Although an able craftsman of the theatre, Melfi has so far failed to pursue his well-worn themes and situations into new territory.

—Walter Bode

MILLAR, (Sir) Ronald (Graeme). British. Born in Reading, Berkshire, 12 November 1919. Educated at Charterhouse School, Surrey; King's College, Cambridge. Served in the Royal Naval Volunteer Reserve, 1940–43: Sub-Lieutenant. Since 1977 Deputy Chairman, Theatre Royal, Haymarket, London. Knighted, 1980. Agent: Ian Bevan, 37 Hill Street, London W1X 8JY. Address: 7 Sheffield Terrace, London W.8, England.

PUBLICATIONS

Plays

Murder from Memory (produced London, 1942).
Zero Hour (produced London, 1944).
The Other Side, adaptation of the novel by Storm Jameson (produced London, 1946).
Frieda (produced London, 1946). London, English Theatre Guild, 1947.
Champagne for Delilah (produced London, 1949).
Waiting for Gillian, adaptation of the novel *A Way Through the Wood* by Nigel Balchin (produced London, 1954). London, French, 1955.
The Bride and the Bachelor (produced London, 1956). London, French, 1958.
A Ticklish Business (produced Brighton, 1958; as *The Big Tickle*, produced London, 1958). London, French, 1959.
The More the Merrier (produced London, 1960). London, French, 1960.
The Bride Comes Back (produced London, 1960). London, French, 1961.
The Affair, adaptation of the novel by C.P. Snow (produced London, 1961; Washington, D.C., 1964). New York, Scribner, 1962; London, French, 1963.
The New Men, adaptation of the novel by C.P. Snow (produced London, 1962). Included in *The Affair, The New Men, The Masters*, 1964.
The Masters, adaptation of the novel by C.P. Snow (produced London, 1963). Included in *The Affair, The New Men, The Masters*, 1964.
The Affair, The New Men, The Masters: Three Plays Based on the Novels and with a Preface by C.P. Snow. London, Macmillan, 1964.
Robert and Elizabeth, music by Ron Grainer, lyrics by Millar, adaptation of the play *The Barretts of Wimpole Street* by Rudolf Besier (produced London, 1964). London, French, 1967.
On the Level, music by Ron Grainer (produced London, 1966).

Number 10, adaptation of the novel by William Clark (produced Glasgow and London, 1967). London, Heinemann, 1967.
They Don't Grow on Trees (produced London, 1968). London, French, 1969.
Abelard and Heloise, based on *Peter Abelard* by Helen Waddell (produced Exeter and London, 1970; New York, 1971). London and New York, French, 1970.
Parents' Day, adaptation of the novel by Edward Candy (produced London, 1972).
Odd Girl Out, adaptation of the novel by Elizabeth Jane Howard (produced Harlow, Essex, 1973).
The Case in Question, adaptation of the novel *In Their Wisdom* by C.P. Snow (produced London, 1975). London, French, 1975.
Once More with Music (produced Guildford, Surrey, 1976).
A Coat of Varnish, adaptation of the novel by C.P. Snow (produced London, 1982). London, French, 1983.

Screenplays: *Frieda*, with Angus Macphail, 1947; *So Evil My Love*, with Leonard Spiegelgass, 1948; *The Miniver Story*, with George Froeschel, 1950; *Train of Events*, with others, 1950; *The Unknown Man*, with George Froeschel, 1951; *Scaramouche*, with George Froeschel, 1951; *Never Let Me Go*, with George Froeschel, 1953; *Rose Marie*, 1954; *Betrayed*, with George Froeschel, 1954.

*

Theatrical Activities:
Actor: **Plays**—in *Swinging the Gate* (revue), London, 1940; Prince Anatole Kuragin in *War and Peace* by David Lucas, London, 1943; Cully in *Mr. Bolfry* by James Bridie, London, 1943; David Marsden in *Murder for a Valentine* by Vernon Sylvaine, London, 1944; Flight Lieutenant Chris Keppel in *Zero Hour*, London, 1944; Penry Bowen in *Jenny Jones* by Ronald Gow, London, 1944; Roy Fernie in *We Are Seven* by Ian Hay, London, 1945; Colin Tabret in *The Sacred Flame* by W. Somerset Maugham, London, 1945; Smith in *Murder on the Nile* by Agatha Christie, London, 1946. **Films**—*The Life and Death of Colonel Blimp*, 1943; *Beware of Pity*, 1945.

* * *

Ronald Millar was born in Reading in 1919. When he was a small boy his mother, an actress, wishing him to be protected from the glamorous uncertainties of stage life, sent him to a good preparatory school to receive a classical education. At the end of his time there he sat for scholarships at several of the great public schools. He was offered one at Harrow, but refused it on the advice of his headmaster, who had his eye on Winchester. At the Winchester examination, however, he happened to be out of sorts and narrowly missed an award; but he did gain one at Charterhouse.

From his mother's point of view this was an unhappy accident; for at that time Charterhouse, of all the great public schools, had the closest connection with the theatre and the largest number of old boys who were actors. And from there young Ronald went on to King's, which of all the colleges in Cambridge had the strongest theatrical tradition.

The outcome was fairly predictable. Millar joined various University acting clubs, showed talent, gained experience—incidentally, he was given the leading part in the triennial Greek play which is traditionally a great dramatic event at Cambridge—and was inevitably attracted to the professional stage. Then service in the Royal Navy delayed his final decision; but by the time he was invalided out he had made up his mind. He did not return to Cambridge to take his degree, but turned actor at once.

However, the years spent with the classics were not wasted. There are many worse forms of training for a writer, and Millar's ambition to be a dramatist was at least as strong as his desire to act, and was to prove much more lasting. His second play, *Zero Hour*, was produced at the Lyric in June 1944, with himself in the cast, and his third, *Frieda* (about a girl escaped from Nazi Germany), at the Westminster in 1946. This had a fair success on the stage and a bigger one as a film.

In 1949 Millar suffered a deep disappointment. Returning to England after an interlude spent writing filmscripts in Hollywood, he brought with him a light comedy, *Champagne for Delilah*, which was instantly accepted for West End production. To all the experts who handled it, it seemed certain to have a huge success, and it was received with acclaim on its prior-to-London tour. But on arrival at the New Theatre it proved a dead failure, and nobody has ever been able to suggest why. Seven years later, however, Millar must have felt compensated by an ironic twist of fate when another play, *The Bride and the Bachelor*, ran for more than 500 performances after having been given a hostile reception by nearly all the critics. Later still, in 1960, a sequel to this piece, *The Bride Comes Back*, also ran very well.

By this time Millar had enough successful work to his credit to prove that one of his outstanding qualities was his versatility. From the seriousness of *Frieda* to the frivolity of the two "Bride" plays was a big step and a vivid contrast in styles; and he now proceeded to demonstrate further uses to which his versatility might be put.

The year 1961 saw the beginning of a whole series of plays adapted by Millar from novels or other literary sources, the first of them being a stage version of C.P. Snow's story of college life at Cambridge, *The Affair*. As a Cambridge man himself, Millar was familiar with the atmosphere so truthfully rendered by the book, and, given a free hand, matched that atmosphere quite perfectly. Then came a setback. Manager after manager refused to believe that a play so local in its application could interest the general public. At last Henry Sherek, who had been Millar's backer for *Frieda* and *Champagne for Delilah*, accepted the risk, and was rewarded with critical favour and a year's run.

A second play from a Snow novel, *The New Men*, followed in 1962 and had no success; but a second Cambridge piece, *The Masters*, was staged in 1963 and ran even longer than *The Affair* had, and in 1975 yet another, *The Case in Question*, ran very well.

The particular talent which carried Millar to his notable successes in this field is an ability to turn a novelist's narrative prose into dialogue without losing his personal flavour, added to which is an ability where necessary to write in scenes of his own invention in a style to fit in with the rest.

This was perhaps not an especially difficult task in the case of the two Cambridge plays, where novelist and adapter had in common a detailed knowledge of and feeling for the atmosphere they wished to convey; but it became a problem of much delicacy in the case of Millar's next, and much more serious play, *Abelard and Heloise*. The main materials for this play were Helen Waddell's book about Peter Abelard and the famous letters, and the task was to find an idiom which would convey both these elements. This was done with such skill that the play drew not only the more serious playgoers but also the general public. Produced in May 1970, it ran into 1972.

One other proof of Millar's versatility should be noted. In 1964 he wrote both the book and lyrics for *Robert and Elizabeth*, the musical version of *The Barretts of Wimpole Street*, which ran for two and a half years.

—W.A. Darlington

MILLER, Arthur. American. Born in New York City, 17 October 1915. Educated at Abraham Lincoln High School, New York, graduated 1932; University of Michigan, Ann Arbor (Hopwood Award, 1936, 1937), 1934–38, A.B. 1938. Married 1) Mary Slattery in 1940 (divorced 1956), one son and one daughter; 2) the actress Marilyn Monroe in 1956 (divorced 1961); 3) the photographer Ingeborg Morath in 1962, one daughter. Worked in automobile supply warehouse, 1932–34; member of the Federal Theatre Project, 1938; writer for CBS and NBC Radio Workshops. Associate Professor of Drama, University of Michigan, 1973–74. International President, PEN, London and New York, 1965–69. Recipient: Theatre Guild award, 1938; New York Drama Critics Circle award, 1947, 1949; Tony award, 1947, 1949, 1953; Pulitzer Prize, 1949; National Association of Independent Schools award, 1954; American Academy Gold Medal, 1959; Brandeis University Creative Arts Award, 1969; Peabody award, for television play, 1981; Bobst Award, 1983. D.H.L.: University of Michigan, 1956; Honorary degree: Hebrew University, Jerusalem, 1959; Litt.D.: University of East Anglia, Norwich, 1984. Member, American Academy, 1981. Lives in Connecticut. Agent: Kay Brown, International Creative Management, 40 West 57th Street, New York, New York 10019, U.S.A.

PUBLICATIONS

Plays

Honors at Dawn (produced Ann Arbor, Michigan, 1936).

No Villain (*They Too Arise*) (produced Ann Arbor, Michigan, 1937).

The Pussycat and the Expert Plumber Who Was a Man, and *William Ireland's Confession*, in *100 Non-Royalty Radio Plays*, edited by William Kozlenko. New York, Greenberg, 1941.

The Man Who Had All the Luck (produced New York, 1944; London, 1960). Published in *Cross-Section 1944*, edited by Edwin Seaver, New York, Fischer, 1944.

That They May Win (produced New York, 1944). Published in *Best One-Act Plays of 1944*, edited by Margaret Mayorga, New York, Dodd Mead, 1945.

Grandpa and the Statue, in *Radio Drama in Action*, edited by Erik Barnouw. New York, Farrar and Rinehart, 1945.

The Story of Gus, in *Radio's Best Plays*, edited by Joseph Liss. New York, Greenberg, 1947.

The Guardsman, radio adaptation of a play by Ferenc Molnár, and *Three Men on a Horse*, radio adaptation of the play by George Abbott and John Cecil Holm, in *Theatre Guild on the Air*, edited by William Fitelson. New York, Rinehart, 1947.

All My Sons (produced New York, 1947; London, 1948). New York, Reynal, 1947; in *Collected Plays*, 1957.

Death of a Salesman: Certain Private Conversations in Two Acts and a Requiem (produced New York and London, 1949). New York, Viking Press, and London, Cresset Press, 1949.

An Enemy of the People, adaptation of a play by Ibsen (produced New York, 1950; Lincoln, 1958). New York, Viking Press, 1951.

The Crucible (produced New York, 1953; Bristol, 1954; London, 1956). New York, Viking Press, 1953; London, Cresset Press, 1956; augmented version (with additional scene, subsequently omitted), New York, Dramatists Play Service, 1954.

A View from the Bridge (produced New York, 1955). With *A Memory of Two Mondays*, New York, Viking Press, 1955; revised version (produced London, 1956), New York, Dramatists Play Service, 1956; London, Cresset Press, 1957.

A Memory of Two Mondays (produced New York, 1955; Nottingham, 1958). With *A View from the Bridge*, New York, Viking Press, 1955; in *Collected Plays*, 1957.

Collected Plays (includes *All My Sons, Death of a Salesman, The Crucible, A Memory of Two Mondays, A View from the Bridge*). New York, Viking Press, 1957; London, Cresset Press, 1958.

After the Fall (produced New York, 1964; Coventry, 1967). New York, Viking Press, 1964; London, Secker and Warburg, 1965.

Incident at Vichy (produced New York, 1964; Brighton and London, 1966). New York, Viking Press, 1965; London, Secker and Warburg, 1966.

The Price (produced New York, 1968; also director: produced London, 1969). New York, Viking Press, and London, Secker and Warburg, 1968.

Fame, and The Reason Why (produced New York, 1970). *Fame* published in *Yale Literary Magazine* (New Haven, Connecticut), March 1971.

The Creation of the World and Other Business (produced New York, 1972; Edinburgh, 1974). New York, Viking Press, 1973; in *Collected Plays 2*, 1981; revised version, as *Up from Paradise*, music by Stanley Silverman (also director: produced Ann Arbor, Michigan, 1974; New York, 1983), New York, French, 1984.

The Archbishop's Ceiling (produced Washington, D.C., 1977; revised version produced Cleveland, 1984; Bristol, 1985; London, 1986). London, Methuen, 1984; New York, Dramatists Play Service, 1985.

The American Clock, adaptation of the work *Hard Times* by Studs Terkel (produced Seattle, 1979; New York, 1980; Birmingham, 1983; London, 1986). New York, Dramatists Play Service, 1982; London, Methuen, 1983.

Playing for Time, adaptation of a work by Fania Fenelon (televised 1980; produced Edinburgh, 1986). New York, Bantam, 1981; in *Collected Plays 2*, 1981.

Collected Plays 2 (includes *The Misfits, After the Fall, Incident at Vichy, The Price, The Creation of the World and Other Business, Playing for Time*). New York, Viking Press, and London, Secker and Warburg, 1981.

Eight Plays (includes *All My Sons, Death of a Salesman, The Crucible, A Memory of Two Mondays, A View from the Bridge, After the Fall, Incident at Vichy, The Price*). New York, Doubleday, 1981.

Two-Way Mirror (includes *Elegy for a Lady* and *Some Kind of Love Story*) (also director: produced New Haven, Connecticut, 1982; Edinburgh, 1984). *Elegy for a Lady* published New York, Dramatists Play Service, 1982; *Some Kind of Love Story* published Dramatists Play Service, 1983; both plays published London, Methuen, 1984.

Danger! Memory! (includes *I Can't Remember Anything* and *Clara*) (produced New York, 1987). London, Methuen, 1986; New York, Grove Press, 1987.

Screenplays: *The Story of G.I. Joe* (uncredited), 1945; *The Witches of Salem*, 1958; *The Misfits*, 1961.

Radio Plays: *The Pussycat and the Expert Plumber Who Was a Man, William Ireland's Confession, Grandpa and the Statue, The Story of Gus, The Guardsman, Three Men on a Horse*, early 1940's; *The Golden Years*, 1987 (UK).

Television Play: *Playing for Time*, 1980.

Novels

Focus. New York, Reynal, 1945; London, Gollancz, 1949.
The Misfits (novelization of screenplay). New York, Viking Press, and London, Secker and Warburg, 1961.

Short Stories

I Don't Need You Any More. New York, Viking Press, and London, Secker and Warburg, 1967.

Other

Situation Normal. New York, Reynal, 1944.
Jane's Blanket (for children). New York, Crowell Collier, and London, Collier Macmillan, 1963.
In Russia, photographs by Inge Morath. New York, Studio, and London, Secker and Warburg, 1969.
The Portable Arthur Miller, edited by Harold Clurman. New York, Viking Press, 1971; London, Penguin, 1977.
In the Country, photographs by Inge Morath. New York, Studio, and London, Secker and Warburg, 1977.
The Theater Essays of Arthur Miller, edited by Robert A. Martin. New York, Viking Press, and London, Penguin, 1978.
Chinese Encounters, photographs by Inge Morath. New York, Farrar Straus, and London, Secker and Warburg, 1979.
"Salesman" in Beijing. New York, Viking, and London, Methuen, 1984.
Timebends (autobiography). New York, Grove Press, and London, Methuen, 1987.

*

Bibliography: "Arthur Miller: The Dimension of His Art: A Checklist of His Published Works," in *Serif* (Kent, Ohio), June 1967, and *Arthur Miller Criticism (1930–1967)*, Metuchen, New Jersey, Scarecrow Press, 1969, revised edition as *An Index to Arthur Miller Criticism*, 1976, both by Tetsumaro Hayashi; *Arthur Miller: A Reference Guide* by John H. Ferres, Boston, Hall, 1979.

Manuscript Collections: University of Texas, Austin; University of Michigan, Ann Arbor; New York Public Library; Library of Congress, Washington, D.C.

Critical Studies (selection): *Arthur Miller*, Edinburgh, Oliver and Boyd, and New York, Grove Press, 1961, and *Miller: A Study of His Plays*, London, Eyre Methuen, 1979, revised edition as *Miller the Playwright*, Methuen, 1983, both by Dennis Welland; *Arthur Miller* by Robert Hogan, Minneapolis, University of Minnesota Press, 1964; *Arthur Miller: The Burning Glass* by Sheila Huftel, New York, Citadel Press, and London, W.H. Allen, 1965; *Arthur Miller: Death of a Salesman: Text and Criticism* edited by Gerald Weales, New York, Viking Press, 1967; *Arthur Miller* by Leonard Moss, New York, Twayne, 1967, revised edition, 1980; *Arthur Miller, Dramatist* by Edward Murray, New York, Ungar, 1967; *Arthur Miller: A Collection of Critical Essays* edited by Robert W. Corrigan, Englewood Cliffs, New Jersey, Prentice Hall, 1969; *Psychology and Arthur Miller* by Richard I. Evans, New York, Dutton, 1969; *The Merrill Guide to Arthur Miller* by Sidney H. White, Columbus, Ohio, Merrill, 1970; *Arthur Miller: Portrait of a Playwright* by Benjamin Nelson, New York, McKay, and London, Owen, 1970; *Arthur Miller* by Ronald Hayman, London, Heinemann, 1970, New York, Ungar, 1972; *Twentieth-Century Interpretations of The Crucible* edited by John H. Ferres, Englewood Cliffs, New Jersey, Prentice Hall, 1972; *Studies in Death of a Salesman* edited by Walter J. Meserve, Columbus, Ohio, Merrill, 1972; *Critical Essays on Arthur Miller* edited by James J. Martine, Boston, Hall, 1979; *Arthur Miller: New Perspectives* edited by Robert A. Martin, Englewood Cliffs, New Jersey, Prentice Hall, 1982; *Arthur Miller* by Neil Carson, London, Macmillan, and New York, Grove Press, 1982; *Twentieth-Century Interpretations of Death of a Salesman* edited by Helene Wickham Koon, Englewood Cliffs, New Jersey, Prentice Hall, 1983; *Conversations with Arthur Miller* edited by Matthew C. Roudané, Jackson, University Press of Mississippi, 1987.

Theatrical Activities:
Director: **Plays**—*The Price*, London, 1969; *Up from Paradise*, Ann Arbor, Michigan, 1974; *Two-Way Mirror*, New Haven, Connecticut, 1982; *Death of a Salesman*, Beijing, 1983.
Actor: **Play**—Narrator in *Up from Paradise*, Ann Arbor, Michigan, 1974.

Arthur Miller comments:

I have, I think, provided actors with some good things to do and say. Beyond that I cannot speak with any certainty. My plays seem to exist and that's enough for me. What people may find in them or fail to find is not in my control anymore; I can only hope that life has not been made less for what I've done, and possibly a bit more.

* * *

How may a man make of the outside world a home?

I am constantly awed by what an individual is, by the endless possibilities in him for good and evil, by his unpredictability, by the possibilities he has for any betrayal, any cruelty, as well as any altruism, any sacrifice.

—Arthur Miller

Arthur Miller writes primarily about man's relationship to society and the issues of personal identity and human dignity. Throughout, he has used the realistic form. His statement of purpose—to write "a drama of the whole-man"—conveys his interest in psychology as well as morality. Miller frequently uses what T.S. Eliot called the "objective correlative" ("a set of objects, a situation, a chain of events which shall be the formula of that *particular* emotion") in order to combine an extraordinarily forceful theater with uncanny psychological insights and lyrical and poetic vision. His aim is a theater that "teaches, not by proposing solutions but by defining problems."

The *Collected Plays* of 1957 portray the individual struggling against the laws of society, family, and even selfhood—torn between either the dreams the dog-eat-dog world has imposed upon him and his essential goodness, or torn between his deepest wishes for the simple life and the needs he feels obliged to meet. Set against a ruthless capitalist system that ignores or uses the common man, his identity frequently consists of merely accommodating himself to an essentially alien universe (society) and the act of painstakingly supporting his family. Sometimes, however, he learns that he never was in fact connected with family or job, let alone society, or that the values of each were equally spurious.

Miller's first successful play, *All My Sons*, portrays the conflict between the idealistic son (Chris) and his materialistically corrupted father (Joe Keller). To retain his business, Keller has shipped out defective plane parts which have ultimately caused the deaths of many fliers. The seeds of the great *Death of a Salesman* are here—from the stage setting (with the Keller's house and the impinging presence of the more successful neighbors) to the use of poetic images (wind, the car), to even specific rhetorical cadences ("Nobody in this house dast take her faith away"). Here is the eternally forgiving, self-deluding wife-mother; her idealistic sons (one has committed suicide for his principles); the poignant and misguided bond between father and son; and the father's suicide to expiate a lifetime of wrong commitment. Here is Miller's vision of the terrible rat-race of ordinary, business reality, and one's better knowledge of the need to love other men. One bears a responsibility to the other, and "can be better! Once and for all you can know there's a universe of people outside and you're responsible to it." This, however, becomes increasingly difficult to enact, as one's love for his family may also tear him apart: "There's nothin' he could do that I wouldn't forgive. Because he's my son. Because I'm his father and he's my son."

Miller's masterpiece, *Death of a Salesman*, measures the enormous gap between America's promise of inevitable success and the devastating reality of one's concrete failure. Commitment to false social values blinds one to the true values of human experience—the comforts of personal relationships, of family and friendship, of love. Identity and commitment are again the subject. Willie Loman, who might well exemplify Miller's definition of the tragic hero (in his important essay "Tragedy and the Common Man"), has completely sold himself to what is at best an anachronistic dream—that anyone can get ahead. This is what he has been brought up to believe, the promise of his mythic (salesmen) heroes. While Willie has pursued this for 40 years and has sold it to his two sons, he is blind to its contemporary meaninglessness and to his own (and their) failure. But Willie *is* a great salesman—of the old American dream—and even his wife, the loyal Linda, lives in a world of self-generating lies and illusions. What Willie comes to realize on this single day of the play—his "recognition scene"—is that he has totally overlooked his true wealth, that he is a deeply loved father. Ironically, armed with this knowledge, he defies the system that has until now defeated him. He commits suicide to give his sons the only thing his society respects—cash. In defiance, irony, and profound bitterness, Miller sends Willie to his death with the same illusion he has lived by—though Willie is now fully aware of and in control of it. This is Miller's most bitter picture of the system that uses the little man—that eats the orange and throws away the peel. As tattered and self-pitying as Willie sometimes appears, he is one of the theater's most poignant and moving figures.

Miller has connected the origins of *The Crucible* with McCarthyism, with the "political, objective knowledgable campaign from the far Right [which] was capable of creating not only a terror, but a new subjective reality, a veritable mystique which was gradually assuming even a holy resonance." Specifically about the Salem witch trials of 1692, the play also treats the national paranoia, hysteria, and general immorality that characterized the McCarthy witch-hunts. Miller bitterly attacks the society that rewards the suppression of freedom in the name of "right" and conformity. Two lines summarize his focus: the rhetorical "Is the accusor always holy?" and "You must understand ... that a person is either with this court or he must be counted against it, there be no road between." Although this has been called a modern morality play, Miller goes beyond black/white characterizations to portray his figures' petty rivalries and moral ambiguities. He probes the political, social, and psychological needs of both those who capitulate and those who resist. Mr. Proctor, after defying the court's demands, finally regains his name (also important to Willie and Keller) and dies in another act of defiance. Once again, Miller illustrates his conviction that one can assert his "personal dignity" and "act against the scheme of things that degrades." As he puts it in *All My Sons*, one can be "better."

A Memory of Two Mondays, which Miller has expressed an especial fondness for, brings back the depression years. It was produced initially with *A View from the Bridge*, which treats the hardworking and likeable Eddie Carbone who, out of blind love toward his niece-ward, informs on the illegal immigrants he is presumably safeguarding; one is his niece's boyfriend. Blind to what really drives him ("You can never have her"), and defiant of community, family, and natural law, he endures public humiliation for his act of treason. His grief is overwhelming as he cries the familiar: "I want my name"; he draws a knife and once again Miller's protagonist precipitates his own death. Although the play is, as Miller intended, simpler than *Salesman*, it recalls it in many ways: two men in conflict with a third, an authority figure; the (surrogate) father's blind worship of his charge ("She's the best"); the ever-supportive and loving wife; it also retains certain expressionistic elements (the narrator functions like a Greek chorus and frames each section in mythic terms).

For the next nine years, Miller wrote short stories, prose essays (the important "The Shadow of Gods"), and the screenplay *The Misfits*. With *After the Fall* he turns from the family and one's obligation to connect with the social world to a more existential statement: the recuperative and regenerative powers of love, the question of personal or universal guilt, and the necessity of man to justify himself to himself (rather than the system)—the need for human community and love, and the fact that one *is* his brother's keeper. Despite the many critical attempts to pigeonhole *After the Fall* autobiographically (with Maggie as Miller's wife, Marilyn Monroe), Miller has said that the play is no more autobiographical than his other work. It treats, he continues, the self-destructiveness of a character who views herself as "pure victim." In this stream-of-consciousness drama, Quentin, the protagonist, subjects all of his values to scrutiny. His statement—"the bench was empty. No judge in sight. And all that remained was the endless argument with oneself, this pointless litigation of existence before any empty bench"—and the tone of the entire piece redefines Miller's conviction that one must come to terms with his own acts and values. As Quentin confronts his parents, wives, and the various situations of his recent and past life, Miller suggests that we all bear the mark of Cain; we are all born after the fall and are responsible for all our acts. After such knowledge *is* forgiveness: the play ends with the affirmative "Hello."

Themes of commitment, responsibility, and integrity continue in *Incident at Vichy*, where the aristocrat Von Berg (the mirror image of Quentin) transfers his own freedom to the Jewish Leduc and accepts his own death. Miller raises questions about sacrifice and guilt ("the soul's remorse for his own hostility"). The play investigates the need we all have for scapegoats and the suffering "other." "You must face your own complicity," he writes, "with ... your own humanity." One must accept not only his own evil (and goodness) but also the sacrifices and kindness of others.

The Price returns to two brothers, the poles of love and money, the sacrifices and selfishness of each, and the terrible lack of relationship that always existed between the two—the terrible "price" that rivalry and lovelessness exact. Unlike Von Berg in *Incident*, the brothers have given nothing, and they therefore have nothing. Gregory Solomon, the antiques dealer, teaches that one must give without expecting repayment; he understands the gratuitousness of love. One must embrace community while realizing the utter isolation that is finally the human condition.

Although in 1972 Miller said that his plays were becoming more mythical, *The Creation of the World and Other Business* (about God's conflict with Lucifer over the behavior of Adam and Eve, and Cain and Abel) is an existential query into the nature of individual responsibility. Miller's most recent works have been less than successful. *The American Clock* is a series of vignettes in which the fate of a Depression family—the not particularly heroic Baums—is intertwined with that of a remarkably heroic nation during the 1930's. An overly ambitious effort, Miller describes it "as though the whole country were really the setting"; it was intended, he explains, to be "a mural for the theater inspired by Studs Terkel's *Hard Times*." The two minidramas of *Two-Way Mirror*, on the other hand, are extremely modest, although they are intended as "passionate voyages through the masks of [agonizing] illusion." *Elegy for a Lady* focuses on a middle-aged man who, while selecting a gift for his dying mistress, indulges in a conversation on the pain of love with the boutique proprietress. In *Some Kind of Love Story* a detective visits an old girlfriend, now a call girl, who may be the key figure in clearing a murder suspect. Although these plays lack the intense characterizations through which Miller typically raises moral and psychological issues, his goal remains steadfast: "Without the belief that man has a choice and without his willingness to take responsibility for that choice, you are unable to rely on conscientious objections to anything. I've been writing about it for a long time."

—Lois Gordon

MILLER, Jason. American. Born John Miller in Long Island City, New York, 22 April 1939. Educated at St. Patrick's High School, Scranton, Pennsylvania; Scranton University, B.A. 1961; Catholic University, Washington, D.C., 1962–63. Married Linda Gleason in 1963 (divorced 1973); one daughter and two sons. Stage and film actor. Recipient: New York Drama Critics Circle award, 1972; Tony award, 1973; Pulitzer Prize, 1973. Address: c/o Screen Actors Guild, 7750 Sunset Boulevard, Los Angeles, California 90046, U.S.A.

PUBLICATIONS

Plays

Three One-Act Plays: Lou Gehrig Did Not Die of Cancer, It's a Sin to Tell a Lie, The Circus Lady (produced New York, 1970). New York, Dramatists Play Service, 1972.

Nobody Hears a Broken Drum (produced New York, 1970). New York, Dramatists Play Service, 1971.

That Championship Season (produced New York, 1972; London, 1974). New York, Atheneum, and London, Davis Poynter, 1972.

Screenplay: *That Championship Season*, 1982.

Television Play: *Reward*, 1980.

Verse

Stone Step. New York, Jadis Yumi, 1968.

*

Theatrical Activities:
Director: **Film**—*That Championship Season*, 1982.
Actor: **Plays**—Champlain Shakespeare Festival, Vermont; Cincinnati Shakespeare Festival; New York Shakespeare Festival; Edmund in *Long Day's Journey into Night* by O'Neill; Tom in *The Glass Menagerie* by Tennessee Williams; Pip in *Pequod* by Roy S. Richardson, New York, 1969; Poker Player in *The Odd Couple* by Neil Simon, Fort Worth, Texas, 1970; Assistant in *The Happiness Cage* by Dennis J. Reardon, New York, 1970; Rogoshin in *Subject to Fits* by Robert Montgomery, New York, 1971; in *Juno and the Paycock* by O'Casey, Washington, D.C., 1971. **Films**—*The Exorcist*, 1972; *The Nickel Ride*, 1975; *The Devil's Advocate*, 1977; *Marilyn—The Untold Story*, 1980; *Twinkle, Twinkle Killer Kane* (*The Ninth Configuration*), 1980; *Monsignor*, 1982; *Toy Soldiers*, 1984. **Television**—*A Home of Our Own*, 1975; *F. Scott Fitzgerald in Hollywood*, 1976; *The Dain Curse*, 1978; *Vampire*, 1979; *The Henderson Monster*, 1980; *The Best Little Girl in the World*, 1981; *A Touch of Scandal*, 1984.

* * *

Jason Miller's *That Championship Season* is a solid, vibrant play. The solidity comes in part from the familiar structure of the play—too familiar, at points—but Miller's freshness of detail saves the evening.

The event that occasions the drama has been used a lot: it is a reunion, in this case of four members of a champion high-school basketball team of twenty years ago. The fifth man on stage is the now-retired coach who has taught them that winning is all that counts—in basketball and in life. As Walter Kerr pointed out, the set itself is familiar—limp lace curtains and a steep staircase that recalls the conventional naturalism of William Inge's *The Dark at the Top of the Stairs*.

In fact, the experienced play-goer knows within two minutes what the arc of things will be: the men have come together to celebrate and live again their triumph, but before the night is out it will be revealed how everything has gone rotten somehow. And so it turns out. One of the players is now mayor of the small Pennsylvania town, and he is proud of it. But underneath he is a loser—and indeed it is obvious he will be thrown out of the forthcoming election.

Another team-mate has been his chief financial backer—a man made rich through the strip-mining that ecologists condemn. But now he sees the mayor will lose, so he wants to shift his backing to another candidate.

A third player is now a school principal who wants to be superintendent. When the mayor tells him that he can't back him because it will hurt his own candidacy, the superintendent angrily blurts out that the strip-miner is sleeping with the mayor's wife, and he says he'll tell the whole town if they don't support him. But he is a mediocrity; he knows it, his own young son knows it, and everyone on stage knows it. The coach calls his bluff, knowing he is even too much of a mediocrity to do something so substantial as tell the town about the mayor's wife.

The fourth player is now an alcoholic but he nevertheless sees things more clearly than the rest. It is he who brings up Martin. In baskbetball there are five players: Martin was the fifth, and at first he is mourned as if dead. Ultimately it is revealed that he has simply gone away, turning his back on the coach and his dogmas. It was Martin who, at the coach's direction, broke the ribs of the "nigger" who was the star of the other team, and it's clear that's the only reason our boys won.

The play uncovers the dark underside of that old triumph and the abject failure beneath any gloss of current success. The coach is shown to be a bigot, a right-wing supporter of Joe McCarthy, a champion of the ugly ethic that to win is to be good.

So the route of the play is familiar and so are the figures. But the figures are not cardboard—Miller fills in their dimension with the rich detail of an orthodox novelist. And the play is not without surprises. In particular it is verbally surprising. Lines are fresh and newly honed. And the humor is painfully superb. Cautioning the mayor not to exploit the fact of his handicapped child, the alcoholic says, "You lose the mongoloid vote right there." And he denies he has a liquor problem: "I can get all I want."

Miller's limitation, at least in this play, is his conventionality, his predictability. But many regard the theatrical experimentation on the American scene as unrewarding, and other traditionalists have lost the vitality that Miller found in this play. It's a somber comment on American theatre that one of the most promising plays of the early 1970's could have been written in the early 1950's.

—Thomas J. McCormack

MILLER, Susan. American. Born in Philadelphia, Pennsylvania, 6 April 1944. Educated at Pennsylvania State University, University Park, B.A. 1965; Bucknell University, Lewisburg, Pennsylvania, M.A. 1970. Instructor in English, Pennsylvania State University, 1969–73; Lecturer in Playwriting, University of California, Los Angeles, 1975–76; playwright-in-residence, Mark Taper Forum Theatre, Los Angeles, 1975. Recipient: Rockefeller grant, 1975; National Endowment for the Arts grant, 1976; Obie award, 1979. Agent: Flora Roberts Inc., 157 West 57th Street, New York, New York 10019, U.S.A.

PUBLICATIONS

Plays

No One Is Exactly 23 (produced University Park, Pennsylvania). Published in *Pyramid 1* (Belmont, Massachusetts), 1968.
Daddy, and A Commotion of Zebras (produced New York, 1970).
Silverstein & Co. (produced New York, 1972).
Confessions of a Female Disorder (produced Hartford, Connecticut, 1973). Published in *Gay Plays*, edited by William M. Hoffman, New York, Avon, 1979.
Denim Lecture (produced Los Angeles, 1974).
Flux (produced New York, 1975; London, 1976; revised version produced New York, 1977).
Cross Country (produced Los Angeles, 1976; New York, 1977). Published in *West Coast Plays* (Berkeley, California), 1978.
Nasty Rumors and Final Remarks (produced New York, 1979).
Arts and Leisure (produced Los Angeles, 1985).

Television Plays: *Home Movie* (*Family* series); *One for the Money, Two for the Show*, with Nedra Deen; *A Whale for the Killing; Visions* series.

*   *   *

With the exception of *Arts and Leisure*, Susan Miller's plays deal with a woman's struggle to find her own definition in contemporary society. This process requires an examination, and often a repudiation, of society's traditional rules and role models for women. Whether conforming to or breaking these rules, Miller's protagonists come to learn both the value of contradiction and difference and the necessity for remaining in the world of work and societal demands; Miller's women do not "drop out," either in thematic or stylistic terms. The conflict that results from this search for a sense of self within a system that often fosters repressive assumptions about gender provides the dramatic movement of Miller's work. Structurally, Miller's work is at its most complex when the plays weave story lines in and out of chronological sequence and naturalistic scenes are juxtaposed with stylized or symbolic ones, as a confusion in time or location parallels the protagonist's own state.

In *Nasty Rumors and Final Remarks*, Raleigh, a woman of 38, suffers a cerebral hemorrhage. The people who have been most important in her life gather at the hospital, to wait for her death. Raleigh, though installed in an intensive care unit (offstage), moves in and out of retrospective and present action, responding to the group in the waiting room or talking directly to the audience. This movement between flashback and present moment results in a complex layering of character histories upon the simple story of Raleigh's accident and the reactions of those close to her. Raleigh emerges as a strong yet difficult woman, very much in a class with Miller's other protagonists: women who begin their adult lives largely defined by traditional female roles and, after some pain and disillusionment at finding these roles antithetical to both creativity and ambition, rebel, emerging finally as independent women. Their rebellion, the source of dramatic tension in the plays, may involve leaving a marriage, taking a lover, forming a lesbian bond, starting a new career, beginning to write.

Confessions of a Female Disorder follows Ronnie from puberty through college and her subsequent marriage. A chorus of cheerleaders and lettermen (later cocktail party guests) moves between or comments upon the narrative scenes. In college Ronnie discovers an odd and disconcerting closeness with her friend Coop. She marries too early; she notices the unhappy women around her as she confronts her own inability to write. The play indicts a culture (and a class) for its eagerness to reinforce sexual stereotypes.

At the beginning of *Cross Country*, Perry, a writer and teacher, is preparing to leave her husband and young son and move to Los Angeles to devote herself to her writing. In a series of scenes that move between third-person narration and dialogue, and between present tense and past, Perry plays out her affair with a young female student and her disappointment with and ultimate understanding of her marriage. She settles in Los Angeles, her son comes to live with her, she battles the crassness of the entertainment industry; the play ends as she begins rehearsals for her new play. As *Cross Country* was developed in workshops (Mark Taper Forum, Los Angeles, and Women's Interart Theatre, New York), the sections in narrative prose were handled by distributing the lines among the four actors. This stylization of the narrative lends a distanced and fragmented quality to the play, as characters comment on their own actions and those of others.

Flux concerns a teacher's rite of passage from a position of naive optimism regarding the student-teacher transaction, through disappointment and pain when that transaction backfires, to a greater self-awareness of her role as teacher and woman. Classroom scenes at times transform into non-realistic, movement-and-sound tableaux as students and an ex-professor turned carnival hustler/philosopher confront the teacher.

Finally, with *Arts and Leisure* Miller breaks from her dramatic pattern somewhat; she moves the focus away from a single female protagonist and centers the play in a naturalistic time progression. An English professor and his girlfriend, a graduate student, hold J.D. Salinger hostage in order to force the release of the writings that he (so the professor believes) has been harboring for the last 15 years. The professor needs to prove (mostly to himself, of course) that the great author can still be admired, that he remains a hero because he has not willfully stopped producing. The play moves in scenes of confrontation and revelation as each character learns something about his or her attachment to an art, a passion, a goal.

—Kathleen Dimmick

MILNER, Ron(ald). American. Born in Detroit, Michigan, 29 May 1938. Educated at Northeastern High School, Detroit; Highland Park Junior College, Detroit; Detroit Institute of Technology; Columbia University, New York. Writer-in-residence, Lincoln University, Pennsylvania, 1966–67; taught at Michigan State University, East Lansing, 1971–72. Founding director, Spirit of Shango theatre company, and Langston Hughes Theatre, Detroit. Recipient: John Hay Whitney fellowship, 1962; Rockefeller grant, 1965. Address: c/o Crossroads Theatre Company, 320 Memorial Parkway, New Brunswick, New Jersey 08901, U.S.A.

PUBLICATIONS

Plays

Who's Got His Own (produced New York, 1966). Published in *Black Drama Anthology*, edited by Milner and Woodie King, New York, New American Library, 1971.

The Monster (produced Chicago, 1969). Published in *Drama Review* (New York), Summer 1968.

The Warning: A Theme for Linda (produced New York, 1969). Published in *A Black Quartet: Four New Black Plays*, New York, New American Library, 1970.

(M)Ego and the Green Ball of Freedom (produced Detroit, 1971). Published in *Black World* (Chicago), April 1971.

What the Wine-Sellers Buy (produced Los Angeles, 1973; New York, 1974). New York, French, 1974.

These Three (produced Detroit, 1974).

Season's Reasons (produced Detroit, 1976; New York, 1977).

Jazz Set, music by Max Roach (produced Los Angeles, 1979; New York, 1982).

Crack Steppin' (produced Detroit, 1981).

Roads of the Mountaintop (produced New Brunswick, New Jersey, 1986).

Other

Editor, with Woodie King, *Black Drama Anthology*. New York, New American Library, 1971.

* * *

Since the production of his first major play, *Who's Got His Own*, in 1966, Ron Milner has been one of the most articulate spokesmen for the Black Arts movement in America. His essays on black theater urge the instructional function of theater for black Americans: theatre is to reveal the historic and contemporary problems that face black people in the United States, and it is meant unabashedly to distinguish between constructive and destructive behavior. Milner's plays, which have often been termed "morality dramas," aptly illustrate and fulfill his aesthetics. Milner's writings in the 1970's stress the African origins of black American theater and culture but also argue that black American artists should illuminate and work in the cities and towns that hold the roots of their own lives. In the 1970's, following his own advice, Milner returned from New York to Detroit, the city of his youth, to initiate his own theater for his own community.

Who's Got His Own was the premiere production of the New Lafayette Theater, the house and company that became the central showcase in the late 1960's for new works of the Black Arts Movement. Like most of his plays, *Who's Got His Own* is set in Detroit and reveals the generational tensions within a family. The setting is a wake, just after the funeral for Tim Sr., the father of the family. The pressure of the context and of the first visit home in some years of Tim Jr. provokes a series of revelations of the truths each member of the family has hidden from others. Tim Jr., who at first appears to be a somewhat stereotypical angry young man on an adolescent quest for truth, initiates the confessions by asserting the family's hypocrisy. While they have been naming the virtues of the deceased father, Tim Jr. has been dwelling in shame at his memories of his father's demeaned and demeaning behavior. The testimonies that follow Tim's explosion suggest the rituals of a participatory church service. Confronted with the blame her children place on their father for their agonies, the mother of the family finally reveals the history behind her husband's apparent cowardice: as a child of eight, Tim Sr. had witnessed hooded white men castrate and murder his own father; a few days after the murder, the child had been forced to endure the same white men's protestations of sympathy for the family. This last revelation raises the possibilities for a reorientation of the family structure and of new points of view for both the members of the family and for us. Instead, the force of melodrama—present throughout the play—takes command. We are distracted from these central testimonies by the information that a man whom Tim Jr. thought he had killed had in fact only suffered a concussion. The play simply stops, and the sigh of relief on stage is neither aesthetically nor politically satisfying for those in the audience.

Milner's next play, *The Warning: A Theme for Linda*, is similar in both its strengths and its weaknesses to *Who's Got His Own*. Again, a series of interrelated personal confessions moves a family closer to each other and to some truth about itself, but, again, a too rapid and facile ending resolves the plot without fully acknowledging the questions raised by the play. *The Warning* is, however, more complex in its dramaturgical gestures and its vision of the larger society than *Who's Got His Own*: major characters in *The Warning* are first presented as Linda's dream visions, then appear within the conscious world of the play. And whereas *Who's Got His Own* labels the white man as the clear source of evil, without exploration of the nature of or counters to that evil, *The Warning* illuminates a black world in which conflicts, confusions, good, and evil all are contained within the world projected. In performance (initially in 1969 as part of *A Black Quartet* that included plays by Ben Caldwell, Bullins, and Baraka as well as Milner), *The Warning* moves powerfully through a series of small eruptions that engage us so thoroughly in the predominantly female world of the play that we have difficulty shaking ourselves loose from the theater.

Many of the same ambiguous issues that occur in Milner's earlier work are reflected transparently in his most controversial play, *What the Wine-Sellers Buy*. As in his other plays, Milner pays particular attention to the black women in the world he creates in *What the Wine-Sellers Buy*, but the attitude behind that attention is troubling. As critics have remarked, Milner repeatedly defines women characters by the men in their lives, and such definition is unavoidably clear in this play of Detroit black family life. Faced with a choice between the "easy" but corrupt role of a pimp and a struggle of indefinite duration to make a more challenging and dignified life for himself, Steve, the young male protagonist of *What the Wine-Sellers Buy*, finally decides to take the moral path and reject the temptations of hustling. The play argues persuasively that the *way* one tries to achieve one's dreams *does* matter; this is a world where morality can be described and where moral people can sustain themselves and be applauded.

Milner's more recent work, especially *Season's Reasons*, produced in Detroit by his own company, continues to affirm the possibilities of discovering new resources for a moral life. The theatrical and social vitality of black music and ritual, apparent in Milner's first plays, becomes emphatic in *Season's Reasons*. With this play, Milner takes still another step towards the goal of which he has repeatedly spoken; his aim is to make the black theater as organic in black American culture as has been the church, and to make theater organic, specifically in black terms. Increasingly, Milner sees music as both the metaphor and the best resource to achieve his goal. In a mid-1970's interview, Milner remarked, "When they took away the drum, we had to become our own drums." His continuing effort is to facilitate that process.

—Helene Keyssar

MINGHELLA, Anthony. British. Born in Ryde, Isle of Wight, 6 January 1954. Educated at the University of Hull, Yorkshire (Reckitt Travel Award), B.A. (honours) 1975. Lecturer in Drama, University of Hull, 1976–81. Recipient. London Theatre Critics award, 1984, 1986. Lives in London. Agent: Judy Daish Associates, 83 Eastbourne Mews, London W2 6LQ, England.

PUBLICATIONS

Plays

Mobius the Stripper, adaptation of the story by Gabriel Josipovici (also director: produced Hull, 1975).
Child's Play (also director: produced Hull, 1978).
Whale Music (also director: produced Hull, 1980; London, 1981). Included in *Whale Music and Other Plays*, 1987.
A Little Like Drowning (produced Hemel Hempstead, Hertfordshire, 1982; London, 1984). Included in *Whale Music and Other Plays*, 1987.
Two Planks and a Passion (produced Exeter, 1983; London, 1984). Included in *Whale Music and Other Plays*, 1987.
Love Bites (produced Derby, 1984).
Made in Bangkok (produced London, 1986). London, Methuen, 1986.
Whale Music and Other Plays. London, Methuen, 1987.

Television Plays: *Studio* series, 1983; *What If It's Raining?*, 1986; *Inspector Morse*, from a novel by Colin Dexter, 1987; *Storyteller* series, 1987 (USA).

Novel

On the Line (novelization of television series). London, Severn House, 1982.

*

Theatrical Activities:
Director: some of his own plays.

* * *

Anthony Minghella has emerged as one of the most consistently adventurous younger British dramatists of the 1980's. He is a writer refreshingly prepared to tackle a wide variety of subjects, and his plays have been marked by an unsentimental humanism and steadily growing technical confidence as he has moved from relatively small-scale work in studio and fringe theatres to wider exposure in the commercial sector.

Whale Music was an early indication of Minghella's original voice; with an all-female cast (Minghella has continued to write superb roles for actresses), it is structured round a diverse group of women waiting in a seaside town for a student friend to have her baby. While the play at times seems over-schematic and, in its succession of short scenes, at points jerkily constructed (the dissolving scenes worked much more surely in a later television version), it still creates a recognisable milieu with understated precision. Tender, ironic, and funny, it contains some memorable writing, particularly a long speech from the drifting Stella, giving room to the pregnant Caroline, savagely corrosive in its picture of the men she encounters in her one-night stands.

A Little Like Drowning is also written in a succession of short scenes, but here ambitiously spanning the years with its fulcrum in the break-up of an Anglo-Italian couple's marriage. Moving between the present on an English beach where the old Leonora recalls her life to her granddaughter, to her 1920's marriage to Alfredo in Italy and Alfredo's affair and later life in Dublin with Julia, the play seamlessly links time and space—a scene in 1939 with Alfredo packing to leave Leonora has both Leonora and Julia on stage, unaware of each other, the scene playing as if their dialogue is totally independent. Minghella continued to explore and celebrate his own Anglo-Italian inheritance, this time on a more epic scale, in *Love Bites*. The first act is set in wartime England, concentrating on two Italian-immigrant brothers, Angelo and Bruno, establishing themselves in the ice-cream business. Particularly impressive in this act is Minghella's handling of Angelo's affair with Elizabeth, a schoolteacher who becomes pregnant by him and to whose love he cannot finally respond; his suggestion of the curiously suspended quality of time during wartime is especially evocative. The second act leaps into the present, set in a convention hotel with Angelo about to be inaugurated as President of the Ice Cream Group of Great Britain. Minghella handles his large cast and canvas here with a sharp sense of focus, painting a vivid picture of the family's tribal relationships among the different generations. Bruno, in disappointed middle age, realises that he has let himself be trapped by the past but comes to realise in a powerfully written late scene that he and Angelo are essentially alike after all; in such scenes, Minghella's control of the play's changes of mood is continuously sure.

He moved completely away from such material in *Two Planks and a Passion*, set in late 14th-century York, where a troubled Richard II, his wife, and his friend the Earl of Oxford have escaped the court's pressures while the workmen's guilds prepare the Mystery Plays for the Feast of Corpus Christi. The play weaves several strands—the royals' mischievous exploitation of local bourgeois snobbery, rivalry among the artisans for patronage, and the workers rehearsing the Crucifixion—including some scenes of high comedy (especially that involving the King mercilessly teasing the fawning mayor during an innovative golf game), gradually drawing them together as the rehearsal becomes a moving performance witnessed by the royal party. The play may occasionally suffer from the lack of one truly dynamic central character but it remains an engaging, grave, and totally individual play.

Two Planks and a Passion gradually brought Minghella into the critical spotlight and a "Most Promising Playwright" award rightly came his way in 1984. That promise was amply confirmed by his first major West End play, *Made in Bangkok*. The play covers a group of English tourists and businessmen in Bangkok; often sharply and satirically funny, its moods keep boldly changing, emerging as a very dark comedy indeed about personal as well as cultural exploitation. He again created a challengingly complex leading female role in Frances, wife of a devious and finally frightening businessman, the only character not tainted by some form of exploitation, and he again demonstrates his ability to handle a multi-scene and intricately interlocking play with accomplished control. He also reaffirmed the theatre's ability to shock, to jolt an audience's moral attitude, as in the scene in which Edward, a repressed homosexual dentist, finally makes a sickeningly pathetic bid for the favours of the hotel-worker guide who has helped him. Minghella's dispassionate (and compassionate) handling of all his characters gave the play a depth of texture that made one intrigued to see in what direction he will travel next.

—Alan Strachan

MITCHELL, Adrian. British. Born in London, 24 October 1932. Educated at Greenways School; Dauntsey's School, West Lavington, Wiltshire; Christ Church, Oxford (editor, *Isis* magazine, 1954–55), 1952–55. Served in the British Army, 1951–52. Reporter, Oxford *Mail*, 1955–57, and *Evening Standard*, London, 1957–59; columnist and reviewer, *Daily Mail*, *Woman's Mirror*, the *Sun*, the *Sunday Times*, *Peace News*, *Black Dwarf*, and the *Guardian*, all London. Instructor, University of Iowa, Iowa City, 1963–64; Granada Fellow in the Arts, University of Lancaster, 1967–69; Fellow, Wesleyan University Center for the Humanities, Middletown, Connecticut, 1971–72; resident writer, Sherman Theatre, Cardiff, 1974–75; visiting writer, Billericay Comprehensive School, Essex, 1978–80; Judith E. Wilson Fellow, Cambridge University, 1980–81; resident writer, Unicorn Theatre for Young People, London, 1982–83. Recipient: Eric Gregory award, 1961; PEN prize for translation, 1966; Tokyo Festival award, for television, 1971. Agent: Fraser and Dunlop Scripts Ltd., 91 Regent Street, London W1R 8RU, England.

PUBLICATIONS

Plays

The Ledge (libretto), music by Richard Rodney Bennett (produced London, 1961).

The Persecution and Assassination of Jean-Paul Marat as Performed by the Inmates of the Asylum of Charenton under the Direction of the Marquis de Sade, adaptation of the play by Peter Weiss (produced London, 1964; New York, 1965). London, Calder, 1965; New York, Atheneum, 1966.

The Magic Flute, adaptation of the libretto by Schikaneder and Giesecke, music by Mozart (produced London, 1966).

US, with others (produced London, 1966). Published as *US: The Book of the Royal Shakespeare Production US/Vietnam/US/Experiment/Politics*..., London, Calder and Boyars, 1968; as *Tell Me Lies*, Indianapolis, Bobbs Merrill, 1968.

The Criminals, adaptation of a play by José Triana (produced London, 1967; New York, 1970).

Tyger: A Celebration of the Life and Work of William Blake, music by Mike Westbrook (produced London, 1971). London, Cape, 1971.

Tamburlane the Mad Hen (for children; produced Devon, 1971).

Man Friday, music by Mike Westbrook (televised 1972; produced London, 1973). With *Mind Your Head*, London, Eyre Methuen, 1974.

Mind Your Head, music by Andy Roberts (produced Liverpool, 1973; London, 1974). With *Man Friday*, London, Eyre Methuen, 1974.

The Government Inspector (as *The Inspector General*, produced Nottingham, 1974; revised version, as *The Government Inspector*, produced London, 1985). London, Methuen, 1985.

A Seventh Man, music by Dave Brown, adaptation of the book by John Berger and Jean Mohr (produced London, 1976).

White Suit Blues, music by Mike Westbrook, adaptation of works by Mark Twain (produced Nottingham and London, 1977).

Houdini: A Circus-Opera, music by Peter Schat (produced Amsterdam, 1977; Aspen, Colorado, 1980). Amsterdam, Clowns, 1977(?).

Uppendown Mooney (produced Welwyn Garden City, Hertfordshire, 1978).

The White Deer (for children), adaptation of the story by James Thurber (produced London, 1978).

Hoagy, Bix, and Wolfgang Beethoven Bunkhaus (produced London, 1979; Indianapolis, 1980).

The Mayor of Zalamea; or, The Best Garrotting Ever Done, adaptation of a play by Calderón (produced London, 1981). Edinburgh, Salamander Press, 1981.
Mowgli's Jungle, adaptation of *The Jungle Book* by Kipling (pantomime; produced Manchester, 1981).
You Must Believe All This (for children), adaptation of "Holiday Romance" by Dickens, music by Nick Bicât and Andrew Dickson (televised 1981). London, Thames Television-Methuen, 1981.
The Wild Animal Song Contest (for children; produced London, 1982).
Life's a Dream, with John Barton, adaptation of a play by Calderón (produced Stratford-on-Avon, 1983; London, 1984).
A Child's Christmas in Wales, with Jeremy Brooks, adaptation of the work by Dylan Thomas (produced Cleveland, 1983).
The Great Theatre of the World, adaptation of a play by Calderón (produced Oxford, 1984).
C'mon Everybody (produced London, 1984).
Animal Farm (lyrics only), book by Peter Hall, music by Richard Peaslee, adaptation of the novel by George Orwell (for children; produced London, 1984; Baltimore, 1986). London, Methuen, 1985.
The Tragedy of King Real (screenplay), in *Peace Plays 1*, edited by Stephen Lowe. London, Methuen, 1985.
Satie Day/Night (produced London, 1986).
The Pied Piper (for children), music by Dominic Muldowney (produced London, 1986).
Mirandolina, adaptation of a play by Goldoni (produced Bristol, 1987).

Screenplays: *Marat/Sade*, 1966; *Tell Me Lies* (lyrics only), 1968; *The Body* (commentary), 1969; *Man Friday*, 1976; *The Tragedy of King Real*, 1983.

Radio Play: *The Island* (libretto), music by William Russo, 1963.

Television Plays: *Animals Can't Laugh*, 1961; *Alive and Kicking*, 1971; *William Blake* (documentary), 1971; *Man Friday*, 1972; *Somebody Down There Is Crying*, 1974; *Daft As a Brush*, 1975; *The Fine Art of Bubble Blowing*, 1975; *Silver Giant, Wooden Dwarf*, 1975; *Glad Day*, music by Mike Westbrook, 1979; *You Must Believe All This*, 1981; *Juno and Avos*, from libretto by Andrei Voznesensky, music by Alexei Rybnikov, 1983.

Initiated and helped write student shows: *Bradford Walk*, Bradford College of Art; *The Hotpot Saga*, *The Neurovision Song Contest*, and *Lash Me to the Mast*, University of Lancaster; *Move Over Jehovah*, National Association of Mental Health; *Poetry Circus*, Wesleyan University; *Mass Media Mash* and *Mud Fair*, Dartington College of the Arts, 1976 and 1977.

Novels

If You See Me Comin'. London, Cape, 1962; New York, Macmillan, 1963.
The Bodyguard. London, Cape, 1970; New York, Doubleday, 1971.
Wartime. London, Cape, 1973.
Man Friday. London, Futura, 1975.

Verse

(*Poems*). Oxford, Fantasy Press, 1955.
Poems. London, Cape, 1964.
Peace Is Milk. London, Peace News, 1966.
Out Loud. London, Cape Goliard Press, and New York, Grossman, 1968; revised edition, as *The Annotated Out Loud*, London, Writers and Readers, 1976.
Ride the Nightmare: Verse and Prose. London, Cape, 1971.
Cease-Fire. London, Medical Aid Committee for Vietnam, 1973.
Penguin Modern Poets 22, with John Fuller and Peter Levi. London, Penguin, 1973.
The Apeman Cometh. London, Cape, 1975.
For Beauty Douglas: Collected Poems 1953–1979. London, Allison and Busby, 1982.
Nothingmas Day (for children). London, Allison and Busby, 1984.
On the Beach at Cambridge: New Poems. London, Allison and Busby, 1984.

Recording: *Poems*, with Stevie Smith, Argo, 1974.

Other

Naked In Cheltenham (miscellany). Cheltenham, Gastoday, 1978.
The Adventures of Baron Munchausen (for children). London, Walker, 1985.
The Baron Rides Out (for children). London, Walker, and New York, Philomel, 1985.
The Baron on the Island of Cheese (for children). London, Walker, and New York, Philomel, 1986.
Leonardo, The Lion from Nowhere (for children). London, Deutsch, 1986.

Editor, with Richard Selig, *Oxford Poetry 1955*. Oxford, Fantasy Press, 1955.
Editor, *Jump, My Brothers, Jump: Poems from Prison*, by Tim Daly. London, Freedom Press, 1970.

Translator, with Joan Jara, *Victor Jara: His Life and Songs*. London, Hamish Hamilton, 1976.

*

Theatrical Activities:
Actor: **Play**—*C'mon Everybody*, London, 1984.

* * *

"A truthful colour supplement. As you turn the pages, conflicting images hit you." Adrian Mitchell's description of his stage show *Mind Your Head* may to some extent be applied to all his dramatic creations. Impossible to pigeon-hole into any one form, they mingle genres indiscriminately, juxtaposing pathos with horror and ribald humour. Instead of adhering to the norms of dramatic artifice, Mitchell appears to seize the chaos and disturbance of modern life and transfer it whole to the stage. Constants of his work are its anarchic individualism and the opposition of its author to establishment mores.

Irony lies at the root of Mitchell's dilemma. A notable "performance" poet, adept in a structured, concentrated medium, he nevertheless strives continually to dispense with the formal restraints of language. Equally, as a playwright, he attempts to eschew established theatrical conventions. While the best of his lyrics impress with their bite and precision, his worst writing betrays a self-indulgent transience. Overall, Mitchell's work recalls the 1960's and its legacy of protest, which had a profound influence on his thinking. Together with his contemporary Christopher Logue, he featured prominently in anti-Vietnam War demonstrations, taking part in the famous public poetry readings and contributing to the radical stage show *US*.

All the same, this aspect of Mitchell's writing may be overstressed. His plays are perhaps more traditional and less orthodox than they appear at first glance. Centuries ago, Aristophanes combined fantasy, social comment, satire, and personal invective against establishment figures, the action interspersed with song and dance routines. In much the same way, Mitchell's dramas blend the 1960's "happening" with elements of pantomime and old-time music hall, their seemingly random progress broken by songs and comic patter from various members of the cast. *Mind Your Head* typifies this approach, a surreal revamping of the Hamlet legend, built around the passengers and crew of a London bus. Mitchell allows his humour a free rein, using parodies of comic and pop song styles for some of the key passages—Hamlet's Soliloquy, for example, is performed as a Frankie Howerd monologue—and bestowing the names of jazz musicians on his characters. The pantomime atmosphere of the show, with its songs and jokes, provides for audience participation, which accords with Mitchell's "performance" style. A similar work is *Tyger*, where scenes from the daily life of the poet William Blake are expanded to include a fantasy moon-voyage, and several establishment "names" are mercilessly caricatured in song-and-dance form. Mitchell's affinity with Blake is spiritual rather than stylistic, and he is able to evoke the nature of the man by judicious quotation, while retaining his own mixed-genre method of presentation.

Mitchell's television plays tend to show more formal organization than his stage dramas. *Glad Day* is an exception, another Blake tribute where Mitchell manages to transfer some of the spontaneous energy of *Tyger* to the small screen. Like several of Mitchell's dramas, *Glad Day* involved the close co-operation of Mike Westbrook, whose musical accompaniments gave an added power to Blake's poetry, not least in the memorable "Song of the Slave" whose lyrics are intensified by the jazz arrangement. More typical of the television plays is *Man Friday*, a significant work which Mitchell later adapted for the stage and as a novel. It embodies many of Mitchell's most profound beliefs on the theory of white supremacy, which he contrasts with the foundations of so-called "primitive" societies. In a series of dialogues between Crusoe and the "savage" Friday, Mitchell adroitly ridicules not only the white man's "civilizing" mission, but also popular concepts of nationalism, crime and punishment, and property ownership. The stage version, which allows for more audience interaction, is a strong work, but the original television play is the more enduring. Ironically, as with other Mitchell creations, its organized structure ensures its success.

The throwaway "instant" quality of some of Mitchell's writing, his ability to create for specific occasions, may perhaps explain his skill in adapting the work of other writers. His earliest success in this field came in the 1960's, with his verse translation of Weiss's *Marat/Sade*, whose blend of social comment and gallows humour evidently appealed to him. Since then, he has produced versions of works by Dickens, Gogol, and more recently Calderón and Goldoni. *You Must Believe All This*, taken from Dickens, shows Mitchell to be an able writer for children, for whom audience participation is a natural response. Mitchell fractures the originals to obtain his desired result, altering language and adding or deleting scenes, often to good effect. His adaptation of Gogol's *The Government Inspector* inserts the famous "troika" scene and speech from *Dead Souls*, and provides Khlestakov with a startling airborne departure, both of which work dramatically and are in keeping with the lurking unease that underlies this particular "comedy." Similarly, his versions of Calderón's *Life's a Dream* and *The Mayor of Zalamea* break with the fluency of the Spanish originals in favour of a popular, slangy English verse-form which has greater impact than a strict translation. Calderón's exploration of the major human themes, his matching of sentiment with grim humour, is clearly to Mitchell's taste, and thus far the results have been interesting. This skill in adaptation is far from the least of Mitchell's talents, and his efforts in this field deserve comparison with his original plays.

—Geoff Sadler

MITCHELL, (Charles) Julian (Humphrey). British. Born in Epping, Essex, 1 May 1935. Educated at Winchester College, 1948–53; Wadham College, Oxford, B.A. 1958; St. Antony's College, Oxford, M.A. 1962. Served in the Royal Naval Volunteer Reserve, 1953–55: Midshipman. Member, Arts Council Literature Panel, 1966–69; formerly, Governor, Chelsea School of Art, London. Recipient: Harkness fellowship, 1959; Rhys Memorial Prize, 1965; Maugham Award, 1966; International Critics Prize, for television play, 1977; Christopher Award, for television play, 1977 (USA); Florio Prize, for translation, 1980; Society of West End Theatre award, 1982. Agent: A.D. Peters Ltd., 10 Buckingham Street, London WC2N 6BU, England. Address: 2 Castle Rise, Llanvaches, Newport, Gwent NP6 3BS, Wales.

PUBLICATIONS

Plays

A Heritage and Its History, adaptation of the novel by Ivy Compton-Burnett (produced London, 1965). London, Evans, 1966.

A Family and a Fortune, adaptation of the novel by Ivy Compton-Burnett (produced Guildford, Surrey, 1966; Seattle, 1974; London, 1975). London, French, 1976.

Shadow in the Sun (televised 1971). Published in *Elizabeth R*, edited by J.C. Trewin, London, Elek, 1972.

Half-Life (produced London, 1977; New York, 1981). London, Heinemann, 1977.

Henry IV, adaptation of the play by Pirandello. London, Eyre Methuen, 1979.

The Enemy Within (produced Leatherhead, Surrey, 1980).

Another Country (produced London, 1981; New Haven, Connecticut, 1983). Ambergate, Derbyshire, Amber Lane Press, 1982; New York, Limelight, 1984.

Francis (produced London, 1983). Oxford, Amber Lane Press, 1984.

After Aida; or, Verdi's Messiah (produced London, 1986). Oxford, Amber Lane Press, 1986.

The Evils of Tobacco, adaptation of a work by Chekhov, translated by Ronald Hingley (produced London, 1987).

Screenplays: *Arabesque*, with Stanley Price and Pierre Marton, 1966; *Another Country*, 1984.

Radio Documentary: *Life and Deaths of Dr. John Donne*, 1972.

Television Plays: *Persuasion*, from the novel by Jane Austen, 1971; *Shadow in the Sun*, 1971; *The Man Who Never Was*, 1972; *A Perfect Day*, 1972; *Fly in the Ointment*, 1972; *A Question of Degree*, 1972; *The Alien Corn*, from story by W. Somerset Maugham, 1972; *Rust*, 1973; *Jennie*, 1974; *Abide with Me*, from the book *A Child in the Forest* by Winifred Foley, 1976; *Staying On*, from the novel by Paul Scott, 1980; *The Good Soldier*, from the novel by Ford Madox Ford, 1981; *The Weather in the Streets*, from the novel by Rosamond Lehmann, 1984; and other adaptations.

Novels

Imaginary Toys. London, Hutchinson, 1961.
A Disturbing Influence. London, Hutchinson, 1962.
As Far as You Can Go. London, Constable, 1963.
The White Father. London, Constable, 1964; New York, Farrar Straus, 1965.
A Circle of Friends. London, Constable, 1966; New York, McGraw Hill, 1967.
The Undiscovered Country. London, Constable, 1968; New York, Grove Press, 1970.

Short Stories

Introduction, with others. London, Faber, 1960.

Other

Truth and Fiction (lecture). London, Covent Garden Press, 1972.
Jennie, Lady Randolph Churchill: A Portrait with Letters, with Peregrine Churchill. London, Collins, 1974; New York, St. Martin's Press, 1975.

Editor, with others, *Light Blue, Dark Blue: An Anthology of Recent Writing from Oxford and Cambridge Universities*. London, Macdonald, 1960.

* * *

Julian Mitchell's success as a playwright makes nonsense of claims for the death of the well-made play. He is a skilful craftsman whose work fits well into a British theatrical tradition as defined by, say, Terence Rattigan. Dialogue is all in his work, and the plays offer audiences an invitation into a world of polite discourse in which if voices are occasionally raised there is always someone present to push the argument forward into its next phase. He is not an innovative writer but he is always a polished one, as might be expected from someone who came late to the stage after an extensive literary apprenticeship. Mitchell's reputation as a writer in the 1960's rested solely on his activities as a novelist. The 1970's saw him established as a regular writer and adaptor for television—including dramatisations of Austen's *Persuasion*, Paul Scott's *Staying On*, and Ford Madox Ford's *The Good Soldier*, as well as a contribution to the *Elizabeth R* series—and it is only comparatively recently that he has begun to receive serious attention as a stage dramatist. Indeed, two of his earliest stage plays, *A Heritage and Its History* and *A Family and a Fortune*, were both adapted from novels by Ivy Compton-Burnett; and it is always apparent that he writes as a novelist converted to the stage.

His first novel was compared by one critic with the work of Aldous Huxley, and his plays all have a dedicated commitment to a series of theatrical debates that makes the comparison only too inviting. At worst the characters serve as convenient mouth-pieces for opposing views—in *Half-Life*, for instance, that most predictable of all West End formats, a country-house weekend, is the venue for a political discussion with an assorted bunch of over-articulate people, and there is scarcely any sense of theatricality about the events depicted. All is wit and verbal swordplay. But when Mitchell is at his best the debate is more open, and nowhere more so than in his most successful play to date, *Another Country*.

In *Another Country* Mitchell offers one of many recent analyses of the "betrayal" of their class by the Cambridge Communists of the 1930's. What makes his account interesting is that he transfers the action back to the penultimate year of their public-schooldays, placing the thoughts of the pro-Stalinist Judd and the flamboyantly gay Bennett (Guy Burgess in a thin disguise, as is made explicit in the film version) in the context of that institution which is intended to mould them for their future roles as statesmen and administrators. The familiar use of the school as metaphor here of the state, not of the country at large but of its ruling class, allows Mitchell to show how an essentially apolitical Bennett might be led into the world of espionage both as a reaction to the brutal punishing of his sexual appetites by an institution which serves only to heighten their appeal; and as an extension of the need to be continually in disguise, leading a double life, which he sees as his fate.

The economic need to restrict the size of the cast (although the play eventually transferred to the West End it started its life at the Greenwich Theatre) does much to increase the sense of enclosure, of claustrophobia, that confronts any boy who cannot, or will not, fit into the system ready-created for him. Bennett actually spends a great deal of time in the play acknowledging the attention of his off-stage and never-seen young lover and peering through binoculars at what is happening outside the particular room he is in—including the early sighting of the removal of the body of a boy who has hanged himself in the bell tower, a victim of the sexual double-standards of the school.

After Aida offers a similarly enclosed stage, in this instance to consider the events leading up to Verdi's agreement to compose *Otello*. It is difficult not to compare this play with Peter Shaffer's *Amadeus*, but it stands up well enough to the exercise, being a far less pretentious re-animation of musical history. A preoccupation with the past is also evident in the previous play, *Francis*, which takes a long sweep through the life of St. Francis and his attempts to hang onto his ideal of poverty in the face of pressure from both the established church and his increasingly wealthy new order. As a character, Francis is Mitchell's most successful creation, and more sense of internal conflict is apparent than in most of his protagonists, who are allowed to dominate the action simply by the superiority of their wit and rhetoric. Francis's attempt to relive the spartan life of his Christ unites in him the rebellious instincts of Bennett with the puritan discipline of Judd in *Another Country*, and here the corrupt oppression of church and papacy takes the place of the school. As in all Mitchell's plays, the voice of the rebel is allowed a place—as it is with the young Prue Hoggart in *Half-Life*—but the resolution of the plays, having suggested a plausible reason for the rebellion, is always to suggest the impossibility of real change.

History, for Mitchell, teaches a lesson of conflict in which the terms of reference remain essentially unchanged. In all his plays there is little sense of new ground being broken, either theatrically or intellectually, but if the mainstream is to continue to demand a steady diet of well-made plays then at least there is always evidence of an articulate intelligence behind Mitchell's work; and that is certainly to be welcomed in the increasingly dull world of contemporary West End theatre.

—John Bull

MITCHELL, Loften. American. Born in Columbus, North Carolina, 15 April 1919. Educated at De Witt Clinton High School, Bronx, New York, graduated 1937; City College, New York, 1937–38; Talladega College, Alabama, B.A. in sociology 1943; Columbia University, New York, 1947–51, M.A. Served in the United States Naval Reserve, 1944–45: Seaman Second Class. Married Helen Marsh in 1948; two sons. Actor, stage manager, and press agent, 115th Street People's Theatre and Harlem Showcase, New York, 1946–52; social worker, with Gypsy families, 1947–58, and in Day Care Center Program for Older Persons, 1959–66, Department of Welfare, New York; Professor of Afro-American Studies and Theatre, State University of New York, Binghamton, 1971–85, now Professor Emeritus. Editor, NAACP *Freedom Journal*, 1964. Recipient: Guggenheim fellowship, 1958; Rockefeller grant, 1961; Harlem Cultural Council award, 1969; State University of New York Research Foundation award, 1974; Audelco award, 1979. Address: 15 McNamara Avenue, Binghamton, New York 13903, U.S.A.

PUBLICATIONS

Plays

Shattered Dreams (produced New York, 1938).
Blood in the Night (produced New York, 1946).
The Bancroft Dynasty (produced New York, 1948).
The Cellar (produced New York, 1952).
A Land Beyond the River (produced New York, 1957). Cody, Wyoming, Pioneer Drama Service, 1963.
The Phonograph (produced New York, 1961).
Tell Pharaoh (televised 1963; produced New York, 1967). Published in *The Black Teacher and the Dramatic Arts*, edited by William R. Reardon and Thomas D. Pawley, Westport, Connecticut, Negro Universities Press, 1970.
Ballad for Bimshire, with Irving Burgie (produced New York, 1963; revised version produced Cleveland, 1964).
Ballad of the Winter Soldiers, with John Oliver Killens (produced New York, 1964).
Star of the Morning: Scenes in the Life of Bert Williams (produced Cleveland, 1965; revised version produced New York, 1985). Published in *Black Drama Anthology*, edited by Woodie King and Ron Milner, New York, New American Library, 1971.
The Final Solution to the Black Problem in the United States; or, The Fall of the American Empire (produced New York, 1970).
Sojourn to the South of the Wall (produced 1973; revised version produced 1983).
The Walls Came Tumbling Down, music by Willard Roosevelt (produced New York, 1976).
Bubbling Brown Sugar, concept by Rosetta LeNoire, music by Danny Holgate, Emme Kemp, and Lillian Lopez (produced New York, 1976; London, 1977).
Cartoons for a Lunch Hour, music by Rudy Stevenson (produced New York, 1978).
A Gypsy Girl (produced Pine Bluff, Arkansas, 1982).
Miss Waters, To You, concept by Rosetta LeNoire (produced New York, 1983).

Screenplays: *Young Man of Williamsburg*, 1954; *Integration: Report One*, 1960; *I'm Sorry*, 1965.

Radio Writing: *Tribute to C.C. Spaulding*, 1952; *Friendly Advisor* program, 1955; *The Later Years* program, 1959–62.

Television Play: *Tell Pharaoh*, 1963.

Novel

The Stubborn Old Lady Who Resisted Change. New York, Emerson Hall, 1973.

Other

Black Drama: The Story of the American Negro in the Theatre. New York, Hawthorn, 1967.

Editor, *Voices of the Black Theatre.* Clifton, New Jersey, James T. White, 1975.

*

Manuscript Collections: State University of New York, Binghamton; Boston University; Talladega College, Alabama; Schomburg Collection, New York.

Critical Studies: *Negro Playwrights in the American Theatre 1925–1959* by Doris E. Abramson, New York, Columbia University Press, 1969; article by Ja A. Jahannes, in *Afro-American Writers after 1955* edited by Thadious M. Davis and Trudier Harris, Detroit, Gale, 1985.

Theatrical Activities:
Actor: **Plays**—with the Progressive Dramatizers and the Rose McClendon Players, both New York; Victor in *Cocktails*, and Aaron in *Having Wonderful Time* by Arthur Kober, 1938; Angel in *The Black Messiah* by Denis Donoghue and James H. Dunmore, 1939.

* * *

For his work as a black theatre historian, the American theatre owes a great debt to Loften Mitchell. His books—*Black Drama* and *Voices of the Black Theatre*—and numerous essays contain invaluable information and insights on Afro-American contributions to the theatre. Mitchell's plays reflect his passionate interest in the black theatre and black American history in general. With few exceptions, his plays and librettos inform the audience of the tribulations and achievements of well known black entertainers and historical figures.

Black pride, unity, and perseverance during times of adversity form recurrent themes in Mitchell's plays. These concepts are often voiced in rhetorical discourses by characters drawn along simplistic, ideological lines. His protagonists based on historical individuals speak and act as though already aware of the significance of their achievements to future generations.

After the black characters have suffered in conflicts with external forces motivated by racial prejudice and self-interests, the plays end on a triumphant note as the blacks learn how to endure the hardships and, in some cases, prevail over their adversaries.

Tell Pharaoh surveys the history of black Americans; the characters speak of their illustrious African heritage, bitter experiences as slaves, and ongoing struggles for the same civil rights and opportunities enjoyed by white Americans. The drama identifies black American heroes and martyrs, and celebrates the contributions of blacks to various aspects of American life. As in most of his works, Mitchell includes a tribute to his beloved Harlem and uses music to set the mood and underscore the sentiments of the play. The concluding harangue against Pharaoh—a symbolic persecutor of blacks, Latins, Asians, Indians, and other groups—dates the work and typifies the rhetoric of the revolutionary activists of the 1960's.

Based on real events, *A Land Beyond the River* depicts the story of a rural, black South Carolina community which through the judicial system sought the right to send its children to any school receiving public funds. In Mitchell's dramatization, a sickly but courageous black woman—Martha Layne—proposes the law suit and her husband—Joseph—rallies the support of other black citizens and a sympathetic white physician. "Uncle Toms" and white bigots attempt to undermine their efforts. Intimidating threats and the burning of the Layne home aggravate Martha's precarious condition and result in her death. The events create dissension among the blacks and encourage most to accept a local court decision to provide a "separate, but equal" school for blacks. However, in a stirring speech punctuated with biblical references, Joseph contends that black children would not receive parity with whites through the ruling. Instead, he convinces his peers to appeal the case to a higher court in order to achieve their original objective of obtaining equal access to services and facilities enjoyed by white students. Despite the clichés and simplistic characterizations, the drama provides a moving historical portrait of valiant individuals bound by a common cause in the civil rights movement.

A more recent work—*Miss Waters, To You*—is based on the life of Ethel Waters. A series of scenes with musical numbers depict Waters's transition from a struggling 17-year-old divorcée to an accomplished actress and singer. The play includes appearances by such noted entertainers as Bessie Smith, Lena Horne, Duke Ellington, and Cab Calloway. These blacks provide each other with moral support and teach Waters how to endure the racial prejudice and indignities of their profession. However, such scenes weaken the credibility of the play as a true portrait of Waters's life. In fact, her animosity toward some black entertainers, such as Miss Horne, is quite well known. The drama also glosses over certain of Waters's ignoble traits which would place her in a less exalted light. As in his other tributes to black entertainers—*Bubbling Brown Sugar* and *Star of the Morning: Scenes in the Life of Bert Williams*—Mitchell chose to portray black role models of high esteem with few, if any, unadmirable attributes.

—Addell Austin

MOLLOY, M(ichael) J(oseph). Irish. Born in Milltown, County Galway, 3 March 1917. Educated at St. Jarlath's College and in a seminary for 4 years. Farmer, 1950–72. Recipient: Irish Arts Council award, 1972. Address: Milltown, Tuam, County Galway, Ireland.

PUBLICATIONS

Plays

Old Road (produced Dublin, 1943). Dublin, Progress House, 1961.

The Visiting House (produced Dublin, 1946). Published in *Seven Irish Plays 1946–1964*, edited by Robert Hogan, Minneapolis, University of Minnesota Press, 1967.

The King of Friday's Men (produced Dublin, 1948; London, 1949; New York, 1951). Dublin, Duffy, 1954; included in *Three Plays*, 1975.

The Wood of the Whispering (produced Dublin, 1953; London, 1963; New York, 1975). Dublin, Progress House, 1961; included in *Three Plays*, 1975.

The Paddy Pedlar (produced Dublin, 1953). Dublin, Duffy, 1954; included in *Three Plays*, 1975.

The Will and the Way (produced Dublin, 1955). Dublin, Bourke, 1957.

A Right Rose Tree (produced Dublin, 1958).

Daughter from over the Water (produced 1962; produced Dublin, 1964). Dublin, Progress House, 1963.

The Wooing of Duvesa (produced Dublin, 1964).

The Bitter Pill, in *Prizewinning Plays of 1964*. Dublin, Progress House, 1965.

Three Plays. Newark, Delaware, Proscenium Press, 1975.

Petticoat Loose (produced Dublin, 1979). Newark, Delaware, Proscenium Press, 1982.

The Bachelor's Daughter (produced Dublin, 1985).

* * *

M. J. Molloy may be Ireland's most genuine folk-dramatist. He is certainly the most distinguished contributor to this genre since Synge. Unlike Synge, who was a stranger to rural Ireland and had to be educated about its culture, Molloy is a native of County Galway and still lives there, in simple circumstances very like those he describes in his plays. Most of his plays have been produced either at the Abbey Theatre or by the Abbey Theatre Company. They represent a 45-year effort to provide for the Irish theater the sort of play Yeats said was needed to make Irish people conscious of their own history. Molloy has singlemindedly written plays which deal with the experience of the Irish countryman. A broadly educated man himself, he has witnessed and understood the changes which in the past 40 years have moved rural Ireland away from what Molloy regards as its feudal traditions and toward a society less certain of its values and more vulnerable to the exploitation of its land and its people.

In all of Molloy's plays there is nostalgia for a time when men had a proper regard for each other and for the land, a time when depopulation had not reduced rural Ireland to a gaggle of testy and self-righteous bachelors, a time before technology and an unscrupulous middle class purloined the land. Not surprisingly, since he is a dramatist rather than an historian, Molloy's plays do not deal with that ancient age of social order, but rather with periods of conflict, of moments when one can observe the old order passing. A self-confessed romantic, Molloy can see no good coming out of this change.

Two of Molloy's early plays, *The King of Friday's Men* and *The Visiting House*, might be regarded as paradigms of the worlds that have been lost. Set in late 18th-century Mayo and

Galway, *The King of Friday's Men* reveals a large society still responsive to the old feudal structure of lord and peasant. The play concerns a lord's obsession with his right to have as his mistresses the unmarried daughters of his tenant farmers. His exploitation of a feudal right provokes disorder in the land and leads ultimately to the violent death of the lord. Molloy is not naive in his romantic attachment to Ireland's feudal past. As a Catholic, he believes that human nature has been self-seeking and violent since the Fall and can never change. Nevertheless, all the characters in *The King of Friday's Men* share the same social and moral values. Lord and tenant both know when privilege has been exploited.

The Visiting House has a contemporary setting and reveals a shrunken social order. Unlike *The King of Friday's Men* in which action ranges all over Galway and Mayo, and an heroic Bartley Dowd wipes out a contingent of the lord's men with a few swipes of his shillelagh, *The Visiting House* is confined to the single setting which Molloy has used for most of his plays. The heroics are rhetorical rather than physical as characters called The Man of Learning and The Verb-to-Be nightly take their positions by the fire and engage in a merry flyting match. Within these narrowed circumstances, however, *The Visiting House* does reveal a social order based on ownership of the land. A once flourishing institution barely more than a memory when Molloy wrote his play, the visiting house was the place where small farmers gathered and where each had respect and a social identity.

Molloy's other plays deal more directly with the breakdown of traditional Irish rural life. *Old Road* is about the depopulation caused by farmers being unable to divide their small farms any further. Only the oldest son may inherit the land. Others must leave the community for Dublin or England. *The Wood of the Whispering* also has depopulation for its theme. Molloy assembles an array of zany and impotent old bachelors who lust after the one or two girls left in the village. Their lives pass in the shadow of ancient Castle D'Arcy, a reminder to Molloy's audience of a time when society was stable. *The Will and the Way* has to do with a rural community whose visiting house is threatened by the arrival of a city-type who has no feeling for community life and nearly succeeds in destroying it.

In his more recent plays Molloy has been unable to maintain the gentle comic spirit and ironic distance which characterize his earlier work. The last traces of genuine rural Irish life are being destroyed by technology, especially by television which gives the Irish a false sense of being a national community while at the same time imposing a radical isolation of one man from another. *A Right Rose Tree* presents a rural Ireland so fraught with social problems that the play is more like documentary than drama. It deals with the period 1921–23, when the Irish countryside rises up against the English only to witness even more bloody battles of brother against brother when the Black and Tans have left. The utter lawlessness which results permits the base to inherit the earth. The lines from Yeats which give the play its title assert the purposefulness of violence—"There's nothing but our own red blood/Can make a right Rose tree." For Molloy violence has no such creative energy. The final horror of *A Right Rose Tree*, the symbolic killing of a landlord by insensitive, ignorant, and cowardly men, leaves nothing of value after it.

—Arthur E. McGuinness

MOORE, (James) Mavor. Canadian. Born in Toronto, Ontario, 8 March 1919. Educated at University of Toronto secondary schools, graduated 1936; University of Toronto, 1936–41 (Leonard Foundation Scholar), B.A. (honours) in philosophy and English 1941. Served in the Canadian Army Intelligence Corps, 1941–45: Captain (Psychological Warfare). Married 1) Darwina Faessler in 1943 (divorced), four daughters; 2) the writer Phyllis Grosskurth in 1969; 3) Alexandra Browning in 1982, one daughter. Feature producer, Toronto, 1941–42, chief producer for the International Service, Montreal, 1944–45, and Pacific Region producer, Vancouver, 1945–46, CBC Radio; teacher, Academy of Radio Arts, Toronto, 1946–49; managing producer, New Play Society, Toronto, 1946–50, 1954–57; radio director, 1946–50, and executive television producer, 1954–60, United Nations Information Division, New York; chief producer, 1950–53, and assistant television program director, 1954, CBC Television, Toronto; drama critic, Toronto *Telegram*, 1958–60; stage director, Canadian Opera Company, Toronto, 1959–61, 1963; general director, Confederation Centre, Charlottetown, Prince Edward Island, 1963–65; founder and artistic director, Charlottetown Festival, 1964–67; general director, St. Lawrence Centre for the Arts, Toronto, 1965–70. Since 1961 President, Mavor Moore Productions Ltd., Toronto; since 1970 Professor of Theatre, York University, Downsview, Ontario; member, 1974, member of the Executive Committee, 1975, and since 1979 Chairman, Canada Council. Since 1953 member of the Board of Directors, later Senator, Stratford Festival, Ontario; Chairman, Canadian Theatre Centre, 1957–58; since 1958 Governor, National Theatre School, Montreal; founding Chairman, Guild of Canadian Playwrights, 1977. Recipient: Peabody award, 1947, 1949, 1957; Canadian Association of Authors and Artists award, for television writing, 1955; Centennial Medal, 1967. D.Litt.: York University, 1969; LL.D.: Mount Allison University, Sackville, New Brunswick, 1982. Officer, Order of Canada, 1973. Agent (Canada): Canadian Speakers and Writers Service, 44 Douglas Crescent, Toronto, Ontario; (U.K. and U.S.A.): ACTAC Ltd., 16 Cadogan Lane, London S.W.1, England. Address: 176 Moore Avenue, Toronto, Ontario M4T 1V8, Canada.

PUBLICATIONS

Plays

Spring Thaw (revue; produced Toronto, 1947 and later versions, 1948–57, 1961–65). Sketch *Togetherness* published in *A Treasury of Canadian Humor*, edited by Robert Thomas Allen, Toronto, McClelland and Stewart, 1967.

Who's Who (also director: produced Toronto, 1949).

The Best of All Possible Worlds, adaptation of the novel *Candide* by Voltaire (broadcast 1952; revised version, as *The Optimist*, broadcast 1954; revised version, as *The Best of All Possible Worlds*, music and lyrics by Moore, produced Toronto, 1956).

The Hero of Mariposa, music and lyrics by Moore, adaptation of *Sunshine Sketches of a Little Town* by Stephen Leacock (broadcast 1953; as *Sunshine Town*, also director: produced Toronto, 1956).

The Ottawa Man, adaptation of a play by Gogol (televised 1958; revised version, also director: produced Toronto, 1961; revised version produced Lennoxville, Quebec, 1972).

Louis Riel (opera libretto), with Jacques Languirand, music by Harry Somers (produced Toronto, 1967; Washington, D.C., 1975).

Yesterday the Children Were Dancing, adaptation of a play by Gratien Gélinas (also co-director: produced Charlottetown, Prince Edward Island, 1967). Toronto, Clarke Irwin, 1969.

Johnny Belinda, lyrics by Moore, musical version of the play by Elmer Harris (produced Charlottetown, Prince Edward Island, 1968).

Getting In (broadcast 1968; as *The Interview*, televised 1973). New York, French, 1972.

The Pile (broadcast 1969). Included in *The Pile, The Store, Inside Out*, 1973.

Man Inc., adaptation of a play by Jacques Languirand (produced Toronto, 1970).

The Argument (broadcast 1970). Published in *Performing Arts in Canada* (Toronto), Winter 1973.

The Store (broadcast 1971). Included in *The Pile, The Store, Inside Out*, 1973.

Inside Out (televised 1971). Included in *The Pile, The Store, Inside Out*, 1973.

Anne of Green Gables (additional lyrics, with Elaine Campbell), book by Donald Harron, music by Norman Campbell, lyrics by Harron and Campbell, adaptation of the novel by L.M. Montgomery (produced Charlottetown, Prince Edward Island, 1971).

Come Away, Come Away (broadcast 1972). Published in *Encounter: Canadian Drama in Four Media*, edited by Eugene Benson, Toronto, Methuen, 1973.

Customs (broadcast 1973). Published in *Cues and Entrances*, edited by Henry Beissel, Toronto, Gage, 1977.

The Pile, The Store, Inside Out. Toronto, Simon and Pierre, 1973.

The Roncarelli Affair, with F.R. Scott (televised 1974). Published in *The Play's the Thing*, edited by Tony Gifford, Toronto, Macmillan, 1976.

Abracadabra, music by Harry Freedman (produced Courtenay, British Columbia, 1979).

Love and Politics, music and lyrics by Moore, adaptation of the play *The Fair Grit* by Nicholas Flood Davin (produced St. Catherines, Ontario, 1979).

Fauntleroy, music and lyrics by Johnny Burke, adaptation of the novel *Little Lord Fauntleroy* by Frances Hodgson Burnett (produced Charlottetown, Prince Edward Island, 1980).

Radio Plays: more than 100 plays, including *The Best of All Possible Worlds*, 1952 (revised as *The Optimist*, 1954); *The Hero of Mariposa*, 1953; *Fast Forward*, 1968; *Getting In*, 1968; *The Pile*, 1969; *The Argument*, 1970; *The Store*, 1971; *A Matter of Timing*, 1971; *Come Away, Come Away*, 1972; *Customs*, 1973 (USA); *Time Frame*, 1974; *Freak*, 1975.

Television Plays: more than 50 plays, including *Catch a Falling Star*, 1957; *The Ottawa Man*, 1958; *The Well*, 1961; *The Man Born to Be King*, 1961; *The Man Who Caught Bullets*, 1962; *Mary of Scotland*, 1966; *Inside Out*, 1971; *The Interview*, 1973; *The Roncarelli Affair*, with F.R. Scott, 1974.

Verse

And What Do You Do? A Short Guide to the Trades and Professions. Toronto and London, Dent, 1960.

Other

4 Canadian Playwrights: Robertson Davies, Gratien Gélinas, James Reaney, George Ryga. Toronto, Holt Rinehart, 1973.

Slipping on the Verge: The Performing Arts in Canada with Theatre as a Case Study. Washington, D.C., Canadian Embassy, 1983.

Editor, *The Awkward Stage: The Ontario Theatre Study.* Toronto, Methuen, 1969.

Editor, *An Anthology of Canadian Plays.* Toronto, New Press, 1973.

*

Theatrical Activities:

Director: **Plays**—*King Lear*, Toronto, 1948; *Heartbreak House* by Shaw, Toronto, 1948; *The Circle* by W. Somerset Maugham, Toronto, 1948; *The Government Inspector* by Gogol, Toronto, 1948; *Who's Who*, Toronto, 1949; *Macbeth*, Toronto, 1949; *The Tempest*, Toronto, 1949; *Sunshine Town*, Toronto, 1956; *The Ottawa Man*, Toronto, 1961, Charlottetown, Prince Edward Island, 1966; *The Fourposter* by Jan de Hartog, Halifax, Nova Scotia, 1963; *Dial M for Murder* by Frederick Knott, Halifax, 1963; *Floradora*, Vancouver, 1964; *Julius Caesar*, Vancouver, 1964; *An Evening with Wayne and Shuster*, Charlottetown, 1965; *Laugh with Leacock*, Charlottetown, 1965; *Yesterday the Children Were Dancing* (co-director), Charlottetown, 1967. **Television and Radio**—productions for CBC, United Nations (New York), CBS and NBC (USA).

Actor: **Plays**—roles with the New Play Society, Toronto, the Crest Theatre, the Charlottetown and Vancouver Festivals, and other theatre companies, including title role in *King Lear*, Toronto, 1948, 1963; title role in *Riel*, Toronto, 1948; Escalus in *Measure for Measure*, Stratford, Ontario, 1954; Caesar in *Caesar and Cleopatra* by Shaw, Toronto and Vancouver, 1962; Undershaft in *Major Barbara* by Shaw, Halifax, 1963. **Television**—starring roles in numerous Canadian drama series. **Radio**—roles in numerous CBC productions, CBS and NBC (USA), etc.

* * *

Mavor Moore is Canada's most ubiquitous man-about-theatre. In the last 40 years he has had great success as actor, producer, director, festival impresario, and theatre administrator. Now, as professor of theatre at York University in Toronto, he has a period of relative calm in which he can once more concentrate on writing. For most of his career as a playwright for the stage, he has mainly adapted the work of other writers and adapted it very often for his own direction. Or he has worked as a librettist in cooperation with composers and co-writers.

In the area of musical drama Moore created a lively version of Mariposa, that sleepy little town which Stephen Leacock wrote about in *Sunshine Sketches*. In *Sunshine Town* Moore wrote a book, music, and lyrics which had the right period feeling; it has had several revivals.

On another occasion, for his Charlottetown Festival, he wrote a musical version of *Johnny Belinda* based on the Broadway play by Elmer Harris. Again, the quality of the writing and the success of his director, Alan Lund, made even the story of a deaf-mute who is raped a good and satisfying musical.

Louis Riel is an opera rather than a musical; with a score composed by Harry Somers, it was a notable addition to the

Canadian Opera Company's repertoire for the Centennial Year of 1967. Moore went to history—Riel is a key figure in the French-English debate which still is a central part of Canada's polity—and managed to create a full-blooded set of characters, even though from time to time the dialogue was more operatic than dramatic. Generally, though, Moore's greatest gift as a dramatist is his skill in dialogue, perhaps because he has written so much for radio—a purely verbal medium.

Moore's best known play is *The Ottawa Man*, an adaptation of Gogol's *The Government Inspector*. Only Moore's talent for dialogue could have made it the success it is because the central situation, which is firmly rooted in the official corruption of czarist Russia, cannot be easily transplanted to the relative honesty of 19th-century pioneer Manitoba. But the fact is that one doesn't question this while the play is being acted; nor is one too aware of the fact that the characters are all stereotypes rather than people. What one is aware of is the farcical encounter between two Irishmen, a French-Canadian Catholic, a German immigrant, and an English remittance man—all of whom speak in an uncannily accurate style and accent.

In recent years Moore has written several one-act plays, mainly for radio and television. Character is not important in them, but ideas and verbal play on those ideas are. In fact, so little character is necessary for embodying the ideas that in some of the plays none of the characters has a name: in *Come Away, Come Away*, which is about an old man facing death and a little girl fascinated by the encounter, the characters are Old Man and Little Girl; in *The Pile*, a fable about modern business and ecology, the characters are X and Y; and in *Getting In*, a play with a really strange resonance, P is the official and T is an applicant.

Perhaps the most significant of these plays is *The Argument* which, through its dialogue alone, establishes characters who are identified only as M—a man—and W—a woman. But their dialogue, their argument, creates an interaction which convinces one that Moore is capable of writing longer and more solid work.

—Arnold Edinborough

MORRISON, Bill. Irish. Born in Ballymoney, County Antrim, Northern Ireland, 22 January 1940. Educated at Dalriada Grammar School, Ballymoney, 1951–58; Queen's University, Belfast, 1958–62, LL.B. (honours) 1962. Married Valerie Lilley in 1968. Actor in Belfast, Dublin, and London, from 1963; resident writer, Victoria Theatre, Stoke-on-Trent, Staffordshire, 1969–71; radio drama producer, BBC, Belfast, 1975–76; resident writer, Everyman Theatre, 1977–78, Lecturer in Creative Writing, C.F. Mott College, 1977–78, drama producer, Radio City, 1979–81, and associate director, 1981–83, and artistic director, 1983–85, Playhouse Theatre, all Liverpool. Since 1978 board member, Merseyside Young People's Theatre, Liverpool, since 1981 board member, Playhouse Theatre, and since 1985 Chairman, Merseyside Arts Drama Panel. Recipient: Ford Foundation grant, 1972; Arts Council bursary, 1975; Pye award, for radio feature, 1981. Agent: Michael Imison Playwrights, 28 Almeida Street, London N1 1TD. Address: 39 Peel Street, Flat 5, Liverpool L8 3SY, England.

PUBLICATIONS

Plays

Love and a Bottle, adaptation of the play by George Farquhar (produced Dublin, 1966; Nottingham, 1969).

Laugh But Listen Well (produced Dublin, 1967).

Conn and the Conquerors of Space (for children; also director: produced Falmer, Sussex, 1969; London, 1971).

Please Don't Shoot Me When I'm Down (produced Manchester, 1969; London, 1972).

Jupiter-5 (for children; produced Stoke-on-Trent, 1970; London, 1971).

Aladdin and His Magic Lamp (for children; also director: produced Stoke-on-Trent, 1971).

Tess of the d'Urbervilles, adaptation of the novel by Hardy (produced Stoke-on-Trent, 1971). London, Macmillan, 1980.

Sam Slade Is Missing (broadcast 1971; produced Derby, 1972; London, 1974). Published in *The Best Short Plays 1973*, edited by Stanley Richards, Radnor, Pennsylvania, Chilton, 1973.

The Time Travellers (for children; produced Stoke-on-Trent, 1971).

Patrick's Day (produced New Haven, Connecticut, 1972).

The Love of Lady Margaret (broadcast 1972; produced London, 1973).

Ellen Cassidy (broadcast 1974; produced Liverpool, 1978).

The Emperor of Ice-Cream, adaptation of the novel by Brian Moore (broadcast 1975; produced Dublin, 1977).

The Irish Immigrants Tale (produced Liverpool, 1976).

Flying Blind (produced Liverpool, 1977; London, 1978; New York, 1979). London, Faber, 1978.

Time on Our Hands (produced Belfast, 1979).

Dr. Jekyll of Rodney Street (produced Liverpool, 1979).

Scrap! (produced Liverpool, 1982; London, 1985).

Cavern of Dreams, with Carol Ann Duffy (produced Liverpool, 1984).

Run, Run, Runaway (for children; produced Liverpool and London, 1986).

Radio Plays: *Sam Slade Is Missing*, 1971; *The Love of Lady Margaret*, 1972; *The Great Gun-Running Episode*, 1974; *Ellen Cassidy*, 1974; *Crime and Punishment*, from a novel by Dostoevsky, 1975; *Crow's Flight*, from a play by Dimitri Kehaidis, 1975; *The Emperor of Ice-Cream*, 1975; *Simpson and Son*, 1977; *The Big Sleep*, *The High Window*, *The Lady in the Lake*, *The Little Sister*, and *The Long Goodbye*, all from the novels by Raymond Chandler, 1977; *Maguire*, 1979; *The Spring of Memory* (feature), 1981.

Television Plays: *McKinley and Sarah*, 1973; *Joggers*, 1978; *Potatohead Blues*, 1982; *Shergar*, 1986.

*

Theatrical Activities:

Director: **Plays**—*On Approval* by Frederick Lonsdale, Dublin, 1967; *The Lion in Winter* by James Goldman, London, 1969; *Two Gentlemen of Verona* by Shakespeare, London, 1969; *Conn and the Conquerors of Space*, Falmer, Sussex, 1969; *Aladdin and His Magic Lamp*, Stoke-on-Trent, 1971; Playhouse Theatre, Liverpool: *A Doll's House* by Ibsen, *Ladies in Waiting* by Ellen Fox, *These Men* by Mayo Simon, *Skirmishes* by Catherine Hayes, *Walking on Walter* by Claire Luckham, *A Lesson from Aloes* by Athol Fugard, *I Want* by Nell Dunn and Adrian Henri, *Breezeblock Park* by Willy Russell, *Alfie*

by Bill Naughton, *Cavern of Dreams*, and *The Divvies Are Coming* by Eddie Braben, 1981–85; *The Beastly Beatitudes of Balthazar B* by J.P. Donleavy, London, 1983.
Actor: **Plays**—roles at Arts Theatre, Belfast, and with Ulster Theatre Company, 1963–65; Nick in *Who's Afraid of Virginia Woolf?* by Edward Albee, Dublin, 1966; Barney Muldoon in *Illuminatus!* by Robert Anton Wilson, Liverpool, 1978. **Film**—*Sinful Davey*, 1969.

Bill Morrison comments:

(1982) I was born in Ireland but I was born in the British part of it. I was born during a war and have lived in the shadow of war since. I am more an Ulster writer than an Irish one. My language has the particular rhythms of that place, my characters and subjects are violently shaped by it, my use of comedy is dictated by it. I write in order to try to make sense of what happens to me and what I see around me and I hope by that to make a record of how people felt and lived in a particular time and place, which I take to be the job of the writer in any society.

I also write for an audience. I am proud of the fact that my work has been performed in twelve countries. The excitement and persistence of theatre is that it is the form which depends on the creative participation of the audience to complete it. The audience always affects and often profoundly alters the quality of the artistic event. To me the theatre is a laboratory of human communication, a place of constant experiment. The glory of the nature of it is that it has to be on the human scale. Technology does change and improve but it barely affects the essential experience. Writing for radio, TV, or film is rewarding because of the audience it reaches but it is not the same. Theatre is the only human activity I have found which embraces and needs all levels of skill and talent in its making and where, despite all its internal conflicts, the need and advantage of co-operating always wins. The event is always greater than the individual. It is always communal.

That is how it should be. It is why I now run a theatre with other writers. However, I regret the fact that, apart from a community tour of a show *Time on Our Hands* which I devised with a company, my work remains unperformed in Northern Ireland.

(1988) The purpose of the writer in society is to record how people feel about the time they live in and the events in it. I try to make sense of what I feel and see around me, and mostly fail—which is why I write comedy and farce. The story of my time is the story of murder exposed as farce.

* * *

Following up his own proposition that since 1969 "the trouble with being an Ulster playwright has been trouble," Bill Morrison wrote in 1977: "the best of my work, or at least the most important to me, has been about my country and the people who try to survive in it. The plays have been about my struggle to understand the disease in my society which caused its intense, unbearably prolonged and homicidal breakdown. But they have also been about my struggle to find a form which would encompass it." This comment conveniently suggests the characteristics which give Morrison's drama its force: his exploration of the problematic relation between cultural and personal spheres in the Ulster context, and the formal experimentation from play to play that such an exploration necessarily entails. Moreover, in a writer who believes, as Morrison does, that "the theatre is ultimately the only way of fully discovering oneself," the "struggle to find a form" makes itself felt as a moral as well as an artistic imperative.

The struggle was complicated for Morrison in the early 1970's by a lack of sympathy he encountered in theatre (and television) for his exploratory treatment of the Ulster situation. Finding an outlet instead in radio, he experimented with the use of stereo in adaptations (notably *Crime and Punishment*) and, in his first original radio play, *The Love of Lady Margaret*, satisfyingly exploited the potential of the medium for narrative ambiguity in the rendering of an isolated consciousness and its labyrinth of ultimately self-thwarting fictions.

The aptness of the radio medium to the playwright's concerns is powerfully (though perhaps not consistently) apparent in *Ellen Cassidy*—a later stage version of which the author considers to have been unsatisfactory. Here the troubled consciousness belongs to the 34-year-old Armagh-born Protestant Ellen. Now in London, estranged from yet still haunted by her Irish husband, and awaiting the arrival of her young lover, she engages with the constraints and outcomes of an Ulster upbringing in a fluid series of recollections, reflective monologues, and flashbacks. The writing is often richly imaged, and at the heart of the play is the symbolic opposition of blood—the issue of menstruation, of sexual and sectarian violence, the pulsing badge of cultural belonging, something *inside* the self and controlling it—and water, an element outside the self which for Ellen promises cool, free-floating identity. As a woman, Ellen has experienced in both her upbringing and her relationships the stifling cultural consequences of the evolutionary determinism expatiated upon by her older lover, the biologist Gorman. When it becomes clear that the men in her life are, in their different ways, all pathetically enslaved by their cultural conditioning and its "stories," she finally proclaims her independence of all three and of "the old old days of pain": "My name is Ellen Cassidy and I live all alone."

Because of—or perhaps despite—the lyrical power of its monologues, *Ellen Cassidy* cannot help but bring to mind Morrison's admission that at this time he was "using plays as a form of psychoanalysis." *Flying Blind* signals a breakthrough for Morrison in its achievement of a decisively *im*personal form for the articulation of his characteristic preoccupations. The brooding and often painful energies of *Ellen Cassidy* are here gathered, shaped, and endowed with a bitter comic trajectory by the crisp dialogue and coolly contrived sudden mayhem of farce. The result is, as one critic has put it, "a world where the laws of farce and tragedy are interchangeable."

The increasingly fevered comings and goings of *Flying Blind* take place in and around the "imaginatively furnished" living room of an Ulster medical rep, Dan Poots, a supplier of "happy pills" who has dedicated himself to survival in an environment he considers to be in the grip of a "perversion of the spirit." He retreats between stereo headphones, listening to the music of his hero, Charlie "Bird" Parker, who "found the terms of membership unacceptable"—as Dan now does. Even before the darkly funny (and, for him, bladder-stretching) incursions of two groups of terrorists—a Protestant murder-squad and vengeful Catholics—Dan's strategy for survival is seriously disturbed by the demands of his concerned wife Liz, and by her old flame the sociologist Michael, who has returned to his native Ulster, laden with simplistic socio-political solutions and a desperation born of childlessness, determined to "save" Liz (or, failing that, her babysitter). Meanwhile the lawyer Boyd, recently forced out of politics by terrorist death-threats, is alarmed to find his sexual impulses arising only in the revolver he brandishes—and even that fails to go off at the climactic moment. In fact sex, that generic stipulation of farce, is here ingeniously invested with a pivotal diagnostic function. The pathetic impotence of the men in the play is symptomatic of a diseased society in which, as Dan realizes, potency exists not in sexual relationships but in the self-destructive violence of history's "blind men," the terrorists. Hence the moral force behind the farce when Dan and his generous (though unfulfilled) neighbour Bertha confront imminent death by undressing to make love right in front of the panic-stricken terrorists who are threatening them. In the end a fatal mêlée (graced by a bucket of piss and a purblind terrorist called Magoo) disrupts the reconciliation of friends and neighbours, and happy ending gives way to familiar stalemate.

Following the success of *Flying Blind* and after a group of Raymond Chandler adaptations for radio, Morrison worked on radio scripts in the U.S.A. and on a number of television projects, most of them either abortive or disappointing, in Britain. His last important stage play before his spell as director at the Liverpool Playhouse (1981–85) was *Scrap!* Here again farce is the formal basis, but the action is rather less riotous than in *Flying Blind*, and there are interwoven elements of the thriller-mode—or even of whodunnit.

Scrap! is centrally concerned with betrayal—personal, cultural, and political. The high-ranking English policeman Cleaver (a.k.a. Butcher) aims "to solve the problems of a whole country" by an appeal to what he considers to be the "eternal verities"—"bribery, blackmail, and betrayal." His plan is to lure the key Protestant terrorist organizer Sidney Mulligan out of Belfast to Liverpool and to deliver him over to the Catholic terrorist leader Madigan as part of a deal involving the military–strategic co-operation with Britain of a prospective non-neutral "new" united Ireland. To this end Cleaver brings over to Liverpool Mulligan's schoolgirl daughter Kate, who has gone to the police with her father's operational notebooks in her possession. Kate, ironically, is glad to escape Belfast, and with it the childhood innocence that makes her a potential blood-sacrifice on the altar of Ulster's history, yet at the same time she is torn at the prospect of betraying her father and all that he stands for. She manages to deposit the vital documents with his cousin, the English scrap-dealer Tommy Atkins (who is unaware of the fact). When Mulligan himself arrives in Liverpool, impelled less by his concern for the notebooks than by the desperation and "black pain" he feels at the disappearance of the child in whose innocence he invests all his surviving values, he is drawn into a deadly, yet also farcical, pattern of intrigue and betrayal. The plainly allegorical design of the play is reinforced by the co-ordination of symbolic structure and setting: the mirror-lined basement bar of the second half realizes visually the darkly oppressive phantom-world of Ulster history which shuts out the "sweet daylight" of freedom and reduces the Protestants to the contorted scrap of Britain. At the climax, Cleaver's underhand plans go grotesquely wrong, and the powerful Protestant Mulligan, having wrapped himself in a waistcoat of dynamite and lit the fuse, grasps the disarmed Catholic Madigan under one arm and the crooked Englishman Cleaver under the other, as he asks: "which among us deserves to be saved?" This final stage-image crystallizes the deadlock Morrison has always sought to confront and to understand through his drama—in the belief that such understanding would also constitute a kind of self-discovery.

—Paul Lawley

MORTIMER, John (Clifford). British. Born in Hampstead, London, 21 April 1923. Educated at Harrow School, Middlesex, 1937–40; Brasenose College, Oxford, 1940–42, B.A. 1947; called to the Bar, 1948; Queen's Counsel, 1966; Master of the Bench, Inner Temple, 1975. Served with the Crown Film Units as scriptwriter during World War II. Married 1) Penelope Dimont (i.e., the writer Penelope Mortimer) in 1949 (divorced 1971), one son and one daughter; 2) Penelope Gollop in 1972, one daughter. Drama critic, *New Statesman*, *Evening Standard*, and *Observer*, 1972, all London. Since 1968 member of the National Theatre Board; since 1984 President, Berkshire, Buckinghamshire, and Oxfordshire Naturalists' Trust; Chairman, League of Dramatists. Recipient: Italia prize, for radio play, 1958; Screenwriters Guild award, for television play, 1970; BAFTA award, for television play, 1980; *Yorkshire Post* award, 1983. D.Litt.: Susquehanna University, Selinsgrove, Pennsylvania, 1985; University of St. Andrews, Fife, 1987; LL.D.: Exeter University, 1986. C.B.E. (Commander, Order of the British Empire), 1986. Agent: A.D. Peters Ltd., 10 Buckingham Street, London WC2N 6BU. Address: Turville Heath Cottage, Henley-on-Thames, Oxfordshire, England.

PUBLICATIONS

Plays

The Dock Brief (broadcast 1957; produced London, 1958; New York, 1961). Included in *Three Plays*, 1958.

I Spy (broadcast 1957; produced Salisbury and Palm Beach, Florida, 1959). Included in *Three Plays*, 1958.

What Shall We Tell Caroline? (produced London, 1958; New York, 1961). Included in *Three Plays*, 1958.

Three Plays. London, Elek, 1958; New York, Grove Press, 1962.

Call Me a Liar (televised 1958; produced London, 1968). Included in *Lunch Hour and Other Plays*, 1960; in *The Television Playwright: Ten Plays for B.B.C. Television*, edited by Michael Barry, New York, Hill and Wang, 1960.

Sketches in *One to Another* (produced London, 1959). London, French, 1960.

The Wrong Side of the Park (produced London, 1960). London, Heinemann, 1960.

Lunch Hour (broadcast 1960; produced Salisbury, 1960; London, 1961; New York, 1977). Included in *Lunch Hour and Other Plays*, 1960; published separately, New York, French, 1961.

David and Broccoli (televised 1960). Included in *Lunch Hour and Other Plays*, 1960.

Lunch Hour and Other Plays. London, Methuen, 1960.

Collect Your Hand Baggage (produced in German, Wuppertal, 1963; televised in English, 1963). Included in *Lunch Hour and Other Plays*, 1960.

Sketches in *One over the Eight* (produced London, 1961).

Two Stars for Comfort (produced London, 1962). London, Methuen, 1962.

A Voyage round My Father (broadcast 1963; produced London, 1970). London, Methuen, 1971.

Sketches in *Changing Gear* (produced Nottingham, 1965).

A Flea in Her Ear, adaptation of a play by Feydeau (produced London, 1966; Tucson, 1979). London and New York, French, 1967.

A Choice of Kings (televised 1966). Published in *Playbill Three*, edited by Alan Durband, London, Hutchinson, 1969.

The Judge (produced Hamburg and London, 1967). London, Methuen, 1967.

Desmond (televised 1968). Published in *The Best Short Plays 1971*, edited by Stanley Richards, Philadelphia, Chilton, 1971.
Cat among the Pigeons, adaptation of a play by Feydeau (produced London, 1969; Milwaukee, 1971). New York, French, 1970.
Come As You Are: Four Short Plays (includes *Mill Hill*, *Bermondsey*, *Gloucester Road*, *Marble Arch*) (produced London, 1970). London, Methuen, 1971.
Five Plays (includes *The Dock Brief*, *What Shall We Tell Caroline?*, *I Spy*, *Lunch Hour*, *Collect Your Hand Baggage*). London, Methuen, 1970.
The Captain of Köpenick, adaptation of a play by Carl Zuckmayer (produced London, 1971). London, Methuen, 1971.
Conflicts, with others (produced London, 1971).
I, Claudius, adaptation of the novels *I, Claudius* and *Claudius the God* by Robert Graves (produced London, 1972).
Knightsbridge (televised 1972). London, French, 1973.
Collaborators (produced London, 1973). London, Eyre Methuen, 1973.
The Fear of Heaven (as *Mr. Luby's Fear of Heaven*, broadcast 1976; as *The Fear of Heaven*, produced with *The Prince of Darkness* as *Heaven and Hell*, London, 1976). London, French, 1978.
Heaven and Hell (includes *The Fear of Heaven* and *The Prince of Darkness*) (produced London, 1976; revised version of *The Prince of Darkness*, as *The Bells of Hell*, produced Richmond, Surrey, and London, 1977). *The Bells of Hell* published London, French, 1978.
The Lady from Maxim's, adaptation of a play by Feydeau (produced London, 1977). London, Heinemann, 1977.
John Mortimer's Casebook (includes *The Dock Brief*, *The Prince of Darkness*, *Interlude*) (produced London, 1982).
When That I Was (produced Ottawa, 1982).
Edwin (broadcast 1982). Included in *Edwin and Other Plays*, 1984.
A Little Hotel on the Side, adaptation of a play by Feydeau and Maurice Desvalliers (produced London, 1984). Included in *Three Boulevard Farces*, 1985.
Edwin and Other Plays (includes *Bermondsey*, *Marble Arch*, *The Fear of Heaven*, *The Prince of Darkness*). London, Penguin, 1984.
Three Boulevard Farces (includes *A Little Hotel on the Side*, *A Flea in Her Ear*, *The Lady from Maxim's*). London, Penguin, 1985.

Screenplays: *Ferry to Hong Kong*, with Lewis Gilbert and Vernon Harris, 1959; *The Innocents*, with Truman Capote and William Archibald, 1961; *Guns of Darkness*, 1962; *I Thank a Fool*, with others, 1962; *Lunch Hour*, 1962; *The Running Man*, 1963; *Bunny Lake Is Missing*, with Penelope Mortimer, 1964; *A Flea in Her Ear*, 1967; *John and Mary*, 1969.

Radio Plays: *Like Men Betrayed*, 1955; *No Hero*, 1955; *The Dock Brief*, 1957; *I Spy*, 1957; *Three Winters*, 1958; *Lunch Hour*, 1960; *The Encyclopedist*, 1961; *A Voyage round My Father*, 1963; *Personality Split*, 1964; *Education of an Englishman*, 1964; *A Rare Device*, 1965; *Mr. Luby's Fear of Heaven*, 1976; *Edwin*, 1982.

Television Plays: *Call Me a Liar*, 1958; *David and Broccoli*, 1960; *A Choice of Kings*, 1966; *The Exploding Azalea*, 1966; *The Head Waiter*, 1966; *Hughie*, 1967; *The Other Side*, 1967; *Desmond*, 1968; *Infidelity Took Place*, 1968; *Married Alive*, 1970; *Swiss Cottage*, 1972; *Knightsbridge*, 1972; *Rumpole of the Bailey*, 1975, and series, 1978, 1979, 1987; *A Little Place off the Edgware Road*, *The Blue Film*, *The Destructors*, *The Case for the Defence*, *Chagrin in Three Parts*, *The Invisible Japanese Gentlemen*, *Special Duties*, and *Mortmain*, all from stories by Graham Greene, 1975–76; *Will Shakespeare*, 1978; *Rumpole's Return*, 1980; *Unity*, from the book by David Pryce-Jones, 1981; *Brideshead Revisited*, from the novel by Evelyn Waugh, 1981; *The Ebony Tower*, from the story by John Fowles, 1984; *Paradise Postponed*, from his own novel, 1986.

Ballet Scenario: *Home*, 1968.

Son et Lumière scripts: *Hampton Court*, 1964; *Brighton Pavilion*, 1965.

Novels

Charade. London, Lane, 1947; New York, Viking, 1987.
Rumming Park. London, Lane, 1948.
Answer Yes or No. London, Lane, 1950; as *The Silver Hook*, New York, Morrow, 1950.
Like Men Betrayed. London, Collins, 1953; Philadelphia, Lippincott, 1954.
The Narrowing Stream. London, Collins, 1954.
Three Winters. London, Collins, 1956.
Will Shakespeare: The Untold Story. London, Hodder and Stoughton, 1977; New York, Delacorte Press, 1978.
Paradise Postponed. London and New York, Viking, 1985.
Like Men Betrayed. London, Viking, 1987.

Short Stories

Rumpole. London, Allen Lane, 1980.
  Rumpole of the Bailey. London, Penguin, 1978; New York, Penguin, 1980.
  The Trials of Rumpole. London, Penguin, 1979; New York, Penguin, 1981.
Regina v. Rumpole. London, Allen Lane, 1981.
  Rumpole's Return. London, Penguin, 1980; New York, Penguin, 1982.
  Rumpole for the Defence. London, Penguin, 1982.
Rumpole and the Golden Thread. London and New York, Penguin, 1983.
The First Rumpole Omnibus (includes *Rumpole of the Bailey*, *The Trials of Rumpole*, *Rumpole's Return*). London, Penguin, 1983.
The Second Rumpole Omnibus (includes *Rumpole for the Defence*, *Rumpole and the Golden Thread*, *Rumpole's Last Case*). London, Viking, 1987.

Other

No Moaning at the Bar (as Geoffrey Lincoln). London, Bles, 1957.
With Love and Lizards (travel), with Penelope Mortimer. London, Joseph, 1957.
Clinging to the Wreckage: A Part of Life. London, Weidenfeld and Nicolson, and New Haven, Connecticut, Ticknor and Fields, 1982.
In Character (interviews). London, Allen Lane, 1983.
The Liberty of the Citizen (lecture), with Franklin Thomas and Lord Hunt of Tanworth. London, Granada, 1983.
Character Parts (interviews). London, Viking, 1986.

Editor, *Famous Trials*, edited by Harry Hodge and James H. Hodge. London, Viking, and New York, Penguin, 1984.

*

Manuscript Collections: Boston University; University of California, Los Angeles.

Critical Study: *Anger and After* by John Russell Taylor, London, Methuen, 1962, revised edition, 1969, as *The Angry Theatre*, New York, Hill and Wang, 1962, revised edition, 1969.

John Mortimer comments:

(1982) Comedy, I remember saying when my plays were first performed, is the only thing worth writing in this despairing age. Twenty years later the world has offered no call for a change of attitude. It may be that only in the most secure and optimistic ages can good tragedies be written. Our present situation, stumbling into a misty future filled with uncertainty and mistrust, is far too serious to be described in terms that give us no opportunity to laugh.

* * *

John Mortimer arrived as a playwright in the heady days of the revolution inaugurated by John Osborne's *Look Back in Anger*. *The Dock Brief*, a radio play for two speakers, had followed half a dozen novels none of which had achieved any startling success though none could be dismissed as a failure. *The Dock Brief*, however, proved to be witty, imaginative, unusual, and cleverly worked out. It was at its best in its original form, as a radio play, and its subsequent disguises—as a television play, a one-act stage play, and, sadly inflated, as a film—did not manage to destroy the odd, quirky personality and originality of the work they dilute.

In *The Dock Brief* Morganhall, an unsuccessful barrister, has to defend Fowle, a confessed murderer, and at once plans to do so by imagining the circumstances under which Fowle might be innocent. This odd, silly-sad conversation has been taken by some critics to indicate that Mortimer lives in an odd relationship to naturalism, as though he can neither escape from nor finally submit to naturalist teaching and practice. Morganhall finds it natural to justify himself and his client by an athletic leap into fantasy; not to make that leap would be to leave himself without any hope of justification, and it is to make his counsel happy that Fowle goes along with him and supports the fantasy, not for a moment imagining that it is of any value; he is simply too nice a man to make his counsel miserable. The couple in *Lunch Hour*, looking for a room in which to commit adultery, have no reason not to carry out their plan; but the fact that it demands a married man's betrayal of his wife, indicates his natural untrustworthiness and his willingness to abandon his dependent children proves to the woman that, although the children do not exist, the light her imagination throws on his character cannot be denied. It is not the sordid mechanics of adultery that dissuades them, but the moral truth of what they imagine.

Mortimer's characters seem to share a common intensity of imagination so that they can walk into each other's fantasies and find themselves either trapped or liberated. When they do not find a way in which to share their fantasies, their capacity for communicating at all seems to be in danger, for to Mortimer's people communication is an exercise of the imagination rather than a matter entirely decided by reason. This, of course, makes him a natural writer of comedy. *What Shall We Tell Caroline?* concerns the attempt of Caroline's parents to decide how to explain to her, now that she is reaching adulthood, the imaginary *ménage-à-trois* in which they are involved with Tony, the assistant master at the school they run. The *ménage-à-trois* is a long-standing pretence, but it has kept the three of them happy, and an unsatisfactory marriage in balance for years. *The Wrong Side of the Park* considers a woman whose first marriage had been apparently flawlessly happy while her present, second marriage (her first husband having lost his life in a road accident) is dull and miserable. But as she thinks of past joy and present discontent it becomes as clear to her as to the audience that the happy memories she associates with her first marriage belong to her second, and that the desperate boredom belongs to the first; by the end of the play, she is beginning to understand herself, her husband, and her situation.

Two Stars for Comfort and *The Judge* are less dependent on characters whose fantasies provide a potentially dangerous sort of alternative reality. *Two Stars for Comfort* concerns two linked episodes in the amorous career of a man who cannot deny the love he thinks others need from him, and his discovery of his own real wishes and desires. Mortimer's plays all share a precise observation of the situation of a declining, embattled middle class driven deeper and deeper into seediness; he writes the elegy of fading prep schools and not very successful hotels, of a world where the only colour left is in personality. *A Voyage round My Father*, which began as a radio play in 1963 and made its way through a television adaptation into the theatre, shows Mortimer moving away from his normal preoccupations. The play is a study of his father, a well-known blind barrister, a man of wit and force, who refused to be handicapped in any way by his blindness; it is funny, affectionate, touching, and beautifully organised for the media through which it has passed.

Mortimer, himself barrister, scriptwriter, novelist, and playwright, has poured out a great deal of work. His revue sketches tend to become expansions of and variations on his favourite themes. He is a master of the one-act play. *A Flea in Her Ear* and *Cat among the Pigeons* are adaptations of farces by Feydeau in which the French master seems to be granted not mere translation but English nationalisation; the same is true of *The Captain of Köpenick*, Mortimer's version of Carl Zuckmayer's German comedy. Among his television plays, *David and Broccoli* centres on David, a weedily unathletic little boy, who contrives an ingenious, merciless revenge on his prep school P.T. instructor, a stupid, well-battered ex-boxer, who makes David's life a misery. In this, as in all Mortimer's comedies, something sad seems to have been going on in the background. In a sense, the *Rumpole* series of television plays, shamelessly exploiting a larger-than-life character, a usually successful defender of hopeless causes, a drinker, untidy smoker, and inveterate quoter of romantic verse, seems to voice a deep-rooted belief of Mortimer's that it is possible to manipulate the law on behalf of one's own sense of justice. Mortimer has said that he rejects the type of play in which comedy is easy because life itself is easy, but that "Comedy is, to my mind, the only thing worth writing in this despairing age, providing the comedy is on the side of the lonely, the neglected and the unsuccessful, and plays its part in the war against established rules and against the imposing of an arbitrary code of behaviour upon individual and unpredictable human beings." In the Introduction to *Three Plays* he makes his aims, if not his techniques, clear.

—Henry Raynor

MOSEL, Tad. American. Born in Steubenville, Ohio, 1 May 1922. Educated at Amherst College, Massachusetts, B.A. 1947; Yale University, New Haven, Connecticut, 1947–49; Columbia University, New York, M.A. 1953. Served in the United

States Army Air Force, 1943–46: Sergeant. Clerk, Northwest Airlines, 1951–53. Visiting Critic in Television Writing, Yale University School of Drama, 1957–58. Member of the Executive Board, *Television Quarterly*, Syracuse, New York; member of the Executive Council, Writers Guild of America. Recipient: Pulitzer Prize, 1961; New York Drama Critics Circle award, 1961. D.Litt.: College of Wooster, Ohio, 1963; D.F.A.: College of Steubenville, 1969. Agent: William Morris Agency, 1350 Avenue of the Americas, New York, New York 10019. Address: 400 East 57th Street, New York, New York 10022, U.S.A.

PUBLICATIONS

Plays

The Happiest Years (produced Amherst, Massachusetts, 1942).
The Lion Hunter (produced New York, 1952).
Madame Aphrodite (televised 1953; revised version, music by Jerry Herman, produced New York, 1962).
My Lost Saints (televised 1955). Published in *Best Television Plays*, edited by Gore Vidal, New York, Ballantine, 1956.
Other People's Houses: Six Television Plays (includes *Ernie Barger Is Fifty*, *The Haven*, *The Lawn Party*, *Star in the Summer Night*, *The Waiting Place*). New York, Simon and Schuster, 1956.
The Out-of-Towners (televised 1956). Published in *Television Plays for Writers: Eight Television Plays*, edited by A.S. Burack, Boston, The Writer, 1957.
The Five-Dollar Bill (televised 1957). Chicago, Dramatic Publishing Company, 1958.
Presence of the Enemy (televised 1958). Published in *Best Short Plays 1957–1958*, edited by Margaret Mayorga, Boston, Beacon Press, 1958.
All the Way Home, adaptation of the novel *A Death in the Family* by James Agee (produced New York, 1960). New York, Obolensky, 1961.
Impromptu (produced New York, 1961). New York, Dramatists Play Service, 1961.
That's Where the Town's Going (televised 1962). New York, Dramatists Play Service, 1962.

Screenplays: *Dear Heart*, 1964; *Up the Down Staircase*, 1967.

Television Plays: *Jinxed*, 1949; *The Figgerin' of Aunt Wilma*, 1953; *This Little Kitty Stayed Cool*, 1953; *The Remarkable Case of Mr. Bruhl*, 1953; *Ernie Barger Is Fifty*, 1953; *Other People's Houses*, 1953; *The Haven*, 1953; *Madame Aphrodite*, 1953; *The Lawn Party*, 1955; *Star in the Summer Night*, 1955; *Guilty Is the Stranger*, 1955; *My Lost Saints*, 1955; *The Waiting Place*, 1955; *The Out-of-Towners*, 1956; *The Five-Dollar Bill*, 1957; *The Morning Place*, 1957; *Presence of the Enemy*, 1958; *The Innocent Sleep*, 1958; *A Corner of the Garden*, 1959; *Sarah's Laughter*, 1959; *The Invincible Teddy*, 1960; *Three Roads to Rome: Venus Ascendant, Roman Fever, The Rest Cure*, from stories by Martha Gellhorn, Edith Wharton, and Aldous Huxley, 1960; *That's Where the Town's Going*, 1962.

Other

Leading Lady: The World and Theatre of Katharine Cornell, with Gertrude Macy. Boston, Little Brown, 1978.

* * *

Tad Mosel gained attention as one of the leading American writers for live television in the 1950's. His scripts were ideally suited for the medium in their restricted scope, focus on intimate details, and Chekhovian naturalism within a thoroughly contemporary American suburban milieu. An earlier one-act play written for the stage, *Impromptu*, has become a minor classic in its treatment of illusion and reality by means of a theatrical metaphor. A group of actors find themselves on a stage to which they have been summoned in order to improvise a play. Their groping efforts point up the recognition that life itself is essentially an improvisation in which roles are assumed and identity is elusive. Mosel handles this potentially trite and sentimental concept with wit and restraint.

Mosel's most successful work, however, was *All the Way Home*, a stage adaptation of James Agee's novel, *A Death in the Family*. Mosel's play captures the essence of the subjective, introspective novel while providing it with an external, theatrical form. In its depiction of several generations of a family and its compassionate rendering of death, birth, and the process of emotional maturing, the work has echoes of Thornton Wilder, an impression that is reinforced by Mosel's fluid handling of time and space. Especially noteworthy is the economy of dialogue, which is related to Mosel's sure sense of the power of the stage to communicate in unverbalized, visual terms.

—Jarka M. Burian

MOWAT, David. British. Born in Cairo, Egypt, 16 March 1943. Educated at Bryanston School, 1956–60; New College, Oxford, 1961–64, B.A. (honours) in English language and literature 1964; University of Sussex, Falmer, 1964–66. Cilcennin Fellow, University of Bristol, 1973–75; director of the Playwrights Workshop, University of Iowa, Iowa City, 1978; Fellow, Virginia Center for Creative Arts, 1979. Since 1984 director of the Playwriting Workshop, Actors Centre, London. Recipient: Arts Council bursary, 1970, 1971, 1976, 1983. Agent: Margaret Ramsay Ltd., 14-A Goodwin's Court, London WC2N 4LL. Address: 8 Folly Bridge Court, Oxford OX1 1SW, England.

PUBLICATIONS

Plays

Jens (produced Falmer, Sussex, 1965; London, 1969). Included in *Anna-Luse and Other Plays*, 1970.
Pearl (produced Brighton, 1966).
1850 (produced London, 1967).
Anna-Luse (produced Edinburgh, 1968; London, 1971; New York, 1972). Included in *Anna-Luse and Other Plays*, 1970.
Dracula, with others (produced Edinburgh, 1969; London, 1973).
Purity (produced Manchester, 1969; London, 1970; New York, 1972). Included in *Anna-Luse and Other Plays*, 1970.
Anna-Luse and Other Plays. London, Calder and Boyars, 1970.
The Normal Woman, and Tyyppi (produced London, 1970).
Adrift, with others (produced Manchester, 1970).
The Others (produced London, 1970). London, Calder and Boyars, 1973.
Most Recent Least Recent (produced Manchester, 1970).

Inuit (produced London, 1970).
Liquid (produced London, 1971).
The Diabolist (produced London, 1971).
John (produced London, 1971).
Amalfi, based on *The Duchess of Malfi* by Webster (produced Edinburgh, 1972).
Phoenix-and-Turtle (produced London, 1972; New York, 1976). Published in *The London Fringe Theatre*, edited by Victor Mitchell, London, Burnham House, 1975.
Morituri (produced London, 1972).
My Relationship with Jayne (produced London, 1973).
Come (produced London, 1973).
Main Sequence (produced Bristol, 1974).
The Collected Works (produced London, 1974; New York, 1977).
The Memory Man (produced Bristol, 1974).
The Love Maker (produced Bristol, 1974).
X to C (produced Bristol, 1975).
Kim (produced Sheffield, 1977; London, 1980).
Winter (produced Iowa City, 1978; London, 1983).
The Guise (produced Birmingham and London, 1979).
Hiroshima Nights (produced Milton Keynes, Buckinghamshire, and London, 1981).
The Midnight Sun (produced London, 1983).
Carmen (produced Chichester, 1984).

Short Stories

New Writers 11, with others. London, Calder and Boyars, 1974.

*

David Mowat comments:

I wrote my first play in 1955, and since then have written about 50, some 20 of which have been performed in Britain, Europe, and the U.S.A. In most of my work my intention has been to enlarge people's notion of reality, and in doing so to extend the dimensions and potential of the field known as "theatre."

The most widely-performed of my plays so far, *Anna-Luse*, written in 1966, is concerned with blindness and the treatment of the physically and mentally handicapped. *Purity*, from the same year, considers the phenomenon of censorship and the plight of the casualties of the "permissive society."

Recent work of mine, from about 1973, looks at questions relating to science, notably time and gravitation (*Come*), light and astrophysics (*Main Sequence*), memory and amnesia (*The Memory Man*). By contrast, *Phoenix-and-Turtle* and *The Collected Works* are centred on poems of Shakespeare and Wyatt respectively for their formal and thematic content. I have written musical scores for many of my plays, such as *The Memory Man*, *The Love Maker*, *X to C*, and the unproduced *Life of Casanova*.

* * *

The name of David Mowat is familiar to those who frequent experimental fringe theatres. He began his career as one of the band of writers who provide much of the repertoire of short plays produced on the lunch-time circuit.

Many of these playwrights seem almost indistinguishable from each other: indeed, some half dozen of them indulge occasionally in corporate efforts. Their methods are free-wheeling, their subject matter often sensational, and their intention to subvert the existing social structure by means of shock effects. They command respect on account of their talent and seriousness of purpose, although their playing out of sadistic and erotic fantasies induces doubt as often as cheers.

From these writers, Mowat stands conspicuously apart. There is present in his work an obsessive search for truth: "What information, useful information for the living of our lives, are we getting from this person?" asks the Narrator in a direct address to the audience in *Phoenix-and-Turtle*. In the same play he also observes "There's no obscenity so obscene as the horrid spectra of untruth lurking in the centre of one's home." The speaker is a Lecturer in English who has been sacked as a result of a liaison with a student; who has just burnt the manuscript of his book on the subject of the eponymous Shakespeare poem; who feels compelled to tell his wife that she has not long to live; and who—after an incestuous attack on his daughter—discovers that the girl is already pregnant. All these lies are brought into the open but, characteristically, the very act of telling the truth by means of the basic lie of theatre is also questioned. The author likens art to putting a frame around lies and, by making them scan or rhyme, pretending to give them a moral purpose.

Fat-Man (from the same period but not yet produced), deals allegorically with the rifts in the political left. Using as a motto a dictum of Mao Tse-tung's—"When the body is healthy, the feelings are correct"—the scene is set in a gymnasium threatened with demolition. The name of three of its four characters—Fatman, Cripple, and Little-Boy—indicate the satirical nature of the problem: each one has passionate convictions regarding the desired use of the gymnasium. The play is subtitled "the exercise of power"; needless to say, Mowat offers no easy solutions. His adaptation of *The Duchess of Malfi* and his approving quotation of Webster's remark that all life is a torture chamber may point to a vein of pessimism, but this, too, could be misleading. There is a quality of nagging obsession in Mowat's plays. His zeal for uncovering the truth has an echo of Ibsen, his haunted, nightmarish fantasies remind one of Strindberg. Of living authors, only Pinter comes to mind: Mowat, too, is a master of mystery and economy and his plays, though often difficult to comprehend at first sight, share with Pinter's the power to keep an audience spellbound.

He has travelled a long way since he wrote *Jens*: a comparatively straightforward piece of symbolism in which animals and humans mingle surrealistically. His most impressive early play was *Anna-Luse*. Here, a blind young girl gets up in the morning, goes through a ritual of stock-taking of her body and her possessions, and is visited by a girlfriend (also blind), a confused young man, and a dubious P.T. instructor. The last was the victim of a gang of thugs on the way over. Drenched but undaunted, he proceeds to give the girls some strange therapy, which induces in Anna-Luse a phantom pregnancy and childbirth. It is, however, the Instructor who is revealed most surprisingly: he ends, curled up like a baby, at Anna-Luse's breast.

Mowat's plays are by no means solemn. In *The Diabolist*, for example, a worried mum is introduced to her daughter's new boyfriend. He is the epitome of the ordinary bloke, but turns out unexpectedly to be a devil-worshipper. Apart from a macabre and not altogether unsuccessful ending, this sketch is as funny as anything produced by the absurdists.

The surface of these plays is in most cases shabbily suburban and lower middle class. They gain from being staged with absolute naturalism; the tension between manner and matter becomes then increasingly menacing. The rug is slowly and unnervingly pulled from under our feet, and we leave the theatre with our heads buzzing with questions which have no easy or formal solutions but which demand to be asked, if not answered.

Mowat's full-length play *John* belongs in this category. Its hero spends the entire play in a catatonic trance. The unease engendered by his silence, and its effect on the other, superficially "ordinary" characters, provides an exciting evening. Sudden irruptions of extreme violence occur regularly in Mowat's work, but they never appear gratuitously.

The short play *Come* seems to me wilfully enigmatic. Here a distraught father attempts to persuade his estranged daughter to return to him. He lies in wait for her in a room adjoining an intellectual party which becomes an orgy. Nothing is achieved, and neither the motives nor the narrative makes any comprehensible sense.

The full-length play *The Collected Works* is Mowat's most lucid and fully realized to date. The setting is a library; the books, like the eyes of accumulated wisdom and disillusion, stare down at the turbulent emotional tangle involving a researcher, a love-sick girl, the sterile Chief Librarian, and his beautiful wife. Taking as his theme the tensions between life and art, Mowat contrasts the messiness and unexpectedness of the former with the unalterable composure of the latter. There is much sly comedy as the characters explain themselves in lengthy monologues. Once again, he writes in a deliberate undertone, but the surface simmers with unease and bubbles with incipient volcanic explosions.

With his sensitivity, his depth, and his increasing technical assurance, there is every chance that he will emerge from his present, somewhat esoteric, milieu and give us a play of real significance, with "useful information for the living of our lives."

—Frank Marcus

MURDOCH, (Jean) Iris. British. Born in Dublin, Ireland, 15 July 1919. Educated at the Froebel Education Institute, London; Badminton School, Bristol; Somerville College, Oxford, 1938–42, B.A. (first class honours) 1942; Newnham College, Cambridge (Sarah Smithson Student in philosophy), 1947–48. Married the writer John Bayley in 1956. Assistant Principal in the Treasury, London, 1942–44; administrative officer with the United Nations Relief and Rehabilitation Administration (UNRRA) in London, Belgium, and Austria, 1944–46; Fellow, St. Anne's College, Oxford, and University Lecturer in Philosophy, Oxford University, 1948–63; Honorary Fellow of St. Anne's College since 1963; Lecturer, Royal College of Art, London, 1963–67. Recipient (for fiction): James Tait Black Memorial Prize, 1974; Whitbread Award, 1974; Booker Prize, 1978. Member, Irish Academy, 1970; Honorary Member, American Academy, 1975, and American Academy of Arts and Sciences, 1982; Honorary Fellow, Somerville College, 1977, and Newnham College, 1986; Companion of Literature, Royal Society of Literature, 1987. C.B.E. (Commander, Order of the British Empire), 1976; D.B.E. (Dame Commander, Order of the British Empire), 1987. Lives in Oxfordshire. Agent: Ed Victor Ltd., 162 Wardour Street, London W1V 4AT, England.

PUBLICATIONS

Plays

A Severed Head, with J.B. Priestley, adaptation of the novel by Murdoch (produced Bristol and London, 1963; New York, 1964). London, Chatto and Windus, 1964.

The Italian Girl, with James Saunders, adaptation of the novel by Murdoch (produced Bristol, 1967; London, 1968). London, French, 1969.

The Servants and the Snow (produced London, 1970). With *The Three Arrows*, London, Chatto and Windus, 1973; New York, Viking Press, 1974.

The Three Arrows (produced Cambridge, 1972). With *The Servants and the Snow*, London, Chatto and Windus, 1973; New York, Viking Press, 1974.

Art and Eros (produced London, 1980).

The Servants (opera libretto), adaptation of her play *The Servants and the Snow*, music by William Mathias (produced Cardiff, 1980).

Radio Play: *The One Alone* (in verse), music by Gary Carpenter, 1987.

Novels

Under the Net. London, Chatto and Windus, and New York, Viking Press, 1954.

The Flight from the Enchanter. London, Chatto and Windus, and New York, Viking Press, 1956.

The Sandcastle. London, Chatto and Windus, and New York, Viking Press, 1957.

The Bell. London, Chatto and Windus, and New York, Viking Press, 1958.

A Severed Head. London, Chatto and Windus, and New York, Viking Press, 1961.

An Unofficial Rose. London, Chatto and Windus, and New York, Viking Press, 1962.

The Unicorn. London, Chatto and Windus, and New York, Viking Press, 1963.

The Italian Girl. London, Chatto and Windus, and New York, Viking Press, 1964.

The Red and the Green. London, Chatto and Windus, and New York, Viking Press, 1965.

The Time of the Angels. London, Chatto and Windus, and New York, Viking Press, 1966.

The Nice and the Good. London, Chatto and Windus, and New York, Viking Press, 1968.

Bruno's Dream. London, Chatto and Windus, and New York, Viking Press, 1969.

A Fairly Honourable Defeat. London, Chatto and Windus, and New York, Viking Press, 1970.

An Accidental Man. London, Chatto and Windus, 1971; New York, Viking Press, 1972.

The Black Prince. London, Chatto and Windus, and New York, Viking Press, 1973.

The Sacred and Profane Love Machine. London, Chatto and Windus, and New York, Viking Press, 1974.

A Word Child. London, Chatto and Windus, and New York, Viking Press, 1975.

Henry and Cato. London, Chatto and Windus, 1976; New York, Viking Press, 1977.

The Sea, The Sea. London, Chatto and Windus, and New York, Viking Press, 1978.

Nuns and Soldiers. London, Chatto and Windus, 1980; New York, Viking Press, 1981.

The Philosopher's Pupil. London, Chatto and Windus, and New York, Viking Press, 1983.

The Good Apprentice. London, Chatto and Windus, 1985; New York, Viking, 1986.

The Book and the Brotherhood. London, Chatto and Windus, 1987; New York, Viking, 1988.

Verse

A Year of Birds. Tisbury, Wiltshire, Compton Press, 1978.

Other

Sartre, Romantic Rationalist. Cambridge, Bowes, and New Haven, Connecticut, Yale University Press, 1953; as *Sartre, Romantic Realist*, Brighton, Harvester Press, 1980.
The Sovereignty of Good over Other Concepts (lecture). Cambridge, University Press, 1967.
The Sovereignty of Good (essays). London, Routledge, 1970; New York, Schocken, 1971.
The Fire and the Sun: Why Plato Banished the Artists. London and New York, Oxford University Press, 1977.
Reynolds Stone (address). London, Warren, 1981.
Acastos: Two Platonic Dialogues. London, Chatto and Windus, 1986; New York, Viking, 1987.

*

Bibliography: *Iris Murdoch and Muriel Spark: A Bibliography* by Thomas T. Tominaga and Wilma Schneidermeyer, Metuchen, New Jersey, Scarecrow Press, 1976.

Manuscript Collection: University of Iowa, Iowa City.

Critical Studies: *Iris Murdoch* by Rubin Rabinovitz, New York, Columbia University Press, 1968; *Iris Murdoch* by Frank Baldanza, New York, Twayne, 1974; *Iris Murdoch* by Donna Gerstenberger, Lewisburg, Pennsylvania, Bucknell University Press, 1974; *Iris Murdoch* by A.S. Byatt, London, Longman, 1976; *Iris Murdoch: The Shakespearian Interest*, New York, Barnes and Noble, and London, Vision Press, 1979, and *Iris Murdoch*, London, Methuen, 1984, both by Richard Todd; *Iris Murdoch: Work for the Spirit* by Elizabeth Dipple, Chicago, University of Chicago Press, and London, Methuen, 1982; *Iris Murdoch's Comic Vision* by Angela Hague, Selinsgrove, Pennsylvania, Susquehanna University Press, 1984; *Iris Murdoch: The Saint and the Artist* by P.J. Conradi, London, Macmillan, and New York, St. Martin's Press, 1986; *Iris Murdoch* edited by Harold Bloom, New York, Chelsea House, 1986; *Iris Murdoch* by Deborah Johnson, Bloomington, Indiana University Press, and Brighton, Harvester Press, 1987.

* * *

Iris Murdoch has published only two original plays, *The Servants and the Snow* and *The Three Arrows*. Her third play, *Art and Eros*, remains unpublished at her wish, though Harold Hobson praised Andrew Cruickshank's performance, saying he conducted "a Socratic enquiry with philosophic zeal and illuminating theatrical skill." Before Murdoch tried her own playwriting, she collaborated with J.B. Priestley in the stage adaptation of her novel *A Severed Head*, and with James Saunders on the adaptation of *The Italian Girl*. The experienced hands of her collaborators made these plays more actable than her own later ones—indeed, *A Severed Head* was a theatrical success.

The play version of *A Severed Head* diminishes the complexity and obscurity of Murdoch's novel while it preserves its zany, quick-paced, very British high comedy. Physical farce, unexpected entrances, surprise discoveries, and unanticipated twists of plot all contribute to the effect. In "Against Dryness" Murdoch described her novel as one in which Sartre's "facile idea of sincerity" is tested against the "Hard idea of truth." When Martin is confronted by his wife's affair with her analyst, he tries broadmindedly to take it in stride. Unwilling to confess his own affair, and himself attracted to the American analyst, he suffers passively as his wife flaunts her infatuation and asks his approval of her plan to move into her lover's home. It takes Honor Klein, the half-sister of the analyst and a Cambridge anthropologist, to function as the "dark god" of this play. Manipulating all the other characters, she forces Martin to submit to irrational and primitive forces, to understand the "hard idea of truth," and to give himself over to his love for her, however temporary and however imperfectly understood. The play rivals Restoration comedy in the variety of its sexual pairings. Martin passes through the stages of outraged husband, latently homosexual lover to his wife's lover, complacent cuckold, violent lover, and lover surrendering to a higher, more mysterious, primitive love. Variations of incest are explored in the relationship between Honor and her half-brother and Antonia and her brother-in-law. In many ways, *A Severed Head* is a modern *The Cocktail Party*. T.S. Eliot's one-eyed Reilley becomes Murdoch's Honor Klein. Both plays examine religious feeling and neurotic obsessions.

Murdoch's other plays confirm that her gifts are as a novelist; nonetheless, the plays are also interesting in their own right. Murdoch the storyteller and Murdoch the moral philosopher struggling with ideas of freedom and contingency, accident and pattern both live fairly comfortably together in her novels. In her plays, the two fight each other and conspire to flatten her characters in a way the novel can accommodate or avoid. She is often unable to find the dialogue that believably captures her hybrid characters—half-mythic, half-natural.

The Servants and the Snow is a compact play which, like Strindberg's *Miss Julie*, depends for its effect on the pressure that the environment and past exert on the characters. The snow madness imprisons the characters; it covers and holds the blood guilt of the past. Basil, a landowner who returns to the isolated country house of his father who has died six months earlier, finds himself accountable for his father's crimes. His pragmatic, spoiled wife, Oriane, understands power. He feels unequal to the task of being master to his two hundred or more servants. Too anxious to play benevolent master, and too scrupulously "sincere" in his efforts to examine his own situation and motives, he finds himself forced to atone for his father's affair with a servant girl, Marina, which led to the death of the girl's husband at the hand of her jealous master. To prevent the erosion of his own authority, Basil is persuaded to re-enact his father's crime—to unflower the servant girl on her nuptial night. Neither Marina nor Oriane can tolerate weak men, but like the girl in Plath's poem "Daddy," prefer the "boot in the face" administered by the brute Daddy/husband. Marina consents to the marriage because it will figuratively give her back her dead master and dead husband. Oriane loathes Basil's sentimentality and misguided sense of guilt, and cannot abide the injury to her pride posed by Marina. In a jealous rage, Oriane kills her husband during Marina's wedding vows and welcomes the arrival of her brother, the General, who knows how to treat servants as swine and to give commands. The play examines the nature of power and the relation of past to present. It also probes moral character. The final action fulfills Murdoch's ideas about accident and free will, but it cannot wholly contain the ideas. The characters in the play are too reductive.

Murdoch's second play depends heavily for its effects upon ritual action and theatricality. Some of its moments are brilliant. Set in medieval Japan, the play explores the choices available to Prince Yorimitsu, a political prisoner held captive by the Emperor and held pawn by the Shogun, the real ruler. Yorimitsu's avowed ambition is to be a leader of the forces of the North and seize the power of the Shogun. The play abounds with deceits and stratagems. Necessity conspires to defeat moral purpose and free will. Yorimitsu is forced to choose between the contemplative life, an honorable death, love, or his ambition for power. The choices he ultimately exercizes are constrained: he acts without properly knowing the motives of those who act against him, or understanding the meaning of the choices put to him. At the end of the play, he is free, the Shogun dead, the princess he loved dead, and the young Emperor the willing accomplice in his escape. Intellectually, the play is fascinating, but its plot unfolds too slowly and the motives behind certain actions are incompletely conceptualized.

—Carol Simpson Stern

MURPHY, Thomas. Irish. Born in Tuam, County Galway, 23 February 1935. Educated at Vocational School, Tuam; Vocational Teachers' Training College, Dublin. Married Mary Hippisley; three children. Apprentice fitter and welder, Tuam, 1953–55; engineering teacher, Vocational School, Mountbellow, County Galway, 1957–62. Actor and director, 1951–62. Member of the Board of Directors, 1972–83, and since 1986 writer-in-association, Irish National Theatre (Abbey Theatre), Dublin; Regents Lecturer, University of California, Santa Barbara, 1981; writer-in-association, Druid Theatre, Galway, 1983–85. Founding member, Moli Productions, Dublin, 1974. Recipient: Irish Academy of Letters award, 1972; Independent Newspapers award, 1983; Harvey's award, 1983, 1986; *Sunday Tribune* award, 1985. Member, Irish Academy of Letters, 1982, and Aosdána, 1984. Agent: Kenneth Ewing, Fraser and Dunlop Scripts, 91 Regent Street, London W1R 8RU, England; or, Bridget Aschenberg, International Creative Management, 40 West 57th Street, New York, New York 10019, U.S.A. Address: 46 Terenure Road West, Dublin 6, Ireland.

PUBLICATIONS

Plays

On the Outside, with Noel O'Donoghue (produced Cork, 1961; New Haven, Connecticut, 1976). With *On the Inside*, Dublin, Gallery Press, 1976.

A Whistle in the Dark (produced London, 1961; New Haven, Connecticut, and New York, 1969). New York, French, 1971.

Famine (produced Dublin, 1966; London, 1969; New York, 1981). Dublin, Gallery Press, 1977.

The Fooleen (as *A Crucial Week in the Life of a Grocer's Assistant*, televised 1967; as *The Fooleen*, produced Dublin, 1969). Dixon, California, Proscenium Press, 1970; Dublin, Gallery Press, 1978.

The Orphans (produced Dublin, 1968; Newark, Delaware, 1971). Newark, Delaware, Proscenium Press, 1974.

The Morning after Optimism (produced Dublin, 1971; New York, 1974). Cork, Mercier Press, 1973.

The White House (produced Dublin, 1972).

On the Inside (also director: produced Dublin, 1974; New Haven, Connecticut, 1976). With *On the Outside*, Dublin, Gallery Press, 1976.

The Vicar of Wakefield, adaptation of the novel by Goldsmith (produced Dublin, 1974).

The Sanctuary Lamp (produced Dublin, 1975; New York, 1980). Dublin, Poolbeg Press, 1976; revised version, Dublin, Gallery Press, 1984.

The J. Arthur Maginnis Story (produced Dublin, 1976).

Conversations on a Homecoming (televised 1976; produced Galway, 1985; New York, 1986; London, 1987). Dublin, Gallery Press, 1986.

Epitaph under Ether (also director: produced Dublin, 1979).

The Blue Macushla (produced Dublin, 1980).

The Informer, adaptation of the novel by Liam O'Flaherty (also director: produced Dublin, 1981; Louisville, 1982).

She Stoops to Conquer, adaptation of the play by Goldsmith (produced Dublin, 1982).

The Gigli Concert (produced Dublin, 1983; Costa Mesa, California, 1984). Dublin, Gallery Press, 1984.

Bailegangáire (produced Galway, 1985; London, 1986; New Haven, Connecticut, 1987). Dublin, Gallery Press, 1986.

A Thief of a Christmas (produced Dublin, 1985).

Television Plays: *The Fly Sham*, 1963; *Veronica*, 1963; *A Crucial Week in the Life of a Grocer's Assistant*, 1967; *Snakes and Reptiles*, 1968; *Young Man in Trouble*, 1970; *The Moral Force*, *The Policy*, *Relief* (trilogy), 1973; *Conversations on a Homecoming*, 1976; *Speeches of Farewell*, 1976; *Bridgit*, 1981; *Fatalism*, 1981.

*

Bibliography: *Ten Modern Irish Playwrights* by Kimball King, New York, Garland, 1979.

Critical Studies: "Thomas Murphy Issue" of *Irish University Review* (Dublin), Spring 1987.

Theatrical Activities:
Director: **Plays**—*On the Outside/On the Inside*, Dublin, 1974; *Famine*, Dublin, 1978; *The Well of the Saints* by J.M. Synge, Dublin, 1979; *Epitaph under Ether*, Dublin, 1979; *The Informer*, Dublin, 1981.

Thomas Murphy comments:

My plays attempt to recreate the feeling or the mood of life rather than to represent it: they attempt to create something that can be identified with, felt or recognised. The emotional and/or spiritual truth is, if anything, more important than the intellectual truth. The mood can be the theme of the play.

* * *

Apart from *A Whistle in the Dark*, which made Kenneth Tynan and other notables sit up in the early 1960's, Thomas Murphy's plays have not won the international recognition they deserve. It is significant that when *Conversations on a Homecoming* was staged by the Galway Druid Theatre Company at the Pepsico International Arts Festival in New York in 1986 he was spoken of in reviews as if he were new on the scene.

The main reason for this unwarranted neglect internationally seems to lie in Murphy's exploration of themes that are particularly (though not exclusively) Irish, in a form that uncompromisingly makes strenuous demands on audiences. A typical Murphy play, while not necessarily set in Dublin and possibly as vague in setting as the dreamlike forest in *The Morning after Optimism*, is occupied with a spiritual deprivation and a social humiliation that are endemically Irish. The grounding, the "objective correlative," is invariably a situation potentially explosive, deriving from feelings powerfully responsive to defects in a particular community, society, or national institution. Unless one is familiar with the grounding, the plays may appear obscure or the level of feeling inexplicably intense, and the language (Murphy's strongest weapon) perhaps in excess of the apparent facts. This is to say that atmosphere and mood are of primary importance. For example, *The Sanctuary Lamp*, to the puzzlement of some British reviewers covering the Dublin Theatre Festival in 1975, caused disturbance among its first audiences at the Abbey Theatre, and comparison was made with the initial impact of O'Casey's *The Plough and the Stars* (1926), when riots occurred. Murphy's play was regarded by some as highly blasphemous. The satiric and iconoclastic feelings released in it arise out of a church setting, taken over by three outcast characters, Harry and Francisco, who used to have a circus act of a sleazy nature, and Maudie, a runaway orphan frightened into believing that Jesus has taken away her baby because she is bad. Francisco has pursued Harry for defecting, and to spring upon him the shattering news that Harry's wife, who formed part of their dubious circus act in rich people's houses, is dead from an overdose of drugs. Harry, for his part, is heart-sick at the death of his little daughter Teresa, and is burning with feelings of revenge against life and God. He takes the job of sacristan and custodian of the lamp that signifies the divine presence. When Francisco arrives, pursuing the fugitive from himself, they argue in the locked church at night over the effects on their lives of the "metaphysical monster" the Catholic Church. With a bottle of altar wine in one hand Francisco delivers from the pulpit his bitter jeremiad against contemporary Catholicism. But when all passion's spent, the three characters settle down for the night in a confession box, forming a fellowship against the dark, and tending the lamp as a gesture of human rather than of divine presence.

Murphy's plays, besides being uncompromising as passionate indictments of hypocrisy of every kind, are also theatrically demanding. Some, such as the historical drama *Famine*, are almost unrelieved Theatre of Cruelty. One of his best and most ambitious plays, *The Gigli Concert*, ran for three and a half hours at the Abbey Theatre, and Murphy refused to cut it. The director and cast of such plays face huge problems, but overcoming them has provided the Irish theatre with some of its greatest achievements in the 1970's and early 1980's. *The Gigli Concert* may be described as a fantastic reworking of the Faust story so as to explore and express in contemporary terms the nature of damnation and of magical release. The plot centres on a self-made Irish millionaire's visit during a mental breakdown to one J.P.W. King, a professed "dynamatologist," actually an abandoned practitioner of an American quasi-science. The "patient" wants to sing like Beniamino Gigli. It is an obsession arising from recurring depression caused by guilt. In this regard he could be compared with Ibsen's Solness (*The Master Builder*) and Osborne's Maitland (*Inadmissible Evidence*). King gets caught up in the pursuit of this impossible ambition and Gigli's voice, on record, begins to fascinate him also. "He's the devil!" the Irish Man warns him. But when the latter backs away, preferring to return to society with all his neuroses intact, and King's Gretchen figure has told him she is dying of cancer, while Helen accuses him of making obscene telephone calls, King feels compelled to go on with the mad scheme of trying himself to sing like Gigli. He turns to conjuring and in a theatrically challenging scene he manages to bring off the impossible: the "magic" of theatre and its illusion allows the audience to believe that this hopeless case has transcended the barriers of the normal. King then plugs in the cassette player once more and pressing the repeat button lets Gigli sing on forever while he takes off elsewhere.

Bailegangáire, Murphy's most recent play (if one discounts its counterpart *A Thief of a Christmas*, staged at the Abbey as a Christmas show in 1985), breaks new ground. Written when Murphy was playwright-in-association at the Druid Theatre in Galway, it has a good deal of Irish (i.e., Gaelic) words and phrases and it deals with Irish tragic material in a style that seems to marry Synge and Beckett. The play combines two levels and two situations in two time periods. On one level an old woman, Mommo, raves in a senile manner in bed, endlessly telling a story of a tragic event in her history, but never finishing the tale. On another level her granddaughters, Mary and Dolly, while caring for her try at the same time to come to terms with their own lives. Often their conversations take place while Mommo raves on at the same time. Each of the women is in fact trying to seize hold of her life, but it happens that Mommo holds the key to the happiness of all three. Mary, the nurse, realising that Mommo's obsession with the story relates to her own need to shape her life, forces her to finish the tale for the first time. It concerns a laughing contest in which Mommo's husband won over a local champion but caused his death and subsequently the death of another grandchild. The full facts have the effect of drawing Mary and Dolly closer to Mommo, and, rather like the three characters who settle down for the night at the end of *The Sanctuary Lamp*, these three women settle down in Mommo's bed and, in knowledge and understanding, find peace. The beautiful and moving ending was powerfully rendered by Siobhan McKenna as Mommo in the first production, which travelled to the Donmar Warehouse, London, in 1986. The play, while being well received, was found to be somewhat mystifying to some English reviewers, who could make sense of it only as allegory, with Mommo as Ireland obsessed with her history.

Murphy stands out among the most challenging and most powerful Irish playwrights since Sean O'Casey. His only rival among his Irish contemporaries is Brian Friel, who writes a more lyrical, more Chekhovian kind of play and who has enjoyed more international attention. Perhaps Murphy's approach to theatre is too uncompromising to win international acclaim, and there is no denying unevennesses in his plays. But their very roughness vouches for their honesty, and what they aspire to constantly is so admirable and so compassionate that their beauty and truth must come to be appreciated worldwide.

—Christopher Murray

MURRELL, John. Canadian. Born in the United States, 15 October 1945. Educated at schools in Alberta; University of Calgary, Alberta, B.A. in drama. Married; one daughter. Schoolteacher for 5 years; playwright-in-residence, Alberta Theatre Projects, Calgary, 1975; associate director, Stratford Festival, Ontario, 1978. Recipient: Clifford E. Lee award, 1975. Address: c/o Talonbooks, 201–1019 East Cordova, Vancouver, British Columbia V6A 1M8, Canada.

PUBLICATIONS

Plays

Metamorphosis. Edmonton, Alberta Department of Culture, 1970.

Haydn's Head (produced Edmonton, 1973).
Power in the Blood (produced Edmonton, 1975).
Arena (produced Calgary, 1975).
Teaser, with Kenneth Dyba (produced Calgary, 1975).
A Great Noise, A Great Light (produced Calgary, 1976).
Waiting for the Parade: Faces of Women in War (produced Calgary, 1977; London, 1979; St. Paul, 1982). Vancouver, Talonbooks, 1980.
Memoir (produced Guelph, Ontario, 1977; London, 1978; revised version produced Calgary, 1981). New York, Avon, 1978.
Uncle Vanya: Scenes from Rural Life, adaptation of a play by Chekhov (produced Stratford, Ontario, 1978; Portsmouth, New Hampshire, 1979; London, 1982). Toronto, Theatrebooks, 1978.
Mandragola, adaptation of the play by Machiavelli (produced Calgary, 1978).
Bajazet, adaptation of the play by Racine (produced Toronto, 1979).
The Seagull, adaptation of a play by Chekhov (produced Stratford, Ontario, 1980).
Farther West (produced Calgary, 1982). With *New World*, Toronto, Coach House Press, 1985.

*

Theatrical Activities:
Director: **Play**—*Mrs. Warren's Profession* by Shaw, Calgary, 1981.

* * *

Though John Murrell has several unpublished scripts and translations to his credit, he is known primarily for the internationally successful works *Memoir* and *Waiting for the Parade*. These were preceded by several other pieces. *Power in the Blood*, loosely about the American evangelist Amy Semple McPherson, was followed by two comedies commissioned by Pleiades Theatre, Calgary, and then by *A Great Noise, A Great Light*, about the late 1930's in Alberta.

Waiting for the Parade interweaves the stories of five women through several years of World War II in Calgary. The eldest, Margaret, is pessimistic, a widow with one son in the navy and one imprisoned for anti-war activities. Catherine, a factory-hand, is a total contrast, a promiscuous extrovert whose husband is a prisoner-of-war. Eve is an idealistic teacher with a husband too old to join the army. They are bossed by the energetic, bigoted Janet, who is compensating for her spouse, a radio announcer who is not contributing to the war effort (she is more thinly characterized than the others). Detached from the foursome is a seamstress, German-born Marta, whose father is interned for supposed Nazi sympathies. These women variously talk, plan, and argue while rolling bandages and taking fruit to troop trains at the station: the detail of wartime life, with appropriate songs, is good. *Waiting for the Parade* is gentle and poignant, sometimes comic.

Memoir is about 77-year-old Sarah Bernhardt in 1922, during the last year of her life, composing her memoirs on an island off the Brittany coast, occasionally acting a fragment of her greatest roles. The only other character is her pedantic, spinsterish, middle-aged male secretary, dubious about theatre, a bad actor, who has to play all the other parts—a manager, a doctor, Oscar Wilde. Bernhardt's biography is obliquely revealed. "Old actors do not die; they simply rehearse their dying," comments Keith Garebian. The play touches on such themes as the relationship between art and life and that between a great artist and lesser mortals. Murrell always writes eloquently, risking over-writing: an early work such as this is marked by lines like "a tall gray woman with a voice like a clay jug thrown against a stone wall." The 1981 version of the play is substantially altered, and improved. *Memoir* has been very successful in many countries.

Two of Murrell's subsequent plays are more ambitious, with larger casts. Though directed by Robin Phillips, neither drew much national or international attention. *Farther West*, which the author labels "a romance," is loosely based on the life and death of an actual Calgary brothel-mistress, May Buchanan. Starting in Rat Portage, Ontario, in 1886, she travels west to Calgary and then has to take refuge in Nose Creek. She is pursued by Seward, an obsessive, puritanical policeman who continues the hunt for her even after leaving the force, and Shepherd, a rancher who loves her and wants to marry her. They pursue her to Vancouver, where in 1892 Shepherd kills her. In a powerful final scene, Seward pushes her corpse in a rowing-boat out into English Bay. The play is strongly charged with sex—the first half ends in what Mark Czarnecki called "the most erotic simulated lovemaking ever to see the Canadian stage"—yet May can perform the sex act while keeping her true self inviolate. She never stops seeking her West: "Thomas Shepherd of Sheep River! That's not the sort of kindling to start fires under me. I've got to travel farther, much farther, before I find anybody." In her West there are "no rules, no laws, no judges." Instead, she seeks her independence: "I prefer my own kind of pleasure, my own kind of peace and my own pennies to anybody else's dimes!" The West as myth, in fact, is partly caught in this drama, though perhaps impossible to embody on the stage.

New World takes place on one summer day on China Beach on Vancouver Island, looking out to the Pacific. The seven characters include an unhappy English woman painter (Old World) and her brother, an American maker of rock videos (New World). Between the two worlds are a third sibling, an ageing photographer (anglophone Canadian) and his assistant, a cook and bisexual (francophone Canadian). The sadness of both the failed painter and the successful photographer is exposed. There's lots of plot: the French-Canadian will go off with the rock-video man's wife, but include him too, while her daughter starts to fall in love with the photographer's young apprentice. Yet *New World* is not centrally a play of character or plot. On the contrary, what matters for Murrell are the references to *The Tempest*, the sea and the sun; the use of Puccini's music; the photographer taking endless self-portraits; a beautiful blue Japanese fishing float, found on the beach, which is admired, broken, mended, and, at the last moment of the third scene, "spontaneously explodes into a thousand bright fragments." Murrell aspires here to write what Jamie Portman called a "tone poem" beyond the banalities of character and plot (it resembles some of Michel Tremblay's later work and David Storey's *Early Days*); he has not achieved this difficult ambition.

Murrell is a fine craftsman in his use of both language and music. After modest, very effective small-scale pieces, he gropes towards a poetic theatre in *New World* and encompasses epic and myth in the audacious *Farther West*.

—Malcolm Page

MUSAPHIA, Joseph. New Zealander. Born in London, England, 8 April 1935. Educated at a primary school in Australia, and at Christchurch Boys' High School, New Zealand. Married Marie Beder in 1966; one son and one daughter. Shop assistant, Ballintyne's, Christchurch, 1950–51; motor mechanic, David Crozier's, Christchurch, 1951–54; commercial artist, Stuart Wearn, Christchurch, 1954–55, Wood and Braddock, Wellington, 1955, John Haddon, London, England, 1956–57, and for agencies, Wellington, 1958–60; cartoonist, New Zealand *Listener*, Wellington, 1958–60; fish and chip shop owner, Wellington, 1971–73. Since 1974 columnist, the *Dominion* and *Sunday Times*, both Wellington. Writing Fellow, Victoria University, Wellington, 1979. Recipient: New Zealand State Literary Fund grant, 1963; New Zealand Arts Council grant, 1974, 1976. Agent: Playmarket, P.O. Box 9767, Wellington. Address: 75 Monro Street, Wellington 3, New Zealand.

PUBLICATIONS

Plays

Free (produced Wellington, 1961). Published in *Landfall 68* (Christchurch), December 1963.
Virginia Was a Dog (broadcast 1963; produced Wellington, 1968).
The Guerilla (produced Sydney, 1971). Sydney, Currency Press, 1976.
Victims (produced Wellington, 1973). Published in *Act 20* (Wellington), August 1973.
Obstacles (produced Wellington, 1974). Published in *Act 25* (Wellington), December 1974.
Mothers and Fathers (produced Wellington, 1975). Sydney, Currency Press, 1977.
Hunting (produced Wellington, 1979).
Shotgun Wedding (produced Wellington, 1980). Wellington, Playmarket, 1981.
The Hangman (produced Wellington, 1983).
Mates (produced Wellington, 1986).

Screenplay: *Don't Let It Get You*, 1966.

Radio Plays: more than 120 plays, including *Out of the Passing Crowd*, 1962; *A Seat in the Sun*, 1963; *Bread Crumbs for the Pigeons*, 1963; *Suddenly It's Tomorrow*, 1963; *Virginia Was a Dog*, 1963; *This Business of Being Alive*, 1963; *The Cause of Something*, 1965; *This Side of Life*, 1965; *The Marriage*, 1965; *See Mr. Roberts*, 1966; *Too Many Cooks*, 1966; *The Listener with the Pop-up Toaster*, 1966; *Be Good If You Could but You Can't*, 1967; *Has Anybody Here Seen Christmas?*, 1967; *Once upon a Blind Date*, 1968; *Think!*, 1968; *A Fair Go for Charlie Wellman*, 1968; *The Spook*, 1968; *A Jolly Roger for Christmas*, 1969; *The Old Man and the Sea and Christmas Dinner*, 1973; *Going On*, 1974; *I Was a Teenage Matchmaker*, 1975; *Sound Furious*, 1976; *Never Let It Be Said*, 1977; *Flotsam and Jetsam*, 1977; *Hello Goodbye*, 1979; *Mind Jogging*, 1980; *Just Desserts*, 1982; *That'll Be the Day*, 1983.

Television Plays: episode in *Buck House* series, 1974; scripts for *Joe's World* and *In View of the Circumstances* series.

*

Joseph Musaphia comments:

While I have tried both serious and comedy writing and acting, I prefer comedy. Receiving an immediate, vocal response from the members of an audience is the one vital peculiarity comedy has that allows its creator conclusive proof that his effort was worthwhile. By the same token, I hope that what the audience initially laughed at supplies them with food for thought for some time after their amusement has died down. If I had to describe my attitude towards my writing, it would probably be best summed up by a description used by a local critic in reviewing *Mothers and Fathers*. Michael Dean referred to me in the New Zealand *Listener* as a "moral democrat." Having checked out his description in as many tomes as are available to me, I have decided that it just might be inoffensive enough to be acceptable to this playwright, who is not at all happy to be categorized or to write about his own work. I don't enjoy being asked what a play of mine "was getting at," because if the play worked on stage the question should not have to be asked. I can say that after a preposterously varied existence, I count myself very lucky indeed to be making such an enjoyable living out of a typewriter. If audiences continue to get half the pleasure out of watching my plays as I get writing them, I have no complaints.

* * *

Joseph Musaphia's plays for the theatre all in a sense develop out of the early one-act piece *Free*, which is about personal freedom. Musaphia has delighted in exploring the ways people hold down and exploit others, especially in sexual relationships, in order to satisfy purely selfish needs of their own. His plays are comedies—in fact, more than any other New Zealand playwright he uses some of the elements of 19th-century farce—but the moral implications seldom leave any doubt that it is his intention, as he would say, to hit his audience hard.

Musaphia found an apt vehicle for this in *The Guerilla*. Adam King, an ordinary man (though the name might suggest Original Egotism), frustrated by all the minor indignities imposed by petty officialdom on suburban life, barricades himself in his house with some hand grenades and his de facto wife and demands to see the Prime Minister. (It is characteristic that King's success in persuading the police to pass in to him an armalite rifle, a farcical detail which seems to remove the play from the world of possibility, actually occurred in the incident on which the play is based.) Musaphia likes to use such a character, apparently harmless, whom life drives into aberration if not madness. In *Obstacles* a bedridden woman sexually teases her father's friend into a position where she can blackmail them both into performing her slightest wish—yet still needs their assistance to reach the loo. Much of the comedy rises out of situations thus extrapolated, so to speak, from ordinary life into the world of farce.

Farce is not often connected with strong moral concern, and it is a sign of Musaphia's not-so-farcical nature that he has more difficulty with his last than with his first acts. He can catch an audience's attention effortlessly. The bickering couple of a dead marriage in *Shotgun Wedding* are interrupted by the entry of the husband's partner from a recent naughty weekend—in full bridal dress! It is a superb *coup de théâtre*. Equally fine is the opening of *Mothers and Fathers*, in which a suburban couple place by telephone the following advertisement: "Mature, liberated, rational, childless couple are willing to pay five thousand dollars to suitable woman prepared to volunteer her body for impregnation by male half of the aforementioned married couple."

Musaphia is unwilling to resolve the complications which arise from such openings with either a wedding or a pistol shot. Life is good for a laugh, but is also a serious matter, and when all passions are spent returns to its habitual grey.

The more complicated plots tend to diverge rather than converge in the last act. *Victims* (which capitalises splendidly on its 1900 setting and parallels the ignorance of strait-laced Victorian puritanism with modern societies for the preservation of community standards) opens with almost the entire cast standing around a grave, but ends with couples separated into three different bedrooms. Even when violence is used, as in the underrated *Hunting*—in which two middle-aged divorcees, feeling their way gingerly towards a relationship they both desperately want, are interrupted by the return of their grown-up children, also the victims of sexual mistakes, clamouring for their parents' undivided protection and attention—nothing is really resolved. This crisis of middle age also dominates Musaphia's latest play, *Mates*, where the same difficulty in finding a satisfying "action" or shape allows the initial power of the piece to drain away.

Mothers and Fathers, by far Musaphia's most successful play, avoids any madness or extreme nastiness, and presents four characters not one of whom is really unsympathetic. Their sexual needs and antagonisms result in a realignment of forces: the two husbands, rendered irrelevant, are left confronting their two ex-wives, who have joined against the common enemy and occupied the house—an example of aggressive feminism to be paralleled in most of the other plays. If Musaphia's men are not quite so rampantly chauvinist as some of his women, no doubt Musaphia would agree that their world is so arranged that they don't need to be so self-centred to get their way.

Musaphia has often contributed to the successful production of his plays as either director or actor. His audiences, though, have been suspicious of the taste shown in exploiting such pitiful and sometimes unpleasant characters for such uproarious farcical laughter. There is not a doubt that Musaphia can make his audiences laugh; but they have not always liked being hit so hard at the same time.

—John Thomson

NAUGHTON, Bill (William John Francis Naughton). British. Born in Ballyhaunis, County Mayo, Ireland, 12 June 1910; grew up in Lancashire, England. Educated at St. Peter and St. Paul School, Bolton, Lancashire. Civil Defence driver in London during World War II. Married to Ernestine Pirolt. Has worked as a lorry driver, weaver, and coal-bagger. Recipient: Screenwriters Guild award, 1967, 1968; Italia prize, for radio play, 1974; Children's Rights Workshop Other Award, 1978. Address: Kempis, Orrisdale Road, Ballasalla, Isle of Man, United Kingdom.

PUBLICATIONS

Plays

My Flesh, My Blood (broadcast 1957). London, French, 1959; revised version, as *Spring and Port Wine* (produced Birmingham, 1964; London, 1965; as *Keep It in the Family*, produced New York, 1967), London, French, 1967.
She'll Make Trouble (broadcast 1958). Published in *Worth a Hearing: A Collection of Radio Plays*, edited by Alfred Bradley, London, Blackie, 1967.
June Evening (broadcast 1958; produced Birmingham, 1966). London, French, 1973.
All in Good Time (as *Honeymoon Postponed*, televised 1961; as *All in Good Time*, produced London, 1963; New York, 1965). London, French, 1964.
Alfie (as *Alfie Elkins and His Little Life*, broadcast 1962; as *Alfie*, produced London, 1963; New York, 1964). London, French, 1964.
He Was Gone When We Got There, music by Leonard Salzedo (produced London, 1966).
Annie and Fanny (produced Bolton, Lancashire, 1967).
Lighthearted Intercourse (produced Liverpool, 1971).

Screenplays: *Alfie*, 1966; *The Family Way*, with Roy Boulting and Jeffrey Dell, 1966; *Spring and Port Wine*, 1970.

Radio Plays: *Timothy*, 1956; *My Flesh, My Blood*, 1957; *She'll Make Trouble*, 1958; *June Evening*, 1958; *Late Night on Watling Street*, 1959; *The Long Carry*, 1959; *Seeing a Beauty Queen Home*, 1960; *On the Run*, 1960; *Wigan to Rome*, 1960; *'30–'60*, 1960; *Jackie Crowe*, 1962; *Alfie Elkins and His Little Life*, 1962; *November Day*, 1963; *The Mystery*, 1973; *A Special Occasion*, 1982.

Television Plays: *Nathaniel Titlark* series, 1957; *Starr and Company* series 1958; *Yorky* series, with Allan Prior, 1960–61; *Looking for Frankie*, 1961; *Honeymoon Postponed*, 1961; *Somewhere for the Night*, 1962; *It's Your Move*, 1967.

Novels

Rafe Granite. London, Pilot Press, 1947.
One Small Boy. London, MacGibbon and Kee, 1957.
Alfie. London, MacGibbon and Kee, and New York, Ballantine, 1966.
Alfie, Darling. London, MacGibbon and Kee, 1970; New York, Simon and Schuster, 1971.

Short Stories

Late Night on Watling Street and Other Stories. London, MacGibbon and Kee, 1959; New York, Ballantine, 1966.
The Goalkeeper's Revenge and Other Stories. London, Harrap, 1961.
The Goalkeeper's Revenge, and Spit Nolan. London, Macmillan, 1974.
The Bees Have Stopped Working and Other Stories. Exeter, Wheaton, 1976.

Other

A Roof over Your Head (autobiography). London, Pilot Press, 1945.
Pony Boy (for children). London, Pilot Press, 1946.
A Dog Called Nelson (for children). London, Dent, 1976.
My Pal Spadger (for children). London, Dent, 1977.
On the Pig's Back: An Autobiographical Excursion. Oxford and New York, Oxford University Press, 1987.

*

Critical Study: introduction by Naughton to *Spring and Port Wine*, London, Heinemann, 1973.

* * *

Bill Naughton's emergence in the 1960's as a major writer for the theatre was primarily seen as a revival of the spirit of the Manchester School, and indeed his two biggest successes—*All in Good Time* and *Spring and Port Wine*, concentrating on the detailed exploration of family crises in working-class Bolton—recall the world of Harold Brighouse. In fact, in these plays Naughton emerges more as the natural successor of intermediary writers in the Manchester tradition such as Walter Greenwood; and to concentrate only on this side of his talents is to overlook the wider range and theatrical development away from realism in plays such as *Alfie* and even in work derived from his favourite Bolton background such as *June Evening*. This work, based on a radio original, is an episodic play covering the stream of life in a Bolton street in 1921 during a pit strike; it is one of Naughton's most interesting plays, though it never achieved commercial success, and has had to date only an abortive provincial tour.

Naughton's earlier work in television and in radio documentary plays such as *The Long Carry* (about coal picking) and *Wigan to Rome* (following a coach-party of Northern tourists) provided much of the content and style of his work in the theatre, although his first stage play, *All in Good Time*, indicates an attempt to establish a more formal construction in contrast with his television and radio plays, which largely avoided orthodox frameworks. However, it similarly examines a basic truth of human behaviour in a context of carefully observed community life. Its basis, the non-consummation of a young couple's marriage, could be the core of any routine Northern comedy, even opening with the familiar situation of a wedding-party, but the human elements in the play outweigh conventionality, and already apparent is the great strength of Naughton's gentle but ironically affectionate and therefore basically unsentimental attitude towards his characters. He is particularly adroit in handling changes of mood as an initial comedy situation graduates into a wider examination of parental problems as well as those of the younger generation. The play suffers somewhat by its rather abruptly contrived final disclosures, revealing a certain lack of cohesion between Naughton's discursive manner and the demands of the three-act play format, and the same pattern occurs in the second of his Bolton comedies, *Spring and Port Wine*. A similarly warm-hearted comedy, it likewise focuses on family stress, with an even stronger paterfamilias central character in Rafe Crompton, a Hobson-like domestic tyrant. Naughton once wrote of the Bolton he knew—"I remember the smells in the homes, the jobs, and everything about the people"—an attitude reflected in the detail of the play and an understanding of his characters which gives them the stamp of authenticity, just as Naughton's acute ear for the occasional deflating truth saves the characters from overwhelming sentimentality. Again, however, the fabric of the play tends to dissolve at the close, in a contrived happy ending of reconciliation, as Crompton crumbles in a surprisingly sudden change of heart.

Alfie reveals further Naughton's gift of creating a dynamic central character and demonstrates that he is not necessarily a playwright of Lancashire comedy only. This history of the amorous adventures of a cockney "spiv" Don Juan had its origin in one of Naughton's best radio plays, *Alfie Elkins and His Little Life*, and its greatest strength, Naughton's extraordinary ability to get under the skin of his protagonist, remains in the stage version. Although the surroundings of the main character and the counterpoint of Alfie's monologues with the action at times seem rather thin, and the transitions in the opening-out of the play occasionally somewhat stiff, Alfie himself remains a superbly realized figure as Naughton explores all his meretricious charm and essential bleak loneliness, especially in a striking scene as Alfie thinks of fatherhood, an idea he finds at once appealing and appalling.

Naughton's work since these three successes has been sporadic. *He Was Gone When We Got There* was in a markedly different vein, a neo-Orwellian social satire probing the clash between computerized bureaucracy and anarchic individualism in the shape of Badger Brown, the last "Free unit" in a Britain entangled in red tape. A promising core is dissipated by the lumbering obviousness of the satire and even more by the surprisingly lukewarm sub-Ealing Films quality of Naughton's comedy. *Lighthearted Intercourse* marked a return to the surer background of his Bolton plays; a gentle, two-character comedy of married life, it has a great deal of poignancy and charm. Its loose structure and use of a shifting time-scale represented a new departure for Naughton in the use of his staple Lancashire material within a freer technique.

—Alan Strachan

NELSON, Richard. American. Born in Chicago, Illinois, 17 October 1950. Educated at Hamilton College, Clinton, New York, 1968–72, B.A. 1972. Married Cynthia B. Bacon in 1972; one daughter. Literary manager, BAM Theater Company, Brooklyn, New York, 1979–81; associate director, Goodman Theatre, Chicago, 1980–83; dramaturg, Guthrie Theatre, Minneapolis, 1981–82. Recipient: Watson fellowship, 1972; Rockefeller grant, 1979; Obie award, 1979, 1980; National Endowment for the Arts fellowship, 1980, 1985; Guggenheim fellowship, 1983; ABC award, 1985; Playwrights USA award, 1986; HBO award, 1986; *Time Out* award (London), 1987. Agent: Peter Franklin, William Morris Agency, 1350 Avenue of the Americas, New York, New York 10019. Address: 32 South Street, Rhinebeck, New York 12572, U.S.A.

PUBLICATIONS

Plays

The Killing of Yablonski (produced Los Angeles, 1975).

Conjuring an Event (produced Los Angeles, 1976; New York, 1978). Included in *An American Comedy and Other Plays*, 1984.

Scooping (produced Washington, D.C., 1977).

Jungle Coup (produced New York, 1978). Published in *Plays from Playwrights Horizons*, New York, Broadway Play Publishing, 1987.

The Vienna Notes (produced Minneapolis, 1978; New York and Sheffield, 1979). Published in *Wordplays 1*, New York, Performing Arts Journal Publications, 1980.

Don Juan, adaptation of a play by Molière (produced Washington, D.C., 1979).

The Wedding, with Helga Ciulei, adaptation of a play by Brecht (produced New York, 1980).

The Suicide, adaptation of a play by Nikolai Erdman (produced Chicago, 1980).

Bal (produced Chicago, 1980). Included in *American Comedy and Other Plays*, 1984.

Rip Van Winkle; or, "The Works" (produced New Haven, Connecticut, 1981). New York, Broadway Play Publishing, 1986.

Il Campiello, adaptation of the play by Goldoni (produced New York, 1981). New York, Theatre Communications Group, 1981.

Jungle of Cities, adaptation of a play by Brecht (produced New York, 1981).
The Marriage of Figaro, adaptation of a play by Beaumarchais (produced Minneapolis, 1982; New York, 1985).
The Return of Pinocchio (produced Seattle, 1983; New York, 1986). Included in *An American Comedy and Other Plays*, 1984.
An American Comedy (produced Los Angeles, 1983). Included in *An American Comedy and Other Plays*, 1984.
Accidental Death of an Anarchist, adaptation of a play by Dario Fo (produced Washington, D.C., and New York, 1984). New York, French, 1987.
Three Sisters, adaptation of a play by Chekhov (produced Minneapolis, 1984).
Between East and West (also co-director: produced Seattle, 1984). Published in *New Plays USA 3*, edited by James Leverett and M. Elizabeth Osborn, New York, Theatre Communications Group, 1986.
An American Comedy and Other Plays. New York, Performing Arts Journal Publications, 1984.
Principia Scriptoriae (produced New York and London, 1986). New York, Broadway Play Publishing, and London, English Theatre Guild, 1986.

Other

Editor, *Strictly Dishonorable and Other Lost American Plays*. New York, Theatre Communications Group, 1986.

*

Theatrical Activities:
Director: **Play**—*Between East and West* (co-director, with Ted D'Arms), Seattle, 1984.

* * *

Richard Nelson is one of a small handful of American playwrights who write "political" plays. His characters wrestle not only with their families and/or their immediate personal concerns, but with complexities of the world in which they struggle to survive. In the tradition of Brecht and Molière, as well as Shakespeare, Nelson's characters live in and deal with a social and political landscape.

The title of a recent work, *Principia Scriptoriae*, translates into "Principles of Writing," and as the plot unfolds it becomes apparent that Nelson is writing about what happens to principles when the individual is forced to confront a not always welcoming society. The story is about two young writers of strong political convictions who must come to terms with how the world uses writers who involve themselves in public life. It is an investigation of human vanity, the abuses and seductions of power, and of an artist's responsibility to live his life according to his convictions. This play about writers and politics, and about individuals in a time of crisis, got little better than a shrug from New York critics when it opened at the Manhattan Theatre Club under the direction of Lynne Meadow. Yet it was enthusiastically received in London when it was presented by the Royal Shakespeare Company, directed by David Jones. A careful reading of the reviews in these two cities is a textbook case in the differences of national tastes and cultures.

The majority of Nelson's work is about how the intellect, as opposed to the emotions, is affected by an issue. When Nelson deals with emotional reactions in characters his writing lacks a smooth flow, and his situations become more fatuous than comical. In *An American Comedy* two successful Broadway playwrights are ending a collaboration of many years because one of them has read *Das Kapital* and is in the process of wrapping himself in Marxism as though it was a red cashmere scarf. Like *Principia Scriptoriae, An American Comedy* is about writers and politics. However, Nelson seems uncomfortable with overt satire, and his comedy is too often contrived to be genuinely funny.

A far more successful satire is *The Return of Pinocchio*, a bitter tale about the American dream as seen from the viewpoint of the poor peasants of a small village in Italy in 1946. In the well known fairy tale, Pinocchio was once a puppet who turned into a real boy. In the play, Pinocchio is now a man in his thirties who, having once starred in a Walt Disney movie, is a wealthy American entertainer touring with the U.S.O. He has returned to this Italian village from America to visit his father, the cabinet maker. Here Nelson uses his pen like a carving knife to slice pieces off the elusive American dream of having it all and making it big. The rest of the world may be starving and may be reduced to theft and prostitution to survive, Nelson says, but Americans continue living their fairy tale existence using innocence more as a mask for vice than as a mark of virtue.

Another revisionist view of an old fable is *Rip Van Winkle; or, "The Works."* Nelson takes Washington Irving's classic tale (about a good-hearted drunk who, after a magical night of revelry with Hendrick Hudson's ghostly crew, is put to sleep for 20 years) and bends it into a savage examination of the place of the individual in an industrialized and dehumanized society.

When Nelson's characters are not confronting their society, they are engaged in making—or realizing they are *not* making—commitments. His characters are either involved and committed, or they are not. In either case they suffer. The American need to do the "right" thing, and the resulting insecurity, are rife in all Nelson's work regardless of the style he is using at the time. And, like any master craftsman, Nelson has a variety of dramatic styles at his command, from comedy, to farce, to bitter tragedy. In many of his plays (*Rip Van Winkle, Principia Scriptoriae, The Return of Pinocchio*) he uses Brechtian surtitles to introduce scenes. The effect is of a frame which enhances the value of the picture within. Other works, such as *Bal* (a play which deals with intellect and non-involvement at the extremes), tell their stories with a point/counterpoint interplay.

Nelson worries about the artist and the intellectual foundering in a world which has little use for the qualities they can offer. His vision is a dark one. His Edenic myth is that of a garden of visual delights in which the plants have been poisoned by toxins from industrial wastes, and the people are plotting to steal one another's fig leaves.

—Leah D. Frank

NGUGI wa Thiong'o. Formerly wrote as James T. Ngugi. Kenyan. Born in Kamiriithu, near Limuru, Kiambu District, 5 January 1938. Educated at Kamaandũra School, Limuru; Karing'a School, Maanguũ; Alliance High School, Kikuyu; University College, Kampala, Uganda (editor, *Penpoint*), 1959–63, B.A. 1963; Leeds University, Yorkshire, 1964–67, B.A. 1964. Married Nyambura in 1961; two sons and three daughters. Columnist ("As I See It"), in early 1960's, and reporter, 1964, Nairobi *Daily Nation*; Lecturer in English, University College, Nairobi, 1967–69; Fellow in Creative Writing, Makerere University, Kampala, 1969–70; Visiting Lecturer, Northwestern University, Evanston, Illinois, 1970–71; Senior Lecturer, Associate Professor, and Chairman of the Department of Literature, University of Nairobi, 1972–77. Imprisoned under Public Security Act, 1977–78. Editor, *Zuka*, Nairobi, 1965–70. Recipient: East African Literature Bureau award, 1964. Address: c/o Heinemann Educational Books, 22 Bedford Square, London WC1B 3HH, England.

PUBLICATIONS

Plays

The Black Hermit (produced Kampala, Uganda, 1962). London, Heinemann, 1968.
This Time Tomorrow (broadcast 1967). Included in *This Time Tomorrow*, 1970.
This Time Tomorrow (includes *The Rebels* and *The Wound in the Heart*). Nairobi, East African Literature Bureau, 1970.
The Trial of Dedan Kimathi, with Micere Mugo (produced London, 1984). Nairobi, Heinemann, 1976; London, Heinemann, 1977.
Ngaahika Ndeenda (in Kikuyu), with Ngugi wa Mirii (produced Limuru, 1977). Nairobi, Heinemann, 1980; as *I Will Marry When I Want*, London, Heinemann, 1982.

Radio Play: *This Time Tomorrow*, 1967.

Novels

Weep Not, Child. London, Heinemann, 1964; New York, Collier, 1969.
The River Between. London, Heinemann, 1965.
A Grain of Wheat. London, Heinemann, 1967.
Petals of Blood. London, Heinemann, 1977; New York, Dutton, 1978.
Caitaani Mutharaba-ini (in Kikuyu). Nairobi, Heinemann, 1980; as *Devil on the Cross*, London, Heinemann, 1982.

Short Stories

Secret Lives and Other Stories. London, Heinemann, and New York, Hill, 1975.

Other

Homecoming: Essays on African and Caribbean Literature, Culture, and Politics. London, Heinemann, 1972; New York, Hill, 1973.
The Independence of Africa and Cultural Decolonisation, with *The Poverty of African Historiography*, by A.E. Afigbo. Lagos, Afrografika, 1977.
Writers in Politics: Essays. London, Heinemann, 1981.
Detained: A Writer's Prison Diary. London, Heinemann, 1981.
Education for a National Culture. Harare, Zimbabwe Publishing House, 1981.
Barrel of a Pen: Resistance to Repression in Neo-Colonial Kenya. London, New Beacon, and Trenton, New Jersey, Africa World Press, 1983.
Decolonising the Mind: The Politics of Language in African Literature. London, Currey, 1986.

*

Critical Studies: *Ngugi wa Thiong'o* by Clifford Robson, London, Macmillan, 1979, New York, St. Martin's Press, 1980; *An Introduction to the Writings of Ngugi* by G.D. Killam, London, Heinemann, 1980; *Ngugi wa Thiong'o: An Exploration of His Writings* by David Cook and Michael Okenimkpe, London, Heinemann, 1983.

* * *

For several years after its production in 1962, Ngugi wa Thiong'o's *The Black Hermit* was the only full-length play in English from East Africa. Written just before Kenya achieved independence, the play is a pessimistic look at the rival claims of traditional and modern ways of life, traditional and modern religions, public service and private fulfilment. Unfortunately, the claims of nation, ideology, family, and love are only touched upon, not explored. The shuffling of the different issues—now one, now another held before us—produces melodrama. The author himself has called the play "very confused."

Remi, the first of his tribe to go to college, loved Thoni, who married his brother while he was away. On the death of his brother, Remi's father urged him to follow tradition and marry his brother's wife. This he did, though he felt that he could never love one who was another's. He fled from her, and from the expectations of the tribe that he would be their political leader, to the city and the love of a white girl. The play opens with the efforts of his mother and wife to get him to return; the pastor will visit Remi on their behalf. Meanwhile, the elders also send emissaries, bearing "medicine." Weighing the bible in one hand, the "medicine" in the other, Remi is moved by these "pieces of superstition" and returns home. He holds a successful political rally, against tribalism, but while he discusses future plans a woman enters with a letter from

> She who was kind.
> She who was true.
> A tender sapling growing straight.
> Though surrounded by weed.

His wife had loved him, and deep down he had loved her, but she had heard him say that he had been wrong to follow custom in marrying her, and so committed suicide, leaving the letter to state that she has always loved him. The play ends with Remi kneeling beside her body and declaring "I came to break Tribe and Custom, Instead, I've broken you and me."

More interesting is a short radio play, *This Time Tomorrow*. A slum, ironically named Uhuru (Freedom) Market, is to be bulldozed because "tourists from America, Britain and West Germany are disgusted with the dirt that is slowly creeping into a city that used to be the pearl of Africa." In the slum live Njango, wife of a freedom fighter, and her dreaming daughter Wanjiro. During the play, Wanjiro's lover persuades her to move into his house, and Njango attends a protest meeting, led by the Stranger, a former freedom fighter who is arrested. A bulldozer razes the hut as Njango ends the play: "If only we had stood up against them! If only we could stand together!" Against the actualities of the situation, caught in a soliloquy of Wanjiro's—"How often have I leaned against this very post, and watched the city awake. Just now, noise is dead in the city. It is so dark outside—the crawling maggots in the drains are hidden"—are set the bland phrases of the journalist, with which the play opens—"The filthy mushrooms—inhabited by human beings—besieging our capital city, came tumbling down yesterday."

As an epigraph to his collection of essays *Writers in Politics*, Ngugi quotes Karl Marx: "The profound hypocrisy and inherent barbarism of bourgeois civilization lies unveiled before our eyes, turning from its home, where it assumes respectable forms, to the colonies, where it goes naked. . . . " The struggle against colonialism is dramatized in *The Trial of Dedan Kimathi*, while *I Will Marry When I Want* attacks the new black bourgeois exploiters. A believer in the collectivization of economic resources and the "release of a people's creative spirit [through] the active work of destroying an inhibitive social structure and building a new one" (*Homecoming*), Ngugi wrote the latter play in Kikuyu originally and it was, he tells us, "really a community product." Both dramatize his views insistently and even stridently; performance of the latter led to his being jailed for a year.

Kimathi was a leader of the Mau Mau rebellion, captured and shot by the British. In Ngugi's play Kimathi's brief arraignment and trial frame four "trials" of his resolution in his cell, reminiscent of the visits of the tempters to Eliot's Becket. The last of these is followed by a flashback to a trial over which Kimathi presided, to judge traitors in the guerrilla ranks. Woven between are scenes which focus on a boy and a girl whom a female colleague of Kimathi's recruits for a rescue attempt. They allow Ngugi to describe the life of the most destitute, stress women's contribution to the liberation struggle, and show the spirit of revolt passed to the next generation. The complexity of the play's structure saves it from being too pietistic or too obviously didactic.

There are flashbacks to the independence struggle in *I Will Marry When I Want*, but they seem to serve more as excuses for the songs and dances that befit a popular piece rather than to have a dramatic purpose. The play has a narrower focus than *The Trial of Dedan Kimathi*, showing the destruction of a simple family bourgeois who are both hypocritically Christian and the black tools of foreign capitalism. The didactic message is spelled out by a neighbor raisonneur.

The Black Hermit is like Soyinka's *A Dance of the Forests* in the caution and pessimism with which it greets independence. With the exception of the ultimately optimistic *The Trial of Dedan Kimathi*, his later plays show an increasing bitterness, a disgust at official and religious cant, and a sense that Uhuru has brought nothing to the common people. Ngugi does not have Soyinka's knowledge of the theatre, nor his ability to give vital energy to his characters, but the social perceptions that inform their plays have undergone parallel developments.

—Anthony Graham-White

NICHOLS, Peter (Richard). British. Born in Bristol, 31 July 1927. Educated at Bristol Grammar School, 1936–44; Bristol Old Vic Theatre School, 1948–50; Trent Park Teachers' Training College, Hertfordshire, 1955–57. Served in the Royal Air Force, 1945–48. Married Thelma Reed in 1959; three daughters (one deceased) and one son. Actor, in repertory, television, and films, 1950–55; teacher in primary and secondary schools, 1957–59; has also worked as a park keeper, English language teacher in Italy, cinema commissionaire, and clerk. Visiting playwright, Guthrie Theatre, Minneapolis, 1977. Governor, Greenwich Theatre, London, 1970–76; member, Arts Council Drama Panel, 1972–75. Recipient: Arts Council bursary, 1961; *Evening Standard* award, 1967, 1969, 1978, 1982; John Whiting Award, 1968; Society of West End Theatre award, 1978, 1982. Fellow, Royal Society of Literature, 1983. Agent: Margaret Ramsay Ltd., 14-A Goodwin's Court, London WC2N 4LL. Address: The Old Rectory, Hopesay, Craven Arms, Shropshire SY7 8HD, England.

PUBLICATIONS

Plays

Promenade (televised 1959). Published in *Six Granada Plays*, London, Faber, 1960.

Ben Spray (televised 1961). Published in *New Granada Plays*, London, Faber, 1961.

The Hooded Terror (televised 1963; produced Bristol, 1964).

A Day in the Death of Joe Egg (produced Glasgow and London, 1967; New York, 1968). London, Faber, 1967; as *Joe Egg*, New York, Grove Press, 1967.

The Gorge (televised 1968). Published in *The Television Dramatist*, edited by Robert Muller, London, Elek, 1973.

The National Health; or, Nurse Norton's Affair (produced London, 1969; Chicago, 1971; New York, 1974). London, Faber, 1970; New York, Grove Press, 1975.

Hearts and Flowers (televised 1970). Included in *Plays 1*, 1987.

Forget-Me-Not Lane (produced London, 1971; New Haven, Connecticut, 1973). London, Faber, 1971.

Neither Up nor Down (produced London, 1972). Included in *Plays 1*, 1987.

The Common (televised 1973). Revised version in *Plays 1*, 1987.

Chez Nous (produced London, 1974; New York, 1977). London, Faber, 1974.

The Freeway (produced London, 1974; Milwaukee, 1978). London, Faber, 1975.

Harding's Luck, adaptation of the novel by E. Nesbit (produced London, 1974).

Privates on Parade (produced London, 1977; New Haven, Connecticut, 1979). London, Faber, 1977.

Born in the Gardens (also director: produced Bristol, 1979; London, 1980). London, Faber, 1980.

Passion Play (produced London, 1981). London, Eyre Methuen, 1981; as *Passion* (produced New York, 1983), New York, French, 1983.

Poppy, music by Monty Norman (produced London, 1982). London, Methuen, 1982.

Privates on Parade (screenplay). London, Star, 1983.

A Piece of My Mind (produced Southampton and London, 1987).

Plays 1 (includes *Forget-Me-Not Lane, Hearts and Flowers, Neither Up nor Down, Chez Nous, The Common* revised version, *Privates on Parade*). London, Methuen, 1987.

Screenplays: *Catch Us If You Can* (*Having a Wild Weekend*), 1965; *Georgy Girl*, with Margaret Forster, 1966; *A Day in the Death of Joe Egg*, 1972; *The National Health*, 1973; *Privates on Parade*, 1983; *Changing Places*, 1984.

Television Plays: *Walk on the Grass*, 1959; *After All*, with Bernie Cooper, 1959; *Promenade*, 1959; *Ben Spray*, 1961; *The Big Boys*, 1961; *The Reception*, 1961; *The Heart of the Country*, 1962; *Ben Again*, 1963; *The Hooded Terror*, 1963; *The Continuity Man*, 1963; *The Brick Umbrella*, 1964; *When the Wind

Blows, 1965; *The Gorge*, 1968; *Majesty*, from a story by F. Scott Fitzgerald, 1968; *Winner Takes All*, from a story by Evelyn Waugh, 1968; *Daddy Kiss It Better*, 1968; *Hearts and Flowers*, 1970; *The Common*, 1973.

Other

Feeling You're Behind: An Autobiography. London, Weidenfeld and Nicolson, 1984.

*

Critical Studies: *The Second Wave* by John Russell Taylor, London, Methuen, and New York, Hill and Wang, 1971; interview in *Playback 2* by Ronald Hayman, London, Davis Poynter, 1973; *The New British Drama* by Oleg Kerensky, London, Hamish Hamilton, 1977, New York, Taplinger, 1979; *British Television Drama* edited by George W. Brandt, London, Cambridge University Press, 1981; *Landmarks of Modern British Drama: The Seventies* edited by Roger Cornish and Violet Ketels, London, Methuen, 1986.

Theatrical Activities:
Director: **Play**—*A Day in the Death of Joe Egg*, London, 1971; *The National Health*, Minneapolis, 1977; *Born in the Gardens*, Bristol, 1979.

* * *

Few dramatists have had more success than Peter Nichols in making their characters reveal their attitudes towards a problem, towards each other, towards society; and in this media age, when everyone's opinion is solicited, known, and categorized, the writer who is an artist at encapsulating attitude is likely to achieve wide popularity.

In, for example, *A Day in the Death of Joe Egg*, Nichols demonstrates admirably his ability to deal with a forbidden subject (in 1967), that of the paraplegic, the spastic, the "vegetable" (referred to in many ways during the course of the play). There was a surge of approval as a new barrier of inhibition was swept away: this is very flattering to an audience. Nichols manages to present an uncomfortable subject in a kind of hectic, hectoring way that is contrived not to offend. He incorporated every possible range of emotional response. We come away feeling there's something in the problem for all of us.

Nichols's jokes always cut near the bone, and in the revival of *Joe Egg*, directed by the author himself, one sometimes had the feeling there was no bone left to cut near. Possibly there may be something too quiescent at the back of the parents' games. They constantly exercise their instantly dismissable feelings at the expense of their "problem." Sometimes, one feels, a sustained and heartfelt cry of pain might be more cathartic. But pain is not an attitude. The main reservation concerns the theme. One looks in vain for some guiding idea to capture the imagination. Here and there Nichols throws in a possibility, as when, for instance, he points out that we are all cripples in some way, all limited. While the peripheries of the problem never relax their hold, a central issue obstinately fails to materialize. Nichols's method is to touch upon all, moving forward with brittle and lighting force in case he loses his audience.

The National Health, produced at the National Theatre in 1969, combines many Anouilhesque qualities and shortcomings. Half of this play is a comic comment on the human race, the conclusion being that each of us is entitled to his own death—half a gallop through every known attitude to health. The result has a lively spontaneous progress, is well-organized, but, ultimately, on the thin side.

In *Forget-Me-Not Lane* the debt to Anouilh appears even greater, as a middle-age man asks himself what went wrong in his marriages and re-examines his childhood and his life with his parents during World War II. The device of shuttling the action back and forth between past and present results in much high comedy and some sharp theatrical moments. *Chez Nous* presents the much-trodden situation of two friendly married couples, Dick and Liz, Diana and Phil, on holiday in the Dordogne, who are driven to the brink of splitting up. The marital tug of war that we have already seen in *Joe Egg* and *Forget-Me-Not Lane* is organized in greater depth and comic intensity than Nichols has used previously, and in his presentation of the boulevard twist of fate—that Dick's daughter has given birth to Phil's son—Nichols pulls off a memorable *coup de théâtre*. Some critics found it highly improbable, but the combination of artificiality and the earthy—even squalid—way the couples express themselves towards each other produces an enjoyable, if not exactly profound, sense of truth.

In *Passion Play* Nichols drives even more relentlessly down the path of adultery by a device of splitting the main characters, Eleanor and James, into double identities (a device similar to that of Brian Friel in *Philadelphia, Here I Come!*). Again it's the many-sidedness of life he attempts to pay tribute to, but what promises much by way of exploring the inner states of the pair never lives up to expectations. No larger vision appears than that of lost apes in pursuit of ultimate sexiness: this may, of course, be sound comment, or may equally point to the shortcoming that virtuosity has become an end in itself.

With minor plays such as *The Freeway* Nichols returns to the episodic comic style of *The National Health*, though with less success. A great motorway (the FI) has been built running North to South, and in a week-end jam a number of marooned motorists commingle in the form of a glorified variety entertainment. Though there is some sharply observed satire, we seem, like the cars themselves, not to arrive anywhere in particular. But by the same token, *Privates on Parade* succeeds admirably. It is a mixture of cynical squaddie comment and concern routines of an army entertainment troupe around 1950, and in it Nichols again demonstrates his skill as pure entertainer. *Harding's Luck* is a straightforward adaptation of E. Nesbit's children's novel, using the author as narrator. The central character is Dickie, the crippled urchin from Deptford. He is elevated by the hospitality of a genteel family, finds out he is well-connected, and finally is submitted to a magical transformation backwards in time—from an Edwardian childhood into a Jacobean youth.

Poppy is an ambitious attempt to do with pantomime convention what *Privates on Parade* did with the concert party, but it is much less successful. Taking as his subject the Opium Wars in mid-19th-century China, Nichols satirizes British imperial commercialism in a mixture of styles, and reveals, ultimately, that he has little that is vitally comic or original to add to what has become a hackneyed target for entertainers in the 1980's.

—Garry O'Connor

NKOSI, Lewis. British. Born in Durban, South Africa, 5 December 1936. Educated at public schools in Durban; Zulu Lutheran High School; M.L. Sultan Technical College, Durban, 1961–62; Harvard University, Cambridge, Massachusetts (Nieman Fellow), 1962–63. Married Bronwyn Ollerenshaw in 1965; twin daughters. Staff member, *Ilanga Lase Natal* (Zulu newspaper), Durban, 1955–56, *Drum* magazine and *Golden*

City Post, Johannesburg, 1956–60, and *South African Information Bulletin*, Paris, 1962–68; radio producer, BBC Transcription Centre, London, 1962–64; National Education Television interviewer, New York, 1963; literary editor, *New African* magazine, London, 1965–68; Regents Lecturer on African Literature, University of California, Irvine, Spring 1971. Currently Professor of English, University of Zambia, Lusaka. Recipient: Dakar Festival prize, for essays, 1965; C. Day Lewis fellowship, 1977; Macmillan Silver Pen award, 1987. Address: Department of English, University of Zambia, P.O. Box 31338, Lusaka, Zambia.

PUBLICATIONS

Plays

The Rhythm of Violence (produced London, 1963). London, Oxford University Press, 1964; in *Plays from Black Africa*, edited by Fredric M. Litto, New York, Hill and Wang, 1968.
Malcolm (televised 1967; produced London, 1972).

Screenplay: *Come Back Africa*, 1959.

Radio Plays: *The Trial*, 1969; *We Can't All Be Martin Luther King*, 1971.

Television Play: *Malcolm*, 1967 (Sweden).

Novel

Mating Birds. Nairobi, East African Publishing House, 1983; London, Constable, and New York, St. Martin's Press, 1986.

Other

Home and Exile (essays). London, Longman, 1965; revised edition, 1983.
The Transplanted Heart: Essays on South Africa. Benin City, Nigeria, Ethiope, 1975.
Tasks and Masks: Themes and Styles of African Literature. London, Longman, 1981.

*

Theatrical Activities:
Actor: **Play**—Father Higgins in *No-Good Friday* by Athol Fugard, Johannesburg, 1958.

* * *

When Lewis Nkosi's *The Rhythm of Violence* was published in 1964 it was hailed as the first play by a black South African to appear in print since Herbert Dhlomo's *The Girl Who Killed to Save* (1935). Because of its sensitive handling of the explosive issues of South African racism the play was widely acclaimed and Nkosi was seen by some as being in the vanguard of a new black South African theatre. Since then Nkosi has published short stories and essays (a form in which he seems to excel), but his visible dramatic output has been limited to three radio and television plays.

Since the mid-1960's the immediacy of the South African situation, the terrific tensions it creates (which Nkosi himself has noted in his speculations on the dearth of recent plays and novels from South Africa), have made it difficult for the black South African writer to do anything other than the personal forms of essay, short story, and autobiography. Drama is written for an audience, and the stricter, though more subtle, laws which developed after the Sharpeville Massacre made it difficult for a mixed audience to come together in South Africa.

Thus we are left with only one major work in theatre on which to judge Nkosi, *The Rhythm of Violence*, an outstanding first play, an important one. There are some weaknesses in the play. Certain of the scenes tend to drag and some of the characters seem static, almost unreal—especially Tula and Sarie, the Zulu boy and Boer girl who are caught in the web of destruction. Nkosi's moral, however, that violence is mindless, that it destroys both the guilty and the innocent, and that violence begets more violence, is effectively acted out. Nkosi also does an excellent job in presenting the two Boer policemen, Jan and Piet, in such a way that we see beyond the harshness of their exterior into their confused souls. They are the most fully realized characters in the play and in one masterful scene, when Jan pretends to be a black politician and is carried away in his part ("You spoke just like a native communist," says Piet in a shocked voice), Nkosi makes it clear that the possibility for understanding between men does exist—unless the rhythm of violence prevents such understanding from developing.

—Joseph Bruchac

NOONAN, John Ford. American. Born in New York City, 7 October 1943. Educated at Fairfield Preparatory School, Connecticut, graduated 1959; Brown University, Providence, Rhode Island, A.B. in philosophy 1964; Carnegie Institute of Technology, Pittsburgh, M.A. in dramatic literature 1966. Married Marcia Lunt in 1962 (divorced 1965); three children. Taught Latin, English, and history at Buckley Country Day School, North Hills, Long Island, New York, 1966–69; stagehand, Fillmore East Rock Theatre, New York, 1969–71; stockbroker, E.F. Hutton Company, New York, 1971–72; Professor of Drama, Villanova University, Pennsylvania, 1972–73. Recipient: Rockefeller grant, 1973. Agent: Joan Scott Inc., 162 West 56th Street, New York, New York 10019. Address: 484 West 43rd Street, New York, New York 10036, U.S.A.

PUBLICATIONS

Plays

The Year Boston Won the Pennant (produced New York, 1969). New York, Grove Press, 1970.
Lazarus Was a Lady (produced New York, 1970).
Rainbows for Sale (produced New York, 1971). Published in *The Off-Off-Broadway Book*, edited by Albert Poland and Bruce Mailman, Indianapolis, Bobbs Merrill, 1972.
Concerning the Effects of Trimethylchloride (produced New York, 1971).
Monday Night Varieties (produced New York, 1972).
Older People (also director: produced New York, 1972).
Good-By and Keep Cold (produced New York, 1973).
A Noonan Night (produced New York, 1973).
A Sneaky Bit to Raise the Blind, and Pick Pack Pock Puck (produced New York, 1974).
Where Do We Go from Here? (produced New York, 1974).

Getting Through the Night (produced New York, 1976).
A Coupla White Chicks Sitting Around Talking (produced New York, 1979; London, 1983). New York, French, 1981.
Listen to the Lions (produced New York, 1979).
Some Men Need Help (produced New York, 1982). New York, French, 1983.

Screenplays: *Septuagenarian Substitute Ball*, 1970; *The Summer the Snows Came*, 1972.

*

Manuscript Collection: Lincoln Center Library of the Performing Arts, New York.

Critical Studies: "Theatre as Mystery," in *Evergreen Magazine* (New York), December 1969, and reviews in *Village Voice* (New York), May 1971 and May 1972, all by John Lahr.

Theatrical Activities:
Director: **Play**—*Older People*, New York, 1972.
Actor: Since 1967 in summer stock, regional and off-Broadway theatres, and in television and films.

John Ford Noonan comments:

In *The Year Boston Won the Pennant*, Marcus Sykowski, a once legendary baseball pitcher who has mysteriously lost his glove arm and is now in search of a chrome limb to take its place, discusses pitching as follows:

> I am a pitcher. Pitching is my job. I have lost an arm, but I will earn it back. I have science on my side. I'm no college man. I never got a degree. I am no thinker, no man whose job it is to lead or be understood. I am a pitcher. I stand on the mound. I hold the ball, smile, get the feel I'm ready. I rear, I fire, and that ball goes exactly where I tell it 'cause I tell it to, 'cause it was me who threw it, the great Sykowski. What else must they know. . . . One strike, two strikes, three strikes, four, five, six, seven, eight, nine . . . the whole side, 'cause when you're pouring rhythm sweet, when you got it, really got it, they can't see it, they can't smell it, they can't touch it, they can't believe it. . . . It's yours, all yours . . . it's magic.

I believe Marcus is speaking of more than throwing a baseball.

* * *

John Ford Noonan's plays veer in style from conventional realism to fantasy and treat a range of American character types from baseball players and firemen to transvestites, gangsters, old people, and deserted wives. They have earned Noonan critical and popular attention since his first full-length play's production in 1969. Themes interweaving his plays encompass Saroyanesque concern for the vulnerability of the world's little people and the need to help one another. While believing in the communion of saints, Noonan largely avoids sentimentality in his work and sees the dark forces lurking in the sunlight. Characters in early plays tend toward caricatures and are often enmeshed in conflicts with mythic implications.

His more recent work discloses characters of realistic dimension while thematically supporting W.H. Auden's thought that "we must love one another or die." *A Coupla White Chicks Sitting Around Talking*, Noonan's deservedly most popular work, is a two-character comedy effectively accenting that good can come from unlikely relationships. In Westchester County suburbia a prim WASP housewife, Maude Mix, angry and lost at the latest desertion by her philandering husband, finds herself called upon by Hannah Mae, a prying Texan wife and new next-door neighbor who forces uninvited daily visits and offers practical but unwelcome advice after deducing Maude's situation. Maude cannot rid herself of the loudmouth do-gooder even when she truthfully reports that Hannah's oafish husband has forced her into bed on a surprise visit. Instead of leaving Maude alone at this news, Hannah leaves her husband and moves in; a symbiotic friendship develops. Maude learns to accept her marriage's futility and after taking Hannah on a pleasure-filled trip to New York City regains self-esteem and the strength to go it alone, while Hannah returns to her now penitent husband but promises to maintain daily visits. The comedy offers a perceptive look at two delightfully defined contemporary women undergoing loss and gain. Although differing in details, a reverse-gender repetition of the above play appears in the more recent but less successful *Some Men Need Help*. A career-disillusioned and wife-deserted young WASP advertising executive, Singleton, is drowning himself in liquor and self-loathing in his Connecticut home when he is visited by an overbearing lower-class ex-Mafioso neighbor who inexplicably insists on saving him. Singleton cannot eject the unwelcome Good Samaritan, even with racist slurs, yet eventually is persuaded to undergo detoxification and to change his self-destructive attitude. While too reminiscent of its predecessor, this well-intentioned comedy about two men who grow to like each other relays Noonan's message that help is possible when you love your neighbor.

More characteristic of his individual voice, Noonan's earlier plays often are less realistic in style and context than these later ones. *The Year Boston Won the Pennant* employs fantasy and Brechtian techniques to chronicle the odyssey through a callous society of the maimed baseball pitcher Marcus Sykowski, who wishes to regain his former fame and the ability he enjoyed before mysteriously losing his arm. Throughout 14 mockingly titled scenes, the impractical but courageously aspiring Sykowski visits family and friends seeking solace and money to buy a prosthetic limb (which cannot restore his prowess), only bewilderingly to encounter attempted exploitation and unprovoked betrayal or violence, while at the same time an anti-war revolution occurs in the streets unnoticed by all. Also constantly pursued by a mysteriously menacing gangster, Sykowski is assassinated when pitching a dream-like comeback game. The accumulating scenes suggest that the victimized hero is a metaphor for a baffled, maimed Vietnam-era America self-destructively pursuing an impossible quest for lost prestige and driven by forces of greed and unconscionable irrationality. This dark comedy, sometimes ambiguously uneven in style and characterization, does more than confirm Leo Durocher's observation that "good guys finish last."

The hysteria and inclination toward fantasy of ordinary people often are subjects in Noonan's work of the 1970's. In *Rainbows for Sale* a boy custodian, preparing a firehouse for a meeting for new recruits, meets his older self to find him a deceased racist fireman who has maniacally gone on a shooting spree in an ethnic neighborhood after witnessing a colleague's death in a fire, and now has come to address the new firemen. The play effectively mixes fantasy with forcibly graphic narrative. The difficulties of aging are well represented with empathy and irony in *Older People*, a cycle of 15 sketch-like short plays with interludes of song—a Noonan characteristic—dealing with the new fears and waning sexual powers of the elderly. While the sketches range in quality, the work's contrast between its sad and wistful subject matter and its farcical form is engaging.

Noonan is a talented dramatist with a zany, acerbic, yet perceptive comic vision of the world. His is an individual voice worthy of our attention.

—Christian H. Moe

NORMAN, Marsha (née Williams). American. Born in Louisville, Kentucky, 21 September 1947. Educated at Durrett High School, Louisville; Agnes Scott College, Decatur, Georgia, B.A. in philosophy 1969; University of Louisville, 1969–71, M.A. 1971. Married 1) Michael Norman in 1969 (divorced 1974); 2) Dann C. Byck, Jr., in 1978 (divorced 1986). Worked with disturbed children at Kentucky Central State Hospital, 1969–71; teacher, Brown School, Louisville, from 1973; book reviewer and editor of children's supplement (*Jelly Bean Journal*), Louisville *Times*, mid-1970's; playwright-in-residence, Actors Theatre, Louisville, 1977–78, and Mark Taper Forum, Los Angeles, 1979. Recipient: American Theater Critics Association prize, 1978; National Endowment for the Arts grant, 1978; Rockefeller grant, 1979; John Gassner Award, 1979; Oppenheimer award, 1979; Susan Smith Blackburn Prize, 1983; Pulitzer Prize, 1983; American Academy award, 1986. Lives in New York City. Agent: Samuel Liff, William Morris Agency, 1350 Avenue of the Americas, New York, New York 10019, U.S.A.

PUBLICATIONS

Plays

Getting Out (produced Louisville, 1977; New York, 1978). New York, Avon, 1980.
Third and Oak: The Laundromat (produced Louisville, 1978; New York, 1979). New York, Dramatists Play Service, 1980.
Third and Oak: The Pool Hall (produced Louisville, 1978). New York, Dramatists Play Service, 1985.
Circus Valentine (produced Louisville, 1979).
Merry Christmas, in *Holidays* (produced Louisville, 1979).
'Night, Mother (produced Cambridge, Massachusetts, 1982; New York, 1983; London, 1985). New York, Hill and Wang, 1983; London, Faber, 1984.
The Holdup (produced San Francisco, 1983). New York, Dramatists Play Service, 1987.
Traveler in the Dark (produced Cambridge, Massachusetts, 1984; revised version produced Los Angeles, 1985).

Television Plays: *It's the Willingness* (*Visions* series), 1978; *In Trouble at Fifteen* (*Skag* series), 1980.

Novel

The Fortune Teller. New York, Random House, 1987.

*

Theatrical Activities:
Director: **Play**—*Semi-Precious Things* by Terri Wagener, Louisville, 1980.

* * *

Marsha Norman's career suggests the importance of regional theater in nurturing and developing the talents of the aspiring American playwright. Growing up in Louisville, Kentucky, she was isolated from classmates and neighbors by her family's religious fundamentalism so that she turned to reading and playing the piano for emotional support. She became such a good amateur musician that at one time she seriously considered studying composition at Juilliard. Her knowledge of rhythm and tone, she claims, comes from music, rather than language. *'Night, Mother* is "written in a sonata form. And works that way." And in *Traveler in the Dark* "there are incredible arpeggios and deep chords that hold all the way through the arpeggios."

She attended Louisville public schools and after graduation from Agnes Scott College where she majored in philosophy, she returned to marry, to pursue a master's degree at the University of Louisville, and to work with gifted as well as emotionally disturbed children in various projects which involved her in administering arts programs, teaching film making, editing a weekly children's supplement for the local newspaper. Her early fascination with the question of Job's suffering, the subject of a prize-winning high school essay, pointed the direction her writing would follow in asking difficult philosophic questions and probing moral issues.

She began writing for the theater when Jon Jory, artistic director of Actors Theatre, asked her to write a docudrama about the issue of busing children to achieve racial balance in Louisville's public schools. She ultimately rejected his request, turning instead for inspiration to her experiences with disturbed adolescents, particularly one difficult girl with whom she could barely communicate and who eventually ended up in prison for murder. This desperate adolescent became the inspiration for Arlie, the violent and rebellious other self of Arlene, the subdued and sensitive heroine of *Getting Out*, Norman's first play. Arlene has just been released from prison and must come to terms with her past, assess the reality of her present and accept the tentativeness of her future. In order to survive, she must reject the seductive voices of her pimp and the prison guard who wish to continue their exploitation. Can one survive by reinventing the self? Arlene, inarticulate and weak, might appear to be a poor candidate for such a transformation, but Norman's strength as a writer comes from her unerring understanding of the "ordinary person" who leads a life of quiet desperation with little chance to achieve even the most minor success. Thus Arlene's survival is a triumph just as Jessie's suicide in *'Night, Mother* is not a defeat but a victory for individual choice. "The choices you make out of freedom," Norman has said, "are the best ones."

Norman's preoccupation with the need to confront life-and-death issues is shown most clearly in *'Night, Mother*, which leads the audience through the dark night of the soul experienced by a mother and daughter as they struggle with the ordinariness of their lives and the extraordinary choice the daughter wishes to make with her mother's reluctant consent. Jessie Cates (in her late thirties or early forties) has only recently "gained control of her mind and body"; her mother Thelma Cates (in her late fifties or early sixties) believes that "things *are* what she says they are and thus there is no room in her universe for Jessie's plan to kill herself. An unhappy marriage, a delinquent son, a failed life haunt Jessie; in making her final choice to end her life, she asks her disbelieving mother to accept suicide as a triumph of individuality. (The play won the 1983 Pulitzer Prize for Drama.)

The success of these two plays eluded *Traveler in the Dark*,

Norman's most ambitious play to date, which describes the struggle between a cerebral doctor/scientist and his minister father for the possession of the doctor's son. The grandfather's simple faith in God transfers in the son's generation to a worship of intelligence. When the brilliant surgeon undergoes a crisis of faith, he seeks a way to protect his son from his failure to synthesize mind and body. As the doctor tries to wean his son from fairy tales by retelling the story of the Donner party's cannibalism, his intellectual arrogance undermines his argument and reinforces the strength of the grandfather's gentleness. Norman appears to be saying that "you cannot protect the people you love." But as Jack Kroll, reviewing the play in *Newsweek*, warned: "Marsha Norman is one of those writers who are natural lightning rods for the shattering assault on faith and hope that come to all of us. The danger is that her moral urgency will drive her into the too-conscious role of crisis laureate."

—Tess Hoffmann

NOWRA, Louis. Australian. Born in Melbourne, Victoria, in 1950. Educated at La Trobe University, Bundoora, Victoria. Married Sarah de Jong in 1974. Writer-in-residence, University of Queensland, Brisbane, 1979, Lighthouse Company, Adelaide, 1982, Playbox Theatre, Melbourne, 1985, and Capricornia Institute, 1987; associate artistic director, Sydney Theatre Company, 1980, and Lighthouse Company, 1983. Recipient: Australian Literature Board fellowship, 1975, 1977–79, 1981, 1983. Agent: Hilary Linstead and Associates, 223 Commonwealth Street, Surry Hills, New South Wales 2010, Australia.

PUBLICATIONS

Plays

Kiss the One-Eyed Priest (produced Melbourne, 1973).
Albert Names Edward (broadcast 1975; produced Melbourne, 1976). Radio version published in *Five Plays for Radio*, edited by Alrene Sykes, Sydney, Currency Press, 1976; stage version published with *Inner Voices*, Currency Press, 1983.
Inner Voices (produced Sydney, 1977; London, 1982). Sydney, Currency Press, 1978.
Visions (produced Sydney, 1978). Sydney, Currency Press, 1979.
The Lady of the Camelias, adaptation of a play by Dumas fils (produced Sydney, 1979).
Inside the Island (produced Sydney, 1980). With *The Precious Woman*, Sydney, Currency Press, 1981.
The Precious Woman (produced Sydney, 1980). With *Inside the Island*, Sydney, Currency Press, 1981.
Cyrano de Bergerac, adaptation of the play by Rostand (produced Sydney, 1980).
The Song Room (broadcast 1980). Stage version published in *Seven One-Act Plays*, edited by Rodney Fisher, Sydney, Currency Press, 1983.
Death of Joe Orton (produced Adelaide, 1980).
Beauty and the Beast (produced Sydney, 1980).
Lulu, adaptation of a play by Frank Wedekind (produced Adelaide, 1981).
Spellbound (produced Adelaide, 1982; London, 1986).
Royal Show (produced Adelaide, 1982).
The Prince of Homburg, adaptation of a play by Heinrich von Kleist (also director: produced Adelaide, 1982).
Sunrise (produced Adelaide, 1983). Sydney, Currency Press, 1983.
The Golden Age (produced Melbourne, 1985). Sydney, Currency Press, 1985.

Radio Plays: *Albert Names Edward*, 1975; *The Song Room*, 1980; *The Widows*, 1986.

Television Plays: *Displaced Persons*, 1985; *Hunger*, 1986; *The Lizard King*, 1987.

Novel

The Misery of Beauty: The Loves of Frogman. Sydney and London, Angus and Robertson, 1976.

Other

Editor, *The Cheated*. Sydney, Angus and Robertson, 1979.

*

Critical Study: *Louis Nowra* edited by Veronica Kelly, Amsterdam, Rodopi, 1987.

Theatrical Activities:
Director: **Plays**—*The Prince of Homburg*, Adelaide, 1982; *The Marriage of Figaro* by Beaumarchais, Adelaide, 1983; *Not about Heroes* by Stephen MacDonald, Melbourne, 1985; *The Lighthouse* by Peter Maxwell Davies, Sydney, 1985.

* * *

When Louis Nowra first began to write plays, in the early 1970's, Australian dramatists were still absorbed in their attempt to define Australianness and build Australian myths. Nowra, seeking detachment for himself and his audience, set *Albert Names Edward* in an unidentified city, *Inner Voices* in 18th-century Russia, *Visions* in 19th-century Paraguay. After *Visions*, with its clear parllels with the Australian experience, he felt sufficiently confident to move his settings to the Australian environment, beginning with *Inside the Island*, set on a wheat-growing property in 1912. Nowra attempts large themes, and his plays, for full impact, demand large stages with setting and production on the grand scale. The importance of pictorial images in the theatre of Nowra cannot be overestimated. (The horrors of *Inside the Island* culminate in a blazing house and the frenzied leaping of ergot-poisoned, murderous, and self-mutilating soldiers.) Neither naturalistic nor cartoon in style, his plays suggest, in fact, opera, with their defined, cumulative scenes, "the enclosure of an emotion within the tableau of a particular scene," to quote Nowra himself, though he was speaking of Shakespeare's plays rather than his own. The scenes are structured not so much to advance plot as to provide different perspectives on theme and narrative, and balance between opposing points of view provides a major tension in Nowra's drama. There is often critical disagreement over what his plays "mean," but paradoxically the first impact of a Nowra play is powerfully emotionally, strikingly visual, rather than cerebral. The questions come later.

Nowra sees his work as evolving in a spiral, and in each coil, plays and other works explore related territory. Several themes recur, one of the most important, to date, being the exploration of the relationship between the world without and the world within. Nowra quotes, as fundamental to his plays, a statement by Novalis: "There are ideal series of events which run parallel with the real ones. They rarely coincide. Men and circumstances generally modify the ideal train of events, so that it seems imperfect, and its consequence equally imperfect." He is interested in the way our dream world is undercut by reality, and the way in which the powerful seek to impose their vision of reality upon the weak. The idea was expressed in its simplest form in *Albert Names Edward*, an early radio play about Edward, who loses his memory, and Albert, old and almost illiterate, who takes Edward in and "teaches" him, imposing on him a vision of a world peopled with figures of menace, images from cheap thrillers, and Albert's own dubious past. The *tabula rasa* figure is a favourite with Nowra. *Inner Voices* begins with a scene in which Ivan, imprisoned heir to the throne of Russia who has been brought up without hearing human speech, is washed, naked, by his guards, while he repeats over and over the one word he knows, his own name. The Empress dies, Ivan's guards teach him to speak and to absorb their values, lead him to the throne, and are then destroyed by him as he moves towards madness (a madness reflecting sympathetically the turmoil of Russia caught up in civil war), defeat, and death. In *Visions* the perspective broadens from individual misuse of power into what Nowra calls "cultural imperialism"; this time, the enforced learning is an attempt by Madame Lynch, the Parisian wife of the president of Paraguay, to impose her culture on the simpler culture of Paraguay; at the end of the play, both President Lopez and Madame Lynch are dead, but an insidious residue of Lynch's totally inappropriate culture remains, expressed in the madness that decends on Juana, the peasant girl who has symbolized the synthesis of the nation. The fate of Paraguay is reflected in her chaos, and her final crazed acceptance of the false visions. In spite of their detachment, Nowra's plays contain considerable violence.

Inside the Island is also concerned with cultural imperialism. Nowra's later plays are unusual, for Australian drama, in having strong roles for women; Nowra sees women as being both strong in themselves and exerting significant cultural influence. *Inside the Island* is dominated by the matriarchal Lillian Dawson, a female version of the socially and mythically complex figure, the squatter, or landowner; her values relate wholly to "the mother country." At the end of the play, her family is dead; most of the 50 soldiers who had camped on her property and eaten the ergot-poisoned flour she gave them are either crazed or dead also; her home has been destroyed by fire; so she turns towards England. In her terms, "The strong forget, the weak remember." The horrendous scenes of the fire and the ergot-maddened soldiers look forward to World War I and Gallipoli; World War II has a significant role in *The Golden Age,* the most attractive of Nowra's recent plays, which moves between Tasmania and Berlin in the last days of the war. Two young men discover in the Tasmanian wilds a "lost tribe" of six people, descended from a group—mostly convict—that went searching for gold in the 1850's; the gold quickly ran out but they decided to stay in the wilderness. Brought back to "civilization," the group, physically impaired and speaking a strange but powerful language derived from their convict ancestors, is confined in an asylum, to avoid publicity about "genetic impurities" which, it is feared, might give ammunition to Nazi propaganda for the Aryan, genetically superior "master race." The play ends with one of the young men, Francis, returning to the wilderness with the only survivor from the group, Bethsheb; she speaks, to him, the hopeful last words of the play, "Nowt more outcastin'." But in spite of the pastoral overtones, this is an uncertain, probably doomed, and immensely moving ending.

Nowra's radio plays include *Albert Names Edward* and *The Song Room*, the latter a sensitive account of a war-disabled man who has lost the power of coherent speech, learns to communicate through singing, and then has this precious outlet brutally withdrawn. (The music for *The Song Room*, as for most of Nowra's stage plays, was composed by Sarah de Jong.) More recently, the ABC has broadcast his telemovies, two concerned with migrants, the powerful *Displaced Persons* and *Hunger.*

—Alrene Sykes

O'MALLEY, Mary (Josephine). British. Born in Bushey, Hertfordshire, 19 March 1941. Resident writer, Royal Court Theatre, London, 1977. Recipient: *Evening Standard* award, 1978; Susan Smith Blackburn Prize, 1978; Pye award, for television play. Agent: Jane Annakin, William Morris Agency, 31–32 Soho Square, London W1V 6AP, England.

PUBLICATIONS

Plays

Superscum (produced London, 1972).
A 'nevolent Society (produced London, 1974).
Oh If Ever a Man Suffered (produced London, 1975).
Once a Catholic (produced London, 1977; New York, 1979). Ashover, Derbyshire, Amber Lane Press, and New York, French, 1978.
Look Out ... Here Comes Trouble (produced London, 1978). Ashover, Derbyshire, Amber Lane Press, 1979.
Talk of the Devil (produced Watford, Hertfordshire, 1986; revised version produced Bristol, 1986).

Television Plays: *Percy and Kenneth*, 1976; *Oy Vay Maria*, 1977; *Shall I See You Now?*, 1978; *On the Shelf*, 1984.

*   *   *

Mary O'Malley came into the public eye with her mischievous play *Once a Catholic*, which premiered at the Royal Court Theatre in 1977, and then transferred to the West End. The play won awards from the London *Evening Standard* and *Plays and Players.* The play is warm but sharply retrospective look at a Catholic girls' convent in the 1950's, with the youth rebellion of that decade given added edge by the repressiveness of the nuns. All the girls are called "Mary," and the play is a witty and perceptive extended sit-com, which is such good fun that it would undoubtedly offend no-one. In its way it even was able to test the taboos of the commercial theatre, in a scene where one of the shocked nuns discovers a packet of Tampax hidden in the lavatory, and a final act of sacrilege when one of the girls affixes a plasticine penis to a statue of Christ in the school chapel—for which Mary the scapegoat (the only one who genuinely wants to become a nun) is blamed.

There is a satirical edge to O'Malley's writing which derives from a sensitivity to the very ordinary pains and ironies of daily life—and also to the iconography of domestic experience, which is so important to people. This latter was the main feature of her play *Look Out . . . Here Comes Trouble*, staged by the Royal Shakespeare Company at the Warehouse in London in 1978. The play was set in a psychiatric ward, but floundered in the material detail, and although the comic pain was a feature in the lives of the characters, it never became part of the structural fabric of the play. Somehow O'Malley appears to be caught between the potentialities of a more ruthless satirical approach and a familiar, lightly comic sit-com approach.

—Michelene Wandor

O'NEILL, Michael. British. Educated at Northampton Grammar School; Cambridge University. Teacher. Agent: Curtis Brown, 162–168 Regent Street, London W1R 5TB, England.

PUBLICATIONS

Plays (with Jeremy Seabrook)

Life Price (produced London, 1969).
Morality (produced London, 1971).
Millennium (produced London, 1973).
Our Sort of People (produced London, 1974).
Sex and Kinship in a Savage Society (produced London, 1975).
Sharing (produced London, 1980).
Black Man's Burden (produced London, 1980).

Radio Plays: *The Bosom of the Family*, 1975; *Living Private*, 1978; *Our Children's Children*, 1980; *Life Skills*, 1985.

Television Plays: *Skin Deep*, 1971; *Soap Opera in Stockwell*, 1973; *Highway Robbery*, 1973; *A Clear Cut Case*, 1973; *A Stab in the Front*, 1973; *Children of the Sun*, 1975; *Beyond the Call of Duty* (*Crown Court* series), 1976; *A State of Welfare*.

* * *

It was Genet whose beliefs about society radically changed when he discovered that, according to the most advanced and accurate statistics available, the percentage of criminals remained the same whichever class or system held power at a particular moment. Michael O'Neill and Jeremy Seabrook's early work suffers from the widespread delusion that it is only as a result of capitalism, the "ceaseless gutting of their body and spirit in the name of enterprise, profits, efficiency," that there is a social sediment at the bottom of society, providing both aggressors and victims for horrible crime. For in their first performed play, *Life Price*, the pre-destined victim, Debbie, and the typical child murderer, George Reginald Dunkley, are both observed against a landscape of "neglected mounds of detritus, crumbling terraces, derelict buildings, and the housing estate itself, all cabbage-stalks and dilapidated creosote fences, maculated concrete, rusting bed-springs and motor-bikes, dead chrysanthemums and dingy paintwork."

A State of Welfare, a television play, is a much better organized work about an American scent spray firm moving into England, and its impact on the household of an average worker. Here the theme of a working-class boy bettering himself, by taking French lessons with an executive's wife, and so coming into conflict with his father—the two sides of industry get together over dinner in a powerful scene reminiscent of Ibsen's *The League of Youth*—forms a substantial and colourful central thread.

Morality is an even more domestic story than *A State of Welfare*. A family called the Pargeters are trying to make their son Nick "get on" by passing his A-level exams and winning a place at university. When it is discovered that Nick is having a homosexual affair with his progressive and sensitive teacher, Larry, the family is up in arms at the scandal this will cause in the neighbourhood. However, when Nick's parents manage to summon up the courage to go and see Larry, Larry calms them down with a hypocritical assertion of "morality." The psychology—and morality—may be crude compared with other plays about divided loyalty, but *Morality* is a lively portrayal of family conflict. As in *Life Price* the authors would seem to be saying it is society which is to blame for the cynicism and destructiveness of young people towards their elders. This is an attitude supported by concrete, almost documentary writing, not by the continual assertion of a doctrinaire point of view.

In *Millennium*, set in a semi-detached house on a Northampton estate, there's a gap of 53 years between the first part and the second. The authors present for comparison the life-style of Florrie's family, and that of Doll her granddaughter, in a broader and more sentimental way than in the earlier plays. In Florrie's family one of the girls is dying of scarlet fever, while about her rage the violences of poverty, the stringencies of life caused by the father's status as a hired man. The rebel son, common to both generations, in the first part merely burns his sister's boots (cost, 8/6), while in the second he has, as part of a gang, tied up a boy, cut his hair, and tried to extort money from his parents. The boot-burning satisfies the instinct for anger at the circumstances, and it is punished and purged within the family unit. The second misdemeanour is a matter for the courts, showing the impersonality of justice and how the family has broken down. The time gap achieves a neat and forceful comparison.

Dramatically striking, too, is the Pirandellian twist by which Florrie's family advance on their petty-minded materialist descendants and engage in a battle of wits. The author's sympathies clearly lie with the earlier brood, on whom a huddled statuesque dignity is conferred. Grim and monochrome as they appear, they have the virtue of discipline and look to the after-life for their reward.

Sex and Kinship in a Savage Society is a less successful treatment of the same theme of family disintegration. In *Black Man's Burden* the family is Jamaican. We hear imposing astral voices with Jamaican accents telling the heroine Melvita her child-to-be is the New Messiah. The family settles in England and the problems of assimilating such a striking notion into a society with a National Health service intent on imposing its own solution on visionaries gives the authors opportunity, once more, for striking contrasts, this time comic, beguiling speech rhythms, and exact evocations of place.

—Garry O'Connor

OSBORNE, John (James). British. Born in London, 12 December 1929. Educated at Belmont College, Devon. Married 1) Pamela Lane in 1951 (marriage dissolved 1957); 2) the actress Mary Ure in 1957 (marriage dissolved 1963); 3) the writer Penelope Gilliatt in 1963 (marriage dissolved 1968), one daughter; 4) the actress Jill Bennett in 1968 (marriage dissolved 1977); 5) Helen Dawson in 1978. Has worked as a tutor, actor, and assistant stage manager. Since 1958 co-director, Woodfall Films; since 1960 director, Oscar Lewenstein Plays Ltd., London. Member of the Council, English Stage Company, London, 1960–82. Recipient: *Evening Standard* award, 1956, 1965, 1968; New York Drama Critics Circle award, 1958, 1965; Tony award, 1963; Oscar, for screenplay, 1964. Honorary Doctor: Royal College of Art, London, 1970. Member, Royal Society of Arts. Agent: Fraser and Dunlop Scripts Ltd., 91 Regent Street, London W1R 8RU, England.

PUBLICATIONS

Plays

The Devil Inside Him, with Stella Linden (produced Huddersfield, Yorkshire, 1950).

Personal Enemy, with Anthony Creighton (produced Harrogate, Yorkshire, 1955).

Look Back in Anger (produced London, 1956; New York, 1957). London, Faber, and New York, Criterion, 1957.

The Entertainer, music by John Addison (produced London, 1957; New York, 1958). London, Faber, 1957; New York, Criterion, 1958.

Epitaph for George Dillon, with Anthony Creighton (produced Oxford, 1957; London and New York, 1958). London, Faber, and New York, Criterion, 1958.

The World of Paul Slickey, music by Christopher Whelen (also director: produced Bournemouth and London, 1959). London, Faber, 1959; New York, Criterion, 1961.

A Subject of Scandal and Concern (as *A Matter of Scandal and Concern*, televised 1960; as *A Subject of Scandal and Concern*, produced Nottingham, 1962; New York, 1966). London, Faber, 1961; Chicago, Dramatic Publishing Company, 1971.

Luther (produced Nottingham and London, 1961; New York, 1963). London, Faber, 1961; New York, Criterion, 1962.

Plays for England: The Blood of the Bambergs, Under Plain Cover (produced London, 1962; New York, 1964–65). London, Faber, 1963; New York, Criterion, 1964.

Tom Jones: A Film Script. London, Faber, 1964; New York, Grove Press, 1965.

Inadmissible Evidence (produced London, 1964; New York, 1965). London, Faber, and New York, Grove Press, 1965.

A Patriot for Me (produced London, 1965; New York, 1969). London, Faber, 1966; New York, Random House, 1970.

A Bond Honoured, adaptation of a play by Lope de Vega (produced London, 1966). London, Faber, 1966.

The Hotel in Amsterdam (produced London, 1968). With *Time Present*, London, Faber, 1968; in *Four Plays*, 1973.

Time Present (produced London, 1968). With *The Hotel in Amsterdam*, London, Faber, 1968; in *Four Plays*, 1973.

The Right Prospectus (televised 1970). London, Faber, 1970.

Very Like a Whale (televised 1980). London, Faber, 1971.

West of Suez (produced London, 1971). London, Faber, 1971; in *Four Plays*, 1973.

Hedda Gabler, adaptation of the play by Ibsen (produced London, 1972; Abingdon, Virginia, 1982). London, Faber, 1972; Chicago, Dramatic Publishing Company, 1974.

The Gift of Friendship (televised 1972). London, Faber, 1972.

A Sense of Detachment (produced London, 1972). London, Faber, 1973.

Four Plays: West of Suez, A Patriot for Me, Time Present, The Hotel in Amsterdam. New York, Dodd Mead, 1973.

A Place Calling Itself Rome, adaptation of *Coriolanus* by Shakespeare. London, Faber, 1973.

The Picture of Dorian Gray: A Moral Entertainment, adaptation of the novel by Oscar Wilde (produced London, 1975). London, Faber, 1973.

Jill and Jack (as *Ms.; or, Jill and Jack*, televised 1974). With *The End of Me Old Cigar*, London, Faber, 1975.

The End of Me Old Cigar (produced London, 1975). With *Jill and Jack*, London, Faber, 1975.

Watch It Come Down (produced London, 1976). London, Faber, 1975.

You're Not Watching Me, Mummy (televised 1980). With *Try a Little Tenderness*, London, Faber, 1978.

A Better Class of Person (An Extract of Autobiography for Television), and God Rot Tunbridge Wells. London, Faber, 1985.

Screenplays: *Look Back in Anger*, with Nigel Kneale, 1959; *The Entertainer*, with Nigel Kneale, 1960; *Tom Jones*, 1963; *Inadmissible Evidence*, 1968; *The Charge of the Light Brigade*, with Charles Wood, 1968.

Television Plays: *Billy Bunter*, 1952, and *Robin Hood*, 1953 (*For the Children* series); *A Matter of Scandal and Concern*, 1960; *The Right Prospectus*, 1970; *The Gift of Friendship*, 1972; *Ms.; or, Jill and Jack*, 1974; *Almost a Vision*, 1976; *You're Not Watching Me, Mummy*, 1980; *Very Like a Whale*, 1980; *A Better Class of Person*, 1985; *God Rot Tunbridge Wells*, 1985.

Other

A Better Class of Person: An Autobiography 1929–1956. London, Faber, and New York, Dutton, 1981.

*

Bibliography: *John Osborne: A Reference Guide* by Cameron Northouse and Thomas P. Walsh, Boston, Hall, 1974.

Critical Studies: *Anger and After* by John Russell Taylor, London, Methuen, 1962, revised edition, 1969, as *The Angry Theatre*, New York, Hill and Wang, 1962, revised edition, 1969, and *Look Back in Anger: A Casebook* edited by Taylor, London, Macmillan, 1968; *John Osborne* by Ronald Hayman, London, Heinemann, 1968, New York, Ungar, 1972; *Osborne* by Martin Banham, Edinburgh, Oliver and Boyd, 1969; *The Plays of John Osborne: An Assessment*, London, Gollancz, and New York, Humanities Press, 1969, and *John Osborne*, London, Longman, 1969, both by Simon Trussler; *John Osborne* by Alan Carter, Edinburgh, Oliver and Boyd, 1969, New York, Barnes and Noble, 1973; *Theatre Language: A Study of Arden, Osborne, Pinter, and Wesker* by John Russell Brown, London, Allen Lane, and New York, Taplinger, 1972; *John Osborne* by Harold Ferrar, New York, Columbia University Press, 1973; *Anger and Detachment: A Study of Arden, Osborne, and Pinter* by Michael Anderson, London, Pitman, 1976; *Coping with Vulnerability: The Achievement of John Osborne* by Herbert Goldstone, Washington, D.C., University

Press of America, 1982; *John Osborne* by Arnold P. Hinchliffe, Boston, Twayne, 1984.

Theatrical Activities:
Director: **Plays**—with the Huddersfield Repertory Company, 1949; *The World of Paul Slickey*, Bournemouth and London, 1959; *Meals on Wheels* by Charles Wood, London, 1965; *The Entertainer*, London, 1974; *Inadmissible Evidence*, London, 1978.
Actor: **Plays**—Mr. Burrells in *No Room at the Inn* by Joan Temple, Sheffield, 1948; on tour and in repertory in Ilfracombe, Bridgwater, Camberwell, Kidderminster, Derby, 1948–56; with the English Stage Company, London: Antonio in *Don Juan* by Ronald Duncan, 1956, Lionel in *The Death of Satan* by Ronald Duncan, 1956, roles in *Cards of Identity* by Nigel Dennis, 1956, Lin To in *The Good Woman of Setzuan* by Brecht, 1956, The Commissionaire in *The Apollo de Bellac* by Giraudoux, 1957, and Donald Blake in *The Making of Moo* by Nigel Dennis, 1957; Claude Hicket in *A Cuckoo in the Nest* by Ben Travers, London, 1964. **Films**—*First Love*, 1970; *Get Carter*, 1971; *Tomorrow Never Comes*, 1978; *Flash Gordon*, 1980. **Television**—*The Parachute* by David Mercer, 1968; *The First Night of Pygmalion* by Richard Huggett, 1969; *Lady Charlotte*, 1977.

* * *

John Osborne's first fortune, and first misfortune, was the tag "angry young man." Fortune because in 1956 it helped to make new writing, and new drama in particular, a talking point, news, in a way it had never been before in the modern British theatre. Misfortune because once landed with such a label it is difficult to grow out of it and even more difficult to convince the public or the critics that you have done so.

Nevertheless, Osborne continued to develop right from the first production of *Look Back in Anger* on 8 May 1956, which was also his first appearance as a dramatist on the London stage, though two earlier plays, written in collaboration, had been briefly shown out of town. At the time he was an actor, 26, and considered something of a juvenile prodigy, at least in comparison with the largely middle-aged strength of the British theatrical establishment. The play had been quite simply sent through the post to the newly founded English Stage Company, a group idealistically devoted to new theatrical writing, and was their first new British play to be produced. It had mixed but on the whole favourable reviews: everyone at least seemed agreed that Osborne's was a distinctive new voice, and before long his hero, Jimmy Porter, became a kind of folk hero for a young generation puzzled by the Hungarian revolution, unhappy about Britain's last imperialist fling at Suez, and dedicated to protest about the Bomb and all manner of questions social and political.

Not that Jimmy Porter, or Osborne himself it would seem, was particularly interested in the larger issues: his contribution was rather a tone of voice, an attitude of private bloodymindedness which set people wondering what exactly he was angry about. Jimmy's marital problems and social contracting-out (he is the graduate keeper of a sweet stall) were acted out in a form which Osborne himself rapidly characterized as "formal, rather old-fashioned," as were the somewhat similar difficulties of George Dillon in *Epitaph for George Dillon* (written in collaboration with Anthony Creighton), a writer with a will to failure as the only thing which will adequately motivate his sense of dissatisfaction. But Osborne was already moving on to new things technically and emotionally in *The Entertainer*, which placed a realistically treated story of a failed comedian and hollow man's last moments of contact with real emotion at the news of his son's death in Cyprus in a non-realistic context of allegorically significant sketches and numbers ostensibly from the tatty show Archie Rice is starring in, but actually reflecting the present state of Britain and relating Archie's personal emotional failure to a wider loss of nerve and purpose. The play also, incidentally, marked the first important marriage of old theatre and new: Laurence Olivier played the lead in its first production.

In the works which followed it sometimes seemed that Osborne was himself suffering from a certain loss of direction. *The World of Paul Slickey*, an ambitious satirical musical about a gossip columnist with a dual personality, was an almost unredeemed failure, and the two historical pieces which followed, *A Subject of Scandal and Concern* (television) and *Luther*, both seemed rather like academic exercises in the dramatization of pre-existent material rather than original creations, though in the latter Osborne did succeed in making over the character of Luther (magnetically played by Albert Finney) into a figure somewhat after the image of Jimmy Porter—or rather, perhaps (since the historical sources were fairly scrupulously adhered to), managed to find in the outlines of the character someone after his own heart. In *Plays for England* some of the best of Osborne and some of the worst were juxtaposed. One of the two plays, *The Blood of the Bambergs*, a feeble satire about a royal wedding, was generally regarded as Osborne's poorest play, but the other, *Under Plain Cover*, opened up an interesting new area by embarking directly on the world of private neurosis, in this case the strange shared fantasy world of a married couple who turn out to be brother and sister.

What had worried some critics about *Look Back in Anger* was that Osborne seemed in it to be dealing with a neurotic character whom he did not fully realize to be neurotic, and anyway he allowed him to win all the arguments and take on a heroic role by virtue of his sheer biting eloquence. *Under Plain Cover* might almost be a fourth act to *Look Back in Anger*, showing what could have happened to Jimmy and Alison a few years after they were reunited. Osborne's next play, and still in many ways his best, *Inadmissible Evidence*, pursues this line of dramatic thinking further. Its central character, Bill Maitland, is a lawyer who could also be Jimmy some years later. But this time he is allowed centre stage for his monologues simply because nobody bothers to listen to him any more; he rails at a world which doesn't care, and his deep sense of dissatisfaction is seen no longer as an objectively justified response to the ills of the world, but as the expression of a mind at the end of its tether. One of an accidental group of "male menopause" dramas of the 1960's (others were Arthur Miller's *After the Fall* and Fellini's *8½*), *Inadmissible Evidence* retains the extra kick of a kind of personal anguish expressed with all the lucidity and technical skill of a born dramatist working at the height of his powers.

Perhaps no play Osborne has written since has quite achieved the same happy balance, but at least there is no doubt possible about his being a born dramatist, one to whom dramatic expression comes with perfect naturalness and ease; it is fair to say that whatever the successes of other dramatists of his generation (and they have been many and varied) he is the only one who has contrived to win through consistently to an ampler public utterance, to remain defiantly a popular dramatist capable of speaking to a mass public, even if some of his plays may individually fail. *A Patriot for Me* failed, if it may be said to have failed, primarily because of a belated tangle with moribund theatrical censorship over its homosexual theme: a large-scale period drama, it recounted the strange history of Alfred Redl, master double spy for Austria and Russia in the period immediately before World War I. *A Bond Honoured* was in a comparison a minor work, a long one-act fantasy on themes from Lope de Vega's *La fianza satisfecha* which made Lope's God-defying hero into almost a parody of Osborne's earlier railers; it was commissioned by the National Theatre.

In 1968 Osborne returned to the wider public stage with two new plays, presented in the first instance together although they have little or no thematic connection, *Time Present* and *The Hotel in Amsterdam.* Both represented in some respects new departures: *Time Present* was Osborne's first play to have a female protagonist, though Pamela, a "resting" actress, could not unfairly be described as a Jimmy Porter in skirts, a feminine variation of the familiar pattern, considering it her right, if not her duty, to bitch at everyone in sight to compensate in some way for her gnawing sense of dissatisfaction. *The Hotel in Amsterdam* seems on the contrary like some sort of answer by Osborne to those of his critics who have complained that he tends to write monologue plays, plays in which only one character is really given a chance to speak. It is much more of an ensemble play, with several characters of almost equal weight, all of them refugees from the unseen presence of the dreaded "K.L.," a film producer around whom, in one fashion or another, all their lives revolve, who have holed up for a weekend of respite/holiday/group therapy in *the* hotel in Amsterdam.

West of Suez, for all its untidiness, its eagerness to pack everything possible into a form suggested by Shaw's *Heartbreak House* and already bursting at the seams, does all the same have passages of Osborne's best writing, a surprising range of rounded, believable characters (in a sense it is another ensemble play), and re-examines many of Osborne's pet themes, from the decline of imperialist Britain through homosexuality and nostalgia for the settled values of the past to a wary acceptence of a new, irrational order of things which may becoming to birth. In this play more than any other, Osborne seems to be deliberately siding with the conservatives, the old values. It is a long way from *Look Back in Anger*, but also by the look of it something very like a new beginning. Since *West of Suez* he has written several slight television plays, adaptations, and a couple of almost defiantly lightweight stage plays. But still we may continue to expect a further development of a dramatist who has through triumph and disaster never ceased to change and grow.

—John Russell Taylor

OSOFISAN, Femi (Babafemi Adeyemi Osofisan). Nigerian. Born 16 June 1946. Educated at schools in Ilesha, Ife, and Erunwon; Government College, Ibadan; University of Dakar, Senegal, D.E.S. 1968; University of Ibadan, B.A. 1969, Ph.D. 1974; University of Paris III, 1971–73. Since 1973, member of the Faculty, currently Senior Lecturer in Theatre Arts, University of Ibadan. Visiting Professor, University of Benin, Lomé, Togo Republic, 1980, University of Pennsylvania, Philadelphia, 1983, University of Benin, Benin City, Nigeria, 1983–85, and University of Ife, Ife-Ife, 1985–86. Founding member of the Editorial Board, the *Guardian*, Lagos, 1984–85. Currently editor, *Opon Ifa: Ibadan Poetry Chapbooks.* Drama consultant, Festac 77, Lagos. Recipient: Association of Nigerian Authors prize, 1983; Fulbright fellowship, 1986. Address: Department of Theatre Arts, University of Ibadan, Ibadan, Nigeria; or *The Guardian*, PMB 1217, Oshodi, Lagos, Nigeria.

Publications

Plays

Odudwa, Don't Go! (produced Ibadan, 1968).
You Have Lost Your Fine Face (produced Ibadan, 1969).
A Restless Run of Locusts (produced Akure, 1970). Ibadan, Onibonoje Press, 1975.
The Chattering and the Song (produced Ibadan, 1974). Ibadan, Ibadan University Press, 1977.
Who's Afraid of Solarin? (produced Ibadan, 1977). Calabar, Scholars Press, 1978.
Once upon Four Robbers (produced Ibadan, 1978). Ibadan, BIO, 1982.
Farewell to a Cannibal Rage (produced Ibadan, 1978; revised version produced Benin City, 1984). Ibadan, Evans, 1986.
Morountodun (produced Ibadan, 1979; revised version produced Ife-Ife, 1980). Included in *Morountodun and Other Plays*, 1982.
Birthdays Are Not for Dying (produced Ibadan, 1981). Ibadan, Evans, 1987.
The Oriki of a Grasshopper (produced Ibadan, 1981; revised version produced Benin City, 1985). Included in *Two Short Plays*, 1986.
No More the Wasted Breed (produced Ibadan, 1982). Included in *Morountodun and Other Plays*, 1982.
Morountodun and Other Plays (includes *No More the Wasted Breed* and *Red Is the Freedom Road*). Ikeja, Longman, 1982.
Midnight Hotel (produced Ibadan, 1982). Ibadan, Evans, 1986.
Altine's Wrath (televised 1983). Included in *Two Short Plays*, 1986.
Esu and the Vagabond Minstrels (produced Benin City, 1984; revised version produced Ife-Ife, 1986). Ibadan, New Horn Press, 1987.
Two Short Plays. Ibadan, New Horn Press, 1986.

Television Plays: *Altine's Wrath, A Debt to the Dead, A Date with Danger, Fires Burn But They Die Not, The New Cathedral, At the Petrol Station, Mission Abandoned, A Hero Comes Home, Operation Rat-Trap, To Kill a Dream* (all in *Visitors* series), 1983.

Novel

Kolera Kolej. Ibadan, New Horn Press, 1975.

Other

Beyond Translation: Tragic Paradigms and the Dramaturgy of Ola Rotimi and Wole Soyinka. Ife-Ife, Ife Monographs on African Literature, 1986.
The Orality of Prose: A Comparatist Look at the Works of Rabelais, Joyce, and Tutuola. Ife-Ife, Ife Monographs on African Literature, 1986.

*

Theatrical Activities:
Director: all of his own plays.

* * *

University professor, theatre director, newspaper columnist, and poet, Femi Osofisan is part of a generation which has experienced Nigerian independence only as an empty slogan. Thus, he fashions a committed literature designed to reawaken a collective, imaginatively self-critical sensibility and break the enduring shackles of religion, custom, and colonialism in favor of a more humane, egalitarian society. Within Nigeria he is often viewed as a radical who would completely destroy the past, but his radicalism actually builds positively upon the best of tradition while seeking to encourage pervasive change.

For analytical convenience, Osofisan's works may be separated into the broad categories of realistic protest plays, satiric adaptations of European models, and a particularly African form of "total theatre." *A Restless Run of Locusts, Red Is the Freedom Road*, and *The Oriki of a Grasshopper* fit into the first category. Here, the playwright registers the widespread political corruption, brutality, intellectual failure, and rhythm of repression, coup, and counter-coup of post-independence Nigeria. His *No More the Wasted Breed* rejects an acceptance of martyrdom, articulated in Wole Soyinka's *The Strong Breed*, and illuminates in persuasive dramatic form aspects of the quarrel—albeit friendly—which many younger intellectuals have with their distinguished mentor.

European dramatic literature provides a ready source for adaptation in such plays as *Who's Afraid of Solarin?* and *Midnight Hotel.* The former play is a loose adaptation of Gogol's *The Inspector General*, and the latter, through its use of farcical complications and acerbic songs, rendered from an oversized songbook, borrows from both Feydeau and Brecht. More importantly for Nigerian audiences which may be unaware of the European originals, these plays satirize the rampant materialism of the upper classes. As such, they may be considered an ingenious contemporary development of the traditional, age-grade satires in which the unempowered expressed their dissatisfaction with privileged.

To date, Osofisan's most conceptually and stylistically complex plays are *The Chattering and the Song, Farewell to a Cannibal Rage, Once upon Four Robbers, Morountodun*, and *Esu and the Vagabond Minstrels.* Illustrative of an African concept of drama, these plays incorporate non-verbal elements like dance and music into a spoken text; insist upon theatre as artifice through frequent role-changes and storytelling techniques; conjoin spatial and temporal frames into a seamless experiential present; and place high value on episodic and open-ended structures which challenge audiences to impose meaning upon the event.

The Chattering and the Song, the first Osofisan play written in this genre, contains many of the themes upon which the playwright subsequently elaborates. The play traces a path whereby university-trained supporters of a farmers' movement move from an unfocused anger about social injustice to an active understanding of the process of social change. Games, or the construction of illusory systems in which the characters invest belief, are the vehicles through which this evolution is accomplished. Thus, the characters play a number of riddling and card games, with each new round being a repetition with significant variation; riddling, which is designed to develop intellectual prowess through experimentation with trope and which epitomises the temporary resolution of apparent paradox, becomes a metaphor for an appropriate revolutionary stance which acknowledges dialectical development yet maintains commitment to an egalitarian ideal.

The initial irony of would-be revolutionaries unwittingly betraying espoused principles within the context of a game is repeated in their later re-enactment of a play-within-the-play, for the most flamboyant radical begins awkwardly in his role of ruler but grows more overbearing the longer he is called upon to defend his privileged position. The historical drama which these characters enact is itself a radical re-interpretation of recorded fact; the alteration enables Osofisan to posit identity as multiple, contextual, and susceptible to change, qualities which in turn necessitate continuous re-evaluation of material circumstances. The confrontational climax of the historical drama is rendered in song, dance, and drumming, sensorially rich devices which satisfy his audiences' inherited expectations concerning aesthetic structures most suited for conveying deep emotion. Yet, this appeal to the senses is followed by an intellectual argument, couched in terms of myth, another popular mode of expression which Osofisan has elsewhere characterized as a "pedagogical explanation of knowledge by means of metaphor." The abrupt disruption of the play-within-the-play offers the audience a graphic image of its potential to reject and redirect a hegemonic social reality; the moment anticipates the final deconstruction of form when the actors jettison their roles entirely and encourage the audience to join in acknowledging the positive thrust of the farmers' movement.

Thus, Osofisan offers in plays like *The Chattering and the Song* what Brecht defines as a "fighting" popular theatre. With sophisticated irreverence, he re-interprets core values, thereby challenging audiences to reclaim for themselves the power to alter their world.

—Sandra L. Richards

OWEN, Alun (Davies). British. Born in Liverpool, Lancashire, 24 November 1925. Educated at Cardigan Grammar School, Wales; Oulton High School, Liverpool. Married Mary O'Keeffe in 1942; two sons. Stage manager, director, and actor, 1942–59. Recipient: Screenwriters and Producers Script of the Year Award, 1960; Screenwriters Guild award, 1961; *Daily Mirror* award, 1961; Golden Star, 1967; Banff International Television Festival prize, 1985. Lives in Dublin. Agent: Julian Friedmann, Blake Friedmann Agency, 37–41 Gower Street, London WC1E 6HH, England.

PUBLICATIONS

Plays

The Rough and Ready Lot (broadcast 1958; produced London, 1959). London, Encore, 1960.

Progress to the Park (broadcast 1958; produced London, 1959). Published in *New English Dramatists 5*, London, Penguin, 1962.

Three T.V. Plays (includes *No Trams to Lime Street; After the Funeral; Lena, Oh My Lena*). London, Cape, 1961; New York, Hill and Wang, 1963.

The Rose Affair (televised 1961; produced Cardiff, 1966). Published in *Anatomy of a Television Play*, London, Weidenfeld and Nicolson, 1962.

Dare to Be a Daniel (televised 1962). Published in *Eight Plays: Book 1*, edited by Malcolm Stuart Fellows, London, Cassell, 1965.

A Little Winter Love (produced Dublin, 1963; London, 1965). London, Evans, 1965.

Maggie May, music and lyrics by Lionel Bart (produced London, 1964).

The Game (includes *The Winner* and *The Loser*) (produced Dublin, 1965).

The Goose (produced Dublin, 1967).
The Wake (televised 1967). Published in *Theatre Choice: A Collection of Modern Short Plays*, edited by Michael Marland, London, Blackie, 1972.
Shelter (televised 1967; produced London, 1971). London, French, 1968.
George's Room (televised 1967). London and New York, French, 1968.
There'll Be Some Changes Made (produced London, 1969).
Norma, in *We Who Are About to . . .*, later title *Mixed Doubles* (produced London, 1969; revised version produced London, 1983). London, Methuen, 1970.
Doreen (televised 1969). Published in *The Best Short Plays 1971*, edited by Stanley Richards, Philadelphia, Chilton, 1971.
The Male of the Species (televised 1969; produced Brighton and London, 1974). Published in *On Camera 3*, edited by Ron Side and Ralph Greenfield, New York, Holt Rinehart, 1972; published separately London, French, 1975.
Lucia (produced Cardiff, 1982).

Screenplays: *The Criminal* (*The Concrete Jungle*), with Jimmy Sangster, 1960; *A Hard Day's Night*, 1964; *Caribbean Idyll*, 1970.

Radio Plays: *Two Sons*, 1957; *The Rough and Ready Lot*, 1958; *Progress to the Park*, 1958; *It Looks Like Rain*, 1959; *Café Society*, 1982; *The Lancaster Gate End*, 1982; *Colleagues*, 1982; *Kisch-Kisch*, 1983; *Soft Impeachment*, 1983; *Tiger*, 1984; *Halt*, 1984; *Earwig* series, 1984; *Widowers*, 1985.

Television Plays: *No Trams to Lime Street*, 1959; *After the Funeral*, 1960; *Lena, Oh My Lena*, 1960; *The Ruffians*, 1960; *The Ways of Love*, 1961; *The Rose Affair*, 1961; *The Hard Knock*, 1962; *Dare to Be a Daniel*, 1962; *You Can't Win 'em All*, 1962; *The Strain*, 1963; *Let's Imagine* series, 1963; *The Stag*, 1963; *A Local Boy*, 1963; *The Other Fella*, 1966; *The Making of Jericho*, 1966; *The Fantasist*, 1967; *The Wake*, 1967; *Shelter*, 1967; *George's Room*, 1967; *Stella*, 1967; *Thief*, 1967; *Charlie*, 1968; *Gareth*, 1968; *Tennyson*, 1968; *Ah, There You Are*, 1968; *Alexander*, 1968; *Minding the Shop*, 1968; *Time for the Funny Walk*, 1968; *The Ladies*, 1969; *Doreen*, 1969; *Spare Time*, 1969; *Park People*, 1969; *You'll Be the Death of Me*, 1969; *The Male of the Species* (U.S. title: *Emlyn, MacNeil, Cornelius*), 1969; *Joan*, 1970; *Hilda*, 1970; *And a Willow Tree*, 1970; *Just the Job*, 1970; *Female of the Species*, 1970; *Joy*, 1970; *Ruth*, 1971; *Funny*, 1971; *Pal*, 1971; *Giants and Ogres*, 1971; *The Piano Player*, 1971; *The Web*, 1972; *Ronny Barker Show* (3 scripts); *Buttons*, 1973; *Flight*, 1973; *Lucky*, 1974; *Left*, 1975; *The Vandy Case*, 1975; *Forget-Me-Not* (6 plays), 1976; *The Fetch*, 1977; *The Look*, 1978; *Passing Through*, 1979 (Ireland); *The Runner*, 1980; *Sealink*, 1980; *Lovers of the Lake*, from the story by Sean O'Faolain, 1984.

*

Theatrical Activities:
Actor: **Plays**—with the Birmingham Repertory Company, 1943–44; Gotti in *The Lonely Falcons* by P.N. Walker-Taylor, London, 1946; Jepson in *Humoresque* by Guy Bolton, London, 1948; Rolph in *Snow White and the Seven Dwarfs*, London, 1951; with Sir Donald Wolfit's Company at the Old Vic, London, 1951: in *Tamburlaine the Great* by Marlowe, Charles in *As You Like It*, Curan and Herald in *King Lear*, Officer in *Twelfth Night*, Salarino in *The Merchant of Venice*, Sexton in *Macbeth*, Gonzales Ferera in *The Wandering Jew* by J. Temple Thurston, a Lord and Joseph in *The Taming of the Shrew*; with the English Stage Company at the Royal Court, London, 1957; Clifford in *Man with a Guitar* by Gilbert Horobin, and Smith in *The Waiting of Lester Abbs* by Kathleen Sully, London, 1957; Reader in *The Samson Riddle* by Wolf Mankowitz, Dublin, 1972. **Films**—*Valley of Song* (*Men Are Children Twice*), 1953; *Every Day Except Christmas*, 1957; *In the Wake of a Stranger*, 1959; *I'm All Right Jack*, 1959; *Jet Storm*, 1959; *The Servant*, 1963.

* * *

The main strengths of Alun Owen's work have always been its accuracy of observation, its depth of characterization, and the power and fluency of its dialogue, sometimes reaching the level of poetry. *Progress to the Park*, set in the Liverpool of the late 1950's, is a vivid and detailed portrait of working-class life in that town at the period. The play's central theme is the vice-like grip that religious intolerance has on the city's inhabitants; and is expressed through the central relationship between Bobby Laughlin, a Protestant boy, and Mag Keegan, a Catholic girl. Their potential love is stifled and destroyed by the bigoted attitudes of their elders. There are a number of sharply defined character studies, including members of the Laughlin and Keegan families; and of Teifion Davies, the detached, ironic young Welshman who has a love-hate relationship to his home town, which is reflected in his commentary on the action. The play teems with vitality and power, each episode flowing effectively and relentessly into and out of each other but related strongly to the central theme.

The Rough and Ready Lot is set in monastery in a Spanish colony in South America a few years after the end of the American Civil War and revolves around four "soldiers of fortune"—Kelly, O'Keefe, Morgan, and the Colonel. They are in a lull between fighting, ostensibly on the side of the Indians in their bid to free themselves from their Spanish oppressors; in the meantime, the four men talk. O'Keefe is a fantical Catholic; Morgan an equally fanatical political revolutionary; the Colonel is a "realist," who thinks he knows the motives for people's actions but is, in fact, incredibly blinkered; while Kelly just takes life as it comes. They argue and try to impose their views on the others, sometimes in bursts of magnificent rhetoric; but in the end only Kelly survives. As Irving Wardle said in a review, "Its dialogue flows beautifully; its characters are conceived in depth and, as embodiments of conflicting principles, they are disposed in a pattern of geometric symmetry; the plot is constructed solidly and attaches itself tenaciously to the governing theme."

In the musical *Maggie May*, written with Lionel Bart, Owen returns to the Liverpool scene and gives us another teeming, vital slice of life. The early and mid-1960's was also the time of his award-winning television plays, also set on Merseyside, *No Trams to Lime Street*, *Lena, Oh My Lena*, and *After the Funeral*; and his sharp and witty script for the Beatles' first and best film, the semi-documentary *A Hard Day's Night*. By contrast, *The Rose Affair*, also a television award-winner, was a modernized version of the fairy-tale *Beauty and the Beast*, the Beast-figure an isolated, high-powered businessman, the Beauty a girl he falls in love with from afar; stylistically, it had some bold innovations for its time and also had some pithy things to say on the split between being a public and a private person.

In recent years, most of Owen's work has been for television, and includes *Shelter*, a play about the confrontation between an aggressive working-class man and an alienated young middle-class woman, and *Dare to Be a Daniel*, in which a young man with a grudge against his former schoolteacher returns to the small town where he comes from to gain his revenge.

Owen adapted his 1969 television play *The Male of the Species* for the stage in 1974. Consisting of three short plays, this work purports to show how women are exploited by men. Mary MacNeil is shown in her encounters with three crucial male figures: her father, a master carpenter; her employer, a suave, urbane barrister; and the "office cad." The trouble is, however, that the men are all depicted as attractive, while Mary is portrayed as the willing victim. The perhaps unconscious male chauvinism of the play is disappointing in a writer of Owen's talent.

—Jonathan Hammond

OWENS, Rochelle. Pseudonym for Rochelle Bass. American. Born in Brooklyn, New York, 2 April 1936. Educated at Lafayette High School, Brooklyn, graduated 1953. Married the writer George Economou in 1962. Worked as clerk, typist, telephone operator. Founding member, New York Theatre Strategy. Visiting Lecturer, University of California, San Diego, 1982; Adjunct Professor, and host of radio program *The Writer's Mind*, University of Oklahoma, Norman, 1984. Recipient: Rockefeller grant, 1965, 1975; Ford grant, 1965; Creative Artists Public Service grant, 1966, 1973; Yale University School of Drama fellowship, 1968; Obie award, 1968, 1971, 1982; Guggenheim fellowship, 1971; National Endowment for the Arts grant, 1974; Villager award, 1982. Agent: Fifi Oscard. Associates, 19 West 44th Street, New York, New York 10036. Address: 1401 Magnolia, Norman, Oklahoma 73069, U.S.A.

PUBLICATIONS

Plays

Futz (produced Minneapolis, 1965; New York, Edinburgh, and London, 1967). New York, Hawk's Well Press, 1961; revised version in *Futz and What Came After*, 1968; in *New Short Plays 2*, London, Methuen, 1969.
The String Game (produced New York, 1965). Included in *Futz and What Came After*, 1968.
Istanboul (produced New York, 1965; London, 1982). Included in *Futz and What Came After*, 1968.
Homo (produced Stockholm and New York, 1966; London, 1969). Included in *Futz and What Came After*, 1968.
Beclch (produced Philadelphia and New York, 1968). Included in *Futz and What Came After*, 1968.
Futz and What Came After. New York, Random House, 1968.
The Karl Marx Play, music by Galt MacDermot, lyrics by Owens (produced New York, 1973). Included in *The Karl Marx Play and Others*, 1974.
The Karl Marx Play and Others (includes *Kontraption, He Wants Shih!, Farmer's Almanac, Coconut Folksinger, O.K. Certaldo*). New York, Dutton, 1974.
He Wants Shih! (produced New York, 1975). Included in *The Karl Marx Play and Others*, 1974.
Coconut Folksinger (broadcast 1976). Included in *The Karl Marx Play and Others*, 1974.
Kontraption (produced New York, 1978). Included in *The Karl Marx Play and Others*, 1974.
Emma Instigated Me, published in *Performing Arts Journal 1* (New York), Spring 1976.
The Widow, and The Colonel, in *The Best Short Plays 1977*, edited by Stanley Richards. Radnor, Pennsylvania, Chilton, 1977.
Mountain Rites, in *The Best Short Plays 1978*, edited by Stanley Richards. Radnor, Pennsylvania, Chilton, 1978.
Chucky's Hunch (produced New York, 1981). Published in *Wordplays 2*, New York, Performing Arts Journal Publications, 1982.
Who Do You Want, Peire Vidal? (produced New York, 1982). With *Futz*, New York, Broadway Play Publishing, 1986.

Screenplay: *Futz* (additional dialogue), 1969.

Radio Plays: *Coconut Folksinger*, 1976 (Germany); *Sweet Potatoes*, 1977.

Television Play (video): *Oklahoma Too: Rabbits and Nuggets*, 1987.

Short Stories

The Girl on the Garage Wall. Mexico City, El Corno Emplumado, 1962.
The Obscenities of Reva Cigarnik. Mexico City. El Corno Emplumado, 1963.

Verse

Not Be Essence That Cannot Be. New York, Trobar Press, 1961.
Four Young Lady Poets, with others, edited by LeRoi Jones. New York, Totem-Corinth, 1962.
Salt and Core. Los Angeles, Black Sparrow Press, 1968.
I Am the Babe of Joseph Stalin's Daughter. New York, Kulchur, 1972.
Poems from Joe's Garage. Providence, Rhode Island, Burning Deck, 1973.
The Joe 82 Creation Poems. Los Angeles, Black Sparrow Press, 1974.
The Joe Chronicles 2. Santa Barbara, California, Black Sparrow Press, 1979.
Shemuel. St. Paul, New Rivers Press, 1979.
French Light. Norman, Oklahoma Press with the Flexible Voice, 1984.
Constructs. Norman, Oklahoma, Poetry Around, 1985.
W.C. Fields in French Light. New York, Contact II, 1986.
How Much Paint Does the Painting Need. New York, Kulchur, 1988.

Recordings: *A Reading of Primitive and Archaic Poetry*, with others, Broadside; *From a Shaman's Notebook*, with others, Broadside; *The Karl Marx Play*, Kilmarnock, 1975; *Totally Corrupt*, Giorno, 1976; *Black Box 17*, Watershed Foundation, 1979.

Other

Editor, *Spontaneous Combustion: Eight New American Plays*. New York, Winter House, 1972.

*

Manuscript Collections: Mugar Memorial Library, Boston University; University of California, Davis; University of Oklahoma, Norman; Lincoln Center Library of the Performing Arts, New York.

Critical Studies: by Harold Clurman and Jerome Rothenberg in *Futz and What Came After*, 1968; review by Jane Augustine in *World 29* (New York), 1974; "Rochelle Owens Symposium" in *Margins 24–26* (Milwaukee), 1975; *American Playwrights: A Critical Survey* by Bonnie Marranca and Gautam Dasgupta, New York, Drama Book Specialists, 1981; *Women in American Theatre* edited by Helen Krich Chinoy and Linda Walsh Jenkins, New York, Crown, 1981; *American Women Writers* by Linda Mainiero, New York, Ungar, 1981; article by Owens in *Contemporary Authors Autobiography Series 2* edited by Adele Sarkissian, Detroit, Gale, 1985; Len Berkman, in *Parnassus* (New York), 1985.

Theatrical Activities:
Director and actress: **Television**—*Oklahoma Too: Rabbits and Nuggets*, 1987.

Rochelle Owens comments:

I am interested in the flow of imagination between the actors and the director, the boundless possibilities of interpretation of a script. Different theatrical realities are created and/or destroyed depending upon the multitudinous perceptions and points of view of the actors and director who share in the creation of the design of the unique journey of playing the play. There are as many ways to approach my plays as there as combinations of people who might involve themselves.

The inter-media video *Oklahoma Too* uses poetry and images juxtaposed. The structures both linguistic and visual offer exciting projections of my continuous investigation of making art.

* * *

Rochelle Owens came to the attention of the theatre public with her first play, *Futz*, whose shocking subject and inventive language launched her theatrical career. Owens's plays are distinguished by intense poetic imagery that springs from primordial human impulses of the subconscious and by the passionate and often violent struggle of her characters to survive within their repressive societies. Although a moralist who satirizes human frailty with parody, dialect, and the comic grotesque, Owens is also a compassionate observer who imbues her characters with tragic dimensions.

Futz is preceded by a quotation from Corinthians: "Now concerning the things whereof ye wrote to me: It is good for a man not to touch a woman." Cyrus Futz loves his pig, Amanda, and is persecuted by the community. Majorie Satz lusts for all men and wheedles an invitation to share Futz's sexual pleasure with his pig. Oscar Loop is driven to madness and murders Ann Fox when they inadvertently witness the Futz-Amanda-Majorie orgy. Majorie kills Amanda for revenge. Oscar is condemned to hang and Futz is sent to prison where he is stabbed by Majorie's brother. Puritanical society punishes innocent sensuality.

The String Game also explores the conflict between puritanism and natural impulse. Greenland Eskimos play the string game to ward off winter boredom. They are admonished for creating erotic images by their Italian priest, Father Bontempo; yet he longs for his own string game: warm spaghetti. Half-breed Cecil tempts Bontempo with a promise of pasta in exchange for the support of Cecil's commercial schemes. While gluttonously feasting, the priest chokes to death. The saddened Eskimos refuse to comply with Cecil's business venture and stoically return to their string games.

Istanboul dramatizes a cultural clash and *Homo* a class struggle. In *Istanboul* Norman men are fascinated by hirsute Byzantine women, and their wives by the smooth-skinned Byzantine men. In a religious frenzy St. Mary of Egypt murders the barbaric Norman, Godfrigh, and sensual Leo makes love to Godfrigh's wife as they wait for the Saracens to attack. *Homo* presents the mutual greed and contempt of Nordic and Asiatic. A surrealistic exploration of racial and class conflict the dramatic energy of the play in which revolution comes and goes, and workers continue their brutality.

Human perversion and bloody primitive rites prevail in Owens's most savage play, *Beclch*. In a fantasy Africa, four white adventurers intrude upon the natural innocence of a village. Queen Beclch, a monster of excess, professes her love for young Jose, then introduces him to the cruelty of cockfighting. She promises Yago Kingship, if he will contract elephantiasis. When Yago cannot transcend the pain of his deformity, he is forced mercilessly by the villagers to strangle himself. Beclch moves further into excess, and Jose flees in disgust. Since a queen cannot rule without a male consort, Beclch prepares herself for death as voluptuously as she lived.

A promise of social progress resides in Owens's first play with music, *The Karl Marx Play*. As in *Homo*, linear time is ignored and through a montage of scenes, past and present, a human portrait of Marx emerges in this, Owens's most joyful play. Her Marx is drained by illness, poverty, and lust for his aristocratic wife. All those who surround him demand that he complete *Das Kapital*, particularly his friend Engels and a 20th-century American black, Leadbelly. Though Marx denies his Jewish heritage, he invokes Yahweh for consolation, but it is finally Leadbelly who actively ignites the man of destiny to fulfill his mission.

He Wants Shih! is an elegant poetic tragedy. Lan, son of the last Empress of the Manchu dynasty, abdicates the warlike legacy of his mother, ignores the adoring Princess Ling, loves his stepbrother Bok, and is enthralled with his stern mentor Feng. Steeped in Eastern philosophy and the supernatural, this surrealistic archetypal myth of individuation is dramatized with ritual, masks, and pseudo-Chinese dialect. The dismembered head of the Empress continues to speak on stage while Western imperialists decimate the Chinese. Acknowledging his homosexuality in the final scene, Lan-he transforms into Lan-she. Total renunciation of sex and empire ends this fantastic play.

As *He Wants Shih!* explores the quest for selfhood, *Kontraption* examines dehumanization in a technological world. On an empty terrain Abdul and Hortten share their lives and sexual fantasies. Abdul's intolerance of their repulsive laundryman, Strauss, drives him to murder, and he is in turn transformed by a magician into a mechanical contraption. When Abdul attempts to transcend his own grotesque condition he falls to his death, leaving behind a disconsolate Hortten.

Owens returns to historical biography in *Emma Instigated Me*. The life of Emma Goldman, the 19th-century anarchist, is juxtaposed against a contemporary Author, Director, and female revolutionaries. Once again linear time is dissolved. The characters change from one to another, from character into actor into bystander. The theatricality of the play becomes its most important objective.

Owens continues to experiment. *Chucky's Hunch* was acclaimed by New York critics as hilarious and impelling. In contrast to her multi-character dramas, the solitary Chucky, a middle-aged failure, narrates a series of recriminating letters to one of his three ex-wives. Similarly, in her most recent play, *Who Do You Want, Peire Vidal?*, two characters assume multiple roles. In this play-within-a-play a Japanese-American professor is among the transformational characters in a series of episodic confrontations. Owens's fantastic imagery, charged language, and daring confrontation with subconscious impulse remains unique in American theatre.

—Elaine Shragge

PAGE, Louise. British. Born in London, 7 March 1955. Educated at High Storrs Comprehensive School, Sheffield; University of Birmingham, 1973–76, B.A. in drama and theatre arts 1976; University of Wales, Cardiff, 1976–77, post-graduate diploma in theatre studies 1977. Yorkshire Television Fellow in Creative Writing, University of Sheffield, 1979–81; resident playwright, Royal Court Theatre, London, 1982–83. Recipient: George Devine Award, 1982; J.T. Grein award, 1985. Agent: Phil Kelvin, Goodwin Associates, 12 Rabbit Row, London W8 4DX. Address: 6-J Oxford and Cambridge Mansions, Old Marylebone Road, London NW1 5EC, England.

PUBLICATIONS

Plays

Want-Ad (produced Birmingham, 1977; revised version produced London, 1979).
Glasshouse (produced Edinburgh, 1977).
Tissue (produced Birmingham and London, 1978; Connecticut, 1985). Published in *Plays by Women 1*, edited by Michelene Wandor, London, Methuen, 1982.
Lucy (produced Bristol, 1979).
Hearing (produced Birmingham, 1979).
Flaws (produced Sheffield, 1980).
House Wives (produced Derby, 1981).
Salonika (produced London, 1982; New York, 1985). London, Methuen, 1983.
Falkland Sound/Voces de Malvinas (produced London, 1983).
Real Estate (produced London, 1984; Washington, D.C., 1985). London, Methuen, 1985.
Golden Girls (produced Stratford-on-Avon, 1984; London, 1985). London, Methuen, 1985.
Beauty and the Beast (produced Liverpool and London, 1985). London, Methuen, 1986.
Goat (produced Croydon, Surrey, 1986).

Radio Plays: *Saturday, Late September*, 1978; *Agnus Dei*, 1980; *Armistice*, 1983.

Television Play: *Peanuts* (*Crown Court* series), 1982.

* * *

Although Louise Page's work may lack the strident militancy expected of modern women writers, her contribution lies in her singling out the experiences of women as keystones to an examination of social conditioning. These women are unexceptional, lacking in unique personality traits. Their right to be the centre of the drama stems from the situations they are in, unremarkable situations in themselves, but personal crises to the characters through whom we see the contradictions between our socially conditioned expectations and our private experience of life. By isolating these ordinary women and their mundane crises, Page explores and exposes the social preconceptions by which people define and judge, analysing the ways in which these assumptions limit our lives, complicate our decisions, and contradict our experiences.

Page adopts different theatrical styles to highlight this tension between socially conditioned expectations and private experience. In plays as different in form as *Tissue*, *Salonika*, and *Real Estate*, the most frequent single word is "expect," and the action of the plays is played out against a background of expectations, making the audience aware of the contradictions and distortions these ingrained preconceptions place upon individual behaviour. *Tissue*, for example, is not so much a play about breast cancer as a play in which the crisis of breast cancer serves as a focus for the examination of assumptions about female sexuality and value.

A straight narrative about a woman fighting breast cancer would, by definition, imply themes of personal heroism. The structure of *Tissue* changes the emphasis from personality and the fact of cancer to the associated ideas that make facing breast cancer more difficult for both victim and associates. Scenes from Sally's life, unconnected by time or space, irrelevant in themselves, are magnetized by Sally's cancer; their juxtaposition highlights the complex socially conditioned assumptions which create the feminine mystique. Their sequence has the logic of memory, setting each other off through association of word, image, or emotional logic and building an analysis of the obsessive connections between breasts and sexuality, sex and love, and the evaluation of women by physical appearance we absorb from childhood. Sally herself is barely a character at all. She displays no individual personality traits; her thoughts and reactions are not so much personal as situational, the responses of a woman who has breast cancer.

Breasts define womanhood. They are assumed to be the measure of attractiveness, synonymous with sexuality and prerequisites for love, happy partnership, and future. The mystique created round the female body is shown through the play to prevent realistic and healthy attitudes towards oneself and others. Sally's mother, who treated Sally's growing breasts as objects of magical impurity, is afraid to touch her own to test for cancer. Sally's boss tells of his wife who "wrecked her life trying to keep her body whole. I did not ask her to be beautiful but to be there." Although we would consciously reject the evaluation of a woman solely on the size of her breasts, the progress of the play illuminates the way these assumptions infiltrate our lives and inform our behaviour.

Through stylistic choices, Page depersonalizes the characters in order to accentuate their situations and responses. All the men and women, except Sally, are meant to be played by the same actor and actress. Direct speeches to the audience and other theatrical devices like the content-related sequence of scenes and the quick-fire lists (the "possible causes" of cancer in Scene 28) serve to demystify by removing the personal elements and emphasizing the situational behaviour and its constriction through preconceptions. The construction of the play encourages audiences to go beyond their fear of cancer and recognize the social conditioning which exacerbates their fears but which, through unravelling and understanding, can be overcome. Cancer, terrifying as it is, becomes not the end of the road, but a pathway through distorted preconceptions of feminity and the examination of the taboos of both cancer and sexuality.

Sally's greatest fear when she finds she has cancer is not that she will die, but that she will cease to be attractive to men and thus be unable to love and be loved. Only at the end, when she has a new lover, and after she has confronted, with us, the moments of her life which make up the fearful, complex confusion between her appearance and her value as a woman does she take joy in the very fact of living.

Salonika, too, celebrates the indefatigable life force which defies physical limitation, while making us aware of our assumptions and their limiting effect on our lives. The play's dream-like quality not only stems from the World War I soldier's ghost rising from the sands; the situation itself flies in the face of expectation. The mother and daughter on holiday to visit the father's grave are 84 and 64 years old. The mother has a 74-year-old lover who has hitch-hiked to Greece to be with her. In a world where love is assumed to be the reserve of the young and beautiful, these very facts cause a sense of unreality and demand that we take note of our preconceptions.

Within the play, too, the characters are constantly evaluating the expectations they held in the light of experience:

Ben —(the ghost)—I didn't think you'd be a daughter.
Enid —Didn't you?
Ben —No. That's why I said to call a girl Enid. Because I thought you'd be a boy.
Leonard —You expect everything in you to shrivel. All the hate and the longing. The lust. You don't expect to have them any more. But there isn't much else so you have them all the more. I could kill now. If I had the strength.... That's not what you expect.

Life as we live it defies expectation. The young man on the beach suddenly dies, leaving the old to bury him.

This dichotomy between social preconceptions and personal experience is elaborated in a more realistic form in *Real Estate*. Here Gwen, a middle-aged woman, lives with Dick, her second husband, outside Didcot where she runs a small estate agency. Her daughter Jenny, a successful London buyer, returns for the first time since she ran away 20 years before. Jenny is pregnant and has come to claim the care and attention mothers are expected, automatically, to provide. Gwen, conventional as she appears, does not revert to type. Although she dreads losing contact with Jenny again, she resists her intrusion into her life.

We assume, without thinking, that the younger, modern woman would introduce a life-style free from preconceptions and conventions. But Jenny, the very image of the modern independent woman, demands conventional responses from others. The "modernness" she brings with her is calloused, self-centred, and totally material. She carelessly lets the dog out; she refuses to marry Eric, the child's father, while demanding his attention. When she insinuates herself into the business Gwen has founded on honesty, loyalty, and personal concern, Jenny's first act is to encourage a client to gazump.

Almost by definition, we expect a middle-aged, middle-class woman's life to be circumscribed by convention and socially approved roles, but, without proselytizing, Gwen and Dick have evolved a life-style that suits them both: "I can't ask you to stay for supper because I don't know if there's enough. Are you expecting to be asked to stay? Dick's province, not mine. He's the one who knows how long the mince has been in the freezer. How many sheets there are which haven't been turned edge to edge." Dick even embroiders tapestries! Indeed, the men in the play could not be more amenable. Eric, though divorced, appears sympathetic to his wife and is actively committed to the care of his daughter. Jenny considers this a liability; when her needs conflict with the child's, she demands priority although she refuses Eric her commitment. While Gwen has no desire to be a mother, again, nor a grandmother, Dick longs for a baby on whom to lavish loving care.

Gwen cannot share her life with Jenny. Their expectations and values are mutually exclusive. Without fuss, leaving to Dick the traditional role she once imagined for herself, Gwen takes the little acorn she planted at the play's start and plants it in the forest; like Jenny, it is well able to continue its growth on its own, though probably more willing. The placing of Gwen at the centre of the play challenges our assumptions. We are led to consider the limitations these preconceptions force upon individual lives and their lack of validity as bases for judgement and the evaluation of human behaviour. While retaining our sympathy, Gwen foils our expectations, setting them in relief so we might evaluate them.

Page structures her plays to call into question our assumptions about character, behaviour, and role and to stress that the roots of these automatic expectations and responses are in social conditioning rather than personality and psychology. Her choice of unexceptional women in unexceptional circumstances places emphasis on the way these preconceptions infiltrate the very fabric of our lives, laying bases for misunderstanding and regret and corrupting moments of crisis and decision.

—Elaine Turner

PARKER, (James) Stewart. British. Born in Belfast, Northern Ireland, 20 October 1941. Educated at Queen's University, Belfast, B.A. 1963, M.A. 1965. Married Kate Ireland in 1964. Instructor in English, Hamilton College, Clinton, New York, 1964–67, and Cornell University, Ithaca, New York, 1967–69. Recipient: *Evening Standard* award, 1977; Thames Television bursary, 1977; Christopher Ewart-Biggs Memorial Prize, 1979; Banff International Television Festival prize, 1985. Agent: Marc Berlin, London Management, 235 Regent Street, London W1A 2JT. Address: 29 Chelverton Road, London SW15 1RN, England.

PUBLICATIONS

Plays

The Iceberg (broadcast 1974). Published in *Honest Ulsterman* (Belfast), 1975.

Spokesong, music by Jimmy Kennedy (produced Dublin, 1975; London, 1976; Waterford, Connecticut, 1978; New York, 1979). New York and London, French, 1980.

The Actress and the Bishop (produced London, 1976).

Catchpenny Twist (televised 1977; produced Dublin, 1977; Hartford, Connecticut, 1978; London, 1980). Dublin, Gallery Press, 1980; New York, French, 1984.

Kingdom Come, music by Shaun Davey (produced London, 1978).

The Kamikaze Ground Staff Reunion Dinner (broadcast 1979). Published in *Best Radio Plays of 1980*, London, Eyre Methuen, 1981.
Tall Girls Have Everything (produced Louisville, 1980).
Nightshade (produced Dublin, 1980; London, 1984). Dublin, Co-op, 1980.
Pratt's Fall (produced Glasgow, 1983).
Northern Star (produced Belfast, 1984).
Heavenly Bodies (produced Birmingham, 1986).
Pentecost (produced Derry, 1987).

Radio Plays: *Speaking of Red Indians*, 1967; *Minnie and Maisie and Lily Freed*, 1970; *Requiem*, 1973; *The Iceberg*, 1974; *I'm a Dreamer, Montreal*, 1976; *The Kamikaze Ground Staff Reunion Dinner*, 1979; *The Traveller*, 1985.

Television Plays: *Catchpenny Twist*, 1977; *Iris in the Traffic, Ruby in the Rain*, 1981; *Joyce in June*, 1982; *Blue Money*, 1984; *Radio Pictures*, 1985; *Lost Belongings*, 1987.

Verse

The Casualty's Meditation. Belfast, Festival, 1967.
Maw. Belfast, Festival, 1968.

Other

Editor, *Over the Bridge*, by Sam Thompson. Dublin, Gill and Macmillan, 1970.

* * *

The most obvious characteristic of Stewart Parker's work is the self-delighting wit of his dialogue. With its alertness to the unconscious felicities and incongruities of everyday speech, and especially of cliché and dead metaphor, his dramatic style can be seen to embody resilience and energy in the midst of deadness and ordinariness. The wit of the characters' language offsets the nagging, though often only vaguely defined, sense of dissatisfaction they feel with their lives, and indeed suggests their ability to break through to a richer existence. Even form and stagecraft reinforce this suggestion, for Parker establishes and develops his themes less by soberly discursive means than by a constant play of symbol and metatheatrical reference operating within a fast-moving, eventful narrative.

The "troubles" are, not unnaturally for an Ulster playwright, ominously present either within or behind most of Parker's work. He sees himself as preoccupied "with the challenge of forging a unifying dramatic metaphor for the Northern Irish human condition." His interest is in psychological consequences rather than political causes—in his earlier work at least: the pressures of circumstances created by sectarian violence and a military presence are felt, in such pieces as *I'm a Dreamer, Montreal* and the "Caribbean-Irish Musical Comedy" *Kingdom Come* (which, like the radio play *The Iceberg*, allegorizes the situation), to stifle the energy of the individual.

Spokesong, Parker's best known piece, was intended as "a play about violence which would ambush the audience with pleasure." It is typical of his work in its treatment of the troubles and in its clever stagecraft. Frank's attempt to woo Daisy (in competition with his "implacably bitter" brother Julian) and to preserve the family bicycle shop in Belfast from the ravages of urban "development" and terrorist bombs is presented concurrently with his grandparents' courtship and his grandfather's service in World War I. The "bicycle-philosophy" of Frank's family is shown to represent physical energy, freedom, health, and beneficial social change amid the chaos and constriction of the "diseased," car-dominated city. Frank is driven almost to despair by the surrounding pressures, but Daisy steps in to save the shop and stand with him. Their united resolve promotes an affirmation not so much of the eccentric "bicycle-philosophy" as of human energy and independence as such.

By remaining in Belfast, Frank and Daisy acknowledge and confront the historical past. But the catchpenny songwriters of *Catchpenny Twist* find themselves with little choice in the same matter. When their exuberance gets them the sack from their teaching jobs, Ray and Martyn are forced to leave Belfast because of terrorist death threats. The threats pursue them, through growing emotional turmoil (caused largely by their singer, Monagh), first to Dublin and then to London. The "twist" comes when, having missed their chance of a break in a European song contest, they are blown up by a parcel bomb at a foreign airport. Their Republican "friend" considers their endeavour puerile because of its lack of connection with the serious business of their country's political past, yet the final effect of the play's wit and the energy of its songs is to question the moral adequacy of a seriousness that inhibits feeling and destroys life.

Nightshade, Parker's most difficult play, moves outside a specifically Ulster context. The themes are characteristic, nonetheless, and there is some virtuoso stagecraft. The central figure is the mortician Quinn, whose daughter comes to realize the connection between his profession and his hobby, magic: in embalming the dead so as to suggest, as if by magic, continuing life, he is "mummifying" the living too, "preserving" them from that confrontation with the reality of death which is necessary for the fullest experience of the reality of *life*.

A concentration on the individual in crisis is typical of Parker's work in the 1980's, but the perspective is now larger than before. His major project has consisted of "a trio of history plays, dealing roughly with the struggle between the individual will and the forces of the Age in which it operates"—of which two parts have so far been produced. In both cases the dramatic format is that of a man near or at the point of death reviewing his life and actions in a series of key flashbacks which counterpoint or parody various dramatic styles or scenes. In the second play, *Heavenly Bodies*, the Victorian Irish playwright Dion Boucicault is put on trial for his afterlife and found guilty of a self-serving opportunism which has led him to exploit his suffering fellow-countrymen for the sake of show-business and a glittering career. "You *are* the Age," Boucicault is authoritatively told within the play, yet the dramatic treatment does not endow the claim with any force, and Boucicault as presented here seems neither interesting enough in himself nor weighty enough as a representative figure to invite sustained scrutiny within the declared thematic frame of the "trio." The trial is conducted by Boucicault's opposite, the Irish singing clown Johnny Patterson, who was murdered by his audience.

Patterson's belief in the "commingling of the Orange and the Green" and his fatal effort to bring it about ally him to the figure of the great Protestant United Irishman Henry Joy McCracken in the much more satisfying first play of the "trio," *Northern Star*. After the "stillborn" attempt of the 1798 rising to bring about the birth of a united Irish nation, McCracken is on the run and being sheltered by his toughly commonsensical mistress Mary Bodle in a semi-ruined farm labourer's cottage outside Belfast. The time is "the continuous past," with "deliberate anachronisms and historical shifts." "McCracken's Night Thoughts" (the play's subtitle) are presented by him, in modern idiom, in a sequence of dramatic scenes that chart the course through seven ironic ages, each age a parody of the style of a famous Irish playwright, of his attempt to forge a united Ireland: Innocence (Sheridan), Idealism (Boucicault), Cleverness (Wilde), Dialectic (Shaw), Heroism (Synge), Compromise (O'Casey), Shame (Behan)—and a monologue after Beckett. The ambition is Joycean—nothing less than an attempt to transform an individual's history, through a virtuoso theatrical digest, into a nation's, and thus to suggest how an escape from the dungeon of history might be effected by way of moral rather than physical force. *Northern Star* is certainly Parker's most interesting, and perhaps his best play, though ultimately it fails to achieve that integration of theatrical perspective with large historical theme towards which its author seems to be reaching.

—Paul Lawley

PATRICK, John. American. Born John Patrick Goggan in Louisville, Kentucky, 17 May 1905. Educated at Holy Cross School, New Orleans; St. Edward's School, Austin, Texas; St. Mary's Seminary, LaPorte, Texas. Served in the American Field Service in India and Burma, 1942–44: Captain. Radio writer, NBC, San Francisco. 1933–36; free-lance writer, Hollywood, 1936–38. Recipient: Pulitzer Prize, 1954; New York Drama Critics Circle award, 1954; Tony award, 1954; Donaldson award, 1954; Foreign Correspondents award, 1957; Screen Writers Guild award, 1957. D.F.A.: Baldwin Wallace College, Berea, Ohio, 1972. Address: Fortuna Mill Estate, Box 2386, St. Thomas, Virgin Islands 00801, U.S.A.

PUBLICATIONS

Plays

Hell Freezes Over (produced New York, 1935).

The Willow and I (produced New York, 1942). New York, Dramatists Play Service, 1943.

The Hasty Heart (produced New York and London, 1945). New York, Random House, 1945.

The Story of Mary Surratt (produced New York, 1947). New York, Dramatists Play Service, 1947.

The Curious Savage (produced New York, 1950; Derby, 1966). New York, Dramatists Play Service, 1951.

Lo and Behold! (produced New York, 1951). New York, French, 1952.

The Teahouse of the August Moon, adaptation of a novel by Vern Sneider (produced New York, 1953; London, 1954). New York, Putnam, 1954; London, Heinemann, 1955; revised version as *Lovely Ladies, Kind Gentlemen*, music and lyrics by Stan Freeman and Franklin Underwood (produced New York, 1970), New York, French, 1970.

Good as Gold, adaptation of a novel by Alfred Toombs (produced New York, 1957).

Juniper and the Pagans, with James Norman (produced Boston, 1959).

Everybody Loves Opal (produced New York, 1961; London, 1964). New York, Dramatists Play Service, 1962.

It's Been Wonderful (produced Albuquerque, 1966). New York, Dramatists Play Service, 1976.

Everybody's Girl (produced Miami, 1967). New York, Dramatists Play Service, 1968.

Scandal Point (produced Albuquerque, 1967). New York, Dramatists Play Service, 1969.

Love Is a Time of Day (produced New York, 1969). New York, Dramatists Play Service, 1970.

A Barrel Full of Pennies (produced Paramus, New Jersey, 1970). New York, Dramatists Play Service, 1971.

Opal Is a Diamond (produced Flat Rock, North Carolina, 1971). New York, Dramatists Play Service, 1972.

Macbeth Did It (produced Flat Rock, North Carolina, 1972). New York, Dramatists Play Service, 1972.

The Dancing Mice (produced Berea, Ohio, 1972). New York, Dramatists Play Service, 1972.

The Savage Dilemma (produced Long Beach, California, 1972). New York, Dramatists Play Service, 1972.

Anybody Out There? New York, Dramatists Play Service, 1972.

Roman Conquest (produced Berea, Ohio, 1973; Altrincham, Cheshire, 1980). New York, French, 1973.

The Enigma (produced Berea, Ohio, 1973). New York, Dramatists Play Service, 1974.

Opal's Baby: A New Sequel (produced Flat Rock, North Carolina, 1973). New York, Dramatists Play Service, 1974.

Sex on the Sixth Floor: Three One Act Plays (includes *Tenacity, Ambiguity, Frustration*). New York, French, 1974.

Love Nest for Three. New York, French, 1974.

A Bad Year for Tomatoes (produced North Royalston, Ohio, 1974). New York, Dramatists Play Service, 1975.

Opal's Husband (produced Flat Rock, North Carolina, 1975). New York, Dramatists Play Service, 1975.

Noah's Animals: A Musical Allegory (produced Berea, Ohio, 1975). New York, French, 1976.

Divorce, Anyone? (produced North Royalston, Ohio, 1975). New York, Dramatists Play Service, 1976.

Suicide, Anyone? (produced St. Thomas, Virgin Islands, 1976). New York, Dramatists Play Service, 1976.

People! Three One Act Plays: Boredom, Christmas Spirit, Aptitude (produced North Royalston, Ohio, 1976). New York, French, 1980.

That's Not My Father! Three One Act Plays: Raconteur, Fettucine, Masquerade (produced St. Thomas, Virgin Islands, 1979). New York, French, 1980.

That's Not My Mother: Three One Act Plays: Seniority, Redemption, Optimism (produced St. Thomas, Virgin Islands, 1979). New York, French, 1980.

Opal's Million Dollar Duck (produced St. Thomas, Virgin Islands, 1979). New York, Dramatists Play Service, 1980.

The Girls of the Garden Club (produced Berea, Ohio, 1979). New York, Dramatists Play Service, 1980.

The Magenta Moth. New York, Dramatists Play Service, 1983.

It's a Dog's Life (includes *The Gift*, *Co-Incidence*, *The Divorce*). New York, French, 1984.

Danny and the Deep Blue Sea (produced Louisville, 1984).

Screenplays: *Educating Father*, with Katharine Kavanaugh and Edward T. Lowe, 1936; *36 Hours to Live*, with Lou Breslow, 1936; *15 Maiden Lane*, with others, 1936; *High Tension*, with others, 1936; *Midnight Taxi*, with Lou Breslow, 1937; *Dangerously Yours*, with Lou Breslow, 1937; *The Holy Terror*, with Lou Breslow, 1937; *Sing and Be Happy*, with Lou Breslow and Ben Markson, 1937; *Look Out, Mr. Moto*, with others, 1937; *Time Out for Romance*, with others, 1937; *Born Reckless*, with others, 1937; *One Mile from Heaven*, with others, 1937; *Big Town Girl*, with others, 1937; *Battle of Broadway*, with Lou Breslow and Norman Houston, 1938; *Five of a Kind*, with Lou Breslow, 1938; *Up the River*, with Lou Breslow and Maurine Watkins, 1938; *International Settlement*, with others, 1938; *Mr. Moto Takes a Chance*, with others, 1938; *Enchantment*,

1948; *The President's Lady*, 1953; *Three Coins in the Fountain*, 1954; *Love Is a Many-Splendored Thing*, 1955; *High Society*, 1956; *The Teahouse of the August Moon*, 1956; *Les Girls*, with Vera Caspary, 1957; *Some Came Running*, with Arthur Sheekman, 1958; *The World of Susie Wong*, 1960; *The Main Attraction*, 1962; *Gigot*, with Jackie Gleason, 1962; *The Shoes of the Fisherman*, with James Kennaway, 1968.

Radio Plays: *Cecil and Sally* series (1100 scripts), 1929–33.

Television Play: *The Small Miracle*, with Arthur Dales, from the novel by Paul Gallico, 1972.

*

Manuscript Collection: Boston University.

* * *

John Patrick began his career as an NBC script writer who became noted for radio dramatizations of novels. He first reached Broadway in 1935 with *Hell Freezes Over*, an unsuccessful and short-lived melodrama concerning polar explorers whose dirigible crash-lands in Antarctica. Patrick continued writing, primarily Hollywood film scripts. His next play, also unsuccessful, was *The Willow and I*, a forced but sensitively written psychological drama about two sisters competing for the love of the same man and destroying each other in the struggle.

During World War II Patrick served as an ambulance driver with the British Army in North Africa, Syria, India, and Burma. His experience furnished the background for *The Hasty Heart*. Set in a military hospital behind the Assam-Burma front, the action centers on a dour Scottish sergeant sent to the convalescent ward unaware that a fatal illness condemns him to early death. His wardmates, knowing the prognosis, extend their friendship. But the Scot's suspicious nature and uncompromising independence nearly wrecks their good intentions. He gradually warms to his companions until he discovers his fatal condition and concludes that their proffered fellowship is merely pity. Ultimately he comes to accept his wardmates' goodwill, poignantly demonstrating Patrick's premise: "the importance of man's acknowledgement of his interdependency." Although some critics doubted that the stubbornly misanthropic protagonist could be capable of change, the majority found the play's effect credible and warming. It enjoyed a substantial run before being made into a motion picture, and evinced its author's growth as a dramatist in dealing more incisively with plot structure, characterization, and the effect of inner states of mind on conduct and character.

Patrick's next three plays failed to win popular approval. Based on historical events, *The Story of Mary Surratt* depicts the trial and conviction of the Washington landlady sentenced to the gallows by a vindictive military tribunal for complicity in the assassination of Abraham Lincoln. Patrick's view was that Mrs. Surratt, whose misguided son had become involved in Booth's plot, was an innocent victim of 1865 postwar hysteria. Although the drama was a compassionate protest against injustice and the vengeful concept of war guilt, playgoers did not want to be reminded of a probable miscarriage of justice in their own history at a time when war crime trials were a present reality. Critical opinion was divided, and the production failed. The drama, despite some turgidity of dialogue and the minor portrait of its title character, still emerges as a substantial work which deserved a better fate.

Patrick turned to comedy in *The Curious Savage*. The story focuses on a charmingly eccentric wealthy widow, insistent on spending her millions on a foundation financing people's daydreams, whose mendacious stepchildren commit her to a sanatorium where she finds her fellow inmates more attractive than her own sane but greedy family; with the help of the former she outwits the latter. While admitting the play's affectionate humor, critics fairly faulted the author for treating his rational "villains" too stridently and his irrational characters too romantically. Although it had only a brief run on Broadway, *The Curious Savage* has been popular with regional theatres. A sequel, *The Savage Dilemma*, was published in 1972, but not presented in New York.

Other comedies followed. *Lo and Behold!* introduces a rich, solitude-loving writer who dies, having stipulated in his will that his house be kept vacant as a sanctuary for his spirit, and returns in ghostly form to find the premises occupied by three incompatible ghosts whom he untimately persuades to leave after all join forces to resolve a stormy courtship between a lingering housemaid and the estate's executor.

In 1953 Patrick achieved a Broadway triumph with *The Teahouse of the August Moon*, based on a novel by Vern Sneider. The play is a satire on the American Army of Occupation's attempts following World War II to bring democracy to the people of Okinawa. Amidst amusing clashes of mores and traditions, a young colonel with a past record of failure abandons standard Occupation procedure, builds the teahouse the villagers have longed for rather than a school-house, and a distillery producing a local brandy which brings them prosperity. His obtuse commanding officer visits the village and hotly orders an end to such unorthodox practices but is overridden by a Congressional declaration that the colonel's methods are the most progressive in Okinawa. Critic John Mason Brown accurately commented that "no plea for tolerance between peoples, no editorial against superimposing American customs on native tradition has ever been less didactic or more persuasive." The comedy captivated audiences and critics alike to become one of America's most successful plays, winning both the Pulitzer Prize and a New York Critics Circle award. Patrick rewrote it as a screenplay and later as a short-lived musical called *Lovely Ladies, Kind Gentlemen*.

Other comedies by Patrick include *Good as Gold* and *Everybody Loves Opal*. The former, a dramatization of a novel by Alfred Toombs, concentrates on a botanist who discovers a formula for changing gold into soil that will grow enormous vegetables but who cannot persuade Congress to give him the contents of Fort Knox. This farcical satire on politics constructed on one joke failed to find support. The title character of *Everybody Loves Opal* is a kindly recluse, living in a dilapidated mansion, who reforms three intruding petty crooks with her faith in the goodness of man. The comedy's fun was intermittent and its run short. Patrick has written several sequels.

Several other Patrick plays, mostly comedies, have been published, but not produced on Broadway. Patrick is a prolific writer of radio, film, and play scripts, but his reputation as a major craftsman in the American theatre rests chiefly on *The Teahouse of the August Moon*, one of the most successful American comedies.

—Christian H. Moe

PATRICK, Robert (Robert Patrick O'Connor). American. Born in Kilgore, Texas, 27 September 1937. Educated at Eastern New Mexico University, Portales, three years.

Host, La Mama, 1965, secretary to Ruth Yorck, 1965, and doorman, Caffe Cino, 1966–68, all New York; features editor and contributor, *Astrology Magazine*, New York, 1971–72; columnist, *Other Stages*, New York, 1979–81. Artist-in-residence, Jean Cocteau Repertory Theater, New York, 1984. Recipient: *Show Business* award, 1969; Rockefeller grant, 1973; Creative Artists Public Service grant, 1976; International Thespians Society award, 1980; Janus award, 1983. Address: c/o La Mama, 74-A East 4th Street, New York, New York 10003, U.S.A.

PUBLICATIONS

Plays

The Haunted Host (produced New York, 1964; London, 1975). Included in *Robert Patrick's Cheep Theatricks!*, 1972; in *Homosexual Acts*, London, Inter-Action, 1976.
Mirage (produced New York, 1965). Included in *One Man, One Woman*, 1978.
Sketches (produced New York, 1966).
The Sleeping Bag (produced New York, 1966).
Halloween Hermit (produced New York, 1966).
Indecent Exposure (produced New York, 1966).
Cheesecake (produced New York, 1966). Included in *One Man, One Woman*, 1978.
Lights, Camera, Action (includes *Lights, Camera Obscura, Action*) (produced New York, 1966; in *My Dear It Doesn't Mean a Thing*, produced London, 1976). Included in *Robert Patrick's Cheep Theatricks!*, 1972.
Warhol Machine (produced New York, 1967).
Still-Love (produced New York, 1968). Included in *Robert Patrick's Cheep Theatricks!*, 1972.
Cornered (produced New York, 1968). Included in *Robert Patrick's Cheep Theatricks!*, 1972.
Un Bel Di (produced New York, 1968). Published in *Performance* (New York), 1972.
Help, I Am (produced New York, 1968). Included in *Robert Patrick's Cheep Theatricks!*, 1972.
See Other Side (produced New York, 1968). Published in *Yale/Theatre* (New Haven, Connecticut), 1969.
Absolute Power over Movie Stars (produced New York, 1968).
Preggin and Liss (produced New York, 1968). Included in *Robert Patrick's Cheep Theatricks!*, 1972.
The Overseers (produced New York, 1968).
Angels in Agony (produced New York, 1968).
Salvation Army (produced New York, 1968).
Joyce Dynel: An American Zarzuela (as *Dynel*, produced New York, 1968; revised version, as *Joyce Dynel*, produced New York, 1969). Included in *Robert Patrick's Cheep Theatricks!*, 1972.
Fog (produced New York, 1969). Published in *G.P.U. News* (Milwaukee), 1980.
The Young Aquarius (produced New York, 1969).
I Came to New York to Write (produced New York, 1969; Edinburgh, 1975). Included in *Robert Patrick's Cheep Theatricks!*, 1972.
Oooooooops! (produced New York, 1969).
Lily of the Valley of the Dolls (produced New York, 1969; Edinburgh, 1972).
One Person: A Monologue (produced New York, 1969; London, 1975). Included in *Robert Patrick's Cheep Theatricks!*, 1972.
Silver Skies (produced New York, 1969).
Tarquin Truthbeauty (produced New York, 1969).
Presenting Arnold Bliss (produced New York, 1969; in *The Arnold Bliss Show*, produced Edinburgh, 1972).
The Actor and the Invader (in *Kinetic Karma*, produced New York, 1969; in *The Arnold Bliss Show*, Edinburgh, 1972).
Hymen and Carbuncle (produced New York, 1970). Included in *Mercy Drop and Other Plays*, 1979.
A Bad Place to Get Your Head (produced New York, 1970).
Bead-Tangle (includes *La Répétition*) (produced New York, 1970).
Sketches and Songs (produced New York, 1970).
I Am Trying to Tell You Something (produced New York, 1970).
Angel, Honey, Baby, Darling, Dear (produced New York, 1970).
The Golden Animal (produced New York, 1970).
Picture Wire (produced New York, 1970).
The Richest Girl in the World Finds Happiness (produced New York, 1970). Included in *Robert Patrick's Cheep Theatricks!*, 1972.
A Christmas Carol (produced New York, 1971).
Shelter (produced New York, 1971).
The Golden Circle (produced New York, 1972). New York, French, 1977(?).
Ludwig and Wagner (produced New York, 1972). Included in *Mercy Drop and Other Plays*, 1979.
Youth Rebellion (produced New York, 1972).
Songs (produced New York, 1972).
Robert Patrick's Cheep Theatricks!, edited by Michael Feingold. New York, Winter House, 1972.
The Arnold Bliss Show (includes *Presenting Arnold Bliss, The Actor and the Invader, La Répétition, Arnold's Big Break*) (produced Edinburgh, 1972). Included in *Robert Patrick's Cheep Theatricks!*, 1972.
Play-by-Play (also director: produced New York, 1972; revised version produced Chicago and London, 1975). New York, French, 1975.
Something Else (produced New York, 1973; in *My Dear It Doesn't Mean a Thing*, produced London, 1976). Included in *One Man, One Woman*, 1978.
Cleaning House (produced New York, 1973). Included in *One Man, One Woman*, 1978.
The Track of the Narwhal (produced Boston, 1973).
Judas (produced New York, 1973). Published in *West Coast Plays 5* (Berkeley, California), Fall 1979.
Mercy Drop; or, Marvin Loves Johnny (produced New York, 1973). Included in *Mercy Drop and Other Plays*, 1980.
The Twisted Root (produced New York, 1973).
Simultaneous Transmissions (produced New York, 1973). Published in *The Scene/2 (Plays from Off-Off-Broadway)*, edited by Stanley Nelson, New York, The Smith/New Egypt, 1974.
Hippy as a Lark (produced New York, 1973).
Imp-Prisonment (produced New York, 1973).
Kennedy's Children (produced New York, 1973; London, 1974). London, French, 1975; New York, Random House, 1976.
Love Lace (produced New York, 1974). Included in *One Man, One Woman*, 1978.
How I Came to Be Here Tonight (produced Los Angeles, 1974).
Orpheus and Amerika, music by Rob Felstein (produced Los Angeles, 1974; New York, 1980).
Fred and Harold, and One Person (produced London, 1975). Published in *Homosexual Acts*, London, Inter-Action, 1976.
My Dear It Doesn't Mean a Thing (includes *Lights, Camera Obscura, Action, Something Else*) (produced London, 1976).

Report to the Mayor (produced New York, 1977).
Dr. Paroo (produced New York, 1981). Published in *Dramatics* (Cincinnati), 1977.
My Cup Ranneth Over (produced New York and London, 1978). New York, Dramatists Play Service, 1979.
Mutual Benefit Life (produced New York, 1978). New York, Dramatists Play Service, 1979.
T-Shirts (produced Minneapolis, 1978; New York, 1980). Published in *Gay Plays*, edited by William M. Hoffman, New York, Avon, 1979.
One Man, One Woman (produced New York, 1979). New York, French, 1978.
Bank Street Breakfast (produced New York, 1979). Included in *One Man, One Woman*, 1978.
Communication Gap (produced Greensboro, North Carolina, 1979; as *All in Your Mind*, produced New York, 1981).
The Family Bar (produced Hollywood, 1979). Included in *Mercy Drop and Other Plays*, 1979.
Mercy Drop and Other Plays (includes *The Family Bar* and *The Loves of the Artists: Ludwig and Wagner*, *Diaghilev and Nijinsky*, and *Hymen and Carbuncle*). New York, Calamus, 1979.
Diaghilev and Nijinsky (produced San Francisco, 1981). Included in *Mercy Drop and Other Plays*, 1979.
Sane Scientist (produced New York, 1981).
Michelangelo's Models (produced New York, 1981). New York, Calamus Press, 1983.
24 Inches, music by David Tice, lyrics by Patrick (produced New York, 1982).
The Spinning Tree (produced Ada, Ohio, 1982; New York, 1983).
They Really Love Roba (produced New York, 1982).
Sit-Com (produced Minneapolis, 1982). Published in *Blueboy* (New York), June 1982.
Willpower, published in *Curtain* (Cincinnati) May 1982.
Blue Is for Boys (produced New York, 1983).
Nice Girl (produced New York, 1983).
Beaux-Arts Ball (produced New York, 1983).
The Comeback (produced New York, 1983).
The Holy Hooker (produced Madison, Wisconsin, 1983).
50's 60's 70's 80's (produced New York, 1984).
Big Sweet, music by LeRoy Dysart (produced Richmond, Virginia, 1984).
That Lovable Laughable Auntie Matter in "Disgustin' Space Lizards" (produced New York, 1985).
Bread Alone (produced New York, 1985).
No Trojan Women, music by Catherine Stornetta (produced Wallingford, Connecticut, 1985).
Left Out (produced Arroyo Grande, California, 1985). Published in *Dramatics* (Cincinnati), 1985.
The Hostages (produced New York, 1985).
The Trial of Socrates (produced New York, 1986).
Bill Batchelor Road (produced Minneapolis, 1986).
On Stage (produced Ralston, Nebraska, 1986).
Why Are They Like That? (produced Spokane, Washington, 1986).
Desert Waste (produced New York, 1986).
La Balance (produced New York, 1987).
The Last Stroke (produced Edinburgh, 1987).

Screenplays: *The Haunted Host*, 1969; *The Credit Game*, 1972.

*

Manuscript Collection: Lincoln Center Library of the Performing Arts, New York.

Theatrical Activities:
Director: **Plays**—*Wonderful, Wonderful*, by Douglas Kahn, and excerpt from *The Approach* by Jean Reavey, La Mama, New York, 1965; artistic director of *Bb Aa Nn Gg!!!*, New York, 1965; created Comic Book Shows at the Caffe Cino, New York, 1966; assistant director to Tom O'Horgan and Jerome Savary, Brandeis University, Waltham, Massachusetts, 1968; originated *Dracula*, Edinburgh, 1968; reopened *Bowery Follies*, New York, 1972; *Silver Queen* by Paul Foster, New York, 1973; directed many of his own plays.

Actor: **Plays**—at Caffe Cino, La Mama, and Old Reliable in his own plays and plays by Powell Shepherd, Soren Agenoux, John Hartnett, Stuart Koch, H.M. Koutoukas, and William M. Hoffman.

Robert Patrick comments:

(1973) My plays are dances with words. The words are music for the actors to dance to. They also serve many other purposes, but primarily they give the actors images and rhythms to create visual expressions of the play's essential relationships. The ideal production of one of my plays would be completely understandable even without sound, like a silent movie. Most of my plays are written to be done with a minimum of scenery, although I have done some fairly lavish productions of them. My plays fall into three general classes: 1) simple histories, like *I Came to New York to Write*; 2) surrealistic metaphors, like *The Arnold Bliss Show, Lights, Camera, Action*, and *Joyce Dynel*; and 3) romances, like *Fog, Female Flower* (unproduced), and both *The Golden Animal* and *The Golden Circle*. Basically, I believe the importance of a play to be this: a play is an experience the audience has together; it is stylized to aid in perception and understanding; and, above all, it is done by live players, and it is traced in its minutest particulars, so that it can serve as a warning (if it is a tragedy or comedy) or as a good example. Nothing must be left out or it becomes merely ritual. The time of the ritual is over. The essential experience must replace it.

* * *

Robert Patrick's conception of theatrical form and purpose was molded at the Caffe Cino. He had been working there at odd jobs in the early 1960's and, influenced by Joe Cino's creative energy along with playwrights like Lanford Wilson, Paul Foster, David Starkweather, and the entire Cino gang, he wrote his first play, *The Haunted Host*. In fact, he got his name with that production in a typical Cino haphazard manner. Marshall Mason (later artistic director of Circle Repertory Company and chief interpreter of Lanford Wilson's dramas) was rushing out to get *The Haunted Host* programs printed. Patrick, who was acting in his own show, asked that Mason break up his name and list Robert Patrick and Bob O'Connor, one for playwright and the other for actor, because he didn't want people concentrating on the fact that the playwright and actor were the same person. When Mr. Mason came back with the program, Robert Patrick O'Connor was known as Robert Patrick, playwright.

The Cino was a place in which theatrical rules did not exist. Experimentation with form and content was common, and wits-only, wing-it living was the norm. Although when the Cino closed it was shrouded in tragedy, for most of its years the key word there was fun. Entertainment was the only guideline anyone followed, and this free-wheeling, fun-obsessed life-style turned a naive young Texan named Bob O'Connor into the most prolific playwright of his generation. As he says of the off-off-Broadway movement which began, in part, at the Cino, "For the first time a theatre movement began, of any scope or duration, in which theatre was considered the equal of the other arts in creativity and responsibility; never before had theatre existed free of academic, commercial, critical, religious, military, and political restraints. For the first time, a playwright wrote from himself, not attempting to tease money, reputation, or licences from an outside authority."

To analyze the numerous plays Patrick has written and produced since 1964 on a script by script basis would be to miss the profound contribution of the overall body of his work. His genius stems not from some artfully crafted style or from deep, intellectual questioning, but rather from an uncanny ability to record and reflect the world around him. *Kennedy's Children*, his best known play, captures the mood of an entire era, and serves as a mirror of morals for a lost decade.

In *Kennedy's Children* the characters, all of whom we now recognize as 1960's stereotypes, sit separately in a bar. We're presented with their interior monologues. The alienation, the loneliness, and the confusion that were so apparent in America's youth throughout the tumultuous years of Vietnam are so accurately portrayed in *Kennedy's Children* that it is difficult to imagine a more perfect example of the crumbling American dream post-Vietnam.

To read Patrick for clues to a specific style is to get trapped. For most of his career, his style has been unique only in its absence, a fact which often drives his critics to despair. It could only be described, perhaps, as Cinoese, or off-off-Broadway eclectic. As he continues to write, he appears to be coalescing his vast mental resources into a genuine effort to produce works which deal with an unchanging human condition. The classical themes of love, greed, pride, and tormented self-doubt abound in all his plays, but never as obviously mirrored as in his most current works. In fact, he now says he is striving to write "classical Greek drama." If his style is elusive, his subject certainly is not. Patrick is pure romantic and in play after play writes primarily about relationships and heterosexual marriage. In recent years he has become known as a gay playwright and, although he is currently using gay themes again, in fact most of his "gay" plays are early works which have been re-discovered in the current rage for gay theatre. Although *Michelangelo's Models* is about how a man and a boy do get together, theirs is a basically traditional relationship, and this play, too, is about how people do or do not form unions. It is this general appeal to the traditional which gives his plays not only an international popularity, but which also accounts for his enormous effect on high school audiences. Young people are drawn to him as to a pied piper and it is to them that he is most expressive about the great excitement the art of theater can generate. He travels extensively to high schools across the country encouraging students to write for and/or to become involved with theater.

Aside from stating the obvious, that his story is the subject of his play, like apples are the subjects of a Cézanne painting, and that his stories are about couples getting together or not getting together and about how society affects a relationship, there is no generalizing about a Patrick play. From the stark classic tragedy of *Judas* to the innovative oratorio of an age, *Kennedy's Children*, to the retrograde Renaissance fantasia of *Michelangelo's Models*, he has been a man in love with playwriting. He has improvised full-scale musicals in four days (*Joyce Dynel* and *A Christmas Carol*), provided occasional entertainments (*The Richest Girl in the World Finds Happiness, Play-by-Play, Halloween Hermit*), whipped out formal experiments (*Lights, Camera, Action; Love Lace; Something Else*), manufactured commercial successes (*My Cup Ranneth Over, Mutual Benefit Life*), helped the developing gay theatre (*Mercy Drop, T-Shirts, The Haunted Host*), and piled up eccentricities (*The Golden Animal, Lily of the Valley of the Dolls* and the unproduced *Female Flower*). His first collection, *Robert Patrick's Cheep Theatricks!*, was only an arbitrary gleaning of the 150 works he had accumulated by 1972; his second, *One Man, One Woman*, ranged from 1964 to 1979; his third, *Mercy Drop and Other Plays*, from 1965 through 1980. Many works are still unpublished and unproduced.

Patrick believes that words are music for the actors to dance to, and that rhythms have to help the actors build up emotions. He is very conscious of vocabulary and of how words give the actors images to act out, tell an audience story facts and plot facts or jokes or bits of poetry. In *Michelangelo's Models* Ignudo, the peasant boy who wants to marry Michelangelo, talks in Okie dialect. And Michelangelo's speech varies between the formal patterns of the other characters and the slang that unites him to Ignudo. Patrick's fascination with words sometimes gets him tangled in verbiage, but it creates a type of security blanket for this off-off-Broadway baby. Playwrights who regularly work off-off-Broadway never know if they're going to have sets, lights, music, or anything, so writing for a bare floor and some actors is a form of artistic self-preservation. Then, if you can get lights and background music to set the mood it's all the better. If Patrick is sometimes overly expository it can be traced directly to the Caffe Cino where the lights sometimes went out and action had to be described to an audience in the dark.

—Leah D. Frank

PHILLIPS, Caryl. British. Born in St. Kitts, West Indies, 13 March 1958; brought to England in 1958. Educated at schools in Leeds; Queen's College, Oxford, 1976–79, B.A. (honours) in English 1979. Founding chairman, 1978, and artistic director, 1979, *Observer* Festival of Theatre, Oxford; resident dramatist, The Factory, London, 1981. Member of the Board of Directors, Bush Theatre, London. Recipient: Arts Council bursary, 1983; British Council fellowship, 1984; Malcolm X Prize, for novel, 1985. Lives in London. Agent: Judy Daish Associates, 83 Eastbourne Mews, London W2 6LQ; or, Aitken and Stone Ltd., 29 Fernshaw Road, London SW10 0TG, England.

PUBLICATIONS

Plays

Strange Fruit (produced Sheffield, 1980; London, 1982). Ambergate, Derbyshire, Amber Lane Press, 1981.
Where There Is Darkness (produced London, 1982). Ambergate, Derbyshire, Amber Lane Press, 1982.
The Shelter (produced London, 1983). Oxford, Amber Lane Press, 1984; New York, Applause, 1986.
The Wasted Years (broadcast 1984). Published in *Best Radio Plays of 1984*, London, Methuen, 1985.
Playing Away (screenplay). London, Faber, 1987.

Screenplay: *Playing Away*, 1986.

Radio Plays: *The Wasted Years*, 1984; *Crossing the River*, 1986; *The Prince of Africa*, 1987.

Television Plays: *The Hope and the Glory*, 1984; *The Record*, 1984.

Novels

The Final Passage. London, Faber, 1985.
A State of Independence. London, Faber, and New York, Farrar Straus, 1986.

Other

The European Tribe (travel). London, Faber, 1987.

*

Caryl Phillips comments:
My dominant theme has been cultural and social dislocation, most commonly associated with a migratory experience.

* * *

Few British dramatists have been equally at home in fiction and in the theatre, but Caryl Phillips is a playwright well on his way to a reputation that overlaps a variety of categories. Most of his work has been concerned with the immigrant experience of blacks in Britain, but his perspective is both historical and international and he has applied his talent with success to drama for the stage, television, radio, and the cinema. In addition, he has made a mark in the demanding form of the novel. Journalism, too, has proved a fruitful form, provoking thoughtful essays on such significant predecessors as James Baldwin. Indeed, Baldwin is an unmistakable model and inspiration, and the clear, passionate view of the United States which was seen in Baldwin's early essays, when he was able to combine a knowledge of the American South with a European perspective, is reflected in Phillips's view of Britain, though Phillips goes further and applies Baldwin's measures to Europe as well. For Phillips, it is Europe that has made him a "black" writer. In the preface to his play in two parts, *The Shelter*, he says: "In Africa I was not black. In Africa I was a writer. In Europe I am black. In Europe I am a black writer. If the missionaries [for which read critics] wish to play the game along these lines then I do not wish to be an honorary white."

Although born in St. Kitts and very conscious of his Caribbean heritage, he is a child of Leeds where he was raised, and his accent is Yorkshire. His plays have persistently explored the conflicts of immigration, looking at the yearning for a homeland which has achieved mythological significance and at the reality of life in a society which views the immigrant as an outsider because of colour. While immigration has remained his major theme, he has maintained an ironic distance that sees slavery as the first immigration, very much an immigration imposed on the African by Europeans and North Americans.

His perspective is finally more mid-Atlantic than Caribbean, and the title of his first play, *Strange Fruit*, is drawn directly and knowingly from the Billie Holiday song about lynching. As in much of his later work, the subject is a West Indian family held together by a single parent but pulled between two hemispheres. Although Vivien has educated her sons in England, they feel drawn to the black culture of the Caribbean.

In his next and more ambitious play, *Where There Is Darkness*, the pull of the islands is felt by a West Indian man, Albert, who 25 years earlier fled his home for the promises of England, first making a girl pregnant so her father would pay their passage to the "motherland." Phillips sets the play on the eve of Albert's return to the Caribbean, during and after a farewell party for the white friends and colleagues he has gathered in his years as a social worker. In his London garden Albert confronts the guilt of his betrayals, including the sacrifice of his first wife to his ambition, and his inability to bring the son he loves into his vision of success.

While remembering that his own father had advised him that the only way out of the gutters and up to the mountains was through exile, and foreign wealth, the sacrifice he was prepared to make was the gift of his son to England. When he took his father-in-law's money for the passage it was to the admonition that "The child belongs to England." His disappointment when his son announces that he is leaving university to marry his pregnant black girlfriend proves the final blow in his struggle for self-justification. At the beginning of the play, Albert's confrontation with his accommodations to white society has driven him into the garden with a raging headache. At the end of the play he has stripped down to his trousers to plunge into an imaginary sea. His Faustian bargain has torn his spirit apart.

Everywhere in Phillips's work he is concerned with the price paid for admission into the white man's world, "the price of a ticket" in Baldwin's phrase. In his novel *The Final Passage*, as in his plays of immigration, it is confrontation with the bitter reality of England that is the revelation. But the final passage is not really a voyage made by choice. It is rather the completion of a journey that began with the "middle passage," the crossing of the Atlantic from Africa to the New World in English slave ships. For the black men and women of his dramas, every choice is the result of a desperate search for a homeland to replace the Africa which they lost generations past when their ancestors were ripped from their tribes. The final passage for the black people of the Commonwealth is the attempt to complete the voyage to English society.

In *The Shelter*, a play which takes on the potent image, taboo for so long, of black men with white women, Phillips first imagines a shipwreck which throws together a freed slave and a white widow on a desert island at the end of the 18th century. His use of the period language is too fussy wholly to express his ideas, and the ex-slave is so demonstrably superior to the English woman in thought and poetic speech that his slow transformation in his mind from ape to man is devalued, but it does nicely prepare the way for the second act, an examination of a sexual relationship between a black immigrant and a white woman in the London of the 1950's. At that key moment in the history of immigration, the man and woman can only meet in a pub by pretending to be strangers. When their relationship is revealed by a kiss they sacrifice their right to sit together, but a more fundamental decision is being made. The woman has chosen to bear the man's child despite his announcement that he wants to return "home," alone.

Radio is a medium which has allowed Phillips the means to explore his ideas with greater ambition, beginning with his prize-winning play *The Wasted Years*. In that piece he was able to recreate the pressures of school and family life on two brothers, products of the wave of immigration so ironically reflected by "news reports" describing the original arrival of the previous generation, "these dashing chaps in their colourful hats and big smiles." His starkly refined short radio play *Crossing the River* looked at the triangle of the slave heritage, from Africa to the United States and Britain, and his most powerful radio piece, *The Prince of Africa*, was the richly imagined story of the crossing of a slave ship. Although the destination of the ship was Boston, Massachusetts, it was a play which was firm in its condemnation of England as a nation of slavers and it gave little sympathy to the guilty captain who refused to take personal responsibility for his cargo.

With a finely disciplined command of language, and wide experience of a world well beyond the triangle of the slave heritage, Phillips promises to be a voice who will continue to broaden the understanding of his audiences, particularly when he is allowed to drop the burden of his label as a "black" writer.

—Ned Chaillet

PIELMEIER, John. American. Born in Altoona, Pennsylvania, 23 February 1949. Educated at Catholic University, Washington, D.C., 1966–70, B.A. (summa cum laude) in speech and drama 1970 (Phil Beta Kappa); Pennsylvania State University, University Park (Shubert Fellow), 1970–73, M.F.A. in playwriting 1978. Married Irene O'Brien in 1982. Actor, 1973–82: numerous roles in regional theatres, including Actors Theatre of Louisville, Guthrie Theatre, Minneapolis, Alaska Repertory Theatre, Anchorage, Center Stage, Baltimore, and Eugene O'Neill Playwrights Conference, Waterford, Connecticut. Recipient: National Endowment for the Arts grant, 1982; Christopher award, for television play, 1984; Humanitas award, for television play, 1984. D.H.L.: St. Edward's University, Austin, Texas, 1984. Agent: Jeannine Edmunds, Artists Agency, 230 West 55th Street, Suite 17-D, New York, New York 10019. Address: R.R. 1, Box 108, Horton Road, Cold Spring, New York 10516, U.S.A.

PUBLICATIONS

Plays

Agnes of God (produced Louisville, 1980; New York, 1982; London, 1983). New York, New American Library, 1985.
Jass (produced New York, 1980).
Chapter Twelve: The Frog (produced Louisville, 1981).
Courage (produced Louisville, 1983; New York, 1984).
Cheek to Cheek (produced Louisville, 1983).
A Gothic Tale (also director: produced Louisville, 1983). Included in *Haunted Lives*, 1984.
Haunted Lives (includes *A Witch's Brew*, *A Ghost Story*, *A Gothic Tale*) (produced Edinburgh, 1986). New York, Dramatists Play Service, 1984.
The Boys of Winter (produced New York, 1985).
Evening (produced Cincinnati, 1986).
In Mortality (produced Louisville, 1986).
Sleight of Hand (produced New York, 1987).

Screenplay: *Agnes of God*, 1985.

Television Play: *Choices of the Heart*, 1983.

*

Theatrical Activities:
Director: **Play**—*A Gothic Tale*, Louisville, 1983.
Actor: **Plays**—Jasmine in *Memphis Is Gone* by Dick Hobson, New York, 1975; Tommy in *Female Transport* by Steve Gooch, Lymon in *Ballad of the Sad Café* by Edward Albee, and Boy in *Welcome to Andromeda* by Ron Whyte, all Louisville, 1975; Junior in *Waterman* by Frank B. Ford, Billy in *The Collected Works of Billy the Kid* by Michael Ondaatje, Burnaby in *The Matchmaker* by Thornton Wilder, and Kid in *Cold* by Michael Casale, all Minneapolis, 1976; Dorcas in *Gazelle Boy* by Ronald Tavel, and Dennis in *Scooter Thomas Makes It to the Top of the World* by Peter Parnell, both Waterford, Connecticut, 1977; roles in *Holidays*, and Mark in *The Shadow Box* by Michael Cristofer, both Louisville, 1979; Mark Levine in *Today a Little Extra* by Michael Kassin, Louisville, 1980; role in *The Front Page* by Ben Hecht and Charles MacArthur, Baltimore, 1980; Lysander in *A Midsummer Night's Dream*, Anchorage, Alaska, 1981; and numerous other roles.

John Pielmeier comments:

I consider myself primarily a writer for actors, and then a theatrical storyteller. I am fascinated with music and the myths of history, though *Agnes of God* is an exception to the latter. Some of my best work (*Jass* and *The Boys of Winter*) illustrates this fascination clearly. I consider writing a collaborative effort with actors and audience, and a play is never finished until it is on its feet for several weeks or for several productions. J.M. Barrie and Thornton Wilder are the playwrights closest to my heart—so in the end I suppose I am something of a theatrical romantic.

* * *

The playwright and actor John Pielmeier is indebted to regional theatre, where much of his work has been developed and presented. National attention was achieved with *Agnes of God*, whose successful Broadway engagement was preceded by nine regional productions. The drama's concern with the conflict between the real and the imagined, the rational and the irrational, is one constantly catching Pielmeier's interest.

In the published play's introduction, Pielmeier confesses that *Agnes of God* sprang from his questioning concern as a lapsed Catholic with the possibility of saints and miracles today, augmented by an evocative headline about a nunnery infanticide. The drama's circumstances are that a stigmatic and emotionally disturbed young nun, who as a child was abused by a sadistic mother, gives birth in her convent to a child later found strangled in a wastepaper basket. The saintly nun Agnes (from Latin "lamb"), who hears divine voices, claims to remember nothing about the child's conception, birth, or death. A court psychiatrist, a lapsed Catholic woman harboring a grudge against nuns, is sent to discover whether Agnes is sufficiently sane to stand trial for manslaughter. Proceeding as a narrator and detective-like investigator, the anticlerical doctor becomes absorbed with Agnes, beginning to question her own pragmatic values in the face of the situation's supernatural overtones. The overt conflict arises between the doctor and the convent's Mother Superior, later revealed to be Agnes's aunt, who is protective of Agnes and believes in the possibility of a parthenogenetic miracle. At the investigation's climax, Sister Agnes re-enacts under hypnosis the child's conception, still leaving unanswered the question of devine or human fatherhood. Yet the psychiatrist's anguished self-questioning emerges as the central issue. Unavoidable is a comparison to Peter Shaffer's *Equus*, whose plot is similar and which is more successful in the depth of its protagonist physician and in the examination of the questions raised. Nonetheless, Pielmeier has written a theatrically powerful play whose well-orchestrated female characters and strong dramatic climaxes provide an exciting theatre experience. The question of faith and miracles initially posed, while understandably not answered, tends to become obscured by the psychological issues triggering the second act's revelations erupting after an exposition-laden first act. The play stimulates the emotions but leaves the intellect confused. Pielmeier also wrote the screen version of the play.

The enigmatic dichotomy of the natural and unnatural interconnects three three-character one-acts collectively titled *Haunted Lives*. In the least effective but still eerie *A Witch's Brew*, a brother engages his doubting sister and her boyfriend in a grisly childhood game (pretending objects passed around in darkness are human body parts) in a semi-dark farmhouse basement where he claims his mother murdered and buried his long-absent father. The brother has played the game in earnest. *A Ghost Story*, a more successfully developed piece, presents two hiking strangers seeking shelter from a wintry blizzard in an isolated Maine cabin where they are joined by a mysterious girl who participates in telling frightening stories, one involving the throat-cutting of hikers by an unknown murderer. One hiker, once his companions fall asleep, tells the audience of a recurring dream, realized at the play's conclusion, in which his dead sister appears and cuts the throat of a hiker whom she first seduces. In *A Gothic Tale*, the final and most chilling tale, a young woman obsessed with the need to be loved and her manservant imprison a young rake in an island mansion tower, warning him that he will die unless admitting love for the woman. At the end of six weeks, depicted in sex scenes, the gradually starved prisoner's aversion turns to terror and capitulation as he dies discovering the skeletons of men preceding him. The drama's cumulative effect of impending doom is strong. *Haunted Lives* is a well-crafted minor work again demonstrating Pielmeier's theatrical skill.

In addition to *Courage*, a monodrama about J.M. Barrie, and *Choices of the Heart*, a teleplay about a religious worker murdered in El Salvador, two other works show an extension of Pielmeier's range. The musical *Jass* (dialect for "jazz"), with story-and-mood songs by the playwright, tells an unfocused story of the demise of a New Orleans Storyville red-light district house facing legal closure in 1917. An anti-war drama short-lived on Broadway, *The Boys of Winter*, delineates seven Marines who are wiped out on a Vietnam hilltop in 1968, except for their lieutenant who on his return cold-bloodedly kills seven innocent Vietnamese civilians. The atrocity is rationalized in the men's monologues, offering the controversial premise that we all are guilty of My Lais. Despite flaws, the play's dialogue projects a salty reality, and its bloody incidents gather theatrical force.

Pielmeier is a dramatist of proven theatrical expertise; the nature of his development and the durability of his plays will be discovered by the future.

—Christian H. Moe

PIÑERO, Miguel (Antonio Gomez, Jr.). American. Born in Gurabo, Puerto Rico, 19 December 1946; brought to New York City, 1950. Educated at public schools in New York; at Otisville State Training School for Boys, New York, two years; Manhattan State Hospital, high school equivalency diploma. Married Juanita Lovette Rameize in 1977 (divorced 1979); one adopted son. Served sentence for burglary, Riker's Island Prison, New York, 1964, and second term for drug possession; served sentence for burglary, Ossining Correctional Facility (Sing Sing prison), Ossining, New York, 1971–73: joining theatre workshop while in prison; founder, Nuyorican Poets Theatre, New York, 1974. Recipient: Obie award, 1974; New York Drama Critics Circle award, 1974. Agent: Neal I. Gantcher, Cohn Glickstein Lurie Ostrin Lubell and Lubell, 1370 Avenue of the Americas, New York, New York 10019, U.S.A.

PUBLICATIONS

Plays

All Junkies (produced New York, 1973).
Short Eyes (produced New York, 1974; London, 1984). New York, Hill and Wang, 1975.
The Sun Always Shines for the Cool (produced New York, 1975). Included in *The Sun Always Shines for the Cool, A Midnight Moon at the Greasy Spoon, Eulogy for a Small-Time Thief*, 1984.
The Guntower (produced New York, 1976).
Eulogy for a Small-Time Thief (produced New York, 1977). Included in *The Sun Always Shines for the Cool, A Midnight Moon at the Greasy Spoon, Eulogy for a Small-Time Thief*, 1984.
Straight from the Ghetto, with Neil Harris (produced New York, 1977).
Paper Toilet (produced Los Angeles, 1979?).
Cold Beer (produced New York, 1979–80).
Nuyorican Nights at the Stanton Street Social Club (produced New York, 1980).
Playland Blues (produced New York, 1980).
A Midnight Moon at the Greasy Spoon (produced New York, 1981). Included in *The Sun Always Shines for the Cool, A Midnight Moon at the Greasy Spoon, Eulogy for a Small-Time Thief*, 1984.
The Sun Always Shines for the Cool, A Midnight Moon at the Greasy Spoon, Eulogy for a Small-Time Thief. Houston, Arte Público Press, 1984.
Outrageous: One-Act Plays. Houston, Arte Público Press, 1986.

Screenplay: *Short Eyes*, 1977.

Television Plays: scripts for *Baretta* series.

Verse

La Bodega Sold Dreams. Houston, Arte Público Press, 1979.

Other

Editor, with Miguel Algarin, *Nuyorican Poetry: An Anthology of Puerto Rican Words and Feelings*. New York, Morrow, 1975.

*

Theatrical Activities:
Actor: **Play**—God in *Steambath* by Bruce Jay Friedman, Philadelphia, 1975. **Films**—*Short Eyes*, 1977; *The Jericho Mile*, 1979; *Fort Apache the Bronx*, 1981.

Television—*Baretta* and *Kojak* series; *Miami Vice* series, 1984.

*   *   *

When Miguel Piñero won a New York Drama Critics Circle award for his play *Short Eyes*, he emerged as the leading Puerto Rican American dramatist. The play, richly imbued with the detail and insight gained from his own prison experiences, is the most ruthlessly authentic and exciting drama with a prison setting so far produced by the American theater. Harrowing, brutal, yet suffused with a transforming, unsettling sensuality, it succeeds in imparting a special kind of understated, deliberately minimal poetic beauty and compassion to the rather terrifying events it dramatizes.

The play, set in the House of Detention, concerns what Piñero calls the "underclass," people who are socially deprived or outside the law, and this group with its own code of justice—for Piñero also to be read "just us"—becomes of course an inverse mirror of that other society without. The highly individualized characters, primarily Puerto Rican and black, with two white prisoners and white prison officers, come together during the play in the "Dayroom" where their unique personalities, social roles, and ethnic backgrounds are forged into the play's community. Each of the characters, Paco, Ice, "El Raheem," "Longshoe," Mr. Nett, and the others, creates believability and plays a role in the personal and social processes the play depicts, but three of them are crucial: the catalyst Clark Davis, the "short eyes" or child molester of the title, who is murdered; Juan, the listener, "Poet," and choral commentator; and Julio, nicknamed "Cupcakes," everyone's idealized youth, whose initiation into silent complicity with the others in the murder costs him his innocence and ironically completes the community. As he leaves the prison, Juan pronounces judgment: "Oye, espera, no corra, just one thing brother, your fear of this place stole your spirit.... And this ain't no pawnshop."

Despite its explosive subject matter, Piñero has constructed his play with carefully calculated and controlling structural clarity. It consists of two perfectly balanced acts, each building toward a climax in physical violence, and a concluding "Epilogue." Each act also includes a dramatic monologue concerned with sexuality and fantasy that makes incandescent the play's emotional tensions. The correspondence between "underclass," prison, and society in general assures the play's potentially poetic dimension, but the process of poetic transformation of the play's realistic details is skillfully assisted in other ways as well. The terms that make up the play's special language—"short eyes," "homey," "bandido," "run it," and many more—become constant conversational metaphors; the "Dayroom" is a common ground for coming together and revelation; and the monologues declare the power of the transcending imagination. Clark Davis's brilliant monologue in particular, in which he recounts to Juan, for the first time to anyone, his dream-like encounters with little girls, has that special ambiguity of "facts" upon which poetry in part depends. The subtle border between intent and action, the imagined and real, is emphasized when the inmates discover that he was not in fact guilty of the offense that led to his arrest and death.

Piñero's other plays retain the authenticity and some of the visceral excitement of *Short Eyes*, but they lack its sharp focus and the structural unity and pressure provided in part by its prison setting with its shock-of-recognition framework for less familiar revelations. In these plays the dramatic situation is reversed. The characters are "out" and seek a kind of stabilizing home, "A bar in a large city" "where the time is NOW" in *The Sun Always Shines for the Cool*, Gerry's and Joe's "small luncheonette in the Times Square area" in *A Midnight Moon at the Greasy Spoon*, a small apartment in North Philadelphia in *Eulogy for a Small-Time Thief*. But the literal dead-end of the journeys is always the same: death. *The Sun Always Shines* is the best and most vivid of these continuing chronicles of the "underclass." Here the "hustlers and players" climax in the deadly triangle composed of Viejo, who commits suicide, his innocent daughter, and her lover Cat Eyes in a world where "Every player is a poet." In all three plays the vivid talk is in the foreground, the characters and action somewhat submerged beneath the verbal surface. The unproduced and unpublished *The Cinderella Ballroom* has particular promise, although its compassionate close-up of homeless teenagers in the New York City area known to habitués as "42 and 8" would have seemed more dramatically informative several years ago when it was written. But Piñero remains an important figure, a writer whose identity and materials are uniquely one.

—Gaynor F. Bradish

PINNER, David. British. Born in Peterborough, Northamptonshire, 6 October 1940. Educated at Deacon's Grammar School, Peterborough; Royal Academy of Dramatic Art, London, 2 years. Married the actress Catherine Henry Griller in 1965; one daughter and one son. Has acted with repertory companies in Sheffield, Coventry, Windsor, and Farnham, and in London. Playwright-in-residence, Peterborough Repertory Theatre, 1974. Recipient: 4 Arts Council bursaries. Agent: Elspeth Cochrane Agency, 11–13 Orlando Road, London SW4 0LE. Address: 18 Leconfield Avenue, London S.W. 13, England.

PUBLICATIONS

Plays

Dickon (produced Hornchurch, Essex, 1966). Published in *New English Dramatists 10*, London, Penguin, 1967.
Fanghorn (produced Edinburgh and London, 1967). London, Penguin, 1966.
The Drums of Snow (televised 1968). Published in *New English Dramatists 13*, London, Penguin, 1968; revised version (produced Stanford, California, 1970; Oxford, 1974), in *Plays of the Year 42*, London, Elek, 1972.
Marriages (also director: produced London, 1969).
Lightning at the Funeral (produced Stanford, California, 1971).
The Potsdam Quartet (produced Guildford, Surrey, 1973; revised version produced London, 1980; New York, 1982). Leominster, Herefordshire, Terra Nova, 1980; New York, French, 1982.
Cartoon (produced London, 1973).
An Evening with the GLC (produced London, 1974).
Hereward the Wake (produced Peterborough, 1974).
Shakebag (produced London, 1976). Published in *Green River Review* (University Center, Michigan), 1976.
Lucifer's Fair (produced London, 1976).
Screwball (produced Plymouth, 1982).
Revelations (produced Grinnell, Iowa, 1986).

Radio Plays: *Lightfall*, 1967; *Cardinal Richelieu*, 1976; *The Ex-Patriot*, 1977; *Keir Hardie*, 1978; *The Square of the Hypotenuse*, 1978; *Talleyrand*, 1978; *Drink to Me Only*, 1978; *The Last Englishman*, 1979; *Fings Ain't What They Used to Be*, 1979.

Television Plays: *The Drums of Snow*, 1968; *Strange Past*, 1974; *Juliet and Romeo* (Germany), 1976; *Leonora*, 1981; *The Sea Horse*, 1982.

Novels

Ritual. London, Hutchinson, 1967.
With My Body. London, Weidenfeld and Nicolson, 1968.
There'll Always Be an England. London, Blond and Briggs, 1985.

*

Manuscript Collection: Grinnell College, Iowa.

Theatrical Activities:
Director: **Plays**—*Marriages*, London, 1969; *All My Sons* by Arthur Miller, London, 1976; *The Three Sisters* by Chekhov, London, 1976; *The American Dream* by Edward Albee, London, 1977; *Suddenly Last Summer* by Tennessee Williams, London, 1977.
Actor: **Plays**—Hornbeck in *Inherit the Wind* by Jerome Lawrence and Robert E. Lee, Perth, Scotland, 1960; Ross in *Macbeth* and Magpie in *Naked Island* by Russell Bladdon, Coventry, 1961; Gratiano in *The Merchant of Venice*, Newcastle upon Tyne, 1963; title role in *Billy Liar* by Keith Waterhouse and Willis Hall, Windsor, 1964; Cassius in *The Man Who Let It Rain* by Marc Brandel, London, 1964; Laertes in *Hamlet*, Bassanio in *The Merchant of Venice*, and Edmund in *King Lear*, Sunderland, 1964–65; Lopahin in *The Cherry Orchard* by Chekhov, Hornchurch, Essex, 1965; Sergeant Trotter in *The Mousetrap* by Agatha Christie, London, 1966; Joseph in *Revelations*, Grinnell, Iowa, 1986. **Film**—*Robbery*, 1967. **Television**—*The Growing Pains of P.C. Penrose* by Roy Clarke, 1975; *The Prince Regent* by Robert Muller, 1979; *Henry V*, 1979; *Fame Is the Spur*, by Howard Spring, 1982; *A Murder Is Announced* by Agatha Christie, 1985.

* * *

David Pinner's *Fanghorn* may have misfired in the 1967 production and it may fail to sustain the comic impact and inventiveness of the first two acts in the third, but the talent is unmistakable. What is remarkable about the writing is its energy. It begins with a middle-aged man beheading roses with a sword, then fencing flirtatiously with his 16-year-old daughter, before switching to making her jump by slashing at her legs. And it sustains a brisk pace in visual surprises and twists in the plot. Occasionally an uncertain note is struck with deliberately over-written lines like "Look at that gull battering his whiteness against the hooks of the wind!" But there are also some very funny lines and plenty of intriguing changes of direction in the dialogue, which builds up to the entrance of Tamara Fanghorn, a tough-talking, leather-clad sophisticate, who arrives before she is expected, and from upstairs. Subsequent developments make it look as though she is in league with the wife to humiliate the husband, who is First Secretary to the Minister of Defence. Act 2 ends with him naked except for his pants, his hands tied with his belt and his feet with the telephone wire. As the curtain falls Tamara is brandishing a cut-throat razor and threatening "Now I am going to cut off what offends me most!" When the curtain rises on Act 3, we find him denuded only of his moustache. The crucial twist comes when his disillusioned wife has walked out on him and we find that this is what he and Tamara had wanted all along.

Dickon is centred more ordinarily on family relationships. It is vitiated by perfunctoriness and superficiality in most of its characterisation, but there is a glowingly affectionate portrait of a lower-middle-class father trying to fight off the awareness of cancer, and then later fighting with pain. But the end piles on the drama too heavily, with one son powdering morphine tablets to put the dying man out of his agony, the other son giving them to him and then the two of them fighting and laughing hysterically.

There is a curious reprise of these themes in *The Potsdam Quartet*. Act 1 ends with the leader revealing to the cellist that for ten years he has been suffering from Parkinson's Disease, and the cellist, who had thought he was going mad, reacts with a joyful demonstration of relief. How the cellist could have remained ignorant of his own condition is never adequately explained and there are only cursory references to the illness in Act 2, in which the biggest climax is provided by a quarrel between the second violin and the viola player, who are lovers, John (second violin) threatens Ronald (viola) that he is going to have the boyfriend of the leader's daughter, and Ronald responds by swallowing a succession of sleeping pills.

The play is set in an ante-room at the Potsdam Conference in 1945. The string quartet (which is based on the Griller Quartet) play two quartets to Churchill, Stalin, and Truman. Act 1 takes place immediately after the first quartet and Act 2 immediately after the second. Apart from the four musicians the only character is a Russian guard who hardly ever speaks. The characters are well contrasted and there is some amusing dialogue, but it is a realistic play in which the action is limited to what can go on in one room between four men who know each other extremely well. Act 1 cannot always avoid the pitfall of making them tell each other things they all know in order to give information to the audience and Act 2 resorts to making them all drunk in order to increase the ratio of action to talk. It lacks the energy and the courage of *Fanghorn* but after writing many unproduced plays in the six intervening years, Pinner cannot be blamed for playing safe, though the theatre can be blamed for failing to nourish the talent he originally showed.

Perhaps his two best plays are two one-acters produced at the Soho Poly. *Cartoon* is about an alcoholic cartoonist drying out in a clinic just up the road from the pub where he customarily spends his lunch-hour drinking grapefruit juice and weeping as he regularly wins money out of the fruit machine. *An Evening with the GLC* is set in a television studio where a Labour Councillor and his wife are exposed to a live interview conducted by their son. They both walk a little too willingly into the traps which are set for them, but the exposure of political dishonesties is nonetheless effective. Written when Pinner was resident playwright at Peterborough, *Hereward the Wake* is another historical play with dialogue in the modern idiom.

—Ronald Hayman

PINTER, Harold. British. Born in Hackney, London, 10 October 1930. Educated at Hackney Downs Grammar School,

1943–47; Royal Academy of Dramatic Art, London, 1948. Conscientious objector: no military service. Married 1) the actress Vivien Merchant in 1956 (divorced 1980), one son; 2) the writer Lady Antonia Fraser in 1980. Professional actor, 1949–60, and occasionally since then; also a director; associate director, National Theatre, London, 1973–83; director, United British Artists, 1983. Recipient: *Evening Standard* award, 1960; Newspaper Guild of New York award, 1962; Italia prize, for television play, 1962; Berlin Film Festival Silver Bear, 1963; Screenwriters Guild award, for television play, 1963, for screenplay, 1963; New York Film Critics award, 1964; BAFTA award, 1965, 1971; Tony award, 1967; Whitbread award, 1967; New York Drama Critics Circle award, 1967, 1980; Shakespeare Prize (Hamburg), 1970; Writers Guild award, 1971; Cannes Film Festival Golden Palm, 1971; Austrian State prize, 1973; Pirandello prize, 1980; Donatello prize, 1982; British Theatre Association award, 1983, 1985; Bobst award, 1984. D.Litt.: universities of Reading, 1970, Birmingham, 1971, Glasgow, 1974, East Anglia, Norwich, 1974, Stirling, 1979, and Hull, 1986; Brown University, Providence, Rhode Island, 1982. Honorary Fellow, Modern Language Association (USA), 1970. C.B.E. (Commander, Order of the British Empire), 1966. Lives in London. Agent: Judy Daish Associates, 83 Eastbourne Mews, London W2 6LQ, England.

PUBLICATIONS

Plays

The Room (produced Bristol, 1957; also director: produced London, 1960; New York, 1964). Included in *The Birthday Party and Other Plays*, 1960.

The Birthday Party (produced Cambridge and London, 1958; San Francisco, 1960; New York, 1967). London, Encore, 1959; included in *The Birthday Party and Other Plays*, 1960; revised version, London, Methuen, 1965.

Sketches in *One to Another* (produced London, 1959). London, French, 1960.

Sketches in *Pieces of Eight* (produced London, 1959). Included in *A Slight Ache and Other Plays*, 1961; in *The Dwarfs and Eight Revue Sketches*, 1965.

A Slight Ache (broadcast 1959; produced London, 1961; New York, 1962). Included in *A Slight Ache and Other Plays*, 1961; in *Three Plays*, 1962.

The Dumb Waiter (produced, in German, Frankfurt 1959; London, 1960; Madison, Wisconsin, and New York, 1962). Included in *The Birthday Party and Other Plays*, 1960.

The Dwarfs (broadcast 1960; also director: produced London, 1963; revised version produced Edinburgh, 1966; Boston, 1967; New York, 1974). Included in *A Slight Ache and Other Plays*, 1961; in *Three Plays*, 1962.

The Birthday Party and Other Plays (includes *The Dumb Waiter* and *The Room*). London, Methuen, 1960; as *The Birthday Party and The Room* (includes *The Dumb Waiter*), New York, Grove Press, 1961.

The Caretaker (produced London, 1960; New York, 1961). London, Methuen, 1960; with *The Dumb Waiter*, New York, Grove Press, 1961.

Night School (televised 1960). Included in *Tea Party and Other Plays*, 1967; in *Early Plays*, 1968.

A Night Out (broadcast 1960; produced Dublin and London, 1961; New York, 1971). Included in *A Slight Ache and Other Plays*, 1961; in *Early Plays*, 1968.

A Slight Ache and Other Plays (includes *The Dwarfs, A Night Out*, and sketches). London, Methuen, 1961.

The Collection (televised 1961; also co-director; produced London, 1962; New York, 1963; revised version, televised 1978). London, French, 1962; in *Three Plays*, 1962.

Three Plays. New York, Grove Press, 1962.

The Lover (televised 1963; also director: produced London, 1963; New York, 1964). Included in *The Collection, and The Lover*, 1963; published separately, New York, Dramatists Play Service, 1965.

The Collection, and The Lover (includes the prose piece *The Examination*). London, Methuen, 1963.

The Compartment (unreleased screenplay), in *Project 1*, with Samuel Beckett and Eugène Ionesco. New York, Grove Press, 1963.

Dialogue for Three, published in *Stand* (Newcastle upon Tyne), vol. 6, no. 3, 1963.

Tea Party (televised 1965; produced New York, 1968; London, 1970). London, Methuen, 1965; New York, Grove Press, 1966; revised version, London, Karnac, 1968.

The Homecoming (produced London, 1965; New York, 1967). London, Methuen, 1965; New York, Grove Press, 1966; revised version, London, Karnac, 1968.

The Dwarfs and Eight Revue Sketches (includes *Trouble in the Works, The Black and White, Request Stop, Last to Go, Applicant, Interview, That's All, That's Your Trouble*). New York, Dramatists Play Service, 1965.

The Basement (televised 1967; produced New York, 1968; London, 1970). Included in *Tea Party and Other Plays*, 1967; in *The Lover, The Tea Party, The Basement*, 1967.

Tea Party and Other Plays. London, Methuen, 1967.

The Lover, The Tea Party, The Basement. New York, Grove Press, 1967.

Early Plays: A Night Out, Night School, Revue Sketches. New York, Grove Press, 1968.

Sketches by Pinter (produced New York, 1969). Included in *Early Plays*, 1968.

Landscape (broadcast 1968; produced London, 1969; New York, 1970). London, Pendragon Press, 1968; included in *Landscape, and Silence*, 1969.

Silence (produced London, 1969; New York, 1970). Included in *Landscape, and Silence*, 1969.

Landscape, and Silence (includes *Night*). London, Methuen, 1969; New York, Grove Press, 1970.

Night, in *Mixed Doubles* (produced London, 1969). Included in *Landscape and Silence*, 1969.

Five Screenplays (includes *The Caretaker, The Servant, The Pumpkin Eater, Accident, The Quiller Memorandum*). London, Methuen, 1971; modified version, omitting *The Caretaker* and including *The Go-Between*, London, Karnac, 1971; New York, Grove Press, 1973.

Old Times (produced London and New York, 1971). London, Methuen, and New York, Grove Press, 1971.

Monologue (televised 1973; produced London, 1973). London, Covent Garden Press, 1973.

No Man's Land (produced London, 1975; New York, 1976). London, Eyre Methuen, and New York, Grove Press, 1975.

Plays 1–4. London, Eyre Methuen, 1975–81; as *Complete Works 1–4*, New York, Grove Press, 1977–81.

The Proust Screenplay: A la Recherche du Temps Perdu. New York, New Directions, 1977; London, Eyre Methuen-Chatto and Windus, 1978.

Betrayal (produced London, 1978; New York, 1980). London, Eyre Methuen, 1978; New York, Grove Press, 1979.
The Hothouse (also director: produced London, 1980). London, Eyre Methuen, and New York, Grove Press, 1980; revised version (produced Providence, Rhode Island, and New York, 1982), Methuen, 1982.
Family Voices (broadcast 1981; produced London and Cambridge, Massachusetts, 1981). London, Next Editions, and New York, Grove Press, 1981.
The Screenplay of The French Lieutenant's Woman. London, Cape, and Boston, Little Brown, 1981.
The French Lieutenant's Woman and Other Screenplays (includes *Langrishe, Go Down* and *The Last Tycoon*). London, Methuen, 1982.
Other Places (includes *Family Voices*, *Victoria Station*, *A Kind of Alaska*) (produced London, 1982). London, Methuen, 1982; New York, Grove Press, 1983; revised version, including *One for the Road* and omitting *Family Voices* (produced New York, 1984; London, 1985).
Precisely (sketch), in *The Big One* (produced London, 1983).
One for the Road (also director: produced London, 1984; in *Other Places*, produced New York, 1984). London, Methuen, 1984; revised version, Methuen, 1985; New York, Grove Press, 1986.

Screenplays: *The Servant*, 1963; *The Guest* (*The Caretaker*), 1964; *The Pumpkin Eater*, 1964; *The Quiller Memorandum*, 1966; *Accident*, 1967; *The Birthday Party*, 1968; *The Go-Between*, 1971; *The Homecoming*, 1976; *The Last Tycoon*, 1976; *The French Lieutenant's Woman*, 1981; *Betrayal*, 1983; *Turtle Diary*, 1985.

Radio Plays: *A Slight Ache*, 1959; *The Dwarfs*, 1960; *A Night Out*, 1960; *Landscape*, 1968; *Family Voices*, 1981; *Players*, 1985.

Television Plays: *Night School*, 1960; *The Collection*, 1961, revised version, 1978; *The Lover*, 1963; *Tea Party*, 1965; *The Basement*, 1967; *Monologue*, 1973; *Langrishe, Go Down*, from the novel by Aidan Higgins, 1978.

Verse

Poems, edited by Alan Clodd. London, Enitharmon Press, 1968; revised edition, 1971.
I Know the Place. Warwick, Greville Press, 1979.

Other

Mac (on Anew McMaster). London, Pendragon Press, 1968.
Poems and Prose 1949–1977. London, Eyre Methuen, and New York, Grove Press, 1978; revised edition, as *Collected Poems and Prose*, Methuen, 1986.

Editor, with John Fuller and Peter Redgrove, *New Poems 1967: A PEN Anthology*. London, Hutchinson, 1968.
Editor, with Geoffrey Godbert and Anthony Astbury, *100 Poems by 100 Poets*. London, Methuen, 1986; New York, Grove Press, 1987.

*

Bibliography: *Pinter: A Bibliography: His Works and Occasional Writings with a Comprehensive Checklist of Criticism and Reviews of the London Productions* by Rudiger Imhof, London, TQ Publications, 1975; *Harold Pinter: An Annotated Bibliography* by Steven H. Gale, Boston, Hall, and London, Prior, 1978.

Critical Studies (selection): *Harold Pinter*, New York, Twayne, 1967, revised edition, 1981, and *Harold Pinter*, New York, St. Martin's Press, 1975, London, Macmillan, 1976, both by Arnold P. Hinchliffe; *Harold Pinter* by Ronald Hayman, London, Heinemann, 1968, New York, Ungar, 1973, revised edition, Heinemann, 1980; *Harold Pinter* by John Russell Taylor, London, Longman, 1969; *Stratagems to Uncover Nakedness: The Dramas of Harold Pinter* by Lois Gordon, Columbia, University of Missouri Press, 1969; *Harold Pinter: The Poetics of Silence* by James H. Hollis, Carbondale, Southern Illinois University Press, 1970; *Harold Pinter* by Alrene Sykes, St. Lucia, University of Queensland Press, and New York, Humanities Press, 1970; *The Peopled Wound: The Plays of Harold Pinter* by Martin Esslin, London, Methuen, and New York, Doubleday, 1970, revised edition, as *Pinter: A Study of His Plays*, Methuen, 1973, New York, Norton, 1976, revised edition, Eyre Methuen, 1977, revised edition, as *Pinter: The Playwright*, Methuen, 1982; *The Dramatic World of Harold Pinter: Its Basis in Ritual* by Katherine H. Burkman, Columbus, Ohio State University Press, 1971; *Pinter: A Collection of Critical Essays* edited by Arthur Ganz, Englewood Cliffs, New Jersey, Prentice Hall, 1972; *The Plays of Harold Pinter: An Assessment* by Simon Trussler, London, Gollancz, 1973; *The Pinter Problem* by Austin E. Quigley, Princeton, New Jersey, Princeton University Press, 1975; *The Dream Structure of Pinter's Plays: A Psychoanalytic Approach* by Lucina Paquet Gabbard, Rutherford, New Jersey, Fairleigh Dickinson University Press, 1976; *Where the Laughter Stops: Pinter's Tragi-Comedy*, Columbia, University of Missouri Press, 1976, and *Harold Pinter*, London, Macmillan, and New York, Grove Press, 1982, both by Bernard F. Dukore; *Butter's Going Up: A Critical Analysis of Harold Pinter's Work* by Steven H. Gale, Durham, North Carolina, Duke University Press, 1977, and *Harold Pinter: Critical Approaches* edited by Gale, Madison, New Jersey, Fairleigh Dickinson University Press, 1986; *Harold Pinter: A Critical Evaluation* by Surendra Sahai, Salzburg, Austria, Salzburg Studies in English Literature, 1981; *Canters and Chronicles: The Use of Narrative in the Plays of Samuel Beckett and Harold Pinter* by Kristin Morrison, Chicago, University of Chicago Press, 1983; *Harold Pinter* by Guido Almansi and Simon Henderson, London, Methuen, 1983; *Pinter: The Player's Playwright* by David T. Thompson, London, Macmillan, and New York, Schocken, 1985; *Pinter's Comic Play* by Elin Diamond, Lewisburg, Pennsylvania, Bucknell University Press, 1985; *Harold Pinter: You Never Heard Such Silence* edited by Alan Bold, London, Vision Press, and New York, Barnes and Noble, 1985; *Making Pictures: The Pinter Screenplays* by Joanne Klein, Columbus, Ohio State University Press, 1985; *Harold Pinter: The Birthday Party, The Caretaker, and The Homecoming: A Casebook* edited by Michael Scott, London, Macmillan, 1986.

Theatrical Activities:
Director: **Plays**—*The Birthday Party*, Oxford and Cambridge, 1958; *The Room*, London, 1960; *The Collection* (co-director, with Peter Hall), London, 1962; *The Lover*, London, 1963; *The Dwarfs*, London, 1963; *The Birthday Party*, London, 1964; *The Man in the Glass Booth* by Robert Shaw, London, 1967, New York, 1968; *Exiles* by James Joyce, London, 1970; *Butley* by Simon Gray, Oxford and London, 1971; *Next of Kin* by John Hopkins, London, 1974; *Otherwise Engaged* by Simon Gray, Oxford and London, 1975, New York, 1977; *Blithe Spirit* by Noël Coward, London, 1976; *The Innocents* by William Archibald, New York, 1976; *The Rear Column* by Simon Gray, London, 1978; *Close of Play* by Simon Gray, London, 1979;

The Hothouse, London, 1980; *Quartermaine's Terms* by Simon Gray, London, 1981; *Incident at Tulse Hill* by Robert East, London, 1981; *The Trojan War Will Not Take Place* by Jean Giraudoux, London, 1983; *The Common Pursuit* by Simon Gray, London, 1984; *One for the Road, and Victoria Station*, London, 1984; *Sweet Bird of Youth* by Tennessee Williams, London, 1985; *Circe and Bravo* by Donald Freed, London, 1986. **Film**—*Butley*, 1976. **Television**—*The Rear Column* by Simon Gray, 1980; *The Hothouse*, 1981.

Actor (as David Baron and Harold Pinter): **Plays**—with Anew McMaster's theatre company in Ireland, 1950–52; with Donald Wolfit's theatre company, Kings Theatre, Hammersmith, London, 1953; numerous provincial repertory companies, 1953–60; Mick in *The Caretaker*, London, 1964; Goldberg in *The Birthday Party*, Cheltenham, 1964; Lenny in *The Homecoming*, Watford, Hertfordshire, 1969; Deeley in *Old Times*, Los Angeles, 1985. **Radio**—*Monologue*, 1975; *Rough for Radio* by Samuel Beckett, 1976; *Two Plays* by Vaclav Havel, 1977. **Films**—*The Servant*, 1963; *Accident*, 1967; *The Rise and Rise of Michael Rimmer*, 1970. **Television**—*Rogue Male*, 1976; *Langrishe, Go Down*, 1978; *The Birthday Party*, 1986.

* * *

In a remarkably prolific period between 1957 and 1965, Harold Pinter established himself as the most gifted playwright in England and the author of a unique dramatic idiom. Popularly labelled "the Pinteresque," Pinter's theater is not "of the absurd"; nor is it a "drama of menace," both of which portray the gratuitous visitation upon innocent victims of external forces of terror or "the absurd." Actually, "the Pinteresque" consists of a much more frightening visitation: Pinter's comfortable people (at least through *Silence* and *Landscape*), unlike the innocents of Kafka's or even Beckett's worlds, are besieged by their own internal fears and longings and their own irrepressible guilts and menacing sexual drives, and it is these which invariably wage successful war against the tidy life-styles they have constructed in order to survive from day to day.

Pinter's characters, usually enclosed in a room, organize their lives with the "games people play." But in their games or role-playing—where each has agreed to a specific scenario with implicit limits and taboos—they often say one thing but really feel and often communicate another. During their exchanges, in fact, the verbal is only the most superficial level of communication. The connotations of their words and their accompanying gestures, or pauses, or *double-entendres*—and their hesitations and silences—really communicate a second level of meaning often opposed to the first. Pinter himself has said of language: "The speech we hear is an indication of that which we don't hear. It is a necessary avoidance, a violent, sly, and anguished or mocking smoke screen which keeps the other in its true place. When true silence falls we are left with echo but are nearer nakedness. One way of looking at speech is to say that it is a constant stratagem to cover nakedness." Indeed, one way of looking at Pinter's plays is to say that they are dramatic stratagems that uncover nakedness.

Into his characters' rooms, and into their ritualized and verbal relationships, a stranger invariably enters, whereupon language begins to disintegrate, and the protection promised by the room becomes threatened. The commonplace room, in fact, becomes the violent scene of mental and physical breakdown. What occurs, in effect, is that the characters *project on to* the stranger—an intruder into their precarious, psychic stability—their deepest fears. The so-called victimizers—Goldberg and McCann in *The Birthday Party*; Riley in *The Room*; the blind, mute matchseller in *A Slight Ache*; the visiting, unfamiliar sister-in-law in *The Homecoming*; the old, garrulous, and admittedly opportunistic Davies in *The Caretaker*; and even the mechanical dumbwaiter in *The Dumb Waiter*—all function as screens upon which the characters externalize their own irrationality, that side of themselves which the games have ultimately been inadequate to hide. Pinter's "intruders" are, in a sense, his technique for leading his characters to expose their true identities. What is, of course, simultaneously funny and horrific is that the games constructed—and even the "intruders" or screens, which are mirror images of the characters—contain within themselves the boring lives already lived *and* the violence struggling for expression.

In Pinter's first play, *The Room*, Rose coddles, feeds, clothes, and emasculates her silent husband, Bert, fittingly portrayed as a child (he has agreed to play the passive child in their relationship), wearing a silly hat and reading comic books. Protective of her precarious stability she admits: "This is a good room. You've got a chance in a place like this.... It's cold out.... It's murder." When a young couple enters (a mirror of Rose and Bert many years before), thinking her flat free, she actually experiences them as potential "murderers." This is exacerbated by her landlord's (Kidd's) retaliatory remarks (because of her earlier putdown) and his mention that a blind, black man in the basement (an obvious image of her subterranean mind) is waiting to "see" her. For the rest of the play, Rose acts out her rage, sexual appetite, and then guilt toward the black Riley, as though re-enacting an earlier Oedipal crime. From her "You're all deaf and dumb and blind, the lot of you," she succumbs to his "Sal [a childhood name].... I want you to come home" and caresses his eyes and head. With Bert's return, following this enactment of her most basic instinctual/tabooed behavior, she becomes blind.

In *The Birthday Party* a young man has similarly secluded himself in order to hide from some lingering childhood guilt. When the two strangers Goldberg and McCann enter his seaside retreat, Stanley becomes violent and projects upon them his own fantasies and guilts: "You stink of sin"; "you contaminate womankind.... Mother defiler.... You verminate the sheet of your birth." Later at a "celebration," his landlady, Meg, with whom Stanley has structured a safe though flirtatious child-lover relationship, and the neighbor, Lulu, along with Goldberg and McCann, act out both Stanley's taboo Oedipal impulses and his repulsion and guilt toward these drives. As Rose became blind, Stanley becomes mute. In *The Dumb Waiter* two hitmen lose control when some actually very funny messages descend on the building's dumb waiter and the w.c. misfunctions, whereupon their carefully measured roles are upset. In *The Caretaker* the intrusion of a harmless (though manipulative and highly verbal) old man threatens the carefully designed relationship of two brothers. In *The Homecoming* a presumably stable all-male household is exposed in all its rage, confused sexuality, and utter precariousness when an unknown woman (the visiting wife of a third son) appears. Her mere presence threatens everyone's identity. In *The Basement* and *Tea Party* Pinter returns to his earlier triangular patterns, and focuses on the breakdown of orderly and controlled behavior for displays of cuckoldry and homosexuality.

Silence and *Landscape* indicate a new direction. The same childless couples inhabit these plays, but they have long ago learned that playing games will not assure their relationship. Nothing is certain in their isolated rooms, and least of all, identity or connection. Each not only fails to understand himself (unable to distinguish fantasy from experience) but he can never know the stranger who calls himself his spouse. There is a kind of finality in these plays but also a poignancy about these people so inextricably locked within themselves.

The plays demand a more poetic reading—for the lyrical sense of the characters' rationalizations, hopes, fears, and fantasies, which are true at one and the same time. Still in the tradition of Joyce, Woolf, and Beckett, Pinter has now moved from earlier explorations of the underside of self (and what Freud called "the seething cauldron" beneath logical thought and act) to a dramatic rendering of the simultaneous levels of fantasy and real experience that equally occupy the individual. He has said of the complexities and ultimate mystery of human behavior: "The desire for verification on the part of us all, with regard to our own experience and the experience of others, is understandable, but cannot always be satisfied. I suggest there can be no hard distinctions between what is real and what is unreal, nor between what is true and what is false. A thing is not necessarily either true or false; it can be both true and false."

The details, characters, and images of *Silence* and *Landscape* are similar, as though each were two halves of a whole. Poetic images of growing old, they tell of brief and unfulfilled love affairs. Their details are of walks in the country, moments in pubs, and flights of birds; recollections are illuminated by memories of fading sunlight or grey clouds or gusts of rain. Speakers interrupt their wistful thoughts with lusty outbursts about the most mundane of matters. Every word, gesture, color, and mood reverberates, and each character's reveries define the others; although their conversations are not directed to the other, each one explains the way in which life has passed the other by, although to him that insight remains unfathomable. Just as these people fail to connect, their poetically connected insights, their common pain and joy, and their repetition of words and gestures suggest a universality about human nature. Pinter has clearly moved toward new, poetic dimensions; interestingly, he also published his first volume of poems at this time, although they were written as early as his first plays.

Old Times returns to issues of possible and real homosexual and heterosexual commitment, fidelity, and friendship. Pinter's triangle (two women and a man) suggests any number of possibilities and combinations: "There are some things one remembers even though they may never have happened. There are things I remember which may never have happened but as I recall them so they take place." *No Man's Land* recreates a male world of potential comforters and predators with each man locked in a precarious linguistic world of identity. "No man's land" is that mysterious realm of truth and self-knowledge, of one's comprehension of oneself and one's world that "never moves, which never changes, which never grows older, but which remains forever, icy and silent."

Almost as though Pinter had begun with a line from *Old Times* (where one man tells another he "proposed" that his wife "betray" him), *Betrayal* treats multiple betrayals among friends, spouses, lovers (and even within the self)—in a fascinating structural manipulation of time. Perhaps inspired by his screenplay of Proust's *A la recherche*, it begins two years after an affair ended and in nine scenes moves back in time. Humor, banality, poetry, violence, diluted passion, and pain merge in a poignant evocation of time and one's eternal separation from both innocence and responsibility.

The Hothouse, written in 1958 but not published until 1980, focuses on the sanatorium in which the mute Stanley in *The Birthday Party* might have been committed. Staff members chatter in banal, funny, and threatening conversations about sex and the variations of power and control. Playing with traditional symbolism—there has been both a birth and death; the play occurs on Christmas; the characters (in this hothouse) are named Roote, Cutts, Lush, and Lamb—Pinter raises serious and ambiguous issues about sanity and insanity, "leaders" and "followers." At the end, a gratuitous mass murder of the staff is committed, but the perpetrator remains ambiguous: is it one of the patients? Is it one of the staff?

The London production of *Other Places* included *Victoria Station, A Kind of Alaska*, and *Family Voices*; in New York, *One for the Road* replaced *Family Voices*, originally a radio play. There is a curious unity in the three remaining works, as they anatomize primitive responses to menace and loyalty. *Tours de force* in concreteness, they are finely chiselled portraits of the contingency of human experience; they simultaneously evoke the most abiding of human encounters with evil or kindness.

The very short *Victoria Station* portrays the conversation between a taxi despatcher and a driver who, after picking up a female passenger, loses all sense of place and identity. The despatcher becomes his brother's keeper. *One for the Road* conveys a series of frightening confrontations between a banal, Goldberg-like torturer (vaguely representative of God and country) and his victims—a tortured man, his brutally assaulted wife, and their eventually murdered son. In the most affecting of the group, *A Kind of Alaska*, a woman in her mid-forties "erupts to life" after nearly 30 years of sleeping sickness. Pinter depicts her rebellious, bewildered, foolish, angry, and gallant responses in a combination of hallucination, childlike language, and erotic wish fulfilment. The reality of her lost youth and lost love, along with her sister's and doctor's unshakable loyalty, create a powerful work.

—Lois Gordon

PLATER, Alan (Frederick). British. Born in Jarrow-on-Tyne, County Durham, 15 April 1935. Educated at Pickering Road Junior and Infant School, Hull, 1940–46; Kingston High School, Hull, 1946–53; King's College, Newcastle upon Tyne (University of Durham), 1953–57; qualified as architect (Associate, Royal Institute of British Architects), 1961. Married 1) Shirley Johnson in 1958 (divorced 1985), two sons and one daughter; 2) Shirley Rubinstein, three stepsons. Worked in an architect's office, Hull, 1957–60. Since 1960 full-time writer. Co-founder, Humberside Theatre (formerly Hull Arts Centre), 1970; Co-Chairman, Writers Guild of Great Britain, 1986–87. Recipient: Writers Guild award, for radio play, 1972; Sony award, for radio play, 1983; Royal Television Society award, 1984; New York and San Francisco film festival awards, 1986. D.Litt.: Hull University, 1985. Honorary Fellow, Hull College of Higher Education, 1983; Fellow, Royal Society of Literature, 1985. Lives in London. Agent: Margaret Ramsay Ltd., 14-A Goodwin's Court, London WC2N 4LL, England.

Publications

Plays

The Referees (televised 1961; produced Stoke-on-Trent, 1963).

The Mating Season (broadcast 1962; produced Stoke-on-Trent, 1963). Published in *Worth a Hearing: A Collection of Radio Plays*, edited by Alfred Bradley, London, Blackie, 1967.

A Smashing Day (televised 1962; revised version, music by Ben Kingsley and Robert Powell, produced Stoke-on-Trent, 1965; London, 1966).
The Rainbow Machine (broadcast 1962; produced Stoke-on-Trent, 1963).
Ted's Cathedral (produced Stoke-on-Trent and London, 1963).
A Quiet Night (televised 1963). Published in *Z Cars: Four Scripts from the Television Series*, edited by Michael Marland, London, Longman, 1968.
See the Pretty Lights (televised 1963; produced London, 1970). Published in *Theatre Choice: A Collection of Modern Short Plays*, edited by Michael Marland, London, Blackie, 1972.
The Nutter (televised 1965; revised version, as *Charlie Came to Our Town*, music by Alex Glasgow, produced Harrogate, Yorkshire, 1966).
Excursion (broadcast 1966). Included in *You and Me*, 1973.
The What on the Landing? (broadcast 1967; produced Coventry, 1968; London, 1971).
On Christmas Day in the Morning (*Softly, Softly* series; televised 1968). Included in *You and Me*, 1973.
Hop Step and Jump (produced Scarborough, Yorkshire, 1968).
Close the Coalhouse Door, music by Alex Glasgow, adaptation of stories by Sid Chaplin (produced Newcastle upon Tyne and London, 1968). London, Methuen, 1969.
Don't Build a Bridge, Drain the River!, music by Michael Chapman and Mike Waterson (produced Hull, 1970; revised version, music by Mike O'Neil, produced Hull, 1980).
Simon Says!, music by Alex Glasgow (produced Leeds, 1970).
And a Little Love Besides (produced Hull, 1970; London, 1977). Included in *You and Me*, 1973.
King Billy Vaudeville Show, with others (produced Hull, 1971).
Seventeen Per Cent Said Push Off (televised 1972). Included in *You and Me*, 1973.
The Tigers are Coming—O.K.? (produced Hull, 1972).
You and Me: Four Plays, edited by Alfred Bradley. London, Blackie, 1973.
Swallows on the Water (produced Hull, 1973).
When the Reds Go Marching In (produced Liverpool, 1973).
Annie Kenney (televised 1974). Published in *Act 3*, edited by David Self and Ray Speakman, London, Hutchinson, 1979.
Tales of Humberside, music by Jim Bywater (produced Hull, 1975).
Trinity Tales, music by Alex Glasgow (televised 1975; produced Birmingham, 1975).
Our Albert (produced Hull, 1976).
The Fosdyke Saga, with Bill Tidy (produced London, 1977). London, French, 1978.
Drums along the Ginnel (produced London, 1977).
Fosdyke 2, with Bill Tidy (produced London, 1977).
Short Back and Sides (televised 1977). Published in *City Life*, edited by David Self, London, Hutchinson, 1980.
Well Good Night Then . . . (produced Hull, 1978).
Skyhooks (produced Oldham, Lancashire, 1982).
On Your Way, Riley!, music by Alex Glasgow (produced London, 1982).
A Foot on the Earth (produced Newcastle upon Tyne, 1984).
Prez, music by Bernie Cash (produced Hull and London, 1985).

Screenplays: *The Virgin and the Gypsy*, 1970; *Juggernaut*, 1974; *It Shouldn't Happen to a Vet* (*All Things Bright and Beautiful*), 1976; *Priest of Love*, 1982; *The Inside Man*, 1984.

Radio Plays: *The Smokeless Zone*, 1961; *Counting the Legs*, 1961; *The Mating Season*, 1962; *The Rainbow Machine*, 1962; *The Seventh Day of Arthur*, 1963; *Excursion*, 1966; *The What on the Landing?*, 1967; *Fred*, 1970; *The Slow Stain*, 1973; *5 Days in '55* (*The Gilberdyke Diaries*), 1976; *Tunes*, 1979; *Swallows on the Water*, 1981; *The Journal of Vasilije Bogdanovic* (*In a Strange Land* series), 1982; *Tolpuddle*, with Vince Hill, 1982; *Who's Jimmy Dickenson?*, from his play *Well Good Night Then . . .*, 1986.

Television Plays: *The Referees*, 1961; *A Smashing Day*, 1962; *So Long Charlie*, 1963; *See the Pretty Lights*, 1963; *Z Cars* series (18 episodes), 1963–65; *Ted's Cathedral*, 1964; *Fred*, 1964; *The Incident*, 1965; *The Nutter*, 1965; *Softly, Softly* series (30 episodes), 1966–76; *To See How Far It Is* (trilogy), 1968; *The First Lady* series (4 episodes), 1968–69; *Rest in Peace, Uncle Fred*, 1970; *Seventeen Per Cent Said Push Off*, 1972; *The Reluctant Juggler* (*The Edwardians* series), 1972; *Tonight We Meet Arthur Pendlebury*, 1972; *It Must Be Something in the Water* (documentary), 1973; *Brotherly Love*, 1973; *The Land of Green Ginger*, 1974; *The Needle Match*, 1974; *Goldilocks and the Three Bears*, 1974; *Wish You Were Here* (documentary), 1974; *Annie Kenney* (*Shoulder to Shoulder* series), 1974; *The Loner* series, 1975; *The Stars Look Down*, from the novel by A.J. Cronin, 1975; *Trinity Tales* series, 1975; *Willow Cabins*, 1975; *Practical Experience*, 1976; *Oh No—It's Selwyn Froggit* series, 1976; *A Tyneside Entertainment* (documentary), 1976; *Seven Days That Shook Young Jim* (*Going to Work* series), 1976; *We Are the Masters Now*, 1976; *There Are Several Businesses Like Show Business*, 1976; *The Bike*, 1977; *Short Back and Sides*, 1977; *Middlemen* series, 1977; *By Christian Judges Condemned*, 1977; *For the Love of Albert* series, 1977; *Give Us a Kiss, Christabel*, 1977; *The Eddystone Lights* (documentary), 1978; *The Party of the First Part*, 1978; *Curriculee Curricula*, music by Dave Greenslade, 1978; *Night People*, 1978; *Flambards*, from works by K.M. Peyton, 1979; *The Blacktoft Diaries*, 1979; *Reunion*, 1979; *The Good Companions*, from the novel by J.B. Priestley, 1980; *Get Lost!* series, 1981; *Barchester Chronicles*, from novels by Trollope, 1981; *The Clarion Van*, from a work by Doris Neild Chew, 1983; *Feet Foremost*, from a story by L.P. Hartley, 1983; *Bewitched*, from the story by Edith Wharton, 1983; *The Consultant*, from the novel *Invitation to Tender* by John McNeil, 1983; *Pride of Our Alley*, 1983; *The Crystal Spirit: Orwell on Jura* (documentary), 1983; *Thank You, Mrs. Clinkscales*, 1984; *The Solitary Cyclist*, from a story by Arthur Conan Doyle, 1984; *Edward Lear: On the Edge of the Sand*, 1985; *The Beiderbecke Affair* series, 1985; *A Murder Is Announced*, from the novel by Agatha Christie, 1985; *Coming Through*, 1985; *The Man with the Twisted Lip*, from a story by Arthur Conan Doyle, 1986; *Death Is Part of the Process*, from a novel by Hilda Bernstein, 1986; *Fortunes of War*, from novels by Olivia Manning, 1987.

Novels

The Beiderbecke Affair. London, Methuen, 1985.
The Beiderbecke Tapes. London, Methuen, 1986.
Misterioso. London, Methuen, 1987.

Other

The Trouble with Abracadabra (for children). London, Macmillan, 1975.

*

Critical Studies: introduction to *Close the Coalhouse Door*,

1969, "What's Going On Behind the Coalhouse Door," in *Sunday Times* (London), 9 February 1969, "The Playwright and His People," in *Theatre Quarterly 2* (London), April-June 1971, "One Step Forward, Two Steps Back," in *New Statesman* (London), 3 November 1972, "Views," in *Listener* (London), 29 November 1973, and "Twenty-Five Years Hard," in *Theatre Quarterly 25* (London), 1977, all by Plater; "The London Show" by Yorick Blumenfeld, in *Atlantic* (Boston), August 1969; *The Second Wave* by John Russell Taylor, London, Methuen, and New York, Hill and Wang, 1971; "Trinity Collage" by Peter Fiddick, in *Guardian* (London), 12 December 1975; article by Albert Hunt, in *British Television Drama* edited by George W. Brandt, London, Cambridge University Press, 1981.

Alan Plater comments:

(1973) Authors introducing their work fill me with gloom, like people explaining jokes: if I didn't laugh or cry before the explanation, nothing is likely to change afterwards. Therefore all I can do is look down the laundry list of my work to date and try to work out why I bothered, apart from what Mr. Perelman calls "the lash of economic necessity."

The clue lies in the place of birth and the present address: I was born and have always lived in industrial communities. I live in a place that works for a living. I never ran barefoot other than from choice. I have always eaten well and have never been deprived of anything that mattered: but I have always been close enough to the inequalities and grotesque injustices of our society to get angry about them.

(1977) Essentially I am writing a segment of the history of a society that was forged by the Industrial Revolution. This is less earnest and painful than it sounds; if an idea is important enough it is worth laughing at and one professional associate defined my method as taking fundamentally serious concepts like Politics and Religion and Life and Death and kicking the Hell out of them with old jokes. At any rate, the evidence of the more-or-less knockabout shows we've done around the regions is that people laugh the louder if the fun is spiced with a couple of centuries of inherited prejudice.

The other thought prompted by the laundry list is that not many writers have tangled with as rich and diverse a company of people and subjects: D.H. Lawrence, Mrs. Pankhurst, Sandy Powell, and Les Dawson would look good on any music-hall poster, though there might be some dispute over billing. At any rate, it underlines my feeling that it's the job of the writer at all times to head for the nearest tightrope and, in the words of Max Miller, Archie Rice, or both: "You've got to admit, lady, I do have a go."

(1982) Very little changes. The inequalities and injustices of 1973 are still there and I'm still heading for the tightrope as in 1977. We've got a new dog called The Duke (after Ellington) and I've had a programme banned by the BBC, which is a distinction of a sort. I copied some words by Jean Rhys and pinned them on the wall behind my desk. She says: "All of writing is a huge lake. There are great rivers that feed the lake, like Tolstoy and Dostoevsky. And there are trickles, like Jean Rhys. All that matters is feeding the lake. I don't matter. The lake matters. Nothing else is important. . . ."

(1988) After all that worthy stuff about living in an industrial community, here I am writing this paragraph in downtown N.W.3. In the famous words of Mr. Vonnegut: so it goes. We grow older, we change, we pursue happiness and sometimes find it. Professionally, I still head for the tightrope and Jean Rhys is still with me. So, for that matter, is The Duke.

* * *

Alan Plater is one of several dramatists whose work has done much to further the cause of British regional theatre. Although some of his plays have been seen in London and he has written widely for national television and the cinema, for many years his energies were directed towards ensuring the success of the ambitious Hull Arts Centre, a small 150-seat theatre. This physical home was also apparently a spiritual one, for his plays are set in the northeast of England and are largely concerned with the particular problems and history of the area. "Central to the greater part of my writing," he once stated, "is man's relationship to his work": and work in this context means particularly coal-mining and deep-sea fishing, two regional industries. Plater admires the "genuine solidarity and craft-consciousness" of those whose jobs involve "hideous physical working conditions": and he has captured the sheer pride in overcoming fear and danger which distinguishes the miners in his highly successful musical documentary, *Close the Coalhouse Door*. Nor is this admiration a skin-enthusiasm, for Plater identifies wholeheartedly with the community he describes: he shares the passion for football, and once, when he was asked about his literary influences, he replied by mentioning the popular music-hall names of his youth—Norman Evans, Mooney and King. He also expresses with great fire many of the social and political attitudes (some might call them prejudices) which characterize the region: a hatred of the bosses, who are usually portrayed as effete Southerners, a respect for Trade Union tradition, a somewhat over-generalized call for revolution which is coupled with a suspicion of change, a brashly extrovert dismissal of all forms of theatre which lack working-class appeal and a socialism which refuses to accept that Labour politicians are better than stooges for capitalistic con-men.

His work falls into two main categories. Plater has written several carefully observed naturalistic plays, such as *See the Pretty Lights* and *A Smashing Day*, which were both rewritten for the stage from television scripts. In 1966 Plater met the composer and songwriter Alex Glasgow and together they have collaborated on several musical documentaries, among them *Charlie Came to Our Town* and *Close the Coalhouse Door*. The documentaries, unlike the naturalistic plays, combine many styles of writing—cross-talk sketches, songs, impassioned oratory, summaries of historical incidents, and much satire—which are all loosely brought together by a general theme, the history of Hull or the struggle of miners to gain decent living standards.

These two styles reveal different qualities. *See the Pretty Lights* is a gentle, warm, and moving account of a meeting between a middle-aged man and a teenage girl at the end of a pier. Both lead dull lives: and the bright lights of the seaside and their momentary friendship helps to relieve—but also to underline—their social frustrations. The hero of *A Smashing Day* is a young man, Lennie, who suffers from bored aimlessness: he meekly accepts his job, the odd nights at the palais with his mates who never become friends, and the routine drink. But he senses that a more exciting life awaits him somewhere if only he could find out where. He goes steady with a girl, Anne, and drifts towards marriage, which he doesn't want: and the social pressures are such that he persists in marrying her even after meeting Liz, an independent and sensitive girl with whom he falls in love. Many critics felt that the increased length of the stage play failed to achieve the concentrated power of the television script, and *A Smashing Day* was not successful in London. But it did provide an excellent part for the then unknown actor, Hywel Bennett, and revealed Plater's ability to describe an apparently uninteresting person in some depth. Lennie is never allowed to be either a pathetic person or an angry young man: and despite his shy insecurity which leaves an impression of spinelessness, his situation is both moving, credible, and strong enough to hold the play together.

If the naturalistic plays are distinguished by restraint and accuracy, the documentaries have entirely the opposite qualities: panache, a cheerful display of class bias, and a loose, anything-goes technique. The best known is *Close the Coalhouse Door*, which was remarkably successful in Newcastle but received only a limited run in London, a fact which could be interpreted in several ways. The episodes of mining history are told within the context of a golden "wedding" reception in the Millburn family, who step out of a photograph to tell stories of strikes and hardships. Some scenes were particularly powerful: the death of a miner, the rivalry between families and men, the bitterness against the blackleg miners who went back to work too soon after the General Strike. Plater stressed the complicated mixture of affection and fear for the pits, together with a scorn of modernization programmes whose effect was to send miners back on the dole. The songs by Alex Glasgow caught the friendly liveliness of music halls and pubs, and in Newcastle it became a cult show. "Workers turned up in their thousands once the word got round," recalled Plater: the large Playhouse Theatre was filled to capacity night after night—the audiences would sit in the aisles, even on the steps to the stage.

Why did the show receive such a tepid reception in London? The answer is a complex one, revealing much about Plater's work. Plater has offered two reasons—that London audiences are prejudiced against working-class plays and that in any case they could not be expected to share the associations of the North. Both may be true: but isn't it the job of a dramatist to convey the importance on his theme to those who do not belong to the background? London critics generally commented on the superficial characterization of the play, on the rather simplistic dialogue and form, and on the one-sided interpretations of history. These objections to Plater's documentaries were confirmed by two subsequent shows which didn't come to London: *Simon Says!*, a wholesale attack on the British ruling classes represented by Lord Thing, the Chairman of the MCC (the governing board of English cricket), and *And a Little Love Besides*, a scathing account of the uncharitable Church. The critical charge against both these plays was that the satire was too sweeping and naive to hit any real targets. Plater's documentaries are seen at their best perhaps either when the subject contains real and deeply felt observations or when the general sense of fun takes over. *Charlie Came to Our Town*, Plater's first documentary with Alex Glasgow, is a delightfully light-hearted musical about an eccentric anarchist.

Plater's two styles complement each other: and it is sad perhaps that they haven't been combined in one play. The naturalistic plays are small-scale and lack the passionate energy of the documentaries: the documentaries are too vaguely polemical and lack the construction of the naturalistic plays. Plater is a prolific writer, whose talents seem hard to control. But his adaptability is shown by the skill with which he has adjusted to the various media: his contributions to the *Z Cars* detective series on television and his screenplay for D.H. Lawrence's *The Virgin and the Gypsy* have been rightly praised. This energetic eagerness to tackle any task which interests him helped revitalize the theatre in the northeast and suggests that in future his many abilities may be contained within undeniably good plays.

—John Elsom

POLIAKOFF, Stephen. British. Born in London, 1 December 1952. Educated at Westminster School, London; King's College, Cambridge, 1972–73. Writer-in-residence, National Theatre, London, 1976–77. Recipient: *Evening Standard* award, 1976; BAFTA award, 1980. Agent: Margaret Ramsay Ltd., 14-A Goodwin's Court, London WC2N 4LL, England.

Publications

Plays

Granny (produced London, 1969).
Bambi Ramm (produced London, 1970).
A Day with My Sister (produced Edinburgh, 1971).
Lay-By, with others (produced Edinburgh and London, 1971). London, Calder and Boyars, 1972.
Pretty Boy (produced London, 1972).
Theatre Outside (produced London, 1973).
Berlin Days (produced London, 1973).
The Carnation Gang (produced London, 1974).
Clever Soldiers (produced London, 1974).
Heroes (produced London, 1975).
Hitting Town (produced London, 1975; New York, 1979). Included in *Hitting Town, and City Sugar*, 1976.
City Sugar (produced London, 1975; New York, 1978). Included in *Hitting Town, and City Sugar*, 1976.
Hitting Town, and City Sugar. London, Eyre Methuen, 1976; revised edition 1978.
Strawberry Fields (produced London, 1977; New York, 1978). London, Eyre Methuen, 1977.
Shout Across the River (produced London, 1978; New York, 1979). London, Eyre Methuen, 1979.
American Days (produced London, 1979; New York, 1980). London, Eyre Methuen, 1979.
The Summer Party (produced Sheffield, 1980). London, Eyre Methuen, 1980.
Caught on a Train (televised 1980). With *Favourite Nights*, London, Methuen, 1982.
Favourite Nights (produced London, 1981). With *Caught on a Train*, London, Methuen, 1982.
Soft Targets (televised 1982). With *Runners*, London, Methuen, 1984.
Breaking the Silence (produced London, 1984). London, Methuen, 1984.
Runners (screenplay). With *Soft Targets*, London, Methuen, 1984.
Coming in to Land (produced London, 1987). London, Methuen, 1987.

Screenplay: *Runners*, 1983.

Television Plays: *Stronger Than the Sun*, 1977; *Bloody Kids*, 1980; *Caught on a Train*, 1980; *Soft Targets*, 1982.

* * *

Although Stephen Poliakoff had tasted early success, he first achieved wide-scale recognition with the two related plays *Hitting Town* and *City Sugar* in 1975. The plays attacked a series of readily identifiable targets—the tackiness and squalor of new inner-city developments, the alienating effects of fast-food shops and discos, the banality of pop radio D.J.s—in a way that suggested an over-rapid ingestion of some mammoth Liberal Studies course. The news about the awfulness and the emptiness of modern urban life was rather stale, and its articulation in the plays was often so glib as to suggest a series of carefully inserted diatribes for the characters to intone.

To dwell on them as plays about public issues is, however, to miss the point, for here, as so often subsequently, the rather crude political context is less the real subject of the drama than a convenient back-drop against which a series of strangely vulnerable odd-ball characters rehearse their particular desperation. Poliakoff's is a theatre of individual gesture rather than generalised political analysis. Although his plays appear to offer a series of thematically related attacks on contemporary society in loosely political terms, it is the emotional subtext that is most important. So, in *Hitting Town* it is the awkward movement of a lonely woman and her waywardly embittered younger brother through a desolate provincial night on the town and towards an incestuous bed that creates most of the dramatic tension; just as in the more recent screenplay for *Runners* it is the tentative efforts of the father to achieve some kind of relationship with his young runaway daughter that holds the attention, rather than the more general theme of hopelessness in the face of mass youth unemployment that the film presents initially as its primary concern. And indeed the daughter is not presented as a passive victim of circumstances. Like so many of Poliakoff's protagonists she is a survivor, shell-shocked but still in possession of a tentative resilience, surviving in a half-glimpsed London world of the dispossessed by distributing advertising literature.

Poliakoff returns continually to city nightlife. It is when his characters can be displayed at their loneliest—a situation which brings about the very existence of the all-night radio phone-in which provides the structural continuity of *City Sugar*. And it is this pervading sense of isolation in supposedly crowded locations that gives his plays their peculiar clarity. For Poliakoff's stage city is a curiously unpopulated one. In *Hitting Town* the sister and brother first visit a Wimpy Bar in which the only other person present is a waitress who will again be the sole witness to their dialogue in the shopping precinct. Whether other people are assumed to be present, and thus a further cause of the sister's worry at her brother's studiedly provocative behaviour, is deiberately left unclear, but no such ambiguity exists by the time the three of them arrive at a disco in which the only direct evidence of the presence of others comes from the voice of the unseen D.J.

Again, in *Favourite Nights* Catherine, a language teacher by day and escort by night, takes her sister and her Austrian businessman-student to a casino in which we otherwise see only a croupier, an American punter, and Alan, an official of the club. The absence of characters who must be understood to be present in night spots such as discos and casinos intensifies the way in which Poliakoff's characters see themselves as a part of, and yet separate from, the contemporary world. Catherine's manic attempts to beat the bank yet again in order to avoid the sexual compromise potentially involved in letting her client pay for their evening out is seen as if in a filmic close-up from which all the extras are excluded; and the attempts to communicate with her lover, Alan, in a locale in which contact between staff and punters is banned, is given a curious intensity by the presence of spy cameras unsupported by any other realised members of the casino management.

Even when Poliakoff moves out of a city environment, as in *Strawberry Fields*, he takes his characters in and out of service stations and lay-bys which are as unpopulated as his all-night bars and casinos. Kevin and Charlotte set off to meet other members of the fascist group to which they belong at pre-arranged points. In this instance the lack of contact with any other characters—with the exception of a police constable and a hitch-hiker, who are shot dead at the end of the first and second acts respectively—stresses their lack of contact with any reality, other than Kevin's half-remembered images of the 1960's, to support their ideology. They see themselves increasingly as latter-day Bonnies and Clydes, but the paranoia of persecution and pursuit on which their stance is built is undercut by the non-appearance of the police who are supposedly chasing them.

This thematic use of the journey is another manifestation of the characters as socially and politically rootless and unconnected to the details of everday life. In his 1980 television play, *Caught on a Train* Poliakoff uses a railway journey across Europe in which a series of characters—from a collection of anarchically politicised football hooligans to a young American thoroughly disenchanted with Europe—meet in transit without ever properly communicating as an informing metaphor for an account of the contemporary malaise. This film marked a major development in his work, and, interestingly, he was to return to the central motif of the train journey in what has been his most impressive stage play to date, *Breaking the Silence*.

For the first time since his earliest work Poliakoff moved the action into the past, Russia in the immediate aftermath of the revolution. Nikolai, a wealthy Jewish aristocrat based loosely on the playwright's own Russian grandfather, is turned out of his spacious accommodation and made Telephone Surveyor of the Northern Railway. To this end he is given a train in order to patrol a region where telephone poles have yet to be erected, all the time working single-mindedly towards his life's ambition of producing the first synchronised talking pictures. He is to be thwarted, finishing the play preparing for exile in England, his pictures as silent as the Northern region's telephone system. It is again a journey of isolation, in which all attempts at communication are literally and metaphorically denied; but it is also again a story of a survivor. Poliakoff for the first time properly united the individual concerns of the narrative with a larger thematic structure, and did so with an intensity of focus which places honestly his own uncertainties about commitment and the possibility of communication. There is reason to await with great interest the work of a writer who is, for all his prolific output, still a comparatively young playwright.

—John Bull

POLLOCK, Sharon (née Chalmers). Canadian. Born in Fredericton, New Brunswick, 19 April 1936. Educated at the University of New Brunswick, Fredericton, 2 years. Married Ross Pollock in 1954; six children. Actress in New Brunswick, and with touring group, Prairie Players, Calgary; head of the playwriting division, Department of Drama, University of Alberta, Edmonton, 1976–77; director of the Playwrights' Colony, Banff School of Fine Arts, Alberta, 1977–81; playwright-in-residence, Alberta Theatre Projects, Calgary, 1977–79,

National Arts Centre, Ottawa, 1981, 1982, and Regina Public Library, Saskatchewan, 1986–87; dramaturge, 1982–83, associate artistic director, 1983–84, and artistic director, 1984, Theatre Calgary. Member, 1979–80, and Chairman, 1980–81, Canada Council Advisory Arts Panel; Vice-Chairman, Playwrights Canada National Executive, 1981–83. Recipient: Dominion Drama Festival award, for acting, 1966; Nellie award, for radio play, 1981; Governor-General's award, 1981, 1986; Alberta Award of Excellence, 1983; Chalmers award, 1984; Canada Council Senior Arts grant, 1984; Alberta Writers Guild award, 1986; Alberta Literary Foundation award, 1987. Honorary Doctorate: University of New Brunswick, 1986. Address: 319 Manora Drive N.E., Calgary, Alberta T2A 4R2, Canada.

PUBLICATIONS

Plays

A Compulsory Option. Edmonton, Department of Culture, Youth, and Recreation, 1970; revised version (produced Vancouver, 1972; as *No! No! No!* produced Toronto, 1977), Vancouver, New Play Centre, 1972.

Walsh (produced Calgary, 1973). Vancouver, New Play Centre, 1972; revised version (produced Stratford, Ontario, 1974), Vancouver, Talonbooks, 1974.

New Canadians (for children; produced Vancouver, 1973).

Superstition Throu' the Ages (for children; produced Vancouver, 1973).

Wudjesay? (for children; produced Vancouver, 1974).

A Lesson in Swizzlery (for children; produced New Westminster, British Columbia, 1974).

The Rose and the Nightingale (for children), adaptation of the story by Oscar Wilde (produced Vancouver, 1974).

The Star-child (for children), adaptation of the story by Oscar Wilde (produced Vancouver, 1974).

The Happy Prince (for children), adaptation of the story by Oscar Wilde (produced Vancouver, 1974).

And Out Goes You? (produced Vancouver, 1975).

The Komagata Maru Incident (produced Vancouver, 1976; London, 1985). Toronto, Playwrights, 1978.

Blood Relations (as *My Name Is Lisbeth*, produced New Westminster, British Columbia, 1976; revised version, as *Blood Relations*, produced Edmonton, 1980; New York, 1983; Derby and London, 1985). Included in *Blood Relations and Other Plays*, 1981; in *Plays by Women 3*, edited by Michelene Wandor, London, Methuen, 1984.

Tracings: The Fraser Story (collective work), with others (produced Edmonton, 1977).

The Wreck of the National Line Car (for children; produced Calgary, 1978).

Mail vs. Female (produced Calgary, 1979).

Chautauqua Spelt E-N-E-R-G-Y (for children; produced Calgary, 1979).

One Tiger to a Hill (produced Edmonton, 1980; revised version produced Lennoxville, Quebec, and New York, 1981). Included in *Blood Relations and Other Plays*, 1981.

Generations (produced Calgary, 1980). Included in *Blood Relations and Other Plays*, 1981.

Blood Relations and Other Plays. Edmonton, NeWest Press, 1981.

Whiskey Six (produced Calgary, 1983).

Doc. Toronto, Playwrights, 1986.

Other Play: *The Great Drag Race; or, Smoked, Choked, and Croaked* (for children).

Radio Plays: *Split Seconds in the Death Of*, 1971; *31 for 2; We to the Gods; Waiting; The B Triple P Plan; In Memory Of; Generation*, 1980; *Sweet Land of Liberty*, 1980; *Intensive Care; Mary Beth Goes to Calgary; Mrs. Yale and Jennifer* (8 episodes); *In the Beginning Was*.

Television Plays: *Portrait of a Pig; The Larsens; Ransom; Free Our Sisters, Free Ourselves; The Person's Case; Country Joy* (6 episodes).

*

Manuscript Collection: University of Calgary, Alberta.

Theatrical Activities:
Director: **Plays**—some of her own plays, and *Betrayal* and *A Slight Ache* by Harold Pinter; *The Mousetrap* by Agatha Christie; *Scapin* by Molière; *The Gingerbread Lady* by Neil Simon; *The Bear* and *A Marriage Proposal* by Chekhov; *Period of Adjustment* by Tennessee Williams; *The Indian Wants the Bronx* by Israel Horovitz; *The Effect of Gamma Rays on Man-in-the-Moon Marigolds* by Paul Zindel; *Buried Child* by Sam Shepard; and others.
Actress: **Plays**—roles in some of her own plays, and title role in *Lysistrata* by Aristophanes; Nancy in *The Knack* by Ann Jellicoe; Amanda in *Private Lives* by Noël Coward; Miss Cooper in *Separate Tables* by Terence Rattigan; Bunny in *The House of Blue Leaves* by John Guare; Nell in *Endgame* by Samuel Beckett; Maddy in *All That Fall* by Arthur Miller; Polina in *The Seagull* by Chekhov; title role in *Miss Julie* by Strindberg; Alison in *Look Back in Anger* by John Osborne; The Psychiatrist in *Anges of God* by John Pielmeier; and others.

* * *

Sharon Pollock's early plays are typical of the large branch of Canadian theatre which directly explores the country's history, employing documents but moving from them in a subjective response to events and an investigation of character and political process. In a note to the text of *The Komagata Maru Incident*, Pollock posits that drama "is a theatrical impression of an historical event seen through the optique of the stage and the mind of the playwright."

Her first play, *A Compulsory Option*, is a rather simple exercise in farce which does not fit this documentary model and which has been overshadowed by the later plays which do. It is, however, an amusing play with witty insights, especially into predictable academic character traits.

In her second play, *Walsh*, Pollock began to experiment with what has been considered her typical form. In the first version of the play, for example, broadcasted speeches taken from historical sources preceded each scene to provide necessary background; this rather awkward attempt at documentation was replaced in the published version by a Prologue which occurs out of time and which shows us the eventual moral decline of the protagonist while simultaneously providing fewer but more easily assimilated historical details. The play recreates the dilemma of Major John Walsh of the Northwest Mounted Police who, in 1876, is caught in the middle between the Canadian government of Sir John A. MacDonald (symbolized by Queen Victoria as Great White Mother) and the American Indian nations as symbolized by Chief Sitting Bull. Sitting Bull is cast as a shamanistic figure, and when critics have sometimes found the character overly pious to the point of unreality, they have ignored the fact that he is intended not as rounded character in a drama but as mystical *exemplum* of his dying race, caught in a modern European world it cannot resist and true to the primitive but doomed values of the "Sacred Hoop" of life. Major Walsh, a strict militarist, attempts to extend white logic to the Indian view of the world and discovers that he does not himself wish to accept the detached political logic of his white superiors. He also discovers that considerations other than reason and fair play motivate the Canadian government. In one short and highly dramatic speech, however, he capitulates in the face of these discoveries, reverting to his background and his sense of duty, and by doing so seals his own moral doom. The young recruit, Clarence, functions in the play as a mirror to Walsh's spiritual decline, learning to see the Indians as human beings even as Walsh forces himself to manage them as political pawns. The interesting discussion which these two figures embody becomes a central theme of the play: the man without responsibility can remain idealistic and humane; the bureaucrat trapped between forces he cannot control but must administer suffers and often falls victim to the events of history. The staging echoes this stark reality—a few representative figures on an almost bare stage play out a tiny portion of the larger event and do so in an unadorned and internalized landscape.

The same trapped figure reappears in *The Komagata Maru Incident* in the person of the spy, William Hopkinson. In this play, Pollock returns to a form similar to that of *Walsh* after an experiment in history seen as burlesque in *And Out Goes You? Komagata Maru* concerns the historic refusal of the turn-of-the-century provincial government to allow a boatload of East Indian refugees to enter the country. The ship remains in harbour for two months, and the play explores the racial and legal aspects of the event. Sent as a spy, Hopkinson is forced to come to terms with his own racial self-image (he is half-East Indian) and with his attempts to survive in a white world by denying his cutural background. The rendering of Hopkinson is rounder than that of Walsh; the issues are not as clear cut and the protagonist fights not only the social values which surround him but the weaker side of his own personality. The stagecraft is similarly more sophisticated than it was in *Walsh*: the action moves back and forth from the ship to other locales; the secondary characters and motives are interesting in themselves; and the thematic action is less directly stated. The theme, though it centres on a serious local problem of a particular time, is universal enough to affect other audiences and its considerations of the roles of fear, envy, and ambition speak to us all.

Although these first plays concern the reactions of men to historical events, the later plays show a growing interest by Pollock in the reactions of women in general and herself in particular. Her most successful play, *Blood Relations*, a re-working of an idea she first wrote as *My Name Is Lisbeth*, is a study of the American murderer Lizzie Borden in the context both of her feminine struggle to resist a role carved out for her by 19th-century society and her attempt to discover her own identity as a agent with Will. The play makes its point not only in the text, but by a powerful staging in which Lizzie switches roles with her Actress friend and watches "herself" repeat the action which led to the murder. The question of her guilt is played out in this mirror world and extended through an elaborate pattern of blood imagery to include the audience. As part of the folklore which condemns her, the play suggests, Americans and even Canadians are as guilty of the murder as is Lizzie. This contention is supported not only in the double action, but in Pollock's most successful writing, a well-designed and intricate web of language which demonstrates a significant leap from the earlier dialogue.

The most recent major play, the semi-autobiographical *Doc*, continues Pollock's search into the feminine memories of family. Although the play has not attracted the critical attention of *Blood Relations*, it has reinforced the notion that Pollock has, in the later plays, found a more literary voice. The writing here is highly compelling, the speeches often beautiful in themselves, and the general tone softer and more intimate. By moving steadily away from the directly documentary and away, as well, from the heroes themselves (be they male or female) into the philosophical implications of her events and characters, Pollock is creating plays which exist beyond the confines of the history they employ; her new plays have become more important than the subjects which have inspired them.

—S. R. Gilbert

POMERANCE, Bernard. American. Born in Brooklyn, New York, in 1940. Educated at the University of Chicago. Co-founder, Foco Novo theatre group, London. Recipient: New York Drama Critics Circle award, Tony award, Obie award, and Outer Circle award, all 1979. Lives in London. Address: c/o Faber and Faber Ltd., 3 Queen Square, London WC1N 3AU, England.

PUBLICATIONS

Plays

High in Vietnam, Hot Damn; Hospital; Thanksgiving Before Detroit (produced London, 1971). Published in *Gambit 6* (London), 1972.

Foco Novo (produced London, 1972).

Someone Else Is Still Someone (produced London, 1974).

A Man's a Man, adaptation of a play by Brecht (produced London, 1975).

The Elephant Man (produced Exeter and London, 1977; New York, 1979). New York, Grove Press, 1979; London, Faber, 1980.

Quantrill in Lawrence (produced London, 1980). London, Faber, 1981.

Melons (produced London, 1985).

* * *

An American living in England, Bernard Pomerance found productions for his early plays in London's fringe theater of the 1970's. Yet it was his play *The Elephant Man*, produced on Broadway in 1979 subsequent to an English premiere and an off-off Broadway presentation, that established Pomerance as a playwright. An immense critical and popular success, the play won several awards including an Obie and one from the New York Drama Critics Circle.

The title of the biography-drama was a sideshow term applied to John Merrick (1863–90), a noted teratoid "freak" of Victorian England, so hideously malformed by an incurable and then unknown disease (now diagnosed as neuro-fibromatosis) that he was cruelly exploited as a traveling show oddity. Rescued from such exhibition by the anatomist Dr. Frederick Treves, he was given safe shelter in London Hospital, Whitechapel, which raised public donations for his maintenance and became his home for six years before his death in 1890. Merrick became a curio studied by science and visited by fashionable society who found him a man of surprising intelligence and sensitivity. Treves's published account of Merrick's life sparked Pomerance's interest in the subject.

In 22 often trenchant short scenes identified by title placard, *The Elephant Man* effectively employs a presentational and Brechtian style to tell its story. In Act 1 Treves encounters Merrick in a sideshow, later offers him shelter after a mob almost kills him, and determines with condescending compassion to create for his patient the illusion of normality. To this purpose, he enlists the actress Mrs. Kendal to befriend Merrick. The second act shifts focus from physician to patient as we watch the progress of Treves's social engineering. The "Elephant Man" fits himself into the role of the correct Victorian gentleman, but not without questioning the rules he is told to obey.

As the metamorphosis continues, fashionable society lionizes him for he lets them see him not as an individual but as a mirror of qualities they like to claim. Noting to Mrs. Kendal that sexual loneliness continues to isolate him from other men and that he has never seen a naked woman, the actress kindly obliges by baring her breasts only to be interrupted by a scandalized Treves who orders her out for her impropriety: she does not return. Interpreting the experience as defining his own limitations, Merrick realizes his normality has been an illusion, and he suicidally lets his huge head drop unsupported, causing strangulation. Simultaneously with his patient's development, Treves comes to question his principles and those of his class and painfully perceives Merrick's subtle exploitation by science and society. Pomerance is concerned with the theme that compassion, society and its conventional morality, and the idea of normality are at bottom destructive illusions.

Pomerance's play is at once theatrically effective, emotionally compelling, and intellectually provoking. Yet the drama has some problems. More ideas are unleashed than are developed, and some of these are overstated in the later scenes. Moreover, the shift in focus from Treves to Merrick and then back to the former near the conclusion unbalances the center of the play: the physician's loss of self-assurance demands more preparation. But such problems are minor when considering the play's overriding strengths.

As John Merrick is an exemplary victim of 19th-century greed, intolerance, and samaritanism, the aging Apache leader Caracol alias John Lame Eagle in *Melons* is a noble-turned-vengeful-savage exploited and oppressed by white civilization. Regarded as a messiah by his southwest Pueblo settlement, Caracol confronts his old U.S. Cavalry adversary now (in 1906) representing an oil company with drilling rights on the Indian's land, recalls past humiliations at white hands, and ultimately reveals his ritual decapitation of two geologists sent by the company to find oil on the reservation. This revelation causes at the climax both his death and that of his white antagonist. Caracol's doomed attempts to hold onto the ancient ways and his white enemy's callous materialism reflect the Indian's inability to accommodate the conquering culture. Pomerance employs as a narrator an Indian activist raised by whites who encompasses the tension between both cultures and is powerless to prevent the conflict's bloody conclusion. The narrator strides back in time to tell us the Caracol story in a fractured narrative burdened with commentary, flashbacks, and a lengthy narrator-Caracol debate which hinders the forward momentum and immediate action of the play. Many critics viewing the 1985 London production by the Royal Shakespeare Company faulted the play's structural and storytelling flaws, and the consequent shortcomings in overall theatrical effectiveness, while praising its ambitions.

Quantrill in Lawrence, an earlier play, displays similar deficiencies in craft and the playwright's characteristic attraction to historical settings and situation. This play combines a plot derived from Euripides's *Bacchae* with the burning of Lawrence, Kansas, in 1863 by the Confederate outlaw Quantrill. The liberation of women and of suppressed desires are the play's thematic concerns.

Pomerance is a talented playwright committed to tackling large themes. His work is notable for its continuing interest in biographical and historical sources as means by which to examine contemporary problems.

—Christian H. Moe

POTTER, Dennis (Christopher George). British. Born in Joyford Hill, Coleford, Gloucestershire, 17 May 1935. Educated at Christchurch Village School; Bell's Grammar School, Coleford; St. Clement Danes Grammar School, London; New College, Oxford (editor, *Isis*, 1958), B.A. (honours) in philosophy, politics and economics 1959. Married Margaret Morgan in 1959; one son and two daughters. Member of the Current Affairs Staff, BBC Television, 1959–61; feature writer, then television critic, *Daily Herald*, London, 1961–64; leader writer, the *Sun*, London, 1964; television critic, *New Statesman*, London, 1967, 1972, 1974–75; book reviewer, the *Times*, London, 1967–73 and the *Guardian*, London, 1973; television critic, *Sunday Times*, London, 1976–78. Labour Candidate for Parliament, East Hertfordshire, 1964. Recipient: Writers Guild award, 1965, 1969; Society of Film and Television Arts award, 1966; BAFTA award, 1979, 1980; Italia prize, 1982; San Francisco Film Festival award, for television play, 1987; Broadcasting Press Guild award, for television play, 1987. Agent: Goodwin Associates, 12 Rabbit Row, London W8 4DX. Address: Morecambe Lodge, Duxmere, Ross-on-Wye, Herefordshire HR9 5BB, England.

Publications

Plays

Vote Vote Vote for Nigel Barton (televised 1965; revised version produced Bristol, 1968). Included in *The Nigel Barton Plays*, 1968.

The Nigel Barton Plays: Stand Up, Nigel Barton, Vote Vote Vote for Nigel Barton: Two Television Plays. London, Penguin, 1968.

Son of Man (televised 1969; produced Leicester and London, 1969). London, Deutsch, 1970.

Follow the Yellow Brick Road (televised 1972). Published in *The Television Dramatist*, edited by Robert Muller, London, Elek, 1973.

Only Make Believe (televised 1973; produced Harlow, Essex, 1974).

Brimstone and Treacle (produced Sheffield, 1978; London, 1979). London, Eyre Methuen, 1978.

Sufficient Carbohydrate (produced London, 1983). London, Faber, 1983.

Waiting for the Boat: Dennis Potter on Television (includes *Joe's Ark*, *Blue Remembered Hills*, and *Cream in My Coffee*). London, Faber, 1984.

The Singing Detective (televised 1986). London, Faber, 1986.

Screenplays: *Pennies from Heaven*, 1982; *Brimstone and Treacle*, 1982; *Gorky Park*, 1983; *Dreamchild*, 1985.

Television Plays: *The Confidence Course*, 1965; *Alice*, 1965; *Stand Up, Nigel Barton*, 1965; *Vote Vote Vote for Nigel Barton*, 1965; *Emergency—Ward 9*, 1966; *Where the Buffalo Roam*, 1966; *Message for Posterity*, 1967; *The Bonegrinder*, 1968; *Shaggy Dog*, 1968; *A Beast with Two Backs*, 1968; *Moonlight on the Highway*, 1969; *Son of Man*, 1969; *Lay Down Your Arms*, 1970; *Angels Are So Few*, 1970; *Paper Roses*, 1971; *Traitor*, 1971; *Casanova* (series of six plays), 1971; *Follow the Yellow Brick Road*, 1972; *Only Make Believe*, 1973; *A Tragedy of Two Ambitions*, from a story by Hardy, 1973; *Joe's Ark*, 1974; *Schmoedipus*, 1974; *Late Call*, from the novel by Angus Wilson, 1975; *Double Dare*, 1976; *Where Adam Stood*, from the book *Father and Son* by Edmund Gosse, 1976; *The Mayor of Casterbridge*, from the novel by Hardy, 1978; *Pennies from Heaven*, 1978; *Blue Remembered Hills*, 1979; *Blade on the Feather*, 1980; *Rain on the Roof*, 1980; *Cream in My Coffee*, 1980; *Tender Is the Night*, from the novel by F. Scott Fitzgerald, 1985; *The Singing Detective*, 1986; *Visitors*, from his play *Sufficient Carbohydrate*, 1987; *Brimstone and Treacle*, 1987.

Novels

Hide and Seek. London, Deutsch, 1973.
Pennies from Heaven (novelization of television series). London, Quartet, 1981.
Ticket to Ride. London, Faber, 1986.
Blackeyes. London, Faber, 1987.

Other

The Glittering Coffin. London, Gollancz, 1960.
The Changing Forest: Life in the Forest of Dean Today. London, Secker and Warburg, 1962.

* * *

Dennis Potter presents, albeit with a great deal of brittle humour and some acerbic comments on present-day life in Britain, an arrestingly grim view of mankind's eternal plight. He shows how beings are condemned to journey through lives which are often physically or psychologically painful as they more or less consciously search for a glory that has departed, for a god whose existence they vaguely intuit though he remains tantalisingly aloof and who might release them from their agonising and incurable sense of disinheritance. Only human relationships can sometimes assuage man's grief, but all too often they only make it worse. Education may well have served to increase Potter's feeling of alienation from certain traditional values that might have supported him, and his attitudes have no doubt been shaped to some degree by prolonged and distressing ill-health. But if he had been a French intellectual, critics would have had little hesitation in referring to Jansenism with its uncompromising condemnation of moral laxness and, above all, to Pascal's doctrine of fallen man's perennial and insatiable craving to know a god who remains hidden despite all the efforts of the reason to discover him. Within such a context, the combination of metaphysical despair with a heartfelt attachment to socialist values would not seem in the least unusual either.

For the most part Potter has written for television, scoring several noted successes, among them the famous *Pennies from Heaven*, and, recently, *The Singing Detective*. Television is a medium that he handles with great skill, notably paring down his dialogue and leaving it to the screen image to convey much of what he has to say about the characters. Even such early works as *The Nigel Barton Plays* show many of his constant themes. *Stand Up, Nigel Barton*, presents the agonies of the bright boy at school, squirming with embarrassment when he finds he is becoming teacher's pet and realising that he is, in two senses, becoming alienated from the fellow members of his class. At home things are little better as Nigel's father, a Nottinghamshire miner, tries to make sense of his son's education, and Oxford is presented more as Babylon than as the new Jerusalem which it had seemed when viewed as the goal of every educational ambition. *Vote Vote Vote for Nigel Barton* takes idealism down another peg, going behind the scenes of contemporary British politics as Nigel stands as Labour candidate in a by-election which he knows he cannot win. Party loyalty and the sheer impossibility of denying the recent past impel him to go forward until at last despair wins the upper hand. Only then are human values reasserted, and in his hour of deepest self-doubt his wife Anne sees that, in a world where compromise is the pre-condition of such limited success as will ever be possible, Nigel has personal qualities that matter. Another television play, *Follow the Yellow Brick Road*, takes dillusionment further. Jack is an actor, and the sense that authenticity has departed from his life is neatly conveyed by his paranoid illusion that he is being continuously photographed, while his disgust at materialist values is expressed by reference to the futile banalities of the dog-food commercials in which he has to play a ridiculous part. In *Cream in My Coffee* the familiar device of juxtaposing two time-sequences as a couple visit a seaside hotel before their marriage and return 30 years later neatly demonstrates, in a play also notable for its evocation of period, another failure in human relations. With *Joe's Ark* Potter tackles the issue of death with a directness uncommon in television drama. As Lucy lies dying of cancer she talks the matter over with her doctor; he admits he has no cure, or explanation either; then he adds that "every doctor eventually expects his patient to *collude* with him," and in the acceptance of the inevitable there is some comfort.

Brimstone and Treacle was written for television in the mid-1970's, but the BBC refused to screen it until 1987. Potter was naturally outraged, but it is not too hard to see why there were doubts about screening a play in which a girl who has long lain in a coma tended by her distraught parents recovers consciousness after being assaulted and raped by a young man with a whiff of Satanism about him. All the same, as well as revealing Potter's theatrical skills, the stage version of the play bravely tackles a taboo subject and offers some paradoxical optimism at the end.

So too does *Sufficient Carbohydrate*. On a Greek Island an English couple are holidaymaking with an ill-assorted American couple who are accompanied by their callow son. The Englishman, Jack, has been forced into selling his food processing company to an American conglomerate, and now manoeuvres are going on to force him to resign the post he was fobbed off with after the merger. Junk food, summed up in vitriolic attacks on sodium monoglutamate, the additive that brings out the flavour, and on efforts to regulate the genes of mushrooms so that they breed identical in shape for easy marketing, is the focus for Jack's attacks on all that the modern world has to offer him. He drinks more than is good for him and equally often gets drunk on words, indulging himself in torrents of abuse about the sins and follies of the modern world. All the frustration of an existence that seems to have no solid purpose is brought out in the sexual tensions that are created, when Jack's wife, her patience exhausted, turns to the American while his wife casts her eyes on his son by a former marriage. Exceedingly funny in its lashing, highly articulate, and allusively literate humour, *Sufficient Carbohydrate* is deftly constructed for the stage, not betraying in any way that its author has had much of his experience in television. Played out amid the beauties of the setting on a Greek island and in a situation where, as it would in a classical drama, no outside force will come to complicate or solve the characters' problems, the human dilemmas hold our attention because the characters are so well observed. At first Jack irritates because of his self-pity, and his idealism seems close to self-indulgence and wishful thinking. Gradually his struggle becomes something grander as he sees, however dimly, a vision of values that will serve to nourish the human spirit in a materialistic age.

—Christopher Smith

POWNALL, David. British. Born in Liverpool, Lancashire, 19 May 1938. Educated at Lord Wandsworth College, Long Sutton, Hampshire, 1949–56; University of Keele, Staffordshire, 1956–60, B.A. (honours) 1960. Married 1) Glenys Elsie Jones in 1961 (divorced 1971), one son; 2) Mary Ellen Ray in 1972, one son. Personnel officer, Ford Motor Co., Dagenham, Essex, 1960–63; personnel manager, Anglo-American, Zambia, 1963–69; resident writer, Century Theatre touring group, 1970–72, and Duke's Playhouse, Lancaster, 1972–75; founder and resident writer, Paines Plough Theatre, Coventry, 1975–80. Recipient: John Whiting Award, 1982, 1986. Agent: Andrew Hewson, John Johnson Ltd., 45–47 Clerkenwell Green, London EC1R 0HT. Address: 136 Cranley Gardens, London N10 3AH, England.

PUBLICATIONS

Plays

As We Lie (produced Cheltenham, 1973). Zambia, Nkana-Kitwe, 1969.
How Does the Cuckoo Learn to Fly? (produced on tour, 1970).
How to Grow a Guerrilla (produced Preston, Lancashire, 1971).
All the World Should Be Taxed (produced Lancaster, 1971).
The Last of the Wizards (for children; produced Windermere, Cumbria, and London, 1972).
Gaunt (produced Lancaster, 1973).
Lions and Lambs (produced on Lancashire tour, 1973).
The Dream of Chief Crazy Horse (for children; produced Fleetwood, Lancashire, 1973). London, Faber, 1975.
Beauty and the Beast, music by Stephen Boxer (produced Lancaster, 1973).
The Human Cartoon Show (produced Lancaster, 1974).
Crates on Barrels (produced on Lancashire tour, 1974; London, 1984).
The Pro (produced London, 1975).
Lile Jimmy Williamson (produced Lancaster, 1975).
Buck Ruxton (produced Lancaster, 1975).
Ladybird, Ladybird (produced Edinburgh and London, 1976).
Music to Murder By (produced Canterbury, 1976; Miami, 1984). London, Faber, 1978.
A Tale of Two Town Halls (produced Lancaster, 1976).
Motocar, and Richard III, Part Two, music by Stephen Boxer (produced Edinburgh and London, 1977). London, Faber, 1979.
An Audience Called Édouard (produced London, 1978). London, Faber, 1979.
Seconds at the Fight for Madrid (produced Bristol, 1978).
Livingstone and Sechele (produced Edinburgh, 1978; London, 1980; New York, 1982).
Barricade (produced on tour, 1979).
Later (produced London, 1979).
The Hot Hello (produced Edinburgh, 1981).
Beef (produced London, 1981; New York, 1986). Published in *Best Radio Plays of 1981*, London, Methuen, 1982.
Master Class (produced Leicester, 1983; London and Washington, D.C., 1984; New York, 1986). London, Faber, 1983.
Pride and Prejudice, adaptation of the novel by Jane Austen (produced Leicester, 1983; New Haven, Connecticut, 1985; London, 1986).
Ploughboy Monday (broadcast 1985). Published in *Best Radio Plays of 1985*, London, Methuen, 1986.
The Viewing (produced London, 1987).
Black Star (produced Bolton, Lancashire, 1987).
The Edge (produced London, 1987).
King John's Jewel (produced Birmingham, 1987).

Radio Plays: *Free Ferry*, 1972; *Free House*, 1973; *A Place in the Country*, 1974; *An Old New Year*, 1974; *Fences*, 1976; *Under the Wool*, 1976; *Back Stop*, 1977; *Butterfingers*, 1981; *The Mist People*, 1981; *Flos*, 1982; *Ploughboy Monday*, 1985; *Beloved Latitudes*, 1986; *The Bridge at Orbigo*, 1987.

Television Plays: *High Tides*, 1976; *Mackerel Sky*, 1976; *Return Fare*, 1978; *Follow the River Down*, 1979; *Room for an Inward Light*, 1980; *The Sack Judies*, 1981; *Love's Labour* (*Maybury* series), 1983; *The Great White Mountain* (*Mountain Men* series), 1987.

Novels

The Raining Tree War. London, Faber, 1974.
African Horse. London, Faber, 1975.
God Perkins. London, Faber, 1977.
Light on a Honeycomb. London, Faber, 1978.
Beloved Latitudes. London, Gollancz, 1981.

Short Stories

My Organic Uncle and Other Stories. London, Faber, 1976.

Verse

An Eagle Each: Poems of the Lakes and Elsewhere, with Jack Hill. Carlisle, Cumbria, Arena, 1972.
Another Country. Liskeard, Cornwall, Harry Chambers/Peterloo Poets, 1978.

Other

Between Ribble and Lune: Scenes from the North-West, photographs by Arthur Thompson. London, Gollancz, 1980.
The Bunch from Bananas (for children). London, Gollancz, 1980; New York, Macmillan, 1981.

Editor, with Gareth Pownall, *The Fisherman's Bedside Book*. London, Windward, 1980.

* * *

David Pownall has written prolifically in the 1970's and 1980's: five novels, and numerous plays for the stage, radio, and television. Partly because few of the plays are published, he had little attention until the success of *Master Class* at the Old Vic in 1984. A second well-known stage work is an adaptation of Jane Austen's novel *Pride and Prejudice*.

A few of Pownall's plays are conventional pieces of storytelling, for instance, *Ladybird, Ladybird*, which shows Miriam's return to Liverpool after 50 years in the United States. A young war widow, she had escaped her environment, leaving a baby son behind. Now she comes back for a first meeting with her grandchildren, two men and a girl in a wheelchair, and the play shows the twists, turns, shifts, and complexities in these new relationships. Other stories set in the present are *Fences*, for radio, in which an upper-class girl falls in love with a stableboy, and two for television, *Return Fare*, in which a discharged mental patient goes to live with his brother, and *Follow the River Down*, where an old man relives his life as he follows a river to its mouth.

In Pownall's most distinctive plays, something quite unexpected breaks through, identifiable reality changing to fantasy or taking on ritualistic aspects. In the early, strange *How to Grow a Guerrilla* an English garden has run wild and turned to jungle. A moronic youth plays soldiers, and a take-over by gangsters is followed by one by black police. *Motocar* is set in Rhodesia ten days before independence (indefinitely in the future when Pownall wrote it in 1976), in a mental hospital run by whites for blacks. A suspected black terrorist, named Motocar, is brought in for psychiatric examination. A poetic ritual eventually develops in which the blacks force the four whites to relive aspects of the black experience of oppression.

Most of this group of plays uses historical events and changes and adapts them. *Richard III, Part Two* ingeniously weaves together George Orwell in 1984 and Richard III in 1484 by way of a board game about Richard, called Betrayal. Games and men must both be properly marketed for success—Richard failed in this, while Orwell knew it. The 30-character *Seconds at the Fight for Madrid* is set in November 1936. The audience meets English, Americans, Germans, a Russian, peasants, beggars, who discuss the fate of three showgirls and a musician who have blundered into this military zone. The picture of the Spanish Civil War is completed with appearances by the king, Franco, Hitler, and, since Pownall is ever imaginative, Don Juan and Don Quixote. *Barricade*, set in the Spanish countryside in May 1937, has anarchists joined by two gypsies and a young English army officer on a cycling holiday. The gypsies, in curious stylized scenes, attempt to awaken the Englishman politically. *An Audience Called Édouard* starts with the pose of two men and two women as in *Le Déjeuner sur l'herbe*; Manet, unseen, is imagined painting this somewhere among the audience. The chatter of the foursome is disturbed by two intruders from the river, one of whom is Karl Marx, indeed a disruptor of the harmony of La Belle Époque. Most difficult of all, in *Music to Murder By* a California woman musicologist conjures up the ghosts of Gesualdo, an Italian Renaissance composer, and Philip Heseltine, alias Peter Warlock, a scholar and composer who killed himself in 1930, as an illustration of links between creativity and violence.

A third group of plays treats historical subjects more objectively. *All the World Should Be Taxed* emphasises political elements in the Nativity story. *The Dream of Chief Crazy Horse*, written for schools with 70 parts, surveys ten thousand years of Red Indian history. In *Livingstone and Sechele* the young missionary David Livingstone makes his first convert, Sechele, chief of the Crocodile people, in South Africa, and is obliged to scrutinize his own faith. The other characters are their wives, submissive Mary and Mokoton, a fifth wife, scheming to keep her man from the outsiders.

Two plays of 20th-century local history were written for Lancaster. *Buck Ruxton* deals with two brutal murders by a Parsee doctor in 1935. *Lile Jimmy Williamson* looks at the man who was the "uncrowned king" of Lancaster from the 1880's to the 1920's. He was a millionaire linoleum manufacturer, and Liberal MP from 1892 on. Pownall explained that Williamson "monopolised the city's industry so that he could pay subsistence wages and control the movement of employment. . . . I wasn't grinding any particular political axe. I was fascinated to find out what happened and why. Especially why it was allowed."

The wide-ranging historical interests and the musical aspect of *Music to Murder By* come together in *Master Class*, set in the Kremlin in 1948. Stalin, shown as a subtle manipulator, and Zhdanov, a bully, summon two famous composers to condemn their kind of music and to require them to meet Communist Party expectations in future. Shostakovich wants to be loyal, to work within the Soviet system, while Prokofiev feels himself outside it. As Stalin has all the power, the conflict is uneven, and, from outside the drama, audiences may know that the composers survived this confrontation. The second half has additional interest when the men try to compose a Georgian folk-cantata to show their conformity. Though some critics have argued that Pownall trivializes the issues, *Master Class* poses important questions about art and politics, elitism and social purpose, and the distance between modern music and the general public.

Pownall is a man overflowing with ideas, eagerly moving on to the next work rather than perfecting the previous one. His difficulty in gaining wider recognition, though, arises from the demands he makes on his audiences, whether to care about controversy in Russia in 1948 or to go more than halfway towards him in the strange world of *Richard III, Part Two*, *An Audience Called Édouard* and *Music to Murder By*.

—Malcolm Page

RABE, David (William). American. Born in Dubuque, Iowa, 10 March 1940. Educated at Loras College, Dubuque, B.A. in English 1962; Villanova University, Pennsylvania, 1963–64, 1967–68, M.A. 1968. Served in the United States Army, 1965–67. Married 1) Elizabeth Pan in 1969, one son; 2) the actress Jill Clayburgh in 1979. Feature writer, New Haven *Register*, Connecticut, 1969–70. Assistant Professor, 1970–72, and from 1972, consultant, Villanova University. Recipient: Rockefeller grant, 1967; Associated Press award, for journalism, 1970; Obie award, 1971; Tony award, 1972; Outer Circle award, 1972; New York Drama Critics Circle citation, 1972, and award, 1976; *Variety* award, 1972; Dramatists Guild Hull-Warriner Award, 1972; American Academy award, 1974; Guggenheim fellowship, 1976. Agent: Ellen Neuwald Inc., 905 West End Avenue, New York, New York 10025. Address: c/o Grove Press, 920 Broadway, New York, New York 10010, U.S.A.

PUBLICATIONS

Plays

Sticks and Bones (produced Villanova, Pennsylvania, 1969; New York, 1971; London, 1978). With *The Basic Training of Pavlo Hummel*, New York, Viking Press, 1973.

The Basic Training of Pavlo Hummel (produced New York, 1971). With *Sticks and Bones*, New York, Viking Press, 1973.

The Orphan (produced New York, 1973). New York, French, 1975.

In the Boom Boom Room (as *Boom Boom Room*, produced New York, 1973; revised version, as *In the Boom Boom Room*, produced New York, 1974; London, 1976). New York, Knopf, 1975; revised version (produced New York, 1986), New York, Grove Press, 1986.

Burning (produced New York, 1974).

Streamers (produced New Haven, Connecticut, and New York, 1976; London, 1978). New York, Knopf, 1977.

Goose and Tomtom (produced New York, 1982). New York, Grove Press, 1987.

Hurlyburly (produced Chicago and New York, 1984). New York, Grove Press, 1985.

Screenplays: *I'm Dancing as Fast as I Can*, 1982; *Streamers*, 1983.

*

Bibliography: *Ten Modern American Playwrights* by Kimball King, New York, Garland, 1982.

Manuscript Collection: Mugar Memorial Library, Boston University.

* * *

David Rabe's corrosive portrait of American life evolves within a series of metaphoric arenas—living rooms, military barracks, disco bars—where his characters collide violently against each other, but where, primarily, they struggle with their own society-fostered delusions. The revised edition of *In the Boom Boom Room*, published in 1986, is mischievously dedicated to "the wolf at the door" but the creature is already well within Rabe's theatrical house and the psyches of those who dwell inside it.

Two Rabe plays, forming with *Streamers* what has come to be known as his Vietnam trilogy, burst onto the New York stage in 1971 when both were produced by Joseph Papp at the Shakespeare Festival Public Theatre. Rabe denies that they are specifically "anti-war" plays, maintaining that he neither expected nor intended them to wield any political effect, that they merely define a condition as endemic to the "eternal human pageant" as family, marriage, or crime. ("A play in which a family looks bad is not called an 'antifamily' play. A play in which a marriage looks bad is not called an 'antimarriage' play. A play about crime is not called an 'anticrime' play.")

But *The Basic Training of Pavlo Hummel* and *Sticks and Bones* portray the dehumanization and senseless horror of the Vietnam era with the sustained raw power now ordinarily associated only with certain films produced well after American troop withdrawal (*Apocalypse Now, The Killing Fields, Platoon, Full Metal Jacket*). Poor Pavlo Hummel's basic training functions as ritual throughout the play, contributing significantly to Rabe's theatrical stylization of an essentially realistic dramatic structure. Rabe's "realism" is invariably a realism heightened, stretched beyond traditional limits through (as in *Sticks and Bones* and *Hurlyburly*) dazzling language-play or (as in *Pavlo Hummel*) surreal fracturing of time and space and the ominous on-and-off-stage drifting of Ardell, a character seen only by Pavlo. Such blending of the real and surreal characterizes Rabe's style and serves both to rattle a viewer's preconceptions and to reinforce (as in *Sticks and Bones*) a given figure's alienation from those closest to him. It also prevents a play with a simple-minded hero from itself becoming simple-minded by complicating the theatrical conventions that develop Pavlo into an Army-trained killer who is ironically killed himself, not on the battlefield but in a brothel squabble. A sense of verisimilitude nevertheless underpins Rabe's stylistic virtuosity, the details of the Vietnam plays clearly emanating not only from the playwright's imagination but from his own Army experience in a hospital support unit at Long Binh as well.

While *Pavlo Hummel* focuses on pre-combat preparation for war, *Sticks and Bones* concerns its grotesque stateside aftermath. The naive Pavlo may be blind to the reality of war but David, the embittered veteran of *Sticks and Bones*, has been literally—physically—blinded *by* it. Torn by the atrocities he has witnessed, tormented by his psychological and physical infirmity, David must be expelled from the bosom of the family whose artificial tranquility he is determined to destroy. Pavlo knows too little, David too much, and both must therefore die.

Despite its intensely serious subject, the method of *Sticks and Bones* is often wildly comic, dependent upon the clichéd conventions of situation comedy which Rabe transforms into a vehicle for macabre parody of American delusion. The play resonates, however, with overtones of American domestic tragedy, notably Miller's *Death of a Salesman* and O'Neill's *Long Day's Journey into Night*. Generically complex, articulated in language that alternates between poetic and vernacular extremes, *Sticks and Bones* remains the most important American play to come out of the Vietnam experience.

Streamers, adapted to the screen by Rabe and the director Robert Altman in 1983, expands the thematic scope of the earlier plays but most resembles *Pavlo Hummel* in its barracks setting. The violence inherent in the military system is here expanded, linked by Rabe to institutionalized racism and homophobia camouflaged in the rhetoric of patriotism.

Hurlyburly, a title that reflects the chaos of its characters' lives, veers in a different direction. The word appears in the opening lines of *Macbeth*, which Rabe considered using in their entirety to name each of his three acts, respectively: "When Shall We Three Meet Again?," "In Thunder Lightning or in Rain?," and "When the Hurlyburly's Done, When the Battle's Lost and Won." Though he rejected the idea, he writes in the Afterword to the play that he "felt for a long time that the play was in many ways a trilogy, each act an entity, a self-contained action however enhanced it might be by the contents of the other acts and the reflections that might be sent back and forth between all three." (Rabe is an astute commentator on the art of playwriting—his own and others'. See also his Introduction to *Pavlo Hummel* and the Author's Note to *Sticks and Bones*.)

Like that of *Streamers* and *Pavlo Hummel*, the world of *Hurlyburly* is male-centered, but the barracks of those plays shifts to the living room of a small house in the Hollywood Hills, inhabited by Rabe's least sympathetic outcasts. Cut off from their wives and children by divorce or separation, the men of *Hurlyburly* waver violently between macho boasting and episodes of confessional self-loathing as they seek solace in drugs, alcohol, and uncommitted affairs. Their hostility toward women, whom they regard as "broads" or "bitches," masks their inability to reconcile male behavior codes learned as children with expectations demanded by their liberated partners.

These boy-men lack a moral center and represent for Rabe a characteristically American rootlessness.

Their anger is articulated in the stylized excesses and violence of the play's language, in the four-letter words that punctuate the dialogue but, more subtly, in the winding convolutions of speech: parenthetical expressions, self-interruptions, thoughts within thoughts, the repetitions and circularity that contribute to the work's considerable length and O'Neillian power. Eddie, Mickey, and Phil fear silence even more than they fear tuning into their own feelings, and thus keep talking, even if doing so runs the risk of accidental self-revelation. In this regard, an early stage direction notes that "in the characters' speeches phrases such as 'whatchamacallit,' 'thingamajig,' 'blah-blah-blah' and 'rapateta' abound. These are phrases used by the characters to keep themselves talking and should be said unhesitatingly with the authority and conviction with which one would have in fact said the missing word." The play's dialogue is extraordinary in its rich mix of funny, vulgar, savagely articulate language.

Rabe maintains that *Hurlyburly* contains no spokesman, that "no one in it knows what it is about." But the Age of Anxiety, documented by the disasters ticked off nightly on the 11 o'clock news, determines how his characters, and his audience, live. Rabe may claim that no single person in his play knows what it means, but *Hurlyburly*'s thematic core is expressed clearly in the drunken Eddie's furious lament for an absent God:

> The Ancients might have had some consolation from a view of the heavens as inhabited by this thoughtful, you know, meditative, maybe a trifle unpredictable and wrathful, but nevertheless UP THERE—this divine onlooker—we have bureaucrats devoted to the accumulation of incomprehensible data—we have connoisseurs of graft and the filibuster—virtuosos of the three-martini lunch for whom we vote on the basis of their personal appearance. The air's bad, the water's got poison in it, and into whose eyes do we find ourselves staring when we look for providence? We have emptied out the heavens and put oblivion in the hands of a bunch of aging insurance salesmen whose jobs are insecure.

Hurlyburly is Rabe's most intricate, verbally dazzling theatrical statement to date.

—Mark W. Estrin

RANSLEY, Peter. British. Born in Leeds, Yorkshire, 10 December 1931. Educated at Pudsey Grammar School, Yorkshire, 1942–49; Queen Mary College, University of London, 1950–52. Married 1) Hazel Rew in 1955 (divorced 1970); 2) Cynthia Harris in 1974, one son. Journalist, social worker, and development manager of a publishing company, then freelance writer. Recipient: First Commonwealth Film and TV Festival Gold Medal, 1980. Agent: A.D. Peters Ltd., 10 Buckingham Street, London WC2N 6BU, England.

PUBLICATIONS

Plays

Disabled (produced Manchester, 1969; as *Dear Mr. Welfare*, televised 1970; revised version, as *Disabled*, produced London, 1971). Published in *Plays and Players* (London), June 1971.

Ellen (produced Manchester, 1970; London, 1971). Published in *Plays and Players* (London), April 1971.

The Thomson Report (produced London, 1972).

Runaway (produced London, 1974).

Nothing Special (produced London, 1981).

Television Plays: *Dear Mr. Welfare*, 1970; *Black Olives*, 1971; *Night Duty*, 1972; *Blinkers*, 1973; *A Fair Day's Work*, 1973; *Bold Face Condensed*, 1974; *Mark Massey Is Dead*, 1974; *Big Annie*, 1974; *Jo and Ann*, 1974; *The House on the Hill*, 1975; *The Healing Hand*, 1975; *Henry and Jean*, 1975; *To Catch a Thief*, 1978; *Couples*, 1978; *Hospital Roulette*, 1979; *Minor Complications*, 1980; *Kate*, 1980; *Bread of Blood*, from the book *A Shepherd's Life* by W.H. Hudson, 1981; *Shall I Be Mother?*, 1983; *The Best Chess Player in the World* (*Tales of the Unexpected* series), from a story by Julian Symons, 1984; *The Price*, 1985; *Inside Story*, 1986.

Novel

The Price (novelization of television series). London, Corgi, 1984.

* * *

Peter Ransley's first two plays, *Ellen* and *Disabled*, are based upon actual persons. For a period Ransley was a social worker, and in his first play, *Disabled*, he writes about one particular old man. In *Ellen* he depicts a playwright from the North who is writing a play about Ellen, a tramp who lives on his doorstep. When the play was staged at the Hampstead Theatre Club the real-life Ellen came to see the play about herself.

The central character in *Disabled*, Barker, is a problem case, dirty, smelly, cantankerous; further, he is in a disputed area where three welfare districts meet, so that responsibility for him is passed from department to department. He alienates all who try to help him, task force, home help, male nurse. But, as Ted, a character in *Ellen*, remarks, "Help is a cruel word." Both plays are concerned with the need to consider individuals as people, and not as "cases." Again, as Ted says in *Ellen*, "Labels. That's what makes people acute cases. The labels people stick on them."

At the end of the first act of *Disabled* a young man enters, an unidentified social worker called Mike. Barker gets him to talk about his marriage, which is on the rocks. He has not had intercourse with his wife for three years (the same length of time that Barker has been without sex since his accident), and after her last miscarriage Mike's wife took up social work. Like the wife Clare in *Ellen*, she is a frigid and sterile person. When she appears at the end of the play she says to Barker, "You are my case," to which he replies, "I am my own case."

Disabled is about the reversal of roles; it probes and poses such questions as who is the helper and who the helped. As Barker begins to tap Mike's dilemma we realize that it is Mike who, psychologically, is disabled. And when at the final curtain Barker is left alone saying "Poor bastard," it is perhaps less of himself that he is thinking than of Mike. In another sense it is also both of them, for in this play, not wholly successfully, Ransley attempts to merge two styles, naturalism and fantasy. In a central scene (finely directed at the Hampstead Theatre Club by Vivian Matalon with Leonard Rossiter as Barker and Peter McEnery as Mike), Barker gets Mike to make up his face like a woman. (Barker used to be a ventriloquist and do an act on the halls with his wife, Maisie.) Empathetically, almost mediumistically, Barker begins to take on the voice of Mike's wife (whom he has never met). By assuming the persona of Mike's wife he is able to uncover Mike's neurosis. At the climax of this curious scene he persuades Mike to lift him out of his wheel chair and to dance with him. As they dance so "Barker's limbs come to life" (author's stage directions). The moment the wife enters the room Barker collapses and falls to the floor.

What the author is trying to convey is that it is Mike whose psychological limbs have been brought to life by Barker's insight and understanding. And in the process of having to think about another human being, Barker finds a role for himself—he, too, comes to life.

Ransley described, in an audience discussion about the play, how at one point in his relationship with the particular old man who provided the play's genesis, he lost his temper and hit the old man. He was at once ashamed of himself but the old man laughed and laughed. For the first time someone had responded to him not as a "case," as a disabled person requiring a special attitude, but as a human begin. By losing his temper Ransley has revealed a true involvement with the old man, they had begun to relate to each other as people.

Ellen is a considerable advance in complexity and skill. While developing further the major theme of *Disabled*, it also touches upon the dilemma of the provincial artist. At one point Ted says to the playwright "We've both come a long way since those old Brummy days. I wasn't sure it was right for you to come to London because it is more of a challenge in the provinces, and you do lose contact with the source of your material—aren't you losing contact with your sources, cockalorum?" to which the playwright replies, "Trust you to go straight to the heart of my neuroses."

One of the arguments for "Drama-in-Education" is that it provides an additional teaching medium, and as such enables any subject from history to geography to English or science, to be taught, or handled, dramatically. Similarly, Ransley's plays are essays in sociology presented through the medium of drama. Carefully and sensitively he dissects aspects of our society. In *Runaway* he brings under his microscope a working-class family in a remote part of Yorkshire who have fallen under the shadow of cancer. The father is an old trade union man who failed to expose the risks of a dangerous chemical used in the manufacture of car tyres in the local factory. The resulting cancer which has crippled his best friend Charlie now threatens him. His 11-year-old grandson, the runaway of the title, and the best written part, is at the centre of the conflicts within this family. The writing is spare, pared to the bone, and beautifully understated.

Ransley's is a quiet and thoughtful talent but one which has a way of lingering on in the memory, of exercising one's conscience in everyday life.

—James Roose-Evans

REANEY, James (Crerar). Canadian. Born in South Easthope, Ontario, 1 September 1926. Educated at Elmhurst Public School, Easthope Township, Perth County; Central Collegiate Vocational Institute, Stratford, Ontario, 1939–44; University College, Toronto (Epstein Award, 1948), B.A. 1948, M.A. 1949, graduate study, 1956–58, Ph.D. in English 1958. Married Colleen Thibaudeau in 1951; two sons (one deceased) and one daughter. Member of the English Department, University of Manitoba, Winnipeg, 1949–56. Since 1960 Professor of English, Middlesex College, University of Western Ontario, London, Founding editor, *Alphabet* magazine, London, 1960–71. Active in little theatre groups in Winnipeg and London: founder, Listeners Workshop, London, 1966. Recipient: Governor-General's award, for poetry 1950, 1959, for drama, 1963; President's Medal, University of Western Ontario, 1955, 1958; Massey award, 1960; Chalmers award, 1975, 1976. D.Litt.: Carleton University, Ottawa, 1975. Fellow, Royal Society of Canada; Officer, Order of Canada. Agent: Sybil Hutchinson, 409 Ramsden Place, 50 Hillsboro Avenue, Toronto, Ontario M5R 1S8. Address: Department of English, University of Western Ontario, London, Ontario N6A 3K7, Canada.

PUBLICATIONS

Plays

Night-Blooming Cereus music by John Beckwith (broadcast 1959; produced Toronto, 1960). Included in *The Killdeer and Other Plays*, 1962.

The Killdeer (produced Toronto, 1960; Glasgow, 1965). Included in *The Killdeer and Other Plays*, 1962; revised version (produced Vancouver, 1970), in *Masks of Childhood*, 1972.

One-Man Masque (also director: produced Toronto, 1960). Included in *The Killdeer and Other Plays*, 1962.

The Easter Egg (produced Hamilton, Ontario, 1962). Included in *Masks of Childhood*, 1972.

The Killdeer and Other Plays. Toronto, Macmillan, 1962.

The Sun and the Moon (produced London, Ontario, 1965). Included in *The Killdeer and Other Plays*, 1962.

Names and Nicknames (produced Winnipeg, 1963). Rowayton, Connecticut, New Plays for Children, 1969.

Aladdin and the Magic Lamp, Apple Butter, Little Red Riding Hood (puppet plays; also director: produced London, Ontario, 1965). *Apple Butter* included in *Apple Butter and Other Plays*, 1973.

Let's Make a Carol (for children), music by Alfred Kunz. Waterloo, Ontario, Waterloo Music, 1965.

Listen to the Wind (also director: produced London, Ontario, 1966). Vancouver, Talonbooks, 1972.

Ignoramus (for children; produced London, Ontario, 1966). Included in *Apple Butter and Other Plays*, 1973.

The Canada Tree (produced Morrison Island, Ontario, 1967).

Colours in the Dark (for children; produced Stratford, Ontario, 1967). Vancouver and Toronto, Talonbooks-Macmillan, 1970.

Geography Match (for children; produced London, Ontario, 1967). Included in *Apple Butter and Other Plays*, 1973.

Three Desks (produced London, Ontario, 1967). Included in *Masks of Childhood*, 1972.

Don't Sell Mr. Aesop (produced London, Ontario, 1968).

Genesis (also director: produced London, Ontario, 1968).

Masque, with Ron Cameron (produced Toronto, 1972). Toronto, Simon and Pierre, 1974.

Masks of Childhood, edited by Brian Parker. Toronto, New Press, 1972.

All the Bees and All the Keys (for children), music by John Beckwith (produced Toronto, 1972). Erin, Ontario, Press Porcépic, 1976.

Apple Butter and Other Plays for Children (includes *Names and Nicknames, Ignoramus, Geography Match*). Vancouver, Talonbooks, 1973.

The Donnellys: A Trilogy. Erin, Ontario, Press Porcépic, 1983.

1. *Sticks and Stones* (produced Toronto, 1973). Erin, Ontario, Press Porcépic, 1975.
2. *The St. Nicholas Hotel* (produced Toronto, 1974). Erin, Ontario, Press Porcépic, 1976.
3. *Handcuffs* (produced Toronto, 1975). Erin, Ontario, Press Porcépic, 1977.

Baldoon, with C.H. Gervais (produced Toronto, 1976). Erin, Ontario, Porcupine's Quill, 1976.

The Dismissal; or, Twisted Beards and Tangled Whiskers (produced Toronto, 1977). Erin, Ontario, Press Porcépic, 1979.

The Death and Execution of Frank Halloway; or, The First Act of John Richardson's Wacousta (produced Timmins, Ontario, 1977). Published in *Jubilee 4* (Wingham, Ontario), 1978; complete version, as *Wacousta!* (produced Toronto, 1978), Erin, Ontario, Press Porcépic, 1979.

At the Big Carwash (puppet play; produced Armstrong, British Columbia, 1979).

King Whistle! (produced Stratford, Ontario, 1979). Published in *Brick 8* (Ilderton, Ontario), Winter 1980.

Antler River (produced London, Ontario, 1980).

Gyroscope (produced Toronto, 1981). Toronto, Playwrights, 1983.

The Shivaree (opera), music by John Beckwith (produced Toronto, 1982).

I the Parade (produced 1982).

The Canadian Brothers (produced Calgary, 1983). Published in *Major Plays of the Canadian Theatre 1934–1984*, edited by Richard Perkyns, Toronto, Irwin, 1984.

Radio Plays: *Night-Blooming Cereus*, 1959; *Wednesday's Child*, 1962; *Canada Dash, Canada Dot* (3 parts), music by John Beckwith, 1965–67.

Verse

The Red Heart. Toronto, McClelland and Stewart, 1949.

A Suit of Nettles. Toronto, Macmillan, 1958.

Twelve Letters to a Small Town. Toronto, Ryerson Press, 1962.

The Dance of Death at London, Ontario. London, Ontario, Alphabet, 1963.

Poems, edited by Germaine Warkentine. Toronto, New Press, 1972.

Selected Shorter [and *Longer*] *Poems*, edited by Germaine Warkentin. Erin, Ontario, Press Porcépic, 2 vols., 1975–76.

Imprecations: The Art of Swearing. Windsor, Ontario, Black Moss Press, 1984.

Other

The Boy with an "R" in His Hand (for children). Toronto, Macmillan, 1965.

14 Barrels from Sea to Sea. Erin, Ontario, Press Porcépic, 1977.

Take the Big Picture (for children). Erin, Ontario, Porcupine's Quill, 1986.

*

Manuscript Collections: University of Toronto; Toronto Public Library.

Critical Studies: *James Reaney* by Alvin A. Lee, New York, Twayne, 1968; *James Reaney* by Ross G. Woodman, Toronto, McClelland and Stewart, 1971; *4 Canadian Playwrights* by Mavor Moore, Toronto, Holt Rinehart, 1973; *James Reaney* by J. Stewart Reaney, Agincourt, Ontario, Gage, 1977; *Approaches to the Work of James Reaney* edited by Stan Dragland, Downsview, Ontario, ECW Press, 1983.

Theatrical Activities:
Director: **Plays**—*One-Man Masque*, Toronto, 1960; *Aladdin and the Magic Lamp, Apple Butter*, and *Little Red Riding Hood*, London, Ontario, 1965; *Listen to the Wind*, London, Ontario, 1966; *Genesis*, London, Ontario, 1968.

Actor: **Plays**—in *One-Man Masque and Night-Blooming Cereus*, Toronto, 1960.

James Reaney comments:

These plays are interested in telling stories. I like using choral and collage techniques. The plays, particularly the children's plays, are based on watching children play on streets and in backyards. So—Plays as play.

* * *

When James Reaney turned to drama in the late 1950's, he had already won well deserved recognition as a poet with the volumes *The Red Heart* (1949) and *A Suit of Nettles* (1958), both awarded Governor General's awards. The early plays show Reaney struggling to master the elements of the dramatist's craft, a struggle that is not always successful. *The Killdeer*, first produced in 1960, reveals weaknesses typical of Reaney's work at this time—a sensational and melodramatic plot (a female prisoner, accused of murder, is made pregnant by the protagonist to save her from the gallows; Madame Fay is unmasked in a final courtroom scene); crude characterization; uncertain motivation. But if the other plays of this period—*The Easter Egg, The Sun and the Moon, Listen to the Wind*, and *Three Desks*—reveal similar weaknesses, they are also plays rich in poetry featuring a non-realistic approach to theatre which relies on non-linear plots, and the representation of mythic patterns through theatrical effects. If the reader or viewer is disconcerted by these early plays it is because there are so many unexpected and unprepared for shifts in Reaney's dramatic voice.

Some of Reaney's best work is represented by his 1960's plays for children—*Names and Nicknames, Geography Match*, and *Ignoramus*. *Colours in the Dark*, commissioned by the Stratford Festival and produced by John Hirsch at the Avon Theatre, Stratford, in 1967, is the best of these children's plays; it also appeals to adult audiences. It dispenses almost entirely with plot, motivation, and conventional structure replacing them with structural elements related to the play's thematic concerns—the letters of the alphabet, the books of the Bible, the seasons. The play's key structural element which gives coherence to the multiple incidents and to the rapid switches in mood is provided by poems which Reaney had already published and which are themselves given coherence by the dominant "Existence" poem. Central to these elements or motifs is the archetypal theme of a Fall and possible redemption.

Many critics regard Reaney's Donnelly trilogy (produced between 1973 and 1975 by Toronto's Tarragon Theatre) as his best work. His recreation of the events surrounding the 1880 murder of the Donnelly family of southwestern Ontario by Orangemen combines in a striking way history, folktales, myth, music, dancing, mime, and an inventive use of props. The first part, *Sticks and Stones*, is a vivid celebration of the Donnelly family and a powerful foreshadowing of their death. While rooted in naturalistic detail, the play suggests that the Donnellys are outsiders, as mythic in stature as Oedipus or the Ancient Mariner. The other two plays of the trilogy—*The St. Nicholas Hotel* and *Handcuffs*—are less effective because they repeat the essential story of the murder of the Donnellys. In them the mythic gives way to the naturalistic and drama is too often subsumed in literal documentary. But if the trilogy is marred by Reaney's excesses and if the published text seems confusing (nine actors must carry more than 70 roles), the true values of the work can best be seen in production where the complex nexus of symbols and the larger-than-life characters carry dramatic conviction. Reaney's plays are best understood *as process* rather than in terms of the printed text.

Following the Donnelly trilogy Reaney turned to dramatizing Canadian historical themes as in *Baldoon* (with C.H. Gervais), *The Dismissal, Wacousta!*, and *The Canadian Brothers*, the last two based on melodramatic novels by Major John Richardson, a deservedly neglected early nineteenth-century writer. These late plays have not been well received. In such 1980's plays as *King Whistle!* and *Antler River* Reaney has further reduced the scope of his themes by dramatizing incidents in the history of his own immediate neighbourhood—Stratford and London, Ontario; these plays have not gained provincial or national attention.

Although Reaney is generally held in high regard as a dramatist, his work is uneven revealing a conflict between his innate academicism and the populist theatricality to which he aspires.

—Eugene Benson

REARDON, Dennis J. American. Born in Worcester, Massachusetts, 17 September 1944. Educated at Tulane University, New Orleans, 1962–63; University of Kansas, Lawrence (Hopkins Award, 1965, 1966), 1963–66, B.A. in English (cum laude) 1966; Indiana University, Bloomington, 1966–67. Served in the United States Army, 1968–69. Married in 1971 (separated); one daughter. Playwright-in-residence, University of Michigan, Ann Arbor (Shubert Fellow, 1970; Hopwood Award, 1971), 1970–71, and Hartwick College, Oneonta, New York. Since 1985 member of the English Department, State University of New York, Albany. Recipient: Creative Artists Public Service grant, 1984; Weissberger Foundation award, 1985; National Play award, 1986; National Endowment for the Arts fellowship, 1986. Lives in Guilderland Center, New York. Agent: Susan Schulman, 454 West 44th Street, New York, New York 10036, U.S.A.

PUBLICATIONS

Plays

The Happiness Cage (produced New York, 1970). New York, French, 1971.

Siamese Connections (produced Ann Arbor, Michigan, 1971; New York, 1972).

The Leaf People (produced New York, 1975). Published in *Plays from the New York Shakespeare Festival*, New York, Broadway Play Publishing, 1986.

The Incredible Standing Man and His Friends (also co-director: produced Oneonta, New York, 1980).

Steeple Jack (produced Portland, Maine, 1983; New York, 1985).

Subterranean Homesick Blues Again (produced Louisville, 1983; New York, 1984).

Comment, music by Merrill Clark (produced New York, 1985).

New Cures for Sunburn (produced Albany, 1986).

*

Manuscript Collection: Lincoln Center Library of the Performing Arts, New York.

Critical Study: *Uneasy Stages* by John Simon, New York, Random House, 1975.

Theatrical Activities:
Director: **Play**—*The Incredible Standing Man and His Friends* (co-director), Oneonta, New York, 1980.

Dennis J. Reardon comments:

The central dynamic in my plays exists in the tension between what is "real" and what is "made up." I often mix carefully researched and recognizably topical material with the stuff of dreams, and I am seldom precise about where one mode leaves off and the other begins. My intent is to push beyond the suffocating ephemera of journalistic facts into a more iconic realm where the only reality is a metaphor.

* * *

Among the plays of America's contemporary dramatists, Dennis J. Reardon's work is distinguished by an energy that assaults the intellect as well as the emotions. With an audacity arising first from his youthful enthusiasm and then from a greater understanding of his craft, Reardon has experimented with theatrical effect in order to enhance his stories and to communicate his vision of man to audiences from whom he clearly demands intellectual involvement while besieging their senses with a variety of staged actions. Yet he remains basically a storyteller, albeit one with a bit of the Irish dark side showing. His subject is the plight of man immemorial, a condition he explores with all of the anxieties, frustrations, and reactions to the violent freedoms of the 1960's that marked his own maturing years. To date, his career divides into two distinct periods. *The Happiness Cage, Siamese Connections*, and *The Leaf People* brought him immediate recognition on Broadway as well as a sense of being both victor and victim in a world he did not fully understand. After a period of "self-willed" oblivion he began writing again in 1980 and has produced a half-dozen plays that reveal the vibrancy of his earlier work accentuated through experience and by the more balanced probing of the demons and saints, facts and fates, that persistently follow the modern Everyman.

The plays of Reardon's early period remain as daringly theatrical as anything he has written. Because he is always idea-oriented, however, his heavy emphasis upon a depressing view of humanity in these plays changes in subsequent work without bringing a complete denial to his philosophical stance. Feeling that he has "the power to bring an untold amount of happiness into this miserable world," Dr. Freytag of *The Happiness Cage* experiments upon his patients to find a cure for schizophrenia. Then one patient questions Freytag's assessment of his condition as "lonely, confused, frightened, and thoroughly unhappy" and asserts that is is simply a man, that he is a unique human being. Moreover, he wants to know what happiness means. Apparently sharing Nathaniel Hawthorne's definition of the "unpardonable sin," Reardon mocks the stupid cruelty of the veteran's hospital where Freytag works and the flagrant hypocrisy of its management toward the lonely, confused, frightened, and thoroughly unhappy doctor. The "brooding, barren immensity" of the Kansas farm in *Siamese Connections* provides a metaphor for the story of two brothers—the favored one who was killed in Vietnam and the one who survived but did not know how to kill the ghosts that made him into a homicidal monster, resentful of his brother, unable to escape, condemned. In *The Leaf People*, a most demanding play for actors and technicians, Reardon underscored one of the ironies of life while dramatizing mankind's murderous pathway to power. The action takes place in the Amazon rain forest where a rock star searches for his father, an Irish apostle named Shaughnessey who has discovered, and wants to save the Leaf People. Internal conflict prevents the Leaf People from protecting themselves from the invisible agreed of the outside world, the apostle dies, the son fails as a messenger of their danger, and disaster results. Eventually, new residents in the area say that they "never heard of any tribe called the Leaf People."

In all of Reardon's plays since 1980 there is a persistent probing of man's sensitivities and sensibilities, but his overall perspective is obviously comic as he writes about the human comedy. Laughter, however, is not his objective; understanding is. If people laugh, it is as likely the laughter of pain or startled hilarity, a dark and improbable humor. *The Incredible Standing Man and His Friends*, "a parody of dysfunction on both the societal and individual levels," may produce such confused laughter with its stereotypical characters in an absurd world. Who helps and what happens to the inarticulate man in a situation people do not understand? *Steeple Jack*, Reardon's most balanced view of life, dramatizes the trials of a young girl, tortured by fears and despairs, who is guided to hope by an illiterate busboy and a self-anointed apostle who preaches at perpetual man as he trudges on toward Armageddon. In *Subterranean Homesick Blues Again* the cavern tour guide, Charon, appropriately delivers his querulous tourists with ironic politeness to that place where "the turbulence and confusion of your days beneath the Sun are ended." Both *Security* and *Club Renaissance* in *Unauthorized Entries* (written 1984; unpublished) show the insubstantiality of modern times where a whimsical fate controls. A darker humor prevails in *New Cures for Sunburn* where the disastrous impulses of family cruelty and morbidity climax in a loss of human dignity for all. In opposition to such bleak pictures of grotesque man, *Sanctuary for Two Violins* (*Under Assault*) (written 1984; unpublished) repeats the hope of *Steeple Jack* as two old violinists heroically resist the assaults of life and survive to create the music described in the final line of the play, "How lovely!"

Having chosen the stage on which to project the conflicts and crises of modern man, Reardon finds that he has a great deal to say—about moral obligations, a mechanical society, illusions of security, destructive cynicism, fraudulence and perversity, the destructive forces of vulgarity. In order to underline his concerns, he is an explorer in contemporary theatre. Music plays an important role in his art—rock music, popular ballads, a sonata for two violins. Like many writers—such as Thornton Wilder whom he appears to admire—Reardon experiments with the concept of time and the complexity of its adequate expression on stage. In *Siamese Connections* the dead and the living exist together; in *The Incredible Standing Man* life hangs waiting for a traffic light to change; dance movements in *Sanctuary for Two Violins* project timeless assaults on life. In these experiments with time, some of Reardon's plays suggest the vertical approach of the Noh drama, unfettered by realistic representation or linear progression of thought. Space—on stage or imagined—also stabs Reardon's consciousness and moves him toward shifting scenes divided by numerous blackouts. His work is also marked by that relentless energy, now carefully orchestrated in such plays as *Steeple Jack*, *Standing Man*, and *Sanctuary for Two Violins*, to produce compelling and thoughtful drama.

—Walter J. Meserve

RECKORD, Barry. Jamaican. Born in Jamaica. Attended Oxford University, 1952. Lived in London until 1970; now lives in Jamaica. Address: c/o Tricycle Theatre, 269 Kilburn High Road, London NW6 7JR, England.

PUBLICATIONS

Plays

Adella (produced London, 1954; revised version, as *Flesh to a Tiger*, produced London, 1958).
You in Your Small Corner (produced Cheltenham, 1960; London, 1961).
Skyvers (produced London, 1963). Published in *New English Dramatists 9*, London, Penguin, 1966.
Don't Gas the Blacks (produced London, 1969).
A Liberated Woman (also director: produced New York, 1970; London, 1971).
Give the Gaffers Time to Love You (produced London, 1973).
X (produced London, 1974).
Streetwise, music and lyrics by Reckord (produced London, 1982).
White Witch (produced London, 1985).

Radio Play: *Malcolm X*, 1973.

Television Plays: *In the Beautiful Caribbean*, 1972; *Club Havana*, 1975.

Other

Does Fidel Eat More Than Your Father: Cuban Opinion. London, Deutsch, and New York, Praeger, 1971.

*

Theatrical Activities:
Director: **Play**—*A Liberated Woman*, New York, 1970.
Actor: **Play**—Guy in *A Liberated Woman*, London, 1971.

* * *

Barry Reckord's studies of the effects of exploitation are thorough and broad-based. In his early play *Flesh to a Tiger* we are let in to the struggle of people in a Jamaican slum trying to emancipate themselves from superstition without falling under white domination. Della is a beautiful but poor woman, and her child is dying. She has to choose between the local "shepherd's" magic and the English doctor's medicine. Half-fearful of magic and half in love with the doctor, she encourages him to be insulted in the end—for what he regards as his "weakness." She finally smothers the baby and stabs the shepherd.

But exploitation is basically a class evil, rather than a racial one, and Reckord illustrates this impressively in his most famous play, *Skyvers*, which is an authentic picture of students in a London comprehensive school just before they drop out. The beautifully preserved "cockney patter" is another triumph of the play. As with *Flesh to a Tiger*, it deals with the incipient violence which results from frustration and limited choice. The children are surrounded by parents and teachers who are social failures; and they dream about football stars, pop singers and big-time criminals. Even if we deny that such schools are "invented" to suppress talent, the effect is the same. And the sight of "criminally ill-educated" uncertain boys suddenly acting with confidence and more than a hint of violence when they get together as a group should be a warning.

Having looked at exploitation of the group, Reckord then examined the other side of the coin—liberation of the individual. In *Don't Gas the Blacks* he introduced a black lover to test the professed liberalism of a middle-class Hampstead couple, and succeeds in exposing the racialism of the one and in destroying the sexual fantasies of the white woman about the black man. In *A Liberated Woman* the experiment is taken one stage further, where it is the husband who is black and the wife's lover white. Does the wife's liberation extend to her having a white lover?

Reckord is also interested in establishing the link between social and economic exploitation and the obsession of blacks to ape white bourgeois values. The aping can be seen in a lighter vein in *You in Your Small Corner*, where it is the black bourgeois family in Brixton who are the custodians of "culture." It is they who are educated, who "talk posh" and the English who are down-trodden and "common." The black mother (the successful owner of a club) doesn't want her son to get serious about the local girls, but to wait until he goes up to Cambridge where he will meet "people of his own class."

In the television play *In the Beautiful Caribbean*, however, the mood is darker. Nothing much seems to have changed in Jamaica since *Flesh to a Tiger* fourteen years earlier, except that now the class and race battles are fought to the death. The society does really seem to be in disintegration because of the many special interests hostile to each other. There's the American exploitation of bauxite, the drugs industry, the subordination of the black working classes by the black middle classes, unemployment, the generation gap, and more.

This is not new in itself; what is new is the people's refusal to be abused indefinitely and this brings about the black power uprising. We trace this from One Son who is fired from his job as captain of a fishing boat, becomes interested in politics, and starts selling a black power newspaper. He is thrown in jail, beaten and killed because the police think he knows where the black power guns are hidden. His friend Jonathan, a barrister, and therefore middle-class, finally manages to forego white power temptations, and becomes a persuasive black power orator instead. And as so often happens, the end is bloodshed and defeat.

—E.A. Markham

RENÉE. New Zealander. Born Renée Gertrude Jones in Napier, 19 July 1929. Educated at primary schools to age 12; extra-mural study at Massey University, Palmerston North, from 1967: B.A. (University of Auckland) 1979. Married in 1949 (divorced); three sons. English and drama teacher in secondary schools, Wairoa, and at Long Bay College, Auckland, 1975–81; member, Womenspirit Collective, 1979–85, and Broadsheet Collective, Auckland, 1982–84; organised and led several writing workshops, 1983–85; playwright-in-residence, Theatre Corporate, Auckland, 1986. Actress and director with Napier Repertory Players, Wairoa Community Theatre, and in Auckland. Recipient: Queen Elizabeth II Arts Council grant, 1982, and award, 1986. Lives in Auckland. Agent: Playmarket, P.O. Box 9767, Wellington, New Zealand.

PUBLICATIONS

Plays

Secrets: Two One-Woman Plays (produced Auckland, 1982; revised version produced Auckland, 1987). With *Setting the Table*, Wellington, Playmarket, 1984.
Breaking Out (produced Wellington, 1982).
Setting the Table (produced Auckland, 1982). With *Secrets*, Wellington, Playmarket, 1984.
What Did You Do in the War, Mummy? (also director: produced Auckland, 1982).
Asking for It (also director: produced Kaikohe, 1983).
Dancing (produced Auckland, 1984).
Wednesday to Come (produced Wellington, 1984). Wellington, Victoria University Press, 1985.
Groundwork (produced Auckland, 1985).
Pass It On (produced Auckland, 1986). Wellington, Victoria University Press, 1986.
Born to Clean, songs by Jess Hawk Oakenstar and Hilary King (produced Auckland, 1987).

Television Plays: *Husbands and Wives* (*Country G.P.* series), 1985; *Beginnings and Endings*, *Strings*, and *Sheppard Street* (*Open House* series), 1986.

*

Manuscript Collection: University of Canterbury, Christchurch; Playmarket, Wellington.

Theatrical Activities:
Director: **Plays**—*What Did You Do in the War, Mummy?*, New Zealand tour, 1982; *Asking for It*, New Zealand tour, 1983.

* * *

Near the end of Renée's first full-length play, *Setting the Table*, a woman underlines both the reasons for the play's title and the metaphorical basis of all her creator's theatrical work: "Look we're setting the table. Right? All those women we know about and the hundreds we don't. Well. They got the ingredients ready and cooked the dinner. And now we've got as far as setting the table. Oh I know it seems as though we'll never sit down to the dinner-party. Well maybe we won't. But we'll get the table ready." The reference to Judy Chicago's extraordinary multi-medium art work proclaiming the achievements of women through centuries of male-dominated history is deliberate, but the day of such celebration in New Zealand is seen as distant. Renée's plays both chart and are part of the struggle that might bring it about, for she is the country's first playwright whose art cannot be separated from her stance as a woman.

Her work is fuelled by a common concern of feminist theatre: "I am interested in writing good roles for women about women we don't see on stage but who are all around us." Her rejection of female stereotypes has led to a theatrically realistic exploration of the domestic details of women's lives. Her first work, *Secrets*, consists of two dramatic monologues by older, poorer women. The first, a cafeteria assistant, sits trapped in her kitchen, brooding over a life obsessed by cleanliness only because she had been dirtied by the secret games her father played with her. The more optimistic side of the story is told with earthy good humour by a woman who walks out on her slavery by trashing the men's lavatory she has spent her life cleaning. It is a little present for her boss, which can be done because she has won a sweepstake. If *Secrets* presents Renée's only defeated woman, it is also the last time solutions are brought about by luck. There is a veiled autobiographical element behind the play for, until she started writing seriously in her forties, Renée had been employed in a host of often menial occupations. She even cleaned the lavatories in the Auckland theatre that was later to stage her plays.

Setting the Table reveals a deepening political vision that will have no truck with the myth that New Zealand is a classless egalitarian society set in a rural paradise. In another kitchen, surrounded by run-down city streets, four women, who have decided to devote a year of their lives to creating a refuge for battered wives, debate with passion ways of changing the world. One has turned violence back upon a rapist by typing a yellow ribbon around his blunt instrument and sending him to hospital with stab wounds. The police may catch her. A moment of powerful vengeance could undo all the gains won by communal love's labours—labours which may always have been lost, because they only patch up victims, while the system that breeds brutalities is left unchallenged. In *Groundwork*, drawing on her own part-Ngati Kahungunu background of which she was taught to feel ashamed as a child, Renée uses the conflicts generated by the 1981 Springbok rugby tour to shatter that other national myth of a racially harmonious land. This is another realistic play of ideas in which the central question is one of priorities. Must the Maori walk tall before the feminist revolution can take place?

With issues fiercely posed, but unresolved in the present, Renée has increasingly turned to traumatic events in the country's past: "It's a hard road remembering, but someone has to." Examining the Depression or the 1951 waterfront lock-out ("the most important struggle that has taken place in this country without exception"), she has focused on what the cracks in the fabric of society have revealed. Everywhere she finds strong women, unmentioned in conventional histories, enduring and triumphing over the bleakest circumstances, but the struggle always engenders the need for another victory. In her most important play, *Wednesday to Come*, four generations of women respond to a husband's suicide caused by the Depression. Speaking for her author, the oldest, Granna, explains to her great-granddaughter "what it's always about": "It's asking and getting no for an answer. And then asking a bit louder and a bit louder. And then—sometimes—if you're lucky—you get a little bit of what you asked for and then—it starts all over again. And you wonder—you do Jeannie—do they ever listen?" *Pass It On*, which presents the dockers' confrontation with the government, shows Jeannie carrying on the struggle 20 years later.

Renée started by writing discussion dramas in which her warm faith in women was presented with striking economy. Her dialogue has remained sparse as characters are born in the silences that surround their words, but progressively her ideas have been incorporated into the theatrical structure of the plays. The fragmentation caused by industrial turmoil breaks *Pass It On* into 29 scenes as action takes place almost simultaneously at different ends of the city. More successfully in *Wednesday to Come*, the audience is shown through a mass of realistic detail that, while women never cease from working (scones are even mixed and baked on stage), men are theatrically prone to make egotistical dramas out of their lives and then to demand the starring roles even after they are dead. The husband was a working-class playboy of his time. Now, defeated by degrading labour in the relief camps, he has killed himself. His coffin is brought home where it dominates the stage until, at the end of the play, it is borne proudly out through the audience. This is a glorious histrionic martyrdom, but the play, like its author, knows that true value lies in the less flashy lives of generations of women who are so often found in a kitchen.

—Sebastian Black

RHONE, Trevor D. Jamaican. Born in Kingston, 24 March 1940. Educated at a school in St. Catherine; Beckford and Smith's School (now Jago High School), Spanish Town, 1952–57; Rose Bruford College, Sidcup, Kent, 1960–63. Has one daughter. Writer, Jamaican Broadcasting Corporation, Kingston, 1958–60; teacher in Jamaica, 1963–64 and 1965–69; actor in England, 1964–65; founder, Theatre '77 (Barn Theatre), Kingston, 1965. Since 1969 free-lance writer. Address: c/o Drumbeat Series, Longman Group Ltd., 5 Bentinck Street, London W1M 5RN, England.

PUBLICATIONS

Plays

Smile Orange (produced Kingston, 1971; Waterford, Connecticut, and London, 1972). Included in *Old Story Time and Other Plays*, 1981.
The Web (produced Waterford, Connecticut, 1972).
School's Out (produced Kingston, 1975; London, 1986). Included in *Old Story Time and Other Plays*, 1981.
Old Story Time (also director: produced Nassau, 1979; London, 1984). Included in *Old Story Time and Other Plays*, 1981.
Old Story Time and Other Plays. London, Longman, 1981.
Two Can Play (produced London, 1983; New York, 1985). With *School's Out*, London, Longman, 1986; published separately, Lexington, Kentucky, KET, 1986.

Screenplay: *Smile Orange*, 1974.

*

Theatrical Activities:
Director: **Play**—*Old Story Time*, Nassau, 1979, and London, 1984. **Film**—*Smile Orange*, 1974.

Actor: **Play**—Russ Dacres in *School's Out*, Kingston, 1975.

*   *   *

Filmmaker, actor, and teacher of acting, Trevor Rhone is Jamaica's best known playwright and one of the few Caribbean dramatists to be often performed outside the region. Having started the Barn Theatre in Kingston, he has a highly professional understanding of theatre economics, and the technical abilities and limitations of most drama groups. Written for small casts, using readily available stage props, requiring few set changes, his plays can be easily and inexpensively performed. They are entertaining while treating serious social problems. Rhone writes good acting parts and has a talent for suggesting dialect without clouding meaning for standard-English speakers. He has a sense of what makes people tick, how they behave towards each other. While he shows people influenced by their environment, their problems are personal and require will to solve. The plays are Jamaican in subject matter and nationalist in perspective, but their themes are universal. Rhone is especially concerned with domination on a personal and national level, and with the ways self-interest destroys communal values.

Rhone's first success, *Smile Orange*, is built upon a contrast between the real and the tourist Jamaica, as found at a third-rate Montego Bay hotel. Language is representative of cultural and racial identification, as is shown by the hotel telephone operator's shift from the standard English she uses on her job to the dialect forms she uses in conversation with friends. "Me see one or two dry-up looking white people but [*hiss*] is today dem say di season start proper." In an impoverished society, both personal and national relationships are established by financial considerations: "Is money I looking. Him have nutten to offer." As the workers feel dependent on the American tourists, they suffer from racial self-hatred: "di boss man have a black man out front as Assistant Manager. Di tourist don't like dat, you know, and I don't blame dem." A satire about the corrupting effect of the tourist economy on Jamaica, *Smile Orange* shows a society in which self-respect and sense of community have been lost, with the result that the characters feel trapped by circumstances, exploit each other, and look towards America for their redemption. "When it get down to di nitty-gritty is each man for himself." Driven rather by self-interest than vocation, dignity, ethics, or sense of community, the hotel employees are unreliable, even malicious. In the background a band plays cheerful music, but tableware is polished with spit and banana skins are left dangerously on the floor.

School's Out, a satirical exposé of the failure of local schools since independence, offers a disillusioned view of Jamaica and of human motives. The missionary school, representative of the nation, is perhaps best symbolized by the non-functioning toilet to which the characters often refer. Overflowing for weeks, its stink pervades the school but no one will have it fixed as it is the responsibility of the apparently absent headmaster, whose unopened door is always present on stage. The teaching staff and chaplain are late to their classes, find excuses to dismiss them early and by not doing their duty have left the school's canteen and other activities in the control of unsupervised students whose hooliganism the teachers then use to justify themselves. When a new white teacher begins to restore order, he is accused of asserting himself and of racial pride. As the play's symbolism suggests, he is a Christ-like leader whose involvement cuts through the stereotypes and who looks after the students' personal and moral welfare. Seeing their sinecures threatened, the other teachers start rumours of his sexual involvement with the students, which lead to his resignation and the return of disorder and incompetence.

In *School's Out* the staff are divided by politics. The conservatives do nothing to prevent a drop in standards while praising the past when the school had high standards and excluded the masses. Meanwhile the semi-literate products of recent mass education drive out the good, and hire others like themselves. The obvious analogy is to Jamaican society since independence. The evil of self-interest triumphs over national reform.

The relationships between the political, racial, moral, and religious aspects of Rhone's writing are clear in *Old Story Time*, where a black mother's initial hatred for and eventual acceptance of her black daughter-in-law is symbolic of Jamaica's coming to terms with itself and overcoming both black and colonial self-hatred. As in the other plays relations between characters are illustrative of the national mentality. The play covers 40 years of Jamaican social history, from a time when anything black was condemned as inferior, to a present when many of the same prejudices linger on under the surface of national independence. The villain is "a high brown man," who ruthlessly pursues his own self-interest and cheats others, especially trusting blacks.

The use of a *conteur* in *Old Story Time* is a technically effective way of moving back and forth in time. While the use of a traditional oral literary frame reinforces the play's concern with the revaluation of blackness, it allows dramatization of revelations about the past. Similarly, the use of obeah by the mother, the highly educated son's belief in its effectiveness, and the exorcism, half-obeah and half-Christian, of the mother's hatred are both psychologically probable and a statement about African survivals in the New World. The ending is sentimental, but the ceremonial exorcism is good spectacle.

Set in Kingston in the late 1970's, when politics has resulted in a near civil war, with people locking themselves into their houses while the sounds of machine guns are heard in the near distance, *Two Can Play* translates women's liberation to a Jamaican context. The national situation has contributed to the crisis of a marriage in which the husband has dominated, exploited, and humiliated his wife, leaving her sexually and emotionally unsatisfied. Unable to jump the legal and financial hurdles to emigrate to America, the husband collapses into futile incompetence, whereas the wife proves to be daring, disciplined, and quick-thinking. Having reached America on her own, she returns to Jamaica, now conscious of her abilities, to demand that her husband treat her better. To a nation where violence appears to have destroyed society, America may seem the promised land, but by the play's conclusion, when the husband and wife can emigrate to the United States, they have learned that American cities are also dangerously violent and marked by racial prejudice and conflict.

—Bruce King

RIBMAN, Ronald (Burt). American. Born in New York City, 28 May 1932. Educated at Brooklyn College, New York, 1950–51; University of Pittsburgh, B.B.A. 1954, M.Litt. 1958, Ph.D. 1962. Served in the United States Army, 1954–56. Married Alice Rosen in 1967; one son and one daughter. Assistant Professor of English, Otterbein College, Westerville, Ohio, 1962–63. Recipient: Obie award, 1966; Rockefeller grant, 1966, 1975; Guggenheim fellowship, 1970; National Endowment for the Arts grant, 1974; Creative Artists Public Service grant, 1976; Dramatists Guild Hull-Warriner Award, 1977; Playwrights U.S.A. award, 1984; National Endowment for the Arts fellowship, 1986. Lives in South Salem, New York. Agent: Flora Roberts Inc., 157 West 57th Street, New York, New York 10019, U.S.A.

PUBLICATIONS

Plays

Harry, Noon and Night (produced New York, 1965). With *The Journey of the Fifth Horse*, Boston, Little Brown, 1967.
The Journey of the Fifth Horse, based in part on "The Diary of a Superfluous Man" by Turgenev (produced New York, 1966; London, 1967). With *Harry, Noon and Night*, Boston, Little Brown, 1967; published separately, London, Davis Poynter, 1974.
The Final War of Olly Winter (televised 1967). Published in *Great Television Plays*, New York, Dell, 1969.
The Ceremony of Innocence (produced New York, 1967). New York, Dramatists Play Service, 1968.
Passing Through from Exotic Places (includes *The Son Who Hunted Tigers in Jakarta, Sunstroke, The Burial of Esposito*) (produced New York, 1969). New York, Dramatists Play Service, 1970.
The Most Beautiful Fish (televised 1969). Published in *New York Times*, 23 November 1969.
Fingernails Blue as Flowers (produced New York, 1971). Published in *The American Place Theatre*, edited by Richard Schotter, New York, Dell, 1973.
A Break in the Skin (produced New Haven, Connecticut, 1972; New York, 1973).
The Poison Tree (produced Philadelphia, 1973; revised version produced Philadelphia, 1975; New York, 1976). New York, French, 1977.
Cold Storage (produced New York, 1977; London, 1986). New York, French, 1978.
Five Plays (includes *Cold Storage; The Poison Tree; The Ceremony of Innocence; The Journey of the Fifth Horse; Harry, Noon and Night*). New York, Avon, 1978.
Buck (produced New York, 1983). New York, Theatre Communications Group, 1983.

Screenplay: *The Angel Levine*, with Bill Gunn, 1970.

Television Plays: *The Final War of Olly Winter*, 1967; *The Most Beautiful Fish*, 1969; *Seize the Day*, from the novella by Saul Bellow, 1985.

*

Bibliography: in *The Work of Ronald Ribman: The Poet as Playwright* by Susan H. Dietz, University of Pennsylvania, unpublished dissertation, 1974.

Manuscript Collection: New York Public Library.

Critical Studies: "Journey and Arrival of a Playwright" by Robert Brustein, in *New Republic* (Washington, D.C.), 7 May 1966; *The Jumping-Off Place*, New York, Harcourt Brace, 1969, and "Ronald Ribman: The Artist of the Failure Clowns," in *Essays on Contemporary American Drama* edited by Hedwig Bock and Albert Wertheim, Munich, Hueber, 1981, both by Gerald Weales; articles by Anne Roiphe, 25 December 1977, and by Leslie Bennetts, 6 March 1983, both in *New York Times* theatre section; *Harvard Guide to Contemporary American Writing* edited by Daniel Hoffman, Cambridge, Massachusetts, Harvard University Press, 1979.

* * *

Ronald Ribman is a difficult playwright to characterize. The surface dissimilarity among his works gives each of his plays a voice of its own, but all are variations on the dramatist's own voice—on his preoccupation with recurrent themes, on his commitment to language that is at once complex and dramatic. Perhaps because he is also a poet (although not so good a poet as he is a playwright), he is essentially a verbal dramatist, fascinated by the nuances of language—the way a well-chosen adverb can alter the first meaning of a sentence, the way an extended metaphor can come to characterize its speaker through both content and style. Yet he is aware of and, often in key scenes, dependent on visual images that give particular force to the words; consider the scene in *Harry, Noon and Night* in which Immanuel cleans a fish while sparring verbally with Archer, the aggressive chop-chop-chop altering seemingly innocent statements.

The chief thematic concern of the playwright is with man caught between aspiration and possibility. "Well, all my characters are crying out against the universe they can't alter," he once told an interviewer, but the inalterable force varies from play to play. Sometimes it seems to lie primarily within the character (Harry of *Harry, Noon and Night*), sometimes to be dictated by the assumptions of society (the prisoners in *The Poison Tree*). More often it is a combination of these two. Finally, in *Cold Storage*, it lies in the fact of human mortality.

His first two plays—*Harry, Noon and Night* and *The Journey of the Fifth Horse*—deal with "failure clowns," "fifth horses," to borrow the "loser" images of the two plays. Underlying *Harry* is a conventional psychological drama about a young man perpetually in the shadow of his successful older brother. Yet, Harry can be victimizer as well as victim, and so can Immanuel, who routs the brother in Scene 2, but is himself the captive clown of Scene 3. Add the German setting with its references to the Nazis, "the Dachau circus," and the metaphor of the failure clown spreads to suggest the human condition. All this in a very funny comedy. The fifth horses of *Journey*, which grows out of Turgenev's "The Diary of a Superfluous Man," are Turgenev's hero and the publisher's reader who finally rejects the manuscript; the second character is only an ironic note in the original story, but Ribman creates him fully, his real and his fantasy lives, and lets him recognize and cry out against the identification he feels with the man whose diary he is reading.

With his television play, *The Final War of Olly Winter*, and *The Ceremony of Innocence*, Ribman seemed to be moving into overt social drama, into a direct pacifist statement brought on by the general distress with the American presence in Vietnam. Similarly *The Poison Tree* seemed to some an explicit commentary on prison conditions and racial bigotry, a reading that perhaps contributed to its commercial failure as the theater moved away from the social/political concerns of the 1960's. Although the social implications of these dramas are real enough, they are plays that deal with familiar Ribman themes and display the complexities of structure and language already familiar from the early plays. *The Ceremony of Innocence* is an historical drama which uses flashback scenes to explain why Ethelred will not come out of seclusion to defend England against the Danish invasion. He prefers to stand aside from a society which, mouthing the rhetoric of honor, chooses war over peace and special privilege over public welfare; still, the failures of his society—so forcefully expressed in a speech of the disillusioned idealist Kent—are reflections of Ethelred's inability to rule even himself, giving way, as he does at crucial moments, to an anger that belies his faith in the rational mind. In *The Poison Tree*, in which the prison is largely peopled by black convicts and white guards, Ribman develops his titular metaphor to show that all the characters are creatures of the situation. The manipulative guard who is his own victim, too easily a caricature in production, is actually the Kent of this play, finally as helpless as the leading prisoner, the one who prefers feeling to dehumanizing theory, but is incapable of non-violent, regenerative action.

With *Cold Storage* Ribman returned to the exuberance, the inventiveness that characterized *Harry, Noon and Night*. Primarily a two-character play, *Cold Storage* is set in the terminal ward of a New York hospital. Given that setting, it is perhaps surprising to find such vitality, so much luxury of language, such wild humor, but these qualities are as important to the play's content as they are to its texture. Parmigian, a dying fruit merchant with an incredible frame of reference and a compulsive need to talk (silence is death), assaults Landau, gets him to release his secret guilt at having survived the Holocaust. As Landau learns to live, Parmigian comes to accept the fact of death. The play ends with a community of two, a conspiracy of sorts against the human condition, and leaves the audience with a marvelously replenishing sense of life.

The "crying out" is more muted in *Buck* and the unproduced *Sweettable at the Richelieu*, but they provide opposition to the inevitable—the one an image, the other a character. The titular protagonist of *Buck*, a director for a sex-and-violence television company, fails to humanize his product, to modify the cruel behavior of his colleagues, to solve his offstage personal problems, but the play ends with the new snow falling, bringing the promise of cleansing even though it will quickly turn to dirt and slush. As the patrons of the Richelieu, a metaphorical luxury spa, exit for the last sleighride, the less self-obsessed of the guests is defined as the Lady of Enduring Hope although she knows that no one can stay long enough to taste all the glories on the sweet table.

—Gerald Weales

RICHARDSON, Jack (Carter). American. Born in New York City, 18 February 1935. Educated at Columbia University, New York, 1954–57, B.A. (summa cum laude) in philosophy 1957 (Phi Beta Kappa); University of Munich (Adenauer Fellow), 1958. Served in the United States Army, in France and Germany, 1951–54. Married Anne Grail Roth in 1957; one daughter. Recipient: Brandeis University Creative Arts Award, 1963. Address: c/o Simon and Schuster, 1230 Avenue of the Americas, New York, New York 10020, U.S.A.

PUBLICATIONS

Plays

The Prodigal (produced New York, 1960). New York, Dutton, 1960.
Gallows Humor (produced New York, 1961; Edinburgh, 1964). New York, Dutton, 1961.
Lorenzo (produced New York, 1963).
Xmas in Las Vegas (produced New York, 1965). New York, Dramatists Play Service, 1966.
As Happy as Kings (produced New York, 1968).
Juan Feldman, in *Pardon Me, Sir, But Is My Eye Hurting Your Elbow?*, edited by Bob Booker and George Foster. New York, Geis, 1968.

Novel

The Prison Life of Harris Filmore. London, Eyre and Spottiswoode, 1961; Greenwich, Connecticut, New York Graphic Society, 1963.

Other

Memoir of a Gambler. New York, Simon and Schuster, 1979; London, Cape, 1980.

*

Theatrical Activities:
Actor: **Film**—*Beyond the Law*, 1968.

* * *

At the outset of the 1960's four young playwrights, Edward Albee, Jack Richardson, Arthur Kopit, and Jack Gelber, held the attention of the American theatre as its best prospects for the future since the postwar emergence of Tennessee Williams and Arthur Miller. The four became acquainted, and in the season of 1962–63 they were simultaneously active in the Playwrights' Unit of the Actors Studio in New York. Jack Richardson's particular position in this rather brilliant quartet was achieved by the success of two splendid plays produced off-Broadway, *The Prodigal*, his retelling in his own contemporary idiom of the Orestes story, and *Gallows Humor*, two linked tragicomic plays in a modern setting. In these plays Richardson stands apart from his three immediate contemporaries for certain defining characteristics unmistakably his own, characteristics that also mark his subsequent and somewhat parallel pair of Broadway plays, *Lorenzo* and *Xmas in Las Vegas*.

The plays, all vividly theatrical, are intentionally intellectual in the French tradition—somewhat unusual in American drama, although less so perhaps for a graduate in philosophy from Columbia University—and for their almost neo-classical emphasis upon verbal precision and formal control. At the same time, the plays share a conscious concern for previous dramatic materials and conventions, classical, medieval, Renaissance, and are unified by Richardson's persistent and strongly held view of the human predicament as man's forced participation in a destructive conflict between fundamental opposites: life, individuality, imaginative illusion, but chaos on the one hand; or death, conformity, reality, and order on the other.

The first pair of plays, *The Prodigal* and *Gallows Humor*, are written with an exhilarating wit and a Shavian exuberance hard to match in recent drama in English, and they are contrasting but complementary in method, with the classically inspired play modern by implication and the modern by medieval allusion universal or timeless in intent. In the former play Richardson personifies his characteristic and paradoxically grouped opposites in the figures of Aegisthus and Agamemnon, and in their conflicting views of man as either lesser or greater than he is Richardson also reflects Aristotle's definitions of comedy and tragedy. Orestes, the perfect tragicomic hero, succeeds for a time in avoiding either view and the destructive oppositions Aegisthus and Agamemnon represent. He seeks instead to "walk along the shore" and adopts the detachment of "laughter." But this modern stance, interestingly prophetic of the disillusion of youth in the later 1960's, proves a precarious stasis which cannot hold, and the murder of his father compels Orestes's participation in the battle of extremes he sought to avoid. The seeming inevitability of his decision is doubly reinforced in the play by the revenge theme of the myth itself and by the return motif of the biblical reference to the prodigal son, and at the play's close Orestes identifies his own decision with the general fate of man:

> The sea will always roar with Electra's cry; the waters will always rush toward Agamemnon's vengeance. It will cleanse or wash away the earth entirely, but it will never change ... I can resist these forces no longer. I will go back, murder, and say it's for a better world.

In *Gallows Humor* the two component plays are linked by their common theme and by the fact that each play exactly reverses the central characters, condemned and executioner, and their points of view, and the effect of reversal is heightened by the appearance of the actors in the first play as their counterpart selves in the second. Walter, the condemned murderer, has a surprising passion for order and conformity, strives to keep his cell immaculate, and to go to his death with his "number patch" in place. But in the last hours, at the imminence of death, he is seduced back toward a celebration of life, illusion, and chaos by the prison prostitute Lucy. In the second play, Phillip the executioner, properly "dressed in the trousers, shirt, and tie of his official uniform," has an irresistible attraction toward revolt and wishes for the coming solemnities "to dress up like a headsman from the Middle Ages" in "a black hood." But his cold and practical wife Martha reasons him back toward conformity and order. The hood, Lucy's face, like a "carnival mask," the essential brutality of the execution itself, and the appearance of Death from the old Morality Plays to deliver the Prologue, give the play its comparative time metaphor. Although modern appearances are confusing, and Death complains that it is now difficult for him to "tell the hangman from the hanged," Richardson's essential oppositions, life or death, order or disorder, conformity or individuality, illusion or reality, and hangman or hanged, are reasserted as Walter and Phillip, modern ambiguities to the contrary, do end up playing their destined roles.

To an extent *Lorenzo* is a Renaissance variation of *The Prodigal*, but with a special emphasis upon illusion and reality, and the gambling metaphor in *Xmas in Las Vegas*, with its insistence upon the either/or of winner and loser, repeats the executioner-condemned contraries of *Gallows Humor* in a zany world and manner reminiscent of Kaufman and Hart and *You Can't Take It with You*. Lorenzo, "director of the theatrical troupe 'Theatre of the First Dove,'" is caught up in the midst of a "small war of the Renaissance" in Italy, and like Orestes he tries vainly not to become involved in the destructive conflict of opposites, polarized here in the impractical Duke, Filippo, and his general, the realist Van Miessen. In *Xmas in Las Vegas* Wellspot is the inveterate gambler condemned to lose, and Olympus, the casino owner, is the financial executioner. Olympus, with his suggestion of the gods, gambling as fate or destiny, and the sacrificial connotations of Christmas all enlarge the dimension of this modern parable.

Although there are important contemporary influences and parallels in his work—Anouilh's wryly detached sense of humor, for example, Genet's concern with illusion, especially Genet's and Beckett's preoccupation with opposites—Richardson's plays (and it is their limiting strength) insist upon his own almost geometrically precise view of the human condition where everything is energized as it is drawn toward its opposite and toward its destruction, and it is this underlying and rather formulaic purity which initiates a sense of tragic inevitability beneath the comic facades of his plays.

More recently in other forms of writing, in periodical essays and in a splendid and revealing book *Memoir of a Gambler*, Richardson has continued to develop with his accustomed precision the preoccupations of his plays. But although this non-dramatic writing has been deservedly successful and represents a high level of accomplishment, one hopes that he will once more be lured back to that special, indeed incurable kind of gambling, theater, in which he has in the past so skillfully played his hand.

—Gaynor F. Bradish

RIDLER, Anne (Barbara, née Bradby). British. Born in Rugby, Warwickshire, 30 July 1912. Educated at Downe House School; King's College, London, diploma in journalism 1932. Married Vivian Ridler in 1938; two sons and two daughters. Member of editorial department, Faber and Faber, publishers, London, 1935–40. Recipient: Oscar Blumenthal prize, 1954, and Union League Civic and Arts Foundation prize, 1955 (*Poetry*, Chicago). Address: 14 Stanley Road, Oxford OX4 1QZ, England.

PUBLICATIONS

Plays

Cain (produced Letchworth, Hertfordshire, 1943; London, 1944). London, Editions Poetry London, 1943.

The Shadow Factory: A Nativity Play (produced London, 1945). London, Faber, 1946.

Henry Bly (produced London, 1947). Included in *Henry Bly and Other Plays*, 1950.

Henry Bly and Other Plays. London, Faber, 1950.

The Mask, and The Missing Bridegroom (produced London, 1951). Included in *Henry Bly and Other Plays*, 1950.

The Trial of Thomas Cranmer, music by Bryan Kelly (produced Oxford, 1956). London, Faber, 1956.

The Departure, music by Elizabeth Maconchy (produced London, 1961). Included in *Some Time After and Other Poems*, 1972.

Who Is My Neighbour? (produced Leeds, 1961). With *How Bitter the Bread*, London, Faber, 1963.

The Jesse Tree: A Masque in Verse, music by Elizabeth Maconchy (produced Dorchester, Oxfordshire, 1970). London, Lyrebird Press, 1972.

Rosinda, translation of the libretto by Faustini, music by Cavalli (produced Oxford, 1973; London, 1975).

Orfeo, translation of the libretto by Striggio, music by Monteverdi (produced Oxford, 1975; London, 1981). London, Faber Music, 1975; revised edition, 1981.

Eritrea, translation of the libretto by Faustini, music by Cavalli (produced Wexford, Ireland, 1975). London, Oxford University Press, 1975.

The King of the Golden River, music by Elizabeth Maconchy (produced Oxford, 1975).
The Return of Ulysses, translation of the libretto by Badoaro, music by Monteverdi (produced London, 1978).
The Lambton Worm, music by Robert Sherlaw Johnson (produced Oxford, 1978). London, Oxford University Press, 1979.
Orontea, translation of the libretto by Cicognini, music by Cesti (produced London, 1979).
Agrippina, translation of the libretto by Grimani, music by Handel (produced London, 1982).
La Calisto, translation of the libretto by Faustini, music by Cavalli (produced London, 1984).
Così fan Tutte, translation of the libretto by da Ponte, music by Mozart (produced London, 1986). Oxford, Perpetua Press, 1987.

Verse

Poems. London, Oxford University Press, 1939.
A Dream Observed and Other Poems. London, Editions Poetry London, 1941.
The Nine Bright Shiners. London, Faber, 1943.
The Golden Bird and Other Poems. London, Faber, 1951.
A Matter of Life and Death. London, Faber, 1959.
Selected Poems. New York, Macmillan, 1961.
Some Time After and Other Poems. London, Faber, 1972.
Italian Prospect: Six Poems. Oxford, Perpetua Press, 1976.
Dies Natalis: Poems of Birth and Infancy. Oxford, Perpetua Press, 1980.
Poems New and Selected. London, Faber, 1988.

Other

Olive Willis and Downe House: An Adventure in Education. London, Murray, 1967.

Editor, *Shakespeare Criticism 1919–1935*. London and New York, Oxford University Press, 1936.
Editor, *A Little Book of Modern Verse*. London, Faber, 1941.
Editor, *Time Passes and Other Poems*, by Walter de la Mare. London, Faber, 1942.
Editor, *Best Ghost Stories*. London, Faber, 1945.
Editor, *The Faber Book of Modern Verse*, revised edition. London, Faber, 1951.
Editor, *The Image of the City and Other Essays*, by Charles Williams. London, Oxford University Press, 1958.
Editor, *Selected Writings*, by Charles Williams. London, Oxford University Press, 1961.
Editor, *Shakespeare Criticism 1935–1960*. London and New York, Oxford University Press, 1963.
Editor, *Poems and Some Letters*, by James Thomson. London, Centaur Press, and Urbana, University of Illinois Press, 1963.
Editor, *Thomas Traherne: Poems, Centuries, and Three Thanksgivings*. London, Oxford University Press, 1966.
Editor, with Christopher Bradby, *Best Stories of Church and Clergy*. London, Faber, 1966.
Editor, *Selected Poems of George Darley*. London, Merrion Press, 1979.
Editor, *The Poems of William Austin*. Oxford, Perpetua Press, 1984.

*

Critical Study: *The Christian Tradition in Modern British Verse Drama* by William V. Spanos, New Brunswick, New Jersey, Rutgers University Press, 1967.

Anne Ridler comments:

(1977) It is a great advantage for a dramatist to know the cast and place he is writing for, the audience he is addressing. Only rarely have I had this opportunity, and this is perhaps why *Thomas Cranmer*, commissioned for performance in the church where Cranmer was tried, has been judged my best play.

Writing words for music, however, gives a rare opportunity for a contemporary poet to use his particular talents in the theatre, and it is in this field (whether by original words, or fitting a translation to a musical line) that I prefer to work at present. Libretto-writing, as W.H. Auden said, gives the poet his one chance nowadays of using the high style.

* * *

Although Anne Ridler has to her credit a number of plays which have their place in the postwar revival of blank verse drama, it is more likely that she will be remembered for her volumes of poetry than for her work in the theatre. She began by tackling the forbidding theme of Cain, presenting the characters from Genesis with the archangels Michael and Gabriel serving as chorus to the tragedy. *The Shadow Factory*, a most unusual nativity play, is altogether more interesting as it juxtaposes reflections on the birth of Christ and some sharp criticisms of contemporary issues. In the factory the workers are reduced almost to robots, endlessly repeating the same pointless actions in the production line. The jingle "The Piece-Work Way/Means Better Pay" sums up the futility of it all, and the director is no doubt intentionally something of an Orwellian Big Brother. He has, however, had the idea of commissioning a large mural painting as an example of corporate sponsorship which will enhance the company's image. The artist who undertakes the work soon sizes up the situation and, having taken the precaution of obtaining a promise that nobody shall see what he is doing until it is finished, paints a picture which portrays the director as a masked figure playing chess heartlessly with the lives of his work people. Meantime, a parson, who is also admitted to the factory as part of a policy of good treatment for the staff, rehearses a nativity play with the workers. The two strands come together as the director swallows his pride and accepts the mural and its message, or rather the message of the nativity. With its concern for social injustice the play strikes a chord, and if the director is a little too wooden in his attitudes and expression, there is certainly life in the portrayal of the workers, especially William, whose reactions to the birth of his first child are observed with affectionate accuracy. All the same, the mixture of realism and allegory is not altogether persuasive, and the optimism, as with many nativity plays, is a little difficult to swallow except on Christmas Eve.

Henry Bly is more successful because its engaging plot, based on the Grimm Brothers' fairy tale "Brother Lustig," is realistic only in its depiction of characters, not of milieu. Henry is a picaresque rogue, always keen to enjoy a drink or to cadge a coin. On his feckless way through life he falls in with a Tramp who never explains himself very fully but whom we soon come to recognise as some sort of Christ-figure when he works miracles without hope of any material reward. For Henry he is at first merely a simpleton to be exploited, but by the end the ne'er-do-well comes to realise that what he is being offered is his chance for salvation. Folklore is also used as the basis for *The Mask* which takes the form of a reworking of the moving Somerset folksong "The Shooting of His Dear" and manages to modernise the tale without destroying its charm.

Ridler turned to history with *The Trial of Thomas Cranmer*, written to mark the 400th aniversary of his death. When played in the University Church, Oxford, near so many of the sites mentioned by the characters, the tragedy must have been particularly moving, but even without local knowledge this simple and yet very sympathetic chronicle of inhumanity strikes home. Ridler's method is first to show Cranmer as a complete human being, naturally anxious to avoid the challenge of martyrdom, so that she can enlist all our sympathies as he goes to his death. His persecutors seem all the more ignoble since hs is not cast in the heroic mould, and his courage and faith impress us all the more since we know he would sooner not be tested. There is, of course, also Cranmer's magnificent control of language, and this, perhaps as much as an obvious Oxford connection and reverence for one of the martyrs of the English church, must have attracted Ridler.

For her, verse drama is not a matter of grand phrases and extravagant imagery. Instead she prefers a sober style, rarely enlivened by metaphor and spiced with just occasional dry wit. She knows the power of mono-syllables and has enough confidence in the power of her verse to avoid gross effects. It is the rhythm, close to that of prose yet subtly more strict, that repeatedly lifts the speeches she puts into the mouths of her characters above the mundane matters they may be discussing and gives her dialogue the extra strengths of poetry. In her plays her constant concern is to present images of redemption within contexts which portray the pains, problems, and little joys of mankind. Her verse serves as one more element in the bridge that she seeks to build between two worlds.

After writing her verse plays Ridler turned to libretti, writing, for instance, *The Departure* and *The King of the Golden River* for setting by Elizabeth Maconchy. In recent years she has also produced translations—or as she likes to call them, "English singing versions"—of the texts of Monteverdi's *The Return of Ulysses*, Cavalli's *La Calisto*, and Handel's *Agrippina*, among others. These meticulously worked versions, which reveal a rare combination of verbal and musical sensitivity, have set high standards and contributed significantly to the growing tendency, exemplified by Kent Opera, of performing the masterpieces of the operatic repertory in English.

—Christopher Smith

ROMERIL, John. Australian. Born in Melbourne, Victoria, 26 October 1945. Educated at Brighton Technical School and High School, South Australia; Monash University, Clayton, Victoria, 1966–71, B.A. (honours) in English 1970. Writer-in-residence, Australian Performing Group, Melbourne, 1974, Western Australian Institute of Technology, Bentley, 1977, University of Newcastle, New South Wales, 1978, Jigsaw Theatre Company, Canberra, 1980, Troupe, Adelaide, 1981, Flinders University, Bedford Park, South Australia, 1984, Magpie, Adelaide, 1985, National University of Singapore, 1986–87; Mathew J. Cody Artist-in-Residence, Victorian Arts Centre, Melbourne, 1985. Also a director and actor. Recipient: Australian Council for the Arts travel grant, 1972; Canada-Australia Prize, 1976. Agent: Almost Managing, P.O. Box 34, Carlton, Victoria 3053, Australia.

PUBLICATIONS

Plays

A Nameless Concern (produced Melbourne, 1968).

The American Independence Hour (produced Melbourne, 1969).

Mr. Big, The Big, Big Pig (produced Melbourne, 1969).

In a Place Somewhere Else (produced Melbourne, 1969).

I Don't Know Who to Feel Sorry For (produced Melbourne, 1969). Sydney, Currency Press, 1973; London, Eyre Methuen, 1975.

Chicago Chicago (produced Melbourne, 1970). Published in *Plays*, Melbourne, Penguin, 1970.

Marvellous Melbourne, with Jack Hibberd (produced Melbourne, 1970). Published in *Theatre Australia* (Potts Point, New South Wales), July–September 1977.

Dr. Karl's Kure (produced Melbourne, 1970).

Whatever Happened to Realism (produced Melbourne, 1971).

Mrs. Thrally F (produced Melbourne, 1971). Published in *Seven One-Act Plays*, edited by Rodney Fisher, Sydney, Currency Press, 1983.

Two Plays (includes *The Kitchen Table* and *Brudder Humphrey*). Clayton, Victoria, Kosmos, 1971.

Rearguard Action (produced Melbourne, 1971).

He Can Swagger Sitting Down (produced Melbourne, 1972).

Bastardy (produced Melbourne, 1972). Montmorency, Victoria, Yackandandah, 1982.

Waltzing Matilda: A National Pantomime with Tomato Sauce, with Tim Robertson (produced Melbourne, 1974). Montmorency, Victoria, Yackandandah, 1984.

The Floating World (produced Melbourne, 1974). Sydney, Currency Press, 1975; London, Eyre Methuen, 1976; revised version, Currency Press, 1982.

The Golden Holden Show (produced Melbourne, 1975).

Dudders, with John Timlin (produced Melbourne, 1976).

The Radio-Active Horror Show (produced Melbourne, 1977).

The Accidental Poke (produced Melbourne, 1977). Published in *Popular Short Plays for the Australian Stage*, edited by Ron Blair, Sydney, Currency Press, 1985.

Mickey's Moomba (produced Melbourne, 1979).

Carboni (produced Melbourne, 1980).

700,000 (produced Canberra, 1980).

Samizdat (produced Adelaide, 1981).

The Kelly Dance (produced Adelaide, 1984). Montmorency, Victoria, Yackandandah, 1986.

Definitely Not the Last (produced Adelaide, 1985).

Jonah, music by Alan John, adaptation of the novel by Louis Stone (produced Sydney, 1985).

Legends, with Jennifer Hill and Chris Anastassiades (produced Melbourne, 1985). Montmorency, Victoria, Yackandandah, 1986.

Other Plays: *Scene One*, with John Minter, 1969; *The Man from Chicago*, 1969; *200 Years*, 1970; *The Magnetic Matian Potato*, 1971; *A Night in Rio and Other Bummerz*, with Tim Robertson, 1972; *Hackett Gets Ahead*, with Bill and Lorna Hannan, 1972; *The Earth, Air, Fire, and Water Show*, 1973; *Centenary Dance*, 1984; *Top End*, 1986; *History of Australia*, 1987; *Koori Radio*, 1987.

Television Plays: *Bonjour Balwyn*, 1969; *The Best of Mates*, 1972; *Charley the Chequer Cab Kid*, 1973; *The Great McCarthy*, from a novel by Barry Oakley, 1975; *6 of the Best* series, 1981–82; *Mr. Steam and Dry*, 1986.

Other

6 of the Best: An Introduction to the Television Drama Series. Melbourne, Transition Education Advisory Committee, 1984.

*

Critical Studies: interview in *Meanjin* (Melbourne), vol. 3, 1978; article by Romeril, in *Theatre Australia* (Potts Point, New South Wales), April 1979.

John Romeril comments:

I take my prime duty as a playwright to be the recording and representation of contemporary Australian reality on the stage. Politically I'm of a left-wing persuasion, hence interested in plays of ideas. However, I operate on the premise that if you want people to entertain ideas you must first entertain people. Thus the kind of theatre I try to make is above all lively, full of colour, movement, wit and style, fused with content of pressing concern.

* * *

Since the late 1960's John Romeril has been the most prolific playwright writing in Australia, and yet much of his work remains unpublished and has had little critical attention. Many of his plays are occasional pieces, written in conjunction with regional, community-based theatre companies, theatre-in-education teams, or groups who have come together for single projects. This is part of a considered "industrial" ethics, whereby Romeril sees himself as a "public servant of the pen," taking his material from the community in which he is working, processing it according to his specific industrial skills, and giving it back to the community.

Like other playwrights of the "New Wave" of Australian playwriting, such as David Williamson, Alexander Buzo, and Jack Hibberd, Romeril first came to prominence as a young "alternative" writer in the late 1960's. His theatre was the Australian Performing Group (APG) in Melbourne, a self-consciously radical company, working as a co-operative, using "consensus creativity" to strive for a distinctively populist Australian way of presenting political material. The company's work was a curious mixture: heavily influenced by the radical American theatre of the 1960's as well as by various modernist dramatic movements such as absurdism, which had hitherto had little influence on Australian playwriting. In its early years, at the small La Mama theatre in Melbourne, the restrictions of a tiny performance space led to an intimate style which the company called (after O'Neill) "supernaturalism." Later, in the larger, rowdier space of the Pram Factory, the company developed a more overtly theatricalist, presentational mode of performance, drawing on the traditions of vaudeville and melodrama.

Of the many writers who cut their theatrical teeth with the APG Romeril remained the most faithful to the theatre's original spirit. For ten years he worked with them, ignoring the attractions of the growing professional theatrical establishment to which many of his fellow writers drifted. When the APG finally closed in 1981 Romeril moved on to work on the series of political and community projects which has ensured him a low profile in the academic histories.

Romeril's unpublished plays make up an impressive body of work. Many of them show the marks of their origins, as pieces written for a specific group or political situation. The writing is often rushed and unrefined, but there are an energy and a theatrical exuberance which are very appealing. Romeril likes to speak of the "10% innovation" whereby the audience is given 90% of the material in a familiar genre or style and 10% new, challenging matter. Many of the occasional pieces are written in established conventions: vaudeville musicals, children's plays, or soap opera, for example, with an injection of original material, often with a political point.

Romeril has also produced a few plays, bearing the marks of a more individual impulse, which have become minor classics of Australian drama of the 1970's. Undoubtedly the most important is *The Floating World*, a comic but finally gruelling study of Australian xenophobia and some of the very real historical events and political considerations which have created it. Major aspects of Australia's involvement in two world wars are seen through the eyes of an old soldier who goes quietly mad reliving his experience as a P.O.W. on the notorious Burma-Thailand railway while on a "Woman's Weekly Cherry Blossom Cruise" to Japan. This central character, Les Harding, is first presented to us as a typically vulgar Australian male, an "ocker" of the sort which became a common theatrical stereotype in the 1970's. The play sets up, in the first half, a series of comic images of Australian aggressive self-assertion. As the cruise ship nears its destination, however, Les's past begins to consume him and we are led into the depths of the frightened insecurity which underlies the stereotyped social mask he has created for himself. The play succeeds particularly well in showing the personal feeling which lies behind the public mask of the clichéd Australian male. It ends with a neat irony, as Les finds himself at last able to describe his personal crisis in the war, a moment when after all the pain of his imprisonment he became physically "well again." As he says it we watch him, strait-jacketed, finally and irrevocably insane.

I Don't Know Who to Feel Sorry For is an earlier work which also examines the individual feeling behind the social masks which the characters use, vainly, in an attempt to control their lives. In this case the central characters, Celia and Lenny, play out their relationship in a series of cannibalistic games which reveal a Strindbergian paranoia as to the possibilities of male-female relationships. *Chicago Chicago* is a rather unwieldy but at times powerful picture of those violent and amoral aspects of American society which, after the Chicago demonstrations of 1968, most terrified radical Australians, especially in the context of the Australian commitment to the war in Vietnam. The play employs a number of expressionist dislocating effects which make it, even now, one of the most formally adventurous of Australian plays of the New Wave. *Bastardy* is a bleak, unrelentingly naturalistic study of the "lower depths" of society. It presents the emotional (and physical) violence which its characters exhibit towards one another as being systematic and socially determined.

These plays, and others unpublished, reveal a dimension to Romeril's writing which seems to belie his modest claim to be a "public servant of the pen," as do the sudden flashes of originality in his formulaic writing for theatre-in-education and community companies, and, recently, for television. More than any other Australian writer, including his intellectual and artistic confrère Stephen Sewell, Romeril has addressed the problem of politically radical writing which aims to make social and political, as well as artistic, statements in a manner which is accessible to audiences who are not part of the normal theatre-going public.

—John McCallum

ROTIMI, Ola. Nigerian. Born in Sapele, 13 April 1938. Educated at Methodist Boys' High School, Lagos, 1952–56; Boston University (President, African Students Union, 1962–63), 1959–63, B.F.A. 1963; Yale University School of Drama, New Haven, Connecticut (Rockefeller scholar, 1963–66; Student Drama prize, 1966), 1963–66, M.F.A. 1966. Married Hazel Mae Gaudreau in 1965; three sons and one daughter. Executive director and artistic director, University of Ife Theatre, 1973–77. Since 1977 director of the university theatre, Dean of Student Affairs, 1979–80, Dean of the Faculty of Humanities, 1982–84, and since 1982 Head of the Department of Creative Arts, all University of Port Harcourt. Recipient: *African Arts* prize, 1969; Oxford University Press prize, 1970; Nigerian National Festival of the Arts prize, 1974. Address: Department of Creative Arts, University of Port Harcourt, P.M.B. 5323, Port Harcourt, Rivers State, Nigeria.

PUBLICATIONS

Plays

Our Husband Has Gone Mad Again (produced Ibadan and New Haven, Connecticut, 1966). Ibadan, Oxford University Press, 1977.
The Gods Are Not to Blame (produced Ife-Ife, 1968; London, 1978). Ibadan, Oxford University Press, 1971.
Kurunmi: An Historical Tragedy (produced Ife-Ife, 1969). Ibadan, Oxford University Press, 1971.
Holding Talks (produced Ife-Ife, 1970). Ibadan, Ibadan University Press-Oxford University Press, 1979.
Ovonramwen Nogbaisi (produced Ife-Ife, 1971). Benin City, Ethiope, and London, Oxford University Press, 1974.
Initiation into Madness, adaptation of a play by Adegoke Durojaiye (produced Ife-Ife, 1973).
Grip Am (produced Ife-Ife, 1973).
Akassa Youmi (produced Port Harcourt, 1977).
If: A Tragedy of the Ruled (produced Port Harcourt, 1979). Ibadan, Heinemann, 1983.
Hopes of the Living-Dead (produced Port Harcourt, 1985).

*

Bibliography: by O. Lalude, in *Bibliographic Series 1*, Port Harcourt, University of Port Harcourt Library, 1984.

Critical Studies: interview in *Dem Say* (Austin, Texas), 1974; *African Theatre Today* by Martin Banham and Clive Wake, London, Pitman, 1976; "Three Dramatists in Search of a Language" by Dapo Adelugba, in *Theatre in Africa* edited by Oyin Ogunba and Abiola Irele, Ibadan, Ibadan University Press, 1978; "Ola Rotimi's Search for Technique" by Akanju Nasiru, in *New West African Literature* edited by Kolawole Ogungbesan, London, Heinemann, 1979; "The Search for a Popular Theatre" by Biodun Jeyifo, in *Drama and Theatre in Nigeria* edited by Yemi Ogunbiyi, Lagos, Nigeria Magazine, 1981; article by Alex C. Johnson, in *African Literature Today 12* edited by Eldred Jones and Eustace Palmer, London, Heinemann, 1981; *Beyond Translation: Tragic Paradigms and the Dramaturgy of Ola Rotimi and Wole Soyinka* by Femi Osofisan, Ife-Ife, Ife Monographs on African Literature, 1986.

Theatrical Activities:
Director: **Plays**—all his own plays; *King Christophe* by Aimé Césaire, Ife-Ife, 1970; *Rere Run* by Dejo Okediji, Ife-Ife, 1973; *Wahala* by Babalola Fatunwase, Ife-Ife, 1973; *The Curse* by Kole Omotosho, Ife-Ife, 1975; *The Family* by Comish Ekiye, Ife-Ife, 1976; *Sizwe Bansi Is Dead* by Athol Fugard, John Kani, and Winston Ntshona, Port Harcourt, 1984; *The Emperor Jones* by Eugene O'Neill, Port Harcourt, 1985; *Behold My Redeemer* by Rasheed Gbadamosi, Port Harcourt, 1986.

Ola Rotimi comments:
My creative passion is for a people's theatre informed by that which also impels it, namely: the spasms of the socio-political tendons of Africa yesterday, today, and tomorrow.

* * *

Of the generation of Nigerian playwrights who began writing in the late 1960's, Ola Rotimi exhibits the surest sense of drama as a plastic, three-dimensional form incorporating the spoken word, dance, music, mime, and the massing of bodies in space for the creation of spectacle. This sense of theatrical possibility is found equally in his high or stylistically elevated dramas and in his more realistic, socio-political plays.

Characteristic of this "high" style are the tragedy *The Gods Are Not to Blame* and the historical dramas *Kurunmi* and *Ovonramwen Nogbaisi.* Each play distances its concerns by locating events in the previous century; treats the gods as an awesome, unseen presence rather than as a physical manifestation; molds music, mime, and ritual elements to create a varied social panorama; employs dance in an efficacious manner designed to enhance collective well-being; and makes extensive use of traditional poetic forms for the expression of values central to the community portrayed. The best known play of this group, *The Gods Are Not to Blame*, is also a good example of the blend of theatre traditions to which Rotimi is heir, for he obtained degrees in directing and playwriting from Boston and Yale universities in the United States and, following his return to Nigeria in 1966, began researching traditional Yoruba performance modes as part of his direction of the Ori Olokun Acting Company.

Adapted from the Oedipus story, *The Gods Are Not to Blame* strives to reject the fatalistic relationship of man to god, contained in the Greek original, by using as a central visual image the shrine of Ogun, the Yoruba god associated with iron and, by implication, with the creation of technologies designed to extend man's manipulation of the environment. In Rotimi's hands the source of the protagonist's downfall becomes the learned, social conditioning of ethnic paranoia.

But this adaptation is not fully successful, for Yoruba attitudes concerning fate only superficially approximate an interpretation of Greek tragedy as attributable to a single character flaw. Furthermore, Rotimi's subsequent explanation that the drama, first produced in 1968 during the Nigerian Civil War, was intended as a direct commentary on current events is not fully satisfactory, for such a position invalidates the centrality of the prophecy imposed by the original, and runs the risk of reducing the war's complex causes to a single issue. Rather, it seems that in this instance the choice of material identifies Rotimi with the period in modern African literatures when writers were eager to validate their cultures in terms which the former colonial masters could appreciate.

A similar borrowing from Western perspectives seems evident in *Kurunmi* and *Ovonramwen Nogbaisi*, for these historical dramas concerning internecine Yoruba wars and the British conquest of the Benin Empire hinge upon the great-man theory of history, antithetical to an African emphasis on personality as collective. While the latter play is not entirely persuasive because the king's failure of will seems insufficiently motivated,

Kurunmi is an impressive evocation of a world under fatal pressure. Through the manipulation in English of Yoruba expressive modes governing the use of proverbs and lyrical structures or the easy movement between the spiritual/tragic realm and the secular/comic world, Rotimi creates an effective defense of tradition and culture as the sole element which distinguishes humans from other life forms. Yet, true to historical accounts and his own contemporary reality, the playwright brings his protagonist to the ironic realization that this defense visits widescale destruction and eventual decline upon the entire nation.

In contrast, later realistic plays like *If: A Tragedy of the Ruled* and *Hopes of the Living-Dead* tackle current social concerns directly and explore the dynamic interplay between leaders and followers. The first play, loosely adapted from Errol John's Caribbean drama *Moon on a Rainbow Shawl*, is an impassioned plea for the rejection of self-interest in favor of a collective vision of national health. The latter play, while conforming to sketchy historial accounts, projects the sobering image of Nigeria as a nation of lepers threatened with sure extinction unless they learn to work collectively for the benefit of all.

In these socio-political plays the playwright achieves a theatrical plasticity similar to that of the stylistically elevated plays. The simultaneous playing of several scenes and massing of actors in such a way as to convey separate foci which momentarily converage and allow for the settling on a common purpose; the successful integration of various Nigerian languages with pidgin and English to capture the dream of a truly pluralistic society; and the use of music to evoke a poignant sense of the possibility of a shared, human grandeur all distinguish Rotimi as one of the best playwrights of contemporary Nigerian drama.

—Sandra L. Richards

RUDKIN, (James) David. British. Born in London, 29 June 1936. Educated at King Edward's School, Birmingham, 1947–55; St. Catherine's College, Oxford, 1957–61, M.A. 1961. Served in the Royal Corps of Signals, 1955–57. Married Sandra Thompson in 1967; two sons and two daughters. Assistant Master of Latin, Greek and music, County High School, Bromsgrove, Worcestershire, 1961–64. Recipient: *Evening Standard* award, 1962; John Whiting Award, 1974; Obie award, 1977. Agent: Margaret Ramsay Ltd., 14-A Goodwin's Court, London WC2N 4LL, England.

PUBLICATIONS

Plays

Afore Night Come (produced Oxford, 1960; London, 1962). Included in *New English Dramatists 7*, London, Penguin, 1963; published separately, New York, Grove Press, 1966.
Moses and Aaron, translation of the libretto, music by Schoenberg (produced London, 1965). London, Friends of Covent Garden, 1965.
The Grace of Todd, music by Gordon Crosse (produced Aldeburgh, Suffolk, and London, 1969). London, Oxford University Press, 1970.
Burglars (for children; produced London, 1970). Published in *Prompt Two*, edited by Alan Durband, London, Hutchinson, 1976.
The Filth Hunt (produced London, 1972).
Cries from Casement as His Bones Are Brought to Dublin (broadcast 1973; produced London, 1973). London, BBC Publications, 1974.
Ashes (produced Hamburg, 1973; London, 1974; Los Angeles and New York, 1976). London, Pluto Press, 1978.
Penda's Fen (televised 1974). London, Davis Poynter, 1975.
No Title (produced Birmingham, 1974).
The Sons of Light (produced Newcastle upon Tyne, 1976; London, 1978). London, Eyre Methuen, 1981.
Sovereignty under Elizabeth (produced London, 1977).
Hippolytus, adaptation of the play by Euripides (produced Stratford-on-Avon, 1978; London, 1979). London, Heinemann, 1980.
Hansel and Gretel (produced Stratford-on-Avon, 1980; London, 1981).
The Triumph of Death (produced Birmingham, 1981). London, Eyre Methuen, 1981.
Peer Gynt, adaptation of the play by Ibsen (produced Stratford-on-Avon, 1982; London, 1983). London, Methuen, 1983.
Space Invaders (produced London, 1984).
Will's Way (produced London, 1985).
The Saxon Shore (produced London, 1986). London, Methuen, 1986.
Deathwatch, and The Maids, adaptations of plays by Jean Genet (produced London, 1987).

Screenplays (additional dialogue, uncredited): *Fahrenheit 451*, 1966; *Mademoiselle*, 1966.

Radio Plays: *No Accounting for Taste*, 1960; *The Persians*, from the play by Aeschylus, 1965; *Gear Change*, 1967; *Cries from Casement as His Bones Are Brought to Dublin*, 1973; *Hecuba*, from the play by Euripides, 1975.

Television Plays: *The Stone Dance*, 1963; *Children Playing*, 1967; *House of Character*, 1968; *Blodwen, Home from Rachel's Marriage*, 1969; *Bypass*, 1972; *Atrocity*, 1973; *Penda's Fen*, 1974; *Pritan* and *The Coming of the Cross* (*Churchill's People* series), 1975; *The Ash Tree*, from the story by M.R. James, 1975; *The Living Grave* (*Leap in the Dark* series), 1981; *Artemis 81*, 1981; *Across the Water*, 1983; *White Lady*, 1987.

Ballet Scenario: *Sun into Darkness*, 1966.

*

Theatrical Activities:
Director: **Television**—*White Lady*, 1987.

* * *

David Rudkin's *Afore Night Come* is one of the most mature and assured first plays of the postwar period, though in retrospect it can be seen to contain its author's chief dramatic preoccupations only (as it were) in solution, uncrystallized. Primitive chthonic forces long repressed by culture and individual psychology reassert themselves with great violence when a group of fruit-pickers on a Midlands farm single out a casual worker—a strange, "educated" Irish tramp—as scapegoat for their personal, moral, and economic failings and carry out his ritual murder in the sinister, though apparently numinous presence of a crop-spraying helicopter. Thematic elements which are to become central in Rudkin's later work—homosexuality, sexual infertility, the threat of nuclear devastation, England's Irish problem—are present but not developed. Indeed, thematic coherence seems less important to Rudkin at this stage of his career than the recognizably Pinteresque menace which can be generated by the rhythms of a judiciously charged dialogue. It is perhaps for this reason that, though the crucial sacrificial event of *Afore Night Come* is obviously two-edged, the energy of the play makes itself felt as essentially destructive.

By contrast, Rudkin's work after his 12-year self-imposed apprenticeship is energized by his passionate commitment to a powerful central *idea*. The primitive impulses of *Afore Night Come* reveal their creative aspect in the concentration on the reintegration and realization of the self that occurs in the gradual, painful liberation from a complex web of repression. On the evidence of his work, Rudkin believes that the power-wielders of modern civilization, and especially the various Christian churches with their capacity for psychological conditioning, function only by burying or perverting for their own dark ends original, natural forces and beliefs. His dramatic response is to affirm the continuity of these forces, on several different levels simultaneously—psychological, sexual, cultural, historical—using those forms which many modern artists have regarded as the enduring repositories of non-rational or even anti-rational values: image, fable, and myth. The quasi-physical impact of Rudkin's dramatic language, with its intense compression and often eccentric syntax, itself reflects these values. Hence also the importance to Rudkin of dialect, the concrete, poetic language of the authentic, geographically rooted self which he repeatedly sets against abstract discourse, the rootless, "Flat Urban Academic" that "will bury our theatre." (The Norwegian acts of his *Peer Gynt* are translated into the "stylized rural Ulster speech" of his own childhood.)

Ashes is a harrowing autobiographical play which rotates the theme of sexual infertility through a series of wider perspectives, political, anthropological, and existential, in handling the problem of free will and determinism. However, the roughly contemporaneous television play *Penda's Fen* offers a more satisfying dramatic realization of his preoccupations. The growth of an adolescent boy in Worcestershire away from social, religious, educational, and sexual constraints into mature selfhood is articulated through images of a local landscape in which the natural forces of Penda's Fen are being perverted, in the modern Pinvin, to menacing scientific ends, through suggestive sequences of music (which, together with sound-effects, has always been more important to Rudkin than scenery or props), and through a series of dream-images which reveal to the boy his homosexuality. Here, as elsewhere in Rudkin's work, homosexuality is important less as a social reality than as an idea: it is the humane "mixed" state which stands as a critique of the conventional phallic "manliness" of society's power-wielders. Having realized that Christianity has "buried" the authentic Jesus—just as "Pinvin" (a real place) has buried Penda's Fen—the boy Stephen rejects power and inherits, in a vision of Penda himself (the last of the English pagan kings) "the sacred demon of ungovernableness."

The key work in Rudkin's oeuvre, at which he worked from 1965 to 1976, is *The Sons of Light*, a massive, multi-layered fable with science-fiction elements and a tripartite mythic structure: "The Division of the Kingdom," "The Pit," "Surrection." The ancient paradigm drawn on by Rudkin is most familiar from the Christian Harrowing of Hell, but the play is hardly less critical of church Christianity and its power-seeking perversions than the more recent (and luridly schematic) *The Triumph of Death*. In *The Sons of Light* a new pastor and his three sons arrive on a Scottish Atlantic island to find it divided and ruled by its "Benefactor" in the name of a religion of wrath. A subterranean industrial complex dehumanizes and mechanizes its workers, allaying any stirrings of discontent with the (purely functional) promise of religious transcendence. Two of the pastor's sons die, but, amid much violence and suffering, the remaining one descends into this "pit," initiates a fresh consciousness of self in the workers and destroys the complex, thus uniting the island and reclaiming it for its inhabitants. Simultaneously the identity of a schizophrenic girl, hitherto an outcast, is reintegrated and she is made whole. The cultural-psychological parallel reveals the essence of Rudkin's sensibility.

In Rudkin's most recent major work, *The Saxon Shore*, an attempted movement from repression into authentic selfhood is represented as failing tragically. In this instance, however, the narrative of an individual is placed firmly within a specific historical context. The context is also implicitly political, and in Rudkin this means (as in *Ashes, Cries from Casement . . .*, and *Across the Water*) the Irish problem. The play is set in the last years of Roman rule in Britain. On the North Sea coast, the displaced native British Celts and a "plantationer" Saxon community face each other across Hadrian's Wall in the presence of a disgruntled and demoralized colonial army. The allegorical "fit" with the Ulster situation (a Saxon Volunteer Force aids the scornful Roman soldiers and Saxons-turned-nocturnal-werewolves compulsively perpetrate acts of terror) is too neat to be exploratory. The dramatization of the cultural-spiritual progress of the (Gyntian) Saxon Athdark is marred by a reliance on narrative cliché and by language that comes near to parodying Rudkin's most effective, lurching as it does between costive ejaculation, imaged and gestural in nature, and a sentimental "poetry." Artaud may be invoked; indeed the physical aspects of the play in production were impressive—and it received respectful reviews. Yet if Rudkin is Britain's most underrated playwright, *The Saxon Shore* hardly seems likely to promote his cause.

—Paul Lawley

RUSSELL, Willy (William Martin Russell). British. Born in Whiston, Lancashire, 23 August 1947. Educated at schools in Knowsley and Rainford, Lancashire; Childwall College of Further Education, Lancashire, 1969–70; St. Katharine's College of Higher Education, Liverpool, 1970–73, Cert.Ed. Married Ann Margaret Seagroatt in 1969; one son and two daughters. Ladies hairdresser, Liverpool and Kirkby, 1963–68; labourer, Bear Brand warehouse, 1968–69, and teacher, Shorefields Comprehensive, 1973–74, Liverpool. Since 1974 freelance writer. Associate director, 1981–83, and since 1983 honorary director, Liverpool Playhouse; since 1982 founding director, Quintet Films, London. Writer-in-residence, C.F. Mott College of Education, Liverpool, 1976; Fellow in Creative Writing, Manchester Polytechnic, 1977–79. Also folk song composer and singer: performances (with group Kirbytown Three) in clubs and on radio and television since 1965. Recipient: Arts Council bursary, 1974; *Evening Standard* award, 1974; London Theatre Critics award, 1974; Society of West End Theatre award, 1980, 1983; Golden Globe award, 1984; Ivor Novello award, 1985. M.A.: Open University, Milton Keynes, Buckinghamshire, 1983. Agent: Margaret Ramsay Ltd., 14-A Goodwin's Court, London WC2N 4LL. Address: W.R. Ltd., 43 Canning Street, Liverpool L8 7NN, England.

PUBLICATIONS

Plays

Keep Your Eyes Down (produced Liverpool, 1971).
Blind Scouse (includes *Keep Your Eyes Down, Playground, Sam O'Shanker*) (produced Liverpool, 1972; revised version of *Sam O'Shanker*, music by Russell, produced Liverpool, 1973).
Tam Lin (for children), music by Russell (produced Liverpool, 1972).
When the Reds, adaptation of the play *The Tigers Are Coming—O.K.?* by Alan Plater (produced Liverpool, 1973).
Terraces, in *Second Playbill 1*, edited by Alan Durband. London, Hutchinson, 1973; collection published as *Terraces*, 1979.
John, Paul, George, Ringo and Bert (produced Liverpool and London, 1974).
The Cantril Tales, with others (produced Liverpool, 1975).
Breezeblock Park (produced Liverpool, 1975; London, 1977). London, French, 1978.
Break In (televised 1975). Published in *Scene Scripts 2*, edited by Michael Marland, London, Longman, 1978.
I Read the News Today (broadcast 1976). Published in *Home Truths*, London, Longman, 1982.
One for the Road (as *Painted Veg and Parkinson*, produced Manchester, 1976; as *Dennis the Menace*, produced Norwich, 1978; as *Happy Returns*, produced Brighton, 1978; as *One for the Road*, produced Nottingham, 1979). London, French, 1980; revised version (produced Liverpool, 1986; London, 1987), 1985.
Our Day Out (televised 1977). Published in *Act 1*, edited by David Self and Ray Speakman, London, Hutchinson, 1979; revised version, songs and music by Bob Eaton, Chris Mellors, and Russell (produced Liverpool and London, 1983), London, Methuen, 1984.
Stags and Hens (produced Liverpool, 1978; London, 1984). London, French, 1985.
Lies (televised 1978). Published in *City Life*, edited by David Self, London, Hutchinson, 1980.
Politics and Terror (televised 1978). Published in *Wordplays 1*, edited by Alan Durband, London, Hutchinson, 1982.
The Boy with the Transistor Radio (televised 1980). Published in *Working*, edited by David Self, London, Hutchinson, 1980.
Educating Rita (produced London, 1980; Chicago and New York, 1987). London, French, 1981.
Blood Brothers (produced Liverpool, 1981; revised version, music and lyrics by Russell, produced Liverpool and London, 1983). London, Hutchinson, 1986.
Educating Rita, Stags and Hens, and Blood Brothers. London, Methuen, 1986.
Shirley Valentine (produced Liverpool, 1986).

Screenplay: *Educating Rita*, 1983.

Radio Play: *I Read the News Today*, 1976.

Television Plays: *King of the Castle*, 1973; *Break In*, 1975; *The Death of a Young, Young Man*, 1975; *Our Day Out*, 1977; *Lies*, 1978; *Politics and Terror*, 1978; *The Daughters of Albion*, 1979; *The Boy with the Transistor Radio*, 1980; *One Summer* series, 1983.

Verse

Sam O'Shanker: A Liverpool Tale. Liverpool, Mersey Yarns, 1978.

Other

Published Music: *I Will Be Your Love* and *OOee boppa OOee boppa*, RSO, 1974; *Dance the Night*, Paternoster, 1980; *Blood Brothers*, Paternoster-Russell Music, 1983; *The Show*, Timeact-Russell Music-Paternoster, 1985; *Mr. Love*, Russell Music-Warner Brothers, 1986.

*

Critical Study: "Willy Russell: The First Ten Years" by Timothy Charles, in *Drama* (London), Summer 1983.

Theatrical Activities:
Director: **Play**—*Educating Rita*, Liverpool, 1981.
Actor: **Plays**—Narrator in *Blood Brothers*, Liverpool, 1985, and *Shirley Valentine*, Liverpool, 1986. **Film**—*Educating Rita*, 1983.

Willy Russell comments:

I am loathe to make any specific statement on the nature of my work as I reserve the right to dismiss on Wednesday the statement I made on Thursday. However, in a letter of 1984, written to a BBC producer to explain why I would not be writing a play I wrote the following (I think for me it will remain as true on a Thursday as it is on a Wednesday):

> To write a play one must passionately believe in something which one wants to communicate. The writer might want to tell of the ills of the world, or of his love for another, of society's folly, of mankind's goodness and baseness. He may want to argue a political cause or just show off his wit. Whatever, it is something which requires a passionate belief in telling what one has to tell. I heard David Edgar say recently that (to paraphrase) writing becomes more difficult as one gets older because as one gets older one gets less certain. Perhaps what he meant was that with age one sees the corollary to every argument, that the radical turns merely liberal. I don't want to be liberal. But *what* do I, personally, want to communicate? What is it that I am deeply concerned with at present? Am I being too heavy on myself? When going through this pre-play torture have I *ever* felt concerned with anything? Is total emptiness a necessary condition in the prelude to writing a play?
>
> I don't want to write what I've already written. I want to learn. I want to write a play which forces me to develop the talent I have. Talent must not go back on itself and stagnate. It is a nerve-wracking process but truly it is better to write nothing than to write something which one has already written. It's only with pushing against the barriers, stretching the boundaries, staring at the abyss that the imagination soars and poetry can be achieved. I believe that no great play was ever written at any significant distance from the abyss—they are all written on the edge. Think of Moss Hart saying that one never learns to be a playwright, only how to write one particular play. The next play, no matter how "successful" the playwright, is something about which he knows nothing. He cannot know how to write it, has no guidelines because, before he has written it, it has never existed. Every play is a trip back to the beginning and a walk through hell all over again.

What do I want to say? What moves me? What story do I want to tell? I believe that every play I have ever written has, ultimately, been one which celebrates the goodness of man; certainly, the plays have included emptiness, despair, possibly even baseness. But it is the goodness that I hope the audience is left with. I really don't want to write plays which are resigned, menopausal, despairing, and whinging. I don't want to use any medium as a platform for displaying the smallness and hopelessness of man. Man is man because madly, possibly stupidly but certainly wonderfully, he kicks against the inevitability of life. He spends his life looking for answers. There probably are no answers but the fact that man asks the questions is the reason I write plays.

* * *

What happens when you grow beyond the class and the culture you were born into? When is freedom real and when is it a fake? What is true knowledge? These are the central questions posed by Willy Russell's major plays since the mid-1970's.

Breezeblock Park is set in the houses of two sisters, Betty and Reeny. It is Christmas and therefore a time for competitive consumption. Betty and Reeny try to outdo each other over costly furniture, bathroom fittings, and central-heating systems. Betty's husband Ted is obsessed with his new car and sees himself as an intellectual with his knowledge of *Mastermind* and his ambitions as an author. Betty's brother Tommy represents a vulgar alternative to this working-class gentility when he gives Betty a vibrator as a Christmas present and prefers to celebrate in the pub rather than in his sister's tasteful front room. Gender roles are strictly defined. The women's territory is the home, particularly the kitchen. Their talk is of clothes, food, children, and relationships. The men work away from the home and their talk is of sport, politics, and general knowledge. Everyone, however, closes ranks over the play's central issue—the pregnancy of Betty's daughter Sandra. Their code demands that she marry the father. There's no shame in "being in the club." As Tommy explains: "It's a bloody secret society they've got goin'. They have a great time." But Sandra is different. She reads, she's interested in ideas, she hangs around with students; in fact, her lover, Tim, is a student. After a strong talking-to by the men, Tim is ready to do the decent thing, but Sandra stands firm. She'll have the child, but she'll live with Tim, unmarried, in a student house. "I want a *good* life, Mother," she shouts at Betty. "I want to sit around and talk about films and—and music." And Betty replies, "You begrudge me every bit of pleasure I have ever had." The two cultures, gentility and bohemianism, are irreconcilable. In a skilful last scene Sandra breaks through the menacing circle of her relations, but only because her mother steps aside. Tim meekly follows her.

Another wedding fails and another escape takes place in *Stags and Hens*. It is stag night for Dave and hen night for Linda before they get married. But both parties have booked into the same dance-hall in Liverpool. On a single set, which consists of the Ladies' and Gents' loos side by side, the differing codes of sex, drink, and clothes are enacted in dialogue which is witty, vulgar, sentimental, and bitter. Linda, we discover, is uneducated but discontented with her girlfriends' cheerful acceptance of the conventions of their class. It isn't so much the consumer world of *Breezeblock Park* that is satirised as the competitive world of grabbing a girl or keeping a man. In a shrewd theatrical move, Dave, the groom at tomorrow's "wedding," stays dead drunk throughout the play, which puts the spotlight even more fiercely on Linda. She finally rejects her world by leaving with Peter, lead singer of the band and an old flame who's made good in London. But the last word is given to Eddy, the leader of Dave's friends. It is he, like Tommy in the earlier play, who organises local solidarity against the outsider. "Don't you come makin' people unhappy," he warns Dave. "She's our mate's tart. We look after our mates. We stick with them." Eddy, however, is younger than Tommy. He has to construct a myth of freedom for his class and culture in the dead wastes of Merseyside. Peter may be a successful artist but Eddy assures everyone, "You could do that, what he does if you wanted to. You can do anythin' he can do. We all can." All they can do is get drunk, draw their names on the toilet walls, and try to chat up women. Eddy is furious when Linda gets out, but still optimistic for the future. The play ends with his staggering out of the Gents carrying the still-oblivious Dave over his shoulder and muttering, "She's gone. Well y've got no baggage weighin' y' down. There's nothin' holdin' us back now Dave. We can go anywhere."

With *Educating Rita* all these themes are very sharply expressed and focussed by Rita herself. She's already outpaced Sandra and Linda by enrolling on an Open University course, but the early encounters between her directness and the cultured evasiveness of her tutor Frank reveal real cultural gulfs. But, as she shows in a series of brilliant observations in Act 1, Scene 4, she knows very well what she's leaving behind and why she wants to change. Her class may have a certain level of affluence but it hasn't got meaning, it hasn't got culture as meaningful life. "I just see everyone pissed, or on the Valium, tryin' to get from one day to the next." Since Rita doesn't believe in a distinct working-class culture—"I've read about that. I've never seen it though"—she wants the knowledge and skills that Frank can give her. "What do you want to know?" he asks her at their first tutorial. "Everything," she replies. By the end she's certainly acquired a poise, a sophistication—"I know what clothes to wear, what plays to see"—and a contempt for Frank she didn't have at the beginning. She's escaped her origins and she knows how much everyone resents this kind of mobility. "They hate it when one of them tries to break away."

In his most recent success, the musical *Blood Brothers*, Russell shifts to men and their life chances. Twin brothers, separated at birth, are brought up by natural and fake mothers, in working-class and middle-class environments. Another Linda shuttles between the two. Each sees advantages in the other's situation, but it is working-class Mickey who suffers unemployment, depression, and jealousy over Linda. Edward goes to university and becomes a local politician. He helps his brother with housing and a job but, in a melodramatic ending, Mickey shoots his brother because he thinks Linda has slept with him and gets shot down himself by the police. So, once again, the women progress as the men go under.

Russell has worked a successful vein of cultural satire and class mobility for the last ten years. But old distinctions and antagonisms have now been elided into the cultural fair that we all partake of. What about working-class bohemianism as the next space for his wit and wisdom?

—Tony Dunn

SAINER, Arthur. American. Born in New York City, 12 September 1924. Educated at Washington Square College, New York University (John Golden Award, 1946), 1942–46, B.A. 1946; Columbia University, New York, 1947–48, M.A. in philosophy 1948. Married 1) Stefanie Janis in 1956 (divorced 1962), two sons and two daughters; 2) Maryjane Treloar in 1981. New York editor, *TV Guide*, New York, 1956–61; film critic, *Show Business Illustrated*, Chicago, 1961; founding editor, *Ikon*, New York, 1967. Book critic since 1961, book editor, 1962, and drama critic, 1961–65 and since 1969, *Village Voice*, New York; since 1986 film and theatre editor, *American Book Review*, New York. Member of the English or Theatre department, C.W. Post College, Brookville, New York, 1963–67, 1974–75, Bennington College, Vermont, 1967–69, Chautauqua Writers' Workshop, New York, 1969, Staten Island Community College, New York, 1974–75, Hunter College, New York, 1974, 1980–81, Adelphi University, Garden City, New York, 1975, Wesleyan University, Middletown, Connecticut, 1977–80, and Middlebury College, Vermont, 1981–83. Member of the Academic Council and program adviser, Campus-Free College, Boston, 1971–74. Co-producer, Bridge Theatre, New York, 1965–66. Recipient: Office for Advanced Drama Research grant, 1967; Ford grant, 1979, 1980; Berman award, 1984. Address: 565 West End Avenue, New York, New York 10024, U.S.A.

PUBLICATIONS

Plays

The Bitch of Waverly Place (produced New York, 1964).
The Game of the Eye (produced Bronxville, New York, 1964).
The Day Speaks But Cannot Weep (produced Bronxville, New York, and New York City, 1965).
The Blind Angel (produced New York, 1965).
Untitled Chase (produced New York, 1965).
God Wants What Men Want (also director: produced New York, 1966).
The Bombflower (also director: produced New York, 1966).
The Children's Army Is Late (produced Brookville, New York, 1967; New York City, 1974).
The Thing Itself (produced Minneapolis, 1967; New York, 1972). Published in *Playwrights for Tomorrow 6*, edited by Arthur H. Ballet, Minneapolis, University of Minnesota Press, 1969.
Noses (produced New York, 1967).
OM: A Sharing Service (produced Boston, 1968).
Boat Sun Cavern, music by George Prideaux and Mark Hardwick (produced Bennington, Vermont, 1969; New York, 1978).
Van Gogh (produced New York, 1970).
I Piece Smash (produced New York, 1970). Published in *The Scene/2 (Plays from Off-Off-Broadway)*, edited by Stanley Nelson, New York, The Smith/New Egypt, 1974.
I Hear It Kissing Me, Ladies (produced New York, 1970).
Images of the Coming Dead (produced New York, 1971).
The Celebration: Jooz/Guns/Movies/The Abyss (produced New York, 1972).
Go Children Slowly (produced New York, 1973).
The Spring Offensive (produced New York, 1974).
Charley Chestnut Rides the I.R.T., music by Sainer (produced New York, 1975).
Day Old Bread: The Worst Good Time I Ever Had (produced New York, 1976).
The Rich Man, Poor Man Play, music by David Tice and Paul Dyer (produced New York, 1976).
Witnesses (also director: produced New York, 1977).
Carol in Winter Sunlight, music by George Prideaux (produced New York, 1977).
After the Baal-Shem Tov (produced New York, 1979).
Sunday Childhood Journeys to Nobody at Home (produced New York, 1980).

Television Plays: *A New Year for Margaret*, 1951; *The Dark Side of the Moon*, 1957; *A Man Loses His Dog More or Less*, 1972.

Other

The Sleepwalker and the Assassin: A Study of the Contemporary Theatre. New York, Bridgehead, 1964.
The Radical Theatre Notebook. New York, Avon, 1975.

*

Theatrical Activities:
Director: **Plays**—several of his own plays, and *Lord Tom Goldsmith* by Victor Lipton, New York, 1979.
Actor: **Plays**—*OM: A Sharing Service*, Boston, 1968; *The Children's Army Is Late*, Parma, Italy, 1974.

Arthur Sainer comments:

(1973) I like to believe I write plays to find out something—about self, about self in cosmos, about the cosmos, I try to make something in order to understand something.

But they're not thinking plays as much as feeling plays. I understand primarily through feeling. So I try to shape something into being so I can feel it, so others can feel it. Sometimes the plays use ideological material but they aren't ideological plays. Ultimately if they work they work as felt experience.

For some time I was fascinated by the juxtaposition of live performers and visual projections, concerned with an enlarged arrested image operating on a level other than that of the "real" performer. That period ran from *The Game of the Eye* (1964) through *Boat Sun Cavern* (written in 1967, produced in 1969). But I've lost interest in projections, I want the magic to be live, immediate, home-made. And I want the mistakes to be live ones.

Language—I've gone from many words, *God Wants What Men Want* (written in 1963), to few words, *The Blind Angel* (1965), *The Bombflower* (1966), to some words, *Images of the Coming Dead* (1971). None of these approaches is superior to the others. It depends on what the play needs and what the playwright needs at that time. Bodies are no more or less useful than the utterances that emerge from them. Only truth is useful.

Words are useful, but so is everything else. I don't hold with Grotowski's belief that every conceivable element other than the performer ought to be stripped away. Everything on God's earth, everything designed or decimated by the hands of man, is potentially viable and important, all of it is a testament to this life. But I've come lately (in *The Spring Offensive*) to believe in an economy of means—forget the lights, forget the setting—to believe in the magic of what is obviously being put together by hand before our eyes.

Much theatre leaves me cold, and most audiences disturb me. I don't want to make audiences happy particularly or excite them anymore. I don't want them to be sitting there judging the play, to be weighing its excellences and faults. I want the audiences to be seized and ultimately to become the play. We like to say that a really fine play changed its audience, but a really fine play also creates the condition where its audience can change it. The play ultimately is the product of this mutual vulnerability.

* * *

Theatre's ability to reproduce the external, everyday details of human life is balanced by its need to incorporate the internal, imaginative reality of its characters. Arthur Sainer's plays combine the two kinds of reality by allowing the characters to retain their unique contributions to life, while linking them into a living whole. Whether describing radical politics of the 1960's, the shifting forces at work in love and marriage, the alienation of the poor and dispossessed, a subway conductor's imminent death, or other contemporary struggles with life, Sainer is sensitive to both the effect of daily routines and rituals, and the pressure of people upon one another. His real subjects are not the events that happen to people in the course of a play, but rather the way people change and are changed by life around them.

This concentration on people produces plays that are plotless in the usual sense, but obey a rigorous internal logic. Louis, the protagonist of *The Thing Itself*, says

> In the theatre to which we are offering our blood, there are no characters to be created. There are no consistencies, no patterns. Instead there are irrelevancies, inconsistencies, mistakes, broken thoughts. There is an impulse toward chaos, another toward assimilation. In our theatre there is no stage and no story, there is only human life pushed into a corner, threatened with extinction. And human life threatened with human life. And always mistakes.

The statement is unusually blunt for Sainer, whose dialogue is most often more oblique and questioning, and *The Thing Itself* unusually pessimistic and bitter, but Louis does describe Sainer's primary attitude toward drama's means and goals. Louis and his friends—Harold, who eats obsessively; Althea, a sympathetic prostitute who is brutal toward her brutal customers—are coping with the thing itself, the degradation of life in an impersonal, almost savage, city environment.

As in most of Sainer's plays, *The Thing Itself* is frequently interrupted by mimed scenes, fantasies, monologues, songs, slides, and films. Sainer has used most of the techniques available to contemporary playwrights—from Brechtian alienation to improvisation and audience participation—quite skillfully, but in every case they are expressions of the contradictory, tumultuously human life of the plays. A trilogy—*Images of the Coming Dead, The Children's Army Is Late*, and *Carol in Winter Sunlight*—follows the growth and evolution of a family: the shifting stresses on David and Carol resulting from David's immersion in filmmaking, Carol's increasing desire to escape the trap of the family, the love both bear for their children, and their concern for their aging parents combine to create a broad and penetrating portrait of the family. In addition, the logic of this portrait calls up a series of mythological and allegorical scenes: a group of figures who begin in naked innocence, gradually become a mindlessly hardworking society, and are beset by aggressive renegades; Hector and Achilles fight their epic combat; and two characters named Allan and Albert re-enact the tragedy of Cain and Abel with a modern twist. The evolution of the human race vibrates against the evolution of the family, and the depiction of the family, sharp and sensitive as it is, is extended and expanded.

Sainer's ability to mesh the intimacy of everyday life and the development of civilization combines with his inquiries into the meaning of Jewish history to focus his plays on death. In *The Children's Army Is Late*, David searches to find and film a dying man. *Charley Chestnut Rides the I.R.T.* is filled with the bewilderment and agony of an ordinary subway conductor who suddenly faces death from a terminal illness. However, the interest in death stems from its use as a reflection of life. *After the Baal-Shem Tov* tells the story of a Jew who survives a German concentration camp to start life anew in the United States. Israel is an innocent, gentle man with an irritating habit of questioning everything. As he makes his way in America, visits a kibbutz in Israel, and becomes the editor of a respected Jewish newspaper, he loses his naivety but not his questions. Recalling his liberation from the concentration camp, he sings

> Here in the new world, the absent
> From the dead take on new life,
> The skeletons take on new flesh.
>
> What's it like now for the absent from the dead?
> What's it like now? Shoving, running,
> Piling up things, looking into faces.
> It's stupid life, it's joyous days.

Israel gives up everything and everyone he has gained in order to "redeem the promises," and there is throughout Sainer's plays an intensely human attempt to redeem the gift of life, to understand the death of people, of ideas, and of relationships in order to appreciate them more fully.

—Walter Bode

SAUNDERS, James A. British. Born in Islington, London, 8 January 1925. Educated at Wembley County School; University of Southampton. Married Audrey Cross in 1951; one son and two daughters. Formerly taught English in London. Since 1962 full-time writer. Recipient: Arts Council bursary, 1960, 1984; *Evening Standard* award, 1963; Writers Guild award, 1966. Lives in Twickenham, Middlesex. Agent: Margaret Ramsay Ltd., 14-A Goodwin's Court, London, WC2N 4LL, England.

PUBLICATIONS

Plays

Cinderella Comes of Age (produced London, 1949).
Moonshine (produced London, 1955).
Dog Accident (broadcast 1958; revised version produced London, 1969). Published in *Ten of the Best*, edited by Ed Berman, London, Inter-Action Imprint, 1979.
Barnstable (broadcast 1959; produced Dublin and London, 1960). London, French, 1965.
Alas, Poor Fred: A Duologue in the Style of Ionesco (produced Scarborough, 1959; London, 1966). Scarborough, Studio Theatre, 1960.
The Ark, music by Geoffrey Wright (produced London, 1959).

Ends and Echoes: Barnstable, Committal, Return to a City (produced London, 1960). *Return to a City* included in *Neighbours and Other Plays*, 1968.

A Slight Accident (produced Nottingham, 1961; London, 1971; Chicago, 1977). Included in *Neighbours and Other Plays*, 1968.

Double, Double (produced London, 1962). London, French, 1964.

Next Time I'll Sing to You, suggested by a theme from *A Hermit Disclosed* by Raleigh Trevelyan (produced London, 1962; revised version produced London and New York, 1963). London, Deutsch, and New York, Random House, 1963.

Who Was Hilary Maconochie? (produced London, 1963). Included in *Savoury Meringue and Other Plays*, 1980.

The Pedagogue (produced London, 1963). Included in *Neighbours and Other Plays*, 1968.

Neighbours (produced London, 1964; New York, 1969). Included in *Neighbours and Other Plays*, 1968.

A Scent of Flowers (produced London, 1964; New York, 1969). London, Deutsch, and New York, Random House, 1965.

Triangle, with others (produced Glasgow, 1965; London, 1983).

Trio (produced Edinburgh, 1967). Included in *Neighbours and Other Plays*, 1968.

The Italian Girl, with Iris Murdoch, adaptation of the novel by Murdoch (produced Bristol, 1967; London, 1968). London, French, 1969.

Neighbours and Other Plays (includes *Trio; Alas, Poor Fred; Return to a City; A Slight Accident; The Pedagogue*). London, Deutsch, 1968.

Haven, later called *A Man's Best Friend*, in *We Who Are about to ...*, later called *Mixed Doubles* (produced London, 1969). London, Methuen, 1970.

The Travails of Sancho Panza, based on the novel *Don Quixote* by Cervantes (produced London, 1969). London, Heinemann, 1970.

The Borage Pigeon Affair (produced London, 1969). London, Deutsch, 1970.

Savoury Meringue (produced London, 1971; New York, 1981). Included in *Savoury Meringue and Other Plays*, 1980.

After Liverpool (broadcast 1971; produced Edinburgh and London, 1971; New York, 1973). London, French, 1973.

Games (produced Edinburgh and London, 1971; New York, 1973). London, French, 1973.

Opus (produced Loughton, Essex, 1971).

Hans Kohlhaas, adaptation of the story by Heinrich von Kleist (produced London, 1972; as *Michael Kohlhaas*, produced London, 1987).

Bye Bye Blues (produced Richmond, Surrey, 1973; London, 1977). Included in *Bye Bye Blues and Other Plays*, 1980.

Poor Old Simon (in *Mixed Blessings*, produced Horsham, Sussex, 1973; produced separately, New York, 1981). Included in *Savoury Meringue and Other Plays*, 1980.

Random Moments in a May Garden (broadcast 1974; produced London, 1977). Included in *Bye Bye Blues and Other Plays*, 1980.

A Journey to London, completion of the play by Vanbrugh (produced London, 1975).

Play for Yesterday (produced Richmond, Surrey, 1975; London, 1983). Included in *Savoury Meringue and Other Plays*, 1980.

The Island (produced London, 1975). Included in *Bye Bye Blues and Other Plays*, 1980.

Squat (produced Richmond, Surrey, 1976).

Mrs. Scour and the Future of Western Civilisation (produced Richmond, Surrey, 1976; London, 1983).

Bodies (produced Richmond, Surrey, 1977; London, 1978; New Haven, Connecticut, 1981). Ashover, Derbyshire, Amber Lane Press, and New York, Dramatists Play Service, 1979.

Over the Wall (produced London, 1977). Published in *Play Ten*, edited by Robin Rook, London, Arnold, 1977.

What Theatre Really Is, in *Play Ten*, edited by Robin Rook. London, Arnold, 1977.

Player Piano, adaptation of the novel by Kurt Vonnegut (produced London, 1978).

The Mountain (produced Bristol, 1979).

The Caucasian Chalk Circle, adaptation of a play by Brecht (produced Richmond, Surrey, 1979).

Birdsong (produced Richmond, Surrey, 1979; New York, 1984). Included in *Savoury Meringue and Other Plays*, 1980.

The Girl in Melanie Klein, adaptation of the novel by Ronald Harwood (produced Watford, Hertfordshire, 1980).

Savoury Meringue and Other Plays. Ambergate, Derbyshire, Amber Lane Press, 1980.

Bye Bye Blues and Other Plays (includes *The Island* and *Random Moments in a May Garden*). Ambergate, Derbyshire, Amber Lane Press, 1980.

Fall (produced Richmond, Surrey, 1981; London, 1984). London, French, 1985.

Nothing to Declare (broadcast 1982; produced Richmond, Surrey, 1983).

Menocchio (broadcast 1985). Published in *Best Radio Plays of 1985*, London, Methuen, 1986.

Radio Plays: *Love and a Limousine*, 1952; *The Drop Too Much*, 1952; *Nimrod's Oak*, 1953; *Women Are So Unreasonable*, 1957; *Dog Accident*, 1958; *Barnstable*, 1959; *Gimlet* (version of *Double, Double*), 1963; *It's Not the Game It Was*, 1964; *Pay As You Go*, 1965; *After Liverpool*, 1971; *Random Moments in a May Garden*, 1974; *The Last Black and White Midnight Movie*, 1979; *Nothing to Declare*, 1982; *The Flower Case*, 1982; *A Suspension of Mercy* (*Murder for Pleasure* series), from the novel by Patricia Highsmith, 1983; *Menocchio*, 1985.

Television Plays: *Just You Wait* (version of *Double, Double*), 1963; *Watch Me I'm a Bird*, 1964; *The White Stocking, New Eve and Old Adam, Tickets Please, Monkey Nuts, Two Blue Birds, In Love*, and *The Blue Moccasins*, all from works by D.H. Lawrence, 1966–67; *The Beast in the Jungle*, from the story by Henry James, 1969; *Plastic People*, 1970; *The Unconquered*, 1970; *Craven Arms*, from a story by A.E. Coppard, 1972; *The Mill*, 1972; *The Black Dog*, 1972; *Blind Love*, from the story by V.S. Pritchett, 1977; *The Healing Nightmare*, 1977; *People Like Us*, with Susan Pieat and Ian Curteis, from the novel by R.F. Delderfield, 1978; *Bloomers* series, 1979; *The Sailor's Return*, from the novel by David Garnett, 1980; *The Captain's Doll*, from the story by D.H. Lawrence, 1983; *The Magic Bathroom*, 1987.

* * *

James Saunders's work is characterized by a diversity of style which is unusual even among the more eclectic of his contemporaries. He can be compared to a startling variety of other writers, and, should his scripts survive without attribution, future generations of scholars might assign them in something like this fashion: to Harold Pinter the revue sketch investment of the commonplace with interest found in *Double, Double* and the schematic exploration of open marriage found in *Bye Bye Blues*; to John Mortimer the charming coincidence of complimentary handicaps which permits two self-pitying people to unite in *Blind Love*; to Samuel Beckett the seemingly plotless philosophizing of *Next Time I'll Sing to You*; to John Arden and Margaretta D'Arcy the episodic structure and satire of inept and hypocritical public officials in *The Borage Pigeon Affair*; to Eugène Ionesco or N.F. Simpson the absurdist farce of such one-acts as *Who Was Hilary Maconochie?, Alas, Poor Fred*, and *A Slight Accident*; to Simon Gray the mutual torment inflicted by sophisticates in extremis found in *Bodies*; to Peter Handke the invitation to spectators to reject the play found in the fragmented *Games*; to Henry Livings the music-hall flavor of *Savoury Meringue*; and to any one of dozens of realistic dramatists the belligerence and bewilderment of the interracial psychological study *Neighbours*.

Although Saunders's stylistic range is breathtaking our 21st-century literary detectives might discover his authorship by recognizing his distinctive situations and themes. His dramatis personae are frequently couples, and he is constantly investigating how people can relate to others, care about others, commit themselves to others, and sustain the relationship long term. The alienated Saunders character often lives close to the edge. He or she finds difficulty wrenching meaning from a life rendered pointless by death and unbearable by loneliness or, paradoxically, by the proximity of people. He probes the false values exemplified in various interpersonal relations, and illuminates the responsibility people assume or evade for the choices they make. He's a humanist sympathetic to the underdog or the rebel, and deeply suspicious of the games people play to keep their emotions at bay or to score points off others. Yet he's expert at dramatizing those often urbane games, and such is the ambiguity of his situations—particularly in his more recent work—that spectators may be forgiven for wondering whether his commiseration for the losers isn't balanced by a certain admiration for the victor's skill.

Saunders has created a constellation of wonderfully ineffectual characters. There's the driver in *Gimlet* whose bus passes through—but is really bypassed by—life. There's the befuddled actor in *Triangle* who's "not quite sure whether I'm trying to play myself or trying not to play myself." There are the musicians in *Trio* who can't perform because they're under attack by flies. There's the teacher in *The Pedagogue* who loses control of his pupils as well as his faith in mankind. There are the men and women in *After Liverpool* who often botch their desultory attempts to talk to each other. There's the wife in *A Slight Accident* who's flustered by her husband's failure to get up off the floor after she's murdered him and poor Pringle's confusion when he's reminded that he killed the title character in *Alas, Poor Fred*. There's the deceased protagonist of *A Scent of Flowers* whose inability to inspire in her family any accessible love has led her to suicide. In *Next Time I'll Sing to You* there's little Lizzie who's lost because she's replacing her twin sister in the role without benefit of either rehearsal or script. There are the ridiculous attempts of the macho men in *The Island* to bully their superiors (the women) into liking them. ("If I had been expecting anything," quips one of the gals, "they'd be a disappointment.") And there are those archetypal sufferers of indignity in *The Travails of Sancho Panza*.

Repeatedly Saunders has dramatized the tension between such poles as independence and dependence or our responsibility for choices versus our lack of control over events. In an early radio play which later became the street theatre piece *Dog Accident*, for instance, Saunders confronts passersby with a dispute between—seemingly—two of their number over a dog who's just been run over. They disagree over whether the dog's demise was its own fault and, later, over whether the dog's really dead or still suffering. Why, argues the indifferent one, should they care about a dying dog when large-scale catastrophe strikes people every day? The other momentarily opts for bothering, then either can't sustain or can't stomach the pain and prefers to go to lunch. Our mutual interdependence and the complex determinants of an event also inform *Bye Bye Blues*, in which three separate couples discuss one or more automobile accidents in which they're all somehow involved or implicated.

Saunders's best known play, *Next Time I'll Sing to You*, picks as its subject a hermit, Jimmy Mason, who died in Essex in 1942. Another writer might have considered Mason's solitary life and death more conventionally and sentimentally. But Saunders suggests the aimlessness of life with a form which itself rambles. This presentational style and non-linear "plot" may communicate subliminally that life is disordered suffering. Ostensibly, however, the play is a comedy in which the characters are actors making disconnected attempts to put on a play about Mason. They crack jokes, discuss whether they're asleep, and confuse the actress who is supposedly a substitute for her sister. Perhaps five minutes is devoted to conveying the facts of Mason's life. Gradually such philosophical issues as the nature of man and the purpose of life are raised. *Next Time I'll Sing to You*, like *Waiting for Godot*, employs off-beat characters and structure to raise fundamental human questions. After we wonder why Mason lived alone—or, indeed, why he lived—we come to wonder whether his solitude differs only superficially from our own. If we're better off than Mason, the reason may only be "One thing about us—at least we're not dead."

Although well known, *Next Time I'll Sing to You* has been regarded by some critics as pretentious or incomprehensible. Neither charge could be levelled at Saunders's best play, *Bodies*. Though seemingly more realistic—because it's set in recognizable contemporary homes—*Bodies* is one of Saunders's many plays which combine presentational and representational styles. It also epitomizes his highly verbal work; hearing it is much more important than seeing it.

In *Bodies* Saunders portrays two couples who many years before had affairs with each others' mates. Act 1 intercuts monologues, in which each of the four recalls the affairs, with duologues on their approaching reunion with their ex-lovers. Act 2 brings them, at that reunion, into present confrontation with their pasts. The couples have handled their mid-life crises—or passages—quite differently. Anne and Merwyn—who have considered themselves unromantic pragmatists—muddle along experiencing their anxiety at reaching middle age, their panic at disillusionment in the things they once held dear, their terror at lack of self-esteem. David and Helen, on the other hand, have reached, by means of a new therapy, a state untroubled by emotions of any kind. They insist people are only bodies, and happiness and unhappiness don't exist.

We are meant to wonder whether feelings are valuable. Especially if these passions are painful, is it preferable, like tranquil and twitchless David and Helen, to be therapeutically freed from suffering, from the insistence on finding meaning in experience? Or is that insensitive, unresponsive to life, and is one therefore better off—as Peter Shaffer's *Equus* and innumerable other contemporary British plays suggest—with one's neuroses intact? But if Saunders initially sets up a dichotomy between detached David and Helen and the troubled teacher

Merwyn, he subtly suggests that the latter also escapes his emotional traumas, though his means is not therapy, but mental agility liberally laced with alcohol. An off-stage student, meanwhile, has left Merwyn's English seminar and fled his feelings still more effectively by killing himself. Ultimately what Saunders has dramatized, then, is alternative routes to wasting one's personal emotional riches.

Saunders has been blessed with sufficient royalties from his German productions to earn a living and the long-term willingness of two London groups (the Questors and the Richmond Fringe at the Orange Tree) to try whatever he happens to write. Free from worry over whether each new work will prove a commercial success, Saunders has been able to write to please himself. Perhaps this has encouraged self-indulgence in scenes sometimes simultaneously cerebral and long-winded. Yet when he avoids verbosity, Saunders succeeds with versatility, ingenuity, whimsy, suspense, wit, and an emotional sensitivity which permits him to touch us without growing maudlin. Both in depth and in range, his plays continue to intrigue longer than might the work of a more uniform playwright.

—Tish Dace

SCHEVILL, James (Erwin). American. Born in Berkeley, California, 10 June 1920. Educated at Harvard University, Cambridge, Massachusetts, B.S. 1942. Served in the United States Army, 1942–46. Married Margot Helmuth Blum in 1966; two daughters by an earlier marriage. Member of the Faculty, California College of Arts and Crafts, Oakland, 1950–59; member of the Faculty, 1959–68, and director of the Poetry Center, 1961–68, San Francisco State College. Since 1969 Professor of English, Brown University, Providence, Rhode Island. Founding member, Wastepaper Theatre, Providence; since 1983 President, Rhode Island Playwrights Theatre. Recipient: National Theatre Competition prize, 1945; Dramatists Alliance Contest prize, 1948; Fund for the Advancement of Education fellowship, 1953; Phelan prize, for biography, 1954, for play, 1958; Ford grant, 1960; Rockefeller grant, 1964; William Carlos Williams award (*Contact* magazine), 1965; Roadstead Foundation award, 1966; Rhode Island Governor's award, 1975; Guggenheim fellowship, 1981; McKnight fellowship, 1984. Agent: Helen Merrill Ltd., 361 West 17th Street, New York, New York 10011. Address: Department of English, Brown University, Providence, Rhode Island 02912, U.S.A.

PUBLICATIONS

Plays

High Sinners, Low Angels, music by Schevill, arranged by Robert Commanday (produced San Francisco, 1953). San Francisco, Bern Porter, 1953.
The Bloody Tenet (produced Providence, Rhode Island, 1956; Shrewsbury, Shropshire, 1962). Included in *The Black President and Other Plays*, 1965.
The Cid, adaptation of the play by Corneille (broadcast 1963). Published in *The Classic Theatre 4*, edited by Eric Bentley, New York, Doubleday, 1961.
Voices of Mass and Capital A, music by Andrew Imbrie (produced San Francisco, 1962). New York, Friendship Press, 1962.
The Master (produced San Francisco, 1963). Included in *The Black President and Other Plays*, 1965.
American Power: The Space Fan, and The Master (produced Minneapolis, 1964). Included in *The Black President and Other Plays*, 1965.
The Black President and Other Plays. Denver, Swallow, 1965.
The Death of Anton Webern (produced Fish Creek, Wisconsin, 1966). Included in *Violence and Glory: Poems 1962–1968*, 1969.
This Is Not True, music by Paul McIntyre (produced Minneapolis, 1967).
The Pilots (produced Providence, Rhode Island, 1970).
Oppenheimer's Chair (produced Providence, Rhode Island, 1970).
Lovecraft's Follies (produced Providence, Rhode Island, 1970). Chicago, Swallow Press, 1971.
The Ushers (produced Providence, Rhode Island, 1971).
The American Fantasies (produced New York, 1972).
Emperor Norton Lives! (produced Salt Lake City, 1972; revised version, as *Emperor Norton*, music by Jerome Rosen, produced San Francisco, 1979).
Fay Wray Meets King Kong (produced Providence, Rhode Island, 1974). Published in *Wastepaper Theatre Anthology*, edited by Schevill, 1978.
Sunset and Evening Stance; or, Mr. Krapp's New Tapes (produced Providence, Rhode Island, 1974). Published in *Wastepaper Theatre Anthology*, edited by Schevill, 1978.
The Telephone Murderer (produced Providence, Rhode Island, 1975). Published in *Wastepaper Theatre Anthology*, edited by Schevill, 1978.
Cathedral of Ice (produced Providence, Rhode Island, 1975). Wood Hole, Massachusetts, Pourboire Press, 1975.
Naked in the Garden (produced Providence, Rhode Island, 1975).
Year after Year (produced Providence, Rhode Island, 1976).
Questioning Woman (produced Providence, Rhode Island, 1980).
Mean Man I (also director: produced Providence, Rhode Island, 1981).
Mean Man II (also director: produced Providence, Rhode Island, 1982).
Edison's Dream (produced Providence, Rhode Island, 1982).
Cult of Youth (produced Minneapolis, 1984).
Galileo, with Adrian Hall, adaptation of the play by Brecht (produced Providence, Rhode Island, 1984).
Mean Man III (also director: produced Providence, Rhode Island, 1985).
Time of the Hand and Eye (produced Providence, Rhode Island, 1986).
The Planner (also director: produced Providence, Rhode Island, 1986).
Collected Short Plays. Athens, Swallow Press-Ohio University Press, 1986.
The Storyville Doll Lady (also director: produced Providence, Rhode Island, 1987).

Radio Plays: *The Sound of a Soldier*, 1945; *The Death of a President*, 1945; *The Cid*, 1963 (Canada).

Novel

The Arena of Ants. Providence, Rhode Island, Copper Beech Press, 1977.

Verse

Tensions. San Francisco, Bern Porter, 1947.

The American Fantasies. San Francisco, Bern Porter, 1951.
The Right to Greet. San Francisco, Bern Porter, 1955.
Selected Poems 1945–1959. San Francisco, Bern Porter, 1960.
Private Dooms and Public Destinations: Poems 1945–1962. Denver, Swallow, 1962.
The Stalingrad Elegies. Denver, Swallow, 1964.
Release. Providence, Rhode Island, Hellcoal Press, 1968.
Violence and Glory: Poems 1962–1968. Chicago, Swallow Press, 1969.
The Buddhist Car and Other Characters. Chicago, Swallow Press, 1973.
Pursuing Elegy: A Poem about Haiti. Providence, Rhode Island, Copper Beech Press, 1974.
The Mayan Poems. Providence, Rhode Island, Copper Beech Press, 1978.
Fire of Eyes: A Guatemalan Sequence. Providence, Rhode Island, Copper Beech Press, 1979.
The American Fantasies: Collected Poems 1: 1945–1981. Athens, Swallow Press-Ohio University Press, 1983.
The Invisible Volcano. Providence, Rhode Island, Copper Beech Press, 1985.
Ambiguous Dancers of Fame: Collected Poems 2: 1945–1986. Athens, Swallow Press-Ohio University Press, 1987.

Recording: *Performance Poems*, Cambridge, 1984.

Other

Sherwood Anderson: His Life and Work. Denver, University of Denver Press, 1951.
The Roaring Market and the Silent Tomb (biographical study of the scientist and artist Bern Porter). Oakland, California, Abbey Press, 1956.

Editor, *Six Historians*, by Ferdinand Schevill. Chicago, University of Chicago Press, and London, Cambridge University Press, 1956.
Editor, *Break Out! In Search of New Theatrical Environments.* Chicago, Swallow Press, 1973.
Editor, *Wastepaper Theatre Anthology.* Providence, Rhode Island, Pourboire Press, 1978.

*

Manuscript Collection: John Hay Library, Brown University, Providence, Rhode Island.

Critical Study: unpublished thesis by Wanda Howard, University of Rhode Island, Providence, 1981.

Theatrical Activities:
Director: **Plays**—Wastepaper Theatre, Providence: *Mean Man I–III*, 1981–85; *The Planner*, 1986; *The Storyville Doll Lady*, 1987.

James Schevill comments:

(1973) My early plays were verse plays. Recently, my plays have been written in prose. However, as a poet, I still believe in poetry as the roots of the theatre, and do my best to upend a theatre that is too literal and prosaic. I want an action that is both theatrical and poetic, that can use the disturbing images of our time to create a new vitality on stage. To achieve this vitality, I like to use dramatic, historical contrasts to give a play depth and perspective. Today the great possibilities of playwriting lie in the recognition that a play can range in time and space as widely as a film, that it can be as exciting in movement as a film, and that the great advantage it continues to have over film is the live actor who is capable of instantaneous, extraordinary transformations in character and situation.

* * *

A lyric poet, James Schevill has been consistently drawn to the theatre, but his plays are written largely in prose. Composed of history, current events, and fantasy, they theatricalize injustice in contemporary America.

The Bloody Tenet takes its title from the self-defense of Roger Williams when he was persecuted for religious unorthodoxy. Schevill's play sets Williams's story as a play within a play, and the outer frame is a dialogue between a middle-aged Journalist and a voluptuous Evangelist. As the inner play dramatizes Williams's condemnation by orthodox authority, the frame play dramatizes a facile orthodoxy paying lip service to liberty. Schevill's play finally confronts his moderns with Williams himself, who refuses to choose between the Journalist's critique of his inadequacies and the Evangelist's idolization of him. In verse Roger Williams re-emphasizes his belief in individual paths to God.

Moving from religion to politics, Schevill paired his next two plays under the title *American Power*. The first play, *The Space Fan*, is subtitled a play of escape, and the second one, *The Master*, a play of commitment. The titular Space Fan is a zany lady who communicates with beings in outer space, and a suspicious government therefore assigns an Investigator to spy on her activities. Through the course of the play the Space Fan converts the Investigator to her free way of life, and as they join in a dance the Investigator declares: "For the first time in my life, I feel that I've become a real investigator."

In the companion play, *The Master*, investigation is more insidious. An attractive young woman, the Candidate, is guided by the Master in examinations which will culminate in a degree of General Mastery. During the examination the Master imposes upon the Candidate various roles, such as Army Officer, Indian squaw, Minute Man, Southern rebel, and finally corpse. Master and Candidate then oppose each other with their respective autobiographies, which erupt into scenes that glorify American power. The subtitles of both plays emerge as ironic: *The Space Fan* is a play of escape from American power, and *The Master*, a play of commitment, satirizes (and implicitly condemns) commitment to American power.

Schevill's next play, *The Black President*, is rooted in American oppression of blacks, but it reaches out to indict the whole white racist world. Moses Jackburn, a black American, is captain of a fascimile slaveship that is manned by the blacks of many countries. He sails the ship up the Thames to London, demanding to speak with the British Prime Minister. He is met with pious platitudes, then mercantile bargaining, and finally threats of force. Rather than surrender the ship, Jackson orders his crew to blow it up. While awaiting extradition to America, he is visited by Spanish Carla with whom he shares a fantasy life in which she helps him campaign for the presidency, to become the first "Black President." Back in the reality of his prison, Jackburn denounces his dream, but still hopes for "a little light."

In *Lovecraft's Follies* Schevill indicates his concern about man's enslavement by technology. H.P. Lovecraft, a Rhode Island recluse, was one of the first science-fiction writers to stress its gothic horrors. The protagonist of Schevill's play, Stanley Millsage, is a physicist at a space center, who has developed a Lovecraft fixation-fear of the horrors that science can perpetrate, which are theatricalized scenically to serve as a cathartic journey for the protagonist. Thus freed from his Lovecraft fixation, Millsage decares: "Well, that's the end of Lovecraft's follies. . . ." But the figure of Lovecraft, alone on stage, says mockingly to the audience: "Maybe!"

That "Maybe" leads to Schevill's next major play, *Cathedral of Ice*, in which technology again brings horror. On stage is a dream machine: "With our machine's modern computer device/We conjure up a vast Cathedral of Ice./ . . . I become Dream-Fuehrer, power to arrange." The drama fancifully traces the results of Hitler's power mania; in seven scenes he confronts historical and imaginary figures. Inspired by Napoleon and Charlemagne, Hitler summons an architect to "create for eternity our famous German ruins." Converting people's weaknesses into cruel and theatrical strengths, Hitler builds on the legends of Karl May and Richard Wagner. He refuses to tarnish his own legend by marrying Eva Braun. Above all he harnesses science to his monstrous destructive dream. But Night and Fog, actual characters, erode his structures. Even as the gas chambers destroy their multitudes, the Nazis are destroyed by their own manias, so that Hitler finally seeks glory in a *Liebestod* in the Cathedral of Ice.

In fantastic theatrical shapes Schevill's drama explores the realities of power and politics. Using music, dance, ritual, projections, Schevill the poet has reached out to embrace many possibilities of theatre.

—Ruby Cohn

SCHISGAL, Murray (Joseph). American. Born in Brooklyn, New York, 25 November 1926. Educated at the Brooklyn Conservatory of Music; Long Island University, New York; Brooklyn Law School, LL.B. 1953; New School for Social Research, New York, B.A. 1959. Served as a radioman in the United States Navy, 1944–46. Married Reene Schapiro in 1958; one daughter and one son. Jazz musician in 1940's; lawyer, 1953–55; English teacher, Cooper Junior High School, East Harlem, and other private and public schools in New York, 1955–59. Since 1960 full-time writer. Recipient: Vernon Rice award, 1963; Outer Circle award, 1963; Los Angeles and New York Film Critics award, National Society of Film Critics award, and Writers Guild award, all for screenplay, 1983. Lives in New York City. Agent: Bridget Aschenberg, International Creative Management, 40 West 57th Street, New York, New York 10019, U.S.A.

PUBLICATIONS

Plays

The Typists, and The Tiger (as *Schrecks: The Typists, The Postman, A Simple Kind of Love*, produced London, 1960; revised versions of *The Typists* and *The Postman* produced as *The Typists, and The Tiger*, New York, 1963; London, 1964). New York, Coward McCann, 1963; London, Cape, 1964.

Ducks and Lovers (produced London, 1961). New York, Dramatists Play Service, 1972.

Luv (produced London, 1963; New York, 1964). New York, Coward McCann, 1965.

Knit One, Purl Two (produced Boston, 1963).

Windows (produced Los Angeles, 1965). Included in *Fragments, Windows and Other Plays*, 1965.

Reverberations (produced Stockbridge, Massachusetts, 1965; as *The Basement*, produced New York, 1967). Included in *Fragments, Windows and Other Plays*, 1965.

Fragments, Windows and Other Plays (includes *Reverberations, Memorial Day, The Old Jew*). New York, Coward McCann, 1965.

The Old Jew, Fragments, and Reverberations (produced Stockbridge, Massachusetts, 1966). Included in *Fragments, Windows and Other Plays*, 1965.

Fragments (includes *The Basement* and *Fragments*) (produced New York, 1967). Included in *Fragments, Windows and Other Plays*, 1965.

Memorial Day (produced Baltimore, 1968). Included in *Fragments, Windows and Other Plays*, 1965.

Jimmy Shine, music by John Sebastian (produced New York, 1968; revised version, as *An Original Jimmy Shine*, produced Los Angeles, 1981). New York, Atheneum, 1969.

A Way of Life (produced New York, 1969; as *Roseland*, produced Berlin, 1975; as *The Downstairs Boys*, produced East Hampton, New York, 1980).

The Chinese, and Dr. Fish (produced New York, 1970). New York, Dramatists Play Service, 1970.

An American Millionaire (produced New York, 1974). New York, Dramatists Play Service, 1974.

All over Town (produced New York, 1974). New York, Dramatists Play Service, 1975.

Popkins (produced Dallas, 1978). New York, Dramatists Play Service, 1984.

The Pushcart Peddlers (produced New York, 1979). Included in *The Pushcart Peddlers, The Flatulist, and Other Plays*, 1980.

Walter, and The Flatulist (produced New York, 1980). Included in *The Pushcart Peddlers, The Flatulist, and Other Plays*, 1980.

The Pushcart Peddlers, The Flatulist, and Other Plays (includes *A Simple Kind of Love Story, Little Johnny, Walter*). New York, Dramatists Play Service, 1980.

Twice Around the Park (includes *A Need for Brussels Sprouts* and *A Need for Less Expertise*) (produced New York, 1982; Edinburgh, 1984). Included in *Luv and Other Plays*, 1983.

Luv and Other Plays (includes *The Typists, The Tiger, Fragments, The Basement, The Chinese, The Pushcart Peddlers, The Flatulist, Twice Around the Park*). New York, Dodd Mead, 1983.

The New Yorkers (produced New York, 1984).

Jealousy (produced New York, 1984). With *There Are No Sacher Tortes in Our Society!*, New York, Dramatists Play Service, 1985.

Closet Madness and Other Plays (includes *The Rabbi and the Toyota Dealer* and *Summer Romance*). New York, French, 1984.

The Rabbi and the Toyota Dealer (produced Los Angeles, 1985). Included in *Closet Madness and Other Plays*, 1984.

Old Wine in a New Bottle (produced in Flemish, Antwerp, 1985). New York, Dramatists Play Service, 1987.

Schneider (produced Stockbridge, Massachusetts, 1986).

Road Show (produced New York, 1987). New York, Dramatists Play Service, 1987.

Screenplays: *The Tiger Makes Out*, 1967; *Tootsie*, with others, 1983.

Television Plays: *The Love Song of Barney Kempinski*, 1966; *Natasha Kovolina Pipishinsky*, 1976.

Novel

Days and Nights of a French Horn Player. Boston, Little Brown, 1980.

* * *

In the mid-1960's, Murray Schisgal's plays were hailed as a step ahead of the avant-garde and more absurd than the work of the absurdists. He was frequently grouped with the new author-stars of American theater—Edward Albee, John Guare, Arthur Kopit, Jack Gelber—whose work, like Schisgal's, was first seen in the United States off-Broadway. As Schisgal notes with irony in the preface to his plays *The Typists, and The Tiger*, this recognition by American critics came only after he had achieved significant success as a playwright in England. *The Typists* and *The Tiger*, two one-acts, and a full-length play, *Ducks and Lovers*, were in fact all first produced in London, and Schisgal's eventual Broadway hit, *Luv*, was optioned in London as early as 1961. After the popular success of *Luv*, which opened in London in 1963 and New York in 1964, Schisgal's career as a playwright seemed assured. He continued to write new plays at a remarkably steady pace through the 1960's and 1970's; most of his new works were produced and published. Critics, however, quickly lost interest in his work, and he has thus become one of the few American playwrights who has genuinely sustained a career in the theater but has no defined place in American culture or drama history.

Much of the oddity of Schisgal's reception can be discovered in the comic constancy and contemporaneity of his work. He is a satirist of daily life in America and of the clichés of that life. His plays evoke a zany world that teeters between lunacy and good sense. In each of his plays, there is at least one character whose social role is ostensibly ordinary but whose manner of inhabiting that role is eccentric and perverse. Nowhere is this disclosure of the volatile, chaotic energy of ordinary people better accomplished than in *The Tiger*. The plot is simply and potentially melodramatic: Ben, a postman, kidnaps Gloria, a surburban housewife; he intends to rape her. We encounter the two as Ben enters his dingy, cluttered basement apartment with Gloria slung over his shoulder. Any expectations we might have of soap-opera melodrama are quickly thwarted by the peculiar behavior of both characters. Ben's notion of rape begins with a peck on Gloria's cheek and includes playing her a recording of Tchaikovsky's first piano concerto; Gloria is so impressed by Ben's quasi-philosophic utterances that she repeatedly forgets that she, not he, is the victim in this situation. Ben's hyperbolic frustration turns out to be the perfect match for Gloria's fertile boredom, and, as we laugh at the two equally naive lovers groping for each other like adolescents, we are finally able to laugh, too, at the self-indulgence of our own overly promoted ennui.

The Tiger delights both because it enables us to laugh at our inflation of contemporary causes and because almost every line is a surprise. While remaining within a recognizable world, Schisgal captures the inanity of our assertions and our memories. Like *The Tiger*, Schisgal's full-length work *Luv* is a comedy of contemporary manners and obsessions. The classic triangle—a man, his wife, and his best friend—erupts and renegotiates its connections in *Luv* with much the same irreverence for marriage and other institutions that emerged in *The Tiger*. Milt, Harry, and Ellen of *Luv* clearly deserve each other; no-one else would take any one of them as seriously as they do each other or themselves. In this play, as in *The Tiger*, Schisgal's magic is that of the true clown; he makes us laugh at every near-catastrophe including the suicide attempts of each character. In the end, however, *Luv* does not sustain its wit, and one is left with the uneasy sense that, having displayed love itself as a false totem, the play's most lasting image is of a dog peeing on someone's leg.

Relentless in his deflation of each new passion in American society, Schisgal's plays since the late 1960's have become less funny and more acute in the social issues they address. Of the plays written since *Luv*, two, *Jimmy Shine* and *All Over Town*, are particularly rich in the experience they provide for an audience. *All Over Town* assaults every facile "solution" that was embraced in the late 1960's and early 1970's: welfare, psychiatry, ecology, liberalism, racial and sexual "liberation" are all reduced to confetti in an upper-class New York apartment that becomes a carnival of errors. Although Schisgal has since written other plays in his distinctive satiric mode, *All over Town* so expands the madness and so multiplies the cast of characters that it conveys an aura of finality—in this mode at least. In contrast, *Jimmy Shine*, while orthodox in dramaturgy, exemplifies a powerful new mode in Schisgal's writing. In *Jimmy Shine* Schisgal quietly controls the tentative, unsatisfied struggles of his artist-hero to find meaning without ornamentation. Schisgal's persistent presentation of the humorous aspects of sexuality and the painful burdens of human love are presented in *Jimmy Shine* without the usual parodic refractions. Perhaps it is the integrity so transparent in *Jimmy Shine* that continues to draw community and academic theater companies to Schisgal's plays.

—Helene Keyssar

SEABROOK, Jeremy. British. Born in Northampton in 1939. Educated at Northampton Grammar School; Gonville and Caius College, Cambridge; London School of Economics, diploma in social administration 1967. Teacher in a secondary modern school for two years; social worker, Inner London Education Authority, 1967–69, and with Elfrida Rathbone Association, 1973–76. Agent: Curtis Brown, 162–168 Regent Street, London W1R 5TB, England.

PUBLICATIONS

Plays

Life Price with Michael O'Neill (produced London, 1969).
Morality, with Michael O'Neill (produced London, 1971).
Millennium, with Michael O'Neill (produced London, 1973).
Our Sort of People, with Michael O'Neill (produced London, 1974).
Sex and Kinship in a Savage Society, with Michael O'Neill (produced London, 1975).
Yesterday's News, with Joint Stock (produced Aldershot, Hampshire, and London, 1976).
Sharing, with Michael O'Neill (produced London, 1980).
Black Man's Burden, with Michael O'Neill (produced London, 1980).

Radio Plays: *Birds in a Gilded Cage*, 1974; *A Change of Life*, 1979; *A Mature Relationship*, 1979; *Golden Opportunities*, 1982; with Michael O'Neill—*The Bosom of the Family*, 1975; *Living Private*, 1978; *Our Children's Children*, 1980; *Life Skills*, 1985.

Television Plays, with Michael O'Neill: *Skin Deep*, 1971; *Soap Opera in Stockwell*, 1973; *Highway Robbery*, 1973; *A Clear Cut Case*, 1973; *A Stab in the Front*, 1973; *Children of the Sun*, 1975; *Beyond the Call of Duty* (*Crown Court* series), 1976; *A State of Welfare*.

Other

The Unprivileged: A Hundred Years of Family Life and Tradition in a Working-Class Street. London, Longman, 1967.
City Close-Up. London, Allen Lane, and Indianapolis, Bobbs Merrill, 1971.
Loneliness. London, Temple Smith, 1971; New York, Universe, 1975.
The Everlasting Feast. London, Allen Lane, 1974.
A Lasting Relationship: Homosexuals and Society. London, Allen Lane, 1976.
What Went Wrong? Working People and the Ideals of the Labour Movement. London, Gollancz, 1978; New York, Pantheon, 1979.
Mother and Son: An Autobiography. London, Gollancz, 1979; New York, Pantheon, 1980.
Working-Class Childhood. London, Gollancz, 1982.
Unemployment. London, Quartet, 1982.
The Idea of Neighbourhood: What Local Politics Should Be About. London, Pluto Press, 1984.
A World Still to Win: The Reconstruction of the Post-War Working Class, with Trevor Blackwell. London, Faber, 1985.
Landscapes of Poverty. Oxford, Blackwell, 1985.

* * *

See the essay on Michael O'Neill and Jeremy Seabrook.

SELBOURNE, David. British. Born in London, 4 June 1937. Educated at Manchester Grammar School; Balliol College, Oxford, B.A. (honours) 1958; Inner Temple, London, called to the Bar, 1959. Lecturer, University of Aston, Birmingham, 1963–65; Tutor in Politics, Ruskin College, Oxford, 1965–86. Recipient: Aneurin Bevan Memorial fellowship, 1975; Southern Arts Association award, 1979; Indian Council of Social Science research award, 1979; Social Science Research Council award, 1980; Periodical Publishers Association award, 1986. Address: c/o Xandra Hardie, 9 Elsworthy Terrace, London NW3 3DR, England.

PUBLICATIONS

Plays

The Play of William Cooper and Edmund Dew-Nevett (produced Exeter, 1968). London, Methuen, 1968.
The Two-Backed Beast (produced Liverpool, 1968). London, Methuen, 1969.
Dorabella (produced Edinburgh, 1969). London, Methuen, 1970.
Samson (produced London, 1970). With *Alison Mary Fagan*, London, Calder and Boyars, 1971.
Alison Mary Fagan (produced Auckland, New Zealand, 1972). With *Samson*, London, Calder and Boyars, 1971.
The Damned. London, Methuen, 1971.
Class Play (produced London, 1972). Published in *Second Playbill 3*, edited by Alan Durband, London, Hutchinson, 1973.
Three Class Plays (for children; produced London, 1973).
What's Acting? and Think of a Story, Quickly! (for children; produced London, 1977). London, Arnold, 1977.
A Woman's Trial (produced in Bengali, as *Shrimatir Bichar*, Calcutta, 1982).

Other

Brook's Dream: The Politics of Theatre. London, Action Books, 1974.
An Eye to China. London, Black Liberator Press, 1975.
An Eye to India: The Unmasking of a Tyranny. London, Penguin, 1977.
Through the Indian Looking-Glass: Selected Articles on India 1976–1980. Bombay, Popular Prakashan, and London, Zed Press, 1982.
The Making of A Midsummer Night's Dream: An Eye-Witness Account of Peter Brook's Production. London, Methuen, 1982.
Against Socialist Illusion: A Radical Argument. London, Macmillan, and New York, Schocken, 1985.
Left Behind: Journeys into British Politics. London, Cape, 1987.

Editor, *In Theory and in Practice: Essays on the Politics of Jayaprakash Narayan.* New Delhi, Oxford University Press, 1985; Oxford and New York, Oxford University Press, 1986.

*

Critical Studies: introductions by John Russell Brown to *The Play of William Cooper and Edmund Dew-Nevett*, 1968, by Stuart Hall to *An Eye to China*, 1975, and by Selbourne to *What's Acting? and Think of a Story, Quickly!*, 1977.

* * *

David Selbourne writes with consistent strategy. He chooses simple actions that involve basic motives with the minimum of complication through story or the representation of the process of everyday living. So he is free to move his characters into ever-changing relationships with each other, and with their own reactions. In the one-act *Samson* a boy tries to break away from his father in twelve short scenes. In *Dorabella* a spinster is attracted to the boyfriend of her hairdresser. In *The Play of William Cooper and Edmund Dew-Nevett* a simpleton and would-be artist seeks happiness and finds corruption.

These are intellectual plays in that they are based on a clear view of how time, power, imagination, thought, and passions work together. But they are realized with a sensual awareness that seeks to create brilliant juxtapositions, activity and language that can take actors and audiences directly to total, undisguised confrontations.

Almost all the dialogue is in a verse form that serves to accentuate thrust and concision. It also holds attention for the echoes from mystical poets and the Old Testament that play a large part in creating the overall impression of the plays. The echoes are purposefully easy to catch and, more than this, they live together with a lively response to ordinary talk and responses. This style with its radiant images offsets the restricted nature of the play's actions, where man is repeatedly shown caught by his own conditions of living. *The Damned* presents self-deception and domination with calculated ruthlessness, but even in this painful drama the words spoken show how the hope of free life is still the characters' true source of energy. At the end of *William Cooper* the simpleton can "fly no more," but he has only just recognized again "Light blazing into my head."

Two plays are in a separate category, for in the one-act *Alison Mary Fagan* and the short *Class Play* Selbourne has placed real people in dramatic forms: in the first an actress who faces herself, her life and her career, and in *Class Play* three pupils and a teacher facing school and life. These are difficult plays to perform, for the dialogue is still shockingly direct and the situations continually changing, but at the centre of the drama is a person who performs or children who are manipulated, and these are to be seen without artifice, recognized as if outside a theatre.

Selbourne is a writer of teeming imagination and clear determination. He has never fallen in with a fashionable mode of writing for the stage. He has worked on his own, confident in the validity of his purpose. He stakes everything he knows; to share that risk is an exhilarating and demanding enterprise that leaves a permanent mark.

—John Russell Brown

SEWELL, Stephen. Australian. Born in Sydney in 1953. Educated at the University of Sydney, B.S. 1975. Writer-in-residence, Nimrod Theatre, Sydney, 1981–82. Recipient: Australian Writers Guild award, 1982; New South Wales Premier's award, 1985. Address: c/o Currency Press, 87 Jersey Road, Woollahra, New South Wales 2025, Australia.

PUBLICATIONS

Plays

The Father We Loved on a Beach by the Sea (produced Brisbane, 1978). Sydney, Currency Press, 1976.
Traitors (produced Melbourne, 1979; London, 1980). Sydney, Alternative Publishing Co-operative, 1983.
Welcome the Bright World. Sydney, Alternative Publishing Co-operative, 1983.
The Blind Giant Is Dancing (produced Adelaide, 1983). Sydney, Currency Press, 1983; revised version, 1985.
Burn Victim, with others (produced Sydney, 1983).
Dreams in an Empty City (produced Adelaide, 1986). Sydney, Currency Press, 1986.

* * *

The first production of *Traitors* in 1979 established Stephen Sewell as one of the most exciting and challenging of the new generation of Australian playwrights. His work is distinctive for the power and complexity of its political vision, and in this sense is perhaps more appropriately compared with recent left-wing British theatre than with the mostly comic, mostly celebratory style of satire which has dominated Australian stages over the past two decades. Two recent plays, *The Blind Giant Is Dancing* and *Dreams in an Empty City*, share some of the central concerns of that local tradition, however, in the ways they present patterns of social (and particularly marital) interaction which offer distinctive images of contemporary Australia. But always in Sewell's work the analysis of interpersonal politics is conducted in the context of structures of power which exist beyond the individual, and beyond the immediate culture. Sewell is a Marxist of a fairly sceptical and speculative kind, and while his plays have provoked a hostile reaction from some critics who find them ponderous and propagandistic, such a view seems to be a response to his overtly ideological approach to theatre rather than to the complex political vision which the plays actually present. Sewell's description of Marxism as a "tenable hypothesis" fairly indicates his own awareness of the complexity of the issues he deals with; it gives no sense, though, of the importance in the disintegrating world which his plays depict of finding some system of value which is "tenable," or of the passion with which such a commitment can be held.

The Father We Loved on a Beach by the Sea, Sewell's first play, was to some extent a dress-rehearsal for the presentation, in the more recent plays, of aspects of the familial culture in terms which attempt as well to define the forces which create them. It also anticipated something of the structural complexity demanded by Sewell's later more elaborate explorations of political cause and effect. *The Father*'s juxtaposition of two time-frames (remembrance of things past as experienced by Joe, a quintessential Aussie "battler," and a hypothetical revolutionary future focussed on Dan, his activist son) entails an ambitious mixture of playing styles which is developed still more challengingly in *The Blind Giant* and *Dreams in an Empty City*. Here these elements are less satisfyingly reconciled than in the later plays; perhaps the absence of a point of present vantage between warmly stereotypical past and coldly nightmarish future contributes to the sense that there is some uncertainty of focus behind the power of the play. Where the treatment of "little people" in Sewell's later work reflects his premise that the political and the personal are inextricable or identical, the image of the family in *The Father* appeals quite directly to the feelings of unresolved guilt, love, and resentment which most of us have for our parents.

Traitors and *Welcome the Bright World* were greeted as distinguished instances of the "new internationalism" in Australian drama which followed the very self-consciously Australian "new wave" of the late 1960's and early 1970's. The settings of the two plays—respectively, Stalinist Russia between world wars and Germany through the 1970's—certainly looked like a conspicuous refusal to be parochial. In the light of the distinctively local emphasis of the two latest plays, that choice might be seen either as having no significance at all beyond Sewell's particular interests at the time, or as a controlling response to the personal dimensions of *The Father*. The relevance of a concept like "internationalism" to Sewell's work can be sought more profitably in the nature of his political analysis and the theatrical company he (metaphorically) keeps than in matters of literal placement.

Traitors is the most concentrated of his plays. The historicity and episodic structure look Brechtian, but there is not much ground for rational reflection; the play's intensity comes from the unrelenting pressure of its depiction of the efforts of individuals to find some place for love and some sense of personal purpose in a society where betrayal and oppression appear to pre-empt such things. Here the personal is the political in a particularly overt and uncomplicated way; although the ideological commitments of all the characters make self-abnegation seem a moral imperative, *Traitors* explores the tensions which that creates.

Soviet factionalism provided a somewhat esoteric base for *Traitors*; the combination of revolutionary politics in Germany, different forms of consciousness of being Jewish, and the state of contemporary physics made a more demanding one for *Welcome the Bright World*. This play confirmed a general critical conception of Sewell as a playwright whose reach, excitingly but rather wilfully, would always exceed his grasp. As in *Traitors*, there is a great deal going on, most of it very powerful and disturbing, and all of it suggesting that this is a writer who will not make theatrical compromises in his mission to address an audience intelligently. The unwieldiness of the structure becomes in a sense an aspect of the play's power, in its seeming guarantee that there are forces here which are beyond containment.

The two most recent plays have found forms of containment which have not been at the expense of the intensity of the idea. In returning to aspects of Australian society as his subject, Sewell has in both cases drawn on a central myth to encompass the action beyond its immediate political reference—the Faust story in *The Blind Giant*, and the Christ story in *Dreams in an Empty City*. *Welcome the Bright World* foreshadowed this development, in its treatment of the effort of much modern nuclear theory to establish the principles which relate the smallest detectable (or imaginable) particle to the largest forms of matter; unification theory became a metaphor not only for the essential interrelatedness of political structures, but for the form of the play itself. But where that central metaphor requires a good deal of explanatory play on blackboards with quarks and neutrinos, *The Blind Giant* and *Dreams* appeal to analogies which are quite as rich and more broadly available.

The Blind Giant deals with political corruption at all levels of Australian society, though its focus is on the corrosiveness of compromise in the development of its central character, a crusader on the Labor left. There is nothing simplistic about this concern, though, since the exploration of power structures from the domestic to the international is complicated in the action by the elusiveness of answers to all questions about the sources of power, and by individual psychological patterns of assertion and submission. It is perhaps in the latter area that the play's major strength lies; its treatment of sexual and familial politics seems to offer more durable insights than the remarkably accurate short-term prophecies which emerge from its presentation of Australian political life.

The force which in *The Blind Giant* threatens to undermine all positions of integrity is cynicism, and no-one in the play (apart from a rather unlikely Chilean freedom-fighter) seems to find an answer to it. In *Dreams* that force is given its full spiritual dimension in the form of corrupting despair; even the most venal of the financial predators in this play appeal at some point to a perception of the world as irredeemably fallen in order to mask their opportunism with moral repugnance. The enemy of political change is not the dominant system in itself, but the sickness which breeds it. *Dreams* ends, like *The Father* and *The Blind Giant*, on a note of apocalyptic fantasy; here it is nothing less than the collapse of international capitalism. But for all the risks involved in its giant subject, and in its allegorical methods which transpose Christian virtue into a context of secular revolution, *Dreams* works, very powerfully and movingly.

Sewell is a young playwright whose achievement is already very impressive. The only thing which can be confidently predicted about the way in which his work might develop in the future is that it is sure to be exciting.

—Peter Fitzpatrick

SEYMOUR, Alan. Australian. Born in Perth, Western Australia, 6 June 1927. Educated at Fremantle State School, Western Australia; Perth Modern School. Free-lance film and theatre critic and educational writer, Australian Broadcasting Commission, Perth and Sydney, 1950's; actor, Perth and Sydney, 1950's; contributor, *Overland* and *Meanjin*, both Melbourne, and Sydney *Bulletin-Observer*, from 1950's; co-founding director, Sydney Opera Group, 1953–58; theatre critic, *London Magazine*, 1962–65; lived in Izmir, Turkey, 1966–71. Recipient: Sydney Journalists' Club prize, 1960; Australian Council for the Arts grant, 1974. Address: 74 Upland Road, London SE22 0DB, England.

PUBLICATIONS

Plays

Swamp Creatures (produced Canberra, 1958).
The One Day of the Year (produced Adelaide, 1960; London, 1961). Sydney, Angus and Robertson, 1962; included in *Three Australian Plays*, London, Penguin, 1963; revised version, in *Three Australian Plays*, edited by Alrene Sykes, Melbourne, Penguin, 1985.
The Gaiety of Nations (produced Glasgow, 1965; London, 1966).
A Break in the Music (produced Perth, 1966).
The Pope and the Pill (produced London, 1968).
Oh Grave, Thy Victory (produced Canberra, 1973).
Structures (produced Perth, 1973).
The Wind from the Plain, adaptation of a novel by Yashar Kemal (produced, in Finnish, Turku, Finland, 1974–75).
The Float (produced Adelaide, 1980).

Radio Plays: *Little Moron*, 1956; *The Man Who Married a Dumb Wife*, from a work by Rabelais, 1956; *A Winter Passion*, 1960; *Donny Johnson*, 1965 (Finland).

Television Plays (UK): *Richard II*, from the play by Shakespeare, 1958 (Australia); *The Runner*, 1960 (Australia); *Lean Liberty*, 1962; *And It Wasn't Just the Feathers*, 1964; *Auto-Stop*, 1965; *The Trial and Torture of Sir John Rampayne*, 1965; *Stockbrokers Are Smashing But Bankers Are Better*, 1965; *Fixation*, from a work by Miles Tripp, 1973; *The Lotus, Tigers Are Better-Looking*, and *Outside the Machine*, from stories by Jean Rhys, 1973–74; *Eustace and Hilda*, from the novels by L.P. Hartley, 1977; *Sara Dane* series, from the novel by Catherine Gaskin, 1981 (Australia); *Frost in May*, from the novel by Antonia White, 1982; *The Tribute*, from a work by Jane Gardam, 1983; *The Ghostly Earl*, from a story by R. Chetwynd-Hayes, 1984; *The Box of Delights* series, from the book by John Masefield, 1984; *Tudawali* (documentary), 1987 (Australia); *The Lion, The Witch, and the Wardrobe* series, from the novel by C.S. Lewis, 1988; *Menace Unseen* series, 1988.

Novels

The One Day of the Year. London, Souvenir Press, 1967.
The Coming Self-Destruction of the United States of America. London, Souvenir Press, 1969; New York, Grove Press, 1971.

*

Manuscript Collection: Mitchell Library, Sydney.

Critical Studies: "Seymour's Anzac Play" by Max Harris, in *Nation* (Sydney), April 1961; introduction by Harry Kippax to *Three Australia Plays*, 1963; *Profile of Australia* by Craig McGregor, London, Hodder and Stoughton, 1966; essay in *On Native Grounds* edited by C.B. Christesen, Sydney, Angus and Robertson, 1967; introduction by Charles Higham to *Australian Writing Today*, London, Penguin, 1968; *The Great Australian Stupor* by Ronald Conway, Melbourne, Sun Books, 1971; article by Alrene Sykes, in *Australian Literary Studies* (Hobart, Tasmania), vol. 6, 1974, and by Sykes and Keith Richardson, in *Australasian Drama Studies* (St. Lucia, Queensland), April 1984; *After "The Doll"* by Peter Fitzpatrick, Melbourne, Arnold, 1979; *Contemporary Australian Playwrights* edited by Jennifer Palmer, Adelaide, Adelaide University Union Press, 1979.

Theatrical Activities:
Director: **Play**—*The One Day of the Year*, Australia tour, 1961. **Operas**—with Sydney Opera Group: *The Telephone, The Medium, Amahl and the Night Visitors*, and *Amelia Goes to the Ball*, all by Menotti; *Impresario* by Mozart; *The Secret of Susanna* by Wolf-Ferrari; *Une Education manquée* by Chabrier; and *The Jumping Frog of Calaveras County* by Lukas Foss, Sydney and Australia tours, 1953–58.

Alan Seymour comments:

(1973) As a theatre critic and student of theatre history and especially modern theatre experiments, I am concerned with the research for new forms. Paradoxically, the play of mine most widely performed in Australia and other countries, *The One Day of the Year*, is least typical of my work and intentions, its simple neo-realist form stemming from a conscious artistic choice as the best means to communicate my feelings on the subject of lingering militarism and a need of national self criticism, in the Australian theatre situation of the late 1950's.

Like many Australian playwrights I have in the last decade lived abroad, although the wisdom of this decision is obviously arguable. It is generally held that writers from theatrically under-developed countries need to live abroad because the more open possibilities in, for instance, London make their professional life easier. In my view, life abroad is more difficult. My creative life had I stayed at home would have developed more smoothly, though on more predictable lines. In London, though moderately successful as a television playwright and critic during the first half of the 1960's, I found that, as a playwright for the theatre, I had lost my national voice and not found a new "international" one to replace it.

By '65 this and other problems drove me to live a more isolated life, to think things through, and after five years in Izmir, Turkey, I feel I have a more complex understanding of contemporary life. Certainly some creative problems have been unblocked. Now returned at least temporarily to London, I am interested in the developing Fringe Theater and the perennial problem of how to reinvigorate the traditional theatre. Radical politics and social problems are a continuing preoccupation.

In 1973 I revisited Australia as a guest of the first Australian National Playwrights' Conference.

(1982) In 1980 the problem referred to above was brought home to me most pointedly. My first new stage play for some years was produced by the State Theatre Company in Adelaide's Festival Centre to positive audience reaction and universally bad critical response. The deliberately theatrical, at times non-naturalistic and jokily satirical style affronted the critics. I'd thought the views of a passionately involved yet geographically and culturally distanced commentator would give Australian audiences an interestingly different slant on their society. The tone and content outraged the critics. The richness and complexity gained from living around the world were somehow excluded from the piece by the choice of a glib stylization, a real error of judgment. Welcome both in the U.K. and Australia as an experienced and dedicated craftsman in television writing, I have yet to develop in the theatre as I'd have wished to.

* * *

Born in Australia, now living in England, Alan Seymour is a cosmopolitan rather than a specifically "Australian" playwright. His earliest plays were for the most part set nominally in Australia, but the setting might have been anywhere. The swamp where two elderly sisters and their servant perform weird experiments in *Swamp Creatures* is supposedly "a dank and fertile part of the Australian bush," but there is no hint of gum leaves, however rank and decayed, in the grim setting. Donny Johnson, the Don Juan hero of the play *Donny Johnson*, could be a pop singer anywhere; it just happens that the play moves from a country town in New South Wales to Sydney. Since Seymour left Australia in 1961, one stage play, *A Break in the Music*, has returned to Australia to deal with family memories of life there in the 1930's and 1940's, but for the rest he has ranged widely. His short play *The Gaiety of Nations* took up the theme of Vietnam; his novel *The Coming Self-Destruction of the United States of America* deals with race conflicts in the U.S., and his television plays have covered a wide range of countries and situations.

Risking over-simplification, one might say that Seymour's plays fall into two broad categories, sometimes of course overlapping: on the one hand, compassionate but comic-satiric observation of ordinary people, plays that are convincingly "real"; and on the other hand, plays which are grotesque, macabre, occasionally bordering on the grand guignol, and with characters larger than life. Included in the first type would be the delightful television drama *And It Wasn't Just the Feathers*, about the short-lived relationship between a frightened, lonely old woman with a passion for feathers, and a tough, drifting young man, and the two specifically Australian plays *A Break in the Music* and *The One Day of the Year*.

The One Day of the Year, though an early play, is still probably Seymour's most important work, and it has become part of Australian theatrical and social history. "The one day of the year" is Anzac Day, 25 April, when Australians traditionally mourn their war dead. For Alf Cook, returned soldier, the day is sacred, fraught with implications of courage, mateship, masculinity; it is the day when, marching with old comrades, he is no longer an ordinary little man who drives a lift but someone of importance, once more part of a group, "They make a fuss of y'for once. The speeches and the march ... and y're all mates." For his son Hughie, now a university student and ironically becoming estranged from his parents by the education they have struggled to give him, the Day is also, though he only half comprehends this, a symbol—a symbol of all that he is struggling to free himself from in his working-class background. Hughie comes into violent conflicts with his father when he and Jan, a girlfriend from a higher social level, collaborate to produce an article and pictures for the university newspaper; the subject is Anzac Day, and the message, loud and clear through Hughie's photographs of drunken "old diggers," is that the real significance of the so-called day of mourning is that it is an excuse for an almost national booze-up.

The play comes to a slightly sentimental conclusion, suggesting that though Alf cannot change, he has gained greater insight into himself, and Hughie for his part has learned a little more tolerance of the father he loves and in some ways resembles. Seymour presents with great insight the strengths and weaknesses of each point of view; the dream as well as the drunkenness in Alf's concept of Anzac Day, and, in Hughie's, idealism combined with lack of understanding and compassion for what he has not experienced, and, of course, the need of youth to assert itself and its values. *The One Day of the Year* is basically not a play about Anzac Day or even conflicting ideas of nationalism, but the conflict of generations, heightened by disparity in education. On its first production the play roused considerable indignation, mostly from older Australians who felt with some justice that the sacred nature of Anzac Day had been assailed. In fact, *The One Day of the Year* is dramatically weighted in favour of the older, more colourful "lower class" characters, Alf, his taciturn wife Dot, and Wacka, the only real Anzac in the play; against these, the better-educated Hughie is pallid and almost priggish, his socially superior girlfriend Jan frankly unreal. Alf, Wacka, and Dot have the advantage of a distinctive idiom—Alf with his intolerable reiteration of "I'm a bloody Australian . . ." which, with all its implications of unthinking complacency, is turned against him when Jan tells him sweetly, "You're so right, Mr. Cook." The automatic invitation, "'ave a cuppa tea" has comedy, kindliness—and finally the horrors of strangling, inescapable banality.

The second category of Seymour plays could be represented by such dramas as *The Shattering, Donny Johnson*, and *Swamp Creatures*. In *Swamp Creatures* two sisters and their servant mate different species of animals, producing obscene monsters which prowl through the swamps at night and finally turn on the human beings who made them. It is a slow, highly theatrical revelation of horrors which also carries a message, clearly embedded in the symbolism, a message a good deal less hackneyed when Seymour wrote the play than it is now; that science may in the end turn and rend its creator.

As with most writers, certain characteristic themes and forms of expression recur in Seymour's plays. There is for instance a touch of caricature about many of his best characters, a surprising number of whom are older women, very like Dot Cook in *The One Day of the Year*. Seymour's plays for the most part end in one of two ways: with the main characters trapped unwillingly in some painful situation (*The One Day of the Year, Donny Johnson, Swamp Creatures,* the unproduced *Screams from a Dark Cellar*) or else in Pinter-like isolation (*A Winter Passion, And It Wasn't Just the Feathers*, the unproduced *The Shattering*). Seymour has himself pointed out two recurring motifs, the conflict of generations which occurs in most of his plays, and the less frequent but still observably repeated situation of someone being kidnapped.

The Float, according to Seymour, is concerned with "the interaction of public and private in people's lives," and its climax is the dismissal of a fictional head of government, Ruff Mottram—a glance back at the controversial sacking of the Australian prime minister, Gough Whitlam, in 1975. The play had a mixed reception in Australia, its bleak portrayal of Australian society being, possibly, a contributing cause.

Some of Seymour's best drama writing has been for television, and particularly noteworthy are his sensitive adaptations of the Jean Rhys stories *The Lotus, Tigers Are Better-Looking*, and *Outside the Machine*. He is also a novelist, a knowledgeable and perceptive drama critic, and the author of many short stories and articles.

—Alrene Sykes

SHAFFER, Anthony (Joshua). British. Born in Liverpool, Lancashire, 15 May 1926; twin brother of Peter Shaffer, *q.v.* Educated at St. Paul's School, London; Trinity College, Cambridge (co-editor, *Granta*), graduated 1950. Conscript coalminer, Kent and Yorkshire, 1944–47. Married 1) Carolyn Soley, two daughters; 2) the actress Diane Cilento, 1985. Barrister, 1951–55; journalist, 1956–58; partner in advertising film production agency, 1959–69. Recipient: Tony award, 1971; Mystery Writers of America Edgar Allan Poe Award, for screenplay, 1973. Agent: Fraser and Dunlop Scripts Ltd., 91 Regent Street, London W1R 8RU, England.

PUBLICATIONS

Plays

The Savage Parade (produced London, 1963; as *This Savage Parade*, produced London, 1987).

Sleuth (produced London and New York, 1970). New York, Dodd Mead, 1970; London, Calder and Boyars, 1971.

Murderer (produced Brighton and London, 1975). London, Boyars, 1979.

Widow's Weeds (produced Brisbane, South Australia, 1977; Plymouth, 1987).

Whodunnit (as *The Case of the Oily Levantine* produced Guildford, Surrey, 1977; London, 1979; revised version, as *Whodunnit*, produced New York, 1982; Brighton, 1987). New York, French, 1983.

Screenplays: *Mr. Forbush and the Penguins*, 1971; *Frenzy*, 1972; *Sleuth*, 1973; *The Wicker Man*, 1974; *Masada*, 1974; *The Moonstone*, 1975; *Death on the Nile*, 1978; *Absolution*, 1981; *Evil Under the Sun*, 1982.

Novels

How Doth the Little Crocodile? (as Peter Antony, with Peter Shaffer). London, Evans, 1952; as Peter and Anthony Shaffer, New York, Macmillan, 1957.

Withered Murder, with Peter Shaffer. London, Gollancz, 1955; New York, Macmillan, 1956.

The Wicker Man (novelization of screenplay), with Robin Hardy. New York, Crown, 1978; London, Hamlyn, 1979.

Absolution (novelization of screenplay). London, Corgi, 1979.

*

Bibliography: *Peter and Anthony Shaffer: A Reference Guide* by Dennis A. Klein, Boston, Hall, 1982.

* * *

It is not often that a writer has the opportunity to create a literary fashion and even a new genre, but theatrical thrillers and mysteries can legitimately be divided into pre-*Sleuth* and post-*Sleuth*, indicating more than their date of composition. The traditional stage or film mystery is a variant on the classic English Country House mystery novel, a whodunnit in which a crime is committed and the audience tries to guess which of several suspects is the criminal, while the author carefully directs our suspicions in the wrong directions. In *Sleuth* Anthony Shaffer created the whodunwhat, where not only the identity of the criminal but the nature of the crime—indeed, the reality and reliability of everything we've seen with our own eyes—is part of the mystery.

Sleuth begins in an orthodox way, as a man enlists the aid of his wife's lover in a complex plot to rob himself; this way lover and wife can afford to run off, husband will be free to marry his own mistress, and the insurance company will pay for everything. No sooner has the audience settled in to see whether they'll pull it off and whether one will doublecross the other than we discover that this isn't what has been going on at all; the whole project is a convoluted cover for a murder. And no sooner is that fact absorbed than we are told that the murder we thought we watched happening didn't really happen. (Oh yes it did, we're told a moment later. Oh no it didn't, we're shown a bit after that.) A policeman has come to arrest the murderer. (Oh no he hasn't. Oh yes he has.) In fact, a second murder entirely has happened offstage (Oh no . . .) and the murderer has planted clues implicating the innocent party, which he dares him to find because the police are really coming this time (Oh no . . .). Even the program and cast list can't be trusted.

Of course *Sleuth* has its antecedents, among them Patrick Hamilton's *Gas Light* and the Hitchcock film *Suspicion* (Is the man really trying to kill his wife or is she imagining it?) and the Clouzot film *Diabolique* (Who of the three main characters are the murderers and who the victims?). But Shaffer concentrates and multiplies the questions and red herrings, and dresses them in an entertaining mix of psychology (the husband is a compulsive games-player), social comment (husband is a snob, lover working class), in-jokes (husband writes mysteries of the classic whodunnit kind), and black humor (one plot twist somehow requires a character to dress as a clown). And everything moves so quickly and effortlessly that there is added delight in the author's skill and audacity in so repeatedly confusing us. *Sleuth* was an immense worldwide success that quickly bred dozens of other thrillers of the new genre, notable among them Ira Levin's *Deathtrap* and Richard Harris's *The Business of Murder*. The Agatha Christie-type whodunnit, with corpses who didn't get up again and a murderer who was Someone In This Room, seemed hopelessly old-fashioned when compared to plays in which the audience had to figure out what was really happening before moving on to the question of who was guilty.

Oddly, Shaffer's own follow-ups in the genre he created are rather limp. *Murderer* opens with a 30-minute silent sequence during which we watch a particularly gruesome murder and dismemberment, followed by the arrival of a policeman, the discovery of the grisly evidence and the confession of the criminal—only to be told then that it was all a fake, the passtime of a crime buff reenacting a famous murder. So far, so good, but when the buff then turns his hand to an actual murder, the plot twists are less inevitable and less delightful than in *Sleuth*. Two actual murders take place, one with the wrong victim and one with the wrong murderer, but everything seems forced and unlikely, and requires extensive advance set-ups or after-the-fact explanations. It is ultimately an unpleasant play, working too hard to shock and surprise, and thus removing the pleasure of shock and surprise.

The Case of the Oily Levantine (revised for America as *Whodunnit*) is openly labelled "A Comedy Thriller," and is lighter and more entertaining than *Murderer* though sometimes just as strained and self-conscious. Its first act is a high-spirited parody of the whodunnit genre, with the title character blackmailing everyone in sight—titled dowager, retired officer, debutante, even the butler—until an unidentified one of them murders him. The best touch, with some of *Sleuth*'s flair, is that we periodically hear the disguised voice of the murderer giving teasing clues; it will refer, for example, to lighting a cigarette, only to have each character onstage light up as our hope of catching the criminal fades. As one might predict by now, Act 2 begins with the discovery that nothing we saw in Act 1 was real, except the murder. This twist owes a debt to the 1973 film *The Last of Sheila*, and the working-out of the new version of the murder is unconvincing and unengrossing, despite forced in-jokes both literary and theatrical. There is a satisfying final joke, though, as the solution is shown to be a twist on one of the traditional whodunnit's oldest clichés.

Shaffer's continuing skill as a craftsman of mystery and thrills is seen in his film work, notably for the film version of *Sleuth* and Hitchcock's *Frenzy*. In the theatre, however, his reputation must rest on *Sleuth* and on the genre it created.

—Gerald M. Berkowitz

SHAFFER, Peter (Levin). British. Born in Liverpool, Lancashire, 15 May 1926; twin brother of Anthony Shaffer, *q.v.* Educated at a preparatory school in Liverpool; Hall School, London; St. Paul's School, London; Trinity College, Cambridge (co-editor, *Granta*), 1947–50, B.A. in history 1950. Conscript coalminer, Chislet colliery, Kent, 1944–47. Worked in Doubleday bookstore, an airline terminal, at Grand Central Station, Lord and Taylors department store, and in the acquisition department, New York Public Library, all New York, 1951–54; staff member, Boosey and Hawkes, music publishers, London, 1954–55; literary critic, *Truth*, London, 1956–57; music critic, *Time and Tide*, London, 1961–62. Recipient: *Evening Standard* award, 1958, 1980; New York Drama Critics Circle award, 1960, 1975; Tony award, 1975, 1981; Outer Critics Circle award, 1981; Vernon Rice award, 1981; Oscar, for screenplay, 1985. C.B.E. (Commander, Order of the British Empire), 1987. Lives in New York City. Agent: Macnaughton Lowe Representation, 200 Fulham Road, London SW10 9PN, England; or, Robert Lantz, The Lantz Office, 888 Seventh Avenue, New York, New York 10106, U.S.A.

PUBLICATIONS

Plays

Five Finger Exercise (produced London, 1958; New York, 1959). London, Hamish Hamilton, 1958; New York, Harcourt Brace, 1959.

The Private Ear, and The Public Eye (produced London, 1962; New York, 1963). London, Hamish Hamilton, 1962; New York, Stein and Day, 1964.

The Merry Roosters' Panto, music and lyrics by Stanley Myers and Steven Vinaver (produced London, 1963; as *It's about Cinderella*, produced London, 1969).

Sketch in *The Establishment* (produced New York, 1963).

The Royal Hunt of the Sun: A Play Concerning the Conquest of Peru (produced Chichester and London, 1964; New York, 1965). London, Hamish Hamilton, and New York, Stein and Day, 1965.
Black Comedy (produced Chichester, 1965; London, 1966; New York, 1967). Included in *Black Comedy, Including White Lies*, 1967.
White Lies (produced New York, 1967). Included in *Black Comedy, Including White Lies*, 1967; as *White Liars* (produced London, 1968), London, French, 1967; revised version (produced London and New York, 1976), London, French, 1976.
Black Comedy, Including White Lies: Two Plays. New York, Stein and Day, 1967; as *White Liars, Black Comedy: Two Plays*, London, Hamish Hamilton, 1968.
Shrivings (as *The Battle of Shrivings,* produced London, 1970; revised version, as *Shrivings*, produced York, 1975). London, Deutsch, 1974; with *Equus*, New York, Atheneum, 1974.
Equus (produced London, 1973; New York, 1974). London, Deutsch, 1973; with *Shrivings*, New York, Atheneum, 1974.
Amadeus (produced London, 1979). London, Deutsch, 1980; revised version (produced New York, 1980; London, 1981), New York, Harper, and London, Penguin, 1981.
The Collected Plays of Peter Shaffer (revised texts; includes *Five Finger Exercise, The Private Ear, The Public Eye, The Royal Hunt of the Sun, White Liars, Black Comedy, Equus, Shrivings, Amadeus*). New York, Harmony, 1982.
Black Mischief (produced Bristol, 1983).
Yonadab (produced London, 1985).
Lettice and Lovage (produced Bath and London, 1987).

Screenplays: *Lord of the Flies*, with Peter Brook, 1963; *The Public Eye* (*Follow Me!*), 1972; *Equus*, 1977; *Amadeus*, 1984.

Radio Play: *The Prodigal Father*, 1957.

Television Plays: *The Salt Land*, 1955; *Balance of Terror*, 1957.

Novels

The Woman in the Wardrobe (as Peter Antony). London, Evans, 1951.
How Doth the Little Crocodile? (as Peter Antony, with Anthony Shaffer). London, Evans, 1952; as Peter and Anthony Shaffer, New York, Macmillan, 1957.
Withered Murder, with Anthony Shaffer. London, Gollancz, 1955; New York, Macmillan, 1956.

*

Bibliography: *Peter and Anthony Shaffer: A Reference Guide* by Dennis A. Klein, Boston, Hall, 1982.

Critical Studies: *Peter Shaffer* by John Russell Taylor, London, Longman, 1974; *Peter Shaffer* by Dennis A. Klein, Boston, Twayne, 1979; *File on Shaffer* edited by Virginia Cooke and Malcolm Page, London, Methuen, 1987.

* * *

When Peter Shaffer's *Five Finger Exercise* achieved critical and commercial acclaim in London in 1958, it was difficult to reconcile its middle-class tone and its formal elements with the breed of theatre that was flourishing in Britain at the time. A well-made drawing-room domestic drama set in the Harringtons' weekend cottage in Suffolk, it probed the marital strife of a sadly mismatched couple and its devastating effects upon their nervous, taut, literary son and the young, secretive German tutor who had been brought into the household to tutor the Harringtons' volatile and imaginative 14-year-old daughter, Pamela. The story line is Lawrentian in the manner of *Sons and Lovers*. The intricately wrought monologues of the five characters are played and replayed against a background of music where frequently the gramophone sticks in the groove, or a simple piece by Bach is played over and over again as Pamela practices. The family relationships are dangerously out of balance and the intrusion of the outsider threatens to destroy them. Only after numerous variations of the same theme have been played again and again does the play conclude with a promise that the music may now flow continuously. This technically well-crafted play placed Shaffer in the traditions of the well-made play and he was briefly coupled with other playwrights of his generation, John Osborne and Harold Pinter. But it was difficult to consider him one of Britain's Angry Young Men. John Russell Taylor examined his writing in the context of Britain's New Drama in *Anger and After*, but concluded in a later essay that Shaffer was a more independent playwright, capable of flexing the drama's form to fit his intellectual ideas, and capable of evolving as a playwright in ways that were undeniably original. His fault, according to Taylor, was that he was too impersonal, standing too completely apart from the passions that consumed his characters and shaped the dramatic conflict in his plays.

Taylor's critique was written in the early 1970's, just after the extraordinary commercial success of *Equus*. He was uncannily prescient when he predicted that we could expect "grand and glorious" yet unpredictable plays from Shaffer in the years to come. His account of Shaffer's evolution, however, seemed to diminish the importance of Shaffer's use of narration in his plays. He did not place Shaffer in the tradition with dramatists employing the epic mode, be they Thornton Wilder, Tennessee Williams, Robert Bolt, or the continental writers in the manner of Brecht. Nor did he anticipate how fully Shaffer's narrators would control the prism through which the play is viewed and would provide a structure which offered Shaffer's play of intellect a richer range. Shaffer's use of the conventions of presentational aesthetics emerge clearly in *Equus* and are taken further in *Amadeus* and *Yonadab*. The epic mode permits him to interrupt the play's action and dart backwards and forwards in time, violating the conventions of the fourth wall and addressing the audience directly, inviting them to engage the play's ideas and participate in the experience of epic theatre as it was articulated by Brecht's director, Erwin Piscator. His discovery of the potential of the epic mode provided him with solutions to some of the technical problems apparent in *Five Finger Exercise* and very much evident in *Shrivings*, a play marred by too much ideological talkiness and an inadequate objective correlative for the play's ideas. Shaffer's plays since *Equus*, namely *Amadeus* and *Yonadab*, demonstrate that Shaffer has come to depend on epic theatre. His brilliantly conceived narrators, whether Old Martin in *The Royal Hunt of the Sun*, or the analyst Dysart in *Equus*, or Salieri, Mozart's rival in *Amadeus*, or Yonadab in the play of that title, rivet the audience's attention while permitting the play the luxury of exploring self-consciously its narration and story line without diminishing its nakedly dramatic elements.

Two other elements of Shaffer's art have been with him since his first play. The musical dimensions of his plays are an integral aspect of their soundscape; elements from detective fiction figure prominently in his plotting and in his development of character. He served for a number of years as music critic for *Time and Tide* in London. Before he became a successful playwright, he co-authored two detective novels with his brother, Anthony Shaffer, author of *Sleuth*. Shaffer's light and playful one-act play *The Public Eye* presents a delicious character, Julian Christoforou, a raisin-and-Yoghurt-eating private eye who meddles in the domestic life of Charles and Belinda Sidley in a manner slightly reminiscent of T.S. Eliot's one-eyed Harcourt-Reilly in *The Cocktail Party* who pries into not only the psyche but the souls of his clients. Christoforou is not capable of the arduous religious quest that consumed Celia, but he is a British eccentric who teaches the couple how to experience love again and how to play. Shaffer uses the character of the detective and the devices of detective fiction—disguised identities, the dreary business of sleuthing, the perfunctory discovery scene, the interrogation scene, the establishing of fees—to structure his one-act frivolous play. Many of the same devices can be found in Shaffer's superbly crafted farce *Black Comedy*, and in *Amadeus*.

In *Black Comedy* the entire play depends for its comic effect on a clever theatrical trick of the eye and mind. While the stage is lit, its fictive world is dark; when the stage is black, the characters are inhabiting a fully lit fictive world. Because of this simple reversal of light and dark elements on the stage, the audience relishes the delight of watching a stage full of characters groping around in the darkness but actually flooded with light as a result of a blown fuse in the London flat of Brindsley Miller in early evening. Miller, a young sculptor, is trying to impress his debutante fiancée's father, Colonel Melkett, by selling one of his sculptures to an elderly, deaf millionaire art collector. To insure the evening's success, Brindsley and his fiancée have swiped numerous pieces of elegant Regency furniture from the flat of his modish neighbor, a closet homosexual and owner of an antique china shop. As the evening advances towards its complete dissolution, Brindsley is forced to drag the furniture from his apartment back to its owner's right before the darkened eyes of the owner, his father-in-law-to-be, his mistress who has paid a surprise visit, a spinster, alcoholic upstairs neighbor, and his silly, spoilt fiancée. The scene is hilarious. Comic timing is essential to its success. Brindsley's misstep which causes him to fall neatly down the entire flight of stairs as he attempts to return calmly from his bedroom requires that the actor display no trace of the knowledge that he is facing an uncomfortable fall. The moment when Brindsley passes under the outstretched arms of his father-in-law and fiancée as they are exchanging a glass of lemonade and he is holding a Regency chair in one hand and a Wedgwood bowl in the other is another brilliant comic moment. All the deft timing of exits and entrances, sudden falls, rapid movements of almost all the major pieces of stage furniture, combined with the sharp white light which blaringly exposes the goings-on to the audience testify to the importance that the genre of detective fiction and film play in Shaffer's imagination. The exposed light bulb and the interrogation scenes of detective fiction probably contributed to the game of hide-and-seek executed in this delightful farce.

In *Amadeus* the debt is even more apparent. The play opens with a chorus of rumor. The word "assassin" is hissed and savagely whispered by the characters on the stage, rising to a crescendo, and punctuated with the names of Mozart and Salieri. By the end of the second scene, Salieri, the narrator, promises the audience one final performance, to be entitled, "The Death of Mozart; or, Did I Do It?" The audience is plunged into the world of a whodunnit. The play's textures thicken, but Shaffer never lets us lose the thread of the mystery story with its villain and detective. We fill the latter role while Salieri, the narrator and fiend, depicts his Iago-like role in the undoing and death of Mozart. Shaffer's revised version of *Amadeus* clarified the London version's dramatic structure, more directly implicating Salieri in Mozart's death and replacing Greybig with Salieri as the Masked Figure and Messenger of Death who appears to Mozart in the penultimate scene of the play. *Yonadab* continues in this tradition. In a review by C.J. Gianakaris, he identifies Dan Jacobson's novel *The Rape of Tamar* (1970) as one of the sources of the play, The Old Testament story provides the other source. Yonadab, the cousin of Amnon and Absalom, David's sons, is the treacherous confidant of both brothers. He plays the one against the other, abetting the scene of Tamar's incestuous rape by her half-brother, Amnon, and later, assisting Absalom in the slaying of Amnon. Yonadab is also the reporter of the steamy, lurid scene to the audience. Again, the play's focus on reporters and news, on a lurid tale of intrigue, ambition, incest, and murder, on the cunning ways such plots transpire, and on the way villains are punished all reflect the sure hand of a writer familiar with the genre of detective fiction.

The place of music in Shaffer's plays is an even more essential aspect of his theatrical talent. It is his signature on almost all of his plays. In his fairly slight one-act comedy *White Lies*, later revised as *White Liars*, Shaffer played with the acoustical space of his play, relying on a tape recording to surround the audience with the inner monologues and dialogues of Sophie, his fortune-telling protagonist. In *The Private Ear* Bob's great passion is music and the gramophone; his failed romance is with a girl he met at a concert. *Five Finger Exercise* depends on the music of Bach and Brahms and the stuck recording of a gramophone repeating over and over a portion from Mahler's Symphony No. 4 to dramatize the suicide attempt of the young German tutor whose father's participation in the Nazi Party has driven him to England and the home of the Harringtons. In *The Royal Hunt of the Sun* the brilliant score of Marc Wilkinson embraces "bird cries; plainchant; a fantasia for organ, freezing sounds for the Mime of the Great Ascent, and frightening ones for the Mime of the Great Massacre." Describing the music further, Shaffer writes: "To me its most memorable items are the exquisitely doleful lament which opens Act II, and, most amazing of all, the final Chant of Resurrection, to be whined and whispered, howled and hooted, over Atahuallpa's body in the darkness, before the last sunrise of the Inca Empire." *Amadeus* soars with the music of Mozart and Salieri, and a score that reflects how Salieri probably imagined Mozart's music. Shaffer's immersion in their music is so complete that it is rumored by those working most closely with him that he came to believe that he himself was Mozart when he worked on the play in its original form in London.

Finally, tribute should be paid to Shaffer as a playwright of ideas. Perhaps his eloquent exposition of them failed in *Shrivings*, but the battle between Dysart and Alan Strang in *Equus*, Pizarro and Atahuallpa in *The Royal Hunt of the Sun*, Salieri and Mozart in *Amadeus*, and between Yonadab and David's brothers all repeat variations of Shaffer's theme of man's struggle for meaning in a world in which death dominates and religion holds no salvation. Alan Strang, the boy who blinded six horses, knows a savage God; Atahuallpa is the Son of the Sun God; Pizarro has no faith, nor, until the very end, love or passion. East and West collide in Shaffer's plays; faithfulness is played against faithlessness, passion and violence against impotence, passivity and Eastern love against scepticism and violence. Shaffer's plays press on the intellect. They tease the mind. To their extraordinary credit, they manage to do it through spectacle, lavish soundscapes, dramatic action, and the power of words.

—Carol Simpson Stern

SHANGE, Ntozake. American. Born Paulette Williams in Trenton, New Jersey, 18 October 1948; took name Ntozake Shange in 1971. Educated at schools in St. Louis and New Jersey; Barnard College, New York, 1966–70, B.A. (cum laude) in American studies 1970; University of Southern California, Los Angeles, 1971–73, M.A. in American studies 1973. Married David Murray in 1977 (2nd marriage); one daughter. Faculty member, Sonoma State College, Rohnert Park, California, 1973–75, Mills College, Oakland, California, 1975, City College, New York, 1975, Douglass College, New Brunswick, New Jersey, 1978, and University of Houston, from 1983. Artist-in-residence, Equinox Theatre, Houston, from 1981. Recipient: New York Drama Critics Circle award, 1977; Obie award, 1977, 1980; Columbia University Medal of Excellence, 1981; Los Angeles *Times* award, for poetry, 1981; Guggenheim fellowship, 1981. Address: c/o St. Martin's Press, 175 Fifth Avenue, New York, New York 10010, U.S.A.

PUBLICATIONS

Plays

For Colored Girls Who Have Considered Suicide When the Rainbow Is Enuf (produced New York, 1975; London, 1980). San Lorenzo, California, Shameless Hussy Press, 1976; revised version, New York, Macmillan, 1977; London, Eyre Methuen, 1978.

A Photograph: Lovers-in-Motion (as *A Photograph: A Still Life with Shadows, A Photograph: A Study of Cruelty* produced New York, 1977; revised version, as *A Photograph: Lovers-in-Motion*, also director: produced Houston, 1979). New York, French, 1981.

Where the Mississippi Meets the Amazon, with Thulani Nkabinda and Jessica Hagedorn (produced New York, 1977).

Spell #7 (produced New York, 1979; London, 1985). Included in *Three Pieces*, 1981; published separately, London, Methuen, 1985.

Black and White Two-Dimensional Planes (produced New York, 1979).

Boogie Woogie Landscapes (produced on tour, 1980). Included in *Three Pieces*, 1981.

Mother Courage and Her Children, adaptation of a play by Brecht (produced New York, 1980).

From Okra to Greens: A Different Kinda Love Story (as *Mouths* produced New York, 1981; as *From Okra to Greens* in *Three for a Full Moon*, produced Los Angeles, 1982). New York, French, 1983.

Three Pieces: Spell #7, A Photograph: Lovers-in-Motion, Boogie Woogie Landscape. New York, St. Martin's Press, 1981.

Three for a Full Moon, and Bocas (produced Los Angeles, 1982).

Educating Rita, adaptation of the play by Willy Russell (produced Atlanta, 1983).

Novels

Sassafrass: A Novella. San Lorenzo, California, Shameless Hussy Press, 1977.

Sassafrass, Cypress and Indigo. New York, St. Martin's Press, 1982; London, Methuen, 1983.

Betsey Brown. New York, St. Martin's Press, and London, Methuen, 1985.

Verse

Melissa and Smith. St. Paul, Bookslinger, 1976.

Natural Disasters and Other Festive Occasions. San Francisco, Heirs, 1977.

Nappy Edges. New York, St. Martin's Press, 1978; London, Methuen, 1987.

A Daughter's Geography. New York, St. Martin's Press, 1983; London, Methuen, 1985.

From Okra to Greens: Poems. St. Paul, Coffee House Press, 1984.

Ridin' the Moon West: Word Paintings. New York, St. Martin's Press, 1987.

Other

See No Evil: Prefaces, Essays, and Accounts 1976–1983. San Francisco, Momo's Press, 1984.

*

Theatrical Activities:

Director: **Plays**—*The Mighty Gents* by Richard Wesley, New York, 1979; *The Spirit of Sojourner Truth* by Bernice Reagon and June Jordan, 1979; *A Photograph: Lovers-in-Motion*, Houston, 1979.

Actress: **Plays**—The Lady in Orange in *For Colored Girls Who Have Considered Suicide When the Rainbow Is Enuf*, New York, 1976; in *Where the Mississippi Meets the Amazon*, New York, 1977; in *Mouths*, New York, 1981.

* * *

The production of *For Colored Girls Who Have Considered Suicide When the Rainbow Is Enuf* established Ntozake Shange as a major force in American theatre. True to the Xhosa name she had received in 1971, she was indeed "one who brings her own things" and "walks with lions." Shange has now moved from the spotlight, but she remains one of the finest English-language verse dramatists, forging a poetry compelling in both its social immediacy and its broad vision.

For Colored Girls is a collage of poems mixed with song and dance celebrating the lives of black girls who previously had not been considered a fit subject for dramatic presentation. Structured around rhythmic pulses, the play charts the passage from the self-conscious bravado of "we waz grown," proclaimed at the moment of high school graduation and loss of virginity, through a variety of alternatively funny and painful experiences with men, to the hard-gained knowledge of one's self-worth found in the closing affirmation, "i found god in myself & i loved her fiercely." Belying the women's anguish and seeming predilection towards the negative is their willingness to dance—dance and music being metaphors for the courage to venture into the world with grace, to seek intimate connections with others, and to celebrate the nearly limitless potentiality of life.

The play unlocked emotional doors rarely touched in American theatre. For many women, experiencing a performance became a quasi-religious moment in which some of their deepest feelings were acknowledged and a healing of wounds achieved. For countless other audiences it energized a highly charged debate about male-female relationships and the image of black men in American literature.

Shange's subsequent plays *A Photograph: Lovers-in-Motion* and *Boogie Woogie Landscapes* continue to use a rites-of-passage theme, but the exploration is carried forth within a more clearly delineated social context and a more conventional dramatic form. Thus, in *A Photograph* the male protagonist's identification with both Alexandre Dumas père and the illegitimate Dumas fils serves as a metaphor for his confusion, and the shedding of this fantasy is an indication of the extent to which he moves towards a healthier creative vision. Similarly, Layla in *Boogie Woogie Landscapes* relives her own emotional geography in order to reconcile the possibility of personal love with social struggle. But given the ways in which society distorts personality, love is tenuous, more often a momentary grasping for, rather than solid achievement of, unity.

With *Spell #7* the playwright moves further into the public arena by tackling the iconography of the "nigger." Manipulating the power of music, minstrel performers banish a huge, all-seeing black-face mask along with their stage personae in order to create a safe space in which secret hopes, fears, and dreams may be articulated. But two confessions centering around the shattering of faith puncture the whimsical or contained quality of most of the fantasies and reveal an almost overwhelming anguish. Although the master of ceremonies intervenes to reassure the audience that it will enjoy his black magic, and although the actors conjure forth the joyous spirit of a black church with the chant, "bein colored and love it," the mask returns. In reading the play we are left to wonder whether the actors and audience have indeed enjoyed the freedom of their own definitions and/or whether Shange has performed a sleight of hand which simply allows the drama to end on a positive note. The answer lies finally in the extent to which the communion between actors and audience creates a countervailing force to the hideous ministrel mask and in the audience members' ability to find within their own lives resolutions to the play's purposeful contradictions.

The most recently published play, *From Okra to Greens: A Different Kinda Love Story*, explores further the intersection of the personal and the political. Present are the now-familiar Shange themes of nearly overwhelming brutalization balanced by the transcendence of dance-music-poetry. But significantly new is the shared articulation of many of these experiences by both a male and female protagonist and the effective merger of the personal and the political into a whole which allows them to move forward. Thus, the play closes with the couple bidding their "children" emerge from the ghettoes, bantustands, barrios, and favelas of the world to fight against the old men who would impose death, to dance in affirmation of their unbreakable bond with nature itself.

Within a black theatre tradition Shange seems to have been influenced most by Amiri Baraka and Adrienne Kennedy. Characteristic of her dramaturgy are an attack upon the English language which she as a black woman finds doubly oppressive; a self-consciousness as a writer linked to a determination to reclaim for oppressed peoples the right of self-definition; and a use of poetry, music, and dance to approximate the power of non-linear, supra-rational modes of experience. A poet, Shange brings to the theatre a commitment to it as a locus of eruptive, often contradictory, and potentially healing forces whose ultimate resolution lie beyond the performance space.

—Sandra L. Richards

SHAWN, Wallace. American. Born in New York City, 12 November 1943; son of the editor William Shawn. Educated at the Dalton School, New York, 1948–57; Putney School, Vermont, 1958–61; Harvard University, Cambridge, Massachusetts, 1961–65, B.A. in history 1965; Magdalen College, Oxford, 1966–68, B.A. in philosophy, politics, and economics 1968, M.A.; studied acting with Katharine Sergava, New York, 1971. Lives with Deborah Eisenberg. English teacher, Indore Christian College, Madhya Pradesh, India, 1965–66; teacher of English, Latin, and drama, Church of Heavenly Rest Day School, New York, 1968–70; shipping clerk, Laurie Love Ltd., New York, 1974–75; Xerox machine operator, Hamilton Copy Center, New York, 1975–76. Recipient: Obie award, 1975, 1986; Guggenheim fellowship, 1978. Agent: Luis Sanjurjo, International Creative Management, 40 West 57th Street, New York, New York 10019, U.S.A.; or, Margaret Ramsay Ltd., 14-A Goodwin's Court, London WC2N 4LL, England.

PUBLICATIONS

Plays

Our Late Night (produced New York, 1975). New York, Targ, 1984.

In the Dark, music by Allen Shawn (also director: produced Lenox, Massachusetts, 1976).

A Thought in Three Parts (as *Three Short Plays: Summer Evening, The Youth Hostel, Mr. Frivolous*, produced New York, 1976; as *A Thought in Three Parts*, produced London, 1977). Published in *Wordplays 2*, New York, Performing Arts Journal Publications, 1982.

The Mandrake, adaptation of a play by Machiavelli (produced New York, 1977; as *Mandragola*, music and lyrics by Howard Goodall, produced London, 1984).

The Family Play (produced New York, 1978).

Marie and Bruce (produced London, 1979; New York, 1980). New York, Grove Press, 1980; with *My Dinner with André* (screenplay), London, Methuen, 1983.

My Dinner with André, with André Gregory (produced London, 1980).

My Dinner with André (screenplay), with André Gregory. New York, Grove Press, 1981; with *Marie and Bruce*, London, Methuen, 1983.

The Hotel Play (produced New York, 1981). New York, Dramatists Play Service, 1982.

Aunt Dan and Lemon (produced London and New York, 1985). London, Methuen, and New York, Grove Press, 1985.

Screenplay: *My Dinner with André*, with André Gregory, 1981.

*

Theatrical Activities:
Director: **Play**—*In the Dark*, Lenox, Massachusetts, 1976.

Actor: **Plays**—in *Alice in Wonderland*, New York, 1974; Prologue and Siro in *The Mandrake*, New York, 1977; Ilya in *Chinchilla* by Robert David MacDonald, New York, 1979; in *My Dinner with André*, London, 1980; Father, Jasper, and Freddie in *Aunt Dan and Lemon*, London and New York, 1985. **Films**—*Manhattan*, 1979; *Starting Over*, 1979; *All That Jazz*, 1980; *Atlantic City*, 1980; *Simon*, 1980; *My Dinner with André*, 1981; *Lovesick*, 1983; *Strange Invaders*, 1983; *Deal of the Century*, 1983; *Micki and Maude*, 1984; *Crackers*, 1984; *The Bostonians*, 1984; *The Hotel New Hampshire*, 1984; *Heaven Help Us*, 1985; *Prick Up Your Ears*, 1987; *Radio Days*, 1987; and other films. **Television**—*Saigon: Year of the Cat*, 1983.

* * *

Shock has always been one side-effect of Wallace Shawn's dramatic writing, a rather curious side-effect when one thinks of the man himself in his amiable and benign intelligence. Joint Stock's 1977 production of *A Thought in Three Parts* at London's ICA Theatre started the forces of oppression on a particularly merry chase. Within 24 hours of the play's opening there were calls for prosecution on the grounds of obscenity and there were detectives sitting in the audience. Within a week the Charity Commissioners had initiated an inquiry into the ICA's charitable status. Within two months, the Government had announced that it was setting up a committee to consider the law of obscenity generally, at the same time specifically declining to prosecute *A Thought in Three Parts*.

After the dust settled, the reputation of the three one-act plays that made up the evening was invisible for the outrage that had been engendered. Rarely had London's critics been so disturbed by a theatrical event, and that event showed the danger of taking sex seriously in the theatre. The clownish romping of such shows as *Oh! Calcutta!* had given way to something considerably more threatening.

A dangerous aura of violence hung over the evening despite the jokey comedy and naked sexual frolicking of the actors in the second of the plays, the one which caused the greatest outrage. Something more akin to horror than joy came through, and rather than real copulation there was real fear. The first part, *Summer Evening*, takes place in a hotel room in a foreign city where a man and a woman exchange trivial words about eating, reading, and card-playing. Underneath the conversation is the spectre of brutal sexuality, and phrases break through the trivia to reveal the real state of play: "I just had a picture. I thought of you strangling me."

Rather than viewing sex as communication, the second play analyses the essentially solitary experience of orgasm. The selfishness of much sexual gratification percolates through the distractions presented of oral foreplay, intercourse, and group masturbation in *The Youth Hostel*. Shawn compresses time and emotional responses so that the blinding number of orgasms signal changing relationships between five young people spending the night together. The comedy of the dialogue, in language suitable for *True Teenage Romances*, is a deceiving technique that sharpens the human isolation of his characters when their sexual energies are exhausted.

Mr. Frivolous, the final play, begins and remains with the isolation of an individual, an elegant man breakfasting alone in an elegant room. His monologue skates through idle sexual fantasy, from basic heterosexuality to images of gropes with a priest and the possibilities of bondage. Shawn's very public musings on sexuality are finally too dour to be erotic. He stimulates the mind, not the body.

Shawn first made an impact on the off-off-Broadway scene when André Gregory directed the play *Our Late Night* for the experimental company called the Manhattan Project. An obvious precursor to *A Thought in Three Parts*, the play dramatized the drifting unconscious thoughts of two young people quietly going to bed. Around the two there was a swirl of couples discussing sexuality, food, and other encounters.

Shawn's collaboration with Gregory on that production led to the remarkable play by Shawn and Gregory called *My Dinner with André*, which was made into a film by Louis Malle. Gregory had spent the best part of two decades exploring the expanding boundaries of the theatrical avant-garde, finally chasing the aesthetic experience into a forest in Poland, to the Findhorn community in Scotland, to India, Tibet, and the Sahara Desert. Shawn had spent those years consolidating a reputation as an actor in films with Woody Allen, and with such plays as *Marie and Bruce* which drew attention to him without intensifying the scandal.

The form of *My Dinner with André* is seductive and misleading. It pretends to be an account of an actual dinner that Shawn had with Gregory, "a man I'd been avoiding literally for years," and Shawn himself became the character who introduces and frames the play, indeed playing the part of Wally Shawn opposite Gregory's André in both the stage version and the film. The play's conflict is Shawn's New York rationality confronted with Gregory's telling of the "para-theatrical" activities he had had since quitting the theatre after directing *Our Late Night* in 1975.

No such dinner occurred, but the conversation actually took place, extended well beyond the 100 or so pages of the final script. Shawn and Gregory taped lengthy meetings where Gregory detailed his adventures and conclusions against the curious and sane encouragement of Shawn's scepticism. Gregory talked of the project he undertook in a Polish forest with 40 musicians, creating "experiences" with the encouragement of his friend the Polish director Jerzy Grotowski. He elaborated on his search by telling of a Japanese monk he befriended, and with whom he ate sand in the desert. Shawn responded that he liked electric blankets and that happiness could be a cup of cold coffee in which no cockroach had drowned during the night.

The piece is an aesthetic debate of great interest and value, and while the bulk of the ideological contribution is Gregory's, Gregory credits Shawn with the dramatic sensibility that shaped the debate and made the unfolding of the story so mesmerizing. It is Shawn's own characterization of himself as a cynic that gives a forum to Gregory's ideas, and it makes for a significant contribution to the search for artistic forms and meaning that followed the explosion of experiment in the 1960's. Shawn's own openness to thoughtful and radical inquiry into the nature of art and human experience is hearteningly matched by his disciplined skills of expression.

The amused cynicism evident in his own plays was reflected in Shawn's translation and adaptation of Machiavelli's *Mandragola*, with its jaundiced view of human relationships, but it was his original play *Aunt Dan and Lemon* which again stirred the audience into shock. In some ways a meditation on the Nazi atrocities, it was most disturbing for the cold way in which it portrayed the spiritually damaged woman called Lemon, the narrator of the piece. Beginning by welcoming the audience, including the "little children. How sweet you are, how innocent," she went on to tell the story of a friend of her parents, an American academic teaching at Oxford called Aunt Dan, who had regaled her with strange tales when she was 11. Aunt Dan's stories were sometimes about the heroism of Henry Kissinger when he ordered bombing attacks on Vietnam, or about a woman who had been Aunt Dan's lesbian lover and who had killed a man by strangling him with her stockings. The lesson that Lemon learns is that comfort is bought by assigning the killing to others, and that it is really hypocritical to condemn the Nazis who, after all, had been very successful against the Jews. Profoundly disturbing, the play is a mesmerizing blend of narration and enactment which tries, with mixed success, to comprehend the nature of human cruelty and the negotiated truce with justice that affects all non-political people.

—Ned Chaillet

SHEPARD, Sam. American. Born Samuel Shepard Rogers in Fort Sheridan, Illinois, 5 November 1943. Educated at Duarte High School, California, graduated 1960; Mount San Antonio Junior College, Walnut, California, 1960–61. Married O-Lan Johnson in 1969, one son; one daughter by the actress Jessica Lange. Worked as hot walker at the Santa Anita Race Track, stable hand, Connolly Arabian Horse Ranch, Duarte, herdsman, Huff Sheep Ranch, Chino, orange picker in Duarte, and sheep shearer in Pomona, all in California; actor with Bishop's Company Repertory Players, Burbank, California, and U.S. tour, 1962; car wrecker, Charlemont, Massachusetts; bus boy, Village Gate, 1963–64, waiter, Marie's Crisis Café, 1965, and musician with the Holy Modal Rounders, 1968, all in New York; lived in England, 1971–74, and in California since 1974. Recipient: Obie award, 1967, 1970, 1973, 1975, 1977, 1978 (twice), 1980, 1984; Yale University fellowship, 1967; Rockefeller grant, 1967; Guggenheim grant, 1968; American Academy grant, 1974; Brandeis University Creative Arts Award, 1976, 1985; Pulitzer Prize, 1979; New York Drama Critics Circle award, 1986; Outer Circle award, 1986; Drama Desk award, 1986. Address: c/o New American Library, 1633 Broadway, New York, New York 10019, U.S.A.

PUBLICATIONS

Plays

Cowboys (produced New York, 1964).
The Rock Garden (produced New York, 1964; excerpt produced in *Oh! Calcutta!*, New York, 1969; London, 1970). Included in *The Unseen Hand and Other Plays*, 1971; in *Angel City and Other Plays*, 1976.
Up to Thursday (produced New York, 1965).
Dog (produced New York, 1965).
Rocking Chair (produced New York, 1965).
Chicago (produced New York, 1965; London, 1976). Included in *Five Plays*, 1967.
Icarus's Mother (produced New York, 1965; London, 1970). Included in *Five Plays*, 1967.
4-H Club (produced New York, 1965). Included in *The Unseen Hand and Other Plays*, 1971.
Fourteen Hundred Thousand (produced Minneapolis, 1966). Included in *Five Plays*, 1967.
Red Cross (produced New York, 1966; Glasgow, 1969; London, 1970). Included in *Five Plays*, 1967.
La Turista (produced New York, 1967; London, 1969). Indianapolis, Bobbs Merrill, 1968; London, Faber, 1969.
Melodrama Play (produced New York and London, 1967). Included in *Five Plays*, 1967.
Forensic and the Navigators (produced New York, 1967). Included in *The Unseen Hand and Other Plays*, 1971.
Five Plays: Chicago, Icarus's Mother, Red Cross, Fourteen Hundred Thousand, Melodrama Play. Indianapolis, Bobbs Merrill, 1967; London, Faber, 1968; as *Chicago and Other Plays*, New York, Urizen, 1981; Faber, 1982.
Cowboys #2 (produced New York, 1967; London, 1980). Included in *Mad Dog Blues and Other Plays*, 1971; in *Angel City and Other Plays*, 1976.
The Holy Ghostly (produced on tour, 1969; New York, 1970; London, 1973). Included in *The Unseen Hand and Other Plays*, 1971.
The Unseen Hand (produced New York, 1969; London, 1973). Included in *The Unseen Hand and Other Plays*, 1971; with *Action*, London, Faber, 1975.
Operation Sidewinder (produced New York, 1970). Indianapolis, Bobbs Merrill, 1970; in *Four Two-Act Plays*, 1980.
Shaved Splits (produced New York, 1970). Included in *The Unseen Hand and Other Plays*, 1971.
Cowboy Mouth, with Patti Smith (produced Edinburgh and New York, 1971; London, 1972). Included in *Mad Dog Blues and Other Plays*, 1971; in *Angel City and Other Plays*, 1976.
Mad Dog Blues (produced New York, 1971; Edinburgh, 1978). Included in *Mad Dog Blues and Other Plays*, 1971; in *Angel City and Other Plays*, 1976.
Back Bog Beast Bait (produced New York, 1971). Included in *The Unseen Hand and Other Plays*, 1971.
The Unseen Hand and Other Plays. Indianapolis, Bobbs Merrill, 1971.
Mad Dog Blues and Other Plays. New York, Winter House, 1971.
The Tooth of Crime (produced London and Princeton, New Jersey, 1972; New York, 1973). With *Geography of a Horse Dreamer*, New York, Grove Press, and London, Faber, 1974.
Blue Bitch (televised 1972; produced New York, 1973; London, 1975).
Nightwalk, with Megan Terry and Jean-Claude van Itallie (produced New York and London, 1973). Published in *Open Theater*, New York, Drama Book Specialists, 1975.
Little Ocean (produced London, 1974).
Geography of a Horse Dreamer (also director: produced London, 1974; produced New Haven, Connecticut, 1974; New York, 1975). With *The Tooth of Crime*, New York, Grove Press, and London, Faber, 1974.
Action (produced London, 1974; New York, 1975). With *The Unseen Hand*, London, Faber, 1975; in *Angel City and Other Plays*, 1976.
Killer's Head (produced New York, 1975; London, 1979). Included in *Angel City and Other Plays*, 1976.
Angel City (also director: produced San Francisco, 1976; New York, 1977; London, 1983). Included in *Angel City and Other Plays*, 1976.
Angel City and Other Plays (includes *Curse of the Starving Class, Killer's Head, Action, Mad Dog Blues, Cowboy Mouth, The Rock Garden, Cowboys #2*). New York, Urizen, 1976; London, Faber, 1978.
Suicide in B Flat (produced New Haven, Connecticut, 1976; New York and London, 1977). Included in *Buried Child and Other Plays*, 1979.
The Sad Lament of Pecos Bill on the Eve of Killing His Wife (produced San Francisco, 1976; New York, 1983). With *Fool for Love*, San Francisco, City Lights, 1983; London, Faber, 1984.

Curse of the Starving Class (produced New York, 1976; London, 1977). Included in *Angel City and Other Plays*, 1976.
Inacoma (produced San Francisco, 1977).
Buried Child (produced San Francisco and New York, 1978; London, 1980). Included in *Buried Child and Other Plays*, 1979.
Seduced (produced Providence, Rhode Island, and New York, 1978; London, 1980). Included in *Buried Child and Other Plays*, 1979.
Tongues, with Joseph Chaikin, music by Shepard, Skip LaPlante, and Harry Mann (produced San Francisco, 1978; Edinburgh, 1987). Included in *Seven Plays*, 1981.
Savage/Love, with Joseph Chaikin, music by Shepard, Skip LaPlante, and Harry Mann (produced New York, 1979; London, 1984). Included in *Seven Plays*, 1981.
Buried Child and Other Plays. New York, Urizen, 1979; as *Buried Child, and Seduced, and Suicide in B Flat*, London, Faber, 1980.
True West (produced San Francisco and New York, 1980; London, 1981). London, Faber, 1981; in *Seven Plays*, 1981.
Jackson's Dance, with Jacques Levy (produced New Haven, Connecticut, 1980).
Four Two-Act Plays (includes *La Turista, The Tooth of Crime, Geography of a Horse Dreamer, Operation Sidewinder*). New York, Urizen, 1980; London, Faber, 1981.
Seven Plays (includes *Buried Child, Curse of the Starving Class, The Tooth of Crime, La Turista, True West, Tongues, Savage/Love*). New York, Bantam, 1981; London, Faber, 1985.
Superstitions, music by Shepard and Catherine Stone (produced New York, 1983).
Fool for Love (also director: produced San Francisco and New York, 1983; London, 1984). With *The Sad Lament of Pecos Bill on the Eve of Killing His Wife*, San Francisco, City Lights, 1983; London, Faber, 1984.
Fool for Love and Other Plays (includes *Angel City, Cowboy Mouth, Suicide in B Flat, Seduced, Geography of a Horse Dreamer, Melodrama Play*). New York, Bantam, 1984.
Paris, Texas (screenplay), with Wim Wenders, edited by Chris Sievernich. Berlin, Road Movies, 1984.
A Lie of the Mind (also director: produced New York, 1985; London, 1987). New York, New American Library, and London, Methuen, 1987.
The War in Heaven (broadcast 1985; produced London, 1987).
The Unseen Hand and Other Plays. New York, Bantam, 1986.

Screenplays: *Me and My Brother*, with Robert Frank, 1969; *Zabriskie Point*, with others, 1970; *Ringaleevio*, 1971; *Paris, Texas*, 1984; *Fool for Love*, 1985.

Radio Play: *The War in Heaven*, 1985.

Television Play: *Blue Bitch*, 1972 (UK).

Other

Hawk Moon: A Book of Short Stories, Poems, and Monologues. Los Angeles, Black Sparrow Press, 1973.
Rolling Thunder Logbook. New York, Viking Press, 1977; London, Penguin, 1978.
Motel Chronicles (includes *Hawk Moon*). San Francisco, City Lights, 1982; as *Motel Chronicles and Hawk Moon*, London, Faber, 1985.

*

Bibliography: *Ten Modern American Playwrights* by Kimball King, New York, Garland, 1982.

Critical Studies: *American Dreams: The Imagination of Sam Shepard* edited by Bonnie Marranca, New York, Performing Arts Journal Publications, 1981; *Sam Shepard, Arthur Kopit, and the Off Broadway Theater* by Doris Auerbach, Boston, Twayne, 1982; *Inner Landscapes: The Theater of Sam Shepard* by Ron Mottram, Columbia, University of Missouri Press, 1984; *Sam Shepard* by Vivian M. Patraka and Mark Siegel, Boise, Idaho, Boise State University, 1985; *Sam Shepard: The Life and Work of an American Dreamer* by Ellen Oumano, New York, St. Martin's Press, 1986, London, Virgin, 1987; *Sam Shepard's Metaphorical Stages* by Lynda Hart, Westport, Connecticut, Greenwood Press, 1987.

Theatrical Activities:
Director: Many of his own plays.
Actor: **Plays**—with Bishop's Company, Burbank, California; role in *Cowboy Mouth*, New York, 1971. **Films**—*Brand X*, 1970; *Days of Heaven*, 1978; *Resurrection*, 1981; *Raggedy Man*, 1981; *Frances*, 1982; *The Right Stuff*, 1983; *Country*, 1984; *Fool for Love*, 1985; *Crimes of the Heart*, 1987.

Sam Shepard comments:

(1973) I'm interested in exploring the writing of plays through attitudes derived from other forms such as music, painting, sculpture, film, all the time keeping in mind that I'm writing for the theatre. I consider theatre and writing to be a home where I bring the adventures of my life and sort them out, making sense or non-sense out of mysterious impressions. I like to start with as little information about where I'm going as possible. A nearly empty space which is the stage where a picture, a sound, a color sneaks in and tells me a certain kind of story. I feel that language is a veil hiding demons and angels which the characters are always out of touch with. Their quest in the play is the same as ours in life—to find those forces, to meet them face to face and end the mystery. I'm pulled toward images that shine in the middle of junk. Like cracked headlights shining on a deer's eyes. I've been influenced by Jackson Pollock, Little Richard, Cajun fiddles, and the Southwest.

* * *

In spite of his prolific output—some 40 plays since the mid-1960's—Sam Shepard's invention never flags, and his achievements sometimes tower high. More than any contemporary American playwright, he has woven into his own dramatic idiom the strands of a youth culture thriving on drugs, rock music, astrology, science fiction, old movies, detective stories, cowboy films, and races of cars, horses, dogs. More recently he strives for mythic dimensions in family plays.

Growing up in Southern California, Shepard fell almost accidentally into playwriting when he went to New York City: "The world I was living in was the most interesting thing to me, and I thought the best thing I could do maybe would be to write about it, so I started writing plays." Since the time was the 1960's and the place was the lower East Side, Shepard's short plays were produced off-off-Broadway. Today he finds it difficult to remember these early efforts, the best of which are published as *Five Plays*. They tend to focus on a single event, the characters often talking past one another or breaking into long monologues. However puzzling the action, these plays already ring out with Shepard's deft rhythms.

Within three years of these first efforts, in 1966, 23-year old Shepard produced his first full-length play, *La Turista*, punning on the Spanish word for tourist and the diarrhea that attacks American tourists in Mexico. Perhaps influenced by Beckett's *Waiting For Godot, La Turista* is also composed of two acts in which the second virtually repeats the first. However, questionable identities and mythic roles are at once more blatant and more realistic than in Beckett. In both of Shepard's acts Kent is sick, and his wife Salem (both named for cigarette brands) sends for a doctor, who, more or less aided by his son, essays a cure. But the first act is set in a Mexican hotel room and the illness is *la turista*, whereas the second act is set in an American hotel room and the illness is sleeping sickness. Playing through film stereotypes, Kent breaks out of the theater and perhaps out of illness as well.

Other plays followed swiftly, some published in 1971 in two volumes aptly named for the first and longest play in each book. In the six plays of *The Unseen Hand* almost all the main characters are threatened by unseen hands. Two plays of *Mad Dog Blues* camp the popular arts they embrace affectionately. In the title play two friends, Kosmo, a rock star, and Yahoudi, a drug dealer, separate to seek their respective fortunes. Kosmo takes up with Mae West, and Yohoudi with Marlene Dietrich. Each pair becomes a triangle when Kosmo annexes Waco, Texas, and Yahoudi Captain Kidd, for whose treasure they all hunt. Tumbling from adventure to adventure, Yahoudi shoots Captain Kidd, Marlene goes off with Paul Bunyan, Kosmo and Mae West find the treasure, but Jesse James makes off with treasure and Mae West. Finally Mae suggests that they all go to the Missouri home of Jesse James, and the play ends in festive song and dance.

A longer play from 1970 also ends in comic celebration. The punning title *Operation Sidewinder* refers to an American army computer in the shape of a sidewinder rattlesnake. By the play's end, however, it becomes an actual snake and Hopi Indian religious symbol through whose symbiotic power a disoriented young couple is integrated into an organic society—even as in New Comedy. To attain this, the pair has to avoid a revolutionary conspiracy, military backlash, several corpses, and their own highly verbal confusion.

It is generally agreed that *The Tooth of Crime* is Shepard's most impressive play. He has commented: "It started with language—it started with hearing a certain sound which is coming from the voice of this character, Hoss." And the play's strength remains in language, a synthesis of the slangs of rock, crime, astrology, and sports. Hoss has played by the code and moved by the charts, but he senses that he is doomed. Gradually, the doom takes the shape and name of Crow, a gypsy killer. Alerted through Eyes, warned by the charts of Galactic Jack, doped by his doctor, comforted by his moll, Hoss prepares for his fate, "Stuck in my image." In Act 2, Hoss and Crow, has-been and would-be, duel with words and music—"Choose an argot"—as a Referee keeps score. In the third Round the Ref calls a TKO, and Hoss kills the Referee. Unable to bend to Crow's wild ways, Hoss prefers to die, in the manner of classical heroes but in contemporary idiom: "A true gesture that won't never cheat on itself 'cause it's the last of its kind."

Ironically, this American tragedy was written when Shepard was living in London, where his *Geography of a Horse Dreamer* sprang from English dog-racing. On home ground in California, Shepard wrote *Action* about two passive American couples, *Killer's Head* about a cowboy in the electric chair, *Angel City* about horror and horror movies in Hollywood, *Suicide in B Flat* about pressures leading to artistic suicide. These plays are at once newly inventive and stylistically consistent in their nonrealistic images, unpredictable characters, and rich language grounded in colloquialism and soaring to manic monologue. Shepard's most mercurial achievement in pure monologue is the creation of two pieces for actor Joseph Chaikin—*Tongues* and *Savage/Love*.

While becoming more involved in his career as a film actor, Shepard has written what he himself calls a "family trilogy," although there is no carryover of characters in *Curse of the Starving Class, Buried Child*, and *True West*. In these plays Shepard follows O'Neill in dramatizing a tragic America, mired in sin. In *Curse* the sin is betrayal of the land to soulless speculators. In *Buried Child* it is incest, cruelty, and murder that stifle freedom and creativity in the young. *True West* is at once funnier on its surface and more focused in its opposition of two brothers with divergent lives and attitudes toward the true West.

The love/hate relation within a pair carries over from *True West* to *Fool for Love*, but the pair is now half-siblings and whole lovers. May and Eddie are alternately ecstatic and sadistic in one another's presence in a tawdry motel room, while their father observes them from an offstage vantage. When, at play's end, the motel room goes up in flames, it is not only the end of their inconclusive incest, but of Shepard's own subjection to conventional play-making, with exposition, plot, and resolution. And perhaps Shepard punctuates this stage of his career by acting the part of Eddie in the movie version, where flashbacks are unfortunately shown.

A Lie of the Mind is still undergoing revision, but, dividing the stage between a rootless and a rooted family, a violent representative of the old West, and a family where the victimized women exude tenderness, Shepard implies that America must look forward with a gentleness that belies its violent past.

Shepard has absorbed American pop art, media myths, and the Southwestern scene to recycle them in many—perhaps too many—image-focused plays in which the characters speak inventive idioms in vivid rhythms. At his best—*La Turista, Mad Dog Blues, The Tooth of Crime, A Lie of the Mind*—Shepard achieves his own distinctive coherence through beautifully bridled fantasy.

—Ruby Cohn

SHERMAN, Martin. American. Born in Philadelphia, Pennsylvania, 22 December 1938. Educated at Boston University, 1956–60, M.F.A. 1960. Playwright-in-residence, Playwrights Horizons, New York, 1976–77. Recipient: Wurlitzer Foundation grant, 1973; National Endowment for the Arts fellowship, 1980; Dramatists Guild Hull-Warriner Award, 1980; Rockefeller fellowship, 1985. Agent: Margaret Ramsay Ltd., 14-A Goodwin's Court, London WC2N 4LL; or, Johnnie Planko, William Morris Agency, 1350 Avenue of the Americas, New York, New York 10019, U.S.A. Address: 35 Leinster Square, London W.2, England.

PUBLICATIONS

Plays

A Solitary Thing, music by Stanley Silverman (produced Oakland, California, 1963).

Fat Tuesday (produced New York, 1966).
Next Year in Jerusalem (produced New York, 1968).
The Night Before Paris (produced New York, 1969; Edinburgh, 1970).
Things Went Badly in Westphalia (produced Storrs, Connecticut, 1971). Published in *The Best Short Plays 1970*, edited by Stanley Richards, Philadelphia, Chilton, 1970.
Passing By (produced New York, 1974; London, 1975). Published in *Gay Plays 1*, edited by Michael Wilcox, London, Methuen, 1984.
Soaps (produced New York, 1975).
Cracks (produced Waterford, Connecticut, 1975; New York, 1976; Oldham, Lancashire, 1981). Published in *Gay Plays 2*, edited by Michael Wilcox, London, Methuen, 1986.
Rio Grande (produced New York, 1976).
Blackout (produced New York, 1978).
Bent (produced Waterford, Connecticut, 1978; London and New York, 1979). Ashover, Derbyshire, Amber Lane Press, 1979; New York, Avon, 1980.
Messiah (produced London, 1982; New York, 1984). Oxford, Amber Lane Press, 1982.
When She Danced (produced Guildford, Surrey, 1985).

*

Theatrical Activities:
Director: **Play**—*Point Blank* by Alan Pope and Alex Harding, London, 1980.

* * *

Although Martin Sherman is an American playwright born and bred, his parentage is Russian, and he displays a European consciousness as well as an unusual sensitivity to the music of language. Small wonder he prefers historical periods (including earlier in this century) to the present-day and European settings to American. Although *Bent* and *Passing By* focus on male-identified men, in the leading roles of *Rio Grande, Messiah, When She Danced*, and *A Madhouse in Goa* (unproduced) Sherman has created remarkably complex and individualized portraits of women. Sherman brings a keen intellect to bear on his materials, yet crafts plays which, far from aridly cerebral, are palpably permeated with the deepest feeling. Generalizations about his work, however, are dangerous, for he does not repeat himself. Equally at home with comedy and drama, Sherman works in styles as diverse as his subjects, and his eccentric characters populate works of often audacious originality.

Sherman's volatile and varied subjects include satire of soap operas (*Soaps*); a dying woman who, when visited by an alien from another planet, is tempted to go off with him in his space ship (*Rio Grande*); charming, light comedy about two gay men who, shortly after meeting, develop hepatitis and care for each other (*Passing By*); and a hippie whodunnit so crazed the killer's identity is never revealed (*Cracks*). That madcap comedy of death, described by a British critic as "Agatha Christie on acid," is a counterculture *Ten Little Indians*, but also a satire of narcissism which Joe Orton might have written had he spent the 1960's in California.

The characters in these and other Sherman plays are outsiders because they are gay or Jewish or foreign or female or strangers in a strange land. In *Messiah*, seeing the Cossacks torture her husband to death has rendered Rebecca mute, while in *A Madhouse in Goa* aphasiac Daniel's language is as dislocated as this gay genius—an "other"—is from his world. Seven languages are spoken in *When She Danced* because nearly everyone in the play is an expatriate from another country. The men in *Bent* represent exiles within their own country, because of their differences thrown into a concentration camp to die.

Although this literal and metaphorical alienation devastates spectators, Sherman's survival kit contains, above all, humor. In *Messiah* his Rachel—a skeptical yet compassionate figure who seems to embody the author's spirit more than any of Sherman's other creations—endures because she is blessed with an ironic sensibility which perceives God's exquisite humor and turns even her denial of God's existence into a scream directed at the Deity.

This dark, personal, and painful play set in 17th-century Poland and Turkey concerns not the title character, who never appears, but a clever yet homely woman whose life the news of the "false Messiah" Sabbatai Sevi profoundly alters. From a claustrophobic village to a barren foreign shore, Rachel and what family remains after her husband dies in a literal leap of faith journey in search of salvation. In liberation from dogma and sexual repression and in self-reliance, however, fear and doubt accompany the removal of boundaries. Such exiles must do without, equally, both restrictions and security. Rich in eroticism, brooding mysticism, and earthy humor, *Messiah* dramatizes a courageous, autonomous woman, a resilient and female Job, experiencing metaphysical conflicts often reserved for male heroes. In her soul, as well as in the play as a whole, doubt, superstition, and disillusionment war against buoyant spirits, wit, kindness, and faith—in God, in the future, and in self.

Whereas religion opposes sexuality in *Messiah*, in *Bent* the source of oppression is governmental. A play which has changed the popular perception of Holocaust victims as solely Jewish, *Bent* has been staged in 35 countries worldwide. Its initial urbane comedy quickly moves into a nightmare about men whom Nazis required to wear, not yellow stars, but pink triangles. Forced into complicity in his lover's murder, in order to survive Max also denies his homosexuality and proves he's not "bent" by having sex with a 13-year-old girl's corpse. Yet Max moves beyond betrayal and self-contempt. In the dehumanizing circumstances of Dachau, his humanity emerges as he affirms the possibility of love and self-sacrifice, embraces his gay identity, and defies those who imprison his soul. In the play's most amazing scene, Max even makes love to another prisoner without their ever making physical contact.

When She Danced finds affirmation, not through intense suffering, but in comedy of wit. This day in the life of Isadora Duncan takes its tone from Preston Sturges's 1940's films because that writer/director grew up around the Duncan household. A touching and amusing valentine to genius, this comedy finds the 46-year-old, improvident, charismatic dancer living in Paris with her young husband Sergei, with whom she shares no common tongue. Much of the humor derives from the troubles communicating experienced by characters speaking in seven languages and from the arrival of a translator. Isadora's instincts that language is highly overrated—"We never had it in America"—prove prophetic, as communication promotes discord and chaos, as well as hilarious misunderstandings.

A Madhouse in Goa moves, like *Bent*, from wit to poignance. Naturally, neither of its two parts takes place in Goa. The brittle, mannered comedy of *A Table for a King* unfolds at a Corfu resort in the 1960's, while the stormy weather of *Keeps Rainin' All the Time* occurs on Santorini "one year from now," after nuclear accidents have altered world weather patterns so drastically that rain continually drenches the Greek isles.

The former's narrator is a gay, Jewish, socially awkward young American whose insecurities are assailed by a garrulous southern matron who mocks and mothers him and whose loneliness is momentarily assuaged by the clever Greek waiter who seduces him.

This fellow's wallowing in melancholy seems only minor self-indulgence when contrasted to the second assortment of self-pitying people all wrapped up in their own needs but none too adept at satisfying them. Only gradually does a spectator appreciate that among this self-absorbed crew is the same American, this time in his forties. Not exactly the same man, though, for it appears Daniel is the *author* of the first part, which dramatizes, not the real events of twenty years ago, but a fictionalization which conveniently omits the painful truths that would have reduced his novel's commercial appeal. That sell-out, however, is minor compared to plans for a musical film version of *A Table for a King* presented by a born-again Hollywood producer, who may be the most mercilessly satirized Sherman creation. The self-preoccupied Daniel's stroke-induced aphasia prevents his communicating to the others surrounding him—his male nurse, his dying friend Heather, her hacker son, the producer's girlfriend. Thus when Heather's fears of religious extremists, carcinogenic food, Aids, and getting nuked require reassurance, Daniel intones "Apple sauce."

The despair underlying Sherman's humor, as well as the imaginative situation and plotting, recall David Mercer, particularly *Duck Song*. Underneath the jokes lurks anguish for a doomed world, a perception which prompted the comical woman of Part 1 to commit herself to the titular Indian asylum. Sherman smashes his other characters' lives, leaving Daniel no audience for his incomprehensible and bitter wit. Unlike the Sherman plays which have dramatized survival, *A Madhouse in Goa*—like Beckett's *Endgame*—distills dread for the very future of humanity.

—Tish Dace

SIMON, (Marvin) Neil. American. Born in the Bronx, New York, 4 July 1927. Educated at De Witt Clinton High School, New York, graduated 1943; New York University, 1944–45; University of Denver, 1945–46. Served in the United States Army Air Force, 1945–46: Corporal. Married 1) Joan Baim in 1953 (died 1973), two daughters; 2) the actress Marsha Mason in 1973 (divorced 1983). Radio and television writer, 1948–60. Recipient: Emmy award, for television writing, 1957, 1959; Tony award, 1965, 1970, 1985; London *Evening Standard* award, 1967; Shubert award, 1968; Writers Guild of America West award, for screenplay, 1969, 1971, 1976; PEN Los Angeles Center award, 1982; New York Drama Critics Circle award, 1983; Outer Circle award, 1983, 1985; New York State Governor's award, 1986. L.H.D.: Hofstra University, Hempstead, New York, 1981. Address: c/o Random House Inc., 201 East 50th Street, New York, New York 10022, U.S.A.

PUBLICATIONS

Plays

Sketches (produced Tamiment, Pennsylvania, 1952, 1953).

Sketches, with Danny Simon, in *Catch a Star!* (produced New York, 1955).

Sketches, with Danny Simon, in *New Faces of 1956* (produced New York, 1956).

Adventures of Marco Polo: A Musical Fantasy, with William Friedberg, music by Clay Warnick and Mel Pahl. New York, French, 1959.

Heidi, with William Friedberg, music by Clay Warnick, adaptation of the novel by Johanna Spyri. New York, French, 1959.

Come Blow Your Horn (produced New Hope, Pennsylvania, 1960; New York, 1961; London, 1962). New York and London, French, 1961.

Little Me, music by Cy Coleman, lyrics by Carolyn Leigh, adaptation of the novel by Patrick Dennis (produced New York, 1962; London, 1964; revised version produced New York, 1982; London, 1983). Included in *Collected Plays 2*, 1979.

Barefoot in the Park (as *Nobody Loves Me*, produced New Hope, Pennsylvania, 1962; as *Barefoot in the Park*, produced New York, 1963; London, 1965). New York, Random House, 1964; London, French, 1966.

The Odd Couple (produced New York, 1965; London, 1966; revised [women's] version produced New York, 1985). New York, Random House, 1966.

Sweet Charity, music by Cy Coleman, lyrics by Dorothy Fields, based on the screenplay *Nights of Cabiria* by Federico Fellini and others (produced New York, 1966; London, 1967). New York, Random House, 1966.

The Star-Spangled Girl (produced New York, 1966). New York, Random House, 1967.

Plaza Suite (includes *Visitor from Mamaroneck, Visitor from Hollywood, Visitor from Forest Hills*) (produced New York, 1968; London, 1969). New York, Random House, 1969.

Promises, Promises, music and lyrics by Burt Bacharach and Hal David, based on the screenplay *The Apartment* by Billy Wilder and I.A.L. Diamond (produced New York, 1968; London, 1969). New York, Random House, 1969.

Last of the Red Hot Lovers (produced New York, 1969; Manchester and London, 1979). New York, Random House, 1970.

The Gingerbread Lady (produced New York, 1970; Windsor and London, 1974). New York, Random House, 1971.

The Prisoner of Second Avenue (produced New York, 1971). New York, Random House, and London, French, 1972.

The Sunshine Boys (produced New York, 1972; London, 1975). New York, Random House, 1973.

The Comedy of Neil Simon (includes *Come Blow Your Horn; Barefoot in the Park; The Odd Couple; The Star-Spangled Girl; Plaza Suite; Promises, Promises; Last of the Red Hot Lovers*). New York, Random House, 1972.

The Good Doctor, music by Peter Link, lyrics by Simon, adaptation of stories by Chekhov (produced New York, 1973; Coventry, 1981). New York, Random House, 1974; London, French, 1975.

God's Favorite (produced New York, 1974). New York, Random House, 1975.

California Suite (includes *Visitor from New York, Visitor from Philadelphia, Visitor from London, Visitor from Chicago*) (produced Los Angeles, New York, and London, 1976). New York, Random House, 1977.

Chapter Two (produced Los Angeles and New York, 1977; London, 1981). New York, Random House, and London, French, 1979.

They're Playing Our Song, music by Marvin Hamlisch, lyrics by Carol Bayer Sager (produced Los Angeles, 1978; New York, 1979; London, 1980). New York, Random House, 1980.

Collected Plays 2 (includes *The Sunshine Boys, Little Me, The Gingerbread Lady, The Prisoner of Second Avenue, The Good Doctor, God's Favorite, California Suite, Chapter Two*). New York, Random House, 1979.
I Ought to Be in Pictures (produced Los Angeles and New York, 1980; Perth, Scotland, 1983; London, 1986). New York, Random House, 1981.
Fools (produced New York, 1981). New York, Random House, 1982.
Actors and Actresses (produced Stamford, Connecticut, 1983).
Brighton Beach Memoirs (produced Los Angeles and New York, 1983; London, 1986). New York, Random House, and London, French, 1984.
Biloxi Blues (produced New York, 1985). New York, Random House, 1986.
Broadway Bound (produced New York, 1986). New York, Random House, 1987.

Screenplays: *After the Fox*, with Cesare Zavattini, 1966; *Barefoot in the Park*, 1967; *The Odd Couple*, 1968; *The Out-of-Towners*, 1970; *Plaza Suite*, 1971; *The Heartbreak Kid*, 1972; *The Last of the Red Hot Lovers*, 1972; *The Prisoner of Second Avenue*, 1975; *The Sunshine Boys*, 1975; *Murder by Death*, 1976; *The Goodbye Girl*, 1977; *The Cheap Detective*, 1978; *California Suite*, 1978; *Chapter Two*, 1979; *Seems Like Old Times*, 1980; *Only When I Laugh*, 1982; *I Ought to Be in Pictures*, 1982; *Max Dugan Returns*, 1983; *The Slugger's Wife*, 1985; *Brighton Beach Memoirs*, 1987.

Radio Writing: scripts for *Robert Q. Lewis Show*.

Television Writing: *Phil Silvers Show*, 1948; *Tallulah Bankhead Show*, 1951; *Your Show of Shows*, 1956; *Sid Caesar Show*, 1956–57; *Jerry Lewis Show; Jacky Gleason Show; Red Buttons Show; Sergeant Bilko* series, 1958–59; *Garry Moore Show*, 1959–60; *The Trouble with People*, 1972; *Happy Endings*, with others, 1975.

*

Bibliography: *Ten Modern American Playwrights* by Kimball King, New York, Garland, 1982.

Critical Studies: *Neil Simon* by Edythe M. McGovern, New York, Ungar, 1979; *Neil Simon* by Robert K. Johnson, Boston, Twayne, 1983.

* * *

In a time of turmoil and despair in the commercial theatre both in Britain and in America, it is encouraging to note that neither Neil Simon nor Alan Ayckbourn has been seriously deterred by dismissive or hostile criticism. Fifty years ago on both sides of the Atlantic, there were a number of playwrights who regularly produced new works, confidently expecting professional productions. Today, writers' grants and play-workshops proliferate, as producers, directors, actors, critics, and even audiences wonder where the interesting new plays are to be found. At least in the commercial sector, some already renowned playwrights find it difficult to get a production. In the United States, Simon is almost alone as a successful dramatist who is expected to continue concocting comedies and musicals which please audiences.

Unlike Ayckbourn, who is able to develop and test his new works at Scarborough's Stephen Joseph Theatre before they are shown in the West End, Simon's scripts are customarily commercially mounted and "tried out" in Los Angeles and elsewhere in regional America before coming to Broadway. It has been suggested that Simon may well be the most successful playwright—in terms of royalties and other income from his varied ventures on stage, in films, and on television—who has ever lived. At various times, he has had three and four productions running simultaneously on Broadway, not to mention touring ensembles, stock and amateur productions, and foreign stagings.

His fortunes with many critics, however, have been rather different. Initially, with early domestic comedies such as *Come Blow Your Horn* and *Barefoot in the Park*, he was welcomed as a fresh new voice, with a particular comic talent for pointing up the pangs and problems of urban family life. He was also fortunate in receiving slickly professional productions with impressive performers to bring his visions of contemporary middle-class angst to life. The fact that most new Simon scripts rapidly became long-running hits, significant commercial money-spinners, helped attract even wider audiences. It's an axiom that people would rather see hits than flops. Once in the theatre, however, spectators were obviously amused by Simon's comic techniques, but they also clearly responded to characters and situations they could recognize.

It has been repeatedly pointed out, by regional and foreign critics and producers, that the farther removed from New York a Simon production is, the less easily do audiences respond and empathize. Some explain this by suggesting that Simon's concerns are largely with urban and suburban New Yorkers, which may well be of interest to audiences elsewhere, without striking any personal sparks of instant recognition. A few of Simon's detractors, however, insist that his comedy is not only one of New York insularity, but more specifically of materialistic, middle-class New York Jews, thus making it less immediately accessible to non-Jews beyond the Hudson. Whatever the merits of this argument, in the mid-1980's such nation-wide American Simon successes as his autobiographical *Brighton Beach Memoirs* and *Biloxi Blues* were produced by Britain's subsidized National Theatre rather than by a West End commercial management.

While some object to what they perceive as a regional, cultural, economic, or even ethnic bias in Simon's choice of subject matter, others—notably critics, rather than audiences—complain about what is often seen as the playwright's major fault: his obvious addiction to the "one-liner" comic comment, which seems to elicit boisterous laughter, regardless of the dramatic context in which it occurs. A cursory reading of Simon's comedies and musical comedy books will readily reveal this penchant for the quick, often sarcastic quip, which in fact is more often to be heard in New York conversations than elsewhere in America. This is a distinctive element in Simon's comic writing, and its genesis can be traced to his early collaboration with his brother, Danny Simon, when they were gag-writers for such television series as the *Phil Silvers Show* and the *Sid Caesar Show*, where the smart retort and the devastating comic put-down were major provokers of laughter. The gift of making people laugh in the theatre is to be prized, but this talent in Simon has been viewed, by critics who would like to admire him more, as rather a curse than a dramatic inspiration.

Despite his commercial success and even such official recognitions as the Tony, Shubert, and *Evening Standard* awards, Simon has been sensitive to critical objections. In conversation, he is an informed, concerned, compassionate, serious human being; a Simon interview is not a barrage of hilarious one-liners. He has repeatedly pointed out—to answer critical charges that his comedies are all artificial constructs, manipulations of stereotypes in stock situations—that the most successful of his works, from the first, have been firmly rooted in his personal experience, or that of close friends and family. That's true of *Come Blow Your Horn* and *The Odd Couple*, in terms of the brothers Simon. As television collaborators, Simon has noted, brother Danny was rumpled and disorganized, while brother Neil was always neat and tidy: out of this experience came the comic conflicts of sloppy Oscar and fussy Felix. *Barefoot in the Park* reprised the New York apartment experiences of the newlywed Neil Simons.

Last of the Red Hot Lovers, a series of amorous miscarriages on the part of a frustrated fish merchant with variously fixated women, was inspired by the so-called Sexual Revolution of the 1960's, when many middle-aged men and women feared the new freedoms were passing them by. (Women in the Broadway audience would shout advice to James Coco, playing the forlorn would-be seducer: "Jimmy! *She's* not right for you!") Whatever demanding critics may say, popular audiences readily respond to Simon's view of man and life.

The Star-Spangled Girl is a construct, as Simon has admitted, acknowledging that it didn't work as he hoped it would. *Plaza Suite*, in which the same suite in the famed New York hotel is the scene of three quite different but amusing encounters, may be viewed as a comic tour de force, but the situations are all based on realities. (In fact, Simon's film *The Out-of-Towners* is a dramatised expansion of an opening *Plaza Suite* monologue, omitted on Broadway.)

When Simon tried to show his critics—and his public—that he was capable of dealing thoughtfully and dramatically with a serious subject, *The Gingerbread Lady* was dismissed or disparaged as having been damaged by his recourse to the familiar device of the comic quip. This play was clearly inspired by the self-destructiveness of Judy Garland. Simon explored the possible reasons for her loss of confidence and bad habits; he also was intrigued by the idea of an often hurt but still loving daughter effectually becoming a mother to her own mother, to protect her from herself. Another show-business situation was probed in *The Sunshine Boys*, exploring the behind-the-scenes hostilities—continuing into old age—of vaudeville teams such as Smith and Dale. *The Prisoner of Second Avenue* continues to excite interest, however, with its mordant humor all the more valid as seemingly successful, highly paid executives are suddenly fired, with no prospects of re-employment. As if to answer those who complain that Simon only writes about New Yorkers, *California Suite* did for Los Angeles what *Plaza Suite* did for Manhattan.

Chapter Two—in which Simon came to terms with the sorrow and rage at the loss of his first wife through cancer and began a new relationship—at last was a serious subject which critics and public could accept as an honest, deeply felt vision of suffering and redemption, leavened with sharp personal satire and comic quips. Curiously, the most recent Simon comedies, the saga of a young playwright's growing up, have been critically praised as a kind of break-through in comic technique. Actually, however, the semi-autobiographical *Brighton Beach Memoirs* (childhood in Brooklyn), *Biloxi Blues* (1940's army experience), and *Broadway Bound* (young man with a typewriter) exemplify one of the oldest known dramatic structures. Simon's alter-ego, Eugene Morris Jerome (*pace* Eugene O'Neill), functions as a genial narrator, who interrupts his first-person story to step into dramatised episodes. It's efficient as a technique, but it's hardly an innovation.

Over the years, Simon has also shown himself a skilled adaptor of other materials, as in the musicals *Little Me* (Patrick Dennis's novel), *Sweet Charity* (Federico Fellini's film), and *Promises, Promises* (Billy Wilder's film), and in the plays *The Good Doctor* (Chekhov's short stories), *God's Favorite* (*The Book of Job* on Long Island's North Shore: Simon's answer to MacLeish's *J.B.*), and *Fools* (suggested by Sholem Aleicheim's stories of Chelm). For the cinema, he has drafted effective screenplays of some of his own plays, as well as some originals, such as *The Goodbye Girl* and *Murder by Death*, the first a popular romantic comedy, the second, a puzzling disaster.

Despite periodic renunciations of Broadway, carping critics, the pace of New York life, or East Coast values, Simon does seem to draw his primary inspiration and stimulation from this scene. And, although some denigrators would insist that with Simon, "Nothing succeeds like *excess*," his large, impressive, continuing body of comedies, endorsed to a greater or lesser degree by audiences at home and abroad, is an undeniable achievement by a distinctive talent with a penetrating intelligence. It is a record all the more impressive in a time when so few playwrights are regularly creating effective comedies.

—Glenn Loney

SIMONS, Beverley (née Rosen). Canadian. Born in Flin Flon, Manitoba, 31 March 1938. Educated at Banff School of Fine Arts, Alberta, 1956; McGill University, Montreal, 1956–57; University of British Columbia, Vancouver, 1958–59, B.A. (honours) in English and theatre 1959. Married to Sidney B. Simons; three sons. Lived in Europe, 1959–61. Recipient: Canada Council grant, 1967, and award, 1972. Lives in Vancouver. Address: c/o Playwrights Union of Canada, 8 York Street, 6th Floor, Toronto, Ontario M5J 1R2, Canada.

PUBLICATIONS

Plays

Twisted Roots (as Beverley Rosen), in *First Flowering*, edited by Anthony Frisch. Toronto, Kingswood House, 1956.
The Birth (produced Montreal, 1957).
A Play (produced Montreal, 1957).
The Elephant and the Jewish Question (produced Vancouver, 1968). Vancouver, New Play Centre, n.d.
Green Lawn Rest Home (produced Burnaby, British Columbia, 1969). Toronto, Playwrights, 1973.
Crabdance (produced Seattle, 1969). Vancouver, In Press, 1969; revised version (produced Vancouver, 1972), Vancouver, Talonbooks, 1972.
Preparing (produced Burnaby, British Columbia, 1973). Included in *Preparing* (collection), 1975.
Preparing (includes *Prologue, Triangle, The Crusader, Green Lawn Rest Home*). Vancouver, Talonbooks, 1975.
Prologue, Triangle, The Crusader (produced Toronto, 1976). Included in *Preparing*, 1975.
If I Turn Around Quick, published in *Capilano Review* (North Vancouver), Summer 1976.
Leela Means to Play (produced Waterford, Connecticut, 1978). Published in *Canadian Theatre Review 9* (Downsview, Ontario), Winter 1976.

Television Play: *The Canary*, 1968.

*

Critical Studies: "Beverley Simons Issue" of *Canadian Theatre Review 9* (Downsview, Ontario), Winter 1976.

* * *

Crabdance is Beverley Simons's best-known work and remains her outstanding achievement. In it the commonplace world is transformed by Sadie Golden's hyper-sensitive perceptions, salesmen becoming sons, lovers, and husband as Sadie projects onto them her feelings about sex, motherhood, and her femaleness. At the critical hour of 3 p.m. she dies out of the lacerating existence in which "Mama's gone a-hunting/She's taken off her own white skin. ..." The salesmen are recognizably objective figures as well as emanations from Sadie, and the play's relation to experience is powerfully present through distorted images. The great success of *Crabdance* lies in the perilous balance between observation and feeling, the known world and Sadie's vision of it.

In an earlier one-act play, *Green Lawn Rest Home*, less ambitious than *Crabdance* but the most finished and unified of her plays, Simons also makes the internal perceptions of the characters modify the presentation of outward reality and brilliantly fuses lyrical and satirical perspectives. Society's prettification of senility and dying is critically observed while, at the same time, the mortifications before death, the leaking away of life in anguish, the tiny passions of the geriatrics, are seen and felt from within. A "date" which consists of a walk to the gate of the rest home becomes, for the old couple subjectively presented, the equivalent of the most violent adolescent sexuality. Simons conveys feelingly the real hardness of the green pebbles which, from a little distance away, give the illusion of lawns.

Leela Means to Play presents, sporadically, clear moral views of the operations of legal justice through a kind of trial-by-encounters of a judge. The play is a full-length aggregation of very short scenes, related in theme but not through plot or sequence—gobbets of allegory in which the representation of modern life is distorted by an intensely feeling consciousness. There is no equivalent of Sadie Golden, however, to give focus and coherence in this play. In this work Simons relies too naively on her audience's recognition of the personality *behind* it. The play seems to have been untimely snatched from the authorial womb, still trailing unsynthesized bits of Beckett, Genet, Albee, and Noh-via-Yeats, unfinished though very much alive.

The title piece of *Preparing* gives us (like *Crabdance*) a dramatization of the passionately sensitive perceptions of Simons. This monologue requires an actress skilled in mime and with a set of voices adequate to portray the several ages of woman. From adolescence to womanhood the speaker undertakes preparations for imposed sexual roles ending with ultimate resistance ("fuck 'em all") to all the impositions. Two other short pieces in this collection are too clamantly "experimental"; one, *Crusader*, employs masks in a novel but clumsy way; in the other, *Triangle*, light and movement give us the geometry of bonding and victimage in the relationships of three characters. In both the moral view is rather heavily imposed and not offset by studious "theatricality."

In an earlier play, *The Elephant and the Jewish Question* (published only in mimeographed form), Simons showed herself capable of handling a conventional structure and natural speech, though the piece is rather stickily embedded in "Jewish atmosphere." The great development from this to *Crabdance* is an indication of Simons's strengths. Her work is marked by her exploration of various ways of presenting lyrical, internalized characters within an objective framework. But her genuine distinctiveness seems to be still overlayed and obscured by studious imitation and anxiety about form.

—Michael Sidnell

SIMPSON, N(orman) F(rederick). British. Born in London, 29 January 1919. Educated at Emanuel School, London, 1930–37; Birkbeck College, University of London, 1950–54, B.A. (honours) 1954. Served in the Royal Artillery, 1941–43, and the Intelligence Corps, 1943–46. Married Joyce Bartlett in 1944; one daughter. Staff member, Westminster Bank, London, 1937–39; teacher, College of St. Mark and St. John, London, 1939–41, and City of Westminster College, London, and extra-mural lecturer, 1946–62; literary manager, Royal Court Theatre, London, 1976–78. Address: c/o Oliver Ray, The Orchards, Hopcraft Lane, Deddington, Oxfordshire OX5 4TD, England.

PUBLICATIONS

Plays

A Resounding Tinkle (produced London, 1957; Bloomington, Indiana, and New York, 1961). Published in *The Observer Plays*, London, Faber, and New York, French, 1958; shortened version included in *The Hole and Other Plays and Sketches*, 1964.

The Hole (produced London, 1958; New York, 1961). London and New York, French, 1958.

One Way Pendulum (produced London, 1959; New York, 1961). London, Faber, 1960; New York, Grove Press, 1961.

Sketches in *One to Another* (produced London, 1959). London, French, 1960.

Sketches in *You, Me and the Gatepost* (produced Nottingham, 1960).

Sketches in *On the Avenue* (produced London, 1961).

Sketches in *One over the Eight* (produced London, 1961).

The Form (produced London, 1961). New York and London, French, 1961.

Oh (produced London, 1961). Included in *The Hole and Other Plays and Sketches*, 1964.

The Hole and Other Plays and Sketches (includes shortened version of *A Resounding Tinkle*, and *The Form, Gladly Otherwise, Oh, One Blast and Have Done*). London, Faber, 1964.

The Cresta Run (produced London, 1965; Louisville, Kentucky, 1968). London, Faber, 1966; New York, Grove Press, 1967.

We're Due in Eastbourne in Ten Minutes (televised 1967; produced London, 1971). Included in *Some Tall Tinkles*, 1968; in *The Best Short Plays 1972*, edited by Stanley Richards, Philadelphia, Chilton, 1972.

Some Tall Tinkles: Television Plays (includes *We're Due in Eastbourne in Ten Minutes, The Best I Can Do by Way of a Gate-Leg Table Is a Hundredweight of Coal, At Least It's a Precaution Against Fire*). London, Faber, 1968.

Playback 625, with Leopoldo Maler (produced London, 1970).

How Are Your Handles? (includes *Gladly Otherwise, Oh, The Other Side of London*) (produced London, 1970).

Was He Anyone? (produced London, 1972; New York, 1979). London, Faber, and Chicago, Dramatic Publishing Company, 1973.

In Reasonable Shape (produced London, 1977). Published in *Play Ten*, edited by Robin Rook, London, Arnold, 1977.

Anyone's Gums Can Listen to Reason, in *Play Ten*, edited by Robin Rook. London, Arnold, 1977.

Inner Voices, adaptation of a play by Eduardo De Filippo (produced London, 1983). Oxford, Amber Lane Press, 1983.

Screenplays: *One Way Pendulum*, 1964; *Diamonds for Breakfast*, with Pierre Rouve and Ronald Harwood, 1968.

Radio Plays: *Something Rather Effective*, 1972; *Sketches for Radio*, 1974.

Television Plays: *Make a Man*, 1966; *Three Rousing Tinkles* series: *The Father by Adoption of One of the Former Marquis of Rangoon's Natural Granddaughters, If Those Are Mr. Heckmondwick's Own Personal Pipes They've Been Lagged Once Already*, and *The Best I Can Do by Way of a Gate-Leg Table Is a Hundredweight of Coal*, 1966; *Four Tall Tinkles* series: *We're Due in Eastbourne in Ten Minutes, In a Punt with Friends Under a Haystack on the River Mersey, A Row of Potted Plants*, and *At Least It's a Precaution Against Fire*, 1967; *World in Ferment* series, 1969; *Charley's Grants* series, 1970; *Thank You Very Much*, 1971; *Elementary, My Dear Watson*, 1973; *Silver Wedding*, 1974; *An Upward Fall* (*Crown Court* series), 1977; *Wainwrights' Law* series, 1980.

Novel

Harry Bleachbaker. London, Harrap, 1976; as *Man Overboard: A Testimonial to the High Art of Incompetence*, New York, Morrow, 1976.

*

Manuscript Collections: Indiana University, Bloomington; University of Texas, Austin; University of California, Berkeley.

Critical Studies: *The Theatre of the Absurd* by Martin Esslin, New York, Doubleday, 1961, London, Eyre and Spottiswoode, 1962, revised edition, London, Penguin, 1968, Doubleday, 1969; *Curtains* by Kenneth Tynan, London, Longman, and New York, Atheneum, 1961; *Dramatic Essays* by Nigel Dennis, London, Weidenfeld and Nicolson, 1962, Westport, Connecticut, Greenwood Press, 1978.

N.F. Simpson comments:

The question that, as a writer, one is asked more frequently than any other is the question as to why of all things it should be plays that one has chosen to bring forth rather than, say, novels or books about flying saucers. The answer in my own case lies, I think, in the fact that there is one incomparable advantage which the play, as a form, has over the novel and the book about flying saucers; and this is that there are not anything like as many words in it. For a writer condemned from birth to draw upon a reservoir of energy such as would barely suffice to get a tadpole from one side of a tea-cup to the other, such a consideration cannot but be decisive. Poetry admittedly has in general fewer words still, and for this reason is on the face of it an even more attractive discipline; but alas I have even less gift for that than I have for writing plays, and if I had the gift for it, it would be only a matter of weeks before I came up against the ineluctable truth that there is just not the money in it that there is in plays. Not that, the way I write them, there is all that much money in those either.

As for methods of work, what I do is to husband with jealous parsimony such faint tremors of psychic energy as can sometimes be coaxed out of the permanently undercharged batteries I was issued with at birth, and when I have what might be deemed a measurable amount, to send it coursing down the one tiny channel where with any luck it might do some good. Here it deposits its wee pile of silt, which I allow to accumulate, with the barely perceptible deliberation of a coral reef to the point where it may one day recognise itself with a start of surprise as the small and unpretentious magnum opus it had all along been tremulously aspiring to.

As for why one does it there are various reasons—all of them fairly absurd. There is one's ludicrously all-embracing sense of guilt mainly. I walk the streets in perpetual fear and trepidation, like someone who expects, round the very next corner, to meet his just deserts at the hands of a lynch mob carried away by fully justified indignation. To feel *personally* responsible not only for every crime, every atrocity, every act of inhumanity that has ever been perpetrated since the world began, but for those as well that have not as yet been so much as contemplated, is something which only Jesus Christ and I can ever have experienced to anything like the same degree. And it goes a long way to account for what I write and why I write it. For not only must one do what one can by writing plays to make amends for the perfidy of getting born; one must also, in the interests of sheer self-preservation, keep permanently incapacitated by laughter as many as possible of those who would otherwise be the bearers of a just and terrible retribution. One snatches one's reprieve quite literally laugh by laugh.

My plays are about life—life as I see it. Which is to say that they are all in their various ways about a man trying to get a partially inflated rubber lilo into a suitcase slightly too small to take it even when *un*inflated. Like most Englishmen, of which I am proud to be one, I have a love of order tempered by a deep and abiding respect for anarchy, and what I would one day like to bring about is that perfect balance between the two which I believe it to be peculiarly in the nature of English genius to arrive at. I doubt very much whether I ever shall, but it is nevertheless what I would like to do.

* * *

By now N.F. Simpson must have grown wary of books on the modern drama in which his special quality—an inexhaustible surge of anarchic verbal invention—is relentlessly overanalysed. In the theatre most audiences are amused by the Simpsonian absurdity without seeking to explain it. Among sterner students this work is part of the Theatre of the Absurd which is by no means what it sounds.

Any discussion of his plays that goes too far into motive and method can make Simpson sound tedious whereas, both in performance and in the text, he is among the most cheerfully original dramatists of his time. One may think of Carroll, Lear, and Gilbert, but Simpson is blissfully his own master.

True, this particular line of humour, depending as it does on the non-sequitur and on the carrying of logic as far as it will go (and further) can worry some of Simpson's listeners and readers. They find him too clever, and they become embarrassed. In *A Resounding Tinkle*, his first play, which was later revised, he makes the dramatist say:

It is together that we must shape the experience which is the play we shall all of us have shared. The actors are as much the audience as the audience themselves, in precisely the same way that the audience are as much the actors as the actors themselves. We are all spectators of one another, mutual witnesses of each other's discomfiture.

Simpson, a Londoner and a former bank clerk, became a teacher after Intelligence Corps service during the war. He was noticed first when his earlier version of *A Resounding Tinkle* won a prize in a competition organised by the *Observer*, a London Sunday newspaper. Another treatment was staged later at the Royal Court; and in 1958 the play returned, this time in company with a one-acter, *The Hole*. It was an evening of wreathing verbal smoke-rings, and nothing is less profitable than to try and fix these in a grave dissertation.

A Resounding Tinkle is presented with the straightest of faces—never an incautious gleam in the eye, a trembling of the lip. The principal characters, who are a suburban couple, the Paradocks, keep an elephant but they think it ought to be exchanged for a snake. Agreed, a snake may be too short; still, they can have it lengthened, though then, of course, they will lose on the thickness. Somebody telephones, bothered by the eyesight of her eagles. "Uncle Ted" drops in and proves to be a charming young woman. And so on. The piece, in any version, is exceedingly funny which seems to be cause enough for its appearance. Here we have to quote the author who observes (as a character in the play): "The retreat from reason means precious little to anyone who has never caught up with reason in the first place. It takes a trained mind to relish a non-sequitur." Maybe; but there is no reason to discuss it in detail, and some critics have become almost like Simpsonian parodies in their endeavour to find every fleck of meaning in the text.

The Hole, which shared the double bill, sounded rather more laboured in performance. But most playgoers remember something from the debate among people who gather speculatively round a hole in the ground, and what they remember is usually different. An early speech may be reminiscent of Lucky's monologue in *Waiting for Godot*, and a wild sporting medley can remind us of Q's "Famous Ballad of the Jubilee Cup." But we should always beware of suggesting influences, for Simpson is very much himself: hunt as we may for resemblances and possible questions, he remains in the long run among the truest originals in the theatre of his period, even if his form of humour—and who can be dogmatic?—must sometimes be an acquired taste.

His major play is *One Way Pendulum* which he called, alarmingly, "an evening of high drung and slarrit." Later he changed this, more recognisably, to "a farce in a new dimension." Here, too, writers have been eager to explain. One has said that the play is "a ferocious comment on contemporary British life." We can doubt whether many of its watchers have seen it like that. Simpson himself has said that, as drama, *One Way Pendulum*, "with its turrets and its high pointed gables, should have a particular appeal for anyone approaching it for the first time with a lasso." Not, perhaps, helpful, but extremely Simpsonian. This dramatist of the non-sequitur governed by absolute logic is either irresistible or one sits unmoved; to explain either reaction is like trying to drain the ocean with the leaky limpet-shell Tregeagle, the Cornish giant, was given for Dozmary Pool.

Briefly, *One Way Pendulum* is set in the living room of the Groomkirbys at an address given as 93 Chundragore Street, Suburbia, a space occupied for most of the night by a replica of an Old Bailey court. Arthur Groomkirby, passionate about the law, has put the court together with a do-it-yourself set. It takes a lot of space; when it is up, there is no room for Aunt Mildred who believes, obsessively, that she is in the Outer Hebrides waiting for a train to St. Pancras. Never mind; there will always be room for Myra who drops in professionally to finish any food left in the house—as the author puts it, to practise "incessant eating in a vocational capacity."

When the Old Bailey is set up, it needs a Judge; it acquires one at once, though not a jury ("They are here in spirit, m'Lord" the usher says). It seems that we are at the trial of the younger Groomkirby for forty-three murders—"he has been fairly regularly taking life," a prosecuting council, also on the spot, observes. But Simpson is most engaged with the evidence of Groomkirby senior. After all, it is his own Old Bailey, and he ought to have a good chance to play with it. Having therefore sworn (by Harriet Beecher Stowe) that he will speak nothing but the truth, he proposes to lie to the Court ("a frank and honest answer" the Judge observes), but wilts under cross-examination. Denying that he is a geographer, he yet admits that, to have been in Chester-le-Street on a given date, he had absented himself from most of the places "only an expert geographer could have thought of." The play goes on like this. There is no reason now to speak of the weighing-machines that must sing the Hallelujah Chorus; the woman who wears her pearls "round her waist for the tightness"; the curious nightmare quality of a game of three-handed whist for two players without cards in the dark; and a line (for Mrs. Groomkirby) that became celebrated: "We've nothing against apes. As such."

Simpson has suggested that the Groomkirbys talk and behave very much as any family might which has been harried for months on end by "a runaway drawbridge in slow motion." Excellent; but a redoubtable commentator has insisted that the play "hints at the connexion between . . . the mutual tolerance that allows each of the Groomkirbys to plant his weird preoccupations in the middle of the living-room, and the deep undercurrents of cruelty and sadism that lie behind such a society."

Each to his choice. In his next full-length play, *The Cresta Run* (which did not arrive for six years), the most wayward of intellectuals continued to work a rich vein, though Simpson added—probably to the annoyance of expert analysts—that his plays in which some had claimed to see the hand of Edward the Confessor were in fact "the work of a little old lady in Dunstable." *The Cresta Run* is, more or less, about the "grim and sinister drama of international espionage" which provokes the author to quite irreverent laughter. It is indeed the type of piece in which someone concludes very seriously—because everyone here is very serious—"I doubt whether they'd send ostriches all the way to Scarborough by submarine to spy upon the Head of Security in London." The movement of the play can loiter; but Simpsonians (far fewer of them for this piece than for *One Way Pendulum*) can applaud passages when the dramatist lets his fancy billow out round him. Just why were sixteen-and-a-half million people out of the country at the time of the Norman Conquest? What causes the wife of the trainee spy to say: "A whole grandfather clock squandered, and nothing to show for it but a wall safe we don't know how to open—and now, chiropody."? And again: "People are very funny about having the secret service run by someone who needs naturalising. Bad for the image."

We may have a feeling that Simpson's later appearances as a television dramatist were bad for the image. In an interview before the first of three short plays in 1966, he said with a kind of mild despair: "I'd never even heard of Ionesco when

I first began to write plays." These brief new pieces took us back to the first *Resounding Tinkle*. Here again were the Paradocks: here again the ferociously logical and straight-gazing absurdity. "Can I interest you," asked a canvasser, "in a collapsible canoe in the form of an ocean-going liner?" "No," Middie Paradock replies, "we're too high above sea-level for that." The name of the play is, simply, *The Father by Adoption of One of the Former Marquis of Rangoon's Natural Granddaughters*.

Although the full-length *Was He Anyone?* had well over thirty characters, it seemed faint in comparison with the earlier plays. Possibly the Simpson form of absurdity, defying all analysis, needs at the moment to be refreshed. It will undoubtedly return at full strength. At its best, in the words of one of the earlier plays, it has been "like some unspecified milk of Paradise." It is no good attempting to specify the exact brand; and probably the graver writers are recognising this.

—J.C. Trewin

SLADE, Bernard. Canadian. Born Bernard Slade Newbound in St. Catherines, Ontario, 2 May 1930. Educated at 13 schools in England and Wales, including John Ruskin School, Croydon, Surrey, and Caernarvon Grammar School. Married Jill Hancock in 1953; one daughter and one son. Moved to Canada in 1948: worked in a customs office, 1948; actor, 1949–57; co-founder, Garden Centre Theatre, Vineland, Ontario, 1954; television writer, 1957–74: wrote scripts for Canadian Broadcasting Corporation, CBS, ABC, and NBC. Recipient: Drama Desk award, 1975. Agent: Jack Hutto, 405 West 23rd Street, New York, New York 10011. Address: 101 Central Park West, Apartment 17-F, New York, New York 10011, U.S.A.

PUBLICATIONS

Plays

Simon Says Get Married (produced Toronto, 1960).
A Very Close Family (produced Winnipeg, 1963).
Same Time, Next Year (produced Boston and New York, 1975; London, 1976). New York, Delacorte Press, 1975.
Tribute (produced Boston and New York, 1978; Northampton, 1984). New York, French, 1978.
Romantic Comedy (produced New York, 1979; Watford, Hertfordshire, and London, 1983). New York, French, 1980.
Fling! New York, French, 1979.
Special Occasions (produced New York, 1982; revised version, also director: produced London, 1983). New York, French, 1982.
Fatal Attraction (produced Toronto, 1984; London, 1985). New York, French, 1986.

Screenplays: *Stand Up and Be Counted*, 1972; *Same Time, Next Year*, 1978; *Tribute*, 1980; *Romantic Comedy*, 1983.

Television Plays: *The Prize Winner*, 1957 (revised version, as *The Long, Long Laugh*); *Men Don't Make Passes, Innocent Deception, The Gimmick, Do Jerry Parker, The Most Beautiful Girl in the World, The Big Coin Sound, The Oddball, The Reluctant Angels, A Very Close Family* and *Blue Is for Boys*, 1958–64; *Bewitched* series (16 episodes), 1963–64; pilot films for series: *Love on a Rooftop, The Flying Nun, The Partridge Family, Bridget Loves Bernie, The Girl with Something Extra, Mr. Deeds Goes to Town, The Bobby Sherman Show*, and *Mr. Angel*, 1964–74; 80 scripts for other series.

*

Critical Studies: article by Robert Berkvist, in *New York Times*, 13 April 1975; article by William A. Davis, in *Critical Survey of Drama* edited by Frank N. Magill, Englewood Cliffs, New Jersey, Salem Press, 1985.

Theatrical Activities:
Director: **Play**—*Special Occasions*, London, 1983.
Actor: **Plays**—roles in 300 plays throughout Canada, and on Canadian television, 1949–57; George in *Same Time, Next Year*, Edmonton, 1977.

* * *

Bernard Slade, while not so prolific as Neil Simon, has been Simon's only serious rival as a consistently commercially successful Broadway dramatist in recent years. His work is ultra-professional and, while occasionally unusually adventurous technically, artfully tailored to prevailing Broadway taste.

He had a phenomenal long-running early hit with *Same Time, Next Year*, a rare example of a successful two-character play, recalling Jan de Hartog's *The Fourposter* with adultery instead of marriage at its centre and similarly spanning the years. It follows the love affair of Doris and George, both happily married to their respective partners and with children, in a California hotel room (hardly changing in the play's six scenes), an affair which occupies one weekend every year between 1951 and 1975. The play is an accomplished laughter-rouser, especially in the scene in which an all-too pregnant Doris appears for the 1961 weekend; although somewhat over-reliant on strings of smart one-liners and with noticeably grinding gear changes at more serious moments, as when George cracks up over the death of his son in Vietnam, it never descends into a sniggering comedy of adultery, and a genuine relationship emerges as Slade traces the changes in the couple over a quarter of a century of shifting middle-class American values.

In *Special Occasions* Slade again used only two characters in a shifting time-scale. In 14 scenes moving from 1970 to 1979 and set in various locales in California, New York, and Colorado, the play uses the "special occasions"—weddings, christenings, anniversaries, funerals—in the lives of a divorced couple, Amy and Michael. Slade often writes with both insight and economy into the different levels of the couple's dependence although, as in *Same Time, Next Year*, the play is at its happiest in the groove of broad mainstream comedy. Technically, in the handling of the time-shifts in an unnaturalistic manner, using almost filmic dissolves and links between the major scenes, the play is adventurous but the technique cannot compensate for a distinct air of predictability in its substance.

Romantic Comedy, a valentine to the kind of charmingly elegant comedy that once dominated Broadway and an unabashed star-vehicle play, cunningly updated an apparently moribund genre, complete with a glimpse of 1970's nudity. Set in the luxurious New York penthouse of Jason Carmichael, a successful Broadway dramatist looking for a new collaborator on the eve of his marriage, setting, style, and tone recall the world of Philip Barry in the developing relationship (again over a period of years—the mid-1960's to 1979 here) between Carmichael and Phoebe Craddock, a classic ugly duckling who develops into a beautiful swan. The play has one memorably funny scene involving the collaborators and Carmichael's sharp female agent after a disastrous opening night, but becomes a good deal too lachrymose instead of the bitter-sweet light comedy intended, as well as stiltedly over-written, in its final scenes. Even more manipulative a star-vehicle was *Tribute*, initially set in a Broadway theatre at a tribute evening to Scottie Templeton, a middle-aged screenwriter (described as "a mixture of Noël Coward, the Marx Brothers, and Peter Pan"), the participants including his agent, his doctor (it transpires that Scottie has terminal cancer), and his son. In the flashback scenes into which the play dissolves behind the scrim of the theatre setting, set in Scottie's townhouse, the complex relationship between father and son comes to be the emotional fulcrum of the evening as the two men, both wary of each other, finally make their peace. The play certainly delivered a juicy central role (performed by Jack Lemmon) and adroitly mixed pathos with slapstick comedy; it never risked alienating its public, however, always recovering with a cleverly timed gag from any hint of over-seriousness, especially evident in its sentimental ending.

Slade may yet come up with a play which charts territory more challenging than that of a skilled Broadway professional, one in which the content matches the interesting variations he has played to date with the actual form of the conventional commercial play. However, that play was certainly not his latest effort; *Fatal Attraction*, a would-be glossy thriller with a famous actress under a death-threat was a disappointingly muddled farrago falling well beneath the standards of models such as *Deathtrap*.

—Alan Strachan

SMITH, Dodie (Dorothy Gladys Smith). British. Born in Whitefield, Lancashire, 3 May 1896. Attended Whalley Range High School, Manchester; St. Paul's Girls' School, London; studied acting at Royal Academy of Dramatic Art, London, 1914–15. Married Alec Macbeth Beesley in 1939 (died 1987). Actress, 1915–22; buyer, Heal and Son, London, 1923–32; then full-time writer. Address: The Barretts, Finchingfield, Essex, England.

PUBLICATIONS

Plays

British Talent (as C.L. Anthony) (produced London, 1923).
Autumn Crocus (as C.L. Anthony) (produced London, 1931; New York, 1932). London, Gollancz, 1931; New York, French, 1933.
Service (as C.L. Anthony) (produced London, 1932). London, Gollancz, 1932.
Touch Wood (as C.L. Anthony) (produced London, 1934). London, Gollancz, 1934; New York, French, 1935.
Call It a Day (produced Glasgow and London, 1935; New York, 1936). London, Gollancz, and New York, French, 1936.
Bonnet over the Windmill (also co-director: produced Leeds and London, 1937). London, Heinemann, 1937.
Dear Octopus (also co-director: produced Newcastle upon Tyne and London, 1938; New York, 1939). London, Heinemann, 1938; New York, French, 1939.
Lovers and Friends (produced New York, 1943). New York, French, 1947.
Letter from Paris, adaptation of the novel *The Reverberator* by Henry James (produced Brighton and London, 1952). London, Heinemann, 1954.
I Capture the Castle, adaptation of her own novel (produced Blackpool and London, 1954). London, Heinemann, 1955.
These People, Those Books (produced Leeds, 1958).
Amateur Means Lover (produced Liverpool, 1961). London, French, 1962.

Screenplays: *Schoolgirl Rebels* (as Charles Henry Percy), 1915; *The Uninvited*, with Frank Partos, 1944; *Darling, How Could You!*, with Lesser Samuels, 1951.

Novels

I Capture the Castle. Boston, Little Brown, 1948; London, Heinemann, 1949.
The New Moon with the Old. London, Heinemann, and Boston, Little Brown, 1963.
The Town in Bloom. London, Heinemann, and Boston, Little Brown, 1965.
It Ends with Revelations. London, Heinemann, and Boston, Little Brown, 1967.
A Tale of Two Families. London, Heinemann, and New York, Walker, 1970.
The Girl from the Candle-Lit Bath. London, W. H. Allen, 1978.

Fiction (for children)

The Hundred and One Dalmations. London, Heinemann, 1956; New York, Viking Press, 1957.
The Starlight Barking: More about the Hundred and One Dalmations. London, Heinemann, and New York, Simon and Schuster, 1967.
The Midnight Kittens. London, W.H. Allen, 1978.

Other

Autobiography:
1. *Look Back with Love: A Manchester Childhood.* London, Heinemann, 1974.
2. *Look Back with Mixed Feelings.* London, W.H. Allen, 1978.
3. *Look Back with Astonishment.* London, W.H. Allen, 1979.
4. *Look Back with Gratitude.* London, Muller Blond and White, 1985.

*

Theatrical Activities:
Director: **Plays**—*Bonnet over the Windmill* (co-director, with Murray Macdonald), London, 1937; *Dear Octopus* (co-director, with Glen Byam Shaw), Newcastle upon Tyne and London, 1938.
Actress: **Plays**—in the sketch *Playgoers* by Pinero, London, 1915; *Kitty Grey* by J.S. Piggott and *Mr. Wu* by H.M. Vernon and Harold Owen, toured, 1915; *Ye Gods* by Stephen Robert

and Eric Hudson, and *Jane and Niobe*, 1916–17; *When Knights Were Bold* by Charles Marlowe, London, 1917; in music-hall sketches, in the Portsmouth Repertory Company, and in a concert party in Dieppe, 1918; Claudine in *Telling the Tale*, 1919–20; *French Leave* by Reginald Berkeley, 1921; *The Shewing Up of Blanco Posnet* and *You Never Can Tell* by Shaw, London, 1921; Ann in *The Pigeon* by Galsworthy, London and Zurich, 1922.

* * *

Cynthia —Is that a teddy-bear there? (*Taking it.*) Why, Its Symp.
Scrap —(*Following Her.*) Symp?
Cynthia —We called him that because he was extra sympathetic. We used to hug him whenever we were miserable—when we were in disgrace or the rabbits died or when nobody understood us.

The quotation is from Dodie Smith's best-known play, *Dear Octopus*, a play about a family, its feuds and friendships, first performed in 1938 with one of those casts publicists call "glittering" (with good reason—included in the Queen's Theatre company were Marie Tempest, John Gielgud, Madge Compton, Angela Baddeley, among others). The theme of sympathy, in fact might be Smith's principal key—in all her plays she seems to comprehend the very well-springs of her characters. She builds them surely and with understanding; they emerge as palpable beings, ordinary people who are more-than-ordinarily believable. And that's quite a talent.

Starting with an early screenplay written while studying at RADA (*Schoolgirl Rebels*—written under a male pseudonym) the playwright first went on stage in 1915 at the age of 19, but it did not bring her the golden fruits her pen was later to harvest for her—after a series of depressing tours she left the stage and became a buyer for Heal's. Fortunately while shopping for toys and pictures for middle-class kids she did not stop writing, and in 1923 *British Talent* was given an amateur airing. In 1931 came *Autumn Crocus*—a huge success—and she was launched. She wrote a number of plays in the 1930's, a gilded era when style and construction were of supreme value and audiences expected a well-made play. Smith constructed her plays like boxes, solid, secure, each line leading to another line, each situation growing and blossoming within the classic three-act mold. In fact as one reads them now it is the strong sense of craftsmanship that still comes across—a professional and enviable ability to forge a story so that the shape of the play, from opening curtain to closing line, is all of a piece. You can read her plays like novels—and with a little imagination see the situations developing before you. It isn't surprising that she turned to novel writing, and her first, *I Capture the Castle*, was later turned into a play. She also adapted a Henry James story, *The Reverberator*, to become *Letter from Paris*. It is a play that, unlike some of the others, has a musty air of datedness, and the characters, although still firmly handled and well presented, have a slight edge of melodrama—which may of course be a Jamesian legacy.

It's not just a lucky chance that makes Smith's work so often the choice of enthusiastic amateur groups, for perhaps more than professional actors they seize quickly onto these ready-formed characters which are so near completion on the printed page. Smith likes to write about good middle-class homes and people with values—taking that sensible but often ignored advice, to write about what one knows. She undoubtedly knows her people and she puts them into human situations which cleverly avoid being sentimental. Her ear for the comfortably-off family in *Dear Octopus* is very sound; indeed her dialogue has an authentic natural running ring that rarely bogs down.

—Michael T. Leech

SMITH, Michael T(ownsend). American. Born in Kansas City, Missouri, 5 October 1935. Educated at the Hotchkiss School, Lakeville, Connecticut, 1951–53; Yale University, New Haven, Connecticut, 1953–55. Married Michele Marie Hawley in 1974; two sons. Theatre critic, 1959–74, and associate editor, 1962–65, *Village Voice*, New York (Obie award judge, 1962–68 and 1972–74); teacher, New School for Social Research, New York, 1964–65, Project Radius, Dalton, Georgia, 1972, and Hunter College, New York, 1972; instrument maker, Zuckermann Harpsichords, Stonington, Connecticut, 1974–77 and 1979–85; arts editor, Taos *News*, New Mexico, 1977–78; music, art, and theatre critic, New London *Day*, Connecticut, 1982–86. Since 1986 assistant press secretary to Edward I. Koch, Mayor of New York City. Also director, lighting designer, and musician: manager, Sundance Festival Theatre, Upper Black Eddy, Pennsylvania, 1966–68; producer, Caffe Cino, New York, 1968; director, Theatre Genesis, New York, 1971–75, and Boston Early Music Festival and Exhibition, 1983–85. Recipient: Brandeis University Creative Arts Award, 1965; Obie award, for directing, 1972; Rockefeller grant, 1975. Address: 463 West Street, Apartment D-604, New York, New York 10014, U.S.A.

PUBLICATIONS

Plays

I Like It (also director: produced New York, 1963). Published in *Kulchur* (New York), 1963.
The Next Thing (produced New York, 1966). Published in *The Best of Off-Off-Broadway*, edited by Smith, New York, Dutton, 1969.
More! More! I Want More!, with John P. Dodd and Remy Charlip (produced New York, 1966).
Vorspiel nach Marienstein, with John P. Dodd and Ondine (also director: produced New York, 1967).
Captain Jack's Revenge (also director: produced New York, 1970; London, 1971). Published in *New American Plays 4*, edited by William M. Hoffman, New York, Hill and Wang, 1971.
A Dog's Love, music by John Herbert McDowell (produced New York, 1971).
Tony (produced New York, 1971).
Peas (also director: produced Denver, 1971).
Country Music (also director: produced New York, 1971). Published in *The Off-Off-Broadway Book*, edited by Albert Poland and Bruce Mailman, Indianapolis, Bobbs Merrill, 1972.
Double Solitaire (also director: produced Denver, 1973).
Prussian Suite (also director: produced New York, 1974).
A Wedding Party (also director: produced Denver, 1974; New York, 1980).
Cowgirl Ecstasy (also director: produced Denver, 1976; New York, 1977).
Life Is Dream, adaptation of a play by Calderón (also director: produced Taos, New Mexico, 1979).

Heavy Pockets (also director: produced Westerly, Rhode Island, 1981).

Verse

American Baby. Westerly, Rhode Island, Fast Books, 1983.
A Sojourn in Paris. Westerly, Rhode Island, Fast Books, 1985.

Other

Theatre Journal, Winter 1967. Columbia, University of Missouri Press, 1968.
Theatre Trip (critical journal). Indianapolis, Bobbs Merrill, 1969.

Editor, with Nick Orzel, *Eight Plays from Off-Off-Broadway*. Indianapolis, Bobbs Merrill, 1966.
Editor, *The Best of Off-Off-Broadway*. New York, Dutton, 1969.
Editor, *More Plays from Off-Off-Broadway*. Indianapolis, Bobbs Merrill, 1972.

*

Theatrical Activities:
Director: **Plays**—many of his own plays, and *Three Sisters Who Are Not Sisters* by Gertrude Stein, New York, 1964; *Icarus's Mother* by Sam Shepard, New York, 1965; *Chas. Dickens' Christmas Carol* by Soren Agenoux, New York, 1966; *Donovan's Johnson* by Soren Agenoux, New York, 1967; *With Creatures Make My Way* by H.M. Koutoukas, New York, 1967; *The Life of Juanita Castro* by Ronald Tavel, Denver, 1968; *Dr. Kheal* by María Irene Fornés, Denver, 1968; *Hurricane of the Eye* by Emmanuel Peluso, New York, 1969; *Eat Cake* by Jean-Claude van Itallie, Denver, 1971; *XXX* by William M. Hoffman, Denver, 1971; *Bigfoot* by Ronald Tavel, New York, 1972; *Tango Palace* by María Irene Fornés, New York, 1973; *Krapp's Last Tape* by Beckett, *The Zoo Story* by Albee, and *West Side Story* by Arthur Laurents, Taos, New Mexico, 1977–78; *A Shot in the Dark* by Harry Kurnitz, Kingston, Rhode Island, 1985; *Curse of the Starving Class* by Sam Shepard, New London, Connecticut, 1985.

Michael T. Smith comments:

Circumstances too narrowly personal to be called historical have more to do with the extent and character of my plays than any political or career agenda I may have chosen and willed. It has seemed to me that the real (as opposed to manifest) content of anything I write produces itself from affinities and perceptions that I haven't much control over. In fact they control me, define me. The challenge is to find a form that transmits them, that enables me to share these infinitely intimate flashes of truth and beauty.

* * *

> It all seems to refer to something else, but it is difficult to figure out what that something else is.
> —*Country Music*

I offer the following tale as a model for the unconscious process that seems to underlie the plays of Michael T. Smith:

He has gone to a lot of trouble to arrange his materials. The plantain was picked while Venus was ascendant, the hair was surreptitiously cut from the sleeping girl, the circle was drawn in clean sand by the flowing stream, and now the words so carefully memorized are pronounced correctly. All these elements must be in order to produce the *event.*

Dutifully he summons demons to aid him. From the inner recesses of his consciousness and the stream, from his spinal column and the beech tree, from his shoulder and his dog, demons fly to him. He is protected from danger by the limits of his circle.

He perceives the demons as scraps of old arguments, flashes of relieved emotions, a slight feeling of unease. Is he coming down with a cold? Why did he think of his mother? Will he stay with his lover?

His experience tells him to say "Get ye hence" to the demon-thoughts. He must go further. He's tired of emotion, bored with dialectic. "There must be something else," he thinks.

What does he want tonight? To be loved? To hate? Make fertile? Kill? None of these. Tonight he wants to be *wise*. He does not want information; he has plenty of facts. He knows that hens lay eggs, soldiers kill, lovers love. No, he wishes to know how and where to stand in relation to all his knowledge.

He throws a little something on the fire. It flares briefly, and suddenly a similar flare lights his mind. He thinks of nothing at all for some moments of eternity. The muscles of his neck relax.

After which he addresses the world as the wind makes his hair fly: "Who are you, Moon? Who are you, Stream? Who are you, Dog? Who are you, Man?"

I certainly do not wish to say that Smith is a practitioner of black or white arts. What I do mean to suggest is that Smith, like many other artists of this time, wants to explore lines of inquiry that in earlier times might have been called religious.

As the magician or priest juxtaposes disparate and often illogical elements toward a magical goal, Smith arranges his material without the superficially logical glue that audiences since Ibsen have come to expect.

Smith's stories often seem discontinuous in characterization and time. The actress playing the daughter in *Peas* is also asked to play her own mother, grandmother, and lover's other girlfriend. In *Country Music* costumes and make-up are changed drastically and abruptly. In *The Next Thing* the sequence of events is arranged aesthetically; reaction does not necessarily follow action, although within any small section time is "normal." In *Point Blank* (as yet unproduced) the opening stage direction reads, "This is a loop play. Begin anywhere, repeat several times, stop anywhere."

Thus in spite of fairly naturalistic dialogue the audience is somewhat disoriented by a Smith play. In fact because the dialogue is so "normal" Smith creates enormous tension by letting his characters play freely with role and time.

Smith's homely subject matter, which is most often the family, also is at variance with his treatment. Unlike most playwrights who write about the family, Smith is uninterested in commenting either unfavorably or favorably about his subject.

As the priest or witch places such ordinary elements as bread, wine, and plants in the context of the cosmos, so Smith exposes his characters to time, nature, and politics.

In *Country Music* two couples are exposed to the vagaries of time and weather. Their loves seem more affected by these elements than by psychology. Change seems to occur the same way buds grow. In *Captain Jack's Revenge* the characters are subject to art and politics. In the first act the people consciously try to order their awareness by means of television, radio, stereo, slide and movie projectors, telephone, and the doorbell. In the second act we see how the minds of these same people have been shaped by the actions of remote figures in American history.

Yet Smith does not tell us that we are doomed by weather, time, politics, psychology, or the media. He is pointing two ways at once, both at the solidity of certain facts, the bread and the wine, and at the cosmic context of these facts.

Yes, the couple in *Country Music* are subject to powerful forces outside their control, but look at the stars, look at the different kinds of light we can see—candlelight, sunshine, moonlight, twilight, dawn. The actors prepare food on stage and then eat it. All these experiences are called for by the author as his characters love, grow apart, leave.

Yes, the white people in *Captain Jack's Revenge* are doomed to the Indians' revenge for the crimes of their ancestors, but notice the beauty of the revenge, the glorious but mind-numbing media, the alluring but confusing drugs.

From Smith's magical (I might say "objective") point of view comes the curiously unemotional language. Rarely do his people lose their cool. They love passionately, they hate, they murder, but their language does not often reflect this. Does the playwright feel that emotion is such a heavy element on stage that the total stage picture would be unduly dominated by it? As the son says in *Peas*, "I want other people to be there without making a point of it."

Smith's plays are not designed to weigh ten tons of emotions. The audience must not be distracted from being aware they are seeing a model, not a slice, of life. The altar or voodoo dolls are not naturalistic representations either. Perhaps the logic of a Smith play is: If you can portray a situation objectively, with the freedom to be playful, if you can see the total picture, if you can arrange the elements of existence, you can induce a state of mind that allows us to see the magic of everyday life.

—William M. Hoffman

SOYINKA, Wole (Akinwande Oluwole Soyinka). Nigerian. Born in Abeokuta, 13 July 1934. Educated at St. Peter's School, Ake, Abeokuta, 1938–43; Abeokuta Grammar School, 1944–45; Government College, Ibadan, 1946–50; University College, Ibadan (now University of Ibadan), 1952–54; University of Leeds, Yorkshire, 1954–57, B.A. (honours) in English. Married; has children. Play reader, Royal Court Theatre, London, 1957–59; Rockefeller Research Fellow in Drama, University of Ibadan, 1961–62; Lecturer in English, University of Ife, Ife-Ife, 1963–64; Senior Lecturer in English, University of Lagos, 1965–67; Head of the Department of Theatre Arts, University of Ibadan, 1969–72 (appointment made in 1967); Professor of Comparative Literature, and Head of the Department of Dramatic Arts, University of Ife, 1975–85. Visiting Fellow, Churchill College, Cambridge, 1973–74; Visiting Professor, University of Ghana, Legon, 1973–74, and Yale University, New Haven, Connecticut, 1979–80. Founding director, 1960 Masks Theatre, 1960, and Orisun Theatre, 1964, Lagos and Ibadan, and Unife Guerilla Theatre, Ife-Ife, 1978; editor, *Transition* (later *Ch'indaba*) magazine, Accra, Ghana, 1975–77. Secretary-General, Union of Writers of the African Peoples, 1975. Tried and acquitted of armed robbery, 1965; political prisoner, detained by the Federal Military Government, Lagos and Kaduna, 1967–69. Recipient: Dakar Festival award, 1966; John Whiting Award, 1967; Jock Campbell Award (*New Statesman*), for fiction, 1968; Nobel Prize for Literature, 1986. D. Litt: University of Leeds, 1973, and Yale University, University of Montpellier, France, and University of Lagos. Fellow, Royal Society of Literature (UK); Member, American Academy, and Academy of Arts and Letters of the German Democratic Republic. Agent: Morton Leavy, Leavy Rosensweig and Hyman, 11 East 44th Street, New York, New York 10017, U.S.A. Address: P.O. Box 935, Abeokuta, Nigeria.

PUBLICATIONS

Plays

The Swamp Dwellers (produced London, 1958; New York, 1968). Included in *Three Plays*, 1963; *Five Plays*, 1964.

The Lion and the Jewel (produced Ibadan, 1959; London, 1966). Ibadan, London, and New York, Oxford University Press, 1963.

The Invention (produced London, 1959).

A Dance of the Forests (produced Lagos, 1960). Ibadan, London, and New York, Oxford University Press, 1963.

The Trials of Brother Jero (produced Ibadan, 1960; Cambridge, 1965; London, 1966; New York, 1967). Included in *Three Plays*, 1963; *Five Plays*, 1964.

Camwood on the Leaves (broadcast 1960). London, Eyre Methuen, 1973; in *Camwood on the Leaves, and Before the Blackout*, 1974.

The Republican and *The New Republican* (satirical revues; produced Lagos, 1963).

Three Plays. Ibadan, Mbari, 1963; as *Three Short Plays*, London, Oxford University Press, 1969.

The Strong Breed (produced Ibadan, 1964; London, 1966; New York, 1967). Included in *Three Plays*, 1963; *Five Plays*, 1964.

Kongi's Harvest (produced Ibadan, 1964; New York, 1968). Ibadan, London, and New York, Oxford University Press, 1967.

Five Plays: A Dance of the Forests, The Lion and the Jewel, The Swamp Dwellers, The Trials of Brother Jero, The Strong Breed. Ibadan, London, and New York, Oxford University Press, 1964.

Before the Blackout (produced Ibadan, 1965; Leeds, 1981). Ibadan, Orisun, 1971; in *Camwood on the Leaves, and Before the Blackout*, 1974.

The Road (produced London, 1965; also director: produced Chicago, 1984). Ibadan, London, and New York, Oxford University Press, 1965.

Rites of the Harmattan Solstice (produced Lagos, 1966).

Madmen and Specialists (produced Waterford, Connecticut, and New York, 1970; revised version, also director: produced Ibadan, 1971). London, Methuen, 1971; New York, Hill and Wang, 1972.

The Jero Plays: The Trials of Brother Jero, and Jero's Metamorphosis. London, Eyre Methuen, 1973.

Jero's Metamorphosis (produced Lagos, 1975). Included in *The Jero Plays*, 1973.

The Bacchae: A Communion Rite, adaptation of the play by Euripides (produced London, 1973). London, Eyre Methuen, 1973; New York, Norton, 1974.

Collected Plays:

1. *A Dance of the Forests, The Swamp Dwellers, The Strong Breed, The Road, The Bacchae*. London and New York, Oxford University Press, 1973.

2. *The Lion and the Jewel, Kongi's Harvest, The Trials of Brother Jero, Jero's Metamorphosis, Madmen and Specialists.* London and New York, Oxford University Press, 1974.

Camwood on the Leaves, and Before the Blackout: Two Short Plays. New York, Third Press, 1974.

Death and the King's Horseman (also director: produced Ife-Ife, 1976; Chicago, 1979; also director: produced New York, 1987). London, Eyre Methuen, 1975; New York, Norton, 1976.

Opera Wonyosi, adaptation of *The Threepenny Opera* by Brecht (also director: produced Ife-Ife, 1977). Bloomington, Indiana University Press, and London, Collings, 1981.

Golden Accord (produced Louisville, 1980).

Priority Projects (revue; produced on Nigeria tour, 1982).

Requiem for a Futurologist (also director: produced Ife-Ife, 1983). London, Collings, 1985.

A Play of Giants (also director: produced New Haven, Connecticut, 1984). London, Methuen, 1984.

Six Plays (includes *The Trials of Brother Jero, Jero's Metamorphosis, Camwood on the Leaves, Death and the King's Horseman, Madmen and Specialists, Opera Wonyosi*). London, Methuen, 1984.

Radio Plays: *Camwood on the Leaves*, 1960; *The Detainee*, 1965; *Die Still, Dr. Godspeak*, 1981.

Television Plays: *Joshua: A Nigerian Portrait*, 1962 (Canada); *Culture in Transition*, 1963 (USA).

Novels

The Interpreters. London, Deutsch, 1965; New York, Macmillan, 1970.

Season of Anomy. London, Collings, 1973; New York, Third Press, 1974.

Verse

Idanre and Other Poems. London, Methuen, 1967; New York, Hill and Wang, 1968.

Poems from Prison. London, Collings, 1969.

A Shuttle in the Crypt. London, Eyre Methuen-Collings, and New York, Hill and Wang, 1972.

Ogun Abibimañ. London, Collings, 1976.

Other

The Man Died: Prison Notes. London, Eyre Methuen-Collings, and New York, Harper, 1972.

In Person: Achebe, Awoonor, and Soyinka at the University of Washington. Seattle, University of Washington African Studies Program, 1975.

Myth, Literature, and the African World. London, Cambridge University Press, 1976.

Aké: The Years of Childhood (autobiography). London, Collings, 1981; New York, Vintage, 1983.

The Critic and Society (essay). Ife-Ife, University of Ife Press, 1981.

Editor, *Poems of Black Africa.* London, Secker and Warburg, and New York, Hill and Wang, 1975.

Translator, *The Forest of a Thousand Daemons: A Hunter's Saga*, by D.O. Fagunwa. London, Nelson, 1968; New York, Humanities Press, 1969.

*

Bibliography: *Wole Soyinka: A Bibliography* by B. Okpu, Lagos, Libriservice, 1984.

Critical Studies: *Wole Soyinka* by Gerald Moore, London, Evans, and New York, Africana, 1971, revised edition, Evans, 1978; *The Writing of Wole Soyinka* by Eldred D. Jones, London, Heinemann, 1973, revised edition, 1983; *The Movement of Transition: A Study of the Plays of Wole Soyinka* by Oyin Ogunba, Ibadan, Ibadan University Press, 1975; *Komik, Ironie, und Satire im Dramatischen Werk von Wole Soyinka* by Rita Bottcher-Wobcke, Hamburg, Buske, 1976; *A Dance of Masks: Sengher, Achebe, Soyinka* by Jonathan Peters, Washington, D.C., Three Continents, 1978; *Notes on Wole Soyinka's The Jero Plays* edited by E.M. Parsons, London, Methuen, 1979; *Critical Perspectives on Wole Soyinka* edited by James Gibbs, Washington, D.C., Three Continents, 1980, London, Heinemann, 1981, and *Wole Soyinka* by Gibbs, London, Macmillan, and New York, Grove Press, 1986; *The Lion and the Jewel: A Critical View* by Martin Banham, London, Collings, 1981; *Theatre and Nationalism: Wole Soyinka and LeRoi Jones* by Alain Ricard, Ife-Ife, University of Ife Press, 1983; *A Writer and His Gods: A Study of the Importance of Yoruba Myths and Religious Ideas in the Writing of Wole Soyinka* by Stephan Larsen, Stockholm, University of Stockholm, 1983; *Wole Soyinka and Modern Tragedy: A Study of Dramatic Theory and Practice* edited by Ketu E. Katrak, Westport, Connecticut, Greenwood Press, 1986.

Theatrical Activities:
Director: **Plays**—by Brecht, Chekhov, Clark, Easmon, Eseoghene, Ogunyemi, Shakespeare, Synge, and his own works; *L'Espace et la Magie*, Paris, 1972; *The Biko Inquest* by Jon Blair and Norman Fenton, Ife-Ife, 1978, and New York, 1980.
Actor: **Plays**—Igwezu in *The Swamp Dwellers*, London, 1958; Obaneji and Forest Father in *A Dance of the Forests*, Lagos and Ibadan, 1960; Dauda Touray in *Dear Parent and Ogre* by R. Sarif Easmon, Ibadan, 1961; in *The Republican*, Lagos, 1963. **Film**—*Kongi's Harvest*, 1970. **Radio**—Konu in *The Detainee*, 1965.

* * *

The ease and power with which, in his adaptation of *The Bacchae* by Euripides, Wole Soyinka makes this foundation of Western tragedy his own conveniently suggest the nature and scale of his dramatic achievement. In his work the conventional forms of Western drama are energized by those of traditional African ritual. As a result there is an insistence upon the ritual origins of all drama, and especially upon those of tragedy. Soyinka's best plays contemplate the "numinous passage" of transition between life and death, the human and the divine, affirming the mediating power of dance ("the movement of transition") and music—the art which, for Soyinka, "contains" tragic reality. His thinking is more truly Nietzschean than that of any native Western tragedian.

Soyinka himself has spoken up vehemently against the "reductionist tendency" to see his work as concerned primarily with the "clash of cultures" in West Africa, maintaining that the "Colonial Factor" is "catalytic" and that his interests are essentially metaphysical. Whatever the case, it is noticeable that those plays in which cultural confrontation is an explicit element, such as the early comedy *The Lion and the Jewel*, *Kongi's Harvest*, and *Death and the King's Horseman*, are less rich and more schematic than the major tragedies. Nevertheless the polarities which emerge from these minor pieces—the rootless modern Christian who fears death as against the traditional ritualist who can rejoice in death, asceticism as against virility and fertility, the mass/political as against the individual/religious, city as against forest—are crucial to a basic understanding of the major plays.

The city-forest (or in this case city-swamp) polarity emerges in Soyinka's first play. *The Swamp Dwellers*, a naturalistic work which (perhaps accordingly) manifests an almost Western scepticism about the efficacy of ritual sacrifice and its attendant symbolism. The swamp here is oppressively real, but the forest of *A Dance of the Forests*, the first of the major plays, is more obviously symbolic and the work correspondingly more accommodating to ritual. Written for the Nigerian Independence celebrations, the play is about the necessity for acknowledgement of the totality of the past, its infamous episodes as well as its glorious ones, on both political and personal levels. Three secretly guilty people flee into the numinous forest away from a "Gathering of the Tribes" ceremony (at which only the glorious ancestors are invoked). There the very human-seeming forest gods force them to witness a historical scene in which their past selves re-enact their crimes and thus, by "torturing awareness from their souls," purge the crimes of the spectators, leaving them chastened and united.

In *A Dance of the Forests* the guilty, as spectators, experience ritual expiation of guilt by proxy, but in *The Strong Breed*, a compressed and powerful tragedy, the hero himself becomes a community's Scapegoat—in the original, ritualistic sense of that word. The dispenser Eman is a "stranger" in a community which at every new year ritually rids itself of the old year's evil by using a Scapegoat chosen from among its "strangers." Outraged at the choice of a pathetic idiot, he surrenders himself as substitute. Flashback and ghostly dialogue between the new Scapegoat and his (apparently dead) father establish that Eman belongs to the "Strong Breed" which, in its home district, was bound to supply every year the ritual "carrier" of the community's evils. Thus only in self-sacrifice can Eman confirm the meaning of the "Strong Breed": "it is not the mouth of the boaster that says he belongs to the strong breed. It is the tongue that is red with pain and black with sorrow."

The Road is Soyinka's most ambitious attempt to combine dense naturalism with ritual significance. Set amid the shabbiness of a colony from which the colonial power has long since withdrawn (a setting which finds its linguistic correlative in pidgin-English) and in which native belief persists as ominous superstition, the play shows "the part psychic, part intellectual grope . . . towards the essence of death" of the strange, half-mad Professor, "proprietor etc. of the driver's haven" and the roadside "Aksident Store." He is a scavenger of the road, both material—hence the "store"—and spiritual—he searches perpetually for signs of "the Word." His quest reaches its climax when he is stabbed to death in the panic as his masked servant—who is dead, and yet also a crucial "transitional" figure between life and death—dances himself into a sacrificial frenzy. The dance suggests that Professor has, in effect, been sacrificed to propitiate the god of the road. In his visionary last speech he proclaims the necessity to "power your hands with the knowledge of death" and thus to "cheat fear, by foreknowledge." "Breathe like the road," he enjoins, "be even like the road itself. . . ."

Dense and problematic though *The Road* is, Soyinka's most difficult work to date is his civil war play *Madmen and Specialists*. This intensely angry piece concerns a medical specialist-turned-political inquisitor whose moral nature his own father tries desperately to lay bare to him by inventing a horrendous cannibalistic cult called As. As seems to function as a moral mirror: it is a savage metaphorical reflection of the inhumanities perpetrated in (civil-) wartime. The "mad" old man is finally shot by his son, apparently as he attempts to purge the son's inhumanity and unnaturalness by ritual re-enactment.

Viewed in the light of his previous work, the special features of Soyinka's adaptation of *The Bacchae* can be seen almost as inevitable. Dionysos becomes the virile, sensual god of natural renewal, exhorting his Bacchae to a frenzy of music and dance which replaces (or perhaps recreates) the Euripidean chorus; Pentheus is the (colonial?) politician advocating order and restraint from his walled city. The death of Pentheus is accordingly presented as a sacrifice in "a communion rite": as Christ transubstantiated wine into blood, Pentheus's severed head sprouts not the blood of death but the Dionysian wine of renewed life. Here, as in his other major works, Soyinka has contributed to the great enterprise of Western tragedy by bringing to the genre an African's sense of the value of ritual.

Soyinka's most recent work shifts the emphasis within a formal strategy similar to that of *The Bacchae*. In *Opera Wonyosi* Brecht's *Threepenny Opera* is appropriated rather than adapted (the biter bit!) to produce a "Nigerian *version*." An expatriate colony is the setting for a portrayal, in the sardonic-satiric mode of *Jero's Metamorphosis*, of the "oil-boom society of the seventies." The megalomaniac dictators of the 1970's in Africa are also a target, but it is in *A Play of Giants*, Soyinka's major work of the 1980's so far, that these figures are most impressively handled. This "Fantasia on the Aminian theme" takes Genet's *The Balcony* for its formal model, and accordingly underscores the gruesome theatricality of the dictators. Four African heads of state, carefully distinguished and easily recognizable, pose in the Bugaran (sic) embassy in New York for a large group sculpture which they intend for a prominent position in the nearby U.N. building. Their power-hunger and brutality are made clear during the course of the play in all their horror and absurdity, as are the attitudes towards them of the superpowers. Diplomatic tensions inevitably develop, and the climax is reached when news of a coup in Bugara is received. Protesters are heard outside the embassy, and in an ecstasy of megalomaniac paranoia, "Field Marshal Dr. Life President" Kamini takes hostages (among them the Secretary-General) and threatens the U.N. building itself. As the action freezes, the sculptor, beaten yet retaining the artistic power of representation, "works on in slow motion."

—Paul Lawley

SPEIGHT, Johnny. British. Born in Canning Town, London, 2 June 1920. Educated at St. Helen's School. Married Constance Barrett in 1956; two sons and one daughter. Worked in a factory, as a jazz drummer and insurance salesman; then writer for BBC radio and television. Recipient: Screenwriters Guild award, 1962, 1966, 1967, 1968; *Evening Standard* award, 1977; Pye award, for television writing, 1983. Address: Fouracres, Heronsgate, Chorleywood, Hertfordshire, England.

PUBLICATIONS

Plays

Mr. Venus, with Ray Galton, music and lyrics by Trevor H. Stanford and Norman Newell (produced London, 1958).
Sketches in *The Art of Living* (produced London, 1960).
The Compartment (televised 1961; produced Pitlochry, Perthshire, 1965).
The Knacker's Yard (produced London, 1962).
The Playmates (televised 1962; as *Games,* produced London, 1971).
If There Weren't Any Blacks You'd Have to Invent Them (televised 1965; produced Loenersloot, Holland, and London, 1965). Loenersloot, Holland, Mickery, 1965; London, Methuen, 1968.
Sketches in *In the Picture* (produced London, 1967).
The Salesman (televised 1970; produced London, 1970).
Till Death Us Do Part. London, Woburn Press, 1973.
The Thoughts of Chairman Alf (produced London, 1976).
Elevenses (sketch), in *The Big One* (produced London, 1983).

Screenplays: *French Dressing*, with others, 1964; *Privilege*, with Norman Bogner and Peter Watkins, 1967; *Till Death Us Do Part*, 1968; *The Alf Garnett Saga*, 1972.

Radio Writing: for the *Edmondo Ros, Morecambe and Wise*, and *Frankie Howerd* shows, 1956–58; *Early to Braden* show, 1957–58; *The Deadly Game of Chess*, 1958; *The April 8th Show (7 Days Early)*, 1958; *Eric Sykes* show, 1960–61.

Television Writing: for the *Arthur Haynes* show; *The Compartment*, 1961; *The Playmates*, 1962; *Shamrot*, 1963; *If There Weren't Any Blacks You'd Have to Invent Them*, 1965; *Till Death Us Do Part* series, 1966–75, 1981; *To Lucifer a Sun*, 1967; *Curry and Chips* series, 1969; *The Salesman*, 1970; *Them* series, 1972; *Speight of Marty* series, 1973; *For Richer . . . For Poorer*, 1975; *The Tea Ladies* series, with Ray Galton, 1979; *Spooner's Patch* series, with Ray Galton, 1980; *The Lady Is a Tramp* series, 1982; *In Sickness and in Health*, 1985.

Other

It Stands to Reason: A Kind of Autobiography. London, Joseph-Hobbs, 1973.
The Thoughts of Chairman Alf: Alf Garnett's Little Blue Book; or, Where England Went Wrong: An Open Letter to the People of Britain. London, Robson, 1973.
Pieces of Speight. London, Robson, 1974.
The Garnett Chronicles: The Life and Times of Alf Garnett, Esq. London, Robson, 1986.

*

Theatrical Activities:
Actor: **Films**—*The Plank*, 1967; *The Undertakers*, 1969; *Rhubarb*, 1970.

* * *

Johnny Speight is one of those writers whose success in television has become a trap. Unlike almost every other writer of comic series for peak-hour viewers, he has been a source of controversy, scandal, and outrage as well as having been rewarded with a popularity which has proved to be less than totally advantageous to him. He was a factory worker before World War II, and it was not until 1955 that his determination to succeed as a writer bore any fruit. His first work was writing scripts for such comedians as Frankie Howerd, Arthur Askey, Cyril Fletcher, Eric Sykes, and others. When he began to write for Arthur Haynes, he showed an ability to create unusual material rather than the power to exploit the familiar gifts of an established comedian. For Haynes, Speight created the character of a tramp whose aggressive, rebarbative personality had a striking originality.

It was through a series of programmes for BBC television, *Till Death Us Do Part*, that Speight became a household name. His work became a battleground over which "permissive" liberals fought the old-fashioned viewers who believe in verbal restraint, the importance of good taste and the banishment of certain topics, notably religion, from light entertainment. What Speight wrote was originally in essence a cartoon, a cockney version of the north country Andy Capp, in which attitudes almost everybody would condemn as anti-social were derided. Four people—husband and wife, their daughter and son-in-law—inhabit the sitting room of a slum house; they have nothing in common except their bitter dislike for each other. The father, Alf Garnett, is barely literate, full of misconceived, misunderstood, and ignorant prejudices about race, politics, and religion; his language is atrocious. His wife is reduced almost to the state of a vegetable, coming to life only when her detestation of her husband finds some opportunity of expressing itself. The son-in-law, as ignorantly and stupidly of the left as Garnett is of the right, is a Liverpool-Irish Roman Catholic, who dresses flamboyantly, wears his hair long, and does no work whatever; his only spell of activity was an inefficient attempt to swindle social security officials. The daughter agrees in all things with her husband, but it is plain that her agreement is the result of his effectiveness as a lover rather than of any intellectual processes of argument.

Through these appalling people, Speight was able for a time to lambast senseless racial and political prejudices while making cheeky fun of the Royal Family, the church, and anything else which drifted into what passes in the Garnett household for conversation, and Garnett for a time was a very effective weapon against bigotry and stupidity. Unfortunately, his effectiveness as a vehicle for satire tended to diminish as the monstrous energy with which he was created slipped out of control and allowed him to take possession of each episode of a series which continued long after the original impetus had exhausted itself and which began to show something dangerously ambivalent in Speight's attack on racialism. The creation of two Garnett films demonstrated that Speight's monsters were at their most popular when there was nothing left to say about them, so that *Till Death Us Do Part* seemed to turn into an incubus from which the author was unable to escape.

Curry and Chips, another effort to stifle racial prejudice by allowing it to be voiced in its most extreme forms by the stupid, lacked the vitality of *Till Death Us Do Part*, and a later series, *Them*, in which two tramps dreamed of grandeur, their dreams contrasted sharply with the reality of their way of life, was notable only for the gentleness of its comedy, proving that Speight was capable of more than the stridency of life with the Garnett family.

Such work, for all the energy of Garnettry, and the strength with which the leading monster had been created, made it seem that Speight had moved a long way in the wrong direction. In 1961, his first television play proper, *The Compartment*, had nothing to do with the sort of writing which later made him notorious. In a compartment of an old-fashioned train which has no corridor, a businessman is alone with a practical joker who persecutes him for the length of the journey; it becomes the joker's amusement to convince his pompous, easily frightened companion that he is helpless in the company of an armed, murderous psychopath. There are no motives, no explanations, no rationalisations; the events simply happen with a sort of uneasy humour. A year later, the same joker, selling "jokes" and tricks from door to door, finds himself sheltered for a night by a strange, psychopathic girl who is the only inhabitant of a big house. *The Playmates*—for the girl wants to join in fun with the traveller's samples—shares the disregard for motives and explanations already shown by *The Compartment*. A third play, offering, it seems, another aspect of the experience of the joker, was equally effective. The ideas were fashionable at the time when it was avant garde and exciting to offer allegiance to The Theatre of the Absurd, but Speight produced his genuine shocks and *frissons*.

Both *The Compartment* and a later television play, *If There Weren't Any Blacks You'd Have to Invent Them*, were adapted for stage performances but, despite some success, proved to belong to the screen rather than the stage. *If There Weren't Any Blacks* exploited Speight's reputation, won from the Garnett series, as a passionate opponent of racialism, and makes its point amusingly and convincingly with none of the ambivalence which crept into *Till Death Us Do Part* when Garnett took control of the series and began to speak as a character in his own right rather than as an instrument designed by his creator to ridicule the politically idiotic. Speight's only genuine play for the theatre, not adapted from television material, *The Knacker's Yard*, won some praise for the vigour and imaginativeness of its dialogue.

It is impossible not to think of Speight as a creator of grotesque, disturbing characters who is trapped by television into a situation which demands that he repeat, with diminishing returns, a success which rapidly lost its inventiveness. Thus, he pays the penalty of his originality.

—Henry Raynor

SPENCER, Colin. British. Born in London, 17 July 1933. Educated at Brighton Grammar School, Selhurst; Brighton College of Art. Served in the Royal Army Medical Corps, 1950–52. Married Gillian Chapman in 1959 (divorced 1969); one son. Paintings exhibited in Cambridge and London; costume designer. Chairman, Writers Guild of Great Britain, 1982–83. Agent: (plays) Margaret Ramsay Ltd., 14-A Goodwin's Court, London WC2N 4LL; (novels) Richard Scott Simon, 32 College Cross, London N1 1PR. Address: 2 Heath Cottages, Tunstall, near Woodbridge, Suffolk IP12 2HQ, England.

PUBLICATIONS

Plays

The Ballad of the False Barman, music by Clifton Parker (produced London, 1966).
Spitting Image (produced London, 1968; New York, 1969). Published in *Plays and Players* (London), September 1968.
The Trial of St. George (produced London, 1972).
The Sphinx Mother (produced Salzburg, Austria, 1972).
Why Mrs. Neustadter Always Loses (produced London, 1972).
Keep It in the Family (also director: produced London, 1978).
Lilith (produced Vienna, 1979).

Television Plays: *Flossie*, 1975; *Vandal Rule OK?* (documentary), 1977.

Novels

An Absurd Affair. London, Longman, 1961.
Generation:
Anarchists in Love. London, Eyre and Spottiswoode, 1963; as *The Anarchy of Love*, New York, Weybright and Talley, 1967.
The Tyranny of Love. London, Blond, and New York, Weybright and Talley, 1967.
Lovers in War. London, Blond, 1969.
The Victims of Love. London, Quartet, 1978.
Asylum. London, Blond, 1966.
Poppy, Mandragora, and the New Sex. London, Blond, 1966.
Panic. London, Secker and Warburg, 1971.
How the Greeks Kidnapped Mrs. Nixon. London, Quartet, 1974.

Other

Gourmet Cooking for Vegetarians. London, Deutsch, 1978.
Good and Healthy: A Vegetarian and Wholefood Cookbook. London, Robson, 1983; as *Vegetarian Wholefood Cookbook*, London, Panther, 1985.
Reports from Behind, with Chris Barlas, illustrated by Spencer. London, Enigma, 1984.
Cordon Vert: 52 Vegetarian Gourmet Dinner Party Menus. Wellingborough, Northamptonshire, Thorsons, 1985.
Mediterranean Vegetarian Cooking. Wellingborough, Northamptonshire, Thorsons, 1986.
The New Vegetarian: The Ultimate Guide to Gourmet Cooking and Healthy Living. London, Elm Tree, 1986.
The Vegetarian's Healthy Diet Book, with Tom Sanders. London, Dunitz, 1986.
Feast for Health: A Gourmet Guide to Good Food. London, Dorling Kindersley, 1987.
Al Fresco: A Feast of Outdoor Entertaining. Wellingborough, Northamptonshire, Thorsons, 1987.
The Romantic Vegetarian. Wellingborough, Northamptonshire, Thorsons, 1988.

Editor, *Green Cuisine: The Guardian's Selection of the Best Vegetarian Recipes*. Wellingborough, Northamptonshire, Thorsons, 1986.

*

Critical Study: interview with Peter Burton, in *Transatlantic Review 35* (London), 1970.

Theatrical Activities:
Director: **Play**—*Keep It in the Family*, London, 1978.

* * *

Harold Hobson, reviewing Colin Spencer's musical play *The Ballad of the False Barman* in the *Sunday Times*, referred to "Mr. Spencer's great and complicated skill ... unified by [his] overwhelming sense of evil. This is its aesthetic strength." Certainly there is something in the play that both attracts and alienates. I recall that, as artistic director of the Hampstead

Theatre Club where it was premiered, I sent it to nine directors before the tenth, Robin Phillips, accepted it. Yet re-reading it now for what must be about the twelfth time I find that my first impression is unchanged. The play still seems to me like an impassioned sermon by John Donne, written with the sensuality of Genet, the cogency (especially in the lyrics) of Brecht, and the high camp of Ronald Firbank. If this sounds like mirroring too many influences it should be remembered that it is, after all, a play about disguises. The setting is a bar in Brighton to which come all the so-called "dregs of society." They are welcomed by an enigmatic barman (played by a woman) who fulfills their needs:

> Give me the right to exploit you,
> Tell me your private dream,
> I can fix anything, just leave it to me.

The play's central theme is the opposition of corruption, in the person of the barman, and goodness, in the person of Josie. As the Barman says to Josie, "Your goodness is a thorn in our flesh."

When Josie's lover, a gigolo and burglar called Bill, is thrown into prison, Josie is shown out of the bar. No one will help her. (En route Spencer makes a scathing attack on conventional morality, on the inhumanity of the professional clergyman, the police, and the judiciary.) Josie is driven to accept the hospitality of a mysterious Duke whose advances she has long resisted. But now she says, "I am too tired to do anything else."

She enters the Duke's house with its many rooms. "Explore them," says Duke, "I will give you thoughts like new children. I will uncover areas of feeling, of rhythm, and motion, which will astonish, amaze, excite . . . ," to which Josie replies, "You have shown me things in myself that I never dreamt were there. . . . You have shown me mirrors." The Duke answers, "The more you know, the greater you will grow."

No critic at the time realized what Spencer was doing here. Brilliantly, more alarmingly than in any Mystery play of York or Wakefield, he has updated the story of the serpent in the Garden of Eden, the temptation to eat of the Tree of Knowledge of good *and* evil. The death of Josie's baby comes in this context as a brutal, dream-potent image of death of innocence, the expulsion from Eden. At the end of the play Josie says to the Duke, "You are all the terror in my soul. You are the darkness that I have always feared but when I was laid in your arms I knew such peace." Throughout Spencer is dealing with the metaphysic of evil, with what Jung calls the *shadow* side of experience. Anyone who has read Jung's *Answer to Job* will recognise that ultimate goodness cannot be separated from the question of ultimate evil. And though there is undoubtedly a force of evil, the powers of darkness, just as there is a force of good, Spencer questions whether what we call evil is necessarily always evil. And whether what we call good is necessarily always good. We have first to come to terms with our shadow side and only then is a transformation possible. It is only when Prospero ceases to call Caliban "a devil, a demi-devil," and says "This thing of darkness I acknowledge as my own," that Caliban, his shadow side, is enabled to say, "Henceforth I'll seek for grace."

Josie comes to see that her goodness was no more than "simplicity, easily destroyed and now quite worthless." She becomes a whore. "I began to do what you all do because I thought you'd understand. How does sin destroy what's good?" Yet she is not corrupted. She merely sheds the shell of naivety which we, all too often and mistakenly, call innocence. For, as Amanda, the militant Christian in the play, remarks, "It's difficult to go naked in this world."

What Josie finally learns is that "You can't act being good. It just exists in itself. Goodness is a thing apart. It is itself." And because she believes this she will not accept the only society she knows, that of the Bar. She cries out, "Are we in this modern world trapped so vilely in our flesh? No, no, no, no!"

It is with this affirmation that the play ends. And it seems to me in retrospect that no production has yet done the play credit. It is all too easy to be carried away by the surface camp (admittedly a part of the play's fabric) and to neglect its deep moral purpose.

For, fundamentally, Spencer is a moralist. What he does, more urgently than any other contemporary writer, more wittily and with refreshing humour, is to question accepted conventions. In *The Sphinx Mother* (a modern version of the Oedipus story) there is a moving scene at the beginning of the second act between Clare (the Jocasta figure) and Owen (the Oedipus figure):

> Clare —There has never been such a partnership of power and goodness.
> Owen —How can that be! Goodness based on corruption?
> Clare —Where was the corruption? I have experienced no cruelty or violence from you, nor given you any. We trod softly through each other's lives and gave freely.

Clare challenges Owen's terrible self-mutilation, "all that he showed was his pathetic weakness." Through her, Spencer challenges,

> our abstract ideas of what life and love ought to be. It is these abstract ideas that cause violence and aggression. Can you not accept that we did love each other, totally? If a son has lain with his mother for a quarter of a lifetime is that as grotesque as we think it is?

In other plays, notably the comedies *The Fruiting Body* (not yet produced) and *Spitting Image*, Spencer continues to question and probe. *Spitting Image*, a "happy play" as Spencer had it billed, revealed, as John Russell Taylor observed in a brilliant review, that the author has learnt from a writer like Firbank that camp nonsense can sometimes cut deep. And though, on the surface, *Spitting Image* is about two homosexuals one of whom gives birth to a baby by the other, he has used this fantastic particular instance in order to illuminate a believable, disturbing reality. "If the birth is fantastic," writes Taylor,

> the opposition Gary and Tom encounter, the ways and means by which the authorities seek to suppress the awkward individual, the special case which obstinately refuses to fit into the nearest convenient pigeon-hole, are all too unforgettably credible. The fantastic particular is made to stand effectively for the host of less eye-catching realities, and the social comment reaches its target unerringly.

If sometimes, as in certain passages from *The Sphinx Mother*, or *The Ballad of the False Barman*, Spencer seems almost florid, baroque in his writing, it is because in these passages (such as Bill's loneliness speech in prison and the Duke's long arias) he is trying to pierce below the external observable reality to that anguish of spirit that cannot really be put into words. In these passages he employs, deliberately, a convoluted, imagistic, surreal style of writing, digging out the kind of uncomfortable and embarrassing images that perhaps occur only in dreams. He is concerned to articulate the lost areas of human experience. In the unproduced *Summer at Camber—39* (the setting is the outbreak of World War II) he has Hester say,

> I feel trapped, Maud. I'm thirty-nine and I feel trapped. I don't think I'll ever get free ... so many things there are battering begging to speak, not just from inside of me, but ... so much ... I don't quite understand. You don't understand. Eddy can't understand, ever ... what am I doing? How long must I stay without ... being able to know ... more?

The intensity of emotion conveyed by those dots, those broken phrases, is what increasingly concerns theatre. As Stanislavsky wrote at the turn of the century, "It is necessary to picture not life itself as it takes place in reality, but as we vaguely feel it in our dreams, our visions, our moments of spiritual uplift." Virginia Woolf said that she wanted to write "books about silence; about the things people do not say," but because she, like Spencer, was a writer, she had to try to use words. How to reach the centre is the shared concern of many different artists. One cry rings through all these explorations, the cry of Josie in *The Ballad of the False Barman*, "Who among you cares enough? Stop all this deceit, please, oh, please. Stop all these disguises!"

—James Roose-Evans

SPURLING, John. British. Born in Kisumu, Kenya, 17 July 1936. Educated at Dragon School, Oxford, 1946–49; Marlborough College, Wiltshire, 1950–54; St. John's College, Oxford, 1957–60, B.A. 1960. Served in the Royal Artillery (national service), 1955–57. Married Hilary Forrest (i.e., the writer Hilary Spurling) in 1961; one daughter and two sons. Plebiscite officer for the United Kingdom in Southern Cameroons, 1960–61; announcer, BBC Radio, London, 1963–66; radio and book reviewer, the *Spectator*, London, 1966–70, and other publications. Henfield Fellow, University of East Anglia, Norwich, 1973. Since 1976, art critic, *New Statesman*, London. Lives in London. Agent: Patricia Macnaughton, Macnaughton Lowe Representation, 200 Fulham Road, London SW10 9PN, England.

PUBLICATIONS

Plays

Char (produced Oxford, 1959).
MacRune's Guevara As Realised by Edward Hotel (produced London, 1969; Walla Walla, Washington, 1971; New York, 1975). London, Calder and Boyars, 1969.
Romance, music and lyrics by Charles Ross (produced Leeds and London, 1971).
In the Heart of the British Museum (produced Edinburgh and London, 1971). London, Calder and Boyars, 1972.
Shades of Heathcliff (produced Sheffield, 1971; London, 1972). With *Death of Captain Doughty*, London, Boyars, 1975.
Peace in Our Time (produced Sheffield, 1972).
Death of Captain Doughty (televised 1973). With *Shades of Heathcliff*, London, Boyars, 1975.
McGonagall and the Murderer (produced Edinburgh, 1974).
On a Clear Day You Can See Marlowe (produced London, 1974).
While Rome Burns (produced Canterbury, 1976).
Antigone Through the Looking Glass (produced London, 1979).
The British Empire, Part One (produced Birmingham, 1980). London, Boyars, 1982.
Coming Ashore in Guadeloupe (produced Harrogate and London, 1982).

Radio Plays: *Where Tigers Roam*, 1976; *The Stage Has Nothing to Give Us*, 1980; *The British Empire: Part One: Dominion over Palm and Pine*, 1982, *Part Two: The Christian Hero*, 1982, *Part Three: Day of Reckoning*, 1985; *Daughters and Sons*, from the novel by Ivy Compton-Burnett, 1985.

Television Plays: *Hope*, 1970; *Faith*, 1971; *Death of Captain Doughty*, 1973; *Silver*, 1973.

Other

Beckett: A Study of His Plays, with John Fletcher. London, Eyre Methuen, and New York, Hill and Wang, 1972; revised edition, Eyre Methuen, 1978; revised edition, as *Beckett the Playwright*, Methuen, and New York, Farrar Straus, 1985.
Graham Greene. London, Methuen, 1983.

Editor, *The Hill Station: An Unfinished Novel, and An Indian Diary*, by J.G. Farrell. London, Weidenfeld and Nicolson, 1981.

*

John Spurling comments:

(1977) *MacRune's Guevara* was written from a desire to create an event in space rather than to turn out something recognisable as a play (I imagined it being performed in an art gallery rather than a theatre); at the same time I wanted to represent to myself my own conflicting reactions to Che Guevara and to attack certain forms of artistic and political cant which were dominant in the theatre at the time—perhaps still persist.

I found the idea for the more complex structure of *In the Heart of the British Museum* in Frances Yates's book on Renaissance theories of *The Art of Memory*, but after completing five scenes I put the play away. I took it up again as a commission for the Traverse Workshop Theatre, under Max Stafford-Clark's direction. The piece, with its emphasis on song and dance, was finished with this particular company in mind, but since I had felt the need for just such a company to perform it even before I knew of the company's existence, the original structure did not have to be altered. The subject matter comprises Aztec and Chinese legend, the recent Chinese Cultural Revolution, the exile of the Roman poet Ovid, and some of the subject matter of Ovid's own poems. The central theme is also Ovid's, the idea of Metamorphosis, and this is an important element in the structure.

Shades of Heathcliff grew directly out of being commissioned for Ed Thomason's Crucible Vanguard Theatre in Sheffield. A play for Sheffield seemed to call for a version of *Wuthering Heights*; the company consisted only of three actors and one actress, and, performing in a small space, dictated that it be a chamber piece and that the characters of the four Brontë children and of the novel itself be melted together.

Peace in Our Time was commissioned by the Crucible Theatre, Sheffield. It is the first part of a larger work called *Ghosts and Monsters of the Second World War*, which I have yet to finish. This first part is set in Hell, where the characters (Hitler, Stalin, Mussolini, Chamberlain, et al.) replay some of the political games of 1935–39.

McGonagall and the Murderer is a short play commissioned by the Pool Theatre, Edinburgh. A man who has failed to assassinate Queen Victoria and is now confined in Broadmoor tries to win a second chance by entering the mind of the poet McGonagall, himself on the road to Balmoral. *On a Clear Day You Can See Marlowe* was first written in 1970 and revised in 1974 for the Major Road Company. The play is something of a companion piece to *MacRune's Guevara*—a collage of the few known facts about the playwright Marlowe, much speculation (both reasonable and ludicrous), and versions of his own work in modern rehearsal.

(1988) *While Rome Burns*, commissioned by the Marlowe Theatre, Canterbury under its then director, David Carson, is a futuristic version of Edgar Allan Poe's story "The Masque of the Red Death." A company of travelling players visits an island off the coast of Britain, the last refuge of a group of well-heeled, middle-class people who have fled from a major catastrophe on the mainland. *Antigone Through the Looking Glass*, also commissioned by David Carson for a production at the King's Head, Islington, London, is roughly the same length as Sophocles' *Antigone* which is being acted off-stage, while we watch the performers coming and going in the green-room.

The British Empire trilogy, covering the period 1820–1911, with a cast of over 200 characters, was intended for the stage. Part One was performed in the studio at Birmingham Rep as a promenade production (directed by Peter Farago with a cast of only 9) and then adapted for BBC Radio 3, which also commissioned Parts Two and Three. I am still hoping to see the whole seven-hour work on the stage, preferably performed in one day or at least on successive evenings.

Coming Ashore in Guadeloupe was started in 1973 for a Dutch company which folded, but substantially revised in 1982 for the Cherub Theatre Company and its director Andrew Visnevski. It is a panorama (in fairly concise form) of the European discovery and conquest of America, featuring Columbus, Cortes, Pizarro, Raleigh, Verrazzano, and others, but viewed much of the time through the eyes of the Indian inhabitants.

* * *

John Spurling's work has veered from the technically innovative and exciting to the commonplace, and some of it is probably best forgotten—for example, the sentimental musical drawing-room comedy *Romance*. However, he has produced three plays which will almost certainly survive: *MacRune's Guevara, In the Heart of the British Museum*, and *While Rome Burns*. Two other plays, *Peace in Our Time* and *The British Empire, Part One* (without a further title), are certainly ambitious, but little can be said about them at present as the other parts of each of these plays have not been completed so far. The two individual parts, however, have in common a concern with large historical questions. In the case of the first, what caused World War II? what were Hitler and Stalin, Mussolini and Chamberlain up to? And in the case of the second, what is the nature of the achievements of the British as against those of the peoples they colonized?

There is, in fact, in most of Spurling's plays a profound concern with history and experience. And indeed with what happens to history. In *MacRune's Guevara* it is suggested that the real Guevara was an enigmatic figure of whom we are unlikely to know anything that finally matters. History, present in the play in the form of press reports, and problematic enough by itself, is only one of the ways in which the audience sees Guevara. Other viewpoints come from the actors in the play, as well as from the narrator, Edward Hotel, who is the supposed dramatist. Hotel has recently occupied a room in which the failed Scots-Irish artist MacRune lived just before his death. MacRune had covered the walls of this room with pencil sketches of some 17 scenes of Guevara's Bolivian campaign. These sketches, now faint and sometimes indistinguishable from other marks on the wall, are a parallel to the press reports about Guevara; and these are thrown into a discussion on the nature of history, with Hotel's own views of the subject, and MacRune's supposed views of it—which we are told, with questionable reliability, are heretical from a Marxist point of view. From all this, Guevara emerges as partly ineffectual and partly valiant, guerrilla hero but also a dupe of higher powers, on the one hand an inspirer of love who does not allow himself to be swayed by it from his cause, and on the other a merely simple-minded killer of bourgeois Belgians in an interlude located in the Congo. At the end of his life, he appears disillusioned, though as brave as ever, a man who did not amount to much in life but who has acquired mythic dimensions in death. One critic called this play "an honest magnification of the author's own confusion"; it is, in fact, the exact opposite: a sophisticated attempt to say "No clothes" about a king. Through Guevara, Spurling is also making a point about all contemporary heroes.

The multi-viewpoint technique of *MacRune's Guevara*, of which Spurling was one of the pioneers, was further elaborated in his next notable play, *In the Heart of the British Museum*. Three narratives are interwoven here: the disgrace and rehabilitation of a Chinese professor during the Cultural Revolution, the exile and death of Ovid, and the temptation and fall of the Aztec god Quetzalcoatl and his succession by the grimmer god Texcatlipoca. These themes elaborate and comment on each other. In contrasting power and war with culture and intelligence, in setting history against myth, reputation against reality, Spurling does not take sides. He makes it quite clear that he is not quarrelling with others: it is of his quarrel with his own multitudinous and contradictory responses to Guevara, myth, history, power, and intelligence, that Spurling makes his artistic work. By his omnivorous, witty plays he hopes to make us experience all of reality and thus progress to that profound understanding which is at the heart of all things.

Yet the understanding towards which he stretches his hands is nothing if not radically critical, especially of contemporary fads and blind spots—witness the concern in the title of *While Rome Burns* (loosely structured on Poe's "The Masque of the Red Death"). In this, a privileged few escape from Britain to an island fortress where they are burdened neither with incomes nor with taxes, and are cottoned from news of the world without. War games and cricket, costume balls and leisured adultery, suggestive of a luxury cruise without a destination, are what constitute their concerns. This island sanctuary is approached by an assassin. Disconnected set-pieces provide mannered comic moments which reveal the butterfly character of the protagonists, and their growing sense of dread. We identify with their fear, and yet we cannot help seeing that this beauty is terrible and deserves to be destroyed.

Spurling has written conventional plays with competence; at his best, however, he avoids the comforts of security. Melodrama and the music hall, comedy and tragedy, the neat plot and the predictable one, are alike eschewed. Sometimes Spurling pares away, peels off layer after layer; at other times he takes strange or unexpected angles, comparing like with what appears at first glance to be wholly unlike. Finally, his work functions as parable, icon, mystic text; and, at his finest, he persuades drama to aspire to the condition of petry.

—Prabhu S. Guptara

STARKWEATHER, David. American. Born in Madison, Wisconsin, 11 September 1935. Educated at the University of Wisconsin, Madison, 1953–57, B.A. in speech 1957. Editor of a visitors newspaper in New York. Recipient: Creative Artists Public Service grant, 1975; Rockefeller grant, 1978. Address: 340 West 11th Street, New York, New York 10014, U.S.A.

PUBLICATIONS

Plays

Maggie of the Bargain Basement, music by Starkweather (ballad opera; produced Madison, Wisconsin, 1956).
Excuse Me, Pardon Me (produced Madison, Wisconsin, 1957).
You May Go Home Again (produced New York, 1963). Published in *The Off-Off-Broadway Book*, edited by Albert Poland and Bruce Mailman, Indianapolis, Bobbs Merrill, 1972.
So Who's Afraid of Edward Albee? (produced New York, 1963).
The Love Pickle (produced New York, 1963; Edinburgh, 1971).
The Family Joke (produced New York, 1965).
The Assent (produced New York, 1967).
Chamber Comedy (produced Washington, D.C., 1969).
A Practical Ritual to Exorcise Frustration after Five Days of Rain, music by Allan Landon (also co-director: produced New York, 1970).
The Poet's Papers: Notes for an Event (produced Boston, 1971). Published in *New American Plays 3*, edited by William M. Hoffman, New York, Hill and Wang, 1970.
The Straights of Messina (produced New York, 1973).
Language (also director: produced New York, 1974).
The Bones of Bacon (produced New York, 1977).

*

Manuscript Collection: Lincoln Center Library of the Performing Arts, New York.

Theatrical Activities:
Director: several of his own plays.

David Starkweather comments:

(1973) Two mirrors facing what do they reflect?

Slice the mind in fives, Consciousness stage center. One way wings of Memory, staging areas of attention seeking self-ordering re-experience, detouring terror into ritual belief: Subconscious. Opposite wings of Appetite, senses drawn to sources of actuation, pulled always into foreign homes: Superconscious. Deeper still surrounding wings as well as centers, forms in the mind's structure beneath conception, containing all potential concepts like the possibilities of a medium; Unconscious. Facing Other Consciousness awareness of other centers of awareness, the possibilities of union/conflict with/within all potential spectators. The boundaries between these modes of mindworks the symbol, always blocking one way, all ways disappearing another.

My current vision of theatre is a head, the bodies of the audience resonating chambers like the jugs beneath the stage in the classic Noh, feeling their behavioral imaginations. Sound surrounds but the eyes are in front perceiving SENSES in terms of each other. Vision is figure to sound's ground and vice versa because each word has an aural and visual component. A noun is a picture (visual/spatial) and a verb is a melody (aural/temporal) relation. The split between being and doing dissolves when nouns are just states verbs are in at a given moment. The central human art form is the spoken word.

We laugh at people who are out of control. We laugh with people who are shoulder to shoulder. And we call it tragedy when a hero who is behind us loses.

If you write a play and do it badly that play is about incompetence. My plays in their forms hope to suggest what competence is. Moving toward an ideal. And I deal this round. Place your bets. It's a show of competence. All plays are about knowing. Being is where they're at. What I seek in a word is Order. In a feeling a release of energy.

For themes I have recognized a clear line of development in my last three plays: 1) there is nothing you can know without limiting your ability to know something equally true; 2) the only thing we need to believe is that there is nothing we need to believe; and 3) the only taboo is on taboos.

I write consistently about changing minds.

A number of works, my most ambitious, are as yet unproduced: *Owey Wishey Are You There?*, 1965, *The Wish-House*, 1967.

* * *

Ham —And where are you?
Noah —I am here and it is now. And all around is mystery.
—*A Practical Ritual to Exorcise Frustration after Five Days of Rain.*

It's not that he hates his family, his religion, or the rest of the society; it's just that he can't stand their noise. Most people he knows participate in the trivia of family life and the charades of state. They believe that somewhere there is *one* person who will solve the riddle of their emotional needs, that the state must be protected, especially from within, that there is a god who sits on a throne, somewhere.

So the young man leaves his home, not to be mean or ornery, but because he'll go crazy if he stays. He goes Downtown, where there are so many people that no one will notice him, or Downtown to the wilderness, where there are no people. And now he is in the Downtown part of his mind, where memories of his former life rise and beckon him to return and resume the old ties. He replies to their telephone calls and to his dreams that their lives are meaningless and their ways are mindless and hold no allure.

But the old ways are alluring to him in his solitude, and part of him wants to go home. However, gradually, painfully, he withdraws into the land of light, and now he's totally alone with his mind. Soon he *is* his mind and alone he's together. At this still point fears arise in their pure form and threaten his sanity. Fears: of pain, of people, of death, of body functions.

He discovers that these fears cannot be conquered in their essence but must be met in their actuality, and so, here he goes, folks, back to the "real world" to conquer his fears.

But this time he's armed: around his waist he carries self-containment; his vest is armored with enlightenment; his helmet is pure reason.

There are no trumpets on his return. People have scarcely noticed he's been gone, so busy have they been with their own wars and marriages. When he approaches the natives he finds that things are as they've always been between him and them: they don't see what he sees. So he withdraws again, and returns again armed with new weapons. The cycle is endless, the man is lonely, but filled with love. His attitude is increasingly ironic.

This portrait of the saintly exile is a composite of the heroes and mock heroes that form the core of David Starkweather's work, the recalcitrant lover Colin of *So Who's Afraid of Edward Albee?*, the errant son David of *You May Go Home Again*, the would-be suicide Alan of *The Assent*, the wandering Poet of *The Poet's Papers*, and both Sonny and Pittsburgh, who together form the hero of *Language*. They are all versions of the Odysseus/Christ/dropout anti-heroes of our time.

Colin, one of Starkweather's earliest creations, is merely disgusted by the System and puzzled by his disgust. David, created later, overwhelmed by his ambiguous feelings toward his family, goes into exile. Alan, guilty in exile, longs for death. The Poet, more comfortable in his separation from society, wanders the earth watching it destroy itself. And Sonny and Pittsburgh, who have in different ways plumbed the mysteries of isolation, now seek a way back into a society they have left.

In all of his plays, but especially in *The Family Joke* and *The Wish-House* (unproduced), Starkweather provides ample reason for self-exile, and incidentally offers savage but concerned criticism of Western society. In *The Family Joke* the nuclear family is seen as the System's breeding factory. Children must be raised, no matter what the cost to the parents. *The Wish-House* presents an almost paranoid view of the methods of mind control that the System is willing to employ. For the enemy, here represented by a Dr. Brill, is in possession of the same knowledge that Starkweather's exile-heroes have struggled so hard to obtain: "All that you consider yourself to be is merely the stopper to contain what you really are. All that you do most easily, by habit and without thought, is only to avoid your most beautiful and dangerous nature."

In counterpoint to some of the most glorious abstractions in contemporary theatre, architectural visions that spring from contemplation of the basic dualities of thought, Starkweather weaves the anxieties that often accompany advanced thought: fears of death, impotence, blood, piss, and shit.

In *The Poet's Papers* the war between the two divisions of mankind, the Orals and the Anals, is conducted in lyrical language. In *The Assent* the System prefers control of urination to control of theft: "Petty theft raises the living standard of the worker ... and stimulates cash flow. Whereas urine ... involves the production of a non-salable commodity and is therefore a general drain on the corporate effort." In *Language* Sonny, a virgin, admits: "I think that potency has something to do with murder."

In the plays of Starkweather we have a most complete view of what in olden times would have been called a saint: the man who leaves his society, goes into physical and psychical exile, searches for his god, and brings back the golden fleece to an indifferent world. In play after play, in growing clarity, Starkweather shows us the dangerous yet exciting journey, the abandoned society, and the funny, heartbreaking return. He even allows us glimpses of the fleece:

He goes away within
miles from the common road
to bring back for this world
something lovely something pure
Thank you, man.

—William M. Hoffman

STAVIS, Barrie. American. Born in New York City, 16 June 1906. Educated at New Utrecht High School, Brooklyn, New York, graduated 1924; Columbia University, New York, 1924–27. Served in the Army Signal Corps, Plans and Training section, 1942–45: Technical-Sergeant. Married 1) Leona Heyert in 1925 (divorced 1939); 2) Bernice Coe, 1950, one son and one daughter. Foreign correspondent in Europe, 1937–38; free-lance journalist after World War II. Co-founder, and member of the Board of Directors, New Stages theatre group, 1947, and United States Institute for Theatre Technology, 1961–64 and 1969–72; Visiting Fellow, Institute for the Arts and Humanistic Studies, Pennsylvania State University, University Park, 1971. Recipient: Yaddo fellowship, 1939; National Theatre Conference award, 1948, 1949. Fellow, American Theatre Association, 1982. Lives in New York City. Address: c/o Benjamin Zinkin, 635 Madison Avenue, New York, New York 10022, U.S.A.

PUBLICATIONS

Plays

In These Times (produced New York, 1932).

The Sun and I (produced New York, 1933; revised version produced New York, 1937).

Refuge: A One-Act Play of the Spanish War (produced London, 1938). New York, French, 1939.

Lamp at Midnight: A Play about Galileo (produced New York, 1947; Bristol, 1956). New York, Dramatists Play Service, 1948; revised version, South Brunswick, New Jersey, A.S Barnes, and London, Yoseloff, 1966; revised version, Chicago, Dramatic Publishing Company, 1974; one-hour school and church version (produced Chicago, 1972; New York, 1973), Dramatic Publishing Company, 1974.

The Man Who Never Died: A Play about Joe Hill (produced St. Paul, 1955; New York, 1958). New York, Haven Press, 1954; revised version, South Brunswick, New Jersey, A.S. Barnes, and London, Yoseloff, 1972.

Banners of Steel: A Play about John Brown (produced Carbondale, Illinois, 1962). South Brunswick, New Jersey, A.S. Barnes, and London, Yoseloff, 1967; revised version, as *Harpers Ferry: A Play about John Brown* (produced Minneapolis, 1967).

Coat of Many Colors: A Play about Joseph in Egypt (produced Provo, Utah, 1966). South Brunswick, New Jersey, A.S. Barnes, and London, Yoseloff, 1968.

Joe Hill (opera libretto), music by Alan Bush, adaptation of the play *The Man Who Never Died* by Stavis (produced Berlin, 1970).

Galileo Galilei (oratorio) music by Lee Hoiby, adaptation of the play *Lamp at Midnight* by Stavis (produced Huntsville, Alabama, 1975).

The Raw Edge of Victory (as *Washington*, produced Midland, Texas, 1976). Published in *Dramatics* (Cincinnati), April and May 1986.

Novels

The Chain of Command (novella). New York, Ackerman, 1945.
Home, Sweet Home! New York, Sheridan House, 1949.

Other

John Brown: The Sword and the Word. South Brunswick, New Jersey, A.S. Barnes, and London, Yoseloff, 1970.

Editor, with W. Frank Harmon, *The Songs of Joe Hill.* New York, People's Artists, 1955.

*

Manuscript Collections: Lincoln Center Library of the Performing Arts, New York; Pennsylvania State University, University Park.

Critical Studies: "Barrie Stavis: The Humanist Alternative" by Herbert Shore, in *Educational Theatre Journal* (Washington, D.C.), December 1973; interview in *Astonish Us in the Morning: Tyrone Guthrie Remembered* by Alfred Rossi, London, Hutchinson, 1977, Detroit, Wayne State University Press, 1981; "Humanism Is the Vital Subject" (interview), in *Dramatics* (Cincinnati), March–April 1978; "A History, A Portrait, A Memory" by Stavis, in *Time Remembered: Alan Bush: An Eightieth Birthday Symposium* edited by Ronald Stevenson, Kidderminster, Worcestershire, Bravura, 1981; "How Broad Should the Theatre's Concerns Be?" by Daniel Larner, in *Dramatics* (Cincinnati), May 1981; "Barrie Stavis Issue" of *Religion and Theatre* (St. Paul), August 1981; *American Theater of the 1960's* by Zoltán Szilassy, Carbondale, Southern Illinois University Press, 1986; "Barrie Stavis: Sixty Years of Craft and Commitment" by Ezra Goldstein, in *Dramatics* (Cincinnati), April 1986.

Barrie Stavis comments:

(1973) I wrote my first full-length play when I was 19 years old. I had my first production when I was 26. Fortunately there are no scripts in existence. About a dozen plays followed—all since destroyed.

The material and form of these early plays were derivative, echoing closely the dominant writing and production modes of the American stage. I refer to the Theatre of Illusion where the play is naturalistic in concept and style, generally romantic in approach. The physical envelope of such plays consist of a box set, usually a four-walled room with the fourth wall removed so that the audience can "peek in" and see what happens to those "real" people on the stage.

I was gradually becoming dissatisfied with this kind of stage and its "imitation of life." It could not contain the statements I was trying to make in the theatre. But at that time I did not know how to break away from the narrow restrictions of the romantic-naturalism and the pseudo-realism of the Theatre of Illusion. I knew (though certainly not as clearly as I know it now) that I was concerned with writing plays where the driving force of the characters was the clash of their *ideas*, not their subjective emotions.

Form is dictated by content and should grow out of function. Thus, I was also searching for a form which would be consonant with my material. I was seeking a freedom and a plastic use of the stage which the box set could not give me. I began studying Shakespeare intensively. Shakespeare was, and remains even to this day, my major theatre influence, followed by the Bible for its style, and its ruthlessly candid and objective way of telling a story. My study of the Elizabethan theatre, along with Greek theatre and the Roman amphitheatre, gradually led me to devise what I designated (1933–34) as "Time-Space Stage"—a stage where both time and space could be used with fluidity.

In 1939 I began to work on *Lamp at Midnight*. It took three years to complete. It was in this play that I first achieved a successful synthesis of content and form. The characters in the play are embattled over basic philosophic concepts; and the plastic use of time and space on the stage proved to be the perfect medium for expressing the conflict of ideas.

It was then that I realized I wanted to write further plays exploring this use of the stage. Although all the plays in the series would have the same major theme, each play would be independent unto itself with the common theme developed from a different axis of observation.

The series proved to be a tetralogy exploring the problems of men who have ushered in new and frequent drastic changes in the existing social order—men who are of their time and yet in advance of their time. And I have been concerned with examining the thrust they exercise on their society, and the counter-thrust society exerts on them.

It is the essence of nature and of man to undergo continual change. New forms evolve from old, mature, and, as the inevitable concomitant of their maturation, induce still newer forms which replace them. This is the historical process.

This process of change is gradual. It is not always perceived nor clearly apparent. Yet it is constant and inexorable. At a given moment when historical conditions are ripe, a catalyst enters and fragments the existing culture, setting into motion a new alignment of forces, a new series of relationships, which gradually become stabilized, codified.

It is this process of change that I endeavor to capture in my plays: the precise moment in history when society, ripe for change, gives birth to the catalyst who sets the dynamics of change into accelerated motion.

The four plays in their order are: *Lamp at Midnight* (Galileo Galilei), *The Man Who Never Died* (Joe Hill), *Harpers Ferry* (John Brown), *Coat of Many Colors* (Joseph in Egypt). In the first of these plays, *Lamp at Midnight*, I dramatize the story of Gailileo Galilei, the first human being to turn his new, powerful telescope to the night skies, there to discover the true motion of our solar system, a discovery unleashing a host of scientific and social consequence which heralded the coming Industrial Age. In *The Man Who Never Died* I dramatize the story of Joe Hill, troubador, folk poet, and trade union organizer, who was framed on a murder charge and who, during the 22 months of his prison stay, grew to heroic proportions. In *Harpers Ferry* I dramatize the story of John Brown's raid on Harpers Ferry, a raid which was the precursor to the Civil War. In *Coat of Many Colors* I dramatize the story of Joseph in Egypt, the world's first great agronomist and social planner, and I explore the theme of power and its uses. These four plays have been so designed that they can be performed by a single basic acting company. Further, all four plays can be produced on the same basic unit set.

Galileo Galilei, Joe Hill, John Brown, Joseph—these men have certain things in common. They were put on trial for their thoughts and deeds, found guilty, and punished. Yet their very ideas and acts achieved their vindication by later generations. Thus does the heresy of one age become the accepted truth of the next.

I have chosen to write plays about men who have an awareness of social and moral responsibility, plays that have faith in man's capacity to resolve his problems despite the monumental difficulties facing him. Why? Because I believe in ethical commitment. I believe that man is capable of ultimately solving the problems of the Nuclear Age.

Today, much theatre writing is obsessed with frustration and defeat. One trend of such playwriting deals with personality maladjustments and sexual aberration. This theatre is preoccupied with such matters as who goes to bed with whom, the gap in communication between parent and adolescent, the need to show that sex is either rape or submission. There is intense concern with subjective, neurotic problems, very little concern with the objective and social conditions of the world in which the characters live and the impact of the world upon them. It is as though the characters were living in a vacuum tube. Outside is the pulsating, throbbing world, but within the tube they function only insofar as their psyches collide with one another. Of the outside world, there is barely a reflection. A second contemporary trend is the writing of plays which explore the thesis that the human condition is hopeless because man is utterly dislocated in his society, that rational thought is a snare, that human life is purposeless, that action is without point for it will accomplish no result. There is in such plays no release for the affirmative emotion of an audience.

However, I believe with Chekhov that "Every playwright is responsible not only for what man is, but for what man can be." With Aristophanes, I seek to banish the "little man and woman affair" from the stage and to replace it with plays which explore ideas with such force and clarity as to raise them to the level of passion. Today especially, it should be the responsibility of the playwright to search out those situations which, by the inherent nature of the material, will capture the emotions and the intellect of an audience and focus it on men and women striving creatively for a positive goal.

(1988) I am now engaged in another tetralogy. The overall thematic examination of these four plays is *War, Revolution, and Peace*. In them, I explore George Washington, Abraham Lincoln, Miguel Hidalgo, and Simon Bolivar. Thus, I deal with the four liberators of the Western Hemisphere. In these plays I am concerned with the movement of colony to nation, of subject to citizen.

The material I handle is historical, but like the four plays of my first tetralogy, they are highly contemporary. We have been living in a century of war. There was the Japanese-Russian war in the first years of the century. Then came the famous/infamous assassination in Sarajevo which ushered in World War I. From then on until today, the world has been embroiled in wars, large and small. At this moment, there are over *50* different wars raging throughout the world. Thus, focusing on the theme of *War, Revolution, and Peace* is very much of our time.

I have completed the first play of the tetralogy: *The Raw Edge of Victory*, which deals with George Washington and the Revolutionary War. I'm half way through the second play, which focuses on Abraham Lincoln and the Civil War. Since I spend approximately five years on each play, it is obvious that I have accounted for the next ten years of my writing life!

* * *

A mere glance at the men Barrie Stavis has chosen to write about is indicative of his own passions, goals, intentions: John Brown, Joe Hill, Galileo, the biblical Joseph, and now in various stages of completion, works about George Washington, Hidalgo, Bolivar, and Lincoln.

There is about Stavis an almost Talmudic fury when he discusses his work and when he writes. This is in strange contrast to the man himself: warm, friendly, hopeful, and eager. Stavis is intellectually always aware ("conscious" might be an even better word) of what he is doing, dramaturgically and theatrically. His experience in theatre goes back further than most, and he has worked with almost every kind of theatre—getting his plays on to stages, everywhere.

Beyond grassroots experiences, there is a playwright, Stavis, who is very like the protagonists in his own plays: a man with a vision. It is a driving, almost monomaniacal vision which he, the artist, holds in careful check.

Just as his first tetralogy dealt with, in his words, "four aspects of mankind," all of his plays are precisely predicated. *Lamp at Midnight* (seen by twenty million in one night on a Hallmark Hall of Fame telecast) is "about Truth" (no small feat to undertake in a single play); *The Man Who Never Died* is "about Human Dignity"; *Harpers Ferry* is "about Freedom"; and *Coat of Many Colors* is "about Power." Stavis writes that kind of play deliberately, and there are abundant audiences and theatres in the United States and abroad eagerly seeking these plays: they have something to say, say it clearly, and are "about" something. As with good textbooks (*good* textbooks, mind), his work is pedantic, fascinating, and satisfying.

Stavis celebrated his 80th birthday shortly after the first play in his projected second tetralogy was published in *Dramatics*. This drama is about George Washington's heroic efforts to hold together the colonial army in the face of foreign intrigues, English military superiority, congressional neglect, domestic opportunism, and defeatism, despair, and dissatisfaction in the ranks. Stavis calls this epic drama *The Raw Edge of Victory*, and it is a potent brew of all the conflicts which raged as the Revolutionary War dragged on and on. The real role of black slaves and women in the war is forcefully demonstrated, as are the grim realities of keeping the troops in line, which Washington does with unflinching severity—even though he understands the reasons for rebellion in the ranks. Unlike the earlier plays, there are touches of humor here—even gallows-humor, as well as contrasts between the roughness of camp life and the sophisticated Court of King Louis XVI. Stavis's extensive research fortunately doesn't parade itself; it is abundantly evident in the dramatic revelation of how Washington and his army won the war and at what cost.

As with any conscientious teacher, Stavis is a superb researcher, who reads and studies about and around the men he will put on stage. Eventually, out of that research comes the spine of the play, the direction dictated by the material. His own humanistic background, of course, controls the aesthetics and even the politics of the play, and his experience controls the shape of the work, but the man and the artist avoid the merely pedantic, the narrowly polemic, the purely didactic. The five years he works on any single play make it fairly inevitable as a work: big, intellectual, more than a little "preachy" but almost always theatrical.

Stavis is a grassroots playwright. Middle America listens to the voice of history, and it is history that Stavis purveys most astutely and clearly. Grandeur and pageantry are second nature to the themes and the shapes of his work. His best work, I think, is *The Man Who Never Died.* It is no small accident that the play deals with an early "liberal," an American labor leader martyred and misplaced in time and place. That this play comes most successfully to the stage finally in the form of a German opera is really no surprise to those most familiar with Stavis's work.

He denies a tendency to romanticism and insists on the classicistic nature of his work. As did Brecht, Stavis claims to be more concerned with the *how* of an action than with the *why*. And in fact, his plays (the Joseph play possibly excepted) tend to Seriousness, with a capital S. There is generally little to amuse one in a Stavis play; the solemnity of the central figure is reflected in the almost complete lack of humor in the play itself. Even love is dealt with clinically and analytically. He leaves it to the total action to *move* his audiences: the themes that last, the appeal to noble if belated stances, the hero out of time.

Stavis, quite seriously and realistically, sees his own work as primarily influenced by both Shakespeare and the Holy Bible. If there are more rabbinic research and prophetic polemicism than there are lyricism and joy, Stavis cannot be faulted: he is after all very much a writer of his time and place, with a keen eye on the lessons of the past.

It might seem overly ambitious or optimistic for a playwright at age 80 to be looking forward to completing three more epics, all linked by the theme *War, Revolution, and Peace.* But Stavis has already been doing his years of research on Bolivar, Miguel Hidalgo, and Lincoln. Indeed, the life of Bolivar—whose own officers betrayed the vision of South American democracy for which he fought the war of liberation from Spain—has obsessed him for some time. The new tetralogy, he says, will explore in depth the "processes of throwing off oppression to gain freedom." He's focussing on "the movement of colony to nation, of subject to citizen," but the processes, as in *The Raw Edge of Victory*, are to be illuminated by the central characters of the liberators. In 1986, he was already halfway through his drama about Lincoln, with 2½ epics to go. Knowing Stavis at all is to know that his plays will indeed deliver.

He is a "pro." Methodical, organized, enthusiastic, and almost pristinely professional as he is, there is a double irony in the fact that he has never really had a hit on Broadway. Yet he represents professional theatre to literally dozens of colleges and repertory companies not only in the United States but around the world. To non-Americans, particularly, as Tyrone Guthrie indicated, Stavis represents the clearest and "most American" voice of the time. As perhaps is still true with O'Neill, Stavis seems most American to those who are least American, and he seems most "universal" to his American audiences.

There is, in any event, no mistaking Stavis's intent and purpose. If heroic drama has gone out of fashion in an era of the anti-hero, Stavis persistently views history and man's passage through that history as essentially Heroic with a capital H.

Finally, Stavis is quite the opposite in one crucial aspect from the heroes of his plays. While each of them is a man *out* of joint with his own time, Stavis is *of* his time and writes for that broadest, most fundamental of audiences: people, not critics.

—Arthur H. Ballet

STOPPARD, Tom. British. Born Tom Straussler in Zlin, Czechoslovakia, 3 July 1937; moved to Singapore, 1939, Darjeeling, India, 1942, and England, 1946. Educated at Dolphin School, Nottinghamshire, 1946–48; Pocklington School, Yorkshire, 1948–54. Married 1) Jose Ingle in 1965 (marriage dissolved 1971), two sons; 2) Miriam Moore-Robinson (i.e., the writer Miriam Stoppard) in 1972, two sons. Journalist, *Western Daily Press*, Bristol, 1954–58, and Bristol *Evening World*, 1958–60; then free-lance journalist and writer: drama critic, *Scene*, London, 1962–63. Recipient: Ford grant, 1964; John Whiting Award, 1967; *Evening Standard* award, 1967, 1973, 1975, 1979, 1983; Italia prize, for radio play, 1968; Tony award, 1968, 1976, 1984; New York Drama Critics Circle award, 1968, 1976, 1984; Shakespeare Prize (Hamburg), 1979; Outer Circle award, 1984; Drama Desk award, 1984. M.Lit.: University of Bristol, 1976; Brunel University, Uxbridge, Middlesex, 1979; University of Sussex, Brighton, 1980; honorary degrees: Leeds University, 1980; University of London, 1982; Kenyon College, Gambier, Ohio, 1984; York University, 1984. Fellow, Royal Society of Literature. C.B.E. (Commander, Order of the British Empire), 1978. Agent: Kenneth Ewing, Fraser and Dunlop Scripts Ltd., 91 Regent Street, London W1R 8RU. Address: Iver Grove, Iver, Buckinghamshire, England.

PUBLICATIONS

Plays

A Walk on the Water (televised 1963; produced Hamburg, 1964); revised version, as *The Preservation of George Riley* (televised 1964); as *Enter a Free Man* (produced London, 1968; New York, 1974). London, Faber, 1968; New York, Grove Press, 1972.

The Dissolution of Dominic Boot (broadcast 1964). Included in *The Dog It Was That Died and Other Plays*, 1983.

"M" Is for Moon among Other Things (broadcast 1964; produced Richmond, Surrey, 1977). Included in *The Dog It Was That Died and Other Plays*, 1983.

The Gamblers (produced Bristol, 1965).

If You're Glad I'll Be Frank (broadcast 1966; produced Edinburgh, 1969; London, 1976). With *Albert's Bridge*, London, Faber, 1969; revised version, published separately, New York and London, French, 1978.

Tango, adaptation of a play by Slawomir Mrozek, translated by Nicholas Bethell (produced London, 1966). London, Cape, 1968.

A Separate Peace (televised 1966). London, French, 1977; in *Albert's Bridge and Other Plays*, 1977.

Rosencrantz and Guildenstern Are Dead (produced Edinburgh, 1966; revised version produced London and New York, 1967). London, Faber, and New York, Grove Press, 1967.

Albert's Bridge (broadcast 1967; produced Edinburgh, 1969; New York, 1975; London, 1976). With *If You're Glad I'll Be Frank*, London, Faber, 1969; in *Albert's Bridge and Other Plays*, 1977.

Teeth (televised 1967). Included in *The Dog It Was That Died and Other Plays*, 1983.

Another Moon Called Earth (televised 1967). Included in *The Dog It Was That Died and Other Plays*, 1983.

Neutral Ground (televised 1968). Included in *The Dog It Was That Died and Other Plays*, 1983.

The Real Inspector Hound (produced London, 1968; New York, 1972). London, Faber, 1968; New York, Grove Press, 1969.

After Magritte (produced London, 1970; New York, 1972). London, Faber, 1971; New York, Grove Press, 1972.

Where Are They Now? (broadcast 1970). With *Artist Descending a Staircase*, London, Faber, 1973; in *Albert's Bridge and Other Plays*, 1977.

Dogg's Our Pet (produced London, 1971). Published in *Ten of the Best*, edited by Ed Berman, London, Inter-Action Imprint, 1979.

Jumpers (produced London, 1972; Washington, D.C., and New York, 1974). London, Faber, and New York, Grove Press, 1972; revised version, Faber, 1986.
Artist Descending a Staircase (broadcast 1972). With *Where Are They Now?*, London, Faber, 1973; in *Albert's Bridge and Other Plays*, 1977.
The House of Bernarda Alba, adaptation of the play by García Lorca (produced London, 1973).
Travesties (produced London, 1974; New York, 1975). London, Faber, and New York, Grove Press, 1975.
Dirty Linen, and New-found-land (produced London, 1976; Washington, D.C., and New York, 1977). London, Faber, and New York, Grove Press, 1976.
The Fifteen Minute Hamlet (as *The [Fifteen Minute] Dogg's Troupe Hamlet*, produced London, 1976). London, French, 1978.
Albert's Bridge and Other Plays (includes *Artist Descending a Staircase, If You're Glad I'll Be Frank, A Separate Peace, Where Are They Now?*). New York, Grove Press, 1977.
Every Good Boy Deserves Favour: A Play for Actors and Orchestra, music by André Previn (produced London, 1977; Washington, D.C., 1978; New York, 1979). With *Professional Foul*, London, Faber, and New York, Grove Press, 1978.
Professional Foul (televised 1977). With *Every Good Boy Deserves Favour*, London, Faber, and New York, Grove Press, 1978.
Night and Day (produced London, 1978; Washington, D.C., and New York, 1979). London, Faber, 1978; New York, Grove Press, 1979; revised version, Faber, 1979.
Albert's Bridge Extended (produced Edinburgh, 1978).
Undiscovered Country, adaptation of a play by Schnitzler (produced London, 1979; Hartford, Connecticut, 1981). London, Faber, 1980.
Dogg's Hamlet, Cahoot's Macbeth (produced Warwick, London, Washington, D.C., and New York, 1979). London, Faber, and New York, French, 1980.
On the Razzle, adaptation of a play by Johann Nestroy (produced Edinburgh and London, 1981; Washington, D.C., 1982). London, Faber, 1981.
The Real Thing (produced London, 1982). London, Faber, 1982; revised version (produced New York, 1984), 1984.
The Dog It Was That Died (broadcast 1982). Included in *The Dog It Was That Died and Other Plays*, 1983.
The Love for Three Oranges, adaptation of the opera by Prokofiev (produced on tour, 1983).
The Dog It Was That Died and Other Plays (includes *The Dissolution of Dominic Boot, "M" Is for Moon among Other Things, Teeth, Another Moon Called Earth, Neutral Ground, A Separate Peace*). London, Faber, 1983.
Rough Crossing, adaptation of a play by Ferenc Molnár (produced London, 1984). London, Faber, 1985.
Squaring the Circle: Poland 1980–81 (televised 1984). With *Every Good Boy Deserves Favour and Professional Foul*, London, Faber, 1984.
Four Plays for Radio (includes *Artist Descending a Staircase, Where Are They Now?, If You're Glad I'll Be Frank, Albert's Bridge*). London, Faber, 1984.
Dalliance, adaptation of a play by Schnitzler (produced London, 1986). With *Undiscovered Country*, London, Faber, 1986.
Largo Desolato, adaptation of the play by Václav Havel (produced Bristol, 1986). New York, Grove Press, 1987.

Screenplays: *The Romantic Englishwoman*, with Thomas Wiseman, 1975; *Despair*, 1978; *The Human Factor*, 1980; *Brazil*, with Terry Gilliam and Charles McKeown, 1985.

Radio Plays: *The Dissolution of Dominic Boot*, 1964; *"M" Is for Moon among Other Things*, 1964; *If You're Glad I'll Be Frank*, 1966; *Albert's Bridge*, 1967; *Where Are They Now?*, 1970; *Artist Descending a Staircase*, 1972; *The Dog It Was That Died*, 1982.

Television Plays: *A Walk on the Water*, 1963 (revised version, as *The Preservation of George Riley*, 1964); *A Separate Peace*, 1966; *Teeth*, 1967; *Another Moon Called Earth*, 1967; *Neutral Ground*, 1968; *The Engagement*, from his radio play *The Dissolution of Dominic Boot*, 1970 (USA); *One Pair of Eyes* (documentary), 1972; *The Boundary* (*Eleventh Hour* series), with Clive Exton, 1975; *Three Men in a Boat*, from the novel by Jerome K. Jerome, 1975; *Professional Foul*, 1977; *Squaring the Circle*, 1984.

Novel

Lord Malquist and Mr. Moon. London, Blond, 1966; New York, Knopf, 1968.

Short Stories

Introduction 2, with others. London, Faber, 1964.

*

Bibliography: *Tom Stoppard: A Reference Guide* by David Bratt, Boston, Hall, 1982.

Critical Studies: *Tom Stoppard* by C.W.E. Bigsby, London, Longman, 1976, revised edition, 1979; *Tom Stoppard* by Ronald Hayman, London, Heinemann, and Totowa, New Jersey, Rowman and Littlefield, 1977, 4th edition, Heinemann, 1982; *Beyond Absurdity: The Plays of Tom Stoppard* by Victor L. Cahn, Madison, New Jersey, Fairleigh Dickinson University Press, 1979; *Tom Stoppard* by Felicia Hardison Londré, New York, Ungar, 1981; *Tom Stoppard: Comedy as a Moral Matrix* by Joan Fitzpatrick Dean, Columbia, University of Missouri Press, 1981; *The Stoppard Plays* by Lucina Paquet Gabbard, Troy, New York, Whitston, 1982; *Tom Stoppard's Plays* by Jim Hunter, London, Faber, and New York, Grove Press, 1982; *Tom Stoppard* by Thomas R. Whitaker, London, Macmillan, and New York, Grove Press, 1983; *Stoppard: The Mystery and the Clockwork* by Richard Corballis, New York, Methuen, 1984, Oxford, Amber Lane Press, 1985; *Tom Stoppard: An Assessment* by Tim Brassell, London, Macmillan, and New York, St. Martin's Press, 1985; *File on Stoppard* edited by Malcolm Page, London, Methuen, 1986; *Tom Stoppard* by Susan Rusinko, Boston, Twayne, 1986; *Stoppard the Playwright* by Michael Billington, London, Methuen, 1987; *The Theatre of Tom Stoppard* by Anthony Jenkins, London and New York, Cambridge University Press, 1987.

Theatrical Activities:
Director: **Plays**—*Born Yesterday* by Garson Kanin, London, 1973; *The Real Inspector Hound*, London, 1985.

* * *

Although *Rosencrantz and Guildenstern Are Dead*—the play that brought Tom Stoppard international renown in 1967—may still be his best-known and most often produced work, it can now be seen as juvenilia within the context of a dramatic talent that has matured rapidly, if a bit self-consciously, since then.

While always retaining his characteristic verbal agility, Stoppard developed his craft by exploring a variety of dramatic modes: plays for radio, television, and motion pictures as well as for the stage, both mainstream and experimental; plays inspired by subjects like philosophy, surrealist painting, orchestral music, soccer, and journalism; plays resulting from challenges he set himself—to examine a political question or, uncomfortable as it may be for him, to give rein to the emotions. Exercising his stylistic virtuosity upon other writers' plot structures, he has also done a number of free adaptations of plays from other languages.

Stoppard began his career as a professional dramatist with a series of radio and television plays, the most interesting of which was *If You're Glad I'll Be Frank*, which has also been produced as a stage play. This half-hour radio play is an absurdist sketch of a world made chaotic by too much regularity. Frank, a bus driver, recognizes the voice of the telephone time girl as that of his long-lost wife Gladys, but their attempts at a reunion are thwarted because he must keep the bus on schedule and she must not lose the clock's beat.

The title characters of *Rosencrantz and Guildenstern Are Dead* are the school chums of Shakespeare's Hamlet, who have been summoned to Elsinore without knowing what is expected of them. Stoppard's play shows the two characters adrift in somebody else's plot, just as the Absurdists focussed upon modern man's rudderlessness in a world he cannot control. While the action of *Hamlet* proceeds in the background, the two innocents play games to pass the time in a manner clearly inspired by Beckett's *Waiting for Godot.* Their desire to overcome the fixity of the work of art in which they must function echoes the premise of Pirandello's *Six Characters in Search of an Author*. The complex interrelationships of life and art are demonstrated with particular theatrical flair in the pair's scenes with the Players who come to perform for Claudius at Elsinore.

Two recurring themes in Stoppard's short plays of the 1960's and early 1970's, as well as in his novel *Lord Malquist and Mr. Moon*, are the relativity of truth and the urge to discern some pattern in the world's chaos. In *Albert's Bridge* a well-educated young man opts to spend his life painting a suspension bridge, because it sets him above the fray of daily existence which can now be perceived as "dots and bricks, giving out a gentle hum." *The Real Inspector Hound* amusingly toys with the boundary between art and life by having two theatre critics get caught up in the murder mystery drama they are watching. The stage picture at the beginning of *After Magritte* is like a surrealist painting, but the action of the play reveals a kind of manic logic behind the visual nonsense. The radio play *Artist Descending a Staircase* is an ingenious search backward and forward in time for the truth about the circumstances of an artist's death, which had been misleadingly captured on a tape recording.

The same concerns reappear in Stoppard's two major mid-career full-length plays *Jumpers* and *Travesties*. Although the philosophical discourse may become a bit heavy-handed in *Jumpers*, it must still be counted among his best plays for the brilliance of its theatrical conceits. The intellectual argument of the play, a dialectic between moral philosophy and logical positivism, is reified in stage metaphors like the human pyramid of middle-aged philosophers in jump suits, whose shaky performance inadvertently demonstrates the false logic of a relativistic philosophical system. However, the search for absolutes by philosopher George Moore is constantly subverted by events in his own household that cannot be understood at face value.

Travesties is a dazzling foray into a crucial moment in political and cultural history—filtered through the self-serving memory of a senile minor figure. Henry Carr, who worked at the British Consulate in Zurich during World War I, comes into contact with Lenin, who is preparing the revolution he will take back to Russia, Tristan Tzara, who seeks through Dada to overthrow 25 centuries of artistic convention, and James Joyce, who is already working on the novel that will revolutionize modern literature. Fitting these characters into the borrowed structure of Wilde's *The Importance of Being Earnest* (which was produced by the English Players under Joyce's direction in Zurich in 1917), Stoppard examines the responsibility of the artist to society.

As a kind of busman's holiday from writing his full-length West End fare, Stoppard has occasionally written short pieces for the various "alternative theatre" projects of director Ed Berman, who had premiered *After Magritte* in 1970. Berman's community service organization Inter-Action included a children's theatre company called Dogg's Troupe, for which Stoppard wrote the one-act farce *Dogg's Our Pet.* In this play, as in the later paired one-acts *Dogg's Hamlet, Cahoot's Macbeth*, Stoppard makes fun of the arbitrariness of language by having some of his characters speak Dogg's language, which is composed of English words used to mean different things. The stage action in these plays is the construction of a speaker's platform or a stage or a wall, using slabs, planks, bricks, and cubes—just as language uses the various parts of speech to construct a meaning. *Dogg's Hamlet* incorporates an earlier playlet, *The (Fifteen Minute) Dogg's Troupe Hamlet*, a very funny condensation of Shakespeare's *Hamlet*, followed by a two-minute version as an encore.

In 1976 the American-born Berman asked Stoppard to write a play that would celebrate both the American Bicentennial and Berman's naturalization as a British citizen. Stoppard responded by sandwiching the brief sketch, *New-found-land*, into his longer farce, *Dirty Linen.* Set in a House of Commons meeting room, *Dirty Linen* shows the foibles of the very members of the Select Committee on Promiscuity in High Places; they finally come to accept the common-sense opinions of the attractive Maddie Gotobed who has been sexually involved with most of them. When that Committee adjourns for fifteen minutes, two new characters enter and use the room for a discussion of Berman's citizenship application, which leads to a long and cleverly evocative panegyric monologue about America as seen through foreign eyes.

Some of Stoppard's best writing has come from his moral outrage at totalitarian violations of human rights. Invited by André Previn to write a play that would involve a collaboration of actors and a live orchestra on the stage, Stoppard realized that by making the orchestra a figment of one character's imagination he could set the play in an insane asylum and write about the Soviet practice of confining political prisoners there along with genuine lunatics. For all its serious subject matter, *Every Good Boy Deserves Favour* contains some supremely witty dialogue. It also features a child, Sacha, whose observation of the system's injustice and of his dissident father's integrity has matured him beyond his years. A boy named Sacha also plays a crucial role in the television play *Professional Foul*, which draws its metaphors from a soccer match that is played in Czechoslovakia while British philosophers attend a conference there. In the course of the tense drama, Sacha courageously helps one of them to smuggle his dissident father's doctoral thesis to England for publication. Another television play, *Squaring the Circle*, traces the 1980–81 workers' Solidarity movement in Poland and makes of that complex history a clear and absorbing narrative for the layman. Stoppard's premise is that the concept of a free trade union like Solidarity is as irreconcilable with the Communist bloc's definition of socialism as is the mathematical impossibility of turning a circle into a square with the same area.

The brilliantly theatrical one-act *Cahoot's Macbeth* must also be classed as one of Stoppard's "plays of commitment." The play was inspired by the creative outlet found by some Czechoslovakian actors who, because of dissident activities, were deprived of the right to work in the theatre: they offered clandestine private living-room performances of abridged classics. In Stoppard's play, a performance of *Macbeth* by five actors is interrupted by an Inspector representing the regime, and later by a truck driver delivering a load of slabs, planks, bricks, and cubes, which are passed hand-to-hand through the window at precisely the moment in the play when Birnam Wood comes to Dunsinane. Although the Inspector appropriates the materials to build a wall, the performers triumph—spiritually, at least—by learning to express themselves in Dogg's language.

Night and Day is a play of transition in Stoppard's development, for it continues his concern for human rights in the face of totalitarianism while it branches into a tentative exploration of emotion. It is above all a play about journalists and journalism, a lively demonstration of the pros and cons of a free press. Ruth Carson is the wife of a British mine owner in a fictitious African country where a British-educated black dictator's rule is challenged by a Soviet-backed rebel countryman. The most idealistic of the three journalists who converge upon the Carson home becomes Ruth's fantasy-lover. Although the play received disappointingly mixed critical notices and is now overshadowed by Stoppard's next play, the very successful *The Real Thing, Night and Day* is deserving of more attention than it has had, both for its skillfully balanced approach to the subject and for its stylistic subtlety.

In *The Real Thing*, for the first time in Stoppard's canon, the human story is unabashedly allowed to take precedence over ideological concerns or stylistic conceits. And yet there is a bit of everything in this romantic comedy that does not shy away from either human pain or politics; there is perhaps even a touch of autobiography in that the protagonist Henry Boot is a playwright. His speech using a cricket-bat metaphor to uphold standards in language and thought is dramatic writing at its best, a stylistic high point in the work of a writer for whom style has always been the long suit.

—Felicia Hardison Londré

STOREY, David (Malcolm). British. Born in Wakefield, Yorkshire, 13 July 1933; brother of the writer Anthony Storey. Educated at Queen Elizabeth Grammar School, Wakefield, 1943–51; Wakefield College of Art, 1951–53; Slade School of Fine Art, London, 1953–56, diploma in fine arts 1956. Married Barbara Rudd Hamilton in 1956; two sons and two daughters. Played professionally for the Leeds Rugby League Club, 1952–56. Associate artistic director, Royal Court Theatre, London, 1972–74. Fellow, University College, London, 1974. Recipient: Rhys Memorial Award, for fiction, 1961; Maugham Award, for fiction, 1963; *Evening Standard* award, 1967, 1970; New York Drama Critics Circle award, 1971, 1973, 1974; Faber Memorial Prize, 1973; Obie award, 1974; Booker Prize, for fiction, 1976. Lives in London. Address: c/o Jonathan Cape Ltd., 32 Bedford Square, London WC1B 3EL, England.

PUBLICATIONS

Plays

The Restoration of Arnold Middleton (produced Edinburgh, 1966; London, 1967). London, Cape, 1967; New York, French, 1968.

In Celebration (produced London, 1969; Los Angeles, 1973; New York, 1984). London, Cape, 1969; New York, Grove Press, 1975.

The Contractor (produced London, 1969; New Haven, Connecticut, 1970; New York, 1973). London, Cape, 1970; New York, Random House, 1971.

Home (produced London and New York, 1970). London, Cape, 1970; New York, Random House, 1971.

The Changing Room (produced London, 1971; New Haven, Connecticut, 1972; New York, 1973). London, Cape, and New York, Random House, 1972.

The Farm (produced London, 1973; Washington, D.C., 1974; New York, 1976). London, Cape, 1973; New York, French, 1974.

Cromwell (produced London, 1973; Sarasota, Florida, 1977; New York, 1978). London, Cape, 1973.

Life Class (produced London, 1974; New York, 1975). London, Cape, 1975.

Mother's Day (produced London, 1976). London, Cape, 1977.

Sisters (produced Manchester, 1978). Included in *Early Days, Sisters, Life Class*, 1980.

Early Days (produced Brighton and London, 1980). Included in *Early Days, Sisters, Life Class*, 1980.

Early Days, Sisters, Life Class. London, Penguin, 1980.

Phoenix (produced London, 1984).

Screenplays: *This Sporting Life*, 1963; *In Celebration*, 1976.

Television Play: *Grace*, from the story by James Joyce, 1974.

Novels

This Sporting Life. London, Longman, and New York, Macmillan, 1960.

Flight into Camden. London, Longman, 1960; New York, Macmillan, 1961.

Radcliffe. London, Longman, 1963; New York, Coward McCann, 1964.

Pasmore. London, Longman, 1972; New York, Dutton, 1974.

A Temporary Life. London, Allen Lane, 1973; New York, Dutton, 1974.

Saville. London, Cape, 1976; New York, Harper, 1977.

A Prodigal Child. London, Cape, 1982; New York, Dutton, 1983.

Present Times. London, Cape, 1984.

Other

Writers on Themselves, with others. London, BBC Publications, 1964.

Edward, drawings by Donald Parker. London, Allen Lane, 1973.

*

Manuscript Collection: Boston University.

Critical Studies: "No Goodness or No Kings" by Susan Shrapnel in *Cambridge Quarterly*, Autumn 1970; *The Second Wave*,

London, Methuen, and New York, Hill and Wang, 1971, and *David Storey*, London, Longman, 1974, both by John Russell Taylor; "David Storey: Novelist or Playwright?" by Mike Bygrave, in *Theatre Quarterly 1* (London), April–June 1971; by Marie Peel, in *Books and Bookmen* (London), March 1972; interview in *Plays and Players* (London), September 1973; "The Ironic Anger of David Storey" by William J. Free, in *Modern Drama* (Toronto), December 1973.

Theatrical Activities:
Director: **Television**—*Portrait of Margaret Evans*, 1963; *Death of My Mother* (D.H. Lawrence documentary), 1963.

*   *   *

David Storey is a Yorkshireman, the son of a miner; he is also highly educated and lives in the south of England. The effects of his social, topographical, intellectual, and (perhaps) moral uprooting are everywhere to be seen in his work (as they were in that of his friend and fellow working-class Yorkshireman, David Mercer). But he has achieved a greater degree of detachment than Mercer, and his plays, consequently, tend to be more universal in their implications. One theme that runs through them is the power the past has over the present: it takes a man of exceptional (indeed, impossible) strength to break away from his background and live a full, first-hand life. Another related theme is implicit in a remark in *The Restoration of Arnold Middleton*, that "disintegration is inimical to the soul." Storey's plays, it may be argued, tacitly build up a vision of integration, of human and social wholeness, by openly concentrating on 20th-century deviations from this ideal: man alienated from his family, his roots, his class, his work, his language, and even from himself—a dissociation of sensibility that divides mind from emotion and hands from mind.

Arnold Middleton, Storey's first play, wasn't performed until 1966, but was actually written in 1959 between two of the novels which originally brought him fame. It was widely praised, and remains an impressive debut: rich and intricate, if also sometimes confused and obscure. We are never sure what has driven the provincial schoolmaster, Arnold Middleton, to the brink of madness. Presumably a combination of factors is responsible: his own immaturity and inability to sustain relationships; female pressure, from a demanding, jealous wife and a mother-in-law with a more than maternal interest in him; the northern parents he rarely sees; the mediocrity and moral listlessness of his milieu, "the passivity of modern society." What cannot be missed, however, is the splendidly humorous rhetoric with which Middleton defends himself. It carries one along, whether he is imagining himself in the part of Robin Hood (the archetypal outsider he is representing in the school play), or pretending he is actually a king (symbol, to him, of moral authority and sure social purpose), or, finally confessing his own ineradicable weaknesses ("scars . . . they inhabit the skin. They grow there after a while like natural features. . . . Remove them, and you remove life itself"). The conclusion seems to be that, assert his individuality as he may, a man must substantially reconcile himself to what experience has made him. "Everything has to be defined. Yet how can you define anything except by its limitations?"

This sort of resilient stoicism also emerges from *In Celebration*, which deals more explicitly with the background Storey himself knows. The Shaws are visited on their 40th wedding anniversary by their three sons: one a teacher, another a solicitor turned artist, the third an industrial relations expert, and all clearly live markedly less adequate and fulfilling lives than their father, though neither he nor Storey attempts to sentimentalise the pits in which he works. As Steven, the unhappiest of the uprooted three, declares: "His work actually has significance for him . . . while the work he's educated us to do . . . is nothing . . . at the best a pastime, at the worst a sort of soulless stirring of the pot . . . honestly, what hope has any of us got?" There is more to the play than this suggests, since Storey is at pains to show the complexities of the participants' motives. Old Shaw wanted the boys to be successful in order to appease his wife, who married beneath her, and whom he impregnated, before them, with a son who later died. Andrew is cynical and angry because they rejected him on his brother's death. Under the skilfully sustained surface of the "celebration" of the title, a dark drama of sin, guilt, and atonement begins to unravel—only to be checked by Steven, the nearest to Storey's mouthpiece in the play. There is, he says, "this feeling of disfigurement, this crushing, bloody sense of injury"; but it was "inflicted by innocent hands." Like Middleton, they must accept their scars and learn to make the best of them.

Storey's career has been much helped by the devotion of Lindsay Anderson, who directed all his early plays with a marvellous feeling for detail and the nuance of character. Nowhere was this more evident than with *The Contractor*, a much more visual and less dramatically explicit play than those before it. In the first half a tent is painstakingly and precisely raised, and in the second lowered: what would be the central event a more conventional piece (a wedding and a reception) occurs in the interval. The "family" wanders in and out, notably Ewbank, the bride's father, a tenting contractor and self-made Yorkshireman; but the action mainly involves the seemingly aimless backchat and banter of the men putting up the tent.

The workmen are obvious misfits, "those that nobody else'll employ," but almost everyone else is out of love with society. Ewbank's son tries hopelessly to identify with the men; Ewbank's father bores them with stories of the good old days before machines; Ewbank himself reverberates with unease beneath a tough exterior. Everything is allusive, understated, and, as Storey himself said, the metaphor of the tent "contains the possibility" of many interpretations. In the light of his previous writing, however, it seems best to regard it primarily as a symbol of the frivolity of contemporary work and the impermanence of its achievement.

Home continues the process, both stylistic and moral. The subject is a still deeper alienation; but its expression is oblique, tentative, and even vague. Two old men exchange smalltalk, using dated expressions like "my word" and "by Jove"; two women join them, talking of sex and suffering; and it becomes apparent that this "home" is in fact an asylum. These people could not function in a scarcely saner outside world, and they are not at peace in this secluded one. And Storey goes further, dropping hints that the madhouse is an impressionistic picture of contemporary Britain, deprived of a secure, authoritative place in the world. In other words, *Home* evokes a more total dislocation than any of the previous plays. Indeed alienation has gone so far that the old men cannot even approximately say what they mean. Their language is all social form, without personal content; speech is separated from feeling. All they can do to express themselves is to let fall the occasional tear—as both do, with great dramatic effect.

The Changing Room is a play so lacking in overt significance that it might be mistaken for pure documentary—and, as such, proved compulsively watchable in the theatre. But, as always with Storey, more occurs than appears on the surface. Not only is there considerable opportunity to speculate on the rugby footballers: there are also moments when individuality disappears, and we are able to see the team as a team, each member giving his all to a cooperative enterprise. On the field, 13 minds, hearts, and pairs of hands have worked as one. Man may be alienated from his work: he is not, it seems, always alienated from his play. There is *some* hope.

—Benedict Nightingale

STOTT, Mike. British. Born in Rochdale, Lancashire, 2 January 1944. Attended Manchester University. Stage manager, Scarborough Library Theatre, Yorkshire, and play-reader, Royal Shakespeare Theatre, 3 years; script editor, BBC Radio, London, 1970–72; Thames Television resident writer, Hampstead Theatre Club, London, 1975. Agent: Michael Imison Playwrights, 28 Almeida Street, London N1 1TD, England.

PUBLICATIONS

Plays

Mata Hari (produced Scarborough, 1965).
Erogenous Zones (produced London, 1969).
Funny Peculiar (produced Bochum, Germany, 1973; Liverpool, 1975; London, 1976). Ashover, Derbyshire, Amber Lane Press, 1978.
Lenz, adaptation of the story by Georg Büchner (produced London, 1974; New York, 1979). Todmorden, Lancashire, Woodhouse, 1979.
Plays for People Who Don't Move Much (produced London, 1974; section produced as *Men's Talk*, Edinburgh, 1974).
Midnight (produced London, 1974).
Other People (produced London, 1974).
Ghosts, adaptation of a play by Wolfgang Bauer (produced London, 1975).
Lorenzaccio, adaptation of the play by Alfred de Musset (produced Exeter, 1976).
Followed by Oysters (produced London, 1976; as *Comings and Goings*, produced Liverpool and London, 1978).
The Scenario, adaptation of a play by Anouilh (produced Bellingham, Northumberland, 1976).
Soldiers Talking, Cleanly (televised 1978). London, Eyre Methuen, 1978.
The Boston Strangler (produced London, 1978).
Grandad (produced Croydon, Surrey, 1978).
Strangers (produced Liverpool, 1979).
Ducking Out, adaptation of a play by Eduardo De Filippo (produced London, 1982).
Dead Men (produced Southampton, 1982).
Pennine Pleasures (produced Oldham, Lancashire, 1984).
The Fling, adaptation of a work by Asher (produced London, 1987).

Radio Plays: *Lucky*, 1970; *When Dreams Collide*, 1970; *Early Morning Glory*, 1972; *Lincoln*, 1973; *Richard Serge*, 1973; *The Bringer of Bad News*, 1973; *The Doubting Thomases*, 1973; *The Fancy Man*, 1987.

Television Plays: *The Flaxton Boys*, 1969; *Susan*, 1973; *Thwum*, 1975; *Our Flesh and Blood*, 1977; *Pickersgill People* series, 1978; *Soldiers Talking, Cleanly*, 1978; *One in a Thousand*, 1981; *The Last Company Car*, 1983; *The Practice* series, 1985–86.

* * *

Mike Stott's 1976 West End success with his comedy *Funny Peculiar* may well represent the culmination of his search for an ideal, or at least clinching, formula for the permissive sex comedy.

His search began with *Erogenous Zones*, a collection of sketches for performance by a company of six, centred round the twin themes of love and homicide. The mixture here is one of strip cartoon wit and woman's magazine cliché, the main charm residing in the way passion is reduced to absurdity through being couched in dumb and deadpan phrases. The types are instantly recognizable—the doughy sweetheart, the sadistic cop, the clean-limbed officer doing press-ups, the big beefy success, the mad gunman, the obsessive lawyer—with the point always clear before the pay-offs. Stott shows cleverness in catching the comedy of the obvious, while managing to avoid repetition.

In *Other People* the form is sometimes laboured though the dialogue is often sharp. It begins with an arresting image of a "flasher" naked under his plastic, see-through mac, and a pretty Czech girl who frightens him away by her eagerness to participate in anything he might suggest. But an arresting image does not make a play, and the web of relationships Stott establishes—between a successful businessman, Dave, who ends by taking an overdose, an out-of-work Italian father-of-five who is given a cheque by the dying man to solve all his problems, a lonely widow of 51 who lacks love, and her daughter, married to Dave's friend Geoff—fails to form a coherent pattern of comic interest. The writing is often vivid, as in the Italian's fantasy of selling underwear to Arabs in hair-covered boxes—"We buy the hair, we comb it, shampoo, and we stick it on the boxes. And those Arabs, those Greeks, they go CRAZY in the shops, just to stroke our sexy hairy boxes. Believe me, Mr. Brock, I know those men, the foreigners, the Aristotles, the Ahmeds. They KILL each other to be stroking a hairy English box." The theme of sexual permissiveness is provocatively explored, with the sound of couples making love upstairs and one couple trying to initiate group sex. But it's hard to make out what Stott's intention is, whether he's attempting genuine social observation or merely exploiting current fashion.

Funny Peculiar has a mock moral ending. The hero, Trevor, a North Country grocer proclaiming the virtues of sexual freedom, falls down into his cellar, pursued by a sex-hungry puritan lady of advanced years, and is consequently rendered helpless in plaster and straps on a hospital bed. There he becomes the passive object of wife and mistress's oral lust. A new and up-to-date version of the "tu l'a voulu, Georges Dandin" idea, Trevor's obsession with sex is kept simmering in naked cavorting among the council-estate flower beds and in his attempts to preach to the unconverted customers of his shop (losing custom as a result).

The best writing is found in the scenes when he tries to convince his wife to leap on to the freedom bandwagon and when he upbraids her for sexual ordinariness. Her defence is so heartfelt and real it really seems that her subsequent conversion to his way of thinking is engineered for the sake of the plot. There's one piece of slapstick—a fight with confectionary between a visiting confectionary salesman and Trevor—which must rate as one of the best scenes of comic anarchy ever seen on the West End stage.

In his versions of Büchner's *Lenz* and Wolfgang Bauer's *Ghosts* Stott demonstrates more fragmented skills as an adaptor and translator from the German. *Lenz*, originally a short story about a Strasbourg intellectual who believes he can raise a girl from the dead, is written in numerous short scenes (in Büchner's own expressionistic manner) which fail to come to grips with any central issue. The original of *Ghosts* is a roughed up rewrite of Brecht's satire on a lower-middle-class wedding party, using socially more sophisticated though dramatically more crude characters.

In recent plays Stott has not shown he can move beyond formula writing. *The Boston Strangler*, for all its rape and murder in intended subtle variations—ensuring constant changes of wigs and underwear in the actress playing all the victims—cumulatively diminishes interest in the crimes of a psychopath. *Comings and Goings* promises to be better. Jan, a teacher, married to a cream-cracker executive, deserts him and arrives in the household of a pair of homosexuals. But development is lost in favour of generalized encounters confirming the rule of licence and ending with vapid literary parallels. The characters have little genuineness and the comings and goings lack dramatic direction. Stott seems to have come to the position of despising the people he writes about. *Grandad*, too, displays a tawdry lack of charity, becoming unrelievedly tedious. Stott returned to formula writing in the television series *The Practice*, an examination of life in a medical centre.

—Garry O'Connor

SUTHERLAND, Efua (Theodora, née Morgue). Ghanaian. Born in Cape Coast, 27 June 1924. Educated at St. Monica's School and Training College, Cape Coast; Homerton College, Cambridge, B.A.; School of Oriental and African Studies, London. Married William Sutherland in 1954; three children. Schoolteacher in Ghana, 1951–54. Since 1958 founding director, Experimental Theatre Players (now Ghana Drama Studio), Accra. Founder, Ghana Society of Writers (now the University of Ghana Writers Workshop) and Kusum Agoromba children's theatre group, Legon. Co-founder, *Okyeame* magazine, Accra. Address: Institute of African Studies, University of Ghana, P.O. Box 25, Legon, Ghana.

PUBLICATIONS

Plays

Foriwa (produced Accra, 1962). Accra, State Publishing Corporation, 1967; New York, Panther House, 1970.

Edufa, based on *Alcestis* by Euripides (produced Accra, 1962). London, Longman, 1967; in *Plays from Black Africa*, edited by Fredric M. Litto, New York, Hill and Wang, 1968.

Anansegoro: You Swore an Oath, in *Présence Africaine 22* (Paris), Summer 1964.

Vulture! Vulture! Two Rhythm Plays (for children; includes *Tahinta*), photographs by Willis E. Bell. Accra, Ghana Publishing House, 1968; New York, Panther House, 1970.

Ananse and the Dwarf Brigade (for children; produced Cleveland, 1971).

The Marriage of Anansewa: A Storytelling Drama (produced Accra, 1971). London, Longman, 1975.

Other plays: *Odasani*, version of *Everyman*; adaptation of Chekhov's *The Proposal; The Pineapple Child; Nyamekye; Tweedledum and Tweedledee*, adaptation of *Alice in Wonderland* by Lewis Carroll.

Verse (for children)

Playtime in Africa, photographs by Willis E. Bell. London, Brown Knight and Truscott, 1960; New York, Atheneum, 1962.

Other (for children)

The Roadmakers, with Willis E. Bell, photographs by Bell. Accra, Ghana Information Services, and London, Neame, 1961.

The Original Bob: The Story of Bob Johnson, Ghana's Ace Comedian, illustrated by Willis E. Bell. Accra, Anowuo, 1970.

* * *

It is impossible to consider Efua Sutherland's plays apart from her work as a founder, organiser, and stimulator of theatres and troupes. This work is probably more important for the development of drama in Africa than are her plays, good as these are. I suspect, indeed, that this would be her own assessment, for several of her plays have never appeared in print.

In the mid-1950's Sutherland set up a writer's society to write for children, and her concern with children has been a continuing one. For them she has written many plays, some based upon traditional tales, one an adaptation of *Alice in Wonderland*. Of these, only *Anansegoro: You Swore an Oath* and "two rhythm plays," *Vulture! Vulture!* and *Tahinta*, have been published. The rhythm plays, consisting of simple one-line statements followed by an unvarying chorus line, mean very little on the page. *Anansegoro* is based upon the common tale of a deer who turns into a woman. Ananse has shot a deer, who turns into a beautiful woman and lives with him, relieving him of his poverty with rich gifts. She has told Ananse of her identity and he has sworn never to tell another. His wife becomes jealous of the deer-woman—with reason—and keeps pressing for Ananse's "relative" to leave. Eventually, Ananse tells her the secret and is stripped of all his riches as the deer-woman departs. "If you rub the face of a blessing in the dirt, it deserts you." The events are set in a narrative framework, with a storyteller and a chorus, whose members also play minor parts. The short play is vigorous, simple, and highly theatrical. Children can take pleasure in the story, the song, and the dance, adults in the sophistication of the presentation.

In 1958 Sutherland founded the Experimental Theatre Players in Accra which became the Ghana Drama Studio. In 1960 a courtyard theatre was built for it, drawing in concept upon traditional performance areas. This was, I believe, the first attempt to design an indigenous form of theatre rather than to copy European proscenium stages. A few years later Sutherland designed another open-air theatre for experiments at blending traditional story-telling and drama. The Ghana Drama Studio has become the base for Kusum Agoromba (Kusum Players), which tours schools and training colleges, incorporating the local schoolchildren into its productions: the Studio also collaborates with the Workers Brigade Drama Group, which tours and tries to reach the ordinary person. Both touring companies play in English and in Akan. Sutherland's concern is less with present success in Accra than with the future development of drama in Ghana as a whole: with reaching the children and the common people, particularly those outside the capital, and, at the same time, establishing the basis for the development of African styles of performance and drama.

She has published some full-length plays. *Edufa* is a re-working of *Alcestis*, in which the Admetus-figure becomes a selfish member of the nouveau riche and the play a tragedy, ending with the wife's death. Such a radical change necessitates a change in the Heracles-character, now a seedy intellectual who hides the emptiness of his life and his ambitions as a writer behind the image of a wandering prankster full of songs. The father, self-centered in Euripides, becomes a sympathetic character, full of dignity, knowledge, and insight. The action is set, with rather heavy irony, against an annual ceremony in which funeral songs are sung as evil is expelled from the town. This ceremony, and various omens in which Edufa, the modern man, professes to disbelieve, create an atmosphere of foreboding. Sutherland has also adapted *Everyman* and Chekhov's *The Proposal*, but they have not been published.

Another full-length play, *Foriwa*, impresses one with its usefulness. It is intended to be performed in the open air in a street in any of many small Ghanaian towns, and it tells how to bring life and vitality to such a place. The central characters are Labaran, a university-educated stranger who is camping in the town and "planting seeds" in the minds of those who are receptive, and Foriwa, a beautiful girl just returned from training as a teacher. By the end of the play, of course, they have fallen in love with each other (Sutherland's rejection of tribalism, since Labaran is a Hausa from the North). Yet Sutherland is careful not to present progress as pressed upon the people by the young and educated. Labaran's ally is the retired postmaster; and Foriwa's mother, the Queen-Mother of the town, has long been working for new ways. The climax of the play is her use of a traditional ceremony—again, Sutherland emphasises the alliance of new and old—to call for a re-birth in the town. The play is without villains, for the message is that all must co-operate; even the elders, Labaran says, "have come as far as they are able."

The tone of the play is set in Labaran's opening soliloquy:

> . . . The town has slept itself to raggedness.
>
> I am keeping vigil here, placing my faith in some daybreak after this long night, when the townsmen shall wake and shake my soul with vibrant talk . . .
>
> I was impatient at the beginning; in haste. Seeing the raggedness of my people's homes, I was ashamed, even angry. I heard it screamed: Progress! Development! I wanted it far and everywhere.

And later in the speech, "This is my office, this street: the people who use it are my work and education." Such patently utilitarian drama may be valuable to contemporary Ghana. But Sutherland's talent as a writer has been subordinated to her theatrical projects and the laudable aims they serve, and it is her endeavour as a whole for which one's admiration is greatest.

—Anthony Graham-White

TABORI, George. British. Born in Budapest, Hungary, 24 May 1914. Educated at Zrinyl Gymnasium. Served in the British Army Middle East Command, 1941–43: Lieutenant. Married 1) Hanna Freund (divorced 1954); 2) the actress Viveca Lindfors (divorced), one son, one daughter, and one stepson. Former artistic director, Berkshire Theatre Festival, Stockbridge, Massachusetts. Recipient: British Film Academy award, 1953. Address: 172 East 95th Street, New York, New York 10028, U.S.A.; or, c/o Suhrkamp Verlag, Lindenstrasse 29–35, Postfach 4229, D-6000 Frankfurt am Main, Federal Republic of Germany.

PUBLICATIONS

Plays

Flight into Egypt (produced New York, 1952). New York, Dramatists Play Service, 1953.

The Emperor's Clothes (produced New York, 1953). New York, French, 1953.

Miss Julie, adaptation of the play by Strindberg (also director: produced New York, 1956).

Brouhaha (produced Brighton and London, 1958; New York, 1960).

Brecht on Brecht (produced New York and London, 1962). New York, French, n.d.

The Resistible Rise of Arturo Ui: A Gangster Spectacle, adaptation of the play by Brecht (produced New York, 1963; Edinburgh, 1968; London, 1969). New York, French, 1972.

Andorra, adaptation of the play by Max Frisch (produced New York, 1963).

The Guns of Carrar, adaptation of a play by Brecht (produced Syracuse, New York, 1963; New York City, 1968). New York, French, 1970.

The Niggerlovers: The Demonstration, and Man and Dog, music by Richard Peaslee (produced New York, 1967).

The Cannibals (produced New York, 1968). Published in *The American Place Theatre*, edited by Richard Schotter, New York, Dell, 1973; published separately, London, Davis Poynter, 1974.

Mother Courage, adaptation of the play by Brecht (produced Washington, D.C., 1970).

Pinkville, music by Stanley Walden (produced Stockbridge, Massachusetts, 1970; New York, 1971).

Clowns (also director: produced Tübingen, 1972).

Talk Show (produced Bremen, 1976).

Changes (produced Munich, 1976).

Screenplays: *I Confess*, with William Archibald, 1953; *The Young Lovers*, with Robin Estridge, 1954; *The Journey*, 1959; *No Exit*, 1962; *Secret Ceremony*, 1968; *Parades*, 1972; *Insomnia*, 1975.

Novels

Beneath the Stone the Scorpion. London, Boardman, 1945; as *Beneath the Stone*, Boston, Houghton Mifflin, 1945.

Companions of the Left Hand. London, Boardman, and Boston, Houghton Mifflin, 1946.

Original Sin. London, Boardman, and Boston, Houghton Mifflin, 1947.

The Caravan Passes. London, Boardman, and New York, Appleton Century Crofts, 1951.

The Journey: A Confession. New York, Bantam, 1958; London, Corgi, 1959.

The Good One. New York, Pocket Books, 1960.

Other

Ich wollte, meine Tochter läge tot zu meinen Füssen und hätte die Juwelen in den Ohren: Improvisationen über Shakespeares Shylock: Dokumentationen einer Theaterarbeit. Munich, Hanser, 1979.

*

Theatrical Activities:
Director: **Plays**—*Miss Julie* by Strindberg, New York, 1956; *Brecht on Brecht*, toured, 1962; *Hell Is Other People*, New York, 1964; *The Cannibals* (co-director, with Marty Fried), Berlin, 1970; *Pinkville*, Berlin, 1971; *Clowns*, Tübingen, 1972; *Kohlhaas*, Bonn, 1974; *Emigrants*, Bonn, 1975; *Afore Night Come* by David Rudkin, Bremen, 1975; *The Trojan Women* by Euripides, Bremen, 1976.

* * *

George Tabori's world recalls the Sherwood Anderson title *Dark Laughter*. What a world—betrayal, repression, violence, cannibalism, and, unlike the Greeks', no redemption. And envisioned more and more as a black comedy. But not quite. The flavor is sardonic, tongue-in-cheek, but beneath this is absolutely no acceptance of the world as is. Beneath the sardonic tone we can apprehend the eyes of an anguished, lacerated soul who has seen mankind in one perversion, one degradation after another, seen Hungary in its fascistic period earlier in the century, Germany in the Nazi era, and America in its growing role as police-butcher of the world, has seen it all, and yet whose outcry marks him as one who still believes in the impossible dream of brotherhood. I have the sense that Tabori is too angry, too disgusted to *want* to believe, but that past his disgust, past his disillusionment, there is a tremendous yearning, a cavernous yearning to believe in the possibility of a decent society.

Early Tabori is represented by *The Emperor's Clothes*, the tale of a "fuzzy-headed idealist" intellectual (my quotes) in Budapest who appears to renounce all his beliefs when he falls into the hands of the secret police, but who emerges as a man with backbone. Under torture he rediscovers his manhood. In short, Tabori at his most idealistic.

But then the world grows darker and Tabori begins to shift from naturalism toward a more abstract, less lyrical, and far harsher theatre. He began adapting Brecht, e.g., *Brecht on Brecht* and *Arturo Ui*, and his own work became more detached, more sardonic, more abstract, more song-and-dance oriented. By the time of *The Cannibals* in 1968, the work was very dry, very dark, very bitter, very removed. In a Nazi concentration camp, the prisoners decide to cook and eat their friend Puffi, the fat man who has just died. Hirschler says:

> (To Uncle who is protesting the cannibalism) Listen, Uncle, let's have some perspective. The cake is too small. Whenever you eat, you take a crumb out of someone else's mouth. At this very moment, while you're making such a fuss, millions are starving to death in India; but today we may have stumbled on the most elegant solution. The graveyards are full of goodies; the chimneys are going full blast, and nice fat suicides come floating down every river and stream. All that perfectly good stuff going to waste.

Shades of Swift's *A Modest Proposal*. And the cannibalism, which Tabori treats both literally and as a metaphor, is painted as inexorable. At the end of the play. The Loudspeakers place the action in historic context:

> . . . some savages eagerly desire the body of a murdered man
> So that his ghost may not trouble them,
> For which reason I recommend, dear brethren in Christ,
> The Jew's heart, in aspic or with sauce vinaigrette,
> So soft it will melt in your mouth.

In *The Niggerlovers* Tabori views the racial tensions that afflict the U.S., but any sympathy is sublimated. No one comes off with any saving grace, the white liberals are stupid or saccharine or slightly perverted, the blacks are corroded with cynicism. No action seems to be of any help, there is no way out.

Pinkville studies the development of an American killer—specifically how the U.S. army takes a non-violent, righteous young man, and using his very righteousness, subverts him into the killer it needs to massacre Vietnamese. Again the action is inexorable. Everything becomes grist for the army's purpose. Again the world is so self-enclosed that there is no way out.

And yet the way out is through the action of Tabori's art. For the very work is a cry. The sardonic element has within it a taint of satisfaction, as if the worst is always somehow satisfying, but the worst is also an indictment of us, ultimately a call. For the early heroes are gone, no heroes left in the later plays, nothing for us to emulate. You and I become the only possible heroes left to Tabori and to the world.

—Arthur Sainer

TALLY, Ted. American. Born in Winston-Salem, North Carolina, 9 April 1952. Educated at Yale University, New Haven, Connecticut (John Golden fellowship 1976–77; Kazan award, 1977; Field prize, 1977), B.A. 1974, M.F.A. 1977. Married. Taught at Yale University; artist-in-residence, Atlantic Center for the Arts, 1983. Member of the Artistic Board, Playwrights Horizons, New York. Recipient: CBS-Yale fellowship, 1977; Creative Artists Public Service grant, 1979; John Gassner Award, 1981; National Endowment for the Arts fellowship, 1983; Obie award, 1984; Guggenheim fellowship, 1985. Lives in New York City. Agent: Helen Merrill Ltd., 361 West 17th Street, New York, New York 10011, U.S.A.

Publications

Plays

Terra Nova (produced New Haven, Connecticut, 1977; Chichester, Sussex, 1980; New York, 1984). London, French, 1981; New York, Dramatists Play Service, 1982.

Night Mail and Other Sketches (produced New York, 1977).

Word of Mouth (revue), with others (produced New York, 1978).

Hooters (produced New York, 1978). New York, Dramatists Play Service, 1978.

Coming Attractions, music by Jack Feldman, lyrics by Feldman and Bruce Sussman (produced New York, 1980). New York, French, 1982.

Silver Linings: Revue Sketches. New York, Dramatists Play Service, 1983.
Little Footsteps (produced New York, 1986; London, 1987). New York, Dramatists Play Service, 1986.

Television Writing: *The Comedy Zone* series, 1984; *Holy Angels*, with others, 1986.

*

Ted Tally comments:

I have sometimes been asked whether my plays share any particular theme. Though they have been diverse both stylistically and in terms of subject matter, I think there are at least two common threads: a fascination with rites of passage, and a concern for the prices one must pay in pursuit of a dream.

* * *

Ted Tally writes in versatile voices. Since 1977 productions of his plays at showcase American theaters (including the Yale Repertory Theater, the O'Neill Theater Center in Waterford, Connecticut, the Mark Taper Forum in Los Angeles, and the audaciously innovative Playwrights Horizons in New York City), in Stockholm, and at the Chichester Festival Theatre have earned him recognition as an important new dramatic talent.

Tally's prodigious promise is revealed stunningly in *Terra Nova*, his most widely produced and justifiably praised work to date. His subject is specific and based in reality: Englishman Robert Scott's doomed 1911–12 race to the Antarctic against the Norwegian Roald Amundsen. But the play's method and implications are mythic and poetic; they free Tally from the confines of a history play and enable him to universalize his literal subject through stylized language, setting, and dramatic structure. Set in the mind of the dying Scott as he records final entries in his diary, *Terra Nova* portrays its hero's hallucinatory evaluation of the sources that have driven him and his unlucky band of men to the Antarctic. The procession of stage images shifts seamlessly, cinematically, within the frozen present, the past, the future—all reflected through the anguished mind of Scott, whose story co-exists as exciting theatrical adventure and as the wellspring for a series of complex moral debates.

Tally dissects the core of heroism even as he concedes the needs of nations to create heroes and the symbiotic needs of special men, sometimes tragic men like Scott, to enact the roles their societies write for them. Related to the play's central, ambivalent issue are the vanishing points between national pride and jingoism, patriotic sacrifice and familial irresponsibility, a shrinking British Empire and a future (toward which the play points) bereft of Old Style Heroes. "The world is changing," Amundsen says in Scott's imagined future. "England, Norway, Europe—The Great War changed everything, you wouldn't know it today [1932]. It's a smaller place, but not a more neighbourly one. A frightened place, a world of shopkeepers and thieves. Where is the heroic gesture in such a world? The man who can keep his bread on the table is a hero. Where on such an earth are men who walk like gods? Dead and gone, with Columbus and Magellan." In his haunted fear of failure and conflicting drive to defy man's ordinary boundaries, Scott resembles Ibsen's Master Builder Solness. Possibly, as Amundsen calls him, "the most dangerous kind of decent man," possibly a true representative of the last breed of genuine hero, possibly a complete sham, Scott is one of the few realized tragic heroes in recent American drama.

In *Coming Attractions* the subject is still celebrity but the mode is wild satire. Amundsen's prediction in *Terra Nova* has come true: no heroes are left. But television and the tabloids, memoir publishers and movie writers, hungry for heroes to feed an insatiable American public, fabricate them out of killers, madmen, and Real People. *Coming Attractions* takes deadly aim at many targets: Miss America contests, television news, talk and variety shows, inept law enforcement, an even more inept judicial system, old time religion, advertising, and—especially—an American society that encourages fleeting fame or infamy to masquerade as authentic accomplishment. To appear on television, even for a moment, is the Promised End. Tally's shift from the poetic voices of *Terra Nova* to the parodies in *Coming Attractions* of show biz vernacular, press agentry, and media hype is dazzling. Outrageous puns (Criminal to Judge: "I demand that you give me the chair!" Judge: "Then where would I sit?"), burlesque routines, movie clichés, and mordantly hilarious situations (the play concludes with the televised musical electrocution of its killer-hero: "Live from Death Row—it's—The Execution of Lonnie Wayne Burke!") combine in a lunatic blend of the Marx Brothers, Artaudian theater of cruelty, Paddy Chayefsky's *Network*, and Sinclair Lewis's *Elmer Gantry*.

Tally's other work reflects his discomfort with stylistic uniformity. *Hooters* is a rites of passage sex comedy. His three film scripts (to date unproduced) also differ from each other in form and content: situation comedy (*Couples Only*); epic (*Empire*, on which Tally worked for a year with director Lindsay Anderson); New York police thriller (*Hush-a-bye*).

Like most serious American playwrights of his generation, Tally deplores the exorbitant costs of Broadway theatre which have resulted in productions "which try more and more desperately to appeal to the widest possible audience . . . [and which] have more and more to do with sensation and effect, less to do with any food for thought." Maintaining that Broadway bears as little resemblance, to the real theatre as Disney World to an actual playground, Tally works primarily with strong regional theatre companies and with Playwrights Horizons in New York City, a company with which he has been associated since his career began and one of the most critically acclaimed off-Broadway groups of the past decade. His most recent play, *Little Footsteps*, comically portrays another in those rites of passage which Tally is so fond of exploring. The teenage courtship rituals of *Hooters* have blossomed into marriage and pregnancy as *Little Footsteps* reveals the mounting terror and gradual maturation of a young couple awaiting the birth of their first child. ("We've got nothing against your religion, Ben; it's you we hate," his mother-in-law casually informs the play's beleaguered hero in a characteristically pungent Tally line.)

"Success is a bitch. Grab her, and have her—but don't stand under her window with a mandolin," says Amundsen, the cynical, pragmatic leveler of Scott's romantic imagination. "Ain't life a bitch?" rationalizes theatrical agent Manny Alter in *Coming Attractions* to the about-to-be electrocuted Lonnie, who pleads for life on the grounds of insanity. In *Terra Nova* heroism comes to an end but genuine myths are born. In *Coming Attractions* travesty is the only legitimate vehicle for a society in which violence and bad taste alone capture the public imagination. Intrinsic to Tally's cinematic eye and discriminating ear are the poet's gift of language and the satirist's inescapable logic.

—Mark W. Estrin

TAVEL, Ronald. American. Born in Brooklyn, New York, 17 May 1941. Educated at Brooklyn College; University of Wyoming, Laramie, B.A., M.A. 1961. Screenwriter, Andy Warhol Films Inc., 1964–66; playwright-in-residence, Play-House of the Ridiculous, New York, 1965–67, Theatre of the Lost Continent, New York, 1971–73, Actors Studio, New York, 1972, Yale University Divinity School, New Haven, Connecticut, 1975, 1977, Williamstown Theatre Festival, Massachusetts, Summer 1977, New Playwrights Theatre, Washington, D.C., 1978–79, Cornell University, Ithaca, New York, 1980–81, Centrum Foundation, Fort Worden State Park, Washington, 1981, and Millay Colony for the Arts, New York, 1986; Lecturer in Foreign Languages, Mahidol University, Thailand, 1981–82; Visiting Professor of Creative Writing, University of Colorado, Boulder, 1986. Since 1984 member of the Education Division, Theater for the New City, New York. Literary adviser, *Scripts* magazine, New York, 1971–72; drama critic, *Stages* magazine, Norwood, New Jersey, 1984; theatre editor, *Brooklyn Literary Review*, 1984–85. Recipient: Obie award, 1969, 1973; American Place Theatre grant, 1970; Creative Artists Public Service grant, 1971, 1973; Rockefeller grant, 1972, 1978; Guggenheim fellowship, 1973; National Endowment for the Arts grant, 1974; New York State Council on the Arts grant, 1975; ZBS Foundation grant, 1976; New York Foundation for the Arts fellowship, 1985; Yaddo fellowship, 1986. Agent: Helen Merrill Ltd., 361 West 17th Street, New York, New York 10011. Address: 780 Carroll Street, Brooklyn, New York 11215; or, 438 West Broadway, Apartment 1, New York, New York 10012, U.S.A.

PUBLICATIONS

Plays

Christina's World, published in *Chicago Review*, Winter-Spring 1963.
The Life of Juanita Castro (produced New York, 1965). Included in *Bigfoot and Other Plays*, 1973.
Shower (produced New York, 1965). Included in *Bigfoot and Other Plays*, 1973.
Tarzan of the Flicks (produced Plainfield, Vermont, 1965). Published in *Blacklist 6* (Maplewood, New Jersey), 1965.
Harlot (scenario), published in *Film Culture* (New York), Spring 1966.
The Life of Lady Godiva (produced New York, 1966). Published in *The New Underground Theatre*, edited by Robert Schroeder, New York, Bantam, 1968.
Indira Gandhi's Daring Device (produced New York, 1966). Included in *Bigfoot and Other Plays*, 1973.
Screen Test (produced New York, 1966).
Vinyl (produced New York, 1967). Published in *Clyde* (New York), vol. 2, no. 2, 1966.
Kitchenette (also director: produced New York, 1967). Included in *Bigfoot and Other Plays*, 1973.
Gorilla Queen (produced New York, 1967). Published in *The Best of Off-Off-Broadway*, edited by Michael T. Smith, New York, Dutton, 1969.
Canticle of the Nightingale (produced Stockholm, 1968).
Cleobis and Bito (oratorio; produced New York, 1968).
Arenas of Lutetia (also director: produced New York, 1968). Published in *Experiments in Prose*, edited by Eugene Wildman, Chicago, Swallow Press, 1969.
Boy on the Straight-Back Chair, music by Orville Stoeber (produced New York, 1969). Included in *Bigfoot and Other Plays*, 1973.
Vinyl Visits an FM Station (produced New York, 1970). Published in *Drama Review* (New York), September 1970.
Bigfoot, music by Jeff Labes (produced New York, 1970). Included in *Bigfoot and Other Plays*, 1973.
Words for Bryan to Sing and Dance (produced New York, 1971).
Arse Long—Life Short (produced New York, 1972).
Secrets of the Citizens Correction Committee (produced New York, 1973). Published in *Scripts 3* (New York), January 1972.
Bigfoot and Other Plays. New York, Winter House, 1973.
Queen of Greece (produced New York, 1973).
The Last Days of British Honduras (produced New York, 1974).
Playbirth (produced New York, 1976).
The Clown's Tail (produced New York, 1977).
Gazelle Boy (produced Waterford, Connecticut, 1977).
The Ovens of Anita Orangejuice: A History of Modern Florida (produced Williamstown, Massachusetts, 1977; New York, 1978).
The Ark of God (produced Washington, D.C., 1978).
The Nutcracker in the Land of Nuts, music by Simeon Westbrooke (produced New York, 1979).
My Foetus Lived on Amboy Street (broadcast 1979; also director: produced New York, 1985).
The Understudy (produced Ithaca, New York, 1981).
Success and Succession (produced New York, 1983).
Notorious Harik Will Kill the Pope (also director: produced New York, 1986).

Screenplays: *Harlot*, 1964; *Phillip's Screen Test*, 1965; *Screen Test*, 1965; *Suicide*, 1965; *The Life of Juanita Castro*, 1965; *Horse*, 1965; *Vinyl*, 1965; *Kitchen*, 1965; *Space*, 1965; *Hedy; or, The 14-Year-Old Girl*, 1966; *Withering Sights*, 1966; *The Chelsea Girls*, 1966; *More Milk Evette*, 1966.

Radio Play: *My Foetus Lived on Amboy Street*, 1979.

Novel

Street of Stairs. New York, Olympia Press, 1968.

*

Manuscript Collections: Mugar Memorial Library, Boston University: Lincoln Center Library of the Performing Arts, New York; University of Wisconsin Center for Theatre Research, Madison.

Critical Studies: "The Pop Scene," in *Tri-Quarterly 6* (Evanston, Illinois), 1966, and "Pop Goes America," in *New Republic* (Washington, D.C.), 9 September 1967, both by Peter Michelson; "Ronald Tavel: Ridiculous Playwright" by Dan Isaac, in *Drama Review* (New York), Spring 1968; "Toward Eroticizing All Thought," in *New York Times*, 5 January 1969, and "Ronald Tavel: Celebration of a Panic Vision," in *Village Voice* (New York), 6 March 1969, both by Gino Rizzo; "A Kid Named Toby" by Jack Kroll, in *Newsweek* (New York),

24 March 1969; *American Playwrights: A Critical Survey* by Bonnie Marranca and Gautam Dasgupta, New York, Drama Book Specialists, 1981.

Theatrical Activities:
Director: **Plays**—*The Life of Juanita Castro*, Chicago, 1967; *Kitchenette*, New York, 1967; *Arenas of Lutetia*, New York, 1968; *Infinity*, New York, 1972; *A Streetcar Named Desire* (in Thai, as *Ourrat*) by Tennessee Williams, Bangkok, 1981; *The Zoo Story* (in Thai) by Edward Albee, Bangkok, 1982; *Clash of the Bra Maidens*, New York, 1984; *My Foetus Lived on Amboy Street*, New York, 1985; *The Tell-Tale Heart*, East Meadow, New York, 1985; *Talent*, East Meadow, New York, 1985; *Notorious Harik Will Kill the Pope*, New York, 1986. **Films**—*Harlot*, 1964; *Phillip's Screen Test*, 1965; *Screen Test*, 1965; *The Life of Juanita Castro*, 1965; *Horse*, 1965; *Vinyl*, 1965; *Space*, 1965; *It Happened in Connecticut*, 1965; *Hedy; or, The 14-Year-Old Girl*, 1966; *Withering Sights*, 1966; *The Chelsea Girls* (*Toby Short* and *Hanoi Hanna* episodes), 1966.
Actor: **Plays**—roles in *In Search of the Cobra Jewels* by Harvey Fierstein, New York, 1972, and in all his directed plays. **Films**—in all his directed films, and in *Fifty Fantasticks*, 1964; *Bitch*, 1965; *Jail*, 1967; *Suicide Notations: Fire Escape*, 1972; *Infinity*, 1974.

Ronald Tavel comments:

(1973) My earliest tales were delivered Homerically. At the age of six or seven I took the first step toward giving them permanent form: comic books. While these comics were shameless imitations of the pictorial styles featured in the funnies we read at that time, there was, I fancy, something more urgent in my stories and characterizations. I wrote my first (verse) play (or fragment of one) in my sophomore year in high school and ten verse plays (or fragments of ones) followed that effort. The last of these have reached print but only one (*Cleobis and Bito*) was ever produced. In 1965, after two years of writing, directing, and acting in films, I turned again to playwriting. These were the one-acters that inaugurated The Theatre of the Ridiculous movement—a term I invented to catch the attention of critics and lower them into a category in order to facilitate their work. The term "Ridiculous" should not be taken too seriously (!) unless you want to re-define that word as Professor Peter Michelson did in his essay on the new American absurdity (*New Republic*, 9 September 1967). I sought in these abstract satires to find a distinctly American language for the stage and that is a continuing preoccupation in my later and mercilessly longer "tragedies." In the early plays I also attempted to destroy plot and character, motivation, cause, event, and logic along with their supposed consequences. The word was All: what was spoken did not express the moment's preoccupation; rather, the preoccupation followed the word. In *The Life of Lady Godiva* I reached, cynically, for the Aristotelian principles of playmaking. While cynicism is the major thrust of *Godiva*, a near decade of concern with *The Poetics* was worming its way, re-evaluated, to the core of my chores. *Gorilla Queen* progresses by building and abolishing, rebuilding and reabolishing, etc., the Aristotelian constructs. The full-length plays after *Gorilla Queen* obey, I believe, without too much objection, the Greek's difficult insights. While I have no single favorite, I am particularly fond of *Shower* because it continues to mystify me, am protective of *Arenas of Lutetia* because no one else will be, and consider *Bigfoot* (if you will allow me to play critic) my most ambitious and best play to date.

(1988) Although my recent fellowships and judging and teaching appointments are apparently for my abstract work in theatre, I have continued to create as many formal pieces: partly because I feel that formal values, following the disappearance of American education, are threatened in serious contemporary theatre; and partly because I believe that our present situation is not more keenly scrutinized by the abstract than the formal. (My previous solution, in larger works, was always to combine the two.)

Because of the growing idiosyncratic nature of serious plays, it has become common in the last decade for American dramatists to direct their own work. Reluctantly, I have joined their ranks. Since directing forces a stronger confrontation with space, time, flesh, clothes, and light than words alone do, and requires no rewards or rejuvenations outside itself, it helps the playwright to that closer understanding of the unity of theatre which he irresponsibly surrendered in the past century and a half.

* * *

Ronald Tavel is one of the originators of the mode Susan Sontag identified as "camp." From the start he writes with an unmistakable voice, relentlessly punning, answering back to his own word-plays, philosophizing, art-conscious, joking, ridiculous as the Marx Brothers, and turning his formidable energy to the service of a passion for justice, with a Cassandra's terror of self-righteousness, a not-to-be-thwarted demand for meaning, self- and God-knowledge.

This thrust is evident even in a pop joke like *The Life of Juanita Castro* which takes its authenticity from *Life* magazine. *Indira Gandhi's Daring Device* drew a swift protest from the government of India, and *How Jacqueline Kennedy Became Queen of Greece* was muted (but in title only) to *Queen of Greece*. These plays are travesty, but Tavel is out for serious game, and has loaded them with real facts and arguments.

Gorilla Queen, his first play on a large scale, is a spoof on jungle movies, unique in its crazy playfulness, rococo, smart-aleck language, outlandishly scrambled sexuality, and self-consciousness about art. From the epilogue (delivered by a gibbon holding a purple rose): ". . . art ain't never 'bout life, but life *is* only 'bout art. Dis rose?—oh, it ain't no symbol like ya mighta thought, an dat's cause it ain't got nothing' to do wit life either. Dis here rose is all 'bout art. Here, take it—(He throws the rose into the audience.)"

In *Bigfoot* the work began to reveal, not just refer to, its depth and power. Here Tavel's subject is brothers, in the image of Jacob and Esau. On a profound level of derangement the one, an intellectual monastic and schoolteacher, suspects the other, a forest ranger, of being not human, confusing him with the Bigfoot, the legendary man-ape of the Pacific Northwest. Set in the majestic forest and the monastery schoolroom, *Bigfoot* is a play of immense complexity. The surface is no longer pop or campy but the post-realist strategies are in flood: a fictional lighting girl gets caught up in the *more real* fiction of the play's far-fetched story; the Playwright's Brother is a character *ex machina*, played in the production Tavel supervised by his own brother—what a thing to do in a play about mythic fratricide!

The Ovens of Anita Orangejuice is a boisterous, savage satire about Anita Bryant's 1977 campaign against gay rights. Subtitled "A History of Modern Florida," it is a wisecrack that turns into a nightmare. For all its frenzied hilarity, it makes a thought-provoking, emotionally compelling case. In *Gazelle Boy* a middle-aged missionary in the north woods loses her head over a wild boy, which leads to tragedy of profoundly unsettling dimensions. It is a beautiful play, dense with religion. Here sex is a reaching for the divine. *The Understudy* is about sex murder: the play's playwright may have done the killings he has written about, which the audience is ultimately shown in literal gore; a demented understudy tries to save him, and steal the writer's being, by recommitting them himself.

My Foetus Lived on Amboy Street takes a far more tender tone. The play appears to be, of all things, a prenatal autobiography. The writer experiments here with an expressionistically abstracted, outwardly geometrical stagecraft. The persona of the play's ego images himself as a spider, while the company of players patch in the various roles as freely as the author counterposes multiple vernaculars of lyricism and melodrama. *Notorious Harik Will Kill the Pope*, which Tavel himself staged at the Theatre for the New City in New York in 1986, crammed the stage with movie types (Turhan Bey and Lana Turner are among the characters) in a flashy complexity of scenes. The frivolity of its trashy satirical style—Tavel never resists a pun—masks a sustained demolition of the religious establishment which, like all his themes, the writer gives every sign of meaning.

—Michael T. Smith

TERRY, Megan. American. Born Marguerite Duffy in Seattle, Washington, 22 July 1932. Educated at Banff School of Fine Arts, Alberta, summers 1950–53, 1956; University of Washington, Seattle, 1950, 1953–56, B.Ed. 1956; University of Alberta, Edmonton, 1951–53. Drama teacher and director of the Cornish Players, Cornish School of Allied Arts, Seattle, 1954–56; founding member, 1963, and director of the playwrights workshop, 1963–68, Open Theatre, New York; writer-in-residence, Yale University School of Drama, New Haven, Connecticut, 1966–67; founding member, Women's Theatre Council, 1971; founding member and treasurer, New York Theatre Strategy, 1971; Bingham Professor of Humanities, University of Louisville, 1981; Hill Professor of Fine Arts, University of Minnesota, Duluth, 1983. Since 1971 resident playwright and literary manager, Omaha Magic Theatre. Recipient: Stanley award, 1965; Office of Advanced Drama Research award, 1965; ABC-Yale University fellowship, 1966; Rockefeller grant, 1968, 1987; Obie award, 1970; National Endowment for the Arts grant, 1972; Earplay award, 1972; Creative Artists Public Service grant, 1973; Guggenheim fellowship, 1978; Dramatists Guild award, 1983. Agent: Elisabeth Marton, 96 Fifth Avenue, New York, New York 10011. Address: 2309 Hanscom Boulevard, Omaha, Nebraska 61805; or, c/o Omaha Magic Theatre, 1417 Farnam Street, Omaha, Nebraska 68102, U.S.A.

PUBLICATIONS

Plays

Beach Grass (also director: produced Seattle, 1955).
Seascape (also director: produced Seattle, 1955).
Go Out and Move the Car (also director: produced Seattle, 1955).
New York Comedy: Two (produced Saratoga, New York, 1961).
Ex-Miss Copper Queen on a Set of Pills (produced New York, 1963; Edinburgh, 1987). With *The People vs. Ranchman*, New York, Dramatists Play Service, 1968.
When My Girlhood Was Still All Flowers (produced New York, 1963).
Eat at Joe's (produced New York, 1964).
Calm Down Mother (produced New York, 1965; London, 1969). Indianapolis, Bobbs Merrill, 1966.
Keep Tightly Closed in a Cool Dry Place (produced New York, 1965; London, 1968). Included in *Four Plays*, 1967.
The Magic Realists (produced New York, 1966). Included in *Three One-Act Plays*, 1972.
Comings and Goings (produced New York, 1966; Edinburgh, 1968). Included in *Four Plays*, 1967.
The Gloaming, Oh My Darling (produced Minneapolis, 1966). Included in *Four Plays*, 1967.
Viet Rock: A Folk War Movie (also director: produced New York, 1966; London, 1977). Included in *Four Plays*, 1967.
Four Plays. New York, Simon and Schuster, 1967.
The Key Is on the Bottom (produced Los Angeles, 1967).
The People vs. Ranchman (produced Minneapolis, 1967; New York, 1968). With *Ex-Miss Copper Queen on a Set of Pills*, New York, Dramatists Play Service, 1968.
Home; or, Future Soap (televised 1968; revised version, as *Future Soap*, produced Omaha, 1987). New York, French, 1972.
Jack-Jack (produced Minneapolis, 1968).
Massachusetts Trust (produced Waltham, Massachusetts, 1968). Published in *The Off-Off-Broadway Book*, edited by Albert Poland and Bruce Mailman, Indianapolis, Bobbs Merrill, 1972.
Changes, with Tom O'Horgan (produced New York, 1968).
Sanibel and Captiva (broadcast 1968). Included in *Three One-Act Plays*, 1972.
One More Little Drinkie (televised 1969). Included in *Three One-Act Plays*, 1972.
Approaching Simone (produced Boston and New York, 1970). Old Westbury, New York, Feminist Press, 1973.
The Tommy Allen Show (also director: produced Los Angeles and New York, 1970). Published in *Scripts 2* (New York), December 1971.
Grooving (produced New York, 1972).
Choose a Spot on the Floor, with Jo Ann Schmidman (produced Omaha, 1972).
Three One-Act Plays. New York, French, 1972.
Couplings and Groupings (monologues and sketches). New York, Pantheon, 1973.
Susan Peretz at the Manhattan Theatre Club (produced New York, 1973).
Thoughts (lyrics only), book by Lamar Alford (produced New York, 1973).
Nightwalk, with Sam Shepard and Jean-Claude van Itallie (produced New York and London, 1973). Published in *Open Theater*, New York, Drama Book Specialists, 1975.
St. Hydro Clemency; or, A Funhouse of the Lord: An Energizing Event (produced New York, 1973).
The Pioneer, and Pro-Game (produced Omaha, 1973; New York, 1974). Holly Springs, Mississippi, Ragnarok Press, 1975.
Hothouse (produced New York, 1974). New York, French, 1975.
Babes in the Bighouse (produced Omaha, 1974; New York, 1976). Omaha, Magic Theatre, 1979.
All Them Women, with others (produced New York, 1974).
We Can Feed Everybody Here (produced New York, 1974).
Hospital Play. Omaha, Magic Theatre, 1974.
Henna for Endurance. Omaha, Magic Theatre, 1974.
The Narco Linguini Bust (produced Omaha, 1974).
100,001 Horror Stories of the Plains, with others (produced

Omaha, 1976). Omaha, Magic Theatre, 1979.
Sleazing Towards Athens. Omaha, Magic Theatre, 1977; revised version (produced Omaha, 1986), 1986.
Willie-Willa-Bill's Dope Garden. Birmingham, Alabama, Ragnarok Press, 1977.
Brazil Fado (produced Omaha, 1977). Omaha, Magic Theatre, 1977; revised version (produced Santa Fe, 1978), 1979.
Lady Rose's Brazil Hide Out (produced Omaha, 1977).
American King's English for Queens (produced Omaha, 1978). Omaha, Magic Theatre, 1978.
Goona Goona (produced Omaha, 1979). Omaha, Magic Theatre, 1985.
Attempted Rescue on Avenue B: A Beat Fifties Comic Opera (produced Chicago, 1979). Omaha, Magic Theatre, 1979.
Fireworks, in *Holidays* (produced Louisville, 1979).
Running Gag (lyrics only), book by Jo Ann Schmidman (produced Omaha, 1979). Omaha, Magic Theatre, 1981.
Objective Love I (produced Omaha, 1980). Omaha, Magic Theatre, 1985.
Scenes from Maps (produced Omaha, 1980). Omaha, University of Nebraska, 1980.
Advances (produced Omaha, 1980). Omaha, Magic Theatre, 1980.
Flat in Afghanistan (produced Omaha, 1981). Omaha, Magic Theatre, 1981.
Objective Love II (produced Omaha, 1981). Omaha, Magic Theatre, 1985.
The Trees Blew Down (produced Los Angeles, 1981). Omaha, Magic Theatre, 1981.
Winners (produced Santa Barbara, California, 1981).
Kegger (produced Omaha, 1982).
Fifteen Million Fifteen-Year-Olds (produced Omaha, 1983). Omaha, Magic Theatre, 1983.
Mollie Bailey's Traveling Family Circus, Featuring Scenes from the Life of Mother Jones, music by Jo Anne Metcalf. New York, Broadway Play Publishing, 1983.
X-rayed-iate (produced Omaha, 1984).
Katmandu, published in *Open Spaces* (Columbia, Missouri), 1985.
Family Talk (produced Omaha, 1986).
Sea of Forms (collaborative work), text and lyrics with Jo Ann Schmidman (produced Omaha, 1986). Omaha, Magic Theatre, 1987.
Walking Through Walls (collaborative work), text and lyrics with Jo Ann Schmidman (produced Omaha, 1987). Omaha, Magic Theatre, 1987.
Dinner's in the Blender (produced Omaha, 1987). Omaha, Magic Theatre, 1987.
Retro (produced Omaha, 1988).
Amtrak (produced Omaha, 1988).
Head Light (produced Little Rock, Arkansas, 1988).

Radio Plays: *Sanibel and Captiva*, 1968; *American Wedding Ritual Monitored/Transmitted by the Planet Jupiter*, 1972.

Television Plays: *The Dirt Boat*, 1955; *Home; or, Future Soap*, 1968; *One More Little Drinkie*, 1969.

*

Manuscript Collections: Kent State University, Kent, Ohio; Hope College, Holland, Michigan; Lincoln Center Library of the Performing Arts, New York; Omaha Public Library.

Critical Studies: "Who Says Only Words Make Great Drama?" by Terry, in *New York Times*, 10 November 1968; "Megan Terry: Mother of American Feminist Theatre," in *Feminist Theatre* by Helene Keyssar, London, Macmillan, 1984, New York, Grove Press, 1985; "(Theoretically) Approaching Megan Terry" by Elin Diamond, in *Art and Cinema 3* (New York), 1987.

Theatrical Activities:
Director: **Plays**—with the Cornish Players, Seattle: *Beach Grass, Seascape*, and *Go Out and Move the Car*, 1955; with the Open Theatre's Playwrights Workshop, New York, 1962–68; *Viet Rock*, New York, 1966; *The Tommy Allen Show*, Los Angeles, 1970; and other plays. **Television**—*The Dirt Book*, 1955.
Actress (as Maggie Duffy): **Plays**—Hermia in *A Midsummer's Night Dream*, title role in *Peter Pan* by J.M. Barrie, Kate in *Taming of the Shrew*, and other roles, Banff School of Fine Arts, Alberta, 1950–53.

Megan Terry comments:

I design my plays to provoke laughter—thought may follow.

* * *

Megan Terry spent the 1960's in the limelight. Doyenne of New York's avant garde, she was a founder member of the Open Theatre, with Sam Shepard and Joseph Chaikin among others. One play, *Viet Rock*, caused the FBI to put her under surveillance. All this is relevant information because Terry's plays were shaped by and responsive to the social unrest of that decade. Discussion of content without context would be meaningless, for it was specifically Terry's experience as a woman in a patriarchal society which provoked her experiments with dramatic technique. The well-made play, with star role and supporting players, was constraining. Rigid structures could only represent rigid world views. Theatre had to be reclaimed: a new form for messages of subversion and liberation.

Cartoon characters, radio impersonators, early 1960's improvisational comedy, children at play—Terry delighted in all of these and noticed that the common feature was rapid role transformation, where one player assumes a series of different identities. Later, the Open Theatre was based on daily workshops for company members using transformation exercises (originally developed by Victoria Spolin). Throughout her early plays Terry appropriates and refines transformational techniques. This resolute anti-naturalism, where the world is seen to be created and then altered in front of the audience, has subsequently become a central convention of American feminist theatre. In retrospect, Terry can be seen as a pioneer of a feminist aesthetic.

The significance of these ideas is exemplified by the play *Comings and Goings*. The play is a circling, permutating duologue. Sometimes a recognisable situation is presented—a couple in bed, a waitress and customer. Sometimes the action is obtuse or surreal. Some scenes are written to be repeated a number of times, often with performers reversing roles. Radically different interpretations of the same situation are juxtaposed. Situations and relationships may change violently or languorously, but in either case the action is galvanised by these transformations, not by linear progression.

In *Comings and Goings* the components of theatre—ritual, role play, improvisation—are taken as mimetic of the roles and power relations defining men and women. The capacity and the need for change are indicated by the transformations. Yet *Comings and Goings* is not written for a mere pair. Terry suggests a company comprising at least six people. As the dialogue comes and goes, so do the players (various strategies are offered for effecting these substitutions). Any actor must be able to play any role at any point. The concept of character is denied and the emphasis is placed on the representative action.

The use of ensemble also moves theatre from hierarchical relationships towards a more collective approach. The very act of performing *Comings and Goings*, where the variables make all the performers mutually dependent and supportive, becomes a critique of the power relations it depicts. Theme and form are inseparable. To quote another 1960's luminary: the medium is the message.

Transformational devices and the use of an ensemble are crucial to the structure and effect of Terry's plays. In *Approaching Simone*—for once, Terry takes the experience of an individual (Simone Weil) as her theme—biographical drama is reinvented. At certain points, the ensemble becomes aspects of Simone's self-doubt, pain, and anguish. By embodying these emotions, Simone's inner torment is made actual. Ultimately, the ensemble cannot divest Simone of her pain and she is left alone, starving, as the light diminishes, then dies.

Simone Weil withdrew from political engagement to seek spiritual salvation. It is tempting to draw parallels with Terry's withdrawal from the careerist structure and male domination of mainstream theatre. To think of Terry as sliding into obscurity is to fall into the trap of equating visibility with success or creativity. The absence of prestige off-Broadway productions, attendant reviews, and subsequent publication have rendered Terry's later plays somewhat inaccessible. But out of the limelight, Terry thrives. She was a founder member of the Women's Theatre Council. Since 1970 she has been involved with Omaha Magic Theatre, a community, primarily of women, working experimentally.

While Terry now eschews the overt political analysis of *Viet Rock* or the epic scale of *Approaching Simone*, she continues to explore a variety of themes. *Babes in the Bighouse* concerns women in prison. *American King's English for Queens* examines the sexist nature of language. More recent plays such as *Running Gag* (about jogging) and *Kegger* (adolescent drinking) suggest that Terry is responding to issues that affect her neighbourhood. Megan Terry is alive and well and living in Omaha, Nebraska.

—Joss Bennathan

TERSON, Peter. Pseudonym for Peter Patterson. British. Born in Newcastle upon Tyne, Northumberland, 24 February 1932. Educated at Heaton Grammar School; Newcastle upon Tyne Technical College; Redland Training College, Bristol, 1952–54. Served in the Royal Air Force, 1950–52. Married Sheila Bailey in 1955; two sons and one daughter. Draughtsman, 1948–50; games teacher, 1953–65. Resident writer, Victoria Theatre, Stoke-on-Trent, Staffordshire, 1966–67; associated with the National Youth Theatre. Recipient: Arts Council bursary, 1966; John Whiting Award, 1968; Writers Guild award, 1971. Agent: Harvey Unna and Stephen Durbridge Ltd., 24–32 Pottery Lane, London W11 4LZ, England.

PUBLICATIONS

Plays

A Night to Make the Angels Weep (produced Stoke-on-Trent, 1964; London, 1971). Published in *New English Dramatists 11*, London, Penguin, 1967.

The Mighty Reservoy (produced Stoke-on-Trent, 1964; London, 1967). Published in *New English Dramatists 14*, London, Penguin, 1970.

The Rat Run (produced Stoke-on-Trent, 1965).

All Honour Mr. Todd (produced Stoke-on-Trent, 1966).

I'm in Charge of These Ruins (produced Stoke-on-Trent, 1966).

Sing an Arful Story, with others (produced Stoke-on-Trent, 1966).

Jock-on-the-Go, adaptation of the story "Jock-at-a-Venture" by Arnold Bennett (produced Stoke-on-Trent, 1966).

Holder Dying (extracts produced Stoke-on-Trent, 1966).

Mooney and His Caravans (televised 1966; produced London, 1968). With *Zigger Zagger*, London, Penguin, 1970.

Zigger Zagger (produced London, 1967). With *Mooney and His Caravans*, London, Penguin, 1970.

Clayhanger, with Joyce Cheeseman, adaptation of the novel by Arnold Bennett (produced Stoke-on-Trent, 1967).

The Ballad of the Artificial Mash (produced Stoke-on-Trent, 1967).

The Apprentices (produced London, 1968). London, Penguin, 1970.

The Adventures of Gervase Beckett; or, The Man Who Changed Places (produced Stoke-on-Trent, 1969). Edited by Peter Cheeseman, London, Eyre Methuen, 1973.

Fuzz (produced London, 1969).

Inside-Outside (produced Nottingham, 1970).

The Affair at Bennett's Hill, (Worcs.) (produced Stoke-on-Trent, 1970).

Spring-Heeled Jack (produced London, 1970). Published in *Plays and Players* (London), November 1970.

The 1861 Whitby Lifeboat Disaster (produced Stoke-on-Trent, 1970; London, 1971). Todmorden, Yorkshire, Woodhouse, 1979.

The Samaritan, with Mike Butler (produced Stoke-on-Trent and London, 1971). Published in *Plays and Players* (London), July 1971.

Cadium Firty (produced London, 1971).

Good Lads at Heart (produced London, 1971; New York, 1979).

Slip Road Wedding (produced Newcastle upon Tyne and London, 1971).

Prisoners of the War (produced Newcastle upon Tyne, 1971; London, 1983).

But Fred, Freud Is Dead (produced Stoke-on-Trent, 1972). Published in *Plays and Players* (London), March 1972.

Moby Dick adaptation of the novel by Melville (produced Stoke-on-Trent, 1972).

The Most Cheerful Man (produced Stoke-on-Trent, 1973).

Geordie's March (produced London, 1973).

The Trip to Florence (produced London, 1974).

Lost Yer Tongue? (produced Newcastle upon Tyne, 1974).

Vince Lays the Carpet, and Fred Erects the Tent (produced Stoke-on-Trent, 1975).

The Ballad of Ben Bagot (televised 1977). Published in *Prompt 2*, edited by Alan Durband, London, Hutchinson, 1976.

Love Us and Leave Us, with Paul Joyce (produced London, 1976).

The Bread and Butter Trade (produced London, 1976; revised version produced London, 1982).

Twilight Joker (produced Brighton, 1977; London, 1978).

Pinvin Careless and His Lines of Force (produced Stoke-on-Trent, 1977).

Family Ties: Wrong First Time; Never Right, Yet Again (produced London, 1977). Published in *Act 2*, edited by David Self and Ray Speakman, London, Hutchinson, 1979.
Forest Lodge (produced Salisbury, 1977).
Tolly of the Black Boy (produced Edinburgh, 1977).
Rattling the Railings (produced London, 1978). London, French, 1979.
The Banger (produced Nottingham, 1978).
Cul de Sac (produced Chichester, 1978; London, 1979).
England, My Own (produced London, 1978).
Soldier Boy (produced London, 1978).
VE Night (produced Chichester, 1979).
The Limes, and I Kid You Not (produced London, 1979).
The Pied Piper, adaptation of the poem by Robert Browning, music by Jeff Parton (produced Stoke-on-Trent, 1980). London, French, 1982.
The Ticket (produced London, 1980).
The Night John (produced London, 1980).
We Were All Heroes (produced Andover, Hampshire, 1981).
Aesop's Fables, music by Jeff Parton (produced Stoke-on-Trent, 1983). London, French, 1986.
Strippers (produced Newcastle upon Tyne, 1984; London, 1985). Oxford, Amber Lane Press, 1985.
Hotel Dorado (produced Newcastle upon Tyne, 1985).

Radio Plays: *The Fishing Party*, 1971; *Play Soft, Then Attack*, 1978; *The First Flame*, 1980; *The Rundle Gibbet*, 1981; *The Overnight Man*, 1982; *The Romany Trip* (documentary), 1983; *The Top Sail at Imberley*, 1983; *Madam Main Course*, 1983; *Poole Harbour*, 1984; *Letters to the Otter*, 1985; *When Youth and Pleasure Meet*, 1986.

Television Plays: *Mooney and His Caravans*, 1966; *The Heroism of Thomas Chadwick*, 1967; *The Last Train Through the Harecastle Tunnel*, 1969; *The Gregorian Chant*, 1972; *The Dividing Fence*, 1972; *Shakespeare—or Bust*, 1973; *Three for the Fancy*, 1973; *Dancing in the Dark*, 1974; *The Rough and the Smooth*, 1975; *The Jolly Swagman*, with Paul Joyce (*Crown Court* series), 1976; *The Ballad of Ben Bagot*, 1977; *The Reluctant Chosen*, 1979; *Put Out to Grass*, 1979; *Atlantis*, 1983; *Salvation Army* series.

* * *

Peter Terson has been called a "primitive," a term which (in its complimentary sense) is intended to mean that his technique is artless, his observation fresh and original, and his naturally prolific talent untainted by too much sophistication. This somewhat backhanded tribute, however, belittles his ability. Few dramatists have the sheer skill to write successfully for both the small "in the round" theatre company at the Victoria, Stoke-on-Trent, and the large casts of the British National Youth Theatre, whose London productions take place in conventional proscenium arch theatres. Nor is Terson unknowledgeable about recent trends in the theatre. He insisted, for example, that Harry Philton in *Zigger Zagger*, the boy who escapes from the mindless enthusiams of a football crowd to learn a trade, should not "mature or have a *Roots*-like vision of himself"—thus pushing aside one cliché of contemporary naturalistic drama. One under-rated aspect of Terson's style is the way in which he either avoids an idea which has become too fashionable or twists it to his own ends. In *The Mighty Reservoy* he plays with the Lawrentian theme of the dark, elemental forces of nature and makes it seem both credible as a psychological obsession and (through this haunting power over the mind) a force indeed to be feared. Terson is, however, ruthless with the pretentiousness of middle-class theatre: on receiving a Promising Playwright's Award from Lord Goodman, he enquired whether Green Shield stamps went with it. This latent cheekiness is also part of his plays. Although he rarely ventures into the class polemic of some of Alan Plater's documentaries, he usually caricatures people in authority: magistrates and social workers (in *Zigger Zagger*), scientists and business tycoons (in *The Ballad of the Artificial Mash*) and the paternalistic firm (in *The Apprentices*). He chooses working-class rather them middle-class themes and environments, and writes with particular passion about his own childhood in Newcastle upon Tyne, the poverty and unemployment of the 1930's. This refusal to accept the normal attitudes of the West End, his strong regional loyalties, may help to account for his reputation as a "primitive": but for this very reason the term is misleading. He doesn't write popular West End comedies because he doesn't choose to do so; he doesn't write about middle-class families in the grip of emotional dilemmas because the problems which he tackles seem to him more important. He is a highly skilled writer with a particular insight into Northern working-class societies and whose plays have, at best, a richness of imagination and an infectious humour.

Terson's first plays were produced at the Victoria Theatre, Stoke-on-Trent, a pioneering Midlands company directed by Peter Cheeseman whose work concentrates on "in the round" productions, plays with local associations and documentary plays. Terson caught immediately the company style and became their resident playwright in 1966. His first plays, *A Night to Make the Angels Weep* and *The Mighty Reservoy*, were naturalistic comedies, but with strong underlying themes, *The Mighty Reservoy* is set in the Cotswolds, on a large reservoir built on a hill, which is guarded by Dron. The reservoir is presented as a passionate force of water, which might at any time swamp the surrounding villages. Dron has an affectionate pride towards it: and he introduces his friend Church to its mysteries, among them that the water demands one human sacrifice before it will be satisfied. Church eventually becomes this sacrifice. But the dialogue between the two men ranges from intimate, slightly drunken chat about their dissatisfactions about life to a passionate yearning for union with nature. *Mooney and His Caravans*, another two-person play written for the Victoria Theatre, represents a different type of "drowning": a couple on a caravan site are gradually driven away from their home by the aggressive commercialism of Mooney, whom they admire and who owns the site. With these small cast, tightly knit naturalistic plays, Terson also wrote several looser, more flexible and easy-going works, such as *Jock-on-the-Go*, a picaresque tale about a lad on the make in 19th-century Yorkshire, and *The Ballad of the Artificial Mash*, a horror story about the effect of hormone poultry foods on a salesman, one of the first and most effective plays about environmental pollution. Both these plays were in the style of the Stoke documentaries: short scenes, mainly satirical, brought together by songs and dances written and performed by the company. Although Terson left the Victoria Theatre in 1967, the influence of its informal atmosphere, the economy of means and the easiness of story-telling (using a narrator and props to indicate change of locale) remained with Terson as a formative inspiration. He has since written other plays for the company, including *But Fred, Freud Is Dead*, an amusing Northern comedy.

In 1966, Michael Croft, the director of the National Youth Theatre, invited Terson to write a play for his largely amateur group of schoolchlidren and young adults. Terson's first play for the company, *Zigger Zagger*, was enormously successful, although its story seems flimsy and episodic. Harry Philton leaves school without distinction, and drifts from one job to another, from his unhappy home to his well-intentioned brother-in-law, sustained at first by his love of football. Eventually, however, this craze for football leaves him and he settles down to a proper trade apprenticeship. Terson sets this story against a background of a (pre-hooligan) football terrace, with fans whose songs and attitudes comment on the main events of the story. The exuberance of the production, the nostalgia and fervour of the football crowds provide an unforgettable image of surging humanity, charged with a youthful energy which only heightened the sad frustrations of Harry's career. *The Apprentices* tackled a somewhat similar theme, but more naturalistically. Bagley, a young tearaway, works reluctantly in a local factory—playing football whenever he has the opportunity. He deliberately scorns all opportunities for promotion, determined to leave the town and his job as soon as he can: but he is trapped into an unwise marriage and at the end of the play he is resigned to a dull frustrating future. *Spring-Heeled Jack* and *Good Lads at Heart*, two other plays written for the National Youth Theatre, explore the frustrations of the misfits in an impoverished society.

Although Terson's plays have a much greater variety and range than is often supposed, he usually limits himself to social surroundings with which he is familiar: and perhaps the least satisfactory part of this limitation is that he shares some stock reactions, say, about the awfulness of progress and the craftsmanship of the past which are expressed rather too often in his plays. He also fails to pare down his documentary plays to the dramatic essentials. But his influence in British regional theatre has been considerable, and more than any other contemporary dramatist he carries forward the ideas of social drama pioneered by Joan Littlewood.

—John Elsom

TESICH, Steve. American. Born Stoyan Tesich in Titovo Uzice, Yugoslavia, 29 September 1943; emigrated to the United States, 1957; became citizen, 1961. Educated at Indiana University, Bloomington, B.A. 1965 (Phi Beta Kappa); Columbia University, New York, M.A. in Russian 1967, and further graduate study. Married Rebecca Fletcher in 1971. Caseworker, Brooklyn Department of Welfare, late 1960's. Recipient: Rockefeller grant, 1972; New York Film Critics award, Writers Guild award, and Oscar, all for screenplay, 1979. Agent: International Creative Management, 40 West 57th Street, New York, New York 10019, U.S.A.

PUBLICATIONS

Plays

The Carpenters (produced New York, 1970). New York, Dramatists Play Service, 1971; London, Davis Poynter, 1976.
Lake of the Woods (produced New York, 1971). Included in *Division Street and Other Plays*, 1981.
Baba Goya (produced New York, 1973). Included in *Division Street and Other Plays*, 1981; as *Nourish the Beast* (produced New York, 1973), New York, French, 1974.
Gorky, music by Mel Marvin (produced New York, 1975). New York, French, 1976.
Passing Game (produced New York, 1977). New York, French, 1978.
Touching Bottom (*The Road, A Life, Baptismal*) (produced New York, 1978). New York, French, 1980.
Division Street (produced Los Angeles and New York, 1980; revised version produced New York, 1987). Included in *Division Street and Other Plays*, 1981.
Division Street and Other Plays (includes *Baba Goya*, *Lake of the Woods*, *Passing Game*). New York, Performing Arts Journal Publications, 1981.

Screenplays: *Breaking Away*, 1979; *Eyewitness* (*The Janitor*), 1981; *Four Friends* (*Georgia's Friends*), 1981; *The World According to Garp*, 1982; *Eleni*, 1986.

Novel

Summer Crossing. New York, Random House, 1982; London, Chatto and Windus, 1983.

* * *

Although Steve Tesich is best known as the screenwriter of *Breaking Away*, *Four Friends*, and *Eleni*, he is a talented playwright. *Division Street*, which concerns the protest movement of the 1960's, was not successful, but his earlier plays, presented at the American Place Theatre, are uncommonly interesting. They share the concerns and some of the technical characteristics of his films and belong to the same creative world. Like many immigrants to America—he arrived from Yugoslavia at 14—he brings to his perceptions a revitalized interest in the promise and sometimes disappointing reality of the American dream. The family or extended family of friends and acquaintances become a social group with symbolic import, and failure, loneliness, and breaking away become an underlying lament and response. As the plays develop, the small details of average experience coalesce into revealing events, and this latter characteristic indicates his dramatic method. By the casual accumulation of at first seemingly unrelated, even confusing, details about the lives and surroundings of rather ordinary people, the characters and their interrelationships become gradually absorbing; a unique, intriguing dramatic pattern emerges; and the mundane becomes extraordinary. This method, augmented by a modern cinematic freedom in the use of setting, he has ascribed to the influence of Chekhov, an influence he shares with Lanford Wilson.

In *The Carpenters* the father, rather like an up-dated Master Builder, cannot provide a suitable setting for domestic life. The house is sinking, flooding, falling in, and his wife and children cannot define for themselves viable family and symbolic identities. *Nourish the Beast*, set "in a large room of an older home," almost the comic reversal of *The Carpenters*, is also a "family" play, now with a matriarch at its head and reverberating with wonderfully funny echoes of such earlier American plays as *You Can't Take It With You*, *Touching Bottom*, consisting of three related one-act plays, is stark, minimal, almost Beckett-like in its analysis of the American scene. In *Passing Game*, its title referring in part to basketball and in part to a pattern of human relationships, three couples work out their destinies at an upstate New York resort with a polluted lake, an almost surreal basketball court, and the vivid aura of past deaths. The play ends with the sudden reality of present death, and the last line, spoken by one of the survivors, summarizes the play's sense of solitude and lonely survival: "There is a way out of this pattern and I must find it on my own."

The ease with which Tesich and a few other recent dramatists move from play to film represents an important development.

It reverses the rather disastrous experiences of a long list of earlier playwrights and novelists whose initial success in theater and fiction was often undermined by an inability to transfer their uniqueness for stage or page to film. The ambidextrous Tesich is clearly, in the increasingly mixed media world of American dramatic writing, an especially important figure in its present and future.

—Gaynor F. Bradish

THOMPSON, Mervyn (Garfield). New Zealander. Born in Kaitangata, 14 June 1936. Educated at schools to age 15; University of Canterbury, Christchurch, 1960–64, M.A. Divorced; one son. Schooteacher, 1964–65; lecturer, University of Canterbury, Christchurch, 1966–71; co-director, Court Theatre, Christchurch, 1971–74; artistic director, Downstage Theatre, Wellington, 1975–76; Senior Lecturer in Drama, University of Auckland, 1977–87. Director of New Zealand Playwrights workshops, 1980 and 1982; advisory associate director, Mercury Theatre, Auckland, 1981–82. Recipient: Margaret Condliffe Memorial Prize, 1976. Agent: Playmarket, P.O. Box 9767, Wellington. Address: 27 Curran Street, Herne Bay, Auckland, New Zealand.

PUBLICATIONS

Plays

O! Temperance! (produced Christchurch, 1972). Christchurch, Christchurch Theatre Trust, 1974.
First Return (produced Christchurch, 1974). Christchurch, Christchurch Theatre Trust, 1974.
Songs to Uncle Scrim, music by Stephen McCurdy (produced Rotorua, 1976; Edinburgh and London, 1979). Wellington, Playmarket, 1983.
A Night at the Races, with Yvonne Blennerhassett Edwards, music by Andrew Glover (produced Auckland, 1977). Wellington, Playmarket, 1981.
New Zealand Childhood (produced 1979).
Songs to the Judges, music by William Dart (produced Auckland, 1980). Wellington, Playmarket, 1983.
Poems for a New Zealand Theatre (produced Auckland, 1981).
The Rise and Fall of King Dimplecheek (produced 1981).
The Great New Zealand Truth Show (produced Auckland, 1982).
Coaltown Blues (produced Auckland, 1984). Wellington, Victoria University Press, 1986.
Selected Plays (includes *First Return*, *O! Temperance!*, *Songs to Uncle Scrim*, *Songs to the Judges*). Dunedin, Pilgrims South Press, 1984.

Other

All My Lives (autobiography). Christchurch, Whitcoulls, 1980.

*

Critical Studies: *New Zealand Drama* by Howard McNaughton, Boston, Twayne, 1981; "Politics and Theatre" by Bruce Jesson, in *Metro Magazine* (Auckland), August 1984; introduction by Sebastian Black to *Selected Plays*, 1984.

Theatrical Activities:
Director: **Plays**—most of his own plays; Court Theatre, Christchurch: *King Lear*, *Mother Courage* by Brecht, *Old Times* by Harold Pinter, *Ghosts* and *Peer Gynt* by Ibsen, and *Awatea* by Bruce Mason, 1969–73; Downstage Theatre, Wellington: *Equus* by Peter Shaffer, 1976, *Three Sisters* by Chekhov, 1977, *Marat/Sade* by Peter Weiss; Mercury Theatre, Auckland: *Comedians* by Trevor Griffiths, 1978, and *Tomorrow Will Be a Lovely Day* by Craig Harrison, 1980; *Foreskin's Lament* by Greg McGee, Auckland, 1980; *Objection Overruled* by Carolyn Burns; *Squatter* by Stuart Hoar; and many other productions.
Actor: **Plays**—Deeley in *Old Times* by Harold Pinter, Christchurch, 1972; Simon in *First Return*, Christchurch, 1974; Singer in *Songs to Uncle Scrim*, Wellington, 1976, and New Zealand tour; Judge in *Songs to the Judges*, Auckland, 1980–81, and New Zealand tour; solo performer in *Poems for a New Zealand Theatre*, Auckland, 1981; solo performer in *Coaltown Blues*, Auckland, 1984–87, and New Zealand tour; title role in *Sweeney Todd* by Hugh Wheeler and Stephen Sondheim, Christchurch, 1986.

Mervyn Thompson comments:

Generally I see myself as a working-class playwright whose work interests itself in the fate of the underdogs and the "losers" of New Zealand society (i.e., those who don't get to write the history books). My work often appeals to people who are not habitual theatregoers. *A Night at the Races* drew the racing fraternity (there was much audience participation, including the chance to have a flutter); *Songs to the Judges* brought in a large Maori audience; *Coaltown Blues* appealed to coalminers; and *The Great New Zealand Truth Show* to the readers of *Truth*.

The thrust of my plays is political, in the sense that my "losers" have grounds for complaint against the society that has rejected them. There is also a strong socialist tendency, along with elements of feminism and anti-racism. I am generally considered to be a "nationalist" playwright whose work opposes the various forces of cultural imperialism that have bedevilled this country for 150 years.

Hardly any of my plays are concerned with "naturalistic" prescriptions. Instead they are unashamedly theatrical, often involving direct contact with their audiences. Their movement is filmic, with quick cutting and sharp juxtapositions of scene and atmosphere. There are also expressionistic and surrealistic elements, although the chief concern of all the plays is to entertain and provoke. Though a darker mood has begun to enter, much of my work is celebratory. New Zealand, we are only now discovering, has a history worth recording. I present that history from the "underside," the point of view of those generally excluded from the national text. Consequently the plays contain a great deal of information, it being my belief that Brecht was absolutely right when he spoke of learning as being a *pleasurable* activity. In this quest for learning and pleasure, songs and music are important elements. Two of my plays consist entirely of songs: I call them "Songplays."

Increasingly my later work has as its main theme the collision between the outer, "political" scene and the inner, private world. In the sense that nothing seems as clear-cut to me as it did a decade ago, the more recent plays embrace a greater complexity of human behaviour and response.

* * *

By the end of Mervyn Thompson's semi-autobiographical play *First Return* the central character has discovered who he is by exorcising both his private ghosts and the spectre of England, which has dominated so much of New Zealand life. In triumph he urges all around him to "dance my *gratitude* that you came and gave me something to celebrate at last. Dance my *belief* that this is where we must all begin—with our nakedness, our jaggedness, our entrapment in the rock of our own history." The author had already started to fulfil this task in his most frequently performed play, *O! Temperance!*: "a consciously 'nationalistic' exercise. I wanted to show that New Zealand history was there to be found, could be dramatised and was fun." The play began as a study of a famous first in the country's history—votes for women—but gradually broadened into an account of the Temperance Movement's struggle to banish the demon drink from the land. Although Thompson's plays deal with many different subjects and are written in a variety of theatrical styles, they are all informed by a quest for a New Zealand in which their author can live and of which he can be proud.

As this one long work unfolds, the people about whom Thompson has written are the large majority of those who have built the country: workers and housewives from the Depression, miners of whom he was once one, rugby players, race-goers, and even the readers of the popular scandal sheet *Truth*. His is a world which he believes artists and intellectuals have for too long contemptuously disregarded. His early plays bubble with optimism. They may end with their collective heroes vanquished as the idealistic and generous-hearted temperance workers were—no puritanical "wowsers" these—but Thompson's faith that the people will determine their future is not shaken by the anatomy of single defeats. Innumerable human triumphs, small and large, make up these plays. The action at the end of *Songs to Uncle Scrim* sums them all up. The unemployed advance slowly on the audience, singing quietly a hymn of challenge:

> We shall come the unemployed,
> The disinherited of this earth....
> On our lips the cry for vengenance,
> In our souls the lust for life.

The theatrical image reveals an irresistible force, which will overcome.

If Thompson's career has shown a concern to destroy the elitist myths of working class "Kiwi philistinism," the professional theatre in which he has worked, as a director and actor as well as a playwright, is rarely visited by those whose existence he has sought to vindicate. One consequence has been his movement from the more literary style of *First Return*—"cranky expressionism"—through the new musical theatre of the songplays—a term he coined for "a set of original songs grouped uncompromisingly round a theme, placed in a coherent order to create a strong sense of narrative"—to an ever more enthusiastic embracing of all forms of popular theatre. These formal developments have attempted with considerable success to forge a theatrical language that reflects its subject matter and which is accessible to all. However, the resulting mixture of music and music-hall, politics and pantomime sits uncomfortably in the country's present professional theatres. Thompson has written himself out of the established theatres and has had to create his own theatrical outlets. This may explain why his latest play, *Coaltown Blues*, is a one-man show which can be performed anywhere more easily than a full-scale play.

It is not only in formal terms that *Coaltown Blues* emphasises a new direction in Thompson's work. It underlines the growing pessimism which marks his recent plays. If the collaboratively created *A Night at the Races* allowed the audience to share the thrills of gambling with Murph the Serf of the Turf, *Songs to the Judges* reminds that same audience of where they are at their weakest—on questions of race. On a bare stage, which underlines the fact that people make up Thompson's world, the Maori is described at the moments of racial crisis that occur "once in a generation." The play is not so much a history as a trial with the audience in the dock. They are found guilty of attempting to alienate the *tangata whenua* (People of the Land) from their history and culture. *The Great New Zealand Truth Show*, written in the aftermath of the 1981 Springbok rugby tour, finally indicts the country's most widely read newspaper for its racist attitudes. This revue-style collage presents the first year of each decade from 1931—half a century of social history—through material printed in the paper's columns. It traces how the newspaper moved from being left-of-centre to the extreme right as during the tour it became "an organ of fascism pure-and-simple." The play's final moments deliberately echo the end of *Songs to Uncle Scrim*. Now figures of authority from the Prime Minister down, wearing huge recognisable masks, move on the audience with martial precision. "The whole 'march' should have the impact of a nightmare, frightening and ritualistic." The more personal *Coaltown Blues* is a second return to Thompson's mining birthplace. Once again he explores the public past through his private experiences as "Blacktown" reasserts its hold over him: "Blacktown will not leave me. It holds me with its black and glittering eye, condemning me for the rest of my life to tell its tale.... O Blacktown, Blacktown ... I grew up in you, and in your face ... I saw the face of the world." However, as the blues melodies running through the play hauntingly indicate, the town and its people are long gone. Their struggles ended in 1951 with the defeat of the miners after the country's most bitter strike and lockout. "Them jokers at the top they just can't be beaten, eh!" The only hope left is that one day the "purpose in our black history" will be discovered.

—Sebastian Black

TOWNSEND, Sue (Susan Townsend). British. Born in Leicester, 2 April 1946. Educated at South Wigston Girls High School, Leicestershire. Has three children from first marriage and one daughter from second. Recipient: Thames Television bursary, 1980. Agent: Anthony Sheil Associates, 43 Doughty Street, London WC1N 2LF, England.

PUBLICATIONS

Plays

In the Club and Up the Spout (produced on tour, 1979).
Womberang (produced London, 1980; as *The Waiting Room*, produced Leicester, 1982). Included in *Bazaar and Rummage, Groping for Words, and Womberang*, 1984.
The Ghost of Daniel Lambert, music by Rick Lloyd (produced Leicester, 1981).
Dayroom (produced Croydon, Surrey, 1981).

Bazaar and Rummage (produced London, 1982). Included in *Bazaar and Rummage, Groping for Words, and Womberang*, 1984.
Captain Christmas and the Evil Adults (produced Leicester, 1982).
Groping for Words (produced Croydon, Surrey, 1983; revised version, as *Are You Sitting Comfortably?*, produced Watford, Hertfordshire, 1986). Included in *Bazaar and Rummage, Groping for Words, and Womberang*, 1984.
Clients (produced Croydon, Surrey, 1983).
Bazaar and Rummage, Groping for Words, and Womberang. London, Methuen, 1984.
The Great Celestial Cow (produced Leicester and London, 1984). London, Methuen, 1984.
The Secret Diary of Adrian Mole Aged 13¾, songs by Ken Howard and Alan Blaikley (produced Leicester and London, 1984). London, Methuen, 1985.

Radio Plays: *The Diary of Nigel Mole Aged 13¾*, 1982; *The Growing Pains of Adrian Mole*, 1984.

Television Plays: *Bazaar and Rummage*, 1984; *The Secret Diary of Adrian Mole* series, 1985; *The Growing Pains of Adrian Mole*, 1987; *The Refuge* series, with Carole Hayman, 1987.

Novels

The Adrian Mole Diaries. London, Methuen, 1985; New York, Grove Press, 1986.
The Secret Diary of Adrian Mole Aged 13¾. London, Methuen, 1982; New York, Avon, 1984.
The Growing Pains of Adrian Mole. London, Methuen, 1984.

*

Sue Townsend comments:

I suppose I write about people who do not live in the mainstream of society. My characters are not educated; they do not earn high salaries (if they work at all). I look beneath the surface of their lives. My plays are about loneliness, struggle, survival, and the possibility of change.

Strangely, they are also comedies. Comedy is the most tragic form of drama.

* * *

Sue Townsend writes compassionate comedy whose power comes from its intermittently hard edge. A comedy with serious intentions is nothing new. But what is distinctive about the sometimes gentle, sometimes tough comedy Townsend writes is her full commitment to her characters, to her chosen issues, and to her audience. The sympathy and goodwill with which Townsend creates her characters is an extension of her desire to bring forgotten people to the stage. In what she has called "problem plays," she presents groups whose troubles are conventionally ignored: agoraphobics, adult illiterates, Asian women immigrants. By buoying spectators with the good feelings of her comedy, Townsend presses everyone in her audience—including the working-class people she hopes to attract—to understand the human problem at hand. She is optimistic that by tenderly encouraging such awareness in a diverse audience, her theatre can contribute to social change.

In *Bazaar and Rummage* genial comedy cushions the revealing and disturbing study of three agoraphobics and their two social workers. Here Townsend refines the tendencies already apparent in her early theatre script *Womberang*, tendencies which characterize most of her plays: a group and not an individual is at the center of the action, the play refuses conventional descriptions of its plot, and the comedy is generated by community and concern. Townsend describes plays like *Bazaar*, which offer a "group against the world," as "closet plays," "enclosed plays," to emphasize her focus on neglected social problems. In *Bazaar* she engages her predilection for dealing with "the change in [such] a group" by presenting a trio of agoraphobics venturing from home for the first time in years, flanked by the two amateur social workers attempting to aid them. Instead of focusing on one of the characters and her progress toward health, Townsend balances the advances and setbacks in the lives of all five women; progress toward self-understanding is not a function of individual awareness but of group members supporting one another through crises. The plot which such communal character development creates is more circular than linear. There is a passing of awareness from one character to another until the group's collected courage allows for a collective exit onto an Acton street. Townsend's approach to comedy in this play occasioned a notable critical debate. The marriage of very funny lines to a feminist message moved some reviewers to dismiss the effort as "glib," "quirky," or "not too seriously meant," and motivated Michael Billington to warn the playwright that laughter "can't be used simply to decorate." But Townsend herself describes the combination of comedy and women as natural. Laughter, she explains, is "how women cope and have coped for centuries." She sees comedy as the most powerful tool available to her as an aid in reaching people; and in *Bazaar*, by allowing her audience to laugh with the agoraphobics, she encourages compassion and enables reflection. While theatre critics have found comedy variously revolutionary or reactionary, Townsend uses it to approach tough social issues and sees it—perhaps for that reason—as "a basic need of the human body."

Townsend's concern turns from women's special problems to the class issue of illiteracy in *Are You Sitting Comfortably?* (an earlier version was called *Groping for Words*). The play shares its class-conscious focus with *The Secret Diary of Adrian Mole Aged 13¾*, the play version of Townsend's successful novel. Both plays portray working-class characters seeking personal and social validation, but to the very light touch of *Adrian Mole* Townsend adds, in *Are You Sitting Comfortably?*, a pointed political message—a condemnation of the British class structure which seems to require illiterates. The play's class conflict is manifest in the encounter of the well-positioned, middle-class Joyce—the novice literacy instructor—and her three working-class students, George, Thelma, and Kevin. As in *Bazaar*, Townsend again keys the play's action to the symbiotic developments within this group. By the end of the play Joyce must acknowledge that her liberalism effects little social change, but Kevin vocalizes what all the others are scared to. In the play's chilling ending, he realizes that the world doesn't "want us to read! There ain't room for all of us is there?" This painful truth gels not just in Kevin, however, but also in the group. The audience, too, must join in this difficult collective realization, for as it laughs, it is being asked, "are *you* sitting comfortably?" This play may be the clearest example of Townsend's comic gifts, but also evidence of her commitment to using comedy to urge re-thinking and re-considering.

One moment beyond what Townsend calls her usual "heightened naturalism" occurs in *Are You Sitting Comfortably?* when, near the end of the play, Joyce and her three students venture into Soho sex shops for a real-life reading lesson. The transcendent quality that comes from this scene's acknowledgment of other places and other realities is influential in the play's aggressive ending, but it is not integral. In *The Great Celestial Cow*, however, through her experimentation with the surreal, the fantastic, and the magical, Townsend not only liberates her play from realistic sets and action, but opens up new possibilities for her communities, her concerns, and her comedy. The stylistic liberation—a product both of the communal production method the play had in its origin with Joint Stock and of Townsend's attraction to Caryl Churchill's modal innovations in *Top Girls*—results in a sophisticated array of non-realistic scenes, including a Kali ritual which brings the goddess to life, a conversation with cows, and a final scene which ignores realistic barriers of time, space, and character. One result of a play punctuated by such magical releases is a plot more episodic and wide-ranging than in Townsend's previous work. Strategies that in earlier plays had been mistaken for careless organization are now crucial in the development of a cultural transition from the cohesion of Indian village life to the displacements of Leicester city existence. Sita's story develops as the tale of an individual finding her strength and voice through the support of a community of women, both inside and outside the family. Various notions of community, in fact, mark the play at every level, from its group birth through Joint Stock to protests made against it by Leicester's Asian women. As in *Bazaar* and *Womberang*, the female community encourages feminist response, but offers its women and its audience more options than dogma. Choice is, in fact, encouraged by the play's very open ending. And while comedy is Townsend's mode once again, the shifting realities of the play highlight new theatrical directions. This play, for example, clearly shows Townsend's affinity for strong visuals and for a quick succession of places and scenes seamed together through a Brechtian storytelling perspective. In *The Great Celestial Cow* Townsend's easy comedy is complicated and enhanced by her engagements with new dramatic modes.

The strength of Townsend's work lies in her fusion of comedy and serious matter. Her feminism and class consciousness have led her to write committed plays about neglected groups, plays which require their own organization and mode. In these plays she has worked, through her comedy, to bring people together both inside and outside of the play's frame.

—Susan Carlson

TREVOR, William. Pseudonym for William Trevor Cox. Irish. Born in Mitchelstown, County Cork, 24 May 1928. Educated at St. Columba's College, Dublin, 1942–46; Trinity College, Dublin, B.A. 1950. Married Jane Ryan in 1952; two sons. History teacher, Armagh, Northern Ireland, 1951–53; art teacher, Rugby, England, 1953–55; sculptor, in Somerset, 1955–60; advertising copywriter, London, 1960–64. Recipient: *Transatlantic Review* prize, for fiction, 1964; Hawthornden prize, for fiction, 1965; Society of Authors travelling fellowship, 1972; Allied Irish Banks prize, for fiction, 1976; Heinemann Award, for fiction, 1976; Whitbread Award, 1976, 1983; Irish Community prize, 1979; BAFTA award, for television play, 1983. D.Litt.: University of Exeter, 1984; Trinity College, Dublin, 1986. Member, Irish Academy of Letters. C.B.E. (Commander, Order of the British Empire), 1977. Lives in Devon, England. Agent: A.D. Peters, 10 Buckingham Street, London WC2N 6BU; or, Literistic Ltd., 264 Fifth Avenue, New York, New York 10001, U.S.A. Address c/o Bodley Head Ltd., 32 Bedford Square, London WC1B 3RP, England.

PUBLICATIONS

Plays

The Elephant's Foot (produced Nottingham, 1965).
The Girl (televised 1967; produced London, 1968). London, French, 1968.
A Night with Mrs. da Tanka (televised 1968; produced London, 1972). London, French, 1972.
Going Home (broadcast 1970; produced London, 1972). London, French, 1972.
The Old Boys, adaptation of his own novel (produced London, 1971). London, Davis Poynter, 1971.
A Perfect Relationship (broadcast 1973; produced London, 1973). London, Burnham House, 1976.
The 57th Saturday (produced London, 1973).
Marriages (produced London, 1973). London, French, 1973.
Scenes from an Album (broadcast 1975; produced Dublin, 1981). Dublin, Co-op, 1981.
Beyond the Pale (broadcast 1980). Published in *Best Radio Plays of 1980*, London, Eyre Methuen, 1981.
Autumn Sunshine (televised 1981; broadcast 1982). Published in *Best Radio Plays of 1982*, London, Methuen, 1983.

Radio Plays: *The Penthouse Apartment*, 1968; *Going Home*, 1970; *The Boarding House*, from his own novel, 1971; *A Perfect Relationship*, 1973; *Scenes from an Album*, 1975; *Attracta*, 1977; *Beyond the Pale*, 1980; *The Blue Dress*, 1981; *Travellers*, 1982; *Autumn Sunshine*, 1982; *The News from Ireland*, from his own story, 1986.

Television Plays: *The Baby-Sitter*, 1965; *Walk's End*, 1966; *The Girl*, 1967; *A Night with Mrs. da Tanka*, 1968; *The Mark-2 Wife*, 1969; *The Italian Table*, 1970; *The Grass Widows*, 1971; *O Fat White Woman*, 1972; *The Schoolroom*, 1972; *Access to the Children*, 1973; *The General's Day*, 1973; *Miss Fanshawe's Story*, 1973; *An Imaginative Woman*, from a story by Thomas Hardy, 1973; *Love Affair*, 1974; *Eleanor*, 1974; *Mrs. Acland's Ghosts*, 1975; *The Statue and the Rose*, 1975; *Two Gentle People*, from a story by Graham Greene, 1975; *The Nicest Man in the World*, 1976; *Afternoon Dancing*, 1976; *Voices from the Past*, 1976; *Newcomers*, 1976; *The Love of a Good Woman*, from his own story, 1976; *The Girl Who Saw a Tiger*, 1976; *Last Wishes*, 1978; *Another Weekend*, 1978; *Memories*, 1978; *Matilda's England*, 1979; *The Old Curiosity Shop*, from the novel by Dickens, 1979; *Secret Orchards*, from works by J.R. Ackerley and Diana Petre, 1980; *The Happy Autumn Fields*, from a story by Elizabeth Bowen, 1980; *Elizabeth Alone*, from his own novel, 1981; *Autumn Sunshine*, from his own story, 1981; *The Ballroom of Romance*, from his own story, 1982; *Mrs. Silly* (*All for Love* series), 1983; *One of Ourselves*, 1983; *Aunt Suzanne*, 1984; *Broken Homes*, from his own story, 1985; *The Children of Dynmouth*, from his own novel, 1987.

Novels

A Standard of Behaviour. London, Hutchinson, 1958.
The Old Boys. London, Bodley Head, and New York, Viking Press, 1964.
The Boarding-House. London, Bodley Head, and New York, Viking Press, 1965.
The Love Department. London, Bodley Head, 1966; New York, Viking Press, 1967.
Mrs. Eckdorf in O'Neill's Hotel. London, Bodley Head, 1969; New York, Viking Press, 1970.
Miss Gomez and the Brethren. London, Bodley Head, 1971.

Elizabeth Alone. London, Bodley Head, 1973; New York, Viking Press, 1974.
The Children of Dynmouth. London, Bodley Head, 1976; New York, Viking Press, 1977.
Other People's Worlds. London, Bodley Head, 1980; New York, Viking Press, 1981.
Fools of Fortune. London, Bodley Head, and New York, Viking Press, 1983.
Nights at the Alexandra (novella). London, Hutchinson, and New York, Harper, 1987.

Short Stories

The Day We Got Drunk on Cake and Other Stories. London, Bodley Head, 1967; New York, Viking Press, 1968.
Penguin Modern Stories 8, with others. London, Penguin, 1971.
The Ballroom of Romance and Other Stories. London, Bodley Head, and New York, Viking Press, 1972.
The Last Lunch of the Season. London, Covent Garden Press, 1973.
Angels at the Ritz and Other Stories. London, Bodley Head, 1975; New York, Viking Press, 1976.
Lovers of Their Time and Other Stories. London, Bodley Head, 1978; New York, Viking Press, 1979.
The Distant Past and Other Stories. Dublin, Poolbeg Press, 1979.
Beyond the Pale and Other Stories. London, Bodley Head, 1981; New York, Viking Press, 1982.
The Stories of William Trevor. London and New York, Penguin, 1983.
The News from Ireland and Other Stories. London, Bodley Head, and New York, Viking, 1986.

Other

Old School Ties (miscellany). London, Lemon Tree Press, 1976.
A Writer's Ireland: Landscape in Literature. London, Thames and Hudson, and New York, Viking, 1984.

*

Manuscript Collection: University of Tulsa, Oklahoma.

* * *

A successful novelist and prolific television and radio dramatist before turning in any real measure towards the theatre, William Trevor has been somewhat unlucky in his career as far as his full-length plays are concerned. *The Elephant's Foot* closed during its prior-to-London tour, and *The Old Boys* had a particularly unfortunate opening in London with its star's first-night nerves hindering the flow of a play whose full effect depended on the subtleties of its verbal nuances; and although the central performance improved immeasurably during its original limited Mermaid Theatre run and throughout a subsequent provincial tour, sadly the play did not find a West End theatre.

The Elephant's Foot (along with his early one-acter *The Girl*) represents something of a false start for Trevor. Both reveal his unusual gift for dialogue, particularly that of characters enmeshed in their own sense of failure and for those verging on the sinister or seedy, but both remain somewhat inert, heavily relying as they do on a central situation, of strange intruders entering domestic scenes, itself something of a cliché-situation in the theatre of the early 1960's. In *The Girl*, set in suburban London (one of Trevor's favourite locales, both in novels and plays), a mysterious teenage girl descends on the Green household, convincingly claiming to be Mr. Green's daughter, the result of a single drunken escapade with a prostitute. Her arrival, not surprisingly, divides the family, until it is revealed, with the near-curtain arrival of the girl's violent young friends, that Green is only the latest in a long list of prostitute mother's clients, to be descended on and terrorised in turn by the loutish teenage gang. It is adroit and suspenseful enough to sustain its length, although the ghost of Pinter looms heavily over the play, even to some extent over the dialogue, particularly in the opening sections between the Green family, laden with pauses and the reiteration of the clichés of suburban small-talk. *The Elephant's Foot* is similarly burdened with a top-heavy plot and reliance on a closing "surprise." An elderly couple, Colonel and Mrs. Pocock, who live apart except for their Christmas reunion with their twin children, in the midst of preparing their Christmas meal are invaded by the bizarre stranger Freer (first-cousin to the splendid con-man Swingler in *The Old Boys*) and his mute associate Tiger. Freer gradually unsettles the Pococks, frightening them by anticipating the non-arrival of their children, but he fails to insinuate Tiger into the household in the twins' place and the play closes with the Pococks again alone preparing to resume their old domestic battle. After a promising opening, with a very funny verbal tussle between the Pococks over the unfortunate selection of the Christmas brussels sprouts, the play collapses in the second act, only sustaining itself to the final curtain by resorting to coincidence and unconvincing metaphysical overtones. Nevertheless, *The Elephant's Foot* revealed that Trevor was capable of an individual dramatic verbal style (which his early novels, largely in dialogue, had pointed towards), a stylized counterpointing of the colloquial with the rhetorical which owes a little to Ivy Compton-Burnett but essentially remains very much his own.

This was further developed in *The Old Boys*, his own adaptation of his Hawthornden Prize-winning novel of the same name, which revealed too Trevor's special understanding of elderly characters, particularly in those scenes set in a London residential hotel populated entirely by old boys of the same minor public school and tyrannised over by a dragoness of a Matron-surrogate. In its study of an old schoolboy rivalry extending from out of the past to influence a struggle over the presidency of the Old Boys' Association, the play is by turns hilarious and deeply touching, although the first act never satisfactorily solves some problems of construction in the adaptation process. But the climatic scene as old Mr. Jaraby at last realises the futility of his grudges and ambitions and, now a widower preparing to join the other old men at the Rimini Hotel, launches into a speech of life-affirming anarchy at the expense of the bullying proprietrix, stands as one of Trevor's finest achievements. Since *The Old Boys* Trevor has enjoyed considerable success with one-act plays often adapted from previous television and radio plays or from short stories. Most of these are acutely observed and tightly written duologues between different kinds of victims—the lonely, deserted, or repressed characters Trevor reveals so compassionately. Some of these, such as *A Night with Mrs. da Tanka*, a hotel encounter between a sad drunken divorcée and a shy bachelor, suffer in the transition to the stage and seem curiously artificial. But the best of them—especially *Going Home*, in which a precocious schoolboy and a spinster Assistant Matron, travelling in a train compartment together for the holidays, painfully realise their mutual loneliness—capture moments of crisis in their characters' lives and give them a genuine life on stage beyond the confines of the original medium from which they were adapted. Likewise, some of the best scenes in *The Old Boys* are those not in or most freely adapted from the original novel; hopefully before long Trevor may emerge with a new full-length play original in all senses of the word.

—Alan Strachan

TSEGAYE GABRE-MEDHIN. Ethiopian. Born in Ambo, Shewa, 17 August 1936. Educated at Zema and Kine Ethiopian Orthodox Church Schools, 1945–48; Ambo Elementary School, 1948–52; General Wingate and Commercial Secondary schools, 1952–56; Blackstone School of Law, Chicago, LL.B. 1959. Married Laketch Bitew in 1961; three daughters. Studied British theatre at the Royal Court Theatre, London, and French theatre at the Comédie Française, Paris, 1959–60; director, 1961–71, and general manager, 1967–74, Haile Selassie I Theatre (now Ethiopian National Theatre), Addis Ababa; editor, Oxford University Press, Addis Ababa, 1971; research fellow, University of Dakar, Senegal, from 1971; Permanent Secretary, Ministry of Culture and Sports, Addis Ababa, 1975–76; Assistant Professor of Theatre Arts, Addis Ababa University, 1977; Secretary General, Ethiopian Peace, Solidarity and Friendship House, 1979. Currently adviser, Ministry of Culture, Addis Ababa. Recipient: Unesco fellowship, 1959; International Theatre Institute fellowship, 1965; Haile Selassie I prize, 1966; Fulbright fellowship, 1966, 1971, 1975, 1985; Gold Mercury award, 1982. Commander, Senegal National Order, 1971. Address: Ministry of Culture, P.O. Box 1907, Addis Ababa, Ethiopia.

PUBLICATIONS

Plays

Belg (Autumn) (produced Addis Ababa, 1957). Addis Ababa, Berhanena Selam, 1962.
Yeshoh Aklil (Crown of Thorns) (produced Addis Ababa, 1958). Addis Ababa, Berhanena Selam, 1959.
Askeyami Lijagered (The Ugly Girl) (produced Addis Ababa, 1959).
Jorodegif (Mumps) (produced Addis Ababa, 1959).
Listro (Shoe Shine Boy) (produced Addis Ababa, 1960).
Igni Biye Metahu (Back with a Grin) (produced Addis Ababa, 1960).
Chulo (Errand Boy) (produced Addis Ababa, 1961).
Kosho Cigara (Cheap Cigarettes) (produced Addis Ababa, 1961).
Yemama Zetegn Melk (Mother's Nine Faces) (produced Addis Ababa, 1961).
Tewodros (in English; produced Addis Ababa, 1962; revised version produced Addis Ababa, 1983; London, 1987). Published in *Ethiopian Observer* (Addis Ababa), vol. 10, no. 3, 1966.
Othello, adaptation of the play by Shakespeare. Addis Ababa, Oxford University Press, 1963.
Tartuffe, adaptation of the play by Molière (produced Addis Ababa, 1963).
The Doctor in Spite of Himself, adaptation of a play by Molière (produced Addis Ababa, 1963).
Oda Oak Oracle: A Legend of Black Peoples, Told of Gods and God, Of Hope and Love, Of Fears and Sacrifices (produced Addis Ababa, 1964). London and New York, Oxford University Press, 1965.
Azmari (in English; produced Addis Ababa, 1964). Published in *Ethiopian Observer* (Addis Ababa), vol. 10, no. 10, 1966.
Yekermo Sew (The Seasoned) (produced Addis Ababa, 1966). Addis Ababa, Berhanena Selam, 1967.
Petros (produced Addis Ababa, 1968).
King Lear, adaptation of the play by Shakespeare (produced in part, Addis Ababa, 1968).
Macbeth, adaptation of the play by Shakespeare (produced in part, Addis Ababa, 1968). Addis Ababa, Oxford University Press, 1972.
Hamlet, adaptation of the play by Shakespeare (produced in part, Addis Ababa, 1968). Addis Ababa, Oxford University Press, 1972.
Kirar Siker (Kirar Tight-Tuned) (produced Addis Ababa, 1969).
Ha Hu Besidist Wer (A-B-C in Six Months) (produced Addis Ababa, 1974). Addis Ababa, Berhanena Selam, 1975.
Enat Alem Tenu (Mother Courage), adaptation of the play by Brecht (produced Addis Ababa, 1975). Addis Ababa, Berhanena Selam, 1975.
Atsim Beyegetsu (Skeleton in Pages) (produced Addis Ababa, 1975).
Abugida Transform (produced Addis Ababa, 1976).
Collision of Altars. London, Collings, 1977.
Melikte Proletarian (produced Addis Ababa, 1979).
Mekdem (Preface) (produced Addis Ababa, 1980).
Gamo (produced Addis Ababa, 1981).
Zeray (produced Asmara, Eritrea, 1981).
Zikegna Abera (produced Addis Ababa, 1986).

Verse

Issat Woy Ababa (Fire of Flower). Addis Ababa, Berhanena Selam, 1973.

Other

Ethiopia: Footprint of Time (travel), photographs by Alberto Tessore. Udine, Italy, Magnus, 1984.

*

Tsegaye Gabre-Medhin comments:

I do not think in English or French but in Ethiopian first. My cultural personality is formed out of a background which consciously resists being re-created in the image of any and all supremacist alien values. I write for a people who for many thousands of years have developed a conscious taste for their own poetic heritage, in one of their own scripts, and in one of their own indigenous languages. In the literature of one of the children of Kam: of Meroe, of Nubia, of Egypt, of Ethiopia—of the cradles of the world's earliest civilization. The people are still the judges of my plays which mirror them. They are still the critics of the poetry and culture that make them, and which in turn they themselves make.

If for instance a British poet *naturally* felt hard put to think or dream his verse in Chinese it is because (a) Chinese is not the natural expression of British culture, (b) Chinese literature forms the Chinese personality, makes and develops first a Chinese universal man and not first a Briton or a British personality, and (c) the said British poet is not yet re-created in the image of the Chinese. Can any African artist-poet or playwright (unless of course his culture is already killed in him and replaced by something else) afford to think or dream his verse in anything less than what is his indigenous African expression FIRST? Just like *no* Chinese literature can make a truly British culture, so there is *no* English, French, Dutch, or Portuguese, etc., literature which can make a truly African culture.

* * *

Tsegaye Gabre-Medhin has written plays in Amharic, and written and directed Amharic versions of *Othello, Macbeth, Hamlet, Tartuffe*, and *The Imaginary Invalid*. In the plays he has written in English, both the phrasing and the poetic conception suggest that he is experimenting with the transferral into English of devices alien to it. For instance, in *Oda Oak Oracle*, Goaa has this speech:

It is not easy, Ukutee,
To speak
Of the gloomy path
Of a lone walker.
Loneliness is
When the ripe fruit fails,
To make the bird
Aware of its existence.
Loneliness is
When the avoided heart,
Growing stale every night,
Wears a mask of bitterness,
While the tense veins
Growing frantic and mad
Scratch at the mask
Of a stricken heart.
Loneliness is
When the aged mule
Rubs its flank
Against the deserted trunk
Of a dead bush.
Loneliness is
When the moon is left cold
Among a glowing
Jungle of stars.

The richness of elaboration and repetition, together with heavy rhetoric and (in two of the plays) musical accompaniment, contributes to florid, torrid melodrama.

In *Oda Oak Oracle* the oracle has decreed marriage between Shanka and Ukutee, and the sacrifice of their first-born to the ancestors. To avoid this, Shanka refuses to consummate the marriage. In humiliation and frustration Ukutee offers herself to Shanka's friend, Goaa. He brings to the play the perspective of another society, for he had once been taken away by strangers and instructed by them in the Gospel. His criticism of the oracle and traditional beliefs feeds Shanka's doubts. By the last act Ukutee is in labour. Cloud darkens the valley and there is perturbation among the elders at the lack of sun. The oracle commands a combat between Goaa and Shanka, the victor to be flogged from the valley by Ukutee. Goaa is killed and Ukutee consents to whip out Shanka because the oracle has promised that she will then bear a fine son. In fact, she dies giving birth to a daughter and the play ends with Shanka holding the child as a mob approaches to stone both of them to death.

This doom-laden play Albert Gerard, in his *Four African Literatures* (1971), finds to be "one of the finest plays to have been written in Africa." Personally, I find the extremely short lines awkward and their divisions of little help to the speaker; moreover the climax of the play seems to pile up punishments over-ingeniously.

More interesting, I believe, are two plays which appeared in the *Ethiopia Observer*. *Tewodros* is an account of a mid-19th-century purgative dealer's son who rose to be Emperor. He had a vison of uniting Ethiopia, but his rule was troubled by various revolts and ended by British invasion. Showing both concern for the welfare of the common people and bloody ruthlessness, Tewodros is an ambiguous figure, and the interest of Tsegaye's play lies not in his Tamburlaine-like career, but in the doubts expressed by his first and second wives and by others around him:

> Washing my hands in other's blood and watching mine flow out has occupied the best years of my life. The one exciting activity I can remember of my only son is the lashing of his paper sword and his shouting of the war-cry "zeraf" . . . until finally I heard him repeat the same thing on the battlefield once and for all . . . then he bled to death in my arms. What has the poor peasant to live for, Princess, if he can't afford to question why his children should sing war songs and not read the Book of Life?

The most successful of his plays is *Azmari. Azmaris* are professional singers, and female *azmaris* are considered little better than courtesans. Tsegaye's play portrays the tensions in a family, in each generation of which a member is called to be "the expressive medium for Nature's passions"—and so Lulu considers herself. The centre of the play is her clash with her mother, who resents her being "out with that moaning harp of hers day and night, and never lifting a finger to help the family," and maintains that a minstrel's is "no decent folk's way of life." Who is betraying whom, the member of the family who rejects the call of music, or the artist who does not help support it?

Unlike Tsegaye's other plays, *Azmari* has only one violent action, the smashing of Lulu's harp. As in Chekhov, the significant action takes place offstage—Lulu has played at the marriage of the man she loved, who has jilted her for a socially acceptable bride—and no resolution is offered. The use of music as an emotional punctuation of the scenes is dramatically relevant. Grandiloquence, too, is used dramatically, for it is set off against the everyday speech of those in the family who refuse music's call.

—Anthony Graham-White

TURNER, David. British. Born in Birmingham, Warwickshire, 18 March 1927. Educated at Moseley Grammar School; Birmingham University, B.A. 1950. Served in an army educational theatre unit, 1945–47. Married to Joan Wilson. Teacher for 9 years. Agent: Harvey Unna and Stephen Durbridge Ltd., 24–32 Pottery Lane, London W11 4LZ, England.

PUBLICATIONS

Plays

The Bedmakers (produced Coventry, 1962).

Semi-Detached (produced Coventry and London, 1962; New York, 1963). London, Heinemann, 1962; New York, Dramatists Play Service, 1964; revised version, London, Evans, 1971.
Believe It or Not, with Edward J. Mason (produced Coventry, 1962).
Trevor (produced Birmingham, 1963).
The Antique Shop (produced Coventry, 1963).
Slap in the Middle, with others (produced Birmingham, 1965).
Bottomley (produced Coventry, 1965).
Way Off Beat (televised 1966). Published in *Conflicting Generations: Five Television Plays*, edited by Michael Marland, London, Longman, 1968.
The Beggar's Opera, music edited by Benjamin Pearce Higgins, adaptation of the play by John Gay (produced London, 1968). London, French, 1982.
The Servant of Two Masters, with Paul Lapworth, music by Benjamin Pearce Higgins, adaptation of a play by Carlo Goldoni (produced London, 1968). London, Evans, 1973.
Quick Quick Slow, music and lyrics by Monty Norman and Julian More (produced Birmingham, 1969).
The Prodigal Daughter (produced Colchester, 1973; Washington, D.C., 1974). New York, French, 1976.
The Miser, adaptation of a play by Molière (produced Birmingham, 1973).
The Only True Story of Lady Godiva, with Paul Lapworth (produced Coventry, 1973).
The Girls (produced London, 1975).

Radio Plays: *Grantham's Outing*, 1956; ... *And Tomorrow*, 1956; *Change of Plan*, 1957; *Me, Me Dad and His'n*, 1957; *Mind Your Own Business*, 1958; *Family Business*, 1959; *Come Back Jack*, 1959; *Any Other Business*, 1961; *Now More Than Ever*, 1961; *The Wizard Who Worked Wonders*, from a play by Calderón, 1977.

Television Plays and Serializations: *Fresh as Paint*, 1956; *The Train Set*, 1961; *Cry from the Depths*, 1961; *The Final Result*, 1961; *On the Boundary*, 1961; *Summer, Autumn, Winter, Spring*, 1961; *Choirboys Unite!*, 1961; *The Chem Lab Mystery*, 1963; *Swizzlewick*, 1964; *This Man Craig* series, 1966; *Way Off Beat*, 1966; *North and South*, from the novel by Elizabeth Gaskell, 1966; *Angel Pavement*, from the novel by J.B. Priestley, 1967; *Treasure Island*, from the novel by Robert Louis Stevenson, 1968; *Père Goriot*, from the novel by Balzac, 1968; *Cold Comfort Farm*, from the novel by Stella Gibbons, 1968; *Olive*, 1970; *Germinal*, from the novel by Zola, 1970; *The Roads to Freedom*, from novels by Jean-Paul Sartre, 1972; *Daisy* (*The Edwardians* series), 1973; *Neighbours*, 1973; *Father*, 1973; *Requiem for a Crown Prince*, 1974; *Harold*, 1975; *Prometheus*, from the novel by André Maurois, 1975; *C2H5OH*, 1980.

*

Critical Study: *Anger and After* by John Russell Taylor, London, Methuen, 1962, revised edition, 1969, as *The Angry Theatre*, New York, Hill and Wang, 1962, revised edition, 1969.

* * *

David Turner's plays are all firmly rooted in the Midlands, where he lives, and nearly all are closely observed pictures of lower-middle-class life and values. *Semi-Detached* is his best known play and satirises those values accurately and cruelly. Fred Midway is a middle-aged insurance agent, living with his family in a semi-detached house in a Midlands town, absolutely obsessed with is status in life and "what the neighbours think." He imposes these preconceptions with near-disastrous results on his wife Hilda, his son Tom, and his daughters Eileen and Avril. Eileen is knocking about with a married man, while Avril's husband, Nigel Hadfield, is in disgrace because he went with a prostitute on his visit to London for a football match.

The play is Jonsonian in almost every particular. The author has an unmitigated loathing and contempt for his characters, whose real-life prototypes he has clearly spent many hours observing, and portrays them as caricatures with a grotesquerie arising from their essential social and individual truth. The names of the characters are a clear guide to their personalities—*Mid*way, *Free*man, Make*piece*—and the plot is beautifully constructed and worked out. The play is also excoriatingly witty and funny; witness lines like Fred's "If only I could have a grandchild who actually went to a Public School" and the behaviour of everyone involved in the row between Avril and Nigel, pretending to be acmes of morality but actually basing their behaviour on the most sordidly commercial considerations.

Bottomley is a portrait of another character from the same social and class background as Midway, this time the real-life Horatio Bottomley, the notorious early 20th-century swindler. Bottomley rises meteorically to fame as a businessman and as a politician. A right-wing populist with a strong appeal to the working-class, not unlike Enoch Powell in some aspects, he comes unstuck only because of his tendency to megalomania. The play convincingly reveals Bottomley within his particular political and social context and, by implication, shows how easy it is for a cunning right-wing demagogue to carve a very powerful niche for himself in our society.

The Bedmakers is a sad picture of an elderly workman, Bill Summers, left behind by the march of technology, unable to adjust himself to the new, more sophisticated demands of society for more trendy goods, geared to a quick obsolescence. He determines to make an old-fashioned iron bed for his grandson and the grandson's wife-to-be, fatally unaware that it will be totally useless to them. Both the bed and Bill end up symbolically on the scrapheap. The play is occasionally moving in the ways it depicts the conflicts between Bill, his family, and his bosses (who are keeping him on for sentimental reasons); but overall it is a little too heavy-handed and obvious.

By contrast, *The Antique Shop* is a study in corruption. A successful young shop-owner, Don Newman, is corrupted by his desire for money without really realizing the source of his infection. He has three girlfriends in tow and plays off one against the other. Predictably, two of them ditch him and the third, the Jonsonianly-named Judy Trader, only makes a fresh start with him when he inadvertently ruins himself and has to start all over again. The play is an ironic and effective picture of the dehumanizing effect of the narrow, commercially based attitudes of lower-middle-class capitalism.

Come Back Jack, a radio play, shows Jack, a lower-middle-class man, unsuccessfully struggling to keep his family firm from going bust, hampered by his idle, useless partner, his brother-in-law Donald. Jack married into the family essentially because his shrewd father-in-law realized his potential as a businessman. The basically commercial attitudes of the family towards Jack distort their inter-relationships, twisting Jack's character and desires, so that he spends his life fulfilling their objectives and not his. It is only when an ex-girlfriend forces Jack to face up to the cipher he has become that he manages to free himself, breaking away from the doomed family firm and starting afresh on a new basis with his wife.

The Train Set, for television, is a wry, well-observed study of the relationship between a working-class father and his young son and how it can be affected and twisted by lack of money. *Quick Quick Slow*, a musical written with Monty Norman and Julian More, is a satirical tilt at the ersatz cultural values, in this case represented by ballroom dancing.

At his best, Turner is a keen and truthful observer of the narrowing, repressive effects that the values of modern industrial capitalism have on human beings, and can express them in suitably socially based styles.

—Jonathan Hammond

USTINOV, Peter (Alexander). British. Born in London, 16 April 1921. Educated at Gibbs Preparatory School, London; Westminster School, London, 1934–37; London Theatre Studio, 1937–39. Served in the Royal Sussex Regiment, Royal Army Ordnance Corps, 1942–46; with Army Kinetograph Service, 1943, and Directorate of Army Psychiatry. Married 1) Isolde Denham in 1940 (divorced 1950), one daughter; 2) Suzanne Cloutier in 1954 (divorced 1971), two daughters and one son; 3) Hélène Lau d'Allemans in 1972. Actor, writer, and director. Co-director, Nottingham Playhouse, 1963. Rector, University of Dundee, 1968–73. Since 1969 Goodwill Ambassador, Unicef. Recipient: Golden Globe award, 1952; New York Drama Critics Circle award, 1953; Donaldson award, 1953; *Evening Standard* award, 1956; Royal Society of Arts Benjamin Franklin Medal, 1957; Emmy award, for acting, 1957, 1966, 1970; Oscar, for acting, 1961, 1965; Peabody award, for acting, 1972; Unicef award, 1978; Jordanian Independence Medal, 1978; Prix de la Butte, 1978; Variety Club award, for acting, 1979. D.M.: Cleveland Institute of Music, 1967; D.L.: University of Dundee, 1969; D.F.A.: La Salle University, Philadelphia, 1971; D.Litt.: University of Lancaster, 1972; University of Toronto, 1984. Fellow, Royal Society of Arts; Fellow, Royal Society of Literature, 1978. C.B.E. (Commander, Order of the British Empire), 1975; Commander, Order of Arts and Letters (France), 1985. Agent: William Morris Agency, 31–32 Soho Square, London W1V 6AP, England. Address: 11 rue de Silly, 92110 Boulogne, France.

PUBLICATIONS

Plays

The Bishop of Limpopoland (sketch; produced London, 1939).

Sketches in *Swinging the Gate* (produced London, 1940).

Sketches in *Diversion* and *Diversion 2* (produced London, 1940, 1941).

Fishing for Shadows, adaptation of a play by Jean Sarment (also director: produced London, 1940).

House of Regrets (produced London, 1942). London, Cape, 1943.

Beyond (produced London, 1943). London, English Theatre Guild, 1944; in *Five Plays*, 1965.

Blow Your Own Trumpet (produced Liverpool and London, 1943). Included in *Plays about People*, 1950.

The Banbury Nose (produced London, 1944). London, Cape, 1945.

The Tragedy of Good Intentions (produced Liverpool, 1945). Included in *Plays about People*, 1950.

The Indifferent Shepherd (produced London, 1948). Included in *Plays about People*, 1950.

Frenzy, adaptation of a play by Ingmar Bergman (produced London, 1948).

The Man in the Raincoat (also director: produced Edinburgh, 1949).

Plays about People. London, Cape, 1950.

The Love of Four Colonels (also director: produced Birmingham and London, 1951; New York, 1953). London, English Theatre Guild, 1951; New York, Dramatists Play Service, 1953.

The Moment of Truth (produced Nottingham and London, 1951). London, English Theatre Guild, 1953; in *Five Plays*, 1965.

High Balcony (produced London, 1952).

No Sign of the Dove (also director: produced Leeds and London, 1953). Included in *Five Plays*, 1965.

Romanoff and Juliet (produced Manchester and London, 1956; New York, 1957). London, English Theatre Guild, 1957; New York, Random House, 1958; revised version, as *R Loves J*, music by Alexander Faris, lyrics by Julian More (produced Chichester, 1973).

The Empty Chair (produced Bristol, 1956).

Paris Not So Gay (produced Oxford, 1958).

Photo Finish: An Adventure in Biography (also director: produced Dublin and London, 1962; New York, 1963). London, Heinemann, 1962; Boston, Little Brown, 1963.

The Life in My Hands (produced Nottingham, 1964).

Five Plays: Romanoff and Juliet, The Moment of Truth, The Love of Four Colonels, Beyond, No Sign of the Dove. London, Heinemann, and Boston, Little Brown, 1965.

Halfway up the Tree (produced on tour, Germany, 1967; also director: produced New York and London, 1967). New York, Random House, 1968; London, English Theatre Guild, 1970.

The Unknown Soldier and His Wife: Two Acts of War Separated by a Truce for Refreshment (produced New York, 1967; also director: produced Chichester 1968; London, 1973). New York, Random House, 1967; London, Heinemann, 1968.

Who's Who in Hell (produced New York, 1974).

Overheard (produced Billingham, County Durham, and London, 1981).

The Marriage, adaptation of an opera libretto by Gogol, music by Mussorgsky (also director: produced Milan, 1981; Edinburgh, 1982).

Beethoven's Tenth (produced Paris, 1982; Birmingham, London, and Los Angeles, 1983; New York, 1984).

Screenplays: *The New Lot* (documentary), 1943; *The Way Ahead*, with Eric Ambler, 1944; *The True Glory* (documentary), with others, 1944; *Carnival*, with others, 1946; *School for Secrets* (*The Secret Flight*), 1946; *Vice Versa*, 1948; *Private Angelo*, with Michael Anderson, 1949; *School for Scoundrels*, with others, 1960; *Romanoff and Juliet*, 1961; *Billy Budd*, with Robert Rossen and DeWitt Bodeen, 1962; *Lady L.*, 1965; *Hot Millions*, with Ira Wallach, 1968; *Memed, My Hawk*, 1984.

Television Plays: *Ustinov ad lib*, 1969; *Imaginary Friends*, 1982.

Novels

The Loser. London, Heinemann, and Boston, Little Brown, 1961.

Krumnagel. London, Heinemann, and Boston, Little Brown, 1971.

Short Stories

Add a Dash of Pity. London, Heinemann, and Boston, Little Brown, 1959.
The Frontiers of the Sea. London, Heinemann, and Boston, Little Brown, 1966.

Other

Ustinov's Diplomats: A Book of Photographs. New York, Geis, 1961.
We Were Only Human (caricatures). London, Heinemann, and Boston, Little Brown, 1961.
The Wit of Peter Ustinov, edited by Dick Richards. London, Frewin, 1969.
Rectorial Address Delivered in the University, 3rd November 1972. Dundee, University of Dundee Press, 1972.
Dear Me (autobiography). London, Heinemann, and Boston, Little Brown, 1977.
Happiness (lecture). Birmingham, University of Birmingham, 1980.
My Russia. London, Macmillan, and Boston, Little Brown, 1983.
Ustinov in Russia. London, O'Mara, 1987; New York, Summit, 1988.

Recordings: writer and performer—*Mock Mozart, and Phoney Folk Lore*, Parlophone; *The Grand Prix of Gibraltar*, Orpheum; narrator—*Peter and the Wolf; The Nutcracker Suite; The Soldier's Tale; Háry János; The Little Prince; The Old Man of Lochnagar*.

*

Critical Studies (includes filmographies and bibliographies): *Peter Ustinov* by Geoffrey Willans, London, Owen, 1957; *Ustinov in Focus* by Tony Thomas, London, Zwemmer, and Cranbury, New Jersey, A.S Barnes, 1971.

Theatrical Activities:
Director: **Plays**—*Fishing for Shadows*, London, 1940; *Squaring the Circle* by Valentine Katayev, London, 1941; *The Man in the Raincoat*, Edinburgh, 1949; *Love in Albania* by Eric Linklater, London, 1949; *The Love of Four Colonels*, Birmingham and London, 1951; *A Fiddle at the Wedding*, by Patricia Pakenham-Walsh, Brighton, 1952; *No Sign of the Dove*, Leeds and London, 1953; *Photo Finish*, Dublin and London, 1962; *Halfway up the Tree*, New York, 1967; *The Unknown Soldier and His Wife*, Chichester, 1968, London, 1973. **Films**—*School for Secrets* (*The Secret Flight*), 1946; *Vice Versa*, 1948; *Private Angelo*, with Michael Anderson, 1949; *Romanoff and Juliet*, 1961; *Billy Budd*, 1962; *Lady L.*, 1965; *Hammersmith Is Out*, 1972; *Memed, My Hawk*, 1984. **Operas**—*L'Heure Espagnole* by Ravel, *Gianni Schicchi* by Puccini, and *Erwartung* by Schoenberg (triple bill), London, 1962; *The Magic Flute* by Mozart, Hamburg, 1968; *Don Quichotte* by Massenet, Paris, 1973; *Don Giovanni* by Mozart, Edinburgh, 1973; *Les Brigands* by Offenbach, Berlin, 1978; *The Marriage* by Mussorgsky, Milan, 1981, Edinburgh, 1982; *Mavra* and *The Flood* by Stravinsky, Milan, 1982; *Katja Kabanowa* by Janáček, Hamburg, 1985.
Actor: **Plays**—Waffles in *The Wood Demon* by Chekhov, Shere, Surrey, 1938; in *The Bishop of Limpopoland*, London, 1939; Aylesbury Repertory Company: in *French Without Tears* by Terence Rattigan, *Pygmalion* by G.B. Shaw, *White Cargo* by Leon Gordon, *Rookery Nook* by Ben Travers, and *Laburnum Grove* by J.B. Priestley, 1939; Reverend Alroy Whittingstall in *First Night* by Reginald Denham, Richmond, Surrey, 1940; *Swinging the Gate* (revue), London, 1940; M. Lescure in *Fishing for Shadows*, London, 1940; *Hermione Gingold Revue*, London, 1940; *Diversion* and *Diversion 2* (revues), London, 1940, 1941; Petrovitch in *Crime and Punishment* by Rodney Ackland, London, 1946; Caligula in *Frenzy*, London, 1948; Sergeant Dohda in *Love in Albania* by Eric Linklater, London, 1949; Carabosse in *The Love of Four Colonels*, London, 1951; The General in *Romanoff and Juliet*, London, 1956, New York, 1957; Sam Old in *Photo Finish*, London, 1962, New York, 1963; Archbishop in *The Unknown Soldier and His Wife*, Chichester, 1968, London, 1973; Boris Vassilevitch Krivelov in *Who's Who in Hell*, New York, 1974; title role in *King Lear*, Stratford, Ontario, 1979, 1980; Stage Manager in *The Marriage*, Milan, 1981, Edinburgh, 1982; Ludwig in *Beethoven's Tenth*, Paris, 1982, Birmingham, London, and Los Angeles, 1983, New York, 1984. **Films**—*Hullo Fame!*, 1941; *Mein Kampf, My Crimes*, 1941; *The Goose Steps Out*, 1942; *Let the People Sing*, 1942; *One of Our Aircraft Is Missing*, 1942; *The New Lot*, 1943; *The Way Ahead*, 1944; *The True Glory*, 1944; *School for Secrets* (*The Secret Flight*), 1946; *Vice Versa*, 1948; *Private Angelo*, 1949; *Odette*, 1950; *Quo Vadis*, 1951; *Hotel Sahara*, 1951; *The Magic Box*, 1951; *Beau Brummell*, 1954; *The Egyptian*, 1954; *Le Plaisir* (*House of Pleasure*) (narrator), 1954; *We're No Angels*, 1955; *Lola Montès* (*Lola Montez, The Sins of Lola Montes*), 1955; *I girovaghi* (*The Wanderers*), 1956; *Un angel paso sobre Brooklyn* (*An Angel over Brooklyn, The Man Who Wagged His Tail*), 1957; *Les Espions* (*The Spies*), 1957; *The Adventures of Mr. Wonderful*, 1959; *Spartacus*, 1960; *The Sundowners*, 1960; *Romanoff and Juliet*, 1961; *Billy Budd*, 1962; *La donna del mondo* (*Women of the World*) (narrator), 1963; *The Peaches* (narrator), 1964; *Topkapi*, 1964; *John Goldfarb, Please Come Home*, 1964; *Lady L.*, 1965; *The Comedians*, 1967; *Blackbeard's Ghost*, 1967; *Hot Millions*, 1968; *Viva Max!*, 1969; *Hammersmith Is Out*, 1972; *Big Truck and Sister Clare*, 1973; *Treasure of Matecumbe*, 1976; *One of Our Dinosaurs Is Missing*, 1976; *Logan's Run*, 1976; *Robin Hood* (voice in animated film), 1976; *Un Taxi mauve* (*The Purple Taxi*), 1977; *The Last Remake of Beau Geste*, 1978; *The Mouse and His Child* (narrator), 1978; *Doppio delitto* (*Double Murders*), 1978; *Death on the Nile*, 1978; *Tarka the Otter* (narrator), 1978; *Winds of Change* (narrator), 1978; *Ashanti*, 1979; *Charlie Chan and the Curse of the Dragon Queen*, 1981; *The Great Muppet Caper*, 1981; *Grendel, Grendel, Grendel* (voice in animated film), 1981; *Evil under the Sun*, 1982; *Memed, My Hawk*, 1984. **Television**—*The Life of Dr. Johnson*, 1957; *Barefoot in Athens*, 1966; *In All Directions* series; *A Storm in Summer*, 1970 (USA); *Lord North*, 1972; *The Mighty Continent* (narrator), 1974; *A Quiet War*, 1976 (USA); *The Thief of Bagdad*, 1978; *Jesus of Nazareth*, 1979; *Einstein's Universe* (narrator), 1979; *Imaginary Friends* (5 roles), 1982; *The Well-Tempered Bach*, 1984; *13 at Dinner*, 1985; *Dead Man's Folly*, 1986; *Peter Ustinov's Russia*, 1986 (Canada); *World Challenge*, 1986 (Canada); *Murder in Three Acts*, 1986; narrator for *History of Europe, The Hermitage*, and *The Ballerinas*.

Peter Ustinov comments:

I believe that theories should emerge as a logical consequence of practice, and not be formulated in a coldly intellectual climate for eventual use. I therefore regard myself as a practical writer who began to write in the period of the proscenium arch, but who survived into the epoch of the arena and platform stages. The theatre, to survive, must do what film and television cannot do, and that is to exploit the physical presence of the audience. Naturalism was the logical reaction against romanticism, but the poetry inherent in all valid works of any school emerges more easily on film and even more easily on television than on the stage, and the time of the "fourth wall" has passed. Also, with the extraordinarily graphic quality of current events diffused by the news media, and the growing public sense of irony and scepticism about the nature and possibilities of government, tragedy and comedy have been chased for ever from their ivory towers. This is the time of the tragic farce, of the comic drama, of the paradox, of the dramatized doubt. In my plays as in my non-dramatic works I have always been interested in the comic side of things tragic and in the melancholy side of things ribald. Life could not exist without its imperfections, just as the human body could not survive without germs. And to the writer, the imperfections of existence are life-blood.

* * *

Like Noël Coward, with whose versatility his own was often compared when he was establishing himself, Peter Ustinov had a dazzling early break in his career. While he was appearing in a Herbert Farjeon revue, Farjeon gave one of Ustinov's manuscripts to James Agate, then at the height of his influence on the *Sunday Times*. Following Agate's lavish praise of *House of Regrets*, it was produced in 1942. It is very much a young man's play; its story of Russian émigrés living in genteel poverty in wartime London is an often self-consciously "atmospheric" piece, but it shows already Ustinov's sympathetic identification with eccentrics and the aged in his picture of the old Admiral and General plotting their coup to re-enter Russia. In the immediately following period Ustinov's plays appeared with impressive frequency, perhaps too frequently for their own good. Too many could be described in the terms he uses to label *Blow Your Own Trumpet*, a fantasy set in an Italian restaurant—"An idea rather than a play in the ordinary sense of the word." *The Tragedy of Good Intentions*, a chronicle play about the Crusades, is unfocused and verbose; *The Indifferent Shepherd*, his closest approach to a conventional well-made West End play, centred round a clergyman's crisis of conscience, is lacklustre despite its sincerity; and *No Sign of the Dove*, a resounding critical failure, a re-working of the Noah legend, despite a fine neo-Firbankian opening of high style, dwindles into a tepid mixture of late Shaw and bedroom-door farce. The initial impetus in these earlier plays is rarely sustained consistently.

At the same time, Ustinov's unique gift for the fantastic was developing more surely. *The Banbury Nose*, tracing a great military family through three generations in reverse order (a kind of *Milestones* backwards), is a technical tour de force, but in the scenes between the wife and the men who have loved her Ustinov also reveals a sure understanding of the threads of response between people. Although his 1950's work produced some oddly muffled efforts—such as *The Moment of Truth*, an over-inflated political drama—he also produced *The Love of Four Colonels* and *Romanoff and Juliet*, at his inventive best in both. *The Love of Four Colonels*, set in a European state disputed by the Allies, enjoyably satirizes national characteristics as the four Colonels try to awaken the Sleeping Beauty's love in pastiche scenes in which they play out their own hopes and ideals, while *Romanoff and Juliet* adapts the Romeo and Juliet story in the Cold War context of rival Russian and American embassies in "the smallest country in Europe." Underneath the fairy tales and Ruritanian trappings there is a shrewd core of humanist understanding of contemporary problems, although with Ustinov's polyglot ancestry this inevitably emerges in an international rather than a local context.

His later output continued to develop earlier themes. *Photo Finish* recalls *The Banbury Nose* in its flashback time-sequence, presenting a famous writer in confrontation with his younger selves as he contemplates the mirror of the past. *The Unknown Soldier and His Wife* is a further exploration of some material in *The Tragedy of Good Intentions* but a much surer play. It sweeps in time from ancient Rome to medieval England to modern times, linked by the same recurring characters who emerge whenever war comes and who control its course. Occasionally it threatens to become a series of admittedly amusing anti-war sketches, but it contains some of Ustinov's most pungent writing.

Certainly few of Ustinov's plays have a tight plot progression; as in his novels he is happier in a more picaresque style. His ancestry perhaps partly explains his drawing on the Russian literary tradition blending tragedy and comedy and his best plays have a strong tension between the two. He once stressed the influence of music on his work and there is indeed a Mozartian strain which informs his best plays which, despite an apparent surface plotlessness, have an internal rhythm which gives them strong theatrical movement. This could hardly be said of a string of disappointing work in more recent years. *Halfway up the Tree*, a tired comedy of the drop-out generation, was sadly jaded, but still not so distressingly feeble as *Who's Who in Hell*. This has a splendid initial idea; it is set in an anteroom of Hell where the ultimate destination of new arrivals (including the U.S. President and the Russian Premier) is decided. But the promise of a sharp political comedy is torpedoed by stale jokes and a woefully jejune level of intellectual argument. *Overheard*, a lachrymose comedy of diplomatic life, was similarly thin, while *Beethoven's Tenth* was not entirely a return to form. Again, there is a hugely promising initial premise—Beethoven materialises as the result of a trance by a psychic au pair in the house of a London music critic and is shortly cured of his deafness, also speaking perfect English. The play seems poised to take off into an exhilarating comedy of ideas but apart from a closing scene to the first act in which the critic's wife, an ex-singer, sings "An die ferne Geliebte" to the composer's accompaniment—as good a scene as anything Ustinov has written—the rest of the play never recovers the buoyancy of the opening.

—Alan Strachan

VALDEZ, Luis (Miguel). American. Born 26 June 1940. Educated at San Jose State University, California. Married Guadalupe Valdez in 1969; three children. Union organizer, United Farmworkers, Delano, California, to 1967. Since 1965 founding director, El Teatro Campesino, Delano, 1965–69, Fresno, 1969–71, and since 1971 San Juan Bautista, California. Recipient: Obie award, 1968; Emmy award, for directing, 1973; Rockefeller grant, 1978. Address: 705 Fourth Street, San Juan Bautista, California 95045, U.S.A.

PUBLICATIONS

Plays

Las dos caras del patroncito (produced Delano, 1965). Included in *Actos*, 1971.
La quinta temporada (produced Delano, 1966). Included in *Actos*, 1971.
Los vendidos (produced Delano, 1967). Included in *Actos*, 1971.
The Shrunken Head of Pancho Villa (produced Delano, 1968).
La conquista de Mexico (puppet play; produced Delano, 1968). Included in *Actos*, 1971.
No saco nada de la escuela (produced Fresno, 1969). Included in *Actos*, 1971.
The Militants (produced Fresno, 1969). Included in *Actos*, 1971.
Vietnam campesino (produced Fresno, 1970). Included in *Actos*, 1971.
Soldado razo (produced Fresno, 1970; New York, 1985). Included in *Actos*, 1971.
Huelguistas (produced Fresno, 1970). Included in *Actos*, 1971.
Bernabé (produced Fresno, 1970). Published in *Contemporary Chicano Theatre*, edited by Roberto Garza, Notre Dame, Indiana, University of Notre Dame Press, 1976.
Actos. San Juan Bautista, Cucaracha, 1971.
El Virgen del Tepeyac (produced San Juan Bautista, 1971).
Dark Root of a Scream (produced Los Angeles, 1971; New York, 1985). Published in *From the Barrio: A Chicano Anthology*, edited by Lillian Faderman and Luis Omar Salinas, San Francisco, Canfield Press, 1973.
Los olivos pits (produced San Juan Bautista, 1972).
Mundo (produced San Juan Bautista, 1973).
La gran carpa de los rasquachis (produced San Juan Bautista, 1973).
El baille de los gigantes (produced San Juan Bautista, 1973).
El fin del mundo (produced San Juan Bautista, 1975).
Zoot Suit (produced Los Angeles, 1978; New York, 1979).
I Don't Have to Show You No Stinking Badgers (produced Los Angeles, 1986).

Screenplays: *Zoot Suit*, 1982; *La Bamba*, 1987.

Other

Pensamiento Serpentino: A Chicano Approach to the Theatre of Reality. San Juan Bautista, California, Cucaracha, 1973.

Editor, with Stan Steiner, *Aztlan: An Anthology of Mexican American Literature*. New York, Knopf, 1972.

*

Theatrical Activities:
Director: **Plays**—most of his own plays. **Films**—*Zoot Suit*, 1982; *La Bamba*, 1987.
Actor: **Film**—*Which Way Is Up?*, 1977. **Television**—*Visions* series, 1976.

* * *

Best known as the founder of the Teatro Campesino (Farmworker's Theatre) in 1965, Luis Valdez is a man of many talents: actor, playwright, screenwriter, essayist, stage and film director, and he is the leading practitioner of Chicano theater in the United States. From the earliest agit-prop pieces he directed and wrote, termed *actos*, to his professionally produced *Zoot Suit*, first a play and then a film, Valdez has attempted to portray the Chicano's reality.

The very term "Chicano" connotes a political attitude, cognizant of a distinctive place in the so-called "American melting-pot," and Valdez became a major proponent of this self-imposed designation when his teatro the country asserting a cultural and political distinction. Valdez has termed *Zoot Suit* an "American play," this in deference to his belief that Chicanos are a part of the American society and should not be excluded from what this society has to offer its citizens. Valdez's dramatic themes always reflect Chicanos in crisis, never pretending that Chicanos have been fully accepted into the American mainstream. His characters are always in conflict with some aspect of the system, and more often than not, that manifestation of the power structure is presented by non-Chicanos, or "Anglos." Although the characters in power find it easy to manipulate the subordinate Chicanos, Valdez's audiences discover that whether the heroes win or lose it is they who can win through collective action.

Las dos caras del patroncito (The Two Faces of the Boss) and *La quinta temporada* (The Fifth Season) are *actos* that reveal the plight of striking farmworkers, solved through unionization. When Valdez decided to leave the union in 1967 he sought an independent theater company, not focussed solely on labor movement and farmworker themes. The next *acto, Los vendidos* (The Sellouts), explored various stereotypes of Chicanos and satirized the "sellout" who attempted to assimilate into a white, racist society. *No saco nada de la escuela* (I Don't Get Anything Out of School) exposed some inequities in the educational process and *La conquista de Mexico* (The Conquest of Mexico) paralleled the fall of the Aztecs with the disunity of Chicano activists of the day. The use of masks, farcical exaggeration, stereotyped characters, improvisation, and social commentary in the *actos* reflects Valdez's work with the San Francisco Mime Troupe prior to his founding the teatro. While the *actos* are brief agit-prop statements, Valdez's plays explore other theatrical forms.

Beginning with his first play, *The Shrunken Head of Pancho Villa*, originally written and produced while he was a student, Valdez has written non-realistic statements, mingling fantasy and farce, comedy and pathos. All of Valdez's plays issue forth from a family structure. *The Shrunken Head of Pancho Villa* pits the assimilationist against the *pachuco* social bandit: two brothers whose life-styles reflect the extremes within the barrio. *Bernabé* revolves around a village idiot who gains a spiritual release when he symbolically marries *La Tierra* (The Earth) who appears to him as a symbol of the Mexican Revolution of 1910.

There is much of the Spanish religious folk theatre in Valdez's plays, combined with a new message of social justice. The playwright uses allegorical and mythological figures to present his messages, combatting the evils of the war in Vietnam in the *actos Vietnam campesino* and *Soldado razo* (Private Soldier) or the expressionist play *Dark Root of a Scream*. He exposes the need for a balance with Mother Nature in the ritualistic *El fin del mundo* (The End of the World), *La gran carpa de los rasquachis* (The Great Tent of the Underdogs), and *Mundo* (a title based on the name of the protagonist, Reimundo, or "king of the world"). Beginning with *Bernabé*, each of the plays combines indigenous mythology with contemporary problems. *La gran carpa de los rasquachis* most notably unites the Virgin of Guadalupe with Quetzalcoatl, the meso-American Christ-figure, calling for unity among all people.

In *Zoot Suit* Valdez unites all the elements of his theater to create a statement that cannot be classified without listing its parts: the *acto*, Living Newspaper, the *corrido* (dramatized Mexican ballads), selective realism, and fantasy. The play is narrated by an archetypal "pachuco," a barrio character type that has always fascinated the playwright. This enigmatic figure glides in and out of the action, a fantastical symbol of the Chicano's defiance and ability to survive between two cultures: the Mexican and the Anglo. *Zoot Suit* was the first Chicano play to reach Broadway, and though the New York critics generally disliked the play, it broke box-office records in Los Angeles. The play reminded its audiences that current Chicano struggles has their precedents in such events as the Sleepy Lagoon Murder Trial, which exposed a biased system of justice in the 1940's. Valdez's hit film *La Bamba*, the story of Chicano pop singer Ritchie Valens, reached the Anglo audience in a big way in 1987.

From *actos* to *Zoot Suit*, Valdez remains a singular example of a Chicano who has consistently recreated the struggles and successes of the Chicanos with a clarity of vision and style, however controversial the themes, that makes him a true man of the theater.

—Jorge A. Huerta

---

van ITALLIE, Jean-Claude. American. Born in Brussels, Belgium, 25 May 1936; moved to the United States, 1940; became citizen, 1952. Educated at Great Neck High School, New York; Deerfield Academy, Massachusetts; Harvard University, Cambridge, Massachusetts, A.B. 1958; New York University, 1959; studied acting at the Neighborhood Playhouse, New York. Editor, *Transatlantic Review*, New York, 1960–63; playwright-in-residence, Open Theatre, New York, 1963–68; free-lance writer on public affairs for NBC and CBS television, New York, 1963–67; taught playwriting at the New School for Social Research, New York, 1967–68, 1972, Yale University School of Drama, New Haven, Connecticut, 1969, 1978, 1984–85, and Naropa Institute, Boulder, Colorado, 1976–83; Lecturer, Princeton University, New Jersey, 1973–86, New York University, 1982–86, University of Colorado, Boulder, Fall 1985, and Columbia University, New York, Spring 1986; Visiting Mellon Professor, Amherst College, Massachusetts, Fall 1976. Recipient: Rockefeller grant, 1962; Vernon Rice award, 1967; Outer Circle award, 1967; Obie award, 1968; Guggenheim fellowship, 1973, 1980; Creative Artists Public Service grant, 1973; National Endowment for the Arts fellowship, 1986. Ph.D.: Kent State University, Kent, Ohio, 1977. Address: Box L, Charlemont, Massachusetts 01339, U.S.A.

PUBLICATIONS

Plays

War (produced New York, 1963; Edinburgh, 1968; London, 1969). Included in *War and Four Other Plays*, 1967; in *America Hurrah*, 1967.

Almost Like Being (produced New York, 1964). Included in *War and Four Other Plays*, 1967; in *America Hurrah*, 1967.

I'm Really Here (produced New York, 1964; London, 1979). Included in *War and Four Other Plays*, 1967.

The Hunter and the Bird (produced New York, 1964). Included in *War and Four Other Plays*, 1967.

Interview (as *Pavane*, produced Atlanta, 1965; revised version, as *Interview*, produced New York, 1966; London, 1967). Included in *America Hurrah*, 1967.

Where Is de Queen? (as *Dream*, produced New York, 1965; revised version, as *Where Is de Queen?*, produced Mineapolis, 1965). Included in *War and Four Other Plays*, 1967.

Motel (as *America Hurrah*, produced New York, 1965; revised version, as *Motel*, produced New York, 1966; London, 1967). Included in *America Hurrah*, 1967.

America Hurrah (includes *Interview, TV, Motel*) (produced New York, 1966; London, 1967). New York, Coward McCann, 1967; with *War* and *Almost Like Being*, as *America Hurrah: Five Short Plays*, London, Penguin, 1967.

The Girl and the Soldier (produced Los Angeles, 1967). Included in *Seven Short and Very Short Plays*, 1975.

War and Four Other Plays. New York, Dramatists Play Service, 1967.

Thoughts on the Instant of Greeting a Friend on the Street, with Sharon Thie (produced Los Angeles, 1967; in *Collision Course*, produced New York, 1968). Included in *Seven Short and Very Short Plays*, 1975.

The Serpent: A Ceremony, with the Open Theatre (produced Rome, 1968; New York, 1970). New York, Atheneum, 1969.

Take a Deep Breath (televised 1969). Included in *Seven Short and Very Short Plays*, 1975.

Photographs: Mary and Howard (produced Los Angeles, 1969). Included in *Seven Short and Very Short Plays*, 1975.

Eat Cake (produced Denver, 1971). Included in *Seven Short and Very Short Plays*, 1975.

Mystery Play (produced New York, 1973). New York, Dramatists Play Service, 1973; revised version, as *The King of the United States*, music by Richard Peaslee (also director: produced New York, 1973), New York, Dramatists Play Service, 1975.

Nightwalk, with Megan Terry and Sam Shepard (produced New York and London, 1973). Published in *Open Theater*, New York, Drama Book Specialists, 1975.

The Sea Gull, adaptation of a play by Chekhov (produced Princeton, New Jersey, 1973; New York, 1975). New York, Harper, 1977.

A Fable, music by Richard Peaslee (produced New York, 1975). New York, Dramatists Play Service, 1976.

Seven Short and Very Short Plays (includes *Photographs, Eat Cake, The Girl and the Soldier, Take a Deep Breath, Rosary, Harold, Thoughts on the Instant of Greeting a Friend on the Street*). New York, Dramatists Play Service, 1975.

The Cherry Orchard, adaptation of a play by Chekhov (produced New York, 1977). New York, Grove Press, 1977.

America Hurrah and Other Plays (includes *The Serpent, A Fable, The Hunter and the Bird, Almost Like Being*). New York, Grove Press, 1978.

Medea, adaptation of the play by Euripides (produced Kent, Ohio, 1979).

Three Sisters (produced New York, 1979). New York, Dramatists Play Service, 1979.

Bag Lady (produced New York, 1979). New York, Dramatists Play Service, 1980.

Uncle Vanya, adaptation of a play by Chekhov (produced New York, 1983). New York, Dramatists Play Service, 1980.

Naropa, music by Steve Gorn (produced New York, 1982). Published in *Wordplays 1*, New York, Performing Arts Journal Publications, 1980.

Early Warnings (includes *Bag Lady, Sunset Freeway, Final Orders*) (produced New York, 1983). New York, Dramatists Play Service, 1983.

The Tibetan Book of the Dead; or, How Not to Do It Again, music by Steve Gorn (produced New York, 1983). New York, Dramatists Play Service, 1983.

Pride, in *Faustus in Hell* (produced Princeton, New Jersey, 1985).

The Balcony, adaptation of a play by Jean Genet (produced Cambridge, Massachusetts, 1986).

The Traveler (produced Los Angeles and Leicester, 1987).

Screenplays: *The Box Is Empty*, 1965; *Three Lives for Mississippi*, 1971.

Television Writing: scripts for *Look Up and Live* series, 1963–65; *Hobbies; or, Things Are All Right with the Forbushers*, 1967; *Take a Deep Breath*, 1969; *Picasso: A Painter's Diary*, 1980.

*

Manuscript Collections: Kent State University, Ohio; Harvard University Library, Cambridge, Massachusetts.

Critical Studies: by Walter Kerr, in *New York Times*, 11 December 1966; "Three Views of America," in *The Third Theatre* by Robert Brustein, New York, Knopf, 1969, London, Cape, 1970; *Up Against the Fourth Wall* by John Lahr, New York, Grove Press, 1970; "Jean-Claude van Itallie Issue" of *Serif* (Kent, Ohio), Winter 1972.

Theatrical Activities:
Director: **Play**—*The King of the United States*, New York, 1973.

Jean-Claude van Itallie comments:

I seem to have been most intent on playing with new forms that might express a clear theatre optic. I have worked as a playwright in solitude. I have adapted and translated into English from a foreign language. I have worked as a poet in collaboration with a theatre director and actors, and with actors alone. I have written for puppets. I have written screenplays and specifically for television. I question theatre but I remain married to it, more or less. I agree that language itself helps to keep us isolated but I continue to write. I want to write with greater clarity, but from the heart. I like to work with other artists in the theatre, and to imagine the audience as a community of friends.

The 1960's were an exciting time of revolt and reformation. In the vanguard, theater destroyed preconceptions and invented new disciplines to express re-found truths underlying the mendacity of the commercial and political world. The 1970's were a time of retrenchment; I worked on new versions of classics making contact with my heritage as a playwright, my lineage. What for the 1980's? In form, working to synthesize the discoveries of the 1960's, and the rediscoveries of the 1970's. In content? Political lies and corruption of power have become mundane; we are concerned now with our self-caused possible destruction of the world. What is the relationship between runaway technology and short-sighted pollution of air, food, and water, on the one hand, and spiritual poverty on the other? This is a time, perhaps the very last possible decade, to clarify and acknowledge the split between body and mind in the individual and the world, and in that acknowledgement to effect a healing.

* * *

The early plays of Jean-Claude van Itallie, in terms of their brevity, wit, and social commentary, may be taken to resemble the early one-acts of Ionesco or, better, Chekhov—and later in his career van Itallie composed luminous American versions of the major Chekhov plays. The decisive difference between van Itallie's drama and that of the classic moderns lies in the realm of form. He is preoccupied with multiple levels of experience, with the mask behind the mask, and with states of awareness outside the province of the everyday. His crystalline perceptions give rise to complex modes of characterization, a concern with indeterminate time, and a montage approach to dramatic activity and language.

Van Itallie's essential stage vocabulary is there at the start, in his off-off-Broadway debut with *War*. He describes the play as a "formal war game, a duel" between two male actors of different generations who metamorphose into father and son. They are visited by the shimmering vision of a nameless great actress of the Edwardian era who addresses them as her children and transforms their gritty New York loft which is crammed with theatrical paraphernalia, into a sunny, cheerful park. At the end the men form an emblem of a two-headed eagle of war, each male identity locked into that of the other.

The rich theatrical implications of this meditation on appearances, on essential conflict, and on the role-nature of personality quickly matured when in the same year van Itallie began writing for the newly organized Open Theatre under the direction of Joseph Chaikin. In its shattering of received theatrical forms, its canonization of the workshop process, and its philosophical daring, the Open Theatre provided van Itallie with a subtle instrument for testing the limits of theatrical representation. For the Open Theatre he contributed numerous sketches, improvisations, and short plays, including *The Hunter and the Bird*; among his most successful are the pop-art Hollywood comedies informally known as "the Doris Day plays": *Almost Like Being* and *I'm Really Here*, with a wacky Doris D. in love with Just Rock and then the deadly Rossano.

Van Itallie's chief works for the Open Theatre came in his last years with the company. A triptych of one-acts under the title *America Hurrah* begins with *Interview*, a rhythmic weaving of ritualized daily behavior and speech that starts and concludes in the anonymous offices of an employment agency where all the applicants are named Smith. *TV* dramatizes the menace and trivializing power of the mass media, with a trio watching television in the viewing room of a television-ratings company: the television images break free of the set and engulf the viewers. *Motel: A Masque for Three Dolls* unfolds within a tacky midwestern motel room where a huge Doll Motel-Keeper spews forth an unctuous monologue about the room and its furnishings which represent the mail-order-catalogue surface of a violent America. Man Doll and Woman Doll enter the room and proceed to tear the place apart, have sex, and destroy the Motel-Keeper.

The theme of violence done to persons through the exigencies of the social contract is taken up again in *The Serpent*. Here, in an even more sophisticated interplay of layered actions, contemporary violence is linked back to its ancient sources and seen as a central aspect of the human condition. As it simultaneously presents and confronts the values in its story, this "ceremony" for actors explores the themes and the events of Genesis, and the Tree of Life is a tangle of men who embody the serpent. God's fixing of limits upon Adam and Eve is viewed as humanity's projection of its own need for limits, and the self-consciousness that results from the Fall leads to Cain and Abel and the unending human battle, in which each is "caught between the beginning and the end" and unable to remake the past.

After leaving the Open Theatre, van Itallie wrote and staged *The King of the United States*, a stark political fable about the need for an office of rule supported by agents of the status quo to give order to life. *Mystery Play* recycles the characters and themes of *The King* and inverts its tone and style in an elegantly paced farce-parody of the whodunnit, presided over by a Mystery Writer who likes to play detective.

In 1975 van Itallie collaborated again with Chaikin on *A Fable*, a folktale for adults. In picaresque episodes a Journeyor leaves her impoverished village in search of help, and in her wanderings over a wide and storied landscape she comes to celebrate the need to transcend the beast within.

With *Early Warnings* van Itallie returned to smaller forms and a second triptych, on the theme of accommodation. The warnings are directed at the audience, for the characters already have made their choices. *Bag Lady* presents a day in the street life of the witty Clara who is organizing her bags and keeping only the essential shards of her identity. The perky actress Judy Jensen in *Sunset Freeway* breezes along in her car at dusk on the L.A. freeway, immersed in her identity of commercial actress. She speaks to her toy giraffe, imagines a nuclear holocaust, spots Warren Beatty, and, looking out upon the glories of consumer culture, she's in heaven. In *Final Orders* space program agents Angus and Mike listen to instructions from a computer and hold on to one another, poised for the holocaust that now is at hand.

Among van Itallie's most ambitious projects is a theatrical version of *The Tibetan Book of the Dead; or, How Not To Do It Again*, a ritual for the dead in which the characters are emanations of the Dead One, speaking, chanting, and dancing within a huge skull and upon a floor mandala. In its style and complexity, and in its debt to an ancient text, it resembles *The Serpent*, but its landscape lies beyond history and legend in an essentialized world of the spirit.

The whole of van Itallie's dramatic universe is dedicated to a process of vital experimentation through the counterpoint of language, mask, and gesture. His is a philosophy of theatrical play underscored with social critique. Central to his vision are the inadequacies of being and a knowledge of exile. And above all, a knowledge too of the brutalities that are visited upon the self as it seeks to make its way in a world almost willfully estranged from organic life.

—William Coco

VIDAL, Gore (Eugene Luther Vidal, Jr.). American. Born in West Point, New York, 3 October 1925. Educated at Los Alamos School, New Mexico, 1939–40; Phillips Exeter Academy, Exeter, New Hampshire, 1940–43. Served in the United States Army, 1943–46: Warrant Officer. Editor, E.P. Dutton, publishers, New York, 1946. Lived in Antigua, Guatemala, 1947–49, and Italy, from 1967. Member, Advisory Board, *Partisan Review*, New Brunswick, New Jersey, 1960–71; Democratic-Liberal candidate for Congress, New York, 1960; member, President's Advisory Committee on the Arts, 1961–63; Co-Chairman, New Party, 1968–71. Recipient: Mystery Writers of America Edgar Allan Poe Award, for television play, 1954; National Book Critics Circle award, for criticism, 1983. Address: La Rondinaia, Ravello, 84010 Salerno, Italy; or c/o Random House Inc., 201 East 50th Street, New York, New York 10022, U.S.A.

PUBLICATIONS

Plays

Visit to a Small Planet (televised 1955). Included in *Visit to a Small Planet and Other Television Plays*, 1956; revised version (produced New York, 1957; London, 1960), Boston, Little Brown, 1957; in *Three Plays*, 1962.

Honor (televised 1956). Published in *Television Plays for Writers: Eight Television Plays*, edited by A.S. Burack, Boston, The Writer, 1957; revised version, as *On the March to the Sea: A Southron Comedy* (produced Bonn, Germany, 1961), in *Three Plays*, 1962.

Visit to a Small Planet and Other Television Plays (includes *Barn Burning, Dark Possession, The Death of Billy the Kid, A Sense of Justice, Smoke, Summer Pavilion, The Turn of the Screw*). Boston, Little Brown, 1956.

The Best Man: A Play about Politics (produced New York, 1960). Boston, Little Brown, 1960; in *Three Plays*, 1962.

Three Plays. London, Heinemann, 1962.

Romulus: A New Comedy, adaptation of a play by Friedrich Dürrenmatt (produced New York, 1962). New York, Dramatists Play Service, 1962.

Weekend (produced New York, 1968). New York, Dramatists Play Service, 1968.

An Evening with Richard Nixon and . . . (produced New York, 1972). New York, Random House, 1972.

Screenplays: *The Catered Affair*, 1956; *I Accuse*, 1958; *The Scapegoat*, with Robert Hamer, 1959; *Suddenly Last Summer*, with Tennessee Williams, 1959; *The Best Man*, 1964; *Is Paris Burning?*, with Francis Ford Coppola, 1966; *Last of the Mobile Hot-Shots*, 1970; *The Sicilian*, 1987.

Television Plays: *Barn Burning*, from the story by Faulkner, 1954; *Dark Possession*, 1954; *Smoke*, from the story by Faulkner, 1954; *Visit to a Small Planet*, 1955; *The Death of Billy the Kid*, 1955; *A Sense of Justice*, 1955; *Summer Pavilion*, 1955; *The Turn of the Screw*, from the story by Henry James, 1955; *Honor*, 1956; *The Indestructible Mr. Gore*, 1960; *Vidal in Venice* (documentary), 1985; *Dress Gray*, from the novel by Lucian K. Truscott IV, 1986.

Novels

Williwaw. New York, Dutton, 1946; London, Panther, 1965.

In a Yellow Wood. New York, Dutton, 1947; London, New English Library, 1967.

The City and the Pillar. New York, Dutton, 1948; London, Lehmann, 1949; revised edition, Dutton, and London, Heinemann, 1965.

The Season of Comfort. New York, Dutton, 1949.

Dark Green, Bright Red. New York, Dutton, and London, Lehmann, 1950.

A Search for the King: A Twelfth Century Legend. New York, Dutton, 1950; London, New English Library, 1967.

The Judgment of Paris. New York, Dutton, 1952; London, Heinemann, 1953; revised edition, Boston, Little Brown, 1965; Heinemann, 1966.

Messiah. New York, Dutton, 1954; London, Heinemann, 1955; revised edition, Boston, Little Brown, 1965; Heinemann 1968.

Three: Williwaw, A Thirsty Evil, Julian the Apostate. New York, New American Library, 1962.

Julian. Boston, Little Brown, and London, Heinemann, 1964.

Washington, D.C. Boston, Little Brown, and London, Heinemann, 1967.

Myra Breckinridge. Boston, Little Brown, and London, Blond, 1968.
Two Sisters: A Memoir in the Form of a Novel. Boston, Little Brown, and London, Heinemann, 1970.
Burr. New York, Random House, 1973; London, Heinemann, 1974.
Myron. New York, Random House, 1974; London, Heinemann, 1975.
1876. New York, Random House, and London, Heinemann, 1976.
Kalki. New York, Random House, and London, Heinemann, 1978.
Creation. New York, Random House, and London, Heinemann, 1981.
Duluth. New York, Random House, and London, Heinemann, 1983.
Lincoln. New York, Random House, and London, Heinemann, 1984.
Empire. New York, Random House, and London, Deutsch, 1987.

Novels as Edgar Box

Death in the Fifth Position. New York, Dutton, 1952; London, Heinemann, 1954.
Death Before Bedtime. New York, Dutton, 1953; London, Heinemann, 1954.
Death Likes It Hot. New York, Dutton, 1954; London, Heinemann, 1955.

Short Stories

A Thirsty Evil: Seven Short Stories. New York, Zero Press, 1956; London, Heinemann, 1958.

Other

Rocking the Boat (essays). Boston, Little Brown, 1962; London, Heinemann, 1963.
Sex, Death, and Money (essays). New York, Bantam, 1968.
Reflections upon a Sinking Ship (essays). Boston, Little Brown, and London, Heinemann, 1969.
Homage to Daniel Shays: Collected Essays 1952–1972. New York, Random House, 1972; as *Collected Essays 1952–1972*, London, Heinemann, 1974.
Matters of Fact and of Fiction: Essays 1973–1976. New York, Random House, and London, Heinemann, 1977.
Sex Is Politics and Vice Versa (essay). Los Angeles, Sylvester and Orphanos, 1979.
Views from a Window: Conversations with Gore Vidal, with Robert J. Stanton. Secaucus, New Jersey, Lyle Stuart, 1980.
The Second American Revolution and Other Essays 1976–1982. New York, Random House, 1982; as *Pink Triangle and Yellow Star and Other Essays*, London, Heinemann, 1982.
Vidal in Venice, edited by George Armstrong, photographs by Tore Gill. New York, Summit, and London, Weidenfeld and Nicolson, 1985.
Armageddon? (essays). London, Deutsch, 1987.

Editor, *Best Television Plays.* New York, Ballantine, 1956.

*

Bibliography: *Gore Vidal: A Primary and Secondary Bibliography* by Robert J. Stanton, Boston, Hall, and London, Prior, 1978.

Manuscript Collection: University of Wisconsin, Madison.

Critical Studies: *Gore Vidal* by Ray Lewis White, New York, Twayne, 1968; *The Apostate Angel: A Critical Study of Gore Vidal* by Bernard F. Dick, New York, Random House, 1974; *Gore Vidal* by Robert F. Kiernan, New York, Ungar, 1982.

Theatrical Activities:
Actor: **Film**—*Roma* (*Fellini Roma*), 1972.

* * *

Eschewing all consideration of Gore Vidal as a novelist and short story writer the critic must associate his theatrical production with its kinship to cinema and television, i.e., Vidal's plays are quite stageable yet are intrinsically cinematographic or televisionistic. They have a modernity about them that facilitates their being restructured for each medium—because they are thematically and linguistically hinged loosely but integrally, and the characters drawn in such a manner that in displacing a character, in changing a tempo, or shifting psychology for a particular medium, Vidal does not violate the play's integrity. Critics have envied Vidal's facile success on television and stage; but his success would not be forthcoming were he not an extremely proficient stylist. True, Vidal has a grudge against a complacent "bourgeois" society and likes to jab at sensitive and vulnerable spots, and he succeeded cinematographically in *Suddenly Last Summer*. The film *Lefthanded Gun* (based on his television play on the Billy the Kid legend) succeeded; but *Myra Breckinridge* failed because the producers were not faithful to Vidal.

His themes—extreme and tabooistic in his novels—are more traditional in his plays, mainly war and politics. But the persistent leitmotiv in all his works is man bereft in the modern world. Should man relinquish certain values? Find new ones? Vidal assigns satire for the first alternative, irony for the second. Vidal the person seems to opt for relative values, and creates types (as do all playwrights) to epitomize these values; yet Vidal the writer, in creating the antagonistic types to exemplify certain absolutes, finds himself with characters possessing more dramatic qualities and effectiveness—which indicates that Vidal the writer is instinctively more sage than Vidal the person. Since the antagonist stands well in his own defence he wins dramatic or tragic sympathy; hence, the thesis comes to no social conclusion and the spectator is left with the unresolved futility of modern life. This is good dramaturgy.

Weekend is the least effective of Vidal's plays. It is an attempt to profit from the topical concern about miscegenation which the author encrusts on a political campaign (not unlike *The Best Man*); but the situation and the characters are not real enough for good satire, nor exaggerated enough to make good farce. Vidal's merit as a playwright, however, is best demonstrated in his trilogy: *Visit to a Small Planet, On the March to the Sea, The Best Man.*

Visit to a Small Planet is the story of a one-man invasion from outer space—an extraterrestrial being who is intent on creating a state of war between his world and ours. This "man" is called Kreton (may all warmongers bear this epithet!) and almost succeeds in creating a war hysteria on earth through certain well-conceived comic situations. It was because of these situations that the play became a very successful television series. However, its anti-war theme is ineffective because we cannot associate the Kreton's world with our own cretin world. After all, it was they who wanted war, not us humans. The audience can't help but feel self-righteous at the end when

Kreton is led off to his celestial kindergarten. In attempting a satire on war Vidal created an excellent science-fiction farce with characterizations that are memorable—the pixie Kreton, the prototype of the war-loving general, Tom Powers, and Roger Felding, an equally ambitious television commentator.

Although the theme of *On the March to the Sea* is shop-worn—the disasters wrought on Southern families, particularly that of John Hinks, by the ravages of the Civil War—this play is poignant and highly dramatic. The characters are all believable, with the possible exception of Captain Taylor of the Union Army—flamboyant, too philosophic (war participants, i.e., soldiers, are never introspective not contemplative, at least about ethical or social problems, during bellicose engagements). Vidal thought a lot of this character and gave him the final words of the play; but the character really caught in the maelstrom of life and war, John Hinks, was the authentic tragic figure of the play. The play is in a war setting and the war pervades all. Yet as the title aptly indicates, the main theme is not Sherman's march to the sea, but a series of incidents that take place *on* the march to the sea. The question of what is human dignity (the answer to one's own conscience) and honor (the answer to social conscience) is put literally through a trial by fire. The characters, even though typified (intentionally so) are all quite well drawn, except for Colonel Thayer, who is the "heavy."

But Colonel Thayer is too celluloidish a character to be really cruel. The cruelty prize goes to Clayton, son of John Hinks, too young and self-centered to understand his father's anguish. Though *Visit to a Small Planet* was intended as a satire on war, *On the March to the Sea* is infinitely more effective as an anti-war drama.

The Best Man is the struggle between two presidential aspirants, jockeying, scratching, and grubbing for the nomination of their party. The play is a well-wrought urn, perfectly structured, containing political characters that emulate Hollywoodian stereotypes (Vidal had every intention of doing this), effective dialogue, with each character keeping to his program. The suspenseful outcome of the nomination is solved by an honorable, classical, and justified theatrical technique: President ex-machina. The solution is not only theatrically perfect, but thematically perfect, in that the person eventually to be nominated is of little importance.

The main theme—does one have to be a demogogue to be successful in political life? Vidal gives us such a selection of presidential aspirants that they seem *inverosimil* and incredible. But as the old Italian quip says, "If it's not a wolf, it's a dog." This is ingeniously planted in the mind of the spectator and this is why *The Best Man* is extremely good satire.

—John V. Falconieri

WALCOTT, Derek (Alton). British. Born in Castries, St. Lucia, West Indies, 23 January 1930. Educated at St. Mary's College, Castries, 1941–47; University College of the West Indies, Mona, Jamaica, 1950–54, B.A. 1953. Married 1) Fay Moyston in 1954 (divorced 1959), one son; 2) Margaret Ruth Maillard in 1962 (divorced), two daughters; 3) Norline Metivier. Teacher, Grenada Boys' Secondary School, St. George's, Grenada, 1953–54, St. Mary's College, Castries, 1954, and Jamaica College, Kingston, 1955; feature writer, *Public Opinion*, Kingston, 1956–57; feature writer, 1960–62, and drama critic, 1963–68, *Trinidad Guardian*, Port-of-Spain. Co-founder, St. Lucia Arts Guild, 1950, and Basement Theatre, Port-of-Spain; founding director, Little Carib Theatre Workshop (later Trinidad Theatre Workshop), 1959–76. Assistant Professor of Creative Writing, Boston University, 1981. Recipient: Rockefeller grant, 1957, 1966, and fellowship, 1958; Arts Advisory Council of Jamaica prize, 1960; Guinness award, for poetry, 1961; Ingram Merrill Foundation grant, 1962; Borestone Mountain award, for poetry, 1964, 1977; Royal Society of Literature Heinemann award, for poetry, 1966, 1983; Cholmondeley award, 1969; Audrey Wood fellowship, 1969; Eugene O'Neill Foundation fellowship, 1969; Gold Hummingbird Medal (Trinidad), 1969; Obie award, 1971; Jock Campbell award (*New Statesman*), 1974; Guggenheim award, 1977; *American Poetry Review* award, 1979; Welsh Arts Council International Writers Prize, 1980; MacArthur fellowship, 1981; *Los Angeles Times* prize, for poetry, 1986. D.Litt.: University of the West Indies, Mona, 1973. Fellow, Royal Society of Literature, 1966; Honorary Member, American Academy, 1979. O.B.E. (Officer, Order of the British Empire), 1972. Address: 165 Duke of Edinburgh Avenue, Diego Martin, Trinidad.

PUBLICATIONS

Plays

Cry for a Leader (produced St. Lucia, 1950).

Senza Alcun Sospetto (broadcast 1950; as *Paolo and Francesca*, produced St. Lucia, 1951?).

Henri Christophe: A Chronicle (also director: produced Castries, 1950; London, 1952). Bridgetown, Barbados Advocate, 1950.

Robin and Andrea, published in *Bim* (Christ Church, Barbados), December 1950.

Three Assassins (produced St. Lucia, 1951?).

The Price of Mercy (produced St. Lucia, 1951?).

Harry Dernier (as *Dernier*, broadcast 1952; as *Harry Dernier*, also director: produced Mona, 1952). Bridgetown, Barbados Advocate, 1952.

The Sea at Dauphin (produced Trinidad, 1954; London, 1960; New York, 1978). Mona, University College of the West Indies Extra-Mural Department, 1954; in *Dream on Monkey Mountain and Other Plays*, 1970.

Crossroads (produced Jamaica, 1954).

The Charlatan (also director: produced Mona, 1954?; revised version, music by Fred Hope and Rupert Dennison, produced Port-of-Spain, 1973; revised version, music by Galt MacDermot, produced Los Angeles, 1974; revised version, produced Port-of-Spain, 1977).

The Wine of the Country (also director: produced Mona, 1956).

The Golden Lions (also director: produced Mona, 1956).

Ione: A Play with Music (produced Kingston, 1957). Mona, University College of the West Indies Extra-Mural Department, 1957.

Ti-Jean and His Brothers (produced Castries, 1957; revised version, also director: produced Port-of-Spain, 1958; Hanover, New Hampshire, 1971; also director: produced New York, 1972; London, 1986). Included in *Dream on Monkey Mountain and Other Plays*, 1970.

Drums and Colours (produced Port-of-Spain, 1958). Published in *Caribbean Quarterly* (Mona), vol. 7, nos. 1 and 2, 1961.

Malcochon; or, The Six in the Rain (produced Castries, 1959; as *Six in the Rain*, produced London, 1960; as *Malcochon*, produced New York, 1969). Included in *Dream on Monkey Mountain and Other Plays*, 1970.

Jourmard; or, A Comedy till the Last Minute (produced St. Lucia, 1959; New York, 1962).

Batai (carnival show; also director: produced Port-of-Spain, 1965).

Dream on Monkey Mountain (also director: produced Toronto, 1967; Waterford, Connecticut, 1969; New York, 1970). Included in *Dream on Monkey Mountain and Other Plays*, 1970.

Franklin: A Tale of the Islands (produced Georgetown, Guyana, 1969; revised version, also director: produced Port-of-Spain, 1973).

In a Fine Castle (also director: produced Mona, 1970; Los Angeles, 1972). Excerpt, as *Conscience of a Revolutionary*, published in *Express* (Port-of-Spain), 24 October 1971.

Dream on Monkey Mountain and Other Plays (includes *Ti-Jean and His Brothers, Malcochon, The Sea at Dauphin*, and the essay "What the Twilight Says"). New York, Farrar Straus, 1970; London, Cape, 1972.

The Joker of Seville, music by Galt MacDermot, adaptation of the play by Tirso de Molina (produced Port-of-Spain, 1974). With *O Babylon!*, New York, Farrar Straus, 1978; London, Cape, 1979.

O Babylon!, music by Galt MacDermot (also director: produced Port-of-Spain, 1976). With *The Joker of Seville*, New York, Farrar Straus, 1978; London, Cape, 1979.

Remembrance (also director: produced St. Croix, U.S. Virgin Islands, 1977; New York, 1979; London, 1980). With *Pantomime*, New York, Farrar Straus, 1980.

The Snow Queen (television play), excerpt published in *People* (Port-of-Spain), April 1977.

Pantomime (produced Port-of-Spain, 1978; London, 1979; Washington, D.C., 1981; New York, 1986). With *Remembrance*, New York, Farrar Straus, 1980.

Marie Laveau, music by Galt MacDermot (also director: produced St. Thomas, U.S. Virgin Islands, 1979). Excerpts published in *Trinidad and Tobago Review* (Tunapuna), Christmas 1979.

The Isle Is Full of Noises (produced Hartford, Connecticut, 1982).

Beef, No Chicken (produced New Haven, Connecticut, 1982). Included in *Three Plays*, 1985.

Three Plays (includes *The Last Carnival*; *Beef, No Chicken*; *A Branch of the Blue Nile*). New York, Farrar Straus, 1986.

Radio Plays: *Senza Alcun Sospetto*, 1950; *Dernier*, 1952.

Verse

25 Poems. Port-of-Spain, Trinidad, Guardian Commercial Printery, 1948.

Epitaph for the Young: XII Cantos. Bridgetown, Barbados Advocate, 1949.

Poems. Kingston, Jamaica, City Printery, 1951.

In a Green Night: Poems 1948–1960. London, Cape, 1962.

Selected Poems. New York, Farrar Straus, 1964.

The Castaway and Other Poems. London, Cape, 1965.

The Gulf and Other Poems. London, Cape, 1969; as *The Gulf*, New York, Farrar Straus, 1970.

Another Life. New York, Farrar Straus, and London, Cape, 1973.

Sea Grapes. London, Cape, and New York, Farrar Straus, 1976.

The Star-Apple Kingdom. New York, Farrar Straus, 1979; London, Cape, 1980.

Selected Poetry, edited by Wayne Brown. London, Heinemann, 1981.

The Fortunate Traveller. New York, Farrar Straus, 1981; London, Faber, 1982.

The Caribbean Poetry of Derek Walcott and the Art of Romare Bearden. New York, Limited Editions Club, 1983.

Midsummer. New York, Farrar Straus, and London, Faber, 1984.

Collected Poems 1948–1984. New York, Farrar Straus, and London, Faber, 1986.

The Arkansas Testament. New York, Farrar Straus, 1987.

*

Bibliography: *Derek Walcott: An Annotated Bibliography of His Works* by Irma E. Goldstraw, New York, Garland, 1984.

Critical Studies: *Derek Walcott: Memory as Vision* by Edward Baugh, London, Longman, 1978; *Derek Walcott: Poet of the Islands* by Ned Thomas, Cardiff, Welsh Arts Council, 1980; *Derek Walcott* by Robert D. Hamner, Boston, Twayne, 1981.

Theatrical Activities:
Director: many of his own plays.

* * *

It may seem surprising that one of the more perceptive and lucid speakers for modern man should emerge from the island of Trinidad in the West Indies. But it is nonetheless true. As a man of the theatre Derek Walcott is that sensitive poet-dramatist who contends with the questions that have concerned thoughtful man since time began. What is man? What is his relationship with God? Always aware of the culture and society which produced the present situation, Walcott also relates man to man and seriously questions the values that modernity has brought to man. Although he is particularly conscious of what he calls the present "African phase," his art at its best—his fears, his fire, his compassion—treats and yet transcends what he describes as "one race's quarrel with another's God" and may be associated with the writing of Camus, Sophocles, and the philosophy found in the Noh and Kabuki drama. He writes of man as well as men.

Both in dramaturgy and expressed ideas Walcott's plays provide levels of audience experience ranging from the simplicity of folk drama and vaudeville to the intellectual and emotional entanglements of highly sophisticated discussion. Essentially, he is a poet concerned with language—its dialectual expression, its varying rhythm, its imagery. Nature is ever present and forceful for him. There is the "sea grinding his teeth" or God, "a big fish eating small ones." Contingent upon his use of nature is that folk quality which in his plays is also illustrated by his frequent use of a *conteur* who directs the action of the play. In *O Babylon!* he makes careful and quite extensive use of the Rastafarian language. People, characters, are of greatest importance in his plays, while his presentation of their actions and his ideas may appear as manipulated as the work of the Greek dramatists or the writers of traditional Japanese drama. Music and song add to the folk or fable dimension of his plays. He also uses soliloquies, dreams, fantasies, or varied experimental techniques such as masks, symbols or symbolic figures, or disguises to express his ideas. In these ways he achieves his theatrical change of pace, interspersing light touches of humor through dialect or folk action. During the action of his plays on stage his use of language and his innovative structure provide theatrical entertainment while his serious concern for man becomes overwhelmingly apparent through his carefully drawn characters and the conflicts in which they are involved.

Walcott's published plays suggest his range. In *The Sea at Dauphin* two fishermen argue about taking to sea with them an old man who commits suicide when he is refused. It is a fearful life for fisherman where "God is a white man" and "his spit on Dauphin people is the sea." People work hard, have nothing, and see only death in a circular despair shown in the play by the fishermen's acceptance of a boy for their trip the next day. *Ti-Jean and His Brothers* is a fable in which three brothers representing physical strength, academic wisdom, and "man-wit, common sense" try to unmask the devil. The Devil fights and even the third brother, Ti-Jean, who argues and therefore defeats the devil by refusing to obey him, is "a fool like all heroes" and must be helped by God. In *Malcochon; or, The Six in the Rain* Walcott brings six people together in various confessions that show their frailty and humanity while exposing views of God and justice. His best play is *Dream on Monkey Mountain*. "In the beginning was the ape, and the ape had no name, so God called him man." In an epic fashion set within a mock trial, Walcott equates man's search for identity, his dream, with a present desire for black brotherhood. Following a Christian theme, the hero of the play is betrayed, confesses that "God dead," and is condemned for attempting to escape from the prison of his life. Materialized for his defense, even the best minds of the past cannot help him. He must personally destroy his God and his dream. But the argument and conflict of the play are also only a dream as the action before the final curtain reverts to the opening scene of the simple man in his squalid life.

Each of Walcott's plays is a penetrating comment on man in that arena in which he must contend with all other men and at a moment of his life when the forces of his destiny must overtake him. *The Joker of Seville* was his first attempt to adapt the work of another author, Tirso de Molina's *El burlador de Sevilla*. On a stage that is an arena such as one would find at a bullfight, Walcott creates the story of Don Juan Tenorio, a knight whose seductive ways with women result in his exile and eventual death. The play is a moment in life, a legend in a new vessel equating Don Juan with the Joker—"the boss who can change to elation each grave situation—sans humanite." The bitter irony of Walcott's picture of this moment is emphasized by the repeated idea that "if there is a resurrection, Death is the Joker." *O Babylon!* is essentially a musical which satirizes the people of Babylon and shows the despair of those who would search for Zion. As the Babylonian people of Jamaica prepare for a visit from Haile Selassie, they must remove a Rasta squatter community whose members accept Selassie as God and want to return with him to Ethiopia. In imaginative theatrical scenes featuring songs and dances the forces of Babylon overwhelm the searchers for Zion—"For once I loved the world, but this world don't want love"—who get to see neither Selassie nor God. *Remembrance* is a satire on remembrance which produces nothing. Like *Pantomime* it also satirizes the concept of independence and the vision of immortality that romance inspires. For the teacher, interviewed on Remembrance Day, seven days after his son was killed by a policeman's stray bullet, there is nothing but his faith in the sweet optimism of Gray's elegy. In reality his life was a disappointment—as teacher, as father, as lover, as friend. For the two vaudevillian characters in *Pantomime* life is as difficult to understand and get involved in as the skit they try to rehearse. The conflicting issues overwhelm them—white/black, master/servant, real/theatrical, cry/laugh. Nothing is ever solved. If life is comedy or tragedy, acting makes it so.

Themes involving God and justice have been persistent in Walcott's plays. During the last half-dozen years his personal despair with both the God of his characters and the social conditions with which they must contend has led him to concentrate upon contemporary issues. His most recently published volume of plays illustrates this concern with *The Last Carnival*, *Beef, No Chicken* and *A Branch of the Blue Nile*. *Haitian Earth* (unproduced) deals with Toussaint l'Overture's revolution; *To Die for Grenada* (unproduced) takes place on that island just prior to the US invasion. Although the hero's "dream touch everyone" in *Dream on Monkey Mountain*, it was only a dream, a bitter irony. As Walcott's association with American theatre develops after a five-year MacArthur fellowship, his voice as a social dramatist becomes super-imposed upon his imaginative theatrical devices to fuse his poet's vision for mankind with a sense of temporal urgency.

—Walter J. Meserve

WALKER, George F(rederick). Canadian. Born in Toronto, Ontario, 23 August 1947. Educated at Riverdale Collegiate, Toronto, graduated 1965. Married Susan Purdy in 1980; two daughters. Playwright-in-residence, 1971–76, and artistic director, 1978–79, Factory Theatre Lab, Toronto; resident playwright, New York Shakespeare Festival, 1981. Recipient: Canada Council grant, 1971 (and 4 subsequent grants); Chalmers award, 3 times; Governor-General's award, 1986. Agent: Great North Artists, 345 Adelaide Street West, Toronto, Ontario M5V 1R5, Canada.

PUBLICATIONS

Plays

The Prince of Naples (produced Toronto, 1971). Toronto, Playwrights, 1972.

Ambush at Tether's End (produced Toronto, 1971). Toronto, Playwrights, 1972.

Sacktown Rag (produced Toronto, 1972). Toronto, Playwrights, 1972.

Bagdad Saloon (produced Toronto and London, 1973). Toronto, Playwrights, 1973.

Demerit (produced Toronto, 1974).

Beyond Mozambique (produced Toronto, 1974). Toronto, Playwrights, 1975.

Ramona and the White Slaves (also director: produced Toronto, 1976). Included in *Three Plays*, 1978.

Gossip (produced Toronto and Chicago, 1977). Toronto, Playwrights, 1980.

Zastrozzi, The Master of Discipline (produced Toronto, 1977; London, 1978; Seattle, 1979; New York, 1982). Toronto, Playwrights, 1977.

Three Plays (includes *Bagdad Saloon*, *Beyond Mozambique*, *Ramona and the White Slaves*). Toronto, Coach House Press, 1978.

Filthy Rich (produced Toronto, 1979; Evanston, Illinois, 1982; London, 1984; New York, 1985). Toronto, Playwrights, 1981.

Rumours of Our Death, music by John Roby, lyrics by Walker and Roby (also director: produced Toronto, 1980). Published in *Canadian Theatre Review* (Downsview, Ontario), Winter 1980.

Theatre of the Film Noir (also director: produced Toronto, 1981; London, 1983). Toronto, Playwrights, 1981.

Science and Madness (produced Toronto, 1982). Toronto, Playwrights, 1982.
The Art of War: An Adventure (also director: produced Toronto, 1983). Toronto, Playwrights, 1983.
Criminals in Love (produced Toronto, 1984). Toronto, Playwrights, 1985.
The Power Plays (includes *Gossip*, *Filthy Rich*, *The Art of War*). Toronto, Coach House Press, 1984.
Better Living (produced Toronto, 1986; Poughkeepsie, New York, 1987). Included in *East End Plays*, 1987.
Beautiful City (produced Toronto, 1987). Included in *East End Plays*, 1987.
East End Plays (includes *Criminals in Love*, *Better Living*, *Beautiful City*). Toronto, Playwrights, 1987.

Radio Plays: *The Private Man*, 1973.

Television Plays: *Sam, Grace, Doug, and the Dog*, 1976; *Overlap*, 1977; *Capital Punishment*, 1977.

*

Critical Studies: *Factory Lab Anthology* edited by Connie Brissenden, Vancouver, Talonbooks, 1974; "Playnotes" by Richard Horenblas, in *Scene Changes* (Toronto) October 1975; in *University of Toronto Quarterly*, Spring 1980.

Theatrical Activities:
Director: **Plays**—some of his own plays; *The Extremist* by Ilya Denykin, Toronto, 1976.

* * *

George F. Walker's origins are in the theatre of the absurd. The earliest plays have situations and humour similar to those of *Waiting for Godot* and Stoppard's plays. In *Ambush at Tether's End* a corpse hangs upstage while Galt and Bush engage in dialogue like that of Vladimir and Estragon or Rosencrantz and Guildenstern as they wait for someone to take responsibility. Notes found on the corpse humorously introduce themes of free will and determinism, liberty and responsibility. Trapped in a situation they did not create, unable to act, the two repeatedly attempt suicide but lack the courage. The play is characterised by verbal wit, idiomatic absurdities ("you're here to put your foot down if it gets out of hand"), and economical development of character.

Written during a time when American legends were becoming the subject matter of literature, *Bagdad Saloon* shows the inappropriateness of American myths to other nations. Such American characters in the play as Henry Miller, Gertrude Stein, and Doc Halliday assume they are famous and act as they wish, whereas the non-Americans seek a formula to imitate. Significantly, the heir to the legendary heroes of the Old West and the American writers of the Left Bank is a soldier who returns from the war in Vietnam, thus ending illusions about America. This period of chaotic, highly fragmented, cartoon-like dramas, with their exaggerated actions and simplified characters, continues with *Beyond Mozambique*, a take-off on art about exotic places. While the natives beat drums and collect arms to rebel, the mad Europeans, like many of Walker's characters, no longer can distinguish reality from fantasy. There are parodies of *The Three Sisters*, *Frankenstein*, Graham Greene's "whisky priest," and Hollywood films. Evil appears to rule; society is in a state of collapse and no one knows what to do or much cares. The starkly bleak vision of *Ramona and the White Slaves* probes the depths of the psyche, its perversions, the nature of power, and the wild instability of emotions. Although the setting is once more exotic, Hong Kong in 1919, we learn that the play may be an opium dream; all the slavery, mutilation, rape, and guilt is metaphoric of "the story of a family." The same characters, situations, and themes recur from play to play, including detectives, whores, incest, harsh family conflict, disguises, and ruined lives.

The investigation of power and evil is central to *Zastrozzi, The Master of Discipline*. A study in obsessive revenge and will to dominate, Zastrozzi appears a creature from the feudal past, with his whips, demand for slave-like obedience, and hatred (in 1896) of Impressionist art. He is driven by a code of honour and refuses introspection of his motives or examination of rights or wrongs. Underlying his brutality is a view of life as arbitrary, which he covers up through activity. Zastrozzi is opposed by Victor, the modern, liberal, rational man, who is unable to kill him even when he has the opportunity and, like many of Walker's voices of conscience, is bound to fail. *Zastrozzi* is more unified than the plays that preceded it. The characters are representative archetypes of western civilization. As Walker's work develops, narrative becomes increasingly important, as is the opposition between the power of evil and the weakness of good. *Zastrozzi* has the grotesque melodrama of Jacobean tragedy, and is visually powerful because of its whippings, sword displays, love-making, and murders.

Walker's aesthetics, based on parody, pastiche, and caricature of popular, exotic, and past art, is a product of postmodernism with its collapse of artistic distinctions. The problem is how to go beyond the limitations of junk art. In the three "Power plays"—*Gossip*, *Filthy Rich*, and *The Art of War*—Walker imitates the conventions of popular art forms for a trilogy mediatating on the nature, use, and misuse of power. Tyrone M. Power (the name ironically alludes to the movie star, although this Tyrone Power is short and balding) is first an investigative reporter (allowing Walker to parody the hard-boiled journalist films of the 1930's) and later a hard-drinking, cynical, but really soft-hearted private detective. *Gossip* and *Filthy Rich* have similarities to Raymond Chandler's stories of Los Angeles political corruption, and the moral corruption of the rich and their influential, attractive daughters. At first a loner, then in *Filthy Rich* joined by Jamie, a young working-class Sancho Panza with a more practical bent, Power quixotically takes on the local political establishment, uncovering their crimes, but earns nothing by it except to lose what friends he has and make himself more cynical. In *Gossip* he finds that he is being used by others, who for revenge want corruption exposed. The romantic individualism of the investigative reporter and private eye pays off neither financially nor emotionally. By the time of *The Art of War* Power has become a Sherlock Holmes fighting a losing battle against his Moriarty, an international master criminal who must win because Power, unwilling to rely on the police, is unwilling to shoot the arch-criminal when he has him at his mercy. While the criminal laughs at him and escapes, Power can only ponder, Hamlet-like, his inaction. The play was originally written for performance before an anti-war group.

The struggle between good and evil continues in *Science and Madness*, with its horror-film conventions, and becomes confused in *Theatre of the Film Noir*, which begins with a French police inspector—in a pastiche of cheap French detective fiction and grade-B film voice-overs—warning that as it is the first days of the liberation of Paris from German occupation all order has broken down and there is no clear standard of morality or absolute guilt. He investigates the recent killing of a young Resistance fighter. The suspects include the Communists who need a martyr, the young man's homosexual lover who is a dangerous psychopath, and the young man's sister, a collaborationist with whom he had incestuous relations and who fears exposure of her German-Nazi officer lover with whom her brother had a homosexual relationship. Walker is concerned with the breakdown of significance, the instability and unpredictability of character. Morality has become a question of circumstance. People make themselves through violence, dominance, and deception.

Walker's characters and situations, filled with insults, violence, surprises, and rapid action, are outrageous and require an unpolished acting style. Everything is stripped down, there is no waste. In *Criminals in Love* two innocent teenagers, trapped by their environment and lacking the will to break free, find themselves eventually transformed from unwilling accomplices of criminals to defiantly armed terrorists. Things always go wrong in Walker's plays for those who allow themselves to be manipulated by the strong and unscrupulous. The play is very funny and visually memorable. It opens in a schoolyard with a young man's head under a girl's sweater while he derives pleasure from her breasts; at the play's conclusion they return to the same posture, but now armed and surrounded by police.

—Bruce King

WALKER, Joseph A. American. Born in Washington, D.C., 23 February 1935. Educated at Howard University, Washington, D.C., B.A. in philosophy 1956; Catholic University, Washington, D.C., M.F.A. 1970. Served in the United States Air Force: 2nd Lieutenant. Married 1) Barbara Brown (divorced 1965); 2) Dorothy A. Dinroe in 1970. Worked as taxi driver, salesman, and postal clerk; English teacher in Washington, D.C., and New York; actor with the Negro Ensemble Company, New York, from 1969; playwright-in-residence, Yale University, New Haven, Connecticut, 1970; taught at City College, New York, 1970's; currently member of the Drama Department, Howard University. Address: Department of Drama, Howard University, 2400 6th Street N.W., Washington, D.C. 20059, U.S.A.

Publications

Plays

The Believers, with Josephine Jackson, music and lyrics by Benjamin Carter and others (produced New York, 1968).

The Harangues (produced New York, 1969). Shortened version, as *Tribal Harangue Two*, in *The Best Short Plays 1971*, edited by Stanley Richards, Philadelphia, Chilton, 1971.

Ododo (also director: produced New York, 1970). Published in *Black Drama Anthology*, edited by Ron Milner and Woodie King, New York, New American Library, 1971.

The River Niger (produced New York, 1972). New York, Hill and Wang, 1973.

Yin Yang, music by Dorothy A. Dinroe-Walker (also director: produced New York, 1973).

Antigone Africanus (produced New York, 1975).

The Lion Is a Soul Brother (also director: produced New York, 1976).

District Line (produced New York, 1984).

Screenplay: *The River Niger*, 1976.

*

Theatrical Activities:
Director: several of his own plays.
Actor: **Plays**—*The Believers*, New York, 1968; *Cities in Bezique* by Adrienne Kennedy, New York, 1969. **Films**—*April Fools*, 1969; *Bananas*, 1971. **Television**—*NYPD* series; *In Black America* (narrator).

* * *

The dramas of Joseph A. Walker explore various aspects of black life such as male-female relationships, interracial strife, and family and community bonds. However, the focus of most of his works is on the psyche of black American males. Cut off from their ancestral home and exploited by whites, these disoriented men are portrayed as lacking a sense of identity, purpose, and self-worth. Efforts by some of these men to obtain power and wealth are most often thwarted by white America's black sycophants. Whether or not one agrees with this simplistic ideology, frequently exhorted in the 1960's and 1970's, Walker's plays are still relevant because of their compelling depictions of those black males stagnated by feelings of impotence, frustration, and hopelessness.

While the black male characters are deftly drawn and complex, Walker's portraits of black women and whites rarely escape the limitations of stereotypes. Black women seldom have any personal goals, but instead function as either supporters or "castrators" of their men. White women serve as sexual playmates and status symbols for their black lovers. White men exploit blacks and destroy those who pose a threat to their way of life. Lacking depth and plausible motivations for their actions, these characters weaken the credibility of Walker's plays.

As its title suggests, *The Harangues* is used as a vehicle for the playwright to vent his opinions. Composed of two episodes and two one-act plays, the work portrays a despairing view of black life. In the first episode, a 15th-century West African man chooses to kill his son rather than subject him to life as a slave in the New World. The second episode mirrors the first by showing a contemporary black American revolutionary who kills his child rather than allow him to grow up in a despondent society. Black women plead for their children's lives in the episodes, but are conspicuously absent in the one-acts. The first one-act, set in Washington, D.C., concerns a black male and his pregnant white fiancée. Incredibly, with little hesitation, the white woman agrees to assist her lover in the murder of her father who will disinherit her if she marries. However, the plan backfires and results in the death of the scheming black man due to the actions of a traitorous black "friend." In the second one-act, unless they can convince him of their worthiness to live, a deranged black man threatens to kill his three captives: a white liberal and an assimilationist black man and his white lover. After exposing their perverted lives, only the white woman who endures several sexual indignities is deemed to be virtuous. However, as the death penalty is being carried out, the woman takes a bullet meant for her contemptible black lover. In an ensuing struggle, the assimilationist gains control of his captor's gun and kills him. As in the first one-act, a desperate black man dies at the hands of a black minion of the white race.

In sharp contrast to the pessimistic outlook which envelopes *The Harangues*, *The River Niger* celebrates the enduring qualities of the black man and offers a hopeful vision of the future. Johnny Williams, a middle-aged house painter and poet living in Harlem, uses liquor to escape the bleak reality of a life stagnated by unrealized dreams. Johnny places his hopes for the future in his son Jeff's career in the air force. But his son's homecoming brings another disappointment to Johnny's life. Jeff admits that he was dismissed from the military which he abhored. He contends his ouster was due to his refusal to be a "supernigger"—a black man who tries to prove he has capabilities comparable to whites. He further announces he will no longer be bound by familial and societal expectations but will instead seek only to fulfill his own needs and desires. Despite his intentions, Jeff soon finds himself involved in the self-destructive affairs of his former gang. When prison terms appear imminent for Jeff and the gang after they are betrayed by one of their members, Johnny has a shoot-out with the traitor which results in both of their deaths. But before Johnny dies, he demands to take the rap for the shooting and the gang's alleged offense. Johnny's wife Mattie admonishes her family and the gang not to fail to cooperate and carry out her husband's wishes. Johnny's heroic gesture provides Jeff and other gang members with a new lease on life and a powerful example of the unconditional selfless love that a father can have for his son.

The portraits of the men are well crafted and realistic. The characters function as representatives of differing moral values, abilities, aspirations, and perspectives within the black community. Johnny emerges as the most eloquent and convincing spokesman who, through his poem "The River Niger," speaks of the need to be cognizant of one's unbreakable link to all people of African descent.

Although the play's black women represent various age groups and cultures, they share similar attitudes toward their men. The women serve their men's needs with little concern for their own desires or ambitions. Mattie even accepts the fact that her husband chooses to confide in his West Indian friend instead of her. Incredibly, during a conversation between Mattie and Jeff's South African lover, Johnny's wife agrees with the younger woman that women are incapable of having a similar type of relationship because "women don't trust one another." Despite this and several other questionable remarks made by the women, their behavior as selfless and loyal supporters of their men foreshadows the concluding message of the play. As Johnny's final actions and his demand for cooperation demonstrate, survival of the race requires a communal effort with little thought of self-interest.

A Washington, D.C. taxi-stand serves as the setting for *District Line*. The play depicts a day in the lives of six cab drivers: two white and three black males and one black female. The drivers reveal their past experiences, present concerns, and aspirations as they interact with each other and their passengers. Black males continue to be Walker's most poignant characterizations. Of greatest interest are the scenes concerning two drivers—Doc, a moonlighting Howard University professor and Zilikazi, an exiled South African revolutionary. Women characters, whether black or white, appear to be gratuitous in the drama and remain stereotypes. However, the playwright does portray white men in roles other than the liberal or oppressor of blacks. Still, the work suffers in comparison to Walker's other plays because of a few fundamental flaws. Dramatic action is not adequately developed and sustained throughout the play and the work lacks a central theme to tie all the scenes together. Consequently, the drama fails to create the intense emotional impact characteristic of Walker's other plays.

—Addell Austin

WANDOR, Michelene (Dinah). British. Born in London, 20 April 1940. Educated at Chingford Secondary Modern School, 1954–56, and Chingford County High School, 1956–59, both Essex; Newnham College, Cambridge, 1959–62, B.A. (honours) in English 1962; University of Essex, Colchester, 1974–75, M.A. in sociology 1975. Married the literary agent Ed Victor in 1963 (divorced 1975); two sons. Poetry editor, *Time Out* magazine, London, 1971–82; regular contributor, *Spare Rib* magazine, London, 1972–77; reviewer, *Plays and Players*, *Listener*, and *New Statesman*, all London, and *Kaleidoscope* programme, BBC Radio. Playwright-in-residence, University of Kent, Canterbury, 1982–83. Recipient: Arts Council bursary, 1974, 1983. Address: 71 Belsize Lane, London NW3 5AU, England.

PUBLICATIONS

Plays

You Too Can Be Ticklish (produced London, 1971).
Brag-a-Fruit (produced London, 1971).
The Day after Yesterday (produced London, 1972).
Spilt Milk, and Mal de Mère (produced London, 1972). Published in *Play Nine*, edited Robin Rook, London, Arnold, 1981.
To Die among Friends (includes *Mal de Mère*, *Joey*, *Christmas*, *Pearls*, *Swallows*) (produced London, 1974). Included in *Sink Songs*, 1975.
Friends and Strangers (produced on tour, 1974).
Sink Songs, with Dinah Brooke. London, Playbooks, 1975.
Penthesilia, adaptation of the play by Heinrich von Kleist (produced London, 1977).
The Old Wives' Tale (produced London, 1977). Included in *Five Plays*, 1984.
Care and Control (produced London, 1977). Published in *Strike While the Iron Is Hot*, edited by Wandor, London, Journeyman Press, 1980.
Floorshow, with others (produced London, 1978).
Whores d'Oeuvres (produced London, 1978). Included in *Five Plays*, 1984.
Scissors (produced London, 1978). Included in *Five Plays*, 1984.
Aid Thy Neighbour (produced London, 1978). Included in *Five Plays*, 1984.
Correspondence (broadcast 1978; produced London, 1979).
Aurora Leigh, adaptation of the poem by Elizabeth Barrett Browning (produced London, 1979). Published in *Plays by Women 1*, edited by Wandor, London, Methuen, 1982.
Future Perfect, with Steve Gooch and Paul Thompson (produced on tour, 1980).
The Blind Goddess, adaptation of a play by Ernst Toller (produced on tour, 1981).
Five Plays (includes *To Die among Friends*, *The Old Wives' Tale*, *Whores d'Oeuvres*, *Scissors*, *Aid Thy Neighbour*). London, Journeyman Press, 1984; New York, Riverrun Press, 1985.

The Wandering Jew, with Mike Alfreds, adaptation of a novel by Eugène Sue (produced London, 1987).

Radio Plays and Serials: *Correspondence*, 1978; *The Unlit Lamp*, from the novel by Radclyffe Hall, 1980; *Precious Bane*, from the novel by Mary Webb, 1981; *Lolly Willowes*, from the novel by Sylvia Townsend Warner, 1983; *An Uncommon Love*, 1984; *Kipps*, from the novel by H.G. Wells, 1984; *Venus Smiles*, from the story by J.G. Ballard, 1985; *The Brothers Karamazov*, from a novel by Dostoevsky, 1986; *The Nine Tailors*, from the novel by Dorothy L. Sayers, 1986; *Persuasion*, from the novel by Jane Austen, 1986–87; *Helbeck of Bannisdale*, from the novel by Mrs. Humphry Ward, 1987; *Gardens of Eden*, 1987; *Whose Body?*, from the novel by Dorothy L. Sayers, 1987.

Television Play: *The Belle of Amherst*, from the play by William Luce, 1987.

Novel

Arky Types, with Sara Maitland. London, Methuen, 1987.

Short Stories

Tales I Tell My Mother, with others. London, Journeyman Press, 1978; Boston, South End Press, 1980.
Guests in the Body. London, Virago Press, 1986.
More Tales I Tell My Mother, with others. London, Journeyman Press, 1987.

Verse

Upbeat: Poems and Stories. London, Journeyman Press, 1982; New York, Riverrun Press, 1985.
Touch Papers, with Judith Kazantzis and Michèle Roberts. London, Allison and Busby, 1982.
Gardens of Eden: Poems for Eve and Lilith. London, Journeyman Press, 1984; New York, Riverrun Press, 1985.

Other

The Great Divide: The Sexual Division of Labour; or, Is It Art?, with others. Milton Keynes, Buckinghamshire, Open University Press, 1976.
Understudies: Theatre and Sexual Politics. London, Eyre Methuen, 1981; revised edition, as *Carry On, Understudies*, London, Routledge, 1986.
Look Back in Gender: Sexuality and the Family in Post-1956 British Drama. London, Methuen, 1987.

Editor, *The Body Politic: Writings from the Women's Liberation Movement in Britain 1969–1972*. London, Stage 1, 1972.
Editor, with Michèle Roberts, *Cutlasses and Earrings* (poetry anthology). London, Playbooks, 1977.
Editor, *Strike While the Iron Is Hot: Three Plays on Sexual Politics*. London, Journeyman Press, 1980.
Editor, *Plays by Women 1–4*. London, Methuen, 4 vols., 1982–85.
Editor, *On Gender and Writing*. London, Pandora Press, 1983.

*

Critical Studies: "The Personal Is Political: Feminism and the Theatre" by Wandor, in *Dreams and Deconstructions* edited by Sandy Craig, Ambergate, Derbyshire, Amber Lane Press, 1980; *Feminist Theatre* by Helene Keyssar, London, Macmillan, 1984, New York, Grove Press, 1985.

Michelene Wandor comments:

I began writing plays in 1969, when the "fringe" began. I also was writing poetry and theatre reviews. For me the activities of fiction/non-fiction have always been complementary. At that time I became aware of, and developed, socialist and feminist convictions. For about ten years I wrote plays just for the stage, in a variety of forms—social realism, collage, surreal, comedy, abstract: whatever. Since 1979 I have written extensively for radio, a stimulating medium. I have dramatised/transposed a number of texts for radio—a way of working with the voices and styles of other writers that is both exciting and rewarding. I have absolutely no pre-conceived ideas about the appropriateness or otherwise of dramatic form. For me the appropriate form arrives as a combination of content an my approach to it. Having said that, I can also be lured by any subject. I have written a lot of female-centred work and male-centred work, and am always as aware as I can be of the way an inevitable (though variable) gender-bias operates in every drama.

* * *

Stylistic versatility combined with clear political commitment define Michelene Wandor's work for the theatre. A feminist and socialist who believes in theatre's potential for kicking away ideological crutches, Wandor produces the pitch and pace of naturalistic dialogue (*Aurora Leigh* the exception) while moving characters through flexible often a-temporal spaces. Conflicts between duty and pleasure, family and self, fear of the unknown and desire for political change, spark or transform situations. And sexual politics—the ways in which culture slots women and men into unequal gender roles and, in particular, fosters a woman's emotional and economic dependency on men to the detriment of her own intellectual and artistic growth—affects a wide social spectrum, from small children to retirees, schoolboy chums to lesbian mothers, assimilated Jews to angry prostitutes. This sympathetic diversity is the key to Wandor's humor, to the lightness and poignancy that her best plays achieve.

To Die among Friends contains five duologues, beginning with *Mal de Mère* for two female performers. "A," trapped in a circle of light, plays the precocious daughter Jenny; "V," outside the circle, ventriloquizes various interlocutors—a neighbor child, Jenny's teacher, Jenny's father, but primarily Jenny's mother. The title refers to gender sickness not just in the possessive neurotic mother who sacrifices her life only to suffocate her daughter, but also in Jenny herself, whose rebellion results in early pregnancy and the beginnings of madness. The circle iconography of entrapment and freedom helps mark identities within stichomythic exchanges and rapid role-switching. *Joey*, the second duologue, shows complicated desire strait jacketed by conventional marriage. As a male and female performer move through adolescence to adulthood, Joey is the object they both desire, or rather Joey stands for desire itself: yearning for which there is only displacement, never fulfillment. However, sexual desire is never innocent of sexual politics. Even in childhood, the female "M" is marginalized by the homoerotic attachment between "J," the male character, and Joey. The orthographic link between Joey and "J", suggests the primacy of homoerotic fantasy, leaving "M" almost powerless: "M: Marry me. J: Where's Joey? M: Marry me. J: Why? M: Marry me and you'll find Joey." Since "J" connects "M" with degrading compromise, he soon leaves her. *Christmas* turns the tables, exposing the sterility of a class-bound male relationship in which sexual desire (this time for women) is an ugly symptom of capitalist consumption and marketplace values. As "A" and "B" grow to manhood, "A" assumes authority of a factory in which "B" works and eventually leads a strike. While "A" marries and whores on the side, "B's" marriage declines then improves with his Marxist re-education: ". . . can't leave our marriage behind all the other changes." *Pearls*, an apt sequel, shows the disintegrating middle-class marriage of He and She whose frustrations mirror the contradictions in mid-1970's sexual politics. In *Swallows*, the beautifully crafted final duologue between O and Y, an older and younger woman, Wandor returns to the territory of *Mal de Mère* but further explores the loss of creativity of the gifted woman unable to fulfill herself in gender roles appropriate to her mother's generation.

Gertie, the humorous old socialist in *The Old Wives' Tale*, reveals the rare strength needed to survive those roles. As a young woman she gave up an illegitimate child and now supports and nurtures her fellow retirees. It is Y's desire in *Swallows* to "die among friends"; Wandor shows that women like Gertie can and do create that kind of solidarity for themselves, if only at the end of their lives. A prominent motif in *The Old Wives' Tale*, an amateur production of *Macbeth* in which the three old ladies are cast as the witches, allows Wandor to develop the double image for aging women of prophetess and freak. *Whores d'Oeuvres*, a strong, surrealistic piece, shows how women who sell their bodies in a male-controlled market become freaks, even the savvy prostitute who chastises her colleague for lack of professionalism while they float down the Thames together on a raft. The unusual setting brings the play's issues into focus; these women are adrift not only on the river, but in the contradictions of their profession which depends on self-alienation and exploitation. *Scissors*, Wandor's tour into comic family realism, takes on the confused attitudes of North London Jews towards contemporary anti-Semitism and the Arab-Israeli struggle. The liberal daughter confronts the misogyny of an Orthodox male who sees her independence as part of his oppression. In *Aid Thy Neighbour* Wandor's comedy is sharper, less hampered by realism. The title puns on the Artificial Insemination by Donor program to which both a lesbian couple and a heterosexual couple apply. Through misunderstandings in their first meetings, the couples' attitudes toward having children emerge. Then Wandor whips up a farcical subplot in which an ambitious journalist pretends to be gay in order to expose the lesbian couple as inadequate for motherhood (*male* gay parents would be acceptable). *Aid Thy Neighbour* successfully weaves feminist commitment into well-plotted comedy to show the light side of the problem of legal prejudice against single and/or lesbian mothers. *Care and Control* reveals the dark side. The first act intercuts three relationships in which a woman's desire for children runs afoul of her need for personal growth. The second act intercuts two custody cases, in which legal interrogations, supposedly in the interests of the child, reveal with terrifying clarity how the judicial system reinforces male resentment and punishes women who choose non-traditional family roles.

In *Aurora Leigh* Wandor daringly departs from spare naturalistic dialogue to write an effective verse drama adaptation of Elizabeth Barrett Browning's feminist epic. Paring down Browning's long poem, Wandor focuses on Aurora's eventual merging of intellect and experience ("the world of books is still the world") in verse that is richly textured, theatrical, and subtly polemical. This fine feminist play, along with most of Wandor's theater work, deserves greater attention and more frequent performance.

—Elin Diamond

WARD, Douglas Turner. American. Born in Burnside, Louisiana, 5 May 1930. Educated at Xavier University Preparatory School, New Orleans, 1941–46; Wilberforce University, Ohio, 1946–47; University of Michigan, Ann Arbor, 1947–48; Paul Mann's Actors Workshop, New York, 1955–58. Married Diana Hoyt Powell in 1966; one son and one daughter. Co-founder, 1967, and artistic director, Negro Ensemble Company, New York. Recipient: Vernon Rice award, 1966; Obie award, 1966, 1970, for acting, 1973; Drama Desk award, for acting, 1970; Boston Theatre Critics Circle award, for directing, 1986. Agent: William Morris Agency, 1350 Avenue of the Americas, New York, New York 10019. Address: Negro Ensemble Company, 165 West 46th Street, Suite 800, New York, New York 10036, U.S.A.

PUBLICATIONS

Plays

Happy Ending, and Day of Absence (produced New York, 1965; *Day of Absence* produced Edinburgh, 1987). New York, Dramatists Play Service, 1966; as *Two Plays*, New York, Third Press-Viking Press, 1971.

The Reckoning (produced New York, 1969). New York, Dramatists Play Service, 1970.

Brotherhood (also director: produced New York, 1970). New York, Dramatists Play Service, 1970.

Redeemer, in *Holidays* (produced Louisville, 1979; in *About Heaven and Earth*, also director: produced New York, 1983).

*

Critical Study: introduction by Sheila Rush to *Two Plays* by Ward, New York, Third Press-Viking Press, 1971.

Theatrical Activities:

Director: **Plays**—*Daddy Goodness* by Richard Wright and Louis Sapin, New York, 1968; *Man Better Man* by Errol Hill, New York, 1969; *Contribution* by Ted Shine, New York, 1969; *Brotherhood and Day of Absence*, New York, 1970; *Ride a Black Horse* by John Scott, New York, 1971; *Perry's Mission* by Clarence Young III, New York, 1971; *The River Niger* by Joseph A. Walker, New York, 1972; *A Ballet Behind the Bridge* by Lennox Brown, New York, 1972; *The Great MacDaddy* by Paul Carter Harrison, New York, 1974, 1977; *The First Breeze of Summer* by Leslie Lee, New York, 1975; *Waiting for Mongo* by Silas Jones, New York, 1975; *Livin' Fat* by Judi Ann Mason, New York, 1976; *The Offering* by Gus Edwards, New York, 1977; *The Twilight Dinner* by Lennox Brown, New York, 1978; *The Raft* by John Pepper Clark, New York, 1978; *Black Body Blues* by Gus Edwards, New York, 1978; *Zooman and the Sign* by Charles Fuller, New York, 1980, 1981; *Home* by Samm-Art Williams, New York, 1980; *Weep Not for Me* by Gus Edwards, New York, 1981; *A Soldier's Play* by Charles Fuller, New York, 1981; *The Isle Is Full of Noises* by Derek Walcott,Hartford, Connecticut, 1982; *About Heaven and*

Earth by Ward, Julie Jensen, and Ali Wadad, New York, 1983; *Manhattan Made Me* by Gus Edwards, New York, 1983; *District Line* by Joseph A. Walker, 1984; *Ceremonies in Dark Old Men* by Lonne Elder III, New York, 1985; *The War Party* by Leslie Lee, New York, 1986; *Jonah and the Wonder Dog* by Judi Ann Mason, New York, 1986; *Louie and Ophelia* by Gus Edwards, New York, 1986.
Actor as Douglas Turner and Douglas Turner Ward: **Plays**—Joe Mott in *The Iceman Cometh* by O'Neill, New York, 1957; Matthew Kumalo in *Lost in the Stars* by Maxwell Anderson, New York; Moving Man, then Walter Younger, in *A Raisin in the Sun* by Lorraine Hansberry, New York, 1959, then tour, 1960–61; Archibald in *The Blacks* by Jean Genet, New York, 1961; Porter in *Pullman Car Hiawatha* by Thornton Wilder, New York, 1962; understudied Fredericks in *One Flew over the Cuckoo's Nest* by Dale Wasserman, New York, 1963; Zachariah Pieterson in *The Blood Knot* by Athol Fugard, New York, 1964 and tour; Fitzroy in *Rich Little Rich Girl* by Hugh Wheeler, Philadelphia, 1964; Roman Citizen in *Coriolanus*, New York, 1965; Arthur in *Happy Ending*, New York, 1965; Mayor and Clan in *Day of Absence*, New York, 1965; with the Negro Ensemble Company, New York—Oba Danlola in *Kongi's Harvest* by Wole Soyinka, 1968, in *Summer of the Seventeenth Doll* by Ray Lawler, 1968, Thomas in *Daddy Goodness* by Richard Wright and Louis Sapin, 1968, Russell B. Parker in *Ceremonies in Dark Old Men* by Lonne Elder III, 1969, 1985, Scar in *The Reckoning*, 1969, Black Man and Asura in *The Harangues* by Joseph A. Walker, 1969, in *Frederick Douglass Through His Own Words*, 1972, Johnny Williams in *The River Niger* by Joseph A. Walker, 1972, Harper Edwards in *The First Breeze of Summer* by Leslie Lee, 1975, Mingo Saunders in *The Brownsville Raid* by Charles Fuller, 1976, Bob Tyrone in *The Offering* by Gus Edwards, 1977, Fletcher in *Black Body Blues* by Gus Edwards, 1978, Flick in *The Michigan* by Dan Owens, 1979, Technical Sergeant Vernon C. Waters in *A Soldier's Play* by Charles Fuller, Edinburgh, 1984, Jonah Howard in *Jonah and the Wonder Dog* by Judi Ann Mason, 1986, and Louie in *Louie and Ophelia* by Gus Edwards, 1986; Papa in *This Isle Is Full of Noises* by Derek Walcott, New Haven, Connecticut, 1982.

Douglas Turner Ward comments:
I am a black playwright, of black sensibilities, primarily utilizing the devices of satire, exaggeration, and mordant humor to explore and express themes of contemporary life, particularly as they relate to black survival.

* * *

Douglas Turner Ward, a black American, is one of those rare individuals who have successfully combined careers as actor, writer, and director. He has twice won Obie awards for plays which he wrote and in which he performed: in 1966 for *Happy Ending* and *Day of Absence*, and in 1970 for *The Reckoning*. Since 1967 he has been artistic director of the Negro Ensemble Company, an important repertory company which he and actor-director Robert Hooks founded.

Despite his success as an actor, Ward is better known as a dramatist, particularly for his first two plays, *Happy Ending* and *Day of Absence*, which treat satirically the relationships between blacks and whites. The history of these award-winning one-acts is almost as ironic as their subject matter. Although both plays were completed by 1960, Ward could not find a producer until, five years later, Robert Hooks, operating on limited financing, arranged to have them produced at St. Mark's Theatre.

As *Happy Ending* opens, two black female domestics are lamenting their employer's decision to divorce his promiscuous wife. Their sorrow is interrupted by their dapper nephew, who rebukes them for pitying people who have overworked and underpaid them. This, he informs them, is their chance to escape from domestic labor. Then, they educate him to the ironies of life: as middle-aged black women, with limited formal education (four strikes against them), they can expect only low-paying jobs which will barely provide subsistence. In contrast, as domestic laborers, though they have received little money, they have provided their nephew with fashionable clothes not missed from the employer's wardrobe and with food smuggled from the employer's larder. As the nephew joins in their sorrows, they receive the happy news that the employers have become reconciled.

Day of Absence is a one-act satirical fantasy about the turmoil in a southern city on a day when all blacks disappear. White couples begin to argue as they discover that they have no experience tending the house or caring for their children. The Ku Klux Klan is bitter because, with black people gone, it no longer has a pretext for existence and victims for sadistic practices. Elected repeatedly on a campaign of keeping blacks in their places, the mayor proves incompetent to manage the affairs of the town. In the midst of the despair, the reappearance of one black reassures the whites that others will return. The play ends, however, with the question of whether the whites have fully learned how much they depend upon blacks.

Ward's first full-length play, *The Reckoning*, produced by the Negro Ensemble Company in 1969, focuses on a confrontation between a black pimp and a southern governor. Ward continued his satire in the one-act *Brotherhood*, in which a white husband and wife try to mask their anti-black sentiments from a middle-class black couple whom they have invited to their house. The blacks are not deceived. In 1966, in an article published in the Sunday *New York Times*, Ward adumbrated the need for a predominantly black audience "to readily understand, debate, confirm, or reject the truth or falsity" of the creations of the black playwright. Ward insisted that whenever a black playwright writes for a predominantly white audience—"least equipped to understand his intentions, woefully apathetic or anesthetized to his experience, often prone to distort his purpose"—that writer must restrict himself to the rudimentary re-education of that audience. Consequently, he has no opportunity to develop artistically. Although he admitted that a black playwright could gain the necessary "theatre of Negro identity" in a black community, Ward saw no possibility for such a theatre prior to massive reconstruction of the urban ghettos.

His hope of such a black-oriented theatre inspired the founding of the Negro Ensemble Company, whose notable successes include Lonne Elder III's *Ceremonies in Dark Old Men* and Charles Fuller's *A Soldier's Play*.

—Darwin T. Turner

WASSERSTEIN, Wendy. American. Attended Yale University School of Drama, New Haven, Connecticut. Agent: Luis Sanjurjo, International Creative Management, 40 West 57th Street, New York, New York 10019, U.S.A.

PUBLICATIONS

Plays

Any Woman Can't (produced New Haven, Connecticut).

Happy Birthday, Montpelier Pizz-zazz (produced New Haven, Connecticut, 1974).

When Dinah Shore Ruled the Earth, with Christopher Durang (produced New Haven, Connecticut, 1975).

Uncommon Women and Others (produced New Haven, Connecticut, 1975; New York, 1977; Edinburgh, 1985). New York, Avon, 1979.

Isn't It Romantic (produced New York, 1981; revised version produced New York, 1983). New York, Dramatists Play Service, 1985.

Tender Offer (produced New York, 1983).

The Man in a Case, adaptation of a story by Chekhov, in *Orchards* (produced Urbana, Illinois, 1985; New York, 1986). New York, Knopf, 1986.

Television Play: *The Sorrows of Gin*, from the story by John Cheever, 1979.

*

Theatrical Activities:
Actress: **Play**—in *The Hotel Play* by Wallace Shawn, New York, 1981.

* * *

Wendy Wasserstein's plays are marked by an unerring ability to see the comic side of life, particularly the life of a woman in today's world. She is an astute observer, a witty humanist, and a cheery optimist.

When Dinah Shore Ruled the Earth is an early play she co-wrote with Christopher Durang, with whom she shares a sense of the outrageous. It is an extended satiric sketch on the worst imaginable beauty pageant, featuring four lovely finalists: a "faculty wife, mother, medical architect and cover girl," a "star of stage and screen," a white "black lesbian mother," and a "secretary-poetess." They discuss their hobbies and ambitions and display their questionable talents, egged on by Peter, the M.C. of the event. Peter also stands in for a series of stars who fail to show up, appears as Dame Peggy Ashcroft, the moderator of the "roundtable discussion on topics of our time," and as the judge, "the Edinburgh Festival." The subjects of mothers, motherhood, sexuality, marriage, work, feminism and feminity, recurring themes in Wasserstein's plays, are bitingly lampooned, but through this inverse approach, they command attention.

Any Woman Can't portrays the struggles of a young woman, Chris, as she tries to secure independence and a job in a threatening, male-dominated world. In *Dinah Shore* Peter the M.C. provided the male-world framework of the play. In *Any Woman Can't* there is a chorus of nine men who wander through the audience and onto the stage, sneering sexual innuendos and obscenities, first at the audience, then at the terrified Chris. Wasserstein's comic sense prevails as she shows Chris failing miserably as a Fred Astaire Dance School instructress and facing total disaster at a tap dance audition for a new musical. Despite her education and her efforts, Chris cannot get a job and succumbs to the "protection" of marriage to a self-absorbed sexist. Typical of Wasserstein's women, however, Chris remains optimistic about future possibilities.

An equally frustrating but comic picture of women's options is presented in *Happy Birthday, Montpelier Pizz-zazz*, a play about the college party scene. Wasserstein includes several songs and calls for scenic backdrops, each portraying "a pop comic blurb from *Heart Throb* or *My Love* comic books." Characters are reduced to comic-strip essentials: the sexy, most popular girl in the class, the sexist, woman-devouring, most popular boy in the class, the most popular girl's overweight best friend and the most popular boy's very smart but unsexy hanger-on. Another character is Frederick of Hollywood with a claim to "twenty-six years of mail-order seduction." Once again the male world dominates and conditions the female world, but the women, even with comic-book treatment, are ultimately the vital and endearing characters who battle on, ever-hopeful of creating a better future.

In *Uncommon Women and Others* Wasserstein reduces the male world to a disembodied voice punctuating the play's 17 scenes between a group of students from a New England women's college. The play emerges as the powerful culmination and refinement of the themes and style of the earlier pieces. Here are the same educated and optimistic women trying to carve out a future, socially and intellectually, but now Wasserstein creates a woman's world, and a real world, in contrast to the comic-strip male-dominated worlds of the early work. The approach is still comedic, but the humor is derived from believable and complex characters and pungently witty dialogue rather than from comic exaggeration.

Wasserstein focuses on five women trying to make choices about their lives as they graduate from college. One happily and confidently chooses marriage; another will go to law school and be a career woman; the radical feminist intends to write her novel; the good-humored overweight young woman dreams of finding a "good root-canal man" to marry; and the fifth is torn between her prince charming and the life of a liberated woman. They all face, as do the other women in the play, the conflicting messages of traditional roles and new possibilities, the tensions of changing sexual and social attitudes. The one certain factor is the bonding between the five women, renewed six years later in a reunion lunch which provides the opening and closing framework of the play. There are few surprises after six years, but faith in themselves and in each other, and a resilience born of optimism, still drive them.

Wasserstein takes the career woman and the overweight under-achiever of *Uncommon Women* and develops them into the heroines of *Isn't It Romantic*. They are now out in the working world and still looking for a man. Harriet, the successful businesswoman settles for a sexist boor (as does Chris in *Any Woman Can't*), but the bubbly, struggling writer, Janie, holds out for her ideals and turns down the kind but unexciting man who loves her. The dialogue is crisp and witty, and humor is derived from character and character contrast. Harriet's sophisticated workaholic mother is a vivid contrast to Janie's, who is addicted to diet, exercise classes, tap dancing, and intruding on her daughter. The boyfriends are sharply different as are the backgrounds of the two women. The parallel courses of Janie and Harriet's career advancement and romances point up the contrast of their final choices.

Tender Offer is an intimate and gently humorous one-act play about a father and his nine-year-old daughter who find a way to break down the barriers and destructive patterns that prescribed roles and modern life set up between them. In most respects it is unlike Wasserstein's other plays, but in its reaffirmation of family bonds it shares a theme of her full-scale musical play, *Miami* (not yet produced).

Miami is also thematically linked with *Uncommon Women* and *Isn't It Romantic* in its depiction of people taking responsibility and making choices about their lives in order to create a future. Wasserstein sets her play in a glitzy Miami resort hotel during the last week of 1959. Here zany characters include the Maidman family who stay at the cheap hotel, but gatecrash the flashy—and decidely tacky—celebrations at the posh one. There is also a blacklisted television celebrity, a winningly vulgar chanteuse-comedienne, a slimy real-estate developer and his Cuban refugee partner, and other assorted staff and visitors at the hotel. Several scenes recall the vaudeville-like techniques of the early plays, especially the night-club scenes; others are closer to the character-rooted comedy of *Uncommon Women* and *Isn't It Romantic*. The main focus of the play is on the Maidman family, particularly their son, Jonathan, who discovers, through an escapade with the real-estate developer's daughter, what he doesn't want from life.

Wasserstein's comic vision and her optimism are the striking features of her work. In the early work she portrays women battling against being stereotyped by a male and unreal world. Later she develops fully rounded complex characters battling for individuality and control of their own lives in a real world they can help to shape. Historically comedy has tended to reaffirm traditional roles for women and portray a male-oriented system of values. Wasserstein's notable contribution to comedic playwriting is her challenge of that vision with her comic worlds of women who do strike out and make a difference.

—Elizabeth Swain

WATERHOUSE, Keith (Spencer). British. Born in Leeds, Yorkshire, 6 February 1929. Educated at Osmondthorpe Council School, Leeds; Leeds College of Commerce. Served in the Royal Air Force 1947–49. Married 1) Joan Foster in 1951 (divorced 1968), one son and two daughters; 2) Stella Bingham in 1984. Since 1950 free-lance journalist and writer in Leeds and London; columnist, *Daily Mirror*, 1970–86, and *Daily Mail* since 1986, both London. Recipient (for journalism): Granada award, 1970, and special award, 1982; IPC award, 1970, 1973; British Press award, 1978. Agent: London Management, 235 Regent Street, London W1A 2JT. Address: 29 Kenway Road, London S.W.5, England.

PUBLICATIONS

Plays

Billy Liar, with Willis Hall, adaptation of the novel by Waterhouse (produced London, 1960; Los Angeles and New York, 1963). London, Joseph, 1960; New York, Norton, 1961.
Celebration: The Wedding and The Funeral, with Willis Hall (produced Nottingham and London, 1961). London, Joseph, 1961.
England, Our England, with Willis Hall, music by Dudley Moore (produced London, 1962). London, Evans, 1964.
Squat Betty, with Willis Hall (produced London, 1962; New York, 1964). With *The Sponge Room*, London, Evans, 1963.
The Sponge Room, with Willis Hall (produced Nottingham and London, 1962; New York, 1964). With *Squat Betty*, London, Evans, 1963; in *Modern Short Plays from Broadway and London*, edited by Stanley Richards, New York, Random House, 1969.
All Things Bright and Beautiful, with Willis Hall (produced Bristol and London, 1962). London, Joseph, 1963.
Come Laughing Home, with Willis Hall (as *They Called the Bastard Stephen*, produced Bristol, 1964; as *Come Laughing Home*, produced Wimbledon, 1965). London, Evans, 1965.
Say Who You Are, with Willis Hall (produced Guildford, Surrey, and London, 1965). London, Evans, 1966; as *Help Stamp Out Marriage* (produced New York, 1966), New York, French, 1966.
Joey, Joey, with Willis Hall, music by Ron Moody (produced Manchester and London, 1966).
Whoops-a-Daisy, with Willis Hall (produced Nottingham, 1968). London, French, 1978.
Children's Day, with Willis Hall (produced Edinburgh and London, 1969). London, French, 1975.
Who's Who, with Willis Hall (produced Coventry, 1971; London, 1973). London, French, 1974.
Saturday, Sunday, Monday, with Willis Hall, adaptation of a play by Eduardo De Filippo (produced London, 1973; New York, 1974). London, Heinemann, 1974.
The Card, with Willis Hall, music and lyrics by Tony Hatch and Jackie Trent, adaptation of the novel by Arnold Bennett (produced Bristol and London, 1973).
Filumena, with Willis Hall, adaptation of a play by Eduardo De Filippo (produced London, 1977; New York, 1980). London, Heinemann, 1978.
Worzel Gummidge (for children), with Willis Hall, music by Denis King, adaptation of stories by Barbara Euphan Todd (produced Birmingham, 1980; London, 1981). London, French 1984.
Steafel Variations (songs and sketches), with Peter Tinniswood and Dick Vosburgh (produced London, 1982).
Lost Empires, with Willis Hall, music by Denis King, adaptation of the novel by J.B. Priestley (produced Darlington, County Durham, 1985).
Mr. and Mrs. Nobody, adaptation of *The Diary of a Nobody* by George and Weedon Grossmith (produced London, 1986).

Screenplays, with Willis Hall: *Whistle Down the Wind*, 1961; *The Valiant*, 1962; *A Kind of Loving*, 1963; *Billy Liar*, 1963; *West Eleven*, 1963; *Man in the Middle*, 1963; *Pretty Polly* (*A Matter of Innocence*), 1967; *Lock Up Your Daughters*, 1969.

Radio Plays: *The Town That Wouldn't Vote*, 1951; *There Is a Happy Land*, 1962; *The Woollen Bank Forgeries*, 1964; *The Last Phone-In*, 1976; *The Big Broadcast of 1922*, 1979.

Television Plays. *The Warmonger*, 1970; *The Upchat Line* series, 1977; *The Upchat Connection* series, 1978; *Charlie Muffin*, from novels by Brian Freemantle, 1979; *West End Tales* series, 1981; *The Happy Apple* series, from play by Jack Pulman, 1983; *This Office Life*, from his own novel, 1984; *Charters and Caldicott*, 1985; *Slip Up*, 1987; *Andy Capp* series, 1988; with Willis Hall—*Happy Moorings*, 1963; *How Many Angels*, 1964; *Inside George Webley* series, 1968; *Queenie's Castle* series, 1970; *Budgie* series, 1971–72; *The Upper Crusts* series, 1973; *Three's Company* series, 1973; *By Endeavour Alone*, 1973; *Billy Liar* series, 1973–74; *Briefer Encounter*, 1977; *Public Lives*, 1977; *Worzel Gummidge* series, from stories by Barbara Euphan Todd, 1979.

Novels

There Is a Happy Land. London, Joseph, 1957.
Billy Liar. London, Joseph, 1959; New York, Norton, 1960.
Jubb. London, Joseph, 1963; New York, Putnam, 1964.

The Bucket Shop. London, Joseph, 1968; as *Everything Must Go*, New York, Putnam, 1969.
Billy Liar on the Moon. London, Joseph, 1975; New York, Putnam, 1976.
Office Life. London, Joseph, 1978.
Maggie Muggins; or, Spring in Earl's Court. London, Joseph, 1981.
In the Mood. London, Joseph, 1983.
Thinks. London, Joseph, 1984.

Other

The Café Royal: Ninety Years of Bohemia, with Guy Deghy. London, Hutchinson, 1955.
How to Avoid Matrimony, with Guy Deghy (as Herald Froy). London, Muller, 1957.
Britain's Voice Abroad, with Paul Cave. London, Daily Mirror Newspapers, 1957.
The Future of Television. London, Daily Mirror Newspapers, 1958.
The Joneses: How to Keep Up with Them, with Guy Deghy (as Lee Gibb). London, Muller, 1959.
The Higher Jones, with Guy Deghy (as Lee Gibb). London, Muller, 1961.
The Passing of the Third-Floor Buck (*Punch* sketches). London, Joseph, 1974.
Mondays, Thursdays (*Daily Mirror* columns). London, Joseph, 1976.
Rhubarb, Rhubarb, and Other Noises (*Daily Mirror* columns). London, Joseph, 1979.
The Television Adventures [and *More Television Adventures*] *of Worzel Gummidge* (for children), with Willis Hall. London, Penguin, 2 vols., 1979; complete edition, as *Worzel Gummidge's Television Adventures*, London, Kestrel, 1981.
Worzel Gummidge at the Fair (for children), with Willis Hall. London, Penguin, 1980.
Worzel Gummidge Goes to the Seaside (for children), with Willis Hall. London, Penguin, 1980.
The Trials of Worzel Gummidge (for children), with Willis Hall. London, Penguin, 1980.
Worzel's Birthday (for children), with Willis Hall. London, Penguin, 1981.
New Television Adventures of Worzel Gummidge and Aunt Sally (for children), with Willis Hall. London, Sparrow, 1981.
Daily Mirror Style. London, Mirror Books, 1981.
Fanny Peculiar (*Punch* columns), illustrated by Michael Heath. London, Joseph, 1983.
Mrs. Pooter's Diary. London, Joseph, 1983.
The Irish Adventures of Worzel Gummidge (for children), with Willis Hall. London, Severn House, 1984.
Waterhouse at Large (journalism). London, Joseph, 1985.
The Collected Letters of a Nobody (Including Mr. Pooter's Advice to His Son). London, Joseph, 1986.
The Theory and Practice of Lunch. London, Joseph, 1986.
Worzel Gummidge Down Under (for children), with Willis Hall. London, Collins, 1987.

Editor, with Willis Hall, *Writers' Theatre*. London, Heinemann, 1967.

* * *

See the essay on Willis Hall and Keith Waterhouse.

WEINSTEIN, Arnold. American. Born in New York City, 10 June 1927. Educated at Hunter College, New York, B.A. in classics 1951 (Phi Beta Kappa); University of London, 1949–50; Harvard University, Cambridge, Massachusetts, A.M. in comparative literature 1952; University of Florence (Fulbright Fellow), 1958–60. Served in the United States Navy, 1944–46. Married Suzanne Burgess in 1969. Visiting Lecturer, New York University, 1955–56, and University of Southern California, Los Angeles; United States Information Service Lecturer, Italy, 1958–60; director of Drama Workshop, Wagner College, Staten Island, New York, summers 1964, 1965; Visiting Professor, Hollins College, Virginia, 1964–65; Professor of Dramatic Literature, New School for Social Research, New York, 1965–66; Chairman of the Department of Playwriting, Yale University, New Haven, Connecticut, 1966–69; Visiting Professor, University of Colorado, Boulder, Summer 1969; Chairman of the Department of Drama, Columbia College, Chicago, 1969–70; Visiting Professor, Southampton College, Southampton, New York, 1978–79, and Columbia University, New York, from 1979. Co-director, with Paul Sills, Second City, and other improvisational groups; director, Free Theatre, Chicago, Actors Studio, New York and Los Angeles, and Rock Theatre and Guerilla Theatre, Los Angeles. Recipient: Guggenheim fellowship, 1965. Agent: Sam Cohn, International Creative Management, 40 West 57th Street, New York, New York 10019. Address: Department of English and Comparative Literature, Columbia University, New York, New York 10027, U.S.A.

PUBLICATIONS

Plays

Red Eye of Love (produced New York, 1958). New York, Grove Press, 1962.
White Cap (produced New York, 1960).
Fortuna, music by Francis Thorne, adaptation of a play by Eduardo De Filippo and Armando Curcio (produced New York, 1962).
The Twenty Five Cent White Hat (in *3 × 3*, produced New York, 1962).
Food for Thought: A Play about Food, with Jay and Fran Landesman (produced St. Louis, 1962).
Dynamite Tonite, music by William Bolcom (produced New York, 1963; revised version produced New York, 1964; revised version produced New Haven, Connecticut, 1966). New York, Trio Music, 1964.
Party (produced New York, 1964; revised version, music by Laurence Rosenthal, produced New York, 1976).
They (produced Philadelphia, 1965).
Reg. U.S. Pat. Off., in *Pardon Me, Sir, But Is My Eye Hurting Your Elbow*, edited by Bob Booker and George Foster. New York, Geis, 1968.
Story Theatre (produced New Haven, Connecticut, 1968).
Greatshot, music by William Bolcom (produced New Haven, Connecticut, 1969).
Ovid, music by The True Brethren, adaptation of *Metamorphoses* by Ovid (produced Chicago, 1969; New York, 1971).
Mahagonny, adaptation of the libretto by Brecht, music by Kurt Weill (produced New York, 1970). Excerpts published in *Yale/Theatre* (New Haven, Connecticut), 1969.
The American Revolution, with Paul Sills, music by Tony Greco, lyrics by Weinstein (produced Washington, D.C., 1973).

More Metamorphoses, adaptation of the work by Ovid (produced Spoleto, Italy, 1973).
Gypsy New York (produced New York, 1974).
Lady Liberty's Ice Cream Cone (produced New York, 1974).
Captain Jinks, adaptation of the play by Clyde Fitch, music arranged by William Bolcom (produced New York, 1976).
America More or Less, music by Tony Greco (produced San Francisco, 1976).
Monkey, with Paul Sills (produced New York, 1978).
Stories for Theatre (produced Southampton, New York, 1979).

Improvisational Material: *Second City*, New York, 1963–64.

Television Plays: *Improvisation*; *Story Theatre*; *The Last Ingredient*, music by David Amram.

Verse

Different Poems by the Same Author. Rome, United States Information Service, 1960.

Recording: lyrics for *Black Max: Cabaret Songs*, music by William Bolcom, RCA, 1985.

*

Manuscript Collection: Yale University, New Haven, Connecticut.

Critical Studies: *American Drama since World War II*, New York, Harcourt Brace, 1962, and *The Jumping-Off Place*, Harcourt Brace, 1969, both by Gerald Weales; *A Theatre Divided*, Boston, Little Brown, 1967, and *Opening Nights*, New York, Putnam, 1969, both by Martin Gottfried; *Common and Uncommon Masks* by Richard Gilman, New York, Random House, 1971.

Theatrical Activities:
Director: **Plays**—*Second City* (co-director, with Paul Sills), and other improvisational groups; his own and other plays at the Free Theatre, Chicago, Actors Studio, New York and Los Angeles, and the Rock Theatre and the Guerilla Theatre, Los Angeles; *A Memory of Two Mondays* by Arthur Miller, Southampton, New York, 1979; *The White House Murder Case* by Jules Feiffer, New York, 1980.

Arnold Weinstein comments:

I try to write the history and mythology of today. The schoolroom, the churchroom, the theatre are one, or all are lost. Drama and karma are one. Look them up. Look them up and down. The audience is half the action, the actors the other half; the author starts the fight. Power. The passing of power. It really is life there in the dark, here. The lightning of television terrifies most. Right in the word the intrusion of fear—fear of loss of control, loss of sale, loss of sorcery. Loss of power. Our fear sends us through the channels, puts us on our tracks. If the trinity does not control the power, what's left? Only everything. Everything running around in formless rampant ranks waiting for daring brutes to pick up the wire reins.

* * *

The generation of American playwrights that followed Arthur Miller and Tennessee Williams was a troubled one, reflecting a country that was emerging from a history of brute domination into a future of questions and complexities. These playwrights were similarly trapped between the theater styles and values of an outgoing past and the uncertainty of a fast-approaching future. Such writers as Jack Gelber and Jack Richardson have never fulfilled their early promise, but Arnold Weinstein's inability to find himself as a playwright is perhaps the most painful, for he is the most artistic, talented, and original of the lot. But he has been hurt by a combination of critical rejection and changing taste, and though the author of charming plays and libretti, his career seems frustrated.

His New York professional debut was a production by the Living Theatre of *Red Eye of Love*, which remains his best known full-length play. The Living Theatre at the time was in its Brecht stage and so was Weinstein, who was to prove too affected by changing fashion and too insecure in his own style. The play is a romantic fable about American capitalism. Its hero is a toy inventor in love with a girl who feels it her "duty to marry money." She turns to the owner of a 13-story meat market, which grows beyond 40 stories as the play progresses. This girl vacillates between the inventor (artist) and the butcher (capitalist) while the play does vaudeville turns to Joycean word games with a whimsicality that would prove a Weinstein signature. The author's stage energy, his antic humor, his feel for America, and his deep love of cheap sentiment are established as they would persist through his subsequent work, but the play is too often precious and almost blatantly Brechtian.

In 1962 he wrote the libretto for an off-Broadway musical of inspired zaniness—*Fortuna* (Weinstein was to become involved with many musical projects, one of America's rare artistic playwrights to appreciate their value, but though several were planned, none reached Broadway). *Fortuna*, adapted from an Italian comedy, told of the impoverished and luckless title character who inherits a fortune on the condition that he have no sons. After a series of farcical complications, Fortuna gets his fortune. Once again, Weinstein was dealing with a Schweikian hero-victim (expressionist and absurdist influences would for too long influence his work and keep him from self-discovery).

His one-act absurdist play, *The Twenty Five Cent White Hat*, opened and closed off-Broadway, unappreciated by New York's critics. Though the play was a trite plea for the importance of individuality, it was filled with Weinstein's lively and poetic comedy writing.

The turning point in the playwright's career came with *Dynamite Tonite*, his "comic opera for actors" written with composer William Bolcom. Though not without relation to Brecht, the work had a brisk originality of its own. For though it was a legitimate opera, it was indeed written for actors—that is, non-singers. Weinstein's libretto was intensely pacifist, yet romantic and comic, tender and suffused with affection for a vulnerable mankind. Its operetta-style hero and heroine sang hilarious Wagnerian parodies in counterpoint to flatfooted soldiers doing soft shoe dances, and set as the work was on the battleground of a neverneverland it had an odd mixture of expressionism and Americana that somehow worked.

Dynamite Tonite is a superb theater work, but it was so brutally criticized that it closed on its first night. Several attempts were made to revive it, first by the Repertory Theatre at Yale Drama School and once more off-Broadway, but it seemed doomed to rejection despite (or perhaps because of) its artistic superiority.

Greatshot, another musical work with Bolcom—also produced at Yale—was in the style of the then-popular self-creative companies (such as his friends at the Living Theatre had developed), but there was no soul to the work, nor clarity of intention. The structured, verbal theater to which the playwright naturally inclined did not mesh with physical, improvisational, anti-verbal theater he was emulating.

Meanwhile, Weinstein had been long preparing a new translation of the great Brecht-Weill opera, *Mahoganny*, and when it was finally produced after many years of effort, his work proved mediocre, though hardly showcased by the disastrous production.

Weinstein's history, then, is one of victimization by the American theater's commercialism, which leaves little room for so creative, artistic, and poetic a playwright; it is a victimization by British-American theater generally, with its overwhelming sense of trend (absurdism, once hailed as *the* style for moderns, was obsolete after no more than five years of fashion); and it is a victimization by rejection. His past shows some fulfillment and great promise; his present is in limbo; his future depends on his own resolve and his treatment at the hands of both the theater and circumstance.

—Martin Gottfried

WELLER, Michael. American. Born in New York City, 26 September 1942. Educated at Stockbridge School; Windham College; Brandeis University, Waltham, Massachusetts, B.A. in music 1965; Manchester University, Lancashire. Recipient: Creative Artists Public Service grant, 1976. Agent: Michael Imison Playwrights, 28 Almeida Street, London N1 1TD, England. Address: 215 East 5th Street, New York, New York 10003, U.S.A.

PUBLICATIONS

Plays

Cello Days at Dixon's Palace (produced Cambridge, Massachusetts, 1965).

Fred, music by Weller, adaptation of the novel *Malcolm* by James Purdy (produced Waltham, Massachusetts, 1965).

How Ho-Ho Rose and Fell in Seven Short Scenes, music by Weller (produced Manchester, 1966; London, 1972).

The Making of Theodore Thomas, Citizen, adaptation of the play *Johnny Johnson* by Paul Green (produced London, 1968).

Happy Valley (produced Edinburgh, 1969).

The Bodybuilders, and Now There's Just the Three of Us (produced London, 1969). Included in *The Bodybuilders, and Tira Tells Everything There Is to Know about Herself*, 1972; in *Off-Broadway Plays 2*, London, Penguin, 1972.

Poison Come Poison (produced London, 1970).

Cancer (produced London, 1970). London, Faber, 1971; as *Moonchildren* (produced Washington, D.C., 1971; New York, 1972), New York, French, 1971.

Grant's Movie (produced London, 1971). With *Tira*, London, Faber, 1972.

Tira Tells Everything There Is to Know about Herself (produced London, 1971). Included in *The Bodybuilders, and Tira Tells Everything There Is to Know about Herself*, 1972; as *Tira* (produced New York, 1975), with *Grant's Movie*, London, Faber, 1972.

The Bodybuilders, and Tira Tells Everything There Is to Know about Herself. New York, Dramatists Play Service, 1972.

More Than You Deserve, music by Jim Steinman, lyrics by Weller and Steinman (produced New York, 1973).

Twenty-Three Years Later (produced Los Angeles, 1973).

Fishing (produced New York, 1975; London, 1976). New York, French, 1975.

Alice, in *After Calcutta* (produced London, 1976).

Split (one-act version; produced London, 1977; New York, 1978). New York, French, 1979; as *Abroad* in *Split* (full-length version), 1981.

Loose Ends (produced Washington, D.C., and New York, 1979; London, 1981). New York, French, 1980.

Barbarians, with Kitty Hunter Blair and Jeremy Brooks, adaptation of a play by Gorky (produced New York, 1980). New York, French, 1982.

Dwarfman, Master of a Million Shapes (produced Chicago, 1981).

At Home (produced London, 1981). Included in *Split* (full-length version), 1981.

Split (full-length version; includes *At Home* [*Split*, part 1] and *Abroad* [*Split*, part 2]). New York, French, 1981.

Five Plays (includes *Moonchildren*, *Fishing*, *At Home*, *Abroad*, *Loose Ends*). New York, New American Library, 1982.

The Ballad of Soapy Smith (produced Seattle, 1983; New York, 1984). New York, French, 1985.

Ghost on Fire (produced La Jolla, California, 1985). New York, Grove Press, 1987.

A Dopey Fairy Tale, adaptation of a story by Chekhov, in *Orchards* (produced Urbana, Illinois, 1985; New York, 1986). New York, Knopf, 1986.

Screenplays: *Hair*, 1979; *Ragtime*, 1982.

*

Theatrical Activities:
Actor: **Play**—Star-Man in *The Tooth of Crime* by Sam Shepard, London, 1972.

* * *

Chronicling his own generation, Michael Weller has sent interim reports from the front lines of bourgeois American youth as students moved from universities into communes, from the city to the country, and from idealism to Madison Avenue competitiveness. Whatever the surrounding environment, his basic concern has been with personal relationships and their vulnerability.

Many of his early plays were introduced to London by the American expatriate Charles Marowitz of the Open Space Theatre, and Weller had an English reputation before he had an American one, despite earning his first production while he was still a student at Brandeis University. His plays generally appeared in a kind of hyper-ventilating realism which matched the extremes of emotion that afflict his characters without detailing too completely their day-to-day existence.

His first play to have a genuine transatlantic impact was the very specifically American drama which was called *Cancer* when it had its premiere at London's Royal Court Theatre. Cancer is, of course, an astrological sign as well as a disease, and the play was retitled *Moonchildren* for its first American performance at Arena Stage in Washington D.C. Although written and first produced in 1970, there was something nostalgic and historical in its portrait of a group of college students sharing an apartment during the heady days of resistance to President Nixon and the war in Vietnam.

Perhaps Weller drew the battle lines too clearly, placing his young people in a sort of drug-armed camp opposing the adult society which was represented by police, landlords, and relatives. The sharp details of the young people's conversational exchanges spoke well for his dramatist's ear, however, and there was an optimism in his writing which suggested that goodwill, high spirits, and visionary certitude would break down the barriers between police and students, an idea which grew sour in the later plays where the broken barriers more often represented a capitulation of idealism. What balanced the comical anarchy in *Cancer* was finally the familial call across generations, the news given to one boy that his mother was dying of cancer—actually, painfully, and beyond the relief of metaphor.

Grant's Movie followed *Cancer* almost immediately, and drew harsher lines between the generations. Police and antiwar demonstrators have come to serious violence, and a policeman is kidnapped by three peace-seeking hippies who believe the man might have murdered the brother of a friend during a demonstration. The friend is Grant and the planned torment of the policeman is according to his script: everybody is in Grant's movie.

Weller's next leap was a review of the hippie alternative as it appeared in 1975: *Fishing*, a play that came to be seen as the second part of an extended trilogy that began with *Cancer*. Three drop-outs are discovered in a backwater of the Pacific Northwest, short on cannabis, short on cash, and exploring a new fantasy of beginning a commercial fishery—if they can raise $1,500 to buy a boat. In the course of the play, real death again enters the fable when the man who was selling the boat dies, and again when the chicken who was becoming a pet is killed, plucked for eating, and pulled apart in rage. Another death is flirted with, when one of the three plans suicide on his motorcycle before changing his mind in favour of the fishing: "Oh you're right, it's a dumb idea, no doubt about it. You and me. Two of the finest minds of our generation. But it's something to do. And, you know, if we approach it just the right way, after a while, if we manage to stick to it, and we don't get seasick and we do catch fish we might find there's a good reason for doing it."

Weller's ear for dialogue had become more acute by then, and the acid wit was refined, but the play that best represented his developing perspective was *Loose Ends*, his 1979 report on the progress of the alternative society of the 1960's. It was panoramic in intention, first evoking an accidental meeting on the hippie road to paradise when a young couple come together on a beach in Bali, he returning to America from a depressing tour in the Peace Corps, and she on her way to enlightenment in India. Weller's comedy and optimism survive his story of that relationship, which stretches forward from 1970 across the decade of Vietnam, Watergate, and disillusion.

With the panoramic structure of *Loose Ends*, Weller constructed a play consisting entirely of dramatic touchpoints: the form remained realistic but every meeting was a contrast to what had gone before and what would have been a gradual evolution of a drop-out into a hip property speculator becomes a comical commentary as the woodsman becomes a long-haired man in a business suit. Gurus and passing fashions are recorded for their worth, then brushed aside while the original couple fall into competition with each other, rejecting then courting financial success. Their path was to divorce instead of enlightenment and although their careers remain on the edge of art, in photography and filmmaking, the world is busy overcoming their ideals.

With *Cancer* and *Fishing* it forms a rounded trilogy of reportage, and the plays make a dramatic document of value. Weller remains a writer for the theatre, contributing new, short pieces such as *Split* and important longer works such as *Ghost on Fire*. With such adaptations for the cinema as his screenplay for E.L. Doctorow's *Ragtime*, his reputation has also been growing elsewhere.

—Ned Chaillet

WERTENBAKER, (Lael Louisiana) Timberlake. British and American. Educated at schools near St. Jean-de-Luz, France; attended university. Journalist in London and New York; teacher of French in Greece, 1 year. Resident writer, Shared Experience, 1983, and Royal Court Theatre, 1985, both London. Recipient: Arts Council of Great Britain bursary, 1981, grant, 1983; Thames Television bursary, 1984, 1985; *Plays and Players* award, 1985. Lives in London. Agent: Michael Imison Playwrights, 28 Almeida Street, London N1 1TD, England.

PUBLICATIONS

Plays

This Is No Place for Tallulah Bankhead (produced London, 1978).
The Third (produced London, 1980).
Second Sentence (produced Brighton, 1980).
Case to Answer (produced London, 1980; Ithaca, New York, 1981).
Breaking Through (produced London, 1980).
New Anatomies (produced London, 1981). Published in *Plays Introduction*, London, Faber, 1984.
Inside Out (produced Stoke-on-Trent, 1982).
Home Leave (produced Ipswich, Suffolk, 1982).
False Admissions, adaptation of a play by Marivaux (produced London, 1983).
Successful Strategies, adaptation of a play by Marivaux (produced London, 1983).
Abel's Sister, based on material by Yolande Bourcier (produced London, 1984; New York, 1985).
The Grace of Mary Traverse (produced London, 1985). London, Faber, 1985.
Léocadia, adaptation of the play by Jean Anouilh (broadcast 1985). Published in *Five Plays*, by Anouilh, London, Methuen, 1987.
Mephisto, adaptation of the play by Ariane Mnouchkine, based on a novel by Klaus Mann (produced London, 1986).

Radio Plays: *Léocadia*, 1985; *La Dispute*, from the play by Marivaux, 1987.

*

Timberlake Wertenbaker comments:

I like monologues. I think they are an unused and rather beautiful form of communication. I do not like naturalism. I find it boring. My plays are an attempt to get away from the smallness of naturalism, from enclosed rooms to open spaces, and also to get ideas away from the restraints of closed spaces to something wider. My plays often start with a very ordinary question: If women had power, would they behave the same way as men? Why do we seem to want to destroy ourselves? Is the personal more important than the political? If someone has behaved badly all of their lives, can they redeem themselves? Parallel to this will be some story I may have heard, some gossip about somebody, a sentence heard or read. A friend of mine once told me his mother had been taught how to be a good hostess by being made to talk to empty chairs. I used that as the opening scene of *The Grace of Mary Traverse*. I once heard about a young couple where the woman, for no apparent reason, had come out of the bath and shot herself. That became *Case to Answer*. Somebody showed me a print of the Japanese courtesan Ono No Komachi. I wrote a play about her. Everything gets collected and used at some point. I'm sure it's the same for all writers, but I haven't asked. Once I have the idea and the people, I do a lot of research. I think plays should be accurate, whatever their subject. Then the imagination can be let free, but only after a solid knowledge of the world, the people, the age, whatever is the world of the play.

I don't think you can leave the theatre and go out and make a revolution. That's the naivety of the 1970's. But I do think you can make people change, just a little, by forcing them to question something, or by intriguing them, or giving them an image that remains with them. And that little change can lead to bigger changes. That's all you can hope for. Nor do I think playwrights should have the answers. A play is like a trial: it goes before the jury, the audience, and they decide—to like or not like the people, to agree or not to agree. If you really have the answers, you shouldn't be a writer but a politician. And if you're only interested in slice of life, then you should make documentaries. The theatre is a difficult place, it requires an audience to use its imagination. You must accept that and not try to make it easy for them. You must give them language, because it is best heard in the theatre and language is a potent manifestation of hope. In some theatres in ancient Greece, the number of seats corresponded to the number of adult males with voting rights. I think that is right: theatre is for people who take responsibility. There is no point in trying to attract idiots. Theatre should never be used to flatter, but to reveal, which is to disturb.

* * *

There is something askance about nearly everything Timberlake Wertenbaker writes. Even in the most straightforward of her plays, such as *Home Leave*, which she wrote about women working in a factory at the end of the World War II, her opening stage directions present her leading character with calculated ambiguity: "She's in overalls, her hair hidden in a cloth cap and it should be impossible to tell she's a woman." Often the tilt of her writing explores a fluidity between the sexes that is far more revolutionary than any declaration of equality and she does not hesitate to subvert legend or history in her examinations of human nature.

Perhaps the most elaborate statements about her intentions appear in *Inside Out*, borrowed from the Japanese legend of Komachi, a famous beauty and poet who was doomed to suffer because of the task undertaken by one of her admirers which led to his death. Unable to match the poetic speech of Komachi in his declaration of love, he vowed to return on an arduous journey every night for 100 nights, but returned only 99 times. In Wertenbaker's version, Komachi first appears as an old woman who has survived into our present, and who has become interchangeable with Shosho, the lover. When the story of the love affair is retold, the old woman becomes Shosho and another actress plays the young Komachi who first rebuffs him and then, through desire, regrets the delay. Shosho remains steadfast in his promise.

As if that were not enough sexual ambiguity, it is by draping Shosho in her clothes and exchanging roles with him that Komachi extracts the promise of the 100 visits. Because it is by imagining himself as Komachi that Shosho has invented the idea of the poetic action, it is forever unclear who really suggested the task, but what remains equally unclear is the function of gender in Wertenbaker's version of the story.

The chorus reports that: "They say a woman is a man turned inside out. Most evident in the genitals, his turned out, hers turned in, hers waiting for his, waiting for completion, that's what they say." But while that may be what "they say," it is obvious that Wertenbaker is not convinced. The chorus also asks: "Question: what is the anatomy of a woman?" and is answered by Komachi's companion Li: "Not what you imagine through your genitals."

Another of Wertenbaker's plays, *New Anatomies*, tackles that issue more directly. It tells the story of Isabelle Eberhardt, a young woman who dresses as a male Arab to find acceptance among the Muslims and, ironically, persecution from the French. In her Arab persona as Si Mahmoud she seeks spiritual enlightenment, and though the Arabs have more than a fair idea that she is actually a woman, they befriend her and accept her own determination of her sex. In the stage version, written for a women's theatrical troupe, all the roles, male and female, are taken by women. That ambiguity is not helpful as the issue of Isabelle's self-determined sexuality is profound, and the dressing-up of other women undermines both the spiritual search and the intended clash of western and oriental cultures. However, as a text it carefully and provocatively defines its arguments.

As a woman of American heritage, educated in France and resident in Britain, Wertenbaker herself juggles cultures and influences, and in addition to her original work she has already made significant contributions to translation, particularly with her translations from Marivaux. His stylish comic knowingness about sexuality and faithlessness has been well reflected in her English versions of *False Admissions*, *Successful Strategies*, and *La Dispute*, where she has maintained a coolly ironical posture which admirably suggests the French originals. Although she has also provided convincing versions of Jean Anouilh's *Léocadia* and Ariane Mnouchkine's *Mephisto*, it is in Marivaux's writing that her own preoccupations are best reflected.

Possibly the most straightforward of her original plays is *Abel's Sister*, written with material provided by Yolande Bourcier. It is none the less emotionally complex. Although set in the English countryside, it has some of the mythical aspirations of Sam Shepard's versions of the American family. Sandra, the spastic twin sister of Howard, has removed herself from the "centre" where she lives to move in on her brother and his girlfriend. When she announces that her favourite story is Cain and Abel, because it was right that Cain should at least kill the brother who suffocated him, she prepares the way for an attack on her brother by an American neighbour who has been led to believe that Howard is dangerously violent.

It is typical of Wertenbaker that she should turn to a basic biblical source, again inverting the sexes, to explain the motivation of her characters. In addition to the Japanese Noh theatre and investigations of Muslim culture, she has also explored the radicalization of Electra in her short (and relatively minor) reshaping of the *Oresteia*, *Agamemnon's Daughter* (not yet produced).

Her own most radical historical revision, and most important play, is her dramatic fantasia *The Grace of Mary Traverse*, in which she portrays Lord Gordon, the disaffected peer accused of treason after the destructive "Gordon Riots" of 1780, as a man who discovers power through the impulsive rape of a woman in the streets. In Wertenbaker's version of events, he is a peripheral character, and the catalyst is Mary Traverse, a young woman trained only in polite conversation by her father. After witnessing the rape by Gordon, she determines not to be a victim and decides to enter Georgian London as an equal of the rapacious men. She gambles with them, hires a male whore to deflower her, makes herself a prostitute for her father, and buys the sexual services of a woman for her own pleasure. She, too, finds power a seduction, and helps re-ignite the hatred for Catholics, though the horrors of mass violence finally chill her. Wertenbaker refrains from a final condemnation of the masculine world her battered heroine has entered, coming to the conclusion, through Mary, that it would be best to forgive history since it cannot be forgotten and learn how to love this world since it is the only one we have.

Subversively, and with increasing dramatic powers, Wertenbaker continues to chip away at the notion of a totally masculine universe, and throws down the challenge of a world undivided by gender.

—Ned Chaillet

WESKER, Arnold. British. Born in Stepney, London, 24 May 1932. Educated at Upton House Technical School, Hackney, London, 1943–48; London School of Film Technique, 1955–56. Served in the Royal Air Force, 1950–52. Married Doreen Bicker in 1958; two sons and one daughter. Furniture-maker's apprentice and carpenter's mate, 1948; bookseller's assistant, 1949 and 1952; plumber's mate, 1952; seed sorter on farm, 1953; kitchen porter, 1953–54; pastry cook, London and Paris, 1954–58; founder and director, Centre 42, 1961–70. Chairman of the British Centre, 1978–83, and President of the Playwrights Permanent Committee, 1981–83, International Theatre Institute. Recipient: Arts Council grant, 1958; *Evening Standard* award, 1959; Encyclopaedia Britannica award, 1959; Marzotto prize, 1964; Best Foreign Play award (Spain), 1979. Address: 37 Ashley Road, London N19 3AG, England.

PUBLICATIONS

Plays

The Wesker Trilogy. London, Cape, 1960; New York, Random House, 1961.
- *Chicken Soup with Barley* (produced Coventry and London, 1958; Cleveland, 1962). Published in *New English Dramatists 1*, London, Penguin, 1959.
- *Roots* (produced Coventry and London, 1959; New York, 1961). London, Penguin, 1959.
- *I'm Talking about Jerusalem* (produced Coventry 1960; revised version produced London, 1960). London, Penguin, 1960.

The Kitchen (produced London, 1959; New York, 1966). Published in *New English Dramatists 2*, London, Penguin, 1960; expanded version (produced Coventry and London, 1961; New York, 1966), London, Cape, 1961; New York, Random House, 1962.

Chips with Everything (produced London, 1962; New York, 1963). London, Cape, 1962; New York, Random House, 1963.

The Nottingham Captain: A Moral for Narrator, Voices and Orchestra, music by Wilfred Josephs and Dave Lee (produced Wellingborough, Northamptonshire, 1962). Included in *Six Sundays in January*, 1971.

Menace (televised 1963). Included in *Six Sundays in January*, 1971; in *The Plays of Arnold Wesker 2*, 1977.

Their Very Own and Golden City (produced Brussels, 1965; revised version produced London, 1966). London, Cape, 1966; revised version (also director: produced Aarhus, Denmark, 1974), in *The Plays of Arnold Wesker 2*, 1977.

The Four Seasons (produced Coventry and London, 1965; New York, 1968). London, Cape, 1966; in *The Plays of Arnold Wesker 2*, 1977.

The Friends (also director: produced Stockholm and London, 1970). London, Cape, 1970; in *The Plays of Arnold Wesker 2*, 1977.

The Old Ones (produced London, 1972; New York, 1974). London, Cape, 1973; revised version, edited by Michael Marland, London, Blackie, 1974; in *The Plays of Arnold Wesker 2*, 1977.

The Wedding Feast, adaptation of a story by Dostoevsky (produced Stockholm, 1974; Leeds, 1977; revised version, produced Birmingham, 1980). Included in *The Journalists, The Wedding Feast, The Merchant*, 1980.

The Journalists (produced Coventry, 1977; Los Angeles, 1979). London, Writers and Readers, 1975.

Love Letters on Blue Paper, adaptation of his own story (televised 1976; produced Syracuse, New York, 1977; also director: produced London, 1978; New York, 1984). London, TQ Publications-Writers and Readers, 1978.

The Plays of Arnold Wesker:
1. *The Kitchen, Chips with Everything, The Wesker Trilogy*. New York, Harper, 1976.
2. *The Four Seasons, Their Very Own and Golden City, Menace, The Friends, The Old Ones*. New York, Harper, 1977.

The Merchant (produced Stockholm, 1976; revised version, produced Philadelphia and New York, 1977; revised version produced Birmingham, 1978). Included in *The Journalists, The Wedding Feast, The Merchant*, 1980; revised version published separately, London, Methuen, 1983.

The Journalists, The Wedding Feast, The Merchant. London, Penguin, 1980.

Caritas (produced London, 1981). London, Cape, 1981.

Mothers: Four Portraits (produced Tokyo, 1982; Colorado, 1985; London, 1987).

Annie, Anna, Annabella (broadcast 1983; as *Annie Wobbler*, also director: produced Birmingham and London, 1983; New York, 1986).

Sullied Hand (produced Edinburgh, 1984).

Yardsale (broadcast 1984; produced Edinburgh, 1985; also director: produced London, 1987). Published in *Plays International* (London), April 1987.

One More Ride on the Merry-Go-Round (produced Leicester, 1985).

Whatever Happened to Betty Lemon (produced Paris, 1986; also director: produced London, 1987). Published in *Plays International* (London), April 1987.

Screenplay: *The Kitchen*, 1961.

Radio Plays: *Annie, Anna, Annabella*, 1983 (Germany); *Yardsale*, 1984; *Bluey*, 1985.

Television Plays: *Menace*, 1963; *Love Letters on Blue Paper*, from his own story, 1976.

Short Stories

Love Letters on Blue Paper. London, Cape, 1974; New York, Harper, 1975.
Said the Old Man to the Young Man: Three Stories. London, Cape, 1978.
Love Letters on Blue Paper and Other Stories. London, Penguin, 1980.

Other

Labour and the Arts: II, or, What, Is to Be Done? Oxford, Gemini, 1960.
The Modern Playwright; or, "O Mother, Is It Worth It?" Oxford, Gemini, 1961.
Fears of Fragmentation (essays). London, Cape, 1970.
Six Sundays in January (miscellany). London, Cape, 1971.
Say Goodbye—You May Never See Them Again: Scenes from Two East-End Backgrounds, paintings by John Allin. London, Cape, 1974.
Words as Definitions of Experience. London, Writers and Readers, 1976.
Journey into Journalism. London, Writers and Readers, 1977.
Fatlips (for children). London, Writers and Readers, and New York, Harper, 1978.
The Journalists: A Triptych (includes the play *The Journalists*, *A Journal of the Writing of "The Journalists,"* and *Journey into Journalism*). London, Cape, 1979.
Distinctions. London, Cape, 1985.

*

Critical Studies: *Mid-Century Drama* by Laurence Kitchin, London, Faber, 1960, revised edition, 1962; *The Writer and Commitment* by John Mander, London, Secker and Warburg, 1961; *Anger and After* by John Russell Taylor, London, Methuen, 1962, revised edition, 1969, as *The Angry Theatre*, New York, Hill and Wang, 1962, revised edition, 1969; "Two Romantics: Arnold Wesker and Harold Pinter" by Clifford Leech, in *Contemporary Theatre*, edited by John Russell Brown and Bernard Harris, London, Arnold, 1962, New York, St. Martin's Press, 1963; *Arnold Wesker* by Harold U. Ribalow, New York, Twayne, 1966; "Arnold Wesker, The Last Humanist?" by Michael Anderson, in *New Theatre Magazine* (Bristol), vol. 8, no. 3, 1968; *Arnold Wesker* edited by Michael Marland, London, Times Newspapers, 1970; *Arnold Wesker* by Ronald Hayman, London, Heinemann, 1970, revised edition, New York, Ungar, 1973, Heinemann, 1979; *The Plays of Arnold Wesker: An Assessment* by Glenda Leeming and Simon Trussler, London, Gollancz, 1971, and *Arnold Wesker*, London, Longman, 1972, and *Wesker the Playwright*, London, Methuen, 1983, both by Leeming, and *Wesker on File* edited by Leeming, Methuen, 1985; "Production Casebook 2: Arnold Wesker's *The Friends*" by Garry O'Connor, in *Theatre Quarterly* (London), April 1971; article by Margaret Drabble, in *New Review* (London), February 1975; *Stages in the Revolution* by Catherine Itzin, London, Eyre Methuen, 1980.

Theatrical Activities:
Director: **Plays**—*The Four Seasons*, Havana, 1968; *The Friends*, Stockholm and London, 1970; *The Old Ones*, Munich, 1973; *Their Very Own and Golden City*, Aarhus, Denmark, 1974; *Love Letters on Blue Paper*, London, 1978, and Oslo, 1980; *Annie Wobbler*, Birmingham and London, 1983, London, 1984; *Yardsale*, Stratford-on-Avon, 1985, London, 1987; *Whatever Happened to Betty Lemon*, London, 1987.

Arnold Wesker comments:

(1982) It is really for others to write about me. I try every so often to explain myself in lectures, articles, interviews. Never satisfactorily. Certain themes and relationships seem to pre-occupy me: the relationship between lovers, husband and wife, parent and child, friends, state and the individual; the themes of injustice, defiance, the power of knowledge.

I have no theories about the theatre writing through which I pursue these themes and relationships. Each play comes to me with its own metaphor, dictates its own form, creates its own atmosphere. All literature contains a mixture of poetry and journalism. Poetry in the theatre is that indefinable *sense* of truth which is communicated when two dissimilar or unrelated moments are placed side by side. "Sense" of truth, not *the* one and only truth. I would like to think my plays and stories have a larger proportion of poetry than journalism, and that if I have any talent it is for identifying the metaphors which life contains for the purpose of illuminating itself.

One day I hope someone may write as generously of me as Ruskin did of Turner:

> This you will find is ultimately the case with every true and right master; at first, while we are tyros in art, or before we have earnestly studied the man in question, we shall see little in him; or perhaps see, as we think, deficiencies; we shall fancy he is inferior to this man in that, and to the other man in the other; but as we go on studying him we shall find that he has got both that and the other; and both in a far higher sense than the man who seemed to possess those qualities in excess. Thus in Turner's lifetime, when people first looked at him, those who liked rainy weather said he was not equal to Copley Fielding; but those who looked at Turner long enough found that he could be much more wet than Copley Fielding when he chose. The people who liked force said that "Turner was not strong enough for them; he was effeminate; they liked De Wint,—nice strong tone;—or Cox—great, greeny, dark masses of colour—solemn feeling of the freshness and depth of nature; they liked Cox—Turner was too hot for them." Had they looked long enough they would have found that he had far more force than De Wint, far more freshness than Cox when he chose,—only united with other elements; and that he didn't choose to be cool, if nature had appointed the weather to be hot . . . And so throughout with all thoroughly great men, their strength is not seen at first, precisely because they united, in due place and measure, every great quality . . .

* * *

In an interview in *Tribune* in 1978, Arnold Wesker characterised himself as "world-weary," "over-whelmed with a sense of frustration and impotence." "For reasons which I don't understand, I do seem to arouse hostilities and irritations." Nevertheless, Wesker continues to write and if he can find no place, or small room, in the British theatre, his plays enjoy a considerable success in other countries. The paradox of a major British writer continually premiering his work abroad, in translation, is heightened when one considers the obsessive concern, in the earlier plays, with the necessity of acting in community to transform and transcend the immediate environment in order to live authentically and fully.

Wesker's plays are plays of ideas, dramatising a debate, expressed in passionate terms, about the complexity and necessity of moral choices, when there is no clear precept to follow. In the earlier plays these moral dilemmas are often laid out in set pieces. In *Roots* Beatie tells the story of the girl in love with one man who deserts her, and loved by another who rejects her because she has given herself to the first. Idealism is seen very early to contain its own negative dialectic. "Tell me your dreams," says Peter, in *The Kitchen*, and unleashes the dream of the man who wants to drop a bomb on the CND marchers, because they hold up the buses.

Ironically, Wesker enjoyed much more success with the earlier plays, in which the dialectics between idealism and frustration were presented more simply, than with the later plays, where the issues are much more complex. Often values which had been seen positively in the earlier plays are revealed to be illusory. The search for "words" through which to apprehend the world, express one's thoughts and feelings, and build "bridges" fails to achieve those aims and becomes a way of obscuring or evading the issues. The realisation of self, through education and culture, which is to be the means of Beatie's liberation, becomes in *The Friends* a source of frustration, isolation, and contempt for others.

Wesker's stature in the theatre declined during the 1960's and 1970's. Until 1964 his battle against apathy and purely materialist values, for the individual's right to life, liberty, and the pursuit of happiness through the orderly and gradual reform of society, could be seen as a feasible, and socialist, course of action. The political and economic crises of the mid-1960's through the 1970's called for either a cynical withdrawal from these aims, a dropping out into anarchistic individualism, or a commitment to a programme, however vague, for mass revolution. Wesker's concern with values that surmount the material has embarrassed his opponents. His concern with the individual has led those who share his own passionate concern for the realisation of working-class potential to brand his work as elitist, subjective, and, ultimately, conformist.

It is very easy to select from Wesker's plays quotations which support a critique of counter-revolutionary idealism. After all, in *The Friends* Manfred has a speech in which he says, "The working class! Hate them! It's coming, Macey. Despise them! I can hear myself, it's coming. Hate them! The working class, my class, offend me. Their cowardly acquiescence, their rotten ordinariness—everything about them—Hate them! There!" Wesker leaves himself open to such criticisms, not because he necessarily agrees with such views but because, recognising that such thoughts and feelings are part of the dialectics of his own make-up, he allows his characters to express them with extreme feeling, without explicitly denying them by suppressing them or taking a committed authorial stance against them. Examined closely, Wesker's later plays present a complex dialectical discourse of contrasting and often contradictory views as to what the central issue involves. Friend and foe alike might condemn this as nit-picking over dead ground or a perverse adherence to idealism in th stern face of reality. Politicos may call for a sword to cut through the Gordian knots with which Wesker becomes enmeshed. He himself relentlessly pursues metaphysical values in an increasingly materialistic world, charting as he goes the deepening frustrations of compromise and the high price exacted for sticking to your beliefs.

What is clear from the line of development through his plays is the continual decrease of the spatial area in which the individual can act. The major shift in his work occurred in the mid-1960's and coincides with his withdrawal from public action, as expressed through his involvement with CND, the Committee of 100, and Centre 42. There are fewer scenes of concerted action in the later plays to mark the potential power of the working-class shown in the first act of *The Kitchen* or the coal-stealing scene in *Chips with Everything*. The size of the community participating in the ritual celebrations becomes smaller and more enclosed. In the first act of *Chicken Soup with Barley* the setting is a room, but there is constant reference to the world outside. The streets of the East End and the battlefields of Spain are arenas of political action. Education will make the world Beatie Bryant's oyster. In *The Old Ones* both the streets and the classroom are potential areas of mindless violence. In *The Merchant* Shylock's actions are confined within the space and rules of the ghetto. The line culminates in the walling up of the nun, Christine, in *Caritas* while she repeats "This is a wall, this is a wall. . . ." The area of the action shrinks and the concerns become more metaphysical.

Wesker's world-weariness and his sense of isolation and impotence are nihilistic only if he sees them subjectively. A move out into the world would reveal them as a common feature of the contemporary human condition. If it is harder to keep faith with Sarah Kahn's injunction to "care," her corollary still stands, "if you don't care you'll die." The struggle might be harder and the issues less clear-cut than they appeared before but the battle must still be waged. But to do this the ghetto has to be broken out of, and being walled up for your beliefs is too high a price to pay for integrity.

Since 1981 Wesker's work has marked time with no major play coming from him. However, there are signs that there is some resurgence of light-heartedness and fun if not optimism. *One More Ride on the Merry-Go-Round* is Wesker's attempt at writing pure comedy but, not unexpectedly, serious themes intrude. The main action of the comedy is the revival of energy and purpose in a 50-year-old academic and his wife. *Annie Wobbler* comprises three character monologues for a solo actress. It has served to remind the world that Wesker is, above all, a great writer of character parts and has had a wide international success. One can only hope that a new major play is just around the corner.

—Clive Barker

WESLEY, Richard (Errol). American. Born in Newark, New Jersey, 11 July 1945. Educated at Howard University, Washington, D.C., 1963–67, B.F.A. 1967. Married Valerie Deane Wilson in 1972; three children. Passenger service agent, United Airlines, Newark, 1967–69; member of the New Lafayette Theatre Company and managing editor of *Black Theatre* magazine, New York, 1969–73; founding member, 1973, and member of the Board of Directors, 1976–80, Frank Silvera Writers Workshop, New York; teacher of black theatre history, Manhattanville College, Purchase, New York, and Wesleyan University, Middletown, Connecticut, 1973–74, and Manhattan Community College, New York, 1980–83; member of the Board of Directors, Theatre of Universal Images, Newark, 1979–82; teacher, Rutgers University, New Brunswick, New Jersey, 1984. Recipient: Drama Desk award, 1972; Rockefeller grant, 1973; Audelco award, 1974, 1977; NAACP Image Award, 1974, 1975. Agent: Jay C. Kramer, 135 East 55th Street, New York, New York 10022. Address: P.O. Box 43091, Upper Montclair, New Jersey 07043, U.S.A.

PUBLICATIONS

Plays

Put My Dignity on 307 (produced Washington, D.C., 1967).
The Street Corner (produced Seattle, 1970; New York, 1972).
Headline News (produced New York, 1970).
Knock Knock, Who Dat (produced New York, 1970).
The Black Terror (produced Washington, D.C., 1970; New York, 1971). Published in *The New Lafayette Theatre Presents*, edited by Ed Bullins, New York, Doubleday, 1974.
Gettin' It Together (produced Roxbury, Massachusetts, 1971; New York, 1972). With *The Past Is the Past*, New York, Dramatists Play Service, 1979.
Strike Heaven on the Face! (produced New York, 1973).
Alicia (produced Waterford, Connecticut, 1973; as *Goin' Thru Changes*, produced New York, 1974).
Eight Ball (produced Waterford, Connecticut, 1973).
The Sirens (produced New York, 1974). New York, Dramatists Play Service, 1975.
The Mighty Gents (produced Waterford, Connecticut, 1974; as *The Last Street Play*, produced New York, 1978; as *The Mighty Gents*, produced New York, 1978). New York, Dramatists Play Service, 1979.
The Past Is the Past (produced Waterford, Connecticut, 1974; New York, 1975). With *Gettin' It Together*, New York, Dramatists Play Service, 1979.
On the Road to Babylon, music and lyrics by Peter Link, based on a concept by Brent Nicholson (produced Milwaukee, 1980).
Butterfly (produced Waterford, Connecticut, 1985).

Screenplays: *Uptown Saturday Night*, 1974; *Let's Do It Again*, 1975; *Fast Forward*, 1985; *Native Son*, 1986.

Television Play: *The House of Dies Drear*, from the novel by Virginia Hamilton, 1974.

*

Manuscript Collection: Dramatists Play Service, New York.

* * *

Richard Wesley writes about the black community of America's urban ghettos. He charts the stoops, poolrooms, and tenements of the inner city and the ways of the people who live there: pimps, prostitutes, derelicts, street gangs. While his sensibility is lyrical, his intentions are political. Wesley questions the values that entrap his characters in aimless days and barren futures. He examines the rules by which they try to survive and the human and social costs when these rules prove inadequate.

While black playwrights such as Ed Bullins and Ron Milner really came from the ghettos they dramatize, Wesley grew up in a middle-class family in Newark, New Jersey. He was, he says, nearly a teenager before he discovered that college wasn't compulsory. At Howard University he not only came under the influence of the fabled Owen Dobson, mentor of many black theatre artists, but also embraced the black nationalist movement which took root on campuses in the 1960's. Upon graduation in 1967, he joined Bullins at the Black Playwrights Workshop of Harlem's New Lafayette Theatre, known for its activist posture and the cross-pollination it encouraged between the stage and the surrounding street culture.

His early play *The Black Terror* is a satire on the contradictions Wesley now detected in cultural nationalism. The playwright introduces us to members of a radical cadre pledged to revolutionary suicide in the service of urban guerrilla warfare. Through the character of Keusi, a pragmatic Vietnam veteran, Wesley debates the movement's tactics and its leaders' image of themselves as a kamikaze vanguard. "To die for the revolution is the greatest thing in life," says one of the militants. "But revolution is about life, I thought," Keusi answers. "Our first duty as revolutionaries is to live.... Why we gotta fight a revolution with a value system directed toward death?"

Although its ideological emphasis is unique among his plays, *The Black Terror* incorporates many stylistic traits, blended impressionistically, that Wesley would refine in his increasingly humanistic later works. Raised more on television than live entertainment, he favors the stage equivalents of filmic cross-fades, superimpositions, and jump cuts to shift locations rapidly, juxtapose moods, and suggest simultaneous action—an approach which subsequently brought him several Hollywood contracts. From the classics he borrows choral and ritualistic elements which he mingles with characters and scenes more typical of contemporary naturalistic drama. His dialogue, a pungent street argot, is expanded by poetic rhythms and refrains, while his monologues approach direct address soliloquies.

For the series of short plays he produced between 1972 and 1974, Wesley muted the stylistic exuberance of *The Black Terror* in favor of compassionate yet unsentimental character studies. In *Gettin' It Together* and *Goin' Thru Changes* polarized young couples struggle both against each other and against cheapening odds to piece together a future. *Strike Heaven on the Face!* brings a war hero home to peacetime defeat. *The Past Is the Past* is set in a poolhall, where a son in search of his heritage confronts the father who long ago abandoned him. Inspired in part by Fellini's *Nights of Cabiria*, a second reunion play, *The Sirens*, probes the life of a prostitute, eventually faced with a choice between her hard won but precarious independence and reconciliation with the husband who vanished a decade before to chase a dream now belatedly come true.

Individually, the plots of these five miniatures are casual, mere hooks on which Wesley hangs family portraits. Taken as montage, however, they together gain a thematic solidarity which presents the scenography of a condition. A number of issues that played supporting roles in *The Black Terror* here become Wesley's preoccupations: the breakdown of family structures, leading to alienation among men and women, parents and children; connections between past and present, through which a legacy of defeat passes from generation to generation; thwarted efforts to wrench self-worth from deluded hopes and to stake out a little turf from which pride can be harvested. How, Wesley asks, can the quest for manhood succeed opposite frustrations that lead to inertia on one hand and savagery on the other?

His cinematic style refined, his ability to draw tenderly detailed characters matured, Wesley assembled his thematic concerns in a full-length drama about the important present and harsh destiny in store for the remnants of an expired Newark street gang. *The Last Street Play* opened to enthusiastic reviews, some of which compared Wesley's inner city tragedy to Kurosawa's *The Seven Samurai* and Fellini's *I vitelloni*, film classics concerning disoriented young toughs, now past their prime, who confront tomorrow with a gallows bravado as deluded as it is fatal. Under the title *The Mighty Gents*, the play transferred to Broadway, a commercial tribute that remains rare for legitimate dramas by black authors, and which italicizes the universality of Wesley's subject: the American dream, examined from a black perspective. Frankie Sojourner, onetime Gents leader, owes a debt to Studs Lonigan, the Irish Catholic title character of James T. Farrell's Depression novel of another squandered youth, another wasted generation. Among fellow playwrights who came of age in the 1970's, Wesley has most in common with David Mamet, whose *American Buffalo* in many ways resembles *The Mighty Gents*. In both plays, might-have-been men cling to a past in which, briefly, they were somebody. In both, desperation ignites violent schemes to regain self-esteem in the eyes of a world where, as Frankie puts it, "The census don't count us and welfare don't even know we alive." More largely, each evaluates American society in our times and the standards we use to govern it.

—C. Lee Jenner

WHITE, John (Sylvester). American. Born in Philadelphia, Pennsylvania, 31 October 1919. Educated at Gonzaga High School, Washington, D.C., 1933–37; University of Notre Dame, Indiana, 1937–41, A.B. in English 1941. Married Vasiliki Sarant in 1966. Actor for 25 years: charter member, Actors Studio, New York. Lives in Hawaii. Address: c/o Greenevine Agency, 9021 Melrose Avenue, Suite 304, Los Angeles, California 90069, U.S.A.

PUBLICATIONS

Plays

Twist (produced New York, 1963).
Bugs (produced New York, 1964). With *Veronica*, New York, Dramatists Play Service, 1966.
Sand (produced New York, 1964).
Veronica (produced New York, 1965). With *Bugs*, New York, Dramatists Play Service, 1966.
Bananas (produced New York, 1968).
The Dog School (produced New York, 1969).
Lady Laura Pritchett, American (produced Southampton, New York, 1969).
Mirage (produced Hanover, New Hampshire, 1969).
The Passing of Milldown Muldern (produced Los Angeles, 1974).
Ombres (produced Paris, 1975).
Les Punaises (produced Paris, 1975).

Screenplay: *Skyscraper*, 1959.

Other

Editor (American version), *Report from Palermo*, by Danilo Dolci. New York, Orion, 1958.

*

Manuscript Collection: Lincoln Center Library of the Performing Arts, New York.

Theatrical Activities:
Actor: **Plays**—as John Sylvester: roles in *Richard III*, New York, 1943; *Sundown Beach* by Bessie Brewer, New York, 1948; *Danny Larkin* by James V. McGee, New York, 1948; *All You Need Is One Good Break* by Arnold Manoff, New York, 1950. **Television**—Mr. Woodman in *Welcome Back, Kotter* series, 1975–79; roles in other television and radio plays.

John White comments:

(1973) Unless writing for hire, I write privately, from within, using for material the backwash of fifty years of existence, sometimes even living. I cannot work from the daily paper or the latest vogue. Indeed, I am turned off by the world. When I think about it, I can't write. I have been accused of being formless and have been applauded, on the other hand, for good form. I detest critics (in the main; there are a few splendid exceptions) and professional "knowers-how." Lonely is the word.

* * *

Though represented by professional productions of just one full-length and a few one-act plays, John White in the 1960's established himself as one of the freshest and most talented playwrights in America. Writing in a strikingly idiosyncratic style—the hallmark of any artist—he applied modern surrealism (less than absurdist, more than naturalist) to find a mythology in American roots. His small body of work is uneven—*Bugs* a good one-act play, *Veronica* a superlative one, and *Bananas* a prematurely produced full-length play that, with polishing, would have been a major work. But like too many playwrights producing in New York during this period, White was hurt by a powerful and ignorant fraternity of critics (it was an era when *Waiting for Godot, Entertaining Mr. Sloane*, and *The Homecoming* by Beckett, Orton, and Pinter were rejected). The playwright fled to Hollywood to seek a living wage at least. Ironically, the style that he plumbed has since become familiar (and therefore palatable) through the work of playwrights from Pinter to Sam Shepard.

Bugs (American vernacular for mad) is about a disturbed young man who has escaped from a hospital and returned to a home where things aren't much saner. His mother and girlfriend are respectively and insanely cheerful and stupid. His father, when not hidden behind a newspaper, is a ranting menace. Though the play might have been more, it gave clear promise of the author's specialness.

Veronica fulfilled the promise. Its central characters are a popular American songwriting team of the 1930's. They are holed up in a hotel room, trying desperately to repeat the huge success they had with a song called "Veronica." They are interrupted by a most peculiar burglar whose very philosophy of life, as it turns out, was inspired by the lyrics of that song.

These lyrics, in accurate satire of the period's popular music, spell out the passé, nostalgic, American dream as once advertised—a dream of beautiful blonds and money and trips to tropical islands. But has this sweet, silly dream now grown obsolete, only to be superseded by mundane social responsibility? One of the songwriters is too absorbed by war and disease to write again about June and moon. His partner is furious—"People haven't changed—a kiss is still a kiss, a sigh is still a sigh."

This yearning for a country once foolish and lovable—this choice of innocence over sophistication—was more deeply explored in the ambitious *Bananas*. The play is set in a period burlesque house during a rehearsal by three comics and an actress. A critic arrives. A series of sketches begins in which the author relates the techniques for burlesque to those of absurdism, suggesting that in a nostalgic, truthful-sardonic way, everything is bananas (another American slangword for madness, obviously White's view of existence). As the play continues, the metaphor of a show as life changes from the burlesque theater to a modern television studio, but everyday conversation remains as a replica of dialogue we have heard on some stage, somewhere.

The idea is excellent and much of the technique is virtuosic, but the play was produced prematurely, and is ultimately confusing, though its argument seems clear enough—a preference for the innocence of actors, entertaining, over the hopeless attempts by intellectuals to make sense of life. Without being repetitious, White—like most fine playwrights—had from the start a consistency to his style and content.

But sadly, a start seems to be all that his playwriting career will have. Like too many in the brutal, competitive, business controlled, and mindlessly commercial and anti-artistic American theater, his sensitivity as a playwright seems to have been beaten down by senseless rejection and unappreciation.

—Martin Gottfried

WHITE, Patrick (Victor Martindale). Australian. Born in London, England, 28 May 1912. Educated at Tudor House, Moss Vale, and other schools in Australia, 1919–25; Cheltenham College, England, 1925–29; King's College, Cambridge, 1932–35, B.A. in modern languages 1935. Served in the Royal Air Force, in the Middle East, 1941–45: Intelligence Officer. Travelled in Europe and the United States, and lived in London, before World War II; returned to Australia in 1948. Recipient: Australian Literature Society Gold Medal, for fiction, 1939; Miles Franklin Award, for fiction, 1958, 1962; W.H. Smith Literary Award, for fiction, 1959; National Conference of Christians and Jews Brotherhood Award, 1962; Nobel Prize for Literature, 1973. A.C. (Companion, Order of Australia), 1975 (returned, 1976). Lives in Sydney. Agent: Barbara Mobbs, 73/35-A Sutherland Crescent, Darling Point, New South Wales 2027, Australia.

PUBLICATIONS

Plays

Bread and Butter Women (produced Sydney, 1935).
The School for Friends (produced Sydney, 1935).
Return to Abyssinia (produced London, 1947).
The Ham Funeral (produced Adelaide, 1961; Crewe, Cheshire, 1969). Included in *Four Plays*, 1965.
The Season at Sarsaparilla (produced Adelaide, 1962). Included in *Four Plays*, 1965.
A Cheery Soul, adaptation of his own story (produced Melbourne, 1963). Included in *Four Plays*, 1965.
Night on Bald Mountain (produced Adelaide, 1964). Included in *Four Plays*, 1965.
Four Plays. London, Eyre and Spottiswoode, 1965; New York, Viking Press, 1966; as *Collected Plays 1*, Sydney, Currency Press, 1985.
Big Toys (produced Sydney, 1977). Sydney, Currency Press, 1978.
The Night the Prowler (screenplay). Melbourne, Penguin, 1977.
Signal Driver: A Morality Play for the Times (produced Adelaide, 1982). Sydney, Currency Press, 1983.
Netherwood (produced Adelaide, 1983). Sydney, Currency Press, 1983.
Shepherd on the Rocks (produced Adelaide, 1983).

Screenplay: *The Night the Prowler*, 1979.

Novels

Happy Valley. London, Harrap, 1939; New York, Viking Press, 1940.
The Living and the Dead. London, Routledge, and New York, Viking Press, 1941.
The Aunt's Story. London, Routledge, and New York, Viking Press, 1948.
The Tree of Man. New York, Viking Press, 1955; London, Eyre and Spottiswoode, 1956.
Voss. New York, Viking Press, and London, Eyre and Spottiswoode, 1957.
Riders in the Chariot. New York, Viking Press, and London, Eyre and Spottiswoode, 1961.
The Solid Mandala. New York, Viking Press, and London, Eyre and Spottiswoode, 1966.
The Vivisector. New York, Viking Press, and London, Cape, 1970.
The Eye of the Storm. London, Cape, 1973; New York, Viking Press, 1974.
A Fringe of Leaves. London, Cape, 1976; New York, Viking Press, 1977.
The Twyborn Affair. London, Cape, 1979; New York, Viking Press, 1980.
Memoirs of Many in One. London, Cape, and New York, Viking Press, 1986.

Short Stories

The Burnt Ones. New York, Viking Press, and London, Eyre and Spottiswoode, 1964.
The Cockatoos: Shorter Novels and Stories. London, Cape, 1974; New York, Viking Press, 1975.
A Cheery Soul and Other Stories. Tokyo, Kenkyusha, 1983.

Verse

Thirteen Poems. Privately printed, 1930(?).
The Ploughman and Other Poems. Sydney, Beacon Press, 1935.

Other

Flaws in the Glass: A Self-Portrait. London, Cape, 1981; New York, Viking Press, 1982.

*

Bibliography: *A Bibliography of Patrick White* by Janette Finch, Adelaide, Libraries Board of South Australia, 1966.

Critical Studies (selection): *Patrick White* by Geoffrey Dutton, Melbourne, Lansdowne Press, 1961, revised edition, Melbourne, London, and New York, Oxford University Press, 1971; *Patrick White* by Robert F. Brissenden, London, Longman, 1966; *Patrick White* by Barry Argyle, Edinburgh, Oliver and Boyd, 1967; *Ten Essays on Patrick White Selected from Southerly* edited by G.A. Wilkes, Sydney and London, Angus and Robertson, 1970; *Fossil and Psyche* by Wilson Harris, Austin, University of Texas, 1974; *Patrick White* by Alan Lawson, Melbourne and New York, Oxford University Press, 1974, London, Oxford University Press, 1975; *Patrick White as Playwright* by J.R. Dyce, St. Lucia, University of Queensland Press, 1974; *Patrick White: A General Introduction* by Ingmar Bjorksten, translated by Stanley Gerson, St. Lucia, University of Queensland Press, and Atlantic Highlands, New Jersey, Humanities Press, 1976; *Patrick White: A Critical Symposium* edited by Ron E. Shepherd and Kirpal Singh, Bedford Park, South Australia, Flinders University Centre for Research, and Washington, D.C., Three Continents, 1978; *Patrick White* by Manly Johnson, New York, Ungar, 1980; *Patrick White* by Brian Kiernan, London, Macmillan, and New York, St. Martin's Press, 1980; *Patrick White* by John Colmer, London, Methuen, 1984; *Patrick White* by John A. Weigel, Boston, Twayne, 1984.

* * *

Patrick White holds a unique, and often paradoxical, place in the history of Australian drama. His earliest published play, *The Ham Funeral*, written at a time (1947) when not only Australian but most English-language theatres were dominated by naturalism, was boldly experimental, consciously theatrical, very close to expressionism; the techniques of the plays that followed, from the suburban rituals of *The Season at Sarsaparilla* to the attempt at what one critic called a return to "classical doom" (*Night on Bald Mountain*), were varied, each one taking a new direction as a literate mind explored the frontiers of theatre. Now that so many playwrights have turned their backs on naturalism, the style of White's early plays no longer seems singular, but he has probably been a forerunner rather than a direct influence. White's plays have always roused great interest, and often controversy, but they have not been widely performed, partly because of the difficulties they present. They need, simply, to be done very well. Jim Sharman's Sydney productions of *The Season at Sarsaparilla* (1976) and in particular of White's most challenging play technically, *A Cheery Soul* (1979), have shown that White's plays can make stunning theatre, the latter play breaking the theatre's box-office records; but companies with more limited resources remain cautious. (White is also notoriously cautious in granting permission for his plays to be performed.)

White is to most people outside Australia better known as a novelist and winner of the Nobel Prize for Literature than as a playwright, and not surprisingly many of the themes of the plays are close to subjects he explores at greater length and in greater complexity in his novels. White's earliest major play, *The Ham Funeral*, is often related to the novel published in 1948, *The Aunt's Story*, and *A Cheery Soul*, which the author describes as being about "the destructive power of good," is in fact a dramatization of one of White's short stories. The focus of *A Cheery Soul* is the painfully superb character Miss Docker, a relentless do-gooder and devout church-goer who wreaks havoc in the lives around her. Miss Docker is almost a tragic character, outcast at the end but unlike so many of White's outcasts apparently gaining no special insight at the end, when even the dog (which "is 'God' turned round") rejects her, pissing on her leg.

The brilliant 1976 production of *The Season at Sarsaparilla* made it clear that of all White's early plays, this was the one closest in technique and spirit to the cartoon style which had emerged and gained popularity in Australian theatres during the late 1960's. Sarsaparilla, White's symbol of middle-class suburbia through a range of novels, stories, and plays, is bedevilled by the howling of a pack of dogs pursuing a bitch on heat, against which intrusive background the human inhabitants pay out their rituals of fertility, sexuality, the will towards creativity, death, and ordinary suburban living. The action moves in counterpoint between the kitchens of three houses, and the passing of time is indicated by a razzle dazzle. The characters are for the most part deliberate stereotypes; one character, Nola Boyle, though still a White stereotype, so far surpasses the other characters in warmth and vitality that most of the interest and sympathy of the play is directed to the Boyle household.

It is possible that the successful revival of *The Season at Sarsaparilla* encouraged White's return to the theatre in 1977 with a new play, *Big Toys*, written, he said, to show "the corrupt state of Sydney society today." Actually *Big Toys* proved to be the first of three plays about men and women adrift in a decaying society; it is possible to read in these plays a growing insistence that our world, increasingly corrupt, alienating, and violent, will end in apocalypse. *Big Toys*, set in the luxury penthouse of Mag and Ritchie Bosanquet, opens with Mag gossiping idly on the phone while she plays with a giant balloon, the first of the "big toys" which engage the wealthy and successful in this play: emeralds, an expensive car, and finally uranium mining, "the biggest, gaudiest toy that ever escaped from a child's hand." Terry Legge, an idealistic trade unionist, is tempted by the big toys, but escapes, thus providing the play with its one hint of optimism. *Signal Driver* follows an ordinary suburban couple through 60 years of groping for fulfilment, of half-hearted, unsuccessful attempts to signal the tram (later a bus) which regularly passes the transport shelter against which the play is set; the two Beings or avatars who watch over them are described as "super deros," filthy, with matted hair and lice. At the end of the play, the brilliant light of the Aurora Australis floods the theatre, and has been interpreted variously as the power of love and the possibility of an apocalypse, perhaps the bomb. These two plays move from a world of the rich and powerful to that of a very ordinary suburban couple. *Netherwood* takes a step further, and its victim-characters are this time outcasts, the mentally unstable who are at the mercy of a ruthless, prejudiced world. This play ends with an actual mini-apocalypse, a totally pointless shoot-out which kills off half the characters.

—Alrene Sykes

WHITEHEAD, Ted (Edward Anthony Whitehead). British. Born in Liverpool, Lancashire, 3 April 1933. Educated at St. Francis Xavier's Jesuit College; Christ's College, Cambridge, B.A. (honours) in English 1955, M.A. Served in the King's Regiment, 1955–57. Married 1) Kathleen Horton in 1958 (marriage dissolved 1976), two daughters; 2) Gwenda Bagshaw in 1976. Milkman, postman, bus conductor, sales promotion writer, salesman, and teacher, 1959–65; advertising copywriter and account executive, 1965–71; resident dramatist, Royal Court Theatre, London, 1971–72; Fellow in Creative Writing, Bulmershe College, Reading, Berkshire, 1975–76. Recipient: George Devine Award, 1971; *Evening Standard* award, 1971. Agent: Judy Daish Associates, 83 Eastbourne Mews, London W2 6LQ, England.

PUBLICATIONS

Plays

The Foursome (produced London, 1971; Washington, D.C., 1972; New York, 1973). London, Faber, 1972.
Alpha Beta (produced London, 1972; New York, 1973). London, Faber, 1972.
The Punishment (televised 1972). Published in *Prompt Three*, edited by Alan Durband, London, Hutchinson, 1976.
The Sea Anchor (produced London, 1974; New York, 1982). London, Faber, 1975.
Old Flames (produced Bristol, 1975; London, 1976; New York, 1980). London, Faber, 1976.
Mecca (produced London, 1977; New York, 1980). London, Faber, 1977.
The Man Who Fell in Love with His Wife, adaptation of his television series *Sweet Nothings* (produced London, 1984). London, Faber, 1984.
Dance of Death, adaptation of a play by Strindberg (produced Oxford, 1984; London, 1985).

Radio Play: *The Old Goat Gone*, 1987.

Television Plays: *Under the Age*, 1972; *The Punishment*, 1972; *The Peddler*, 1976; *The Proofing Session*, 1977; *The Irish Connection* (*Crown Court* series), 1979; *Sweet Nothings* series, 1980; *World's End* series, 1981; *The Detective* serial, from the novel by Paul Ferris, 1985; *The Life and Loves of a She-Devil* serial, from the novel by Fay Weldon, 1986.

Novel

World's End (novelization of television series). London, BBC Publications, 1981.

* * *

Ted Whitehead's chosen dramatic territory is marriage and the impossible demands the institution makes on love and fidelity. His principal characters are most often drawn from the white-collar working class. They are witty and articulate but not intellectuals. His dialogue is a rapid verbal sparring, which frequently breaks down into hysteria or physical violence. His writing drives towards as plainstyle a statement as possible of emotions and sexuality, although he is capable of occasional passages of lyrical beauty. "Escape" and "freedom" are key positives in his vocabulary, but they turn out to be chimeras for both men and women. His plays chart accurately the major debates around the family, sex, and marriage since the early 1960's and, while he has little interest in plot or character-development, his ear is very sharp for the changing discourses of male and female in this area.

A comparison between his first stage success, *Alpha Beta*, and his latest original play, *The Man Who Fell in Love with His Wife*, is immediately instructive. *Alpha Beta* has only two characters, Mr. and Mrs. Elliot, and covers the years 1962 to 1971. Mr. Elliot is a manager on the Liverpool docks and his wife is a housewife. When the play opens he is 29 and she is 26. They have two children who remain as an off-stage audience to the bickering, fighting, violence, and hysteria which make up the play. Mr. Elliot already has a mistress, Eileen, and wants a divorce. His wife won't give him one. Although marriage has turned into a bitter trap for both of them, Mrs. Elliot stands by the moral law of until death us do part. For Mr. Elliot they're dead already. He wants the freedom to "fuck a thousand women." He's no different, he claims, from all his male friends, except they sublimate their desires in blue movies and dirty jokes. "I'm sick of fantasy," he says, "I want reality." Elliot's view is that he married too young and too early for the permissive 1960's. Marriage is changing, he warns his wife, and even a woman like her, in the future, will "want a bit of what's going, for herself." A mutual enslavement like theirs shouldn't last. "Man and women are going to share free and equal unions that last because they want them to last. Not because they're forced!" Mrs. Elliot has only contempt for his "honesty" and his sociology. In her view he's retarded. He's never grown out of the role of working-class bucko, tomcatting around after eternal youth. She won't let him escape his duties as head of the household. Over the years of the play they evolve a kind of compromise. Mr. Elliot pays the bills and resides in the house but pursues his extra-marital affairs. His wife runs the house and just about hangs onto her sanity. The play ends with a suicide threat by Mrs. Elliot which her husband takes half seriously but which fires no buried love or affection in him. It's an unsatisfactory ending because there can be no ending to a war on these terms. As the title suggests, this couple must go down through the alphabet of their hatred and then start all over again.

The Man Who Fell in Love with His Wife begins with just that change in women's status that Mr. Elliot foresaw. Mary Fearon, in her late thirties, has got her first job, in the Civil Service. Her husband Tom, aged 41, is also employed as a dock manager in Liverpool. Mary's office life causes him extreme jealousy but also refuels his sexual passion for her. Suspender-belts and instamatic photos play their part in maintaining an ardour that Mary, who still loves him deeply, cannot match. Love in marriage can be as stifling as hatred. Tom wants to replay their adolescence and courtship. The Platters and Ike and Tina Turner are his favourite music. He drags his wife out to a freezing session on a favourite beach near Liverpool. Mary wants to move on and eventually she moves out. By then Tom has given up his job to monitor his wife throughout the day. The roles and emotions of *Alpha Beta* have been reversed, and there is now a chance for the kind of freedom for both sexes that Mr. Elliot prophesied. For this is the 1980's, and between the Fearons and their daughter intervenes a new role-model, the divorcée in her thirties. She is Julia, an office friend of Mary's, who supports her bid for independence and counters Tom's arguments with reason and confidence. "Is it selfish for me to want my wife to love me?" he asks. "It's selfish to damand it regardless of what she wants," Julia replies. In the end they have to settle for separate lives, although old connections can't be broken. "I love you—even if I can't live with you," says Mary, and Tom, now a cab driver, has to become adult out of his own resources.

Glimpses of this comparative optimism can be seen in other Whitehead plays in the 1970's. In *The Sea Anchor* men and women friends wait, on Dublin Bay, for the arrival of daredevil Nick after his solo voyage across the Irish Sea for Liverpool in a ten-foot dinghy. The play is also about the other side of marriage, since all the characters are engaged in adulterous relationships. Nick is their hero since he "does exactly what he wants to do" while the others all cover up in various ways. Whitehead's theme of the trapped, randy male is complemented by that of the calculating, randy female and in the character of Jean we see a coarser precursor to Julia. The backchat is vulgar and witty, but Andy is given two lyrical passages, when he recalls a shoal of mackerel at night," a giant ripple, V-shaped... it came hissing along beside the boat," and the time he and Nick heard black bodies barking in the silver sea and discovered they were porpoises, which sharply contrast with the brutality of the sexual relationships. Nick's boat comes in, empty. His sea anchor, "a kind of parachute, keeps you steady," hasn't saved him. A lost hero is useless and the sea is a false escape from domestic complexity.

Nor is abroad any solution. The group of English tourists in *Mecca* brings its marital conflicts and emotions intact to Morocco. Middle-aged Andrew sublimates his desire for the 20-year-old Sandy into a false fatherly protectiveness. His wife, Eunice, isn't fooled, but her verbal barbs have an articulacy which Mrs. Elliot lacked. Ian is young and fancy-free and Martin is the gay protector for the defensive bravado of Jill, 38, divorced, and feeling herself caught between the insouciance of Sandy and the certainties of Eunice. "She's not afraid of sex," says Jill to Eunice," and neither is her generation. That's why they don't get used-up like us." But Sandy's innocence leads her, dressed only in a towel, outside the compound where the tourists live into the poor and violent world of Arab North Africa. She gets raped, a boy who hangs round the compound is suspected, and when he's cornered Andrew beats him to death. His menopausal desire is displaced into murderous aggression. The police and courts are finally bought off, and the tourists take off with relief for "civilization." But back home, as Whitehead's other plays show, the war goes on.

—Tony Dunn

WHITEMORE, Hugh (John). British. Born in Tunbridge Wells, Kent, 16 June 1936. Educated at Judd School, Tunbridge Wells, 1945–51; King Edward VI School, Southampton, 1951–55; Royal Academy of Dramatic Art, London, 1956–57. Married 1) Jill Brooke in 1961 (marriage dissolved); 2) Sheila Lemon in 1976; one son. Free-lance writer: drama critic, *Harpers and Queen*, London, 1970. Recipient: Emmy award, 1970, 1984; Writers Guild award, 1971, 1972; RAI prize, 1979; Italia prize, 1979; Neil Simon Jury award, 1984. Lives in London. Agent: Judy Daish Associates, 83 Eastbourne Mews, London W2 6LQ, England; or, Phyllis Wender, Rosenstone and Wender, 3 East 48th Street, 4th Floor, New York, New York 10017, U.S.A.

PUBLICATIONS

Plays

Horrible Conspiracies (televised 1971). Published in *Elizabeth R*, edited by J.C. Trewin, London, Elek, 1972.
Stevie: A Play from the Life and Work of Stevie Smith (produced Richmond, Surrey, and London, 1977; New York, 1979). London, French, 1977; New York, Limelight, 1984.
Pack of Lies (produced Brighton and London, 1983; New York, 1985). Oxford, Amber Lane Press, 1983; New York, Applause, 1986.
Breaking the Code, adaptation of the book *Alan Turing: The Enigma of Intelligence* by Andrew Hodges (produced London, 1986; New York, 1987). Oxford, Amber Lane Press, 1987.

Screenplays: *Decline and Fall... of a Birdwatcher!*, with Ivan Foxwell and Alan Hackney, 1968; *All Neat in Black Stockings*, with Jane Gaskell, 1968; *Man at the Top*, with John Junkin, 1973; *All Creatures Great and Small*, 1975; *The Blue Bird*, 1976; *Stevie*, 1978; *The Return of the Soldier*, 1983; *84 Charing Cross Road*, 1987.

Television Plays: *The Full Chatter*, 1963; *Dan, Dan the Charity Man*, 1965; *Angus Slowly Sinking*, 1965; *The Regulator*, 1965; *Application Form*, 1965; *Mrs. Bixby and the Colonel's Coat*, from a story by Roald Dahl, 1965; *Macready's Gala*, 1966; *Final Demand*, 1966; *Girl of My Dreams*, 1966; *Frankenstein Mark II*, 1966; *Amerika*, from the novel by Kafka, 1966; *What's Wrong with Humpty Dumpty?*, 1967; *Party Games*, 1968; *The Last of the Big Spenders*, 1968; *Hello, Good Evening, and Welcome*, 1968; *Mr. Guppy's Tale*, from a story by Dickens, 1969; *Unexpectedly Vacant*, 1970; *The King and His Keeper*, 1970; *Killing Time*, 1970; *Cider with Rosie*, from the book by Laurie Lee, 1971; *Horrible Conspiracies* (*Elizabeth R* series), 1971; *An Object of Affection*, 1971; *Act of Betrayal*, 1971; *Breeze Anstey* (*Country Matters* series), from the story by H.E. Bates, 1972; *The Strange Shapes of Reality*, 1972; *The Serpent and the Comforter*, 1972; *At the Villa Pandora*, 1972; *Eric*, 1972; *Disappearing Trick*, 1972; *Good at Games*, 1972; *Bedtime*, 1972; *Intruders*, 1972; *The Adventures of Don Quixote*, from novel by Cervantes, 1973; *Deliver Us from Evil*, 1973; *The Pearcross Girls*, 1973; *A Thinking Man as Hero*, 1973; *Death Waltz*, 1974; *Outrage*, 1974; *David Copperfield*, from the novel by Dickens, 1974; *Trilby*, from the novel by George du Maurier, 1975; *Goodbye*, 1975; *84 Charing Cross Road*, from the book by Helene Hanff, 1975; *Moll Flanders*, from the novel by Defoe, 1975; *The Eleventh Hour*, with Brian Clark and Clive Exton, 1975; *Censors*, with David Edgar and Robert Muller, 1975; *Brensham People*, from novels by John Moore, 1976; *William Wilson*, from the story by Poe, 1976; *Moths*, from the novel by Ouida, 1977; *Exiles*, from a book by Michael J. Arlen, 1977; *Dummy*, 1977; *Mrs. Ainsworth*, from a novel by E.F. Benson, 1978; *Losing Her*, 1978; *Rebecca*, from the novel by Daphne du Maurier, 1979; *Contract*, 1981; *A Dedicated Man*, from the story by Elizabeth Taylor, 1982; *I Remember Nelson*, 1982; *A Bit of Singing and Dancing*, from the story by Susan Hill, 1982; *Lovers of Their Time*, from the story by William Trevor, 1982; *My Cousin Rachel*, from the novel by Daphne du Maurier, 1983; *Office Romances*, from stories by William Trevor, 1983; *Down at the Hydro*, from a story by William Sansom, 1983; *Concealed Enemies*, 1984; *The Boy in the Bush*, from a story by D.H. Lawrence, 1984.

* * *

Hugh Whitemore is best known as a writer for television, and from 1963 he has had a prolific list of plays to his credit both as parts of series and as individual efforts. His adaptation of Laurie Lee's *Cider with Rosie* won him a Writers Guild Award, as did his contribution to *Country Matters*; and *Elizabeth R*—a series of six plays, one of which, *Horrible Conspiracies*, was provided by Whitemore—received an Emmy award. *Horrible Conspiracies* deals with events surrounding the execution of Mary Queen of Scots, and its fascination with the world of spying and conspiracy was to become a recurrent theme in his work. The Gloriana is presented as an aging ruler, ruled by superstition and fear, obsessively fixated on thoughts of death, and her court as far from magnificent.

The predominant style of *Horrible Conspiracies* is that of conventional television naturalism—although the play is prefaced by a grim masque portending death—and the piece jumps quickly through a series of locations which suggest the complexities of espionage and counter-espionage that lurk immediately beneath the outward display of power. Whitemore showed little interest in the intricacies of psychological behaviour or in any larger political context, and the play seemed very much a part of a larger series in which each individual writer was considerably restrained by the overall structure. Over the years

Whitemore has shown himself adept at meeting the strictures of such demands and able to turn out a consistently well-crafted piece.

The influence of his work for television is evident in his belated stage entrance. *Stevie*—a play based on the life and works of the poet Stevie Smith—makes few bows in the direction of the stage. Information is given in the conventional format of recalled anecodotes raised in the course of a series of conversations between Stevie and the aunt she lived with for most of her life. The atmosphere of suburban London comes across well, as does Stevie's delight in the absurdity of her life there, but we gain little insight into her obsession with death and her failed attempt at suicide. It is a well-made play, offering the kind of "coffee-table" approach to biography so frequently to be found on television. Its chief virtue is Whitemore's success in creating in the central character a plausible human being, even if we learn little more than surface things about her. That this was done in a beautifully realised suburban set does little to take the edge off a feeling that *Stevie* is essentially a television play put on stage.

His next stage play, *Pack of Lies*, was exactly this, being based on material in Whitemore's successful BBC "Play for Today" *Act of Betrayal*. The play concerns the intrusion into a suburban family of the paraphernalia of the British Secret Service, intent on trapping as Russian spies their close friends and neighbours, the Krogers. The play, based on real events in 1960–61, again captures well the restrictions and niceties of suburban life and builds to a traditional theatrical climax as the host family becomes increasingly and ambivalently involved in the enquiry; but again it is difficult to see what exactly is added to the piece by its adaptation to the stage. The direct narrative asides to the audience apart, its predominant tone is still that of a safe naturalism. It asks no questions that cannot be contained within the confines of plot and set, and it is hard not to think that the chief reason for its appearance in the West End is the latest bout of interest in Burgess, Philby, & Co., and it was indeed followed by his 1984 television play, *Concealed Enemies*, about Alger Hiss.

However, Whitemore's third stage play, *Breaking the Code*, does succeed in making the break from the small screen to the stage. Far more ambitious than the two earlier efforts, it presents the story of Alan Turing, the man who broke the German Enigma code in World War II and pioneered the development of computers. Taking on board the difficult task of elucidating the theory behind Turing's work—and succeeding surprisingly well—the play blends the theme of scientific exploration with its depiction of an establishment England that could have the scientist's name obliterated from the record book because he was a practicing homosexual—the two sets of broken codes in conflict. Whitemore was fortunate in having Derek Jacobi play his protagonist, but it says much for the play's superiority to its predecessors that the actor was able to fill the part so well. *Breaking the Code* is, no less than all Whitemore's work, a classically well-made play, produced to a given West End formula, but the difference is that here for the first time the formula has been stretched to fit what the writer wants to say rather than acting as a straitjacket. It will be interesting to see how, and indeed if, Whitemore continues as a stage dramatist.

—John Bull

WILKINSON, Christopher. British. Born 4 May 1941. Address: c/o Independent Bookshop Ltd., 67–69 Surrey Street, Sheffield, Yorkshire S1 2LH, England.

PUBLICATIONS

Plays

Their First Evening Alone Together (produced Sheffield, 1969; London, 1971).
Wally, Molly and Polly (produced Sheffield, 1969).
Teasdale's Follies, with Frank Hatherly, music by Jeremy Barlow (produced Sheffield, 1970).
Strip Jack Naked (produced Sheffield, 1970; London, 1971).
Dynamo (produced London, 1971).
Plays for Rubber Go-Go Girls (produced London, 1971).
I Was Hitler's Maid (also director: produced Sheffield and London, 1971).
Sawn Off at the Knees, with Veronica Thirlaway (produced Sheffield, 1978).

*

Theatrical Activities:
Director: **Play**—*I Was Hitler's Maid*, Sheffield and London, 1971.

* * *

Christopher Wilkinson is best known for his work with two fringe companies—the touring Portable Theatre, and the Vanguard Theatre Club, which is attached to Sheffield's main repertory theatre, the Crucible. These close associations have influenced his work. Wilkinson has written ordinary scripts, such as *Strip Jack Naked*, which revealed his wit, his ear for a good line of dialogue, and his delight in a Grand Guignol situation. But he later chose not to write formal scripts, but rather to suggest themes and games for the acting companies to explore—in improvisation and other ways. *I Was Hitler's Maid* is an example of this non-scripted play. Wilkinson offered the actors some stories taken from semi-pornographic men's magazines: blood, sex, and action. These magazines were of a type distributed to American troops in Vietnam, and were therefore considered to relate in some way to a real political situation. The stories were all exceptionally violent. Some were set in World War II—among SS officers and patriots of the French resistance—others in South America—among guerrilla bands and the forces of Law and Order. But the settings were almost irrelevant, for the situations were pointedly similar. A girl was tortured and repeatedly raped by the Enemy, before being rescued by the Hero. In the opening scene, she is whipped by "Hitler"; in a later scene, she becomes "Calamity Jane," the whipping Wild West heroine. The dialogue is based on the clichés of the genre: and the actors were encouraged to break up the story patterns, the snatches of rehearsed scenes, even the moments of violence, in order to emphasize the arbitrary lack of logic of the fantasies. The production progresses towards two main climaxes—an orgy scene (three men raping one girl) and a disembowelling scene, where three soldiers attack a lifelike (female) doll hanging in a cupboard.

Some critics thought that *I Was Hitler's Maid* was not so much a comment on pornography as pornography itself, while others deplored the deliberate lack of construction. But few productions could have achieved such a telling diatribe against sex-and-violence comics without seeming lofty and puritanical. Wilkinson, by presenting the stories on stage—where actors leapt up in astonishing health after being beaten senseless—and by denying the elementary logic which kept the stories credible, brought out the full sado-masochistic absurdity of the genre. A somewhat similar production, *Dynamo*, was less successful perhaps because Wilkinson's moral intentions had to be more overtly expressed. *Dynamo* is set in a strip club, and the first section consists of ordinary dull strip routines performed by gum-chewing, bored girls. We watch them preparing to go on stage, collecting their props and records, adjusting their hair: then we see the routines. But after a time the strip club becomes an interrogation cell, where a girl is tortured by a police chief, kicked around the floor, and finally hung up naked. Wilkinson wished to draw the parallel between ordinary pornographic fantasies and the political torture of an Algerian suspect by the French police: but the play failed because the association the two events seemed at best clichéd and at worst tenuous and unconvincing. If Wilkinson meant to imply that in both cases women were treated like mere objects of male desire, the theme is convincing enough but rather obvious and could have been developed in many other ways. If he was suggesting that pornography leads to political violence, then the fact that there was no logical connecting link between the scenes damaged his argument.

Wilkinson's most successful work, however, is *Plays for Rubber Go-Go Girls*. These are sketch sequences, loosely linked by an attack on American imperialism and on the sexual fantasies supporting repression. The first half of the production consists of various sex-and-violence stories in the style of *I Was Hitler's Maid*: but the deliberate disorganization of the earlier plays is replaced by a solemn burlesque treatment—high camp. The stories could come from an outrageous adventure story, in the style of James Bond, with beautiful girls from Vietnam and Latin America, submitting with delight to Commie-hating G.I.s. The second half is an amusing skit on childhood training in America. A cop warns his daughter, Fuzz Child, against everything, from drugs to long hair, which might threaten the purity of American middle-class life. The juxtaposition of the repressed fantasies with the formal teaching are related to the Vietnam war, until the war itself is shown to be an effect of various cultural forces. Among these forces is perhaps Wilkinson's most typical preoccupation—the maltreatment of women by men. Women are presented as rubber girls who can be endlessly stabbed either with a phallus or a bayonet. This serious theme is treated with an immense satirical verve and accuracy: the fantasies are funny, familiar, and, shocked out of their usual contexts, have been presented to the public as grotesque art objects, as representative of our civilization as the pyramids were of ancient Egypt. Wilkinson's great achievement as a writer is to make us look afresh at the clichés surrounding our lives.

—John Elsom

WILLIAMS, Heathcote. British. Born in Helsby, Cheshire, 15 November 1941. Associate editor, *Transatlantic Review*, London and New York; founding editor, *Suck*, Amsterdam. Recipient: *Evening Standard* award, 1970; George Devine Award, 1970; John Whiting Award, 1971; Obie award, 1971. Agent: Judy Daish Associates, 83 Eastbourne Mews, London W2 6LQ, England.

PUBLICATIONS

Plays

The Local Stigmatic (produced Edinburgh, and London, 1966; Boston, 1967; New York, 1969). Published in *Traverse Plays*, London, Penguin, 1965; with *AC/DC*, New York, Viking Press, 1973.
AC/DC (produced London, 1970; New York, 1971). London, Calder and Boyars, 1972; with *The Local Stigmatic*, New York, Viking Press, 1973.
Remember the Truth Dentist, music by Bob Flagg (produced London, 1974). With *The Speakers*, London, Calder, 1980.
The Speakers (produced Birmingham, 1974). With *Remember the Truth Dentist*, London, Calder, 1980.
Very Tasty—A Pantomine (produced London, 1975).
An Invitation to the Official Lynching of Michael Abdul Malik (produced Newcastle upon Tyne, 1975).
Anatomy of a Space Rat (produced London, 1976).
Hancock's Last Half-Hour (produced London, 1977; Huntington Station, New York, 1978). London, Polytantric Press, 1977.
Playpen (produced London, 1977).
The Immortalist (produced London, 1977). London, Calder, 1978.
At It, in *Breach of the Peace* (produced London, 1982; produced separately, Edinburgh and London, 1983).
Whales (produced Liverpool and London, 1986).

Screenplay: *Malatesta*, 1969.

Television Play: *What the Dickens!*, 1983.

Verse

Whale Nation. London, Cape, 1988.

Other

The Speakers. London, Hutchinson, 1964; New York, Grove Press, 1967.
Manifestoes, Manifesten. Rotterdam, Cold Turkey Press, 1975.
Severe Joy. London, Calder, 1979.
Elephants. London, Knockabout Comics, 1983.

*

Critical Study: "Heathcote Williams Issue" of *Gambit 18–19* (London), 1971.

Theatrical Activities:
Actor: **Film**—*The Tempest*, 1980.

* * *

Often regarded as a one-play dramatist, Heathcote Williams merits praise not only for his acknowledged counter-culture classic of the 1960's, *AC/DC*, but also for plays that have received only cursory critical treatment. All his plays center on social misfits, who either hope for the reformation of a corrupt society or erect barriers against the void that threatens to engulf them.

The spectacular setting and visceral (and often unintelligible) dialogue of *AC/DC* dazzled audiences of the 1960's. In an amusement arcade, three hippies meet two schizophrenics,

Maurice and Perowne; all are trying to shed media-induced personalities. Maurice helps Perowne achieve this goal by speaking long fantastic monologues. Maurice's monologues so intimidate two of the hippies, a couple, that, silenced, they drop out of the play altogether.

Such bludgeoning dialogues thread through *AC/DC*, though they are not of thematic importance. Sadie, the remaining hippie, competes with Maurice for control of Perowne. Like Maurice, she relies on long, unrelated fantasies to free Perowne from his enslavement to the video-screens, television, and radio, which are the environment for the second half of the play. Besides fantasizing to Perowne, she also trepans him, thus freeing him from media personalities. Sadie thereby overwhelms Maurice, and she dismisses him for being "into the same territory-sex-adrenalin-bullshit" as everyone else. Sadie looks for a revolution that will destroy such alienation.

Like *AC/DC, The Local Stigmatic*, an earlier play, dramatizes a Pinteresque struggle for dominance. Ray often contradicts and challenges Graham, but ultimately he accedes to the latter's game of assaulting strangers. These games lend form to their otherwise pointless existence.

Hancock's Last Half-Hour, like *The Local Stigmatic*, pits an individual against meaninglessness, but in this play the individual loses. Hancock, a former clown, desperately performs comedy to keep the silence from deafening him. He has locked himself in a hotel-room and there engages in the performance that is the play. The performer's fear of audience indifference drives Hancock and accounts for the desperation of his monologue that includes jokes, readings from encyclopedias, Freud's *Jokes*, and press clippings, and parodies of such set-pieces as Hamlet's soliloquy. This fear also accounts for his self-mockery and for his final suicide.

The Immortalist is not as compressed or exciting a play as *AC/DC*, nor does it question existence as do *The Local Stigmatic* and *Hancock's Last Half-Hour*. The play is essentially and atypically didactic. The Immortalist will not die of natural causes, but he *can* be killed. Consequently, he would preserve the earth and its inhabitants from human desecration. He argues against passivity: "Listen, people foul up because they stay in the same place. They've traded Utopia for reality... Consuming as a substitute for being... You have radio as a substitute for telepathy, television as a substitute for astral projection. Aeroplanes are a substitute for inner fire."

Williams's freaks indict a society that fosters passivity and consumerism through its mass media. As individuals, they can find no structures or values by which to order and give meaning to their lives.

—Frances Rademacher Anderson

WILLIAMS, Nigel. British. Born in Cheadle, Cheshire, 20 January 1948. Educated at Highgate School, London; Oriel College, Oxford. Married; three sons. Recipient: Somerset Maugham Award, for fiction, 1978. Agent: Judy Daish Associates, 83 Eastbourne Mews, London W2 6LQ. Address: c/o Faber and Faber, 3 Queen Square, London WC1N 3AU, England.

PUBLICATIONS

Plays

Double Talk (produced London, 1976).

Snowwhite Washes Whiter, and Deadwood (produced Bristol, 1977).

Class Enemy (produced London, 1978; New York, 1979). London, Eyre Methuen, 1978.

Easy Street (produced Bristol, 1979).

Sugar and Spice (produced London, 1980). With *Trial Run*, London, Eyre Methuen, 1980.

Line 'em (produced London, 1980). London, Eyre Methuen, 1980.

Trial Run (produced Oxford and London, 1980). With *Sugar and Spice*, London, Eyre Methuen, 1980.

W.C.P.C. (produced London, 1982). London, Methuen, 1983.

The Adventures of Jasper Ridley (produced Hull, 1982; London, 1983).

My Brother's Keeper (produced London, 1985). London, Faber, 1985.

Deathwatch, adaptation of a play by Jean Genet (produced Birmingham and London, 1985).

Country Dancing (produced Stratford-on-Avon, 1986; London, 1987). London, Faber, 1987.

As It Was, adaptation of a book by Helen Thomas (produced Edinburgh, 1987).

Television Plays: *Talkin' Blues*, 1977; *Real Live Audience*, 1978; *Baby Talk*, 1981; *Let 'em Know We're Here*, 1981; *Johnny Jarvis* series, 1983; *George Orwell* (documentary), 1983; *Charlie*, 1984; *Breaking Up*, 1986.

Novels

My Life Closed Twice. London, Secker and Warburg, 1977.

Jack Be Nimble. London, Secker and Warburg, 1980.

Charlie (novelization of television play). London, Methuen, 1984.

Star Turn. London, Faber, 1985.

Witchcraft. London, Faber, 1987.

Other

Johnny Jarvis (for children). London, Penguin, 1983.

*

Theatrical Activities:
Director: **Television**—*George Orwell*, 1983; *Cambodian Witness* (documentary) by James Fenton, 1987.

* * *

The close structural similarity and thematic parallelism of Nigel Williams's major stage plays suggest that his work to date is best seen not in terms of a development but rather as a patient and thorough working-out of a single vein of dramatic material. The Williams play explores the interaction of and relations between a handful of sharply distinguished individuals who have been isolated by some circumstance, or who isolate themselves, to form a closed group. A convincing (and relishful) rendering of Cockney speech rhythms enables Williams to generate considerable claustrophobic intensity within this dramatic framework. The intensity, however, is largely negative. The plays are dominated by variations on one particular figure: an overbearingly voluble and physically aggressive embodiment of destructive energy. He (or she) stands outside every recognizable position, whether social, sexual, or political, and aims to discredit and destroy those positions (represented by the other characters) by violence both verbal and physical. Though the theme of each play, be it class, race, or sex, is at least *implicitly* political, the presence of this central figure ensures that the dramatic treatment is less political than psychological. The figure catalyzes and externalizes hidden tensions, sometimes with self-destructive consequences, tearing away "civilized" constraints in such a way as to lay bare not political or economic causes but atavistic, tribal impulses.

The tribal emerges clearly in *Class Enemy*. The growing tension and final conflict here take place not between groups but within a single group. Six fifth-formers in a London school fill up an unsupervised afternoon by each "teaching a lesson" on his pet subject. The friction between Iron, the voluble, violent representative of inner-city despair who cherishes his pessimism and seems to relish debasement, and Sky-Light (the nicknames are of course significant), who despite the social circumstances retains trust in the essential goodness of human nature and a radiant perception of the world, erupts into a fight for leadership of the group. Iron wins the fight but, as Sky-Light realizes, the self-directed violence of his moral nature and the frustration of his fevered demand for an indefinable "knowledge" reveal him as the real victim, the "loser."

Sky-Light stands against and illuminates the moral collapse of Iron, but in *Sugar and Spice*, which focusses on sex-hatred as *Class Enemy* focusses on class-hatred, neither the prostitute Suze nor the lovers Carol and Steve are strong enough to counter the disruptive force of the lesbian Sharon and her male counterpart, the Iron-like John. Each contrives the ritual sexual humiliation (by stripping) of a member of the other sex and each addresses a savage climactic speech to the naked victim's genitals. The hatred embodied in Sharon and John represents not just a critique of society's distortion of sexuality but a mutual revulsion of the sexes which seems to extend to a revulsion from sexuality itself.

Though they are no less bleak in tone than the previous plays, *Trial Run* and *Line 'em* both conclude more decisively. In *Trial Run* a young Sikh, Gange, and Billy, who is of mixed parentage, stage a mock trial with hostages they have taken while holed up waiting for the police to surrender a Special Patrol Group man upon whom Gange wants revenge. But the disruptive Billy, with his hatred of society in general, wants more than *personal* revenge. After Gange has been killed by police marksmen Billy mysteriously (and unexpectedly) assumes that posture of inner stillness and blank patience of his Eastern ancestors. His abandonment of the social will makes itself felt as an affirmation, yet in *Line 'em* it is precisely this social will, represented by a solidarity that seems less political than tribal, which is finally affirmed. The anarchistic Foreman mocks and undermines the picket line organized by the old-style union man Sam, yet when soldiers arrive to break the picket he reunites his own ranks by causing insubordination in those of the enemy, and by questioning the validity of the Commanding Officer's values. In the final tableau the two "armies" confront one another.

It will be apparent from these accounts that the power of Williams's drama is cumulative: each play concentrates on a single situation and builds up to an explosive climax. His two comic-satiric plays of the early 1980's, *W.C.P.C.* and *The Adventures of Jasper Ridley* (Williams's most explicitly political play), depart from this pattern in adopting a more obviously scenic form for the presentation of the experiences of their naive-innocent central figures within their respective milieux. However *My Brother's Keeper* again focusses intensely on a single—but this time familial and significantly middle-class—situation. As an old actor lies dying in hospital after a severe stroke, he is visited by his immediate family. His will to live is insistently provoked by his playwright son Tony, whose own thwarted energy arises out of a sense of life wasted through the withholding of feelings, especially love, within this "ordinary" middle-class family. Though vehemently opposed by his brother Sam, a successful businessman with an enduring sense of exclusion from the aesthetic side of the family, Tony attempts to break the maternal domination which he sees as having crippled the family emotionally by encouraging a confrontation (between his parents especially) and a purgation, a speaking out. A point of resolution is reached only when the dying actor-father stumblingly articulates the necessity for mutual *acceptance* within a family of relationships as "states of conflict." Unusually for Williams—and this could be seen as a significant shift of emphasis in his drama—the energies of the play, and of its central figure Tony, make themselves felt as positive. Yet one does suspect here, more strongly than with Williams's previous work, that a great deal of dramatic heat is being expended in the generation of a rather ordinary light.

—Paul Lawley

WILLIAMSON, David (Keith). Australian. Born in Melbourne, Victoria, 24 February 1942. Educated at Monash University, Clayton, Victoria, B.E. in mechanical engineering 1964; Melbourne University. Married 1) Carol Anne Cranby in 1965 (divorced 1972), two children; 2) Kristin Ingrid Lofvén in 1974, two foster children. Design engineer, General Motors-Holden's, Melbourne, 1965; Lecturer, Swinburne College of Technology, Melbourne, 1966–72. Visiting Professor, University of Aarhus, Denmark, 1978. Commissioner, Australian Broadcasting Corporation, 1978–79; Chairman, Australian National Playwrights Conference, 1979–80; President, Australian Writers Guild, 1979–86. Recipient: George Devine Award, 1971; Australian Writers Guild award, 1972, 1973, 1977, 1979, 1980; London *Evening Standard* award, 1974; Australian Film Institute award, 1975, 1977. Officer, Order of Australia, 1983. Agent: Anthony Williams Management, The Basement, 55 Victoria Street, Potts Point, New South Wales 2011, Australia.

PUBLICATIONS

Plays

The Coming of Stork (produced Melbourne, 1970). Included in *The Coming of Stork, Jugglers Three, What If You Died Tomorrow*, 1974.

The Removalists (produced Melbourne, 1971; London and Cleveland, 1973; New York, 1974). Sydney, Currency Press, 1972; London, Eyre Methuen, 1973.

Don's Party (produced Melbourne, 1971; London, 1975). Sydney, Currency Press, and London, Eyre Methuen, 1973.

Jugglers Three (produced Melbourne, 1972). Included in *The Coming of Stork, Jugglers Three, What If You Died Tomorrow*, 1974.

What If You Died Tomorrow (produced Melbourne, 1973; London, 1974). Included in *The Coming of Stork, Jugglers Three, What If You Died Tomorrow*, 1974.

The Coming of Stork, Jugglers Three, What If You Died Tomorrow. Sydney, Currency Press, and London, Eyre Methuen, 1974.
The Department (produced Adelaide, 1974). Sydney, Currency Press, 1975; London, Eyre Methuen, 1976.
A Handful of Friends (produced Adelaide, 1976). Sydney, Currency Press, 1976.
The Club (produced Melbourne, 1977; London, 1980; as *Players*, produced New York, 1978; as *The Team*, produced Toronto, 1981). Sydney, Currency Press, 1978.
Travelling North (produced Sydney, 1979; London, 1980). Sydney, Currency Press, 1980.
Celluloid Heroes (produced Sydney, 1980).
Gallipoli (screenplay), in *The Story of Gallipoli*, by Bill Gammage. Melbourne, Penguin, 1981.
The Perfectionist (produced Melbourne, 1982; London, 1983). Sydney, Currency Press, 1983.
Sons of Cain (also director: produced Melbourne, 1985; London, 1986). Sydney, Currency Press, 1985.
Collected Plays 1 (includes *The Coming of the Stork, The Removalists, Don's Party, Jugglers Three, What If You Died Tomorrow*). Sydney, Currency Press, 1986.
Emerald City (produced Sydney, 1987). Sydney, Currency Press, 1987.

Screenplays: *Stork*, 1971; *The Family Man* (episode in *Libido*), 1972; *Petersen*, 1974; *The Removalists*, 1975; *Don's Party*, 1976; *Mrs. Eliza Fraser*, 1976; *The Club*, 1980; *Gallipoli*, 1981; *The Year of Living Dangerously*, with Peter Weir and C.J. Koch, 1983; *Phar Lap*, 1983.

Television Play: *The Perfectionist*, 1985.

Other

Counterpointforum: The Australian Image, with Geoffrey Bolton. Murdoch, Western Australia, Murdoch University, 1981.

*

Critical Studies: "Mask and Cage: Stereotype in Recent Drama" by Margaret Williams, in *Meanjin* (Melbourne), September 1972; in *Southerly* (Sydney), June 1973; "*The Removalists*: A Conjunction of Limitations" by Williamson, in *Meanjin* (Melbourne), no. 4, 1974; "Australian Bards and British Reviewers" by Alrene Sykes, in *Australian Literary Studies* (Hobart, Tasmania), May 1975; "The Games People Play: The Development of David Williamson," in *Contemporary Australian Drama* edited by Peter Holloway, Sydney, Currency Press, 1981, and "David Williamson's Plays since *The Department*," in *Southerly* (Sydney), March 1986, both by Brian Kiernan; *Modern Australian Styles* by Mark O'Connor, Townsville, Queensland, Foundation for Australian Literary Studies, 1982; "A New Map for Australia: The Plays of David Williamson" by John McCallum, in *Australian Literary Studies* (St. Lucia, Queensland), May 1984; interview with Paul Kavanagh and Peter Kuch, in *Southerly* (Sydney), June 1986.

Theatrical Activities:
Director: **Play**—*Sons of Cain*, Melbourne, 1985.

David Williamson comments:

I would regard my early plays as mounting a satiric-ironic attack, albeit with a modicum of ambivalent affection, on the conformist philistine, materialist, sexist, and aggressive aspects of the Australian social ethos. In my later plays the personal as distinct from the sociological observations are accorded more weight but the ironic-satiric stance of the earlier plays is, I think, maintained.

* * *

David Williamson's plays probably owed their almost instant popularity with Australian audiences to two things: their forceful and amusing dialogue, and the fact that audiences could readily recognise themselves in the characters on stage—oddly, until the late 1960's, Australian dramatists had very little success in portraying urban, middle-class Australia. Like most Australian dramatists since then, Williamson is fascinated by the patterns and pressures of society. Talking of the group which later became the Australian Performing Group he said: "What brought us together . . . was a desire to write about this Australia we all grew up in. No one had got it all right before." Williamson did indeed get it right; but—as is not always recognised when the plays are performed outside Australia—his plays are heightened naturalism, rather than the literal transcript of slice-of-life. Few in the audiences of his early plays would use quite so many four-letter words or as much violence as they observed on stage, but they would certainly recognise beneath this dramatic heightening their own tensions and frustrations. Williamson is interestingly aware of much Australian speech and manner as a deliberate style. Speaking of *Don's Party*, he said: "The fact that most of the characters in the play are patently aware of the un-English bluntness of their social manners and are using this bluntness as a *style* is quite clear . . . The scene in which Don and Mal shout abuse at each other in apparent fury, dissolves into laughter. They have been using an archetypal Australian style. Belligerence without real resentment. Real resentment in this country tends to be wreathed in polite smiles."

The first Williamson play to reach a wide audience was *The Removalists* (later made into a film) in which a young policeman goes beserk and beats a man to death. The play is not, Williamson says, an attack on the police force, but a drama about authoritarianism and its effects, and it shows clear-sighted understanding of both the policemen and their victim, and an understanding of the pressures and problems on both sides which lead inevitably to murder. This refusal by the author to make overt moral judgements on his characters was to prove one of the constant distinguishing characteristics of the Williamson play: nevertheless, there is an implied judgment on the society which has conditioned their violent, primitive reactions, and for this reason *The Removalists* comes closer to taking a visible moral stance than most Williamson plays.

Williamson's later plays have matured and modified, but without undergoing fundamental change. His characters have grown older, richer, more successful in their careers, but they continue to struggle against insecurity, and seek better ways to shape their lives. Audiences still recognise themselves in the characters on stage, and still laugh—though for a popular playwright and master of the one-liner, Williamson's themes are surprisingly bleak: guilt, self-discovery, failure to recognise one's potential, power struggles, materialism, sexual insecurity and violence, with the latter becoming less overt.

The later plays confirm that Williamson's interest is in group interaction rather than in psychological probing of the individual. *A Handful of Friends*, his bleakest play, and one of his best, has five characters: an academic and his wife, a filmmaker and his wife (an actress), and the academic's journalist sister. By the end of the play, this handful of friends has successfully clawed each other's lives apart, apparently in the name of ruthless ambition, though the causes may lie deeper. The plot unfolds in classic onion-peeling style, but what is revealed is not so much the hidden layers of individual personality as the past relationships of the characters and the threads, subtle and unsubtle, which bind them still.

Audience self-recognition goes beyond habits of speech and mannerism; Williams has also an acute awareness of what his audience is likely to be concerned with at any given moment. In the early play *Don's Party* the guests are mostly university graduates, one-time radicals now in their thirties, aware of the failed promise of their youth and now caught up in a world of bigger houses, larger swimming pools—ultimately a timeless theme, but particularly relevant to a fairly large segment of Australian society in the 1970's. This sensitivity to the moment may in the end help to date Williamson's plays, but it may also be one reason why Williamson has continued to develop (leaving aside the disappointing and apparently hurried *Celluloid Heroes*) when too many of the dramatists who emerged with him in the late 1960's seemed to become caught in a groove of trying to repeat what was successful in those early years.

Williamson confessed in an interview in 1977 that he was less committed to social change than he used to be, but he still insists that there is a serious moral concern in his plays: "Amid all the nonsense about bad language and sex in my work, there is a tendency to lose sight of the fact that a moral concern underlies all my plays." Of his play *What If You Died Tomorrow* (an evening of abrasive revelation when all the wrong people arrive unexpectedly at the home of doctor-turned-novelist Andrew and Kirsty, his journalist wife) the author commented: "The play is, if you like, a gentle lament for the death of, and impossibility of regaining, definite value systems. It's a theme that permeates my work."

In Williamson's recent play *Sons of Cain*, there is a return to social commitment at least in the inspiration of the play: in his own words, "the blatant evidence of massive high-level corruption revealed by *The Age/National Times* tapes and the inactivity of the [Australian] Government in investigating what was on those tapes." The play is set in a newspaper office, where the leading characters are the editor, Kevin (an aggressive, obsessive, and finally unsuccessful crusader against the politicians, police, and businessmen involved in drug trafficking), and the three women journalists making up his investigative team: Crystal (a feminist) Nicole (tough career-woman), and Bronwen (as yet young and idealistic). The play sets out, with Williamson's usual clarity and fairness, the moral intricacies of a situation where some members of a government which has achieved desirable social reform are shown to be corrupt; bring down that government in righteous indignation, and it will probably be replaced by another equally corrupt and less compassionate and progressive. The subject could lend itself to raw indignation and violence, but Williamson handles it at one remove; *Sons of Cain* is a social comedy about the impact of an investigation into corruption in high places on both reporters and those who control the paper rather than the corruption itself, and no one involved seems to suffer too profoundly, no one is destroyed or even beaten up. The play clarifies the issues without rousing the emotions.

Williamson is also known increasingly for his film and television scripts. Several of his own plays have been filmed, but his best cinema work to date is the script for the internationally acclaimed Peter Weir film *Gallipoli*, in which Williamson, following distinguished precedent, made a brief, slightly anxious appearance, playing football in front of an Egyptian pyramid.

—Alrene Sykes

WILLIS, Ted (Edward Henry Willis; Baron Willis of Chislehurst). British. Born in Tottenham, Middlesex, 13 January 1918. Educated at state schools, including Tottenham Central School, 1923–33. Served in the Royal Fusiliers, 1940; writer for the War Office and Ministry of Information. Married Audrey Hale in 1944; one son and one daughter. Artistic director, Unity Theatre, London, 1945–48. Director, World Wide Pictures since 1967, and Vitalcall since 1983. Executive member, League of Dramatists, London, 1948–74; Chairman, 1958–63, and President, 1963–68 and 1976–79, Writers Guild of Great Britain; President, International Writers Guild, 1967–69. Since 1964 Governor, Churchill Theatre Trust, Bromley, Kent; member of the Board of Governors, National Film School, London, 1970–73. Recipient: Berlin Festival award, for screenplay, 1957; Edinburgh Festival award; Writers Guild award, 1964, 1967, 1974; Royal Society of Arts Silver Medal, 1967; Variety Guild of Great Britain award, 1976; Pye Trophy, for television writing, 1983. Fellow, Royal Society of Arts. Life Peer, 1963. Agent: Elaine Greene Ltd., 31 Newington Green, London N16 9PU; or, Harvey Unna and Stephen Durbridge Ltd., 24–32 Pottery Lane, London W11 4LZ. Address: 5 Shepherds Green, Chislehurst, Kent BR7 6PB, England.

PUBLICATIONS

Plays

Sabotage (as John Bishop) (produced London, 1943).
Buster (produced London, 1943). London, Fore, 1943.
All Change Here (produced London, 1944).
"God Bless the Guv'nor": A Moral Melodrama in Which the Twin Evils of Trades Unionism and Strong Drink Are Exposed, "After Mrs. Henry Wood" (produced London, 1945). London, New Theatre Publications, 1945.
The Yellow Star (also director: produced London, 1945).
What Happened to Love? (produced London, 1947).
No Trees in the Street (produced London, 1948).
The Lady Purrs (produced London, 1950). London, Deane, and Boston, Baker, 1950.
The Magnificent Moodies (produced London, 1952).
The Blue Lamp, with Jan Read (produced London, 1952).
A Kiss for Adele, with Talbot Rothwell, adaptation of the play by Barillet and Grédy (produced London, 1952).
Kid Kenyon Rides Again, with Allan Mackinnon (produced Bromley, Kent, 1954).
George Comes Home. London, French, 1955.
Doctor in the House, adaptation of the novel by Richard Gordon (produced London, 1956). London, Evans, and New York, French, 1957.
Woman in a Dressing Gown (televised 1956). Included in *Woman in a Dressing Gown and Other Television Plays*, 1959; revised version (produced Bromley, Kent, 1963; London, 1964), London, Evans, 1964.

The Young and the Guilty (televised 1956). Included in *Woman in a Dressing Gown and Other Television Plays*, 1959.

Look in Any Window (televised 1958). Included in *Woman in a Dressing Gown and Other Television Plays*, 1959.

Hot Summer Night (produced Bournemouth and London, 1958). London, French, 1959.

Woman in a Dressing Gown and Other Television Plays. London, Barrie and Rockliff, 1959.

Brothers-in-Law, with Henry Cecil, adaptation of the novel by Cecil (produced Wimbledon, Surrey, 1959). London, French, 1959.

When in Rome, with Ken Ferry, music by Kramer, lyrics by Eric Shaw, adaptation of a play by Garinei and Giovannini (produced Oxford and London, 1959).

The Eyes of Youth, adaptation of the novel *A Dread of Burning* by Rosemary Timperley (as *Farewell Yesterday*, produced Worthing, Sussex, 1959; as *The Eyes of Youth*, produced Bournemouth, 1959). London, Evans, 1960.

Mother, adaptation of the novel by Gorky (produced Croydon, Surrey, 1961).

Doctor at Sea, adaptation of the novel by Richard Gordon (produced Bromley, Kent, 1961; London, 1966). London, Evans, and New York, French, 1961.

The Little Goldmine. London, French, 1962.

A Slow Roll of Drums (produced Bromley, Kent, 1964).

A Murder of Crows (produced Bromley, Kent, 1966).

The Ballad of Queenie Swann (televised 1966; revised version, music by Dick Manning and Marvin Laird, lyrics by Willis, produced Guildford, Surrey, 1967; as *Queenie*, produced London, 1967).

Dead on Saturday (produced Leatherhead, Surrey, 1972).

Mr. Polly, music by Michael Begg and Ivor Slaney, lyrics by Willis, adaptation of the novel by H.G. Wells (produced Bromley, Kent, 1977).

Stardust (produced Bromley, Kent, 1983).

Screenplays: *The Waves Roll On* (documentary), 1945; *Holiday Camp*, with others, 1947; *Good Time Girl*, with Muriel and Sydney Box, 1948; *A Boy, A Girl, and a Bike*, 1949; *The Huggetts Abroad*, with others, 1949; *The Undefeated* (documentary), 1950; *The Blue Lamp*, with others, 1950; *The Wallet*, 1952; *Top of the Form*, with John Paddy Carstairs and Patrick Kirwan, 1953; *Trouble in Store*, with John Paddy Carstairs and Maurice Cowan, 1953; *The Large Rope*, 1953; *One Good Turn*, with John Paddy Carstairs and Maurice Cowan, 1954; *Burnt Evidence*, 1954; *Up to His Neck*, with others, 1954; *It's Great to Be Young*, 1956; *The Skywalkers*, 1956; *Woman in a Dressing Gown*, 1957; *The Young and the Guilty*, 1958; *No Trees in the Street*, 1959; *Six Men and a Nightingale*, 1961; *Flame in the Streets*, 1961; *The Horsemasters*, 1961; *Bitter Harvest*, 1963; *Last Bus to Banjo Creek*, 1968; *Our Miss Fred*, 1972; and other documentaries.

Radio Plays: *Big Bertha*, 1962; *And No Birds Sing*, 1979; *The Buckingham Palace Connection*, from his own novel, 1981; *The Left-Handed Sleeper*, from his own novel, 1982; *Obsession*, 1983; *Death May Surprise Us*, from his own novel, 1984.

Television Plays: *The Handlebar*, *The Pattern of Marriage*, *Big City*, *Dial 999*, *The Sullavan Brothers*, *Lifeline*, and *Taxi* series; *Dixon of Dock Green* series, 1954, and later series; *The Young and the Guilty*, 1956; *Woman in a Dressing Gown*, 1956; *Look in Any Window*, 1958; *Strictly for the Sparrows*, 1958; *Scent of Fear*, 1959; *Days of Vengeance*, with Edward J. Mason, 1960; *Flowers of Evil* series, with Mason, 1961; *Outbreak of Murder*, with Mason; *Sergeant Cork* series, 1963; *The Four Seasons of Rosie Carr*, 1964; *Dream of a Summer Night*, 1965; *Mrs. Thursday* series, 1966; *The Ballad of Queenie Swann*, 1966; *Virgin of the Secret Service* series, 1968; *Crimes of Passion* series, 1970–72; *Copper's End* series, 1971; *Hunter's Walk* series, 1973, 1976; *Black Beauty* series, from the novel by Anna Sewell, 1975; *Barney's Last Battle*, 1976; *Street Party*, 1977; *The Long Way to Shiloh*, 1977; *Man-Eater*, from his own novel, 1980; *Eine Heim für Tiere* series, from 1984 (Germany); *Mrs. Harris M.P.*, 1985; *Mrs. Harris Goes to New York*, 1987; *The Iron Man*, 1987; *Racecourse* series, 1987; *The Valley of Dream*, 1987; *Mrs. Harris Goes to Monte Carlo*, 1988.

Novels

The Blue Lamp. London, Convoy, 1950.

Dixon of Dock Green: My Life, with Charles Hatton. London, Kimber, 1960.

Dixon of Dock Green: A Novel, with Paul Graham. London, Mayflower, 1961.

Black Beauty. London, Hamlyn, 1972.

Death May Surprise Us. London, Macmillan, 1974; as *Westminster One*, New York, Putnam, 1975.

The Left-Handed Sleeper. London, Macmillan, 1975; New York, Putnam, 1976.

Man-Eater. London, Macmillan, 1976; New York, Morrow, 1977.

The Churchill Commando. London, Macmillan, and New York, Morrow, 1977.

The Buckingham Palace Connection. London, Macmillan, and New York, Morrow, 1978.

The Lions of Judah. London, Macmillan, 1979; New York, Holt Rinehart, 1980.

The Naked Sun. London, Macmillan, 1980.

The Most Beautiful Girl in the World. London, Macmillan, 1982.

Spring at the Winged Horse: The First Season of Rosie Carr. London, Macmillan, and New York, Morrow, 1983.

The Green Leaves of Summer: The Second Season of Rosie Carr. London, Macmillan, 1987.

Other

Fighting Youth of Russia. London, Russia Today Society, 1942.

The Devil's Churchyard (for children). London, Parrish, 1957.

Seven Gates to Nowhere (for children). London, Parrish, 1958.

Whatever Happened to Tom Mix? The Story of One of My Lives. London, Cassell, 1970.

A Problem for Mother Christmas (for children). London, Gollancz, 1986.

*

Manuscript Collection: Boston University.

Theatrical Activities:
Director: **Plays**—Unity Theatre, London: *The Yellow Star*, 1945; *Boy Meets Girl* by Bella and Sam Spewack, 1946; *All God's Chillun Got Wings* by Eugene O'Neill, 1946; *Golden Boy* by Clifford Odets, 1947; *Anna Christie* by Eugene O'Neill.

Ted Willis comments:

I am a good example of what can be done by hard work. I've taken a small talent, honed and sharpened it into a good professional instrument. Might have been a better writer if I'd stuck to one area and kept out of politics (both writing and national) but that's the way I am.

* * *

There is no doubt in my mind that Ted Willis owes his success in life to his quite extraordinary power of concentration. At a very early age he decided that he was going to be a writer. When he left school finally at 15 and confided to the Headmaster his determination to write, the crisp comment was "Don't be a fool. You've no literary gift whatever. Much better learn a trade." But to waste time and energy in learning a trade was no part of the Willis plan. He was teaching himself one, and making progress. His intensive study of the cinema was encouraging him to try his hand at that medium, and television; so he took the kind of ill-paid jobs that were open to an unskilled man, and went on writing.

His pen was by now a very well-tempered instrument; but it was through his politics, not his fiction, that this first became publicly known. His views were of the extreme left-wing order, and he expressed them with a force and pungency that made him a valuable asset to the Labour Party. But it was during army service in World War II that he was given the chance to write his first screenplays. This decided his future—for when he went back into civil life in 1945 and was invited to stand for a safe Labour seat in Parliament, he refused. He was still a writer.

He is an inventive storyteller, and his high standard of craftsmanship and severe self-discipline have lead inevitably to success, especially in such compositions as his television series *Dixon of Dock Green* and *Mrs. Thursday*. What it does not necessarily lead to is artistry; and one gathers that Willis knows this very well himself, for he once said modestly to an interviewer, "There are hundreds of better writers with much greater talent than mine. But less ability to work hard."

That honest, if overstated, attempt at self-assessment has a modicum of truth in it, and it is remarkable that not one of his productions has ever induced West End audiences to show much enthusiasm. Even *Woman in a Dressing Gown* (by common consent his best play) caused little stir.

So evident an effect must have a definable cause; but to say simply that Willis has a better talent for screen and television plays than for stage plays is merely to define the matter without explaining it. There could be a dozen explanations but one is fundamental. The world of the living theatre was unknown to the boy who played truant from school to revel in the glories of the cinema. When Willis first encountered the stage in his mid-twenties it was in the spirit not of a lover but of an immensely industrious student. He learned much; but it is not thus that a dramatist acquires that mysterious sense of the theatre which enables him to serve the art of the actor. The hard-working student may well deserve success, but in the theatre he cannot command it.

—W.A. Darlington

WILSON, August. American. Born in Pittsburgh, Pennsylvania, 27 April 1945. Educated at Gladstone High School, Pittsburgh, 1960–61. Married Judy Oliver in 1981; one daughter. Founder, Black Horizons Theatre Company, St. Paul, 1968. Since 1980 associate playwright, Playwrights Center, Minneapolis; since 1982 member, New Playwrights, New York. Recipient: Jerome fellowship, 1980; Bush fellowship, 1982; Rockefeller fellowship, 1984; McKnight fellowship, 1985; New York Drama Critics Circle award, 1985, 1987; Guggenheim fellowship, 1986; Whiting Foundation award, 1986; American Theatre Critics award, 1986; Outer Circle award, 1987; Drama Desk award, 1987; John Gassner Award, 1987; Tony award, 1987; Pulitzer Prize, 1987. Agent (attorney): John Breglio, Paul Weiss Rifkind Wharton and Garrison, 1285 Avenue of the Americas, New York, New York 10019. Address: 469 Selby Avenue, St. Paul, Minnesota 55102, U.S.A.

PUBLICATIONS

Plays

Black Bart and the Sacred Hills (produced St. Paul, 1981).
Jitney (produced Pittsburgh, 1982).
The Mill Hand's Lunch Bucket (produced New York, 1983).
Ma Rainey's Black Bottom (produced New Haven, Connecticut, and New York, 1984). New York, New American Library, 1985.
Fences (produced New Haven, Connecticut, 1985; New York, 1987). New York, New American Library, 1986.
Joe Turner's Come and Gone (produced New Haven, Connecticut, 1986).

*

August Wilson comments:

I write about the black experience in America and try to explore in terms of the life I know best those things which are common to all cultures. I see myself as answering James Baldwin's call for a profound articulation of the black experience, which he defined as "that field of manners and ritual of intercourse that can sustain a man once he has left his father's house." I try to concretize the values of the black American and place them on stage in loud action to demonstrate the existence of the above "field of manners" and point to some avenues of sustenance.

* * *

August Wilson shot to prominence in 1984, when *Ma Rainey's Black Bottom* had its Broadway premiere. That play and his subsequent work have identified him as a writer of exceptional eloquence in expressing the black experience in the United States.

Ma Rainey is the first of a projected cycle of dramas by Wilson, each one dealing with black life in America in a different decade of the 20th century. In *Ma Rainey* the time is the 1920's, in a studio in Chicago where the imperious blues singer Ma Rainey is about to record a new batch of songs for her white bosses. The focus of the play is on a side room, however, where her black musicians—a few scarred veterans and a fiery new horn player—have gathered to wait for the recording session to begin. The talk of these musicians—the resigned old men who invented a vital popular music but lost economic power over it to the white merchandisers, and the young firebrand who wants to take control of his art in new, forceful ways—is at the heart of the play. Their conflict, escalating into sudden violence, is contrasted to the railings of old Ma Rainey as she makes petty demands for her immediate personal comfort.

Fences, set in the 1950's, presents another black hero of near-tragic proportions, Troy Maxson, a baseball player whose career came just before black men had cracked the white major leagues, and who has since settled into family life as a garbage man in "a Northeastern city" that is clearly Wilson's home town of Pittsburgh. An ex-convict, a hard drinker, and a womanizer, still railing against the white men who denied him his big chance, Maxson is common clay indeed, but he is, in Wilson's simple statement, "doing the best he can," and it is his inherent nobility, ground down by the life he has led, that shines through, despite the crippling flaws of character so vividly delineated in the scenes with his long-suffering wife and rebellions, aspiring son. *Fences* won the 1987 Pulitzer Prize.

Joe Turner's Come and Gone, which takes place in 1911 in a Pittsburgh boarding house, reveals yet another aspect of the black experience, focusing on the lot of the dispossessed post-Civil War generation who had lost their ties to Africa, been cut loose from the south, and were migrating north with no sense of identity. *The Piano Lesson* (unproduced), set in the 1930's, examines the legacy of black history in America, using as a metaphor the fate of a cherished old piano that has been in a family for many years. The sister wants to hang on to it for sentimental reasons; the brother insists on selling it to gain money for his shot at a better life.

Wilson's plays are significant for the scope of their ambition in trying to capture, through striking dramatic examples, the causes and effects of the rage, alienation, and frustration of black men and women in America. Individually, the plays are often marked by flaws in structure, notably in the awkwardness of transitions. But these problems are more than balanced by the power and beauty of Wilson's dialogue which transforms the common speech of poor, ignorant men and women into flights of amazing grace.

—Richard Christiansen

WILSON, Doric. American. Born in Los Angeles, California, 24 February 1939. Studied with Lorraine Larson, Tri-Cities, Washington, 1955–58; apprenticed to Richland Players, Washington, 1952–58; attended University of Washington, Seattle, 1958–59. Founding member and playwright-in-residence, Barr/Wilder/Albee Playwrights Unit, New York, 1963–65; artistic director, Ensemble Project, New York, 1965–68; founding member and playwright-in-residence, Circle Repertory Company, New York, 1969–71; founding artistic director, TOSOS Theatre Company, New York, 1973–77; playwright-in-residence, The Glines, New York, 1978–82, and Jerry West's Funtastic Shows, Portland, Oregon, 1983–84; director, New City Theatre Playwright's Workshop, Seattle, 1985. Since 1986 director and playwright-in-residence, Pioneer Square Theater, Seattle. Recipient: San Francisco Cable Car award, 1981; Chambers-Blackwell award, 1982; Villager award, 1983; Newsmaker award, 1984. Agent: Terry Helbing, JH Press, P.O. Box 294 Village Station, New York, New York 10014. Address: 1019 East Pike Street, Apartment V, Seattle, Washington 98122, U.S.A.

PUBLICATIONS

Plays

And He Made a Her (produced New York, 1961).
Babel, Babel, Little Tower (produced New York, 1961).
Now She Dances! (produced New York, 1961; revised version produced New York, 1975).
Pretty People (produced New York, 1961).
In Absence (produced New York, 1968).
It Was a Very Good Year (produced New York, 1970).
Body Count (produced New York, 1971).
The West Street Gang (also director: produced New York, 1977). Included in *Two Plays*, New York, Sea Horse Press, 1979.
Ad Hoc Committee (produced New York, 1978).
Surprise (produced New York, 1978).
Turnabout (as Howard Aldon) (produced Richland, Washington, 1979).
A Perfect Relationship (produced New York, 1979). Included in *Two Plays*, New York, Sea Horse Press, 1979.
Forever After: A Vivisection of Gaymale Love, Without Intermission (also director: produced New York, 1980). New York, JH Press, 1980.
Street Theater: The Twenty-Seventh of June, 1969 (produced New York, 1981). New York, JH Press, 1983.
Saints on a Secret Mission (produced Seattle, 1986).

*

Manuscript Collection: Lincoln Center Library of the Performing Arts, New York.

Critical Studies: introduction by William M. Hoffman to *Gay Plays*, New York, Avon, 1979; *Lavender Culture* by Karla Jay and Allen Young, New York, Jove, 1979; "Caffe Cino" by Wilson, in *Other Stages* (New York), 8 March 1979; interview with Robert Chesley, in *Advocate* (San Francisco), 5 April 1979; "Gay Plays, Gay Theatre, Gay Performance" by Terry Helbing, in *Drama Review* (New York), March 1981.

Theatrical Activities:
Director: **Plays**—many productions in New York, most recently *The Madness of Lady Bright* by Lanford Wilson, 1974; *The Hostage* by Brendan Behan, 1975; *What the Butler Saw* by Joe Orton, 1975; *Now She Dances!*, 1976; *The West Street Gang*, 1977; *Forever After*, 1980.

* * *

Doric Wilson is a quintessentially urban dramatist who grew up in rural Washington State but lived in New York City for more than two decades. He specializes in stylish farce, ironic comedy of wit, and urbane satire. His combination of fantasy and whimsy and his intellectual dialectic may suggest the touch of a Giraudoux or a Shaw, a Wilder or a Wycherley. Yet underlying his often caustic comedy is a surprisingly romantic sensibility which finds him subtly rooting for happy ever afters.

And He Made a Her (1961) may have been the first play written specifically for Caffe Cino—and therefore for off-off-Broadway. Like many of the Cino writers, Wilson is gay, and, after stints as an original member of both the Barr/Wilder/Albee Playwrights Unit and the Circle Repertory Company, in 1973 he formed the first professional gay company, TOSOS (The Other Side of Silence), which he founded with his income as a bartender.

Wilson excels at accurate observation of life, particularly gay life, which he satirizes but with which he also sympathizes. He has displayed unusual courage in his insistence on writing openly about gay characters who are neither sick nor miserable.

Although he dislikes the word "gay," this is a linguistic rather than a political stance. A pioneer in his efforts to write about gay subjects and produce for gay audiences, Wilson has been a leader among up-front homosexuals combating gay self-hatred, and his sharpest satire is reserved for homophobes, whether straight or gay. Wilson's plays speak particularly to gay spectators, but they promote tolerance, affection, honesty, and understanding among people of any sexuality.

Wilson's work is characterized by its playfulness, its fantasy, and its feminism. *And He Made a Her*, for example, dramatizes the displeasure among Adam and the angels caused by Eve's creation. The angelic host—including one described as "of liberal size and liberal party but not left winged enough to fly—or fall—with Lucifer"—worry about Eve, who's disturbing the natural animosity of the animals, domesticating the plants, and intent upon reproduction. Clearly superior to Adam, she provokes amazement "that woman is able to look up at someone shorter than she is." More surprising, perhaps, as early as 1961 is Wilson's substitution—for the response "Amen"—of "A Women." Other early Wilson one-acts which exemplify these characteristics are his satire of narcissism *Pretty People*, set in a museum displaying live people, and the political satire *Babel, Babel, Little Tower*, in which the narcissists are warmongers and religious freaks from several historical periods.

Although these early Wilson plays are not specifically gay in subject, another piece from that period which is concerned with homosexuality has been expanded into a full-length play. *Now She Dances!* comments upon both Oscar Wilde's imprisonment and contemporary America by dramatizing the Salome story according to the dramatic conventions of *The Importance of Being Earnest*. As Lane the butler ("with excellent references from another play") puts it, *Now She Dances!* gives us "farce fencing force over tea." In both versions, Lady Herodias's daughter, Miss Salome, demands and finally receives a man's head on a tray covered with a tea cozy; in the full-length version the word "head" is subject to double entendre which may go over the heads of some. In the original, Wilde is the prisoner, and he won't come out of the closet; in the rewrite, the prisoner is an unashamed and clever contemporary American homosexual whom Salome tries to seduce. The words she speaks as she unbuttons her bodice typify Wilson's simultaneous accomplishment of more than one objective: "In years to come, when you talk of this, and you will, be kind."

Those famous lines directed, in Robert Anderson's *Tea and Sympathy*, toward a boy who is sympathetic because he is *not* gay, serve as implicit critique of years of theatrical treatment of the homosexual, who, until recently, is usually ignored or despised or pitied. Wilson hardly misses an opportunity to mix in comments on the theatre with his wider political satire. Among jabs at animal symbols of women (seagull, wild duck), Actors Studio nonsense about an actress who plays a maid "identifying" with the soup she's serving, and tedious first scenes ("a lovely bouquet of blue expositions"), Wilson spoofs gay dramatists such as Genet and Wilde who do not give us a reasonable facsimile of the life thousands of homosexuals actually live.

In *Street Theater*, his play about the hours preceding the Stonewall riots (which gave birth to the gay rights movement), Wilson mocks the self-contemptuous pair from *The Boys in the Band* and a closet queen as well as the heterosexual mobster bar owner who exploits his "queer" customers and a couple of Vice Squad cops, one of whom arrests the other. Set on the street near the Stonewall gay bar, this comedy offers politically provocative wit plus an array of New York homosexuals deftly characterized and suggests what sort of homophobic treatment prompted them to turn on their tormentors in revolt.

Another treatment of the street-bar scene by one of its own aficionados is *The West Street Gang*, which likewise dramatizes the victimization of gays by homophobes, opportunists, and each other. Set in a downtown west-side leather bar, it was also performed in one (the Spike). It shows the bar's patrons threatened by a gang of teenage fag bashers of the type who regularly try to murder gays with baseball bats and tire chains. Their efforts at self-protection are led by a transvestite and are hampered by a so-called gay rights leader, by Arthur Klang (a thinly disguised Arthur Bell of the *Village Voice*), and Bonita Aryant (a still more thinly disguised Anita Bryant, then waging a nationwide anti-homosexuality crusade). *The West Street Gang* offers more than just appropriate politics. It's a hilarious treatment of some familiar New Yorkers, who turn out to be more than mere stereotypes. There's the hustler who gets rolled, the pacifist who urges violence, and, best of all, the drag queen who leads the fight against the marauding street gang. "She" initially follows the butch dress code on her entrance, then heads for the head and simpers back on in a dress. Whether hero or heroine, she stands up very well not only to the homophobic cops and bar owner and to Bonita (who mistakes the bar's patrons for longshoremen) but to her less than broadminded gay fellow bar patrons. Indeed, the varied characters lead us to conclude that tolerance, cooperation, and mutual respect are the qualities Wilson most admires.

Among his domestic love stories, *Turnabout* is one of several Wilson satires of straight relationships; *A Perfect Relationship* depicts the friendship of two men who don't recognize that they ought to be lovers; and *Forever After* is both a romantic comedy and a parody of same.

Written under the pseudonym "Howard Aldon" *Turnabout* is a suburban sit com in which a wife teaches her adulterous husband a lesson without actually sleeping with other men. A play in which non-stop one-liners compete with very funny situations as sources of humor, *Turnabout* devastates the complacent husband's double standard. It demonstrates Wilson's capacity for exactly the sort of heterosexual commercial comedy with which he could regale Broadway if he weren't more interested in a different kind of dramaturgy. He has, however, written several other satires of heterosexual relations, including *In Absence, It Was a Very Good Year, Body Count*, and *Surprise*.

In *A Perfect Relationship* the protagonists, Ward and Greg, are roommates whose lifestyle is built upon a commitment to non-commitment. Both thrive on cruising, which Greg practices at discos and ward at backroom bars. Although they aren't lovers, they bicker as though they were—over who does the laundry, or cooks dinner, or takes the first shower. They even keep score, as though it were an organized sport, while denigrating each other's masculinity. They have a "perfect" relationship until both sleep with the same trick, a young opportunist who uses this one-night stand to acquire Ward and Greg's desirable Christopher Street apartment. Along the way to discovering that they ought to be lovers, Ward and Greg deal with the kooky heterosexual woman from whom they are subletting. She and her boyfriends behave as though they're at a zoo and the young men are the animals, yet her preconceptions about gays aren't much sillier than their own. Although she outdoes them in promiscusous non-involvement, she helps the roommates to recognize that they share a lot more than the rent.

The kind of love story which Wilson writes in *A Perfect Relationship* he sets out to parody in *Forever After*, yet he maintains an effective tension in the latter between amusement at romanticism and acceptance of long-term commitment between men. Tom and David's amorous remarks are jeered by two mocking muses in drag seated in proscenium boxes. Actually it's Melpomene, the tragic muse, who sets out to destroy the affair. It is her descent into the fray to coach the lovers in suspicion and disharmony which prompts the comic muse Thalia to follow and defend the playwright's prerogative to give the young men a happy-ever-after conclusion. Something of a descendant of Sheridan's *The Critic* or the Duke of Buckingham's *The Rehearsal*, *Forever After* mixes presentational and representational styles while lampooning such theatrical targets as Sam Shepard's *Buried Child*, Martin Sherman's *Bent*, Edward Albee's *The Lady from Dubuque*, Robert Patrick's *T-Shirts*, general negativity in drama, and the claims made by performers in gay plays that they're straight. The particular object of Wilson's wrath—and wisecracks—however, is melodramas in which the homosexual is a tormented degenerate.

Wilson's ear for the varieties of gay attitudes, jargon, and quips is as good as ever in *Forever After*, and his penchant for punning is true to his best form. The dialogue is among his most raunchy and real. As to his appraisal of the dispute between the muses, Wilson shares Thalia's views; he sees the funny and playful side of everything, including love, but on the subjects of human relations and aesthetics he's no cynic. Although *Forever After* demonstrates it's easier to fight than to sustain a relationship, Wilson sets us to cheering those who succeed at commitment.

—Tish Dace

WILSON, Lanford (Eugene). American. Born in Lebanon, Missouri, 13 April 1937. Educated at Ozark High School, Missouri; Southwest Missouri State College, Springfield, 1955–56; San Diego State College, California, 1956–57; University of Chicago, 1957–58. Worked at various jobs, and in advertising, Chicago, 1957–62; director, actor, and designer for Caffe Cino and Cafe La Mama theatres, New York, and other theatres. Since 1969 co-founder and resident playwright, Circle Repertory Company, New York. Recipient: Rockefeller grant, 1967, 1974; Vernon Rice award, 1968; ABC-Yale University fellowship, 1969; New York Drama Critics Circle award, 1973, 1980; Obie award, 1973, 1975, 1983; Outer Circle award, 1973; American Academy award, 1974; Pulitzer Prize, 1980. Agent: Bridget Aschenberg, International Creative Management, 40 West 57th Street, New York, New York 10019. Address: c/o Hill and Wang, 19 Union Square West, New York, New York 10003, U.S.A.

PUBLICATIONS

Plays

So Long at the Fair (produced New York, 1963).
No Trespassing (produced New York, 1964).
Home Free! (also director: produced New York, 1964; London, 1968). Included in *Balm in Gilead and Other Plays*, 1965; with *The Madness of Lady Bright*, London, Methuen, 1968.
Balm in Gilead (produced New York, 1964; Edinburgh, 1986). Included in *Balm in Gilead and Other Plays*, 1965.
The Madness of Lady Bright (also director: produced New York, 1964; London, 1968). Included in *The Rimers of Eldritch and Other Plays*, 1967; with *Home Free!*, London, Methuen, 1968.
Ludlow Fair (produced New York, 1965; Edinburgh, 1967; London, 1977). Included in *Balm in Gilead and Other Plays*, 1965.
Balm in Gilead and Other Plays. New York, Hill and Wang, 1965.
Sex Is Between Two People (produced New York, 1965).
The Rimers of Eldritch (also director: produced New York, 1965). Included in *The Rimers of Eldritch and Other Plays*, 1967.
This Is the Rill Speaking (also director: produced New York, 1965). Included in *The Rimers of Eldritch and Other Plays*, 1967.
Days Ahead (produced New York, 1965). Included in *The Rimers of Eldritch and Other Plays*, 1967.
The Sand Castle (produced New York, 1965). Included in *The Sand Castle and Three Other Plays*, 1970.
Wandering: A Turn (produced New York, 1966). Included in *The Rimers of Eldritch and Other Plays*, 1967.
The Rimers of Eldritch and Other Plays. New York, Hill and Wang, 1967.
Miss Williams: A Turn (produced New York, 1967).
Untitled Play, music by Al Carmines (produced New York, 1967).
The Gingham Dog (produced Washington, D.C., 1968; New York, 1969; Manchester, 1970). New York, Hill and Wang, 1970.
The Great Nebula in Orion (produced Manchester, 1970; New York, 1972; London, 1981). Included in *The Great Nebula in Orion and Three Other Plays*, 1973.
Lemon Sky (produced Buffalo and New York, 1970). New York, Hill and Wang, 1970.
Serenading Louie (produced Washington, D.C., 1970; New York, 1976). New York, Dramatists Play Service, 1976; revised version (produced New York, 1984), New York, Hill and Wang, 1985.
The Sand Castle and Three Other Plays (includes *Wandering, Stoop: A Turn, Sextet (Yes): A Play for Voices*). New York, Dramatists Play Service, 1970.
Sextet (Yes): A Play for Voices (produced New York, 1971). Included in *The Sand Castle and Three Other Plays*, 1970.
Summer and Smoke, music by Lee Hoiby, adaptation of the play by Tennessee Williams (produced St. Paul, 1971; New York, 1972). New York, Belwin Mills, 1972.
Ikke, Ikke, Nye, Nye, Nye (produced New Haven, Connecticut, 1971; New York, 1972; London, 1981). Included in *The Great Nebula in Orion and Three Other Plays*, 1973.
The Family Continues (produced New York, 1972). Included in *The Great Nebula in Orion and Three Other Plays*, 1973.
The Great Nebula in Orion and Three Other Plays (includes *Ikke, Ikke, Nye, Nye, Nye*; *The Family Continues*; *Victory on Mrs. Dandywine's Island*). New York, Dramatists Play Service, 1973.
The Hot l Baltimore (produced New York, 1973; London, 1976). New York, Hill and Wang, 1973.
The Mound Builders (produced New York, 1975). New York, Hill and Wang, 1976.

Brontosaurus (produced New York, 1977; London, 1982). New York, Dramatists Play Service, 1978.
5th of July (produced New York, 1978; Bristol, 1987). New York, Hill and Wang, 1979.
Talley's Folly (produced New York, 1979; London, 1982). New York, Hill and Wang, 1980.
Bar Play, in *Holidays* (produced Louisville, 1979).
Talley and Son (as *A Tale Told*, produced New York, 1981; revised version, as *Talley and Son*, produced New York, 1985). New York, Hill and Wang, 1986.
Angels Fall (produced New York, 1982). New York, Hill and Wang, 1983.
Thymus Vulgaris (produced New York, 1982). New York, Dramatists Play Service, 1982.
Three Sisters, adaptation of a play by Chekhov (produced Hartford, Connecticut, 1985; New York, 1986).
Say deKooning (produced Southampton, New York, 1985).
Sa-Hurt? (produced New York, 1986).
A Betrothal (produced London, 1986).
Burn This (produced Los Angeles and New York, 1987). New York, Hill and Wang, 1988.

Screenplay: *One Arm*, 1970.

Television Plays: *The Migrants*, from a story by Tennessee Williams, 1974; *Taxi!*, 1979.

*

Bibliography: *Ten Modern American Playwrights* by Kimball King, New York, Garland, 1982.

Theatrical Activities:
Director: **Plays**—many of his own plays, including *Home Free!*, New York, 1964; *The Madness of Lady Bright*, New York, 1964; *The Rimers of Eldritch*, New York, 1965; *This Is the Rill Speaking*, New York, 1965; *Indecent Exposure* by Robert Patrick, New York, 1968; *Not to Worry* by A.E. Santaniello, New York, 1975; *In Vienna* by Roy London, New York, 1980. Actor: **Plays**—in *The Clown*, New York, 1968; *Wandering*, New York, 1968; *Him* by E.E. Cummings, New York, 1974.

* * *

Lanford Wilson's plays are deeply concerned with the conflict between the traditional values of the past and the insidious pressures of modern life. While he has been only intermittently successful at resolving this conflict, it has provided him with dramatic material of great variety and interest. The eccentric characters of *Balm in Gilead* and *The Madness of Lady Bright* fight or flee convention, and their desperation is sharply and sympathetically drawn. *The Rimers of Eldritch* or *This Is the Rill Speaking* ridicule the hypocrisy, bigotry, and convention of a small town while they rejoice in the confused innocence and energy of its adolescents. These "collage" plays, in which different strands of dialogue interweave, scenes overlap, and actors double their roles, allowed Wilson deftly to juxtapose the rooted strengths and values of the old with the energy and explorations of the young.

Wilson's experiments with the collage style resolved themselves in *The Hot l Baltimore*, set in a deteriorating flophouse (whose sign has lost its "e") peopled by whores, retirees, outcasts, and deadbeats. At the Hotel Baltimore, however, it is the old who have rejected convention, and the young Girl who fights to recover the past. This callgirl is as dismayed that no one will fight to save the hotel—"That's why nothing gets done anymore. Nobody's got the conviction of their passions"—as she is furious that a young stranger gives up the search for his grandfather too easily. More naturalistic than earlier plays, *The Hot l Baltimore* uses a clear and simple prose and the physical symbol of the hotel to focus on Wilson's basic concerns.

Wilson's trilogy about the Talley family again used buildings as the symbol of an emotional and social conflict between past and present. *5th of July*, set in the present, reunites the scattered Talleys: Aunt Sally Talley, her nephew Ken and his homosexual lover, and Sally's niece June and her illegitimate daughter. Since Ken (whose legs were paralyzed in Vietnam) and June are offering the house to two old friends who were fellow radicals in the 1960's, the play was frequently described as an evaluation of the decade's politics. However, the politics are not deeply felt, and quickly become secondary to the sale of the house, which comes to represent the rejection of the family's roots in favor of a future they don't want or like. *Talley and Son* (set in World War II but the last play to be written) hinges on the struggle between Sally Talley's father and grandfather over control of the family business. While this play was excessively (and clumsily) complex, *Talley's Folly* (whose action is concurrent with that of *Talley and Son*) concerns the elegantly compact and dramatically clear courtship of Sally Talley by a New York lawyer, Matt Friedmann. Described as "a valentine" by Matt (who frequently and non-naturalistically addresses the audience), the play unites tradition and progress through Matt's warm, obstinately honest, and ultimately successful wooing of Sally.

While *Talley's Folly* avoided topical issues to its benefit, *Angels Fall* used an accident at a nearby nuclear plant to trap characters in a small Catholic church (compare *Bus Stop*). Parallelling a young, intelligent Navaho's rejection of his responsibility to his community with an art historian's sudden and violent rejection of his life's work, the play's pretext seems gratuitous and its resolution of the characters' spiritual crises mechanical.

A talented craftsman of dialogue, Wilson often fails to weld his situations seamlessly to his deepest concerns. However, when his primary values—honesty and the love of friends, family, and home—are tied closely to his dramatic situations, his plays enact crucial questions about how the fabric of society is woven and cared for over generations.

—Walter Bode

WILSON, Robert M. American. Born in Waco, Texas, 4 October 1941. Educated at the University of Texas, Austin, 1959–62; Pratt Institute, Brooklyn, New York, 1962–65, B.F.A. 1965; studied painting with George McNeil, Paris, 1962; apprentice in architecture to Paolo Soleri, Acrosanti community, Phoenix, Arizona, 1966. Since 1970 artistic director, Byrd Hoffman Foundation, New York; frequent lecturer at seminars and workshops from 1970. Artist: individual shows since 1971 (retrospective exhibition at Laguna Gloria Museum, Austin, Texas, 1986). Recipient: Best Foreign Play award (France), 1970; Guggenheim fellowship, 1971, 1980; Obie award, for directing, 1974, 1986; Rockefeller fellowship, 1975, and award, 1981; Maharam award, for design, 1975; Lumen award, for design, 1977; French Critics award, for musical theatre, 1977; German Press award, 1979; San Sebastian Film

Festival award, 1984; Berlin Theatre Festival award, 1984; Malaga Theatre Festival Picasso Award, 1986; Boston Theatre Critics Circle award, 1986. Address: Byrd Hoffman Foundation, 325 Spring Street, New York, New York 10013, U.S.A.

PUBLICATIONS

Plays

Dance Event (produced New York, 1965).
Solo Performance (produced New York, 1966).
Theater Activity (produced New York, 1967).
ByrdwoMAN (produced New York, 1968).
The King of Spain (produced New York, 1969). Published in *New American Plays 3*, edited by William M. Hoffman, New York, Hill and Wang, 1970.
The Life and Times of Sigmund Freud (produced New York, 1969).
Deafman Glance (produced Iowa City, 1970; New York, 1971).
Program Prologue Now, Overture for a Deafman (produced Paris, 1971; New York, 1972).
Overture (produced New York, 1972).
Ka Mountain and GUARDenia Terrace: A Story about a Family and Some People Changing (produced Shiraz, Iran, 1972).
King Lyre and Lady in the Wasteland (produced New York, 1973).
The Life and Times of Joseph Stalin (produced Copenhagen and New York, 1973).
A Mad Man a Mad Giant a Mad Dog a Mad Urge a Mad Face (produced Rome and Washington, D.C., 1974).
The Life and Times of Dave Clark (produced Sao Paulo, 1974).
"Prologue" to A Letter for Queen Victoria (produced Spoleto, Italy, 1974).
A Letter for Queen Victoria (produced Spoleto, Italy, and tour, 1974; New York, 1975). New York, Byrd Hoffman Foundation, 1974.
To Street (produced Bonn, 1975).
The $ Value of Man (produced New York, 1975).
Dia Log, with Christopher Knowles (produced New York, 1975).
Spaceman, with Ralph Hilton (produced New York, 1976).
Einstein on the Beach, music and lyrics by Philip Glass (produced New York, 1976). New York, EOS Enterprises, 1976.
I Was Sitting on My Patio This Guy Appeared I Thought I Was Hallucinating (produced Ypsilanti, Michigan, and New York, 1977). New York, Byrd Hoffman Foundation, 1978.
Dia Log/Network (produced Boston, 1978).
"Prologue" to the Fourth Act of Deafman Glance (produced East Hampton, New York, 1978).
Death, Destruction, and Detroit (produced Berlin, 1979). New York, Gnome Baker, 1978.
Dialog/Curious George (produced Brussels, 1979; New York, 1980).
Edison (produced Lyon, France, and New York, 1979).
The Man in the Raincoat (produced Cologne, 1981).
Great Day in the Morning, with Jessye Norman (produced Paris, 1982).
The Golden Windows (produced Munich, 1982; New York, 1985). Munich, Hanser, 1982.
the CIVIL warS: a tree is best measured when it is down (sections produced Rotterdam, 1983; with Heiner Müller, Cologne, 1984; with Maita di Niscemi, Rome, 1984; *Knee Plays* music and lyrics by David Byrne, Minneapolis, 1984; Tokyo, 1984; Marseille, 1984; Cambridge, Massachusetts, 1985). Sections published Amsterdam, Meulenhoff Landshoff, 1983; Frankfurt, Suhrkamp, 1984; Rome, Edizioni del Teatro dell 'Opera, 1984; Los Angeles, Otis Art Institute, 1984; *Knee Plays*, with David Byrne, Minneapolis, Walker Art Center, 1984; with Heiner Müller, Cambridge, Massachusetts, American Repertory Theater, 1985.
Medea, with Gavin Bryars (produced Lyon, 1984).
King Lear (produced Hollywood, 1985).
Alcestis, with Heiner Müller (produced Cambridge, Massachusetts, 1986).

Screenplay: *Overture for a Deafman*, 1971.

Video Works: *Spaceman*, 1976; *Video 50*, 1978; *Deafman Glance*, 1981; *Stations*, 1982.

Recordings: *The Life and Times of Joseph Stalin*, Byrd Hoffman Foundation, 1973; *Einstein on the Beach*, music and lyrics by Philip Glass, CBS, 1979; *the CIVIL warS: Knee Plays*, music and lyrics by David Byrne, Warner Brothers, 1985.

*

Critical Studies: *The Theatre of Visions: Robert Wilson* by Stefan Brecht, Frankfurt, Suhrkamp, 1979, London, Methuen, 1982; *Robert Wilson: The Theater of Images* edited by Craig Nelson, Cincinnati, Contemporary Arts Center, 1980, revised edition, New York, Harper, 1984.

Theatrical Activities:
Director: **Plays**—all his own plays; *Medée* by Marc-Antoine Charpentier, Lyon, France, 1984; *Hamletmachine* by Heiner Müller, New York, 1986, London and Paris, 1987. **Films**—*The House*, 1963; *Slant*, 1963; *Overture for a Deafman*, 1971.
Set Designer: **Plays**—*America Hurrah* by Jean-Claude van Itallie, New York, 1966; *A Letter to Queen Victoria*, New York, 1975.

* * *

Robert M. Wilson is not a dramatist if by this term one means playwright. He is a highly resourceful visual artist whose working materials are not paint, canvas, metal, whatever, but instead the varied resources of theater, including teams of lesser collaborators. The works themselves, including *The Life and Times of Joseph Stalin*, *Einstein on the Beach*, and *the CIVIL warS*, are stately processions of visual images, metaphors if you will, that reverberate in presentation into suppressed text, slow-motion movement or dance, and minimalist music. He increasingly chooses to call these extravaganzas, especially in connection with his association with composer Philip Glass, "operas," and with their unfamiliar-familiar worlds, improbable juxtapositions, evolving repetitions, and time distortions these "motion pictures" achieve the mysterious fascination of dreams.

The announcement of a planned production of *Parsifal* in 1990 to be directed by Wilson is especially apt since no one in today's theater better exemplifies Wagner's famous esthetic, the merger of text, music, and the visual. Or Wagner's prodigious ambition. Or his dedication to interminable length. Wilson's current work has been gradually coalescing into the five-act *the CIVIL warS*, with a connecting section which has been separately performed as *Knee Plays*. Although the whole was intended to be mounted in parts in different countries with international collaborators and presented at the 1984 Olympics, it has thus far been performed only in sections. With

Zeus and Wagner's generous King Ludwig unavailable, assembling this olympian enterprise has thus far not been financially feasible. But although the Wagnerian scope of his concept is undeniable, Wilson's starting point is undoubtedly modern painting, particularly Magritte, whose wonderful juxtapositions suggest a sub-text that continues to intrigue and elude. The surreal Dali of *The Pervasiveness of Memory* with its melting of time, the "hallucinatory succession of contradictory images" of Max Ernst, Dubuffet, collages and assemblages, and Mondrian come inevitably to mind. Wilson's de-emphasis of the third dimension and stress upon horizontals and verticles as in *Knee Plays*, or the felling of the tree totem Abraham Lincoln in the Prologue and Act 5 of *the CIVIL warS* particularly suggests the latter. Pageants, parades with their floats and occasional inflated airborne characters, and variations of the *tableau vivant* also seem to have made their contributions by intent or unconscious coincidence.

Certainly specific personal experiences, such as his slowing down of speech to overcome stuttering and his well known work with the autistic and the Byrd Hoffman Foundation, have played an important role in shaping Wilson's artistic tendencies, especially toward what might be called his technique of suppression and repetition. In his work not only is time slowed down, text frequently absent or incomprehensible, but melody, in the musical accompaniments by Glass, is also simplified and endlessly repeated. The slowing whirling mammies, the long-distance runner who seems to move in water in the first act of *The Life and Times of Joseph Stalin*, and the monologue of the old lady after long silence in its brilliant second act, "The Victorian Bedroom," a verbal explosion quite remarkable in recent drama, are examples of the method's triumph.

Of course, the question of "meaning" naturally poses itself. The international and communal reach of his endeavors; the earlier use of such figures as Stalin, Einstein, and Freud as presiding icons; and the preoccupation of *the CIVIL warS* with other historical characters and various world myths suggest an answer. Since the outset, Wilson seems to have been striving for a communal and timeless synthesis of compelling images, a kind of contradictory slow-motion shorthand of the history of human experience. The conscious strategy for expressing this dramatic *Finnegans Wake* Wilson has best explained himself in discussing that forthcoming *Parsifal*, an opera also infused with myth. He pointed out that what the audience will see on stage is not necessarily what the work is "about." What one sees or hears in a Wilson work, in other words, is not what one gets. What one "gets" is really what by subliminal inference these sights and sounds suggest.

A brilliant and overreaching artist, Wilson has perhaps the most original and controversial sensibility at work in modern theater.

—Gaynor F. Bradish

WILSON, Snoo (Andrew Wilson). British. Born in Reading, Berkshire, 2 August 1948. Educated at Bradfield College, Berkshire, 1962–66; University of East Anglia, Norwich, 1966–69, B.A. (upper second) in English and American studies 1969. Married Ann McFerran in 1976; two sons and one daughter. Founding director, Portable Theatre, Brighton and London, 1968–75; script editor, *Play for Today* series, BBC Television, 1972; dramaturge, Royal Shakespeare Company, 1975–76; director, Scarab Theatre, 1975–80. Henfield Fellow, University of East Anglia, 1978. Recipient: John Whiting Award, 1978; US Bicentennial fellowship, 1980. Agent: Jenne Casarotto, Douglas Rae Ltd., 28 Charing Cross Road, London WC2H 0DB. Address: 41 The Chase, London SW4 0NP, England.

PUBLICATIONS

Plays

Girl Mad As Pigs (produced Norwich, 1967).
Ella Daybellfesse's Machine (produced Norwich, 1967).
Between the Acts, adaptation of the novel by Virginia Woolf (produced Canterbury, 1969).
Charles the Martyr (produced Southampton, 1970).
Device of Angels (produced Edinburgh and London, 1970).
Pericles, The Mean Knight (also director: produced London, 1970).
Pignight (also director: produced Leeds and London, 1971). With *Blowjob*, London, Calder, 1975.
Blowjob (produced Edinburgh and London, 1971). With *Pignight*, London, Calder, 1975.
Lay By, with others (also director: produced Edinburgh and London, 1971). London, Calder and Boyars, 1972.
Reason (as *Reason the Sun King*, produced Edinburgh, 1972; as *Reason: Boswell and Johnson on the Shores of the Eternal Sea*, in *Point 101* produced London 1972; as *Reason*, produced Chicago, 1975). Published in *Gambit* (London), vol. 8, no. 29, 1976.
England's Ireland, with others (also director: produced Amsterdam and London, 1972).
Vampire (produced London, 1973). Published in *Plays and Players* (London), July 1973; revised version (produced London, 1977; New York, 1979), Ashover, Derbyshire, Amber Lane Press, 1979.
The Pleasure Principle: The Politics of Love, The Capital of Emotion (produced London, 1973). London, Eyre Methuen, 1974.
The Beast (produced London, 1974; New York, 1977). Published in *Plays and Players* (London), December 1974 and January 1975; revised version, as *The Number of the Beast* (produced London, 1982), with *Flaming Bodies*, London, Calder, and New York, Riverrun Press, 1983.
The Everest Hotel (also director: produced London, 1975). Published in *Plays and Players* (London), March 1976.
A Greenish Man (televised 1975; produced London, 1978). London, Pluto Press, 1979.
The Soul of the White Ant (produced London, 1976). London, TQ Publications, 1978; New York, French, 1983.
Elijah Disappearing (produced London, 1977).
England-England, music by Kevin Coyne (produced London, 1977).
The Glad Hand (produced London, 1978). London, Pluto Press, 1979.
In at the Death, with others (produced London, 1978).
The Language of the Dead Is Tongued with Fire (produced London, 1978).
Flaming Bodies (produced London, 1979). With *The Number of the Beast*, London, Calder, and New York, Riverrun Press, 1983.
Magic Rose (produced London, 1979).
Spaceache, music by Nick Bicât (produced Cheltenham and London, 1980).
Salvation Now (produced Seattle, 1981).

The Grass Widow (produced Seattle, 1982; London, 1983). London, Methuen, 1983.
Our Lord of Lynchville (produced New York, 1983).
Loving Reno (produced New York, 1983; also co-director: produced London, 1983).
La Colombe, music by Gounod, adaptation of the libretto by Barbier and Carré (produced Buxton, Derbyshire, 1983).
Hamlyn (produced Loughborough, Leicestershire, 1984).
Orpheus in the Underworld, with David Pountney, music by Offenbach, adaptation of the libretto by Crémieux and Halévy (produced London, 1985).
More Light (also co-director: produced London, 1987).

Screenplay: *Shadey*, 1986.

Television Plays: *The Good Life*, 1971; *Swamp Music*, 1972; *More about the Universe*, 1972; *The Barium Meal*, 1974; *The Trip to Jerusalem*, 1975; *A Greenish Man*, 1975; *Don't Make Waves* (*Eleventh Hour* series), with Trevor Griffiths, 1975.

Novels

Spaceache. London, Chatto and Windus, 1984.
Inside Babel. London, Chatto and Windus, 1985.

*

Critical Study: interview in *Theatre Quarterly* (London), Spring 1980.

Theatrical Activities:
Director: **Plays**—*Pericles, The Mean Knight*, London, 1970; *Pignight*, Leeds and London, 1971; *Lay By*, Edinburgh and London, 1971; *England's Ireland*, Amsterdam and London, 1972; *Bodywork* by Jennifer Phillips, London, 1974; *The Everest Hotel*, London, 1975; *Loving Reno* (co-director, with Simon Callow), London, 1983; *More Light* (co-director, with Simon Stokes), London, 1987.
Actor: **Plays**—*Lay By*, London, 1971; The Porpoise in *Freshwater* by Virginia Woolf, London, 1983.

Snoo Wilson comments:

(1973) More than anything else the proscenium arch theatre suggests the success of drawing room conversation as a mirror for a mature civilization. In these mirrors, the even keel of the state slices through the waters of unconsciousness, and very few playwrights have managed to knock any holes in the boat, though a number have suggested that the ship was sinking without their assistance, and others, like the stewards on the *Titanic*, bicycle gaily round the first-class gym, declaring that there is no list to the ship. These last are the ones most likely to be rewarded by the first-class passengers for their élan vital, even while the bilge water is rising round the ankles of the steerage families. The bicycling stewards are most likely to be able to command support that is quite independent of anything except people's gratitude at being amused, and many of them die peacefully in their beds declaring that there was always a slight list to port anyhow, and their reward was plainly a just one since people came and gave willingly, and were briefly happy.

A different brand of steward feels considerable unease at the condition of the ship, and his actions are likely to be much less popular at first than the bicyclists, though as time passes and his costume becomes charmingly archaic his pieces will be revived as Art, safe now from the Life he tried to redirect, which will have moved on in a lateral, unexpected direction. Television in Britain created a brand of "responsible" playwrights whose reputations at first were large and abrasive but now have stabilised in characteristic and therefore unsurprising because recognisable positions of social dynamism, and there the matter rests, a compromise acceptable both to producers who would like to produce more radical plays but have taken "Grandmother's footsteps" as far as they think the head of drama will let them, and to an audience stunned by tedium and kept alive by a feeling they ought to watch plays, sustained by tiny whiffs of excellence that occur in the smog of apathy. Both television and the theatre with one or two exceptions had failed either to make any formal advances in technique or to investigate areas of emotion which would force advances on them: I say "failed" because I believe that there must always be a technical evolution in theatre if only to remind audiences that they are watching a particular genre: playwrights who are adept at naturalism can take the edge off the most workmanlike oeuvre by making its naturalism subliminal.

The small groups who started with very little assistance at first—sometimes none—from the Arts Council in the late 1960's had a different sort of audience, a different sort of motive, and were a growth outside the conventional structure of theatre in Britain largely because it was dull and extremely conservative and did not provide outlets for the sort of things they wanted to do, or, in the case of Portable Theatre, a writer's theatre first, to write. Since there was very little money anyway the opportunity to write what the writer wanted to write and put it on in the way he wanted was possible, and a series of one night stands provided continuous platforms for plays which in the beginning we were prepared to take anywhere.

Now, there are a large number of studio theatres, almost a circuit, round the country. The success of *Lay By*, a group play written round a newspaper story, at the Edinburgh Festival, suggested that it was desirable and possible to launch a play about contemporary events to tour large theatres round England and Scotland. After six months of extreme difficulty we managed to set up a tour of a play about Northern Ireland, called *England's Ireland*, which had its first three weeks in Holland because we were unable to find theatres in England in sufficiently large numbers prepared to take the risk of an unknown play by a previously, quote, experimental group.

When we did bring the play to England, sadly it was in Chalk Farm at the Roundhouse rather than in Glasgow where it drew a significant response, and Lancaster and Nottingham were the only large repertory companies which would have it.

This demonstrates, among other things, the self-stultifying conservatism of the control of British theatre boards who believe that their audiences should be fed what they are accustomed to consume, either the costume drama of Ibsen's Choice, or on plays which by ignoring all but the most trivial of human difficulties and miseries close minds rather than open them in a stuffy two hours at the theatre.

The title I would choose for this essay, *The Freudian Landscape and the Proscenium Mind*, suggests that the middle-class mind is firmly ensconced on stage; this is true only by its being a self-perpetuating situation: it is not true that if we want to widen the range of theatrical experience we have to abandon the theatre. The theatre has always been a whore to safe fashion, but at the moment there is a pressure for a particular sort of awareness and articulacy which hopefully may lead to the good lady opening her legs to a different position, and renewed and enlarged clientele being the result. The plangent cries of either the affronted audience or management should not be an invitation to a secondary dialogue, whose end is respectability. Nor should this secondary dialogue be mistaken for a play, for the theatre is not that self-sufficient, being old, and bloated with the worst vices of time serving and sycophancy: and these will show through shallow devices. It is ourselves, finally, rather than the civilisation, who we have to prove mature; so, paradoxically, the struggle for exposure which shapes the ideas must not dent them, any more than an achieved articulacy within theatrical convention supplants the need for further thought.

* * *

Snoo Wilson began his writing career in the late 1960's with Portable Theatre, of which he was a founding director along with two friends from Cambridge, David Hare and Tony Bicât—Wilson himself studied at the then new University of East Anglia. His earlier plays, particularly *Pignight* and *Blowjob*, are extremely clever and dark works which reflect a good many of Wilson's general preoccupations. Though never an overtly "political" dramatist Wilson has always been concerned with problems of individual psychology, in particular schizophrenia, with moral anarchy, and most specifically with the threat of pollution on a planet which, like the absurdists with whom he has so much in common, he shows to be in direct if often comic opposition to man's dreams and aspirations. In *Pignight* a Lincolnshire farm is taken over by a sinister gangster and turned into a machine for the organized butchering and processing of the animals in question. Underneath this surface violence runs a thread of eerieness—Smitty, a psychopathic farm labourer inherited by the new owners, is a running reminder of the war (he suffers from mysterious brain damage) and takes delight in committing acts of savagery (including the blowing up of the farm dog, Robby). *Blowjob* is an equally violent exercise in alienation, with two skinheads planning to blow up a safe in a factory, an act which they bungle. During their travels they meet up with a homosexual security guard who tries unsuccessfully to pick them up and with a girl student who, typically for the time of the play, is alienated from her academic environment—the whole play acting as a caustic comment on role-playing and its stultifying effect on personality.

Both *Vampire* and *The Pleasure Principle* are plays which further develop Wilson's preoccupation with external ethical codes and their effect on individual freedom. *Vampire*, which has been both revived and revised by Wilson, has a conventional three-act structure which moves from a late 19th-century Presbyterian parsonage and a scene of astral sex in an Edwardian cricket pavilion to a contemporary scene of youthful disquiet (the setting has been altered in a subsequent version from a secular funeral parlour to the pagoda in Kew Gardens), and finishes with Enoch Powell, risen vampire-like from the coffin and delivering his famous "Rivers of Blood" speech. The second act of *Vampire* is a neat example of Wilson's developing style.

In tune with a belief that the stage is the freest medium, he concentrates on sharp juxtapositions which transcend conventional unities of time and place, and—despite Wilson's often underestimated gift for composition—continually upstage the dialogue spoken by his characters. Sarah, an upper-class girl, is wooed by a handsome young cricketer called Henry, killed in World War I. He returns in his astral form to try and make love to Sarah who is frightened of being seen—Freud and Jung suddenly appear on stilts to discuss her hang-up in their own jargonistic fashion, while a talking ox grunts "Let's go to my place and fuck." *The Pleasure Principle* concentrates on the almost undefined relationship between two characters whose opposing ideas of pleasure prevent them from consummating their mutual attraction until the last act. Robert and Gale in fact make it after a seduction sequence played out in a cardboard swan, while the nervous breakdown of Robert, an aggressive businessman with a great belief in capitalism, is prefigured by the entrance of a pair of dancing gorillas bearing messages.

Wilson is by now something of grand old man of the British fringe but still refuses or is unable to be assimilated into the mainstream despite a belief on his own part that his plays are designed to be both popular and fun. Indeed he has developed an eclectic and mercurial interest in occult subjects and in trendy pseudo-science. In *The Beast* and *The Soul of the White Ant*, the latter a quite breathtaking short play, he has explored the worlds of two dead cult figures, the satanist Aleister Crowley and the South African naturalist Eugène Marais, whose reputation, part visionary's, part charlatan's, is tested by the methods of free association that characterise Wilson's work at its best. The title of the play derives from one of Marais's works about the corporate soul which Wilson employs as a metaphor for the collective insanity of his characters, a group of white South Africans who congregate in and around a bar run by a boozy eccentric, Mabel. In typical Wilsonian fashion, the bar is mud-caked and threatened by etymological disaster while Marais himself enters as a back-street abortionist, white-suited, visionary, and also corrupt, a combination of killer and life-giver, as symbolized by an act which he performs when Mabel goes mad and shoots her houseboy, whose carefully collected sperm is now filling her freezer. When the stuff is thrown into the local river two of Mabel's friends, Edith and June, are impregnated and it is Marais who saves them, but only after Mabel's bizarre act of racial and sexual mutilation.

Wilson's most ambitious and perfectly realised play to date is probably *The Glad Hand* which works on many levels both as a political thriller and as a bizarre and often whacky study in synchronisation. On the surface the piece concerns the attempt of one Ritsaat, a South African fascist, to locate and confront the anti-Christ whom Ritsaat claims to have been present on earth during a cowboy strike in Wyoming in 1886. Ritsaat's plan is simple: he will charter an oil tanker and by time-travel via the Bermuda Triangle confront the anti-Christ in person. In fact Ritsaat, through ingenuously offering "cowboy fun" in his recruiting advertisement, acquires two camp actors as part of the crew, along with a family of stock "Paddy" Irish, a portly American scriptwriter, a Cuban cook, a CIA agent, and a dubious psychic surgeon who performs an operation on board. Indeed the ship acts as setting for the recreated cowboy strike which includes passages of riveting documentary description of conditions prevailing at the time of the "real" incident (which did in fact happen). There's also the arrival on board of a raunchy American lesbian who sparks off several more of the play's coincidences until a final mutiny against Ritsaat's rule develops into an alliance of Cuban cook and chauvinist Irishman. Before dying Ritsaat manages to utter: "Between you and your perceptions is the mirror which you think reflects reality." It's a comment which sums up a good deal of Wilson's own intentions. Indeed in showing that "reality" is something which can be changed or at least rearranged he is making both a theatrical point about naturalism and a political point about the world as it exists, although how much real substance there is behind the technique is open to serious questioning.

In *A Greenish Man* Wilson employs his associative powers on the subject of Northern Ireland. Troy Phillips, a half-Irish Liverpudlian, is sent to Kilburn on an errand of revenge and encounters an IRA dinner being organized by the local Irish publican and a bedraggled factory owner who has perfected a formula for green paint made entirely from grass clippings, as well as a battered divorée with a liberal conscience and a tax lawyer. It's a play which fell down in production because the knots with which Wilson tied up the different strands of his ideas didn't survive the tug of live performance.

Flaming Bodies is set in the smart and characterless office of a Los Angeles film producer, whose overweight, compulsively hungry script editor, Mercedes, has just been sacked but refuses to leave the office. Again, Wilson uses this Hockneyesque setting as a launching pad for a trip in which Mercedes rediscovers herself, but only after experiencing such events as a Chevy from another film crashing through the window of the office block, King Herod discovering his love of small boys (the film she's working on at the time of her sacking is a life of Christ), Mary and Joseph (both pregnant) turning up on an inflatable donkey, and her mother's ashes turning up in a film producer's lunch! Indeed Mercedes spends a good deal of the time on the phone, talking to her mother to whom she protests her lesbianism, and to her psychiatrist, to whom she protests her sanity. In the flip, weight-conscious world of California film production, Mercedes is attacked on all sides—even by her dead father who hovers in the air outside the office's huge picture window.

In the cartoon play *Spaceache* Wilson created an Orwellian world where the unwanted and unemployed are cryogenically freeze-dried and reduced to milk-bottle size before being sent into orbit until their time comes for resurrection. This play certainly does not exhibit Wilson's talents at their most representative, unlike those in which surface organization is being continually broken up and recreated and, in an often mundane theatrical terrain, supernatural forces or natural powers are often the real arbiters of the proceedings.

Unfortunately as he reaches maturity Wilson's refusal to compromise on his chosen artistic progression has continued to cause him problems. Though he has moved with some success into novels, films, and opera, his work refuses to find a home on the main stages of any of Britain's premier subsidised companies despite initial plans and interest from both the National and the Royal Shakespeare Company. His last play for the Royal Court, *The Grass Widow*, was a rather unsuccessful jumble of ideas and effects inspired by a year's sabbatical in California. *The Number of the Beast* was an effectively reworked version of *The Beast*. Wilson's obsession with Aleister Crowley still produces dividends, and the piece was an immensely entertaining essay on Crowley's bizarrely revolutionary life, and is soon to be filmed. Wilson's other film, *Shadey*, with Anthony Sher as the eponymously sexually confused character, was well reviewed. But his single most stunning recent success was the libretto for David Pountney's production of Offenbach's *Orpheus in the Underworld*, a much-seen version for the English National Opera. Here it seemed that Wilson's ability to challenge accepted notions of taste and presentation, his impressive grasp of theatrical metaphor, were welded to a firm base. Sadly, though his work is increasingly produced abroad, notably in America, he remains an exciting playwright still to realise his enormous potential at home.

—Steve Grant

WOOD, Charles (Gerald). British. Born in St. Peter Port, Guernsey, Channel Islands, 6 August 1932. Educated at Chesterfield Grammar School, 1942–45; King Charles I School, Kidderminster, 1945–48; Birmingham College of Art, 1948–50. Served in the 17/21st Lancers, 1950–55: Corporal. Married Valerie Elizabeth Newman in 1954; one son and one daughter. Factory worker, 1955–57; designer, scenic artist, and stage manager, Theatre Workshop, London, 1957–59; staff member, Bristol *Evening Post*, 1959–62. Recipient: *Evening Standard* award, 1963, 1973; Screenwriters Guild award, 1965. Fellow, Royal Society of Literature, 1985. Agent: Fraser and Dunlop Scripts Ltd., 91 Regent Street, London W1R 8RU. Address: The Manor, Milton, Banbury, Oxfordshire OX15 4HH, England.

PUBLICATIONS

Plays

Prisoner and Escort (televised 1961; produced in *Cockade*, London, 1963).
Cockade (includes *Prisoner and Escort, John Thomas, Spare*) (produced London, 1963). Published in *New English Dramatists 8*, London, Penguin, 1965; published separately, New York, Grove Press, 1967.
Tie Up the Ballcock (produced Bristol, 1964; New York, 1986). Published in *Second Playbill 3*, edited by Alan Durband, London, Hutchinson, 1973.
Don't Make Me Laugh (produced London, 1965).
Meals on Wheels (produced London, 1965; shortened version produced Liverpool, 1971).
Fill the Stage with Happy Hours (produced Nottingham, 1966; London, 1967). Published in *New English Dramatists 11*, London, Penguin, 1967.
Dingo (produced Bristol and London, 1967). London, Penguin, and New York, Grove Press, 1969.
Labour (produced Bristol, 1968).
H, Being Monologues at Front of Burning Cities (produced London, 1969). London, Methuen, 1970.
Colliers Wood (produced Liverpool, 1970; London, 1971).
Welfare (includes *Tie Up the Ballcock, Meals on Wheels, Labour*) (produced Liverpool, 1971).
Veterans; or, Hairs in the Gates of the Hellespont (produced Edinburgh and London, 1972). London, Eyre Methuen, 1972.
The Can Opener, adaptation of a play by Victor Lanoux (produced London, 1974).
Jingo (produced London, 1975).
The Script (produced London, 1976).
Has "Washington" Legs? (produced London, 1978; Cambridge, Massachusetts, 1981). With *Dingo*, London, Eyre Methuen, 1978.
The Garden (produced Sherborne, Dorset, 1982).
Red Star (produced London, 1984).
Across from the Garden of Allah (produced Guildford, Surrey, and London, 1986).
Tumbledown: A Screenplay. London, Penguin, 1987.

Screenplays: *The Knack*, with Richard Lester, 1965; *Help!*, with Mark Behm, 1965; *Tie Up the Ballcock*, 1967; *How I Won the War*, 1967; *The Charge of the Light Brigade*, with John Osborne, 1968; *The Long Day's Dying*, 1968; *The Bed-Sitting Room*, with John Antrobus, 1969; *Fellini Satyricon* (English dialogue), 1969; *Cuba*, 1980; *Vile Bodies*, 1981.

Radio Plays: *Cowheel Jelly*, 1962; *Next to Being a Knight*, 1972.

Television Plays: *Prisoner and Escort*, 1961; *Traitor in a Steel Helmet*, 1961; *Not at All*, 1962; *Drill Pig*, 1964; *Drums along the Avon*, 1967; *A Bit of a Holiday*, 1969; *The Emergence of Anthony Purdy, Esq.*, 1970; *A Bit of Family Feeling*, 1971; *A Bit of Vision*, 1972; *Death or Glory Boy*, 1974; *Mützen ab*, 1974; *A Bit of an Adventure*, 1974; *Love Lies Bleeding*, 1976; *Do As I Say*, 1977; *Don't Forget to Write!* series, 1977, 1979; *Red Monarch*, from stories by Yuri Krotkov, 1983; *Wagner*, 1984; *Puccini*, 1984; *Dust to Dust* (*Time for Murder* series), 1985; *Company of Adventurers* series, 1986 (Canada); *My Family and Other Animals*, from the book by Gerald Durrell, 1987.

*

Critical Studies: *The Second Wave* by John Russell Taylor, London, Methuen, and New York, Hill and Wang, 1971; *Revolutions in Modern English Drama* by Katharine J. Worth, London, Bell, 1973.

Theatrical Activities:
Director: **Film**—*Tie Up the Ballcock*, 1967.
Actor: **Film**—*The Knack*, 1965.

* * *

All art is presumably the transmutation of personal experience; but, in the case of Charles Wood, the two are unusually closely linked. He served in the army: two of his major plays, and two of his shorter ones, concern it. He worked in the theatre: *Fill the Stage with Happy Hours* takes place in and around the bar and offices of a small-town rep. He has written scripts for, and worked on the sets of, several films: *Veterans* is reportedly based on the shooting of *The Charge of the Light Brigade*, and its main character bears an uncanny likeness to Sir John Gielgud, who in fact starred in both film and play. Such a method of functioning has its advantages, notably a more thorough comprehension of the subject in question, and its obvious dangers, notably the lack of perspective that often results from an author being emotionally too close to his material. But Wood is very far from being an unreflective, impetuous writer, and, as it turns out, succumbs to no such danger. In all, or nearly all, his plays, we can safely say that he has transmuted autobiography into art, "art" being defined in this context as work of some general validity, speaking effectively to the minds, hearts, and spirits of more than the odd, isolated individual.

Wood first came to notice with *Cockade*, and, particularly, with *Prisoner and Escort*, the principal of the three short plays that constituted it. The other two, *John Thomas* and *Spare*, were intellectually fuzzier, linguistically less striking and generally less memorable: this was clearly the voice of a young writer with an individual command of language and a strong sense of theatre. Briefly, it concerns two crude and disagreeable soldiers escorting a third, Jupp, in a train back to the prison from which he has apparently absconded, having disgraced himself and his unit by publicly urinating on the boots of a visiting German general. They handcuff him to the luggage rack: he bears the discomfort stoically, but is clearly not altogether the righteous and sympathetic figure we might believe him, as is suggested not only by what is rightly diagnosed as his "high and mighty" manner, but by the instinctive disgust with which he hears that a girl fellow-traveller is in fact sexually attached to a black. There is a moral ambivalence about Jupp and his situation characteristic of Wood, and several other idiosyncracies which make the piece helpful as an introduction to his later work. There is the strong, fascinated grasp of a particular milieu, in this case, military, with its distinctive manners and slang, and, in the fascination, some evidence of nostalgia and affection, notwithstanding its ugliness. There is the transformation of informal English, including (and perhaps especially) the slang, into a distinctive dramatic poetry, imaginative, metaphoric, rhythmic, and yet persuasively "real," even naturalistic. And there is a hint of what may be seen as the overriding theme of his work to date, that of the gulf between pretension and fact. By humiliating a German general in so decided a fashion, Jupp (and his author) is not only drawing attention to the supposed hypocrisy of fêting a recent enemy: he is, he says, "shooting it up the kilt of every stupid bastard as braces up to the beat of a drum... every twat as thinks it's more than just a great carve-up." He is, if you like, protesting against the ceremony and sentiment that make some forget that an army is essentially designed to kill people.

Such ideas are most evident, however, in *Dingo*, which was described by a major critic as "one of those milestones at which a younger generation overthrows the taste and beliefs of an older one." It is a bitter play, poised, calculated, and yet fiercer than anything written in the period of the "angry young men," ten years earlier; an attack on all who would tend to glamourize, not just war, but a particular war that most of us still think justified, World War II. Satiric scenes are juxtaposed with painfully real ones. On the one hand, we catch a British officer in the act of doltishly hero-worshipping Rommel, as many actually did, a parody of General Montgomery describing the war as a tennis match, and prisoners, dressed as chorus girls for a camp concert, tunnelling out of German territory in a burlesque of British escape films. On the other, we see soldiers kicked to death by their fellow-soldiers, bayonetted by guards, and screaming as they burn in tanks. "That's enemy," says the cynical protagonist, Dingo, as a crazed private cuddles the charred corpse of his friend, "You won't find a photograph, a statue, a painting of a British soldier like that"; and he and his mate take bets on the time of the death of an officer they direct into a minefield, and then they masturbate. Once again, the gulf between what has been called "the aftermyth of war" and the truth about it is shown to be total; and so captivated by this aperçu is Wood that he neglects to answer satisfactorily what seems a vital question, whether it was right to fight Hitler at all. Churchill, says Dingo, "pissed" on us; the war was fought "for all the usual reasons"; and that is that.

The piece does, however, have the power of its overstatement, and proved more theatrically gripping than the thematically somewhat similar *H* did, though this may have been partly due to the latter's awkward first production at the National Theatre. *H* is ambitious and prolix, taking us, as it does, from the beginning of the Indian mutiny to the evacuation of Lucknow: it is beautifully written, in dialogue that capitalizes on the concreteness, the slight primness, and the marginally incorrect grammar the author finds in idiomatic Victorian speech: it is also considerably more subtle than *Dingo*. General Havelock, the "H" of the title, is warmer, more humane and considerate, than General Neill, the ferocious "scourge of the Lord," who would slaughter every Sepoy if he could. Nevertheless, he allows his troops to revel and loot, he shoots rebels from guns, and he is, as Wood sees it, fighting a palpably unjust colonial war: all of which is hard to reconcile with his high principles, religious convictions, and tendency to use most human encounters for a proselytizing homily. His way of life is designed to disprove "the vile falsehood that it is never possible to be a soldier and a Christian at the once"; the sad irony is that it tends to prove exactly that. The truest (because most open and unpretentious) representative of British military might is probably not New Testament Havelock, nor even Old Testament Neill, but the character Wood has said the play is "about": a genial, rather stupid, totally unselfquestioning Welsh captain who idealizes the war as much as any, but is mainly interested in securing himself a higher rank and more pay. The "holy" crusade against the mutineers was really about the advancement of the British nation and of individual members of the British army. Anything else is mere camouflage and self-deception.

Self-deception is also the theme of one of Wood's most successful pieces, *Fill the Stage with Happy Hours*. Its characters are the members and hangers-on of a run-down theatre, desperate for its next Arts Council grant; and most of them speak a theatrical language all their own, full of the obvious "loves" and "darlings," but put together by Wood with his usual style and imagination. These people no longer know what, if anything, they feel, and they have constructed a rhetoric which rarely does more than approximate to emotions either true or untrue. "You bitch; you're talking about our son; have a heart, love," says the manager's wife to the actress who is supposed to have seduced her son, and it is as if she were experimenting with three different methods of expressing the same, vague anger. First, there is melodrama, "bitch"; then something straighter and more factual; then a sentimental appeal; and all in the same sentence. Some people in the play are taken in by these verbal mis-hits and a few correctly diagnose them as "slab emotions—you can only laugh at them." The trouble, of course, is that not all "slab emotions" deserve laughter. Every now and then the manager's wife mentions she has had cancer confirmed, and may only have a short time to live, and by the end, it is clear that this may indeed be the case. But who can take it seriously? Even she seems to find it difficult to do so, having lived too far from reality for too long a time. The moral, which would seem to be that pretension rots the mind and heart, is put sadly and sympathetically by Wood, who is (as before) half in love with the verbose, chaotic, pathetic milieu he is so carefully recording.

Of his other plays, two deserve mention: *Meals on Wheels*, unusual in that it is not about the army or show business, but about old age, and *Veterans*, which touches on all three of these subjects. The first, which is repetitive, ill-organized, and generally agreed to be the least successful of the longer plays, does, however, have a certain vigour and ebullience in its satiric attempts to dispose (characteristically) of some of the myths that attach to the aged and supposedly venerable. Its characters spend their waning years shut away and full of vague resentments, pretending to one another they look more spry and youthful than they do and, mainly, expressing impotent lust in a salacious rhetoric which, as always, Wood handles with invention and wit. Indeed, it is possible that the piece is most memorable for the extraordinary variety of idiom with which the sexual act is invoked.

Veterans is slighter, but better: an entertaining account of life on location, and marked by a genuine affection for the main character, Sir Geoffrey Kendle, a kindly, gentle man, given to upsetting those around him with a devastating, but entirely unintended, tactlessness. Possibly the play is best seen as an act of homage to him, or rather to Sir John Gielgud, with whom he appears to have more than coincidental affinities. Most of the other characters are vulgar, selfish, and tedious by comparison, and the actual process of filming what seems to be a screenplay of Wood's own *H* is shown to be indescribably enervating, very far from the image of such events put about by the fan magazines. The horses are made of wood, and the young male heroes are neurotically concerned with their own uncertain virility. Yet, finally, the play does not achieve that general validity most of Wood's others do. The milieu, far from proving a satisfactory metaphor for human illusion and disillusion, as in *H* and *Fill the Stage with Happy Hours*, remains simply a well-depicted milieu: the insistence on its detail seems tantamount to a sustained in-joke about the British film industry: the total effect is nearer memoir than "art" in the sense postulated earlier. It goes without saying that a writer who has proved himself at once so intellectually questioning, verbally gifted, and dramatically assured is capable of much more than this.

—Benedict Nightingale

WRIGHT, Nicholas. British. Born in Cape Town, South Africa, 5 July 1940. Educated at Rondebosch Boys' School, Cape Town; London Academy of Music and Dramatic Art. Director, Theatre Upstairs, Royal Court Theatre, London, 1970–75; joint artistic director, Royal Court Theatre, 1976–77. Since 1984 associate director of new writing, National Theatre, London. Recipient: Arts Council bursary, 1981. Agent: Judy Daish Associates, 83 Eastbourne Mews, London W2 6LQ. Address: 33 Navarino Road, London E.8, England.

PUBLICATIONS

Plays

Changing Lines (also director: produced London, 1968).
Treetops (produced London, 1978).
The Gorky Brigade (produced London, 1979).
One Fine Day (produced London, 1980; New York, 1986).
The Crimes of Vautrin, adaptation of a novel by Balzac (produced Stockton-on-Tees, County Durham, and London, 1983). London, Joint Stock, 1983.
The Custom of the Country (produced London, 1983). London, Methuen, 1983.
The Desert Air (produced Stratford-on-Avon, 1984; London, 1985). London, Methuen, 1985.
Six Characters in Search of an Author, adaptation of a play by Pirandello (produced London, 1987).

* * *

Nicholas Wright's first play appeared as far back as 1968, but although he has spent most of his professional life in the theatre, he has not produced a large body of work. It is not yet possible to speak of a development in his writing, yet certain definite shifts of emphasis can be discerned within a drama which is notable for combining a careful eclecticism of form and mode with steady concentration on a large but well-defined thematic territory.

Wright's work focuses on periods of social and political change or transition and seeks to explore, in a wide range of ways, the relation of the individual, whether as agent or as victim, to the large historical movement. *Treetops*, his earliest success, is typical in its (South) African setting—Cape

Town in the year of the death of George VI and of the accession of Elizabeth II, 1952. The action is basically naturalistic, but the sunstroke-induced hallucination which prompts the disillusioned English liberal "Rusty" Walker to leave home and family, secede from the reactionary Torch Commando organization for ex-servicemen, and make an illegal gesture is presented surrealistically: Rusty realizes that he is standing within the footprint of a giant, and a chimpanzee on a bicycle brings an enigmatic message from the dead king which nonetheless makes it clear that the giant is the British Empire, within whose soon-to-be-dismembered body Rusty has been living. Rusty's political activism is a matter of quasi-physical impulse rather than of "correct analysis," but his liberal gestures serve to awaken the hitherto dormant energies of the friend to whom he appeals for help and advice, Leo Skiba, an émigré Lithuanian socialist ideologue and organizer. The personal and political symbiosis which moves Leo finally to action and which affords Rusty "moments of the most intense joy" is throughout paralleled, indeed partly articulated, by the movingly realized relationship—one of affection and provocation, need and violence—between Rusty's son Rupert and Leo's son Mark.

The debt to Brecht evident in Wright's formal strategies throughout his work is most clearly felt in *The Gorky Brigade*, which again scrutinizes the relation between political organization, energy for action, and individual dissent at a time of historical change. In Year Three of the Soviet revolution (1920–21), the revolutionary teacher Ekaterina undertakes the supervision and instruction of a colony of teenage "bourgeois anarchists." In Act 1 her initial despair, her new "scientific" (dialectical) teaching methods, and her eventual success in enabling the colonists to form themselves into the "Gorky Brigade" (under which banner they rob rich peasants in order to further their own revolutionary purposes), are presented in a series of scenes after the Brechtian epic model, some of them attached to rubrics taken from Gorky. However, the Gorky sentences are rotated ironically in Act 2 when Ekaterina's star student Minnie, who has been away at university for six years, returns to the colony. Gorky himself is at last to visit his admirers, and she has come to request his help and influence in the case of a professor of hers who is being condemned and persecuted for his work in genetics. The colony, once in the vanguard of the revolution but now isolated and out of touch by virtue of its very idealism, humiliates and rejects Minnie; and Gorky, feeling himself (after his sojourn in Italy) "europeanized" into doubt and non-commitment, can respond to her appeals, despite his climactic public reaffirmation of Soviet aims and thinking, only with gestures of impotence and bad faith. Yet Minnie will not *retreat* into individual dissent. She refuses to leave the colony again, and as the play ends she is trying to call a meeting of all the colonists in order to regalvanize revolutionary principles and action.

In both *Treetops* and *The Gorky Brigade*, different though they are formally and stylistically, the exploration of the role of individual dissent in the process of political change is clearly shaped and underwritten by a commitment to socialism. In his plays of the 1980's, however, Wright's dramatic attitude towards the individual as a motive force in history is firmly ironic, and his treatment less direct than in those of the late 1970's. The tendency, already apparent in the earlier plays, to make a character represent or embody an attitude or class or group emerges with increasing strength through a more obvious stylization of action. In reference to Wright's latest original play, *The Desert Air*, "embody" is emphatically the word. The enormous central figure (memorably incarnated in the Royal Shakespeare Company production by Geoffrey Hutchings), a caricature on a heroic scale, is Colonel—later Brigadier—"Hippo" Gore, a "vulgar toad" in whose "swollen and distended" gut is embodied a whole social movement and moral attitude. Put in charge of a Secret Service unit in wartime Cairo (1942–43), the Hippo dedicates himself to "wangling" his way up through the class-determined hierarchy of the British army, a "stumpy" intent on toppling "those long, tall, *pointy* bastards." Thus the class war cuts across and usurps in importance the World War, and the transference of British support in occupied Yugoslavia from the royalist Chetniks to the communist-led Partisans is effected not by principle or decisive strategic thinking but by the Hippo's self-interested wangling. The physical state figures forth the moral one, often hilariously, sometimes painfully, in the Hippo and his agents, and although he is eventually disgraced, Gore is allowed a final "apotheosis" through a self-interested self-sacrifice, his distended body blown apart at last for the sake of glory in posterity as the man who had "the *guts* to change" British policy—literally.

Wright's handling of the ironic interaction of representative figures is even more impressive in *The Custom of the Country*—all the more so as it is negotiated within the strict generic framework of romantic comedy. Title and plot both derive from Fletcher and Massinger, and there is an authentically Jacobean relish of pace and event in the conduct of a narrative charged with the pathos of yearning and unfulfilment. Wright's decision to set the play in the cultural melting-pot of the southern Africa of the 1890's (mostly Johannesburg) serves to introduce a political dimension into the comedic action. It is the plot's several plotters, rather than the young-married lovers they manipulate, who are the central representative figures: the self-deluding "entrepreneuse," brothel-keeper Daisy Bone, who is persuaded to cast the missionary hero Paul as her "perfect love"; her business manager, the Eastern European Jewish intellectual Lazarus, who looks forward to a moral apocalypse and finds union in death with Daisy; the Afrikaner goldmine owner Henrietta van Es, whose hitherto frustrated femininity finds its sexual object in Paul's "gentleman of leisure" brother Roger, and its maternal project in the reclamation of her errent "zombie" son Willem; and Dr. Jamieson, the agent of British imperialist designs on the African interior whose ultimate success ensures the preparation and impending dispatch of a Pioneer Column to the territory which will eventually become Rhodesia. Happy ending and historical implication are thus posed in an ironic counterpoint which is emphasized by the innocently portentous curtain speech of Paul's African bride Tendai. Such precision of dramatic nuance is characteristic of this play, and indeed of Wright's work at its best.

—Paul Lawley

WYMARK, Olwen (Margaret, née Buck). American. Born in Oakland, California, 14 February 1932. Educated at Pomona College, Claremont, California, 1949–51; University College, London, 1951–52. Married the actor Patrick Wymark in 1950 (died 1970); two daughters and two sons. Writer-in-residence, Unicorn Theatre for Young People, London, 1974–75, and Kingston Polytechnic, Surrey, 1977; script consultant, Tricycle Theatre, London; Lecturer in Playwriting, New York University. Member, Arts Council of Great Britain Drama Panel, 1980–84. Recipient: Zagreb Drama Festival prize, 1967. Lives in London. Agent: Harvey Unna and Stephen Durbridge Ltd., 24–32 Pottery Lane, London W11 4LZ, England.

PUBLICATIONS

Plays

Lunchtime Concert (produced Glasgow, 1966). Included in *Three Plays*, 1967; in *The Best Short Plays 1975*, edited by Stanley Richards, Radnor, Pennsylvania, Chilton, 1975.
Three Plays (as *Triple Image: Coda, Lunchtime Concert, The Inhabitants*, produced Glasgow, 1967; *The Inhabitants*, produced London, 1974). London, Calder and Boyars, 1967.
The Gymnasium (produced Edinburgh, 1967; London, 1971). Included in *The Gymnasium and Other Plays*, 1971.
The Technicians (produced Leicester, 1969; London, 1971). Included in *The Gymnasium and Other Plays*, 1971.
Stay Where You Are (produced Edinburgh, 1969; London, 1973). Included in *The Gymnasium and Other Plays*, 1971; in *The Best Short Plays 1972*, edited by Stanley Richards, Philadelphia, Chilton, 1972.
No Talking (for children; produced London, 1970).
Neither Here nor There (produced London, 1971). Included in *The Gymnasium and Other Plays*, 1971.
Speak Now (produced Edinburgh, 1971; revised version produced Leicester, 1975).
The Committee (produced London, 1971). Included in *Best Friends, The Committee, The Twenty-Second Day*, 1984.
The Gymnasium and Other Plays. London, Calder and Boyars, 1971.
Jack the Giant Killer (produced Sheffield, 1972). Included in *The Gymnasium and Other Plays*, 1971.
Tales from Whitechapel (produced London, 1972).
Daniel's Epic (for children), with Daniel Henry (produced London, 1972).
Chinigchinich (for children; produced London, 1973).
Watch the Woman, with Brian Phelan (produced London, 1973).
The Bolting Sisters (for children; produced London, 1974).
Southwark Originals (collaborative work for children; produced London, 1975).
The Twenty-Second Day (broadcast 1975; produced London, 1975). Included in *Best Friends, The Committee, The Twenty-Second Day*, 1984.
Starters (collaborative work for children; includes *The Giant and the Dancing Fairies, The Time Loop, The Spellbound Jellybaby, The Robbing of Elvis Parsley, I Spy*) (produced London, 1975; Wausau, Wisconsin, 1976).
Three For All (collaborative work for children; includes *Box Play, Family Business, Extended Play*) (produced London, 1976).
We Three, and After Nature, Art (produced London, 1977). Published in *Play Ten*, edited by Robin Rook, London, Arnold, 1977.
Find Me (produced Richmond, Surrey, 1977; Louisville, 1979). London, French, 1980.
The Winners, and Missing Persons (for children; produced London, 1978).
Loved (produced London, 1978; Syracuse, New York, 1979). London, French, 1980.
The Child (broadcast 1979). London, BBC Publications, 1979.
Please Shine Down on Me (produced London, 1980).
Female Parts: One Woman Plays (includes *Waking Up, A Woman Alone, The Same Old Story, Medea*), adaptations of plays by Dario Fo and Franca Rame, translated by Margaret Kunzle and Stuart Hood (produced London, 1981). London, Pluto Press, 1981.
Best Friends (produced Richmond, Surrey, 1981). Included in *Best Friends, The Committee, The Twenty-Second Day*, 1984.
Buried Treasure (produced London, 1983).
Best Friends, The Committee, The Twenty-Second Day. London, Calder, and New York, Riverrun Press, 1984.
Lessons and Lovers (produced York, 1985).
Nana, adaptation of the novel by Zola (produced London, 1987).

Radio Plays: *The Ransom*, 1957; *The Unexpected Country*, 1957; *California Here We Come*, 1958; *The Twenty-Second Day*, 1975; *You Come Too*, 1977; *The Child*, 1979; *Vivien the Blockbuster*, 1980; *Mothering Sunday*, 1980; *Sea Changes*, 1984; *A Wreath of Roses*, from the novel by Elizabeth Taylor, 1985; *Mothers and Shadows*, from a novel by Marta Traba, 1987.

Television Plays: *Mrs. Moresby's Scrapbook*, 1973; *Vermin*, 1974; *Marathon*, 1975; *Mother Love*, 1975; *Dead Drunk*, 1975; and *Her Father's Daughter*, 1984 (all in *Crown Court* series); *Oceans Apart*, 1984; *Not That Kind of People*, 1984.

* * *

Olwen Wymark has written some three dozen plays for radio, television, and stage. These range from one-act plays through full-length ones, and her children's plays typify the playful side of her personality. Indeed smallness figures again and again in her work—though, like so much else, one has to unmask it from her work even as she herself relies on a series of unmasking for dramatic effect. *Find Me*, for example, is a documentary play about a mentally disturbed girl who had, in real life, died in a special hospital. Those expecting the play to concentrate sympathy on the little girl must have been disappointed: it is far easier to sympathize with the restaurant owners, friends, and family who have their peace and property destroyed by the girl's predilection for starting fires. Indeed, though she died in the hospital, viewers find themselves sympathizing with the desperate hospital authorities rather than with Verity. She is so small as to disappear in the maelstroms she creates. It is difficult to find her, let alone love her. For the play was sparked off by letters which the girl had written, and which her family had allowed Wymark to read; one began, "Dear Whoeveryouare. Please find me and have me as your beloved." Here, in Wymark's view, is everyman's dilemma: you feel unsure of yourself, and yet it is precisely that self-doubt which fuels creativity. At least it is so in her own case.

Her early plays are exteriorizations of internal anguish, games devised by the characters to reflect and exercise their griefs and dissatisfactions. In *The Gymnasium*, two friends begin a friendly boxing match, with the elderly and gentlemanly one requesting his pretty cockney partner not to talk. They have hardly commenced sparring when the boy turns on a stream of vitriolic abuse. There is plenty of time to attempt puzzling this through, before one realizes that this is a regular marriage therapy session, in which the cockney plays the gentleman's wife and incites his partner to beat him up instead of the wife who is protected by the fine walls of custom and civility.

Most of Wymark's plays are about boringly familiar situations, rooted as they are in the emotional hothouse of upper-middle-class life. What makes the plays dramatic is a lively sense of timing; she offers to her audience the pleasure of solving marvellously constructed puzzles. It is not always possible to sort out the stories, however; and, as in *Neither Here nor There*, "a series of false certainties recede in infinite perspective. Her characters fall through one trapdoor to the solid ground beneath, only to find that collapsing beneath them as well" (Irving Wardle's review in the *Times*). Is the play a comment on the nightmarish quality of experience? Hardly, because the schoolgirls are inventing the whole game themselves.

Situation and theme; anxieties, tensions, and emotional states; guilt, futility, and desperation—these come across in her bizarre and intense plays much more strongly than characters and situations, though these are presented starkly enough. Whenever it is possible to piece her stories together, one begins to care for her characters. Otherwise her plays remain merely ingenious. Witty, arresting at their best, their lack of shape reflects a deeper problem. *Stay Where You Are* shows us a girl at the mercy of two people who appear to be lunatics. Their lunacy turns out, however, to be designed to wake her from her complacency. Quasi-existentialism no longer brings the excitement it did in the 1960's, and this is Wymark's biggest problem: she needs to find something new or fresh or more substantial that she can say through the pressure and sparkle of her work.

What saves her work is that she is aware of this, and that she laughs at herself: *The Technicians* is a marvellous attack on technical cunning which operates in a moral vacuum. Modern experimental theatre is here hoist with its own petard, and what makes the attack poignant is that Wymark loves modern theatre; in it she lives and moves and has her being.

—Prabhu S. Guptara

YANKOWITZ, Susan. American. Born in Newark, New Jersey, 20 February 1941. Educated at Sarah Lawrence College, Bronxville, New York, B.A. 1963; Yale University School of Drama, New Haven, Connecticut, M.F.A. 1968. Married Herbert Leibowitz in 1978; one son. Recipient: Vernon Rice award, 1970; MacDowell Colony fellowship, 1971, 1973; National Endowment for the Arts fellowship, 1972, 1979; Rockefeller grant, 1973; Guggenheim fellowship, 1974; Creative Artists Public Service grant, 1974; New York State Council on the Arts grant, 1984; Japan/US Friendship Commission grant, 1985. Agent: Gloria Loomis, Watkins/Loomis Agency, 150 East 35th Street, New York, New York 10016. Address: 205 West 89th Street, New York, New York 10024, U.S.A.

PUBLICATIONS

Plays

The Cage (produced New York, 1965).
Nightmare (produced New Haven, Connecticut, 1967; New York, 1968).
Terminal (produced New York, 1969). Published in *Three Works by the Open Theatre*, edited by Karen Malpede, New York, Drama Book Specialists, 1974.
The Ha-Ha Play (produced New York, 1970). Published in *Scripts 10* (New York), October 1972.
The Lamb (produced New York, 1970).
Slaughterhouse Play (produced New York, 1971). Published in *New American Plays 4*, edited by William M. Hoffman, New York, Hill and Wang, 1971.
Transplant (produced Omaha, 1971).
Basics, in *Tabula Rasa* (produced New York, 1972).
Positions, in *Up* (produced New York, 1972).
Boxes (produced New York, 1972). Published in *Playwrights for Tomorrow 11*, edited by Arthur H. Ballet, Minneapolis, University of Minnesota Press, 1973.
Acts of Love (produced Atlanta, 1973).
Monologues for *Wicked Women Revue* (produced New York, 1973).
Wooden Nickels (produced New York, 1973).
America Piece, with the Provisional Theatre (produced Los Angeles, 1974).
Still Life (produced New York, 1977).
True Romances, music by Elmer Bernstein (produced Los Angeles, 1977).
Qui Est Anna Marks? (Who Done It?) (produced Paris, 1978).
A Knife in the Heart (produced Williamstown, Massachusetts, 1983).
Baby (original story), book by Sybille Pearson, music by David Shire, lyrics by Richard Maltby, Jr. (produced New York, 1983).
Alarms (produced London, 1987).

Screenplays: *Danny AWOL*, 1968; *The Land of Milk and Funny*, 1968; *Silent Witness*, 1979.

Radio Plays: *Rats' Alley*, 1969; *Kali*, 1969.

Television Writing: *The Prison Game* (*Visions* series), 1976; *The Forerunner: Charlotte Perkins Gilman*, 1979; *Arrow to the Sun: The Poetry of Sylvia Plath*, 1987.

Novel

Silent Witness. New York, Knopf, 1976.

*

Manuscript Collection: Kent State University, Kent, Ohio.

Critical Studies: interviews with Erika Munk in *Performance* (New York), December 1971, and Arthur Sainer in *The Radical Theatre Notebook* edited by Sainer, New York, Avon, 1975.

Susan Yankowitz comments:

(1973) Most of my work for the theatre has been an attempt to explore what is intrinsically unique in the theatrical situation. That is, I've been interested in sound, gesture, and movement as a corollary to language; in the interaction between the visual and verbal elements of stage life; in the fact of live performers engaged with live audience members in an exchange; and in the development of a theatrical vocabulary. My work has been generally informed by the social and political realities which impinge on all our lives; these, to a large extent, influence and shape my plays. In addition, I have been interested in a collective or collaborative approach to evolving works for the theatre and in working improvisationally with actors and directors to "find" a play which is a creative expression of our shared concerns.

At present, I am growing more concerned with the question of language—its limits and possibilities—and am moving into the realm of fiction which I feel is a more appropriate medium for that adventure.

* * *

Susan Yankowitz enlivens non-realistic, highly theatrical images of sociological problems with music, dance, pantomime, patterned speech, bold sets and costumes. These devices reinforce her verbal attacks on such contemporary social sins as conformity, alienation, racism, and sexism. These devices also enable her to avoid didacticism. Yankowitz's emphasis on *theatre* was undoubtedly encouraged by the Open Theatre, whose ensemble work contributed to the several versions of the published text of *Terminal*. *Terminal* cannot be understood apart from the Open Theatre production; the text merely suggests the performance and may be altered by other groups.

Terminal achieves unity through ritual rather than through coherent plot. It argues that people must face their deaths, and satirizes people who do not. The dying in *Terminal* turn to "Team Members" who offer them a mass-produced panacea for death. The living conduct this impersonal ritual; they also embalm and touch up the dead to hide the fact of death. The dead pierce the subterfuge practiced by and upon the dying; they "come through" the dying to judge the living and themselves. The enactment of necrophilia or the graphic description of embalming involves the audience in this common human fate.

As ritual is the binding thread in *Terminal*, so the structure of a parable unifies *The Ha-Ha Play*. Like *Terminal*, this play exposes a general human failing, but emphasizes rectification rather than exposure. Children, abducted to a woods (in which the audience sits) by hyenas wearing masks, learn to communicate through laughter. Communication is thus not only possible between groups, but it also dissolves enmity between them.

In contrast to *Terminal* and *The Ha-Ha Play, Slaughterhouse Play* traces the growth of consciousness of a unifying character, the black slaughterhouse worker, Junius. *Slaughterhouse Play* attacks racism: its central symbol is the slaughterhouse, which whites run and in which blacks work, slaughtering black troublemakers and selling their "meat" to whites. As in *Terminal*, action and dialogue involve the audience. The most prized black meat is that of the male genitals, which a white butcher displays in his shop, and which Junius and other rebellious black steal to wear around their necks as symbols of their rebellion. *Slaughterhouse Play* ends with a sequence in which blacks stab whites and whites shoot blacks repeatedly.

Not only is *Boxes* in a much lighter vein than *Slaughterhouse Play*, but literal boxes function theatrically as a fictional slaughterhouse cannot. Characters carve windows in boxes, and from within those boxes define themselves according to type and speak in clichés. Yankowitz underlines this conformity by having the characters wear hats with boxes that match their box dwellings. People in their separate boxes perform their daily chores at the same time that others experience great pain or joy. Such caricature unifies *Boxes*. Ultimately the boxes become coffins.

Yankowitz dramatizes individual or social problems and involves her audience either by shock or mimicry. Once engaged, the audience is forced to admit its responsibility for such failures as avoiding death, alienation, conformity, and racism. And this is Yankowitz's aim.

—Frances Rademacher Anderson

ZINDEL, Paul. American. Born in Staten Island, New York, 15 May 1936. Educated at Port Richmond High School, Staten Island; Wagner College, New York, B.S. in chemistry 1958, M.Sc. 1959. Married Bonnie Hildebrand in 1973; one son and one daughter. Technical writer for chemical company, New York, 1959; chemistry teacher, Tottenville High School, New York, 1960–69; playwright-in-residence, Alley Theatre, Houston, 1967. Recipient: Ford grant, 1967; Obie award, 1970; Vernon Rice award, 1970; New York Drama Critics Circle award, 1970; Pulitzer Prize, 1971. D.H.L.: Wagner College, 1971. Lives in New York City. Agent: Curtis Brown, 10 Astor Place, New York, New York 10003. Address: c/o Harper and Row, 10 East 53rd Street, New York, New York 10022, U.S.A.

PUBLICATIONS

Plays

Dimensions of Peacocks (produced New York, 1959).
Euthanasia and the Endless Hearts (produced New York, 1960).
A Dream of Swallows (produced New York, 1964).
The Effect of Gamma Rays on Man-in-the-Moon Marigolds (produced Houston, 1965; New York, 1970; Guildford, Surrey, and London, 1972). New York, Harper, 1971; in *Plays and Players* (London), December 1972.
And Miss Reardon Drinks a Little (produced Los Angeles, 1967; New York, 1971; London, 1976). New York, Random House, 1972.
Let Me Hear You Whisper (televised 1969). New York, Harper, 1974.
The Secret Affairs of Mildred Wild (produced New York, 1972). New York, Dramatists Play Service, 1973.
The Ladies Should Be in Bed (produced New York, 1978). With *Let Me Hear You Whisper*, New York, Dramatists Play Service, 1973.
Ladies at the Alamo (also director: produced New York, 1975).
A Destiny with Half Moon Street (produced Coconut Grove, Florida, 1983).

Screenplays: *Up the Sandbox*, 1973; *Mame*, 1974; *Maria's Lovers*, with others, 1984; *Runaway Train*, with Djordje Milicevic and Edward Bunker, 1985.

Television Play: *Let Me Hear You Whisper*, 1969.

Novel

When a Darkness Falls. New York, Bantam, 1984.

Fiction (for children)

The Pigman. New York, Harper, 1968; London, Bodley Head, 1969.
My Darling, My Hamburger. New York, Harper, 1969; London, Bodley Head, 1970.
I Never Loved Your Mind. New York, Harper, 1970; London, Bodley Head, 1971.
I Love My Mother. New York, Harper, 1975.
Pardon Me, You're Stepping on My Eyeball! New York, Harper, and London, Bodley Head, 1976.
Confessions of a Teenage Baboon. New York, Harper, 1977; London, Bodley Head, 1978.
The Undertaker's Gone Bananas. New York, Harper, 1978; London, Bodley Head, 1979.
The Pigman's Legacy. New York, Harper, and London, Bodley Head, 1980.

A Star for the Latecomer, with Bonnie Zindel. New York, Harper, and London, Bodley Head, 1980.
The Girl Who Wanted a Boy. New York, Harper, and London, Bodley Head, 1981.
To Take a Dare, with Crescent Dragonwagon. New York, Harper, 1982.
Harry and Hortense at Hormone High. New York, Harper, 1984; London, Bodley Head, 1985.
The Amazing and Death-Defying Diary of Eugene Dingman. New York, Harper, and London, Bodley Head, 1987.

*

Manuscript Collection: Boston University.

Theatrical Activities:
Director: **Play**—*Ladies at the Alamo*, New York, 1975.

* * *

Most parts in most plays are male. In realist and humorist Paul Zindel's work, however, almost all the roles are for women. They aren't very nice women, to be sure. They tend, like so many of Tennessee Williams's women, to be neurotic freaks. The tormented women who people his plays are dumpy and defensive, lonely and lacerating, bitter and—psychologically, at least—brutal. Yet Zindel stirs our compassion by imparting to them a vulnerability which guarantees that they must endure at least as much pain as they inflict.

Not all of Zindel's characters are adults. Perhaps because he was initially a high school chemistry teacher on his native Staten Island, he has taken an interest in the distress of young people, not only in his best known play, *The Effect of Gamma Rays on Man-in-the-Moon Marigolds*, but also in such teen novels as *My Darling, My Hamburger, The Pigman*, and *The Pigman's Legacy*. He likewise introduces animals in his scripts with considerable frequency.

Regardless of who their victims may be, Zindel's characters damage those for whom they have reason to feel affection and to whom they are bound, either by blood or in other ways. Where the relationship is familial or a surrogate for the sibling, parental, or conjugal bond, the suffocating initimacies create a dramatic tension familiar from the work of such other American writers of domestic drama as Inge, Williams, O'Neill, and Miller. Most of Zindel's characters are sexually unfulfilled. Despite their tenacity in surviving, his creations are clinging to unlived lives or, in the nuclear terminology of *Marigolds*, half lives, which in some of the plays are shadowed by the dead and the doomed. Yet the terrible plight in which Zindel's characters find themselves is relieved by considerable humor.

The melodrama *Marigolds* has enjoyed far more success than any other of Zindel's plays. Its original New York production ran for over two years and won its author several prizes. This play takes its remarkable title from the project on this subject which withdrawn Tillie, a girl in her early teens, has prepared for her school science fair. Tillie finds solace in the perspective of her place in the whole history of evolution beginning with the creation of the universe. Understanding the continuity of life, of energy and matter, encourages her to look beyond her own squalid surroundings. Her attitude contrasts sharply to the narcissism shared by her crude older sister Ruth and cynical mother Beatrice.

Beatrice is at once eccentric, selfish, and pathetic. She forces Tillie to miss school and then lies about it to the teacher. When she's angry at the other kids' derision of Tillie, her resentment stems not from sympathy with her daughter but from a suspicion they're really ridiculing her. She flirts with the teacher on the phone but insults him behind his back, talks constantly of hairbrained get-rich-quick schemes, taunts and torments her helpless senile boarder and her emotionally crippled daughers. And she kills the girls' pet rabbit.

Yet we grow fond of Beatrice, and of Ruth too, in spite of her resemblance to her mother, with whom she shares lipstick, cigarettes, hostilities, and neuroses. We observe Ruth's dread of thunder and death and her mother's fear of failure and life, we watch them wounded and comfort each other, and we find Zindel's craft compelling us to care for women who might well have seemed monsters. When Ruth destroys her mother's confidence and makes her miss the science fair in which Tillie's project wins first prize, we even appreciate the agony out of which she chloroforms Ruth's rabbit.

Marigolds dramatizes a recurrent Zindel subject, disturbed women, and a recurrent Zindel theme, the suffering friends and relatives inflict on their "loved ones." All three women are "crazies" whose behavior reflects that of more controlled but no less destructive "normal" people. Just as the marigolds have been exposed to gamma rays, these women have been subjected to high concentrations of anguish; Ruth and Beatrice corresponds to the dwarfed plants and Tillie to the rare mutants made beautiful by more moderate radiation.

In *And Miss Reardon Drinks a Little*, another play which depicts women who both cause pain and suffer from it, Zindel sides with the vulnerable but abnormal against the ruthless or insensitive but normal. Each Miss Reardon—one alcoholic, the other depressive—is harmless compared to their executive sistei and her unsupportive husband. In one respect, that couple resemble Mildred and her spouse in *The Secret Affairs of Mildred Wild*. The sexual repression which is mostly implicit in the earlier play, however, becomes an explicit issue in the latter. Mildred absorbs herself in movie magazines and cinematic fantasies instead of her marriage, and her husband in his turn fails to consummate an extra-marital affair because he's distracted by his sweet tooth. While Mildred watches day and night, her diabetic candy-store owner of a husband is swallowing all his merchandise. Naturally both the business and the relationship are bankrupt. Yet somehow the pair survive their eccentricities and—more importantly—their disillusionment with each other to subscribe to the further fantasy of reconciliation.

The farce of *Mildred Wild*—complete with a modernization of the screen scene from *The School for Scandal*—is less successful than the acerbic wit—replete with profanity and obscenity—of *Ladies at the Alamo*. More of a cat fight than a literal shoot-out, this play does take place in Texas, where control of a regional theatre constitutes the battle's stakes. Even though the Alamo is only a theatre, a massacre of sorts does occur, with devastating destruction wrought to each of the five women's egos. Funny, foul-mouthed insults fly amid women feuding over whether the Artistic Director, Dede, will continue to run the theatre she's built from a little box into an empire. The loyalities are complex, the betrayals still more so. Dede is far from admirable and probably wins because she's the biggest bully, but when the dust settles we're somehow glad she's survived. *Alamo* is another Zindel triumph in manipulation of audience sympathies.

The drunken neurotics of that play resemble the bridge players of a short work, *The Ladies Should Be in Bed*. The principal action in this play forms a minor incident as well in *Alamo*, when one of the women maliciously phones parents of teenagers and reports sexual activity with a "pervert." But it's the ladies themselves who are sex obsessed and therefore "should be in bed." Sexuality is likewise the subject of *A Destiny with Half Moon Street*, in which a teenage boy unsure of his sexual preference is thrust temporarily by his mother's employment as a nurse into a gay male household.

Social responsibility becomes the focus in the dramatization of Zindel's *The Pigman* (by F. Andrew Leslie) and in *Let Me Hear You Whisper*. In the former, teenagers behave with a mixture of compassion and lack of integrity towards a lonely old man. When he dies, however, they come to accept their own complicity in the messed up, grown-up world. In the latter, a cleaning woman and a talking dolphin behave with more awareness of their responsibility to others than do the geniuses who control their world. The heroine in this play, in her humane responses to the pathetic plight of the experimental animal, demonstrates a degree of maturity and unselfish commitment to others which is unusual in Zindel's menagerie of female misfits.

—Tish Dace

SCREENWRITERS

"Unless a picture was exceptionally interesting he never rented sound equipment. He had found that lip-reading and guesswork gave the picture an added dimension, and anyhow the dialogue was usually offensively banal" ("Three Stories" by John Cheever). The attitude of Cheever's character toward film dialogue and, by implication, toward screenwriting in general represents a view of the profession popular since the days when adolescent Anita Loos began writing titles for Biograph. Surprisingly, three recent films, the American *The Stunt Man* and *Sweet Liberty*, and the Russian *A Slave of Love*, though they carry vastly different aesthetic and ideological burdens, present the familiar portraits of harried, confused, apologetic screenwriters. *The Stunt Man* and *Sweet Liberty* may allot more time to their characters' artistic and social anxieties, but both films follow the traditional view of the screenwriter as hack, writing to order, and, even when talented, sacrificing his vision to the more commercial goals of the others involved in the filmmaking process. These insider portraits suggest familiar questions: what did Faulkner contribute to *Land of the Pharaohs*, and where is Nathanael West's voice in *Five Came Back*? Or, conversely, to what extent does *The Godfather* represent the vision of a minor talent like Mario Puzo? Of major writers, perhaps only Graham Greene in *The Fallen Idol* and, to a lesser extent, in *The Third Man* succeeded in translating his recognizable world to the screen, though the final script for *The Third Man* owes a great deal to Orson Welles and Joseph Cotten (when Greene had no voice in adaptations of his novels like *Ministry of Fear*, the results were less happy). Greene benefitted from both a film sense derived from years of motion picture reviewing and the enthusiastic collaboration of the director Carol Reed. The screenwriters in *The Stunt Man, Sweet Liberty*, and *A Slave of Love*, however, reflect the traditional view of the profession expressed in the 1950 *Sunset Boulevard*: "Audiences don't know somebody sits down and *writes* a picture. They think the actors make it up as they go along." This view seems especially surprising today because of widespread interest in the screenwriter as rival to the director for title of *auteur*. The influential critic Pauline Kael has emphasized the importance of Herman Mankiewicz's script contributions against those who see *Citizen Kane* as primarily the work of director Orson Welles, and she has suggested that the writer Jules Furthman's image of the good-bad girl was as crucial to films like *Morocco* and *To Have and Have Not* as were the contributions of their *auteur* directors von Sternberg and Hawks. Other critics have judged *Atlantic City* to be more the work of dramatist John Guare than of director Louis Malle. (Conversely, a few years ago most critics assumed that *The Long Goodbye* was essentially the creation of director Robert Altman and not of veteran writer Leigh Brackett.) Even Andrew Sarris, the chief classifier of *auteur* directors, acknowledged that Mae West, like other film comedians, had a crucial role in the form of her films because of her comic persona, an image fostered by the scripts she wrote for herself. Screenwriters have recently begun to assert their celebrity status even further by choosing camp (Babaloo Mandel) or macho (L. M. Kit Carson) professional names. This current tendency has reached its apotheosis in the career of Oliver Stone. Even before he directed his scripts for *Salvador* and *Platoon*, he had promoted a Hemingwayesque image as a man of action whose Vietnam and drug experiences authenticated his flashy, often implausible scripts for *Midnight Express* and *Scarface*. The publicity he garnered suggested that the films were his visions and minimized their directors' contributions, a startling reversal of the auteurist trend of the past 30 years.

A wealth of published screenplays and memoirs by, and interviews with, screenwriters attests to the profession's growing prestige. Yet, however impressive these publications, they frequently raise unanswerable questions about the contribution of the writer to the completed film. Only a few of these screenplays, like Susan Sontag's for *Brother Carl* and *Duet for Cannibals*, provide detailed shot-by-shot directions, and information about such elements as clothing and decor. But then Sontag directed her scripts and was able to exercise the kind of total control writers can only aspire to; most screenplays are sparer and leave items like costumes to the director, actor, or designer. Because producers traditionally assigned several writers to a script, sometimes without each other's knowledge, it is difficult to assess the contribution of a single author to the final screenplay and to evaluate his style. Even when one author receives sole credit, others may have written dialogue or designed entire sequences. Despite the deliberations of the Writers Guild of America to resolve disputes among contributers, the official credits for a film are often misleading. The admirable series of Warner Brothers screenplays published by the University of Wisconsin Press with useful introductions on the provenance of the final script illuminates some of the problems inherent in assessing screenwriting. For example, the writers receiving official credit for *Yankee Doodle Dandy* apparently made a less significant contribution than did uncredited collaborators who polished the dialogue and created much of the atmosphere and tone. In addition, differences between the final screenplay and the completed film stem partly from last-minute changes by director Curtiz and star Cagney. In these days of even greater financial rewards and prestige for screenwriters, Guild arbitrations can become very complex and controversial. It is difficult to separate the contributions to *The Rose* of the talented Bo Goldman from those of Bill Kerby, to whom the Guild awarded co-screenplay and story credit.

A larger problem than assessing an individual author's role in a completed film involves understanding the hybrid nature of screenwriting—how much art compared to how much craft? The bleakest pronouncement from a serious writer (who ironically wrote none of the many film versions of his novels) is perhaps Raymond Chandler's: "as a result of [the Hollywood system] there is no such thing as an art of the screenplay, and there never will be as long as the system lasts, for it is the essence of this system that it seeks to exploit a talent without permitting it the right to be a talent" (*Atlantic Monthly*, August 1945). Chandler's bitterness, however, stems partly from circumstances for which Hollywood was not totally to blame: wartime Navy Department pressure caused him to change the murderer in his original screenplay for *The Blue Dahlia* from an unbalanced veteran to a civilian; the director, George Marshall, altered a sequence to accommodate an injured actor. Ideally, Paramount might have resisted government pressure even during World War II and might also have extended the shooting schedule, or replaced the actor. But surely Chandler's difficulties with this film (he had experiences equally humiliating to his artistic sense some years later when he worked with Hitchcock on *Strangers on a Train*) resulted from more than traditional Hollywood crassness. A more insightful account of the screenwriting process is Samson Raphaelson's memoir of his long collaboration with director Ernst Lubitsch ("Freundschaft," *New Yorker*, 11 May 1981). Raphaelson stressed the productivity of the daily script meetings during which the two frequently changed roles: Lubitsch "wrote some of my best lines, and I supplied some typical Lubitsch touches." In an interview of the PBS program *Creativity*, Raphaelson acknowledged that though none of his screenwriting "represented something that I profoundly stood for," he felt pride in his craftsmanship and gratitude for the opportunity to work closely with Lubitsch, whose talent he admired. Though such Lubitsch-Raphaelson works as *Trouble in Paradise* and *The Shop Around the Corner* do not reach the highest levels of screenwriting art, they reveal that the collaboration of complementary talents can produce wit and emotional nuance even in a medium directed to a mass audience.

Considerations of the screenwriter's status depend on whether he functions as the shaper of the entire film or primarily as a supplier of dialogue, often two distinct abilities. Even when a single writer is responsible for both elements, audiences often assume that the author of flat dialogue (the more noticeable element) could not have developed the interesting plot or design of the film: the visual impact of Joseph Losey's *Secret Ceremony* makes most of writer George Tabori's lines superfluous and threatens to undermine his important contribution to the film. *Possessed*, a 1947 Joan Crawford vehicle, fosters the illusion that the star, the cameraman, and the director, Curtis Bernhardt, had created the film without the help of its writers, Sylvia Richards and Ranald MacDougall. Certainly, tedious explanations of mental illness, and unrestrained romantic effusions impede the non-verbal elements that carry the film. Ironically, inept dialogue on a sufficiently grand scale can transform dull films into camp classics: *The Spectre of the Rose*, *Youngblood Hawke*, and *The Sandpiper*.

If film dialogue sometimes seems an attempt to underline the obvious or to condescend to the mass audience, this dialogue has been, at its best, one of the modest glories of talking pictures and the single element that sometimes redeems otherwise doomed projects. During early talkie days, despite awkward "stage" diction and actors trapped by cumbersome recording equipment into static postures, the dialogue frequently had an authentic verve—the writers seemed to be exulting in their new tool. A number of early sound films convey this exultation while dramatizing the consequences of overreliance on dialogue. A revelatory moment occurs in *The Big House* (1930, screenplay by Frances Marion), as battling prison guards and convicts suddenly vacate the screen, leaving the image of an empty and increasingly darkening corridor and the sound of off-camera voices shouting their anger. Though this film may talk, it no longer seems to move or even convey a clear picture. (The wonderful range of male and female squeaks through the microphone in the opening sequence of Chaplin's otherwise silent *City Lights* [1931] brilliantly demonstrates the importance of sound but mocks the concept of meaningful screen dialogue.) After the establishment of the rather strict motion picture code in 1933, dialogue seemed increasingly to fool unaware censors by innuendo and *double entendre*. The dialogue associated with writers like Dorothy Parker and Anita Loos (who had progressed beyond her silent titles) seemed especially sophisticated, and even today ageing film fans savor the same lines that delighted them as children. A fine example of the multiple shadings possible in a few skillful words is shady lady Glenda Farrell's initially offended, then questioning, and finally elated, "A cultured kiss!" as reluctant, dignified Supreme Court nominee Ronald Colman busses her forehead in the 1942 *The Talk of the Town* (screenplay by Irwin Shaw and Sidney Buchman). In recent films perhaps George Axelrod's dialogue in *The Manchurian Candidate* (1962) and *Lord Love a Duck* (1966) comes closest to the controlled irrationality of the best of 1930's and 1940's films. In *Lord Love a Duck* cocktail waitress Lola Albright attempts to allay daughter Tuesday Weld's fears: "Honey, you know I never go out with married men . . . on the first date." With the apparent near-total abandonment of censorship in the 1960's, film dialogue no longer has to rely on wit or grace to evade censors. Though occasionally this greater freedom creates an authentic sense of real language raised to almost surrealistic heights in a film like *M*A*S*H* (1970), too often it seems to punctuate the dialogue with vulgarities for easy laughs during otherwise dull stretches. Poor Mae West in the 1970 *Myra Breckenridge* seemed pathetically old-fashioned in contrast to the other actors, yet curiously crude when measured against her earlier triumphs of innuendo.

Of modern screenwriters responsible for the total design of the material as well as for the dialogue, the late Paddy Chayefsky had perhaps the most identifiable style, if only because his characters frequently indulged in shouting matches on ideological or social issues (English versus American values in *The Americanization of Emily*, conflicting medical attitudes in *Hospital*). Another signature component was his stress on the healing powers of marriage and other traditional institutions: among the healed are pathetic Bronxite Ernest Borgnine in *Marty*, confused office-worker Don Murray in *Bachelor Party*, and bruised adulterer William Holden in *Network* (though Chayefsky gradually evolved from being a recorder of the lives of "little" men, his themes remained constant). And the professional integrity and commitment of Chayefsky's protagonists often shade into madness, as in Melvyn Douglas's deranged admiral in *The Americanization of Emily*, Peter Finch's television newsman in *Network*, and William Hurt's scientist in *Altered States*. The production of *Altered States* dramatizes the precarious status of even today's established screenwriters. Chayefsky had early in his career become involved in the production of his films, and his contract for *Altered States* gave him approval of any script changes. This power caused a conflict with director Ken Russell, who was so unhappy with what he regarded as the inflated dialogue and pretensions of the screenplay that he undercut Chayefsky's intentions by having characters deliver their lines while eating or being drowned out by other dialogue or background noises. When John Huston decided that some of Walter Huston's speeches in *The Treasure of the Sierra Madre* (1948) were similarly inflated, he had the actor recite them without his teeth, a device that ironically strengthened the characterization while defeating the rhetoric. As writer-director, Huston was able to balance his two roles, while Chayefsky, in anger over the sabotage of his writing, retreated into the pseudonym of Sidney Aaron.

In an industry where the moneymen have the ultimate power, even an established writer-director like Orson Welles found it impossible to get his scripts to the screen. Billy Wilder, presumably because of his successes of the 1950's and 1960's and the admiration of bankable stars like Walter Matthau and Jack Lemmon, has continued to direct his screenplays (written with various collaborators), though his recent films disappoint and earn little or no money, and his fabled cynicism seems increasingly petulant. Another old-guard writer-director, Richard Brooks, no longer seems to be atoning for his early Maria Montez scripts with high-culture projects like *Lord Jim* or *The Brothers Karamazov*; after his successes with adaptations of polemical but popular bestsellers like *In Cold Blood* and *Looking for Mr. Goodbar*, Brooks now focuses on less successful issue-oriented adventures like *Wrong Is Right.* But whatever his materials, a familiar liberal stridency makes him an identifiable voice among practicing screenwriters.

Though Chayefsky's experience indicates that even powerful writers believe their visions betrayed, and though inflated costs make film financing very difficult today, talented writers still desert other media for motion pictures. Aside from wanting to share the tremendous commercial potential from television sales and "novelizations" of scripts, these authors apparently see screenwriting as capable of conferring critical prestige and opportunities for directing, a goal suggesting that some writers still regard the director as final arbiter of the film. The careers of Robert Benton and David Newman, whose screenplay for *Bonnie and Clyde* signaled the arrival of impressive talents, reveal these two chief directions for writers. After further collaborations with Benton, Newman continued to work with other writers on vast projects like *Superman* and *Superman II*. Though Benton had a part in the Superman collaborations, he gradually moved toward smaller films and assumed fuller control by directing his scripts for *The Late Show* (producer Robert Altman may have helped establish the tone of this film), and the rather thin *Kramer vs. Kramer*, and *Places in the Heart*, which became great commercial hits. Benton, however, seems to need a director less conventional than himself to strike sparks from his material. Woody Allen made successful transitions from producing material for nightclubs and Broadway, to screenwriting (sometimes in collaboration), to directing, though his films reveal their origins in nightclub routines and sometimes exhibit the same self-indulgence they attempt to parody. Even the recent *Hannah and Her Sisters* achieves its best moments in Allen's comic bits, which are related only tangentially to the "serious" themes of the film and which expose the fiftyish actor as increasingly ill-suited to his little-boy-lost antics. Robert Towne's debut directing his script for *Personal Best* was impressive. After making solid writing contributions to the elegant private-eye drama *Chinatown* and the sexual comedy *Shampoo*, in both of which he overstressed and weakened the political implications of his material, Towne created in *Personal Best* a sports film in which the physical grace of his protagonists suggests qualities of character that the script does not explicate. Unique among current writer-directors, Towne does not elevate his dialogue over the other filmic elements. The ambitious Paul Schrader, an astute film critic, has also become a writer-director, but has difficulty translating elements from Ozu and Bresson to his melodramatic plots. Schrader's loving direction of his script for *American Gigolo* was frequently exasperating as his camera lingered on Los Angeles settings out of Antonioni to point up the soullessness of the urban landscape. And inflated dialogue seemed ludicrous in the mouths of his demi-monde characters. But Schrader's serious commitment to films, even in flawed attempts to embody his *angst* in the persona of pop idol Michael J. Fox (*Light of Day*), suggests that the elements will one day fuse into a successful film. Another current *wunderkind* among writer-directors is Lawrence Kasdan, whose work on both the *Star Wars* sequel *The Empire Strikes Back* and *Raiders of the Lost Ark* must surely have gained him one of the largest audiences in film history. More a sympathetic recreator of past Hollywood genres than an innovator, Kasdan knows how to balance the serious and ironic treatment of movie serial material in *Raiders of the Lost Ark* and to give its heroine some modern anxieties. Similarly, *The Empire Strikes Back* smoothly blends cartoon adventure with hip jargon for its youthful audience. It is difficult to know how much of the film represents the contribution of the original writer, Leigh Brackett, or of the powerful producer, George Lucas, creator of the original *Star Wars*; it is equally difficult to assess the role of the writer on a project like *Raiders of the Lost Ark*, since the producer, Lucas, and the gifted director, Steven Spielberg, had worked on the film long before bringing in Kasdan. Thus, even today, when his profession seems especially prestigious, the screenwriter may still be the traditional "hired hand." Attempting to escape this category, however, Kasdan directed his screenplay for *Body Heat*, and his competent handling of the script only emphasizes the inadequacies of his conception. The guilty lovers meet to the strains of "That Old Feeling," a clue to Kasdan's desire to recreate the atmosphere of a 1940's film. But though his script has clever twists, his explicit dialogue and frequent images of sweating bodies and symbolic fires make obvious (and occasionally laughable) what seemed powerful in the *film noir* originals because it had to be suppressed. Since the lovers act out their sexual desires, their explosion into violence seems implausible in a world which affords total gratification. *Continental Divide* continued Kasdan's romance with earlier films, but the Tracy-Hepburn battle of the sexes seems anachronistic in the 1980's. Though *The Big Chill* was a commercial success, its melodramatic structure did not support its attempted portrait of middle-ageing 1960's radicals. And *Silverado* made a ludicrous effort to infuse 1980's liberalism into a classic western theme. However, Kasdan's command of film vocabulary and his apparent dedication to putting his vision on the screen make him worthy of future attention.

Among the non-directors, Bo Goldman, who was also involved with a major popular success as co-author of *One Flew over the Cuckoo's Nest*, revealed an authentic voice in scripts for *Melvin and Howard* and *Shoot the Moon*. His work creates the texture of family life, working class in *Melvin and Howard*, and Marin County sophisticated in *Shoot the Moon* (author Albert Finney cannot forget his anti-bourgeois bias even during a tense scene with estranged wife Diane Keaton: "You had dinner with an insurance man!"). Working in *Melvin and Howard* with folk-epic material reminiscent of Capra, Goldman believably rooted it in a 1970's milieu. Both these films offer remarkably tough-minded portraits of children, and both scripts tightly control their deceptively casual, episodic materials. Bo Goldman seems the most talented of a group of non-directors like William Goldman, whose commercially successful *Butch Cassidy and the Sundance Kid* and *All the President's Men* have earned him considerable power in Hollywood. Despite the pretensions to seriousness of *All the President's Men*, it remains, like *Butch Cassidy*, essentially an adolescent fantasy of two guys against the establishment, and too slick for the issues it treats. Steve Tesich, after the charming *Breaking Away*, crudely tangled politics and mystery in *Eyewitness*, and 1960's radicalism with a traditional coming-of-age story in *Four Friends*. But his idiosyncratic viewpoint is welcome among the hordes of anonymous Hollywood writers.

Tennessee Williams produced nothing significant during his tenure as an MGM screenwriter, and the playwrights David Mamet (*The Postman Always Rings Twice, The Verdict*) and David Rabe (*I'm Dancing as Fast as I Can*) have recently made less than impressive screenwriting debuts, though they exhibited enough skill to deserve additional screen opportunities. With greater success, Harold Pinter has worked steadily in films while continuing his important stage work. Pinter's scripts have been uneven: his best were those with director Joseph Losey; his disappointments include the adaptation of *The French Lieutenant's Woman*. But the witty screenwriting lesson that Robert De Niro gives Donald Pleasence in Pinter's version of *The Last Tycoon* reveals a fascination with the medium and an awareness of its limitations (the publication of Pinter's screenplay for *Remembrance of Things Past* is perhaps a tacit admission of its unsuitability for the screen). First-rate dramatists and novelists have rarely made successful transitions to screenwriting, though Pinter and Graham Greene may balance the failures. And then there are those special writers who have never produced a novel or a play but who combine visual imagination with verbal power to create those rare moments, or even hours, when the motion picture does faithfully and powerfully reflect a fine writer's vision and justify all those compromises, frustrations, and inevitable failures inherent in the screenwriting process.

—Burton Kendle

* * *

ALLEN, Jay Presson. Screenplays: *Marnie*, 1964; *The Prime of Miss Jean Brodie*, 1969; *Cabaret*, 1972; *Travels with My Aunt*, 1972; *Funny Lady*, 1975; *Just Tell Me What You Want*, 1980; *Prince of the City*, 1981; *Deathtrap*, 1982; *The Morning After*, 1986. Stage plays: *The Prime of Miss Jean Brodie*, from the novel by Muriel Spark, 1966 (published 1969); *Forty Carats*, from a play by Pierre Barillet and Jean-Pierre Grédy, 1968 (published 1969); *I and Albert*, music by Charles Strouse, lyrics by Lee Adams, 1972; *A Little Family Business*, from a play by Barillet and Grédy, 1982 (published 1983). Television writing: *The Borrowers*, 1973. Film producer and novelist.

ALLEN, Woody. Screenplays: *What's New Pussycat?*, 1965; *What's Up, Tiger Lily* (English version), with others, 1966; *Take the Money and Run*, with Mickey Rose, 1969; *Bananas*, with Rose, 1971 (published 1978); *Play It Again, Sam*, 1972 (published 1977); *Everything You Always Wanted to Know about Sex But Were Afraid to Ask*, 1972; *Sleeper*, with Marshall Brickman, 1973 (published 1978); *Love and Death*, 1975 (published 1978); *Annie Hall*, with Brickman, 1977 (Oscar; published 1978); *Interiors*, 1978 (published 1982); *Manhattan*, 1979 (published 1982); *Stardust Memories*, 1980 (published 1982); *A Midsummer Night's Sex Comedy*, 1982; *Zelig*, 1983 (published 1987); *Broadway Danny Rose*, 1984; *The Purple Rose of Cairo*, 1985 (published 1987); *Hannah and Her Sisters*, 1986 (Oscar); *Radio Days*, 1987. Stage plays: sketches in *From A to Z*, 1960, and *Graham Crackers*, 1963; *Don't Drink the Water*, 1966 (published 1967); *Play It Again, Sam*, 1969 (published 1969); *The Floating Light Bulb*, 1981 (published 1982). Radio plays include *God* (published 1975; staged 1979) and *Death* (published 1975; staged as *Death Knocks*, 1975). Actor and director; also novelist and musician.

ANHALT, Edward. Screenplays: *Strange Voyage*, with Edna Anhalt, 1946; *Avalanche*, with Edna Anhalt, 1946; *Bulldog Drummond Strikes Back*, with Lawrence Edmund Taylor and Edna Anhalt, 1947; *The Gentleman from Nowhere*, 1948; *The Crime Doctor's Diary*, 1949; *Panic in the Streets*, with others, 1950 (Oscar); *The Sniper*, with Edna Anhalt and Harry Brown, 1952; *The Member of the Wedding*, with Edna Anhalt, 1952; *Not as a Stranger*, with Edna Anhalt, 1955; *The Pride and the Passion*, with Edna Anhalt, 1957; *The Young Lions*, 1958; *In Love and War*, 1958; *The Restless Years*, 1959; *The Sins of Rachel Cade*, 1961; *The Young Savages*, with J.P. Miller, 1961; *Girls! Girls! Girls!*, with Allan Weiss, 1962; *A Girl Named Tamiko*, 1962; *Wives and Lovers*, 1963; *Becket*, 1964 (Oscar); *The Satan Bug*, with James Clavell, 1965; *Boeing, Boeing*, 1965; *Hour of the Gun*, 1967; *The Boston Strangler*, 1968; *In Enemy Country*, with Alfred Hayes, 1969; *The Madwoman of Chaillot*, 1969; *The Salzburg Connection*, 1971; *Jeremiah Johnson*, 1972; *Luther*, 1974; *The Man in the Glass Booth*, 1975; *Escape to Athena*, 1977; *Green Ice*, 1981; *The Holcroft Covenant*, with George Axelrod and John Hopkins, 1982. Stage play: *Thomas and the King*, music by John Williams, 1975. Television writing includes *A Time for Killing*, 1965; *QB VII*, from the novel by Leon Uris, 1974; *Contract on Cherry Street*, 1977; *Nowhere to Hide*, 1977; *The Day Christ Died*, 1980; *Madame X*, 1981; *Peter the Great*, from a book by Robert K. Massie, 1987. Writer of documentary films, and producer.

AXELROD, George. See his dictionary entry.

BENTON, Robert. Screenplays: *Bonnie and Clyde*, with David Newman, 1967; *There Was a Crooked Man*, with Newman, 1970; *What's Up, Doc?*, with Newman and Buck Henry, 1972; *Bad Company*, with Newman, 1972; *The Late Show*, 1977; *Superman*, with Newman and others, 1978; *Kramer vs. Kramer*, 1979; *Still of the Night*, with Newman, 1982; *Places in the Heart*, 1984 (Oscar). Stage plays: *It's a Bird ... It's a Plane ... It's Superman*, with Newman, music by Charles Strouse, lyrics by Lee Adams, 1966; sketch, with Newman, in *Oh! Calcutta!*, 1969. Film director.

BODEEN, DeWitt. Screenplays: *Cat People*, 1942; *The Seventh Victim*, with Charles O'Neal, 1943; *The Yellow Canary*, with Miles Malleson and P.M. Bower, 1943; *The Curse of the Cat People*, 1944; *The Enchanted Cottage*, with Herman J. Mankiewicz, 1945; *Night Song*, with Frank Fenton and Dick Irving Hyland, 1947; *I Remember Mama*, 1948; *Mrs. Mike*, with Alfred Lewis Levitt, 1949; *The Girl in the Kremlin*, with others, 1957; *Twelve to the Moon*, with Fred Gebhardt, 1960; *Billy Budd*, with Peter Ustinov and Robert Rossen, 1962. Stage plays include: *Romances by Emma* (published 1938); *First Dance* (published 1939); *Harvest of Years*, 1948. Novelist and writer on film and theatre.

BOLT, Robert. See his dictionary entry.

BROOKS, Richard. Screenplays: *Men of Texas*, with Harold Shumate, 1942; *Don Winslow of the Coast Guard*, with others, 1942; *White Savage*, 1943; *Cobra Woman*, 1944; *My Best Gal*, 1944; *Swell Guy*, 1946; *Brute Force*, 1947; *To the Victor*, 1948; *Key Largo*, with John Huston, 1948; *Any Number Can Play*, 1949; *Mystery Street*, 1950; *Crisis*, 1950; *Storm Warning*, with Daniel Fuchs, 1951; *The Light Touch*, 1951; *Deadline—USA* (*Deadline*), 1952; *Battle Circus*, 1953; *The Last Time I Saw Paris*, with Julius Epstein, 1954; *The Blackboard Jungle*, 1955; *The Last Hunt*, 1956; *Something of Value*, 1957; *The Brothers Karamazov*, with Julius Epstein, 1958; *Cat on a Hot Tin Roof*, with James Poe, 1958; *Elmer Gantry*, 1960 (Oscar); *Sweet Bird of Youth*, 1962; *Lord Jim*, 1965; *The Professionals*, 1966; *In Cold Blood*, 1967; *The Happy Ending*, 1969; *$*, 1971; *Bite the Bullet*, 1975; *Looking for Mr. Goodbar*, 1977; *Wrong Is Right*, 1982. Film director and novelist.

BUCKNER, Robert. Screenplays: *Gold Is Where You Find It*, with Warren Duff, 1938; *Love, Honor, and Behave*, with others, 1938; *Comet over Broadway*, with Mark Hellinger, 1938; *The Oklahoma Kid*, with others, 1939; *Dodge City*, 1939; *You Can't Get Away with Murder*, with Don Ryan and Kenneth Gamet, 1939; *Angels Wash Their Faces*, with others, 1939; *Espionage Agent*, with others, 1939; *Virginia City*, 1940; *Knute Rockne—All American*, 1940; *Santa Fe Trail*, 1940; *My Love Came Back*, with others, 1940; *Dive Bomber*, with Frank Wead, 1941; *Yankee Doodle Dandy*, with Edmund Joseph, 1942 (published 1981); *Rogue's Regiment*, with Robert Florey, 1948; *Sword in the Desert*, 1949; *Deported*, with Lionel Shapiro, 1950; *Free for All*, with Herbert Clyde Lewis, 1950; *Bright Victory*, 1951; *When in Rome*, with Charles Schnee and Dorothy Kingsley, 1952; *The Man Behind the Gun*, with John

Twist, 1953; *A Prize of Gold*, with John Paxton, 1955; *To Paris with Love*, with Sterling Noel, 1955; *Safari*, with Anthony Veiller, 1956; *House of Secrets* (*Triple Deception*), with Bryan Forbes, 1956; *Love Me Tender*, with Maurice Geraghty, 1957; *From Hell to Texas*, with Wendell Mayes, 1958; *Moon Pilot*, with Maurice Tombragel, 1962. Television writing includes *Return of the Gunfighter*, 1967. Film producer and novelist.

CASSAVETES, John. Screenplays: *Shadows*, 1959; *Too Late Blues*, with Richard Carr, 1962; *Faces*, 1968 (published 1970); *Husbands*, 1970; *Minnie and Moscowitz*, 1971 (published 1973); *A Woman under the Influence*, 1974; *The Killing of a Chinese Bookie*, 1976; *Opening Night*, 1978; *Gloria*, 1980; *Love Streams*, with Ted Allan, 1984. Stage play: *Knives* (published in *On Stage*, 1978). Film director and actor.

CLARKE, T.E.B. Screenplays: *For Those in Peril*, with Harry Watt and J.O.C. Orton, 1944; *Dead of Night*, with Angus MacPhail and John Baines, 1945; *Johnny Frenchman*, 1945; *Half-way House*, 1945; *Hue and Cry*, 1947; *Against the Wind*, with Michael Pertwee and Paul Vincent Carroll, 1948; *Passport to Pimlico*, with Henry Cornelius, 1949; *Train of Events*, with others, 1950; *The Blue Lamp*, with others, 1950; *The Magnet*, 1950; *The Lavender Hill Mob*, 1951; *The Ant and the Grasshopper*, in *Encore*, 1951 (published 1951); *The Titfield Thunderbolt*, 1953; *The Rainbow Jacket*, 1954; *Who Done It?*, 1956; *Barnacle Bill* (*All at Sea*), 1957; *Law and Disorder*, with Patrick Campbell, 1958; *A Tale of Two Cities*, 1958; *Gideon's Day* (*Gideon of Scotland Yard*), 1958; *Sons and Lovers*, with Gavin Lambert, 1960; *The Horse Without a Head*, 1963; *A Man Could Get Killed*, 1966; *A Hitch in Time*, 1979; *High Rise Donkey*, 1980. Novelist; autobiography: *This Is Where I Came In*, 1974.

DALRYMPLE, Ian. Screenplays: *The Good Companions*, with W.P. Lipscomb and Angus MacPhail, 1933; *Her Last Affaire*, 1935; *Jury's Evidence*, 1936; *The Brown Wallet*, with Stace Aumonier, 1936; *Radio Lover*, 1936; *Action for Slander*, with Miles Malleson, 1937; *Storm in a Teacup*, with Donald Bull, 1937; *The Divorce of Lady X*, with Lajos Biro and Arthur Wimperis, 1938; *Pygmalion*, with others, 1938 (Oscar); *South Riding*, with Donald Bull, 1938; *The Citadel*, with others, 1938; *Q Planes* (*Clouds over Europe*), with others, 1939; *French Without Tears*, with Terence Rattigan and Anatole de Grunwald, 1939; *The Lion Has Wings*, with Adrian Brunel and E.V.H. Emmett, 1939; *A Window in London* (*Lady in Distress*), with Brigid Cooper, 1939; *Old Bill and Son*, with Bruce Bairnsfather, 1940; *Sea Fort* (short), 1940; *"Pimpernel" Smith*, with others, 1941; *The Woman in the Hall*, with G.B. Stern and Jack Lee, 1947; *Dear Mr. Prohack*, with Donald Bull, 1949; *The Heart of the Matter*, with Lesley Storm, 1952; *Three Cases of Murder*, with others, 1955; *Raising a Riot*, with Hugh Perceval and James Matthews, 1955; *A Hill in Korea*, with Anthony Squire and Ronald Spencer, 1956; *Hunted in Holland*, with Derek Williams, 1961; *Mix Me a Person*, with Roy Kerridge, 1962. Film producer.

DASSIN, Jules. Screenplays: *Rififi*, 1954; *He Who Must Die*, 1957; *Where the Hot Wind Blows*, 1958; *Never on Sunday*, 1959; *Phaedra*, 1962; *10.30 P.M., Summer*, with Marguerite Duras, 1966; *Uptight*, with Ruby Dee and Julian Mayfield, 1968; *Promise at Dawn*, 1970; *A Dream of Passion*, 1978. Stage play (musical): *Illya Darling*, music by Manos Hadjidakis, lyrics by Joe Darion, 1967. Film director.

DIAMOND, I.A.L. Screenplays: *Murder in the Blue Room*, with Stanley Davis, 1944; *Never Say Goodbye*, with others, 1946; *Two Guys from Milwaukee* (*Royal Flush*), with Charles Hoffman, 1946; *Love and Learn*, with others, 1946; *Always Together*, with Henry and Phoebe Ephron, 1947; *Romance on the High Seas* (*It's Magic*), with others, 1948; *Two Guys from Texas* (*Two Texas Knights*), with Allen Boretz, 1948; *The Girl from Jones Beach*, with Allen Boretz, 1949; *It's a Great Feeling*, with Jack Rose and Mel Shavelson, 1949; *Love Nest*, 1951; *Let's Make It Legal*, with F. Hugh Herbert and Mortimer Braus, 1951; *Monkey Business*, with others, 1952; *Something for the Birds*, with others, 1952; *That Certain Feeling*, with others, 1956; *Love in the Afternoon*, with Billy Wilder, 1957; *Merry Andrew*, with Isobel Lennart, 1958; *Some Like It Hot*, with Wilder, 1959 (published 1959); *The Apartment*, with Wilder, 1960 (Oscar; published 1971); *One, Two, Three*, with Wilder, 1961; *Irma La Douce*, with Wilder, 1963 (published 1963); *Kiss Me, Stupid*, with Wilder, 1964; *The Fortune Cookie* (*Meet Whiplash Willie*), with Wilder, 1966 (published 1971); *Cactus Flower*, 1969; *The Private Life of Sherlock Holmes*, with Wilder, 1970; *Avanti!*, with Wilder, 1972; *The Front Page*, with Wilder, 1974; *Fedora*, with Wilder, 1978; *Buddy Buddy*, with Wilder, 1981. Stage plays: *You've Got Something There*, music by Lee Wainer, lyrics by Lupin Fein, 1938; *Life Begins in '40*, music by Lee Wainer, 1940; sketches in *Alive and Kicking*, 1950. Film producer.

DUNNE, Philip. Screenplays: *Student Tour*, 1933; *The Count of Monte Cristo*, 1934; *The Melody Lingers On*, 1935; *The Last of the Mohicans*, with others, 1936; *Lancer Spy*, 1937; *Breezing Home*, with Philip Finley Dunne, Jr., and Charles Grayson, 1937; *Suez*, with Julien Josephson and Sam Duncan, 1938; *The Rains Came*, with Julien Josephson, 1939; *Swanee River*, with John Taintor Foote, 1939; *Stanley and Livingstone*, with Julien Josephson, 1939; *Johnny Apollo*, with others, 1940; *How Green Was My Valley*, 1941 (published in *Twenty Best Film Plays*, 1943); *Son of Fury*, 1942; *The Late George Apley*, 1947; *Forever Amber*, with Ring Lardner, Jr., and Jerome Cady, 1947; *The Ghost and Mrs. Muir*, 1947; *The Luck of the Irish*, 1948; *Escape*, 1948; *Pinky*, with Dudley Nichols, 1949; *Anne of the Indies*, with Arthur Caesar, 1951; *David and Bathsheba*, 1951; *Lydia Bailey*, with Michael Blankfort, 1952; *Way of a Gaucho*, 1952; *The Robe*, with Gina Kaus, 1953; *Demetrius and the Gladiators*, 1954; *The Egyptian*, with Casey Robinson, 1954; *The View from Pompey's Head*, 1955; *Hilda Crane*, 1956; *Three Brave Men*, 1957; *Ten North Frederick*, 1958; *Blue Denim* (*Blue Jeans*), with Edith Sommer, 1958; *The Agony and the Ecstasy*, 1965; *Blindfold*, with W.H. Menger, 1966. Film director. Autobiography: *Take Two*, 1980.

EPSTEIN, Julius. Screenplays (in collaboration with his brother Philip Epstein, 1939–54): *Living on Velvet*, 1935; *In Caliente*, 1935; *Little Big Shot*, 1935; *I Live for Love*, 1935; *Stars over Broadway*, 1935; *Broadway Gondolier*, 1935; *Sons o' Guns*, with Jerry Wald, 1936; *Confession*, with Hans Rameau and Margaret Le Vino, 1937; *Secrets of an Actress*, with Milton Krims and Rowland Leigh, 1938; *Daughters Courageous*, 1939; *Four Wives*, with Maurice Hanline, 1939; *Saturday's Children*, 1940; *No Time for Comedy*, 1940; *Strawberry Blonde*, 1941; *The Bride Came C.O.D.*, with others, 1941; *The Man Who Came to Dinner*, 1941; *Honeymoon for Three*, with Earl Baldwin, 1941; *The Male Animal*, with Stephen Morehouse Avery, 1942; *Casablanca*, with Howard Koch, 1943 (Oscar; published in *The Best Film Plays of 1943–1944*, 1945); *Mr. Skeffington*, 1944; *Arsenic and Old Lace*, 1944; *One More Tomorrow*, with others, 1944; *Romance on the High Seas* (*It's Magic*), with others, 1948; *My Foolish Heart*, 1949; *Take Care of My Little Girl*, 1951; *Forever Female*, 1953; *The Last Time*

I Saw Paris, with Richard Brooks, 1954; *Young at Heart* (Julius only), with Lenore Coffee and Liam O'Brien, 1954; *The Tender Trap*, 1955; *Kiss Them for Me*, 1957; *The Brothers Karamazov*, with Richard Brooks, 1958; *Take a Giant Step*, with Louis S. Peterson, 1959; *Tall Story*, 1960; *Fanny*, 1961; *The Light in the Piazza*, 1962; *Send Me No Flowers*, 1964; *Return from the Ashes*, 1965; *Any Wednesday*, 1966; *Pete 'n' Tilly*, 1972; *Once Is Not Enough*, 1975; *House Calls*, 1978; *Reuben, Reuben*, 1983. Stage plays: *And Stars Remain*, with Philip Epstein, 1936 (published 1937); *Chicken Every Sunday*, with Philip Epstein, from a novel by Rosemary Taylor, 1944; *That's the Ticket*, with Philip Epstein, 1948; *But, Seriously*, 1969 (published 1969). Film producer.

FORBES, Bryan. Screenplays: *The Black Knight*, with Alec Coppel and Dennis O'Keefe, 1954; *Cockleshell Heroes*, with Richard Maibaum, 1955; *House of Secrets* (*Triple Deception*), with Robert Buckner, 1956; *The Black Tent*, with Robin Maugham, 1956; *The Baby and the Battleship*, with Jay Lewis and Gilbert Hackforth-Jones, 1956; *I Was Monty's Double*, 1958; *Danger Within*, with Frank Harvey, 1959; *The Captain's Table*, with John Whiting and Nicholas Phipps, 1959; *The Angry Silence*, with Michael Craig and Richard Gregson, 1960; *Man in the Moon*, with Michael Relph, 1960; *The League of Gentlemen*, 1960; *Only Two Can Play*, 1962; *Station Six—Sahara*, with Bryan Clements, 1962; *The L-Shaped Room*, 1962; *Séance on a Wet Afternoon*, 1964; *The High Bright Sun* (*McGuire Go Home*), with Ian Stuart Black, 1964; *Of Human Bondage*, 1964; *King Rat*, 1965; *The Whisperers*, 1966; *Deadfall*, 1967; *The Raging Moon* (*Long Ago Tomorrow*), 1970; *The Slipper and the Rose*, 1976; *International Velvet*, 1978. Film director and actor; also novelist, biographer, and author of *Notes for a Life*, 1974.

FRANK, Melvin, and Norman PANAMA. Screenplays in collaboration: *My Favorite Blonde*, with others, 1942; *Star Spangled Rhythm*, with others, 1942; *Happy Go Lucky*, with others, 1942; *Thank Your Lucky Stars*, with others, 1943; *And the Angels Sing*, with Claude Binyon, 1944; *Duffy's Tavern*, 1945; *Our Hearts Were Growing Up*, with Frank Waldman, 1946; *Monsieur Beaucaire*, 1946; *Road to Utopia*, 1946; *It Had to Be You*, with others, 1947; *Mr. Blandings Builds His Dream House*, 1948; *A Southern Yankee* (*My Hero*), with Harry Tugend, 1948; *The Return of October* (*A Date with Destiny*), with others, 1949; *The Reformer and the Redhead*, 1950; *Strictly Dishonorable*, 1951; *Callaway Went Thataway*, 1952; *Above and Beyond*, with Beirne Lay, Jr., 1953; *Knock on Wood*, 1954; *White Christmas*, with Norman Krasna, 1954; *The Court Jester*, 1956; *That Certain Feeling*, with others, 1956; *Li'l Abner*, 1959; *The Facts of Life*, 1960; *The Road to Hong Kong*, 1962; *Strange Bedfellows*, with Michael Pertwee, 1965; *A Funny Thing Happened on the Way to the Forum* (Frank only), with Michael Pertwee, 1966; *Not with My Wife You Don't*, with others, 1966; *Buona Sera, Mrs. Campbell* (Frank only), with Denis Norden and Sheldon Keller, 1968; *A Touch of Class* (Frank only), with others, 1973; *Coffee, Tea, or Me* (Frank only), with others, 1973; *The Duchess and the Dirtwater Fox* (Frank only), with others, 1976; *I Will, I Will . . . for Now* (Panama only), with others, 1976. Stage plays: sketches in *Keep Off the Grass*, 1940; *A Free Hand*, 1954; *Li'l Abner*, music by Gene de Paul, lyrics by Johnny Mercer, based on characters by Al Capp, 1956; *A Talent for Murder* (Panama only), with Jerome Chodorov, 1981 (published 1982). Film producers and directors; Panama is also a novelist.

FRY, Christopher. See his dictionary entry.

GILLIAT, Sidney. Screenplays: *A Gentleman of Paris*, with Sewell Collins, 1931; *A Night in Marseilles* (*Night Shadows*), 1931; *Rome Express*, with others, 1932; *Sign Please* (short), 1933; *Post Haste* (short), 1933; *Facing the Music*, with others, 1933; *Falling for You*, with Jack Hulbert, 1933; *Orders Is Orders*, with Leslie Arliss and James Gleason, 1933; *Friday the Thirteenth*, with G.H. Moresby-White and Emlyn Williams, 1933; *Jack Ahoy!*, with others, 1934; *Chu-Chin-Chow*, with Edward Knoblock and L. DuGarde Peach, 1934; *My Heart Is Calling*, with others, 1934; *Bulldog Drummond* (*Alias Bulldog Drummond*), with others, 1935; *King of the Damned*, with Charles Bennett and A.R. Rawlinson, 1935; *Where There's a Will*, with others, 1936; *Seven Sinners* (*Doomed Cargo*), with others, 1936; *Twelve Good Men*, with Frank Launder, 1936; *The Man Who Changed His Mind* (*The Man Who Lived Again*), with John L. Balderston and L. DuGarde Peach, 1936; *Strangers on a Honeymoon*, with Ralph Spence and Bryan Wallace, 1936; *Take My Tip*, with Michael Hogan and Jack Hulbert, 1937; *A Yank at Oxford*, with others, 1937; *Strange Boarders*, with A.R. Rawlinson, 1938; *The Lady Vanishes*, with Launder and Alma Reville, 1938; *The Gaunt Stranger* (*The Phantom Strikes*), 1938; *Ask a Policeman*, with others, 1939; *Jamaica Inn*, with Joan Harrison and J.B. Priestley, 1939; *Inspector Hornleigh on Holiday*, with Launder, 1939; *They Came by Night*, with others, 1940; *Night Train to Munich* (*Night Train*), with Launder, 1940; *The Girl in the News*, with Launder, 1940; *Kipps* (*The Remarkable Mr. Kipps*), with Launder, 1941; *Mr. Proudfoot Shows a Light* (short), 1941; *You're Telling Me!* (short), 1941; *The Young Mr. Pitt*, with Launder, 1942; *Partners in Crime* (short), with Launder, 1942; *Millions Like Us*, with Launder, 1943; *Waterloo Road*, with Val Valentine, 1945; *The Rake's Progress* (*The Notorious Gentleman*), with Launder and Valentine, 1945; *Green for Danger*, with Claude Guerney, 1946; *I See a Dark Stranger* (*The Adventuress*), with Launder and Wolfgang Wilhelm, 1946; *Captain Boycott*, with others, 1947; *London Belongs to Me* (*Dulcimer Street*), with J.B. Williams, 1948; *The Blue Lagoon*, with Michael Hogan and John Baines, 1949; *State Secret* (*The Great Manhunt*), 1950; *The Happiest Days of Your Life*, with John Dighton, 1950; *The Story of Gilbert and Sullivan* (*The Great Gilbert and Sullivan*), with Leslie Bailey and Vincent Korda, 1953; *The Belles of St. Trinian's*, with Launder and Valentine, 1954; *The Constant Husband*, with Valentine, 1955; *Geordie* (*Wee Geordie*), with Launder, 1955; *The Green Man*, with Launder, 1956; *Fortune Is a Woman* (*She Played with Fire*), with Launder and Valentine, 1957; *Blue Murder at St. Trinian's*, with Launder and Valentine, 1957; *Left, Right, and Centre*, with Valentine, 1959; *The Pure Hell of St. Trinian's*, with Launder and Valentine, 1960; *Endless Night*, 1972. Stage plays: *The Body Was Well Nourished*, with Launder, 1940, revised version, as *Meet a Body*, 1954 (published in *Plays of the Year 10*, 1954); *The Green Man*, 1954. Radio writing: *Crooks Tour* and *Secret Mission 609* series, c. 1939. Film producer and director.

GOLDMAN, Bo. Screenplays: *One Flew over the Cuckoo's Nest*, 1975; *End of the Game*, with others, 1976; *The Rose*, with Bill Kerby, 1979; *Melvin and Howard*, 1979; *Shoot the Moon*, 1982. Stage play: *First Impressions*, with Glenn Paxton, 1959.

GOLDMAN, William. Screenplays: *Masquerade*, with Michael Relph, 1964; *Harper* (*The Moving Target*), 1966; *Butch Cassidy and the Sundance Kid*, 1969 (published 1969);

The Hot Rock (*How to Steal a Diamond in Four Uneasy Lessons*), 1972; *The Stepford Wives*, 1974; *The Great Waldo Pepper*, 1975 (published 1975); *Marathon Man*, 1976; *All the President's Men*, 1976; *A Bridge Too Far*, 1977; *Magic*, 1978. Stage plays: *Blood, Sweat, and Stanley Poole*, with James Goldman, 1961 (published 1962); *A Family Affair*, with James Goldman, music by John Kander, 1962. Television play: *Mr. Horn*, 1979. Author of several novels and other books, including *Adventures in the Screen Trade: A Personal View of Hollywood and Screenwriting*, 1983.

GREENE, Graham. See his dictionary entry.

HACKETT, Albert. Screenplays (with Frances Goodrich): *The Secret of Madame Blanche*, 1933; *Penthouse* (*Crooks in Clover*), 1933; *Fugitive Lovers*, 1934; *The Thin Man*, 1934; *Hide-Out*, 1934; *Naughty Marietta*, with John Lee Mahin, 1935; *Ah, Wilderness!*, 1935; *Rose Marie*, with Alice Duer Miller, 1936; *Small Town Girl*, with others, 1936; *After the Thin Man*, with Dashiell Hammett, 1936; *The Firefly*, with Ogden Nash, 1937; *Another Thin Man*, with Dashiell Hammett, 1939; *Society Lawyer*, with others, 1939; *Doctors at War* (short), 1943; *Lady in the Dark*, 1944; *The Hitler Gang*, 1944; *The Virginian*, with Howard Estabrook, 1946; *It's a Wonderful Life*, with others, 1946 (published 1986); *The Pirate*, 1948; *Easter Parade*, with Sidney Sheldon, 1948; *In the Good Old Summertime*, with Ivan Tors, 1949; *Father of the Bride*, 1950; *Father's Little Dividend*, 1951; *Too Young to Kiss*, with Everett Freeman, 1951; *Give a Girl a Break*, with Vera Caspary, 1954; *Seven Brides for Seven Brothers*, with Dorothy Kingsley, 1954; *The Long, Long Trailer*, 1954; *Gaby*, with Charles Lederer, 1956; *A Certain Smile*, 1958; *The Diary of Anne Frank*, 1959 (television version, 1980); *Five Finger Exercise*, 1962. Stage plays (with Frances Goodrich): *Up Pops the Devil*, 1930 (published 1933); *Bridal Wise*, 1932; *Western Union, Please* (published 1942); *The Great Big Doorstep*, from a novel by E.P. O'Donnell, 1942 (published 1943); *The Diary of Anne Frank*, 1955 (published 1958).

HARRISON, Joan. Screenplays: *Young and Innocent* (*A Girl Was Young*), with others, 1937; *Jamaica Inn*, with Sidney Gilliat and J.B. Priestley, 1939; *Rebecca*, with others, 1940; *Foreign Correspondent*, with Charles Bennett, 1940; *Suspicion*, with Samson Raphaelson and Alma Reville, 1941; *Saboteur*, with Peter Viertel and Dorothy Parker, 1942; *Dark Waters*, with Marian Cockrell, 1945; *Phantom Lady*, 1945. Film producer.

HAYES, John Michael. Screenplays: *Red Ball Express*, 1952; *Thunder Bay*, with others, 1953; *Torch Song*, with Jan Lustig, 1953; *War Arrow*, 1954; *Rear Window*, 1954; *To Catch a Thief*, 1955; *It's a Dog's Life*, 1955; *The Trouble with Harry*, 1956; *The Man Who Knew Too Much*, with others, 1956; *Peyton Place*, 1957; *The Matchmaker*, 1958; *But Not for Me*, 1959; *Butterfield 8*, with Charles Schnee, 1960; *The Children's Hour*, with Lillian Hellman, 1961; *The Chalk Garden*, 1964; *The Carpetbaggers*, 1964; *Where Love Has Gone*, 1964; *Harlow*, 1965; *Judith*, with others, 1966; *Nevada Smith*, 1966 (television version, 1975).

HENRY, Buck. Screenplays: *The Troublemaker*, with Theodore Flicker, 1964; *The Graduate*, with Calder Willingham, 1967; *Candy*, 1968; *Catch-22*, 1970; *The Owl and the Pussycat*, 1970; *What's Up, Doc?*, with Robert Benton and David Newman, 1972; *The Day of the Dolphin*, 1973; *First Family*, 1980; *Protocol*, 1984. Television writing includes *Get Smart* series, with Mel Brooks, 1965; *Captain Nice* series, 1966; *Three's a Crowd*, 1969; *Quark* series, 1978. Film and stage actor.

KANIN, Garson. See his dictionary entry.

KASDAN, Lawrence. Screenplays: *The Empire Strikes Back*, with Leigh Brackett, 1979; *Raiders of the Lost Ark*, 1981; *Body Heat*, 1981; *Continental Divide*, 1981; *The Big Chill*, with Barbara Benedek, 1983; *Silverado*, 1985. Film director.

KOCH, Howard. Screenplays: *The Letter*, 1940; *Virginia City* (uncredited), 1940; *The Sea Hawk*, with Seton I. Miller, 1940; *Shining Victory*, with Anne Froelick, 1941; *Sergeant York*, with John Huston, Abem Finkel, and Harry Chandlee, 1941; *In This Our Life*, with Huston, 1942; *Mission to Moscow*, 1943 (published 1980); *Casablanca*, with Julius and Philip Epstein, 1943 (Oscar; published in *The Best Film Plays of 1943–1944*, 1945); *In Our Time*, with Ellis St. Joseph, 1944; *Rhapsody in Blue*, with Elliot Paul and Sonya Levien, 1945; *Three Strangers*, with Huston, 1946; *Letter from an Unknown Woman*, with Max Ophüls, 1948; *No Sad Songs for Me*, 1950; *The Thirteenth Letter*, 1951; *The Greengage Summer* (*Loss of Innocence*), 1961; *The War Lover*, 1962; *633 Squadron*, with James Clavell, 1964; *The Fox*, with Lewis John Carlino, 1967; *Journey Out of Darkness*, with James Trainor, 1967; *The Woman of Otowi Crossing*, 1974. Stage plays: *Great Scott!*, 1929; *Give Us This Day*, 1933; *The Lonely Man*, 1935; *In Time to Come*, with Huston, 1941 (published in *The Best Plays of 1941–1942*, 1942); *The Albatross*, 1963; *Dead Letters*, 1971. Radio play: *Invasion from Mars*, 1938 (published in *The Panic Broadcast*, 1970). Film and television director. Autobiography: *As Time Goes By*, 1979.

KUBRICK, Stanley. Screenplays: *Day of the Fight* (documentary), 1950; *Flying Padre* (documentary), 1951; *Killer's Kiss*, 1955; *The Killing*, 1956; *Paths of Glory*, with Calder Willingham and Jim Thompson, 1957; *Dr. Strangelove; or, How I Learned to Stop Worrying and Love the Bomb*, with Terry Southern and Peter George, 1963; *2001: A Space Odyssey*, with Arthur C. Clarke, 1968; *A Clockwork Orange*, 1971 (published 1972); *Barry Lyndon*, 1975; *The Shining*, with Diane Johnson, 1980; *Full Metal Jacket*, with Gustav Hasford and Michael Herr, 1987. Film director.

LARDNER, Ring, Jr. Screenplays: *Meet Dr. Christian*, with Ian McLellan Hunter and Harvey Gates, 1940; *The Courageous Dr. Christian*, with Ian McLellan Hunter, 1940; *Arkansas Judge* (*False Witness*), with others, 1941; *Woman of the Year*, with Michael Kanin, 1942 (Oscar); *The Cross of Lorraine*, with others, 1943; *Tomorrow the World*, with Leopold Atlas, 1944; *Brotherhood of Man* (short), 1946; *Forever Amber*, with Philip Dunne and Jerome Cady, 1947; *The Forbidden Street* (*Britannia Mews*), 1948; *Four Days Leave* (*Swiss Tour*), with others, 1948; *The Hollywood Ten* (short), 1950; *The Big Night*, with Stanley Ellin, 1951; *Virgin Island* (as Philip Rush), with Pat Jackson, 1958; *A Breath of Scandal*, 1958; *The Cincinnati Kid*, with Terry Southern, 1965; *M*A*S*H*, 1970 (Oscar); *La mortadella* (*Lady Liberty*), 1971; *The Greatest*, 1977. Stage play: *Foxy*, with Ian McLellan Hunter, music by Robert Emmett Dolan, lyrics by Johnny Mercer, suggested by *Volpone* by Jonson, 1964. Television writing includes *The Adventures of Robin Hood* and *Sir Lancelot* series (UK). Novelist; memoirs: *The Lardners: My Family Remembered*, 1976.

LEHMAN, Ernest. Screenplays: *The Inside Story* (*The Big Gamble*), with others, 1948; *Executive Suite*, 1954; *Sabrina*, with Billy Wilder and Samuel Taylor, 1954; *Somebody Up There Likes Me*, 1956; *The King and I*, 1956; *Sweet Smell of Success*, with Clifford Odets, 1957; *North by Northwest*, 1959 (published 1972); *From the Terrace*, 1960; *West Side Story*, 1961; *The Prize*, 1963; *The Sound of Music*, 1965; *Who's Afraid of Virginia Woolf?*, 1966; *Hello, Dolly!*, 1969; *Portnoy's Complaint*, 1972; *Family Plot*, 1976; *Black Sunday*, 1977. Film producer and director; also novelist and short story writer.

MADDOW, Ben. Screenplays: *Frames*, with Jack Patrick, 1947; *Kiss the Blood Off My Hands* (*Blood on My Hands*), with Leonardo Bercovici and Walter Bernstein, 1948; *The Man from Colorado*, with Robert D. Andrews and Borden Chase, 1948; *Intruder in the Dust*, 1949; *The Asphalt Jungle*, with John Huston, 1950 (published 1980); *Shadow in the Sky*, 1952; *Johnny Guitar* (uncredited), 1954; *The Naked Jungle* (uncredited), 1954; *Men in War* (uncredited), 1957; *God's Little Acre* (uncredited), 1958; *The Unforgiven*, 1960; *Two Loves*, 1961; *The Balcony*, 1963; *An Affair of the Skin* (*Love as Disorder*), 1964; *The Way West*, with Mitch Lindeman, 1967; *The Chairman*, 1969; *The Secret of Santa Vittoria*, with William Rose, 1969; *Storm of Strangers*, 1970; *The Mephisto Waltz*, 1971. Also writer and director of documentaries (including *The Savage Eye*, 1960). Stage plays: *In a Cold Hotel*, 1963 (published in *New Theatre in America 1*, 1965); *The Ram's Horn*, 1963 (published as *The Great Right Horn of the Ram*, 1967); *Soft Targets*, with others, 1981. Novelist, and writer on photography.

MAMET, David. See his dictionary entry.

MANKIEWICZ, Joseph L. Screenplays: titles for silent versions of *The Dummy, Close Harmony, The Man I Love, The Studio Murder Mystery, Thunderbolt, River of Romance, The Mysterious Dr. Fu Manchu, The Saturday Night Kid*, and *The Virginian*, 1929; *Fast Company*, with others, 1929; *Slightly Scarlet*, with Howard Estabrook and Percy Heath, 1930; *The Social Lion*, with Agnes Brand Leahy, 1930; *Only Saps Work*, with Sam Mintz and Heath, 1930; *Paramount on Parade*, with others, 1930; *Sap from Syracuse* (uncredited), 1930; *Dude Ranch* (uncredited), 1931; *Touchdown* (uncredited), 1931; *The Gang Buster*, with Heath, 1931; *Finn and Hattie*, with Mintz, 1931; *June Moon*, with Keene Thompson and Vincent Lawrence, 1931; *Skippy*, with others, 1931; *Newly Rich*, with Norman McLeod and Edward Paramore, Jr., 1931; *Sooky*, with McLeod and Mintz, 1931; *This Reckless Age*, with Frank Tuttle, 1932; *Sky Bride*, with Leahy and Grover Jones, 1932; *Million Dollar Legs*, with Henry Myers, 1932; *If I Had a Million*, with others, 1932; *Diplomaniacs*, with Myers, 1933; *Emergency Call*, with John B. Clymer and James Ewens, 1933; *Too Much Harmony*, with Harry Ruskin, 1933; *Alice in Wonderland*, with William Cameron Menzies, 1933; *Manhattan Melodrama*, with Oliver H.P. Garrett, 1934; *Our Daily Bread*, with Elizabeth Hill Vidor, 1934; *Forsaking All Others*, 1934; *I Live My Life*, with Gottfried Reinhardt and Ethel B. Borden, 1935; *Fury* (uncredited), 1936; *The Keys of the Kingdom*, with Nunnally Johnson, 1944; *Dragonwyck*, 1946; *Somewhere in the Night*, with Howard Dimsdale and Lee Strasberg, 1946; *A Letter to Three Wives*, with Vera Caspary, 1949; *House of Strangers* (uncredited), 1949; *No Way Out*, with Lesser Samuels, 1950; *All about Eve*, 1950 (published 1951); *People Will Talk*, 1951; *Five Fingers* (uncredited), 1952; *Julius Caesar*, 1953; *The Barefoot Contessa*, 1954; *Guys and Dolls*, 1955; *The Quiet American*, 1958; *Cleopatra*, with Ranald MacDougall and Sidney Buchman, 1963; *The Honey Pot* (*It Comes Up Murder*), 1967; *Sleuth*, 1972. Film, opera, and television director and producer.

MANKOWITZ, Wolf. See his dictionary entry.

MAY, Elaine. Screenplays: *Such Good Friends* (as Esther Dale), 1971; *A New Leaf*, 1971; *Mikey and Nicky*, 1976; *Heaven Can Wait*, with Warren Beatty, 1978; *Ishtar*, 1987. Stage plays: *An Evening with Mike Nichols and Elaine May*, 1960; *A Matter of Position*, 1962; *Not Enough Rope*, 1962 (published 1964); *Name of a Soup*, 1963; *Adaptation*, 1969 (published 1971); *Hot Line*, 1983. Cabaret, stage, and film actress; stage and film director.

NEWMAN, David. Screenplays: *Bonnie and Clyde*, with Robert Benton, 1967; *There Was a Crooked Man*, with Benton, 1970; *What's Up, Doc?*, with Benton and Buck Henry, 1972; *Bad Company*, with Benton, 1972; *Superman*, with Benton and others, 1978; *Superman II*, with Mario Puzo and Leslie Newman, 1981; *Jinxed*, with Bert Blessing, 1982; *Still of the Night*, with Benton, 1982; *Santa Claus*, 1985. Stage plays: *It's a Bird . . . It's a Plane . . . It's Superman*, with Benton, music by Charles Strouse, lyrics by Lee Adams, 1966; sketch, with Benton, in *Oh! Calcutta!*, 1969. Film director.

OSBORNE, John. See his dictionary entry.

PANAMA, Norman. See **FRANK, Melvin, and Norman PANAMA.**

PINTER, Harold. See his dictionary entry.

POLONSKY, Abraham. Screenplays: *Golden Earrings*, with Helen Deutsch and Frank Butler, 1946; *Body and Soul*, 1947; *Force of Evil*, with Ira Wolfert, 1949; *I Can Get It for You Wholesale*, with Vera Caspary, 1951; *Madigan* with Harry Kleiner, 1968; *Tell Them Willie Boy Is Here*, 1969; *Romance of a Horse Thief*, 1971; *Avalanche Express*, 1979; *Monsignor*, with Wendell Mayes, 1982. Radio and television writer, novelist, and film director.

POWELL, Michael. Screenplays: *My Friend the King*, 1931; *The Fire Raisers*, with Jerome Jackson, 1933; *Red Ensign* (*Strike!*), with Jackson and L. DuGarde Peach, 1934; *The Edge of the World*, 1937; *Contraband* (*Blackout*), with Brock Williams, 1940; *Honeymoon*, 1958; with Emeric Pressburger—*One of Our Aircraft Is Missing*, 1942, *The Life and Death of Colonel Blimp*, 1943, *The Volunteer*, 1943, *A Canterbury Tale*, 1944, *I Know Where I'm Going*, 1945, *A Matter of Life and Death* (*Stairway to Heaven*), 1946, *Black Narcissus*, 1947, *The Small Back Room* (*Hour of Glory*), 1949, *The Elusive Pimpernel* (*The Fighting Pimpernel*), 1950, *Gone to Earth* (*The Wild Heart*), 1950, *The Tales of Hoffmann*, 1951, *Oh Rosalinda* (*Fledermaus '55*), 1955, *The Battle of the River Plate* (*Pursuit of the Graf Spee*), 1956, and *Ill-Met by Moonlight* (*Night Ambush*), 1957; *Trikimia* (*The Tempest*), 1974. Film and television producer and director; also novelist.

RABE, David. See his dictionary entry.

RAPHAEL, Frederic. Screenplays: *Bachelor of Hearts*, with Leslie Bricusse, 1958; *Don't Bother to Knock* (*Why Bother to Knock*), with Denis Cannan and Frederic Gotfurt, 1961; *Nothing But the Best*, 1963; *Darling*, with John Schlesinger and Joseph Janni, 1965; *Two for the Road*, 1967 (published 1967); *Far from the Madding Crowd*, 1967; *A Severed Head*, 1970; *Daisy Miller*, 1974; *Richard's Things*, 1981. Stage plays: *Lady at the Wheel*, with Lucienne Hill, music and lyrics by Leslie Bricusse and Robin Beaumont, 1958; *A Man on the Bridge*, 1961; *The Island* (for children), in *Eight Plays 2* edited by Malcolm Fellows, 1965; *An Early Life*, 1979; *From the*

Greek, 1979. Radio documentaries: *The Daedalus Dimension*, 1979; *Death in Trieste*, 1981. Television plays: *The Executioners*, 1961; *Image of a Society*, from the novel by Roy Fuller, 1963; *The Trouble with England*, from his own novel, 1964; *The Glittering Prizes*, 1976; *Rogue Male*, from the novel by Geoffrey Household, 1976; *Something's Wrong*, 1978; *The Serpent Son*, with Kenneth McLeish, from the *Oresteia* by Aeschylus, 1979 (published 1979); *Of Mycenae and Men*, with McLeish, 1979; *School Play*, 1979; *The Best of Friends*, 1980; *Byron: A Personal Tour* (documentary), 1981; *Oxbridge Blues* series, 1984. Author of several books of fiction, and other works.

RAVETCH, Irving. Screenplays (with Harriet Frank from 1955): *Living in a Big Way*, with Gregory La Cava, 1947; *The Outriders*, 1950; *Vengeance Valley*, 1951; *Ten Wanted Men*, with Kenneth Gamet, 1955; *Run for Cover*, with Winston Miller, 1955; *The Long Hot Summer*, 1958; *The Dark at the Top of the Stairs*, 1960; *Home from the Hill*, 1960; *Hud*, 1963; *Hombre*, 1967; *House of Cards* (as James P. Bonner), 1969; *The Reivers*, 1969; *The Cowboys*, 1972; *Conrack*, 1974; *The Spikes Gang*, 1974; *Norma Rae*, 1979; *Murphy's Romance*, 1985. Stage play: *The Glad and Sorry Season*, with Harriet Frank, 1962. Film producer.

SANGSTER, Jimmy. Screenplays: *A Man on the Beach*, 1956; *X the Unknown*, 1956; *The Curse of Frankenstein*, 1957; *Dracula* (*Horror of Dracula*), 1958; *The Snorkel*, with Peter Myers, 1958; *Intent to Kill*, 1958; *Blood of the Vampire*, 1958; *The Revenge of Frankenstein*, with Hurford James, 1958; *The Trollenberg Terror* (*The Crawling Eye*), 1958; *The Man Who Could Cheat Death*, 1959; *Jack the Ripper*, 1959; *The Mummy*, 1959; *The Brides of Dracula*, with Peter Bryan and Edward Percy, 1960; *The Criminal* (*The Concrete Jungle*), with Alun Owen, 1960; *The Siege of Sidney Street*, with Alexander Baron, 1960; *The Hellfire Club*, with Leon Griffiths, 1961; *Taste of Fear* (*Scream of Fear*), 1961; *The Terror of the Tongs*, 1961; *The Pirates of Blood River*, with John Gilling and John Hunter, 1962; *Maniac*, 1962; *Paranoiac*, 1963; *Nightmare*, 1963; *Hysteria*, 1964; *The Devil-Ship Pirates*, 1964; *The Nanny*, 1965; *Deadlier Than the Male*, with David Osborn and Liz Charles-Williams, 1966; *The Anniversary*, 1967; *Crescendo*, with Alfred Shaughnessy, 1969; *The Horror of Frankenstein*, with Jeremy Burnham, 1970; *Who Slew Aunty Roo?*, 1971; *Fear in the Night*, 1972; *Leadbelly*, 1976; *Phobia*, 1980; *The Devil and Max Devlin*, 1981. Television writing includes *Motive for Murder* and *The Assassin* series, and *The Big Deal*, 1961; *The Spy Killer*, 1969; *Foreign Exchange*, 1970; *A Taste of Money*, 1971; *Maneaters*, 1973; *Scream, Pretty Peggy*, 1973; *Murder in Music City*, 1979; *The Billion Dollar Threat*, 1979; *Ebony, Ivory, and Jade*, 1979; *The Concrete Cowboys*, 1979; *Once upon a Spy*, 1980; *No Place to Hide*, 1980; *The Toughest Man in the World*, 1984. Film producer; also a novelist.

SARGENT, Alvin. Screenplays: *Gambit*, with Jack Davies, 1966; *The Stalking Moon*, with Wendell Mayes, 1968; *The Sterile Cuckoo* (*Pookie*), 1969; *I Walk the Line*, 1970; *The Effects of Gamma Rays on Man-in-the-Moon Marigolds*, 1972; *Love and Pain and the Whole Damn Thing*, 1972; *Paper Moon*, 1973; *Bobby Deerfield*, 1977; *Julia*, 1977; *Straight Time*, 1978; *The Electric Horseman*, 1979; *Ordinary People*, 1980. Television writing includes scripts for *The Man from UNCLE* series, 1968, and *The Impatient Heart*, 1971.

SAYLES, John. Screenplays: *Piranha*, 1978; *The Lady in Red* (*Kiss Me and Die; Bullets, Sin, and Bathtub Gin*), 1979; *Battle Beyond the Stars*, 1980; *The Return of the Secaucus Seven*, 1980; *Alligator*, 1980; *The Howling*, 1981; *The Challenge*, 1982; *Lianna*, 1983; *Baby It's You*, 1983; *The Brother from Another Planet*, 1984; *Enormous Changes at the Last Minute*, 1985; *The Clan of the Cave Bear*, 1986. Stage plays: *Turnbuckle*, and *New Hope for the Dead*, 1981. Television writing includes *A Perfect Match*, 1980. Film director and novelist.

SCHRADER, Paul. Screenplays: *The Yakuza*, with Robert Towne, 1975; *Taxi Driver*, 1976; *Obsession*, 1976; *Rolling Thunder*, with Heywood Gould, 1977; *Blue Collar*, with Leonard Schrader, 1978; *Old Boyfriends*, 1979; *Hardcore*, 1979; *American Gigolo*, 1979; *Raging Bull*, with Mardik Martin, 1981; *Mishima*, with Leonard Schrader, 1985; *The Mosquito Coast*, 1986. Film director.

SCHULBERG, Budd. Screenplays: *Little Orphan Annie*, with Samuel Ornitz and Endre Bohem, 1938; *Winter Carnival*, with Maurice Rapf and Lester Cole, 1939; *Weekend for Three*, with Dorothy Parker and Alan Campbell, 1941; *Government Girl*, with Dudley Nichols, 1943; *City Without Men*, with Martin Berkeley and W.L. River, 1943; *On the Waterfront*, 1954 (Oscar; published 1980); *A Face in the Crowd*, 1957 (published 1957); *Wind Across the Everglades*, 1958 (published 1958); *Joe Louis—For All Time*, 1984. Stage plays: *The Disenchanted*, with Harvey Breit, from the novel by Schulberg, 1958 (published 1959); *What Makes Sammy Run?*, with Stuart Schulberg, music by Ervin Drake, from the novel by Budd Schulberg, 1964. Radio plays include *Hollywood Doctor* (published in *The Writer's Radio Theatre*, 1941), and *Tomorrow* (published in *Free World Theatre*, 1944). Television plays include *The Pharmacist's Mate* (published in *The Best Television Plays 1950–1951*, 1952), and *A Question of Honor*, 1982. Fiction writer, and author of other books; autobiography: *Moving Pictures: Memories of a Hollywood Prince*, 1981.

SEMPLE, Lorenzo, Jr. Screenplays: *Batman*, 1966; *Fathom*, 1967; *Pretty Poison*, 1968; *Daddy's Gone A-Hunting*, with Larry Cohen, 1969; *The Sporting Club*, 1971; *The Marriage of a Young Stockbroker*, 1971; *Papillon*, 1973; *The Super Cops*, 1974; *The Parallax View*, 1974; *The Drowning Pool*, 1975; *Three Days of the Condor*, 1975; *King Kong*, 1976; *Hurricane*, 1979; *Flash Gordon*, 1980; *Never Say Never Again*, 1983; *Sheena*, 1984. Stage plays: *Tonight in Samarkand*, with Jacques Deval, 1955; *Golden Fleecing*, 1959 (published 1958). Television writing includes scripts for *Burke's Law* series, 1964–66, *Batman* series, 1966, and *Rearview Mirror*, 1984.

SIMON, Neil. See his dictionary entry.

SIODMAK, Curt. Screenplays: *Menschen am Sonntag* (*People on Sunday*) (documentary), with Billy Wilder, 1929; *Le Bal*, 1931; *Der Mann der seinen Mörder sucht* (*Looking for His Murderer*), with Billy Wilder, 1931; *F. P. 1 antwortet nicht*, 1933; *Girls Will Be Boys*, with Clifford Grey and Roger Burford, 1934; *La Crise est finie* (*The Slump Is Over*), 1934; *I Give My Heart*, with others, 1935; *The Tunnel* (*Transatlantic Tunnel*), with L. DuGarde Peach and Clemence Dane, 1935; *It's a Bet*, with Frank Miller and Peach, 1935; *Non-Stop New York*, with others, 1937; *Her Jungle Love*, with others, 1938; *The Invisible Man Returns*, with Lester Cole and Joe May, 1940; *The Ape*, with Richard Carroll, 1940; *Black Friday*, with Eric Taylor, 1940; *The Wolf Man*, with Gordon Kann, 1940; *The Invisible Woman*, with others, 1941; *Pacific Blackout*, with others, 1941; *Aloma of the South Seas*, with others, 1941; *Midnight Angel*, with others, 1941; *London Blackout Murders*,

1942; *The Invisible Agent*, 1942; *I Walked with a Zombie*, with Ardel Wray and Inez Wallace, 1943; *Frankenstein Meets the Wolf Man*, 1943; *The Mantrap*, 1943; *Son of Dracula*, with Eric Taylor, 1943; *False Faces*, 1943; *The Purple "V,"* with Bertram Millhauser, 1943; *House of Frankenstein*, with Edward T. Lowe, 1944; *The Climax*, with Lynn Starling, 1944; *Frisco Sal*, with Gerald Geraghty, 1945; *Shady Lady*, with others, 1945; *The Return of Monte Cristo*, with others, 1946; *The Beast with Five Fingers*, with Harold Goldman, 1947; *Berlin Express*, with Harold Medford, 1948; *Tarzan's Magic Fountain*, with Harry Chandlee, 1949; *Four Days Leave*, with others, 1950; *Bride of the Gorilla*, 1951; *The Magnetic Monster*, with Ivan Tors, 1953; *Riders to the Stars*, 1954; *Creature with the Atom Brain*, 1955; *Earth vs. Flying Saucers*, with George Worthing Yates and Raymond Marcus, 1956; *Curucu, Beast of the Amazon*, 1956; *Love Slaves of the Amazon*, 1957; *The Devil's Messenger*, 1962; *Ski Fever*, with Robert Joseph, 1967. Television writing includes *13 Demon Street* series, 1959 (Sweden); *Hauser's Memory*, 1970. Film director; also fiction writer (in German, 1930–37, and English).

SONTAG, Susan. Screenplays: *Duet for Cannibals*, 1970 (published 1970); *Brother Carl*, 1974 (published 1974). Novelist, critic, and director.

SOUTHERN, Terry. Screenplays: *Candy Kisses*, with David Burnett, 1955; *Dr. Strangelove; or, How I Learned to Stop Worrying and Love the Bomb*, with Stanley Kubrick and Peter George, 1963; *The Loved One*, with Christopher Isherwood, 1965; *The Cincinnati Kid*, with Ring Lardner, Jr., 1965; *Casino Royale* (uncredited), 1967; *Barbarella*, with others, 1968; *Easy Rider*, with Peter Fonda and Dennis Hopper, 1969 (published 1969); *The End of the Road*, with Aram Avakian, 1969; *The Magic Christian*, with others, 1969; *Meetings with Remarkable Men*, 1979. Television play: *The Emperor Jones*, from the play by Eugene O'Neill, 1958 (UK). Novelist.

STERN, Stewart. Screenplays: *Teresa*, 1951; *Benjy*, 1951; *Rebel Without a Cause*, 1955; *The Rack*, 1956; *The James Dean Story*, 1957; *Thunder in the Sun*, 1958; *The Outsider*, 1961; *The Ugly American*, 1963; *Rachel, Rachel*, 1968; *The Last Movie*, 1971; *Summer Wishes, Winter Dreams*, 1973. Television writing: *Thunder Silence*, 1954; *Sybil*, 1976; *A Christmas to Remember*, 1978.

STONE, Oliver. Screenplays: *Salvador*, 1976; *Midnight Express*, 1978; *Scarface*, 1983; *Platoon*, 1987. Film director.

SWERLING, Jo. Screenplays: *Ladies of Leisure*, with Dudley Early, 1930; *Sisters*, with Ralph Graves, 1930; *Rain or Shine*, with Dorothy Howell, 1930; *Hell's Island*, with Thomas Buckingham, 1930; *The Last Parade*, 1931; *Dirigible*, 1931; *Ten Cents a Dance*, 1931; *The Miracle Woman*, 1931; *Platinum Blonde*, with Robert Riskin, 1931; *Forbidden*, 1932; *Behind the Mask*, 1932; *War Correspondent*, 1932; *Washington Merry-Go-Round*, 1932; *Below the Sea*, 1933; *Man's Castle*, 1933; *No Greater Glory*, 1934; *The Defense Rests*, 1934; *Lady by Choice*, 1934; *The Whole Town's Talking*, with Robert Riskin and W.R. Burnett, 1935; *Love Me Forever*, with Sidney Buchman, 1935; *The Music Goes Round*, with Sidney Buchman, 1936; *Pennies from Heaven*, with William Rankin, 1936; *Double Wedding*, 1937; *I Am the Law*, 1938; *Doctor Rhythm*, with Richard Connell, 1938; *Made for Each Other*, with Rose Franken, 1939; *The Real Glory*, with Robert Presnell, Sr., 1939; *The Westerner*, with Niven Busch and Stuart N. Lake, 1940; *Blood and Sand*, 1941; *New York Town*, with Lewis Meltzer, 1941; *Confirm or Deny*, with Henry Wales and Samuel Fuller, 1941; *Pride of the Yankees*, with Herman J. Mankiewicz and Paul Gallico, 1942; *Crash Dive*, with W.R. Burnett, 1943; *A Lady Takes a Chance*, with Robert Ardrey, 1943; *Lifeboat*, with John Steinbeck, 1944; *Leave Her to Heaven*, 1945; *It's a Wonderful Life*, with others, 1946 (published 1986); *Thunder in the East*, with others, 1953; *King of the Roaring Twenties*, 1961. Stage plays: *One of Us*, with Jack Lait, 1918; *One Helluva Night*, 1924; *The New Yorkers*, with Henry Myers, 1927; *Kibitzer*, with Edward G. Robinson, 1929 (published 1929); *Guys and Dolls*, with Abe Burrows, music by Frank Loesser, based on a story and characters by Damon Runyon, 1950 (published in *The Modern Theatre 4*, 1956).

TARADASH, Daniel. Screenplays: *Golden Boy*, with others, 1939; *For Love or Money*, with others, 1939; *A Little Bit of Heaven*, with others, 1940; *The Noose Hangs High*, with others, 1948; *Knock on Any Door*, with John Monks, Jr., 1949; *Rancho Notorious*, with Sylvia Richards, 1952; *Don't Bother to Knock*, 1952; *From Here to Eternity*, 1953 (Oscar); *Desiree*, 1954; *Picnic*, 1955; *Storm Center*, with Elick Moll, 1956; *Bell, Book, and Candle*, 1958; *Morituri* (*Saboteur: Code Name Morituri*), 1965; *Hawaii*, with Dalton Trumbo, 1966; *Castle Keep*, with David Rayfiel, 1969; *Doctors' Wives*, 1971; *The Other Side of Midnight*, 1977. Stage plays: *Red Gloves*, from a play by Sartre, 1948; *There Was a Little Girl*, from a novel by Christopher Davis, 1960. Television writing includes *Bogie*, 1980. Film director.

TESICH, Steve. See his dictionary entry.

TOWNE, Robert. Screenplays: *The Last Woman on Earth*, 1960; *Tomb of Ligeia*, 1965; *Villa Rides*, with Sam Peckinpah, 1968; *The Last Detail*, 1973 (published 1987); *Chinatown*, 1974 (published 1987); *Shampoo*, with Warren Beatty, 1975 (published 1987); *The Yakuza*, with Paul Schrader, 1975; *Personal Best*, 1982; *Greystoke: The Legend of Tarzan, Lord of the Apes*, with Michael Austin, 1984. Television writer.

WILDER, Billy. Screenplays: *Menschen am Sonntag* (*People on Sunday*) (documentary), with Curt Siodmak, 1929; *Der Teufelsreporter*, 1929; *Seitensprünge*, 1930; *Ihre Hoheit befiehlt*, 1931; *Der falsche Ehemann*, 1931; *Emil und die Detektive* (*Emil and the Detectives*), 1931; *Der Mann der seinen Mörder sucht* (*Looking for His Murderer*), with Siodmak, 1931; *Es was einmal ein Walzer*, 1932; *Ein blonder Traum*, 1932; *Scampolo, ein Kind der strasse*, 1932; *Das Blaue von Himmel*, 1932; *Madame wünscht keine Kinder*, 1933; *Was Frauen träumen*, 1933; *Music in the Air*, with Howard I. Young, 1934; *Lottery Lover*, with others, 1935; *Champagne Waltz*, with others, 1937; *Bluebeard's Eighth Wife*, with Charles Brackett, 1938; *Midnight*, with Brackett and others, 1939; *What a Life*, with Brackett, 1939; *Ninotchka*, with Brackett and others, 1939 (published 1972); *Arise My Love*, with Brackett and others, 1940; *Rhythm on the River*, with Jacques Théry and Dwight Taylor, 1940; *Hold Back the Dawn*, with Brackett and Ketti Frings, 1941; *Ball of Fire*, with Brackett and Thomas Monroe, 1941; *The Major and the Minor*, with Brackett, 1942; *Five Graves to Cairo*, with Brackett, 1943; *Double Indemnity*, with Raymond Chandler, 1944 (published in *Best Film Plays 1945*, 1946); *The Lost Weekend*, with Brackett, 1945 (Oscar; published in *Best Film Plays 1945*, 1946); *The Emperor Waltz*, with Brackett, 1948; *A Foreign Affair*, with Brackett and others, 1948; *Sunset Boulevard*, with Brackett and D.M. Marshman, Jr., 1950; *Ace in the Hole* (*The Big Carnival*), with Walter Newman and Lesser Samuels, 1951; *Stalag 17*, with Edwin Blum, 1953;

Sabrina, with Ernest Lehman and Samuel Taylor, 1954; *The Seven Year Itch*, with George Axelrod, 1955; *The Spirit of St. Louis*, with Wendell Mayes, 1957; *Love in the Afternoon*, with I.A.L. Diamond, 1957; *Witness for the Prosecution*, with Harry Kurnitz, 1958; *Some Like It Hot*, with Diamond, 1959 (published 1959); *The Apartment*, with Diamond, 1960 (Oscar; published 1971); *One, Two, Three*, with Diamond, 1961; *Irma La Douce*, with Diamond, 1963 (published 1963); *Kiss Me, Stupid*, with Diamond, 1964; *The Fortune Cookie* (*Meet Whiplash Willie*), with Diamond, 1966 (published 1971); *The Private Life of Sherlock Holmes*, with Diamond, 1970; *Avanti!*, with Diamond, 1972; *The Front Page*, with Diamond, 1974; *Fedora*, with Diamond, 1978; *Buddy Buddy*, with Diamond, 1981. Film producer and director.

RADIO WRITERS

In the early 1980's it was possible to be more optimistic, however guardedly, about the future of radio drama in the world than it is today. In Britain the position has not deteriorated greatly and radio drama continues to hold its own, whereas in most English-speaking countries as well as a number of European countries the outlook is less promising than it recently appeared to be. Perhaps the limited revival of radio drama in the 1970's, especially in the United States, will prove to have been a false dawn, but in retrospect the doom-laden prophecies made in the 1950's and 1960's about its inevitable decline and fall, even in its last great bastion, the BBC, have not yet come true and are extremely unlikely to in the closing years of this century. Twenty years ago it did seem safe to predict that radio drama was in a terminal condition. Death might be by millimetres and take decades, but to many people it looked as though an irreversible process was under way. W.H. Auden's famous comment in his preface to a posthumous collection of radio plays (1969) by his friend Louis MacNeice, "radio drama is probably a dying art," was more tentative than many, but it illustrates the valedictory nostalgia with which not only radio drama but the entire medium of radio was being viewed. Phrases such as "the Golden Age of radio" became commonplace to describe the period before television usurped—or was thought to have usurped—the role of radio. Two books published in the early 1970's, both by distinguished radio men, convey in their very titles this sense of a lost world, of an irrecoverable past, of the glory having departed: D.G. Bridson's *Prospero and Ariel: The Rise and Fall of Radio*, and John Snagge and Michael Barsley's *Those Vintage Years of Radio*. The future, it seemed, could only continue the downhill slide.

It is certainly the case that in the entirely commercial and free-enterprise broadcasting system of the United States, television had killed off radio drama by 1960, although the eventual demise had been obvious since the late 1940's when a steady decline began. Had it not been for World War II, which delayed the widespread introduction of television, radio drama might have been eliminated by 1950. In countries with either a monopoly of public-service broadcasting (such as the United Kingdom) or a mixed system (such as Canada and Australia), the advent of television was much less catastrophic, since the BBC, CBC, and ABC, with their commitments to serve minority interests, ensured the survival of radio drama as a public service. Yet the slump in audiences from the days when many millions tuned into the BBC's *Saturday Night Theatre* every week has been massive. Furthermore, in countries with a mixed system, commercial radio has often been dominant; in Australia, for example, the ABC's proportion of the national audience is and always has been small. In Canada, according to recent figures, only 9% of the population ever tune in to a CBC radio programme, the rest always choosing commercial stations.

So has radio drama been kept artificially alive in countries with public-service broadcasting during the age of television? If natural selection had operated, as one might argue it did in the US, would radio drama not have gone the way of the dodo by now? Were the prophets of doom not, after all, right in forecasting a quick extermination in the commercial system and slow strangulation in the public-service system? The most surprising thing about radio drama during the 1970's was not its tenacity in the face of the competition provided by television (the British experience), but the signs of resurrection and new growth in the least expected quarters. In the US radio drama actually began making a comeback, admittedly on a very small scale compared with the heyday of the 1930's and 1940's when directors of the stature of Arch Oboler, Norman Corwin, and Orson Welles were the colossi of the airwaves; but its re-emergence at all well over a decade after it had apparently been laid to rest was close to miraculous. At the forefront of this revival was Elliott Lewis, the last major writer-director of the so-called Golden Age until his short but prolific career between the late 1940's and the mid-1950's was terminated by television. His suspense series, *The Zero Hour*, launched in 1973, is a milestone in the history of American mass communications, an extraordinary breakthrough after the years of silence. After this, there were further developments which looked back to the Golden Age, including the *Earplay* series on National Public Radio (masterminded by Fletcher Markle, who rose to fame via CBC radio and television drama in Canada), *CBS Mystery Theatre* (created by Himan Brown, a former Golden Age director), and *Sears Radio Theatre* (involving both Lewis and Markle). Sadly, the financial problems that have afflicted broadcasting internationally in the 1980's have seriously threatened this American rebirth; National Public Radio, which made radio drama possible again in the US, suffered a nearly fatal crisis in 1983. All is not lost, however, as Richard Imison of the BBC points out in his Preface to *Best Radio Plays of 1983*, and American radio drama has not been completely snuffed out for the second time in 25 years.

What made this act of resuscitation possible in the US, even if it should turn out to be of limited duration? On the part of the commercial sponsors, there was a recognition that, although radio audiences are very much smaller than they were, they are still to be measured in statistically significant quantities. Considering the extraordinary cheapness of radio production compared with the constantly escalating costs of television, sponsors have been tempted to reconsider the possibility of financing radio drama even though it is relatively expensive by radio standards. But they have decided to do so only because they realize that there is an audience for something entertaining on radio apart from the nonstop diet of pop music, news reports, and chat shows of the television age. The assumption of the first television generation that no one would want to listen to drama if they could watch it failed to take account of the fact that listening is possible in situations and at times of the day when watching is out of the question. The first television generation were so captivated by the new medium, as though by magic, that they also failed to foresee that later generations brought up with television would find it as routine and unmagical as two or three cars in every garage and half a dozen chickens in every pot. If one reason for the revival of radio drama in the US was nostalgia on the part of older people (and of younger people too), another reason was that for those younger people radio drama was a completely novel experience, unlike television drama, with which they have been saturated since early childhood. Predictably, much of this new radio drama has been popular and lightweight rather than serious, but that is exactly how it was in the Golden Age too.

Is the experience of the US since 1973 unique, or are there analogues in other countries with different broadcasting systems? One of the most surprising developments in British commercial radio since Independent Local Radio was established in 1973 has been its flirtation with drama. Considering the half-century monopoly which the BBC held in radio drama until 1973 and the size of its output, this commercial sponsorship has struck some people as poaching on BBC preserves, but it indicates that among habitual listeners to ILR stations there is an audience for something other than the usual fare. The largest and most profitable of these stations, Capital Radio in London, has been particularly adventurous in this respect, but other stations, notably Piccadilly Radio in Manchester, Radio City in Liverpool, and Metro Radio in Newcastle, have followed suit, broadcasting serials, series, and single plays. While much of this output is undemanding and unreservedly popular in appeal, as you would expect from the entire American experience of commercial radio, some of it is more ambitious and serious (Strindberg on Metro Radio). Cynics would put this more prestigious broadcasting down to an attempt by ILR to improve its image and make itself culturally respectable, but this would be a malign interpretation of what is happening.

In countries such as Canada and Australia where commercial and public-service radio have coexisted for much longer than in the UK, there has been little sign of commercial stations following the American example of revitalizing radio drama. Nevertheless, in both these countries there is evidence that a new, young audience has emerged for serious radio who are prepared to listen to drama. Concomitant with this has been the interest shown in the medium by the younger generation of writers during the 1970's and 1980's. In neither country, unlike the US, has there been an actual break in drama output on radio, because CBC and ABC respectively have continued to foster it during the television age, but the arrival of television has, of course, acted as a major depressant. The Golden Age of Canadian radio may have gone forever, but the fact that a significant number of recent Canadian radio plays have been published in magazines, anthologies, and single-author collections speaks for itself and cannot be dismissed as part of a desperate attempt by Canadians to convince themselves that they possess a national literature. Among the younger Canadian writers to have been attracted to radio are Michael Cook, Gwendolyn MacEwen, and the prolific J. Michael Yates, but they are indebted to older figures such as Mavor Moore, John Reeves, and George Woodcock for keeping radio drama so alive while television captured the mass audience. In Australia, too, there have been signs of new vitality and new interest in recent years. The publication in 1975 of an anthology of outstanding contemporary radio drama, *Nightmares of the Old Obscenity Master and Other Plays* (edited with a substantial introduction by Alrene Sykes) is a landmark, since the usual fate of radio plays is to be transmitted once and then never heard or seen again. Sykes's anthology made a number of good works readily available, including two by Colin Free, probably the most gifted Australian writer to have found radio a rewarding medium in the last two decades. He is the author of the anthology's title play, a sophisticated and original piece of dramatic writing, superbly crafted for the medium. Nevertheless, all this good news is currently being qualified by the bad: in the difficult financial climate of the mid-1980's both CBC and ABC are under considerable pressure to save money by cutting back radio drama production, and the immediate future may be bleak.

Evidence of a totally different kind can be cited to indicate a new wave of interest in radio drama since the early 1970's. Although coverage of radio drama in the daily, weekly, and monthly press has shrunk, even in the UK, to occasional discussion in one of the remaining columns devoted to radio (such as David Wade in the *Times*, Gillian Reynolds in the *Daily Telegraph*, and Paul Ferris in the *Observer*), academic interest in the subject has been growing after decades of almost total neglect. The establishment and expansion of courses in drama and mass communication are undoubtedly partly responsible for this long overdue development. Students who have assumed that there was not much in radio for them have been astounded to find such a wealthy heritage of imaginative work, and this has made them aware of the expressive possibilities of the medium today.

The first international conference devoted to radio drama, the brainchild of the radio writer and critic Ian Rodger, was held in England in 1977 and attracted a surprisingly large number of people from all over the world, including some undergraduates. Conspicuous at the conference was a group of German academics, most of whom had been studying and teaching British radio plays during the 1970's. This strong German interest, further illustrated by the publication in 1977 of two major studies of British radio drama (one by Horst Priessnitz and the other edited by him), may or may not have put British academics to shame, but it acted as a stimulus. If German professors could find so much to admire in British radio drama and were busy writing about it, why were their British counterparts ignoring it so assiduously? No important study of radio drama had been published in England since the late 1950's when Val Gielgud's *British Radio Drama 1922–1956* (1957) and Donald McWhinnie's *The Art of Radio* (1959) appeared, and both of these were by senior members of the BBC Radio Drama Department. Furthermore, very few radio plays were published unless by established writers of poetry, novels, or stage plays, such as Louis MacNeice, Samuel Beckett, Harold Pinter, and Tom Stoppard. In the wake of the 1977 conference, though not necessarily a consequence of it, publication of radio plays and of books about radio drama has been decidedly on the increase after the dearth of material in the fairly recent past. In addition to the *Papers of the Radio Literature Conference 1977* (1978), there have been Barbara Coulton's *Louis MacNeice in the BBC* (1980), two large and complementary collections of essays, *British Radio Drama* and *Radio Drama*, both published in 1981, and another book called *Radio Drama*, by Ian Rodger, also in 1981. The publications department of the BBC has also been active in promoting radio drama by making texts available, either on its own or, as in the case of the Giles Cooper Award winners, in conjunction with Methuen. The annual Giles Cooper awards (named after one of the finest of all radio dramatists) are themselves new, being established in 1978 under joint BBC and Methuen sponsorship to encourage and reward writers of radio drama, and so far nine volumes of award-winning plays (in a series commencing with *Best Radio Plays of 1978*) have been published.

The BBC's own strong commitment to radio drama suffered a setback in 1980 when the Corporation was forced to make substantial cuts in expenditure. Throughout the 1970's, after the major reorganization of the BBC in 1970, the Radio Drama Department maintained a considerable output, ranging from popular daily serials with audiences of between one and a half and three million (*The Archers* and *Waggoners' Walk*) through the standard Radio 4 slots with audiences sometimes rising to more than half a million (*Saturday Night Theatre*, which used to attract nearly a third of the entire population in the 1940's) to the minority productions of Radio 3, averaging audiences of 50,000. Such figures may look paltry compared with viewing figures for television, but they are far from negligible, and in comparison with audiences for stage plays are remarkably high. How many avant-garde theatrical productions achieve an audience of 5,000, let alone 50,000? In addition to the many hours which BBC Radio devoted to adaptations, translations, features, and dramatized readings, it succeeded in producing about 500 original plays a year. The 1980 cutback dented the Radio Drama Department, but did not hole it amidships. By far its most popular programme, *Waggoners' Walk*, was soon phased out, and two of its new departures of the late 1970's, *Hi-Fi-Theatre* and a more exciting development in fifteen-minute plays, *Just Before Midnight*, disappeared, but there is still a great deal of drama to be heard on Radios 3 and 4. The number of original plays produced has dropped significantly, but remains very high by international standards, averaging six a week, the majority receiving daytime transmission on Radio 4, especially in *Afternoon Theatre*. Drama on Radio 4, though not on Radio 3, has virtually ceased to go out in the later evening, so that such venerable programmes as *Saturday Night Theatre* and the Sunday Classic Serial are now broadcast in the early evening, not at their traditional times. Many changes have been and are taking place, but change is not necessarily for the worse. Those who have followed closely the fortunes and misfortunes of BBC Radio over the past 20 years, notably David Wade, are convinced that there has been a considerable improvement in the quality of radio writing, especially at the more popular end of the spectrum.

Radio drama has also benefitted from the new vitality in BBC Radio as a whole during recent years, in spite of all the economic difficulties. It is television, not radio, which now looks stale, unadventurous, and in urgent need of a massive blood transfusion. The BBC Radio Drama Department, with its low production costs and high output, can afford to take risks in a way that the Television Drama Department cannot. "Safety First" is not the motto of Broadcasting House as it probably has to be of Television Centre. An experiment such as Andrew Sachs's wordless radio play *The Revenge* (1978), consisting only of sound effects and inarticulate human noises, is almost unthinkable on television. Admittedly, some short experimental work by Samuel Beckett has been shown on television, but only in the case of a writer of such monumental stature as Beckett would this occur. Radio, on the other hand, is willing to try things out by unknown or little-known writers, and *The Revenge*, to take an extreme case, succeeded in attracting an enormous amount of attention for a radio play. Or consider a great success story, Douglas Adams's *The Hitch-Hiker's Guide to the Galaxy*, which achieved cult status and joined the bestseller lists. Would this have stood a chance as a television series or a stage play or a published book if it had not won a considerable following on radio first? Radio took the gamble in 1978 and, when it paid off handsomely, television followed, knowing it had a sure winner. The great popularity of *The Hitch-Hiker's Guide to the Galaxy* on radio, where it was much more at home than in any other medium, was itself indicative that 25 years after the Goons and *Under Milk Wood* radio could still originate something of a dramatic nature which was able to ignite the national imagination. If new writers are attracted to radio, it is partly because they know that work of promise has a good chance of being accepted, whereas very few plays written for television ever reach the small screen just as very few film scripts ever reach the large one. In any case, contemporary television drama in the UK has to a great extent settled down to predictable formulas (e.g., BBC's *Play for Today*) and is much less interesting and innovative than it was in the heady days of 20 years ago. Because of the current epidemic of series and serials afflicting television drama, there is less and less space for single plays. Radio, on the other hand, relies heavily on the single play, while maintaining its long-standing commitment to serials, whether daily (*The Archers*) or weekly (popular crime and spy thrillers, as well as the Sunday Classic).

One factor working to the advantage of radio drama today is a proper though belated acknowledgement that at its best it is an autonomous form, not an inferior substitute for the real thing, namely live theatre on the stage (or even film or television drama). For much of its history, the radio play has been treated as the Cinderella of drama because it lacks a visual dimension. The silent cinema was a quarter of a century old before radio drama was born, only a couple of years before the "talkies" arrived. Television did not become the dominant medium until after World War II—Coronation Day in 1953, as far as the UK is concerned—but television transmissions began several years before the war. In such an unprecedently visual culture, radio drama had to struggle on unequal terms. Yet in the early days of radio, pioneering figures such as Lance Sieveking and Tyrone Guthrie in the BBC recognized that radio had to develop dramatic forms unique to itself, not borrow those of the stage. Nevertheless, there is a fundamental ambiguity in the term "radio drama" itself—does it mean "drama on radio" or "drama for radio"? There is a world of difference here, and it is worth remembering that, in the early days of radio, attempts were made to transmit live stage performances. These were so unsatisfactory that studio productions soon replaced them, but the policy of putting "drama on radio" has remained a cornerstone of BBC planning. It was the now-defunct Features Department of the BBC rather than the Drama Department which really developed the distinctive expressive possibilities of radio as a dramatic medium, and such radio classics as Louis MacNeice's *The Dark Tower* (1946) and Dylan Thomas's *Under Milk Wood* (1954) were products of Features, like many other fictional works.

Quite a lot of radio drama remains "drama on radio" rather than "drama for radio." Many playwrights hope for a television or stage production of their work, since the financial rewards and critical esteem can be so much greater, and fall back on radio if rejected elsewhere. This means that they are not thinking in radio terms from the outset and that their plays would be more at home in a medium other than radio. A fairly recent attempt to encourage radio drama (in which the BBC was a joint sponsor) backfired because the various dramatists commissioned to write plays suitable for both staging and broadcasting obviously found the task virtually insuperable. Their plays may have worked in the theatre, but most did not succeed on radio. It is perhaps surprising that such a scheme should have been tried out in 1981, since the success of television as a medium of mass communication has, strangely enough, had the effect of defining very clearly the peculiarly untheatrical characteristics and advantages of radio as a dramatic medium, especially its freedom from visual consistency and continuity. If television tends towards orthodox realism, even naturalism, radio is extraordinarily flexible and accommodates fantasy and surrealism as easily as the well-made play. The natural home for the Theatre of the Absurd is radio.

It is hardly a coincidence that radio drama had a new lease of life in the years immediately following television's great breakthrough in 1953. Samuel Beckett's main period as a radio writer lasted from 1957 until 1964. Four of the outstanding and most dedicated radio dramatists of the postwar period, Giles Cooper, Rhys Adrian, Frederick Bradnum, and Barry Bermange, developed their individual styles at about the same time. Indeed, Cooper's major achievements of the mid- and late-1950's, including *Mathry Beacon* (1956) and *Under the Loofah Tree* (1958), inaugurated a new phase in the history of British radio drama, following the achievement of writers such as MacNeice, Thomas, and Henry Reed, and acted as a stimulus to a new generation of radio writers for whom the apparent limitations of the medium are, in fact, advantages to be exploited to the full. Yet however attractive the medium is artistically—in spite of the technological wizardry now available to the producer, radio remains very much a writer's medium—few dramatists become totally or almost totally dedicated to it. Kudos, fame, and money lie elsewhere—television, stage, films—so radio can be the first rung on the ladder for a budding playwright. Historians of the radio play often draw attention to the fact that several dramatists who have made names for themselves as stage writers, such as Joe Orton and Tom Stoppard, began their careers and achieved their initial successes on radio. Cooper, on the other hand, while writing for the stage and television, was really a committed radio dramatist, as are Rhys Adrian, Frederick Bradnum, Don Haworth, and R.C. Scriven, whereas Beckett, Pinter, Stoppard, David Rudkin, and John Arden are not, even though their radio plays are among the best work ever written for the medium. It is significant that those who have devoted all or most of their creative energy to radio are much less well known to the public than the others, even though Cooper, Adrian, and Scriven must be ranked among the finest dramatic writers since the war.

Considering the number of radio plays broadcast and that few are repeated or published (although the situation is improving on both counts), even the most conscientious critic is hard put to it to keep track of developments. Radio drama attracts so little informed discussion that it is not inconceivable for a masterpiece to slip through without being recognized for what it is except by the BBC Radio Drama Department. During the 1970's and 1980's some of the established radio dramatists, such as Adrian, Bradnum, Scriven, and James Saunders, have continued to write regularly for the medium, but a number of other dramatists—some new, some not so new—have come to prominence. Peter Everett is an example of a dramatist who has been writing for radio for more than twenty years but who has achieved his best work since the mid-1970's. The novelist Susan Hill, on the other hand, came to radio only in 1970 and wrote prolifically for the medium until 1975 when she came to a temporary standstill; more recently she contributed scripts for *The Archers*. Among other writers who have made a notable contribution to radio drama during the last 15 years are Rachel Billington, Howard Barker, Peter Barnes, Angela Carter, Stephen Davis, Ian Dougall, John Fletcher, Shirley Gee, Gabriel Josipovici, Anne Leaton, Jennifer Phillips, David Pownall, Jonathan Raban, Derek Raby, Peter Redgrove, Michael Sadler, Rose Tremain, William Trevor, Elizabeth Troop, and Fay Weldon.

There is plenty of good listening available, yet none of the young or new recruits to radio writing has yet produced work of the stature of Rudkin's *Cries from Casement as His Bones Are Brought to Dublin* (1973) and Arden's *Pearl* (1978). Both of these plays are long, complex, ambitious pieces of writing with wide-ranging social and political implications, and both made excellent radio. In comparison with these, so much broadcast drama, however skilful and radiogenic, seems narrow in focus, limited in range, and content to work within a small circumference, though not necessarily short in duration. Radio drama does, of course, lend itself to the depiction of rigidly circumscribed worlds, whether mental or social. Yet the success of both *Cries from Casement* and *Pearl* establishes how artistically and thematically modest most radio plays are. A comparison between *Pearl* and the other winners of the first Giles Cooper awards in 1978 makes this point clear. 1978 was not a great year for radio drama, but the six award-winning plays apart from *Pearl*, including works by Don Haworth, Jennifer Phillips, and Fay Weldon, are not negligible. Nevertheless, these six plays, anthologized as *Best Radio Plays of 1978* (appropriately enough, *Pearl* was published separately), seem decidedly puny when placed beside Arden's, another of whose radio dramas, *The Old Man Sleeps Alone*, won a Giles Cooper award in 1982. Since the mid-1950s an orthodoxy has developed that radio drama is essentially minimalist—it should hint, not state; work in shades of grey, not primary colours; look inward, not outward; be verbally austere, not rhetorical. The achievements in subtlety and refinement have been numerous, but orthodoxies almost always end up inhibiting new growth and possibilities, and radio dramatists should be encouraged to take up the challenge presented by *Cries from Casement* and *Pearl*.

Best Radio Plays of 1978 was not an impressive advertisement for British radio drama, but subsequent volumes in the series have gone a long way to redeem its reputation. Three of the six winners in 1979, Shirley Gee's *Typhoid Mary*, Carey Harrison's *I Never Killed My German*, and Barrie Keeffe's fifteen-minute *Heaven Scent*, exploited the medium extraordinarily well, making admirable use of narrative voices, while the four award winners for 1980, Stewart Parker's *The Kamikaze Ground Staff Reunion Dinner*, Martyn Read's *Waving to a Train*, Peter Redgrove's *Martyr of the Hives*, and William Trevor's *Beyond the Pale*, also succeeded very well on radio in their different ways. During the 1980's some of the most memorable instances of radio drama have been adaptations, such as that of Mervyn Peake's *Gormenghast* trilogy (written by Brian Sibley), but there has been no shortage of good original plays. Peter Barnes has rightly attracted considerable attention with three brilliant series in arithmetical progression, the first of monologues, the second of duologues, and the third of trios; there may well be more of *Barnes' People* to come, in increasingly complex configurations. Established figures, including Adrian (*Watching the Plays Together*, 1982; *Outpatient*, 1985), Haworth (*Talk of Love and War*, 1981; *Daybreak*, 1984), Stoppard (*The Dog It Was That Died*, 1982), Trevor (*Autumn Sunshine*, 1982), and Pinter (*Family Voices*, 1981), have also added to their stature as radio writers with award-winning plays, and younger, less well known writers of proven quality, such as Shirley Gee (*Never in My Lifetime*, 1983), David Pownall (*Beef*, 1981; *Ploughboy Monday*, 1985), Martyn Read (*Scouting for Boys*, 1983), and Barry Collins (*King Canute*, 1985), have consolidated their achievement in the same way. *Never in My Lifetime* is an outstanding example of the drama inspired by the current situation in Northern Ireland, a popular subject for radio writers in the last few years, vividly treated by the Irish playwright John P. Rooney in *The Dead Image* (1981). Among the most exciting radio drama of the 1980's are plays by even younger writers, such as Martin Crimp, Stephen Dunstone, Steve May, Christopher Russell, and Michael Wall, not necessarily new to the medium but now developing into masters of it. Dunstone's *Who Is Sylvia?* and Russell's *Swimmer* (both first broadcast in 1984) and Crimp's *Three Attempted Acts* (1985) are distinguished plays by any standard, and exemplify the continuing vitality of British radio drama in these hard times for broadcasting.

—Peter Lewis

* * *

ADAMS, Douglas. Radio play: *The Hitch-Hiker's Guide to the Galaxy*, 1978 (staged 1979; novel version 1979; radio scripts published 1985). Television writing: *Doctor Who* series. Novelist.

ADRIAN, Rhys. Radio plays: *The Man on the Gate*, 1956; *The Passionate Thinker*, 1957; *The Prizewinner*, 1960; *Betsie*, 1960; *The Bridge*, 1961; *No Licence for Singing*, 1961; *Too Old for Donkeys*, 1963; *A Room to Let*, 1963; *A Nice Clean Sheet of Paper*, 1963 (published in *New Radio Drama*, 1966); *Sunday, The First of May*, 1964; *Between the Two of Us*, 1967; *Ella*, 1968; *Echoes*, 1969; *Evelyn*, 1969; *I'll Love You Always*,

Always, 1970; *The Gardeners of My Youth*, 1970 (staged 1976); *Mr. and Mrs. Squirrel*, 1971; *A Chance Encounter*, 1972; *Memoirs of a Sly Pornographer*, 1972; *Angle*, 1975; *The Night Nurse Slept in the Day Room*, 1976; *Buffet*, 1976; *The Clerks*, 1978 (published in *BBC Radio Playscripts*, 1979); *Prix Futura '79*, 1979; *Passing Through*, 1981; *Watching the Plays Together*, 1982 (published in *Best Radio Plays of 1982*, 1983); *Passing Time*, 1983; *Outpatient*, 1985 (published in *Best Radio Plays of 1985*, 1986); *Crossroads*, 1985. Television plays: *The Protest*, 1960 (published in *New Granada Plays*, 1961); *Helen and Edward and Henry*, 1965; *Stan's Day Out*, 1967; *The Drummer and the Bloke*, 1968; *The Foxtrot*, 1971; *No Charge for Extra Service*, 1971; *Thrills Galore*, 1972; *The Withered Arm*, from a story by Thomas Hardy, 1973; *The Joke* and *The Cafeteria*, from stories by Isaac Bashevis Singer, 1974; *Tea at Four*, 1975; *Mr. and Mrs. Bureaucrat*, 1978; *Getting It on Concorde*, 1979; *Passing Through*, 1982.

ARDEN, John. See his dictionary entry.

BARKER, Howard. See his dictionary entry.

BARNES, Peter. See his dictionary entry.

BECKETT, Samuel. See his dictionary entry.

BERMANGE, Barry. See his dictionary entry.

BILLINGTON, Rachel. Radio plays: *Mrs. Bleasdale's Lodger*, 1976; *Mary Mary*, 1977; *Sister, Sister*, 1978; *Have You Seen Guy Fawkes?*, 1979. Television plays: *Don't Be Silly*, 1979; *Life after Death*, 1982. Novelist.

BRADNUM, Frederick. Radio plays include *No Commemorating Stone*, 1954; *The Pity of Love*, 1955; *No Going Home*, 1957; *Private Dreams and Public Nightmares*, 1957; *Chloroform for Mr. Bartlett*, 1957; *Mr. Goodjohn and Mr. Badjack*, 1958; *The Cave and the Grail*, 1959; *Hedgehog*, 1961; *The Fist*, 1963; *The Crack of Doom*, 1964; *Appearances Deceive*, 1964; *Rimbaud at Harar*, 1965; *Pennicotte's Truth*, 1966; *A Lonely Place in a Dark Wood*, 1967; *A Storm on the Nile Basin*, 1967; *The Pallingham Depression*, 1969; *Goose with Pepper*, 1970; *Alive and Well and Living in London*, 1971; *A Terribly Strange Man*, 1971; *The Recruiter*, 1971; *A Putney Christmas*, 1971; *Enigmatic Conversations with Eminent Sociologists*, 1972; *You Are Not Alone in the House*, 1972; *The Final Solution*, 1973; *The Questionable Child*, from a work by Terence Tiller, 1973; *The Young Lady from Midhurst*, 1974; *A Dead Man on Leave*, 1974; *Degas, Cellini, Ming*, 1975; *Who Am I Now?*, 1975; *The Dream of George Crabbe*, 1976; *Springer's England*, 1976; *Craven's Stone*, 1977; *Creepers*, 1977; *The Girl Who Didn't Want to Be . . .*, 1978; *Cirrhosis Park*, 1979; *Other Days Around Me*, 1980; *The Man Who Lived among Eskimos*, 1981; *The Autonomous Murder Complex*, 1981; *Rosenberg in the Trenches*, 1982; *I Do It Exceptionally Well*, 1983; *Comrades*, 1983; *A Small Speck of Evil*, 1984; *Alice's Tea Party*, 1984; *The Bishop's Wife*, 1985; *Game of Chance*, 1985; *Deceptions*, 1985; *The Death of Robert De Cerilley*, 1986; *The Mote in the Eye*, 1987; *Death Duties*, 1987; and many radio adaptations of plays and novels. Television play: *The Defector*, 1975. Stage plays: *In at the Kill*, 1963; *Minerva Alone*, 1963; *Liselotte*, from a work by Duchesse d'Orléans, 1973, as *Diary of a Madame*, 1975. Book: *The Long Walks: Journeys to the Sources of the White Nile*, 1969.

CARTER, Angela. Radio plays: *Vampirella*, 1976; *Come unto These Yellow Sands*, 1979 (published 1984); *The Company of Wolves*, from her own story, 1980; *Puss in Boots*, 1982; *A Self-Made Man* (on Ronald Firbank), 1984. Screenplays: *The Company of Wolves*, with Neil Jordan, 1984; *The Magic Toyshop*, 1987. Novelist and writer of short stories and non-fiction.

COLLINS, Barry. See his dictionary entry.

COOK, Michael. See his dictionary entry.

COOPER, Giles. See his appendix entry.

CRIMP, Martin. Radio plays: *Three Attempted Acts*, 1985 (published in *Best Radio Plays of 1985*, 1986); *Six Figures at the Base of a Crucifix*, 1986. Stage plays: *Living Remains*, 1982; *Four Attempted Acts*, 1984; *A Variety of Death-Defying Acts*, 1985; *Definitely the Bahamas*, 1987; *A Kind of Arden*, 1987; *Spanish Girls*, 1987. Novelist and short story writer.

DAVIS, Stephen. Radio plays: *The Dissolution of Marcus Fleischmann*, 1976; *Events in Heroes Square*, 1976; *Man in Space*, 1978; *Yorkshire Rubbish*, 1979; *Trouble with Gregory*, 1980; *Dialogues on a Broken Sphere*, 1987. Television plays: *Busted*, 1983; *Cargo Kings*, 1983; *Floating Off*, 1983. Stage plays: *The Last Elephant*, 1981; *A View of Kabul*, 1982; *Love Field*, 1987.

DOUGALL, Ian. Radio plays: *The Immortal Young Ladies of Avignon*, 1970; *Extra-Terrestrial Objects*, 1974; *Concrete*, 1976; *Ann*, 1977; *Badbury Rings*, 1980.

DUNSTONE, Stephen. Radio plays: *Who Is Sylvia?*, 1984 (published in *Best Radio Plays of 1984*, 1985); *Arrived Safe, Writing Later*, 1985; *Oenanthe and the Beanstalk*, 1986. Stage play: *Dwarfs*, 1987. Novelist and children's writer.

EVERETT, Peter. Radio plays: *Night of the March Hare*, 1959; *Day at Izzard's Wharf*, 1959 (staged 1962); *Private View*, 1966; *The Cookham Resurrection*, 1975; *Me and Mr. Blake*, 1976; *Buffo*, 1976; *Harmonium*, 1978; *Martyr of the Hive*, 1980. Television plays: *The Girl Who Loved Robots*, 1965; *Hurt Hawks*, 1974; *Hoodwink*, 1975; *Freedom of the Dig*, 1978. Screenplays: *Negatives*, 1968; *The Last of the Long-Haired Boys*, 1971. Stage play: *The Daguerrotypes*, 1963. Novelist.

FLETCHER, John. Radio plays: *Wandering in Eden*, 1974; *The View from the Mountain*, 1975; *The Tragedie of Charles, Lord Stourton*, 1979; *The Trumpet Shall Sound*, 1979; *The Mendip Demoniack*, 1980; *Taptoe Through the Telephones*, 1981; *The Mansion of the Mighty*, 1982; *Babylon Has Fallen*, 1984 (published in *Plays Introduction*, 1984); *Deep Six*, 1984; *Suddenly*, 1985; *Some Mother's Son* serial, 1987; *The Glory of the Lord*, 1987; *The Price of Gold*, 1987. Television plays: *Silence*, 1974; *Stargazy on Zummerdown*, 1978; *The Various Ends of Mrs. F's Friends*, 1981. Stage plays: *The Marvellous Boy*, 1982; *Sedgmoor*, 1985.

FREE, Colin. Radio plays include *A Walk among the Wheeneys*, 1966 (staged 1966; published 1975); *Nightmares of the Old Obscenity Master*, 1973 (published 1975); *Murders*, 1981. Novelist.

GEE, Shirley. See her dictionary entry.

HARRISON, Carey. Radio plays: *I Never Killed My German*, 1979 (published in *Best Radio Plays of 1979*, 1980); *The Anatolian Head*, 1980; *The Levitation at St. Michael's*, 1980. Television plays: *The Bequest*, 1970; *The New Life*, 1973; *A Tale* *of Two Paintings*, 1973; *The Jensen Code*, 1974; *Lot 23*, 1975; *Nanny* series, 1981; *Freud*, 1984 (novelization 1984). Stage plays: *Dante Kaputt*, 1966; *Twenty-Six Efforts at Pornography*, 1967 (published in *New Short Plays 1*, 1968); *Lovers* (published in *New Short Plays 2*, 1969); *In a Cottage Hospital*, 1969; *Shakespeare Farewell*, 1969; *Manoeuvres*, with Jeremy Paul, 1974; *Who's Playing God?*, 1979; *Visitors*, with Paul, 1980; *A Night on the Tor*, 1987.

HAWORTH, Don. Radio plays: *The Man with the Red Door*, 1965; *There's No Point in Arguing the Toss*, 1967 (published 1972); *We All Come to It in the End*, 1968 (published 1972); *A Time in Cloud Cuckoo Land*, 1969; *The Prisoner*, 1969 (published 1972); *Where Is This Here Building—By What Route Do I Get There?*, 1970 (published 1972); *Simcocks Abound Across the Earth*, 1971; *The Illumination of Mr. Shannon*, 1971 (published 1972; staged 1973); *The Enlightenment of the Strawberry Gardener*, 1972 (published 1972; staged 1974); *The Eventful Deaths of Mr. Fruin*, 1972; *A Damsel and Also a Rough Bird*, 1974; *Mr. Bruin Who Once Drove the Bus*, 1975 (published in *Act 1*, edited by David Self and Ray Speakman, 1979); *Events at the Salamander Hotel*, 1975; *On a Day in a Garden in Summer*, 1976 (published in *Contemporary One-Act Plays*, 1976); *Memories of a Childhood Friendship*, 1976; *Fun Balloons*, 1977; *Episode on a Thursday Evening*, 1978 (published in *Best Radio Plays of 1978*, 1979); *The Last Ride of Walter Enderby, Motorist and Amorist*, 1979 (published 1979); *Talk of Love and War*, 1981 (published in *Best Radio Plays of 1981*, 1982); *Summer at Apendorf*, 1982; *Dragon*, 1982; *Daybreak*, 1984 (published in *Best Radio Plays of 1984*, 1985); *Solo Across the Atlantic*, 1987; *A View from the Mountain*, 1987. Television plays and documentaries: *Time on Our Hands*, 1962; *Ein Haus Voll Zeit*, 1972 (Germany); *A Brisk Dip Sagaciously Considered*, 1974; *Len Ward: The Rest of the Story*, 1980; *A Man of the Black Mountains*, 1981; *A Brush with Mr. Porter on the Road to El Dorado*, 1981. Stage play: *A Hearts and Mind Job*, 1971 (published 1971). Non-fiction: *Figures in a Bygone Landscape: A Lancashire Childhood*, 1986.

HILL, Susan. Radio plays: *Taking Leave*, 1971; *The End of Summer*, 1971 (published 1975); *Lizard in the Grass*, 1971 (published 1975); *The Cold Country*, 1972 (published 1975); *Winter Elegy*, 1973; *Consider the Lilies*, 1973 (published 1975); *A Window on the World*, 1974; *Strip Jack Naked*, 1974 (published 1975); *Mr. Proudham and Mr. Sleight*, 1974; *On the Face of It*, 1975 (published in *Act 1*, edited by David Self and Ray Speakman, 1979); *The Summer of the Giant Sunflower*, 1977; *The Sound That Time Makes*, 1980; *Here Comes the Bride*, 1980; *Chances*, 1981 (staged 1983); *Out in the Cold*, 1982; *Autumn*, 1985; *Winter*, 1985. Television play: *Last Summer's Child*, from her own story "The Badness Within Him," 1981. Stage play: *The Ramshackle Company* (for children), 1981. Writer of fiction and non-fiction, and books for children.

JOSIPOVICI, Gabriel. Radio plays: *Playback*, 1973; *A Life*, 1973; *Ag*, 1976; *Vergil Dying*, 1979 (published 1981); *Majorana: Disappearance of a Physicist*, with Sacha Rabinovitch, 1981; *The Seven*, with Jonathan Harvey, 1983; *Metamorphosis*, from the story by Kafka, 1985; *Ode for St. Cecilia*, 1986. Stage plays: *Dreams of Mrs. Fraser*, 1972 (published 1974); *Evidence of Intimacy*, 1972; *Flow*, 1973 (published 1974); *Echo*, 1975 (published in *Proteus 3*, 1978); *Marathon*, 1977 (published in *Adam*, 1980); *A Moment*, 1979. Author of novels, short stories, and essays.

KEEFFE, Barrie. See his dictionary entry.

LEATON, Anne. Radio plays: *The Sound of the Planet Dissolving*, 1974; *The Heathcliffe Data*, 1975; *My Name Is Bird McKai*, 1976; *Monsters and Other Events*, 1977. Novelist.

MacEWEN, Gwendolyn. Radio plays include: *Terror and Erebus*, 1965 (published in *Tamarack Review*, October 1974); *The World of Neshiah*, 1967; *The Last Night of James Pike*, 1976. Stage play: *The Trojan Women*, from a play by Euripides, 1978 (published 1979). Poet, novelist, and writer for children.

MAY, Steve. Radio plays: *Down among the Umalogas*, 1982; *Poisoned Apples*, 1982; *Jack*, 1983; *No Exceptions*, 1983 (published in *Best Radio Plays of 1983*, 1984); *Mirror Signal Manoeuvre*, 1984; *Keeping Faith*, 1985; *False Pretences*, 1986; *On a Plate*, 1987.

MOORE, Mavor. See his dictionary entry.

ORTON, Joe. See his appendix entry.

PARKER, Stewart. See his dictionary entry.

PHILLIPS, Jennifer. Radio plays: *Fault on the Line*, 1966; *The Trouble with William*, 1967; *Stone Boy*, 1969; *The Trouble with You, Lillian*, 1969; *Arms and Legs*, 1972; *Henry Enjoying Himself*, 1974; *The Fixed Smile*, 1975; *Birdman*, 1975; *The Antique Baby*, 1975; *Your Tiny Hand Is Frozen*, 1976; *Blow Your House In*, 1977; *Venus at the Seaside*, 1977; *Daughters of Men*, 1978 (published in *Best Radio Plays of 1978*, 1979); *The Camera Often Lies*, 1979; *Past Appearances*, 1979; *A Very Nuclear Family*, 1980; *The Joy of the Worm*, 1980; *Miss Lambert's Last Dance?*, 1981; *The Glass Extension*, 1987; *Miss Lamb to the Slaughter*, 1987. Television plays: *View by Appointment*, 1968; *The Back Handed Kiss*, 1968; *Wink to Me Only*, 1969. Stage plays: *Bodywork*, 1972; *Instrument for Love*, 1973; *A Dog Called Samson* (for puppets), 1980; *The Canonization of Suzie*, 1980. Novelist.

PINTER, Harold. See his dictionary entry.

POWNALL, David. See his dictionary entry.

RABAN, Jonathan. Radio plays: *A Game of Tombola*, 1972; *At the Gate*, 1973; *The Anomaly*, 1974; *The Day Trip*, 1976; *Will You Accept the Call?*, 1977; *The English Department*, 1977; *Falling*, 1979; *Possibilities*, 1980. Television plays: *Snooker*, 1975; *Water Baby*, 1975. Stage play: *The Sunset Touch*, 1977. Travel writer, critic, and novelist.

RABY, Derek. Radio plays: *The Office*, 1973; *Tiger*, 1974; *A Cat Called Willie*, 1974; *Bandstand*, 1975; *Put an Egg in Your Tank*, 1977; *Letter to the Editor*, 1979; *Night Shift*, 1979; *Robinson*, 1979; *To Kill a Town*, 1981.

RAPHAEL, Frederic. See his screenwriters entry.

READ, Martyn. Radio plays: *Thank You for Your Support*, 1979; *Waving to a Train*, 1980 (published in *Best Radio Plays of 1980*, 1981); *Where Were You the Night They Shot the President?*, 1982; *Scouting for Boys*, 1983 (published in *Best Radio Plays of 1983*, 1984). Stage play: *221–B*, 1983.

REDGROVE, Peter. Radio plays: *The White Monument*, 1963; *The Sermon*, 1964 (published 1966); *The Anniversary*, 1964; *In the Country of the Skin*, 1973 (published 1973); *The Holy Sinner*, from a novel by Thomas Mann, 1975; *Dance the*

Putrefact, music by Anthony Smith-Masters, 1975; *The God of Glass*, 1977 (published 1979); *Martyr of the Hives*, 1980 (published in *Best Radio Plays of 1980*, 1981); *Florent and the Tuxedo Millions*, 1982; *The Sin-Doctor*, 1983; *Dracula in White*, 1984; *The Scientists of the Strange*, 1984; *Time for the Cat-Scene*, 1985; *The Valley of Trelamia*, 1986; *Ashiepaddle*, *The Three Feathers*, *The Juniper Tree*, *The One Who Set Out to Study Fear*, *The Master Thief*, and *The Flounder*, all from stories by the Grimm Brothers, 1987. Television play: *Jack Be Nimble* (*Leap in the Dark* series), 1980. Stage plays: *Miss Carstairs Dressed for Blooding and Other Plays* (published 1977); *The Hypnotist*, 1978. Poet, novelist, and writer of non-fiction.

REEVES, John. Radio plays: *A Beach of Strangers*, 1959 (published 1961; staged 1967); *Triptych*, 1971 (published 1972); *The Arithmetic of Love*, 1971.

ROONEY, John P. Radio plays: *The Summer Madness*, 1980; *The Dead Image*, 1981 (published in *Best Radio Plays of 1981*, 1982); *Hitler's the Boy*, 1984; *Born Again*, 1985; *Second Opinion*, 1986; *John Higgins Galway Macguigan Smith*, 1987; *Summit of Desire*, 1987. Stage play: *The Queen's O'Neill*, 1980.

RUDKIN, David. See his dictionary entry.

RUSSELL, Christopher. Radio plays: *Harvey's Festival*, 1975; *A Game of Sin*, 1977; *The Devil and David Dobbs*, 1977; *Vetchley 900*, 1977; *C'est la Shoestrings*, 1978; *Sweets on Sunday*, 1978; *Getting Out*, 1979; *Cold Bath Fields*, 1979; *Shelling Peas*, 1979; *Brandy for the Parson*, 1979; *The Last Witch*, 1979; *The Last Christmas*, 1980; *Tidal Race*, 1981; *Love and Futility*, 1983; *The Knighties*, 1984; *Swimmer*, 1984 (published in *Best Radio Plays of 1984*, 1985); *Armada Rock* (for children), 1985 (novelization 1984); *Navyman God*, 1985; *Screaming Alice*, 1985. Television plays: *Citizens* (*Crown Court* series), 1984; *This Little Pig*, 1985.

SACHS, Andrew. Radio plays: *Till Death Us Do Join*, 1964; *Flat to Let*, 1964; *Pie and Pea Supper*, 1966; *Kidnapped*, 1967; *Time for a Coat*, 1967; *Philately Will Get You Nowhere*, 1971; *Made in Heaven*, 1971 (staged 1975); *Home from Home*, 1972; *Cash Me a Portrait*, 1972; *The Revenge*, 1978; *The Grimm Tale of an Old Master*, 1985; *The Art Lovers*, 1985. Television play: *The Galactic Garden*, with John Dewkey, 1985. Actor.

SADLER, Michael. Radio plays: *Gulliver's Way*, 1970; *The Bull of La Plata*, 1970; *Hopcraft into Europe*, 1972; *South Coast Twilight Serenade*, 1975. Television plays: *Mrs. Pool's Preserves*, 1973; *Pigeon-Hawk or Dove?*, 1974; *Cork and Bottle*, 1976; *Miss*, 1977; *And Things That Go Bump in the Night*, 1977. Stage play: *And Was Jerusalem*, 1967.

SAUNDERS, James. See his dictionary entry.

SCRIVEN, R.C. Radio plays: *The Peacock City of P'Tzan King*, 1947; *A Single Taper*, 1948 (published 1953); *The Inward Eye: Boy—13*, 1948 (published 1953); *The Island of White Birds*, 1948; *Baron Bear and the Little Prince*, with Phyllis Scriven, 1949; *Little Jan Pandrum*, with Phyllis Scriven, 1950; *Vi'lets Sweet Vi'lets*, with Phyllis Scriven, 1950; *The Snow Queen*, with Phyllis Scriven, 1950; *Poet and Englishman*, 1950; *One Man's City: Leeds*, 1951; *The Runaway Rocking Horse*, with Phyllis Scriven, 1952; *Bluecap and the Singing Wheel*, with Phyllis Scriven, 1953; *Joy of Angels*, 1954; *The Night and the Shadow*, 1955; *The Year of the Phoenix*, 1955 (published 1959); *The Lamp and the Flame*, 1956; *Writing a Pantomime—The Babes in the Wood*, 1961; *Reynard the Fox*, 1965; *The Blue Cloak*, 1966; *Jack and the Beanstalk*, 1968; *The Prospect of Whitby*, 1968 (published 1971); *Fiddler's Green*, 1968; *The Seasons of the Blind*, 1968 (published 1974); *The Poltergoose*, 1969 (published 1973); *All Early in the April*, 1970 (published 1974); *The Peacock Screamed One Morning*, 1970 (published 1974); *Dandelion and Parsnip, Vintage 1920*, 1971 (published 1974); *The House of Houses*, 1971; *Summer with Flowers That Fell*, 1972 (published 1974); *Claudia Procula*, 1972; *Give Me London Weather*, 1974; *A Measure of Sliding Sand*, 1974; *Nocturne of Provincial Spring*, 1975; *A Blind Understanding*, 1977. Writer of poetry and non-fiction; autobiography: *Edge of Darkness, Edge of Light*, 1977.

STOPPARD, Tom. See his dictionary entry.

TREMAIN, Rose. Radio plays: *The Wisest Fool*, 1976; *Dark Green*, 1977; *Blossom*, 1977; *Don't Be Cruel*, 1978; *Leavings*, 1978; *Down the Hill*, 1979; *Half Time*, 1980; *Hell and McLafferty*, 1982; *Temporary Shelter*, 1984 (published in *Best Radio Plays of 1984*, 1985); *The Birdcage*, 1984; *Will and Lou's Boy*, 1986; *The Kite Flyer*, 1987. Television plays: *Halleluiah, Mary Plum*, 1978; *Findings on a Late Afternoon*, 1980; *A Rose for Winter*, 1981; *Moving on the Edge*, 1983; *Daylight Robbery*, 1986. Stage plays: *Mother's Day*, 1980; *Yoga Class*, 1981. Novelist and short story writer.

TREVOR, William. See his dictionary entry.

TROOP, Elizabeth. Radio plays: *A Little Like Orson Who?*, 1974; *P.S. Wish You Were Here*, 1974; *Send Up*, 1976; *A Fine Country*, 1976; *The Year of the Great Betrayal*, 1977; *Not Waving*, 1978; *Night*, 1980; *Sludge*, 1980; *Bea Backwards*, 1980; *Comic Cuts*, 1980; *Woolworth Madonna*, 1980; *Abba Dabba Honeymoon*, 1982; *Slipping Away*, from her own novel, 1984; *Daddy's Girl*, 1985. Novelist and short story writer.

WALL, Michael. Radio plays: *Why Don't You Go Back Where You Came From?*, 1982; *Tom*, 1984; *Hiroshima: The Movie*, 1985 (published in *Best Radio Plays of 1985*, 1986); *The Wide-Brimmed Hat*, 1987. Television play: *Japanese Style*, 1983 (staged 1984). Stage plays: *Drawn Away*, 1983; *Branded*, 1985; *Blue Days*, 1985; *Imaginary Wars in England*, 1987.

WELDON, Fay. Radio plays: *Spider*, 1973; *Housebreaker*, 1973; *Mr. Fox and Mr. First*, 1974; *The Doctor's Wife*, 1975; *Polaris*, 1978 (published in *Best Radio Plays of 1978*, 1979); *Weekend*, 1979; *All the Bells of Paradise*, 1979; *I Love My Love*, 1981 (staged 1982; published 1984). Television plays: *Wife in a Blonde Wig*, 1966; *A Catching Complaint*, 1966; *The Fat Woman's Tale*, 1966; *What About Me*, 1967; *Dr. De Waldon's Therapy*, 1967; *Goodnight Mrs. Dill*, 1967; *The 45th Unmarried Mother*, 1967; *Fall of the Goat*, 1967; *Ruined Houses*, 1968; *Venus Rising*, 1968; *The Three Wives of Felix Hull*, 1968; *Hippy Hippy Who Cares*, 1968; *£13083*, 1968; *The Loophole*, 1969; *Smokescreen*, 1969; *Poor Mother*, 1970; *Office Party*, 1970; *On Trial* (*Upstairs, Downstairs* series), 1971; *Old Man's Hat*, 1972; *A Splinter of Ice*, 1972; *Hands*, 1972; *The Lament of an Unmarried Father*, 1972; *A Nice Rest*, 1972; *Comfortable Words*, 1973; *Desirous of Change*, 1973; *In Memoriam*, 1974; *Poor Baby*, 1975; *The Terrible Tale of Timothy Bagshott*, 1975; *Aunt Tatty*, from the story by Elizabeth Bowen, 1975;

Act of Rape, 1977; *Married Love* (*Six Women* series), 1977; *Act of Hypocrisy* (*Jubilee* series), 1977; *Chickabiddy* (*Send in the Girls* series), 1978; *Pride and Prejudice*, from the novel by Jane Austen, 1980; *Honey Ann*, 1980; *Life for Christine*, 1980; *Watching Me, Watching You* (*Leap in the Dark* series), 1980; *Little Mrs. Perkins*, from a story by Penelope Mortimer, 1982; *Redundant! or, The Wife's Revenge*, 1983; *Out of the Undertow*, 1984; *Bright Smiles* (*Time for Murder* series), 1985; *Zoe's Fever* (*Ladies in Charge* series), 1986; *A Dangerous Kind of Love* (*Mountain Men* series), 1986; *Heart of the Country* serial, 1987. Stage plays: *Permanence*, in *Mixed Doubles*, 1969 (published 1970); *Time Hurries On* (published in *Scene Scripts* edited by Michael Marland, 1972); *Words of Advice*, 1974 (published 1974); *Friends*, 1975; *Moving House*, 1976; *Mr. Director*, 1978; *Action Replay*, 1978 (published 1980; staged as *Love among the Women*, 1982); *After the Prize*, 1981 (as *Wood Worm*, 1984); *Jane Eyre*, from the novel by Charlotte Brontë, 1986; *The Hole in the Top of the World*, 1987. Novelist and short story writer.

WOODCOCK, George. Radio plays: *Maskerman*, 1960 (published in *Prism*, Winter 1961); *The Island of Demons*, 1962 (published 1977); *The Benefactor*, 1963 (published 1982); *The Empire of Shadows*, 1964; *The Floor of the Night*, 1965; *The Brideship*, music by Robert Turner, 1967; *Six Dry Cakes for the Hunted*, 1975 (published as *Gabriel Dumont and the Northwest Rebellion*, 1975). Poet, critic, and historian.

YATES, J. Michael. Radio plays: *The Broadcaster*, 1968 (published 1971); *Theatre of War*, 1968 (published 1971); *The Calling*, 1968 (published 1975); *Night Freight*, 1968 (staged 1972; published 1972); *The Panel*, 1969 (published 1971); *The Abstract Beast*, 1969 (published 1971); *Smokestack in the Desert*, 1970 (published 1971); *Poet in an Arctic Landscape*, 1970; *The Border*, 1971 (published 1971); *Realia*, 1975; *The Net*, 1975 (published 1975); *Search for the Tse-Tse Fly*, 1975 (published 1975); *Sinking of the North West Passage*, 1975; *The Secret of State*, 1976. Screenplay: *The Grand Edit*, 1966. Stage play: *Subjunction*, 1965. Poet and short story writer.

TELEVISION WRITERS

Television is more an access system than an aesthetic form, and its drama does not take easily to capsule definitions. Some of Britain's finest films have been made for the medium, as well as some of the worst. That much-reviled hybrid, the studio play, has, from time to time, given us work of extraordinary imagination and power, although, in general, dramatists look on it as an imprecise and slovenly form, too technologically preoccupied to give sufficient weight and authority to an author's text. And the long-running serials of television's history—whether they are expensively and leisurely paced adaptations of famous books, or weekly episodes of some continuous crime story or soap opera—have, more frequently than might be admitted, proved to be real achievements of dramatic writing and invention.

It has been customary, for some years now, to lament the dominance over television drama of naturalism—the journalistic type of writing in which the surface of things is marked out in almost obsessive detail, while the interior landscape of the imagination is left largely to its own devices. Dennis Potter's expansive body of work is correctly seen as a huge criticism of naturalism, a plea for tough-minded poetry in a medium which appears to drift naturally toward prosaic sentimentality. The late David Mercer began his television career, almost by chance, in the likeness of a 1950's naturalistic socialist, and became, very quickly, an anarchic poet of imaginative non-conformity, a writer who used the studio more as a mental than a physical space. But, since the late 1960's and early 1970's, writers who have imaginative territory to explore seem to crave the resources of film, when they can get it. Tape, and the studio, so the argument runs, run counter to the precision and control which a scrupulously written text requires. David Hare, David Rudkin, Stephen Poliakoff, Jack Rosenthal, and Alan Bennett seem to belong on film, and have reputations which can command the much-coveted film slots. Other, less established writers are less squeamish. And there are a few who remain perennially fascinated by the stylistic challenge of tape.

Dennis Potter always maintained, for instance, that the studio play, when properly exploited, had its own strength and integrity. Howard Schuman, who has never been much drawn toward the imitative monotony of naturalism and the documentary style, has deliberately written for video tape in order to explore the collision between daydream and everyday, to show us that one of the functions of imagination is to remake experience in stylised shapes and patterns. His *Rock Follies* and *Rock Follies of '77*—as well as the untransmitted play *Censored Scenes from King Kong*—give us a world infected by high-coloured glamour and farce, a romance of sex, success, and power which nevertheless has its feet on the ground. For a long time Schuman dreamed of a drama serial that would mix videotape and film, the heightened and the naturalistic, for aesthetic rather than budgetary reasons. His projected multi-part drama, *The Ann Lovington Hour*, twice came very close to production, only to be dropped, through a combination of executive-level dislike and programming contingencies by both Thames Television and the BBC. The early scripts are a fascinating mix of film-rooted reality and video dream, with the suburban heroine of the title inhabiting two separate worlds which are subtly and hypnotically drawn together as the story progresses.

It may be sensible to conjecture than an early exposure to the hard-edged and dream-bound qualities of videotape helped both Potter and Schuman to a subject. Potter's famous *Pennies from Heaven* used the tinsel romance of popular song to mark out its own imaginative territory. Arthur Parker, the raunchy and wide-eyed sheet music salesman, knew that life never quite lived up to the promise of the ballads he peddled, and dreamed of a world where the songs might come true. For Potter, show-business is not merely a lie or a fiction or an escape; as he confesses, its gilded fantasies give us a popular version of the consolation once offered by religion and the psalms, and its collective romantic ideals embody the best and deepest feeling in us, as well as the worst. Potter's early, taped plays—such as *Moonlight on the Highway* or *Follow the Yellow Brick Road*—reveal an absorption in daydream, a concern with the intensity of our longing for love and grandeur and poetry, which lead straight to the large, wise and complex canvases of *Pennies from Heaven* and *The Singing Detective*. Here, the pop mythology of television, its stream of jingles, songs, glamorous people, picturesque landscapes, sex, melodrama, burlesque, and parody, becomes the language for what are really novels conceived in dramatic terms for the small screen. Audiences who might balk at the somewhat literary and esoteric visual grammar of a filmmaker like Tarkovsky have no difficulties with the kaleidoscope of scenes and images which makes up *The Singing Detective*. Potter's televisual style, so eloquent and so moving, has been crafted from the slipstream of trivia that pours out of the TV set each night.

Schuman's work shares a similar understanding of the emotive power of those fantasies which are the bright and gaudy language of television. *Rock Follies*, *The Ann Lovington Hour*, and *Up Line*, derive their style, momentum, and vocabulary not from the stage, or from literature, but from the effervescent makeshift of the TV studio. On several occasions, Schuman has deplored the fact that television seemingly refuses to encourage and rear its own writers, that it prefers to lure them in from more "respectable" forms, like stage drama or the novel. Television, Schuman believes, should seek writers who want, primarily, to write for television, instead of making the small screen a consolation prize for aspiring cinema writers, or a prestigious new outlet for well known novelists. And it's true that few writers have really been television's children. David Mercer broke in with a play originally conceived for the stage, *Where the Difference Begins*, although he acclimatised himself to the new medium with an extraordinary artistic and intellectual glee. David Hare and Stephen Poliakoff, whose films *Licking Hitler* and *Caught on a Train* won their respective authors BAFTA awards, had defected from the stage and were, in any case, using the small screen to host filmic ambitions. Frederic Raphael, the university wit whose six-part sequence of plays, *The Glittering Prizes*, caught the public imagination in the mid-1970's began as a novelist and Oscar-winning screenwriter. Alan Bleasdale, who wrote the Thatcherite dole saga, *Boys from the Blackstuff*, was, until this immense success, regarded primarily as a stage dramatist. Practised adaptors like Julian Mitchell, Fay Weldon, and Christopher Hampton had acquired their skills elsewhere. Again and again, the credit for television drama's success seems to go to the Script Editor, that dogsbody-cum-literary-manager who has so often sought out writers in other media and lured them into the studio.

As we near the end of the 1980's, we must admit that no single writer in this decade has seized the opportunity of television to produce a body of work like that of Potter or Mercer in the 1960's or Schuman in the 1970's. And the advent of a predominantly filmic kind of television drama, the sense that television is now hosting the screenplay rather than the tape-play, is the inevitable consequence of Channel Four's *Film on Four* slot. Once the new channel had accustomed viewers to the idea that, in dramatic terms, the TV set was merely a scaled-down version of a cinema screen, that TV's dramatists and directors were to give us films and not plays, almost everyone accepted the change with a sigh of relief. The BBC replied to Channel Four's innovation with a new and successful slot of their own—*Screen Two*—and the old *Play for Today*, with its associations of word-bound taped drama, slipped quietly from our screens. In the 1960's and 1970's filmed drama, so far as the single play was concerned, had remained relatively rare, and highly prized. Writers like David Rudkin, Tom Clarke, and Robert Holles gave us superb screenplays, which were realised on film, and David Hare waited a year in order to secure one of the film slots for *Licking Hitler*. But the majority of television's plays and serials were made on tape, and dramatists like Potter and Mercer did not abandon it easily. And the dramatic language of the films, the sovereignty of the text and the central creative position conceded to the writer, was surely the legacy of the studio, where the playwright was, theoretically at least, at the heart of the process.

Taped drama has often been seen as a hopelessly compromised system, and it may be instructive briefly to examine why. The whole notion of drama on videotape is the result of a historical accident, by which it effectively became possible to store drama that was transmitted live. In the early days of television, the medium was used primarily as a relay system, a way of taking a stage play and beaming it into the home of the viewer. The earliest kind of studio play was, therefore, simply a stage play acted out in front of the TV cameras, and it was subject to most of the formal restrictions of the theatre. It might be done with greater variety of sets than the stage would allow but, as it was being transmitted live, the author had to resort to the stagecraft which could contrive intermediary scenes so that leading actors could change costumes or move unobtrusively from one set to another. These studio dramas were tackled by directors in much the way that outside broadcasts of "live" events like opera are still produced. There is no single director's camera angle, as there is in film, since four or five television cameras are strategically positioned to cover the action from different points of view, and the director, who has access to the live pictures from all of them, selects his angles—or "calls the shots"—as he goes along. The invention of videotape simply made it possible to record this sequence of events, to provide a more or less permanent record of the "live" recording. Incredibly, this is essentially the method still in use today. Studio drama is acted out on sets in front of up to four cameras, and the actors and set are lit to favour all angles equally. Most directors still monitor the recording from a control room where they face a bank of screens. Most actors are obliged to give scaled-down versions of a stage performance, since they are not playing to any one camera specifically. The fundamental difference is that, since the drama is no longer live, actors, directors, and writers are freed from the tyranny of continuous time. Plays can be taped in short segments, and can thus inherit some of the mobility of film. But on film the director chooses each angle with a meticulousness and care alien to the impartial multi-camera method of tape. And on film, for obvious enough reasons, far greater stress is laid on the purely visual aspect of things.

The best writer's case against the studio is made by David Hare in an essay called "Ah, Mischief!", where he describes the unsatisfactory way in which *Brassneck*, the stage play he co-authored with Howard Brenton, was produced for television. But this most persuasive piece of argument is to some extent refuted by Howard Brenton's magnificent *Play for Today*, *A Desert of Lies*, where a nightmarish version of the baking wastes of the Kalahari desert was achieved in the studio by director Piers Haggard, or, earlier, by Mercer's Robert Kelvin trilogy or Potter's superlative *Joe's Ark*. Mercer, in particular, became a master of the studio psychodrama, becoming a sort of anarchic English Strindberg.

In his Robert Kelvin plays, *On the Eve of Publication*, *The Cellar and the Almond Tree*, and *Emma's Time*, he showed that it was possible to construct drama of impressive emotional austerity and weight in the confined spaces of the studio. Although television has since become a medium through which to make films, where the single play slot is earmarked for largely cinematic kinds of drama, it is difficult to resist the conclusion that these elegant and good-looking films have rarely had the power, impact, and authority of those word-bound dramas written by Potter and Mercer. And the shift toward film seems, to me, to have been largely a shift back to naturalism, a revamping of that journalistic form of scriptwriting from which Potter, Mercer, and Schuman had so invigoratingly freed themselves.

In an introduction to the published text of his film *The Imitation Game* (1981), Ian McEwan wrote, "Television was, and is, dominated by the powerful, cohesive conventions of its naturalism. The programme maker who departs radically from these conventions can be sure of at least irritating or surprising the audience—there is a base line of expectation .... Naturalism is a common language of television, not the language we speak, but the one we are accustomed to listen to." This statement still stands, despite the intervening years and the innovation of *Film on Four* and *Screen Two*. The most influential dramatic success of the early 1980's, Alan Bleasdale's *Boys from the Blackstuff*, took its conventions from the naturalistic mainstream, the "social conscience" plays of the 1950's and 1960's, from Jeremy Sandford's *Cathy Come Home* and *Edna, The Inebriate Woman*, from the anecdotal Merseyside sharp-wittedness that was a hallmark of the police series *Z Cars*, from that most tough-minded of naturalistic writers, Trevor Griffiths, from Colin Welland and Jim Allen. *Boys from the Blackstuff* was 1960's naturalism with a whiff of Hogarth and Gillray, a fantastical dimension and defiantly dark humour that was entirely lacking in, say, Nell Dunn's *Up the Junction*. Naturalism had rarely been so dream-bound and fatalistic, so dislocatingly funny in its depiction of an outwardly mundane, inwardly barbaric day-to-day life. The best of Bleasdale's five-play sequence, *Yosser's Story*, was the most imaginatively ambitious and, to make it, director Philip Saville exchanged light, mobile outside broadcast video equipment for film.

Naturalism remains the dominant dramatic form of a medium whose bias is journalistic, which is, at least in part, a newspaper. It lends a cutting edge of superficial immediacy to subjects that might otherwise be stage-built or literary. Again and again, it trades on a documentary veracity in order to lend the plots and situations of romance and melodrama an air of up-to-date authenticity. The claims of naturalism, namely that it offers us people talking not as people talk in plays but as they actually talk in "real life," have tended to make it the foremost aesthetic style of socially conscious drama, and, in dramatic terms, have introduced clichés into the texture of working-class experience which make it formally indistinguishable from those abhored upper-class country-house meloldramas of life among the rich. The sheen of proletarian naturalism has persuaded us to tolerate sentimental excesses from the socialist end of the political spectrum which would be laughed out of the court if they were deployed in the service of some faint, laissez-faire conservatism. Even Trevor Griffiths, who has written two outstanding multi-episode serials of power and responsibility, *Bill Brand* and *The Last Place on Earth*, and the exceptional single plays, *Through the Night* and *Country*, is capable of what was, to me, a wholly preposterous melodrama like *All Good Men*. Naturalism must take some of the blame, too, for the surfeit of slackly platitudinous morality plays written around the Ulster of the Troubles, where, in most cases, mere soap opera is justified by its dauntingly serious political allegiances. Some of the best—as well as some of the worst—plays in this currently fashionable genre have been written by Graham Reid, who followed his *Billy* trilogy for the BBC with a further six Irish stories, *Ties of Blood*. Of the recent work which seems to me to have made some attempt to demolish the lazier assumptions of television naturalism, while staying relatively close to its style and subject, I would single out David Hare's *Dreams of Leaving*, a metropolitan love story lent an air of surreal, dream-fraught poetry by voiceover and gravely austere camera work; David Rudkin's tantalisingly brief—it was heavily cut for transmission—but mesmerising Irish play, *Across the Water*; Howard Brenton's *Desert of Lies*; Trevor Griffiths's rigorously analytical critique of the country-house play, *Country*; Michael Wall's simple but elegiac studio play, *Japanese Style*, which was transmitted live in a rare and experimental break with tradition; the delightful science-fiction romance, *The Flipside of Dominick Hide*, which was scripted by Jeremy Paul and director Alan Gibson; Ian McEwan's *The Imitation Game*; Jim Allen's meandering but corrosively intelligent state-of-England film, *United Kingdom*; Stephen Poliakoff's films *Soft Targets* and *Runners*; Richard Eyre's emotionally luminous adaptation of David Storey's novel, *Pasmore*.

The single play or film remains television's most prestigious form. In the 1960's, and through the 1970's, the BBC's *Wednesday Play* and its successor, *Play for Today*, kept the one-off play at the forefront of both the audience's and the critic's imagination. Soap operas, situation comedies, format series like *Z Cars* or *Doctor Who*, and adapted books frequently made the reputation of actors or programme makers but they rarely brought the same public recognition to their writers. And, in the 1980's as budgets grew tighter, and television executives began to rely more and more on easily packaged, crowd-pleasing blockbusters, the single play looked like an endangered species. In hindsight, Channel Four and its programme of relatively low budget films probably arrived at an opportune moment, allowing the programme makers to abandon the run-down and by then unpopular studio play in favour of well-crafted televisual screenplays. Today, drama production values are arguably of a higher standard than they were during the final years of *Play for Today*, but the financial logistics involved in making films has cut back television's demand for what the BBC's former Head of Plays Christopher Morahan called "the single work of the imagination." And financial considerations, the fact that, in many cases, films have to be jointly funded by different companies with different interests and, often, different cultures, will no doubt prove to be the decisive artistic factor in the years that lie ahead.

This is already proving to be the case as far as television's juggernaut serials are concerned. For years, the expensive episodic drama serial, the famous novel adapted into six or 13 instalments, or a similarly divided life of some colourful historical figure, has been a popular and attractive method of winning both audiences and critical prestige. The BBC's *The Forsyte Saga* (written by Donald Wilson) paved the way for those two beautifully produced adaptations from Granada, *Brideshead Revisited* (written by John Mortimer) and *The Jewel in the Crown* (written by Ken Taylor). Both were taken from respected minor novels, and turned into lush and seductive pageants. Of the two, *Brideshead Revisited* seemed to me incomparably the more original and intelligent, an adapted book which took enormous pains not to lose the texture of Evelyn Waugh's exquisitely cadenced prose. *The Jewel in the Crown*, which drew its long story from Paul Scott's Raj Quartet, was, in contrast, a straightforward romantic melodrama in a style inherited from Hollywood and films like *Gone with the Wind*. But it would be ridiculous to claim these huge endeavours as writer's achievements. The adapted book is, with rare exceptions, a pretext for soap opera from a popular or respected source, a way of recycling Dickens or Hardy, or plundering a bestseller for its dramatic riches. In recent years, Arthur Hopcraft wrote a very fine screen version of John le Carré's *Tinker, Tailor, Soldier, Spy*, which turned an engrossing but somewhat pedestrian espionage whodunnit into an incisive examination of Britain's capacity for upper-middle-class treachery, the most convincing dramatic account yet given of the generation which created Philby, Burgess, and Maclean. Dennis Potter has brought a caustic dramatic flair and insight to adaptations of Hardy's *The Mayor of Casterbridge* and Fitzgerald's *Tender Is the Night*. But the writing in these long-running pageants is generally either reverent or dull, dutiful but uninspired, and it sometimes seems that it is only second-rate books which afford dramatists any real imaginative freedom. Ted Whitehead had a great deal of fun with Paul Ferris's *The Detective*, and Hopcraft seems to have found a Promethean spark in le Carré's erudite thrillers.

The format series, those continuous stories built around a loose and infinitely variable dramatic situation, have often presented writers with a more profitable challenge. Troy Kennedy Martin, who freely adapted Angus Wilson's *The Old Men at the Zoo* and then went on to create his own, six-part nuclear thriller, *Edge of Darkness*, learnt many of his skills as a *Z Cars* scriptwriter. Eccentric and inspired comic dramatists like David Nobbs (*The Fall and Rise of Reginald Perrin*) and Mike Stott (*The Practice*) have used situation comedy almost as if it was a single play, working within television as farceurs like Ben Travers once worked in the theatre. But, as any insider will know, these subdivisions of episodic drama have mostly produced specialists of their own, reliable but on the whole uninspired writers who can set their hands efficiently enough to the genre in question. The crime series, the weekly soaps like *Crossroads*, *Coronation Street*, *Eastenders*, and *Brookside*, science-fiction or mystery formats like *Doctor Who* or the old *Blake's Seven*, all call on a pool of dramatists who understand the form and who can write scripts quickly, properly, and to the right specifications. Even a somewhat higher class of format drama—a continuing saga like *Upstairs, Downstairs* or the historical anthology sequences *The Six Wives of Henry VIII* and *Elizabeth R*—takes its scripts not so much from established "name" dramatists as from a collection of highly skilled dramatic storytellers whose work is somehow both incisive and self-effacing, intelligent but a little bland. There have been a number of intriguing exceptions to this rule—Fay Weldon wrote the first episode of *Upstairs, Downstairs*, Howard Schuman and David Rudkin both contributed episodes to the giant historical saga, *Churchill's People*, and Dennis Potter wrote a six-part life of Casanova—but, on the whole, the authorial demarcation lines remain dismayingly rigid. And, as more and more serials are created for transatlantic consumption, and backed financially in some measure by these outside interests, the reliance on a combination of pedestrian script and high-profile production values will probably grow.

This leaves to last what is, to me, television's most potentially enthralling dramatic form: the "single work of the imagination" which unfolds in many episodes and occupies hours of screen time. Here, television drama can give us something very close to a screen novel, created by a single imagination but not limited to the two-hour duration of the one-off slot. Potter's *Pennies from Heaven* and *The Singing Detective* were gigantic pieces of work, gripping because of their scale and breadth as well as for the moment-to-moment detail of their dialogue and characterisation. Schuman gave us *Rock Follies* and *Rock Follies of '77* in this form, as well as the recent *Up Line*. It was the achievement, too, of Frederic Raphael's *The Glittering Prizes*, of Arthur Hopcraft's *The Nearly Man*, of Trevor Griffiths's *Bill Brand* and his magnificent reappraisal of the historical blockbuster, *The Last Place on Earth*. There have, for obvious enough reasons, been failures or semi-successes in the form, large canvases whose very ambition seems to have exposed a capacity for the banal or sentimental in the dramatist: Farrukh Dhondy's *King of the Ghetto* struck me as an honourable failure, with all the weaknesses of the naturalistic studio play simply extended over four exceptionally well directed episodes of location drama. And the long narrative of *Paradise Postponed* surely promised a quiet epic of British society in the years since 1945, while what John Mortimer gave us was a genteel soap opera of quaint amiability. But the central difficulty with this most challenging and rewarding of dramatic forms is simply its scarcity, the fact that programme makers are rarely prepared to entrust the colossal resources it requires to a single imagination. This explains, I would guess, the strongly thematic flavour of most of these projects, the fact that they have a well-defined subject which, in itself, may prove attractive both to television executives and, theoretically, to the huge audience which it has to satisfy. *The Glittering Prizes* was about the Cambridge generation of the 1950's whose prodigious success in the media world of the 1960's made them famous; *The Last Place on Earth* was, in narrative terms, the story of Scott and Amundsen's race for the South Pole; *The Nearly Man* and *Bill Brand* were, on the surface, tales of political ruthlessness and ambition, with roughly the same subject as the enjoyable Westminster soap opera of Jeffrey Archer's *First among Equals* (written by Derek Marlowe).

As we look forward into the 1990's, we must assume that the large demands of financing worthwhile television drama, the necessity to package the product and sell it abroad, will remain the decisive factor in the minds of commissioning editors. The difficulty of producing "single works of the imagination" will be the difficulty of selling them, of convincing the money-men, in advance, that these projects will bring in a sufficient return. The best British drama has, in one sense, always been the most parochial, the plays or films which came directly and unmistakably out of the experience of living in *this* culture, at a specific time. Inevitably, the increasingly high financial stakes may jeopardise this, as dramatists with a taste for scale and length will continually have to convince the commissioning executives that the appeal of their work will be more than parochial, that quality rather than subject can draw an audience. It is foolish to predict, but I suspect many of the best British writers will be forced to work with a nervous, backward glance at American and worldwide sales.

—Andrew Rissik

* * *

ALLEN, Jim. Television plays: *Coronation Street* series (35 episodes), 1965–67; *The Hard Word*, 1966; *The Lump*, 1967; *The Man Beneath*, 1967; *The Pub Fighter*, 1968; *The Big Flame*, 1969; *The Talking Head*, 1969; *The Rank and File*, 1971; *Walt, King of the Dumper*, 1971; *The Punchy and the Fairy*, 1973; *In the Heel of the Hunt*, 1973; *Days of Hope*, 1975 (novelization 1975); *The Extremist, Tell the Truth and Shame the Devil*, and *Those in Peril* (*Crown Court* series), 1975–76; *A Choice of Evils*, 1977; *The Spongers*, 1978; *United Kingdom*, 1981; *Willie's Last Stand*, 1982; *The Gathering Seed*, 1983. Stage play: *Perdition* (published 1987).

BENNETT, Alan. See his dictionary entry.

BLEASDALE, Alan. See his dictionary entry.

BRENTON, Howard. See his dictionary entry.

CHAPMAN, Robin. Television plays include: *A Deathly Hush*, 1963; *Confidence Class*, 1964; *The Fellows*, 1967; *Spindoe*, 1968; *Big Breadwinner Hog*, 1969; *The Father of the Regiment*, 1970; *By the Pricking of My Thumbs*, from the novel by Agatha Christie, 1971; *Holly*, 1972; *A Picture of Katherine Mansfield*, 1973; *Remember Me*, 1975; *Beata Beatrix*, 1975; *Bellamira*, from the play by Charles Sedley, 1975; *Haunted Poor Girl*, from a story by Elizabeth Taylor, 1975; *Grease Monkey*, 1976; *Dream of a Strange Land* and *Under the Garden*, from stories by Graham Greene, 1976; *Jumping Bean Bag*, 1976; *The Author of Beltraffio*, from the story by Henry James, 1976; *Come the Revolution*, 1977; *Poison*, from a story by Roald Dahl, 1980; *Vicious Circle*, from a work by Donald Honig, 1981; *Completely Foolproof*, from a work by Robert Arthur, 1981; *Death of an Expert Witness*, from the novel by P.D. James, 1983; *The Vorpal Blade*, from a story by Edward D. Hoch, 1983; *Caleb Williams*, from the novel by William Godwin, 1983; *The Aerodrome*, from the novel by Rex Warner, 1983; *Shroud for a Nightingale*, from the novel by P.D. James, 1984; *Killer Contract*, 1985; *Cover Her Face*, from the novel by P. D. James, 1985; *Galloping Foxley*, from a story by Roald Dahl, 1985; *The Boy Who Talked with Animals*, from a story by Roald Dahl, 1986; *Blunt*, 1987. Radio play: *Rift Valley Blues*, 1982 (staged 1982). Stage plays: *High Street China*, with Richard Kane, 1963 (published in *Plays and Players*, March 1963); *How to Kill a Dandy*, 1969; *One of Us*, 1986 (published 1986). Novelist.

CHURCHILL, Donald. Television plays: *Always Something Hot*, 1962; *Sharp at Four*, 1964; *The Cherry on the Top*, 1964; *The Hothouse*, 1964; *The Paraffin Season*, 1965; *The Man Without a Mortgage*, 1966; *Comrades in Arms*, 1966; *The Happy Sacking*, 1967; *Floating Population*, 1967; *A Second Look*, 1968; *Never a Cross Word*, 1968; *Return Match*, 1968; *Room in Town*, 1970; *The Loving Lesson*, 1971; *You Don't Know Me But . . .*, 1972; *A Fluid Arrangement*, 1972; *The Leftovers*, 1972; *Feeling the Pinch*, 1973; *Harriet's Back in Town*, 1973; *A Bit of a Lift*, 1974; *A Girl's Best Friend*, 1974; *Moody and Peg* series, with Julia Jones, 1974–75; *Feeling His Way*, 1975; *The Five Pound Orange*, 1975; *Pie in the Sky*, 1975; *Distant Islands*, with Jones, 1975; *Ron*, 1975; *Our Mutual Friend*, with Jones, from the novel by Dickens, 1976; *She, The Diplomat*, with Jones, 1976; *Hearts and Minds*, with Ted Childs (*The Sweeney* series), 1978; *An Honourable Retirement*, 1979; *Alice Trying*, 1980; *Last Knockings*, 1980; *The Wisdom of Patrick*, 1980; *Goodnight and God Bless* series, 1983; *Mr. Pye*, from the novel by Mervyn Peake, 1986. Radio plays: *The Expenses*, 1967; *The Party Piece*, 1969; *Lines from My Grandfather's Forehead*, with others; *The Prodigal Grandfather*, 1984. Stage plays: *Gestures*; *A Woman on Friday*; *The Performing Husband*, 1972; *A Far Better Husband*, with Peter Yeldham, 1975; *Fringe Benefits*, with Yeldham, 1976 (published 1977); *Past Tense*, 1980; *Mixed Feelings*, 1980; *My Friend Miss Flint*, with Yeldham, 1983 (published 1984); *The Decorator*, 1985. Screenplays: *The Spare Tyres*, 1967; *Zeppelin*, with Arthur Rowe, 1971. Actor.

CLARKE, Tom. Television plays: *A Game for Eskimos*, 1958; *The Escape of RD7*, 1961; *A Matter of Conscience*, from a work by Tolstoy, 1962; *A Little Temptation*, 1965 (published 1966); *Don't Go Down the Bingo, Mother, Father's Home to Tea*, 1966; *Everyone's Rich Except Us*, 1967; *A Brilliant Future Behind Him*, 1967; *Haven't You People Got Homes*, 1967; *Mad Jack*, 1970; *The Moonlighters*, 1971; *A Settled Sort of Life*, 1971; *Stocker's Copper*, 1972 (published in *The Television Play*, 1976); *Feet Together, Hands to the Sides*, 1973; *Billion Dollar Bubble*, 1976; *Victims of Apartheid*, 1978 (published 1978); *Muck and Brass* series, 1982; *Past Caring*, 1986.

DHONDY, Farrukh. Television plays: *Maids in the Mad Shadow*, 1981; *No Problem* series, with Mustapha Matura, 1983; *Good at Art*, 1983; *Dear Manju*, 1983; *The Bride*, 1983 (published 1985); *Salt on a Snake's Tail*, 1983; *Come to Mecca*, 1983; *Romance, Romance*, 1983 (published 1985); *The Empress of the Munshi*, 1984; *Tandoori Nights* series, 1985; *King of the Ghetto*, 1986; *To Turn a Blind Eye*, 1986. Stage plays: *Mama Dragon*, 1980; *Trojans*, from a play by Euripides, 1982; *Kipling Sahib*, 1982; *Vigilantes*, 1985 (published 1987); *Film, Film, Film*, 1986; *All the Fun of the Fair*, with John McGrath and others, 1986. Writer of fiction for children.

DUNN, Nell. See her dictionary entry.

EXTON, Clive. Television plays: *No Fixed Abode*, 1959 (published in *Six Granada Plays*, 1960); *The Silk Purse*, 1959; *Kipps* series, 1960; *Where I Live*, 1960; *Some Talk of Alexander*, 1960; *Hold My Hand, Soldier*, 1960; *On the Spot*, from the novel by Edgar Wallace, 1960; *I'll Have You to Remember*, 1960; *Rain*, from the play by John Colton and Clemence Randolph, 1960; *The Big Eat*, 1962; *The Trial of Doctor Fancy*, 1963; *The Land of My Dreams*, 1964; *The Close Prisoner*, 1964; *The Boneyard*, 1966; *Are You Ready for the Music?*, 1966; *The Dream of Timothy Evans*, 1970; *Mother and Child*, 1970; *Conversation Piece*, 1970; *The Rainbirds*, 1971; *Legacies* (3 plays), 1973; *The Boundary*, with Tom Stoppard, 1975; *Breakthrough*, from a story by Daphne du Maurier, 1975; *When Greek Meets Greek* and *The Root of All Evil*, 1975, and *A Chance for Mr. Lever* and *The Over-night Bag*, 1976, from stories by Graham Greene; *The Killers* series, 1976; *The Creez* series, 1976; *The Spanish Succession*, 1976; *Stigma*, 1977; *The Battle of Harvey Street*, 1978; *Pitman's Folly*, 1978; *Dick Barton, Special Agent* series, 1979; *Casting the Runes*, from a story by M.R. James, 1979; *Henry Intervening*, 1979; *Wolf to the Slaughter*, from the novel by Ruth Rendell, 1987. Radio play: *The Old Boys*, from the novel by William Trevor, 1967. Screenplays: *Night Must Fall*, 1963; *A Place to Go*, with Michael Relph, 1963; *Isadora*, with Melvyn Bragg and Margaret Drabble, 1969; *Entertaining Mr. Sloane*, 1970; *Ten Rillington Place*, 1970; *Doomwatch*, 1972; *Running Scared*, with David Hemmings and Hugo Butler, 1972; *The House in Nightmare Park*, with Terry Nation, 1973; *The Awakening*, with Allan Scott and Chris Bryant, 1980. Stage play: *Have You Any Dirty Washing, Mother Dear?*, 1969 (published 1970).

EYRE, Richard. Television play: *Pasmore*, from the novel by David Storey, 1980. Stage plays: sketches in *Cambridge Circus* (revue), 1963; *The Ha-Ha*, from the novel by Jennifer Dawson, 1967; *High Society*, music and lyrics by Cole Porter, from *The Philadelphia Story* (play by Philip Barry and screenplay by Donald Ogden Stewart and Waldo Salt), 1987. Stage, film, and television director.

FINCH, John. Television plays: *Dark Pastures*, 1963; *The Villains* series, 1964; *The Old Man of Chelsea Reach*, 1965; *Brothers*, 1966; *Wanted*, 1967; *Victims*, 1968; *The Visitors*, 1968; *Them Down There*, 1968; *It's Dearer after Midnight*, 1968; *The House That Jigger Built*, 1968; *A Family at War* series, 1970; *Sam* series, 1973–75; *Spivvy*, 1975; *This Year, Next Year* series, 1977; *End of Season*, 1978; *Flesh and Blood* series, 1980 (novelization 1980); *The Spoils of War* series, 1980; *The Hard Word* series, 1983. Stage play: *Brigade*, 1976. Novelist.

GREATOREX, Wilfred. Television plays: *The Plane Makers* series, 1963; *The Power Game* series, 1965; *The Curtis Affair*, 1968; *The Eleventh Commandment*, 1970; *Dying Gets You Nowhere*, 1970; *Hine* series, 1971; *Night of the Tanks*, 1972; *The Man from Haven* series, 1972; *The Inheritors*, 1974; *Did Machiavelli Have Welch Blood?*, 1974; *The Mackinnons* series, 1977; *Creed of Slaves* series, 1977; *1990* series, 1977 (published 1978); created *Airline* series, 1982. Screenplays: *Nobody Runs Forever* (*The High Commissioner*), 1968; *Battle of Britain*, with James Kennaway, 1969. Novelist.

GRIFFITHS, Trevor. See his dictionary entry.

HAMPTON, Christopher. See his dictionary entry.

HARE, David. See his dictionary entry.

HOLLES, Robert. Television plays: *The Mating Age*, 1961; *Behind the Line*, 1962; *June Fall*, 1963; *Andersen*, 1963; *The Wedding of Smith Seven-Nine*, 1963; *Across the Border*, 1964; *The Big Toe*, 1964; *The Apprentices*, 1964; *The Taming of Trooper Tanner*, 1965; *The Reluctant Witness*, 1966; *Conduct to the Prejudice*, 1966; *The Hunting of Aubrey Hopkiss*, 1966; *The Education of Corporal Holliday*, 1967; *First of the Nightingales*, 1967; *The Wind in a Tall Paper Chimney*, 1968; *Natural Justice*, 1968; *Night of Talavera*, 1968; *The Discharge of Trooper Lusby*, 1969; *There's Always a First Time*, 1970; *Brown Skin Gal Stay Home*, 1971; *Michael Regan*, 1971; *Old Comrades*, 1972; *The Birdwatcher*, 1972; *Bye Bye Mrs. Bly*, 1972; *The Breaking of Colonel Keyser*, 1972; *The Sterile Weapons*, 1973; *Death of Glory*, 1973; *A Little Local Knowledge*, 1973; *Comrades in Arms*, 1973; *Cherryripe and the Lugworm Digger*, 1974; *The Vanishing Army*, 1978; *Fothergill*, from the book *An Innkeeper's Diary* by John Fothergill, 1981. Screenplay: *Guns at Batasi*, 1964. Radio play: *I'll Walk Beside You*, from his own novel, 1981. Stage play: *The Siege of Battersea*, 1962. Novelist.

HOPCRAFT, Arthur. Television plays: *The Mosedale Horseshoe*, 1971; *The Panel*, 1971; *The Birthday Run*, 1971; *The Reporters*, 1972; *Said the Preacher*, 1972; *Buggins' Ermine*, 1972; *Katapult*, 1973; *Humbug, Finger or Thumb?*, 1973; *Jingle Bells*, 1973; *Baa Baa Blacksheep*, from a story by Kipling, 1974; *The Nearly Man*, 1974, and series, 1975; *Nightingale's Boys* series (2 episodes), 1975; *A Journey to London*, completion of the play by John Vanbrugh, 1975; *Wednesday Love*, 1975; *Tweety*, 1975; *Hannah* (*Victorian Scandals* series), 1976; *Hard Times*, from the novel by Dickens, 1977; *Tinker, Tailor, Soldier, Spy*, from the novel by John le Carré, 1979; *Bleak House*, from the novel by Dickens, 1985; *A Perfect Spy*, from the novel by John le Carré, 1987. Screenplay: *Agatha*, with Kathleen Tynan, 1979. Author of novels and non-fiction.

JONES, Julia. Television plays: *The Navigators*, 1965; *Common Ground*, 1965; *The Spoken Word*, 1965; *A Designing Woman*, 1965; *Up and Down*, 1966; *Trapped*, 1966; *First Catch Your Hare*, 1966; *Two's Company*, 1966, and *As You Were*,

1973 (*Love Story* series); *Tickle Times*, 1967; *Love with a Few Hairs*, from the novel by Mohammed Mrabet, translated by Paul Bowles, 1967; *Give and Take*, 1967; *A Bit of a Crucifixion, Father*, 1968; *Penny Wise*, 1968; *The Piano Tuner*, 1969; *Faith and Henry*, 1969 (published 1983); *Devon Violets, Heart's Ease, Sweet Basil*, and *Roses round the Door* (*Take Three Girls* series), 1970; *The Piano*, 1971 (published in *The Pressures of Life*, 1977); *Home and Away* (7 plays), 1972; *Still Waters*, 1972 (published 1983); *Anne of Green Gables*, from the novel by L. M. Montgomery, 1972; *The Stretch*, 1973; *This Quiet Half Hour*, 1973; *Hearty Crafty*, 1974; *Back of Beyond*, 1974 (published 1983); *Moody and Peg* series, with Donald Churchill, 1974–75; *Shouts and Murmurs* (*Churchill's People* series), 1975; *A Free Woman* (*Within These Walls* series), 1975; *Old Fogey*, 1975; *Nuts and Bolts*, 1975; *Distant Islands*, with Churchill, 1975; *Our Mutual Friend*, with Churchill, from the novel by Dickens, 1976; *She, The Diplomat*, with Churchill, 1976; *Lottie's Boy*, 1976, and *Where There's a Will*, 1977 (*Duchess of Duke Street* series); *High Noon*, from the novel by Ruby M. Ayres, 1977; *Pipe Dreams*, 1977; *The Peppermint Pig*, from the novel by Nina Bawden, 1977; *Poor Little Rich Girl*, 1977; *Quiet as a Nun*, from the novel by Antonia Fraser, 1978; *Country Dance*, from a work by Margiad Evans, 1979; *The Swish of the Curtain*, from the story by Pamela Brown, 1980; *We the Accused*, from the novel by Ernest Raymond, 1980; *A Little Silver Trumpet*, from the novel by L.T. Meade, 1980; *Hearth and Home*, 1981; *Avril* (*Take Three Women* series), 1982; *Sisters*, 1982; *Grown Up Girlie*, 1983; *The Moving Finger*, from the novel by Agatha Christie, 1985; *The Shadow* (*Ladies in Charge* series), 1986; *The Cuckoo Sister*, from the novel by Vivien Alcock, 1986. Radio plays: *The H'arrogance of Youth*, 1965; *Honey and Bread* and *A Time to Laugh*, from stories by Rhys Davies, 1969; *The Piano Tuner*, 1970; *Hobble de Hoys*, 1973; *The Day of the Tortoise*, 1973; *This Football Lark*, 1977; *Vegetating*, 1979 (stage version, as *Country Way*, 1983); *Over and Done With*, 1979; *London, Look You*, 1980; *Dear Aunt*, 1983; *A Little Learning*, 1984. Stage plays: *Sleeping Partners*, 1967; *Had We Never Loved So Kindly*, 1969; *The Garden*, 1972; *A Few Kind Words* (*Dear Winnie*), 1973.

KNEALE, Nigel. Television plays: *The Quatermass Experiment*, 1953 (published 1959); *Nineteen Eighty-Four*, from the novel by George Orwell, 1954; *The Creature*, 1955; *Quatermass II*, 1955 (published 1960); *Mrs. Wickens in the Fall*, 1956 (published 1971); *Quatermass and the Pit*, 1959 (published 1960); *The Road*, 1963 (published 1976); *The Crunch*, 1964; *The Year of the Sex Olympics*, 1967 (published 1976); *Bam! Pow! Zapp!*, 1969; *Wine of India*, 1970; *The Chopper*, 1971; *The Stone Tape*, 1972 (published 1976); *Jack and the Beanstalk*, 1974; *Murrain*, 1975; *Buddyboy*, 1976; *During Barty's Party*, 1976; *Special Offer*, 1976; *The Dummy*, 1976; *Baby*, 1976; *What Big Eyes*, 1976; *Quatermass*, 1979; *Kinvig* series, 1981. Screenplays: *Quatermass II* (*Enemy from Space*), with Val Guest, 1957; *The Abominable Snowman*, 1957; *Look Back in Anger*, with John Osborne, 1959; *The Entertainer*, with John Osborne, 1960; *HMS Defiant* (*Damn the Defiant*), with Edmund North, 1962; *First Men in the Moon*, with Jan Read, 1964; *The Witches*, 1966; *Quatermass and the Pit* (*5,000,000 Years to Earth*), 1967; *The Quatermass Conclusion*, 1979. Novelist and short story writer.

MARLOWE, Derek. Television plays: *A Requiem for Modigliani*, 1970; *The Search for the Nile* (documentary), with Michael Hastings, 1971; *The Knight* series, 1978; *Nancy Astor*, 1982; *A Married Man*, from the novel by Piers Paul Read, 1983; *Jamaica Inn*, from the novel by Daphne du Maurier, 1983; *First among Equals*, from the novel by Jeffrey Archer, 1986. Screenplays: *A Dandy in Aspic*, 1968; *Universal Soldier*, with Joseph Massot, 1972; *A Single Summer*, 1979; *The Knight*, 1979. Stage plays: *The Seven Who Were Hanged*, from a novel by Leonid Andreyev, 1961 (as *The Scarecrow*, 1964); *The Lower Depths*, from a play by Gorky, 1962; *How Disaster Struck the Harvest*, 1964; *How I Assumed the Role of a Popular Dandy for Purposes of Seduction and Other Base Matters*, 1965. Novelist.

MARTIN, Troy Kennedy. Television plays: *Incident at Echo Six*, 1958; *Element of Doubt*, from the story by Bernard Newman, 1961; *The Interrogator*, 1961; scripts for *Z Cars* series, 1962–78; *Diary of a Young Man* series, with John McGrath, 1964; *Corporal McCann's Private War*, 1965; *The Pistol*, with Roger Smith, from the novel by James Jones, 1965; *If It Moves, File It*, 1970; *The Appointment*, 1974; *Thin Ice*, 1975, *Night Out*, 1975, *Hard Men*, 1978, and *Selected Target*, 1984 (*The Sweeney* series); *Visiting Fireman*, 1976; *Fear of God*, from the novel by Derry Quinn, 1980; *Reilly—Ace of Spies* series, 1983; *The Old Men at the Zoo*, from the novel by Angus Wilson, 1983; *Edge of Darkness*, 1985.

McDOUGALL, Peter. Television plays: *Just Your Luck*, 1972; *Just Another Saturday*, 1975; *The Elephants' Graveyard*, 1976; *A Wily Couple*, 1976; *Choices*, 1977; *Loyalties*, 1978 (published in *Act Two*, edited by David Self and Ray Speakman, 1979); *Tary Dan, Tary Dan*, 1978; *Jackie McCafferty's Romance*, 1978; *Just a Boy's Game*, 1979; *A Sense of Freedom*, 1981; *Shoot for the Sun*, 1987.

McEWAN, Ian. Television plays: *Jack Flea's Birthday Celebration*, 1976 (published 1981); *The Imitation Game*, 1980 (published 1981); *Solid Geometry* (published 1981); *The Last Day of Summer*, from his own story, 1984. Radio play: *Conversation with a Cupboardman*, 1975. Screenplay: *The Ploughman's Lunch*, 1983 (published 1985). Stage play: *Or Shall We Die?* (oratorio), music by Michael Berkeley, 1983 (published 1983). Novelist and short story writer.

MERCER, David. See his appendix entry.

MITCHELL, Julian. See his dictionary entry.

MORTIMER, John. See his dictionary entry.

NOBBS, David. Television plays: scripts for *That Was the Week That Was* and *Not So Much of a Programme* series, with Peter Tinniswood; *Lance at Large* series, with Tinniswood, 1964; *The Signal Box of Grandpa Hudson*, with Tinniswood, 1966; *The Fall and Rise of Reginald Perrin* series, 1976–80; *Our Young Mr. Wignall*, 1976; *The Sun Trap*, 1980; *The Glamour Girls* series, 1980; *Cupid's Darts*, 1981; *Second from Last in the Sack Race*, 1984; *The Hello Goodbye Man*, 1984; *Fairly Secret Army*, 1984; *Dogfood Dan and the Carmarthen Cowboy*, 1985. Radio plays: *Hardluck Hall* series, with Tinniswood, 1964.

PAUL, Jeremy. Television plays: *Mr. Morecombe*, 1960; *Room for Justice*, 1962; *A Travelling Woman*, from the novel by John Wain, 1964; *Cobb*, 1965; *A Fair Swap*, 1966; *How Well Do You Know This Man?*, 1968; *Father's Day*, 1968; *Charge!*, with Robert Morley, 1969; *A Man for Loving*, 1970; *Love Doesn't Grow on Trees*, 1971; *Husband and Friend*, 1971; *Return of Favours*, 1971; *A Suitable Marriage*, 1971; *A Voice from the Past*, 1972; *Consequences*, 1972; script for *Country*

Matters series, 1972; *Alice*, 1972; *Conan Doyle* (*The Edwardians* series), 1972; *Touch and Go*, 1973; *A Dangerous Point of View*, 1973; *What the Footman Saw*, 1973; *A Perfect Stranger*, 1974; *Home Fires*, 1974, and *The Beastly Hun*, 1977 (*Upstairs, Downstairs* series); *Missing, Believed Killed*, 1974; *The Little Match Girl*, with Leslie Stewart, from a story by Hans Christian Andersen, 1974 (stage version, as *Scraps*, music by Keith Strachan, 1977); *Nine Day Wonder*, 1975; *The Understudy*, 1975; *All the King's Horses*, 1975; *A Walk in the Forest*, 1980; *The Flipside of Dominick Hide*, 1980, and *Another Flip for Dominick*, 1982, both with Alan Gibson; *A Chamber of Horrors* (*Jemima Shore Investigates* series), from a story by Antonia Fraser, 1983; scripts for *By the Sword Divided* series, 1983–85; *Rose's Pigeon*, 1984; *Sorrell and Son*, from the novel by Warwick Deeping, 1984. Stage plays: *Manoeuvres*, with Carey Harrison, 1974; *David Going Out*, 1975; *Gumba Gumba*, with others, 1978; *Visitors*, with Harrison, 1980; *Can You Help?*, 1986.

POLIAKOFF, Stephen. See his dictionary entry.

POTTER, Dennis. See his dictionary entry.

RAPHAEL, Frederic. See his screenwriters entry.

REID, Graham (early plays as J. Graham Reid). Television plays: *Billy* series: *Too Late to Talk to Billy*, 1982, *A Matter of Choice for Billy*, 1983, and *A Coming to Terms for Billy*, 1984 (all published 1984), and *Lorna*, 1987 (published 1987); *Easter 2016*, 1982; *Ties of Blood*, 1985 (published 1986). Radio play: *Sweet Sixteen*, 1982. Stage plays: *The Death of Humpty Dumpty*, 1979 (published 1980); *Dorothy*, 1980; *The Closed Door*, 1980 (published 1980); *The Hidden Curriculum*, 1982; *Remembrance*, 1984 (published 1985); *Callers*, 1985.

ROSENTHAL, Jack. Television plays include scripts for *Bootsie and Snudge* series, 1960–64; *Green Rub*, 1963; *Pie in the Sky*, 1963; *The Night Before the Morning After*, 1966; *Compensation Alice*, 1967; *There's a Hole in Your Dustbin, Delilah*, 1968; *The Dustbinmen* series, 1969; *Your Name's Not God, It's Edgar*, 1969; *The Lovers* series, 1971; *Another Sunday and Sweet F.A.*, 1972 (published in *The Television Dramatist*, 1973); *And for My Next Trick*, 1973; *Hot Fat*, 1974; *Polly, Put the Kettle On*, 1974 (published 1984); *Mr. Ellis Versus the People*, 1974 (published 1984); *There'll Almost Always Be an England*, 1974; *Sadie, It's Cold Outside* series, 1975; *Big Sid*, 1975; *The Evacuees*, 1975 (published 1978); *Ready When You Are, Mr. McGill* (published 1986) and *Well, Thank You, Thursday* (published 1984) (*Red Letter Day* series), 1976; *Bar Mitzvah Boy*, 1976 (staged 1978; published 1978); *Spend, Spend, Spend*, from the book by Vivian Nicholson, 1977 (published 1978); *Auntie's Niece* (*Velvet Glove* series), 1977; *Spaghetti Twostep*, 1977; *The Knowledge*, 1979 (published 1986); *P'Tang Yang Kipperbang*, 1982 (published 1984); *Those Glory Glory Days*, 1983; *The Devil's Lieutenant*, from a novel by Maria Fagyas, 1984; *Mrs. Capper's Birthday*, from a story by Noël Coward, 1985; *The Fools on the Hill*, 1986; *London's Burning*, 1986; *A Day to Remember*, 1986. Screenplays: *The Lovers*, 1973; *Forever Young*, 1984; *Yentl*, with Barbra Streisand, 1984; *The Chain*, 1985 (published 1986). Stage plays: *Smash!*, 1981; *Dear Anyone*, 1983; *Our Gracie*, 1984.

RUDKIN, David. See his dictionary entry.

SANDFORD, Jeremy. Television plays include scripts for *Z Cars* series; *Cathy Come Home*, 1966 (published 1967); *Edna, The Inebriate Woman*, 1971 (published 1971); *Don't Let Them Kill Me on Wednesday* (*Lady Killers* series), 1980. Radio plays: *The Whelks and the Chromium*, 1958 (published in *New English Dramatists 12*, 1968); *Not Wanting to Return*, 1968; *Oluwale*, 1973 (published as *Smiling David: The Story of David Oluwale*, 1974); *Till the End of the Plums*, 1979; also radio documentaries. Stage plays: *Dreaming Bandsmen*, based on *The Whelks and the Chromium*, 1960; *The Motor Heist*, 1976; *The Fatted Calf*, 1980; *Dream Topping*, with Philippa Finnis, 1980. Novelist and writer of works of social history.

SCHUMAN, Howard. Television plays: *Vérité*, 1973; *Captain Video's Story*, 1973; *Carbon Copy*, 1975; *Amazing Stories*, 1975; *The Helping Hand*, 1975; script for *Churchill's People* series, 1975; *Rock Follies* series, 1976; *Rock Follies of '77*, 1977; *Anxious Anne*, 1977; *Bouncing Back*, 1983; *Videostars*, 1983; *Up Line*, 1987. Stage play (originally for television): *Censored Scenes from King Kong*, 1977 (published in *Gambit 26–27*, 1975).

STOTT, Mike. See his dictionary entry.

TAYLOR, Ken. Television plays: *China Doll*, 1960; *The Long-Distance Blue*, 1961; *The Slaughter Men*, 1962; *Parkin's Primitives*, 1962; *Into the Dark*, 1962; *The Tin Whistle Man*, 1963; *Mr. Big*, from a story by Ray Bradbury, 1963; *The Devil and John Brown*, 1964; *The Seekers* (trilogy; includes *The Heretics, The Idealists, The Materialists*), 1964 (published 1970); *The Bachelors*, from the novel by Muriel Spark, 1965; *Days to Come*, from a work by H.G. Wells, 1966; *Dr. Dee Kelly and the Spirits, Incantation of Casanova*, and *Edward Gurney and the Brighton Mesmerist* (*Magicians* series), 1967; *Sally for Keeps*, 1970; *E. Nesbit* (*The Edwardians* series), 1972; *The Solarium*, 1973; *The Melancholic Hussar*, from a story by Hardy, 1973; *Sylvia Pankhurst*, 1974; *The Girls of Slender Means*, from the novel by Muriel Spark, 1975; *The Poisoning of Charles Bravo*, 1975 (stage version, as *The Strange Affair of Charles Bravo*, 1979); *Death or Liberty* (*Churchill's People* series), 1975; *The Birds Fall Down*, from the novel by Rebecca West, 1978; *If All the World Were Mine*, 1978; *The Member for Chelsea*, 1981; *The Maze*, from a work by C.H.B. Kitchin, 1983; *Seaton's Aunt* (*Shades of Darkness* series), from a story by Walter de la Mare, 1983; *Mansfield Park*, from the novel by Jane Austen, 1983; *The Jewel in the Crown*, from the novels by Paul Scott, 1984. Screenplays: *Beyond This Place* (*Web of Evidence*), 1959; *Let's Get Married*, 1960; *Alfred the Great*, with James R. Webb, 1969. Stage plays: *This Is the End*, 1962 (published in *Coventry Porch Plays*, 1965); *Who Is Bobby Valentine?* (published in *Second Playbill 1* edited by Alan Durband, 1973).

WALL, Michael. See his radio writers entry.

WELDON, Fay. See her radio writers entry.

WELLAND, Colin. Television plays: *Bangelstein's Boys*, 1968; *Slattery's Mounted Foot*, 1970; *Say Goodnight to Your Grandma*, 1970 (as *Say Goodnight to Grandma*, staged 1971; published 1973); *Catherine Wheel*, 1970; *Roll On Four O'Clock*, 1970 (staged 1981); *The Hallelujah Handshake*, 1970; *A Roomful of Holes*, 1971 (published 1971); *Kisses at Fifty*, 1973 (published in *The Television Play*, 1976); *Jack Point*, 1973; *Leeds—United!*, 1974; *The Wild West Show* series, 1975; *Your Man from Six Counties*, 1976; *Saints Alive*, 1976; *Bank Holiday*, 1977. Screenplays: *Yanks*, with Walter Bernstein, 1979; *Chariots of Fire*, 1981 (Oscar); *Twice in a Lifetime*, 1987. Stage, television, and film actor.

WHITEHEAD, Ted. See his dictionary entry.

WILSON, Donald. Television plays: *The Six Proud Walkers*, 1954; *The Flight of the Dove*, 1957 (published in *The Television Playwright*, 1960); *The Royalty*, with Michael Voysey, 1958; *No Wreath for the General*, 1960; *The Intervener*, 1961; *Rupert of Hentzau*, from the novel by Anthony Hope, 1964; *Witch Wood*, from the novel by John Buchan, 1964; *The Forsyte Saga*, from the novels by John Galsworthy, 1967; *The First Churchills*, 1969; *Anna Karenina*, from the novel by Tolstoy, 1978. Stage play: *Out of Bounds* (published 1954). Television script editor and producer.

MUSICAL LIBRETTISTS

Gilbert and Sullivan notwithstanding, the librettist (the book writer, as he is still called outside histories of musical comedy) seldom gets equal billing with the composer. There are contemporary instances of shared eminence (Rodgers and Hammerstein), some of which, as in the case of Gilbert and Sullivan, put the librettist first—Lerner and Loewe. Where the librettist is considered half a famous team, he is always the lyricist as well, and it is that function that elevates him to an equal position with the composer. It is, after all, the music, the songs, by which musical comedies are known, celebrated, remembered. That does not mean that the book is unimportant, but that it is the librettist's job to provide the skeleton for the show and, then, to get out of the way and let the musical numbers do their work. As the musical has become more serious in its dramatic intentions, particularly since World War II, it has tried to introduce believable characters in recognizable milieus and—following the conventional drama of the period—to provide psychological studies, social commentary, satiric significance. Although the new seriousness of the musical has attracted many writers with a reputation in drama and in fiction, the librettist, unlike the playwright, must forego the most telling lines and the best scenes because, in a good musical, the songs do the exposition, provide the characterization, embody the conflict. For instance "Rose's Turn," the musical number that brings *Gypsy* to a close, is a moment of revelation as dramatically important as the one in Arthur Laurents's *Home of the Brave* in which the paralyzed veteran is forced to walk. Yet, Laurents, as librettist, had to step back and let Jule Styne and Stephen Sondheim, as composer and lyricist, do the scene. The total effect of *Gypsy*, however—and it is one of the best American musicals—depends on a carefully conceived book which provides the occasion for the songs that define Rose, one of the most fully realized characters in musical comedy.

George Abbott, whose first play was produced the year after W.S. Gilbert died, has been active in the American theater—as director, as actor, as author—through the years in which the musical and its book changed shape, a process to which he contributed. He wrote *The Boys from Syracuse* (1938), an adaptation of *The Comedy of Errors, Where's Charley?* (1948), based on *Charley's Aunt*, and *New Girl in Town* (1957), a version of *Anna Christie*. Although he may have had William Shakespeare, Brandon Thomas, and Eugene O'Neill as silent collaborators on those shows, he worked directly with the authors of the original material when he helped Betty Smith write *A Tree Grows in Brooklyn* (1951), Richard Bissell convert *7½ Cents* into *The Pajama Game* (1954) and Douglass Wallop turn *The Year the Yankees Lost the Pennant* into *Damn Yankees* (1955). Jerome Weidman joined Abbott in two musicals which looked back at an innocently corrupt New York, *Fiorello!* (1959) and the less successful *Tenderloin* (1960); perhaps emboldened by his work with Abbott, Weidman went solo and adapted his novel *I Can Get It for You Wholesale* (1962) for the musical stage.

The image of the director turned author, or more often co-author, is hardly an unusual one on the Broadway musical stage. As early as 1940, Joshua Logan joined Gladys Hurlbut to provide the book for the Rodgers-and-Hart show *Higher and Higher*. His most famous collaboration is with Oscar Hammerstein II on *South Pacific* (1949), which in its day was considered the last word in serious musical books, particularly by critics for whom seriousness is equated with liberal sentiments and solemn sentimentality. No such artistic claims were, or can be, made for Logan's commercial successes such as *Wish You Were Here* (1952), which he and Arthur Kober adapted from Kober's *Having Wonderful Time*, and *Fanny* (1954), which he and S.N. Behrman carved out of the Marcel Pagnol trilogy, *Marius, Fanny*, and *César*.

The late Bob Fosse, a director-choreographer often praised for imposing final shape on a show—for instance, *Pippin* (1972), which has a book by Roger O. Hirson—emerged as co-author, with Fred Ebb, of *Chicago* (1975), "a musical vaudeville" based on Maurine Watkins's popular 1920's comedy melodrama about Roxie Hart. Ebb, best known as a lyricist, had already turned librettist, with Norman L. Martin, on *70 Girls 70* (1971), a tough-minded, much underrated musical about American attitudes toward aging and death. It is James Lapine as director, rather than as playwright, who seems to be dominant in the book of *Sunday in the Park with George* (1984); the stage re-creation of George Seurat's *A Sunday Afternoon on the Island of La Grande Jatte* was much more impressive than the conventional theme about artistic obsession.

Practicing playwrights have always been attracted to musical comedy, but with the increasing importance of the book in the post-World War II theater, a great many serious dramatists turned to the musical. Arthur Laurents has sometimes come a cropper as a librettist—the over-elaborate *Anyone Can Whistle* (1964)—but with *Gypsy* (1959) and *West Side Story* (1957), in which he uses *Romeo and Juliet* as a jumping-off place for his own romantic story of lovers beset by the prejudices of their society, he has written two musical books that are more effective dramatically than any of his straight plays. Arthur Miller has persisted in trying to turn *The Creation of the World and Other Business* into a musical ever since his first attempt, *Up from Paradise* (1974). Arthur Kopit, working from Mario Fratti's adaptation from the Italian, tried to retain in *Nine* (1981) some of the philosophical implications of *8½*, the Fellini film on which it is based, but the musical is primarily a girlie show dressed in psychological cliché. In *La Cage aux Folles* (1983), Harvey Fierstein sticks close to the plot of Jean Poiret's play, as it is better known in the successful film version, offering a celebration of homosexuality which is also a sentimental tale of a (male) mother wronged. Terrence McNally is less successful with his mother-daughter conflict in the sentimental *The Rink* (1984). Tom Eyen, using a conventional backstage story, made an effective book for *Dreamgirls* (1981), one which is not only about the use and misuse of a vulnerable performer but about the vulgarization of art for the mass market.

A playwright of a different kind but of equal eminence in her own genre is Bella Spewack, who with her husband Sam wrote the book for Cole Porter's *Leave It to Me!* (1938). For the show, the Spewacks, leading American farceurs, turned out a libretto which, at least in setting (a slapstick Soviet Russia), suggests their earlier farce, *Clear All Wires*. Their best known libretto, however, is the one for the postwar Porter show, *Kiss Me, Kate* (1948), in which they mix *The Taming of the Shrew* with a fairly typical backstage story. The Spewacks, working in farce and the musical at the same time, were following a Broadway tradition that is still carried on by Neil Simon, the most successful comic writer of the postwar period. His libretti are a great deal less tightly written than his plays; the best of them, *Promises, Promises* (1968) owes as much to the Billy Wilder-I.A.L. Diamond film *The Apartment*, on which it is based, as it does to Simon's invention.

Another adaptation from film, *Sweet Charity* (1966), an Americanization of *Nights of Cabiria*, has unhappily none of the quality of the Fellini original. The very successful *They're Playing Our Song* (1978) is a romantic comedy about a songwriter (male) and his lyricist (female). Garson Kanin, whose work falls somewhere near the serious side of Simon's kind of comedy, wrote *Do Re Mi* (1960), based on his own novella, a musical which begins as broad caricature but which collapses as the central figure demands that we take him seriously as a victim of the American success dream.

Perhaps the most impressive librettists—in industry if not always in final product—are those jack-of-all-trades who insist on writing music, lyrics, and book. Several English writers who fall into this category have achieved transoceanic success in recent years: Sandy Wilson, who is best known for *The Boy Friend* (1953), a delightful parody of the 1920's musical at its most fatuous; Lionel Bart, whose *Oliver!* (1960) tried to hold on to some of the scariness of the Dickens original; Leslie Bricusse and Anthony Newley, whose pretentious and sentimental excursions into the symbolic parable—*Stop the World—I Want to Get Off* (1961) and *The Roar of the Greasepaint—The Smell of the Crowd* (1964)—found audiences that were willing to take them at their mask value; Richard O'Brien, whose infantile pop-culture parody, *The Rocky Horror Show* (1973), has become—particularly in its film version—a cult show for backward teenagers. There were American composers who wrote their own books, of course. Peter Link and C.C. Courtney shared credit for book, music, and lyrics of a rock examination of the ways toward the need for *Salvation* (1969), although Link's more recent work suggests that he was the composer of the show. In *Ain't Supposed to Die a Natural Death* (1971) and *Don't Play Us Cheap* (1972), Melvin Van Peebles drew affectionate caricatures of Harlem life which have, among other things, helped to change the character of American audiences by drawing large numbers of blacks into the theatres. His more recent *Waltz of the Stork* (1982), autobiographical monologues pretending to be a "comedy with music," proved less successful. Al Carmines, the singing clergyman, has been touted as a latter-day Noël Coward, off-off-Broadway variation, but his best works are not those like *Joan* (1972), for which he did his own book, but those in which he had the help of librettists such as María Irene Fornés, whose *Promenade* (1969) is a full-length version of an earlier play, and Tim Reynolds, who went to Aristophanes for *Peace* (1969). William Finn made music out of husbands who come out of the closet in *March of the Falsettos* (1981) and, less effectively, *In Trousers* (revised version, 1985). Rupert Holmes used a combination of music hall and audience-participation show to make a very amusing musical from Dickens's *The Mystery of Edwin Drood* (1985). John Gray, with help from Eric Peterson, came up with an exportable Canadian musical in *Billy Bishop Goes to War* (1978).

At this point, pressed, pressed by lack of space, I had best resort to a catalogue of sorts:

Betty Comden and Adolph Green, having begun as lyricists and performers, wrote their first book for Leonard Bernstein—*On the Town* (1944), a wartime salute to New York. They are at their most characteristic—sly, wry, and a little soft-hearted—when they stick to New York—*Bells Are Ringing* (1956)—or to show business—*Applause* (1970)—but the same two subjects can go soft in their hands, as in *Subways Are for Sleeping* (1961) and *Fade Out—Fade In* (1964). *Singin' in the Rain* (1983), their adaptation of their 1952 screenplay, never quite managed the exuberance of the original.

Jerome Chodorov and Joseph Fields, after turning their *My Sister Eileen* into Leonard Bernstein's *Wonderful Town* (1953)—lyrics inevitably by Comden and Green—tried, with less success, to create an earlier New York by building *The Girl in Pink Tights* (1954) around the story of America's first musical, *The Black Crook*.

Joseph Stein has tried, with varying degrees of failure, to be convincingly Pennsylvania Dutch in *Plain and Fancy* (1955) and black in *Mr. Wonderful* (1956), both with Will Glickman's help, and, on his own, Irish in *Juno* (1959) and Greek in *Zorbá* (1968). His best book is clearly *Take Me Along* (1959), adapted with Robert Russell from O'Neill's *Ah, Wilderness!*, but he is most famous for having reduced Sholom Aleichem's Tevye to a lovable figure with a message in *Fiddler on the Roof* (1964).

Peter Stone, after having written a very workable libretto, *1776* (1969), in which American history shares space with stereotypical comedy as the United States is born, went on to make very weak adaptations of Clifford Odets's *The Flowering Peach—Two by Two* (1970)—the Wilder-Diamond film *Some Like it Hot—Sugar* (1972)—and George Stevens's film of the same name—*Woman of the Year* (1981). With Timothy S. Mayer he concocted an amiable 1920's-style book for *My One and Only* (1983), an excuse to recycle some attractive George Gershwin songs.

Tom Jones's best libretto, the phenomenally successful *The Fantasticks* (1959, revised 1960), is a bittersweet adaptation of Rostand's *Les Romanesques*. *I Do! I Do!* (1966), his adaptation of Jan de Hartog's *The Fourposter*, is a much more conventional libretto. He and composer Harvey Schmidt have been experimenting with small studio musicals—*Portfolio Revue* (1974), *Philemon* (1975)—which, although they have not been well received, suggest a return to the production intimacy that led to *The Fantasticks*.

Beverley Cross, who is known in the United States primarily for *Half a Sixpence* (1963), an adaptation of H.G. Wells's *Kipps* which retained much of the charm but little of the social comment of the original, has written libretti for almost a dozen musicals, including the opera *The Mines of Sulphur* (1965).

Philip Rose and Peter Udell, who helped Ossie Davis turn his caricature comedy *Purlie Victorious* into *Purlie* (1970), joined James Lee Barrett on *Shenandoah* (1975), an occasionally sentimental, sometimes serious musical with a Civil War setting.

Joe Masteroff fashioned a libretto from Christopher Isherwood's *Berlin Stories* and John van Druten's *I Am a Camera*, spongey in plot and character, but distinguished in its presentation of the titular *Cabaret* (1966), the setting for the most acid of the Fred Ebb-John Kander songs. His *She Loves Me* (1963) was an effective translation of the sentimental movie favorite, *The Shop Around the Corner*.

Tim Rice, working in the tradition that retells biblical stories in the vernacular, sentimentalized Genesis in *Joseph and His Amazing Technicolour Dreamcoat* (1968) and redid the Gospels for the rock generation in *Jesus Christ Superstar* (1970). His *Evita* (1976) pretended to be satiric about Eva Perón but was in fact celebratory. More recently and with less success, he has been involved with the twelfth century—*Blondel* (1983)—and the contemporary Cold War—*Chess* (1984).

Thomas Meehan made a musical comedy star of Harold Gray's Little Orphan Annie—*Annie* (1977)—and then proved that he should have stayed with the funny papers by falling down the treacle well with the maudlin *I Remember Mama* (1979).

George Furth examined and finally recommended marriage in the occasionally satiric *Company* (1970); his *Merrily We Roll Along* (1981), based on the George S. Kaufman-Moss Hart play, closed quickly, but, as so often happens with Stephen Sondheim shows, it developed an underground reputation and has found its way back to the stage (*Pacific Overtures* [1976], with a very clever book by John Weidman, is another example).

Dick Vosburgh's *A Day in Hollywood/A Night in the Ukraine* (1980) had fun with Chekhov and the Marx Brothers; although his *Windy City* (1982) was based on the popular Ben Hecht-Charles MacArthur farce-melodrama *The Front Page*, it found its success in England.

Garry Trudeau discovered that the characters of his satiric comic strip lost their bite in *Doonesbury* (1983), but he tried again in 1984 with *Rap Master Ronnie*, a revue that was reworked in 1986.

Mention should be made of a number of authors whose reputations, as librettists at least, depend on a single show, sometimes because they worked on no more than one. Here they are, alphabetically. Don Appell used a cross-the-cultures romance in *Milk and Honey* (1961), but it was the Israeli setting that made the show. Howard Ashman found broad comedy in the Roger Corman film *Little Shop of Horrors* (1982). Mark Bramble reaffirmed the popularity of the carnival with *Barnum* (1980). William F. Brown wrote *The Wiz* (1975), a black version of *The Wizard of Oz* that turned out to be more Broadway show-biz than American fantasy. Gretchen Cryer used a hapless hero to make comments, mostly amiable, on contemporary social phenomena in *The Last Sweet Days of Isaac* (1970). Donald Driver gave a vaguely mod touch to *Twelfth Night* as the title *Your Own Thing* (1968) indicates. William Gibson was presumably largely responsible for *Golden Boy* (1964), which, not very satisfactorily, transferred Clifford Odets's play to a Harlem setting. James Goldman imposed soap-opera romance on show business reminiscence in *Follies* (1971). Peggy Harmon and Polly Pen had off-Broadway success with their adaptation of Christina Rossetti's poem *Goblin Market* (1986). William Hauptman provided a somewhat sanitized version of *Huckleberry Finn* for *Big River* (1984). Jim Jacobs and Warren Casey made the profitable discovery, with *Grease* (1971), that the 1950's were ready for the nostalgia treatment. Larry L. King, with the help of director Peter Masterson, expanded a magazine article into *The Best Little Whorehouse in Texas* (1978), the show that discovered the American longing for innocent, institutional sin. Jerome Lawrence and Robert E. Lee turned a very successful pig's ear into a still more successful pig's ear when they carpentered *Mame* (1966) out of their earlier play *Auntie Mame*. Stephen Longstreet used his novel *Some Like Them Handsome* as the basis for *High Button Shoes* (1947), one of the most charming of the nostalgia-for-the-American-past shows so popular just after World War II. Robert Nemiroff, with Charlotte Zaltzberg, continued his theatrical resurrection of Lorraine Hansberry's literary remains, this time by softening her *A Raisin in the Sun* into *Raisin* (1973). Sybille Pearson celebrated birth in *Baby* (1983), working from a story developed by Susan Yankowitz. John R. Powers adapted his own novel for *Do Black Patent Leather Shoes Really Reflect Up?* (1978), a fun-and-games-in-parochial-school show that was very popular outside New York. Gerome Ragni and James Rado wrote a conventional pacifist plot for *Hair* (1967), but they increased its popularity by decorating it with the minutiae of high-school hippie acts and attitudes. Bob Randall concocted a tacky backstage story for *The Magic Show* (1974), an excuse to bring a talented magician on stage. Budd Schulberg, with his brother Stuart, made a workable but less astringent libretto of the novel that made his reputation as a writer, *What Makes Sammy Run?* (1964). Maurice Sendak transferred some of his children's book characters to the stage in the much too cunning *Really Rosie* (1978). Richard Stilgoe planted a love story in *Starlight Express* (1984), a celebration of trains which was little more than an excuse for special effects. Samuel Taylor wrote an interracial love story for *No Strings* (1962) which was unusual only in that the libretto, on the page, gives no indication that the girl is black. Dale Wasserman, working from his own television adaptation of *Don Quixote*, wrote an essay in uplift called *Man of La Mancha* (1965), beloved by everyone except admirers of Cervantes. Aubrey Woods, perhaps because he is primarily a performer and perhaps because the Victorian theater specialist George Rowell had a hand in the show, saw that his *Trelawney* (1972) not only borrowed the sentimental love-across-the-classes plot of *Trelawney of the Wells* but retained the serious point about changing theatrical conventions that was so important in the Arthur Wing Pinero original.

For some historians of the musical, such as composer Alec Wilder (*American Popular Song*), the musical's best days came before World War II when a group of talented and witty composers regularly turned out sophisticated scores. If one thinks in terms of complete shows rather than songs, however, the richest years are almost certainly the late 1940's and early 1950's in which the librettos moved away from the pre-war formulas in search of more complicated material. In the 1960's and 1970's, the musical was suffering the consequences of that move. There was something exciting, at first, when the librettists turned to other genres—novels, plays—in search of adaptable stories. The borrowing which began as a release for the writer's imagination has become a trap, a crutch. The current musical listings in New York or London still turn up adaptations, but even the most successful of these shows, commercially, tend to be pedestrian. It is not simply that the surprise has gone out of adaptation as a device, but that other elements which helped define the musical—irreverence and a sense of fun—have disappeared almost completely. The formula writing now lies in the feel, the tone of the librettos rather than in the plots and their comic devices. Now that the Broadway musical—and its West End counterpart, to a lesser extent—has become so expensive to produce, each one is an institution before the curtain rises with all the heaviness of heart that the word *institution* implies. That may help account for the growing number of revivals on Broadway. There is as yet a minimum of evidence, but I suspect that the hope for the libretto, for musical comedy itself, lies in the small musical which is a reaction, often of young writers and composers, to the overstuffed output of their elders. After all, isn't the history of theatre a string of small revolutions?

—Gerald Weales

* * *

ABBOTT, George. See his dictionary entry.

APPELL, Don. Musicals: *Milk and Honey*, music and lyrics by Jerry Herman, 1961. Other plays: *This Too Shall Pass*, 1946; *Lullaby*, 1954 (as *And Mama Makes Three*, 1962); *A Girl Could Get Lucky*, 1964; *Hot Shot*, 1977 (published 1977); *Kindling*, 1978 (published 1978). Stage and television director.

ASHMAN, Howard. Musicals: *Dreamstuff*, music by Marsha Malamet, lyrics by Dennis Green, from *The Tempest* by Shakespeare, 1976; *God Bless You, Mr. Rosewater*, music by Alan Menken, from the novel by Kurt Vonnegut, Jr., 1979 (published 1980); *Real Life Funnies*, songs by Alan Menken, from the comic strip by Stan Mack, 1981; *Little Shop of Horrors*, music by Alan Menken, from the film by Roger Corman (screenplay by Charles B. Griffith), 1982 (published 1985). Other play: *The Confirmation*, 1977. Stage director.

BART, Lionel. Musicals: *Fings Ain't Wot They Used T'Be* (lyrics and music only), book by Frank Norman, 1959; *Lock Up Your Daughters* (lyrics only), book by Bernard Miles, music by Laurie Johnson, 1959; *Oliver!*, music and lyrics by Bart, 1960; *Blitz*, with Joan Maitland, music and lyrics by Bart, 1962; *Maggie May*, book by Alun Owen, music and lyrics by Bart, 1964; *Twang*, with Harvey Orkin, music and lyrics by Bart, 1965; *La Strada*, book by Charles K. Peck Jr., music and lyrics by Bart, 1969; *Costa Packet*, book by Frank Norman, music and lyrics by Bart and Alan Klein, 1972; *The Londoners*, 1972. Film scores: *The Tommy Steele Story* (*Rock Around the World*), 1957; *The Duke Wore Jeans*, 1958; *Tommy the Toreador*, 1959; *Serious Charge*, 1959; *The Heart of a Man*, 1959; *In the Nick*, 1960; *Let's Get Married*, 1960; *Light Up the Sky*, 1960; *Sparrows Can't Sing*, 1963; *From Russia with Love*, 1963; *Man in the Middle*, 1963.

BRAMBLE, Mark. Musicals: *T*ts D*amond*, music by Lee Pockriss, lyrics by Steve Brown, 1977; *Pal Joey '78*, with Jerome Chodorov, music and lyrics by Richard Rodgers and Lorenz Hart, from the play by John O'Hara, 1978; *Elizabeth and Essex*, with Michael Stewart, music by Doug Katsaros, lyrics by Richard Engquist, from the play *Elizabeth the Queen* by Maxwell Anderson, 1978; *The Grand Tour*, with Stewart, music and lyrics by Jerry Herman, from the play *Jacobowsky and the Colonel* by S.N. Behrman, 1979; *Barnum*, music by Cy Coleman, lyrics by Stewart, 1980; *42nd Street*, with Stewart, music and lyrics by Harry Warren and Al Dubin, from the novel by Bradford Ropes, 1980; *The Three Musketeers*, music by Rudolf Friml, lyrics by P.G. Wodehouse and Clifford Grey, from the play by William Anthony McGuire based on a novel by Dumas père, 1983; *Fat Pig*, music by Henry Krieger, lyrics by Jenny Hawkesworth, from a story by Colin McNaughton, 1987.

BROWN, William F. Sketches and lyrics for *Dime a Dozen*, 1962; *Baker's Dozen*, 1964; *Bits and Pieces*, 1964; *Pick a Number XV*, 1965; *Leonard Sillman's New Faces of 1968*, 1968. Musicals: *How to Steal an Election*, music and lyrics by Oscar Brand, 1968; *The Wiz*, music by Charlie Smalls, from the novel *The Wizard of Oz* by L. Frank Baum, 1975; *A Broadway Musical*, music by Charles Strouse, lyrics by Lee Adams, 1978. Other plays: *The Girl in the Freudian Slip*, 1967; *A Single Thing in Common*, 1978. Television writer and cartoonist.

CARMINES, Al. Musicals and librettos include *The Journey of Snow White*, 1970; *Joan*, 1972; *Christmas Rappings*, 1972 (and annually); *A Look at the Fifties*, 1972; *The Life of a Man*, 1972; *Faggot*, 1973; *Religion*, 1973; *The Future*, 1974; *Sacred and Profane Love*, 1975; *The Beast*, 1976; *Camp Meeting 1840*, 1976, revised 1977; *In Praise of Death*, 1978; *Someone's in the Kitchen with Dinah*, 1979; *The Agony of Paul*, 1980; *T.S. Eliot: Midwinter Vigil(ante)*, 1981; *The Evangelist*, 1982; *The Gospel According to Al*, 1982. Composer for many plays. Director of the Judson Poets Theatre, New York.

CASEY, Warren. Musicals (with Jim Jacobs): *Grease*, 1971; *Island of the Lost Co-eds*, 1979. Actor.

CHODOROV, Jerome. Musicals: *Pretty Penny*, music and lyrics by Harold Rome, 1949; *Wonderful Town*, with Joseph Fields, music by Leonard Bernstein, lyrics by Betty Comden and Adolph Green, 1953; *The Girl in Pink Tights*, with Fields, music by Sigmund Romberg, lyrics by Leo Robin, 1954; *I Had a Ball*, music and lyrics by Jack Lawrence and Stan Freeman, 1964; *The Great Waltz*, music by Johann Strauss adapted by Erich Korngold and others, from the book by Moss Hart and Milton Lazarus, 1965; *Dumas and Son*, music and lyrics by Robert Wright and George Forrest, 1967; *Pal Joey '78*, with Mark Bramble, music and lyrics by Richard Rodgers and Lorenz Hart, from the play by John O'Hara, 1978; *Boffola!*, 1984. Other plays: *Schoolhouse on the Lot*, with Fields, 1938; *My Sister Eileen*, with Fields, 1940; *Junior Miss*, with Fields, 1941; *Barnaby and Mr. O'Malley*, 1945; *The French Touch*, with Fields, 1945; *Anniversary Waltz*, with Fields, 1954; *The Ponder Heart*, with Fields, 1956; *Tunnel of Love*, with Fields, 1957; *The Happiest Man Alive*, 1962; *Three Bags Full*, 1966; *A Community of Two*, 1974; *Culture Caper*, from the novel *Bech: A Book* by John Updike, 1975; *A Talent for Murder*, with Norman Panama, 1981 (published 1982). Screenplays: some of his own plays, and *Case of the Lucky Legs*, 1935; *Dancing Feet*, 1936; *Gentleman from Louisiana*, 1936; *Devil's Playground*, 1937; *Reported Missing*, 1937; *All over Town*, 1937; *Rich Man, Poor Girl*, 1938; *Conspiracy*, 1939; *Two Girls on Broadway*, 1940; *Louisiana Purchase*, 1941; *Murder in the Big House*, 1942; *Those Endearing Young Charms*, 1945; *Man from Texas*, 1948; *Happy Anniversary*, 1959. Stage director.

COMDEN, Betty. Musicals (with Adolph Green): *The Revuers*, 1944; *On the Town*, music by Leonard Bernstein, 1944; *Billion Dollar Baby*, music by Morton Gould, 1945; *Bonanza Bound*, music by Saul Chaplin, 1947; *Two on the Aisle* (revue), with others, music by Jule Styne 1951; *Wonderful Town* (lyrics only), book by Joseph Fields and Jerome Chodorov, music by Bernstein, 1953; *Peter Pan* (some lyrics only), music by Mark Charlap, lyrics by Carolyn Leigh, musical version of the play by J.M. Barrie, 1954; *Bells Are Ringing*, music by Styne, 1956; *Say Darling* (lyrics only), book by Abe Burrows and Richard and Marian Bissell, music by Styne, 1958; *Do Re Mi* (lyrics only), book by Garson Kanin, music by Styne, from the novel by Kanin, 1960; *Subways Are for Sleeping*, music by Styne, 1961; *Fade Out—Fade In*, music by Styne, 1964; *Hallelujah, Baby!* (lyrics only), book by Arthur Laurents, music by Styne, 1967; *Applause*, music by Charles Strouse, lyrics by Lee Adams, 1970; *Lorelei; or, Gentlemen Still Prefer Blondes* (lyrics only), book by Kenny Solms and Gail Parent, music by Styne, from the musical *Gentlemen Prefer Blondes* by Fields and Anita Loos, 1974; *By Bernstein*, music by Leonard Bernstein, 1975; *On the Twentieth Century*, music by Cy Coleman, from the play *Twentieth Century* by Ben Hecht and Charles MacArthur, 1978; *A Doll's Life*, music by Larry Grossman, 1982 (published 1983). Screenplays and film lyrics (with Adolph Green): some of their own musicals, and *Good News*, 1947; *The Barkleys of Broadway*, 1949; *Take Me Out to the Ball Game*, 1949; *Singin' in the Rain*, 1952 (staged 1983; published 1986); *The Band Wagon*, 1953 (published 1986); *It's Always Fair Weather*, 1955; *Auntie Mame*, 1958; *What a Way to Go*, 1964. Actress and singer.

COURTNEY, C.C. Musicals: *Salvation*, with Peter Link, 1969; *East of Ruston*, with Ragan Courtney, music by Link, 1971.

CROSS, Beverley. See his dictionary entry.

CRYER, Gretchen. Musicals: *Now Is the Time for All Good Men*, music by Nancy Ford, 1967; *The Last Sweet Days of Isaac: The Elevator, and I Want to Talk to San Francisco*, music by Nancy Ford, 1970; *The Wedding of Iphigenia, and Iphigenia in Concert*, with Doug Dyer and Peter Link, music by Link,

1971; *Shelter*, music by Ford, 1972; *I'm Getting My Act Together and Taking It on the Road*, music by Ford, 1978 (published 1980); *Hang On to the Good Times* (revue), with Richard Maltby, Jr., and Ford, songs by Cryer and Ford, 1985; *Eleanor*, music by Ford, 1986.

DAVIS, Ossie. See his dictionary entry.

DRIVER, Donald. Musicals: *Your Own Thing*, music and lyrics by Hal Hester and Danny Apolinar, from *Twelfth Night* by Shakespeare, 1968; *Broadway Follies*, music and lyrics by Walter Marks, 1981; *Oh, Brother!*, music by Michael Valenti, 1981 (published 1982). Other plays: *From Paris with Love*, 1962; *Status Quo Vadis*, 1973; *In the Sweet Bye and Bye*, 1983; *A Walk Out of the Water*, 1985. Stage director and actor.

EBB, Fred. Lyrics for *From A to Z*, 1960; *Vintage 60*, 1960; *Put It in Writing*, 1963; *Flora, The Red Menace* by George Abbott and Robert Russell, music by John Kander, 1965; *Cabaret*, by Joe Masteroff, music by Kander, 1966; *By Jupiter* (additional material) by Richard Rodgers and Lorenz Hart, 1967; *The Happy Time* by N. Richard Nash, music by Kander, 1968; *Zorbá* by Joseph Stein, music by Kander, 1968; *The Act* by George Furth, music by Kander, 1977; *Two by Five*, conceived by Seth Glassman, music by Kander, 1981; *Woman of the Year* by Peter Stone, music by Kander, from the screenplay by Ring Lardner, Jr., and Michael Kanin, 1981; *The Rink* by Terrence McNally, music by Kander, 1984 (published 1985). Musicals: *Morning Sun*, music by Paul Klein, 1963; *70 Girls 70*, with Norman L. Martin and Masteroff, music by Kander, lyrics by Ebb, from the play *Breath of Spring* Peter Coke, 1971; *Chicago*, with Bob Fosse, music by Kander, from the play by Maurine Dallas Watkins, 1975. Television: *Liza*, 1970 (staged 1974); *Mama Malone*, music by Kander, 1983.

EYEN, Tom. See his dictionary entry.

FIERSTEIN, Harvey. See his dictionary entry.

FINN, William. Musicals: *In Trousers*, 1979, revised version, 1985 (published 1986); *March of the Falsettos*, 1981 (published 1981); *America Kicks Up Its Heels* (music and lyrics), book by Charles Rubin, 1984. Composer of music for *Benny Leonard and the Brooklyn Bridge* by Paul Leaven, 1977, and other plays.

FURTH, George. See his dictionary entry.

GIBSON, William. See his dictionary entry.

GOLDMAN, James. See his dictionary entry.

GRAY, John. See his dictionary entry.

GREEN, Adolph. See the entry for Betty Comden above.

HARMON, Peggy. Musical: *Goblin Market*, with Polly Pen, music by Pen, from the poem by Christina Rossetti, 1986. Actress.

HAUPTMAN, William. See his dictionary entry.

HOLMES, Rupert. Musical: *The Mystery of Edwin Drood*, from the novel by Dickens, 1985. Songwriter and performer; composer of film music.

JACOBS, Jim. Musicals (with Warren Casey): *Grease*, 1971; *Island of the Lost Co-eds*, 1979. Other play: *Bats in the Belfry*, with Jim Weston, 1982. Actor.

JONES, Tom. Sketches in *Four Below*, 1956; *Shoestring '57*, 1956; *Kaleidoscope*, 1957; *Demi-Dozen*, 1958. Musicals with music by Harvey Schmidt: *The Fantasticks*, 1959, expanded version, 1960; *110 in the Shade* (lyrics only) by N. Richard Nash, 1963; *I Do! I Do!*, 1966; *Celebration*, 1969; *Colette* (lyrics only) by Elinor Jones, 1970, revised version (book and lyrics), 1982; *Portfolio Revue*, 1974; *Philemon*, 1975; *The Bone Room*, 1975. Television writing: *New York Scrapbook*, 1961.

KANIN, Garson. See his dictionary entry.

KING, Larry L. Musical: *The Best Little Whorehouse in Texas*, with Peter Masterson, music and lyrics by Carol Hall, 1978 (screenplay version 1982). Other play: *The Kingfish*, with Ben Z. Grant, 1979. Journalist and novelist.

KOPIT, Arthur. See his dictionary entry.

LAPINE, James. Musicals: *Sunday in the Park with George*, music and lyrics by Stephen Sondheim, 1984 (published 1986); *Into the Woods*, music and lyrics by Sondheim, 1987. Other plays: *Photograph*, from a poem by Gertrude Stein, 1977; *Twelve Dreams*, 1978 (published 1982); *Table Settings*, 1979 (published 1980). Stage director.

LAURENTS, Arthur. See his dictionary entry.

LAWRENCE, Jerome, and **Robert E. LEE.** See their dictionary entries.

LOGAN, Joshua. Musicals: *Higher and Higher*, with Gladys Hurlbut, music by Richard Rodgers, lyrics by Lorenz Hart, 1940; *South Pacific*, with Oscar Hammerstein II, music by Rodgers, lyrics by Hammerstein, 1949; *Wish You Were Here*, with Arthur Kober, music and lyrics by Harold Rome, from a play by Kober, 1952; *Fanny*, with S.N. Behrman, music and lyrics by Rome, from plays by Marcel Pagnol, 1954; *Miss Moffat*, with Emlyn Williams, music by Albert Hague, lyrics by Williams, from the play *The Corn Is Green* by Williams, 1974. Other plays: *Mister Roberts*, with Thomas Heggen, 1948; *The Wisteria Trees*, 1950; *Rip Van Winkle*, with Ralph Allen, 1976. Screenplay: *Ensign Pulver*, 1964. Memoirs: *Josh*, 1976, and *Movie Stars, Real People, and Me*, 1978. Stage and film director.

LONGSTREET, Stephen. Musical: *High Button Shoes*, music by Jule Styne, lyrics by Sammy Kahn, 1947. Other play: *Gauguin*, 1948. Screenplays: *The Gay Sisters*, 1942; *Stallion Road*, 1943; *The Jolson Story*, 1946; *Duel in the Sun*, 1946; *Silver River*, 1948; *The Greatest Show on Earth*, 1952; *The Helen Morgan Story*, 1957; and others. Author of novels and radio and television scripts; painter and cartoonist; journalist.

MASTEROFF, Joe. Musicals: *She Loves Me*, music by Jerry Bock, lyrics by Sheldon Harnick, 1963; *Cabaret*, music by John Kander, lyrics by Fred Ebb, 1966; *70 Girls 70*, with Ebb and Norman L. Martin, music by Kander, lyrics by Ebb, from the play *Breath of Spring* by Peter Coke, 1971; *Jane White, Who? . . .*, 1980. Other play: *The Warm Peninsula*, 1959.

MASTERSON, Peter. Musical: *The Best Little Whorehouse in Texas*, with Larry L. King, music and lyrics by Carol Hall, 1978 (screenplay version 1982). Stage and film actor and director.

MAYER, Timothy S. Musical: *My One and Only*, with Peter Stone, music by George Gershwin, lyrics by Ira Gershwin,

1983. Other plays: *Prince Erie*, 1967; *Red Eye*, 1979; *Aladdin in Three Acts*, 1981. Stage director.

McNALLY, Terrence. See his dictionary entry.

MEEHAN, Thomas. Musicals: *Annie*, music by Charles Strouse, lyrics by Martin Charnin, from the comic strip *Little Orphan Annie* by Harold Gray, 1977; *Oh, Kay!*, music by George Gershwin, lyrics by Ira Gershwin, from the musical by Guy Bolton and P.G. Wodehouse, 1978; *I Remember Mama*, music by Richard Rodgers, lyrics by Charnin, from the play by John van Druten, 1979. Journalist and television writer.

MILLER, Arthur. See his dictionary entry.

NEMIROFF, Robert. Musicals (with Charlotte Zaltzberg): *The Sign in Sidney Brustein's Window*, music by Gary William Friedman, lyrics by Ray Errol Fox, from the play by Lorraine Hansberry, 1972; *Raisin*, music by Judd Woldin, lyrics by Robert Brittan, from the play *A Raisin in the Sun* by Hansberry, 1973. Other plays: *Postmark Zero*, 1965 (U.K. version as *Last Letters from an Eastern Front*, 1966); *To Be Young, Gifted and Black*, from writings by Hansberry, 1969; *Les Blancs*, from the play by Hansberry, 1970.

NEWLEY, Anthony. Musicals: *Stop the World—I Want to Get Off*, with Leslie Bricusse, 1961; *The Roar of the Greasepaint—The Smell of the Crowd*, with Bricusse, 1964; *The Good Old Bad Old Days*, with Bricusse, 1972; *Royalty Folies*, music by Newley and John Taylor, 1974; *The Travelling Music Show*, with Bricusse, 1978; *Chaplin*, with Stanley Ralph Ross, 1983. Music and songs: for the films *Willie Wonka and the Chocolate Factory*, 1971, and *Mr. Quilp*, 1975, and the television production of *Peter Pan*, 1976. Stage and film actor and director.

O'BRIEN, Richard. Musicals: *The Rocky Horror Show: A Rock Musical*, 1973 (published 1983); *T. Zee*, music by Richard Hartley, based on characters by Edgar Rice Burroughs, 1976; *Disaster*, music by Hartley, 1978. Other play: *Top People*, 1984. Television play: *A Hymn from Jim*, 1977. Screenplay: *Shock Treatment*, 1981. Actor.

PEARSON, Sybille. Musical: *Baby*, music by David Shire, lyrics by Richard Maltby, Jr., from a story by Susan Yankowitz, 1983. Other plays: *Sally and Marsha*, 1981 (published 1985); *A Little Going Away Party*, 1984.

PEN, Polly. Musicals: *Goblin Market*, with Peggy Harmon, music by Pen, from the poem by Christina Rossetti, 1986; *Songs on a Shipwrecked Sofa*, with James Milton, music by Pen, from poems by Mervyn Peake, 1987. Musician, composer, and actress.

POWERS, John R. Musical: *Do Black Patent Leather Shoes Really Reflect Up?*, music and lyrics by James Quinn and Alaric Jans, from the novel by Powers, 1978. Novelist and journalist.

RADO, James. Musicals: *Hair*, with Gerome Ragni, music by Galt MacDermot, 1967; *Rainbow*, with Ted Rado, music and lyrics by James Rado, 1972, revised version, 1974; *Jack Sound*, with Ragni, music by Steve Margoshes, 1978.

RAGNI, Gerome. Musicals: *Hair*, with James Rado, music by Galt MacDermot, 1967; *Dude*, music by MacDermot, 1972; *Jack Sound*, with Rado, music by Steve Margoshes, 1978. Actor.

RANDALL, Bob. Musical: *The Magic Show*, music by Stephen Schwartz, 1974. Other plays: *6 Rms Riv Vu*, 1972 (published 1973); *Odd Infinitum*, 1974. Television writing: *Mo and Joe*, 1974; *On Our Own* series, 1977; *Kate and Allie* series, from 1984. Screenplay: *Zorro, The Gay Blade*, 1981. Novelist.

RICE, Tim. Musicals: *Joseph and His Amazing Technicolour Dreamcoat*, music by Andrew Lloyd Webber, 1968, expanded version, 1973; *Jesus Christ Superstar*, music by Lloyd Webber, 1970; sketches in *Hullabaloo* (revue), 1972; *Evita*, music by Lloyd Webber, 1976, revised version, 1978; *Blondel*, music by Stephen Oliver, 1983; *Chess*, music by Benny Andersson and Björn Ulvaeus, 1984, revised version, 1986. Writer on cricket and popular music.

ROSE, Philip. Musicals: *Purlie*, with Peter Udell and Ossie Davis, music by Gary Geld, lyrics by Udell, from the play *Purlie Victorious* by Davis, 1970; *Shenandoah*, with James Lee Barrett and Udell, music by Geld, lyrics by Udell, from the screenplay by Barrett, 1975; *Comin' Uptown*, with Udell, music by Garry Sherman, lyrics by Udell, from the story *A Christmas Carol* by Dickens, 1979 (published as *Christmas Is Comin' Uptown*, 1982); *Amen Corner*, with Udell, music by Sherman, lyrics by Udell, from the play by James Baldwin, 1983. Stage producer and director.

SCHULBERG, Budd. See his screenwriters entry.

SENDAK, Maurice. Musicals: *Really Rosie*, music by Carole King, from the television version of his stories *The Sign on Rosie's Door* and *Nutshell Library*, 1978 (published 1985); *Where the Wild Things Are*, music by Oliver Knussen, from the story by Sendak, 1984. Author and illustrator of books for children; opera designer.

SHERRIN, Ned. Musicals: with Caryl Brahms—*Cindy-Ella; or, I Gotta Shoe*, broadcast 1957, musical version, music by Peter Knight and Ron Grainer, 1963; *No Bed for Bacon*, from the novel by Brahms and S.J. Simon, 1959, musical version, music by Sherrin, 1964; *The Spoils*, from the novel *The Spoils of Poynton* by Henry James, 1968; *Sing a Rude Song*, additional material by Alan Bennett, music by Ron Grainer, 1969; *Liberty Ranch!* (concept and lyrics only), book by Dick Vosburgh, music by John Cameron, from the play *She Stoops to Conquer* by Goldsmith, 1972; *Nickleby and Me*, music by Ron Grainer, 1975, revised version, 1981; *The Mitford Girls*, music by Peter Greenwell, 1981; other musicals—continuity for *Side by Side with Sondheim*, 1976; *Only in America*, based on songs by Jerry Leiber and Mike Stoller, 1980; *Oh, Kay!*, with Tony Geiss, music by George Gershwin, lyrics by Ira Gershwin, from the musical by Guy Bolton and P.G. Wodehouse, 1984; *The Ratepayers' Iolanthe*, with Alistair Beaton, from an opera by Gilbert and Sullivan, 1984; *The Metropolitan Mikado*, with Alistair Beaton, from an opera by Gilbert and Sullivan, 1985; *Small Expectations*, with Alistair Beaton, music by Gerard Kenny, from works by Dickens, 1986. Other plays: with Brahms—*Fish Out of Water*, from a play by Feydeau, 1971; *Let's Go to Bed*, from a play by Feydeau, 1976; *Hush and Hide*, 1978; *Beecham*, 1979; with Neil Shand—*The Sloane Ranger Revue*, 1985. Radio plays (with Brahms): *Duchess Don't Allow*, 1958; *The Haven*, 1958; *Bigger Beggars*, 1958; *Shut Up and Sing*, 1960; *Mr. Tooley Tried*, 1960; *The Italian Straw Hat*, from a play by Labiche and Michel, 1960; *The Sunday Market*, 1961; *Justice for Johnny*, 1962; *The People in the Park*, 1963; *Those Cowardly Captains!*, 1963. Television plays (with Brahms): *Take It Away*, 1955; *Benbow Was His Name*,

1964 (staged 1969); *Ooh La La!* series, from plays by Feydeau, 1968–73 (*Paying the Piper* published 1972); *The Great Inimitable Mr. Dickens*, 1970. Screenplay: *Girl/Stroke/Boy*, with Brahms, 1971. Film, theatre, and television producer and director; also writer of fiction and non-fiction; memoirs: *A Small Thing—Like an Earthquake*, 1983.

SIMON, Neil. See his dictionary entry.

SPEWACK, Bella. Musicals (with Sam Spewack): *Leave It to Me!*, music by Cole Porter, 1938; *Kiss Me, Kate,* music by Cole Porter, 1948. Other plays (with Sam Spewack): *The Solitaire Man*, 1926; *Poppa*, 1928; *The War Song*, 1928; *Clear All Wires*, 1932; *Spring Song*, 1934; *Boy Meets Girl*, 1935; *Miss Swan Expects*, 1939; *Woman Bites Dog*, 1946; *My Three Angels*, 1953; *Festival*, 1955. Television play: *Enchanted Nutcracker*, 1963. Screenplays: several of her own plays, and *When Ladies Meet*, 1933; *Should Ladies Behave?*, 1933; *The Nuisance*, 1933; *The Cat and the Fiddle*, 1934; *Rendezvous*, 1935; *Vogues of 1938*, 1937; *The Chaser*, 1938; *Three Loves Has Nancy*, 1938; *My Favorite Wife*, 1940; *Weekend at the Waldorf*, 1945.

STEIN, Joseph. Contributor to revues: *Lend an Ear*, 1948; *Inside USA*, 1948; *Mrs. Gibbons' Boys*, 1949; *Alive and Kicking*, 1950. Musicals: *Plain and Fancy*, with Will Glickman, music by Albert Hague, lyrics by Arnold B. Horwitt, 1955; *Mr. Wonderful*, with Glickman, music and lyrics by Jerry Bock, Larry Holofcener, and George Weiss, 1956; *The Body Beautiful*, with Glickman, music by Bock, lyrics by Sheldon Harnick, 1958; *Juno*, music and lyrics by Marc Blitzstein, 1959, revised version, as *Darlin' Juno*, 1976; *Take Me Along*, with Robert Russell, music and lyrics by Robert Merrill, from the play *Ah, Wilderness!* by Eugene O'Neill, 1959; *Fiddler on the Roof*, music by Bock, lyrics by Harnick, 1964; *Zorbá*, music by John Kander, lyrics by Fred Ebb, 1968; *Irene*, with Hugh Wheeler, music by Harry Tierney, lyrics by Joseph McCarthy, adaptation by Harry Rigby of the play by James Montgomery, 1973; *So Long, 174th Street*, music and lyrics by Stan Daniels, from his own play *Enter Laughing*, 1976; *The Baker's Wife*, music and lyrics by Stephen Schwartz, from a play and film by Marcel Pagnol and Jean Giono, 1976; *King of Hearts*, music by Peter Link, lyrics by Jacob Brackman, from the film by Philippe de Broca, Maurice Bessy, and Daniel Boulanger, 1978; *Carmelina*, with Alan Jay Lerner, music by Burton Lane, lyrics by Lerner, 1979; *Rags*, music by Charles Strouse, lyrics by Schwartz, 1986. Other plays: *Enter Laughing*, from the novel by Carl Reiner, 1963; *Before the Dawn*, from a play by Aleksandr Borshchgovsky, 1985. Radio and television writer.

STILGOE, Richard. Musicals: *Cats* (additional lyrics only, with Trevor Nunn), from poems by T.S. Eliot, music by Andrew Lloyd Webber, 1981 (published 1981); *Starlight Express*, music by Lloyd Webber, 1984; *Who Plays Wins*, music by Peter Skellern, 1985; *The Phantom of the Opera*, with Lloyd Webber, music by Lloyd Webber, lyrics by Charles Hart (additional lyrics by Stilgoe), from a novel by Gaston Leroux, 1986. Other play: *Bodywork*, 1987. Radio play: *Peace, Brotherly Love, and a Punch in the Jaw*, 1985. Television writing: *A Class by Himself* series, 1972. Actor.

STONE, Peter. Musicals: *Kean*, music and lyrics by Robert Wright and George Forrest, 1959; *Skyscraper*, music by James Van Heusen, lyrics by Sammy Kahn, 1965; *1776*, music and lyrics by Sherman Edwards, 1969; *Two by Two*, music by Richard Rodgers, lyrics by Martin Charnin, 1970; *Sugar*, music by Jule Styne, lyrics by Bob Merrill, from the film *Some Like It Hot* by Billy Wilder and I.A.L. Diamond, 1972; *Woman of the Year*, music by John Kander, lyrics by Fred Ebb, from the screenplay by Ring Lardner, Jr., and Michael Kanin, 1981; *My One and Only*, with Timothy S. Mayer, music by George Gershwin, lyrics by Ira Gershwin, 1983. Other plays: *Friend of the Family*, 1958; *Full Circle*, from a play by Erich Maria Remarque, 1973. Screenplays: some of his own plays, and *Charade*, 1963; *Father Goose*, 1964; *Mirage*, 1965; *Arabesque*, 1966; *The Secret War of Harry Frigg*, 1968; *Jigsaw* (as Quentin Werty), 1968; *Dark of the Sun* (as Werty), 1968; *Sweet Charity*, 1969; *The Skin Game*, 1971; *The Taking of Pelham 123*, 1974; *Silver Bears*, 1976; *Who Is Killing the Great Chefs of Europe?* (*Too Many Chefs*), 1978; *Why Would I Lie?*, 1980. Television writer.

TAYLOR, Samuel. Musical: *No Strings*, with Richard Rodgers, 1962. Other plays: *The Happy Time*, 1950; *Nina*, 1951; *Sabrina Fair*, 1953; *The Pleasure of His Company*, with Cornelia Otis Skinner, 1958; *First Love*, 1961; *Beekman Place*, 1964; *Avanti!*, 1968 (as *A Touch of Spring*, 1975); *Legend*, 1976; *Perfect Pitch*, 1976; *Gracious Living*, 1978.

TRUDEAU, Garry. Musicals: *Doonesbury*, music by Elizabeth Swados, 1983; *Rap Master Ronnie*, music by Swados, 1984, revised version, 1986. Writer of *Doonesbury* comic strip from 1970, and of several *Doonesbury* books.

UDELL, Peter. Musicals: *Purlie*, with Philip Rose and Ossie Davis, music by Gary Geld, lyrics by Udell, from the play *Purlie Victorious* by Davis, 1970; *Shenandoah*, with Rose and James Lee Barrett, music by Geld, lyrics by Udell, from the screenplay by Barrett, 1975; *Angel*, with Ketti Frings, music by Geld, from the play *Look Homeward, Angel* by Frings, 1978; *Comin' Uptown*, with Rose, music by Garry Sherman, lyrics by Udell, from the story *A Christmas Carol* by Dickens, 1979 (published as *Christmas Is Comin' Uptown*, 1982); *Amen Corner*, with Rose, music by Sherman, lyrics by Udell, from the play by James Baldwin, 1983.

VAN PEEBLES, Melvin. Musicals (author and composer): *Ain't Supposed to Die a Natural Death*, 1971; *Don't Play Us Cheap*, 1972; *Reggae*, with others, 1980; *Waltz of the Stork*, 1982 (as *Waltz of the Stork Boogie*, 1984); *Champeen!*, 1983. Screenplay: *Greased Lightning*, 1977. Director and novelist.

VOSBURGH, Dick. Musicals: *Liberty Ranch!* (book), concept and lyrics by Caryl Brahms and Ned Sherrin, music by John Cameron, from the play *She Stoops to Conquer* by Goldsmith, 1972; *A Day in Hollywood/A Night in the Ukraine*, lyrics by Vosburgh and others, music by Frank Lazarus and others, 1980 (published 1984); *Steafel Variations* (songs and sketches), with Peter Tinniswood and Keith Waterhouse, 1982; *Windy City*, music by Tony Macaulay, from the play *The Front Page* by Ben Hecht and Charles MacArthur, 1982; *Jerome Kern Goes to Hollywood* (book for revue), conceived by David Kernan, music by Kern, 1986.

WASSERMAN, Dale. Musical: *Man of La Mancha*, music by Mitch Leigh, lyrics by Joe Darion, 1965. Other plays: *Livin' the Life*, with Bruce Geller, 1955; *The Pencil of God*, 1961; *998*, 1962; *One Flew over the Cuckoo's Nest*, from the novel by Ken Kesey, 1963; *The Shining Mountains*, 1977; *Play with Fire*, 1978. Screenplays: *The Vikings*, 1958; *Quick Before It Melts*, 1965; *Mister Buddwing*, 1965; *A Walk with Love and Death*, 1969; *Man of La Mancha*, 1972. Television writer.

WEIDMAN, Jerome. Musicals: *Fiorello!*, with George Abbott, music by Jerry Bock, lyrics by Sheldon Harnick, 1959 (published 1960); *Tenderloin*, with Abbott, music by Bock, lyrics by Harnick, from the work by Samuel Hopkins Adams, 1960 (published 1961); *I Can Get It for You Wholesale*, music by Harold Rome, from the novel by Weidman, 1962 (published 1961); *Cool Off!*, music by Howard Blackman, 1964; *Pousse-Café*, music by Duke Ellington, lyrics by Marshall Barer and Frank Tobias, 1966. Other plays: *Ivory Tower*, with James Yaffe, 1968 (published 1969); *The Mother Lover*, 1969 (published 1969); *Asterisk! A Comedy of Terrors*, 1969 (published 1969). Screenplays: *The Damned Don't Cry*, with Harold Medford, 1950; *The Eddie Cantor Story*, with Ted Sherdeman and Sidney Skolsky, 1953; *Slander*, 1957. Television writing: *The Reporter* series, 1964. Novelist and short story writer; autobiography: *Praying for Rain*, 1986.

WEIDMAN, John. Musicals: *Pacific Overtures*, music and lyrics by Stephen Sondheim, additional material by Hugh Wheeler, 1976; *America's Sweetheart*, with Alfred Uhry, music by Robert Waldman, lyrics by Uhry, from the book *Capone* by John Kobler, 1985.

WILSON, Sandy. Contributor to revues: *Slings and Arrows*, 1948; *Oranges and Lemons*, 1949; *See You Later*, 1951; *See You Again*, 1952; *Pieces of Eight*, 1959. Musicals (author and composer): *The Boy Friend*, 1953; *The Buccaneer*, 1953; *Valmouth*, from the novel by Ronald Firbank, 1959; *Call It Love* (songs only), book by Robert Tanitch, 1960; *Divorce Me, Darling!*, 1965; *As Dorothy Parker Once Said* (music only), 1969; *His Monkey Wife*, from the novel by John Collier, 1971; *Sandy Wilson Thanks the Ladies* (one-man show), 1971; *The Clapham Wonder*, from a novel by Barbara Comyns, 1978; *Aladdin*, 1979. Television scores: *The World of Wooster*, 1965; *Danny La Rue's "Charley's Aunt"*, 1970. Author of several works of non-fiction; autobiography: *I Could Be Happy*, 1975.

WOODS, Aubrey. Musical: *Trelawney*, music by Julian Slade, from the play *Trelawney of the Wells* by Arthur Wing Pinero, 1972. Other plays: *Make Way for Lucia*, from works by E.F. Benson, 1980; *Roughover Golf Course 1936*, 1983. Radio plays: *As Long as Ye Both Shall Live*, 1974; *And on the Seventh Day*, 1974; *Lucia in London*, from the novel by E.F. Benson, 1985.

ZALTZBERG, Charlotte. See the entry for Robert Nemiroff.

THEATRE GROUPS

Theatre Groups in Britain

At any one time, throughout Britain, there are well over 200 working theatre groups, using any number of different techniques, with widely varying approaches to their work, playing to audiences of all classes and milieus. Generally, they do not have their own theatre buildings. Many tour to a variety of venues up and down the country; others mount work at one or another venue on a one-off basis. Naturally, in the limited space of this article, only a handful of these groups can be discussed and the picture given is bound to be selective.

The late 1960's and early 1970's are often referred to as boom years for the growth of new groups outside the mainstream of the large building-based theatres. These were the years which gave birth to the fringe—so-called on the model of the unofficial Fringe at the Edinburgh Festival. For all the disparity between groups, this period was remarkable for certain shared attitudes towards theatrical experimentation, and towards the artist's relationship with society and with a given audience. There was a vision of collective creation and responsibility in the theatre which notably shifted perceptions of what could be done on a stage and for whom; the pioneering spirit brought about new forms and discovered new audiences. Very often, the terms "stage" and "audience" themselves became obsolete.

Some of this vision persists, but much diluted. It is still true among many groups that joint responsibility for the process of creating a work of art rests on a bedrock of broadly progressive belief and outlook. The urge to improve society still pervades a great deal of work, but its edges are blurred, its impact smoothed. In 1973 it was possible for one writer on fringe theatre to speculate that political pressures on society at large could mount to such an extent "that the fringe may really have to go underground, and become the one surviving democratic means of communication" ("A Potted History of the Fringe" by Jonathan Hammond, in *Theatre Quarterly*, October–December 1973). Whether or not this perhaps inflated prognosis could have been extended to theatre groups at large, 15 years later we can see that rather than go underground groups have undergone a process of consolidation while at the same time being subjected to a number of pressures. Some work has been very popular, and the standards of the best work in all departments has been very high, but at all times companies are struggling for their share of a diminishing number of available dates, financial resources that are steadily contracting in real terms, and audiences that have not grown as much as had been hoped in the palmy early days.

Some groups have reached the point where the boundaries between their work and that of more established, building-based companies are no longer as sharply defined as they used to be. Unionisation, improvement of conditions (marginal though it has been in so many cases), and higher standards of administration have brought the different areas of professional theatre much closer together. As always, there is a continual movement of people from small theatre groups into the larger, more prestigious and better-funded theatres. There is no doubt that some playwrights, such as Howard Brenton, David Hare, and Caryl Churchill, have had a profound influence on forms of theatre more conventional than those in which their work originated. This is even more true of a handful of directors such as Mike Leigh, Mike Bradwell, Max Stafford-Clark, and Mike Alfreds. But, for all that, one of the more remarkable characteristics of British theatre of the last twenty-odd years is the way in which established theatre has usually failed to learn from the artistic successes of its smaller kindred, particularly in the area of visual and performance work. Alongside this is the failure of British writers on theatre to adapt and develop their critical vocabulary, or at least their critical responses, to meet the challenge of some of the more innovative new work.

For the purposes of discussion it is helpful to divide the wide variety of theatre groups into loose areas of activity or aim. There are perhaps four such areas, though they inevitably overlap and shade into each other: 1) script-based production, whether through revival of plays (classical or otherwise) or the staging of new ones; 2) constituency-based drama—that is, for or out of particular sections of the population (women's theatre, black or gay, for instance); 3) issue- and community-based theatre (work on issues of the day or addressing the experience of certain communities); 4) autonomously creative work, often experimental and innovative.

The degree to which these areas can overlap is perhaps best illustrated by Joint Stock Theatre Group. Probably this company's major influence has been in the techniques developed by its founders (Max Stafford-Clark, David Hare, David Aukin, and, later, William Gaskill). A group of actors, led by a director, a writer, and a designer, spend several weeks in workshops developing an idea, improvising on it and carrying out research in various ways. At the end of the first period, the writer withdraws to prepare a script, which is then brought to rehearsals for the final production. This method has resulted in some of the landmarks of British theatre. Joint Stock has been vitally important in its encouragement of the work of writers such as Caryl Churchill, Howard Brenton, and Hanif Kureishi. But the company is also remarkable in its collective organization, in which it is governed at any one time by a committee of actors, directors, writers, designers, and technicians, always including the company currently in production. While Joint Stock epitomises some significant aspects of British theatre groups, its collaboration with major theatres such as the Royal Court, Leicester Haymarket, and Birmingham Rep also points to the blurring of boundaries between "established" and "alternative" companies.

Many companies began life playing one-night stands in small venues. It is significant that some now look for larger venues and more extended audiences. Foco Novo, originally committed to new plays on themes of social importance, has since moved on to quite large revivals of modern classics, only to return to its first aims and mode of operation in recent years. Directed by Roland Rees, Foco Novo exemplifies a number of groups who rely on the talents of a single director, often the group's founder. Shared Experience was founded by Mike Alfreds, who directed several brilliant adaptations of literary works, originating a form of narrative theatre based on the actor which has been immensely influential. This company, too, moved on to productions of classical plays, in recent years on a fairly substantial scale. A significant aspect of this increase in scale in the work of some companies has been their resultant subjection to market demands for comparatively well-known titles and accessible or popular work, generally because of the need to attract large audiences and because audiences and venue managers have become more rather than less conservative in their tastes.

The production of classics in pared-down, sharply theatrical productions, playing in often small venues up and down the country, is typified by ATC (Actors Touring Company) and Cheek by Jowl. The former was founded by director John Retallack and is now led by Mark Brickman. The latter boasts the extremely effective partnership of director Declan Donnellan and designer Nick Ormerod. Companies devoted to new writing, whose founders have successfully handed over to new directors, are Hull Truck Theatre Company and Paines Plough. Having for ten years been led by Mike Bradwell with his accomplished vein of improvised plays, Hull Truck now concentrates on the work of its writer-director John Godber. Paines Plough (founded by director John Adams and writer David Pownall) is now led by director Pip Broughton and has begun to develop the work of a series of young writers on contemporary themes. It is also among the few to tackle acutely important current political issues, as it did in *Joyriders* (1986) by Christina Reid, set in embattled Belfast.

Because by their nature and philosophy groups playing to particular constituencies stand outside the mainstream, often in considered opposition to it, their work has from time to time been a source of theatrical innovation. This has been true of women's theatre. Monstrous Regiment, a feminist group that nevertheless does not confine its collective solely to women, has often in the past encouraged new forms, whether in the plays of Caryl Churchill and Bryony Lavery or in works such as *Shakespeare's Sister* (1980). This last, directed by Hilary Westlake of Lumiere and Son, assimilated the approach of performance theatre to enriching effect. A 1987 production, *Alarms* by Susan Yankowitz, deals with the issue of nuclear pollution.

While Monstrous Regiment preserves a core of founder members who still share in the group's decisions and policy, the personnel of Women's Theatre Group, though confined as of principle to women only, has changed completely over the years. Like many younger women's groups, it reflects the growth of a new generation of politically and socially aware women performers and the encouragement of new women writers. Chief among these writers of late has been Deborah Levy who, in work such as the "blasphemous thriller" *Our Lady* (1986), has been forging a style which marries expressionist and performance theatre.

It is perhaps natural that a gay group such as Gay Sweatshop should stage work that is both issue-based and innovatory. This a company which at one stage discovered an entirely new audience among the homosexual community. Understandably, much of its work has explored themes germane to male and female gay people.

Yet another constituency, of both performers and audiences, is that of the handicapped. The dual demand for opportunities for handicapped performers often excluded from conventional theatre and for work accessible to handicapped audiences has led to the growth of companies such as Graeae. This group has shown not only what can be done when talented performers in this area get together, but has also begun to show what theatrical possibilities are opened up when handicapped performers are used. Interesting, too, is Graeae's involvement in theatre-in-education.

One of the most important fields of development in British theatre over the last few years has been in the work of black and Asian groups. Temba, founded by Alton Kumalo and now directed by Alby James, was an early pioneer in black theatre in Britain. Its policy now entails not only the encouragement of new writing, but the revival of black plays such as *Scrape Off the Black* by Tunde Ikoli (1985) and *Woza Albert!* (1986). Black Theatre Co-operative, operating along collective lines, has followed a similar policy, staging the work of Mustapha Matura, Edgar White, and others, and mounting excellent revivals such as Lorraine Hansberry's *A Raisin in the Sun* (1985).

While the innovation in the work of these companies largely stems from the reflection of the experience of a generation and community not generally represented on the British stage before now, the work of the Asian Tara Arts Group may have more far-reaching impact. By combining work on the experience of young Asians in Britain (such as *Chilli In Yor Eyes* in 1984) with versions of classical Indian drama such as *The Broken Thigh* (1986), Tara shows a gradual development towards a theatre which could merge influences from both East and West to fascinating effect. Possibly its most interesting experiment to date has been *This Story's Not for Telling* (1985), which in non-realistic form, using techniques learned from Indian folk theatre, staged tales of the traumas of the Partition of the Indian subcontinent, giving each episode its own distinctive shape and theatrical mode. The result had a daring simplicity and expressiveness seen only occasionally in the more accomplished of the European experimental groups.

The field of issue-based work and community theatre is a wide one, ranging from well-established companies to small local groups that are only semi-professional. The work of the larger professional groups in itself covers various different forms and approaches. Both 7:84 (England) and 7:84 (Scotland)—the name based on the statistic that at one time 7% of the population owned 84% of the country's wealth—share the talents of their founder, John McGrath. Their work is overtly and sometimes powerfully socialist, though even in the 1980's agitprop shows its unsubtle influence. Generally speaking, these two related companies tour throughout their respective countries. But some of the more fruitful work in this field is confined to a particular region, often resolutely local in its appeal.

Red Ladder Theatre concentrates on Leeds, its base, and other parts of Yorkshire, often with shows—like *On the Line* (1986) about the origins of racism—aimed at young audiences, with the express intention of making them think about central issues in their lives and environment. Another Yorkshire company, DAC (Doncaster Arts Centre) Theatre Company, performs shows about local and national issues, some specially for youngsters and touring to schools and youth clubs, others for adults in miners' clubs, village halls, and so on. At the other end of the country, Avon Touring Theatre Company confines itself to Bristol and the county of Avon, performing not only youth and issue-based shows, but also productions of wider theatrical appeal such as its recent adaptation of Dickens's *Little Dorrit* (1986).

In London, one of the veteran agitprop companies, CAST, has branched out in the last few years into the area of "alternative cabaret," for the most part functioning as a producer for numerous variety acts, largely with a political and satirical message. It has now refurbished an old variety theatre, the Hackney Empire, as a base for its programmes. The development of this kind of work is also symptomatic of a strong recent trend among many groups to produce musical entertainment more akin to variety than drama. While this may reflect the growth of musical skills among performers, it also stems from two opposing tendencies in alternative theatre since the 1960's. There is a tendency to cater for a much-reduced audience attention span; to simplify drama down to the sketch; to fillet issues down to their barest bones; to sugar the pill with catchy tunes. However, this style of work also has something in common with the total theatre of some more experimental groups, where music is actually used to extend the medium's range and possibilities. An array of theatrical techniques, from mime to improvisation, allied to the use of music—often specially composed—and an eclectic and frequently highly sophisticated use of concepts learned from the visual arts distinguish work that can be only loosely grouped under the heading of the autonomously creative. That is, theatre that often originates not from a prewritten script, not from the verbal or the literary, but from an open-ended search for particular solutions to particular artistic questions, with a highly flexible use of a variety of means to achieve those solutions. There are in fact as many different approaches as there are groups; and some would consider the term "theatre" as inapposite to their work as they would the term "drama."

Many of these companies share a group ethos which has an effect both on their way of life and on the work they perform. The members of the former Cornish company, Footsbarn Theatre Company, now based on the Continent, live and travel together as a commune encompassing performers, friends, and children—virtually as an extended family. Their work—unlike that of most other groups discussed in this section—is based on texts, most recently Shakespeare's *King Lear* (1985) and *Macbeth* (1986). But the approach is that of group interpretation, exuberant, free-ranging in its humanism, and strikingly theatrical. Footsbarn found the scope for its work in Britain contracting and eventually left the country. Other companies have been seriously affected by a combination of changing cultural attitudes and financial constrictions in the 1980's. A prime example is the Pip Simmons Theatre Group, whose brand of subversion was too individual and too disturbing to be accommodated into any of the prevailing fashions in the twenty years of its existence. The group's basically pop approach in its early years—using rock music, bold comic-strip presentation, and shock tactics of various kinds—was always qualified by an uncanny ability to undermine its audience's expectations. *George Jackson's Black and White Minstrel Show* in 1972 subverted white liberal complacency, just as in 1980 *Towards a Nuclear Future* impugned our complicity in the death of Karen Silkwood. But Pip Simmons's increasing urge to distance himself from coterie audiences while addressing larger canvasses has conflicted with a reduced demand for adventurous theatre. His work is more and more confined to the Continent, where audiences and funds for this kind of theatre are more abundant.

Another company whose work was affected by changing times is Natural Theatre. Though of late its work has been more akin to cabaret theatre, this group grew out of an involvement with the community on the one hand (originally as part of Bath Arts Workshop, a community arts organization) and the impetus to make fun of its environment on the other. The Natural Theatre "normals," strange anonymous bowler-hatted figures, their faces obscured in silver lurex stocking fabric, would flit noiselessly in formation through public events, observing, accompanying, commenting by default, but never intervening. On other occasions, members of the company would appear at gala events as spoof representatives of the ruling classes, wryly offsetting the pomposity around them by their very presence. Natural Theatre became expert at highly polished and often sophisticated street theatre, but eventually suffered from legal constraints on this sort of performance and lack of funds for it.

Terms frequently used for some of the work we have called autonomously creative are "performance theatre" or "visual theatre." This is work in which the performance often exists for itself; where rather than being "about" or "for" something, it simply "is." It uses a series of actions or images; sometimes random, sometimes repetitive; sometimes aleatory, sometimes meticulously controlled. It constitutes an experience complete in itself, at its most idealistically abstract without reference to external meanings, messages, or stories. The veteran company in this field is The People Show, which has been a seminal influence for most of its twenty years. Continuity and significance in a given People Show (some shows have titles, but each is invariably given a number; the latest at the time of writing was People Show 92 in 1987) are provided by the visual and aural impact of the performance, but first and foremost by the personalities of those involved, who create each show through a lengthy process of discussion and trial and error. While the work at its peak created a world of disturbing and deceptively anarchic mystery, a period spent performing the wildly funny People Show Cabaret has now resulted in a more popular approach. Music continues to be a vital element, but it is allied to wry humour and a discernible, though tenuous, narrative.

The growing use of music even led another company, Lumiere and Son, to create the opera *Senseless* in 1983. This group, founded by director Hilary Westlake and writer David Gale in 1973, differs from most others in relying on original scripts of considerable complexity, elaboration, and wit to deal with the unexpected, the extreme, and the numinous. Its work has ranged from the brilliant black humour of *Circus Lumiere* (1980) to the mass spectacle of *Deadwood* (1986). The company has often used non-professional performers, and shares with others a possibly contradictory hankering to both disturb the spectator and appeal to a wider, more popular audience.

It is characteristic of some performance theatre that there is a sustained attempt to deal with the darker side of human nature, with images that belong to the subconscious, the surreal, and the mythical. The work of IOU Theatre contrasts with that of Lumiere and Son in that until recently it was largely non-verbal and made extensive use of found objects and deliberately rough costumes to determine the physical and visual aspects of the shows. The group is a collective of visual artists and musicians (originally an offshoot of Welfare State International, of whom more later) and its non-theatre shows entail the transformation of particular sites to create special environments in which outlandish creatures appear and perform. Weird and wonderful music is integral to the performances and is played on unorthodox combinations of instruments, with sung lyrics of surreal irrationality. The original solemnity of the work has of recent years been tempered with a quirky humour and the use of occasional written passages.

The eccentric has never been far from the field of British theatre and one of the groups that might be so described is Forkbeard Fantasy, actually the brothers Tim and Chris Britton. Here strange quixotic quests and sibling battles are allied to the construction of bizarre machines and intricately surprising sets, often using incidental films. The use of words and intrusion of narrative or rational meaning are ancillary to the hilarious impact of the whole. The influence of the visual artist, so evident in this area, was taken even further in some of the work of Hidden Grin (originally part of Rational Theatre), in which shows were created in collaboration with leading artists—as in *Parasite Structures* (1984) which articulated on stage the work of the sculptor Denis Masi.

A great deal of the work of performance or visual theatre groups stemmed from the ideas of artists teaching or studying in the 1970's at a number of art schools, most notably at the Fine Art Department of Leeds Polytechnic. This was the origin of the work of Hesitate and Demonstrate (now sadly defunct). Its director, Geraldine Pilgrim, evolved a style in which personal and public fantasies found expression in elaborate visual spectacle, where the action was interwoven with complex sound tapes and was usually without words. Extraordinary juxtapositions and startling images were hallmarks of the performances, which were given with polished technical precision. The source material was usually the hinterland of middle-class English and European life, often in bygone days—a world of tea-dances, midnight steam trains, and politely suppressed passion. The company's most successful show was *Goodnight Ladies!* (1981), which created enthralling images of enigma and betrayal in a world of postwar European émigrés. The precision of Hesitate and Demonstrate's work can be seen reflected in that of a more recent company, Intimate Strangers, where there is a tight alliance of extreme technical control with powerful emotional substance.

Impact Theatre Co-operative (now no longer in operation) was itself originally based in Leeds. This company, perhaps more than any other, showed the influence of European performance theatre and aspired to work in that context. Its most successful creations, directed by Pete Brooks on the basis of the group's joint efforts, were *A Place in Europe* (1983) and *The Carrier Frequency* (1984). The former was devised as a British-Italian co-production and had a strong musical content, all but one of its performers playing instruments. The latter, originally based on work-in-progress by the writer Russell Hoban, created a desolate and shattering image of a post-nuclear holocaust world.

The "Leeds connection" came at first from the work of John Fox, in 1971 a senior lecturer at Leeds Polytechnic. In 1968 he had founded Welfare State International, which remains the most uncompromisingly non-establishment and freely creative of the groups. In its attempt to reinvigorate popular culture and revivify communal myths, it has resolutely steered clear of theatrical orthodoxies of any kind, remaining committed to enriching the imaginative lives of people mostly outside Britain's presumed cultural centres. Based in Ulverston, Cumbria, Welfare State works within its local community and in other communities in the country, bringing a celebratory joy that attempts to resist the dehumanising ravages of modern society. The company mounts its events and performances outdoors or in community venues. They range from the comparatively contained naming ceremonies for new-born infants to major one-off celebrations attracting up to 15,000 people. For several years, each time at a different site, the group would celebrate Guy Fawkes Night with a tremendous event in which, after giant puppet shows, music, and feasting, a phantasmagorical replica of the Houses of Parliament was set alight to the crack and thud of fireworks. The group brings its barn dances to villages and towns, involving entire communities in celebrations of their common humanity and life-affirming uniqueness. The fusion of performance, music, dancing, and spectacle found one of its most comprehensive expressions in *The Raising of the Titanic* (1983), which managed to affirm hope for humankind while giving poignant vent to disgust at its follies.

British theatre is often praised for its technical accomplishment and the power of its actors. It is also known for its stamina in the face of parsimonious government funding and steadily dwindling resources. All this is evident in the work of the groups discussed here. But these groups also demonstrate an overwhelming ground for hope in their surviving impetus towards innovation, growing at its best out of a faith in the vigour of human imagination.

—Jonathan Lamede

Theatre Groups in the United States

Over the last twenty years the transformations in American theatre have come fast and furious, reflecting the gyrations of a society in continual transition. The rules of the game—for young creative artists on the brink of performance careers, and for audiences who attend the theatre—are very different now from what they were two or three decades ago, and are changing all the time.

This is particularly evident when one surveys the state of American "fringe" theatre ensembles dedicated to forging distinctive performance styles and exploring thematic or aesthetic territory not usually covered in mainstream popular culture. These alternative companies exist apart from (and sometimes in direct opposition to) the beleaguered commercial Broadway and off-Broadway establishment, and also apart from the growing phalanx of institutionalized regional repertory theatres around the country.

Most critics date the modern American avant garde fringe movement back to the late 1960's, when a number of influential ensembles erupted into prominence. During that era maverick groups like the Living Theatre founded by Julian Beck and Judith Malina, the Open Theatre under the direction of Joseph Chaikin, and the Performance Group led by Richard Schechner were responsible for a passionate, fiercely partisan "new wave" which didn't just aim to entertain: it zealously promoted social transformation, artistic experimentation, and the politics of collectivity. In the rehearsal studio and on the stage, these groups and their progeny channeled the burning concerns of a widespread youth counterculture movement: opposition to the war in Vietnam, eagerness to experiment with mind-altering drugs and communal lifestyles, fascination with non-Western religion and art, and rejection of the prevailing middle-class consumerist-materialist value system.

Rebelling against the aesthetic confines of conventional American theatre, such groups felt free to draw inspiration from an array of multi-cultural sources—Asian theatre forms, diverse religious texts and practices, visual art media (video, film, sculpture), the epic theatre theories of Brecht, Theatre of Cruelty theories of Artaud, the Poor Theatre of Grotowski. Performers studied yoga, acrobatics, and martial arts to create more physicalized acting techniques. Directors experimented with unorthodox staging and multi-media visual effects.

The area of script development ceased to be solely the domain of playwrights. In many groups texts were created collectively over extended rehearsal periods through acting improvisations and incorporation of material from many documentary and literary sources. Actors were no longer mere interpreters of pre-existing roles, but key collaborators in the writing and directing process as well.

There was also a serious rethinking of the formal actor-spectator relationship which has dominated much of Western theatre, a determined breaking down of "the fourth wall." In the Living Theatre's *Paradise Now* (1968) the audience was vigorously encouraged to participate in an erotic "Rite of Universal Intercourse" and led into the streets to incite a "non-violent anarchist revolution." The performances of Peter Schumann's Bread and Puppet Theatre often occurred in churches and other public spaces, culminating in the ritualistic sharing of food. As Artaud and others had envisioned, contemporary theatre was reclaiming its early tribal roots of pageantry and communion, while large-scale rock music festivals, mass peace marches, and psychedelic "Be-Ins" achieved similar effects in other contexts.

Some theatre ensembles that emerged in the 1960's and 1970's promoted specific political goals, drawing more inspiration from Brecht and Piscator than from Artaud. These companies—the San Francisco Mime Troupe, the Free Southern Theatre, the Gay Theatre Collective, El Teatro Campesino, and others—mounted frontal attacks on issues confronting oppressed social groups such as blacks, Hispanics, Asians, homosexuals, and women. The goal was to raise the political consciousness of these particular constituencies, while also creating awareness within the society at large.

By the early 1980's many of the seminal fringe groups had disbanded, the victims of significant shifts within their own companies, and within American culture at large. They had created the context and vocabulary for a new theatrical aesthetic, but were unable to survive as ongoing institutions. All were forced to grapple with a swiftly changing financial climate. During the relatively prosperous Vietnam War era, dedicated young theatre artists could eke out a spare but adequate income by living communally, sharing basic expenses, and taking advantage of federal social programs like food stamps, unemployment benefits, and CETA (Comprehensive Education and Training Act) grants. Many also eventually derived funding from the National Endowment for the Arts (NEA) and from state and local arts councils, whose budgets increased dramatically during the 1970's—thanks in part to Richard Nixon's interest in becoming a "modern day Medici." Though public arts agencies had, in earlier times, funnelled money primarily to "establishment" opera, symphony, and ballet groups, the institution of peer review panels and a nationwide explosion of populist arts activity resulted in more grants to grassroots and experimental theatres. The most prominent ensembles could also rely on touring, finding a national and international market for their performances.

But massive worldwide inflation in the 1970's and substantial cuts in U.S. government spending since Ronald Reagan became president in 1980 have taken a harsh toll on many nonprofit arts organizations. Tougher restrictions and cutbacks gave fewer artists access to social subsidies like food stamps. The NEA and state arts council budgets have been reduced or frozen at pre-inflation levels, and there is a renewed emphasis on directing public and corporate funds toward "major" institutions. The costs of domestic and international touring rose astronomically, as did basic production costs.

Beyond simple arithmetic, many artists no longer nurse romantic notions about "voluntary poverty." Some of the mavericks of two decades ago now have families to support and very real fears about financial insecurity; the younger artists just entering the field can't help but be influenced by the renewed emphasis on materialism pervading American society at all levels. Without a unifying spirit of political and social commitment to propel them into a life "on the fringe," many ambitious young artists are more attracted to the lucrative pastures of mainstream television, film, and popular music than to the precarious world of experimental and political theatre.

Theatre artists are also absorbing the effects of a highly accelerated computer and mass media revolution that began in the 1950's and shows no signs of slowing down. By the 1980's the average American home had a television set turned on for more then seven hours each day. Television, with its small screen, heightened naturalism, fragmented pace, and ability immediately to interpret and disseminate current events and consumer trends, has had a far-reaching impact on live performance. Furthermore, in large sectors of the population entertainment is becoming a strictly private rather than communal activity. For many, the very idea of attending a live, "unmediated" event seems rather obsolete: why venture out to the cinema at night when it has become easier and cheaper to rent a movie on video and watch it at home? Why go to hear a concert when the sound of a compact disc player improves on the real thing? Why participate actively with strangers when you can access information and stimulate yourself with your home computer? Why attend live theatre at all, with its higher ticket prices, slower pace, and musty "highbrow" connotations?

Indeed, theatre must justify itself anew to endure within the frantic marketplace of American culture. The current alternative ensembles are vigorously working on various fronts to make live theatre—and new hybrids synthesizing theatre, visual art, and music—relevant to a younger audience with little awareness of the form. They are also designing more flexible collaboratives so that individual members have the freedom to develop solo projects and take on higher paid work in other media when necessary.

Unsurprisingly, the most embattled sector within alternative theatre involves those collective ensembles dedicated to addressing political and social issues in a direct, topical, person-to-person fashion. Since 1980 many of the oldest, most prominent groups in this camp have slowed down their activities or ceased producing altogether. While founder-director Luis Valdez grows more intrigued with film possibilities, El Teatro Campesino (a Chicano ensemble founded during a migrant workers' strike) no longer maintains an ongoing acting company, and mounts live productions infrequently. The future of the Living Theatre has been unclear since the death of its dynamic co-founder, Julian Beck. Lilith, the Free Southern Theatre, Dakota Theatre Caravan, the Provisional Theatre, and other important "people's theatre" groups have disbanded entirely.

Some political and grassroots collectives do persist, however. Their durability reflects a willingness to evolve artistically and thematically, an ongoing commitment by key original members, and the financial and moral support of their immediate communities. One of the hardiest survivors is the San Francisco Mime Troupe, a racially integrated company founded in 1959 which still performs radical agitprop musicals each summer in the parks of San Francisco, and tours in the U.S. and abroad. The Troupe is slowly evolving from an ongoing collective to a looser production group, but it still examines current political issues from a radical-socialist perspective. Recent productions have included *Steeltown* (1984), about the failure of American unions to prevent plant closings, *Crossing Borders* (1985), which considers the plight of illegal Central American refugees, and *The Mozamgola Caper* (1986), concerning the aftermath of socialist revolutions in Africa. Other interracial political collectives such as Modern Times Theater and the New York Street Theater Caravan also continue to produce and tour, though more sporadically.

Various rurally-based companies also endure; they live far from the increasingly expensive and competitive urban cultural centers. The venerable Bread and Puppet Theatre still holds its vibrant Domestic Resurrection Fair and Circus annually on founder-director Peter Schumann's rural Vermont farm, and makes regular forays to New York to present socially oriented mask-and-puppet works. The Dell'Arte Players of Blue Lake, California runs an internationally known school of mime and clowning while producing and touring "new vaudeville" satires on social issues. Their *Malpractice* (1984) converted a Molière comedy into an acrobatic skewering of the modern medical establishment; *The Road Not Taken* (1985) dramatized the confrontation between the Northwest logging industry and environmental activists in a mock murder mystery. Roadside Theater remains rooted in the small Appalachian town of Whitesburg, Kentucky under the direction of founder Dudley Cocke. In pieces like *South of the Mountain* (1981), *Mountain Tales and Music* (1975), and *Red Fox/Second Hangin'* (1977) they take a folkloric approach, blending down-home bluegrass music with Appalachian legend and contemporary oral histories.

In the midwest, playwright Megan Terry (a veteran of the Open Theatre) remains an important figure in the ongoing

Omaha Magic Theatre. The feminist collective At The Foot of the Mountain, based in Minneapolis, keeps on producing shows related to the sociopolitical concerns of women, including the docu-drama *Raped* (1976) and the anti-nuclear *Ashes, Ashes, We All Fall Down* (1982).

In the area of ethnically oriented ensembles, the San Francisco-based A Traveling Jewish Theatre remains committed to the theatrical investigation of contemporary and ancient Jewish experience. Their *Coming from a Great Distance* (1979) and *The Last Yiddish Poet* (1980) delved into the literary and musical traditions of Eastern European Jewry; *Berlin, Jerusalem, and the Moon* (1985) examined the condition of Jewish intellectuals in Nazi Germany and in modern Israel. Recently their three core members (Naomi Newman, Albert Greenberg, and Corey Fischer) have experimented with solo efforts. El Teatro de la Esperanza is one of the few remaining Chicano collectives; though many of its original members have moved on, the company continues under new leadership. Their 1984 adaptation of *We Won't Pay! We Won't Pay!* relocated Dario Fo's satire on food prices from the slums of Rome to the Hispanic barrios of Southern California.

The companies mentioned above are stylistically diverse, but all are actor-oriented, work primarily with narrative texts, are rooted in the traditions of theatre, and aim to be accessible to a broad-based audience. In striking counterpoint, there is a growing crop of alternative companies who emanate a very different sensibility—one that is, in some ways, more in tune with the tenor and tempo of the 1980's. For these ensembles, the conventional boundaries between the visual and performing arts are dissolving. By juxtaposing video, film, and electronic music with live performance, they are creating technologically sophisticated new "crossover" forms which exert a strong appeal on the television generation. Though their work can appear abstract and fragmented, many of these artists still harbor radical motives: they want to stimulate a new dialetic between electronic and live imagery which will "deconstruct" the media code and challenge audiences to examine the complex nature of modern experience. In a sense they are adopting the tools of conventional mass media for subversive purposes. And, in harmony with the general thrust of postmodernism, they are not timid about mingling ancient and modern forms, high culture and pop culture, expressionism and surrealism.

Mabou Mines is one of the most prominent and prolific of such collaboratives. The nine member artists do multiple duty as performers, directors, filmmakers, and writers, working within the company and on individual outside projects as well. Mabou Mines' diverse offerings reflect a range of viewpoints and styles: their 1984 productions of Franz Xaver Kroetz's play *Through the Leaves* and Samuel Beckett's *Imagination Dead Imagine* strongly emphasized text and acting, while *Dead End Kids: A History of Nuclear Power* (1980), directed and written by JoAnne Akalaitis, and Lee Breuer's *Hajj* in 1983 were more technically complex multi-media excursions. Most of Mabou Mines' pieces pivot on provocative social concerns—nuclear power, the savagery of the Civil War (*Cold Harbor*, 1983), homosexuality (Greg Mehrten's *Pretty Boy*, 1984)—but these issues are explored elliptically, forcing the viewer to draw his or her own conclusions from an elegant array of words and images.

The Wooster Group also makes its audience sort out their own perceptions, but their barrage of imagery is more frenetic and outrageous. Founded by former members of the Performance Group in 1975 under the artistic leadership of Elizabeth LeCompte, the Wooster Group concocts explosively ironic critiques of American culture by blending video, flamboyant live acting, and fragments of many texts in startling and often controversial ways. In particular, the repertory pieces *Route 1 & 9* (1981) and *L.S.D.* (1984) have catalyzed heated debate among critics, audiences, and other theatre artists. *Route 1 & 9* contrasts the repressive smalltown white America of Thornton Wilder's play, *Our Town* with exaggerated images of blacks as a method of exposing and confronting racism—at least, that's what supporters contend. Detractors find a sequence where actors in blackface re-enact a crude comedy routine by black vaudevillian Pigmeat Markham far too offensive to be defended on aesthetic grounds. In *L.S.D.* fragments from Arthur Miller's play *The Crucible*, quotations from Timothy Leary and Allen Ginsberg, and pieces of other existing texts are orchestrated in a dissonant examination of American culture and counterculture of the 1950's and 1960's; blackface is employed here as well. Arthur Miller objected to the "deconstructed" use of his play in this context and threatened to sue; the company's response was to perform the speeches from *The Crucible* in gibberish.

The unsettling manipulation of text, performance, and visual effects combined with fierce (though deliberately unprogrammatic) social critique also informs the work of Squat Theatre, which emigrated to the U.S. from Hungary in 1977. Squat's surrealistic film-theatre pieces have emphasized the absurb, the taboo, the perverse, and the mysterious. The long-running *Mr. Dead and Mrs. Free* (1981) represented American culture as an 11-foot high baby with video-screen eyes blazing with television images, and the live action included simulated acts of graphic violence. The well-regarded *Dreamland Burns* in 1986 (created by some Squat members after the original group's break-up) examined the tenuous nature of love and human contact through a series of distanced encounters with film characters, dummies, and live actors.

Several other companies conjure similarly disturbing images of dissociation and fragmentation while concentrating entirely on live performance. Their work conveys the sensibility of cinema, but remains intensely actor-centered and language oriented. No Theater of Northampton, Massachusetts, led by Roy Faudree, employed *camera obscura* effects with giant mirrors to convey the psychic distortions of a motel-based movie crew in the 1985 piece *Atokadakota* (part of *Last Resort*). Theatre X in Milwaukee (under the direction of John Schneider and John Kishline) and the Blake Street Hawkeyes of Berkeley, California (founded by former members of the Iowa Theatre Lab) investigate personal and cultural history through idiosyncratic language and wordplay, and intensely physical acting.

But there are other experimental groups who are pointedly de-emphasizing language and acting in favor of elaborate visuals and music. They tend to view the stage as a painter views an empty canvas; consequently, much of their work is strikingly two-dimensional, and the abstract imagery is highly subjective rather than overtly political. Most of these groups are centered around a strong, auteur-style director, and some are attracting a young audience that identifies more with New Wave music and rock videos than with theatre.

A number of such outfits are based in San Francisco, including George Coates's Performanceworks. Coates (a veteran of the Blake Street Hawkeyes) devises sumptuous, audio-visual spectacles that blend experimental music, opera singing, mime, slide projections, and other elements into a seamless, non-narrative montage. With abstract names like *The Way of How* (1982), *See Hear* (1984), and *Rare Area* (1985), Coates's pieces are post-literary phantasias which some classify as "new opera" because of their epic scale and reliance on music for mood and pacing.

Soon 3, under the direction of Alan and Bean Finneran, works with some of the same elements, but takes an even cooler, more distanced approach. The Finnerans' "performance landscapes" are highly composed arrangements of music, live actors, mobile sculptures, lighting sources, and clear containers of sand and water. Soon 3 does work with specific themes, but the result is still a perceptual rather than political exploration. Their 1981 piece, *Renaissance Radar* investigated the area of film violence and pornography with nude actresses passively enduring simulated drownings, stabbings, and shootings—much to the dismay of many feminists in the audience. *Magi* (1986) envisioned a desert-like aftermath of nuclear holocaust, with archeologists clinically "excavating" film legacies of the dead from their sculptural remains.

Nightletter Theatre also concocts highly intricate visual landscapes, but this collective of artists from various disciplines concentrates on the psychic terrain of personal memory and childhood. Works like their 1985 piece *Ulterior Rooms* incorporate concrete poetry, puppetry, and toy-like props as well as film and live action.

Antenna Theater and Nightfire, the two offshoots of the now-defunct Snake Theater, have each veered off into new directions. While Snake Theater specialized in "location" pieces performed in public locales, Antenna (directed by Christopher Hardman) equips its audiences with earphones and taped narratives, and leads them through animated theatrical environments that resemble funhouses. *Amnesia* (1983) was a guided tour through someone's deranged memory; *Adjusting the Idle* (1984) featured a carnival-like series of exhibits and vignettes about automobile culture. In *Dracula in the Desert* (1986) an updated vampire story is conveyed via infrared sound and 3-D visual effects. Laura Farabough's Nightfire balances live action with video performance; in the 1985 piece *Baseball Zombie* the stage was dominated by a dozen television monitors.

For financial and aesthetic reasons, some veteran experimental performers are finding more opportunities and challenges now as solo artists. Spalding Gray, Eric Bogosian, Paul Zaloom, Bill Talen, Danitra Vance, and Whoopi Goldberg are all successful writer-actors who have deftly meshed theatrical storytelling with stand-up comedy and performance art. Their humorous emphasis on character and personal biography makes them highly accessible to a mainstream audience, and easily translatable to the "talking heads" medium of television. Interestingly, some of them alternate solo pieces with ensemble work and commercial television and film roles—a pluralistic approach that was unimaginable for most alternative artists of the 1960's.

Indeed, creating and maintaining "pure" avant garde theatre ensembles in the mid-1980's is a problematic venture for all the economic, sociological, and aesthetic reasons outlined here. But as American society becomes more individualistic and mass media-oriented, many dedicated artists are continually inventing new ways to express their adventurous visions directly to the public. In a sense, making live theatre happen at all has become a radical act. The ensembles that continue to do so—despite all the counter-pressures—constitute a humanistic front in an increasingly dehumanized age.

—Misha Berson

* * *

ANTENNA THEATER. Founded by Christopher Hardman in Sausalito, California, in 1980 (a division of Snake Theater, founded by Laura Farabough and Hardman in Sausalito in 1977). Productions presented by Snake: *Dead Play*, 1977; *24th Hour Cafe, Somewhere in the Pacific*, and *Her Building*, 1978; *Sub-Division*, and *Auto*, 1979; *Ride Hard/Die Fast*, 1980; productions presented by Antenna: *Vacuum*, and *High School*, 1981; *Pink Prom, Moving Sculptures*, and *Artery*, 1982; *Amnesia*, 1983; *Radio Active Theater*, and *Adjusting the Idle*, 1984; *Russia*, 1985; *Dracula in the Desert*, and *The New Season*, 1986. References: *Drama Review 91* and *100* (New York), 1981–83; *Theater Heute* (Hannover, Germany), October 1981; *American Alternative Theatre* by Theodore Shank, London, Macmillan, and New York, Grove Press, 1982; *Esquire* (New York), December 1985 and March 1986; *Theatre Crafts* (New York), January 1986.

AT THE FOOT OF THE MOUNTAIN. Founded by a group of women and men in Minneapolis in 1974; in 1976 became a women's theatre. Productions include: *Pimp* and *The Gelding* both by Martha Boesing, 1974; *River Journal* by Boesing, 1975; *Love Song for an Amazon* and *Raped* both by Boesing, 1976; *Babes in the Bighouse* by Megan Terry, and *The Moon Tree* by Boesing, 1977; *The Story of a Mother* by Boesing, and *The Clue in the Old Birdbath* by Kate Kasten and Sandra de Helen, 1978; *The Life* by Martha Roth, and *Prehistoric Visions for Revolting Hags* by Boesing, 1979; *Dora Dufran's Wild West Extravaganza; or, The Real Lowdown on Calamity Jane* by Boesing, and *Pizza* by Michelle Linfante, 1980; *Junkie!* by Boesing, 1981; *Ashes, Ashes, We All Fall Down* by Boesing, 1982; *Low Life on a High Plane* by Chris Cinque, *Haunted by the Holy Ghost* by Jan Magrane, and *Antigone Too: Rites of Love and Defiance* by Boesing, 1983; *Las Gringas* by Boesing, and *The Girls Room* and *Head over Heels* both by Magrane, 1984; *Going to Seed* by Nancy Rawles, *The Ladies Who Lunch* by Marilyn Seven, and *Neurotic Erotic Exotic* (collaboration with Spiderwoman Theater), 1985; *Fefu and Her Friends* by María Irene Fornés, and *Funnyhouse of a Negro* by Adrienne Kennedy, 1986. References: *Feminist Theatre Groups* by Dinah Luise Leavitt, Jefferson, North Carolina, McFarland, 1980; *Women in the American Theatre* edited by Helen Krich Chinoy and Linda Walsh Jenkins, New York, Crown, 1981; *Women in Theatre: Compassion and Hope* by Karen Malpede, New York, Drama Book Specialists, 1983; *Women and Performance* (New York), Spring-Summer 1983.

ATC (Actors Touring Company). Founded by John Retallack in London in 1978; Mark Brickman took over as artistic director in 1985. Productions: *Don Juan* by Byron, 1978; *Measure for Measure*, 1979; *Quixote* from the novel by Cervantes, and *The Tempest*, 1981; *Berlin/Berlin* by Retallack, and *The Provoked Wife* by Sir John Vanbrugh, 1982; *Ubu the Vandalist* from a play by Alfred Jarry, and *Don Juan* by Molière, 1983; *Twelfth Night*, and *A Doll's House* by Ibsen, 1984; *Peer Gynt* by Ibsen, *Ubu and the Clowns* from a play by Jarry, and *Bourgeois Gentleman* by Molière, 1985; *Hamlet*, 1986; *Faustus* from a play by Marlowe, 1987.

AVON TOURING THEATRE COMPANY. Founded in Bristol in 1974. Productions: *At Last the M5 Show, E for Environment Show*, and *Pickets* all by David Illingworth, and *It Used to Be Fun*, 1974; *A Tale of Three Bristols* (*Smokescreen* by Illingworth, *Concorde* by David Edgar, and *Welcome to Buckhill* by Chris Allen), *The Football King, The Wild West Show*, and *The Godmother* all by Illingworth, and *Sea, Stag and Chips* and *Trouble and Strife*, 1975; *Learning the Game* and *Ernie Bevin's Workers Playtime* by Illingworth, and *Roadshow, The Breadshop* by Brecht, *Regina v. Stevens* by Illingworth and John Caird, and *Prostitutes* by A.C.H. Smith, 1976; *Snowwhite*

Washes Whiter and *Deadwood* by Nigel Williams, *Face Value* by A.C.H. Smith, and *Nolly's Drinking Contest*, 1977; *Measure for Measure*, and *Riff Raff Rules* and *Allez-Oop* by Vince Foxall, 1978; *Diaries* by Donna Franceschild, *Paradise* by Foxall, and *Women Beware Women* by Middleton, 1979; *Brittle Glory* by Foxall, and *The Good Woman of Setzuan* by Brecht, 1980; *Kept In/Kept Out* by Foxall, *Riot Sellers* by Kate Phelps, and *Gulliver's Travels*, 1981; *Rabbit in a Trap* by Sue Jamieson, *The Crooked Scythe* by Melissa Murray, *War Story* by Tony Robinson and Paul Unwin, and *A Pinch of Salt* by Robert Johnson, 1982; *Break Out* by Johnson and Roger McKern, *Great Expectations* by Phil Smith, and *The Egg* by Angie Farrow, 1983; *Horror Story* by Phil Smith, *Shadow of a Doubt* by Johnson, and *Escape Artists* by Foxall, 1984; *Half Hearts and Quarter Measures* by Cindy Artiste, and *Little Dorrit* from the novel by Dickens, 1986.

BLACK THEATRE CO-OPERATIVE. Founded by Mustapha Matura and Charlie Hanson in London in 1978. Productions: *More, More* and *Another Tuesday* by Matura, 1978; *Welcome Home Jacko* by Matura, 1979; *Mama Dragon* by Farrukh Dhondy, and *Snatch* by Peter Cox, 1980; *One Rule* by Matura, 1981; *Trojans* by Dhondy, *Trinity* by Edgar White, and *Fingers Only* by Yemi Ajibade, 1982; *The Nine Night* by White, *The Tooth of Crime* (reggae version) by Sam Shepard, and *Nevis Mountain Dew* by Steve Carter, 1983; *No Place to Be Nice* by Frank McField, *Redemption Song* by White, and *Money to Live* by Jacqueline Rudet, 1984; *A Raisin in the Sun* by Lorraine Hansberry, 1985; *Waiting for Hannibal* by Ajibade, 1986.

BREAD AND PUPPET THEATRE. Founded by Peter Schumann in Germany; in New York from 1963; in Plainfield, Vermont, 1970–74, and since 1974 in Glover, Vermont. Productions include Mime and Mask Plays, Giant Puppet Shows, Sidewalk Shows, Puppet Plays, Children's Shows, Political Pageants, Crankys, and Parades: *Totentanz, The Battle*, and *Fire I*, 1962; *Neither; The Cry; Dance of Death* (first U.S. play); *The Dead Man Rises; Apocalypse; Chicken Little; Johnny; The Good King; Blue Raven Beauty; Leaf Feeling the Moonlight; Christmas Story; Death, Narrator and the Great Warrior*, 1967; *A Man Says Goodbye to His Mother; The Cry of the People for Meat*, 1969; *The Difficult Life of Uncle Fatso*, 1970; *Birdcatcher in Hell, Emilia, The Quest*, and *Attica*, 1971; *Grey Lady Cantata; The Fourteen Stations of the Cross, Laos, Hallelujah, The Coney Island Cycle*, and *That Simple Light May Rise Out of Complicated Darkness*, 1972; *Three Yells, Trouble*, and *Attica Memorial*, 1973; *Christmas Story, Easter's Stations of the Cross*, and *Our Domestic Resurrection Fair and Circus*, annually since 1974; *A Monument for Ishi—An Anti-Bicentennial Pageant*, 1975; *Domestic Resurrection*, 1976; *White Horse Butcher; Joan of Arc; Masaniello; Ave Maris Stella; St. Francis Preaches to the Birds; Wolkenstein; Ah! or, The First Washerwoman Cantata*, 1980; *The Washerwoman Nativity; Goya, Rising from the Water, Woyzeck*, and *The Story of One Who Set Out to Study Fear*, 1981; *The Thunderstorm of the Youngest Child, The Fight Against the End of the World Pageant and June 12 Parade*, and *Diagonal Man (Theory and Practice)*, 1982; *The Insurrection Opera and Oratorio*, and *The End Falls Before the Beginning*, 1983; *Rites of Winter Pagaent, Josephine the Singer, The Nativity, Crucifixion, and Resurrection of Archbishop Romero of El Salvador*, and *The Guilty Bystander Oratorio*, 1984; *The Door, Bach Cantata, Mozart's Requiem*, and *Ex Voto 1*, 1985; *Ex Voto 2–5, The Hunger of the Hungry and the Hunger of the Overfed*, and *Stravinsky's Symphony of Psalms*, 1986. References: *Drama Review 38, 47, 55*, and *61* (New York), 1968–74; *Le Bread and Puppet Theatre* by François Kourilsky, Paris, Le Cité Editeur, 1971; *Theatre Quarterly 20–21* (London), 1975; *Performing Arts Journal* (New York), Spring 1977; *Black and White Shows/Spectacles en noir et blanc* by Christian Dupavillon and Etienne George, Paris, Les Loges, 1978; *American Alternative Theatre* by Theodore Shank, London, Macmillan, and New York, Grove Press, 1982; "Puppeteers with a Passion" by Steve Hagar, in *Geo*, March 1983; *Bread and Puppet: Stories of Struggle and Faith* edited by Greg Guma, Burlington, Vermont, Green Valley, 1985.

CAST. Founded by Claire and Roland Muldoon in London in 1965; re-formed in 1981, and now mainly performs variety and cabaret shows. Productions include: *Goodbye Union Jack*, 1976; *Confessions of a Socialist*, and *What Happens Next*, 1978; *Killer on the Loose*, and *Waiting for Lefty*, 1979; *Full Confessions of a Socialist*, and *From One Strike to Another*, 1980; *Sedition 81*, and *Hotel Sunshine*, 1981; *The Return of Sam the Man M.P.*, and *Sedition UK*, 1982; *The Bottom Line*, and *Reds under the Bed*, 1983; *London Live Show*, 1984.

CHEEK BY JOWL. Founded by Declan Donnellan and Nick Ormerod in London in 1981. Productions: *The Country-Wife* by Wycherley, 1981; *Othello, Rack Abbey* by Colin Sell and Donnellan, and *Gotcha* by Barrie Keeffe, 1982; *Vanity Fair* by Ormerod and Donnellan, from the novel by Thackeray, 1983; *Pericles*, and *Andromache* by Racine, 1984; *A Midsummer Night's Dream*, and *The Man of Mode* by Etherege, 1985; *Twelfth Night*, and *The Cid* by Corneille, 1986; *Macbeth*, 1987.

DAC THEATRE COMPANY. Founded in Doncaster, Yorkshire, in 1979. Productions include: *Two Men from Derby* by Barry Hines, and *Oi for England* by Trevor Griffiths, 1982; *Billy's Last Stand* by Hines, *Bread and Roses* by Ron Rose, and *Slow Bowler* by Ian McMillan and David Harmer, 1984; *The Enemies Within* by Rose, *Tilly Mint and the Dodo* by Berly Doherty, and *Never the Same Again*, 1985; *Fun City* by Hines, *Flying* by McMillan and Martin Wiley, and *Stronger Than Superman*, 1986; *Cat and Man* by McMillan and Rose, 1987.

DELL'ARTE PLAYERS COMPANY. Founded by Joan Schirle and others in 1977 as a touring company; now based in Blue Lake, California. Productions: *The Loon's Rage* by Joan Holden, Steve Most, and Jael Weisman, 1977; *Under Glass* (*The Greenfields* by Jael Weisman, *Infancy* by Thornton Wilder, *The Gloaming, Oh My Darling* by Megan Terry, and *Save Me a Place at Forest Lawn* by Lorees Yerby), and *Refried Brains* (*Bittersweet Blues* by Joan Schirle, *Birds of a Feather* by Stan Laurel, and *The Amazing Zoroasters* by Jael Weisman), 1978; *Intrigue at Ah-Pah*, 1979; *Whiteman Meets Bigfoot*, 1980; *Performance Anxiety*, 1982; *Malpractice*, 1984; *The Road Not Taken*, 1985; *Going to Waste* by Schirle, 1986. References: *Theatre Crafts* (New York), Spring 1980; *West Coast Plays 8* (Berkeley, California), 1981; article by Misha Berson, in *Drama Review 98* (New York), 1983.

FOCO NOVO THEATRE COMPANY. Founded by David Aukin, Bernard Pomerance, and Roland Rees in London in 1972. Productions include: *Foco Novo* by Pomerance, 1972; *Drums in the Night* by Brecht, 1973; *Someone Else Is Still Someone* by Pomerance, and *Cock Artist* by Fassbinder, 1974; *A Man's a Man* by Brecht, *Death of a Black Man* by Alfred Fagon, and *The Arthur Horner Show* by Phil Woods, 1975; *The Nine Days and Saltley Gates* by Jon Chadwick and John Hoyland, and *A Seventh Man* by Adrian Mitchell, 1976; *Tighten Your Belt* by Chadwick and Hoyland, and *The Elephant*

Man by Pomerance, 1977; *Withdrawal Symptoms* by C.P. Taylor, *On the Out* by Tunde Ikoli, and *The Free Fall* by Colin Mortimer, 1978; *Independence* by Mustapha Matura, *Landscape of Exile* by David Zane Mairowitz, and *The Guise* by David Mowat, 1979; *Woyzeck* by Büchner, *Quantrill in Lawrence* by Pomerance, and *Please Shine Down on Me* by Olwen Wymark, 1980; *Snap* by Nigel Gearing, and *Citizen Ilyushin* by Kevin Mandry, 1981; *Four Hundred Pounds* by Fagon, and *Edward II, Conversations in Exile*, and *Mr. Puntilla and His Servant Matti* all by Brecht, and *Sink or Swim* by Ikoli, 1982; *Sleeping Policemen* by Howard Brenton and Ikoli, 1983; *Play Mas* by John Constable, and *Bloody Poetry* by Brenton, 1984; *Deathwatch* by Genet, *Week In, Week Out* by Ikoli, and *The Ass* by Mike and Kate Westbrook, 1985; *The Lower Depths* by Gorky, and *Banged Up* by Ikoli, 1986; *Needles of Light* by James Pettifer, and *The Cape Orchard* by Michael Picardie, 1987.

FOOTSBARN THEATRE COMPANY. Founded in Cornwall in 1971; since 1980 based mainly in Europe. Recent productions: *Chinese Puzzle*, and *King Lear*, 1985; *Macbeth*, and *Circus Tosov*, 1986.

FORKBEARD FANTASY. Founded by Chris and Tim Britton in Edinburgh in 1974; now based in Devon. Productions include: *The Rubber God Show*, 1976; *The Cranium Show*, and *The Great British Square Dance* by Simon Britton, 1977; *Men Only, Desmond Fairybreath, The Government Warning Show*, and *The Single Grey Hair Salami* by Ian Hinchliffe, 1978; *The Grid Reference Show*, and *The Splitting Headache Show*, 1979; *The Clone Show*, 1980; *Seal of the Walrus*, and *The Library Ssshow*, 1981; *The Cold Frame*, and *Headquarters*, 1982; *The Brontosaurus Show*, 1983; *Springtime*, 1984; *Ghosts, High Tech*, and *The Brittonioni Bros.*, 1985; *Myth*, and *The Corridor of Doors*, 1986; *Hypochondria*, 1987. References: *Southern Arts* (Winchester), no. 45, 1978; *Art and Artists* (London), September 1979; *Performance Magazine* (London), no. 7, 1980; *Peninsula Voice*, September 1986.

GAY SWEATSHOP. Founded in London in 1975. Productions: *Mister X* by Roger Baker and Drew Griffiths, 1975; *Any Woman Can* by Jill Posener, *The Fork* by Ian Brown, *Randy Robinson's Unsuitable Relationship* by Andrew Davies, *Stone* by Edward Bond, *Indiscreet* by Baker and Griffiths, *Jingleball*, parts 1 and 2, by the company and Griffiths, and *Age of Consent* by the company, 1976; *Care and Control* by Michelene Wandor, and *As Time Goes By* by Noel Greig and Griffiths, 1977; *Iceberg* and *Warm* by the company, and *What the Hell Is She Doing Here?* by the women of the company, 1978; *The Dear Love of Comrades* by Greig, *I Like Me Like This* by Sharon Nassauer and Angela Stewart-Park, and *Who Knows?* by Philip Timmins, Sarah Hardy, and Bruce Bayley, 1979; *Blood Green* by Greig and Stewart-Park, 1980; *Poppies* by Greig, 1983; *Telling Tales* by Philip Osment, and *Raising the Wreck* by Sue Frumin, 1985; *Skin Deep* by Nigel Pugh, *Julie* by Catherine Kilcoyne, *More* by Maro Green and Caroline Griffin, and *Compromised Immunity* by Andy Kirby, 1986.

GRAEAE. Founded by Nabil Shaban and Richard Tomlinson in London in 1980; theatre company of performers with disabilities. Productions: *Sideshow*, 1980; *3-D*, and *M3 Junction 4*, both by Tomlinson, 1982; *Endless Variety Show* by Chris Speyer, *Not Much to Ask* by Patsy Rodenburg, and *Casting Out* by Nigel Jamieson, 1983; *A Cocktail Cabaret*, and *Frankenstein* by Geoff Parker, from the novel by Mary Shelley, 1984; *Working Hearts* by Noel Greig, 1986; *A Private View* by Tasha Fairbanks, 1987. References: *Disability, Theatre and Education* by Tomlinson, London, Souvenir Press, 1982; *People's Minds* (television documentary), 1984.

HESITATE AND DEMONSTRATE. Founded by Geraldine Pilgrim and Janet Goddard in 1975. Productions: *Points of Departure*, and *Ha Ha*, 1977; *Horrid Things, Minutes*, and *No Regrets*, 1978; *Scars*, and *Excuse Me*, 1979; *Do Not Disturb* 1980; *Goodnight Ladies!*, 1981; *Shangri-La*, and *So, No More Songs of Love*, 1984.

HIDDEN GRIN. Founded by members of the Rational Theatre Co-operative in London in 1984. Productions: *The Hidden Grin*, and *Parasite Structures*, 1984; *Overseen, Overheard, Overlooked* (installation), 1985; *The Suburbs of Hell*, 1986.

HULL TRUCK THEATRE COMPANY. Founded by Mike Bradwell in Hull in 1971; Pam Brighton was artistic director, 1982–83; since 1984 John Godber is artistic director. Productions (devised and directed by Bradwell through 1981, unless noted otherwise): *The Children of the Lost Planet, The Land of Woo*, and *The Last of the Great Love Goddesses*, 1972; *The Weekend after Next, The Mackintosh Cabaret, Joe Flash and the Singing Caterpillar from Venus*, and *Wimbo the Wonderdog*, 1973; *The Knowledge*, 1974; *Oh What, The Writing on the Wall* (television), and *Granny Sorts It Out*, 1975; *Bridget's House*, and *The Melody Bandbox Rhythm Roadshow*, 1976; *A Bed of Roses*, and *Bunny Scruff's Disc Date*, 1977; *The Great Caper* by Ken Campbell, *The New Garbo* by Doug Lucie, *The Dalkey Archive*, and *The Cockroach That Ate Cincinnati* by Alan Williams, 1978; *Ship Ahoy*, and *Ooh La La!*, 1979; *The Gorgon* by Mike Absalom, and *Mean Streaks* and *The Cockroach Trilogy* by Alan Williams, 1980; *The Day War Broke Out* by Peter Tinniswood, *In Dreams* by Alan Williams, and *Still Crazy after All These Years*, 1981; *Diary of a Hunger Strike* by Peter Sheridan, and *The Adventure of Jasper Ridley* by Nigel Williams, 1982; *The Fosdyke Saga* by Bill Tidy and Alan Plater, 1983; *September in the Rain, Cramp, Bouncers*, and *Up 'n' Under* all by John Godber, and *A Christmas Carol* by Dickens, 1984; *Shakers* by Godber and Jane Thornton, *Up 'n' Under II* by Godber, and *Toad of Toad Hall* by A.A. Milne, 1985; *Blood, Sweat and Tears* by Godber and *Cramp* (revised version, music by Tom Robinson and Hereward K), *Cut and Dried* by Thornton, and *The Lion, The Witch, and the Wardrobe* from the novel by C.S. Lewis, 1986; *The Dock* by Phil Woods, and *Teechers* by Godber, 1987.

IMPACT THEATRE CO-OPERATIVE. Founded in Leeds in 1978. Productions include: *Parsifal*, 1982; *A Place in Europe, Useful Vices*, and *No Weapons for Mourning*, 1983; *The Carrier Frequency*, with Russell Hoban, 1984; *Songs of the Claypeople* by Andrew Poppy and Pete Brooks, and *Repeat Frame Echo*, 1985.

INTIMATE STRANGERS. Founded by Paul Roylance and Melanie Thompson in 1983. Productions: *Rendezvous*, 1984; *Same River Twice*, 1985; *Den Trettende Tango* (*The Thirteenth Tango*), and *Chine*, 1986.

IOU THEATRE. Founded in 1976 as a co-operative of visual artists and musicians. Productions: *Log, Haunted Lift*, and *Captain Goat's Parrot*, 1976; *The Rape of the Tea Goose, Towers, Untitled*, and *Nutrimenta*, 1977; *Wet Maps, Dry Seas, Les Loups du Lac, Journey of the Tree Man, Mayhem and Violins*, and *Between the Floods—The Churning of the Milky*

Ocean, 1978; *Rub-a-Dub-Dub, Images of Flesh, Bread, and Wax, An Example of Zeal* (film), *Arable Parable, Forced Landings*, and *Agog*, 1979; *The Universe (Simplified), Forbidden Riddles, A Clock Sculpture, Odd Descending, Walk a Deathly Dog*, and *Large Door*, 1980; *Double Geography, Eyepiece, From Hell, Hull and Halifax*, and *The Trumpet Rat and Other Curiosities*, 1981; *A Musical Meal, The House*, and *I Could Have Sworn I Saw Feathers*, 1982; *The Patience of Fossils, The Lost Wax Process*, and *The Sleep of Reason*, 1983; *A Drop in the Ocean, The See Saw Red, Table Talk*, and *The Gift*, 1984; *The Attraction of Things, Distance No Object, This Is the Edge, The Other Foot*, and *Three Storeys and a Dark Cellar*, 1986; *Pocket Atlas*, 1987. Publication: *Dangerous Lullaby*, 1984.

JOINT STOCK THEATRE GROUP. Founded by Max Stafford-Clark, David Hare, and David Aukin in 1973. Productions include: *The Speakers*, 1974; *Fanshen* by Hare, 1975; *Yesterday's News*, and *Light Shining in Buckinghamshire* by Caryl Churchill, 1976; *Epsom Downs* by Howard Brenton, *A Mad World, My Masters* by Barrie Keeffe, *Devil's Island* by Tony Bicât, and *A Thought in Three Parts* by Wallace Shawn, 1977; *The Ragged Trousered Philanthropists* by Stephen Lowe, 1978; *Cloud Nine* by Caryl Churchill, and *The House* by David Halliwell, 1979; *An Optimistic Thrust*, 1980; *Say Your Prayers* by Nick Darke, and *Borderline* by Hanif Kureishi, 1981; *Real Time*, 1982; *Fen* by Churchill, *Victory* by Howard Barker, and *The Crimes of Vautrin* by Nicholas Wright, 1983; *The Great Celestial Cow* by Sue Townsend, and *The Power of the Dog* by Barker, 1984; *Deadlines* by Stephen Wakelam, *Amid the Standing Corn* by Jane Thornton, and *Fire in the Lake* by Karim Alrawi, 1985; *A Mouthful of Birds* by Churchill and David Lan, 1986; *Sanctuary* by Ralph Brown, 1987. Reference: *The Joint Stock Book: The Making of a Theatre Collective* edited by Rob Ritchie, London, Methuen, 1987.

THE LIVING THEATRE. Founded by Judith Malina and Julian Beck (died 1985) in New York in 1947; formally launched in 1951; moved to Europe in mid-1960's, toured U.S. in 1968, in Brazil, 1970–71, U.S., 1971–75, based in Italy, touring Europe, 1975–83; returned to New York, 1984. First play presented in a theatre was *Dr. Faustus Lights the Lights* by Gertrude Stein, 1951; later productions: *He Who Says Yes and He Who Says No* by Brecht, *Childish Jokes* by Paul Goodman, *Dialogue of the Young Man and the Mannikin* by Lorca, *Ladies' Voices* by Stein, and *Beyond the Mountains* by Kenneth Rexroth, 1951; *Desire Trapped by the Tail* by Picasso, *Sweeney Agonistes* by T.S. Eliot, *Faustina* by Goodman, and *The Heroes* by John Ashbery, 1952; *The Age of Anxiety* by Auden, *The Spook Sonata* by Strindberg, *Orpheus* by Cocteau, and *The Idiot King* by Claude Fredericks, 1954; *Tonight We Improvise* by Pirandello, *Phèdre* by Racine, and *The Young Disciple* by Goodman, 1955; *Many Loves* by William Carlos Williams, *The Cave at Machpelah* by Goodman, and *The Connection* by Jack Gelber, 1959; *Women of Trachis* by Pound, *The Marrying Maiden* by Jackson Mac Low, and *In the Jungle of Cities* by Brecht, 1960; *The Apple* by Gelber, 1961; *Man Is Man* by Brecht, 1962; *The Brig* by Kenneth H. Brown, 1963; *Mysteries and Smaller Pieces*, 1964; *The Maids* by Genet, and *Frankenstein*, 1965; *The Antigone of Sophokles* by Brecht, 1967; *Paradise Now*, 1968; *The Legacy of Cain, Christmas Cake for the Hot Hole and the Cold Hole*, and *Rites and Visions of Transformation*, 1970; *Six Dreams about Mother*, 1971; *Seven Meditations on Political Sado-Masochism*, and *Strike Support Oratorium*, 1973; *Turning the Earth, Six Public Acts*, and *The Destruction of the Money Tower*, 1975; *Turning the Violence, The End of the World, Where Does the Violence Come From?, Why Are We Afraid of Sexual Freedom?, The New World, Where Have We Come From? Why Are We Here? Where Are We Going?, Monday, Tuesday, Wednesday, Is There Something Wrong with the Way We Work?, Breaking Our Silence*, and *Unemployment, Work, Power, and Exploitation*, 1976; *Brothers, Don't Shoot!, The Body of Giuseppe Pinelli, Free Theatre, Workers Working, Lovers Loving, Workers Not Working, Lovers Not Loving*, and *Can I Kill You?*, 1977; *Fear and Flying, The Box Play*, and *Prometheus*, 1978; *Antigone*, 1979; *The One and the Many*, and *Masse Mensch* by Ernst Toller, 1980; *The Yellow Methuselah* by Hanon Reznikov, 1982; *The Archeology of Sleep*, 1983. References: *The Drama Review 43, 51*, and *62* (New York), 1969–74; *The Living Theatre/USA* by Renfreu Neff, Indianapolis, Bobbs Merrill, 1970; *We, The Living Theatre* by Aldo Rostagno, Beck, and Malina, New York, Ballantine, 1970; *Scripts 1* (New York), November 1971; *The Living Theatre* by Pierre Biner, New York, Avon, 1972; *The Life of the Theatre* by Beck, San Francisco, City Lights, 1972; *The Enormous Despair* by Malina, New York, Random House, 1972; *Praxis* (Berkeley, California), Spring 1975; *Julian Beck e Judith Malina: Il Lavoro del Living Theatre: Materiali 1952–1969*, Milan, Ubulibri, 1982; *The Diaries of Judith Malina 1947–1957*, New York, Grove Press, 1984; "Julian Beck: Il Living Theatre," in *Quaderni di Teatro* (Florence), 1986; "Julian Beck, Businessman" by Jack Gelber, in *Drama Review 110* (New York), 1986.

LUMIERE AND SON. Founded by David Gale and Hilary Westlake in 1973. Productions written by Gale and directed by Westlake: *Jack ... The Flames*, and *Trickster*, 1974; *Pest Cure and Molester, White Men Dancing, The Sleeping Quarters of Sophia*, and *Indications Leading to ...*, 1975; *Dogs* and *Special Forces*, 1976; *Passionate Positions*, 1977; *Night Fall*, 1978; *The Dancers, Glazed*, and *Jean Pool*, 1979; *Circus Lumiere*, 1980; *Slips*, 1981; *Son of Circus Lumiere*, and *The Final Order, and The Appeal* (television), 1982; *Senseless*, and *Beauty and the Beast*, 1983; Westlake devised and directed *Tip Top Condition*, 1974; *Icing*, 1977; *Giants*, and *String of Perils* and *Ship Shape* (with Trevor Stuart), 1980; *Blood Pudding*, 1981; *Vulture Culture*, and *Brightside*, 1984; *The Rotherham Project, Entertaining Strangers, Deadwood*, and *The Bosworth Project*, 1986; *Panic*, 1987.

MABOU MINES. Formally founded by JoAnne Akalaitis, Lee Breuer, Philip Glass, Ruth Maleczech, and David Warrilow in New York in 1970 after years of shared work in San Francisco and Paris; in residence at Ellen Stewart's La Mama Experimental Theatre Club, New York, 1970–73; since 1975 in residence at Joseph Papp's Public Theatre, New York. Productions: *The Red Horse Animation* by Breuer, 1970; *Play* and *Come and Go* both by Beckett, 1971; *The B-Beaver Animation* by Breuer, 1974; *The Saint and the Football Players* by Breuer, and *Cascando* by Beckett, 1976; *The Lost Ones* and *The Shaggy Dog Animation* both by Breuer, and *Dressed Like an Egg* by Akalaitis, 1977; *Southern Exposure* by Akalaitis, and *Mercier and Camier* by Frederick Neumann, 1979; *A Prelude to Death in Venice* by Breuer, *Vanishing Pictures* by Maleczech, *Dead End Kids: A History of Nuclear Power* by Akalaitis, and *Keeper* (radio) by Dale Worsley, 1980; *Wrong Guys* by Maleczech, and *The Joey Schmerda Story* (radio) by Jim Strahs, 1981; *Lies* (videotape); *Hajj* by Breuer, *Cold Harbor*, and *Company*, 1983; *Through the Leaves* by Franz Xaver Kroetz, *Pretty Boy* by Greg Mehrten, and *Imagination Dead Imagine* by Maleczech, 1984; *Starcock* by Apple Vail, 1985; *Help Wanted* by Kroetz, and *Worstward Ho*, 1986.

MODERN TIMES THEATER. Based in New York. Productions include: *Tell Me a Riddle* by Denny Partridge, from the story by Tillie Olsen, 1978; *Homeland* by Selaelo Maredi and Steve Friedman, 1979; *The Bread and Roses Play* by Steve Friedman, 1981; *Hibakusha: Stories from Hiroshima*, 1982; *Freedom Days*, 1984.

MONSTROUS REGIMENT. Founded by a group of women performers in London in 1975. Productions: *Scum* by Chris Bond and Claire Luckham, and *Vinegar Tom* by Caryl Churchill, 1976; *Kiss and Kill* by Susan Todd and Ann Mitchell, 1977; *Floorshow*, and *Time Gentlemen Please*, 1978; *Teendreams* by David Edgar and Todd, 1979; *Gentlemen Prefer Blondes* by Bryony Lavery, *Dialogue Between a Prostitute and One of Her Clients* by Dacia Maraina, and *Shakespeare's Sister*, 1980; *Mourning Pictures* by Honor Moore, and *Yoga Class* by Rose Tremain, 1981; *The Execution* by Melissa Murray, 1982; *The Fourth Wall* by Franca Rame and Dario Fo, 1983; *Calamity* and *Origin of the Species* by Lavery, and *Enslaved by Dreams* by Chris Bowler, 1984; *Point of Convergence* by Bowler, 1985; *My Song Is Free* by Jorge Diaz, 1986; *Alarms* by Susan Yankowitz, and *My Sister in This House* by Wendy Kesselman, 1987.

NATURAL THEATRE. Founded in Bath in 1969, an offshoot of the Bath Arts Workshop. Indoor productions include: *The Rocky Ricketts Show; Phil Grimm's Progress* by M. Banks; *Blood Weekend* by J.C. Wood, B. Vaughan, and R. Jerrom; *The Air Apparent* by Wood and Jerrom; *Macbeth by Norman Grimethorpe and W. Shakespeare* by Wood; *Prairie Oysters; Eat Me; The Four Sidneys: Executive Street Theatre* (outdoor); *Wet Sheets; Scarlatti's Birthday Party; Her Majesty's Pleasure; Spy Society.*

NEW YORK STREET THEATER CARAVAN. Productions include: *Sacco and Vanzetti* by Marketa Kimbrell, 1976; *Bitter Harvest*, 1977; *Molly Maguire* by Kimbrell, 1980; *Gold*, 1986.

NIGHTFIRE. Founded by Laura Farabough in Sausalito, California, in 1980 (a division of Snake Theater, founded by Farabough and Christopher Hardman in Sausalito in 1977). For productions presented by Snake, see listing under Antenna Theater; productions presented by Nightfire (all by Farabough): *Femme Fatale: The Invention of Personality*, and *Surface Tension*, 1981; *Obedience School*, and *Locker Room*, 1982; *Sea of Heartbreak*, and *Beauty Science*, 1983; *Liquid Distance/Timed Approach*, and *Under Construction*, 1984; *Baseball Zombie*, 1985; installations: *Soundings*, 1985; *Twelve Stations of the Latrine*, and *U2 & I: Take a Walk*, 1986. References: *American Alternative Theatre* by Theodore Shank, London, Macmillan, and New York, Grove Press, 1982; *West Coast Plays 11–12* (Berkeley, California), 1982.

NIGHTLETTER THEATRE. Based in San Francisco. Productions include: *Ulterior Rooms*, 1985.

NO THEATER. Founded in Northampton, Massachusetts, in 1974. Productions include: *Hotel Motel* by Roy Faudree, 1974; *The Elephant Man* by Faudree, 1975; *The Duel* from a story by Chekhov, 1977; *And Now We Are Fiction* by Rosemary Quinn, 1978; *DFS (De Fiance Suction)* by Faudree, and *A Man, A Dictionary* by Franz Xaver Kroetz, 1979; *Husbands and Wives* by Linda Patnode and Mike Mullin, and *The Story of Your Life* and *Nothing Yet* both by Mullin, 1980; *Last Resort* (5 plays; includes *Take One, L/R SF, Not Just Another Kodak Hula Show, Left/Right: A Dyslexic Comedy, Atokadakota: It's Only a Movie*) by Faudree, 1981–85; *The Glass Mayonnaise Jar* from a play by Karel and Josef Capek, 1982; *Kitchen Heat* by Patnode, 1983; *I C Men* by Faudree, 1984; *Furniture Boy* by Marty Maceda, 1985.

OMAHA MAGIC THEATRE. Founded by Jo Ann Schmidman in 1968; Megan Terry joined the theatre in 1971 as resident playwright and literary manager. Productions include: *The Artaud Anthology*, 1968; *Man's a Man* by Brecht, 1969; *The Tommy Allen Show* by Terry, and *How to Make a Woman* by the Caravan Theatre, 1970; *Transplant* by Susan Yankowitz, and *The Unknown Chinaman* by Kenneth Bernard, 1971; *The Pioneer* and *Pro-Game* both by Terry, 1973; *Babes in the Bighouse* by Terry, 1974; *Temporary Insanity* by Judith Katz, 1975; *100,001 Horror Stories of the Plains* by Terry and the company, and *Walking into the Dawn: A Celebration* by Rochelle Holt, 1976; *Astral White* by Mimi Loring, and *Brazil Fado* by Terry, 1977; *American King's English for Queens* by Terry, 1978; *Running Gag* by Schmidman, and *Goona Goona* by Terry, 1979; *Tix Tox, Yellow Strapping, White Out, Blue Tube*, and *Reflected Light* all by Sora Kim and Schmidman, and *Objective Love I* by Terry, 1980; *Kegger* by Terry, and *Aliens under Glass* by Schmidman, 1982; *Room 17-C* by Rosalyn Drexler, and *Fifteen Million Fifteen-Year-Olds* by Terry, 1983; *X-rayed-iate* by Terry, *An Unexpected Evening with June Havoc*, and *Astro-Bride* by Schmidman, 1984; *Mud* by María Irene Fornés, 1985; *Family Talk* and *Sleazing Toward Athens* both by Terry, and *Sea of Forms* text by Terry and Schmidman, 1986. References: *Women in the American Theatre* edited by Helen Krich Chinoy and Linda Walsh Jenkins, New York, Crown, 1981; "Omaha Magic Theatre Merges Art and Social Concern," in *Plainswoman* (Grand Forks, North Dakota), January 1982; "Making Magic," in *Heartwomen* by Sandy Boucher, New York, Harper, 1983; article in *Performing Arts Journal* (New York), vol. 7, no. 3, 1983; *Feminist Theatre* by Helene Keyssar, London, Macmillan, 1984, New York, Grove Press, 1985; article in *Esquire* (New York), December 1984; *Interviews with Contemporary Women Playwrights* edited by Kathleen Betsko and Rachel Koenig, Long Beach, California, Beechtree, 1986.

PAINES PLOUGH. Founded by John Adams, Chris Crooks, and David Pownall in Coventry in 1975. Productions: *Crates on Barrels* by Pownall, 1975; *Ladybird, Ladybird*, and *Music to Murder By* by Pownall, 1976; *Motocar*, and *Richard III, Part Two* by Pownall, and *Fungus* by Mike Yates, 1977; *Inuit* by David Mowat, and *Dorothy and the Bitch* by Marcella Evaristi, 1978; *Six Feet Apart* and *The Messiah of Ismir* by Elisabeth Bond, and *Barricade* and *Later* by Pownall, 1979; *Jubilee Too* by Stephen Jeffreys, and *Rise of the Old Cloud* by Mike Dorrell, 1980; *Beef* by Pownall, *Days Here So Dark* by Terry Johnson, and *The Decameron* by Justin Greene and Steve Cook, 1981; *Breach of the Peace*, 1982; *Master Class* by Pownall, *Welcome Home* by Tony Marchant, and *Red Saturday* by Martin Allen, 1983; *Mr. Hyde* by Alan Drury, and *The Key to the World* by Doug Lucie, 1984; *Songs for Stray Cats* by Donna Franceschild, and *Returning Fire* by Jeffreys, 1985; *Goat* by Louise Page, *Joyriders* by Christina Reid, and *Pinocchio Boys* by Jim Morris, 1986; *Thatcher's Women* by Kate Adshead, *The Way to Go Home* by Rona Munro, and *Berlin Days, Hollywood Nights* by Nigel Gearing, 1987.

THE PEOPLE SHOW. Founded by Mark Long and others at the Abbey Arts Centre, London in 1966. Originally produced new scripts (several by Jeff Nuttall). Later material originates within the groups with all members contributing and working without a director. Recent work has involved much music, acrobatics, and comedy. Each production bears a number and occasionally a name (e.g., 79 was also called the Hamburg Show because it was devised for a festival in that city). Show numbers are now into the nineties as well as the long-running, much-travelled Cabaret Show. References: *Gambit 16* (London) 1969; *The Drama Review 52* and *62* (New York) 1971, 1974; *Plays and Players* (London) 1979.

PERFORMANCE GROUP. See **THE WOOSTER GROUP.**

PERFORMANCEWORKS. Founded by George Coates in San Francisco. Productions include: *The Way of How*, 1982; *See Hear*, 1984; *Rare Area*, 1985.

RED LADDER THEATRE (originally Agit-Prop Theatre, later The Big Red Ladder Show). Founded as a political theatre co-operative in London in 1968; since 1976 in Leeds. Indoor and outdoor productions include: *Housing Play; Race Play; Productivity Play; Unemployment Play; Happy Robots*; since mid-1970's the group has concentrated on indoor productions: *A Woman's Work Is Never Done*, 1974; *It Makes You Sick*, 1976; *Anybody Sweating?*, and *Would Jubilee've It?*, 1977; *Taking Our Time*, and *Where There's Brass*, 1978; *Nerves of Steel*, and *Power Mad*, 1979; *Mild and Bitter*, and *Ladders to the Moon*, 1980; *Circus*, and *The Blind Goddess*, 1981; *Playing Apart, Best of British*, and *Preparations*, 1982; *Dumb Blonde*, and *Bring Out Your Dead*, 1983; *Happy Jack, The Beano*, and *This Story of Yours*, 1984; *Safe with Us*, 1985; plays for young people: *State Agent*, 1985; *Back to the Walls*, and *On the Line*, 1986. References: *Drama Review 44* (New York), 1969; *New Edinburgh Review*, August 1975; *Plays and Players* (London), May 1976; *Travail Théâtral* (Paris), Winter 1976; *Socialist Review* (London), September 1978; *Stages in the Revolution* by Catherine Itzin, London, Eyre Methuen, 1980; *Wedge Magazine* (New York), no. 1–2, 1982.

ROADSIDE THEATER. Founded by Dudley Cocke and others in Whitesburg, Kentucky in 1975, as part of Appalshop, an Appalachian arts organization. Productions: *Mountain Tales and Music*, 1975; *Red Fox/Second Hangin'* by Don Baker and Cocke, 1977; *Brother Jack* by Baker and Ron Short, 1979; *South of the Mountain* by Short, 1981; *Pretty Polly* by Baker and Short, 1985; *Leaving Egypt* by Short, 1986. References: *Smithsonian Magazine* (Washington, D.C.), vol. 12, 1981; *Commonwealth* (Norfolk, Virginia), vol. 49, 1982; *Drama Review 98* (New York), 1983; *Theatre Profiles 6* by Laura Ross, 1984, and *Theatre Profiles 7* by Ross and John Istel, 1986, New York, Theatre Communications Group; *Southern Exposure* (Durham, North Carolina), vol. 14, 1986; *Southern* (Little Rock, Arkansas), vol. 1, 1986.

SAN FRANCISCO MIME TROUPE. Founded by R.G. Davis in 1959; reorganized in 1970 as a collective. Early productions were mainly *commedia dell'arte* pieces based on Molière and Goldoni, and include *Mime and Words*, 1959; *Man with a Stick*, 1960; *Event I*, 1961; *The Dowry*, 1962; *The Root* by Machiavelli, and *Ubu King* by Jarry, 1963; *Tartuffe* by Molière, 1964; *The Exception and the Rule* by Brecht, 1965; *Olive Pits* by Lope de Vega, 1966; *L'Amant Militaire*, 1967; *Ruzzante*, 1968; *Congress of the Whitewashers* by Brecht, 1969; since the reorganization in 1970, productions include: *The Independent Female, or, A Man Has His Pride, Seize the Time*, and *Eco-Man*, 1970; *Soledad, The G.I. Show, The Car Acto*, and *The Dragon Lady's Revenge*, 1971; *High Rises*, and *Frozen Wages*, 1972; *The Mother* by Brecht, and *San Fran Scandals*, 1973; *The Great Air Robbery*, 1974; *Frijoles*, and *Power Play*, 1975; *False Promises/Nos Engañaron*, 1976; *The Hotel Universe*, 1977; *Electrobucks*, 1978; *Squash, We Can't Pay, We Won't Pay* by Dario Fo, and *TV Dinner* (for children), 1979; *Factperson*, 1980; *Americans, or, Last Tango in Huahuatenango*, and *Factwino Meets the Moral Majority*, 1981; *Factwino vs. Armageddonman*, 1982; *Secrets in the Sand*, 1983; *Steeltown*, 1984; *Factwino: The Opera*, 1985; *Crossing Borders*, 1985; *Spain/36*, 1986; *The Mozamgola Caper*, 1986. References: *Drama Review 32, 61, 66*, and *86* (New York), 1966–80; *Theatre Quarterly* (London), Fall 1975, Autumn 1977; *The San Francisco Mime Troupe: The First Ten Years* by R.G. Davis, Palo Alto, California, Ramparts Press, 1975; *By Popular Demand: Plays and Other Works by the San Francisco Mime Troupe*, San Francisco, San Francisco Mime Troupe, 1980.

7:84 THEATRE COMPANY. Founded by John McGrath in 1971; divided into 7:84 (England) and 7:84 (Scotland) in 1973. Productions include works by McGrath, John Burrows, Barrie Keeffe, Peter Cox, Ena Lamont Stewart, Archie Hind, and Joe Corrie.

SHARED EXPERIENCE. Founded by Mike Alfreds in London in 1975. Productions: *Arabian Nights*, 1975; *Bleak House* by Dickens, 1977; *Science Fictions*, 1978; *Gothic Horrors*, and *Cymbeline*, 1979; *The Merchant of Venice*, 1980; *The Seagull* by Chekhov, and *The Maids* by Genet, 1981; *La Ronde* by Arthur Schnitzler, *The Insomniac in Morgue Drawer 9* by Andy Smith, and *A Handful of Dust* by Evelyn Waugh, 1982; *The Comedy Without a Title* by Ruzante, and *Successful Strategies* and *False Admissions* both by Marivaux, 1983; *Marriage* by Gogol, and *Happy Days* by Beckett, 1984; *Pamela* by Samuel Richardson, 1985; *Three Sisters* by Chekhov, and *Too True to Be Good* by Shaw, 1986; *The Heat of the Day* by Elizabeth Bowen, *Paradise Lost* by Milton, and *Nana* by Zola, 1987. Reference: *Shared Experience 1975–1984*, London, Shared Experience, 1985.

PIP SIMMONS THEATRE GROUP. Founded by Pip Simmons in London in 1968. Productions include plays by Jean Tardieu and Arrabal and group-developed pieces *The Pardoner's Tale*, 1969; *Superman*, 1970; *Do It!*, and *Alice*, 1971; *George Jackson's Black and White Minstrel Show*, 1972; *Dracula*, 1974; *An die Musik*, and *The Dream of a Ridiculous Man*, 1975; *The Masque of the Red Death*, and *Woyzeck*, 1977; *The Tempest*, 1978; *We, Towards a Nuclear Future*, and *Rien ne Va Plus*, 1980; *Beauty and the Beast*, and *Peter Pan*, 1981; *Can't Sit Still*, 1982; *Snuff*, 1984; *Ballista*, 1985; *Aschenputtel*, 1985; *In the Penal Colony* from a story by Kafka, 1985; *Die Troerinnen*, 1986. References: *Superman* script published in *New Short Plays*, London, Methuen, 1972; *Drama Review 68* and *78* (New York), 1975, 1978; *Disrupting the Spectacle* by Peter Ansorge, London, Pitman, 1975; *Travail Théâtral* (Paris), Winter 1976; *Dreams and Deconstructions* edited by Sandy Craig, Ambergate, Derbyshire, Amber Lane Press, 1980.

SOON 3. Founded by Alan Finneran in San Francisco in 1972. Productions: *Desire Circus*, and *One by One*, 1975; *Over and Over*, and *Killers of a False Midnight*, 1976; *Tactics: Five Task Activated Performance Landscapes, Black Water Echo*, and *The Woman in the Water/The Woman in the Seven Rooms*, 1977; *A Wall in Venice/3 Women/Wet Shadows*, and *Rainbow Echoes*, 1978; *The White Woman*, and *Tropical Proxy*, 1979; *The Man in the Nile at Night*, 1980; *Renaissance Radar: A Performance Landscape*, 1981; *Chrome Pastoral*, 1982; *Voodoo Automatic, Red Rain*, and *Artifacts/Echoes*, 1983; *Glass*

Shadows, and *Outcalls/Riptides*, 1984; *blindSite/Iguana Hotel*, 1985; *Swoon, Winter Gaze*, and *Magi*, 1986. References: *Drama Review 75, 79, 91, 100* (New York), 1977–83; *Teatro del Novecento* edited by Antonio Ottisani, Milan, Feltrinelli, 1980; *Performing Arts Journal* (New York), vol. 4, no. 3, 1980; *American Alternative Theatre* by Theodore Shank, London, Macmillan, and New York, Grove Press, 1982; article by Bernard Weiner, in *Theatre Communications*, March 1982; *Off Off and Away* by Ruggero Bianchi, Turin, Tirrenia, 1983; *West Coast Plays 13–14* (Berkeley, California), May 1983.

SQUAT THEATRE. Founded in Budapest in 1970; banned from public performances in 1971: gave private performances, 1971–76; toured Western Europe, 1976–77; since 1977 based in New York. Productions: *Skanzen Killers* by Peter Halasz, Stephan Balint, and Peter Lajtai, 1971; *Breznyik and a Woman* by Peter Berg, 1972; *King Kong, Clown Stories* by Balint, and *Puppet Show* by Halasz, 1973; *Guido and Tyrius* by Eva Buchmuller and Halasz, *House*, and *Children Killer of Bethlehem*, 1974; *The Three Sisters* by Chekhov, and *Don Juan von Leporello* and *Eight Days in a Sand Mine* (films), 1975; *Pig, Child, Fire!*, 1977; *Andy Warhol's Last Love*, and *Cool King Kong*, 1978; *Mr. Dead and Mrs. Free*, 1981; *Dreamland Burns*, 1986. References: *Travail Théâtral* (Paris), Autumn 1977; *Drama Review 79* (New York), 1978; article by Anne-Marie Duguet, in *Theater Heute* (Hannover, Germany), May 1979; *American Alternative Theatre* by Theodore Shank, London, Macmillan, and New York, Grove Press, 1982.

TARA ARTS GROUP. Founded in London in 1976 to perform plays by and about Asians in Britain. Productions (original plays or adaptations of Indian classics by Jatinder Verma) include: *Vilayat; or, England Your England*, and *Diwaali*, 1981; *Scenes in the Life of, The Lion's Raj*, and *The Shape of Dreams*, 1982; *Meet Me*, 1983; *Chilli in Yor Eyes*, 1984; *This Story's Not for Telling*, 1985; *The Broken Thigh, The Little Clay Cart*, and *Tejo Vanio* and *Zanda Zulan* both by Asaitha Thakar, 1986; *1919: An Incident, Exile in the Forest*, and *Bicharo!*, 1987.

EL TEATRO CAMPESINO (The Farmworker's Theatre). See the dictionary entry for Luis Valdez.

EL TEATRO DE LA ESPERANZA (The Theatre of Hope). Founded by Jorge A. Huerta in Santa Barbara, California, in 1971. Productions include: *Guadalupe*, 1974; *La Víctima*, 1977; *We Won't Pay! We Won't Pay!* from a play by Dario Fo, 1984. Reference: "El Teatro de la Esperanza: Keeping in Touch with the People" by Huerta, in *Drama Review 73* (New York), 1977.

TEMBA. Founded by Alton Kumalo in 1972. Productions: *Temba* by Kumalo, 1972; *Rhythm of Violence* by Lewis Nkosi, 1973; *Dutchman* by Amiri Baraka, 1974; *Sherry and Wine* by Jimi Rand, 1975; *The Blood Knot* by Athol Fugard, and *Caliban Lives* by Richard Drain, 1976; *Black Slaves, White Chains* and *More, More* by Mustapha Matura, and *Sizwe Bansi Is Dead* by Fugard, 1977; *Prejudice* by David Halliwell, and *Mister Biko* by Peter Rodda, Andrew Carr, and Kumalo, 1978; *Teresa* by Kumalo, 1979; *Black Lear* by Barrie Keeffe, 1980; *Exodus* by Jamal Ali, Kumalo, and Ian Giles, 1981; *City Jungle* by Kumalo, and *The Island* by Fugard, John Kani, and Winston Ntshona, 1982; *Bitter Milk* by David Clough, and *Getting Plenty* by Peter Speyer, 1983; *The Boot Dance* by Edgar White, 1984; *Scrape Off the Black* by Tunde Ikoli, *Chameleon* by Michael Ellis, *Pantomime* by Derek Walcott, *All You Deserve* by Debbie Horsfield, *Basin* by Jacqueline Rudet, and *Mamma Decemba* by Nigel D. Moffatt, 1985; *The Pirate Princess* by Barbara Gloudon, and *Woza Albert!* by Percy Mtwa, Mbongeni Ngemi, and Barney Simon, 1986.

A TRAVELING JEWISH THEATRE. Founded by Corey Fischer, Albert Greenberg, and Naomi Newman in Los Angeles in 1978; now based in San Francisco. Productions include: *Coming from a Great Distance*, 1979; *The Last Yiddish Poet*, 1980; *A Dance of Exile*, 1982; *Berlin, Jerusalem, and the Moon*, 1985. References: article by Tina Margolis and Susan Weinacht, in *Drama Review 87* (New York), 1980; Joel Rosenberg, in *Moment* (Boston), November 1980; Deena Metzger, in *Parabola* (New York), vol. 4, no. 4; Leslie Kelen, in *Westigan Review* (Kalamazoo, Michigan), vol. 4, no. 1.

WELFARE STATE INTERNATIONAL (formerly Welfare State). Formed by John Fox in Bradford in 1968, now based in Ulverston, Cumbria; consortium of visual artists, performers, and musicians. Performances include seasonal ceremonies and celebrations for events such as marriage and the naming of children: *The Tide Is OK for the 30th*, 1968; *Earthrise*, 1969; *Circus Time*, and *Dr. Strangebrew's Plastic Hand*, 1970; *The Sweet Misery of Life Show*, 1971; *The Travels of Sir Lancelot Quail*, 1972; *Beauty and the Beast*, 1973; *Ringmaen*, 1974; *Slug City, Harbinger*, and *Anacrusus*, 1975; *Secrets of the Iron Egg*, and *Island of the Lost World*, 1976; *Fountain of Change*, 1977; *Uppendown Mooney*, 1978; *Volcano Junction*, 1979; *Eye of the Peacock*, 1980; *Parliament in Flames*, 1981; *Wild Windmill Gala, Doomsday Colouring Book*, and *Scarecrow Zoo*, 1982; *King Real and the Hoodlums*, and *The Raising of the Titanic*, 1983; *Nutcracker*, 1985; *False Creek: A Visual Symphony*, 1986. References: *Theatre Quarterly* (London), October 1972; *Engineers of the Imagination: The Welfare State Handbook* edited by Tony Coult and Baz Kershaw, London, Methuen, 1983; *Drama Review 107* (New York), 1985.

WOMEN'S THEATRE GROUP. Formed in London in 1973. Productions: *Fantasia*, 1973; *My Mother Says I Never Should*, 1974; *Work to Role*, 1975; *Out on the Costa del Trico*, and *Pretty Ugly*, 1977; *In Our Way* and *Hot Spot* by Eileen Fairweather and Melissa Murray, 1978; *The Soap Opera* by Donna Franceschild, and *The Wild Bunch* by Bryony Lavery, 1979; *Better a Live Pompey Than a Dead Cyril* by Clare McIntyre and Stephanie Nunn, *My Mkinga* by Kate Phelps, and *Breaking Through* by Timberlake Wertenbaker, 1980; *New Anatomies* by Wertenbaker, 1981; *Time Pieces*, and *Double Vision*, 1982; *Love and Dissent* by Elisabeth Bond, and *Dear Girl* by Tierl Thompson and Libby Mason, 1983; *Trade Secrets* by Jacqui Shapiro, and *Pax* by Deborah Levy, 1984; *Witchcraze* by Lavery, and *Anywhere to Anywhere* by Joyce Holiday, 1985; *Fixed Deal* by Tasha Fairbanks, and *Our Lady* by Levy, 1986.

THE WOOSTER GROUP. Founded by Elizabeth LeCompte and Spalding Gray in New York in 1975; included several members of the Performance Group, founded by Richard Schechner in New York in 1967. Performance Group productions included: *Dionysus in 69*, 1968; *Makbeth*, 1969; *Commune*, 1970 (and subsequent versions); *Concert for T.P.G.*, 1971; *The Tooth of Crime* by Sam Shepard, 1972; *The Beard* by Michael McClure, 1973; *Mother Courage* by Brecht, *A Wing and a Prayer* by LeCompte, and *The Marilyn Project*, 1975. Wooster Group productions: *Three Places in Rhode Island: Sakonnet Point, Rumstick Road, Nayatt School* by Gray and LeCompte, 1975–78; *Point Judith: An Epilog* by Gray, 1979; *The Road to Immortality: Route 1 & 9, L.S.D. (... Just the High*

Points . . .), Saint Anthony, 1981–87; *Hula*, 1981; *For the Good Times*, 1982; *North Atlantic* by Jim Strahs, 1984; *And That's How the Rent Gets Paid, Part IV* by Jeff Weiss, 1984; *Swimming to Cambodia*, parts 1 and 2 by Gray, 1984; *Seventeen, At That Time I Was Studying Carole Lombard*, and *The Father* all by Beatrice Roth, 1985; *Miss Universal Happiness* by Richard Foreman, 1985. References: *Drama Review 39, 43, 50, 51, 81, 91, 106* (New York), 1968–85; *Theatre Quarterly* (London), 1971; *The Wooster Group 1975–1985: Breaking the Rules* by David Savran, Ann Arbor, Michigan, UMI Research Press, 1986; *Performing Arts Journal 26–27* (New York), 1986. See the dictionary entry for Spalding Gray.

APPENDIX

BEHAN, Brendan (Francis). Irish. Born in Dublin, 9 February 1923. Educated at the French Sisters of Charity School, Dublin, 1928–34; Christian Brothers School, Dublin, 1934–37; Day Apprentice School, 1937. Married Beatrice ffrench-Salkeld in 1955; one daughter. Joined the Irish Republican Army in 1937; apprentice housepainter, 1937–39; sent to Hollesley Bay Borstal, England, 1939–41, and deported; served terms in Mountjoy, Arbour Hill, and Curragh prisons, 1942–46; housepainter, journalist, and seaman, 1946–50; broadcaster, Radio Eireann, 1951–53; columnist, *Irish Press*, Dublin, 1954–55. Recipient: Obie award, 1958; Paris Festival award, 1958; French Critics award, 1962. *Died 20 March 1964.*

PUBLICATIONS

Plays

Moving Out, and A Garden Party (broadcast 1952). Edited by Robert Hogan, Dixon, California, Proscenium Press, 1967; included in *The Complete Plays*, 1978.

The Quare Fellow (produced Dublin, 1954; London, 1956; New York, 1958). London, Methuen, and New York, Grove Press, 1956.

The Big House (broadcast 1957; produced Dublin, 1958; London, 1963). Included in *The Complete Plays*, 1978.

An Giall (in Irish; produced Dublin, 1958). Included in *Poems and a Play in Irish*, Dublin, Gallery Press, 1981; revised version, translated by Behan as *The Hostage* (produced London, 1958; New York, 1960), London, Methuen, 1958; New York, Grove Press, 1959; revised version, Methuen, 1962.

The New House (stage version of *Moving Out* and *A Garden Party*) (produced Dublin, 1958). Published in *Best Short Plays of the World Theatre 1958–1967*, edited by Stanley Richards, New York, Crown, 1968.

Richard's Cork Leg, edited and completed by Alan Simpson (produced Dublin and London, 1972). London, Eyre Methuen, 1973; New York, Grove Press, 1974.

Time for a Gargle (produced Leicester, 1973).

The Complete Plays (includes *The Quare Fellow, The Hostage, The Big House, Moving Out, A Garden Party, Richard's Cork Leg*). London, Eyre Methuen, and New York, Grove Press, 1978.

Radio Plays: *Moving Out*, 1952; *A Garden Party*, 1952; *The Big House*, 1957.

Novel

The Scarperer. New York, Doubleday, 1964; London, Hutchinson, 1966.

Verse

Life Styles: Poems, with Nine Translations from the Irish of Brendan Behan, translated by Ulick O'Connor. Dublin, Dolmen Press, and London, Hamish Hamilton, 1973.

Poems and Stories, edited by Denis Cotter. Dublin, Liffey Press, 1978.

Poems and a Play in Irish. Dublin, Gallery Press, 1981.

Other

Borstal Boy (autobiography). London, Hutchinson, 1958; New York, Knopf, 1959.

Brendan Behan's Island: An Irish Sketch-Book. London, Hutchinson, and New York, Geis, 1962.

Hold Your Hour and Have Another (articles). London, Hutchinson, 1963; Boston, Little Brown, 1964.

Brendan Behan's New York. London, Hutchinson, and New York, Geis, 1964.

Confessions of an Irish Rebel. London, Hutchinson, 1965; New York, Geis, 1966.

The Wit of Brendan Behan, edited by Sean McCann. London, Frewin, 1968.

After the Wake: Twenty-One Prose Works, edited by Peter Fallon. Dublin, O'Brien Press, 1981; London, Allison and Busby, 1983.

Brendan Behan: Interviews and Recollections, edited by E. H. Mikhail. London, Macmillan, and New York, Barnes and Noble, 2 vols., 1982.

*

Bibliography: *Ten Modern Irish Playwrights* by Kimball King, New York, Garland, 1979; *Brendan Behan: An Annotated Bibliography of Criticism* by E. H. Mikhail, London, Macmillan, and New York, Barnes and Noble, 1980.

Critical Studies: *Beckett and Behan and a Theatre in Dublin* by Alan Simpson, London, Routledge, 1962; *With Breast Expanded* by Brian Behan, London, MacGibbon and Kee, 1964; *My Brother Brendan* by Dominic Behan, London, Frewin, 1965, New York, Simon and Schuster, 1966; *The World of Brendan Behan* edited by Sean McCann, London, New English Library, 1965; *Brendan Behan: Man and Showman* by Rae Jeffs, London, Hutchinson, 1966, Cleveland, World, 1968; *Brendan Behan* by Ted E. Boyle, New York, Twayne, 1969; *Brendan Behan* by Ulick O'Connor, London, Hamish Hamilton, 1970, as *Brendan*, Englewood Cliffs, New Jersey, Prentice hall, 1971; *Brendan Behan: A Memoir* by Séamus de Búrca, Newark, New Jersey, Proscenium Press, 1971; *The Major Works of Brendan Behan* by Peter R. Gerdes, Berne, Switzerland, Lang, 1973; *My Life with Brendan* by Beatrice Behan, Des Hickey, and Gus Smith, London, Frewin, 1973, Los Angeles, Nash, 1974; *Brendan Behan* by Raymond Porter, New York, Columbia University Press, 1973; *The Writings of Brendan Behan* by Colbert Kearney, Dublin, Gill and Macmillan, London, Macmillan, and New York, St. Martin's Press, 1977; *The Art of Brendan Behan* edited by E. H. Mikhail, London, Vision Press, 1979, New York, Barnes and Noble, 1980; *With Brendan Behan* by Peter Arthurs, New York, St. Martin's Press, 1981, London, Routledge, 1982.

* * *

Formidable obstacles bar a just appreciation of Brendan Behan as dramatist. First is his "legend," live enough to prompt a biography staged in New York as recently as 1975. Then the post-O'Casey Irish fantasies tend to assimilate a writer with a superficial relationship to them. But Behan is not reducible to publicity sprung from self-destructive alcoholism or to spin-off from Abbey Theatre tradition. A look at *The Hostage* in the context of political and terrorist activity some 30 years later will identify an original talent.

Synge's *The Playboy of the Western World* provoked riots. In certain locations *The Hostage* would be likely to do so now. If not, it would be because dramatized controversy is no longer a monopoly of the theatre. "The IRA and the War of Independence are as dead as the Charleston," "The IRA is out of date." That only for starters. Equally insolent remarks are directed at: the Gaelic language, Padraic Pearse, the St. Vincent de Paul Society ("all ex-policemen"), the RAF, Irish patriots, gunmen, de Valera, Handel, Protestant bishops, puritanical Catholics, the Royal Family as reported in the popular press ("you might almost be in the yacht there with them"), Evelyn Waugh, the Queen, and, as a component of cockney rhyming slang, the Holy Ghost.

These and countless equally subversive comments revolve round the inhabitants of a lodging house and grotesque visitors ranging from a Polish communist sailor to an evangelical whore. Its caretaker, claiming to be a survivor of the Troubles and the Easter Rising, lives on the immoral earnings of his abrasive wife. Yeats once proclaimed the birth of "a terrible beauty," and this community is its tawdry old age. Wildly farcical collisions of stereotypes occur without probing or development of character. Then what is there to mould chaotic action into shape? A catalyst, the hostage himself. In retaliation for the sentencing of a young activist due to be hanged in Belfast, the IRA has kidnapped a British soldier outside a dance hall. He arrives under escort at the end of the first act, and in view of Behan's experience of imprisonment in England it's a proof of artistic detachment that this Londoner commands more sympathy than anyone else in the play. Those lucky enough to have seen Murray Melvin's performance can attest that the role skirts "cockney sparrer" clichés without falling into them. Surprisingly from an Irish playwright, the soldier is perhaps the most authentic working-class character in English drama. Information about the boy's social background, for example, is uncommonly precise, and the same is true of Teresa, a devout Roman Catholic servant girl in the lodging house. Between these two, one reared in a convent and other in the Old Kent Road, a love affair of great delicacy and pathos illuminates the second act.

Parallels with the situation in Cyprus and an awareness of imperial decline, along with a prophetic sense of youth's indifference to such issues, can be had from *The Hostage* over and above its mature attitude to the conflict in Northern Ireland. That, and unflagging satirical energy, ought to preserve the play. The ending, though, defaces it. To have the young soldier killed in error during a shoot-out with government agents is evasively casual. "He died in a strange land and at home he has no one," says Teresa finely, then ruins the gravity by adding that she'll never forget him, "never till the end of time." A jaunty song by the resurrected soldier unwisely includes fragments from the burial service. These draw attention to a profundity which the action has been steadily working towards and finally shirked.

There are no such flaws in *The Quare Fellow*, a durable masterpiece if ever there was one, hard-edged and classical for all its colloquial idiom and gallows humour. The play is about hanging and could serve as polemic worthy of Swift. But it is more than that. An entire prison community is brought to life, from the novice alert to education in crime ("Do you think Triplex or celluloid is best for yale locks, sir?") to the Governor intent on providing a good breakfast for the hangman, who renders "The Rose of Tralee" before calculating the condemned man's weight in relation to the law of gravity. Nothing frivolous here, because the grisly ritual from night watch to burial has been realized cumulatively by convicts' and warders' conversation.

Within the austere dramatic structure there is profuse variety of incident. One warder is outspokenly disgusted; it is taboo to name the hangman other than as "himself"; an old lag bets his bacon ration against reprieve. All that and more is geared to the classical unities of action and time. Unity of place is relaxed for episodes in the prison yard, the digging and filling up of an incorrectly numbered grave. And the condemned man, though he dominates the drama, is never heard or seen.

—Laurence Kitchin

COOPER, Giles (Stannus). Irish. Born in Carrickmines, County Dublin, 9 August 1918. Educated at Lancing College, Sussex; Grenoble University, France; Webber Douglas Academy of Dramatic Art, London. Served in the British Army, 1939–46, including four years with the West Yorkshire Regiment in Burma; joined the London Irish Rifles (Territorial Army), 1949. Married Gwyneth Lewis in 1947. Actor in repertory in London and the provinces, 1946–52; assistant script editor, BBC Television, 1953, and Associated Rediffusion Television, 1955. Recipient: Guild of Television Producers award, 1961; Czech International prize, for radio drama, 1966. O.B.E. (Officer, Order of the British Empire), 1960. Giles Cooper Award established, 1978. *Died 2 December 1966.*

PUBLICATIONS

Plays

Never Get Out (produced Edinburgh and London, 1950).
Haddock's Eyes (produced London, 1950).
Mathry Beacon (broadcast 1956; produced Edinburgh, 1968). Published in *Six Plays for Radio*, 1966.
Unman, Wittering, and Zigo (broadcast 1958). London, Macmillan, 1971.
Everything in the Garden (produced London, 1962). London, Evans, 1963.
Out of the Crocodile (produced Oxford and London, 1963). London, Evans, 1964.
The Lady of the Camellias, adaptation of the play by Dumas fils, adapted by Terrence McNally (produced New York, 1963).
The Object (broadcast 1964). Published in *New English Dramatists 12*, London, Penguin, 1968.
Happy Family (produced London, 1966). London, French, 1984.
The Spies Are Singing (produced Nottingham, 1966).
Six Plays for Radio (includes *Mathry Beacon; Unman, Wittering, and Zigo; The Disagreeable Oyster; Without the Grail; Before the Monday; Under the Loofah Tree*). London, BBC Publications, 1966.

Radio Plays: *Thieves Rush In*, 1950; *The Forgotten Rotten Borough*, 1950; *The Timbimbo Craze, or, New Games for Old*, 1950; *Small Fortune*, 1951; *The Private Line*, 1951; *The Owl and the Pussycat*, 1953; *The Sound of Cymbals*, 1955; *Mathry Beacon*, 1956; *The Volunteer*, 1956; *The Disagreeable Oyster*, 1957; *Unman, Wittering, and Zigo*, 1958; *Without the Grail*, 1958; *Under the Loofah Tree*, 1958; *All for Three Days: A Story of the Hungarian Revolution* (*With Courage* series), 1958; *Dangerous Word*, 1958; *Before the Monday*, 1959; *Caretaker*, 1959; *Part of the View*, 1959; *A Crown of Gold*, 1959; *Pig in the Middle*, 1960; *General Forefinger*, 1961; *The Return of General Forefinger*, 1961; *A Perfectly Ghastly Joke*, 1962; *I Gotta Universe*, 1963; *All the Way Home*, 1963; *The Object*, 1964; *The Lonesome Road*, 1964; *Something from the Sea*, 1966; *Brass Farthing*, from the novel by Rupert Croft-Cooke, 1966; *The Day of the Triffids*, from the novel by John Wyndham, 1968; *Oliver Twist*, from the novel by Dickens, 1970;

The Private Patient, 1970; *The Wrong Box*, from the story by Robert Louis Stevenson, 1972.

Television Plays: *The No-Man*, 1955; *General Confusion*, 1955; *Liberty Hall*, 1958; *Maigret and the Lost Life*, 1959, and the *Maigret* series, 1960, from novels by Simenon; *Point of Humour*, 1960; *Where the Party Ended*, 1960; *The Night of the Big Heat*, from the novel by John Lymington, 1960; *Love and Penguins*, 1961; *The Power of Zero*, 1962; *The Double Doll*, 1963; *True Love and Limbeck*, 1963; *Loop*, 1963; *The Freewheelers*, 1963; *A Wicked World*, 1964; *The Other Man*, 1964; *Carried by Storm*, 1964; *Madam Bovary*, from the novel by Flaubert, 1965; *The Six Napoleons*, from the story by Arthur Conan Doyle, 1965; *The Way of All Flesh*, from the novel by Samuel Butler, 1965; *The Canterville Ghost*, from the story by Oscar Wilde, 1965; *Lost Hearts*, from the story by M. R. James, 1965; *Seek Her Out*, 1965; *The Long House*, 1965; *For Whom the Bell Tolls*, 1965, and *A Farewell to Arms*, 1966, from the novels by Ernest Hemingway; *I Am Osango*, 1967; *Sword of Honour*, from the novels by Evelyn Waugh, 1967; *Kittens Are Brave*, 1967; *To the Frontier*, 1968; *A Man in the Zoo*, from the novel by David Garnett, 1975.

Novel

The Other Man (novelization of television play). London, Panther, 1964.

* * *

When the curtain rose on Giles Cooper's plays for the stage—well, they had the appearance of being the sort of plays on which curtains *would*, eternally, rise. But in the expanding imaginative universe of his work for radio and television one might find oneself transported anywhere from the ur-world spawned under his eponymous *Carboy* (unproduced) to the more prosaic but no less microcosmic bathtub of *Under the Loofah Tree*. Beneath a proscenium arch, it was as if Cooper (not unlike those established novelists who were coerced into trying their hands at the theatre in the early days of the Royal Court) felt constrained by conventions of well-made construction which, in his more accustomed medium, he had long ago transcended.

Donald McWhinnie, who directed much of Cooper's work for all three media, commented on the "drawbacks" of his stage techniques: "the audience cannot afford to take its eye, or its ear, off the machine, if it wants to see how the wheels go round." This is because Cooper's plays have "a terseness of expression, an elliptical form . . . the result of years of thinking in terms of the rapid interconnections and swift, understated action" of radio and television drama. No wonder that theatre audiences, lulled into a false sense of security by the comfortable settings of the plays, found their burgeoning ambiguities not only disturbing but profoundly puzzling.

Everything in the Garden thus opens with a sunlit vignette of suburban affluence; *Out of the Crocodile* with a glimpse of bland metropolitan sophistication; and *Happy Family* in the slightly shabby gentility of the governing classes in rural retreat.

Each proceeds to expode its particular myth, showing an acquisitive society ready to sell itself body and soul in the first play; self-deception taken to an extreme of conditioned solipsism in the second; and "breeding" turned viciously in upon itself in the third. Charges by some critics of random motivation and of arbitrary endings usually reveal only their own lulled awareness; scrupulously, perhaps over scrupulously, all the causes and effects are *there* in the writing, its sheer density and comic deceptiveness tempting audiences into the half-attention the conventions seem to permit.

In the plays for television and, more especially, for radio, Cooper fashioned his own conventions. Whether in the surrealistic progress of a piece like *The Disagreeable Oyster* (in which a night out "on the town" turns into a nightmare progressing with its own unreasonable yet irresistible momentum), or the psychological realism of the male-female encounter in *Before the Monday*, he allowed his material to forge its appropriate formal medium. Both plays, however, also typify the pessimism of Cooper's world view. It is true that his targets are almost invariably of the middle classes, or of the more ossified establishment institutions: but he does not offer even an implicit alternative, whether to the kind of facile human relationships he shows to be empty, or to the bourgeois values he reveals as a worthless facade. Even the obvious outsiders—the artist who suffers for being a social misfit in *Everything in the Garden*, for example—achieve only the enigmatic affirmation of martyrdom.

Cooper was essentially a writer for voices. Not that he was unable to handle stage pictures, or to think in televisual terms: but he was at his best when the emphasis could fall most naturally upon verbal modulation and counterpoint. Hence the insidious menace behind probably his best known work for radio, *Unman, Wittering, and Zigo*, where the quasi-naturalistic struggle for authority between a schoolmaster and his pupils is constantly underpinned by that almost liturgical feeling for the force of words resonant even in the play's title. The accidental rhythm beaten out by three surnames at the end of an alphabetical roll can utters a threat at once in its arbitrariness, its elusive associative quality, and its self-sustaining assonance.

Thus Cooper worked both by highlighting the unexpectedly "normal" in the fantastic, and by exposing the absurdity of the ostensibly commonplace. Often, he was able to make one faintly ashamed of one's own laughter, as what had seemed to be no more than a ludicrous boil on society's rump was laid bare as a terminal growth. Another reason, no doubt, why theatre audiences, reluctant to laugh lest laughter echo their own poor taste, found his plays so disconcerting, while the listener to the radio plays could relate to Cooper and his world directly—and alone.

In one of those radio plays, *Without the Grail*, Cooper used a "realistic" conflict of character to expose the opposing but equal failures of imperialism, communism, tribalism, and pragmatism. Not content with creating this vacuum of communal ideals, he allowed condemnation and catastrophe also to overtake the one character totally immersed in his own self. The only redemptive feature in this as in almost all his work is its humour—which is never a matter of light relief, but itself embodies an attitude towards his material and so, surely, an attitude to life. If Cooper left humanity without a shred of illusion, at least he allowed it the gift of laughter, and the perverse relief of total comic catharsis.

—Simon Trussler

HANSBERRY, Lorraine (Vivian). American. Born in Chicago, Illinois, 19 May 1930. Educated at the Art Institute, Chicago; University of Wisconsin, Madison, 1948–50. Married Robert Nemiroff in 1953 (divorced 1964). Journalist, 1950–51, and associate editor after 1952, *Freedom*, New York. Recipient: New York Drama Critics Circle award, 1959. *Died 12 January 1965.*

PUBLICATIONS

Plays

A Raisin in the Sun (produced New York and London, 1959). New York, Random House, 1959; London, Methuen, 1960.
The Sign in Sidney Brustein's Window (produced New York, 1964). New York, Random House, 1965; in *Three Negro Plays*, London, Penguin, 1969.
To Be Young, Gifted, and Black: A Portrait of Lorraine Hansberry in Her Own Words, adapted by Robert Nemiroff (produced New York, 1969). New York, French, 1971.
Les Blancs, edited by Robert Nemiroff (produced New York, 1970). Included in *Les Blancs* (collection), 1972.
Les Blancs: The Collected Last Plays of Lorraine Hansberry (includes *Les Blancs, The Drinking Gourd, What Use Are Flowers?*), edited by Robert Nemiroff. New York, Random House, 1972; as *The Collected Last Plays*, New York, New American Library, 1983.

Screenplay: *A Raisin in the Sun*, 1961.

Other

The Movement: Documentary of a Struggle for Equality. New York, Simon and Schuster, 1964; as *A Matter of Colour*, London, Penguin, 1965.
To Be Young, Gifted, and Black: A Portrait of Lorraine Hansberry in Her Own Words, edited by Robert Nemiroff. Englewood Cliffs, New Jersey, Prentice Hall, 1969.

*

Critical Studies: "Lorraine Hansberry Issue" of *Freedomways* (New York), vol. 19, no. 4, 1979; *Lorraine Hansberry* by Anne Cheney, Boston, Twayne, 1984.

Theatrical Activities:
Director: **Play**—*Kicks and Co.*, Chicago, 1960.

* * *

"Presume no commitment, disavow all engagement, mock all great expectations," says Sidney in *The Sign in Sidney Brustein's Window*, Lorraine Hansberry's second play, the last one that she finished before her death in 1965. In contrast, the playwright, speaking at a Negro Writers Conference shortly before the opening of her first play in 1959, stood out against the fashionable angst of the time: "man is unique in the universe, the only creature who has in fact the powers to transform the universe ... man might just do what the apes never will—*impose* the reason for life on life." A far cry from an easy optimist ("*Despair?*" she once wrote, " ... listen to the sons of those who have known little else"), she spoke in a persistently positive voice, directly in speeches and articles, dramatically through her protagonists.

A Raisin in the Sun is a realistic family play set on Chicago's Southside. A black play, in its characters and its concerns, it is also a combination of two pervasive American subjects, a maturation play containing a critique of the American Dream. The leading character, Walter Lee Younger, is at once a product and a victim of American attitudes toward success. A chauffeur who feels trapped by his job, his home, even his family, he is convinced that all he needs is a little money, a push that will propel him into the big time. Using the familiar insurance-policy plot, Hansberry gives Walter the money and a chance to lose it, reminding the audience once again that, whatever popular mythology may say, success is not inevitable. Nor need it be material, for at this point the other play takes over. Lena, the strong mother figure in the play, has used part of the insurance money to make a down payment on a house in a white neighborhood, a tentative first step on that journey out of the ghetto which Walter expected to make in a flamboyant single leap, and, in his new despair, Walter is willing to sell out to the white neighborhood association, to take the money and run. Or—as his Uncle Tom routine indicates—to take the money and shuffle. When the moment comes, he cannot demean himself; he makes a rambling, painful, but effective speech on family pride and, as Lena says, comes "into his manhood."

Sidney Brustein is unusual among plays by black dramatists in that most of its characters are white, but its middle-class Jewish hero is cousin-german to Walter, although Sidney is not so much an innocent who must find himself as a perennial loser-of-innocence who regularly refinds himself. A "modern bourgeois intellectual," as one character puts it, suffering from "the great sad withdrawal from the affairs of men," Sidney begins the play with a failed business and a failing marriage, commits himself to a reform political campaign and, after a descent into drunken and murderous despair when his white knight turns out to be conventionally tarnished, he recommits himself to social and personal possibility—to political action and his uncertain marriage.

Les Blancs, Hansberry's African play, was unfinished when she died, and the play as we have it must be taken as an attempt by Robert Nemiroff (her husband and literary executor) and Charlotte Zaltzberg to give a workable final shape to a drama that was still in process. Yet, its protagonist, Tshembe Matoseh, is so clearly a character in the Sidney Brustein mold, that the play, in its essentials, is clearly Hansberry's work. Tshembe returns from England to a fictional African colony, an ironic outsider, neither African nor European, and is claimed by the rebellion in process. A speech invoking Orestes and Hamlet and the recurrent use of a symbolic dancer suggest that, unlike Walter and Sidney, Tshembe is more chosen than choosing. Although Tshembe's commitment is the culmination of *Les Blancs*, much of its power lies in his reluctance to declare himself and in the pain of his final decision.

In discussing Hansberry's work ideationally, I have been unfair to her if I have implied that her social and philosophical concerns led her to sacrifice art to argument. Her strengths as a playwright lie in her ability to create an almost tangible milieu—particularly out of Chicago and the Greenwich Village settings that she knew so well—and in her understanding of and affection for human complexity. This last is most apparent in Walter and Sidney, her two finest creations, characters so rich that the affirmative endings, however important to the playwright, almost come as impositions—saved, of course, by the fact that Hansberry, too, knew that they were tentative.

—Gerald Weales

INGE, William (Motter). American. Born in Independence, Kansas, 3 May 1913. Educated at Montgomery County High School, Independence, graduated 1930; University of Kansas, Lawrence, 1930–35, A.B. 1935; Peabody Teachers College, Nashville, Tennessee, 1935–36, M.A. 1938; Yale University, New Haven, Connecticut, 1940. Announcer, KFH Radio, Wichita, Kansas, 1936–37; teacher at Columbus High School, Kansas, 1937–38, Stephens College, Columbia, Missouri, 1938–43, and Washington University, St. Louis, 1946–

49; arts critic, St. Louis *Star-Times*, 1943–46; story consultant, *Bus Stop* television series, 1961–62; Lecturer, University of North Carolina, Chapel Hill, 1969, and University of California, Irvine, 1970. Recipient: George Jean Nathan Award, 1951; Pulitzer Prize, 1953; New York Drama Critics Circle award, 1953; Donaldson Award, 1953; Oscar, for screenplay, 1962. *Died (suicide) 10 June 1973.*

PUBLICATIONS

Plays

The Dark at the Top of the Stairs (as *Farther Off from Heaven*, produced Dallas, 1947; revised version, as *The Dark at the Top of the Stairs*, produced New York, 1957; London, 1961). New York, Random House, 1958; in *Four Plays*, 1958.
Come Back, Little Sheba (produced Westport, Connecticut, 1949; New York, 1950; London, 1952). New York, Random House, 1950; in *Four Plays*, 1958.
Picnic: A Summer Romance (produced New York, 1953; London, 1962). New York, Random House, 1953; in *Four Plays*, 1958; revised version, as *Summer Brave* (produced Hyde Park, New York, 1962; New York City, 1973), included in *Summer Brave and Eleven Short Plays*, 1962.
Bus Stop (produced New York, 1955; Leatherhead, Surrey, 1958; London, 1976). New York, Random House, 1955; in *Four Plays*, 1958.
Four Plays. New York, Random House, 1958; London, Heinemann, 1960.
Glory in the Flower (produced New York, 1959). Published in *24 Favorite One-Act Plays*, edited by Bennett Cerf and Van H. Cartmell, New York, Doubleday, 1958.
The Tiny Closet (produced Spoleto, Italy, 1959). Included in *Summer Brave and Eleven Short Plays*, 1962.
A Loss of Roses (produced New York, 1959). New York, Random House, 1960.
Splendor in the Grass: A Screenplay. New York, Bantam, 1961.
Natural Affection (produced Phoenix, 1962; New York, 1963). New York, Random House, 1963.
Summer Brave and Eleven Short Plays (includes *To Bobolink, For Her Spirit; A Social Event; The Boy in the Basement; The Tiny Closet; Memory of Summer; The Rainy Afternoon; The Mall; An Incident at the Standish Arms; People in the Wind; Bus Riley's Back in Town; The Strains of Triumph*). New York, Random House, 1962.
Where's Daddy? (as *Family Things, Etc.*, produced Falmouth, Massachusetts, 1965; as *Where's Daddy?*, produced New York, 1966). New York, Random House, 1966.
The Disposal (as *Don't Go Gentle*, produced Los Angeles, 1968; as *The Last Pad*, produced Phoenix, 1972). Published in *Best Short Plays of the World Theatre 1958–1967*, edited by Stanley Richards, New York, Crown, 1968; revised version, as *The Disposal*, music by Anthony Caldarella, lyrics by Judith Gero (produced New York, 1973).
Two Short Plays: The Call, and A Murder. New York, Dramatists Play Service, 1968.
Midwestern Manic (in *The Love Death Plays*, produced New York, 1975). Published in *The Best Short Plays 1969*, edited by Stanley Richards, Philadelphia, Chilton, 1969.
Overnight (produced Los Angeles, 1969; New York, 1974).
Caesarian Operations (produced Los Angeles, 1972).
The Love Death Plays: Dialogue for Two Men, Midwestern Manic, The Love Death, Venus and Adonis, The Wake, The Star (produced New York, 1975).

Screenplays: *Splendor in the Grass*, 1961; *All Fall Down*, 1962; *Bus Riley's Back in Town*, 1965.

Television Play: *Out on the Outskirts of Town*, 1964.

Novels

Good Luck, Miss Wyckoff. Boston, Little Brown, and London, Deutsch, 1971.
My Son Is a Splendid Driver. Boston, Little Brown, 1972.

*

Bibliography: *William Inge: A Bibliography* by Arthur F. McClure, New York, Garland, 1982.

Manuscript Collections: Humanities Research Center, University of Texas, Austin; Independence Community College, Kansas; University of Kansas, Lawrence.

Critical Study: *William Inge* by R. Baird Shuman, New York, Twayne, 1966.

Theatrical Activities:
Actor: **Film**—*Splendor in the Grass*, 1961.

* * *

> But the aristocracy of Freedom, Kansas, was not that of eighteenth-century France.
> —*Good Luck, Miss Wyckoff*

William Inge's plays epitomize the weaknesses inherent in American society. Even in those works set outside the dreary Kansas-Oklahoma area of the 1920's and 1930's that is Inge's usual world, his characters, lacking authority figures within the family or community, frequently turn to actors for models, or for emotional and aesthetic satisfaction: Bobolink, whose devotion to autograph hunting raises her to "professional" status in the early one-acter *To Bobolink, For Her Spirit*; Pinky, whose recollections of the stage performances of Ina Claire and Ethel Barrymore are indices to a vanished civilization superior to the one he inhabits in *Where's Daddy?* In general, the personal styles of the stars and the clichés of their films are criteria against which characters measure their own situations. Even the hard-boiled Rosemary Sidney in *Picnic* (and its revision *Summer Brave*) cries to her unromantic lover: "I want to drive into the sunset, Howard! I want to drive into the sunset!"

Given the pantheon of film stars and the American thrust for upward mobility and popularity, Inge's characters often aspire disastrously toward theatrical careers, or give impromptu amateur performances. In *Picnic*, Hal claims to have failed as a film star only because he would not have his teeth fixed; in *Where's Daddy?* and *Midwestern Manic* the protagonists are serious young actors who must earn their living in television commercials. Though occasionally someone like Millie in *Picnic* reads Carson McCullers, hangs a Picasso reproduction in her room, and plans on a writing career, the bartender in *Glory in the Flower* best summarizes Inge's young: "They're all ambitious but they all wanta be movie stars or bandleaders, or disc-jockeys. They're too *good* for plain, ordinary, everyday work. And what's gonna happen to us if everyone becomes a bandleader, I'd like to know."

Democratic egalitarianism, a post-frontier product of the unchallenging geography of the midwest, created a tyranny of the majority, the female majority, that controlled every area of life, especially sexual life. Inge's women, who function within the family and the community as the standard-bearers of morality (often equated to mutilating naked statues of Roman gladiators, and making men obey the prescripts of etiquette in the bathroom), attempt to repress sex in others and, ironically, deny the drive in themselves, often with disastrous results. Mrs. Loomis in Inge's screenplay *Splendor in the Grass* convinces her daughter Deanie that "a woman doesn't enjoy these things like a man does," a conviction that helps drive Deanie into a lengthy spell of madness, like Jackie in *Bus Riley's Back in Town.*

With these problems of normal sexuality in Inge's work, it is predictable that those outside this range will suffer even further. Spencer Scranton, the middle-aged undertaker of *The Boy in the Basement*, must restrict his homosexual activities to furtive weekends in Pittsburgh, while his mother dominates his life back home and taunts him when she learns the truth. The basement suggests not only the literal headquarters of Spencer's undertaking business, but also the semi-acknowledged arena of his sexuality. The two meanings fuse when Spencer can touch the body of the delivery boy, Joker Evans, whom he loves, only in the basement when he prepares the drowned youth for burial. Similarly, *The Tiny Closet* hides the secret transvestism of another middle-aged homosexual, the floorwalker Mr. Newbold, but the play deals less with the nature of Newbold's fixation than with the repressive activities of his landlady, Mrs. Crosby, determined to invade here boarder's privacy, lest it conceal political and moral unorthodoxy. (Communism and sexual aberrations are interchangeable examples of the non-conformity in Inge's world.) Many of his characters, especially schoolteachers, lead lonely boardinghouse existences subject to the tyranny of their landladies; Inge's one-acter *A Murder* carries roominghouse restrictions to their absurd extreme, as the protagonist desperately tries to get a lock on a closet: "I have some *things* I want to keep quite safe." (Another middle-aged neurotic, in *The Call*, carries his secrets around in a suitcase.) The male desire for privacy is, of course, impossible in a world in which the unrestricted petty tyrannies of women assume enormous proportions.

Male tyrants, inside and outside the family, are rarer in Inge. Ace Stamper in *Splendor in the Grass* is a self-made oilman who dominates the town's economy and his son Bud's life. Another self-made millionaire, Del Loomis in *Bus Riley's Back in Town*, runs the community and imprisons his daughter's lover primarily because he is poor and half-Mexican: "But I guess all that money and all that power kinda went to his head. He was actin' kinda crazy around here, like he was Nero or one of those Roman emperors." Ultimately, both Stamper and Loomis lose their wealth and authority. Thus, the traditional American aspiration to rise in society produces tyrannies, however short-lived, as oppressive as those democracy supposedly replaced.

From the infantile worship of the film stars, through the submission to the petty absolutism of landladies, to the perversion of the American dream, Inge's characters dramatize the spiritual poverty and emotional repression of democratic life. Though Freudianism is obviously crucial in Inge's work, and explains especially the mother-son relationships and the dangers of repressed sexuality, the psychological exploration of character seems less an end in itself than a means of assessing the larger social context. Despite their greater power, even the domineering women seem more the products of this society than its ultimate shapers.

Despite Inge's frequent revisions and variant versions of his works, it is possible to assess chronologically both the development of his major dramatic concerns and the worth of individual plays. The immediate problem of *Come Back, Little Sheba* is Lola's attempt to control the drinking of her husband, Doc Delaney, with the help of Alcoholics Anonymous. What prevents the play becoming merely an A.A. tract are the garrulous Lola, simultaneously ludicrous and touching, desperately talking to whomever will listen, and Inge's deft use of a subplot involving the Delaneys' roomer, Marie, to parallel and contrast with their situation. Doc is infatuated with Marie, whose relationship with a virile college student seems a recapitulation of Lola's past, while Lola identifies childishly with Marie's affair. The Delaneys' involvement with Marie helps clarify their own lives through the illusion of two time levels; both Doc and Lola are trapped in the past as they work desperately to resolve their current dilemma. Doc's attraction to Marie indicates that he wants to repeat the mistake that created his initial disaster. However, when Lola finally accepts the loss of her dog that has dominated her thoughts and her dreams, she is presumably ready to be an adequate wife and has conquered her desire to relive her youth: "I don't think Little Sheba's ever coming back, Doc. I'm not going to call her any more." The symbolism is effective without becoming obtrusive, though the suddenly mature Lola and sober Doc are not totally convincing. The play works best dramatizing the link between impoverished social values (puritanical sex codes, concern with job and financial status) and the impoverished lives they produce.

Picnic and its revision *Summer Brave* are Inge's most ambitious and successful works. Both plays attempt to endow the central figure Hal, an out-of-work wanderer, with mythical sexual qualities, as he changes the lives of the women he encounters in the Kansas town where he seeks help from his wealthy college friend, Alan Seymour. Hal's jeans-clad appearance transforms Millie Owens from a tomboy, while her sister Madge either runs off with Hal to a life of romantic improvidence (*Picnic*) or loses both her virtue and her chance to marry Alan (*Summer Brave*), after a dance with Hal that "has something of the nature of a primitive rite that could mate the young people." Such over-reaction to male bodies is, of course, typical of many Inge women: Jackie Loomis in *Bus Riley's Back in Town* and *Glory in the Flower* sees Bus as a kind of sexual "god" and submits appropriately, though she later frees herself from this kind of worship in *Glory*; but sometimes women like Cora, in *The Dark at the Top of the Stairs*, who is obsessed with her husband's physicality, spend their lives fighting this passion and attempt to make the male conform to female notions of "decency." Rosemary Sidney's attraction to Hal is so strong, perhaps because she tries to deny it, that in her stimulated state she gives herself to her suitor Howard and persuades him to marry her. The Labor Day setting reinforces Rosemary's now-or-never desperation, since her teaching chores will resume the next day, along with the restricted life of a teacher in a small Kansas town. Madge's mother, though she sees Hal as an obvious threat to her daughter's future, also reponds to his charms in a way that recalls her reluctant emotional and physical dependence on her husband. Sixtyish Helen Potts whose unconsummated marriage had been annulled forty years before by the tyrannical mother she still serves slavishly, reacts sentimentally to Hal when he performs odd jobs for her: "Everything he did reminded me there was a man in the house, and it seemed good." Thus, all the women in the play respond to Hal's fertility god appeal, though perhaps the Fall Kansas setting explains the muted reaction of some females. The theme seems to demand the intensity and exalted language of Lorca works like *Blood Wedding*, but stifled passion and prosaic language are more suited to Kansas. *Picnic* seems a gentler version of Ugo Betti's *The Crime on Goat Island*; while Betti's stranger seduces all three women in the community he invades, and then dies in the appropriately symbolic well into which they have tricked him, Hal's behavior is comparatively guileless, and Inge's women, dominated by their feelings, if not their hormones, lack the cunning and intellectual force of Betti's and embody the very limited development their society permits. In a "dry" state like Kansas, where even adults must drink secretly, schoolteachers like Rosemary, the strongest woman in the play, deny their physical drives and study during the summer only to satisfy the Board of Education requirements. And just as the women conform to a concept of femininity that limits both body and mind, Hal lacks any real freedom—the women force him to put on his shirt, and the exploits of which he boasts, notably encounters with sexually aggressive females, have degraded him. Though he excites women, they fear this excitement so much they wish to control its source. Hal is a victim of society that can cast a well-built, but poor and not overly bright young man only as a purely physical object: his fraternity tolerated him as long as they thought his athletics would bring them prestige. Alan's attempt to use his father's power to run Hal out of town reinforces Inge's view that the perversion of democracy in American society denies the humanity of the individual.

Bus Stop brings together a group of characters in a small Kansas town to contrast various male/female encounters: Grace and the busdriver who have a brief sexual union in her apartment above the restaurant/bus stop; Elma, the young waitress, more observer than participant in the adult world she is about to join, and Dr. Lyman, failed college professor and semi-pathological pursuer of young girls, who tries to establish a bond with her by quoting Shakespeare; and, more important, Bo Decker, returning to his Montana ranch with Cherie, an unsuccessful *chanteuse*, as his unwilling companion. Having had his first sex experience with Cherie while he was in Kansas City for a rodeo, Bo tries to force her to marry him. Though she resists and tries to run away, her pathetic past and uncertain future make it inevitable that she will marry and presumably love him, especially since she acknowledges his physical appeal. With an actress capable of the right blend of toughness and pathos, the role of Cherie can be the emotional focus of the play. The easily satisfied longings of Grace, and the terrifying loneliness of Dr. Lyman offer the only possible alternatives to marrying Bo. Because of Bo's vitality and Cherie's comic uncertainty, *Bus Stop* is the most cheerful of Inge's works, despite Dr. Lyman, and Virgil, Bo's lifelong companion and substitute father, who chooses to stay behind, once Bo has won Cherie. When Grace tells Virgil there is no place to wait after the bus stop has closed: "... you're just left out in the cold," he replies, "Well ... that's what happens to some people." Though the play says nothing of Virgil's private life and presents him only as unnecessarily noble, since he could presumably work on Bo's ranch even after the wedding, the implied motivation links him with Pinky, the homosexual college professor in *Where's Daddy?*, who picks up 15-year-old Tom and raises him as a combination son and lover. Thus, Virgil's solitary stance at the climax adds another dimension to the pervasive loneliness which most of the characters confront (the bus stop offers even less permanence than Inge's familiar boardinghouse). Depending on emphases of staging and performance, Virgil's final line can turn the play into a study of those excluded from any conventional relationship, or merely suggest that Inge was unready to face this theme in the early 1950's. Since Inge provides no convincing explanation of the psychology of his characters, *Bus Stop* remains primarily a study of emotionally impoverished lower-middle-class people who, like those in other Inge works, are willing to settle for less than an ideal life.

Of the four major Inge works that had successful Broadway runs and film versions, *The Dark at the Top of the Stairs* is the most persistent attempt to probe the psychology of its characters, Cora and Rubin Flood, and their children, 10-year-old Sonny, and 16-year-old Reenie, in an Oklahoma town of the 1920's. The play explores Sonny's oedipal involvement and suggests that he is rather miraculously outgrowing his attachment to his mother as "he avoids her embrace," at the climax of Act 3, when he and Reenie leave for the movies, and Cora climbs the stairs for a reunion with her husband; "we see Rubin's naked feet standing in the warm light at the top." However, neither Sonny's rapid independence nor Cora's acceptance of the masculinity in Rubin that she has continuously fought, seems convincing, and the ending lacks the irony to make clear the impermanence of these resolutions. What dominates the play, despite character analysis and the lengthy sexual confession of Cora's sister, Lottie, is the sense of the changing economy which caused Rubin to lose his financial and emotional bearings. Cora tells Sonny that Rubin "and his family were pioneers. They fought Indians and buffalo, and they settled in this country when it was just a wilderness." However, at the play's conclusion, Rubin confesses to his fears:

> I s'pose all this time you been thinkin' you was married to one a them movin'-pitcher fellas that jump off bridges and hold up trains and shoot Indians, and are never a scared a nothin'. Times are changin', Cora, and I dunno where they're goin' .... Men becomin' millionaires overnight, drivin' down the street in big limousines, goin' out to the country club and gettin' drunk, acting like they was lords of creation. I dunno what to think of things now, Cora. I'm a stranger in the very land I was born in.

Thus, the economic situation seems the root of the other problems in the play—Rubin's travelling job and insecurity cause his infidelities; his enforced absence from home increases Sonny's dependence on Cora, and Reenie's lack of confidence with men. The money shortage prevents Cora taking the children to Oklahoma City, as does her inadequate job training. The play makes the general inadequacy of the society more crucial than the psychology of the characters. Ironically, though Sammy Goldenbaum, the unloved son of a film actress, commits suicide, surely a sign that stars may be unworthy of the adulation and intense interests of Sonny, and even Lottie, the play ends as Sonny and Reenie leave for the movies, presumably to worship the players as well as the fantasies they enact.

A Loss of Roses, Inge's first major failure, another study of a strong mother-son relationship, seems, despite this psychological core, to link with the problem plays of the 1930's (Odets's *Paradise Lost*, for example), which stress the economic and social origins of democratic inadequacies. Kenny Baird's attachment to his mother, Helen, is more serious than Sonny's, since Kenny is 21, and Mr. Baird has been dead for a number of years, having drowned saving Kenny. The appearance of Lila Green, a 32-year-old friend of Helen's and Kenny's former baby-sitter, triggers Kenny's attempt to assert himself, ironically with a woman who is a substitute mother. When Kenny proves unable to marry her, Lila returns to a former lover and a downhill theatrical career that will continue her exploitation. Though the play seems uncertain who is the protagonist, in the revised version Inge published Lila dominates the final scene and delivers the curtain line, "No one's gonna porteck me," a speech linking her with Virgil in *Bus Stop* and Inge's world of loners and outsiders. Typically, the characters eke out near-subsistence livings (Helen is a nurse and Kenny a filling-station attendant) or perpetually face starvation, like Lila and her fellow performers. That these actors display no interest in the theater, no commitment to anything but sex and survival, reveals the intellectual vacuity of Inge's society.

Inge's last Broadway plays, both failures, seem partially attempts to keep up with trends toward violence and sexually explicit dialogue. *Natural Affection*, another mother-son study, focusing on Sue Barker and her 17-year-old son Donnie, home for Christmas from reform school, opens with Sue and her lover Bernie in bed and contains some racy dialogue, especially from their neighbor, Vince Brinkman (both he and his wife Claire are attracted to Bernie, a situation raising the already high temperature). Donnie's involvement with his mother expresses itself in ardent caresses, as he pleads with her to keep him at home so he can avoid returning to the school. Sue's refusal causes Donnie to explode in a fit of rage and kill a young woman who innocently wanders into the apartment from a holiday party and makes the mistake of flirting with him. Despite Inge's belief that "The terror of rejection seemed to me the cause of violence everywhere" (Preface), neither the characters nor the audience achieves any illumination into the nature of the society shaping violent behavior or the psychology of the violent. The characters remain personifications of an emotional flatness that never deserts them, even when they deliver long confessions or commit murder. *Where's Daddy?* tries, through the introduction of the homosexual father figure, Pinky, to make contemporary the familiar story of a young man's maturing and accepting responsibility as a parent. The Manhattan setting, the sympathetic portrayal of a black couple, and some peripheral banter about the state of the theater in a hip society fail to disguise the sentimentality of the material.

Despite his Hollywood activity and two late novels, Inge continued to produce new plays and rewrite old ones (a revised *Summer Brave* appeared briefly in New York in 1973). The new plays try not only to embody recent fashions in sexual frankness, but also to create characters who, unlike the trapped and inarticulate victims of the earlier works, convey political and philosophical insights. The symbolic Houseman in *A Murder*, the archetypal boardinghouse play, uses existentialist formulae to give resonance to his observations: "When we consider that the things we think are absurd are just as true as the things we don't think are absurd, then you have to believe that *everything* is absurd, or *nothing* is absurd." Predictably, the harried would-be boarder is called simply The Man, and the landlady The Landlady, to eliminate details that might detract from the significance of the actions. *The Disposal*, an attack on capital punishment, set on death row, is more successful, despite the rambling speculations and embarrassing self-doubts of the prison chaplain. What generates the chief interest is not the plight of the condemned man, Jess, who having "absurdly" murdered his pregnant wife, awaits a meaningful, but ultimately empty meeting with his long absent father. Though "Jess loses control of his bowels," as the guards carry him off, he is upstaged by Archie, another condemned man, a homosexual, whose bitchy and obscene comments, and wide-ranging quotations, convey the pervasive hysteria absent from Jess's character. Archie, an apparent fusion of Vince in *Natural Affection* and Pinky in *Where's Daddy?*, with a touch of some Genet criminals, suggests that Inge should have devoted a play to such a character. Most successful of Inge's later plays is *Midwestern Manic*, which opens, like *Natural Affection*, with a sleeping couple who will presumably appear naked in this scene and others. The play, one of a contemplated series on life in a housing development in the East, begins with a focus on George Krimm's embarrassment, when his vulgar Oklahoman sister, brother-in-law, and nephew arrive unexpectedly at his New York apartment, while George and his mistress Diane are in bed. The play seems a traditional bedroom farce, as George tries to keep Diane's presence and his lost virginity a secret from his sister, but ultimately turns into a comic allegory of eastern liberalism versus southwestern conservatism, as Diane and the brother-in-law, Harley, clash. The two are amusing caricatures, and even the inevitability of Harley's violent seduction of Diane (liberals are traditionally stimulating) reinforces the implied meaning of the rival social philosophies. These last three plays indicate that Inge might profitably have pursued his gifts as a delineator of the bizarrely comic and foregone the serious issues.

Any appraisal of Inge's work must both acknowledge and question the immense popularity and critical acclaim he shared in the 1950's with Arthur Miller and Tennessee Williams. Certainly, Inge's dialogue is undistinguished. The folksy, unstylized colloquialisms, appropriate for the characters, fail to generate much excitement or convey nuances of feeling. The many recitations from Shakespeare in the plays (Archie in *The Disposal* also quotes from Shaw, Wilde, Housman, and Millay) emphasize the inadequacies of Inge's language more than is necessary to reinforce a sense of midwestern flatness. Perhaps Inge's success stemmed from his single sets and concentrated time that produce tight, uninnovative drama, and from his technical expertise in using secondary characters to reinforce and counterpoint the protagonists' situations, as in *Bus Stop* and *Come Back, Little Sheba*. Perhaps, more important, was Inge's confronting what were, for the period, somewhat daring themes and providing happy, though occasionally wistful, endings. Inge's world contains no Willy Loman, who escaped the weaknesses of Miller's style and sociology into the realm of authentic American myth, and Inge's plays convey little of the psychological power, often obsessive, of Williams, but perhaps Inge's schoolteachers and other forlorn seekers of privacy, if not fulfillment, will remain part of the American consciousness. Inge's bleak world does offer the comfort of dramatic control, concern for the displaced, and the limited insight that "If you expect happy endings anywhere outside the movies, you're fooled" (*Summer Brave*). Thus, it is possible to accept the shallow Howard's verdict in the same play: "It's not a very lively part of the country but a person learns to like it."

—Burton Kendle

MERCER, David. British. Born in Wakefield, Yorkshire, 27 June 1928. Educated at King's College, Newcastle upon Tyne, B.A. (honours) in fine art (Durham University) 1953. Served as a laboratory technician in the Royal Navy, 1945–48. Married twice; one daughter. Laboratory technician, 1942–45; lived in Paris, 1953–54; supply teacher, 1955–59; teacher, Barrett Street Technical College, 1959–61. Recipient: Writers

Guild award, for television play, 1962, 1967, 1968; *Evening Standard* award, 1965; BAFTA award, 1966; French Film Academy César Award, for screenplay, 1977; Emmy award, for television play, 1980. *Died 8 August 1980.*

PUBLICATIONS

Plays

The Governor's Lady (broadcast 1960). Published in *Stand* (Newcastle upon Tyne), Spring 1962; revised version (produced London, 1965), London, Methuen, 1968; in *Best Short Plays of the World Theatre 1958–1967*, edited by Stanley Richards, New York, Crown, 1968.
The Buried Man (produced Manchester, 1962).
The Generations: A Trilogy of Plays (includes *Where the Difference Begins, A Climate of Fear, The Birth of a Private Man*). London, Calder, and New York, Fernhill, 1964; as *Collected TV Plays 1*, 1981.
Ride a Cock Horse (produced Nottingham and London, 1965; New York, 1979). London, Calder and Boyars, and New York, Hill and Wang, 1966.
Belcher's Luck (produced London, 1966). London, Calder and Boyars, and New York, Hill and Wang, 1967.
Three TV Comedies (includes *A Suitable Case for Treatment, For Tea on Sunday, And Did Those Feet*). London, Calder and Boyars, 1966.
In Two Minds (televised 1967; produced London, 1973). Included in *The Parachute with Two More TV Plays*, 1967.
The Parachute with Two More TV Plays: Let's Murder Vivaldi, In Two Minds. London, Calder and Boyars, 1967.
Let's Murder Vivaldi (televised 1968; produced London, 1972). Included in *The Parachute with Two More TV Plays*, 1967; in *The Best Short Plays 1974*, edited by Stanley Richards, Radnor, Pennsylvania, Chilton, 1974.
On the Eve of Publication and Other Plays (television plays; includes *The Cellar and the Almond Tree* and *Emma's Time*). London, Methuen, 1970; *On the Eve of Publication* published in *Scripts 8* (New York), June 1972.
White Poem (produced London, 1970).
Flint (produced Oxford and London, 1970; Buffalo, 1974). London, Methuen, 1970.
After Haggerty (produced London, 1970). London, Methuen, 1970.
Blood on the Table (produced London, 1971).
Duck Song (produced London and New York, 1974). London, Eyre Methuen, 1974.
The Arcata Promise (televised 1974; produced New York, 1982; London, 1983). Included in *Huggy Bear and Other Plays*, 1977.
The Bankrupt and Other Plays (includes *You and Me and Him, An Afternoon at the Festival, Find Me*). London, Eyre Methuen, 1974.
Huggy Bear and Other Plays (includes *The Arcata Promise* and *A Superstition*). London, Eyre Methuen, 1977.
Shooting the Chandelier (televised 1977). With *Cousin Vladimir*, London, Eyre Methuen, 1978.
Cousin Vladimir (produced London, 1978). With *Shooting the Chandelier*, London, Eyre Methuen, 1978.
Then and Now (produced London, 1979). With *The Monster of Karlovy Vary*, London, Eyre Methuen, 1979.
No Limits to Love (produced London, 1980). London, Eyre Methuen, 1981.
Collected TV Plays 1–2 (includes *Where the Difference Begins, A Climate of Fear, The Birth of a Private Man, A Suitable Case for Treatment, For Tea on Sunday, And Did Those Feet, The Parachute, Let's Murder Vivaldi, In Two Minds*). London, Calder, 2 vols., 1981.

Screenplays: *90 Degrees in the Shade* (English dialogue), 1965; *Morgan! A Suitable Case for Treatment*, 1966; *Family Life*, 1972; *A Doll's House*, with Michael Meyer, 1973; *Providence*, 1978.

Radio Plays: *The Governor's Lady*, 1960; *Folie à Deux*, 1974.

Television Plays: *Where the Difference Begins*, 1961; *A Climate of Fear*, 1962; *A Suitable Case for Treatment*, 1962; *The Birth of a Private Man*, 1963; *The Buried Man*, 1963; *For Tea on Sunday*, 1963; *A Way of Living*, 1963; *And Did Those Feet*, 1965; *In Two Minds*, 1967; *The Parachute*, 1968; *Let's Murder Vivaldi*, 1968; Robert Kelvin trilogy: *On the Eve of Publication*, 1968, *The Cellar and the Almond Tree*, 1970, and *Emma's Time*, 1970; *The Bankrupt*, 1972; *You and Me and Him*, 1973; *An Afternoon at the Festival*, 1973; *Barbara of the House of Grebe*, from a story by Hardy, 1973; *The Arcata Promise*, 1974; *Find Me*, 1974; *Huggy Bear*, 1976; *A Superstition*, 1977; *Shooting the Chandelier*, 1977; *The Ragazza*, 1978; *A Rod of Iron*, 1980.

Short Story

The Long Crawl Through Time, in *New Writers 3*. London, Calder and Boyars, 1965.

*

Bibliography: *The Quality of Mercer: A Bibliography of Writings by and about the Playwright David Mercer* by Francis Jarman, John Noyce, and Malcolm Page, Brighton, Smoothie, 1974.

Critical Studies: *The Second Wave* by John Russell Taylor, London, Methuen, and New York, Hill and Wang, 1971; *David Mercer: Where the Difference Begins* edited by Paul Madden, London, British Film Institute, 1981.

* * *

The closing image of David Mercer's television play *The Birth of a Private Man* shows the central character, Colin, shot on the Berlin Wall, marking the boundary between an East and West equally unacceptable. Throughout his plays Mercer constructed a gallery of characters driven to despair, suicide, and feelings of total impotence. His characters thrash around in the middle of contradictions inherent in their lives, never at home anywhere, painfully aware of their displacement, and often driven to madness as a way of coping.

The contradictions which Mercer faced were symptomatic of a whole generation of déclassé, auto-didactic intellectuals from working-class backgrounds, which released more than its fair share of major playwrights into the British theatre. Mercer appears to have felt these contradictions more keenly than most of his contemporaries, and his writing, although not strictly autobiographical, is nevertheless exceptionally close to his personal heart. To a large extent he wore his heart upon his sleeve.

Brought up in the restricting, puritanical atmosphere of a family who were, in Mercer's words, "upper-working class, highly respectable—and very ambitious for their children," and further restricted by a childhood illness which for a time kept him literally encased in a total plaster cast, Mercer became subsequently retarded in his education and in his relationships with other people. Leaving school early, he went to work at the age of 14, helping at autopsies in a pathology laboratory. Towards the end of the war, he volunteered for the Navy from an "utterly mistaken patriotism" and "as a kind of self-proof . . . that I could go in there and fight," and ended up treating sailors for VD in a ship's pathology lab.

The Navy awakened Mercer's desire for education, and he studied fine art at university after his release, accompanied by voracious reading. Alienating himself from his working-class roots by his education and surpassing his father's Labour Party politics in his political studies, Mercer became a committed Marxist at the time when the atrocities and repression of Stalin's regime were becoming clear to the world. He became a communist who never joined a party or organisation because "I couldn't see any development of communism to which I could give my allegiance." In the 1960's Mercer presented the anomaly of being the writer who most protested his Marxist beliefs and spent most of his time attacking the socialist system. At certain times during his career either one or both of these aspects of Mercer's work was unfashionable and he left himself wide open to attacks from left, right, and centre.

Mercer's personal political crisis was further complicated by factors in his personal life and relationships. ". . . I think I was already dimly Women's Lib years and years before it became a social carry-on—partly because I was one of the great guilty, and probably still am. The trouble is that however intellectually men recognise the complicatedly awful position of women in society, the more primitive male instincts and assumptions, and the whole weight of history and tradition, still urge men to relate to women in a primitive way. My personal life has been a history of wrecked and failed relationships with women . . . ."

Undergoing analysis and finding in the work of R.D. Laing some objectivisation of his suffering, Mercer came to a concept of madness as a "psychological revolution," "attempts by individuals to reclaim for sanity whole areas of human experience whose validity is rigorously denied by society." In their madness, some of Mercer's characters at least have their moment of triumph, like Morgan Delt in *A Suitable Case for Treatment*, the hero of *Flint*, and Nicholas in *For Tea on Sunday*. These are anarchic lunatics, who pervert through their non-conformism the accepted pattern of behaviour expected by a repressive society and its institutions. Mercer values these gestures highly: ". . . the only possible revolution is the individual revolution; any expression of individuality, however small, is a revolutionary gesture. Anything in fact that helps us to escape from categories . . . . Now the 'lunatic' fascinated me, I think, because he is the man who, almost by definition, escapes from categories."

Although Mercer's writing proceeds from his personal position, what prevents his work from being indulgent or "therapeutic" is his philosophical concern and the rigorous honesty with which he dramatises his explorations of the contradictions and absurdities of being caught between the ideal, the possible, and the actual. "I was looking for a synthesis between the problems of the individual in society and the problems of the society that produces the individual."

Anyone coming fresh to Mercer's work will find it difficult to assess his importance as a writer for lack of evidence. By the sort of tragic irony which ran through his plays, Mercer's pioneer work in television, which lifted the level of drama in that medium to a new level of maturity and introduced a number of important technical advances in editing, fragmentation of the narrative line, and use of fantasy, was destroyed as a result of a crass administrative decision in the BBC. His stage plays were less successful than his television work, having to rely more on the power of the word than the selective image and denied the fluidity of changes of time and place that his pioneering use of cutting and editing allowed him in television. He died tragically early in 1980 at the age of 52 when the question of the individual's conscience and the need to assert the rights of the individual against the convenience of the stage were again becoming a major theme in European thought, East and West. His late play *Cousin Vladimir* is scathing in its view of the repressions of Soviet society but sees more hope there than in the West. A new field of enquiry was opening up which Mercer was uniquely qualified to examine.

—Clive Barker

ORTON, Joe (John Kingsley Orton). British. Born in Leicester, 1 January 1933. Educated at Clark's College, Leicester, 1945–47; Royal Academy of Dramatic Art, London (Leicester Educational Committee grant), 1951–53, diploma 1953. Amateur actor, Leicester and London, 1949–51; assistant stage manager, Ipswich Repertory Company, Suffolk, 1953; worked part-time in Cadbury's chocolate factory, London, 1957–59. Served six-month prison term (for theft of and malicious damage to library books), Wormwood Scrubs Prison, London, and Eastchurch Prison, Sheerness, Kent, 1962. Recipient: *Evening Standard* award, 1967. *Died (murdered) 9 August 1967.*

PUBLICATIONS

Plays

Entertaining Mr. Sloane (produced London, 1964; New York, 1965). London, Hamish Hamilton, 1964; New York, Grove Press, 1965.

The Ruffian on the Stair (broadcast 1964). Published in *New Radio Drama*, London, BBC Publications, 1966; revised version (produced London, 1966; New York, 1968), in *Crimes of Passion*, 1967; in *The Complete Plays*, 1976.

Loot (produced Cambridge, 1965; revised version produced London, 1966; New York, 1968). London, Methuen, and New York, Grove Press, 1967.

Crimes of Passion: The Ruffian on the Stair, and The Erpingham Camp (*The Erpingham Camp* televised 1966; *Crimes of Passion* produced London, 1967; New York, 1969). London, Methuen, 1967; in *The Complete Plays*, 1976.

The Good and Faithful Servant (televised 1967; produced London, 1971). With *Funeral Games*, London, Methuen, 1970; in *The Complete Plays*, 1976.

Funeral Games (televised 1968; produced London, 1970; New York, 1973). With *The Good and Faithful Servant*, London, Methuen, 1970; in *The Complete Plays*, 1976.

What the Butler Saw (produced London, 1969; New York, 1970). London, Methuen, 1969; New York, Grove Press, 1970.

Until She Screams (sketch), in *Oh! Calcutta!* (produced London, 1970). Published in *Evergreen Review* (New York), May 1970.

The Complete Plays. London, Eyre Methuen, 1976; New York, Grove Press, 1977.

Up Against It: A Screenplay for the Beatles (produced London, 1985). London, Eyre Methuen, and New York, Grove Press, 1979.

Radio Play: *The Ruffian on the Stair*, 1964.

Television Plays: *The Erpingham Camp*, 1966; *The Good and Faithful Servant*, 1967; *Funeral Games* (*The Seven Deadly Virtues* series), 1968.

Novel

Head to Toe. London, Blond, 1971.

Other

The Orton Diaries, edited by John Lahr. London, Methuen, and New York, Harper, 1986.

*

Critical Studies: *Prick Up Your Ears: The Biography of Joe Orton* by John Lahr, London, Allen Lane, and New York, Knopf, 1978; *Joe Orton* by C.W.E. Bigsby, London, Methuen, 1982; *Joe Orton* by Maurice Charney, London, Macmillan, and New York, Grove Press, 1984.

* * *

Joe Orton made West End audiences laugh about sodomy, casual murder, nymphomania, sexual blackmail, vicarious incest, and something approaching necrophilia—all this, just a few years after the nation's jurists had deemed *Lady Chatterley's Lover* fit reading for their wives and servants. But Orton's bland outrageousness has tended to make us overlook the fact that he was actually working within very traditional forms of English comedy. Lady Wishfort in Congreve's *The Way of the World* only embodies in an ennobled form the thwarted, middle-aged sexuality in Kath in *Entertaining Mr. Sloane*—and, long before *Loot*, Ben Travers had recognized in *Plunder* that criminal self-interest was a fit subject for manipulative comedy. In between, Oscar Wilde had shown, often in more predictably inverted clichés, that the technique of the epigram lies as much in its disappointment of verbal expectation as in its own actual felicity. And, visually, the world of Joe Orton is not far from that of Donald McGill.

At the same time, it is impossible to forget that the man who wrote with such apparent brutality about being done to death was himself brutally done to death by his own longstanding homosexual partner, who then committed suicide—so far as one can understand, as a result of feeling outcast by Orton's sudden rise to fame. The fragile line that divides fantasy from reality, here so tragically breached, points to the necessity for Orton's purgative kind of art. He laughed us out of violence: those incapable of laughter had, surely, the greater capacity for violence.

Orton's first stage play, *Entertaining Mr. Sloane*, was first produced in May 1964: he was murdered in August 1967. During that brief period he had already achieved a rare combination of "serious" critical acclaim and solid commercial success. But he was, and is, overpraised. His was the assured kind of craftsmanship that matures with practice, not the instant genius that stretches with the years: thus, by normal standards the three full-length and handful of shorter pieces by which we must judge him would have represented exciting but exploratory early work. Indeed, *Entertaining Mr. Sloane* is still groping to find its form: where *Loot* and *What the Butler Saw* are unashamed farces, *Sloane* keeps a hiccuping hold on naturalism, and this occasionally raises irrelevant questions for its audiences.

Poetic justice triumphs in *Sloane*—its eponymous young biter well and truly bitten, and his attempt to manipulate poor Kath and gullible Ed for his own comfort nearly inverted, to leave him the object of their evenly apportioned sexual appetites. But poetic justice seldom has logic or probability on its side, where farce demands both—not in any pedantic sense, but in the same way that tragedy, not so far away along the generic axis, needs to be sufficient unto itself. The world of farce, as of tragedy, is one in which the circumstances and the people one instinctively keeps apart suddenly converge, and control of events is lost. Granted the coincidental conventions such a convergence assumes, if the farceur wishes to add mortality and murder to his usual themes of adultery and fraud, the loss of control is rather more likely to be tragic than comic in its implications. Orton triumphantly transcends that likelihood, and in *Loot* makes mortality (and an embarrassingly omnipresent corpse) hilariously funny—yet somehow incidental to the sense of impending catastrophe he was able to evoke with an impish integrity that was all his own.

"We must keep up appearances" is the last line of *Loot*: it typifies at once the social propriety which Orton's characters are so often concerned to assert (in the face of their every action), and his turning of linguistic cliché against itself. His characters distil their speech quite unconsciously from their media-saturated experience—using, say, the idiom of a holiday brochure to defend their moral probity, or of a civil service footnote to make an amorous advance. The resulting dissonance can be very funny: there is a danger that it may also become baffling, as the prose it parodies accretes unto itself new kinds of jargon. This may be why Orton was feeling his way in *What the Butler Saw* towards a comedy in which language and action are much more closely integrated. Socially a cut above the characters of the earlier plays, his characters here are more conscious of verbal facility in the face of the multiple disasters of the action—often using it as their only defence against those disasters. The play points the way towards a quite unique blend of comedy of manners and broad farce with a richness of invention that is more reminiscent of, say, *Bartholomew Fair* than Congreve. So it is no dismissal with faint praise to suggest that Orton left us with the finest body of apprentice work in English drama: rather, it is to mourn the lost comic masterpieces that would surely have been the products of his developing genius.

—Simon Trussler

WHITING, John (Robert). British. Born in Salisbury, Wiltshire, 15 November 1917. Educated at Taunton School, Somerset, 1930–34; Royal Academy of Dramatic Art, London, 1935–37. Served in the Royal Artillery, 1939–44: Lieutenant. Married Asthore Lloyd Mawson in 1940; two sons and two daughters. Actor in repertory, and in London, 1936–38, 1944–52; drama critic, *London Magazine*, 1961–62. Member, Arts Council Drama Panel, 1955–63. Recipient: Festival of Britain award, 1951. John Whiting Award established, 1965. *Died 16 June 1963.*

PUBLICATIONS

Plays

Paul Southman (broadcast 1946; produced London, 1965).
A Penny for a Song (produced Wimbledon and London, 1951). Included in *The Plays of John Whiting*, 1957; revised version (produced London, 1962), London, Heinemann, 1964.
Saint's Day (produced London, 1951). Included in *The Plays of John Whiting*, 1957.
Marching Song (produced Cardiff and London, 1954; New York, 1959). London, French, 1954.
Sacrifice to the Wind, adaptation of a play by André Obey (televised 1954; produced London, 1955). Published in *Plays for Radio and Television*, edited by Nigel Samuels, London, Longman, 1959.
The Gates of Summer (produced Oxford, 1956). Included in *The Collected Plays 2*, 1969.
The Plays of John Whiting (includes *Saint's Day, A Penny for a Song, Marching Song*). London, Heinemann, 1957.
Madame de ..., and Traveller Without Luggage, adaptation of plays by Jean Anouilh (produced London, 1959). London, French, 1959.
A Walk in the Desert (televised 1960). Included in *The Collected Plays 2*, 1969.
The Devils, adaptation of the book *The Devils of Loudun* by Aldous Huxley (produced London, 1961; New York, 1965). London, Heinemann, 1961; New York, Hill and Wang, 1962.
No Why (produced London, 1964). London, French, 1961.
Conditions of Agreement (as *The Conditions of Agreement*, produced Bristol, 1965; New York, 1972). Included in *The Collected Plays 1*, 1969.
The Nomads (produced London, 1965). Included in *The Collected Plays 2*, 1969.
The Collected Plays, edited by Ronald Hayman. London, Heinemann, and New York, Theatre Arts Books, 1969.
1. *Conditions of Agreement, Saint's Day, A Penny for a Song, Marching Song.*
2. *The Gates of Summer, No Why, A Walk in the Desert, The Devils, Noman, The Nomads.*
No More A-Roving (broadcast 1979; produced Richmond, Surrey, 1987). London, Heinemann, 1975.

Screenplays: *The Ship That Died of Shame*, with Michael Relph and Basil Dearden, 1955; *The Good Companions*, with T.J. Morrison and J.L. Hodgson, 1957; *The Captain's Table*, with Bryan Forbes and Nicholas Phipps, 1959; *Young Cassidy*, 1965.

Radio Plays: *Paul Southman*, 1946; *Eye Witness*, 1949; *The Stairway*, 1949; *Love's Old Sweet Song*, 1950; *No More A-Roving*, 1979.

Television Plays: *Sacrifice to the Wind*, 1954; *A Walk in the Desert*, 1960.

Other

John Whiting on Theatre. London, Alan Ross, 1966.
The Art of the Dramatist and Other Pieces, edited by Ronald Hayman. London, London Magazine Editions, 1970.

*

Manuscript Collection: British Theatre Museum, London.

Critical Studies: *John Whiting* by Ronald Hayman, London, Heinemann, 1969; *The Plays of John Whiting: An Assessment* by Simon Trussler, London, Gollancz, 1972; *The Dark Journey: John Whiting as Dramatist* by Eric Salmon, London, Barrie and Jenkins, 1979.

Theatrical Activities:
Actor: **Plays**—with New Garden Theatre Company, Bideford, Devon, 1937; Croydon Repertory Theatre, 1938; in Peterborough, 1944–45; with White Rose Players, Harrogate, Yorkshire, 1945–46; in York, 1947; with Scarborough Repertory Theatre, Yorkshire, 1950; at Phoenix Theatre, London (with John Gielgud's company), 1951.

* * *

John Whiting was and remains an enigma. Although he was consistently championed by men of the theatre rather than by armchair critics, he only once achieved the conventional success of a prolonged London run—and that with his least characteristic, final play, *The Devils*. Previously he had all but abandoned working in the live theatre in order to make the livelihood it denied him by scripting films. Yet his three early plays, together with the long *Conditions of Agreement* and *The Gates of Summer* (which never reached London), represent the most considerable body of writing from any British dramatist of the immediate post-war period, Fry, Eliot, and Rattigan notwithstanding.

Not that Whiting *did* withstand them: he was a highly allusive dramatist as well as an elusive one, and something of Eliot's metaphysical spirituality, of Fry's often downbeat whimsy, and even of Rattigan's over-structured colloquialism is there in his plays for the finding. These echoes are often disconcerting, but they only partially explain the opacity of his work. Whiting wrote public plays from the raw material of intensely private experience, and so occasionally gave images—or themes, or tones of voice—a significance disproportionate to their actual, dramatic function. Yet it is in part because of this that his plays take on something of the baffling totality and infinitely tangential quality of "real" life, in which any individual's experience is a sum that defies neat, objective encapsulation.

Hence, *Conditions of Agreement* and *Saint's Day* create closely felt, individual worlds of elliptic human relationships, and of occasionally warped causality; but those worlds are total, complex, and—the ultimate test—capable of being fully achieved by actors on a stage. They are, in these plays, childhood worlds—in the sense that *Conditions of Agreement* is "about" the adult struggling to repudiate adolescence, and *Saint's Day* "about" the second childhood of senility. Similarly, Whiting's last three plays, the one-acters *No Why* and *A Walk in the Desert*, and *The Devils*, are "about" apparently unmotivated cruelties which are, directly or allusively, childish.

A Penny for a Song is, in these terms, child*like*—a joyous, unequivocal celebration of happiness which is unique in Whiting's work, and which lacks (in its original, more satisfactory version) the dark corners of the adult world. Oddly, when Whiting tried to fill in those dark corners for the Royal Shakespeare Company's revival of the play, it appeared suddenly loose at the seams. Even *Marching Song* and *The Gates of Summer*, while far from childlike, are curiously innocent—their life-and-death debates somehow abstracted from the stuff of life and death.

Whiting felt that much of his work was about self-destruction. This is so, in the sense that he was characteristically concerned with the inward-turning of sensibility—a reversion, one might say, to the selfishness of infancy—that makes a man or woman a spiritual cripple. And this points to another paradox of his work: for he wrote, he claimed, for an elite, and he certainly always wrote *about* an elite, stressing the irrationality of the common people transformed into a threatening mob. Yet his aristocrats and his artists were invariably in the grip of decadence, and in the process of self-destruction, while his most nearly happy and fulfilled characters were refugees from the slums. He sought to elevate resignation into stoicism, yet affirmed that love was the only viable line of communication. He explored and created character through incongruous, sometimes ridiculous actions, yet made these actions so self-sufficient dramatically that they seemed, after all, to *matter*.

Thus, Whiting's best plays are most readily understood as parables, infinitely extensible rather than particular in reference, and paradigms of human behaviour rather than enquiries into its idiosyncrasies—though these may be superficially prominent. Perhaps it is because actors and directors can fully explore the multiple possibilities during the rehearsal process, and choose the line which their own interpretation will take, that they have been so much more responsive to Whiting's work than front-of-house critics, always in search of a particular, literal-minded explanation.

Similarly, those familiar with the whole of Whiting's work will find individual plays more rewarding for their awareness of his recurrent motifs and preoccupations. Saints and nomads, cripples and clowns, childishness and self-destruction: when these continuing concerns are seen within the total context of Whiting's work, their significance, or apparent lack of it, is less baffling for the knowledge that they are a matter of personal vocabulary—of Whiting's way of seeing the world—rather than precise points of reference within a particular play. It is no more possible to take in at a first sitting a play by Whiting than *Hamlet*. This does not make Whiting a bad or, intrinsically, a difficult dramatist: it means that he demands and repays our full and continuing attention.

—Simon Trussler

TITLE INDEX

The following list includes the titles of all stage, screen, radio, and television plays cited in the main entries, the supplements, and the appendix. The name in parenthesis is meant to direct the reader to the appropriate entry where fuller information is given. The date is that of first production or publication. These abbreviations are used:

scr	screenplay
radio	radio play
tv	television play
suppl 1	Screenwriters supplement
suppl 2	Radio Writers supplement
suppl 3	Television Writers supplement
suppl 4	Musical Librettists supplement
suppl 5	Theatre Groups supplement

A (Fratti), 1959
A la Recherche du Temps Perdu (Pinter), 1977
A-A-America (E. Bond), 1976
Abba Dabba Honeymoon (Troop suppl 2), 1982
Abelard and Heloise (Millar), 1970
Abel's Sister (Wertenbaker), 1984
Abide with Me (Keeffe), 1976
Abide with Me (tv J. Mitchell), 1976
Abigail's Party (Leigh), 1977
Abingdon Square (Fornés), 1984
Able's Will (tv Hampton), 1977
Abominable Snowman (Kneale suppl 3), 1957
Abortive (radio Churchill), 1971
About Heaven and Earth (Ward), 1983
About Time (Hailey), 1982
Above and Beyond (Frank & Panama suppl 1), 1953
Abracadabra (Moore), 1979
Abroad (Weller), 1981
Absence of Emily (tv Cannan), 1982
Absent Friends (Ayckbourn), 1974
Absolute Beginners (tv Griffiths), 1974
Absolute Hell! (Ackland), 1987
Absolute Power over Movie Stars (R. Patrick), 1968
Absolution (scr A. Shaffer), 1981
Abstract Beast (Yates suppl 2), 1969
Absurd Person Singular (Ayckbourn), 1972
Abugida Transform (Tsegaye), 1976
AC/DC (H. Williams), 1970
Academic Murders (Koch), 1966
Academy (Fratti), 1963
Acapulco (Berkoff), 1986
Accademia (Fratti), 1964
Access to the Children (tv Trevor), 1973
Accident (scr Pinter), 1967
Accidental Death of an Anarchist (Nelson), 1984
Accidental Poke (Romeril), 1977
According to the Book (Campton), 1979
Ace in the Hole (Wilder suppl 1), 1951
Aces High (scr Barker), 1976
Aces Wild (Hendry), 1972
Aces Wild (scr Hendry), 1974
Achilles Heel (tv B. Clark), 1973
Acid (Edgar), 1971
Acrobats (Horovitz), 1968
Acrobats (scr Horovitz), 1972
Across from the Garden of Allah (Wood), 1986
Across the Border (Holles suppl 3), 1964
Across the River and into the Jungle (Kopit), 1958
Across the Water (tv Rudkin), 1983
Act (Ebb suppl 4, Furth), 1977
Act of Betrayal (tv Whitemore), 1971
Act of Hypocrisy (Weldon suppl 2), 1977
Act of Rape (Weldon suppl 2), 1977
Act Without Words (Beckett), 1958
Act Without Words II (Beckett), 1959
Acte (Durrell), 1961
Acte sans paroles (Beckett), 1957
Action (R. Patrick), 1966
Action (Shepard), 1974
Action for Slander (Dalrymple suppl 1), 1937
Action Replay (Weldon suppl 2), 1978
Actor (tv Lawrence, Lee), 1978
Actor and the Alibi (tv Leonard), 1974
Actor and the Invader (R. Patrick), 1969
Actors and Actresses (Simon), 1983
Actors' Delicatessen (Mednick), 1984
Actor's Nightmare (Durang), 1981
Actos (Valdez), 1971
Actress and the Bishop (Parker), 1976
Acts of Love (Yankowitz), 1973
Ad Hoc Committee (D. Wilson), 1978
Adam (Carter), 1966
Adam Adamant (tv Frisby), 1966
Adam and Eve and Pinch Me (Laffan), 1974
Adam Smith (tv Griffiths, as Rae), 1972
Adams County, Illinois (Mac Low), 1963
Adam's Game (tv Hastings), 1964
Adam's Rib (scr Kanin), 1949
Adaptation (May suppl 1), 1969
Adelaise (radio Forsyth), 1951
Adella (Reckord), 1954
Adjusting the Idle (Antenna suppl 5), 1984
Adrian (Birimisa), 1974
Adrift (Mowat), 1970
Advances (Terry), 1980
Adventures of a Black Girl (Howarth), 1980
Adventures of Don Quixote (tv Whitemore), 1973
Adventures of Frank (tv J. McGrath), 1979
Adventures of Gervase Beckett (Terson), 1969
Adventures of Jasper Ridley (N. Williams), 1982
Adventures of Marco Polo (Simon), 1959
Adventures of Robin Hood (Lardner suppl 1)

Precious Bane (radio Wandor), 1981
Precious Sons (Furth), 1986
Precious Woman (Nowra), 1980
Precisely (Pinter), 1983
Preggin and Liss (R. Patrick), 1968
Prehistoric Visions for Revolting Hags (At the Foot of the Mountain suppl 5), 1979
Prejudice (Halliwell), 1978
Prelude to Death in Venice (Breuer), 1980
Prelude to Fame (scr Boland), 1950
Prelude to Fury (Dyer), 1959
Preparations (Red Ladder suppl 5), 1982
Preparing (Simons), 1973
Presbyterian Wooing (Gallacher), 1976
Presence of the Enemy (tv Mosel), 1958
Present Tense (Gilroy), 1972
Presenting Arnold Bliss (R. Patrick), 1969
Preservation of George Riley (tv Stoppard), 1964
President's Lady (scr J. Patrick), 1953
Pressures of Life (Jones suppl 3), 1977
Pretty Boy (Mabou Mines suppl 5), 1984
Pretty Boy (Poliakoff), 1972
Pretty English Girls (tv Hopkins), 1964
Pretty Penny (Chodorov suppl 4), 1949
Pretty People (D. Wilson), 1961
Pretty Poison (Semple suppl 1), 1968
Pretty Polly (scr W. Hall, Waterhouse), 1967
Pretty Polly (Roadside suppl 5), 1985
Pretty Ugly (Women's Theatre Group suppl 5), 1977
Previous Tenant (radio Gallacher), 1986
Prez (Plater), 1985
Price (A. Miller), 1968
Price (tv Ransley), 1985
Price of Gold (Fletcher suppl 2), 1987
Price of Mercy (Walcott), 1951(?)
Prick Up Your Ears (scr Bennett), 1987
Pride (van Itallie), 1985
Pride and Prejudice (Pownall), 1983
Pride and Prejudice (Weldon suppl 2), 1980
Pride and the Passion (Anhalt suppl 1), 1957
Pride of Our Alley (tv Plater), 1983
Pride of the Yankees (Swerling suppl 1), 1942
Priest of Love (scr Plater), 1982
Primary English Class (Horovitz), 1975
Prime of Miss Jean Brodie (J. Allen suppl 1), 1966
Primitive World (Baraka), 1984
Primrose Path (radio Barnes), 1984
Prince Erie (Mayer suppl 4), 1967
Prince of Africa (radio Phillips), 1987
Prince of Darkness (Mortimer), 1976
Prince of Homburg (Nowra), 1982
Prince of Naples (G. Walker), 1971
Prince of Peasantmania (Gagliano), 1968
Prince of the City (J. Allen suppl 1), 1981
Princess (tv Simon Gray), 1970
Principia Scriptoriae (Nelson), 1986
Priority Projects (Soyinka), 1982
Prison Game (tv Yankowitz), 1976
Prisoner (Boland), 1954
Prisoner (scr Boland), 1955
Prisoner (Haworth suppl 2), 1969
Prisoner and Escort (tv Wood), 1961
Prisoner of Second Avenue (Simon), 1971
Prisoner of Second Avenue (scr Simon), 1975
Prisoners of Mother England (R. Hall), 1979
Prisoners of the War (J. McGrath), 1972
Prisoners of the War (Terson), 1971
Pritan (tv Rudkin), 1975
Private Angelo (scr Ustinov), 1949
Private Club (Herbert), 1962
Private Dreams and Public Nightmares (Bradnum suppl 2), 1957
Private Ear (P. Shaffer), 1962
Private Eye of Hiram Bodoni (Gagliano), 1978
Private Function (scr Bennett), 1984
Private Life of Sherlock Holmes (Diamond suppl 1, Wilder suppl 1), 1970
Private Line (radio Cooper appendix), 1951
Private Man (radio G. Walker), 1973
Private Parts (Barker), 1972
Private Patient (radio Cooper appendix), 1970
Private Place (tv Campton), 1968
Private Places (scr Hendry), 1976
Private Potter (tv Harwood), 1961
Private Potter (scr Harwood), 1962
Private View (Everett suppl 2), 1966
Private View (Graeae suppl 5), 1987
Private View (T. McGrath), 1987
Privates on Parade (Nichols), 1977
Privates on Parade (scr Nichols), 1983
Privilege (scr Speight), 1967
Prix Future '79 (Adrian suppl 2), 1979
Prize (Lehman suppl 1), 1963
Prize of Gold (Buckner suppl 1), 1955
Prize Winner (tv Slade), 1957
Prizewinner (Adrian suppl 2), 1960
Pro (Pownall), 1975
Probation (tv Leigh), 1982
Problem (Gurney), 1968
Process of Elimination (Halliwell), 1975
Prodigal (Richardson), 1960
Prodigal Daughter (Turner), 1973
Prodigal Father (radio P. Shaffer), 1957
Prodigal Grandfather (Churchill suppl 3), 1984
Producer, The Director (radio Cook), 1976
Productivity Play (Red Ladder suppl 5)
Professional Foul (tv Stoppard), 1977
Professionals (scr Barnes), 1960
Professionals (Brooks suppl 1), 1966
Pro-Game (Terry), 1973
Program Prologue Now (R. Wilson), 1971
Progress (Lucie), 1984
Progress to an Exile (radio Gallacher), 1970
Progress to the Park (radio Owen), 1958
Progs (Halliwell), 1975
Project (Gems), 1976
Prologue (Simons), 1975
"Prologue" to A Letter for Queen Victoria (R. Wilson), 1974
"Prologue" to the Fourth Act of Deafman Glance (R. Wilson), 1978
Promenade (Fornés), 1965
Promenade (tv Nichols), 1959
Prometheus (Living Theatre suppl 5), 1978
Prometheus (tv Turner), 1975
Promise at Dawn (Dassin suppl 1), 1970
Promises, Promises (Simon), 1968
Promontory Point Revisited (tv Kopit), 1969
Proofing Session (tv Whitehead), 1977
Proposal (Sutherland)
Prospect of Whitby (Scriven suppl 2), 1968
Prostitutes (Avon Touring Theatre suppl 5), 1976
Protest (Adrian suppl 2), 1960

Vandal Rule OK? (tv Spencer), 1977
Vandaleur's Folly (Arden), 1978
Vandy Case (tv Owen), 1975
Vanishing Army (Holles suppl 3), 1978
Vanishing Pictures (Mabou Mines suppl 5), 1980
Vanity (Crane), 1980
Vanity Fair (radio Anderson)
Vanity Fair (Cheek by Jowl suppl 5), 1983
Variable Lengths (Livings), 1967
Variable Lengths and Longer (Livings), 1969
Varieties of Love (radio Bowen), 1968
Variety Inc. Show (tv Antrobus), 1957
Variety Night (Dunn, Gems), 1982
Variety of Death-Defying Acts (Crimp suppl 2), 1985
Various Ends of Mrs. F's Friends (Fletcher suppl 2), 1981
VD Blues (tv Feiffer, Horovitz), 1972
VE Night (Terson), 1979
Vedova Bianca (Fratti), 1963
Vegetating (Jones suppl 3), 1979
Velvet Edge (McClure), 1982(?)
Velvet Glove (Rosenthal suppl 3), 1977
Vendidos (Valdez), 1967
Vengeance of the Gang (Gow), 1933
Vengeance Valley (Ravetch suppl 1), 1951
Venus and Adonis (Inge appendix), 1975
Venus and Superkid (Crane), 1975
Venus Ascendant (tv Mosel), 1960
Venus at the Seaside (Phillips suppl 2), 1977
Venus Observed (Fry), 1950
Venus Rising (Weldon suppl 2), 1968
Venus Smiles (radio Wandor), 1985
Verdict (scr Mamet), 1982
Verdurous Sanguinaria (Mac Low), 1961
Vergil Dying (Josipovici suppl 2), 1979
Vérité (Schuman suppl 3), 1973
Vermin (tv Wymark), 1974
Vermont Sketches (Mamet), 1984
Veronica (tv Murphy), 1963
Veronica (J. White), 1965
Vertical Mobility (Foreman), 1974
Very Close Family (tv Slade), 1958
Very Close Family (Slade), 1963
Very Important Business (T. McGrath), 1981
Very Last Lover of the River Cane (McLure), 1985
Very Like a Whale (tv Osborne), 1971
Very Nuclear Family (Phillips suppl 2), 1980
Very Tasty (H. Williams), 1975
Vetchley 900 (Russell suppl 2), 1977
Veterans (Wood), 1972
Vet's Daughter (radio Gee), 1976
Vibrations (Eveling), 1969
Vicar of Wakefield (Murphy), 1974
Vice Versa (scr Ustinov), 1948
Vicious Circle (Chapman suppl 3), 1981
Vicki Madison Clocks Out (Buzo), 1976
Victim (Fratti), 1968
Víctima (El Teatro de la Esperanza suppl 5), 1977
Victims (Conn), 1970
Victims (Finch suppl 3), 1968
Victims (tv McCabe), 1976
Victims (Musaphia), 1973
Victims of Amnesia (Ferlinghetti), 1963
Victims of Apartheid (Clarke suppl 3), 1978
Victor (radio Campton)
Victoria Fellows (Carter), 1978
Victoria Station (Pinter), 1982
Victorian Scandals (Hopcraft suppl 3), 1976
Victory (Barker), 1983
Victory (Cross), 1970
Victory on Mrs. Dandywine's Island (L. Wilson), 1973
Videostars (Schuman suppl 3), 1983
Vienna (tv Frayn), 1977
Vienna Notes (Nelson), 1978
Viet Rock (Terry), 1966
Vietnam campesino (Valdez), 1970
Vietnamese Wedding (Fornés), 1967
Vietnamization of New Jersey (Durang), 1977
View by Appointment (Phillips suppl 2), 1968
View from Here (Campton), 1982
View from Pompey's Head (Dunne suppl 1), 1955
View from Sorrento (Koutoukas), 1967
View from the Bridge (A. Miller), 1955
View from the Brink (Campton), 1960
View from the Mountain (Fletcher suppl 2), 1975
View from the Mountain (Haworth suppl 2), 1987
View from the Obelisk (tv Leonard), 1964
View of Kabul (Davis suppl 2), 1982
Viewing (Pownall), 1987
Vigilantes (Dhondy suppl 3), 1985
Vikings (Wasserman suppl 4), 1958
Vilayat (Tara Arts suppl 5), 1981
Vile Bodies (scr Wood), 1981
Vi'lets Sweet Vi'lets (Scriven suppl 2), 1950
Villa Maroc (tv W. Hall), 1972
Villa Rides (Towne suppl 1), 1968
Village (Fuller), 1968
Villains (tv Bowen, Dewhurst, Finch suppl 3)
Villon (Forsyth), 1981
Vince Lays the Carpet, and Fred Erects the Trent (Terson), 1975
Vinegar Tom (Churchill), 1976
Vingt-cinquième Heure (scr Mankowitz), 1967
Vint (Mamet), 1985
Vintage 60 (Ebb suppl 4), 1960
Vinyl (scr Tavel), 1965
Vinyl (Tavel), 1967
Vinyl Visits an FM Station (Tavel), 1970
Violent Moment (scr Barnes), 1959
Violenze (Fratti), 1972
Viols (Fratti), 1983
Virgen del Tepeyac (Valdez), 1971
Virgin and the Gypsy (scr Plater), 1970
Virgin Island (Lardner as Rush suppl 1), 1958
Virgin of the Secret Service (tv Willis), 1968
Virgin Soldiers (scr Hopkins, J. McGrath), 1969
Virginia City (Buckner suppl 1, Koch suppl 1), 1940
Virginia Was a Dog (radio Musaphia), 1963
Virginian (Hackett suppl 1), 1946
Virginian (Mankiewicz suppl 1), 1929
Virgins (tv Leonard), 1972
Visions (tv Jenkin, S. Miller, Norman, Yankowitz)
Visions (Nowra), 1978
Visions of Kerouac (Duberman), 1976
Visit (Fornés), 1981
Visit from Miss Prothero (tv Bennett), 1978
Visit to a Small Planet (tv Vidal), 1955
Visiting Fireman (Martin suppl 3), 1976
Visiting House (Molloy), 1946
Visitor (Ableman), 1974
Visitor from Chicago (Simon), 1976
Visitor from Forest Hills (Simon), 1968

ADVISERS AND CONTRIBUTORS

ADAMS, Elizabeth. Member of the Department of English, State University of New York, Albany. Author of fiction and reviews in *Massachusetts Review*, *Theater*, and other journals. **Essay:** Mark Medoff.

ANDERSON, Frances Rademacher. Free-lance writer, Sacramento, California. **Essays:** Heathcote Williams; Susan Yankowitz.

AUSTIN, Addell. Assistant Professor of Theater, State University of New York, Oneonta. **Essays:** Loften Mitchell; Joseph A. Walker.

BALLET, Arthur H. Professor Emeritus of Theatre, University of Minnesota, Minneapolis. Formerly director, Office for Advanced Drama Research, dramaturg, Guthrie Theatre, Minneapolis, and consultant and program director, National Endowment for the Arts, Washington, D.C. Editor of *Playwrights for Tomorrow* series, 13 vols. **Essays:** Lee Kalcheim; Barrie Stavis.

BARKER, Clive. Senior Lecturer in Theatre Studies, University of Warwick, Coventry; joint editor of *New Theatre Quarterly*, Cambridge. Author of *Theatre Games*, 1977. **Essays:** David Mercer (appendix); Arnold Wesker.

BARLOW, Judith E. Associate Professor of English, State University of New York, Albany; associate editor of *Theatre Survey*. Author of *Final Acts: The Creation of Three Late O'Neill Plays*, 1985. Editor of *Plays by American Women 1900–1930*, 1985. **Essay:** Tina Howe.

BARNETT, Gene A. Professor of English, Fairleigh Dickinson University, Teaneck, New Jersey. Author of *Denis Johnston*, 1978, a forthcoming book on Lanford Wilson, and articles on Hawthorne, Shaw, and Robert Bolt. **Essay:** Thomas Kilroy.

BEAMS, David W. Free-lance writer. Author of articles on Lotte Lenya and Brechtian theatre, Hochhuth, James Huneker, and matinee idols, in *Theatre Arts*, *Criticism*, and other journals. **Essay:** Mart Crowley.

BENEDIKT, Michael. Author of several books of poetry—the most recent being *Night Cries*, 1976, and *The Badminton at Great Barrington*, 1980—and three plays. Editor of anthologies of French, German, American, and Spanish plays, and anthologies of poetry. Has taught at several American universities.

BENNATHAN, Joss. Free-lance writer, drama teacher, and actor. **Essays:** Harry Kondoleon; Doug Lucie; Megan Terry.

BENSON, Eugene. Professor of English, University of Guelph, Ontario; editor of *Canadian Drama/L'Art dramatique canadien*. Author of *J.M. Synge*, 1983, and numerous articles and reviews. Editor of an anthology of Canadian plays and co-editor of *The Oxford Companion to Canadian Theatre* (forthcoming). **Essay:** James Reaney.

BENTLEY, Eric. See his own entry.

BERKOWITZ, Gerald M. Professor of English, Northern Illinois University, De Kalb. Author of *David Garrick: A Reference Guide*, 1980, *Sir John Vanbrugh and the End of Restoration Comedy*, 1981, and *New Broadways: Theatre Across America 1950–1980*, 1982. Editor of *The Plays of David Garrick*, 1981. **Essays:** Tom Kempinski; Anthony Shaffer.

BERSON, Misha. Free-lance writer, San Francisco; staff member, National Endowment for the Arts. Theatre critic, *San Francisco Bay Guardian*, and executive director, Bay Area Theatre Communications Center. **Essay:** Theatre Groups in the United States.

BERTIN, Michael. Free-lance writer; Washington correspondent for *Plays International*, London. Author of a forthcoming book on Eric Bentley and articles in *Times Literary Supplement*, *Theater*, and *Shakespeare Quarterly*. Editor of *The Play and Its Critic: Essays for Eric Bentley*, 1986. **Essay:** Eric Bentley.

BIGSBY, C.W.E. Professor of American Studies, University of East Anglia, Norwich. Author of *Confrontation and Commitment: A Study of Contemporary American Drama*, 1967, *Edward Albee*, 1969, *Tom Stoppard*, 1976 (revised 1979), *The Second Black Renaissance*, 1980, *Contemporary English Drama*, 1981, *Joe Orton*, 1982, *A Critical Introduction to Twentieth-Century American Drama*, 3 vols., 1982–85, *David Mamet*, 1985, and a television play, *The After Dinner Game* (with Malcolm Bradbury), 1975. Editor of *Three Negro Plays*, 1969, *The Black American Writer*, 1970, *Dada and Surrealism*, 1972, *Superculture*, 1974, *Edward Albee: A Collection of Critical Essays*, 1976, *Approaches to Popular Culture*, 1976, *The Radical Imagination and the Liberal Tradition* (with Heide Ziegler), 1982, *Cultural Change in the United States since World War II*, 1986, and *The Plays of Susan Glaspell*, 1987. **Essays:** Robert Anderson; Henry Livings.

BILLINGTON, Michael. Drama critic, the *Guardian*, London; contributor to numerous radio and television arts programs. Author of *The Modern Actor*, 1972, *How Tickled I Am*, 1977, *The Guinness Book of Theatre Facts and Feats*, 1982, *Alan Ayckbourn*, 1983, and *Stoppard the Playwright*, 1987. **Essays:** Denis Cannan; Nigel Dennis.

BLACK, Sebastian. Senior Lecturer in English, University of Auckland; theatre critic, *New Zealand Listener* and *Act* magazine. Author of articles on British and New Zealand drama. **Essays:** Renée; Mervyn Thompson.

BLAU, Herbert. Distinguished Professor of English, University of Wisconsin, Milwaukee; formerly artistic director of Kraken, co-founding director of the Actors Workshop, San Francisco, and co-director of the Repertory Theater of Lincoln Center, New York. Director of the American premieres of *Mother Courage*, *Serjeant Musgrave's Dance*, and *The Condemned of Altona*. Author of *The Impossible Theater*, 1964, *Take Up the Bodies: Theater at the Vanishing Point*, 1982, *Blooded Thought*, 1982, *Telegraph Hill* and *A Gift of Fury* (plays), and texts for Kraken.

BODE, Walter. Editor, Grove Press, New York. Editor of *Audition Pieces: Monologues for Student Actors*. **Essays:** Thomas Babe; Richard Foreman; Michael McClure; Leonard Melfi; Arthur Sainer; Lanford Wilson.

BOWEN, John. See his own entry. **Essays:** John Hale; David Lan; Stephen Lowe.

BRADISH, Gaynor F. Adjunct Associate Professor, Union College, Schenectady, New York. Author of the introduction to Arthur Kopit's *Oh Dad, Poor Dad . . .*, 1960. Director of *Asylum* by Kopit, New York, 1963, and of many plays for drama workshops and university groups. **Essays:** Edward

Albee; Michael Cristofer; Jack Gelber; Albert Innaurato; Terrence McNally; Miguel Piñero; Jack Richardson; Steve Tesich; Robert M. Wilson.

BRISBANE, Katharine. Founding Managing Editor of Currency Press Pty. Ltd., Sydney. Author of introductions to works by Alexander Buzo, Peter Kenna, Jim McNeil, Katharine Susannah Prichard, John Romeril, Patrick White, and David Williamson, the drama section of *The Literature of Australia*, 1976, a chapter in Allardyce Nicoll's revised version of *World Drama*, 1976, and articles in *Contemporary Australian Drama*, 1981. **Essays:** Janis Balodis; Alexander Buzo; Jack Davis; Dorothy Hewett; Peter Kenna.

BRISSENDEN, Constance. Free-lance writer and editor. Formerly, dramaturge, Playwrights Canada, editor of *Toronto Theatre Review*, and managing editor, EXPO 86, Vancouver. **Essays:** Carol Bolt (with Sandra Souchotte); Michael Cook.

BROWN, John Russell. Professor of Theatre, and artistic director of Project Theatre, University of Michigan, Ann Arbor; associate director, National Theatre, London. Has directed many plays. Author of *Shakespeare's Plays in Performance*, 1966, *Effective Theatre*, 1969, *Theatre Language*, 1972, *Free Shakespeare*, 1974, *Discovering Shakespeare*, 1981, *Shakespeare and His Theatre*, 1982, and *A Short Guide to Modern British Drama*, 1982. Editor of plays by Shakespeare and other dramatists, several anthologies of criticism, and *Modern British Dramatists*, 1984. **Essays:** Shelagh Delaney; David Selbourne.

BRUCHAC, Joseph. Editor of *Greenfield Review*, Greenfield Center, New York. Author of 12 collections of poetry (the most recent being *Near the Mountains*, 1986), several novels, and four collections of retellings of Native American stories. Editor of numerous anthologies including *Breaking Silence: Asian American Poetry*, 1984, and of *Survival This Way: Interviews with American Indian Poets*, 1987. **Essays:** R. Sarif Easmon; Obi B. Egbuna; James Ene Henshaw; Lewis Nkosi.

BULL, John. Lecturer in English Literature and Drama, Sheffield University. Author of *New British Political Dramatists*, 1984, and *Stage Right: The Recovery of the Mainstream* (forthcoming). Co-editor of *The Penguin Book of English Pastoral Verse*, 1974. **Essays:** Peter Barnes; John Godber; John McGrath; Julian Mitchell; Stephen Poliakoff; Hugh Whitemore.

BURIAN, Jarka M. Professor of Theatre, State University of New York, Albany. Has been active as actor, producer, and director. Author of *The Scenography of Josef Svoboda*, 1971, and *Svoboda: Wagner: Josef Svoboda's Scenography for Richard Wagner's Operas*, 1983. **Essay:** Tad Mosel.

CARLSON, Susan. Associate Professor of English, Iowa State University, Ames. Author of *Women of Grace: Henry James and the Comedy of Manners*, 1985, and articles in *Modern Drama*, *Midwest Quarterly*, *Themes in Drama*, *New Theatre Quarterly*, and other journals. **Essay:** Sue Townsend.

CARRAGHER, Bernard. Free-lance writer. **Essays:** Lonnie Carter; Charles Dizenzo.

CHAILLET, Ned. Editor, Radio 3 Plays, BBC, London. **Essays:** Steven Berkoff; Richard Crane; Athol Fugard; Barrie Keeffe; Hugh Leonard; Tom McGrath; Caryl Phillips; Wallace Shawn; Michael Weller; Timberlake Wertenbaker.

CHAMBERS, D.D.C. Associate Professor of English, Trinity College, Toronto. **Essays:** Jack Gray; John Herbert.

CHRISTIANSEN, Richard. Entertainment editor, Chicago *Tribune*. **Essays:** David Mamet; August Wilson.

CLURMAN, Harold. Critic and lecturer. Author of *The Fervent Years: The Story of the Group Theatre*, 1945, *Lies Like Truth: Theatre Essays and Reviews*, 1958, *All People Are Famous: Instead of an Autobiography*, 1974, *The Divine Pastime: Theatre Essays*, 1974, and *Ibsen*, 1977. Producer and director of many plays, starting in the 1920's. Died 1980.

COCO, William. Contributing editor of *Performing Arts Journal*, and member of the drama faculty, Columbia University, New York; dramaturg for Joseph Chaikin and the Living Theatre. Author of articles in *Theatre Journal*, *Performing Arts Journal*, *Drama Review*, and *Performance*. Currently editing the papers of Joseph Chaikin. **Essays:** Lee Breuer; Jean-Claude van Itallie.

COHN, Ruby. Professor of Comparative Drama, University of California, Davis; co-editor of *Modern Drama*, *Theatre Journal*, and *Cambridge Guide to World Drama*. Author of *Samuel Beckett: The Comic Gamut*, 1962, *Currents in Contemporary Drama*, 1969, *Edward Albee*, 1969, *Dialogue in American Drama*, 1971, *Back to Beckett*, 1971, *Modern Shakespeare Offshoots*, 1976, *Just Play: Beckett's Theatre*, 1980, *New American Dramatists 1960–1980*, 1982, and *From Desire to Godot*, 1987. **Essays:** Samuel Beckett; Edward Bond; Rick Cluchey; Lawrence Ferlinghetti; Christopher Hampton; Joan Holden; James Schevill; Sam Shepard.

COLOMBO, John Robert. Free-lance writer. Author of many books of poetry (*Selected Poems*, 1982), and several books about Canada. Editor of collections of Canadian writing and of anthologies; translator of works by Robert Zend, Andrei Germanov, Dora Gabe, Marin Sorescu, George Faludy, and others.

COLVIN, Clare. Free-lance writer; member of the Editorial Board, *Drama*, London. Reviewer and critic for the *Times*, *Observer*, *Sunday Times*, *Daily Telegraph*, and other newspapers and magazines. **Essays:** Nell Dunn; Hanif Kureishi.

COOK, Albert. Professor of Classics, English, and Comparative Literature, and Ford Foundation Professor, Brown University, Providence, Rhode Island. Author of several plays, a book of poetry, and many critical works, including *Enactment: Greek Tragedy*, 1971, *Shakespeare's Enactment*, 1972, *Myth and Language*, 1980, *French Tragedy*, 1981, *Changing the Signs: The Fifteenth-Century Breakthrough*, 1985, and *Thresholds: The Romantic Experience*, 1985.

COOKE, Judy. Editor of *Fiction Magazine*, London, and of the anthology *The Best of Fiction Magazine*, 1986. **Essays:** Lawrence Durrell; Wolf Mankowitz.

COPELIN, David. Adjunct Associate Professor of Dramatic Writing, New York University. Author of *Ubu Rex* (translation of *Ubu Roi* by Alfred Jarry), 1973, and articles in *Drama Review*, *Performing Arts Journal*, *West Coast Plays*, and other journals. Has been dramaturg at Mark Taper Forum, Los Angeles, Phoenix Theatre and New Dramatists, New York, and Arena Stage, Washington, D.C. **Essay:** Horton Foote.

CORRIGAN, Robert W. Dean, School of Arts and Humanities, University of Texas at Dallas. Author of *Theatre in Search* *of a Fix*, 1973, *The World of the Theatre*, 1979, and *The Making of Theatre*, 1980. Editor of *Arthur Miller: A Collection of Critical Essays*, 1969, several anthologies of plays, and volumes on comedy and tragedy. Founding editor of *Tulane Drama Review* (later *Drama Review*).

DACE, Tish. Professor of English, Southeastern Massachusetts University, North Dartmouth; theatre critic for *Plays International*, *Stages*, *Village Voice*, *Plays and Players*, *New York Times*, *New York Magazine*, *American Theatre*, *Playbill*, and other publications. Author of *LeRoi Jones (Imamu Amiri Baraka): A Checklist of Works by and about Him*, 1971, and *The Theatre Student: Modern Theatre and Drama*, 1973. **Essays:** Spalding Gray; Bernard Kops; James Saunders; Martin Sherman; Doric Wilson; Paul Zindel.

DARLINGTON, W.A. Member of the editorial staff, and chief drama critic, 1920–68, *Daily Telegraph*, London. Author of *Alf's Button*, 1919 (novel), 1924 (play); *I Do What I Like*, 1947; *The Actor and His Audience*, 1949; and *Six Thousand and One Nights*, 1960. C.B.E. 1963. Died 1979. **Essays:** Ronald Gow; Ronald Millar; Ted Willis.

DAWSON, Terence. Free-lance writer; contributor to *New Comparison* and other journals. Former lecturer in French, University of East Anglia, Norwich. **Essay:** Peter Luke.

DIAMOND, Elin. Assistant Professor of English, Rutgers University, New Brunswick, New Jersey. Author of *Pinter's Comic Play*, 1985, and articles on Pinter, Beckett, Churchill, Benmussa, and Duras in *Theatre Journal*, *Modern Drama*, and *Comparative Drama*. **Essays:** Adrienne Kennedy; Michelene Wandor.

DIMMICK, Kathleen. Assistant to the Publisher, Grove Press, New York. Author of articles in *Theater*. Theatre director in California and New York, and dramaturge, Yale Repertory Theatre, New Haven, Connecticut. **Essay:** Susan Miller.

DOUGLAS, Reid. University teacher and free-lance writer; former editor of *Contemporary Theatre*. **Essay:** Ray Mathew.

DUNN, Tony. Senior Lecturer in Cultural Studies, Portsmouth Polytechnic, Hampshire; editor of *Gambit*, London. Author of articles on Howard Barker, political plays, and reviews and features in *Gambit*, *Drama*, *New Socialist*, and *Plays and Players*. **Essays:** Howard Barker; Alan Bleasdale; Willy Russell; Ted Whitehead.

EDINBOROUGH, Arnold. President of the Council for Business and the Arts in Canada; member of the Board of Governors of the Stratford Festival, Ontario. Author of *Canada*, 1962, *Some Camel . . . Some Needle*, 1974, *The Enduring Wood*, 1978, *The Festivals of Canada*, 1981, and articles in the *Financial Post*, *Canadian Churchman*, and other periodicals. **Essay:** Mavor Moore.

ELSOM, John. Senior Lecturer, City University, London. Author of *Theatre Outside London*, 1972, *Post-War British Theatre*, 1976 (revised 1979), *The History of the National Theatre*, with Nicholas Tomalin, 1978, and *Post-War British Theatre Criticism*, 1981. **Essays:** Barry Bermange; Chris Bond; J.P. Donleavy; John Grillo; Wilson John Haire; Willis Hall and Keith Waterhouse; Alan Plater; Peter Terson; Christopher Wilkinson.

ESTRIN, Mark W. Professor of English and Director of Film Studies, Rhode Island College, Providence. Author of *Lillian Hellman: Plays, Films, Memoirs: A Reference Guide*, 1980, and essays in *Modern Drama*, *Literature/Film Quarterly*, *Journal of Narrative Technique*, and *The International Dictionary of Films and Filmmakers*. **Essays:** David Rabe; Ted Tally.

FALCONIERI, John V. Vice-President and Academic Dean, American University of Rome; editor of *Theatre Annual*; member of the Editorial Board, *International Drama*; Director, Academy of Social and Humanistic Studies. Editor of works by José Lopez-Rubio. **Essay:** Gore Vidal.

FEINGOLD, Michael. Drama critic, *Village Voice*, New York. Director: productions include plays by John Arden and Lanford Wilson. Translator of plays by Brecht, Ibsen, Molière, Prévert, Diderot, Bernhard, and others. Literary director of the Guthrie Theatre, Minneapolis, 1970–79. **Essay:** Kenneth Bernard.

FITZPATRICK, Peter. Senior Lecturer in English, Monash University, Clayton, Victoria. Author of *After "The Doll": Australian Drama since 1955*, 1979, and a number of articles on Australian drama, including the critical survey and chronology on recent theatre in Australia in *New Theatre Quarterly*, February 1986. **Essay:** Stephen Sewell.

FLEISCHER, Leonard. Senior executive staff writer, RCA, New York; member of the New York Bar. Author of articles and reviews in *Saturday Review*, *London Jewish Quarterly*, *Congress Bi-Weekly*, and other publications. **Essay:** Oliver Hailey.

FRANK, Leah D. Theatre critic, *New York Times* Long Island Supplement; theatre critic and feature writer for many newspapers and magazines, including *New York Times*, New York *Daily News*, *Elle*, *Other Stages* (founding editor), Stamford *Advocate*, Connecticut, and *New York Theater Review*. **Essays:** Harvey Fierstein; Frank D. Gilroy; Richard Nelson; Robert Patrick.

FRIEDMAN, Melvin J. Professor of Comparative Literature, University of Wisconsin, Milwaukee; advisory editor of *Journal of Popular Culture*, *Studies in the Novel*, *Renascence*, *Journal of American Culture*, *Studies in American Fiction*, *Fer de Lance*, *Contemporary Literature*, *Journal of Beckett Studies*, *International Fiction Review*, *Arete*, and *Yiddish*. Author of *Stream of Consciousness: A Study in Literary Method*, 1955. Author or editor of works about Beckett, Flannery O'Connor, Styron, Catholic novelists, and Ionesco. **Essay:** Bruce Jay Friedman.

GALE, Steven H. Professor of English, and Director of the Honors Program, Missouri Southern State College, Joplin. Author of *Butter's Going Up: A Critical Analysis of Harold Pinter's Work*, 1977, *Harold Pinter: An Annotated Bibliography*, 1978, *Readings for Today's Writers* (textbook), 1982, *S.J. Perelman: An Annotated Bibliography*, 1985, *S.J. Perelman: A Critical Study*, 1987, and articles on Hare, Pinter, Mamet, Gelber, Simon Gray, Kopit, and other writers; also author of plays, poems, and fiction. **Essay:** John Guare.

GILBERT, S.R. Professor of Drama and Coordinator, Department of English, Capilano College, North Vancouver, British Columbia. Author of the play *A Glass Darkly*, 1972, and numerous articles and reviews in *Canadian Drama*, *Canadian Theatre Review*, *Capilano Review*, and other periodicals, and in the Profiles in Canadian Literature series. **Essays:** David

Fennario; David Freeman; John Gray; Tom Hendry; Sharon Pollock.

GILMAN, Richard. Professor of Drama, Yale University, New Haven, Connecticut. Author of *The Confusion of Realms*, 1970, *Common and Uncommon Masks*, 1971, *The Making of Modern Drama*, 1975, *Decadence*, 1979, and *Faith, Sex, Mystery: A Memoir*, 1987. Former literary editor of *New Republic* and drama critic for *Commonweal* and *Newsweek*.

GORDON, Lois. Professor and Chair, Department of English and Comparative Literature, Fairleigh Dickinson University, Teaneck and Rutherford, New Jersey. Author of *Stratagems to Uncover Nakedness: The Dramas of Harold Pinter*, 1969, *Donald Barthelme*, 1981, *Robert Coover: The Universal Fictionmaking Process*, 1983, *American Chronicle: Six Decades in American Life 1920–1980*, 1987, and articles on Arthur Miller, Tennessee Williams, Samuel Beckett, T.S. Eliot, William Faulkner, Randall Jarrell, Philip Roth, Elizabeth Bishop, William Gaddis, and other writers. **Essays:** Arthur Miller; Harold Pinter.

GOTTFRIED, Martin. Free-lance writer and drama critic. Author of *A Theater Divided*, 1968, *Opening Nights*, 1970, *Broadway Musicals*, 1979, *Jed Harris: The Curse of Genius*, 1984, and *In Person: The Great Entertainers*, 1986. **Essays:** Lewis John Carlino; Arnold Weinstein; John White.

GRAHAM-WHITE, Anthony. Professor, Department of Communication and Theater, University of Illinois, Chicago. Author of *The Drama of Black Africa*, 1974, and articles in *Yale/Theatre* and *Das Englische Drama nach 1945*, 1980. Former editor of *Educational Theatre Journal* (now *Theatre Journal*). **Essays:** Ama Ata Aidoo; David Campton; John Pepper Clark; David Cregan; Len Jenkin; Ngugi wa Thiong'o; Efua Sutherland; Tsegaye Gabre-Medhin.

GRANT, Steve. Assistant editor of *Time Out*, London. Author of four plays, essays on fringe theatre in *Dreams and Deconstructions*, 1980, and articles in the *Guardian*, *Observer*, *Morning Star*, and other periodicals. **Essays:** John Byrne; David Hare; Mike Leigh; Snoo Wilson.

GRAY, Frances. Lecturer in English, Sheffield University. Author of *John Arden*, 1982, and *Noël Coward*, 1987. **Essays:** Sarah Daniels; Shirley Gee; Tony Marchant.

GUERNSEY, Otis L., Jr. Author of *Curtain Times: The New York Theater 1965–1987*, 1987. Editor of *The Best Plays of 1964–1965* through *1984–1985* (The Burns Mantle Yearbook; now co-editor with Jeffrey Sweet), *The Directory of American Theater 1894–1971*, 1971, *Playwrights, Lyricists, Composers on Theater*, 1974, and *Broadway Song and Story: Playwrights/Lyricists/Composers Discuss Their Hits*, 1986.

GUPTARA, Prabhu S. Free-lance writer, lecturer, and broadcaster. Author of two books of poetry, *Beginnings*, 1975, and *Continuations*, 1976, and articles in *Encyclopaedia Iranica*, *The Oxford Companion to English Literature*, 1985, and the *Times Literary Supplement* and other journals. **Essays:** Michael Abbensetts; John Antrobus; Michael Hastings; John Spurling; Olwen Wymark.

HAMMOND, Jonathan. Late Vice-President, National Union of Journalists; former editor, Penguin Books, London. Author of articles in *Culture and Agitation* and *Plays and Players*. Died 1983. **Essays:** John Burrows and John Harding; Stewart Conn; Roger Howard; Alun Owen; David Turner.

HAYMAN, Carole. Actress and director. Has acted at the Bristol Old Vic, the Traverse Theatre Workshop, Edinburgh, with Joint Stock Theatre Group, and in more than 20 productions at the Royal Court Theatre, London. Since 1980 has directed plays by Sue Townsend, Jane Thornton, Andrea Dunbar, and Sarah Daniels at the Royal Court, Soho Poly, and for Joint Stock. Author of *Letters from Kim* (radio play), 1986. Editor, with Dale Spender, of *How the Vote Was Won and Other Suffragette Plays*, 1985. **Essay:** Andrea Dunbar.

HAYMAN, Ronald. Free-lance writer and director. Author of *Techniques of Acting*, *The Set-Up: An Anatomy of British Theatre*, *British Theatre since 1955*, *Theatre and Anti-Theatre*, *Fassbinder, Film-maker*, studies of Beckett, Pinter, Osborne, Arden, Whiting, Robert Bolt, Wesker, Miller, Albee, Stoppard, Ionesco, Leavis, Artaud, de Sade, Nietzsche, Tolstoy, and John Gielgud, and biographies of Kafka, Brecht, and Sartre. Director of plays by Peter Handke, Martin Walser, Rainer Werner Fassbinder, and others. **Essays:** Ted Allan; Bridget Boland; David Caute; Nick Darke; Donald Howarth; Doris Lessing; David Pinner.

HIGGINS, Dick. Free-lance writer and publisher. Author of five stage plays, several radio plays, and more than 40 books, including *Jefferson's Birthday/Postface*, 1964, *Die fabelhafte Geträume von Taifun-Willi*, 1969, *Le petit cirque au fin du monde*, 1973, *A Dialectic of Centuries: Notes Towards a Theory of the New Arts*, 1978, *Selected Early Works*, 1982, and *Horizons: The Poetics and Theory of the Intermedia*, 1983. Artist: individual exhibitions in Europe and the U.S.A. since 1973. **Essay:** Jackson Mac Low.

HILL, Errol. See his own entry. **Essay:** Amiri Baraka.

HIRSCH, Foster. Professor of Film, Brooklyn College, New York. Author of books on the Actors Studio, Laurence Olivier, Williams, Albee, O'Neill, film noir, George Kelly, Elizabeth Taylor, Edward G. Robinson, Woody Allen, Joseph Losey, and forthcoming studies of American theatre in the 1920's and American musical theatre. **Essay:** George Abbott.

HOBSON, Harold. Special writer for the *Sunday Times*, London. Author of *The First Three Years of the War*, 1942, *The Devil in Woodford Wells* (novel), 1946, *Theatre*, 1948, *Theatre II*, 1950, *Verdict at Midnight*, 1952, *The Theatre Now*, 1953, *The French Theatre of Today*, 1953, *Ralph Richardson*, 1958, *The French Theatre since 1830*, 1978, *Indirect Journey* (autobiography), 1978, and *Theatre in Britain: A Personal View*, 1984. Editor of five volumes of *International Theatre Annual*. Knighted 1977. **Essay:** Charles Dyer.

HOFFMAN, William M. See his own entry. **Essays:** Michael T. Smith; David Starkweather.

HOFFMANN, Tess. Professor of English, Rhode Island College, Providence. **Essay:** Marsha Norman.

HUERTA, Jorge A. Associate Professor of Drama, University of California, San Diego. Author of *A Bibliography of Chicano and Mexican Dance, Drama, and Music*, 1971, *Chicano Theater: Themes and Forms*, 1982, and many articles. Editor of *El Teatro de la Esperanza: An Anthology of Chicano Drama*, 1973. Producer and director of several plays. **Essay:** Luis Valdez.

JENNER, C. Lee. Free-lance writer, New York. **Essays:** William M. Hoffman (with Michael T. Smith); Richard Wesley.

KAUFFMANN, Stanley. Visiting Professor of Theater, City University of New York Graduate Center; film critic, *New Republic*. Author of several books of film criticism, including *A World of Film*, 1966, *Figures of Light*, 1971, *Living Images*, 1975, *Before My Eyes*, 1980, and *Field of View*, 1986, theatre criticism—*Persons of the Drama*, 1976, and *Theater Criticisms*, 1984—and *Albums of Early Life* (memoirs), 1980.

KENDLE, Burton. Professor of English, Roosevelt University, Chicago. Author of articles on D.H. Lawrence, John Cheever, William March, Tennessee Williams, and others. **Essays:** Alan Bennett; James Leo Herlihy; William Inge (appendix); Screenwriters.

KEYSSAR, Helene. Associate Professor of Communications and Drama, University of California, San Diego. Author of *The Curtain and the Veil: Strategies in Black Drama*, 1981, *Feminist Theatre*, 1985, and articles in *Educational Theatre Journal*, *Prospects*, and other journals. Has directed and acted with the Eureka Ensemble and other groups. **Essays:** Charles Gordone; Ron Milner; Murray Schisgal.

KHAN, Naseem. Free-lance writer; member of the Editorial Board, *Drama*, London. Author of *The Arts Britain Ignores: The Arts of Ethnic Minorities in Britain*, 1976, and many articles and reviews.

KING, Bruce. Editor of Macmillan English Dramatists series, and co-editor of Macmillan Modern Dramatists series. Author of *Dryden's Major Plays*, 1966, *Marvell's Allegorical Poetry*, 1977, *New English Literatures: Cultural Nationalism in a Changing World*, 1980, and *History of Seventeenth-Century English Literature*, 1982. Editor of *Introduction to Nigerian Literature*, 1971, *Literatures of the World in English*, 1974, *A Celebration of Black and African Writing*, 1976, *West Indian Literature*, 1979, and *Modern Indian Poetry in English*, 1988. **Essays:** Francis Ebejer; Yulisa Amadu Maddy; Trevor Rhone; George F. Walker.

KITCHIN, Laurence. Former Professor of Liberal Arts, City University of New York; has taught at Bristol, Tufts, Stanford, and Simon Fraser universities. Author of *Len Hutton*, 1953, *Three on Trial*, 1959, *Mid-Century Drama*, 1960 (revised 1962), *Drama in the Sixties*, 1966, and numerous radio scripts. **Essay:** Brendan Behan (appendix).

KLAUS, H. Gustav. Part-time Reader in English, University of Osnabrück, West Germany. Author of *Caudwell im Kontext*, 1978, and *The Literature of Labour*, 1985. Editor of *Marxistische Literaturkritik in England*, 1973, *The Socialist Novel in Britain*, 1982, and *The Rise of Socialist Fiction 1880–1914*, 1987. **Essay:** Trevor Griffiths.

KOSTELANETZ, Richard. Writer and artist. Author of radio plays, several books of poetry (most recently *Arenas Fields Pitches Turfs*, 1982), collections of short stories (most recently *More Short Fictions*, 1980, and *Epiphanies*, 1983), volumes of experimental prose (*Aftertexts/Prose Pieces*, 1986), and critical works including *The Theatre of Mixed-Means*, 1968, *The End of Intelligent Writing*, 1974, *Twenties in the Sixties*, 1979, *The Old Poetries and the New*, 1981, and *The Old Fictions and the New*, 1986. Editor of many collections and anthologies of experimental writing. Visual poetry and related language art exhibited at galleries and universities since 1975. **Essays:** Robert Hivnor; Kenneth Koch.

KUHN, John G. Professor of English and Theater, and Chairman of the Division of English, Theater, and Classics, Rosemont College, Pennsylvania. **Essay:** María Irene Fornés.

LAMEDE, Jonathan. General Manager, Shared Experience theatre group, London; free-lance writer. **Essay:** Theatre Groups in Britain.

LANGE, Bernd-Peter. Professor of English, University of Braunschweig, West Germany; co-editor of *Gulliver: German-English Yearbook*. Author of *George Orwell: Nineteen Eighty-Four*, 1982, *Cultural Studies*, 1984, and *Die Utopie in der anglo-amerikanischen Literatur*, 1984. **Essay:** Steve Gooch.

LAWLEY, Paul. Lecturer in English, Rolle College, Exmouth, Devon. Author of essays and reviews in *Journal of Beckett Studies*, *Modern Drama*, *Modern Fiction Studies*, *Theatre Journal*, and *Modern Language Review*. **Essays:** Brian Clark; David Edgar; Ron Hutchinson; Terry Johnson; Bill Morrison; Stewart Parker; David Rudkin; Wole Soyinka; Nigel Williams; Nicholas Wright.

LEECH, Michael T. Free-lance writer. Author of *Italy*, 1974 (revised 1987), *Amsterdam*, 1985, and *Exploring Rural Italy*, 1988. **Essays:** Jerome Lawrence and Robert E. Lee; Dodie Smith.

LEWIS, Peter. Senior Lecturer in English, University of Durham. Author of *The Beggar's Opera* (critical study), 1976, *John le Carré*, 1984, and *Fielding's Burlesque Drama*, 1987. Editor of *The Beggar's Opera* by John Gay, 1973, *Poems '74* (anthology of Anglo-Welsh poetry), 1974, *Papers of the Radio Literature Conference 1977*, 1978, and *Radio Drama*, 1981. **Essay:** Radio Writers.

LONDRÉ, Felicia Hardison. Professor of Theatre, University of Missouri, Kansas City. Author of *Tennessee Williams*, 1980, *Tom Stoppard*, 1981, *Federico García Lorca*, 1984, articles on French and Russian theatre, and plays, including the libretto for the opera *Duse and D'Annunzio*, composed by Gerald Kemner, 1984. Associate editor of *Shakespeare Around the Globe: A Guide to Notable Postwar Revivals*, 1986; translator of *The Show-Man* by Andrée Chedid. **Essays:** William Hauptman; Tom Stoppard.

LONEY, Glenn. Professor of Theatre, City University of New York; editor of *Art Deco News*. Author or editor of many books, including *The Shakespeare Complex*, 1972, *Peter Brook's Royal Shakespeare Company Production of A Midsummer Night's Dream*, 1974, *The House of Mirth: The Play of the Novel*, 1980, *Your Future in the Performing Arts*, 1980, *Twentieth-Century Theatre* (chronology), 2 vols., 1983, *California Gold-Rush Plays*, 1983, *Musical Theatre in America*, 1984, *Unsung Genius: Jack Cole*, 1984, and articles and reviews in *Opera News*, *Dance*, *Stages*, *Theatre Crafts*, *Performing Arts Journal*, and other journals. **Essays:** William Alfred; William Mastrosimone; Neil Simon.

MARCUS, Frank. See his own entry. **Essays:** Maureen Duffy; David Mowat.

MARKHAM, E.A. Free-lance writer. Author of several books of poetry—*The Lamp*, 1978, *Pierrot*, 1979, *Love Poems*,

1979, *Games and Penalties*, 1980, *Human Rites*, 1984, *Living in Disguise*, 1986, and *Lambchops in Papua/New Guinea*, 1986—*Love, Politics, and Food*, 1982, and *Something Unusual* (stories), 1986. **Essays:** Douglas Archibald; Errol John; Barry Reckord.

MARKUS, Thomas B. Artistic Director, Theatre by the Sea, Portsmouth, New Hampshire. Author of *The Professional Actor: From Audition to Performance*, 1980, and essays on Genet and Albee. Has been a director and actor in New York and Hollywood. **Essays:** Ron Cowen; Martin Duberman.

MARRANCA, Bonnie. Publisher and editor, with Gautam Dasgupta, *Performing Arts Journal* and Performing Arts Journal Publications, New York. Author of *American Playwrights: A Critical Survey*, with Dasgupta, 2 vols., 1981, *Theatre-writings*, 1984, and numerous essays. Editor of *The Theatre of Images*, 1977, and *American Dreams: The Imagination of Sam Shepard*, 1981.

McCALLUM, John. Senior Lecturer in Drama, University of New England, Armidale, New South Wales. Author of forthcoming books on Alexander Buzo and Stephen Sewell, and many articles on recent Australian drama. **Essays:** Ray Lawler; John Romeril.

McCORMACK, Thomas J. Chairman of St. Martin's Press, New York; director of Macmillan Publishers, London. Author of the play *American Roulette*, 1969. Editor of *Afterwords*, 1969. **Essay:** Jason Miller.

McGUINNESS, Arthur E. Professor of English, University of California, Davis. Author of *Henry Home, Lord Kames*, 1970, *George Fitzmaurice*, 1975, and articles in *Eire-Ireland*, *Irish University Review*, *Themes in Drama*, *Studies in Short Fiction*, *Texas Studies in Literature and Language*, and *Studies in Scottish Literature*. **Essays:** John B. Keane; M.J. Molloy.

McNAUGHTON, Howard. Reader in English, University of Canterbury, Christchurch. Author of *Bruce Mason*, 1976, and *New Zealand Drama*, 1981. Editor of *Contemporary New Zealand Plays*, 1976, and *James K. Baxter: Collected Plays*, 1982. **Essays:** John Bowen; Barry Collins; Rosalyn Drexler; Paul Foster; Peter Gill; Clem Gorman; Roger Hall; Greg McGee.

MESERVE, Walter J. Professor of Theatre and Drama, and Director of the Institute for American Theatre Studies, Indiana University, Bloomington. Author of *An Outline History of American Drama*, 1965, *Robert Sherwood: Reluctant Moralist*, 1970, *An Emerging Entertainment: The Drama of the American People to 1828*, 1977, *American Drama* (vol. 8 of the Revels History), with others, 1977, *American Drama to 1900: A Guide to Reference Sources*, 1980, and *Heralds of Promise: The Drama of the American People During the Age of Jackson 1829–1849*, 1986. Editor of *The Complete Plays of William Dean Howells*, 1960, *Discussions of Modern American Drama*, 1966, *American Satiric Comedies*, 1969, *Modern Drama from Communist China*, 1970, *The Rise of Silas Lapham* by Howells, 1971, *Studies in Death of a Salesman*, 1972, and *Modern Literature from China*, 1974. **Essays:** George Axelrod; Herb Gardner; William Hanley; Beth Henley; Garson Kanin; Arthur Laurents; Dennis J. Reardon; Derek Walcott.

MITCHELL, Louis D. Associate Professor of English, University of Scranton, Pennsylvania. Author of songs and lyrics for *Star of the Morning*, 1971, and many articles in *Theatre Notebook*, *Eighteenth Century Studies*, *Crisis*, and other journals. **Essays:** Ossie Davis; Errol Hill.

MOE, Christian H. Professor of Theatre, Southern Illinois University, Carbondale; member of the Advisory Board, Institute of Outdoor Drama; bibliographer for the American Theatre Association. Author or co-author of *Creating Historical Drama*, 1965, an essay on D.H. Lawrence, and several plays for children. Joint editor of *The William and Mary Theatre: A Chronicle*, 1968, and *Six New Plays for Children*, 1971. **Essays:** Christopher Durang; William Gibson; Dusty Hughes; Romulus Linney; James McLure; John Ford Noonan; John Patrick; John Pielmeier; Bernard Pomerance.

MORDDEL, Anne. Free-lance writer, London. **Essay:** Bryony Lavery.

MURRAY, Christopher. Statutory Lecturer in English, University College, Dublin; member of the Executive Board, *Irish University Review*. Author of *Robert William Elliston, Manager*, 1975. Editor of *St. Stephen's Green* (an Irish Restoration comedy), 1980, and *Selected Plays of Lennox Robinson*, 1982. **Essays:** Eugene McCabe; Thomas Murphy.

NIGHTINGALE, Benedict. Free-lance writer; drama critic, *New Statesman*, London, 1969–86; Professor of English, University of Michigan, Ann Arbor, 1986–87. Author of *An Introduction to Fifty Modern British Plays*, 1982 (as *A Reader's Guide to Fifty Modern British Plays*, 1982), and *Fifth Row Center: A Critic's Year On and Off Broadway*, 1986. **Essays:** Paul Ableman; Beverley Cross; John Hopkins; David Storey; Charles Wood.

O'CONNOR, Garry. Playwright and biographer. Author of *French Theatre Today*, 1975, *The Pursuit of Perfection* (biography of Maggie Teyte), 1979, *Darlings of the Gods: One Year in the Lives of Laurence Olivier and Vivien Leigh*, 1984, *Ralph Richardson: An Actor's Life*, revised edition 1986, *The Life of Sean O'Casey*, 1987, and seven stage and radio plays, including *The Musicians*, *Semmelweis*, and *The Kingdom of Allemonde*. Editor of *Laurence Olivier: In Celebration*, 1987. **Essays:** Robert Bolt; Michael Frayn; Peter Nichols; Michael O'Neill and Jeremy Seabrook; Mike Stott.

O'CONNOR, Marion. Lecturer in English, University of Kent, Canterbury. **Essay:** Tom Gallacher.

PAGE, Malcolm. Professor of English, Simon Fraser University, Burnaby, British Columbia. Author of *John Arden*, 1984, *Richard II* (critical study), 1987, and several articles and bibliographies. Editor or co-editor of *Arden on File*, 1985, *File on Stoppard*, 1986, and *File on Shaffer*, 1987. Past President of the Association for Canadian Theatre History. **Essays:** Alan Ayckbourn; Ann Jellicoe; Mustapha Matura; John Murrell; David Pownall.

PARKER, Dorothy. Associate Professor of English, Victoria College, University of Toronto. Editor of *Modern American Drama: Williams, Miller, Albee, and Shepard*, 1986. **Essay:** David French.

POUNTNEY, Rosemary. Lecturer in English, Jesus College, Oxford. Author of a forthcoming book on Beckett, and articles and reviews in *Modern Drama*, *Journal of Beckett Studies*, *Biography*, *Irish University Review*, *Review of Contemporary Fiction*, and other journals. **Essay:** Howard Brenton.

RAYNOR, Henry. Schoolmaster and free-lance writer. Author of *Joseph Haydn*, 1962, *Wagner*, 1970, *Radio and Television*, 1970, *A Social History of Music from the Middle Ages to Beethoven*, 1972, *Mahler*, 1975, *Music and Society since 1815*, 1976, *The Orchestra*, 1978, *Mozart*, 1978, and *Music in England*, 1980. **Essays:** Terence Frisby; Graham Greene; Kevin Laffan; John Mortimer; Johnny Speight.

REILLY, John M. Professor of English, State University of New York, Albany. Author of many articles on Afro-American literature, popular crime writing and social fiction, and bibliographical essays in *Black American Writers*, 1978, and *American Literary Scholarship*. Editor of *Twentieth-Century Interpretations of Invisible Man*, 1970, *Richard Wright: The Critical Reception*, 1978, and the reference book *Twentieth-Century Crime and Mystery Writers*, 1980 (2nd edition 1985). **Essay:** Ed Bullins.

RICHARDS, Sandra L. Assistant Professor of Drama, and Director of the Committee on Black Performing Arts, Stanford University, California. Author of the introduction to *Center Stage: An Anthology of Twenty-one Black American Plays*, 1981, and articles on Amiri Baraka, the actor Bert Williams, and Nigerian playwrights in *Theatre Journal*, *Mime*, and *San Francisco Theatre*. **Essays:** Charles Fuller; Femi Osofisan; Ola Rotimi; Ntozake Shange.

RISSIK, Andrew. Free-lance writer; regular contributor of articles on theatre, film, and television to the *Independent*, *New Statesman*, *Times*, and other periodicals. Author of *Friends and Other Lovers* (television play), 1981, and several radio plays, including *Louise and the Puppet Man*, 1984, *Blue Pacific Island*, 1985, *A Man Alone* (trilogy; *Anthony* published in *Best Radio Plays of 1986*, 1987), 1986, and *King Priam*, 1987. **Essay:** Television Writers.

ROOSE-EVANS, James. Director, author, and lecturer; founder of the Hampstead Theatre Club and the Stage Two Theatre Workshop, London. Author of plays (most recently *Augustus*, *A Peepshow into Paradise*, and an adaptation of Helene Hanff's *84 Charing Cross Road*), radio documentaries, several books for children, and *Directing a Play*, 1968, *Experimental Theatre from Stanislavsky to Today*, revised 1973 and 1984, *London Theatre: From the Globe to the National*, 1977, and *Inner Journey: Outer Journey* (novel), 1987. Director of many plays, most recently works by Shakespeare, Noël Coward, George Axelrod, and Gyles Brandreth and Julian Slade. **Essays:** James Forsyth; Peter Ransley; Colin Spencer.

SADDLEMYER, Ann. Professor of English, and Director of the Graduate Centre for the Study of Drama, University of Toronto; co-editor, *Theatre History in Canada*. Author of *In Defence of Lady Gregory, Playwright*, 1966, and *Synge and Modern Comedy*, 1968. Editor of *The World of W.B. Yeats* (with Robin Skelton), 1965 (revised 1967), *The Plays of J.M. Synge*, 2 vols., 1968, *The Collected Plays of Lady Gregory*, 4 vols., 1971, *Theatre Business: The Correspondence of the First Abbey Theatre Directors*, 1982, and *The Collected Letters of J.M. Synge*, 2 vols., 1983–84. **Essay:** Margaret Hollingsworth.

SADLER, Geoff. Assistant Librarian, Local Studies, Chesterfield, Derbyshire. Author of nine western novels (as Jeff Sadler), including, most recently, *Throw of a Rope*, 1984, and *Manhunt in Chihuahua*, 1984, and the *Justus* trilogy of plantation novels (as Geoffrey Sadler), 1982. **Essays:** Dannie Abse; Ray Cooney; Adrian Mitchell.

SAINER, Arthur. See his own entry. **Essays:** Julie Bovasso; Ruth Krauss; George Tabori.

SCHECHNER, Richard. Founding director, the Performance Group, New York; Professor of Performance Studies, New York University. Author of *Public Domain*, 1968, *Environmental Theatre*, 1973, *Theatres, Spaces, and Environments* (with Jerry N. Rojo and Brooks McNamara), 1975, *Essays in Performance Theory*, 1977, *The End of Humanism*, 1982, *Performative Circumstances*, 1983, and *Between Theater and Anthropology*, 1986. Joint editor of *Free Southern Theatre*, 1969, and *Ritual, Play, and Performance*, 1976. Director for the Wooster Group.

SCHIFF, Ellen. Professor of French and Comparative Literature, North Adams State College, Massachusetts. Author of *From Stereotype to Metaphor: The Jew in Contemporary Drama*, 1982, and articles in the *New York Times*, *Massachusetts Review*, *Holocaust Studies Annual*, and *Anti-Semitism in American History*. **Essay:** Emily Mann.

SCHNEIDER, Alan. Late Professor of Drama, University of California, San Diego. Director of Broadway and off-Broadway plays by Albee, Beckett, Edward Bond, Grass, Preston Jones, Pinter, Saroyan, Ted Whitehead, Tennessee Williams, Elie Wiesel, and Lanford Wilson. Died 1984.

SHRAGGE, Elaine. Free-lance writer, San Francisco. **Essay:** Rochelle Owens.

SIDNELL, Michael. Professor of English, Trinity College, University of Toronto; actor and director. Co-author of *Druid Craft* (on Yeats), 1971, and *The Secret Rose*, 1981, and author of *Dances of Death: A History of the London Group Theatre*, 1984, and articles on Irish and theatre subjects. **Essay:** Beverley Simons.

SMITH, Christopher. Senior Lecturer, School of Modern Languages and European History, University of East Anglia, Norwich; editor of *Seventeenth-Century French Studies*. Author of *Alabaster, Bikinis and Calvados: An ABC of Toponymous Words*, 1985, a forthcoming study of Jean Anouilh, and many articles and reviews of the performing arts. Editor of works by Antoine de Montchrestien, Jean de la Taille, and Pierre Matthieu. **Essays:** Keith Dewhurst; William Douglas-Home; Dennis Potter; Anne Ridler.

SMITH, Michael T. See his own entry. **Essays:** George Birimisa; Tom Eyen; William M. Hoffman (with C. Lee Jenner); H.M. Koutoukas; Murray Mednick; Ronald Tavel.

SOGLIUZZO, A. Richard. Theatre critic, historian, and professor of drama; assistant editor, *Theatre Annual*. Author of *Luigi Pirandello, Director*, 1982, and articles on Italian theatre, Arthur Miller, and Eugene O'Neill, in *A Handbook of Modern Drama*, *A History of the Theatre*, and in periodicals. **Essays:** Mario Fratti; Frank Gagliano; Israel Horovitz.

SOUCHOTTE, Sandra. Free-lance journalist and theatre critic, Yellowknife, Northwest Territories, Canada. **Essay** (with Constance Brissenden): Carol Bolt.

SPURLING, John. See his own entry. **Essays:** Rodney Ackland; Barry England; Stanley Eveling; David Halliwell.

STERN, Carol Simpson. Professor and Chair, Department of Performance Studies, Northwestern University, Evanston,

Illinois; member of the advisory board, *Literature in Performance*. Author of articles and theatre and book reviews in *Victorian Studies* and *Literature in Performance.* **Essays:** Kenneth H. Brown; James Goldman; Simon Gray; Iris Murdoch; Peter Shaffer.

STRACHAN, Alan. Artistic director, Greenwich Theatre, London. Productions in London include *The Watched Pot* by Saki, 1970; *John Bull's Other Island*, 1971, and *Misalliance*, 1973, by Shaw; *The Old Boys* by William Trevor, 1971; *A Family and a Fortune* by Julian Mitchell, 1975; *Just Between Ourselves* by Alan Ayckbourn, 1977; devised or co-devised *Cowardy Custard*, 1972, *Cole*, 1974, *Shakespeare's People*, 1975, and *Yahoo*, 1976; at Greenwich Theatre since 1978: many new plays, including *An Audience Called Édouard* by David Pownall, *The Paranormalist* by Jonathan Gems, and *One of Us* by Robin Chapman, and revivals including *Private Lives* and *Present Laughter* by Noël Coward, and *A Streetcar Named Desire* and *The Glass Menagerie* by Tennessee Williams. **Essays:** George Furth; A.R. Gurney, Jr.; Keith Johnstone; Anthony Minghella; Bill Naughton; Bernard Slade; William Trevor; Peter Ustinov.

STYAN, J.L. Franklyn Bliss Snyder Professor of English, and Professor of Theatre, Northwestern University, Evanston, Illinois. Author of *The Elements of Drama*, 1960, *The Dark Comedy*, 1962 (revised 1968), *The Dramatic Experience*, 1965, *Shakespeare's Stagecraft*, 1967, *Chekhov in Performance*, 1971, *The Challenge of the Theatre*, 1972, *Drama, Stage and Audience*, 1975, *The Shakespeare Revolution*, 1977, *Modern Drama in Theory and Practice*, 3 vols., 1981, *Max Reinhardt*, 1982, *The State of Drama Study*, 1984, and *Restoration Comedy in Performance*, 1986. Editor of *Shakespeare in Performance: All's Well That Ends Well*, 1984. **Essay:** Christopher Fry.

SWAIN, Elizabeth. Adjunct Assistant Professor in Theatre, Barnard College, New York. Author of *David Edgar: Playwright and Politician*, 1986, an article on women in the American theatre, and theatre criticism for *Stages* and other journals. Actress in Broadway, repertory, and television productions. **Essays:** Wendy Kesselman; Wendy Wasserstein.

SYKES, Alrene. Senior Lecturer in English, University of Queensland, Brisbane. Formerly editor in the Drama Department, Australian Broadcasting Commission. Author of *Harold Pinter*, 1970, and articles on modern drama and Australian fiction. Editor of *Five Plays for Radio* and four other anthologies of Australian plays. **Essays:** Jack Hibberd; Louis Nowra; Alan Seymour; Patrick White; David Williamson.

TAUBMAN, Howard. Drama critic, 1960–66, and critic at large, 1966–75, *New York Times*. Adviser to the Exxon Corporation on its "Theatre in America" series and other arts programs. Author of *The Making of American Theatre*, 1965, and several books on music.

TAYLOR, John Russell. Art critic, the *Times*, London. Author of many books, including *Anger and After*, 1962 (revised 1969, as *The Angry Theatre*, 1962, revised 1969), *The Second Wave*, 1971, *Directors and Directions*, 1975, *Hitch: The Life and Work of Alfred Hitchcock*, 1978, and *Strangers in Paradise*, 1981, and studies of Pinter, David Storey, Peter Shaffer, Ingrid Bergman, Alec Guinness, Vivien Leigh, Orson Welles, Edward Wolfe, the television play, and various aspects of film and art. Editor of *Look Back in Anger: A Casebook*, 1968, and the film criticism of Graham Greene. **Essay:** John Osborne.

THOMSON, John. Senior Lecturer in English, Victoria University, Wellington. Author of *New Zealand Drama 1930–1980*, 1984. **Essays:** Robert Lord; Joseph Musaphia.

TREWIN, J.C. Drama critic, *Illustrated London News*, *The Lady*, and the Birmingham *Post*. Author of more than 40 books, including *Mr. Macready*, 1955, *Benson and the Bensonians*, 1960, *Shakespeare on the English Stage 1900–1964*, 1964, *Peter Brook: A Biography*, 1971, *Theatre Bedside Book*, 1974, *The Edwardian Theatre*, 1976, *Going to Shakespeare*, 1978, *Companion to Shakespeare*, 1981, and *Five and Eighty Hamlets*, 1987; co-devised *Farjeon Reviewed*, 1975. Editor of *Plays of the Year* series, 1949–81, and many other books. O.B.E. 1981. **Essays:** Brian Friel; Ronald Harwood; N.F. Simpson.

TRUSSLER, Simon. Senior Lecturer in Drama, Goldsmiths' College, University of London; editor of *New Theatre Quarterly*, Cambridge. Author of several books on theatre and drama, including studies of Osborne, Wesker, Whiting, Pinter, and Edward Bond, and articles on theatre bibliography and classification. Editor of two collections of 18th-century plays, *Royal Shakespeare Company Yearbook*, annually since 1978, *New Theatre Voices of the Seventies* (interviews), 1982, and the Swan Theatre Plays and Writers on File series. **Essays:** Giles Cooper (appendix); Joe Orton (appendix); John Whiting (appendix).

TURNER, Darwin T. University of Iowa Foundation Professor of English, and Head of Afro-American World Studies, University of Iowa, Iowa City. Author of *Katharsis* (poetry), 1964, *Nathaniel Hawthorne's The Scarlet Letter*, 1967, *Afro-American Writers*, 1970, *In a Minor Chord: Three Afro-American Writers*, 1971, and *The Teaching of Literature by Afro-American Writers*, 1972. Editor of several books, including *Images of the Negro in America*, 1965, *Black American Literature*, 3 vols., 1969, *Black Drama in America*, 1971, *Voices from the Black Experience*, 1972, *The Wayward and the Seeking: A Collection of Writings by Jean Toomer*, 1980, and *The Art of Slave Narrative*, 1982. **Essays:** James Baldwin; Alice Childress; Lonne Elder III; Douglas Turner Ward.

TURNER, Elaine. Lecturer and tutor, University of Warwick, Coventry, and Central School of Speech and Drama, London; assistant editor of *New Theatre Quarterly*, Cambridge. **Essays:** John Arden; Louise Page.

WANDOR, Michelene. See her own entry. **Essays:** Caryl Churchill; Pam Gems; Mary O'Malley.

WARDLE, Irving. Drama critic, the *Times*, London. Author of *The Houseboy* (play), 1974, and *The Theatres of George Devine*, 1978.

WATERMEIER, Daniel J. Professor and Chair, Department of Theatre, University of Toledo, Ohio. Editor of *Between Actor and Critic: Letters of Edwin Booth and William Winter*, 1971, and *Shakespeare Around the Globe: A Guide to Notable Postwar Revivals*, 1986. **Essay:** Robertson Davies.

WEALES, Gerald. Professor of English, University of Pennsylvania, Philadelphia; drama critic for the *Reporter* and *Commonweal*. Author of *Religion in Modern English Drama*, 1961, *American Drama since World War II*, 1962, *A Play and Its Parts*, 1964, *Tennessee Williams*, 1965, *The Jumping-Off Place: American Drama in the 1960's*, 1969, *Clifford Odets*, 1971 (revised 1985), and *Canned Goods as Caviar: American Film Comedy in the 1930's*, 1985. Editor of several collections of plays and essays and of *The Complete Plays of William Wycherley*, 1966. **Essays:** Phillip Hayes Dean; Jules Feiffer; Lorraine Hansberry (appendix); David Henry Hwang; Arthur Kopit; Ronald Ribman; Musical Librettists.

YOUNG, B.A. Drama critic, *Financial Times*, London. Author of several radio and television plays, and books including *Cabinet Pudding* (novel), 1967, *The Colonists from Space* (novel), 1979, *The Mirror Up to Nature: A Review of the Theatre 1964–1982*, 1982, and *The Rattigan Version* (biography), 1986. **Essay:** Frank Marcus.